With love
Debs x

Best wishes
Simon x

God bless

Mark.

Jeremiah 29 v11-13

PRESENTED TO

Alex

BY

J2 & Youth Group, FCC

ON

4ᵗʰ Oct. 2015

AUTHENTIC
YOUTH BIBLE

ERV

A
Authentic

Writers: Nick Page, Claire Page, Liza Hoeksma, Chip Kendall, Helen Kendall, Alistair Metcalfe, Becci Brown, Stephanie Bushell, Alistair Gordon, Chris Juby, Hannah Juby.
Designers: David McNeill, Beth Wilcox, David Marklund.
Editors and proofreaders: Liz Williams, Louise Stenhouse, Su Box, Martin Street, Nathan Burley.
Easy-to-Read Version™ consultants: Brian McLemore, Ervin Bishop.

Text design and typesetting by Bookprint Creative Services, www.bookprint.co.uk
Published by Authentic Media Limited, 52 Presley Way, Crownhill, Milton Keynes, MK8 0ES.
Printed and bound by CPI Group (UK) Ltd, Croydon, CR0 4YY.

CONTENTS

The Old Testament

The New Testament

ABOUT THE EASY-TO-READ VERSION™

This version of the Bible has been prepared especially for people who want an English translation that accurately expresses the full meaning of the original text in a style that is clear and easy to understand. It is especially helpful for those who have limited experience with English, including children and people who are just learning English. It is designed to help such people overcome or avoid the most common difficulties to reading with understanding.

The writers of Scripture, especially those who produced the New Testament writings, showed by the language style they used that they were interested in good communication. The translators of this English version considered this an important example to follow. So they worked to express the meaning of the biblical text in a form that would be simple and natural. They used language that, instead of working as a barrier to understanding, would provide a key to unlock the truths of the Scriptures for a large segment of the English-speaking world.

The translation is based directly on the original languages of Scripture. In the case of the Old Testament, the translators followed the Hebrew Masoretic Text as it is found in the latest printed edition of *Biblia Hebraica Stuttgartensia* (1984), while referring occasionally to some earlier readings in the Dead Sea Scrolls. In some cases, they also followed the *Septuagint* (LXX), the Greek translation of the Old Testament, where it has readings that are actually earlier than any known Hebrew manuscript. For the New Testament, the source text was that which is found in both the United Bible Societies' *Greek New Testament* (fourth revised edition, 1993) and the Nestle-Aland *Novum Testamentum Graece* (twenty-seventh edition, 1993). The occasional variation from these printed editions was guided by reference to the findings of more recent scholarship.

Several special features are used to aid understanding. Brief explanations or synonyms (italicized within parentheses) sometimes follow difficult or unusual words in the text. If a word or phrase needs fuller explanation, it is specially marked in one of two ways: *(1)* If its usage is unique or unusual, it is marked by a letter of the alphabet (°) linking it to a footnote that provides an explanation or important information. Included in such footnotes are references to Scripture quotations and information about alternative readings when significant differences occur in the ancient manuscripts. *(2)* If it is a word that occurs frequently with the same meaning an explanation can be found in a Word List at the end of the Bible.

As in all translations, words that are implied by the context are often supplied in the text to make the meaning clear. For example, the phrase that in Greek is simply "David of Jesse" is always translated into English as "David the son of Jesse". If such explanatory words or phrases are extensive or unusual, they may be marked by half brackets. For example, in the translation, "The Lord gave this command to Moses ⌊for the people⌋," the phrase in half brackets is added to avoid any misunderstanding that the Lord's command was intended only for Moses and not for all the people.

In the Old Testament two different words are translated "Lord". When "Lord" is printed with small capital letters (Lord), it represents the Hebrew *YHWH*, which in some versions has been transliterated into English as "Jehovah" or "Yahweh". In a few cases, where *YHWH* is obviously used as the name of God or in place names, it is translated "Yahweh". When the word "Lord" contains lower case letters, it represents the Hebrew word *adonai* or a pronoun that refers to either *adonai* or *YHWH*. When *adonai* occurs together with *YHWH*, it is translated "Lord" and *YHWH* is translated God, as in "the Lord God". In cases where the speaker does not recognize that the one being addressed is God, *adonai* may be translated "Sir". The same is true in the New Testament for the Greek word *kurios*, which may be translated either "Lord" or "Sir", depending on the context.

Finally, in the Gospels, the first four books of the New Testament, the section headings are often followed by cross references. These identify where the same or similar material is found in one or more of the other Gospels.

ABOUT THE BIBLE

The Bible is the most important book ever written. No book has exerted more influence on the world – certainly the Western world. Art, literature, politics, architecture, history, law – they've all been influenced by the Bible. More importantly, its writings are considered sacred. Christians believe that the Bible is inspired by God, which means that the people who wrote it were passing on messages from God – messages that were not only for the people of their time, but for all people, everywhere and in any time.

Having said all that, exploring the Bible can be a bit daunting for the modern reader. We're put off by its size: 66 books, 1,189 chapters, over 750,000 words. We're also put off by its age: we're talking about a book written by many different authors, across thousands of years, and completed around 2,000 years ago.

And maybe we're put off by the content itself. There are passages in the Bible that lift and inspire – and there are parts that disgust and shock. It can also be dull: long family trees, even longer lists of laws, all those strange names of people and countries . . .

But if you do venture in, if you do try to explore, then there are wonderful things to be found. You get great poetry, stirring stories, thought-provoking wisdom, life-changing truths. You get love, sex, violence, faithfulness, bravery, cowardice, triumph and disaster.

The Bible is all about the big issues in life. It tells us why we're here, what we're supposed to be doing on earth, where we all came from. It tells us how we should live our lives and how we should treat other people. It talks about real people with real problems – and although they lived a long time ago, they faced exactly the same kind of problems that we face today.

Most of all, Christians believe the Bible speaks to us. It is one of the ways that we hear from God and understand more about him.

The Bible is the most revolutionary, most exciting, most important book ever written. What more do you need to know?

What is it?

The title comes from the Greek *ta biblia* meaning "the books". And that's the first thing to recognize about the Bible. It's not one book – it's a collection of many different kinds of book or writing, including history, poetry, stories, legal codes, proverbs and sayings, apocalyptic visionary descriptions, hymns, letters . . .

These are split into two sections:

The Old Testament or Hebrew Scriptures contains writings sacred to both Jews and Christians. This section contains History, Prophecy, Wisdom and what some people call the "Pentateuch" or the "Books of the Law".

The New Testament contains only Christian Scriptures. The New Testament is divided into two main sections: the Gospels and Acts, and the Letters, from people such as Paul, John and Peter.

"Testament" means "promise". Christians believe that the Old Testament tells the story of God's promise to the Israelites, while the New Testament of his promise to all people.

The Bible was written in two main languages – Hebrew and Greek – with bits of Aramaic and Latin. The Old Testament was written almost entirely in Hebrew, with some small parts in Aramaic. Although Jesus and his disciples spoke Aramaic, the New Testament was written in Greek. Most people around the Mediterranean region spoke Greek. The type of Greek they spoke – and which is found in the New Testament – has since been called *koine* or "common Greek". This was the ordinary language of everyday folk: traders, housewives, shopkeepers. People like Paul and Luke and Mark wrote in Greek, the common language of the Roman Empire. There are also occasional Latin words in the New Testament, but these are mainly technical terms such as names, e.g. *kentyrion*, the Greek version of the Latin centurion; *denarius*, the Roman coinage and *mille*, the Roman mile. They reflect the fact that when the New Testament was written the Roman Empire was the major power in the region.

We should remember that the first Christians did not have "the Bible" as we know it. When the early Christians talked about scripture, they were talking about the Hebrew Scriptures, or what we know as the Old Testament. The early Church probably sang psalms and read the writings of the prophets to see how they pointed to Jesus.

But they also told stories and shared memories of Jesus' life and teaching, passing on these memories from group to group. After a while, the early Church had grown and the original eyewitnesses began to die. So people began to write down their own accounts, drawing on their own observations and the memories of the people who were there. These became the Gospels. At the same time, leaders such as Paul, Peter and John wrote letters to churches helping them to solve problems and offering spiritual advice. These Letters were collected and copied and passed around the early Church. Eventually, the Gospels and the Letters were brought together to form the New Testament, but this didn't happen until some time around AD 400.

How is it Organized?

So, the Bible is in two parts: the **Old Testament** and the **New Testament**. Each section is made up of different numbers of **books** of the Bible. (For example, the Gospels and Acts section contains Matthew, Mark, Luke, John and Acts). Some books are huge, some are just one page long. They are written in different styles. Psalms, for instance, contain collections of poems; Kings is a long history. With some books, such as Corinthians, there are more than one with the same name, and these are distinguished by a number in front of the book name e.g. 1 Corinthians and 2 Corinthians.

Each book of the Bible is broken down into numbered **chapters**. Some bits of these appear in more than one book; Kings and Chronicles share a lot of the same content, told from different viewpoints, as do Matthew, Mark, Luke and John. Some books only have one chapter and so don't have a chapter number.

Finally, the chapters are split into individual, numbered **verses**. Some verses are found in more than one book of the Bible.

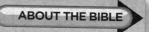

To find our way around the Bible we use Bible **references** – a bit like an address. So, for example:

Exodus 3 means – Exodus chapter 3 (the whole chapter)

John 3:16 means – the book of John, chapter 3, verse 16

Genesis 1:1–17 means – the book of Genesis, chapter 1, verses 1 to 17

James 4:13,15; 5:6 means – the book of James, chapter 4, verse 13, verse 15 and chapter 5, verse 6

2 Kings 2:23 – 3:12 means – the second book of Kings, chapter 2, verse 23 through to chapter 3, verse 12

THE BIBLE: AN OVERVIEW

The Old Testament

In the beginning, God creates the heavens and the earth. He creates a world that is good and fills it with plants and animals. He creates Adam and Eve – the first man and woman – and gives them a garden to inhabit. Even though they are only given one rule to obey, they choose to disobey and turn away from God. They have to leave the garden. Sin and evil have polluted God's creation.

As humanity spreads throughout the earth, so does evil. So God decides to start again by sending a flood to wipe out humanity. As Noah is a good man and trusts in God he and his family alone are saved. God makes a solemn promise never to destroy humanity again.

God chooses Abram – who later becomes Abraham. God makes a promise to Abraham that his descendants will be a great nation and they will inhabit the land of Canaan. He also says that all of humanity will be blessed by Abraham's descendants. Although Abraham is in his nineties, God keeps his promises, and Abraham's wife Sarah gives birth to Isaac.

Isaac is the father to twins, Esau and Jacob. After a dramatic encounter with God, Jacob's name is changed to Israel, and it is by this name that the people will come to be known.

Jacob has 12 children, one of whom, Joseph, ends up in Egypt after falling out with his brothers. Jacob's family flee to Egypt to escape famine where they are reunited with Joseph. The descendants of Jacob's 12 children become the 12 tribes of Israel.

In Egypt the Israelites multiply, and after a few hundred years the entire nation is in slavery. So God selects a leader called Moses, who helps the Israelites escape. This escape is known as "the exodus". They make their way back to Canaan. On the way God gives them ten commandments and detailed instructions on how to live and worship him. However, when they get to the borders of Canaan, the people are too scared to cross into it. God punishes this lack of faith by making them live in the desert for 40 years.

Moses never makes it into Canaan, the "promised land". He hands the leadership to Joshua, who takes the Israelites across the River Jordan and into the land. God gives his people instructions to conquer the whole land, but the Israelites don't finish the task. Some of the old inhabitants – the Canaanites – remain and, with them, their own ways of worship. For the next 800 years, Israel's history is a battle between the worship of God and the worship of false gods.

After Joshua's death comes a time when the people of Israel did what was evil in the sight of the Lord and everyone did what was right in his own eyes. The Judges – leaders like Deborah, Gideon and Samson – bring only occasional light into the darkness. In the end, the Israelites ask the prophet Samuel to appoint a king and Saul becomes the first king of Israel. He is succeeded by David, Israel's greatest king. David captures Jerusalem and defeats the enemies of Israel while his son and successor, Solomon, builds a magnificent Temple.

On Solomon's death, however, civil war breaks out, and the nation splits into two: Israel in the north and Judah in the south. For the next 300 years, the two nations are continually threatened by powerful enemies, while a succession of evil and foolish kings stray from worshipping God to follow false gods. God sends a series of prophets – like Elijah, Elisha, Isaiah, Jeremiah and Ezekiel – who warn the kingdoms of what will happen to them if they don't change. They also talk of a Messiah – a "chosen one" – a mighty leader whom God would send to save his people.

In 722 BC the northern kingdom of Israel is captured and the inhabitants taken into captivity in Assyria, never to be heard of again. About a hundred years later, the southern kingdom of Judah falls to another empire, the Babylonians, and all the people are exiled to Babylon. This period – known as the exile – lasts 70 years.

Then the Babylonian empire falls and the exiles from Judah return to Israel. They rebuild Jerusalem and the Temple, but the glory days have gone. God doesn't send any more prophets and the people of Israel place their hopes in the long-awaited Messiah.

The New Testament

Four hundred years later, a teenage girl called Mary who is still a virgin becomes pregnant and gives birth to a son. She is told by an angel that the baby is very special – he is God's son – and that she should call him Jesus.

After John the Baptist warns people that someone special is coming, Jesus' public work begins, when he is around 30 years old. With his disciples he travels through Roman Palestine, preaching, teaching and performing miracles. He makes claims for himself that go beyond those of a teacher or even a prophet. He forgives people their sins and raises the dead; he challenges the establishment. He enters Jerusalem in triumph. Then it all seems to go wrong. Betrayed by one of his followers, Jesus is tried by the authorities, taken outside the city and crucified.

Three days later, his followers start to make remarkable claims. They claim that Jesus has risen from the dead, that many of them have seen him. More, they claim that Jesus is the Messiah, that his death has changed the world and that he has sent them a new helper, the Holy Spirit, to empower them.

These followers become known as Christians. New leaders emerge: Peter, the fisherman who was one of Jesus' first followers; and Paul, who began his career persecuting Jesus' followers and who, after a dramatic vision of Jesus, becomes one of his most outspoken followers. Gradually the stories about Jesus are written down as gospels and sent around the world. The followers set up local churches. People of all nationalities start to believe in this Messiah.

Increasingly, Christians face persecution from the Jewish and Roman authorities. One such follower is John, who is sentenced to exile on a small island. While there, he has a vision of the end of time. Jesus will return and gain the final victory. The world will end as it began – with creation, with God creating a new heaven and a new earth, where all his followers will live in peace. It is an end, but also a new beginning.

THE BIBLE: HOW TO READ IT

The reason so many of us find it difficult to read the Bible is that we don't always approach it in the right way. We look at it a bit like going to the dentist: we know we have to go, but we don't expect to actually enjoy the experience.

Well the good news is that the Bible is not like that! It's more like exploring another country. So it helps to approach the Bible with the spirit of an explorer, excited by the knowledge that there is always so much more to discover!

Having said that, all explorers need the right attitude and the right tools. So here are a few tips to help you make the most of your journey.

Work to a Plan

The Bible is big. It contains around 750,000 words. So you need to have a plan of action to help you explore. You can work through a particular book, or follow a particular person and study their life. Or you could study a topic such as "prayer" or "forgiveness" or "justice".

Give it Time

Take your time. You can't see anything clearly if you're zooming through it at 120 miles per hour. Read carefully and you'll find loads to fascinate you. It often helps to read the passage aloud. Make time for it. You can get a good grip of what the Bible is all about by reading it for five or ten minutes a day. That's probably less than the time you spend watching adverts on TV! Try not to concentrate on just one verse, but look at the passages that surround it.

Ask Questions

This is really important. A lot of people feel that they shouldn't ask questions about the Bible, as if it's "too sacred" for that. In fact, the Bible is full of people who asked God challenging questions. If you don't ask, you won't find out.

Write Notes

Keep a traveller's journal as you explore. Write down your thoughts and observations. Make maps, draw diagrams. You can keep a notebook for this purpose or you can make notes in the margins of your Bible. Underline or highlight important bits. Write down how God has spoken to you.

Use Some Guidebooks

When you go travelling you take some things like guidebooks, maps and phrase books. When you explore the Bible it's good to get some help as well. There are some parts where we need an expert to give us a bit of help. You can use Bible guides and commentaries to help you delve deeper.

Learn About the History

If there is one thing that really helps people understand the Bible, it's a broad understanding of Bible history. Each book of the Bible was written at a different point in time; understanding this can help our understanding of the entire book.

Understand the Culture

They did things differently in Bible times. They had different attitudes to war, women, families, relationships and other such things. If you spend a little time trying to grasp the culture it will help you understand the passage a lot better.

Don't Expect to Understand Everything

There are bits in the Bible that even the experts don't understand. So if you find a difficult part, work at it, ask questions and then, if it's still baffling, move on. Just because we don't understand something, doesn't mean we should stop exploring.

Use Your Common Sense

God has given us wisdom. Some of us could do with a little more, admittedly, but we all have it. So, when you read the Bible, try to use the wisdom God has given you. Don't fly off into fanciful theories and ideas based on one verse. Try to identify whether the writer is speaking metaphorically or literally. Use your common sense.

Be Creative

Try reading the Bible in different ways. Exploring a story? Draw a picture, write it as a play or turn it into a comic book. Act it out with a friend. You'll find a lot more in there if you look at something from a different perspective.

MAPPING THE ADVENTURE

In this Youth Bible there are a number of special features designed to help you find your way around.

Do you ever wonder how the Bible works as a whole? What part does each book play and why aren't they in chronological order? There are **Introductions** to both the Old and New Testaments, an explanation of what happened in-between the two and **Overviews** of each of the sections within the testaments, which will help you to work out where you are.

Do you want to get an idea of what each Bible book is about? Would you like to have someone help you navigate your way through, pointing out the scenery, giving you the history, helping you understand? Each book starts with a short **Guide** explaining who wrote it, when, and what it is about. It also gives a **Quick Tour** of the main events, so that you can find the bits you want to read quickly.

Are there specific areas of particular interest to you? Want to explore them straight away? Take a look at the colour **Topical** pages and find out what the Bible has to say on important issues.

Do you find some bits difficult to understand? Wonder how they apply to you today? As you read through each book, you'll find short **Insights** which give a bit of background information or help explain the meaning or context of certain verses or passages.

Would you like to explore some parts of the Bible in more depth but don't know where to start? There are 164 **Bible Bits** to help you dig in and find out more. Many have suggestions for how you can dig even deeper and find out more by searching further afield if you want to.

At the back you'll find details of local **Weights and Measures**, a **Dictionary** of unfamiliar words and phrases you'll come across, and **Maps** of the Bible lands showing some of the important journeys that were taken.

Happy exploring!

BIBLE BITS

BIBLE BITS

WHERE CAN I FIND HELP WHEN I'M . . . ?

Angry
Matthew 5:22; Ephesians 4:25–27; 1 Timothy 2:8

Ashamed
Psalms 32; 51; Isaiah 55:7–13; Micah 7:18; Acts 13:38–39

Bitter
Psalm 37; Proverbs 3:11–12; Ephesians 4:31–32; James 3:13–18

Confused
Psalms 25:4–5; 32:8–9; Proverbs 3:1–6; Isaiah 42:16; John 14:1–14; Ephesians 5:6–16

Depressed
Psalms 30; 34; Isaiah 35

Discouraged
Genesis 15:1–6; Psalms 23; 41:5–11; 55:22; Matthew 5:11–12; 2 Corinthians 4:8–18; Philippians 4:4–7

Discriminated against
Matthew 7:1–5,12; 20:1–16; Galatians 3:26–29; Ephesians 2:11–22; Colossians 3:11; James 2:1–13

Doubting
Judges 6:36–40; Matthew 8:23–27; John 20:24–29; Jude 21–22

Feeling a failure
Psalm 73:25–26; Jeremiah 30:18–22; Romans 3:23–24; 8:31–39; 2 Corinthians 12:9; Ephesians 2:8–9

Feeling alone
Psalms 22; 23; 40:1–3; 68:5–6; Matthew 28:20; Hebrews 13:5–6

Feeling let down
Matthew 18:21–25; Luke 17:3–4; Romans 12:14–21

Feeling rejected
Deuteronomy 31:6; Psalm 86; Acts 4:11–12; Romans 8:28,31–39; Hebrews 13:5b–6

Finding it tough going
Exodus 18:17–23; Numbers 11:10–23; 1 Kings 19:1–8; 1 Samuel 30:6; Job 19:1–27; Psalm 43:1–4;
    Matthew 11:28–30; Galatians 6:9–10; Hebrews 12:1–13

Frightened

Psalm 27; 34:4–6; Isaiah 12:1–2; Matthew 10:28–31; 1 Peter 3:13–14

Grieving

Psalm 23; Matthew 5:4; 1 Thessalonians 4:13–18; Revelation 21:4

Hating myself

Psalm 139; Jeremiah 1:4–10; 1 Corinthians 1:26–31; 12:12–27; Colossians 3:12; 1 Peter 2:9

In need of protection

Numbers 6:24–26; Psalms 27:1–6,14; 56:8–13; 91; Nahum 1:7; Malachi 3:17–18

Leading others

1 Timothy 3:1–7; 2 Timothy 2:14–26; Titus 1:5–9

Needing patience

Proverbs 14:29; 19:11; Romans 12:12; 1 Corinthians 13:4; Galatians 5:22–23; Colossians 3:12–14; Hebrews 10:36

Needing peace

Isaiah 26:3; Luke 1:78–79; John 14:27; Romans 5:1–5; Philippians 4:6–7; Colossians 3:15

Needing to prioritize

Proverbs 12:11; 28:19; Ecclesiastes 3:1–8; Haggai 1:5–9; Matthew 6:19–21; Luke 21:34–36; Titus 3:14

Sad

Ecclesiastes 3:1–13; Isaiah 53:3–10; 61:1–7; Jeremiah 31:16–17; Matthew 5:4; 2 Corinthians 1:3–7; Revelation 21:3–4

Sick

Proverbs 18:14; Matthew 14:34–36; Mark 5:21–43; 7:31–37; Acts 3:1–10; James 5:14–15; Revelation 21:4

Suffering

Psalm 102; Lamentations 3:21–24; 2 Corinthians 12:9–10; Colossians 1:24 – 2:5; 1 Peter 4:12–13,19

Tempted

Psalms 1; 139:23–24; 1 Corinthians 10:12–13; Hebrews 2:14–18; James 4:7; 2 Peter 3:17–18

Thankful

Psalms 100; 118:27–29; 136; Philippians 4:6; Colossians 3:16–17; 1 Thessalonians 5:18

Worried

Psalms 46; 94:18–19; Matthew 6:19–34; John 14:27; Philippians 4:6; 1 Peter 5:6–7

Worried about money

Ecclesiastes 5:10–20; Matthew 6:24–34; Mark 10:17–30; Luke 12:13–21; 1 Timothy 6:6–10

Worried about work

Proverbs 11:3; Ecclesiastes 10:4; Romans 12:3–11; 1 Thessalonians 5:12–18; 2 Thessalonians 3:6–13

THE OLD TESTAMENT

The Old Testament covers a long period of time and contains a lot of different material. It takes us from the beginning of creation to around 400 BC. It is made up of a huge mixture of different kinds of writing split into four main sections: The Law (or Pentateuch), History, Wisdom and Prophecy (split into the Major and Minor Prophets).

Although it varies in style and content, it tells one overall story: the story of God's relationship with human beings. It tells how humans were created by God, how they rebelled against him and how he put in place a plan to save them. You can't understand what happened in the New Testament unless you get a grip on what happened in the Old Testament.

There is a lot of great, inspiring, uplifting stuff. But as anyone who reads it soon finds out, it also contains some confusing, strange and even downright horrible stuff. So here are a few reasons why, at times, the Old Testament doesn't seem very "Christian":

- They weren't Christians. The people in the Old Testament lived hundreds or even thousands of years before Jesus arrived. Some had great faith – and there is a lot that we can learn from their experiences and their lives. But they weren't Christians. They didn't have the whole picture.

- The people in the Old Testament lived a long time ago. The Old Testament covers a huge period of time and took around 1,500 years to put together. So, naturally, the cultures of those times were hugely different. That will affect the way they behave and the social "rules" of the time. Generally speaking, the Old Testament times were tougher. In warfare, for example, there was no such thing as the United Nations or the International Courts – there were just a load of big people with swords. So if it seems at times more brutal, that's because it actually was more brutal.

- The Old Testament is packed with real people. That's why they behave so badly. Real people sometimes do stupid, dangerous and evil things. Sometimes they just make mistakes, sometimes they do things deliberately but this stuff happens. (And it still happens today.)

And if there is some strange and horrible stuff, there are many more moments of great beauty, majesty and wonder.

QUICK TOUR  **OLD TESTAMENT**

Creation Genesis 1:1–31
The origin of sin Genesis 3:1–24
The promise Genesis 17:1–27
Moses meets God Exodus 3:1–22
Escape! Exodus 12:31–41
The Ten Commandments Exodus 19:1 – 20:21
Entering the land Joshua 1:1–16

We want a king 1 Samuel 8:1–22
Samuel anoints David 1 Samuel 16:1–13
The Lord's promise to David 2 Samuel 7:1–29
Elijah v. Baal 1 Kings 18:1–46
Justice Amos 5:10–15
The coming king Isaiah 11:1–9
A new promise Jeremiah 31:31–4

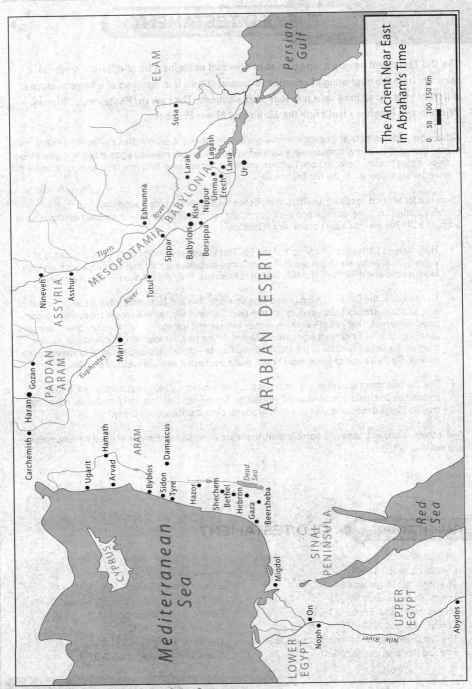

The Ancient Near East
in Abraham's Time

0 50 100 150 km

Persian Gulf

ELAM

Susa

Lagash
Larak
Nippur
Umma
Erech
Larsa
Ur

MESOPOTAMIA BABYLONIA

Eshnunna
Kish
Sippar
Babylon
Borsippa

Tigris River

ASSYRIA

Nineveh
Asshur
Tutul

ARABIAN DESERT

PADDAN ARAM

Gozan
Haran
Carchemish
Mari

Euphrates River

ARAM

Hamath
Ugarit
Arvad
Byblos
Sidon
Damascus
Tyre
Hazor
Shechem
Bethel
Hebron
Gaza
Beersheba

Dead Sea

CYPRUS

Mediterranean Sea

SINAI PENINSULA

Migdol

Red Sea

LOWER EGYPT

On
Noph

Nile River

UPPER EGYPT

Abydos

The first five book of the Bible are known as the "Books of the Law". In fact they have a number of different names. Sometimes these are called "the Pentateuch" from the Greek word *pentateuchos*, meaning "five-volumed book"; sometimes they are called the "Books of Moses". The Jewish name for this section is the "Torah" which means "law", "teachings" or "instruction". In the New Testament when Jesus talks about "the law" this is what he's talking about. We get an idea of how important this was for Israel from Exodus 12:49: "The same rules are for everyone. It doesn't matter if they are citizens or foreigners living among you."

The books cover a wide variety of subjects and take us from the origins of creation itself to the Israelites' forty years in the desert. But they are important because they introduce some really big themes of the Bible, such as creation, sin, and the agreement between man and God.

Genesis is the book of beginnings. It traces the origins of the people of Israel from creation through to people like Abraham, Isaac and Jacob. It also tells of God's promises – or agreements – with his people. By the end of Genesis, the people of Israel are in slavery in Egypt.

Exodus tells of the Israelites' escape from Egypt. The book ends with Moses receiving the Ten Commandments and the instructions for the building of the Holy Tent.

Leviticus is mainly about the laws the Israelites were supposed to follow to show that they were true followers of God. Many people find it a difficult book, but there are gems inside, such as the amazing Jubilee legislation.

Numbers is so called because it's full of numbers. Amazing! But, along with a record of how many Israelites left Egypt, it also tells how the Israelites rebelled against God and ended up spending forty years in the wilderness.

Deuteronomy is a kind of summary of the other four books. It's Moses' farewell speech, given just before his death and before the Israelites' entry to the land God has promised them.

Who
The book is traditionally ascribed to Moses. The traditional view is that Moses wrote all the books of the Law, the "Pentateuch". He may well have had a hand in it, but there are signs of other writers as well.

 When
Genesis was written over a long period of time. It was probably begun in the time of Moses, but later generations added other material and edited the book together. The book probably reached its final form around the time of Solomon (970–930 BC).

 What
Genesis is really a "why" book. It tells us where we came from and why we are here. It is one of the most important books of the Bible as it introduces all the major themes of the Bible – creation, sin and rebellion, love, grace and mercy.

The book is structured around the lives of several key figures such as Adam, Noah, Abraham, Jacob and Joseph. These are known as the "patriarchs", which means "the fathers". They are not only the fathers of the Israelite nation, but also our spiritual ancestors. There are, of course, interludes which cover other topics, but these are the key characters.

Their stories remind us that the Bible is not just a book about God: it is a book about God and man. God is personal. He speaks, he thinks, he relates to humans. This is not some impersonal "life-force", still less some distant, alien being. This is a "someone" who wants to communicate with the world he has created. Indeed, the whole of the Bible is about God's attempts to make himself known to his creations, to inspire, cajole, correct and above all to love these people he made.

Most importantly, God makes promises to his people. These promises are known as "covenants" which means a solemn promise or legal agreement. God promises Noah that he will never again wipe out the human race; he promises Abraham that, even though he is old and childless, he will be the father of a mighty nation. These promises underpin God's relationship with his people throughout the rest of the Bible. God has promised to be with them – and he keeps his promises.

QUICK TOUR **GENESIS**

"God looked at everything he had made. And he saw that everything was very good."

Genesis 1:31

The Beginning of the World

1 In the beginning, when God created the earth and sky,[a] ²the earth was without form and not yet useful for anything. Deep waters covered the earth, and darkness covered the water. God's Spirit[b] was moving like a storm over the surface of the water.

The First Day—Light

³Then God said, "Let there be light!" And light began to shine. ⁴He saw the light, and he knew that it was good. Then he separated the light from the darkness. ⁵God named the light "day", and he named the darkness "night".

There was evening, and then there was morning. This was the first day.

The Second Day—Sky

⁶Then God said, "Let there be a space[c] to separate the water into two parts!" ⁷So God made the space and separated the water. Some of the water was above it, and some of the water was below it. ⁸God named that space "sky". There was evening, and then there was morning. This was the second day.

The Third Day—Dry Land and Plants

⁹Then God said, "Let the water under the sky be gathered together so that the dry land will appear." And it happened. ¹⁰God named the dry land "earth", and he named the water that was gathered together "seas". And God saw that this was good.

¹¹Then God said, "Let the earth grow grass, plants that make grain and fruit trees. The fruit trees will make fruit with seeds in them. And each plant will make its own kind of seed. Let these plants grow on the earth." And it happened. ¹²The earth grew grass and plants that made grain. And it grew trees that made fruit with seeds in them. Every plant made its own kind of seeds. And God saw that this was good.

¹³There was evening, and then there was morning. This was the third day.

The Fourth Day—Sun, Moon and Stars

¹⁴Then God said, "Let there be lights in the sky to separate the day from the night. These lights will mark the beginning and end of days and years. And they will be used to mark the times for festivals.[d] ¹⁵They will be in the sky to shine light on the earth." And it happened.

¹⁶So God made the two large lights. He made the larger light to rule during the day and the smaller light to rule during the night. He also made the stars. ¹⁷God put these lights in the sky to shine on the earth. ¹⁸He put them in the sky to rule over the day and over the night. They separated the light from the darkness. And God saw that this was good.

¹⁹There was evening, and then there was morning. This was the fourth day.

The Fifth Day—Fish and Birds

²⁰Then God said, "Let the water be filled with many living things, and let there be birds to fly in the air over the earth." ²¹So God created the large sea animals.[e] He created all the many living things in the sea and every kind of bird that flies in the air. And God saw that this was good.

²²God blessed all the living things in the sea and told them to have many babies and fill the seas. And he blessed the birds on land and told them to have many more babies.

²³There was evening, and then there was morning. This was the fifth day.

The Sixth Day—Land Animals and People

²⁴Then God said, "Let the earth produce many kinds of living things. Let there be many different kinds of animals. Let there be large animals and small crawling animals of every kind. And let all these animals produce more animals." And all these things happened.

²⁵So God made every kind of animal. He made the wild animals, the tame animals and all the small crawling things. And God saw that this was good.

²⁶Then God said, "Now let's make humans[f] who will be like us.[g] They will rule over all the fish in the sea and the birds in the air. They will rule over all the large animals and all the little things that crawl on the earth."

²⁷So God created humans in his own image. He created them to be like himself.[h] He created them male and female. ²⁸God blessed them and said to

---

[a] **1:1** Or "In the beginning God created the heavens and the earth." "God" in this first section (1:1 – 2:3) is the most general word for God in the Old Testament. It is a plural form. See verse 26.

[b] **1:2 God's Spirit** Or "A wind from God".

[c] **1:6 space** Or "firmament". The Hebrew word can refer to a piece of metal that has been hammered into the shape of a bowl.

[d] **1:14 festivals** The Israelites used the sun and moon to decide when the months and years began. Many Israelite festivals and special meetings began at the time of the new moon or full moon.

[e] **1:21 large sea animals** Or "sea monsters".

[f] **1:26 humans** The Hebrew word means "man", "people" or the name "Adam". It is like the word meaning "earth" or "red clay".

[g] **1:26 Now let's make . . . like us** Or "Now let's make humans in our image and in our likeness."

[h] **1:27 So God created humans . . . himself** Or "So God created them in his image. In the image of God he created them." Compare Gen. 5:1,3.

BEGINNINGS

Look out of your window. Can you imagine there being no world out there? Nothing to see, hear or touch. No trees, or birds or animals. No mates, no parents and no teachers. No chocolate, TV, sport or art. It is impossible to imagine, but Genesis tells us there was a time when this was the case – everything that we see and experience now had a beginning.

DIG IN

READ Genesis 1:1 – 2:25

- Have a look at verse 1. Who was there in the beginning? How do we know?
- Go through chapter 1 and make a note of all the things that started to exist.
- Look through the chapter again and find out *how* all these things started to exist.

Amazingly, just by the word of God, our beautiful world began. Christians disagree about whether this happened in six days or more, but what is important is that God is the creator of everything.

- What did God think about each thing when he had made it?
- Who do you think owns the world and why?

When God looked at all the things that he had made he saw they were exactly as he wanted – perfect. And because God made the world, it belongs to him. He is the king, he's in charge. That means nothing can exist without him and no one is bigger or better than him. And what a good, generous and powerful ruler he is in making such a beautiful, awesome and exciting world!

- Read verse 26. What is special about human beings?
- What job are they given to do?

How exciting to read about the beginning of humankind! Not only that, but human beings are made like God! This doesn't really mean we look like God, but that we are like God in nature, and able to have a relationship with him. And because of this God has given people the special task of looking after the world, under his rule.

DIG THROUGH

- Think about the ways in which God is a better ruler than any other monarch or prime minister. Think about his power, his generosity and creativity – because he rules we should obey him, but because he's so good, hopefully we want to as well!
- Why not write down some of your favourite things in the world around us and tell God how amazing he is for making them.
- Thank God that he wanted human beings to have a relationship with him and ask him to help you have a relationship with him.

DIG DEEPER

- Read Psalm 95:3–7 and Revelation 4:11 to see some ways to respond to the fact that God made the world.
- Genesis is the book of beginnings. Having described the beginning of the world, the rest of the book tells the story of things happening for the first time. Why not keep reading and look out for the very first time that all sorts of thing happened: conversation between God and those he had created, marriage, humanity *disobeying God, clothes, punishment, sacrifice, family, farming, murder, change in language, city, promise, mention of faith . . .*

them, "Have many children. Fill the earth and take control of it. Rule over the fish in the sea and the birds in the air. Rule over every living thing that moves on the earth."

29God said, "I am giving you all the grain bearing plants and all the fruit trees. These trees make fruit with seeds in it. This grain and fruit will be your food. 30And I am giving all the green plants to the animals. These green plants will be their food. Every animal on earth, every bird in the air and all the little things that crawl on the earth will eat that food." And all these things happened.

31God looked at everything he had made. And he saw that everything was very good.

There was evening, and then there was morning. This was the sixth day.

The Seventh Day—Rest

2 So the earth, the sky and everything in them were finished. 2God finished the work he was doing, so on the seventh day he rested from his work. 3God blessed the seventh day and made it a holy day. He made it special because on that day he rested from all the work he did while creating the world.

The First Man and the Garden of Eden

4This is the story about the creation of the sky and the earth. This is what happened when the LORD God made the earth and the sky. 5This was before there were plants on the earth. Nothing was growing in the fields because the LORD God had not yet made it rain on the earth, and there was no one to care for the plants.

6So water*a* came up from the earth and spread over the ground. 7Then the LORD God took dust from the ground and made a man.*b* He breathed the breath of life into the man's nose, and the man became a living thing. 8Then the LORD God planted a garden in the East,*c* in a place named Eden. He put the man he made in that garden. 9Then the LORD God caused all the beautiful trees that were good for food to grow in the garden. In the middle of the garden, he put the tree of life and the tree that gives knowledge about good and evil.

10A river flowed from Eden and watered the garden. The river then separated and became four smaller rivers. 11The name of the first river was Pishon. This river flowed around the entire country of Havilah.*d* 12(There is gold in that

country, and that gold is pure. A kind of expensive perfume and onyx are also found there.) 13The name of the second river was Gihon. This river flowed around the whole land of Cush.*e* 14The name of the third river was Tigris. This river flowed east of Assyria. The fourth river was the Euphrates.

15The LORD God put the man in the Garden of Eden to work the soil and take care of the garden. 16The LORD God gave him this command: "You may eat from any tree in the garden. 17But you must not eat from the tree that gives knowledge about good and evil. If you eat fruit from that tree, on that day you will certainly die!"

A Companion for Adam

18Then the LORD God said, "I see that it is not good for the man to be alone. I will make the companion he needs, one just right for him."

19The LORD God used dust from the ground and made every animal in the fields and every bird in the air. He brought all these animals to the man, and the man gave them all a name. 20The man gave names to all the tame animals, to all the birds in the air and to all the wild animals. He saw many animals and birds, but he could not find a companion that was right for him. 21So the LORD God caused the man to sleep very deeply. While he was asleep, God took one of the ribs from the man's body. Then he closed the man's skin where the rib had been. 22The LORD God used the rib from the man to make a woman. Then he brought the woman to the man. 23And the man said,

"Finally! One like me,
    with bones from my bones
    and a body from my body.
She was taken out of a man,
    so I will call her 'woman'."

24That is why a man leaves his father and mother and is joined to his wife. In this way two people become one. 25The man and his wife were naked, but they were not ashamed.

The Beginning of Sin

3 The snake was the most clever of all the wild animals that the LORD God had made. The snake spoke to the woman and said, "Woman, did God really tell you that you must not eat from any tree in the garden?"

---

a **2:6 water** Or "a mist".
b **2:7 man** The Hebrew word means "man", "people" or the name "Adam". It is like the word meaning "earth" or "red clay".
c **2:8 East** This usually means the area between the Tigris and Euphrates rivers as far east as the Persian Gulf.
d **2:11 Havilah** The land along the west coast of the Arabian Peninsula and possibly, the part of Africa south of Ethiopia.
e **2:13 Cush** Usually this means Ethiopia, but here, it probably refers to the area north and east of the Tigris River.

WHERE DID IT ALL GO WRONG?

Can you imagine walking around naked? Would you blush and feel ashamed? Genesis 2:25 says, "The man and his wife were naked, but they were not ashamed." Reading this may make us giggle, but it shows that things were so good that Adam and Eve had nothing to hide from each other or from God. They weren't ashamed, everything was perfect. So where did it all go wrong?

DIG IN

READ Genesis 3:1–24

We are not told exactly where the snake comes from, but other bits of the Bible tell us that this is Satan, God's enemy, trying to undermine and destroy God's loving rule.

- What tactics does the snake use when he talks to Eve (vv.1–2,5)?
- What does Eve do?

The snake makes God sound harsh, he questions God's word and he makes God sound like a spoilsport (vv.1, 4–5). By choosing to eat the fruit, Eve (followed by Adam) decides to do what God told her not to. It seems weird that there's a problem with eating fruit, but God had told them that they could eat from any tree except for the tree "that gives knowledge about good and evil" (2:17). By disobeying God and choosing to eat the forbidden fruit they begin to experience and know good and evil, which they were never meant to do.

- What happens to Adam and Eve's relationship (vv.7,12)?
- What happens to Adam and Eve's relationship with God (vv.8–11)?

Yikes! What a mess. Adam and Eve had been totally open with each other but now they suddenly feel ashamed. Adam speaks as if he no longer likes Eve, blaming her for their sin. And saddest of all is their relationship with God; they hide from him, they have chosen to disobey him and are afraid.

- Read verses 14–19 and see if you can pick out some of the punishments and consequences God tells both Adam and Eve, and the snake that they face.

The world is spoilt – now there's going to be work to do (and it won't be easy), relationships will be difficult and there's going to be pain and suffering. God forces them out of the beautiful garden so that they cannot eat from the tree of life (v.24). Now they will die, just as God said they would (2:17).

- Verse 15 is interesting. Who do you think the "child" (descendant) might be that will crush the snake's head?

The exciting thing about Genesis 3 is that even though there's so much sadness as a result of their disobedience, God seems to be promising that one day evil will be ended by a descendant of Eve. Could this be Jesus?

DIG THROUGH

- Adam blames Eve and Eve blames the snake, but each, individually, had chosen to disobey God. How often are you tempted to blame someone or something else when you do something wrong?
- Why not say sorry to God for the times you may have made a wrong choice and chosen not to follow him.

DIG DEEPER

- Read Genesis 4:1–15, 5:1–32, 6:5–8 and 11:1–9 to see how sin and death spread.

²The woman answered the snake, "No, we can eat fruit from the trees in the garden. ³But there is one tree we must not eat from. God told us, 'You must not eat fruit from the tree that is in the middle of the garden. You must not even touch that tree, or you will die.'"

⁴But the snake said to the woman, "You will not die. ⁵God knows that if you eat the fruit from that tree you will learn about good and evil, and then you will be like God!"

INSIGHT

We often talk of Adam and Eve eating an apple from the tree of the knowledge of good and evil but the type of fruit is not mentioned in the Bible. It could have been a banana! However, it doesn't sound as though it was any ordinary fruit.

Genesis 3:6

⁶The woman could see that the tree was beautiful and the fruit looked so good to eat. She also liked the idea that it would make her wise. So she took some of the fruit from the tree and ate it. Her husband was there with her, so she gave him some of the fruit, and he ate it.

⁷Then it was as if their eyes opened, and they saw things differently. They saw that they were naked. So they got some fig leaves, sewed them together and wore them for clothes.

⁸During the cool part of the day, the Lord God was walking in the garden. The man and the woman heard him, and they hid among the trees in the garden. ⁹The Lord God called to the man and said, "Where are you?"

¹⁰The man said, "I heard you walking in the garden, and I was afraid. I was naked, so I hid."

¹¹God said to the man, "Who told you that you were naked? Did you eat fruit from that special tree? I told you not to eat from that tree!"

¹²The man said, "The woman you put here with me gave me fruit from that tree. So I ate it."

¹³Then the Lord God said to the woman, "What have you done?"

She said, "The snake tricked me, so I ate the fruit."

¹⁴So the Lord God said to the snake,

"You did this very bad thing,
  so bad things will happen to you.
It will be worse for you
  than for any other animal.
You must crawl on your belly
  and eat dust all the days of your life.
¹⁵I will make you and the woman enemies to
  each other.
  Your children and her children will be
  enemies.
You will bite her child's foot,
  but he will crush your head."

¹⁶Then God said to the woman,

"I will cause you to have much trouble
  when you are pregnant.
And when you give birth to children,
  you will have much pain.
You will want your husband very much,
  but he will rule over you."ᵃ

¹⁷Then God said to the man,

"I commanded you not to eat from that tree.
  But you listened to your wife and ate from it.
So I will curse the ground because of you.
  You will have to work hard all your life for
  the food the ground produces.
¹⁸The ground will grow thorns and weeds for
  you.
  And you will have to eat the plants that
  grow wild in the fields.ᵇ
¹⁹You will work hard for your food,
  until your face is covered with sweat.
You will work hard until the day you die,
  and then you will become dust again.
I used dust to make you,
  and when you die, you will become dust
  again."

²⁰Adamᶜ named his wife Eve.ᵈ He gave her this name because Eve would be the mother of everyone who ever lived.

²¹The Lord God used animal skins and made some clothes for the man and his wife. Then he put the clothes on them.

²²The Lord God said, "Look, the man has become like us—he knows about good and evil. And now the man might take the fruit from the tree of life. If the man eats that fruit, he will live forever."

ᵃ **3:16 You will . . . over you** Or "You will want to rule your husband, but he will rule over you." In Hebrew this is like the last part of Gen. 4:7.
ᵇ **3:18** See Gen. 1:28–29.
ᶜ **3:20 Adam** This name means "man" or "people". It is like the word meaning "earth" or "red clay".
ᵈ **3:20 Eve** This name is like the Hebrew word meaning "life".

²³So the LORD God forced the man out of the Garden of Eden to work the ground he was made from. ²⁴God forced the man to leave the garden. Then he put Cherub angels and a sword of fire at the entrance to the garden to protect it. The sword flashed around and around, guarding the way to the tree of life.

The First Family

4 Adam's wife Eve became pregnant, and they had a son. Eve said, "With the LORD's help, I have made a child!" So she named him Cain.*ᵃ*

²Eve gave birth again to Cain's brother Abel. Abel became a shepherd, and Cain became a farmer.

The First Murder

³⁻⁴At harvest time,*ᵇ* Cain brought a gift to the LORD. He brought some of the food that he grew from the ground, but Abel brought some animals from his flock. He chose some of his best sheep and brought the best parts from them.*ᶜ*

The LORD accepted Abel and his gift. ⁵But he did not accept Cain and his offering. Cain was sad because of this, and he became very angry. ⁶The LORD asked Cain, "Why are you angry? Why does your face look sad? ⁷You know that if you do what is right, I will accept you. But if you don't, sin is ready to attack you. That sin will want to control you, but you must control it."*ᵈ*

⁸Cain said to his brother Abel, "Let's go out to the field."*ᵉ* So they went to the field. Then Cain attacked his brother Abel and killed him.

⁹Later, the LORD said to Cain, "Where is your brother Abel?"

Cain answered, "I don't know. Is it my job to watch over my brother?"

¹⁰⁻¹¹Then the LORD said, "What have you done? You killed your brother and the ground opened up to take his blood from your hands. Now his blood is shouting to me from the ground. So you will be cursed from this ground. ¹²Now when you work the soil, the ground will not help your plants grow. You will not have a home in this land. You will wander from place to place."

¹³Then Cain said to the LORD, "This punishment is more than I can bear! ¹⁴You are forcing me to leave the land, and I will not be able to be near you or have a home! Now I must wander from place to place, and anyone I meet could kill me."

¹⁵Then the LORD said to Cain, "No, if anyone kills you, I will punish that person much, much more." Then the LORD put a mark on Cain to show that no one should kill him.

Cain's Family

¹⁶Cain went away from the LORD and lived in the land of Nod.*ᶠ*

¹⁷Cain's wife became pregnant, and they had a son named Enoch. Cain built a city and gave the city the same name as his son Enoch.

¹⁸Enoch had a son named Irad. Irad had a son named Mehujael. Mehujael had a son named Methushael. And Methushael had a son named Lamech.

¹⁹Lamech married two women. One wife was named Adah, and the other was named Zillah. ²⁰Adah gave birth to Jabal. Jabal was the father*ᵍ* of people who live in tents and earn their living by keeping cattle. ²¹Jabal was Jubal's brother. Jubal was the father of people who play the harp and flute. ²²Zillah gave birth to Tubal-Cain. Tubal-Cain was the father of people who work with bronze and iron. The sister of Tubal-Cain was named Naamah.

²³Lamech said to his wives,

"Adah and Zillah, hear my voice!
　You wives of Lamech, listen to me.
A man hurt me, so I killed him.
　I even killed a child for hitting me.
²⁴The punishment for killing Cain was very
　　bad.
But the punishment for killing me will be
　　many times worse!"

Adam and Eve Have a New Son

²⁵Adam and his wife Eve had another son. Eve named him Seth. She said, "God has given me another son. Cain killed Abel, but now I have Seth."*ʰ* ²⁶Seth also had a son. He named him Enosh. At that time people began to pray to the LORD.*ⁱ*

ᵃ **4:1** *Cain* This name is like the Hebrew word meaning "make" or "get".
ᵇ **4:3–4** *At harvest time* Literally, "at the end of days".
ᶜ **4:3–4** *He chose . . . from them* Literally, "He brought some of his firstborn sheep, especially their fat."
ᵈ **4:7** *But if you . . . control it* Or "But if you don't do right, sin is crouching at your door. It wants you, but you must rule over it."
ᵉ **4:8** *Let's go . . . field* This sentence is found in the ancient versions but not in the standard Hebrew text.
ᶠ **4:16** *Nod* This name means "wandering".
ᵍ **4:20** *father* This probably means that this man invented these things or was the first one to use them.
ʰ **4:25** *Seth* This is like a Hebrew word meaning "to give".
ⁱ **4:26** *people . . . the LORD* Literally, "people began calling on the name YAHWEH".

The History of Adam's Family

5 This is the history of Adam's[a] family. When God created people, he made them like himself.[b] [2]He created them male and female. And on the same day he made them, he blessed them and called them "humans".[c]

[3]After Adam was 130 years old, he had another son. This son looked just like Adam.[d] Adam named his son Seth. [4]After Seth was born, Adam lived 800 years and had other sons and daughters. [5]So Adam lived a total of 930 years; then he died.

[6]After Seth was 105 years old, he had a son named Enosh. [7]After Enosh was born, Seth lived 807 years and had other sons and daughters. [8]So Seth lived a total of 912 years; then he died.

[9]After Enosh was 90 years old, he had a son named Kenan. [10]After Kenan was born, Enosh lived 815 years and had other sons and daughters. [11]So Enosh lived a total of 905 years; then he died.

[12]After Kenan was 70 years old, he had a son named Mahalalel. [13]After Mahalalel was born, Kenan lived 840 years and had other sons and daughters. [14]So Kenan lived a total of 910 years; then he died.

[15]When Mahalalel was 65 years old, he had a son named Jared. [16]After Jared was born, Mahalalel lived 830 years and had other sons and daughters. [17]So Mahalalel lived a total of 895 years; then he died.

[18]After Jared was 162 years old, he had a son named Enoch. [19]After Enoch was born, Jared lived 800 years and had other sons and daughters. [20]So Jared lived a total of 962 years; then he died.

[21]After Enoch was 65 years old, he had a son named Methuselah. [22]After Methuselah was born, Enoch walked with God for 300 years and had other sons and daughters. [23]So Enoch lived a total of 365 years. [24]One day Enoch was walking with God, and he disappeared. God took him.[e]

[25]After Methuselah was 187 years old, he had a son named Lamech. [26]After Lamech was born, Methuselah lived 782 years and had other sons and daughters. [27]So Methuselah lived a total of 969 years; then he died.

[28]When Lamech was 182 years old, he had a son. [29]Lamech named his son Noah.[f] Lamech said, "We work very hard as farmers because God cursed the ground. But Noah will bring us rest."

[30]After Noah was born, Lamech lived 595 years and had other sons and daughters. [31]So Lamech lived a total of 777 years; then he died.

[32]After Noah was 500 years old, he had sons named Shem, Ham and Japheth.

People Become Evil

6 The number of people on earth continued to increase. When these people had daughters, [2]the sons of God saw how beautiful they were. So they chose the women they wanted. They married them, and the women had their children.

[3]Then the LORD said, "People are only human. I will not let my Spirit be troubled by them forever. I will let them live only 120 years."[g]

[4]During this time and also later, the Nephilim people lived in the land. They have been famous as powerful soldiers since ancient times.

[5]The LORD saw that the people on the earth were very evil. He saw that they thought only about evil things all the time. [6]The LORD was sorry that he had made people on the earth. It made him very sad in his heart. [7]So the LORD said, "I will destroy all the people I created on the earth. I will destroy every person and every animal and everything that crawls on the earth. And I will destroy all the birds in the air, because I am sorry that I have made them."

[8]But Noah pleased the LORD.

Noah and the Great Flood

[9]This is the history of Noah's family. He was a good man all his life, and he always followed God. [10]Noah had three sons: Shem, Ham and Japheth.

[11–12]When God looked at the earth, he saw that people had ruined it. Violence was everywhere, and it had ruined their life on earth.

[13]So God said to Noah, "Everyone has filled the earth with anger and violence. So I will destroy all living things. I will remove them from the earth. [14]Use cypress wood[h] and build a boat for yourself. Make rooms in the boat and cover it with tar inside and out.

[15]"This is the size I want you to make the boat: 133 metres[i] long, 22 metres wide and 13 metres

---

[a] **5:1 Adam** This name means "man" or "people". It is like the word meaning "earth" or "red clay".
[b] **5:1 When God . . . like himself** Literally, "He made him in the image of God." See Gen. 1:27; 5:3.
[c] **5:2 humans** The Hebrew word means "Adam", "man" or "people".
[d] **5:3 he had . . . like Adam** Or "he fathered a son in his image and likeness". In Hebrew this is like Gen. 1:27; 5:1.
[e] **5:24** Or "Enoch pleased God. Enoch disappeared. God took him."
[f] **5:29 Noah** This name is like the Hebrew word meaning "to rest", "to be sorry" or "comfort".
[g] **6:1–4 People . . . 120 years** Or "The spirit from me will not live in people forever, because they are flesh. They will live only 120 years." Or "My Spirit will not judge people forever, because they will all die in 120 years."
[h] **6:14 cypress wood** In Hebrew, "gopher timbers". It is uncertain what kind of wood this is. It might be a kind of tree or squared timbers.
[i] **6:15 133 metres** Literally, "300 cubits".

high. [16]Make a window for the boat about half a metre below the roof. Put a door in the side of the boat. Make three floors in the boat: a top deck, a middle deck and a lower deck.

[17]"Understand what I am telling you. I will bring a great flood of water on the earth. I will destroy all living things that live under heaven. Everything on the earth will die. [18]I will make a special agreement with you. You, your wife, your sons and their wives will all go into the boat. [19]Also, you will take two of every living thing on the earth with you into the boat. Take a male and female of every kind of animal so that they might survive with you. [20]Two of every kind of bird, animal and creeping thing will come to you so that you might keep them alive. [21]Also bring every kind of food into the boat, for you and for the animals."

[22]Noah did everything God commanded him.

The Flood Begins

7 Then the LORD said to Noah, "I have seen that you are a good man, even among the evil people of this time. So gather your family, and go inside the boat. [2]Get seven pairs (seven males and seven females) of every kind of clean animal. And get one pair (one male and one female) of every other animal on the earth. Lead all these animals into the boat with you. [3]Get seven pairs (seven males and seven females) of all the birds. This will allow all these animals to continue living on the earth after the other animals are destroyed. [4]Seven days from now, I will send much rain on the earth. It will rain for 40 days and 40 nights, and I will wipe everything off the face of the earth. I will destroy everything I made." [5]Noah did everything the LORD told him to do.

[6]Noah was 600 years old at the time the rains came. [7]He and his family went into the boat to be saved from the flood. His wife and his sons and their wives were on the boat with him. [8]All the clean animals, all the other animals on the earth, the birds and everything that crawls on the earth [9]went into the boat with Noah. These animals went into the boat in groups of two, male and female, just as God commanded. [10]Seven days later the flood started. The rain began to fall on the earth.

[11-13]On the seventeenth day of the second month, when Noah was 600 years old, the springs under the earth broke through the ground, and water flowed out everywhere. The sky also opened like windows and rain poured down. The rain fell on the earth for 40 days and 40 nights. That same day Noah went into the boat with his wife, his sons Shem, Ham and Japheth and their wives. [14]They and every kind of animal on the earth were in the boat. Every kind of cattle, every kind of animal that crawls on the earth and every kind of bird were in the boat. [15]All these animals went into the boat with Noah. They came in groups of two from every kind of animal that had the breath of life. [16]All these animals went into the boat in groups of two, just as God had commanded Noah. Then the LORD closed the door behind Noah.

[17]Water flooded the earth for 40 days. The water began rising and lifted the boat off the ground. [18]The water continued to rise, and the boat floated on the water high above the earth. [19]The water rose so much that even the highest mountains were covered by the water. [20]The water continued to rise above the mountains. The water was about seven metres[a] above the highest mountain.

[21-22]Every living thing on earth died—every man and woman, every bird and every kind of animal. All the many kinds of animals and all the things that crawl on the ground died. Every living, breathing thing on dry land died. [23]In this way God wiped the earth clean—he destroyed every living thing on the earth—every human, every animal, everything that crawls and every bird. All that was left was Noah and his family and the animals that were with him in the boat. [24]The water continued to cover the earth for 150 days.

The Flood Ends

8 But God did not forget about Noah. God remembered him and all the animals that were with him in the boat. God made a wind blow over the earth, and all the water began to disappear.

[2]Rain stopped falling from the sky, and water stopped flowing from under the earth. [3-4]The water that covered the earth began to go down. After 150 days the water was low enough that the boat touched land again. The boat stopped on one of the mountains of Ararat. This was the seventeenth day of the seventh month. [5]The water continued to go down, and by the first day of the tenth month, the tops of the mountains were above the water.

[6]Forty days later Noah opened the window he had made in the boat. [7]Then he sent out a raven. The raven flew from place to place until the ground was dry and the water had gone. [8]Noah also sent out a dove. He wanted it to find dry ground. He wanted to know if water still covered the earth.

---

[a] 7:20 *about seven metres* Literally, "15 *cubits*".

INSIGHT

Most doves (unlike pigeons) do not have a homing instinct. When let out of a cage, they are unlikely to return unless there is no other source of food. This helps explain the actions of the dove Noah sent out from the ark. At first it returned with an olive leaf, but when the waters finally dried up the dove didn't return to him.

Genesis 8:8–12

⁹The dove could not find a place to rest because water still covered the earth, so the dove came back to the boat. Noah reached out his hand and caught the dove and brought it back into the boat. ¹⁰After seven days Noah again sent out the dove. ¹¹And that afternoon the dove came back to Noah. The dove had a fresh olive leaf in its mouth. This was a sign to show Noah that there was dry ground on the earth. ¹²Seven days later Noah sent the dove out again. But this time the dove didn't come back.

¹³After that, Noah opened the door*ᵃ* of the boat. He looked and saw that the ground was dry. This was the first day of the first month of the year. He was 601 years old. ¹⁴By the twenty-seventh day of the second month, the ground was completely dry.

¹⁵Then God said to Noah, ¹⁶"Leave the boat. You, your wife, your sons and your sons' wives should go out now. ¹⁷Bring every living animal out of the boat with you—all the birds, animals and everything that crawls on the earth. These animals will make many more animals, and they will fill the earth again."

¹⁸So Noah went out with his sons, his wife and his sons' wives. ¹⁹All the animals, everything that crawls and every bird left the boat. All the animals came out of the boat in family groups.

²⁰Then Noah built an altar to honour the LORD. Noah took some of all the clean birds and some of all the clean animals and burned them on the altar as a gift to God.

²¹The LORD smelled these sacrifices, and it pleased him. The LORD said to himself, "I will never again curse the earth as a way to punish people. People are evil from the time they are young, but I will never again destroy every living thing on the earth as I did this time. ²²As long as the earth continues, there will always be a time for planting and a time for harvest. There will always be cold and hot, summer and winter, day and night on earth."

The New Beginning

9 God blessed Noah and his sons and said to them, "Have many children. Fill the earth with your people. ²Every animal on earth, every bird in the air, every animal that crawls on the ground and every fish in the sea will be afraid of you. All of them will be under your control. ³In the past, I gave you the green plants to eat. Now every animal will also be food for you. I give you everything on earth—it is yours. ⁴But I give you one command. You must not eat meat that still has its life (blood) in it. ⁵Also, I will demand your blood for your lives. That is, I will demand the life of any person or animal that takes a human life.

⁶"God made humans to be like himself.
    So whoever kills a person must be killed by
        another person.

⁷"Have many children and fill the earth with your people."

⁸Then God said to Noah and his sons, ⁹"I now make my promise to you and to your people who will live after you. ¹⁰I make my promise to all the birds, and to all the cattle, and to all the animals that came out of the boat with you. I make my promise to every living thing on earth. ¹¹This is my promise to you: All life on the earth was destroyed by the flood. But that will never happen again. A flood will never again destroy all life on the earth."

¹²And God said, "I will give you something to prove that I made this promise to you. It will continue forever to show that I have made an agreement with you and every living thing on earth. ¹³I am putting a rainbow in the clouds as proof of the agreement between me and the earth. ¹⁴When I bring clouds over the earth, you will see the rainbow in the clouds. ¹⁵When I see this rainbow, I will remember the agreement between me and you and every living thing on the earth. This agreement says that a flood will never again destroy all life on the earth. ¹⁶When I look and see the rainbow in the clouds, I will remember the agreement that continues forever. I will remember the agreement between me and every living thing on the earth."

¹⁷So God said to Noah, "This rainbow is proof of the agreement that I made with all living things on earth."

ᵃ **8:13 opened the door** Literally, "removed the covering".

INSIGHT

The original word for rainbow used here comes from the word meaning "bow" as in "bow and arrow". When God made his agreement with humankind and promised never to destroy the earth with water again, he literally laid down his "bow" of judgement – the rainbow!

Genesis 9:13–17

Problems Begin Again

18Noah's sons came out of the boat with him. Their names were Shem, Ham and Japheth. (Ham was the father of Canaan.) 19These three men were Noah's sons. And all the people on earth came from these three sons.

20Noah became a farmer and planted a vineyard. 21One day Noah made some wine. He got drunk, went into his tent and took off all his clothes. 22Ham, the father of Canaan, saw that his father was naked and told his brothers who were outside the tent. 23Shem and Japheth took a robe, put it across their shoulders and walked backwards into the tent. Then they covered their father without looking at him.

24Later, Noah woke up. (He was sleeping because of the wine.) When he learned what his youngest son Ham had done to him, 25he said,

"May there be a curse on Canaan!a
　May he be a slave to his brothers."

26Noah also said,

"May the LORD, the God of Shem, be praised!
　May Canaan be Shem's slave.
27May God give more land to Japheth.
　May God live in Shem's tents,
　and may Canaan be their slave."

28After the flood Noah lived 350 years. 29He lived a total of 950 years; then he died.

Nations Grow and Spread

10 This is the history of the families of Shem, Ham and Japheth. They are Noah's sons. These men had children after the flood.

Japheth's Descendants

2Japheth's sons were Gomer, Magog, Madai, Javan, Tubal, Meshech and Tiras.
3Gomer's sons were Ashkenaz, Riphath and Togarmah.
4Javan's sons were Elishah, Tarshish, Kittim and Dodanim.b

5All the people who lived in the area around the Mediterranean Sea came from these sons of Japheth. The people separated and went to different countries according to languages, families and nations.

Ham's Descendants

6Ham's sons were Cush,c Mizraim,d Put and Canaan.
7Cush's sons were Seba, Havilah, Sabtah, Raamah and Sabteca.
Raamah's sons were Sheba and Dedan.

8Cush also had a son named Nimrod who became a very powerful man on earth. 9He was a great hunter before the LORD. That is why people compare other men to him and say, "That man is like Nimrod, a great hunter before the LORD."

10Nimrod's kingdom spread from Babylon to Erech, to Akkad and then to Calneh in the land of Babylonia.e 11Nimrod also went into Assyria. In Assyria, Nimrod built the cities of Nineveh, Rehoboth Ir, Calah and 12Resen. (Resen is the city between Nineveh and Calah, the big city.)

13Mizraim was the father of the people of Lud, Anam, Lehab, Naphtuh, 14Pathrus, Casluh and Caphtor. (The Philistine people came from Casluh.)
15Canaan was the father of Sidon. Sidon was Canaan's first son. Canaan was also the father of the Hittites, 16Jebusites, Amorites, Girgashites, 17Hivites, Arkites, the Sinites, 18Arvadites, Zemarites and Hamathites.

The families of Canaan spread to different parts of the world. 19The land where the Canaanites lived went from Sidon down along the coast to Gerar and from Gaza as far east as Sodom and Gomorrah and from Admah and Zeboiim as far north as Laish.
20All these people were descendants of Ham. They are arranged by families, languages, countries and nations.

---

a 9:25 **Canaan** Ham's son. The people of Canaan lived along the coast of Palestine, Lebanon and Syria. Later, God gave this land to the Israelites.
b 10:4 **Dodanim** Or "Rodanim, the people of Rhodes."
c 10:6 **Cush** Another name for Ethiopia.
d 10:6 **Mizraim** Another name for Egypt. Also in verse 13.
e 10:10 **Babylonia** Literally, "Shinar", which may be a form of the name Sumer. Also in 11:2; 14:1.

Shem's Descendants

21Shem was Japheth's older brother. One of Shem's descendants was Eber, the father of all the Hebrew people.*a*

22Shem's sons were Elam, Asshur, Arphaxad, Lud and Aram.
23Aram's sons were Uz, Hul, Gether and Mash.
24Arphaxad was the father of Shelah.
Shelah was the father of Eber.
25Eber was the father of two sons. One son was named Peleg.*b* He was given this name because the earth was divided during his life. The other son was named Joktan.
26Joktan was the father of Almodad, Sheleph, Hazarmaveth, Jerah, 27Hadoram, Uzal, Diklah, 28Obal, Abimael, Sheba, 29Ophir, Havilah and Jobab. All these people were Joktan's sons. 30They lived in the area between Mesha and the hill country in the East.*c* Mesha was towards the country of Sephar.

31These are the people from the family of Shem. They are arranged by families, languages, countries and nations.
32This is the list of the families from Noah's sons. They are arranged according to their nations. From these families came all the people who spread across the earth after the flood.

The Tower of Babel

11 There was a time when the whole world spoke one language. Everyone used the same words. 2Then people began to move from the East. They found a plain in the land of Babylonia and stayed there to live. 3Then they said to each other, "Let's make some bricks of clay and bake them in the fire." Then they used these bricks as stones, and they used tar as mortar.
4Then the people said, "Let's build ourselves a city and a tower that will reach to the sky. Then we will be famous. This will keep us together so that we will not be scattered all over the earth."
5Then the LORD came down to see the city and the tower. 6The LORD said, "These people all speak the same language. And I see that they are joined together to do this work. This is only the beginning of what they can do. Soon they will be able to do anything they want. 7Let's go down and confuse their language. Then they will not understand each other."

8So people stopped building the city, and the LORD scattered them all over the earth. 9That is the place where the LORD confused the language of the whole world. That is why it is called Babel.*d* And it was from there that the LORD caused the people to spread out to all the other places on earth.

The History of Shem's Family

10This is the history of Shem's family. Two years after the flood, when Shem was 100 years old, his son Arphaxad was born. 11After that, Shem lived 500 years. He had other sons and daughters.
12When Arphaxad was 35 years old, his son Shelah was born. 13After Shelah was born, Arphaxad lived 403 years. During that time he had other sons and daughters.
14After Shelah was 30 years old, his son Eber was born. 15After Eber was born, Shelah lived 403 years. During that time he had other sons and daughters.
16After Eber was 34 years old, his son Peleg was born. 17After Peleg was born, Eber lived another 430 years. During that time he had other sons and daughters.
18After Peleg was 30 years old, his son Reu was born. 19After Reu was born, Peleg lived another 209 years. During that time he had other sons and daughters.
20After Reu was 32 years old, his son Serug was born. 21After Serug was born, Reu lived another 207 years. During that time he had other sons and daughters.
22After Serug was 30 years old, his son Nahor was born. 23After Nahor was born, Serug lived another 200 years. During that time he had other sons and daughters.
24After Nahor was 29 years old, his son Terah was born. 25After Terah was born, Nahor lived another 119 years. During that time he had other sons and daughters.
26After Terah was 70 years old, his sons Abram, Nahor and Haran were born.

The History of Terah's Family

27This is the history of Terah's family. Terah was the father of Abram, Nahor and Haran. Haran was the father of Lot. 28Haran died in his home town, Ur of Babylonia,*e* while his father Terah was still alive. 29Abram and Nahor both married. Abram's wife was named Sarai. Nahor's wife was named Milcah. Milcah was the daughter of Haran. Haran was the father of Milcah and

---

a **10:21** *One . . . Hebrew people* Literally, "To Shem was born the father of Eber's sons."
b **10:25** *Peleg* This name means "division".
c **10:30** *East* This usually means the area between the Tigris and Euphrates rivers as far east as the Persian Gulf. Also in 11:2.
d **11:9** *Babel* Or "Babylon". This is like a word meaning "confuse".
e **11:28** *Ur of Babylonia* Literally, "Ur of the Chaldeans". A city in southern Babylonia. Also in verse 31.

Iscah. ³⁰Sarai did not have any children because she was not able to have children.

³¹Terah took his family and left Ur of Babylonia. They planned to travel to Canaan. Terah took his son Abram, his grandson Lot (Haran's son) and his daughter-in-law Sarai (Abram's wife). They travelled to the city of Haran and decided to stay there. ³²Terah lived to be 205 years old. He died in Haran.

God Calls Abram

12 The LORD said to Abram, "Leave your country and your people. Leave your father's family and go to the country that I will show you.

²"I will build a great nation from you.
I will bless you
and make your name famous.
People will use your name
to bless other people.
³I will bless those who bless you,
and I will curse those who curse you.
I will use you to bless
all the people on earth."

Abram Goes to Canaan

⁴So Abram left Haran just like the LORD said, and Lot went with him. Abram was 75 years old when he left Haran. ⁵He took his wife Sarai, his nephew Lot, all the slaves and all the other things he had got in Haran. Then he and his group moved to the land of Canaan. ⁶Abram travelled through the land as far as the town of Shechem and then to the big tree at Moreh. The Canaanites were living in the land at that time.

⁷The LORD appeared*ᵃ* to Abram and said, "I will give this land to your descendants."

Abram built an altar to honour the LORD who appeared to him there. ⁸Then he left that place and travelled to the mountains east of Bethel. He set up his tent there. Bethel was to the west, and Ai*ᵇ* was to the east. Abram built another altar at that place to honour the LORD, and he worshipped the LORD there. ⁹Then he moved on towards the Negev, stopping for a time at several places on the way.

Abram in Egypt

¹⁰During this time there was not enough food in the land, so Abram went down to Egypt to live. ¹¹Just before they arrived in Egypt, Abram told Sarai, "Look, I know that you are a very beautiful woman. ¹²When the Egyptian men see you, they will say, 'This woman is his wife.' Then they will kill me and keep you alive because they want you. ¹³So tell them that you are my sister. Then they will be good to me because of you. In this way you will save my life."

¹⁴So when Abram went into Egypt, the Egyptian men saw that Sarai was a very beautiful woman. ¹⁵Even some of Pharaoh's officials noticed her and told Pharaoh how beautiful she was. So they took her to Pharaoh's house. ¹⁶Pharaoh was kind to Abram because he thought Abram was Sarai's brother. He gave Abram sheep, cattle, donkeys, camels and men and women servants.

¹⁷Pharaoh took Abram's wife, so the LORD caused Pharaoh and all the people in his house to have very bad diseases. ¹⁸Pharaoh called Abram and said to him, "You have done a very bad thing to me! Why didn't you tell me Sarai was your wife? ¹⁹You said, 'She is my sister.' Why did you say that? I took her so that she could be my wife, but now I give your wife back to you. Take her and go!" ²⁰Then Pharaoh commanded his men to lead Abram out of Egypt. So Abram and his wife left that place and took everything they had with them.

Abram Returns to Canaan

13 So Abram left Egypt. He travelled through the Negev with his wife and everything he owned. Lot was also with them. ²At this time Abram was very rich. He had many animals and much silver and gold.

³Abram continued travelling around. He left the Negev and went back to Bethel. He went to the place between the city of Bethel and Ai, where he and his family had camped before. ⁴This was where Abram had built an altar earlier. So he worshipped the LORD there.

Abram and Lot Separate

⁵During this time Lot was also travelling with Abram. Lot had many animals and tents. ⁶Abram and Lot had so many animals that the land could not support both of them together. ⁷(The Canaanites and the Perizzites were also living in this land at the same time.) The shepherds of Abram and Lot began to argue.

⁸So Abram said to Lot, "There should be no arguing between you and me or between your people and my people. We are all brothers. ⁹We should separate. You can choose anywhere you want. If you go to the left, I will go to the right. If you go to the right, I will go to the left."

¹⁰Lot looked and saw the whole Jordan Valley. He saw that there was much water there. (This

---

ᵃ **12:7** *The LORD appeared* God often used special shapes so that people could see him. Sometimes he was like a man, an angel, a fire or a bright light.
ᵇ **12:8** *Ai* The name of this town means "the ruins". Also in 13:3.

PROMISES, PROMISES, PROMISES

Do you ever make promises to people? Are they easy to keep? What sorts of promises do you think God makes? Sometimes God's promises are surprising but he always keeps them. In Genesis chapters 3 – 11 people seem to be sinning more and following God less. What will happen to them? What will God do about the situation? Will they ever live in a proper relationship with him?

DIG IN

READ Genesis 12:1–9 and 17:1–8

- God makes some promises to Abram in these passages. Can you spot what they are? (Clue: there are three main ones!)

This is all so strange! God speaks to a random guy living in a random place and makes some seemingly odd promises.

READ Genesis 12:2 and 17:4–8

- What would the people become?
- Who would they belong to?
- What land will God give them?
- Why do you think God changed Abram's name?

God promises that Abram's family will become a great nation and that they would belong to God. At this point Abram's wife could not have children – it was going to take a lot for Abram to believe this one! It's interesting to see that God changed Abram's name to Abraham, which means "father of many" (17:4–7).

By giving his people the land of Canaan God would make it obvious that he was blessing his people. Bear this in mind – it's going to come up again later in the Bible!

READ Genesis 12:3

This is an exciting promise – a promise of blessings. God is promising that just as when Adam and Eve ate the fruit sadness and death entered the world, so through Abram he is beginning to undo the effects of what sin has done. It's exciting because the rest of the Bible shows how God does this.

- Check out Genesis 15:6. Why did God choose Abram? Was there anything special about him?
- Do you think it would have been easy for Abram to believe God's promises?

There was nothing special about Abram but God wanted to show his undeserved love, kindness and generosity to the people. God accepted Abram not because he was particularly good but because he believed (had faith) in God's promises (even the one about being a nation, although he had no children). This is good news and it is the same for us too!

DIG THROUGH

- Why not thank God that he wants people to be his even though, like Adam and Eve, we may sometimes want to run from him (Genesis 3:8).
- Do you find it hard to believe that what God says is true? Just as Abraham believed God, why not ask God to help you to trust him.

DIG DEEPER

- Read more of Genesis and why not write down every time you see God keeping the promises he made to Abraham.
- Read the stories of Isaac (Genesis chapters 22 – 27, particularly chapter 26) and Jacob (Genesis 28, particularly verses 10–17) and see if you can spot God making the same promises.

was before the LORD destroyed Sodom and Gomorrah. At that time the Jordan Valley all the way to Zoar was like the LORD's Garden. This was good land, like the land of Egypt.) ¹¹So Lot chose to live in the Jordan Valley. The two men separated, and Lot began travelling east. ¹²Abram stayed in the land of Canaan, and Lot lived among the cities in the valley. Lot moved as far as Sodom and made his camp there. ¹³The LORD knew that the people of Sodom were very evil.

¹⁴After Lot left, the LORD said to Abram, "Look around you. Look north, south, east, west. ¹⁵All this land that you see I will give to you and your people who live after you. This will be your land forever. ¹⁶I will make your people so many that they will be like the dust of the earth. If people could count all the particles of dust on earth, they could count your people. ¹⁷So go. Walk through your land. I now give it to you."

¹⁸So Abram moved his tents. He went to live near the big trees of Mamre. This was near the city of Hebron. There he built an altar to honour the LORD.

Lot Is Captured

14 Amraphel was the king of Babylonia, Arioch was the king of Ellasar, Kedorlaomer was the king of Elam and Tidal was the king of Goiim. ²All these kings fought a war against King Bera of Sodom, King Birsha of Gomorrah, King Shinab of Admah, King Shemeber of Zeboiim and the king of Bela. (Bela is also called Zoar.) ³All these kings joined their armies in the Valley of Siddim. (The Valley of Siddim is now the Salt Sea.) ⁴These kings had served Kedorlaomer for twelve years. But in the thirteenth year, they all rebelled against him. ⁵So in the fourteenth year, King Kedorlaomer and the kings with him came to fight against them. Kedorlaomer and the kings with him defeated the Rephaites in Ashteroth Karnaim. They also defeated the Zuzites in Ham. They defeated the Emites in Shaveh Kiriathaim. ⁶And they defeated the Horites who lived in the area from the hill country of Seir*ᵃ* to El Paran.*ᵇ* (El Paran is near the desert.) ⁷Then King Kedorlaomer turned back, went to En Mishpat (that is, Kadesh), and defeated the Amalekites. He also defeated the Amorites living in Hazazon Tamar.

⁸At that time the kings of Sodom, Gomorrah, Admah, Zeboiim and Bela (Zoar) joined together to fight against their enemies in the Valley of Siddim.*ᶜ* ⁹They fought against King Kedorlaomer of Elam, King Tidal of Goiim, King Amraphel of Babylonia and King Arioch of Ellasar. So there were four kings fighting against five.

¹⁰There were many holes filled with tar in the Valley of Siddim. When the kings of Sodom and Gomorrah and their armies ran away, some of the soldiers fell into these holes, but the others ran away to the mountains.

¹¹So Kedorlaomer and his armies took everything that the people of Sodom and Gomorrah owned. They took all their food and clothing and left. ¹²Lot, the son of Abram's brother, was living in Sodom, and they captured him. They also took everything he owned and left. ¹³One of the men who had escaped went to Abram the Hebrew and told him what happened. Abram was camped near the trees of Mamre the Amorite. Mamre, Eshcol and Aner*ᵈ* had made an agreement to help each other, and they had also signed an agreement to help Abram.

Abram Rescues Lot

¹⁴When Abram learned that Lot had been captured, he called together 318 trained soldiers. He led the men and chased the enemy all the way to the town of Dan. ¹⁵That night he and his men made a surprise attack against the enemy. They defeated them and chased them to Hobah, north of Damascus. ¹⁶Then Abram brought back everything the enemy had stolen, as well as the women and servants, his nephew Lot and everything Lot owned.

¹⁷Then Abram went home after he had defeated Kedorlaomer and the kings with him. On his way home, the king of Sodom went out to meet him in the Valley of Shaveh. (This is now called King's Valley.)

Melchizedek

¹⁸Melchizedek, the king of Salem and a priest of God Most High, also went to meet Abram. He brought bread and wine. ¹⁹He blessed Abram and said,

"Abram, may you be blessed by God Most
   High,
   the one who made heaven and earth.
²⁰And we praise God Most High,
   who helped you defeat your enemies."

Abram gave Melchizedek one-tenth of everything he had taken during the battle. ²¹Then the

---

ᵃ **14:6** *Seir* Or "Edom".
ᵇ **14:6** *El Paran* Probably the town Elath, at the southern tip of Israel near the Red Sea.
ᶜ **14:8** *Valley of Siddim* The valley or plain along the eastern or south-eastern side of the Dead Sea.
ᵈ **14:13** *Mamre . . . Aner* Literally, "Mamre . . . was a brother of Eshcol and a brother of Aner."

king of Sodom told Abram, "Give me my people who were captured. But you can keep everything else."

²²But Abram said to the king of Sodom, "I make this promise to the LORD, the God Most High, the one who made heaven and earth. ²³I promise that I will not keep anything that is yours—not even a thread or a sandal strap! I don't want you to say, 'I made Abram rich.' ²⁴The only thing I will accept is the food that my young men have eaten, but you should give the other men their share. Take what we won in battle and give some to Aner, Eshcol and Mamre. These men helped me in the battle."

God's Agreement With Abram

15 After all these things happened, the word of the LORD came to Abram in a vision. God said, "Abram, don't be afraid. I will defend you and give you a great reward."

²But Abram said, "Lord GOD, there is nothing you can give me that will make me happy, because I have no son. My slave Eliezer from Damascus will get everything I own after I die." ³Abram said, "You have given me no son, so a slave born in my house will get everything I have."

⁴Then the LORD spoke to Abram and said, "That slave will not be the one to get what you have. You will have a son who will get everything you own."

⁵Then God led Abram outside and said, "Look at the sky. See the many stars. There are so many you cannot count them. Your family will be like that."

⁶Abram believed the LORD, and because of this faith the Lord accepted him as one who has done what is right. ⁷He said to Abram, "I am the LORD who led you from Ur of Babylonia.ᵃ I did this so that I could give you this land. You will own this land."

⁸But Abram said, "Lord GOD, how can I be sure that I will get this land?"

⁹God said to Abram, "We will make an agreement. Bring me a three-year-old cow, a three-year-old goat, a three-year-old ram, a dove and a young pigeon."

¹⁰Abram brought all these to God. Abram killed these animals and cut each of them into two pieces. Then he laid each half opposite the other half. He did not cut the birds into two pieces.

¹¹Later, large birds flew down to eat the animals, but Abram chased them away.

¹²The sun began to go down and Abram got very sleepy. While he was asleep, a very terrible darkness came over him. ¹³Then the Lord said to Abram, "You should know this: Your descendants will live in a country that is not their own. They will be strangers there. The people there will make them slaves and be cruel to them for 400 years. ¹⁴But then I will punish the nation that made them slaves. Your people will leave that land, and they will take many good things with them.

¹⁵"You yourself will live to be very old. You will die in peace and will be buried with your family. ¹⁶After four generations your people will come to this land again and defeat the Amorites. That will happen in the future because the Amorites are not yet guilty enough to lose their land."

¹⁷After the sun went down, it got very dark. The dead animals were still on the ground, each animal cut into two pieces. Then a smoking firepotᵇ and a flaming torch passed between the halves of the dead animals.ᶜ

¹⁸So on that day the LORD made a promise and an agreement with Abram. He said, "I will give this land to your descendants. I will give them the land between the river of Egyptᵈ and the great river Euphrates. ¹⁹This is the land of the Kenites, Kenizzites, Kadmonites, ²⁰Hittites, Perizzites, Rephaites, ²¹Amorites, Canaanites, Girgashites and Jebusites."

Hagar the Servant Girl

16 Sarai was Abram's wife, but she did not have any children. She had an Egyptian slave named Hagar. ²Sarai told Abram, "The LORD has not allowed me to have children, so sleep with my slave. Maybe she can have a son, and I will accept him as my own." Abram did what Sarai said.

³So after living ten years in the land of Canaan, Sarai gave her Egyptian slave to Abram as a second wife. ⁴Abram slept with Hagar, and she became pregnant. When Hagar realized this, she became very proud and began to feel that she was better than Sarai her owner. ⁵Then Sarai said to Abram, "My slave girl now hates me, and I blame you for this. I gave her to you, and she became pregnant. Then she began to feel that she is better than I am. I want the LORD to judge which of us is right."

ᵃ **15:7** *Ur of Babylonia* Literally, "Ur of the Chaldeans". A city in southern Babylonia.
ᵇ **15:17** *firepot* A clay pot in which burning coals were placed to be used for starting new fires.
ᶜ **15:17** *passed between . . . animals* This showed that God "signed" or "sealed" the agreement he made with Abram. People showed that they were sincere in making an agreement by walking between the parts of animals that had been cut into pieces and saying something like, "May this same thing happen to me if I don't keep the agreement."
ᵈ **15:18** *river of Egypt* That is, the stream called "Wadi El-Arish".

⁶But Abram said to Sarai, "She is your slave. You can do anything you want to her." So Sarai was cruel to Hagar, and Hagar ran away.

Hagar's Son Ishmael

⁷The angel of the LORD found Hagar near a spring of water in the desert. The spring was by the road to Shur. ⁸The angel said, "Hagar, Sarai's slave girl, why are you here? Where are you going?"

Hagar said, "I am running away from Sarai."

⁹The angel of the LORD said to her, "Sarai is your owner. Go home to her and obey her." ¹⁰The angel of the LORD also said, "From you will come many people—too many people to count."

¹¹Then the angel of the LORD said,

"Hagar, you are now pregnant,
    and you will have a son.
You will name him Ishmael,ᵃ
    because the LORD has heard your crying.
¹²Ishmael will be wild and free
    like a wild donkey.
He will be against everyone,
    and everyone will be against him.
He will move from place to place
    and camp near his brothers."

¹³The LORD talked to Hagar. She began to use a new name for God. She said to him, "You are 'God Who Sees Me'." She said this because she thought, "I see that even in this place God sees me and cares for me!" ¹⁴So the well there was called Beer Lahai Roi.ᵇ It is between Kadesh and Bered.

¹⁵Hagar gave birth to Abram's son, and Abram named the son Ishmael. ¹⁶Abram was 86 years old when Ishmael was born from Hagar.

Circumcision—Proof of the Agreement

17 When Abram was 99 years old, the LORD appeared to him. He said, "I am God All-Powerful.ᶜ Obey me and live the right way. ²If you do this, I will prepare an agreement between us. I will promise to make your people a great nation."

³Then Abram bowed down before God. God said to him, ⁴"This is my part of our agreement: I will make you the father of many nations. ⁵I will change your name from Abramᵈ to Abraham,ᵉ because I am making you the father of many nations. ⁶I will give you many descendants. New nations and kings will come from you. ⁷And I will prepare an agreement between me and you. This agreement will also be for all your descendants. It will continue forever. I will be your God and the God of all your descendants. ⁸And I will give this land to you and to all your descendants. I will give you the land you are travelling through—the land of Canaan. I will give you this land forever, and I will be your God."

⁹Then God said to Abraham, "Now, this is your part of the agreement: You and all your descendants will obey my agreement. ¹⁰This is my agreement that you must obey. This is the agreement between me and you and all your descendants. Every male must be circumcised. ¹¹You will cut the skin to show that you follow the agreement between me and you. ¹²When the baby boy is eight days old, you will circumcise him. Every boy born among your people and every boy who is a slave of your people must be circumcised. ¹³So every baby boy in your nation will be circumcised. Every boy who is born from your family or bought as a slave will be circumcised. ¹⁴Abraham, this is the agreement between you and me: Any male who is not circumcised will be cut off from his peopleᶠ because he has broken my agreement."

Isaac—the Promised Son

¹⁵God said to Abraham, "I will give Sarai,ᵍ your wife, a new name. Her new name will be Sarah.ʰ ¹⁶I will bless her. I will give her a son, and

---

ᵃ **16:11 Ishmael** This name means "God hears".
ᵇ **16:14 Beer Lahai Roi** This means "the well of the Living One who sees me".
ᶜ **17:1 God All-Powerful** Literally, "El Shaddai".
ᵈ **17:5 Abram** This name means "honoured father".
ᵉ **17:5 Abraham** This name means "great father" or "father of many".
ᶠ **17:14 cut off from his people** This means he must be separated from his family and lose his share of the inheritance.
ᵍ **17:15 Sarai** A name, probably Aramaic, meaning "princess".
ʰ **17:15 Sarah** A Hebrew name meaning "princess".

you will be the father. She will be the mother of many new nations. Kings of nations will come from her."

¹⁷Abraham bowed his face to the ground to show he respected God. But he laughed and said to himself, "I am 100 years old. I cannot have a son, and Sarah is 90 years old. She cannot have a child."

¹⁸Then Abraham said to God, "I hope Ishmael will live and serve you."

¹⁹God said, "No, I said that your wife Sarah will have a son. You will name him Isaac.*ᵃ* I will make my agreement with him that will continue forever with all his descendants.

²⁰"You mentioned Ishmael, and I heard you. I will bless him, and he will have many children. He will be the father of twelve great leaders. His family will become a great nation. ²¹But I will make my agreement with Isaac, the son who Sarah will have. He will be born at this same time next year."

²²After God finished talking with Abraham, God went up into heaven. ²³Then Abraham gathered together Ishmael and all the slaves born in his house. He also gathered all the slaves he had bought. Every man and boy in Abraham's house was gathered together, and they were all circumcised. Abraham circumcised them that day, just as God had told him to do.

²⁴Abraham was 99 years old when he was circumcised. ²⁵And Ishmael, his son, was 13 years old when he was circumcised. ²⁶Abraham and his son were circumcised on the same day. ²⁷Also, on that day all the men in Abraham's house were circumcised. All the slaves born in his house and all the slaves he had bought were circumcised.

The Three Visitors

18 Later, the Lᴏʀᴅ again appeared to Abraham near the oak trees of Mamre. It was the hottest part of the day, and Abraham was sitting at the door of his tent. ²He looked up and saw three men standing in front of him. When he saw the men, he ran to them and bowed before them. ³Abraham said, "Sirs,*ᵇ* please stay a while with me, your servant. ⁴I will bring some water to wash your feet. You can rest under the trees. ⁵I will get some food for you, and you can eat as much as you want. Then you can continue your journey."

The three men said, "Do as you wish."

⁶Abraham hurried to the tent. He said to Sarah, "Quickly, prepare enough flour for three loaves of bread." ⁷Then Abraham ran to his cattle. He took his best young calf and gave it to the servant

there. He told the servant to quickly kill the calf and prepare it for food. ⁸Abraham brought the meat and some milk and cheese and set them down in front of the three men. Then he stood near the men, ready to serve them while they sat under the tree and ate.

⁹Then the men said to Abraham, "Where is your wife Sarah?"

Abraham said, "She is there, in the tent."

¹⁰Then one of them said, "I will come again in the spring. At that time your wife Sarah will have a son."

Sarah was listening in the tent and heard these things. ¹¹Abraham and Sarah were very old. Sarah was past the right age for women to have children. ¹²So she laughed to herself and said, "I am old, and my husband is old. I am too old to have a baby."

¹³Then the Lᴏʀᴅ said to Abraham, "Sarah laughed and said she was too old to have a baby. ¹⁴But is anything too hard for the Lᴏʀᴅ? I will come again in the spring, just as I said I would, and your wife Sarah will have a son."

¹⁵Sarah said, "I didn't laugh!" (She said this because she was afraid.)

Then the Lord said, "No, I know that is not true. You did laugh!"

¹⁶Then the men got up to leave. They looked towards Sodom and began walking in that direction. Abraham walked with them to send them on their way.

Abraham's Bargain With God

¹⁷The Lᴏʀᴅ said to himself, "Should I tell Abraham what I am going to do now? ¹⁸Abraham will become a great and powerful nation, and all the nations on earth will be blessed because of him. ¹⁹I have made a special agreement with him. I did this so that he would command his children and his descendants to live the way the Lᴏʀᴅ wants them to. I did this so that they would do what is right and be fair. Then I, the Lᴏʀᴅ, can give him what I promised."

²⁰Then the Lᴏʀᴅ said, "I have heard many times that the people of Sodom and Gomorrah are very evil. ²¹I will go and see if they are as bad as I have heard. Then I will know for sure."

²²So the men turned and started walking towards Sodom while Abraham stood there before the Lᴏʀᴅ. ²³Then Abraham approached him and asked, "Will you destroy the good people while you are destroying those who are evil? ²⁴What if there are fifty good people in that city? Will you still destroy it? Surely you will save the city for the fifty good people living there. ²⁵Surely

---

ᵃ **17:19 Isaac** This name means "he laughs" or "he is happy".
ᵇ **18:3 Sirs** This Hebrew word can mean "sirs" or "Lord". This might show that these were not ordinary men.

you would not destroy the city. You would not destroy fifty good people to kill those who are evil. If that happened, those who are good would be the same as those who are evil—both would be punished. As the judge of the whole world, surely you would do the right thing!"

²⁶Then the LORD said, "If I find fifty good people in the city of Sodom, I will save the whole city."

²⁷Then Abraham said, "Compared to you, Lord, I am only dust and ashes. But let me bother you again and ask you this question. ²⁸What if there are five less than fifty? Will you destroy a whole city because of just five people?"

The Lord said, "If I find forty-five good people there, I will not destroy the city."

²⁹Abraham spoke again. He said, "And if you find only forty good people there, will you destroy the city?"

The Lord said, "If I find forty good people, I will not destroy the city."

³⁰Then Abraham said, "Lord, please don't be angry with me, but let me ask you this. If only thirty good people are in the city, will you destroy it?"

The Lord said, "If I find thirty good people there, I will not destroy the city."

³¹Then Abraham said, "Lord, may I bother you again and ask, what if there are twenty good people?"

The Lord answered, "If I find twenty good people, I will not destroy the city."

³²Then Abraham said, "Lord, please don't be angry with me, but let me bother you this one last time. If you find ten good people there, what will you do?"

The Lord said, "If I find ten good people in the city, I will not destroy it."

³³The LORD finished speaking to Abraham and left. Then Abraham went back home.

Lot's Visitors

19 That evening the two angels came to the city of Sodom. Lot was sitting near the city gates and saw them. He got up and went to them. He bowed to show respect and said, ²"Sirs, please come to my house, and I will serve you. There you can wash your feet and stay the night. Then tomorrow you can continue your journey."

The angels answered, "No, we will stay the night in the city square."

³But Lot continued to ask them to come to his house, so they agreed and went with him. Lot gave them something to drink. He baked some bread for them, and they ate it.

⁴That evening, just before bedtime, men from every part of town came to Lot's house. They stood around the house and called to Lot. They said, ⁵"Where are the two men who came to you tonight? Bring them out to us. We want to have sex with them."

⁶Lot went outside and closed the door behind him. ⁷He said to the men, "No, my friends, I beg you, please don't do this evil thing! ⁸Look, I have two daughters who have never slept with a man before. I will give my daughters to you. You can do anything you want with them. But please don't do anything to these men. They have come to my house, and I must protect them."^a

⁹The men surrounding the house answered, "Get out of our way!" They said to themselves, "This man Lot came to our city as a visitor. Now he wants to tell us how we should live!" Then the men said to Lot, "We will do worse things to you than to them." So the men started moving closer and closer to Lot. They were about to break down the door.

¹⁰But the two men staying with Lot opened the door, pulled him back inside the house and closed the door. ¹¹Then they did something to the men outside the door—they caused all these evil men, young and old, to become blind. So the men trying to get in the house could not find the door.

The Escape From Sodom

¹²The two men said to Lot, "Are there any other people from your family living in this city? Do you have any sons-in-law, sons, daughters or any other people from your family here? If so, you should tell them to leave now. ¹³We are going to destroy this city. The LORD heard how evil this city is, so he sent us to destroy it."

¹⁴So Lot went out and spoke to his sons-in-law, the men who had married his other daughters. He said, "Hurry and leave this city! The LORD will soon destroy it!" But they thought he was joking.

¹⁵The next morning at dawn, the angels were trying to make Lot hurry. They said, "This city will be punished, so take your wife and your two daughters who are still with you and leave this place. Then you will not be destroyed with the city."

¹⁶When Lot did not move fast enough, the two men grabbed his hand. They also took the hands of his wife and his two daughters. The two men led Lot and his family safely out of the city. The LORD was kind to Lot and his family. ¹⁷So after the two men brought Lot and his family out of the city, one of the men said, "Now run to save your life! Don't look back at the city, and don't stop anywhere in the valley. Run until you are in the mountains. If you stop, you will be destroyed with the city!"

---

^a **19:8 I must protect them** Whoever invited a traveller in as a guest was also promising to protect the traveller.

¹⁸But Lot said to the two men, "Sirs, please don't force me to run so far! ¹⁹You have been very kind to me, your servant. You have been very kind to save me, but I cannot run all the way to the mountains. What if I am too slow and something happens? I will be killed! ²⁰Look, there is a very small town near here. Let me run to that town. I can run there and be safe."

²¹The angel said to Lot, "Very well, I'll let you do that. I will not destroy that town. ²²But run there quickly. I cannot destroy Sodom until you are safely in that town." (That town is named Zoar,^a because it is a small town.)

Sodom and Gomorrah Destroyed

²³Lot was entering the town as the sun came up, ²⁴and the LORD began to destroy Sodom and Gomorrah. He caused fire and burning sulphur to fall from the sky. ²⁵He destroyed the whole valley—all the cities, the people living in the cities and all the plants in the valley.

INSIGHT

When God destroyed the cities of Sodom and Gomorrah he made sure that they could never be rebuilt. Archaeological evidence shows that something happened in the plain around the Dead Sea c.2000 BC, probably an earthquake, which caused the area to become underwater.

Genesis 19:23–29

---

²⁶Lot's wife was following behind him and looked back at the city. When she did, she became a block of salt.

²⁷Early the next morning, Abraham got up and went to the place where he stood before the LORD. ²⁸Abraham looked down into the valley towards the cities of Sodom and Gomorrah. He saw clouds of smoke rising from the land, like smoke from a furnace.

²⁹God destroyed the cities in the valley, but he remembered what Abraham had said. So God sent Lot away from those cities before destroying them.

Lot and His Daughters

³⁰Lot was afraid to stay in Zoar, so he and his two daughters went to live in the mountains in a cave. ³¹One day the older daughter said to the younger, "Everywhere on the earth, men and women marry and have a family. But our father is old, and there are no men around here to give us children. ³²So let's get our father drunk with wine. Then we can have sex with him. That way we can use our father to keep our family alive!"

³³So that night they gave their father plenty of wine to make him drunk. Then the older daughter went and had sex with him. He did not even know when she came to bed or when she got up.

³⁴The next day the older daughter said to the younger daughter, "Last night I went to bed with my father. Let's get him drunk with wine again tonight. Then you can go and have sex with him. In this way we can use our father to have children, and our family will not come to an end." ³⁵So that night they gave their father enough wine to make him drunk. Then the younger daughter went and had sex with him. Again, Lot did not know when she came to bed or when she got up.

³⁶Both of Lot's daughters became pregnant. Their father was the father of their babies. ³⁷The older daughter gave birth to a son. She named him Moab.^b Moab is the ancestor of all the Moabites living today. ³⁸The younger daughter also gave birth to a son. She named him Ben-Ammi.^c Ben-Ammi is the ancestor of all the Ammonites living today.

Abraham Goes to Gerar

20 Abraham left that place and travelled to the Negev. He settled in the city of Gerar, between Kadesh and Shur. While in Gerar, ²Abraham told people that Sarah was his sister. King Abimelech of Gerar heard this. Abimelech wanted Sarah, so he sent some servants to take her. ³But one night God spoke to Abimelech in a dream and said, "You will die. The woman you took is married."

⁴But Abimelech had not yet slept with Sarah, so he said, "Lord, I am not guilty. Would you kill an innocent man? ⁵Abraham himself told me, 'This woman is my sister,' and she also said, 'This man is my brother.' I am innocent. I did not know what I was doing."

⁶Then God said to Abimelech in a dream, "Yes, I know that you are innocent and that you did not know what you were doing. I saved you. I did not allow you to sin against me. I was the one who did not allow you to sleep with her. ⁷So give Abraham his wife again. He is a prophet. He will pray for you, and you will live. But if you don't

---

^a **19:22** *Zoar* This name means "small".
^b **19:37** *Moab* In Hebrew this name sounds like "from father".
^c **19:38** *Ben-Ammi* In Hebrew this name sounds like "son of my father" or "son of my people".

give Sarah back to him, I promise that you will die. And all your family will die with you."

⁸So very early the next morning, Abimelech called all his servants and told them about the dream. The servants were very afraid. ⁹Then Abimelech called Abraham and said to him, "Why have you done this to us? What wrong did I do to you? Why did you lie and say that she was your sister? You brought great trouble to my kingdom. You should not have done this to me. ¹⁰What were you afraid of? Why did you do this to me?"

¹¹Then Abraham said, "I thought no one in this place respected God. I thought someone would kill me to get Sarah. ¹²She is my wife, but she is also my sister. She is the daughter of my father but not the daughter of my mother. ¹³God led me away from my father's house. He led me to wander to many different places. When that happened, I told Sarah, 'Do something for me. Wherever we go, tell people you are my sister.'"

¹⁴So Abimelech gave Sarah back to Abraham. Abimelech also gave Abraham some sheep, cattle and slaves. ¹⁵And Abimelech said, "Look all around you. This is my land. You may live anywhere you want."

¹⁶Abimelech said to Sarah, "I gave your brother Abraham 1,000 pieces of silver. I did this to show that I am very sorry. I want everyone to see that I did the right thing."

¹⁷⁻¹⁸The LORD made all the women in Abimelech's family not able to have children. God did this because Abimelech had taken Sarah, Abraham's wife. But Abraham prayed to God, and God healed Abimelech, his wife and his servant girls.

Finally, a Baby for Sarah

21 The LORD came back to visit Sarah as he said he would, and he kept his promise to her. ²At exactly the time God said it would happen, Sarah became pregnant and gave birth to a son for Abraham in his old age. ³Abraham named his son Isaac.ᵃ ⁴Abraham did what God commanded and circumcised Isaac when he was eight days old.

⁵Abraham was 100 years old when his son Isaac was born. ⁶Sarah said, "God has made me happy, and everyone who hears about this will be happy with me. ⁷No one thought that I, Sarah, would be able to have Abraham's child. But I have given Abraham a son, even though he is old."

Trouble at Home

⁸Isaac continued to grow, and soon he was old enough to begin eating solid food. So Abraham gave a big party. ⁹Sarah saw Hagar's son playing. (Hagar was the Egyptian slave woman who gave birth to Abraham's first son.) ¹⁰Sarah said to Abraham, "Get rid of that slave woman and her son. Send them away! When we die, our son Isaac will get everything we have. I don't want that slave woman's son sharing these things with my son Isaac!"

¹¹This upset Abraham very much. He was worried about his son Ishmael. ¹²But God said to Abraham, "Don't worry about the boy and the slave woman. Do what Sarah wants. Your descendants will be those who come through Isaac. ¹³But I will also bless the son of your slave woman. He is your son, so I will make a great nation from his family also."

¹⁴Early the next morning Abraham took some food and water and gave them to Hagar. She carried them and left with her boy. She left that place and wandered in the desert of Beersheba.

¹⁵After some time, when all their drinking water was gone, Hagar put her son under a bush. ¹⁶Then she walked a short distance away and sat down. She thought her son would die because there was no water. She did not want to watch him die. She sat there and began to cry.

¹⁷God heard the boy crying, and God's angel called to Hagar from heaven. He said, "What is wrong, Hagar? Don't be afraid! God has heard the boy crying there. ¹⁸Go and help the boy. Hold his hand and lead him. I will make him the father of many people."

¹⁹Then God allowed Hagar to see a well of water. So she went to the well and filled her bag with water. Then she gave water to the boy to drink.

²⁰God continued to be with the boy while he grew up. Ishmael lived in the desert and became a hunter. He learned to shoot a bow very well. ²¹His mother found a wife for him in Egypt. They continued to live in the Paran desert.

Abraham's Bargain With Abimelech

²²Then Abimelech and Phicol spoke with Abraham. Phicol was the commander of Abimelech's army. They said to Abraham, "God is with you in everything you do. ²³So make a promise to me here before God. Promise that you will be fair with me and with my children. Promise that you will be kind to me and this country where you have lived. Promise that you will be as kind to me as I have been to you."

²⁴And Abraham said, "I promise to treat you the same way you have treated me." ²⁵Then Abraham complained to Abimelech because Abimelech's servants had captured a well of water.

ᵃ **21:3 Isaac** This name means "he laughs" or "he is happy".

26But Abimelech said, "I don't know who did this. You did not tell me about this before today!"

27So Abraham and Abimelech made an agreement. Abraham gave Abimelech some sheep and cattle as proof of the agreement. 28Abraham also put seven[a] female lambs in front of Abimelech.

29Abimelech asked Abraham, "Why did you put these seven female lambs by themselves?"

30Abraham answered, "When you accept these lambs from me, it will be proof that I dug this well."

31So after that, the well was called Beersheba.[b] Abraham gave the well this name because it was the place where they made a promise to each other.

32So Abraham and Abimelech made an agreement at Beersheba. Then Abimelech and Phicol, his military commander, went back to the country of the Philistines.

33Abraham planted a special tree at Beersheba and prayed to the LORD, the God who lives forever. 34And Abraham lived as a stranger for a long time in the country of the Philistines.

Abraham, Kill Your Son

22 After these things God decided to test Abraham's faith. God said to him, "Abraham!"

And he said, "Yes!"

2Then God said, "Take your son to the land of Moriah and kill your son there as a sacrifice for me. This must be Isaac, your only son, the one you love. Use him as a burnt offering on one of the mountains there. I will tell you which mountain."

3In the morning Abraham got up and saddled his donkey. He took Isaac and two servants with him. He cut the wood for the sacrifice. Then they went to the place where God told them to go. 4After they had travelled for three days, Abraham looked up, and in the distance he saw the place where they were going. 5Then he said to his servants, "Stay here with the donkey. The boy and I will go to that place and worship. Then we will come back to you later."

6Abraham took the wood for the sacrifice and put it on his son's shoulder. Abraham took the special knife and fire. Then both he and his son went together to the place for worship.

7Isaac said to his father Abraham, "Father!"

Abraham answered, "Yes, son?"

Isaac said, "I see the wood and the fire. But where is the lamb we will burn as a sacrifice?"

8Abraham answered, "God himself is providing the lamb for the sacrifice, my son."

So both Abraham and his son went together to that place. 9When they came to the place where God told them to go, Abraham built an altar. He carefully laid the wood on the altar. Then he tied up his son Isaac and laid him on the altar on top of the wood. 10Then Abraham reached for his knife to kill his son.

11But the angel of the LORD stopped him. The angel called from heaven and said, "Abraham, Abraham!"

Abraham answered, "Yes?"

12The angel said, "Don't kill your son or hurt him in any way. Now I can see that you do respect and obey God. I see that you are ready to kill your son, your only son, for me."

13Then Abraham noticed a ram whose horns were caught in a bush. So Abraham went and took the ram. He offered it, instead of his son, as a sacrifice to God. 14So Abraham gave that place a name, "The LORD Provides".[c] Even today people say, "On the mountain of the LORD, he will give us what we need."[d]

15The angel of the LORD called to Abraham from heaven a second time. 16The angel said, "You were ready to kill your only son for me. Since you did this for me, I make you this promise: I, the LORD, promise that 17I will surely bless you and give you as many descendants as the stars in the sky. There will be as many people as sand on the seashore. And your people will live in cities that they will take from their enemies. 18Every nation on the earth will be blessed through your descendants. I will do this because you obeyed me."

19Then Abraham went back to his servants. They all travelled back to Beersheba, and Abraham stayed there.

20After all these things happened, a message was sent to Abraham. It said, "Your brother Nahor and his wife Milcah have children now. 21The first son is Uz. The second son is Buz. The third son is Kemuel, the father of Aram. 22Then there are Kesed, Hazo, Pildash, Jidlaph and Bethuel." 23Bethuel was the father of Rebekah. Milcah was the mother of these eight sons, and Nahor was the father. Nahor was Abraham's brother. 24Also Nahor had four other sons from his slave woman Reumah. The sons were Tebah, Gaham, Tahash and Maacah.

---

a **21:28** *seven* The Hebrew word for "seven" is like the Hebrew word for "oath" or "promise", and it is like the last part of the name Beersheba. The seven animals were proof of this promise.
b **21:31** *Beersheba* This name means "well of the oath".
c **22:14** *The LORD Provides* Hebrew, "*Yahweh Yireh*", which can mean "the LORD sees" or "the LORD gives".
d **22:14** *On the mountain . . . need* Or "On this mountain the LORD can be seen."

Sarah Dies

23 Sarah lived to be 127 years old. ²She died in the city of Kiriath Arba (Hebron) in the land of Canaan. Abraham was very sad and cried for her there. ³Then he left his dead wife and went to talk to the Hittites. He said, ⁴"I am only a foreigner staying in your country. I have no place to bury my wife. Please give me some land so that I can bury her."

⁵The Hittites answered Abraham, ⁶"Sir, you are a great leader*ᵃ* among us. You can have the best place we have to bury your dead. You can have any of our burying places that you want. None of us will stop you from burying your wife there."

⁷Abraham got up and bowed to the people. ⁸He said to them, "If you really want to help me bury my dead wife, speak to Ephron the son of Zohar for me. ⁹I would like to buy the cave of Machpelah, which belongs to Ephron. It is at the end of his field. I will pay him the full price. I want all of you to be witnesses that I am buying it as a burial place."

¹⁰Ephron was sitting there among the people. He answered Abraham, ¹¹"No, sir. Here in front of my people, I give you that land and the cave on it so that you can bury your wife."

¹²Abraham bowed before the Hittites. ¹³He said to Ephron before all the people, "But I want to give you the full price for the field. Accept my money, and I will bury my dead."

¹⁴Ephron answered Abraham, ¹⁵"Sir, listen to me. 400 pieces of silver mean nothing to you or me. Take the land and bury your dead wife."

¹⁶Abraham understood that Ephron was telling him the price of the land.*ᵇ* So Abraham paid him for the land. He weighed out 400 pieces of silver for Ephron and gave it to the merchant.*ᶜ*

¹⁷⁻¹⁸So the field of Ephron changed owners. This field was in Machpelah, near Mamre. Abraham became the owner of the field, the cave in it and all the trees in the field. Everyone in the city saw the agreement between Ephron and Abraham. ¹⁹After this, Abraham buried his wife Sarah in the cave of that field near Mamre (Hebron) in the land of Canaan. ²⁰Abraham bought the field and the cave in it from the Hittites. So this became his property to be used as a burial place.

A Wife for Isaac

24 Abraham lived to be a very old man. The LORD blessed him and everything he did. ²Abraham's oldest servant was in charge of everything he owned. Abraham called that

servant to him and said, "Put your hand under my leg.*ᵈ* ³Now I want you to make a promise to me. Promise to me before the LORD, the God of heaven and earth, that you will not allow my son to marry a girl from Canaan. We live among these people, but don't let him marry a Canaanite girl. ⁴Go back to my country, to my own people, to find a wife for my son Isaac. Bring her here to him."

⁵The servant said to him, "Maybe this woman will not want to come back with me to this land. If that happens, should I take your son with me to your homeland?"

⁶Abraham said to him, "No, don't take my son to that place. ⁷The LORD, the God of heaven, brought me from my homeland to this place. That place was the home of my father and the home of my family, but he promised that this new land would belong to my family. May he send his angel before you so that you can choose a wife for my son. ⁸If the girl refuses to come with you, you will be free from this promise. But you must not take my son back to that place."

⁹So the servant put his hand under his master's leg and made the promise.

The Search Begins

¹⁰The servant took ten of Abraham's camels and left that place. The servant carried with him many different kinds of beautiful gifts. He went to Mesopotamia, to Nahor's city. ¹¹In the evening, when the women come out to get water, he went to the water well outside the city. He made the camels kneel down at the well.

¹²The servant said, "LORD, you are the God of my master Abraham. Please show your kindness to my master by helping me find a wife for his son Isaac. ¹³Here I am, standing by this well of water, and the young women from the city are coming out to get water. ¹⁴I will say to one of them, 'Please put your jar down so that I can drink.' Let her answer show whether she is the one you have chosen for your servant Isaac. If she says, 'Drink, and I will also give water to your camels,' I will know that she is the right one. It will be proof that you have shown kindness to my master."

A Wife Is Found

¹⁵Before the servant finished praying, a young woman named Rebekah came to the well. She was the daughter of Bethuel. (Bethuel was the son of Milcah and Nahor, Abraham's brother.) Rebekah came to the well with her water jar on

---

ᵃ **23:6 great leader** Literally, "God's prince".
ᵇ **23:16 Abraham understood . . . the land** Literally, "Abraham heard".
ᶜ **23:16 merchant** Someone who earns their living by buying and selling things. Here, this is probably a person who was helping Abraham and Ephron write the contract in verses 17 and 18.
ᵈ **24:2 Put your hand under my leg** This was a sign of a very important promise that Abraham trusted his servant to keep.

her shoulder. ¹⁶She was a very pretty young woman, still a virgin. She went down to the well, filled her jar and went back up towards the city. ¹⁷Then the servant ran to her and said, "Please give me a little water to drink from your jar."

¹⁸Rebekah quickly lowered the jar from her shoulder and gave him a drink. She said, "Drink this, sir." ¹⁹As soon as she finished giving him something to drink, Rebekah said, "I will also pour some water for your camels." ²⁰So Rebekah quickly poured all the water from her jar into the drinking trough for the camels. Then she ran to the well to get more water, and she gave water to all the camels.

²¹The servant quietly watched her. He wanted to be sure that the LORD had given him an answer and had made his trip successful. ²²After the camels finished drinking, he gave Rebekah a small gold ring.ᵃ He also gave her two large gold arm bracelets.ᵇ ²³The servant asked, "Who is your father? And is there a place in your father's house for me and my men to sleep?"

²⁴Rebekah answered, "My father is Bethuel, the son of Milcah and Nahor." ²⁵Then she said, "Yes, we have straw and other food for your camels and a place for you to sleep."

²⁶The servant bowed and worshipped the LORD. ²⁷He said, "Praise be to the LORD, the God of my master Abraham. The LORD has been kind and loyal to him by leading me to his own people."

²⁸Then Rebekah ran and told her family about all these things. ²⁹⁻³⁰She had a brother named Laban. She told him what the man had said to her. Laban was listening to her. And when he saw the ring and the bracelets on his sister's arms, he ran out to the well. There the man was, standing by the camels at the well. ³¹Laban said, "Sir, you are welcome to come in!ᶜ You don't have to stand outside here. I have prepared a room for you to sleep in and a place for your camels."

³²So Abraham's servant went into the house. Laban unloaded his camels and gave them straw and feed. Then he gave Abraham's servant water so that he and the men with him could wash their feet. ³³Laban then gave him food to eat, but the servant refused to eat. He said, "I will not eat until I have told you why I came."

So Laban said, "Then tell us."

Bargaining for Rebekah

³⁴The servant said, "I am Abraham's servant. ³⁵The LORD has greatly blessed my master in everything. My master has become a great man. The Lord has given him many flocks of sheep and herds of cattle. He has much silver and gold and many servants. He has many camels and donkeys. ³⁶Sarah was my master's wife. When she was very old, she gave birth to a son, and my master has given everything he owns to that son. ³⁷My master forced me to make a promise to him. He said to me, 'You must not allow my son to marry a girl from Canaan. We live among these people, but I don't want him to marry one of the Canaanite girls. ³⁸So you must promise to go to my father's country. Go to my family and choose a wife for my son.' ³⁹I said to my master, 'Maybe the woman will not come back to this place with me.' ⁴⁰But my master said to me, 'I serve the LORD, and he will send his angel with you and help you. You will find a wife for my son among my people there. ⁴¹But if you go to my father's country, and they refuse to give you a wife for my son, you will be free from this promise.'

⁴²"Today I came to this well and said, 'LORD, God of my master Abraham, please make my trip successful. ⁴³I will stand by this well and wait for a young woman to come to get water. Then I will say, "Please give me water from your jar to drink." ⁴⁴The right woman will answer in a special way. She will say, "Drink this water, and I will also get water for your camels." That way I will know that she is the one the LORD has chosen for my master's son.'

⁴⁵"Before I finished praying, Rebekah came out to the well to get water. She had her water jar on her shoulder as she went to get water from the well. I asked her to give me some water. ⁴⁶She quickly lowered the jar from her shoulder and poured me some water. Then she said, 'Drink this, and I'll get some water for your camels.' So I drank the water, and she gave water to my camels. ⁴⁷Then I asked her, 'Who is your father?' She answered, 'My father is Bethuel the son of Milcah and Nahor.' Then I gave her the ring and bracelets for her arms. ⁴⁸I bowed my head and worshipped the LORD. I praised the LORD, the God of my master Abraham. I thanked him for leading me straight to the granddaughter of my master's brother. ⁴⁹Now, tell me, will you be kind and loyal to my master and give him your daughter? Or will you refuse to give her to him? Tell me so that I will know what I should do."

⁵⁰Then Laban and Bethuel answered, "We see that this is from the LORD, so there is nothing we can say to change it. ⁵¹Here is Rebekah. Take her and go. Let her marry your master's son. This is what the LORD wants."

⁵²When Abraham's servant heard this, he bowed to the ground before the LORD. ⁵³Then he

---

ᵃ **24:22 a small gold ring** Literally, "a gold ring weighing 1 *beka*".
ᵇ **24:22 large gold arm bracelets** Literally, "arm bracelets weighing 10 *shekels*", about 115 grammes each.
ᶜ **24:31 Sir, you are welcome to come in** Literally, "Come in, blessed of the LORD!"

gave Rebekah the gifts he brought. He gave her beautiful clothes and gold and silver jewellery. He also gave expensive gifts to her mother and brother. [54]Then he and his men had something to eat and drink, and they spent the night there. Early the next morning they got up and the servant said, "Now we must go back to my master."

[55]Rebekah's mother and her brother said, "Let Rebekah stay with us for a short time. Let her stay with us for ten days. After that, she can go."

[56]But the servant said to them, "Don't make me wait. The LORD has made my trip successful. Now let me go back to my master."

[57]Rebekah's brother and mother said, "We will call Rebekah and ask her what she wants to do." [58]They called her and asked her, "Do you want to go with this man now?"

Rebekah said, "Yes, I will go."

[59]So they allowed Rebekah to go with Abraham's servant and his men. Her nurse also went with them. [60]While Rebekah was leaving they said to her,

"Our sister, may you be
    the mother of millions of people,
and may your descendants defeat
    their enemies and take their cities."

[61]Then Rebekah and her nurse got on the camels and followed the servant and his men. So the servant took Rebekah and left.

[62]Isaac had left Beer Lahai Roi and was now living in the Negev. [63]One evening he went out to the field to think.[a] He looked up and saw the camels coming from far away.

[64]Rebekah also looked and saw Isaac. Then she jumped down from the camel. [65]She said to the servant, "Who is that young man walking in the field to meet us?"

The servant said, "That is my master's son." So Rebekah covered her face with her veil.

[66]The servant told Isaac everything that had happened. [67]Then Isaac brought the girl into his mother's tent. Rebekah became his wife that day. Isaac loved her very much. So he was comforted after his mother's death.

Abraham's Family

25 Abraham married again. His new wife was named Keturah. [2]She gave birth to Zimran, Jokshan, Medan, Midian, Ishbak and Shuah. [3]Jokshan was the father of Sheba and Dedan. The people of Asshur,[b] Leum and Letush were descendants of Dedan. [4]The sons of Midian were Ephah, Epher, Hanoch, Abida and Eldaah. All these sons came from the marriage of Abraham and Keturah. [5-6]Before Abraham died, he gave some gifts to his sons who were from his slave women. He sent them to the East,[c] away from Isaac. Then Abraham gave everything he owned to Isaac.

[7]Abraham lived to be 175 years old. [8]Then he grew weak and died. He had lived a long and satisfying life. He died and went to be with his people. [9]His sons Isaac and Ishmael buried him in the cave of Machpelah. This cave is in the field of Ephron, the son of Zohar. It was east of Mamre. [10]This is the same cave that Abraham bought from the Hittites. He was buried there with his wife Sarah. [11]After Abraham died, God blessed Isaac. Isaac was living at Beer Lahai Roi.

[12]This is the list of Ishmael's family. Ishmael was Abraham and Hagar's son. (Hagar was Sarah's Egyptian maid.) [13]These are the names of Ishmael's sons, the oldest to the youngest: Nebaioth, Kedar, Adbeel, Mibsam, [14]Mishma, Dumah, Massa, [15]Hadad, Tema, Jetur, Naphish and Kedemah. [16]These were the names of Ishmael's sons. Each son had his own camp that became a small town. The twelve sons were leaders over their own people. [17]Ishmael lived to be 137 years old. Then he died and went to be with his people. [18]His descendants settled throughout the desert area from Havilah to Shur. This area begins near Egypt and goes towards Assyria. Ishmael's people were often at war with[d] the other descendants of Abraham.

Isaac's Family

[19]This is the story of Isaac. Abraham had a son named Isaac. [20]When Isaac was 40 years old, he married Rebekah. Rebekah was from Paddan Aram. She was Bethuel's daughter and the sister of Laban the Aramean. [21]Isaac's wife could not have children. So Isaac prayed to the LORD for her. The LORD heard Isaac's prayer, and he allowed Rebekah to become pregnant.

[22]While Rebekah was pregnant, the babies inside her struggled with one another. She prayed to the LORD and said, "What is happening to me?" [23]The LORD said to her,

"The leaders of two nations are in your body.
    Two nations will come from you,
    and they will be divided.
One of them will be stronger,
    and the older will serve the younger."

---

[a] **24:63** *think* Or "to go for a walk".
[b] **25:3** *Asshur* Or "Assyria".
[c] **25:5** *East* This usually means the area between the Tigris and Euphrates rivers as far east as the Persian Gulf.
[d] **25:18** *were often at war with* Or "lived away from".

²⁴When the right time came, Rebekah gave birth to twins. ²⁵The first baby was red. His skin was like a hairy robe. So he was named Esau.ᵃ ²⁶When the second baby was born, he was holding tightly to Esau's heel. So that baby was named Jacob.ᵇ Isaac was 60 years old when Jacob and Esau were born.

²⁷The boys grew up. Esau became a skilled hunter, who loved to be out in the fields. But Jacob was a quiet man, who stayed at home. ²⁸Isaac loved Esau. He liked to eat the animals Esau killed. But Rebekah loved Jacob.

²⁹One day Esau came back from hunting. He was tired and weak from hunger. Jacob was boiling a pot of soup. ³⁰So Esau said to Jacob, "I am weak with hunger. Let me have some of that red soup." (That is why people call him "Red".ᶜ)

³¹But Jacob said, "You must sell me your rights as the firstborn son."

³²Esau said, "I am almost dead with hunger, so what good are these rights to me now?"

³³But Jacob said, "First, promise me that you will give them to me." So Esau made an oath to him and sold his rights as the firstborn son to Jacob. ³⁴Then Jacob gave Esau bread and lentilᵈ soup. Esau ate the food, had something to drink and then left. So Esau showed that he did not care about his rights as the firstborn son.

Isaac Lies to Abimelech

26 Now there was a famine. This was like the famine that happened during Abraham's life. So Isaac went to the town of Gerar, to King Abimelech of the Philistines. ²The LORD spoke to Isaac and said, "Don't go down to Egypt. Live in the land that I commanded you to live in. ³Stay in this land, and I will be with you. I will bless you. I will give you and your family all these lands. I will do what I promised to Abraham your father. ⁴I will make your family as many as the stars of heaven, and I will give all these lands to your family. Through your descendantsᵉ every nation on earth will be blessed. ⁵I will do this because your father Abraham obeyed my words and did what I said. He obeyed my commands, my laws and my rules."

⁶So Isaac settled in Gerar. ⁷His wife Rebekah was very beautiful. The men of that place asked Isaac about Rebekah. He said, "She is my sister." He was afraid to tell them Rebekah was his wife. He was afraid the men would kill him so that they could have her.

⁸After Isaac had lived there for a long time, Abimelech looked out of his window and saw Isaac and his wife enjoying one another. ⁹Abimelech called for Isaac and said, "This woman is your wife. Why did you tell us that she was your sister?"

Isaac said to him, "I was afraid that you would kill me so that you could have her."

¹⁰Abimelech said, "You have done a bad thing to us. One of our men might have had sex with your wife. Then he would be guilty of a great sin."

¹¹So Abimelech gave a warning to all the people. He said, "No one must hurt this man or this woman. If anyone hurts them, they will be killed."

Isaac Becomes Rich

¹²Isaac planted fields in that place, and that year he gathered a great harvest. The LORD blessed him very much. ¹³Isaac became rich. He gathered more and more wealth until he became a very rich man. ¹⁴He had many flocks and herds of animals. He also had many slaves. All the Philistines were jealous of him. ¹⁵So they destroyed all the wells that Isaac's father Abraham and his servants had dug many years before. They filled them with sand. ¹⁶Abimelech said to Isaac, "Leave our country. You have become much more powerful than we are."

¹⁷So Isaac left that place and camped near the little river of Gerar. He stayed there and lived. ¹⁸Long before this time, Abraham had dug many wells. After he died, the Philistines filled the wells with sand. So Isaac went back and dug those wells again. He gave them the same names his father had given them. ¹⁹Isaac's servants also dug a well near the little river and found fresh water.ᶠ ²⁰But the men who herded sheep in the Valley of Gerar argued with Isaac's servants. They said, "This water is ours." So Isaac named that well Esek.ᵍ He gave it that name because it was the place where they had argued with him.

²¹Then Isaac's servants dug another well. But there was an argument over this well too. So Isaac named that well Sitnah.ʰ

²²Isaac moved from there and dug another well. No one came to argue about this well. So Isaac named it Rehoboth.ⁱ He said, "Now the LORD has found a place for us. We will grow and be successful in this place."

²³From there Isaac went to Beersheba. ²⁴The LORD spoke to him that night and said, "I am the God of your father Abraham. Don't be afraid. I am

---

ᵃ **25:25 Esau** This name is like the word meaning "hairy".
ᵇ **25:26 Jacob** This name is like the Hebrew word meaning "heel". It also means "the one who follows" or "dishonest".
ᶜ **25:30 Red** Literally, "Edom", a name that means "red".
ᵈ **25:34 lentil** A type of bean.
ᵉ **26:4 Descendants** Or "Descendant". See Gal. 3:16.
ᶠ **26:19 fresh water** Or "an underground stream". Literally, "living water".
ᵍ **26:20 Esek** This means "argument" or "fight".
ʰ **26:21 Sitnah** This means "hatred" or "being an enemy".
ⁱ **26:22 Rehoboth** This means "open place" or "crossroads".

with you, and I will bless you. I will make your family great. I will do this because of my servant Abraham." 25So Isaac built an altar and worshipped the LORD in that place. He set up camp there, and his servants dug a well.

26Abimelech came from Gerar to see Isaac. He brought with him Ahuzzath, his advisor, and Phicol, the commander of his army.

27Isaac asked, "Why have you come to see me? You were not friendly to me before. You even forced me to leave your country."

28They answered, "Now we know that the LORD is with you. We think that we should make an agreement. We want you to make a promise to us. 29We did not hurt you; now you should promise not to hurt us. We sent you away, but we sent you away in peace. Now it is clear that the LORD has blessed you."

30So Isaac gave a party for them. They all ate and drank. 31Early the next morning each man made a promise and a vow. Then the men left in peace.

32On that day Isaac's servants came and told him about the well they had dug. The servants said, "We found water in that well." 33So Isaac named it Shibah.[a] And that city is still called Beersheba.[b]

Esau's Wives

34When Esau was 40 years old, he married two Hittite women. One was Judith the daughter of Beeri. The other was Basemath the daughter of Elon. 35These marriages made Isaac and Rebekah very unhappy.

INSIGHT

Esau had two wives, which was fairly common during Old Testament times. Other well-known figures, including Abraham, Jacob, David and Solomon, had multiple wives too. However, this wasn't God's design for marriage (see Genesis 2:18–25), and in the New Testament having just one wife is a sign of being a responsible man (1 Timothy 3:2,12; Titus 1:6).

Genesis 26:34

Jacob Tricks Isaac

27 Isaac grew old, and his eyes became so weak that he could not see clearly. One day he called his older son Esau to him and said, "Son!"

Esau answered, "Here I am."

2Isaac said, "I am old. Maybe I will die soon. 3So take your bow and arrows and go hunting. Kill an animal for me to eat. 4Prepare the food that I love. Bring it to me, and I will eat it. Then I will bless you before I die." 5So Esau went hunting.

Rebekah was listening when Isaac told this to his son Esau. 6Rebekah said to her son Jacob, "Listen, I heard your father talking to your brother Esau. 7Your father said, 'Kill an animal for me to eat. Prepare the food for me, and I will eat it. Then, with the LORD as witness, I will bless you before I die.' 8So listen, son, and do what I tell you. 9Go out to our goats and bring me two young ones. I will prepare them the way your father loves them. 10Then you will carry the food to your father, and he will bless you before he dies."

11But Jacob told his mother Rebekah, "My brother Esau is a hairy man. I am not hairy like him. 12If my father touches me, he will know that I am not Esau. Then he will not bless me—he will curse me because I tried to trick him."

13So Rebekah said to him, "I will accept the blame if there is trouble. Do what I said. Go and get the goats for me."

14So Jacob went out and got two goats and brought them to his mother. His mother cooked the goats in the special way that Isaac loved. 15Then Rebekah took the clothes that her older son Esau loved to wear. She put these clothes on the younger son Jacob. 16She took the skins of the goats and put them on Jacob's hands and on his neck. 17Then she got the food she had cooked and gave it to Jacob.

18Jacob went to his father and said, "Father."

His father answered, "Yes, son. Who are you?"

19Jacob said to his father, "I am Esau, your first son. I have done what you told me. Now sit up and eat the meat from the animals that I hunted for you. Then you can bless me."

20But Isaac said to his son, "How have you hunted and killed the animals so quickly?"

Jacob answered, "Because the LORD your God allowed me to find the animals quickly."

21Then Isaac said to Jacob, "Come near to me so that I can feel you, my son. If I can feel you, I will know if you are really my son Esau."

22So Jacob went to Isaac his father. Isaac felt him and said, "Your voice sounds like Jacob's voice, but your arms are hairy like the arms of Esau." 23Isaac did not know it was Jacob, because his arms were hairy like Esau's. So Isaac blessed Jacob.

24Isaac said, "Are you really my son Esau?"

Jacob answered, "Yes, I am."

---

[a] 26:33 Shibah A Hebrew word meaning "seven" or "oath".
[b] 26:33 Beersheba This name means "well of the oath".

The Blessing for Jacob

25Then Isaac said, "Bring me the food. I will eat it and bless you." So Jacob gave him the food, and he ate it. Then Jacob gave him some wine, and he drank it.

26Then Isaac said to him. "Son, come near and kiss me." 27So Jacob went to his father and kissed him. When Isaac smelled Esau's clothes, he blessed him and said,

"My son smells like the fields
the LORD has blessed.
28May God give you plenty of rain,
good crops, and wine.
29May the nations serve you
and many people bow down to you.
You will rule over your brothers.
Your mother's sons will bow down to you
and obey you.
Whoever curses you will be cursed.
Whoever blesses you will be blessed."

Esau's "Blessing"

30Isaac finished blessing Jacob. Then, just as Jacob left his father Isaac, Esau came in from hunting. 31Esau prepared the food in the special way his father loved. He brought it to his father and said, "Father, I am your son. Get up and eat the meat from the animals that I killed for you. Then you can bless me."

32But Isaac said to him, "Who are you?"

He answered, "I am your son—your first son—Esau."

33Then Isaac became so upset that he began to shake. He said, "Then who was it that cooked and brought me food before you came? I ate it all, and I blessed him. Now it is too late to take back my blessing."

34When Esau heard his father's words, he became very angry and bitter. He cried out and said to his father, "Then bless me also, father!"

35Isaac said, "Your brother tricked me! He came and took your blessing!"

36Esau said, "His name is Jacob.a That is the right name for him. He has tricked me twice. He took away my rights as the firstborn son. And now he has taken away my blessing." Then Esau said, "Have you saved any blessing for me?"

37Isaac answered, "I have already given Jacob the power to rule over you. And I said all his brothers would be his servants. I have given him the blessing for much grain and wine. There is nothing left to give you, my son."

38But Esau continued to beg his father. "Do you have only one blessing, father? Bless me also, father!" Esau began to cry.

39Then Isaac said to him,

"You will not live on good land.
You will not have much rain.
40You will have to fight to live,
and you will be a slave to your brother.
But when you fight to be free,
you will break away from his control."

Jacob Leaves the Country

41After that, Esau hated Jacob because of this blessing. Esau said to himself, "My father will soon die, and after we have mourned for him, I will kill Jacob."

42Rebekah heard about Esau's plan to kill Jacob. She sent for Jacob and said to him, "Listen, your brother Esau is planning to kill you. 43So, son, do what I say. My brother Laban is living in Haran. Go to him and hide. 44Stay with him for a short time until your brother stops being angry. 45When your brother forgets what you did to him, I will send a servant to bring you back. I don't want to lose both of my sons the same day."

46Then Rebekah said to Isaac, "Your son Esau married Hittite women. I am very upset about this, because they are not our people. I'll have nothing to live for if Jacob marries one of these women!"

28 Isaac called Jacob and blessed him. Then Isaac gave him a command and said, "You must not marry a Canaanite woman. 2So leave this place and go to Paddan Aram. Go to the house of Bethuel, your mother's father. Laban, your mother's brother, lives there. Marry one of his daughters. 3I pray that God All-Powerfulb will bless you and give you many children. I pray that you will become the father of a great nation 4and that God will bless you and your children the same way he blessed Abraham. And I pray that you will own the land where you live. This is the land God gave to Abraham."

5So Isaac sent Jacob to Rebekah's brother in Paddan Aram. Jacob went to Laban, son of Bethuel the Aramean. Laban was the brother of Rebekah, the mother of Jacob and Esau.

6Esau learned that his father Isaac had blessed Jacob and sent him away to Paddan Aram to find a wife there. He also learned that Isaac had commanded Jacob not to marry a Canaanite woman. 7Esau learned that Jacob had obeyed his father and

---

a **27:36 Jacob** This name is like the Hebrew word meaning "heel". It also means "the one who follows" or "dishonest".
b **28:3 God All-Powerful** Literally, "El Shaddai".

his mother and had gone to Paddan Aram. [8]Esau saw from this that his father did not want his sons to marry Canaanite women. [9]Esau already had two wives, but he went to Abraham's son Ishmael and married another woman, Mahalath, the daughter of Ishmael. Mahalath was Nebaioth's sister.

Jacob's Dream at Bethel

[10]Jacob left Beersheba and went to Haran. [11]The sun had already set when he came to a good place to spend the night. He found a stone there and laid his head on it to sleep. [12]Jacob had a dream. He dreamed there was a ladder that was on the ground and reached up into heaven. He saw the angels of God going up and down the ladder. [13]And then Jacob saw the LORD standing by the ladder. He said, "I am the LORD, the God of your grandfather Abraham. I am the God of Isaac. I will give you the land that you are lying on now. I will give this land to you and to your children. [14]You will have as many descendants as there are particles of dust on the earth. They will spread east and west, north and south. All the families on earth will be blessed because of you and your descendants.

[15]"I am with you, and I will protect you everywhere you go. I will bring you back to this land. I will not leave you until I have done what I have promised."

[16]Then Jacob woke up and said, "I know that the LORD is in this place, but I did not know he was here until I slept."

[17]Jacob was afraid and said, "This is a very great place. This is the house of God. This is the gate to heaven."

[18]Jacob got up very early in the morning. He took the rock he had slept on and set it up on its edge. Then he poured oil on the rock. In this way he made it a memorial to God. [19]The name of that place was Luz, but Jacob named it Bethel.[a]

[20]Then Jacob made a promise. He said, "If God will be with me, and if he will protect me on this trip, and if he gives me food to eat and clothes to wear, [21]and if I return in peace to my father's house—if he does all these things—then the LORD will be my God. [22]I am setting this stone up as a memorial stone. It will show that this is a holy place for God, and I will give God one-tenth of all he gives me."

Jacob Meets Rachel

29 Then Jacob continued his journey. He went to the country in the East. [2]He looked and saw a well in the field. There were three flocks of sheep lying near the well, where the sheep drank water. There was a large rock covering the mouth of the well. [3]When all the flocks were gathered there, the shepherds would roll the rock away from the well. Then all the sheep could drink from the water. After the sheep were full, the shepherds would put the rock back in its place.

[4]Jacob said to the shepherds there, "Brothers, where are you from?"

They answered, "We are from Haran."

[5]Then Jacob said, "Do you know Laban, the son of Nahor?"

The shepherds answered, "We know him."

[6]Then Jacob said, "How is he?"

They answered, "He is well. Look, that is his daughter Rachel coming now with his sheep."

[7]Jacob said, "Look, it is still day and long before the sun sets. It is not yet time for the animals to be gathered together for the night. So give them water and let them go back into the field."

[8]But they said, "We cannot do that until all the flocks are gathered together. Then we will move the rock from the well, and all the sheep will drink."

[9]While Jacob was talking with the shepherds, Rachel came with her father's sheep. (It was her job to take care of the sheep.) [10]Rachel was Laban's daughter. Laban was the brother of Rebekah, Jacob's mother. When Jacob saw Rachel, he went and moved the rock and gave water to the sheep. [11]Then Jacob kissed Rachel and cried. [12]He told her that he was from her father's family. He told her that he was the son of Rebekah. So Rachel ran home and told her father.

[13]When Laban heard the news about his sister's son Jacob, he ran to meet him. Laban hugged him and kissed him and brought him to his house. Jacob told Laban everything that had happened. [14]Then Laban said, "This is wonderful! You are from my own family." So Jacob stayed with Laban for a month.

Laban Tricks Jacob

[15]One day Laban said to Jacob, "You are a relative of mine. It is not right for you to continue working for me without pay. What should I pay you?"

[16]Now Laban had two daughters. The older was Leah and the younger was Rachel. [17]Leah's eyes were gentle,[b] but Rachel was beautiful. [18]Jacob loved Rachel, so he said to Laban, "I will work seven years for you if you will allow me to marry your daughter Rachel."

[19]Laban said, "It would be better for her to marry you than someone else. So stay with me."

---

[a] **28:19** *Bethel* A town in Israel. This name means "God's house".

[b] **29:17** *Leah's eyes were gentle* This might be a polite way of saying Leah was not very pretty.

²⁰So Jacob stayed and worked for Laban for seven years. But it seemed like a very short time because he loved Rachel very much.

²¹After seven years, Jacob said to Laban, "Give me Rachel so that I can marry her. My time of work for you is finished."

²²So Laban gave a party for all the people in that place. ²³That night Laban brought his daughter to Jacob to be his wife. But he brought Leah, not Rachel, and Jacob slept with her. ²⁴Laban also gave his maid Zilpah to Leah to be her maid.

²⁵In the morning Jacob saw that it was Leah he had slept with, and he said to Laban, "Why did you do this to me? I worked hard for you so that I could marry Rachel. Why did you trick me?"

INSIGHT

How was Jacob tricked into marrying the wrong sister? You'd think he'd have noticed! In ancient wedding ceremonies the bride was entirely covered from head to toe. The man was not allowed to see the woman's face during the ceremony.

Genesis 29:16–30

²⁶Laban said, "In our country we don't allow the younger daughter to marry before the older daughter. ²⁷Continue for the full week of the marriage ceremony, and I will also give you Rachel to marry. But you must serve me for another seven years."

²⁸So Jacob did this and finished the week. Then Laban gave him his daughter Rachel as a wife. ²⁹(Laban gave his maid Bilhah to his daughter Rachel to be her maid.) ³⁰So Jacob also had sex with Rachel, and he loved her more than Leah. He then worked for Laban another seven years.

Jacob's Family Grows

³¹The LORD saw that Jacob loved Rachel more than Leah, so he made it possible for Leah to have children. But Rachel did not have any children.

³²Leah gave birth to a son, and she named him Reuben.ᵃ She named him this because she said, "The LORD has seen my troubles. My husband does not love me. So now maybe my husband will love me."

³³Leah became pregnant again and had another son. She named this son Simeon.ᵇ She said, "The LORD has heard that I am not loved, so he gave me this son."

³⁴Leah became pregnant again and had another son. She named this son Levi.ᶜ She said, "Now, surely my husband will love me. I have given him three sons."

³⁵Then Leah gave birth to another son. She named this son Judah.ᵈ Leah named him this because she said, "Now I will praise the LORD." Then Leah stopped having children.

30 Rachel saw that she was not giving Jacob any children. She became jealous of her sister Leah. So Rachel said to Jacob, "Give me children, or I will die!"

²Jacob became angry with Rachel and said, "I am not God. He is the one who has caused you to not have children."

³Then Rachel said, "You can have my maid Bilhah. Sleep with her, and she will have a child for me.ᵉ Then I can be a mother through her."

⁴So Rachel gave Bilhah to her husband Jacob. He had sex with Bilhah. ⁵She became pregnant and gave birth to a son for Jacob.

⁶Rachel said, "God has listened to my prayer. He decided to give me a son." So she named this son Dan.ᶠ

⁷Bilhah became pregnant again and gave Jacob a second son. ⁸Rachel said, "I have fought hard to compete with my sister, and I have won." So she named that son Naphtali.ᵍ

⁹Leah saw that she could have no more children. So she gave her slave girl Zilpah to Jacob. ¹⁰Then Zilpah had a son. ¹¹Leah said, "I am lucky." So she named the son Gad.ʰ ¹²Zilpah gave birth to another son. ¹³Leah said, "I am very happy! Now women will call me happy." So she named that son Asher.ⁱ

¹⁴During the wheat harvest Reuben went into the fields and found some special flowers.ʲ He brought them to his mother Leah. But Rachel said

---

ᵃ **29:32 Reuben** This is like the Hebrew word meaning "Look, a son."
ᵇ **29:33 Simeon** This is like the Hebrew word meaning "He hears."
ᶜ **29:34 Levi** This is like the Hebrew word meaning "accompany", "be joined together" or "become close".
ᵈ **29:35 Judah** This name is like the word meaning "He is praised."
ᵉ **30:3 she will have a child for me** Literally, "she will give birth on my knees, and I, too, will have a son through her".
ᶠ **30:6 Dan** This is like the Hebrew word meaning "to decide" or "to judge".
ᵍ **30:8 Naphtali** This is like the Hebrew word meaning "my struggle".
ʰ **30:11 Gad** This is like the Hebrew word meaning "lucky" or "fortunate".
ⁱ **30:13 Asher** This is like the Hebrew word meaning "blessed" or "happy".
ʲ **30:14 special flowers** Or "mandrakes". The Hebrew word means "love plant". People thought these plants could help women have babies.

to Leah, "Please give me some of your son's flowers."

[15]Leah answered, "You have already taken away my husband. Now you are trying to take away my son's flowers."

But Rachel answered, "If you will give me your son's flowers, you can sleep with Jacob tonight."

[16]Jacob came in from the fields that night. Leah saw him and went out to meet him. She said, "You will sleep with me tonight. I have paid for you with my son's flowers." So Jacob slept with Leah that night.

[17]Then God allowed Leah to become pregnant again. She gave birth to a fifth son. [18]She said, "God has given me a reward because I gave my slave to my husband." So she named her son Issachar.[a]

[19]Leah became pregnant again and gave birth to a sixth son. [20]She said, "God has given me a fine gift. Now surely Jacob will accept me, because I have given him six sons." So she named this son Zebulun.[b]

[21]Later, Leah gave birth to a daughter. She named her Dinah.

[22]Then God heard Rachel's prayer and made it possible for Rachel to have children. [23]She became pregnant and gave birth to a son. She said, "God has taken away my shame." [24]Rachel named the son Joseph,[c] saying, "May the Lord give me another son."

Jacob Tricks Laban

[25]After the birth of Joseph, Jacob said to Laban, "Now let me go back to my own homeland. [26]Give me my wives and my children. I have earned them by working for you. You know that I served you well."

[27]Laban said to him, "Please, let me say something. I know[d] that the LORD has blessed me because of you. [28]Tell me what I should pay you, and I will give it to you."

[29]Jacob answered, "You know that I have worked hard for you. Your flocks have grown and been well while I cared for them. [30]When I came, you had little. Now you have much, much more. Every time I did something for you, the LORD blessed you. Now it is time for me to work for myself—it is time to do things for my family."

[31]Laban asked, "Then what should I give you?"

Jacob answered, "I don't want you to give me anything! I only want you to let me do this one thing: I will go back and take care of your sheep. [32]But let me go through all your flocks today and take every sheep with spots or stripes. Let me

take every black young lamb and every goat with stripes or spots. That will be my pay. [33]In the future you can easily see if I am honest. You can come to look at my flocks. If I have any goat that isn't spotted or any lamb that isn't black, you will know that I stole it."

[34]Laban answered, "I agree to that. We will do what you ask." [35]But that day Laban hid all the male goats that had spots. And he hid all the female goats that had spots on them. He also hid all the black sheep. Laban told his sons to watch these sheep. [36]So the sons took all the spotted animals and led them to another place. They travelled for three days. Jacob stayed and took care of all the animals that were left.

[37]Then Jacob cut green branches from poplar and almond trees. He stripped off some of the bark so that the branches had white stripes on them. [38]He put the branches in front of the flocks at the watering places. When the animals came to drink, they also mated in that place. [39]Then when the goats mated in front of the branches, the young that were born were spotted, striped or black.

[40]Jacob separated the spotted and the black animals from the other animals in the flock. He kept his animals separate from Laban's. [41]Any time the stronger animals in the flock were mating, Jacob put the branches before their eyes. The animals mated near those branches. [42]But when the weaker animals mated, Jacob did not put the branches there. So the young animals born from the weak animals were Laban's. And the young animals born from the stronger animals were Jacob's. [43]In this way Jacob became very rich. He had large flocks, many servants, camels and donkeys.

Time to Leave—Jacob Runs Away

31 One day Jacob heard Laban's sons talking. They said, "Jacob has taken everything that our father owned. He has become rich—and he has taken all this wealth from our father." [2]Then Jacob noticed that Laban was not as friendly as he had been in the past. [3]The LORD said to Jacob, "Go back to your own land where your ancestors lived. I will be with you."

[4]So Jacob told Rachel and Leah to meet him in the field where he kept his flocks of sheep and goats. [5]He said to them, "I notice that your father is not as friendly with me as he used to be. But the God of my father has been with me. [6]You both know that I have worked as hard as I could for your father. [7]But he cheated me. He has changed my pay ten times. But during all this time, God protected me from Laban's tricks.

---

[a] **30:18** *Issachar* This is like the Hebrew word meaning "reward" or "salary".
[b] **30:20** *Zebulun* This is like the Hebrew word meaning "praise" or "honour".
[c] **30:23–24** *Joseph* This is like the Hebrew word meaning "to add".
[d] **30:27** *know* Or "guessed", "divined" or "concluded".

8"At one time Laban said, 'You can keep all the goats with spots. This will be your pay.' After he said this, all the animals gave birth to spotted goats, so they were all mine. But then Laban said, 'I will keep the spotted goats. You can have all the striped goats. That will be your pay.' After he said this, all the animals gave birth to striped goats. 9So God has taken the animals away from your father and has given them to me.

10"I had a dream during the time when the animals were mating. I saw that the only male goats that were mating were the ones with stripes and spots. 11The angel of God spoke to me in that dream. The angel said, 'Jacob!'

"I answered, 'Yes!'

12"The angel said, 'Look, only the striped and spotted goats are mating. I am causing this to happen. I have seen all the wrong things Laban has been doing to you. I am doing this so that you can have all the new baby goats. 13I am the God who came to you at Bethel, and there you made an altar, poured olive oil on it, and made a promise to me. Now I want you to be ready to go back to the country where you were born.'"

14Rachel and Leah answered Jacob, "Our father has nothing to give us when he dies. 15He treated us like strangers. He sold us to you, and then he spent all the money that should have been ours. 16God took all this wealth from our father, and now it belongs to us and our children. So you should do whatever God told you to do."

17So Jacob prepared for the journey. He put his children and his wives on camels. 18Then they began travelling back to the land of Canaan, where his father lived. All the flocks of animals that Jacob owned walked ahead of them. He carried everything with him that he had got while he lived in Paddan Aram.

19While Laban was gone to cut the wool from his sheep, Rachel went into his house and stole the false gods that belonged to her father. 20Jacob tricked Laban the Aramean. He did not tell Laban he was leaving. 21Jacob took his family and everything he owned and left quickly. They crossed the Euphrates River and travelled towards the hill country of Gilead.

22Three days later Laban learned that Jacob had run away. 23So he gathered his men together and began to chase Jacob. After seven days, Laban found Jacob near the hill country of Gilead. 24That night God came to Laban in a dream and said, "Be careful! Be careful of every word you say to Jacob."

The Search for the Stolen Gods

25The next morning Laban caught up with Jacob. Jacob had set up his camp on the mountain, so Laban and all his men set up their camp in the hill country of Gilead.

26Laban said to Jacob, "Why did you trick me? Why did you take my daughters as if they were women you captured during war? 27Why did you run away without telling me? If you had told me, I would have given you a party. There would have been singing and dancing with music. 28You did not even let me kiss my grandchildren and my daughters goodbye. You were very foolish to do this! 29I have the power to really hurt you. But last night the God of your father came to me in a dream. He warned me not to hurt you in any way. 30I know that you want to go back to your home. That is why you left. But why did you steal the gods from my house?"

31Jacob answered, "I left without telling you, because I was afraid. I thought you would take your daughters away from me. 32But I did not steal your gods. If you find anyone here with me who has taken your gods, they will be killed. Your men will be my witnesses. You can look for anything that belongs to you. Take anything that is yours." (Jacob did not know that Rachel had stolen Laban's gods.)

33So Laban went and looked through Jacob's camp. He looked in Jacob's tent and then in Leah's tent. Then he looked in the tent where the two slave women stayed, but he did not find the gods from his house. Then he went into Rachel's tent. 34Rachel had hidden the gods inside her camel's saddle, and she was sitting on them. Laban looked through the whole tent, but he did not find the gods.

35And Rachel said to her father, "Father, don't be angry with me. I am not able to stand up before you. I am having my monthly period of bleeding." So Laban looked through the camp, but he did not find the gods from his house.

36Then Jacob became very angry and said, "What wrong have I done? What law have I broken? What right do you have to chase me and stop me? 37You looked through everything I own and found nothing that belongs to you. If you found something, show it to me. Put it here where our men can see it. Let our men decide which one of us is right. 38I have worked for you for 20 years. During all that time none of the baby sheep and goats died during birth. And I have not eaten any of the rams from your flocks. 39Any time a sheep was killed by wild animals, I always paid for the loss myself. I did not take the dead animal to you and say that it was not my fault. But I was robbed day and night. 40In the daytime the sun took away my strength, and at night sleep was taken from my eyes by the cold. 41I worked for 20 years like a slave for you. For the first 14 years I worked to win your two daughters. The last six years I worked to earn your animals. And during that time you changed my pay ten times. 42But the God of my ancestors, the God of

Abraham and the Fear of Isaac,[a] was with me. If God had not been with me, you would have sent me away with nothing. But he saw the trouble that I had and the work that I did, and last night God proved that I am right."

Jacob and Laban's Treaty

43Laban said to Jacob, "These women are my daughters. These children belong to me, and these animals are mine. Everything you see here belongs to me, but I can do nothing to keep my daughters and their children. 44So I am ready to make an agreement with you. We will set up a pile of stones to show that we have an agreement."

45So Jacob found a large rock and put it there to show that he had made an agreement. 46He told his men to find some more rocks and to make a pile of rocks. Then they ate beside the pile of rocks. 47Laban named that place Yegar Sahadutha.[b] But Jacob named that place Galeed.[c]

48Laban said to Jacob, "This pile of rocks will help us both remember our agreement." That is why Jacob called the place Galeed.

49Then Laban said, "Let the LORD watch over us while we are separated from each other." So that place was also named Mizpah.[d]

50Then Laban said, "If you hurt my daughters, remember that God will punish you. If you marry other women, remember that God is watching. 51Here are the rocks that I have put between us, and here is the special rock to show that we made an agreement. 52This pile of rocks and this one special rock both help us to remember our agreement. I will never go past these rocks to fight against you, and you must never go on my side of these rocks to fight against me. 53May the God of Abraham, the God of Nahor, and the God of their ancestors judge us guilty if we break this agreement."

Jacob's father, Isaac, called God "Fear". So Jacob used that name to make the promise. 54Then Jacob killed an animal and offered it as a sacrifice on the mountain. And he invited his men to come and share a meal. After they finished eating, they spent the night on the mountain. 55Early the next morning Laban kissed his grandchildren and his daughters goodbye. He blessed them and went back home.

Jacob Prepares to Meet Esau

32 Jacob also left that place. While he was travelling, he saw God's angels. 2When he saw them, he said, "This is God's camp!" So Jacob named that place Mahanaim.[e]

3Jacob's brother Esau was living in the area called Seir in the hill country of Edom. Jacob sent messengers to Esau. 4He told them, "Tell this to my master Esau: 'Your servant Jacob says, I have lived with Laban all these years. 5I have many cattle, donkeys, flocks and servants. Sir, I am sending you this message to ask you to accept us.'"

6The messengers came back to Jacob and said, "We went to your brother Esau. He is coming to meet you. He has 400 men with him."

7Jacob was very frightened and worried. He divided the people who were with him and all the flocks, herds and camels into two groups. 8Jacob thought, "If Esau comes and destroys one group, the other group can run away and be saved."

9Then Jacob said, "God of my father Abraham! God of my father Isaac! LORD, you told me to come back to my country and to my family. You said that you would do good to me. 10You have been very kind to me. You did many good things for me. The first time I travelled across the Jordan River, I owned nothing—only my walking stick. But now I own enough things to have two full groups. 11I ask you to please save me from my brother Esau. I am afraid that he will come and kill us all, even the mothers with the children. 12Lord, you said to me, 'I will be good to you. I will increase your family and make your children as many as the grains of sand on the seashore. There will be too many to count.'"

13Jacob stayed in that place for the night. He prepared some things to give to Esau as a gift. 14He took 200 female goats and 20 male goats, 200 female sheep and 20 male sheep. 15He took 30 camels and their colts, 40 cows and 10 bulls, 20 female donkeys and 10 male donkeys. 16He gave each flock of animals to his servants. Then he said to them, "Separate each group of animals. Go ahead of me and keep some space between each herd." 17Jacob gave them their orders. To the servant with the first group of animals he said, "When Esau my brother comes to you and asks you, 'Whose animals are these? Where are you going? Whose servant are you?' 18then you should answer, 'These animals belong to your servant Jacob. He sent them as a gift to you, my master Esau. And he also is coming behind us.'"

19Jacob also ordered the second servant, the third servant and all the other servants to do the same thing. He said, "You will say the same thing to Esau when you meet him. 20You will say,

---

a **31:42** *Fear of Isaac* A name for God.
b **31:47** *Yegar Sahadutha* Aramaic words meaning "rock pile of the agreement".
c **31:47** *Galeed* Another name for Gilead. This Hebrew name means "rock pile of the agreement".
d **31:49** *Mizpah* This means "a place to watch from".
e **32:2** *Mahanaim* This name means "two camps".

'This is a gift to you, and your servant Jacob is behind us.'"

Jacob thought, "If I send these men ahead with gifts, maybe Esau will forgive me and accept me." 21So Jacob sent the gifts to Esau, but he stayed that night in the camp.

22During the night, Jacob got up and began moving his two wives, his two maids and his eleven sons across the Jabbok River at the crossing. 23After he sent his family across the river, he sent across everything he had.

The Fight With God

24Jacob was left alone, and a man came and wrestled with him. The man fought with him until the sun came up. 25When the man saw that he could not defeat Jacob, he touched Jacob's leg and put it out of joint.

26Then the man said to Jacob, "Let me go. The sun is coming up."

But Jacob said, "I will not let you go. You must bless me."

27And the man said to him, "What is your name?"

And Jacob said, "My name is Jacob."

28Then the man said, "Your name will not be Jacob. Your name will now be Israel.*a* I give you this name because you have fought with God and with men, and you have won."

29Then Jacob asked him, "Please tell me your name."

But the man said, "Why do you ask my name?" Then the man blessed Jacob at that place.

30So Jacob named that place Peniel.*b* He said, "At this place, I saw God face to face, but my life was spared." 31Then the sun came up as Jacob left Peniel. He was limping because of his leg. 32So even today, the people of Israel don't eat the muscle that is on the hip joint of any animal, because this is the muscle where Jacob was hurt.

Jacob Meets Esau

33 Jacob looked and saw Esau coming with 400 men. Jacob divided his family into four groups. Leah and her children were in one group, Rachel and Joseph were in one group, and the two maids and their children were in two groups. 2Jacob put the maids with their children first. Then he put Leah and her children behind them, and he put Rachel and Joseph in the last place.

3Jacob himself went out before them. While he was walking towards his brother Esau, he bowed down to the ground seven times.

4When Esau saw Jacob, he ran to meet him. He put his arms around Jacob, hugged his neck, and kissed him. Then they both cried. 5Esau looked up and saw the women and children. He said, "Who are all these people with you?"

Jacob answered, "These are the children that God has given me. God has been good to me."

6Then the two maids and the children with them went to Esau. They bowed down before him. 7Then Leah and the children with her went to Esau and bowed down. And then Rachel and Joseph went to him and bowed down.

8Esau said, "Who were all those people I saw while I was coming here? And what were all those animals for?"

Jacob answered, "These are my gifts to you so that you might accept me."

9But Esau said, "You don't have to give me gifts, brother. I have enough for myself."

10Jacob said, "No, I beg you! If you really accept me, please accept the gifts I give you. I am very happy to see your face again. It is like seeing the face of God. I am very happy to see that you accept me. 11So I beg you to also accept the gifts I give you. God has been very good to me. I have more than I need." Because Jacob begged Esau to take the gifts, he accepted them.

12Then Esau said, "Now you can continue your journey. I will go with you."

13But Jacob said to him, "You know that my children are weak. And I must be careful with my flocks and their young animals. If I force them to walk too far in one day, all the animals will die. 14So you go on ahead. I will follow you slowly. I will go slowly enough for the cattle and other animals to be safe and so that my children will not get too tired. I will meet you in Seir."

15So Esau said, "Then I will leave some of my men to help you."

But Jacob said, "That is very kind of you, but there is no need to do that." 16So that day Esau started on his journey back to Seir. 17But Jacob went to Succoth.*c* There he built a house for himself and small barns for his cattle. That is why the place was named Succoth.

18Jacob safely ended his journey from Paddan Aram when he came to the town of Shechem in Canaan. He made his camp in a field near the city. 19He bought the field where he camped from the family of Hamor, father of Shechem. He paid 100 pieces of silver for it. 20He built an altar there to honour God. He named the place "El,*d* the God of Israel".

---

a **32:28** *Israel* This name might mean "he fights for God", "he fights with God" or "God fights".
b **32:30** *Peniel* A name that means "the face of God".
c **33:17** *Succoth* A town east of the Jordan River. This name means "temporary shelters".
d **33:20** *El* A Hebrew name for God.

The Rape of Dinah

34 One day, Dinah, the daughter of Leah and Jacob, went out to see the women of that place. [2]She was seen by Shechem, the son of Hamor the Hivite, who ruled that area. Shechem took Dinah and raped her. [3]But he was so attracted to her that he fell in love and began expressing his feelings to her. [4]He told his father, "Please get this girl for me so that I can marry her."

[5]Jacob learned that Shechem had done this very bad thing to his daughter. But all his sons were out in the fields with the cattle. So he did nothing until they came home. [6]Then Shechem's father, Hamor, came out to talk with Jacob.

[7]In the fields Jacob's sons heard the news about what had happened. They were very angry because Shechem had brought shame to Israel by raping Jacob's daughter. They came in from the fields as soon as they heard about the terrible thing Shechem had done.

[8]But Hamor talked to Dinah's brothers and said, "My son Shechem wants Dinah very much. Please let him marry her. [9]This marriage will show we have a special agreement. Then our men can marry your women, and your men can marry our women. [10]You can live in the same land with us. You will be free to own the land and to trade here."

[11]Shechem also talked to Jacob and to Dinah's brothers and said, "Please accept me. I will do anything you ask me to do. [12]I will give you any gift[a] you want if you will only allow me to marry Dinah. I will give you anything you ask, but let me marry her."

[13]Jacob's sons decided to lie to Shechem and his father because Shechem had done such a bad thing to their sister Dinah. [14]The brothers said to them, "We cannot allow our sister to marry you because you are not yet circumcised. That would bring us shame. [15]But we will allow you to marry her if you do this one thing: Every man in your town must be circumcised like us. [16]Then your men can marry our women, and our men can marry your women. Then we will become one people. [17]If you refuse to be circumcised, we will take Dinah away."

[18]This agreement made Hamor and Shechem very happy. [19]Shechem was very happy to do what Dinah's brothers asked.

Shechem was the most honoured man in his family. [20]Hamor and Shechem went to the meeting place of their city. They spoke to the men of the city and said, [21]"These people want to be friends with us. We want to let them live in our land and be at peace with us. We have enough land for all of us. We are free to marry their women, and we are happy to give them our women to marry. [22]But there is one thing that all our men must agree to do. They must agree to be circumcised as they are. [23]If we do this, we will become rich from all their cattle and other animals. We should make this agreement with them so that they will stay here with us." [24]All the men who heard this in the meeting place agreed with Hamor and Shechem. And every man was circumcised at that time.

[25]Three days later the men who were circumcised were still sore. Two of Jacob's sons, Simeon and Levi, knew that the men would be weak at this time. So they went to the city and killed all the men there. [26]Dinah's brothers, Simeon and Levi, killed Hamor and his son Shechem. Then they took Dinah out of Shechem's house and left. [27]Jacob's sons went to the city and stole everything that was there because of what Shechem had done to their sister. [28]So the brothers took all their animals, all their donkeys and everything else in the city and in the fields. [29]The brothers took everything those people owned. They even took their wives and children.

[30]But Jacob said to Simeon and Levi, "You have caused me a lot of trouble. All the people in this place will hate me. All the Canaanites and the Perizzites will turn against me. There are only a few of us. If the people in this place gather together to fight against us, I will be destroyed. And all our people will be destroyed with me."

[31]But the brothers said, "Should we let these people treat our sister like a prostitute? They were wrong to do that to our sister!"

Jacob in Bethel

35 God said to Jacob, "Go to the town of Bethel.[b] That is where I appeared to you when you were running away from your brother Esau. Live there and make an altar to honour me as El,[c] the God who appeared to you."

[2]So Jacob told his family and all the other people with him, "Destroy all these foreign gods that you have. Make yourselves pure. Put on clean clothes. [3]We will leave here and go to Bethel. There I will build an altar to the God who has always helped me during times of trouble. He has been with me wherever I have gone."

[4]So the people gave Jacob all the foreign gods they had, and they gave him all the rings they were wearing in their ears. He buried everything under an oak tree near the town called Shechem.

---

[a] **34:12 gift** Or "dowry". Here, the money a man paid for a wife.
[b] **35:1 Bethel** A town in Israel. This name means "God's house".
[c] **35:1 El** A Hebrew name for God.

⁵Then Jacob and his sons left that place. The people in the surrounding cities wanted to follow and kill them, but God filled them with such great fear that they did not go after them. ⁶So Jacob and his people went to Luz, which is now called Bethel. It is in the land of Canaan. ⁷Jacob built an altar there. He named the place "El Bethel".ᵃ Jacob chose this name because that is the place where God first appeared to him when he was running from his brother.

⁸Deborah, Rebekah's nurse, died there. They buried her under the oak tree at Bethel. They named that place Allon Bacuth.ᵇ

Jacob's New Name

⁹When Jacob came back from Paddan Aram, God appeared to him again. God blessed Jacob ¹⁰and said to him, "Your name is Jacob, but I will change that name. You will no longer be called Jacob. Your new name will be Israel."ᶜ So God named him Israel.

¹¹God said to him, "I am God All-Powerful,ᵈ and I give you this blessing: Have many children and grow into a great nation. Other nations and other kings will come out of you. ¹²I gave Abraham and Isaac some special land. Now I give the land to you and to all your people who will live after you." ¹³Then God left that place. ¹⁴⁻¹⁵Jacob set up a memorial stone there. He made the rock holy by pouring wine and oil on it. This was a special place because God spoke to Jacob there, and Jacob named the place Bethel.

Rachel Dies Giving Birth

¹⁶Jacob and his group left Bethel. Before they came to Ephrath, Rachel began giving birth to her baby. ¹⁷She was having a lot of trouble with this birth. She was in great pain. When her nurse saw this, she said, "Don't be afraid, Rachel. You are giving birth to another son."

¹⁸Rachel died while giving birth to the son. Before dying, she named the boy Benoni.ᵉ But Jacob called him Benjamin.ᶠ

¹⁹Rachel was buried on the road to Ephrath (that is, Bethlehem). ²⁰Jacob put a special rock on Rachel's grave to honour her. That special rock is still there today. ²¹Then Israel continued his journey. He camped just south of Eder tower.ᵍ

²²Israel stayed there for a short time. While he was there, Reuben slept with Israel's slave woman Bilhah. Israel heard about this, and he was very angry.ʰ

The Family of Israel (Jacob)

These are the names of Jacob's twelve sons:

²³His firstborn son was Reuben, whose mother was Leah. Jacob's other sons by Leah were Simeon, Levi, Judah, Issachar and Zebulun. ²⁴His sons by Rachel were Joseph and Benjamin. ²⁵His sons by Bilhah, Rachel's maid, were Dan and Naphtali. ²⁶His sons by Zilpah, Leah's maid, were Gad and Asher.

These were Jacob's sons who were born in Paddan Aram.

²⁷Jacob went to his father Isaac at Mamre in Kiriath Arba (Hebron). This is where Abraham and Isaac had lived. ²⁸Isaac was 180 years old ²⁹when he died. By the time he took his last breath, he had lived a long and satisfying life. And now he joined his ancestors who had gone before him. His sons Esau and Jacob buried him.

Esau's Family

36 This is the history of the family of Esau (Edom). ²Esau married women from the land of Canaan. His wives were Adah, the daughter of Elon the Hittite, Oholibamah, the daughter of Anah, the son of Zibeon the Hivite, and ³Basemath, Ishmael's daughter, the sister of Nebaioth. ⁴Esau and Adah had a son named Eliphaz. Basemath had a son named Reuel. ⁵Oholibamah had three sons: Jeush, Jalam and Korah. These were Esau's sons who were born in the land of Canaan.

⁶⁻⁸Jacob and Esau's families became too big for the land in Canaan to support them all, so Esau moved away from his brother Jacob. He took his wives, sons, daughters, all his slaves, cattle and other animals, and everything else that he had got in Canaan and moved to the hill country of Seir.ⁱ He is also known as Edom.

ᵃ **35:7 El Bethel** A name that means "the God of Bethel".
ᵇ **35:8 Allon Bacuth** This name means "the oak tree of sadness".
ᶜ **35:10 Israel** This name might mean "he fights for God", "he fights with God" or "God fights".
ᵈ **35:11 God All-Powerful** Literally, "El Shaddai".
ᵉ **35:18 Benoni** This name means "son of my suffering".
ᶠ **35:18 Benjamin** This name means "right-hand son" or "favourite son".
ᵍ **35:21 Eder tower** Or "Migdal Eder".
ʰ **35:22 and he was very angry** This is from the ancient Greek translation. They are not in the standard Hebrew text. See Gen. 49:4.
ⁱ **36:6–8 Seir** A mountain range in Edom.

⁹Esau is the father of the people of Edom. These are the names of Esau's family living in the hill country of Seir:

¹⁰Esau and Adah's son was Eliphaz. Esau and Basemath's son was Reuel.
¹¹Eliphaz had five sons: Teman, Omar, Zepho, Gatam and Kenaz.
¹²Eliphaz also had a slave woman named Timna. Timna and Eliphaz had a son named Amalek.
¹³Reuel had four sons: Nahath, Zerah, Shammah and Mizzah.
These were Esau's grandsons from his wife Basemath.
¹⁴Esau's third wife was Oholibamah, the daughter of Anah. (Anah was the son of Zibeon.) Esau and Oholibamah's children were Jeush, Jalam and Korah.

¹⁵These are the family groups that came from Esau:
Esau's first son was Eliphaz. From Eliphaz came Teman, Omar, Zepho, Kenaz, ¹⁶Korah, Gatam and Amalek.
All these family groups came from Esau's wife Adah.
¹⁷Esau's son Reuel was the father of these families: Nahath, Zerah, Shammah and Mizzah.
All these families came from Esau's wife Basemath. They were born in the territory of Edom.
¹⁸Esau's wife Oholibamah, daughter of Anah, gave birth to Jeush, Jalam and Korah. These three men were the leaders of their families.
¹⁹They were all sons of Esau and leaders of the family groups of Edom.[a]

²⁰Seir, a Horite man, lived in Edom before Esau. These are the sons of Seir:
Lotan, Shobal, Zibeon, Anah, ²¹Dishon, Ezer and Dishan. These sons were all Horite family leaders from Seir in Edom.
²²Lotan was the father of Hori and Heman.[b] (Timna was Lotan's sister.)
²³Shobal was the father of Alvan, Manahath, Ebal, Shepho and Onam.
²⁴Zibeon had two sons, Aiah and Anah. Anah is the man who found the springs in the desert while he was caring for his father's donkeys.

²⁵Anah was the father of Dishon and Oholibamah.
²⁶Dishon had four sons. They were Hemdan, Eshban, Ithran and Keran.
²⁷Ezer had three sons. They were Bilhan, Zaavan and Akan.
²⁸Dishan had two sons. They were Uz and Aran.
²⁹These are the names of the leaders of the Horite families: Lotan, Shobal, Zibeon, Anah, ³⁰Dishon, Ezer and Dishan. These men were the leaders of the families that lived in the country of Seir.

³¹At that time there were kings in Edom. Edom had kings a long time before Israel did.
³²Bela son of Beor was a king who ruled in Edom. He ruled over the city of Dinhabah.
³³When Bela died, Jobab became king. Jobab was the son of Zerah from Bozrah.
³⁴When Jobab died, Husham ruled. Husham was from the land of the Temanites.
³⁵When Husham died, Hadad ruled that area. Hadad was the son of Bedad. (He was the man who defeated Midian in the country of Moab.) Hadad was from the city of Avith.
³⁶When Hadad died, Samlah ruled that country. Samlah was from Masrekah.
³⁷When Samlah died, Shaul ruled that area. Shaul was from Rehoboth by the Euphrates River.
³⁸When Shaul died, Baal Hanan ruled that country. Baal Hanan was the son of Acbor.
³⁹When Baal Hanan died, Hadad[c] ruled that country. Hadad was from the city of Pau. His wife's name was Mehetabel, the daughter of Matred. (Mezahab was Matred's father.)

⁴⁰⁻⁴³Esau was the father of the Edomite families:

Timna, Alvah, Jetheth, Oholibamah, Elah, Pinon, Kenaz, Teman, Mibzar, Magdiel and Iram. Each of these families lived in an area that was called by the same name as their family.

Joseph the Dreamer

37 Jacob lived in the land of Canaan, where his father had lived. ²This is the story of Jacob's family.

---

[a] **36:19** *Esau . . . Edom* Two names for the man Esau and the country Edom.
[b] **36:22** *Heman* Or "Homam".
[c] **36:39** *Hadad* Or "Hadar".

DESPISED AND REJECTED

Have you ever had something really good only to have it taken away from you? Maybe it was a favourite toy that broke or a best friend who moved away? Joseph was a character pretty familiar with losing good things.

Jacob, the grandson of Abraham, is living in Canaan, the land God has given and is trying to bring up his very large family (Genesis 35:22–29). He doesn't seem to be doing a great job of treating all his sons equally.

DIG IN

READ Genesis 37:1–36

- How did Jacob treat his son, Joseph (v.3)?
- How did Joseph's dreams make his brothers feel (vv.4,8,11)?
- How do Joseph's brothers get even (vv.18–36)?

We might expect the brothers to act up, shout at their dad and maybe make life hard for Joseph, but throwing him in a pit, selling him into slavery and then telling Jacob he was dead?! It's a pretty extreme reaction, isn't it?

This story should get us asking some questions – was Joseph just being arrogant, or would the dreams actually come true? Having been taken out of the land God promised to Abraham, it wasn't looking great for Joseph – what would happen to him?

READ Genesis 39:1–23

- What do we learn about Joseph?
- What do we learn about God and his plans?
- How would you feel if you were Joseph?

It all starts off so well. The Lord is with Joseph and he is quickly given a good job in Egypt. But it all goes pear-shaped when Potiphar's wife starts to fancy him – before he knows it he is slammed up behind bars. Having been sold by his brothers and shipped far away from home, he now finds himself in prison, having done nothing wrong. It might look like a disaster, but God is still with him (v.21).

READ Genesis 40:1–23

- Who gives Joseph the ability to interpret dreams?
- How would you feel if you were Joseph?

Joseph must have been pretty excited – he could finally see a way out of the prison. But wait a minute, the wine server was so excited about getting out of prison that he forgot to mention Joseph. He must have been gutted.

DIG THROUGH

- Is life tough? Does God feel far away? Just as God was still with Joseph in a grim place like prison, he is with you whatever you're going through. He has a perfect plan for your life; keep hanging on to him.
- Are you tempted to give up when things feel hard? What about when Joseph's brothers betrayed him? Or when Potiphar's wife wanted to sleep with him? He could have given in. What about when he was in prison? He could have made the job of the guards really tough. What can you learn from Joseph?

DIG DEEPER

- Up to this point Joseph has been rejected by his family, sold for a few pieces of silver and been treated like an enemy, being thrown into prison. Fast-forward almost 2,000 years and another man, Jesus, faces similar things. Throughout the Old Testament there are many references to Jesus (though they do not use his name). Sometimes they are in what the prophets say, sometimes they are in the way certain characters experience life – the writers want us to know that someone special is coming who will fulfil all those promises God made to Abraham. Check out Isaiah 53:3–6, Zechariah 11:12–13 and 13:7–9.

INSIGHT

The special coat Jacob gave to Joseph was probably a long robe with sleeves, and may have been richly embroidered. This would set him apart as special and superior, as labourers wore shorter, sleeveless garments.

Genesis 37:3

When Jacob's son Joseph was 17 years old, his job was to take care of the sheep and the goats. Joseph did this work with his brothers, the sons of Bilhah and Zilpah, his father's wives. Joseph told his father about some bad things his brothers had done. ³Joseph was born at a time when his father Israel was very old, so Israel loved him more than he loved his other sons. Jacob gave him a special coat, which was long and very beautiful.ᵃ ⁴When Joseph's brothers saw that their father loved Joseph more than he loved them, they hated their brother because of this. They refused to say nice things to him.

⁵One night Joseph had a special dream. When he told his brothers about this dream, they hated him even more.

⁶Joseph said, "I had a dream. ⁷We were all working in the field, tying bundles of wheat together. Then my bundle got up. It stood there while all your bundles of wheat made a circle around mine and bowed down to it."

⁸His brothers said, "Do you think this means that you will be a king and rule over us?" His brothers hated Joseph even more because of the dreams he had about them.

⁹Then Joseph had another dream, and he told his brothers about it. He said, "I had another dream. I saw the sun, the moon and eleven stars bowing down to me."

¹⁰Joseph also told his father about this dream, but his father criticized him. His father said, "What kind of dream is this? Do you believe that your mother, your brothers and I will bow down to you?" ¹¹Joseph's brothers continued to be jealous of him, but his father thought about all these things and wondered what they could mean.

¹²One day Joseph's brothers went to Shechem to care for their father's sheep. ¹³Jacob said to Joseph, "Go to Shechem. Your brothers are there with my sheep."

Joseph answered, "I will go."

¹⁴His father said, "Go and see if your brothers are safe. Come back and tell me if my sheep are all fine." So Joseph's father sent him from the Valley of Hebron to Shechem.

¹⁵At Shechem, Joseph got lost. A man found him wandering in the fields. The man said, "What are you looking for?"

¹⁶Joseph answered, "I am looking for my brothers. Can you tell me where they are with their sheep?"

¹⁷The man said, "They have already gone away. I heard them say that they were going to Dothan." So Joseph followed his brothers and found them in Dothan.

Joseph Sold Into Slavery

¹⁸Joseph's brothers saw him coming from far away. They decided to make a plan to kill him. ¹⁹They said to each other, "Here comes Joseph the dreamer. ²⁰We should kill him now while we can. We could throw his body into one of the empty wells and tell our father that a wild animal killed him. Then we will show him that his dreams are useless."

²¹But Reuben wanted to save Joseph. He said, "Let's not kill him. ²²We can put him into a well without hurting him." Reuben planned to save Joseph and send him back to his father. ²³When Joseph came to his brothers, they attacked him and tore off his long and beautiful coat. ²⁴Then they threw him into an empty well that was dry.

²⁵While Joseph was in the well, the brothers sat down to eat. They looked up and saw a group of tradersᵇ travelling from Gilead to Egypt. Their camels were carrying many different spices and riches. ²⁶So Judah said to his brothers, "What profit will we get if we kill our brother and hide his death? ²⁷We will profit more if we sell him to these traders. Then we will not be guilty of killing our own brother." The other brothers agreed. ²⁸When the Midianite traders came by, the brothers took Joseph out of the well and sold him to the traders for 20 pieces of silver. The traders took him to Egypt.

²⁹Reuben had been away, but when he came back to the well, he saw that Joseph was not there. He tore his clothes to show that he was upset. ³⁰Reuben went to the brothers and said, "The boy is not in the well! What will I do now?" ³¹The brothers killed a goat and put the goat's blood on Joseph's beautiful coat. ³²Then the brothers showed the coat to their father. And the brothers said, "We found this coat. Is this Joseph's coat?"

³³His father saw the coat and knew that it was Joseph's. He said, "Yes, that is his! Maybe some

---

ᵃ **37:3** *beautiful* The Hebrew means "striped" or possibly "many coloured".
ᵇ **37:25** *traders* Literally, "Ishmaelites".

wild animal has killed him. My son Joseph has been eaten by a wild animal!" ³⁴Jacob was so upset about his son that he tore his clothes. Then Jacob put on special clothes to show that he was sad. He continued to be sad about his son for a long time. ³⁵All of Jacob's sons and daughters tried to comfort him, but Jacob was never comforted. He said, "I will be sad about my son until the day I die." So Jacob continued to mourn his son Joseph.

³⁶The Midianite traders later sold Joseph in Egypt. They sold him to Potiphar, an officer of the king of Egypt and the captain of his palace guards.

Judah and Tamar

38 About that time, Judah left his brothers and went to stay with a man named Hirah from the town of Adullam. ²Judah met a Canaanite girl there and married her. The girl's father was named Shua. ³The Canaanite girl gave birth to a son and named him Er. ⁴Later, she gave birth to another son and named him Onan. ⁵Then she had another son named Shelah. Judah lived in Kezib when his third son was born.

⁶Judah chose a woman named Tamar to be the wife of his first son Er. ⁷But Er did many bad things. The LORD was not happy with him, so the LORD killed him. ⁸Then Judah said to Er's brother Onan, "Go and sleep with your dead brother's wife.ᵃ Become like a husband to her. If children are born, they will belong to your brother Er."

⁹Onan knew that the children would not belong to him. So when he had sex with Tamar, he pulled away before he finished. By doing this, he kept Tamar from getting pregnant and having a child for his brother. ¹⁰This made the LORD angry. So he killed Onan also. ¹¹Then Judah said to his daughter-in-law Tamar, "Go back to your father's house. Stay there and don't marry until my young son Shelah grows up." Judah was afraid that Shelah would also be killed like his brothers. So Tamar went back to her father's home.

¹²Later, Judah's wife, the daughter of Shua, died. After Judah's time of sadness, he went to Timnah with his friend Hirah from Adullam. Judah went to Timnah to have the wool cut from his sheep. ¹³Tamar learned that Judah, her father-in-law, was going to Timnah to cut the wool from his sheep. ¹⁴Tamar always wore clothes that showed that she was a widow. So she put on some different clothes and covered her face with a veil. Then she sat down near the road going to Enaim, a town near Timnah. Tamar knew that Judah's younger son Shelah was now

grown up, but Judah would not make plans for her to marry him.

¹⁵Judah travelled on that road and saw her, but he thought that she was a prostitute. (Her face was covered with a veil like a prostitute.) ¹⁶So he went to her and said, "Let me have sex with you." (Judah did not know that she was Tamar, his daughter-in-law.)

She said, "How much will you give me?"

¹⁷Judah answered, "I will send you a young goat from my flock."

She answered, "I agree to that. But first you must give me something to keep until you send me the goat."

¹⁸Judah asked, "What do you want me to give you as proof that I will send you the goat?"

Tamar answered, "Give me your seal and its stringᵇ and your walking stick." Judah gave these things to her. Then Judah and Tamar had sex, and she became pregnant. ¹⁹Then Tamar went home, took off her veil that covered her face, and again put on the special clothes that showed she was a widow.

²⁰Later, Judah sent his friend Hirah to Enaim to give the prostitute the goat he had promised her. Judah also told Hirah to get the special seal and the walking stick from her, but Hirah could not find her. ²¹He asked some of the men at the town of Enaim, "Where is the prostitute who was here by the road?"

The men answered, "There has never been a prostitute here."

²²So Judah's friend went back to Judah and said, "I could not find the woman. The men who live in that place said that there was never a prostitute there."

²³So Judah said, "Let her keep the things. I don't want people to laugh at us. I tried to give her the goat, but we could not find her. That is enough."

Tamar Is Pregnant

²⁴About three months later, someone told Judah, "Your daughter-in-law Tamar sinned like a prostitute, and now she is pregnant."

Then Judah said, "Take her out and burn her."

²⁵The men went to Tamar to kill her, but she sent a message to her father-in-law that said, "The man who made me pregnant is the man who owns these things. Look at them. Whose are they? Whose special seal and string is this? Whose walking stick is this?"

²⁶Judah recognized these things and said, "She is right. I was wrong. I did not give her my son

---

ᵃ **38:8 Go and sleep . . . wife** In Israel if a man died without children, one of his brothers would take the widow. If a child was born, it would be considered the dead man's child.

ᵇ **38:18 seal . . . string** People wrote a contract, folded it, tied it with string, put wax or clay on the string, and pressed the seal onto it to seal it. This was like signing the agreement. Also in verse 25.

Shelah like I promised." And Judah did not sleep with her again.

27The time came for Tamar to give birth. She was going to have twins. 28While she was giving birth, one baby put his hand out. The nurse tied a red string on the hand and said, "This baby was born first." 29But that baby pulled his hand back in, so the other baby was born first. So the nurse said, "You were able to break out first!" So they named him Perez.*a* 30After this, the other baby was born. This was the baby with the red string on his hand. They named him Zerah.*b*

Joseph Is Sold to Potiphar in Egypt

39 The traders*c* who bought Joseph took him down to Egypt. They sold him to Potiphar, an officer of the king of Egypt and the captain of his palace guards. 2The LORD helped Joseph become a successful man. Joseph lived in the house of his master, Potiphar the Egyptian.

3Potiphar saw that the LORD was with Joseph and that the LORD helped Joseph to be successful in everything he did. 4So Potiphar was very happy with Joseph. He allowed Joseph to work for him and to help him rule the house. Joseph was the ruler over everything Potiphar owned. 5After Joseph was made the ruler over the house, the LORD blessed the house and everything that Potiphar owned. The LORD also blessed everything that grew in Potiphar's fields. The Lord did this because of Joseph. 6So Potiphar allowed Joseph to take responsibility for everything in the house. Potiphar did not have to worry about anything except deciding what to eat.

Joseph Refuses Potiphar's Wife

Joseph was a very handsome, good-looking man. 7After some time, the wife of Joseph's master began to pay special attention to him. One day she said to him, "Sleep with me."

8But Joseph refused. He said, "My master trusts me with everything in his house. He has given me responsibility for everything here. 9My master has made me almost equal to him in his house. I cannot sleep with his wife! That is wrong! It is a sin against God."

10The woman talked with Joseph every day, but he refused to sleep with her. 11One day Joseph went into the house to do his work. He was the only man in the house at the time. 12His master's wife grabbed his coat and said to him, "Come to bed with me." But Joseph ran out of the house so fast that he left his coat in her hand.

13The woman saw that Joseph had left his coat in her hand and had run out of the house. 14She called to the men outside and said, "Look! This Hebrew slave was brought here to make fun of us. He came in and tried to attack me, but I screamed. 15My scream scared him and he ran away, but he left his coat with me." 16Then she kept his coat until her husband, Joseph's master, came home. 17She told her husband the same story. She said, "This Hebrew slave you brought here tried to attack me! 18But when he came near me, I screamed. He ran away, but he left his coat."

19Joseph's master listened to what his wife said, and he became very angry. 20So Potiphar put Joseph into the prison where the king's enemies were held, and that is where Joseph remained.

Joseph in Prison

21The LORD was with Joseph and continued to show his kindness to him, so the commander of the prison guards began to like Joseph. 22The commander of the guards put Joseph in charge of all the prisoners. Joseph was their leader, but he still did the same work they did. 23The commander of the guards trusted Joseph with everything in the prison. This happened because the LORD was with Joseph. The LORD made him successful in everything he did.

Joseph Explains Two Dreams

40 Later, two of Pharaoh's servants did something wrong to Pharaoh. These servants were the baker and the man who served wine to Pharaoh. 2Pharaoh became angry with his baker and wine server, 3so he put them in the same prison as Joseph. Potiphar, the commander of Pharaoh's guards, was in charge of this prison. 4The commander put the two prisoners under Joseph's care. The two men continued to stay in prison for some time. 5One night both of the prisoners had a dream. The baker and the wine server each had his own dream, and each dream had its own meaning. 6Joseph went to them the next morning and saw that the two men were worried. 7He asked them, "Why do you look so worried today?"

8The two men answered, "We both had dreams last night, but we don't understand what we dreamed. There is no one to explain the dreams to us."

Joseph said to them, "God is the only one who can understand and explain dreams. So I beg you, tell me your dreams."

---

a **38:29** *Perez* This name is like the word meaning "to break out".
b **38:30** *Zerah* This name is like the word meaning "bright".
c **39:1** *traders* Literally, "Ishmaelites".

The Wine Server's Dream

9So the wine server told Joseph his dream. The server said, "I dreamed I saw a vine. 10On the vine there were three branches. I watched the branches grow flowers and then become grapes. 11I was holding Pharaoh's cup, so I took the grapes and squeezed the juice into the cup. Then I gave the cup to Pharaoh."

12Then Joseph said, "I will explain the dream to you. The three branches mean three days. 13Before the end of three days, Pharaoh will forgive you and allow you to go back to your work. You will do the same work for Pharaoh as you did before. 14But when you are free, remember me. Be good to me and help me. Tell Pharaoh about me so that I can get out of this prison. 15I was kidnapped and taken from the land of my people, the Hebrews. I have done nothing wrong! I should not be in prison."

The Baker's Dream

16The baker saw that the other servant's dream was good, so he said to Joseph, "I also had a dream. I dreamed there were three baskets of bread on my head. 17In the top basket there were all kinds of baked food for the king, but birds were eating this food."

18Joseph answered, "I will tell you what the dream means. The three baskets mean three days. 19Before the end of three days, the king will take you out of this prison and cut off your head! He will hang your body on a pole, and the birds will eat it."

Joseph Is Forgotten

20Three days later it was Pharaoh's birthday. He gave a party for all his servants. At the party Pharaoh allowed the wine server and the baker to leave the prison. 21He freed the wine server and gave him his job back, and once again the wine server put a cup of wine in Pharaoh's hand. 22But Pharaoh hanged the baker, and everything happened the way Joseph said it would. 23But the wine server did not remember to help Joseph. He said nothing about him to Pharaoh. The wine server forgot about Joseph.

Pharaoh's Dreams

41 Two years later Pharaoh dreamed that he was standing by the Nile River. 2In the dream, seven cows came out of the river and stood there eating grass. They were healthy, good-looking cows. 3Then seven more cows came out of the river and stood on the bank of the river by the healthy cows. But these cows were thin and looked sick. 4The seven sick cows ate the seven healthy cows. Then Pharaoh woke up.

5Pharaoh went back to sleep and began dreaming again. This time he dreamed that he saw seven heads of grain growing on one plant. They were healthy and full of grain. 6Then he saw seven more heads of grain sprouting, but they were thin and scorched by the hot wind. 7The thin heads of grain ate the seven good heads of grain. Then Pharaoh woke up again and realized it was only a dream. 8The next morning Pharaoh was worried about these dreams, so he sent for all the magicians and wise men of Egypt. Pharaoh told these men the dreams, but none of them could explain the dreams.

The Servant Tells Pharaoh About Joseph

9Then the wine servant remembered Joseph and said to Pharaoh, "I remember something that happened to me. 10You were angry with the baker and me, and you put us in prison. 11Then one night he and I had a dream. Each dream had a different meaning. 12There was a young Hebrew man in prison with us. He was a servant of the commander of the guards. We told him our dreams, and he explained them to us. He told us the meaning of each dream, 13and what he said came true. He said I would be free and have my old job back, and it happened. He also said the baker would die, and it happened!"

Joseph Is Called to Explain the Dreams

14So Pharaoh called Joseph from the prison. The guards quickly got Joseph out of prison. Joseph shaved, put on some clean clothes, and went to see Pharaoh. 15Pharaoh said to Joseph, "I had a dream, and no one can explain it for me. I heard that you can explain dreams when someone tells you about them."

16Joseph answered, "I cannot! But God can explain the dream for you, Pharaoh."

17Then Pharaoh said to Joseph, "In my dream I was standing by the Nile River. 18Seven cows came up out of the river and stood there eating the grass. They were healthy, good-looking cows. 19Then I saw seven more cows come up out of the river after them, but these cows were thin and looked sick. They were the worst cows I had ever seen anywhere in Egypt! 20The thin, sick cows ate the first healthy cows, 21but they still looked thin and sick. You couldn't even tell they had eaten the healthy cows. They looked as thin and sick as they did in the beginning. Then I woke up.

22"In my next dream I saw seven heads of grain growing on one plant. They were healthy and full of grain. 23And then seven more heads of grain grew after them, but they were thin and scorched by the hot wind. 24Then the thin heads of grain ate the seven good heads of grain.

"I told these dreams to my magicians. But no one could explain the dreams to me. What do they mean?"

Joseph Explains the Dreams

25Then Joseph said to Pharaoh, "Both of these dreams have the same meaning. God is telling you what will happen soon. 26The seven good cows and the seven good heads of grain are seven good years. 27And the seven thin, sick-looking cows and the seven thin heads of grain mean that there will be seven years of hunger in this area. These seven bad years will come after the seven good years. 28God has shown you what will happen soon. He will make these things happen just as I told you. 29For seven years there will be plenty of food in Egypt. 30But then there will be seven years of hunger. The people will forget how much food there had been in Egypt before. This famine will ruin the country. 31It will be so bad that people will forget what it was like to have plenty of food.

32"Pharaoh, you had two dreams about the same thing. This means that God has decided he will make this happen, and he will do it soon! 33So, Pharaoh, you should choose a wise, intelligent man and put him in charge of Egypt. 34Then you should choose other men to collect food from the people. During the seven good years, the people must give them one-fifth of all the food they grow. 35In this way, these men will collect all the food during the seven good years and store it in the cities until it is needed. Pharaoh, this food will be under your control. 36Then during the seven years of hunger, there will be food for the country of Egypt. And Egypt will not be destroyed by the famine."

37This seemed like a very good idea to Pharaoh, and all his officials agreed. 38Then Pharaoh told them, "I don't think we can find anyone better than Joseph to take this job! God's Spirit is in him, making him very wise!"

39So Pharaoh said to Joseph, "God showed these things to you, so you must be the wisest man. 40I will put you in charge of my country, and the people will obey all your commands. I will be the only one more powerful than you."

41Pharaoh said to Joseph, "I now make you governor over all the land of Egypt." 42Then Pharaoh gave his special ring to Joseph. The royal seal was on this ring. Pharaoh also gave Joseph a fine linen robe and put a gold chain around his neck. 43Then he told Joseph to ride in his second chariot. Pharaoh's officials said, "Let him be the governor over the whole land of Egypt!"[a]

INSIGHT

In Old Testament times those who lived in the Middle East depended on rain for the success of their crops. If it didn't rain, people didn't have enough to eat and often went to Egypt where the Nile flooded each year, making the ground rich and fertile. If it didn't rain in Egypt it would be disastrous, so Joseph's prediction of seven years of famine was taken very seriously.

Genesis 41:25–43

44Then Pharaoh said to him, "I am Pharaoh, the king over everyone in Egypt, but no one else in Egypt can lift a hand or move a foot unless you say he can." 45Then Pharaoh gave Joseph another name, Zaphenath Paneah.[b] He also gave Joseph a wife named Asenath. She was the daughter of Potiphera, a priest in the city of On. So Joseph became the governor over the whole country of Egypt.

46Joseph was 30 years old when he began serving the king of Egypt. He travelled throughout the land. 47During the seven good years, the crops in Egypt grew very well. 48Joseph saved the food in Egypt during those seven years and stored the food in the cities. In every city he stored grain that grew in the fields around the city. 49Joseph stored so much grain that it was like the sand on the seashore. He stored so much grain that it could not be measured.

50Joseph's wife, Asenath, was the daughter of Potiphera, the priest in the city of On. Before the first year of hunger came, Joseph and Asenath had two sons. 51Joseph named the first son Manasseh.[c] He was given this name because Joseph said, "God made me forget all my hard work and everything back home in my father's house." 52Joseph named the second son Ephraim.[d] Joseph gave him this name because he said, "I had great troubles, but God has made me successful in everything."

---

[a] **41:43** Or "Then Pharaoh had Joseph ride in the chariot of his second-in-command, and they said, 'Bow before Joseph.' In this way Joseph became the governor over all the land of Egypt."
[b] **41:45** *Zaphenath Paneah* This Egyptian name probably means "sustainer of life", but it is like Hebrew words meaning "a person who explains secret things".
[c] **41:51** *Manasseh* This is like the Hebrew word meaning "to forget".
[d] **41:52** *Ephraim* This name is like the Hebrew word meaning "twice fruitful".

The Famine Begins

[53]For seven years people had all the food they needed, but those years ended. [54]Then the seven years of famine began, just as Joseph had said. No food grew anywhere in any of the countries in that area. But in Egypt people had plenty to eat because Joseph had stored the grain. [55]When the famine began, the people cried to Pharaoh for food. Pharaoh said to the Egyptian people, "Go and ask Joseph what to do."

[56]There was famine everywhere, so Joseph gave the people grain from the warehouses. He sold the stored grain to the people of Egypt. Not only was the famine bad in Egypt, [57]it was bad everywhere. So people from the countries around Egypt had to come to Joseph in Egypt to buy grain.

The Dreams Come True

42 During the famine in Canaan, Jacob learned that there was grain in Egypt. So he said to his sons, "Why are you sitting here doing nothing? [2]I have heard that there is grain for sale in Egypt. Go there and buy grain for us so that we will live and not die!"

[3]So ten of Joseph's brothers went to Egypt to buy grain. [4]Jacob did not send Benjamin. (Benjamin was Joseph's only full brother.a) Jacob was afraid that something bad might happen to Benjamin.

[5]The famine was very bad in Canaan, so there were many people from Canaan who went to Egypt to buy grain. Among them were the sons of Israel.

[6]Joseph was the governor of Egypt at the time. He was the one who checked the sale of grain to people who came to Egypt to buy it. Joseph's brothers came to him and bowed before him. [7]Joseph saw his brothers and recognized them, but he acted as if he did not know them. He was rude when he spoke to them. He said, "Where do you come from?"

The brothers answered, "We have come from the land of Canaan to buy food."

[8]Joseph recognized his brothers, but they did not know who he was. [9]Then Joseph remembered the dreams that he had dreamed about his brothers.

Joseph said to his brothers, "You have not come to buy food! You are spies. You came to learn where we are weak."

[10]But the brothers said to him, "No, sir, we come as your servants. We come only to buy food. [11]We are all brothers—we all have the same father. We are honest men. We have come only to buy food."

[12]Then Joseph said to them, "No, you have come to spy on us!"

[13]And the brothers said, "No, sir, we come as servants from Canaan. We are all brothers, sons of the same father. There were twelve brothers in our family. Our youngest brother is still at home with our father, and the other brother died a long time ago."

[14]But Joseph said to them, "No! I can see that I am right. You are spies. [15]But I will let you prove that you are telling the truth. In the name of Pharaoh, I swear that I will not let you go until your youngest brother comes here. [16]One of you must go back to get your youngest brother while the rest of you stay here in prison. Then we can prove whether you are telling the truth or not. If you are not telling the truth, then by Pharaoh, I swear that you are spies!" [17]Then Joseph put them all in prison for three days.

The Troubles Begin

[18]After three days, Joseph said to them, "I am a God-fearing man. Do this, and I will let you live. [19]If you are honest men, one of your brothers can stay here in prison, and the others can go and carry grain back to your people. [20]But then you must bring your youngest brother back here to me. Then I will know that you are telling the truth, and you will not have to die."

The brothers agreed to this. [21]They said to each other, "We are being punished for the bad thing we did to our younger brother Joseph. We saw the trouble he was in. He begged us to save him, but we refused to listen. So now we are in trouble."

[22]Then Reuben said to them, "I told you not to do anything bad to that boy, but you refused to listen to me. Now we are being punished for his death."

[23–24]Joseph was using an interpreter to talk to his brothers, so the brothers did not know that he understood their language. He heard and understood everything they said, and that made him want to cry. So he turned away and left the room. When he came back, he took one of the brothers, Simeon, and tied him up while the others watched. [25]Joseph told the servants to fill the bags with grain. The brothers had given Joseph the money for the grain, but he did not keep the money. He put the money in their bags of grain. Then he gave them what they would need for their journey back home.

[26]So the brothers put the grain on their donkeys and left. [27]That night the brothers stopped at a place to spend the night. One of the brothers opened his sack to get some grain for his donkey.

---

a **42:4 full brother** Literally, "brother". Joseph and Benjamin had the same mother.

YOU PLANNED
TO DO SOMETHING BAD TO ME

How do you feel when things get tough? Unloved? Forgotten about? As if your life is one massive mistake? Joseph would have been forgiven for feeling like that . . .

DIG IN — READ Genesis 41:1-57

- Why not draw some pictures of Pharaoh's dreams.
- What did the dreams mean?
- How can you see God at work through all the events here?

Who would have thought a dream could be so significant? For Joseph it was the difference between rotting away in prison and becoming a powerful official in Egypt. The wine server may have forgotten him for two years – but God certainly hadn't and was organizing everything in just the right way.

READ Genesis 42:1 – 44:34

Things are getting pretty dramatic – the famine hits Canaan pretty badly and Joseph's brothers are sent to Egypt to buy food. As the story unfolds they come face to face with Joseph but don't realize who he is. These chapters give the full story. Ask as you read:

- How is God sorting everything out so that he keeps the promises he made to Abraham (Genesis 12:1–9)?

READ Genesis 45:1-28

- Who does Joseph say sent him to Egypt (v.5)?
- Why is it important that Joseph was in Egypt?

It's amazing isn't it? Not only does Joseph not have a go at his brothers but he is also full of forgiveness. He's aware of a bigger plan! God used the brothers' jealousy as a means of sending Joseph to Egypt. Why? Because if one of God's people hadn't been in Egypt to sort out the food stores when the famine hit, then God's people in Canaan would have been wiped out! Joseph was placed in Egypt by God so that God could keep his promises to Abraham. Amazing or what?!

READ Genesis 50:15-26

- What does verse 20 tell us about God's plans?
- Where does Joseph want to be buried? Why?

All along, God was using Joseph to fulfil his plan to save his people. Does that sound familiar? Joseph is a "prefiguring" (a picture) of Jesus – he also is used by God (even in a painful, difficult way) to save others. And, understanding God's promises, Joseph asks to be buried not in Egypt, but in the land that God promised his people.

DIG THROUGH

It's pretty mind-boggling to think that God was doing all this stuff to ensure his people didn't die out when the famine hit. At the end of his life, Joseph could see that God was behind it all – despite how rubbish it all must have felt at the time.

- Check out Romans 8:28 and think over the events in your life – can you trust God that no matter what you're going through it is for good?
- Check out Genesis 50:20 again – through one man, Joseph, God saved many. Once more, does that sound familiar? Why not thank God for Jesus, and for the way he used other Old Testament characters to show us more of Jesus.

And there in the sack, he saw his money! ²⁸He said to the other brothers, "Look! Here is the money I paid for the grain. Someone put the money back in my sack." The brothers were very afraid. They said to each other, "What is God doing to us?"

The Brothers Report to Jacob

²⁹The brothers went back to their father Jacob in the land of Canaan. They told him about everything that had happened. ³⁰They said, "The governor of that country spoke rudely to us. He thought that we were spies! ³¹We told him, 'We are honest men, not spies. ³²There are twelve of us brothers, all from the same father. But one of our brothers is no longer living, and the youngest is still at home with our father in Canaan.' ³³"Then the governor of that country said to us, 'Here is a way to prove that you are honest men: Leave one of your brothers here with me. Take your grain back to your families. ³⁴Bring your youngest brother to me. Then I will know if you are honest men or if you were sent from an army to destroy us. If you are telling the truth, I will give your brother back to you. I will give him to you, and you will be free to buy grain in our country.'"

³⁵Then the brothers started taking the grain out of their sacks, and every brother found his bag of money in his sack of grain. When the brothers and their father saw the money, they were afraid. ³⁶Jacob said to them, "Do you want me to lose all my children? Joseph is gone. Simeon is gone, and now you want to take Benjamin away too!"

³⁷But Reuben said to his father, "Father, you may kill my two sons if I don't bring Benjamin back to you. Trust me. I will bring him back to you."

³⁸But Jacob said, "I will not let Benjamin go with you. His brother is dead, and he is the only son left from my wife Rachel. It would kill me if anything happened to him during the trip to Egypt. You would send me to the grave*ᵃ* a very sad, old man."

Jacob Lets Benjamin Go to Egypt

43 The famine was very bad in the land of Canaan. ²The people ate all the grain they had brought from Egypt. When that grain was gone, Jacob said to his sons, "Go to Egypt and buy some more grain for us to eat."

³But Judah said to Jacob, "But the governor of that country warned us. He said, 'If you don't bring your brother back to me, I will refuse to talk to you.' ⁴If you send Benjamin with us, we will go down and buy grain. ⁵But if you refuse to send

Benjamin, we will not go. The man warned us not to come back without him."

⁶Israel said, "Why did you tell him you had another brother? Why did you do such a bad thing to me?"

⁷The brothers answered, "He asked lots of questions. He wanted to know all about us and about our family. He asked us, 'Is your father still alive? Do you have another brother at home?' We only answered his questions. We did not know he would ask us to bring our brother to him!"

⁸Then Judah said to his father Israel, "Let Benjamin go with me. I will take care of him. We have to go to Egypt to get food. If we don't go, we will all die—including our children. ⁹I will make sure he is safe. I will be responsible for him. If I don't bring him back to you, you can blame me forever. ¹⁰If you had let us go before, we could already have made two trips for food."

¹¹Then their father Israel said, "If it is really true, take Benjamin with you. But take some gifts to the governor. Take some of the things we have been able to gather in our land. Take him some balm,*ᵇ* honey, pistachio nuts, almonds, spices and myrrh. ¹²Take twice as much money with you this time. Take the money that was given back to you after you paid last time. Maybe the governor made a mistake. ¹³Take Benjamin, and go back to the man. ¹⁴I pray that God All-Powerful will help you when you stand before the governor. I pray that he will let Benjamin, and also Simeon, come back safely. If not, I will again be sad from losing my children."

¹⁵So the brothers took the gifts to give to the governor. And the brothers took twice as much money with them as they took the first time. This time Benjamin went with the brothers to Egypt.

The Brothers at Joseph's House

¹⁶When Joseph saw Benjamin with them, he said to his servant, "Bring these men into my house. Kill an animal and cook it. They will eat with me at noon today." ¹⁷The servant did as he was told. He brought the men into Joseph's house.

¹⁸The brothers were afraid when they were taken to Joseph's house and said, "We have been brought here because of the money that was put back in our sacks the last time. They will use this as proof against us and steal our donkeys and make us slaves."

¹⁹So the brothers went to the servant in charge of Joseph's house. ²⁰They said, "Sir, I promise this is the truth. The last time we came, we came to buy food. ²¹⁻²²On the way home, we opened our

---

ᵃ **42:38** *grave* Or "Sheol", the place of death.
ᵇ **43:11** *balm* An ointment from some kinds of trees and plants. It is used as medicine.

sacks and found our money in every sack. We don't know how it got there, but we brought that money with us to give it back to you. And we have brought more money to pay for the food that we want to buy this time."

23But the servant answered, "Don't be afraid; believe me. Your God, the God of your father, must have put the money in your sack as a gift. I remember that you paid me for the grain the last time."

Then the servant brought Simeon out of the prison. 24The servant led the men into Joseph's house. He gave them water, and they washed their feet. Then he fed their donkeys.

25The brothers heard that they were going to eat with Joseph, so they worked until noon preparing their gifts for him.

26When Joseph came home, the brothers gave him the gifts they had brought with them. Then they bowed down to the ground in front of him.

27Joseph asked them how they were doing. Then he said, "How is your elderly father you told me about? Is he still alive and well?"

28The brothers answered, "Yes, sir, our father is still alive." And they again bowed before Joseph.

29Then Joseph saw his brother Benjamin. (Benjamin and Joseph had the same mother.) Joseph said, "Is this your youngest brother that you told me about?" Then Joseph said to Benjamin, "God bless you, my son!"

30Joseph felt a strong desire to show his brother Benjamin that he loved him. He was about to cry and did not want his brothers to see him, so he ran into his private room and cried there. 31Then Joseph washed his face and came out. He regained control of himself and said, "Now it is time to eat."

32The servants seated Joseph at a table by himself. His brothers were at another table by themselves, and the Egyptians were at a table by themselves. The Egyptians believed that it was wrong for them to eat with Hebrews.ᵃ 33Joseph's brothers were seated at a table facing him. The brothers were looking at each other because, to their surprise, they had been seated in order, from the oldest to the youngest. 34Servants were taking food from Joseph's table and bringing it to them. But the servants gave Benjamin five times more than the others. The brothers continued to eat and drink with Joseph until they were drunk.

Joseph Sets a Trap

44 Then Joseph gave a command to his servant. He said, "Fill the men's sacks with as much grain as they can carry. Then put each man's money into his sack with the grain. 2Put the youngest brother's money in his sack too. But also put my special silver cup in his sack." So the servant obeyed Joseph.

3Early the next morning the brothers and their donkeys were sent back to their country. 4After they had left the city, Joseph said to his servant, "Go and follow the men. Stop them and say to them, 'We were good to you! So why have you been bad to us? Why did you steal my master's silver cup?ᵇ 5My master drinks from that cup, and he uses it to learn secret things. What you did was wrong!'"

6So the servant obeyed. He rode out to the brothers and stopped them. The servant said to them what Joseph had told him to say.

7But the brothers said to the servant, "Why does the governor say these things? We wouldn't do anything like that! 8We brought back the money that we found in our sacks before. So surely we wouldn't steal silver or gold from your master's house. 9If you find the silver cup in any of our sacks, let that man die. You can kill him, and we will be your slaves."

10The servant said, "I agree, except that only the man who is found to have the cup will be my slave. The others will be free."

The Trap Is Sprung; Benjamin Is Caught

11Then every brother quickly opened his sack on the ground. 12The servant started looking in the sacks. He started with the oldest brother and ended with the youngest. He found the cup in Benjamin's sack. 13The brothers were very sad. They tore their clothes to show their sadness. They put their sacks back on the donkeys and went back to the city.

14When Judah and his brothers went back to Joseph's house, Joseph was still there. The brothers fell to the ground and bowed down before him. 15Joseph said to them, "Why have you done this? Didn't you know that I have a special way of learning secrets? No one is better at this than I am!"

16Judah said, "Sir, there is nothing we can say. There is no way to explain. There is no way to show that we are not guilty. God has judged us guilty for something else we have done. So all of us, even Benjamin, will be your slaves."

17But Joseph said, "I will not make you all slaves! Only the man who stole the cup will be my slave. You others can go in peace to your father."

Judah Pleads for Benjamin

18Then Judah went to Joseph and said, "Sir, please let me speak plainly with you. Please don't

---

ᵃ 43:32 *The Egyptians . . . Hebrews* The Egyptians would not eat with them because they were shepherds and ate meat from cattle, sheep and goats. To the Egyptians, these animals represented some of their gods. See Gen. 46:34.
ᵇ 44:4 *Why did . . . silver cup* This is from the ancient Greek version.

be angry with me. I know that you are like Pharaoh himself. [19]When we were here before, you asked us, 'Do you have a father or a brother?' [20]And we answered you, 'We have a father—he is an old man. And we have a younger brother. Our father loves him because he was born while our father was old. This youngest son's brother is dead, so he is the only son who is left from that mother. Our father loves him very much.' [21]Then you said to us, 'Bring that brother to me. I want to see him.' [22]And we said to you, 'That young boy cannot come. He cannot leave his father. If his father loses him, his father will be so sad that he will die.' [23]But you said to us, 'You must bring your youngest brother, or I will not sell you grain again.' [24]So we went back to our father and told him what you said.

[25]"Later, our father said, 'Go back and buy us some more food.' [26]We said to our father, 'We cannot go without our youngest brother. The governor said he will not sell us grain again until he sees our youngest brother.' [27]Then my father said to us, 'You know that my wife Rachel gave me two sons. [28]I let one son go away, and he was killed by a wild animal. And I haven't seen him since. [29]If you take my other son away from me, and something happens to him, I will be sad enough to die.' [30]Now, imagine what will happen when we go home without our youngest brother—he is the most important thing in our father's life! [31]Our father will die if he sees that the boy isn't with us—and it will be our fault. We will send our father to his grave a very sad man.

[32]"I took responsibility for the young boy. I told my father, 'If I don't bring him back to you, you can blame me for the rest of my life.' [33]So now I beg you, please let the boy go back with his brothers, and I will stay and be your slave. [34]I cannot go back to my father if the boy is not with me. I am very afraid of what would happen to my father."

Joseph Reveals Who He Is

45 Joseph could not control himself any longer. He cried in front of all the people who were there. Joseph said, "Tell everyone to leave here." So all the people left. Only the brothers were left with Joseph. Then he told them who he was. [2]Joseph continued to cry, and all the Egyptian people in Pharaoh's house heard it. [3]He said to his brothers, "I am your brother Joseph. Is my father doing well?" But the brothers did not answer him because they were confused and afraid.

[4]So Joseph said to his brothers again, "Come here to me. I beg you, come here." When the brothers went to him, he said to them, "I am your brother Joseph. I am the one you sold as a slave to Egypt. [5]Now don't be worried. Don't be angry

with yourselves for what you did. It was God's plan for me to come here. I am here to save people's lives. [6]This terrible famine has continued for two years now, and there will be five more years without planting or harvest. [7]So God sent me here ahead of you so that I can save your people in this country. [8]It was not your fault that I was sent here. It was God's plan. God made me like a father to Pharaoh. I am the governor over all his house and over all the land of Egypt."

Israel Invited to Egypt

[9]Joseph said, "Hurry up and go to my father. Tell him his son Joseph sent this message: 'God made me the governor of Egypt. So come here to me quickly. Don't wait. [10]You can live near me in the land of Goshen. You, your children, your grandchildren, and all your animals are welcome here. [11]I will take care of you during the next five years of hunger. So you and your family will not lose everything you own.'

[12]"Surely you can see that I really am Joseph. Even my brother Benjamin knows it is me, your brother, talking to you. [13]So tell my father about the honour I have received here in Egypt. Tell him about everything you have seen here. Now hurry, go and bring my father back to me." [14]Then Joseph hugged his brother Benjamin, and they both began crying. [15]Then Joseph cried as he kissed all his brothers. After this, the brothers began talking with him.

[16]Pharaoh learned that Joseph's brothers had come to him. This news spread throughout Pharaoh's house. Pharaoh and his servants were very excited! [17]So Pharaoh told Joseph, "Tell your brothers to take all the food they need and go back to the land of Canaan. [18]Tell them to bring your father and their families back here to me. I will give you the best land in Egypt to live on. And your family can eat the best food we have here. [19]Also give your brothers some of our best carts. Tell them to go to Canaan and bring your father and all the women and children back in the carts. [20]Don't worry about bringing all their belongings. We can give them the best of Egypt."

[21]So the sons of Israel did this. Joseph gave them good carts just as Pharaoh had promised. And Joseph gave them enough food for their journey. [22]He gave each brother a suit of beautiful clothes. But to Benjamin he gave five suits of beautiful clothes and 300 pieces of silver. [23]Joseph also sent gifts to his father. He sent ten donkeys with bags full of many good things from Egypt. And he sent ten female donkeys loaded with grain, bread and other food for his father on his journey back. [24]Then Joseph told his brothers to go. While they were leaving, he said to them, "Go straight home, and don't fight on the way."

²⁵So the brothers left Egypt and went to their father in the land of Canaan. ²⁶They told him, "Father, Joseph is still alive! And he is the governor over the whole country of Egypt."

Their father did not know what to think. At first he did not believe them. ²⁷But then they told him everything Joseph had said. Then their father saw the carts that Joseph had sent to bring him back to Egypt, and he became excited and very happy. ²⁸Israel said, "Now I believe you. My son Joseph is still alive! I am going to see him before I die!"

God Assures Israel

46 So Israel began his journey to Egypt. First he went to Beersheba. There he worshipped God, the God of his father Isaac. He offered sacrifices. ²During the night God spoke to Israel in a dream and said, "Jacob, Jacob."

Israel answered, "Here I am."

³Then God said, "I am God, the God of your father. Don't be afraid to go to Egypt. In Egypt I will make you a great nation. ⁴I will go to Egypt with you, and I will bring you out of Egypt again. You will die there, but Joseph will be with you. His own hands will close your eyes when you die."

Israel Goes to Egypt

⁵Then Jacob left Beersheba and travelled to Egypt. His sons, the sons of Israel, brought their father, their wives, and all their children to Egypt. They travelled in the carts the Pharaoh had sent. ⁶They also had their cattle and everything they owned in the land of Canaan. So Israel went to Egypt with all his children and his family. ⁷With him were his sons and his grandsons, his daughters and his granddaughters. His whole family went with him.

The Family of Jacob (Israel)

⁸These are the names of Israel's sons and family who went to Egypt with him:

Reuben was Jacob's first son. ⁹Reuben's sons were Hanoch, Pallu, Hezron and Carmi. ¹⁰Simeon's sons were Jemuel, Jamin, Ohad, Jakin and Zohar. There was also Shaul. (Shaul was born from a Canaanite woman.) ¹¹Levi's sons were Gershon, Kohath and Merari. ¹²Judah's sons were Er, Onan, Shelah, Perez and Zerah. (Er and Onan died while still in Canaan.) Perez's sons were Hezron and Hamul. ¹³Issachar's sons were Tola, Puah, Job and Shimron. ¹⁴Zebulun's sons were Sered, Elon and Jahleel.

¹⁵Reuben, Simeon, Levi, Judah, Issachar and Zebulun were Jacob's sons from his wife Leah. Leah had these sons in Paddan Aram. She also had a daughter named Dinah. There were 33 people in this family.

¹⁶Gad's sons were Zephon, Haggi, Shuni, Ezbon, Eri, Arodi and Areli. ¹⁷Asher's sons were Imnah, Ishvah, Ishvi, Beriah and their sister Serah. Also there were Beriah's sons, Heber and Malkiel.

¹⁸All these were Jacob's sons from his wife's servant, Zilpah. (Zilpah was the maid that Laban had given to his daughter Leah.) There were 16 people in this family.

¹⁹Benjamin was also with Jacob. Benjamin was Jacob and Rachel's son. (Joseph was also Rachel's son, but he was already in Egypt.) ²⁰In Egypt, Joseph had two sons, Manasseh and Ephraim. (Joseph's wife was Asenath, the daughter of Potiphera, the priest in the city of On.) ²¹Benjamin's sons were Bela, Beker, Ashbel, Gera, Naaman, Ehi, Rosh, Muppim, Huppim and Ard.

²²These were the sons of Jacob from his wife Rachel. There were 14 people in this family.

²³Dan's son was Hushim. ²⁴Naphtali's sons were Jahziel, Guni, Jezer and Shillem.

²⁵These were the sons of Jacob and Bilhah. (Bilhah was the maid that Laban had given to his daughter Rachel.) There were seven people in this family.

²⁶The total number of Jacob's direct descendants who went with him to Egypt was 66 people. (The wives of Jacob's sons were not counted in this number.) ²⁷Also, Joseph had two sons in Egypt. With these two grandsons, Jacob's family in Egypt numbered 70 people in all.

Israel Arrives in Egypt

²⁸Jacob sent Judah ahead to speak to Joseph. Judah went to Joseph in the land of Goshen. Then Jacob and his people followed into the land. ²⁹Joseph learned that his father was coming. So he prepared his chariot and went out to meet his father, Israel, in Goshen. When Joseph saw his father, he hugged his neck and cried for a long time. ³⁰Then Israel said to Joseph, "Now I can die in peace. I have seen your face, and I know that you are still alive."

[31]Joseph said to his brothers and to the rest of his father's family, "I will go and tell Pharaoh that you are here. I will say to Pharaoh, 'My brothers and the rest of my father's family have left the land of Canaan and have come here to me. [32]They are a family of shepherds. They have always kept sheep and cattle. They have brought all their animals and everything they own with them.' [33]When Pharaoh calls you, he will ask, 'What work do you do?' [34]You tell him, 'We are shepherds. All our lives we have been shepherds, and our ancestors were shepherds before us.' Then Pharaoh will allow you to live in the land of Goshen. Egyptians don't like shepherds, so it is better that you stay in Goshen."

Israel Settles in Goshen

47 Joseph went in to Pharaoh and said, "My father and my brothers and all their families are here. They have all their animals and everything they own from the land of Canaan with them. They are now in the land of Goshen." [2]Joseph chose five of his brothers to be with him before the Pharaoh.

[3]Pharaoh said to the brothers, "What work do you do?"

The brothers said to Pharaoh, "Sir, we are shepherds, just as our ancestors were shepherds before us." [4]They said to Pharaoh, "The famine is very bad in Canaan. There are no fields left with grass for our animals, so we have come to live in this land. We ask you to please let us live in Goshen."

[5]Then Pharaoh said to Joseph, "Your father and your brothers have come to you. [6]You can choose anywhere in Egypt for them to live. Give your father and your brothers the best land. Let them live in the land of Goshen. And if they are skilled shepherds, they can also care for my cattle."

[7]Then Joseph called his father Jacob to come in to meet Pharaoh. Jacob blessed Pharaoh.

[8]Then Pharaoh said to him, "How old are you?"

[9]Jacob said to Pharaoh, "I have had a short life with many troubles. I am only 130 years old. My father and his ancestors lived to be much older than I am."

[10]Then Jacob blessed Pharaoh and left from his meeting with him.

[11]Joseph did what Pharaoh said and gave his father and brothers land in Egypt. It was the best land in Egypt, in the eastern part of the country, around Rameses. [12]Joseph also gave his father, his brothers, and all their people the food they needed.

Joseph Buys Land for Pharaoh

[13]The famine got worse; there was no food anywhere in the land. Egypt and Canaan became very poor because of this bad time. [14]People in the land bought more and more grain. Joseph saved the money and brought it to Pharaoh's house. [15]After some time, the people in Egypt and Canaan had no money left. They had spent all their money to buy grain. So the people of Egypt went to Joseph and said, "Please give us food. Our money is gone. If we don't eat, we will die while you are watching."

[16]But Joseph answered, "Give me your cattle, and I will give you food." [17]So the people used their cattle and horses and all their other animals to buy food. And that year, Joseph gave them food and took their animals.

[18]But the next year the people had no animals and nothing to buy food with. So they went to Joseph and said, "You know that we have no money left, and all our animals belong to you. So we have nothing left—only what you see—our bodies and our land. [19]Surely we will die while you are watching. But if you give us food, we will give Pharaoh our land, and we will be his slaves. Give us seed so that we can plant. Then we will live and not die, and the land will grow food for us again."

[20]So Joseph bought all the land in Egypt for Pharaoh. All the people in Egypt sold Joseph their fields. They did this because they were very hungry. [21]And everywhere in Egypt all the people became Pharaoh's slaves. [22]The only land Joseph did not buy was the land that the priests owned. The priests did not need to sell their land because Pharaoh paid them for their work. So they used this money to buy food to eat.

[23]Joseph said to the people, "Now I have bought you and your land for Pharaoh. So I will give you seed, and you can plant your fields. [24]At harvest time, you must give one-fifth of your crops to Pharaoh. You can keep four-fifths for yourselves. You can use the seed you keep for food and planting the next year. Now you can feed your families and your children."

[25]The people said, "You have saved our lives. We are happy to be slaves to Pharaoh."

[26]So Joseph made a law at that time in the land, and that law continues today. The law says that one-fifth of everything from the land belongs to the Pharaoh who owns all the land. The only land he does not own is the land of the priests.

Don't Bury Me in Egypt

[27]Israel stayed in Egypt. He lived in the land of Goshen. His family grew and became very large. They became landowners there and did very well.

[28]Jacob lived in Egypt for 17 years, so he was 147 years old. [29]The time came when Israel knew

he would soon die, so he called his son Joseph to him. He said, "If you love me, put your hand under my leg and make a promise.[a] Promise that you will do what I say and that you will be truthful with me. When I die, don't bury me in Egypt. ³⁰Bury me in the place where my ancestors are buried. Carry me out of Egypt and bury me in our family grave."

Joseph answered, "I promise that I will do what you say."

³¹Then Jacob said, "Make a vow to me." And Joseph vowed to him that he would do this. Then Israel laid his head back down on the bed.[b]

Blessings for Manasseh and Ephraim

48 Some time later, Joseph learned that his father was very sick. So he took his two sons, Manasseh and Ephraim, and went to his father. ²When Joseph arrived, someone told Israel, "Your son Joseph has come to see you." Israel was very weak, but he tried hard and sat up in his bed.

³Then Israel said to Joseph, "God All-Powerful appeared to me at Luz in the land of Canaan. God blessed me there. ⁴He said to me, 'I will make you a great family. I will give you many children and you will be a great people. Your family will own this land forever.' ⁵Now you have two sons. These two sons were born here in the country of Egypt before I came. Your two sons, Ephraim and Manasseh, will be like my own sons. They will be like Reuben and Simeon to me. ⁶So these two boys will be my sons. They will share in everything I own. But if you have other sons, they will be your sons. But they will also be like sons to Ephraim and Manasseh—that is, in the future, they will share in everything that Ephraim and Manasseh own. ⁷On the journey from Paddan Aram, Rachel died in the land of Canaan. This made me very sad. We were still travelling towards Ephrath. I buried her there on the road to Ephrath (which is now called Bethlehem).

⁸Then Israel saw Joseph's sons. Israel said, "Who are these boys?"

⁹Joseph said to his father, "These are my sons. These are the boys God gave me."

Israel said, "Bring your sons to me. I will bless them."

¹⁰Israel was old and his eyes were not good. So Joseph brought the boys close to his father. Israel kissed and hugged the boys. ¹¹Then Israel said to Joseph, "I never thought I would see your face again. But look! God has let me see you and your children."

¹²Then Joseph took the boys off Israel's lap, and they bowed down in front of his father. ¹³Joseph put Ephraim on his right side and Manasseh on his left side. (So Ephraim was on Israel's left side, and Manasseh was on Israel's right side.) ¹⁴But Israel crossed his hands and put his right hand on the head of the younger boy Ephraim. Then he put his left hand on Manasseh, even though Manasseh was the firstborn. ¹⁵And Israel blessed Joseph and said,

"My ancestors, Abraham and Isaac,
    worshipped our God,
    and that God has led me all my life.
¹⁶He was the Angel who saved me from all my
    troubles.
    And I pray that he will bless these boys.
Now they will have my name
    and the name of our ancestors, Abraham
    and Isaac.
I pray that the earth will be filled
    with their descendants."

¹⁷Joseph saw that his father put his right hand on Ephraim's head. This did not make Joseph happy. Joseph took his father's hand because he wanted to move it from Ephraim's head and put it on Manasseh's head. ¹⁸Joseph said to his father, "You have your right hand on the wrong boy. Manasseh is the firstborn. Put your right hand on him."

¹⁹But his father refused and said, "I know, son. I know. Manasseh is the firstborn. He will be great and will be the father of many people. But his younger brother will be greater than he is. And the younger brother's family will be much larger."

²⁰So Israel blessed them that day. He said,

"The Israelites will use your names
    whenever they bless someone.
They will say, 'May God make you
    like Ephraim and Manasseh.'"

In this way Israel made Ephraim greater than Manasseh.

²¹Then Israel said to Joseph, "Look, my time to die is almost here, but God will still be with you. He will lead you back to the land of your ancestors. ²²I have given you one portion more than I gave to your brothers. I gave you the land that I won from the Amorites. I used my sword and bow to take that land."

---

[a] **47:29 *put your hand . . . make a promise*** This was a sign of a very important promise that Jacob trusted Joseph to keep.
[b] **47:31 *Then Israel . . . on the bed*** Or "Then Israel bowed down at the head of his bed" or "Then Israel worshipped on the head of the staff."

Jacob Blesses His Sons

49 Then Jacob called all his sons to him. He said, "My sons, come here to me. I will tell you what will happen in the future.

2"Children of Jacob, gather around.
  Come, listen to Israel, your father.

Reuben

3"Reuben, my first son, you are my strength,
  the first proof of my manhood.
You were the most honoured
  and powerful of all my sons.
4But your passion was like a flood you couldn't
    control.
  So you will not remain my most honoured
    son.
You climbed into your father's bed
  and slept with one of his wives.
You brought shame to my bed,
  to the bed you lay on.

Simeon and Levi

5"Simeon and Levi are brothers.
  They are violent with their swords.
6I will not join their secret meetings.
  I will not take part in their evil plans.
They have killed people out of anger
  and crippled animals for fun.
7Their anger is so strong that it is a curse.
  They are too cruel when they are angry.
They will not get their own land in the land of
    Jacob.
  They will be spread throughout Israel.

Judah

8"Judah, your brothers will praise you.
  You will defeat your enemies.
  Your brothers will bow down to you.
9Judah is like a young lion.
  My son, you are like a lion standing over
    the animal it killed.
Like a lion, Judah lies down to rest,
  and no one is brave enough to disturb
    him.
10King after king will come from Judah's family.
  They will hold the authority of the throne
until the real king comes,*a*
  and all people honour and obey him.
11Judah's land is so rich,
  his donkeys feed on the best grapevines.

And his vineyards produce so much wine,
  he could use it for washing his clothes.
12He has so much wine to drink,
  his eyes are red.
And he has so much milk to drink,
  his teeth are white.

Zebulun

13"Zebulun will live near the sea.
  His seashore will be a safe place for ships.
  His land will continue as far as the city of
    Sidon.

Issachar

14"Issachar is like a donkey that has worked
    too hard.
  He will lie down under his heavy load.
15He will see his land is pleasant
  and that his resting place is good.
But he will agree to carry heavy loads;
  he will agree to work as a slave.

Dan

16"Dan*b* will rule his people
  as one of the tribes of Israel.
17His tribe will be small but dangerous,
  like a snake by the roadside
that strikes a horse's heel
  and makes the rider fall off.
18"Lord, I am waiting for your salvation.

Gad

19"A group of robbers will attack*c* Gad,
  but Gad will chase them away.

Asher

20"Asher's land will grow much good food.
  He will have food fit for a king!

Naphtali

21"Naphtali is like a deer running free,
  a doe with beautiful young fawns."*d*

Joseph

22"Joseph is like a wild donkey,
  like a young donkey by a spring,
  like colts grazing in a pasture.*e*
23Men with bows attacked him,
  shooting their arrows and chasing him.
24But he aimed his bow well,
  and his arms were strong.

---

a 49:10 *until the real king comes* Or "until Shiloh comes", "until the man it belongs to comes" or "until his tribute comes".
b 49:16 *Dan* This name means "judge" and is a wordplay with "rule".
c 49:19 *A group of robbers will attack* The Hebrew words for "group of robbers" and "attack" sound like the name Gad.
d 49:21 *a deer . . . fawns* Or "a terebinth tree that has spread out and gives excellent fruit". The Hebrew text is not clear.
e 49:22 Or "Joseph is very successful. Joseph is like a vine covered with fruit, like a vine growing by a spring, like a vine growing along a fence."

His power came from the Mighty One of
    Jacob,
  from the Shepherd, the Rock of Israel.
25May the God of your father help you.
    May God All-Powerful bless you.
  May he bless you with rain from the sky
    above
    and with springs from the earth below.
  May your wives have many babies to nurse
    and your animals produce many young
    ones.
26My parents had many good things happen to
    them.
  And I, your father, enjoyed even more
    blessings.
  Joseph, you are the leader of your brothers,
    so with my hand on your head,
    I pray that all my blessings will be yours.

Benjamin

27"Benjamin is like a hungry wolf.
  In the morning he kills and eats.
  In the evening he shares what is left."

28These are the twelve families of Israel. And
this is what their father said to them. He gave
each son a blessing that was right for him. 29Then
Israel gave them a command. He said, "When I
die, I want to be with my people. I want to be
buried with my ancestors in the cave in the field
of Ephron the Hittite. 30That cave is in the field of
Machpelah near Mamre in the land of Canaan.
Abraham bought that field from Ephron so that he
could have a burying place. 31Abraham and his
wife Sarah are buried in that cave. Isaac and his
wife Rebekah are buried in that cave. I buried
my wife Leah in that cave. 32That cave is in
the field that was bought from the Hittites."
33After Jacob finished talking to his sons, he lay
back down on the bed. Then he took his last
breath and joined his ancestors who had gone
before him.

Jacob's Funeral

50 When Israel died, Joseph was very sad.
He hugged his father and cried over him
and kissed him. 2Joseph commanded his servants
to prepare his father's body. (These servants were
doctors.) The doctors prepared Jacob's body to be
buried. They prepared the body in the special way
of the Egyptians. 3When the Egyptians prepared
the body in this special way, they waited 40 days
before they buried the body. Then the Egyptians
had a special time of sadness for Jacob. This time
was 70 days.

4After the time of sadness was finished, Joseph
spoke to Pharaoh's officers and said, "Please tell
this to Pharaoh: 5'When my father was near
death, I made a promise to him. I promised that I
would bury him in a cave in the land of Canaan.
This is the cave that he prepared for himself. So
please let me go and bury my father. Then I will
come back here to you.'"
6Pharaoh answered, "Keep your promise. Go
and bury your father."
7So Joseph went to bury his father. All Pharaoh's
officials, personal advisors, and all the leaders of
Egypt went with Joseph. 8All the people in
Joseph's family, his brothers, and all the people
in his father's family went with him. Only the
children and the animals stayed in the land of
Goshen. 9So there was a large crowd of people
with him. There was even a group of soldiers
riding in chariots and some on horses.
10They went to Goren Atad,[a] east of the Jordan
River. There they had a long funeral service for
Israel, which continued for seven days. 11When
the people who lived in Canaan saw the funeral
service at Goren Atad, they said, "This is a time of
great sorrow for those Egyptians." So now that
place across the Jordan River is named Abel
Mizraim.[b]
12So Jacob's sons did as their father commanded.
13They carried his body to Canaan and buried it in
the cave at Machpelah. This was the cave near
Mamre in the field that Abraham bought from
Ephron the Hittite. Abraham bought that cave to
use as a burial place. 14After Joseph buried his
father, he and everyone in the group with him
went back to Egypt.

The Brothers Are Still Afraid of Joseph

15After Jacob died, Joseph's brothers were
worried. They were afraid that Joseph would still
be angry about what they had done years before.
They said, "Maybe Joseph still hates us for what
we did." 16So the brothers sent this message to
Joseph: "Before your father died, he told us to
give you a message. 17He said, 'Tell Joseph that I
beg him to please forgive his brothers for the bad
things they did to him.' So now, Joseph, we beg
you, please forgive us for the bad things we did
to you. We are the servants of God, the God of
your father."
That message made Joseph very sad, and he
cried. 18His brothers went to him and bowed
down in front of him. They said, "We will be your
servants."
19Then Joseph said to them, "Don't be afraid. I
am not God! I have no right to punish you. 20It is

---

true that you planned to do something bad to me. But really, God was planning good things. God's plan was to use me to save the lives of many people. And that is what happened. [21]So don't be afraid. I will take care of you and your children." And so Joseph said kind things to his brothers, and this made them feel better.

[22]Joseph continued to live in Egypt with his father's family. He died when he was 110 years old. [23]During Joseph's life Ephraim had children and grandchildren. And his son Manasseh had a son named Makir. Joseph lived to see Makir's children.

The Death of Joseph

[24]When Joseph was near death, he said to his brothers, "My time to die is almost here. But I know that God will take care of you and lead you out of this country. God will lead you to the land he promised to give Abraham, Isaac and Jacob."

[25]Then Joseph asked his people to make a promise. Joseph said, "Promise me that you will carry my bones with you when God leads you out of Egypt."

[26]Joseph died in Egypt when he was 110 years old. Doctors prepared his body for burial and put the body in a coffin in Egypt.

Who
The traditional view is that this book was written by Moses: Joshua mentions the "*Book of the Law of Moses*" (Joshua 8:31) and the New Testament claims that Moses was responsible for certain passages. Probably other, later writers had a hand in shaping and editing the original materials.

 When
If we accept Moses started it off, it would mean that the book probably dates from the thirteenth century BC.

 What
The title of the book means "exit". It comes from the Greek title *Exodos Aigyptou* which means "departure from Egypt". And that's what it is all about: the rescue of the Israelites from slavery in Egypt. The Hebrew title of the book *Shemot* is an abbreviation of "These are the names", which is how the book begins.

The book deals with the escape of the Israelites from slavery in Egypt. It includes lots of religious ceremony and legal issues but, more importantly, some vital insights into the nature of God and the relationship between God and his people. At the centre of all this is Moses, the Israelite raised as an Egyptian, the first freedom fighter of his people.

Exodus tells the story of how a group of escaping slaves turned into the people of God. This is shaped by two events: the rescue from slavery in Egypt and God's agreement with his people. Because God rescues them from the Egyptians he asks them to follow him and be his people. He gives them laws to follow, including the famous Ten Commandments and many other laws for regulating their daily life and worship.

Exodus also contains some of the deepest, most mysterious passages of the Bible, giving us a unique insight into what God is like. He is not a distant, remote God, but one who cares for his people, who rescues them and who wants to show them how best to live. And he reveals to Moses his name: Yahweh or "I am".

So maybe it is the book of names after all.

 QUICK TOUR ➤ **EXODUS**

Slavery 1:1–14	Final punishment 11:1–10; 12:29–30
Moses' birth 1:15 – 2:10	Passover 12:1–28
Murder 2:11–25	Escape 12:31–42
Burning bush 3:1–21	Over the sea 14:1–31
Instructions 4:1–17	Manna 16:1–26
Moses v. Pharaoh 5:1–21	Ten Commandments 19:16 – 20:17
Plagues 7:14 – 8:32	The Holy Box and the Holy Tent 25:1–22

"Then God said to Moses, 'Tell them, "I AM WHO I AM." When you go to the Israelites, tell them, "I AM" sent me to you.' And God said, 'Tell the Israelites that you were sent by YAHWEH, the God of your ancestors – the God of Abraham, the God of Isaac, the God of Jacob. This will always be my name. It is how I want the people to remember me from now on.'"

Exodus 3:14–15

Jacob's Family in Egypt

1 When Jacob (Israel) went to Egypt, his sons and their families went with him. These are the names of those sons: ²Reuben, Simeon, Levi, Judah, ³Issachar, Zebulun, Benjamin, ⁴Dan, Naphtali, Gad and Asher. ⁵Another son, Joseph, was already in Egypt. So Jacob's whole family was with him in Egypt—70 descendants in all.

⁶Later, Joseph, his brothers and all the people of that generation died. ⁷But the Israelites had many children, and their number grew until the country of Egypt was filled with them.

Trouble for the Israelites

⁸Then a new king began to rule Egypt. He did not know Joseph. ⁹This king said to his people, "Look at the Israelites. There are too many of them, and they are stronger than we are! ¹⁰We must make plans to stop them from growing stronger. If there is a war, they might join our enemies, defeat us and escape from the land!"

¹¹The Egyptians decided to make life hard for the Israelites, so they put slave masters over the people. These masters forced the Israelites to build the cities of Pithom and Rameses for the king. The king used these cities to store grain and other things. ¹²The Egyptians forced the Israelites to work harder and harder. But the harder they worked, the more they grew and spread, and the more the Egyptians became afraid of them. ¹³So the Egyptians made them work even harder. ¹⁴They made life hard for the Israelites. They forced the Israelites to work hard at making bricks and mortar and to work hard in the fields. The Egyptians showed no mercy in all the hard work they made the Israelites do!

The Nurses Who Trusted God

¹⁵There were two Hebrew*a* nurses who helped the Israelite women give birth. They were named Shiphrah and Puah. The king of Egypt said to the nurses, ¹⁶"You will continue to help the Hebrew women give birth to their children. If a girl baby is born, let the baby live. But if the baby is a boy, you must kill him!"

¹⁷But the nurses trusted*b* God, so they did not obey the king's command. They let all the baby boys live.

¹⁸The king of Egypt called for the nurses and asked them, "Why did you do this? Why did you let the baby boys live?"

¹⁹The nurses said to the king, "The Hebrew women are much stronger than the Egyptian women. They give birth to their babies before we can go to help them." ²⁰⁻²¹The nurses trusted God, so he was good to them and allowed them to have their own families.

The Hebrews continued to have more children, and they became very strong. ²²So Pharaoh gave this command to his own people: "If the Hebrew women give birth to a baby girl, let it live. But if they have a baby boy, you must throw it into the Nile River."

Baby Moses

2 There was a man from the family of Levi who decided to marry a woman from the tribe of Levi.*c* ²She became pregnant and gave birth to a baby boy. The mother saw how beautiful the baby was and hid him for three months. ³She hid him for as long as she could. After three months she made a basket and covered it with tar so that it would float. Then she put the baby in the basket and put the basket in the river in the tall grass. ⁴The baby's sister stayed and watched to see what would happen to the baby.

⁵Just then, Pharaoh's daughter went to the river to bathe. She saw the basket in the tall grass. Her servants were walking beside the river, so she told one of them to go and get the basket. ⁶The king's daughter opened the basket and saw a baby boy. The baby was crying and she felt sorry for him. Then she noticed that it was one of the Hebrew*d* babies.

⁷The baby's sister was still hiding. She stood and asked the king's daughter, "Do you want me to go and find a Hebrew woman who can nurse the baby and help you care for it?"

⁸The king's daughter said, "Yes, please."

So the girl went and brought the baby's own mother.

⁹The king's daughter said to the mother, "Take this baby and feed him for me. I'll pay you to take care of him."

So the woman took her baby and cared for him. ¹⁰The baby grew, and after some time, the woman gave the baby to the king's daughter. The king's daughter accepted the baby as her own son. She named him Moses*e* because she had pulled him from the water.

Moses Helps His People

¹¹Moses grew and became a man. He saw that his own people, the Hebrews, were forced to work very hard. One day he saw an Egyptian

---

a **1:15 Hebrew** Or "Israelite". This name might also mean "descendants of Eber" (read Gen. 10:25–31) or "people from beyond the Euphrates River". Also in verse 19.
b **1:17 trusted** Literally, "feared" or "respected". Also in verses 20–21.
c **2:1 woman . . . Levi** Literally, "the daughter of Levi". See Exod. 6:20; Num. 26:59.
d **2:6 Hebrew** Or "Israelite". Also in verses 7,11,13.
e **2:10 Moses** This name is like a Hebrew word meaning "to pull or draw out".

man beating a Hebrew man. [12]Moses looked around and saw that no one was watching, so he killed the Egyptian and buried him in the sand.

[13]The next day Moses saw two Hebrew men fighting each other. He saw that one man was wrong and said to him, "Why are you hurting your neighbour?"

[14]The man answered, "Did anyone say you could be our ruler and judge? Tell me, will you kill me as you killed the Egyptian yesterday?"[a]

Then Moses was afraid. He thought to himself, "Now everyone knows what I did."

[15]Pharaoh heard about what Moses did, so he decided to kill him. But Moses ran away from Pharaoh and went to the land of Midian.

Moses in Midian

Moses stopped near a well in Midian. [16]There was a priest there who had seven daughters. These girls came to that well to get water for their father's sheep. They were trying to fill the water trough with water. [17]But there were some shepherds there who chased the girls away and would not let them get water. So Moses helped the girls and gave water to their animals.

[18]Then they went back to their father, Reuel.[b] He asked them, "Why have you come home early today?"

[19]The girls answered, "The shepherds chased us away, but an Egyptian rescued us. He got water for us and gave it to our animals."

[20]So Reuel said to his daughters, "Where is this man? Why did you leave him? Go and invite him to eat with us."

[21]Moses was happy to stay with that man. Reuel let Moses marry his daughter, Zipporah. [22]Zipporah became pregnant and had a son. Moses named him Gershom[c] because Moses was a stranger in a land that was not his own.

God Decides to Help Israel

[23]A long time passed and that king of Egypt died. But the Israelites were still forced to work very hard. They cried for help, and God heard them. [24]God heard their painful cries and remembered the agreement he made with Abraham, Isaac and Jacob. [25]God saw the troubles of the Israelites, and he knew that he would soon help them.

The Burning Bush

3 Moses' father-in-law was named Jethro.[d] Jethro was a priest of Midian. Moses took care of Jethro's sheep. One day, Moses led the sheep to the west side of the desert. He went to a mountain called Horeb,[e] the mountain of God. [2]On that mountain, Moses saw the angel of the LORD in a burning bush.

Moses saw a bush that was burning without being destroyed. [3]So he decided to go closer to the bush and see how a bush could continue burning without being burned up.

[4]The LORD saw Moses was coming to look at the bush. So he called to him from the bush. He said, "Moses, Moses!"

Moses said, "Yes, Lord."

[5]Then God said, "Don't come any closer. Take off your sandals. You are standing on holy ground. [6]I am the God of your ancestors. I am the God of Abraham, the God of Isaac and the God of Jacob."

Moses covered his face because he was afraid to look at God.

[7]Then the LORD said, "I have seen the troubles my people have suffered in Egypt, and I have heard their cries when the Egyptians hurt them. I know about their pain. [8]Now I will go down and save my people from the Egyptians. I will take them from that land and lead them to a good land where they can be free from these troubles.[f] It is a land filled with many good things.[g] Many different people live in that land: the Canaanites, Hittites, Amorites, Perizzites, Hivites and Jebusites. [9]I have heard the cries of the Israelites, and I have seen the way the Egyptians have made life hard for them. [10]So now I am sending you to Pharaoh. Go! Lead my people, the Israelites, out of Egypt."

[11]But Moses said to God, "I am not a great man! How can I be the one to go to Pharaoh and lead the Israelites out of Egypt?"

[12]God said, "You can do it because I will be with you. This will be the proof that I am sending you: After you lead the people out of Egypt, you will come and worship me on this mountain."

[13]Then Moses said to God, "But if I go to the Israelites and say to them, 'The God of your ancestors sent me,' then the people will ask, 'What is his name?' What should I tell them?"

[14]Then God said to Moses, "Tell them, 'I AM WHO I AM.'[h] When you go to the Israelites, tell them, 'I AM' sent me to you." [15]And God said,

---

[a] **2:14 yesterday** This is from the ancient Greek version.

[b] **2:18 Reuel** He is also called Jethro.

[c] **2:22 Gershom** This name is like the Hebrew words meaning "a stranger there".

[d] **3:1 Jethro** He is also called Reuel.

[e] **3:1 a mountain called horeb** That is, "Mount Sinai".

[f] **3:8 land . . . troubles** Or "a spacious land".

[g] **3:8 land . . . things** Literally, "land flowing with milk and honey". Also in verse 17.

[h] **3:14 I AM WHO I AM** The Hebrew words are like the name YAHWEH ("LORD").

THERE ARE NO GODS LIKE YOU

Have you ever wondered what God is like and what it's like to have a relationship with him? Well, Exodus is all about coming to know God. In this action-packed book the drama centres on God rescuing the people from Egypt and bringing them into a relationship with him.

DIG IN

READ Exodus 3:1–22

It's been a difficult time for God's people (the Israelites) who have been in Egypt since all of Joseph's family moved there at the end of Genesis. Over the years their numbers have increased dramatically, which has freaked out the Egyptians – as a means of population control they have made Israelites do back-breaking work and now they are killing their infant boys. The people cry out to God, wanting his help. Enter Moses . . .

- What do we learn about God in 3:5–6 and 14–15?
- What is God going to do in 3:8? What does this tell us about God?

Do you get a sense of the power of God speaking in 3:14–15? The name "YAHWEH" means "I will be what I have always been" – he's the same God worshipped by Abraham, Isaac and Jacob. This is more significant than it might seem. God made promises to them that they would belong to him, that he would give them a safe land to live in (not Egypt!) and would bless them. As God meets with Moses he is telling him he will keep to the things he promised. He is a holy, faithful God who doesn't change.

- What are the Egyptians going to see about God (3:19–21)?

SKIM through Exodus 7:1 – 12:51

- What does God display?

Through horrible plagues Pharaoh and the Egyptians come to discover that God is powerful and awesome. He is passionate about rescuing his people and passionate that people know who he is and worship him (Exodus 14:17–18).

READ Exodus 14:1–31

- What does God do for the people?
- What is their response?

Dramatic stuff! God rescues his people, he brings them through the sea, killing their enemies, and makes them his own. If you have time, check out Moses' awesome song about God in Exodus 15:1–18.

DIG THROUGH

- The people were in a bad way in Egypt but God kept his promises to rescue them. Is there a promise God has made in the Bible that you find hard to believe when you're having a tough time? Ask God to help you believe it and to trust in his faithfulness and his powerful passion for your rescue. You might like to chew over Exodus 15:11 to remind yourself what an awesome God you have.
- Just as God rescued the people from the Egyptians (their enemies) so, if you follow Jesus, God has rescued you from your enemies, from every power that stops you enjoying God's goodness, especially Satan. Just as God rescued Israel through the Red Sea, he's rescued you through the death of Jesus on the cross. Thank God for Jesus! Write a song or poem, like the people did when God rescued them, telling God how great he is.

DIG DEEPER

- Read Exodus 16:1 – 17:16. What does this show us about God and his relationship with the people?
- The Psalms often talk about the way God rescues his people. Check out Psalms 77 and 78, which talk specifically about this story. Note down all the things the psalmist says God does for his people. How do the people seem to act despite all these things? In what ways are we similar?

"Tell the Israelites that you were sent by YAHWEH, the God of your ancestors—the God of Abraham, the God of Isaac, the God of Jacob. This will always be my name. It is how I want the people to remember me from now on.

INSIGHT

Whenever God's Hebrew name YHWH or YAHWEH is translated, our English Bibles simply say "the LORD". But for a Hebrew reader this name is a grammatical wonder. Its tense is ambiguous, so the same word can be translated both past, present and future. Moses really did encounter a God who was, is and is to come! (See Revelation 4:8.)

Exodus 3:13–15

16"Now go and call together the leaders of the people. Tell them that YAHWEH, the God of your ancestors—the God of Abraham, Isaac and Jacob—appeared to you. Give them this message from me: 'I have been watching over you and have seen what people in Egypt have done to you. 17And I have decided that I will take you away from the troubles you are suffering in Egypt. I will lead you to the land that now belongs to others—the Canaanites, Hittites, Amorites, Perizzites, Hivites and Jebusites. I will lead you to a land filled with many good things.'

18"The leaders will listen to you. And then you and the leaders will go to the Pharaoh. You will tell him, 'YAHWEH*a* is the God of the Hebrews.*b* He came to us and told us to travel three days into the desert. There we must offer sacrifices to YAHWEH our God.'

19"But I know that the Pharaoh will not let you go. Only a great power will force him to let you go, 20so I will use my great power against Egypt. I will cause amazing things to happen in that land. After I do this, he will let you go. 21And I will cause the Egyptians to be kind to the Israelites. They will give many gifts to your people when they leave Egypt.

22"All the Hebrew women will ask their Egyptian neighbours and the Egyptian women living in their houses for gifts. And those Egyptian women will give them gifts of silver, gold and fine clothing. Then you will put those gifts on your children. In this way you will take away the wealth of the Egyptians."

Proof for Moses

4 Then Moses said to God, "But the Israelites will not believe me when I tell them that you sent me. They will say, 'The LORD*c* did not appear to you.'"

2But the LORD said to Moses, "What is that you have in your hand?"

Moses answered, "It is my walking stick."

3Then God said, "Throw your walking stick on the ground."

So Moses threw his walking stick on the ground, and it became a snake. Moses ran from it, 4but the LORD said to him, "Reach out and grab the snake by its tail."

When Moses reached out and caught the snake's tail, the snake became a walking stick again. 5Then God said, "Use your stick in this way, and the people will believe that you saw the LORD, the God of your ancestors, the God of Abraham, the God of Isaac and the God of Jacob."

6Then the LORD said to Moses, "I will give you another proof. Put your hand under your robe."

So Moses opened his robe and put his hand inside. Then he brought his hand out of the robe and it was changed. His hand was covered with spots that were white like snow.

7Then God said, "Now put your hand into your robe again." So Moses put his hand into his robe again. Then he brought his hand out, and his hand was changed. Now his hand was good again, as it was before.

8Then God said, "If the people don't believe you when you use your walking stick, then they will believe you when you show them this sign. 9If they still refuse to believe after you show them both of these signs, then take some water from the Nile River. Pour the water on the ground, and as soon as it touches the ground, it will become blood."

10Then Moses said to the LORD, "But, Lord, I am telling you, I am not a good speaker. I have never been able to speak well. And that hasn't changed since you started talking to me. I am still not a good speaker. You know that I speak slowly and don't use the best words."*d*

11Then the LORD said to him, "Who made a person's mouth? And who can make someone deaf or not able to speak? Who can make a person blind? Who can make a person able to see? I am the one. I am the LORD. 12So go. I will be with you when you speak. I will give you the words to say."

13But Moses said, "My Lord, I beg you to send someone else, not me."

---

a 3:18 *YAHWEH* Or "the LORD". See "YAHWEH" in the Word List.
b 3:18 *Hebrews* Or "Israelites". Also in verse 22.
c 4:1 *The LORD* Or "YAHWEH". See "YAHWEH" in the Word List.
d 4:10 *I Speak . . . words* Or "I stutter and don't speak clearly."

[14]Then the LORD became angry with Moses and said, "All right! I'll give you someone to help you. Aaron the Levite is your brother, isn't he? He is a good speaker. In fact, Aaron is already coming to meet you, and he will be happy to see you. [15]I will tell you what to say. Then you will tell Aaron, and I will help him say it well. I will tell both of you what to do. [16]So Aaron will speak for you. Like God, you will speak to him, and he will tell the people what you say. [17]So go and carry your walking stick with you. Use it and the other miracles to show the people that I am with you."

Moses Leaves Midian

[18]Then Moses went back to Jethro, his father-in-law. Moses said to him, "Please let me go back to Egypt. I want to see if my people are still alive."

Jethro said to Moses, "Go in peace."

[19]Then, while Moses was still in Midian, the LORD said to him, "It is safe for you to go back to Egypt now. The men who wanted to kill you are now dead."

[20]So Moses put his wife and children on the donkey and returned to Egypt. He carried his walking stick with him—the walking stick with the power of God.

[21]While Moses was travelling back to Egypt, the LORD spoke to him, "When you talk to Pharaoh remember to show him all the miracles that I have given you the power to do. But I will cause Pharaoh to be very stubborn. He will not let the people go. [22]Then you should say to Pharaoh, 'This is what the LORD says: Israel is my firstborn son. [23]And I am telling you to let my son go and worship me. If you refuse to let Israel go, then I will kill your firstborn son.'"

Moses' Son Circumcised

[24]On the way to Egypt, Moses stopped at a place to spend the night. The LORD met Moses at that place and tried to kill him.[a] [25]But Zipporah took a flint knife[b] and circumcised her son. She took the skin and touched his feet. Then she said to Moses, "You are a bridegroom of blood to me." [26]Zipporah said this because she had to circumcise her son. So God let Moses live.[c]

Moses Arrives in Egypt

[27]The LORD had spoken to Aaron and told him, "Go out into the desert and meet Moses." So Aaron went and met Moses at the Mountain of God.[d] He saw Moses and kissed him. [28]Moses told Aaron everything the LORD had commanded him to say and all the miracles he must do to prove that God had sent him.

[29]So Moses and Aaron went and gathered together all the leaders of the Israelites. [30]Then Aaron spoke to the people and told them everything the LORD had told Moses. Then Moses did the miracles for all the people to see, [31]and they believed what they had heard. Then the Israelites understood that the LORD had seen their troubles and had come to help them. So they bowed down and worshipped God.

Moses and Aaron Before Pharaoh

5 After Moses and Aaron talked to the people, they went to Pharaoh and said, "The LORD,[e] the God of Israel, says, 'Let my people go into the desert so that they can have a festival to honour me.'"

[2]But Pharaoh said, "Who is the LORD? Why should I obey him? Why should I let Israel go? I don't even know who this LORD is, so I refuse to let Israel go."

[3]Then Aaron and Moses said, "The God of the Hebrews[f] has talked with us. So we beg you to let us travel three days into the desert. There we will offer a sacrifice to the LORD our God. If we don't do this, he might become angry and destroy us. He might make us die from sickness or war."

[4]But Pharaoh said to them, "Moses and Aaron, you are bothering the workers. Let them do their work. Go back to your own work! [5]There are very many workers, and you are keeping them from doing their jobs."

Pharaoh Punishes the People

[6]That same day Pharaoh gave a command to the slave masters and Hebrew foremen. [7]He said, "You have always given the people straw to use to make bricks. But now, tell them they have to go and find their own straw to make bricks. [8]But they must still make the same number of bricks as they did before. They have become lazy. That is why they are asking me to let them go. They don't have enough work to do. That is why they asked me to let them make sacrifices to their God. [9]So make these people work harder. Keep them busy. Then they will not have enough time to listen to the lies of Moses."

[10]So the Egyptian slave masters and the Hebrew foremen went to the Israelites and said,

---

[a] 4:24 *tried to kill him* Or possibly, "wanted to circumcise him".
[b] 4:25 *flint knife* A sharp knife made from flint rock.
[c] 4:26 Or "And he was healed. She said, 'You are a bridegroom of blood' because of the circumcision."
[d] 4:27 *Mountain of God* That is, Mount Horeb (Sinai).
[e] 5:1 *The LORD* Or "YAHWEH". See "YAHWEH" in the Word List.
[f] 5:3 *Hebrews* Or "Israelites". Also in verses 10,14,15,19.

"Pharaoh has decided that he will not give you straw for your bricks. ¹¹You must go and get the straw for yourselves. So go and find straw, but you must still make as many bricks as you made before."

INSIGHT

The children of Israel had been slaves in Egypt for hundreds of years and at the end of their captivity they were forced to do a considerable amount of manual labour. This included making bricks out of mud and straw and helping with the construction of two great cities, Pithom and Rameses. Without straw to bind them together it was virtually impossible to make useable bricks.

Exodus 5:7

---

¹²So the people went everywhere in Egypt looking for straw. ¹³The slave masters forced the people to work even harder. They forced the people to make as many bricks as before. ¹⁴The Egyptian slave masters had chosen the Hebrew foremen and had made them responsible for the work the people did. The Egyptian slave masters beat these foremen and said to them, "Why aren't you making as many bricks as you made in the past? If you could do it then, you can do it now!"

¹⁵Then the Hebrew foremen went to Pharaoh. They complained and said, "We are your servants. Why are you treating us like this? ¹⁶You give us no straw, but you tell us to make as many bricks as before. And now our masters are beating us. Your people are wrong for doing this."

¹⁷Pharaoh answered, "You are lazy, and you don't want to work! That is why you ask me to let you go. And that is why you want to leave here and make sacrifices to the LORD. ¹⁸Now, go back to work! We will not give you any straw. And you must still make as many bricks as you did before."

¹⁹The Hebrew foremen knew they were in trouble, because the Pharaoh had told them, "You must still make as many bricks as you made before."

²⁰When they were leaving the meeting with Pharaoh, they passed Moses and Aaron. Moses and Aaron were waiting for them. ²¹So they said to Moses and Aaron, "May the LORD judge and punish you for what you did! You made Pharaoh and his rulers hate us. You have given them an excuse to kill us."

Moses Complains to God

²²Then Moses prayed to the LORD and said, "Lord, why have you done this terrible thing to your people? Why did you send me here? ²³I went to Pharaoh and said what you told me to say. But since that time he has made the people suffer, and you have done nothing to help them!"

6 Then the LORD said to Moses, "Now you will see what I will do to Pharaoh. I will use my great power against him, and he will let my people go. In fact, when he sees my power he will force them to go."

²Then God said to Moses, "I am the LORD. ³I appeared to Abraham, Isaac and Jacob. They called me God All-Powerful. They did not know my name, the LORD. ⁴I made an agreement with them. I promised to give them the land of Canaan. They lived in that land, but it was not their own. ⁵Now, I have heard their painful cries. I know that they are slaves in Egypt. And I remember my agreement. ⁶So tell the Israelites that I say to them, 'I am the LORD. I will save you. You will no longer be slaves of the Egyptians. I will use my great power to make you free, and I will bring terrible punishment to the Egyptians. ⁷You will be my people and I will be your God. I am the LORD your God, and you will know that I made you free from Egypt. ⁸I made a great promise to Abraham, Isaac and Jacob. I promised to give them a special land. So I will lead you to that land. I will give you that land. It will be yours. I am the LORD.'"

⁹So Moses told this to the Israelites, but the people would not listen to him. They were working so hard that they were not patient with Moses.

¹⁰Then the LORD said to Moses, ¹¹"Go and tell Pharaoh that he must let the Israelites leave his land."

¹²But Moses answered, "LORD, the Israelites refuse to listen to me. So surely Pharaoh will also refuse to listen. I am a very bad speaker."[a]

¹³But the LORD talked with Moses and Aaron and commanded them to go and talk to the Israelites and to Pharaoh, the king of Egypt. He commanded them to lead the Israelites out of the land of Egypt.

Some of the Families of Israel

¹⁴These are the names of the leaders of the families of Israel:

Israel's first son, Reuben, had four sons. They were Hanoch, Pallu, Hezron and Carmi.

---

[a] *6:12 I am a very bad speaker* Or "I sound like a foreigner." Literally, "I have uncircumcised lips."

¹⁵Simeon's sons were Jemuel, Jamin, Ohad, Jakin, Zohar and Shaul. (Shaul was the son from a Canaanite woman).
¹⁶Levi lived 137 years. His sons were Gershon, Kohath and Merari.
¹⁷Gershon had two sons, Libni and Shimei.
¹⁸Kohath lived 133 years. His sons were Amram, Izhar, Hebron and Uzziel.
¹⁹Merari's sons were Mahli and Mushi.

All these families were from Israel's son Levi.

²⁰Amram lived 137 years. He married his father's sister, Jochebed. Amram and Jochebed gave birth to Aaron and Moses.
²¹Izhar's sons were Korah, Nepheg and Zicri.
²²Uzziel's sons were Mishael, Elzaphan and Sithri.
²³Aaron married Elisheba. (Elisheba was the daughter of Amminadab, and the sister of Nahshon.) Aaron and Elisheba gave birth to Nadab, Abihu, Eleazar and Ithamar.
²⁴The sons of Korah (that is, the ancestors of the Korahites) were Assir, Elkanah and Abiasaph.
²⁵Aaron's son, Eleazar, married a daughter of Putiel. She gave birth to Phinehas.

All these people were from Israel's son, Levi.
²⁶Aaron and Moses were from this tribe. And they are the men the LORD spoke to and said, "Lead my people out of Egypt in groups."ᵃ ²⁷Aaron and Moses are the men who talked to Pharaoh, the king of Egypt, and told him to let the Israelites leave Egypt.

God Repeats His Call to Moses

²⁸The LORD spoke to Moses again in the land of Egypt. ²⁹He said, "I am the LORD. Tell the king of Egypt everything I tell you."

³⁰But Moses, standing there before the LORD, said, "You know me. I'm a very bad speaker. How will I make the king listen to me?"

7 The LORD said to Moses, "See how important I have made you? In speaking to Pharaoh, you will be like God, and your brother Aaron will be your prophet. ²You will tell Aaron everything that I command you. Then he will tell the king what I say. And Pharaoh will let the Israelites leave this country. ³But I will make Pharaoh stubborn so that he will not do what you tell him. Then I will do many miracles in Egypt to prove who I am. ⁴But he will still refuse to listen. So then I will punish Egypt very much. And I will lead my army, my people, out of that land. ⁵I will punish the people of Egypt, and they will learn that I am the LORD. Then I will lead my people out of their country."

⁶Moses and Aaron did what the LORD told them. ⁷Moses was 80 years old at the time, and Aaron was 83.

Aaron's Walking Stick Becomes a Snake

⁸The LORD said to Moses and Aaron, ⁹"Pharaoh will ask you to prove your power. He will ask you to do a miracle. Tell Aaron to throw his walking stick on the ground. While Pharaoh is watching, the stick will become a snake."

¹⁰So Moses and Aaron went to Pharaoh and obeyed the LORD. Aaron threw his walking stick down. While Pharaoh and his officers watched, the stick became a snake. ¹¹So Pharaoh called for his wise men and magicians. These men used their magic, and they were able to do the same thing as Aaron. ¹²They threw their walking sticks on the ground, and their sticks became snakes. But then Aaron's walking stick ate theirs. ¹³Pharaoh still refused to let the people go, just as the LORD had said. Pharaoh refused to listen to Moses and Aaron.

The Water Becomes Blood

¹⁴Then the LORD said to Moses, "Pharaoh is being stubborn. He refuses to let the people go. ¹⁵In the morning, Pharaoh will go out to the river. Go to him by the edge of the Nile River. Take the walking stick that became a snake. ¹⁶Tell him this: 'The LORD, the God of the Hebrews, sent me to you. He told me to tell you to let his people go and worship him in the desert. Until now you have not listened to the Lord. ¹⁷So the LORD says that he will do something to show you that he is the LORD. I will hit the water of the Nile River with this walking stick in my hand, and the river will turn into blood. ¹⁸The fish in the river will die, and the river will begin to stink. Then the Egyptians will not be able to drink the water from the river.'"

¹⁹The LORD said to Moses: "Tell Aaron to hold the walking stick in his hand over the rivers, canals, lakes and every place where they store water. When he does this, all the water will turn into blood. All the water, even the water stored in wood and stone jars, will turn into blood."

²⁰So Moses and Aaron did what the LORD commanded. Aaron raised the walking stick and hit the water in the Nile River. He did this in front of Pharaoh and his officials. So all the water in the river changed into blood. ²¹The fish in the river died, and the river began to stink. So the Egyptians could not drink water from the river. The blood was everywhere in Egypt.

ᵃ 6:26 groups Or "divisions". This is a military term. It shows that Israel was organized like an army.

²²The magicians used their magic to do the same thing. So Pharaoh refused to listen to Moses and Aaron. This happened just as the LORD said. ²³Pharaoh ignored what Moses and Aaron had done. He turned and went into his house.

²⁴The Egyptians could not drink the water from the river, so they dug wells around the river for water to drink.

The Frogs

²⁵Seven days passed after the LORD changed the Nile River.

8 Then the LORD told Moses, "Go to Pharaoh and tell him that the LORD says, 'Let my people go to worship me! ²If you refuse to let my people go, then I will fill Egypt with frogs. ³The Nile River will be filled with frogs. They will come from the river and enter your houses. They will be in your bedrooms and in your beds. They will be in the houses of your officials and in your ovens and in your jars of water. ⁴The frogs will be all over you, your people and your officials.'"

⁵Then the LORD said to Moses, "Tell Aaron to hold the walking stick in his hand over the canals, rivers and lakes. Then the frogs will come out onto the land of Egypt."

⁶So Aaron raised his hand over the waters of Egypt, and the frogs began coming out of the water and covered the land of Egypt.

⁷The magicians used their magic to do the same thing—so even more frogs came out onto the land in Egypt!

⁸Pharaoh called for Moses and Aaron and said, "Ask the LORD to remove the frogs from me and my people. I will let the people go to offer sacrifices to the LORD."

⁹Moses said to Pharaoh, "I will pray for you, your people and your officials. Then the frogs will leave you and your houses. They will remain only in the river. When do you want the frogs to go away?"

¹⁰Pharaoh said, "Tomorrow."

Moses said, "It will happen as you say. In this way you will know that there is no god like the LORD our God. ¹¹The frogs will leave you, your house, your officials and your people. They will remain only in the river."

¹²Moses and Aaron left Pharaoh. Moses prayed to the LORD about the frogs he had sent against Pharaoh. ¹³And the LORD did what Moses asked. The frogs died in the houses, in the yards and in the fields. ¹⁴They began to rot, and the whole country began to stink. ¹⁵But when Pharaoh saw that they were free of the frogs, he again became stubborn. Pharaoh did not do what Moses and Aaron had asked him to do. This happened just as the LORD had said.

The Lice

¹⁶Then the LORD said to Moses, "Tell Aaron to raise his stick and hit the dust on the ground, and everywhere in Egypt dust will become lice."

¹⁷They did this. Aaron raised the stick in his hand and hit the dust on the ground, and everywhere in Egypt the dust became lice. The lice got on the animals and the people.

¹⁸The magicians used their magic and tried to do the same thing. But the magicians could not make lice come from the dust. The lice remained on the animals and the people. ¹⁹So the magicians told Pharaoh that the power of God did this. But Pharaoh refused to listen to them. This happened just as the LORD had said.

The Flies

²⁰The LORD said to Moses, "Get up in the morning and go to Pharaoh. He will go out to the river. Tell him that the LORD says, 'Let my people go and worship me! ²¹If you don't let my people go, then flies will come into your houses. The flies will be on you and your officials. The houses of Egypt will be full of flies. They will be all over the ground too! ²²But I will not treat the Israelites the same as the Egyptians. There will not be any flies in Goshen, where my people live. In this way you will know that I, the LORD, am in this land. ²³So tomorrow I will treat my people differently from your people. This will be my proof.'"

²⁴So the LORD did just what he said. Millions of flies came into Egypt. The flies were in Pharaoh's house, and they were in all his officials' houses. They were all over Egypt. The flies were ruining the country. ²⁵So Pharaoh called for Moses and Aaron and told them, "Offer sacrifices to your God here in this country."

²⁶But Moses said, "It would not be right to do that. The Egyptians think it is terrible to kill animals as sacrifices for the LORD our God. If we do this here, the Egyptians will see us and throw stones at us and kill us. ²⁷Let us go three days into the desert and offer sacrifices to the LORD our God. This is what he told us to do."

²⁸So Pharaoh said, "I will let you go and offer sacrifices to the LORD your God in the desert, but you must not go very far. Now, go and pray for me."

²⁹Moses said, "Look, I will leave and ask the LORD to remove the flies from you, your people and your officials tomorrow. But you must not stop the people from offering sacrifices to the LORD."

³⁰So Moses left Pharaoh and prayed to the LORD. ³¹And the LORD did what Moses asked. He removed the flies from Pharaoh, his officials and his people. None of the flies remained. ³²But Pharaoh again became stubborn and did not let the people go.

The Disease of the Farm Animals

9 Then the LORD told Moses to go to Pharaoh and tell him: "The LORD, the God of the Hebrews, says, 'Let my people go to worship me!' [2]If you continue to hold them and refuse to let them go, [3]then the LORD will use his power against your animals in the fields. He will cause all your horses, donkeys, camels, cattle and sheep to get sick with a terrible disease. [4]But the LORD will treat Israel's animals differently from the animals of Egypt. None of the animals that belong to the Israelites will die. [5]The LORD has set the time for this to happen. He said, 'Tomorrow the LORD will make this happen in this country.'"

[6]The next morning the LORD did what he said. All the farm animals of the Egyptians died, but none of the animals that belonged to the Israelites died. [7]Pharaoh sent people to see if any of the animals of Israel had died. Not one of them had died. But Pharaoh remained stubborn and did not let the people go.

The Boils

[8]The LORD said to Moses and Aaron, "Fill your hands with the ashes from a furnace. Moses, you throw the ashes into the air in front of Pharaoh. [9]This will become dust that will go throughout the land of Egypt. Whenever the dust touches a person or an animal in Egypt, sores will break out on the skin."

[10]So Moses and Aaron took ashes from a furnace and went and stood before Pharaoh. Moses threw the ashes into the air, and sores began breaking out on people and animals. [11]The magicians could not stop Moses from doing this, because even the magicians had the sores. This happened everywhere in Egypt. [12]But the LORD made Pharaoh stubborn, so he refused to listen to Moses and Aaron, just as the LORD had said.

The Hail

[13]Then the LORD said to Moses, "Get up in the morning and go to Pharaoh. Tell him that the LORD, the God of the Hebrews, says, 'Let my people go to worship me! [14]This time, I will use my full power against you, your officials and your people. Then you will know that there is no god in the world like me. [15]I could use my power and cause a disease that would wipe you and your people off the earth. [16]But I have put you here for a reason. I have put you here so that I could show you my power. Then people all over the world will learn about me! [17]You are still against my people. You are not letting them go free. [18]So at this time tomorrow, I will cause a very bad hailstorm. There has never been a hailstorm like this in Egypt, not since Egypt became a nation.

[19]Now, you must put your animals in a safe place. Everything you own that is now in the fields must be put in a safe place. Any person or animal that remains in the fields will be killed. The hail will fall on everything that is not gathered into your houses.'"

[20]Some of Pharaoh's officials paid attention to the LORD's message. They quickly put all their animals and slaves into houses. [21]But other people ignored the LORD's message and lost all their slaves and animals that were in the fields.

[22]The LORD told Moses, "Raise your hand into the air and the hail will start falling all over Egypt. The hail will fall on all the people, animals and plants in all the fields of Egypt."

[23]So Moses raised his walking stick into the air, and the LORD sent hail with thunder and lightning down on the earth. The LORD caused hail to fall all over Egypt. [24]The hail was falling, and lightning was flashing all through it. It was the worst hailstorm that had ever hit Egypt since it had become a nation. [25]The storm destroyed everything in the fields in Egypt. The hail destroyed people, animals and plants. The hail also broke all the trees in the fields. [26]The only place that did not get hail was the land of Goshen, where the Israelites lived.

[27]Pharaoh sent for Moses and Aaron and told them, "This time I have sinned. The LORD is right, and I and my people are wrong. [28]We have had enough of this hail and thunder! Ask the LORD to stop the storm, and I will let you go. You don't have to stay here."

[29]Moses told Pharaoh, "When I leave the city, I will lift my hands in prayer to the LORD, and the thunder and hail will stop. Then you will know that the LORD is in this land. [30]But I know that you and your officials don't really fear and respect the LORD yet."

[31]The flax had already developed its seeds, and the barley was already blooming. So these plants were destroyed. [32]But wheat and spelt ripen later than the other grains, so these plants were not destroyed.

[33]Moses left Pharaoh and went outside the city. He lifted his hands in prayer to the LORD. And the thunder and hail stopped, and even the rain stopped.

[34]When Pharaoh saw that the rain, hail and thunder had stopped, he again did wrong. He and his officials became stubborn again. [35]Pharaoh refused to let the Israelites go free, just as the LORD had said through Moses.

The Locusts

10 The LORD said to Moses, "Go to Pharaoh. I have made him and his officials stubborn. I did this so that I could show them my powerful miracles. [2]I also did this so that you could tell your children and your grandchildren about the miracles and other wonderful things that I have done in Egypt. Then all of you will know that I am the LORD."

³So Moses and Aaron went to Pharaoh. They told him, "The LORD, the God of the Hebrews,ª says, 'How long will you refuse to obey me? Let my people go to worship me! ⁴If you refuse to let my people go, then tomorrow I will bring locusts into your country. ⁵The locusts will cover the land. There will be so many locusts that you will not be able to see the ground. Anything that was left from the hailstorm will be eaten by the locusts. The locusts will eat all the leaves from every tree in the field. ⁶They will fill all your houses, and all your officials' houses, and all the houses in Egypt. There will be more locusts than your fathers or your grandfathers have ever seen. There will be more locusts than there have ever been since people began living in Egypt.'" Then Moses turned and left Pharaoh.

⁷Then the officials asked Pharaoh, "How long will we be trapped by these people? Let the men go to worship the LORD their God. If you don't let them go, before you know it, Egypt will be destroyed!"

⁸So Pharaoh told his officials to bring Moses and Aaron back to him. Pharaoh said to them, "Go and worship the LORD your God. But tell me, just who is going?"

⁹Moses answered, "All of our people, young and old, will go. And we will take our sons and daughters and our sheep and cattle with us. We will all go because the LORD's festival is for all of us."

¹⁰Pharaoh said to them, "The LORD really will have to be with you before I let you and all your children leave Egypt. Look, you are planning something evil. ¹¹The men can go and worship the LORD. That is what you asked for in the beginning. But all your people cannot go." Then Pharaoh sent Moses and Aaron away.

¹²The LORD told Moses, "Raise your hand over the land of Egypt and the locusts will come! They will spread all over the land of Egypt and will eat all the plants that the hail did not destroy."

¹³So Moses raised his walking stick over the land of Egypt, and the LORD caused a strong wind to blow from the east. The wind blew all that day and night. When morning came, the wind had brought the locusts to the land of Egypt. ¹⁴The locusts flew into the country of Egypt and landed on the ground. There were more locusts than there had ever been in Egypt. And there will never again be that many locusts there. ¹⁵They

covered the ground, and the whole country became dark. The locusts ate every plant on the ground and all the fruit in the trees that the hail had not destroyed. There were no leaves left on any of the trees or plants anywhere in Egypt.

¹⁶Pharaoh quickly called for Moses and Aaron. Pharaoh said, "I have sinned against the LORD your God and against you. ¹⁷Now, forgive me for my sins this time. Ask the LORD to remove this 'death' from me."

¹⁸Moses left Pharaoh and prayed to the LORD. ¹⁹So the LORD changed the wind. He made a very strong wind blow from the west, and it blew the locusts out of Egypt and into the Red Sea.ᵇ Not one locust was left in Egypt! ²⁰But the LORD caused Pharaoh to be stubborn again, and Pharaoh did not let the Israelites go.

The Darkness

²¹Then the LORD told Moses, "Raise your hand into the air and darkness will cover Egypt. It will be so dark you can feel it!"

²²So Moses raised his hand into the air and a cloud of darkness covered Egypt. The darkness stayed in Egypt for three days. ²³None of the people could see each other, and no one got up to go anywhere for three days. But there was light in all the places where the Israelites lived.

²⁴Again Pharaoh called for Moses. He said, "Go and worship the LORD! You can take your children with you. But you must leave your sheep and cattle here."

²⁵Moses said, "No, we will take them all. In fact, you will give us offerings and sacrifices for us to use in worshipping the LORD our God. ²⁶Yes, we will take our animals with us to worship the LORD our God. Not one hoof will be left behind. We don't know yet exactly what we will need to worship the LORD. We will learn that only when we get there."

²⁷The LORD made Pharaoh stubborn again, so he refused to let them go. ²⁸Then Pharaoh told Moses, "Get out of here. I don't want you to come here again. The next time you come to see me, you will die!"

²⁹Then Moses told Pharaoh, "You are right about one thing. I will not come to see you again."

The Death of the Firstborn

11 Then the LORD told Moses, "I have one more disaster to bring against Pharaoh and Egypt. After this he will ask you to leave Egypt. In fact, he will force you to leave this country. ²You must give this message to the Israelites: 'Men and women, you must ask your neighbours to give

---

ª **10:3** *Hebrews* Or "Israelites". This name might also mean "descendants of Eber" (read Gen. 10:25–31) or "people from beyond the Euphrates River".
ᵇ **10:19** *Red Sea* Or "Reed Sea". See 1 Kgs 9:26.

you things made of silver and gold.'" ³The LORD caused the Egyptians to be kind to the Israelites. The Egyptians, even Pharaoh's own officials, already considered Moses to be a great man.

⁴Moses said to the king, "The LORD says, 'At midnight tonight, I will go through Egypt, ⁵and every firstborn son in Egypt will die, from the firstborn son of Pharaoh, the ruler of Egypt, to the firstborn son of the slave girl grinding grain. Even the firstborn animals will die. ⁶The crying in Egypt will be worse than at any time in the past or any time in the future. ⁷But none of the Israelites or their animals will be hurt—not even a dog will bark at them.' Then you will know that the LORD has treated Israel differently from Egypt. ⁸All these officials of yours will come down and bow to me. They will say, 'Leave and take all your people with you.' Only then will I leave!" Then in anger, Moses left the meeting with Pharaoh.

⁹Then the LORD told Moses, "The reason Pharaoh did not listen to you is so that I could show my great power in Egypt." ¹⁰That is why Moses and Aaron did all these great miracles in front of Pharaoh. And that is why the LORD made Pharaoh so stubborn that he would not let the Israelites leave his country.

Passover

12 While Moses and Aaron were still in Egypt, the LORD spoke to them. He said, ²"This monthᵃ will be the first month of the year for you. ³This command is for the whole community of Israel: On the tenth day of this month each man must get one lamb for the people in his house. ⁴If there are not enough people in his house to eat a whole lamb, then he should invite some of his neighbours to share the meal. There must be enough lamb for everyone to eat. ⁵The lamb must be a one-year-old male, and it must be completely healthy. This animal can be either a young sheep or a young goat. ⁶You should watch over the animal until the fourteenth day of the month. On that day, all the people of the community of Israel must kill these animals just before dark. ⁷You must collect the blood from these animals and put it on the top and sides of the doorframe of every house where the people eat this meal.

⁸"That night you must roast the lamb and eat all the meat. You must also eat bitter herbs and bread made without yeast. ⁹You must not eat the lamb raw or boiled in water. You must roast the whole lamb over a fire. The lamb must still have

its head, legs and inner parts. ¹⁰You must eat all the meat that night. If any of the meat is left until morning, you must burn it in the fire.

¹¹"When you eat the meal, you must be fully dressed and ready to travel. You must have your sandals on your feet and your walking stick in your hand. You must eat in a hurry, because this is the LORD's Passover.

¹²"That night I will go through Egypt and kill every firstborn man and animal in Egypt. In this way I will judge all the gods of Egypt and show that I am the LORD. ¹³But the blood on your houses will be a special sign. When I see the blood, I will pass overᵇ your house. I will cause bad things to happen to the people of Egypt. But none of these bad diseases will hurt you.

¹⁴"You will always remember that night—it will be a special festival for you. Your descendants will honour the LORD with this festival forever. ¹⁵For this festival you will eat bread made without yeast for seven days. On the first day, you will remove all the yeast from your houses. No one should eat any yeast for the full seven days of this festival. Anyone who eats yeast must be separated from the rest of Israel. ¹⁶There will be holy assemblies on the first day and the last day of the festival. You must not do any work on these days. The only work you can do is preparing the food for your meals. ¹⁷You must remember the Festival of Unleavened Bread, because on this day I took all your people out of Egypt in groups.ᶜ All of your descendants must remember this day. This is a law that will last forever. ¹⁸So on the evening of the fourteenth day of the first month, you will begin eating bread without yeast. You will eat this bread until the evening of the twenty-first day of the same month. ¹⁹For seven days there must not be any yeast in your houses. Anyone, either a citizen of Israel or a foreigner living among you,ᵈ who eats yeast at this time must be separated from the rest of Israel. ²⁰During this festival you must not eat any yeast. You must eat bread without yeast wherever you live."

²¹So Moses called all the leaders together and told them, "Get the lambs for your families. Kill the lambs for Passover. ²²Take bunches of hyssop and dip them in the bowls filled with blood. Paint the blood on the sides and top of each doorframe. No one must leave their house until morning. ²³At the time the LORD goes through Egypt to kill the firstborn, he will see the blood on the sides and top of each doorframe. Then he will protectᵉ

ᵃ **12:2** *month* Abib (or Nisan). See "ABIB" in the Word List.
ᵇ **12:13** *pass over* Or "protect". Also in verse 27.
ᶜ **12:17** *groups* Or "divisions". This is a military term. It shows that Israel was organized like an army. Also in verse 51.
ᵈ **12:19** *foreigner living among you* That is, someone who has chosen to live among the Israelites and obey their laws and customs. Also in verse 48.
ᵉ **12:23** *protect* Or "pass over".

that house and not let the Destroyer come into any of your houses and hurt you. 24You must remember this command. This law is for you and your descendants forever. 25You must remember to do this even when you go to the land the LORD is giving you. 26When your children ask you, 'Why are we doing this ceremony?' 27you will say, 'This Passover is to honour the LORD, because when we were in Egypt, he passed over the houses of Israel. He killed the Egyptians, but he saved the people in our houses.'"

Then the people bowed down and worshipped the Lord. 28The LORD had given this command to Moses and Aaron, so the Israelites did what the Lord commanded.

29At midnight the LORD killed all the firstborn sons in Egypt, from the firstborn son of Pharaoh (who ruled Egypt) to the firstborn son of the prisoner sitting in jail. Also all the firstborn animals died. 30That night someone died in every house in Egypt. Pharaoh, his officials and all the people of Egypt began to cry loudly.

Israel Leaves Egypt

31So that night Pharaoh called for Moses and Aaron and said to them, "Get up and leave my people. You and your people can do as you say. Go and worship the LORD. 32Take all your sheep and cattle with you, just as you said you would. Go! And say a blessing for me too." 33The people of Egypt also asked them to hurry and leave. They said, "If you don't leave, we will all die!"

34The Israelites did not have time to put the yeast in their bread. They just wrapped the bowls of dough with cloth and carried them on their shoulders. 35Then the Israelites did what Moses asked them to do. They went to their Egyptian neighbours and asked for clothing and things made from silver and gold. 36The LORD caused the Egyptians to be kind to the Israelites, so the Egyptians gave their riches to the Israelites.

37The Israelites travelled from Rameses to Succoth. There were about 600,000 men, not counting the small boys. 38A great number of people who were not Israelites went with them, along with many sheep, cattle and other livestock. 39The people did not have time to put yeast in their bread or make any special food for their journey. So they had to bake their bread without yeast.

40The Israelites had lived in Egypt[a] for 430 years. 41After 430 years, to the very day, all the armies of the LORD[b] left Egypt. 42The night they left, the LORD watched over them to bring them safely out of Egypt. So on this same night each year, the Israelites will always celebrate to remember what the LORD did.

43The LORD told Moses and Aaron, "These are the rules for Passover: No foreigner[c] is allowed to eat the Passover meal. 44-45A foreigner who is only a hired worker or is only staying in your country is not allowed to eat the meal. But if someone buys a slave and circumcises him, then the slave can eat the Passover meal.

46"Each family must eat the meal in one house. None of the food is to be taken outside the house. Don't break any of the lamb's bones. 47The whole community of Israel must celebrate this special night. 48If a foreigner living among you wants to share in the LORD's Passover, he must be circumcised. Then he can share in the meal like any other citizen of Israel. But a man who is not circumcised cannot eat the Passover meal. 49The same rules are for everyone. It doesn't matter if they are citizens or foreigners living among you."

50So all the Israelites obeyed the commands that the LORD gave to Moses and Aaron. 51On that same day the LORD led all the Israelites out of the country of Egypt. The people left in groups.

13 Then the LORD said to Moses, 2"You must give me every male in Israel who is his mother's first child. That means that every firstborn baby boy and every firstborn male animal will be mine."

3Moses said to the people, "Remember this day. You were slaves in Egypt, but on this day the LORD used his great power and made you free. You must not eat bread with yeast. 4Today, in the month of Abib, you are leaving Egypt. 5The LORD made a special promise to your ancestors. He promised to give you the land of the Canaanites, Hittites, Amorites, Hivites and Jebusites. After the Lord leads you to the land filled with many good things,[d] then you must remember this day. You must have a special day of worship on this day during the first month of every year.

6"For seven days you must eat only bread without yeast. On the seventh day, there will be a great festival to show honour to the LORD. 7So for seven days you must not eat any bread made with yeast. There must be no bread with yeast anywhere in your land. 8On this day you should tell your children, 'We are having this festival because the LORD took me out of Egypt.'

---

a 12:40 **Egypt** The ancient Greek and Samaritan versions say "Egypt and Canaan". This would mean they counted the years from about Abraham's time, not from Joseph's. See Gen. 15:12–16 and Gal. 3:17.

b 12:41 **armies of the LORD** The Israelites.

c 12:43 **foreigner** Here, this means someone who has not agreed to follow the laws and customs of Israel.

d 13:5 **land . . . things** Literally, "land flowing with milk and honey".

⁹"This festival will help you remember; it will be like a string tied on your hand. It will be like a sign before your eyes.ᵃ This festival will help you remember the LORD's teachings. It will help you remember that the LORD used his great power to take you out of Egypt. ¹⁰So remember this festival every year at the right time.

¹¹"The LORD will lead you into the land he promised to give you. The Canaanites live there now. But God promised your ancestors that he would give you this land. When that happens, ¹²you must remember to give the LORD every firstborn boy. And you must also give to the LORD every male animal that is the firstborn. ¹³Every firstborn donkey can be bought back. You can offer a lamb and keep the donkey. If you don't want to buy back the donkey like this, then you must break its neck to kill it. But every firstborn baby boyᵇ must be bought back from the Lord.

¹⁴"In the future your children will ask why you do this. They will say, 'What does all this mean?' And you will answer, 'The LORD used his great power to save us from Egypt. We were slaves in that place, but he led us out and brought us here. ¹⁵In Egypt, Pharaoh was stubborn and refused to let us leave. So the LORD killed every firstborn in all the land. (The Lord killed the firstborn males—animal and human.) That is why I give every firstborn male animal to the LORD, and that is why I buy back each of my firstborn sons from him.' ¹⁶This is like a string tied on your hand, like a sign in front of your eyes. It helps you remember that the LORD brought us out of Egypt with his great power."

The Journey Out of Egypt

¹⁷Pharaoh made the people leave Egypt. God did not let them take the road that goes through the land of the Philistines. That road along the coast is the shortest way, but God said, "If the people go that way they will have to fight. Then they might change their minds and go back to Egypt." ¹⁸So God led them another way through the desert by the Red Sea.ᶜ The Israelites were dressed for war when they left Egypt.

Joseph Goes Home

¹⁹Moses carried the bones of Joseph with him. Before Joseph died, he made the Israelites promise to do this for him. He said, "When God saves you, remember to carry my bones with you out of Egypt."

The LORD Leads His People

²⁰The Israelites left Succoth and camped at Etham. Etham was near the desert. ²¹The LORD led the way. During the day, he used a tall cloud to lead the people. And during the night, he used a tall column of fire to lead the way. This fire gave them light so that they could also travel at night. ²²The cloud was always with them during the day, and the column of fire was always with them at night.

14 Then the LORD said to Moses, ²"Tell the people to go back to Pi Hahiroth. Tell them to spend the night between Migdol and the Red Sea, near Baal Zephon. ³Pharaoh will think that the Israelites are lost in the desert and that the people will have no place to go. ⁴I will make Pharaoh brave, and he will chase you. But I will defeat Pharaoh and his army. This will bring honour to me. Then the people of Egypt will know that I am the LORD." So the Israelites did what he told them.

Pharaoh Chases the Israelites

⁵Pharaoh received a report that the Israelites had escaped. When he heard this, he and his officials changed their minds about what they had done. Pharaoh said, "Why did we let the Israelites leave? Why did we let them run away? Now we have lost our slaves!"

⁶So Pharaoh prepared his chariot and took his men with him. ⁷He took 600 of his best men and all his chariots. There was an officer in each chariot.ᵈ ⁸The Israelites were leaving with their arms raised in victory. But the LORD caused Pharaoh, the king of Egypt, to become brave. And Pharaoh chased the Israelites.

⁹The Egyptian army had many horsemen and chariots. They chased the Israelites and caught up with them while they were camped near the Red Sea at Pi Hahiroth, east of Baal Zephon.

¹⁰When the Israelites saw Pharaoh and his army coming towards them, they were very frightened and cried to the LORD for help. ¹¹They said to Moses, "Why did you bring us out of Egypt? Did you bring us out here in the desert to die? We could have died peacefully in Egypt; there were plenty of graves in Egypt. ¹²We told you this would happen! In Egypt we said, 'Please don't bother us. Let us stay and serve the Egyptians.' It would have been better for us to stay and be slaves than to come out here and die in the desert."

ᵃ **13:9 string . . . eyes** Literally, "a mark on your hands and a reminder between your eyes". This might refer to the special things an Israelite ties to his arm and forehead to help him remember God's laws for him. Also in verse 16.
ᵇ **13:13 baby boy** Or "baby".
ᶜ **13:18 Red Sea** Or "Reed Sea". Also in 14:2,9,16,21,30. See 1 Kgs 9:26.
ᵈ **14:7 there was . . . chariot** Or "There were three soldiers in each chariot."

¹³But Moses answered, "Don't be afraid! Don't run away! Stand where you are and watch the LORD save you today. You will never see these Egyptians again. ¹⁴You will not have to do anything but stay calm. The LORD will do the fighting for you."

¹⁵Then the LORD said to Moses, "Why are you still crying to me? Tell the Israelites to start moving. ¹⁶Raise the walking stick in your hand over the Red Sea, and the sea will split. Then the people can go across on dry land. ¹⁷I have made the Egyptians brave, so they will chase you. But I will show you that I am more powerful than Pharaoh and all of his horses and chariots. ¹⁸Then Egypt will know that I am the LORD. They will honour me when I defeat Pharaoh and his horsemen and chariots."

The LORD Defeats the Egyptian Army

¹⁹Then the angel of God moved to the back of the people. (The angel was usually in front of the people, leading them.) So the tall cloud moved from in front of the people and went to the back of the people. ²⁰In this way the cloud stood between the Egyptians and the Israelites. There was light for the Israelites. But there was darkness for the Egyptians. So the Egyptians did not come any closer to the Israelites that night.

²¹Moses raised his hand over the Red Sea, and the LORD caused a strong wind to blow from the east. The wind blew all night long. The sea split, and the wind made the ground dry. ²²The Israelites went through the sea on dry land. The water was like a wall on their right and on their left. ²³Then all of Pharaoh's chariots and horsemen followed them into the sea. ²⁴Early that morning the LORD looked down from the tall cloud and column of fire at the Egyptian army. Then he made them panic. ²⁵The wheels of the chariots became stuck. It was very hard to control the chariots. The Egyptians shouted, "Let's get out of here! The LORD is fighting against us. He is fighting for the Israelites."

²⁶Then the LORD told Moses, "Raise your hand over the sea to make the water fall and cover the Egyptian chariots and horsemen."

²⁷So just before daylight, Moses raised his hand over the sea. And the water rushed back to its proper level. The Egyptians were running as fast as they could from the water, but the LORD swept them away with the sea. ²⁸The water returned to its normal level and covered the chariots and horsemen. Pharaoh's army had been chasing the Israelites, but that army was destroyed. None of them survived!

²⁹But the Israelites crossed the sea on dry land. The water was like a wall on their right and on their left. ³⁰So that day the LORD saved the Israelites from the Egyptians. Later, the Israelites saw the dead bodies of the Egyptians on the shore of the Red Sea. ³¹The Israelites saw the great power of the LORD when he defeated the Egyptians. So the people feared and respected the LORD, and they began to trust the LORD and his servant Moses.

The Song of Moses

15 Then Moses and the Israelites began singing this song to the LORD:

"I will sing to the LORD!
  He has done great things.
He took the enemy's horses and riders
  and threw them all into the sea.
²The LORD is my strength,
  the reason I sing for joy![a]
He is the one who saved me.
He is my God,
  and I praise him.
He is the God of my ancestors,
  and I honour him.
³The LORD is a great soldier.
  The LORD is his name.
⁴He threw Pharaoh's chariots
  and soldiers into the sea.
Pharaoh's very best soldiers
  drowned in the Red Sea.[b]
⁵The deep water covered them,
  and they sank to the bottom like rocks.

⁶"LORD, your right hand is amazingly
    strong.
  With your right hand, LORD, you broke
    the enemy to pieces.
⁷In your great majesty you destroyed
  those who stood against you.
Your anger destroyed them,
  like fire burning straw.
⁸The wind you sent in anger
  piled the water high.
The flowing water became a wall,
  solid to its deepest parts.

⁹"The enemy said,
  'I will chase them and catch them.
I will take all their riches.
  I will take it all with my sword.
  I will take everything for myself.'
¹⁰But you blew on them
  and covered them with the sea.

---

[a] **15:2 the reason . . . joy** Literally, "my song" or possibly, "my power".
[b] **15:4 Red Sea** Or "Reed Sea". Also in verse 22. See 1 Kgs 9:26.

They sank like lead
   into the deep sea.

11"Are there any gods like the LORD?
   No, there are no gods like you—
   you are wonderfully holy!
   You are amazingly powerful!
   You do great miracles!
12You raised your right hand to punish the
     enemy,
   and the ground opened up to swallow
     them.
13But with your kindness
   you led the people you saved.
And with your strength
   you led them to your holy land.*a*

14"The other nations will hear this story,
   and they will be frightened.
   The Philistines will shake with fear.
15The commanders of Edom will tremble.
   The leaders of Moab will be afraid.
   The people of Canaan will lose courage.
16They will be filled with fear
   when they see your strength.
   They will be as still as a rock, LORD,
   while your people, the ones you made, pass
     by.
17You will lead your people into the land
   and let them settle on your own
     mountain,
   the place that you, LORD, chose for your
     home,
   the Temple, Lord, that you yourself built.

18"The LORD will rule for ever and ever!"

19Yes, it really happened! Pharaoh's horses and riders, and chariots went into the sea. And the LORD brought all the water of the sea down on top of them. But the Israelites walked through that sea on dry land. 20Then Aaron's sister, the woman prophet Miriam, took a tambourine. She and the women began singing and dancing. 21Miriam repeated the words,

"Sing to the LORD!
   He has done great things.
He took the enemy's horses and riders
   and threw them all into the sea."

Israel Goes Into the Desert

22Moses led the Israelites away from the Red Sea and into the desert of Shur. They travelled for three days in the desert. They could not find any water. 23Then they came to Marah.*b* There was water at Marah, but it was too bitter to drink. (That is why the place was named Marah.) 24The people began complaining to Moses. They said, "Now what will we drink?" 25So Moses called to the LORD, and the LORD showed him a large piece of wood. When Moses put the wood in the water, the water became good to drink.

There the LORD put in place a law and a command for him and tested him to see if he would obey.*c* 26He said to him, "I am the LORD your God. If you listen to me and do what I say is right, and if you obey all my commands and laws, then I will not give you any of the sicknesses that I gave the Egyptians. I am the LORD who heals you."

27Then the people travelled to Elim. At Elim there were twelve springs of water and 70 palm trees. So the people made their camp there near that water.

Israel Complains, So God Sends Food

16 Then all the Israelites left Elim. They reached the western Sinai Desert,*d* between Elim and Mount Sinai, on the fifteenth day of the second month*e* after leaving Egypt. 2There in the desert the Israelites all began complaining to Moses and Aaron. 3They said, "It would have been better if the LORD had just killed us in the land of Egypt. At least there we had plenty to eat. We had all the food we needed. But now you have brought us out here into this desert to make us all die from hunger."

4Then the LORD said to Moses, "I will cause food to fall from the sky. This food will be for you to eat. Every day the people should go out and gather the food they need that day. I will do this to see if they will do what I tell them. 5Every day the people will gather only enough food for one day. But on Friday, when the people prepare their food, they will see that they have enough food for two days."*f*

6So Moses and Aaron said to the Israelites, "This evening you will see the power of the LORD, and you will know that he is the one who brought you out of Egypt. 7And in the morning you

---

a **15:13** *holy land* Israel, the special land God set apart for the Israelites.
b **15:23** *Marah* This name means "Bitter" or "Sad".
c **15:25** *There . . . he would obey* Or "There the LORD put in place a law and a command for them and tested them to see if they would obey."
d **16:1** *western Sinai Desert* Literally, "desert of Sin".
e **16:1** *fifteenth day of the second month* That is, the fifteenth of Iyyar. The Israelites had been travelling for a month.
f **16:5** *Friday, . . . two days* This happened so that the people would not have to work on the Sabbath (Saturday), the day of rest.

will see the Glory of the Lord because he has heard your complaining against him. Yes, your complaining is against the LORD, not us. We do only what he tells us to do, so you had no reason to complain against us."

⁸Then Moses said, "In the evening the LORD will give you meat to eat, and in the morning you will have all the bread you want. The LORD will do this because he has heard your complaining, which was against him, not us. What can we do? We do only what he tells us to do, so your complaints are really against the LORD."

⁹Then Moses said to Aaron, "Tell the whole community of Israelites to come together before the LORD, because he has heard their complaints."

¹⁰So Aaron spoke to all the Israelites. While he was talking, the people turned and looked into the desert. And they saw the Glory of the LORD appear in a cloud.

¹¹The LORD said to Moses, ¹²"I have heard the complaints of the Israelites. So tell them, 'This evening you will eat meat. And in the morning you will have all the bread you want. Then you will know you can trust the LORD, your God.'"

¹³That evening, flocks of quail came and filled the camp, and in the morning dew lay on the ground all around it. ¹⁴After the dew was gone, something like thin flakes of frost was on the ground. ¹⁵When the Israelites saw it, they asked each other, "What is that?" because they did not know what it was. So Moses told them, "This is the food the LORD is giving you to eat. ¹⁶The LORD says, 'Each of you should gather what you need, 2 litres ᵃ of manna for everyone in your family.'"

¹⁷So that is what the Israelites did. Some people gathered a large amount, some people gathered a little. ¹⁸But when they measured what they had gathered, there was no shortage and there was none left over. Everyone gathered just what they needed.

¹⁹Moses told them, "Don't save that food to eat the next day." ²⁰But some of the people did not obey Moses. They saved their food for the next day. But worms got into the food and it began to stink. Moses was angry with the people who did this.

²¹Every morning the people gathered as much food as they could eat, but by noonᵇ the food had melted and was gone.

²²On Friday the people gathered twice as much food—4 litresᶜ for every person. So all the leaders of the people came and told this to Moses.

²³Moses told them, "This is what the LORD said would happen. It happened because tomorrow is the Sabbath, the special day of rest to honour the LORD. You can cook all the food you need to cook for today, but save the rest of this food for tomorrow morning."

²⁴So the people saved the rest of the food for the next day, as Moses had commanded, and none of the food spoiled or had worms in it.

²⁵On Saturday, Moses told the people, "Today is the Sabbath, the special day of rest to honour the LORD. So none of you should be out in the fields. Eat the food you gathered yesterday. ²⁶You should gather the food for six days. But the seventh day of the week is a day of rest—so there will not be any of the special food on the ground."

²⁷On Saturday, some of the people went out to gather some of the food, but they could not find any. ²⁸Then the LORD said to Moses, "How long will you people refuse to obey my commands and teachings? ²⁹Look, the LORD has made the Sabbath a day of rest for you. So on Friday he will give you enough food for two days. Then, on the Sabbath, each of you should sit down and relax. Stay where you are." ³⁰So the people rested on the Sabbath.

³¹The people called the special food "manna".ᵈ It was like small white coriander seeds and tasted like thin cakes made with honey. ³²Moses told the people what the LORD said: "Save a basket of this food for your descendants. Then they can see the food that I gave to you in the desert when I took you out of Egypt."

³³So Moses told Aaron, "Take a jar and fill it with 2 litres of manna. Save this manna to put before the LORD. Save it for our descendants." ³⁴(Aaron did what the LORD had commanded Moses. Aaron put the jar of manna in front of the Box of the Agreement.) ³⁵The people ate the manna for 40 years, until they came to the land of rest, that is, until they came to the edge of the land of Canaan. ³⁶(The measure they used for the manna was an *omer*. An *omer* was about two litres.ᵉ)

Water From the Rock

17 The Israelites left the western Sinai Desert.ᶠ They all travelled together from place to place as the LORD commanded. They camped at Rephidim, but there was no water there for the people to drink. ²So they turned against Moses and started arguing with him. They said, "Give us water to drink."

ᵃ **16:16 2 litres** Literally, "1 *omer*". Also in verse 33.
ᵇ **16:21 noon** Literally, "the heat of the day".
ᶜ **16:22 4 litres** Literally, "2 *omers*".
ᵈ **16:31 manna** This name is like the Hebrew phrase in verse 15 meaning "What is that?"
ᵉ **16:36 about two litres** Literally, "⅒ of an *ephah*".
ᶠ **17:1 western Sinai Desert** Literally, "desert of Sin".

Moses said to them, "Why have you turned against me? Why are you testing the LORD?"

³But the people were very thirsty, so they continued complaining to Moses. They said, "Why did you bring us out of Egypt? Did you bring us out here so that we, our children, and our cattle will all die without water?"

⁴So Moses cried to the LORD, "What can I do with these people? They are ready to kill me."

⁵The LORD said to Moses, "Go before the Israelites. Take some of the leaders of the people with you. Carry your walking stick with you. This is the stick that you used when you hit the Nile River. ⁶I will stand before you on a rock at Horeb.ᵃ Hit that rock with the walking stick and water will come out of it. Then the people can drink."

Moses did these things and the leaders of Israel saw it. ⁷Moses named that place Meribahᵇ and Massah,ᶜ because this was the place that the Israelites turned against him and tested the LORD. The people wanted to know if the LORD was with them or not.

War With the Amalekites

⁸At Rephidim the Amalekites came and fought against the Israelites. ⁹So Moses said to Joshua, "Choose some men and go and fight the Amalekites tomorrow. I will stand on the top of the hill and watch you. I will be holding the walking stick God gave me."

¹⁰Joshua obeyed Moses and went to fight the Amalekites the next day. At the same time Moses, Aaron and Hur went to the top of the hill. ¹¹Any time Moses held his hands in the air, the men of Israel would start winning the fight. But when Moses put his hands down, the men of Israel began to lose the fight.

¹²After some time, Moses' arms became tired. So they put a large rock under Moses for him to sit on. Then Aaron and Hur held Moses' hands in the air. Aaron was on one side of Moses and Hur was on the other side. They held his hands up like this until the sun went down. ¹³So Joshua and his men defeated the Amalekites in this battle.

¹⁴Then the LORD said to Moses, "Write about this battle. Write these things in a book so that people will remember what happened here. And be sure to tell Joshua that I will completely destroy the Amalekites from the earth."

¹⁵Then Moses built an altar and named it, "The LORD is My Flag." ¹⁶Moses said, "I lifted my hands

towards the LORD's throne. So the LORD fought against the Amalekites, as he always has."

Advice From Moses' Father-in-Law

18 Jethro, Moses' father-in-law, was a priest in Midian. He heard about the many ways that God helped Moses and the Israelites. He heard about the LORD leading the Israelites out of Egypt. ²So Jethro went to Moses while Moses was camped near the mountain of God.ᵈ Jethro brought Moses' wife, Zipporah, with him. (Zipporah was not with Moses, because Moses had sent her home.) ³Jethro also brought Moses' two sons with him. The first son was named Gershom,ᵉ because when he was born, Moses said, "I am a stranger in a foreign country." ⁴The other son was named Eliezer,ᶠ because when he was born, Moses said, "The God of my father helped me and saved me from the king of Egypt." ⁵So Jethro went to Moses while Moses was camped in the desert near the mountain of God. Moses' wife and his two sons were with Jethro.

⁶Jethro sent a message to Moses that said, "This is your father-in-law Jethro. I am bringing your wife and her two sons to you."

⁷So Moses went out to meet his father-in-law. Moses bowed down before him and kissed him. The two men asked about each other's health. Then they went into Moses' tent to talk more. ⁸Moses told Jethro everything the LORD had done for the Israelites. He told his father-in-law what the Lord had done to Pharaoh and the people of Egypt. He told him about all the problems they had along the way. And he told him how the LORD saved the Israelites every time there was trouble.

⁹Jethro was happy when he heard all the good things the LORD had done for Israel. He was glad that the Lord had freed the Israelites from the Egyptians. ¹⁰He said, "Praise the LORD! He freed you from the power of Egypt. He saved you from Pharaoh. ¹¹Now I know the LORD is greater than all the gods. They thought they were in control, but look what God did!"

¹²Jethro got some sacrifices and offerings to honour God. Then Aaron and all the leaders of Israel came to eat with Moses' father-in-law Jethro. They all ate together there with God.

¹³The next day, Moses had the special job of judging the people. There were so many people that they had to stand before him all day.

¹⁴Jethro saw Moses judging the people. He asked, "Why are you doing this? Why are you

---

ᵃ **17:6 Horeb** Another name for Mount Sinai.
ᵇ **17:7 Meribah** This name means "argument" or "rebellion".
ᶜ **17:7 Massah** This name means "trial", "temptation" or "test".
ᵈ **18:2 mountain of God** That is, Mount Horeb (Sinai).
ᵉ **18:3 Gershom** This name is like the Hebrew words meaning "a stranger there".
ᶠ **18:4 Eliezer** This name means "my God helps".

the only judge? And why do people come to you all day?"

¹⁵Then Moses said to his father-in-law, "The people come to me and ask me to ask for God's decision for their problem. ¹⁶If people have an argument, they come to me, and I decide which person is right. In this way I teach the people God's laws and teachings."

¹⁷But Moses' father-in-law said to him, "This isn't the right way to do this. ¹⁸It is too much work for you to do alone. You cannot do this job by yourself. It wears you out. And it makes the people tired too. ¹⁹Now, listen to me. Let me give you some advice. And I pray God will be with you. You should continue listening to the problems of the people. And you should continue to speak to God about these things. ²⁰You should explain God's laws and teachings to the people. Warn them not to break the laws. Tell them the right way to live and what they should do. ²¹But you should also choose some of the people to be judges and leaders.

"Choose good men you can trust—men who respect God. Choose men who will not change their decisions for money. Make these men rulers over the people. There should be rulers over 1,000 people, 100 people, 50 people and even over ten people. ²²Let these rulers judge the people. If there is a very important case, then they can come to you and let you decide what to do. But they can decide the other cases themselves. In this way these men will share your work with you, and it will be easier for you to lead the people. ²³If you do this as God directs you, then you will be able to do your job without tiring yourself out. And the people can still have all their problems solved before they return home."

²⁴So Moses did what Jethro told him. ²⁵Moses chose good men from among the Israelites. He made them leaders over the people. There were rulers over 1,000 people, 100 people, 50 people and ten people. ²⁶These rulers were judges for the people. The people could always bring their arguments to these rulers, and Moses had to decide only the most important cases.

²⁷After a short time, Moses said goodbye to his father-in-law Jethro, and Jethro went back to his own home.

God's Agreement With Israel

19 In the third month of their journey from Egypt, the Israelites reached the desert of Sinai. ²They had travelled there from Rephidim. They camped in the desert near Mount Sinai. ³Then Moses climbed up the mountain to meet with God. The LORD spoke to him on the mountain and said, "Tell this to the Israelites, the great family of Jacob: ⁴'You people saw what I did to the people of Egypt. You saw that I carried you out of Egypt like an eagle

and brought you here to me. ⁵So now I tell you to obey my commands and keep my agreement. So if you do this, you will be my own special people. The whole world belongs to me, but I am choosing you to be my own special people. ⁶You will be a special nation—a kingdom of priests.' Moses, you must tell the Israelites what I have said."

INSIGHT

Here God makes an agreement, sometimes called a "covenant", with Moses. And throughout the Bible God makes similar agreements with other individuals and groups of people.

Exodus 19:5

---

⁷So Moses climbed down the mountain and called the leaders of the people together. Moses told the leaders everything the LORD had commanded him to tell them. ⁸All the people spoke at the same time and said, "We will obey everything the LORD says."

Then Moses went back up the mountain and told the Lord that the people would obey him. ⁹Then the LORD said to Moses, "I will come to you in the thick cloud. I will speak to you. All the people will hear me talking to you. I will do this so that they will always believe what you tell them."

Then Moses told God everything the people had said.

¹⁰And the LORD said to Moses, "Today and tomorrow you must prepare the people for a special meeting. They must wash their clothes ¹¹and be ready for me on the third day. On the third day, the LORD will come down to Mount Sinai. And all the people will see me. ¹²⁻¹³But you must tell the people to stay away from the mountain. Make a line and don't let them cross it. Any person or animal that touches the mountain must be killed with stones or shot with arrows. But don't let anyone touch them. The people must wait until the trumpet blows. Only then can they go up the mountain."

¹⁴So Moses climbed down the mountain and went to the people. He got them ready for the special meeting and they washed their clothes. ¹⁵Then Moses said to the people, "Be ready for the meeting with God in three days. Do not have sex during that time."

¹⁶On the morning of the third day, a thick cloud came down onto the mountain. There was thunder and lightning and a very loud sound from a trumpet. All the people in the camp were frightened. ¹⁷Then Moses led the people out of

the camp to a place near the mountain to meet God. [18]Mount Sinai was covered with smoke. Smoke rose off the mountain like smoke from a furnace. This happened because the LORD came down to the mountain in fire. Also the whole mountain began to shake. [19]The noise from the trumpet became louder and louder. Every time Moses spoke to God, God answered him with a voice like thunder.

[20]So the LORD came down to Mount Sinai. He came from heaven to the top of the mountain. Then he called Moses to come up to the top of the mountain with him. So Moses went up the mountain.

[21]The LORD said to Moses, "Go down and warn the people not to come near me and look at me. If they do, many will die. [22]Also tell the priests who come near the LORD that they must prepare themselves for this special meeting. If they don't, I, the LORD, will punish them."

[23]Moses said to the LORD, "But the people cannot come up the mountain. You yourself told us to make a line and not allow the people to cross the line to holy ground."

[24]The LORD said to him, "Go down to the people. Get Aaron and bring him back with you. But don't let the priests or the people come near me. I will punish them if they come too close."

[25]So Moses went down to the people and told them these things.

The Ten Commandments

20
These are the things God told his people:

[2]"I am the LORD your God. I am the one who freed you from the land of Egypt, where you were slaves.

[3]"You must not worship any other gods except me.

[4]"You must not make any idols. Don't make any statues or pictures of anything up in the sky or of anything on the earth or of anything down in the water. [5]Don't worship or serve idols of any kind, because I, the LORD, am your God. I hate my people worshipping other gods.[a] People who sin against me become my enemies, and I will punish them. And I will punish their children, their grandchildren and even their great-grandchildren. [6]But I will be very kind to people who love me and obey my commands. I will be kind to their families for thousands of generations.[b]

[7]"You must not use the name of the LORD your God to make empty promises. If you do, the LORD will not let you go unpunished.

[8]"You must remember to keep the Sabbath a special day. [9]You may work six days a week to do your job. [10]But the seventh day is a day of rest in honour of the LORD your God. So on that day no one should work—not you, your sons and daughters or your men and women slaves. Even your animals and the foreigners living in your cities must not work! [11]That is because the LORD worked six days and made the sky, the earth, the sea and everything in them. And on the seventh day, he rested. In this way the LORD blessed the Sabbath—the day of rest. He made that a very special day.

[12]"You must honour and respect your father and your mother. Do this so that you will have a full life in the land that the LORD your God gives you.

[13]"You must not murder anyone.

[14]"You must not commit adultery.

[15]"You must not steal anything.

[16]"You must not tell lies about other people.[c]

[17]"You must not want to take your neighbour's house. You must not want his wife. And you must not want his men and women servants or his cattle or his donkeys. You must not want to take anything that belongs to another person."

The People Are Afraid of God

[18]During all this time, the people in the valley heard the thundering and saw the lightning on the mountain. They saw smoke rising from the mountain and heard the sound of the trumpet. They were afraid and shook with fear. They stood away from the mountain and watched. [19]Then the people said to Moses, "If you want to speak to us, then we will listen. But please don't let God speak to us. If this happens, we will die."

[20]Then Moses said to them, "Don't be afraid! God has come to test you. He wants you to respect him so that you will not sin."

[21]The people stood far away from the mountain while Moses went to the dark cloud where God was. [22]Then the LORD told Moses to say this to the Israelites: "You people have seen that I talked with you from heaven. [23]So you must not make idols using gold or silver to compete with me. You must not make these false gods.

[24]"Make a special altar for me. You should use dirt to make this altar. Offer sheep and cattle as burnt offerings and fellowship offerings on this altar. Do this in every place where I tell you to remember me. Then I will come and bless you. [25]But if you use stones to make an altar, then

---

[a] 20:5 *I hate ... gods* Or "I am El Kanah—the Jealous God."
[b] 20:6 Or "But I will show mercy to thousands of people who love me and obey my commands."
[c] 20:16 Or "You must not be a false witness against your neighbour."

YOU WILL BE MY SPECIAL PEOPLE

What do you think about rules? Do you find them hard to keep? Are they annoying and do they stop you having fun? God's people were about to receive some rules . . . what would they make of them?

DIG IN   READ Exodus 19:1–25

- What had God already done for the people (v.4)?
- What does God promise (vv.5–6)?

Having rescued and looked after his people, God now makes an agreement with them to become his special people, with a special role to play in his plan for the earth. Amazingly this relationship is brought about by God's power and faithfulness, not because of anything strong or good in the people. But because God is holy he demands obedience from the people to maintain the relationship.

- What preparations do the people need to make (vv.10–15)? Why?
- How do you think the people would be feeling (look at vv.16–19)?
- What do these verses tell us about God?

God asked the people to get themselves clean and stay at a safe distance – probably a reassuring thing once the thunder, lightning and shaking started! It must have been scary and yet wonderful to know this powerful God wanted to make them his special people. God isn't someone to be messed around with – the relationship was to be taken seriously.

READ Exodus 20:1–26

- Why do you think God gave the people these commands (vv.2–3,20)?
- Do you think these commandments would be easy to obey?

When a couple get married they make vows to one another; these rituals make the marriage formal and the agreement the couple make is out of love for one another. Similarly, God makes his relationship with the people formal and the rules he gives them are to be obeyed out of love. Yet they were never going to keep them perfectly, so would that mean the relationship was over before it was begun?

DIG THROUGH

- Here we see that God is powerful, holy . . . (add more descriptions of your own), yet he also says, "I carried you out of Egypt like an eagle and brought you here to me" (Exodus 19:4). Do you think of God in this way? Do you find it hard to remember that God is holy and a loving rescuer? Ask God to help you remember that both are true of him.
- God's standards for obedience are so high! The people failed straight away and often that's just what we do. We soon find we can't obey God's commandments by ourselves; we need someone who is perfect to do it for us. This was Jesus (Galatians 3:13). Thank God that, if we follow Jesus, he is satisfied with Jesus' perfect keeping of the commandments in our place.
- Whilst the commandments show us we fall short of God's standards, as God's people now, we still want to act in a way that shows we belong to him. Choose one commandment that you find particularly hard and ask God to help you with this and to help you live more as he wants you to.

DIG DEEPER

- Read Exodus chapters 21 – 24 for the rest of the details about the relationship agreement. From looking at these rules, what things do you think God is passionate about?
- Read Galatians 3:21–25. Do the laws give us new life? What does? What is the purpose of the law?

don't use stones that were cut with an iron tool.*a* If you do that, it will make the altar unacceptable. 26And you must not make steps leading up to the altar. If there are steps, when people look up to the altar, they will be able to see under your clothes."

Other Laws and Commands

21 Then God said to Moses, "These are the other laws that you will give to the people: 2"If you buy a Hebrew*b* slave, then that slave will serve for only six years. After six years, he will be free, and he will have to pay nothing. 3If he is not married when he becomes your slave, when he becomes free, he will leave without a wife. But if the man is married when he becomes your slave, then he will keep his wife at the time he is made free. 4If the slave is not married, the master can give him a wife. If that wife gives birth to sons or daughters, she and her children will belong to the master. After the slave is finished with his years of service, he will be made free.

5"But if the slave decides that he wants to stay with the master, he must say, 'I love my master. I love my wife and my children. I will not become free—I will stay.' 6If this happens, the master will bring the slave before God.*c* The master will take the slave to the door or the doorpost and pierce the slave's ear using a sharp tool to show that the slave will serve that master for all his life.

7"A man might decide to sell his daughter as a slave. If this happens, the rules for making her free are not the same as the rules for making the men slaves free. 8If the master who chose her for himself is not pleased with her, then he can sell the woman back to her father. If the master broke his promise to marry her, he loses the right to sell her to other people. 9If the master promised to let the slave woman marry his son, he must treat her like a daughter, not like a slave.

10"If the master marries another woman, he must not give less food or clothing to the first wife. And he must continue to give her what she has a right to have in marriage. 11The man must do these three things for her. If he does not, the woman is made free, and it will cost her nothing. She owes no money to the man.

12"Whoever hits and kills someone must be killed too. 13But if an accident happens, and a person kills someone without planning it, then God allowed that thing to happen. I will choose some special places where people can run to for safety. So that person can run to one of those places. 14But whoever plans to kill someone out of anger or hatred must be punished. Take them away from my altar and kill them.

15"Whoever hits their father or their mother must be killed.

16"Whoever steals someone to sell them as a slave or to keep them for their own slave must be killed.

17"Whoever curses their father or mother must be killed.

18"Two men might argue and one might hit the other with a rock or with his fist. If the man who was hurt is not killed, the man who hurt him should not be killed. 19If the man was hurt and must stay in bed for some time, the man who hurt him must support him. The man who hurt him must pay for the loss of his time. He must support him until he is completely healed.

20"Sometimes people beat their slaves. If the slave dies after being beaten, the killer must be punished. 21But if the slave gets up after a few days, then the master will not be punished.*d* That is because someone paid their money for the slave, and the slave belongs to them.

22"Two men might be fighting and hurt a pregnant woman. This might make the woman give birth to her baby before its time. If the woman was not hurt badly,*e* the man who hurt her must pay a fine. The woman's husband will decide how much the man must pay. The judges will help the man decide how much the fine will be. 23But if the woman was hurt badly, then the man who hurt her must be punished. The punishment must fit the crime. You must trade one life for another life. 24You must trade an eye for an eye, a tooth for a tooth, a hand for a hand, a foot for a foot, 25a burn for a burn, a bruise for a bruise, a cut for a cut.

26"If a man hits a slave in the eye, and the slave is blinded in that eye, then the slave will be allowed to go free. His eye is the payment for his freedom. This is the same for a man or a woman slave. 27If a master hits his slave in the mouth, and the slave loses a tooth, then the slave will be allowed to go free. The slave's tooth is payment for the slave's freedom. This is the same for a man or a woman slave.

28"If a man's bull kills a man or woman, then you should kill that bull with stones. You should not eat the bull. The owner of the bull is not guilty. 29But if the bull had hurt people in the past, and if the owner was warned, then the owner is guilty. That is because he did not keep the bull

a **20:25 iron tool** Literally, "sword".
b **21:2 Hebrew** Or "Israelite".
c **21:6 before God** Or "before the judges".
d **21:21 punished** Or "punished for murder".
e **21:22 hurt badly** Or "killed".

tied or locked in its place. So if the bull is allowed to be free and kills someone, the owner is guilty. You should kill the bull with stones and also kill the owner. ³⁰But the family of the dead man may accept money. If they accept money, the man who owned the bull should not be killed. But he must pay as much money as the judge decides.

³¹"This same law must be followed if the bull kills someone's son or daughter. ³²But if the bull kills a slave, the owner of the animal must pay the master 30 pieces of silver.ᵃ And the bull must also be killed with stones. This law will be the same for men and women slaves.

³³"A man might take a cover off a well or dig a hole and not cover it. If another man's animal comes and falls into that hole, the man who owns the hole is guilty. ³⁴The man who owns the hole must pay for the animal. But after he pays for the animal, he will be allowed to keep the body of that animal.

³⁵"If one man's bull kills another man's bull, they should sell the bull that is alive. Both men will get half of the money that comes from selling the bull, and both men will also get half of the bull that was killed. ³⁶But if a man's bull has hurt other animals in the past, that owner is responsible for his bull. If his bull kills another bull, he is guilty because he allowed the bull to be free. That man must pay bull for bull. He must trade his bull for the bull that was killed.

22 "How should you punish someone who steals a bull or a sheep? If he kills the animal or sells it, then he cannot give it back. So he must pay five bulls for the one he stole. Or he must pay four sheep for the one he stole. He must pay for stealing. ²⁻⁴If he owns nothing, then he will be sold as a slave. But if he still has the animal and you find it, he must give the owner two animals for every animal he stole. It doesn't matter if the animal was a bull, a donkey or a sheep.

"If a thief is killed while trying to break into a house at night, then no one will be guilty for killing him. But if this happens during the day, the one who killed him will be guilty of murder.

⁵"Someone's cattle might wander from his own field or vineyard and graze in a field that belongs to someone else. If that happens, the owner must pay the other person for what the cattle ate. And the payment must come from the best of his crop.

⁶"Someone might start a fire to burn thorn-bushes on his field. But if the fire grows and burns his neighbour's crops or the grain growing on the

neighbour's field, the person who started the fire must pay for what he burned.

⁷"Someone might give some money or tools to a neighbour for safekeeping. What should you do if someone steals those things from the neighbour's house? If you find the one who stole them, then that thief must pay twice as much as the things are worth. ⁸If you don't find the thief, then the owner of the house must go before the judgesᵇ who will decide if that person is guilty.

⁹"What should you do if two men disagree about a bull or a donkey or sheep or clothing or something that is lost? One man says, 'This is mine,' and the other says, 'No, it is mine.' Both men should go before the judges who will decide who is guilty. The one who was wrong must pay the other man twice as much as the thing is worth.

¹⁰"A man might ask his neighbour to take care of an animal for a short time. It might be a donkey, a bull or a sheep. But what should you do if that animal is hurt or dies or someone takes the animal while no one is looking? ¹¹That neighbour must explain that he did not steal the animal. If this is true, the neighbour will promise to the LORD that he did not steal it. The owner of the animal must accept this promise. The neighbour does not have to pay the owner for the animal. ¹²But if the neighbour stole the animal, then he must pay the owner for the animal. ¹³If wild animals killed the animal, then the neighbour should bring the body as proof. The neighbour will not have to pay the owner for the animal that was killed.

¹⁴"If a man borrows an animal from his neighbour, and the animal is hurt or dies, then the neighbour must pay the owner for the animal. The neighbour is responsible, because the owner was not there himself. ¹⁵But if the owner was there, then the neighbour does not have to pay. Or if the neighbour was paying money to use the animal for work, he will not have to pay if the animal dies or is hurt. The money he paid to use the animal will be enough payment.

¹⁶"If a man has sex with a virgin who he is not engaged to,ᶜ then he must pay her father the full amount necessary to marry her. ¹⁷If the father refuses to allow his daughter to marry him, then the man must still pay the full amount for her.

¹⁸"You must not allow any woman to do evil magic. If she does magic, you must not let her live.

¹⁹"You must not allow anyone to have sex with an animal. If this happens, that person must be killed.

ᵃ **21:32 *30 pieces of silver*** The price for a new slave.
ᵇ **22:8 *judges*** Or "God". Also in verse 9.
ᶜ **22:16 *a virgin . . . engaged to*** Literally, "a virgin who is not engaged".

²⁰"Whoever makes a sacrifice to a false god should be destroyed. The Lord is the only one you should make sacrifices to.

²¹"Remember, in the past you were foreigners in the land of Egypt. So you should not cheat or hurt anyone who is a foreigner in your land.

²²"You must never do anything bad to women whose husbands are dead or to orphans. ²³If you do anything wrong to these widows or orphans, I will know it. I will hear about their suffering. ²⁴And I will be very angry. I will kill you with a sword. Then your wives will become widows, and your children will become orphans.

²⁵"If you loan money to any of my people, that is, the poor among you, don't be like a moneylender and charge them interest. ²⁶You might take their cloak to make sure they pay the money back, but you must give that cloak back to them before sunset. ²⁷That cloak might be their only protection against the cold when they lie down to sleep. If they call to me for help, I will listen because I am kind.

²⁸"You must not curse God or the leaders of your people.

²⁹"At harvest time you should give me the first grain and the first juice from your fruit. Don't wait until late in the year.

"Give me your firstborn sons. ³⁰Also, give me your firstborn cattle and sheep. Let the firstborn stay with its mother for seven days. Then on the eighth day, give him to me.

³¹"You are my special people. So don't eat the meat from something that was killed by wild animals. Let the dogs eat that dead animal.

23 "Don't tell lies against other people. If you are a witness in court, don't agree to help a bad person tell lies.

²"Don't do something just because everyone else is doing it. If you see a group of people doing wrong, don't join them. You must not let them persuade you to do wrong things—you must do what is right and fair.

³"In court, don't treat a person in a special way simply because that person is poor.

⁴"If you see a lost bull or donkey, then you must return it to its owner—even if the owner is your enemy.

⁵"If you see an animal that cannot walk because it has too much to carry, you must stop and help that animal. You must help that animal even if it belongs to one of your enemies.

⁶"In court, don't let anyone take advantage of a person simply because that person is poor.

⁷"Be very careful if you say that someone is guilty of something. Don't make false charges against a person. Never allow innocent people to be killed as punishment for something they did not do. Whoever kills an innocent person is evil, and I will not treat a guilty person as innocent.

⁸"If someone tries to pay you to agree with them when they are wrong, don't accept that payment. A payment like that can blind judges so that they cannot see the truth. It can make good people tell lies.

⁹"You must never do wrong things to a foreigner. Remember, you know what it is like to be a foreigner because at one time you were foreigners in the land of Egypt.

The Special Festivals

¹⁰"Plant seeds, harvest your crops and work the ground for six years. ¹¹But the seventh year must be a special time of rest for the land. Don't plant anything in your fields. If any food grows there, allow the poor to have it. And allow the wild animals to eat the food that is left. You should do the same with your vineyards and with your fields of olive trees.

¹²"Work for six days, but on the seventh day, rest! This will allow your slaves and other workers a time to rest and relax. And your bulls and donkeys will also have a time of rest.

¹³"Be sure that you obey all these laws. Don't worship false gods. You should not even speak their names!

¹⁴"You will have three special festivals each year. You must come to my special place to worship me during these festivals. ¹⁵The first festival is the Festival of Unleavened Bread. This is as I commanded you. During this time you will eat bread that is made without yeast. This will continue for seven days. You will do this during the month of Abib, because this is the time when you came out of Egypt. Everyone must bring a sacrifice to me at that time.

¹⁶"The second festival will be the Festival of Harvest. This festival will be during the early summer when you begin harvesting the first crops that you planted in your fields.

"The third festival will be the Festival of Shelters. This will be in the autumn, when you finish gathering the rest of the crops from your fields.

¹⁷"So three times each year all the men will come to the special place to be with the Lord God.

¹⁸"When you kill an animal and offer its blood as a sacrifice, you must not include anything that has yeast in it. And when you burn the fat from my sacrifice, don't let any of it remain until morning.

¹⁹"When you gather your crops at harvest time, you should bring the first of everything you harvest to the house[a] of the Lord your God.

---

[a] **23:19** *house* The "Holy Tent" where the people went to meet with God. See Exod. 25:8–9.

"You must not eat the meat from a young goat that is boiled in its mother's milk."

God Will Help Israel Take Their Land

20"I am sending an angel before you to protect you along the way and to lead you to the place that I have prepared for you. 21Obey the angel and follow him. Be careful in his presence, and don't rebel against him. The angel will not forgive the wrong things you do to him. He has my power*a* in him. 22If you listen to what he says and do everything I tell you, then I will be an enemy to all your enemies. I will be against everyone who is against you.

23"My angel will lead you through the land. He will lead you against many different people—the Amorites, Hittites, Perizzites, Canaanites, Hivites and Jebusites. But I will defeat all of them.

24"Don't worship their gods. Don't ever bow down to those gods. You must never live the way those people live. You must destroy their idols. And you must break the stones that help them remember their gods.*b* 25You must serve the LORD your God. If you do this, I will bless you with plenty of bread and water. I will take away all sickness from you. 26Your women will all be able to have babies. None of their babies will die at birth. And I will allow you to live long lives.

27"When you fight against your enemies, I will send my great power before you.*c* I will help you defeat all your enemies. The people who are against you will become confused in battle and run away. 28I will send the hornet*d* in front of you. He will force your enemies to leave. The Hivites, Canaanites and Hittites will leave your country. 29But I will not force all of them out in just one year. If the people leave too quickly, the land will be left empty. Then the wild animals will multiply, and you will be unable to control them all. 30So I will force the people out slowly, until there are enough of you to take over the land.

31"I will give you all the land from the Red Sea*e* to the Mediterranean Sea,*f* and from the desert of Sinai to the Euphrates River. I will let you defeat the people living there and force them all to leave.

32"You must not make any agreements with any of those people or their gods. 33Don't let them stay in your country. If you let them stay, they will be like a trap to you—they will cause you to sin against me. And you will begin worshipping their gods."

God and Israel Make Their Agreement

24 The LORD told Moses, "You, Aaron, Nadab, Abihu and the 70 leaders of Israel must come up the mountain and worship me from a distance. 2Then only Moses will come close to the LORD. The other men must not come close, and the rest of the people must not even come up the mountain."

3Moses told the people all the rules and commands from the LORD. Then all the people said, "We will obey all the commands that the LORD has spoken."

4So Moses wrote down all the commands of the LORD. The next morning he got up and built an altar near the bottom of the mountain. And he set up twelve stones—one for each of the twelve tribes of Israel. 5Then Moses sent young men of Israel to offer sacrifices. These men offered bulls to the LORD as burnt offerings and fellowship offerings.

6Moses saved the blood from these animals. He put half of the blood in bowls, and he poured the other half of the blood on the altar.*g*

7Moses read the scroll with the special agreement written on it. He read the agreement so that all the people could hear him. And the people said, "We have heard the laws that the LORD has given us. And we agree to obey them."

8Then Moses held the bowls full of the blood from the sacrifices. He threw that blood on the people. He said, "This blood shows that the LORD has made a special agreement with you. The laws God gave you explain the agreement."

9Then Moses, Aaron, Nadab, Abihu and the 70 leaders of Israel went up the mountain. 10On the mountain, these men saw the God of Israel. He was standing on something that looked like blue sapphires, as clear as the sky! 11All the leaders of Israel saw God, but God did not destroy them.*h* They all ate and drank together.

Moses Goes to Get God's Law

12The LORD said to Moses, "Come to me on the mountain. I have written my teachings and laws on two stone tablets. These teachings and laws

---

a **23:21 *my power*** Literally, "my name".
b **23:24 *stones . . . gods*** Or "memorials". Here, these were stone markers that people used in worshipping their gods.
c **23:27 *When you fight . . . you*** Or "News of my power will go before you, and your enemies will be frightened."
d **23:28 *hornet*** A stinging insect like a large wasp or bee. Here, it might mean "God's angel" or "his great power".
e **23:31 *Red Sea*** Or "Reed Sea", probably the part known as the Gulf of Aqaba. See 1 Kgs 9:26.
f **23:31 *Mediterranean Sea*** Literally, "Philistine Sea".
g **24:6** The blood was used to seal the agreement between God and the people. It was poured on the altar to show that God shared in the agreement.
h **24:11 *saw God . . . destroy them*** In other places, the Bible says that people cannot see God. But God wanted these leaders to know what he was like, so he allowed them to see him in some special way.

are for the people. I will give these stone tablets to you."

¹³So Moses and his helper, Joshua, went up the mountain of God. ¹⁴Moses said to the leaders, "Wait here for us until we come back to you. While I am gone, Aaron and Hur will rule over you. Go to them if anyone has a problem."

Moses Meets With God

¹⁵Then Moses went up the mountain, and the cloud covered the mountain. ¹⁶The Glory of the LORD came down on Mount Sinai. The cloud covered the mountain for six days. On the seventh day, the LORD spoke to Moses from the cloud. ¹⁷The Israelites could see the Glory of the LORD. It was like a fire burning on top of the mountain.

¹⁸Then Moses went higher up the mountain into the cloud. He was on the mountain for 40 days and 40 nights.

Gifts for the Holy Tent

25 The LORD said to Moses, ²"Tell the Israelites to bring me gifts. You will accept gifts for me from everyone who is willing to give. ³Here is the list of the things that you should accept from the people: gold, silver and bronze; ⁴blue, purple and red yarn and fine linen; goat hair, ⁵ram skins dyed red and fine leather; acacia wood; ⁶oil for the lamps; spices for the anointing oil and spices for the sweet-smelling incense. ⁷Also accept onyx stones and other jewels to be put on the ephod and the judgement pouch.

The Holy Tent

⁸"Tell the people to build a special place for me, and I will live among them. ⁹I will show you a plan for this Holy Tent. Make the tent and everything in it look exactly like this plan.

The Box of the Agreement

¹⁰"Use acacia wood and build a special box. This Holy Box must be 110 centimetres*a* long, 66 centimetres*b* wide and 66 centimetres high. ¹¹Use pure gold to cover it inside and out, and put gold trim around the edges. ¹²Make four gold rings and attach them by the four corners, two rings on each side. ¹³Then make poles to put through the rings. They should be made from acacia wood and covered with gold. ¹⁴Put the poles through

the rings on the sides of the Holy Box, and use these poles to carry it. ¹⁵The poles should always stay in the rings of the Box. Never take them out.

¹⁶"I will give you the Agreement. Put it into this Box. ¹⁷Then make a lid, the mercy-cover. Make it from pure gold. Make it 110 centimetres long and 66 centimetres wide. ¹⁸Then make two winged creatures and put them on each end of the mercy-cover. Hammer gold to make these angels. ¹⁹Put one creature on each end of the mercy-cover. Join the creatures together with the mercy-cover to make one piece. ²⁰The wings of these creatures should spread up towards the sky. They should cover the Box with their wings and should face each other, looking towards the mercy-cover.

²¹"I will give you the Agreement. Put it in the Box, and put the mercy-cover on the Box. ²²When I meet with you, I will speak from between the winged creatures on the mercy-cover that is on the Box of the Agreement. From that place, I will give all my commands to the Israelites.

The Table

²³"Make a table from acacia wood. The table must be 88 centimetres*c* long, 44 centimetres*d* wide and 66 centimetres high. ²⁴Cover the table with pure gold and put gold trim around it. ²⁵Then make a frame 75 millimetres*e* wide around the table. And put gold trim on the frame. ²⁶Then make four gold rings and put them on the four corners of the table, where the four legs are. ²⁷Put the rings close to the frame around the top of the table. These rings will hold the poles used to carry the table. ²⁸Use acacia wood to make the poles, and cover them with gold. The poles are for carrying the table. ²⁹Make the plates, the spoons, the pitchers and the bowls from pure gold. The pitchers and bowls will be used for pouring the drink offerings. ³⁰Put the special bread*f* before me on the table. It must always be there in front of me.

The Lampstand

³¹"Then you must make a lampstand. Use pure gold and hammer it to make the base and the shaft.*g* Make flowers, buds and petals from pure gold. Join all these things together into one piece.

³²"The lampstand must have six branches—three branches on one side and three branches on

a 25:10 *110 centimetres* Literally, "2½ *cubits*". Also in verse 17.
b 25:10 *66 centimetres* Literally, "1½ *cubits*". Also in verses 17,23.
c 25:23 *88 centimetres* Literally, "2 *cubits*".
d 25:23 *44 centimetres* Literally, "1 *cubit*".
e 25:25 *75 millimetres* Literally, "1 *handbreadth*". The width of 4 fingers.
f 25:30 *special bread* Also called "bread of the Presence". Every day this bread was put before God on the special table in the Holy Place.
g 25:31 *base and the shaft* Or "flared base".

the other. ³³Each branch must have three flowers. Make these flowers like almond flowers with buds and petals. ³⁴Make four more flowers for the lampstand. These flowers must be made like almond flowers with buds and petals. ³⁵There will be six branches on the lampstand—three branches coming out from each side of the shaft. Make a flower with buds and petals below each of the three places where the branches join the shaft. ³⁶The whole lampstand with the flowers and branches must be made from pure gold. All this gold must be hammered and joined together into one piece. ³⁷Then make seven lamps[a] to go on the lampstand. These lamps will give light to the area in front of the lampstand. ³⁸Use pure gold to make the lamp snuffers and trays. ³⁹Use 35 kilogrammes[b] of pure gold to make the lampstand and the things to be used with it. ⁴⁰Be very careful to make everything exactly the way I showed you on the mountain.

The Holy Tent

26 "The Holy Tent should be made from ten curtains. These curtains must be made from fine linen and blue, purple and red yarn. A skilled worker should sew pictures of winged creatures into the curtains. ²Make each curtain the same size. Each curtain should be 12 metres[c] long and 2 metres[d] wide. ³Join the curtains together into two groups. Join five curtains together to make one group and join five curtains together to make the other group. ⁴Use blue cloth to make loops along the edge of the end curtain in one group. Do the same on the end curtain in the other group. ⁵There must be 50 loops on the end curtain of the first group. And there must be 50 loops on the end curtain of the other group. These loops must be opposite each other. ⁶Then make 50 gold rings to join the curtains together. This will join the Holy Tent together into one piece.

⁷"Make another tent that will cover the Holy Tent. Use eleven curtains to make this tent. Make these curtains from goat hair. ⁸All these curtains must be the same size. They must be 13 metres[e] long and 2 metres wide. ⁹Join five of the curtains together into one group. Then join the other six curtains together into another group. Fold back half of the sixth curtain at the front of the Tent. ¹⁰Make 50 loops down the edge of the end curtain of one group. Do the same for the end curtain of the other group. ¹¹Then make 50

bronze rings to join the curtains together. This will join the tent together into one piece. ¹²Half of the end curtain of this tent will hang down below the back edge of the Holy Tent. ¹³On the sides, the curtains of this tent will hang down 44 centimetres[f] below the bottom edges of the Holy Tent. So this tent will completely cover the Holy Tent. ¹⁴Make two coverings to go over the outer tent. One covering should be made from ram skins dyed red. The other covering should be made from fine leather.

¹⁵"Use acacia wood to make frames to support the Holy Tent. ¹⁶The frames should be 4 metres[g] high and 66 centimetres[h] wide. ¹⁷Two side poles should be joined together with cross pieces to make each frame. All the frames for the Holy Tent must be the same. ¹⁸Make 20 frames for the south side of the Holy Tent. ¹⁹And make 40 silver bases for the frames. Each frame should have two silver bases to go under it—one base for each side pole. ²⁰Make 20 more frames for the other side, the north side, of the Holy Tent. ²¹And make 40 silver bases for these frames—two bases under each frame. ²²Make six more frames for the back, the west side, of the Holy Tent. ²³Make two frames for the corners at the back of the Holy Tent. ²⁴The frames at the corners should be joined together at the bottom. At the top a ring will hold the frames together. Do the same for both corners. ²⁵There will be a total of eight frames for the west end of the Tent. There will be 16 silver bases—two bases under each frame.

²⁶"Use acacia wood and make braces for the frames of the Holy Tent. There should be five braces for the first side of the Holy Tent. ²⁷And there should be five braces for the frames on the other side of the Holy Tent. And there should be five braces for the frames at the back, the west side, of the Holy Tent. ²⁸The middle brace should pass through the frames from one end to the other.

²⁹"Cover the frames with gold. And make rings for the frames to hold the braces. Make these rings from gold. Also cover the braces with gold. ³⁰Build the Holy Tent the way I showed you on the mountain.

Inside the Holy Tent

³¹"Use fine linen and make a special curtain for the inside of the Holy Tent. Use blue, purple and red yarn and sew pictures of winged creatures into

---

[a] **25:37 *lamps*** Small bowls filled with oil. A wick was put in the bowl and lit to produce light.
[b] **25:39 *35 kilogrammes*** Literally, "1 *talent*".
[c] **26:2 *12 metres*** Literally "28 *cubits*".
[d] **26:2 *2 metres*** Literally "4 *cubits*". Also in verse 8.
[e] **26:8 *13 metres*** Literally "30 *cubits*".
[f] **26:13 *44 centimetres*** Literally "1 *cubit*".
[g] **26:16 *4 metres*** Literally "10 *cubits*".
[h] **26:16 *66 centimetres*** Literally "1 ½ *cubits*".

the curtain. [32]Make four posts from acacia wood, and cover the posts with gold. Put hooks made from gold on the four posts. Put four silver bases under the posts. Then hang the curtain on the gold hooks. [33]Put the curtain under the gold rings.[a] Then put the Box of the Agreement behind the curtain. This curtain will separate the Holy Place from the Most Holy Place. [34]Put the mercy-cover on the Box of the Agreement in the Most Holy Place.

[35]"Put the special table you made outside the curtain. The table should be on the north side of the Holy Tent. Then put the lampstand on the south side, opposite the table.

The Door of the Holy Tent

[36]"Then make a curtain to cover the entrance to the Holy Tent. Use blue, purple and red yarn and fine linen to make this curtain. Weave pictures into it. [37]Make gold hooks for this curtain. Make five posts using acacia wood covered with gold and make five bronze bases for the five posts.

The Altar for Burning Offerings

27 "Use acacia wood and build an altar. The altar should be square. It must be 2.2 metres[b] long, 2.2 metres wide and 1.3 metres[c] high. [2]Make a horn for each of the four corners of the altar. Join each horn to its corner so that everything is one piece. Then cover the altar with bronze.

[3]"Use bronze to make all the tools and dishes that will be used on the altar. Make pots, shovels, bowls, forks and pans. These will be used for cleaning ashes from the altar. [4]Make a grating for the altar. This grating will be shaped like a net. And make a bronze ring at each of the four corners of the grating. [5]Put the grating under the ledge at the bottom of the altar. The grating will go halfway up into the altar from below.

[6]"Use acacia wood to make poles for the altar, and cover them with bronze. [7]Put the poles through the rings on both sides of the altar. Use these poles for carrying the altar. [8]Make the altar like an empty box with the sides made from boards. Make the altar just as I showed you on the mountain.

The Courtyard Around the Holy Tent

[9]"Make a courtyard for the Holy Tent. The south side should have a wall of curtains 44 metres[d] long. These curtains must be made from

fine linen. [10]Use 20 posts and 20 bronze bases under the posts. The hooks for the posts and the curtain rods[e] should be made from silver. [11]The north side must also have a wall of curtains 44 metres long. It must have 20 posts and 20 bronze bases. The hooks for the posts and the curtain rods must be made from silver.

[12]"On the west side of the courtyard there must be a wall of curtains 22 metres[f] long. There must be ten posts and ten bases. [13]The east side of the courtyard must also be 22 metres long. [14]Here at the entrance to the courtyard, one side must have curtains 6.6 metres[g] long. There must be three posts and three bases on this side. [15]The other side of the entrance must also have curtains 6.6 metres long. There must be three posts and three bases on that side.

[16]"Make a curtain 9 metres[h] long to cover the entrance to the courtyard. Make that curtain from fine linen and blue, purple and red yarn. Weave designs into that curtain. There must be four posts and four bases for that curtain. [17]All the posts around the courtyard must be joined with silver curtain rods. The hooks on the posts must be made from silver and the bases for the posts must be bronze. [18]The courtyard should be 44 metres long and 22 metres wide. The wall of curtains around the courtyard should be 2.2 metres high. The curtains must be made from fine linen. The bases under the posts must be bronze. [19]All the tools, tent pegs and other things used in the Holy Tent must be made from bronze. And all the pegs for the curtains around the courtyard must be made from bronze.

Oil for the Lamp

[20]"Command the Israelites to bring their best olive oil for the lamp that must be lit each evening. [21]This lamp is in the first room of the Meeting Tent, outside the curtain for the room where the Agreement is. Aaron and his sons will make sure this lamp is burning before the LORD every day from evening until morning. The Israelites and their descendants must obey this law forever.

Clothes for the Priests

28 "Tell your brother Aaron and his sons, Nadab, Abihu, Eleazar and Ithamar, to come to you from the Israelites. These men will serve me as priests.

---

[a] **26:33** *under the gold rings* The 50 gold rings that joined together the two parts of the Holy Tent. See Exod. 26:6.
[b] **27:1** *2.2 metres* Literally, "5 *cubits*". Also in verse 18.
[c] **27:1** *1.3 metres* Literally, "3 *cubits*".
[d] **27:9** *44 metres* Literally, "100 *cubits*". Also in verses 11,18.
[e] **27:10** *curtain rods* These were either rods that joined the posts together or grommets (rings) sewn into the curtains.
[f] **27:12** *22 metres* Literally, "50 *cubits*". Also in verse 18.
[g] **27:14** *6.6 metres* Literally, "15 *cubits*".
[h] **27:16** *9 metres* Literally, "20 *cubits*".

2"Make special clothes for your brother Aaron. These clothes will give him honour and respect. 3I have given special wisdom to some of the skilled men. Tell them to make the clothes for Aaron. These clothes will show that he serves me in a special way. Then he can serve me as a priest. 4These are the clothes the men should make: the judgement pouch, the ephod, a blue robe, a white woven robe, a turban and a cloth belt. They must make these special clothes for your brother Aaron and his sons. Then Aaron and his sons can serve me as priests. 5Tell the men to use gold thread, fine linen and blue, purple and red yarn.

The Ephod and the Cloth Belt

6"Use gold thread, fine linen and blue, purple and red yarn to make the ephod. This must be the work of a very skilled person. 7At each shoulder of the ephod, there should be a shoulder piece. These shoulder pieces should be tied to the two corners of the ephod.

8"The men will very carefully weave a cloth belt for the ephod. This belt must be made the same way as the ephod—use gold threads, fine linen and blue, purple and red yarn.

9"Take two onyx stones. Write the names of the twelve sons of Israel on these jewels. 10Write six names on one jewel and six names on the other jewel. Write the names in order, from the oldest son to the youngest. 11Cut the names of the sons of Israel into these stones. Do this the way a worker makes a seal. Put the jewels in gold settings. 12Then put these two jewels on the shoulder pieces of the ephod. Aaron will wear this special coat when he stands before the LORD. And the two stones with the names of the sons of Israel will be on the ephod. These jewels will cause the Lord to remember the Israelites. 13Use fine gold to hold the stones on the ephod. 14Twist chains of pure gold together like a rope. Make two of these gold chains and fasten them to the gold settings.

The Judgement Pouch

15"Make the judgement pouch for the high priest. Skilled workers should make this pouch just as they made the ephod. They must use gold threads, fine linen and blue, purple and red yarn. 16The judgement pouch should be folded double to make a square pocket. It should be 22 centimetresa long and 22 centimetres wide. 17Put four rows of beautiful jewels on the judgement pouch. The first row of jewels should have a ruby, a topaz and a beryl. 18The second row should have a turquoise, a sapphire and an emerald. 19The third row should have a jacinth,

an agate and an amethyst. 20The fourth row should have a chrysolite, an onyx and a jasper. Set all these jewels in gold. 21There will be twelve jewels on the judgement pouch—one stone for each of the sons of Israel. Each stone will be like a seal with the name of one of the twelve tribes cut into it.

22"Make chains of pure gold for the judgement pouch. These chains must be braided like a rope. 23Make two gold rings and put them on two corners of the judgement pouch. 24Put the two gold chains through the two rings at the corners of the judgement pouch. 25Fasten the other ends of the gold chains to the two settings. This will fasten them to the two shoulder pieces of the ephod on the front. 26Make two more gold rings and put them on the other two corners of the judgement pouch. This will be on the inside edge of the judgement pouch next to the ephod. 27Make two more gold rings and put them on the bottom of the shoulder pieces on the front of the ephod. Put the gold rings above the cloth belt of the ephod. 28Use blue ribbon to tie the rings of the judgement pouch to the rings of the ephod. In this way the judgement pouch will rest close to the cloth belt and will be held against the ephod.

29"When Aaron enters the Holy Place, he must wear the judgement pouch. In this way he will wear the names of the twelve sons of Israel over his heart. And the LORD will always be reminded of them. 30Put the Urim and Thummim inside the judgement pouch. They will be over Aaron's heart when he goes before the LORD. So Aaron will always carry with him a way of judging for the Israelites when he is before the LORD.

Other Clothes for the Priests

31"Make a blue robe for the ephod. 32Make a hole in the centre for the head. And sew a piece of cloth around the edge of this hole. This cloth will be like a collar that keeps the hole from tearing. 33Use blue, purple and red yarn to make cloth pomegranates. Hang these pomegranates around the bottom edge of the robe, and hang gold bells between the pomegranates. 34So around the bottom edge of the robe there should be bells and pomegranates. There should be a bell following each pomegranate. 35Aaron will wear this robe when he serves as a priest. The bells will ring as Aaron goes into the Holy Place to stand before the LORD, and the bells will ring as he leaves the Holy Place. This way Aaron will not die.

36"Make a strip of pure gold and carve these words into the gold like the writing on a seal: ONLY FOR THE LORD. 37Fasten the gold strip to a blue ribbon. Tie the blue ribbon around the turban.

---

a **28:16** *22 centimetres* Literally, "1 *span*". The distance from the tip of the thumb to the tip of the little finger.

The gold strip should be on the front of the turban. [38]Aaron will wear this on his head. In this way he will remove the guilt if anything is wrong with the gifts that the Israelites[a] give to God. Aaron will always wear this on his head so that the LORD will accept the gifts of the people.

[39]"Use fine linen to make the white woven robe and the turban. The cloth belt should have designs sewn into it. [40]Also make coats, belts and special caps for Aaron's sons. This will give them honour and respect. [41]Put the clothes on your brother Aaron and his sons. Then pour the special oil on them to make them priests. This will make them holy, and they will serve me as priests.

[42]"Use linen to make underclothes for the priests. These underclothes will cover them from the waist to the thighs. [43]Aaron and his sons must wear these clothes whenever they enter the Meeting Tent. They must wear these clothes when they come near to the altar to serve as priests in the Holy Place. If they don't wear these clothes, they will be guilty of wrong and will have to die. All this should be a law that continues forever for Aaron and all his family after him.

The Ceremony for Appointing the Priests

29 "Now I will tell you what you must do to show that Aaron and his sons serve me in a special way as priests. Find one young bull and two rams that have nothing wrong with them. [2]Then use fine wheat flour without yeast to make bread. And use the same things to make cakes mixed with olive oil. Make small thin cakes spread with oil. [3]Put this bread and the cakes in a basket. Then give the basket to Aaron and his sons. At the same time, give them the bull and the two rams.

[4]"Then bring Aaron and his sons to the entrance of the Meeting Tent. Wash them with water. [5]Put the special clothes on Aaron. Put on him the white woven robe and the blue robe that is worn with the ephod. Put the ephod and the judgement pouch on him. Then tie the beautiful cloth belt on him. [6]Put the turban on his head and the special crown around the turban. [7]Take the anointing oil and pour it on Aaron's head. This will show that he is chosen for this work.

[8]"Then bring Aaron's sons to that place. Put the white woven robes on them. [9]Then tie cloth belts around their waists, and give them special caps to wear. At that time they will begin to be priests. They will be priests because of the special law that will continue forever. This is the way you will make Aaron and his sons priests.

[10]"Then bring the bull to that place at the front of the Meeting Tent. Aaron and his sons must put their hands on the bull's head. [11]Then kill the bull there in the LORD's presence at the entrance to the Meeting Tent. [12]Then take some of the bull's blood and go to the altar. Use your finger to put some blood on the horns of the altar. Pour out all the blood that is left at the bottom of the altar. [13]Then take all the fat from inside the bull, the fatty part of the liver, both kidneys and the fat around them. Burn this fat on the altar. [14]Then take the bull's meat, his skin and his other parts and go outside your camp and burn them. This bull is an offering to take away the sins of the priests.

[15]"Then tell Aaron and his sons to put their hands on the head of one of the rams. [16]Kill that ram and save the blood. Throw the blood against the altar on all four sides. [17]Then cut the ram into several pieces. Wash all the parts from inside the ram and the legs. Put these things with the head and the other pieces of the ram. [18]Then burn everything on the altar. It is a burnt offering to the LORD. It is a sweet-smelling gift to the LORD.

[19]"Tell Aaron and his sons to put their hands on the other ram. [20]Kill that ram and save some of its blood. Put that blood on the right ear lobes of Aaron and his sons. Also put some of the blood on the thumbs of their right hands and on the big toes of their right feet. Then throw blood against all four sides of the altar. [21]Then take some of the blood from the altar. Mix it with the special oil and sprinkle it on Aaron and his clothes. And sprinkle it on his sons and their clothes. This will show that Aaron and his sons serve me in a special way. And it will show that their clothes are used only at special times.

[22]"Then take the fat from the ram. (This is the ram that will be used in the ceremony to make Aaron the high priest.) Take the fat from around the tail and the fat that covers the organs inside the body. Then take the fat that covers the liver, both kidneys and the fat on them and the right leg. [23]Then take the basket of bread that you made without yeast. This is the basket you put before the LORD. Take these things out of the basket: one loaf of bread, one cake made with oil and one small thin cake. [24]Give them to Aaron and his sons. Tell them to hold these things in their hands before the Lord. This will be a special offering to the LORD. [25]Then take them from Aaron and his sons and put them on the altar with the ram. Then burn everything on the altar. It is a burnt offering to the LORD. It is a sweet-smelling gift to the LORD.

[26]"Then take the breast from the ram. (This is the ram that will be used in the ceremony to make Aaron the high priest.) Hold the breast of the ram before the LORD as a special offering. Then

---

[a] **28:38** *In this way . . . Israelites* Literally, "It will keep him holy when he bears the guilt from the gifts of the Israelites."

take it back and keep it. This part of the animal will be for you. ²⁷Take the breast and the leg of the ram that was used to make Aaron the high priest and make these parts holy. Then give these special parts to Aaron and his sons. ²⁸The Israelites will always give Aaron and his sons these parts. These parts will always belong to the priests when the Israelites make an offering to the LORD. When they give these parts to the priest, it will be the same as giving them to the Lord.

²⁹"Save these special clothes that were made for Aaron and his descendants. They will wear these clothes when they are chosen to be priests. ³⁰Aaron's son will become the next high priest after him. That son will wear these clothes for seven days when he comes to the Meeting Tent to serve in the Holy Place.

³¹"Cook the meat from the ram that was used to make Aaron the high priest. Cook that meat in a holy place. ³²Then Aaron and his sons must eat the meat at the front door of the Meeting Tent. And they must also eat the bread that is in the basket. ³³These offerings were used to take away their sins when they were made priests. Now they should eat these offerings. ³⁴If any of the meat from that ram or any of the bread is left the next morning, then it must be burned. You must not eat that bread or the meat because it should be eaten only in a special way at a special time.

³⁵"You must do all these things for Aaron and his sons. You must do them exactly as I told you. The ceremony for appointing them to be priests must continue for seven days. ³⁶You must kill one bull every day for seven days. This will be an offering for the sins of Aaron and his sons. You will use these sacrifices to make the altar pure, and pour olive oil on the altar to make it holy. ³⁷You will make the altar pure and holy for seven days. At that time the altar will be most holy. Anything that touches the altar will also be holy.

³⁸"Every day you must make an offering on the altar. You must kill two lambs that are one year old. ³⁹Offer one lamb in the morning and the other in the evening. ⁴⁰⁻⁴¹When you kill the first lamb, also offer 1 kilogramme[a] of fine wheat flour. Mix that flour with 1 litre[b] of the best oil. Also offer 1 litre of wine as an offering. When you kill the second lamb in the evening, also offer the 1 kilogramme of fine flour mixed with 1 litre of the best oil and offer 1 litre of wine. This is the same as you did in the morning. This will be a sweet-smelling gift to the LORD. When you burn this offering, he will smell it, and it will please him.

⁴²"You must burn these things as an offering to the Lord every day. Do this at the entrance of the Meeting Tent before the LORD. Continue to do this for all time. When you make the offering, I will meet you there and speak to you. ⁴³I will meet with the Israelites at that place, and my Glory will make that place holy.

⁴⁴"So I will make the Meeting Tent and the altar holy. I will also make Aaron and his sons holy so that they can serve me as priests. ⁴⁵I will live with the Israelites. I will be their God. ⁴⁶The people will know that I am the LORD their God. They will know that I am the one who led them out of Egypt so that I could live with them. I am the LORD their God.

The Altar for Burning Incense

30 "Make an altar from acacia wood. You will use this altar for burning incense. ²You must make the altar square—44 centimetres[c] long and 44 centimetres wide. It must be 88 centimetres[d] high. There will be horns at the four corners. These horns must be made as one piece with the altar. ³Cover the top, the horns and all four sides of the altar with pure gold. Then put gold trim all around the altar. ⁴Below this trim there should be two gold rings. There should be two gold rings on opposite sides of the altar. These gold rings will be used with poles to carry the altar. ⁵Make the poles from acacia wood and cover them with gold. ⁶Put the altar just outside the special curtain that hangs in front of the Box of the Agreement. So the altar will be in front of the mercy-cover that is above the Agreement. This is the place where I will meet with you.

⁷"Aaron must burn sweet-smelling incense on the altar every morning. He will do this when he comes to care for the lamps. ⁸He must burn incense again when he checks the lamps in the evening so that incense will be burned before the LORD every day forever. ⁹Don't use this altar for offering any other kind of incense or burnt offering or for any kind of grain offering or drink offering.

¹⁰"Once a year Aaron must make a special sacrifice. He will use the blood of the sin offering to erase the sins of the people. He will do this at the horns of this altar. This day will be called the Day of Atonement, and it will be a very special day for the LORD."

The Temple Tax

¹¹The LORD said to Moses, ¹²"Count the Israelites so that you will know how many people there

---

ᵃ **29:40–41** *1 kilogramme* Literally, "¹⁄₁₀ of a *ephah*".
ᵇ **29:40–41** *1 litre* Literally, "¼ *hin*".
ᶜ **30:2** *44 centimetres* Literally, "1 *cubit*".
ᵈ **30:2** *88 centimetres* Literally, "2 *cubits*".

are. Every time this is done, each man must make a payment for himself to the LORD so that nothing terrible will happen to the people. [13]Each man who is counted must pay 5 grammes[a] of silver. (That is by the official measure, which is 11.5 grammes.[b]) These 5 grammes of silver are an offering to the LORD. [14]Every man who is at least 20 years old must be counted. And every man who is counted must give the LORD this offering. [15]The rich must not give more than 5 grammes, and the poor must not give less. All people will make the same offering to the LORD. This will be a payment for your life. [16]Gather this money from the Israelites. Use the money for the service in the Meeting Tent. This payment will be a way for the LORD to remember his people. They will be paying for their own lives."

The Washing Bowl

[17]The LORD said to Moses, [18]"Make a bronze bowl and put it on a bronze base. You will use this for washing. Put the bowl between the Meeting Tent and the altar. Fill the bowl with water. [19]Aaron and his sons must wash their hands and feet with the water from this bowl. [20]Every time they enter the Meeting Tent, they must wash with that water so that they will not die. They must also wash every time they come near the altar to burn incense or to offer gifts to the LORD. [21]They must wash their hands and their feet so that they will not die. This will be a law that continues forever for Aaron and his people who will live in the future."

The Anointing Oil

[22]Then the LORD said to Moses, [23]"Find the finest spices. Get 6 kilogrammes[c] of liquid myrrh, half that amount (that is, 3 kilogrammes[d]) of sweet-smelling cinnamon, and 6 kilogrammes of sweet-smelling cane, [24]and 6 kilogrammes of cassia. Use the official measure to measure all these things. Also get 4 litres[e] of olive oil.

[25]"Mix all these things to make a special sweet-smelling anointing oil. [26]Pour this oil on the Meeting Tent and on the Box of the Agreement. This will show that these things have a special purpose. [27]Pour the oil on the table and on all the dishes on the table. And pour this oil on the lamp and on all its tools. Pour the oil on the incense altar. [28]Also, pour the oil on the altar for burning offerings to God. Pour this oil on everything on that altar. Pour this oil on the bowl and on the base under the bowl. [29]You will make all these things holy. They will be very special to the Lord. Anything that touches these things will also become holy.

[30]"Pour the oil on Aaron and his sons to show that they are separated from the rest of the people to serve as priests. [31]Tell the Israelites that the anointing oil is holy—it must always be used only for me. [32]This oil is holy and you must treat it as something special. Don't use the same formula for making perfume and don't let people use this oil like an ordinary perfume. [33]Whoever makes a perfume like that and puts it on anyone except a priest[f] must be separated from the people."

The Incense

[34]Then the LORD said to Moses, "Get these sweet-smelling spices: resin, onycha, galbanum and pure frankincense. Be sure that you have equal amounts of these spices. [35]Mix the spices together to make a sweet-smelling incense. Do this the same as a perfume maker would do it. Also mix salt with this incense. This will make it pure and special. [36]Grind some of the incense until it becomes a fine powder. Put the powder in front of the Holy Box that holds the Agreement in the Meeting Tent. This is the place where I meet with you. You must use this incense powder only for its very special purpose. [37]You must use it only in this special way for the LORD. You must also make it in a special way. Don't make any other incense in this way. [38]There may be people who will want to make some of this incense for themselves so that they can enjoy the smell. But whoever does this must be separated from their people."

Bezalel and Oholiab

31 Then the LORD said to Moses, [2]"I have chosen a man from the tribe of Judah to do some special work for me. His name is Bezalel son of Uri son of Hur. [3]I have filled Bezalel with the Spirit of God—I have given him the skill and knowledge to do all kinds of things. [4]He is a very good designer. And he can make things from gold, silver and bronze. [5]He can cut and set beautiful jewels. And he can work with wood. He can do all kinds of work. [6]I have also chosen Oholiab to work with him. Oholiab is the son of Ahisamach from the tribe of Dan. And I have given skills to all the other workers so that they can make everything that I have commanded you:

---

[a] **30:13** *5 grammes* Literally, "½ *shekel*".
[b] **30:13** *11.5 grammes* Literally, "20 *gerahs*".
[c] **30:23** *6 kilogrammes* Literally, "500 measures".
[d] **30:23** *3 kilogrammes* Literally, "250 measures".
[e] **30:24** *4 litres* Literally, "a *hin*".
[f] **30:33** *priest* Literally, "stranger".

[7]the Meeting Tent;
the Box of the Agreement;
the mercy-cover that is on it;
[8]the table and everything on it;
the pure gold lampstand and everything used
with it;
the altar for burning incense;
[9]the altar for burning offerings and the things
used at the altar;
the bowl and the base under it;
[10]the special clothes for Aaron the priest;
the special clothes for Aaron's sons when they
serve as priests;
[11]the sweet-smelling anointing oil;
the sweet-smelling incense for the Holy
Place.

These workers must make everything the way
that I have commanded you."

The Sabbath

[12]Then the LORD said to Moses, [13]"Tell the
Israelites this: 'You must follow the rules about
my special days of rest. You must do this because
they will be a sign between you and me for all
generations. This will show you that I, the LORD,
have made you my special people.

[14]"'Make the Sabbath a special day. If someone
treats the Sabbath like any other day, that person
must be killed. Whoever works on the Sabbath day
must be separated from their people. [15]There are
six other days in the week for working. But the
seventh day is a very special day of rest. That is the
special day to honour the LORD. Anyone who works
during the Sabbath must be killed. [16]The Israelites
must remember the Sabbath and make it a special
day. They must continue to do this forever. It is an
agreement between them and me that will
continue forever. [17]The Sabbath will be a sign
between me and the Israelites forever.'" (The LORD
worked six days and made the sky and the earth,
and on the seventh day, he rested and relaxed.)

[18]When God finished speaking to Moses on
Mount Sinai, he gave him the two stone tablets of
the agreement. God had written on the stones
with his finger.

The Golden Calf

32 The people saw that a long time had
passed and Moses had not come down
from the mountain. So they gathered around
Aaron. They said to him, "Look, Moses led us out
of the land of Egypt, but we don't know what has
happened to him. So make us some gods to go
before us and lead us."

[2]Aaron said to the people, "Bring me the gold
earrings that belong to your wives, sons and
daughters."

[3]So the people collected all their gold earrings
and brought them to Aaron. [4]He took the gold
from the people and used it to make an idol.
Using a special tool, he shaped the gold into a
statue of a calf.

Then the people said, "Israel, here are your
gods! These are the gods that brought you out of
the land of Egypt!"[a]

[5]Aaron saw all these things, so he built an altar
in front of the calf. Then Aaron made an
announcement. He said, "Tomorrow will be a
special festival to honour the LORD."

[6]The people woke up very early the next
morning. They killed animals and offered them as
burnt offerings and fellowship offerings. They sat
down to eat and drink. Then they got up and had
a wild party.

[7]At the same time, the LORD said to Moses, "Go
down from this mountain. Your people, the people
you brought out of the land of Egypt, have
committed a terrible sin. [8]They have very quickly
turned away from what I commanded them to do.
They made a calf from melted gold for themselves.
They are worshipping that calf and making
sacrifices to it. The people have said, 'Israel, these
are the gods that led you out of Egypt.'"

[9]The LORD said to Moses, "I have seen these
people, and I know that they are very stubborn.
They will always turn against me. [10]So now let
me destroy them in anger. Then I will make a
great nation from you."

[11]But Moses begged the LORD his God, "LORD,
don't let your anger destroy your people. You
brought them out of Egypt with your great power
and strength. [12]But if you destroy your people,
the Egyptians will say, 'God planned to do bad
things to his people. That is why he led them out
of Egypt. He wanted to kill them in the mountains.

---

[a] **32:4 Israel . . . Egypt** This shows that the people worshipped the calf as a special symbol for the LORD, and even this was
forbidden. See 1 Kgs 12:26–30.

He wanted to wipe them off the earth.' So don't be angry with your people. Please change your mind! Don't destroy them. 13Remember Abraham, Isaac and Israel. These men served you, and you used your name to make a promise to them. You said, 'I will make your people as many as the stars in the sky. I will give your people all this land as I promised. This land will be theirs forever.'"

14So the LORD felt sorry for the people. He did not do what he said he might do—he did not destroy them.

15Then Moses went down the mountain. He had the two stone tablets with the agreement on them. The commandments were written on both sides of the stone, front and back. 16God himself made the stones, and God himself wrote the commandments on them.

17Joshua heard the noise from the party in camp. He said to Moses, "It sounds like war down in the camp!"

18Moses answered, "It is not the noise of an army shouting for victory. And it is not the noise of an army crying from defeat. The noise I hear is the sound of music."a

19When Moses came near to the camp, he saw the gold calf and the people dancing. He became very angry, and he threw the stone tablets on the ground. The stones broke into several pieces at the bottom of the mountain. 20Then Moses destroyed the calf that the people had made. He melted it in the fire. Then he ground the gold until it became dust and threw it into the water. Then he forced the Israelites to drink that water.

21Moses said to Aaron, "What did these people do to you that would make you do this? Why did you lead them to do such a terrible sin?"

22Aaron answered, "Don't be angry, sir. You know that these people are always ready to do wrong. 23The people said to me, 'Moses led us out of Egypt, but we don't know what has happened to him. So make us some gods to lead us.' 24So I told the people, 'If you have any gold rings, then give them to me.' The people gave me their gold. I threw the gold into the fire, and out of the fire came this calf!"

25Moses saw that Aaron had let the people get out of control. They were being wild, and all their enemies could see them acting like fools. 26So Moses stood at the entrance to the camp and said, "Anyone who wants to follow the LORD should come to me." Everyone from the tribe of Levi ran to Moses.

27Then Moses said to them, "I will tell you what the LORD, the God of Israel, says: 'Every man must get his sword and go from one end of the camp to the other. You men must kill ⌊those who are against the Lord⌋, even if they are your brothers, friends or neighbours.'"

28The people from the tribe of Levi obeyed Moses. That day about 3,000 of the people died. 29Then Moses said, "Take your role today as special servants of the LORD because you were willing to fight against even your own sons and brothers. You will receive a blessing for this."b

30The next morning Moses told the people, "You have committed a terrible sin! But now I will go up to the LORD, and maybe I can do something so that he will forgive you for your sin." 31So Moses went back to the LORD and said, "Please listen! These people committed a terrible sin and made a god from gold. 32Now, forgive them of this sin. If you will not forgive them, then erase my name from your book."c

33But the LORD said to Moses, "The only people I erase from my book are those who sin against me. 34So now, go down and lead the people where I tell you to go. My angel will go before you and lead you. When the time comes to punish those who sinned, they will be punished." 35So the LORD caused a terrible sickness to come to the people. He did this because they told Aaron to make the gold calf.

I Will Not Go With You

33 Then the LORD said to Moses, "You and the people you brought out of Egypt must leave this place. Go to the land that I promised to give to Abraham, Isaac and Jacob. I promised them that I would give that land to their descendants. 2So I will send an angel to go before you, and I will defeat the Canaanites, Amorites, Hittites, Perizzites, Hivites and Jebusites. I will force them to leave your land. 3So go to the land filled with many good things,d but I will not go with you. You people are very stubborn. If I go with you, I might destroy you along the way."

4The people heard this bad news and became very sad, so they stopped wearing jewellery. 5This was because the LORD said to Moses, "Tell the Israelites, 'You are a stubborn people. I might destroy you even if I travel with you only a short time. So take off all your jewellery while I decidee what to do with you.'" 6So the Israelites stopped wearing their jewellery at Mount Horeb.

a 32:18 *music* Or "singing".
b 32:29 *Take your role . . . blessing for this* This seems to be the point when the priesthood changed. Before this time, the priests came from the firstborn sons; after this time, they came from the sons of Aaron of the tribe of Levi.
c 32:32 *your book* The book of life, in which God has written the names of his chosen people. See Rev. 3:5; 21:27.
d 33:3 *land . . . things* Literally, "land flowing with milk and honey".
e 33:5 *jewellery . . . decide* This is a wordplay in Hebrew, but people often wore jewellery to remind them of their false gods.

The Temporary Meeting Tent

⁷Moses used to take a tent a short way outside the camp. He called it "the meeting tent".ᵃ Anyone who wanted to ask something from the LORD would go to the meeting tent outside the camp. ⁸Whenever Moses went out to the tent, all the people watched him. They stood at the entrance of their tents and watched Moses until he entered the meeting tent. ⁹Whenever Moses went into the tent, the tall cloud would come down and stay at the entrance to the tent. And the Lord would speak with Moses. ¹⁰So when the people saw the cloud at the entrance of the tent, they would go to the entrance of their own tents and bow down to worship God.

¹¹In this way the LORD spoke to Moses face to face like a man speaks with his friend. Then Moses would go back to the camp, but his helper, Joshua son of Nun, always stayed in the tent.

Moses Sees the Glory of the LORD

¹²Moses said to the LORD, "You told me to lead these people, but you did not say who you would send with me. You said to me, 'I know you very well, and I am pleased with you.' ¹³If I have really pleased you, then teach me your ways. I want to know you. Then I can continue to please you. Remember that these people are your nation."

¹⁴The Lord answered, "I myself will go with you. I will lead you."ᵇ

¹⁵Then Moses said to him, "If you don't go with us, then don't make us leave this place. ¹⁶Also, how will we know if you are pleased with me and these people? If you go with us, we will know for sure. If you don't go with us, these people and I will be no different from any other people on the earth."

¹⁷Then the LORD said to Moses, "I will do what you ask. I will do this because I am pleased with you and because I know you very well."ᶜ

¹⁸Then Moses said, "Now, please show me your Glory."

¹⁹Then the Lord answered, "I will show my love and mercy to anyone I want to. So I will cause my perfect goodness to pass by in front of you, and I will speak my name, YAHWEH, so that you can hear it. ²⁰But you cannot see my face. No one can see me and continue to live."

²¹Then the LORD said, "Here is a place for you to stand by me on this large rock. ²²I will put you in a large crack in that rock. Then I will cover you with my hand, and my Glory will pass by. ²³Then I will take away my hand, and you will see my back. But you will not see my face."

The New Stone Tablets

34

Then the LORD said to Moses, "Make two more stone tablets like the first two that were broken. I will write the same words on these stones that were written on the first two stones. ²Be ready tomorrow morning and come up on Mount Sinai. Stand before me there on the top of the mountain. ³No one will be allowed to come with you. No one should even be seen anywhere on the mountain. Even your herds of animals or flocks of sheep will not be allowed to eat grass at the bottom of the mountain."

⁴So Moses made two more stone tablets like the first ones. Early the next morning Moses went up Mount Sinai, just as the LORD had commanded. Moses carried the two stone tablets with him. ⁵Then the LORD came down to him in a cloud, stood there with Moses, and spoke his own name. ⁶That is, the LORD passed in front of Moses and said,

"I am YAHWEH, the LORD,
  the God who is kind and merciful.
I am slow to become angry,
  full of unfailing love and forever loyal.
⁷My faithful love for my people never ends.
  I forgive even sinners, who turn against me
    and do wrong.
But I do not fail to punish people who are
    guilty.
  Even the children suffer because of their
    parents' sins,
  as well as their grandchildren and great-
    grandchildren."

⁸Then Moses quickly bowed to the ground and worshipped the Lord. Moses said, ⁹"Lord, if you are pleased with me, please go with us. I know that these are stubborn people, but forgive us for the bad things we did. Accept us as your people."

¹⁰Then the Lord said, "I am making this agreement with all of your people. I will do amazing things that have never before been done for any other nation on earth. The people with you will see that I, the LORD, am very great. They will see the wonderful things that I will do for you. ¹¹Obey what I command you today, and I will force your enemies to leave your land. I will force out the Amorites, Canaanites, Hittites, Perizzites, Hivites and Jebusites. ¹²Be careful! Don't make any agreement with the people who live in the land where you are going. If you make an agreement with them, it will bring you trouble. ¹³So destroy their altars, break the stones

---

ᵃ **33:7 meeting tent** This is probably a tent that Moses used only until the real Meeting Tent was built.
ᵇ **33:14 lead you** Or "give you rest".
ᶜ **33:17 I know you very well** Literally, "I know you by name".

they worship, and cut down their idols.[a] ¹⁴Don't worship any other god. I am YAHWEH KANAH—the jealous God. That is my name. I hate it when my people worship other gods.[b]

¹⁵"Be careful not to make any agreements with the people who live in that land. If you do this, you might join them when they worship their gods. They will invite you to join them, and you will eat their sacrifices. ¹⁶You might choose some of their daughters as wives for your sons. Those daughters serve false gods. They might lead your sons to do the same thing.

¹⁷"Don't make idols.

¹⁸"Celebrate the Festival of Unleavened Bread. For seven days eat the bread made without yeast as I commanded you before. Do this during the month I have chosen, the month of Abib, because that is the month you came out of Egypt.

¹⁹"A woman's first baby always belongs to me. Even the first animals that are born from your cattle or sheep belong to me. ²⁰If you want to keep a donkey that is the first born, then you can buy it with a lamb. But if you don't buy that donkey with a lamb, you must break the donkey's neck. You must buy back all of your firstborn sons from me. No one should come before me without a gift.

²¹"You will work for six days, but on the seventh day, you must rest. You must rest even during the times of planting and harvesting.

²²"Celebrate the Festival of Harvest. Use the first grain from the wheat harvest for this festival. And in the autumn[c] celebrate the Festival of Shelters.

²³"Three times each year all your men must go to be with the Lord GOD, the God of Israel.

²⁴"When you go into your land, I will force your enemies out of that land. I will expand your borders—you will get more and more land. You will go before the LORD your God three times each year. At that time no one will try to take your land from you.

²⁵"When you kill an animal and offer its blood as a sacrifice, you must not include anything that has yeast in it.

"Don't let any of the meat from the Passover meal remain until morning.

²⁶"Give the Lord the very first crops that you harvest. Bring them to the house[d] of the LORD your God.

"Never cook a young goat in its mother's milk."

²⁷Then the LORD said to Moses, "Write everything that I have told you. This is the agreement that I made with you and the Israelites."

²⁸Moses stayed there with the LORD for 40 days and 40 nights. Moses did not eat any food or drink any water. And he wrote the words of the agreement (the Ten Commandments) on the two stone tablets.

Moses' Shining Face

²⁹When Moses came down from Mount Sinai, he carried the two stone tablets of the agreement. Because he had talked with the Lord, his face was shining, but he did not know it. ³⁰Aaron and all the people of Israel saw that Moses' face was shining bright. So they were afraid to go near him. ³¹But Moses called to them. So Aaron and all the leaders of the people went to him. Moses talked with them. ³²After that, all the Israelites came near Moses, and he gave them the commands that the LORD had given him on Mount Sinai.

³³When Moses finished speaking to the people, he put a covering over his face. ³⁴Any time Moses went before the LORD to speak with him, Moses took off the covering. Then Moses would come out and tell the Israelites what the Lord commanded. ³⁵The people would see that Moses' face was shining bright, so he would cover his face again. He kept his face covered until the next time he went in to speak with the Lord.

Rules About the Sabbath

35 Moses gathered all the Israelites together and said to them, "I will tell you what the LORD has commanded you to do:

²"There are six days for working, but the seventh day will be a very special day of rest for you. You will honour the LORD by resting on that special day. Anyone who works on the seventh day must be killed. ³On the Sabbath you should not even light a fire in any of the places where you live."

Things for the Holy Tent

⁴Moses said to all the Israelites, "This is what the LORD commanded: ⁵Gather special gifts for the LORD. Each of you should decide in your heart what you will give. And then you should bring that gift to the LORD. Bring gold, silver and bronze; ⁶blue, purple and red yarn and fine linen; goat hair; ⁷ram skins dyed red and fine leather; acacia wood; ⁸oil for the lamps; spices for the anointing oil and spices for the sweet-smelling incense. ⁹Also, bring onyx stones and other jewels to be put on the ephod and the judgement pouch.

---

[a] **34:13** *stones . . . idols* Literally, "memorials . . . Asherah poles". These were stone markers and wood poles that the people set up to help them remember and honour false gods.

[b] **34:14** *I hate . . . gods* Or "I am El Kanah—the Jealous God."

[c] **34:22** *autumn* Literally, "at the changing of the year".

[d] **34:26** *house* The "Holy Tent" where the people went to meet with God. See Exod. 25:8–9.

WILL YOU GO WITH US?

Things hadn't got off to a good start for the Israelites. God had rescued them from Egypt and made them his special people. Yet before Moses had even come down from the mountain to tell them all the things God had for his people, they'd built a golden calf to worship instead (check out Exodus chapter 32). It's really bad news.

DIG IN

READ Exodus 33:1-6

- What is God no longer going to do for the people?
- Why does he say this?
- What do the people remove and how do they feel?

It doesn't get more miserable than this. God tells Moses he can't go with the people any longer – he's so angry at their sin that he might destroy them if he does. It must have been pretty scary for them – how could they go alone? To make it worse, God asks the people to remove the jewellery that he'd given them when they'd left Egypt. It had been a sign of his rescuing love, and removing it symbolized the relationship had broken.

READ Exodus 33:7-23

- What does Moses want for himself from God (v.13)?
- In verses 15 and 16 what was Moses asking God for?
- Why was God's presence so important for the people (v.16)?
- What's the good news (v.17)?

What an amazing relationship Moses has with God! Moses is desperate for God's presence to remain with them – he's afraid of the consequences if he doesn't. Who would help him lead? How will they be any different from the other nations? He asks God to remember that these are his people. Can you imagine Moses' relief as God agrees to go with them (v.14)!

READ Exodus 40:1-38

- Try drawing a picture of the Meeting Tent (or Holy Tent) and all its furnishings.
- What filled the Holy Tent (vv.34–35)?
- How did God's presence guide the people (vv.36–38)?

Did you notice that Moses couldn't enter the Holy Tent when the Lord was there? If there's one thing we learn in Exodus it's that God is holy and we aren't! The next book, Leviticus, will show us how the priests had to offer sacrifices to pay for the people's sin – and only then can Moses and the priests enter the Meeting Tent (see Leviticus 9:23). For now, the Lord is with his people and guiding them through the cloud and fire – that's pretty awesome!

DIG THROUGH

- Moses was desperate to know that God was going with them. How desperate are you to know God more?
- Because of Jesus we no longer have to go to a tent to meet with God and offer sacrifices for our sins. By the Holy Spirit, God lives in us! Praise God for that!

DIG DEEPER

- Check out John 1:1,14. Jesus (the Word) lived in the world and fulfilled all that the original Holy Tent did. See if you can figure out how.
- Look back over Exodus chapters 36 – 40. Can you spot a) what item symbolized God's presence? b) what some of the other items in the Holy Tent were used for?

10"All of you who are skilled workers should make all the things the LORD commanded: 11the Holy Tent, its outer tent and its covering; the hooks, boards, braces, posts and bases; 12the Holy Box, its poles, the mercy-cover and the curtain that covers the area where the Box stays; 13the table and its poles, all the things on the table and the special bread on the table; 14the lampstand that is used for light and the things used with the lampstand, the lamps and oil for the light; 15the altar for burning incense and its poles; the anointing oil and the sweet-smelling incense; the curtain that covers the door at the entrance to the Holy Tent; 16the altar for burning offerings and its bronze grating, the poles and all the things used at the altar; the bronze bowl and its base; 17the curtains around the courtyard, their posts and bases and the curtain that covers the entrance to the courtyard; 18the pegs used to support the Tent and the wall of curtains around the courtyard, and the ropes that tie to the pegs; 19and the special woven clothes for the priest to wear in the Holy Place. These are the special clothes for Aaron the priest and his sons to wear when they serve as priests."

The Great Offering From the People

20Then all the Israelites went away from Moses. 21All the people who wanted to give came and brought a gift to the LORD. These gifts were used for making the Meeting Tent, everything in the Tent and the special clothes. 22All the men and women who wanted to give brought gold jewellery of all kinds. They brought pins,a earrings, rings and other jewellery. They all gave their jewellery as a special offering to the LORD. 23Everyone who had fine linen and blue, purple and red yarn brought it to the Lord. Anyone who had goat hair or ram skins dyed red or fine leather brought it to the Lord. 24Everyone who wanted to give silver or bronze brought that as a gift to the LORD. Everyone who had acacia wood came and gave it to the Lord. 25Every skilled woman made fine linen and blue, purple and red yarn. 26And all the women who were skilled and wanted to help made cloth from the goat hair.

27The leaders brought onyx stones and other jewels. These stones and jewels were put on the ephod and judgement pouch of the priest. 28The people also brought spices and olive oil. These things were used for the sweet-smelling incense, the anointing oil and the oil for the lamps.

29All the Israelites who wanted to help brought gifts to the LORD. They gave these gifts freely, because they wanted to. These gifts were used to make everything the LORD had commanded Moses and the people to make.

Bezalel and Oholiab

30Then Moses said to the Israelites, "Look, the LORD has chosen Bezalel son of Uri, from the tribe of Judah. (Uri was the son of Hur.) 31And he has filled Bezalel with the Spirit of God—he gave Bezalel special skill and knowledge to do all kinds of things. 32He can design and make things with gold, silver and bronze. 33He can cut and set stones and jewels. He can work with wood and make all kinds of things. 34The Lord has given Bezalel and Oholiab special skills to teach other people. (Oholiab was the son of Ahisamach from the tribe of Dan.) 35He has given both of these men special skills to do all kinds of work. They are able to do the work of carpenters and metalworkers. They can weave cloth with designs in it from blue, purple and red yarn and fine linen. And they are able to weave things with wool.

36 "So Bezalel, Oholiab and all the other skilled men must do the work the LORD has commanded. The LORD has given these men the wisdom and understanding to do all the skilled work needed to build this holy place."

2Then Moses called Bezalel, Oholiab and all the other skilled men who the LORD had given special skills to. And they came because they wanted to help with the work. 3Moses gave them everything the Israelites had brought as gifts, and they used these things to build this holy place. The people continued to bring gifts each morning. 4Finally, all the skilled workers left the work they were doing, and they went to speak to Moses. 5They said, "The people have brought too much. We have more than we need to finish the work the LORD told us to do."

6Then Moses sent this message throughout the camp: "No man or woman should make anything else as a gift for this holy place." So the people were stopped from giving more. 7The people had brought more than enough things to finish the work.

The Holy Tent

8Then the skilled workers began making the Holy Tent. They made the ten curtains from fine linen and blue, purple and red yarn. And they sewed pictures of winged creatures into the curtains. 9Each curtain was the same size—12 metresb long and 2 metresc wide. 10The workers joined the curtains together into two groups of

---

a 35:22 *pins* Or "hooks". These were like safety pins and were used like buttons to fasten their robes.
b 36:9 *12 metres* Literally, "28 *cubits*".
c 36:9 *2 metres* Literally, "4 *cubits*".

curtains. They joined five curtains together to make one group and five curtains together to make the other group. ¹¹Then they used blue cloth to make loops along the edge of the end curtain of one group. And they did the same on the end curtain in the other group. ¹²There were 50 loops on the end curtain in one group and 50 loops on the end curtain in the other group. The loops were opposite each other. ¹³Then they made 50 gold rings to join the two curtains together. So the Holy Tent was joined together into one piece.

> ## INSIGHT
>
> Goat hair was probably chosen for the curtains because when it was dry it would have been open and airy, making it cooler inside the tent but when wet it would have expanded, keeping the rain out.
>
> **Exodus 36:14**

¹⁴Then the workers made another tent to cover the Holy Tent. They used goat hair to make eleven curtains. ¹⁵All the curtains were the same size— 13 metres*ᵃ* long and 2 metres wide. ¹⁶The workers joined five curtains together into one group and six curtains together into another group. ¹⁷They put 50 loops along the edge of the end curtain of one group. And they did the same on the end curtain of the other group. ¹⁸The workers made 50 bronze rings to join the two groups of curtains together to form one tent. ¹⁹Then they made two more coverings for the Holy Tent. One covering was made from ram skins dyed red. The other covering was made from fine leather.

²⁰Then the workers made frames from acacia wood to support the Holy Tent. ²¹Each frame was 4 metres*ᵇ* long and 66 centimetres*ᶜ* wide. ²²There were two side poles joined together with cross pieces to make each frame. Every frame for the Holy Tent was made the same. ²³They made 20 frames for the south side of the Holy Tent. ²⁴Then they made 40 silver bases for the frames. There were two bases for each frame—one base for each side pole. ²⁵They also made 20 frames for the other side, the north side, of the Holy Tent. ²⁶They made 40 silver bases for the frames—two bases for each frame. ²⁷They made six more frames for the back, the west side, of the Holy

Tent. ²⁸They also made two frames for the corners at the back of the Holy Tent. ²⁹These frames were joined together at the bottom. And at the top a ring held the corner frames together. They did the same for both corners. ³⁰There were eight frames for the west side of the Holy Tent. And there were 16 silver bases—two bases for each frame.

³¹Then the workers used acacia wood to make the braces for the frames—five braces for the first side of the Holy Tent, ³²five braces for the other side, and five braces for the back, the west side, of the Holy Tent. ³³They made the middle brace so that it passed through the frames from one end to the other. ³⁴They covered these frames with gold. Then they used gold to make the rings to hold the braces, and they covered the braces with gold.

³⁵They used fine linen and blue, purple and red yarn to make the special curtain for the entrance to the Most Holy Place. And they sewed pictures of winged creatures into the curtain. ³⁶They made four posts using acacia wood, and they covered the posts with gold. Then they made gold hooks for the posts and four silver bases for the posts. ³⁷Then they made the curtain to cover the entrance to the Tent. They used blue, purple and red yarn and fine linen to make this curtain. And they wove pictures into it. ³⁸Then they made the five posts and the hooks for this curtain over the entrance. They covered the tops of the posts and the curtain rods*ᵈ* with gold. And they made the five bronze bases for the posts.

The Box of the Agreement

37 Bezalel made the Holy Box from acacia wood. The Box was 110 centimetres*ᵉ* long, 66 centimetres*ᶠ* wide and 66 centimetres high. ²He covered the inside and outside of the Box with pure gold. Then he put gold trim around the Box. ³He made four rings of gold and put them on the four corners. These rings were used for carrying the Box. There were two rings on each side. ⁴Then he made the poles for carrying the Box. He used acacia wood and covered the poles with pure gold. ⁵He put the poles through the rings on each side of the Box. ⁶Then he made the mercy-cover from pure gold. It was 110 centimetres long and 66 centimetres wide. ⁷Then Bezalel hammered gold to make two winged creatures. He put the winged creatures on each end of the mercy-cover. ⁸He put one angel on one end and the other angel on the other end. The angels were joined together with the mercy-cover to make one piece. ⁹The wings of the angels were

---

ᵃ **36:15** *13 metres* Literally, "30 *cubits*".
ᵇ **36:21** *4 metres* Literally, "10 *cubits*".
ᶜ **36:21** *66 centimetres* Literally, "1½ *cubits*".
ᵈ **36:38** *curtain rods* Or "fasteners".
ᵉ **37:1** *110 centimetres* Literally, "2½ *cubits*".
ᶠ **37:1** *66 centimetres* Literally, "1½ *cubits*". Also in verse 10.

spread up towards the sky. The angels covered the Box with their wings and faced each other, looking towards the mercy-cover.

The Special Table

[10]Then he made the table from acacia wood. The table was 88 centimetres[a] long, 44 centimetres[b] wide and 66 centimetres high. [11]He covered it with pure gold and put gold trim around it. [12]Then he made a frame 75 millimetres[c] wide around the table. He put gold trim on the frame. [13]Then he made four gold rings and put them at the four corners of the table, where the four legs were. [14]He put the rings close to the frame. The rings were to hold the poles used to carry the table. [15]Then he used acacia wood to make the poles for carrying the table. He covered the poles with pure gold. [16]Then he made everything that was used on the table. He made the plates, the spoons, the bowls and the pitchers from pure gold. The bowls and pitchers are used for pouring the drink offerings.

The Lampstand

[17]Then he made the lampstand. He used pure gold and hammered it to make the base and the shaft.[d] Then he made flowers, buds and petals and joined everything together into one piece. [18]The lampstand had six branches—three branches on one side and three branches on the other side. [19]Each branch had three flowers on it. These flowers were made like almond flowers with buds and petals. [20]The shaft of the lampstand had four more flowers. They were also made like almond flowers with buds and petals. [21]There were six branches—three branches coming out from each side of the shaft. And there was a flower with buds and petals below each of the three places where the branches joined the shaft. [22]The whole lampstand, with the flowers and branches, was made from pure gold. All this gold was hammered and joined together into one piece. [23]He made seven lamps for this lampstand. Then he made lamp snuffers and trays from pure gold. [24]He used 35 kilogrammes[e] of pure gold to make the lampstand and the things used with it.

The Altar for Burning Incense

[25]He made the altar for burning incense from acacia wood. The altar was square. It was 44 centimetres long, 44 centimetres wide and 88 centimetres high. There were four horns on the altar. There was one horn on each corner. These horns were joined together with the altar to make one piece. [26]He covered the top, all the sides and the horns with pure gold. Then he put gold trim around the altar. [27]He made two gold rings for the altar. He put the gold rings below the trim on each side of the altar. These gold rings held the poles for carrying the altar. [28]He made the poles from acacia wood and covered them with gold.

[29]Then he made the holy anointing oil. He also made the pure, sweet-smelling incense. These things were made the same way that a perfume maker would make them.

The Altar for Burning Offerings

38 Then Bezalel used acacia wood to build the altar. This was the altar used for burning offerings. The altar was square. It was 2.2 metres[f] long, 2.2 metres wide and 1.3 metres[g] high. [2]He made a horn for each of the four corners of the altar. He joined each horn to its corner so that everything was one piece. He covered the altar with bronze. [3]Then he used bronze to make all the tools to be used on the altar. He made the pots, shovels, bowls, forks and pans. [4]Then he made a bronze grating for the altar. This grating was shaped like a net. The grating was put under the ledge at the bottom of the altar. It went halfway up into the altar from below. [5]Then he made bronze rings to hold the poles for carrying the altar. He put the rings at the four corners of the grating. [6]Then he used acacia wood to make the poles and covered them with bronze. [7]He put the poles through the rings on the sides of the altar to carry it. He used boards to make the sides of the altar. It was hollow, like an empty box.

[8]He made the bowl and its base with bronze. He used the bronze mirrors that the women gave. These were the women who served at the entrance to the Meeting Tent.

The Courtyard Around the Holy Tent

[9]Then he made a wall of curtains around the courtyard. On the south side, he made a wall of curtains 44 metres[h] long. The curtains were made from fine linen. [10]The curtains on the south side were supported by 20 posts. The posts were on 20 bronze bases. The hooks for the posts and

---

[a] 37:10 **88 centimetres** Literally, "2 *cubits*". See also in verse 25.
[b] 37:10 **44 centimetres** Literally, "1 *cubit*". Also in verse 25.
[c] 37:12 **75 millimetres** Literally, "1 *handbreadth*". The width of 4 fingers.
[d] 37:17 **base and the shaft** Or "flared base".
[e] 37:24 **35 kilogrammes** Literally, "1 *talent*".
[f] 38:1 **2.2 metres** Literally, "5 *cubits*". Also in verse 18.
[g] 38:1 **1.3 metres** Literally, "3 *cubits*".
[h] 38:9 **44 metres** Literally, "100 *cubits*".

the curtain rods[a] were made from silver. [11]The north side of the courtyard also had a wall of curtains 44 metres long. There were 20 posts with 20 bronze bases. The hooks for the posts and the curtain rods were made from silver.

[12]On the west side of the courtyard, the wall of curtains was 22 metres[b] long. There were 10 posts and 10 bases. The hooks for the posts and the curtain rods were made from silver.

[13]The east side of the courtyard was 22 metres wide. The entrance to the courtyard was on this side. [14]On one side of the entrance, the wall of curtains was 6.6 metres[c] long. There were three posts and three bases on this side. [15]The wall of curtains on the other side of the entrance was also 6.6 metres long. There were three posts and three bases on that side. [16]All the curtains around the courtyard were made from fine linen. [17]The bases for the posts were made from bronze. The hooks and the curtain rods were made from silver. The tops of the posts were covered with silver also. All the posts in the courtyard had silver curtain rods.

[18]The curtain for the entrance of the courtyard was made from fine linen and blue, purple and red yarn. Designs were woven into that curtain. The curtain was 9 metres[d] long and 2.2 metres high. It was the same height as the curtains around the courtyard. [19]The curtain was supported by four posts and four bronze bases. The hooks on the posts were made from silver. The tops on the posts were covered with silver, and the curtain rods were also made from silver. [20]All the tent pegs for the Holy Tent and for the curtains around the courtyard were made from bronze.

[21]Moses commanded the Levites to write down everything that was used to make the Holy Tent, that is, the Tent of the Agreement. Ithamar son of Aaron was in charge of keeping the list.

[22]Bezalel son of Uri, the son of Hur, from the tribe of Judah, made everything the LORD commanded Moses. [23]Also Oholiab son of Ahisamach, from the tribe of Dan, helped him. Oholiab was a skilled worker and designer. He was skilled at weaving fine linen and blue, purple and red yarn.

[24]The people gave 1,000 kilogrammes[e] of gold as an offering to the Lord for his holy place. (This was weighed using the official measure.)

[25-26]All the men 20 years old or older were counted. Each man had to pay a tax of 1 *beka* of silver. (Using the official measure, 1 *beka* is ½ *shekel.[f]*) There were 603,550 men. So they collected about 3,420 kilogrammes of silver. [27]They used 3,400 kilogrammes of that silver to make 100 bases for the Holy Tent and its curtains. They used 34 kilogrammes[g] of silver for each base. [28]They used the remaining 20 kilogrammes[h] of silver to make the hooks, the curtain rods and the silver covers for the posts.

[29]They gave more than 2,425 kilogrammes[i] of bronze. [30]That bronze was used to make the bases at the entrance of the Meeting Tent. They also used the bronze to make the altar and the bronze grating. And the bronze was used to make all the tools and dishes for the altar. [31]It was also used to make the bases for the curtains around the courtyard and the bases for the curtains at the entrance. And the bronze was used to make the tent pegs for the Holy Tent and for the curtains around the courtyard.

The Priests' Special Clothes

39 The workers used the blue, purple and red yarn to make special clothes for the priests to wear when they served in the holy place. They also made the special clothes for Aaron as the LORD had commanded Moses.

The Ephod

[2]They made the ephod from gold thread, fine linen and blue, purple and red yarn. [3](They hammered the gold into thin strips and cut the gold into long threads. They wove the gold into the blue, purple and red yarn and fine linen. This was the work of a very skilled person.) [4]They made the shoulder pieces for the ephod. They tied these shoulder pieces to the two corners of the ephod. [5]They wove the cloth belt and fastened it to the ephod. It was made the same way as the ephod—they used gold thread, fine linen and blue, purple and red yarn, just as the LORD commanded Moses.

[6]The workers put the onyx stones for the ephod in gold settings. They wrote the names of the sons of Israel on these stones. [7]Then they put these jewels on the shoulder pieces of the ephod. These jewels were to help God to remember the

---

a 38:10 *curtain rods* Or "fasteners". Also in verses 12,17,19,28.
b 38:12 *22 metres* Literally, "50 cubits".
c 38:14 *6.6 metres* Literally, "15 cubits".
d 38:18 *9 metres* Literally, "20 cubits".
e 38:24 *1,000 kilogrammes* Literally, "29 *talents* and 730 *shekels*".
f 38:25–26 *beka . . . shekel* See Table of Weights and Measurements.
g 38:27 *34 kilogrammes* Literally, "1 *talent*".
h 38:28 *20 kilogrammes* Literally, "1,775 *shekels*".
i 38:29 *2,425 kilogrammes* Literally, "70 *talents* and 2,400 *shekels*".

Israelites. This was done as the LORD commanded Moses.

The Judgement Pouch

8Then they made the judgement pouch. It was the work of a skilled person, just like the ephod. It was made from gold threads, fine linen and blue, purple and red yarn. 9The judgement pouch was folded in half to make a square pocket. It was 22 centimetres*a* long and 22 centimetres wide. 10Then the workers put four rows of beautiful jewels on the judgement pouch. The first row had a ruby, a topaz and a beryl. 11The second row had a turquoise, a sapphire and an emerald. 12The third row had a jacinth, an agate and an amethyst. 13The fourth row had a chrysolite, an onyx and a jasper. All these jewels were set in gold. 14There were twelve jewels on the judgement pouch— one jewel for each of the sons of Israel. Each stone had the name of one of the sons of Israel carved onto it, like a seal.

15The workers made two chains from pure gold for the judgement pouch. The chains were braided like a rope. 16The workers made two gold rings and fastened them to two corners of the judgement pouch. Then they made two gold settings for the shoulder pieces. 17They fastened the gold chains to the rings at the corners of the judgement pouch. 18They fastened the other ends of the gold chains to the settings on the shoulder pieces. They fastened these to the front of the ephod. 19Then they made two more gold rings and put them on the other two corners of the judgement pouch. This was on the inside edge of the judgement pouch next to the ephod. 20They also put two gold rings on the bottom of the shoulder pieces on the front of the ephod. These rings were near the fastener, just above the cloth belt. 21Then they used a blue ribbon and tied the rings of the judgement pouch to the rings of the ephod. In this way the judgement pouch would rest close to the cloth belt and would be held tight against the ephod. They did everything just as the LORD commanded.

Other Clothes for the Priests

22Then they made the robe for the ephod from blue cloth. It was woven by a skilled worker. 23They made a hole in the centre of the robe and sewed a piece of cloth around the edge of this hole. This cloth kept the hole from tearing. 24Then they used fine linen and blue, purple and red yarn to make the cloth pomegranates. They hung these pomegranates around the bottom edge of the robe. 25Then they made bells from pure gold. They hung these bells around the bottom edge of the robe between the pomegranates. 26Around the bottom edge of the robe, there were bells and pomegranates. There was a bell following each pomegranate. This robe was for the priest to wear when he served the Lord. It was made just as the LORD commanded Moses.

27Skilled workers wove shirts for Aaron and his sons. These shirts were made from fine linen. 28And the workers made a turban from fine linen. They also used fine linen to make special caps and underclothes. 29Then they made the cloth belt from fine linen and blue, purple and red yarn. Designs were sewn into the cloth. These things were made as the LORD had commanded Moses.

30Then they made a strip of pure gold for the holy crown. They carved these words into the gold like the writing on a seal: ONLY FOR THE LORD. 31They fastened the gold strip to a blue ribbon. Then they tied the blue ribbon around the turban like the LORD had commanded Moses.

Moses Inspects the Holy Tent

32So all the work on the Holy Tent, that is, the Meeting Tent, was finished. The Israelites did everything just as the LORD had commanded Moses. 33Then they showed the Holy Tent and everything in it to Moses. They showed him the rings, the frames, the braces, the posts and the bases. 34They showed him the covering of the Tent that was made from ram skins dyed red and the covering that was made from fine leather. And they showed him the curtain that covered the entrance to the Most Holy Place.

35They showed Moses the Box of the Agreement, the poles used for carrying it and the mercy-cover. 36They showed him the table with everything on it and the special bread.*b* 37They showed him the pure gold lampstand and the lamps on it, the oil, and all the other things that were used with the lamps. 38They showed Moses the golden altar, the anointing oil, the sweet-smelling incense and the curtain that covered the entrance to the Tent. 39They showed him the bronze altar, the bronze grill, the poles used for carrying the altar and everything that was used on the altar. They showed him the bowl and the base under the bowl.

40They showed Moses the wall of curtains around the courtyard with the posts and bases. They showed him the curtain that covered the entrance to the courtyard. They showed him the ropes and the tent pegs. They showed him

---

a **39:9** *22 centimetres* Literally, "1 *span*". The distance from the tip of the thumb to the tip of the little finger.
b **39:36** *special bread* Also called "bread of the Presence". Every day this bread was put before God on the special table in the Holy Place.

everything in the Holy Tent, that is, the Meeting Tent.

⁴¹Then they showed Moses the clothes that were made for the priests serving in the holy area.ᵃ They showed him the special clothes for Aaron the priest and his sons to wear when they served as priests.

⁴²The Israelites did all this work exactly as the LORD had commanded Moses. ⁴³Moses looked closely at all the work and saw that it was done exactly as the LORD had commanded. So Moses blessed them.

Moses Sets Up the Holy Tent

40 Then the LORD said to Moses, ²"On the first day of the first month, set up the Holy Tent, that is, the Meeting Tent. ³Put the Box of the Agreement in the Holy Tent, and hang the curtain so that the Box is behind it. ⁴Then bring in the table. Put the things on the table that should be there. Then put the lampstand in the Tent. Put the lamps on the lampstand in the right places. ⁵Put the golden altar for offering incense in the Tent in front of the Box of the Agreement. Then put the curtain at the entrance to the Holy Tent.

⁶"Put the altar for burning offerings in front of the entrance of the Holy Tent, that is, the Meeting Tent. ⁷Put the bowl between the Meeting Tent and the altar. Put water in the bowl. ⁸Set up the wall of curtains around the courtyard. Then put the curtain at the entrance to the courtyard.

⁹"Use the anointing oil and anoint the Holy Tent and everything in it. When you put the oil on these things, you will make them holy. ¹⁰Anoint the altar for burning offerings. Anoint everything on the altar. You will make the altar holy. It will be very holy. ¹¹Then anoint the bowl and the base under it to make these things holy.

¹²"Bring Aaron and his sons to the entrance of the Meeting Tent. Wash them with water. ¹³Then put the special clothes on Aaron. Anoint him with the oil and make him holy. Then he can serve me as a priest. ¹⁴Then put the clothes on his sons. ¹⁵Anoint the sons in the same way you anointed their father. Then they can also serve me as priests. When you anoint them, they will become priests. That family will continue to be priests for all time to come." ¹⁶Moses obeyed the Lord. He did everything that the LORD commanded him.

¹⁷So the Holy Tent was set up at the right time. It was the first day of the first month during the second year from the time they left Egypt. ¹⁸Moses set up the Holy Tent just as the Lord had said. He put the bases down first. Then he put the frames on the bases. Then he put the braces on and set up the posts. ¹⁹After that, Moses put the outer tent over the Holy Tent. Then he put the covering over the outer tent. He did these things just as the LORD had commanded.

²⁰Moses took the Agreement and put it in the Holy Box. He put the poles on the Box and put the mercy-cover on it. ²¹Then Moses put the Holy Box into the Holy Tent. He hung the curtain in the right place to protect it. In this way he protected the Box of the Agreement behind the curtain just as the LORD had commanded him. ²²Then Moses put the table in the Meeting Tent on the north side of the Holy Tent. He put it in the Holy Place, in front of the curtain. ²³Then he put the bread on the table before the LORD. He did this just as the LORD had commanded him. ²⁴Then Moses put the lampstand in the Meeting Tent on the south side of the Tent, opposite the table. ²⁵Then Moses put the lamps on the lampstand before the LORD. He did this just as the LORD had commanded him.

²⁶Then Moses put the golden altar in the Meeting Tent, in front of the curtain. ²⁷Then he burned sweet-smelling incense on the altar. He did this as the LORD had commanded him. ²⁸Then Moses put the curtain at the entrance to the Holy Tent.

²⁹Moses put the altar for burning offerings at the entrance to the Holy Tent, that is, the Meeting Tent. Then Moses offered a burnt offering on that altar. He also offered grain offerings to the Lord. He did these things just as the LORD had commanded him.

³⁰Then Moses put the bowl between the Meeting Tent and the altar. He put water in the bowl for washing. ³¹Moses, Aaron and Aaron's sons used this bowl to wash their hands and feet. ³²They washed themselves every time they entered the Meeting Tent. They also washed themselves every time they went near the altar. They did these things just as the LORD commanded Moses.

³³Then Moses set up the curtains around the courtyard of the Holy Tent. He put the altar in the courtyard. Then he put the curtain at the entrance to the courtyard. So he finished all the work.

INSIGHT

When the Holy Tent was finished God filled it with his Glory and such power that no man could enter. From then on God travelled with the Israelites wherever they went, dwelling among them and leading them to the promised land.

Exodus 40:34–38

ᵃ **39:41** *holy area* A restricted area that was considered sacred (special) because of God's presence.

The Glory of the LORD

34Then the cloud covered the Meeting Tent and the Glory of the LORD filled the Holy Tent. 35Moses could not go into the Meeting Tent because the cloud had settled on it, and the Glory of the LORD had filled the Holy Tent.

36When the cloud rose from the Holy Tent, the Israelites would begin to travel. 37But when the cloud stayed on the Holy Tent, the people did not try to move. They stayed in that place until the cloud rose. 38So the cloud of the LORD was over the Holy Tent during the day, and at night there was a fire in the cloud. So all the Israelites could see the cloud while they travelled.

LEVITICUS

 Who

Modern experts tend to think that Leviticus is the work of someone writing much later in a "priestly" tradition. The book, however, is full of explicit references to Moses being given the law. So, as with the other books of the Pentateuch, there is probably a core of ancient material.

 When

If you view it as the work of a priestly editor or writer then it would probably have been written around 600 BC. If you view it as primarily Moses' work, then it probably dates from the thirteenth century BC.

 What

Leviticus takes its name from the Levites, the tribe from which all the priests for Israel came. This is essentially their handbook – a book full of the rules which they and the people are supposed to follow, covering subjects from sacrifice to skin diseases, criminal justice to clothing manufacture, health and safety to holiness.

Leviticus is a book that aims to tell the Israelites how to be holy enough to approach God. In our culture we might find some of the methods of achieving this holiness strange or even unpleasant. For example, there is an emphasis on physical perfection which means that no one with any blemish can serve at the Holy Tent. Sores, burns, skin diseases, even a woman's monthly period, were supposed to make a person unclean and force them to leave the camp.

Why, we might think, should God look down on women and those suffering from illnesses and disabilities? Why should he need all this rigmarole? The culture of the time, however, believed that only the perfect was good enough for God: perfect sacrifices, perfect animals, perfect priests.

While our culture is different and while Jesus has meant that we don't have to follow all this ritual any more, there is a lot in Leviticus which should affect our behaviour. There is stuff about behaving honestly, not making fun of blind or deaf people and respecting the elderly (19:13–17,23). Most of all, Leviticus includes radical social laws to help the poor and the needy – especially the Jubilee, a revolutionary economic and political concept which was so far ahead of its time that even now it is used to challenge nations in the way that they treat each other.

QUICK TOUR ▶ **LEVITICUS**

The priests are appointed 8:1–36
The first sacrifice 9:1–24
Clean and unclean animals 11:1–47
Rules about sex 18:1–30

Good ways to behave 19:9–37
The festivals 23:1–44
The Jubilee 25:1–55

"Be special. Make yourselves holy, because I am the LORD your God. Remember and obey my laws. I am the LORD."

Leviticus 20:7–8

Voluntary Sacrifices and Offerings

1 [a] So the LORD called out to Moses from inside the Meeting Tent and said, [2]"Tell the Israelites: When you bring an offering to the LORD, the offering must be one of your tame animals—it can be a sheep, a goat or one of your cattle.

[3]"If you offer one of your cattle as a burnt offering, it must be a bull that has nothing wrong with it. You must take the animal to the entrance of the Meeting Tent where the LORD will accept the offering. [4]You must put your hand on the animal's head while it is being killed. Then the Lord will accept it as your burnt offering to make you pure.

INSIGHT

God refused to accept anything less than a perfect sacrifice. This wasn't because he was picky or snobbish! It's because he was and is a perfectly pure and holy God, and he wants the best his people have to offer.

Leviticus 1:3–4

---

[5]"You[b] must kill the young bull in front of the LORD. Then Aaron's sons, the priests, will bring the blood to the altar that is near the entrance of the Meeting Tent. He will splash the blood on all four sides of the altar. [6]You must remove the skin from that animal and then cut the animal into pieces. [7]Aaron's sons, the priests, will put the fire on the altar and arrange the wood on the fire. [8]They will lay the pieces of the animal, including the head and fat, on top of the burning wood. [9]You must wash the legs and inner parts of the animal with water. Then the priest will bring all these parts to the altar to be offered as a burnt offering, a sweet-smelling gift to the LORD.

[10]"If you offer a sheep or a goat as a burnt offering, it must be a male that has nothing wrong with it. [11]You must kill the animal on the north side of the altar in front of the LORD. Then Aaron's sons, the priests, will splash the animal's blood on all four sides of the altar. [12]You must cut the animal into pieces and remove the head and the fat. The priest will then lay them on the wood that is on the fire of the altar. [13]You must wash the legs and inner parts of the animal with water. Then the priest will bring all these parts to the altar to be offered as a burnt offering, a sweet-smelling gift to the LORD.

[14]"If you offer a bird as a burnt offering to the LORD, that bird must be a dove or a young pigeon. [15]The priest will bring the offering to the altar. There the priest will remove the bird's head, drain out the blood on the side of the altar and burn the bird on the altar. [16]He will remove the bird's tail and inner parts[c] and throw them onto the pile of ashes east of the altar. [17]Then the priest will tear the bird open by its wings, but he must not divide it completely into two parts. So he will bring the bird to the altar to be offered as a burnt offering, a sweet-smelling gift to the LORD.

Grain Offerings

2 "When you give a grain offering to the LORD, your offering must be made from fine flour. You must pour oil on this flour and put frankincense on it. [2]Then you must bring it to Aaron's sons, the priests. One of them will take a handful of the fine flour with oil and frankincense in it. He will bring this part, which represents the whole grain offering, to the altar. There it will be burned up as a sweet-smelling gift to the LORD. [3]The rest of that grain offering will belong to Aaron and his sons. This gift to the LORD is very holy.

Baked Grain Offerings

[4]"If you give a grain offering that was baked in the oven, it must be bread without yeast made from fine flour mixed with oil, or it must be wafers with oil poured over them. [5]If you bring a grain offering cooked in a baking pan, it must be made from fine flour without yeast and mixed with oil. [6]You must break it into pieces and pour oil over it. It is a grain offering. [7]If you bring a grain offering cooked in a frying pan, it must be made from fine flour mixed with oil.

[8]"When you bring grain offerings made from these things to the LORD, you must give them to the priest, and he will take them to the altar. [9]Then the priest will take part of the grain offering and lift it up as a memorial offering. He will bring it to the altar to be burned up as a sweet-smelling gift to the LORD. [10]The rest of that grain offering will belong to Aaron and his sons. This gift to the LORD is very holy.

[11]"You must not give any grain offering to the LORD that has yeast in it. You must not burn yeast or honey as a gift to the LORD. [12]You may bring yeast and honey to the LORD as an offering from the first harvest, but they must not be put on the

---

[a] **1:1** This continues the story in Exod. 40:34–35 where the Glory of the Lord filled the Meeting Tent and Moses was unable to enter. See "GLORY" in the Word List.
[b] **1:5** *You* Or "They (the priests)". Also in verse 11.
[c] **1:16** *tail . . . inner parts* Or "crop and its feathers".

altar to be burned as a sweet smell. [13]Also, you must put salt on every grain offering you bring. You must not forget to add salt, because it represents God's agreement with you. Always put salt on these offerings.

Grain Offerings From the First Harvest

[14]"When you offer the first part of your grain harvest, roast the fresh grain and grind it. Then you may bring it as a grain offering to the Lord. [15]You must put oil and frankincense on it. It is a grain offering. [16]The priest must burn part of the crushed grain, the oil and all the frankincense on it as a memorial offering. It is a gift to the Lord.

Fellowship Offerings

3 "If you offer one of your cattle as a fellowship offering, it can be a bull or a cow. But the animal you offer to the Lord must have nothing wrong with it. [2]You must put your hand on the animal's head and kill the animal at the entrance of the Meeting Tent. Then Aaron's sons, the priests, will splash the blood on all four sides of the altar. [3]The priest will take a part of that fellowship offering as a gift to the Lord. He will take the fat that is over and around the inner parts. [4]He will take the two kidneys and the fat covering them near the lower back muscle. He will also remove the fat part of the liver that is near the kidneys. [5]Then Aaron's sons will bring the fat to the altar and put it on the burnt offering that is on the wood on the fire. It is a sweet-smelling gift to the Lord.

[6]"If you offer a sheep or a goat as a fellowship offering to the Lord, whether it is a male or a female, it must have nothing wrong with it. [7]If you bring a lamb as an offering to the Lord, [8]you must put your hand on the animal's head and kill it in front of the Meeting Tent. Then Aaron's sons will splash the animal's blood on all four sides of the altar. [9]The priest will take part of the fellowship offering to the altar as a gift to the Lord. The priest must cut off the tail close to the backbone. Then he will offer the tail with all its fat and the fat that is over and around the animal's inner parts. [10]He will also offer the two kidneys and the fat covering them near the lower back muscles. He will also offer the fat part of the liver. He must remove it with the kidneys. [11]Then the priest will take that part to the altar to be burned up as food, a gift to the Lord.

[12]"If the offering is a goat, you must bring it before the Lord. [13]You must put your hand on the goat's head and kill it in front of the Meeting Tent. Then Aaron's sons, the priests, must splash the goat's blood on all four sides of the altar. [14]The priest will give part of the fellowship offering as a gift to the Lord. He will offer the fat that is over and around the animal's inner parts. [15]He will offer the two kidneys and the fat covering them near the lower back muscle. He will also offer the fat part of the liver. He will remove it with the kidneys. [16]Then the priest will burn these parts on the altar as food offered by fire. The smoke will be a sweet-smelling gift to the Lord. All the best part, the fat, belongs to the Lord. [17]This rule will continue forever through all your generations. Wherever you live, you must never eat fat or blood."

Offerings for Accidental Sins

4 The Lord spoke to Moses and said, [2]"Tell the Israelites this: A person might sin without meaning to and do something that the Lord commanded should not be done. For example:

[3]"The anointed priest[a] might make a mistake while he is making an offering for the sin of the people. If that happens, the people will still be guilty for their sin. In that case, he must offer a young bull to the Lord as an offering for his own sin.[b] The bull must have nothing wrong with it. [4]The anointed priest must bring the bull to the entrance of the Meeting Tent in front of the Lord. He must put his hand on the bull's head and kill the bull in front of the Lord. [5]Then the anointed priest must get some of the blood from the bull and take it into the Meeting Tent. [6]He must put his finger in the blood and sprinkle the blood seven times before the Lord in front of the curtain of the Most Holy Place. [7]The priest must put some of the blood on the corners of the incense altar. (This altar is in the Meeting Tent, in front of the Lord.) He must pour out the rest of the bull's blood at the base of the altar of burnt offering. (This altar is at the entrance of the Meeting Tent.) [8]Then the priest must take all the fat from the bull of the sin offering. He must take the fat that is on and around the inner parts. [9]He must take the two kidneys and the fat covering them near the lower back muscle. He must also take the fat part of the liver. He must remove it with the kidneys. [10]The priest must lift up these things and burn them on the altar for burnt offerings, just as he does for the fellowship offering.[c] [11–12]But the priest must carry out the bull's skin, inner parts and body waste and all the meat, including the

---

[a] **4:3 anointed priest** Special oil was poured on the priest's head to show that God chose him to serve. Here, this refers to the high priest. Also in verse 16.
[b] **4:3 an offering for his own sin** Literally, "as a sin offering". After making this offering, the priest would then make the offering for the sin of the people. Compare 16:14,15. See also Heb. 9:7.
[c] **4:10 just as . . . fellowship offering** See Lev. 3:1–5.

AT ONE WITH GOD

Sometimes it seems that rules are just there to be broken. It looks as though that's what the Israelites thought, anyway – not a great idea when the rules come from a God who makes the mountains shake (Exodus 19:18). But God is gracious and merciful. He gave them a way to stay pure even if they did break the rules.

DIG IN
READ Leviticus 1:1–17

God gives the people and priests some detailed instructions. These show his people how to make five different sacrifices – grain offerings, fellowship offerings, guilt offerings, burnt offerings and sin offerings.

- Why do you think the person making the offering puts their hands on the animal's head before sacrificing them (vv.3–4)?
- What are the rules for the type of animals offered (v.10)?
- How does the offering appear to God (vv.13,17)?

READ Leviticus 16:1–34

These verses describe the events on the first Day of Atonement.

- What is the Day of Atonement for?
- Which animals are used and what for?
- Who carries out the sacrifices, and where?
- What words are missing below?

The first goat offered for the Israelites' sins is a _____ offering (v.15), and its blood used to purify the _____ (v.16) from all the _____ (v.16). The second goat is sent into the _____, carrying all the Israelites' _____ (vv.21–22) away with it. (We still use the word "scapegoat" to talk about an innocent person who is blamed for what someone else did.)

It seems a bit brutal to kill animals, doesn't it? But death is a natural consequence of sin. The sacrificial system was God's way of saving the Israelites from death. The animals died in their place, and their blood atoned for their sins, making them at one *with God.*

- These days, we don't need to sacrifice animals in order to be at one with God. Why not?

DIG THROUGH

- Can you imagine how bloody the tent must have become after a few years?! The sacrifices had to be made continuously. But one day, God sent his son Jesus to die, to be a final sacrifice. Check out 1 Peter 2:24 and Hebrews 9:26b–28. Can you see how they explain that Jesus died to carry our sins so that we no longer have to sacrifice lots of animals?
- When Christians celebrate Holy Communion (also known as the Lord's Supper or the Eucharist) they are remembering this sacrifice that Jesus made. If you take communion why not thank God that your sins have been paid for by Christ when he died on the cross and that you have been raised to a new life with him. Jesus has made "atonement" for you. This is an opportunity for you to offer yourself back to God as a "living sacrifice" in worship and thanks to him (Romans 12:1).

DIG DEEPER

Jesus fulfils the old sacrificial system. That means that he has provided everything that the old system provided, and more.

- Can you see some similarities between Jesus' sacrifice and the Israelites' sacrifices of the goats?
- Can you think of a way in which Jesus' sacrifice is even better than that? Write some thoughts and then have a look at Hebrews 9.

head and legs. He must carry those parts outside the camp to the special place where the ashes are poured out. He must put those parts on the wood and burn them there on the ash pile.

INSIGHT

Just as the sin of someone in a high position would bring guilt upon the entire community, so one sacrifice could bring forgiveness to that same community. This was a foreshadowing of the significance of Jesus' sacrificial death on the cross.
Leviticus 4:1–21

[13]"The whole nation of Israel might sin without knowing it. They might break one of the commands of the LORD and become guilty of doing something he said must not be done. [14]When they learn about that sin, the community of Israel must offer a young bull as a sin offering for the whole nation. They must bring the bull to the Meeting Tent. [15]The leaders of the people must put their hands on the bull's head in front of the LORD. Then they must kill the bull in front of the LORD. [16]The anointed priest must get some of the bull's blood and take it into the Meeting Tent. [17]He must put his finger in the blood and sprinkle it seven times in front of the curtain before the LORD. [18]He must put some of the blood on the corners of the altar. (This altar is inside the Meeting Tent, in front of the LORD.) He must then pour out all the blood at the base of the altar of burnt offering. (This altar is at the entrance of the Meeting Tent.) [19]Then he must take all the fat from the animal and bring it to the altar. [20]He must offer these parts, just as he offered the bull of the sin offering. In this way the priest will make the people pure, and God will forgive them. [21]The priest must carry this bull outside the camp and burn it, just as he burned the other bull. This is the sin offering for the whole community.

[22]"A ruler might do something that the LORD his God has said must not be done. Even if he did not realize at the time that he was committing a sin, he is still guilty. [23]As soon as he learns that he has sinned, he must bring a male goat that has nothing wrong with it as his offering. [24]The ruler must put his hand on the goat's head and kill the goat at the place where they kill the burnt offering before the LORD. The goat is a sin offering. [25]The priest will take some of the blood of the sin offering on his finger and put it on the corners of the altar of burnt offering. He will pour out the rest of the blood at the base of the altar. [26]The priest will burn all the goat's fat on the altar, just as he does for the fellowship offerings. In this way the priest will make the ruler pure, and God will forgive him.

[27]"Finally, one of you common people might sin without meaning to. You might break one of the commands of the LORD and become guilty of doing something he said must not be done. [28]If you learn about that sin, you must bring a female goat that has nothing wrong with it as your sin offering. [29]You must put your hand on the animal's head and kill it at the place for the burnt offering. [30]Then the priest will take some of the goat's blood on his finger and put it on the corners of the altar of burnt offering. He will pour out the rest of its blood at the base of the altar. [31]The priest will then remove all of its fat, just as he does for the fellowship offerings. Then he will bring it to the altar as a sweet smell to the LORD. The priest will do this to make you pure, and God will forgive you.

[32]"If you bring a lamb as your sin offering, then you must bring a female lamb that has nothing wrong with it. [33]You must put your hand on the animal's head and kill it as a sin offering in the place where people kill the burnt offering. [34]The priest will take some of the blood from the sin offering on his finger and put it on the corners of the altar of burnt offering. He will pour out the rest of the lamb's blood at the base of the altar. [35]He will then remove all the lamb's fat, just as he does for the fellowship offerings. Then he will bring it to the altar as a gift to the LORD. The priest will do this to make you pure, and God will forgive you.

Different Accidental Sins

5 "You might be called as a witness and take an oath to tell the truth. If you saw something or knew something but did not tell it, you are guilty of doing wrong and must bear the responsibility for your guilt.

[2]"You might touch something unclean. It might be the dead body of any kind of animal. You might not know that you touched these things, but you will still become unclean and must pay a fine.

[3]"You might touch any of the many things that can make a person unclean. You might touch something unclean, but not know about it. When you learn that you have touched something unclean, you must pay a fine.

[4]"You might make a quick promise to do something—it makes no difference if it is bad or good. People make many kinds of quick promises. You might make such a promise and forget it.[a] When you remember[b] your promise, you must

---

[a] 5:4 **forget it** Literally, "it is hid from him".
[b] 5:4 **remember** Literally, "know of".

pay a fine because you did not keep it. ⁵If you are guilty of any of these things, you must confess whatever you did wrong. ⁶Then you must bring your guilt offering to the Lord for your sin. You must bring a female lamb or a female goat as a sin offering. The priest will offer this sacrifice to make you pure from your sin.

⁷"If you cannot afford a lamb, you must bring two doves or two young pigeons to the Lord. These will be the guilt offering for your sin. One bird must be for a sin offering, and the other must be for a burnt offering. ⁸Take them to the priest. First, the priest will offer one bird for the sin offering. The priest will pull the bird's head from its neck but he will not pull it off completely. ⁹The priest will sprinkle the blood from the sin offering on the side of the altar. Then he will pour out the rest of the blood at the base of the altar. It is a sin offering. ¹⁰Then he will offer the second bird according to the rules for a burnt offering. The priest will do this to make you pure from your sin, and God will forgive you.

¹¹"If you cannot afford two doves or two pigeons, you must bring 1 kilogramme[a] of fine flour as your sin offering. You must not put oil or frankincense on the flour because it is a sin offering. ¹²You must bring the flour to the priest. The priest will take a handful of the flour as the memorial offering and bring it to the altar as a gift to the Lord. It is a sin offering. ¹³The priest will do this to make you pure, and God will forgive you. The part that is left will belong to the priest, just as with the regular grain offering."

Guilt Offerings for Other Sins

¹⁴The Lord gave this command to Moses for the people: ¹⁵"You might promise to give something to the Lord. You might sin against me without meaning to by not giving what you promised. If you do that, you must bring a ram that has nothing wrong with it (or the same amount in silver using the official measure) as a guilt offering. ¹⁶You must give what you promised and add one-fifth of that amount as a fine. Give it to the priest and he will use the ram to make you pure, and God will forgive you.

¹⁷"If you sin by doing any of the things that the Lord said must not be done, you are guilty. Even if you did not know about it, you are still responsible for your sin. ¹⁸You must bring a ram that has nothing wrong with it (or the same amount in silver) to the priest. The priest will offer the ram, and God will forgive you for the sin you did without knowing it. ¹⁹You are

guilty, and you must pay the guilt offering to the Lord."

> ## INSIGHT
>
> *Today we may not think much about paying for our sins, unless we've actually broken the law. But imagine if you had to do all the things listed here every time you did something wrong!*
>
> **Leviticus 5 – 6**

6 The Lord said to Moses, ²"You people are guilty of sin against the Lord when you do any of these things: when you lie about what happened to something you were taking care of for someone else; when you lie about a deposit[b] you received; when you steal something; when you cheat someone; ³when you find something that was lost and lie about having it; when you fail to keep a promise; or when you do any other bad things like these. ⁴If you do any of these things, you are guilty of doing wrong. You must give back whatever you stole or whatever you took by cheating. You must return whatever you accepted as a security deposit, or whatever you found and lied about having, ⁵or whatever you made a false promise about. You must pay the full price and then add one-fifth of that amount as a fine and give it all to the true owner. ⁶You must also bring a ram to the Lord that has nothing wrong with it (or the same amount in silver) to the priest. ⁷Then the priest will go to the Lord to make you pure, and God will forgive you for whichever of these things you did that made you guilty."

Burnt Offerings

⁸The Lord said to Moses, ⁹"Give this command to Aaron and his sons: This is the law of the burnt offering. The burnt offering must stay on the hearth[c] of the altar all night until morning. The altar's fire must be kept burning. ¹⁰The priest must change clothes and put on the special linen underwear and linen robe. Then he must gather up the ashes from the fire and burnt offerings and set them down by the altar. ¹¹Then he must take off the special clothes and put on the other clothes and carry the ashes outside the camp to a special place that is pure. ¹²The fire that was started on the altar must never be allowed to stop burning. Every morning the

---

[a] **5:11 1 kilogramme** Literally, "¹⁄₁₀ of an *ephah*".
[b] **6:2 deposit** Literally, "pledge" or "security". This is something like a down payment given as proof that something more important will be done.
[c] **6:9 hearth** The place on an altar or in a fireplace where a fire is burned.

priests must put wood on the altar. They must arrange the burnt offerings on the wood, and they must burn the fat of the fellowship offerings on it. [13]That fire must always be kept burning on the altar. It must never be allowed to stop burning.

Grain Offerings

[14]"This is the law for the grain offering: The sons of Aaron will bring it to the front of the altar as an offering to the LORD. [15]There must be some oil and frankincense on the grain offering. The priest will take a handful of fine flour from the grain offering and burn it on the altar as a sweet-smelling memorial offering to the LORD.

[16]"Aaron and his sons will use the rest of that grain to make bread without yeast. This must be eaten in a holy place—in the courtyard around the Meeting Tent. [17]I have given this part of the grain offering as the priests' share of the gifts offered to me. Like the sin offering and the guilt offering, it is most holy. It must not be baked with yeast. [18]Any male descendant of Aaron may eat from these gifts to the LORD. This is their share forever throughout your generations. Whatever touches these offerings will be made holy."

The Priests' Grain Offering

[19]The LORD said to Moses, [20]"This is the offering that Aaron and his sons must bring to the LORD when Aaron is anointed to be the high priest. They must bring 1 kilogramme[a] of fine flour for a grain offering. This will be offered at the times of the daily offering—half of it in the morning and half of it in the evening. [21]The fine flour must be mixed with oil and baked on a pan. After it is cooked, you must bring it in, break it into pieces and offer it as a sweet-smelling gift to LORD. [22]"In the future, when Aaron's descendants take their place as the anointed priests,[b] they will continue to make this grain offering to the Lord. This rule will continue forever. The grain offering must be completely burned for the LORD. [23]Every grain offering that a priest gives must be completely burned. It must not be eaten."

The Law of the Sin Offering

[24]The LORD said to Moses, [25]"Tell Aaron and his sons: This is the law of the sin offering. The sin offering must be killed in the place where the burnt offering is killed before the LORD. It is most holy. [26]The priest who offers the sin offering must eat it. But he must eat it in a holy place, in the courtyard around the Meeting Tent. [27]Touching

the meat of the sin offering makes a person or a thing holy.

"If any of the sprinkled blood falls on a person's clothes, you must wash the clothes in a holy place. [28]If the sin offering was boiled in a clay pot, the pot must be broken. If the sin offering was boiled in a bronze pot, the pot must be washed and rinsed in water.

[29]"Any male in a priest's family may eat the sin offering. It is very holy. [30]But if the blood of the sin offering was taken into the Meeting Tent and used in the Holy Place to make people pure, that sin offering must not be eaten. It must be completely burned in the fire.

Guilt Offerings

7 "These are the rules for the guilt offering, which is very holy: [2]A priest must kill the guilt offering in the same place where they kill the burnt offerings. Then he must sprinkle the blood from the guilt offering around the altar.

[3]"The priest must offer all the fat from the guilt offering. He must offer the fat tail and the fat that covers the inner parts. [4]He must offer the two kidneys and the fat covering them at the lower back muscle. He must also offer the fat part of the liver. He must remove it with the kidneys. [5]He must bring these things to the altar as a gift to the LORD. It is a guilt offering.

[6]"Any male in a priest's family may eat the guilt offering. It is very holy, so it must be eaten in a holy place. [7]The guilt offering is like the sin offering. The same rules are for both offerings. The priest who does the sacrificing will get the meat for food. [8]He will also get the skin[c] from the burnt offering. [9]Every grain offering belongs to the priest who offers it. That priest will get the grain offerings that were baked in an oven, or cooked on a frying pan or in a baking dish. [10]The grain offerings will belong to Aaron's sons. It doesn't make any difference if the grain offerings are dry or mixed with oil. The sons of Aaron will all share this food.

Fellowship Offerings

[11]"This is the law of the sacrifice of fellowship offerings that you bring to the LORD: [12]People can bring fellowship offerings to show their thanks to God. If you bring your sacrifice to give thanks, you should also bring bread without yeast mixed with oil, wafers with oil poured over them and loaves of fine flour mixed with oil. [13]You must also bring loaves of bread made with yeast to go with your fellowship offering. [14]Offer one each of

---

[a] **6:20 1 kilogramme** Literally, "¹⁄₁₀ of an *ephah*".
[b] **6:22 anointed priests** Special oil was poured on the priest's head to show that God chose him to serve. Here, this refers to the high priest.
[c] **7:8 skin** This was used for making leather.

these different kinds of bread as a gift to the LORD. Then it will belong to the priest who sprinkles the blood of the fellowship offerings. [15]The meat of the fellowship offering must be eaten on the same day it is offered as a way of showing thanks to God. None of the meat should remain until the next morning.

[16]"If you bring a fellowship offering simply because you want to give a gift to God or because it is part of a special promise you made to him, the sacrifice should be eaten the same day you offer it. But if there is any left, it must be eaten the next day. [17]If any meat from this sacrifice is still left over on the third day, it must be burned in the fire. [18]If anyone eats the meat from the fellowship offering on the third day, the Lord will not accept it as a sacrifice. It will have no value for that person, and to the Lord it will be like rotten meat! Whoever eats it will be responsible for their sin.

[19]"People must not eat any of the meat that touches anything unclean. They must burn this meat in the fire. Whoever is clean may eat the meat from the fellowship offering. [20]But anyone who is unclean and eats the meat from the fellowship offerings that was offered to the LORD must be separated from their people.

[21]"You can become unclean by touching something that is unclean. It may be unclean because of an unclean person, an unclean animal or any other sickening unclean thing. It doesn't matter how it became unclean. If you touch it, you will become unclean. And then if you eat any of the meat from the fellowship offerings that was given to the LORD, you must be separated from your people."

[22]The LORD said to Moses, [23]"Tell the Israelites: You must not eat any fat from your cattle, sheep or goats. [24]You may use the fat from any animal that has died by itself or was torn by other animals, but you must never eat it. [25]Whoever eats the fat from an animal that was offered as a gift to the LORD must be separated from their people.

[26]"No matter where you live, you must never eat blood from any bird or any animal. [27]Anyone who eats blood must be separated from their people."

Rules for the Offerings Presented to God

[28]The LORD said to Moses, [29]"Tell the Israelites: If you bring a fellowship offering to the LORD, you must present that gift to the LORD yourself. [30]You must bring the fat and the breast of the animal to the priest. Then he will lift up the breast in front

of the LORD to show it was presented to God. [31]The priest will burn the fat on the altar, but the breast of the animal will belong to Aaron and his sons. [32]You must also give the right thigh from the fellowship offering as a gift to the priest. [33]That part of the fellowship offering will belong to the priest[a] who carries the blood and fat to the altar. [34]I will accept the breast that was lifted up and the gift of the right thigh from the Israelites. Then I will give these things to Aaron and his sons. This is their share from the fellowship offerings of the Israelites forever."

[35]Those parts from the gifts offered to the LORD were given to Aaron and his sons. Whenever Aaron and his sons serve as the LORD's priests, they get that share of the sacrifices. [36]The LORD commanded the Israelites to give those parts to the priests once they have been anointed. That will be their share from the Israelites forever.

[37]These are the laws about burnt offerings, grain offerings, sin offerings, guilt offerings, fellowship offerings and offerings for when the priests are appointed. [38]The LORD gave these laws to Moses on Mount Sinai when he commanded the Israelites to bring their offerings to the LORD in the desert of Sinai.

Moses Appoints the Priests

8 The LORD said to Moses, [2]"Take Aaron and his sons and their clothes, the anointing oil, the bull of the sin offering, the two rams, and the basket of bread without yeast. [3]Then gather the people together at the entrance of the Meeting Tent."

[4]Moses did what the LORD commanded him. The people met together at the entrance of the Meeting Tent. [5]Then Moses said to them, "This is what the LORD has commanded must be done."

[6]Moses brought Aaron and his sons forward and washed them with water. [7]Moses put the woven shirt on Aaron and tied the cloth belt around him. Then Moses put the robe and the ephod on Aaron and tied the beautiful cloth belt around him. [8]Moses put the judgement pouch on Aaron and put the Urim and Thummim inside its pocket. [9]He also put the turban on Aaron's head. He put the strip of gold on the front of the turban. This strip of gold is the holy crown. Moses did this just as the LORD had commanded.

[10]Then Moses took the anointing oil and sprinkled it on the Holy Tent and on everything in it. In this way he made them holy. [11]He sprinkled some of the anointing oil on the altar seven times. He sprinkled the oil on the altar, on all its tools and dishes and on the bowl and its base. In this

---

[a] **7:33** *the priest* Literally, "him of the sons of Aaron".

way he made them holy. ¹²He poured some of the anointing oil on Aaron's head to make him holy. ¹³Then Moses brought Aaron's sons forward. He put their woven shirts on them, tied belts around them and put special caps on their heads. He did everything just as the LORD had commanded.

¹⁴Then Moses brought out the bull of the sin offering. Aaron and his sons put their hands on the bull's head. ¹⁵Then Moses killed the bull and collected its blood. He used his finger to put some of the blood on all the corners of the altar. In this way he made the altar ready for sacrifices. Then he poured out the blood at the base of the altar to make the altar ready for sacrifices to make the people pure. ¹⁶Moses took all the fat from the inner parts of the bull. He took the fat part of the liver with the two kidneys and the fat on them. Then he burned them on the altar. ¹⁷Moses took the bull's skin, its meat and its body waste outside the camp. He burned these things in a fire outside the camp. He did everything just as the LORD commanded him.

¹⁸Then Moses brought the ram of the burnt offering. Aaron and his sons put their hands on the ram's head. ¹⁹Then Moses killed the ram. He sprinkled the blood around on the altar. ²⁰⁻²¹He cut the ram into pieces. He washed the inner parts and legs with water. Then he burned the whole ram on the altar. He burned the head, the pieces and the fat as a burnt offering. It was a sweet-smelling gift to the LORD. Moses did everything just as the LORD commanded.

²²Then Moses brought the other ram. This ram was used for appointing Aaron and his sons to become priests. Aaron and his sons put their hands on the ram's head. ²³Then Moses killed the ram. He put some of its blood on the tip of Aaron's ear, on the thumb of his right hand and on the big toe of his right foot. ²⁴Then Moses brought Aaron's sons close to the altar. He put some of the blood on the tip of their right ears, on the thumb of their right hands and on the big toe of their right feet. Then he sprinkled the blood around on the altar. ²⁵He took the fat, the fat tail, all the fat on the inner parts, the fat covering of the liver, the two kidneys and their fat and the right thigh. ²⁶A basket of bread without yeast is put before the LORD each day. Moses took one of those loaves of bread, one loaf of bread mixed with oil and one wafer. He put these pieces of bread on the fat and on the right thigh of the ram. ²⁷Then he put all of it in the hands of Aaron and his sons. Moses lifted these pieces to show he was offering them before the LORD. ²⁸Then Moses took these things from the hands of Aaron and his sons and burned them on the altar on top of the burnt offering. So this was the offering for appointing Aaron and his sons as priests. It was a sweet-smelling

gift to the LORD. ²⁹Moses took the breast and lifted it to show he had presented it to the LORD. It was Moses' share of the ram for appointing the priests. This was just as the LORD had commanded him.

³⁰Moses took some of the anointing oil and some of the blood that was on the altar. He sprinkled some on Aaron and on Aaron's clothes. He sprinkled some on Aaron's sons who were with Aaron and on their clothes. In this way Moses made Aaron, his clothes, his sons and his sons' clothes holy.

³¹Then Moses said to Aaron and his sons, "I told you, 'Aaron and his sons must eat these things.' So take the basket of bread and meat from the ceremony for appointing the priests. Boil that meat at the entrance of the Meeting Tent. Eat the meat and bread at that place. Do this as I told you. ³²If any of the meat or bread is left, burn it. ³³The ceremony for appointing the priests will last for seven days. You must not leave the entrance of the Meeting Tent until that time is finished. ³⁴Everything we did today was what the LORD commanded us to do in order to make you pure. ³⁵You must stay at the entrance of the Meeting Tent day and night for seven days. If you don't obey the LORD's commands, you will die! The LORD gave me these commands."

³⁶So Aaron and his sons did everything that the LORD had commanded Moses.

God Accepts the Priests

9 On the eighth day, Moses called for Aaron and his sons and the leaders of Israel. ²He said to Aaron, "Take a bull and a ram. There must be nothing wrong with them. The bull will be a sin offering, and the ram will be a burnt offering. Offer these animals to the LORD. ³Tell the Israelites, 'Take a male goat for a sin offering, and take a calf and a lamb for a burnt offering. The calf and the lamb must each be one year old. There must be nothing wrong with them. ⁴Take a bull and a ram for fellowship offerings. Take these animals and a grain offering mixed with oil for an offering to the LORD. Do this because the LORD will appear to you today.'"

⁵So all the people came to the Meeting Tent. They all brought the things that Moses had commanded. All the people stood before the LORD. ⁶Moses said, "You must do what the LORD commanded. Then the Glory of the LORD will appear to you."

⁷Then Moses told Aaron: "Go and do what the LORD commanded. Go to the altar and offer sin offerings and burnt offerings. Do what will make you and the people pure. Take the people's sacrifices and make them pure."

⁸So Aaron went to the altar. He killed the bull for the sin offering. This sin offering was for

himself. ⁹Then the sons of Aaron brought the blood to Aaron. Aaron put his finger in the blood and put it on the corners of the altar. Then he poured out the blood at the base of the altar. ¹⁰He took the fat, the kidneys and the fat part of the liver from the sin offering. He burned them on the altar just as the Lord had commanded Moses. ¹¹Then Aaron burned the meat and skin on a fire outside the camp.

¹²Next, Aaron killed the animal for the burnt offering. His sons brought the blood to him, and he sprinkled the blood around on the altar. ¹³Aaron's sons gave the pieces and head of the burnt offering to Aaron, and he burned them on the altar. ¹⁴He also washed the inner parts and the legs of the burnt offering and burned them on the altar.

¹⁵Then Aaron brought the people's offering. He killed the goat of the sin offering that was for the people. He offered the goat for sin, like the earlier sin offering. ¹⁶He brought the burnt offering and offered it in the way the Lord had commanded. ¹⁷He brought the grain offering to the altar. He took a handful of the grain and put it on the altar beside that morning's daily sacrifice.

¹⁸Aaron also killed the bull and the ram that were the fellowship offerings from the people. His sons brought the blood to him, and he sprinkled this blood around on the altar. ¹⁹Aaron's sons also brought him the fat of the bull and the ram. They brought the fat tail, the fat covering the inner parts, the kidneys and the fat part of the liver. ²⁰Aaron's sons put these fat parts on the breasts of the bull and the ram. Aaron burned them on the altar. ²¹He lifted the breasts and the gift of the right thigh to show he was offering them before the Lord, just as Moses had commanded.

²²Then Aaron lifted up his hands towards the people and blessed them. After he finished offering the sin offering, the burnt offering and the fellowship offerings, he came down from the altar.

²³Moses and Aaron went into the Meeting Tent. They came out and blessed the people. Then the Glory of the Lord appeared to all the people. ²⁴Fire came out from the Lord and burned the burnt offering and fat on the altar. When all the people saw this, they shouted with joy and then bowed to the ground to show their respect.

God Destroys Nadab and Abihu

10 Then Aaron's sons Nadab and Abihu made a mistake. They took their incense dishes and put some fire and incense in them. But they did not use the fire that was on the altar—they took fire from another place and brought it to the Lord. This was not what he had commanded. ²So fire came from the Lord and destroyed Nadab and Abihu, and they died there in front of the Lord.

³Then Moses said to Aaron, "The Lord says, 'The priests who come near me must respect me. I must be holy to them and to all the people.'" So Aaron did not say anything about his sons dying.

⁴Aaron's uncle Uzziel had two sons. They were Mishael and Elzaphan. Moses said to these sons, "Come here and get your cousins' bodies and carry them away from this holy place and take them outside the camp."

⁵So Mishael and Elzaphan obeyed Moses. They carried the bodies of Nadab and Abihu outside the camp. Nadab and Abihu were still wearing their special woven shirts.

⁶Then Moses spoke to Aaron and his other sons Eleazar and Ithamar. He said, "Don't show any sadness! Don't tear your clothes or mess up your hair!ᵃ If you do anything to show your sadness, you will be killed, and the Lord will show his anger against everyone. But let all the other people of Israel, your relatives, cry for those the Lord destroyed with fire. ⁷But you must not even leave the entrance of the Meeting Tent. If you leave, you will die because the Lord's anointing oil is on you." So Aaron, Eleazar and Ithamar obeyed Moses.

⁸Then the Lord said to Aaron, ⁹"You and your sons must not drink wine or beer when you come into the Meeting Tent. If you do, you will die. This law continues forever through each generation. ¹⁰You must be able to clearly tell the difference between what is holy and what is not holy, between what is clean and what is unclean. ¹¹And you must teach the people about all the laws that the Lord gave them through Moses."

¹²Aaron had two sons who were still alive, Eleazar and Ithamar. Moses said to Aaron and his two sons, "When people give sacrifices as a gift to the Lord, some of the grain offering is not burned. Use that grain to make bread without yeast. You priests must eat that bread near the altar because that grain is very holy. ¹³The portion of food for you and your sons will come from the special gifts to the Lord, so you must eat that food in a holy place. ¹⁴"You, your sons and your daughters may all eat the breast and thigh that were lifted up before the Lord as an offering. But you must eat these in a place that is clean because they come from the fellowship offerings. They are your share of those offerings that the Israelites give to God. ¹⁵The people must bring the gifts of fat from their

---

ᵃ **10:6** *tear . . . hair* Torn clothes and messed up hair showed that a person was mourning (see "MOURN" in the Word List) for a dead person.

animals as part of the sacrifice. They must also bring the thigh of the fellowship offering and the breast that is lifted up to show it is offered in front of the LORD. Then it will be your share of the offering. It will belong to you and your children. That part of the sacrifices will be your share forever, just as the LORD said."

16Moses looked for the goat of the sin offering, but it had already been burned up. Moses became very angry with Aaron's other sons Eleazar and Ithamar. Moses said, 17"Why did you not eat the sin offering in the holy area! That meat is very holy! God gave it to you to carry away the guilt of the people—to make the people pure before the LORD. 18That goat's blood was not brought into the Holy Place. So you should have eaten the meat in the holy area, just as I commanded!"

19But Aaron said to Moses, "Look, today they brought their sin offering and burnt offering before the LORD. But you know what happened to me today! Do you think the LORD would have been happy if I had eaten the sin offering today?"

20When Moses heard this, he agreed.

Rules About Eating Meat

11 The LORD said to Moses and Aaron, 2"Tell the Israelites: These are the animals you can eat: 3If an animal has hooves that are split into two parts, and if that animal also chews the cud, then you may eat the meat from that animal.

4-6"Some animals chew the cud, but they don't have split hooves. Don't eat these animals. Camels, rock badgers and rabbits are like that, so they are unclean for you. 7Other animals have hooves that are split into two parts, but they don't chew the cud. Don't eat these animals. Pigs are like that, so they are unclean for you. 8Don't eat the meat from these animals. Don't even touch their dead bodies! They are unclean for you.

Rules About Sea Food

9"You may eat everything that lives in the sea or in a river that has fins and scales. 10-11But you must not eat anything that lives in the sea or in a river and does not have fins and scales. Just the thought of eating such a creature should make you sick. This will never change. So don't ever eat meat from anything like that. Don't even touch its dead body! 12It is a sickening thought for you to touch anything that lives in the water and does not have fins and scales.

Birds That Must Not Be Eaten

13"You must also treat some birds as things that are wrong to eat. Stay away from them. It is a sickening thought for you to eat any of these birds: eagles, vultures, buzzards, 14kites, all kinds of falcons, 15all kinds of black birds, 16ostriches, nighthawks, seagulls, all kinds of hawks, 17little owls, great owls, 18white owls, ospreys, pelicans, cormorants, 19storks, all kinds of herons, hoopoes and bats.

Rules About Eating Insects

20"Don't eat insects that have wings and crawl.*a* Even the thought of eating them should make you sick! 21But you may eat insects if they have legs with joints above their feet so that they can jump. 22You may also eat all kinds of locusts, all kinds of winged locusts, all kinds of crickets and all kinds of grasshoppers.

23"But stay away from all the other insects that have wings and crawl. 24They will make you unclean. If you touch the dead bodies of these insects, you will become unclean until evening. 25If you pick up one of these dead insects, you must wash your clothes. You will be unclean until evening.

More Rules About Animals

26-27"Some animals have split hooves, but the hooves don't make exactly two parts. Some animals don't chew the cud. Some animals don't have hooves—they walk on their paws.*b* All these animals are unclean for you. If you touch them, you will become unclean until evening. 28If you pick up the dead bodies of these unclean animals, you must wash your clothes. You will be unclean until evening. These animals are unclean for you.

Rules About Crawling Animals

29"These small animals are unclean for you: moles, mice, all kinds of great lizards, 30geckos, crocodiles, lizards, sand reptiles and chameleons. 31Whoever touches their dead bodies will be unclean until evening.

Rules About Unclean Animals

32"If any of these unclean animals dies and falls on something, that thing will become unclean. It might be something made from wood, cloth, leather or sackcloth. Whatever it is or is used for, it must be washed with water. It will be unclean until evening. Then it will become clean again. 33If any of these unclean animals dies and falls into a clay dish, anything in the dish will become unclean. And you must break the dish. 34If water from the unclean clay dish touches any food, that food will become unclean. Any drink in the unclean dish will become unclean. 35If any part of

---

a dead, unclean animal falls on something, that thing is unclean. It may be a clay oven or a clay baking pan. It must be broken into pieces. These things will remain unclean. They will always be unclean for you.

36"A spring or a well that collects water will remain clean, but anyone who touches the dead bodies of any unclean animal ⌊in that water⌋ will become unclean. 37If any part of a dead, unclean animal falls on seed that is to be planted, that seed is still clean. 38But if you put water on some seed and if any part of a dead, unclean animal falls on those seeds, they are unclean for you.

39"Also, if an animal which you use for food dies, whoever touches its dead body will be unclean until evening. 40If you eat meat from this animal's body, you must wash your clothes. You will be unclean until evening. If you pick up the dead body of the animal, you must wash your clothes. You will be unclean until evening.

41"You must not eat anything that crawls on the ground. It is a sickening thought for you to eat such a creature. 42You must not eat any of the reptiles that crawl on their bellies or that walk on all four feet or that have many feet. It is a sickening thought for you to eat such things! 43Don't let them make you filthy.*a* You must not become unclean, 44because I am the LORD your God. I am holy, so you should keep yourselves holy. Don't make yourselves unclean with these crawling things. 45I, the LORD, brought you out of Egypt so that you could be my special people and I could be your God. I am holy, so you must be holy too."

46These are the rules about all the tame animals, birds, all the animals in the sea and all the animals that crawl on the ground. 47These rules will help the people know which animals are unclean and which animals are allowed to eat and which ones they cannot eat.

Rules for New Mothers

12 The LORD said to Moses, 2"Tell the Israelites:

"When a woman gives birth, she will be unclean, just as she is during her monthly period of bleeding. If the baby is a boy, the mother will be unclean for seven days. 3The baby boy must be circumcised on the eighth day. 4Because of the blood from childbirth, another 33 days must pass before she can touch anything that is holy. She must not enter the Holy Place until the time of her purification*b* is finished. 5But if she gives birth to a girl, the mother will be unclean for 14 days, just as she is during her monthly period. Because

of the blood from childbirth, another 66 days must pass before she becomes clean.

6"After the time of her purification is finished, the new mother of a baby girl or boy must bring special sacrifices to the Meeting Tent. She must give her sacrifices to the priest at the entrance of the Meeting Tent. She must bring a one-year-old lamb for a burnt offering and a dove or young pigeon for a sin offering. 7-8If the woman cannot afford a lamb, she may bring two doves or two young pigeons. One bird will be for a burnt offering and one for a sin offering. The priest will offer them before the LORD. In this way the priest will make her pure, and she will be clean from the blood of childbirth. These are the rules for a woman who gives birth to a baby boy or a baby girl."

Rules About Skin Diseases

13 The LORD said to Moses and Aaron, 2"Someone might have a swelling on their skin, or it may be a rash or a bright spot. If the sore looks like the disease of leprosy, the person must be brought to Aaron the priest or to one of his sons, the priests. 3The priest must look at the sore on the person's skin. If the hair in the sore has become white, and if the sore seems deeper than the person's skin, it is leprosy. When the priest has finished looking at the person, he must announce that the person is unclean.

4"Sometimes there is a white spot on a person's skin that does not seem deeper than the skin. If that is true, the priest must separate that person from other people for seven days. 5On the seventh day, the priest must look at the person again. If the priest sees that the sore has not changed and has not spread on the skin, he must separate the person for seven more days. 6Seven days later the priest must look at the person again. If the sore has faded and has not spread on the skin, the priest must announce that the person is clean. The sore is only a rash. After washing the clothes, that person will be clean again.

7"But if the rash spreads over the skin after the person has shown himself to the priest to be made clean again, that person must come again to the priest. 8The priest must look, and if the rash has spread, he must announce that the person is unclean. The disease is leprosy.

9"Whoever has leprosy must be brought to the priest. 10He must look at that person. If there is a white swelling on the skin, if the hair has become white and if the skin looks raw in the swelling, 11it is leprosy that has been there for a long time. The priest must announce that the person is

---

a **11:43 filthy** Or "hated". Not pure or not acceptable to God for worship.
b **12:4 purification** Being made clean or acceptable to God for worship.

unclean. He does not have to wait until after a period of separation, because he already knows that the person is unclean.

[12]"Sometimes a skin disease will spread all over a person's body, covering the skin from head to foot. The priest must look at that person's whole body. [13]If the priest sees that the skin disease covers the whole body and that it has turned all the skin white, the priest must announce that the person is clean. [14]But if the skin is raw, that person is not clean. [15]When the priest sees the raw skin, he must announce that the person is unclean. The raw skin is not clean. It is leprosy.

[16]"If the raw skin changes and becomes white, the person must come to the priest. [17]The priest must look at the person. If the skin has become white, the person who had the infection is clean, and the priest must announce this.

[18]"Someone might get a boil on their skin that heals over. [19]Then that boil might become a white swelling or a bright, white spot with red streaks in it. If this happens, the person must show that spot to the priest. [20]The priest must look at it. If the swelling is deeper than the skin, and the hair on it has become white, the priest must announce that the person is unclean. The spot is leprosy that has broken out from inside the boil. [21]But if the priest looks at the spot, and there are no white hairs in it, and the spot is not deeper than the skin but is faded, the priest must separate the person for seven days. [22]If the spot spreads on the skin, the priest must announce that the person is unclean; it is an infection. [23]But if the bright spot stays in its place and does not spread, it is only the scar from the old boil. The priest must announce that the person is clean.

[24-25]"Someone might get a burn on the skin. If the raw skin becomes a white spot or a white spot with red streaks in it, the priest must look at it. If that white spot seems to be deeper than the skin, and the hair at that spot has become white, it is leprosy that has broken out in the burn. The priest must announce that the person is unclean. [26]But if the priest looks at the spot, and there is no white hair in the bright spot, and the spot is not deeper than the skin but is faded, the priest must separate the person for seven days. [27]On the seventh day, the priest must look at the person again. If the spot has spread on the skin, the priest must announce that the person is unclean. It is leprosy. [28]But if the bright spot has not spread on the skin but has faded, it is only a scar from the burn. The priest must announce that the person is clean.

[29]"Someone might get an infection on the scalp[a] or beard. [30]A priest must look at the infection. If the infection seems to be deeper than the skin, and if the hair around it is thin and yellow, the priest must announce that the person is unclean. It is a serious skin disease. [31]If the disease does not seem deeper than the skin, but there is no dark hair in it, the priest must separate that person for seven days. [32]On the seventh day, the priest must look at it again. If the disease has not spread, and there are no yellow hairs growing in it, and the disease does not seem deeper than the skin, [33]the person must shave. But the diseased area should not be shaved. The priest must separate that person for seven more days. [34]On the seventh day, the priest must look at it again. If the disease has not spread, and it does not seem deeper than the skin, the priest must announce that the person is clean. After washing those clothes, that person will be clean. [35]But if the disease spreads on the skin after the person has become clean, [36]then the priest must look at the person again. If the disease has spread, the priest does not need to look for yellow hair. The person is unclean. [37]But if the priest thinks that the disease has stopped, and black hair is growing in it, the disease has healed. The person is clean, and the priest must announce this.

[38]"If anyone has white spots on the skin, [39]a priest must look at them. If the spots on that person's skin are dull white, the disease is only a harmless rash. That person is clean.

[40]"A man might begin to lose the hair on his head. It is only baldness, so he is clean. [41]A man might lose hair from the sides of his head. He is clean. It is only another kind of baldness. [42]But if there is a red and white infection on his scalp, it is a skin disease. [43]A priest must look at him. If the swelling of the infection is red and white and looks like the leprosy on other parts of his body, [44]then he has leprosy on his scalp. The person is unclean. The priest must announce that he is unclean.

[45]"People with leprosy must warn other people. They must shout, 'Unclean, unclean!' They must tear their clothes at the seams. They must let their hair grow wild,[b] and they must cover their mouth. [46]They are unclean the whole time that they have the infection. They are unclean and must live outside the camp.

[47-48]"Some clothing might have mildew on it. The cloth could be linen or wool, woven or knitted. Or the mildew might be on a piece of leather or on something made from leather. [49]If

---

[a] **13:29** *scalp* The skin on a person's head. Also in verse 42.
[b] **13:45** *They must tear . . . wild* This also showed that a person was very sad about something.

the mildew is green or red, it must be shown to the priest. 50The priest must look at it and put it in a separate place for seven days. 51–52On the seventh day, he must look at it again. It doesn't matter if the mildew is on leather or cloth or if the cloth is woven or knitted. And it doesn't matter what the leather was used for. If the mildew has spread, the object is unclean because of the infection. The priest must burn it.

53"If the priest sees that the mildew did not spread on the object, it must be washed. It doesn't matter if it is leather or cloth, or if the cloth is knitted or woven, it must be washed. 54He must order the people to wash it. Then he must separate the clothing for seven more days. 55After that time, the priest must look at it again. If the mildew still looks the same, the object is unclean. It doesn't matter if the infection has not spread; you must burn that cloth or piece of leather.

56"But if the priest looks at that piece of leather or cloth, and the mildew has faded, he must tear the infected spot out of the piece of leather or cloth. It doesn't matter if the cloth is woven or knitted. 57But the mildew might come back to that piece of leather or cloth. If that happens, the mildew is spreading, and the object must be burned. 58If the mildew did not come back after washing, that piece of leather or cloth is clean, whether the cloth was woven or knitted."

59These are the rules for mildew on pieces of leather or cloth, whether the cloth is woven or knitted.

Rules for Those With Skin Diseases

14 The LORD said to Moses, 2"These are the rules for people who have had a skin disease and have been made well. These rules are for making them clean.

"A priest must look at those who had the skin disease. 3The priest must go to them outside the camp and look to see if the skin disease is healed. 4If they are healthy, the priest will tell them to do these things: They must bring two clean birds that are still alive, a piece of cedar wood, a piece of red cloth and a hyssop plant. 5Then the priest must order one bird to be killed in a clay bowl over running water. 6He must take the other bird that is still alive and the piece of cedar wood, the piece of red cloth and the hyssop plant and dip them in the blood of the bird that was killed over the running water. 7He must sprinkle the blood seven times on those who had the skin disease. Then he must announce that they are clean. After that, the priest must go to an open field and let the live bird go free.

8"The people going through this purification ceremony must wash their clothes, shave off all their hair and wash with water. Then they will be clean. They may then go into the camp, but they must stay outside their tent for seven days. 9On the seventh day, they must shave off all their hair. They must shave their head, their beard and their eyebrows—yes, all their hair. Then they must wash their clothes and bathe their bodies in water. Then they will be clean.

10"On the eighth day, anyone who had a skin disease must take two male lambs that have nothing wrong with them and a one-year-old female lamb that has nothing wrong with it. They must also take 3 kilogrammes*a* of fine flour mixed with oil for a grain offering and a third of a litre*b* of olive oil. 11The priest must bring that person and those sacrifices before the LORD at the entrance of the Meeting Tent. (This must be the same priest who announced that the person is clean.) 12The priest will take one of the lambs and the oil as a guilt offering. He will lift them in front of the LORD to show they were presented to God. 13Then the priest will kill the male lamb in the holy place where they kill the sin offering and the burnt offering. Like the sin offering, the guilt offering belongs to the priest. It is very holy.

14"The priest will take some of the blood of the guilt offering. He will put some of this blood on the tip of the right ear of the person to be made clean. The priest will put some of this blood on the thumb of the right hand and on the big toe of the right foot of that person. 15The priest will also take some of the oil and pour it into his own left palm. 16Then the priest will dip the finger of his right hand into the oil that is in his left palm. He will use his finger to sprinkle some of the oil seven times before the LORD. 17Then he will put

---

a **14:10** *3 kilogrammes* Literally, "$\frac{3}{10}$", probably meaning $\frac{1}{10}$ of an *ephah*.

b **14:10** *a third of a litre* Literally, "1 *log*". Also in verse 21.

some of the oil that is in his palm on the person to be made clean. He will put that oil on the same places he put the blood of the guilt offering. The priest will put some of the oil on the tip of the person's right ear, on the thumb of the right hand and on the big toe of the person's right foot. ¹⁸He will put the oil that is left in his palm on the head of the person to be made clean. In this way he will make that person pure before the LORD.

¹⁹"Then the priest must offer the sin offering to make that person pure. After that, he will kill the animal for the burnt offering. ²⁰He will then offer up the burnt offering and the grain offering on the altar. In this way the priest will make that person pure, and that person will become clean.

²¹"A poor person might not be able to afford all these offerings. So that poor person can use one male lamb as a guilt offering. It will be presented to God so that the priest can make that person pure. The poor person must take 1 kilogramme*a* of fine flour mixed with oil. This flour will be used for a grain offering. The poor person must also take a third of a litre of olive oil ²²and two doves or two young pigeons. Even poor people can afford these things. One bird will be a sin offering, and the other will be a burnt offering.

²³"On the eighth day, that person will bring these things to the priest at the entrance of the Meeting Tent. These things will be offered before the LORD so that the person can become clean. ²⁴The priest will take the lamb for the guilt offering and the oil, and he will lift them up to show they were offered before the LORD. ²⁵Then he will kill the lamb of the guilt offering, take some of its blood and put it on the tip of the right ear of the person to be made clean. The priest will put some of this blood on the thumb of the right hand and on the big toe of the right foot of this person. ²⁶He will also pour some of this oil into his own left palm. ²⁷He will use the finger of his right hand to sprinkle some of the oil that is in his left palm seven times before the LORD. ²⁸Then he will put some of the oil that is in his palm on the same places he put the blood from the guilt offering. He will put some of the oil on the tip of the right ear of the person to be made clean. The priest will put some of the oil on the thumb of the right hand and on the big toe of the person's right foot. ²⁹He will put the oil that is left in his palm on the head of the person to be made clean. In this way he will make that person pure before the LORD.

³⁰"Then the priest must offer one of the doves or young pigeons. (He must offer whichever the person can afford.) ³¹He must offer one of these birds as a sin offering and the other bird as a burnt offering. He must offer the birds with the grain offering. In this way the priest will make that person pure before the LORD, and that person will become clean."

³²These are the rules for making people clean after they become well from a skin disease. These are the rules for those who cannot afford the regular sacrifices for becoming clean.

Rules for Mildew in a House

³³The LORD also said to Moses and Aaron, ³⁴"I am giving the land of Canaan to your people. Your people will enter that land. At that time I might cause mildew to grow in someone's house. ³⁵The person who owns that house must come and tell the priest, 'I see something like mildew in my house.'

³⁶"Then the priest must order the people to take everything out of the house before he goes in to look at the mildew. Then the priest will not have to say everything in the house is unclean. After the people have taken everything out of the house, the priest will go in to look at the house. ³⁷He will look at the mildew. If the mildew on the walls of the house has holes that are a green or red colour, and if the mildew goes into the wall's surface, ³⁸he must go out of the house and lock the house for seven days.

³⁹"On the seventh day, the priest must come back and check the house. If the mildew has spread on the walls of the house, ⁴⁰then he must order the people to tear out the stones with the mildew on them and throw them away. They must put these stones at a special unclean place outside the city. ⁴¹Then the priest must have the entire house scraped inside. The people must throw away the plaster that was scraped off the walls. They must put that plaster at a special unclean place outside the city. ⁴²Then new stones must be put in the walls, and the walls must be covered with new plaster.

⁴³"Maybe someone took away the old stones and plaster and put in new stones and plaster. And maybe mildew again appears in that house. ⁴⁴Then the priest must come in and check the house. If the infection has spread in the house, it is a disease that spreads quickly to other places. So the house is unclean. ⁴⁵The house must be torn down. All the stones, plaster and pieces of wood must be taken to the special unclean place outside the city. ⁴⁶Anyone who goes into that house will be unclean until evening. ⁴⁷Anyone who eats in that house or lies down in there must wash their clothes.

⁴⁸"After new stones and plaster are put in a house, the priest must check the house. If the

---

a **14:21** *1 kilogramme* Literally, "¹⁄₁₀ of an *ephah*".

mildew has not spread through the house, the priest will announce that the house is clean, because the mildew is gone.

⁴⁹"Then, to make the house clean, the priest must take two birds, a piece of cedar wood, a piece of red cloth and a hyssop plant. ⁵⁰He will kill one bird in a clay bowl over running water. ⁵¹Then he will take the cedar wood, the hyssop, the piece of red cloth and the live bird and dip them in the blood of the bird that was killed over running water. Then he will sprinkle that blood on the house seven times. ⁵²In this way he will use these things to make the house clean. ⁵³He will go to an open field outside the city and let the live bird go free. In this way the priest will make the house pure. The house will be clean."

⁵⁴These are the rules for any infection of leprosy, ⁵⁵for mildew on pieces of cloth or in a house. ⁵⁶These are the rules for swellings, rashes or bright spots on the skin. ⁵⁷These rules teach when something is clean and when something is unclean. These are the rules about these kinds of diseases.

Rules for Discharges From the Body

15 The Lord also said to Moses and Aaron, ²"Say to the Israelites: Whoever has a genital discharge is unclean. ³The person is unclean whether the discharge continues to flow or whether it stops.

⁴"If a man with a discharge lies on a bed, that bed becomes unclean. Everything he sits on will become unclean. ⁵If you touch that bed, you must wash your clothes and bathe in water. You will be unclean until evening. ⁶If you sit on anything that he sat on, you must wash your clothes and bathe in water. You will be unclean until evening. ⁷If you touch him, you must wash your clothes and bathe in water. You will be unclean until evening. ⁸If he spits on you, you must wash your clothes and bathe in water. You will be unclean until evening. ⁹If that man sits on a saddle, it will become unclean. ¹⁰If you touch or carry anything that was under him, you will be unclean until evening. ¹¹If he touches you, you must wash your clothes and bathe in water. You will be unclean until evening.

¹²"If a man with a discharge touches a clay bowl, that bowl must be broken. If he touches a wooden bowl, that bowl must be washed in water. ¹³"When the time comes for a man with a discharge to be made clean, he must wait seven days. Then he must wash his clothes and bathe his body in running water. Then he will become clean. ¹⁴On the eighth day, he must take for himself two doves or two young pigeons and come before the Lord at the entrance of the Meeting Tent. He will give the two birds to the priest. ¹⁵The priest will offer the birds, one for a sin offering, and the other for a burnt offering. In this way the priest will make that man pure before the Lord.

¹⁶"If a man has a flow of semen, he must bathe his whole body in water. He will be unclean until evening. ¹⁷If the semen is on any clothing or leather, that clothing or leather must be washed with water. It will be unclean until evening. ¹⁸If a woman has sex with a man, and he has a flow of semen, both the man and the woman must bathe in water. They will be unclean until evening.

¹⁹"If a woman has a discharge from her monthly period of bleeding, she will be unclean for seven days. Anyone who touches her will be unclean until evening. ²⁰Everything she lies on during her monthly period will be unclean. And everything she sits on during that time will be unclean. ²¹Whoever touches her bed must wash their clothes and bathe in water. They will be unclean until evening. ²²Whoever touches anything she has sat on must wash their clothes and bathe in water. They will be unclean until evening. ²³It doesn't matter if they touched the woman's bed or if they touched something she sat on, they will be unclean until evening.

²⁴"If a man has sex with a woman during her monthly period, he will be unclean for seven days. Every bed he lies on will be unclean.

²⁵"If a woman has a discharge of blood for many days, not during her monthly period, or if she has a discharge after that time, she will be unclean, just as during the time of her monthly period. She will be unclean for as long as she has a discharge. ²⁶Any bed she lies on during the time of her discharge will be like her bed during the time of her monthly period. Everything she sits on will be unclean, just as it is during the time she is unclean from her monthly period. ²⁷Whoever touches these things will be unclean until evening. They must wash their own clothes and bathe in water. ²⁸After the woman's discharge stops, she must wait seven days. After that, she will be clean. ²⁹Then on the eighth day, she must bring two doves or two young pigeons to the priest at the entrance of the Meeting Tent. ³⁰Then the priest must offer one bird for a sin offering and the other bird for a burnt offering. In this way the priest will make her pure before the Lord.

³¹"So you must warn the Israelites about being unclean. If you don't warn the people, they might make my Holy Tent unclean. And then they would have to die!"

³²These are the rules for anyone with a discharge from the body. These rules are for men who become unclean from a flow of semen. ³³And these rules are for women who become unclean from their monthly period. And these are

the rules for anyone who becomes unclean by sleeping with another person who is unclean.

The Day of Atonement

16 Two of Aaron's sons died while offering incense to the LORD.*a* After that time, the LORD spoke to Moses. 2The LORD said, "Talk to your brother Aaron. Tell him that he cannot go behind the curtain into the Most Holy Place any time he wants to. The mercy-cover is in the room behind that curtain on top of the Holy Box, and I appear in a cloud over that mercy-cover. If Aaron goes into that room, he will die!

3"Before Aaron enters the Most Holy Place, he will offer a bull for a sin offering and a ram for a burnt offering. 4Aaron will wash his whole body with water and put on the special clothes. He will put on the linen underwear next to his body, the linen robe, the linen belt and then he will put the linen turban on his head.

5"From the whole community of Israel, Aaron will accept two male goats for a sin offering and one ram for a burnt offering. 6Then he will offer the bull for the sin offering. This sin offering is for himself. He will do this to purify*b* himself and his family.

7"Then Aaron will take the two goats and bring them before the LORD at the doorway of the Meeting Tent. 8Aaron will throw lots for the two goats. One lot will be for the LORD. The other lot will be for Azazel.*c*

9"Then Aaron will offer the goat chosen by the lot for the LORD. Aaron will make this goat a sin offering. 10But the goat chosen by the lot for Azazel will be brought alive before the LORD. Then this goat will be sent out to Azazel in the desert. This is to make the people pure.

11"Then Aaron will offer the bull as a sin offering for himself. He will purify himself and his family. He will kill the bull for the sin offering for himself. 12Then he will take a firepan full of coals of fire from the altar before the LORD. Aaron will take two handfuls of sweet incense that has been ground into powder and take it into the room behind the curtain. 13He will put the incense on the fire before the LORD. Then the cloud of incense will hide the mercy-cover that is over the Box that holds the Agreement.*d* This way Aaron will not die. 14Aaron will dip his finger into the bull's blood and sprinkle it on the front of the Holy Box. Then he will sprinkle the blood seven times onto the front of the mercy-cover.

15"Then Aaron will kill the goat of the sin offering for the people. He will bring this goat's blood into the room behind the curtain. He will do with the goat's blood as he did with the bull's blood. He will sprinkle the goat's blood on the mercy-cover and in front of it. 16In this way Aaron will purify the Most Holy Place from all the uncleanness and sins of the Israelites. He will also purify the Meeting Tent, because it stands in the middle of people whose sins have made them unclean.

17"No one must be in the Meeting Tent when Aaron goes in to purify the Most Holy Place. No one is to go in there until Aaron comes out after purifying himself, his family and all the Israelites. 18Then Aaron will go out to the altar that is before the LORD. Aaron will make the altar pure. He will take some of the blood from the bull and from the goat and put it on the corners of the altar on all four sides. 19Then he will dip his finger in the blood and sprinkle it on the altar seven times. In this way Aaron will make the altar holy and clean from all the sins of the Israelites.

20"So Aaron will make the Most Holy Place, the Meeting Tent and the altar pure. Then he will bring the live goat to the front of the tent. 21He will put both his hands on the head of the goat. Then he will confess the sins and crimes of the Israelites over the goat. In this way Aaron will lay the people's sins on the goat's head. Then he will send the goat away into the desert. A man will be standing by, ready to lead this goat away. 22So the goat will carry all the people's sins on itself into the empty desert. The man who leads the goat will let it loose in the desert.

23"Then Aaron will enter the Meeting Tent. He will take off the linen clothes that he put on when he went into the Holy Place. He will leave these clothes there. 24He will wash his whole body with water in a holy place. Then he will put on his clothes. He will come out and offer his burnt offering and the people's burnt offering. He will make himself and the people pure. 25Then he will burn the fat of the sin offering on the altar.

26"The man who led the goat to Azazel must wash his clothes and his whole body with water. After that, he may come into the camp. 27"The bull and the goat for the sin offerings will be taken outside the camp. (The blood from these animals was brought into the Holy Place to make ⌊the holy things⌋ pure.) The skins, bodies and body waste of those animals will be burned in

---

a **16:1 Two of Aaron's sons . . . LORD** See Lev. 10:1–2.

b **16:6 purify** Or "make atonement". The Hebrew word means "to cover" or "to erase" a person's sins. Also in verses 11,16,17,34.

c **16:8 Azazel** This name means "scapegoat", "the goat for God" or "the goat demon". This might be the name of a particular place in the desert where the goat was released. Also in verse 10,26.

d **16:13 Box that holds the Agreement** Literally, "Testimony". See "AGREEMENT" in the Word List.

the fire. 28Then the man who burns them must wash his clothes and bathe his whole body with water. After that, he may come into the camp.

29"This law will always continue for you: On the tenth day of the seventh month, you must not eat food.*a* You must not do any work. None of the travellers or foreigners living in your land can do any work either. 30Because on this day, the priest will do this to make you pure and wash away your sins. Then you will be clean to the LORD. 31You must humble yourselves*b* because this day is a very important day of rest for you. This law will continue forever.

32"In the future this ceremony will be done by the priest who will be anointed and appointed to serve after his father. That priest will put on the holy linen clothes 33and make the Most Holy Place, the Meeting Tent and the altar pure. He will also make the priests and all the people pure. 34That law will continue forever. Once every year you will purify the Israelites from all their sins."

So they did everything that the LORD had commanded Moses.

Rules About Killing and Eating Animals

17 The LORD said to Moses, 2"Speak to Aaron and to his sons, and to all the Israelites. Tell them this is what the LORD has commanded: 3Any one of you Israelites might kill a bull, a lamb or a goat. You might be in the camp or outside the camp. 4It doesn't matter; you must bring that animal to the entrance of the Meeting Tent. You must give a part of that animal as a gift to the LORD. You spilled blood, so you must take a gift to the LORD's Holy Tent. If you don't take part of the animal as a gift to the LORD, you must be separated from your people! 5This rule is so that you will bring your fellowship offering to the LORD. You must bring any animal that you kill in the field to the LORD at the entrance of the Meeting Tent. Bring those animals to the priest. 6Then the priest will throw their blood onto the LORD's altar near the entrance of the Meeting Tent. And the priest will burn the fat from those animals on the altar as a sweet-smelling gift to the LORD. 7In this way you will stop being unfaithful to me by offering sacrifices to your 'goat gods'. This law will continue forever.

8"Tell the people: Any citizen of Israel, traveller or foreigner living among you might want to offer a burnt offering or some other sacrifice. 9They must take the sacrifice to the entrance of the Meeting Tent and offer it to the LORD. Whoever does not do this will be separated from their people.

10"I will turn against those who eat blood whether they are citizens of Israel or foreigners living among you, I will separate them from their people. 11This is because the life of the body is in the blood. I have told you that you must pour the blood on the altar to purify yourselves. It is the blood that makes a person pure. 12That is why I am telling you Israelites and the foreigners living among you that you must not eat blood.

13"If any of you, whether Israelite or foreigner living among you, goes hunting and kills a wild animal or bird that you are allowed to eat, you must pour the blood of that animal on the ground and cover it with dirt. 14This is because the life of every kind of animal is in its blood. So I give this command to the Israelites: Don't eat meat that still has blood in it! Whoever eats blood must be separated from their people.

15"If any of you, whether Israelite or foreigner living among you, eats an animal that died by itself or was killed by some other animal, you will be unclean until evening. You must wash your clothes and bathe your whole body with water. 16If you don't wash your clothes and bathe your whole body, you will be responsible for your guilt."

Rules About Sex

18 The LORD said to Moses, 2"Tell the Israelites: I am the LORD your God. 3You must not follow the customs of Egypt where you lived, and you must not follow the customs of the Canaanites where I am leading you. You must not live the way they do. 4You must obey my rules and follow my laws. Be sure to follow my rules because I am the LORD your God. 5You must obey my rules and my laws, because whoever obeys them will live. I am the LORD.

6"You must never have sex with*c* your close relatives. I am the LORD.

7"You must never have sex with your father or mother. She is your mother, so you must not have sex with her. 8You must not have sex with your father's wife, even if she is not your mother, because that is like having sex with your father.*d*

9"You must not have sex with your sister. It doesn't matter if she is the daughter of your father or your mother. And it doesn't matter if your sister was born in your house*e* or somewhere else.

---

a **16:29** *not eat food* Literally, "humble yourselves".

b **16:31** *humble yourselves* This also means that the people were not supposed to eat any food on this day.

c **18:6** *have sex with* Literally, "uncover the nakedness of". Also in verses 7,9–12,15–19.

d **18:8** *sex . . . father* Literally, "She is the nakedness of your father." Husband and wife are like one person. See Gen. 2:24.

e **18:9** *sister was born in your house* Or "household". If a man had many wives, each wife and her children had their own tent or part of the house. So this probably means a man was not supposed to have sex with any of his father's daughters, whether sister or half-sister.

¹⁰"You must not have sex with your granddaughter. It doesn't matter whether she is the daughter of your son or the daughter of your daughter—they are all a part of you!

¹¹"If your father and his wife*ᵃ* have a daughter, she is your sister. You must not have sex with her.

¹²"You must not have sex with your father's sister. She is your father's close relative. ¹³You must not have sex with your mother's sister. She is your mother's close relative. ¹⁴You must not have sex with the wife of your father's brother. You must not go near your uncle's wife for sex. She is your aunt.

¹⁵"You must not have sex with your daughter-in-law. She is your son's wife, so you must not have sex with her.

¹⁶"You must not have sex with your brother's wife. That would be like having sex with your brother.*ᵇ*

¹⁷"You must not have sex with a mother and her daughter or her granddaughter. It doesn't matter if this granddaughter is the daughter of this woman's son or daughter. Her granddaughters are her close relatives. It is wrong to do this.

¹⁸"While your wife is still living, you must not take her sister as another wife. This will make the sisters become enemies. You must not have sex with your wife's sister.

¹⁹"You must not go near a woman to have sex with her during her monthly period of bleeding. She is unclean during this time.

²⁰"You must not have sex with your neighbour's wife. This will only make you filthy.*ᶜ*

²¹"You must not give any of your children through the fire to Molech. If you do this, you will show that you don't respect the name of your God. I am the LORD.

²²"Men, you must not have sex with another man as with a woman. That is a sickening sin!

²³"Men, you must not have sex with any animal. This will make you filthy. And women, you must not have sex with any animal. It is against nature!

²⁴"Don't make yourself unclean by doing any of these wrong things! I am throwing nations off their land and giving it to you because they did those terrible sins. ²⁵They made the land filthy. Now the land is sick of those things, and it will vomit out the people who live there.

²⁶"So you must obey my laws and rules. You must not do any of these sickening sins. These rules are for the citizens of Israel and the people living among you. ²⁷Those who lived in the land

before you have done all these terrible things. So the land became filthy. ²⁸If you do these things, you will make the land filthy. And it will vomit you out as it vomited out the nations that were there before you. ²⁹Whoever does any of these terrible sins must be separated from their people! ³⁰Other people have done these sickening sins, but you must obey my laws. You must not do any of these sins. Do not make yourself filthy with them. I am the LORD your God."

Israel Belongs to God

19 The LORD said to Moses, ²"Tell all the Israelites: I am the LORD your God. I am holy, so you must be holy.

³"Each of you must honour your mother and father and keep my special days of rest.*ᵈ* I am the LORD your God!

⁴"Do not worship idols. Do not make statues of gods for yourselves. I am the LORD your God.

⁵"When you offer a sacrifice of fellowship offerings to the LORD, you must offer it in the right way so that you will be accepted. ⁶You may eat it the same day you offer it and on the next day. But if any of that sacrifice is left on the third day, you must burn it in the fire. ⁷You must not eat any of that sacrifice on the third day. It will be unclean, and it will not be accepted. ⁸You will be guilty of sin if you do that, because you did not respect the holy things that belong to the LORD. If you do that you will be separated from your people.

INSIGHT

In Bible times they didn't have a government benefit system in place to look after the poor, but farmers were expected to leave grain round the edges of their fields and fallen grapes in their vineyards so that poor people or travellers could collect the leftovers (see Ruth 2:2–9).

Leviticus 19:9–10

⁹"When you cut your crops at harvest time, don't cut all the way to the corners of your fields. And if grain falls on the ground, you must not gather up that grain. ¹⁰Don't pick all the grapes in your vineyard or pick up the grapes that fall to the

---

ᵃ **18:11** *his wife* This probably means "your stepmother".
ᵇ **18:16** *sex . . . brother* Literally, "She is the nakedness of your brother".
ᶜ **18:20** *filthy* Or "polluted" or "unclean". Also in verses 23,25,27.
ᵈ **19:3** *special days of rest* Or "Sabbaths". This might mean Saturday, or it might mean all the special days when the people were not supposed to work. Also in verse 30.

LIVING THE RIGHT WAY

"Be special. Make yourselves holy, because I am the LORD your God" (Leviticus 20:7).

Think of some of your family "rules", like what you do at meal times, or shared family activities. The particular rules held by your own family mark you out as being one of them. They show that you belong, are wanted and are loved.

DIG IN   READ Leviticus 19:1–37

- What do you think of these laws? Can you see the goodness in them?
- Why do you think God gave the Israelites these laws?
- How many times are the words "I am the LORD" repeated in this chapter?
- Why should the Israelites obey God's commands?

In order to live out their lives as God's people, the Israelites had to be holy. This is because God is holy.

- Have you ever tried mixing a little cooking oil with a glass of water? It doesn't work, does it! The oil forms a layer on top and stays separate. That is what it is like with sin and holiness: the two just can't mix. So, in order to have a relationship with God, sinful people have to become holy.
- What does it mean to be holy? Read the verses below and look for these words and phrases related to the word "holy": separate, right with God, blameless, without any fault, clean, set apart, pleasing to God, dedicated. Leviticus 20:24–26; 27:14; Romans 12:1; Galatians 3:6; Ephesians 1:4; Colossians 1:22; 2 Timothy 2:21.

DIG THROUGH

- Have you ever suffered from the "brick wall" syndrome? Did you feel as if God was far away? Or did you feel he wasn't listening?

Sometimes that happens because our sin spoils the closeness we have to God. The writer of Psalm 139 knew that God was close no matter how he felt or where he went and that God knew his every thought. Remember that if you put your trust in Jesus, God is always close to you because of him – no matter how it feels!

- Talk to God. Ask him to show you if you have done anything wrong or if you have any wrong thoughts, and ask him to help you (Psalm 139:23–24).

DIG DEEPER

God is gracious as well as holy. Although the Israelites disobeyed God time and time again, he still wanted to have a relationship with them. That's why he told them to make sacrifices and gave them laws so that they could be holy and enjoy closeness with him. But this system wasn't perfect – people still disobeyed, and there was still a distance between God and them: only the priests could approach him, and only in very strict circumstances. That's why he sent Jesus. He extended his grace out to all people through Jesus, and now we don't have to make these sacrifices or follow these laws any more.

- So, can we just behave however we like?
- Read Romans 6:15–23.

Because of Jesus, we are free from God's anger at our sin. But that doesn't mean we can do whatever we like, because that is not freedom. We are free to do right, because to do right in the eyes of God is to be free, to be fully ourselves as he created us to be.

- Where do we get the power to live out this freedom?
- Read Romans 8:1–17. If we believe in Jesus, we have the Spirit in us. Ask God to guide you, with his word and by his Spirit so that you can live right.

ground. You must leave those things for poor people and for people travelling through your country. I am the Lord your God.

¹¹"You must not steal. You must not cheat people. You must not lie to each other. ¹²You must not use my name to make false promises. If you do that, you will show that you don't respect the name of your God. I am the Lord!

¹³"You must not cheat or rob your neighbour. You must not hold a hired worker's salary overnight until morning.*ᵃ*

¹⁴"You must not curse anyone who is deaf. You must not do anything to make a blind person fall. But you must respect your God. I am the Lord.

¹⁵"You must be fair in judgement. You must not show special favour to the poor. And you must not show special favour to important people. You must be fair when you judge your neighbour. ¹⁶You must not go around spreading false stories against other people. Don't do anything that would put your neighbour's life in danger. I am the Lord.

¹⁷"Don't secretly hate any of your neighbours. But tell them openly what they have done wrong. Then you will not be just as guilty of sin as they are. ¹⁸Forget about the wrong things people do to you. Don't try to get even. Love your neighbour as yourself. I am the Lord.

¹⁹"You must obey my laws. You must not let your animals mate with animals of a different kind. You must not sow your field with two kinds of seed. You must not wear clothing made from two kinds of material mixed together.

²⁰"It may happen that a man has sex with a woman who is the slave of another man. But this slave woman has not been bought or given her freedom. If this happens, there must be punishment. But they will not be put to death because the woman was not free. ²¹The man must bring his guilt offering to the Lord at the entrance of the Meeting Tent. He must bring a ram for a guilt offering. ²²The priest will make him pure by offering the ram as a guilt offering before the Lord. The offering is for the man's sins, which will then be forgiven.

²³"In the future, when you enter your country, you will plant many kinds of trees for food. After planting a tree, you must wait three years before you can use any of the fruit from that tree. You must not use that fruit. ²⁴In the fourth year, the fruit from that tree will belong to the Lord, a holy offering of praise to him. ²⁵Then, in the fifth year, you can eat the fruit from that tree. And the tree will produce more and more fruit for you. I am the Lord your God.

²⁶"You must not eat any meat with blood still in it.

"You must not try to use different kinds of magic to tell the future.

²⁷"You must not round off the hair that grows on the side of your face. You must not cut your beard that grows on the side of your face. ²⁸You must not cut your body as a way to remember the dead. You must not make any tattoo marks on yourselves. I am the Lord.

²⁹"Do not dishonour your daughters by making them become prostitutes. If you do that, your whole country will turn away from God and be filled with all kinds of sinful things.

³⁰"You must not work on my special days of rest. You must honour my holy place. I am the Lord.

³¹"Do not try to contact ghosts or the spirits of the dead for advice or secret knowledge. This will make you unclean. I am the Lord your God.

³²"Show honour to old people. Stand up when they come into the room. And show respect to your leaders.*ᵇ* I am the Lord.

³³"Do not do bad things to foreigners living in your country. ³⁴You must treat them the same as you treat your own citizens. Love them as you love yourselves. Remember, you were foreigners in Egypt. I am the Lord your God!

³⁵"You must be fair when you judge people, and you must be fair when you measure and weigh things. ³⁶Your baskets should be the right size. Your jars should hold the right amount of liquids. Your weights and balances should weigh things correctly. I am the Lord your God. I brought you out of the land of Egypt.

³⁷"You must remember all my laws and rules. And you must obey them. I am the Lord."

Warning Against Worshipping Idols

20 The Lord said to Moses, ²"You must also tell the Israelites these things: Anyone living in Israel who gives one of their children to the false god Molech must be killed! It doesn't matter if they are a citizen of Israel or a foreigner, you must throw stones at them and kill them. ³I will be against them and separate them from their people, because they gave their children to Molech. They showed that they did not respect my holy name. And they made my holy place unclean. ⁴Maybe the common people will ignore them. Maybe they will not kill those who gave their children to Molech. ⁵But I will be against these people and their families. I will separate them from their people. I will separate anyone who is unfaithful to me and chases after Molech.

ᵃ **19:13** Workers were paid at the end of each day for the work they did that day. See Matt. 20:1–16.
ᵇ **19:32** *leaders* Or "God".

⁶"I will turn against anyone who tries to contact ghosts or spirits of the dead for advice or secret knowledge. Whoever does this is being unfaithful to me. So I will separate them from their people.

⁷"Be special. Make yourselves holy, because I am the LORD your God. ⁸Remember and obey my laws. I am the LORD. And I have made you my special people.

⁹"Whoever curses their father or mother must be put to death. They cursed their father or mother, so they are responsible for their own death!ᵃ

Punishments for Sexual Sins

¹⁰"If a man has sex with his neighbour's wife, both the man and the woman are guilty of adultery and must be put to death! ¹¹If a man has sex with his father's wife, both the man and the woman must be put to death. They are responsible for their own death.ᵇ It is as if that man had sex with his father!ᶜ

¹²"If a man has sex with his daughter-in-law, both of them must be put to death. They have committed a terrible sexual sin! They are responsible for their own death.

¹³"If a man has sex with another man as with a woman, both of them have committed a sickening sin. They must be put to death. They are responsible for their own death.

¹⁴"It is a terrible sin if a man has sex with a woman and her mother. The people must burn that man and the two women in fire! Don't let this terrible sin happen among your people.

¹⁵"If a man has sex with an animal, both the man and the animal must be put to death. ¹⁶If a woman has sex with an animal, you must kill the woman and the animal. They must be put to death. They are responsible for their own death.

¹⁷"It is a shameful thing for a brother and his sister or half-sister to marry each other and have sex with each other.ᵈ They must be punished in public. They must be separated from their people. The man who has sex with his sister must be punished for his sin.ᵉ

¹⁸"If a man has sex with a woman during her monthly period of bleeding, both the woman and the man must be separated from their people. They sinned because they exposed her source of blood.

¹⁹"You must not have sex withᶠ your mother's sister or your father's sister. That is a sin of incest.ᵍ You must be punished for your sins.ʰ

²⁰"A man must not have sex with his uncle's wife. It would be like having sex with his uncle. That man and his uncle's wife will be punished for their sins. They will die without children.ⁱ

²¹"It is wrong for a man to take his brother's wife. It would be like having sex with his brother! They will have no children.

²²"You must remember all my laws and rules. And you must obey them. I am leading you to your land. You will live in that country. If you obey my laws and rules, that land will not vomit you out. ²³I am forcing other people to leave that country because they committed all those sins. I hate those sins! So don't live the way those people lived. ²⁴But I have told you that you will get their land. I will give their land to you. It will be your land! It is a land filled with many good things.ʲ I am the LORD your God.

"I have treated you differently from other people. ²⁵So you must treat clean animals differently from unclean animals. You must also treat clean birds differently from unclean birds. Don't eat any of these unclean birds or animals or things that crawl on the ground. I have made these things unclean. ²⁶I have separated you from other nations to be my own special people. So you must be holy because I am the LORD, and I am holy.

²⁷"It is wrong for any man or woman to contact a ghost or the spirit of a dead person and allow that spirit to take control of them. Anyone who does this must be put to death. You must kill them with stones. And they are responsible for their own death."

Rules for Priests

21 The LORD said to Moses, "Tell these things to Aaron's sons, the priests: A priest must not make himself unclean by touching a dead person. ²But if the dead person was one of his close relatives, he can touch the dead body. The

---

ᵃ 20:9 they . . . death Literally, "his blood is on him".
ᵇ 20:11 They . . . death Literally, "Their blood is on them." Also in verses 12,13,16,27.
ᶜ 20:11 man . . . father Literally, "he uncovered his father's nakedness".
ᵈ 20:17 sex with each other Literally, "he sees her nakedness, and she sees his nakedness."
ᵉ 20:17 The man . . . sin Literally, "He will carry his guilt".
ᶠ 20:19 have sex with Literally, "uncover the nakedness of". Also in verse 21.
ᵍ 20:19 incest Having sex with a close relative.
ʰ 20:19 You . . . sins Literally, "You will carry your guilt."
ⁱ 20:20 That man . . . children Literally, "They must bear their childlessness. They will die."
ʲ 20:24 land . . . things Literally, "land flowing with milk and honey".

priest can make himself unclean if the dead person is his mother or father, his son or daughter, his brother or ³his unmarried*a* sister. (This sister is close to him because she has no husband. So the priest may make himself unclean for her if she dies.) ⁴But a priest must not make himself unclean if the dead person was only one of his slaves.*b*

⁵"Priests must not shave their heads bald. They must not shave off the edges of their beards. They must not make any cuts in their bodies. ⁶Priests must be holy for their God. They must show respect for God's name. They offer the bread and special gifts to the LORD, so they must be holy.

⁷"A priest serves God in a special way, so he must not marry a woman who has had sex with any other man. He must not marry a prostitute or a divorced woman. ⁸A priest serves God in a special way. So you must treat him in a special way, because he carries holy things. He brings the holy bread to me, and I am holy. I am the LORD, and I make you holy.

⁹"If a priest's daughter becomes a prostitute, she ruins her reputation and brings shame to her father. She must be burned to death in the fire!

¹⁰"The high priest was chosen from among his brothers. The anointing oil was poured on his head. In this way he was chosen for the special job of being high priest. He was chosen to wear the special clothes, so he must not do things to show his sadness in public. He must not let his hair grow wild. He must not tear his clothes. ¹¹He must not make himself unclean by touching a dead body. He must not go near a dead body, even if it is his own father or mother. ¹²The high priest must not leave God's holy place, because he might become unclean and then make God's holy place unclean. The anointing oil was poured on the high priest's head. This separated him from the rest of the people. I am the LORD.

¹³"The high priest must marry a woman who is a virgin. ¹⁴He must not marry a woman who has had sex with any man. He must not marry a prostitute, a divorced woman or a widow. The high priest must marry a virgin from his own people. ¹⁵In this way people will show respect for his children.*c* I, the LORD, have separated the high priest for his special work."

¹⁶The LORD said to Moses, ¹⁷"Tell Aaron: If any of your descendants have anything wrong with them, they must not carry the special bread to God. ¹⁸Any man who has something wrong with him must not serve as priest and bring sacrifices to me. These men cannot serve as priests: blind men, lame men, men with bad scars on their faces, men with arms or legs that are too long, ¹⁹men with broken feet or hands, ²⁰men with bent backs, men who are dwarfs,*d* men who are cross-eyed, men with rashes or bad skin diseases and men with crushed testicles.

²¹"If one of Aaron's descendants has something wrong with him, he cannot approach the altar to bring gifts to the LORD. And he cannot carry the special bread to God. ²²He is from the family of priests, so he can eat the holy bread. He can also eat the very holy bread. ²³But he cannot go through the curtain into the Most Holy Place and he cannot go near the altar. This is because he has something wrong with him. He must not make my holy places unholy. I am the LORD, and I make these places holy."

²⁴So Moses told these things to Aaron, Aaron's sons and all the Israelites.

22 The LORD God said to Moses, ²"Tell Aaron and his sons: The gifts that the Israelites bring to me become holy. They belong to me, so you priests must show respect for these gifts. If you don't, you will show that you don't respect my holy name. I am the LORD. ³If any one of your descendants touches these things, that person will become unclean and must be separated from me. The Israelites gave these things to me. I am the LORD.

⁴"If any of Aaron's descendants has a serious skin disease*e* or a discharge, he cannot eat the holy food until he becomes clean. This rule is for any priest who becomes unclean. That priest can become unclean from a dead body or from his own semen. ⁵He can also become unclean if he touches any unclean crawling animal. And he can become unclean if he touches an unclean person. It doesn't matter what made that person unclean. ⁶If he touches any of these things, he will become unclean until evening. He must not eat any of the holy food. Even if he washes with water, he cannot eat the holy food. ⁷He will be clean only after the sun goes down. Then he can eat the holy food because it is his share.

⁸"A priest must not eat any animal that died by itself or that was killed by wild animals. If he eats that animal, he will be unclean. I am the LORD.

⁹"The priests must be very careful when it comes time to serve me. They must be careful not to dishonour the holy things. If they are careful,

---

a 21:3 *unmarried* Literally, "virgin", a girl who was never married and never had sex.
b 21:4 Or "A master must not become unclean for his people".
c 21:15 *people . . . children* Or "his children will not become unclean from the people".
d 21:20 *dwarfs* A small person whose body stopped growing properly.
e 22:4 *serious skin disease* This could be leprosy, or it could be another kind of contagious skin disease. Also in verse 22.

they will not die. I, the LORD, have separated them from the rest of the people for this special job. [10]Only a priest's family can eat the holy food. A visitor staying with the priest or a hired worker must not eat any of the holy food. [11]But if the priest buys a person as a slave with his own money, that person may eat some of the holy things. Slaves who were born in the priest's house may also eat some of the priest's food. [12]A priest's daughter might marry a man who is not a priest. If she does that, she cannot eat any of the holy offerings. [13]A priest's daughter might become a widow, or she might be divorced. If she does not have any children to support her, and she goes back to her father's house where she lived as a child, she can eat some of her father's food. But only people from a priest's family can eat this food.

[14]"Whoever eats some of the holy food by mistake must give the priest the price of that food and add another one-fifth of the price as a fine.

[15]"The Israelites will bring offerings to the LORD. These offerings become holy, so the priests must not let them be used in a wrong way. [16]They must not let the people eat these offerings. If they do, they are guilty of doing wrong, and they must pay for it. I am the LORD, the one who makes these offerings holy."

[17]The LORD God said to Moses, [18]"Tell Aaron and his sons and all the Israelites: A citizen of Israel or a foreigner might want to bring an offering. It might be because of a promise that person made, or it might just be a special sacrifice that person wanted to give to the LORD as a burnt offering. [19-20]These are gifts that the people bring because they really want to give a gift to God. If the gift is a bull or a sheep or a goat, the animal must be a male. And it must not have anything wrong with it. You must not accept any offering that has anything wrong with it. I will not accept that gift.

[21]"You might bring a fellowship offering to the LORD. That fellowship offering might be payment for a special promise that you made. Or maybe it is a special gift that you wanted to give to the Lord. It can be a bull or a sheep, but it must be healthy. There must be nothing wrong with that animal. [22]You must not offer to the LORD any animal that is blind, that has broken bones or is lame, or that has a discharge or a serious skin disease. You must not offer sick animals as a gift to the LORD. You must not put anything like that on his altar.

[23]"Sometimes a bull or lamb will have a leg that is too long, or a foot that did not grow right. If you want to give that animal as a special gift to the Lord, it will be accepted. But it will not be accepted as payment for a special promise that you made.

[24]"If an animal has bruised, crushed or torn testicles, you must not offer that animal to the LORD. You must not do this anywhere in your land.

[25]"You must not accept animals from foreigners to offer as a sacrifice to your God. The animals might have been hurt in some way. They might have something wrong with them, so they will not be accepted."

[26]The LORD said to Moses, [27]"When a calf or a sheep or a goat is born, it must stay seven days with its mother. Then from the eighth day on, this animal will be accepted as a sacrifice offered as a gift to the LORD. [28]But you must not kill the animal and its mother on the same day. This rule is the same for cattle and sheep.

[29]"If you want to offer some special offering of thanks to the LORD, you are free to offer that gift. But you must do it in a way that pleases God. [30]You must eat the whole animal that day. You must not leave any of the meat for the next morning. I am the LORD.

[31]"Remember my commands, and obey them. I am the LORD. [32]Show respect for my holy name. I must be very special to the Israelites. I, the LORD, have made you my special people. [33]I brought you out of Egypt in order to be your God. I am the LORD."

The Special Festivals

23 The LORD said to Moses, [2]"Tell the Israelites: You will announce the LORD's chosen festivals as holy meetings. These are my special festivals.

Sabbath

[3]"Work for six days, but the seventh day, the Sabbath, will be a special day of rest, a holy meeting. You must not do any work. It is a day of rest to honour the LORD in all your homes.

INSIGHT

The Sabbath actually begins the evening before the day itself, as do the other Jewish festivals and holidays. Why? It's based on the Jewish tradition that each 24-hour period begins at sunset. This comes from their understanding of the creation (Genesis 1:31).

Leviticus 23:3

Passover

[4]"These are the LORD's chosen festivals. You will announce the holy meetings at the times

chosen for them. ⁵The Lord's Passover is on the fourteenth day of the first month*ᵃ* just before dark.

Festival of Unleavened Bread

⁶"The Lord's Festival of Unleavened Bread is on the fifteenth day of the same month. You will eat bread without yeast for seven days. ⁷On the first day of this festival, you will have a special meeting. You must not do any work on that day. ⁸For seven days, you will bring sacrifices offered as gifts to the Lord. Then there will be another special meeting on the seventh day. You must not do any work on that day."

Festival of the First Harvests

⁹The Lord said to Moses, ¹⁰"Tell the Israelites: You will enter the land that I will give you and reap its harvest. At that time you must bring in the first sheaf*ᵇ* of your harvest to the priest. ¹¹The priest will lift the sheaf to show it was offered before the Lord. Then you will be accepted. The priest will present the sheaf on Sunday morning.*ᶜ*

¹²"On the day when you present the sheaf, you will offer a one-year-old male lamb. There must be nothing wrong with that lamb. That lamb will be a burnt offering to the Lord. ¹³You must also offer a grain offering of 2 kilogrammes*ᵈ* of fine flour mixed with olive oil. You must also offer 1 litre*ᵉ* of wine. The smell of that offering will please the Lord. ¹⁴You must not eat any of the new grain or fruit or bread made from the new grain until you bring that offering to your God. This law will always continue through your generations, wherever you live.

Festival of Harvest

¹⁵"From that Sunday morning (the day you bring the sheaf to be presented to God), count seven weeks. ¹⁶On the Sunday following the seventh week (that is, 50 days later), you will bring a new grain offering to the Lord. ¹⁷On that day, bring two loaves of bread from your homes. That bread will be lifted up to show it was offered to God. Use yeast and 2 kilogrammes of flour to make those loaves of bread. That will be your gift to the Lord from your first harvest.

¹⁸"With these grain offerings bring one bull, one ram and seven one-year-old male lambs for burnt offerings to the Lord. There must be nothing wrong with these animals. Offer them

together with the grain offerings and the drink offerings. The smell of these offerings made by fire will be pleasing to the Lord. ¹⁹You will also offer one male goat for a sin offering and two one-year-old male lambs as a fellowship offering.

²⁰"The priest will lift them up with the bread from the first harvest to show they were offered with the two lambs before the Lord. They are holy to the Lord. They will belong to the priest. ²¹On that same day you will call a holy meeting. You must not do any work. This law continues forever in all your homes.

²²"Also, when you harvest the crops on your land, don't cut all the way to the corners of your field. Don't pick up the grain that falls on the ground. Leave it for poor people and for foreigners travelling through your country. I am the Lord your God."

Festival of Trumpets

²³Again the Lord said to Moses, ²⁴"Tell the Israelites: On the first day of the seventh month, you must have a special day of rest. Blow the trumpet to remind the people that this is a holy meeting. ²⁵You must not do any work. You must bring an offering as a gift to the Lord."

Day of Atonement

²⁶The Lord said to Moses, ²⁷"The Day of Atonement will be on the tenth day of the seventh month. There will be a holy meeting. You must not eat food,*ᶠ* and you must bring an offering as a gift to the Lord. ²⁸You must not do any work on that day, because it is the Day of Atonement. On that day the priests will go before the Lord and perform the ceremony that makes you pure.

²⁹"Anyone who refuses to fast on this day must be separated from their people. ³⁰If anyone does any work on this day, I will destroy that person from among the people. ³¹You must not do any work at all. This is a law that continues forever for you, wherever you live. ³²It will be a special day of rest for you. You must not eat food. You will start this special day of rest on the evening following the ninth day of the month.*ᵍ* This special day of rest continues from that evening until the next evening."

Festival of Shelters

³³Again the Lord said to Moses, ³⁴"Tell the Israelites: On the fifteenth day of the seventh

---

ᵃ **23:5** *first month* Abib (or Nisan). See "Aʙɪʙ" in the Word List.
ᵇ **23:10** *sheaf* A bundle of corn. Also in verses 12,15.
ᶜ **23:11** *Sunday morning* Literally, "the morning after the Sabbath". Also in verse 15.
ᵈ **23:13** *2 kilogrammes* Literally, "⅒ of an *ephah*". Also in verse 17.
ᵉ **23:13** *1 litre* Literally, "¼ *hin*".
ᶠ **23:27** *You must not eat food* Literally, "You must humble yourselves." Also in verse 32.
ᵍ **23:32** *evening following . . . month* A day starts at sunset.

month is the Festival of Shelters. This festival to the LORD will continue for seven days. 35There will be a holy meeting on the first day. You must not do any work. 36You will bring offerings as gifts to the LORD for seven days. On the eighth day, you will have another holy meeting. You must not do any work. You will bring an offering as a gift to the LORD.

37"These are the LORD's special festivals. There will be holy meetings during these festivals. You will bring offerings as gifts to the LORD—burnt offerings, grain offerings, sacrifices and drink offerings. You will bring these gifts at the right time. 38You will celebrate these festivals in addition to remembering the LORD's Sabbath days. You will offer these gifts in addition to your other gifts and any offerings you give as payment for your special promises. They will be in addition to any special offerings you want to give to the LORD.

39"On the fifteenth day of the seventh month, when you have gathered in the crops of the land, you will celebrate the LORD's festival for seven days. The first day will be a special day of rest, and the eighth day will also be a special day of rest. 40On the first day you will take good fruit from fruit trees. And you will take branches from palm trees, poplar trees and willow trees by the brook. You will celebrate before the LORD your God for seven days. 41You will celebrate this festival to the LORD for seven days each year. This law will continue forever. You will celebrate this festival in the seventh month. 42You will live in temporary shelters for seven days. All the people born in Israel will live in them. 43Why? So all your descendants will know that I made the Israelites live in temporary shelters during the time I brought them out of Egypt. I am the LORD your God."

44So Moses told the Israelites about all the special meetings to honour the LORD.

The Lampstand and the Holy Bread

24 The LORD said to Moses, 2"Command the Israelites to bring to you pure oil from crushed olives. That oil is for the lamps that must burn without stopping. 3Aaron will keep the light burning in the Meeting Tent before the LORD from evening until morning. This light will be outside the curtain that hangs in front of the Box that holds the Agreement.a This law will continue forever. 4Aaron must always keep the lamps burning on the lampstand of pure gold before the LORD.

5"Take fine flour and bake twelve loaves with it. Use 2 kilogrammesb of flour for each loaf. 6Put them in two rows on the golden table before the LORD. Six loaves will be in each row. 7Put pure frankincense on each row. This will help the LORD remember the gift. 8Every Sabbath day Aaron will put the bread in order before the LORD. This must be done forever. This agreement with the Israelites will continue forever. 9That bread will belong to Aaron and his sons. They will eat the bread in a holy place, because that bread is one of the special gifts to the LORD. It is Aaron's share forever."

The Man Who Cursed God

10There was a son of an Israelite woman and an Egyptian father. He was walking among the Israelites, and he started fighting in camp. 11The Israelite woman's son began cursing, using the Lord's name in a bad way, so the people brought him to Moses. (The name of the man's mother was Shelomith, the daughter of Dibri, from the tribe of Dan.) 12The people held him as a prisoner and waited for the LORD's command to be made clear to them.

13Then the LORD said to Moses, 14"Bring the man who cursed to a place outside the camp. Then bring together everyone who heard him curse. They will put their hands on his head.c And then all the people must throw stones at him and kill him. 15You must tell the Israelites: Anyone who curses their God must be punished. 16Anyone who speaks against the name of the LORD must be put to death. All the people must stone him. Any foreigner or anyone born in Israel who uses the Lord's name in a bad way must be put to death.

17"And whoever kills another person must be put to death. 18Whoever kills an animal that belongs to another person must give another animal to take its place.d

19"And whoever causes an injury to their neighbour must be given the same kind of injury: 20a broken bone for a broken bone, an eye for an eye and a tooth for a tooth. The same kind of injury a person gives another person must be given that person. 21Whoever kills an animal must pay for the animal. But whoever kills another person must be put to death.

22"The law will be the same for foreigners and for people from your own country. This is because I am the LORD your God."

23Then Moses spoke to the Israelites, and they took the man who cursed to a place outside the

---

a 24:3 *Box that holds the Agreement* Literally, "Testimony". See "AGREEMENT" in the Word List.
b 24:5 *2 kilogrammes* Literally, "⅒ of an *ephah*".
c 24:14 *put their hands on his head* To show that all these people were sharing in punishing the man.
d 24:18 *give . . . its place* Literally, "pay for it, life for life".

camp. Then they killed him with stones. So the Israelites did just what the LORD had commanded Moses.

A Time of Rest for the Land

25 The LORD spoke to Moses at Mount Sinai. He said, ²"Tell the Israelites: When you enter the land that I am giving to you, you must let the land have a special time of rest. This will be a special time of rest to honour the LORD. ³You will plant seed in your field for six years. You will trim your vineyards for six years and bring in its fruits. ⁴But during the seventh year, you will let the land rest. This will be a special time of rest to honour the LORD. You must not plant seed in your field or trim your vineyards. ⁵You must not cut the crops that grow by themselves after your harvest. You must not gather the grapes from your vines that are not trimmed. The land will have a year of rest.

⁶"The land will have a year of rest, but you will still have enough food. There will be enough food for your men and women servants. There will be food for your hired workers and for the foreigners living in your country. ⁷And there will be enough food for your cattle and other animals to eat.

Jubilee—the Year of Release

⁸"You will also count seven groups of seven years. This will be 49 years. During that time there will be seven years of rest for the land. ⁹On the Day of Atonement, you must blow a ram's horn. That will be on the tenth day of the seventh month. You must blow the ram's horn through the whole country. ¹⁰You will make the fiftieth year a special year. You will announce freedom for everyone living in your country. This time will be called 'Jubilee'. Each of you will go back to your own property.ᵃ And each of you will go back to your own family. ¹¹The fiftieth year will be a special celebrationᵇ for you. Don't plant seeds, don't harvest the crops that grow by themselves and don't gather grapes from the vines that are not trimmed. ¹²That year is Jubilee. It will be a holy time for you. You will eat the crops that come from the field. ¹³In the year of Jubilee, you will go back to your own property.

¹⁴"Don't cheat your neighbours when you sell your land to them. Don't cheat each other when you buy or sell land. ¹⁵If you want to buy your neighbour's land, count the number of years since the last Jubilee, and use that number to decide the right price. You are only buying the rights for harvesting crops until the next Jubilee. ¹⁶If there are many years before the next Jubilee, the price will be high. If the years are few, the price will be lower. So your neighbour is really only selling a number of crops to you.ᶜ ¹⁷You must not cheat each other. You must honour your God. I am the LORD your God.

¹⁸"Remember my laws and rules. Obey them and you will live safely in your country. ¹⁹And the land will produce good crops for you. Then you will have plenty of food, and you will live safely on the land.

INSIGHT

The year of Jubilee came once every fifty years. In that year debts were cancelled, grievances forgiven and slaves and prisoners set free. Christ's birth was the start of a new Jubilee – a lifetime of debts cancelled, sins forgiven and freedom.

Leviticus 25:8–22

²⁰"But maybe you will say, 'If we don't plant seeds or gather our crops, we will not have anything to eat during the seventh year.' ²¹I will order my blessing to come to you during the sixth year. The land will continue growing crops for three years. ²²When you plant in the eighth year, you will still be eating from the old crop. You will eat the old crop until the harvest of the ninth year.

Property Laws

²³"The land really belongs to me, so you cannot sell it permanently. You are only foreigners and travellers living on my land with me. ²⁴People might sell their land, but the family will always get their land back. ²⁵If someone in your country becomes very poor and must sell their property, a close relative must come and buy it back. ²⁶If there is not a close relative to buy back the land, the person might get enough money to buy it back. ²⁷Then the years must be counted since the land was sold. That number must be used to decide how much to pay for the land. The person must then buy back the land, and it will be their property again. ²⁸But if this first owner cannot find enough money to buy the land back, it will

---

ᵃ **25:10 own property** In Israel, the land belonged to the family or tribe. A person might sell his land, but at Jubilee that land again belonged to the family and tribe that it was originally given to.
ᵇ **25:11 special celebration** Literally, "Jubilee". See "JUBILEE" in the Word List.
ᶜ **25:16** At the next Jubilee the land will again belong to that family.

stay in the hands of the one who bought it until the year of Jubilee. Then during that special celebration, the land will go back to the first owner's family. So the property will again belong to the right family.

²⁹"Anyone who sells a home in a walled city still has the right to get it back until a full year after it was sold. Their right to get the house back will continue for one year. ³⁰But if the owner does not buy back the house before a full year is finished, the house that is in the walled city will belong to the one who bought it and to their descendants. The house will not go back to the first owner at the time of Jubilee. ³¹Towns without walls around them will be treated like open fields. So houses built in these small towns will go back to the first owners at the time of Jubilee.

³²"But about the cities of the Levites: The Levites can buy back at any time their houses in the cities that belong to them. ³³If someone buys a house from a Levite, that house in the Levites' city will again belong to the Levites at the time of Jubilee. This is because houses in Levite cities belong to those from the tribe of Levi. The Israelites gave these cities to the Levites. ³⁴Also, the fields and pastures around the Levite cities cannot be sold. They belong to the Levites forever.

Rules for Slave Owners

³⁵"If anyone from your own country becomes too poor to support themselves, you must let them live with you like a visitor. ³⁶Don't charge them any interest on money you might loan to them. Respect your God and let those from your own country live with you. ³⁷Don't charge them interest on any money you lend them. And don't try to make a profit from the food you sell them. ³⁸I am the LORD your God. I brought you out of the land of Egypt to give the land of Canaan to you and to become your God.

³⁹"If anyone from your own country becomes so poor that they must sell themselves to you, don't make them work like slaves. ⁴⁰They will be like hired workers or foreigners living with you until the year of Jubilee. ⁴¹Then they can leave you, take their children, and go back to their family. They can go back to the property of their ancestors, ⁴²because they are my servants. I brought them out of slavery in Egypt. They must not become slaves again. ⁴³You must not be a cruel master to them. You must respect your God.

⁴⁴"About your men and women slaves: You may get men and women slaves from the other nations around you. ⁴⁵Also, you may get children as slaves if they come from the families of the foreigners living in your land. These child slaves will belong to you. ⁴⁶You may even pass these foreign slaves on to your children after you die so that they will belong to them. They will be your slaves forever. You may make slaves of these foreigners. But you must not be a cruel master over your own brothers, the Israelites.

⁴⁷"Maybe a foreigner or visitor among you becomes rich. Or maybe someone from your own country becomes so poor that they sell themselves as slaves to a foreigner living among you or to a member of a foreigner's family. ⁴⁸These people have the right to be bought back and become free. Someone from their own country can buy them back. ⁴⁹Or their uncle, their cousin or one of their close relatives from their family can buy them back. Or if they get enough money, they can pay the money themselves and become free again.

⁵⁰"You must count the years from the time they sold themselves to the foreigner up to the next year of Jubilee. Use that number to decide the price, because really the person only 'hired' them for a few years. ⁵¹If there are still many years before the year of Jubilee, the one sold must give back a large part of the price. It all depends on the number of years. ⁵²If only a few years are left until the year of Jubilee, the one who was sold must pay a small part of the original price. ⁵³But that person will live like a hired worker with the foreigner every year. Don't let the foreigner be a cruel master over that person.

⁵⁴"Those who sold themselves will become free, even if no one buys them back. At the year of Jubilee, they and their children will become free. ⁵⁵This is because the Israelites are my servants. They are the servants who I brought out of slavery in Egypt. I am the LORD your God!

Rewards for Obeying God

26 "Don't make idols for yourselves. Don't set up statues or memorial stones in your land to bow down to, because I am the LORD your God!

²"Remember my special days of rest^a and honour my holy place. I am the LORD.

³"Remember my laws and commands, and obey them. ⁴If you do these things, I will give you rains at the time they should come. The land will grow crops and the trees of the field will grow their fruit. ⁵Your threshing will continue until it is time to gather grapes. And your grape gathering will continue until it is time to plant. Then you will have plenty to eat. And you will live safely in your land. ⁶I will give peace to your country. You

---

^a **26:2 special days of rest** Or "Sabbaths". This might mean Saturday, or it might mean all the special days when the people were not supposed to work.

will lie down in peace. No one will come to make you afraid. I will keep harmful animals out of your country. And armies will not come through your country.

7"You will chase your enemies and defeat them. You will kill them with your swords. 8Five of you will chase 100 men, and 100 of you will chase 10,000 men. You will defeat your enemies and kill them with your sword.

9"Then I will turn to you. I will let you have many children. I will keep my agreement with you. 10You will have enough crops to last for more than a year. You will harvest the new crops. But then you will have to throw out the old crops to make room for the new crops. 11Also, I will place my Holy Tent among you. I will not turn away from you. 12I will walk with you and be your God. And you will be my people. 13I am the LORD your God. You were slaves in Egypt, but I brought you out of Egypt. You were bent low from the heavy weights you carried as slaves, but I broke the poles that were on your shoulders. I let you walk proudly again.

Punishment for Not Obeying God

14"But if you don't obey me and all my commands, bad things will happen to you. 15If you refuse to obey my laws and commands, you have broken my agreement. 16If you do that, I will cause terrible things to happen to you. I will cause you to have disease and fever. They will destroy your eyes and take away your life. You will not have success when you plant your seed. And your enemies will eat your crops. 17I will be against you, so your enemies will defeat you. These enemies will hate you and rule over you. You will run away even when no one is chasing you.

18"After these things, if you still don't obey me, I will punish you seven times more for your sins. 19And I will also destroy the great cities that make you proud. The skies will not give rain, and the earth will not produce crops.*a* 20You will work hard, but it will not help. Your land will not give any crops, and your trees will not grow their fruit.

21"If you still turn against me and refuse to obey me, I will beat you seven times harder! The more you sin, the more you will be punished. 22I will send wild animals against you. They will take your children away from you. They will destroy your animals. They will kill many of your people. The roads will all be empty.

23"If you don't learn your lesson after all this, and if you still turn against me, 24then I will also turn against you. I—yes, I myself—will punish you seven times for your sins. 25You will have broken my agreement, so I will punish you. I will bring armies against you. You will go into your cities for safety, but I will cause diseases to spread among you. And your enemies will defeat you. 26I will give you a share of the grain left in that city. But there will be very little food to eat. Ten women will be able to cook all their bread in one oven. They will measure each piece of bread. You will eat, but you will still be hungry.

27"If you still refuse to listen to me, and if you still turn against me, 28I will really show my anger! I—yes, I myself—will punish you seven times for your sins. 29You will become so hungry that you will eat the bodies of your sons and daughters. 30I will destroy your high places. I will cut down your incense altars. I will put your dead bodies on the dead bodies of your idols. You will be sickening to me. 31I will destroy your cities. I will make your holy places empty. I will stop smelling your offerings. 32I will make your land empty. And your enemies who come to live there will be shocked at it. 33I will scatter you among the nations. I will pull out my sword and destroy you. Your land will become empty, and your cities will be destroyed.

34"You will be taken to your enemy's country. Your country will be empty. So your land will finally get its rest. The land will enjoy its time of rest. 35During the time that the land is empty, it will get the time of rest that you did not give it while you lived there. 36The survivors will lose their courage in the land of their enemies. They will be afraid of everything. They will run around like a leaf blown by the wind. They will run as if someone is chasing them with a sword. They will fall even when no one is chasing them. 37They will run as if someone is chasing them with a sword. They will fall over each other—even when no one is chasing them.

"You will not be strong enough to stand up against your enemies. 38You will be lost in other nations. You will disappear in the land of your enemies. 39So the survivors will rot away in their sin in their enemies' countries. They will rot away in their sins just as their ancestors did.

There Is Always Hope

40"But maybe the people will confess their sins. And maybe they will confess the sins of their ancestors. Maybe they will admit that they turned against me. Maybe they will admit that they sinned against me. 41Maybe they will admit that I turned against them and brought them into the land of their enemies. These people will be like

---

a 26:19 **The skies . . . crops** Literally, "Your skies will be like iron, your land like bronze."

strangers to me. But maybe they will become humble[a] and accept the punishment for their sin. [42]If they do, I will remember my agreement with Jacob. I will remember my agreement with Isaac. I will remember my agreement with Abraham, and I will remember the land.

[43]"The land will be empty. The land will enjoy its time of rest. Then the survivors will accept the punishment for their sins. They will learn that they were punished because they hated my laws and refused to obey my rules. [44]They have sinned. But if they come to me for help, I will not turn away from them. I will listen to them, even if they are in the land of their enemies. I will not completely destroy them. I will not break my agreement with them, because I am the LORD their God. [45]For them, I will remember the agreement with their ancestors. I brought their ancestors out of the land of Egypt so that I could become their God. The other nations saw these things. I am the LORD."

[46]These are the laws, rules and teachings that the LORD gave to the Israelites. These laws are the agreement between the Lord and the Israelites. The Lord gave these laws to Moses at Mount Sinai.

Gifts Promised to the LORD

27 The LORD said to Moses, [2]"Tell the Israelites: You might promise to give someone to the LORD as a servant. The priest must set a price for that person. [3]The price for a man from 20 to 60 years old is 50 pieces[b] of silver. (You must use the official measure for the silver.) [4]The price for a woman who is 20 to 60 years old is 30 pieces of silver. [5]The price for a man from 5 to 20 years old is 20 pieces of silver. For a woman the price is 10 pieces. [6]The price for a boy from one month to five years old is 5 pieces of silver. For a girl, the price is 3 pieces. [7]The price for a man who is 60 years old or older is 15 pieces of silver. The price for a woman is 10 pieces.

[8]"If anyone is too poor to pay the price, bring that person to the priest. The priest will decide how much money the person can afford to pay.

Other Gifts to the LORD

[9]"You might promise to give an animal to the Lord. If it is a clean animal—one that is acceptable as an offering to the LORD—then the animal you bring will become holy. [10]You must not put any other animal in its place. Don't try to trade a good animal for a bad one or a bad animal for a good one. If you try to change animals, both animals will become holy—they will both belong to the Lord.

[11]"The animal you promised might be one that is not acceptable as an offering to the LORD. If you promised one of these unclean animals, you must bring it to the priest. [12]The priest will decide a price for that animal. The price will be whatever the priest decides, whether good or bad. [13]If you want to buy back the animal,[c] then you must add one-fifth to the price.

The Value of a House

[14]"If you dedicate your house as holy to the LORD, the priest must decide its price. It doesn't make any difference if the house is good or bad. If the priest decides on a price, that is the price for the house. [15]But if you want to get the house back, you must add one-fifth to the price. Then you will get the house back.

The Value of a Field

[16]"If you dedicate a field to the LORD, the value of this field will depend on how much seed is needed to plant it. It will be 10 pieces of silver for 20 kilogrammes[d] of barley seed. [17]If you give your field to God during the year of Jubilee, its value will be whatever the priest decides. [18]But if you give your field after the Jubilee, the priest must decide its exact price. He must count the number of years to the next year of Jubilee and use that number to decide the price. [19]If you want to buy the field back, you must add one-fifth to that price. Then you will get the field back. [20]If you don't buy the field back and the land is sold to someone else, you cannot get the land back. [21]If you don't buy the land back by the year of Jubilee, the field will remain holy to the LORD—it will belong to the priest forever. It will be treated like any other thing that was given completely to the Lord.

[22]"If you dedicate a field to the LORD that you had bought, and it is not a part of your family's property,[e] [23]then the priest must count the years to the year of Jubilee and decide the price for the land. Then that land will belong to the LORD. [24]At the year of Jubilee, the land will go to the family that originally owned the land.

[25]"You must use the official measure in paying these prices, which is 11.5 grammes[f] for each piece.

---

[a] **26:41** *These people . . . humble* Literally, "If they humble their uncircumcised heart".
[b] **27:3** *50 pieces* Literally, "50 *shekels*". Also in verse 16.
[c] **27:13** *buy back the animal* See Exod. 13:1–16 for the laws about giving to God or "buying back" firstborn children or animals.
[d] **27:16** *20 kilogrammes* Literally, "*homer*".
[e] **27:22** *family's property* In ancient Israel, land was given by God to the family, not the individual. Usually it could not be sold, only leased for up to 50 years.
[f] **27:25** *11.5 grammes* Literally, "20 *gerahs*".

The Value of Animals

26"You can give cattle and sheep as special gifts to the LORD. But if the animal is the firstborn, it already belongs to the LORD. So you cannot give these animals as special gifts. 27If the firstborn animal is an unclean animal, you must buy back that animal. The priest will decide the price of the animal, and you must add one-fifth to that price. If you don't buy that animal back, the priest will sell the animal for whatever price he decides.

Special Gifts

28"There is a special kind of gift[a] that people give to the LORD. It belongs only to him, and it cannot be bought back or sold. This gift belongs to the LORD. This type of gift includes people, animals and fields from the family property. 29If this gift is a person, that person cannot be bought back. That person must be killed.

30"A tenth of all crops belongs to the LORD. This means the crops from fields and the fruit from trees—a tenth belongs to the LORD. 31So if you want to get back your tenth, you must add one-fifth to its price and then buy it back.

32"The priests will take every tenth animal from a person's cattle or sheep. Every tenth animal will belong to the LORD. 33The owner should not worry if the chosen animal is good or bad or trade it for another animal. If this happens, then both animals will belong to the LORD. They cannot be bought back."

34These are the commands that the LORD gave Moses at Mount Sinai for the Israelites.

---

a 27:28 *special kind of gift* This usually means things taken in war. These things (gifts) belonged only to the Lord, so they could not be used for anything else.

Who
Traditionally authorship is ascribed to Moses, writing during the final year of his life, but (as with Leviticus) there are also passages that indicate a later writer was involved.

 When
If Moses was responsible it was only because he ordered the information to be gathered together, which would mean it probably dates from the thirteenth century BC. If you view it as the work of a priestly editor or writer then it would have been written c.600 BC.

 What
Numbers is largely just that: a book of statistics and accounts, a list of the tribes of Israel and the number of people in each tribe. The Hebrew title is *Bemidbar* – meaning "In the wilderness" – which sounds a lot more exciting.

Numbers tells of Israel's journey to the edge of – and failure to enter – the "promised land". It's the story of God's faithfulness to a bickering, grumbling, disobedient group of people. God enabled them to escape from Egypt; their own sin meant that they were never to escape the desert.

But along the way there are some exciting bits. If Leviticus tells how Israel became a worshipping people, Numbers tells how they became an army. After the giving of the law and the creation of the Holy Tent at Sinai, the Israelites march out to conquer the lands about them.

Leviticus only covers a timescale of about a month. Numbers covers forty years. Leviticus takes place in one location. Numbers zooms around the desert like a camel on steroids.

We see the jealousy of Moses' family and encounter the strange tale of Balaam and the talking donkey. We even see Moses' disobedience, and God's decision that he, too, will not enter the land God has promised to them.

So there is a lot more in Numbers than just, well, a load of numbers.

QUICK TOUR ▷ NUMBERS

The Nazirites 6:1–21
The Israelites begin their journey 10:11–35
Complaints 11:1–35
Jealousy in Moses' family 12:1–15
The twelve spies 13:1–33

The punishment of the Israelites 14:1–45
Korah's rebellion 16:1 – 17:13
Moses' disobedience 20:1–13
Balaam's donkey 22:1 – 23:12
Israel's journey to the Canaan border 33:1–56

"None of the people I led out of Egypt will ever see the land of Canaan. They saw my glory and the great signs that I did in Egypt and in the desert. But they disobeyed me and tested me ten times. I promised their ancestors I would give them that land. But none of those people who turned against me will ever enter that land!"

Numbers 14:22–23

Moses Counts the Israelites

1 The LORD spoke to Moses in the Meeting Tent. This was in the desert of Sinai. It was on the first day of the second month of the second year after the Israelites left Egypt. He said to Moses: [2]"Count all the Israelites. List the name of each man with his family and his family group. [3]You and Aaron must count the men of Israel who are 20 years old or older. (These are all the men who are able to serve in the army of Israel.) List them by their divisions. [4]One man from each tribe will help you. This man will be the leader of his tribe. [5]These are the names of the men who will stand with you and help you:

from the tribe of Reuben—Elizur son of Shedeur;
[6]from the tribe of Simeon—Shelumiel son of Zurishaddai;
[7]from the tribe of Judah—Nahshon son of Amminadab;
[8]from the tribe of Issachar—Nethanel son of Zuar;
[9]from the tribe of Zebulun—Eliab son of Helon;
[10]from the descendants of Joseph:
from the tribe of Ephraim—Elishama son of Ammihud;
from the tribe of Manasseh—Gamaliel son of Pedahzur;
[11]from the tribe of Benjamin—Abidan son of Gideoni;
[12]from the tribe of Dan—Ahiezer son of Ammishaddai;
[13]from the tribe of Asher—Pagiel son of Ocran;
[14]from the tribe of Gad—Eliasaph son of Deuel;[a]
[15]from the tribe of Naphtali—Ahira son of Enan."

[16]All these men were the leaders of their families. The people also chose them to be leaders of their tribes. [17]Moses and Aaron took the men who had been chosen to be leaders [18]and called all the Israelites together on the first day of the second month. Then the people were listed by their families and their family groups. All the men who were 20 years old or older were listed. [19]Moses did exactly what the LORD commanded—he counted the people while they were in the desert of Sinai.

[20]The tribe of Reuben was counted. (Reuben was the firstborn son of Israel.) The names of all the men who were 20 years old or older and able to serve in the army were listed. They were listed with their families and family groups. [21]The total number of men counted from the tribe of Reuben was 46,500.

[22]The tribe of Simeon was counted. The names of all the men who were 20 years old or older and able to serve in the army were listed. They were listed with their families and family groups. [23]The total number of men counted from the tribe of Simeon was 59,300.

[24]The tribe of Gad was counted. The names of all the men who were 20 years old or older and able to serve in the army were listed. They were listed with their families and family groups. [25]The total number of men counted from the tribe of Gad was 45,650.

[26]The tribe of Judah was counted. The names of all the men who were 20 years old or older and able to serve in the army were listed. They were listed with their families and family groups. [27]The total number of men counted from the tribe of Judah was 74,600.

[28]The tribe of Issachar was counted. The names of all the men who were 20 years old or older and able to serve in the army were listed. They were listed with their families and family groups. [29]The total number of men counted from the tribe of Issachar was 54,400.

[30]The tribe of Zebulun was counted. The names of all the men who were 20 years old or older and able to serve in the army were listed. They were listed with their families and family groups. [31]The total number of men counted from the tribe of Zebulun was 57,400.

[32]The tribe of Ephraim was counted. (Ephraim was Joseph's son.) The names of all the men who were 20 years old or older and able to serve in the army were listed. They were listed with their families and family groups. [33]The total number of men counted from the tribe of Ephraim was 40,500.

[34]The tribe of Manasseh was counted. (Manasseh was also Joseph's son.) The names of all the men who were 20 years

[a] **1:14** *Deuel* Or "Reuel".

READY, STEADY, GO!

Have you ever been on an expedition somewhere? What do you need to get ready? Who do you need to listen to?

DIG IN

READ Numbers 1:1

- Where were the people?
- Who spoke?

If you've followed the Bible story up until this point you will know that God rescued his people from Egypt and promised them he would take them to a land where they would live in safety and with his blessing. It is time for the people to move towards the promised land, but before they set off they have some preparations to make and they need to listen to God through the chosen leader, Moses.

READ Numbers 1:1 – 9:23

- See if you can spot some of the things God gets Moses to do so the people will be ready to enter the land. For example, instructions for who was to camp where, the jobs of the priests and Levites, getting clean, instructions about the Holy Tent and the festival of the Passover.
- What sort of thing is really important to God?

All these things might seem strange, but they teach us that God takes holiness really seriously. The priests and Levites are mentioned a lot because they act as important go-betweens for God and the people. The priests would offer sacrifices for the sins of the people (Leviticus chapters 1 – 7) and the Levites would camp around the Holy Tent so God's anger might be stopped (Numbers 1:50–53). Only the priests and Levites were able to touch the holy things of God.

READ Numbers 6:22–27

You may be familiar with the words of this blessing.

- Who provides the blessing?
- What things will the people be blessed with?

Because the people have been obedient, God gives this awesome blessing. Did you notice it contains everything about their special relationship? For example, they will remain his people and he'll remain their God; this relationship was free and constant despite their sin, and it provided an answer to their prayers for peace. God would be on their side and keep them safe as they entered the land.

READ Numbers 9:15–23

- How did God show the people when to move?
- What did the people do (v.23)?

We might use an alarm clock to know when to get up and a sat nav to know where to go – God, however, appeared as cloud or fire, depending on the time of day, and moved when it was time to pack up and go! The people obeyed and did as the Lord asked, which meant they could enjoy his continued presence.

DIG THROUGH

- The people listened to and obeyed God's words in getting everything ready to go. How are you doing with listening to and obeying God?
- The people needed the priests and Levites to do their jobs so they could be forgiven and have peace with God. Just to remind you why we don't sacrifice any more, God sent Jesus to offer himself as a sacrifice for us. Say thanks to God that we can be forgiven and have a relationship with God through Jesus.

old or older and able to serve in the army were listed. They were listed with their families and family groups. ³⁵The total number of men counted from the tribe of Manasseh was 32,200.

³⁶The tribe of Benjamin was counted. The names of all the men who were 20 years old or older and able to serve in the army were listed. They were listed with their families and family groups. ³⁷The total number of men counted from the tribe of Benjamin was 35,400.

³⁸The tribe of Dan was counted. The names of all the men who were 20 years old or older and able to serve in the army were listed. They were listed with their families and family groups. ³⁹The total number of men counted from the tribe of Dan was 62,700.

⁴⁰The tribe of Asher was counted. The names of all the men who were 20 years old or older and able to serve in the army were listed. They were listed with their families and family groups. ⁴¹The total number of men counted from the tribe of Asher was 41,500.

⁴²The tribe of Naphtali was counted. The names of all the men who were 20 years old or older and able to serve in the army were listed. They were listed by name with their families and family groups. ⁴³The total number of men counted from the tribe of Naphtali was 53,400.

⁴⁴Moses, Aaron and the twelve leaders of Israel counted these men. (There was one leader from each tribe.) ⁴⁵They counted every man who was 20 years old or older and able to serve in the army. Each man was listed with his family. ⁴⁶The total number of men counted was 603,550 men.

⁴⁷The families from the tribe of Levi were not counted with the other Israelites. ⁴⁸The LORD had told Moses: ⁴⁹"Don't count the men from the tribe of Levi or include them with the other Israelites. ⁵⁰Tell the Levites that they are responsible for the Tent of the Agreement. They must take care of that tent and everything that is with it. They must carry the Holy Tent and everything in it. They must make their camp around it and take care of it. ⁵¹Whenever the Holy Tent is moved, the Levites must do it. Whenever the Holy Tent is set up, the Levites must do it. They are the men who will take care of the Holy Tent. Anyone else who tries to take care of the tent must be killed. ⁵²The Israelites will make their camps in separate divisions. Everyone must camp near their family flag. ⁵³The Levites will set up their tents so that they surround the Tent of the Agreement. They will serve as guards and keep the people away from the Tent. This will protect the Israelites from the Lord's anger."

⁵⁴The LORD had given these commandments to Moses. So the Israelites did everything he commanded.

The Camp Arrangement

2 The LORD said to Moses and Aaron: ²"The Israelites should make their camps around the Meeting Tent. Each division will have its own special flag, and everyone will camp near their group's flag.

³"The flag of the camp of Judah will be on the east side, where the sun rises. The people of Judah will camp near its flag. The leader of the people of Judah is Nahshon son of Amminadab. ⁴There are 74,600 men in his division.

⁵"The tribe of Issachar will camp next to the tribe of Judah. The leader of the tribe of Issachar is Nethanel son of Zuar. ⁶There are 54,400 men in his division.

⁷"The tribe of Zebulun will also camp next to the tribe of Judah. The leader of the tribe of Zebulun is Eliab son of Helon. ⁸There are 57,400 men in his division.

⁹"The total number of men in Judah's camp is 186,400. All these men are divided into their different tribes. Judah will be the first group to move when the people travel from one place to another.

¹⁰"The flag of Reuben's camp will be south of the Holy Tent. Each group will camp near its flag. The leader of the tribe of Reuben is Elizur son of Shedeur. ¹¹There are 46,500 men in this division.

¹²"The tribe of Simeon will camp next to the tribe of Reuben. The leader of the tribe of Simeon is Shelumiel son of Zurishaddai. ¹³There are 59,300 men in this division.

¹⁴"The tribe of Gad will also camp next to the tribe of Reuben. The leader of the tribe of Gad is Eliasaph son of Deuel.ᵃ ¹⁵There are 45,650 men in this division.

¹⁶"The total number of men in all the divisions of Reuben's camp is 151,450. His camp will be the second group to move when the people travel from place to place.

ᵃ **2:14 Deuel** Or "Reuel".

17"When the people travel, Levi's camp will move next. The Meeting Tent will be with them between the other camps. The people will make their camps in the same order that they move.

18"The flag of the camp of Ephraim will be on the west side. The division of Ephraim will camp there. The leader of the tribe of Ephraim is Elishama son of Ammihud. 19There are 40,500 men in this division. 20"The tribe of Manasseh will camp next to Ephraim's family. The leader of the tribe of Manasseh is Gamaliel son of Pedahzur. 21There are 32,200 men in this division. 22"The tribe of Benjamin will also camp next to Ephraim's family. The leader of the tribe of Benjamin is Abidan son of Gideoni. 23There are 35,400 men in this division. 24"The total number of men in Ephraim's camp is 108,100. They will be the third family to move when the people travel from one place to another.

25"The flag of Dan's camp will be on the north side. The tribes of Dan will camp there. The leader of the tribe of Dan is Ahiezer son of Ammishaddai. 26There are 62,700 men in this division. 27"The people from the tribe of Asher will camp next to the tribe of Dan. The leader of the tribe of Asher is Pagiel son of Ocran. 28There are 41,500 men in this division. 29"The tribe of Naphtali will also camp next to the tribe of Dan. The leader of the tribe of Naphtali is Ahira son of Enan. 30There are 53,400 men in this division. 31"There are 157,600 men in Dan's camp. They will be the last to move when the people travel from place to place. Each group will have its own flag."

32So these were the Israelites. They were counted by families. The total number of Israelite men in the camps, counted by divisions, is 603,550. 33Moses obeyed the LORD and did not count the Levites with the other Israelites.

34So the Israelites did everything the LORD told Moses. Each group camped under its own flag. And everyone stayed with their own family and family group.

Aaron's Family, the Priests

3 This is the family history of Aaron and Moses at the time the LORD talked to Moses on Mount Sinai.

2Aaron had four sons. Nadab was the firstborn son. Then there were Abihu, Eleazar and Ithamar. 3These sons were the chosen[a] priests. They were given the special work of serving the LORD as priests. 4But Nadab and Abihu died while serving the LORD. They used fire that the LORD did not allow when they made an offering to him. So Nadab and Abihu died there, in the desert of Sinai. They had no sons, so Eleazar and Ithamar took their place and served the Lord as priests. This happened while their father Aaron was still alive.

Levites—the Priests' Helpers

5The LORD said to Moses, 6"Bring all the men from the tribe of Levi. Bring them to Aaron the priest. These men will be his helpers. 7The Levites will help him when he serves at the Meeting Tent. And they will help all the Israelites when they come to worship at the Holy Tent. 8The Israelites should protect everything in the Meeting Tent; it is their duty. But the Levites will serve the Israelites by caring for these things. This will be their way of serving at the Holy Tent.

9"Give the Levites to Aaron and his sons. The Levites were chosen from all the Israelites to help Aaron and his sons.

10"Appoint Aaron and his sons to be priests. They must do their duty and serve as priests. Anyone else who tries to come near the holy things[b] must be killed."

11The LORD also said to Moses, 12–13"I destroyed all the firstborn in Egypt. At that time I chose all the firstborn from every family in Israel to be mine in a special way. That included all the firstborn men and animals. But now I am choosing the Levites to take their place. Now they will be my special servants. I, the LORD, give this command!"

14The LORD again said to Moses in the desert of Sinai, 15"Count all the families and family groups in the tribe of Levi. Count every man or boy who is one month old or older." 16So Moses obeyed the LORD. He counted them all.

17Levi had three sons. Their names were Gershon, Kohath and Merari.
18Each son was the leader of several family groups.
The Gershon family groups were Libni and Shimei.
19The Kohath family groups were Amram, Izhar, Hebron and Uzziel.
20The Merari family groups were Mahli and Mushi.

---

[a] **3:3 chosen** Or "anointed". See "ANOINT" in the Word List.
[b] **3:10 tries . . . holy things** Or "tries to serve as a priest".

These are the families that belonged to Levi's family group.

21The families of Libni and Shimei belonged to the family of Gershon. They were the Gershonite family groups. 22There were 7,500 men and boys over one month old in these two family groups. 23The Gershonite family groups were told to camp in the west. They made their camp behind the Holy Tent. 24The leader of the family groups of the Gershonites was Eliasaph son of Lael. 25In the Meeting Tent, the Gershonites had the job of taking care of the Holy Tent, the outer tent and the covering. They also took care of the curtain at the entrance of the Meeting Tent. 26They cared for the curtain in the courtyard. And they cared for the curtain at the entrance of the courtyard. This courtyard was around the Holy Tent and the altar. And they cared for the ropes and for everything that was used with the curtains.

27The families of Amram, Izhar, Hebron and Uzziel belonged to the family of Kohath. They were the Kohathite family groups. 28In this family group there were 8,300*a* men and boys a month old or over. The Kohathites were given the job of taking care of the things in the Holy Place. 29The Kohathite family groups were given the area to the south of the Holy Tent. This was the area where they camped. 30The leader of the Kohathite family groups was Elizaphan son of Uzziel. 31Their job was to take care of the Holy Box, the table, the lampstand, the altars and the dishes of the Holy Place. They also cared for the curtain and all the things that were used with the curtain.

32The leader over the leaders of the Levites was Eleazar son of Aaron the priest. Eleazar was in charge of everyone who took care of the holy things.

33-34The family groups of Mahli and Mushi belonged to the Merari family. There were 6,200 men and boys who were one month old or older in the Merari family group. 35The leader of the Merari family group was Zuriel son of Abihail. This family group was given the area to the north of the Holy Tent. This is the area where they camped. 36The people from the Merari family were given the job of caring for the frames of the Holy Tent. They cared for all the braces, posts, bases and everything that was used with the frames of the Holy Tent. 37They also cared for all the posts in the courtyard around the Holy Tent. This included all the bases, tent pegs and ropes.

38Moses, Aaron and his sons camped east of the Holy Tent, in front of the Meeting Tent. They were given the work of caring for the Holy Place. They did this for all the Israelites. Anyone else who came near the Holy Place was to be killed.

39The LORD commanded Moses and Aaron to count all the men and boys one month old or older in Levi's family group. The total number was 22,000.

Levites Take the Place of the Firstborn

40The LORD said to Moses, "Count all the firstborn men and boys in Israel who are at least one month old. Write their names on a list. 41I am the LORD. I will take the Levites instead of all the firstborn men and boys of Israel. I will also take the animals from the Levites instead of taking all the firstborn animals from the other people in Israel."

42So Moses did what the LORD commanded. He counted all the firstborn children of the Israelites. 43He listed all the firstborn men and boys who were one month old or older. There were 22,273 names on that list.

44The LORD also said to Moses, 45"I, the LORD, give this command: Take the Levites instead of all the firstborn men from the other families of Israel. And I will take the animals of the Levites instead of the animals of the other people. The Levites are mine. 46There are 22,000 Levites, but there are 22,273 firstborn sons from the other families. This leaves 273 more firstborn sons than Levites. 47Using the official measure, collect five pieces*b* of silver for each of the 273 people. (Each piece of silver by the official measure weighs 11.5 grammes.*c*) Collect that silver from the Israelites. 48Give the silver to Aaron and his sons as payment for the 273 Israelites."

49There were not enough Levites to take the place of all the men from the other family groups, so Moses gathered the money for them. 50Moses collected the silver from the firstborn men of the Israelites. He collected 1,365 pieces*d* of silver, using the official measure. 51Moses obeyed the LORD's command and gave the silver to Aaron and his sons. He did it just as the LORD had told him.

The Jobs of the Kohath Family

4 The LORD said to Moses and Aaron, 2"Count the men in the families of the Kohath family group. (The Kohath family group is a part of Levi's family group.) 3Count all the men from 30 to

---

a **3:28 8,300** Some copies of the ancient Greek version have "8,300". The Hebrew copies have "8,600". See Num. 3:22,28,34,39.

b **3:47 five pieces** Literally, "five *shekels*".

c **3:47 11.5 grammes** Literally, "20 *gerahs*".

d **3:50 1,365 pieces** Literally, 1,365 *shekels*".

50 years old who come to serve. These men will work in the Meeting Tent. [4]Their job is to take care of the most holy things in the Meeting Tent.

[5]"When the Israelites travel to a new place, Aaron and his sons must go into the Meeting Tent and take down the curtain and cover the Box of the Agreement with it. [6]Then they must cover all of this with covering made from fine leather. Then they must spread the solid blue cloth over the leather and put the poles in the rings on the Holy Box.

[7]"Then they must spread a blue cloth over the holy table. Then they must put the plates, spoons, bowls and the jars for drink offerings on the table. Put the special bread on the table. [8]Then you must put a red cloth over all these things, cover everything with fine leather and put the poles in the rings of the table.

[9]"Then they must cover the lampstand and its lamps with a blue cloth. They must also cover all the things used to keep the lamps burning and all the jars of oil that are used in the lamps. [10]Then wrap everything in fine leather. Then they must put all these things on poles used for carrying them.

[11]"They must spread a blue cloth over the golden altar. They must cover that with fine leather. Then they must put the poles for carrying it in the rings on the altar.

[12]"Then they must gather together all the special things that are used for worship in the Holy Place. They must gather them together and wrap them in a blue cloth. Then they must cover that with fine leather. They must put these things on a frame for carrying them.

[13]"They must clean the ashes out of the bronze altar and spread a purple cloth over it. [14]Then they must gather together all the things that are used for worship at the altar. These are the firepans, forks, shovels and the bowls. They must put these things on the bronze altar. Then they must spread a covering of fine leather over the altar and put the poles for carrying it in the rings on the altar.

[15]"Aaron and his sons must finish covering all the holy things in the Holy Place. Then the men from the Kohath family can go in and begin carrying these things. In this way they will not touch the holy things and die.

[16]"Eleazar son of Aaron the priest will be responsible for the Holy Tent. He will be responsible for everything in it, including the holy things. He will be responsible for the oil for the lamp, the sweet-smelling incense, the daily offering,[a] and the anointing oil."

[17]The LORD said to Moses and Aaron, [18]"Be careful! Don't let these Kohathite men be des-troyed. [19]You must do these things so that the Kohathite men can go near the most holy things and not die. Aaron and his sons must go in and show each Kohathite man what to do and what to carry. [20]If you don't do this, the Kohathite men might go in and look at the holy things. If they look at these things, even for a moment, they must die."

The Jobs of the Gershon Family

[21]The LORD said to Moses, [22]"Count all the people of the Gershon family. List them by family and family group. [23]Count all the men who are from 30 to 50 years old who come to serve. These men will have the job of caring for the Meeting Tent.

[24]"This is what the Gershonite family must do and the things they must carry: [25]They must carry the curtains of the Holy Tent, the Meeting Tent, its covering and the covering made from fine leather. They must also carry the curtain at the entrance of the Meeting Tent. [26]They must carry the curtains of the courtyard that are around the Holy Tent and the altar. And they must carry the curtain for the entrance of the courtyard. They must also carry all the ropes and all the things that are used with the curtains. The Gershonite men will be responsible for anything that needs to be done with these things. [27]Aaron and his sons will watch all the work that is done. Everything the Gershonites carry and the other work they do will be watched by Aaron and his sons. You must tell them what they are responsible for carrying. [28]This is the work that the men of the Gershonite family group must do for the Meeting Tent. Ithamar son of Aaron the priest will be responsible for their work.

The Jobs of the Merari Family

[29]"Count all the men in the families and family groups in the Merari family group. [30]Count all the men who are from 30 to 50 years old and come to serve. These men will do a special work for the Meeting Tent. [31]When you travel, it is their job to carry the frames of the Meeting Tent. They must carry the braces, the posts and the bases. [32]They must also carry the posts that are around the courtyard. They must carry the bases, the tent pegs, the ropes and everything that is used for the poles around the courtyard. List the names and tell each man exactly what he must carry. [33]This is what the people from the Merari family will do to serve in the work for the Meeting Tent. Ithamar son of Aaron the priest will be responsible for their work."

---

[a] 4:16 *daily offering* Offerings that were made twice each day as a gift to God.

The Levite Families

³⁴Moses, Aaron and the leaders of the Israelites counted the Kohathites. They counted them by families and family groups. ³⁵They counted all the men from 30 to 50 years old who were able to serve. These men were given special work to do for the Meeting Tent.

³⁶There were 2,750 men in the Kohath family group who were qualified to do this work. ³⁷So these men from the Kohath family group were given their special work to do for the Meeting Tent. Moses and Aaron counted them just as the Lord had commanded.

³⁸Also, the Gershonite family group was counted. ³⁹All the men from 30 to 50 years old who qualified to serve were counted. These men were given their special work to do for the Meeting Tent. ⁴⁰There were 2,630 men in the families of the Gershon family group who were qualified. ⁴¹So these men from the Gershon family group were given their special work to do for the Meeting Tent. Moses and Aaron counted them just as the Lord had commanded.

⁴²Also, the men in the families and family groups of the Merari family were counted. ⁴³All the men from 30 to 50 years old who qualified to serve were counted. These men were given their special work to do for the Meeting Tent. ⁴⁴There were 3,200 men in the families of the Merari family group who were qualified. ⁴⁵So these men from the Merari family group were given their special work. Moses and Aaron counted them just as the Lord had commanded.

⁴⁶So Moses, Aaron and the leaders of the Israelites counted all the people in Levi's family group. They had counted each family and each family group. ⁴⁷All the men between the ages of 30 and 50 who qualified to serve were counted. These men were given a special work to do for the Meeting Tent. They did the work of carrying the Meeting Tent when they travelled. ⁴⁸The total number was 8,580. ⁴⁹Each man was counted just as the Lord commanded Moses. Each man was given his own work and told what he must carry just as the Lord had said.

Rules About Cleanliness

5 The Lord said to Moses, ²"Tell the people to send away from the camp anyone who is unclean, that is, anyone who has a serious skin diseaseᵃ or discharge and anyone who has touched a dead body. ³Whether they are a man or a woman, send them away so that the camp where I am living among you will not be made unclean."

⁴So the Israelites obeyed God's command. They sent those people outside the camp. They did what the Lord had told Moses.

Paying for Doing Wrong

⁵The Lord said to Moses, ⁶"Tell this to the Israelites: You might do something wrong to another person. When you do that, you are really sinning against God. So you are guilty of doing wrong. ⁷You must confess that sin. Then you must fully pay for that wrong thing you did. You must add one-fifth to the payment and give it all to the person you had done wrong to. ⁸But maybe the person is dead and does not have any close relatives to accept the payment. In that case, you will give the payment to the Lord. That is, you will give the full payment to the priest. The priest must sacrifice the ram that makes people pure. This ram will be sacrificed to cover over your sins, but the priest will keep the rest of the payment.

⁹"If any of you Israelites gives a special gift to God, the priest who accepts that gift can keep it. It is his. ¹⁰You don't have to give these special gifts, but if you do, the gifts belong to the priest."

Jealous Husbands

¹¹Then the Lord said to Moses, ¹²"Tell the Israelites this: A man's wife might be unfaithful to him. ¹³She might have sex with another man and hide this from her husband. And there might not be anyone to tell him that his wife committed this sin. Her husband might never know about the wrong thing she did, and she might not tell her husband about her sin. ¹⁴But the husband might begin to think that his wife has sinned against him, whether she has or not. He might become jealous. He might begin to believe that she is not pure and true to him. ¹⁵If that happens, he must take his wife to the priest. The husband must also take an offering of 1 kilogrammeᵇ of barley flour. He must not pour oil or incense on the barley flour. This barley flour is a grain offering to the Lord that is given because the husband is jealous. This offering will show that he thinks his wife has been unfaithful to him.

¹⁶"The priest will take the woman before the Lord and make her stand there. ¹⁷Then he will take some special water and put it in a clay jar. He will put some dirt from the floor of the Holy Tent into the water. ¹⁸He will force the woman to stand before the Lord. Then he will loosen her hair and put the grain offering in her hand. This is the barley flour that her husband gave because he was jealous. At the same time, he will hold the

---

ᵃ **5:2 serious skin disease** This could be leprosy, or it could be another kind of contagious skin disease.
ᵇ **5:15 1 kilogramme** Literally, "¹⁄₁₀ of an *ephah*".

clay jar of special water. This is the special water that can bring trouble to the woman.

19"Then the priest will make the woman promise to tell the truth and say to her: 'If you have not slept with another man, and if you have not sinned against your husband while you were married to him, then this water that causes trouble will not hurt you. 20But if you have sinned against your husband—if you had sex with a man who is not your husband—then you are not pure. 21If that is true, you will have much trouble when you drink this special water. You will not be able to have children. And if you are pregnant now, your baby will die.*a* And the LORD will cause your people to speak evil of you and curse you.'

"Then the priest must tell the woman to make an oath. She must agree for the LORD to cause these things to happen to her if she lies. 22The priest must say, 'You must drink this water that causes trouble. If you have sinned, you will not be able to have children. Any baby you have will die before it is born.' And the woman should say, 'I agree to do as you say.'

23"The priest should write these warnings on a scroll. Then he should wash the words off into the water. 24Then the woman must drink the water that brings trouble. This water will enter her and, if she is guilty, it will cause her much suffering.

25"Then the priest will take the grain offering from her (the offering for jealousy) and raise it before the LORD. Then he will carry it to the altar. 26The priest will fill his hands with some of the grain and put it on the altar and let it burn there. After that, he will tell the woman to drink the water. 27If the woman has sinned against her husband, the water will bring her trouble. The water will go into her body and cause her much suffering. Any baby that is in her will die before it is born, and she will never be able to have children. All the people will turn against her.*b* 28But if the woman has not sinned against her husband and she is pure, the priest will say that she is not guilty. Then she will be normal and able to have children.

29"So this is the law about jealousy. This is what you should do when a woman sins against her husband while she is married to him. 30Or if the man becomes jealous and thinks his wife has sinned against him, this is what the man should do. The priest must tell her to stand before the LORD. Then the priest will do all these things. This is the law. 31The husband will not be guilty of

doing anything wrong, but the woman will suffer if she has sinned."

Nazirites

6 The LORD said to Moses, 2"Tell the Israelites this: If there are people, men or women, who want to make a vow dedicating themselves to the LORD as Nazirites for a time, this is what they must do: 3They must stay away from wine or other strong drink. They must not drink vinegar that is made from wine or from other strong drink. They must not drink grape juice or eat grapes or raisins. 4During that special time of dedication, they must not eat anything that comes from grapes. They must not even eat the seeds or the skins from grapes.

5"The whole time of their Nazirite vow they must not cut their hair. They must be holy until this time of special dedication to the LORD is ended. They must let their hair grow long.

6"They must not go near someone who is dying*c* at any time during the period for which they have given themselves fully to the LORD. 7They must not let themselves be made unclean in this way, even if it is their own father, mother, brother or sister who is dying.*d* This is because they have the hair that they dedicated to God on their head! 8They are holy because they have given themselves fully to the LORD for the full time of that dedication. 9So if they are with someone when they suddenly die, they will be unclean and will have to shave the hair from their head. They must do that on the seventh day of their purification ceremony when they are made clean. 10Then on the eighth day, they must bring two doves or two young pigeons and give them to the priest at the entrance of the Meeting Tent. 11Then the priest will offer one bird as a sin offering and the other one as a burnt offering. The burnt offering will be a payment for the sin of touching a dead body during the special time of dedication. Then they must again promise to give the hair on their head as a gift to God. 12This means they must again give themselves to the LORD for another time of dedication. They must bring a one-year-old male lamb to offer as a guilt offering. They must start again from the beginning with a new time of dedication because they touched a dead body during their time of dedication.

13"After their time of dedication is over, Nazirites must go to the entrance of the Meeting Tent 14and give their offering to the LORD. Their offering must be:

---

a **5:21** *You will . . . die* Literally, "Your loins will fall and your belly will swell."
b **5:27** *All . . . against her* Literally, "She will be like a curse among the people."
c **6:6** *someone who is dying* Or "a dead person".
d **6:7** *is dying* Or "has died".

a one-year-old male lamb that has nothing
wrong with it for a burnt offering;
a one-year-old female lamb that has nothing
wrong with it for a sin offering;
a ram that has nothing wrong with it for a
fellowship offering;
15a basket of bread made without yeast—bread
made with fine flour mixed with oil and
wafers with oil spread on top;
and the grain offerings and drink offerings that
are a part of these gifts.

16"The priest will give these things to the LORD,
and then the priest will make the sin offering and
the burnt offering. 17He will give the basket of
bread without yeast to the LORD. Then he will kill
the ram as a fellowship offering to the Lord. He
will give it to the Lord with the grain offering and
the drink offering.

18"The Nazirites must go to the entrance of the
Meeting Tent. There they must shave off their
hair that they grew as a dedication to the Lord.
That hair will be put in the fire that is burning
under the sacrifice of the fellowship offering.

19"After the Nazirites have cut off their hair,
the priest will give them a boiled shoulder from
the ram and a large and a small cake from the
basket. Both of these cakes are made without
yeast. 20Then the priest will lift these things up to
show that they were presented before the LORD.
These things are holy and belong to the priest.
Also, the ram's breast and thigh that were lifted
up and presented belong to the priest. After that,
the Nazirites can drink wine.

21"These are the rules for those who decide to
make the Nazirite vow. They must give all these
gifts to the LORD. But they might be able to give
much more. If they promise to do more, they
must keep their promise. But they must give at
least all the things listed in these rules for the
Nazirite vow."

The Priests' Blessings

22The LORD said to Moses, 23"Tell Aaron and his
sons that when they bless the Israelites, this is
what they should say:

24"May the LORD bless you
and keep you safe.
25May the LORD smile down on you[a]
and show you his kindness.

26May the LORD answer your prayers[b]
and give you peace.'

27In this way Aaron and his sons will use my
name to give a blessing to the Israelites, and I will
bless them."

Dedicating the Holy Tent

7 Moses finished setting up the Holy Tent. On
that day he dedicated it to God. Moses
anointed the Tent and everything in it. He also
anointed the altar and all the things used with it.
2Then the leaders of Israel gave offerings to
God. These men were the heads of their families
and leaders of their tribes. These were the same
men who were in charge of counting the people.
3These leaders brought gifts and gave them to the
LORD in front of the Holy Tent. They brought six
covered carts and twelve oxen for pulling the
carts. Each leader gave an ox and joined with
another leader to give a cart.
4The LORD said to Moses, 5"Accept these gifts
from the leaders. These gifts can be used in the
work of the Meeting Tent. Give them to the
Levites to help them do their work."
6So Moses accepted the carts and the oxen and
gave them to the Levites. 7He gave two carts
and four oxen to the men in Gershon's group.
They needed the carts and the oxen for their
work. 8Then Moses gave four carts and eight
oxen to the men in Merari's group. They needed
the carts and oxen for their work. Ithamar son
of Aaron the priest was responsible for the work
of all these men. 9Moses did not give any oxen
or carts to the men in Kohath's group, because
their job was to carry the holy things on their
shoulders.
10When Moses anointed the altar, the leaders
brought offerings for its dedication. They gave
their offerings to the Lord at the altar. 11The LORD
told Moses, "Each day one leader must bring his
gift for the dedication of the altar."
12–83c Each of the twelve leaders brought these
gifts:
Each leader brought one silver plate that weighed
about 1.5 kilogrammes.[d] Each leader brought one
silver bowl that weighed almost 1 kilogramme.[e]
Both of these gifts were weighed by the official
measure. The bowl and the plate were each filled
with fine flour mixed with oil. This was to be used
as a grain offering. Each leader also brought a large

---

[a] **6:25 May . . . on you** Literally, "May the LORD make his face shine on you."
[b] **6:26 May . . . prayers** Literally, "May the LORD lift his face to you," that is, "May he accept you into his presence and grant your request."
[c] **7:12–83** In the Hebrew text each leader's gift is listed separately. But the text is the same for each gift, so these verses have been combined for easier reading.
[d] **7:12–83 about 1.5 kilogrammes** Literally, "130 *shekels*". Also in verse 85.
[e] **7:12–83 almost 1 kilogramme** Literally, "70 *shekels*". Also in verse 85.

gold spoon that weighed 115 grammes.ᵃ The spoon was filled with incense.

Each leader also brought 1 young bull, 1 ram and 1 male lamb a year old. These animals were for a burnt offering. Each leader also brought 1 male goat to be used as a sin offering. Each leader brought 2 cattle, 5 rams, 5 male goats and 5 male lambs a year old. All of them were sacrificed for a fellowship offering.

On the first day, the leader of the tribe of Judah, Nahshon son of Amminadab brought his gifts.

On the second day, the leader of the tribe of Issachar, Nethanel son of Zuar brought his gifts.

On the third day, the leader of the tribe of Zebulun, Eliab son of Helon brought his gifts.

On the fourth day, the leader of the tribe of Reuben, Elizur son of Shedeur brought his gifts.

On the fifth day, the leader of the tribe of Simeon, Shelumiel son of Zurishaddai brought his gifts.

On the sixth day, the leader of the tribe of Gad, Eliasaph son of Deuelᵇ brought his gifts.

On the seventh day, the leader of the tribe of Ephraim, Elishama son of Ammihud brought his gifts.

On the eighth day, the leader of the tribe of Manasseh, Gamaliel son of Pedahzur brought his gifts.

On the ninth day, the leader of the tribe of Benjamin, Abidan son of Gideoni brought his gifts.

On the tenth day, the leader of the tribe of Dan, Ahiezer son of Ammishaddai brought his gifts.

On the eleventh day, the leader of the tribe of Asher, Pagiel son of Ocran brought his gifts.

On the twelfth day, the leader of the tribe of Naphtali, Ahira son of Enan brought his gifts.

84So all these things were the gifts from the leaders of the Israelites. They brought them during the time that Moses dedicated the altar by anointing it. They brought 12 silver plates, 12 silver bowls and 12 gold spoons. 85Each silver plate weighed about 1.5 kilogrammes. And each bowl weighed almost 1 kilogramme. The silver plates and the silver bowls together all weighed 27 kilogrammes,ᶜ using the official measure. 86The 12 gold spoons filled with incense weighed 110 grammes each, using the official measure. The 12 gold spoons all together weighed about 1.5 kilogrammes.ᵈ

87The total number of animals for the burnt offering was 12 bulls, 12 rams and 12 one-year-old male lambs. There were also the grain offerings that must be given with these offerings. And there were 12 male goats to be used for a sin offering. 88The leaders also gave animals to be killed and used as a fellowship offering. The total number of these animals was 24 bulls, 60 rams, 60 male goats and 60 one-year-old male lambs. In this way they dedicated the altar after Moses had anointed it.

89When Moses went into the Meeting Tent to speak to the Lord, he heard the Lord's voice speaking to him. The voice was coming from the area between the two winged creatures on the mercy-cover on top of the Box of the Agreement. In this way the Lord spoke to Moses.

The Lampstand

8 The Lord said to Moses, 2"Tell Aaron to put the seven lamps in the place I showed you. These lamps will light the area in front of the lampstand."

INSIGHT

The seven lamps mentioned here are referred to today as a "menorah" – a large branched candlestick with seven candles.

Numbers 8:1–4

3Aaron did this. He put the lamps in the right place so that they lighted the area in front of the lampstand. He obeyed the command that the Lord gave Moses. 4This is how the lampstand was made: It was made from hammered gold, all the way from the gold base at the bottom to the gold flowers at the top. It looked just like the pattern that the Lord had shown to Moses.

Dedicating the Levites

5The Lord said to Moses, 6"Separate the Levites from the other Israelites. Make these Levites clean. 7This is what you should do to make them clean: Sprinkle the special water from the sin offering on them. This water will make them clean. Then they must shave their bodies and

---

ᵃ 7:12–83 *115 grammes* Literally, "10 *shekels*". Also in verse 86.
ᵇ 7:12–83 *Deuel* Or "Reuel".
ᶜ 7:85 *27 kilogrammes* Literally, "2,400 *shekels*".
ᵈ 7:86 *about 1.5 kilogrammes* Literally, "120 *shekels*".

wash their clothes. This will make their bodies clean.

8"They must take a young bull and the grain offering that must be offered with it. This grain offering will be flour mixed with oil. Then take another young bull for a sin offering. 9Bring the Levites to the area in front of the Meeting Tent. Then bring all the Israelites together at that place. 10Bring the Levites before the LORD. The Israelites will put their hands on them.*a* 11Aaron will give the Levites to the LORD as an offering from the Israelites. Then the Levites will be ready to do their special work for the LORD.

12"Tell the Levites to put their hands on the heads of the bulls. One bull will be a sin offering and the other bull will be used as a burnt offering to the LORD. These offerings will make the Levites pure. 13Tell the Levites to stand in front of Aaron and his sons. Then give the Levites to the LORD. They will be like an offering. 14This will make the Levites holy. They will be different from the other Israelites. The Levites will belong to me.

15"So make the Levites pure and give them to the Lord as a special offering.*b* After you do this, they can come and do their work at the Meeting Tent. 16The Israelites will give me the Levites. They will belong to me. In the past I told every Israelite family to give me their firstborn son. But now I am taking the Levites in place of these firstborn sons from the other families in Israel. 17Every firstborn in Israel—man or animal—is mine, because I killed all the firstborn children and animals in Egypt. And I chose to take the firstborn sons to belong to me. 18But now I will take the Levites in their place. I will take the Levites in place of all the firstborn sons from the other families in Israel. 19I chose the Levites from among all the Israelites. And I give them as gifts to Aaron and his sons. I want them to do the work at the Meeting Tent. They will serve for all the Israelites. They will help make the sacrifices that make the Israelites pure. Then no great sickness or trouble will come to the Israelites when they come near the holy place."

20So Moses, Aaron and all the Israelites obeyed the LORD. They did with the Levites everything that the Lord commanded Moses. 21The Levites washed themselves and their clothes. Then Aaron gave them to the LORD as special offerings. Aaron gave the offerings that covered their sins and made them pure. 22After that, the Levites came to the Meeting Tent to do their work. Aaron and his sons watched them. They were responsible for the work of the Levites. Aaron and his sons did what the LORD commanded Moses.

23Then the LORD said to Moses, 24"This is a special command for the Levites: Every Levite man who is 25 years old or older must come and share in the work at the Meeting Tent. 25But when a man is 50 years old, he will retire from this hard work. 26Men who are at least 50 years old will be on duty to help their brothers, but they will not do the work themselves. That is what you must do for the Levites so that they can do their duty."

Passover

9 The LORD spoke to Moses in the desert of Sinai. This was during the first month of the second year after the Israelites came out of Egypt. He said to Moses, 2"Tell the Israelites to celebrate Passover at the chosen time. 3They must eat the Passover meal just before dark on the fourteenth day of this month. They must do this at the chosen time, and they must follow all the rules about Passover."

4So Moses told the Israelites to celebrate Passover. 5The people did this in the desert of Sinai just before dark on the fourteenth day of the first month. The Israelites did everything just as the LORD commanded Moses.

6But some of the people could not celebrate Passover that day. They were unclean because they had touched a dead body. So they went to Moses and Aaron that day 7and said to Moses, "We touched a dead body and became unclean. But why must we be kept from offering our gifts to the LORD at the chosen time with the rest of the Israelites?"

8Moses said to them, "I will ask the LORD what he says about this."

9Then the LORD said to Moses, 10"Tell the Israelites this: It might happen sometimes that you or your descendants cannot celebrate the LORD's Passover at the right time. Someone might be unclean because they touched a dead body, or they might be away on a trip. They will still be able to celebrate Passover at another time. 11They must celebrate Passover just before dark on the fourteenth day of the second month. At that time they must eat the lamb, the bread made without yeast and the bitter herbs. 12They must not leave any of that food until the next morning. And they must not break any of the bones of the lamb. They must follow all the rules about Passover. 13But anyone who is able must celebrate Passover at the right time. If they are clean and they are not away on a trip, there is no excuse for them not to do it. If they don't celebrate Passover at the right time, they must be separated from their

---

a **8:10 put their hands on them** This showed that the people shared in appointing the Levites to their special work.
b **8:15 special offering** Literally, "a lifted offering". Also in verse 21.

people. They are guilty and must be punished, because they did not give the LORD his gift at the right time.

[14]"A foreigner living among you might want to share in the LORD's Passover with you. This is allowed, but that person must follow all the rules about Passover. The same rules are for everyone."

The Cloud and the Fire

[15]On the day the Holy Tent, the Tent of the Agreement, was set up, a cloud covered it. At night the cloud over the Holy Tent looked like fire. [16]The cloud stayed over the Holy Tent all the time. And at night the cloud looked like fire. [17]When the cloud moved from its place over the Holy Tent, the Israelites followed it. When the cloud stopped, that is the place where the Israelites camped. [18]This was the way the LORD showed the Israelites when to move and when to stop and set up camp. While the cloud stayed over the Holy Tent, the people continued to camp in that same place. [19]Sometimes the cloud would stay over the Holy Tent for a long time. The Israelites obeyed the LORD and did not move. [20]Sometimes the cloud was over the Holy Tent for only a few days. So the people obeyed the LORD's command—they followed the cloud when it moved. [21]Sometimes the cloud stayed only during the night—the next morning the cloud moved. So the people gathered their things and followed it. If the cloud moved, during the day or during the night, they followed it. [22]If the cloud stayed over the Holy Tent for two days, a month or a year, the people stayed at that place. They did not leave until the cloud moved. When the cloud rose from its place and moved, they also moved. [23]So the people obeyed the LORD's commands. They camped when the LORD told them to, and they moved when he told them to. They watched carefully and obeyed the LORD's commands to Moses.

The Silver Trumpets

10 The LORD said to Moses, [2]"Make two trumpets. Use silver and hammer it to make the trumpets. These trumpets will be for calling the people together and for telling them when it is time to move the camp. [3]If you blow long blasts on both trumpets, all the people must meet together at the entrance of the Meeting Tent. [4]But if you blow long blasts on only one trumpet, only the leaders will come to meet with you. (These are the leaders of the twelve tribes of Israel.)

[5]"Short blasts on the trumpets will be the way to tell the people to move the camp. The first time

you blow a short blast on the trumpets, the tribes camping on the east side of the Meeting Tent must begin to move. [6]The second time you blow a short blast on the trumpets, the tribes camping on the south side of the Meeting Tent will begin to move. [7]But if you want to gather the people together for a special meeting, blow the trumpets in a different way—blow a long steady blast on the trumpets. [8]Only Aaron's sons, the priests, should blow the trumpets. This is a law for you that will continue forever, for generations to come.

[9]"If you are fighting an enemy in your own land, blow loudly on the trumpets before you go to fight them. The LORD your God will hear you, and he will save you from your enemies. [10]Also blow these trumpets for your special meetings, New Moon celebrations and all your happy times together. Blow the trumpets when you give your burnt offerings and fellowship offerings. This will be a special way for your God to remember you. I command you to do this; I am the LORD your God."

The Israelites Move Their Camp

[11]On the twentieth day of the second month of the second year after the Israelites left Egypt, the cloud rose from above the Tent of the Agreement. [12]So the Israelites began their journey. They left the desert of Sinai and travelled until the cloud stopped in the desert of Paran. [13]This was the first time the people moved their camp. They moved it the way the LORD commanded Moses.

[14]The three divisions from Judah's camp went first. They travelled under their flag. The first group was the tribe of Judah. Nahshon son of Amminadab was the commander of that group. [15]Next came the tribe of Issachar. Nethanel son of Zuar was the commander of that group. [16]And then came the tribe of Zebulun. Eliab son of Helon was the commander of that group.

[17]Then the Holy Tent was taken down. And the men from the Gershon and the Merari families carried the Holy Tent. So the people from these families were next in line.

[18]Then came the three divisions from Reuben's camp. They travelled under their flag. The first group was the tribe of Reuben. Elizur son of Shedeur was the commander of that group. [19]Next came the tribe of Simeon. Shelumiel son of Zurishaddai was the commander of that group. [20]And then came the tribe of Gad. Eliasaph son of Deuel[a] was the commander of that group. [21]Then came the Kohath family. They carried the holy things from inside the Holy Tent. These people came at this time so that the other people could

---

[a] **10:20** *Deuel* Or "Reuel".

set up the Holy Tent and make it ready at the new camp before these people arrived.

²²Next came the three groups from Ephraim's camp. They travelled under their flag. The first group was the tribe of Ephraim. Elishama son of Ammihud was the commander of that group. ²³Next came the tribe of Manasseh. Gamaliel son of Pedahzur was the commander of that group. ²⁴Then came the tribe of Benjamin. Abidan son of Gideoni was the commander of that group.

²⁵The last three tribes in the line were the rear guard for all the other tribes. These were the groups from Dan's camp. They travelled under their flag. The first group was the tribe of Dan. Ahiezer son of Ammishaddai was their commander. ²⁶Next came the tribe of Asher. Pagiel son of Ocran was the commander of that group. ²⁷Then came the tribe of Naphtali. Ahira son of Enan was the commander of that group. ²⁸That was the way the Israelites marched when they moved from place to place.

²⁹Hobab was the son of Reuel, the Midianite. (Reuel was Moses' father-in-law.) Moses said to Hobab, "We are travelling to the land that the LORD promised to give to us. Come with us and we will be good to you. The LORD has promised good things to the Israelites."

³⁰But Hobab answered, "No, I will not go with you. I will go back to my homeland and to my own people."

³¹Then Moses said, "Please don't leave us. You know more about the desert than we do. You can be our guide. ³²If you come with us, we will share with you all the good things that the LORD gives us."

³³So they began travelling from the mountain of the LORD. The priests took the Box of the LORD's Agreement and walked in front of the people. They carried the Holy Box for three days, looking for a place to camp. ³⁴And when they left their camp every morning, the cloud was there to lead them.

³⁵When the people lifted the Holy Box to move the camp, Moses always said,

"Get up, LORD!
    May your enemies be scattered.
    May your enemies run away from you."

³⁶And when the Holy Box was put in its place, Moses always said,

"Come back, LORD,
    to the millions of Israelites."

The People Complain Again

11 The people started complaining about their troubles. The LORD heard their complaints. He heard these things and became angry. Fire from the LORD burned among the people. The fire burned some of the areas at the edge of the camp. ²So the people cried to Moses for help. He prayed to the LORD and the fire stopped burning. ³So that place was called Taberah.ᵃ The people gave the place that name because the LORD caused a fire to burn in their camp.

The 70 Leaders

⁴The foreigners who had joined the Israelites began wanting other things to eat. Soon all the Israelites began complaining again. The people said, "We want to eat meat! ⁵We remember the fish we ate in Egypt. That fish cost us nothing. We also had good vegetables like cucumbers, melons, chives, onions and garlic. ⁶But now we have lost our strength. We never eat anything—only this manna!" ⁷(The manna was like small coriander seeds, and it looked like sap from a tree. ⁸The people gathered the manna. Then they used rocks to crush it and cooked it in a pot. Or they ground it into flour and made thin cakes with it. The cakes tasted like sweet cakes cooked with olive oil. ⁹The manna fell on the ground each night when the ground became wet with dew.)

¹⁰Moses heard the people complaining. People from every family were sitting by their tents and complaining. The LORD became very angry, and this made Moses very upset. ¹¹He asked the LORD, "Why did you bring this trouble on me? I am your servant. What did I do wrong? What did I do to upset you? Why did you give me responsibility over all these people? ¹²You know that I am not the father of all these people. You know that I did not give birth to them. But I must take care of them, like a nurse carrying a baby in her arms. Why do you force me to do this? Why do you force me to carry them to the land that you promised to our fathers? ¹³I don't have enough meat for all these people! And they continue complaining to me. They say, 'Give us meat to eat!' ¹⁴I cannot take care of all these people alone. The burden is too heavy for me. ¹⁵If you plan to continue giving me their troubles, kill me now. If you accept me as your servant, let me die now. Then I will be finished with all my troubles!"

¹⁶The LORD said to Moses, "Bring to me 70 of the leaders of Israel who everyone respects. Bring them to the Meeting Tent. Let them stand there with you. ¹⁷Then I will come down and speak with you there. The Spiritᵇ is on you now. But I will also give some of that Spirit to them. Then

---

ᵃ **11:3 Taberah** This name means "burning".
ᵇ **11:17 Spirit** Or "spirit". Also in verses 25,29.

they will help you take care of the people. In this way you will not have to be responsible for these people alone.

18"Tell the people this: Make yourselves ready for tomorrow. Tomorrow you will eat meat. The LORD heard you when you cried out and said, 'We need meat to eat! It was better for us in Egypt!' So now the LORD will give you meat. And you will eat it. 19You will eat it for more than one, or two, or five, or ten or even twenty days! 20You will eat that meat for a whole month until you are sick of it. This will happen to you because you complained against the LORD. He lives among you and knows what you need, but you cried and complained to him! You said, 'Why did we ever leave Egypt?'"

21Moses said, "There are 600,000 soldiers here, and you say, 'I will give them enough meat to eat for a whole month!' 22If we were to kill all the sheep and cattle, that would still not be enough to feed this many people for a month. And if we caught all the fish in the sea, it would not be enough for them!"

23But the LORD said to Moses, "Don't limit my power! You will see that I can do what I say I can do."

24So Moses went out to speak with the people. He told them what the LORD said. Then he gathered 70 of the leaders together and told them to stand around the Tent. 25Then the LORD came down in the cloud and spoke to Moses. He put on the 70 leaders some of the same Spirit that was on Moses. After the Spirit came down on them, they began to prophesy.ᵃ But that was the only time they ever did this.

26Two of the leaders, Eldad and Medad, did not go out to the Tent. Their names were on the list of leaders, but they stayed in the camp. But the Spirit also came on them, and they began prophesying in the camp. 27A young man ran and told Moses. The man said, "Eldad and Medad are prophesying in camp."

28Joshua son of Nun said to Moses, "Moses, sir, you must stop them!" (Joshua had been Moses' helper since Joshua was a boy.)

29But Moses answered, "Are you afraid the people will think that I am not the leader now? I wish that all the LORD's people were able to prophesy. I wish that the LORD would put his Spirit on all of them!" 30Then Moses and the leaders of Israel went back to the camp.

The Quail Come

31Then the LORD made a powerful wind blow in from the sea, and it blew quail into the area all around the camp. There were so many birds that the ground was covered. They were about three feet deep on the ground. There were quail in every direction as far as a man can walk in one day. 32They went out and gathered quail all that day and all that night. And they gathered quail all the next day too! The smallest amount anyone gathered was at least 1,000 kilogrammes. Then the people spread the quail meat all around the camp to dry in the sun.

33People began to eat the meat, but the LORD became very angry. While the meat was still in their mouths, before the people could finish eating it, the LORD caused the people to become very sick and die. 34So the people named that place Kibroth Hattaavah,ᵇ because there they buried those who had the strong desire for meat.

35From Kibroth Hattaavah the people travelled to Hazeroth and stayed there.

Miriam and Aaron Criticize Moses

12 Miriam and Aaron began to talk against Moses. They criticized him because he married an Ethiopianᶜ woman. 2They said to themselves, "Moses is not the only one the LORD has used to speak to the people. He has also spoken through us!"

The LORD heard this. 3(Moses was a very humble man. He was more humble than any other man on earth.) 4Suddenly, the LORD came and spoke to Moses, Aaron and Miriam. He said, "You three, come to the Meeting Tent, now!"

So Moses, Aaron and Miriam went to the Tent. 5The LORD came down in the tall cloud and stood at the entrance to the Tent. He called out, "Aaron and Miriam!" They went to him. 6God said, "Listen to me! You will have prophets. I, the LORD, will let them learn about me through visions. I will speak to them in dreams. 7But Moses is not like that. He is my faithful servant—I trust him with everyone in my house. 8When I speak to him, I talk face to face with him. I don't use stories with hidden meanings—I show him clearly what I want him to know. And Moses can look at the very image of the LORD. So why were you brave enough to speak against my servant Moses?"

9The LORD was very angry with them, and he left them. 10The cloud rose from the Tent. Aaron turned and looked at Miriam. Her skin was white like snow—she had a terrible skin disease!

11Then Aaron said to Moses, "Please, sir, forgive us for our foolish sin. 12Don't let her lose her skin like a baby who is born dead."

ᵃ **11:25 prophesy** Usually this means "to speak for God". But here, it might mean that God's Spirit took control of these men in some special way. Also in verse 26.

ᵇ **11:34 Kibroth Hattaavah** This name means "Graves of Strong Desire".

ᶜ **12:1 Ethiopian** Or "Cushite", a person from Ethiopia, in Africa.

(Sometimes a baby will be born like that, with half of its skin eaten away.)

13So Moses prayed to the LORD, "God, please heal her from this sickness!"

14The LORD answered Moses, "If her father had spat in her face, she would be shamed for seven days. So put her outside the camp for seven days. After that, she can come back into the camp."

15So they took Miriam outside the camp for seven days. And the people did not move from that place until she had been brought in again. 16After that, the people left Hazeroth and travelled to the desert of Paran where they set up camp.

The Spies Go to Canaan

13 The LORD said to Moses, 2"Send some men to explore the land of Canaan. I will give this land to the Israelites. Send one leader from each of the twelve tribes."

3So Moses obeyed the LORD's command and sent out the Israelite leaders while the people were camped in the desert of Paran. 4These are their names:

from the tribe of Reuben—Shammua son of Zaccur;
5from the tribe of Simeon—Shaphat son of Hori;
6from the tribe of Judah—Caleb son of Jephunneh;
7from the tribe of Issachar—Igal son of Joseph;
8from the tribe of Ephraim—Hoshea[a] son of Nun;
9from the tribe of Benjamin—Palti son of Raphu;
10from the tribe of Zebulun—Gaddiel son of Sodi;
11from the tribe of Manasseh (a tribe from Joseph)—Gaddi son of Susi;
12from the tribe of Dan—Ammiel son of Gemalli;
13from the tribe of Asher—Sethur son of Michael;
14from the tribe of Naphtali—Nahbi son of Vophsi;
15from the tribe of Gad—Geuel son of Maki.

16These are the names of the men Moses sent to look at and study the land. (Moses called Hoshea son of Nun by another name. Moses called him Joshua.)

17When Moses was sending them out to explore Canaan, he said, "Go through the Negev and then into the hill country. 18See what the land looks like. Learn about the people who live there. Are they strong or are they weak? Are they few or are they many? 19Learn about the land that they live in. Is it good land or bad land? What kind of towns do they live in? Do the towns have walls protecting them? Are the towns strongly defended? 20And learn other things about the land. Is the soil good for growing things, or is it poor soil? Are there trees on the land? Try to bring back some of the fruit from that land." (This was during the time when the first grapes should be ripe.)

21So they went to explore the country. They explored the area from the desert of Zin to Rehob and Lebo Hamath. 22They entered the country through the Negev and went to Hebron. (The town of Hebron was built seven years before the town of Zoan in Egypt.) Ahiman, Sheshai and Talmai lived there. These men were descendants of Anak. 23Then the men went to Eshcol Valley. There they cut off a branch from a grapevine that had a bunch of grapes on it. They put that branch on a pole, and two men carried it between them. They also carried some pomegranates and figs. 24That place is called the Eshcol[b] Valley, because there the men of Israel cut off the bunch of grapes.

25The men explored that country for 40 days, and then they went back to the camp. 26The Israelites were camped near Kadesh, in the desert of Paran. The men went to Moses and Aaron and all the Israelites. They told Moses, Aaron and all the people what they had seen and showed them the fruit from the land. 27The men told Moses, "We went to the land where you sent us. It is a land filled with many good things![c] Here is some of the fruit that grows there. 28But the people living there are very powerful. The cities are very large and strongly defended. We even saw some Anakites there. 29The Amalekites live in the Negev. The Hittites, Jebusites and Amorites live in the hill country. The Canaanites live near the sea and by the Jordan River."

30Caleb told the people near Moses to be quiet. Then Caleb said, "We should go up and take that land for ourselves. We can easily take that land."

31But the men who had gone with him said, "We cannot fight those people! They are much stronger than we are." 32So those men gave a report that discouraged the people. They said, "The land we saw is full of strong people. They are strong enough to easily defeat anyone who goes there. 33We saw the giant Nephilim people there! (The descendants of Anak come from the

---

a **13:8 Hoshea** Or "Joshua".
b **13:24 Eshcol** This name is like the Hebrew word meaning "a bunch of grapes".
c **13:27 land . . . things** Literally, "land flowing with milk and honey". Also in 14:8.

DEAD ENDS

Finally God's people have reached the edge of the land that God had promised would be theirs. All that remains is to go and check it out. An excited few are picked to be spies. What adventures will they have? What report will they bring back?

DIG IN

READ Numbers 13:1–33

Oh. Not quite so exciting any more. More like terrifying!
- What was the land like (vv.23–27)?
- What were the people like (vv.28–29)?
- How did the spies feel (vv.31–33)?

READ Numbers 14:1–10
- What is the people's response to the spies' report?
- Caleb and Joshua had a different view. What did they remind the people about (vv.8–9)?

The people start complaining and moaning; they even say it would have been better if they had stayed in Egypt – are they mad?! They were slaves in Egypt, their baby boys were killed in Egypt. Despite all that God has done for them, they still think they will be killed. However, Joshua and Caleb get it right: if the Lord wants them to be there, he will sort it!

- What do the people try to do (v.10)?

It's downright chaos! The people have deliberately turned their backs on God and are now thinking of murdering their own people!

READ Numbers 14:10–35
- What does God say is the people's sin (vv.11,22,31)?

They had knowledge of God – they'd seen his glory and the great signs he did, yet they refused to trust him. Now they're rejecting the land he'd given by refusing to enter it. They couldn't show more unbelief if they tried. Can you feel God's pain and anger in verse 11?

- What was the punishment (vv.23,33–35)?

The people must have been gutted. They had been looking forward to the day when a beautiful land would be theirs. It was going to be the place where they could stop travelling and enjoy food, peace and safety. And now they would live the rest of their days in the desert – only their children would see the promised land. There was no way back, this was it. This is how seriously God takes the deliberate, rejecting sin of the people.

DIG THROUGH

- The people had all the evidence that God was real and to be trusted and yet they refused to believe him, disobeying him and rejecting the wonderful promise of the land. Is this how you treat God? Those who continually reject God and sin deliberately will one day find they will not enter "the land" either. (Check out Hebrews 10:26–31.)

DIG DEEPER

- The people had been in a special relationship with God – they had privileged knowledge and yet deliberately rebelled against him. And so they weren't allowed to go into the land. Check out Numbers 15:22–31. What are the differences between sin that's deliberate and sin that's unintentional?

Nephilim.) We felt like little grasshoppers. Yes, we were like grasshoppers to them!"

The People Complain Again

14 That night all the people in the camp began shouting loudly. ²The Israelites complained against Moses and Aaron. All the people came together and said to Moses and Aaron, "We should have died in Egypt or in the desert. ³Did the LORD bring us to this new land to be killed in war? The enemy will kill us and take our wives and children! It would be better for us to go back to Egypt."

⁴Then the people said to each other, "Let's choose another leader and go back to Egypt."

⁵Moses and Aaron bowed low to the ground in front of all the people gathered there. ⁶Joshua and Caleb became very upset. (Joshua son of Nun and Caleb son of Jephunneh were two of the men who explored the land.) ⁷These two men said to all the Israelites gathered there, "The land that we saw is very good. ⁸It is a land filled with many good things. If the LORD is pleased with us, he will lead us into that land. And he will give that land to us. ⁹So don't turn against the LORD! Don't be afraid of the people in that land. We can defeat them. They have no protection, nothing to keep them safe. But we have the LORD with us, so don't be afraid!"

¹⁰All the people began talking about killing Joshua and Caleb with stones. But the Glory of the LORD appeared over the Meeting Tent where all the people could see it. ¹¹The LORD spoke to Moses and said, "How long will these people continue to turn against me? They show that they don't trust me or believe in my power, in spite of the many miracles I have done among them. ¹²I will kill them all with a terrible sickness. I will destroy them, and I will use you to make another nation. Your nation will be greater and stronger than these people."

¹³Then Moses said to the LORD, "If you do that, the Egyptians will hear about it! They know that you used your great power to bring your people out of Egypt. ¹⁴The Egyptians have already told the people in Canaan about it. They already know you are the LORD. They know that you are with your people. They know that the people saw you. Those people know about the special cloud. They know you use the cloud to lead your people during the day. And they know the cloud becomes a fire to lead your people at night. ¹⁵So you must not kill these people now. If you kill them, all the nations who have heard about your power will say, ¹⁶'The LORD was not able to bring them into the land he promised them. So he killed them in the desert.'

¹⁷"So now, Lord, show your strength! Show it the way you said you would. ¹⁸You said, 'The

LORD is slow to become angry. He is full of great love. He forgives[a] those who are guilty and break the law. But he always punishes those who are guilty. He punishes them, and he also punishes their children, their grandchildren and even their great-grandchildren for those bad things.' ¹⁹Now, show your great love to these people. Forgive their sin. Forgive them the same way you have been forgiving them since the time they left Egypt until now."

²⁰The LORD answered, "Yes, I will forgive the people as you asked. ²¹But I tell you the truth. As surely as I live and as surely as the Glory of the LORD fills the whole earth, I make you this promise: ²²None of the people I led out of Egypt will ever see the land of Canaan. They saw my glory and the great signs that I did in Egypt and in the desert. But they disobeyed me and tested me ten times. ²³I promised their ancestors I would give them that land. But none of those people who turned against me will ever enter that land! ²⁴But my servant Caleb was different. He follows me completely. So I will bring him into the land that he has already seen, and his people will get that land. ²⁵The Amalekites and the Canaanites are living in the valley. So tomorrow you must leave this place. Go back to the desert on the road to the Red Sea."

The LORD Punishes the People

²⁶The LORD said to Moses and Aaron, ²⁷"How long will these evil people continue to complain against me? I have heard their complaints and their grumbling. ²⁸So tell them, 'The LORD says that he will surely do all those things to you that you complained about. This is what will happen to you: ²⁹You will die in this desert. Every person who is 20 years old or older and was counted as one of my people will die. You complained against me. ³⁰So none of you will ever enter and live in the land that I promised to give you. Only Caleb son of Jephunneh and Joshua son of Nun will enter that land. ³¹You were afraid and complained that your enemies in that new land would take your children away from you. But I tell you that I will bring them into the land. They will enjoy what you refused to accept. ³²As for you people, you will die in this desert.

³³"'Your children will wander around like shepherds here in the desert for 40 years. They will suffer because you were not faithful to me. They must suffer until all of you lie dead in the desert. ³⁴For 40 years you will suffer for your sins. (That is one year for each of the 40 days that the men explored the land.) You will know that it is a terrible thing for me to be against you.'

---

[a] **14:18** *forgives* Or "spares".

³⁵"I am the LORD, and I have spoken. And I promise that I will do these things to all these evil people. They have come together against me. So they will all die here in this desert."

INSIGHT

Of the twelve spies, only two, Joshua and Caleb, were confident they could take the promised land. As a result, the children of Israel had to wander in the desert for forty years – until the generation of doubters had died – before they could enter Canaan.

Numbers 14:26–38

³⁶The men Moses sent to explore the new land were the ones who came back complaining about him to all the Israelites. They said that the people were not strong enough to enter that land. ³⁷The men were responsible for spreading the trouble among the Israelites. So the LORD caused a sickness to kill all those men. ³⁸But Joshua son of Nun and Caleb son of Jephunneh were among the men who were sent out to explore the land. They are the only ones who did not get the sickness that caused the others to die.

The People Try to Go Into Canaan

³⁹When Moses told the Israelites this, they were very sad. ⁴⁰Early the next morning the people started to go up to the high hill country. They said, "We have sinned. We are sorry that we did not trust the Lord. We will go to the place that the LORD promised."

⁴¹But Moses said, "Why are you not obeying the LORD's command? You will not be successful! ⁴²Don't go into that land. The LORD is not with you, so your enemies will easily defeat you. ⁴³The Amalekites and Canaanites will fight against you there. You have turned away from the LORD, so he will not be with you when you fight them. And you will all be killed in battle."

⁴⁴But the people did not believe Moses. They went towards the high hill country. But Moses and the Box of the LORD's Agreement did not go with the people. ⁴⁵The Amalekites and the Canaanites living in the hill country came down

and attacked the Israelites and easily defeated them and chased them all the way to Hormah.

Rules About Sacrifices

15 The LORD said to Moses, ²"Speak to the Israelites and tell them this: I am giving you a land to be your home. When you enter that land, ³you must give special gifts to the LORD. Their smell will please the LORD. You will use your cattle, sheep and goats for burnt offerings, sacrifices, special promises, special gifts, fellowship offerings or at your special festivals.

⁴"At the time someone brings their offering, they must also give a grain offering to the LORD. The grain offering will be 1 kilogramme^a of fine flour mixed with 1 litre^b of olive oil. ⁵Each time you offer a lamb as a burnt offering or sacrifice, you must also prepare a litre of wine as a drink offering.

⁶"If you are giving a ram, you must also prepare a grain offering. This grain offering should be 2 kilogrammes^c of fine flour mixed with 1.5 litres^d of olive oil. ⁷And you must prepare 1.5 litres of wine as a drink offering. Its smell will please the LORD.

⁸"You might prepare a young bull as a burnt offering, a sacrifice, a fellowship offering or to keep a special promise to the LORD. ⁹At that time you must also bring a grain offering with the bull. That grain offering should be 3 kilogrammes^e of fine flour mixed with 2 litres^f of olive oil. ¹⁰Also bring 2 litres of wine as a drink offering as a sweet-smelling gift to the LORD. ¹¹Each bull or ram or lamb or young goat that you give must be prepared in this way. ¹²Do this for every one of these animals that you give.

¹³"This is the way every citizen of Israel must give gifts to please the LORD. ¹⁴Foreigners will live among you. If they give gifts to please the LORD, they must offer them the same way you do. ¹⁵The same rules will be for everyone—the Israelites and the foreigners living among you. This law will continue forever. You and the people living among you will be the same before the LORD. ¹⁶This means that you must follow the same laws and the same rules. These laws and rules are for you Israelites and for the other people who are living among you."

¹⁷The LORD said to Moses, ¹⁸"Tell the Israelites this: I am taking you to another land. ¹⁹When you eat the food that grows in that land, you must give part of that food as an offering to the LORD. ²⁰You will gather grain and grind it into flour to make dough for bread. You must give the first

---

^a 15:4 *1 kilogramme* Literally, "¹/₁₀ of an *ephah*".
^b 15:4 *1 litre* Literally, "¹/₄ *hin*".
^c 15:6 *2 kilogrammes* Literally, "²/₁₀ of an *ephah*".
^d 15:6 *1.5 litres* Literally, "¹/₃ *hin*".
^e 15:9 *3 kilogrammes* Literally, "³/₁₀ of an *ephah*".
^f 15:9 *2 litres* Literally, "¹/₂ *hin*".

bread from that flour as a gift to the Lord. It will be like the grain offering that comes from the threshing floor. 21You and all your descendants must give part of the first dough you make from that flour as a gift to the LORD.

22"As you try to obey all the commands that the LORD gave Moses, you might fail and make a mistake. 23The LORD gave you those commands through Moses, and they have been in effect from the day they were given throughout the generations until today. 24If you made this mistake where everyone could see it, the whole community must offer a young bull as a burnt offering, as a sweet-smelling gift to the LORD. You must also offer the grain offering and the drink offering with the bull. And you must also give a male goat as a sin offering.

25"So the priest will make purification for the whole community of Israel, and they will be forgiven for the mistake they made. Since they made the mistake, they must bring a gift and a sin offering to the LORD. 26Then the whole community of Israel and any foreigners among them will be forgiven for the mistake.

27"But if only one person makes a mistake and sins, that person must bring a female goat that is one year old. That goat will be the sin offering. 28The priest will make purification before the LORD for the one who sinned, and that person will be forgiven. 29This law is for everyone who makes a mistake and sins. The same law is for the people born in the family of Israel and for the foreigners living among you.

30"If someone sins and knows they are doing wrong, they are insulting the LORD. They must be separated from their people. The same law applies to citizens of Israel and to foreigners living among you. 31They thought the LORD's word was not important, so they broke his commands. That is why they must be separated from their people—they must bear the responsibility for their guilt."

A Man Works on the Day of Rest

32While the Israelites were in the desert, some of them saw a man gathering firewood on the Sabbath day. 33The people who saw him gathering the wood brought him to Moses and Aaron and the whole community of Israel. 34They guarded the man carefully because they did not know how they should punish him.

35Then the LORD said to Moses, "The man must die. All the people must throw stones at him outside the camp." 36So the people took him outside the camp and killed him with stones. They did this just as the LORD commanded Moses.

A Way to Remember God's Commands

37The LORD said to Moses, 38"Speak to the Israelites. Tell them this: Tie several pieces of thread together and tie them in the corner of your clothes. Put a piece of blue thread in each one of these tassels. You must wear these things now and forever. 39You will be able to look at these tassels and remember all the commands that the LORD has given you. Then you will obey the commands. You will not do wrong by forgetting about the commands and doing the things that your own bodies and eyes want. 40You will remember to obey all my commands. Then you will be God's special people. 41I am the LORD your God. I am the one who brought you out of Egypt. I did this to be your God. I am the LORD your God."

Some Leaders Turn Against Moses

16 Korah, Dathan, Abiram and On turned against Moses. (Korah was the son of Izhar. Izhar was the son of Kohath, and Kohath was the son of Levi. Dathan and Abiram were brothers, the sons of Eliab. And On was the son of Peleth. Dathan, Abiram and On were descendants of Reuben.) 2These four men gathered 250 other men from Israel together and came against Moses. They were leaders who had been chosen by the people. All the people knew them. 3They came as a group to speak against Moses and Aaron and said, "You have gone too far—you are wrong! All the Israelites are holy—the LORD still lives among them. You are making yourselves more important than the rest of the LORD's people."

4When Moses heard this, he bowed his face to the ground to show he was not being proud. 5Then Moses said to Korah and all his followers, "Tomorrow morning the LORD will show who belongs to him. He will show who is holy, and he will bring that man near to him. He will choose him and bring that man near to him. 6So Korah, you and all your followers should do this: 7Tomorrow put fire and incense in some special pans. Then bring those pans before the LORD. He will choose the man who is holy. You Levites have gone too far—you are wrong!"

8Moses also said to Korah, "You Levites, listen to me. 9You should be happy that the God of Israel chose you to be different from the rest of the Israelites. He lets you come near to him to do the special work in the LORD's Holy Tent to help the Israelites worship him. Isn't that enough? 10He brought you Levites near to him to help the priests, but now you are trying to become priests also. 11You and your followers have joined together and turned against the LORD! Did Aaron do anything wrong? No, so why are you complaining against Aaron?"

12Then Moses called Dathan and Abiram, the sons of Eliab. But the two men said, "We will not come! 13You have brought us out of a land filled with many good things.ᵃ You brought us to the desert to kill us. And now you want to show that you have even more power over us. ¹⁴Why should we follow you? You promised to bring us into a new land filled with many good things. But where is it? You have not given us the land with fields and vineyards that you said would be ours. Do you think you can keep on fooling these people? No! We will not come."

¹⁵So Moses became very angry. He said to the LORD, "I have not done anything wrong to these people. I have never taken anything from them—not even a donkey! Don't accept their gifts!"

¹⁶Then Moses said to Korah, "You and all your followers will stand before the LORD tomorrow. Aaron will also be there with you and your followers. ¹⁷Each of you must bring a pan, put incense in it, and present it to the LORD. There will be 250 pans for the leaders and one pan for you and one pan for Aaron."

¹⁸So each man got a pan and put burning incense in it. Then they stood at the entrance of the Meeting Tent. Moses and Aaron also stood there. ¹⁹Korah also gathered all the people together at the entrance of the Meeting Tent. Then the Glory of the LORD appeared to everyone there.

²⁰The LORD said to Moses and Aaron, ²¹"Move away from these men! I want to destroy them now!"

²²But Moses and Aaron bowed to the ground and cried out, "God, you know what people are thinking.ᵇ Please don't be angry with all these people. Only one man really sinned."

²³Then the LORD said to Moses, ²⁴"Tell the people to move away from the tents of Korah, Dathan and Abiram."

²⁵Moses stood and went to Dathan and Abiram. All the leaders of Israel followed him. ²⁶Moses warned the people, "Move away from the tents of these evil men. Don't touch anything that belongs to them! If you do, you will be destroyed because of their sins."

²⁷So the men moved away from the tents of Korah, Dathan and Abiram. Dathan and Abiram went to their tents. They stood outside of their tents with their wives, children and little babies.

²⁸Then Moses said, "I will show you proof that the LORD sent me to do all the things I told you. I will show you that all these things were not my own idea. ²⁹These men will die, but if they die in a normal way—the way people always die—then that will show that the LORD did not really send me. ³⁰But if the LORD causes them to die in a different way, then you will know that these men

have sinned against the LORD. This is the proof: The earth will open and swallow them. They will go down to their grave still alive. And everything that belongs to these men will go down with them."

³¹When Moses finished saying these things, the ground under the men opened. ³²It was as if the earth opened its mouth and swallowed them. All of Korah's men, their families, and everything they owned went down into the earth. ³³They went down into their grave alive. Everything they owned went with them. Then the earth closed over them. They were finished—gone from the camp!

³⁴The Israelites heard the cries of the men being destroyed. So they all ran in different directions and said, "The earth will swallow us too!"

³⁵Then a fire came from the LORD and destroyed the 250 men who were offering the incense.

³⁶The LORD said to Moses, ³⁷⁻³⁸"Tell Eleazar son of Aaron the priest to get all the incense pans from the fire. Tell him to scatter the coals and ashes. These men sinned against me, and their sin cost them their lives. But the incense pans are still holy. The pans became holy when people gave them to the LORD. Hammer the pans into flat sheets. Use the metal sheets to cover the altar. This will be a warning to all the Israelites."

³⁹So Eleazar the priest gathered together all the bronze pans that the men had brought. These men had all been burned up, but the pans were still there. Then Eleazar told some men to hammer the pans into flat metal. Then he put the metal sheets on the altar. ⁴⁰He did this the way the LORD commanded him through Moses. This was a sign to help the Israelites remember that only someone from the family of Aaron should burn incense before the LORD. Any other person who burns incense before the Lord will die like Korah and his followers.

Aaron Saves the People

⁴¹The next day all the Israelites complained against Moses and Aaron. They said, "You killed the LORD's people."

⁴²Moses and Aaron were standing at the entrance of the Meeting Tent. The people gathered together at that place to complain against Moses and Aaron. But when they looked towards the Meeting Tent, the cloud covered it and the Glory of the LORD appeared there. ⁴³Then Moses and Aaron went to the front of the Meeting Tent.

⁴⁴The LORD said to Moses, ⁴⁵"Move away from these people so that I can destroy them now." So

---

ᵃ **16:13 land . . . things** Literally, "land flowing with milk and honey".
ᵇ **16:22 God, . . . thinking** Literally, "God, the God of the spirits of all people."

Moses and Aaron bowed with their faces to the ground.

⁴⁶Then Moses said to Aaron, "Get your bronze pan and some fire from the altar. Then put incense in it. Hurry to the people and do the things that will make them pure. The LORD is angry with them. The trouble has already started."

⁴⁷⁻⁴⁸So Aaron got the incense and the fire, and he ran to the middle of the people. But the sickness had already started among them. So Aaron stood between the dead and those who were still alive. He did as Moses said, and the sickness stopped there. ⁴⁹But 14,700 people died from that sickness—and that is not counting the people who died because of Korah. ⁵⁰So the terrible sickness was stopped, and Aaron went back to Moses at the entrance of the Meeting Tent.

God Proves Aaron Is the High Priest

17 The LORD said to Moses, ²"Speak to the Israelites. Get twelve wooden walking sticks from them. Get one from the leader of each of the twelve tribes. Write the name of each man on his walking stick. ³On the stick from Levi, write Aaron's name. There must be one stick for the head of each of the twelve tribes. ⁴Put these walking sticks in the Meeting Tent in front of the Box of the Agreement. This is the place where I meet with you. ⁵I will choose one man to be the true priest. You will know which man I choose because his walking stick will begin to grow new leaves. In this way I will stop the people from always complaining against you and me."

⁶So Moses spoke to the Israelites. Each of the leaders gave him a walking stick. There were twelve walking sticks. There was one stick from each leader of each tribe. One of the walking sticks belonged to Aaron. ⁷Moses put the walking sticks before the LORD in the Tent of the Agreement.

⁸The next day Moses entered the Tent. He saw that Aaron's walking stick, the stick from the family of Levi, was the one that had grown new leaves. That walking stick had even grown branches and made almonds. ⁹So Moses brought out all the sticks from the LORD's place. He showed the walking sticks to the Israelites. They all looked at the sticks, and each man took his own stick back.

¹⁰Then the LORD said to Moses, "Put Aaron's walking stick back in front of the Box that holds the Agreement.ᵃ This will be a warning for these people who are always turning against me. This will stop their complaining against me so that I will not destroy them." ¹¹So Moses did what the LORD commanded him.

¹²The Israelites said to Moses, "We know that we will die! We are lost! We will all be destroyed! ¹³Anyone who even comes near the LORD's holy place will die. Is it true that we will all die?"

The Work of the Priests and Levites

18 The LORD said to Aaron, "You, your sons and all the people in your father's family must bear the responsibility for any wrong that is done against the holy place or against the priests. ²To prevent that from happening, you must bring the rest of the men from the tribe of Levi to join you. These Levites will help you and your sons do your work in the Tent of the Agreement. ³These Levites will be under your control. They will do all the work that needs to be done in the Tent. But they must not go near the things in the Holy Place or the altar. If they do, they will die—and you also will die. ⁴They will join you and work with you. They will be responsible for caring for the Meeting Tent. All the work that must be done in the Tent will be done by them. No one else may come near the place where you are.

⁵"You are responsible for caring for the holy place and the altar. I don't want to become angry with the Israelites again. ⁶I myself chose the Levites from among all the Israelites. They are as a gift to you. I gave them to you to serve the LORD and work in the Meeting Tent. ⁷But, Aaron, only you and your sons may serve as priests. You are the only ones who can go near the altar or behind the curtain into the Most Holy Place. I am giving you a gift—your service as a priest. Anyone else who tries to come too close must be killed."

⁸Then the LORD said to Aaron, "I myself gave you responsibility over all the special gifts people give to me. All the holy gifts that the Israelites give to me, I give to you. You and your sons can share in these gifts. They will always belong to you. ⁹The people will bring gifts, grain offerings, sin offerings and guilt offerings. These offerings are most holy. Your share in the most holy offerings will come from the parts that are not burned. All these things will be for you and your sons. ¹⁰Eat these things only in a very holy place. Every male in your family may eat them, but you must remember that these offerings are holy.

¹¹"The Israelites will bring special gifts that you will lift up to me. I give these gifts to you and your sons and daughters. That is your share. Everyone in your family who is clean will be able to eat it.

¹²"And I give you all the best olive oil and all the best new wine and grain. These are the things that the Israelites give to me, the LORD. These are the first things that they gather in their harvest.

ᵃ **17:10** *Box that holds the Agreement* Literally, "Testimony". See "AGREEMENT" in the Word List.

¹³When the people gather a harvest, they bring all the first things to the LORD. So these things I will give to you. And everyone in your family who is clean may eat it.

¹⁴"Anything in Israel that is a special gift to God[a] belongs to you.

¹⁵"A woman's first baby and an animal's first baby must be given to the LORD. That baby will belong to you. If the firstborn animal is unclean, then it must be bought back. If the baby is a child, that child must be bought back. ¹⁶They must make the payment when the baby is one month old. The cost will be 5 pieces[b] of silver. You must use the official measure to weigh this silver. Each piece of silver by the official measure is 11.5 grammes.[c]

¹⁷"But you must not make a payment for the firstborn cow, sheep or goat. These animals are holy. Sprinkle their blood on the altar and burn their fat as a sweet-smelling gift to the LORD. ¹⁸But the meat from these animals will be yours. And also the breast that was lifted up to the Lord will be yours. And the right thigh from other offerings will be yours. ¹⁹I, the LORD, give you everything that the people offer as holy gifts. This is your share. I give it to you and your sons and daughters. This law will continue forever. It is an agreement with the LORD that cannot be broken.[d] I make this promise to you and to your descendants."

²⁰The LORD also said to Aaron, "You will not get any of the land. And you will not own anything that the other people own. I myself will be yours. The Israelites will get the land that I promised, but I am my gift to you.

²¹"The Israelites will give one-tenth of everything they have. So I give that one-tenth to the Levites. This is their payment for the work that they do while they serve at the Meeting Tent. ²²But the other Israelites must never go near that Meeting Tent. If they do, they must be put to death! ²³The Levites will do the work of caring for the Meeting Tent. They must bear the responsibility for anything done against it. This is a law that will continue forever. The Levites will not get any of the land that I promised to the other Israelites. ²⁴But the Israelites will give one-tenth of everything they have to the LORD, and I will give that one-tenth to the Levites. That is why I said these words about the Levites: They will not get the land that I promised the Israelites."

²⁵The LORD said to Moses, ²⁶"Speak to the Levites and tell them: The Israelites will give one-tenth of everything they own to the LORD. That one-tenth will belong to the Levites. But you must give one-tenth of that to the Lord as your offering. ²⁷That tenth will be your offering to the Lord. It will be like grain from your own threshing floor or wine from your own winepress. ²⁸In this way you will also give an offering to the LORD just as the other Israelites do. You will get the one-tenth that the Israelites give to the LORD, and then you will give one-tenth of that to Aaron the priest. ²⁹When the Israelites give you one-tenth of everything that they own, then you must give the best and the holiest part of these things as your gift to the LORD.

³⁰"Moses, tell this to the Levites: When you give the best part of what you receive to the Lord, it will be the same as grain from your own threshing floor and wine from your own winepress. ³¹You and your families can eat all that is left. This is your payment for the work you do in the Meeting Tent. ³²And if you always give the best part of it to the Lord, you will never be guilty. You will always remember that these gifts are the holy offerings from the Israelites. And you will not die."

The Ashes of the Red Cow

19 The LORD spoke to Moses and Aaron. He said, ²"These are the laws from the teachings that the LORD gave to the Israelites. Get a red cow that has nothing wrong with it. That cow must not have any bruises. And it must never have worn a yoke. ³Give that cow to Eleazar, and he will take it outside the camp and kill it there. ⁴Then Eleazar the priest must put some of its blood on his finger and sprinkle some of the blood towards the Holy Tent. He must do this seven times. ⁵Then the whole cow must be burned in front of him; the skin, the meat, the blood and the intestines must all be burned. ⁶Then the priest must take a cedar stick, a hyssop branch and some red string. He must throw these things into the fire where the cow is burning. ⁷Then the priest must wash himself and his clothes with water. Then he must come back into the camp. He will be unclean until evening. ⁸The man who burns that cow must wash himself and his clothes in water. He will be unclean until evening.

⁹"Then someone who is clean will collect the ashes from the cow and put them in a clean place outside the camp. These ashes will be used when someone must keep a special ceremony to

---

[a] **18:14** *special gift to God* Anything offered to God that could not be bought back. See Lev. 27:28–29.
[b] **18:16** *5 pieces* Literally, "5 *shekels*".
[c] **18:16** *11.5 grammes* Literally, "20 *gerahs*".
[d] **18:19** *It is an agreement . . . broken* Literally, "It is an eternal, salt agreement before the LORD."

become clean. These ashes will also be used to remove a person's sins.

¹⁰"The man who collected the cow's ashes must wash his clothes. He will be unclean until evening.

"This rule will continue forever. This rule is for the citizens of Israel and for the foreigners living with you. ¹¹Those who touch a dead body will be unclean for seven days. ¹²They must wash themselves with the special water on the third day and again on the seventh day. If they don't do this, they will remain unclean. ¹³Those who touch the body of someone who has died are unclean. If they stay unclean and then go to the LORD's Holy Tent, they make it unclean. So they must be separated from the Israelites. Because the special water was not thrown on them, they remain unclean.

¹⁴"This is the rule about those who die in their tents: If someone dies in the tent, everyone in the tent will be unclean for seven days. ¹⁵And every jar or pot without a lid becomes unclean. ¹⁶If there is a dead body out in a field, whether the person died in battle or for some other reason, whoever touches that dead body, or its bones, or even its grave will be unclean for seven days.

¹⁷"If you have become unclean, someone must use the ashes from the burned cow to make you clean again. He must pour fresh water*ᵃ* over the ashes into a jar. ¹⁸And then someone who is clean must take a hyssop branch and dip it into the water. He must sprinkle it over the tent, the dishes, and any people who were in the tent. The same must be done for anyone who touches a dead body, its bones or even a grave.

¹⁹"The one who is clean must sprinkle this water on you on the third day and again on the seventh day to make you clean. Then you must wash your clothes and bathe yourself in water, and that evening you will be clean.

²⁰"Whoever becomes unclean and does not make themselves clean again must be separated from the community. If they are not sprinkled with the special water for cleansing, they remain unclean and will be guilty of making the LORD's Holy Tent unclean. ²¹This rule will never change. And whoever sprinkled the special water must also wash his clothes. And anyone else who touches that water will be unclean until evening. ²²And if an unclean person touches anything, it becomes unclean, and anyone else who touches it will be unclean until evening."

Miriam Dies

20 The Israelites arrived at the desert of Zin in the first month of the year. The people stayed at Kadesh. Miriam died and was buried there.

Moses Makes a Mistake

²There was not enough water for the people at that place. So the people met together to complain against Moses and Aaron. ³The people argued with Moses and said, "Maybe we should have died in front of the LORD like our brothers did. ⁴Why did you bring the LORD's people into this desert? Do you want us and our animals to die here? ⁵Why did you bring us from Egypt? Why did you bring us to this bad place? There is no grain. There are no figs, grapes or pomegranates, and there is no water to drink."

⁶So Moses and Aaron left the crowd of people and went to the entrance of the Meeting Tent. They bowed down to the ground, and the Glory of the LORD appeared to them.

⁷The LORD spoke to Moses and said, ⁸"Get the special walking stick. Take your brother Aaron and the crowd of people and go to that rock. Speak to the rock in front of the people. Then water will flow from the rock, and you can give that water to the people and to their animals."

⁹The walking stick was in the Holy Tent, in front of the LORD. Moses took the walking stick as the Lord said. ¹⁰Moses and Aaron told the people to meet together in front of the rock. Then Moses said, "You people are always complaining. Now listen to me. I will cause water to flow from this rock." ¹¹Moses lifted his arm and hit the rock twice. Water began flowing from the rock, and the people and their animals drank that water.

¹²But the LORD said to Moses and Aaron, "You did not trust me enough to honour me and show the people that I am holy. You did not show the Israelites that the power to make the water came from me. So you will not lead the people into the land that I have given them."

¹³This place was called the waters of Meribah.*ᵇ* This is where the Israelites argued with the LORD and where he showed them that he was holy.

Edom Will Not Let Israel Pass

¹⁴While Moses was at Kadesh, he sent some men with a message to the king of Edom. The message said,

"This is what your brothers, the Israelites, say to you: You know about all the troubles we have had. ¹⁵Many years ago our ancestors went down into Egypt, and we lived there for many years. The people of Egypt were cruel to us. ¹⁶But we asked the LORD for help,

---

ᵃ **19:17** *fresh water* Literally, "living water". This means fresh, flowing water.
ᵇ **20:13** *Meribah* This name means "argument" or "rebellion".

and he heard us and sent an angel to help us. The Lord has brought us out of Egypt.

"Now we are here at Kadesh, where your land begins. [17]Please let us travel through your country. We will not travel through any fields or vineyards. We will not drink water from any of your wells. We will travel only along King's Road. We will not leave that road to the right or to the left. We will stay on the road until we have travelled through your country."

[18]But the king of Edom answered, "You may not travel through our land. If you try to travel through our land, we will come and fight you with swords."

[19]The Israelites answered, "We will travel along the main road. If our animals drink any of your water, we will pay you for it. We only want to walk through your country. We don't want to take it for ourselves."

[20]But again the king of Edom answered, "We will not allow you to come through our country." Then the king of Edom gathered a large and powerful army and went out to fight against the Israelites. [21]The king of Edom refused to let the Israelites travel through his country, so the Israelites turned around and went another way.

Aaron Dies

[22]All the Israelites travelled from Kadesh to Mount Hor. [23]Mount Hor was near the border of Edom. The LORD said to Moses and Aaron, [24]"It is time for Aaron to die and go to be with his ancestors. Aaron will not enter the land that I promised to the Israelites. Moses, I say this to you because both you and Aaron did not fully obey the command I gave you at the waters of Meribah.

[25]"Now, bring Aaron and his son Eleazar up to Mount Hor. [26]Take Aaron's special clothes from him and put these clothes on his son Eleazar. Aaron will die there on the mountain. And he will go to be with his ancestors."

[27]Moses obeyed the LORD's command. Moses, Aaron and Eleazar went up on Mount Hor. All the Israelites watched them go. [28]Moses removed Aaron's special clothes and put them on Aaron's son Eleazar. Then Aaron died there on top of the mountain. Moses and Eleazar came back down the mountain. [29]All the Israelites learned that Aaron was dead. So everyone in Israel mourned for 30 days.

War With the Canaanites

21 The Canaanite king of Arad lived in the Negev. He heard that the Israelites were coming on the road to Atharim, so the king went out and attacked the Israelites. Arad captured some of the people and made them prisoners. [2]Then the Israelites made a special promise to the LORD: "Please help us defeat these people. If you do this, we will give their cities to you. We will totally destroy them."

[3]The LORD listened to the Israelites and helped them defeat the Canaanites. They completely destroyed the Canaanites and their cities. So that place was named Hormah.[a]

The Bronze Snake

[4]The Israelites left Mount Hor and travelled on the road that goes to the Red Sea. They did this to go around the country of Edom. But the people became impatient. [5]They began complaining against God and Moses. The people said, "Why did you bring us out of Egypt? We will die here in the desert! There is no bread and no water! And we hate this terrible food!"

[6]So the LORD sent poisonous snakes among the people. The snakes bit the people, and many of the Israelites died. [7]The people came to Moses and said, "We know that we sinned when we spoke against the LORD and against you. Pray to the LORD. Ask him to take away these snakes." So Moses prayed for them.

[8]The LORD said to Moses, "Make a bronze snake and put it on a pole. If anyone is bitten by a snake, that person should look at the bronze snake on the pole. Then that person will not die." [9]So Moses made a bronze snake and put it on a pole. Then when a snake bit anyone, that person looked at the bronze snake on the pole and lived.

The Journey to Moab

[10]The Israelites left that place and camped at Oboth. [11]Then they left Oboth and camped at Iye Abarim in the desert east of Moab. [12]They left that place and camped in Zered Valley. [13]Then they moved and camped opposite the Arnon River in the desert. This river started at the Ammonite border. The valley was the border between Moab and the Amorites. [14]That is why these words are written in the *Book of the Wars of the LORD*:

"Waheb in Suphah, and the Valleys of the Arnon, [15]and the hills by the valleys that lead to the town of Ar. These places are at the border of Moab."

[16]The Israelites left that place and travelled to Beer.[b] There is a well in Beer, where the LORD said to Moses, "Bring the people together here, and I

---

[a] 21:3 *Hormah* This name means "completely destroyed" or "a gift given totally to God". See Lev. 27:28–29.
[b] 21:16 *Beer* This Hebrew name means "well".

will give them water." 17Then the Israelites sang this song:

"Well, flow with water!
   Sing about it!
18This is the well that princes dug.
   It was opened up by our great leaders,
   using their staffs and walking sticks."

From the desert the Israelites travelled to the town of Mattanah. 19And from Mattanah they went to Nahaliel. Then from Nahaliel they went to Bamoth. 20From Bamoth they travelled to the Valley of Moab. In this place the top of the Pisgah Mountain looks over the desert.

Sihon and Og

21The Israelites sent some men to King Sihon of the Amorites. The men said to the king,

22"Allow us to travel through your country.
We will not go through any field or vineyard.
We will not drink water from any of your
   wells. We will travel only along King's Road.
We will stay on that road until we have
   travelled through your country."

23But King Sihon would not allow the Israelites to travel through his country. He gathered together his army and marched out to the desert to fight against the Israelites. The king's army fought against the Israelites at Jahaz. 24But the Israelites defeated the king and took his land from the Arnon River to the Jabbok River. The Israelites took the land as far as the Ammonite border. They stopped at that border because it was strongly defended by the Ammonites. 25Israel took all the Amorite cities and began living in them. They even defeated the city of Heshbon and all the small towns around it. 26Heshbon was the city where Sihon, the Amorite king, lived. In the past Sihon had fought with the king of Moab. Sihon had taken the land as far as the Arnon River. 27That is why the singers sing this song:

"Go in and rebuild Heshbon!
   Make Sihon's city strong.
28A fire began in Heshbon.
   That fire began in Sihon's city.
The fire destroyed Ar in Moab.
   It burned the hills above Arnon River.
29It is bad for you, Moab!
   Chemosh, your god, has left you in ruins!
He has let Sihon, king of the Amorites,
   chase away your men
   and take your women as prisoners.

30But we defeated those Amorites.
   We destroyed their towns from Heshbon to
      Dibon,
   from Nashim to Nophah, near Medeba."

31So the Israelites made their camp in the land of the Amorites. 32Moses sent some men to look at the town of Jazer. Then the Israelites captured that town and the small towns that were around it. They forced the Amorites who were living there to leave.

33Then the Israelites travelled on the road towards Bashan. King Og of Bashan got his army and marched out to meet the Israelites. He fought against them at Edrei. 34But the LORD said to Moses, "Don't be afraid of that king. I will allow you to defeat him. You will take his whole army and all his land. Do the same to him as you did to Sihon, the Amorite king who lived in Heshbon." 35So the Israelites defeated Og and his army. They killed him, his sons, and all his army. Then the Israelites took all his land.

Balaam and the King of Moab

22 Then the Israelites travelled to the Jordan Valley in Moab. They camped near the Jordan River, opposite Jericho.

2-3Balak son of Zippor saw everything the Israelites had done to the Amorites. The king of Moab was very frightened of the Israelites because there were so many of them. He was very afraid. 4The king of Moab said to the leaders of Midian, "This large group of people will destroy everything around us, the way an ox eats all the grass in a field."

Balak son of Zippor was the king of Moab at this time. 5He sent some men to Balaam son of Beor. Balaam was at Pethor, near the Euphrates River. This was where Balaam's people lived.a This was Balak's message:

"A new nation of people has come out of
Egypt. There are so many people that they
cover all the land. They have camped next to
me. 6Come and help me. These people are too
powerful for me. I know that you have great
power. If you bless people, good things happen
to them. And if you curse people, bad things
happen to them. So come and curse these
people. Maybe then I will be able to defeat
them and force them to leave my country."

7The leaders of Moab and Midian left. They went to talk to Balaam. They carried with them

---

a **22:5 This . . . lived** Or "This was the land of the Ammonites."

money to pay him for his service.[a] Then they told him what Balak had said.

[8]Balaam said to them, "Stay here for the night. I will talk to the LORD and tell you the answer he gives me." So the leaders of Moab stayed there with Balaam that night.

[9]God came to Balaam and asked, "Who are these men with you?"

[10]Balaam said to God, "The king of Moab, Balak son of Zippor, sent them to give me a message. [11]This is the message: A new nation of people has come out of Egypt. There are so many people that they cover the land. So come and curse these people. Then maybe I will be able to fight them and force them to leave my land."

[12]But God said to Balaam, "Don't go with them. You must not curse those people. They are my people."

[13]The next morning Balaam got up and said to leaders from Balak, "Go back to your own country. The LORD will not let me go with you."

[14]So the leaders of Moab went back to Balak and told him this. They said, "Balaam refused to come with us."

[15]So Balak sent other leaders to Balaam. This time he sent many more than the first time. And these leaders were much more important than the first ones he sent. [16]They went to Balaam and said, "This is what Balak son of Zippor says to you: Please don't let anything stop you from coming. [17]I will pay you very well,[b] and I will do whatever you ask. Come and curse these people for me."

[18]Balaam gave Balak's officials his answer. He said, "I must obey the LORD my God. I cannot do anything, great or small, against his command. Even if King Balak offers to give me his beautiful home filled with silver and gold, I will not do anything against the Lord's command. [19]But you can stay here tonight like the other men did, and during the night I will learn what the LORD wants to tell me."

[20]That night, God came to Balaam. God said, "These men have come again to ask you to go with them. So you can go with them. But do only what I tell you to do."

Balaam and His Donkey

[21]The next morning, Balaam got up, put a saddle on his donkey, and went with the Moabite leaders. [22]Balaam was riding on his donkey. Two of his servants were with him. While Balaam was travelling, God became angry. So the angel of the LORD stood in the road in front of Balaam to stop[c] him.

[23]When Balaam's donkey saw the angel of the LORD standing in the road with a sword in his hand, the donkey turned from the road and went into the field. Balaam could not see the angel, so he was very angry at the donkey. He hit the donkey and forced it to go back on the road.

[24]Later, the angel of the LORD stood at a place where the road became narrow. This was between two vineyards. There were walls on both sides of the road. [25]Again the donkey saw the angel of the LORD. So the donkey walked very close to one wall. This crushed Balaam's foot against the wall. So Balaam hit his donkey again.

[26]Later, the angel of the LORD stood at another place where the road became narrow. There was no place where the donkey could go around him. It could not turn to the left or to the right. [27]The donkey saw the angel of the LORD. So the donkey lay down with Balaam sitting on top of it. Balaam was very angry at the donkey. So he hit it with his walking stick.

[28]Then the LORD caused the donkey to speak. The donkey said to Balaam, "Why are you angry at me? What have I done to you? You have hit me three times!"

INSIGHT

Apart from the serpent in the garden of Eden, this is the only reference to an animal speaking in the entire Bible. Which is more surprising – the donkey talking or the fact that Balaam talks back as if this was an everyday occurrence?
Numbers 22:28–30

[29]Balaam answered the donkey, "You have made me look foolish. If I had a sword in my hand, I would kill you right now!"

[30]But the donkey said to Balaam, "Look, I am your donkey. You have ridden me for so many years. And you know that I have never done this to you before!"

"That is true," Balaam said.

[31]Then the LORD allowed Balaam to see the angel. The LORD's angel was standing in the road,

---

[a] **22:7 for his service** Or "for the things he needed to make curses". In ancient times, when people asked bad things to happen to other people, they often wrote the curses on special bowls and used them in ceremonies. They did this to try to force these bad things to happen. See Deut. 18:10.

[b] **22:17 I will pay you very much** Or "I will honour you very much."

[c] **22:22 stop** Or "oppose" or "accuse". Also in verse 32.

holding a sword in his hand. Balaam bowed low to the ground. ³²Then the angel of the LORD asked Balaam, "Why did you hit your donkey three times? I am the one who came to stop you. But just in time,^a ³³your donkey saw me and turned away from me. That happened three times. If the donkey had not turned away, I probably would have killed you already. And I would have let your donkey live."

³⁴Then Balaam said to the angel of the LORD, "I have sinned. I did not know that you were standing in the road. If I am doing wrong, I will go back home."

³⁵Then the angel of the LORD said to Balaam, "No, you can go with these men. But be careful. Speak only the words that I will tell you to say." So Balaam went with the leaders that Balak had sent.

³⁶Balak heard that Balaam was coming. So Balak went out to meet him at the Moabite town^b near the Arnon River. This was at the northern border of his country. ³⁷When Balak saw Balaam, he said to him, "I asked you before to come. I told you it was very important. Why didn't you come to me? Did you think I might not be able to pay you?"

³⁸Balaam answered, "Well, I am here now. I came, but I might not be able to do what you asked. I can only say the words God tells me to say."

³⁹Then Balaam went with Balak to Kiriath Huzoth. ⁴⁰Balak killed some cattle and some sheep as his sacrifice. He gave some of the meat to Balaam and some to the leaders who were with him.

⁴¹The next morning Balak took Balaam to the town of Bamoth Baal. From there they could see part of the Israelite camp.

Balaam's First Message

23 Balaam said, "Build seven altars here. And prepare seven bulls and seven rams for me." ²Balak did what Balaam asked. Then Balak and Balaam killed a ram and a bull on each of the altars.

³Then Balaam said to Balak, "Stay here near this altar. I will go to another place. Then the LORD will come to me, and he will tell me what I must say." Then Balaam went away to a higher place.

⁴God came to Balaam at that place, and Balaam said, "I have prepared seven altars. And I have killed a bull and a ram as a sacrifice on each altar."

⁵Then the LORD gave Balaam a message for Balak and said, "Go back to Balak and say the things that I have given you to say."

⁶So Balaam went back to Balak. Balak was still standing near the altar, and all the leaders of Moab were standing there with them. ⁷Then Balaam spoke, and this was his message:

"Balak, the king of Moab,
    brought me here from the eastern
        mountains of Aram.
Balak said to me,
    'Come, curse Jacob for me.
    Come, speak against the Israelites.'
⁸But God is not against them,
    so I cannot speak against them either!
The LORD has not asked for bad things to
        happen to these people.
    So I cannot do that either.
⁹I see these people from the mountain.
    I see them from the high hills.
They live alone.
    They are not part of another nation.
¹⁰Counting Jacob's people is like counting
        dust!
    No one could count even a fourth of the
        Israelites.
When I die, may people say such good things
        about me.
    Let my life end as happily as theirs!"

¹¹Balak said to Balaam, "What have you done to me? I brought you here to curse my enemies, but you have blessed them!"

¹²But Balaam answered, "I must say the things that the LORD tells me to say."

¹³Then Balak said to him, "So come with me to another place. At that place you can see more of these people. You cannot see all of them—you can only see part of them. Maybe from that place you can curse them for me." ¹⁴So Balak led Balaam to Watchmen Hills.^c This was on top of Mount Pisgah. There Balak built seven altars and killed a bull and a ram on each altar as a sacrifice.

¹⁵Then Balaam said to Balak, "Stay here by this altar while I go and meet with God over there."

¹⁶So the LORD came to Balaam and told Balaam what to say. Then he told Balaam to go back to Balak and say these things. ¹⁷So Balaam went to Balak. Balak was still standing near the altar. The leaders of Moab were there with him. Balak saw Balaam coming and said, "What did the LORD say?"

---

^a **22:32** *But just in time* Or "You should not be going this way", or "You are not doing right." The Hebrew text is not clear.
^b **22:36** *Moabite town* Or possibly, "Ar Moab".
^c **23:14** *Watchmen Hills* Or "the fields of Zophim".

Balaam's Second Message

18Then Balaam said this:

"Stand up, Balak, and listen to me.
  Hear me, Balak son of Zippor.
19God is not a man;
  he will not lie.
God is not a human being;
  his decisions will not change.
If he says he will do something,
  then he will do it.
If he makes a promise,
  then he will do what he promised.
20He told me to bless them.
  He blessed them, so I cannot change that.
21God saw no wrong in the people of Jacob.
  He saw no sin in the Israelites.
The LORD their God is with them,
  The Great King is with them!
22God brought them out of Egypt.
  They are as strong as a wild ox.
23There is no power that can defeat the people
    of Jacob.
  There is no magic that can stop the
    Israelites.
People will say this about Jacob and the
    Israelites
  'Look at the great things God did!'a
24The people are as strong as lions,
  and they fight like lions.
And a lion will not rest until it eats what it has
    caught,
  until it drinks the blood of what it has
    killed."

25Then Balak said to Balaam, "You didn't ask for good things to happen to these people, but you didn't ask for bad things to happen to them either!"

26Balaam answered, "I told you before that I can only say what the LORD tells me to say."

27Then Balak said to Balaam, "So come with me to another place. Maybe God will be pleased and will allow you to curse them from that place." 28So Balak led Balaam to the top of Mount Peor, which looks out over the desert.

29Balaam said, "Build seven altars here. Then prepare seven bulls and seven rams for the altars." 30Balak did what Balaam asked. Balak offered the bulls and rams on the altars.

Balaam's Third Message

24 Balaam saw that the LORD wanted to bless Israel, so he did not try to change that by using any kind of magic. But Balaam turned and looked towards the desert. 2He saw all the Israelites with each tribe in a separate camp. Then the Spirit of God came on him, 3and he gave this message:

"This message is from Balaam son of Beor.
  I am speaking about things I see clearly.
4These are the words I heard from God.
  I saw what God All-Powerfulb showed me.
  I humbly tell what I clearly see.

5"People of Jacob, your tents are beautiful!
  Israelites, your homes are beautiful!
6You are like rows of palm trees planted by the
    streams.
  You are like gardens growing by the rivers.
You are like sweet-smelling bushes planted by
    the LORD.
  You are like cedar trees growing by the
    water.
7You will always have enough water,
  enough water for your seeds to grow.
Your king will be greater than King Agag.
  Your kingdom will be very great.

8"God brought them out of Egypt.
  They are as strong as a wild ox.
They will defeat all their enemies.
  They will break their bones and shatter
    their arrows.
9Israel is like a lion,
  curled up and lying down.
Yes, they are like a young lion,
  and no one wants to wake him!
Anyone who blesses you will be blessed.
  And anyone who curses you will have great
    troubles."

10When Balak heard this, he angrily struck his fist against his hand and said to Balaam, "I called you to come and curse my enemies. But you have blessed them. You have blessed them three times. 11Now leave and go home! I told you that I would give you a very good payment, but the LORD has caused you to lose your reward."

12Balaam said to Balak, "You sent men to ask me to come. Don't you remember what I told them? I said, 13'Even if Balak gives me his most beautiful house filled with silver and gold, I can still say only what the LORD commands me to say. I cannot do anything myself, good or bad. I must say what the LORD commands.' 14Now I am going back to my own people. But I will give you this warning. I will tell you what these Israelites will do to you and your people in the future."

---

a **23:23** Or "There is no fortune-telling in Jacob, no magic in Israel. God tells them immediately what he plans to do."
b **24:4 God All-Powerful** Hebrew, "El Shaddai". Also in verse 16.

Balaam's Last Message

¹⁵Then Balaam gave this message:

"This message is from Balaam son of Beor.
I am speaking about things I see clearly.
¹⁶I heard this message from God.
I learned what God Most High taught me.
I saw what God All-Powerful showed me.
I humbly tell what I clearly see.

¹⁷"I see him coming, but not now.
I see him coming, but not soon.
A star will come from the family of Jacob.
A new ruler will come from the Israelites.
He will smash the heads of the Moabites
and crush the heads of all the sons of
Sheth.^a
¹⁸Israel will grow strong!
He will get the land of Edom.
He will get the land of Seir,^b his enemy.

¹⁹"A new ruler will come from the family of
Jacob.
That ruler will destroy the people left alive
in that city."

²⁰Then Balaam saw the Amalekites and said
this:

"Amalek is the strongest of all nations,
but even Amalek will be destroyed!"

²¹Then Balaam saw the Kenites and said this:

"You believe your country is safe,
like a bird's nest high on a mountain.
²²But you Kenites will be destroyed
when Assyria takes you away as prisoners."

²³Then Balaam said this:

"No one can live when God does this.
²⁴ Ships will come from Cyprus.
They will defeat Assyria and Eber,^c
but those ships will also be destroyed."

²⁵Then Balaam got up and went back home,
and Balak went his own way.

Israel at Peor

25 While the Israelites were camped near
Acacia, the men committed sexual sins^d
with Moabite women. ²⁻³The Moabite women
invited the men to come and join in their sacrifices
to their false gods. So the Israelites joined in
worshipping these false gods—they ate the
sacrifices and worshipped these gods. There the
Israelites began worshipping the false god, Baal of
Peor. And the LORD became very angry with them.
⁴The LORD said to Moses, "Get all the leaders of
these people. Then kill them so that all the people
can see.^e Lay their bodies before the LORD. Then
the LORD will not show his anger against all the
Israelites."

⁵So Moses said to Israel's judges, "Each of you
must find the men in your tribe who have led
people to worship the false god, Baal of Peor.
Then you must kill these men."

⁶At the time Moses and all the leaders of Israel
were gathered together at the entrance to the
Meeting Tent. An Israelite man brought a
Midianite woman home to his brothers.^f He did
this where Moses and all the leaders could see.
Moses and the leaders were very sad. ⁷Phinehas
was the son of Eleazar and the grandson of Aaron
the priest. Phinehas saw this man bring the
woman into camp. So he left the meeting and
got his spear. ⁸He followed the Israelite into the
tent. Then he used the spear to kill the Israelite
man and the Midianite woman in her tent.^g
He pushed the spear through both of their
bodies. At that time there was a great sickness
among the Israelites. But when Phinehas killed
these two people, the sickness stopped. ⁹A total
of 24,000 people died from that sickness.

¹⁰The LORD said to Moses, ¹¹"I was so angry
with the Israelites that I wanted to kill them. But
Phinehas, son of Eleazar and grandson of Aaron
the priest, has saved them from my anger. He
did this by showing that he feels strongly, just as
I do, that my people must worship only me. ¹²Tell
Phinehas that I am making a peace agreement
with him. ¹³This is the agreement: He and his
whole family who live after him will always be
priests, because he had strong feelings for his
God. And he did what was needed to make the
Israelites pure."

---

^a **24:17 sons of Sheth** Or "Seth." Seth was Adam's third son. This might be like the phrases "son of Man" (Adam) and "son of
Enosh" and mean simply "all these people".
^b **24:18 Seir** Another name for Edom.
^c **24:24 Eber** This might mean the people living west of the Euphrates River, or it might mean the "Hebrews", the descendants of
Eber. See Gen. 10:21.
^d **25:1 sexual sins** Sexual sin was often connected with temples for false gods. So this can mean that the men were unfaithful to
their wives and also that they were unfaithful to God by going to their temples.
^e **25:4 so that all the people can see** Literally, "before the sun".
^f **25:6 brothers** Or "family".
^g **25:8 her tent** This was probably a special tent that showed this woman was a prostitute serving the false god, Baal of Peor.

[14] The Israelite man who was killed with the Midianite woman was named Zimri son of Salu. He was the leader of a family in the tribe of Simeon. [15] And the name of the Midianite woman who was killed was Cozbi.[a] She was the daughter of Zur. Zur was the head of a family and leader of a Midianite tribe.

[16] The LORD said to Moses, [17] "The Midianites are your enemies. You must kill them. [18] They have already made you their enemies. They tricked you at Peor. And they tricked you with the woman named Cozbi. She was the daughter of a Midianite leader, but she was killed when the sickness came to the Israelites. That sickness was caused because the people were tricked into worshipping the false god Baal of Peor."

The People Are Counted

26 After the great sickness, the LORD spoke to Moses and Eleazar son of Aaron the priest. [2] He said, "Count the Israelites. Count all the men who are 20 years old or older and list them by families. These are the men who are able to serve in the army of Israel."

[3] At this time the people were camped in the Jordan Valley in Moab. This was near the Jordan River, opposite Jericho. So Moses and Eleazar the priest spoke to the people. They said, [4] "You must count every man who is 20 years old or older. The LORD gave Moses this command."

Here is the list of the Israelites who came out of Egypt:

[5] These were the people from the tribe of Reuben (the firstborn son of Israel):
Hanoch—the Hanochite family group;
Pallu—the Palluite family group;
[6] Hezron—the Hezronite family group;
Carmi—the Carmite family group.
[7] The total number of men in these family groups from the tribe of Reuben was 43,730.

[8] Pallu's son was Eliab. [9] Eliab had three sons—Nemuel, Dathan and Abiram. Remember, Dathan and Abiram were the two leaders who turned against Moses and Aaron. They followed Korah when Korah turned against the LORD. [10] That was the time when the earth opened and swallowed Korah and all of his followers. And 250 men died! That was a warning to all the Israelites. [11] But the other people who were from the family of Korah did not die.

[12] These were the family groups from the tribe of Simeon:

Nemuel—the Nemuelite family group;
Jamin—the Jaminite family group;
Jakin—the Jakinite family group;
[13] Zerah—the Zerahite family group;
Shaul—the Shaulite family group.
[14] The total number of men in these family groups from the tribe of Simeon was 22,200.

[15] These were the family groups from the tribe of Gad:
Zephon—the Zephonite family group;
Haggi—the Haggite family group;
Shuni—the Shunite family group;
[16] Ozni—the Oznite family group;
Eri—the Erite family group;
[17] Arodi—the Arodite family group;
Areli—the Arelite family group.
[18] The total number of men in these family groups from the tribe of Gad was 40,500.

[19-20] These were the family groups from the tribe of Judah:
Shelah—the Shelanite family group;
Perez—the Perezite family group;
Zerah—the Zerahite family group.
(Two of Judah's sons, Er and Onan, died in Canaan.)
[21] These were the family groups from Perez:
Hezron—the Hezronite family group;
Hamul—the Hamulite family group.
[22] These were the family groups from the tribe of Judah. The total number of men was 76,500.

[23] These were the family groups from the tribe of Issachar:
Tola—the Tolaite family group;
Puah—the Puite family group;
[24] Jashub—the Jashubite family group;
Shimron—the Shimronite family group.
[25] These were the family groups from the tribe of Issachar. The total number of men was 64,300.

[26] These were the family groups from the tribe of Zebulun:
Sered—the Seredite family group;
Elon—the Elonite family group;
Jahleel—the Jahleelite family group.
[27] These were the family groups from the tribe of Zebulun. The total number of men was 60,500.

[28] Joseph's two sons were Manasseh and Ephraim. Each son became a tribe with its own family groups.
[29] These were the family groups of Manasseh:
Makir—the Makirite family groups. (Makir was the father of Gilead.)
Gilead—the Gileadite family groups.

---

[a] 25:15 *Cozbi* This name is like the Hebrew word meaning "my lie".

30These were the family groups from Gilead:
Iezer—the Iezerite family group;
Helek—the Helekite family group;
31Asriel—the Asrielite family group;
Shechem—the Shechemite family group;
32Shemida—the Shemidaite family group;
Hepher—the Hepherite family group.
33Zelophehad was the son of Hepher. But he had no sons—only daughters. His daughters' names were Mahlah, Noah, Hoglah, Milcah and Tirzah.
34These are all the family groups from the tribe of Manasseh. The total number of men was 52,700.

35These were the family groups from the tribe of Ephraim:
Shuthelah—the Shuthelahite family group;
Beker—the Bekerite family group;
Tahan—the Tahanite family group.
36Eran was from Shuthelah's family group;
Eran—the Eranite family group.
37These were the family groups from the tribe of Ephraim. The total number of men was 32,500.

These family groups of Manasseh and Ephraim are all the descendants of Joseph.

38These were the family groups from the tribe of Benjamin:
Bela—the Belaite family group;
Ashbel—the Ashbelite family group;
Ahiram—the Ahiramite family group;
39Shupham—the Shuphamite family group;
Hupham—the Huphamite family group.
40The family groups from Bela were:
Ard—the Ardite family group;
Naaman—the Naamanite family group.
41These were all the family groups from the tribe of Benjamin. The total number of men was 45,600.

42These were the family groups from the tribe of Dan:
Shuham—the Shuhamite family group.
That was the family group from the tribe of Dan.
43There were many family groups in the Shuhamite tribe. The total number of men was 64,400.

44These were the family groups from the tribe of Asher:
Imnah—the Imnite family group;
Ishvi—the Ishvite family group;
Beriah—the Beriite family group.

45These were the family groups from Beriah:
Heber—the Heberite family group;
Malkiel—the Malkielite family group.

46(Asher also had a daughter named Serah.)
47These were the family groups in the tribe of Asher. The total number of men was 53,400.

48These were the family groups from the tribe of Naphtali:
Jahzeel—the Jahzeelite family group;
Guni—the Gunite family group;
49Jezer—the Jezerite family group;
Shillem—the Shillemite family group.
50These were the family groups from the tribe of Naphtali. The total number of men was 45,400.

51So the total number of men of Israel was 601,730.

52The LORD said to Moses, 53"The land will be divided and given to these people. Each tribe will get enough land for all the people who were counted. 54A large tribe will get much land, and a small tribe will get less land. The land that they get will be equal to the number of people who were counted. 55But you must use lots to decide which tribe gets which part of the land. Each tribe will get its share of the land, and that land will be given the name of that tribe. 56Land will be given to each tribe—large and small. And you will throw lots to make the decisions."

57They also counted the tribe of Levi. These are the family groups from the tribe of Levi:
Gershon—the Gershonite family group;
Kohath—the Kohathite family group;
Merari—the Merarite family group.

58These are also family groups from the tribe of Levi:
the Libnite family group;
the Hebronite family group;
the Mahlite family group;
the Mushite family group;
the Korahite family group.

Amram was from the Kohath family group. 59Amram's wife was named Jochebed. She was also from the tribe of Levi. She was born in Egypt. Amram and Jochebed had two sons, Aaron and Moses. They also had a daughter, Miriam.
60Aaron was the father of Nadab, Abihu, Eleazar and Ithamar. 61But Nadab and Abihu died. They died because they made an offering to the LORD with fire that was not allowed.
62The total number of males one month or older from the tribe of Levi was 23,000. But these men were not counted with the other Israelites. They did not get a share of the land that the Lord gave to the other people.

HE IS STILL FAITHFUL

The people of Israel had deliberately disobeyed God and didn't believe he would be faithful to all his promises – to protect them and lead them into Canaan, the promised land. For this, they were punished – they wandered in the desert for forty years.

DIG IN
READ Numbers 26:63–65

- How many people had died since the last census of the people of Israel in Numbers 1?

There were still hundreds of thousands of Israelites (can you spot how many men in total?) but only four of the originals remained who were faithful to God. How sad is that? Apart from Moses, Aaron, Joshua and Caleb everyone who had been there at the previous census had now died, leaving only their children (v.65).

READ Numbers 33:50–56
- Who speaks to Moses?
- What are the people finally able to do?
- What did the people have to do when they got there?

God's words here bring good news – the people are finally allowed to cross the Jordan River into the land of Canaan. God promised that this land would belong to his people and he never breaks his promises.

READ Numbers 36:1–13
Some guys from the family tribe of Manasseh are a little concerned. Zelophehad (what a name!) had no sons to receive his inheritance when he died and so God had told Moses to allow Zelophehad's daughters to inherit their father's land (see Numbers 27:1–11). The guys that went to see Moses (in chapter 36) were anxious that if Zelophehad's daughters married men from other tribes then the land would pass to those men and out of their tribe.

- What is God's answer to this problem (v.6–9)?
- What would the result be?

It may seem like a small thing but the consequences are massive. If all the people married out of their own tribes then the land would no longer belong to them. God was in this – making sure the land was kept by its rightful owners. However, the Bible tells us the land of Canaan was never intended to be the full and forever fulfilment of the promise for land – there is a greater land to come. The people of God who follow him are promised a place in heaven forever. This is a promise of God that he will always remain faithful to (John 6:37–40).

DIG THROUGH

- God promises that if you love him you have an inheritance like that of the people in Numbers and just as the law ensured they didn't lose their inheritance (Numbers 36:9), so yours is kept for you. Check out 1 Peter 1:3–5 for more about this.
- Why not think about the ways you have known God to be faithful to you even though you have not always loved him as you should. Why not say sorry, if you need to, and thank God for sticking with you.

DIG DEEPER

- Throughout the book of Numbers God gives sets of laws with which to govern the people. Often these laws relate to the people's sin or something that has happened to them. Check out the laws for entering the land: there are some interesting examples in chapters 34 – 36. What other laws can you spot in Numbers, and can you see what happened to provoke God to give them?

⁶³Moses and Eleazar the priest counted all these people. They counted the Israelites while they were in the Jordan Valley in Moab. This was near the Jordan River, opposite Jericho. ⁶⁴Many years before, in the desert of Sinai, Moses and Aaron the priest counted the Israelites. But all these people were dead. Not one of them was still alive, ⁶⁵because the LORD told them that they would all die in the desert. The only two men who were left alive were Caleb son of Jephunneh and Joshua son of Nun.

Zelophehad's Daughters

27 Zelophehad was the son of Hepher. Hepher was the son of Gilead. Gilead was the son of Makir. Makir was the son of Manasseh. Manasseh was the son of Joseph. Zelophehad had five daughters. Their names were Mahlah, Noah, Hoglah, Milcah and Tirzah. ²These five women went to the Meeting Tent and stood before Moses, Eleazar the priest, the leaders, and all the Israelites.

The five daughters said, ³"Our father died while we were travelling through the desert. He died a natural death. He was not one of the men who joined Korah's group. (Korah was the man who turned against the LORD.) But our father had no sons. ⁴This means that our father's name will not continue. It is not fair that our father's name will not continue. His name will end because he had no sons. So we ask you to give us some of the land that our father's brothers will get."

⁵So Moses asked the LORD what he should do. ⁶The LORD said to him, ⁷"The daughters of Zelophehad are right. They should share the land with their father's brothers. So give them the land that you would have given to their father.

⁸"So tell the Israelites, 'If a man has no son, when he dies everything he owns will be given to his daughter. ⁹If he has no daughter, everything he owns will be given to his brothers. ¹⁰If he has no brothers, everything he owns will be given to his father's brothers. ¹¹If his father had no brothers, everything he owns will be given to the closest relative in his family. This will be a law among the Israelites. The LORD has given this command to Moses.'"

Joshua Is the New Leader

¹²Then the LORD said to Moses, "Go up on one of mountains in the desert east of the Jordan River. There you will see the land that I am giving to the Israelites. ¹³After you have seen this land, you will die like your brother Aaron. ¹⁴Remember when the people became angry at the water in the desert of Zin. Both you and Aaron refused to obey my command. You did not honour me and show the people that I am holy." (This was at the water of Meribahᵃ near Kadesh in the desert of Zin.)

¹⁵Moses said to the LORD, ¹⁶"LORD, you are the God who knows what people are thinking. I pray that you will choose a leader for these people.ᵇ ¹⁷I pray that you will choose a leader who will lead them out of this land and bring them into the new land. Then your people will not be like sheep without a shepherd."

¹⁸So the LORD said to Moses, "Joshua son of Nun is very wise.ᶜ You will place your hand on him and make him the new leader. ¹⁹Tell him to stand in front of Eleazar the priest and all the people. Then make him the new leader. ²⁰"Show the people that you are making him leader,ᵈ then all the people will obey him. ²¹If Joshua needs to make a decision, he will go to Eleazar the priest. Eleazar will use the Urim to learn the LORD's answer. Then Joshua and all the Israelites will do the things God says. If he says, 'go to war,' they will go to war. And if he says, 'go home,' they will go home."

²²Moses obeyed the LORD. Moses told Joshua to stand before Eleazar the priest and all the Israelites. ²³Then Moses put his hands on him to show that he was the new leader. He did this just as the LORD told him to.

Daily Offerings

28 Then the LORD spoke to Moses. He said, ²"Give this command to the Israelites. Tell them to be sure to give the grain offerings and sacrifices to me at the right time as sweet-smelling gifts. ³These are gifts that they must give to the LORD. Every day they must give 2 lambs that are one year old. There must be nothing wrong with them. ⁴Offer one of the lambs in the morning and the other lamb just before dark. ⁵Also give a grain offering of 1 kilogrammeᵉ of fine flour mixed with 1 litreᶠ of olive oil." ⁶(They started giving the daily offerings at Mount Sinai as sweet-smelling gifts to the LORD.) ⁷"The people must also give the drink offerings that go with the gifts. They must give 1 litre of wine with every lamb. Pour that drink

---

ᵃ **27:14 water of Meribah** Or "water of rebellion".
ᵇ **27:16 LORD, . . . these people** Literally, "May the LORD, the God of the spirits of all people, appoint a man for this community."
ᶜ **27:18 Joshua . . . is very wise** Literally, "Take Joshua son of Nun. He is a man with a spirit in him." This might mean that Joshua was very wise, or it might mean that God's Spirit was with him.
ᵈ **27:20 Show . . . leader** Literally, "Give him some of your glory."
ᵉ **28:5 1 kilogramme** Literally, "¹⁄₁₀ of an *ephah*". Also in verses 13,20–21,29.
ᶠ **28:5 1 litre** Literally, "¹⁄₄ *hin*". Also in verse 14.

offering on the altar in the Holy Place. This is a gift to the LORD. ⁸Offer the second lamb just before dark. Offer it just as the morning offering. Also give the drink offering that goes with it. This will be a sweet-smelling gift to the LORD.

Sabbath Offerings

⁹"On the Sabbath you must give 2 lambs that are one year old. There must be nothing wrong with them. You must also give a grain offering of 2 kilogrammes*ᵃ* of fine flour mixed with olive oil, and a drink offering. ¹⁰This is a special offering for the day of rest. This offering is in addition to the regular daily offering and drink offering.

Monthly Meetings

¹¹"On the first day of each month you will offer a special burnt offering to the LORD. This offering will be 2 male bulls, 1 ram and 7 lambs that are one year old. There must be nothing wrong with them. ¹²With each bull, you must give a grain offering of 3 kilogrammes*ᵇ* of fine flour mixed with olive oil. And with the ram, you must give a grain offering of 2 kilogrammes of fine flour mixed with olive oil. ¹³Also give a grain offering of 1 kilogramme of fine flour mixed with olive oil with each lamb. This will be a sweet-smelling gift to the LORD. ¹⁴The drink offering will be 2 litres*ᶜ* of wine with each bull, 1.5 litres*ᵈ* of wine with the ram, and 1 litre of wine with each lamb. That is the burnt offering that must be offered each month of the year. ¹⁵In addition to the regular daily burnt offering and drink offering, you must also give 1 male goat to the LORD. That goat will be a sin offering.

Passover

¹⁶"The LORD's Passover will be on the fourteenth day of the first month. ¹⁷The Festival of Unleavened Bread begins on the fifteenth day of that month. This festival lasts for seven days. The only bread you can eat is bread made without yeast. ¹⁸You must have a special meeting on the first day of this festival. You will not do any work on that day. ¹⁹You will give burnt offerings to the LORD. The burnt offerings will be 2 bulls, 1 ram and 7 lambs that are one year old. There must be nothing wrong with them. ²⁰⁻²¹You must also give a grain offering of 3 kilogrammes of fine flour mixed with olive oil with each bull, and

2 kilogrammes of fine flour mixed with oil with the ram, and 1 kilogramme of fine flour mixed with oil for each lamb. ²²You must also give a male goat as a sin offering to make you pure. ²³You must give these offerings in addition to the morning burnt offerings that you give every day.

²⁴"In this way, each day for seven days, you must bring the food that is offered by fire. The smell of these offerings will please the LORD. You must give these offerings in addition to the daily burnt offering and the drink offering that goes with it.

²⁵"Then, on the seventh day of this festival, you will have another special meeting. You will not do any work on that day.

Festival of Harvest

²⁶"The first day of the Festival of Harvest is the day you bring the first of your new crops and give them as a grain offering to the LORD. At that time you must also call a special meeting. You must not do any work on that day. ²⁷You must offer a burnt offering as a sweet-smelling gift to the LORD. You must offer 2 bulls, 1 ram and 7 lambs that are one year old. There must be nothing wrong with them. ²⁸You must also give 3 kilogrammes of fine flour mixed with oil with each bull, and 2 kilogrammes with each ram, ²⁹and 1 kilogramme with each lamb. ³⁰You must also sacrifice a male goat to make you pure. ³¹You must give these offerings in addition to the daily burnt offerings and the grain offering you give with them. Be sure there is nothing wrong with the animals or the drink offerings that you give with them.

Festival of Trumpets

29 "There will be a special meeting on the first day of the seventh month. You will not do any work on that day. That is the day for blowing the trumpets.*ᵉ* ²You will offer burnt offerings. Their smell will please the LORD. You will offer 1 bull, 1 ram and 7 lambs that are one year old. There must be nothing wrong with them. ³You will also offer 3 kilogrammes*ᶠ* of fine flour mixed with oil with the bull, 2 kilogrammes*ᵍ* with the ram, ⁴and 1 kilogramme*ʰ* with each of the 7 lambs. ⁵Also offer a male goat as a sin offering to make you pure. ⁶These offerings are in addition to the New Moon sacrifice and its grain offering. And they are in addition to the daily

---

ᵃ **28:9 2 kilogrammes** Literally, "²⁄₁₀ of an *ephah*". Also in verses 12,20–21,28.
ᵇ **28:12 3 kilogrammes** Literally, "³⁄₁₀ of an *ephah*". Also in verses 20–21,28.
ᶜ **28:14 2 litres** Literally, "½ *hin*".
ᵈ **28:14 1.5 litres** Literally, "⅓ *hin*".
ᵉ **29:1 blowing the trumpets** Or "shouting". This might mean this is a day for shouting and being happy.
ᶠ **29:3 3 kilogrammes** Literally, "³⁄₁₀ of an *ephah*". Also in verses 9,14.
ᵍ **29:3 2 kilogrammes** Literally, "²⁄₁₀ of an *ephah*". Also in verses 9,14.
ʰ **29:4 1 kilogramme** Literally, "¹⁄₁₀ of an *ephah*". Also in verses 10,15.

sacrifice and its grain offerings and drink offerings. These must be done according to the rules. They will be sweet-smelling gifts to the LORD.

The Day of Atonement

7"There will be a special meeting on the tenth day of the seventh month. During that day you must not eat any food,[a] and you must not do any work. 8You will offer burnt offerings. Their smell will please the LORD. You must offer 1 bull, 1 ram and 7 lambs that are one year old. There must be nothing wrong with them. 9You must also offer 3 kilogrammes of fine flour mixed with olive oil with the bull, 2 kilogrammes with the ram, 10and 1 kilogramme with each of the 7 lambs. 11You will also offer 1 male goat as a sin offering. This will be in addition to the sin offering for the Day of Atonement. This will also be in addition to the daily sacrifice and its grain offerings and drink offerings.

Festival of Shelters

12"There will be a special meeting on the fifteenth day of the seventh month.[b] You must not do any work on that day. You must celebrate a special festival for the LORD for seven days. 13You will offer burnt offerings as sweet-smelling gifts to the LORD. You will offer 13 bulls, 2 rams and 14 lambs that are one year old. There must be nothing wrong with them. 14You must also offer 3 kilogrammes of fine flour mixed with oil with each of the 13 bulls, 2 kilogrammes with each of the 2 rams 15and 1 kilogramme with each of the 14 lambs. 16You must also offer 1 male goat. This must be in addition to the daily sacrifice and its grain offerings and drink offerings.

17"On the second day of this festival, you must offer 12 bulls, 2 rams and 14 lambs that are one year old. There must be nothing wrong with them. 18You must also give the right amount of grain and drink offerings with the bulls, rams and lambs. 19You must also offer 1 male goat as a sin offering. This must be in addition to the daily sacrifice and its grain offerings and drink offerings.

20"On the third day of this festival, you must offer 11 bulls, 2 rams and 14 lambs that are one year old. There must be nothing wrong with them. 21You must also give the right amount of grain and drink offerings with the bulls, rams and lambs. 22You must also give 1 goat as a sin offering. This must be in addition to the daily sacrifice and its grain offerings and drink offerings.

23"On the fourth day of this festival, you must offer 10 bulls, 2 rams and 14 lambs that are one year old. There must be nothing wrong with them. 24You must also give the right amount of grain and drink offerings with the bulls, rams and lambs. 25You must also give 1 male goat as a sin offering. This must be in addition to the daily sacrifice and its grain offerings and drink offerings.

26"On the fifth day of this festival, you must offer 9 bulls, 2 rams and 14 lambs that are one year old. There must be nothing wrong with them. 27You must also give the right amount of grain and drink offerings with the bulls, rams and lambs. 28You must also give 1 male goat as a sin offering. This must be in addition to the daily sacrifice and its grain offerings and drink offerings.

29"On the sixth day of this festival, you must offer 8 bulls, 2 rams and 14 lambs that are one year old. There must be nothing wrong with them. 30You must also give the right amount of grain and drink offerings for the bulls, rams and lambs. 31You must also give 1 male goat as a sin offering. This must be in addition to the daily sacrifice and its grain offerings and drink offerings.

32"On the seventh day of this festival, you must offer 7 bulls, 2 rams and 14 lambs that are one year old. There must be nothing wrong with them. 33You must also give the right amount of grain and drink offerings with the bulls, rams and lambs. 34You must also give 1 male goat as a sin offering. This must be in addition to the daily sacrifice and its grain offerings and drink offerings.

35"The eighth day of this festival is a very special meeting for you. You must not do any work on that day. 36You must offer a burnt offering as a sweet-smelling gift to the LORD. You must offer 1 bull, 1 ram and 7 lambs that are one year old. There must be nothing wrong with them. 37You must also give the right amount of grain and drink offerings with the bull, ram and lambs. 38You must also give 1 male goat as a sin offering. This must be in addition to the daily sacrifice and its grain offerings and drink offerings.

39"At the special festivals you must bring your burnt offerings, grain offerings, drink offerings and fellowship offerings. You must give these offerings to the LORD. They are in addition to any special gift you might want to give him and any offering that is part of a special promise you make."

40Moses told the Israelites everything the LORD had commanded him.

Vows and Promises

30 Moses spoke with all the leaders of the Israelite tribes and told them about these commands from the LORD:

2"If a man makes a vow to the LORD or makes a promise with an oath, he must not break his

---

[a] **29:7 you . . . food** Literally, "you will humble your souls".
[b] **29:12 fifteenth day of the seventh month** This is the Festival of Shelters. See "FESTIVAL OF SHELTERS" in the Word List.

promise. He must do everything he said he would do.

[3] "A young woman might still be living in her father's house. She might make a vow to the LORD or promise something with an oath. [4] If her father hears about the vow or promise and says nothing against it, the young woman must do what she promised. [5] But if her father hears about it and does not agree for her to do it, she is free from her vow or any promise she made. She does not have to do what she said. Her father stopped her, so the LORD will forgive her.

[6] "A woman might make a vow, or she might make a promise with an oath without thinking enough about it. If she then gets married, [7] and her husband hears about her vow or promise and says nothing against it, the woman must keep it. She must do whatever she said she would do. [8] But if the husband hears about her vow or promise and does not agree for her to do it, the wife does not have to keep her vow or the careless promise she made with an oath. If her husband is against it, this ends her duty to keep it. So the LORD will forgive her.

[9] "But a woman who is a widow or divorced must keep any vow or promise she makes. She must do everything she said she would do.

[10] "A married woman living with her husband might make a vow or a promise with an oath. [11] If her husband hears about it and says nothing against it, she must keep any vow or promise she made. She must do everything she said she would do. [12] But if her husband hears about her vows or promises and refuses to let her keep them, she does not have to keep them. It doesn't matter what she promised to do; if her husband is against it, this ends her duty to do it. And the LORD will forgive her. [13] When a married woman makes a vow or promises to do without something,[a] her husband can allow her to keep her vows or promises, or he can stop her from keeping them. [14] If he hears about them and does not stop them, he is allowing her to keep them. She must then do everything she said she would do. By saying nothing against her vows or promises the husband agreed for her to keep them. [15] But if the husband says nothing when he hears about them, but then later stops her from keeping them, he is the one responsible for breaking her promises."[b]

[16] These are the commands the LORD gave to Moses. These are the commands about a man and his wife, and about a father and his daughter who is still young and living at home in her father's house.

Israel Fights Back Against the Midianites

31 [1] The LORD spoke to Moses and said, [2] "Moses, tell the Israelites to go and attack the Midianites and do to them what they did to you. After that, you will die."[c]

[3] So Moses spoke to the people. He said, "Choose some of your men to be soldiers. The LORD will use these men to do to the Midianites what they did to you. [4] Choose 1,000 men from each of the tribes of Israel. [5] There will be a total of 12,000 soldiers from the tribes of Israel."

[6] Moses sent these 12,000 men to war. He sent Phinehas son of Eleazar with them as the priest. Phinehas took the holy things and the horns and trumpets with him. [7] The Israelites fought the Midianites as the LORD had commanded. They killed all the Midianite men. [8] Among the people who they killed were Evi, Rekem, Zur, Hur and Reba—the five kings of Midian. They also killed Balaam son of Beor with a sword.

[9] The Israelites took the Midianite women and children as prisoners. They also took all their sheep, cattle and other things. [10] Then they burned all their towns and villages. [11] They took all the people and animals [12] and brought them to Moses, Eleazar the priest, and all the other Israelites. They brought all the things they took in war to the camp of Israel. The Israelites were camped in the Jordan Valley in Moab, on the east side of the Jordan River, opposite Jericho. [13] Then Moses, Eleazar the priest and the leaders of the people went out of the camp to meet with the soldiers.

[14] Moses was very angry with the leaders of the army, the commanders of 1,000 men and the commanders of 100 men, who came back from the war. [15] Moses said to them, "Why did you let the women live? [16] These are the women who listened to Balaam and caused the men of Israel to turn away from the LORD that time at Peor. The disease will come to the LORD's people again. [17] Now, kill all the Midianite boys, and kill all the Midianite women who have had sex with a man. [18] You can let all the young girls live—but only if they never had sex with any man. [19] And then, all you men who killed other people must stay outside the camp for seven days. You must stay outside the camp even if you just touched a dead body. On the third day, you and your prisoners must make yourselves pure. You must do the same thing again on the seventh day. [20] You must wash all of your clothes. You must wash anything made with leather, wool or wood. You must purify yourselves."

---

[a] **30:13 do without something** Literally, "humble her soul". Usually this means to make the body suffer in some way, such as by not eating food.

[b] **30:15 he . . . her promises** Literally, "he carries her guilt".

[c] **31:2 you will die** Literally, "you will be gathered to your people".

21Then Eleazar the priest spoke to the soldiers. He said, "These are the rules that the LORD gave to Moses for soldiers coming back from war. 22-23You must put gold, silver, bronze, iron, tin or lead into the fire and then wash these things with the special water to make them pure. If something can be put in the fire, you must put it in fire to purify it. If things cannot be put in fire, you must still wash them with the special water. 24On the seventh day, you must wash all your clothes. Then you will be pure. After that, you can come into camp."

25Then the LORD said to Moses, 26"You, Eleazar the priest, and all the leaders should count all the prisoners, animals and everything the soldiers took in war. 27Then divide these things between the soldiers who went to war and the rest of the Israelites. 28Take part of these things from the soldiers who went to war. That part will belong to the LORD. His share is one from every 500 items. This includes people, cattle, donkeys and sheep. 29Take that share from the soldiers' half of the things they took in war. Then give these things to Eleazar the priest. That part will belong to LORD. 30And then, from the people's half, take one thing for every 50 items. This includes people, cattle, donkeys, sheep or any other animal. Give that share to the Levites, because they take care of the LORD's Holy Tent."

31So Moses and Eleazar did what the LORD commanded Moses. 32The soldiers had taken 675,000 sheep, 3372,000 cattle, 3461,000 donkeys 35and 32,000 women. (These are only the women who had not had sex with any man.) 36The soldiers who went to war got 337,500 sheep. 37They gave 675 sheep to the LORD. 38The soldiers got 36,000 cattle. They gave 72 cattle to the LORD. 39The soldiers got 30,500 donkeys. They gave 61 donkeys to the LORD. 40The soldiers got 16,000 women. They gave 32 women to the LORD. 41Moses gave all these gifts for the LORD to Eleazar the priest, as the LORD had commanded him.

42Then Moses counted the people's half. This was their share that Moses had taken from the soldiers who had gone to war. 43The people got 337,500 sheep, 4436,000 cattle, 4530,000 donkeys 46and 16,000 women. 47Moses took one out of every 50 women and animals. He gave them to the Levites because they took care of the LORD's Holy Tent. Moses did this as the LORD had commanded.

48Then the leaders of the army (the leaders over 1,000 men and the leaders over 100 men)

came to Moses. 49They told Moses, "We, your servants, have counted our soldiers. We have not missed any of them. 50So we are bringing the LORD's gift from every soldier. We are bringing things that are made of gold—armbands, bracelets, rings, earrings and necklaces. This gift to the LORD is to make us pure."

51So Moses and Eleazar the priest accepted all these gold items from them. 52The gold that the commanders*a* and captains*b* gave to the LORD weighed almost 200 kilogrammes.*c* 53The soldiers kept the rest of their share of the things they took in war. 54Moses and Eleazar the priest took the gold from the commanders and captains and then put that gold in the Meeting Tent. This present was a memorial*d* before the LORD for the Israelites.

Tribes East of the Jordan River

32 The tribes of Reuben and Gad had many cattle. These people looked at the land near Jazer and Gilead. They saw that this land was good for their cattle. 2So the people from the tribes of Reuben and Gad came to Moses. They spoke to Moses, Eleazar the priest and the leaders of the people. 3-4They said, "We, your servants, have many cattle. And the land that the LORD let the people of Israel capture is good land for cattle. This land includes the area around Ataroth, Dibon, Jazer, Nimrah, Heshbon, Elealeh, Sibmah,*e* Nebo and Beon. 5If it pleases you, we would like this land to be given to us. Don't take us to the other side of the Jordan River."

6Moses told the people from the tribes of Reuben and Gad, "Will you let your brothers go and fight while you settle here? 7Why are you trying to discourage the Israelites? You will make them not want to cross the river and take the land that the LORD has given to them! 8Your fathers did the same thing to me. In Kadesh Barnea I sent spies to look at the land. 9These men went as far as Eshcol Valley. They saw the land, and they discouraged the Israelites. These men made the Israelites not want to go into the land that the LORD had given to them. 10The LORD became very angry with the people. He made this promise: 11'None of the people who came from Egypt and are 20 years old or older will be allowed to see this land. I made a promise to Abraham, Isaac and Jacob. I promised to give this land to these people, but they did not really follow me. 12Only Caleb son of Jephunneh the Kenizzite and Joshua son of Nun really followed the LORD!'

---

a **31:52 commanders** Literally, "leaders of 1,000 men".
b **31:52 captains** Literally, "leaders of 100 men".
c **31:52 200 kilogrammes** Literally, "16,750 *shekels*".
d **31:54 memorial** Something that helps people remember things that happened in the past.
e **32:3–4 Sibmah** Or "Sebam".

GUIDANCE

HAVE you read the book of Jeremiah recently? In a nutshell, God says to Jeremiah, "I've known you inside out since before you were born; I know everything about you. I know you are young but I'm calling you to be a prophet, to speak for me internationally. Even if you don't feel you have the skills, I will give them to you and tell you what to say and I will save you from anyone who comes against you."

Wouldn't you just love to have God lay it all out there for you like that? No more wondering "What career am I supposed to do?" "What

> ## "I KNOW THE PLANS THAT I HAVE FOR YOU . . . I HAVE GOOD PLANS FOR YOU. I DON'T PLAN TO HURT YOU. I PLAN TO GIVE YOU HOPE AND A GOOD FUTURE." (JEREMIAH 29:11)

exams should I take?" "What is my calling?" Just a direct word from God, clear and to the point. Of course God does still speak to some people in the way he spoke to Jeremiah, but for many people, finding God's guidance and direction is not so black and white. Sometimes we can feel as if unless we've seen something written in the sky or heard a booming voice from heaven then we haven't heard God.

The truth is God made you and he knows you, just like he knew Jeremiah. He has a plan for your life: "I know the plans that I have for you . . . I have good plans for you. I don't plan to hurt you. I plan to give you hope and a good future" (Jeremiah 29:11). Sometimes he will tell you these plans in advance, but sometimes you will have to go step by step, testing things out. Follow your God-inspired desires, use the skills and talents that he has given you, listen to one small instruction from God at a time, and you will find that you end up exactly where he wants you.

To find out more, check out: 1 Chronicles 16:11; Psalms 25:9; 32:8. ←

If you want to, you can pray:

Father, help me not to worry about my life but to trust that you have an amazing plan for me. Help me to hear your voice and follow your guidance when I need it most.

Amen

TRUSTING GOD

TODAY was the big day that Joel had spent the last three months preparing for. Most of his sponsorship money had already come in, and now there was no turning back. He smiled at the six other passengers aboard the tiny twin-engine plane that was quickly climbing to 14,000 feet. In moments, he would be jumping out. This was his first tandem skydive.

Strangely, Joel didn't feel very nervous. Instead his thoughts centred on an illustration his youth leader had made the previous night, comparing his tandem skydive to a very important verse in the Bible. "When people sin, they earn what sin pays – death. But God gives his people a free gift – eternal life in Christ Jesus our Lord" (Romans 6:23). The youth leader pointed out that the law of gravity, that says what goes up must come down, is a bit like the law of sin and death mentioned in that verse. All sin is ultimately punishable by death. But there's good news for Christians. We can beat sin and death!

How does a tandem skydiver beat the law of gravity? With two things: an instructor and a parachute. How do we beat the law of sin and death? With two things: Jesus and eternal life. He's our life instructor and eternal life is our parachute.

It suddenly occurred to Joel just how much trust he had in the man he hardly knew who was strapped to his back. "I want to trust God this much with the way I live my life," he thought. After all, Jesus has already successfully overcome every temptation

There would be times in his life when he might feel a million miles from God, but all he needed to do was remember that God promised never to leave us or abandon us (Hebrews 13:5). And that included Joel. God would "have his back", no matter what.

THERE WOULD BE TIMES IN HIS LIFE WHEN HE MIGHT FEEL A MILLION MILES FROM GOD, BUT ALL HE NEEDED TO DO WAS REMEMBER THAT GOD PROMISED NEVER TO LEAVE US OR ABANDON US.

known to humankind. He even overcame death when he rose again. Who better to give your life over to, especially when it comes to some of the tougher struggles we all face in terms of living a true life of faith? Joel began to think about how the closer he was to God, the more of an adventure his life would become.

Just then, Joel's thoughts were interrupted by a tap on his shoulder from the instructor. They'd reached the correct altitude and it was their turn to jump. A smile spread across Joel's face as he shouted, "Let's do it!"

The Christian life is meant to be lived as an adventure – and not necessarily a "safe" one at that. Discover more in: Psalm 37:5,7; 1 Timothy 1:19; Hebrews 11. ←

Why not pray this prayer:

Father God, you have promised that you are with me and will never leave me, no matter what. Help me to trust you at all times: when things get difficult, as well as when life seems easy. I want my journey to be an adventure with you.

Amen

SEX and RELATIONSHIPS

SO . . . How far can you go?

Over the years there have been all sorts of witty guidelines presented by youth leaders, for example, "Always stay vertical, not horizontal" and "Don't do anything you wouldn't do if Jesus was watching". But is asking "How far can I go?" really the right question?

Imagine you break down at the side of the motorway. You and your girlfriend or boyfriend end up walking down the edge of the road with cars and lorries speeding past at 70 mph. Would you both walk as close as you could to the speeding vehicles to see how close you could get without getting hit? I doubt it. You'd want the person you love to stay as far away from danger as possible so they were guaranteed to be safe. Asking "How far can we go?" is like saying "How close to the speeding cars can we go without getting run over?" By the time you've learned the answer to the question you may have been run over and it's too late.

Instead, how about asking, "How can I stay the purest possible?" or "How much can I save for my future husband/wife?" or "How can I honour God most in this situation?" or "Would I want my future wife/husband to be doing this with someone else?" At the end of

AT THE END OF THE DAY, GOD MADE SEX AS A GREAT GIFT FOR YOU AND YOUR FUTURE HUSBAND OR WIFE; HE DOESN'T WANT IT TO BE SPOILED OR FOR YOU TO GET HURT.

the day, God made sex as a great gift for you and your future husband or wife; he doesn't want it to be spoiled or for you to get hurt. When we turn against God and sin it breaks his heart, especially when we misuse a gift he made so carefully for us.

To find out more, check out: Matthew 5:27–28; 1 Corinthians 7:9; Philippians 4:8; 2 Timothy 2:22. ←

You might want to pray a prayer like this:

Lord, I give you my body and my life. Please help me to stay pure and live in a way that truly honours you.

Amen

[13]"The LORD was very angry with the Israelites. So he made the people stay in the desert for 40 years. He made them stay there until all the people who had sinned against the LORD were dead. [14]And now you are doing the same thing that your fathers did. You sinful people, do you want the LORD to be even more angry with his people? [15]If you stop following the Lord, he will make Israel stay even longer in the desert. Then you will destroy all these people!"

[16]But the people from the tribes of Reuben and Gad went to Moses. They said, "We will build cities for our children and barns for our animals here. [17]Then our children can be safe from the other people who live in this land. But we will gladly come and help the other Israelites. We will bring them to their land. [18]We will not come back home until everyone in Israel has taken his part of the land. [19]We will not take any of the land west of the Jordan River. No, our part of the land is east of the Jordan River."

[20]So Moses told them, "If you do all these things, this land will belong to you. But your soldiers must go before the LORD into battle. [21]Your soldiers must cross the Jordan River and be ready to fight for the LORD until he forces the enemy to leave. [22]After the LORD helps us all take the land, you can go back home. Then the LORD and Israel will not think that you are guilty. And the LORD will let you have this land. [23]But if you don't do these things, you will be sinning against the LORD. And know for sure that you will be punished for your sin. [24]Build cities for your children and barns for your animals. But then, you must do what you promised."

[25]Then the people from the tribes of Gad and Reuben said to Moses, "We are your servants. You are our master, so we will do what you say. [26]Our wives, children and all our animals will stay in the cities of Gilead. [27]But we, your servants, will cross the Jordan River. We will march before the LORD into battle, as our master says."

[28]So Moses, Eleazar the priest, Joshua son of Nun, and all the leaders of the tribes of Israel heard them make that promise. [29]Moses said to them, "The people of Gad and Reuben will cross the Jordan River. They will march before the LORD into battle. They will help you take the land. And you will give the land of Gilead as their part of the country. [30]But if they do not cross the river with you ready to fight, they will not be given any land on this side. They will get only a share of the land of Canaan with the rest of you."

[31]The people of Gad and Reuben answered, "We promise to do what the LORD commanded. [32]We will cross the Jordan River and march before the LORD into the land of Canaan. And our part of the country is the land east of the Jordan River."

[33]So Moses gave that land to the people of Gad, to the people of Reuben, and to half the tribe of Manasseh. (Manasseh was Joseph's son.) That land included the kingdom of Sihon the Amorite and the kingdom of King Og of Bashan and all the cities around that area.

[34]The people of Gad built the cities of Dibon, Ataroth, Aroer, [35]Atroth Shophan, Jazer, Jogbehah, [36]Beth Nimrah and Beth Haran. They built cities with strong walls, and they built barns for their animals.

[37]The people of Reuben built Heshbon, Elealeh, Kiriathaim, [38]Nebo, Baal Meon and Sibmah. They used the names of the cities that they rebuilt. But they changed the names of Nebo and Baal Meon.

[39]People from Makir's family group went to Gilead.[a] (Makir was Manasseh's son.) They defeated the city. They defeated the Amorites who lived there. [40]So Moses gave Gilead to Makir from the tribe of Manasseh, and his family settled there. [41]Jair, from the family of Manasseh, defeated the small towns there. Then he called them Towns of Jair. [42]Nobah defeated Kenath and the small towns near it. Then he called that place by his own name.

Israel's Journey From Egypt

33 Here is a list of the places the Israelites went when they left Egypt. They were organized in groups like an army and were led by Moses and Aaron. [2]Following the LORD's command, Moses kept a record of each place they stayed before moving on to the next place. These are all the places they went:

[3]On the fifteenth day of the first month, they left Rameses. That morning after Passover, the Israelites marched out of Egypt with their arms raised in victory. All the people of Egypt saw them. [4]The Egyptians

INSIGHT

For the Israelites, it was important to remember their journey from slavery to the promised land. For them, every detail carried significance. Equally, it is important for Christians today not to forget their spiritual journey, to remember where they have come from.

Numbers 33

---

[a] **32:39** *Gilead* Here, this seems to refer to a city, perhaps Ramoth Gilead. But it might refer to the whole area. See Hos. 6:8.

were burying all the people the LORD killed. They were burying all their firstborn sons. The LORD had shown his judgement against the gods[a] of Egypt.

⁵The Israelites left Rameses and travelled to Succoth. ⁶From Succoth they travelled to Etham. They camped there at the edge of the desert. ⁷They left Etham and went to Pi Hahiroth. This was near Baal Zephon. They camped near Migdol.

⁸They left Pi Hahiroth and walked through the middle of the sea. They went towards the desert. Then they travelled for three days through the desert of Etham. The people camped at Marah.

⁹They left Marah and went to Elim and camped there. There were 12 springs of water and 70 palm trees there.

¹⁰They left Elim and camped near the Red Sea.[b]

¹¹They left the Red Sea and camped in the western Sinai Desert.[c]

¹²They left there and camped at Dophkah.

¹³They left Dophkah and camped at Alush.

¹⁴They left Alush and camped at Rephidim. There was no water for the people to drink at that place.

¹⁵They left Rephidim and camped in the desert of Sinai.

¹⁶They left the desert of Sinai and camped at Kibroth Hattaavah.

¹⁷They left Kibroth Hattaavah and camped at Hazeroth.

¹⁸They left Hazeroth and camped at Rithmah.

¹⁹They left Rithmah and camped at Rimmon Perez.

²⁰They left Rimmon Perez and camped at Libnah.

²¹They left Libnah and camped at Rissah.

²²They left Rissah and camped at Kehelathah.

²³They left Kehelathah and camped at Mount Shepher.

²⁴They left Mount Shepher and camped at Haradah.

²⁵They left Haradah and camped at Makheloth.

²⁶They left Makheloth and camped at Tahath.

²⁷They left Tahath and camped at Terah.

²⁸They left Terah and camped at Mithcah.

²⁹They left Mithcah and camped at Hashmonah.

³⁰They left Hashmonah and camped at Moseroth.

³¹They left Moseroth and camped at Bene Jaakan.

³²They left Bene Jaakan and camped at Hor Haggidgad.

³³They left Hor Haggidgad and camped at Jotbathah.

³⁴They left Jotbathah and camped at Abronah.

³⁵They left Abronah and camped at Ezion Geber.

³⁶They left Ezion Geber and camped at Kadesh, in the desert of Zin.

³⁷They left Kadesh and camped at Hor. This was the mountain at the border of the country of Edom. ³⁸Aaron the priest obeyed the LORD and went up Mount Hor. Aaron died at that place on the first day of the fifth month. That was the fortieth year after the Israelites had left Egypt. ³⁹Aaron was 123 years old when he died on Mount Hor.

⁴⁰Arad was a town in the Negev, in the land of Canaan. The Canaanite king in that place heard that the Israelites were coming. ⁴¹The people left Mount Hor and camped at Zalmonah.

⁴²They left Zalmonah and camped at Punon.

⁴³They left Punon and camped at Oboth.

⁴⁴They left Oboth and camped at Iye Abarim. This was at the border of the country of Moab.

⁴⁵They left Iye Abarim and camped at Dibon Gad.

⁴⁶They left Dibon Gad and camped at Almon Diblathaim.

⁴⁷They left Almon Diblathaim and camped on the mountains of Abarim near Nebo.

⁴⁸They left the mountains of Abarim and camped in the Jordan Valley in Moab. This was near the Jordan River, opposite Jericho. ⁴⁹They camped by the Jordan River in the Jordan Valley in Moab. Their camp went from Beth Jeshimoth to Acacia Field.

⁵⁰There, the LORD spoke to Moses and said, ⁵¹"Speak to the Israelites and tell them this: You will cross the Jordan River. You will go into the land of Canaan. ⁵²You will take the land from the people you find there. You must destroy all of their carved statues and idols. You must destroy all of their high places. ⁵³You will take the land and you will settle there, because I am giving this

---

[a] **33:4 gods** This might be the false gods of Egypt. Or here, it might mean the king and other powerful leaders in Egypt.
[b] **33:10 Red Sea** Or "Reed Sea", but see 1 Kgs 9:26.
[c] **33:11 western Sinai Desert** Literally, "desert of Sin".

land to you. It will belong to your family groups. [54]Each of your family groups will get part of the land. You will throw lots to decide which family group gets each part of the country. Large family groups will get large parts of the land. Small family groups will get small parts of the land. The lots will show which family group gets which part of the land. Each tribe will get its part of the land.

[55]"You must force these other people to leave the country. If you let them stay in your country, they will bring many troubles to you. They will be like a needle[a] in your eye and a thorn in your side. They will bring many troubles to the country where you will be living. [56]I showed you what I would do—and I will do that to you!"

The Borders of Canaan

34 The LORD spoke to Moses. He said, [2]"Speak to the Israelites and tell them this: You will soon enter the land of Canaan. I am giving you that land to be your very own. These will be its borders: [3]On the south, you will get part of the desert of Zin near Edom. Your southern border will start at the south end of the Dead Sea. [4]It will cross south of Scorpion Pass. It will go through the town of Zin to Kadesh Barnea and then to Hazar Addar, and then it will pass through Azmon. [5]From Azmon the border will go to the river of Egypt,[b] and it will end at the Mediterranean Sea. [6]Your western border will be the Mediterranean Sea. [7]Your northern border will begin at the Mediterranean Sea and go to Mount Hor. [8]From Mount Hor it will go to Lebo Hamath, and then to Zedad. [9]Then that border will go to Ziphron and it will end at Hazar Enan. So that will be your northern border. [10]Your eastern border will begin at Enan and it will go to Shepham. [11]From Shepham the border will go east of Ain to Riblah. The border will continue along the hills by Lake Galilee.[c] [12]Then the border will continue along the Jordan River. It will end at the Dead Sea. These are the borders around your country."

[13]So Moses gave this command to the Israelites, "That is the land that you will get. You will throw lots to divide the land among the nine tribes and half the tribe of Manasseh, as the LORD commanded. [14]The tribes of Reuben and Gad, and half the tribe of Manasseh have already taken their land. [15]These two and a half tribes took the land near Jericho—they took the land east of the Jordan River."

[16]Then the LORD spoke to Moses. He said, [17]"These are the men who will help you divide the land: Eleazar the priest, Joshua son of Nun, [18]and the leaders of all the tribes. There will be one leader from each tribe. These men will divide the land. [19]These are the names of the leaders:

from the tribe of Judah—Caleb son of Jephunneh;
[20]from the tribe of Simeon—Shemuel son of Ammihud;
[21]from the tribe of Benjamin—Elidad son of Kislon;
[22]from the tribe of Dan—Bukki son of Jogli;
[23]from the descendants of Joseph;
from the tribe of Manasseh—Hanniel son of Ephod;
[24]from the tribe of Ephraim—Kemuel son of Shiphtan;
[25]from the tribe of Zebulun—Elizaphan son of Parnach;
[26]from the tribe of Issachar—Paltiel son of Azzan;
[27]from the tribe of Asher—Ahihud son of Shelomi;
[28]from the tribe of Naphtali—Pedahel son of Ammihud."

[29]The LORD chose these men to divide the land of Canaan among the Israelites.

The Levites' Towns

35 The LORD spoke to Moses. This was in the Jordan Valley in Moab, near the Jordan River, opposite Jericho. He said, [2]"Tell the Israelites that they should give some of the cities in their part of the land to the Levites. The Israelites should give these cities and the pastures around them to the Levites. [3]The Levites will be able to live in them. And all the cattle and other animals that belong to the Levites will be able to eat from the pastures around these cities. [4]⌊How much of your land should you give to the Levites?⌋ From the walls of the cities, go out 450 metres[d]— all that land will belong to the Levites. [5]Measure off an area around the city for the Levites. Start at the north-east corner and measure 900 metres[e] to the south. Then from this corner, measure 900 metres to the west. From there measure 900 metres to the north and from that corner, 900 metres to the east. The city will be in the centre of this area. [6]Six of those cities will be cities of

---

[a] **33:55** *needle* A thin barb or thorn from a plant.
[b] **34:5** *river of Egypt* That is, the stream called "Wadi El-Arish".
[c] **34:11** *Lake Galilee* Literally, "Kinnereth Lake".
[d] **35:4** *450 metres* Literally, "1,000 *cubits*". The people probably let their sheep and cattle use this land.
[e] **35:5** *900 metres* Literally, "2,000 *cubits*". The Levites probably used this land for gardens and vineyards.

safety. If a person accidentally kills someone, that person can run to those towns for safety. In addition to those six cities, you will also give 42 more cities to the Levites. ⁷So you will give a total of 48 cities to the Levites. You will also give them the land around those cities. ⁸The large tribes of Israel will get large pieces of land. The small tribes of Israel will get small pieces of land. So the large tribes will give more cities and the small tribes will give fewer cities to the Levites."

⁹Then the LORD said to Moses, ¹⁰"Tell the people this: You will cross the Jordan River and go into the land of Canaan. ¹¹You must choose towns to be cities of safety. If someone accidentally kills another person, that person can run to one of those towns for safety. ¹²That person will be safe from anyone from the dead man's family who wants to punish the killer until that person is judged in court. ¹³There will be six cities of safety. ¹⁴Three of them will be east of the Jordan River and three of them will be in the land of Canaan, west of the Jordan River. ¹⁵These cities will be places of safety for citizens of Israel and for foreigners and travellers. Any of these people will be able to run to one of these cities if they accidentally kill someone.

¹⁶"If you use an iron weapon[a] to kill someone, you are a murderer, and you must die. ¹⁷If you use a rock large enough to kill someone and you kill another person, you are a murderer, and you must die. ¹⁸If you use a piece of wood large enough to kill someone and you kill another person, you are a murderer, and you must die. ¹⁹A member of the dead person's family[b] can chase you and kill you.

²⁰⁻²¹"You might hit someone with your hand or push someone or throw something at them and kill them. If you did that from hate, you are a murderer, and you must be killed. A member of the dead person's family can chase you and kill you.

²²"You might accidentally kill someone, maybe by pushing or by accidentally hitting them with a tool or weapon. ²³Perhaps you threw a rock that was large enough to kill, but it hit someone you didn't see and killed them. You didn't plan to kill anyone. You didn't hate the person you killed—it was only an accident. ²⁴If that happens, the community must decide what to do. The court must decide if a member of the dead person's family can kill you. ²⁵If the community decides to protect you from the dead person's family, the community must take you back to your city of safety. You must stay there until the official high priest[c] dies.

²⁶⁻²⁷"You must never go outside the limits of your city of safety. If you do and if a member of the dead person's family catches you and kills you, that family member will not be guilty of murder. ²⁸Whoever accidentally killed someone must stay in their city of safety until the high priest dies. After the high priest dies, that person can go back to their own land. ²⁹These rules will be the law forever in all the towns of your people.

³⁰"A killer should be put to death as a murderer only if there are witnesses. No one can be put to death if there is only one witness.

³¹"A murderer must be put to death. Don't take money to change the punishment. That murderer must be killed.

³²"If a person killed someone and then ran to one of the cities of safety, don't take money to let that person go home. That person must stay in that city until the high priest dies.

³³"Don't let your land be polluted with innocent blood. If a person murders someone, the only payment for that crime is that the murderer must be killed! There is no other payment that will free the land from that crime. ³⁴I am the LORD. I will be living in your country with the Israelites, so don't make it unclean with the blood of innocent people."

INSIGHT

God appoints cities of refuge where people who have accidentally killed someone (manslaughter) could be protected. However, if that person left a city of refuge the dead person's family could take revenge.

Numbers 35:6–28

The Land of Zelophehad's Daughters

36 Manasseh was Joseph's son. Makir was Manasseh's son. Gilead was Makir's son. The leaders of Gilead's family went to talk to Moses and the leaders of the tribes of Israel. ²They said, "Sir, the LORD commanded us to get our land by throwing lots. And sir, the LORD commanded that the land of Zelophehad our brother be given to his daughters. ³Maybe a man from one of the other tribes will marry one of Zelophehad's daughters. Will that land leave our family? Will the people of that other tribe

---

[a] **35:16 iron weapon** This shows that the murderer chose a weapon he knew could kill the other person.
[b] **35:19 member of the dead person's family** Literally, "the blood avenger". Also in verses 20–21,24,26–27.
[c] **35:25 official high priest** Literally, "the high priest who was anointed with the holy oil".

get the land? Will we lose the land that we got by throwing lots? ⁴People might sell their land, but in the year of Jubilee, all the land is returned to the tribe that really owns it. At that time who will get the land that belongs to Zelophehad's daughters? Will our tribe lose that land forever?"

⁵Moses gave this command from the LORD to the Israelites: "The men from this tribe of Joseph's people are right. ⁶This is the LORD's command to Zelophehad's daughters: If you want to marry someone, you must marry someone from your own tribe. ⁷In this way land will not be passed from tribe to tribe among the Israelites. Each Israelite will keep the land that belonged to their own ancestors. ⁸And if a woman gets her father's

land, she must marry someone from her own tribe. That way everyone will keep the land that belonged to his ancestors. ⁹So the land must not be passed from tribe to tribe among the Israelites. Each Israelite will keep the land that belonged to their own ancestors."

¹⁰So Zelophehad's daughters obeyed the LORD's command to Moses. ¹¹Zelophehad's daughters— Mahlah, Tirzah, Hoglah, Milcah and Noah— married their cousins on their father's side of the family. ¹²Their husbands were from Manasseh's family groups, so their land remained within their father's family group and tribe.

¹³So these are the laws and commands that the LORD gave to Moses in the Jordan Valley in Moab, by the Jordan River, opposite Jericho.

DEUTERONOMY

Who
Deuteronomy is Moses' farewell speech. The traditional view is that Moses wrote it, although obviously the introduction and the account of Moses' death were by a different hand.

When
If Moses was involved, it probably dates from around the thirteenth century BC, although it was probably compiled sometime later.

What
It is a reminder of all that had happened to the Israelites, of how God brought them out of slavery and, despite their own lack of faith, brought them to the verge of the promised land. Indeed, the name Deuteronomy means "repetition of the law".

At the time of this speech, Moses and the Israelites are in Moab, just where the Jordan flows into the Dead Sea. The leadership has been handed over to Joshua, and Moses is saying "farewell". He reminds the people of the things that have happened to them and the laws they are to obey. He issues promises of blessings if Israel obeys God, and dire warnings of the consequences should they disobey. These warnings look far ahead, to a time when the Israelites would be in exile and when all the dreams of a "promised land" seemed to have turned to dust. The Lord warns of punishment, but he also promises that he will bring his people back (30:1–10).

The God that comes across in Deuteronomy is more caring and personal than he often seems in the other books of the Pentateuch. He teaches his people through their trials. In all their wanderings they never go hungry, their clothes don't wear out and they don't even get swollen feet! Now this loving God has led them to a land of plenty (8:1–9).

Moses knows he isn't going to make it into the land God has promised them. So these speeches are his farewell gifts to the people he has led all these years. He can't go with them. He can't fight their battles any more; but he can remind them of who God is and all that he has done for them.

The New Testament regards Deuteronomy highly – there are nearly one hundred quotations from Deuteronomy in the New Testament.

QUICK TOUR ▶ DEUTERONOMY

First speech 1:1–46
No entry 3:1–29
Ten Commandments 5:1–33
Best rule 6:1–25
Holy Box and tablets 10:1–9

False gods 12:29 – 13:18
Blessings 28:1–14
Joshua 31:1–8
Moses' song 31:30 – 32:47
Moses' death 34:1–12

"Today I have given you a choice between life and death, success and disaster."
Deuteronomy 30:15

Moses Talks to the Israelites

1 These are the commands that Moses gave the Israelites while they were in the Jordan Valley, in the desert east of the Jordan River. This was opposite Suph, between the desert of Paran and the cities Tophel, Laban, Hazeroth and Dizahab.

²The journey from Mount Horeb through the mountains of Seir to Kadesh Barnea takes only eleven days. ³But it was 40 years from the time the Israelites left Egypt until the time they came to this place. On the first day of the eleventh month of the fortieth year, Moses spoke to the people and told them everything the LORD commanded. ⁴This was after he defeated Sihon and Og. Sihon was the king of the Amorites and lived in Heshbon. Og was the king of Bashan and lived in Ashtaroth and in Edrei. ⁵The Israelites were in Moab on the east side of the Jordan River when Moses began to explain what God had commanded:

⁶"At Mount Horeb the LORD our God spoke to us. He said, 'You have stayed at this mountain long enough. ⁷Go to the hill country where the Amorites live and to all the neighbouring areas in the Jordan Valley, the hill country, the western slopes, the Negev and the coast. Go throughout the land of Canaan and Lebanon as far as the great river, the Euphrates. ⁸Look, I am giving you this land. Go and take it. It is the land that I, the LORD, promised to give to your ancestors— Abraham, Isaac and Jacob. I promised to give this land to them and to their descendants.'

Moses Chooses Leaders

⁹"At that time I told you, 'I can't take care of you by myself. ¹⁰And now, there are even more of you. The LORD your God has added more and more people, so that today you are as many as the stars in the sky. ¹¹May the LORD, the God of your ancestors, give you 1,000 times more people than you are now! May he bless you as he promised. ¹²But I cannot take care of you and solve all your arguments by myself. ¹³So choose some men from each tribe, and I will make them leaders over you. Choose wise men with experience who understand people.'

¹⁴"And you said, 'That is a good thing to do.'

¹⁵"So I took the wise, experienced men you chose from your tribes, and I made them your leaders. In this way I gave you leaders over 1,000 people, over 100 people, over 50 people and over 10 people. I also gave you officers for each of your tribes.

¹⁶"At that time I told these judges, 'Listen to the arguments between your people. Be fair when you judge each case. It doesn't matter if the problem is between two Israelites or between an Israelite and a foreigner. You must judge each case fairly. ¹⁷You must treat everyone the same when you judge. You must listen carefully to everyone— whether they are important or not. Don't be afraid of anyone, because your decision is from God. But if there is a case too hard for you to judge, bring it to me and I will judge it.' ¹⁸At that same time I also told you everything you must do.

The Spies Go to Canaan

¹⁹"So we obeyed the LORD our God. We left Mount Horeb and went to the hill country of the Amorites. You remember that big, terrible desert that we walked through. We came as far as Kadesh Barnea. ²⁰Then I said to you, 'You have now come to the hill country of the Amorites. The LORD our God will give us this country. ²¹Look, there it is! Go up and take the land for your own. The LORD, the God of your ancestors, told you to do this, so don't be afraid or worry about anything.'

²²"But all of you came to me and said, 'Let's send some men to look at the land first. They can spy out the land and come back and tell us the way we should go and which cities we will come to.'

²³"I thought that was a good idea. So I chose twelve men from among you, one man from each tribe. ²⁴Then they left and went up to the hill country. They came to the Valley of Eshcol and explored it. ²⁵They took some of the fruit from that land and brought it back to us. They told us about the land and said, 'The LORD our God is giving us a good land.'

²⁶"But you refused to go into the land. You refused to obey the LORD your God. ²⁷You went to your tents and began to complain. You said, 'The LORD hates us! He brought us out of the land of Egypt just to let the Amorites destroy us. ²⁸Where can we go now? The men we sent have frightened us with their report. They said, "The people there are bigger and taller than we are. The cities are big and have walls as high as the sky. And we saw giants*ᵃ* there!"'

²⁹"So I said to you, 'Don't be upset or afraid of those people. ³⁰The LORD your God is in front, leading you. He will fight for you just as he did in Egypt. ³¹You saw what happened in the desert. You saw how the LORD your God carried you like a man carries his child. He brought you safely all the way to this place.' ³²"You didn't trust the LORD your God then either. ³³But he was always in front, going ahead to find a place for you to camp. At night, he was

---

ᵃ **1:28** *giants* Literally, "Anakites", descendants of Anak, a family famous for tall and powerful fighting men. See Num. 13:33.

in the fire that showed you where to go. And during the day, he was in the cloud.

People Not Allowed to Enter Canaan

34"The LORD heard what you said, and he was angry. He made a vow. He said, 35'Not one of you evil people who are alive now will go into the good land that I promised to your ancestors. 36Only Caleb son of Jephunneh will see that land. I will give Caleb the land he walked on, and I will give that land to his descendants, because he did all that I, the LORD, commanded.'

37"The LORD was also angry with me because of you. He said to me, 'Moses, you cannot enter the land, either. 38But your helper, Joshua son of Nun, will go into the land. Encourage Joshua, because he will lead the Israelites to take the land for their own. 39You thought your little children would be taken by your enemies. But those children, who are still too young to know right from wrong, will go into the land. I will give it to them. Your children will take the land for their own. 40But you—you must turn around, take the road to the Red Sea and go back into the desert.'

41"Then you said, 'Moses, we sinned against the LORD, but now we will do what the LORD our God commanded us before—we will go and fight.'

"Then each of you put on your weapons. You thought it would be easy to go and take the hill country. 42But the LORD said to me, 'Tell the people not to go up there and fight, because I will not be with them. Their enemies will defeat them!'

43"I spoke to you, but you did not listen. You refused to obey the LORD's command. You thought you could use your own power, so you went up into the hill country. 44The Amorites who lived there came out like a swarm of bees and chased you all the way from Seir to Hormah. 45Then you came back crying to the LORD for help, but the LORD refused to listen to you. 46So you stayed at Kadesh for a long time.

Moses Remembers Israel's Wanderings

2 "Then we did what the LORD told me to do. We went back into the desert on the road that leads to the Red Sea. We travelled for many days to go around the mountains of Seir.*a* 2Then the LORD said to me, 3'You have travelled around these mountains long enough. Turn north. 4Tell the people this: You will pass through the land of Seir. This land belongs to your relatives, the descendants of Esau. They will be afraid of you. Be very careful. 5Don't fight them. I will not give

you any of their land—not even a foot of it, because I gave the hill country of Seir to Esau to keep as his own. 6You must pay the people of Esau for any food you eat or water you drink there. 7Remember that the LORD your God has blessed you in everything you have done. He knows about everything that happened on the journey through this great desert. The LORD your God has been with you these 40 years. You have always had everything you needed.'

8"So we passed by our relatives, the people of Esau living there in Seir. We left the road that leads from the Jordan Valley to the towns of Elath and Ezion Geber. We turned onto the road that goes to the desert in Moab.

Moses Tells What Happened at Ar

9"The LORD said to me, 'Don't bother the Moabites. Don't start a war against them. I will not give you any of their land. They are the descendants of Lot,*b* and I gave them the city of Ar.'"

10(In the past, the Emites lived in Ar. They were strong people, and there were many of them. They were very tall, like the Anakites. 11The Anakites were part of the Rephaites. People thought the Emites were also Rephaites, but the people of Moab called them Emites. 12The Horites also lived in Seir in the past. Then Esau's people destroyed the Horites, took their land and settled there, just as the Israelites did to the people in the land that the LORD gave them.)

13"The Lord said to me, 'Now go to the other side of Zered Valley.' So we crossed Zered Valley. 14It was 38 years from the time we left Kadesh Barnea until the time we crossed Zered Valley. As the LORD had vowed, all the fighting men in our camp from that generation had died. 15The LORD had opposed those men until they were all dead and gone from our camp.

16"After all the fighting men were dead and gone, 17the LORD said to me, 18'Today you must cross the border at Ar and go into Moab. 19You will be very close to the Ammonites. Don't bother them or fight with them, because I will not give you their land. They are descendants of Lot, and I have given that land to them.'"

20(That country is also known as the Land of Rephaim. The Rephaites lived there in the past. The people of Ammon called them the Zamzummites. 21There were many Rephaites, and they were very strong and tall like the Anakites. But the LORD helped the Ammonites destroy them. The Ammonites took that land and live there now. 22God did the same thing for

---

a 2:1 **Seir** Another name for Edom.
b 2:9 **descendants of Lot** Lot's sons were Moab and Ammon. See Gen. 19:30–38.

Esau's people. In the past the Horites lived in Seir.[a] But Esau's people destroyed the Horites, and Esau's descendants still live there today. [23]God did the same thing for some people from Crete. The Avvites lived in the towns around Gaza, but the Cretans destroyed them, took the land and live there now.)

Defeat of the Amorites

[24]"The Lord said to me, 'Get ready to go across Arnon Valley. I will let you defeat Sihon the Amorite, the king of Heshbon. I will let you take his country. So fight against him and take his land. [25]Today I will make all people everywhere afraid of you. They will hear the news about you, and they will be afraid and shake with fear.'

[26]"While we were in the desert of Kedemoth, I sent messengers to King Sihon of Heshbon. The messengers offered peace to Sihon. They said, [27]'Let us go through your land. We will stay on the road. We will not turn off the road to the right or to the left. [28]We will pay you in silver for any food we eat or any water we drink. We only want to march through your country. [29]Let us go through your land until we go across the Jordan River into the land that the LORD our God is giving us. Other people have let us go through their land—the people of Esau living in Seir and the Moabites living in Ar.'

[30]"But King Sihon of Heshbon would not let us pass through his country. The LORD your God had made him very stubborn and ready to fight. The Lord did this so that he could help you defeat King Sihon. And today we know that is what happened.

[31]"The LORD said to me, 'I am giving King Sihon and his country to you. Now, go and take his land!' [32]"Then King Sihon and all his people came out to fight against us at Jahaz. [33]But the LORD our God gave him to us. We defeated King Sihon, his sons and all his people. [34]We captured all the cities that belonged to King Sihon at that time. We completely destroyed the people in every city—the men, women and children. We did not leave anyone alive! [35]We took only the cattle and the valuable things from those cities. [36]We defeated the town of Aroer on the edge of the Arnon Valley and the other town in the middle of that valley. The LORD let us defeat all the cities between the Arnon Valley and Gilead. No city was too strong for us. [37]But you did not go near the land that belongs to the people of Ammon. You did not go near the shores of the Jabbok River or the cities of the hill country. You did not go near any place that the LORD our God would not let us have.

Fighting the People of Bashan

3 "We turned and went on the road to Bashan. King Og of Bashan and all his men came out to fight against us at Edrei. [2]The LORD said to me, 'Don't be afraid of Og. I have decided to give him to you. I will give you all his men and his land. You will defeat him just as you defeated Sihon, the Amorite king who ruled in Heshbon.'

[3]"So the LORD our God let us defeat King Og of Bashan. We destroyed him and all his men. Not one of them was left. [4]Then we took all the cities that belonged to Og at that time. We took all the cities from Og's people—60 cities in the area of Argob, Og's kingdom in Bashan. [5]All these cities were very strong. They had high walls, gates and strong bars on the gates. There were also many towns that did not have walls. [6]We destroyed them just as we destroyed the cities of King Sihon of Heshbon. We completely destroyed every city and all the people in them, even the women and the babies. [7]But we kept all the cattle and the valuable things from the cities for ourselves.

[8]"In that way we took the land from the two Amorite kings. We took that land on the east side of the Jordan River, from Arnon Valley to Mount Hermon. [9](The people from Sidon call Mount Hermon, Sirion, but the Amorites called it Senir.) [10]We took all the cities in the high plain and all of Gilead. We took all of Bashan, all the way to Salecah and Edrei. Salecah and Edrei were cities of Og's kingdom of Bashan."

[11](Og was the king of Bashan. He was one of the few Rephaites still alive. His bed was made from iron, and it was over 4 metres long and almost 2 metres wide.[b] The bed is still in the city of Rabbah, where the Ammonites live.)

The Land East of the Jordan River

[12]"So we took that land to be ours. I gave part of this land to the tribes of Reuben and Gad. I gave them the land from Aroer in the Arnon Valley to the hill country of Gilead with the cities in it. They got half of the hill country of Gilead. [13]I gave the other half of Gilead and the whole area of Bashan to half the tribe of Manasseh."

(Bashan was Og's kingdom. Part of Bashan was called Argob. It was also called the Land of Rephaim. [14]Jair, from the tribe of Manasseh, took the whole area of Argob. That area went all the way to the border of the Geshurites and the Maacathites. It was named for Jair, and even today people call Bashan the Towns of Jair.)

---

[a] *2:22* *Seir* The hill country of Edom.
[b] *3:11* **4 metres long and almost 2 metres wide** Literally, "9 *cubits* long and 4 *cubits* wide, following the measure of a man's *cubit*".

¹⁵"I gave Gilead to Makir. ¹⁶And to the tribe of Reuben and the tribe of Gad, I gave the land that begins at Gilead and goes from the Arnon Valley to the Jabbok River. The middle of the valley is one border. The Jabbok River is the border for the Ammonites. ¹⁷The Jordan River near the desert is their western border. Lake Galilee*a* is north of this area and the Dead Sea*b* is to the south. It is at the bottom of the cliffs of Pisgah, which are to the east.

¹⁸"At that time I gave those tribes this command: 'The LORD your God has given you the land on this side of the Jordan River to live in. But now your fighting men must take their weapons and lead the other Israelite tribes across the river. ¹⁹Your wives, your little children and your cattle (I know you have many cattle) will stay here in the cities I have given you. ²⁰But you must help your Israelite relatives until they take the land that the LORD is giving them on the other side of the Jordan River. Help them until the LORD gives them peace, just as he did for you here. Then you may come back to this land that I have given you.'

²¹"Then I told Joshua, 'You have seen all that the LORD your God has done to these two kings. The LORD will do the same thing to all the kingdoms you will enter. ²²Don't fear the kings of these lands, because the LORD your God will fight for you.'

Moses Not Allowed into Canaan

²³"Then I begged the LORD to do something special for me. I said, ²⁴'Lord GOD, I am your servant. I know that you have shown me only a small part of the wonderful and powerful things you will do. There is no god in heaven or earth that can do the great and powerful things you have done. ²⁵Please let me go across the Jordan River and see the good land on the other side. Let me see the beautiful hill country and Lebanon.'

²⁶"But the LORD was angry with me because of you and refused to listen to me. The LORD said to me, 'That's enough! Don't say another word about this. ²⁷Go up to the top of Mount Pisgah. Look to the west, to the north, to the south and to the east. You may see these things with your eyes, but you can never go across the Jordan River. ²⁸You must give instructions to Joshua. Encourage him. Make him strong, because Joshua must lead the people across the Jordan River. You can see the land, but Joshua will lead them into that land. He will help them take the land and live in it.'

²⁹"So we stayed in the valley opposite Beth Peor.

Moses' Warning to Obey God's Laws

4 "Now, Israel, listen to the laws and to the commands that I teach you. Obey them and you will live. Then you can go in and take the land that the LORD, the God of your ancestors, is giving you. ²You must not add to what I command you. And you must not take anything away. You must obey the commands of the LORD your God that I have given you.

³"You have seen what the LORD did at Baal Peor. The LORD your God destroyed all your people who followed the false god Baal at that place. ⁴But all of you who stayed with the LORD your God are alive today.

⁵"I taught you the laws and rules that the LORD my God commanded me. I did this so you could obey them in the land you are ready to enter and take for your own. ⁶Obey these laws carefully. This will show the people of the other nations that you are wise and sensible. They will hear about these laws and say, 'Truly, the people of this great nation are wise and sensible.'

⁷"The LORD our God is near when we ask him to help us. No other nation has a god like that! ⁸And no other nation is great enough to have laws and rules as good as the teachings I give you today. ⁹But you must be careful! Be sure that as long as you live you never forget what you have seen. You must teach these things to your children and grandchildren. ¹⁰Remember the day you stood before the LORD your God at Mount Horeb. The LORD said to me, 'Gather the people together to listen to what I have to say. Then they will learn to respect me as long as they live on earth. And they will teach these things to their children.' ¹¹You came near and stood at the bottom of the mountain. The mountain burned with fire that reached up to the sky. There were thick black clouds and darkness. ¹²Then the LORD spoke to you from the fire. You heard the sound of someone speaking, but you did not see any form. There was only a voice. ¹³The Lord told you about his agreement, which he commanded you to obey. He told you about the Ten Commandments, which he wrote on two stone tablets. ¹⁴At that time the LORD also commanded me to teach you the other laws and rules that you must follow in the land you are going to take and live in.

¹⁵"On the day the LORD spoke to you from the fire at Mount Horeb, you did not see him—there was no shape for God. ¹⁶So be careful! Don't sin and destroy yourselves by making false gods or statues in the shape of any living thing. Don't make an idol that looks like a man or a woman, ¹⁷or like an animal on the earth or like a bird that

---

a **3:17** *Lake Galilee* Literally, "Kinnereth Lake".
b **3:17** *Dead Sea* Literally, "Arabah Sea". Also called the "Salt Sea".

flies in the sky. [18]And don't make an idol that looks like anything that crawls on the ground or like a fish in the sea. [19]And be careful when you look up and see the sun, the moon and the stars—all the many things in the sky. Be careful that you are not tempted to worship and serve them. The LORD your God lets the other people in the world do this. [20]But the LORD brought you out of Egypt to make you his own special people. He saved you from Egypt. It was as if he pulled you from a hot furnace.[a] And now you are his people.

[21]"The LORD was angry with me because of you. He swore that I could not go across the Jordan River into the good land that the LORD your God is giving you. [22]So I must die here in this land. I cannot go across the Jordan River, but you will soon go across it and take that good land and live there. [23]You must be careful not to forget the agreement that the LORD your God made with you. You must obey the LORD's command. Don't make any idols in any form, [24]because the LORD your God hates it when his people worship other gods. And he can be like a fire that destroys!

[25]"You will live in the country for a long time. You will have children and grandchildren there. After all that time, be sure that you do not then ruin your lives by making any kind of idol! That is something the LORD your God considers evil, and it would make him very angry! [26]So I am warning you now. Heaven and earth are my witnesses! If you do such an evil thing, you will quickly be destroyed! You are crossing the Jordan River now to take that land. But if you make any idols, you will not live there for very long. No, you will be destroyed completely! [27]The LORD will scatter you among the nations. And only a few of you will be left alive to go to the countries where the LORD will send you. [28]There you will serve gods made by men—things made of wood and stone that cannot see or hear or eat or smell! [29]But there in these other lands you will look for the LORD your God. And if you look for him with all your heart and soul, you will find him. [30]When you are in trouble—when all these things happen to you— then you will come back to the LORD your God and obey him. [31]The LORD your God is a merciful God! He will not leave you there or destroy you completely. He will not forget the agreement that he made with your ancestors.

Think About the Great Things God Did

[32]"Has anything this great ever happened before? Never! Look at the past. Think about everything that happened before you were born. Go all the way back to the time when God made people on the earth. Look at everything that has happened anywhere in the world. Has anyone ever heard about anything as great as this? No! [33]You people heard God speaking to you from a fire, and you are still alive. Has that ever happened to anyone else? No! [34]Has any other god ever tried to go and take a people for himself from inside another nation? No! But you yourselves have seen everything that the LORD your God did for you. He showed you his power and strength. You saw the troubles that tested the people. You saw miracles and wonders. You saw war and the terrible things that happened.

[35]"The LORD showed you all this so that you would know that he is God. There is no other god like him. [36]He let you hear his voice from heaven so that he could teach you a lesson. On earth he let you see his great fire, and he spoke to you from it. [37]He loved your ancestors. That is why he chose you, their descendants. And that is why he brought you out of Egypt. He was with you and brought you out with his great power. [38]When you moved forward, he forced out nations that were greater and more powerful than you. And he led you into their land. He gave you their land to live in, as he is still doing today.

[39]"So today you must remember and accept that the LORD is God. He is God in heaven above and on the earth below. There is no other god! [40]And you must obey his laws and commands that I give you today. Then everything will go well with you and your children who live after you. And you will live a long time in the land the LORD your God is giving you—it will be yours forever."

Moses Chooses the Cities of Safety

[41]Then Moses chose three cities on the east side of the Jordan River. [42]Any person who killed someone by accident and not out of hate could run away to one of these three cities and not be put to death. [43]The three cities that Moses chose were Bezer in the high plains for the tribe of Reuben, Ramoth in Gilead for the tribe of Gad and Golan in Bashan for the tribe of Manasseh.

Introduction to the Law of Moses

[44]Moses gave God's law to the Israelites. [45]Moses gave these teachings, laws and rules to the people after they came out of Egypt. [46]He gave them these laws while they were on the east side of the Jordan River, in the valley opposite Beth Peor. They were in the land of Sihon, the Amorite king who lived at Heshbon. Moses and the Israelites had defeated Sihon when they came out of Egypt. [47]They took Sihon's land to keep. They also took the land of King Og of Bashan. These two Amorite kings lived on the east side of

---

[a] **4:20** *furnace* Literally, "iron furnace", that is, a furnace hot enough to soften iron.

the Jordan River. 48This land goes from Aroer on the edge of the Arnon Valley all the way to Mount Sirion,*a* that is, Mount Hermon. 49This land also included the whole Jordan Valley on the east side of the Jordan River. To the south, this land reached to the Dead Sea.*b* To the east, it reached to the foot of Mount Pisgah.

The Ten Commandments

5 Moses called together all the Israelites and said to them, "Israelites, listen to the laws and rules that I tell you today. Learn these laws and be sure to obey them. 2The LORD our God made an agreement with us at Mount Horeb. 3The LORD did not make this agreement with our ancestors, but with us—yes, with all of us who are alive here today. 4The LORD spoke with you face to face at that mountain. He spoke to you from the fire. 5But you were afraid of the fire. And you did not go up the mountain. So I stood between you and the LORD to tell you what the LORD said. He said,

6"I am the LORD your God. I am the one who freed you from Egypt, where you were slaves.

7"You must not worship any other gods except me.

8"You must not make any idols. Don't make any statues or pictures of anything up in the sky or of anything on the earth or of anything down in the water. 9Don't worship or serve idols of any kind, because I am the LORD your God. I hate it when my people worship other gods.*c* People who sin against me become my enemies. And I will punish them, and their children, their grandchildren and even their great-grandchildren. 10But I will be very kind to people who love me and obey my commands. I will be kind to their families for thousands of generations!*d*

11"You must not use the name of the LORD your God to make empty promises. If you do, the LORD will not let you go unpunished.

12"You must keep the Sabbath a special day like the LORD your God commanded. 13Work six days a week and do your job, 14but the seventh day is a day of rest in honour of the LORD your God. So on that day no one should work—not you, your sons and daughters, foreigners living in your cities or your men and women slaves. Not even your cattle, donkeys and other animals should do any work! Your slaves should be able to rest just as you do. 15Don't forget that you were

slaves in the land of Egypt. The LORD your God brought you out of Egypt with his great power and made you free. That is why the LORD your God commands you to always make the Sabbath a special day.

16"You must honour your father and your mother. The LORD your God has commanded you to do this. If you follow this command, you will live a long time, and everything will go well for you in the land that the LORD your God gives you.

17"You must not murder anyone.

18"You must not commit the sin of adultery.

19"You must not steal.

20"You must not tell lies about other people.*e*

21"You must not want another man's wife. You must not want his house, his fields, his men and women servants, his cattle or his donkeys. You must not want to take anything that belongs to another person."

The People Were Afraid of God

22Moses said, "The LORD gave these commands to all of you when you were together there at the mountain. He spoke in a loud voice that came from the fire, the cloud and the thick darkness. After he gave us these commands, he didn't say any more. He wrote his words on two stone tablets and gave them to me.

23"You heard the voice from the darkness while the mountain was burning with fire. Then all the chiefs and the other leaders of your tribes came to me. 24They said, 'The LORD our God has shown us his Glory and his greatness! We heard him speak from the fire. We have seen today that it is possible to continue living even after God speaks to us. 25But if we hear the LORD our God speak to us again, surely we will die! That terrible fire will destroy us. We don't want to die. 26We heard the living God speak from the fire! Has anyone ever done that and lived through it? 27Moses, you go near and listen to everything the LORD our God says. Then tell us what the LORD tells you. We will listen and do everything he says.'

The LORD Speaks to Moses

28"The LORD heard what you said and told me, 'I heard what the people said. And that is fine. 29I only wanted to change their way of thinking—I wanted them to respect me and obey all my commands from the heart. Then everything would be fine with them and with their descendants forever.

---

a **4:48** *Sirion* Or "Siyon".
b **4:49** *Dead Sea* Literally, "Arabah Sea".
c **5:9** *I hate . . . gods* Or "I am El Kanah—the Jealous God."
d **5:10** Or "But I will show mercy to thousands of people who love me and obey my commands."
e **5:20** Or "You must not be a false witness against your neighbour."

[30]"'Go and tell the people to go back to their tents, [31]but you stand here near me. I will tell you all the commands, laws and rules that you must teach them. They must do these things in the land that I am giving them to live in.'

[32]"So you people must be careful to do everything the LORD commanded you. Do not stop following God! [33]You must live the way the LORD your God commanded you. Then you will continue to live, and everything will be fine with you. You will live a long life in the land that will belong to you.

Always Love and Obey God

6 "These are the commands, the laws and the rules that the LORD your God told me to teach you. Obey these laws in the land that you are entering to live in. [2]You and your descendants must respect the LORD your God as long as you live. You must obey all his laws and commands that I give you. If you do this, you will have a long life in that new land. [3]Israelites, listen carefully and obey these laws. Then everything will be fine with you. You will have many children, and you will get the land filled with many good things[a]—just as the LORD, the God of your ancestors, promised.

INSIGHT

For practising Jews these verses called the Shema are as important as the Lord's Prayer is to Christians and they are recited or sung at least twice a day. Parents teach it to their children before they go to sleep at night, and traditionally Jews will say it as their last words on their deathbed.

Deuteronomy 6:4–9

[4]"Listen, people of Israel! The LORD is our God. The LORD is the only God. [5]You must love the LORD your God with all your heart, with all your soul and with all your strength. [6]Always remember these commands that I give you today. [7]Be sure to teach them to your children. Talk about these commands when you sit in your house and when you walk along the road. Talk about them when you lie down and when you get up. [8]Tie them on your hands and wear them on your foreheads to help you remember my

teachings. [9]Write them on the doorposts of your houses and on your gates.

[10]"The LORD your God made a promise to your ancestors, Abraham, Isaac and Jacob. He promised to give you this land, and he will give it to you. He will give you great and rich cities that you did not build. [11]He will give you houses full of good things that you did not put there. He will give you wells that you did not dig. He will give you vineyards and olive trees that you did not plant, and you will have plenty to eat.

[12]"But be careful! Don't forget the LORD. You were slaves in Egypt, but he brought you out of the land of Egypt. [13]Respect the LORD your God and serve only him. You must use only his name to make promises. [14]You must not follow other gods. You must not follow the gods of the people who live around you. [15]The LORD your God is always with you, and he hates it when his people worship other gods![b] So if you follow those other gods, the Lord will become very angry with you. He will destroy you from the face of the earth.

[16]"You must not test the LORD your God like you tested him at Massah. [17]You must be sure to obey the commands of the LORD your God. You must follow all the teachings and laws he has given you. [18]You must do what is right and good—what pleases the LORD. Then everything will go well for you, and you can go in and take the good land that the LORD promised your ancestors. [19]And you will force out all your enemies, just as the LORD said.

Teach Your Children the Things God Did

[20]"In the future your children might ask you, 'The LORD our God gave you teachings, laws and rules. What do they mean?' [21]Then you will say to them, 'We were Pharaoh's slaves in Egypt, but the LORD brought us out of Egypt with his great power. [22]The LORD did great and amazing things. We saw him do these things to the Egyptian people, to Pharaoh and to the people in Pharaoh's house. [23]He brought us out of Egypt so that he could give us the land that he promised our ancestors. [24]The LORD commanded us to follow all these teachings. We must respect the LORD our God. Then he will always keep us alive and doing well, as we are today. [25]If we carefully obey the whole law, exactly as the LORD our God told us to, he will say that we have done a very good thing.'[c]

Israel, God's Special People

7 "The LORD your God will lead you into the land that you are entering to take for your

---

[a] **6:3 land . . . things** Literally, "land flowing with milk and honey".

[b] **6:15 he . . . gods** Or "The LORD your God is El Kanah—the Jealous God."

[c] **6:25** Or "The LORD our God will credit us with righteousness if we carefully obey the whole law, exactly as he commanded us."

JUST THE ONE WILL DO

There's excitement and tension in the air – the days of wandering and waiting, the forty long years of punishment for not believing God's promises in the desert are almost over (Deuteronomy 8:1–5) – as Moses gathers the people for some final instructions . . .

DIG IN

READ Deuteronomy 6:1–5

- How is God described? (Check out Deuteronomy 4:7 too.)
- What are the people to do?

Whenever the word "Lord" is used for God at this time, the people would remember the time he appeared to Moses at the burning bush (Exodus 3), keeping his promises to rescue them. When the people hear this name in Deuteronomy it reminds them of all their history.

There's no getting around what Moses says here. There is only one God and that God is the Lord. There's no other God like him, so worship him with everything you are: it's easy to say, not exactly easy to do . . .

READ Deuteronomy 4:32–40

Moses a little earlier on had retraced some of that history with the people. Check out Moses' passion and enthusiasm for God and all he's done.

- What has God done for the people?
- How is God described?
- What should the people do in response?

Can you imagine all the people standing there nodding their heads in agreement? Maybe some even shed a few tears – it's pretty convincing stuff. If you read chapters 10 – 12 it gets even better . . . They are his special people, chosen and loved, rescued and cared for. He is the only God they should want to love and worship. The question is, do they?

READ Deuteronomy 7:1–11 and 10:12–22

Going into the new land is going to be a bit like walking into a sweet shop – there will be so much choice: lots of other religions, gods and ways of thinking which will threaten to take their love away from God.

- What should the people do to the false gods (v.5)?
- Why (vv.6–7)?
- What does God want (chapter 10)?

It's radical and violent – chucking the statues in the dustbin isn't going to cut it – they have to totally destroy anything that takes the place of God. The other gods are all rubbish anyway!

Did you notice how closely the people's freedom from Egypt is linked to their worship of God alone? Belonging to God and worshipping him, including obeying his rules, is the most freeing thing anyone can do.

DIG THROUGH

- How do you think about God – is he the only one worth worshipping? Why not read Isaiah 44:6–28 and see how God compares other things that get worshipped with himself.
- We may not have actual carved images these days but there are plenty of things that take God's place of importance – money, friends, relationships, doing what I want when I want . . . What gods do you have in your life? What do you need to do?

own. He will force out many nations for you—the Hittites, Girgashites, Amorites, Canaanites, Perizzites, Hivites and Jebusites—seven nations greater and more powerful than you. ²The Lord your God will put these nations under your power. And you will defeat them. You must destroy them completely. Don't make an agreement with them or show them mercy. ³Don't marry any of them, and don't let your sons or daughters marry any of the people from those other nations. ⁴If you do, they will turn your children away from following me. Then your children will serve other gods, and the Lord will be very angry with you. He will quickly destroy you!

Destroy False Gods

⁵"This is what you must do to those nations: You must smash their altars and break their memorial stones into pieces. Cut down their Asherah poles and burn their statues. ⁶Do this because you are the Lord's own people. From all the people on earth, the Lord your God chose you to be his special people—people who belong only to him. ⁷Why did the Lord love and choose you? It was not because you are such a large nation. You had the fewest of all people! ⁸But the Lord brought you out of Egypt with great power and made you free from slavery. He freed you from the control of Pharaoh, the king of Egypt. The Lord did this because he loves you and he wanted to keep the promise he made to your ancestors.

⁹"So remember that the Lord your God is the only God, and you can trust him! He keeps his agreement. He shows his love and kindness to all people who love him and obey his commands. He continues to show his love and kindness through a thousand generations, ¹⁰but the Lord punishes people who hate him. He will destroy them. He will not be slow to punish those who hate him. ¹¹So you must be careful to obey the commands, laws and rules that I give you today.

The Lord Promises to Help His People

¹²"If you listen to these laws, and if you are careful to obey them, the Lord your God will keep his agreement of love with you. He promised this to your ancestors. ¹³He will love you and bless you. He will make your nation grow. He will bless your children. He will bless your fields with good crops and will give you grain, new wine and oil. He will bless your cows with calves and your sheep with lambs. You will have all these blessings in the land that he promised your ancestors to give you.

¹⁴"You will be blessed more than all people. Every husband and wife will be able to have children. Your cows will be able to have calves. ¹⁵The Lord will take away all sickness from you and he will not let you catch any of the terrible diseases that you had in Egypt. But he will make your enemies catch those diseases. ¹⁶You must destroy all the people the Lord your God helps you defeat. Don't feel sorry for them, and don't worship their gods! They will trap you—they will ruin your life.

¹⁷"Don't say in your heart, 'These nations are stronger than we are. How can we force them out?' ¹⁸You must not be afraid of them. You must remember what the Lord your God did to Pharaoh and to all the people of Egypt. ¹⁹You saw the great troubles he gave them and the amazing things he did. You saw the Lord use his great power and strength to bring you out of Egypt. The Lord your God will use that same power against all the people you fear.

²⁰"The Lord your God will send the hornet[a] against them. He will do this until he destroys all the people who escaped and tried to hide. ²¹Don't be afraid of them, because the Lord your God is with you. He is a great and awesome God. ²²The Lord your God will force those nations to leave your country little by little. You will not destroy them all at once. If you did, the wild animals would grow to be too many for you. ²³But the Lord your God will let you defeat those nations. He will confuse them in battle, until they are destroyed. ²⁴He will help you defeat their kings. You will kill them, and the world will forget they ever lived. No one will be able to stop you. You will destroy them all!

²⁵"You must throw the statues of their gods into the fire and burn them. Don't even think about wanting or keeping the silver or gold on those statues for yourselves. That's like walking into a trap—it will ruin your life. The Lord your God hates those idols. ²⁶You must not bring any of those hated idols into your homes, or you will be destroyed just as they will be. You must hate them as the sickening things they are! They are sure to be destroyed.

Remember the Lord

8 "You must obey all the commands that I give you today, because then you will live and grow to become a great nation. You will get the land that the Lord promised to your ancestors. ²And you must remember the entire journey that the Lord your God has led you through these 40 years in the desert. He was testing you. He wanted to make you humble. He wanted to know

---

ᵃ **7:20 hornet** A stinging insect like a large wasp or bee. Here, it might mean God's angel or his great power.

what is in your heart. He wanted to know if you would obey his commands. 3He humbled you and let you be hungry. Then he fed you with manna—something you did not know about before. It was something your ancestors had never seen. Why did the Lord do this? Because he wanted you to know that it is not just bread that keeps people alive. People's lives depend on what the Lord says. 4These past 40 years, your clothes did not wear out, and your feet did not swell. 5You must remember that the Lord your God teaches and corrects you as a father teaches and corrects his son.

6"You must obey the commands of the Lord your God. Follow him and respect him. 7The Lord your God is bringing you into a good land—a land with rivers and pools of water. Water flows out of the ground in the valleys and hills. 8It is a land with wheat and barley, grapevines, fig trees and pomegranates. It is a land with olive oil and honey. 9There you will have plenty of food and everything you need. It is a land where the rocks are iron. You can dig copper out of the hills. 10You will have all you want to eat. Then you will praise the Lord your God for the good land he has given you.

Don't Forget What the Lord Has Done

11"Be careful. Don't forget the Lord your God! Be careful to obey the commands, laws and rules that I give you today. 12Then you will have plenty to eat, and you will build good houses and live in them. 13Your cattle, sheep and goats will grow large. You will get plenty of gold and silver. You will have plenty of everything. 14When that happens, you must be careful not to become proud. You must not forget the Lord your God. You were slaves in Egypt, but he made you free and brought you out of that land. 15He led you through that great and terrible desert where there were poisonous snakes and scorpions. The ground was dry, and there was no water anywhere. But he gave you water out of a solid rock. 16In the desert he fed you manna—something your ancestors had never seen. He tested you to make you humble so that everything would go well for you in the end. 17Don't ever say to yourself, 'I got all this wealth by my own power and ability.' 18Remember the Lord your God is the one who gives you power to do these things. He does this because he wants to keep the agreement that he made with your ancestors, as he is doing today! 19"Don't ever forget the Lord your God. Don't ever follow other gods or worship and serve them. If you do that, I warn you today: You will surely be destroyed! 20The Lord is destroying other nations for you. But if you stop listening to the Lord your God, you will be destroyed just like them!

The Lord Will Be With Israel

9 "Listen, you Israelites! You will go across the Jordan River today. You will go into that land to force out nations greater and stronger than you. Their cities are big and have walls as high as the sky! 2The people there are tall and strong. They are the Anakites. You know about them. You heard our spies say, 'No one can win against the Anakites.' 3But you can be sure that it is the Lord your God who goes across the river before you—and God is like a fire that destroys! He will destroy those nations and make them fall before you. You will force those nations out and quickly destroy them. The Lord has promised you that this will happen.

INSIGHT

Moses associates God with fire. Other people in the Bible do the same, including: Elijah (1 Kings 18), Asaph (Psalm 50:3), the writer of the letter to the Hebrews (Hebrews 12:29) and the apostle John (Revelation 2:18).

Deuteronomy 9:3

4"The Lord your God will force those nations out for you. But don't say to yourselves, 'The Lord brought us to live in this land because we are such good people.' No, the Lord forced those nations out because they were evil, not because you were good. 5You are going in to take their land, but not because you are good and do what is right. You are going in, and the Lord your God is forcing those people out because of the evil way they lived. And the Lord wants to keep the promise he made to your ancestors, Abraham, Isaac and Jacob. 6The Lord your God is giving you that good land to live in, but you should know that it is not because you are good. The truth is that you are very stubborn people!

Remember the Lord's Anger

7"Remember how you made the Lord your God angry in the desert. Never forget that! From the day you left the land of Egypt to the day you came to this place, you have refused to obey the Lord. 8You made the Lord angry at Mount Horeb. The Lord was angry enough to destroy you! 9I went up the mountain to get the stone tablets. The agreement that the Lord made with you was written on those stones. I stayed on the mountain 40 days and 40 nights. I did not eat any food or drink any water. 10The Lord gave me the two stone tablets. He wrote his commands on the stones with his finger. The LORD wrote everything he said to you from the fire when you were gathered together at the mountain. ¹¹"So at the end of 40 days and 40 nights, the LORD gave me two stone tablets—the stones of the agreement. ¹²Then the LORD said to me, 'Get up and quickly go down from here. The people you brought out of Egypt have ruined themselves. They stopped obeying my commands so quickly. They melted gold and made an idol for themselves.'

¹³"The LORD also said to me, 'I have watched these people. They are very stubborn! ¹⁴Let me destroy these people completely, so no one will even remember their names. Then I will make another nation from you that is stronger and greater than these people.'

The Golden Calf

¹⁵"Then I turned and came down from the mountain. The mountain was burning with fire. And the two stone tablets of the agreement were in my hands. ¹⁶I looked and I saw you had sinned against the LORD your God. I saw the calf you made from melted gold! You stopped obeying the LORD so quickly. ¹⁷So I took the two stone tablets and threw them down. There before your eyes I broke the stones into pieces. ¹⁸Then I bowed down before the LORD with my face to the ground for 40 days and 40 nights, as I did before. I did not eat any food or drink any water. I did this because you had sinned so badly. You did what the LORD considers evil, and you made him angry. ¹⁹I was afraid of the LORD's terrible anger. He was angry enough to destroy you, but the LORD listened to me again. ²⁰The LORD was very angry with Aaron—enough to destroy him! So I also prayed for Aaron at that time. ²¹I took that terrible thing, the calf you made, and burned it in the fire. I broke it into small pieces. And I crushed the pieces until they were dust. Then I threw the dust into the river that came down from the mountain.

Moses Asks God to Forgive Israel

²²"Also, at Taberah, Massah and Kibroth Hattaavah you made the LORD angry. ²³And you did not obey when the LORD told you to leave Kadesh Barnea. He said, 'Go up and take the land I am giving you.' But you refused to obey the LORD your God. You did not trust him. You did not listen to his command. ²⁴All the time that I have known you, you have refused to obey the LORD.

²⁵"So I bowed down before the LORD 40 days and 40 nights, because the LORD said he would destroy you. ²⁶I prayed to the LORD. I said, 'Lord GOD, don't destroy your people. They belong to you. You freed them and brought them out of Egypt with your great power and strength. ²⁷Remember your promise to your servants Abraham, Isaac and Jacob. Forget how stubborn these people are. Don't look at their evil ways or their sins. ²⁸If you punish your people, the Egyptians might say, "The LORD was not able to take his people into the land he promised them. And he hated them. So he took them into the desert to kill them." ²⁹But they are your people, Lord. They belong to you. You brought them out of Egypt with your great power and strength.'

New Stone Tablets

10 "At that time the LORD said to me, 'You must cut out two stone tablets like the first two stones. Then you must come up to me on the mountain. Also make a wooden box. ²I will write on the stone tablets the same words that were on the first stones—the stones you broke. Then you must put these new stones in the Box.'

³"So I made a box from acacia wood. I cut two stone tablets like the first two stones. Then I went up on the mountain. I had the two stone tablets in my hand. ⁴And the LORD wrote on the stones the same words he had written before—the Ten Commandments he spoke to you from the fire, when you were gathered together at the mountain. Then the LORD gave the two stone tablets to me. ⁵I came back down from the mountain. I put the stones in the Box I had made. The LORD commanded me to put them there. And the stones are still there in that Box."

⁶(The Israelites travelled from the wells of the people of Jaakan to Moserah. There Aaron died and was buried. Aaron's son Eleazar served in Aaron's place as priest. ⁷Then the Israelites went from Moserah to Gudgodah. And they went from Gudgodah to Jotbathah, a land of rivers. ⁸At that time the LORD separated the tribe of Levi from the other tribes for his special work. They had the work of carrying the Box of the LORD's Agreement. They also served as priests before the LORD. And they had the work of blessing people in the LORD's name. They still do this special work today. ⁹That is why the people from the tribe of Levi did not get any share of land like the other tribes did. They have the LORD for their share. That is what the LORD your God promised them.)

¹⁰"I stayed on the mountain 40 days and 40 nights, like the first time. The LORD also listened to me at that time. He decided not to destroy you. ¹¹The LORD said to me, 'Go and lead the people on their journey. They will go in and live in the land that I promised to give to their ancestors.'

What the LORD Really Wants

12"Now, Israelites, listen! What does the LORD your God really want from you? The LORD your God wants you to respect him and do what he says. He wants you to love him and to serve the LORD your God with all your heart and with all your soul. 13So obey the laws and commands of the LORD that I am giving you today. These laws and commands are for your own good.

14"Everything belongs to the LORD your God. The heavens, even the highest heavens, belong to him. The earth and everything on it belong to him. 15The LORD loved your ancestors very much. He loved them so much that he chose you, their descendants, to be his people. He chose you instead of any other nation, and you are still his chosen people today.

16"Stop being stubborn. Give your hearts to God. 17The LORD is your God. He is the God of gods and the Lord of lords. He is the great God. He is the amazing and powerful fighter. To him everyone is the same. He does not accept money to change his mind. 18He defends widows and orphans. He loves even the foreigners living among us. He gives them food and clothes. 19So you must also love them, because you yourselves were foreigners in the land of Egypt.

20"You must respect the LORD your God and worship only him. Never leave him. When you make promises, you must use his name only. 21He is the one you should praise. He is your God. He has done great and amazing things for you. You have seen them with your own eyes. 22When your ancestors went down into Egypt, there were only 70 people. Now the LORD your God has made you as many as the stars in the sky.

Remember the LORD

11 "So you must love the LORD your God. You must do what he tells you to do and always obey his laws, rules and commands. 2Remember today all the great things the LORD your God has done to teach you. It was you, not your children, who saw those things happen and lived through them. You saw how great he is. You saw how strong he is, and you saw the powerful things he does. 3You, not your children, saw the miracles he did in Egypt. You saw what he did to Pharaoh, the king of Egypt and to his whole country. 4You, not your children, saw what he did to the Egyptian army—to their horses and chariots. They were chasing you, but you saw him cover them with the water from the Red Sea. You saw how the LORD completely destroyed them. 5It was you, not your children, who saw everything he did for you in the desert until you came to this place. 6You saw what he did to Dathan and Abiram, the sons of Eliab from Reuben's family. All the Israelites watched as the ground opened up like a mouth and swallowed them, their families, their tents and all their servants and animals. 7It was you, not your children, who saw all the great things the LORD did.

8"So you must obey every command I tell you today. Then you will be strong. And you will be able to go across the Jordan River and take the land that you are ready to enter. 9Then you will live a long life in that country. The LORD promised to give that land to your ancestors and all their descendants. It is a land filled with many good things.a 10The land that you will get is not like the land of Egypt that you came from. In Egypt you planted your seeds and used your feet to pump water from the canals to water your fields like a vegetable garden. 11But the land that you will soon get is not like that. In Israel there are mountains and valleys, and the land gets its water from the rain that falls from the sky. 12The LORD your God cares for that land. The LORD your God watches over it, from the beginning to the end of the year.

13"The Lord says, 'You must listen carefully to the commands I give you today: You must love the LORD your God, and serve him with all your heart and all your soul. If you do that, 14I will send rain for your land at the right time. I will send the autumn rain and the spring rain. Then you can gather your grain, your new wine and your oil. 15And I will make grass grow in your fields for your cattle. You will have plenty to eat.'

16"He says, 'Be careful! Don't be fooled. Don't turn away from me to serve other gods and to bow down to them.' 17If you do that, the LORD will become very angry with you. He will shut the skies, and there will be no rain. The land will not make a harvest, and you will soon die in the good land that the LORD is giving you.

INSIGHT

Some Jews still take these verses literally. They tie "phylacteries" (small boxes which contain passages from the law) to their arms or foreheads. They also attach small boxes called "mezuzot" to the doorframes of their houses.

Deuteronomy 11:18–21

18"Remember these commands I give you. Keep them in your hearts. Write them down and

---

a 11:9 land . . . things Literally, "land flowing with milk and honey".

tie them on your hands and wear them on your foreheads as a way to remember my laws. [19]Teach these laws to your children. Talk about these things when you sit in your houses, when you walk along the road, when you lie down, and when you get up. [20]Write these commands on the doorposts of your houses and on your gates. [21]Then both you and your children will live a long time in the land that the LORD promised to give to your ancestors. You will live there as long as the skies are above the earth.

[22]"Be careful to obey every command I have told you to follow: Love the LORD your God, follow all his ways and be faithful to him. [23]Then, when you go into the land, the LORD will force all those other nations out. You will take the land from nations that are larger and more powerful than you. [24]Wherever you go, the land will be yours—from the desert in the south all the way to Lebanon in the north and from the Euphrates River in the east all the way to the Mediterranean Sea in the west. [25]No one will be able to stand against you. The LORD your God will make the people fear you wherever you go in that land. That is what he promised you before.

Israel's Choice: Blessings or Curses

[26]"Today I am giving you a choice. You may choose the blessing or the curse. [27]You will get the blessing if you listen and obey the commands of the LORD your God that I have told you today. [28]But you will get the curse if you refuse to listen and obey the commands of the LORD your God. So don't stop living the way I command you today, and don't follow other gods that you don't know.

[29]"The LORD your God will lead you to your land. You will soon go in and take that land. At that time you must go to the top of Mount Gerizim and read the blessings to the people from there. And then you must go to the top of Mount Ebal and read the curses to the people from there. [30]These mountains are on the other side of the Jordan River in the land of the Canaanites living in the Jordan Valley. These mountains are towards the west, not far from the oak trees of Moreh near the town of Gilgal. [31]You will go across the Jordan River. You will take the land that the LORD your God is giving you. This land will belong to you. When you are living in this land, [32]you must carefully obey all the laws and rules I give you today.

The Place for Worshipping God

12 "These are the laws and rules that you must obey in your new land. You must carefully obey them as long as you live in that land. The LORD is the God of your ancestors, and he is giving that land to you. [2]You will take that land from the nations that live there now. You must completely destroy all the places where the people of those nations worship their gods. Those places are on high mountains, on hills and under green trees. [3]You must smash their altars and break their memorial stones into pieces. You must burn their Asherah poles and cut down the statues of their gods. Wipe out everything that would remind you of those gods.

[4]"You must not worship the LORD your God in the same way those people worship their gods. [5]The LORD your God will choose a special place among your tribes. That will be the home for his name. You must go to that place to worship him. [6]There you must bring your burnt offerings, your sacrifices, one-tenth of your crops and animals,[a] your special gifts, any gifts you promised to him, any special gift you want to give and the first animals born in your herds and flocks. [7]You and your families will eat together at that place, and the LORD your God will be there with you. You will enjoy sharing the things you worked for there. You will remember that the LORD your God blessed you and gave you these good things.

[8]"You must not continue to worship the way we have been worshipping. Until now everyone has been worshipping God any way they wanted. [9]That's because you have not yet entered the peaceful land that the LORD your God is giving you. [10]But you will go across the Jordan River and live in the land that the LORD your God is giving you. There he will give you rest from all your enemies, and you will be safe. [11]Then the LORD your God will choose a place that will be the home for his name. You must bring everything I command you to that place. Bring your burnt offerings, your sacrifices, one-tenth of your crops and animals, your special gifts and any gifts that you promised to give to the LORD. [12]Come to that place with all your people—your children, all your servants and the Levites living in your towns. (These Levites will not have a share of the land for their own.) Enjoy yourselves together there with the LORD your God. [13]Be sure you don't offer your burnt offerings in just any place you see. [14]The LORD will choose his special place among your tribes. Offer your burnt offerings and do everything else I told you only in that place.

[15]"Whenever you want to eat meat, you can enjoy that blessing from the LORD your God wherever you live. You can butcher the animal just as you do gazelles and deer and anyone, clean or unclean, can eat it. [16]But you must not

---

[a] 12:6 *one-tenth . . . animals* Or "tithes". Also in verse 11.

eat the blood. You must pour the blood on the ground like water.

¹⁷"Also, the things you are offering to God must not be eaten where you live. These include the part of your grain that belongs to God, the part of your new wine and oil that belongs to God, the first animals born in your herd or flock, any gift that you promised to God, any special gifts you want to give or any other gifts for God. ¹⁸You must eat these offerings only in his presence at the special place that the LORD your God will choose. You must go there and eat together with your sons, your daughters, all your servants and the Levites living in your towns. Enjoy yourselves there with the LORD your God. Enjoy what you have worked for. ¹⁹But be sure that you always share these meals with the Levites. Do this as long as you live in your land.

²⁰⁻²¹"The LORD your God promised to make your country larger. When he does this, you might live too far from the place the LORD your God chooses to be the home for his name. If it is too far, and you are hungry for meat, you may eat any meat you have. You may kill any animal from the herd or flock that he has given you. Do this the way I have commanded you. You may eat this meat there where you live any time you want. ²²You may eat this meat the same as you would eat gazelle or deer meat. Anyone can do this—people who are clean and people who are unclean. ²³But be especially careful not to eat the blood, because the life is in the blood. You must not eat meat that still has its life in it. ²⁴Don't eat the blood. Pour it out like water onto the ground. ²⁵So don't eat blood. You must do what the LORD says is right, and good things will happen to you and to your descendants.

²⁶"If you decide to give something special to God, you must go to the special place that the LORD your God will choose. And if you make a special promise, you must go to that place to give that gift to God. ²⁷You must offer your burnt offerings in that place. Offer the meat and the blood of your burnt offerings on the altar of the LORD your God. For your other sacrifices, you must pour the blood on the altar of the LORD your God. Then you may eat the meat. ²⁸Carefully obey all the commands that I give you. When you do what is good and right—what pleases the LORD your God—then everything will go well for you and for your descendants forever.

²⁹"You are going to take your land from other people. The LORD your God will destroy these people for you. You will force them out of that land, and then you will live there. ³⁰But be careful that you don't fall into the same trap they did! Don't go to their false gods for help. Don't say to yourself, 'They worshipped these gods, so I will

worship them too.' ³¹Don't do that to the LORD your God! These people do all kinds of bad things that the LORD hates. They even burn their children as sacrifices to their gods!

³²"You must be careful to do everything I command you. Don't add anything to what I tell you, and don't take anything away.

Don't Serve Other Gods

13 "A prophet or someone who explains dreams might come to you and tell you that they will show you a sign or a miracle. ²And the sign or miracle they told you about might come true. Then they might ask you to follow other gods (gods you don't know) and say to you, 'Let's serve these gods!' ³Don't listen to them, because the LORD your God is testing you. He wants to know if you love him with all your heart and all your soul. ⁴You must follow the LORD your God. Respect him. Obey his commands and do what he tells you. Serve the LORD your God, and never leave him. ⁵Also, you must kill that prophet or person who explains dreams, because they told you to turn against the LORD your God. And it was the LORD your God who brought you out of the land of Egypt, where you were slaves. They tried to pull you away from the life he commanded you to live, so you must kill them to remove this evil from your people.

⁶"Someone close to you might secretly persuade you to worship other gods. It might be your own brother, your son, your daughter, the wife you love or your closest friend. They might say, 'Let's go and serve other gods.' (These are gods that you and your ancestors never knew. ⁷They are the gods of the people who live in the other lands around you, some near and some far away.) ⁸You must not agree with them. Don't listen to them or feel sorry for them. Don't let them go free or protect them. ⁹⁻¹⁰No, you must kill them with stones. You be the first one to pick up stones and throw at them. Then everyone must throw stones to kill them, because they tried to pull you away from the LORD your God. And it was the Lord who brought you out of the land of Egypt, where you were slaves. ¹¹Then all the Israelites will hear about it and be afraid. And they will not do those evil things any more.

¹²"The LORD your God has given you cities to live in. Sometimes you might hear some bad news about one of these cities. You might hear that ¹³some troublemakers from your own nation are persuading the people of their city to do bad things. They might say to the people of their city, 'Let's go and serve other gods.' (These would be gods that you never knew before.) ¹⁴If you hear this kind of news, you must do all you can to learn if it is true. If you learn that it is true,

if you prove that such a terrible thing really did happen, [15]then you must kill all the people of that city and their animals too. You must destroy that city completely. [16]You must gather up everything of value and take it to the centre of the city. Burn the whole city and everything in it as a burnt offering to the LORD your God. You must turn that city into an empty pile of rocks forever, and that city must never be rebuilt. [17]Everything in that city must be destroyed as an offering to God. So you must not keep any of the things for yourselves. If you follow this command, the LORD will stop being so angry with you. He will be kind to you. He will feel sorry for you. He will let your nation grow larger, as he promised your ancestors. [18]This will happen if you listen to the LORD your God—if you obey all his commands that I give you today. You must do what the LORD your God says is right.

Israel, God's Special People

14 "You are the children of the LORD your God. When someone dies, you must not cut yourselves or shave your heads[a] to show your sadness. [2]This is because you are different from other people. You belong to the LORD your God. From all the people in the world, the LORD chose you to be his own special people.

Food the Israelites Are Allowed to Eat

[3]"Don't eat anything that the Lord hates. [4]You may eat these animals: cattle, sheep, goats, [5]deer, gazelles, roe deer, ibex, wild goats, antelopes and mountain sheep. [6]You may eat any animal that has hooves divided into two parts and that chews the cud. [7]But don't eat camels, rabbits or rock badgers. These animals chew the cud, but they don't have split hooves. So these animals are not a clean food for you. [8]And you must not eat pigs. Their hooves are divided, but they don't chew the cud. So pigs are not a clean food for you. Don't eat any meat from pigs. Don't even touch a pig's dead body.

[9]"You may eat any kind of fish that has fins and scales. [10]But don't eat anything living in the water that does not have fins and scales. It is not a clean food for you.

[11]"You may eat any clean bird. [12]But don't eat any of these birds: eagles, vultures, buzzards, [13]red kites, falcons, any kind of kite, [14]any kind of raven, [15]horned owls, screech owls, seagulls, any kind of hawk, [16]little owls, great owls, white owls, [17]desert owls, ospreys, cormorants, [18]storks, any kind of heron, hoopoes or bats.

[19]"All insects with wings are unclean, so don't eat them. [20]But you may eat any clean bird.

[21]"Don't eat any animal that has died by itself. You may give the dead animal to the foreigner in your town, and he can eat it. Or you may sell the dead animal to a foreigner. But you yourselves must not eat the dead animal, because you belong to the LORD your God. You are his special people.

"Don't cook a baby goat in its mother's milk.

Giving One-Tenth

[22]"Every year you must be sure to save one-tenth of all the crops that grow in your fields. [23]Then you must go to the place the Lord chooses to be the home for his name. You will go there to be with the LORD your God. At that place you will eat the tenth of your crops—one-tenth of your grain, your new wine, your oil and the first animals born in your herds and flocks. In this way you will always remember to respect the LORD your God. [24]But that place might be too far for you to travel to. Maybe you will not be able to carry one-tenth of all the crops that the LORD has blessed you with. If that happens, [25]sell that part of your crops and take the money with you to the special place the LORD has chosen. [26]Use the money to buy anything you want—cattle, sheep, wine or beer or any other food. Then you and your family should eat and enjoy yourselves there in that place with the LORD your God. [27]But don't forget the Levites living in your town. Share your food with them because they don't get a share of the land the way you do.

[28]"At the end of every three years, you must gather one-tenth of your harvest for that year. Store this food in your towns. [29]Keep this food for the Levites, because they don't have any land of their own. Also keep this food for the foreigners, orphans and widows who live in your towns. This will provide enough for them to come and eat all they want. If you do this, the LORD your God will bless you in everything you do.

The Special Year of Cancelling Debts

15 "At the end of every seven years, you must cancel debts. [2]This is the way you must do this: Everyone who has lent money to another Israelite must cancel the debt. He should not ask a fellow Israelite to repay the debt, because the LORD told you to cancel debts during that year. [3]You may require a foreigner to repay you, but you must cancel any debt another Israelite owes you. [4]There should not be any poor people in your country, because the LORD your God is giving you this land. And the LORD will greatly bless you. [5]But this will happen only if you obey the LORD your God. You must be careful to obey every command that I have told you today. [6]Then

---

[a] **14:1** *shave your heads* Literally, "shave between your eyes".

the LORD your God will bless you, as he promised. And you will have enough money to make loans to many nations. But you will not need to borrow from anyone. You will rule over many nations. But none of these nations will rule over you.

7"When you are living in the land the LORD your God is giving you, there might be some poor people living among you. You must not be selfish. You must not refuse to give help to them. 8You must be willing to share with them. You must lend them whatever they need.

9"Don't ever refuse to help someone simply because the seventh year, the year for cancelling debts, is near. Don't let an evil thought like that enter your mind. You must never have bad thoughts about someone who needs help. You must not refuse to help them. If you don't help the poor, they might complain to the LORD, and he will judge you guilty of sin.

10"So be sure to give to the poor. Don't hesitate to give to them, because the LORD your God will bless you for doing this good thing. He will bless you in all your work and in everything you do. 11There will always be poor people in the land. That is why I command you to be ready to help your brother or sister. Give to the poor in your land who need help.

Letting Slaves Go Free

12"You might buy a Hebrew man or woman to serve you as a slave. You may keep that person as a slave for six years. But in the seventh year, you must let that person go free. 13But when you let your slave go free, don't send him away with nothing. 14You must give him some of your animals, grain and wine. The LORD your God blessed you and gave you plenty of good things. In the same way, you must give plenty of good things to your slave. 15Remember, you were slaves in Egypt. And the LORD your God set you free. So that is why I am giving you this command today.

16"But one of your slaves might say to you, 'I will not leave you.' He might say this because he loves you and your family and because he has a good life with you. 17Make this servant put his ear against your door and use a sharp tool to make a hole in his ear. This will show that he is your slave forever. You must do this even to the women slaves who want to stay with you.

18"Don't regret letting your slave go free. Remember, he served you for six years for half of what you would have paid a hired worker.*a* The LORD your God will bless you in everything you do.

Rules About Firstborn Animals

19"All the first male animals born in your herd and flock are special. You must give them to the LORD. Don't use any of these animals for your work and don't cut wool from any of these sheep. 20Every year you must take these animals to the place the LORD your God will choose. There with the LORD, you and your family will eat these animals.

21"But if an animal has something wrong with it—if it is lame or blind or has something else wrong with it—then you must not sacrifice that animal to the LORD your God. 22But you may eat the meat from that animal at home. Anyone may eat it—people who are clean and people who are unclean. The rules for eating this meat are the same as the rules for eating gazelles and deer. 23But you must not eat the blood from the animal. You must pour the blood out on the ground like water.

Passover

16 "Remember, in the month of Abib you must celebrate Passover to honour the LORD your God. It was that night in Abib when the LORD your God brought you out of Egypt. 2You must go to the place the LORD your God will choose to be the home for his name. There you must offer the Passover sacrifice to honour the LORD. You must offer the cattle and goats. 3Don't eat bread that has yeast in it with this sacrifice. You must eat bread without yeast for seven days. This bread is called 'Bread of Trouble'. It will help you remember the troubles you had in Egypt. Remember how quickly you had to leave that country. You must remember that day as long as you live. 4There must be no yeast in anyone's house anywhere in the country for seven days. And all the meat you sacrifice on the evening of the first day must be eaten before morning.

5"You must not sacrifice the Passover animal in any of the towns that the LORD your God gives you. 6You must sacrifice the Passover animal only at the place that the LORD your God will choose to be the home for his name. There you must sacrifice the Passover animal in the evening when the sun goes down. This is the festival when you remember that God brought you out of Egypt. 7You must cook the meal and eat it at the place the LORD your God will choose. The next morning you may go back home. 8You must eat bread without yeast for six days. On the seventh day, you must not do any work. On this day the people will come together for a special meeting to honour the LORD your God.

---

a **15:18 Remember . . . hired worker** Or "Remember, he served you for six years for the same amount you would have paid a hired worker."

Festival of Harvest

9"You must count seven weeks from the time you begin to harvest the grain. 10Then celebrate the Festival of Harvest for the LORD your God. Do this by bringing him some special gift you want to bring. Decide how much to give by thinking about how much the LORD your God has blessed you. 11Go to the place the LORD will choose to be the home for his name. You and your people should enjoy yourselves together there with the LORD your God. Take all your people with you— your sons, your daughters and all your servants. And take the Levites, foreigners, orphans and widows living in your towns. 12Remember, you were slaves in Egypt. So be sure to obey these laws.

Festival of Shelters

13"Seven days after you have gathered your harvest in from your threshing floor and from your winepress, you should celebrate the Festival of Shelters. 14Enjoy yourselves at this festival— you, your sons, your daughters, all your servants and the Levites, foreigners, orphans and widows living in your towns. 15Celebrate this festival for seven days at the special place the LORD will choose. Do this to honour the LORD your God. The LORD your God blessed your harvest and all the work you did, so be very happy!

16"Three times a year all your men must come to meet with the LORD your God at the special place he will choose. They must come for the Festival of Unleavened Bread, the Festival of Harvest and the Festival of Shelters. Everyone who comes to meet with the LORD must bring a gift. 17Each man should give as much as he can. He should decide how much to give by thinking about how much the LORD has given him.

Judges and Officers for the People

18"Choose men to be judges and officers in every town that the LORD your God gives you. Every tribe must do this. And these men must be fair in judging the people. 19You must always be fair. You must not favour some people over other

people. You must not take money to change your mind in judgement. Money blinds the eyes of wise people and changes what a good person will say. 20Goodness and Fairness! You must try very hard to be good and fair all the time. Then you will live and keep the land that the LORD your God is giving you.

God Hates Idols

21"When you set up an altar for the LORD your God, you must not place beside the altar any of the wooden poles that honour the goddess Asherah. 22You must not set up special stones for worshipping false gods. The LORD your God hates them.

Use Only Good Animals for Sacrifices

17 "You must not sacrifice to the LORD your God an ox or sheep that has anything wrong with it. The LORD your God would hate that.

Punishment for Worshipping Idols

2"You might hear about an evil thing that happens in one of the cities that the LORD your God is giving you. You might hear that a man or woman in your group has sinned against the LORD your God. You might hear that they have broken his agreement or 3that they have worshipped other gods or maybe the sun, the moon or the stars. I told you never to do that! 4If you hear bad news like this, you must check it carefully. You must learn if it is true that this terrible thing has really happened in Israel. If you prove that it is true, 5you must punish the person who did this evil thing. You must take that man or woman out to a public place near the city gates and kill them with stones. 6But no one should be punished with death if only one witness says that person did this evil thing. But if two or three witnesses say it is true, the person must be killed. 7The witnesses must throw the first stones to kill that person. Then the other people should throw stones to finish killing that person. In this way you will remove this evil from your group.

Difficult Court Decisions

8"There might be some problems that are too hard for your courts to judge. It might be a murder case or an argument between two people. Or it might be a fight in which someone was hurt. When these cases are argued in your towns, your judges there might not be able to decide what is right. Then you must go to the special place that the LORD your God will choose. 9You must go to the Levite priests and to the judge on duty at that time. They will decide what to do about that problem. 10There at the LORD's special place they

---

INSIGHT

Justice is a major theme throughout the Bible. It encompasses the virtues of honesty, integrity, righteousness, fairness and impartiality, all characteristics of God that are revealed in Scripture.

Deuteronomy 16:18–20

will tell you their decision. You must do whatever they say. Be sure to do everything they tell you to do. ¹¹You must accept their decision and follow their instructions exactly—don't change anything!

¹²"You must punish anyone who refuses to obey the judge or the priest who is there at that time serving the LORD your God. That person must die. You must remove this evil person from Israel. ¹³All the people will hear about this punishment and be afraid. Then they will not be stubborn any more.

How to Choose a King

¹⁴"You will enter the land that the LORD your God is giving you. You will take that land and live in it. Then you will say, 'We will put a king over us, like all the nations around us.' ¹⁵When that happens, you must be sure to choose the king that the LORD your God chooses. The king over you must be one of your own people. You must not make a foreigner your king. ¹⁶The king must not get more and more horses for himself. And he must not send people to Egypt to get more horses, because the LORD has told you, 'You must never go back that way.' ¹⁷Also, the king must not have too many wives, because that will make him turn away from the Lord. And he must not make himself rich with silver and gold.

¹⁸"When the king begins to rule, he must write a copy of the law for himself in a book. He must make that copy from the books that the priests from the tribe of Levi keep. ¹⁹He must keep that book with him and read from it all his life, because he must learn to respect the LORD his God. He must learn to completely obey everything the law commands. ²⁰Then the king will not think that he is better than any of his own people. He will not turn away from the law, but he will follow it exactly. Then he and his descendants will rule the kingdom of Israel for a long time.

Supporting the Priests and Levites

18 "The people from the tribe of Levi, that is, the priests and all the other Levites, will not get any share of land in Israel. They will eat some of the offerings that people bring to be burned on the altar as gifts to the LORD. This will be their share ²instead of receiving land like the other tribes. Their share is whatever belongs to the LORD himself, as he said before.

³"When you kill one of your sheep or cattle for a sacrifice, you must give the priests these parts: the shoulder, both cheeks and the stomach. ⁴You must give the priests the first part of your harvest.

You must give them the first part of your grain, your new wine and your oil. You must give the Levites the first wool cut from your sheep. ⁵This is because the LORD your God looked at all your tribes and chose Levi and his descendants to serve him as priests forever.

⁶"Any Levite living in any town anywhere in Israel may leave his home and come to the LORD's special place. He may do this any time he wants. ⁷And this Levite may serve in the name of the LORD his God, the same as all his brother Levites who are on duty before the LORD. ⁸And that Levite will get an equal share with the other Levites, in addition to the share his family normally gets.ᵃ

Israel Must Not Live Like Other Nations

⁹"When you come into the land that the LORD your God is giving you, don't learn to do the terrible things the people of the other nations there do. ¹⁰Don't sacrifice your sons or daughters in the fires on your altars. Don't try to learn what will happen in the future by talking to a fortune-teller or by going to a magician, a witch or a sorcerer. ¹¹Don't let anyone try to put magic spells on people. And don't let anyone try to get advice or secret knowledge from a ghost or the spirit of a dead person. No one should ever try to talk with someone who has died. ¹²The LORD hates anyone who does these things. And because these other nations do these terrible things, the LORD your God will force them out of the land as you enter it. ¹³You must be faithful to the LORD your God, never doing anything he considers wrong.

The LORD's Special Prophet

¹⁴"You will force the other nations out of your land. They listen to people who use magic and try to tell the future. But the LORD your God will not let you do these things. ¹⁵The LORD your God will send to you a prophet. This prophet will come from among your own people, and he will be like me. You must listen to him. ¹⁶God will send you this prophet because that is what you asked him to do. When you were gathered together at Mount Horeb, you became frightened and said, 'Don't let us hear the voice of the LORD our God again! Don't let us see that great fire or we will die!'

¹⁷"The LORD said to me, 'What they ask for is good. ¹⁸I will send them a prophet like you. This prophet will be one of their own people. I will tell him what he must say, and he will tell the people everything I command. ¹⁹This prophet will speak for me, and I will punish anyone who refuses to

---

ᵃ **18:8 in addition . . . gets** Or "without regard to gifts from family and friends."

listen to my commands. ²⁰But a prophet might say something that I did not tell him to say. And he might tell people that he is speaking for me. If this happens, that prophet must be killed. Also a prophet might come that speaks for other gods. That prophet must also be killed.'

²¹"You might be thinking, 'How can we know if something a prophet says is not from the LORD?' ²²If a prophet says he is speaking for the LORD, but what he says does not happen, you will know that the LORD did not say it. You will know that this prophet was speaking his own ideas. You don't need to be afraid of him.

Cities of Safety

19 "The LORD your God is giving you land that belongs to other nations. The LORD your God will destroy those nations. You will live where these people lived. You will take their cities and their houses. When that happens, ²⁻³you must divide the land that the LORD your God is giving you. Divide it into three parts and choose a city in the middle of each part that can be a place of safety. You must also build good roads to these cities. Then whoever kills another person may run to the closest city of safety.

⁴"This is the rule for someone who kills another person and runs to one of these three cities for safety: It must be someone who killed another person accidentally, not out of hatred. ⁵Here is an example: A man goes into the forest with another person to cut wood. The man swings his axe to cut down a tree, but the head of the axe separates from the handle. The axe head hits the other person and kills him. The man who swung the axe may then run to one of these three cities and be safe. ⁶But if the city is too far away, he might not be able to run there fast enough. A close relative*ᵃ* of the person he killed might run after him and catch him before he reaches the city. The relative might kill the man in anger, even though he did not deserve to die because he did not mean to harm anyone. ⁷That is why I commanded you to choose three special cities.

⁸"The LORD your God promised your fathers that he would make your land larger. He will give you all the land that he promised to give to your ancestors. ⁹He will do this if you completely obey his commands that I give you today—if you love the LORD your God and always live the way he wants. Then, when he gives you more land, you should choose three more cities for safety. They should be added to the first three cities. ¹⁰Then innocent people will not be killed in the land that the LORD your God is giving you. And you will not be guilty for any such deaths.

¹¹"But suppose there is a man who hates his neighbour. That man might hide and wait to kill the person he hates. If he kills that person and runs to one of these cities of safety, ¹²the leaders in his home town must send someone to get him and take him away from the city of safety. These leaders must hand him over to the close relative. He is a murderer and he must die. ¹³Don't feel sorry for him. He is guilty of killing an innocent person, and you must remove that guilt from Israel. Then everything will go well for you.

Property Lines

¹⁴"You must not move the stones that mark your neighbour's property. People put them there in the past to mark each person's property. These stones mark the land that the LORD your God gave you.

Witnesses

¹⁵"If someone is accused of doing something against the law, one witness is not enough to prove that the person is guilty. There must be two or three witnesses to prove that the person really did wrong.

¹⁶"A witness might try to hurt another person by lying and saying that this person did wrong. ¹⁷If that happens, both of them must go to the LORD's special house and be judged by the priests and judges who are on duty at that time. ¹⁸When the judges carefully ask their questions, they might find that the witness lied against the other person. If the witnesses tell lies, ¹⁹you must punish them with the same punishment the other person would have received. In this way you will remove this evil from your group. ²⁰Other people will hear about this and be afraid, and people will not do evil things like that again.

²¹"Don't feel sorry about punishing someone who does wrong. If a life is taken, a life must be paid for it. The rule is an eye for an eye, a tooth for a tooth, a hand for a hand, a foot for a foot— the punishment must equal the crime.

Rules for War

20 "When you go out to battle against your enemies, and you see horses, chariots and many more people than you have, you must not be afraid of them. The LORD your God is with you—and he brought you out of Egypt.

²"When you go to the battle, the priest must go to the soldiers and speak to them. ³The priest will say, 'Men of Israel, listen to me! Today you are

---

ᵃ **19:6 *close relative*** Literally, "avenger of blood". When a person was killed, his relative had to be sure the killer was punished. Also in verse 12.

going against your enemies in battle. Don't lose your courage. Don't be troubled or upset. Don't be afraid of the enemy. 4The LORD your God is going with you to help you fight against your enemies. He will help you win!'

5"The Levite officials will say to the soldiers, 'Is there any man here who has built a new house but has not yet dedicated it? That man should go back home. He might be killed in the battle, and then another person will dedicate that man's house. 6Is there any man here who has planted a vineyard but has not yet gathered any of the grapes? That man should go back home. If that man dies in the battle, someone else will enjoy the fruit from his field. 7Is there any man here who is engaged to be married? That man should go back home. If he dies in the battle, another man will marry the woman he is engaged to.'

8"These Levite officials must also say to the people, 'Is there any man here who has lost his courage and is afraid? He should go back home. Then he will not cause the other soldiers to lose their courage too.' 9Then, after the officers have finished speaking to the army, they must choose captains to lead the soldiers.

10"When you go to attack a city, you must first offer peace to the people there. 11If they accept your offer and open their gates, all the people in that city will become your slaves and be forced to work for you. 12But if the city refuses to make peace with you and fights against you, you should surround the city. 13And when the LORD your God lets you take the city, you must kill all the men in it. 14But you may take for yourselves the women, the children, the cattle and everything else in the city. You may use all these things. The LORD your God has given these things to you. 15That is what you must do to all the cities that are far away from you—the cities that are not in the land where you will live.

16"But when you take cities in the land that the LORD your God is giving you, you must kill everyone. 17You must completely destroy all the people—the Hittites, Amorites, Canaanites, Perizzites, Hivites and Jebusites. The LORD your God has commanded you to do this. 18So then they will not be able to teach you to sin against the LORD your God or to do any of the terrible things they do when they worship their gods.

19"When you are making war against a city, you might surround that city for a long time. You must not cut down the fruit trees around that city. You may eat the fruit from these trees, but you must not cut them down. These trees are not the enemy, so don't make war against them. 20But you may cut down the trees that you know are not fruit trees. You may use these trees to build weapons for making war against that city. You may use them until the city falls.

If Someone Is Found Murdered

21 "In the land that the LORD your God is giving you, you might find a dead body in a field, but no one knows who killed that person. 2Your leaders and judges must come out and measure the distance to the towns around the dead body. 3When you learn which town is nearest to the dead body, the leaders of that town must take a cow from their herds. It must be a cow that never had a calf and that has never been used for work. 4The leaders of that town must then bring the cow down to a valley with running water. It must be a valley that has never been ploughed or had anything planted in it. Then the leaders must break the cow's neck there in that valley. 5The priests, the descendants of Levi, must also go there. (The LORD your God has chosen these priests to serve him and to bless people in the name of the LORD. The priests will decide who is right in every lawsuit and whenever someone is hurt.) 6All the leaders of the town nearest the dead body must wash their hands over the cow that had its neck broken in the valley. 7These leaders must say, 'We did not kill this person, and we did not see it happen. 8LORD, you saved your people Israel. Now make us pure. Don't blame us for killing an innocent person.' In this way these men will not be blamed for killing an innocent person. 9In this way you will remove that guilt from your group by doing what the LORD said.

Women Captured in War

10"You might fight against your enemies, and the LORD your God might let you defeat them and take them as captives. 11You might see a beautiful woman among the captives who you want to be your wife. 12You must then bring her into your house where she will shave her head and cut her nails. 13She must change her clothes and take off the clothes she was wearing when she was captured in war. She will stay in your house and be sad about losing her father and her mother for a full month. After that, you may go to her to be her husband, and she will be your wife. 14If you are not pleased with her and choose to divorce her, set her free. You cannot sell her. You had sex with her, so you must not treat her like a slave.

The Oldest Son

15"A man might have two wives. He might love one wife more than the other. Both wives might have children for him, but the firstborn son might be from the wife he does not love. 16When the man divides his property among his children, he cannot give the rights of the firstborn to the son of his favourite wife. 17The man must accept the firstborn son from the wife he does not love. The man must give that son a double share of everything he owns because that son is his first child. The right of the firstborn belongs to that son.

Children Who Refuse to Obey

18"A man might have a son who is stubborn and refuses to obey. This son does not obey his father or mother. They punish the son, but he still refuses to listen to them. 19His father and mother must then take him to the leaders of the town at the town meeting place. 20They must say to the leaders of the town: 'Our son is stubborn and refuses to obey. He does not do anything we tell him to do. He eats and he drinks too much.' 21Then the men in the town must kill the son with stones. By doing this you will remove this evil from your group. Everyone in Israel will hear about this and be afraid.

Criminals Killed and Hanged on a Tree

22"A man might be guilty of a sin that must be punished by death. People might kill him and hang his body on a tree. 23You must not let that body stay on the tree overnight. You must be sure to bury this man on the same day, because the one who hangs on a tree is cursed by God, and you must not let the land that the LORD your God is giving you become unclean.

Other Laws

22 "If you see that your neighbour's ox or sheep is loose, you must not ignore it. Be sure to take it back to its owner. 2If the owner does not live near you or if you don't know who it belongs to, take the ox or sheep to your house. Keep it there until the owner comes looking for it; then give it back. 3You must do the same thing when you find anything that your neighbour might have lost. Don't try selling it to your neighbour—you must give it back.

4"If your neighbour's donkey or ox has fallen down on the road, you must not ignore it. You must help your neighbour lift it up again.

5"A woman must not wear men's clothes, and a man must not wear women's clothes. The LORD your God hates this.

6"You might be walking along a path and find a bird's nest in a tree or on the ground. If the mother bird is sitting with her baby birds or on the eggs, you must not take the mother bird with the babies. 7You may take the babies for yourself, but you must let the mother go. If you obey these laws, things will go well for you, and you will live a long time.

8"When you build a new house, you must build a wall around your roof.*a* Then you will not be guilty for the death of a person who falls from the house.

Things That Must Not Be Put Together

9"You must not plant seeds of grain in the same fields as your grapevines. Why? Because then they become useless*b*—both the grapes and the grain produced by the seeds you planted.

10"You must not plough with an ox and a donkey together.

11"You must not wear clothes made by weaving together wool and linen.

12"Tie several pieces of thread together. Then put these tassels*c* on the four corners of the robes you wear.

Marriage Laws

13"A man might marry a woman and have sex with her. Then he might decide that he does not like her. 14He might accuse her of doing wrong and say, 'I married this woman, but when we had sex, I found she was not a virgin.' By saying this against her, people might think bad things about her. 15If this happens, the girl's father and mother must bring the proof that the girl was a virgin to the town leaders at the meeting place of the town. 16The girl's father must say to the leaders, 'I gave my daughter to this man to be his wife, but now he does not want her. 17This man accused my daughter of doing wrong and said, "I did not find the proof that your daughter is a virgin." But here is the proof that my daughter was a virgin.' Then they should show the cloth*d* to the town leaders. 18Then the leaders of that town must take that man and punish him. 19They must fine him 100 pieces of silver.*e* They will give the money to the girl's father because her husband brought shame to an Israelite girl. And the girl will continue to be the man's wife. He cannot divorce her for the rest of his life.

20"But what the husband said about his wife might be true. The wife's parents might not have the proof that she was a virgin. If this happens,

---

a **22:8 wall around your roof** In ancient Israel, houses had flat roofs that were used as an extra room. This law made the roof a safer place.

b **22:9 they become useless** Literally, "they become holy". This means these things belonged only to God, so they couldn't be used by the people.

c **22:12 tassels** These pieces of string were made from different materials, so they became holy. This helped the people remember God and his commands.

d **22:17 cloth** The bloodstained bed cover that the bride kept from her wedding night to prove she was a virgin when she married.

e **22:19 100 pieces of silver** This is probably twice the amount of money that a man usually paid the father of the bride to seal the marriage agreement. See Deut. 22:29.

21the town leaders must bring the girl to the door of her father's house. Then the men of the town must kill her with stones. She has done a shameful thing in Israel by having sex before she was married. You must remove this evil from your group.

Sexual Sins

22"If a man is found having sex with another man's wife, both of them must die—the woman and the man who had sex with her. You must remove this evil from Israel.

23"A man might meet a virgin girl engaged to another man. He might have sex with her. If this happens in the city, 24you must bring them both out to the public place near the gate of that city, and you must kill them with stones. You must kill the man, because he used another man's wife for sexual sin. And you must kill the girl, because she was in the city but did not call for help. You must remove this evil from your people.

25"But if a man finds an engaged girl out in the field and forces her to have sex with him, only the man must die. 26You must do nothing to the girl. She did nothing that deserves the punishment of death. This is like someone attacking their neighbour and killing them. 27The man found the engaged girl out in the field and attacked her. Maybe she called for help, but there was no one to help her.

28"A man might find a virgin girl who is not engaged and force her to have sex with him. If other people see this happen, 29he must pay the girl's father 50 pieces of silver.*a* And the girl will become the man's wife, because he used her for sexual sin. He cannot divorce her all his life.

30"A man must not bring shame to his father by marrying his father's wife.

People Who Cannot Join in Worship

23 "A man with a crushed testicle or part of his sex organ cut off may not join with the men of Israel to worship the LORD. 2If a man's parents were not legally married, that man may not join with the men of Israel to worship the LORD. And none of his descendants to the tenth generation—may join in that group.

3"An Ammonite or Moabite may not join with the men of Israel when they gather to worship the LORD. And none of their descendants, to the tenth generation, may join in the worship of the LORD. 4The Ammonites and Moabites refused to give you bread and water on your journey at the time you came from Egypt. They also tried to hire Balaam, the son of Beor from the Mesopotamian city of Pethor, to curse you. 5But the LORD your God refused to do what Balaam asked. Instead, the LORD changed the curse into a blessing for you because he loves you. 6You must never try to make peace with the Ammonites or Moabites. As long as you live, don't do anything to help them.

People the Israelites Must Accept

7"You must not hate Edomites, because they are your relatives. You must not hate Egyptians, because you were a stranger in their land. 8The children of the third generation born to the Edomites and Egyptians may join with the people of Israel to worship the LORD.

Keeping the Army Camp Clean

9"When your army goes to fight against your enemies, stay away from everything that would make you unclean. 10If there is any man who is unclean because he had a flow of semen during the night, he must go out of the camp. He must stay away from the camp. 11Then, when evening comes, the man must bathe himself in water. And when the sun goes down, he may come into the camp again.

12"You also must have a place outside the camp where people can go to relieve themselves. 13Among your weapons, you must also carry a stick to dig with. Then, when you relieve yourself, you must dig a hole and cover it up. 14This is because the LORD your God is there with you in your camp to save you and to help you defeat your enemies. So the camp must be holy. He must not see anything unclean among you, or he will leave you.

Other Laws

15"If slaves run away and come to you, don't force them to go back to their masters. 16Runaway slaves may live with you wherever they like in whatever city they choose. You must not trouble them.

17"An Israelite man or woman must never become a temple prostitute. 18The money earned by a prostitute, either a male or female, must not be brought to the special house of the LORD your God. That money cannot be used to pay for a gift that was promised to the LORD your God because he hates what prostitutes do.

19"When you loan something to another Israelite, you must not charge interest. Don't charge interest on money, on food or on anything that may earn interest. 20You may charge interest to a foreigner. But you must not charge interest to another Israelite. If you follow these rules, the

---

a **22:29** *50 pieces of silver* This money became the dowry, the money a man paid to a woman's father to seal the marriage agreement. Often the father saved this money to take care of the woman if something happened to her husband.

LORD your God will bless you in everything you do in the land where you are going to live.

21"When you make a promise to the LORD your God, don't be slow to pay everything you promised. The LORD your God will demand that you pay it. You will sin if you don't pay what you promised. 22If you don't make a promise, you are not sinning. 23But you must do what you say you will do. If you choose to make a promise to the LORD your God, you must do what you promised.

24"When you go through another person's vineyard, you may eat as many grapes as you want. But you cannot put any of the grapes in your basket. 25When you go through another person's field of grain, you may eat all the grain you can pick with your hands. But you cannot use a sickle to cut that person's grain and take it with you.

24 "A man might marry a woman, and then find some secret thing about her that he does not like. If that man is not pleased with her, he must write the divorce papers and give them to her. Then he must send her from his house. 2When she has left his house, she may go and become another man's wife. 3-4But suppose the new husband also does not like her and sends her away. If that man divorces her, the first husband may not take her again to be his wife. Or if the new husband dies, her first husband may not take her again to be his wife. She has become unclean to him. If he married her again, he would be doing something the LORD hates. You must not sin like this in the land that the LORD your God is giving you.

5"When a man is newly married, he must not be sent into the army. And he must not be given any other special work. For one year he must be free to stay at home and make his new wife happy.

6"When you lend someone something, you must not take as security*a* any part of the stones used to grind flour. That would be the same as taking away their food.

7"Someone might kidnap another Israelite— one of their own people. And that kidnapper might sell that person as a slave. If that happens, that kidnapper must be killed. You must remove this evil from your group.

8"When you have a very bad skin disease, be very careful to follow everything the Levite priests teach you. You must follow carefully what I told the priests to do. 9Remember what the LORD your God did to Miriam*b* on your journey out of Egypt.

10"When you give someone any kind of loan, you can keep something they own until they pay you back. But you must not go into their house to get what you will keep as the security. 11You must wait outside for the person to bring the security to you. 12If he is poor and gives you his only coat as security, you must not keep it overnight. 13You must give that security back to him every evening. Then he will have a coat to sleep in. He will bless you, and the LORD your God will accept this as living right and doing good.

14"You must not cheat a hired servant who is poor and needy. It does not matter if he is an Israelite or if he is a foreigner living in one of your cities. 15Give him his pay every day before sunset, because he is poor and depends on the money. If you don't pay him, he will complain against you to the LORD, and you will be guilty of sin.

16"Parents must not be put to death for something their children did. And children must not be put to death for something their parents did. People should be put to death only for a bad thing that they themselves did.

17"You must make sure that foreigners and orphans are treated fairly. And you must never take clothes from a widow as security. 18Remember, you were poor slaves in Egypt. And the LORD your God took you from that place and set you free. That is why I tell you to do these things for the poor.

19"You might be gathering your harvest in the field, and you might forget and leave some grain there. You must not go back to get it. It will be for the foreigners, the orphans and the widows. If you leave some grain for them, the LORD your God will bless you in everything you do. 20When you beat your olive trees, you must not go back to check the branches. The olives you leave will be for the foreigners, the orphans and the widows. 21When you gather the grapes from your vineyard, you must not go back to gather the grapes you left. They will be for the foreigners, the orphans and the widows. 22Remember you were poor slaves in Egypt. That is why I tell you to do these things for the poor.

25 "When two people have an argument, they should go to the court. The judges will decide which person is right and which is wrong. 2If the judge decides a person must be beaten with a whip, the judge must make that person lie face down. Someone will beat the guilty person while the judge watches. The number of times he must be hit depends on the crime. 3Don't hit anyone more than 40 times during punishment, because more than that means that their life is not important to you.

4"When an animal is being used to separate grain, you must not cover its mouth to stop it from eating.

---

a **24:6** *security* Anything someone gives as a promise to repay a loan. If the loan is not repaid, the lender keeps whatever was given. Also in verses 10,17.
b **24:9** *Miriam* See Num. 12:1–15.

5"If two brothers live together, and one of them dies without a son, the wife of the dead man must not marry a stranger outside the family. Her husband's brother must take her as his wife and have sex with her. He must do the duty of a husband's brother for her. 6Then the first son she has will be considered the dead man's son in order to keep the dead man's name alive in Israel. 7If the man does not want to take his brother's wife, she must go to the town meeting place and tell the leaders, 'My husband's brother refuses to keep his brother's name alive in Israel. He will not do the duty of a husband's brother to me.' 8Then the leaders of the city must call the man and talk to him. If the man is stubborn and says, 'I don't want to take her,' 9then his brother's wife must come to him in front of the leaders. She must take his sandal off his foot and spit in his face. She must say, 'This is being done to the man who will not give his brother a son!' 10From then on, the brother's family will be known in Israel as, 'the family of the man whose sandal was removed'.

11"Two men might be fighting against each other. One man's wife might come to help her husband, but she must not grab the other man's private parts. 12If she does that, cut off her hand. Don't feel sorry for her.

13"Don't use weights that are too heavy or too light. 14Don't keep measures in your house that are too large or too small. 15You must use weights and measures that are correct and accurate. Then you will live a long time in the land that the LORD your God is giving you. 16The LORD your God hates people who cheat with false weights and measures. Yes, he hates all people who do wrong.

The Amalekites Must Be Destroyed

17"Remember what the Amalekites did to you when you were coming from Egypt. 18The Amalekites did not respect God. They attacked you when you were weak and tired. They killed all your people who were slow and walking behind everyone else. 19That is why you must destroy the memory of the Amalekites from the world. You will do this when you enter the land that the LORD your God is giving you. There he will give you rest from all the enemies around you. But do not forget to destroy the Amalekites!

The First Harvest

26 "You will soon enter the land that the LORD your God is giving you. You will take that land and live there. 2You will gather the crops that grow in the land the LORD your God is giving you. You must take some of the first crops you gather and put them in baskets. Then take that part of your harvest to the place that the LORD your God chooses to be the home for his name. 3Go to the priest who is serving at that time. Tell him, 'The LORD promised our ancestors that he would give us some land. Today I come to announce to the LORD your God that I have come to that land.'

4"Then the priest will take the basket from you. He will put it down in front of the altar of the LORD your God. 5Then there before the LORD your God you will say: 'My ancestor was a wandering Aramean.*a* He went down into Egypt and stayed there. When he went there, he had only a few people in his family. But in Egypt he became a great nation—a powerful nation with many people. 6The Egyptians treated us badly. They made us slaves. They hurt us and forced us to work very hard. 7Then we prayed to the LORD, the God of our ancestors. And the LORD heard us. He saw our trouble, our hard work and our suffering. 8Then the LORD brought us out of Egypt with his great power and strength. He used great miracles and wonders and did amazing things. 9So he brought us to this place. He gave us this land, a land filled with good things.*b* 10Now, LORD, I bring you the first harvest from the land that you gave me.'

"Then you must put the harvest down before the LORD your God and bow down to worship him. 11Then you must have a meal together and enjoy all the good things that the LORD your God has given to you and your family. You must share them with the Levites and the foreigners living among you.

12"Every third year is the Year of Tithes. In that year, you must give one-tenth of your harvest to the Levites, to the foreigners living in your country, and to the widows and orphans. Then they will have plenty to eat in every city. 13You must say to the LORD your God, 'I have taken out of my house the holy part of my harvest. I have given it to the Levites, to the foreigners, and to the orphans and widows. I have followed all the commands you gave me. I have not refused to obey any of your commands. I have not forgotten them. 14I have not eaten this food when I was sad.*c* I was not unclean when I collected this food.*d* I have not offered any of this food for dead people. I have obeyed you, LORD my God. I have

---

a **26:5 Aramean** A person from ancient Syria. Here, this might be Abraham, Isaac or probably Jacob (Israel).
b **26:9 land . . . things** Literally, "land flowing with milk and honey". Also in verse 15.
c **26:14 I have . . . sad** People ate this food to be happy about the many things God gave them, so it could not be from food used during a time of sadness.
d **26:14 I was . . . food** This would mean other people could not eat this food during the celebration to honour the Lord.

done everything you commanded me. ¹⁵Look down from your holy home, from heaven, and bless your people Israel. And bless the land that you gave us. You promised our ancestors to give us this land—a land filled with many good things.'

Obey the LORD's Commands

¹⁶"Today the LORD your God commands you to obey all these laws and rules. Be careful to follow them with all your heart and soul. ¹⁷Today you have said that the LORD is your God. You have promised to live the way he wants. You promised to follow his teachings and to obey his laws and commands. You said you would do everything he tells you to do. ¹⁸And today the LORD has accepted you to be his own people. He has promised you this. The LORD also said that you must obey all his commands. ¹⁹The LORD will make you greater than all the nations he made. He will give you praise, fame and honour. And you will be his own special people, as he promised."

Stone Memorials for the People

27 Moses and the leaders of Israel spoke to the people. Moses said, "Obey all the commands that I give you today. ²You will soon go across the Jordan River into the land that the LORD your God is giving you. On that day you must put up large stones. Cover them with plaster. ³Then write on the stones all these commands and teachings. You must do this when you go across the Jordan River. Then you may go into the land that the LORD your God is giving you—a land filled with many good things.ᵃ The LORD, the God of your ancestors, promised to give you this land.

⁴"After you go across the Jordan River, you must do what I command you today. You must set up the stones on Mount Ebal. You must cover these stones with plaster. ⁵Also, use some stones there to build an altar to the LORD your God. Don't use iron tools to cut the stones. ⁶You must not use cut stones to build the altar for the LORD your God. Offer burnt offerings on this altar to the LORD your God. ⁷And you must sacrifice and eat fellowship offerings there. Eat and enjoy yourselves there together with the LORD your God. ⁸You must write all these teachings on the stones that you set up. Write clearly so that they are easy to read."

The People Must Agree to God's Rules

⁹Moses and the Levite priests spoke to all the Israelites. Moses said, "Be quiet and listen, Israel!

Today you have become the people of the LORD your God. ¹⁰So you must do everything that the LORD your God tells you. You must obey his commands and his laws that I am giving you today."

¹¹That day Moses also told the people, ¹²"After you have gone across the Jordan River, these tribes will stand on Mount Gerizim to read the blessings to the people: Simeon, Levi, Judah, Issachar, Joseph and Benjamin. ¹³And these tribes will stand on Mount Ebal to read the curses: Reuben, Gad, Asher, Zebulun, Dan and Naphtali.

¹⁴And the Levites will say to all the Israelites in a loud voice:

¹⁵"'Cursed is the one who makes a false god and puts it in its secret place. These false gods are only statues that some worker makes from wood, stone or metal. The LORD hates these things!'

"Then all the people will answer, 'Amen!' ¹⁶"The Levites will say, 'Cursed is the one who does not show respect to their father or their mother!'

"Then all the people will answer, 'Amen!' ¹⁷"The Levites will say, 'Cursed is the one who moves a neighbour's landmark!ᵇ'

"Then all the people will say, 'Amen!' ¹⁸"The Levites will say, 'Cursed is the one who tricks a blind man into going the wrong way!'

"Then all the people will say, 'Amen!' ¹⁹"The Levites will say, 'Cursed is the one who does not give fair judgement for the foreigners, orphans and widows!'

"Then all the people will say, 'Amen!' ²⁰"The Levites will say, 'Cursed is the one who shames his father by having sex with his father's wife.'

"Then all the people will say, 'Amen!' ²¹"The Levites will say, 'Cursed is the one who has sex with any kind of animal!'

"Then all the people will say, 'Amen!' ²²"The Levites will say, 'Cursed is the one who has sex with his sister or half-sister!'

"Then all the people will say, 'Amen!' ²³"The Levites will say, 'Cursed is the one who has sex with his mother-in-law!'

"Then all the people will say, 'Amen!' ²⁴"The Levites will say, 'Cursed is the one who kills anyone, even if he is not caught!'

"Then all the people will say, 'Amen!'

ᵃ **27:3 land . . . things** Literally, "land flowing with milk and honey".
ᵇ **27:17 landmark** A stone or sign that showed where the limits of a person's property were.

25"The Levites will say, 'Cursed is the one who takes money to kill an innocent person!'

"Then all the people will say, 'Amen!'

26"The Levites will say, 'Cursed is the one who does not support this law and agree to obey it.'

"Then all the people will say, 'Amen!'

Blessings for Obeying the Law

28 "Now, if you will be careful to obey the LORD your God and follow all his commands that I tell you today, the LORD your God will put you high above all the nations on earth. 2If you will obey the LORD your God, all these blessings will come to you and be yours:

3"He will bless you
in the city and in the field.
4He will bless you
and give you many children.
He will bless your land
and give you good crops.
He will bless your animals
and let them have many babies.
He will bless you with calves and lambs.
5He will bless your baskets and pans
and fill them with food.
6He will bless you at all times
in everything you do.

7"The LORD will help you defeat your enemies who come to fight against you. Your enemies will come against you one way, but they will run away from you seven different ways!

8"The LORD will bless you and fill your barns. He will bless everything you do. The LORD your God will bless you in the land that he is giving you. 9If you follow the LORD your God and obey his commands, he will do what he promised. The LORD will make you his own special people. 10Then all the people in that land will see that you are called to be the LORD's people, and they will be afraid of you.

11"And the LORD will give you many good things. He will give you many children. He will give your cows many calves. He will give you a good harvest in the land that the LORD promised your ancestors to give you. 12The LORD will open his storehouse where he keeps his rich blessings. He will send rain at the right time for your land. He will bless everything you do. You will have money to lend to many nations. And you will not need to borrow anything from them. 13The LORD will make you be like the head, not the tail. You will be on top, not on the bottom. This will happen if you listen to the commands of the LORD your God that I tell you today. You must carefully obey these commands. 14You must not turn away from any of the teachings that I give you today. You must not turn away to the right or to the left. You must not follow other gods to serve them.

Curses for Not Obeying the Law

15"But if you don't listen to what the LORD your God tells you—if you don't obey all his commands and laws that I tell you today—then all these bad things will happen to you:

16"The Lord will curse you
in the city and in the field.
17He will curse what you use to make
bread,
and you will not have enough to eat.
18He will curse your families,
and you will not have many children.
He will curse your land,
and you will not have good crops.
He will curse your herds and flocks,
and you will not have many calves and
lambs.
19He will curse you at all times
in everything you do.

20"If you do evil and turn away from the LORD, he will make bad things happen to you. You will have frustration and trouble in everything you do. He will continue to do this until you are quickly and completely destroyed. He will do this because you turned away from him and left him. 21The LORD will send you terrible diseases until you no longer exist, until you are completely gone from the land. 22The LORD will punish you with diseases, fever and swelling. He will send you terrible heat and you will have no rain. Your crops will die from the heat and disease.ᵃ All these bad things will happen until you are destroyed! 23There will be no clouds in the sky—the sky will look like polished brass. And the ground under you will be hard like iron. 24The LORD will not send rain—only sand and dust will fall from the sky. It will come down on you until you are destroyed.

25"The LORD will let your enemies defeat you. You will go to fight against your enemies one way, but you will run away from them seven different ways. The bad things that happen to you will make all the people on earth afraid. 26Your dead bodies will be food for the wild birds and animals. There will be no one to scare them away from your dead bodies.

ᵃ 28:22 *disease* This might be mildew, a disease that turns the heads of grain yellow and stops them from growing seeds.

CHOOSE LIFE

Every day we have to make choices – Weetabix or Frosties, to go out or stay in, do homework or play on the Xbox, chat to our friends online or check in with our parents . . .

The people of Israel had a choice to make. To love and live for God or not . . . God had given them good laws for loving him, the smooth running of the land and a happy society – would they choose this way? Would they choose life?

DIG IN

READ Deuteronomy 30:11–20

These verses are like the renewal of the agreement that God had made with the people back in Exodus – now all these years later, as they are finally about to enter the land, God wants to lay out the choices before them.

- What is the command given to the people?
- What things are they to choose between?
- What are the consequences of each option?

God hadn't kept his message hidden away, or made it overly difficult for them. Rather he had come and spoken with them, urging them to choose truth (v.14), love (vv.16,20), life (vv.15,20), success (v.15) and blessing (v.15). All stuff every human wants, right? And God is offering it! It makes choosing the other options – death, destruction and punishment – sound ridiculous doesn't it?

A little earlier on God, through Moses, unpacked what each option would look like . . .

READ Deuteronomy 28:1–14

- Jot down the different ways God wants to bless the people.
- What does it show about where all good things come from?

There's not a single area of life that the blessing of God doesn't touch when the people love and obey him. And notice the description of blessing comes first – this is what God longs to do for his people.

READ Deuteronomy 28:15–68

- What will happen to their land? Their relationships? Their bodies?
- What happens to their relationship with God?

Does reading that make you shudder? It's a hideous picture of complete and utter destruction, misery and pain. All the way through Deuteronomy God urges the people to obey him so that things will go well with them – choosing to love God means choosing freedom and life.

The worst punishment of all is that the people would be uprooted from the land God has given them to be turned into slaves and made to worship other gods. It's almost as if God will give them what they want – gods other than him – yet when they get it they'll be worse off than before.

DIG THROUGH

- God's promises of blessing were bound up in the actual piece of land the people were about to enter. The Bible tells us that now those promises are fulfilled for us in Jesus – he is our place of rest where we can find truth, life and love. One day we will enter another land – the new heaven and earth.
- God asks us to make the same decision that he asked the people – will you choose life?
- Do you believe that everything you need, every good thing, can be found in Jesus? Or are you tempted to look elsewhere?

27"The LORD will punish you with boils, like those he sent on the Egyptians. He will punish you with tumours, sores that run, and an itch that cannot be cured. 28The LORD will punish you by making you crazy. He will make you blind and confused. 29In daylight you will have to feel your way like a blind man. You will fail in everything you do. Again and again people will hurt you and steal from you. And there will be no one to save you.

30"You will be engaged to a woman, but another man will have sex with her. You will build a house, but you will not live in it. You will plant a vineyard, but you will not gather anything from it. 31People will kill your cattle in front of you, but you will not eat any of the meat. People will take your donkeys, and they will not give them back to you. Your enemies will get your sheep, and there will be no one to help you.

32"Other people will be allowed to take your sons and your daughters. Day after day you will look for your children. You will look for them until your eyes become weak and blind—but you will not find them. And God will not help you.

33"A nation that you don't know will take all your crops and everything you worked for. People will treat you badly and abuse you. 34The things you see will make you go crazy. 35The LORD will punish you with sore boils that cannot be healed. These boils will be on your knees and legs. The boils will be on every part of your body—from the bottom of your feet to the top of your head.

36"The LORD will send you and your king away to a nation you don't know. You and your ancestors have never seen that nation. There you will serve false gods made of wood and stone. 37In the countries where the LORD will send you, the people will be shocked at the terrible things that happen to you. They will laugh at you and say bad things about you.

The Curse of Failure

38"Your fields will produce plenty of grain. But your harvest will be small, because the locusts will eat your harvest. 39You will plant vineyards and work hard in them. But you will not gather the grapes or drink the wine from them, because the worms will eat them. 40You will have olive trees everywhere on your land. But you will not have any of the oil to use, because the olives will drop to the ground and rot. 41You will have sons and daughters. But you will not be able to keep them, because they will be captured and taken away. 42Locusts will destroy all your trees and the crops in your fields. 43The foreigners living among you will get more and more power, and you will lose the power you had. 44The foreigners will have money to loan you, but you will not have any money to loan them. They will control you the way the head controls the body. You will be like the tail.

45"All these curses will come on you. They will keep chasing you and catching you, until you are destroyed, because you did not listen to what the LORD your God told you. You did not obey the commands and laws that he gave you. 46These curses will show people that God judged you and your descendants forever. People will be amazed at the terrible things that happen to you.

47"The LORD your God gave you many blessings. But you did not serve him with joy and a glad heart. 48So you will serve the enemies the LORD will send against you. You will be hungry, thirsty, naked and poor. He will put a load on you that cannot be removed. You will carry that load until he destroys you.[a]

The Curse of an Enemy Nation

49"The LORD will bring a nation from far away to fight you. You will not understand their language. They will come quickly, like an eagle coming down from the sky. 50These people will be cruel. They will not care about old people or show mercy to young children. 51They will take your animals and the food you grow. They will take everything until they destroy you. They will not leave you any grain, wine, oil, cattle, sheep or goats. They will take everything, until they destroy you.

52"That nation will surround and attack your cities. You think that the tall, strong walls around your cities will protect you. But those walls will fall down. The enemy will surround all your cities everywhere in the land the LORD your God is giving you. 53You will suffer very much. The enemy will surround your cities. They will not let you have any food. You will get very hungry. You will be so hungry that you will eat your own sons and daughters—you will eat the bodies of the children the LORD your God gave you.

54"Even the most kind and gentle man among you will become cruel. He will be cruel to his family, and he will be cruel to his wife he loves so much. And he will be cruel to his children who are still alive. 55He will have nothing left to eat, so he will eat his own children. And he will not share that meat with anyone—not even the other people in his own family. All these bad things will happen when your enemy comes to surround your cities and make you suffer.

---

[a] **28:48 He . . . destroys you** Literally, "He will put an iron yoke on your neck until he destroys you."

⁵⁶"Even the most kind and gentle woman among you will become cruel. She might be a lady so gentle and delicate that she never put her feet on the ground to walk anywhere. But she will become cruel to her husband she loves so much. And she will be cruel to her own son and daughter. ⁵⁷She will hide and give birth to a baby. And she will eat the baby and everything that comes out of her body with it. All these bad things will happen when your enemy comes to surround your cities and make you suffer.

⁵⁸"You must obey all the commands and teachings that are written in this book. And you must respect the wonderful and awesome name of the LORD your God. If you don't obey, ⁵⁹the LORD will punish you and your descendants with terrible diseases. He will cause you to suffer illnesses that have no cure. And you will find no relief for your misery! ⁶⁰He will bring on you all the diseases you saw in Egypt that filled you with fear, and you will not be able to avoid them. ⁶¹The LORD will even bring troubles and diseases that are not written in this *Book of Teachings*. He will continue to do this until you are destroyed. ⁶²You might have as many people as the stars in the sky. But only a few of you will be left, because you did not listen to the LORD your God.

⁶³"The LORD was happy to be good to you and to make your nation grow. In the same way, the LORD will be happy to ruin and destroy you. You are entering that land to make it yours. But you will be forced to leave it! ⁶⁴The LORD will scatter you among all the people in the world. He will scatter you from one end of the earth to the other. There you will serve false gods made of wood and stone, gods that you or your ancestors never worshipped before.

⁶⁵"Among those nations you will find no peace. You will have no place to rest. The LORD will fill your mind with worry. Your eyes will feel tired. You will lose all hope. ⁶⁶You will live in constant danger. You will be full of fear day and night, never sure if you will live or not. ⁶⁷In the morning you will say, 'I wish it were evening!' In the evening you will say, 'I wish it were morning!' This will happen because of the fear in your heart and the terrible things you will see. ⁶⁸The LORD will send you back to Egypt in ships. I said you would never have to go to that place again, but he will send you there. In Egypt you will try to sell yourselves as slaves to your enemies, but no one will buy you."

The Agreement in Moab

29 The LORD made an agreement with the Israelites at Mount Horeb. In addition to that agreement, he also commanded Moses to make another agreement with them while they were in Moab. This is that agreement.

²Moses called together all the Israelites. He said to them, "You saw everything the LORD did in the land of Egypt. You saw what he did to Pharaoh, to Pharaoh's officers, and to his whole country. ³You saw the great troubles he gave them. You saw the miracles and amazing things he did. ⁴But even today, you still don't understand what happened. The LORD has not let you really understand what you saw and heard. ⁵He led you through the desert for 40 years, and in all that time, your clothes and sandals did not wear out. ⁶You did not have any food with you. You did not have any wine or anything else to drink. But he took care of you so that you would understand that he is the LORD your God.

⁷"You came to this place, and King Sihon of Heshbon and King Og of Bashan came out to fight against us. But we defeated them. ⁸Then we took their land and gave it to the people in the tribes of Reuben and Gad and to half the tribe of Manasseh. ⁹If you obey all the commands in this agreement, you will continue to succeed in everything you do.

¹⁰"Today all of you are standing here before the LORD your God. Your chiefs, your officials, your other leaders and all the other men are here. ¹¹Your wives and children are here and also the foreigners living among you—the people who cut your wood and bring you water. ¹²You are all here to enter into an agreement with the LORD your God. The LORD your God is making this agreement with you today. ¹³With this agreement he is making you his own special people, and he himself will become your God. He told you this. He promised this to your ancestors—Abraham, Isaac and Jacob. ¹⁴The LORD is making this agreement with its promises with you people, but not only with you. ¹⁵Yes, he is making this agreement with all of you who stand here with us today before the LORD our God. But this agreement is also for our descendants who are not here with us today. ¹⁶You remember how we lived in the land of Egypt. And you remember how we travelled through the countries that were on our way here. ¹⁷You saw their hated things—the idols they had made from wood, stone, silver and gold. ¹⁸Be sure that there is no man, woman, family or tribe here today who turns away from the LORD our God. No one should go and serve the gods of the other nations. People who do that are like a plant that grows bitter and poisonous fruit.

¹⁹"Some people might hear these curses and comfort themselves by saying, 'I will continue doing what I want. Nothing bad will happen to me.' But that attitude will bring total disaster.

20-21The LORD will not forgive them for that. No, the LORD will be angry and upset with them and punish them. The LORD will separate them from the tribes of Israel. He will completely destroy them. All the curses that are written in this book will happen to them. They are a part of the agreement that is written in this *Book of Teachings.*

22"In the future your descendants and foreigners from faraway countries will see how the land has been ruined. They will see the diseases that the LORD has brought to it. 23All the land will be useless—destroyed by burning sulphur and covered with salt. The land will have nothing planted in it. Nothing will be growing—not even weeds. The land will be destroyed like Sodom, Gomorrah, Admah and Zeboiim, the cities the LORD destroyed when he was very angry.

24"All the other nations will ask, 'Why did the LORD do this to this land? Why was he so angry?' 25The answer will be, 'This happened because the Israelites left the agreement of the LORD, the God of their ancestors. They stopped following the agreement he made with them when he brought them out of Egypt. 26They started serving other gods. They began worshipping gods they had never worshipped before, gods that the Lord never allowed them to worship. 27That is why the LORD became very angry with the people of this land. So he brought to them all the curses that are written in this book. 28The LORD became very angry and upset with them. So he took them out of their land. He put them in another land, where they are today.'

29"There are some things that the LORD our God has kept secret. Only he knows these things. But he told us about some things. And these teachings are for us and our descendants forever. And we must obey all the commands in that law.

The Israelites Will Return to Their Land

30 "Everything that I have mentioned will happen to you—both the blessings and the curses. And you will remember these words when the LORD your God sends you away to other nations. 2Then you and your descendants will turn back to the LORD your God. You will follow him with all your heart and completely obey all his commands that I have given you today. 3Then the LORD your God will be kind to you. The LORD your God will make you free again! He will bring you back from the nations where he sent you. 4Even if you were sent to the farthest parts of the earth, the LORD your God will gather you from there and bring you back. 5The LORD your God

will bring you into the land your ancestors had, and the land will become yours. He will do good to you, and you will have more than your ancestors had. You will have more people in your nation than they ever had. 6The LORD your God will make you and your descendants want to obey him.*a* Then you will love the LORD your God with all your heart. And you will live!

7"Then the LORD your God will make all these bad things happen to your enemies, who hate you and cause you trouble. 8And you will again obey the LORD. You will obey all his commands that I give you today. 9The LORD your God will make you successful in everything you do. He will bless you with many children. He will bless your cows—they will have many calves. He will bless your fields—they will grow many good crops. He will be good to you. The LORD will again enjoy doing good for you, the same as he enjoyed doing good for your ancestors. 10But you must do what the LORD your God tells you to do. You must obey his commands and follow the rules that are written in this *Book of Teachings.* You must obey the LORD your God with all your heart and with all your soul. Then these good things will happen to you.

Life or Death

11"This command that I give you today is not too hard for you. It is not a secret hidden in some faraway land. 12This command is not in heaven so that you should say, 'Who will go up to heaven for us and bring it to us, so that we can hear and do it?' 13This command is not on the other side of the sea so that you should say, 'Who will go across the sea for us and bring it to us, so that we can hear it and do it?' 14No, the word is very near to you. It is in your mouth and in your heart. So you can obey it.

15"Today I have given you a choice between life and death, success and disaster.*b* 16I command you today to love the LORD your God. I command you to follow him and to obey his commands, laws and rules. Then you will live, and your nation will grow larger. And the LORD your God will bless you in the land that you are entering to take for your own. 17But if you turn away from your God and refuse to listen, if you are led away to worship and serve other gods, 18you will be destroyed. I am warning you today, if you turn away from God, you will not live long in that land across the Jordan River that you are ready to enter and take for your own.

19"Today I am giving you a choice of two ways. And I ask heaven and earth to be witnesses of

---

a **30:6 make you ... obey him** Literally, "circumcise the hearts of you and your seed."
b **30:15 success and disaster** Or "good and evil".

your choice. You can choose life or death. The first choice will bring a blessing. The other choice will bring a curse. So choose life! Then you and your children will live. 20You must love the LORD your God and obey him. Never leave him, because he is your life. And he will give you a long life in the land that he, the LORD, promised to give to your ancestors—Abraham, Isaac and Jacob."

Joshua Will Be the New Leader

31 Then Moses went and spoke these words to all the Israelites. 2Moses said to them, "I am now 120 years old. I cannot lead you any more. The LORD said to me, 'You will not go across the Jordan River.' 3But the LORD your God will lead you people into that land. He will destroy these nations for you. You will take their land away from them. The LORD said that Joshua must lead you.

4"The LORD destroyed Sihon and Og. He destroyed those Amorite kings, and he will do the same for you! 5The LORD will help you defeat these nations. But you must do to them everything I told you to do. 6Be strong and brave. Don't be afraid of those people, because the LORD your God is with you. He will not fail you or leave you."

7Then Moses called Joshua. All the Israelites watched while Moses said to Joshua, "Be strong and brave. You will lead these people into the land that the LORD promised to give to their ancestors. You will help the Israelites take that land and divide it among them. 8The LORD will lead you. He himself is with you. He will not fail you or leave you. Don't worry. Don't be afraid!"

The Teachings Written Down for the Future

9Then Moses wrote down these teachings in a book and gave it to the priests and the leaders of Israel. The priests, who were from the tribe of Levi, carried the Box of the LORD's Agreement. 10Then Moses spoke to these leaders. He said, "At the end of every seven years, in the Year of Freedom,*a* read these teachings at the Festival of Shelters. 11At that time all the Israelites must come to meet with the LORD your God at the special place he will choose. Then you must read the teachings to the people so that they can hear them. 12Bring together all the people—the men, the women, the little children and the foreigners living in your cities. They will hear the teachings, and they will learn to respect the LORD your God. Then they will be able to do everything in this *Book of Teachings.* 13If their descendants don't know the teachings, they will hear them, and

they will learn to respect the LORD your God. They will respect him as long as you live in your country. You will soon go across the Jordan River and take that land to be your own."

The LORD Calls Moses and Joshua

14The LORD said to Moses, "Now the time is near for you to die. Get Joshua and come to the Meeting Tent. I will tell Joshua what he must do." So Moses and Joshua went to the Meeting Tent.

15The LORD appeared at the Tent in a tall cloud. The tall cloud stood over the entrance of the Tent. 16The LORD said to Moses, "You will die soon. And after you have gone to be with your ancestors, these people will not continue to be faithful to me. They will break the agreement I made with them. They will leave me and begin worshipping other gods—the false gods of the land where they are going. 17At that time I will become very angry with them, and I will leave them. I will refuse to help them, and they will be destroyed. Terrible things will happen to them, and they will have many troubles. Then they will say, 'These bad things happened to us because our God is not with us.' 18And I will refuse to help them, because they have done evil and worshipped other gods.

19"So write down this song, and teach it to the Israelites. Teach them to sing this song. Then this song will be a witness for me against the Israelites. 20I will take them into the land that I promised to give to their ancestors—a land filled with many good things.*b* And they will have all they want to eat. They will have a rich life. But then they will turn to other gods and serve them. They will turn away from me and break my agreement. 21Then many terrible things will happen to them. They will have many troubles. At that time their descendants will still know this song, and it will show them how wrong they are. I have not yet taken them into the land I promised to give them. But I already know what they are planning to do there."

22So that same day Moses wrote down the song and taught it to the Israelites.

23Then the Lord spoke to Joshua son of Nun and said, "Be strong and brave. You will lead the Israelites into the land I promised them, and I will be with you."

Moses Warns the Israelites

24Moses carefully wrote all these teachings in a book. When he finished, 25he gave this command to the Levites in charge of the Box of the LORD's Agreement: 26"Take this *Book of Teachings* and

---

a **31:10** *Year of Freedom* That is, the year for cancelling debts.
b **31:20** *land . . . things* Literally, "land flowing with milk and honey".

ENDING SPOILER

Have you ever watched a film with a mate who has seen it before and halfway through they let slip what's going to happen in the end? It's pretty annoying!

In the last chapters of Deuteronomy we're told the ending of the people's story – except it's not the ending, it's really just the beginning . . .

DIG IN

READ Deuteronomy 31:1-13

- Describe how Joshua might be feeling.
- How might Moses be feeling?

These are exciting and daunting times. Joshua is chosen to lead the people into the promised land – a time they have been waiting for for forty years. Joshua must have been feeling a mixture of fear (vv.5–6), strength (vv.7–8) and anticipation. They were both probably pretty excited about the relationship they, and the people, had with God.

READ Deuteronomy 31:14-29

- What's the bad news?
- What sort of thing will the people do?
- Why will they do this (v.27)?

Nothing much changes does it? The people have always been stubborn and disobedient and God knows that they will be again. What they hear acts like a cold shower on a hot day – wakes them up to a harsh reality.

READ Deuteronomy 32:1-52

- How does the song describe God – who he is, what he's done (vv.4,6,8–14,39–41)?
- How does the song describe the people – what they're like, how they've responded to God (vv.5–6,15–18, 28–33)?
- Why does the song bring up the past so much?

Have you ever heard a song like this in the charts? Probably not. It's packed full of the highs and lows of the nation's history and isn't shy in pointing out the people's failures.

It's a sad ending to the highs of Deuteronomy and not a very positive note on which to start heading into the land. Before the people even start out to conquer the land we know they're going to fail.

- What will God do to his people? Why (vv.23–27,34–38)?
- What will God do for his people (vv.39–43)?

This could be a chart topper – it's got the best and worst of news in every line: God will judge, but he will also rescue his people when they say sorry. It's a "look at how wrong you are, come back to me" song . . . he is desperate to make them pure.

DIG THROUGH

Do you ever feel as though you already know the ending of every day of your life – repeated failure and an inability to live for God? You're in good company – the people constantly failed and so do we all. God knew the bad stuff the people were going to do in the future, and he knows all we're going to do too. It's really humbling and yet at the same time, really reassuring. Nothing we might do will surprise God – he already knows we're going to stuff up – that's why he sent Jesus so that we could be forgiven.

- At the end of the song, God promises deliverance to make the land and people pure – do you long for purity in your life? In Jesus, God has already made you pure before him (check out Colossians 1:21–22). But there's more! One day we will actually be completely pure and perfect. Hoorah!

put it by the side of the Box of the Agreement of the Lord your God. Then it will be a witness against you. 27I know you are very stubborn. I know you want to live your own way. Look, you refused to obey the Lord while I was with you. So I know you will refuse to obey him after I die. 28Bring together all the officers and leaders of your tribes. I will tell them these things. And I will call heaven and earth to be witnesses against them. 29I know that after my death you will become evil. You will turn from the way I commanded you to follow. Terrible things will happen to you in the future, because you want to do what the Lord says is wrong. You will make him angry because of the evil things you do."

The Song of Moses

30All the Israelites were gathered together, and Moses sang this whole song for them:

32

"Skies, listen and I will speak.
Earth, hear the words of my mouth.
2My teachings will come like the rain,
like a mist falling to the ground,
like a gentle rain on the soft grass,
like rain on the green plants.
3I will openly praise the Lord's name.
And you should all say how great our
God is!

4"The Lord is the Rock,
and his work is perfect!
Yes, all his ways are right!
God is true and faithful.
He is good and honest.
5And you are not really his children.
You are completely unfaithful to him.
You are crooked liars.
6Is this the way you repay the Lord for all he
has done for you?
You are stupid, foolish people.
He is your Father and your Creator.
He made you, and he supports you.

7"Remember the days of the past.
Think about what happened so long ago.
Ask your father; he will tell you.
Ask your older leaders; they will tell you.
8God Most High separated the people on earth
and gave each nation its land.
He set up borders for all people.
He made as many nations as there are
angels.a
9The Lord chose his people to be his own.
The people of Jacob belong to him.

10"The Lord found them in the desert,
in an empty, windy land.
He surrounded them and watched over them.
He protected them like the pupil of his eye,
11like an eagle when she makes her young leave
the nest to fly.
She stays close to them, ready to help.
She spreads her wings to catch them when
they fall
and carries them to a safe place.
12The Lord alone led his people.
They had no help from any foreign god.
13The Lord helped them take control of the hill
country.
They took the harvest in the fields.
He gave them honey from the cliffs
and olive oil from the rocky ground.
14He gave his people butter from the herd and
milk from the flock.
He gave them lambs and goats.
They had the best rams from Bashan and the
finest wheat.
They drank the best wine made from the
juice of red grapes.

15"But Jeshurunb became fat and kicked like a
bull.
(Yes, you people were fed well and became
full and fat.)
They left the God who made them!
They ran away from the Rock who saved
them.
16They made him jealous by worshipping other
gods.
They made him angry with those disgusting
idols.
17They offered sacrifices to demons, not God,
to gods they had not known before.
They had just learned about these new
gods,
gods their ancestors never worshipped.
18You people left the Rock who made you;
you forgot the God who gave you life.

19"The Lord saw this and became upset.
His sons and daughters made him angry!
20So he said, 'I will turn away from them;
then let's see what happens!
They are a rebellious people.
They are like children who will not learn
their lessons.
21They made me jealous with things that are not
really gods.
They made me angry with their worthless
idols.

---

a 32:8 angels This is from the ancient Greek version. Some Hebrew copies at Qumran have "sons of God", which can also mean "angels". The standard Hebrew text has "sons of Israel" (see Exod. 1:5).
b 32:15 Jeshurun Another name for Israel. It means "good" or "honest".

So I will use people who are not really a
   nation to make them jealous.
I will use a worthless[a] nation to make them
   angry.
[22]My anger will become a flaming fire
   that burns down to the deepest grave.
It will destroy the earth and all it produces,
   burning deep down under the mountains.

[23]"'I will bring troubles to the Israelites.
   I will shoot all my arrows at them.
[24]They will become thin from hunger.
   Terrible diseases will destroy them.
I will send wild animals against them.
   Poisonous snakes and lizards will bite them.
[25]In the streets, soldiers will kill them.
   In their houses, terrible things will
      happen.
Soldiers will kill young men and women.
   They will kill babies and old people.

[26]"'I thought about destroying the Israelites
   so that people would forget them
      completely!
[27]But I know what their enemies would say.
   The enemy would not understand.
They would boast and say,
   "The LORD did not destroy Israel.
   We won by our own power!"'

[28]"They are foolish.
   They don't understand.
[29]If they were wise,
   they would understand;
   they would know what would happen to
      them.
[30]Can one man chase away 1,000 men?
   Can two men cause 10,000 men to run
      away?
This will happen only if the LORD gives them
   to their enemy.
It will happen only if their Rock sells them
   like slaves.
[31]The 'rock' of our enemies is not strong like
   our Rock.
   Even our enemies know that.
[32]They are as evil as Sodom and Gomorrah.
   They are like grapevines planted there.
Their grapes are full of poison.
   The fruit they produce is bitter.
[33] Their wine is as deadly
      as the poison of snakes.

[34]"The Lord says, 'I am saving that
   punishment.

I have it locked up in my storehouse!
[35]I will punish them for what they have done.
   One day they will slip and fall.
Their time of trouble is near.
   Their punishment will come quickly.'

[36]"The LORD will judge his people.
   They are his servants, and he will show
      them mercy.
He will see that their power is gone.
   He will see that they are all helpless—
   the slaves and free people too.
[37]Then the Lord will say, 'Where are the false
      gods?
   Where is the "rock" you ran to for
      protection?
[38]Those gods ate the fat of your sacrifices.
   And they drank the wine of your offerings.
So let them get up and help you!
   Let them protect you!

[39]"'Now, see that I, and only I, am God!
   There is no other God!
I put people to death,
   and I let people live.
I can hurt people,
   and I can make them well.
No one can save another person from my
      power!
[40]I raise my hand towards heaven and make this
      promise.
   As surely as I live forever, these things will
      happen!
[41]I swear,
   I will sharpen my flashing sword.
I will use it to punish my enemies.
   I will give them the punishment they
      deserve.
[42]My enemies will be killed and taken as
      prisoners.
   My arrows will be covered with their blood.
   My sword will cut off the heads of their
      soldiers.'

[43]"The whole world should be happy for God's
      people!
   God punishes people who kill his servants.
He gives his enemies the punishment they
      deserve.
   And he makes his land and people pure."

Moses Teaches the People His Song

[44]Moses and Joshua son of Nun came and sang
all the words of this song for the Israelites to hear.
[45]When Moses finished giving these teachings to

---

[a] **32:21 worthless** Literally, "foolish" used as a wordplay because in Hebrew it sounds like the word "worthless" used earlier in this verse.

the people, ⁴⁶he said to them, "You must be sure to pay attention to all the commands I tell you today. And you must tell your children to obey completely the commands in this Law. ⁴⁷Don't think these teachings are not important. They are your life! Through these teachings you will live a long time in the land across the Jordan River that you are ready to take."

Moses on Mount Nebo

⁴⁸The LORD spoke to Moses that same day. He said, ⁴⁹"Go to the Abarim Mountains. Go up on Mount Nebo in the land of Moab opposite the city of Jericho. Then you can look at the land of Canaan that I am giving to the Israelites to live in. ⁵⁰You will die on that mountain. You will go to be with your people, just as your brother Aaron died on Mount Hor. ⁵¹This is because you both sinned against me. You were at the waters of Meribah near Kadesh, in the desert of Zin. There, in front of the Israelites, you did not honour me and show that I am holy. ⁵²So now you may see the land that I am giving to the Israelites. But you cannot go into that land."

Moses Blesses the People

33 This is the blessing that Moses, the man of God, gave the Israelites before he died:

²"The LORD came from Sinai,
　like a light shining at dawn over Seir,
　like a light shining from Mount Paran.
He came with 10,000 holy ones.^a
　God's mighty soldiers were by his side.^b
³Yes, the Lord loves his people.
　All his holy people are in his hand.
They sit at his feet
　and learn his teachings!
⁴Moses gave us the law.
　These teachings are for Jacob's people.
⁵At that time the Israelites
　and their leaders met together,
　and the Lord became Israel's king!^c

Blessing on Reuben's People

⁶"Let Reuben live, and not die!
　But let there be only a few people in his
　　tribe!"

Blessing on Judah's People

⁷Moses said this about the people of Judah:

"LORD, hear the prayer of Judah's tribe.
　Bring them back together with your people.
Make them strong,
　and help them defeat their enemies!"

Blessing on Levi's People

⁸Moses said this about Levi and his people:

"Levi is your true follower.
　He keeps the Urim and Thummim.
At Massah you tested the people of Levi.
　At the waters of Meribah,^d you challenged
　　them.
⁹Obeying your commands was more important
　　to them
　than caring for their own fathers and
　　mothers.
They gave more attention to keeping your
　　agreement
　than to their brothers or even their own
　　children.
¹⁰They teach your rules to the people of Jacob;
　they give your teachings to Israel.
They burn incense before you.
　They offer burnt offerings on your altar.

¹¹"LORD, bless everything Levi has.
　Accept what he does.
Destroy those who attack him!
　Defeat his enemies so that they will never
　　attack again."

Blessing on Benjamin's People

¹²Moses said this about Benjamin and his people:

"Benjamin is loved by the LORD
　and lives close to him in safety.
The LORD protects him all the time
　like a child at rest on its mother's back."^e

Blessing on Joseph's People

¹³Moses said this about Joseph and his people:

"May the LORD bless Joseph's land
　with rain from the skies above
　and water from the ground below.
¹⁴Let the sun cause good fruit to grow.
　Let each month bring a rich harvest.
¹⁵Let the hills and ancient mountains
　produce their best crops.

^a **33:2 holy one** Here, this probably means an angel.
^b **33:2 He came . . . side** Or "He came from 10,000 holy angels where his troops were by his right side."
^c **33:5 Israel's king** Literally, "king in Jeshurun." Jeshurun is another name for the people of Israel. It means "good" or "honest." Also in verse 26.
^d **33:8 Massah . . . Meribah** See Num. 20:1–13 for the story.
^e **33:12 like a child . . . back** Literally, "and he rests between his shoulders". The metaphor may refer to the custom of a mother carrying her baby tied on her back as she works. See Ps. 131:2.

¹⁶May the Lord who appeared in the burning
    bush show that he is pleased
    and cause the earth to provide them with
        the best it has.
May these blessings come down on the people
    of Joseph,
    who was the leader among his brothers.
¹⁷He is like a powerful young bull,
    and his two sons are like a bull's horns.
They will attack other people
    and push them to the ends of the earth!
Yes, Manasseh has thousands of people,
    and Ephraim has ten thousands."

Blessing on the People of Zebulun and Issachar

¹⁸Moses said this about Zebulun and his people:

"Zebulun, be happy when you go out.
    And you, Issachar, be happy in your tents at
        home.
¹⁹They will call the people to their mountain.
    There they will offer good sacrifices.
They will take riches from the sea
    and treasures from the shore."

Blessing on Gad's People

²⁰Moses said this about Gad and his people:

"Praise God who gave Gad more land!
    Gad is like a lion that lies down and
        waits,
    then attacks and tears an animal to pieces.
²¹He chose the best part for himself.
    He took the king's share.
The leaders of the people come to him.
    He did what the LORD says is good.
    He did what is right for the Israelites."

Blessing on Dan's People

²²Moses said this about Dan and his people:

"Dan is a lion's cub
    that jumps out from Bashan."

Blessing on Naphtali's People

²³Moses said this about Naphtali and his people:

"Naphtali, you will get all you want.
    The LORD will really bless you.
    You will get the land by Lake Galilee."

Blessing on Asher's People

²⁴Moses said this about Asher and his people:

"Asher[a] is the most blessed of the sons.
    Let him be the favourite of his brothers.
    And let him wash his feet in olive oil.
²⁵Your gates will have locks made from iron and
        bronze.
    You will be strong all your life."

Moses Gives Praise to God

²⁶"There is no one like the God of Israel!
    He rides on the clouds in his divine
        greatness.
    He comes riding through the skies to help
        you.
²⁷God lives forever.
    He is your place of safety.
His power continues forever!
    He is protecting you.
He will force your enemies to leave your land.
    He will say, 'Destroy the enemy!'
²⁸So Israel will live in safety.
    Jacob's well belongs to them.
They will get a land of grain and wine.
    And that land will get plenty of rain.
²⁹Israel, you are blessed.
    No other nation is like you.
The LORD saved you.
    He is like a strong shield protecting you.
    He is like a powerful sword.
Your enemies will be afraid of you,
    and you will put your foot on their backs!"[b]

INSIGHT

*Moses believed God would keep his
promise to Israel, even though he knew
that he wouldn't be around to see it
happen. He stood on the mountaintop and
saw the promised land, but never entered
it. Hebrews 11 is full of heroes of the faith
who died before seeing their promises
fulfilled.*

Deuteronomy 34

Moses Dies

34 Moses climbed Mount Nebo. Moses went
from the Jordan Valley in Moab to the top
of Mount Pisgah. This was across the Jordan River
from Jericho. The LORD showed Moses all the
land from Gilead to Dan. ²He showed him all
the land of Naphtali, Ephraim and Manasseh. He

---

[a] **33:24 Asher** This name means "blessed" or "happy".
[b] **33:29 and you . . . backs** Or "You will trample their holy places."

showed him all the land of Judah as far as the Mediterranean Sea. ³He showed Moses the Negev and the valley that goes from Zoar to Jericho, the city of palm trees. ⁴The Lord said to Moses, "This is the land I promised to Abraham, Isaac and Jacob. I said to them, 'I will give this land to your descendants.' I have let you see the land, but you cannot go there."

⁵Then the Lord's servant Moses died there in the land of Moab. The Lord had told Moses this would happen. ⁶He buried Moses in Moab. This was in the valley opposite Beth Peor. But even today no one knows exactly where Moses' grave is. ⁷Moses was 120 years old when he died. He was as strong as ever, and his eyes were still good. ⁸The Israelites cried for Moses for 30 days. They stayed in the Jordan Valley in Moab until the time of sadness was finished.

Joshua Becomes the New Leader

⁹Moses had put his hands on Joshua and appointed him to be the new leader. Then Joshua son of Nun was filled with the spirit of wisdom. So the Israelites began to obey Joshua, and they did what the Lord had commanded Moses.

¹⁰Israel never had another prophet like Moses: The Lord knew Moses face to face. ¹¹The Lord sent Moses to do powerful miracles in the land of Egypt. Pharaoh, all his officers, and all the people in Egypt saw those miracles. ¹²No other prophet ever did as many powerful and amazing things as Moses did for the Israelites to see.

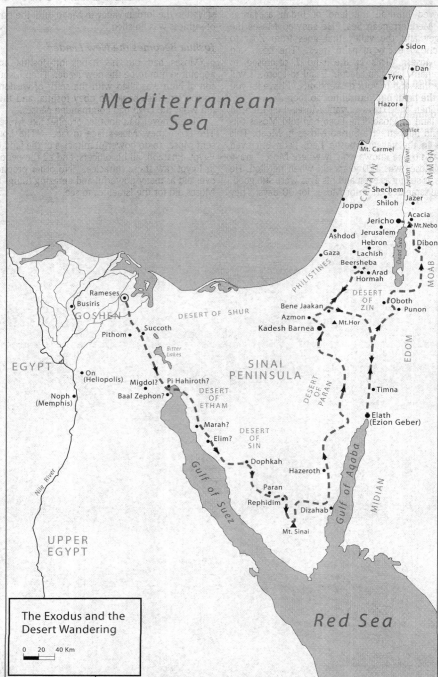

The Exodus and the
Desert Wandering

0   20   40 Km

Copyright © 2005 by World Bible Translation Center

All the books in the Old Testament contain some history, but the twelve books in this section are specifically about the history of Israel. They take the story on from the conquest of the promised land, through the decline of the monarchy, into exile under foreign powers and finally to the return from exile of the Jewish nation. They are full of stories, in fact: love stories, war stories, hero stories, gory stories, stories of human beings and all the things they do, good and bad.

Joshua was the successor to Moses. Moses never got to enter the promised land – it was Joshua who led the Israelites across the Jordan. This book tells of the invasion and conquest of the land, and the division of the territory between the twelve tribes of Israel.

Judges is one of the bleakest books of the Bible. It tells of the dark, anarchic era that followed the conquest, when every man acted as he thought fit, and violence and barbarism ruled. The only exceptions were the "judges", leaders raised by God who brought occasional order to the chaos.

Ruth is a small book telling the moving story of Ruth who, despite being a "foreigner" from Moab, shows great faithfulness and love and is rewarded.

1 and 2 Samuel tell the story of the first kings of Israel: Saul and David. The title of the books comes from Samuel, the prophet who anointed both kings.

1 and 2 Kings starts with the reign of Solomon and then goes downhill as the kingdom splits in two, with "Israel" in the north and "Judah" in the south. Kings tell of the downfall of Israel, as a succession of bad kings get their hands on the thrones. Eventually, both kingdoms are destroyed and their inhabitants taken into slavery by foreign powers.

1 and 2 Chronicles are a condensed version of the Samuel/Kings story. The books concentrate mainly on the kings of Judah and have a particular focus on the building of the Temple and the religious ceremonies.

Ezra and Nehemiah are two books telling of the return of the Jews from exile in Babylon, their struggles to rebuild the shattered city of Jerusalem, the re-establishment of the Temple and the rediscovery of the books of the law.

Esther is the story of Queen Esther, a Jew who became Queen of Persia and saved her people from extermination at the hands of their enemies.

Who Although Joshua orders his men to make a survey of the land (Joshua 18:8) and he draws up commands and laws (24:25), we don't know who the author was. However, the book appears to contain eyewitness testimony.

When Some believe that the book was written about 800 years after the events it describes. But a lot of the descriptions of the cities use the kind of names and details which would have been prevalent at the time, for example, "the Jebusite city" for Jerusalem (15:8). So it probably dates from around 900 BC, but includes material that was added later.

What The book takes its name from the leading character, Joshua, son of Nun, who took over the leadership of the Israelites from Moses. After their years of wandering in the desert, the Israelites finally make it across the Jordan and conquer Canaan, the land that God had given them.

Joshua tells of the invasion of Canaan by the Israelites, conquering city-state after city-state. In this, they are helped by God – sometimes miraculously, as in the defeat of Jericho and the battle at Gibeon where the Amorites are hailstoned to death (10:1–15)! Cities were either destroyed or occupied until, finally, there was peace in the land (11:23).

When the Israelites come to settle the land, each tribe is allocated territory in which to live, with the exception of the Levites, who are given towns scattered throughout the country. Joshua leads the people in swearing allegiance to God.

However, there is more to Joshua than meets the eye. Hidden in this list of military victories, you'll find the seeds of Israel's future problems. For it's not quite the triumph it seems; the Israelites never complete the job of clearing out the previous inhabitants and removing the false gods; some of the previous inhabitants remain, and their gods would be a temptation and a downfall for Israel for many years to come.

QUICK TOUR ▶ JOSHUA

Instructions 1:1–16
Rahab 2:1–24
Miracle at the Jordan River 3:1–17
The fall of Jericho 6:1–27
Achan 7:1–26

The sun stands still 10:1–27
Israel takes over the land 10:40–43; 11:12–20
The safe cities 20:1–9
Farewell 23:1–16; 24:29–33

"So the LORD kept the promise that he had made to the Israelites and gave the people all the land that he had promised. The people took the land and lived there."

Joshua 21:43

God Chooses Joshua to Lead Israel

1 Moses was the LORD's servant, and Joshua son of Nun was Moses' helper. After Moses died, the LORD spoke to Joshua and said, 2"My servant Moses is dead. Now you and all these people must go across the Jordan River. You must go into the land I am giving to the Israelites. 3I promised Moses that I would give you this land, so I will give you all the land wherever you go. 4All the land from the desert in the south to Lebanon in the north will be yours. It will reach to the great river, the Euphrates, including all the land of the Hittites. And all the land from here to the Great Sea in the west will be yours. 5Just as I was with Moses, I will be with you. No one will be able to stop you all your life. I will not abandon you. I will never leave you.

INSIGHT

God commanded Joshua to be strong and courageous in the face of overwhelming odds. Some scholars estimate that by the time Joshua was leading the children of Israel they numbered in excess of a million people. That's a big responsibility!

Joshua 1:9

6"Joshua, you must be strong and brave! You must lead these people so that they can take their land. I promised their fathers that I would give them this land. 7But you must be strong and brave about obeying the commands my servant Moses gave you. If you follow his teachings exactly, you will be successful in everything you do. 8Always remember what is written in that Book of the Law. Speak about that book and study it day and night. Then you can be sure to obey what is written there. If you do this, you will be wise and successful in everything you do. 9Remember, I commanded you to be strong and brave. Don't be afraid, because the LORD your God will be with you wherever you go."

Joshua Takes Command

10So Joshua gave orders to the leaders of the people: 11"Go through the camp and tell the people to get some food ready. Three days from now we will go across the Jordan River and take the land that the LORD our God is giving us."

12Then Joshua said to the tribes of Reuben, Gad and half the tribe of Manasseh, 13–14"Remember what the LORD's servant Moses told you. He said that the LORD your God would give you a place to live. So he has given you this land east of the Jordan River. But now you must help your relatives get their land. Your wives and children can stay here with your animals. But all your fighting men must prepare for battle and lead the men of the other tribes across the river. 15The LORD has given you a place to live, and he will do the same for your brothers. But you must help them until they take control of the land the LORD your God is giving them. Then you can come back and settle here on the east side of the river. This is the land that the LORD's servant Moses said would be yours."

16Then the people answered Joshua, "We will do whatever you command us to do. We will go wherever you tell us to go. 17We will obey whatever you say, just as we obeyed Moses. We only ask that the LORD your God be with you just as he was with Moses. 18Then anyone who refuses to obey your commands or turns against you will be killed. Just be strong and brave!"

Spies in Jericho

2 Joshua son of Nun and all the people were camped at Acacia.ᵃ Joshua sent out two spies. No one knew that Joshua had sent out these men. Joshua said to them, "Go and look at the land, especially the city of Jericho."

So the men went to the city of Jericho and stayed at the house of a prostitute named Rahab.

2But someone told the king of Jericho, "Last night some men from Israel came to look for weaknesses in our country."

3So the king of Jericho sent this message to Rahab: "Do not hide the men who came and stayed in your house. Bring them out. They have come to spy on our country."

4Rahab had hidden the two men, but she said, "They did come here, but I didn't know where they came from. 5In the evening, when it was time to close the city gate, the men left. I don't know where they went. But if you go quickly, maybe you can catch them." 6(Rahab said this, but really she had taken the men up to the roof and had hidden them in the flaxᵇ that she had piled up there.)

7So the king's men went out of the city, and the people closed the city gates. The king's men went to look for the two men from Israel. They went to the Jordan River and looked at all the places where people cross the river.

8The two men were ready to sleep for the night, but Rahab went to the roof to talk to them. 9She

---

ᵃ **2:1** *Acacia* Or "Shittim", a town east of the Jordan River. Also in 3:1.
ᵇ **2:6** *flax* A plant used to make linen.

said, "I know that the LORD has given this land to your people. You frighten us. Everyone living in this country is afraid of you. [10]We are afraid because we have heard about the ways that the LORD helped you. We heard that he dried up the Red Sea when you came out of Egypt. We also heard what you did to the two Amorite kings, Sihon and Og. We heard how you destroyed those kings living east of the Jordan River. [11]When we heard about this, we were very afraid. And now, not one of our men is brave enough to fight you, because the LORD your God rules the heavens above and the earth below! [12]So now, I want you to make a promise to me. I was kind to you and helped you. So promise me before the LORD that you will be kind to my family. Please tell me that you will do this. [13]Tell me that you will allow my family to live—my father, mother, brothers, sisters and all their families. Promise me that you will save us from death."

[14]The men agreed and said, "We will trade our lives for yours. Don't tell anyone what we are doing. Then, when the LORD gives us the land, we will be kind to you. You can trust us."

[15]Rahab's house was built into the city wall, so she used a rope to let the men down through a window. [16]Then she said to them, "Go into the hills so that the king's men will not accidentally find you. Hide there for three days. After the king's men come back, you can go on your way."

[17]The men said to her, "We made a promise to you. But you must do one thing, or we will not be responsible for our promise. [18]When we come back to this land, you must tie in your window this red rope you are using to help us escape. You must bring your father, your mother, your brothers and all your family into your house with you. [19]We will protect everyone who stays in this house. If anyone in your house is hurt, we will be responsible. But if they go out of your house and are killed, we will not be responsible. It will be their own fault. [20]We are making this agreement with you. But if you tell anyone about what we are doing, we will be free from this agreement."

[21]Rahab answered, "I will do just what you said." She said goodbye, and the men left her house. Then she tied the red rope in the window.

[22]The men left her house and went into the hills. They stayed there for three days. The king's men looked all along the road. After three days, they stopped looking and went back to the city. [23]Then the two men went back to Joshua. They left the hills and crossed the river. They went to Joshua and told him everything that they had learned. [24]They said to him, "The LORD really has given us all the land. All the people in that country are afraid of us."

Miracle at the Jordan River

3 Early the next morning, Joshua and all the Israelites got up and left Acacia. They travelled to the Jordan River and camped there before they crossed it. [2]After three days the leaders went through the camp. [3]They told the people, "When you see the Box of the Agreement of the LORD your God being carried by the Levite priests, follow it. [4]You have not gone this way before, but if you follow the Box of the Agreement, you will see where to go. But do not follow too closely. Stay about a kilometre[a] behind it."

[5]Then Joshua told the people, "Make yourselves pure. Tomorrow the LORD will do amazing things among us."

[6]Then Joshua said to the priests, "Take the Box of the Agreement and go across the river in front of the people." So the priests lifted the Box and carried it in front of the people.

[7]Then the LORD said to Joshua, "Today I will begin to make you a great man for all the Israelites to see. Then the people will know that I am with you just as I was with Moses. [8]The priests will carry the Box of the Agreement. Tell them this, 'Walk to the shore of the Jordan River and stop just before you step into the water.'"

[9]Then Joshua said to the Israelites, "Come and listen to the words of the LORD your God. [10]Here is proof that the living God is really with you and that he will surely defeat your enemies. He will defeat the Canaanites, Hittites, Hivites, Perizzites, Girgashites, Amorites and Jebusites; he will force them to leave their land. [11]The Box of the Agreement of the Lord of the whole world will go before you as you cross the Jordan River. [12]Now choose twelve men, one from each of the twelve tribes of Israel. [13]The priests will carry the Holy Box of the LORD. He is the Lord of the whole world. They will carry that Box in front of you into the Jordan River. When they enter the water, the water of the Jordan River will stop flowing and fill behind that place like at a dam."

[14]The priests carried the Box of the Agreement, and the people left the place they had camped. The people started going across the Jordan River. [15](During harvest time the Jordan River overflows its banks, so the river was at its fullest.) The priests who were carrying the Box came to the shore of the river. When they stepped into the water, [16]immediately the water stopped flowing and piled up like a wall. The water piled up high a long way up the river—all the way to Adam, a town near Zarethan. And the water flowing down to the Dead Sea was completely cut off. The people crossed the river near Jericho. [17]The ground at that place became dry, and the priests

---

[a] **3:4 a kilometre** Literally, "2,000 *cubits*".

carried the Box of the LORD's Agreement to the middle of the river and stopped. They waited there while all the Israelites walked across the Jordan River on dry land.

Rocks to Remind the People

4 After all the people had crossed the Jordan River, the LORD said to Joshua, 2"Choose twelve men, one from each tribe. 3Tell them to look in the river where the priests were standing and get twelve rocks from that place. Carry these rocks with you and put them where you stay tonight."

4So Joshua chose one man from each tribe. Then he called the twelve men together. 5He said to them, "Go out into the river where the Holy Box of the LORD your God is. Each of you must find one rock. There will be one rock for each of the twelve tribes of Israel. Carry that rock on your shoulder. 6These rocks will be a sign for you. In the future your children will ask you, 'What do these rocks mean?' 7You will tell them that the Lord stopped the water from flowing in the Jordan River. When the Box of the LORD's Agreement crossed the river, the water stopped flowing. These rocks will help the Israelites remember this forever."

8So the Israelites obeyed Joshua. They carried twelve rocks from the middle of the Jordan River. There was one rock for each of the twelve tribes of Israel. They did this the way the LORD had commanded Joshua. The men carried the rocks with them. Then they put the rocks at the place where they made their camp. 9Joshua also put twelve rocks in the middle of the Jordan River. He put them at the place where the priests had stood while carrying the Holy Box. These rocks are still there today.

10The LORD had commanded Joshua to tell the people what to do. This is what Moses had said Joshua must do. So the priests carrying the Holy Box stood in the middle of the river until everything was done. Meanwhile, the people hurried across the river. 11After the people finished crossing the river, the priests carried the LORD's Holy Box to the front of the people.

12The men from the tribes of Reuben, Gad and half the tribe of Manasseh obeyed Moses. These men crossed the river in front of the other people. These men were prepared for war. They were going to help the rest of the Israelites take the land God had promised to give them. 13About 40,000 soldiers, prepared for war, passed before the LORD. They were marching towards the plains of Jericho.

14That day the LORD made Joshua a great man to all the Israelites. From that time on, they respected Joshua just as they had Moses.

15Then the LORD said to Joshua, 16"Command the priests carrying the Box that holds the Agreement[a] to come out of the river."

17So Joshua commanded the priests, "Come out of the Jordan River."

18The priests obeyed Joshua. They carried the Box of the LORD's Agreement with them and came out of the river. When their feet touched the land on the other side of the river, the water in the river began flowing again. The water again overflowed its banks just as it had before the people crossed.

19The people crossed the Jordan River on the tenth day of the first month and camped at Gilgal, east of Jericho. 20They carried with them the twelve rocks that they had taken from the Jordan River, and Joshua set them up at Gilgal. 21Then Joshua told the Israelites, "In the future your children will ask you, 'What do these rocks mean?' 22Tell them, 'These rocks help us remember the way the people of Israel crossed the Jordan River on dry land.' 23The LORD your God caused the water in the Jordan River to stop flowing so that you could cross it on dry land—just as the LORD had stopped the water at the Red Sea so that we could cross it on dry land. 24The LORD did this so that all the people in this country would know that he is very powerful. Then they will always be afraid of the LORD your God."

INSIGHT

For the children of Israel, crossing the Jordan River was hugely significant. After 40 years of wandering, they were finally entering the land God had promised them. Building a memorial was their way of ensuring they'd never forget that momentous event.

Joshua 4

5 So the LORD dried up the Jordan River until the Israelites finished crossing it. The kings of the Amorites living west of the Jordan River and the Canaanites living along the coast heard about this and became very frightened. After that, they were not brave enough to stand and fight against the Israelites.

---

a 4:16 **Box that holds the Agreement** Literally, "Testimony". See "AGREEMENT" in the Word List.

Do you like watching films with big battle scenes? If so, why? Do you like the blood and gore? Or maybe you like witnessing justice as the goodies win and the baddies lose? Maybe it's the way we get to know a strong leader or a frightened citizen . . . Whatever it is, the book of Joshua has it all.

The people have been given the promised land by God, but there's a problem – it's filled with people who don't love God and want to stay in their cities. Let battle commence!

DIG IN

READ Joshua 5:13–15

- Who appears to Joshua?
- What words can you think of to describe how Joshua might have felt?

Joshua's on an emotional rollercoaster – one minute he's grabbing his sword to defend himself, the next he's on his face worshipping the commander of the Lord's army! But Joshua can breathe a sigh of relief (as much as anyone can when they're about to do battle with a city of God-hating people). God is with them; it's his fight.

READ Joshua 6:1–24

- Read the story carefully and try to imagine (or draw) the scenes.
- Who gives the orders?

It's a strange strategy with a miserable outcome for the enemies of God. Just as God commanded, the priests blew the trumpets and the people shouted and the walls of the city fell down – it's God's work as the people obey (Numbers 27:18–21).

- How does the ending make you feel (vv.20–21)?

Much like a lot of the book of Joshua, if this story were made into a film it wouldn't be suitable for young children! It's a gruesome tale of the destruction of a whole city – men, women and children. These people were the enemies of God – they worshipped false gods and would have encouraged the Israelites to do the same. Destroying them and forcing them out of the land was always God's plan (check out Leviticus 18:26–30 and Deuteronomy 7:1–5). All this mirrors the promise that one day God will judge all people, destroying those who hate him and bringing those who love him into a land with him forever.

- Who did God save (v.17)?
- What made Rahab different (check out Joshua 2)?

These stories can leave us feeling afraid of God, even if we understand that punishment is just and fair. But look at Rahab – was she a model citizen? Morally, she was pretty much as low as it gets, but she was not destroyed! It's an amazing story of the way God saves those who believe in him (Joshua 2:9–12).

DIG THROUGH

- "It's not fair!" How often have you said that? Everyone wants life to be fair. These stories may be uncomfortable, but God is just; it is fair that one day all those who hate him will be punished. Ask him to help you get your head round that.
- What isn't "fair" is that those of us who believe in him are granted forgiveness – we don't deserve it! Praise God for his grace.

DIG DEEPER

Trumpet blowing and shouting doesn't seem to be the normal way to do battle! There are other interesting tactics in Joshua (chapters 8 and 10).

- Every time the Israelites go to battle they have to obey God. Check out what happens when they don't obey (Joshua 7) and have a look at Joshua's priority after defeating the people of Ai (Joshua 8).

The Israelites Are Circumcised

²At that time the LORD said to Joshua, "Make knives from flint rocks and circumcise the men of Israel."

³So Joshua made knives from flint rocks and circumcised the men of Israel at Gibeath Haaraloth.*ᵃ*

⁴⁻⁷This is why Joshua circumcised the men: After the Israelites left Egypt, all the men who were able to serve in the army were circumcised. While in the desert, many of the fighting men did not listen to the LORD. So the LORD vowed that they would not see the "land where much food grows". The LORD had promised our ancestors that he would give us that land. But because of those men, he forced the people to wander in the desert for 40 years. During that time all the fighting men died, and their sons took their place. But none of the boys who were born in the desert on the journey from Egypt had been circumcised. So Joshua circumcised them.

⁸Joshua finished circumcising all the men. The people camped at that place until all the men were healed.

First Passover in Canaan

⁹Then the LORD said to Joshua, "You were slaves in Egypt, and this made you ashamed. But today I have taken away that shame." So Joshua named that place Gilgal.*ᵇ* And that place is still named Gilgal today.

¹⁰The Israelites celebrated Passover while they were camped at Gilgal on the plains of Jericho. This was on the evening of the fourteenth day of the month. ¹¹The day after Passover, the people ate food that grew in that land. They ate bread made without yeast and roasted grain. ¹²The next morning, the manna from heaven stopped coming. This happened the first day after the people ate the food that grew in the land of Canaan. From that time on, the Israelites did not get the manna from heaven.

The Commander of the LORD's Army

¹³When Joshua was near Jericho, he looked up and saw a man standing in front of him. The man had a sword in his hand. Joshua went to the man and asked, "Are you a friend to our people or are you one of our enemies?"

¹⁴The man answered, "I am not an enemy. I am the commander of the LORD's army. I have just now come to you."

Then Joshua bowed his face to the ground to show respect and said, "I am your servant. Does my master have a command for me?"

¹⁵The commander of the LORD's army answered, "Take off your sandals. The place where you are standing is holy." So Joshua obeyed him.

6 The gates of the city of Jericho were closed. The people in the city were afraid because the Israelites were near. No one went into the city, and no one came out.

²Then the LORD said to Joshua, "Look, I will let you defeat the city of Jericho. You will defeat the king and all the fighting men in the city. ³March around the city with your army once every day for six days. ⁴Tell seven of the priests to carry trumpets made from the horns of male sheep and to march in front of the priests who are carrying the Holy Box. On the seventh day, march around the city seven times and tell the priests to blow the trumpets while they march. ⁵They will make one loud noise from the trumpets. When you hear that noise, tell all the people to begin shouting. When you do this, the walls of the city will fall down and your people will be able to go straight into the city."

The Battle Against Jericho

⁶So Joshua son of Nun called the priests together and said to them, "Carry the Holy Box of the LORD. Tell seven priests to carry the trumpets and march in front of it."

⁷Then Joshua ordered the people, "Now go! March around the city. The soldiers with weapons will march in front of the Holy Box of the LORD."

⁸After Joshua had finished speaking to the people, the seven priests with the trumpets began marching before the LORD, blowing the trumpets as they marched. The priests carrying the Box of the LORD's Agreement followed them. ⁹The soldiers with weapons marched in front of the priests who were blowing the horns. And the rest of the men walked behind the Holy Box, marching and blowing their trumpets. ¹⁰Joshua had told the people not to give a war cry. He said, "Don't shout. Don't say a word until the day I tell you. Then you will shout."

¹¹So Joshua made the priests carry the Holy Box of the LORD around the city once. Then they went back to the camp and spent the night there.

¹²Early the next morning Joshua got up, and the priests carried the LORD's Holy Box again. ¹³The seven priests with the trumpets marched in front of the LORD's Holy Box, blowing their trumpets. The soldiers with weapons marched in front of them. The rest of the people marched behind the LORD's Holy Box. During the whole

---

ᵃ **5:3 Gibeath Haaraloth** This name means "Circumcision Hill".
ᵇ **5:9 Gilgal** This name is like the Hebrew word meaning "to roll away".

time they marched, the priests were blowing the trumpets. [14]On the second day, they all marched around the city once. And then they went back to the camp. They continued to do this every day for six days.

[15]On the seventh day, they got up at dawn and marched around the city seven times. They marched in the same way they had marched on the days before, but on that day they marched around the city seven times. [16]The seventh time they marched around the city, the priests blew their trumpets. Then Joshua gave the command: "Now, shout! The LORD is giving you this city! [17]The city and everything is to be destroyed as an offering to the LORD. Only Rahab the prostitute and everyone in her house will be left alive. They must not be killed because she helped the two spies we sent. [18]Remember, you must destroy everything else. Don't take anything. If you see something you want and take it,[a] you will cause great trouble for the whole Israelite camp. You will put us all in danger of being destroyed. [19]All the things made from silver, gold, bronze and iron belong to the LORD. They must be put in the LORD's treasury."

INSIGHT

Jericho would have been more like a strong fortress with high walls than a huge modern city. The Israelites marched outside the city walls for a week without encountering any resistance – perhaps those guarding the city did not think they were a serious threat?

Joshua 6:20

[20]So then the priests blew the trumpets. When the people heard the trumpets, they began shouting. The walls fell down, and the people ran up into the city. So the Israelites defeated that city. [21]The people destroyed everything in the city. They destroyed everything that was living there. They killed the young and old men, the young and old women, and the cattle, sheep and donkeys.

[22]Joshua talked to the two spies. He said, "You made a promise to the prostitute. So go to her house and bring her out and all those who are with her."

[23]So the two men went into the house and brought out Rahab, her father, mother, brothers, all her family and all those who were with her. They put all the people in a safe place outside the camp of Israel.

[24]Then the Israelites burned the whole city and everything in it except for the things made from silver, gold, bronze and iron. They put these things in the LORD's treasury. [25]Joshua saved Rahab the prostitute, her family and all those who were with her. Joshua let them live because Rahab helped the spies Joshua had sent out to Jericho. Rahab still lives among the Israelites today.

[26]At that time Joshua made this important promise. He said:

"Whoever rebuilds Jericho
  will be in danger from the LORD.
When he lays the foundation,
  he will lose his oldest son.
When he sets up the gates,
  he will lose his youngest son."[b]

[27]So the LORD was with Joshua, and Joshua became famous throughout the whole country.

Achan's Sin

7 But the Israelites did not obey God. There was a man from the tribe of Judah named Achan son of Carmi, grandson of Zimri, great-grandson of Zerah. Achan kept some of the things that should have been destroyed. So the LORD became very angry with the Israelites.

[2]After they defeated Jericho, Joshua sent some men to Ai.[c] Ai was near Beth Aven, east of Bethel. He told them, "Go to Ai and look for weaknesses in that area." So the men went to spy on that land.

[3]Later, the men came back to Joshua. They said, "Ai is a weak area. We will not need all our people to defeat them. Send 2,000 or 3,000 men to fight there. There is no need to use the whole army. There are only a few men there to fight against us."

[4-5]So about 3,000 men went to Ai, but the people of Ai killed about 36 men of Israel. And the Israelites ran away. The people of Ai chased them from the city gates all the way to the quarries.[d] The people of Ai beat them badly.

When the people from Israel saw this, they became very frightened and lost their courage. [6]When Joshua heard about this, he tore his clothes to show his sadness. He bowed down to the ground before the Holy Box and stayed there

[a] **6:18** *If . . . take it* This is from the ancient Greek version. The Hebrew text has "When you are setting anything aside to be destroyed, if you take it . . .".
[b] **6:26** *When he . . . son* See 1 Kgs 16:34.
[c] **7:2** *Ai* The name of this town means "the ruins".
[d] **7:4–5** *quarries* Places where people cut stones from the solid rock.

until evening. The leaders of Israel did the same thing. They also threw dirt on their heads to show their sadness.

7Joshua said, "Lord GOD, you brought our people across the Jordan River. Why did you bring us this far and then allow the Amorites to destroy us? We should have been satisfied and stayed on the other side of the Jordan River. 8I promise by my life, Lord! There is nothing I can say now. Israel has surrendered to the enemy. 9The Canaanites and all the other people in this country will hear about what happened. Then they will attack us and kill us all! Then what will you do to protect your great name?"

10The LORD said to Joshua, "Why are you down there with your face on the ground? Stand up! 11The Israelites sinned against me. They have broken the agreement that I commanded them to obey. They took some of the things that I commanded them to destroy. They have stolen from me. They have lied. They have taken those things for themselves. 12That is why the army of Israel turned and ran away from the fight. They did that because they have done wrong. They should be destroyed. I will not continue to help you or be with you unless you destroy everything I commanded you to destroy.

13"Now go and make the people pure. Tell them, 'Make yourselves pure. Prepare for tomorrow. The LORD, the God of Israel, says that some people are keeping things that he commanded to be destroyed. You will never be able to defeat your enemies until you throw away those things.

14"'Tomorrow morning you must all stand before the LORD. All the tribes will stand before the LORD, and he will choose one tribe. Only that tribe will stand before him. Then the LORD will choose one family group from that tribe. Only that family group must stand before him. Then he will look at each family in that family group, and the LORD will choose one family. Then he will look at each man in that family. 15The man who is keeping those things that we should have destroyed will be caught. Then he will be destroyed by fire, and everything that he owns will be destroyed with him. He broke the agreement with the LORD. He has done a very bad thing to the Israelites!'"

16Early the next morning, Joshua led out all the Israelites. Each tribe came forward to stand before the LORD, and he chose the tribe of Judah. 17So then all the family groups of Judah stood before

the LORD, and he chose the Zerah family group. Then all the families of the Zerah group stood before the LORD, and he chose the family of Zimri. 18Then Joshua told all the men in that family to come before the LORD. He chose Achan the son of Carmi. (Carmi was the son of Zimri. And Zimri was the son of Zerah.)

19Then Joshua said to Achan, "Son, you must honour the LORD, the God of Israel. Praise him and confess your sins to him. Tell me what you have done, and don't try to hide anything from me."

20Achan answered, "It is true! I have sinned against the LORD, the God of Israel. This is what I did: 21In Jericho, I saw a beautiful coat from Babylonia,a about two kilogrammesb of silver, and about a half a kilogrammec of gold. I wanted these things for myself, so I took them. You will find them buried in the ground under my tent. The silver is under the coat."

22So Joshua sent some men to the tent. They ran to the tent and found the things hidden there. The silver was under the coat. 23The men brought the things out of the tent and took them to Joshua and all the Israelites. They threw them on the ground before the LORD.

24Then Joshua and all the people led Achan son of Zerah to the Valley of Achor. They also took the silver, the coat, the gold, Achan's sons and daughters, his cattle, his donkeys, his sheep, his tent and everything he owned. They took all these things to the Valley of Achor with Achan. 25Then Joshua said, "You caused much trouble for us, but now the LORD will bring trouble to you." Then all the people threw stones at Achan and his family until they died. Then the people burned them and everything he owned. 26After they burned Achan, they put many rocks over his body. The rocks are still there today. That is why it is called the Valley of Achor.d After this the LORD was not angry with the people.

Ai Destroyed

8 Then the LORD said to Joshua, "Don't be afraid; don't give up. Lead all your fighting men to Ai.e I will help you defeat the king of Ai. I am giving you his people, his city and his land. 2You will do to Ai and its king the same thing you did to Jericho and its king. Only this time you can take all the wealth and animals and keep it for yourselves. You will share the wealth with your people. Now, tell some of your soldiers to hide behind the city."

a 7:21 **Babylonia** Literally, "Shinar", which may be a form of the name Sumer.
b 7:21 **about two kilogrammes** Literally, "200 shekels".
c 7:21 **about half a kilogramme** Literally, "50 shekels".
d 7:26 **Achor** This name means "trouble".
e 8:1 **Ai** See Josh. 7:2. The name of this town means "the ruins".

³So Joshua led his whole army towards Ai. Then Joshua chose 30,000 of his best fighting men and sent them out at night. ⁴Joshua gave them this command: "Listen carefully to what I tell you. You must hide in the area behind the city. Wait for the time to attack. Don't go far from the city. Continue to watch and be ready. ⁵I will lead the men with me; we will march towards the city. The men in the city will come out to fight against us. We will turn and run away from them as we did before. ⁶These men will chase us away from the city, so we will run away. They will think that we are running away from them as we did before. ⁷Then you should come out of your hiding place and take control of the city. The LORD your God will give you the power to win.

⁸"When you have taken control of the city, you must do what the LORD said. You must burn it. Now go! These are my orders."

⁹Then Joshua sent them to their hiding place and waited. They went to a place west of Ai, between Bethel and Ai. But Joshua stayed the night with his people.

¹⁰Early the next morning Joshua gathered the men together. Then Joshua and the leaders of Israel led the men to Ai. ¹¹All the soldiers who were with Joshua marched to Ai. They stopped in front of the city. The army made its camp north of the city. There was a valley between the army and Ai.

¹²Then Joshua chose about 5,000 men. He sent these men to hide in the area west of the city, between Bethel and Ai. ¹³So Joshua had prepared his men for the fight. The main camp was north of the city. The other men were hiding to the west. That night Joshua went down into the valley.

¹⁴Later, the king of Ai saw the army of Israel. The king and his people hurried out to fight the army of Israel. The king of Ai went out the east side of the city towards the Jordan Valley, so he did not see the soldiers hiding behind the city.

¹⁵Joshua and all the men of Israel let the army of Ai push them back. Joshua and his men began running east towards the desert. ¹⁶The people in the city began to shout and started to chase them. All the people left the city. ¹⁷All the men of Ai and Bethel chased the army of Israel. The city was left open—no one stayed to protect the city.

¹⁸Then the LORD said to Joshua, "Hold your spear towards the city of Ai, because I will give you that city." So Joshua held his spear towards the city of Ai. ¹⁹When the Israelites who were hiding saw this, they quickly came out from their hiding place and hurried towards the city. They entered the city and took control of it. Then the soldiers started fires to burn the city.

²⁰The men from Ai looked back and saw their city burning. When they saw the smoke rising into the sky, they lost their strength and courage. They stopped chasing the men of Israel. The Israelites stopped running away. They turned and went to fight the men from Ai. There was no safe place for the men from Ai to run to. ²¹When Joshua and his men saw that his army had taken control of the city and that smoke was rising from it, they stopped running away and turned to fight the men of Ai. ²²Then the men who were hiding came out of the city to help with the fight. The army of Israel was on both sides of the men of Ai—the men of Ai were trapped. Israel defeated them. They fought until none of the men from Ai were left alive—none of the enemy escaped. ²³But the king of Ai was left alive. Joshua's men brought him to Joshua.

A Review of the Fighting

²⁴During the fighting, the army of Israel chased the men from Ai into the fields and into the desert. So the army of Israel finished killing all the men from Ai in the fields and in the desert. Then the Israelites went back to Ai and killed all the people who were still alive in the city. ²⁵All the people of Ai died that day; there were 12,000 men and women. ²⁶Joshua had held his spear towards Ai as a sign to his people to destroy the city. And he did not stop until all the people of Ai were destroyed. ²⁷The Israelites kept the animals and other things from the city for themselves. This is what the LORD said they could do when he gave Joshua the commands.

INSIGHT

There's no denying that certain parts of the Bible are fairly gruesome, and this passage is no exception. God has reasons for his actions throughout history, even if we don't fully understand them. He is all about justice for his people, but he is also full of mercy.

Joshua 8:24–29

²⁸Then Joshua burned the city of Ai. That city became an empty pile of rocks. It is still like that today. ²⁹Joshua hanged the king of Ai on a tree and left him hanging there until evening. At sunset, Joshua told his men to take the king's body down from the tree. They threw his body down at the city gate. Then they covered the body with many rocks. That pile of rocks is still there today.

Reading the Blessings and Curses

³⁰Then Joshua built an altar for the Lord, the God of Israel. He built the altar on Mount Ebal. ³¹The Lord's servant Moses told the Israelites how to build altars. So Joshua built the altar the way it was explained in the *Book of the Law*ᵃ *of Moses*. The altar was made from stones that were not cut. No tool had ever been used on those stones. They offered burnt offerings to the Lord on that altar. They also gave fellowship offerings.

³²There Joshua copied onto the stones the law Moses had written down. This was for all the people of Israel to see. ³³The leaders, officers, judges and all the Israelites were standing around the Box of the Lord's Agreement. They were standing in front of the Levite priests, who carried the Holy Box. The Israelites and the other people with them were all standing there. Half of the people stood in front of Mount Ebal and the other half of the people stood in front of Mount Gerizim. The Lord's servant Moses had told the people to do this. He told them to do this to be blessed.

³⁴Then Joshua read all the words from the law. He read the blessings and the curses. He read everything the way it was written in the *Book of the Law*. ³⁵All the Israelites were gathered together there. All the women and children and all the foreigners who lived with the Israelites were there. And Joshua read every command that Moses had given.

The Gibeonites Trick Joshua

9 All the kings west of the Jordan River heard about these things. They were the kings of the Hittites, Amorites, Canaanites, Perizzites, Hivites and Jebusites. They lived in the hill country and in the plains. They also lived along the coast of the Great Sea as far as Lebanon. ²All these kings came together and made plans to fight against Joshua and the Israelites.

³The people from the city of Gibeon heard about the way Joshua had defeated Jericho and Ai. ⁴So they decided to try to trick the Israelites. This was their plan: They gathered together old wineskins that were cracked and broken. They put these old wineskins on the backs of their animals. They put old pieces of cloth on their animals to look as if they had travelled from far away. ⁵The men put old sandals on their feet and wore old clothes. They found some old bread that was dry and mouldy. ⁶Then they went to the camp of the Israelites. This camp was near Gilgal.

The men went to Joshua and said to him, "We have travelled from a faraway country. We want to make a peace agreement with you."

⁷The men of Israel said to these Hivite men, "Maybe you are trying to trick us. Maybe you live near us. We cannot make a peace agreement with you until we know where you are from."

⁸The Hivite men said to Joshua, "We are your servants."

But Joshua asked, "Who are you? Where do you come from?"

⁹The men answered, "We are your servants. We have come from a faraway country. We came because we heard of the great power of the Lord your God. We heard about what he has done and about everything he did in Egypt. ¹⁰And we heard that he defeated the two kings of the Amorites east of the Jordan River. This was King Sihon of Heshbon and King Og of Bashan in the land of Ashtaroth. ¹¹So our leaders and our people said to us, 'Take enough food for your journey. Go and meet with the Israelites.' Tell them, 'We are your servants. Make a peace agreement with us.'

¹²"Look at our bread. When we left home, it was warm and fresh. But now you can see that it is dry and old. ¹³Look at our wineskins. When we left home, they were new and filled with wine. But now you can see that they are cracked and old. Look at our clothes and sandals. You can see that the long journey has almost destroyed the things we wear."

¹⁴The men of Israel wanted to know if these men were telling the truth. So they tasted the bread—but they did not ask the Lord what they should do. ¹⁵Joshua agreed to make peace with them. He agreed to let them live. The leaders of Israel agreed by making a promise with an oath.

¹⁶Three days later the Israelites learned that these men lived very near their camp. ¹⁷So the Israelites went to the place where they lived. On the third day, the Israelites came to the cities of Gibeon, Kephirah, Beeroth and Kiriath Jearim. ¹⁸But the army of Israel did not try to fight against those cities. They had made a peace agreement with them. They had made a promise to them before the Lord, the God of Israel.

All the people complained against the leaders who had made the agreement. ¹⁹But the leaders answered, "We have given our promise with an oath before the Lord, the God of Israel. We cannot fight against them now. ²⁰This is what we must do. We must let them live. We cannot hurt them or God will be angry with us because we broke the promise we made to them. ²¹So let them live, but they will be our servants. They will cut wood for us and carry water for all our people." So the leaders did not break their promise of peace to them.

²²Joshua called the Gibeonites together. He said, "Why did you lie to us? Your land was near

---

ᵃ **8:31** *Law* Or "Teachings". Also in verses 32,34.

our camp. But you told us you were from a faraway country. 23Now, your people will have many troubles. All your people will be slaves— they will have to cut wood and carry water for the house of God."*a*

24The Gibeonites answered, "We lied to you because we were afraid you would kill us. We heard that God commanded his servant Moses to give you all this land. And God told you to kill all the people who lived in this land. That is why we lied to you. 25Now we are your servants. You can do whatever you think is right."

26So the Gibeonites became slaves, but Joshua let them live. He did not allow the Israelites to kill them. 27He made them slaves of the Israelites. They cut wood and carried water for the Israelites and for the altar of the LORD—wherever the LORD chose it to be. They are still slaves today.

The Day the Sun Stood Still

10 At this time Adoni Zedek was the king of Jerusalem. He heard that Joshua had defeated Ai and completely destroyed it. The king learned that Joshua had done the same thing to Jericho and its king. He also learned that the Gibeonites had made a peace agreement with Israel and that they lived very near Jerusalem. 2So Adoni Zedek and his people were very frightened. Gibeon was not a small town like Ai. It was a very big city—as big as any royal city.*b* And all the men in that city were good fighters, so the king was afraid. 3King Adoni Zedek of Jerusalem talked with King Hoham of Hebron. He also talked with King Piram of Jarmuth, King Japhia of Lachish and King Debir of Eglon. The king of Jerusalem begged these men, 4"Come with me and help me attack Gibeon. Gibeon has made a peace agreement with Joshua and the Israelites."

5So these five Amorite kings joined their armies together. (The five kings were the king of Jerusalem, the king of Hebron, the king of Jarmuth, the king of Lachish and the king of Eglon.) Their armies went to Gibeon, surrounded the city and began fighting against it.

6The people in the city of Gibeon sent a message to Joshua at his camp at Gilgal: "We are your servants! Don't leave us alone. Come and help us! Hurry! Save us! All the Amorite kings from the hill country have brought their armies together to fight against us."

7So Joshua marched out of Gilgal with his whole army. His best fighting men were with him. 8The LORD said to Joshua, "Don't be afraid of those armies. I will allow you to defeat them. None of them will be able to defeat you."

9Joshua and his army marched all night to Gibeon, so it was a complete surprise when he attacked them.

10The LORD caused those armies to be very confused when Israel attacked. So Israel defeated them and won a great victory. Israel chased the enemy from Gibeon along the road going up to Beth Horon. The army of Israel killed men all the way to Azekah and Makkedah. 11Then they chased the enemy down the road from Beth Horon to Azekah. While they were chasing the enemy, the LORD caused large hailstones to fall from the sky. Many of the enemy were killed by these large hailstones. More men were killed by the hailstones than by the swords of the soldiers of Israel.

12On that day the LORD gave Israel the victory against the Amorites. Joshua stood before all the Israelites and said to the LORD:

"Sun, stop over Gibeon.
    Moon, stand still over the Valley of Aijalon."

13So the sun did not move, and the moon stopped until the people had defeated their enemies. This story is written in the *Book of Jashar*. The sun stopped in the middle of the sky. It did not move for a full day. 14That had never happened before, and it has never happened again. That was the day the LORD obeyed a man. The LORD really was fighting for Israel!

15After this, Joshua and his army went back to the camp at Gilgal. 16But during the fight, the five kings ran away. They hid in a cave near Makkedah, 17but someone found them hiding in that cave. Joshua learned about this. 18He said, "Cover the entrance to the cave with large rocks. Put some men there to guard the cave. 19But don't stay there yourselves. Continue chasing the enemy and attacking them from behind. Don't let the enemy get back to their cities. The LORD your God has given you the victory over them."

20So Joshua and the Israelites killed the enemy. But some of them were able to go to their cities that had tall walls around them and hide. These men were not killed. 21After the fighting, Joshua's men came back to him at Makkedah. Not one of the people in that country was brave enough to say anything against the Israelites.

22Joshua said, "Move the rocks that are covering the entrance to the cave. Bring the five kings to me." 23So Joshua's men brought the five kings out of the cave—the kings of Jerusalem, Hebron, Jarmuth, Lachish and Eglon. 24When they brought the five kings to Joshua, he called all

---

a **9:23 house of God** This might mean the "family of God" (Israel), "the Holy Tent" or "the Temple".
b **10:2 royal city** A strong, well-protected city that controlled smaller towns nearby.

his men to come to that place. He said to the officers of his army, "Come here! Put your feet on the necks of these kings." So the officers of Joshua's army came close and put their feet on the necks of the kings.

²⁵Then Joshua said to his men, "Be strong and brave! Don't be afraid. I will show you what the LORD will do to all the enemies you will fight in the future."

²⁶Then Joshua killed the five kings and hung their bodies on five trees. He left them hanging in the trees until evening. ²⁷At sunset Joshua told his men to take the bodies down from the trees. So they threw the bodies into the cave where the kings had been hiding and covered the entrance of the cave with large rocks. Their bodies are still in that cave today.

²⁸That day Joshua defeated Makkedah. He killed the king and the people in that city. No one was left alive. Joshua did the same thing to the king of Makkedah that he had done to the king of Jericho.

Taking the Southern Cities

²⁹Then Joshua and all the Israelites travelled from Makkedah to Libnah and attacked that city. ³⁰The LORD allowed the Israelites to defeat that city and its king. They killed everyone in the city. No one was left alive. And they did the same thing to that king as they had done to the king of Jericho.

³¹Then Joshua and all the Israelites left Libnah and went to Lachish. Joshua and his army camped around that city and attacked it. ³²The LORD allowed them to defeat the city of Lachish. They defeated it on the second day. The Israelites killed everyone in the city, just as they had done in Libnah. ³³King Horam of Gezer came to help Lachish, but Joshua also defeated him and his army. No one was left alive.

³⁴Then Joshua and all the Israelites travelled from Lachish to Eglon. They camped around Eglon and attacked it. ³⁵That day they captured the city and killed everyone in the city. This was the same thing they had done to Lachish.

³⁶Then Joshua and all the Israelites travelled from Eglon to Hebron and attacked it. ³⁷They captured the city and all the small towns near Hebron. The Israelites killed everyone in the city, just as they did to Eglon. No one was left alive there. They destroyed the city and killed all the people in it as an offering to the Lord.

³⁸Then Joshua and all the Israelites went back to Debir and attacked it. ³⁹They captured the city, its king and all the towns near Debir. They killed

everyone in the city, just as they had done to Libnah and its king. No one was left alive there. They destroyed the city and killed all the people in it as an offering to the Lord.

⁴⁰So Joshua defeated all the kings of the cities of the hill country, the Negev, the western foothills and the eastern foothills. The LORD, the God of Israel, had told Joshua to kill all the people, so Joshua did not leave anyone alive in those places.

⁴¹Joshua captured all the cities from Kadesh Barnea to Gaza. He captured all the cities from Goshenᵃ to Gibeon. ⁴²Joshua captured all these cities and their kings in one series of battles. He did this because the LORD, the God of Israel, was fighting for Israel. ⁴³Then Joshua and all the Israelites returned to their camp at Gilgal.

Defeating the Northern Cities

11 King Jabin of Hazor heard about everything that had happened. So he decided to call together the armies of several kings. He sent a message to King Jobab of Madon to the king of Shimron, to the king of Acshaph, ²and to the kings of the north in the hill country and in the desert. Jabin sent the message to the kings of the Kinnereth,ᵇ the Negev and the western foothills. He also sent the message to the king of Naphoth Dor in the west. ³Jabin sent the message to the kings of the Canaanites in the east and in the west. He sent the message to the Amorites, Hittites, Perizzites and Jebusites living in the hill country. He also sent the message to the Hivites living below Mount Hermon near Mizpah. ⁴So the armies of all these kings came together. There were many fighting men and many horses and chariots. It was a very large army—it looked as if there were as many men as grains of sand on the seashore.

⁵All these kings met together at the small river of Merom. They joined their armies together into one camp and made plans for the battle against Israel.

⁶Then the LORD said to Joshua, "Don't be afraid of that army, because I will allow you to defeat them. By this time tomorrow, you will have killed them all. You will cut the legs of the horses and burn all their chariots."

⁷So Joshua and his whole army surprised the enemy and attacked them at the river of Merom. ⁸The LORD allowed Israel to defeat them. The army of Israel defeated them and chased them to Greater Sidon, Misrephoth Maim and the Valley of Mizpah in the east. The army of Israel fought until none of the enemy was left alive. ⁹Joshua

---

ᵃ **10:41 Goshen** The north-eastern part of Egypt.
ᵇ **11:2 Kinnereth** The area near the Sea of Galilee.

did what the LORD had told him to do; he crippled their horses and burned their chariots.

¹⁰Then Joshua went back and captured the city of Hazor and killed its king. (Hazor was the leader of all the kingdoms that fought against Israel.) ¹¹The army of Israel killed everyone in that city and completely destroyed all the people. There was nothing left alive. Then they burned the city. ¹²Joshua captured all these cities and killed all their kings. He completely destroyed everything in these cities—just as the LORD's servant Moses had commanded. ¹³But the army of Israel did not burn any cities that were built on hills. The only city built on a hill that they burned was Hazor. This is the city Joshua burned. ¹⁴The Israelites kept for themselves all the things and all the animals they found in the cities. But they killed all the people there. They left no one alive. ¹⁵Long ago the LORD commanded his servant Moses to do this. Then Moses commanded Joshua to do this. So Joshua obeyed God. He did everything that the LORD had commanded Moses.

¹⁶So Joshua defeated all the people in that whole area. He had control over the hill country, the Negev, all the area of Goshen, the western foothills, the Jordan Valley and the mountains of Israel and all the hills near them. ¹⁷Joshua had control of all the land from Mount Halak near Seir to Baal Gad in the Valley of Lebanon below Mount Hermon. He captured all the kings in that land and killed them. ¹⁸Joshua fought against them for many years. ¹⁹Only one city in all the land made a peace agreement with Israel. That was the Hivite city of Gibeon. All the other cities were defeated in war. ²⁰The LORD made those people feel brave enough to fight against Israel. This was so that Israel could destroy them completely without mercy just as the LORD had commanded Moses to do.

²¹The Anakites lived in the hill country in the area of Hebron, Debir, Anab and Judah. Joshua fought them and completely destroyed all the people and their towns. ²²There were no Anakites left living in the land of Israel. The only Anakites who were left alive were in Gaza, Gath and Ashdod. ²³Joshua took control of the whole land of Israel as the LORD had told Moses long ago. The Lord gave that land to Israel as he promised. And Joshua divided the land among the tribes of Israel. Finally, the fighting ended and there was peace in the land.

Kings Defeated by Israel

12 The Israelites had taken control of the land east of the Jordan River. They had all the land from Arnon Ravine to Mount Hermon and all the land along the eastern side of the Jordan Valley. These are all the kings the Israelites defeated to take this land:

²They defeated King Sihon of the Amorites living in the city of Heshbon. He ruled the land from Aroer at the Arnon Ravine to the Jabbok River. His land started in the centre of that ravine. This was their border with the Ammonites. Sihon ruled over half of the land of Gilead. ³He also ruled over the eastern side of the Jordan Valley from Lake Galilee to the Dead Sea (Salt Sea). And he ruled from Beth Jeshimoth to the south to the hills of Pisgah.

⁴They also defeated King Og of Bashan. Og was from the Rephaites. He ruled the land in Ashtaroth and Edrei. ⁵Og ruled over Mount Hermon, Salecah and all the area of Bashan. His land ended where the people of Geshur and Maacah lived. Og also ruled half of the land of Gilead. This land ended at the land of King Sihon of Heshbon.

⁶The LORD's servant Moses and the Israelites defeated all these kings. And Moses gave that land to the tribe of Reuben, the tribe of Gad and half the tribe of Manasseh. Moses gave them this land to be their own.

⁷Joshua and the Israelites defeated the kings of the land west of the Jordan River. This land was in the area west of Baal Gad in the Lebanon Valley as far as Mount Halak that rises towards Seir. Joshua divided it among the tribes. ⁸This included the hill country, the western foothills, the Jordan Valley, the eastern mountains, the desert and the Negev. This was where the Hittites, Amorites, Canaanites, Perizzites, Hivites and Jebusites had lived. These are the kings the Israelites defeated:

⁹the king of Jericho,
  the king of Ai near Bethel,
¹⁰the king of Jerusalem,
  the king of Hebron,
¹¹the king of Jarmuth,
  the king of Lachish,
¹²the king of Eglon,
  the king of Gezer,
¹³the king of Debir,
  the king of Geder,
¹⁴the king of Hormah,
  the king of Arad,
¹⁵the king of Libnah,
  the king of Adullam,
¹⁶the king of Makkedah,
  the king of Bethel,
¹⁷the king of Tappuah,
  the king of Hepher,
¹⁸the king of Aphek,
  the king of Sharon,
¹⁹the king of Madon,
  the king of Hazor,
²⁰the king of Shimron Meron,
  the king of Acshaph,

²¹the king of Taanach,
  the king of Megiddo,
²²the king of Kedesh,
  the king of Jokneam in Carmel,
²³the king of Dor at Mount Dor,
  the king of Goyim in Gilgal,
²⁴and the king of Tirzah.

The total number of kings was 31.

Land Not Yet Taken

13 When Joshua was very old, the LORD said to him, "Joshua you have grown old, but there is still much land for you to take control of. ²You must still take the land of the Philistines and the Geshurites. ³This includes the land that begins at the Shihor River on the east side of Egypt and reaches north to the border of Ekron, which belongs to the Canaanites. It also includes the area that belongs to the five Philistine rulers of Gaza, Ashdod, Ashkelon, Gath and Ekron. You must also defeat the Avvites ⁴who live south of the Canaanite land. And you must go north to take Mearah, which the Sidonians control. From there you must go as far as Aphek on the Amorite border. ⁵And you still have to take the land of the Gebalites and all Lebanon east of Baal Gad below Mount Hermon to Lebo Hamath.

⁶"The people of Sidon are living in the hill country from Lebanon to Misrephoth Maim. But I will force them out for the Israelites. Be sure to remember this land when you divide the land among the Israelites. Do this as I told you. ⁷Now divide the land among the nine tribes and half the tribe of Manasseh."

Dividing the Land

⁸The tribes of Reuben, Gad and the other half of the tribe of Manasseh had already received all their land. The LORD's servant Moses gave them the land east of the Jordan River. ⁹Their land started at Aroer by the Arnon Ravine and continued to the town in the middle of the ravine. And it included the whole plain from Medeba to Dibon. ¹⁰All the towns that King Sihon of the Amorites ruled were in that land. He ruled in the city of Heshbon. The land continued to the area where the Ammonites lived. ¹¹Also the town of Gilead was in that land. And the area where the people of Geshur and Maacah lived was in that land. All Mount Hermon and all Bashan as far as Salecah was in that land. ¹²The whole kingdom of King Og of Bashan was in that land. Og, one of the last Rephaites, had once ruled in Ashtaroth and Edrei. Moses had defeated those people and had taken their land. ¹³But the Israelites did not force the people of Geshur and Maacah to leave the land. So they still live among the Israelites today.

¹⁴The tribe of Levi is the only tribe that did not get any land. Instead, the Levites were given all the animals offered by fire to the LORD, the God of Israel. That is what the Lord promised them.

¹⁵Moses had given each family group from the tribe of Reuben some land. This is the land they received: ¹⁶It was the land from Aroer near the Arnon Ravine to the town of Medeba. This included the whole plain and the town in the middle of the ravine. ¹⁷The land continued to Heshbon. It included all the towns on the plain. Those towns were Dibon, Bamoth Baal, Beth Baal Meon, ¹⁸Jahaz, Kedemoth, Mephaath, ¹⁹Kiriathaim, Sibmah, Zereth Shahar on the hill in the valley, ²⁰Beth Peor, the hills of Pisgah and Beth Jeshimoth. ²¹So that land included all the towns on the plain and all the area that King Sihon of the Amorites had ruled. He ruled in the town of Heshbon, but Moses had defeated him and the leaders of the Midianites. Those leaders were Evi, Rekem, Zur, Hur and Reba. (They all fought together with Sihon.) They all lived in that country. ²²The Israelites defeated Balaam son of Beor. (Balaam tried to use magic to tell the future.) The Israelites killed many people during the fighting. ²³The land that was given to Reuben stopped at the shore of the Jordan River. So the land that was given to the family groups of Reuben included all these towns and their fields that were listed.

²⁴This is the land Moses gave to the tribe of Gad. He gave this land to each family group:

²⁵He gave them the land of Jazer, all the towns of Gilead and half of the land of the Ammonites that went as far as Aroer near Rabbah. ²⁶Their land included the area from Heshbon to Ramath Mizpah and Betonim, from Mahanaim to the land of Debir, ²⁷the valley of Beth Haram, Beth Nimrah, Succoth and Zaphon, including the rest of the kingdom of King Sihon of Heshbon, along the Jordan all the way up to Lake Galilee on the eastern side of the river. ²⁸All this land is the land Moses gave the family groups of Gad. That land included all the towns that were listed. Moses gave that land to each family group.

²⁹This is the land Moses gave to half the tribe of Manasseh. Half of all the families in the tribe of Manasseh got this land:

³⁰The land started at Mahanaim. The land included all of Bashan, all the land ruled by King Og of Bashan and all the towns of Jair in Bashan. (In all, there were 60 cities.) ³¹The land also included half of Gilead, Ashtaroth and Edrei. (Gilead, Ashtaroth and Edrei were the cities where King Og had lived.) All this land was given to the family of Makir son of Manasseh. Half of all his sons got this land.

³²Moses gave all this land to these tribes. He did this while the people were camped on the

plains of Moab. This was across the Jordan River, east of Jericho. ³³Moses did not give any land to the tribe of Levi. The Lord, God of Israel, promised that he himself would be the gift for the tribe of Levi.

14 Eleazar the priest, Joshua son of Nun, and the leaders of all the tribes of Israel decided what land in Canaan to give to the people. ²The Lord had commanded Moses long ago how he wanted the people to choose their land. The people of the nine and a half tribes threw lots to decide which land they would get. ³Moses had already given the two and a half tribes their land east of the Jordan River. The tribe of Levi did not receive any land like the other tribes. ⁴The descendants of Joseph had divided into two tribes—Manasseh and Ephraim. Each of these tribes received some land; the tribe of Levi was not given any land. They were given only some towns scattered throughout the other tribes and some fields around those towns for their animals. ⁵The Lord had told Moses how to divide the land among the tribes of Israel. The Israelites divided the land the way the Lord had commanded.

Caleb Gets His Land

⁶One day some people from the tribe of Judah went to Joshua at Gilgal. One of them was Caleb, the son of Jephunneh the Kenizzite. Caleb said to Joshua, "You remember what the Lord said at Kadesh Barnea. The Lord was speaking to Moses, his servant.ᵃ The Lord was talking about you and me. ⁷The Lord's servant Moses sent me to look at the land where we were going. I was 40 years old at that time. When I came back, I told Moses what I thought about the land. ⁸The other men who went with me told the people things that made them afraid. But I really believed that the Lord would allow us to take that land. ⁹So that day Moses made a promise to me. He said, 'The land where you went will become your land. Your children will own that land forever. I will give you that land because you really believed in the Lord, my God.'

¹⁰"Now the Lord has kept me alive for 45 more years—as he said he would. During that time we all wandered in the desert. Now, here I am, 85 years old. ¹¹I am still as strong today as I was the day Moses sent me out. I am as ready to fight as I was then. ¹²So give me the hill country that the Lord promised me that day long ago. At that time you heard that the strong Anakites lived there and the cities were very big and well protected. But now, maybe the Lord will be with me, and I will take that land just as the Lord said."

¹³Joshua blessed Caleb son of Jephunneh. Joshua gave him the city of Hebron as his own. ¹⁴And that city still belongs to the family of Caleb son of Jephunneh the Kenizzite. That land still belongs to his people because he trusted and obeyed the Lord, God of Israel. ¹⁵In the past that city was called Kiriath Arba. It was named for the greatest man among the Anakites—a man named Arba.

After this there was peace in the land.

Land for Judah

15 The land that was given to Judah was divided among the families of that tribe. That land went to the border of Edom and south all the way to the desert of Zin at the edge of Teman. ²The southern border of Judah's land started at the south end of the Dead Sea. ³The border went south to Scorpion Pass and continued on to Zin. Then the border continued south to Kadesh Barnea. It continued past Hezron to Addar, then turned towards Karka. ⁴From there it went to Azmon, then to the brook of Egypt, which it followed to the Mediterranean Sea. That was the southern border of Judah and all the tribes of Israel.

⁵Their eastern border was the shore of the Dead Sea to the area where the Jordan River flowed into it.

Their northern border started at the area where the Jordan River flowed into the Dead Sea. ⁶Then the northern border went to Beth Hoglah and continued north of Beth Arabah. The border continued to the stone of Bohan, the son of Reuben. ⁷Then the northern border went through the Valley of Achor to Debir. There the border turned to the north and went to Gilgal. Gilgal is opposite the road that goes through the mountain of Adummim. It is on the south side of the brook. The border continued along the waters of En Shemesh. The border stopped at En Rogel. ⁸Then the border went through the Valley of Ben Hinnom beside the southern side of the Jebusite city (that is, Jerusalem). There the border went to the top of the hill on the west side of Hinnom Valley. This was at the northern end of Rephaim Valley. ⁹From there the border went to the spring of water of Nephtoah. Then the border went to the cities near Mount Ephron. There the border turned and went to Baalah. (Baalah is also called Kiriath Jearim.) ¹⁰At Baalah the border turned west and went to the hill country of Seir. The border continued along the north side of Mount Jearim (Kesalon) and continued down to Beth Shemesh. From there the border went past Timnah. ¹¹Then the border went to the hill north

---

ᵃ **14:6 his servant** Literally, "the man of God".

GOING HOME

Can you imagine the responsibility – you've just led millions of Israelites like a big army into this huge land, you've killed thousands of people and destroyed many cities with them, and have got to know them like family as they've been born and grown up in the desert. How on earth are you going to decide who gets what bit of land and city so that it's fair and everyone's happy?!

DIG IN

READ Joshua 14:1–5

- Who decided how the land should be divided?
- Who didn't get any land?

We often let coins make decisions for us that we might not be able to make fairly ourselves without a big argument! It's not clear what "throwing lots" is specifically but it's generally agreed that it's not dissimilar to tossing a coin or rolling a dice. But did you notice who was behind how the "lots" fell? This was all God's doing – he decided which tribe should have which bit of land. Does it seem unfair that the Levites didn't get any land? (See below.)

READ Joshua 14:6–15

Remember Caleb? He and Joshua were the only people from amongst the millions of Israelites who actually believed God was more powerful than a bunch of tall, strong men living in the promised land (read the story in Numbers 13).

- How does Caleb get his land?
- What was his request based on (vv.6–9)?
- What does this teach us about Caleb and about God?

Did you notice how many times it said Caleb believed God? Caleb's land isn't decided by throwing lots but was given to him as God had promised to Joshua. God had not forgotten that Caleb hadn't gone along with the crowd and instead had chosen to believe in God.

DIG THROUGH

- Caleb believed and trusted God even when everyone else didn't, which couldn't have been easy. But his faith was rewarded. How about you? Do you go along with the crowd? Ask God to help you believe like Caleb even when everything is stacked against you.

God promised the people this gift of land, and God delivered! As we've seen earlier, the land is an image for our salvation – rest in Jesus now (Matthew 11:28–30) and even more so in the future. One day there will be a new heaven and a new earth for us to enjoy – a land that's a billion times better than anything Joshua and the Israelites enjoyed.

- Check out Revelation chapters 21 – 22 for other exciting stuff about the future!

DIG DEEPER

- The Levites may not have got any land but they were no less important than the rest of God's people. Can you find out:
  - » Who they are (Numbers 3:40–43; 8:12 onwards)?
  - » What they do (Numbers 3:5–8)?
  - » Why they were chosen (Exodus 32:25 onwards)?
  - » Why they don't get land (Joshua 18:7)?
  - » What they did get (Deuteronomy 18:1–4; Joshua 21:1 onwards; Numbers 35:1–5)?

of Ekron. From there it turned to Shikkeron and went past Mount Baalah. It continued on to Jabneel and ended at the sea. [12]And the Great Sea was the western border. The families of Judah lived inside these four borders.

[13]The LORD had commanded Joshua to give Caleb son of Jephunneh part of the land in Judah. So Joshua gave Caleb the land God had commanded. Joshua gave him the town of Kiriath Arba, that is, Hebron. (Arba was the father of Anak.) [14]Caleb forced the three Anakite families living in Hebron to leave there. Those families were Sheshai, Ahiman and Talmai. They were from the family of Anak. [15]Then Caleb fought against the people living in Debir. (In the past, Debir was also called Kiriath Sepher.) [16]Caleb said, "I will give my daughter in marriage to the man who attacks and conquers Kiriath Sepher."

[17]Othniel, the son of Caleb's brother Kenaz, defeated the city. So Caleb gave his daughter Acsah to Othniel as his wife. [18]After Acsah and Othniel were married, she told him they should ask her father for some land. So Acsah went to her father. As she was getting off her donkey, Caleb asked her, "What are you doing here?"

[19]Acsah answered, "I came to ask you for a favour. You gave me dry desert land in the Negev. Please give me some land with water on it." So Caleb gave her what she wanted. He gave her the upper and lower pools of water in that land.

[20]The tribe of Judah got the land that God promised them. Each family group got part of the land.

[21]The tribe of Judah got all the towns in the southern part of the Negev. These towns were near the border of Edom. Here is a list of the towns:

Kabzeel, Eder, Jagur, [22]Kinah, Dimonah, Adadah, [23]Kedesh, Hazor, Ithnan, [24]Ziph, Telem, Bealoth, [25]Hazor Hadattah, Kerioth Hezron (Hazor), [26]Amam, Shema, Moladah, [27]Hazar Gaddah, Heshmon, Beth Pelet, [28]Hazar Shual, Beersheba, Biziothiah, [29]Baalah, Iim, Ezem, [30]Eltolad, Kesil, Hormah, [31]Ziklag, Madmannah, Sansannah, [32]Lebaoth, Shilhim, Ain and Rimmon. In all, there were 29 towns and all their fields.

[33]The tribe of Judah also got these towns in the western foothills:

Eshtaol, Zorah, Ashnah, [34]Zanoah, En Gannim, Tappuah, Enam, [35]Jarmuth, Adullam, Socoh, Azekah, [36]Shaaraim, Adithaim and Gederah (Gederothaim). In all, there were 14 towns and all their fields.

[37]The tribe of Judah was also given these towns: Zenan, Hadashah, Migdal Gad, [38]Dilean, Mizpah, Joktheel, [39]Lachish, Bozkath, Eglon, [40]Cabbon, Lahmas, Kitlish, [41]Gederoth, Beth Dagon, Naamah and Makkedah. In all, there were 16 towns and all the fields around them.

[42]The people of Judah also got these towns: Libnah, Ether, Ashan, [43]Iphtah, Ashnah, Nezib, [44]Keilah, Aczib and Mareshah. In all, there were nine towns and all the fields around them. [45]The people of Judah also got the town of Ekron and all the small towns and fields near it. [46]They also got the area west of Ekron and all the fields and towns near Ashdod. [47]All the area around Ashdod and the small towns there were part of the land of Judah. The people of Judah also got the area around Gaza and the fields and towns that were near it. Their land continued to the brook of Egypt and followed it to the coast of the Great Sea.

[48]The people of Judah were also given these towns in the hill country:

Shamir, Jattir, Socoh, [49]Dannah, Kiriath Sannah (Debir), [50]Anab, Eshtemoh, Anim, [51]Goshen, Holon and Giloh. In all, there were eleven towns and all the fields around them.

[52]The people of Judah were also given these towns:

Arab, Dumah, Eshan, [53]Janim, Beth Tappuah, Aphekah, [54]Humtah, Kiriath Arba (Hebron) and Zior. There were nine towns and all the fields around them.

[55]The people of Judah were also given these towns:

Maon, Carmel, Ziph, Juttah, [56]Jezreel, Jokdeam, Zanoah, [57]Kain, Gibeah and Timnah. In all, there were ten towns and all the fields around them.

[58]The people of Judah were also given these towns:

Halhul, Beth Zur, Gedor, [59]Maarath, Beth Anoth and Eltekon. In all, there were six towns and all the fields around them.

[60]The people of Judah were also given the two towns of Rabbah and Kiriath Baal (Kiriath Jearim).

[61]The people of Judah were also given these towns in the desert:

Beth Arabah, Middin, Secacah, 62Nibshan, Salt City and En Gedi. In all, there were six towns and all the fields around them.

63The army of Judah was not able to force out the Jebusites living in Jerusalem. So today there are still Jebusites living among the people of Judah in Jerusalem.

Land for Ephraim and Manasseh

16 This is the land that the family of Joseph received. This land started at the Jordan River near Jericho and continued to the waters of Jericho. (This was just east of Jericho.) The border went up from Jericho to the hill country of Bethel. 2Then the border continued from Bethel (Luz) to the Arkite border at Ataroth. 3Then the border went west to the border of the Japhletites. It continued to Lower Beth Horon, then went to Gezer and continued to the Mediterranean Sea.

4So the people of Manasseh and Ephraim got their land. (Manasseh and Ephraim were sons of Joseph.)

5This is the land that was given to the people of Ephraim: Their eastern border started at Ataroth Addar near Upper Beth Horon. 6And the western border started at Micmethath. The border turned to the east to Taanath Shiloh and continued east to Janoah. 7Then it went from Janoah down to Ataroth and to Naarah. The border continued until it touched Jericho and ended at the Jordan River. 8The border went from Tappuah west to Kanah Ravine and ended at the sea. This is all the land that was given to the Ephraimites. Each family in that tribe got a part of this land. 9Many of the border towns of Ephraim were actually in Manasseh's borders, but the Ephraimites got the towns and the fields around them. 10But the Ephraimites were not able to force the Canaanites to leave the town of Gezer. So the Canaanites still live among the Ephraimites today, although they did become slaves of the Ephraimites.

17 Then land was given to the tribe of Manasseh. Manasseh was Joseph's first son. Manasseh's first son was Makir, the father of Gilead.ᵃ Makir was a great soldier, so the areas of Gilead and Bashan were given to his family. 2Land was also given to the other families in the tribe of Manasseh. These families were Abiezer, Helek, Asriel, Shechem, Hepher and Shemida. All these men were the other sons of Manasseh, the son of Joseph. The families of these men got their share of the land.

3Zelophehad was the son of Hepher. Hepher was the son of Gilead. Gilead was the son of Makir, and Makir was the son of Manasseh. Zelophehad did not have any sons, but he had five daughters. The daughters were named Mahlah, Noah, Hoglah, Milcah and Tirzah. 4The daughters went to Eleazar the priest, Joshua son of Nun and all the leaders. The daughters said, "The LORD told Moses to give us land the same as our male relatives." So Eleazar obeyed the LORD and gave the daughters some land, just like their uncles.

5So the tribe of Manasseh had ten areas of land west of the Jordan River and two more areas of land, Gilead and Bashan, on the other side of the Jordan River. 6So these women from the tribe of Manasseh got land the same as the men. The land of Gilead was given to the rest of the families of Manasseh.

7The lands of Manasseh were in the area between Asher and Micmethath. This is near Shechem. The border went south to the En Tappuah area. 8The land around Tappuah belonged to Manasseh, but the town itself did not. The town of Tappuah was at the border of Manasseh's land, and it belonged to the people of Ephraim. 9The border of Manasseh continued south to Kanah Ravine. This area belonged to the tribe of Manasseh, but the cities belonged to the people of Ephraim. Manasseh's border was on the north side of the river and it continued west to the Mediterranean Sea. 10The land to the south belonged to Ephraim. And the land to the north belonged to Manasseh. The sea was the western border. The border touched Asher's land in the north and Issachar's land in the east.

INSIGHT

Although the land was divided and allotted to the eleven tribes, the land of Canaan was not yet fully conquered. The individual tribes were left to finish off the job and fully unite their areas. But some cities remained Canaanite and the inhabitants were used as forced labour. Because of this, their culture and religion remained a constant lure to the Israelites.
Joshua 17:11–13

11The people of Manasseh had towns in the area of Issachar and Asher. Beth Shean, Ibleam

---

ᵃ **17:1** *father of Gilead* Or "the leader of the area of Gilead".

and the small towns around them also belonged to them. The people of Manasseh also lived in Dor, Endor, Taanach, Megiddo and the small towns around these cities. They also lived in the three towns of Naphoth. 12The people of Manasseh were not able to defeat those cities. So the Canaanites continued to live there. 13But the Israelites grew strong. When this happened, they forced the Canaanites to work for them. But they did not force them to leave that land.

14The descendants of Joseph came to Joshua and said, "Why did you give us only one area of land? We need more than that because the LORD has continued to bless us with so many people."

15Joshua answered them, "If you have too many people, go up to the wooded area in the hill country and clear that land for a place to live. That land now belongs to the Perizzites and the Rephaites. But if the hill country of Ephraim is too small for you, go and take that other land."

16The people of Joseph said, "Even if we had all the hill country, it is not large enough for us. And the Canaanites living down in the valley are too powerful for us with their iron chariots! They control Jezreel Valley, Beth Shean and all the small towns in that area."

17Then Joshua said to the people of Joseph, the tribes of Ephraim and Manasseh, "You have many people and you are very strong, so you should get more than one share of the land. 18You will take these mountains. It is a forest, but you can cut down the trees and make it a good place to live. You can take it from the Canaanites and force them to leave. You can defeat them, even if they are strong and have iron chariots."

Dividing the Rest of the Land

18 All the Israelites gathered together at Shiloh where they set up the Meeting Tent. The Israelites controlled that country. They had defeated all the enemies in that land. 2But at this time there were still seven tribes of Israel that had not yet received their land.

3So Joshua said to the Israelites, "Why do you wait so long to take your land? The LORD, the God of your ancestors, has given this land to you. 4So each of your tribes should choose three men. I will send them out to study the land. They will describe that land, and then they will come back to me. 5They will divide the land into seven parts. The people of Judah will keep their land in the south. The people of Joseph will keep their land in the north. 6But you should describe the land and divide it into seven parts. Bring the map to me and we will throw lots to let the LORD our God decide how to divide the land among the tribes. 7The Levites don't get a share of the land. Their share is to serve the LORD as priests. Gad, Reuben

and half the tribe of Manasseh have already received the land that was promised to them. They are on the east side of the Jordan River. The LORD's servant Moses gave them that land."

8So the men who were chosen went to look at the land and write down what they saw. Joshua told them, "Go through the land and describe it in writing. Then come back to me at Shiloh. I will throw lots and let the LORD decide how you will share the land."

9So the men went into the land. As they walked through it, they wrote down what they saw. They listed all the cities and divided the land into seven parts. Then they went back to Joshua at Shiloh. 10Joshua threw lots for them in front of the LORD at Shiloh. In this way Joshua divided the land and gave each tribe its part of the land.

Land for Benjamin

11The tribe of Benjamin was given the land that was between the areas of Judah and Joseph. Each family in the tribe of Benjamin got its land. This is the land that was chosen for Benjamin: 12The northern border started at the Jordan River. It went along the northern edge of Jericho. Then the border went west into the hill country. It continued until it was just east of Beth Aven. 13Then the border went south to Luz (Bethel), then down to Ataroth Addar. Ataroth Addar is on the hill south of Lower Beth Horon. 14At the hill south of Beth Horon, the border turned south and went along the west side of the hill. The border went to Kiriath Baal (also called Kiriath Jearim). This town belonged to the people of Judah. This was the western border.

15The southern border started near Kiriath Jearim and went to the River of Nephtoah. 16Then the border went down to the bottom of the hill near the valley of Ben Hinnom, north of Rephaim Valley. It continued down Hinnom Valley just south of the Jebusite city. Then the border went on to En Rogel. 17There it turned north, went to En Shemesh and then continued on to Geliloth. (Geliloth is near the Adummim Pass in the mountains.) The border went down to the Great Stone that was named for Bohan, the son of Reuben. 18It continued to the northern part of Beth Arabah. Then the border went down into the Jordan Valley. 19Then it went to the northern part of Beth Hoglah and ended at the north shore of the Dead Sea. This is where the Jordan River flows into that sea. That was the southern border.

20The Jordan River was the eastern border. So this was the land that was given to the tribe of Benjamin. These were the borders on all sides. 21Each family got its land. These are their cities: Jericho, Beth Hoglah, Emek Keziz, 22Beth Arabah, Zemaraim, Bethel, 23Avvim, Parah, Ophrah,

24Kephar Ammoni, Ophni and Geba. There were twelve cities and the fields around them.

25The tribe of Benjamin also got Gibeon, Ramah, Beeroth, 26Mizpah, Kephirah, Mozah, 27Rekem, Irpeel, Taralah, 28Zelah, Haeleph, the Jebusite city (that is, Jerusalem), Gibeah and Kiriath. There were 14 cities and the fields around them. The tribe of Benjamin got all these areas.

Land for Simeon

19 Then Joshua gave all the families in the tribe of Simeon their share of the land. The land they got was inside the area that belonged to Judah. 2This is the land that was given to that tribe: Beersheba (also called Sheba), Moladah, 3Hazar Shual, Balah, Ezem, 4Eltolad, Bethul, Hormah, 5Ziklag, Beth Marcaboth, Hazar Susah, 6Beth Lebaoth and Sharuhen. There were 13 towns and all the fields around them.

7They also got the towns of Ain, Rimmon, Ether and Ashan. There were four towns and all the fields around them. 8They also got all the fields around the cities as far as Baalath Beer (Ramah in the Negev). So this was the area that was given to the tribe of Simeon. Each family got its land. 9Simeon's share of land was within the area that Judah got. The people of Judah had more land than they needed, so the people of Simeon got part of their land.

Land for Zebulun

10The next tribe to get their land was Zebulun. Each family in Zebulun got the land that was promised to them. The border of Zebulun went as far as Sarid. 11Then the border went west to Maralah and just touched Dabbesheth. Then it went along the ravine near Jokneam. 12Then the border turned to the east. It went from Sarid to Kisloth Tabor. Then it went on to Daberath and to Japhia. 13Then the border continued to the east to Gath Hepher and Eth Kazin. It ended at Rimmon. Then it turned and went to Neah. 14At Neah the border turned again, went north to Hannathon and then continued to the Valley of Iphtah El. 15Inside this border were the cities of Kattath, Nahalal, Shimron, Idalah and Bethlehem. In all, there were twelve towns and all the fields around them.

16So these are the towns and fields around them that were given to Zebulun. Each family in Zebulun got its part of the land.

Land for Issachar

17The fourth part of the land was given to the tribe of Issachar. Each family in that tribe got its part of the land. 18This is the land that was given to that tribe: Jezreel, Kesulloth, Shunem, 19Hapharaim, Shion, Anaharath, 20Rabbith, Kishion, Ebez, 21Remeth, En Gannim, En Haddah and Beth Pazzez.

22The border of their land touched Tabor, Shahazumah and Beth Shemesh. It ended at the Jordan River. In all, there were 16 towns and the fields around them. 23These cities and towns were part of the land that was given to the tribe of Issachar. Each family got its part of the land.

Land for Asher

24The fifth part of land was given to the tribe of Asher. Each family in that tribe got its part of the land. 25This is the land that was given to that tribe: Helkath, Hali, Beten, Acshaph, 26Allammelech, Amad and Mishal.

The western border continued to Mount Carmel and Shihor Libnath. 27Then the border turned to the east. It went to Beth Dagon. The border touched Zebulun and the Valley of Iphtah El. Then it went north of Beth Emek and Neiel. It passed north of Cabul. 28Then the border went to Abdon,*a* Rehob, Hammon and Kanah. It continued to the Greater Sidon area. 29Then the border went back south to Ramah. It continued to the strong city of Tyre. Then the border turned and went to Hosah. It ended at the sea, near Aczib, 30Ummah, Aphek and Rehob.

In all there were 22 towns and the fields around them. 31These cities and the fields around them were given to the tribe of Asher. Each family in that tribe got its share of the land.

Land for Naphtali

32The sixth part of land was given to the tribe of Naphtali. Each family in that tribe got its share of the land. 33The border of their land started at the large tree near Zaanannim. This is near Heleph. Then the border went through Adami Nekeb and Jabneel. It continued to Lakkum and ended at the Jordan River. 34Then the border went to the west through Aznoth Tabor. It ended at Hukkok. The southern border touched Zebulun and the western border touched Asher. The border went to Judah, at the Jordan River to the east. 35There were some very strong cities inside these borders. They were Ziddim, Zer, Hammath, Rakkath, Kinnereth, 36Adamah, Ramah, Hazor, 37Kedesh, Edrei, En Hazor, 38Iron, Migdal El, Horem, Beth Anath and Beth Shemesh. In all, there were 19 towns and all the fields around them.

39These cities and the fields around them were given to the tribe of Naphtali. Each family in that tribe got its land.

---

a **19:28** *Abdon* Or "Ebron".

Land for Dan

⁴⁰Then land was given to the tribe of Dan. Each family in that tribe got its land. ⁴¹This is the land that was given to them: Zorah, Eshtaol, Ir Shemesh, ⁴²Shaalabbin, Aijalon, Ithlah, ⁴³Elon, Timnah, Ekron, ⁴⁴Eltekeh, Gibbethon, Baalath, ⁴⁵Jehud, Bene Berak, Gath Rimmon, ⁴⁶Me Jarkon, Rakkon and the area near Joppa.

⁴⁷But the people of Dan had trouble taking their land. There were strong enemies there and the people of Dan could not easily defeat them. So the people of Dan went to the northern part of Israel and fought against Laish.ᵃ They defeated Laish and killed the people who lived there. So the people of Dan lived in the town of Laish. They changed the name to Dan because that was the name of the father of their tribe. ⁴⁸All these cities and fields around them were given to the tribe of Dan. Each family got its share of the land.

Land for Joshua

⁴⁹So the leaders finished dividing the land and giving it to the different tribes. After they finished, all the Israelites decided to give Joshua son of Nun some land too. This was land that was promised to him. ⁵⁰The LORD had commanded that he get this land. So they gave Joshua the town of Timnath Serahᵇ in the hill country of Ephraim. This was the town that Joshua told them he wanted. So he built the town stronger and lived there.

⁵¹All these lands were given to the different tribes of Israel. Eleazar the priest, Joshua son of Nun and the leaders of each tribe met together at Shiloh to divide the land. They met before the LORD at the entrance of the Meeting Tent. So they finished dividing the land.

Cities of Safety

20 Then the LORD said to Joshua: ²"Through Moses, I told you to choose some cities to be cities of safety. ³Anyone who kills someone accidentally can go to a city of safety to hide from the relatives who want to kill him.

⁴"If you accidentally kill someone and you run away to one of those cities, you must stop at the entrance of the city and tell the leaders of the people what happened. Then the leaders can allow you to enter the city. They will give you a place to live among them. ⁵If someone chases you and follows you to that city, the leaders of the city must not give you up. They must protect you because you came to them for safety after killing someone by accident—you were not angry and did not plan to kill the person. It was something that just happened. ⁶You should stay in that city

until the court has judged you and until the high priest dies. Then you may go back to your home town."

⁷So the Israelites chose some cities to be called cities of safety. These are the cities: Kedesh in Galilee in the hill country of Naphtali; Shechem in the hill country of Ephraim; Kiriath Arba (Hebron) in the hill country of Judah; ⁸Bezer, east of the Jordan River opposite Jericho, in the desert area in the land of Reuben; Ramoth in Gilead in the land of Gad; and Golan in Bashan in the land of Manasseh.

⁹All Israelites or any foreigners living among them who killed someone by accident were allowed to run away to one of these cities of safety. They could be safe there and not be killed by anyone chasing them. The court in that city would judge them.

Towns for Priests and Levites

21 The family rulers of the Levite tribe went to talk to Eleazar the priest, to Joshua son of Nun and to the rulers of the other tribes of Israel. ²At Shiloh in the land of Canaan, the Levite rulers said to them, "The LORD gave Moses a command. He commanded that you give us towns to live in and that you give us fields where our animals can eat." ³So the Israelites obeyed this command from the LORD and gave the Levites these towns and the land around them for their animals:

⁴The Kohath family groups were descendants of Aaron the priest from the tribe of Levi. Part of the Kohath family was given 13 towns in the areas that belonged to Judah, Simeon and Benjamin.

⁵The other Kohath families were given ten towns in the areas that belonged to Ephraim, Dan and half of Manasseh.

⁶The people from the Gershon family were given 13 towns. These towns were in the areas that belonged to Issachar, Asher, Naphtali and the half of Manasseh that was in Bashan.

⁷The people from the Merari family were given twelve towns. These towns came from the areas that belonged to Reuben, Gad and Zebulun.

⁸So the Israelites gave the Levites these towns and the fields around them, just as the LORD had told Moses.

⁹These are the names of the towns that were in the areas that belonged to Judah and Simeon. ¹⁰The first choice of towns was given to the Levites from the Kohath family group. ¹¹They gave them Kiriath Arba. (This is Hebron. It was named for a man named Arba. Arba was the father of Anak.)

ᵃ **19:47 Laish** Or "Leshem".
ᵇ **19:50 Timnath Serah** Or "Timnath Heres".

They also gave them some land near the town for their animals. [12]But the fields and the small towns around the city of Kiriath Arba belonged to Caleb son of Jephunneh. [13]So they gave the city of Hebron to Aaron's descendants. (Hebron was a city of safety.) They also gave Aaron's descendants the towns of Libnah, [14]Jattir, Eshtemoa, [15]Holon, Debir, [16]Ain, Juttah and Beth Shemesh. They also gave them some of the land near these towns for their animals. These two tribes gave them nine towns.

[17]They also gave Aaron's descendants cities that belonged to the tribe of Benjamin. These cities were Gibeon, Geba, [18]Anathoth and Almon. They gave them these four towns and some of the land near the towns for their animals. [19]In all, they gave 13 towns to the priests. (All priests were descendants of Aaron.) They also gave them some land near each town for their animals.

[20]The other people from the Kohathite family groups were given towns that were in the areas that belonged to the tribe of Ephraim. They got these towns: [21]the city of Shechem from the hill country of Ephraim (which was a city of safety), Gezer, [22]Kibzaim and Beth Horon. In all, Ephraim gave them four towns and some land around each town for their animals.

[23]The tribe of Dan gave them Eltekeh, Gibbethon, [24]Aijalon and Gath Rimmon. In all, Dan gave them four towns and some land around each town for their animals.

[25]Half the tribe of Manasseh gave them Taanach and Gath Rimmon. In all, this half of Manasseh gave them two towns and some land around each town for their animals.

[26]In all, the rest of the people from the Kohath family groups got ten towns and some land around each town for their animals.

[27]The Gershon family groups were also from the tribe of Levi. They got these towns:

Half the tribe of Manasseh gave them Golan in Bashan. (Golan was a city of safety.) Manasseh also gave them Be Eshtarah. In all, this half of Manasseh gave them two towns and some land around each town for their animals.

[28]The tribe of Issachar gave them Kishion, Daberath, [29]Jarmuth and En Gannim. In all, Issachar gave them four towns and some land around each town for their animals.

[30]The tribe of Asher gave them Mishal, Abdon, [31]Helkath and Rehob. In all, Asher gave them four towns and some land around each town for their animals.

[32]The tribe of Naphtali gave them Kedesh in Galilee. (Kedesh was a city of safety.) Naphtali also gave them Hammoth Dor and Kartan. In all, Naphtali gave them three towns and some land around each town for their animals.

[33]In all, the Gershon family groups got 13 towns and some land around each town for their animals.

[34-39]The other Levite group was the Merari family group. They were given these towns: The tribe of Zebulun gave them Jokneam, Kartah, Dimnah and Nahalal. In all, Zebulun gave them four towns and some land around each town for their animals. The tribe of Reuben gave them Bezer, Jahaz, Kedemoth and Mephaath. In all, Reuben gave them four towns and some land around each town for their animals. The tribe of Gad gave them Ramoth in Gilead. (Ramoth was a city of safety.) They also gave them Mahanaim, Heshbon and Jazer. In all, Gad gave them four towns and some land around each town for their animals.

[40]In all, the last family of Levites, the Merari family, got twelve towns.

[41]So the Levites were given a total of 48 towns and some land around each town for their animals. All these towns were in areas that belonged to the other tribes. [42]Each of these towns had some land in it for their animals. That was true for every town.

[43]So the LORD kept the promise that he had made to the Israelites and gave the people all the land that he had promised. The people took the land and lived there. [44]And the LORD allowed them to have peace on all sides of their land, just as he had promised their ancestors. None of their enemies defeated them. The LORD allowed the Israelites to defeat every enemy. [45]The LORD kept every promise that he made to the Israelites. There were no promises that he failed to keep. Every promise came true.

Three Tribes Go Home

22 Then Joshua called a meeting of all the people from the tribes of Reuben, Gad and half the tribe of Manasseh. [2]Joshua said to them, "Moses was the LORD's servant. You obeyed everything that Moses told you to do. And you also obeyed all my commands. [3]All this time you have supported all the other Israelites. You carefully obeyed all the commands that the LORD your God gave you. [4]The LORD your God promised to give the Israelites peace. And now, he has kept his promise, so now you can go home. The LORD's servant Moses gave you the land on the east side of the Jordan River. Now you can go home to that land. [5]But remember—continue to obey the law that the LORD's servant Moses gave you. You must love the LORD your God and obey his commands. You must continue to follow him and serve him the very best that you can."

[6]Then Joshua said goodbye to them, and they left and went home. [7]Moses had given the land of

BLAZING GUNS

What do you do when you think a Christian friend is disobeying God? Does it even bother you? Or are you the opposite – judgemental and in there with all guns blazing? Some of the Israelites were faced with exactly this dilemma . . .

DIG IN

READ Joshua 22:1–6

The time had come for three of the tribes to head to their land – away from everyone else, on the other side of the River Jordan! Reuben and Gad had asked to live here (Numbers 32:1–5) and Moses had given land there to the tribe of Manasseh because of their role in battle (Numbers 32:39–42).

- What's the big command as the tribes go home?

READ Joshua 22:9–19

- What do the tribes of Reuben, Gad and Manasseh do?
- What are the other tribes worried about (vv.16–19)?

The big command is to love God and obey his laws. For example, only the priests can sacrifice and only in the Holy Tent. But what have these tribes done?! They've only gone and built an altar! Uh oh!

- Can you see the way in which the Israelites respond to what they think the three tribes have done?
  - » Look at verses 13 and 14. Who did they send? Why is this good?
  - » What do they show by being willing to fight (v.12)?
  - » What is their main concern (vv.18–19)?
- From this, what can we learn about resolving issues?

The people of Israel are so concerned about the purity and obedience of the tribes that they don't bury their heads in the sand, but are willing to risk even their lives to ensure they remain a nation committed to the Lord. However, they don't go in with all guns blazing and shooting their mouths off – they send their wisest men to speak with the tribes, urging them to follow God and not turn against him. And they were willing to share their land if it meant the others wouldn't sin any more.

READ Joshua 22:21–34

- What were the three tribes actually doing by building this altar?
- What is the response of all the people of Israel (vv.33–34)?

It's all good – the three tribes wanted all their children to be able to keep worshipping God, and they were worried that being on the other side of the river might cause the other tribes to forget they all belonged together. They weren't going to sacrifice on the altar at all – it was a reminder for all the generations to come that they belonged to the Lord, that they offer the same sacrifices as those from the other side of the river. What a brilliant act of worship!

DIG THROUGH

- How committed are you to obeying God? Do you think it's worth risking your life for?
- Phew! Can you imagine the disaster if the other tribes had started killing before talking? Fortunately, when they took action they were gentle. What can you learn from this the next time a Christian friend of yours seems not to care about God?
- The three tribes were doing something new in their worship of God. There was nothing wrong with what they did, and once the initial confusion had been cleared up, the other tribes thought it was great. How do you respond when someone worships God in a different way to you?

Bashan to half of the Manasseh tribe. Joshua gave land on the west side of the Jordan River to the other half of the Manasseh tribe. Joshua blessed them and sent them home. ⁸He said, "You have become very rich. You have many animals. You have gold, silver and expensive jewellery. You have many beautiful clothes. You have taken many things from your enemies. Go home and divide these things among yourselves."

⁹So the people from the tribes of Reuben, Gad and Manasseh left the Israelites at Shiloh in Canaan. They went back home to Gilead. This was their own land, the land that Moses gave them, as the LORD had commanded.

¹⁰They went to the place called Geliloth, near the Jordan River in the land of Canaan. There they built a beautiful altar. ¹¹The Israelites heard about this altar at Geliloth. They heard that it was on the border of Canaan near the Jordan River on Israel's side. ¹²When the Israelites heard this, they all gathered at Shiloh to go to war against these three tribes.

¹³The Israelites sent some men to talk to the people of Reuben, Gad and Manasseh. The leader of these men was Phinehas, son of Eleazar the priest. ¹⁴They also sent ten of the leaders of the tribes there. There was one man from each family group of Israel who was at Shiloh.

¹⁵So these eleven men went to Gilead. They went to talk to the people of Reuben, Gad and Manasseh. The eleven men said to them, ¹⁶"All the LORD's people sent us to ask why you did this thing against the God of Israel. Why did you stop following the LORD? Why did you build an altar for yourselves? You know that this is against the LORD's command. ¹⁷Remember what happened at Peor? Was the sin we committed there not bad enough? Because of that sin, the LORD punished his people with a terrible sickness. And we are still suffering from that sin. ¹⁸And now you are doing the same thing. You are turning against the LORD. Will you refuse to follow the LORD? If you don't stop what you are doing, he will be angry with everyone in Israel.

¹⁹"If your land is not a good place to worship God, come over to the LORD's land. This is where the LORD's Tent is. You can have some of the land and live here. But don't turn against the LORD or against us by building another altar. We already have the altar of the LORD our God at the Meeting Tent.

²⁰"Remember how Achan son of Zerah refused to obey the command about things that must be destroyed. Because that one man broke God's law, all the Israelites were punished. Achan died because of his sin, but also many other people died."

²¹The people from the tribes of Reuben, Gad and Manasseh answered the eleven men. They said, ²²"The LORD is our God!ᵃ Again we say that the LORD is our God! And God knows why we did this. We want you to know too. You can judge what we did. If you think we did it because we are against the LORD or refuse to obey him, you can kill us today. ²³Do you think we built our own altar because we want to turn away from the LORD? Do you think we built another altar for burnt offerings, grain offerings and fellowship offerings? If that is why we built this altar, we ask the LORD himself to punish us. ²⁴But that is not why we built it. We built it because we were afraid that in the future your descendants might not accept us as part of God's people. So your children might say to our children, 'You people have no reason to worship the LORD, the God of Israel. ²⁵The LORD separated you people of Reuben and Gad from us by giving you the land on the other side of the Jordan River. So you are not part of the LORD's people.' If your children said that, it might make our children stop worshipping the LORD.

²⁶"So we decided to build this altar. But we did not plan to use it for burning offerings and sacrifices. ²⁷We built it to be a reminder for us and for you and for our descendants. We want it to remind them that we, too, have the right to worship the LORD at his holy place. We can take our sacrifices, grain offerings and fellowship offerings there and offer them to the LORD. Then your descendants will not be able to say to ours, 'You are not part of the LORD's people.' ²⁸In the future, if it happens that your children say that we don't belong to Israel, then our children can say, 'Look, our fathers who lived before us made an altar. That altar is exactly like the LORD's altar at the Holy Tent. We don't use this altar for sacrifices—this altar is proof that we are part of Israel.'

²⁹"The truth is, we don't want to be against the LORD. We don't want to stop following him now. We know that the only true altar is the one that is in front of the Holy Tent. That altar belongs to the LORD our God."

³⁰Phinehas the priest and the leaders with him heard what the people from Reuben, Gad and Manasseh said. They were satisfied that they were telling the truth. ³¹So Phinehas the priest said, "Now we know that the LORD is with us and that you did not turn against him. We are happy that the Israelites will not be punished by the LORD."

³²Then Phinehas and the leaders left that place and went home. They left the people of Reuben

---

ᵃ 22:22 The LORD is our God Or "YAHWEH is the true God!" Hebrew, "El Elohim YAHWEH!"

and Gad in the land of Gilead and went back to Canaan. They went back to the Israelites and told them what had happened. 33The Israelites were also satisfied. They were happy and thanked God. They decided not to go and fight against the people of Reuben, Gad and Manasseh. They decided not to destroy the land where those people live.

34The people of Reuben and Gad gave the altar this name: "A Reminder to Us All That the LORD Is Our God."

Joshua Encourages the People

23 The LORD gave Israel peace from their enemies around them. He made Israel safe. Many years passed and Joshua became very old. 2At this time Joshua called a meeting of all the leaders, heads of families, judges and officers of the Israelites. Joshua said, "I have grown very old. 3You have seen what the LORD did to our enemies. He did this to help us. The LORD your God fought for you. 4Remember that I told you that your people could have the land between the Jordan River and the Great Sea in the west. I promised to give you that land, but you don't control it yet. I have taken the land away from those nations, but they are still living there. 5But the LORD your God will force the people living there to leave. You will take that land. The LORD will force them to leave, just as he promised.

6"You must be careful to obey every command written in the *Book of the Law*[a] *of Moses*. Never turn away from that law. 7There are still some people living among us who are not Israelites. They worship their own gods. Don't become friends with them. Don't serve or worship their gods. 8You must continue to follow the LORD your God. You have done this in the past and you must continue to do it.

9"The LORD helped you defeat many great and powerful nations. He forced them to leave. No nation has been able to defeat you. 10With his help, one man from Israel could defeat 1,000 enemy soldiers, because the LORD your God fights for you, as he promised. 11So you must continue to love the LORD your God.

12"Never stop following him. Don't become friends with those people who did not leave when you took the land. They are not part of Israel. Don't marry any of their people. If you become friends with those people, 13the LORD your God will not help you defeat your enemies. They will become like a trap for you. They will cause you pain—like smoke and dust in your eyes. And you will be forced to leave this good land. The LORD your God gave you this land. But you can lose it if you don't obey this command.

14"It is almost time for me to die. You know and really believe that the Lord has done many great things for you. You know that the LORD your God has not failed in any of his promises. He has kept every promise that he has made to us. 15Every good promise that the LORD your God made to us has come true. But in the same way, the LORD will make his other promises come true: If you do wrong, bad things will happen to you. You will be forced to leave this good land that the LORD your God has given to you. 16This will happen if you refuse to keep your agreement with the LORD your God. You will lose this land if you go and serve other gods. You must not worship those other gods. If you do, the LORD will become very angry with you. Then you will quickly be forced to leave this good land that he gave you."

Joshua Says Goodbye

24 Joshua called all the tribes of Israel to meet together at Shechem. Then Joshua called the leaders, heads of the families, judges and the officers of Israel. These men stood before God.

2Then Joshua spoke to all the people. He said, "I am telling you what the LORD, the God of Israel, says to you: 'A long time ago, your ancestors lived on the other side of the Euphrates River. I am talking about men like Terah, the father of Abraham and Nahor. At that time they worshipped other gods. 3But I took your father Abraham out of the land on the other side of the River. I led him through the land of Canaan and gave him many children. I gave Abraham his son Isaac. 4And I gave Isaac two sons, Jacob and Esau. To Esau, I gave the land around the mountains of Seir. Jacob and his sons did not live there. They went to live in the land of Egypt.

5"'Then I sent Moses and Aaron to Egypt. I wanted them to bring my people out of Egypt. I caused many terrible things to happen to the people of Egypt. Then I brought your people out of Egypt. 6When I brought your ancestors out of Egypt, they came to the Red Sea and the men of Egypt were chasing them. There were chariots and men on horses. 7So the people asked me, the LORD, for help. And I caused great trouble to come to the men of Egypt. I caused the sea to cover them. You yourselves saw what I did to the army of Egypt.

"'After that, you lived in the desert for a long time. 8Then I brought you to the land of the Amorites, east of the Jordan River. Those people fought against you, but I allowed you to defeat

---

[a] **23:6** *Law* Or "Teachings".

them. I gave you the power to destroy them, and you took control of that land.

⁹"Then Balak, the son of Zippor, the king of Moab, prepared to fight against the Israelites. The king sent for Balaam the son of Beor to curse you, ¹⁰but I refused to listen to Balaam's prayer. So he asked me to bless you, and I saved you from the enemy.

¹¹"Then you went across the Jordan River to the city of Jericho. The people in Jericho fought against you. Also, the Amorites, Perizzites, Canaanites, Hittites, Girgashites, Hivites and Jebusites fought against you. But I allowed you to defeat them all. ¹²As your army went forward, I sent fearᵃ ahead of you and drove out the two kings of the Amorites. It was not your swords and bows that brought you victory.

¹³"I, the Lord, gave you that land. You did not work for it—I gave it to you! And I gave you cities you did not build. Now you live in those cities, and you enjoy food from vineyards and olive trees that you did not plant.'"

¹⁴Then Joshua said to the people, "So now you must respect the LORD and sincerely serve him. Throw away the false gods that your ancestors worshipped. That was something that happened a long time ago on the other side of the Euphrates River and in Egypt. Now you must serve only the LORD.

¹⁵"But maybe you don't want to serve the LORD. You must choose for yourselves today. Today you must decide who you will serve. Will you serve the gods that your ancestors worshipped when they lived on the other side of the Euphrates River? Or will you serve the gods of the Amorites who lived in this land? You must choose for yourselves. But as for me and my family, we will serve the LORD."

¹⁶Then the people answered, "We will never stop following the LORD. We will never serve other gods! ¹⁷We know that it was the LORD God who brought our people out of Egypt. We were slaves in that land, but he did great things for us there. He brought us out of that land and protected us while we travelled through other lands. ¹⁸The LORD helped us defeat the people living in these lands. He helped us defeat the Amorites who lived in this land where we are now. So we will continue to serve the LORD, because he is our God."

¹⁹Then Joshua said, "You will not be able to continue serving the LORD. God is holy. And God hates his people worshipping other gods. He will not forgive you if you turn against him like that. ²⁰If you leave the LORD and serve other gods, he will cause terrible things to happen to you. He

will destroy you. He has been good to you, but if you turn against him he will destroy you."

²¹Then the people said to Joshua, "No, we will serve the LORD!"

²²Then Joshua said, "Look around at yourselves and the people with you. Do you all know and agree that you have chosen to serve the LORD? Are you all witnesses to this?"

The people answered, "Yes, it is true. We all see that we have chosen to serve the LORD."

²³Then Joshua said, "So throw away the false gods that you have among you. Love the LORD, the God of Israel, with all your heart."

²⁴Then the people said to Joshua, "We will serve the LORD our God. We will obey him."

²⁵So that day Joshua made an agreement for the people. He made this agreement at the town called Shechem. It became a law for them to follow. ²⁶Joshua wrote these things in the *Book of the Law of God.* Then he found a large stone for the proof of this agreement. He put the stone under the oak tree near the LORD's Holy Tent.

²⁷Then Joshua said to all the people, "This stone will help you remember what we said today. This stone was here when the LORD was speaking to us today. So this stone will be something that helps you remember what happened today. The stone will be a witness against you. It will stop you from turning against your God."

²⁸Then Joshua told the people to go home. So everyone went back to his own land.

INSIGHT

When people died in Bible times, they weren't buried in a hole in the ground or cremated as they are nowadays. They were placed in a family cave or tomb cut from rock, which was large enough for several family members. The entrance was sealed with a large boulder.

Joshua 24:29–33

Joshua Dies

²⁹After that, the LORD's servant Joshua son of Nun died. He was 110 years old. ³⁰Joshua was buried on his own land at Timnath Serah, in the hill country of Ephraim, north of Mount Gaash.

³¹The Israelites served the LORD during the time Joshua was living. After Joshua died, the people continued to serve the Lord while their

---

ᵃ **24:12** *fear* Or "The Hornet", a stinging insect like a large wasp or bee. The meaning of the Hebrew word is uncertain.

leaders were alive. These were the leaders who had seen what the LORD had done for Israel.

Joseph Comes Home

32When the Israelites left Egypt, they carried the bones from the body of Joseph with them. They buried the bones of Joseph at Shechem on the land that Jacob had bought from the sons of Hamor, the father of the man named Shechem. Jacob had bought that land for 100 pieces of pure silver. This land belonged to Joseph's children.

33Aaron's son, Eleazar, died and was buried at Gibeah in the hill country of Ephraim. Gibeah had been given to Eleazar's son Phinehas.

Who
Tradition says that the book is by Samuel, but there's no evidence of this. It is possible that he assembled some of it, but Judges is more likely the work of several hands.

 When
The book probably dates from the time of the monarchy (hence the constant refrain about Israel having no king), in which case it would be the tenth century BC. The events described in Judges take place following the death of Joshua.

 What
Its title comes from the phrase "Then the LORD chose leaders called judges" (2:16). These judges were not only leaders in battle; they decided legal cases and even performed religious rituals; they were a mix of law-makers and tribal chieftains.

Judges takes us from the time of Joshua to the establishment of the monarchy. It starts with a captured king having his thumbs and big toes cut off (1:6–7) and goes downhill from there. This is one of the grimmest places to visit in the entire Bible, a picture of what happens to a society when it abandons God, when everyone lives by their own laws, when "In those days the Israelites did not have a king, so everyone did whatever they thought was right" (21:25).

Judges is the story of a nation who managed to forget the God who had led them to safety and turned, time and time again, to other gods. It's like a dreadful recurring dream: the people turn away from God; God sends a foreign nation to punish them; the people cry out to God for deliverance; God sends them a "judge" to deliver them. Then the people turn away again . . .

Thankfully, it's not all despair and anarchy. There are heroes like Samson and Deborah, Ehud the left-handed assassin and Gideon. Judges is not only about the faithlessness of the people, it's also about the faithfulness of God.

QUICK TOUR ▶ JUDGES

Israel doesn't finish the task 1:27–35	Gideon is chosen 6:11–40
Israel is punished 2:6–19	The army is chosen 7:1–25
Ehud and Eglon 3:12–30	Samson's birth 13:1–25
Deborah and Barak 4:1–24	Samson's strength 15:1–20
Deborah's song 5:1–31	Samson and Delilah 16:4–31

"In those days the Israelites did not have a king, so everyone did whatever they thought was right."

Judges 21:25

Judah Fights the Canaanites

1 After Joshua died, the Israelites prayed to the LORD, "Which of our tribes should be the first to go and fight for us against the Canaanites?"

[2]The LORD said to the Israelites, "The tribe of Judah will go. I will let them take this land."

[3]The men of Judah went to their relatives from the tribe of Simeon and asked for help. They said, "Brothers, if you will come and help us fight for the land God gave us, we will go and help you fight for your land." The men of Simeon agreed and went with them.

[4]The LORD helped the men of Judah defeat the Canaanites and the Perizzites. They killed 10,000 men at the city of Bezek. [5]In the city of Bezek, they found the ruler of Bezek[a] and fought him, and they defeated the Canaanites and the Perizzites.

[6]The ruler of Bezek tried to escape, but the men of Judah chased him and caught him. When they caught him, they cut off his thumbs and big toes. [7]Then the ruler of Bezek said, "I cut off the thumbs and big toes of 70 kings. And they had to eat pieces of food that fell from my table. Now God has paid me back for what I did to them." The men of Judah took the ruler of Bezek to Jerusalem, and he died there.

[8]The men of Judah fought against Jerusalem and captured it. They used their swords to kill the people of Jerusalem. Then they burned the city. [9]Later, they went down to fight against some more Canaanites who lived in the hill country, in the Negev and in the western foothills.

[10]Then the men of Judah went to fight against the Canaanites who lived in the city of Hebron. (Hebron used to be called Kiriath Arba.) They defeated the men named Sheshai, Ahiman and Talmai.[b]

Caleb and His Daughter

[11]The men of Judah left that place. They went to the city of Debir to fight against the people there. (In the past, Debir was called Kiriath Sepher.) [12]Before they started to fight, Caleb made a promise to the men. He said, "I will give my daughter Acsah in marriage to the man who attacks and conquers Kiriath Sepher."

[13]Othniel, the son of Caleb's brother Kenaz, defeated the city. So Caleb gave his daughter Acsah to Othniel as his wife.

[14]After Acsah and Othniel were married, she told him they should ask her father for some land.

So Acsah went to her father. As she was getting off her donkey, Caleb asked her, "What are you doing here?"

[15]Acsah answered, "I came to ask you for a favour. You gave me dry desert land in the Negev. Please give me some land with water on it." So Caleb gave her what she wanted. He gave her the upper and lower pools of water in that land.

[16]The Kenites left the City of Palm Trees[c] and went with the men of Judah. They went to the desert of Judah to live with the people there. This was in the Negev near the city Arad. (The Kenites were from the family of Moses' father-in-law.)

[17]Some Canaanites lived in the city of Zephath. The men of Judah and men from the tribe of Simeon attacked them and completely destroyed the city. So they named the city Hormah.[d]

[18]The men of Judah also captured the cities of Gaza, Ashkelon and Ekron and all the small towns around them.

[19]The LORD was on the side of the men of Judah when they fought. They took the land in the hill country, but they failed to take the land in the valleys, because the people living there had iron chariots.

[20]Moses had promised to give the land near Hebron to Caleb, so that land was given to Caleb's family. The men of Caleb forced the three sons of Anak[e] to leave that place.

[21]The tribe of Benjamin could not force the Jebusites to leave Jerusalem. So even today,[f] the Jebusites live with the people of Benjamin in Jerusalem.

Joseph's Descendants Capture Bethel

[22]The descendants of Joseph went to fight against the city of Bethel, and the LORD was with them. [23]They sent some spies to the city of Bethel (which was then called Luz). [24]While the spies were watching, they saw a man come out of the city. They said to the man, "Show us a secret way into the city. If you help us, we will not hurt you."

[25]The man showed the spies the secret into the city. The men of Joseph used their swords to kill the people of Bethel. But they did not hurt the man who helped them or anyone in his family. The man and his family were allowed to go free. [26]He went to the land where the Hittites lived and built a city. He named it Luz, and that city is still called Luz today.

---

[a] **1:5 ruler of Bezek** Or "Adoni Bezek".

[b] **1:10 Sheshai, Ahiman and Talmai** Three sons of a man named Anak. They were giants. See Num. 13:22.

[c] **1:16 City of Palm Trees** Another name for Jericho.

[d] **1:17 Hormah** This name means "completely destroyed" or "a gift given totally to God". See Lev. 27:28–29.

[e] **1:20 three sons of Anak** Sheshai, Ahiman and Talmai, mentioned above in verse 10.

[f] **1:21 even today** That is, at the time the book was written.

Other Tribes Fight the Canaanites

27There were Canaanites living in the cities of Beth Shean, Taanach, Dor, Ibleam, Megiddo and the small towns around the cities. The people from the tribe of Manasseh could not force those people to leave their towns. So the Canaanites stayed. They refused to leave their homes. 28Later, the Israelites grew stronger and forced the Canaanites to work as slaves for them. But the Israelites could not force all the Canaanites to leave their land.

29There were Canaanites living in Gezer. And the Ephraimites did not make all the Canaanites leave their land. So they continued to live in Gezer with the Ephraimites.

30Some Canaanites lived in the cities of Kitron and Nahalol. The people of Zebulun did not force those people to leave their land. They stayed and lived with the people of Zebulun. But the people of Zebulun made them work as slaves.

31The people of Asher did not force the other people to leave the cities of Acco, Sidon, Ahlab, Aczib, Helbah, Aphek and Rehob. 32The people of Asher did not force those Canaanites to leave their land, so the Canaanites continued to live with them.

33The people of Naphtali did not force the people to leave the cities of Beth Shemesh and Beth Anath, so the people of Naphtali continued to live with the people in those cities. Those Canaanites worked as slaves for the people of Naphtali.

34The Amorites forced the tribe of Dan to live in the hill country. They had to stay in the hills because the Amorites would not let them come down to live in the valleys. 35The Amorites decided to stay in Mount Heres, Aijalon and Shaalbim. Later, when the descendants of Joseph grew stronger, they made the Amorites work as slaves for them. 36The land of the Amorites was from Scorpion Pass to Sela and up into the hill country past Sela.

The Angel of the LORD at Bokim

2 The angel of the LORD went up to the city of Bokim from the city of Gilgal. The angel spoke this message from the Lord to the Israelites: "I brought you out of Egypt and led you to the land that I promised to give to your ancestors. I told you I would never break my agreement with you. 2But in return, you must never make any agreement with the people living in that land. You must destroy their altars. I told you that, but you didn't obey me.

3"Now I will tell you this, 'I will not force the other people to leave this land any longer. These people will become a problem for you. They will be like a trap to you. Their false gods will become like a net to trap you.'"

4After the angel gave the Israelites this message from the LORD, the people cried loudly. 5So they named the place Bokim.*a* There they offered sacrifices to the LORD.

Disobedience and Defeat

6Then Joshua told the people to go home, so each tribe went to take their area of land. 7The Israelites served the LORD as long as Joshua was alive, and they continued serving the Lord during the lifetimes of the leaders who lived after Joshua had died. These old men had seen all the great things the LORD had done for the Israelites. 8Joshua son of Nun, the servant of the LORD, died at the age of 110 years. 9The Israelites buried Joshua on the land that he had been given. That was at Timnath Heres, in the hill country of Ephraim, north of Mount Gaash.

10After that whole generation died, the next generation grew up. This new generation did not know about the LORD or what he had done for the Israelites. 11So the Israelites did something the LORD considered evil: They began serving the false god Baal. 12It was the LORD, the God their ancestors worshipped, who had brought the Israelites out of Egypt. But they stopped following him and began to worship the false gods of the people living around them. This made the LORD angry. 13The Israelites stopped following the LORD and began worshipping Baal and Ashtoreth.

14The LORD was angry with the Israelites, so he let enemies attack them and take their possessions. He let their enemies who lived around them defeat them. The Israelites could not protect themselves from their enemies. 15When the Israelites went out to fight, they always lost. They lost because the LORD was not on their side. He had already warned them that they would lose if they served the gods of the people living around them. The Israelites suffered very much.

16Then the LORD chose leaders called judges. These leaders saved the Israelites from the enemies who took their possessions. 17But the Israelites did not listen to these judges and were unfaithful to God. Instead of worshipping him, they worshipped other gods. For a short time they had followed the example of their ancestors, obeying the LORD's commands. But then they turned away from him.

18Many times the enemies of Israel did bad things to them, so the Israelites would cry for help. And each time, the LORD felt sorry for the people and sent a judge to save them from their enemies. The LORD was always with those judges.

---

a **2:5 Bokim** This name means "people crying".

ARE YOU JUDGING ME?!

How often do you hear your parents say, "I've told you once and I'm not going to tell you again!"? It's quite easy to forget the things we've been told – especially when we didn't want to hear something in the first place!

It's been a number of years since the Israelites entered the promised land excited and buoyed up by dreams of a future in a beautiful place, somewhere they could build a just and peaceful society, serving God. Given all that God had done for and through them, you'd think they'd remember him . . . Not so . . .

DIG IN

READ Judges 2:10–13

- How long had it taken for the people to forget God?
- What did they do instead?
- What was the consequence?

It makes me wonder . . . Hadn't the parents even told their kids about all the awesome things God had done? Maybe they'd just got too comfortable; maybe it all got a bit boring. Either way the stories hadn't been passed on, with the result that idols had become more interesting and stolen the people's hearts.

God doesn't let the people's disobedience go unpunished – he lets their enemies have a pop at them without his protection. It was a pretty bad time for the Israelites, but it was all their own doing.

READ Judges 2:16–19

- How does God show his undeserved love for the people?
- What is the role of the "judges"?
- How do the people respond to the judges?

How typical! God's unfailing devotion to the people causes him to come to their rescue when they cry out to him. Their punishment over, he sends judges who are to lead the people both spiritually (v.17) and in war (v.16). But do they listen? It's pretty typical of the Israelites – no sooner has God helped them than they forget him again. It's pretty typical of me too . . .

READ Judges 3:7–11

What do we know about Othniel? Not much, but what we are told is important. He is Caleb's younger brother and has already done things for God (Joshua 15:17). On top of this, God puts his Spirit upon him and he faithfully leads the people for forty years. Not much to know – but we know the Lord was with him and Othniel obeyed him fearlessly. As the first judge, he set the benchmark for the other judges to follow and it's not a bad description of good leadership for today.

DIG THROUGH

- It was a disastrous time for the Israelites because they chose to ignore God, but every time they cried out, God sent a judge to help them – that's how faithful he is! Do you feel you've started ignoring God? Cry out to him – he never stops loving you.
- Othniel was a great leader of the people, but only because the Lord was with him and he obeyed. Why not pray for your leaders to be like Othniel? Not all the judges were like him – and as good a leader as Othniel was he wouldn't have been perfect. But, as you'll see, God uses anyone who will serve him. Does that include you?

DIG DEEPER

- The Judges are a motley crew. As you read Judges ask yourself, "When will there be a perfect leader to save the people? Where is God?" Judges is like walking round and round down a spiral staircase – the history of the people is depressing and repetitive and takes you lower and lower. But it's definitely worth reading and seeing what happens when people stop following God and doing what he says is right. However, the whole problem in Judges is that the people are doing what *they* think is right (Judges 21:25)!

As long as the judges lived, the Israelites were saved from their enemies. ¹⁹But when each judge died, the Israelites again sinned and started worshipping the false gods. They became worse than their ancestors. The Israelites were very stubborn and refused to change their evil ways.

²⁰So the LORD became angry with the Israelites, and he said, "This nation has broken the agreement that I made with their ancestors. They have not listened to me. ²¹So I will no longer defeat the nations and clear the way for the Israelites. Those nations were still in this land when Joshua died, and I will let them stay in this land. ²²I will use them to test the Israelites. I will see if the Israelites can keep the LORD's commands as their ancestors did." ²³The LORD allowed those nations to stay in the land. He did not quickly force them to leave the country. He did not help Joshua's army defeat them.

3 The LORD did not force all the other nations to leave Israel's land. He wanted to test the Israelites. None of the Israelites living at this time had fought in the wars to take the land of Canaan. So he let those other nations stay in their country. ²(He did this to teach the Israelites who had not fought in those wars.) These are the nations the Lord left in the land: ³the five rulers of the Philistines, all the Canaanites, the people of Sidon and the Hivites who lived in the Lebanon mountains from Mount Baal Hermon to Lebo Hamath. ⁴He left those nations in the land to test the Israelites. He wanted to see if the Israelites would obey the LORD's commands that he had given to their ancestors through Moses.

⁵The Israelites lived with the Canaanites, Hittites, the Amorites, Perizzites, Hivites and Jebusites. ⁶The Israelites began to marry the daughters of those people. They allowed their own daughters to marry the sons of those people. The Israelites also began to worship their gods.

Othniel, the First Judge

⁷The Israelites did something the LORD considered evil: They forgot about the LORD their God and served the false gods Baal and Asherah. ⁸The LORD was angry with the Israelites, so he allowed King Cushan Rishathaim of Aram Naharaim[a] to defeat the Israelites and to rule over them. The Israelites were under that king's rule for eight years. ⁹But the Israelites cried to the LORD for help, and the LORD sent a man named Othniel to save them. He was the son of Kenaz,

who was Caleb's younger brother. Othniel saved the Israelites. ¹⁰The Spirit of the LORD filled Othniel, and he became a judge for the Israelites. He led the Israelites to war. The LORD helped Othniel defeat King Cushan Rishathaim of Aram. ¹¹So the land was at peace for 40 years, until Othniel son of Kenaz died.

Ehud, the Judge

¹²Again the Israelites did things the LORD considered evil, and the LORD saw them doing these things. So the LORD gave King Eglon of Moab power to defeat the Israelites. ¹³Eglon got help from the Ammonites and the Amalekites. They joined him and attacked the Israelites. Eglon and his army defeated the Israelites and forced them to leave the City of Palm Trees.[b] ¹⁴King Eglon of Moab ruled over the Israelites for 18 years.

¹⁵The Israelites cried to the LORD for help, so he sent a man named Ehud son of Gera to save them. Ehud was from the tribe of Benjamin and was trained to fight with his left hand. The Israelites sent Ehud with a gift to King Eglon of Moab. ¹⁶Ehud made himself a sword with two sharp edges that was about 30 centimetres[c] long. He tied the sword to his right thigh and hid it under his uniform.

¹⁷So Ehud brought the gift to King Eglon of Moab. Eglon was a very fat man. ¹⁸After offering the gift, Ehud left the palace with the men who had carried the gift. ¹⁹When Ehud reached the statues[d] near Gilgal, he turned and went back to King Eglon and said, "King, I have a secret message for you."

The king told him to be quiet and then sent all the servants out of the room. ²⁰Ehud went to King Eglon. The king was sitting all alone in the upper room of his palace.

Then Ehud said, "I have a message from God for you." The king stood up from his throne. He was very close to Ehud. ²¹As the king was getting up from his throne,[e] Ehud reached with his left hand and took out the sword that was tied to his right thigh. Then he pushed the sword into the king's belly. ²²The sword went into Eglon's belly so far that even the handle sank in and the fat closed around it. The point of the blade came out of his back. Ehud left the sword inside Eglon.

²³Then Ehud went out of the private room, closed the doors to the upper room, and locked the king inside. ²⁴Ehud then left the main room, and the servants went back in. The servants found the doors to the upper room locked, so they said,

---

[a] **3:8 Aram Naharaim** The area in northern Syria between the Tigris and Euphrates rivers.
[b] **3:13 City of Palm Trees** Another name for Jericho.
[c] **3:16 30 centimetres** Literally, "1 gomed". The exact length of a gomed is uncertain.
[d] **3:19 statues** These were probably statues of gods or animals that "protected" the entrance to the city. Also in verse 26.
[e] **3:20–21 He was very close . . . throne** This section of the text is found in the ancient Greek version but not in the standard Hebrew text.

"The king must be relieving himself in his private toilet." 25The servants waited for a long time, but the king never opened the doors to the upper room. Finally the servants got worried. They got the key and unlocked the doors. When they went inside, they saw their king lying dead on the floor.

26While the servants were waiting for the king, Ehud had time to escape. He passed by the statues and went towards the place named Seirah. 27When Ehud came to Seirah, he blew a trumpet there in the hill country of Ephraim. The Israelites heard the trumpet and went down from the hills with Ehud leading them. 28He said to the Israelites, "Follow me! The LORD has helped us defeat our enemies, the Moabites."

So the Israelites followed Ehud. They went down with him to take control of the places where people could easily cross the Jordan River into the land of Moab. The Israelites did not allow anyone to go across the Jordan River. 29They killed about 10,000 strong and brave men from Moab. Not one Moabite man escaped. 30So on that day the Israelites began to rule over the Moabites, and there was peace in the land for 80 years.

Shamgar, the Judge

31After Ehud saved the Israelites, another man saved Israel. That man's name was Shamgar son of Anath.*a* Shamgar used an ox goad to kill 600 Philistine men.

Deborah, the Judge

4 After Ehud died, the people again did what the LORD considered evil. 2So the LORD allowed King Jabin of Canaan to defeat the Israelites. Jabin ruled in a city named Hazor. A man named Sisera was the commander of King Jabin's army. Sisera lived in a town called Harosheth Haggoyim. 3Sisera had 900 iron chariots, and he was very cruel to the Israelites for 20 years. So they cried to the LORD for help.

4There was a woman prophet named Deborah. She was the wife of a man named Lappidoth. She was judge of Israel at that time. 5One day Deborah was sitting under the Palm Tree of Deborah, and the Israelites came up to her to ask what to do about Sisera. (The Palm Tree of Deborah is between the cities of Ramah and Bethel in the hill country of Ephraim.) 6Deborah sent a message to a man named Barak and asked him to come and meet with her. Barak was the son of a man named Abinoam. Barak lived in the city of Kedesh, which is in the area of Naphtali. Deborah said to Barak,

"The LORD, the God of Israel, commands you: 'Go and gather 10,000 men from the tribes of Naphtali and Zebulun. Lead them to Mount Tabor. 7I will make Sisera, the commander of King Jabin's army, come to you. I will make Sisera, his chariots and his army come to the Kishon River.*b* I will help you defeat Sisera there.'"

8Then Barak said to Deborah, "I will go and do this if you will go with me. But if you will not go with me, I will not go."

9"Of course I will go with you," Deborah answered. "But because of your attitude, you will not be honoured when Sisera is defeated. The LORD will allow a woman to defeat Sisera."

So Deborah went with Barak to the city of Kedesh. 10At the city of Kedesh, Barak called together the tribes of Zebulun and Naphtali. He gathered 10,000 men to follow him from these tribes, and Deborah also went with him.

11There was a man named Heber who was from the Kenites. The Kenites were descendants of Moses' father-in-law,*c* Hobab. Heber had left the other Kenites and had made his home by the oak tree in Zaanannim, near the city of Kedesh.

12Someone told Sisera that Barak son of Abinoam was at Mount Tabor. 13So Sisera gathered his 900 iron chariots and all the men with him, and they marched from the city of Harosheth Haggoyim to the Kishon River.

14Then Deborah said to Barak, "Today the LORD will help you defeat Sisera. Surely you know that the LORD has already cleared the way for you." So Barak led the 10,000 men down from Mount Tabor. 15Barak and his men attacked Sisera. During the battle, the LORD confused Sisera and his army and chariots. They did not know what to do. Barak and his men defeated Sisera's army, but Sisera left his chariot and ran away on foot. 16Barak continued fighting Sisera's army. He and his men chased Sisera's chariots and army all the way to Harosheth Haggoyim. They used their swords to kill all of Sisera's men. Not one of Sisera's men was left alive.

17But Sisera ran away to the tent where a woman named Jael lived. Jael was the wife of Heber the Kenite. His family was at peace with King Jabin of Hazor. That is why Sisera ran to Jael's tent. 18Jael saw him coming, so she went out to meet him and said, "Sir, come into my tent. Come in. Don't be afraid." So Sisera went into Jael's tent, and she covered him with a blanket.

19But first, Sisera asked Jael for a drink of water. Jael had some milk in a bottle made from animal

---

a **3:31** *Anath* The Canaanite goddess of war. Here, this might be Shamgar's father or mother, or it might mean "Shamgar the great soldier" or "Shamgar from the town of Anath".
b **4:7** *Kishon River* A river about ten miles from Mount Tabor.
c **4:11** *father-in-law* Or possibly, "son-in-law".

WHO'S THE HERO?

Over the next eighty years, the people of Israel continued in this pattern of messing up, getting rescued by God and then messing up again.

DIG IN
READ Judges 4:1–3

This time it's Jabin, king of Canaan, who gets used by God to oppress the people. It requires imagination to think what cruel things Jabin was up to, but someone who is mighty enough to have 900 chariots could probably do a lot of damage. As before, the people cry out to God.

READ Judges 4:1–10
- Who is Deborah?
- What does verse 6 show us about what God is up to?

We're told that Deborah is the judge at the time and no doubt has been praying, crying out to God for the deliverance of the people. Somehow God speaks to her (though we're not told how) and tells her his plan for the rescue of Israel.

- What is the plan?
- How do you think Barak is feeling (especially considering v.3)?
- How do the people of Israel respond (v.10 and also 5:2,9)?

Coming up against 900 chariots is not going to be the cushiest job in the kingdom and it's hardly surprising he asks Deborah to go with him. Yet, having had a direct word from God, surely he should have shown a bit more faith? However, as Barak sends the message out, 10,000 men hear the call and join him for the fight of their lives.

READ Judges 4:11–24
- Who's the real hero of the story?
- What do these verses tell us about Jael?

Jael is pretty special as far as women of God go, right? Her husband had made peace with Sisera (v.17) which was never going to be a good idea. But as Jael drove that tent peg into Sisera's head it was as if she was declaring whose side she was on . . . and it wasn't the same side as her husband! Jael might be awesome (Deborah even sings about her, see Judges 5:24) but don't be fooled into thinking she's the hero of this story. Our lead characters have only won the fight and secured rest for the nation (5:31) for one reason – God has been behind it all (4:14–15,23). As Deborah sings in the next chapter her words are full of praise to God, the real hero.

DIG THROUGH

- God used Deborah as an administrator, Barak as the commander, the people as an army and Jael as the assassin. It's great how God uses people to accomplish his plans, but he is the real hero of the story and once again he's rescued the people from their enemies. Thank God for being the kind of God who rescues his people even when they're in trouble through their own mistakes.
- Barak was probably a bit weedy for wanting Deborah to go with him (and he lost out on delivering the final blow on Sisera because of it, 4:9), but God's word was strong enough to rally the troops and confuse the biggest army. I wonder how Barak felt after seeing that? What, in your life, does God want you to do that seems difficult? Will you trust that he is powerful enough to take care of you?

Jael was an ordinary woman who did something extraordinarily brave for God's people. Sometimes we need to stand up against what is wrong, just like she did. (I wonder how her husband felt about that?) The choices we make for God and the things we say may not always be popular, but God is with us when we make the right choices for him.

skin. So she gave him a drink of the milk and then covered him up.

²⁰Then Sisera said to Jael, "Go and stand at the entrance to the tent. If anyone comes by and asks you, 'Is anyone in there?' say, 'No.'"

²¹But Jael found a tent peg and a hammer. She quietly went to Sisera. Sisera was very tired, so he was sleeping. She put the tent peg to the side of Sisera's head and hit it with a hammer. The tent peg went through the side of his head and into the ground. Sisera died.

²²Just then Barak came by Jael's tent, looking for Sisera. Jael went out to meet Barak and said, "Come in here, and I will show you the man you are looking for." So Barak entered the tent with Jael. There Barak found Sisera lying dead on the ground, with the tent peg through the side of his head.

²³On that day God made the army of King Jabin of Canaan unable to defend themselves against the Israelites. ²⁴The Israelites fought harder and harder against Jabin, the Canaanite king, until they finally destroyed him.

The Song of Deborah

5 ᵃ On the day that the Israelites defeated Sisera, Deborah and Barak son of Abinoam sang this song:

²"The men of Israel prepared for battle.ᵇ
    They volunteered to go to war.
  Praise the LORD!

³"Listen, kings.
    Pay attention, rulers.
  I will sing.
    I myself will sing to the LORD.
  I will make music to the LORD,
    to the God of the Israelites.

⁴"LORD, in the past you came from Seir.ᶜ
    You marched from the land of Edom.
  You marched and the earth shook.
    The skies rained.
    The clouds dropped water.
  ⁵The mountains shook before the LORD, the
      God of Mount Sinai,
    before the LORD, the God of Israel!

⁶"In the days of Shamgar son of Anath,ᵈ
    and in the days of Jael, the main roads
      were empty.
    Caravans and travellers travelled on the
      back roads.

⁷"There were no soldiers in Israel
    until you came, Deborah,
    until you came to be a mother to Israel.ᵉ

⁸"God chose new leaders
    to fight at the city gates.ᶠ
  No one could find a shield or a spear
    among the 40,000 soldiers of Israel.

⁹"My heart is with the commanders of
      Israel.
    They volunteered to go to war.
  Praise the LORD!

¹⁰"Pay attention you people riding on white
      donkeys,
    sitting on saddle blankets,ᵍ
    and walking along the road.
  ¹¹At the watering holes for the animals,
    we hear the music of cymbals.
  People sing about the victories of the LORD,
    the victories of his soldiers in Israel.
  That is when the LORD's people
    went down to the city gates.

¹²"Wake up, wake up, Deborah!
    Wake up, wake up, sing the song!
  Get up, Barak!
    Go and capture your enemies, son of
      Abinoam!

¹³"Now, survivors, go to the leaders.
    People of the LORD, come with me and the
      soldiers.

¹⁴"The men of Ephraim came from the hill
      country of Amalek.ʰ
    Benjamin, those men followed you and
      your people.
  And there were commanders from the family
      of Makir.ⁱ

ᵃ **5:1 Chapter 5** This is a very old song, and many of the lines are not clear in the standard Hebrew text.
ᵇ **5:2 The men . . . battle** This might also mean "When leaders led in Israel" or "When men wore long hair in Israel." Soldiers often dedicated their hair as a special gift to God.
ᶜ **5:4 Seir** Another name for the land of Edom.
ᵈ **5:6 Shamgar son of Anath** A judge of Israel. See Judg. 3:31.
ᵉ **5:7 until you . . . to Israel** Or "until I came, Deborah, until I came, mother of Israel". Or "until I established you, Deborah, until I established you, mother of Israel".
ᶠ **5:8 God chose . . . gates** Or "They chose to follow new gods. So they had to fight at their city gates." The Hebrew text is not clear.
ᵍ **5:10 saddle blankets** The meaning of this Hebrew word is uncertain.
ʰ **5:14 hill country of Amalek** The area settled by the tribe of Ephraim. See Judg. 12:15.
ⁱ **5:14 Makir** This family was part of the tribe of Manasseh that settled in the area east of the Jordan River.

Leaders from the tribe of Zebulun came
with their bronze clubs.
¹⁵The leaders of Issachar were with Deborah.
The family of Issachar was true to Barak.
Those men marched to the valley on foot.

"Reuben, there are many brave soldiers in
your army groups.
¹⁶So why did you sit there against the walls of
your sheep pens?^a
The brave soldiers of Reuben thought hard
about war.
But they stayed home listening to the music
they played for their sheep.
¹⁷The people of Gilead^b stayed in their camps on
the other side of the Jordan River.
As for you, people of Dan, why did you stay
by your ships?
The people of Asher remained by the sea,
camped near their safe harbours.

¹⁸"But the men of Zebulun and Naphtali risked
their lives
fighting on those hills.
¹⁹The kings of Canaan came to fight,
but they didn't carry any treasures home.
They fought at the city of Taanach,
by the waters of Megiddo.
²⁰The stars fought them from heaven.
From their paths across the sky, they fought
against Sisera.
²¹The Kishon River, that ancient river,
swept Sisera's men away.
My soul, march on with strength!^c
²²The horses' hooves hammered the ground.
Sisera's mighty horses ran and ran.

²³"The angel of the LORD said, 'Curse the city of
Meroz.
Curse its people!
They did not come to help the LORD fight.'
They did not help the LORD against his
powerful enemies.
²⁴Jael was the wife of Heber the Kenite.
She will be blessed above all women.
²⁵Sisera asked for water.
Jael gave him milk.
In a bowl fit for a ruler,
she brought him cream.
²⁶Then Jael reached out and took a tent peg.
Her right hand reached for a workman's
hammer.
She put the peg against the side of Sisera's head
and hit it with the hammer.

²⁷He sank down between Jael's feet.
He fell, and there he lay.
He sank down between her feet.
He fell there.
Where Sisera sank, he fell,
and there he lay, dead!

²⁸"There is Sisera's mother, looking out of the
window,
looking through the curtains and crying,
'Why is Sisera's chariot so late?
Why can't I hear his horses?'
²⁹Her wisest servant girl answers her.
Yes, the servant gives her an answer:
³⁰'I'm sure they won the war,
and they are now taking things from the
people they defeated.
They are dividing those things among
themselves.
Each soldier is taking a girl or two.
Maybe Sisera found a piece of dyed cloth.
That's it! Sisera found a piece of fancy cloth,
or maybe two, to wear around his neck in
victory.'

³¹"May all your enemies die like this, LORD!
But may all those who love you be as strong
as the rising sun!"

And there was peace in the land for 40 years.

The Midianites Fight Israel

6 Again the Israelites did what the LORD considered evil. So for seven years the LORD
allowed the Midianites to defeat the Israelites.
²The Midianites were very powerful and were
cruel to the Israelites. So the Israelites made
many hiding places in the mountains. They hid
their food in caves and places that were hard
to find. ³They did that because the Midianites
and Amalekites from the east always came and
destroyed their crops. ⁴They camped in the land
and destroyed the crops that the Israelites had
planted. They ruined the crops of the Israelites as
far as the land near the city of Gaza. They did not
leave anything for the Israelites to eat. They did
not even leave them any sheep, cattle or donkeys.
⁵The Midianites came with their families, animals
and tents. They were like a swarm of locusts! They
and their camels were too many to count. They
came into the land and ruined it. ⁶The Israelites
became very poor because of the Midianites.
So the Israelites cried to the LORD for help.

^a 5:16 *walls of your sheep pens* Or "campfires" or "saddlebags".
^b 5:17 *Gilead* This area was east of the Jordan River.
^c 5:21 *My soul . . . strength* Or with some changes it could be, "His mighty charging horses marched forward."

[7a] The Midianites did all these bad things, so the Israelites cried to the LORD for help. [8] The LORD sent a prophet to them. He said, "This is what the LORD, the God of Israel, says: 'You were slaves in the land of Egypt. I made you free and brought you out of that land. [9] I saved you from the powerful Egyptians. Then the Canaanites hurt you, so I saved you again. I made them leave their land. And I gave their land to you.' [10] Then I said to you, 'I am the LORD your God. You will live in the land of the Amorites, but you must not worship their false gods.' But you did not obey me."

The Angel of the LORD Visits Gideon

[11-12] One day the angel of the LORD came to a place called Ophrah and sat under an oak tree. This oak tree belonged to a man named Joash from the Abiezer family. His son Gideon was threshing wheat[b] in a winepress. He was hiding so that the Midianites could not see the wheat. The angel of the LORD appeared to Gideon and said, "The LORD be with you, brave soldier."

[13] Then Gideon said, "Pardon me, sir, but if the LORD is with us, why are we having so many troubles? We heard that he did wonderful things for our ancestors. They tell us that the LORD took them out of Egypt. But now it seems the LORD has left us and is letting the Midianites defeat us."

[14] The LORD turned towards Gideon and said, "Then use your great power and go and save the Israelites from the Midianites. I am sending you to save them."

[15] But Gideon answered and said, "Pardon me, sir.[c] How can I save Israel? My family group is the weakest in the tribe of Manasseh, and I am the youngest one in my family."

[16] The LORD answered Gideon and said, "I will be with you, so you can defeat the Midianites as easily as if they were only one man."

[17] Then Gideon said to him, "If you would, please give me some proof that you really are the LORD. [18] Please wait here. Don't go away until I come back to you. Let me bring my offering and set it down before you."

And the LORD said, "I will wait until you come back."

[19] So Gideon went in and cooked a young goat in boiling water. He also took about 10 kilogrammes[d] of flour and made bread without yeast. Then he put the meat into a basket and the broth from the meat into a pot. He brought out the meat, the broth and the bread without yeast and gave them to the LORD under the oak tree.

[20] The angel of God said to Gideon, "Put the meat and the bread on that rock over there. Then pour the broth on it." Gideon did as he was told.

[21] The angel of the LORD had a walking stick in his hand. He touched the meat and the bread with the end of the stick, and fire jumped up out of the rock and burned up the meat and the bread. Then the angel of the LORD disappeared.

[22] Then Gideon realized that he had been talking to the angel of the LORD. So he shouted, "Oh Lord GOD! I have seen the angel of the LORD face to face!"

[23] But the LORD said to Gideon, "Calm down![e] Don't be afraid! You will not die!"[f]

[24] So Gideon built an altar there to worship the LORD and named it "The LORD is Peace". It still stands in the city of Ophrah, where the Abiezer family lives.

Gideon Tears Down the Altar of Baal

[25] That same night the LORD said to Gideon, "Choose your father's best bull, the one that is seven years old.[g] First, use it to pull down the altar your father built to worship Baal. Also, cut down the Asherah pole beside the altar. [26] Then build the right kind of altar for the LORD your God. Build it on this high ground. Then kill and burn the bull on this altar. Use the wood from the Asherah pole to burn your offering."

[27] So Gideon took ten of his servants and did what the LORD had told him to do. But Gideon was afraid that his family and the men of the city might see what he was doing, so he did it all at night, not in the daytime.

[28] The men of the city got up the next morning and saw that the altar for Baal had been destroyed! They also saw that the Asherah pole had been cut down. It had been sitting next to the altar for Baal. They also saw the altar that Gideon had built. And they saw the bull that had been sacrificed on that altar.

[29] The men of the city looked at each other and asked, "Who pulled down our altar? Who cut down our Asherah pole? Who sacrificed this bull

---

[a] **6:7–10** These verses do not appear in the oldest Hebrew copy of the book of Judges, the Dead Sea Scroll fragment, 4QJudgesA.
[b] **6:11–12** *threshing some wheat* That is, separating the grains of wheat from the husks. Usually this is done near the top of a hill.
[c] **6:15** *sir* Or "LORD", a title for God.
[d] **6:19** *10 kilogrammes* Literally, "1 *ephah*".
[e] **6:23** *Calm down* Literally, "Peace".
[f] **6:23** *You will not die* Gideon thought he would die because he had seen the LORD face to face.
[g] **6:25** *Choose . . . seven years old* This translation follows one ancient Greek version. The standard Hebrew text has "Take the bull of the bull[s], the second bull, the seven-year-old one." Adding different vowels to the Hebrew text gives a meaning similar to that in the translation above.

on this new altar?" They asked many questions and tried to learn who did this.

Someone told them, "Gideon son of Joash did this."

30So the men of the city came to Joash and said, "You must bring your son out. He pulled down the altar for Baal, and he cut down the Asherah pole that was beside it. So your son must die."

31Then Joash spoke to the crowd that was standing around him. Joash said, "Are you going to take Baal's side? Are you going to rescue Baal? If anyone takes Baal's side, let him be put to death by morning. If Baal really is a god, let him defend himself when someone pulls down his altar." 32Joash said, "If Gideon pulled Baal's altar down, let Baal argue with him." On that day Joash gave Gideon a new name. He called him Jerub-Baal.*a*

Gideon Defeats the Midianites

33The Midianites, Amalekites and other people from the east joined together to fight against the Israelites. They went across the Jordan River and camped in the Jezreel Valley. 34The Spirit of the LORD filled Gideon. So Gideon blew a trumpet to call the family of Abiezer to follow him. 35He sent messengers to all the people of the tribe of Manasseh and told them to get their weapons and prepare for battle. Gideon also sent messengers to the tribes of Asher, Zebulun and Naphtali. The messengers took the same message to them. So they also went up to meet Gideon and his men.

36Then Gideon said to God, "You said that you would help me save the Israelites. Give me proof. 37I will put a sheepskin on the threshing floor. If there is dew only on the sheepskin, while all the ground is dry, I will know that you will use me to save Israel, as you said."

INSIGHT

The fleece Gideon used would have been from either a sheep or a goat. Because of his slowness to trust God, Gideon twice asked God to prove his promise to him by doing something miraculous, and amazingly God did!

Judges 6:36–40

38And that is exactly what happened. Gideon got up early the next morning and squeezed the sheepskin. He was able to drain a bowl full of water from it.

39Then Gideon said to God, "Don't be angry with me. Let me ask just one more thing. Let me test you one more time with the sheepskin. This time let the sheepskin be dry, while the ground around it gets wet with dew."

40That night God did that very thing. Just the sheepskin was dry, but the ground around it was wet with dew.

7 Early in the morning, Jerub-Baal (Gideon) and all his men set up their camp at the spring of Harod. The Midianites were camped in the valley at the bottom of the hill called Moreh, north of Gideon and his men.

2Then the LORD said to Gideon, "I am going to help your men defeat the Midianites, but you have too many men. I don't want the Israelites to forget me and boast that they saved themselves. 3So make an announcement to your men. Tell them, 'Anyone who is afraid may leave Mount Gilead and go back home.'"

At that time 22,000 men left Gideon and went back home, but 10,000 still remained.

4Then the LORD said to Gideon, "There are still too many men. Take the men down to the water, and I will test them for you there. If I say, 'This man will go with you,' he will go. But if I say, 'That one will not go with you,' then he will not go."

5So Gideon led the men down to the water. There the LORD said to him, "Separate the men like this: Those who drink the water by using their tongue to lap it up like a dog will be in one group. And those who bend down to drink will be in the other group."

6There were 300 men who used their hands to bring water to their mouth and lapped it like a dog does. All the other people bent down and drank the water. 7The LORD said to Gideon, "I will use the 300 men who lapped the water like a dog. I will use them to save you, and I will allow you to defeat the Midianites. Let the other men go home."

8So Gideon sent the other men of Israel home. He kept the 300 men with him. Those 300 men kept the supplies and the trumpets of the other men who went home.

The Midianites were camped in the valley below Gideon's camp. 9During the night the LORD spoke to Gideon and said, "Get up. I will let you defeat the Midianite army. Go down to their camp. 10If you are afraid to go alone, take your servant Purah with you. Go into the camp of the Midianites. 11Listen to what they are saying. After that, you will not be afraid to attack them."

So Gideon and his servant Purah went down to the edge of the enemy camp. 12The Midianites,

---

a **6:32 Jerub-Baal** This is like the Hebrew words meaning "Let Baal argue". The same verb is translated "take one's side" and "defend" in verse 31.

the Amalekites and all the other people from the east were camped in that valley. There were so many people that they seemed like a swarm of locusts. It seemed as if they had as many camels as there are grains of sand on the seashore.

13Gideon came to the enemy camp, and he heard a man talking. That man was telling his friend about a dream. He said, "I dreamed that a round loaf of bread came rolling into the camp of the Midianites. That loaf of bread hit the tent so hard that the tent turned over and fell flat."

14The man's friend knew the meaning of the dream. He said, "Your dream can only have one meaning. Your dream is about that man from Israel. It is about Gideon son of Joash. It means that God will let Gideon defeat the whole army of Midian."

15After he heard the men talking about the dream and what it meant, Gideon bowed down to God. Then Gideon went back to the camp of the Israelites and called out to the people, "Get up! The LORD will help us defeat the Midianites." 16Then Gideon divided the 300 men into three groups. He gave each man a trumpet and an empty jar with a burning torch inside it. 17Then Gideon told the men, "Watch me and do what I do. Follow me to the edge of the enemy camp. When I get to the edge of the camp, do exactly what I do. 18You men surround the enemy camp. I and all the men with me will blow our trumpets. When we blow our trumpets, you blow your trumpets too. Then shout these words: 'For the LORD and for Gideon!'"

19So Gideon and the 100 men with him went to the edge of the enemy camp. They arrived there just after the enemy changed guards. It was during the middle watch of the night. Gideon and his men blew their trumpets and smashed their jars. 20All three groups of Gideon's men blew their trumpets and smashed their jars. The men held the torches in their left hands and the trumpets in their right hands. As they blew their trumpets, they shouted, "A sword for the LORD and a sword for Gideon!"

21Gideon's men stayed where they were. But inside the camp, the men of Midian began shouting and running away. 22When Gideon's 300 men blew their trumpets, the LORD caused the men of Midian to kill each other with their swords. The enemy army ran away to the city of Beth Shittah, which is towards the city of Zererah. They ran as far as the border of the city of Abel Meholah, which is near the city of Tabbath.

23Then soldiers from the tribes of Naphtali, Asher and all of Manasseh were told to chase the Midianites. 24Gideon sent messengers through all the hill country of Ephraim. The messengers said, "Come down and attack the Midianites. Take control of the river as far as Beth Barah and the Jordan River. Do this before the Midianites get there."

So they called all the men from the tribe of Ephraim. They took control of the river as far as Beth Barah. 25The men of Ephraim caught two of the Midianite leaders named Oreb and Zeeb. They killed Oreb at a place named the Rock of Oreb and Zeeb at a place named the Winepress of Zeeb. They continued chasing the Midianites, but first they cut off the heads of Oreb and Zeeb and took the heads to Gideon. Gideon was at the place where people cross the Jordan River.

8 The men of Ephraim were angry with Gideon. When they found him, they asked, "Why did you treat us this way? Why didn't you call us when you went to fight against the Midianites?"

2But Gideon answered the men of Ephraim, "I have not done as well as you. You people of Ephraim have a much better harvest than my family, the Abiezers. At harvest time you leave more grapes in the vineyard than my family gathers! Isn't that true? 3In the same way, you have a better harvest now. God allowed you to capture Oreb and Zeeb, the leaders of Midian. How can I compare my success with what you did?" When the men of Ephraim heard Gideon's answer, they were not as angry as they had been.

Gideon Captures Two Kings of Midian

4Then Gideon and his 300 men came to the Jordan River and went across to the other side, but they were tired and hungry.*a* 5Gideon said to the men of the city of Succoth, "Give my soldiers something to eat. They are very tired. We are still chasing Zebah and Zalmunna, kings of Midian."

6But the leaders of the city of Succoth said to Gideon, "Why should we give your soldiers something to eat? You haven't caught Zebah and Zalmunna yet."

7Then Gideon said, "The LORD will help me capture Zebah and Zalmunna. And since you would not give us any food, I will come back and beat you with thorns and briers from the desert."

8Gideon left the city of Succoth and went to the city of Penuel. He asked the men of Penuel for food, just as he had asked the men of Succoth. But the men of Penuel gave Gideon the same answer that the men of Succoth had given. 9So Gideon said to the men of Penuel, "After I win the victory, I will come back here and pull this tower down."

---

a **8:4** *hungry* This is from the ancient Greek version. The standard Hebrew text has "chasing".

¹⁰Zebah and Zalmunna and their army were in the city of Karkor. Their army had 15,000 soldiers in it. These soldiers were all who were left of the army of the people of the east. 120,000 strong soldiers of that army had already been killed. ¹¹Gideon and his men used Tent Dwellers' Road, which is east of the cities of Nobah and Jogbehah and attacked the enemy at Karkor. The enemy army did not expect the attack. ¹²Zebah and Zalmunna, kings of the Midianites, ran away. But Gideon chased and caught them. Gideon and his men defeated the enemy army.

¹³Then Gideon son of Joash returned from the battle. He and his men returned by going through a mountain pass called the Pass of Heres. ¹⁴Gideon captured a young man from the city of Succoth. He asked the young man some questions. The young man wrote down some names for Gideon. The young man wrote down the names of the leaders and officials of the city of Succoth. He gave Gideon the names of 77 men.

¹⁵When Gideon came to the city of Succoth, he said to the men of that city, "Here are Zebah and Zalmunna. You made fun of me by saying, 'Why should we give food to your tired soldiers? You have not caught Zebah and Zalmunna yet.'" ¹⁶Gideon took the leaders of the city of Succoth and beat them with thorns and briers from the desert. ¹⁷Gideon also pulled down the tower in the city of Penuel and killed the men living in that city. ¹⁸Then Gideon said to Zebah and Zalmunna, "You killed some men on Mount Tabor. What were the men like?"

Zebah and Zalmunna answered, "They were like you. Each one of them seemed like a prince." ¹⁹Gideon said, "Those men were my brothers, my mother's sons! As the LORD lives, if you had not killed them, I would not kill you now." ²⁰Then Gideon turned to Jether, his oldest son, and said, "Kill these kings." But Jether was only a boy and was afraid, so he would not take out his sword.

²¹Then Zebah and Zalmunna said to Gideon, "Come on, kill us yourself. You are a man and strong enough to do the job." So Gideon got up and killed Zebah and Zalmunna. Then he took the decorations shaped like a half-moon off their camels' necks.

Gideon Makes an Ephod

²²The Israelites said to Gideon, "You saved us from the Midianites. So now rule over us. We want you, your son and your grandson to rule over us."

²³But Gideon told the Israelites, "The LORD will be your ruler. I will not rule over you, and my son will not rule over you."

²⁴Some of the people who the men of Israel defeated were Ishmaelites. And the Ishmaelite men wore gold earrings. So Gideon said to the Israelites, "I want you to do this one thing for me. I want each of you to give me a gold earring from the things you took in the battle."

²⁵The Israelites said to Gideon, "We will gladly give you what you want." So they put a coat down on the ground, and each man threw an earring onto the coat. ²⁶When the earrings were gathered up, they weighed about 20 kilogrammes.^a This did not include the other gifts the Israelites gave to Gideon. They also gave him jewellery shaped like the moon and jewellery shaped like teardrops. And they gave him purple robes. The kings of the Midianites had worn these things. They also gave him the chains from the camels of the Midianite kings.

²⁷Gideon used the gold to make an ephod, which he put in his home town, the town called Ophrah. All the Israelites became unfaithful to God by worshipping the ephod. It became a trap that caused Gideon and his family to sin.

The Death of Gideon

²⁸The Midianites were forced to be under the rule of the Israelites. The Midianites did not cause trouble any more. And the land was at peace for 40 years, as long as Gideon was alive.

²⁹Gideon^b son of Joash went home. ³⁰Gideon had 70 sons of his own. He had so many sons because he had many wives. ³¹He had a slave woman who lived in the city of Shechem. He had a son by her. He named that son Abimelech.

³²So Gideon son of Joash died at a good old age. He was buried in the tomb that Joash, his father, owned. That tomb is in the city of Ophrah, where the family of Abiezer lives. ³³As soon as Gideon died, the Israelites again became unfaithful to God by worshipping Baal. They made Baal Berith^c their god. ³⁴The Israelites did not remember the LORD their God, who had saved them from all their enemies living around them. ³⁵The Israelites were not loyal to the family of Jerub-Baal (Gideon), even though he had done many good things for them.

Abimelech Becomes King

9 Abimelech was the son of Gideon. Abimelech went to his uncles who lived in the city of Shechem. He said to his uncles and all his mother's family, ²"Ask the leaders of the city of

^a **8:26 20 kilogrammes** Literally, "1,700 *shekels*".
^b **8:29 Gideon** Literally, "Jerub-Baal", a nickname given to Gideon earlier (see 6:32). Also throughout chapter 9.
^c **8:33 Baal Berith** A name that means "Lord of the Agreement". It shows that the people were confusing the worship of the true God with the worship of local idols. Also in 9:4.

Shechem if it is better to be ruled by the 70 sons of Gideon or to be ruled by only one man. Remember, I am your relative."

³Abimelech's uncles spoke to the leaders of Shechem and asked them that question. The leaders of Shechem decided to follow Abimelech. They said, "After all, he is our brother." ⁴So the leaders of Shechem gave Abimelech 70 pieces of silver. That silver was from the temple of the god Baal Berith. Abimelech used the silver to hire some men. These men were worthless, reckless men. They followed Abimelech wherever he went.

⁵Abimelech went to his father's house at Ophrah and murdered his brothers. He killed the 70 sons of his father Gideon. He killed them all at the same time,ᵃ but Gideon's youngest son hid from Abimelech and escaped. The youngest son's name was Jotham.

⁶Then all the leaders in Shechem and the officials of Beth Milloᵇ came together. Everyone gathered beside the big tree of the pillar in Shechem and made Abimelech their king.

Jotham's Story

⁷Jotham heard that the leaders of the city of Shechem had made Abimelech king. When he heard this, he went and stood on the top of Mount Gerizimᶜ and shouted out this story to the people:

"Listen to me you leaders of the city of Shechem. Then let God listen to you.

⁸"One day the trees decided to choose a king to rule over them. The trees said to the olive tree, 'You be king over us.'

⁹"But the olive tree said, 'My oil is used to honour gods and humans. Should I stop making my oil just to go and sway over the other trees?'

¹⁰"Then the trees said to the fig tree, 'Come and be our king.'

¹¹"But the fig tree answered, 'Should I stop making my good, sweet fruit just to go and sway over the other trees?'

¹²"Then the trees said to the vine, 'Come and be our king.'

¹³"But the vine answered, 'My wine makes men and kings happy. Should I stop making my wine just to go and sway over the trees?'

¹⁴"Finally all the trees said to the thornbush, 'Come and be our king.'

¹⁵"But the thornbush said to the trees, 'If you really want to make me king over you, come and find shelter in my shade. But if you don't want to do this, let fire come out of the thornbush. Let the fire burn even the cedar trees of Lebanon.'

INSIGHT

Cedars of Lebanon were famous for being the tallest, strongest and most beautiful trees of their time. They were the kind of trees imported by kings to be used in the construction of palaces. In this story they are being contrasted with a bramble which is much smaller.

Judges 9:15

¹⁶"Now if you were completely honest when you made Abimelech king, may you be happy with him. And if you have been fair to Gideon and his family, and if you have treated him as you should, this is also good. ¹⁷But remember what my father did for you. He fought for you and risked his life when he saved you from the Midianites. ¹⁸But now you have turned against my father's family. You have killed 70 of his sons all at the same time. You made Abimelech the new king over the city of Shechem. He is only the son of my father's slave girl. But you made him king because he is your relative. ¹⁹So if you have been completely honest to Gideon and his family today, then may you be happy with Abimelech as your king. And may he be happy with you. ²⁰But leaders of Shechem and Beth Millo, if you have not acted right, may Abimelech destroy you. And may Abimelech be destroyed too!"

²¹After Jotham had said this, he ran away and escaped to the city named Beer. He stayed there because he was afraid of his brother Abimelech.

Abimelech Fights Against Shechem

²²Abimelech ruled the Israelites for three years. ²³–²⁴Abimelech had killed Gideon's 70 sons—and they were his own brothers. The leaders of Shechem had supported him in doing this evil thing. So God caused trouble between Abimelech and the leaders of Shechem. And they began planning ways to hurt Abimelech. ²⁵The leaders

---

ᵃ **9:5 all at the same time** Literally, "on one stone". Also in verse 18.
ᵇ **9:6 officials of Beth Millo** Or "House of Millo". Also in verse 20. Beth Millo may have been a well-protected part of the city, perhaps the location of the pagan temple mentioned in verse 46.
ᶜ **9:7 Mount Gerizim** This mountain is right beside the city of Shechem.

of the city of Shechem did not like Abimelech any more. They put men on the hilltops to attack and rob everyone who went by. Abimelech found out about the attacks.

26A man named Gaal son of Ebed and his brothers moved to the city of Shechem. The leaders of the city of Shechem decided to trust and follow Gaal.

27One day the people of Shechem went out to the vineyards to pick grapes. They squeezed the grapes to make wine. And then they had a party at the temple of their god. The people ate and drank and cursed Abimelech.

28Gaal son of Ebed said, "Why should we serve Abimelech? He's not one of our people. He's the son of Gideon! So we should not have to obey Abimelech or his officer Zebul. Our leader should be someone from the family of Hamor, the ancestor of Shechem. 29If you make me the commander of these people, I will destroy Abimelech. I will say to him, 'Get your army ready and come out to battle.'"

30Zebul was the governor of the city of Shechem. Zebul heard what Gaal son of Ebed said, and he became very angry. 31Zebul sent messengers to Abimelech in the city of Arumah.a This is the message:

"Gaal son of Ebed and Gaal's brothers have come to the city of Shechem. They are making trouble for you. Gaal is turning the whole city against you. 32So now you and your men should come tonight and hide in the fields outside the city. 33When the sun comes up in the morning, attack the city. Gaal and his men will come out of the city to fight you. When they come out to fight, do what you can to them."

34So Abimelech and all his soldiers got up during the night and went to the city. The soldiers separated into four groups. They hid near the city of Shechem. 35Gaal son of Ebed went out and was standing at the entrance to the gate of the city of Shechem. While Gaal was standing there, Abimelech and his soldiers came out of their hiding places.

36When Gaal saw the soldiers, he said to Zebul, "Look, there are people coming down from the mountains."

But Zebul said, "You are only seeing the shadows of the mountains. The shadows just look like people."

37But again Gaal said, "Look, there are some people coming down from that place over there by Land's Navel. And there! I saw someone's head over by Magician's Tree."b 38Zebul said to Gaal, "Why aren't you boasting now? You said, 'Who is Abimelech? Why should we obey him?' You made fun of these men. Now go out and fight them."

39So Gaal led the leaders of Shechem out to fight Abimelech. 40Abimelech and his men chased Gaal and his men. Gaal's men ran back towards the gate of the city of Shechem, but many were killed before they could get back to the gate.

41Then Abimelech returned to the city of Arumah. Zebul forced Gaal and his brothers to leave the city of Shechem.

42The next day the people of Shechem went out to the fields to work. Abimelech found out about it. 43So Abimelech separated his men into three groups. He wanted to surprise the people of Shechem, so he hid his men in the fields. When he saw the people coming out of the city, he jumped up and attacked them. 44Abimelech and his group ran to a place near the gate to Shechem. The other two groups ran out to the people in the fields and killed them. 45Abimelech and his men fought against the city of Shechem all that day. They captured the city of Shechem and killed its people. Then Abimelech tore down the city and threw salt over the ruins.

46There were some people who lived at the Tower of Shechem.c When they heard what had happened to Shechem, they gathered together in the safest roomd of the temple of the god El Berith.e

47Abimelech heard that all the leaders of the Tower of Shechem had gathered together. 48So Abimelech and all his men went up to Mount Zalmon.f Abimelech took an axe and cut off some branches and carried them on his shoulders. Then Abimelech said to the men with him, "Hurry! Do the same thing that I have done." 49So all the men cut branches and followed Abimelech. They piled the branches against the safest room of the temple of the god El Berith. Then they set the branches on fire and burned the people in the room. About 1,000 men and women living near the Tower of Shechem died.

a 9:31 in the city of Arumah Or "secretly" or "in Tormah", the town where Abimelech lived as king. It was probably about eight miles south of Shechem.
b 9:37 Land's Navel . . . Magician's Tree Two places in the hills near Shechem.
c 9:46 Tower of Shechem This was probably a place near Shechem but not actually part of the city.
d 9:46 safest room The meaning of this Hebrew word is uncertain. Also in verse 49.
e 9:46 El Berith Another name for the god Baal Berith mentioned in verses 4 and 8:33. The name here means "God of the Agreement". Also in verse 49.
f 9:48 Mount Zalmon This is probably another name for Mount Ebal, a mountain near Shechem.

Abimelech's Death

⁵⁰Then Abimelech and his men went to the city of Thebez and captured that city. ⁵¹But inside the city there was a strong tower, so all the leaders and other men and women of that city ran to the tower. When the people were inside the tower, they locked the door behind them. Then they climbed up to the roof of the tower. ⁵²Abimelech and his men came to the tower to attack it. Abimelech went up to the door of the tower to burn it. ⁵³But, while Abimelech was standing at the door of the tower, a woman on the roof dropped a grinding stone on his head. The grinding stone crushed his skull. ⁵⁴Abimelech quickly said to the servant who carried his weapons, "Take out your sword and kill me. I want you to kill me so that people will not say that a woman killed Abimelech." So the servant stabbed Abimelech with his sword, and he died. ⁵⁵The Israelites saw that Abimelech was dead, so they all went back home.

⁵⁶In that way God punished Abimelech for all the bad things he had done. Abimelech sinned against his own father by killing his 70 brothers. ⁵⁷God also punished the men of the city of Shechem for the bad things they had done. So the things said by Jotham son of Gideon came true.

Tola, the Judge

10 After Abimelech died, God sent another judge to save the Israelites. His name was Tola. He was the son of Puah, who was the son of Dodo. Tola was from the tribe of Issachar and lived in the city of Shamir, in the hill country of Ephraim. ²Tola was a judge for the Israelites for 23 years. Then he died and was buried in the city of Shamir.

Jair, the Judge

³After Tola died, God sent another judge. His name was Jair, and he lived in the area of Gilead. He was a judge for the Israelites for 22 years. ⁴Jair had 30 sons who rode 30 donkeys.ᵃ These 30 sons controlled 30 towns in the area of Gilead. These towns are called the Towns of Jair to this very day. ⁵Jair died and was buried in the city of Kamon.

The Ammonites Fight Against Israel

⁶Again the Israelites did what the LORD considered evil: They began worshiping the false gods Baal and the Ashtoreth. They also worshiped the gods of the people of Aram, the gods of the people of Sidon, the gods of the Moabites, the gods of the Ammonites and the gods of the Philistines. The Israelites left the LORD and stopped serving him.

⁷So the LORD became angry with the Israelites and allowed the Philistines and the Ammonites to defeat them. ⁸In that same year those people destroyed the Israelites who lived on the east side of the Jordan River, in the area of Gilead. That is the land where the Amorites had lived. The Israelites suffered for 18 years. ⁹The Ammonites then went across the Jordan River to fight against the people of Judah, Benjamin and Ephraim. The Ammonites brought many troubles to the Israelites.

¹⁰So the Israelites cried to the LORD for help. They said, "God, we have sinned against you. We left our God and worshiped the false god Baal."

¹¹The LORD answered the Israelites, "You cried to me when the Egyptians, the Amorites, the Ammonites and the Philistines hurt you. I saved you from these people. ¹²You cried to me when the people of Sidon, the Amalekites and the Midianitesᵇ hurt you. I also saved you from those people. ¹³But you left me and started worshiping other gods, so I refuse to save you again. ¹⁴You like worshiping those gods, so go and call to them for help. Let them save you when you are in trouble."

¹⁵But the Israelites said to the LORD, "We have sinned. Do whatever you want to do to us, but please save us today." ¹⁶Then the Israelites threw away the foreign gods and began to worship the LORD again. So he felt sorry for them when he saw them suffering.

Jephthah Is Chosen as a Leader

¹⁷The Ammonites gathered together for war. Their camp was in the area of Gilead. The Israelites gathered together. Their camp was at the city of Mizpah. ¹⁸The leaders of the people living in the area of Gilead said, "Whoever leads us in the attack against the Ammonites will become the head of all the people living in Gilead."

11 Jephthah was from the tribe of Gilead. He was a strong soldier. But Jephthah was the son of a prostitute. His father was a man named Gilead. ²Gilead's wife had several sons. When they grew up, they did not like Jephthah. They forced Jephthah to leave his home town. They said to him, "You will not get any of our father's property, because you are the son of another woman." ³So Jephthah went away because of his brothers and lived in the land of Tob. In the land of Tob, some rough men began to follow Jephthah.

ᵃ **10:4** *30 sons who rode 30 donkeys* This showed that these men were important leaders, possibly the mayors of the 30 towns in Gilead.
ᵇ **10:12** *Midianites* This is from the ancient Greek version. The standard Hebrew text has "The Maonites".

[4]After a time the Ammonites fought with the Israelites. [5]The Ammonites were fighting against Israel, so the leaders in Gilead went to Jephthah. They wanted Jephthah to leave the land of Tob and come back to Gilead.

[6]The leaders said to Jephthah, "Come and be our leader so that we can fight the Ammonites."

[7]But Jephthah said to the leaders of the land of Gilead, "You forced me to leave my father's house. You hate me. So why are you coming to me now that you are having trouble?"

[8]The leaders from Gilead said to Jephthah, "That is the reason we have come to you now. Please come with us and fight against the Ammonites. You will be the commander over all the people living in Gilead."

[9]Then Jephthah said to the leaders from Gilead, "If you want me to come back to Gilead and fight the Ammonites, I will do it. But if the Lord helps me win, I will be your new leader."

[10]The leaders from Gilead said to Jephthah, "The Lord is listening to everything we are saying. And we promise to do everything you tell us to do."

[11]So Jephthah went with the leaders from Gilead, and the people made him their leader and commander. Jephthah repeated all his words in front of the Lord at the city of Mizpah.

Jephthah Warns the King of Ammon

[12]Jephthah sent messengers to the king of the Ammonites with this message: "What is the problem between the Ammonites and the Israelites? Why have you come to fight in our land?"

[13]The king of the Ammonites said to the messengers of Jephthah, "We are fighting Israel because the Israelites took our land when they came up from Egypt. They took our land from the Arnon River to the Jabbok River to the Jordan River. Now, tell the Israelites to give our land back to us without fighting for it."

[14]So the messengers of Jephthah took this message back to Jephthah.[a] Then Jephthah sent the messengers to the king of the Ammonites again. [15]They took this message:

"This is what Jephthah says: Israel did not take the land of the Moabites or the land of the Ammonites. [16]When the Israelites came out of the land of Egypt, they went into the desert. They went to the Red Sea. Then they went to Kadesh. [17]The Israelites sent messengers to the king of Edom. The messengers asked for a favour. They said, 'Let the Israelites cross through your land.' But the king of Edom didn't let us go through his land. We also sent the same message to the king of Moab. But the king of Moab would not let us go through his land either. So the Israelites stayed at Kadesh.

[18]"Then the Israelites went through the desert and around the edges of the land of Edom and the land of Moab. They travelled east of the land of Moab. They made their camp on the other side of the Arnon River. They did not cross the border of the land of Moab. (The Arnon River was the border of the land of Moab.)

[19]"Then the Israelites sent messengers to King Sihon of the Amorites. Sihon was the king of the city of Heshbon. The messengers asked Sihon, 'Let the Israelites pass through your land. We want to go to our land.' [20]But King Sihon of the Amorites would not let the Israelites cross his borders. So Sihon gathered all his people and made a camp at Jahaz. Then the Amorites fought with the Israelites. [21]But the Lord, the God of Israel, helped the Israelites defeat Sihon and his army. So the land of the Amorites became the property of the Israelites. [22]The Israelites got all the land of the Amorites from the Arnon River to the Jabbok River. The land also went from the desert to the Jordan River.

[23]"It was the Lord, the God of Israel, who forced the Amorites to leave their land. And he gave the land to the Israelites. Do you think you can make the Israelites leave this land? [24]Surely you can live in the land that your god Chemosh has given to you. So we will live in the land that the Lord our God has given to us. [25]Are you any better than Balak son of Zippor?[b] He was the king of the land of Moab. Did he argue with the Israelites? Did he actually fight with the Israelites? [26]The Israelites have lived in the city of Heshbon and the towns around it for 300 years. They have lived in the city of Aroer and the towns around it for 300 years. They have lived in all the cities along the side of the Arnon River for 300 years. Why have you not tried to take these cities in all that time? [27]The Israelites have not sinned against you. But you are doing a very bad thing to them. May the Lord, the true Judge, decide whether the Israelites or the Ammonites are right."

[28]The king of the Ammonites refused to listen to this message from Jephthah.

---

[a] **11:14 *So the messengers . . . Jephthah*** This is from the ancient Greek version.
[b] **11:25 *Balak son of Zippor*** See Num. 22–24 for his story.

Jephthah's Promise

29Then the Spirit of the LORD came on Jephthah, and he passed through the area of Gilead and Manasseh. He went through the city of Mizpah in Gilead on his way to the land of the Ammonites.

INSIGHT

Jephthah must have regretted making this promise to God. He may have expected to see an animal come out of his house, as houses then often included space for cattle. However, he honoured his promise, even though it meant death for his only daughter. A very different outcome to Abraham and Isaac in Genesis 22.

Judges 11:29–40

30Jephthah made a promise to the LORD. He said, "If you will let me defeat the Ammonites, 31I will give you the first thing that comes out of my house when I come back from the victory. I will give it to the LORD as a burnt offering."

32Then Jephthah went to the land of the Ammonites. He fought the Ammonites, and the LORD helped him defeat them. 33He defeated them from the city of Aroer to the city of Minnith. Jephthah captured 20 cities. Then he fought the Ammonites to the city of Abel Keramim. The Israelites defeated them. It was a very great defeat for the Ammonites.

34Jephthah went back to Mizpah. He went to his house, and his daughter came out to meet him. She was playing a tambourine and dancing. She was his only daughter, and Jephthah loved her very much. He did not have any other sons or daughters. 35When Jephthah saw that his daughter was the first thing to come out of his house, he tore his clothes to show his sadness. Then he said, "Oh, my daughter! You have ruined me! You have made me very sad! I made a promise to the LORD, and I cannot change it!"

36Then his daughter said to Jephthah, "Father, you have made a promise to the LORD, so keep your promise. Do what you said you would do. After all, the LORD did help you defeat your enemies, the Ammonites."

37Then Jephthah's daughter said to her father, "But do this one thing for me first. Let me be alone for two months. Let me go to the mountains. I will not marry and have children, so let me and my friends go and cry together."

38Jephthah said, "Go." He sent her away for two months. Jephthah's daughter and her friends stayed in the mountains. They cried for her because she would not marry and have children.

39At the end of two months, Jephthah's daughter returned to her father, and Jephthah did what he had vowed to do. His daughter never had sex with anyone. So this became a custom in Israel. 40Every year the young women of Israel would go out for four days to remember the daughter of Jephthah from Gilead and to cry for her.

Jephthah and Ephraim

12 The men from the tribe of Ephraim called all their soldiers together. Then they went across the river to the city of Zaphon. They said to Jephthah, "Why didn't you call us to help you fight the Ammonites? We will burn your house down with you in it."

2Jephthah answered them, "The Ammonites have been giving us many problems. So my people and I fought against them. I called you, but you didn't come to help us. 3I saw that you would not help us, so I risked my own life. I went across the river to fight against the Ammonites. The LORD helped me defeat them. Now why have you come to fight against me today?"

4Then Jephthah called the men of Gilead together. They fought against the men from the tribe of Ephraim because they had insulted the men of Gilead. They had said, "You men of Gilead are nothing but survivors of the men of Ephraim. Part of you belongs to Ephraim, and part of you belongs to Manasseh." The men of Gilead defeated the men of Ephraim.

5The men of Gilead captured the places where people cross the Jordan River. Those places led to the country of Ephraim. Any time a survivor from Ephraim came to the river and said, "Let me cross," the men of Gilead would ask him, "Are you from Ephraim?" If he said, "No," 6they would say, "Say the word 'Shibboleth'." The men of Ephraim could not say that word correctly. They pronounced the word "Sibboleth". So if the man said, "Sibboleth," then the men of Gilead knew he was from Ephraim. So they would kill him at the crossing place. They killed 42,000 men from Ephraim.

7Jephthah was a judge for the Israelites for six years. Then Jephthah from Gilead died and was buried in his town in Gilead.

Ibzan, the Judge

8After Jephthah, a man named Ibzan was a judge for the Israelites. Ibzan was from the city of Bethlehem. 9Ibzan had 30 sons and 30 daughters. He told his 30 daughters to marry men who were not his relatives. And he found 30 women who were not his relatives, and his sons married these women. Ibzan was a judge for the Israelites for seven years. [10]Then Ibzan died and was buried in the city of Bethlehem.

Elon, the Judge

[11]After Ibzan, a man named Elon was a judge for the Israelites. Elon was from the tribe of Zebulun. He was a judge for the Israelites for ten years. [12]Then Elon from the tribe of Zebulun died and was buried in the city of Aijalon in the land of Zebulun.

Abdon, the Judge

[13]After Elon died, a man named Abdon son of Hillel was a judge for the Israelites. Abdon was from the city of Pirathon. [14]Abdon had 40 sons and 30 grandsons. They rode on 70 donkeys.[a] Abdon was a judge for the Israelites for eight years. [15]Then Abdon son of Hillel died and was buried in the city of Pirathon. Pirathon is in the land of Ephraim in the hill country where the Amalekites lived.

The Birth of Samson

13 Again the people did what the LORD considered evil. So the LORD allowed the Philistines to rule over them for 40 years.

[2]There was a man named Manoah from the city of Zorah. He was from the tribe of Dan. Manoah had a wife, but she was not able to have children. [3]The angel of the LORD appeared to Manoah's wife and said, "You have not been able to have children. But you will become pregnant and have a son. [4]Don't drink any wine or any other strong drink. Don't eat any food that is unclean, [5]because you are pregnant, and you will have a son. He will be dedicated to God in a special way. He will be a Nazirite. So you must never cut his hair. He will be God's special person from before he is born. He will save the Israelites from the power of the Philistines."

[6]Then the woman went to her husband and told him what had happened. She said, "A man of God came to me. He looked like the angel of God. He frightened me. I didn't ask him where he was from, and he didn't tell me his name. [7]But he said to me, 'You are pregnant and will have a son. Don't drink any wine or other strong drink. Don't eat any food that is unclean, because the boy will be dedicated to God in a special way. The boy will be God's special person from before he is born until the day he dies.'"

[8]Then Manoah prayed to the LORD. He said, "Lord, I beg you to send the man of God to us again. We want him to teach us what we should do for the boy who will soon be born."

[9]God heard Manoah's prayer. The angel of God came to the woman again. She was sitting in a field and her husband Manoah was not with her. [10]So the woman ran to tell her husband, "The man is back! The man who came to me the other day is here."

[11]Manoah got up and followed his wife. When he came to the man, he said, "Are you the same man who spoke to my wife before?"

The angel said, "I am."

[12]So Manoah said, "May what you say happen. Tell me, what kind of life will the boy live? What will he do?"

[13]The angel of the LORD said to Manoah, "Your wife must do everything I told her. [14]She must not eat anything that grows on a grapevine. She must not drink any wine or strong drink. She must not eat any food that is unclean. She must do everything that I have commanded her to do."

[15]Then Manoah said to the angel of the LORD, "We would like you to stay for a while. We want to cook a young goat for you to eat."

[16]The angel of the LORD said to Manoah, "Even if you keep me from leaving, I will not eat your food. But if you want to prepare something, offer a burnt offering to the LORD." (Manoah did not understand that the man was really the angel of the LORD.)

[17]Then Manoah asked the angel of the LORD, "What is your name? We want to know so that we can honour you when what you have said really happens."

[18]The angel of the LORD said, "Why do you ask my name? It is too amazing for you to believe."[b]

[19]Then Manoah sacrificed a young goat on a rock. He offered the goat and a grain offering as a gift to the LORD and to the One Who Does Amazing Things.[c] [20]Manoah and his wife were watching what happened. As the flames went up to the sky from the altar, the angel of the LORD went up to heaven in the fire.

When Manoah and his wife saw that, they bowed down with their faces to the ground. [21]He finally understood that the man was really the angel of the LORD. The angel of the LORD did not appear to Manoah and his wife again. [22]Manoah said to his wife, "We have seen God. Surely we will die because of this."

[23]But his wife said to him, "The LORD does not want to kill us. If he wanted to kill us, he would

---

[a] **12:14 They rode on 70 donkeys** This showed that they were important leaders, possibly mayors of their towns.
[b] **13:18 It is . . . believe** Or "It is Pelei". This means "amazing" or "wonderful". This is like the name "Wonderful Counsellor" in Isa. 9:6.
[c] **13:19 the LORD . . . Amazing Things** Or "the LORD Who Does Amazing Things". Both of these are names for God, but Manoah didn't know the man was really the angel of the LORD.

MAN OF MYSTERY

What things make a great leader? A man able to kill a lion with his hands, dedicated to the Lord from birth? Someone strong and brave? Or a man who has an eye for the women, does what God tells him not to do and ends up a blind slave? Samson is all of these and more . . .

DIG IN

READ Judges 13:1–25

"Again the people did what the LORD considered evil" (v.1). Pretty depressing huh? But maybe there's hope . . .
- What was Samson destined to be?
- What was Samson not to do?

Here are some slightly weird things to say about a baby! Samson was "a Nazirite" (check out the rules for these in Numbers 6) and had to say no to some pretty good, normal things such as alcohol and cutting his hair in order that he might be God's special person. Samson was hand-picked by God to save the people from the Philistines – things are looking up!

READ Judges 14:1–9; 15:15–20; 16:1–3
- What sort of thing does Samson do that
  - » God has told him not to do?
  - » God has told all Israelites not to do?
  - » shows God is using him (14:4;15:18)?

It's all quite mysterious really. On the one hand Samson is having success in sorting out the Philistines, he's being used by God and he's calling out to God, and yet on the other Samson is really pushing the boundaries. He's doing things that either as a Nazirite or an Israelite he knows he shouldn't such as hanging out in a vineyard, touching a dead lion and sleeping with forbidden women.
- How is this like the Israelites (Judges 3:5–6)?
- In what ways is this like you?

READ Judges 16:4–31

Women – they'll be the death of Samson! Oh, wait . . .
- Write Delilah's biography.
- What is the result for Samson (vv.19–21)?
- How do verses 22 and 28 give us hope?

Delilah was probably not the best choice of partner. Not only was she manipulative, pulling out the "You don't love me" card (v.15), but she was also willing to sell Samson's secret, and therefore his life (v.5). And the Samson conundrum continues – on one hand, he's self-centred and weak, and yet he also calls out to God, willing to make the ultimate sacrifice (v.30).

DIG THROUGH

- Check out Hebrews 11:32–33. How encouraging is that! Despite frequent screw-ups, Samson is used by God and his faith is mentioned in the hall of fame. No one is too messed up for God to use. Why not ask him to use you?

God had a plan to rescue his people from the Philistines and even in the mistakes of Samson, God was working for the good of his people. It's mysterious how this works – but be comforted. God is always in control and always works for the good of his people.

DIG DEEPER

The Israelites needed a leader to rescue them from the Philistines and judge wisely. Samson wasn't exactly the ideal model for this and he makes us long for someone to lead the people perfectly. Yet in so many ways he reminds us, in his birth and death, of the perfect leader to come.

not have accepted our burnt offering and grain offering. He would not have shown us all these things or told us this."

²⁴So the woman had a boy. She named him Samson. He grew and the LORD blessed him. ²⁵The Spirit of the LORD began to work in Samson while he was in the city of Mahaneh Dan. That city is between the cities of Zorah and Eshtaol.

Samson's Marriage

14 Samson went down to the city of Timnah. He saw a young Philistine woman there. ²When he returned home, he said to his father and mother, "I saw a Philistine woman in Timnah. I want you to get her for me. I want to marry her."

³His father and his mother answered, "But surely there is a woman from the Israelites you can marry. Do you have to marry a woman from the Philistines? Their men are not even circumcised."

But Samson said, "Get that woman for me! She is the one I want!" ⁴(Samson's parents did not know that the LORD wanted this to happen. He was looking for a way to challenge the Philistines. They were ruling over the Israelites at that time.)

⁵Samson went down with his father and mother to the city of Timnah. They went as far as the vineyards near that city. There a young lion suddenly roared and jumped at Samson! ⁶The Spirit of the LORD came on Samson with great power. He tore the lion apart with his bare hands. It seemed easy to him. It was as easy as tearing apart a young goat. But Samson did not tell his father or mother what he had done.

⁷So Samson went down to the city and talked to the Philistine woman. She pleased him. ⁸Several days later, Samson went back to marry her. On his way, he went over to look at the dead lion. He found a swarm of bees in its body. They had made some honey. ⁹Samson got some of the honey with his hands. He walked along eating the honey. When he came to his parents, he gave them some of the honey, and they ate it too. But Samson did not tell his parents that he had taken the honey from the body of the dead lion.

¹⁰Samson's father went down to see the Philistine woman. The custom was for the bridegroom to give a party. So Samson gave a party. ¹¹When the Philistines saw that he was having a party, they sent 30 men to be with him.

¹²Then Samson said to the 30 men, "I want to tell you a riddle. This party will last for seven days. Try to find the answer during that time. If you can answer the riddle in that time, I will give you 30 linen shirts and 30 changes of clothes. ¹³But if you cannot find the answer, you must give me 30 linen shirts and 30 changes of clothes." So the 30 men said, "Tell us your riddle, we want to hear it."

¹⁴Samson told them this riddle:

"Out of the eater came something to eat.
  Out of the strong came something sweet."

The 30 men tried for three days to find the answer, but they couldn't.

¹⁵On the fourth day,ᵃ the men came to Samson's wife. They said, "Did you invite us here just to make us poor? You must trick your husband into telling us the answer to the riddle. If you don't get the answer for us, we will burn you and everyone in your father's house to death."

¹⁶So Samson's wife went to him and began crying. She said, "You just hate me! You don't really love me! You told my people a riddle, and you will not tell me the answer."

Samson said to her, "Look, I have not even told my father and mother. So why should I tell you?"

¹⁷Samson's wife cried for the rest of the seven days of the party. So he finally gave her the answer to the riddle on the seventh day. He told her because she kept bothering him. Then she went to her people and told them the answer to the riddle.

¹⁸So before the sun went down on the seventh day of the party, the Philistine men had the answer. They came to Samson and said,

"What is sweeter than honey?
  What is stronger than a lion?"

Then Samson said to them,

"If you had not ploughed with my cow,
  you would not have solved my riddle!"

¹⁹Samson was very angry. The Spirit of the LORD came on Samson with great power. He went down to the city of Ashkelon and killed 30 Philistine men. He took all the clothes and property from the dead bodies and gave them to the men who had answered his riddle. Then he went to his father's house. ²⁰So Samson's wife was given to his best man.

Samson Makes Trouble for the Philistines

15 At the time of the wheat harvest, Samson went to visit his wife. He took a young goat with him as a gift. He said, "I am going to my wife's room."

ᵃ **14:15 *fourth day*** This is from the ancient Greek version. The standard Hebrew text has "seventh day".

But her father would not let Samson go in. ²He said, "I thought you hated her, so I let her marry the best man at the wedding. Her younger sister is more beautiful. Take her younger sister."

³But Samson said to him, "Now I have a good reason to hurt you Philistines. No one will blame me now."

⁴So Samson went out and caught 300 foxes. He took two foxes at a time and tied their tails together to make pairs. Then he tied a torch between the tails of each pair of foxes. ⁵He lit the torches that were between the foxes' tails and let them run through the fields of the Philistines. In this way he burned up the plants growing in their fields and the bundles of corn they had cut. He also burned up their vineyards and their olive trees.

⁶The Philistines asked, "Who did this?"

Someone told them, "Samson, the son-in-law of the man from Timnah, did this. He did this because his father-in-law gave Samson's wife to the best man at his wedding." So the Philistines burned Samson's wife and her father to death.

⁷When Samson heard about this, he went and told the Philistines, "You must pay for this terrible thing you have done! I will not rest until I get revenge on you!"

⁸So he attacked the Philistines and killed many of them. Then he went and stayed in a cave in a place called the Rock of Etam.

⁹The Philistines went to the land of Judah and stopped near a place named Lehi. Their army camped there. ¹⁰The men of the tribe of Judah asked them, "Why have you Philistines come here to fight us?"

They answered, "We have come to get Samson. We want to make him our prisoner. We want to punish him for what he has done to our people."

¹¹Then 3,000 men from the tribe of Judah went to the cave near the Rock of Etam and said to Samson, "What have you done to us? Don't you know that the Philistines rule over us?"

Samson answered, "I only punished them for what they did to me."

¹²Then they said to Samson, "We have come to tie you up. We will give you to the Philistines."

Samson said to the men from Judah, "Promise me that you yourselves will not hurt me."

¹³The men from Judah said, "We agree. We will just tie you up and give you to the Philistines. We promise that we will not kill you." So they tied Samson with two new ropes and led him up from the cave in the rock.

¹⁴When Samson came to the place called Lehi, the Philistines came to meet him. They were shouting with joy. Then the Spirit of the Lord came on Samson with great power. Samson broke the ropes—they were like burned strings falling from his arms and the ropes on his hands seemed to melt away. ¹⁵Samson found a jawbone of a dead donkey and killed 1,000 Philistine men with it.

¹⁶Then Samson said,

"With a donkey's jawbone,
   I killed 1,000 men!
With a donkey's jawbone,
   I piled*a* them into a tall pile."

¹⁷When Samson finished speaking, he threw the jawbone down. So that place was named Ramath Lehi.*b*

¹⁸Samson was very thirsty. So he cried to the Lord. He said, "I am your servant. You gave me this great victory. Please don't let me die from thirst now. Please don't let me be captured by men who are not even circumcised."

¹⁹There is a hole in the ground at Lehi. God made that hole crack open, and water came out. Samson drank the water and felt better. He felt strong again. So he named that water spring En Hakkore.*c* It is still there in the city of Lehi today.

²⁰Samson was a judge for the Israelites for 20 years during the time of the Philistines.

INSIGHT

God had a special plan for Samson set out before he was born, but Samson kept getting distracted by relationships with the wrong women. Despite all his mistakes, Samson was still used to fulfil God's purposes.

Judges 16

Samson Goes to the City of Gaza

16 One day Samson went to the city of Gaza. He saw a prostitute there and went in to stay the night with her. ²Someone told the people of Gaza, "Samson has come here." They wanted to kill him, so they surrounded the city. They hid near the city gate and waited all night for him. They were very quiet all night long. They had said to each other, "When morning comes, we will kill Samson."

---

a **15:16 *piled*** In Hebrew, the word "pile" is like the word "donkey".
b **15:17 *Ramath Lehi*** This name means "Jawbone Heights".
c **15:19 *En Hakkore*** This name means "the spring of the one who calls".

³But Samson only stayed with the prostitute until midnight. Then he got up and grabbed the doors of the city gate and pulled them loose from the wall. He pulled down the doors, the two posts and the bars that lock the doors shut. He put them on his shoulders and carried them to the top of the hill near the city of Hebron.

Samson and Delilah

⁴Later, Samson fell in love with a woman named Delilah, who was from Sorek Valley. ⁵The rulers of the Philistines went to Delilah and said, "We want to know what makes Samson so strong. Try to trick him into telling you his secret. Then we will know how to capture him and tie him up. Then we will be able to control him. If you do this, each one of us will give you 1,100 pieces*ᵃ* of silver."

⁶So Delilah said to Samson, "Tell me why you are so strong. How could someone tie you up and make you helpless?"

⁷Samson answered, "Someone would have to tie me up with seven fresh, new bowstrings.*ᵇ* If someone did that, I would be as weak as any other man."

⁸Then the rulers of the Philistines brought seven fresh, new bowstrings to Delilah, and she tied Samson with the bowstrings. ⁹Some men were hiding in the next room. Delilah said to Samson, "Samson, the Philistine men are going to capture you!" But Samson easily broke the bowstrings. They snapped like a string when it comes too close to a flame. So the Philistines did not find out the secret of Samson's strength.

¹⁰Then Delilah said to Samson, "You lied to me. You made me look foolish. Please tell me the truth. How could someone tie you up?"

¹¹Samson said, "Someone would have to tie me up with new ropes. They would have to tie me with ropes that have not been used before. If someone did that, I would become as weak as any other man."

¹²So Delilah took some new ropes and tied up Samson. Some men were hiding in the next room. Then Delilah called out to him, "Samson, the Philistine men are going to capture you!" But he broke the ropes easily as if they were threads.

¹³Then Delilah said to Samson, "You lied to me again. You made me look foolish. Now, tell me how someone could tie you up."

Samson said, "If you use the loom to weave the seven braids of hair on my head and tighten it with a pin, I will become as weak as any other man."

¹⁴Later, Samson went to sleep, so Delilah used the loom to weave the seven braids of hair on his head.*ᶜ* Then Delilah fastened the loom to the ground with a tent peg. Again she called out to him, "Samson, the Philistine men are going to capture you!" Samson pulled up the tent peg, the loom and the shuttle.*ᵈ*

¹⁵Then Delilah said to Samson, "How can you say, 'I love you,' when you don't even trust me? You refuse to tell me your secret. This is the third time you made me look foolish. You haven't told me the secret of your great strength." ¹⁶She kept bothering Samson day after day. He got so tired of her asking him about his secret that he felt as if he was going to die. ¹⁷Finally, Samson told Delilah everything. He said, "I have never had my hair cut. I was dedicated to God before I was born. If someone shaved my head, I would lose my strength. I would become as weak as any other man."

¹⁸Delilah saw that Samson had told her his secret. She sent a message to the rulers of the Philistines. She said, "Come back again. Samson has told me everything." So the rulers of the Philistines came back and brought the money that they had promised to give her.

¹⁹Delilah got Samson to go to sleep with his head lying in her lap. Then she called in a man to shave off the seven braids of Samson's hair. In this way she made Samson weak, and his strength left him. ²⁰Then Delilah called out to him, "Samson, the Philistine men are going to capture you!" He woke up and thought, "I will escape as I did before and free myself." But Samson did not know that the LORD had left him.

²¹The Philistine men captured Samson. They tore out his eyes and took him down to the city of Gaza. Then they put chains on him to keep him from running away. They put him in prison and made him work grinding grain. ²²But his hair began to grow again.

²³The Philistine rulers came together to celebrate. They were going to offer a great sacrifice to their god Dagon. They said, "Our god helped us defeat Samson our enemy." ²⁴When the Philistines saw Samson, they praised their god. They said,

"This man ruined our land
   and killed many of our people!
But our god helped us,
   and we defeated our enemy!"

²⁵The people were having a good time at the celebration. So they said, "Bring Samson out. We

---

ᵃ **16:5** *1,100 pieces* Literally, "1,100 *shekels*".
ᵇ **16:7** *fresh, new bowstrings* Bowstrings were often made from sinew (tendons) which is brittle after it becomes old and dry.
ᶜ **16:14** *so Delilah . . . head* This is found in the ancient Greek version but not in the standard Hebrew text.
ᵈ **16:14** *shuttle* The tool used to pull the threads back and forth on a loom to make cloth.

want to make fun of him." So they brought Samson from the prison and made fun of him. They made him stand between the columns in the temple of the god Dagon. 26A servant was holding his hand. Samson said to him, "Put me where I can feel the columns that hold this temple up. I want to lean against them."

27The temple was crowded with men and women. All the Philistine rulers were there. There were about 3,000 men and women on the roof of the temple. They were laughing and making fun of Samson. 28Then Samson said a prayer to the LORD, "Lord GOD, remember me. God, please give me strength one more time. Let me do this one thing to punish these Philistines for tearing out both of my eyes!" 29Then Samson took hold of the two columns in the centre of the temple that supported the whole temple. He braced himself between the two columns. One column was at his right side and the other at his left side. 30Samson said, "Let me die with these Philistines!" Then he pushed as hard as he could, and the temple fell on the rulers and everyone in it. In this way Samson killed many more Philistines when he died than when he was alive.

31Samson's brothers and all the people in his father's family went down to get his body. They brought him back and buried him in his father's tomb, which is between the cities of Zorah and Eshtaol. Samson was a judge for the Israelites for 20 years.

Micah's Idols

17 There was a man named Micah who lived in the hill country of Ephraim. 2Micah said to his mother, "Do you remember that someone stole 1,100 pieces*a* of silver from you? I heard you say a curse about that. Well, I have the silver. I took it."

His mother said, "The LORD bless you, my son."

3Micah gave the 1,100 pieces of silver back to his mother. Then she said, "I will give this silver as a special gift to the LORD. I will give it to my son so that he can make a statue and cover it with the silver. So now, son, I give the silver back to you."

4But Micah gave the silver back to his mother. So she took about 200 pieces*b* of the silver and gave them to a silversmith.*c* He used the silver to make a statue covered with silver. The statue was put in Micah's house. 5Micah had a temple for worshipping idols. He made an ephod and some house idols. Then Micah chose one of his sons to be his priest. 6(At that time the Israelites did not

have a king, so everyone did what they thought was right.)

7There was a young man who was a Levite from the city of Bethlehem in Judah. He had been living among the tribe of Judah. 8He left Bethlehem to look for another place to live. As he was travelling, he came to Micah's house in the hill country of the land of Ephraim. 9Micah asked him, "Where have you come from?"

The young man answered, "I am a Levite from the city of Bethlehem in Judah. I am looking for a place to live."

10Then Micah said to him, "Live with me. Be my father and my priest. I will give you ten pieces*d* of silver each year. I will also give you clothes and food."

The Levite did what Micah asked. 11The young Levite agreed to live with Micah. He became like one of Micah's own sons. 12Micah chose him to be his priest. So the young man became a priest and lived in Micah's house. 13And Micah said, "Now I know that the LORD will be good to me. I know this because I have a man from the tribe of Levi to be my priest."

Dan Captures the City of Laish

18 At that time the Israelites did not have a king. And the tribe of Dan was still looking for a place to live. They did not have their own land yet. The other tribes of Israel already had their land, but the tribe of Dan had not taken their land yet.

2So the tribe of Dan sent five soldiers to look for some land. They went to search for a good place to live. These five men were from the cities of Zorah and Eshtaol. They were chosen because they were from all the families of Dan. They were told, "Go, look for some land."

The five men came to the hill country of Ephraim. They came to Micah's house and spent the night there. 3When the five men came close to Micah's house, they heard the voice of the young Levite. They recognized his voice, so they stopped at Micah's house. They asked the young man, "Who brought you to this place? What are you doing? Why are you here?"

4The young man told them what Micah had done for him. "Micah hired me," he said. "I am his priest."

5So they said to him, "Please ask God if our search for a place to live will be successful."

6The priest said to the five men, "Yes. Go in peace. The LORD will lead you on your way."

7So the five men left. They came to the city of Laish and saw that the people of that city lived in

---

a **17:2 *1,100 pieces*** Hebrew, "1,100 *shekels*". Also in verse 3.
b **17:4 *200 pieces*** Literally, "200 *shekels*".
c **17:4 *silversmith*** A person who makes things from silver.
d **17:10 *ten pieces*** Literally, "ten *shekels*."

safety. They were ruled by the people of Sidon. Everything was peaceful and quiet. The people had plenty of everything, and they didn't have any enemies nearby to hurt them. Also they lived a long way from the city of Sidon, and they did not have any agreements with the people of Aram.[a]

[8] The five men went back to the cities of Zorah and Eshtaol. Their relatives asked them, "What did you learn?"

[9] The five men answered, "We have found some land, and it is very good. We should attack them. Don't wait! Let's go and take that land! [10] When you come to that place, you will see that there is plenty of land. There is plenty of everything there. You will also see that the people are not expecting an attack. Surely God has given that land to us."

[11] So 600 men from the tribe of Dan left the cities of Zorah and Eshtaol. They were ready for war. [12] On their way to the city of Laish, they stopped near the city of Kiriath Jearim in the land of Judah. They set up a camp there. That is why the place west of Kiriath Jearim is named Mahaneh Dan[b] to this very day. [13] From there the 600 men travelled on to the hill country of Ephraim. Then they came to Micah's house.

[14] So the five men who had explored the land around Laish spoke. They said to their relatives, "There is an ephod in one of these houses. And there are also household gods, a carved statue and a silver idol. You know what to do." [15] So they stopped at Micah's house, where the young Levite lived. They asked the young man how he was. [16] The 600 men from the tribe of Dan stood at the entrance of the gate. They all had their weapons and were ready for war. [17-18] The five spies went into the house. The priest stood just outside by the gate with the 600 men who were ready for war. The men took the carved idol, the ephod, the household idols and the silver idol. The young Levite priest said, "What are you doing?"

[19] The five men answered, "Be quiet! Don't say a word. Come with us. Be our father and our priest. You must choose. Is it better for you to be a priest for just one man or for a whole tribe of Israelites with many family groups?"

[20] This made the Levite happy. So he took the ephod, the household idols and the idol. He went with the men from the tribe of Dan.

[21] Then the 600 men from the tribe of Dan and the Levite priest turned and left Micah's house. They put their little children, their animals and all their things in front of them.

[22] The men from the tribe of Dan had gone a long way from that place. But the people living near Micah met together. Then they began chasing the men of Dan and caught up with them. [23] The men with Micah were shouting at the men of Dan. The men of Dan turned around and said to Micah, "What's the problem? Why are you shouting?"

[24] Micah answered, "You men from Dan took my idols. I made them for myself. You have also taken my priest. What do I have left now? How can you ask me, 'What's the problem?'"

[25] The men from the tribe of Dan answered, "You had better not argue with us. Some of our men become angry easily. If you shout at us, they will attack you. You and your families will be killed."

[26] Then the men of Dan turned around and went on their way. Micah knew that these men were too strong for him, so he went back home.

[27] So the men of Dan took the idols that Micah had made. They also took the priest who had been with Micah. Then they came to Laish. They attacked the people living in Laish. Those people were at peace. They were not expecting an attack. The men of Dan killed them with their swords and then burned the city. [28] The people living in Laish did not have anyone to rescue them. They lived too far from the city of Sidon for the people there to help. And the people of Laish did not have any agreements with the people of Aram—so they did not help them. The city of Laish was in a valley, which belonged to the town of Beth Rehob. The people from Dan built a new city in that place, and it became their home. [29] The people of Dan gave the city a new name. That city had been called Laish, but they changed the name to Dan. They named the city after their ancestor Dan, one of the sons of Israel.

[30] The people of the tribe of Dan set up the idol in the city of Dan. They made Jonathan son of Gershom their priest. Gershom was the son of Moses.[c] Jonathan and his sons were priests for the tribe of Dan until the time when the Israelites were taken into captivity. [31] The people of Dan set up for themselves the idol that Micah had made. That idol was there the whole time that the house of God was in Shiloh.

A Levite and His Woman Servant

19

At that time the Israelites did not have a king.

There was a Levite who lived far back in the hill country of Ephraim. He had taken as a wife a slave woman. She was from the city of Bethlehem

---

[a] **18:7 they did not have . . . Aram** Or "they did not have any dealings with people".
[b] **18:12 Mahaneh Dan** This name means "The Camp of Dan".
[c] **18:30 Moses** Or "Manasseh".

in the country of Judah. ²But his slave woman had an argument with him. She left him and went back to her father's house in Bethlehem in Judah. She stayed there for four months. ³Then her husband went after her. He wanted to speak kindly to her so that she would come back to him. He took with him his servant and two donkeys. The Levite came to her father's house. Her father saw the Levite and came out to greet him. The father was very happy. ⁴The woman's father led the Levite into his house. The Levite's father-in-law invited him to stay. So he stayed for three days. He ate, drank and slept in his father-in-law's house.

⁵On the fourth day, they got up early in the morning. The Levite was getting ready to leave. But the young woman's father said to his son-in-law, "Eat something first. After you eat, you can go." ⁶So the Levite and his father-in-law sat down to eat and drink together. After that, the young woman's father said to the Levite, "Please stay tonight. Relax and enjoy yourself." So the two men ate together. ⁷The Levite got up to leave, but his father-in-law persuaded him to stay the night again.

⁸Then, on the fifth day, the Levite got up early in the morning. He was ready to leave. But the woman's father said to his son-in-law, "Eat something first. Relax and stay until this afternoon." So they both ate together again.

⁹Then the Levite, his slave woman and his servant got up to leave. But the young woman's father said, "It is almost dark. The day is almost gone. So stay the night here and enjoy yourself. Tomorrow morning you can get up early and go on your way."

¹⁰But the Levite did not want to stay another night. He took his two donkeys and his slave woman. He travelled as far as the city of Jebus (that is, Jerusalem). ¹¹The day was almost over. They were near the city of Jebus. So the servant said to his master, the Levite, "Let's stop at this Jebusite city. Let's stay the night here."

¹²But his master, the Levite man, said, "No, we will not go inside a strange city. Those people are not Israelites. We will go to the city of Gibeah."ᵃ ¹³The Levite said, "Come on. Let's try to make it to Gibeah or Ramah. We can stay the night in one of those cities."

¹⁴So the Levite and those with him travelled on. The sun was going down just as they entered the city of Gibeah. Gibeah is in the area that belongs to the tribe of Benjamin. ¹⁵They planned to stop there and stay the night. They came to the city square and sat down, but no one invited them home to stay the night.

¹⁶That evening an old man came into the city from the fields. His home was in the hill country of Ephraim, but now he was living in the city of Gibeah. (The men of Gibeah were from the tribe of Benjamin.) ¹⁷The old man saw the traveller in the public square and asked, "Where are you going? Where did you come from?"

¹⁸The Levite answered, "We have come from Bethlehem in Judah, where I went for a visit. Now I am on my way home,ᵇ which is a long way into the hill country of Ephraim. I expected that someone here would invite us in for the night, but no one has. ¹⁹We already have straw and food for our donkeys. There is also bread and wine for me, the young woman and my servant. We don't need anything else."

²⁰The old man said, "You are welcome to stay at my house. I will give you anything you need, but don't stay the night in the public square." ²¹Then the old man took the Levite and the people with him to his house. He fed their donkeys. They washed their feet and then had something to eat and drink.

²²While the Levite and those who were with him were enjoying themselves, some very bad men from the city surrounded the house. They began beating on the door. They shouted at the old man who owned the house. They said, "Bring out the man who came to your house. We want to have sex with him."

²³The old man went outside and said to them, "My friends, don't do such an evil thing! This man is a guest in my house.ᶜ Don't commit this terrible sin. ²⁴Look, here is my daughter. She has never had sex before. I will bring her out to you now. This man also has a slave woman. You can use them any way you want, but don't do such a terrible sin against this man."

²⁵But those evil men would not listen to the old man. So the Levite took his slave woman and put her outside with them. They hurt her and raped her all night long. Then, at dawn, they let her go. ²⁶At dawn, the woman came back to the house where her master was staying. She fell down at the front door and lay there until it was daylight.

²⁷The Levite got up early the next morning. He wanted to go home. He opened the door to go outside, and a hand fell across the threshold of the door. There was his slave woman. She had

---

ᵃ **19:12** *Gibeah* Gibeah was a few miles north of Jebus. Jebus was the old name for Jerusalem.
ᵇ **19:18** *home* This is from the ancient Greek version, which has "to my house". The standard Hebrew text has "to the LORD's house".
ᶜ **19:23** *This man . . . my house* At this time, it was a custom that if you invited people to be your guests, you had to protect and care for those people.

fallen down against the door. 28The Levite said to her, "Get up; let's go." But there was no answer.

The Levite put her body on his donkey and went home. 29When he arrived at his house, he took a knife and cut her body into 12 parts. Then he sent the 12 parts of the woman to each of the areas where the Israelites lived. 30Everyone who saw this said, "Nothing like this has ever happened in Israel before. We haven't seen anything like this from the time we came out of Egypt. Discuss this and tell us what to do."

The War Between Israel and Benjamin

20 So all the Israelites joined together. They all came together to stand before the LORD in the city of Mizpah. People came from everywhere in Israel.*ᵃ* Even the Israelites from Gilead*ᵇ* were there. 2The leaders of all the tribes of Israel were there. They took their places in the public meeting of God's people. There were 400,000 soldiers with swords in that place. 3The people from the tribe of Benjamin heard that the Israelites were meeting together in Mizpah. The Israelites said, "Tell us how this terrible thing happened."

4So the Levite, the husband of the woman who had been murdered, told them the story. He said, "My slave woman and I came to the city of Gibeah in the area of Benjamin. We spent the night there. 5But during the night the men of the city of Gibeah came to the house where I was staying. They surrounded the house, and they wanted to kill me. They raped my slave woman, and she died. 6So I took her and cut her into pieces. Then I sent one piece to each of the tribes of Israel. I sent the 12 pieces to the lands we have received. I did that because the people of Benjamin have done this terrible thing in Israel. 7Now, all you men of Israel, speak up. Give your decision about what we should do."

8Then all the people stood up at the same time. They said together, "None of us will go home. No, not one of us will go back to his house. 9Now this is what we will do to the city of Gibeah. We will throw lots to let God show us who will lead the attack. 10In this way we will choose men from every tribe of Israel—ten men from every hundred, a hundred men from every thousand and a thousand men from every ten thousand. These men will get supplies for the army. Then the army will go to the Benjamite city of Gibeah and punish those people for the terrible thing they did among the Israelites."

11So all the men of Israel gathered together at the city of Gibeah, united together and in agreement about what should happen. 12They sent men to the tribe of Benjamin with this message: "What about this terrible thing that some of your men have done? 13Send the bad men from the city of Gibeah to us so that we can put them to death. We must remove the evil from among the Israelites."

But the people from the tribe of Benjamin would not listen to the messengers from their relatives, the other Israelites. 14The people from the tribe of Benjamin left their cities and went to the city of Gibeah. They went to Gibeah to fight against the other tribes of Israel. 15The people from the tribe of Benjamin got 26,000 soldiers together who were trained for war. They also had 700 trained soldiers from the city of Gibeah. 16There were also 700 trained soldiers who were trained to fight with their left hand.*ᶜ* Each one of them could use a sling with great skill. They all could use a sling to throw a stone at a hair and not miss!

17All the tribes of Israel, except Benjamin, gathered together 400,000 fighting men with swords. Each one was a trained soldier. 18The Israelites went up to the city of Bethel. At Bethel they asked God, "Which tribe will be first to attack the tribe of Benjamin?"

The LORD answered, "The tribe of Judah will go first."

19The next morning the Israelites got up. They made a camp near the city of Gibeah. 20Then the army of Israel took their positions for battle against the army of Benjamin at the city of Gibeah. 21Then the army of Benjamin came out of the city of Gibeah. The army of Benjamin killed 22,000 men in the army of Israel during the battle that day.

22-23The Israelites went to the LORD and cried until evening. They asked the LORD, "Should we go to fight the people of Benjamin again? They are our relatives."

The LORD answered, "Go and fight against them." The men of Israel encouraged each other. So they again went out to fight, as they had done the first day.

24Then the army of Israel came near the army of Benjamin. This was the second day of the war. 25The army of Benjamin came out of the city of Gibeah to attack the army of Israel on the second day. This time, the army of Benjamin killed another 18,000 men from the army of Israel. All the men in the army of Israel were trained soldiers.

26Then all the Israelites went up to the city of Bethel. There they sat down and cried to the LORD. They did not eat anything all day, until

---

ᵃ **20:1** *from everywhere in Israel* Literally, "from Dan to Beersheba".
ᵇ **20:1** *Gilead* This area was east of the Jordan River.
ᶜ **20:16** *trained . . . left hand* Literally, "restrained in their right hand".

evening. They also offered burnt offerings and fellowship offerings to the LORD. [27]The men of Israel asked the LORD a question. (In those days God's Box of the Agreement was there at Bethel. [28]Phinehas was the priest who served God there. Phinehas was the son of Eleazar. Eleazar was the son of Aaron.) The Israelites asked, "The people of Benjamin are our relatives. Should we again go to fight against them? Or should we stop fighting?"

The LORD answered, "Go. Tomorrow I will help you defeat them."

[29]Then the army of Israel hid some men all around the city of Gibeah. [30]The army of Israel went to fight against the city of Gibeah on the third day. They got ready for battle as they had done before. [31]The army of Benjamin came out of the city of Gibeah to fight the army of Israel. The army of Israel backed up and let the army of Benjamin chase them. In this way the army of Benjamin was tricked into leaving the city far behind them.

The army of Benjamin began to kill some of the men in the army of Israel, as they had done before. They killed about 30 men from Israel. They killed some of them in the fields, and they killed some of them on the roads. One road led to the city of Bethel. The other road led to the city of Gibeah. [32]The men of Benjamin said, "We are winning as before!"

The men of Israel were running away, but it was a trick. They wanted to lead the men of Benjamin away from their city and onto the roads. [33]So all the men ran away. They stopped at a place named Baal Tamar. Some of the men of Israel were hiding west of Gibeah. They ran from their hiding places. [34]10,000 of Israel's best-trained soldiers attacked the city of Gibeah. The fighting was very heavy. But the army of Benjamin did not know that a terrible thing was about to happen to them.

[35]The LORD used the army of Israel and defeated the army of Benjamin. On that day, the army of Israel killed 25,100 soldiers from Benjamin. All of them had been trained for war. [36]So the people of Benjamin saw that they were defeated.

The army of Israel had moved back because they were depending on the surprise attack. They had men hiding near Gibeah. [37]The men who were hiding rushed into the city of Gibeah. They spread out and killed everyone in the city with their swords. [38]Now the men of Israel had made a plan with the men who were hiding. The men who were hiding were supposed to send a special signal. They were supposed to make a big cloud of smoke. [39-41]The army of Benjamin had killed about 30 Israelite soldiers. So the men of Benjamin were

saying, "We are winning, as before." But then a big cloud of smoke began to rise from the city. The men of Benjamin turned around and saw the smoke. The whole city was on fire. Then the army of Israel stopped running away. They turned around and began to fight. The men of Benjamin were afraid because they knew that a terrible thing had happened to them.

[42]So the army of Benjamin ran away from the army of Israel. They ran towards the desert. But they could not escape the fighting. And the men of Israel came out of the cities and killed them. [43]The men of Israel surrounded the men of Benjamin and began chasing them. They did not let them rest. They defeated them in the area east of Gibeah. [44]So 18,000 brave and strong fighters from the army of Benjamin were killed.

[45]The army of Benjamin turned around and ran towards the desert. They ran to a place called the Rock of Rimmon, but the army of Israel killed 5,000 soldiers from Benjamin along the roads. They kept chasing the men of Benjamin. They chased them as far as a place named Gidom. The army of Israel killed 2,000 more men from Benjamin in that place.

[46]On that day, 25,000 men of the army of Benjamin were killed. They all fought bravely with their swords. [47]But 600 men from Benjamin ran into the desert to the place called the Rock of Rimmon and stayed there for four months. [48]The men of Israel went back to the land of Benjamin. They killed the people and all the animals in every city. They destroyed everything they could find and burned every city they came to.

Getting Wives for the Men of Benjamin

21 At Mizpah, the men of Israel made a promise. This was their promise: "Not one of us will let his daughter marry a man from the tribe of Benjamin."

[2]The Israelites went to the city of Bethel. There they sat before God until evening. They cried loudly as they sat there. [3]They said to God, "LORD, you are the God of the Israelites. Why has this terrible thing happened to us? Why has one tribe of the Israelites been taken away?"

[4]Early the next day, the Israelites built an altar. They put burnt offerings and fellowship offerings to God on that altar. [5]Then the Israelites said, "Are there any tribes of Israel who did not come here to meet with us before the LORD?" They asked this question because they had vowed that anyone who did not come together with the other tribes at the city of Mizpah would be killed.

[6]Then the Israelites felt sorry for their relatives, the people of Benjamin. They said, "Today, one tribe has been separated from Israel. [7]We made a promise with an oath before the LORD. We

promised not to allow our daughters to marry a man from Benjamin. How can we make sure that the men of Benjamin will have wives?"

⁸Then the Israelites asked, "Which one of the tribes of Israel did not come here to Mizpah? We have come together before the LORD. Surely one family was not here!" Then they found that no one from the city of Jabesh Gilead had met together with the other Israelites. ⁹The Israelites counted everyone to see who was there and who was not. They found that no one from Jabesh Gilead was there. ¹⁰So the Israelites sent 12,000 soldiers to the city of Jabesh Gilead. They told the soldiers, "Go to Jabesh Gilead, and use your swords to kill everyone who lives there, even the women and children. ¹¹You must do this! You must kill every man in Jabesh Gilead and every woman who has had sex with a man. But do not kill any woman who has never had sex with a man." So the soldiers did these things.ᵃ ¹²The 12,000 soldiers found 400 young women in the city of Jabesh Gilead who had never had sex with a man. They brought these women to the camp at Shiloh in the land of Canaan.

¹³Then the Israelites sent a message to the men of Benjamin. They offered to make peace with the men of Benjamin. The men of Benjamin were at the place named the Rock of Rimmon. ¹⁴So the men of Benjamin came back to Israel. The Israelites gave them the women from Jabesh Gilead who they had not killed. But there were not enough women for all the men of Benjamin.

¹⁵The Israelites felt sorry for the men of Benjamin. They felt sorry for them because the LORD had separated them from the other tribes of Israel. ¹⁶The leaders of the Israelites said, "The women of the tribe of Benjamin have been killed. Where can we get wives for the men of Benjamin who are still alive? ¹⁷The men of Benjamin who are still alive must have children to continue their families. This must be done so that a tribe in Israel will not die out! ¹⁸But we cannot allow our daughters to marry the men of Benjamin. We have made this promise: Bad things will happen to anyone who gives a wife to a man of Benjamin.

¹⁹We have an idea! This is the time for the festival of the LORD at the city of Shiloh. This festival is celebrated every year there." (The city of Shiloh is north of the city of Bethel and east of the road that goes from Bethel to Shechem. And it is also to the south of the city of Lebonah.)

²⁰So the leaders told the men of Benjamin about their idea. They said, "Go and hide in the vineyards. ²¹Watch for the time during the festival when the young women from Shiloh come out to join the dancing. Then run out from where you are hiding in the vineyards. Each of you should take one of the young women from the city of Shiloh. Take them to the land of Benjamin and marry them. ²²The fathers or brothers of the young women will come and complain to us. But we will say, 'Be kind to the men of Benjamin. Let them marry the women. We could not get wives for each of them during the war. And you did not willingly give the women to the men of Benjamin, so you did not break your promise.'"

INSIGHT

As a way of preserving their family lineage, the children of Israel literally ambushed their own cousins while they were dancing and then carried them off to be their wives.

Judges 21:20–23

---

²³So that is what the men of the tribe of Benjamin did. While the young women were dancing, each man caught one of them. They took them away and married them. Then they went back to their land. The men of Benjamin built cities again in that land, and they lived in them. ²⁴Then the Israelites went home. They went to their own land and tribe.

²⁵In those days the Israelites did not have a king, so everyone did whatever they thought was right.

ᵃ **21:11** *But do not kill . . . these things* This is from the ancient Greek version.

Who This is the story of Ruth, great-grandmother of King David. The author is unknown, though some experts believe that it could have been written by the prophet Samuel, along with Judges.

When Set in the time of the Judges, during a period of peace between Israel and Moab. As the book records an incident in the history of the family of David, it is likely that it was written during the time of the monarchy – sometime between 950 and 700 BC.

What Ruth is a story about family duty, affection and friendship. In the story the three main characters Ruth, Naomi and Boaz show a loyalty and commitment that go beyond the boundaries of duty or legal obligation. Ruth sticks with Naomi; Naomi looks after Ruth; Boaz is kind to both women.

Importantly, the person who most embodies selfless love in this book is not an Israelite, but "Ruth, the Moabite woman" – a woman from Moab, a despised and hated enemy of Israel. Ruth shows that participation in the kingdom of God is nothing to do with nationality, but a matter of loving God and following his commands.

In particular, Ruth is about redemption. Redemption means paying a price to save someone from evil. This is an important theme in the Bible because it describes what God does for all humans through Jesus. Through the death of Jesus we have been bought back, "redeemed", from our slavery to sin. Through the selfless love of Ruth and Boaz, Naomi is redeemed. She is given a grandson, and through that, a future. She is bought back from hunger and homelessness to security and contentment.

The other hero of this story is Boaz, who protects Ruth, provides for her and eventually marries her. Boaz buys back the family property. He is described by Naomi as "one of our relatives . . . one of our protectors" (2:20). He is their "redeemer", someone who rescues his relatives.

Indeed, the marriage of Ruth and Boaz leads to King David and then, eventually, to Jesus. So this story of redemption leads ultimately to the great redeemer himself. Indeed, Ruth is so honoured that she, a foreign woman, is mentioned in the family tree of Christ (Matthew 1:2–16).

QUICK TOUR ▶ RUTH

Naomi and Ruth go to Bethlehem 1:1–22
Ruth meets Boaz 2:1–23

Naomi's plan 3:1–18
Ruth and Boaz are married 4:1–22

"But Ruth said, 'Don't force me to leave you! Don't force me to go back to my own people. Let me go with you. Wherever you go, I will go. Wherever you sleep, I will sleep. Your people will be my people. Your God will be my God.'"

Ruth 1:16

Famine in Judah

1 Long ago, during the time the judges ruled, there was a famine in the land, and a man named Elimelech left the town of Bethlehem in Judah. He, his wife and his two sons moved to the country of Moab. ²The man's wife was named Naomi, and his two sons were named Mahlon and Kilion. They belonged to the family of Ephrathah from Bethlehem, but they went to Moab to live for a while.

³Later, Naomi's husband, Elimelech, died, so only Naomi and her two sons were left. ⁴Her sons married women from the country of Moab. One wife's name was Orpah, and the other wife's name was Ruth. They lived in Moab about ten years; ⁵then Mahlon and Kilion also died. So Naomi was left alone without her husband or her two sons.

Naomi Goes Home

⁶While Naomi was in the country of Moab, she heard that the Lord had helped his people by giving them food. So she decided to leave the hill country of Moab and go back home. Her daughters-in-law decided to go with her. ⁷They left the place where they had been living and started walking back to the land of Judah.

⁸Then Naomi told her daughters-in-law, "Each of you should go back home to your mother. You have been very kind to me and my sons who are now dead. So I pray that the Lord will be just as kind to you. ⁹I pray that the Lord will help each of you find a husband and a good home." Naomi kissed her daughters-in-law, and they all started crying.

¹⁰Then the daughters said, "But we want to come with you and go to your family."

¹¹But Naomi said, "No, daughters, go back to your own homes. Why should you go with me? I can't have any more sons to be your husbands. ¹²Go back home. I am too old to have a new husband. Even if I thought I could be married again, I could not help you. If I became pregnant tonight and had two sons, ¹³you would have to wait until they grew to become men before you could marry them. I cannot make you wait that long for husbands. That would make me very sad. And I am already sad enough—the Lord has done many things to me!"

¹⁴So again they cried very much. Then Orpah kissed Naomi goodbye, but Ruth hugged her and stayed.

¹⁵Naomi said, "Look, your sister-in-law has gone back to her own people and her own gods. You should do the same."

¹⁶But Ruth said, "Don't force me to leave you! Don't force me to go back to my own people. Let me go with you. Wherever you go, I will go. Wherever you sleep, I will sleep. Your people will be my people. Your God will be my God. ¹⁷Where you die, I will die, and that is where I will be buried. I ask the Lord to punish me if I don't keep this promise: Only death will separate us."[a]

INSIGHT

Ruth volunteered to leave everything and everyone she knew to follow her mother-in-law to her home country. This was before the days of easy transport or communication, so she was really saying goodbye to her friends and family forever.

Ruth 1:16–17

The Homecoming

¹⁸Naomi saw that Ruth wanted very much to go with her. So Naomi stopped arguing with her. ¹⁹Naomi and Ruth travelled until they came to the town of Bethlehem. When the two women entered Bethlehem, all the people were very excited. They said, "Is this Naomi?"

²⁰But Naomi told the people, "Don't call me Naomi;[b] call me Marah.[c] Use this name because God All-Powerful has made my life very sad. ²¹I had everything I wanted when I left, but now, the Lord brings me home with nothing. The Lord has made me sad, so why should you call me 'Happy'?[d] God All-Powerful has given much trouble to me."

²²So Naomi and her daughter-in-law Ruth, the Moabite, came back from the hill country of Moab. These two women came to Bethlehem at the beginning of the barley harvest.

Ruth Meets Boaz

2 There was a rich man named Boaz living in Bethlehem. Boaz was one of Naomi's close relatives[e] from Elimelech's family.

---

a 1:17 *I ask . . . separate us* Literally, "May the Lord do this to me, and even more, unless death separates us!"
b 1:20 *Naomi* This name means "Happy" or "Pleasant".
c 1:20 *Marah* This name means "Bitter" or "Sad".
d 1:21 *Happy* This is the meaning of the name Naomi.
e 2:1 *close relatives* If a man died without children, one of his close relatives would take the dead man's wife so that she could have children. He would care for this family, but this family and their property would not belong to him. They would all be in the dead man's name.

NAOMI'S PAIN AND RUTH'S REWARD

Are you sometimes tempted to think that God is not involved in all of your life, both in the good and the bad? Here is a story that illustrates how God works everything for good – nothing happens that is beyond his control.

DIG IN   READ Ruth 1:1–16

- List all the sad things that had happened to Naomi.
- Why does she tell Ruth and Orpah to turn back?
- What is Ruth's response?

This story only makes sense when we remember that God had told his people not to move to foreign lands like Moab and not to marry foreigners. This isn't racist anti-Jewishness; God didn't want his people to start worshipping the gods of the non-Israelites. Elimelech and Naomi disobeyed God by leaving Judah, moving to Moab and allowing their sons to marry Moabite women.

Can you imagine how devastating the events described in verses 3–5 are for Naomi? Yet as she returns home to die, one of her daughters-in-law, who seems to have come to know God, promises to stick with her.

READ Ruth 1:17–22

- How do you feel about what Naomi says about God in verses 20 and 21?

Naomi means "blessed"; Marah means "bitter". That's how awful Naomi feels – she wants a new name! Naomi's views of God, as uncomfortable as they might be, are spot on. He is all-powerful and nothing that happens to her is out of his control. Therefore, he has allowed all these bad things to happen. But what Naomi doesn't see is that things are going to work out for good: God is at work in her pain and misery, working out a plan in incredible ways. You'll have to keep reading to see this happen.

READ Ruth 2:1–23

- What do verses 1–7 show about Ruth's character?
- What is significant about Boaz (v.1)?
- How does Boaz treat Ruth?

Do you remember how, in chapter 1, Naomi urges Ruth to go back to Moab because there is no one left for her to marry in Naomi's family? How wrong Naomi is ... Hardworking, humble Ruth just "happened" (did you notice that word in verse 3?) to come into the field belonging to Boaz, who is a relative of Naomi's husband (and therefore of Naomi). In those days relatives had a responsibility to marry widows to keep the family name going – check out Deuteronomy 25:5–10. The writer of Ruth may have used the word "happened", but with God nothing just "happens" ...

- Why does Boaz say he is treating her kindly (v.12)?

Boaz's kindness and generosity shock Ruth – she doesn't deserve any of this! After all, she's a foreigner; she doesn't belong with the Lord's people. But Boaz knows of all the good things she has done because of her faith. Humbly, Ruth left the gods she would have been taught about at home in Moab and went to the Lord God looking for safety and protection in him. She believed and trusted the God of these people and her faith was rewarded.

DIG THROUGH

- Read Romans 8:28. As the rest of the story unfolds we will see that all Naomi's pain is turned into something beautiful. Ask God to help you see that this can be true for you too.
- Finding refuge in God means trusting him above everything else in our lives. How do you think Ruth felt when she first learnt to trust God, despite all the stuff going wrong in her life? Read Psalm 91 and ask God to help you take refuge in him, maybe for the first time, or specifically for something tough you are facing.

[2]One day Ruth, the Moabite, said to Naomi, "I think I will go to the fields. Maybe I can find someone who will be kind to me and let me gather the grain they leave in their field."

Naomi said, "Fine, daughter, go ahead."

[3]So Ruth went to the fields. She followed the workers who were cutting the grain and gathered the grain that was left.[a] It happened that part of the field belonged to Boaz, the man from Elimelech's family.

[4]Later, Boaz came to the field from Bethlehem and greeted his workers. He said, "The LORD be with you!"

And the workers answered, "And may the LORD bless you!"

[5]Then Boaz spoke to his servant who was in charge of the workers. He asked, "Whose girl is that?"

[6]The servant answered, "She is the Moabite woman who came with Naomi from the country of Moab. [7]She came early this morning and asked me if she could follow the workers and gather the grain that was left on the ground. And she has been working ever since. She rested only a short time in that shelter."[b]

[8]Then Boaz said to Ruth, "Listen, child. Stay here in my field to gather grain for yourself. There is no need for you to go to any other field. Continue following behind my women workers. [9]Watch to see which fields they go into to cut the grain and follow them. I have warned the young men not to bother you. When you are thirsty, go and drink from the same water jug my men drink from."

[10]Then Ruth bowed very low to the ground. She said to Boaz, "I am a foreigner, so I am surprised you even noticed me."

[11]Boaz answered her, "I know about all the help you have given to your mother-in-law Naomi. I know you helped her even after your husband died. And I know that you left your father and mother and your own country and came here to this country. You did not know anyone from this country, but you came here with Naomi. [12]The LORD will reward you for all the good things you have done. The LORD, the God of Israel, will pay you in full. You have come to him for safety,[c] and he will protect you."

[13]Then Ruth said, "I hope I can continue to please you, sir. You are very kind. I am only a servant and not even one of your own servants.

But you have said kind words to me and comforted me."

[14]At mealtime, Boaz told Ruth, "Come and eat some of our bread. Here, dip your bread in our vinegar."

So Ruth sat down with the workers. Boaz gave her some roasted grain. Ruth ate until she was full, and there was some food left. [15]Then Ruth got up and went back to work.

Then Boaz told his servants, "Let Ruth gather even around the piles of grain. Don't stop her. [16]And make her work easier by dropping some full heads of grain for her. Let her gather that grain. Don't tell her to stop."

Naomi Hears About Boaz

[17]Ruth worked in the fields until evening. Then she separated the grain from the chaff. There was about 10 kilogrammes[d] of barley. [18]Ruth carried the grain into town to show her mother-in-law what she had gathered. She also gave her the food that was left from lunch.

[19]Her mother-in-law asked her, "Where did you gather all this grain? Where did you work? Bless the man who noticed you."

Then Ruth told her about the man she had worked with. She said, "The man I worked with today is named Boaz."

[20]Naomi told her daughter-in-law, "The LORD bless him! He has continued showing his kindness to the living as well as the dead." Then Naomi told her daughter-in-law, "Boaz is one of our relatives. He is one of our protectors."[e]

[21]Then Ruth said, "Boaz also told me to come back and continue working. He said that I should work closely with his servants until the harvest is finished."

[22]Then Naomi said to her daughter-in-law Ruth, "It is good for you to continue working with his women servants. If you work in another field, some man might hurt you." [23]So Ruth continued working closely with the women servants of Boaz. She gathered grain until the barley harvest was finished. She also worked there until the end of the wheat harvest. Ruth continued living with her mother-in-law Naomi.

The Threshing Floor

3 Then Naomi, Ruth's mother-in-law, said to her, "My daughter, maybe I should find a husband and a good home for you. That would be good for

---

[a] **2:3** There was a law that a farmer must leave some grain in his field during harvest, so poor people and travellers could find something to eat. See Lev. 19:9; 23:22.
[b] **2:7 She . . . shelter** Or "That is her house over there."
[c] **2:12 You have . . . for safety** Literally, "You have come under his wings for safety."
[d] **2:17 10 kilogrammes** Literally, "one *ephah*".
[e] **2:20 protectors** Or "redeemers", those who cared for and protected the family of a dead relative. Often they bought back (redeemed) the poor relatives from slavery, making them free again.

GOD'S PLAN

Ah, Boaz – rich, eligible, loves God and very, very kind – what a great lead character for a romantic film!

DIG IN

READ Ruth 3:1–18

- What's Naomi's plan for Ruth?
- What is Boaz's response to Ruth?
- What is Boaz going to do for Ruth?

Phew, Boaz is a man who loves God and treats Ruth honourably – but can you feel the tension? Love is most definitely in the air but it's not a done deal. This is where it gets a bit complicated. As Boaz says, Ruth could have had anyone, someone closer to her age, perhaps, but she considers other things a higher priority. One of God's laws was that a family member of a dead man should be given his wife and children so that the name and any land remains in the family. This is where Boaz comes in, although there's someone more closely related than him. And clearly Ruth likes Boaz or Naomi wouldn't have told her to be patient. Oh, the drama!

We're on the edge of our seats. Will Ruth get the man she loves? Will Naomi be happy again? How will God work all of this out?

READ Ruth 4:1–12

- Here we see how land and family were so closely tied together in Old Testament times. Can you see why (v.10)?
- Who gets the land and the girl in the end?

And everyone rejoices! The closer relative did not want the land and so he allowed Boaz to have it – which meant marrying Ruth. This all might seem weird to us, but the rules were there to protect women and to ensure that the land God had given the people was fairly apportioned.

READ Ruth 4:13–22

- Do you remember Naomi's sadness in chapter 1? How does her story end?
- What's so great about what we learn in verse 22? (Check out Matthew 1:1–16.)

At the beginning of the book, Naomi had no grandchildren and her husband and both her sons were dead. Worried that Ruth would not re-marry she urged her to return to Moab. Yet by the close of the book, Naomi is blessed by God in a way that she could never have imagined. Ruth was to become the great-grandmother of David and it is from the line of David that Jesus was born! Naomi is related to the Saviour of the world!

DIG THROUGH

- What's more important to you when you think about relationships – doing what God wants or being with whoever you want? Ask God to help you have his priorities.
- Throughout this story God is working his purposes out – even to sorting out who Ruth will marry. Trust him for your future too.
- Think back over the story of Ruth (or re-read it) and how all the little details fell into place in just the right way so that Ruth and Boaz could marry, have a child and be part of the family tree of Jesus.

you. ²Boaz is our close relative.*ᵃ* You worked with his women servants. Tonight he will be working at the threshing floor. ³Go and wash yourself and get dressed. Put on a nice dress, and go down to the threshing floor. But don't let Boaz see you until he has finished eating his dinner. ⁴After he eats, he will lie down to rest. Watch him so that you will know where he lies down. Go there and lift the cover off his feet.*ᵇ* Then lie down there with Boaz. He will tell you what to do next."

⁵Then Ruth answered, "I will do what you say."

⁶So Ruth went down to the threshing floor and did everything that her mother-in-law told her to do. ⁷After eating and drinking, Boaz was very satisfied. He went to lie down near the pile of grain. Then Ruth went to him very quietly and lifted the cover from his feet and lay down by his feet.

⁸About midnight, Boaz rolled over in his sleep and woke up. He was very surprised to see a woman lying near his feet. ⁹Boaz said, "Who are you?"

She said, "I am Ruth, your servant girl. You are our family's protector. So spread your cover over me."*ᶜ*

¹⁰Then Boaz said, "May the Lᴏʀᴅ bless you, young woman. You have been very kind to me. Your kindness to me is even greater than the kindness you showed to Naomi in the beginning. You could have looked for a young man to marry, rich or poor. But you did not. ¹¹Now, young woman, don't be afraid. I will do what you ask. All the people in our town know that you are a very good woman. ¹²And it is true that I am a close relative. But there is a man who is a closer relative to you than I am. ¹³Stay here tonight. In the morning we will see if he will help*ᵈ* you. If he decides to help you, that is fine. If he refuses to help, I promise, as surely as the Lᴏʀᴅ lives, I will marry you and buy back Elimelech's land for you.*ᵉ* So lie here until morning."

¹⁴So Ruth lay near Boaz's feet until morning. She got up while it was still dark, before it was light enough for people to recognize each other.

Boaz said to her, "We will keep it a secret that you came here to me last night." ¹⁵Then he said, "Bring that cloak you are wearing and hold it out."

So Ruth held it out, and Boaz poured six measures of barley into it. He lifted it up for her to carry. Then he returned to the city.

¹⁶When Ruth came back to her mother-in-law's house, Naomi asked her what had happened.

Ruth told Naomi everything Boaz had done for her. ¹⁷She said, "Boaz gave me this barley and said, 'You must not go home without taking this as a gift for your mother-in-law.'"

¹⁸Naomi said, "My daughter, be patient until we see what happens next. Boaz will not rest until he has done all that he should do. We will know something before the end of the day."

Boaz and Naomi's Close Relative

4 Boaz went to the place where people gather near the city gates. He sat there until the close relative he had told Ruth about passed by. Boaz called to him, "Come and sit here, friend."

²Boaz also gathered ten of the leaders of the city. He told them, "Sit here!" So they sat down.

³Then Boaz spoke to Naomi's close relative. He said, "Naomi came back from the hill country of Moab. She wants to sell the land that belonged to our relative Elimelech. ⁴I decided to tell you about this in front of the leaders living here and in front of the leaders of our people. If you want to pay the widow for the land and keep it in the family, then pay her for it. If you don't want to buy the land, tell me, because I am the next one in the family who has the right to buy it. If you don't buy the land from her, I will."

Naomi's closest relative said, "I will buy the land from her."

⁵Then Boaz said, "If you buy the land from her, you must also marry the dead man's wife, Ruth, the Moabite woman. Then the first child will get the land, and it will stay in the dead man's family."

⁶The close relative answered, "Then I cannot buy the land. If I do, I might lose my own land. So I cannot do it. You buy the land." ⁷Then he gave Boaz something to show that he was serious. During that time in Israel, when people bought property, one person took off a sandal and gave it to the other person. This was like signing an agreement. ⁸So when the close relative said to Boaz, "You buy the land," he took off his sandal and gave it to Boaz.*ᶠ*

ᵃ **3:2 *close relative*** A close relative who could marry Ruth so that she could have children. This man would care for this family, but this family and their property would not belong to him. They would belong to Ruth's dead husband. Also in 3:9,12; 4:1,3,6.
ᵇ **3:4 *lift the cover off his feet*** Literally, "uncover his legs". This was a way of asking Boaz to be her husband and protector.
ᶜ **3:9 *spread your cover over me*** Or "spread your wing over me". With these words Ruth was asking Boaz to be her husband and protector. See Ruth 2:12.
ᵈ **3:13 *help*** Or "redeem". This meant the close relative would care for and protect the dead man's family and property, but that property would not be his.
ᵉ **3:13 *I will marry . . . you*** Literally, "I will redeem you".
ᶠ **4:8 *and gave it to Boaz*** This is from the ancient Greek version.

INSIGHT

"Setting foot" on land has long been used to describe taking possession and dominion over property. This could be why in ancient Israel the giving of a sandal was used to mark the transfer in ownership of land.

Ruth 4:8

⁹Then Boaz said to the leaders and all the people, "You are witnesses today that I am buying from Naomi everything that belonged to Elimelech, Kilion and Mahlon. ¹⁰I also take Ruth to be my wife. Then the dead man's property will continue to belong to his family. And he will always be remembered by his family and the people in his home town. You are all witnesses of what I am doing today."

¹¹So all the leaders and the people who were near the city gates said, "We are witnesses to this. And may the LORD bless this woman who is coming into your home to be like Rachel and Leah. They are the ones who had many children to make the people of Israel strong. And may you become powerful in the family of Ephrathah and famous in Bethlehem! ¹²May the LORD bless you with many children through Ruth. May your family become great like the family of Perez,ᵃ the son Tamar bore for Judah."

¹³So Boaz married Ruth. The LORD allowed Ruth to become pregnant, and she had a son. ¹⁴The women there said to Naomi, "Praise the LORD who gave you this child.ᵇ May he become famous in Israel. ¹⁵He will make you alive again and care for you in your old age. Your daughter-in-law made it happen because she bore this child for you. She loves you, and she is better for you than seven sons."

¹⁶Naomi took the boy, held him in her arms, and cared for him. ¹⁷The neighbours gave the boy his name. These women said, "Naomi has a son now!"ᶜ They named him Obed. Obed was the father of Jesse, and Jesse was the father of David.

The Family of Ruth and Boaz

¹⁸This is the family history of Perez:

Perez was the father of Hezron.
¹⁹Hezron was the father of Ram.
Ram was the father of Amminadab.
²⁰Amminadab was the father of Nahshon.
Nahshon was the father of Salmon.
²¹Salmon was the father of Boaz.
Boaz was the father of Obed.
²²Obed was the father of Jesse.
Jesse was the father of David.

ᵃ 4:12 *Perez* A famous ancestor in Boaz's family.
ᵇ 4:14 *child* Literally, "protector" or "redeemer". This might refer to Boaz, or the women might have used this name for the baby because he would be the one to care for Naomi and her family and to carry on the name of Elimelech.
ᶜ 4:17 *Naomi . . . now* Literally, "A son was born for Naomi."

Who It is not known who the author was but the book is named after Samuel the prophet and parts of it may have been written by Samuel himself (1 Chronicles 29:29).

When Whoever the author was, he probably lived after the death of Solomon since he refers to the two kingdoms of Israel and Judah, which only came into existence after Solomon's death.

What Samuel is actually one book, which was originally divided into two parts simply because you couldn't fit the whole thing on one scroll. The two cover about one hundred years, from the close of the time of the Judges to the establishment of the kingdom under David.

It may well have been edited together from a variety of original sources. Samuel mentions one such source – *The Book of Jashar* (2 Samuel 1:18) – but there are others mentioned elsewhere, such as *The History of King David* (1 Chronicles 27:24), and the books of "Samuel the seer", "Nathan the prophet" and "Gad the seer" (1 Chronicles 29:29).

The stories in the first book of Samuel really revolve around three people: Samuel, Saul and David.

Samuel is one of the great prophets of Israel and the last of the judges. He is the man who has the job of appointing the kings of Israel. Saul is Samuel's first appointment: the first king of Israel. He's a man who should have had it all, but who constantly relied on his own judgement, rather than obeying God's commands. So Saul is rejected, to be replaced by David, the young shepherd/ harpist/giant slayer. David is a strong leader and a fierce warrior, a great poet with a deep sense of justice and honour. But for all that he has some serious flaws, which come out in the second part of this book.

The first book centres mainly on the kingship of Saul and the emergence of David. Saul starts well, but as the book continues, he becomes an increasingly unstable figure, prone to wild mood swings and ever more desperate to hold on to his kingdom. But God has already promised it to someone else and the first part ends with Saul and his son Jonathan dying on the slopes of Mount Gilboa, killed during the battle against the Philistines.

QUICK TOUR **1 SAMUEL**

"But Samuel answered, 'Which pleases the Lᴏʀᴅ more: burnt offerings and sacrifices or obeying his commands? It is better to obey the Lᴏʀᴅ than to offer sacrifices to him. It is better to listen to him than to offer the fat from rams.'"

1 Samuel 15:22

Elkanah's Family Worships at Shiloh

1 There was a man named Elkanah from the Zuph family who lived in Ramah in the hill country of Ephraim. Elkanah was the son of Jeroham, the son of Elihu, the son of Tohu, the son of Zuph from the tribe of Ephraim.
²Elkanah had two wives. One wife was named Hannah and the other wife was named Peninnah. Peninnah had children, but Hannah did not.
³Every year Elkanah left his town of Ramah and went up to Shiloh. He worshipped the LORD All-Powerful at Shiloh and offered sacrifices to the Lord there. Shiloh was where Eli's sons, Hophni and Phinehas, served as priests of the LORD.
⁴Whenever Elkanah offered his sacrifices, he always gave one share of the food to his wife Peninnah and a share of the food to each of Peninnah's children. ⁵Elkanah always gave an equal share*ᵃ* of the food to Hannah. He did this because he loved her very much, even though the LORD had not let Hannah have any children.

Peninnah Upsets Hannah

⁶Peninnah always upset Hannah and made her feel bad because the LORD had not made her able to have children. ⁷This happened every year when their family went to the LORD's house at Shiloh. Peninnah would upset Hannah so much that she would begin to cry and would not eat anything. One year when this happened, ⁸her husband Elkanah said to her, "Hannah, why are you crying? Why won't you eat? Why are you so sad? You have me. Isn't that better than having even ten sons?"

Hannah's Prayer

⁹After eating and drinking, Hannah quietly got up and went to pray to the Lord.*ᵇ* Eli the priest was sitting on a chair near the door of the LORD's Holy Building.*ᶜ* ¹⁰Hannah was so sad that she cried the whole time she was praying to the LORD.
¹¹She made a special promise to God and said, "LORD All-Powerful, you can see how sad I am. Remember me. Don't forget me. If you will give me a son, I will give him to you. He will be yours his whole life, and as a Nazirite, he will not drink wine or strong drink,*ᵈ* and no one will ever cut his hair."

¹²Hannah prayed to the LORD for a long time. Eli was watching her mouth while she was praying. ¹³Hannah was praying in her heart. Her lips were moving, but since she did not say the words out loud, Eli thought she was drunk. ¹⁴He said to her, "You have had too much to drink. It is time to put away the wine."
¹⁵Hannah answered, "Sir, I have not drunk any wine or beer. I am deeply troubled, and I was telling the LORD about all my problems. ¹⁶Don't think I am a bad woman. I have been praying so long because I have so many troubles and am very sad."
¹⁷Eli answered, "Go in peace. May the God of Israel give you what you asked for."
¹⁸Hannah said, "May you be happy with me." Then she left and ate something. She was not sad any more.
¹⁹Early the next morning Elkanah's family got up. They worshipped the LORD and then went back home to Ramah.

Samuel's Birth

Elkanah had sex with his wife Hannah, and the LORD remembered Hannah. ²⁰By that time the following year, Hannah had become pregnant and had a son. She named him Samuel.*ᵉ* She said, "His name is Samuel because I asked the LORD for him."
²¹Elkanah went to Shiloh to offer the sacrifice for that year and the gift he had promised to the LORD. He took his family with him. ²²But Hannah did not go. She told Elkanah, "When the boy is old enough to eat solid food, I will take him to Shiloh. Then I will give him to the LORD. He will become a Nazirite.*ᶠ* He will stay at there at Shiloh."
²³Hannah's husband Elkanah said to her, "Do what you think is best. You may stay at home until the boy is old enough to eat solid food. May the LORD do what you*ᵍ* have said." So Hannah stayed at home to nurse her son until he was old enough to eat solid food.

Hannah Takes Samuel to Eli at Shiloh

²⁴When the boy was old enough to eat solid food, Hannah took him to the LORD's house at Shiloh. She also took a bull that was three years old, 10 kilogrammes*ʰ* of flour and a bottle of wine.

ᵃ **1:5 equal share** Or "double share".
ᵇ **1:9 went to pray to the Lord** This is from the ancient Greek version.
ᶜ **1:9 Holy Building** This could mean the Holy Tent at Shiloh where people went to worship the Lord or a larger area where they put the Holy Tent.
ᵈ **1:11 he . . . strong drink** This is found in the ancient Greek version and a Hebrew scroll from Qumran but not in the standard Hebrew text.
ᵉ **1:20 Samuel** This name means "His name is El (God)". But in Hebrew it is like "heard by God".
ᶠ **1:22 He will become a Nazirite** This is found in the ancient Greek version and a Hebrew scroll from Qumran but not in the standard Hebrew text.
ᵍ **1:23 you** This is from the ancient Greek version and a Hebrew scroll from Qumran. The standard Hebrew text has "he".
ʰ **1:24 10 kilogrammes** Literally, "an *ephah*".

25They went before the Lord. Elkanah killed the bull as a sacrifice to the Lord as he usually did.a Then Hannah gave the boy to Eli. 26She said to him, "Pardon me, sir. I am the same woman who stood near you praying to the LORD. I promise that I am telling the truth. 27I prayed for this child, and the LORD answered my prayer. He gave me this child. 28And now I give this child to the LORD. He will serveb the LORD all his life."

Then Hannah left the boy therec and worshipped the LORD.

Hannah Gives Thanks

2 Hannah said:

"My heart is happy in the LORD.
   I feel very strongd in my God.
I laugh at my enemies.e
   I am very happy in my victory.

2"There is no holy God like the LORD.
   There is no God but you.
   There is no Rock like our God.

3"Don't continue boasting.
   Don't speak proud words,
because the LORD God knows everything.
   He leads and judges people.
4The bows of strong soldiers break,
   and weak people become strong.
5People who had plenty of food in the past
   must now work to get food.
But those who were hungry in the past
   now grow fat on food.
The woman who was not able to have
      children
   now has seven children.
But the woman who had many children
   is sad because her children are gone.

6"The LORD causes people to die,
   and he causes them to live.
He sends people down to the grave,
   and he can raise them up to live again.
7The LORD makes some poor,
   and he makes others rich.

He humbles some people,
   and he honours others.
8He raises the poor from the dust,
   and he takes away their sadness.f
He makes them important
   and seats them with princes and at the
      places for honoured guests.
The LORD made the whole world,
   and the whole world belongs to him.g

9"He protects his holy people.
   He keeps them from stumbling.
But evil people will be destroyed.
   They will fall in the darkness.
   Their power won't help them win.
10The LORD destroys his enemies.
   He will thunder in heaven against them.
The LORD will judge even the lands that are far
      away.
   He will give power to his king
   and make his chosen kingh strong."

11Elkanah and his family went home to Ramah, but the boy stayed in Shiloh and served the LORD under Eli the priest.

Eli's Evil Sons

12Eli's sons were evil men who did not care about the LORD. 13They did not care about how priests were supposed to treat people. Whenever someone brings a sacrifice, priests are supposed to put the meat in a pot of boiling water. Then their servant is supposed to get the three-pronged fork 14and use it to get some meat out of the pot or kettle. The priest is supposed to take whatever his helper removes from the pot with the special fork. This is what the priests should have done for the Israelites who came to offer sacrifices at Shiloh. 15But that is not what the sons of Eli did. Even before the fat was burned on the altar, their servant would go to the people offering sacrifices and say, "Give the priest some meat to roast. The priest won't accept boiled meat from you."

16Maybe the man offering the sacrifice would say, "Burn the fati first, and then you can take whatever you want." But the servant would

---

a **1:25 They went . . . he usually did** This is found in the ancient Greek version and a Hebrew scroll from Qumran but not in the standard Hebrew text.
b **1:28 serve** Or "belong to".
c **1:28 left the boy there** This is found in a Hebrew scroll from Qumran but not in the standard Hebrew text.
d **2:1 I feel very strong** Literally, "In the LORD my horn is lifted high." The horn is a symbol of strength.
e **2:1 I laugh at my enemies** Literally, "My mouth is wide open over my enemies."
f **2:8 he . . . sadness** Literally, "he picks up the poor from the ashes".
g **2:8 The LORD made . . . to him** Literally, "The whole world, even to its foundations, belongs to the LORD. He set the world on those pillars."
h **2:10 chosen king** Literally, "anointed one".
i **2:16 Burn the fat** The fat was the part of the animal that belonged only to God. It was supposed to be burned first as an offering to him.

answer: "No, give me the meat now. If you don't give it to me, I'll take it from you!"

¹⁷In this way Hophni and Phinehas showed that they did not respect the offerings made to the Lord. This was a terrible sin against the Lord.

¹⁸But Samuel served the Lord. He was a helper who wore the linen ephod. ¹⁹Every year Samuel's mother made a robe for Samuel. She took the little robe to Samuel when she went up to Shiloh with her husband for the sacrifice every year.

²⁰Eli would bless Elkanah and his wife. He would say, "May the Lord give you more children through Hannah who will take the place of the boy she prayed for and gave to the Lord."

Elkanah and Hannah went home. ²¹The Lord was kind to Hannah, and she had three sons and two daughters. The boy Samuel grew up at the holy place near the Lord.

Eli Fails to Control His Evil Sons

²²Eli was very old. He heard about the bad things his sons were doing to the Israelites at Shiloh and how his sons were having sex with the women who served at the door of the Meeting Tent.

²³Eli said to his sons, "The people here told me about the evil things you have done. Why are you doing such things? ²⁴Sons, stop that! The Lord's people are saying bad things about you. ²⁵If you sin against other people, God might protect you. But who can help you if you sin against the Lord?"

Eli's sons refused to listen to him, so the Lord decided to kill them.

²⁶The boy Samuel kept growing. He was pleasing to the Lord and to the people.

The Terrible Prophecy About Eli's Family

²⁷A man of God came to Eli and said, "The Lord says, 'I appeared to your ancestors[a] when they were slaves of Pharaoh. ²⁸From all the tribes of Israel, I chose your tribe to be my priests. I chose them to offer sacrifices on my altar, to burn incense and wear the ephod. I also let your tribe have the meat from the sacrifices that the Israelites give to me. ²⁹So why don't you respect these gifts and sacrifices? You become fat eating the best parts of the meat that the Israelites bring to me.'

³⁰"The Lord, the God of Israel, promised that your father's family would serve him forever. But now the Lord says, 'That will never be! I will honour people who honour me, but bad things will happen to those who refuse to respect me. ³¹The time is coming when I will destroy all your descendants. No one in your family will live to be an old man. ³²Good things will happen to Israel, but you will see bad things happening at home.[b] No one in your family will live to be an old man. ³³There is only one man I will save to serve as priest at my altar. He will live until his eyes wear out and his strength is gone. But all your descendants will die by the sword.[c] ³⁴I will give you a sign to show that these things will come true. Your two sons, Hophni and Phinehas, will die on the same day. ³⁵I will choose a priest I can trust. This priest will listen to me and do what I want. I will make his family strong, and he will always serve before my chosen king.[d] ³⁶Then whoever is left in your family will come and bow down before this priest and beg for a little money or a piece of bread. They will say, "Please give me a job as priest so that I can have some food to eat."'"

God Calls Samuel

3 The boy Samuel was Eli's helper and served the Lord with him. At that time the Lord did not speak directly to people very often. There were very few visions.

²Eli's eyes were getting so weak that he was almost blind. One night he went to his room to go to bed. ³The special lamp in the Lord's temple[e] was still burning, so Samuel lay down in the temple near where the Holy Box was. ⁴The Lord called Samuel, and Samuel answered, "Here I am." ⁵Samuel thought Eli was calling him, so he ran to Eli and said, "Here I am. You called me."

But Eli said, "I didn't call you. Go back to bed."

So Samuel went back to bed. ⁶Again the Lord called, "Samuel!" Again Samuel ran to Eli and said, "Here I am. You called me."

Eli said, "I didn't call you. Go back to bed."

⁷Samuel did not know it was the Lord because the Lord had not spoken directly to him before.[f]

⁸The Lord called Samuel the third time. Again Samuel got up and went to Eli and said, "Here I am. You called me."

Finally, Eli understood that the Lord was calling the boy. ⁹Eli told Samuel, "Go to bed. If he

---

[a] **2:27 ancestors** Literally, "father's house". See "ANCESTOR" in the Word List.
[b] **2:32 but you . . . at home** These words are not in the ancient Greek version or the Hebrew scrolls from Qumran.
[c] **2:33 by the sword** This is found in the ancient Greek version and a Hebrew scroll from Qumran. The standard Hebrew text has "like men".
[d] **2:35 chosen king** Literally, "anointed one".
[e] **3:3 temple** This could mean the Holy Tent at Shiloh where people went to worship the Lord or a larger area where they put the Holy Tent.
[f] **3:7 the Lord . . . him before** Literally, "the word of the Lord had not yet been revealed to him".

calls you again, say, 'Speak, LORD. I am your servant, and I am listening.'"

So Samuel went back to bed. [10]The LORD came and stood there. He called as he did before, saying, "Samuel, Samuel!"

Samuel said, "Speak. I am your servant, and I am listening."

[11]The LORD said to Samuel, "I will soon do things in Israel that will shock anyone who hears about them. [12]I will do everything I said I would do against Eli and his family, everything from the beginning to the end. [13]I told Eli I would punish his family forever. I will do this because Eli knew his sons were saying and doing bad things against God. But he failed to control them. [14]That is why I swore an oath that sacrifices and offerings will never take away the sins of the people in Eli's family."[a]

[15]Samuel lay down in bed until the morning came. He got up early and opened the doors of the LORD's house. Samuel was afraid to tell Eli about the vision.

[16]But Eli said to Samuel, "Samuel, my son."

Samuel answered, "Yes, sir."

[17]Eli asked, "What did God say to you? Don't hide it from me. God will punish you if you hide anything from the message he spoke to you."

[18]So Samuel told Eli everything. He did not hide anything from him.

Eli said, "He is the LORD. Let him do whatever he thinks is right."

[19]The LORD was with Samuel as he grew up. He made everything happen just as Samuel said it would. [20]Then all Israel, from Dan to Beersheba, knew that Samuel was a true prophet of the LORD. [21]And the LORD continued to appear to Samuel at Shiloh. There he told Samuel what he wanted.

INSIGHT

At this time it was rare for God to speak directly to people, so when people realized that God was speaking regularly to Samuel news soon spread that he was someone worth listening to.

1 Samuel 3:1 – 4:1

4 Then Samuel would announce the LORD's message to all the people of Israel. When Eli was very old, his sons did more and more things that the LORD considered evil.[b]

The Philistines Defeat the Israelites

At that time the Israelites went out to fight against the Philistines. The Israelites made their camp at Ebenezer. The Philistines made their camp at Aphek. [2]The Philistines lined up their soldiers in front of the Israelites and began the attack.

The Philistines defeated the Israelites. They killed about 4,000 soldiers from Israel's army. [3]The rest of the Israelite soldiers went back to their camp. The leaders of Israel asked, "Why did the LORD let the Philistines defeat us? Let's bring the Box of the LORD's Agreement from Shiloh. God will go with us into battle and save us from our enemies."

[4]So the people sent men to Shiloh. The men brought back the Box of the Agreement of the LORD All-Powerful. On top of the Box are the winged creatures. They are like a throne where the Lord sits. Eli's two sons, Hophni and Phinehas, came with the Box.

[5]When the Box of the LORD's Agreement came into the camp, all the Israelites gave a great shout loud enough to make the ground shake. [6]The Philistines heard Israel's shout and asked, "Why are the people so excited in the Hebrew[c] camp?"

Then the Philistines learned that the LORD's Holy Box had been brought into Israel's camp. [7]They became afraid and said, "Gods have come to their camp! We're in trouble. This has never happened before. [8]We are worried. Who can save us from these powerful gods? These gods are the same ones that gave the Egyptians those diseases and terrible sicknesses. [9]Be brave, Philistines. Fight like men. In the past they were our slaves, so fight like men or you will become our slaves."

[10]So the Philistines fought very hard and defeated the Israelites. The Israelite soldiers ran away and went home. It was a terrible defeat for Israel. 30,000 Israelite soldiers were killed. [11]The Philistines took God's Holy Box and killed Eli's two sons, Hophni and Phinehas.

[12]One of the men who ran from the battle was a man from the tribe of Benjamin. He tore his clothes and put dust on his head to show his great sadness. [13]Eli was worried about the Holy Box, so he was sitting there by the city gate waiting and watching when the Benjamite man came into Shiloh and told the bad news. All the people in town began to cry loudly. [14-15]Eli was 98 years old. He was blind, so he could not see what was happening, but he could hear the loud noise of the people crying. Eli asked, "Why are the people making this loud noise?"

---

[a] 3:14 Or "That is why I swore an oath that Eli's family would not be forgiven for their sins against the offerings and sacrifices."
[b] 4:1 *When Eli . . . evil* The ancient Greek version adds these words at the end of chapter 3.
[c] 4:6 *Hebrew* Or "Israelite".

The Benjamite man ran to Eli and told him what had happened. [16]He said, "I am the man who just came from the battle. I ran away from the battle today."

Eli asked, "What happened, son?"

[17]The Benjamite man answered, "Israel ran away from the Philistines. The Israelite army has lost many soldiers. Your two sons are both dead, and the Philistines took God's Holy Box."

[18]When the Benjamite man mentioned God's Holy Box, Eli fell backwards off his chair near the gate and broke his neck. Eli was old and fat, so he died. He had led Israel for 20 years.[a]

The Glory Is Gone

[19]Eli's daughter-in-law, the wife of Phinehas, was pregnant. It was nearly time for her baby to be born. She heard the news that God's Holy Box had been taken. She also heard that her father-in-law Eli and her husband Phinehas were both dead. As soon as she heard the news, her pain started and she began giving birth to her baby. [20]She was about to die when the women who were helping her said, "Don't worry, you have given birth to a son."

But she did not answer or pay attention. [21]She named the baby Ichabod, meaning, "Israel's glory has been taken away." She did this because God's Holy Box had been taken away and because both her father-in-law and her husband were dead. [22]She said, "Israel's glory has been taken away" because the Philistines had taken God's Holy Box.

The Holy Box Troubles the Philistines

5 The Philistines carried God's Holy Box, from Ebenezer to Ashdod. [2]They carried God's Holy Box into the temple of Dagon and put it next to the statue of Dagon. [3]The next morning, the people of Ashdod got up and found Dagon lying face down on the ground before the LORD's Box.

The people of Ashdod put the statue of Dagon back in its place. [4]But the next morning when the people of Ashdod got up, they found Dagon on the ground again. Dagon had fallen down before the LORD's Holy Box. This time, Dagon's head and hands were broken off and were lying in the doorway. Only his body was still in one piece. [5]That is why, even today, the priests or other people refuse to step on the threshold when they enter Dagon's temple at Ashdod.

[6]The LORD made life hard for the people of Ashdod and their neighbours. He gave them many troubles and caused them to get tumours. He also sent mice to them. The mice ran all over their ships and then onto their land. The people in the city were very afraid.[b] [7]They saw what was happening and said, "The Holy Box of the God of Israel can't stay here. God is punishing us and Dagon our god."

[8]The people of Ashdod called the five Philistine rulers together and asked them, "What must we do with the Holy Box of the God of Israel?"

The rulers answered, "Move the Holy Box of the God of Israel to Gath." So the Philistines moved God's Holy Box.

[9]But after the Philistines had moved God's Holy Box to Gath, the LORD punished that city. The people became very frightened. God caused many troubles for all the people—young and old. He caused the people in Gath to have tumours. [10]So the Philistines sent God's Holy Box to Ekron.

But when God's Holy Box came into Ekron, the people of Ekron complained. They said, "Why are you bringing the Box of the God of Israel to our city Ekron? Do you want to kill us and our people?" [11]The people of Ekron called all the Philistine rulers together and said to the rulers, "Send the Box of the God of Israel back home before it kills us and our people!"

The people of Ekron were deathly afraid because God severely punished them there. [12]Many people died, and those who did not, had tumours. The people of Ekron cried loudly to heaven.

God's Holy Box Is Sent Back Home

6 The Philistines kept the LORD's Holy Box in their land for seven months. [2]The Philistines called their priests and magicians and said, "What must we do with the LORD's Box? Tell us how to send it back home."

[3]The priests and magicians answered, "If you send back the Holy Box of the God of Israel, don't send it away empty. You must offer gifts to the God of Israel. Then you will be healed. You must do this so that God will stop punishing you."[c]

[4]The Philistines asked, "What kind of gifts should we send for Israel's God to forgive us?"

The priests and magicians answered, "There are five Philistine leaders, one leader for each city. All of you and your leaders had the same problems. So you must make five gold models to look like five tumours. And you must make five gold models to look like five mice. [5]So make models of the tumours and models of the mice

---

[a] 4:18 *20 years* This is found in the ancient Greek version and Josephus. The standard Hebrew text has "40 years".
[b] 5:6 *He also sent . . . afraid* This is from the ancient Greek version.
[c] 6:3 *You must do . . . punishing you* This is found in the ancient Greek version and a Hebrew scroll from Qumran. The standard Hebrew text has "Then you will know why God did not stop punishing you."

that are ruining the country. Give these gold models to the God of Israel as payment. Then maybe the God of Israel will stop punishing you, your gods and your land. ⁶Don't be stubborn like Pharaoh and the Egyptians. God punished the Egyptians. That is why the Egyptians let the Israelites leave Egypt.

⁷"You must build a new cart and get two cows that have just had calves. These must be cows that have never worked in the fields. Tie the cows to the cart so that they can pull it. Then take the calves back home and put them in their pen. Don't let them follow their mothers.ᵃ ⁸Put the LORD's Holy Box on the cart. You must put the gold models in the bag beside the Box. They are your gifts for God to forgive your sins. Send the cart straight on its way. ⁹Watch the cart. If the cart goes towards Beth Shemesh in Israel's own land, then it is their God who has given us this great sickness. But if the cows don't go straight to Beth Shemesh, we will know it was not their God who brought this sickness to us. It was just one of those things that sometimes happen."

¹⁰The Philistines did what the priests and magicians said. They found two cows that had just had calves and tied them to the cart. But they kept the calves at home in a pen. ¹¹Then the Philistines put the LORD's Holy Box on the cart along with the bag that held the gold models of the tumours and mice. ¹²The cows went straight to Beth Shemesh. The cows stayed on the road, mooing all the way. They did not turn right or left. The Philistine rulers followed the cows as far as the city limits of Beth Shemesh.

¹³The people of Beth Shemesh were harvesting their wheat in the valley. They looked up and saw the Holy Box. They were very happy to see it again. They ran to get it. ¹⁴⁻¹⁵The cart came to the field that belonged to Joshua of Beth Shemesh and stopped there near a large rock.

Some Levites took down the LORD's Holy Box and the bag that had the gold models. The Levites put the LORD's Box and the bag that was with it on the large rock.

The people of Beth Shemesh cut up the cart and killed the cows. That day, they sacrificed the cows as burnt offerings to the LORD.

¹⁶The five Philistine rulers watched the people of Beth Shemesh do this and then went back to Ekron that same day.

¹⁷In this way the Philistines sent gold models of tumours as gifts for their sins to the LORD. They sent one gold model of a tumour for each of the Philistine towns of Ashdod, Gaza, Ashkelon, Gath and Ekron. ¹⁸The Philistines also sent gold models of mice. The number of these gold mice was the same number as the towns that belonged to the five Philistine rulers. These towns had walls around them, and each town had villages around it.

The LORD's Holy Box was put on a large rock. That rock is still in the field of Joshua from Beth Shemesh. ¹⁹When the men of Beth Shemesh first saw the LORD's Holy Box coming, they began to celebrate. But there were no priests there to take charge. So the LORD killed 70 of the men there. The people of Beth Shemesh cried loudly because of this hard punishment. ²⁰They said, "Where can we find a priest who can take care of the Holy Box? Where should it go from here?"

²¹There was a priest at Kiriath Jearim, so the people of Beth Shemesh sent messengers there. They said, "The Philistines have brought back the LORD's Holy Box. Come down and take it to your city."

7 The men of Kiriath Jearim came and took the LORD's Holy Box up the hill to the house of Abinadab the priest. They performed a special ceremony to prepare Abinadab's son, Eleazar, to guard the LORD's Holy Box. ²The Box stayed there at Kiriath Jearim for a long time.

The LORD Saves the Israelites

Twenty years passed while the Holy Box was in Kiriath Jearim, and the Israelites began to follow the LORD again. ³Samuel told the Israelites, "If you are really coming back to the LORD with all your heart, you must throw away your foreign gods and your idols of Ashtoreth. You must give yourselves fully to the LORD and serve only him. Then he will save you from the Philistines."

⁴So the Israelites threw away their statues of Baal and Ashtoreth. The Israelites served only the LORD.

⁵Samuel said, "All Israel must meet at Mizpah. I will pray to the LORD for you."

⁶The Israelites met together at Mizpah. They got water and poured it out before the LORD. In this way they began a time of fasting. They did not eat any food that day, and they confessed their sins. They said, "We have sinned against the LORD." So Samuel served as a judge of Israel at Mizpah.

⁷When the Philistines heard that the Israelites were meeting at Mizpah, they went to fight them. The Israelites were frightened when they heard the Philistines were coming ⁸and said to Samuel, "Don't stop praying to the LORD our God for us. Ask him to save us from the Philistines."

ᵃ **6:7 Don't let . . . mothers** The Philistines thought if the cows did not try to find their calves it would prove that God was leading them and that he had accepted their gifts.

9Samuel took a baby lamb and offered it as a whole burnt offering to the LORD. He prayed to the LORD for Israel, and the LORD answered his prayer. 10The Philistines came closer and closer to fight the Israelites while Samuel offered the sacrifice. But then, the LORD caused a loud clap of thunder to hit near the Philistines. The thunder scared the Philistines, and they became confused, so the Israelites defeated them in battle. 11The men of Israel ran out of Mizpah and chased the Philistines all the way to Beth Car. They killed Philistine soldiers all along the way.

Peace Comes to Israel

12After this Samuel set up a special stone to help people remember what God did. Samuel put the stone between Mizpah and Shen[a] and named the stone "Stone of Help".[b] Samuel said, "The LORD helped us all the way to this place."

13The Philistines were defeated and did not enter the land of Israel again. The LORD was against the Philistines during the rest of Samuel's life. 14The Philistines had taken some cities from Israel, but the Israelites won them back. They recovered those cities throughout the Philistine area, from Ekron to Gath.

There was also peace between Israel and the Amorites.

15Samuel led Israel all his life. 16He went from place to place judging the Israelites. Every year he travelled around the country. He went to Bethel, Gilgal and Mizpah and he judged the Israelites in all these places. 17But Samuel always went back to his home in Ramah. There he built an altar to the LORD and judged Israel.

Israel Asks for a King

8 When Samuel was old, he appointed his sons to be judges for Israel. 2Samuel's first son was named Joel. His second son was named Abijah. Joel and Abijah were judges in Beersheba. 3But Samuel's sons did not live the same way he did. Joel and Abijah accepted bribes. They took money secretly and changed their decisions in court. They cheated people in court. 4So all the leaders of Israel met together and went to Ramah to meet with Samuel. 5The leaders said to Samuel, "You're old, and your sons don't do what is right. They are not like you. Now, give us a king to rule us like all the other nations."

6So the leaders asked for a king to lead them. Samuel thought this was a bad idea, so he prayed to the LORD. 7The LORD told Samuel, "Do what the people tell you. They have not rejected you.

They have rejected me. They don't want me to be their king. 8They are doing the same thing they have always done. I took them out of Egypt, but they left me and served other gods. They are doing the same to you. 9So listen to the people and do what they say. But give them a warning. Tell the people what a king will do to them. Tell them how a king rules people."

10Those people asked for a king. So Samuel told them everything the LORD said. 11Samuel said, "If you have a king ruling over you, this is what he will do: He will take away your sons and force them to serve him. He will force them to be soldiers—they must fight from his chariots and become horsemen in his army. Your sons will become guards running in front of the king's chariot.

12"A king will force your sons to become soldiers. He will choose which of your sons will be officers over 1,000 men and which will be officers over 50 men.

"A king will force some of your sons to plough his fields and gather his harvest. He will force some of your sons to make weapons for war and to make things for his chariots.

13"A king will take your daughters and force some of them to make perfume for him and some to cook and bake for him.

14"A king will take your best fields, vineyards and olive groves. He will take them from you and give them to his officers. 15He will take one-tenth of your grain and grapes, and he will give them to his officers and servants.

16"A king will take your men and women servants. He will take your best cattle[c] and your donkeys. He will use them all for his own work. 17He will take one-tenth of your flocks.

"And you yourselves will become slaves of this king. 18When that time comes, you will cry because of the king you chose. But the LORD won't answer you at that time."

INSIGHT

Israel wanted to be like the other nations around them and have a king, even though they really already had one – God. Although it wasn't God's plan, he gave the people what they wanted and even though the kings were all fallible, he worked through them.

1 Samuel 8:19–22

---

[a] **7:12 Shen** Or "Jeshanah", a town about 17 miles north of Jerusalem.
[b] **7:12 Stone of Help** Or "Ebenezer".
[c] **8:16 cattle** This is from the ancient Greek version. The standard Hebrew text has "young men".

BE CAREFUL WHAT YOU WISH FOR

"I want more!" is one of the first phrases little children learn how to say. One piece of chocolate cake is never enough. The only thing that's going to make them happy is eating another, then another, then another.

There's an old saying, "Be careful what you wish for, because it might come true." From time to time a parent might just give in to the child and let them loose on the whole plate. They know that the resulting stomach ache will teach the child everything they need to know about the value of moderation!

DIG IN
READ 1 Samuel 8:1–22

- What are the people asking for (v.5)?
- What reasons do they give – and what others could you imagine?
- What does Samuel say to the people to try to put them off (vv.11–18)?

Samuel is a special figure in the Bible whose work bridged the gap between the judges and the prophets. Actually, 1 and 2 Samuel is really a single book with one long story that tells us some amazing things about the character of God.

Samuel may not be the "star of the show" but he's important because he starts off a chain of events that changes the history of God's people. Up until this point, Israel had been led, through good times and bad, by patriarchs (like Abraham and Jacob), by prophets (like Moses and Samuel) or by Judges (like Othniel and Deborah). It had been that way for a thousand years. But during Samuel's term of office, the people started asking for a different kind of leadership. They saw what other nations had and demanded the same: a king (v.20).

Samuel tries to deter the people by giving them reasons why a king would not be popular. These seem to be mainly financial reasons – after all, "money talks"! And yet the people will not be swayed.

- What is God's response to the request (v.22)?

Even though Samuel saw it would be bad for them, God gave in to their request for a king.

DIG THROUGH

- Have you ever found yourself longing for something just because your friends have one? Was this influence a good thing or a bad thing?
- Why does God give in to the people's request? Think back to the earlier example of the parent who gives in to the greedy child.

DIG DEEPER

The Bible teaches that leadership is really important to God. But he knows that human leaders are always flawed and subject to compromise. We'll see throughout the books of Samuel that Israel's kings are only ever pointers to the perfect king that God plans for his people: King Jesus.

- In Psalm 145, David shows a special understanding of his heavenly "God and King" (v.1). Read this psalm and try making it your own.
- Look ahead to 1 Samuel chapter 12, which is Samuel's farewell message to the people. It contains a summary of God's dealings with the Hebrew people throughout history to that time. What is Samuel's closing point? How does it apply today?

¹⁹But the people would not listen to Samuel. They said, "No, we want a king to rule over us. ²⁰Then we will be the same as all the other nations. Our king will lead us. He will go before us and fight our battles."

²¹Samuel listened to the people and then repeated their words to the LORD. ²²The LORD answered, "Listen to them and give them a king."

Then Samuel told the Israelites, "You will have a king. Now go home."

Saul Looks for His Father's Donkeys

9 Kish was an important man from the tribe of Benjamin. He was the son of Abiel. Abiel was the son of Zeror. Zeror was the son of Becorath. Becorath was the son of Aphiah, a man from Benjamin. ²Kish had a son named Saul, who was a handsome young man. There was no one more handsome than Saul. He stood a head taller than any other man in Israel.

³One day Kish's donkeys got lost. So he said to his son Saul, "Take one of the servants and go and look for the donkeys." ⁴Saul went to look for the donkeys. He walked through the hills of Ephraim and through the area around Shalisha. But Saul and the servant could not find Kish's donkeys. So they went to the area around Shaalim, but the donkeys were not there either. Then Saul travelled through the land of Benjamin, but he and the servant still could not find the donkeys.

⁵Finally, Saul and the servant came to the town named Zuph. Saul said to his servant, "Let's go back. My father will stop worrying about the donkeys and start worrying about us."

⁶But the servant answered, "A man of God is in this town. People respect him. Everything he says comes true, so let's go into town. Maybe the man of God will tell us where we should go next."

⁷Saul said to his servant, "Sure, we can go into town, but what can we give him? We have no gift to give the man of God. Even the food in our bags is gone. What can we give him?"

⁸Again the servant answered Saul. "Look, I have a little bit of money.ᵃ Let's give it to the man of God. Then he will tell us where we should go."

⁹⁻¹¹Saul said to his servant, "That is a good idea. Let's go." So they went to the town where the man of God was.

Saul and the servant were walking up the hill towards the town when they met some young women on the road. The young women were coming out to get water. Saul and the servant asked the young women, "Is the seer here?" (In the past, people in Israel called a prophet a "seer". So if they wanted to ask something from God, they would say, "Let's go to the seer.")

¹²The young women answered, "Yes, the seer is here. He is just up the road. He came to our town today. Some people are meeting together today to share in a fellowship offering at the place for worship.ᵇ ¹³So go into town and you will find him. If you hurry, you can catch him before he goes up to eat at the place for worship. The seer blesses the sacrifice, so the people won't begin eating until he gets there. If you hurry, you can find him."

¹⁴Saul and the servant started walking up the hill to the town. Just as they came into the town, they saw Samuel coming out of the town, walking towards them. He was on his way to the place for worship.

¹⁵The day before, the LORD had told Samuel, ¹⁶"At this time tomorrow I will send a man to you. He will be from the tribe of Benjamin. You must anoint him and make him the new leader over my people Israel. This man will save my people from the Philistines. I have seen my people suffering,ᶜ and I have heard their cries for help."

¹⁷When Samuel saw Saul, the LORD said to Samuel, "This is the man I told you about. He will rule my people."

¹⁸Saul went up to a man near the gate to ask directions. This man just happened to be Samuel. Saul said, "Excuse me. Could you tell me where the seer's house is?"

¹⁹Samuel answered, "I am the seer. Go on up ahead of me to the place for worship. You and your servant will eat with me today. I will let you go home tomorrow morning. I will answer all your questions. ²⁰And don't worry about the donkeys that you lost three days ago. They have been found. Now, there is something that everyone in Israel is looking for and that something is you and your family."

²¹Saul answered, "But I am a member of the tribe of Benjamin. It is the smallest tribe in Israel. And my family is the smallest in the tribe of Benjamin. Why do you say Israel wants me?"

²²Then Samuel took Saul and his servant to the eating area. About 30 people had been invited to eat together and share the sacrifice. Samuel gave Saul and his servant the most important place at the table. ²³Samuel said to the cook, "Bring the meat I gave you. It is the share I told you to save."

²⁴The cook brought out the thighᵈ and put it on the table in front of Saul. Samuel said, "Eat the meat that was put in front of you. It was saved for

---

ᵃ *9:8 a little bit of money* Literally, "¼ *shekel* of silver".
ᵇ *9:12 place for worship* Or "high place". See "HIGH PLACE" in the Word List. Also in verses 14,19,25.
ᶜ *9:16 suffering* This is from the ancient Greek version.
ᵈ *9:24 thigh* This was probably the left thigh that was reserved for important guests. The right thigh was reserved for the priest who sacrificed the animal. This priest helped kill the animal and put the fat from the animal on the altar as a gift to God.

you for this special time when I called the people together." So Saul ate with Samuel that day.

25After they finished eating, they came down from the place for worship and went back to town. Samuel made a bed for Saul on the roof, 26and Saul went to sleep.*a*

Early the next morning, Samuel shouted to Saul on the roof and said, "Get up. I will send you on your way." Saul got up and went out of the house with Samuel.

27Saul, his servant and Samuel were walking together near the edge of the town. Samuel said to Saul, "Tell your servant to go on ahead of us. I have a message for you from God." So the servant walked ahead of them.

Samuel Anoints Saul

10 Samuel took a jar of the special oil and poured the oil on Saul's head. Samuel kissed Saul and said, "The LORD has anointed you to be the leader over the people who belong to him. You will control the people. You will save them from the enemies that are all around them. He has anointed you to be ruler over his people. Here is a sign that will prove this is true:*b* 2After you leave me today, you will meet two men near Rachel's tomb on the border of Benjamin at Zelzah. The two men will say to you, 'Someone found the donkeys you were looking for. Your father stopped worrying about his donkeys. Now he is worrying about you. He is saying: What will I do about my son?'"

3Samuel said, "Then you will go until you come to the large oak tree at Tabor. Three men will meet you there. They will be on their way to worship God at Bethel. One man will be carrying three young goats. The second man will be carrying three loaves of bread. And the third man will have a leather bag full of wine. 4These three men will say hello to you. They will offer you two loaves of bread, and you will accept the two loaves. 5Then you will go to Gibeath Elohim. There is a Philistine fortress in that place. When you come to this town, a group of prophets will come out. These prophets will come down from the place for worship.*c* They will be prophesying.*d* They will be playing harps, tambourines, flutes and lyres. 6Then the LORD's Spirit will come on you with great power. You will be changed. You will be like a different man. You will begin to

prophesy with these prophets. 7After that happens, you can do whatever you choose to do, because God will be with you.

8"Go to Gilgal before me. Then I will come there to you. And I will offer burnt offerings and fellowship offerings. But you must wait seven days. Then I will come and tell you what to do."

Saul Becomes Like the Prophets

9Just as Saul turned to leave Samuel, God turned Saul's life around. All these things happened that day. 10When Saul and his servant came to Gibeath Elohim, Saul met a group of prophets. God's Spirit came on Saul with great power, and Saul prophesied with the prophets. 11Some of the people who had known Saul before saw him prophesying with the prophets. So they asked each other, "What has happened to Kish's son? Is Saul also one of the prophets?"

12A man living in Gibeath Elohim said, "Yes, and it seems that he is their leader."*e* That is why this became a famous saying: "Is Saul also one of the prophets?"

Saul Arrives Home

13After Saul finished prophesying, he went to the place of worship.

14Saul's uncle asked Saul and his servant, "Where have you been?"

Saul said, "We were looking for the donkeys. When we couldn't find them, we went to see Samuel."

15Saul's uncle said, "Please tell me, what did Samuel say to you?"

16Saul answered, "Samuel told us the donkeys were already found." He did not tell his uncle everything. Saul did not tell him what Samuel had said about the kingdom.

Samuel Announces Saul as King

17Samuel told all the Israelites to meet together with the LORD at Mizpah. 18Samuel told the Israelites, "The LORD, the God of Israel says, 'I led Israel out of Egypt. I saved you from Egypt's control and from the other kingdoms that tried to hurt you.' 19But today you have rejected your God. Your God saves you from all your troubles and problems. But you said, 'No, we want a king to rule us.' Now come, stand before the LORD in your family groups and tribes."

---

a **9:25–26 made . . . to sleep** This is from the ancient Greek version. The standard Hebrew text has "Samuel spoke with Saul on the roof." In ancient Israel, houses had flat roofs that were used as an extra room.

b **10:1 You will control . . . true** This is from the ancient Greek version.

c **10:5 place for worship** Or "high places", places for worshipping God or false gods. These places were often on the hills and mountains.

d **10:5 prophesying** This usually means "speaking for God". But here, this also means that the Spirit of God took control of people, causing them to sing and dance. Also in verses 11,13.

e **10:12 Yes . . . leader** Literally, "And who is their father?" Often the man who taught and led other prophets was called "father".

²⁰Samuel brought all the tribes of Israel near. Then Samuel began to choose the new king. First, the tribe of Benjamin was chosen. ²¹Samuel told each family in the tribe of Benjamin to pass by. Matri's family was chosen. Then Samuel told each man in Matri's family to walk by. Saul son of Kish was chosen.

But when the people looked for Saul, they could not find him. ²²Then they asked the LORD, "Has Saul come here yet?"

The LORD said, "Saul is hiding behind the supplies."

²³The people ran and took Saul out from behind the supplies. Saul stood up among the people. He was a head taller than anyone else.

²⁴Samuel said to all the people, "See the man the LORD has chosen. There is no one like Saul among the people."

Then the people shouted, "Long live the king!"

²⁵Samuel explained the rules of the kingdom to the people. He wrote the rules in a book and put the book before the LORD. Then Samuel told the people to go home.

²⁶Saul also went to his home in Gibeah. God touched the hearts of brave men who then began to follow Saul. ²⁷But some troublemakers said, "How can this man save us?" They said bad things about Saul and refused to bring gifts to him. But Saul said nothing.

Nahash, King of the Ammonites

King Nahash of the Ammonites had been hurting the tribes of Gad and Reuben. Nahash poked out the right eye of each of the men and did not allow anyone to help them. He poked out the right eye of every Israelite man living in the area east of the Jordan River. But 7,000 Israelite men ran away from the Ammonites and came to Jabesh Gilead.[a]

11 About a month later, Nahash the Ammonite and his army surrounded Jabesh Gilead. All the people of Jabesh said to Nahash, "If you will make a treaty with us, we will serve you."

²But he answered, "I will make a treaty with you people only if I can poke out the right eye of each person. Then all Israel will be ashamed."

³The leaders of Jabesh said to Nahash, "Let us have seven days. We will send messengers through all Israel. If no one comes to help us, we will come up to you and surrender to you."

Saul Saves Jabesh Gilead

⁴The messengers came to Gibeah where Saul lived. They told the news to the people. The people cried loudly. ⁵Saul had been out in the field with his oxen. When he came in from the field he heard the people crying and asked, "What's wrong with the people? Why are they crying?"

Then the people told Saul what the messengers from Jabesh said. ⁶Saul listened to their story. Then God's Spirit came on him with great power. Saul became very angry. ⁷He took a pair of oxen and cut them in pieces. Then he gave the pieces of the oxen to messengers. He ordered the messengers to carry the pieces throughout the land of Israel. He told them to give this message to the Israelites: "Come and follow Saul and Samuel. If anyone doesn't come and help them, this same thing will happen to his oxen."

A great fear from the LORD came on the people. They all came together like one person. ⁸Saul gathered the men together at Bezek. There were 300,000 men from Israel and 30,000 men from Judah.

⁹Saul and his army told the messengers from Jabesh, "Tell the people at Jabesh in Gilead that by noon tomorrow, you will be saved."

The messengers told Saul's message to the people at Jabesh, and they were very happy. ¹⁰Then the people of Jabesh said to Nahash the Ammonite, "Tomorrow we will come to you, and you can do whatever you want to us."

¹¹The next morning Saul separated his soldiers into three groups. At sunrise, Saul and his soldiers entered the Ammonite camp. Saul attacked while they were changing guards that morning. He and his soldiers defeated the Ammonites before noon. The Ammonite soldiers all ran away in different directions—no two soldiers stayed together.

¹²Then the people said to Samuel, "Where are the people who said they didn't want Saul to rule as king? Bring them here, and we will kill them."

¹³But Saul said, "No, don't kill anyone today! The LORD saved Israel today."

¹⁴Then Samuel said to the people, "Come, let's go to Gilgal. At Gilgal we will again make Saul the king."

¹⁵All the people went to Gilgal. There, in front of the LORD, the people made Saul king. They offered fellowship offerings to the LORD. Saul and all the Israelites had a great celebration.

Samuel Speaks About the King

12 Samuel said to all Israel: "I have done everything you wanted me to do. I have put a king over you. ²Now you have a king to lead you. I am old and grey, but my sons are here with you. I have been your leader since I was young.

---

[a] **10:27 Nahash . . . came to Jabesh Gilead** This is found in some ancient versions and in a Hebrew scroll from Qumran but not in the standard Hebrew text.

[3]Here I am. If I have done anything wrong, you must tell these things to the LORD and his chosen king.[a] Did I steal anyone's ox or donkey? Did I hurt or cheat anyone? Did I ever take money, or even a pair of sandals, to do something wrong? If I did any of these things, I will make it right."

[4]The Israelites answered, "No, you never did anything bad to us. You never cheated us or took things from us."

[5]Samuel said to the Israelites, "The LORD and his chosen king are witnesses today. They heard what you said—that you found nothing wrong with me." The people answered, "Yes, the Lord is witness!"

[6]Then Samuel said to the people, "The LORD has seen what happened. He is the one who chose Moses and Aaron and brought your ancestors out of Egypt. [7]So now you take your place and I will present my arguments against you before the LORD. I will tell about all the great things the LORD has done to save you and your ancestors.

[8]"Jacob went to Egypt. Later, the Egyptians made life hard for his descendants. So they cried to the LORD for help. The LORD sent Moses and Aaron, and they took your ancestors out of Egypt and led them to live in this place.

[9]"But your ancestors forgot the LORD their God. So he let them become the slaves of Sisera, the commander of the army at Hazor. Then the Lord let them become the slaves of the Philistines and the king of Moab. They all fought against your ancestors. [10]But your ancestors cried to the LORD for help. They said, 'We have sinned. We left the LORD, and we served the false gods Baal and Ashtoreth. But now save us from our enemies, and we will serve you.'

[11]"So the LORD sent Gideon,[b] Barak,[c] Jephthah and Samuel.[d] He saved you from your enemies around you, and you lived in safety. [12]But then you saw King Nahash of the Ammonites coming to fight against you. You said, 'No, we want a king to rule over us!' You said that, even though the LORD your God was already your king. [13]Now, here is the king you chose. The LORD put this king over you. [14]You must fear and respect the LORD. You must serve him and obey his commands. You must not turn against him. You and the king

ruling over you must follow the LORD your God. If you do, God will save you.[e] [15]But if you don't listen to the LORD, if you refuse to do what the LORD says, he will be against you. The LORD will destroy you and your king.

[16]"Now stand still and see the great thing the LORD will do before your eyes. [17]Now is the time of the wheat harvest.[f] I will pray to the LORD and ask him to send thunder and rain. Then you will know you did a very bad thing against the LORD when you asked for a king."

[18]So Samuel prayed to the LORD. That same day the LORD sent thunder and rain. And the people became very afraid of the LORD and Samuel. [19]All the people said to Samuel, "Pray to the LORD your God for us, your servants. Don't let us die! We have sinned many times. And now we have added to these sins—we have asked for a king."

[20]Samuel answered, "Don't be afraid. It is true that you did all these bad things, but don't stop following the LORD. Serve the LORD with all your heart. [21]Idols are only statues—they can't help you. So don't worship them. Idols can't help you or save you. They are nothing!

[22]"But the LORD won't leave his people. No, the LORD was pleased to make you his own people. So for his own good name, he won't leave you. [23]And as for me, I would never stop praying for you. If I stopped praying for you, I would be sinning against the LORD. I will continue to teach you the right way to live a good life. [24]But you must honour the LORD. You must serve him sincerely with all your heart. Remember the wonderful things he has done for you. [25]But if you are stubborn and do evil, God will throw you and your king away, like dirt swept out with a broom."

Saul Causes Trouble for Israel

13 Saul was 30[g] years old when he became king. He ruled over Israel for 42 years.[h] [2]Saul chose 3,000 men from Israel. There were 2,000 men who stayed with him at Micmash in the hill country of Bethel. There were 1,000 men who stayed with Jonathan at Gibeah in Benjamin. Saul sent the other men in the army back home.

[3]Jonathan defeated the Philistines at their camp in Geba. The Philistines heard about this. They said, "The Hebrews have rebelled."[i]

---

[a] **12:3 chosen king** Literally, "anointed one". Also in verse 5.
[b] **12:11 Gideon** Literally, "Jerub-Baal", a nickname given to Gideon earlier. (See Judg. 6:32.)
[c] **12:11 Barak** This is found in the ancient Greek and Syriac versions. The Hebrew has "Bedan".
[d] **12:11 Samuel** The Syriac version and some copies of the Greek version have "Samson".
[e] **12:14 If you do, God will save you** This is from the ancient Greek version.
[f] **12:17 time of . . . harvest** This was the dry time of year when no rains fell.
[g] **13:1 30** This first number and part of the second number in this verse are missing in the Hebrew text. The whole verse is missing from most copies of the ancient Greek version, but a few late Greek copies have the numbers 30 and 42. Acts 13:21 says that Saul was king for 40 years.
[h] **13:1 He ruled . . . 42 years** Or "After he had ruled over Israel for 2 years, . . .".
[i] **13:3 They said . . . rebelled** This is from the ancient Greek version.

Saul said, "Let the Hebrew people hear what happened." So Saul told the men to blow trumpets through all the land of Israel. 4All the Israelites heard this news: "Saul has killed the Philistine leader. Now the Philistines will really hate the Israelites!"

The Israelites were called to join Saul at Gilgal. 5The Philistines gathered to fight Israel. The Philistines camped at Micmash, east of Beth Aven. They had 3,000*a* chariots and 6,000 horsemen. There were so many Philistines that they were like sand on the seashore.

6The Israelites saw that they were in trouble. They felt trapped. They ran away to hide in caves and cracks in the rock. They hid among the rocks, in wells and in other holes in the ground. 7Some Hebrews even went across the Jordan River to the land of Gad and Gilead. Saul was still at Gilgal. All the men in his army were shaking with fear.

8Samuel said he would meet Saul at Gilgal. Saul waited there seven days. But Samuel had not yet come to Gilgal, and the soldiers began to leave Saul. 9So Saul said, "Bring me the burnt offerings and the fellowship offerings." Then Saul offered the burnt offering. 10As soon as Saul finished offering that sacrifice, Samuel arrived. Saul went out to meet him.

11Samuel asked, "What have you done?"

Saul answered, "I saw the soldiers leaving me. You were not here on time, and the Philistines were gathering at Micmash. 12I thought to myself, 'The Philistines will come here and attack me at Gilgal, and I haven't asked the LORD to help us yet.' So I forced myself to offer the burnt offering."

13Samuel said, "You did a foolish thing. You did not obey the LORD your God. If you had done what he commanded, the LORD would have let your family rule Israel forever. 14But now your kingdom won't continue. The LORD was looking for a man who wants to obey him.*b* He has found that man—and the LORD has chosen him to be the new leader of his people, because you didn't obey his command." 15Then Samuel got up and left Gilgal.

The Battle at Micmash

Saul and the rest of his army left Gilgal*c* and went to Gibeah in Benjamin. Saul counted the men who were still with him. There were about 600. 16Saul, his son Jonathan and the soldiers went to Geba in Benjamin.

The Philistines were camped at Micmash. 17So their best soldiers began the attack. The Philistine army split into three groups. One group went north on the road to Ophrah, near Shual. 18The second group went south-east on the road to Beth Horon, and the third group went east on the road to the border. That road looks over the Valley of Zeboim towards the desert.

19There were no blacksmiths in Israel. The Philistines would not allow them because they were afraid the Israelites would make iron swords and spears. 20Only the Philistines could sharpen iron tools. So if the Israelites needed to sharpen their ploughs, hoes, axes or sickles, they had to go to the Philistines. 21The Philistine blacksmiths charged 8 grammes*d* of silver for sharpening ploughs and hoes and 4 grammes*e* of silver for sharpening picks, axes and the iron tip on ox goads. 22So on the day of battle, none of the Israelite soldiers with Saul had iron swords or spears. Only Saul and his son Jonathan had such weapons.

23A group of Philistine soldiers guarded the mountain pass at Micmash.

Jonathan Attacks the Philistines

14 That day, Saul's son Jonathan was talking with the young man who carried his weapons. Jonathan said, "Let's go to the Philistine camp on the other side of the valley." But Jonathan did not tell his father.

2Saul was sitting under a pomegranate tree at the threshing floor*f* at the edge of the hill.*g* Saul had about 600 men with him. 3One of the men was named Ahijah. Ahijah was a son of Ichabod's brother Ahitub. Ahitub was the son of Phinehas. Phinehas was the son of Eli. Eli had been the LORD's priest at Shiloh. Now Ahijah was the priest who wore the ephod.

These men did not know that Jonathan had left. 4Jonathan was planning to go through a pass to get to the Philistine camp. There was a large rock on each side of the pass. The large rock on one side was named Bozez. The large rock on the other side was named Seneh. 5One of the rocks faced north towards Micmash, and the other faced south towards Geba.

---

a **13:5 3,000** This is found in some copies of the ancient Greek version and the Syriac version. The standard Hebrew text has "30,000".

b **13:14 a man who wants to obey him** Literally, "a man according to his heart". This could also mean "a man of his own choosing".

c **13:15 Saul and the rest of his army left Gilgal** This is found in the ancient Greek version but not in the standard Hebrew text.

d **13:21 8 grammes** Literally, "1 *pim*".

e **13:21 4 grammes** Literally, "½ *shekel*".

f **14:2 at the threshing floor** Or "in Migron".

g **14:2 edge of the hill** Or "the edge of Gibeah".

⁶Jonathan said to his young helper who carried his weapons, "Come on, let's go to the camp of those foreigners.ᵃ Maybe the LORD will use us to defeat them. Nothing can stop the LORD—it doesn't matter if we have many soldiers or just a few soldiers."

⁷The young man who carried Jonathan's weapons said to him, "Do what you think is best. Whatever you decide, I am with you all the way."

⁸Jonathan said, "Let's go! We'll cross the valley and go to the Philistine guards. We'll let them see us. ⁹If they say to us, 'Stay there until we come to you,' we will stay where we are. We won't go up to them. ¹⁰But if the Philistine men say, 'Come up here,' then we will climb up to them. That will be a sign from God. That will mean that the LORD will allow us to defeat them."

¹¹So Jonathan and his helper let the Philistines see them. The Philistine guards said, "Look! The Hebrews are coming out of the holes they were hiding in." ¹²The Philistines in the fortress shouted to Jonathan and his helper, "Come up here. We'll teach you a lesson."

Jonathan said to his helper, "Follow me up the hill. The LORD is letting Israel defeat the Philistines."

¹³⁻¹⁴So Jonathan climbed up the hill with his hands and feet, and his helper was right behind him. Jonathan and his helper attacked them. In the first attack, they killed 20 Philistines in an area about a quarter of a hectare in size. Jonathan fought the men who attacked from the front. His helper came behind him and killed the men who were only wounded.

¹⁵Great fear spread among the Philistine soldiers—those in the field, in the camp and at the fortress. Even the bravest soldiers were afraid. The ground began to shake, and they were completely overcome with fear.

¹⁶Saul's guards at Gibeah in the land of Benjamin saw the Philistine soldiers running away in different directions. ¹⁷Saul said to the army with him, "Count the men. I want to know who left camp."

They counted the men. Jonathan and his helper were gone.

¹⁸Saul said to Ahijah, "Bring God's Holy Box!" (At that time God's Holy Box was there with the Israelites.)ᵇ ¹⁹Saul was talking to Ahijah the priest ⌊waiting for advice from God⌋. But the noise and confusion in the Philistine camp was growing and

growing. Saul was becoming impatient. Finally, he said to Ahijah the priest, "That's enough. Put your hand down ⌊and stop praying⌋."

²⁰Saul gathered his army together and went to the battle. The Philistine soldiers were very confused. They were even fighting each other with their swords. ²¹There were Hebrews who had served the Philistines in the past and who stayed in the Philistine camp. But now these Hebrews joined the Israelites with Saul and Jonathan. ²²All the Israelites who had hidden in the hill country of Ephraim heard the Philistine soldiers were running away. So these Israelites also joined in the battle and began chasing the Philistines.

²³So the LORD saved the Israelites that day. The battle moved on past Beth Aven. The whole army was with Saul—he now had about 10,000 men. The battle spread to every city in the hill country of Ephraim.ᶜ

Saul Makes Another Mistake

²⁴But Saul made a big mistake that day.ᵈ He made this oath: "If any man eats food before evening comes, before I finish defeating my enemies, he will be under a curse." He made the soldiers promise not to eat. So none of them ate anything.

²⁵⁻²⁶Because of the fighting, the people went into some woods. Then they saw a honeycomb on the ground. The Israelites went up to the honeycomb, but they didn't eat any of it. They were afraid to break the promise. ²⁷But Jonathan didn't know about the oath. He didn't hear his father make the soldiers promise not to eat. Jonathan had a stick in his hand, so he dipped the end of the stick into the honeycomb and pulled out some honey. He ate the honey and began to feel much better.

²⁸One of the soldiers told Jonathan, "Your father forced the soldiers to make a special promise. He said that any man who eats today will be under a curse. So the men have not eaten anything. That's why they are weak."

²⁹Jonathan said, "My father has brought a lot of trouble to the land. See how much better I feel after tasting just a little of this honey. ³⁰It would have been much better for the men to eat the food that they took from their enemies today. We could have killed more Philistines."

³¹That day the Israelites defeated the Philistines. They fought them all the way from

---

ᵃ **14:6 foreigners** Literally, "uncircumcised". This means people who did not share in the agreement God made with Israel. See "CIRCUMCISE, CIRCUMCISION" in the Word List.

ᵇ **14:18** The ancient Greek and Latin versions have "Saul said to Ahijah, 'Bring the ephod!' (At that time Ahijah was wearing the ephod.)"

ᶜ **14:23 The whole army . . . Ephraim** This is from the ancient Greek version.

ᵈ **14:24 But Saul . . . that day** This is from the ancient Greek version. The standard Hebrew text has "The Israelites were very tired and hungry that day."

Micmash to Aijalon. So the people were very tired and hungry. [32]They had taken sheep, cattle and calves from the Philistines. Now they were so hungry that they killed the animals on the ground and ate them. And the blood was still in the animals.

[33]Someone said to Saul, "Look, the men are sinning against the LORD. They're eating meat that still has blood in it!"

Saul said, "You have sinned. Roll a large stone over here now!" [34]Then Saul said, "Go to the men and tell them that each one must bring his bull and sheep to me. Then the men must kill their bulls and sheep here. Don't sin against the LORD! Don't eat meat that still has blood in it."

That night everyone brought their animals and killed them there. [35]Then Saul built an altar for the LORD. Saul himself began building that altar for the LORD.

[36]Saul said, "Let's go after the Philistines tonight. We will take everything from them. We will kill them all!"

The army answered, "Do whatever you think is best."

But the priest said, "Let's ask God."

[37]So Saul asked God, "Should I go chase the Philistines? Will you let us defeat the Philistines?" But God did not answer Saul that day.

[38]So Saul said, "Bring all the leaders to me! Let's find who committed the sin today. [39]I swear by the LORD who saves Israel, that even if my own son Jonathan sinned, he must die." None of the people said a word.

[40]Then Saul said to all the Israelites, "You stand on this side. I and my son Jonathan will stand on the other side."

The soldiers answered, "As you wish, sir."

[41]Then Saul prayed, "LORD, God of Israel, why haven't you answered me today? Show us who sinned. If it was I or my son Jonathan, give Urim. But if it was your people Israel who sinned, give Thummim."[a]

Saul and Jonathan were shown to be the ones who sinned, and the people went free. [42]Saul said, "Throw them again to show the guilty one—me or my son Jonathan." Jonathan was shown to be the one.

[43]Saul said to Jonathan, "Tell me what you have done."

Jonathan told Saul, "I only tasted a little honey from the end of my stick. Should I die for doing that?"

[44]Saul said, "I made an oath and asked God to punish me if I didn't keep it. Jonathan, you must die."

[45]But the soldiers said to Saul, "Jonathan led Israel to a great victory today. Must Jonathan die? Never! As surely as the LORD lives, not one hair of Jonathan's head will fall to the ground! God helped Jonathan fight against the Philistines today." So the people saved Jonathan from death.

[46]Saul did not chase the Philistines. The Philistines went back to their land.

Saul Fights Israel's Enemies

[47]Saul took full control of Israel and fought all the enemies who lived around Israel. Saul fought Moab, the Ammonites, Edom, the king of Zobah and the Philistines. He defeated Israel's enemies wherever he went. [48]Saul was very brave. He saved Israel from all the enemies who tried to take things from the Israelites. He even defeated the Amalekites.

[49]Saul's sons were Jonathan, Ishvi and Malki Shua. Saul's older daughter was named Merab. Saul's younger daughter was named Michal. [50]Saul's wife was named Ahinoam. Ahinoam was the daughter of Ahimaaz.

The commander of Saul's army was named Abner son of Ner. Ner was Saul's uncle. [51]Saul's father Kish and Abner's father Ner were sons of Abiel.

[52]Saul was brave all his life. He fought hard against the Philistines. Any time Saul saw a man who was strong or brave, he took that man and put him into the group of soldiers who stayed near the king and protected him.

Saul Destroys the Amalekites

15 One day Samuel said to Saul, "The LORD sent me to anoint you king over his people Israel. Now listen to his message. [2]The LORD All-Powerful says, 'When the Israelites came out of Egypt, the Amalekites tried to stop them from going to Canaan. I saw what the Amalekites did. [3]Now go and fight against the Amalekites. You must completely destroy the Amalekites and everything that belongs to them. Don't let anything live; you must kill all the men and women and all their children and little babies. You must kill all their cattle and sheep and all their camels and donkeys.'"

[4]Saul gathered the army together at Telaim. There were 200,000 foot soldiers and 10,000 other men, including the men from Judah. [5]Then Saul went to the city of Amalek and waited in the valley. [6]He said to the Kenites, "Go away! Leave the Amalekites. Then I won't destroy you with the Amalekites. You showed kindness to the

---

[a] **14:41** *Then Saul prayed . . . give Thummim* This is found in the ancient Greek version. The standard Hebrew text has "Then Saul prayed to the Lord, God of Israel, 'Give the right answer.'"

A FALSE START, A NEW HOPE

Do you ever wonder if God is really taking much notice of you? Can you look back on situations where it seemed he just wasn't paying attention? Do you feel that way now?

We've already seen how God sometimes chooses to use history to teach the people he loves the things he needs them to know (see the Bible Bit "Be Careful What You Wish For" on 1 Samuel chapter 8). Sometimes God will let a situation rumble on, waiting for just the right time to act. But he's always aware of what's going on – and he's always in control.

DIG IN
READ 1 Samuel 15:10–35

- What had Saul done wrong in God's eyes (v.11)?
- What are the consequences going to be (v.28)?

Saul was the man God chose to be Israel's first king. He had a lot going for him, and things started well – he got an early military victory and at first seemed to be walking closely with God. But it didn't last. He turned out to be flawed in many ways. This passage is where God finally gives up on Saul and names his replacement.

- What impression do you get of Saul from the way he defends himself and his actions to Samuel (vv.15, 20–21,24,30)?
- What's noticeable about the way Saul refers to God in those verses?

Saul's account of what happened doesn't cut it with Samuel. First he tries to change the subject to sacrifices (which, Samuel reminds him, is not what God is really after: he wants heartfelt obedience). Then Saul reveals that he's much more interested in pleasing people than pleasing God (v.24).

You might also have picked up on the way he talks about God – he repeatedly calls him "the Lᴏʀᴅ your God", not "my God" or "our God". This contrasts sharply with the way David (the next king) speaks to and about God later in the books of Samuel and in the Psalms. You get the feeling that the Lord is a close personal friend to David. That's not the case with Saul.

READ 1 Samuel 16:1–13

God sends Samuel on a secret mission to find Saul's successor and he has to avoid anything that might look suspicious to Saul. Nothing's public yet – this is between Samuel and God.

DIG THROUGH

- Do you have any sympathy for poor old Saul? Can you recognize aspects of yourself in the way he behaves? It's not as simple as Saul = bad, David = good. Both rulers attract the favour of God at times; both come crashing down because of their characters' flaws at other times.
- How do you think God felt about the way things worked out with Saul? Samuel says that "[God] is not like a man who is always changing his mind" (15:29) yet he still says God "was very sorry that he had made Saul king" (15:35). God has a plan for history – bigger than any of us can get our heads around. Yet, amazingly, it still matters to him how individual situations turn out.

DIG DEEPER

- As you read 1 Samuel, it might be useful to have a notebook and pen handy so you can jot down the different character traits of Saul and David. What obvious differences are there? What clear contrasts between the two men can you detect?

Israelites when they came out of Egypt." So the Kenites left the Amalekites.

⁷Saul defeated the Amalekites. He fought them and chased them all the way from Havilah to Shur, at the border of Egypt. ⁸Agag was the king of the Amalekites. Saul captured Agag alive. Saul let Agag live, but he killed all the men in Agag's army. ⁹Saul and the Israelite soldiers felt bad about destroying everything. So they let Agag live. They also kept the fat cattle, the best sheep and the lambs. They kept everything that was worth keeping. They didn't want to destroy those things. They destroyed only what was not worth keeping.

Samuel Tells Saul About His Sin

¹⁰Then Samuel received this message from the LORD: ¹¹"Saul has stopped following me, so I am sorry that I made him king. He is not doing what I tell him." Samuel became angry and cried to the LORD all night.

¹²Samuel got up early the next morning and went to meet Saul. But the people told Samuel, "Saul went to Carmel. He went there to set up a stone monument to honour himself. Then he left there and went down to Gilgal."

So Samuel went to Saul. Saul had just offered the first part of the things he took from the Amalekites as a burnt offering to the Lord.ᵃ ¹³When Samuel came near to Saul, Saul greeted him and said, "The LORD bless you! I have obeyed the LORD's commands."

¹⁴But Samuel said, "Then what is that sound I hear? Why do I hear sheep and cattle?"

¹⁵Saul said, "The soldiers took them from the Amalekites. They saved the best sheep and cattle to burn as sacrifices to the LORD your God. But we destroyed everything else."

¹⁶Samuel said to Saul, "Stop! Let me tell you what the LORD told me last night."

Saul answered, "Tell me what he said."

¹⁷Samuel said, "In the past you didn't think that you were important, but the LORD chose you to be the king. So you became the leader of the tribes of Israel. ¹⁸The LORD sent you on a special mission. He said, 'Go and destroy all the Amalekites. They are evil people. Destroy them all! Fight them until they are completely finished.' ¹⁹So why didn't you listen to the LORD? You did what the LORD said is wrong because you wanted to keep what you took in battle."

²⁰Saul said, "But I did obey the LORD! I went where the LORD sent me. I destroyed all the Amalekites. I brought back only one—their king, Agag. ²¹And the soldiers took the best sheep and cattle to sacrifice to the LORD your God at Gilgal."

²²But Samuel answered,

"Which pleases the LORD more:
    burnt offerings and sacrifices
    or obeying his commands?
It is better to obey the Lord than to offer
    sacrifices to him.
It is better to listen to him than to offer the
    fat from rams.
²³Refusing to obey is as bad as the sin of
    sorcery.
Being stubborn and doing what you want is
    like the sin of worshipping idols.
You refused to obey the LORD's command,
    so he now refuses to accept you as king."

²⁴Then Saul said to Samuel, "I have sinned. I did not obey the LORD's commands, and I did not do what you told me. I was afraid of the people, and I did what they said. ²⁵Now I beg you, forgive me for committing this sin. Come back with me, so I may worship the LORD."

²⁶But Samuel said to Saul, "I won't go back with you. You rejected the LORD's command, and now the LORD rejects you as king of Israel."

²⁷When Samuel turned to leave, Saul caught Samuel's robe. The robe tore. ²⁸Samuel said to Saul, "In this same way the LORD has torn the kingdom of Israel from you today. He has given the kingdom to one of your friends, a man who is a better person than you. ²⁹The one who lives forever, the God of Israel, does not lie and will not change his mind. He is not like a man who is always changing his mind."

³⁰Saul answered, "It is true that I sinned! But please come back with me. Show me some respect in front of the leaders and the Israelites. Come with me so that I may worship the LORD your God." ³¹Samuel went back with Saul, and Saul worshipped the LORD.

³²Samuel said, "Bring King Agag of the Amalekites to me."

Agag came to Samuel. Agag was tied with chains and thought, "Surely he won't kill me."ᵇ

³³But Samuel said to Agag, "Your sword took babies from their mothers. So now, your mother will have no children." And Samuel cut Agag to pieces before the LORD at Gilgal.

³⁴Then Samuel left and went to Ramah. And Saul went up to his home in Gibeah. ³⁵After that, Samuel never saw Saul again. Samuel was very sad for Saul. And the LORD was very sorry that he had made Saul king of Israel.

ᵃ **15:12 Saul had just offered . . . Lord** This is from the ancient Greek version.
ᵇ **15:32 Surely . . . kill me** The ancient Greek version has "This treatment is worse than death."

Samuel Goes to Bethlehem

16 The LORD said to Samuel, "How long will you feel sorry for Saul? I have rejected him as king of Israel. Fill your horn[a] with oil and go to Bethlehem. I am sending you to Jesse who lives in Bethlehem, because I have chosen one of his sons to be the new king."

²But Samuel said, "If I go, Saul will hear the news and try to kill me."

The LORD said, "Go to Bethlehem. Take a young calf with you and tell them, 'I have come to make a sacrifice to the LORD.' ³Invite Jesse to the sacrifice. Then I will show you what to do. You must anoint the person I show you."

⁴Samuel did what the LORD told him to do and went to Bethlehem. The leaders of Bethlehem shook with fear. They met Samuel and asked, "Do you come in peace?"

⁵Samuel answered, "Yes, I come in peace. I come to make a sacrifice to the LORD. Prepare yourselves and come to the sacrifice with me." Samuel prepared Jesse and his sons. Then he invited them to come and share the sacrifice.

⁶When Jesse and his sons arrived, Samuel saw Eliab and thought, "Surely this is the man who the LORD has chosen."

⁷But the LORD said to Samuel, "Eliab is tall and handsome, but don't judge by things like that. God doesn't look at what people see. People judge by what is on the outside, but the LORD looks at the heart. Eliab is not the right man."

⁸Then Jesse called his second son, Abinadab. Abinadab walked by Samuel. But Samuel said, "No, this is not the man who the LORD chose."

⁹Then Jesse told Shammah to walk by Samuel. But Samuel said, "No, the LORD did not choose this man, either."

¹⁰Jesse showed seven of his sons to Samuel. But Samuel said to Jesse, "The LORD has not chosen any of these men."

¹¹Then he asked Jesse, "Are these all the sons you have?"

Jesse answered, "No, I have another son—my youngest, but he is out taking care of the sheep."

Samuel said, "Send for him. Bring him here. We won't sit down to eat until he arrives."

¹²Jesse sent someone to get his youngest son. This son was a good-looking, healthy[b] young man. He was very handsome.

The LORD said to Samuel, "Get up and anoint him. He is the one."

¹³Samuel took the horn with the oil in it, and poured the special oil on Jesse's youngest son in front of his brothers. The Spirit of the LORD came on David with great power from that day on. Then Samuel went back home to Ramah.

INSIGHT

David was just a young man when Samuel anointed him to lead God's people, but that wasn't a problem for God. The Bible is full of stories that show God using young people.

1 Samuel 16:11–13

An Evil Spirit Bothers Saul

¹⁴The LORD's Spirit left Saul. Then the LORD sent an evil spirit to Saul that caused him much trouble. ¹⁵Saul's servants said to him, "An evil spirit from God is bothering you. ¹⁶Give us the command and we will look for someone who can play the harp. If the evil spirit from God comes on you, this person will play music for you. Then you will feel better."

¹⁷So Saul said to his servants, "Find someone who plays music well and bring him to me."

¹⁸One of the servants said, "There is a man named Jesse living in Bethlehem. I saw Jesse's son. He knows how to play the harp. He is also a brave man and fights well. He is smart and handsome, and the LORD is with him."

¹⁹So Saul sent messengers to Jesse. They told Jesse, "You have a son named David. He takes care of your sheep. Send him to me."

²⁰So Jesse got some things as a gift for Saul. Jesse got a donkey, some bread and a leather bag full of wine and a young goat. He gave them to David and sent him to Saul. ²¹So David went to Saul and stood in front of him. Saul loved David very much. David became the helper who carried Saul's weapons. ²²Saul sent a message to Jesse. "Let David stay and serve me. I like him very much."

²³Any time the evil spirit from God came on Saul, David would take his harp and play it. The evil spirit would leave Saul and he would begin to feel better.

Goliath Challenges Israel

17 The Philistines gathered their armies together for war. They met at Socoh in Judah. Their camp was between Socoh and Azekah, at a town called Ephes Dammim. ²Saul and the Israelite soldiers also gathered together. Their camp was in the Valley of Elah.

---

[a] 16:1 *horn* An animal's horn is hollow and often used like a bottle.
[b] 16:12 *healthy* The Hebrew word means "red", "ruddy" or "red-haired". Also in 17:42.

Saul's soldiers were lined up and ready to fight the Philistines. ³The Philistines were on one hill. The Israelites were on the other hill. The valley was between them.

⁴The Philistines had a champion fighter named Goliath, who was from Gath. He was almost 3 metres*a* tall. Goliath came out of the Philistine camp. ⁵He had a bronze helmet on his head. He wore a coat of armour that was made like the scales on a fish. This armour was made of bronze and weighed about 57 kilogrammes.*b* ⁶Goliath wore bronze protectors on his legs. He had a bronze javelin tied on his back. ⁷The wooden part of his spear was as big as a weaver's rod. The spear's blade weighed 7 kilogrammes.*c* Goliath's helper walked in front of him, carrying Goliath's shield.

⁸Each day Goliath would come out and shout a challenge to the Israelite soldiers. He would say, "Why are all your soldiers lined up ready for battle? You are Saul's servants. I am a Philistine. So choose one man and send him to fight me. ⁹If that man kills me, he wins and we Philistines will become your slaves. But if I kill your man, then I win, and you will become our slaves. You will have to serve us."

¹⁰The Philistine also said, "Today I stand and make fun of the army of Israel. I dare you to send me one of your men and let us fight."

¹¹Saul and the Israelite soldiers heard what Goliath said, and they were very afraid.

David Goes to the Battle Front

¹²*d* David was the son of Jesse, who belonged to the family of Ephrathah from Bethlehem in Judah. Jesse had eight sons. In Saul's time Jesse was an old man. ¹³Jesse's three oldest sons went with Saul to the war. The first son was Eliab, the second was Abinadab, and the third was Shammah. ¹⁴David was the youngest son. The three oldest sons were in Saul's army, ¹⁵but David left Saul from time to time to take care of his father's sheep at Bethlehem.

¹⁶The Philistine came out every morning and evening and stood before the Israelite army. Goliath insulted Israel like this for 40 days.

¹⁷One day Jesse said to his son David, "Take this basket*e* of cooked grain and these ten loaves of bread to your brothers in the camp. ¹⁸Also take these ten pieces of cheese for the officer who commands your brothers' group of 1,000 soldiers. See how your brothers are doing. Bring back something to show me your brothers are all right. ¹⁹Your brothers are with Saul and all the Israelite soldiers in the Valley of Elah. They are there to fight against the Philistines."

²⁰Early in the morning, David got another shepherd to take care of the sheep while he took the food and left as Jesse had told him to. When David arrived at the camp, the soldiers were going out to their battle positions. The soldiers began shouting their war cry. ²¹The Israelites and Philistines were lined up and ready for battle.

²²David left the food with the man who kept supplies. Then he ran to the place where the Israelite soldiers were and asked about his brothers. ²³While David was talking with his brothers, the Philistine champion fighter came out from the Philistine army. This was Goliath, the Philistine from Gath. Goliath shouted things against Israel as usual. David heard what he said.

²⁴The Israelite soldiers saw Goliath and ran away. They were all afraid of him. ²⁵One of the Israelite men said, "Did you see that man? Look at him! He comes out each day and makes fun of Israel. Whoever kills him will get rich. King Saul will give him a lot of money. Saul will also let his daughter marry the man who kills Goliath. He will also make that man's family free from taxes in Israel."

²⁶David asked the men standing near him, "What did he say? What is the reward for killing this Philistine and taking away this shame from Israel? Who is this Goliath anyway? He is only some foreigner,*f* nothing but a Philistine. Why does he think he can speak against the army of the living God?"

²⁷So the Israelite told David about the reward for killing Goliath. ²⁸David's oldest brother Eliab heard David talking with the soldiers and became angry. Eliab asked David, "Why did you come here? Who did you leave those few sheep with in the desert? I know why you came down here. You didn't want to do what you were told to do. You just wanted to come down here to watch the battle."

²⁹David said, "What have I done now? I haven't done anything wrong! I was only talking." ³⁰He turned to some other people and asked them the

---

a **17:4 almost 3 metres** Literally, "6 *cubits* and 1 *span*". Josephus, most copies of the ancient Greek version, and a Hebrew scroll from Qumran all have "4 *cubits* and 1 *span*".
b **17:5 57 kilogrammes** Literally, "5,000 *shekels*".
c **17:7 7 kilogrammes** Literally, "600 *shekels*".
d **17:12** The oldest copies of the ancient Greek version do not have 17:12–31,41,48b, 50,55–58; 18:1–5,10–11,17–19,29b-30.
e **17:17 basket** Literally, "*ephah*" (10 kilogrammes).
f **17:26 foreigner** Literally, "uncircumcised". This means a person who did not share in the agreement God made with Israel. See "CIRCUMCISE, CIRCUMCISION" in the Word List. Also in verse 36.

same questions. They gave him the same answers as before.

[31] Some men heard David talking. They took David to Saul and told him what David had said. [32] David said to Saul, "People shouldn't let Goliath discourage them. I am your servant. I will go and fight this Philistine."

INSIGHT

David was only visiting the battlefield to take supplies to his brothers; he wasn't old enough to be in the army. Yet he used the skills and confidence God had given him through his life experiences to win in what seemed an impossible situation with God's help.

1 Samuel 17:32–54

---

[33] Saul answered, "You can't go out and fight against this Philistine. You're not even a soldier![a] Goliath has been fighting in wars since he was a boy."

[34] But David said to Saul, "There were times when I was taking care of my father's sheep that wild animals came to take some sheep from the flock. Once there was a lion and another time, a bear. [35] I chased that wild animal, attacked it, and took the sheep from its mouth. The wild animal jumped on me, but I caught it by the fur under its mouth. And I hit it and killed it. [36] I killed both a lion and a bear like that! And I will kill that foreigner, Goliath, just like them. Goliath will die because he made fun of the army of the living God. [37] The Lord saved me from the lion and the bear. He will also save me from this Philistine."

Saul said to David, "Go and may the Lord be with you." [38] Saul put his own clothes on David. He put a bronze helmet on David's head and armour on his body. [39] David put on the sword and tried to walk around. He tried to wear Saul's uniform, but David was not used to all those heavy things.

David said to Saul, "I can't fight in these things. I'm not used to them." So David took them all off. [40] He took his walking stick in his hand and went to find five smooth stones from the stream. He put the five stones in his shepherd's bag and held his sling in his hand. Then he went out to meet the Philistine.

David Kills Goliath

[41] The Philistine slowly walked closer and closer to David. Goliath's helper walked in front

of him, carrying a large shield. [42] Goliath looked at David and saw that he was nothing more than a handsome, healthy boy. Showing no respect for David, Goliath made fun of him. [43] He said, "What is that stick for? Did you come to chase me away like a dog?" Then Goliath used the names of his gods to say curses against David. [44] He said to David, "Come here, and I'll feed your body to the birds and wild animals."

[45] David said to the Philistine, "You come to me using sword, spear and javelin. But I come to you in the name of the Lord All-Powerful, the God of the armies of Israel. You have said bad things about him. [46] Today the Lord will let me defeat you. I will kill you. I will cut off your head and feed your body to the birds and wild animals. And we will do the same thing to all the other Philistines too. Then all the world will know there is a God in Israel. [47] All the people gathered here will know that the Lord doesn't need swords or spears to save people. The battle belongs to the Lord, and he will help us defeat all of you."

[48] Goliath the Philistine started to attack David. He slowly walked closer and closer towards David, but David ran out to meet Goliath.

[49] David took out a stone from his bag. He put it in his sling and swung the sling. The stone flew from the sling and hit Goliath right between the eyes. The stone sank deep into his head, and Goliath fell to the ground—face down.

[50] So David defeated the Philistine with only a sling and one stone! He hit the Philistine and killed him. David didn't have a sword, [51] so he ran and stood beside the Philistine. Then David took Goliath's own sword out of its sheath and used it to cut off his head. That is how David killed the Philistine.

When the other Philistines saw their hero was dead, they turned and ran. [52] The soldiers of Israel and Judah shouted and started chasing the Philistines. The Israelites chased them all the way to the city limits of Gath and to the gates of Ekron. They killed many of the Philistines. Their bodies were scattered along the Shaaraim road all the way to Gath and Ekron. [53] After chasing the Philistines, the Israelites came back to the Philistine camp and took many things from that camp.

[54] David took the Philistine's head to Jerusalem, but he kept the Philistine's weapons at home.

Saul Begins to Fear David

[55] Saul watched David go out to fight Goliath. Saul spoke to Abner, the commander of the army. "Abner, who is that young man's father?"

---

[a] **17:33 You're not even a soldier** Or "You are only a boy!" The Hebrew word for "boy" often means "servant" or "the helper who carries a soldier's weapons".

Abner answered, "I swear I don't know, sir."
⁵⁶King Saul said, "Find out who his father is."
⁵⁷When David came back after killing Goliath, Abner brought him to Saul. David was still holding the Philistine's head.
⁵⁸Saul asked him, "Young man, who is your father?"

David answered, "I am the son of your servant Jesse, from Bethlehem."

David and Jonathan Become Friends

18 Saul decided to take David with him. He would not let David go back home to his father. ²After David finished talking with Saul, Jonathan developed a strong friendship with David.ᵃ ³Jonathan loved David as much as himself, so they made a special agreement. ⁴Jonathan took off the coat he was wearing and gave it to David. In fact, Jonathan gave David his whole uniform—including his sword, his bow and even his belt.

Saul Notices David's Success

⁵David went to fight wherever Saul sent him. He was very successful, so Saul put him in charge of the soldiers. This pleased everyone, even Saul's officers. ⁶David would go out to fight against the Philistines. On the way home after the battles, women in every town in Israel would come out to meet him. They sang and danced for joy as they played their tambourines and lyres. They did this right in front of Saul! ⁷The women sang,

"Saul has killed his thousands,
    but David has killed tens of thousands."

⁸This song upset Saul and he became very angry. Saul thought, "The women give David credit for killing tens of thousands of the enemy, and they give me credit for only thousands. A little more of this and they will give him the kingdom itself!"ᵇ ⁹So from that time on, Saul watched David very closely.

Saul Is Afraid of David

¹⁰The next day, an evil spirit from God took control of Saul and he went wildᶜ in his house. David played the harp to calm him as he usually did, ¹¹but Saul had a spear in his hand. He thought, "I'll pin David to the wall." Saul threw the spear twice, but David jumped out of the way both times.

¹²The LORD had left Saul and was now with David, so Saul was afraid of David. ¹³Saul sent David away and made him a commander over 1,000 soldiers. This put David out among the men even more as they went into battle and returned. ¹⁴The LORD was with David, so he was successful in everything. ¹⁵Saul saw how successful David was and became even more afraid of him. ¹⁶But all the people in Israel and Judah loved David because he was out among them and led them into battle.

Saul Wants His Daughter to Marry David

¹⁷One day Saul said to David, "Here is my oldest daughter, Merab. I will let you marry her. Then you will be like a son to me and you will be a real soldier.ᵈ Then you will go and fight the LORD's battles." Saul was really thinking, "Now I won't have to kill David. I will let the Philistines kill him for me."

¹⁸But David said, "I am not an important man from an important family. I can't marry the king's daughter."

¹⁹So when the time came for David to marry Saul's daughter, Saul let her marry Adriel from Meholah.

²⁰People told Saul that his daughter Michal loved David. This made Saul happy. ²¹He thought, "I will use Michal to trap David. I will let Michal marry David, and then I will let the Philistines kill him." So Saul said to David a second time, "You can marry my daughter today."

²²Saul commanded his officers to speak to David in private. He told them to say, "Look, the king likes you. His officers like you. You should marry his daughter."

²³Saul's officers said these things to David, but David answered, "Do you think it is easy to become the king's son-in-law? I am just a poor, ordinary man."

²⁴Saul's officers told Saul what David said. ²⁵Saul told them, "Say this to David, 'David, the king doesn't want you to pay money for his daughter.ᵉ He wants to get even with his enemy, so the price for marrying his daughter is 100 Philistine foreskins.'" That was Saul's secret plan. He thought the Philistines would kill David.

²⁶Saul's officers told this to David. David was happy that he had a chance to become the king's son-in-law, so immediately ²⁷he and his men went out to fight the Philistines. They killed 200ᶠ

ᵃ **18:1–2 Jonathan . . . with David** Literally, "Jonathan's soul was tied to David's soul".
ᵇ **18:8 A little more . . . itself** This is not in one of the oldest and best copies of the ancient Greek version.
ᶜ **18:10 Saul . . . wild** Or "Saul prophesied". The Hebrew word means that the person lost control of what they said and did. Usually this meant God was using them to give a special message to other people.
ᵈ **18:17 real soldier** That is, a member of the warrior class. They were free from certain duties of ordinary citizens.
ᵉ **18:25 money for his daughter** In Bible times a man usually had to give money to a woman's father before he could marry her.
ᶠ **18:27 200** The ancient Greek version has "100".

Philistines. David took the Philistine foreskins and gave them to Saul. He did this because he wanted to become the king's son-in-law.

Saul let David marry his daughter Michal. 28He saw that the LORD was with David and he also saw that his daughter, Michal, loved David. 29So Saul became even more afraid of David and was against him all that time.

30The Philistine commanders continued to go out to fight the Israelites, but David defeated them every time. He became famous as Saul's best officer.

Jonathan Helps David

19 Saul told his son Jonathan and his officers to kill David. But Jonathan liked David very much, 2-3so he warned him. "Be careful! Saul is looking for a chance to kill you. In the morning go into the field and hide. I will go out into the field with my father. We will stand in the field where you are hiding. I will talk to my father about you, and I will tell you what I learn."

4Jonathan talked to his father Saul. Jonathan said good things about David. He said, "You are the king. David is your servant. David hasn't done anything wrong to you, so don't do anything wrong to him. He has always been good to you. 5He risked his life when he killed the Philistine. The LORD won a great victory for all Israel. You saw it, and you were happy. Why do you want to hurt David? He's innocent. There is no reason to kill him."

6Saul listened to Jonathan and made a promise. He said, "As surely as the LORD lives, David won't be put to death."

7So Jonathan called David and told him everything that was said. Then Jonathan brought David to Saul, and David was with Saul as before.

Saul Tries Again to Kill David

8Once again there was war with the Philistines, and David went out to fight. He defeated them badly, and they ran away. 9Later, in Saul's house, David was playing the harp. Saul was there with his spear in his hand. Then an evil spirit from the LORD came on Saul. 10Saul threw his spear at David and tried to pin him to the wall. David jumped out of the way, so the spear missed him and stuck in the wall. That night, David ran away.

11Saul sent men to watch David's house. They stayed there all night. They were waiting to kill David in the morning, but David's wife Michal warned him. She said, "You must run away tonight and save your life. If you don't, you will be killed tomorrow." 12Then Michal let David down out of a window, and he escaped and ran away. 13Michal took the household god, put clothes on it and put goats' hair on its head. Then she put the statue in the bed.

14Saul sent messengers to take David prisoner. But Michal said, "David is sick."

15The men went and told Saul, but he sent the messengers back to see David. Saul told these men, "Bring David to me. Bring him lying on his bed if you must, even if it kills him."

16The messengers went to David's house. They went inside to get him, but they saw it was only a statue and that its hair was only goats' hair.

17Saul said to Michal, "Why did you trick me like this? You let my enemy escape, and now he is gone."

Michal answered Saul, "David told me he would kill me if I didn't help him escape."

David Goes to the Camps at Ramah

18David escaped and ran away to Samuel at Ramah. He told Samuel everything that Saul had done to him. Then David and Samuel went to the camps where the prophets stayed. David stayed there.

19Saul heard that David was there in the camps near Ramah. 20So he sent some men to arrest David. But when they came to the camps, there was a group of prophets prophesying.*a* Samuel was standing there leading the group. The Spirit of God came on Saul's messengers and they began prophesying.

21Saul heard about this, so he sent other messengers, but they also began prophesying. So Saul sent messengers a third time, and they also began prophesying. 22Finally, Saul himself went to Ramah. Saul came to the big well by the threshing floor at Secu. He asked, "Where are Samuel and David?"

The people answered, "In the camps near Ramah."

23So Saul went out to the camps near Ramah. The Spirit of God came on Saul, and he also began prophesying. He prophesied all the way to the camps at Ramah. 24Saul even took off his clothes. He lay there naked all day and through the night. So even Saul prophesied there in front of Samuel.

That is why people say, "Is Saul also one of the prophets?"

David and Jonathan Make an Agreement

20 David ran away from the camps at Ramah and went to Jonathan and asked him, "What have I done wrong? What is my crime? Why is your father trying to kill me?"

---

a **19:20 prophesying** This usually means "speaking for God". But here, this also means that the Spirit of God took control of the people, causing them to sing and dance. Also in verse 23.

2Jonathan answered, "That can't be true! My father isn't trying to kill you. My father doesn't do anything without first telling me. It doesn't matter how important it is, my father always tells me. Why would my father refuse to tell me that he wants to kill you? No, it is not true!"

3But David answered, "Your father knows very well that I am your friend. Your father said to himself, 'Jonathan must not know about it. If he knows, he will tell David.'a But as surely as you and the LORD are alive, I am very close to death."

4Jonathan said to David, "I will do anything you want me to do."

5Then David said, "Look, tomorrow is the New Moon celebration. I am supposed to eat with the king, but let me hide in the field until the evening. 6If your father notices I am gone, tell him, 'David wanted to go home to Bethlehem. His family is having its own feast for this monthly sacrifice. David asked me to let him run down to Bethlehem and join his family.' 7If your father says, 'Fine,' then I am safe. But if your father becomes angry, you will know that he wants to hurt me. 8Jonathan, be kind to me. I am your servant. You have made an agreement with me before the LORD. If I am guilty, you may kill me yourself, but don't take me to your father."

9Jonathan answered, "No, never! If I learn that my father plans to hurt you, I will warn you."

10David said, "Who will warn me if your father says bad things to you?"

11Then Jonathan said, "Come, let's go out into the field." So Jonathan and David went together into the field.

12Jonathan said to David, "I make this promise before the LORD, the God of Israel. I promise that I will learn how my father feels about you. I will learn if he feels good about you or not. Then, in three days, I will send a message to you in the field. 13If my father wants to hurt you, I will let you know. I will let you leave in safety. May the LORD punish me if I don't do this. May the LORD be with you as he has been with my father. 14-15As long as I live, show me the same kindness the LORD does. And if I die, never stop showing this kindness to my family. Be faithful to us, even when the LORD destroys all your enemiesb from the earth." 16So Jonathan made this agreement with David and his family, and he asked the LORD to hold them responsible for keeping it.c

17Jonathan loved David as himself, and because of this love, he asked David to repeat this agreement for himself.

18Jonathan said to David, "Tomorrow is the New Moon celebration. Your seat will be empty, so my father will see that you are gone. 19On the third day, go to the same place you hid when this trouble began. Wait by that hill. 20On the third day, I will go to that hill and shoot three arrows as if I am shooting at a target. 21Then I will tell the boy to go and find the arrows. If everything is fine, I will tell the boy, 'You went too far! The arrows are closer to me. Come back and get them.' If I say that, you can come out of hiding. I promise, as surely as the LORD lives, you are safe. There is no danger. 22But if there is trouble, I will say to the boy, 'The arrows are farther away. Go and get them.' If I say that, you must leave. The LORD is sending you away. 23Remember this agreement between you and me. The LORD is our witness forever."

24Then David hid in the field.

Saul's Attitude at the Celebration

The time for the New Moon celebration came, and the king sat down to eat. 25He sat next to the wall where he usually sat, and Jonathan sat opposite him. Abner sat next to Saul, but David's place was empty. 26That day Saul said nothing. He thought, "Maybe something has happened to David so that he is not clean."

27On the next day, the second day of the month, David's place was empty again. Then Saul said to his son Jonathan, "Why didn't Jesse's son come to the New Moon celebration yesterday or today?"

28Jonathan answered, "David asked me to let him go to Bethlehem. 29He said, 'Let me go. Our family is having a sacrifice in Bethlehem. My brother ordered me to be there. Now if I am your friend, please let me go and see my brothers.' That is why David has not come to the king's table."

30Saul was very angry with Jonathan and said to him, "You son of a twisted, rebellious woman! I know that you have chosen to support that son of Jesse.d This will bring shame to you and to your mother. 31As long as Jesse's son lives, you will never be king over this land. Now, bring him to me! He is a dead man."

32Jonathan asked his father, "Why should David be killed? What did he do wrong?"

33But Saul threw his spear at Jonathan and tried to kill him. So Jonathan knew that his father wanted very much to kill David. 34Jonathan became angry and left the table. He was so upset

---

a **20:3** *he will tell David* This is from the ancient Greek version. The standard Hebrew text here has "he will be upset".

b **20:14–15** *enemies* Or "descendants".

c **20:14–16** The Hebrew text is not clear, and several different translations are possible.

d **20:30** *that son of Jesse* Saul refers to David by his father's name, intending it as an insult.

and angry with his father that he refused to eat any food on the second day of the festival. He was angry because Saul humiliated him and because Saul wanted to kill David.

David and Jonathan Say Goodbye

[35]The next morning Jonathan went out to the field to meet David as they had agreed. Jonathan brought a little boy with him. [36]He said to the boy, "Run. Go and find the arrows I shoot." The boy began to run, and Jonathan shot the arrows over his head. [37]The boy ran to the place where the arrows fell, but Jonathan called, "The arrows are farther away." [38]Then he shouted, "Hurry! Go and get them. Don't just stand there." The boy picked up the arrows and brought them back to his master. [39]The boy knew nothing about what this meant. Only Jonathan and David knew. [40]Jonathan gave his bow and arrows to the boy and told him to go back to town.

[41]When the boy left, David came out from his hiding place on the other side of the hill. David gave a formal greeting by bowing to the ground three times to show his respect for Jonathan. But then David and Jonathan kissed each other and cried together. It was a very sad goodbye, especially for David.

[42]Then Jonathan said to David, "Go in peace. We have taken an oath in the LORD's name to be friends forever. We have asked the LORD to be a witness between us and our descendants forever."

David Goes to See Ahimelech the Priest

21 Then David left and Jonathan went back to the town. David went to the town named Nob[a] to see Ahimelech the priest.

Ahimelech went out to meet David. He was afraid of David and asked, "Why are you alone? Why isn't anyone with you?"

[2]David answered him, "The king gave me a special order. He told me, 'Don't let anyone know about this mission. No one must know what I told you to do.' I told my men where to meet me. [3]Now, what food do you have with you? Give me five loaves of bread or whatever you have to eat."

[4]The priest said to David, "I don't have any ordinary bread here, but I do have some of the holy bread. Your officers can eat it if they have not had sex with any women."[b]

[5]David answered the priest, "We have not been with any women. My men keep their bodies[c] holy every time we go out to fight, even on ordinary missions.[d] And this is especially true today."

[6]There was no bread except the holy bread, so the priest gave David this bread. This was the bread that the priests put on the holy table before the LORD. Each day they took this bread away and put fresh bread in its place.

[7]One of Saul's officers was there that day. He was Doeg the Edomite, the leader of Saul's shepherds.[e] He had been kept there before the LORD.[f]

[8]David asked Ahimelech, "Do you have a spear or sword here? The king's business is very important. I had to leave quickly, and I didn't bring my sword or any other weapon."

[9]The priest answered, "The only sword here is the sword of Goliath the Philistine. It is the sword you took from him when you killed him in the Valley of Elah. That sword is behind the ephod, wrapped in a cloth. You may take it if you want to."

David said, "Goliath's sword—there's not another one like it. Give it to me."

David Runs Away to the Enemy at Gath

[10]That day David ran away from Saul and went to King Achish of Gath. [11]Achish's officers said, "Isn't this David, the king of the land of Israel? He is the one the Israelites sing about. They dance and sing this song about him:

"Saul has killed thousands of enemies,
    but David has killed tens of thousands."

[12]David paid close attention to what they said. He was afraid of King Achish of Gath, [13]so he pretended to be crazy in front of Achish and his officers. While David was with them, he acted like a crazy man. He spat on the doors of the gate. He let spit fall down his beard.

[14]Achish said to his officers, "Look at the man! He is crazy. Why did you bring him to me? [15]I have enough crazy men. I don't need you to bring this man to my house to act like this in front of me. Don't let this man come into my house again."

---

[a] **21:1 Nob** A city near Ramah where many priests lived. See 1 Sam. 22:19.
[b] **21:4 Your officers . . . women** This would make the men unclean and not able to eat any food that had been made holy by offering it to God. See Lev. 7:21; 15:1–33.
[c] **21:5 bodies** Literally, "vessels" or "weapons".
[d] **21:5 My men . . . missions** See 2 Sam. 11:11 and the rules in Deut. 23:9–14.
[e] **21:7 shepherds** Or "messengers".
[f] **21:7 kept there before the LORD** This might mean that Doeg was there as part of a special promise to God or some other religious reason. Or it might mean he was being held there because of some crime, such as accidentally killing a man.

David Goes to Different Places

22 David left Gath and ran away to the cave[a] of Adullam. David's brothers and relatives heard that David was at Adullam and went to see him there. [2]Many people joined David. There were men who were in some kind of trouble, men who owed a lot of money, and men who were just not satisfied with life. All kinds of people joined David, and he became their leader. He had about 400 men with him.

[3]David left Adullam and went to Mizpah in Moab. David said to the king of Moab, "Please let my father and mother come and stay with you until I learn what God is going to do to me." [4]So David left his parents with the king of Moab. They stayed with the king of Moab while David was at the fortress.

[5]But the prophet Gad said to David, "Don't stay in the fortress. Go to the land of Judah." So David left and went to Hereth Forest.

Saul Destroys Ahimelech's Family

[6]Saul heard the report about David and his men while sitting under the tree on the hill at Gibeah. Saul had his spear in his hand. All his officers were standing around him. [7]Saul said to his officers who were standing around him, "Listen, men of Benjamin. Do you think that son of Jesse[b] will give you fields and vineyards? He is not one of us, so don't think he will give you anything or make you officers over 1,000 or even 100 men! [8]No, but you are all plotting against me. None of you told me about my son Jonathan and the agreement he made with the son of Jesse. None of you cared enough about me to tell me what was happening—that my son Jonathan encouraged one of my own men to turn against me. And today that man is looking for a way to kill me!"

[9]Doeg the Edomite was standing there with Saul's officers. Doeg said, "I saw Jesse's son at Nob. He came to see Ahimelech son of Ahitub. [10]Ahimelech prayed to the LORD for David and gave him some food. He even gave David the sword of Goliath the Philistine."

[11]Then King Saul ordered some men to bring the priest to him. Saul told them to bring Ahimelech son of Ahitub and all his relatives who were priests at Nob. So they all came to the king. [12]Saul said to Ahimelech, "Listen now, son of Ahitub."

Ahimelech answered, "Yes, sir."

[13]Saul said to him, "Why did you and Jesse's son make secret plans against me? You gave David bread and a sword. You prayed to God for him. And right now, David is waiting to attack me."

[14]Ahimelech answered, "David is very faithful to you. Not one of your other officers is as faithful as David. He is your own son-in-law and the captain of your bodyguards. Your own family respects David. [15]That was not the first time I prayed to God for David. Not at all! Don't blame me or any of my relatives. We are your servants. I know nothing about what is happening."

[16]But the king said, "Ahimelech, you and all your relatives must die." [17]Then the king told the guards at his side, "Go and kill the priests of the LORD because they are on David's side too. They knew he was running away, but they didn't tell me."

The king's officers refused to hurt the priests of the LORD. [18]So the king gave the order to Doeg. Saul said, "Doeg, you go kill the priests." So Doeg the Edomite went and killed the priests. That day he killed 85 men who were priests.[c] [19]Nob was the city of the priests. Doeg killed all the people of Nob. He used his sword and killed men, women, children and babies. He even killed their cattle, donkeys and sheep.

[20]But Abiathar son of Ahimelech escaped. He ran away and joined David. [21]Abiathar told David that Saul had killed the LORD's priests. [22]Then David told Abiathar, "I saw Doeg the Edomite at Nob that day. I knew he would tell Saul! I am responsible for the death of your father's family. [23]Stay with me. Don't be afraid, because the man who tried to kill you is the same man who wants to kill me. I will protect you if you stay with me."

David at Keilah

23 People told David, "Look, the Philistines are fighting against the city of Keilah. They are robbing grain from the threshing floors."

[2]David asked the LORD, "Should I go and fight these Philistines?"

The LORD answered David, "Yes, go attack the Philistines. Save Keilah."

[3]But David's men said to him, "Look, our men are afraid here in Judah. Just think how afraid we will be if we go to Keilah, where the Philistine army is lined up and ready for battle."

[4]David again asked the LORD. And the LORD answered David, "Go down to Keilah. I will help you defeat the Philistines." [5]So David and his men went to Keilah. David's men fought the Philistines. They defeated them and took their cattle. In this way David saved the people of Keilah. [6]Abiathar

---

[a] **22:1 cave** Or possibly, "fortress".
[b] **22:7 that son of Jesse** As usual, Saul refers to David by his father's name, intending it as an insult.
[c] **22:18 priests** Literally, "men who wore the linen ephod".

son of Ahimelech was the man who had run away from Saul and was now in Keilah with David. Abiathar had brought an ephod with him.

⁷People told Saul that David was now at Keilah. Saul said, "God has given David to me. David trapped himself when he went into a city surrounded by a wall with gates and bars to lock them." ⁸Saul called all his army together for battle. They prepared to go down to Keilah to attack David and his men.

⁹David learned that Saul was making plans against him. David then said to Abiathar the priest, "Bring the ephod."

¹⁰David prayed, "LORD, God of Israel, I have heard that Saul plans to come to Keilah and destroy the town because of me. ¹¹Will Saul come to Keilah? Will the people of Keilah give me to Saul? LORD, God of Israel, I am your servant. Please tell me!"

The LORD answered, "Saul will come."

¹²Again David asked, "Will the people of Keilah give me and my men to Saul?"

The LORD answered, "They will."

¹³So David and his men left Keilah. There were about 600 men who went with David. They kept moving from place to place. Saul learned that David had escaped from Keilah, so he did not go to that city.

Saul Chases David

¹⁴David went into the desert of Ziph and stayed in the mountains and fortresses there. Saul kept looking for David, but the Lord[a] didn't let Saul catch him.

¹⁵David was at Horesh in the desert of Ziph. He was afraid because Saul was coming to kill him. ¹⁶But Saul's son Jonathan went to see David at Horesh and encouraged him to have a stronger faith in God. ¹⁷Jonathan told David, "Don't be afraid. My father Saul won't hurt you. You will become the king of Israel, and I will be second to you. Even my father knows this."

¹⁸Jonathan and David both made an agreement before the LORD. Then Jonathan went home, and David stayed at Horesh.

The People of Ziph Tell Saul About David

¹⁹Some people from Ziph went to Saul at Gibeah and told him, "David is hiding in our area. He is at the fortresses of Horesh on Hakilah Hill, south of Jeshimon. ²⁰Now, King, come down any time you want. It is our duty to give David to you."

²¹Saul answered, "May the LORD bless you for helping me. ²²Go and learn more about David.

Keep track of where he goes and who goes to see him. I am told that David is smart and that he is trying to trick me. ²³Find all the hiding places that David uses. Then come back to me and tell me everything. Then I'll go with you. If David is in the area, I will find him, even if I must go to every family group in Judah."

²⁴So those people went back to Ziph before Saul.

David and his men were in the desert of Maon, south of Jeshimon. ²⁵Saul and his men went to look for David, but the people warned him. They told David that Saul was looking for him. So David then went down to "The Rock" in the desert of Maon. Saul heard that David had gone there, so Saul went to that place to find him.

²⁶Saul was on one side of the mountain. David and his men were on the other side of the same mountain. David was moving as quickly as possible to get away from Saul. But Saul and his soldiers were going around the mountain to cut them off and trap David and his men.

²⁷Then a messenger arrived and told Saul, "Come quickly! The Philistines are attacking."

²⁸So Saul stopped chasing David and went to fight the Philistines. That is why people call this place "Slippery Rock".[b] ²⁹David left the desert of Maon and went to the fortresses near En Gedi.

David Shames Saul

24 After Saul had chased the Philistines away, people told him, "David is in the desert area near En Gedi."

²So Saul chose 3,000 men from all over Israel and began searching for David and his men. They looked near Wild Goat Rocks. ³Saul came to some sheep pens beside the road. There was a cave near there, so Saul went in to relieve himself. David and his men were deep inside that same cave. ⁴David's men told him, "This is the day the LORD told you about when he said, 'I will give your enemy to you, and you can do whatever you want to him.'"

So David crawled closer and closer to Saul and cut off a corner of Saul's robe. Saul didn't notice what happened. ⁵Later, David felt bad about what he did. ⁶He said to his men, "I pray that the LORD never lets me do anything like that to my master again. I must not do anything against Saul, because he is the LORD's chosen king."[c] ⁷David said these things to stop his men. He would not let his men hurt Saul.

Saul left the cave and went on his way. ⁸Later, David came out of the cave and called out to Saul, "My lord the king!"

---

[a] **23:14 the Lord** From the ancient Greek version and a Hebrew copy from Qumran. The standard Hebrew text has "God".
[b] **23:28 Slippery Rock** Or "Sela Hammahlekoth".
[c] **24:6 chosen king** Literally, "anointed one". Also in verse 10.

INSIGHT

Saul became jealous when the people praised David's continued victories in battle and so he kept trying to kill him. However, David trusted that God would protect him and make him king at the right time. He refused to take either this or another chance to kill Saul (see 1 Samuel 26:22–24).

1 Samuel 24:4–7

Saul looked back. David bowed with his face to the ground to show his respect. 9David said to Saul, "Why do you listen when people say, 'David plans to hurt you'? 10You can see with your own eyes that is not true. The LORD put you within my grasp today in the cave, but I refused to kill you. I was merciful to you. I said, 'I won't hurt my master. Saul is the LORD's chosen king.' 11Look at this piece of cloth in my hand. I cut off the corner of your robe. I could have killed you, but I didn't. Now, I want you to understand this. I want you to know that I am not planning anything against you. I did nothing wrong to you, but you are hunting me and trying to kill me. 12Let the LORD be the judge. I hope the LORD will punish you for the wrong you did to me, but I won't fight you myself. 13There is an old saying:

'Bad things come from bad people.'

"I haven't done anything bad, and I won't hurt you. 14Why are you chasing me anyway? Should the king of Israel be out chasing someone no more important than a dying dog or a little flea? 15Let the LORD be the judge. Let him decide between you and me. He will support me and show that I am right. He will save me from you."

16When David finished speaking, Saul asked, "Is that your voice, David my son?" Then Saul lifted his voice and began to cry. 17He said, "You are right, and I am wrong. You were good to me, even though I have been bad to you. 18You yourself said it when you told me about the good things you did. The LORD put my life in your hands, but you did not kill me. 19This shows that you are not my enemy. A man doesn't catch his enemy and then just let him go. He doesn't do good things for his enemy. May the LORD reward you for being good to me today. 20Now I know that you will become the new king. You will rule the kingdom of Israel. 21Now make a promise to me with an oath using the LORD's name. Promise that you will not kill my descendants, even after I die. Promise me that you will not erase my name from my father's family."

22So David made this promise to Saul with an oath. Then Saul went home. But David and his men went back up to the fortress.

David and Nabal the Fool

25 Samuel died. All the Israelites met together and mourned his death. They buried him at his home in Ramah.

Then David moved to the desert of Maon.*a* 2There was a very rich man living in Maon. He had 3,000 sheep and 1,000 goats. That man was in Carmel taking care of some business. He went there to cut the wool from his sheep. 3This man's name was Nabal.*b* He was from Caleb's family. Nabal's wife was named Abigail. She was a wise and beautiful woman, but Nabal was a mean and cruel man.

4David was in the desert when he heard that Nabal was cutting the wool from his sheep. 5David sent ten young men to talk to Nabal. He told them, "Go to Carmel. Find Nabal and tell him 'Hello' for me." 6David gave them this message for Nabal: "May you and your family be well and all that you own be well. 7I heard that you are cutting wool from your sheep. Your shepherds were with us for a while, and we did nothing wrong to them. We never took anything from your shepherds while they were at Carmel. 8Ask your servants and they will tell you this is true. Please be kind to my young men. We come to you now, at this happy time. Please give these young men anything you can. Please do this for me, your friend*c* David."

9David's men went to Nabal. They gave his message to Nabal, 10but Nabal said, "Who is David? Who is this son of Jesse? There are many slaves who have run away from their masters these days. 11I have bread and water, and I have the meat I killed for my servants who cut the wool from my sheep. But I won't give them to men I don't even know."

12David's men went back and told him everything that Nabal had said. 13David told them, "Put on your swords." So David and his men put on their swords. About 400 men went with David while 200 of them stayed with the supplies.

---

a **25:1 *Maon*** This is from the ancient Greek version. The standard Hebrew text has "Paran".
b **25:3 *Nabal*** This name means "foolish".
c **25:8 *friend*** Literally, "son".

Abigail Prevents Trouble

¹⁴One of Nabal's servants spoke to Nabal's wife Abigail. The servant said, "David sent messengers from the desert to meet our master, but Nabal was rude to them. ¹⁵These men were very good to us while we were out in the fields with the sheep. David's men were with us the whole time, and they never did anything wrong to us. They did not take anything from us. ¹⁶His men protected us night and day. They were like a wall around us—they protected us while we were with them caring for the sheep. ¹⁷Nabal was foolish to say what he did. Terrible trouble is coming to our master and all his family. You need to think of something to do."

¹⁸Abigail quickly gathered up 200 loaves of bread, two full wine bags, five cooked sheep, 17 kilogrammes*ᵃ* of cooked grain, 1 kilogramme*ᵇ* of raisins, and 200 cakes of pressed figs. She put them on donkeys. ¹⁹Then Abigail told her servants, "Go on. I'll follow you." But she did not tell her husband.

²⁰Abigail rode her donkey down to the other side of the mountain. She met David and his men coming from the other direction.

²¹David was saying, "I protected Nabal's property in the desert. I made sure not one of his sheep was missing. I did all that for nothing. I was good to him, but he was rude to me. ²²I swear,*ᶜ* I won't let even one man in Nabal's family live until tomorrow morning."

²³Just then Abigail arrived. When she saw David, she quickly got off her donkey and bowed down with her face to the ground in front of him. ²⁴Abigail fell at his feet and said, "Sir, please let me talk to you. Listen to what I say. Blame me for what happened. ²⁵I didn't see the men you sent. Sir, don't pay any attention to that worthless man, Nabal. His name means 'Foolish', and that is what he is. ²⁶The LORD has kept you from killing innocent people. As surely as the LORD lives and you as well, may your enemies and anyone else who wants to harm you be as cursed as Nabal is. ²⁷Now, I am bringing this gift to you. Please give these things to your men. ²⁸Please forgive me for doing wrong. I know the LORD will make your family strong because you fight his battles. People will never find anything bad about you as long as you live. ²⁹If someone chases you to kill you, the LORD your God will save your life. But he will throw away your enemies like a stone from a sling. ³⁰The LORD promised to do many good things for you, and he will keep his promises. He

will make you leader over Israel. ³¹So don't do anything that would make you guilty of killing innocent people. Please don't fall into that trap. Please remember me when the LORD blesses you."

³²David answered Abigail, "Praise the LORD, the God of Israel. Praise God for sending you to meet me. ³³God bless you for your good judgement. You kept me from killing innocent people today. ³⁴As surely as the LORD, the God of Israel, lives, if you hadn't come quickly to meet me, not one man in Nabal's family would have lived until tomorrow morning. But the Lord prevented me from hurting you."

³⁵Then David accepted Abigail's gifts. He told her, "Go home in peace. I have listened to your request, and I will do what you asked."

Nabal's Death

³⁶Abigail went back to Nabal, who was in the house. He had been eating like a king, and he was drunk and feeling good. So Abigail told Nabal nothing until the next morning. ³⁷The next morning, Nabal was sober, so his wife told him everything. He had a heart attack and became as stiff as a rock. ³⁸About ten days later, the LORD gave him a stroke and Nabal died.

³⁹When David heard that Nabal was dead, he said, "Praise the LORD! He judged Nabal to be wrong for insulting me and kept me from doing something wrong. The LORD made Nabal pay for what he did."

Then David sent a message to Abigail and asked her to be his wife. ⁴⁰His servants went to Carmel with this message, "David sent us to get you. He wants you to be his wife."

⁴¹Abigail bowed her face to the ground. She said, "I am willing to be your slave woman, even if it is only to wash the feet of my master's servants."

⁴²Abigail quickly got on a donkey and brought five of her maids with her. They followed David's messengers. So Abigail became David's wife. ⁴³David had also married Ahinoam of Jezreel. Both Ahinoam and Abigail were David's wives. ⁴⁴David was also married to Saul's daughter Michal, but Saul had taken her away from him and had given her to a man named Palti, son of Laish. Palti was from the town named Gallim.

David and Abishai Enter Saul's Camp

26 The people of Ziph went to see Saul at Gibeah and said to him, "David is hiding on Hakilah Hill, opposite Jeshimon."

ᵃ **25:18** *17 kilogrammes* Literally, "5 *seahs*".
ᵇ **25:18** *1 kilogramme* Literally, "1 *omer*". This is from the ancient Greek translation. The Hebrew has "100 cakes".
ᶜ **25:22** *I swear* Literally, "May God do so and so for David's enemies if . . .".

²Saul gathered 3,000 of the best soldiers in Israel and went down to the desert of Ziph to search for David there. ³Saul set up his camp by the road at Hakilah Hill, opposite Jeshimon.

David was out in the desert and saw that Saul had come out into the desert after him. ⁴So David sent out spies to know for certain that Saul had come after him again. ⁵Then David went to where Saul had set up his camp. David saw where Saul and Abner were sleeping. (Abner son of Ner was the commander of Saul's army.) Saul was sleeping in the centre of a circle of men that surrounded him.

⁶David talked to Ahimelech the Hittite and Abishai son of Zeruiah. (Abishai was Joab's brother.) He asked them, "Who would like to go down into the camp with me after Saul?"

Abishai answered, "I'll go with you."

⁷When night came, David and Abishai went into Saul's camp. Saul was asleep in the middle of the circle of men. His spear was stuck in the ground near his head. Abner and the other soldiers were asleep around Saul. ⁸Abishai said to David, "Today God has given your enemy to you. Let me pin Saul to the ground with his spear. I'll only do it once!"

⁹But David said to Abishai, "Don't kill Saul! Anyone who hurts the LORD's chosen king[a] must be punished. ¹⁰As surely as the LORD lives, the LORD himself will punish Saul. Maybe Saul will die naturally or maybe he will be killed in battle. ¹¹But I pray that the LORD never lets me hurt the LORD's chosen king. Now pick up the spear and water jug by Saul's head and let's go."

¹²So David took the spear and water jug that were near Saul's head, and then David and Abishai left Saul's camp. No one knew what had happened. No one saw it. No one even woke up. Saul and all his soldiers slept because the LORD had put them into a deep sleep.

David Shames Saul Again

¹³David crossed over to the other side of the valley. He stood on top of the mountain across the valley from Saul's camp. David and Saul's camp were far apart. ¹⁴David shouted to the army and to Abner son of Ner, "Answer me, Abner!"

Abner answered, "Who are you? Why are you calling the king?"

¹⁵David said, "You are an important man, aren't you? You are better than any other man in Israel. Is that right? So why didn't you guard your master, the king? An ordinary man came into your camp to kill your master, the king. ¹⁶You made a big mistake. As surely as the LORD is alive, you and your men should die, because you didn't protect your master, the LORD's chosen king. Look for the king's spear and the water jug that was near Saul's head. Where are they?"

¹⁷Saul knew David's voice and said, "Is that your voice, David my son?"

David answered, "Yes, it is my voice, my lord the king. ¹⁸Sir, why are you chasing me? What wrong have I done? What am I guilty of? ¹⁹My lord the king, listen to me. If the LORD caused you to be angry with me, let him accept an offering. But if men caused you to be angry with me, I ask the LORD to curse them because they forced me to leave the land that the LORD gave me and told me to go and serve other gods. ²⁰Now don't make me die far away from the LORD's presence. The king of Israel has come out looking for a flea. You are like a man hunting partridges in the mountains."[b]

²¹Then Saul said, "David, my son! I have sinned. Come back. Today you showed me that my life is important to you, so I won't try to hurt you. I have acted foolishly. I have made a big mistake."

²²David answered, "Here is the king's spear. Let one of your young man come here and get it. ²³The LORD pays every man for what he does—he rewards him if he does right, and he punishes him if he does wrong. The LORD gave you to me today, but I wouldn't harm the LORD's chosen king. ²⁴Today I showed you that your life is important to me. In the same way, the LORD will show that my life is important to him. He will save me from every trouble."

²⁵Then Saul said to David, "God bless you, David my son. You will do great things and you will win."

David went on his way, and Saul went back home.

David Lives With the Philistines

27 But David thought to himself, "Saul will catch me some day. The best thing I can do is to escape to the land of the Philistines. Then Saul will give up looking for me in Israel. That way I will escape from Saul."

²So David and his 600 men left Israel and went to Achish son of Maoch. Achish was king of Gath. ³David, his men and their families lived in Gath with Achish. David had his two wives with him—Ahinoam of Jezreel and Abigail of Carmel. Abigail was the widow of Nabal. ⁴People told Saul

---

[a] **26:9 *chosen king*** Literally, "anointed one". Also in verses 16,23.
[b] **26:20 *hunting partridges in the mountains*** People hunted these birds until the birds became too tired to go on. Then they killed the birds. Saul was chasing David the same way. This is also a wordplay. The Hebrew word for "partridge" is like the word for "calling" in verse 14.

that David had run away to Gath, so Saul stopped looking for him.

⁵David said to Achish, "If you are pleased with me, give me a place in one of the country towns. I am only your servant. I should live there, not here with you in this royal city."

⁶That day Achish gave David the town of Ziklag. And Ziklag has belonged to the kings of Judah ever since. ⁷David lived with the Philistines for one year and four months.

David Fools King Achish

⁸David and his men went to fight the Amalekites and Geshurites who lived in the area from Telem*ᵃ* near Shur all the way to Egypt. David's men defeated them and took their wealth. ⁹David defeated the people in that area. He took all their sheep, cattle, donkeys, camels and clothes and brought them back to Achish. But David didn't let any of those people live.

¹⁰David did this many times. Each time Achish asked David where he had fought and taken those things. David said, "I fought against the southern part of Judah", or "I fought against the southern part of Jerahmeel", or "I fought against the southern part of the Kenizzites."*ᵇ* ¹¹David never brought a man or woman alive to Gath. He thought, "If we let anyone live, they might tell Achish what I really did."

David did this all the time he lived in the Philistine land. ¹²Achish began to trust David and said to himself, "Now David's own people hate him. The Israelites hate him very much. Now he will serve me forever."

The Philistines Prepare for War

28 Later, the Philistines gathered their armies to fight against Israel. Achish said to David, "Do you understand that you and your men must go with me to fight against Israel?"

²David answered, "Certainly, then you can see for yourself what I can do."

Achish said, "Fine, I will make you my permanent bodyguard."

Saul and the Woman at Endor

³After Samuel died, all the Israelites mourned for him and buried him in Ramah, his home town.

Now Saul had made a law in Israel against anyone trying to contact ghosts*ᶜ* or spirits of the dead for advice or secret knowledge.

⁴The Philistines prepared for war. They came to Shunem and made their camp at that place. Saul gathered all the Israelites together and made his camp at Gilboa. ⁵Saul saw the Philistine army, and he was afraid. His heart pounded with fear. ⁶He prayed to the LORD, but the LORD did not answer him. God did not talk to Saul in dreams. God did not use the Urim to give him an answer, and God did not use prophets to speak to Saul. ⁷Finally, Saul said to his officers, "Find me a woman who contacts ghosts. Then I can go and ask her what will happen."

His officers answered, "There is a woman at Endor*ᵈ* who contacts ghosts."

⁸That night, Saul put on different clothes so that no one would know who he was. Then Saul and two of his men went to see the woman. Saul said to her, "I want you to bring up a ghost who can tell me what will happen in the future. You must call for the ghost of the person I name."

⁹But the woman said to him, "I'm sure you know what Saul did. He made a law in Israel against anyone trying to contact ghosts or spirits of the dead for advice or secret knowledge. Are you trying to trap me and get me killed?"

¹⁰Saul used the LORD's name to make a promise to the woman. He said, "As surely as the LORD lives, you won't be punished for doing this."

¹¹The woman asked, "Who do you want me to bring up for you?"

Saul answered, "Bring up Samuel."

¹²And it happened—the woman saw Samuel and screamed. She said to Saul, "You tricked me! You are Saul."

¹³The king said to the woman, "Don't be afraid! What do you see?"

The woman said, "I see a spirit coming up out of the ground."*ᵉ*

¹⁴Saul asked, "What does he look like?"

The woman answered, "He looks like an old man wearing a special robe."

Then Saul knew it was Samuel, and he bowed down. His face touched the ground. ¹⁵Samuel said to Saul, "Why did you bother me? Why did you bring me up?"

ᵃ **27:8 Telem** This is found in copies of the ancient Greek version. The standard Hebrew text has "long ago".
ᵇ **27:10 Judah, Jerahmeel, Kenizzites** All these places belonged to Israel. David made Achish think he had fought against his own people, the Israelites.
ᶜ **28:3 contact ghosts** One way people in the ancient Near East tried to contact ghosts, spirits, or gods who lived underground was to dig a pit and call for the spirit to come up through it. Also, they might offer sacrifices or other gifts to attract or persuade the spirits to come.
ᵈ **28:7 Endor** A town around the mountain from Shunem, where the Philistines were camped. Saul had to go around them to get to Endor.
ᵉ **28:13 ground** Or "Sheol", the place of death.

Saul answered, "I am in trouble! The Philistines have come to fight me, and God has left me. God won't answer me any more. He won't use prophets or dreams to answer me, so I called you. I want you to tell me what to do."

[16]Samuel said, "The LORD left you and is now your enemy, so why are you asking me for advice? [17]The LORD used me to tell you what he would do, and now he is doing what he said he would do. He is tearing the kingdom out of your hands and giving it to your neighbour, David. [18]The LORD was angry with the Amalekites and told you to destroy them. But you did not obey him. That's why the LORD is doing this to you today. [19]The LORD will let the Philistines defeat you and the army of Israel today. Tomorrow, you and your sons will be here with me."

[20]Saul quickly fell to the ground and lay stretched out there. Saul was afraid because of what Samuel said. Saul was also very weak because he had not eaten any food all that day and night.

[21]The woman came over to Saul and saw how afraid he was. She said, "Look, I am your servant. I have obeyed you. I risked my life and did what you told me to do. [22]Please, listen to me. You need to eat. Let me get you some food. Then you will have enough strength to go on your way."

[23]But Saul refused. He said, "I won't eat."

Saul's officers joined the woman and begged him to eat. Finally, Saul listened to them. He got up from the ground and sat on the bed. [24]The woman had a calf that she had been fattening. She quickly killed the calf. She took some flour and pressed it with her hands. Then she baked some bread without yeast. [25]The woman put the food before Saul and his officers and they ate. Then they got up and left during the night.

David Can't Come With Us

29 Meanwhile, the Philistines had gathered all their army camps at Aphek. The Israelites were camped by the spring near Jezreel. [2]The Philistine rulers were marching in divisions of 100 and 1,000 men. David and his men were at the back with Achish.

[3]The Philistine captains asked, "What are these Hebrews doing here?"

Achish told the Philistine captains, "This is David. He was one of Saul's officers, but he has been with me for a long time. I have found nothing wrong in David since the time he left *Saul* and came to me."

[4]But the Philistine captains were angry with Achish. They said, "Send him back. Let him go back to the city you gave him, but he can't go into battle with us. As long as he is here, we have an enemy in our own camp. He would make his king happy by killing our men. [5]Isn't David the one the Israelites sing about? They dance and sing this song:

'Saul has killed thousands of enemies,
    but David has killed tens of thousands.'"

[6]So Achish called David and said, "As surely as the LORD lives, you are loyal to me. I would be pleased to have you serve in my army. I haven't found anything wrong with you since the day you came to me. The Philistine rulers also think you are a good man.[a] [7]Go back in peace. Don't do anything to upset the Philistine rulers."

[8]David asked, "What have I done wrong? Have you found anything wrong with me since the day I came to you? So why won't you let me go to fight the enemies of my lord the king?"

[9]Achish answered, "I believe that you are a good man. You are like an angel from God. But the Philistine captains still say, 'David can't go with us into battle.' [10]Early in the morning, you and your men should go back to the city I gave you. Don't pay attention to the bad things the captains say about you. You are a good man, but you must leave in the morning as soon as there is enough light."

[11]So David and his men got up early in the morning and went back to the country of the Philistines, and the Philistines went up to Jezreel.

The Amalekites Attack Ziklag

30 As soon as David and his men arrived at Ziklag on the third day, they saw that the Amalekites had attacked Ziklag. The Amalekites invaded the Negev area, attacked Ziklag and burned the city. [2]They took all the women in Ziklag, both young and old, as prisoners. They didn't kill anyone; they only took them as prisoners.

[3]When David and his men came to Ziklag, they found the city burning. Their wives, sons and daughters had all gone. The Amalekites had taken them. [4]David and the other men in his army cried loudly until they were too weak to cry any more. [5]The Amalekites had taken David's two wives, Ahinoam of Jezreel and Abigail, who had been the wife of Nabal from Carmel.

---

[a] **29:6 The Philistine . . . man** This is from the ancient Greek version. The Philistine rulers were pleased with David. It was the Philistine army commanders who were against him. The standard Hebrew text has "The Philistine rulers do not think you are a good man."

[6]All the men in the army were sad and angry because their sons and daughters had been taken as prisoners. The men were talking about killing David with stones. This upset David very much, but he found strength in the LORD his God. [7]David said to Abiathar the priest, "Let's use the ephod to see what God wants us to do." So Abiathar brought the ephod to David.

[8]Then David prayed to the LORD. "Should I chase the people who took our families? Will I catch them?"

The Lord answered, "Chase them. You will catch them, and you will save your families."

David Finds an Egyptian Slave

[9-10]David took the 600 men with him and went to Besor Ravine. About 200 of his men stayed there because they were too weak and tired to continue. But David and the other 400 men continued to chase the Amalekites.

[11]David's men found an Egyptian in a field and took him to David. They gave the Egyptian some water to drink and some food to eat. [12]The Egyptian had not had any food or water for three days and nights, so they gave him a piece of fig cake and two clusters of raisins. He felt better after eating.

[13]David asked the Egyptian, "Who is your master? Where do you come from?"

The Egyptian answered, "I am an Egyptian, the slave of an Amalekite. Three days ago I got sick, and my master left me behind. [14]We had attacked the Negev area where the Kerethites[a] live. We also attacked Judah and the Negev area where Caleb's people live. We burned Ziklag."

[15]David asked the Egyptian, "Will you lead me to the people who took our families?"

The Egyptian answered, "If you make a special promise before God, I will help you find them. But you must promise that you will not kill me or give me back to my master."

David Defeats the Amalekites

[16]The Egyptian led David to the Amalekites. They were lying around on the ground, eating and drinking. They were celebrating with the many things they had taken from the Philistines and from Judah. [17]David attacked them and killed them. They fought from sunrise until the evening of the next day. None of the Amalekites escaped, except for 400 young men who jumped onto their camels and rode away.

[18]David got back everything the Amalekites had taken, including his two wives. [19]Nothing was missing. They found all the children and old people, all their sons and daughters and all their valuables. They got back everything the Amalekites had taken. David brought everything back. [20]He took all the sheep and cattle. His men led these animals to the front of the group and said, "This is David's prize."

All Men Will Share Equally

[21]David came to the 200 men who had stayed at Besor Ravine. These were the men who were too weak and tired to follow David. They came out to meet him and the soldiers who went with him. They greeted David and his army as they approached. [22]There were some troublemakers in the group who went with David who started complaining, "These 200 men didn't go with us, so why should we give them any of the things we took. These men get nothing but their own wives and children."

[23]David answered, "No, my brothers. Don't do that! Think about what the LORD gave us. He let us defeat the enemy that attacked us. [24]No one will listen to what you say. The share will be the same for the man who stayed with the supplies and for the man who went into battle. Everyone will share alike." [25]David made this an order and rule for Israel. This rule continues even today.

[26]When David got to Ziklag, he sent some of the things he took from the Amalekites to his friends, the leaders of Judah. David said, "Here is a present for you that we took from the LORD's enemies."

[27]David sent some of the gifts to the leaders in Bethel, Ramoth in the Negev, Jattir, [28]Aroer, Siphmoth, Eshtemoa, [29]Racal, the cities of the Jerahmeelites and the cities of the Kenites, [30]Hormah, Bor Ashan, Athach [31]and Hebron, and to all the other places where David and his men had stayed.

The Death of Saul

31 Meanwhile, the Philistines fought against the Israelites, and the Israelites ran from them. There were many dead bodies that fell at Mount Gilboa. [2]The Philistines fought hard against Saul and his sons. They killed Jonathan, Abinadab and Malki Shua.

[3]The battle grew even more intense around Saul. The archers closed in on Saul and wounded him with many arrows. [4]Saul told the boy who carried his armour, "Take your sword and kill me or else these foreigners will do it and torment me as well!" But Saul's helper was afraid and refused to kill him. So Saul took out his own sword and fell on it.

---

[a] **30:14 Kerethites** Or "people from Crete". These were one of the groups of Philistines. Some of David's best soldiers were Kerethites.

[5]When the helper saw that Saul was dead, he took out his own sword, fell on it and died there with Saul. [6]So Saul, his three sons and the boy who carried his armour all died together that day.

The Philistines Rejoice at Saul's Death

[7]The Israelites who lived on the other side of the valley saw the Israelite army running away. They saw that Saul and his sons were dead, so they left their cities and ran away. Then the Philistines came and lived in their cities.

[8]The next day, the Philistines went back to take things from the dead bodies. They found Saul and his three sons dead on Mount Gilboa. [9]The Philistines cut off Saul's head and took all his armour. They carried the news to the Philistines and to all the temples of their idols. [10]They put Saul's armour in the temple of Ashtoreth. The Philistines also hung Saul's body on the wall of Beth Shan.[a]

[11]The people living in Jabesh Gilead heard what the Philistines had done to Saul. [12]So all the soldiers of Jabesh went to Beth Shan. They marched all night, went to the wall of Beth Shan and took down the bodies of Saul and his sons. Then they carried them to Jabesh. There the people of Jabesh burned the bodies of Saul and his three sons. [13]Later, they buried the bones of Saul and his three sons under the big tree in Jabesh. Then the people of Jabesh showed their sadness—they did not eat for seven days.

---

[a] 31:10 **Beth Shan** Or possibly, "Beth Shean". Also in verse 12.

Who
As with 1 Samuel (this is the second part of that book), though it is named after the prophet Samuel we don't know who the author was. Portions of it may have been written by Samuel himself.

When
The book must have been written after the death of Solomon since the writer refers to the two kingdoms of Israel and Judah, which only came into existence after Solomon's death.

What
The second book of Samuel concentrates on the reign of King David. It is the story of David's triumph, and of his downfall – the tale of how Israel's greatest king gained control of the kingdom, only to lose control of himself and his family. Yet it also tells how he discovered new depths of God's love and forgiveness.

The first seven years of David's reign are spent in civil war. David battles against Saul's supporters, led by the late king's son, Ish Bosheth. Finally, David defeats Ish Bosheth, captures Jerusalem from the Jebusites and becomes king of the united kingdom of Israel.

But he doesn't leave it there. He goes on to defeat the enemy nations around Israel and develop the nation into a kind of small empire. He transforms Jerusalem into the capital of the country, puts the Box of the Agreement in place and starts to plan a magnificent Temple.

And then it all goes wrong. David commits adultery, tries to cover it up with murder and his family is torn apart by the consequences. He ends up fighting a civil war against his own son, and his kingdom suffers from famine and plague. But right at the end he purchases a piece of land which will eventually be the site of the Temple.

Perhaps that's the key message of 2 Samuel. Yes, it's about national success and glory, but it's also about personal failure and forgiveness. Faced with his own actions, he throws himself on God's mercy. David defeated Israel's enemies, but he also discovered more about Israel's God, a God who promised that his family would reign in the land forever.

QUICK TOUR ▶ 2 SAMUEL

David becomes king 5:1–12
David brings the Holy
    Box to Jerusalem 6:1–23
God's promise 7:1–29
David and Bathsheba 11:1–27

Nathan reveals the truth 12:1–23
Absalom rebels 15:1–37
Absalom is killed 18:1–33
David's final sin 24:1–25

"I promise that I will make your family a family of kings. When your life is finished, you will die and be buried with your ancestors. But then I will make one of your own children become the king."
                                                                    2 Samuel 7:11–12

David Learns About Saul's Death

1 After David defeated the Amalekites, he went back to Ziklag. This was just after Saul had been killed. David had been there for two days. [2]Then, on the third day, a young soldier from Saul's camp came to Ziklag. His clothes were torn, and he had dirt on his head.[a] He came to David and bowed with his face to the ground.

[3]David asked him, "Where have you come from?"

The man answered, "I have just come from the Israelite camp."

[4]David asked him, "Please tell me, who won the battle?"

The man answered, "Our people ran away from the battle. Many of them were killed in the battle. Even Saul and his son Jonathan are dead."

[5]David said to the young soldier, "How do you know Saul and his son Jonathan are dead?"

[6]The young soldier said, "I happened to be on Mount Gilboa. I saw Saul leaning on his spear. The Philistine chariots and horsemen were coming closer and closer to Saul. [7]Saul looked back and saw me. He called to me and I answered him. [8]Then Saul asked me who I was. I told him that I was an Amalekite. [9]Then Saul said, 'Please kill me. I am hurt badly. And I am about to die anyway.' [10]He was hurt so badly that I knew he wouldn't live. So I stopped and killed him. Then I took the crown from his head and the bracelet from his arm and brought them here to you, my lord."

INSIGHT

In ancient times tearing the clothes was a sign of mourning and grief, and often the mourner would wear sackcloth for a period of time (see Genesis 37:34; 2 Samuel 3:31). The tearing of clothes still takes place today as part of some traditional Jewish funerals.

2 Samuel 1:11

---

[11]Then David tore his clothes to show he was very sad. All the men with him did the same thing. [12]They were very sad and cried. They did not eat until evening. They cried because Saul and his son Jonathan were dead. David and his men cried for the Lord's people, and they cried for Israel. They cried because Saul, his son Jonathan and many Israelites had been killed in battle.

David Gives Orders for the Amalekite to be Killed

[13]Then David talked with the young soldier who had told him about Saul's death. David asked, "Where are you from?"

The young soldier answered, "I am the son of a foreigner. I am an Amalekite."

[14]David said to the young soldier, "Why were you not afraid to kill the Lord's chosen king?"[b]

[15-16]Then David told the Amalekite, "You are responsible for your own death. You said you killed the Lord's chosen king, so your own words prove you are guilty." Then David called one of his young servants and told him to kill the Amalekite. So the young Israelite killed him.

David's Song About Saul and Jonathan

[17]David sang a sad song about Saul and his son Jonathan. [18]David told his men to teach the song to the people of Judah. This song is called "The Bow", and it is written in the *Book of Jashar.*[c]

[19]"Israel, your beauty was ruined on your hills.
   Oh, how those heroes fell!
[20]Don't tell the news in Gath.[d]
   Don't announce it in the streets of
     Ashkelon.[e]
Those Philistine cities would be happy!
   Those foreigners[f] would be glad.

[21]"May no rain or dew fall
   on you, mountains of Gilboa.
May there be no offerings
   coming from your fields.
The shields of the heroes rusted there.
   Saul's shield was not rubbed with oil.
[22]Jonathan's bow killed its share of enemies,
   and Saul's sword killed its share!
They have spilled the blood of men now dead.
   They cut into the fat of strong men.

[23]"Saul and Jonathan—how dear they were
     to us!
In life they loved being together,
   and even death did not separate them!
They were faster than eagles
   and stronger than lions.

---

[a] **1:2 clothes . . . head** This showed that the man was very sad.
[b] **1:14 chosen king** Literally, "anointed one".
[c] **1:18 Book of Jashar** An ancient book about the wars of Israel.
[d] **1:20 Gath** The Philistine capital city.
[e] **1:20 Ashkelon** One of the five major Philistine cities.
[f] **1:20 foreigners** Literally, "uncircumcised". This shows that the Philistines had not shared in Israel's agreement with God.

²⁴Daughters of Israel, cry for Saul!
  Saul gave you beautiful red dresses
  and covered them with gold
  jewellery!

²⁵"Strong men have fallen in the battle.
  Jonathan is dead on Gilboa's hills.
²⁶Jonathan, my brother, I miss you!
  I enjoyed your friendship so much.
  Your love for me was wonderful,
  stronger than the love of women.
²⁷Heroes have fallen in battle.
  Their weapons of war are lost."

David Is Anointed King of Judah

2 Later David asked the LORD for advice. David said, "Should I take control*a* of any of the cities of Judah?"

The LORD said to David, "Yes."

David asked, "Where should I go?"

The Lord answered, "To Hebron."

²So David and his two wives moved to Hebron. (His wives were Ahinoam from Jezreel and Abigail, who had been the wife of Nabal from Carmel.) ³David also brought his men and their families. All of them made their homes in Hebron and the towns nearby.

⁴The men of Judah came to Hebron and anointed David to be the king of Judah. Then they told David, "The men of Jabesh Gilead buried Saul."

⁵David sent messengers to the men of Jabesh Gilead. These messengers told the men in Jabesh: "The LORD bless you, because you have shown kindness to your lord Saul by burying him.*b* ⁶The LORD will be kind and true to you, and so will I. ⁷Now be strong and brave. Your lord, Saul, is dead, but the tribe of Judah has anointed me to be their king."

Ish Bosheth Becomes King

⁸Abner son of Ner was the captain of Saul's army. Abner took Ish Bosheth*c* son of Saul to Mahanaim ⁹and made him king of Gilead, Asher, Jezreel, Ephraim, Benjamin and all Israel.*d*

¹⁰Ish Bosheth son of Saul was 40 years old when he began to rule over Israel. He ruled Israel for two years, but the tribe of Judah followed David. ¹¹David ruled over the tribe of Judah from Hebron for seven years and six months.

The Deadly Contest

¹²Abner son of Ner and the officers of Ish Bosheth son of Saul left Mahanaim and went to Gibeon. ¹³Joab, Zeruiah's son and the officers of David also went to Gibeon. They met Abner and Ish Bosheth's officers at the pool of Gibeon. Abner's group sat on one side of the pool. Joab's group sat on the other side.

¹⁴Abner said to Joab, "Let's have the young soldiers get up and have a contest here."

Joab said, "Yes, let's have a contest."

¹⁵So the young soldiers got up. The two groups counted their men for the contest. They chose twelve men from the tribe of Benjamin to fight for Ish Bosheth son of Saul, and they chose twelve men from David's officers. ¹⁶Each of the men grabbed his opponent's head and stabbed him in the side with his sword, and then they fell down together. That is why this place in Gibeon is called "The Field of the Sharp Knives".*e* ¹⁷That contest turned into a terrible battle and David's officers defeated Abner and the Israelites that day.

Abner Kills Asahel

¹⁸Zeruiah had three sons, Joab, Abishai and Asahel. Asahel was a fast runner, as fast as a wild deer. ¹⁹Asahel ran straight towards Abner and began chasing him. ²⁰Abner looked back and asked, "Is that you, Asahel?"

Asahel said, "Yes, it's me."

²¹Abner didn't want to hurt Asahel, so he said to Asahel, "Stop chasing me—go after one of the young soldiers. You could easily take his armour for yourself." But Asahel refused to stop chasing Abner.

²²Abner again said to Asahel, "Stop chasing me, or I will have to kill you. Then I will not be able to look your brother Joab in the face again."

²³But Asahel refused to stop chasing Abner. So Abner used the back end of his spear and pushed it into Asahel's stomach. The spear went deep into Asahel's stomach and came out of his back. Asahel died right there.

Joab and Abishai Chase Abner

Asahel's body lay on the ground. Everyone who came that way stopped to look at Asahel, ²⁴but Joab and Abishai*f* continued chasing Abner. The sun was just going down when they came to Ammah Hill. (Ammah Hill is in front of Giah on

---

a **2:1 take control** Literally, "go up against".

b **2:5 burying him** The bodies of both Saul and Jonathan were burned and their bones were buried. See 1 Sam. 31:12.

c **2:8 Ish Bosheth** In the ancient Greek version and 1 Chr. 8:33; 9:39, his name is Ish Baal or Eshbaal. Later Hebrew scribes substituted Bosheth ("shame") for Baal ("Lord"), because Baal was also the name for a Canaanite god.

d **2:9 Israel** Sometimes this means the whole country, Judah and Israel. Here, it means only the tribes that were not united with Judah.

e **2:16 The Field of the Sharp Knives** Or "Helkath Hazzurim".

f **2:24 Joab and Abishai** Brothers of Asahel, the man who Abner killed. See verse 18.

the way to the desert of Gibeon.) 25The men from the tribe of Benjamin gathered around Abner at the top of the hill.

26Abner shouted to Joab and said, "Must we fight and kill each other forever? Surely you know that this will only end in sadness. Tell the people to stop chasing their own brothers."

27Then Joab said, "As surely as God is alive, if you had not said something, people would still be chasing their brothers in the morning." 28So Joab blew a trumpet, and his people stopped chasing the Israelites. They did not try to fight the Israelites any more.

29Abner and his men marched all night through the Jordan Valley. They crossed the Jordan River and then marched all day until they came to Mahanaim.

30Joab stopped chasing Abner and turned back. Joab had gathered his men and learned that 19 of David's officers were missing, including Asahel. 31But David's officers had killed 360 of Abner's men from the tribe of Benjamin. 32David's officers took Asahel and buried him in the tomb of his father at Bethlehem.

Joab and his men marched all night. The sun came up just as they reached Hebron.

War Between Israel and Judah

3 There was war for a long time between Saul's family and David's family. David became stronger and stronger, but Saul's family became weaker and weaker.

David's Six Sons Born at Hebron

2These are David's sons who were born at Hebron:

The first son was Amnon. Amnon's mother was Ahinoam from Jezreel.
3The second son was Kileab. His mother was Abigail, who had been the wife of Nabal from Carmel.
The third son was Absalom. Absalom's mother was Maacah daughter of King Talmai of Geshur.
4The fourth son was Adonijah. Adonijah's mother was Haggith.
The fifth son was Shephatiah. Shephatiah's mother was Abital.
5The sixth son was Ithream. Ithream's mother was David's wife Eglah.

These sons were all born at Hebron.

Abner Decides to Join David

6As the families of Saul and David fought each other, Abner became more and more powerful in Saul's army. 7Saul had a slave woman named Rizpah daughter of Aiah. Ish Bosheth said to Abner, "Why did you have sex with my father's servant woman?"

8This made Abner very angry. He said, "I have been loyal to Saul and his family. I did not give you to David. I am not a traitor working for Judah.*a* But now you are saying that I did this bad thing. 9–10The LORD promised with an oath that he would take the kingdom away from Saul's family and give it to David. And I swear I will make sure that happens. God will make David king of Judah and Israel. He will rule from Dan to Beersheba.*b*" 11Ish Bosheth was too afraid of Abner to say anything in response.

12Abner sent messengers to David and said, "Who do you think should rule this country? Make an agreement with me, and I will help you become the ruler of all the people of Israel."

13David answered, "Good! I will make an agreement with you. But I ask you only one thing: I will not meet with you until you bring Saul's daughter Michal to me."

14David sent messengers to Saul's son Ish Bosheth. David said, "Give me my wife Michal. She was promised to me. I killed 100 Philistines to get her."*c*

15Then Ish Bosheth told the men to go and take Michal from a man named Paltiel son of Laish. 16Michal's husband, Paltiel, followed them, crying all the way to Bahurim. Finally, Abner said to him, "Go back home." So Paltiel went back home.

17Abner sent this message to the leaders of Israel. He said, "For a long time you have wanted to make David your king. 18Now do it! The LORD was talking about David when he said, 'I will save my people the Israelites from the Philistines and all their other enemies. I will do this through my servant David.'"

19Abner said these things to David in Hebron, and he said these things to the people of the tribe of Benjamin. The things Abner said sounded good to the tribe of Benjamin and to all the people of Israel.

20Then Abner came up to David at Hebron. Abner brought 20 men with him. David gave a party for Abner and for all the men who came with him.

21Abner said to David, "My lord and king, let me go and bring all the Israelites to you. Then

---

a **3:8 *I am not . . . Judah*** Literally, "Am I a dog's head of Judah?"
b **3:9–10 *Dan to Beersheba*** This means the whole nation of Israel, north and south. Dan was a town in the northern part of Israel and Beersheba was in the southern part of Judah.
c **3:14 *I killed . . . to get her*** Literally, "I paid for her with 100 Philistine foreskins." See 1 Sam. 18:20–30; 25:44.

they will make an agreement with you, and you will rule over all Israel, as you wanted."

So David let Abner leave in peace.

Abner's Death

²²Joab and David's officers came back from battle. They had many valuable things that they had taken from the enemy. David had just let Abner leave in peace. So Abner was not there in Hebron with David. ²³Joab and all his army arrived at Hebron. The army said to Joab, "Abner son of Ner came to King David, and David let Abner leave in peace."

²⁴Joab came to the king and said, "What have you done? Abner came to you, but you sent him away without hurting him! Why? ²⁵You know Abner son of Ner. He came to trick you. He came to learn all about what you are doing."

²⁶Joab left David and sent messengers to Abner at the well of Sirah. The messengers brought Abner back, but David did not know this. ²⁷When Abner arrived at Hebron, Joab met him in the gateway, pulled him aside to talk in private, and then stabbed him in the stomach. So he got his revenge against Abner. Joab killed Abner because Abner had killed Joab's brother Asahel.

David Cries for Abner

²⁸Later David heard the news and said, "My kingdom and I are innocent of the death of Abner son of Ner. The Lord knows this. ²⁹Joab and his family are responsible for this, and they will be cursed. Many troubles will come to his family. His people will be sick with leprosy, lame, killed in war and not have enough food to eat!"

³⁰Joab and his brother Abishai killed Abner because Abner had killed their brother Asahel in the battle at Gibeon.

³¹⁻³²David said to Joab and to all the people with Joab, "Tear your clothes and put on sackcloth. Cry for Abner." They buried Abner in Hebron. David went to the funeral. King David and all the people cried at Abner's grave.

³³King David sang this sad song at Abner's funeral:

"Did Abner die like some foolish criminal?
³⁴   Abner, your hands were not tied.
    Your feet were not put in chains.
No, Abner, evil men killed you!"

Then all the people cried again for Abner. ³⁵All day long people came to encourage David to eat food. But David had made a special promise. He said, "May God punish me and give me many troubles if I eat bread or any other food before the sun goes down." ³⁶All the people saw what happened, and they were pleased with what King David had done. ³⁷All the people of Judah and Israel understood that King David had not killed Abner son of Ner.

³⁸King David said to his officers, "You know that a very important leader died today in Israel. ³⁹And it was on the very same day that I was anointed to be the king. These sons of Zeruiah have caused me a lot of trouble. May the Lord give them the punishment they deserve."

Troubles Come to Saul's Family

4 Saul's son Ish Bosheth heard that Abner had died at Hebron. Ish Bosheth and all his people became very afraid. ²Two men went to see to Saul's son. These two men were captains in the army. They were Recab and Baanah, the sons of Rimmon from Beeroth. (They were Benjamites because the town Beeroth belonged to the tribe of Benjamin. ³But all the people in Beeroth ran away to Gittaim, and they are still living there today.)

⁴Saul's son Jonathan had a son named Mephibosheth. He was five years old when the news came from Jezreel that Saul and Jonathan had been killed. The woman who cared for Mephibosheth picked him up and ran away. But while running away, she dropped the boy, and he became lame in both feet.

⁵Recab and Baanah, sons of Rimmon from Beeroth, went to Ish Bosheth's house at noon. Ish Bosheth was resting because it was hot. ⁶⁻⁷Recab and Baanah came into the house as if they were going to get some wheat. Ish Bosheth was lying on his bed in his bedroom, and they stabbed and killed him. Then they cut off his head and took it with them. They travelled all night on the road through the Jordan Valley. ⁸When they arrived at Hebron, they gave Ish Bosheth's head to David.

Recab and Baanah said to King David, "Here is the head of your enemy, Ish Bosheth son of Saul. He tried to kill you, but the Lord has punished Saul and his family for you today."

⁹But David told Recab and his brother Baanah, "As surely as the Lord lives, he is the one who has rescued me from all my troubles! ¹⁰Once before a man thought he would bring me good news. He told me, 'Look! Saul is dead.' He thought I would reward him for bringing me the news. But I grabbed this man and killed him at Ziklag. ¹¹I will kill you too and remove this evil from our land because you evil men killed a good man sleeping on his own bed, in his own house."

¹²So David commanded his young helpers^a to kill Recab and Baanah. The young men cut off the hands and feet of Recab and Baanah and hanged

---

^a **4:12 young helpers** Young men who carried a soldier's weapons into battle but were not yet soldiers themselves.

them by the pool of Hebron. Then they took the head of Ish Bosheth and buried it where Abner was buried at Hebron.

The Israelites Make David King

5 All the tribes of Israel came to David at Hebron. They said to David, "Look, we are one family![a] [2]Even when Saul was our king, you were the one who led us into battle. And you were the one who brought Israel back home from war. The LORD himself said to you, 'You will be the shepherd of my people, the Israelites. You will be the ruler over Israel.'"

INSIGHT

David could have killed Saul, seizing power and becoming king whenever he wanted to, but instead he waited for God's timing. When the people came and asked him to be king it was the fulfilment of a prophecy that had been made many years earlier (1 Samuel 16).

2 Samuel 5:1–5

---

[3]So all the leaders of Israel came to meet with King David at Hebron. He made an agreement with them in Hebron in front of the LORD, and they anointed David to be the king of Israel. [4]David was 30 years old when he began to rule. He was king for 40 years. [5]In Hebron he ruled over Judah for 7 years and 6 months, and in Jerusalem he ruled over all Israel and Judah for 33 years.

David Captures Jerusalem

[6]The king and his men went to fight against the Jebusites living in Jerusalem. The Jebusites said to David, "You cannot come into our city.[b] Even our blind and lame people can stop you." (They said this because they thought that David would not be able to enter their city. [7]But David did take the fortress of Zion. This fortress became the City of David.)

[8]That day David said to his men, "Whenever you strike at the Jebusites, aim for the throat and kill them."[c] David said this because he hated to have people left who were lame and blind. That is

why people now say, "The lame and blind are not allowed in the temple."[d]

[9]David lived in the fortress and called it "The City of David". David built up the city from the Millo inwards.[e] [10]He became stronger and stronger because the LORD All-Powerful was with him.

[11]King Hiram of Tyre sent messengers to David. He also sent cedar trees, carpenters and stonemasons. They built a house for David. [12]Then David knew that the LORD had really made him king of Israel and had made him ruler over his kingdom for the good of his people, Israel.

[13]David moved from Hebron to Jerusalem. In Jerusalem, he got more slave women and wives. So David had more children who were born in Jerusalem. [14]David's sons who were born in Jerusalem are Shammua, Shobab, Nathan, Solomon, [15]Ibhar, Elishua, Nepheg, Japhia, [16]Elishama, Eliada and Eliphelet.

David Fights Against the Philistines

[17]When the Philistines heard that the Israelites had anointed David to be the king of Israel, all the Philistines went up to kill him. David heard about this and went down into the fortress at Jerusalem. [18]The Philistines came and camped in Rephaim Valley.

[19]David asked the LORD, "Should I go up to fight against the Philistines? Will you help me defeat them?"

The LORD answered, "Yes, I certainly will help you defeat the Philistines."

[20]Then David went to Baal Perazim and defeated the Philistines in that place. He said, "The LORD broke through my enemies like water breaking through a dam." That is why David named that place "Baal Perazim".[f] [21]The Philistines left the statues of their gods behind at Baal Perazim. David and his men took them away.

[22]Again the Philistines came up and camped in Rephaim Valley.

[23]David prayed to the LORD again and got this answer: "Don't go up the valley. Go around them to the other side of their army. Attack them from the other side of the balsam trees. [24]When you hear the sound of marching in the tops of the balsam trees, you must act quickly because that is the sign that the LORD has gone out in front of you to defeat the Philistines."[g]

---

[a] **5:1 one family** Literally, "your flesh and blood".

[b] **5:6 You cannot come . . . city** The city of Jerusalem was built on a hill. It had high walls around it, making it hard to capture.

[c] **5:8 Whenever . . . kill them** Or "Whoever wants to attack the Jebusites must go through the shaft." This might refer to a tunnel or shaft leading up into the city through Gihon Spring, which was outside the city walls.

[d] **5:8 temple** Or "the king's palace".

[e] **5:9 inward** Or "towards the Temple".

[f] **5:20 Baal Perazim** This name means "the LORD breaks through".

[g] **5:24** Or "From the top of the balsam trees you will be able to hear them marching into battle. Then you must act quickly, because at that time the LORD will go ahead of you and defeat the Philistines for you."

25David did what the Lord commanded him to do, and he defeated the Philistines. He chased them from Geba to Gezer, killing them all along the way.

God's Holy Box Is Moved to Jerusalem

6 David again gathered all the best soldiers in Israel. There were 30,000 men. 2Then David and all his men went to Baalah in Judah[a] to take God's Holy Box there. [The Holy Box is like God's throne]—people go there to call on the name of the Lord All-Powerful who sits as king above the Cherub angels that are on that Box. 3David's men brought the Holy Box out of Abinadab's house on the hill. Then they put God's Holy Box on a new cart. Uzzah and Ahio, sons of Abinadab, were driving the new cart.

4So they carried the Holy Box out of Abinadab's house on the hill. The sons of Abinadab, Uzzah and Ahio, drove the new cart. Ahio was walking in front of the Holy Box. 5David and all the Israelites were dancing in front of the Lord and playing all kinds of musical instruments. There were lyres, harps, drums, rattles, instruments made from cypress wood and cymbals. 6When David's men came to the threshing floor of Nacon, the oxen stumbled and God's Holy Box began to fall off the cart. Uzzah caught the Holy Box. 7But the Lord was angry with Uzzah and killed him for that mistake. Uzzah showed that he did not honour God when he touched the Holy Box, so he died there by God's Holy Box. 8David was upset because the Lord had killed Uzzah. David called that place "Perez Uzzah".[b] It is still called Perez Uzzah today.

9David became afraid of the Lord that day, and he said, "How can I bring God's Holy Box here now?" 10So David would not move the Lord's Holy Box into the City of David. He put the Holy Box at the house of Obed Edom from Gath.[c] 11The Lord's Holy Box stayed in Obed Edom's house for three months. The Lord blessed Obed Edom and all his family.

12Later people told David, "The Lord has blessed the family of Obed Edom and everything he owns, because God's Holy Box is there." So David went and brought God's Holy Box from Obed Edom's house. David was very happy and excited. 13When the men who carried the Lord's Holy Box had walked six steps, they stopped and David sacrificed a bull and a fat calf. 14David was dancing in front of the Lord. He was wearing a linen ephod.

15David and all the Israelites were excited—they shouted and blew trumpets as they brought the Lord's Holy Box into the city. 16Saul's daughter Michal was looking out of the window. While the Lord's Holy Box was being carried into the city, David was jumping and dancing before the Lord. Michal saw this, and she was upset at David.

17David put up a tent for the Holy Box. The Israelites put the Lord's Holy Box in its place under the tent. Then David offered burnt offerings and fellowship offerings before the Lord. 18After David had finished offering the burnt offerings and the fellowship offerings, he blessed the people in the name of the Lord All-Powerful. 19He also gave a share of bread, a raisin cake and some date bread to every man and woman of Israel. Then all the people went home.

Michal Scolds David

20David went back to bless his house, but Saul's daughter Michal came out to meet him. She said, "The king of Israel did not honour himself today! You took off your clothes in front of your servants' girls. You were like a fool who takes off his clothes without shame!"

21Then David said to Michal, "The Lord chose me, not your father or anyone from his family. The Lord chose me to be leader of his people, the Israelites. So I will continue dancing and celebrating in front of the Lord. 22I might do things that are even more embarrassing! Maybe you will not respect me, but the girls you are talking about are proud of me!"

23Saul's daughter Michal never had a child. She died without having any children.

David Wants to Build a Temple

7 After King David moved into his new house the Lord gave him some relief from all his enemies around him. 2King David said to Nathan the prophet, "Look, I am living in a fancy house made of cedar wood, but God's Holy Box is still kept in a tent!"

3Nathan said to King David, "Do whatever you want to do. The Lord will be with you."

4But that night, the Lord's word came to Nathan:

5"Go and tell my servant David, 'This is what the Lord says: You are not the one to build a house for me to live in. 6I did not live in a house at the time I took the Israelites out of Egypt. No, I travelled around in a tent. I used the tent for my home. 7I never told any of the tribes of Israel to build me a fancy house made from cedar wood.'

---

[a] 6:2 Baalah in Judah Another name for Kiriath Jearim. See 1 Chr. 13:6.
[b] 6:8 Perez Uzzah This name means "The Punishment of Uzzah."
[c] 6:10 Obed Edom from Gath A person from the tribe of Levi who lived near Jerusalem.

THE PROMISE OF A KING

What makes a great leader? Think about some of the people whose leadership you respect. Maybe you've already got first-hand experience of what it means to lead others in some way. If so, what's it like to be the person others look to for guidance and inspiration?

DIG IN

READ 2 Samuel 6:16–23

- What do David's actions in verses 16–19 say about this king?
- In what ways does David express worship here?

David is a central figure in the "big story" of the Bible. As well as being a faithful and successful king, David was also a poet – he wrote a large chunk of the Bible's songbook, The Psalms. David knew something about worship from the heart, and that spilled into his singing, his songwriting, his generosity – and his dancing!

- What motivates David's wife Michal to react the way she does in verse 20?

Michal clearly thought that David was not behaving like a king. But God thought otherwise! He measured David's suitability for the job as king not by his courage, his talent or his leadership ability (though he certainly had all three) but by his heart. There's another reason David is central to God's plans. Here in 2 Samuel, David receives an enormous promise, but one that he'll never see fulfilled in his lifetime.

READ 2 Samuel 7:1–29

- How do you think David must have felt hearing God's words in verses 8–11?
- What is God promising to do with David's family?
- What does David's prayer of response tell us about him?
- How does David express worship here?

David wanted to do something for God – he wanted to build God a house (vv.1–2). But God tells him he doesn't need to – God will build David a family "house" instead! What God is promising David here is that from his family line will come another king – one much greater than him and whose rule would last forever. Although his name isn't spoken here, the king being talked about is the Messiah, King Jesus.

David is chosen as one of the people in the Bible who will point to the hero of the whole book – Jesus Christ. The good qualities of David – his heart of worship, his faithfulness, his good leadership and more – are all foretastes of the qualities of Jesus.

DIG THROUGH

- David had a lot of things going for him, but what God was most interested in wasn't his gifts but his heart. In your heart, is there any trace of you trying to impress God with what you can do for him? Forget that idea – God wants to do great things for you!
- How is your worship life? Are you bothered by what other people think of you or do you feel free to worship God however that looks?

DIG DEEPER

- In the New Testament, Matthew 1:1–17 shows where David fits into the genealogy (family line) of Jesus. Check it out to see how many of the names you recognize. It's amazing to see how God worked through generation after generation to bring about his purposes.
- David is the author of about half the book of Psalms. Most are short and can be read in a few minutes. Why not read a few to get a feel for the way David talked to God? Start with Psalm 19 or 24.

8"You must say this to my servant David: 'This is what the LORD All-Powerful says: I chose you while you were out in the pasture following the sheep. I took you from that job and made you the leader of my people, the Israelites. 9I have been with you everywhere you went. I have defeated your enemies for you. I will make you one of the most famous people on earth. 10–11And I chose a place for my people, the Israelites. I planted the Israelites. I gave them their own place to live so that they will not have to move from place to place any more. In the past, I sent judges to lead my people, but evil people gave them many troubles. That will not happen now. I am giving you peace from all your enemies. I promise that I will make your family a family of kings.*a*

12"When your life is finished, you will die and be buried with your ancestors. But then I will make one of your own children become the king. 13He will build a house for my name, and I will make his kingdom strong forever. 14I will be his father, and he will be my son.*b* When he sins, I will use other people to punish him. They will be my whips. 15But I will never stop loving him. I will continue to be loyal to him. I took away my love and kindness from Saul. I pushed Saul away when I turned to you. 16Your family of kings will continue—you can depend on that! For you, your kingdom will continue forever! Your throne will stand forever!'"

17Nathan told David about that vision. He told David everything God had said.

David Prays to God

18Then King David went in and sat in front of the LORD. David said,

"Lord GOD, why am I so important to you? Why is my family important? Why have you made me so important? 19I am nothing but a servant, but Lord GOD, you have also said these kind things about my future family. Lord GOD, you don't always talk like this to people, do you? 20How can I continue talking to you? Lord GOD, you know that I am only a servant. 21You will do all these wonderful things because you said you would do them and because you want to do them. And you decided to let me know about all these things. 22Lord GOD, this is

why you are so great! There is no one like you. There is no god except you! We know that because of what we ourselves have heard about what you did.

INSIGHT

David's prayer is one of utter gratitude. He gives God the full credit for all his achievements and asks his blessing for the future of his work and for his family. God fulfilled this spectacularly through the eventual birth of Jesus into David's family line.

2 Samuel 7:18–29

23"And there is no nation on earth like your people, Israel. They are a special people. They were slaves, but you took them out of Egypt and made them free. You made them your people. You did great and wonderful things for the Israelites and for your land. 24You made the people of Israel your very own people forever, and LORD, you became their God.

25"Now, LORD God, you promised to do something for me, your servant, and for my family. Now please do what you promised—make my family a family of kings forever! 26Then your name will be honoured forever. People will say, 'The LORD God All-Powerful rules Israel! And may the family of your servant David continue to be strong in serving you.'

27"You, LORD All-Powerful, the God of Israel, have shown things to me. You said, 'I will make your family great.' That is why I, your servant, decided to pray this prayer to you. 28Lord GOD, you are God, and I can trust what you say. And you said that these good things would happen to me, your servant. 29Now, please, bless my family. Let them stand before you and serve you forever. Lord GOD, you yourself said these things. You yourself blessed my family with a blessing that will continue forever."

David Wins Many Wars

8 Later David defeated the Philistines and took control of a large area of land around Gath.*c*

---

a 7:10–11 *make . . . family of kings* Literally, "make a house for you".
b 7:14 *father . . . son* God "adopted" the kings from David's family, and they became his "sons". See Ps. 2:7.
c 8:1 *area of land around Gath* Or "villages controlled by the mother city" or "Metheg-Ammah". See 1 Chr. 18:1.

[2]He also defeated the Moabites. He forced them to lie on the ground in a long row. Using a rope to measure, those within two lengths of the rope were killed and those within every third length were allowed to live. So the Moabites became servants of David and paid tribute to him.

[3]David went to an area near the Euphrates to set up a monument for himself.[a] At that time he defeated the king of Zobah, Hadadezer son of Rehob. [4]David took 1,000 chariots, 7,000 horsemen,[b] and 20,000 foot soldiers from Hadadezer. He crippled all but 100 of the chariot horses.[c]

[5]Arameans from Damascus came to help King Hadadezer of Zobah, but David defeated those 22,000 Arameans. [6]Then David put his soldiers in Damascus, Aram. The Arameans became David's servants and brought tribute. The LORD gave victory to David wherever he went.

[7]David took the gold shields[d] that had belonged to Hadadezer's servants and brought them to Jerusalem. [8]David also took many things made of bronze from Tebah[e] and Berothai. (Tebah and Berothai were cities that had belonged to Hadadezer.)

[9]King Toi of Hamath heard that David had defeated Hadadezer's whole army. [10]Hadadezer had fought against Toi in the past, so Toi sent his son Joram to King David. Joram greeted him and blessed him because David had fought against Hadadezer and defeated him. Joram brought gifts of silver, gold and bronze. [11]David took these things and dedicated them to the LORD, as he had done with all the other things he had taken from the nations he had defeated: [12]Aram, Moab, Ammon, Philistia and Amalek. He had also defeated Hadadezer son of Rehob, king of Zobah. [13]David had defeated 18,000 Edomites[f] in Salt Valley. He was famous when he came home. [14]He put teams of soldiers throughout Edom, and the whole nation became his servants. The LORD gave victory to him wherever he went.

David's Rule

[15]David ruled over all Israel, and he made good and fair decisions for all his people. [16]Joab son of Zeruiah was the captain over the army. Jehoshaphat son of Ahilud was the historian. [17]Zadok son of Ahitub and Ahimelech son of Abiathar were priests. Seraiah was secretary. [18]Benaiah son of Jehoiada was in charge of the Kerethites and Pelethites,[g] and David's sons were priests.[h]

David Is Kind to Saul's Family

9 David asked, "Is there anyone still left in Saul's family? I want to show kindness to this person. I want to do it for Jonathan."

[2]There was a servant named Ziba from Saul's family. David's servants called Ziba to David. King David said to Ziba, "Are you Ziba?"

Ziba said, "Yes, I am your servant Ziba."

[3]The king said, "Is there anyone left in Saul's family? I want to show God's kindness to this person."

Ziba said to King David, "Jonathan has a son still living. He is lame in both feet."

[4]The king said to Ziba, "Where is this son?"

Ziba said to the king, "He is at the house of Makir son of Ammiel in Lo Debar."

[5]Then King David sent some of his officers to Lo Debar to bring Jonathan's son from the house of Makir son of Ammiel. [6]Jonathan's son Mephibosheth came to David and bowed with his face low to the floor.

David said, "Mephibosheth?"

Mephibosheth said, "Yes sir, it is I, your servant Mephibosheth."

[7]David said to Mephibosheth, "Don't be afraid. I will be kind to you because of your father Jonathan. I will give back to you all the land of your grandfather Saul. And you will always be able to eat at my table."

[8]Mephibosheth bowed to David again and he said, "I am no better than a dead dog, but you are being very kind to me."

[9]Then King David called Saul's servant Ziba and said, "I have given Saul's family and everything he owns to your master's grandson, Mephibosheth. [10]You will farm the land for Mephibosheth. Your sons and servants will do this for him. You will harvest the crops. Then your master's grandson will have plenty of food to eat, but Mephibosheth will always be allowed to eat at my table."

Ziba had 15 sons and 20 servants. [11]He said to King David, "I am your servant. I will do everything that my lord the king commands."

---

[a] **8:3 David went . . . for himself** Or "David went to take control of the area near the Euphrates River."
[b] **8:4 David . . . horsemen** This is found in the ancient Greek version and a Hebrew scroll from Qumran. The standard Hebrew text has "1,700 horsemen".
[c] **8:4 He crippled . . . horses** Or "He destroyed all but 100 chariots."
[d] **8:7 shields** Or "bow cases".
[e] **8:8 Tebah** This is found in some ancient Greek copies. The standard Hebrew text has "Betah". See 1 Chr. 18:8.
[f] **8:13 Edomites** This is found in the ancient Greek and Syriac versions and a few Hebrew copies. The standard Hebrew text has "Arameans".
[g] **8:18 Kerethites and Pelethites** These were David's special bodyguards. An ancient Aramaic version has "the archers and stone throwers". This would mean these men were specially trained in using bows and arrows and slings.
[h] **8:18 priests** Or "important leaders".

So Mephibosheth ate at David's table like one of the king's sons. 12Mephibosheth had a young son named Mica. All the people in Ziba's family became Mephibosheth's servants. 13Mephibosheth lived in Jerusalem. He was lame in both feet, and every day he ate at the king's table.

Hanun Shames David's Men

10 Later King Nahash of the Ammonites died. His son Hanun became the new king after him. 2David said, "Nahash was kind to me, so I will be kind to his son Hanun." So David sent his officers to comfort Hanun about his father's death.

David's officers went to the land of the Ammonites. 3But the Ammonite leaders said to Hanun, their lord, "Do you think that David is trying to honour your father by sending some men to comfort you? No, David sent these men to spy on your city. They plan to make war against you."

4So Hanun took David's officers and shaved off one half of their beards. He cut off their clothes at the hips. Then he sent them away.

5When the people told David, he sent messengers to meet his officers. He did this because these men were very ashamed. King David said, "Wait at Jericho until your beards grow again. Then come back home."

War Against the Ammonites

6The Ammonites saw that they had become David's enemies, so they hired Arameans from Beth Rehob and Zobah. There were 20,000 Aramean foot soldiers. The Ammonites also hired the king of Maacah with 1,000 men and 12,000 men from Tob.

7David heard about this, so he sent Joab and the whole army of powerful men. 8The Ammonites came out and got ready for the battle. They stood at the city gate. The Arameans from Zobah and Rehob and the men from Tob and Maacah did not stand together with the Ammonites in the field.

9Joab saw that there were enemies in front of him and behind him. So he chose some of the best Israelite soldiers and lined them up for battle against the Arameans. 10Then Joab gave the other men to his brother Abishai to lead against the Ammonites. 11Joab said to Abishai, "If the Arameans are too strong for me, you will help me. If the Ammonites are too strong for you, I will come and help you. 12Be strong, and let us fight bravely for our people and for the cities of our God. The LORD will do what he decides is right." 13Then Joab and his men attacked the Arameans. The Arameans ran away from Joab

and his men. 14The Ammonites saw that the Arameans were running away, so they ran away from Abishai and went back to their city.

So Joab came back from the battle with the Ammonites and went back to Jerusalem.

The Arameans Decide to Fight Again

15When the Arameans saw that the Israelites had defeated them, they came together into one big army. 16Hadadezer[a] sent messengers to bring the Arameans who lived on the other side of the Euphrates River. These Arameans came to Helam. Their leader was Shobach, the captain of Hadadezer's army.

17When David heard about this, he gathered all the Israelites together. They crossed over the Jordan River and went to Helam.

There the Arameans prepared for battle and attacked, 18but David defeated them, and they ran from the Israelites. David killed 700 chariot drivers and 40,000 horsemen as well as Shobach, the captain of the Aramean army.

19The kings who served Hadadezer saw that the Israelites had defeated them, so they made peace with the Israelites and became their servants. The Arameans were afraid to help the Ammonites again.

David Meets Bathsheba

11 In the spring, when kings go out to war, David sent Joab, his officers and all the Israelites out to destroy the Ammonites. Joab's army surrounded their capital city, Rabbah.

David stayed in Jerusalem. 2One evening he got up from his bed and walked around on the roof of his house. From there he saw a woman bathing. She was very beautiful, 3so David sent for his officers and asked them who she was. An officer answered, "That is Bathsheba, daughter of Eliam. She is the wife of Uriah the Hittite."

4David sent messengers to go and bring Bathsheba to him. She had just purified herself after her monthly period of bleeding. She went to David, he had sex with her and then she went back to her house. 5Later, Bathsheba became pregnant. She sent word to him saying, "I am pregnant."

David Tries to Hide His Sin

6David sent a message to Joab. "Send Uriah the Hittite to me."

So Joab sent Uriah to David. 7When Uriah came, David asked him how Joab was, how the soldiers were and how the war was going. 8Then David said to Uriah, "Go home and relax."[b]

---

[a] 10:16 **Hadadezer** The ancient Greek version has "Hadarezer". Also in verse 19.
[b] 11:8 **relax** Literally, "wash your feet".

TEMPTATION, SIN AND CONSEQUENCES

What do you think of David so far? In one man, we have a successful king, a great warrior and a prolific songwriter – a guy who not only looked good on a horse but sounded like a rock star too. What a man!

David is also crucial to the story of the Bible as part of the family line of Jesus and, more than that, as someone whose good qualities actually showed God's people what to expect from the coming Messiah (see more in the Bible Bit "The Promise of a King" on 2 Samuel chapters 6 and 7).

But David was not Jesus. He was human like us; he didn't get it all right all the time. And at one point, he messed up royally.

DIG IN
READ 2 Samuel 11:1–27

- Can you see a way David might have avoided the whole sorry situation (v.1)?
- How does David make matters worse (vv.14–17)?
- What's God's reaction (v.27)?

David's affair with Bathsheba is wrong in so many ways. He shouldn't have been hanging around in Jerusalem – he should have been on the battlefield with his troops (v.1). His act of adultery was bad enough. But when he realizes how much trouble he's got himself into, David makes it worse with deceit and an elaborate murder conspiracy to try and clean up the mess. Five of the Ten Commandments broken in one sorry incident! God is not happy (11:27).

READ 2 Samuel 12:1–23

- How does God uncover David's sin (vv.1–7)?
- What is David's response (vv.13–23)?
- What does it remind you of about David's character?

The fact is, once we've sinned, we can't hide it from God. And sometimes, like David, we won't be able to escape the consequences. What matters most is what David does once he's been found out (vv.1–13). He acknowledges his guilt and gets right with God straight away.

DIG THROUGH

- We're all vulnerable to temptation. What things do you need to do (or avoid doing) to make sure that you don't find yourself caught out like David?
- God always sees our sin, even when others don't. That ought to make us think twice about our "secret sins". Are there sins you're elaborately trying to hide from God and from others – sins you need to give up?
- Sometimes the consequences of our wrongdoing affect other people. Again, that shows how much even our "secret sins" matter. Are you quick to ask God for forgiveness when you know you've hurt someone by your selfish actions? Is there anyone you need to get right with?
- Why does the Bible include this story at all? Wouldn't the king's PR people rather have edited it out? No, this incident is crucial because it leaves God's people longing for a king who will not fail or compromise – as even David did – King Jesus.

DIG DEEPER

- Psalm 51 is one of David's great psalms of confession and heartfelt repentance. Read it to get an insight into how he was feeling after Nathan convicted him of his sin. We all have a need to be continually convicted of our wrongdoing and resolve to turn away from it. Our hearts are desensitized by the effects of repeated sin; we need the Holy Spirit to "wash [us] . . . whiter than snow" (Psalm 51:7) and "create a pure heart" (v.10) in us. Thank God that "the blood sacrifice of Jesus, God's Son, washes away every sin and makes us clean" (1 John 1:7).
- Both 1 Corinthians 6:18–20 and 1 Thessalonians 4:3–8 give good advice on how to deal with sexual temptation.

So Uriah left the king's palace. The king also sent a gift to Uriah. ⁹But Uriah did not go home. He slept outside the door of the king's palace, as the rest of the king's servants did. ¹⁰The servants told David, "Uriah did not go home."

Then David said to Uriah, "You came from a long journey. Why did you not go home?"

¹¹Uriah said to David, "The Holy Box and the soldiers of Israel and Judah are staying in tents. My lord Joab and my lord's officers are camping out in the field. So it is not right for me to go home to eat and drink and sleep with my wife. As surely as you live, I will not do this."

¹²David said to Uriah, "Stay here today. Tomorrow I will send you back to the battle." Uriah stayed in Jerusalem until the next morning. ¹³Then David called Uriah to come and see him. Uriah ate and drank with David. David got him drunk, but Uriah still did not go home. That evening, Uriah again slept at the palace with the rest of the king's servants.

David Plans Uriah's Death

¹⁴The next morning David wrote a letter to Joab and made Uriah carry the letter. ¹⁵In the letter David wrote: "Put Uriah on the front lines where the fighting is the hardest. Then leave him there alone, and let him be killed in battle."

¹⁶Joab watched the city and saw where the bravest Ammonites were. He chose Uriah to go to that place. ¹⁷The men of the city came out to fight against Joab. Some of David's men were killed. Uriah the Hittite was one of them.

¹⁸Then Joab sent a report to David about what happened in the battle. ¹⁹Joab told the messenger to tell King David what had happened in the battle. ²⁰"The king might get upset and ask, 'Why did Joab's army go that close to the city to fight? Surely he knows that there are men on the city walls who can shoot arrows down at his men? ²¹Surely he remembers that at Thebez a woman killed Abimelech son of Jerub Besheth when she threw the top part of a grinding stone down from the wall. So why did he go that close to the wall?' If King David says something like that, tell him, 'Your officer, Uriah the Hittite, also died.'"

²²The messenger went in and told David everything Joab told him to say. ²³The messenger told David, "The men of Ammon attacked us in the field. We fought them and chased them all the way to the city gate. ²⁴Then the men on the city wall shot arrows at your officers. Some of your officers were killed, including Uriah the Hittite."

²⁵David said to the messenger, "Give this message to Joab: 'Don't be too upset about this. A sword can kill one person as well as the next. Make a stronger attack against Rabbah and you will win.' Encourage Joab with these words."

David Marries Bathsheba

²⁶Bathsheba heard that her husband Uriah had died, so she mourned for him. ²⁷After her time of sadness, David sent servants to bring her to his house. She became David's wife and gave birth to a son for David. But the LORD did not like what David had done.

Nathan Speaks to David

12 The LORD sent Nathan to David. Nathan went to him and said, "There were two men in a city. One man was rich, but the other man was poor. ²The rich man had lots of sheep and cattle. ³But the poor man had nothing except one little female lamb that he bought. The poor man fed the lamb, and the lamb grew up with this poor man and his children. She ate from the poor man's food and drank from his cup. The lamb slept on the poor man's chest. The lamb was like a daughter to the poor man.

⁴"Then a traveller stopped to visit the rich man. The rich man wanted to give food to the traveller, but he did not want to take any of his own sheep or cattle to feed the traveller. No, the rich man took the lamb from the poor man and cooked it for his visitor."

⁵David became very angry with the rich man. He said to Nathan, "As the LORD lives, the man who did this should die! ⁶He must pay four times the price of the lamb because he did this terrible thing and because he had no mercy."

Nathan Tells David About His Sin

⁷Then Nathan said to David, "You are that rich man! This is what the LORD, the God of Israel, says: 'I chose[a] you to be the king of Israel. I saved you from Saul. ⁸I let you take his family and his wives, and I made you king of Israel and Judah. As if that had not been enough, I would have given you more and more. ⁹So why did you ignore my command? Why did you do what I say is wrong? You let the Ammonites kill Uriah the Hittite, and you took his wife. It is as if you yourself killed Uriah in war. ¹⁰So your family will never have peace! When you took Uriah's wife, you showed that you did not respect me.'

¹¹"This is what the LORD says: 'I am bringing trouble against you. This trouble will come from your own family. I will take your wives from you and give them to someone who is very close to you. He will have sex with your wives, and

---

[a] **12:7 *chose*** Literally, "anointed". See "ANOINT" in the Word List.

everyone will know it!ᵃ ¹²You had sex with Bathsheba in secret, but I will punish you so that all the people of Israel can see it.'"ᵇ

¹³Then David said to Nathan, "I have sinned against the LORD."

Nathan said to David, "The LORD will forgive you, even for this sin. You will not die. ¹⁴But you did things that made the LORD's enemies lose their respect for him, so your new baby son will die."

> ## INSIGHT
>
> David repented of his sin with Bathsheba, but the consequences of his actions continued to ripple through his family. Their baby died and David's son Amnon abused his power and raped his stepsister Tamar. This act resulted in a family feud and caused David to go to war against his own son.
>
> **2 Samuel 12:13–14**

David and Bathsheba's Baby Dies

¹⁵Then Nathan went home. And the LORD caused the baby boy who was born to David and Uriah's wife to become very sick. ¹⁶David prayed to God for the baby. David refused to eat or drink. He went into his house and stayed there and lay on the ground all night.

¹⁷The leaders of David's family came and tried to pull David up from the ground, but he refused to get up. He refused to eat with these leaders. ¹⁸On the seventh day the baby died. David's servants were afraid to tell him that the baby was dead. They said, "Look, we tried to talk to David while the baby was alive, but he refused to listen to us. If we tell David that the baby is dead, he might do something bad to himself."

¹⁹David saw his servants whispering and understood that the baby was dead. So David asked his servants, "Is the baby dead?"

The servants answered, "Yes, he is dead."

²⁰Then David got up from the floor. He washed himself. He changed his clothes and got dressed. Then he went into the LORD's house to worship. After that, he went home and asked for something

to eat. His servants gave him some food, and he ate.

²¹David's servants asked him, "Why are you doing this? When the baby was alive, you cried and refused to eat. But when the baby died you got up and ate food."

²²David said, "While the baby was still living, I cried and refused to eat because I thought, 'Who knows? Maybe the LORD will feel sorry for me and let the baby live.' ²³But now the baby is dead, so why should I refuse to eat? Can I bring the baby back to life? No. Some day I will go to him, but he cannot come back to me."

Solomon Is Born

²⁴Then David comforted Bathsheba his wife. He slept with her and had sex with her. Bathsheba became pregnant again and had another son. David named the boy Solomon. The LORD loved Solomon ²⁵and sent word for Nathan the prophet to give Solomon the name Jedidiah.ᶜ So Nathan did this for the LORD.

David Captures Rabbah

²⁶Rabbah was the capital city of the Ammonites. Joab fought against Rabbah and captured it. ²⁷Joab sent messengers to David and said, "I have fought against Rabbah and have captured its water supply. ²⁸Now bring the rest of the army together and attack Rabbah. Capture this city before I do, or else it will be called by my name."

²⁹So David gathered all the soldiers together and went to Rabbah. He fought against Rabbah and captured the city. ³⁰David took the crown off their king's head.ᵈ The crown was gold and weighed about 34 kilogrammes.ᵉ This crown had precious stones in it. They put the crown on David's head. David took many valuable things out of the city.

³¹David also brought out the people of the city of Rabbah and made them work with saws, iron picks and axes. He also forced them to build things with bricks. He did the same thing to all the Ammonite cities. Then David and the army went back to Jerusalem.

Amnon and Tamar

13 David had a son named Absalom. Absalom had a very beautiful sister named Tamar. Another one of David's sons, Amnon,ᶠ was in love

---

ᵃ **12:11 and everyone will know it** Literally, "in the sight of the sun".

ᵇ **12:12 so that all . . . can see it** Literally, "before all Israel and before the sun".

ᶜ **12:25 Jedidiah** This name means "loved by the LORD".

ᵈ **12:30 their king's head** Or "Milcom's head". Milcom was a false god that the Ammonites worshipped.

ᵉ **12:30 34 kilogrammes** Literally, "1 talent".

ᶠ **13:1 Amnon** Amnon was half-brother to Absalom and Tamar. They all had David as their father, but Amnon had a different mother. See 2 Sam. 3:2–3.

with Tamar. ²She was a virgin. Amnon wanted her very much, but he did not think it was possible for him to have her. He thought about her so much that he made himself sick.ᵃ

³Amnon had a friend named Jonadab son of Shimeah. (Shimeah was David's brother.) Jonadab was a very clever man. ⁴He said to Amnon, "You are the king's son. So why do you always look so sad? Tell me what the trouble is!"

Amnon told Jonadab, "I love Tamar. But she is the sister of my half-brother Absalom."

⁵Jonadab said to Amnon, "Go to bed. Pretend you are sick. Then your father will come to see you. Tell him, 'Please let my sister Tamar come in and give me food to eat. Let her make the food in front of me. Then I will see it and eat it from her hand.'"

⁶So Amnon lay down in bed and pretended to be sick. King David came in to see Amnon. He said to King David, "Please let my sister Tamar come in. Let her make two cakes for me while I watch. Then I can eat from her hands."

⁷David sent messengers to Tamar's house. They told her, "Go to your brother Amnon's house and make some food for him."

⁸So Tamar went to the house of her brother Amnon. He was in bed. Tamar took some dough, pressed it together with her hands and cooked the cakes. She did this while he watched. ⁹Then Tamar took the cakes out of the pan and set them out for him. But he refused to eat. He said to his servants, "Get out of here. Leave me alone!" So all his servants left the room.

Amnon Rapes Tamar

¹⁰Then Amnon said to Tamar, "Bring the food into the bedroom and feed me by hand."

So Tamar took the cakes she had made and went into her brother's bedroom. ¹¹She started to feed Amnon, but he grabbed her hand. He said to her, "Sister, come and sleep with me."

¹²Tamar said to Amnon, "No, brother! Don't force me to do this. Don't do this shameful thing! Terrible things like this should never be done in Israel! ¹³I would never get rid of my shame, and people would think that you are just a common criminal. Please, talk with the king. He will let you marry me."

¹⁴But Amnon refused to listen to Tamar. He was stronger than she was, so he forced her to have sex with him. ¹⁵Then Amnon began to hate

Tamar. He hated her much more than he had loved her before. Amnon said to her, "Get up and get out of here!"

¹⁶Tamar said to Amnon, "No! Don't send me away like this. That would be even worse than what you did before!"

But Amnon refused to listen to Tamar. ¹⁷He called his servant and said, "Get this girl out of this room, now! And lock the door after her."

¹⁸So Amnon's servant led Tamar out of the room and locked the door.

Tamar was wearing a long robe with many colours.ᵇ The king's virgin daughters wore robes like this. ¹⁹Tamar tore her robe of many colours and put ashes on her head. Then she put her hand on her head and began crying.ᶜ

²⁰Then Tamar's brother Absalom said to her, "Have you been with your brother Amnon? Did he hurt you? Now, calm down sister. Amnon is your brother, ⌊so we will take care of this⌋. Don't let it upset you too much." So Tamar did not say anything. She quietly went to live at Absalom's house.ᵈ

²¹King David heard the news and became very angry, but he did not want to say anything to upset Amnon, because he loved him since he was his firstborn son.ᵉ ²²Absalom began to hate Amnon. Absalom did not say one word, good or bad, to Amnon, but he hated him because Amnon had raped his sister Tamar.

Absalom's Revenge

²³Two years later, Absalom had some men come to Baal Hazor near Ephraim to cut the wool from his sheep. He invited all the king's sons to come and watch. ²⁴Absalom went to the king and said, "I have some men coming to cut the wool from my sheep. Please come with your servants and watch."

²⁵King David said to Absalom, "No, son. We will not all go. It will be too much trouble for you."

Absalom begged David to go. David did not go, but he did give his blessing.

²⁶Absalom said, "If you don't want to go, please let my brother Amnon go with me."

King David asked Absalom, "Why should he go with you?"

²⁷Absalom kept begging David. Finally, David let Amnon and all the king's other sons go with Absalom.

ᵃ 13:2 He thought . . . sick Or "Amnon thought of a plan to pretend he was sick."
ᵇ 13:18 many colours Or "stripes".
ᶜ 13:19 Tamar tore . . . crying This was the way people showed how very sad and upset they were.
ᵈ 13:20 She . . . Absalom's house Or "She lived in her brother Absalom's house, a ruined woman."
ᵉ 13:21 but he did not . . . son This is found in the ancient Greek version and a Hebrew scroll from Qumran but not in the standard Hebrew text.

Amnon Is Murdered

²⁸Then Absalom gave this command to his servants, "Watch Amnon. When he is drunk and feeling good from the wine, I will give you the command. You must attack Amnon and kill him. Don't be afraid of being punished. After all, you will only be obeying my command. Now, be strong and brave."

²⁹So Absalom's young soldiers did what he said. They killed Amnon. But all of David's other sons escaped. Each son got on his mule and escaped.

David Hears About Amnon's Death

³⁰While the king's sons were still on their way into the town, King David got a message about what had happened. The message was, "Absalom has killed all the king's sons! Not one of the sons was left alive."

³¹King David tore his clothes and lay on the ground.ᵃ All of David's officers standing near him also tore their clothes.

³²But then Jonadab, the son of David's brother Shimeah, said, "Don't think that all the king's sons were killed! Only Amnon is dead. Absalom has been planning this from the day that Amnon raped his sister Tamar. ³³My lord and king, don't think that all your sons are dead. Only Amnon is dead."

³⁴Absalom ran away.

There was a guard standing on the city wall. He saw many people coming from the other side of the hill, and went to tell the king. ³⁵So Jonadab said to King David, "Look, I was right! The king's sons are coming."

³⁶The king's sons came in just after Jonadab said that. They were crying loudly. David and all his officers began crying. They all cried very hard. ³⁷David cried for his son every day.

Absalom Escapes to Geshur

Absalom ran away to Talmai son of Ammihud, the king of Geshur.ᵇ ³⁸After Absalom had run away to Geshur, he stayed there for three years. ³⁹King David was comforted after Amnon died, but he missed Absalom very much.

Joab Sends a Wise Woman to David

14 Joab son of Zeruiah knew that King David missed Absalom very much. ²So Joab sent messengers to Tekoa to bring a wise woman from there. Joab said to this wise woman, "Please pretend to be very sad. Put on sackcloth. Don't dress up. Act like a woman who has been crying many days for someone who died. ³Go to the king and talk to him using these words that I tell you." Then Joab told the wise woman what to say.

⁴Then the woman from Tekoa talked to the king. She bowed with her face to the ground. Then she said, "King, please help me!"

⁵King David said to her, "What's your problem?"

The woman said, "I am a widow. My husband is dead. ⁶I had two sons. They were out in the field fighting. There was no one to stop them. One son killed the other son. ⁷Now the whole family is against me. They said to me, 'Bring us the son who killed his brother and we will kill him, because he killed his brother.' My son is like the last spark of a fire. If they kill my son, that fire will burn out and be finished. He is the only son left alive to get his father's property. So my dead husband's property will go to someone else and his name will be removed from the land."

⁸Then the king said to the woman, "Go home. I will take care of things for you."

⁹The woman of Tekoa said to the king, "Let the blame be on me, my lord and king. You and your kingdom are innocent."

¹⁰King David said, "If anyone is saying bad things to you, bring them to me. They will not bother you again."

¹¹The woman said, "Please, use the name of the LORD your God and swear that you will stop these people. They want to punish my son for murdering his brother. Swear that you will not let them destroy my son."

David said, "As the LORD lives, no one will hurt your son. Not even one hair from your son's head will fall to the ground."

¹²The woman said, "My lord and king, please let me say something else to you."

The king said, "Speak."

¹³Then the woman said, "Why have you planned these things against the people of God? When you say these things, you show you are guilty because you have not brought back the son who you forced to leave home. ¹⁴We will all die some day. We will be like water that is spilled on the ground. No one can gather this water back from the ground. You know God forgives people. God made plans for people who are forced to run away for safety—God does not force them to run away from him! ¹⁵My lord and king, I came to say these words to you, because the people made me afraid. I said to myself, 'I will talk to the king. Maybe the king will help me. ¹⁶The king will listen to me and save me from the man who wants to kill me and my son. That man just wants to keep us from getting what God gave us.'

ᵃ **13:31** *tore his clothes . . . ground* This showed that he was very sad and upset.
ᵇ **13:37** *Talmai . . . king of Geshur* Talmai was Absalom's grandfather. See 2 Sam. 3:3.

17I know that the words of my lord the king will give me rest, because you are like an angel from God. You know what is good and what is bad. And the LORD your God is with you."

18King David answered the woman, "You must answer the question I will ask you."

The woman said, "My lord and king, please ask your question."

19The king said, "Did Joab tell you to say all these things?"

The woman answered, "As you live, my lord and king, you are right. Your officer Joab did tell me to say these things. 20Joab did this so that you would see things differently. My lord, you are as wise as God's angel. You know everything that happens on earth."

Absalom Returns to Jerusalem

21The king said to Joab, "Look, I will do what I promised. Now please bring back the young man Absalom."

22Joab bowed with his face on the ground. He blessed King David, and said, "Today I know that you are pleased with me. I know because you have done what I asked."

23Then Joab got up and went to Geshur and brought Absalom to Jerusalem. 24But King David said, "Absalom must go back to his own house. He cannot come to see me." So Absalom went back to his own house, but he could not go to see the king.

25People really boasted about how good-looking Absalom was. No man in Israel was as handsome as Absalom. Every part of his body was perfect—from his head to his feet. 26At the end of every year, Absalom cut the hair from his head and weighed it. The hair weighed about 2 kilogrammes.a 27Absalom had three sons and one daughter. Her name was Tamar, and she was a beautiful woman.

Absalom Forces Joab to Go and See Him

28Absalom lived in Jerusalem for two full years without being allowed to visit King David. 29Absalom sent a message to Joab, asking for permission to see the king, but Joab refused to go and see him. So Absalom sent a second message to Joab. Again, Joab refused to go and see him.

30Then Absalom said to his servants, "Look, Joab's field is next to my field. He has barley growing in that field. Go and burn the barley."

So Absalom's servants went and started a fire in Joab's field. 31Joab got up and came to Absalom's house. He said to him, "Why did your servants burn my field?"

32Absalom said to Joab, "I sent a message to you. I asked you to come here. I wanted to send you to the king to ask him why he asked me to come home from Geshur. I cannot see him, so it would have been better for me to stay in Geshur. Now let me see the king. If I have sinned, he can kill me!"

Absalom Visits King David

33Then Joab went to the king and told him what Absalom had said. The king called for Absalom. Absalom went to the king and bowed low on the ground before the king. The king kissed him.

Absalom Makes Many Friends

15 After this, Absalom got a chariot and horses for himself. He had 50 men run in front of him while he drove the chariot. 2Absalom would get up early and stand near the gate.b He would watch for anyone with problems who was going to King David for judgement. Then Absalom would talk to them and say, "What city are you from?" They would say they were from such and such tribe in Israel. 3Then Absalom would say, "Look, you are right, but King David will not listen to you."

4Absalom would also say, "Oh, I wish someone would make me a judge in this country! Then I could help everyone who comes to me with a problem. I would help them get a fair solution to their problem."

5And if anyone came to Absalom and started to bow down to him, Absalom would treat him like a close friend—he would reach out and touch him and kiss him. 6Absalom did that to all the Israelites who came to King David for judgement. In this way Absalom won the hearts of all the people of Israel.

Absalom Plans to Take David's Kingdom

7After four years,c Absalom said to King David, "Please let me go to Hebron to complete a special promise that I made to the LORD. 8I made that promise while I was still living in Geshur in Aram. I said, 'If the LORD brings me back to Jerusalem, I will serve the LORD in a special way.'"

9King David said, "Go in peace."

Absalom went to Hebron. 10But he also sent spies to all the tribes of Israel. They told the people, "When you hear the trumpet, say, 'Absalom is king in Hebron!'"

11Absalom invited 200 men to go with him. They left Jerusalem with him, but they did not know what he was planning. 12Ahithophel was

---

a **14:26 2 kilogrammes** Literally, "200 shekels by the king's weight".

b **15:2 gate** This was where people came to do all their business. This was also where many court cases were held.

c **15:7 four years** This is found in several ancient versions. The standard Hebrew text has "40 years".

one of David's advisors. He was from the town of Giloh. While Absalom was offering sacrifices, he invited Ahithophel to join. Absalom's plans were working very well and more and more people began to support him.

David Learns About Absalom's Plans

13A man came in to tell the news to David. The man said, "The people of Israel are beginning to follow Absalom."

14Then David said to all his officers who were still in Jerusalem with him, "Come on, we cannot let him trap us here in Jerusalem. Hurry up, before he catches us. He will destroy us all, and Jerusalem will be destroyed in the battle."

15The king's officers told him, "We will do whatever you tell us."

David and His People Escape

16King David left with everyone in his family, except ten of his slave women. He left them to take care of the house. 17The king left with everyone in his house following him on foot. They stopped at the last house in the city. 18All the king's officers passed by him. And all the Kerethites, all the Pelethites and the Gittites (600 men from Gath) passed by the king.

19The king said to Ittai from Gath, "Why are you also going with us? You are a foreigner; this is not your homeland. Go back and stay with the new king. 20You came to join me only yesterday. You don't need to wander from place to place with me. Take your brothers and go back. Go with my faithful, loving kindness."

21But Ittai answered the king, "As the LORD lives, and as long as you live, I will stay with you, in life or death!"

22David said to Ittai, "Then come, let's cross Kidron Brook."

So Ittai from Gath and all his people and their children crossed over Kidron Brook. 23All the people*a* were crying loudly. Then King David crossed over Kidron Brook, and all the people went out to the desert. 24Zadok and all the Levites with him were carrying the Box of God's Agreement. They set down God's Holy Box, and Abiathar said prayers*b* until all the people had left Jerusalem.

25King David said to Zadok, "Take God's Holy Box back to Jerusalem. If the LORD is pleased with me, he will bring me back and let me see Jerusalem and his Temple. 26But if he says he is not pleased with me, let him do whatever he wants to me."

27The king said to Zadok the priest, "You are a seer. Go back to the city in peace.*c* Take your son Ahimaaz and Jonathan the son of Abiathar. 28I will be waiting near the places where people cross the river into the desert. I will wait there until I hear from you."

29So Zadok and Abiathar took God's Holy Box back to Jerusalem and stayed there.

David's Prayer Against Ahithophel

30David walked up the path to the Mount of Olives. He was crying, his head was covered and he went without sandals on his feet. All the people with David also covered their heads and were crying as they walked with him.

31Someone told David, "Ahithophel is one who joined in Absalom's plot against you." Then David prayed, "LORD, I ask you to make Ahithophel give only foolish advice." 32When David got to the top of the mountain, he bowed down to worship God. Then David noticed Hushai the Arkite. Hushai's coat was torn, and there was dust on his head.*d*

33David said to Hushai, "If you go with me, you will be just one more person to care for. 34But if you go back to Jerusalem, you can disagree with Ahithophel and make his advice useless. Tell Absalom, 'King, I am your servant. I served your father, but now I will serve you.' 35The priests Zadok and Abiathar will be with you. You must tell them everything you hear in the king's palace. 36Zadok's son Ahimaaz and Abiathar's son Jonathan will be with them. You can send them to tell me everything you hear."

37So David's friend Hushai went back to the city, just as Absalom arrived in Jerusalem.

Ziba Meets David

16 David went a short way over the top of the Mount of Olives and met Ziba, the servant of Mephibosheth. Ziba had two donkeys with saddles on them. The donkeys also carried 200 loaves of bread, 100 bunches of raisins, 100 summer fruits and a wineskin full of wine. 2King David said to Ziba, "What are these things for?"

Ziba answered, "The donkeys are for the king's family to ride on. The bread and the summer fruit are for the servants to eat. And the wine is refreshment for whoever begins to feel weak in the desert."

---

a **15:23** *people* Literally, "country".

b **15:24** *said prayers* Literally, "went up". This could mean "burn incense", "offer sacrifices" or it might mean simply that Abiathar stood to one side, by the Holy Box, until all the people passed by.

c **15:27** *You are a seer . . . peace* Or "You do see, don't you, that you should go back to the city in peace."

d **15:32** *coat was torn . . . head* This showed that he was very sad.

³Then the king asked, "And where is Mephibosheth?"ᵃ

Ziba answered the king, "Mephibosheth is staying in Jerusalem. He said, 'Today the Israelites will give my father's kingdom back to me.'"

⁴Then the king said to Ziba, "All right, I now give you everything that belonged to Mephibosheth."

Ziba said, "I bow to you. I pray I will always be able to please you."

Shimei Curses David

⁵As David came to Bahurim, a man from Saul's family, Shimei son of Gera, came out cursing David again and again.

⁶Shimei began throwing stones at David and his officers. Both the people and the soldiers gathered around David to protect him—they were all around him. ⁷Shimei cursed David. He said, "Get out, get out, you no-good murderer!ᵇ ⁸The LORD is punishing you because you killed people in Saul's family. You stole Saul's place as king. But now the same bad things are happening to you. The LORD has given the kingdom to your son Absalom, because you are a murderer."

⁹Abishai son of Zeruiah said to the king, "Why should this dying dog curse you, my lord the king? Let me go over and cut off Shimei's head."

¹⁰But the king answered, "What can I do, sons of Zeruiah? Yes, Shimei is cursing me, but the LORD told him to curse me. And who can ask him why he did that?" ¹¹David also said to Abishai and all his servants, "Look, my very own son is trying to kill me, so why shouldn't this man from the tribe of Benjamin want to do the same? Leave him alone. Let him continue to curse me. The LORD told him to do this. ¹²Maybe the LORD will see the wrong things that are happening to me and give me something good for every bad thing that Shimei says today."

¹³So David and his men went on their way down the road. Shimei kept following David. He walked on the other side of the road by the side of the hill. He kept cursing David on his way. Shimei also threw stones and dirt at David.

¹⁴King David and all his people came to the Jordan River. They were tired, so they rested and refreshed themselves there.

¹⁵Meanwhile, Absalom, Ahithophel and all the Israelites came to Jerusalem. ¹⁶David's friend, Hushai the Arkite, came to Absalom and told him, "Long live the king! Long live the king!"

¹⁷Absalom answered, "Why are you not loyal to your friend David? Why did you not leave Jerusalem with your friend?"

¹⁸Hushai said, "I belong to the one that the LORD chooses. These people and the people of Israel chose you. I will stay with you. ¹⁹In the past, I served your father. So now I will serve you, David's son."

Absalom Asks Ahithophel for Advice

²⁰Absalom said to Ahithophel, "Please tell us what we should do."

²¹Ahithophel said to Absalom, "Your father left some of his slave women here to take care of the house. Go and have sex with them. Then all the Israelites will hear how you humiliated your father, and they will be encouraged to give you more support."

²²Then they put up a tent for Absalom up on the roof of the house. Absalom had sex with his father's wivesᶜ so that all the Israelites could see what happened. ²³So in those days Ahithophel's advice was very important. Both David and Absalom accepted his advice as though it were the word of God.

Ahithophel's Advice About David

17 Ahithophel also said to Absalom, "Now, let me choose 12,000 men to chase David tonight. ²I will catch him while he is tired and weak. I will frighten him, and all his people will run away. But I will kill only King David. ³Then I will bring all the people back to you. If David is dead, all the people will come back in peace."

⁴This plan seemed good to Absalom and all the leaders of Israel. ⁵But Absalom said, "Now call Hushai the Arkite. I also want to hear what he says."

Hushai Ruins Ahithophel's Advice

⁶Hushai came to Absalom. Absalom said to Hushai, "This is the plan Ahithophel gave. Should we follow it? If not, tell us."

⁷Hushai said to Absalom, "Ahithophel's advice is not good this time." ⁸Hushai added, "You know that your father and his men are strong men. They are as dangerous as a wild bear when something has taken its cubs. Your father is a skilled fighter. He will not stay all night with the people. ⁹He is probably already hiding in a cave or some other place. If your father attacks your men first, people will hear the news and think, 'Absalom's followers are losing!' ¹⁰Then even your bravest men will be frightened, because all the Israelites know that your father is a powerful soldier and that his men are very brave.

ᵃ **16:3 Mephibosheth** Literally, "your master's grandson".

ᵇ **16:7 murderer** Literally, "man of blood".

ᶜ **16:22 wives** Or "concubines". See "SLAVE WOMAN" in the Word List.

¹¹"This is what I suggest: You must gather all the Israelites together from Dan to Beersheba.ᵃ Then there will be many people, like the sand by the sea. Then you yourself must go into the battle. ¹²We will catch David wherever he is hiding and attack him with so many soldiers that they will be like the dew that covers the ground. We will kill David and all his men—no one will be left alive. ¹³But if David escapes into a city, all the Israelites can bring ropes to that city and pull its walls down into the valley. Not even a small stone will be left in that city."

¹⁴Absalom and all the Israelites said, "Hushai's advice is better than Ahithophel's." Actually, Ahithophel's advice was good, but they said this because the LORD had decided to make Ahithophel's advice useless. He did this to punish Absalom.

Hushai Sends a Warning to David

¹⁵Hushai told the priests, Zadok and Abiathar, what was said. He told them what Ahithophel suggested to Absalom and the leaders of Israel. Hushai also told them what he himself had suggested. He said, ¹⁶"Send a message to David now! Tell him not to spend the night at the places where people cross into the desert. Tell him to go across the Jordan River at once. If he crosses the river, the king and all his people will not be caught."

¹⁷The priests' sons, Jonathan and Ahimaaz, did not want to be seen going into the town, so they waited at En Rogel. A servant girl went out to them and gave them the message. Then Jonathan and Ahimaaz carried the message to King David.

¹⁸But a boy saw Jonathan and Ahimaaz and ran to tell Absalom. Jonathan and Ahimaaz ran away quickly. They arrived at a man's house in Bahurim. The man had a well in his courtyard.ᵇ Jonathan and Ahimaaz went down into this well. ¹⁹The man's wife spread a sheet over the mouth of the well and covered it with grain. The well looked like a pile of grain, so no one would know to look there. ²⁰Absalom's servants came to the woman at the house. They asked, "Where are Ahimaaz and Jonathan?"

The woman said to Absalom's servants, "They have already crossed over the brook."

Absalom's servants then went to look for Jonathan and Ahimaaz, but they could not find them. So Absalom's servants went back to Jerusalem.

²¹After Absalom's servants left, Jonathan and Ahimaaz climbed out of the well and went to King David. They said to David, "Hurry, go across the river. Ahithophel is planning to do something to you."

²²So David and his people crossed over the Jordan River. By sunrise, all of David's people had crossed the Jordan River. No one was left behind.

Ahithophel Kills Himself

²³When Ahithophel saw that the Israelites did not do what he suggested, he saddled his donkey and went back to his home town. He made plans for his family and then hanged himself. They buried him in his father's tomb.

Absalom Crosses the Jordan River

²⁴David arrived at Mahanaim just as Absalom and the Israelites who were with him crossed over the Jordan River. ²⁵⁻²⁶Absalom and the Israelites made their camp in the land of Gilead. Absalom had made Amasa the new captain of the army. He took Joab's place.ᶜ Amasa was the son of Ithra the Ishmaelite.ᵈ His mother was Abigail, the daughter of Nahash, the sister of Joab's mother, Zeruiah.ᵉ

Shobi, Makir and Barzillai

²⁷When David arrived at Mahanaim, Shobi, Makir and Barzillai were there. Shobi son of Nahash was from the Ammonite town of Rabbah. Makir son of Ammiel was from Lo Debar. Barzillai was from Rogelim in Gilead. ²⁸⁻²⁹These three men said, "The people are tired, hungry and thirsty from the desert." So they brought many things to David and those with him. They brought beds, bowls and other kinds of dishes. They also brought wheat, barley, flour, roasted grain, beans, lentils, dried seeds, honey, butter, sheep and cheese made from cow's milk.

David Gets Ready for Battle

18 David counted his men and chose captains over 1,000 and captains over 100 to lead them. ²He separated the people into three groups and sent them out. Joab led a third of the men. Joab's brother, Abishai son of Zeruiah, led another third. And Ittai from Gath led the last third.

ᵃ **17:11** *Dan to Beersheba* This means the whole nation of Israel, north and south. Dan was a town in the northern part of Israel, and Beersheba was in the southern part of Judah.
ᵇ **17:18** *courtyard* An open area outside the house. Many houses were built around courtyards so that people could work, cook or eat outside.
ᶜ **17:25–26** *He took Joab's place* Joab still supported David. Joab was one of the three captains in David's army when David was running away from Absalom. See 2 Sam. 18:2.
ᵈ **17:25–26** *Ishmaelite* This is from the ancient Greek version. The standard Hebrew text has "Israelite," but see 1 Chr. 2:17.
ᵉ **17:25–26** *His mother . . . Zeruiah* Literally, "Ithra had sex with Abigail, the daughter of Nahash sister of Zeruiah."

King David said to the people, "I will also go with you."

³But they said, "No! You must not go with us. If we run away in the battle, Absalom's men will not care. No, even if only half of us are killed, Absalom's men will not care. But you are worth 10,000 of us! It is better for you to stay in the city. Then, if we need help, you can come to help us."

⁴The king said to them, "I will do what you think is best."

Then the king stood by the gate as the army went out in groups of 100 and 1,000.

⁵The king gave a command to Joab, Abishai and Ittai. He said, "Do this for me: Be gentle with young Absalom!" Everyone heard the king's orders about Absalom to the captains.

David's Army Defeats Absalom's Army

⁶David's army went out into the field against Absalom's Israelites. They fought in the forest of Ephraim. ⁷David's army defeated the Israelites. It was a great defeat because 20,000 men were killed that day. ⁸The battle spread throughout the country, but more men died in the forest than by the sword.

⁹It so happened that David's officers found Absalom. Absalom jumped on his mule and tried to escape, but the mule went under the branches of a large oak tree. The branches were thick, and Absalom's head got caught in the tree. His mule ran out from under him, so Absalom was left hanging above the ground.ᵃ

¹⁰Someone saw this happen and told Joab, "I saw Absalom hanging in an oak tree."

¹¹Joab said to the man, "Why didn't you kill him and let him fall to the ground? I would have given you a belt and ten pieces of silver!"

¹²The man said to Joab, "I would not try to hurt the king's son even if you gave me 1,000 pieces of silver. We heard the king's command to you, Abishai and Ittai. The king said, 'Be careful not to hurt young Absalom.' ¹³If I had killed Absalom, the king himself would find out, and you would punish me."ᵇ

¹⁴Joab said, "I will not waste my time here with you!"

Absalom was still alive and hanging in the oak tree. Joab took three sticks in his hand and stabbed him in the heart. ¹⁵Ten of Joab's young helpers gathered around Absalom and killed him.

¹⁶Joab blew the trumpet and called the people to stop chasing Israelites. ¹⁷Then Joab's men took Absalom's body and threw it into a large hole in the forest and covered it with stones.

All the Israelites ran away and went home.

¹⁸While Absalom was alive he put up a memorial stone in King's Valley. He said, "I have no son to keep my name alive." So he named that monument after himself. It is called "Absalom's Monument" even today.

Joab Sends the News to David

¹⁹Ahimaaz the son of Zadok said to Joab, "May I run and take the news to King David? I'll tell him the LORD has destroyed the enemy for him."

²⁰Joab answered Ahimaaz, "No, you will not carry the message today. You can do it some other time, but not today because it is the king's son who is dead."

²¹Then Joab said to a man from Ethiopia, "Go and tell the king what you have seen."

So the Ethiopian bowed to Joab and ran to tell David.

²²But Ahimaaz son of Zadok begged Joab again, "No matter what happens, please let me also run after the Ethiopian!"

Joab said, "Son, why do you want to carry the news? You will not get any reward for the news you bring."

²³Ahimaaz answered, "No matter what happens, I will run to David."

Joab said to Ahimaaz, "All right, run to David!"

Then Ahimaaz ran through Jordan Valley and passed the Ethiopian.

David Hears the News

²⁴David was sitting between the two gates of the city. The watchman went up to the roof over the gate walls and saw a man running alone. ²⁵The watchman shouted to tell King David.

King David said, "If the man is alone, he is bringing news."

The man came closer and closer to the city. ²⁶But then the watchman saw another man running. He called to the gatekeeper, "Look! Another man is running alone."

The king said, "He is also bringing news."

²⁷The watchman said, "I think the first man runs like Ahimaaz son of Zadok."

The king said, "Ahimaaz is a good man, he must be bringing good news."

²⁸Ahimaaz called to the king, "All is well!" Ahimaaz bowed with his face to the ground in front of the king and said, "Praise the LORD your God! The LORD has defeated the men who were against you, my lord and king."

²⁹The king asked, "Is young Absalom all right?"

ᵃ 18:9 *above the ground* Literally, "between heaven and earth".
ᵇ 18:13 *you would punish me* Or "you would have opposed me".

Ahimaaz answered, "When Joab sent me, I saw some great excitement, but I don't know what it was."

³⁰Then the king said, "Step over here and wait." Ahimaaz went there and stood waiting.

³¹The Ethiopian arrived and said, "News for my lord and king. Today the Lord has punished all those who were against you!"

³²The king asked the Ethiopian, "Is young Absalom all right?"

The Ethiopian answered, "May your enemies, or whoever tries to hurt you, suffer the same as this young man did."

³³So the king knew Absalom was dead and he became very upset. He went upstairs to the room over the gate, crying, "O my son Absalom! My son Absalom, I wish I had died instead of you! O Absalom, my son, my son!"

Joab Scolds David

19 People told Joab what had happened, "Look, the king is crying and mourning for Absalom." ²So the joy of victory turned to sadness for everyone. It was a very sad day because the people heard, "The king is mourning for his son."

³The people came into the city quietly as if they were the ones who had been defeated in battle. ⁴The king had covered his face and was crying loudly, "O my son Absalom, O Absalom, my son, my son!"

⁵Joab came into the king's palace and said to the king, "You are humiliating every one of your officers! Look, they saved your life today and the lives of your sons and daughters and your wives and slave women. ⁶It seems that you love those who hate you, and you hate those who love you! Today you have made it clear to your officers and men that they mean nothing to you. It appears as if you would have been perfectly happy if Absalom had lived and the rest of us had been killed today! ⁷Now get up and go and encourage your officers. I swear by the Lord, if you don't go out and do that right now, not one man will be with you tonight. And that will be worse for you than all the trouble you have had since you were a child."

⁸So the king went to the city gate.ᵃ The news spread that the king was at the gate, so all the people came to see him, except for the Israelites who had run away to their homes.

David Is King Again

⁹The tribes of Israel began discussing what to do next. They said, "King David saved us from the Philistines and our other enemies. David left the country because he was running away from Absalom. ¹⁰We anointed Absalom to be the king, but he was killed in battle. So we should bring David back to be the king again."

¹¹King David sent a message to Zadok and Abiathar the priests. David said, "Speak to the leaders of Judah and tell them, 'Why are you the last tribe to bring King David back home? See, all the Israelites are talking about bringing the king back home. ¹²You are my brothers, my family, so why are you the last tribe to bring the king back?' ¹³Also tell Amasa, 'You are part of my family. I swear that I will make you captain of the army in Joab's place.'"

¹⁴David touched the hearts of the people of Judah, and they all agreed as one. The people of Judah sent a message to the king, saying, "You and all your officers come back!"

¹⁵King David came to the Jordan River. The people of Judah came to Gilgal to meet the king and take him across the Jordan River.

Shimei Asks David to Forgive Him

¹⁶Shimei son of Gera, from the tribe of Benjamin, lived in Bahurim. Shimei rushed down to meet King David, with the rest of the people of Judah. ¹⁷About 1,000 people from the tribe of Benjamin came with Shimei. Ziba the servant from Saul's family also came. Ziba brought his 15 sons and 20 servants with him. All these people hurried to the Jordan River to meet King David.

¹⁸The people went across the Jordan River to help bring the king's family back to Judah. They did whatever the king wanted. While the king was crossing the river, Shimei son of Gera came to meet him. He bowed down to the ground in front of the king. ¹⁹Shimei said to the king, "My lord, don't think about the wrong things I did. My lord and king, don't remember the bad things I did when you left Jerusalem. ²⁰I know that I sinned. That is why today I am the first person from Joseph's familyᵇ to come down and meet you, my lord and king."

²¹Abishai son of Zeruiah said, "Let's kill him for all the bad things he said about the Lord's chosen king."ᶜ

²²David said, "What should I do with you, sons of Zeruiah? Are you trying to cause me trouble? No one will be put to death in Israel today! Today I know that I am king over Israel."

²³Then the king said to Shimei, "You will not die." The king made a promise to Shimei that he himself would not kill Shimei.ᵈ

ᵃ **19:8** *city gate* This was where the public meetings were held.
ᵇ **19:20** *Joseph's family* This probably means the Israelites who followed Absalom. Many times the name Ephraim (a son of Joseph) is used for all the tribes in northern Israel.
ᶜ **19:21** *chosen king* Literally, "anointed one".
ᵈ **19:23** David did not kill Shimei. But a few years later, David's son Solomon ordered Shimei to be put to death. See 1 Kgs 2:44–46.

Mephibosheth Goes to See David

²⁴Saul's grandson,ᵃ Mephibosheth, came down to meet King David. Mephibosheth had not cared for his feet, trimmed his moustache or washed his clothes since the day the king left Jerusalem. ²⁵When he met the king at Jerusalem, the king said, "Mephibosheth, why didn't you go with me when I ran away from Jerusalem?"

²⁶Mephibosheth answered, "My lord and king, my servant tricked me. I am lame so I said to my servant, Ziba, 'Go and saddle a donkey for me so that I can go with the king.' ²⁷But my servant tricked me and said bad things about me. My lord and king, you are like an angel from God. Do whatever you think is right. ²⁸You could have killed all my grandfather'sᵇ family, but you did not do that. Instead, you included me among the people who eat at your own table. So I don't have a right to complain to the king about anything."

²⁹The king said to Mephibosheth, "Don't say anything more about your problems. This is what I have decided: You and Ziba will divide the land."

³⁰Mephibosheth said to the king, "My lord and king, it is enough that you have come home in peace. Let Ziba have the land."

David Asks Barzillai to Come With Him

³¹Barzillai of Gilead came down from Rogelim to cross the Jordan River with King David and send him on his way home. ³²Barzillai was a very old man, 80 years old. He had given the king food and other things when David was staying at Mahanaim. Barzillai could do this because he was a very rich man. ³³David said to Barzillai, "Come across the river with me. I will take care of you if you will live in Jerusalem with me."

³⁴But Barzillai said to the king, "Do you know how old I am? Do you think I can go with you to Jerusalem? ³⁵I am 80 years old! I am too old to tell what is bad or good. I cannot taste what I eat or drink or hear the voices of men and women singers. Why should you want to be bothered with me? ³⁶I don't need any of the things that you want to give me. I will cross the Jordan River with you. ³⁷Then please let me go back so that I can die in my own town and be buried in the grave of my father and mother. But here is Kimham; take him back with you as a servant, my lord and king. Do whatever you want with him."

³⁸The king answered, "Kimham will go back with me. I will be kind to him for you. I will do anything for you."

David Goes Back Home

³⁹The king kissed Barzillai and blessed him. Barzillai went back home, and the king and all the people went across the river.

⁴⁰The king crossed the Jordan River to Gilgal. Kimham went with him. All the people of Judah and half the people of Israel led David across the river.

Israelites Argue With the People of Judah

⁴¹All the Israelites came to the king and said to him, "Why did our brothers, the people of Judah, steal you away? Why did they bring you and your family back across the Jordan River with your men?"

⁴²All the people of Judah answered the Israelites, "We did it because the king is our close relative. Why are you angry with us about this? We have not eaten food at the king's expense. The king did not give us any gifts."

⁴³The Israelites answered, "We have ten shares in David,ᶜ so we have more right to David than you do. Why did you ignore us? We were the first ones to talk about bringing our king back."

But the people of Judah replied with words that were even louder and angrier than those of the Israelites.

Sheba Leads Israel Away From David

20 At that place there was a man named Sheba son of Bicri. Sheba was a worthless troublemaker from the tribe of Benjamin. He blew a trumpet to gather the people together and said,

"We have no share in David.
 We have no part in the son of Jesse.
Israel, let's all go home."

²So all the Israelitesᵈ left David and followed Sheba son of Bicri. But the people from Judah stayed with their king all the way from the Jordan River to Jerusalem.

³David went back to his house in Jerusalem. He had left ten of his slave women to take care of the house. He put these women in a special house.ᵉ Then he put guards around the house.

ᵃ **19:24 grandson** Literally, "son".

ᵇ **19:28 grandfather's** Literally, "father's".

ᶜ **19:43 ten shares in David** Judah and Benjamin were two of the tribes that later became the kingdom of Judah after the kingdom split. The other ten tribes were in the kingdom of Israel.

ᵈ **20:2 Israelites** Here, this means the tribes not united with Judah.

ᵉ **20:3 David . . . special house** David's son Absalom had ruined David's concubines by having sex with them. See 2 Sam. 16:21–22.

They stayed in this house until they died. David took care of the women and gave them food, but he did not have sex with them. They lived like widows until they died.

⁴The king told Amasa, "Tell the people of Judah to meet with me in three days. You must be here, too."

⁵So Amasa called the people of Judah together, but he took longer than the king had told him.

David Tells Abishai to Kill Sheba

⁶David said to Abishai, "Sheba son of Bicri is more dangerous to us than Absalom was. So take my officers and chase Sheba. Hurry before he gets into cities with walls. If he gets into the well-protected cities, we will not be able to get him."

⁷So Joab took the Kerethites and Pelethites*ᵃ* and the other soldiers with him and left Jerusalem to chase after Sheba son of Bicri.

Joab Kills Amasa

⁸When Joab and the army came to Big Rock at Gibeon, Amasa came out to meet them. Joab was wearing his uniform with a belt that held a knife. As he walked towards Amasa, the knife on the belt came out. ⁹Joab asked Amasa, "How are you doing, brother?" Joab reached out with his right hand and grabbed Amasa by the beard to greet him with a kiss. ¹⁰Amasa didn't see the knife that was now in Joab's other hand. Joab stabbed him in the stomach, and Amasa's intestines spilled out on the ground. There was no need for Joab to stab him again; he was already dead.

David's Men Continue to Look for Sheba

Then Joab and his brother Abishai resumed the chase after Sheba son of Bicri. ¹¹One of Joab's young soldiers stood by Amasa's body and said, "All of you who support Joab and David, let's follow Joab."

¹²Amasa was there in the middle of the road, lying in his own blood. The young soldier noticed that all the people kept stopping to look at the body, so he rolled the body off the road and into the field and covered it with a cloth. ¹³Once the body was out of the way, the people simply passed it by and joined up with Joab to go after Sheba son of Bicri.

Sheba Escapes to Abel Beth Maacah

¹⁴Sheba son of Bicri passed through all the tribes of Israel on his way to Abel Beth Maacah. All the Berites*ᵇ* joined together and followed Sheba.

¹⁵When Joab and his men came to Abel Beth Maacah, they surrounded the town. They piled dirt up against the city wall and began breaking stones out of the wall to make it fall down.

¹⁶But there was a very wise woman in that city who shouted to them and said, "Listen to me! Tell Joab to come here. I want to talk with him."

¹⁷Joab went to talk with the woman. She asked him, "Are you Joab?"

Joab answered, "Yes, I am."

Then the woman said, "Listen to me."

Joab said, "I am listening."

¹⁸Then the woman said, "In the past people would say, 'Ask for help in Abel and you will get what you need.' ¹⁹I am one of many peaceful, loyal people in this town. You are trying to destroy an important city of Israel. Why do you want to destroy something that belongs to the LORD?"

²⁰Joab answered, "I don't want to destroy anything. I don't want to ruin your city. ²¹But there is a man in your city from the hill country of Ephraim. He is named Sheba son of Bicri. He rebelled against King David. Bring him to me, and I will leave the city alone."

The woman said to Joab, "All right. His head will be thrown over the wall to you."

²²Then the woman spoke very wisely to all the people of the city. They cut off the head of Sheba son of Bicri and threw it over the city wall to Joab.

So Joab blew the trumpet and the army left the city. The soldiers went home, and Joab went back to the king in Jerusalem.

The People on David's Staff

²³Joab was captain of the whole army of Israel. Benaiah son of Jehoiada led the Kerethites and Pelethites. ²⁴Adoniram led the men who were forced to do hard work. Jehoshaphat son of Ahilud was the historian. ²⁵Sheva was the secretary. Zadok and Abiathar were the priests. ²⁶And Ira from Jair was David's personal priest.*ᶜ*

Saul's Family Punished

21 While David was king, there was a famine that continued for three years. So David prayed to the LORD. And the LORD answered, "Saul and his family of murderers*ᵈ* are the reason for the famine, because he killed the Gibeonites." ²(The Gibeonites were not Israelites. They were a group of Amorites. The Israelites had promised not to hurt them,*ᵉ* but Saul tried to kill the Gibeonites. He did this because of his strong feelings for the people of Israel and Judah.)

ᵃ **20:7 Kerethites and Pelethites** David's special group of fighting men. Also in verse 23.
ᵇ **20:14 Berites** The Greek and Latin versions have "Bicrites".
ᶜ **20:26 personal priest** Or "chief servant" or "advisor".
ᵈ **21:1 family of murderers** Literally, "house of blood".
ᵉ **21:2 The Israelites . . . them** This happened in Joshua's time when the Gibeonites tricked the Israelites. Read Josh. 9:3–15.

King David called the Gibeonites together and talked to them. [3]David said to the Gibeonites, "What can I do for you? What can I do to take away Israel's sin, so that you can bless the LORD's people?"

[4]The Gibeonites said to David, "There isn't enough gold and silver for Saul's family to pay for what they did. But we don't have the right to kill anyone else in Israel."

David said, "Well, what can I do for you?"

[5]The Gibeonites said to King David, "The person who plotted against us was Saul. He is the one who tried to destroy all our people living in the land of Israel. [6]Give us seven of Saul's sons. Saul was the LORD's chosen king, so we will hang his sons in front of the LORD on Mount Gibeah of Saul."

King David said, "All right, I will give them to you." [7]But the king protected Jonathan's son, Mephibosheth. Jonathan was Saul's son, and David had made a promise in the LORD's name to Jonathan.[a] So the king did not let them hurt Mephibosheth. [8]David gave them Armoni and Mephibosheth.[b] These were the sons of Saul and Rizpah. Saul also had a daughter named Merab who was married to Adriel son of Barzillai, from Meholah. David took the five sons of Merab and Adriel. [9]David gave these seven men to the Gibeonites who then brought them to Mount Gibeah and hanged them in front of the LORD. Those seven men died together in the spring, during the first days of the barley harvest.

David and Rizpah

[10]Rizpah the daughter of Aiah took a mourning cloth and put it on the rock.[c] That cloth stayed on the rock from the time the harvest began until the rains came. Rizpah watched the bodies day and night. She protected them from the wild birds during the day and the wild animals at night.

[11]People told David what Saul's slave woman Rizpah was doing. [12]Then David took the bones of Saul and Jonathan from the men of Jabesh Gilead. (The men of Jabesh Gilead got these bones after Saul and Jonathan were killed at Gilboa. The Philistines had hanged the bodies of Saul and Jonathan on a wall in Beth Shan.[d] But the men of Jabesh Gilead had gone there and stolen the bodies from that public area.) [13]David brought the bones of Saul and his son Jonathan from Jabesh Gilead and buried them with the bodies of the seven men who were hanged. [14]They buried the bones of Saul and his son Jonathan in the area of Benjamin, in one of the tunnels in the grave of Saul's father Kish, as the king commanded. After that, God again listened to the prayers of the people in that land.

War With the Philistines

[15]The Philistines started another war with Israel. David and his men went out to fight the Philistines, but David became very tired and weak. [16]Ishbi-Benob was one of the giants.[e] His spear weighed about 3.5 kilogrammes.[f] He put on new armour and thought he would be able to kill David. [17]But Abishai son of Zeruiah killed this giant Philistine and saved David's life.

Then David's men made him promise that he would not go out to battle any more. They said, "If you do, Israel might lose its brightest leader."

[18]Later, there was another battle with the Philistines at Gob. Sibbecai the Hushathite killed Saph, another one of the giants.

[19]Later, there was another battle at Gob against the Philistines. Elhanan the son of Jaare Oregim from Bethlehem killed ⌊Lahmi, the brother of⌋ Goliath from Gath.[g] His spear was as big as a post.[h]

[20]There was another battle at Gath. There was a very large man who had six fingers on each hand and six toes on each foot. He had 24 fingers and toes in all. This man was also one of the giants. [21]This man challenged Israel and made fun of them, but Jonathan killed this man. (This was Jonathan, the son of David's brother Shimei.)

[22]All four of these men were giants from Gath. They were killed by David and his men.

David's Song of Praise to the LORD

22 [i] David sang this song to the LORD when the LORD saved him from Saul and all his other enemies.

[2]The LORD is my Rock, my fortress, my place of safety.

---

[a] **21:7 David had made . . . to Jonathan** David and Jonathan promised each other they would not harm each other's families. Read 1 Sam. 20:12–23,42.

[b] **21:8 Mephibosheth** This is another man named Mephibosheth, not Jonathan's son.

[c] **21:10 rock** This might be the Big Rock at Gibeon (read 2 Sam. 20:8), the rock that the bodies were lying on, or a rock that marked the place where her sons were buried.

[d] **21:12 Beth Shan** Or possibly, "Beth Shean".

[e] **21:16 one of the giants** Or "a son of Rapha (Rephaim)". Also in verses 18,20,22.

[f] **21:16 about 3.5 kilogrammes** Literally, "300 shekels of bronze".

[g] **21:19 Lahmi . . . Gath** See 1 Chr. 20:5.

[h] **21:19 post** Literally, "a weaver's rod", the large beam across a loom.

[i] **22:1 Chapter 22** This song is also found in Ps. 18.

3   He is my God, the Rock I run to for
       protection.
  He is my shield; by his power I am saved.[a]
     He is my hiding place,
     my place of safety, high in the hills.
  He is my saviour,
     the one who rescues me from the cruel
       enemy.
4I called to the LORD for help,
   and he saved me from my enemies.
   He is worthy of my praise!

5Waves of death were crashing around me.
   A deadly flood was carrying me
     away.
6The ropes of the grave wrapped around me.
   Death set its trap right there in front of me.
7In my trouble I called to the LORD.
   Yes, I cried out to my God for help.
  There in his temple he heard my voice.
   He heard my cry for help.
8The earth shook and shivered.
   The foundations of heaven trembled.
   They shook because he was angry!
9Smoke came from his nose.
   Burning flames came from his mouth.
   Red-hot coals fell from him.
10He tore open the sky and came down.
   He stood on a thick, dark cloud.
11He flew across the sky, riding on a Cherub
     angel,
   gliding on the wings of the wind.
12He wrapped himself in darkness that covered
     him like a tent.
   He was hidden by dark clouds filled with
     water.
13Out of the brightness before him,
   flashes of lightning came down.
14The LORD thundered from the sky.
   God Most High let his voice be heard.
15He scattered the enemy with his arrows—
   the lightning bolts that threw them into
     confusion.

16The LORD shouted his command,
   and a powerful wind began to blow.[b]
  Then the bottom of the sea could be seen,
   and the earth's foundations were
     uncovered.

17The Lord reached down from above and
     grabbed me.
   He pulled me from the deep water.
18He saved me from my powerful enemies, who
     hated me.

They were too strong for me, so he
     saved me.
19They attacked me in my time of trouble,
   but the LORD was there to support me.
20He was pleased with me, so he rescued me.
   He took me to a safe place.
21The LORD rewarded me for doing what is
     right.
   He was good to me because I am innocent.
22The LORD did this because I have obeyed
     him.
   I have not turned against my God.
23I always remembered his laws.
   I never stopped following his rules.
24He knows I did nothing that was wrong.
   I have kept myself from sinning.
25So the LORD rewarded me for doing what is
     right.
   He could see that I am innocent.

26Lord, you are faithful to those who are
     faithful.
   You are good to those who are good.
27You never do wrong to those who have done
     no wrong.
   But you outsmart the wicked,
     no matter how clever they are.
28You help those who are humble,
   but as soon as you see the proud, you
     humiliate them.
29LORD, you are my lamp.
   You, LORD, turn the darkness around me
     into light.
30With your help I can defeat an army.
   If my God is with me,
   I can climb over enemy walls.

31God's way is perfect.
   The LORD's promise always proves to be
     true.
   He protects those who trust in him.
32There is no God except the LORD.
   There is no Rock except our God.
33God is my strong fortress.
   He clears the path I need to take.
34He makes my feet as steady as those of a
     deer.
   Even on steep mountains he keeps me from
     falling.
35He trains me for war
   so that my arms can bend the most
     powerful bow.

36Lord, you have given me your shield to
     protect me.

---

[a] **22:3 by his power I am saved** Literally, "He is the horn of my salvation."
[b] **22:16 and . . . blow** Or "and a blast of breath came from his nose".

It is your help that has made me great.
³⁷You cleared a path for my feet
    so that I could walk without stumbling.

INSIGHT

David was confident that God had given him everything he needed to face his enemies. Those who put their trust in God today can be sure that he will protect and guide them too – whatever they're up against from day to day.

2 Samuel 22:35–37

---

³⁸I chased my enemies and defeated them.
    I did not stop until they were destroyed.
³⁹I destroyed my enemies.
    I struck them down.
They did not get up again.
    They fell under my feet.

⁴⁰Lord, you made me strong in battle.
    You made my enemies fall before me.
⁴¹You made my enemies turn and run away.
    I destroyed those who hated me.
⁴²They looked for help,
    but there was no one to save them.
They cried out to the Lord,
    but he did not answer them.
⁴³I beat my enemies to pieces
    like dust on the ground.
I smashed them and walked on them
    like mud in the streets.

⁴⁴You saved me from those who fought
    against me.
    You made me the ruler over nations.
    People I never knew now serve me.
⁴⁵Foreigners fall helpless before me!
    As soon as they heard about me,
    they were ready to obey.
⁴⁶They lose all their courage
    and come out of their hiding places shaking
      with fear.

⁴⁷The Lord lives!
    I praise my Rock!
How great is my God, the Rock who saves
    me!
⁴⁸He is the God who punishes my enemies
    for me,

the one who puts people under my rule.
⁴⁹He saves me from my enemies!

You help me defeat those who attack me.
    You save me from cruel people.
⁵⁰Lord, that is why I praise you among the
    nations.
    That is why I sing songs of praise to your
      name.

⁵¹You help your king win battle after battle.
    You show your faithful love to your chosen
      one,^a
    to David and his descendants forever!

David's Last Words

23 These are the last words of David:

"This message is from David son of Jesse.
    This message is from the man God made
      great.
He is the king chosen by the God of Jacob,
    the sweet singer of Israel.^b
²The Lord's Spirit spoke through me.
    His word was on my tongue.
³The God of Israel spoke.
    The Rock of Israel said to me,
'Whoever rules people fairly,
    who rules with respect for God,
⁴is like the morning light at dawn,
    like a morning without clouds.
He is like sunshine after a rain
    that makes tender grass grow from the
      ground.'

⁵"God made my family strong and secure.^c
    He made an agreement with me forever.
God made sure this agreement was
    good and secure in every way.
So surely he will give me every victory.
    He will give me everything I want!

⁶"But evil people are like thorns.
    People don't hold thorns.
    They throw them away.
⁷If someone touches them,
    it hurts like a spear made of wood and iron.
Yes, evil people are like thorns.
    They will be thrown into the fire,
    and they will be completely burned."

The Three Heroes

⁸These are the names of David's special
soldiers:

---

^a **22:51** *your chosen one* Literally, "his anointed one".
^b **23:1** *the sweet singer of Israel* Or "The most pleasant of the songs of Israel".
^c **23:5** *God . . . secure* Or "Hasn't God made my family strong?"

Josheb Basshebeth the Tahkemonite*ª* was captain of the king's special forces.*ᵇ* He used his spear to kill 800 men at one time.*ᶜ*

⁹Next, there was Eleazar son of Dodai*ᵈ* who was there with David when he challenged the Philistines who had gathered for battle. The Israelites ran away, ¹⁰but Eleazar stood and fought the Philistines until his hand became so tired that it cramped around his sword handle. The LORD won a great victory that day. The people of Israel came back, but only to take things from the dead.

¹¹Next there was Shammah son of Agee from Harar. The Philistines came together to fight. They fought in a field of lentils.*ᵉ* The people ran away from the Philistines. ¹²But Shammah stood in the middle of the field and defended it. He defeated the Philistines. The LORD gave Israel a great victory that day.

¹³Once during harvest time David was at the cave of Adullam, and three of the Thirty Heroes*ᶠ* went down to meet him there. At the same time the Philistine army was camped in the Valley of Rephaim.*ᵍ*

¹⁴Another time David was in the fortress, and a group of Philistine soldiers was stationed in Bethlehem. ¹⁵David was thirsty for some water from his home town, so he said, "Oh, if only I could have some water from that well by the gate in Bethlehem." ¹⁶So the Three Heroes*ʰ* fought their way through the Philistine army and got some water from the well near the city gate in Bethlehem. They took it to David, but he refused to drink it. He poured it on the ground as an offering to the LORD. ¹⁷David said, "LORD, I cannot drink this water. It would be like drinking the blood of the men who risked their lives for me." This is why David refused to drink the water. The Three Heroes did many brave things like that.

Other Brave Soldiers

¹⁸Abishai was the brother of Joab son of Zeruiah. Abishai was the leader of the Three Heroes. He used his spear against 300 enemies and killed them. He became as famous as the Three. ¹⁹Abishai was as famous as the Three Heroes. He became their leader, even though he was not one of them.

²⁰Then there was Benaiah son of Jehoiada, from Kabzeel. He was the son of a powerful man.*ⁱ* Benaiah did many brave things. He killed two of the best soldiers in Moab. One day when it was snowing, Benaiah went down into a hole in the ground and killed a lion. ²¹Benaiah also killed a big Egyptian soldier. The Egyptian had a spear in his hand, and Benaiah only had a club. He grabbed the spear in the Egyptian's hands and took it away from him. Then Benaiah killed the Egyptian with his own spear. ²²Benaiah son of Jehoiada did many more brave things like that. He was as famous as the Three Heroes. ²³Benaiah was even more famous than the Thirty Heroes, but he did not become a member of the Three Heroes. David made Benaiah the leader of his bodyguards.

The Thirty Heroes

²⁴The following men were among the Thirty Heroes:

Asahel, the brother of Joab;
Elhanan son of Dodo from Bethlehem;
²⁵Shammah the Harodite;
Elika the Harodite;
²⁶Helez the Paltite;
Ira son of Ikkesh from Tekoa;
²⁷Abiezer from Anathoth;
Mebunnai the Hushathite;
²⁸Zalmon the Ahohite;
Maharai from Netophah;
²⁹Heled son of Baanah from Netophah;
Ithai son of Ribai from Gibeah of Benjamin;
³⁰Benaiah the Pirathonite;
Hiddai from the Brooks of Gaash;
³¹Abi Albon the Arbathite;
Azmaveth the Barhumite;
³²Eliahba the Shaalbonite;
the sons of Jashen;
Jonathan ³³the son of Shammah from Harar;
Ahiam son of Sharar from Harar;
³⁴Eliphelet son of Ahasbai the Maacathite;
Eliam son of Ahithophel the Gilonite;
³⁵Hezro the Carmelite;
Paarai the Arbite;

ª **23:8** *Josheb Basshebeth the Tahkemonite* Or "Jashobeam the Hacmonite". See 1 Chr. 11:11.

ᵇ **23:8** *king's special forces* A special group of soldiers who formed three-man squads and went on special missions for the king.

ᶜ **23:8** *Josheb Basshebeth . . . time* The Hebrew text here is unclear. The translation follows 1 Chr. 11:11 and the ancient Greek version.

ᵈ **23:9** *Eleazar son of Dodai* Or "Eleazar his cousin".

ᵉ **23:11** *lentils* Small round beans.

ᶠ **23:13** *Thirty Heroes* Or "the king's special forces". These men were David's famous group of very brave soldiers. Also in verses 23,24.

ᵍ **23:13** *three . . . Rephaim* The Hebrew text here is hard to understand, but compare 1 Chr. 11:15.

ʰ **23:16** *Three Heroes* These were David's three bravest soldiers. Also in verses 18,22.

ⁱ **23:20** *powerful man* That is, a man from the warrior class. He is ready to protect his people in war.

³⁶Igal son of Nathan of Zobah;
Bani the Gadite;
³⁷Zelek the Ammonite;
Naharai from Beeroth (Naharai carried the armour for Joab son of Zeruiah);
³⁸Ira the Ithrite;
Gareb the Ithrite;
³⁹and Uriah the Hittite.

There were 37 in all.

David Decides to Count His Army

24 The LORD was angry with Israel again. He caused David to turn against the Israelites. He told David, "Go and count the people of Israel and Judah."

²King David said to Joab, the captain of the army, "Go through all the tribes of Israel from Dan to Beersheba,*ᵃ* and count the people. Then I will know how many people there are."

³But Joab said to the king, "May the LORD your God give you 100 times as many people, no matter how many there are! And may your eyes see this thing happen. But why do you want to do this?"

⁴King David strongly commanded Joab and the other captains of the army to count the people. So they went out from the king to count the people of Israel. ⁵After they crossed the Jordan River, they began counting at Aroer, the city in the middle of the valley of the Gadites, near the town of Jazer.

⁶Then they went east to Gilead, all the way to Tahtim Hodshi. Then they went north to Dan Jaan and around to Sidon. ⁷They went to the fortress of Tyre. They went to all the cities of the Hivites and of the Canaanites. Then they went south to Beersheba in the southern part of Judah. ⁸It took them nine months and 20 days for them to go through the country. After nine months and 20 days they came back to Jerusalem.

⁹Joab gave the list of the people to the king. There were 800,000 men in Israel who could use the sword. And there were 500,000 men in Judah.

The LORD Punishes David

¹⁰David felt ashamed after he had counted the people and said to the LORD, "I have sinned greatly in what I did! LORD, I beg you, forgive me for my sin. I have been very foolish."

¹¹When David got up in the morning, the LORD gave this message to Gad, David's seer: ¹²"Go and tell David, 'This is what the LORD says: There are three ways you can be punished. Choose the one you want.'"

¹³So Gad went to David and said to him, "Choose one of these three: seven*ᵇ* years of famine for you and your country, being chased by your enemies for three months or three days of disease in your country. Think about it, and decide which one you want. I must give your answer to the one who sent me."

¹⁴David said to Gad, "This is a terrible situation to be in. But it would be better to be punished by the LORD than by anyone else, because he is very merciful."

¹⁵So the LORD sent a disease against Israel. It began in the morning and continued until the chosen time to stop. From Dan to Beersheba 70,000 people died. ¹⁶The angel raised his arm over Jerusalem and was ready to destroy it, but the LORD felt very sorry about the bad things that had happened. He said to the angel who destroyed the people, "That's enough! Put down your arm." The LORD's angel was by the threshing floor of Araunah*ᶜ* the Jebusite.*ᵈ*

David Buys Araunah's Threshing Floor

¹⁷When he saw the angel who killed the people, David spoke to the LORD. David said, "I sinned! I did wrong! And these people only did what I told them—they only followed me like sheep. They did nothing wrong. Please let your punishment be against me and my father's family."

¹⁸That day Gad came to David and said, "Go and build an altar to the LORD on the threshing floor of Araunah the Jebusite." ¹⁹So David did what Gad told him to. David did what the LORD wanted and went to see Araunah. ²⁰Araunah looked and saw King David and his officers coming to him. Araunah went out and bowed his face to the ground. ²¹He said, "Why has my lord and king come to me?"

David answered, "I came to buy the threshing floor from you. Then I can build an altar to the LORD. Then the disease will stop."

²²Araunah said to David, "My lord and king, you can take anything you want for a sacrifice. Here are some oxen for the burnt offering, and the threshing boards and the yokes for the wood. ²³O King, I give everything to you!" Araunah also said to the king, "May the LORD your God be pleased with you."

²⁴But the king said to Araunah, "No! I must pay you for everything. I will not offer burnt

---

ᵃ **24:2 Dan to Beersheba** This means the whole nation of Israel, north and south. Dan was a town in the northern part of Israel, and Beersheba was in the southern part of Judah. Also in verse 15.
ᵇ **24:13 seven** 1 Chr. 21:12 and the ancient Greek version have "three".
ᶜ **24:16 Araunah** Also spelled "Ornan". Also in verses 18,22,24.
ᵈ **24:16 Jebusite** A person who lived in Jerusalem before the Israelites took the city. "Jebus" was the old name for Jerusalem.

offerings to the LORD my God that cost me nothing."

So David bought the threshing floor and the oxen for 50 pieces[a] of silver. 25Then David built an altar to the LORD there and offered burnt offerings and peace offerings.

The LORD answered his prayer for the country. He stopped the disease in Israel.

---

[a] **24:24** *pieces* Literally, "shekels".

Who The author of Kings is not known but, whoever he was, he worked from a wide variety of sources and was familiar with Old Testament books such as Deuteronomy.

When Kings was probably written sometime after 561 BC, when the Jews were in exile in Babylon.

What Like Samuel, Kings is really one book, split into two parts because, originally, you couldn't fit it all on one scroll. The first part covers the period from the accession of Solomon (965 BC) to the split of the kingdom after his death.

The first book of Kings focuses mainly on Solomon. The first eleven chapters focus on his ascent to the throne, his wise reign, his establishment of Israel as a powerful kingdom and his building of the magnificent Temple in Jerusalem. But his reign ends badly, with this wise king lured by his many wives into worshipping foreign gods.

After his death, the kingdom of Israel splits into two (due mainly to the way Solomon used the northern tribes as forced labour in the building of the Temple). The southern part is called Judah, and is made up of the two tribes of Judah and Benjamin. The northern part contains the other ten tribes and retains the name Israel.

Kings goes on to tell the tale of the many rulers who governed these two kingdoms. In each case, the author decides whether they are a good king or a bad king, which is decided not by military success, foreign policy or expanding trade, but whether they stayed faithful to God. Every king is measured according to whether he obeyed the commands of the Lord. Mostly, the kings chose to worship foreign gods instead.

The other major characters in Kings are the prophets. In particular, 1 Kings introduces Elijah and Elisha. Elijah is the greatest prophet in Israel's history. He opposes King Ahab and Queen Jezebel of Israel, the northern kingdom. At the time he seems almost a lone voice – it's Elijah v. the rest. It shows what a difficult job it was to be a prophet. It took courage, commitment and huge faith in God to confront wickedness and speak out for God in a world that did not wish to hear what its maker had to say.

QUICK TOUR 1 KINGS

The death of David 1:1 – 2:12	The split of the kingdom 12:1–20
Solomon's wisdom 3:1–28	Asa – a good king 15:9–24
The building of the Temple 5:1 – 6:38	Enter Elijah 17:1–24
The dedication of the Temple 8:1–66	Elijah v. the prophets of Baal 18:1–46
Solomon's stupidity 11:1–13,41–43	The Lord appears to Elijah 19:1–21

"Elijah came to all the people and said, 'You must decide what you are going to do. How long will you keep jumping from one side to the other? If the LORD is the true God, follow him. But if Baal is the true God, then follow him!' The people said nothing."

1 Kings 18:21

Adonijah Wants to Be King

1 King David was very old and could not keep warm. His servants covered him with blankets, but he was still cold. ²So they said to him, "We will find a young woman to care for you. She will lie next to you and keep you warm." ³So the king's servants began looking everywhere in the country of Israel for a beautiful young woman to keep the king warm. They found a young woman named Abishag, from the town of Shunem, and brought her to the king. ⁴She was very beautiful. She cared for the king and served him, but King David did not have sex with her.

⁵⁻⁶Adonijah was the son of King David and his wife Haggith. He was born after Absalom. Adonijah was a very handsome man. King David never corrected his son Adonijah, and he never made him explain his actions. Adonijah became very proud and decided that he would be the next king. He wanted very much to be the king, so he got himself a chariot, horses and 50 men to run ahead of him.

⁷Adonijah talked with Joab son of Zeruiah and Abiathar the priest. They decided to help make him the new king, ⁸but several important men did not join Adonijah. They were Zadok the priest, Benaiah son of Jehoiada, Nathan the prophet, Shimei, Rei and King David's special guard.^a

⁹One day, at Zoheleth Rock near En Rogel,^b Adonijah sacrificed some sheep, cattle and fat calves as a fellowship offering. He invited his brothers, the other sons of King David and all the officers from Judah. ¹⁰But he did not invite his brother Solomon, Nathan the prophet, Benaiah or the men in the king's special guard.

Nathan Advises Bathsheba

¹¹When Nathan heard about this, he went to Solomon's mother Bathsheba and asked her, "Have you heard what Haggith's son, Adonijah, is doing? He is making himself king. And our master, King David, knows nothing about it. ¹²You and your son Solomon are in danger, but I will tell you what to do to save yourself. ¹³Go to King David and tell him, 'My lord and king, you promised me that my son Solomon would be the next king after you. So why is Adonijah becoming the new king?' ¹⁴Then while you are still talking with him, I will come in. After you leave I will tell the king what has happened. This will show that what you said is true."

¹⁵So Bathsheba went in to see the king in his bedroom. The king was very old. Abishag, the girl from Shunem, was caring for him there.

¹⁶Bathsheba bowed down before the king. The king asked, "What can I do for you?"

¹⁷Bathsheba answered, "Sir, you used the name of the LORD your God and made a promise to me. You said, 'Your son Solomon will be the next king after me. He will sit on my throne.' ¹⁸Now, you don't know this, but Adonijah is making himself king. ¹⁹He is giving a big fellowship meal. He has killed many cattle and the best sheep, and he has invited all your sons to the meal. He also invited Abiathar the priest and Joab, the commander of your army, but he did not invite your faithful son Solomon. ²⁰Now, my lord and king, all the Israelites are watching you. They are waiting for you to decide who will be the next king after you. ²¹If you don't decide, then after you are buried, these men will say that Solomon and I are criminals."

²²While Bathsheba was still talking with the king, Nathan the prophet came to see him. ²³The servants told the king, "Nathan the prophet is here." Nathan went in to speak to the king. He bowed down before the king ²⁴and said, "My lord and king, did you announce that Adonijah will be the new king after you? Have you decided that he will rule the people now? ²⁵Today he went down into the valley to offer many cattle and the best sheep as fellowship offerings. He invited all your other sons, the commanders of the army and Abiathar the priest. They are now eating and drinking with him. And they are saying, 'Long live King Adonijah!' ²⁶But he did not invite me, or Zadok the priest, or Benaiah son of Jehoiada or your son Solomon. ²⁷My lord and king, did you do this without telling us? Please tell us, who will be the next king after you?"

²⁸Then King David said, "Tell Bathsheba to come in!" So she came in and stood before the king.

²⁹Then the king made a promise: "The LORD has saved me from every danger. As surely as he lives, I make this promise to you. ³⁰Today I will do what I promised you in the past. I made that promise by the power of the LORD, the God of Israel. I promised that your son Solomon would be the next king after me. I promised that he would take my place on my throne, and I will keep my promise!"

³¹Then Bathsheba bowed down before the king and said, "Long live King David!"

Solomon Is Anointed King

³²Then King David said, "Tell Zadok the priest, Nathan the prophet and Benaiah son of Jehoiada to come in here." So the three men came in to meet with the king. ³³Then the king said to them,

---

^a **1:8** *Shimei, Rei . . . guard* Or "Shimei and his friends, the Heroes".
^b **1:9** *En Rogel* A spring of water in the valley south of Jerusalem, about 400 metres from Gihon Spring.

"Take my officers with you. Put my son Solomon on my mule and take him to Gihon Spring.[a] ³⁴There Zadok the priest and Nathan the prophet will anoint him to be the new king of Israel. Blow the trumpet and announce, 'This is the new king, Solomon!' ³⁵Then come back here with him. Solomon will sit on my throne and be the new king in my place. I have chosen him to be the ruler of Israel and Judah."

³⁶Benaiah son of Jehoiada answered the king, "Amen! It is as true as if the LORD God himself had said it, my lord and king. ³⁷My lord and king, the LORD has been with you, and now I pray that he will be with Solomon! And I pray that King Solomon's kingdom will grow and be even more powerful than yours, my lord and king."

³⁸So Zadok, Nathan, Benaiah and the king's officers obeyed King David. They put Solomon on David's mule and went with him down to Gihon Spring. ³⁹Zadok the priest carried the oil from the Holy Tent and poured it on Solomon's head to show that he was the new king. They blew the trumpet and all the people shouted, "Long live King Solomon!" ⁴⁰Then all the people followed Solomon back into the city. They were very happy and excited. They were playing flutes and making so much noise that the ground shook.

⁴¹Meanwhile, Adonijah and his guests were just finishing their meal. They heard the sound of the trumpet, and Joab asked, "What is that noise? What is happening in the city?"

⁴²While Joab was still speaking, Jonathan, son of Abiathar the priest, arrived. Adonijah said, "Come here! You are a good man,[b] so you must be bringing good news."

⁴³But Jonathan answered, "No, it is not good news for you! King David has made Solomon the new king. ⁴⁴King David sent Zadok the priest, Nathan the prophet, Benaiah son of Jehoiada and all the king's officers with Solomon out to Gihon Spring. They put Solomon on the king's mule. ⁴⁵Zadok the priest and Nathan the prophet anointed Solomon at Gihon Spring and then went back into the city. The people followed them, and now everyone in the city is celebrating. That is the noise you hear. ^{46–47}Solomon is sitting on the king's throne and the king's officers are congratulating King David, saying, 'King David, you are a great king!' And now we pray that your God will make Solomon a great king too. We pray your God will make him even more famous than you. And we pray that his kingdom will be even greater than yours is! Even King David was there. From his bed, the king bowed before Solomon

⁴⁸and said, 'Praise the LORD, the God of Israel. He has put one of my own sons on my throne, and he has let me live to see it.'"

⁴⁹All of Adonijah's guests were afraid and left very quickly. ⁵⁰Adonijah was also afraid of Solomon, so he went to the altar and held onto the horns of the altar. ⁵¹Then someone told Solomon, "Adonijah is afraid of you, King Solomon. He is at the Holy Tent holding onto the horns of the altar, and he refuses to leave. Adonijah says, 'Tell King Solomon to promise that he will not kill me.'"

⁵²So Solomon answered, "If Adonijah shows that he is a good man, I promise that not a hair on his head will be hurt. But if he does anything wrong, he will die." ⁵³Then King Solomon sent some men to get Adonijah and brought him in. He approached the king and bowed before him. Then Solomon said, "Go home."

King David Dies

2 The time came for David to die, so he gave these commands to Solomon, ²"I am about to die, like all men must. But you are growing stronger and becoming a man. ³Now, carefully obey all the commands of the LORD your God. Carefully obey all his laws, commands, decisions and agreements. Obey everything that is written in the Law of Moses. If you do this, you will be successful at whatever you do and wherever you go. ⁴And if you obey the LORD, he will keep his promise about me. He said, 'If your sons carefully live the way I tell them, sincerely, with all their heart, the king of Israel will always be a man from your family.'"

⁵David also said, "You remember what Joab son of Zeruiah did to me. He killed two of the commanders of Israel's army, Abner son of Ner and Amasa son of Jether. Remember, it was during a time of peace when he spilled the blood that splattered onto his sword belt and army boots. I should have punished him then. ⁶Use your wisdom, but don't let him die peacefully of old age.

⁷"Also, be kind to the children of Barzillai from Gilead. Be friends with them, and let them eat at your table, because they helped me when I ran away from your brother Absalom.

⁸"And remember, Shimei son of Gera is still around. He is the Benjamite from Bahurim who cursed me when I ran away to Mahanaim. But when he came down to meet me at the Jordan River, I made a promise to him before the LORD that I would not kill him. ⁹Now, don't leave him unpunished. You are a wise man. You will know what you must do, but don't let him die peacefully of old age."

---

[a] **1:33 Gihon Spring** A spring of water just outside the city walls in the valley east of Jerusalem. It was the main source of water for the city of Jerusalem.
[b] **1:42 good man** Or "important man". This Hebrew word means a person from an important family.

[10]Then David died and was buried in the City of David. [11]David ruled Israel for 40 years. He ruled seven years in Hebron and 33 years in Jerusalem.

Solomon and Adonijah

[12]Now Solomon was king. He sat on the throne of his father David and was in complete control of his kingdom.

[13]One day Adonijah, the son of Haggith, went to Solomon's mother, Bathsheba. She asked him, "Do you come in peace?"

Adonijah answered, "Yes, this is a peaceful visit. [14]I have something to ask you."

Bathsheba said, "Then speak."

[15]Adonijah said, "You know that at one time the kingdom was mine. All the people of Israel wanted me to be their king. But things have changed, and now my brother is the king. The Lord chose him to be king. [16]But now I have one thing to ask you. Please don't refuse me."

Bathsheba answered, "What do you want?"

[17]Adonijah said, "I know that King Solomon will do whatever you ask. So please ask him to let me marry Abishag, the woman from Shunem."

[18]Then Bathsheba said, "Very well, I will speak to the king for you."

[19]So Bathsheba went to King Solomon to talk with him. When the king saw her, he stood up, bowed before her, and then sat back down. He told some servants to bring another throne for his mother, and she sat down at his right side.

[20]Bathsheba said to him, "I have one small thing to ask you. Please don't refuse me."

The king answered, "Ask whatever you want, mother. I will not refuse you."

[21]So Bathsheba said, "Let your brother Adonijah marry Abishag, the woman from Shunem."

[22]King Solomon answered his mother, "Why are you asking me to give Abishag to Adonijah? Why don't you just ask me to give him the whole kingdom! After all, he is my older brother, and both Abiathar the priest and Joab support him!"

[23]Then Solomon said, "By the Lord, I swear I'll make Adonijah pay for this with his life! [24]The Lord made me the king of Israel. He gave me the throne of my father David. The Lord kept his promise and gave the kingdom to me and my family. Now, as surely as the Lord lives, I swear Adonijah will die today!"

[25]King Solomon gave the command to Benaiah, and Benaiah went out and killed Adonijah.

[26]Then King Solomon said to Abiathar the priest, "I should kill you, but I will let you go back to your home in Anathoth. I will not kill you now because you helped carry the Holy Box of the Lord God while marching with my father David. And I know that you shared in the hard times with my father." [27]So Solomon told Abiathar that he could not continue to serve as a priest of the Lord. This happened as the Lord said it would when he told Eli the priest what would happen to him and his family.[a]

INSIGHT

Denying his own mother's dodgy request and instead having Adonijah killed was difficult for Solomon, but it was necessary in order to establish his rule as king. His maturity was marked by his obedience to God rather than being influenced by the people around him.

1 Kings 2:13–25

[28]Joab had supported Adonijah, but not Absalom. But when Joab heard what had happened to Abiathar, he was frightened and ran to the tent of the Lord to hold onto the horns of the altar. [29]Someone told King Solomon that Joab was at the altar in the Lord's Tent. So Solomon ordered Benaiah to go and kill him.

[30]Benaiah went into the Lord's Tent and said to Joab, "The king says, 'Come out!'"

But Joab answered, "No, I will die here."

Benaiah went back to the king and told him what Joab had said. [31]The king commanded Benaiah, "Do as he says! Kill him there and take him out to bury him. Then my family and I will be free of Joab's guilt from killing innocent people. [32]Joab killed two men who were much better than he was. He killed Abner son of Ner, the commander of the army of Israel and Amasa son of Jether, the commander of the army of Judah. He did this without my father's knowledge. But now the Lord will punish Joab for the men he killed. [33]He and his family will always be guilty for their deaths. But the Lord will bring peace to David, his descendants, his family of kings and his kingdom forever."

[34]So Benaiah son of Jehoiada killed Joab, and he was buried near his home in the desert. [35]Solomon then made Benaiah son of Jehoiada the commander of the army in Joab's place. Solomon also made Zadok the new high priest in Abiathar's place. [36]Next, the king sent for Shimei and said to him, "Build yourself a house here in Jerusalem to live in and don't leave the city. [37]If you leave the city and go any further than Kidron

---

[a] **2:27** *This . . . family* See 1 Sam. 2:27–36.

Brook, you will be killed, and it will be your own fault."

³⁸Shimei answered, "Yes, my king. I will obey you." So Shimei lived in Jerusalem for a long time. ³⁹But three years later, two of Shimei's slaves ran away. They went to King Achish of Gath, who was the son of Maacah. Shimei heard that his slaves were in Gath, ⁴⁰so he saddled his donkey and went to King Achish at Gath to find them. He found them there and brought them back home.

⁴¹But someone told Solomon that Shimei had left Jerusalem and gone to Gath and back. ⁴²So Solomon sent for him and said, "I made you promise in the LORD's name not to leave Jerusalem. And I warned you that if you went anywhere, you would die. And you agreed to what I said. You said that you would obey me. ⁴³So why didn't you obey me? Why did you break your promise to the LORD? ⁴⁴You know all the bad things you did to my father David. Now the LORD will punish you for it. ⁴⁵But the LORD will bless me and keep David's throne before him forever."

⁴⁶Then the king ordered Benaiah to kill Shimei, and he did. So Solomon had full control of his kingdom.

Solomon Asks for Wisdom

3 Solomon made a peace treaty with Pharaoh, the king of Egypt, by marrying his daughter. Solomon brought her to the City of David. This was when Solomon was still building his palace, the Temple of the LORD and the wall around Jerusalem. ²The Temple to honour the LORD had not yet been finished, so people were still making animal sacrifices on altars at the high places. ³Solomon showed that he loved the LORD by obeying everything his father David told him to do, except that Solomon continued to go to the high places to offer sacrifices and to burn incense.

⁴King Solomon went to Gibeon to offer a sacrifice because that was the most important high place. He offered a thousand burnt offerings on that altar. ⁵While Solomon was at Gibeon, the LORD came to him at night in a dream. God said, "Solomon, ask for whatever you want me to give you."

⁶Solomon answered, "You were very kind and loyal to your servant, my father David. He was faithful to you and lived a good, honest life. And you showed him the greatest kindness when you let his son take his place as king. ⁷LORD my God, you have made me the king in my father's place, but I am like a small child. I don't have the wisdom I need to do what I must do. ⁸I am your servant here among your chosen people. There are so many that they cannot be counted. ⁹So I ask you to give me the wisdom to rule and judge them well and to help me know the difference between

right and wrong. Without such great wisdom, it would be impossible to rule this great nation."

¹⁰The LORD was happy that Solomon asked for wisdom. ¹¹So God said to him, "You did not ask for long life and riches for yourself. You did not ask for the death of your enemies. You asked for the wisdom to listen and make the right decisions. ¹²So I will give you what you asked for. I will make you wise and intelligent. I will make you wiser than anyone who ever lived or ever will live. ¹³And I will also give you what you did not ask for. You will have riches and honour all your life. There will be no other king in the world as great as you. ¹⁴And I will give you a long life if you follow me and obey my laws and commands as your father David did."

¹⁵Solomon woke up and knew that God had spoken to him in the dream. Then Solomon went to Jerusalem and stood before the Box of the LORD's Agreement. He offered a burnt offering and fellowship offerings to the Lord and then gave a party for all his officials.

Proof of Solomon's Wisdom

¹⁶One day two prostitutes came to Solomon and stood before the king. ¹⁷One of the women said, "Sir, this woman and I live in the same house. We were both pregnant and ready to give birth to our babies. I had my baby while she was there with me. ¹⁸Three days later she also gave birth to her baby. There was no one else in the house with us, just the two of us. ¹⁹One night while this woman was asleep with her baby, the baby died. ²⁰That night while I was asleep, she took my son from my bed and carried him to her bed. Then she put the dead baby in my bed. ²¹In the morning I woke up and was about to feed the baby when I saw he was dead. When I looked at him more closely, I saw that he was not my baby."

²²But the other woman said, "No! The dead baby is yours, and the one still alive is mine!"

But the first woman said, "No, you are wrong! The dead baby is yours! The one that is still alive is mine." So the two women argued in front of the king.

THE WISDOM OF SOLOMON

If you could ask God for just one thing, what would it be? A Bill Gates-sized bank account? Movie star looks? A private jet with your name on it?

King Solomon found himself in that place soon after he became king over Israel. The Lord comes to him in a dream and invites him to ask for whatever he wants.

DIG IN
READ 1 Kings 3:5–14

- How does Solomon see himself as king (vv.7–8)?
- What does he ask God for and why (v.9)?
- What does this say about Solomon?

Solomon may be king but his starting point is as a servant and as "a small child". He sees the enormity of the task of being king (maybe he watched his father, David, at work) and knows he can't blag it. He will need extraordinary wisdom to do a good job.

By humbly asking God for an understanding mind, Solomon already proves himself wise. It's a good idea to go into positions of responsibility not trusting in your own abilities, but in God.

READ 1 Kings 3:16–28

- What do these two women want from Solomon (vv.16–22)?
- What is Solomon's inspired solution (vv.23–25)?

The fact that this case has made it all the way to Solomon suggests that it was too hard or too sensitive for any other court to solve. The women's competing claims are so heartfelt and personal – who would want to be responsible for separating a baby from its mother?

His solution is breathtakingly insightful: the real mother would put the life of her child ahead of her own right to keep it. How could a young man see inside the heart of a mother like that? This is clear evidence that God is already answering Solomon's bold prayer for wisdom (an understanding mind).

DIG THROUGH

- How do you feel about some of the big decisions facing you: what shall I do after school? Which university should I apply to? Should I go out with this person? Are you trying to find the answers yourself when you most need to be asking God for help?
- God loved to answer Solomon's prayer for wisdom and will answer yours too (that's a promise – see James 1:5). In what ways might you see God answering that prayer in your life? Getting help from a mentor perhaps? Being around other people who need your help? The Bible itself (see below)?

DIG DEEPER

- The story of the two prostitutes is one tiny but powerful example of the wisdom God gave to Solomon. Check out the Bible books of Proverbs, Ecclesiastes and Song of Songs for much more of Solomon's wisdom.
- Solomon's reign as king runs through chapters 1 – 11 of 1 Kings. It is a time of amazing prosperity for Israel. Everything looks as if it's clicking into place. But it doesn't end well. Read on until you reach 1 Kings 10 and 11 (and look at the Bible Bit on 1 Kings chapters 4 and 10 "Spanner in the Works").

23Then King Solomon said, "Each of you says that the living baby is your own and that the dead baby belongs to the other woman." 24Then King Solomon sent his servant to get a sword. 25He told the servant, "Cut the living baby in two and give one half of the baby to each woman."

26The second woman said, "Yes, cut him in two. Then neither of us will have him." But the first woman, the real mother, loved her son and said to the king, "Please, sir, don't kill the baby! Give him to her."

27Then King Solomon said, "Stop, don't kill the baby. Give him to this woman. She is the real mother."

28The people of Israel respected the king when they heard about this decision. They saw he had the wisdom of God[a] to make the right decisions.

Solomon's Kingdom

4 King Solomon ruled over all Israel. 2These are the names of his leading officials:

Azariah son of Zadok was the priest;
3Elihoreph and Ahijah, sons of Shisha, had the job of writing notes about what happened in the courts;
Jehoshaphat son of Ahilud wrote notes about the history of the people;
4Benaiah son of Jehoiada was the commander of the army;
Zadok and Abiathar were priests;
5Azariah son of Nathan was in charge of the district governors;
Zabud son of Nathan was a priest and an advisor to King Solomon;
6Ahishar was responsible for everything in the king's palace;
Adoniram son of Abda was in charge of the slaves.

7Israel was divided into twelve districts. Solomon chose governors to rule over each district. These governors were ordered to gather food from their districts and give it to the king and his family. Each of the twelve governors was responsible for giving food to the king for one month each year. 8These are the names of the twelve governors:

Ben Hur was governor of the hill country of Ephraim.
9Ben Deker was governor of Makaz, Shaalbim, Beth Shemesh and Elon Bethhanan.

10Ben Hesed was governor of Arubboth, Socoh and Hepher.
11Ben Abinadab was governor of Naphoth Dor. He was married to Taphath, daughter of Solomon.
12Baana son of Ahilud was governor of Taanach and Megiddo and all of Beth Shean next to Zarethan. This was below Jezreel, from Beth Shean to Abel Meholah across to Jokmeam.
13Ben Geber was governor of Ramoth Gilead. He was governor of all the towns and villages of Jair son of Manasseh in Gilead. He was also governor of the district of Argob in Bashan. In this area there were 60 cities with big walls around them. These cities also had bronze bars on the gates.
14Ahinadab son of Iddo was governor of Mahanaim.
15Ahimaaz was governor of Naphtali. He was married to Basemath the daughter of Solomon.
16Baana son of Hushai was governor of Asher and Aloth.
17Jehoshaphat son of Paruah was governor of Issachar.
18Shimei son of Ela was governor of Benjamin.
19Geber son of Uri was governor of Gilead. There had been two kings in this area, King Sihon of the Amorites and King Og of Bashan, but Solomon appointed only one governor for that district.

20In Judah and Israel there were as many people as sand on the seashore. The people were happy and had plenty to eat and drink.

21Solomon ruled over all the kingdoms from the Euphrates River to the land of the Philistines. His kingdom went as far as the border of Egypt. These countries sent gifts to Solomon, and they obeyed him all his life.[b]

22–23This is the amount of food that Solomon needed each day for himself and for everyone who ate at his table: 6,600 litres[c] of fine flour, 13,200 litres[d] of meal, 10 cattle that were fed grain, 20 cattle that were reared in the fields, 100 sheep, wild animals such as deer, gazelles, roe deer and game birds.

24Solomon ruled over all the countries west of the Euphrates River, from Tiphsah to Gaza. And Solomon had peace along all the borders of his kingdom. 25During Solomon's life everyone in Judah and Israel, all the way from Dan to

---

[a] 3:28 *the wisdom of God* Or "very great wisdom".
[b] 4:21 *sent gifts . . . life* This showed that these countries had made peace agreements with Solomon because of his great power.
[c] 4:22–23 *6,600 litres* Literally, "30 *cors*".
[d] 4:22–23 *13,200 litres* Literally, "60 *cors*".

SPANNER IN THE WORKS

Sometimes everything looks as if it's coming together.

Solomon's reign (roughly 975–935 BC) was really a "golden age" for Israel. Following in the footsteps of his father, David, Solomon has ruled wisely and well. In 1 Kings 10 we see how word of his wisdom has gone around the ancient world (v.24) and resulted in vast wealth for the nation (v.27).

But the wise king was about to make some unwise choices.

DIG IN

READ 1 Kings 4:20-25; 10:23-29

- How does the writer sum up Solomon's rule in these two readings?
- What specific things does he point to?

In many ways, it looked as though the promises made to Israel were all coming true. Just as God had promised Abraham in Genesis 22:17 and Jacob in Genesis 32:12, the people were thriving and numerous. Just as God had promised to Moses in Exodus 23:31, the whole land was under the rule of God's choice of leader. At no other time would Israel extend so far and have so much wealth, prestige and power.

And, Solomon had personally overseen the fulfilment of another promise: God coming down to live among his people as the Box of the LORD's Agreement is placed inside the Temple he builds (1 Kings 8:1–21). As Solomon himself says, "So the LORD has kept his promises" (v.20).

But by the end of his life, God says he is taking Solomon's kingdom away from him. What went wrong?

READ 1 Kings 11:1-13

- What leads to Solomon's downfall?
- What is it that God particularly dislikes about all these wives?

God's ideal is that one man should be faithful to one woman for the whole of their marriage, but in some cases in the Old Testament God allowed polygamy (where one man can have many wives). However, here we can see why God's ideal is the best for everyone. Solomon's wives led him to be unfaithful to God; he worshipped and built temples to the foreign gods his wives worshipped. The Lord is not happy and promises judgement will come.

DIG THROUGH

- God absolutely hates it when we turn towards other "gods". He specifically focuses on this in the first two commandments given to Moses (Exodus 20:3–4). What other gods are we drawn to worship with our minds, our money and our time today?
- There was a big difference between King Solomon and David, his famous father: Solomon's heart was not wholly true or committed to God (1 Kings 11:4–6). And yet David got it wrong sometimes too (see 2 Samuel 11). What is God really looking for?

DIG DEEPER

Sin always has consequences. As a result of Solomon's disobedience, the golden age of Israel is about to come to an end, giving way to civil war and the division of Israel into two parts. Solomon's son, Rehoboam, keeps hold of the southern part of the kingdom, known as Judah, but the rest of Israel separates itself under a new king from within Solomon's army, Jeroboam. From here on, the Israel–Judah story is all about decline.

- You can read about the planning, building and the dedication of the Temple in 1 and 2 Chronicles.

Beersheba, lived in peace and security. The people were at peace sitting under their own fig trees and grapevines.

²⁶Solomon had places to keep 4,000ᵃ horses for his chariots and he had 12,000 horses for riding. ²⁷And each month one of the twelve district governors gave King Solomon everything he needed for all the people who ate at the king's table. ²⁸The district governors also gave the king enough straw and barley for the chariot horses and the riding horses. Everyone brought this grain to the necessary places.

Solomon's Wisdom

²⁹God made Solomon very wise. Solomon could understand more than you can imagine. ³⁰He was wiser than anyone in the Eastᵇ or in Egypt. ³¹He was wiser than anyone on earth, even Ethan the Ezrahite and the sons of Mahol—Heman, Calcol and Darda. King Solomon became famous in all the surrounding countries. ³²By the end of his life, he had writtenᶜ 3,000 proverbs and 1,005 songs.

³³Solomon also knew much about nature. He taught about many different kinds of plants—everything from the great cedar trees of Lebanon to the little vines that grow out of the walls. He also taught about animals, birds and snakes.ᵈ ³⁴People from every nation came to listen to Solomon's wisdom. Kings all over the world sent their people to listen to him.

Solomon and Hiram

5 Hiram was the king of Tyre. He had always been David's friend. So when Hiram heard that Solomon had become the new king after David, he sent his servants to Solomon. ²This is what Solomon said to King Hiram:

³"You remember that my father, King David, had to fight many wars all around him. So he was never able to build a temple to honour the LORD his God. King David was waiting until the LORD allowed him to defeat all his enemies. ⁴But now the LORD my God has given me peace along all the borders of my country. I have no enemies, and my people are in no danger.

⁵"The LORD made a promise to my father David. He said, 'I will make your son king

after you, and he will build a temple to honour me.' So now I plan to build that temple to honour the LORD my God. ⁶And so I ask you to help me. Send your men to Lebanon to cut down cedar trees for me. My servants will work with yours. I will pay you any price that you decide as your servants' wages, but I need your help. Our carpentersᵉ are not as good as the carpenters of Sidon."

⁷Hiram was very happy when he heard what Solomon asked. He said, "I praise the LORD today for giving David a wise son to rule this great nation!" ⁸Then Hiram sent this message to Solomon:

"I heard what you asked for. I will give you all the cedar trees and the pine trees you want. ⁹My servants will bring them down from Lebanon to the sea. Then I will tie them together and float them down the shore to the place you choose. There I will separate the logs, and you can take them from there. As payment for this, you will give food to all those who live in my palace."

¹⁰So Hiram gave Solomon all the cedar and fir logs that he wanted.

¹¹Solomon gave Hiram about 2,000 tonnesᶠ of wheat and about 440,000 litres,ᵍ of pure olive oil every year for his family.

¹²The LORD made Solomon wise as he had promised. Hiram and Solomon made a treaty between themselves and were at peace with each other.

¹³King Solomon forced 30,000 men of Israel to help in this work. ¹⁴He chose a man named Adoniram to be in charge of them. Solomon divided the men into three groups with 10,000 men in each group. Each group worked for one month in Lebanon and then went home for two months. ¹⁵Solomon also forced 80,000 men to work in the hill country cutting stone. There were also 70,000 men to carry the stones. ¹⁶There were 3,300 men to supervise the workers. ¹⁷King Solomon commanded them to cut large, expensive stones for the foundation of the Temple. ¹⁸Then Solomon and Hiram's builders and the men from Byblosʰ carved the stones and prepared them and the logs for use in building the Temple.

ᵃ **4:26 4,000** This is found in some copies of the ancient Greek version. The standard Hebrew text has 40,000, but see 2 Chr. 9:25.
ᵇ **4:30 East** The area between the Tigris and Euphrates rivers as far east as the Persian Gulf.
ᶜ **4:32 written** Literally, "spoken".
ᵈ **4:33 snakes** Literally, "creeping things". These can be anything: insects, lizards, snakes or fish.
ᵉ **5:6 carpenters** People who work with wood. In ancient times, this also meant that they cut the trees.
ᶠ **5:11 2,000 tonnes** Literally, "20,000 *cors*".
ᵍ **5:11 440,000 litres** Literally, "20,000 *baths*".
ʰ **5:18 Byblos** Literally, "Gebal".

Solomon Builds the Temple

6 So in the month of Ziv, the second month of the year, during Solomon's fourth year as king, he began work on the Temple for the LORD. This was 480 years after the Israelites left Egypt.[a] 2The Temple was 27 metres[b] long, 9 metres[c] wide and 13.5 metres[d] high. 3The porch across the front of the Temple was 9 metres long, the same as the width of the Temple. It was 4.5 metres[e] deep. 4There were narrow windows in the Temple. These windows were smaller on the inside of the wall than on the outside.[f] 5A row of rooms was built against the outside wall of the main part of the Temple. These rooms were all the way around this part of the building. 6This row of rooms was three storeys high. The beams on top of each storey rested on ledges around the Temple wall, so there was no need for holes to be cut into the wall. The Temple wall was thinner at the top, so the rooms on the upper floors were larger than the ones below them. The rooms on the bottom floor were just over 2 metres[g] wide. The rooms on the middle floor were almost 3 metres[h] wide. The rooms on top were just over 3 metres[i] wide. 7The stones were completely finished before they were brought into the Temple area, so there was no noise of hammers, axes or any other iron tools in the Temple.

8The entrance to these rooms was on the bottom floor at the south side of the Temple. Inside there were stairs that went up to the second floor and from there to the third floor.

9Solomon had the workers put up a ceiling to complete the main part of the Temple building. The ceiling was made from cedar beams and planks. 10Then they finished building the rooms around the Temple. Each of the three stories was just over 2 metres tall. The cedar beams above these rooms rested on edges around the Temple wall.

11The LORD said to Solomon, 12"If you obey all my laws and commands, I will do for you what I promised your father David. 13I will live among the children of Israel in this Temple that you are building, and I will never leave the people of Israel."

14When the stonework on the Temple was finished, Solomon had 15the stone walls inside the Temple covered with cedar boards from floor to ceiling. Then the stone floor was covered with pine boards. 16The workers built an inner room 9 metres long in the back part of the Temple. It was called the Most Holy Place. They covered the walls with cedar boards from floor to ceiling. 17In front of the Most Holy Place was the main part of the Temple. This room was 18 metres[j] long. 18They covered the walls in this room with cedar boards so that none of the stones could be seen. They carved designs of flowers and gourds into the cedar.

19The inner room at the back of the Temple was for the Box of the LORD's Agreement. 20This room was 9 metres long, 9 metres wide and 9 metres high. Solomon had the walls covered with pure gold. The cedar altar was also covered with gold, 21as was the inside of the Temple. He had gold chains put across the entrance to the Most Holy place, which was also covered with pure gold. 22So the inside of the Temple was completely covered with gold, including the altar in front of the Most Holy Place.

23The workers made two statues of winged creatures. They made the statues from olive wood and put them in the Most Holy Place. Each angel was 4.5 metres tall. 24-26Both winged creatures were the same size and built the same way. Each one had two wings. Each wing was just over 2 metres long. From the end of one wing to the end of the other wing was 4.5 metres. And each winged creature was 4.5 metres tall. 27They put the winged creatures beside each other in the Most Holy Place. Their wings touched each other in the middle of the room. The other two wings touched each side wall. 28The two winged creatures were covered with gold.

29The walls around the main room and the inner room were carved with designs of winged creatures, palm trees and flowers. 30The floor of both rooms was covered with gold.

31The workers made two doors from olive wood. They put these doors at the entrance of the Most Holy Place. The frame around the doors was made with five sides.[k] 32They made the two doors from olive wood. The workers carved designs of winged creatures, palm trees and flowers on the doors. Then they covered the doors with gold.

---

[a] 6:1 **480 years . . . Egypt** This was about 960 BC.
[b] 6:2 **27 metres** Literally, "60 *cubits*".
[c] 6:2 **9 metres** Literally, "20 *cubits*". Also in verses 16,20.
[d] 6:2 **13.5 metres** Literally, "30 *cubits*". The ancient Greek version has "25 *cubits*".
[e] 6:3 **4.5 metres** Literally, "10 *cubits*". Also in verses 23,24–26.
[f] 6:4 **These windows . . . outside** Or "These windows had lattice work over them."
[g] 6:6 **just over 2 metres** Literally, "5 *cubits*". Also in verses 10,24–26.
[h] 6:6 **almost 3 metres** Literally, 6 *cubits*".
[i] 6:6 **just over 3 metres** Literally, "7 *cubits*".
[j] 6:17 **18 metres** Literally, "40 *cubits*".
[k] 6:31 **The frame . . . sides** This probably means there were three sections that formed an arch at the top of the door.

³³They also made doors for the entrance to the main room. They used olive wood to make a square doorframe. ³⁴There were two doors made from pine. Each door had two parts that folded together. ³⁵They carved designs of winged creatures, palm trees and flowers on the doors. Then they covered them with gold.

INSIGHT

Solomon built an extravagant Temple in Jerusalem to provide a permanent home for the Box of the Agreement. The Temple was one of the largest buildings in Israel at the time but wasn't very large by today's standards. Having only about 250 metres of floor space it was smaller than a school gym.

1 Kings 6:2–38

³⁶Then they built a wall around the inner courtyard. Each wall was made from three rows of cut stones and one row of cedar timbers.

³⁷They started working on the LORD's Temple in the month of Ziv, the second month of the year. This was during Solomon's fourth year as king of Israel. ³⁸The Temple was finished in the month of Bul, the eighth month of the year, in Solomon's eleventh year as king. It took seven years to build the Temple. It was built exactly as planned.

Solomon's Palace

7 King Solomon also built a palace for himself. It took 13 years to build Solomon's palace. ²One building, called the Forest-of-Lebanon House, was 44 metres*ᵃ* long, 22 metres*ᵇ* wide and 13.5 metres*ᶜ* high. It had four rows of cedar columns. On top of each column was a cedar capital. ³There were cedar beams going across the rows of columns. There were 15 beams for each section of columns, making a total of 45 beams. On top of these beams there were cedar boards for the ceiling. ⁴There were three rows of windows opposite each other on the side walls. ⁵There were three doors at each end. All the door openings and frames were square.

⁶Solomon also built the Hall of Columns. It was 22 metres long and 13.5 metres wide. Along the front was a porch with a covering supported by columns.

⁷He also built a throne room where he judged people. He called this the Judgement Hall. The room was covered with cedar from floor to ceiling.

⁸Behind the Judgement Hall was a courtyard. The palace where Solomon lived was built around that courtyard and looked like the Judgement Hall. He also built the same kind of palace for his wife, the daughter of the king of Egypt.

⁹All these buildings were made with expensive blocks of stone. The stones were cut to the right size and then smoothed on the front and back. These expensive stones went from the foundation all the way up to the top layer of the wall. Even the wall around the courtyard was made with expensive blocks of stone. ¹⁰The foundations were made with large, expensive stones. Some of the stones were 4.5 metres*ᵈ* long and the others were 3.5 metres*ᵉ* long. ¹¹On top of these stones there were other expensive stones and cedar beams. ¹²There were walls around the palace courtyard and around the courtyard and porch of the LORD's Temple. The walls were built with three rows of stone and one row of cedar timbers.

¹³King Solomon sent for a man named Huram*ᶠ* who lived in Tyre and brought him to Jerusalem. ¹⁴Huram's mother was an Israelite from the tribe of Naphtali. His dead father was from Tyre. Huram made things from bronze. He was a very skilled and experienced builder. So King Solomon asked him to come, and Huram accepted. King Solomon put him in charge of all the bronze work, and Huram did all the work he was given to do.

¹⁵Huram made two bronze columns for the porch. Each column was 8 metres*ᵍ* tall and more than 5 metres*ʰ* around. The columns were hollow and their metal walls were 75 millimetres,*ⁱ* thick.*ʲ* ¹⁶He also made two bronze capitals that were just over 2 metres*ᵏ* tall. He put these capitals on top of the columns. ¹⁷He made two nets of chain to cover the capitals on top of the two columns. ¹⁸Then he made two rows of bronze pomegranates.

ᵃ **7:2 44 metres** Literally, "100 *cubits*".
ᵇ **7:2 22 metres** Literally, "50 *cubits*". Also in verse 6.
ᶜ **7:2 13.5 metres** Literally, "30 *cubits*". Also in verses 6,23.
ᵈ **7:10 4.5 metres** Literally, "10 *cubits*". Also in verse 23.
ᵉ **7:10 3.5 metres** Literally, "8 *cubits*".
ᶠ **7:13 Huram** Or "Hiram". Also in verses 15,23,27,37,38,40–45.
ᵍ **7:15 8 metres** Literally, "18 *cubits*".
ʰ **7:15 more than 5 metres** Literally, "12 *cubits*".
ⁱ **7:15 75 millimetres** Literally, "1 *handbreadth*". Also in verse 26.
ʲ **7:15 The columns . . . 75 millimetres thick** This is from the ancient Greek version.
ᵏ **7:16 just over 2 metres** Literally, "5 *cubits*". Also in verse 23.

He put the bronze pomegranates on the nets of each column to cover the capitals at the top of the columns. [19]The capitals on top of the columns were shaped like flowers and were almost 2 metres[a] tall. [20]The capitals were on top of the columns, above the bowl-shaped net. There were 200 pomegranates in rows all around the capitals. [21]Huram put these two bronze columns at the porch of the Temple. One column was put on the south side of the entrance and one was put on the north side of it. The column on the south was named Jakin. The column on the north was named Boaz. [22]They put the flower-shaped capitals on top of the columns, and the work on the two columns was finished.

[23]Then Huram melted bronze to make a large round basin called the Sea. It was about 13.5 metres across from rim to rim. It was 4.5 metres across and just over 2 metres deep. [24]Below the rim of the basin were images of gourds in two rows all the way around. They were moulded in place as part of the basin, six gourds every 44 centimetres. [25]The large basin rested on top of twelve large statues of bulls. Three bulls looked towards the north, three towards the west, three towards the south and three towards the east. The large basin was on top of these bulls, which all faced out from the centre. [26]The sides of the basin were 75 millimetres thick. The rim was like the rim of a cup or the flower of a lily. The basin held 44,000 litres[b] of water.

[27]Then Huram made ten bronze stands. Each stand was almost 2 metres long, almost 2 metres wide and almost 1.5 metres[c] high. [28]The stands were made with square panels set in frames. [29]On the panels and frames were bronze bulls, lions and winged creatures. There were designs of flowers hammered into the bronze above and below the bulls and lions. [30]Each stand had four bronze wheels with bronze axles. At the corners there were bronze supports for a large bowl. The supports had designs of flowers hammered into the bronze. [31]There was a frame around the top with an opening for the bowl. The frame was 44 centimetres[d] tall, and the opening was 66 centimetres[e] in diameter. There were designs carved into the bronze on the frame. The frame was square, not round. [32]There were four wheels under the frame. The wheels were 66 centimetres in diameter. The axles between the wheels were made as one piece with the stand. [33]The wheels were like the wheels on a chariot. Everything on the wheels—the axles, the rims, the spokes and the hubs were made from bronze.

[34]There were supports at each of the four corners of the stands. They were made as one piece with the stand. [35]There was a strip of bronze around the top of each stand. It was made as one piece with the stand. [36]The sides of the stand and the frames were covered with carved designs of winged creatures, lions and palm trees, surrounded with flower designs. [37]Huram made ten stands, and they were all the same. Each stand was made from bronze. The bronze was melted and poured into a mould. So all the stands were the same size and shape.

[38]Huram also made ten bowls. There was one bowl for each of the ten stands. Each bowl was almost 2 metres across and could hold about 800 litres.[f] [39]He put five stands on the south side of the Temple and five stands on the north side. He put the large basin at the south-east corner of the Temple. [40-45]He also made the pots, shovels and bowls.

So Huram finished everything King Solomon wanted him to make for the Temple of the Lord:

2 columns;
2 bowl-shaped capitals for the top of the columns;
2 nets made of bronze chains to decorate the capitals;
400 pomegranates to make two rows around each net covering the capitals;
10 stands with a bowl on each stand;
the large basin with 12 bulls under it;
the pots, shovels and bowls.

These were all the things King Solomon wanted Huram to make for the Lord's Temple. He made them all from polished bronze. [46-47]Solomon never weighed the bronze that was used to make these things. There was too much to weigh. So the total weight of all the bronze was never known. The king ordered these things to be made near the Jordan River between Succoth and Zarethan. They made them by melting the bronze and pouring it into moulds in the ground.

[48-50]Solomon also commanded that all these things be made from gold for the Temple:

the golden altar;
the golden table that held the special bread offered to God;

---

[a] **7:19 *almost 2 metres*** Literally, "4 *cubits*". Also in verses 27,38.
[b] **7:26 *44,000 litres*** Literally, "2,000 *baths*".
[c] **7:27 *almost 1.5 metres*** Literally, "3 *cubits*".
[d] **7:31 *44 centimetres*** Literally, "1 *cubit*".
[e] **7:31 *66 centimetres*** Literally, "1½ *cubits*".
[f] **7:38 *800 litres*** Literally, "40 *baths*".

the lampstands of pure gold, five on the south
   side and five on the north side in front of
   the Most Holy Place;
the gold flowers, lamps and tongs;
the pure gold bowls, lamp snuffers, small
   bowls, dishes for incense and pans for
   carrying coals;
the gold hinges for the doors to the inner
   room (the Most Holy Place) and for the
   doors to the main room of the Temple.

51When all the work was completed on the
LORD's Temple, Solomon brought in everything
his father David had set aside for the Temple.
Solomon put the silver, the gold and the utensils
into the storage rooms in the LORD's Temple.

The Box of the Agreement in the Temple

8 Then King Solomon told all the leaders of
Israel, the heads of the tribes and the leaders
of the families of Israel to come together in
Jerusalem. Solomon wanted them to join in
moving the Box of the LORD's Agreement from
the City of David up to the Temple. 2So during
the special festival[a] in the month of Ethanim, the
seventh month of the year, all the men of Israel
came to the meeting with King Solomon.

3–4When all the leaders of Israel arrived, the
priests and Levites carried the Holy Box of
the LORD up to the Temple. They also carried the
Meeting Tent and all the holy things that were in
it up to the Temple. 5King Solomon and all Israel
met together before the Box of the Agreement
and sacrificed so many sheep and cattle that no
one was able to count them all. 6The priests
carried the Box of the LORD's Agreement to its
proper place inside the Most Holy Place in the
Temple, under the wings of the winged creatures.
7The wings of the winged creatures spread out
over the Holy Box, and they covered the Holy
Box and its carrying poles. 8The poles are still
there today. They are too long for the Most Holy
Place, so anyone standing in the Holy Place can
see the ends of the poles, although no one outside
can see them. 9The only things inside the Holy
Box are the two tablets that Moses put there at
Mount Horeb. This is where the LORD made his
agreement with the Israelites after they came out
of Egypt.
10When the priests came out of the Holy
Place, the cloud[b] filled the LORD's Temple. 11The
priests could not continue their work because

the Temple was filled with the Glory of the LORD.
12Then Solomon said:

"The LORD caused the sun to shine in the sky,
   but he chose to live in a dark cloud.[c]
13Now, Lord, I have built a beautiful Temple
   for you,
   where you may live forever."

14Then King Solomon turned towards all the
Israelites who were standing there and asked
God to bless them. 15He prayed this long prayer
to the Lord:

"The LORD, the God of Israel, is great. He has
done what he promised my father David. He
told my father, 16'I brought my people, Israel,
out of Egypt, but I had not yet chosen a city
from among the tribes of Israel for a temple
to honour me. And I had not chosen a man
to be leader over my people, Israel. But now
I have chosen Jerusalem to be the city where
I will be honoured.[d] And I have chosen
David to rule over my people, Israel.'
17"My father David wanted very much to
build a temple to honour the LORD, the God
of Israel. 18But the LORD said to my father,
'I know that you want very much to build
a temple to honour me, and it is good that
you want to build it. 19But you are not the
one to build my temple. Your son will build
my temple.'
20"So the LORD has kept his promises. I am
the king now in place of my father David.
I rule the people of Israel as the LORD
promised. And I have built the Temple for
the LORD, the God of Israel. 21I have made a
place in the Temple for the Holy Box. Inside
that Holy Box is the agreement that the
LORD made with our ancestors when he
brought them out of Egypt."

22Then Solomon stood in front of the whole
assembly of Israel and faced the LORD's altar. He
lifted his hands towards heaven 23and said:

"LORD, God of Israel, there is no other god
like you in heaven or on the earth. You keep
the agreement that you made with your
people. You are kind and loyal to those who
follow you with all their heart. 24You made a
promise to your servant, my father David,

---

[a] **8:2 the special festival** That is, the Festival of Shelters. See "FESTIVAL OF SHELTERS" in the Word List.
[b] **8:10 cloud** The special sign that showed God was with his people.
[c] **8:12 The LORD . . . dark cloud** This is from the ancient Greek version, which places verses 12–13 after verse 53. In verse 12
the standard Hebrew text has only "The LORD said he would live in darkness."
[d] **8:16 And I . . . honoured** This is from the ancient Greek version. It is found in the standard Hebrew text of 2 Chr. 6:5–6, but
not here.

and you kept that promise. You made that promise with your own mouth, and with your own hands you made it come true today. 25Now, Lord, God of Israel, keep the other promises you made to your servant David, my father. You said, 'David, if your sons carefully obey me as you did, you will always have someone from your family ruling the people of Israel.' 26Again, God of Israel, I ask you to keep the promise you made to your servant, my father David.

27"But, God, will you really live here with us on the earth? The whole sky and the highest heaven cannot contain you. Certainly this Temple that I built cannot contain you either. 28But please listen to my prayer and my request. I am your servant, and you are the Lord my God. Hear this prayer that I am praying to you today. 29In the past you said, 'I will be honoured there.' So please watch over this Temple, night and day. And please listen to my prayer as I turn towards this Temple and pray to you. 30And please listen to our prayers in the future when I and your people Israel turn to this place and pray to you. We know that you live in heaven. We ask you to hear our prayer there and forgive us.

31"Those who wrong others will be brought to this altar. If they are not guilty, they will make an oath and promise that they are innocent. 32Please listen from heaven and judge them. If they are guilty, please show us that they are guilty. And if they are innocent, please show us that they are not guilty.

33"Sometimes your people Israel will sin against you, and their enemies will defeat them. Then the people will come back to you and praise you. They will pray to you in this Temple. 34Please listen in heaven to the prayers of your people Israel. Forgive them for their sins and let them have their land again. You gave this land to their ancestors.

35"Sometimes they will sin against you, and you will stop the rain from falling on their land. Then they will pray towards this place and praise your name. You make them suffer, and they will be sorry for their sins. 36So please listen in heaven to their prayer. Then forgive us for our sins. Teach the people the right way to live. Then, Lord, please send rain to the land you gave them.

37"The land might become so dry that no food will grow on it. Or maybe a great sickness will spread among the people. Maybe all the food that is growing will be destroyed by insects. Or your people might be attacked in some of their cities by their enemies. Or many of your people might become sick.

38When any of these things happen, and people feel compelled in their hearts to spread their hands in prayer towards this Temple, 39please listen to their prayer. Listen while you are in your home in heaven and forgive them and help them. Only you know what people are really thinking, so only you can judge them fairly. 40Do this so that your people will fear and respect you all the time that they live in this land that you gave to our ancestors.

41–42"People from other places will hear about your greatness and your power. They will come from far away to pray at this Temple. 43From your home in heaven, please listen to their prayers. Please do everything the people from other places ask you. Then they will fear and respect you just as your people in Israel do. Then all people everywhere will know that I built this Temple to honour you.

44"Sometimes you will command your people to go and fight against their enemies. Then your people will turn towards the city that you have chosen and the Temple that I built in your honour, and they will pray to you, Lord. 45Please listen to their prayers from your home in heaven, and help them.

46"Your people will sin against you. I know this because everyone sins. And you will be angry with your people. You will let their enemies defeat them. Their enemies will make them prisoners and carry them to some faraway land. 47In that faraway land, your people will think about what happened. They will be sorry for their sins, and they will pray to you. They will say, 'We have sinned and done wrong.' 48They will be in that faraway land of their enemies, but they will turn back to you. They will be sorry for their sins with their whole heart and soul. They will turn towards the land you gave their ancestors. They will look towards the city you chose and towards the Temple I built, and they will pray to you. 49Please listen to their prayers from your home in heaven, and do what is right. 50Forgive your sinful people for all the things they have done against you. Make their enemies be kind to them. 51Remember that they are your people and that you brought them out of Egypt. It was as if you saved them by pulling them out of a hot oven!

52"Please listen to my prayers and to the prayers of your people Israel. Listen to their prayers any time that they ask you for help. 53You have chosen them from all the peoples of the earth to be your own special people. Lord God, you promised to do that for us. You used your servant Moses to make that promise when you brought our ancestors out of Egypt."

54When Solomon prayed this prayer to the LORD, he was on his knees in front of the LORD's altar and his arms were raised towards heaven. When he finished praying, he stood up. 55Then, in a loud voice, he asked God to bless all the people of Israel. Solomon said:

56"Praise the LORD! He promised to give rest to his people, Israel. And he has given us rest! He used his servant Moses and made many good promises to the people of Israel. And he has kept every one of them! 57I pray that the LORD our God will be with us, as he was with our ancestors. I pray that he will never leave us. 58I pray that we will turn to him and follow him. Then we will obey all the laws, decisions and commands that he gave our ancestors. 59I pray that the LORD our God will always remember this prayer and what I have asked. I pray that he will do these things for his servant, the king and for his people, Israel. I pray that he will do this every day. 60If he will do these things, all the people of the world will know that the LORD is the only true God. 61You people must be loyal and true to the LORD our God. You must always follow and obey all his laws and commands. You must continue to obey in the future as you do now."

62Then King Solomon and all the Israelites with him offered sacrifices to the LORD. 63Solomon killed 22,000 cattle and 120,000 sheep as fellowship offerings to the LORD. In this way the king and the people showed that they had dedicated the Temple to the LORD.

64King Solomon also dedicated the courtyard right in front of the LORD's Temple. He offered burnt offerings, grain offerings and the fat from the animals that were used as fellowship offerings. King Solomon made these offerings there in the courtyard. He did this because the bronze altar in front of the LORD was too small to hold them all.

65So there at the Temple, King Solomon and all the people of Israel celebrated the festival.*a* People came from as far away as Hamath Pass in the north and the border of Egypt in the south. This huge crowd of people ate, drank and enjoyed themselves together with the LORD for seven days. Then they stayed for another seven days. They celebrated for a total of 14 days.*b* 66The next day Solomon told the people to go home. All the people thanked the king, said goodbye and went home. They were happy because of all the good things that the LORD had done for David his servant and for his people Israel.

God Comes to Solomon Again

9 So Solomon finished building the LORD's Temple and his own palace. Solomon built everything that he wanted to build. 2Then the LORD appeared to Solomon again, just as he did at Gibeon. 3The LORD said to him,

"I heard your prayer and what you asked me to do. You built this Temple, and I have made it a holy place. So I will be honoured there forever. I will watch over it and think of it always. 4You must serve me with a pure and honest heart, just as your father David did. You must obey my laws and do everything that I commanded you. 5If you do, I will make sure that your family will always rule Israel, just as I promised your father David when I told him that Israel would always be ruled by one of his descendants.

6-7"But if you or your children stop following me, and don't obey the laws and commands that I have given you, and if you serve and worship other gods, I will force Israel to leave the land that I have given to them. Israel will be an example to other people. Other people will make jokes about Israel. I made the Temple holy. It is the place where people honour me. But I will tear it down. 8This Temple will be destroyed. Everyone who sees it will be amazed. They will ask, 'Why did the LORD do this terrible thing to this land and to this Temple?' 9People will say, 'This happened because they left the LORD their God. He brought their ancestors out of Egypt, but they decided to follow other gods. They worshipped and served those gods. That is why the LORD caused all these bad things to happen to them.'"

10It took 20 years for King Solomon to build the LORD's Temple and the king's palace. 11Hiram supplied Solomon with all the cedar, pine and gold that he wanted, so Solomon gave him 20 cities in Galilee. 12So Hiram travelled from Tyre to see the cities that Solomon had given him. But Hiram was not pleased when he saw them. 13King Hiram said, "What are these towns that you have given me, my brother?" King Hiram named that land the Land of Cabul.*c* And that area is still called Cabul today.

a 8:65 *festival* The Festival of Shelters. See verse 2.
b 8:65 *Then . . . 14 days* This is not in the ancient Greek version.
c 9:13 *Cabul* This name is like the Hebrew word meaning "worthless".

¹⁴Hiram had sent King Solomon more than 4,000 kilogrammes*a* of gold to use in building the Temple. ¹⁵King Solomon forced slaves to work for him to build the Temple and his palace. Then he used these slaves to build many other things. He built the Millo and the city wall around Jerusalem. Then he rebuilt the cities of Hazor, Megiddo and Gezer. ¹⁶In the past the king of Egypt had fought against the city of Gezer and burned it. He killed the Canaanites who lived there. When Solomon married Pharaoh's daughter, Pharaoh gave him that city as a wedding present. ¹⁷Solomon rebuilt Gezer and the city of Lower Beth Horon. ¹⁸He also built the cities of Baalath and Tamar in the Judean Desert. ¹⁹He also built cities where he could store grain, and he built places for his chariots and his horses. King Solomon also built whatever he wanted in Jerusalem, Lebanon and all the places he ruled.

²⁰There were people left in the land who were not Israelites. There were Amorites, Hittites, Perizzites, Hivites and Jebusites. ²¹The Israelites had not been able to destroy them, but Solomon forced them to work for him as slaves. They are still slaves today. ²²Solomon did not force any Israelites to be his slaves. The Israelites were soldiers, government officials, officers, captains and chariot commanders and drivers. ²³There were 550 supervisors over Solomon's projects. They supervised the men who did the work.

²⁴Pharaoh's daughter moved from the City of David to the palace that Solomon had built for her. Then he built the Millo.

²⁵Three times each year Solomon offered burnt offerings and fellowship offerings on the altar he built for the LORD. King Solomon also burned incense before the LORD and supplied what was needed for the Temple.

²⁶King Solomon also built ships at Ezion Geber. This town is near Elath on the shore of the Red Sea, in the land of Edom. ²⁷King Hiram had some skilled sailors who knew the sea well. He sent them to serve in Solomon's navy and work with Solomon's men. ²⁸Solomon's ships went to Ophir and brought back more than 14,000 kilogrammes*b* of gold for him.

The Queen of Sheba Visits Solomon

10 The queen of Sheba heard about Solomon, so she came to test him with hard questions. ²She travelled to Jerusalem with a very large group of servants. There were many camels carrying spices, jewels and a lot of gold. She met Solomon and asked him all the questions that she could think of. ³Solomon answered all the questions. None of her questions were too hard for him to explain. ⁴The queen of Sheba saw that Solomon was very wise. She also saw the beautiful palace he had built. ⁵She saw the food at the king's table. She saw his officials meeting together. She saw the servants in the palace and the good clothes they wore. She saw his parties and the sacrifices that he offered in the LORD's Temple. She was so amazed, she could hardly breathe!

⁶Then she said to King Solomon, "The stories I heard in my country about your great works and your wisdom are true. ⁷I did not believe it until I came and saw it with my own eyes. Now I see that it is even greater than I had heard. Your wealth and wisdom are much greater than people told me. ⁸Your wives*c* and officers are very fortunate, because they serve you and hear your wisdom every day. ⁹Praise the LORD your God! He was pleased to make you king of Israel. Because of the LORD's unending love for Israel, he has made you king to rule with justice and fairness."

¹⁰Then the queen of Sheba gave King Solomon more than 4,000 kilogrammes*d* of gold, a huge amount of spices and precious stones. She gave him more spices than anyone has ever brought into Israel since.

¹¹Hiram's ships brought gold from Ophir. They also brought jewels and a special kind of wood.*e* ¹²Solomon used this special wood to build supports in the Temple and the palace as well as harps and lyres for the singers. That was the last time such a large shipment of that kind of wood was brought to Israel. There hasn't been any seen around here since then.*f*

¹³King Solomon gave the queen of Sheba everything she asked for. He gave her more than she brought to give him. Then the queen of Sheba

---

a **9:14 more than 4,000 kilogrammes** Literally, "120 *talents*".
b **9:28 more than 14,000 kilogrammes** Literally, "420 *talents*".
c **10:8 wives** This is from the ancient Greek version. The Hebrew text has "men".
d **10:10 more than 4,000 kilogrammes** Literally, "120 *talents*".
e **10:11 special . . . wood** Literally, "almug". No one knows exactly what type of wood this was, but it might have been sandalwood.
f **10:12 since then** Literally, "to this day", that is, when the book of Kings was written.

and her servants left and went back to their own country.

Solomon's Great Wealth

[14]Every year King Solomon received almost 23,000 kilogrammes[a] of gold. [15]In addition to the gold brought in by the travelling merchants and traders, all the kings of Arabia and the governors of the land also brought gold and silver to Solomon.

[16]King Solomon made 200 large shields of hammered gold. He used about 7 kilogrammes[b] of gold for each shield. [17]He also made 300 smaller shields of hammered gold. He used about 2 kilogrammes[c] of gold for each shield. The king put them in the Forest-of-Lebanon House.[d]

[18]King Solomon also built a large throne with ivory decorations. It was covered with pure gold. [19]There were six steps leading up to the throne. The back of the throne was round at the top. There were armrests on both sides of the throne, and there were lions in the sides of the throne under the armrests. [20]There were also two lions on each of the six steps, one at each end. There was nothing like it in any other kingdom.

[21]All of Solomon's cups and glasses were made of gold, and all the dishes[e] in the Forest-of-Lebanon House were made from pure gold. Nothing in the palace was made from silver. There was so much gold that in Solomon's time people did not think silver was important.

[22]The king also had many cargo ships[f] that he sent out to trade things with other countries. These were Hiram's ships. Every three years the ships would come back with a new load of gold, silver, ivory and apes and baboons.

[23]King Solomon became greater in riches and wisdom than any other king on earth. [24]People everywhere wanted to see King Solomon and listen to the great wisdom that God had given him. [25]Every year people came to see the king and brought gifts made from gold and silver, clothes, weapons, spices, horses and mules.

[26]Solomon had a great number of chariots and horses. He had 1,400 chariots and 12,000 horses. He built special cities for these chariots. So the chariots were kept in these cities. King Solomon also kept some of the chariots with him in Jerusalem. [27]The king made Israel very rich. In the city of Jerusalem, silver was as common as rocks and cedar wood was as common as the

many fig trees growing on the hills. [28]Solomon brought horses from Egypt and Kue. His traders bought them in Kue and brought them to Israel. [29]A chariot from Egypt cost about 600 pieces of silver, and a horse cost 150 pieces[g] of silver. Solomon sold horses and chariots to the kings of the Hittites and the Arameans.

Solomon and His Many Wives

11 King Solomon loved many foreign women, including the daughter of Pharaoh and women from Moab, Ammon, Edom, Sidon and the Hittites. [2]In the past the LORD had said to the Israelites, "You must not marry people from other nations. If you do, they will cause you to follow their gods." But Solomon fell in love with these women. [3]He had 700 wives who were the daughters of leaders from other nations. He also had 300 slave women who were like wives to him. His wives caused him to turn away from God. [4]When Solomon was old, his wives caused him to follow other gods, so he did not follow the LORD completely as his father David had done. [5]Solomon worshipped Ashtoreth, the goddess of Sidon, and Milcom, the horrible god of the Ammonites. [6]So Solomon did what the LORD said was wrong. He did not follow the LORD completely as his father David had done.

[7]On the mountain next to Jerusalem, Solomon built a place for worshipping Chemosh, that horrible idol of the Moabites. On the same mountain, Solomon built a place for worshipping Molech, that horrible idol of the Ammonites. [8]Solomon did the same thing for all his other foreign wives who burned incense and gave sacrifices to their gods.

[9]So Solomon did not remain faithful to the LORD, the God of Israel, even though God had appeared to him twice. The LORD became angry with him. [10]He had told Solomon that he must not follow other gods, but Solomon did not obey the LORD's command. [11]So the LORD said to Solomon, "You have chosen to break your agreement with me. You have not obeyed my commands. So I promise that I will tear your kingdom away from you and give it to one of your servants. [12]But I loved your father David, so I will not take your kingdom away from you while you are alive. I will wait until your son becomes king. Then I will take it from him. [13]Still, I will not tear away all the kingdom from your son. I will leave

---

[a] **10:14 almost 23,000 kilogrammes** Literally, "666 *talents*".
[b] **10:16 about 7 kilogrammes** Hebrew, "600 shekels". Also in verse 29.
[c] **10:17 2 kilogrammes** Hebrew, "3 *minas*".
[d] **10:17 Forest-of-Lebanon House** The largest of king Solomon's palace buildings. See 1 Kgs 7:2–5.
[e] **10:21 dishes** The Hebrew word can mean "dishes", "tools" or "weapons".
[f] **10:22 cargo ships** Literally, "ships of Tarshish".
[g] **10:29 150 pieces** Literally, "150 *shekels*".

him one tribe to rule. I will do this for my servant David and for Jerusalem, the city I chose."

Solomon's Enemies

[14]Then the LORD raised up Hadad the Edomite to become Solomon's enemy. Hadad was from the royal family of Edom. [15]This is how it happened. In the past David had fought against Edom. Joab was the commander of David's army. Joab went to Edom to bury his dead soldiers. While there Joab killed all the Edomite men who were still alive. [16]Joab and the men of Israel stayed in Edom for six months until they had killed all the men of Edom. [17]At the time Hadad was only a young boy. He and some of his father's servants ran away to Egypt. [18]They left Midian and went to Paran. In Paran some other people joined them and the whole group went to Egypt. They went to Pharaoh, the king of Egypt, and asked for help. Pharaoh gave Hadad a house, some land and food to eat.

[19]Pharaoh liked Hadad so much that he gave Hadad a wife. She was Pharaoh's sister-in-law. (Pharaoh's wife was Queen Tahpenes.) [20]Hadad and the sister of Tahpenes had a son named Genubath. Queen Tahpenes let Genubath grow up in Pharaoh's house with his children.

[21]In Egypt Hadad heard that David had died and that Joab, the commander of the army, was dead. So Hadad said to Pharaoh, "Let me go home to my own country."

[22]But Pharaoh answered, "I have given you everything you need here. Why do you want to go back to your own country?"

Hadad answered, "Please, just let me go home."

[23]God also raised up another man to become one of Solomon's enemies. This man was Rezon, son of Eliada. Rezon ran away from his master, King Hadadezer of Zobah. [24]After David defeated the army of Zobah, Rezon gathered some men and became the leader of a small army. He went to Damascus and stayed there to rule from Damascus. [25]Rezon became the king of Aram. He was an enemy of Israel throughout Solomon's life and added to the trouble that Hadad created for Israel.

[26]There was also another person who became an enemy of Solomon. He was Jeroboam son of Nebat. He was an Ephraimite from the town of Zeredah. His mother was a widow named Zeruah. He was one of Solomon's servants, but he rebelled against the king.

[27]This is the story of how Jeroboam turned against the king. Solomon was building the Millo and repairing the wall around the city of David, his father. [28]Jeroboam was a free man.[a] Solomon saw that this young man was a skilled worker, so he made him the supervisor over all the workers from the tribes that descended from Joseph. [29]One day as Jeroboam was leaving Jerusalem, the prophet Ahijah from Shiloh met him on the road. They were alone out in the country, and Ahijah was wearing a new coat.

[30]Ahijah took his new coat and tore it into twelve pieces. [31]Then he said to Jeroboam, "Take ten pieces of this coat for yourself because the LORD, the God of Israel, says, 'I will tear the kingdom away from Solomon, and I will give you ten of the tribes. [32]I will let David's family keep only one tribe. I will do this because of my servant David and because of Jerusalem, the city that I chose from among all the tribes of Israel. [33]I will take the kingdom from Solomon because he stopped following me and began worshipping Ashtoreth, the goddess of Sidon; Chemosh, the god of Moab; and Milcom, the god of the Ammonites. Solomon stopped following my ways and doing what I say is right. He does not obey my laws and commands as his father David did. [34]So I will take the kingdom away from Solomon's family. I chose David because he obeyed all my laws and commands. So for my servant David, I will let Solomon be the king for the rest of his life. [35]But Jeroboam, I will take the ten tribes away from his son and give them to you. [36]I will let Solomon's son keep one tribe to rule over. I will do this for my servant David, so he will always have someone to rule near me in Jerusalem, the city that I chose to be my own. [37]But I will make you king of Israel.[b] You will rule over everything you want. [38]If you do what is right and obey all my commands, as David did, I will be with you and make your family a family of kings, just as I did for David. And you will have Israel as your kingdom. [39]I will punish David's descendants because of what Solomon did, but not forever.'"

Solomon's Death

[40]Solomon tried to kill Jeroboam, but Jeroboam ran away to Egypt. He went to King Shishak of Egypt and stayed there until Solomon died.

[41]Everything else Solomon did, from the beginning to the end, is written in the book, *The History of Solomon.* [42]Solomon ruled in Jerusalem over all Israel for 40 years. [43]Then he died[c] and was buried in the city of David, his father. Then Solomon's son, Rehoboam, became the next king after him.

---

[a] **11:28 free man** Or "a nobleman", someone who could be called to war to protect his people.
[b] **11:37 Israel** That is, the northern ten tribes.
[c] **11:43 died** Literally, "slept with his ancestors".

Civil War

12 Jeroboam son of Nebat was still in Egypt where he had run away from Solomon. ²When he heard about Solomon's death, he returned to his city, Zeredah, in the hills of Ephraim.*ᵃ*

³Rehoboam went to Shechem, where all the Israelites had gone to make him the king. The people said to Rehoboam,*ᵇ* ⁴"Your father forced us to work very hard. Now, make it easier for us. Stop the heavy work that your father forced us to do and we will serve you."

⁵Rehoboam answered, "Come back to me in three days, and I will answer you." So the people left.

⁶There were some older men who had helped Solomon make decisions when he was alive. So King Rehoboam asked these men what he should do. He said, "How do you think I should answer the people?"

⁷They answered, "If you are like a servant to them today, they will sincerely serve you. If you speak kindly to them, they will always work for you."

⁸But Rehoboam did not listen to the advice from the older men. He asked the young men who were his friends. ⁹Rehoboam asked them, "The people said, 'Give us easier work than your father gave us.' How do you think I should answer them? What should I tell them?"

¹⁰Then the young men who grew up with him answered, "Those people came to you and said, 'Your father forced us to work very hard. Now make our work easier.' So you should tell them, 'My little finger is stronger than my father's whole body. ¹¹My father forced you to work hard, but I will make you work much harder! My father punished you with whips, but I will punish you with whips that have sharp metal tips.'"

¹²Rehoboam had told the people to come back to him on the third day. So, three days later, all the Israelites*ᶜ* came back. ¹³King Rehoboam did not listen to the advice from the older men, and he was rude to the people. ¹⁴He did what his friends told him to do and said, "My father forced you to work hard, but I will make you work much harder! My father punished you with whips, but I will punish you with whips that have sharp metal tips." ¹⁵So the king did not do what the people wanted. The Lᴏʀᴅ caused this to happen. He did this in order to keep the promise he made to Jeroboam son of Nebat when

he sent the prophet Ahijah from Shiloh to speak to him.

¹⁶The Israelites saw that the new king refused to listen to them, so they said to him,

> "We are not part of David's family are we?
>   We don't get any of Jesse's land, do we?
> So, people of Israel, let's go home
>   and let David's son rule his own people!"

So the Israelites went home. ¹⁷But Rehoboam still ruled over the Israelites who lived in the cities of Judah.

¹⁸A man named Adoniram was one of the men who directed the workers. King Rehoboam sent Adoniram to talk to the people, but the Israelites threw stones at him until he died. King Rehoboam ran to his chariot and escaped to Jerusalem. ¹⁹So Israel rebelled against the family of David, and this is how things are even today.

²⁰When all the Israelites heard that Jeroboam had come back, they called him to a meeting and made him king over all Israel. The tribe of Judah was the only tribe that continued to follow the family of David.

²¹Rehoboam went back to Jerusalem and gathered together an army of 180,000 men from the families of Judah and the tribe of Benjamin. Rehoboam wanted to go and fight against the Israelites and take back his kingdom. ²²But God spoke to a prophet named Shemaiah. He said, ²³"Talk to Rehoboam, the son of Solomon, king of Judah, and to all the people of Judah and Benjamin and the rest of the people. ²⁴Say to them, 'The Lᴏʀᴅ says that you must not go to war against your brothers. Everyone, go home! I made all this happen.'" So all the men in Rehoboam's army obeyed the Lᴏʀᴅ. They went home, just as the Lᴏʀᴅ had commanded.

²⁵Jeroboam rebuilt the city of Shechem, in the hill country of Ephraim, and lived there. Later he went to the city of Penuel*ᵈ* and rebuilt it.

²⁶⁻²⁷Jeroboam said to himself, "If the people keep going to Jerusalem to offer sacrifices at the Lᴏʀᴅ's Temple, someday they will want to be ruled by their old masters. They will want to be ruled by King Rehoboam of Judah. And then they will kill me." ²⁸So the king asked his advisors what to do. They gave him their advice, and King Jeroboam made two gold calves. He said to the people, "You don't have to go to Jerusalem to worship any more. Israel, these are the gods that

---

ᵃ **12:2 *to his city . . . Ephraim*** This is from the ancient Greek version.
ᵇ **12:3 *The people said to Rehoboam*** This is from the ancient Greek version. The standard Hebrew text has "They sent and called him, and Jeroboam and all the assembly of Israel came and said to Rehoboam".
ᶜ **12:12 *all the Israelites*** This is from the ancient Greek version. The standard Hebrew text has "Jeroboam and all the people".
ᵈ **12:25 *Penuel*** Or "Peniel".

brought you out of Egypt."[a] 29King Jeroboam put one gold calf in Bethel and the other one in the city of Dan.[b] 30What a terrible sin this was, because the Israelites started going to the cities of Dan and Bethel[c] to worship the calves.

31Jeroboam also built temples at the high places and chose priests from among the different tribes of Israel. (He did not choose priests only from the tribe of Levi.) 32Then King Jeroboam started a new festival that was like the festival[d] in Judah, but it was on the fifteenth day of the eighth month. At this time the king offered sacrifices on the altar at Bethel. He and the priests he chose offered the sacrifices to the calves that he had set up at the high places he had made. 33So King Jeroboam chose his own time for a festival for the Israelites, the fifteenth day of the eighth month. And during that time he offered sacrifices and burned incense on the altar he had built at Bethel.

God Speaks Against Bethel

13 The LORD commanded a man of God from Judah to go to the city of Bethel. King Jeroboam was standing at the altar offering incense when the man of God arrived. 2The LORD had commanded the man of God to speak against the altar. He said,

"Altar, the LORD says to you: 'David's family will have a son. His name will be Josiah. The priests of the high places are now burning incense on you, but Josiah will offer the priests on you and burn human bones on you, so you can never be used again!'"

3The man of God gave proof to the people that this would happen. He said, "This is the proof that the LORD told me about. He said, 'This altar will break apart, and the ashes on it will fall onto the ground.'"

4When King Jeroboam heard the message from the man of God about the altar in Bethel, he took his hand off the altar and pointed at the man. He said, "Arrest that man!" But when the king said this, his arm became paralysed. He could not move it. 5Then the altar broke into pieces, and all its ashes fell onto the ground. This proved that what the man of God had said came from the LORD. 6Then King Jeroboam said to the man of God, "Please pray to the LORD your God for me. Ask him to heal my arm."

So the man of God prayed to the LORD, and the king's arm was healed, as it was before. 7Then the king said to the man of God, "Please come

home with me. Come and eat with me. I will give you a gift."

8But the man of God said to the king, "I will not go home with you, even if you give me half of your kingdom! I will not eat or drink anything in this place. 9The LORD commanded me not to eat or drink anything here. He also commanded me not to go back the same way I came." 10So he took a different road home. He did not go back the same way.

11There was an old prophet living in Bethel. His sons came and told him what the man of God had done in Bethel and what he said to King Jeroboam. 12The old prophet said, "Which way did he go when he left?" So the sons showed their father which road the man of God from Judah had taken. 13The old prophet told his sons to saddle his donkey. They put the saddle on the donkey, and the prophet left.

14The old prophet went after the man of God. He found him sitting under an oak tree and asked him, "Are you the man of God who came from Judah?"

The man of God answered, "Yes, I am."

15So the old prophet said, "Please come home and eat with me."

16But the man of God said, "I cannot go home with you. I cannot eat or drink anything in this place. 17The LORD said to me, 'You must not eat or drink anything in that place, and you must go back on a different road.'"

18The old prophet lied to him and said, "But I am a prophet like you. And an angel from the LORD came to me and told me to bring you home and give you something to eat and drink."

19So the man of God went to the old prophet's house and ate and drank with him. 20While they were sitting at the table, the LORD spoke to the old prophet, 21and the old prophet spoke to the man of God from Judah. He said, "The LORD said that you did not obey him! You did not do what he commanded. 22He told you not to eat or drink anything in this place, but you came back here and ate and drank. So your body will not be buried in your family grave."

23The man of God finished eating and drinking. Then the old prophet saddled the man's donkey for him and the man left. 24On the way home, a lion attacked and killed the man of God. His body was lying on the road while the lion stood next to it. The donkey stood nearby. 25Some people came walking by and saw the body and the lion standing by it. They went into the city where the

---

HARD TIMES AND SUFFERING

HOW do you react when a situation in life just reaches out and smacks you in the face? What gets squeezed out of you when the pressure is on? We can easily think that our good times, when people see us succeeding in life and prospering, represent God's best. But how we react during difficult times can be even more important. When something bad

HOW WE RESPOND IN HARD TIMES IS WHERE THE RUBBER MEETS THE ROAD IN OUR RELATIONSHIP WITH GOD.

happens, do you wallow in grief or self-pity? Do you keep busy so you can avoid thinking about it? Do you turn away from God because things aren't going well?

How we respond in hard times is where the rubber meets the road in our relationship with God. Will we make a decision to praise him even though we don't feel like it? Will we believe what the Bible says even though our experience doesn't always match up with it?

And will we pray and forgive even when it's the last thing in the world we want to do?

If you are going through something tough right now, give yourself some space to breathe and to grieve. You might be grieving the death of a friend or relative; the loss of a dream; the betrayal of a friendship; or you may be suffering because of something else. Get past your first, natural reaction and take time alone with God. Be with him, and if it hurts, tell him. If you think life is unfair, tell him. If you need to shout and scream, cry and wail, or sit and stare, make sure you do it. But when you have done that, get into the word of God because when we are suffering and we feel as if no one understands or can help, God can speak the words we need to hear through the Bible. You might find Psalm 139 is a great place to start to see what God is telling you in your hard times. You could also check out Matthew 5:4 and Romans 8:29–39. ←

Pray and ask God to meet you in your time of struggle and to strengthen and encourage you.

ETERNAL LIFE

WHEN you hear the words "eternal life" do you automatically think of heaven and hell? What happens after you die?

Pictures of heaven and hell created for us by popular culture are fairly stereotypical: God with a white beard, pearly gates and your name on a list, harps and clouds; or fire and a devil in red lycra with a pitchfork and horns! You'd be surprised how many of those images have nothing to do with what the Bible says and are just myth and legend. We know that the Bible speaks of both a heaven and a hell: one place where there is communion with God and another place of eternal separation from God. It mentions angels and demons, a God of truth and a devil who is the father of lies. However, whether God has a white beard and the devil is red and carries a pitchfork is really irrelevant. There's actually much more to eternal life than heaven and hell.

Just before he died Jesus said, "And this is eternal life: that people can know you, the only true God, and that they can know Jesus Christ, the one you sent" (John 17:3). So basically, when we begin to know Jesus we begin to experience eternal life. That's what the Bible says. Do you have to wait until you die to get to know God? No. There are millions of people who already have a friendship with him right now. They're talking with him, reading his promises to them in the Bible and putting his words into action every day. By living in relationship with God through Jesus, they've already begun to have eternal life.

After you die, it just keeps getting better, because we will see God more clearly. The apostle Paul puts it like this: "Now we see God as if we are looking at a reflection in a mirror. But then, in the future, we will see him right before our eyes. Now I know only a part, but at that time I will know fully, as God has known me" (1 Corinthians 13:12). So there's definitely a deeper level of knowing God reserved for you once your earthly life comes to an end. That must mean that eternal life gets better too!

"WON'T ETERNAL LIFE GET A BIT BORING . . . I MEAN, IT'S JUST SO ETERNAL?"

I think most people have wondered at some point, "Won't eternal life get a bit boring . . . I mean, it's just so *eternal*?" Ask anyone mature enough in their faith, and they'll tell you that their relationship with Jesus just gets better with time. It's not like a job, where the excitement wears off after a while. "No one has ever heard of such a God. No one has ever heard such a story. No one has ever seen any God except you, who does such great things for those who trust him" (Isaiah 64:4). See? It's mind-blowing! It's a gift from God, obviously, but more specifically, the Holy Spirit is the one who produces eternal life in us. "If you live to satisfy your sinful self, the harvest you will get from that will be eternal death. But if you live to please the Spirit, your harvest from the Spirit will be eternal life. We must not get tired of doing good. We will receive our harvest of eternal life at the right time. We must not give up" (Galatians 6:8–9).

So, eternal life starts now. Enjoy it, and look forward to everything that's still to come! ←

IMAGE AND SELF-ESTEEM

HAVE you ever noticed how easy it is to see the good in other people and only the bad in ourselves? We look at one friend and see their great smile, their talent for sport and their popularity. We look at ourselves and can only think about our slightly wonky nose, our complete inability to understand maths and how we put our foot in our mouth every time we open it.

It doesn't help that society tells us to measure our worth by how perfect we look, how much money we have, whether we look old enough to get into clubs while we're under age, or whether we own the latest gadgets and most fashionable labels. God has a different way of measuring us. When God first created humankind we were made in his image and he said we were "very good" (Genesis 1:31). In fact, the Bible tells us a lot about who we really are. We read that we are known by God (John 10:14–15); we are his sons and daughters (Galatians 3:26–27); we are his friends (John 15:13–15); and we are loved utterly and completely no matter what (Romans 8:35–39).

HE WILL HELP US UNDERSTAND THAT WE TRULY ARE "VERY GOOD" IN HIS EYES.

If we try to work out our worth by the world's standards we'll always feel that we come up short. But in God's view we don't need to do anything else to be loved. He accepts us as we are and as we get to know him he will help us understand that we truly are "very good" in his eyes. ←

Spend some time reading Psalm 139 and ask God to speak to you about the fact that he made you in such an amazing way (see especially verse 14). You may also like to read Romans 8:31–39 and 1 Samuel 16:7.

old prophet lived and told people what they had seen on the road.

26The old prophet heard the story and said, "This is the man of God who did not obey the LORD's command, so the LORD sent a lion to attack him. The lion has killed him, just as the LORD said would happen." 27Then the prophet told his sons to saddle his donkey, and they did so. 28The old prophet went to find the body lying on the road. The donkey and the lion were still standing near it. The lion had not eaten the body or hurt the donkey.

29The old prophet put the body on his donkey and carried it back to the city to cry for him and bury him. 30The old prophet buried the man in his own family grave. The old prophet cried for him and said, "Oh, my brother, I am sorry for you." 31So the old prophet buried the body. Then he said to his sons, "When I die, bury me in this same grave. Put my bones next to his. 32The LORD used him to speak against the altar at Bethel and against the high places in the other towns in Samaria. And what he said will certainly happen."

33King Jeroboam did not change. He continued doing evil. He continued to choose people from different tribes to serve as priests[a] at the high places. Whoever wanted to be a priest was allowed to be one. 34This is the sin that caused the ruin and destruction of his kingdom.

Jeroboam's Son Dies

14 At that time Jeroboam's son Abijah became very sick. 2Jeroboam said to his wife, "Go to Shiloh and see the prophet Ahijah. He is the one who said that I would become king of Israel. Dress yourself so that people will not know that you are my wife. 3Give the prophet ten loaves of bread, some cakes and a jar of honey. Then ask him what will happen to our son, and he will tell you."

4So the king's wife did what he said. She went to the home of Ahijah the prophet in Shiloh. Ahijah was very old and had become blind. 5But the LORD said to him, "Jeroboam's wife is coming to ask you about her son because he is sick. I will tell you what to say to her."

When she came to Ahijah's house, she pretended to be someone else. 6But when Ahijah heard her coming to the door, he said, "Come in! I know who you are. You are Jeroboam's wife. Why are you pretending to be someone else? I have some bad news for you. 7Go back and tell Jeroboam that this is what the LORD, the God of Israel, says: 'Jeroboam, I chose you from among all the Israelites. I made you the ruler of my people. 8David's family was ruling the kingdom of Israel, but I took the kingdom away from them and gave

it to you. But you are not like my servant David. He always obeyed my commands and followed me with his whole heart. He did only what I accepted. 9But you have sinned more than anyone who ruled before you. You stopped following me and made other gods for yourself. You made those statues to make me angry. 10So Jeroboam, I will bring troubles to your family. I will kill all the men in your family. I will destroy your family completely, like fire burning up dung. 11Anyone from your family who dies in the city will be eaten by dogs. And anyone from your family who dies in the fields will be eaten by birds. The LORD has spoken.'"

12Then Ahijah said, "Now, go home. Your son will die as soon as you enter the city. 13All Israel will cry for him. They will bury him, but he is the only one from Jeroboam's family who will be buried. This is because he is the only one in Jeroboam's family who pleased the LORD, the God of Israel. 14Soon, the LORD will put a new king over Israel who will destroy Jeroboam's family. 15Then the LORD will punish Israel. The Israelites will be so full of fear that they will shake like tall grass in the water. He will pull Israel up from this good land that he gave their ancestors. He will scatter them to the other side of the Euphrates River. The LORD will do this because the people made him angry when they built sacred poles.[b] 16He will let the Israelites be defeated because Jeroboam sinned, and then he made the Israelites sin."

17Jeroboam's wife went back to Tirzah. As soon as she stepped into the house, the boy died. 18They buried him and all the people of Israel cried for him. This happened just as the LORD said it would through his servant, the prophet Ahijah.

19The rest of what King Jeroboam did is written in the book, *The History of the Kings of Israel.* It includes the wars he fought and the way he ruled. 20Jeroboam ruled as king for 22 years. Then he died and was buried with his ancestors. His son Nadab became the new king after him.

Rehoboam, King of Judah

21Solomon's son, Rehoboam, was 41 years old when he became king of Judah. Rehoboam ruled for 17 years in Jerusalem, the city the LORD chose for his own. He chose this city from all the other tribes of Israel. Rehoboam's mother was Naamah. She was an Ammonite.

22The people of Judah did things that the LORD considered evil. They made him angry with all their sins—more than any of their ancestors had done. 23They built high places, memorial stones and sacred poles.[c] They built them on every high hill and under every green tree. 24There were also

---

[a] **13:33 people . . . priests** The Law taught that only people from the tribe of Levi could become priests.
[b] **14:15 sacred poles** People used these things to worship false gods.
[c] **14:23 high places, memorial stones and sacred poles** People used these things to worship false gods.

men who served other gods by selling their bodies for sex.[a] So the people of Judah were worse than the people who had lived in the land before them. And the LORD took the land away from those people to give it to the Israelites.

25In the fifth year that Rehoboam was king, King Shishak of Egypt came to attack Jerusalem. 26He took the treasures from the LORD's Temple and from the king's palace. He even took the gold shields that David had taken from the officers of King Hadadezer of Aram and put on the walls of Jerusalem.[b] 27King Rehoboam made more shields to put in their places, but they were made from bronze. He gave them to the guards on duty at the palace gates. 28Every time the king went to the LORD's Temple, the guards took out the shields and went with him. Afterwards, they put the shields back on the wall in the guardroom.

29The rest of what King Rehoboam did is written in the book, *The History of the Kings of Judah.* 30Rehoboam and Jeroboam were always fighting against each other.

31Rehoboam died[c] and was buried with his ancestors in the City of David. (His mother was Naamah. She was an Ammonite.) Rehoboam's son Abijah became the next king after him.

Abijah, King of Judah

15 Abijah became the new king of Judah during the eighteenth year that Jeroboam son of Nebat ruled Israel. 2Abijah ruled in Jerusalem for three years. His mother's name was Maacah. She was Absalom's daughter.

3He did all the same sins that his father before him had done. Abijah was not faithful to the LORD his God. In this way he was not like his great-grandfather, David. 4But for David's sake, the LORD gave Abijah a kingdom in Jerusalem and allowed him to have a son. He also kept Jerusalem safe. 5David had always done what the LORD said was right. He had always obeyed his commands. The only time David did not obey the Lord was when he sinned against Uriah the Hittite.

6Rehoboam and Jeroboam were always fighting against each other.[d] 7The rest of what Abijah did is written in the book, *The History of the Kings of Judah.*

There was war between Abijah and Jeroboam during the whole time that Abijah was king. 8When Abijah died, he was buried in the City of David. Abijah's son Asa became the new king after him.

Asa, King of Judah

9During Jeroboam's twentieth year as king over Israel, Asa became king of Judah. 10He ruled in Jerusalem for 41 years. His grandmother's name was Maacah, and she was the daughter of Absalom.

11Asa did what the LORD said was right, as his ancestor David did. 12During Asa's time there were men who served other gods by selling their bodies for sex. Asa forced them to leave the country. He took away the idols that his ancestors had made. 13King Asa also took away the right of his mother Maacah to be queen mother. He did this because she had set up one of those awful Asherah poles. Asa cut down the pole and burned it in the Kidron Valley. 14Asa did not destroy the high places, even though he was faithful to the LORD all his life. 15Asa and his father had given some special gifts to God. Asa put these gifts of gold, silver and other things in the LORD's Temple.

16King Asa and King Baasha of Israel were always at war with each other. 17Once Baasha attacked Judah and then built up the city of Ramah to keep Asa from leaving Judah on any kind of military campaign. 18So Asa took gold and silver from the treasuries of the LORD's Temple and the king's palace. He gave it to his officials and sent them to King Ben-Hadad of Aram. Ben-Hadad was the son of Tabrimmon. Tabrimmon was the son of Hezion. Damascus was Ben-Hadad's capital city. 19Asa sent this message: "My father and your father had a peace agreement. Now I want to make a peace agreement with you. I am sending you this gift of gold and silver. Please break your treaty with King Baasha of Israel and make him leave us alone."

20King Ben-Hadad made the agreement with King Asa and sent his army to fight against the Israelite towns of Ijon, Dan, Abel Beth Maacah, the towns near Lake Galilee and the area of Naphtali. 21When Baasha heard about these attacks, he stopped building up Ramah and went back to Tirzah. 22Then King Asa gave an order to all the men in Judah. Everyone had to help. They had to go to Ramah and carry out all the stone and wood that Baasha was using to build up the city. They carried the material to Geba in Benjamin and to Mizpah and used it to strengthen those two cities.

23All the other things about Asa—the great things he did and the cities he built—are written in the book, *The History of the Kings of Judah.* When Asa became old, his feet became infected.

---

a 14:24 men . . . for sex Sexual sins like this were a part of the way people worshipped the Canaanite gods.

b 14:26 He even took . . . Jerusalem This is from the ancient Greek version. The standard Hebrew text has "He even took the gold shields that Solomon made."

c 14:31 died Literally, "slept with his ancestors".

d 15:6 This is not in the ancient Greek version. A few Hebrew copies have "Abijah" instead of "Rehoboam".

²⁴He died and was buried in the City of David, his ancestor. Then Asa's son Jehoshaphat became the new king after him.

Nadab, King of Israel

²⁵During Asa's second year as king of Judah, Jeroboam's son Nadab became king of Israel. Nadab ruled over Israel for two years. ²⁶He did what the LORD said was wrong. He sinned just as his father Jeroboam did when he caused the Israelites to sin.

²⁷Baasha was the son of Ahijah. They were from the tribe of Issachar. Baasha made a plan to kill King Nadab. Nadab and all Israel were fighting against the Philistine town of Gibbethon. And that is where Baasha killed Nadab. ²⁸This happened during Asa's third year as king of Judah. So Baasha became the next king of Israel.

Baasha, King of Israel

²⁹When Baasha became the new king, he killed everyone in Jeroboam's family. He left no one in Jeroboam's family alive. This happened just as the LORD said it would when he spoke through his servant Ahijah at Shiloh. ³⁰This happened because King Jeroboam had committed many sins and had caused the Israelites to sin. This made the LORD, the God of Israel, very angry.

³¹The other things that Nadab did are written in the book, *The History of the Kings of Israel.* ³²Throughout the time that Baasha ruled over Israel, he was fighting wars against King Asa of Judah.

³³Ahijah's son Baasha became king of Israel during the third year that Asa ruled over Judah. Baasha ruled in Tirzah for 24 years, ³⁴but he did what the LORD said was wrong. He committed the same sins as Jeroboam, which caused the Israelites to sin.

16 Then the LORD spoke against King Baasha through the prophet, Jehu son of Hanani. He said, ²"I made you an important prince over my people Israel. But you have done the same things Jeroboam did. You have caused my people Israel to sin. Their sins have made me angry. ³So Baasha, I will destroy you and your family, just as I did Jeroboam son of Nebat and his family. ⁴Dogs will eat the bodies of those in your family who die in the city. And wild birds will eat the bodies of those who die out in the fields."

⁵The rest of the story about Baasha and the great things he did are written in the book, *The History of the Kings of Israel.* ⁶Baasha died and was buried in Tirzah. His son Elah became the new king after him.

⁷That book also has the story about the time the LORD gave the message to Jehu the prophet about Baasha and his family. Baasha did many things the LORD said were wrong, just as Jeroboam and his family had done. This and the fact that Baasha had killed everyone in Jeroboam's family made the Lord very angry.

Elah, King of Israel

⁸Elah son of Baasha became king during the twenty-sixth year that Asa was the king of Judah. He ruled in Tirzah for two years.

⁹Zimri was one of King Elah's officers. Zimri commanded half of Elah's chariots, but Zimri plotted against Elah. King Elah was in Tirzah, drinking and getting drunk at Arza's home. Arza was the man in charge of the palace at Tirzah. ¹⁰Zimri went into the house and killed King Elah. Then Zimri became the new king of Israel after Elah. This was during the twenty-seventh year that Asa was king in Judah.

Zimri, King of Israel

¹¹After Zimri became the new king, he killed all of Baasha's family and friends. He did not let any male in Baasha's family live. ¹²So Zimri destroyed Baasha's family just as the LORD said he would when he spoke against Baasha through the prophet Jehu. ¹³This happened because of all the sins of Baasha and his son, Elah. They sinned and they caused the Israelites to sin. They worshipped worthless idols, and this made the LORD angry.

¹⁴The rest of what Elah did is written in the book, *The History of the Kings of Israel.*

¹⁵Zimri became king of Israel during the twenty-seventh year that Asa was king of Judah. Zimri ruled in Tirzah for only seven days. This is what happened: The army of Israel was at Gibbethon, which was under Philistine control. ¹⁶Omri was the commander of the army of Israel. The men in the camp heard that Zimri had made secret plans against King Elah and killed him. So in the camp all the soldiers made Omri the new king. ¹⁷Then Omri and all the soldiers of Israel left Gibbethon and went to Tirzah. They surrounded the city and attacked it. ¹⁸When Zimri saw the city had been captured, he ran to the palace fortress, but the soldiers burned it down with him still in it. ¹⁹So Zimri died because he sinned and did what the LORD said was wrong, just as Jeroboam did when he caused the Israelites to sin.

²⁰The story about Zimri's secret plans and the other things that he did are written in the book, *The History of the Kings of Israel.*

Omri, King of Israel

²¹Then the Israelites were divided. Half of the people followed Tibni the son of Ginath and wanted to make him king. The other half of the people followed Omri. ²²But Omri's followers

were stronger than the followers of Tibni son of Ginath. Tibni died, and Omri became king.

²³Omri became king of Israel during Asa's thirty-first year as the king of Judah. Omri ruled over Israel for 12 years. Six of those years he ruled from Tirzah. ²⁴Then Omri bought the hill of Samaria from Shemer for 6,000 pieces[a] of silver. Omri built a city on that hill. He named the city Samaria after the name of its owner, Shemer.

²⁵Omri did what the LORD said was wrong. He was worse than all the kings who were before him. ²⁶He committed all the sins that Jeroboam son of Nebat had committed when he caused the Israelites to sin. They worshipped worthless idols, and this made the LORD, the God of Israel, very angry.

²⁷The rest of the story about Omri and the great things he did are written in the book, *The History of the Kings of Israel.* ²⁸Omri died and was buried in Samaria. His son Ahab became the new king after him.

Ahab, King of Israel

²⁹Ahab son of Omri became king of Israel during the thirty-eighth year that Asa was king of Judah. Ahab ruled Israel from the town of Samaria for 22 years. ³⁰He did what the LORD said was wrong. Ahab was worse than all the kings who were before him. ³¹It was not enough for Ahab to commit the same sins that Jeroboam, son of Nebat, had done. Ahab also married Jezebel, daughter of King Ethbaal of Sidon. Then Ahab began to serve and worship Baal. ³²He built a temple and an altar in Samaria for worshipping Baal. ³³He also set up a sacred pole.[b] Ahab did more to make the LORD, the God of Israel, angry than all the other kings who were before him.

³⁴During Ahab's time, Hiel from Bethel rebuilt the town of Jericho. When Hiel started work on the city, his oldest son Abiram died. And when Hiel built the gates of the city, his youngest son Segub died. This happened just as the LORD said it would happen when he spoke through Joshua son of Nun.[c]

Elijah and the Time Without Rain

17 Elijah was a prophet from the town of Tishbe in Gilead. He said to King Ahab, "I serve the LORD, the God of Israel. By his power, I promise that no dew or rain will fall for the next few years. The rain will fall only when I command it to fall."

²Then the LORD said to Elijah, ³"Leave this place and go east. Hide near Kerith Ravine, east of the Jordan River. ⁴You can get your water from that stream, and I have commanded ravens to bring food to you there." ⁵So Elijah did what the LORD told him to do. He went to live near Kerith Ravine, east of the Jordan River. ⁶Ravens brought Elijah food every morning and every evening, and he drank water from the stream.

⁷There was no rain, so after a while the stream became dry. ⁸Then the LORD said to Elijah, ⁹"Go to Zarephath in Sidon and stay there. There is a widow there that I have commanded to take care of you."

¹⁰So Elijah went to Zarephath. He went to the town gate and saw a woman there gathering wood for a fire. She was a widow. Elijah said to her, "Would you bring me a small cup of water to drink?" ¹¹As she was going to get the water, Elijah said, "Bring me a piece of bread too, please."

¹²The woman answered, "I promise you, before the LORD your God, that I have nothing but a handful of flour in a jar and a little bit of olive oil in a jug. I came here to gather a few pieces of wood for a fire to cook our last meal. My son and I will eat it and then die from hunger."

¹³Elijah said to the woman, "Don't worry. Go home and cook your food as you said. But first make a small piece of bread from the flour that you have and bring it to me. Then cook some for yourself and your son. ¹⁴The LORD, the God of Israel, says, 'That jar of flour will never be empty and the jug will always have oil in it. This will continue until the day the LORD sends rain to the land.'"

¹⁵So the woman went home and did what Elijah told her to do. And Elijah, the woman and her son had enough food for a long time. ¹⁶The jar of flour and the jug of oil were never empty. This happened just as the LORD had said through Elijah.

¹⁷Some time later the woman's son became sick. He grew worse and worse until he stopped breathing. ¹⁸Then the woman said to Elijah, "You are a man of God. Can you help me? Or did you come here only to remind me of my sins and to make my son die?"

¹⁹Elijah said to her, "Give me your son." He took the boy from her and carried him upstairs. He laid him on the bed in the room where he was staying. ²⁰Then Elijah cried out to the LORD. He said, "LORD my God, this widow is letting me stay in her house. Will you do this terrible thing to her? Will you cause her son to die?" ²¹Then Elijah lay on top of the boy three times. He prayed, "LORD my God, let this boy live again!"

²²The LORD answered Elijah's prayer. The boy began breathing again and was alive. ²³Elijah

---

[a] 16:24 *6,000 pieces* Literally, "2 *talents*".
[b] 16:33 *sacred pole* People used these to worship false gods.
[c] 16:34 *This happened . . . Joshua son of Nun* See Josh. 6:26.

carried the boy downstairs, gave him to his mother, and said, "Look, your son is alive!"

²⁴The woman answered, "Now I know that you really are a man from God. I know that the LORD really speaks through you!"

Elijah and the Prophets of Baal

18 During the third year that no rain fell, the LORD said to Elijah, "Go and meet with King Ahab, and I will make it rain." ²So Elijah went to meet with Ahab.

The famine was very bad in Samaria. ³So King Ahab told Obadiah to come to him. Obadiah was the man in charge of the king's palace. (Obadiah was a true follower of the LORD. ⁴Once when Jezebel was killing all the LORD's prophets, Obadiah hid 100 prophets in two caves. He put 50 prophets in one cave and 50 prophets in another cave. Then he brought them food and water.) ⁵King Ahab said to Obadiah, "Come with me. We will look at every spring and every stream in the land. We will see if we can find enough grass to keep our horses and mules alive. Then we will not have to kill our animals." ⁶They decided where each of them would go to look for water. Ahab went in one direction by himself, and Obadiah went in another direction by himself. ⁷As Obadiah was walking along the road by himself, he looked up, and there was Elijah. Obadiah recognized him and bowed down to show his respect. He said, "Elijah? Is it really you, master?"

⁸Elijah answered, "Yes, it is me. Now, go and tell your master, the king, that I am here."

⁹Obadiah said, "If I tell Ahab that I know where you are, he will kill me! I have done nothing wrong to you. Why do you want me to die? ¹⁰As surely as the LORD your God lives, the king has been looking for you everywhere. He has sent people to every country to find you. He even made the rulers of those countries swear that you were not there. ¹¹Now you want me to go and tell him that you are here! ¹²If I go and tell King Ahab that you are here, the Spirit of the LORD might carry you away. Then when King Ahab comes here and cannot find you, he will kill me! I have followed the LORD since I was a boy. ¹³Surely you have heard what I did when Jezebel was killing the LORD's prophets. I hid 100 of the LORD's prophets in caves. I put 50 prophets in one cave and 50 in another. I brought them food and water. ¹⁴Now you want me to go and tell the king that you are here. The king will kill me!"

¹⁵Elijah answered, "I serve the LORD All-Powerful. As surely as he lives, I promise that I will stand before the king today."

¹⁶So Obadiah went to King Ahab and told him where Elijah was. King Ahab went to meet Elijah.

¹⁷When Ahab saw Elijah he said, "Is that really you, the troublemaker of Israel?"

¹⁸Elijah answered, "I have not made trouble for Israel. You and your father's family caused all the problems when you stopped obeying the LORD's commands and began following the false gods. ¹⁹Now tell all the people of Israel to meet me at Mount Carmel. Also bring the 450 prophets of Baal and the 400 prophets of the goddess Asherah that Queen Jezebel supports."ᵃ

²⁰So Ahab called all the Israelites and those prophets to Mount Carmel. ²¹Elijah came to all the people and said, "You must decide what you are going to do. How long will you keep jumping from one side to the other? If the LORD is the true God, follow him. But if Baal is the true God, then follow him!"

The people said nothing. ²²So Elijah said, "I am the only prophet of the LORD here, but there are 450 prophets of Baal. ²³So bring us two bulls. Let the prophets of Baal have one bull. Let them kill it, cut it into pieces and then put the meat on the wood. But don't start the fire. I will do the same with the other bull, and I will not start the fire either. ²⁴Prophets of Baal, pray to your god, and I will pray to the LORD. Whichever god answers the prayer and starts the fire is the true God."

All the people agreed that this was a good idea.

²⁵Then Elijah said to the prophets of Baal, "There are many of you, so you go first. Choose a bull and prepare it, but don't start your fire."

²⁶So the prophets took the bull that was given to them and prepared it. They started praying to Baal and prayed until noon. They said, "Baal, please answer us!" But there was no sound. No one answered. Then they began jumping around on the altar they had built.

²⁷At noon Elijah began to make fun of them. He said, "If Baal really is a god, maybe you should pray louder! Maybe he is busy. Maybe he is thinking about something, or maybe he stepped out for a moment! He could be sleeping! Maybe you should pray louder and wake him up!" ²⁸So the prophets prayed louder. They cut themselves with swords and spears. (This was the way they worshipped.) They cut themselves until they were bleeding all over. ²⁹The afternoon passed but the fire still had not started. The prophets were out of control and continued to behave this way until the time came for the evening sacrifice. But nothing happened—there was no answer from Baal. There was no sound. There was no one listening.

³⁰Then Elijah said to all the people, "Now come here." So they gathered around Elijah. The

---

ᵃ **18:19 Queen Jezebel supports** Literally, "Those prophets eat at Jezebel's table."

WAKE-UP CALLS

Elijah is one of the Bible's most famous prophets, even though we don't have whole books of his prophecies in our Bibles like, say, Isaiah or Jeremiah. In fact all we know about him is contained in 1 and 2 Kings.

But like all the Bible's prophets, he brought a challenge to the Israelites – to remind them of their identity and their responsibilities as God's special people. And Elijah had to be courageous, often taking very unpopular messages to people who didn't want to listen.

DIG IN

READ 1 Kings 18:1–2,17–40

- What's the reason for the famine in Israel (v.18)?
- How does Elijah challenge the people (v.21)?
- Why does Elijah set up the two altars?

Elijah was a prophet sent by God to the northern kingdom, which at this time was ruled by King Ahab. It wasn't a happy time for the land as there had been no rain for about three years.

What's the reason for the drought? Well, Ahab has it wrong. He's blaming Elijah, who speaks for the God of Israel. So Elijah sets him straight. It is the worship of false gods (including Baal) that's to blame.

Elijah very dramatically puts God to a public test: it's God versus the false god Baal in a barbecue cook-off. He hopes that this will once and for all turn his people from the idolatry that God hates so much.

- What kind of god is Baal, according to the story (v.28)?
- What does Elijah do to his altar (vv.30–35)?
- Why does Elijah go to such lengths?

Elijah's motives are pure. He wants to honour God (v.32), prove his power and discredit the prophets of Baal. God comes through for him and the people see once again that the Lord is the true God. They bow down to worship him.

DIG THROUGH

- Look again at the behaviour of the prophets of Baal (vv.28–29). Can you see any connection between their actions and those of many young people, perhaps even some of your friends, today spending loads of time, money and effort trying to get approval, security and love? Is there any sense that they are trying to get a response from a "god" who isn't listening?
- Everyone worships some sort of god, whether they realize it or not. How much respect does Elijah have for those worshipping a god other than the real God – the Lord, the God of Israel (v.27)? Look again at the behaviour of the prophets of Baal (vv.28–29). What might it feel like to worship a false god? How hard might it be? What benefit would we get in the end? What do verses 30–39 tell us about the power of the real God and the importance of listening to his words?

DIG DEEPER

- Elijah and the other prophets do sometimes get a response from the people, like on this occasion (v.39). But their message is soon lost. As you read about the prophets you will see that God gives his people lots of warnings, but they rarely listen for long.
- Elijah's fiery personality and fearless preaching were legendary in Israel's history. So when another preacher emerges in Nazareth in Jesus' day, it's no surprise he attracts a comparison. Do you know who we're talking about? Clue: look up Luke 1:5–17 to read the prophecy about the birth of one man which says he will be "powerful like Elijah and will have the same spirit".

LORD's altar had been torn down, so Elijah repaired it. ³¹Elijah found twelve stones. There was one stone for each of the twelve tribes. These twelve tribes were named for the twelve sons of Jacob, the man who the LORD had named Israel. ³²Elijah used these stones to repair the altar to honour the LORD. He dug a small ditch around the altar. It was wide enough and deep enough to hold about 14 litres*a* of water. ³³Then Elijah put the wood on the altar. He cut the bull into pieces and laid the pieces on the wood. ³⁴Then he said, "Fill four jars with water. Pour the water on the pieces of meat and on the wood." Then Elijah said, "Do it again." Then he said, "Do it a third time." ³⁵The water ran down off the altar and filled the ditch.

³⁶At about the time for the evening sacrifice, the prophet Elijah approached the altar and prayed, "LORD, the God of Abraham, Isaac and Jacob, I ask you now to prove that you are the God of Israel and that I am your servant. Show these people that it was you who commanded me to do all these things. ³⁷LORD, answer my prayer. Show these people that you, LORD, are God and that you are the one who is bringing them back to you."

³⁸Then fire came down from the LORD and burned the sacrifice, the wood, the stones and the ground around the altar. Then it dried up all the water in the ditch. ³⁹All the people saw this happen and bowed down to the ground and began saying, "The LORD is God! The LORD is God!"

⁴⁰Then Elijah said, "Get the prophets of Baal! Don't let any of them escape!" So the people captured all the prophets. Then Elijah led them down to Kishon Creek and killed them all.

The Rain Comes Again

⁴¹Then Elijah said to King Ahab, "Now go, eat and drink. A heavy rain is coming." ⁴²So King Ahab went to eat. At the same time Elijah climbed to the top of Mount Carmel. At the top of the mountain, Elijah bent down. He put his head between his knees. ⁴³Then Elijah said to his servant, "Go up higher and look towards the sea."

The servant went and looked. He came back and said, "I saw nothing." Elijah told him to go and look again. This happened seven times. ⁴⁴The seventh time, the servant came back and said, "I saw a small cloud the size of a man's fist that was coming in from the sea."

Elijah told the servant, "Go and tell King Ahab to get his chariot ready and go home now. If he does not leave now, the rain will stop him."

⁴⁵After a short time the sky was covered with dark clouds. The wind began to blow, and a heavy rain began to fall. Ahab got into his chariot and started back to Jezreel. ⁴⁶The power of the LORD came to Elijah. He used his belt to hold up the bottom of his robe away from his feet. Then he ran ahead of King Ahab all the way to Jezreel.

Elijah at Mount Horeb (Sinai)

19 King Ahab told Jezebel everything that Elijah had done and how Elijah had killed all the prophets of Baal with a sword. ²So Jezebel sent a messenger to Elijah and said, "I swear that by this time tomorrow, you will be just as dead as those prophets. If I don't succeed, may the gods do the same or worse to me."

³When Elijah heard this, he was afraid. So he ran away to save his life. He took his servant with him, and they went to Beersheba in Judah. Then Elijah left his servant in Beersheba ⁴and walked for a whole day into the desert. Then he sat down under a bush and asked to die. He said, "I have had enough, LORD! Take my life. I am no better than my ancestors."

> ## INSIGHT
>
> *Having just called down fire from heaven it might seem strange that Elijah is so scared of Jezebel. However, the Old Testament shows that many of the prophets were most open to attack right after winning a major battle for God.*
>
> **1 Kings 19:3–4**

⁵Then Elijah lay down under the bush and went to sleep. An angel came to him and touched him. The angel said, "Get up and eat!" ⁶Elijah looked around, and by his head there was a cake that had been baked over coals and a jar of water. He ate and drank and then went back to sleep.

⁷Later the angel of the LORD came to him again, touched him, and said, "Get up and eat! If you don't, you will not be strong enough to make the long journey." ⁸So Elijah got up. He ate and drank and felt strong. Then Elijah walked for 40 days and nights to Mount Horeb, the mountain of God. ⁹There Elijah went into a cave and spent the night.

Then the LORD said to him, "Elijah, why are you here?"

¹⁰Elijah answered, "LORD God All-Powerful, I have always served you the best I can, but the Israelites have broken their agreement with you. They have destroyed your altars and killed your

---

a **18:32** *about 14 litres* Literally, "2 *seahs* of seed".

prophets. I am the only prophet left alive, and now they are trying to kill me!"

[11]Then the LORD said to Elijah, "Go, stand in front of me on the mountain. I, the LORD, will pass by you."[a] Then a very strong wind blew. The wind caused the mountains to break apart. It broke large rocks in front of the LORD. But that wind was not the LORD. After the wind, there was an earthquake. But that earthquake was not the LORD. [12]After the earthquake, there was a fire. But that fire was not the LORD. After the fire, there was a quiet, gentle voice.[b]

[13]When Elijah heard the voice, he used his coat to cover his face and went to the entrance of the cave and stood there. Then a voice said to him, "Elijah, why are you here?"

[14]Elijah said, "LORD God All-Powerful, I have always served you the best I can, but the Israelites broke their agreement with you. They destroyed your altars and killed your prophets. I am the only prophet left alive, and now they are trying to kill me."

[15]The LORD said, "Go back. Take the road that leads to the desert around Damascus. Go into Damascus and anoint Hazael as king over Aram. [16]Then anoint Jehu son of Nimshi as king over Israel. Next, anoint Elisha son of Shaphat from Abel Meholah. He will be the prophet who takes your place. [17]Jehu will kill anyone who escapes Hazael's sword, and Elisha will kill anyone who escapes from Jehu's sword. [18]I still have 7,000 people in Israel who have never bowed down to Baal or kissed that idol."

Elisha Becomes a Prophet

[19]So Elijah left that place and went to find Elisha son of Shaphat. Elisha was ploughing a field with a team of oxen. He had 11 other men in front of him, each ploughing with one of his teams of oxen. Elijah went to Elisha and put his coat[c] on Elisha. [20]Elisha immediately left his oxen and ran after Elijah. Elisha said, "Let me kiss my mother and father goodbye. Then I will follow you."

Elijah answered, "You can do that. I will not stop you."[d]

[21]Elisha turned away from him and went back. He killed the oxen and used the yoke for firewood. He boiled the meat, gave it to the people, and they all ate together. Then Elisha went to follow Elijah and became his helper.

Ben-Hadad and Ahab Go to War

20 King Ben-Hadad of Aram gathered his army together. There were 32 kings with him and many horses and chariots. They surrounded Samaria and attacked it. [2]The king sent messengers to King Ahab of Israel who was inside the city. [3]The message was, "Ben-Hadad says, 'Your silver and your gold are mine, and so are the best of your wives and children.'"

[4]The king of Israel answered, "Yes, my lord and king, I am yours now, and everything I have belongs to you."

[5]Then the messengers came again to Ahab. They said, "Ben-Hadad says, 'I told you before that all your silver and gold and your wives and children belong to me. So give them to me! [6]Tomorrow I will send my men to search through your house and through the houses of your officials. Give my men all your valuables, and they will bring them back to me.'"

[7]So King Ahab called a meeting of all the leaders of his country and said, "Look, Ben-Hadad is looking for trouble. First he told me that I must give him my wives and children and my silver and gold. I agreed to give them to him."

[8]But the leaders and all the people said, "Don't obey him or do what he says."

[9]So Ahab sent a message to Ben-Hadad that said, "I will do what you said at first, but I cannot obey your second command."

King Ben-Hadad's men carried the message to the king. [10]Then they came back with another message from Ben-Hadad that said, "I will completely destroy Samaria. I promise that there will be nothing left of that city! There will not be enough of that city left for my men to find any souvenirs[e] to take home. May the gods destroy me if I don't do this!"

[11]King Ahab answered, "Tell Ben-Hadad that the man who puts on his armour should not boast as much as the man who lives long enough to take it off."

[12]King Ben-Hadad was drinking in his tent with the other rulers when the messengers came back and gave him the message from King Ahab. King Ben-Hadad commanded his men to prepare to attack the city, so the men moved into their places for the battle.

[13]Then a prophet went to King Ahab and said, "King Ahab, the LORD says to you, 'Do you see that great army? I will defeat that army

---

[a] **19:11** *Go, stand . . . you* This is like the time God appeared to Moses. See Exod. 33:12–23.
[b] **19:12** *voice* Or "sound".
[c] **19:19** *coat* A special robe that prophets wore. Elijah put his coat on Elisha to show that Elisha would take his place as a prophet.
[d] **19:20** *I will not stop you* Literally, "What have I done to you?" or "What will I do to you?"
[e] **20:10** *souvenirs* Things that help people remember places they have been. Literally, the Hebrew text has "handfuls of dust".

for you today. Then you will know that I am the LORD.'"

¹⁴Ahab said, "Who will you use to defeat them?"

The prophet answered, "The LORD says, 'The young men who carry the weapons for the government officials.'"

Then the king asked, "Who should command the main army?"

The prophet answered, "You will."

¹⁵So Ahab gathered the young helpers of the government officials. There were 232 of these young men. Then the king called together the army of Israel. The total number was 7,000.

¹⁶King Ahab began his attack at noon, while King Ben-Hadad and the 32 kings were drinking and getting drunk in their tents. ¹⁷The young helpers went out first. King Ben-Hadad's men told him that some soldiers had come out of Samaria. ¹⁸So Ben-Hadad said, "They might be coming to fight, or they might be coming to ask for peace. Capture them alive."

¹⁹The young men of King Ahab were the first to come out, but the rest of the army of Israel was following them. ²⁰Each of the men of Israel killed the man who had come against him. So the men from Aram began to run away and the army of Israel chased them. King Ben-Hadad escaped on a horse with the chariots. ²¹King Ahab led the army and attacked all the horses and chariots. So King Ahab made the Arameans suffer a great defeat.

²²Then the prophet went to King Ahab and said, "The king of Aram will come back to fight again next spring. So go back and strengthen your army and make careful plans to defend yourself against him."

Ben-Hadad Attacks Again

²³King Ben-Hadad's officers said to him, "The gods of Israel are mountain gods. We fought in a mountain area, so the Israelites won. If we fight them on level ground, we will win. ²⁴Also, don't let the 32 kings command the armies. Put your commanders in charge of the armies. ²⁵Let's gather an army like the one that was destroyed. Gather as many men, horses and chariots as before, and fight the Israelites on level ground. Then we will win." Ben-Hadad followed their advice and did what they said.

²⁶So in the spring, Ben-Hadad gathered the men of Aram and went to Aphek to fight against Israel.

²⁷The Israelites also prepared for war and went to fight the army of Aram. They made their camp opposite the camp of Aram. The Aramean soldiers filled the land, but Israel's army looked like two small flocks of goats.

²⁸A man of God came to the king of Israel with this message: "The LORD said, 'The people of Aram said that I, the LORD, am a god of the mountains and not a god of the valleys. So I will let you defeat this great army. Then you will all know that I am the LORD, wherever you are!'"

²⁹The armies were camped opposite each other for seven days. On the seventh day the battle began. The Israelites killed 100,000 Aramean soldiers in one day. ³⁰The survivors ran away to the city of Aphek. The wall of the city fell on 27,000 of those soldiers. Ben-Hadad also ran away to the city and hid in a room. ³¹His servants said to him, "We heard that the kings of Israel are merciful. Let's dress in rough cloth with ropes on our heads.ᵃ Then let's go to the king of Israel. Maybe he will let us live."

³²They dressed in rough cloth with ropes on their heads. They came to the king of Israel. They said, "Your servant, Ben-Hadad, says, 'Please let me live.'"

Ahab said, "Is he still alive? He is my brother."ᵇ

³³Ben-Hadad's men wanted King Ahab to say something to show that he would not kill King Ben-Hadad. When Ahab called Ben-Hadad his brother, the advisors quickly said, "Yes! Ben-Hadad is your brother."

Ahab said, "Bring him to me." So Ben-Hadad came to King Ahab. King Ahab asked him to get in the chariot with him.

³⁴Ben-Hadad said to him, "Ahab, I will give you the towns that my father took from your father. And you can put shops in Damascus, as my father did in Samaria."

Ahab answered, "If you agree to this, I will let you go free." So the two kings made a peace agreement. Then King Ahab let King Ben-Hadad go free.

A Prophet Speaks Against Ahab

³⁵One of the prophets told another prophet, "Hit me!" He said that because the LORD had commanded it. But the other prophet refused to hit him. ³⁶So the first prophet said, "You did not obey the LORD's command. So a lion will kill you when you leave this place." When the second prophet left, a lion killed him.

³⁷The first prophet went to another man and said, "Hit me!"

This man hit him and hurt the prophet. ³⁸So the prophet wrapped his face with a cloth. This way no one could see who he was. The prophet went and waited for the king by the road.

ᵃ **20:31** *rough cloth . . . heads* This showed that they were being humble and that they wanted to surrender.
ᵇ **20:32** *brother* People who signed peace agreements often called each other "brother". It was as if they were one family.

³⁹When King Ahab came by, the prophet said to him, "I went to fight in the battle. One of our men brought an enemy soldier to me. The man said, 'Guard this man. If he runs away, you will have to give your life in his place or you will have to pay a fine of 3,000 pieces*ª* of silver.' ⁴⁰While I was busy doing other things, the man ran away."

The king of Israel answered, "You admitted that you are guilty, so you know the answer. You must do what the man said."

⁴¹Then the prophet quickly took the cloth from his face, and the king of Israel saw that he was one of the prophets. ⁴²Then the prophet said to the king, "The LORD says to you, 'You set free the man I said should die. So you will take his place—you and your people will die!'"

⁴³Then the king went back home to Samaria. He was worried and upset.

Naboth's Vineyard

21 There was a vineyard near King Ahab's palace in Samaria. A man from Jezreel named Naboth owned it. ²One day Ahab said to Naboth, "Give me your vineyard that is near my palace. I want to make it a vegetable garden. I will give you a better vineyard in its place. Or, if you prefer, I will pay you for it."

³Naboth answered, "By the LORD, I will never give my land to you. This land belongs to my family."

⁴So Ahab went home angry and upset because Naboth told him, "I will not give you my family's land." Ahab went to bed, turned away from everyone, and refused to eat.

⁵His wife Jezebel went to him and asked him, "Why are you upset? Why do you refuse to eat?"

⁶Ahab answered, "I asked Naboth from Jezreel to give me his vineyard. I told him that I would pay him the full price. Or, if he preferred, I would give him another vineyard. But he refused to give it to me."

⁷Jezebel answered, "But you are the king over Israel! Get out of bed and eat something, and you will feel better. I will get Naboth's vineyard for you."

⁸Then Jezebel wrote some letters. She signed Ahab's name on them and used his seal to seal the letters. Then she sent them to the leaders and important men who lived in the same town as Naboth. ⁹This is what the letter said:

"Announce that there will be a day of fasting when the people will eat nothing. Then call all the people of the town together for a meeting. At the meeting we will talk about Naboth. ¹⁰Find some men who will tell lies about Naboth. They should say that they heard Naboth speak against the king and against God. Then take Naboth out of the city and kill him with stones."

¹¹So the leaders and important men of Jezreel obeyed the command. ¹²The leaders announced that there would be a day when all the people would eat nothing. On that day they called all the people together for a meeting. They put Naboth in a special place before the people. ¹³Then two men told the people that they heard Naboth speak against God and the king. So the people carried Naboth out of the city and killed him with stones. ¹⁴Then the leaders sent a message to Jezebel that said: "Naboth has been killed."

¹⁵When Jezebel heard this, she said to Ahab, "Naboth is dead. Now you can go and take the vineyard that you wanted." ¹⁶So Ahab went to the vineyard and took it for his own.

¹⁷Then the LORD spoke to Elijah, the prophet from Tishbe: ¹⁸"Go to King Ahab in Samaria. He will be at Naboth's vineyard. He is there to take the vineyard as his own. ¹⁹Tell Ahab that I, the LORD, say to him, 'Ahab! You killed the man Naboth and now you are taking his land. So I, the LORD, tell you this: Where the dogs licked up the blood of Naboth, they will lick up your blood as well.'"

²⁰So Elijah went to Ahab. When Ahab saw him, he said, "Well, my enemy has found me again!"

Elijah answered, "Yes, I found you, because you have again sold yourself to do what the LORD says is evil. ²¹So this is what he says to you: 'I will make something bad happen to you. I will kill you and every male in your family. ²²I will destroy your family just as I destroyed the families of King Jeroboam son of Nebat and King Baasha. I will do this to you because you have made me angry and you have caused the Israelites to sin.' ²³The LORD also says this about your wife Jezebel: 'Dogs will eat the body of Jezebel by the wall of the city of Jezreel. ²⁴As for the family of Ahab, whoever dies in the city will be eaten by dogs, and whoever dies in the fields will be eaten by birds.'"

²⁵So Ahab sold himself out to do what the LORD says is evil. There is no one who did as much evil as Ahab and his wife Jezebel, who caused him to do these things. ²⁶Ahab committed the terrible sin of worshipping those filthy idols, just as the Amorites did. And that is why the LORD took the land from them and gave it to the Israelites.

²⁷When Ahab heard what Elijah said, he tore his clothes to show how sad he was. Then he put on sackcloth and refused to eat. He even slept in these clothes. He was very sad and upset.

ª **20:39** *3,000 pieces* Literally, "1 *talent*".

²⁸The LORD said to the prophet Elijah from Tishbe, ²⁹"Look, Ahab has humbled himself before me. So I will not make that disaster happen during his lifetime. I will wait until his son is king. Then I will destroy his family."

Micaiah Warns King Ahab

22 For the next two years there was peace between Israel and Aram. ²Then during the third year, King Jehoshaphat of Judah went to visit King Ahab of Israel.

³Ahab asked his officials, "Remember when the king of Aram took Ramoth Gilead from us? That city is ours, so why have we done nothing to get it back?" ⁴So Ahab asked King Jehoshaphat, "Will you join with us to go and fight the Arameans at Ramoth Gilead?"

Jehoshaphat answered, "Yes, you and I will be as one—my men and my horses will be as yours. ⁵But first let's ask the LORD for advice."

⁶So Ahab called a meeting of the prophets. There were about 400 prophets at that time. Ahab asked the prophets, "Should I go and attack the Arameans at Ramoth Gilead or not?"

The prophets answered Ahab, "Yes, because the Lord will let you defeat Ramoth Gilead."

⁷But Jehoshaphat said, "Doesn't the LORD have another prophet here? Let's ask him the same question."

⁸King Ahab answered, "Yes, there is another prophet. His name is Micaiah son of Imlah. But I hate him because he will not say anything good about me when he speaks for the LORD. He always says things that I don't like."

Jehoshaphat said, "The king should not say that!"

⁹So King Ahab told one of his officers to go and find Micaiah.

¹⁰At that time the two kings were sitting on their thrones, with their royal robes on, at the judgement place near the gates of Samaria. All the prophets were standing before them, prophesying. ¹¹One of the prophets was named Zedekiah son of Kenaanah. Zedekiah made some iron horns[a] and said to Ahab, "The LORD says, 'You will use these iron horns to fight against the army of Aram. You will defeat them and destroy them.'" ¹²All the other prophets agreed with Zedekiah and said, "Your army should march now to go and fight against the Arameans at Ramoth Gilead. You will win the battle. The LORD will let you defeat them."

¹³While this was happening, the officer went to find Micaiah. When he found him, the officer told him, "All the other prophets have said that the king will succeed, so you should say the same thing."

¹⁴But Micaiah answered, "As surely as the LORD lives, I can say only what the LORD says."

¹⁵Micaiah went and stood before King Ahab. The king asked him, "Micaiah, should we go and attack the Arameans at Ramoth Gilead or not?"

Micaiah answered, "Yes, go and be successful! The LORD will let you take the city."

¹⁶But Ahab answered, "How many times do I have to tell you? Tell me the truth. What does the LORD say?"

¹⁷So Micaiah answered, "I can see the army of Israel scattered all over the hills, like sheep with no one to lead them. This is what the LORD says, 'These men have no leaders. Let them go home in peace.'"

¹⁸Then Ahab said to Jehoshaphat, "See, I told you! This prophet never says anything good about me. He always says something bad."

¹⁹But Micaiah said, "Listen to this message from the LORD: I saw the LORD sitting on his throne. All of heaven's army was standing around him, some on his left side and some on his right side. ²⁰The LORD said, 'Which of you will go and fool Ahab into attacking the Arameans at Ramoth Gilead so that he will be killed?' The angels discussed many different plans. ²¹Then a spirit[b] went and stood before the LORD and said, 'I will fool him!' The LORD asked, 'How will you do it?' ²²The spirit answered, 'I will go to Ahab's prophets and cause them to tell lies.' So the Lord said, 'Yes, that will fool Ahab. Go out and do that.'

²³"So that is what has happened here. The LORD made your prophets lie to you. The LORD himself decided to bring this disaster to you."

²⁴Then the prophet Zedekiah went to Micaiah and hit him on the face. Zedekiah said, "How is it that the Spirit of the LORD left me to speak through you?"

²⁵Micaiah answered, "Look, what I said will happen! And you will see it one day when you are in a secret room somewhere hiding."

²⁶Then King Ahab ordered one of his officers to arrest Micaiah. Ahab said, "Arrest him and take him to Amon the governor of the city and prince Joash. ²⁷Tell them to put Micaiah in prison. Give him nothing but bread and water to eat. Keep him there until I come home from the battle."

²⁸Micaiah said, "Listen to me, everyone! Ahab, if you come back alive from the battle, the LORD has not spoken through me."

The Battle at Ramoth Gilead

²⁹King Ahab of Israel and King Jehoshaphat of Judah went to fight the Arameans at Ramoth Gilead. ³⁰Ahab said to Jehoshaphat, "Disguise yourself when you go into battle, but wear your

---

[a] 22:11 *iron horns* These were a symbol of great strength.
[b] 22:21 *a spirit* Or "the Spirit".

own clothes. And I will disguise myself." The king of Israel went into battle dressed like an ordinary soldier.

³¹The king of Aram had 32 chariot commanders. He gave them this command, "Don't go after anyone except the king of Israel, no matter how important they are." ³²When the commanders saw King Jehoshaphat, they thought he was the king of Israel, and so they went to kill him. Jehoshaphat started shouting. ³³When the commanders saw that he was not King Ahab, they stopped chasing him.

³⁴Then a soldier in the distance pulled back as far as he could on his bow and shot an arrow into the air. The arrow happened to hit the king of Israel in a small hole where his armour was fastened together. King Ahab said to his chariot driver, "I've been hit! Turn the chariot around and take me off the battlefield!"

³⁵The armies continued to fight while King Ahab was propped up in his chariot. He was leaning against the sides of the chariot, looking out towards the Arameans. His blood ran down onto the floor of the chariot. Later in the evening, he died. ³⁶At sunset all the Israelites cheered when they were told to go home. So they all went back to their home towns.

³⁷And that is how King Ahab died. Some men carried his body to Samaria and buried him there. ³⁸They took his chariot to the large pool in Samaria to clean it. The dogs licked up Ahab's blood while the prostitutes washed the chariot. This happened just as the Lord said it would.

³⁹The rest of what King Ahab did during the time he ruled is written in the book, *The History of the Kings of Israel*. That book tells about all the cities he built and about all the ivory that he used to decorate his palace. ⁴⁰Ahab died and was buried with his ancestors. His son Ahaziah became the next king after him.

Summary of Jehoshaphat's Rule

⁴¹Jehoshaphat son of Asa became the king of Judah in Ahab's fourth year as king of Israel.

⁴²Jehoshaphat was 35 years old when he became king, and he ruled in Jerusalem for 25 years. His mother was Azubah, the daughter of Shilhi. ⁴³Like his father Asa, Jehoshaphat was good and did everything that the Lord wanted, but he did not destroy the high places. The people continued offering sacrifices and burning incense there.

⁴⁴Jehoshaphat made a peace agreement with the king of Israel. ⁴⁵Jehoshaphat was very brave and fought many wars. The rest of what he did is written in the book, *The History of the Kings of Judah*.

⁴⁶Jehoshaphat forced all the men and women who sold their bodies for sex to leave the places of worship. They had served in these places of worship while his father Asa was king.

⁴⁷In those days Edom did not have a king; it was ruled by a governor who was chosen by the king of Judah.

⁴⁸King Jehoshaphat built some cargo ships. He wanted the ships to sail to Ophir for gold, but they never set sail—they were destroyed in their home port at Ezion Geber. ⁴⁹Then King Ahaziah of Israel offered to put some of his own sailors with Jehoshaphat's men,ᵃ but Jehoshaphat refused to accept his help.

⁵⁰Jehoshaphat died and was buried with his ancestors in the City of David. Then his son Jehoram became the next king.

Ahaziah, King of Israel

⁵¹Ahaziah was the son of Ahab. He became king of Israel during the seventeenth year that King Jehoshaphat ruled Judah. Ahaziah ruled in Samaria for two years. ⁵²He sinned against the Lord just as his parents, Ahab and Jezebel, had done. He caused Israel to sin just as Jeroboam son of Nebat had done. ⁵³Ahaziah served the false god Baal and worshipped him, just as his father had done before him. He did all the things that his father had done to make the Lord, the God of Israel, angry.

ᵃ **22:49 King Ahaziah . . . men** Jehoshaphat controlled the port of Ezion Geber which was Israel's only way to the Red Sea and the coasts of Africa, the Arabian Peninsula and the coasts leading to the Persian Gulf and India. Ahaziah thought he could get control of that area by "helping" Jehoshaphat.

Who
We don't know who wrote the book of Kings. But we know that he worked from a wide range of sources and was familiar with Old Testament books such as Deuteronomy.

 When
Kings was probably written sometime after 561 BC, when the Jews were in exile in Babylon.

 What
The second book of Kings continues the story of the long plunge to disaster. It begins with the departure of Elijah – taken away from earth in a manner that convinced the Jews that he would one day return to them. (In Jesus' day the people thought that John the Baptist was Elijah, come back to earth.)

Elijah is succeeded by Elisha, but even a prophet as great as him can't bring the nations back to the straight and narrow. After Elisha departs from the scene, Israel and Judah pretty much go into free fall.

King after king ignores God and follows false and evil gods. Despite the many warnings from the prophets, they refuse to change their ways. They're not all bad though. Among the thirty-six or so kings of Judah and Israel after Solomon, there are a couple of glimmers of hope in the form of King Hezekiah and King Josiah. However, they're more or less the only good ones. (And let's face it, two out of thirty-six is not a good ratio.)

The first kingdom to fall is the northern kingdom of Israel. In 722 BC the Assyrians invade and completely conquer the kingdom. The capital city of Samaria is demolished and all the people are taken into captivity. They are never heard of again.

Judah, the southern kingdom, staggers on for another 150 years or so. But in 586 BC another huge and powerful empire – the Babylonian – invades and systematically dismantles the entire country. Jerusalem is completely destroyed and the majority of the population taken away to Babylon.

During this period prophets such as Isaiah, Jeremiah, Ezekiel, Amos and Hosea were at work. Although they are rarely mentioned in the text of Kings, we can supplement the tale told here by looking at the writings they left behind.

QUICK TOUR **2 KINGS**

Elijah departs 2:1–18
Naaman 5:1–27
Elisha v. the Syrian Army 6:8–23
The tears of a prophet 8:7–15
The death of Jezebel 9:1–37

Elisha dies 13:14–21
Destruction of Israel 17:1–23
Hezekiah 18:1–4; 19:1–37
King Josiah and the Law 22:1–20; 23:21–30
The destruction of Jerusalem 25:1–30

"The LORD became so angry with Jerusalem and Judah that he completely rejected them and sent them all away."

2 Kings 24:20

A Message for Ahaziah

1 After King Ahab died, Moab broke away from Israel's rule.

²One day Ahaziah was on the roof of his house in Samaria. He fell down through the wooden bars on top of his house and was badly hurt. He called messengers and told them, "Go to the priests of Baal Zebub, the god of Ekron, and ask them if I will get well from my injuries."

³But the angel of the LORD said to Elijah the Tishbite, "King Ahaziah has sent some messengers from Samaria. Go and meet those men and ask them, 'There is a God in Israel, so why are you men going to ask questions of Baal Zebub, the god of Ekron? ⁴Since you did this, the LORD says, You will not get up from your bed. You will die!'" Then Elijah left.

⁵When messengers came back to Ahaziah, he asked them, "Why did you come back so soon?"

⁶The messengers said to Ahaziah, "A man came up to meet us and told us to go back to the king who sent us and tell him what the LORD says: 'There is a God in Israel, so why did you send messengers to ask questions of Baal Zebub, the god of Ekron? Since you did this, you will not get up from your bed. You will die!'"

⁷Ahaziah said to the messengers, "What did the man look like who met you and told you this?"

⁸They answered Ahaziah, "This man was wearing a hairy coat[a] with a leather belt around his waist."

Then Ahaziah said, "That was Elijah the Tishbite."

Ahaziah Calls for Elijah

⁹Ahaziah sent a captain and 50 men to Elijah. The captain went to Elijah, who was sitting on top of a hill. The captain said to Elijah, "Man of God, the king says, 'Come down!'"

¹⁰Elijah answered the captain of 50, "If I am a man of God, let fire come down from heaven and destroy you and your 50 men!"

So fire came down from heaven and destroyed the captain and his 50 men.

¹¹Ahaziah sent another captain with 50 men to Elijah. He said to Elijah, "Man of God, the king says, 'Come down quickly!'"

¹²Elijah told the captain and his 50 men, "If I am a man of God, let fire come down from heaven and destroy you and your 50 men!"

Then God's fire came down from heaven and destroyed the captain and his 50 men.

¹³Ahaziah sent a third captain with 50 men. The third captain came to Elijah. He fell down on his knees and begged Elijah, saying to him, "Man of God, I ask you, please let my life and the lives of your 50 servants be valuable to you. ¹⁴Fire came down from heaven and destroyed the first two captains and their 50 men. But now, have mercy and let us live!"

¹⁵The LORD's angel said to Elijah, "Go with the captain. Don't be afraid of him."

So Elijah went with the captain to see King Ahaziah.

¹⁶Elijah told Ahaziah, "This is what the LORD says: 'There is a God in Israel, so why did you send messengers to ask questions of Baal Zebub, the god of Ekron? Since you did this, you will not get up from your bed. You will die!'"

Joram Takes Ahaziah's Place

¹⁷Ahaziah died, just as the LORD said through Elijah. Ahaziah did not have a son, so Joram became the new king after Ahaziah. He began to rule during the second year that Jehoram son of Jehoshaphat was the king of Judah.

¹⁸The other things that Ahaziah did are written in the book, *The History of the Kings of Israel.*

The LORD Makes Plans to Take Elijah

2 It was near the time for the LORD to take Elijah by a whirlwind up into heaven. Elijah and Elisha started to leave Gilgal.

²Elijah said to Elisha, "Please stay here, because the LORD told me to go to Bethel."

But Elisha said, "I promise, as the LORD lives and as you live, I will not leave you." So the two men went down to Bethel.

³The group of prophets[b] at Bethel came to Elisha and said to him, "Do you know that the LORD will take your master away from you today?"

Elisha said, "Yes, I know. Don't talk about it."

⁴Elijah said to Elisha, "Please stay here, because the LORD told me to go to Jericho."

But Elisha said, "I promise, as the LORD lives and as you live, I will not leave you!" So the two men went to Jericho.

⁵The group of prophets at Jericho came to Elisha and said to him, "Do you know that the LORD will take your master away from you today?"

Elisha answered, "Yes, I know. Don't talk about it."

⁶Elijah said to Elisha, "Please stay here, because the LORD told me to go to the Jordan River."

---

[a] **1:8 This man . . . coat** Or "This man was a hairy man."
[b] **2:3 group of prophets** Literally, "sons of the prophets". These were prophets and people studying to become prophets. Also in verses 5,7,15,17; 4:1,38,39,44; 5:22; 6:1,24; 9:1.

Elisha answered, "I promise, as the LORD lives and as you live, I will not leave you!" So the two men went on.

[7]There were 50 men from the group of prophets who followed them. Elijah and Elisha stopped at the Jordan River. The 50 men stood far away from Elijah and Elisha. [8]Elijah took off his coat, folded it and hit the water with it. The water separated to the right and to the left. Then Elijah and Elisha crossed the river on dry ground.

[9]After they crossed the river, Elijah said to Elisha, "What do you want me to do for you before God takes me away from you?"

Elisha said, "I ask you for a double share of your spirit on me."

[10]Elijah said, "You have asked a hard thing. If you see me when I am taken from you, it will happen. But if you don't see me when I am taken from you, it will not happen."

INSIGHT

At the end of his life Elijah was dramatically taken straight up into heaven in a whirlwind by chariots and horses of fire. Other miraculous "passings" include Enoch, who "walked with God"; Moses, whose burial place was known only to God; and, of course, Jesus, who ascended to heaven in a cloud.

2 Kings 2:11–12

The LORD Takes Elijah Into Heaven

[11]Elijah and Elisha were walking and talking together. Suddenly, some horses and a chariot came and separated Elijah from Elisha. The horses and the chariot were like fire. Then Elijah was carried up into heaven in a whirlwind.

[12]Elisha saw it, and shouted, "My father! My father! The chariot of Israel and his horses!"[a]

Elisha never saw Elijah again. Elisha grabbed his own clothes and tore them in two to show his sadness. [13]Elijah's coat had fallen to the ground, so Elisha picked it up. He went back and stood at the edge of the Jordan River. [14]He hit the water and said, "Where is the LORD, the God of Elijah?" Just as Elisha hit the water, the water separated to the right and to the left! Then Elisha crossed the river.

The Prophets Ask for Elijah

[15]When the group of prophets at Jericho saw Elisha, they said, "Elijah's spirit is now on Elisha!"

They came to meet Elisha. They bowed very low to the ground before him. [16]They said, "Look, we have 50 good men. Please let them go and look for your master. Maybe the LORD's Spirit has taken Elijah up and dropped him on some mountain or in some valley."

But Elisha answered, "No, don't send men to look for Elijah!"

[17]The group of prophets begged Elisha until he was embarrassed. Then Elisha said, "Send the men to look for Elijah."

The group of prophets sent the 50 men to look for Elijah. They looked for three days, but they could not find him. [18]So the men went to Jericho where Elisha was staying and told him. Elisha said to them, "I told you not to go."

Elisha Makes the Water Good

[19]The men of the city said to Elisha, "Sir, you can see this city is in a nice place, but the water is bad. That is why the land cannot grow crops."

[20]Elisha said, "Bring me a new bowl and put salt in it."

They brought the bowl to Elisha. [21]Then he went out to the place where the water began flowing from the ground. Elisha threw the salt into the water and said, "The LORD said, 'I am making this water pure! From now on this water will not cause any more death or keep the land from growing crops.'"

[22]The water became pure and is still good today. It happened just as Elisha had said.

Some Boys Make Fun of Elisha

[23]Elisha went from that city to Bethel. He was walking up the hill to the city, and some boys were coming down out of the city. They began making fun of him. They said, "Go away, you baldheaded man! Go away, you baldheaded man!"

[24]Elisha looked back and saw them. He asked the LORD to cause bad things to happen to them. Then two bears came out of the forest and attacked the boys. There were 42 boys ripped apart by the bears.

[25]Elisha left Bethel and went to Mount Carmel and from there he went back to Samaria.

Joram Becomes King of Israel

3 Joram son of Ahab became king over Israel at Samaria. He began to rule during Jehoshaphat's eighteenth year as king of Judah. Joram ruled for 12 years. [2]He did what the LORD said was wrong. But he was not like his father and mother, because he removed the pillar that his father had made for worshiping Baal. [3]But he continued to sin like Jeroboam son of Nebat who had caused the

---

[a] *2:12 chariot . . . horses* Or "the Chariot of Israel and his horsemen". This may mean "God and his heavenly army".

Israelites to sin. Joram did not stop the sins of Jeroboam.

Moab Breaks Away From Israel

⁴Mesha was the king of Moab. He owned many sheep. He gave the wool of 100,000 lambs and 100,000 rams to the king of Israel. ⁵But when Ahab died, the king of Moab broke away from the rule of the king of Israel.

⁶Then King Joram went out of Samaria and gathered together all the men of Israel. ⁷Joram sent messengers to Jehoshaphat, the king of Judah. Joram said, "The king of Moab has broken away from my rule. Will you go with me to fight against Moab?"

Jehoshaphat said, "Yes, I will go with you. We will join together as one army. My people will be like your people, and my horses will be like your horses."

The Three Kings Ask Elisha for Advice

⁸Jehoshaphat asked Joram, "Which way should we go?"

Joram answered, "We should go through the desert of Edom."

⁹So the king of Israel went with the king of Judah and the king of Edom. They travelled around for seven days. There was not enough water for the army or for their animals. ¹⁰Finally the king of Israel said, "I think the LORD really brought the three of us together only to let the Moabites defeat us!"

¹¹But Jehoshaphat said, "Surely one of the LORD's prophets is here. Let's ask the prophet what the LORD says we should do."

One of the servants of the king of Israel said, "Elisha son of Shaphat is here. Elisha was Elijah's servant."ᵃ

¹²Jehoshaphat said, "The LORD's word is with Elisha."

So the king of Israel, Jehoshaphat and the king of Edom went down to see Elisha.

¹³Elisha said to the king of Israel, "What do you want from me? Go to the prophets of your father and mother."

The king of Israel said to Elisha, "No, we have come to see you because the LORD called the three of us together to let the Moabites defeat us."

¹⁴Elisha said, "I respect King Jehoshaphat of Judah, and I serve the LORD All-Powerful. As surely as he lives, I came here only because of Jehoshaphat. I tell you the truth, if he were not here, I would not pay any attention to you.

I would ignore you completely. ¹⁵But now bring me someone who plays the harp."

When the person played the harp, the LORD's powerᵇ came on Elisha. ¹⁶Then Elisha said, "This is what the LORD says: 'Dig holes in the valley.' ¹⁷Yes, this is what the LORD says: 'You will not see wind or rain, but that valley will be filled with water. Then you and your cattle and other animals will have water to drink.' ¹⁸This is an easy thing for the LORD to do. He will also help you defeat the Moabites. ¹⁹You will attack every strong city and every good city. You will cut down every good tree. You will stop up all the springs of water. You will ruin every good field with stones."

²⁰In the morning, at the time for the morning sacrifice, water began flowing from the direction of Edom and filled the valley.

²¹The Moabites heard that the kings had come up to fight against them. So they gathered together all the men old enough to wear armour and waited at the border. ²²The Moabites got up early that morning. The rising sun was shining on the water in the valley, and it looked like blood to the Moabites. ²³They said, "Look at the blood! The kings must have fought against each other. They must have destroyed each other. Let's go and take the valuable things from the dead bodies!"

²⁴The Moabites came to the Israelite camp, but the Israelites came out and attacked the Moabite army. The Moabites ran away from the Israelites. The Israelites followed them into Moab to fight them. ²⁵The Israelites destroyed the cities. They threw their stonesᶜ at every good field in Moab. They stopped up all the springs of water and cut down all the good trees. The Israelites fought all the way to Kir Hareseth. The soldiers surrounded Kir Hareseth and attacked it too.

²⁶The king of Moab saw that the battle was too strong for him, so he took 700 men with swords to break through to the king of Edom. But they were not able to do it. ²⁷Then the king of Moab took his oldest son, who would become the next king after him. On the wall around the city, the king of Moab offered his son as a burnt offering. This upset the Israelites very much. So the Israelites left the king of Moab and went back to their own land.

A Prophet's Widow Asks Elisha for Help

4 A man from the group of prophets had a wife. This man died, and his wife cried out to Elisha, "My husband was like a servant to you. Now he is dead! You know he honoured the

---

ᵃ **3:11 Elisha was Elijah's servant** Literally, "Elisha poured water over Elijah's hands."
ᵇ **3:15 power** Literally, "hand".
ᶜ **3:25 threw their stones** These were probably the stones soldiers threw with slings in war.

A WOMAN OF FAITH

Elisha was Elijah's protégé and, like him, a prophet and miracle worker. The Spirit of God – given only to certain people for specific purposes in those days – was powerfully at work in both these men.

What's great about the stories of Elisha is that they are so "ordinary". It seems as though God just breaks in right in the middle of normal life, while everyone is just going about their business. This story even starts "One day . . ."!

DIG IN   READ 2 Kings 4:8-17

- What can you tell about the Shunammite woman from these verses?
- Why does Elisha want to bless her (v.13)?
- What idea do he and Gehazi have (v.14–17)?

Here's a truly "sorted" woman: happy, despite the fact that she doesn't have a son – a big deal in those days in order to protect her property. This is what Elisha is getting at when he offers to speak to the king or the captain of the army for her (v.13).

But the Shunammite woman is so content with her life, she declines the generous offer, making Elisha and Gehazi think harder for a way to return her kindness.

Almost without second thought, their solution involves an incredible miracle: "Let's ask God to give her a son!" So Elisha prophesies – and it happens.

READ 2 Kings 4:18-37

- What does the woman's action in verse 21 say about her faith?
- How about in verse 26? And verse 30?

It's now a few years later. The son is taken ill and dies very quickly. But rather than going into mourning, the woman acts in faith – she goes to get Elisha. When she arrives, she doesn't panic – she assures them that everything is okay (v.26). But she is firm that she's not going anywhere unless Elisha comes too (v.30).

We see that this is not just a story of a great man of God, but of a great woman of faith. She acts, she remains calm and confident, she perseveres. And because of her faith, the miracle comes.

DIG THROUGH

- What can this story teach us about faith? How did the woman show persevering faith in God and what he could do?
- What can you learn about the woman's contentment with her life? How do you think this attitude affected her reaction when her promised child died?

DIG DEEPER

- Bible scholars often compare Elisha to Jesus, as aspects of his life are echoed in Jesus' life. For example, around 800 years after this event, Jesus would raise a boy from the dead in the village of Nain, which was very close to Shunem (Luke 7:11–17). Elisha also fed a crowd of a hundred men with a few barley loaves (4:42–44). Does this remind you of anything? (Clue: Luke 9:10–17.)

Lord. But he owed money to a man. Now that man is coming to take my two boys and make them his slaves!"

²Elisha answered, "How can I help you? Tell me, what do you have in your house?"

The woman said, "I don't have anything in the house except a small bottle of olive oil."

³Then Elisha said, "Go and borrow jars from all your neighbours. They must be empty. Borrow plenty of jars. ⁴Then go to your house and close the doors. Only you and your sons will be in the house. Then pour the oil into all the jars. Fill them, and put them in a separate place."

⁵So the woman left Elisha, went into her house, and shut the door. Only she and her sons were in the house. Her sons brought the jars to her and she poured oil. ⁶She filled many jars. Finally, she said to her son, "Bring me another jar."

But all the bowls were full. One of the sons said to her, "There aren't any more jars." Then the oil in the jar was finished!

⁷When she told the man of God what had happened, Elisha said to her, "Go, sell the oil and pay your debt. You and your sons can live on the money that is left."

A Woman in Shunem Gives Elisha a Room

⁸One day Elisha went to Shunem, where an important woman lived. She asked Elisha to stop and eat at her house. So every time Elisha went through that place, he stopped there to eat.

⁹The woman said to her husband, "Look, I can see that Elisha is a holy man of God. He passes by our house all the time. ¹⁰Please, let's make a little room on the roof[a] for him. Let's put a bed in this room and a table, a chair and a lampstand. Then when he comes to our house, he can have this room for himself."

¹¹One day Elisha came to the woman's house. He went to this room and rested there. ¹²Elisha said to his servant Gehazi, "Call this Shunammite woman."

The servant called the Shunammite woman, and she stood in front of Elisha. ¹³Elisha told his servant, "Now say to her, 'Look, you have done your best to take care of us. What can we do for you? Do you want us to speak to the king for you, or to the captain of the army?'"

She answered, "I am fine living here among my own people."

¹⁴Elisha said to Gehazi, "What can we do for her?"

He answered, "I know! She does not have a son, and her husband is old."

¹⁵Then Elisha said, "Call her."

So Gehazi called the woman. She came and stood at his door. ¹⁶Elisha said, "About this time next spring, you will be holding your own baby boy in your arms."

The woman said, "No, sir! Man of God, don't lie to me!"

The Woman in Shunem Has a Son

¹⁷But the woman did become pregnant and gave birth to a son that next spring, just as Elisha had said.

¹⁸The boy grew. One day the boy went out into the fields to see his father and the men cutting the grain. ¹⁹The boy said to his father, "Oh, my head! My head hurts!"

The father said to his servant, "Carry him to his mother!"

²⁰The servant took the boy to his mother. The boy sat on his mother's lap until noon. Then he died.

The Woman Goes to See Elisha

²¹The woman laid the boy on the bed of Elisha, the man of God. Then she shut the door to that room and went outside. ²²She called to her husband and said, "Please send me one of the servants and a donkey. Then I will go quickly to get the man of God and come back."

²³The woman's husband said, "Why would you want to go to the man of God today? It isn't the New Moon or Sabbath day."

She said, "Goodbye!"[b]

²⁴Then she put a saddle on a donkey and said to her servant, "Let's go, and hurry! Go slowly only when I tell you to."

²⁵The woman went to Mount Carmel to get the man of God.

The man of God saw the Shunammite woman coming from far away and said to his servant Gehazi, "Look, there's the Shunammite woman! ²⁶Please run now to meet her! Say to her, 'Are you all right? Is your husband all right? Is the child all right?'"

She answered, "Everything is all right."[c]

²⁷But the Shunammite woman went up the hill to the man of God. She bowed down and touched Elisha's feet. Gehazi came near to pull her away. But the man of God said to Gehazi, "Leave her alone! She's very upset, and the Lord didn't tell me about it. He hid this news from me."

²⁸Then she said, "Sir, I never asked for a son. I told you, 'Don't trick me!'"

---

[a] 4:10 *room on the roof* In ancient Israel, houses had flat roofs that were used as an extra room.
[b] 4:23 *Goodbye* Or "Everything is all right." Literally, "Peace."
[c] 4:26 *Everything is all right* Or "Hello". Literally, "Peace."

²⁹Then Elisha said to Gehazi, "Get ready to go. Take my walking stick and go! If you meet anyone along the way, don't even stop to say hello to him. If anyone says hello to you, don't answer. Put my walking stick on the child's face."

³⁰But the child's mother said, "I promise, as the LORD lives and as you live, I will not leave without you!"

So Elisha got up and followed her.

³¹Gehazi arrived at the house before Elisha and the Shunammite woman. Gehazi laid the walking stick on the child's face, but the child did not talk or show any sign that he heard anything. Then Gehazi came back to meet Elisha and said, "The child will not wake up!"

The Woman's Son Comes Back to Life

³²Elisha went into the house, and there was the child, lying dead on his bed. ³³Elisha went into the room and shut the door. He and the child were alone in the room now. Then he prayed to the LORD. ³⁴Elisha went to the bed and lay on the child. He put his eyes on the child's eyes, his mouth on the child's mouth and his hands on the child's hands. He lay there on top of the child until the child's body became warm.

³⁵Then Elisha turned away and walked around the room. He went back and lay on the child until the child sneezed seven times and opened his eyes.

³⁶Elisha called Gehazi and said, "Call the Shunammite woman!"

Gehazi called her, and she came to Elisha. Elisha said, "Pick up your son."

³⁷Then the Shunammite woman went into the room and bowed down at Elisha's feet. Then she picked up her son and went out.

Elisha and the Poisoned Soup

³⁸Elisha went to Gilgal again. There was a famine in the land. The group of prophets was sitting in front of Elisha. Elisha said to his servant, "Put the large pot on the fire, and make some soup for the group of prophets."

³⁹One man went out into the field to gather herbs. He found a wild vine and picked the fruit from it. He put that fruit in his robe and brought it back. He cut up the wild fruit and put it into the pot. But the group of prophets did not know what kind of fruit it was.

⁴⁰Then they poured some of the soup for the men to eat. But when they began to eat the soup, they shouted out, "Man of God! There's poison in the pot!" The food tasted like poison, so they could not eat that food.

⁴¹But Elisha said, "Bring some flour." He threw the flour into the pot. Then he said, "Pour the soup for the people so that they can eat."

And there was nothing wrong with the soup.

Elisha Feeds the Group of Prophets

⁴²A man from Baal Shalishah came and brought bread from the first harvest to the man of God. This man brought 20 loaves of barley bread and fresh grain in his sack. Then Elisha said, "Give this food to the people, so that they can eat."

⁴³Elisha's servant said, "What? There are 100 men here. How can I give this food to all those men?"

But Elisha said, "Give the food to the people to eat. The LORD says, 'They will eat and there will still be food left over.'"

⁴⁴Then Elisha's servant put the food in front of the group of prophets. The group of prophets had enough to eat, and they even had food left over. This happened just as the LORD had said.

Naaman's Problem

5 Naaman was the captain of the army of the king of Aram. He was very important to his king[a] because the LORD used him to lead Aram to victory. Naaman was a great and powerful man, but he was also sick with leprosy.

²The Aramean army sent many groups of soldiers to fight in Israel. Once they took a little girl from the land of Israel. This girl became a servant of Naaman's wife. ³She said to his wife, "I wish that my master would meet the prophet who lives in Samaria. He could cure him of his leprosy."

⁴Naaman went to the king and told him what the Israelite girl had said.

⁵Then the king of Aram said, "Go now, and I will send a letter to the king of Israel."

So Naaman went to Israel. He took 30,000 pieces[b] of silver, 6,000 pieces[c] of gold and ten changes of clothes as gifts. ⁶Naaman took the letter from the king of Aram to the king of Israel. The letter said: "Now this letter is to show that I am sending my servant Naaman to you. Cure his leprosy."

⁷When the king of Israel had read the letter, he tore his clothes to show he was sad and upset. He said, "Am I God? I don't have the power over life and death. So why did the king of Aram send a man sick with leprosy for me to heal? Think about it, and you will see that it is a trick. The king of Aram is trying to start a fight."

⁸Elisha, the man of God, heard that the king of Israel had torn his clothes. So Elisha sent this

---

[a] 5:1 king Literally, "master".
[b] 5:5 30,000 pieces Literally, "10 talents".
[c] 5:5 6,000 pieces Literally, "2 talents". Also in verse 23.

message to the king: "Why did you tear your clothes? Let Naaman come to me. Then he will know there is a prophet in Israel."

⁹So Naaman came with his horses and chariots to Elisha's house and stood outside the door. ¹⁰Elisha sent a messenger to Naaman who said, "Go and wash in the Jordan River seven times. Then your skin will be healed, and you will be pure and clean."

¹¹Naaman became angry and left. He said, "I thought Elisha would at least come out and stand in front of me and call on the name of the LORD his God. I thought he would wave his hand over my body and heal the leprosy. ¹²Abana and Pharpar, the rivers of Damascus, are better than all the water in Israel. Why can't I wash in those rivers in Damascus and become clean?" He was very angry and turned to leave.

¹³But Naaman's servants went to him and talked to him. They said, "Father,ᵃ if the prophet told you to do some great thing, you would do it, wouldn't you? But he said, 'Wash, and you will be pure and clean.'"

¹⁴So Naaman did what the man of God said. He went down and dipped himself in the Jordan River seven times, and he became pure and clean. His skin became soft like the skin of a baby.

¹⁵Naaman and his whole group came back to the man of God. He stood before Elisha and said, "Look, I now know there is no God in all the earth except in Israel. Now please accept a gift from me."

¹⁶But Elisha said, "The LORD is the one I serve, and as surely as he lives, I will not accept any gift."

Naaman tried hard to make Elisha take the gift, but he refused. ¹⁷Then Naaman said, "If you will not accept this gift, at least do this for me. Let me have enough dirt from Israel to fill the baskets on two of my mules.ᵇ I ask this because I will never again offer any burnt offering or sacrifice to any other gods. I will offer sacrifices only to the LORD! ¹⁸And I pray that the LORD will forgive me for this: When my master goes to the temple of Rimmon to worship that false god, he will want to lean on me for support. So I must bow down in the temple of Rimmon. I ask the LORD now to forgive me when that happens."

¹⁹Then Elisha said to Naaman, "Go in peace."

So Naaman left Elisha and went a short way.

²⁰But Gehazi, the servant of Elisha the man of God, thought, "Look, my master has let Naaman the Aramean go without accepting the gift that he brought. As the LORD lives, I will run after

Naaman and get something from him." ²¹So Gehazi ran to Naaman.

Naaman saw someone running after him. He stepped down from the chariot to meet Gehazi. Naaman said, "Is everything all right?"

²²Gehazi said, "Yes, everything is all right. My master has sent me. He said, 'Look, two young men came to me from the group of prophets in the hill country of Ephraim. Please give them 3,000 piecesᶜ of silver and two changes of clothes.'"

²³Naaman said, "Please, take 6,000 pieces." He persuaded Gehazi to take the silver. Naaman put the silver in two bags and took two changes of clothes. Then he gave these things to two of his servants. The servants carried these things for Gehazi. ²⁴When Gehazi came to the hill, he took these things from the servants. He sent the servants away, and they left. Then he hid those things in the house.

²⁵Gehazi came in and stood before his master. Elisha said to Gehazi, "Where have you been Gehazi?"

Gehazi answered, "I didn't go anywhere."

²⁶Elisha said to him, "That is not true! My heart was with you when the man turned from his chariot to meet you. This is not the time to take money, clothes, olives, grapes, sheep, oxen or men and women servants. ²⁷Now you and your children will catch Naaman's disease. You will have leprosy forever!"

When Gehazi left Elisha, his skin was as white as snow! He was sick with leprosy.

Elisha and the Axe Head

6 The group of prophets said to Elisha, "We are staying in that place over there, but it is too small for us. ²Let's go to the Jordan River and cut some wood. Each of us will get a log and we will build a place to live there."

Elisha answered, "Go and do it."

³One of them said, "Please go with us."

Elisha said, "Yes, I will go with you."

⁴So Elisha went with the group of prophets. When they arrived at the Jordan River, they began to cut down some trees. ⁵But when one man was cutting down a tree, the iron axe head slipped from the handle and fell into the water. He shouted, "Oh, master! I borrowed that axe!"

⁶The man of God said, "Where did it fall?"

The man showed Elisha the place where the axe head fell. Then Elisha cut a stick and threw the stick into the water. The stick made the iron

---

ᵃ **5:13 Father** Slaves often called their masters "father" and the masters often called their slaves "children".
ᵇ **5:17 Let me have . . . my mules** Naaman probably thought the ground in Israel was holy, so he wanted to take some with him to help him worship the Lord in his own country.
ᶜ **5:22 3,000 pieces** Literally, "1 *talent*".

axe head float. [7]Elisha said, "Pick up the axe head." Then the man reached out and took the axe head.

INSIGHT

In the Iron Age, axe heads were immensely valuable and the man in this story could have been in big trouble for losing one. Elisha's actions may have saved this man's livelihood and even his life.

2 Kings 6:1–6

Aram Tries to Trap Israel

[8]The king of Aram was making war against Israel. He had a council meeting with his army officers. He said, "Go to such and such a place and prepare to attack the Israelites when they come past."

[9]But the man of God sent a message to the king of Israel. Elisha said, "Be careful! Don't go past that place, because the Aramean soldiers are hiding there!"

[10]The king of Israel sent a message to his men at the place that the man of God warned him about. And the king of Israel saved quite a few men.[a]

[11]The king of Aram was very upset about this. He called his army officers and said to them, "Tell me who is spying for the king of Israel."

[12]One of the officers of the king of Aram said, "My lord and king, not one of us is a spy. Elisha, the prophet from Israel, can tell the king of Israel many secret things—even the words that you speak in your bedroom!"

[13]The king of Aram said, "Find Elisha, and I will send men to catch him."

The servants told the king of Aram, "Elisha is in Dothan."

[14]Then the king of Aram sent horses, chariots and a large army to Dothan. They arrived at night and surrounded the city. [15]Elisha's servant got up early that morning. When he went outside, he saw an army with horses and chariots all around the city.

The servant said to Elisha, "Oh, my master, what can we do?"

[16]Elisha said, "Don't be afraid. The army that fights for us is larger than the army that fights for Aram."

[17]Then Elisha prayed and said, "Lord, I ask you, open my servant's eyes so that he can see."

The Lord opened the eyes of the young man, and the servant saw the mountain was full of horses and chariots of fire. They were all around Elisha.

[18]These horses and chariots of fire came down to Elisha. He prayed to the Lord and said, "I pray that you will cause these people to become blind."

So God did what Elisha asked. He caused the Aramean army to become blind. [19]Elisha said to the Aramean army, "This is not the right way. This is not the right city. Follow me. I will lead you to the man you are looking for." Then Elisha led them to Samaria.[b]

[20]When they arrived at Samaria, Elisha said, "Lord, open the eyes of these men so that they can see."

Then the Lord opened their eyes, and the Aramean army saw they were in the city of Samaria! [21]The king of Israel saw the Aramean army and said to Elisha, "My father, should I kill them? Should I kill them?"

[22]Elisha answered, "No, don't kill them. They are not soldiers you captured in battle. Give them some bread and water. Let them eat and drink. Then let them go home to their leader."

[23]So the king prepared a big meal for the Aramean army. After they had finished eating and drinking, he sent them back home to their leader. The Arameans did not send any more soldiers into the land of Israel to make raids.

A Time of Terrible Hunger Hits Samaria

[24]After this happened, King Ben-Hadad of Aram gathered all of his army and went to surround and attack the city of Samaria. [25]The soldiers would not let people bring food into the city, so there was a time of terrible hunger in Samaria. It was so bad in Samaria that a donkey's head was sold for 80 pieces of silver and 200 grammes[c] of dove's dung sold for five pieces of silver.

[26]The king of Israel was walking on the wall around the city. A woman shouted out to him. She said, "My lord and king, please help me!"

[27]The king of Israel said, "If the Lord does not help you, how can I help you? I cannot give you grain from the threshing floor or wine from the winepress." [28]Then he said to her, "What is your trouble?"

She answered, "This woman said to me, 'Give me your son so that we can eat him today. Then we will eat my son tomorrow.' [29]So we boiled my son and ate him. Then the next day, I said to this woman, 'Give me your son so that we can eat him.' But she has hidden her son!"

---

[a] 6:10 *quite a few men* Literally, "not one or two".
[b] 6:19 *Samaria* This was the capital city of Israel—the enemy of Aram.
[c] 6:25 *200 grammes* Literally, "⅓ *cab*".

[30]When the king heard the woman's words, he tore his clothes to show he was upset. As he passed by on the wall, the people saw the king was wearing the rough cloth under his clothes to show he was sad and upset.

[31]The king said, "May God punish me if the head of Elisha son of Shaphat is still on his body at the end of this day!"

[32]The king sent a messenger to Elisha. Elisha was sitting in his house, and the leaders were sitting with him. Before the messenger arrived, Elisha said to the leaders, "Look, that son of a murderer is sending men to cut off my head. When the messenger arrives, shut the door. Hold the door and don't let him in. I hear the sound of his master's feet coming behind him."

[33]While Elisha was still talking with the leaders, the messenger[a] came to him. This was the message: "This trouble has come from the LORD. Why should I wait for the LORD any longer?"

7 Elisha said, "Listen to the message from the LORD! The LORD says, 'About this time tomorrow, there will be plenty of food, and it will be cheap again. A person will be able to buy 3 kilogrammes[b] of fine flour or 6 kilogrammes of barley for only one piece[c] of silver in the marketplace by the city gates of Samaria.'"

[2]Then the officer who was close to the king[d] answered the man of God. The officer said, "Even if the LORD made windows in heaven, this could not happen."

Elisha said, "You will see it with your own eyes, but you will not eat any of that food."

Lepers Find the Aramean Camp Empty

[3]There were four men sick with leprosy near the city gate. They said to each other, "Why are we sitting here waiting to die? [4]There is no food in Samaria. If we go into the city, we will die there. If we stay here, we will also die. So let's go to the Aramean camp. If they let us live, we will live. If they kill us, we will just die."

[5]So that evening the four lepers went to the Aramean camp. When they came to the edge of the camp, no one was there! [6]The Lord had caused the Aramean army to hear the sound of chariots, horses and a large army. So the soldiers said to each other, "The king of Israel has hired the kings of the Hittites and Egyptians to come against us."

[7]The Arameans ran away early that evening. They left everything behind. They left their tents, horses and donkeys and ran for their lives.

The Lepers in the Enemy Camp

[8]When these lepers came to where the camp began, they went into one tent. They ate and drank. Then they carried silver, gold and clothes out of the camp and hid them. Then they came back and entered another tent. They carried things out from this tent and went out and hid them. [9]Then they said to each other, "We are doing wrong! Today we have good news, but we are silent. If we wait until the sun comes up, we will be punished. Now let's go and tell the people who live in the king's palace."

The Lepers Share the Good News

[10]So the lepers came and called to the gatekeepers of the city. They told the gatekeepers, "We went to the Aramean camp, but we did not hear anyone. No one was there, but the horses and donkeys were still tied up, and the tents were still standing."

[11]Then the gatekeepers of the city shouted out and told the people in the king's palace. [12]It was night, but the king got up from bed and said to his officers, "I will tell you what the Aramean soldiers are doing to us. They know we are hungry. They left the camp to hide in the field. They are thinking, 'When the Israelites come out of the city, we will capture them alive. And then we will enter the city.'"

[13]One of the king's officers said, "Let some men take five of the horses that are still left in the city. The horses will soon die anyway, as will all the Israelites who are still left in the city.[e] Let's send these men to see what happened."

[14]So the men took two chariots with horses. The king sent these men after the Aramean army. He told them, "Go and see what has happened."

[15]The men went after the Aramean army as far as the Jordan River. All along the road there were clothes and weapons. The Arameans had thrown these things down when they hurried away. The messengers went back to Samaria and told the king.

[16]Then the people ran out to the Aramean camp and took valuable things from there. So it happened just as the LORD had said. A person could buy 3 kilogrammes of fine flour or 6 kilogrammes of barley for only one piece of silver.

[17]There was one officer who always stayed close by the king to help him. The king sent this officer to guard the gate, but the people knocked him down and trampled him, and he died. So everything happened just as the man of God had

---

[a] **6:33** *messenger* Or possibly, "king".
[b] **7:1** *3 kilogrammes* Literally, "*seah*". Also in verses 16,18.
[c] **7:1** *one piece* Literally, "one *shekel*". Also in verses 16,18.
[d] **7:2** *who was close to the king* Literally, "on whose arm the king leaned".
[e] **7:13** *The horses . . . city* The Hebrew text is not clear.

said when the king came to Elisha's house. [18]Elisha had said, "A person will be able to buy 3 kilogrammes of fine flour or 6 kilogrammes of barley for only one piece of silver in the marketplace by the city gates of Samaria." [19]But that officer had answered the man of God, "Even if the LORD made windows in heaven, this could not happen!" And Elisha had told the officer, "You will see it with your own eyes, but you will not eat any of that food." [20]It happened to the officer just that way. The people knocked him down at the gate and trampled him, and he died.

The King and the Shunammite Woman

8 Elisha had talked to the woman whose son he had brought back to life. He had said, "You and your family should move to another country, because the LORD has decided that there will be a famine here. It will last for seven years."

[2]So the woman did what the man of God said. She went with her family to stay in the land of the Philistines for seven years. [3]After seven years she returned from the land of the Philistines.

She went to speak with the king to ask him to help her get back her house and land.

[4]The king was talking with Gehazi, the servant of the man of God. The king said to Gehazi, "Please tell me all the great things Elisha has done."

[5]Just as Gehazi was telling the king about Elisha bringing a dead person back to life, the woman whose son Elisha had brought back to life went to the king. She wanted to ask him to help her get back her house and land. Gehazi said, "My lord and king, this is the woman, and this is the son who Elisha brought back to life."

[6]The king asked the woman what she wanted, and she told him.

Then the king chose an officer to help her. The king said, "Give to the woman all that belongs to her. And give her all the harvest of her land from the day she left the country until now."

Ben-Hadad Sends Hazael to Elisha

[7]Elisha went to Damascus. King Ben-Hadad of Aram was sick. Someone told Ben-Hadad, "The man of God has come here."

[8]Then the King Ben-Hadad said to Hazael, "Take a gift and go and meet the man of God. Ask him to ask the LORD if I will get well from my sickness."

[9]So Hazael went to meet Elisha. Hazael brought a gift with him. He brought all kinds of good things from Damascus. It took 40 camels to carry everything. Hazael came to Elisha and said, "Your follower,[a] King Ben-Hadad of Aram, sent me to you. He asks if he will get well from his sickness."

[10]Then Elisha said to Hazael, "Go and tell Ben-Hadad, 'You will live.' But really the LORD told me, 'He will die.'"

Elisha Makes a Prophecy About Hazael

[11]Elisha began to stare. He stared for an embarrassingly long time. Then the man of God began to cry. [12]Hazael said, "Sir, why are you crying?"

Elisha answered, "I am crying because I know the bad things you will do to the Israelites. You will burn their strong cities and kill their young men with swords. You will kill their babies and split open their pregnant women."

[13]Hazael said, "I am not a powerful man![b] How can I do these great things?"

Elisha answered, "The LORD showed me that you will be king over Aram."

[14]Then Hazael left Elisha and went to his king.[c] Ben-Hadad said to Hazael, "What did Elisha say to you?"

He answered, "Elisha told me that you will live."

Hazael Murders Ben-Hadad

[15]But the next day Hazael took a thick cloth and dipped it in water. Then he held it on Ben-Hadad's face until he died. Then Hazael became the new king.

Jehoram Begins His Rule

[16]Jehoram son of Jehoshaphat was the king of Judah. He began to rule in the fifth year that Joram son of Ahab was king of Israel.[d] [17]Jehoram was 32 years old when he began to rule. He ruled

---

[a] 8:9 *follower* Literally, "son".
[b] 8:13 *I . . . powerful man* Literally, "Your servant is only a dog!"
[c] 8:14 *king* Literally, "master".
[d] 8:16 The standard Hebrew text adds "while Jehoshaphat was still king of Judah". That is, according to the Hebrew, father and son ruled Judah together for a time.

for eight years in Jerusalem. ¹⁸But Jehoram lived as the kings of Israel had and did what the LORD saw as evil. He lived as the people from Ahab's family had done, because his wife was Ahab's daughter. ¹⁹But the LORD would not destroy Judah because of the promise to his servant David. He had promised David that someone from his family would always be king.

²⁰In Jehoram's time Edom broke away from Judah's rule. The people of Edom chose a king for themselves.

²¹Then Jehoram and all his chariots went to Zair. The Edomite army surrounded them, but Jehoram and his officers attacked them and escaped. Jehoram's soldiers all ran away and went home. ²²So the Edomites broke away from the rule of Judah. And they have been free from the rule of Judah until today.

At the same time Libnah also broke away from Judah's rule.

²³All the things Jehoram did are written in the book, *The History of the Kings of Judah.*

²⁴Jehoram died and was buried with his ancestors in the City of David. Jehoram's son Ahaziah became the new king.

Ahaziah Begins His Rule

²⁵Ahaziah son of Jehoram became the king of Judah in the twelfth year that Joram son of Ahab was king of Israel. ²⁶Ahaziah was 22 years old when he began to rule. He ruled for one year in Jerusalem. His mother's name was Athaliah. She was the daughter of King Omri of Israel. ²⁷Ahaziah did what the LORD said was wrong. He did many bad things, just as the people from Ahab's family had done. He lived like this because his wife was from Ahab's family.

Joram Is Hurt in the War Against Hazael

²⁸Joram was from Ahab's family. Ahaziah went with Joram to fight against King Hazael of Aram at Ramoth Gilead. The Arameans wounded Joram. ²⁹King Joram went back to Israel so that he could get well from those wounds. He went to the area of Jezreel. Ahaziah son of Jehoram was the king of Judah. Ahaziah went to Jezreel to see Joram.

Elisha Tells a Prophet to Anoint Jehu

9 Elisha the prophet called one of the men from the group of prophets and said to him, "Get ready and take this small bottle of oil in your hand. Go to Ramoth Gilead. ²When you arrive, find Jehu son of Jehoshaphat, the son of Nimshi. Then go in and make him get up from among his brothers. Take him to an inner room. ³Take the small bottle of oil and pour the oil on Jehu's head. Say, 'This is what the LORD says: I have anointed

you to be the new king over Israel.' Then open the door and run away. Don't wait!"

⁴So this young man, the prophet, went to Ramoth Gilead. ⁵When the young man arrived, he saw the captains of the army sitting. He said, "Captain, I have a message for you."

Jehu asked, "Which one of us is the message for?"

The young man said, "For you, sir."

⁶Jehu got up and went into the house. Then the young prophet poured the oil on Jehu's head and said to him, "The LORD, the God of Israel, says, 'I am anointing you to be the new king over the LORD's people, Israel. ⁷You must destroy the family of Ahab your king. In this way I will punish Jezebel for the deaths of my servants, the prophets, and the deaths of all the LORD's servants who were murdered. ⁸So all Ahab's family will die. I will not let any male child in Ahab's family live. It doesn't matter if that male child is a slave or a free person in Israel. ⁹I will make Ahab's family like the family of Jeroboam son of Nebat and like the family of Baasha son of Ahijah. ¹⁰The dogs will eat Jezebel in the area of Jezreel, and she will not be buried.'"

Then the young prophet opened the door and ran away.

The Servants Announce Jehu as King

¹¹Jehu went back to his king's officers. One of the officers said to Jehu, "Is everything all right? Why did this madman come to you?"

Jehu answered the servants, "You know the man and the crazy things he says."

¹²The officers said, "No, tell us the truth. What did he say?" Jehu told the officers what the young prophet said. Jehu said, "He said a few things and then he said, 'This is what the LORD says: I have anointed you to be the new king over Israel.'"

¹³Then each officer quickly took his robe off and put it on the steps in front of Jehu. Then they blew the trumpet and made the announcement, "Jehu is king!"

Jehu Goes to Jezreel

¹⁴So Jehu son of Jehoshaphat, son of Nimshi, made plans against Joram.

At that time Joram and the Israelites had been trying to defend Ramoth Gilead from King Hazael of Aram. ¹⁵King Joram had fought against King Hazael of Aram. But the Arameans wounded King Joram, and he went to Jezreel to get well from those injuries.

So Jehu told the officers, "If you agree that I am the new king, don't let anyone escape from the city to tell the news in Jezreel."

¹⁶Joram was resting in Jezreel, so Jehu got in his chariot and drove to Jezreel. King Ahaziah of Judah had also come to Jezreel to see Joram.

¹⁷A guard was standing on the tower in Jezreel. He saw Jehu's large group coming. He said, "I see a large group of people!"

Joram said, "Send someone on a horse to meet them. Tell this messenger to ask if they come in peace."

¹⁸So the messenger rode on a horse to meet Jehu. The messenger said, "King Joram says, 'Do you come in peace?'"

Jehu said, "You have nothing to do with peace. Come and follow me."

The guard told Joram, "The messenger went to the group, but he has not come back yet."

¹⁹Then Joram sent out a second messenger on a horse. This man came to Jehu's group and said, "King Joram says, 'Peace.'"ᵃ

Jehu answered, "You have nothing to do with peace. Come and follow me."

²⁰The guard told Joram, "The second messenger went to the group, but he has not come back yet. There is a man driving his chariot like a mad man. He is driving like Jehu son of Nimshi."

²¹Joram said, "Get me my chariot!"

So the servant got Joram's chariot. Both King Joram of Israel and King Ahaziah of Judah got their chariots and drove out to meet Jehu. They met him at the property of Naboth from Jezreel.

²²Joram saw Jehu and asked, "Do you come in peace, Jehu?"

Jehu answered, "There is no peace as long as your mother Jezebel does many acts of prostitution and witchcraft."

²³Joram turned the horses to run away. He said to Ahaziah, "It is a trick, Ahaziah!"

²⁴But Jehu grabbed his bow and shot Joram in the middle of his back, through the heart. Joram fell dead in his chariot.

²⁵Jehu said to his chariot driver Bidkar, "Take Joram's body up and throw it into the field of Naboth from Jezreel. Remember when you and I rode together with Joram's father Ahab, the LORD said this would happen to him. ²⁶The LORD said, 'Yesterday I saw the blood of Naboth and his sons. And I, the LORD, am telling you that I will punish Ahab in this field.' So take Joram's body and throw it into the field, just as the LORD said."

²⁷King Ahaziah of Judah saw this and ran away. He tried to escape through the garden house, but Jehu followed him. Jehu had said, "Shoot Ahaziah too!"

Ahaziah was wounded when he was in his chariot on the road to Gur near Ibleam. He got as far as Megiddo, but he died there. ²⁸Ahaziah's servants carried his body in the chariot to Jerusalem. They buried him in his tomb with his ancestors in the City of David.

²⁹Ahaziah had become king over Judah during Joram'sᵇ eleventh year as king of Israel.

The Terrible Death of Jezebel

³⁰When Jehu came to Jezreel, Jezebel heard the news. She put her make-up on and fixed her hair. Then she stood by the window and looked out. ³¹Jehu entered the city. Jezebel said, "Hello, you Zimri.ᶜ You killed your master just as he did."

³²Jehu looked up at the window and said, "Who is on my side? Who?"

Two or three eunuchs looked out at Jehu. ³³Jehu said, "Throw Jezebel down!"

Then the eunuchs threw her down. Some of her blood splashed on the wall and on the horses that trampled her body. ³⁴Jehu went into the house and ate and drank. Then he said, "Now see about this cursed woman. Bury her, because she is a king's daughter."

³⁵The men went to bury Jezebel, but they could not find her body. They could only find her skull, her feet and the palms of her hands. ³⁶When the men came back and told Jehu, he said, "The LORD told his servant Elijah the Tishbite to give this message: 'Dogs will eat the body of Jezebel in the area of Jezreel. ³⁷Her body will be like dung on the field in the area of Jezreel. No one will be able to recognize her body!'"

Jehu Writes to the Leaders of Samaria

10 Ahab had 70 sons in Samaria. Jehu wrote letters and sent them to Samaria to the rulers and leaders of Jezreel.ᵈ He also sent the letters to the people who raised Ahab's sons saying, ²⁻³"As soon as you get this letter, choose the one who is the best and most worthy among your master's sons. You have chariots and horses. And you are living in a strong city. You also have weapons. Put the son you choose on his father's throne. Then fight for your master's family."

⁴But the rulers and leaders of Jezreel were very afraid. They said, "The two kings could not stop Jehu. So we cannot stop him either!"

⁵The palace manager, the official in charge of the city, the leaders and the people who raised the king's children sent a message to Jehu. "We are your servants and we will do whatever you tell us. We will not make anyone king; you may do whatever you think is best."

ᵃ **9:19** *Peace* A way of saying "hello".

ᵇ **9:29** *Joram's* Literally, "Joram son of Ahab".

ᶜ **9:31** *Zimri* Zimri killed Elah and the family of Baasha in Israel many years before. Read 1 Kgs 16:8–12.

ᵈ **10:1** *leaders of Jezreel* The ancient Greek and Latin versions have "leaders of the city".

Leaders of Samaria Kill Ahab's Children

⁶Then Jehu wrote a second letter to these leaders. He said, "If you support me and obey me, cut off the heads of Ahab's sons. Bring them to me at Jezreel about this time tomorrow."

Ahab had 70 sons. They were with the leaders of the city who raised them. ⁷When the leaders of the city received the letter, they took the king's sons and killed all 70 of them. Then the leaders put the heads of the king's sons in baskets and sent the baskets to Jehu at Jezreel. ⁸The messenger came to Jehu and told him, "They have brought the heads of the king's sons."

Then Jehu said, "Lay the heads in two piles at the city gate until morning."

⁹In the morning Jehu went out and stood before the people. He said to them, "You are innocent. Look, I made plans against my master. I killed him. But who killed all these sons of Ahab? You killed them. ¹⁰You should know that everything the LORD says will happen. The LORD used Elijah to say these things about Ahab's family. Now the LORD has done what he said he would do."

¹¹So Jehu killed all the people in Ahab's family living in Jezreel. He killed all the important men, close friends and priests. None of Ahab's people were left alive.

Jehu Kills Ahaziah's Relatives

¹²Jehu left Jezreel and went to Samaria. On the way he stopped at a place called Shepherd's Camp. ¹³There he met with the relatives of King Ahaziah of Judah. Jehu asked, "Who are you?"

They answered, "We are the relatives of King Ahaziah of Judah. We have come down to visit the king's children and the queen mother's*ᵃ* children."

¹⁴Then Jehu said, "Take them alive!"

Jehu's men captured Ahaziah's relatives alive. There were 42 of them. Jehu killed them at the well near Beth Eked. He did not leave anyone alive.

Jehu Meets Jehonadab

¹⁵After Jehu left there, he met Jehonadab son of Recab. Jehonadab was on his way to meet Jehu. Jehu greeted Jehonadab and said to him, "Are you a faithful friend to me, as I am to you?"*ᵇ*

Jehonadab answered, "Yes, I am a faithful friend to you."

Jehu said, "If you are, give me your hand."

Then Jehu reached out and pulled Jehonadab up into the chariot.

¹⁶Jehu said, "Come with me. You can see how strong my feelings are for the LORD."

So Jehonadab rode in Jehu's chariot. ¹⁷Jehu came to Samaria and killed all of Ahab's family who were still alive in Samaria. He killed them all. He did what the LORD had told Elijah.

Jehu Calls the Worshippers of Baal

¹⁸Then Jehu gathered all the people together and said to them, "Ahab served Baal a little, but Jehu will serve Baal much. ¹⁹Now call together all the priests and prophets of Baal. And call everyone who worships Baal. Don't let anyone miss this meeting. I have a great sacrifice to give to Baal. I will kill anyone who does not come to this meeting."

But Jehu was tricking them. He wanted to destroy the worshippers of Baal. ²⁰Jehu said, "Prepare a holy meeting for Baal." So the priests announced the meeting. ²¹Then Jehu sent a message through all the land of Israel. All the worshippers of Baal came. Not one stayed home. The Baal worshippers came into the temple of Baal. The temple was filled with people.

²²Jehu said to the man who kept the robes, "Bring out the robes for all the worshippers of Baal." So that man brought out the robes for the Baal worshippers.

²³Then Jehu and Jehonadab son of Recab went into the temple of Baal. Jehu said to the worshippers of Baal, "Look around and be sure that there are no servants of the LORD with you. Be sure there are only people who worship Baal." ²⁴The worshippers of Baal went into the temple of Baal to offer sacrifices and burnt offerings.

But outside, Jehu had 80 men waiting. He told them, "Don't let anyone escape. If any man lets one person escape, that man must pay with his own life."

²⁵As soon as Jehu had finished offering the burnt offering, he said to the guards and to the captains, "Go in and kill the worshippers of Baal! Don't let anyone come out of the temple alive!"

So the captains used thin swords and killed the worshippers of Baal. They threw the bodies of the worshippers of Baal out. Then the guards and the captains went to the inner room*ᶜ* of the temple of Baal. ²⁶They brought out the memorial stones that were in the temple of Baal and burned that temple. ²⁷Then they smashed the memorial stones of Baal. They also smashed the temple of Baal. They made the temple of Baal into a public toilet, which is still used today.

ᵃ **10:13** *queen mother* The mother of the king.
ᵇ **10:15** *Are you a faithful friend . . . you* Literally, "Is your heart true to me? My heart is true to your heart."
ᶜ **10:25** *inner room* Literally, "the city of the temple of Baal."

[28]So Jehu destroyed Baal worship in Israel, [29]but he did not completely turn away from the sins of Jeroboam son of Nebat that caused Israel to sin. Jehu did not destroy the gold calves in Bethel and in Dan.

Jehu's Rule Over Israel

[30]The LORD said to Jehu, "You have done well. You have done what I say is good. You destroyed Ahab's family the way I wanted you to, so your descendants will rule Israel for four generations." [31]But Jehu was not careful to follow the Law of the LORD with all his heart. Jehu did not stop committing the sins of Jeroboam that caused Israel to sin.

Hazael Defeats Israel

[32]At that time the LORD began to cut away sections of Israel and give them to other nations. King Hazael of Aram defeated the Israelites on every border of Israel. [33]He won the land east of the Jordan River—all the land of Gilead, including the land that belonged to the tribes of Gad, Reuben and Manasseh. He won all the land from Aroer by the Arnon Valley to Gilead and Bashan.

The Death of Jehu

[34]All the other great things that Jehu did are written in the book, *The History of the Kings of Israel.* [35]Jehu died and was buried with his ancestors. The people buried him in Samaria. His son Jehoahaz became the new king of Israel after him. [36]Jehu ruled over Israel in Samaria for 28 years.

Athaliah Kills the King's Sons in Judah

11 Athaliah was Ahaziah's mother. She saw that her son was dead, so she got up and killed all the king's family.

[2]Jehosheba was King Joram's daughter and Ahaziah's sister. Joash was one of the king's sons. While the other children were being killed, Jehosheba took Joash and hid him. She put him and his nurse in her bedroom, so Jehosheba and the nurse hid Joash from Athaliah. That way Joash was not killed.

[3]Then Joash and Jehosheba hid in the LORD's Temple. Joash hid there for six years. During that time Athaliah ruled over the land of Judah.

[4]In the seventh year Jehoiada the high priest sent for the captains of the Carites[a] and guards.[b] He brought them together in the LORD's Temple and made an agreement with them. There in the Temple of the LORD he forced them to make a promise. Then he showed the king's son to them.

[5]Then Jehoiada gave them a command. He said, "This is what you must do. One-third of you, from those who go on duty on the Sabbath day, must stand guard at the royal palace. [6]Another third will be at the Sur Gate, and the other third will be at the gate behind the guard. This way you will stand guard over the palace on all sides. [7]Your two divisions who go off duty on the Sabbath day will stand guard at the LORD's Temple and protect King Joash. [8]You must stay with him wherever he goes. The whole group must surround the king. Each guard must have his weapon in his hand, and you must kill anyone who comes too close to you."

[9]The captains obeyed everything that Jehoiada the priest commanded. Each captain took his men, both those who were going on duty on the Sabbath day and those who were going off duty. All these men went to Jehoiada the priest, [10]and he gave spears and shields to the captains. These were the spears and shields David put in the LORD's Temple. [11]These guards stood with their weapons in their hands from the right corner of the Temple to the left corner. They stood around the altar and the Temple and around the king when he went to the Temple. [12]These men brought out Joash. They put the crown on him and gave him a copy of the agreement.[c] Then they anointed him and made him the new king. They clapped their hands and shouted, "Long live the king!"

[13]Queen Athaliah heard the noise from the guards and the people, so she went to them at the LORD's Temple. [14]Athaliah saw the king by the column where new kings usually stood. She also saw the leaders and men playing the trumpets for him. She saw that all the people were very happy. She heard the trumpets, and she tore her clothes to show she was upset. Then Athaliah shouted, "Treason! Treason!"

[15]Jehoiada the priest gave a command to the captains who were in charge of the soldiers. Jehoiada told them, "Take Athaliah outside of the Temple area. Kill any of her followers, but don't kill them in the LORD's Temple."

[16]So the soldiers grabbed Athaliah and killed her as soon as she went through the horse's entrance to the palace.

[17]Then Jehoiada made the agreement between the LORD and the king and the people. This agreement showed that the king and the people

---

[a] **11:4 Carites** Or "Kerethites", special soldiers hired to serve the king.

[b] **11:4 guards** Literally, "runners" or "messengers".

[c] **11:12 a copy of the agreement** Literally, "testimony". This could be a copy of the Law of Moses (see Deut. 17:18) or a special agreement between God and the king (see verse 17 and 1 Sam. 10:25).

belonged to the LORD. Jehoiada also made the agreement between the king and the people.

[18] Then all the people went to the temple of Baal. They destroyed the statue of Baal and his altars. They broke them into many pieces. They also killed Baal's priest, Mattan, in front of the altars.

So Jehoiada the priest put men in charge of maintaining the LORD's Temple. [19] The priest led all the people. They went from the LORD's Temple to the king's palace. The king's special guards and the captains went with the king, and all the other people followed them. They went to the entrance to the king's palace. Then King Joash sat on the throne. [20] All the people were happy, and the city was peaceful. And Queen Athaliah was killed with a sword near the king's palace.

[21] Joash was seven years old when he became king.

Joash Begins His Rule

12 Joash began to rule during Jehu's seventh year as king of Israel. Joash ruled for 40 years in Jerusalem. His mother was named Zibiah of Beersheba. [2] For as long as he lived, Joash did what the LORD considered right. He did what Jehoiada the priest taught him. [3] But he did not destroy the high places. The people still made sacrifices and burned incense at those places of worship.

Joash Orders the Repair of the Temple

[4-5] Joash said to the priests, "There is much money in the LORD's Temple. People have given things to the Temple and have paid the Temple tax when they were counted. And they have given money simply because they wanted to. You priests should take that money and repair the LORD's Temple. Each priest should use the money he gets from the people he serves. He should use that money to repair the damage to the Temple."

[6] In the twenty-third year that Joash was king, the priests still had not repaired the Temple, [7] so King Joash called for Jehoiada and the other priests. Joash said to them, "Why haven't you repaired the Temple? Stop taking money from the people you serve. That money must be used to repair the Temple."

[8] The priests agreed to stop taking money from the people, but they also decided not to repair the Temple. [9] So Jehoiada the priest took a box and made a hole in the top of it. Then he put the box on the south side of the altar. This box was by the door where people came into the LORD's Temple. Some of the priests were there to guard this doorway.[a] They took the money that people brought for the LORD's Temple and put it into this box.

[10] Whenever the king's secretary and the high priest saw that the box was full, they counted all the money that had been given for the LORD's Temple and put it in bags. [11] Then they paid the men who were in charge of the work on the LORD's Temple. They paid the carpenters and other builders who worked on the LORD's Temple. [12] They used that money to pay the stoneworkers and stonecutters, and they used it to buy timber, cut stone and everything else to repair the LORD's Temple.

[13-14] People gave money for the LORD's Temple, but the priests could not use this money to make silver cups, snuffers, basins, trumpets or any of the gold and silver dishes that were to be used inside the LORD's Temple. This money was used only to pay the workers who repaired the LORD's Temple. [15] Those who were in charge of paying the workers did not have to give a report of how they spent the money, because they could be trusted.

[16] People gave money when they offered guilt offerings and sin offerings, but that money was not used for the LORD's Temple. It belonged to the priests.

Joash Saves Jerusalem From Hazael

[17] Hazael was the king of Aram. He went to fight against the city of Gath and defeated it. Then he made plans to go and fight against Jerusalem.

[18] Joash[b] and his ancestors—Jehoshaphat, Jehoram and Ahaziah—had all been kings of Judah. They had given many things to the LORD that were kept in his Temple. Joash gathered all these things and all the gold that was stored in the Temple and in his palace. He sent all this treasure to King Hazael of Aram, who then commanded his army to leave Jerusalem.

The Death of Joash

[19] All the great things that Joash did are written in the book, *The History of the Kings of Judah*.

[20] Joash's officers made plans against him. They killed Joash at the house of Millo on the road that goes down to Silla. [21] Jozabad son of Shimeath and Jehozabad son of Shomer were Joash's officers. These men killed Joash.

The people buried Joash with his ancestors in the City of David. His son Amaziah became the new king after him.

Jehoahaz Begins His Rule

13 Jehoahaz son of Jehu became king over Israel in Samaria. This was during the twenty-third year that Joash son of Ahaziah was king in Judah. Jehoahaz ruled for 17 years.

---

[a] **12:9 doorway** Literally, "threshold".
[b] **12:18 Joash** Or "Jehoash", the long form of the name "Joash".

²Jehoahaz did what the LORD considered wrong. Like Jeroboam son of Nebat, he committed sins that also caused the people of Israel to sin. And he never stopped doing those things. ³Then the LORD was angry with Israel. He let King Hazael of Aram and Hazael's son Ben-Hadad gain control of Israel.

The LORD Has Mercy on Israel

⁴Then Jehoahaz begged the LORD to help them. The LORD listened to him because he had seen the terrible troubles that the king of Aram had caused the Israelites.

⁵So the LORD sent a man to save Israel. The Israelites were free from the Arameans. So the Israelites went to their own homes, as they did before.

⁶But the Israelites still did not stop committing the sins of the family of Jeroboam that caused Israel to sin. The Israelites continued committing the sins of Jeroboam. They also kept the Asherah poles in Samaria.

⁷The king of Aram defeated Jehoahaz's army and destroyed most of the men in the army. He left only 50 horsemen, 10 chariots and 10,000 foot soldiers. Jehoahaz's soldiers were like chaff blown away by the wind at the time of threshing.

⁸All the great things that Jehoahaz did are written in the book, *The History of the Kings of Israel.* ⁹Jehoahaz died and was buried with his ancestors. The people buried Jehoahaz in Samaria. His son Jehoash became the new king after him.

Jehoash's Rule Over Israel

¹⁰Jehoash son of Jehoahaz became king over Israel in Samaria. This was during the thirty-seventh year that Joash was king of Judah. Jehoash ruled Israel for 16 years. ¹¹He did what the LORD said was wrong. He did not stop committing the sins of Jeroboam son of Nebat who caused Israel to sin. Jehoash continued to commit those sins. ¹²All the great things that Jehoash did and his wars against King Amaziah of Judah are written in the book, *The History of the Kings of Israel.* ¹³Jehoash died and was buried with his ancestors. Jeroboam became the new king and sat on Jehoash's throne. Jehoash was buried at Samaria with the kings of Israel.

Jehoash Visits Elisha

¹⁴Elisha became sick, and later he died from this sickness. King Jehoash of Israel went to visit Elisha. Jehoash cried for him and said, "My father, my father! Is it time for the chariot of Israel and its horses?"[a]

¹⁵Elisha said to Jehoash, "Take a bow and some arrows."

Jehoash took a bow and some arrows. ¹⁶Then Elisha said to the king of Israel, "Put your hand on the bow." Jehoash put his hand on the bow. Then Elisha put his hands on the king's hands. ¹⁷Elisha said, "Open the east window." Jehoash opened the window. Then Elisha said, "Shoot."

Jehoash shot. Then Elisha said, "This is the LORD's arrow of victory over Aram! You will defeat the Arameans at Aphek until you destroy them."

¹⁸Elisha said, "Take the arrows." Jehoash took the arrows. Then Elisha said to him, "Hit them on the ground."

Jehoash hit them on the ground three times. Then he stopped. ¹⁹The man of God was angry with Jehoash. Elisha said, "You should have hit five or six times! Then you would have defeated Aram until you destroyed it! But now, you will defeat Aram only three times."

An Amazing Thing at Elisha's Grave

²⁰Elisha died, and the people buried him.

Once in the spring, a group of Moabite soldiers came to fight against Israel. ²¹Some Israelites were burying a dead man when they saw that group of soldiers. The Israelites quickly threw the dead man into Elisha's grave. As soon as the dead man touched the bones of Elisha, he came back to life and stood up on his feet.

Jehoash Wins Back Cities of Israel

²²During all the days that Jehoahaz ruled, King Hazael of Aram caused trouble to Israel. ²³But the LORD was kind to the Israelites. He had mercy and showed his care for them because of his agreement with Abraham, Isaac and Jacob. He did not want them to be destroyed. He has never completely rejected them.

²⁴King Hazael of Aram died, and Ben-Hadad became the new king after him. ²⁵Before he died, Hazael had taken some cities in war from Jehoahaz, Jehoash's father. But now Jehoash took back these cities from Hazael's son Ben-Hadad. Jehoash defeated Ben-Hadad three times and took back the cities of Israel.

Amaziah Begins His Rule in Judah

14 Amaziah son of King Joash of Judah became king in the second year that Jehoash son of Jehoahaz was king of Israel. ²Amaziah was 25 years old when he began to rule. He ruled for 29 years in Jerusalem. His mother was Jehoaddin from Jerusalem. ³Amaziah did what the LORD said was right, but he did not follow God completely like David his ancestor. Amaziah did everything that Joash his father had done. ⁴He did not destroy

---

ᵃ **13:14** *Is it time . . . horses* This means "Is it time for God to come and take you?" See 2 Kgs 2:12.

the high places. The people still sacrificed and burned incense at those places of worship.

⁵At the time that Amaziah had strong control of the kingdom, he killed the officers who had killed his father. ⁶But he did not kill the children of the murderers because of the rules written in the book, *The Law of Moses.* The LORD gave this command in there: "Parents must not be put to death for something their children did. And children must not be put to death for something their parents did. People should be put to death only for what they themselves did."*ᵃ*

⁷Amaziah killed 10,000 Edomites in the Valley of Salt. In war Amaziah took Sela and called it "Joktheel". It is still called "Joktheel" today.

Amaziah Wants to Fight Jehoash

⁸Amaziah sent messengers to Jehoash son of Jehoahaz, son of King Jehu of Israel. Amaziah's message said, "Come on, let's meet together face to face and fight."

⁹King Jehoash of Israel sent an answer to King Amaziah of Judah. Jehoash said, "The thornbush in Lebanon sent a message to the cedar tree in Lebanon. It said, 'Give your daughter for my son to marry.' But a wild animal from Lebanon passed by and trampled down the thornbush. ¹⁰True, you have defeated Edom. But you have become proud because of your victory over Edom. But stay at home and boast! Don't make trouble for yourself. If you do this, you will fall, and Judah will fall with you!"

¹¹But Amaziah would not listen to Jehoash's warning. So King Jehoash of Israel went to fight against King Amaziah of Judah at Beth Shemesh in Judah.*ᵇ* ¹²Israel defeated Judah. Every man of Judah ran home. ¹³At Beth Shemesh, King Jehoash of Israel captured King Amaziah of Judah, the son of Joash, the son of Ahaziah. Jehoash took Amaziah to Jerusalem. Jehoash broke down the wall of Jerusalem from the Gate of Ephraim to the Corner Gate, almost 200 metres.*ᶜ* ¹⁴Then Jehoash took all the gold and silver and all the dishes in the LORD's Temple and in the treasuries of the king's palace. Jehoash also took people to be his prisoners. Then he went back to Samaria.

¹⁵All the great things that Jehoash did, including how he fought against King Amaziah of Judah, are written in the book, *The History of the Kings of Israel.* ¹⁶Jehoash died and was buried with his ancestors. He was buried in Samaria with the kings of Israel. Jehoash's son Jeroboam became the new king after him.

The Death of Amaziah

¹⁷King Amaziah son of Joash of Judah lived for 15 years after the death of King Jehoash son of Jehoahaz of Israel. ¹⁸All the great things that Amaziah did are written in the book, *The History of the Kings of Judah.* ¹⁹The people made a plan against Amaziah in Jerusalem, so he ran away to Lachish. But the people sent men after Amaziah to Lachish, and they killed him there. ²⁰The people brought Amaziah's body back on horses. He was buried at Jerusalem with his ancestors in the City of David.

Azariah Begins His Rule Over Judah

²¹Then all the people of Judah made Azariah the new king. Azariah was 16 years old. ²²So King Amaziah died and was buried with his ancestors. Then Azariah rebuilt Elath and got it back for Judah.

Jeroboam II Begins His Rule Over Israel

²³King Jeroboam son of King Jehoash of Israel began to rule in Samaria during the fifteenth year that Amaziah son of Joash was king of Judah. Jeroboam ruled for 41 years. ²⁴Jeroboam did what the LORD said was wrong. He did not stop committing the sins of Jeroboam son of Nebat who caused Israel to sin. ²⁵Jeroboam took back Israel's land between Lebo Hamath and the Dead Sea. This happened as the LORD of Israel had told his servant Jonah son of Amittai, the prophet from Gath Hepher. ²⁶The LORD saw that all the Israelites, both slaves and free men, had many troubles. No one was left who could help Israel. ²⁷The LORD did not say that he would take away the name of Israel from the world. So he used Jeroboam son of Jehoash to save the Israelites.

²⁸All the great things that Jeroboam did are written in the book, *The History of the Kings of Israel.* This includes the story about Jeroboam winning back Damascus and Hamath for Israel. (These cities had belonged to Judah.) ²⁹Jeroboam died and was buried with his ancestors, the kings of Israel. Jeroboam's son Zechariah became the new king after him.

Azariah's Rule Over Judah

15 King Azariah son of Amaziah of Judah became king in the twenty-seventh year that Jeroboam was king of Israel. ²Azariah was 16 years old when he began to rule. He ruled for 52 years in Jerusalem. His mother was named Jecoliah of Jerusalem. ³Azariah did what the LORD said was right, just as his father Amaziah had

---

ᵃ **14:6** *Parents must . . . did* See Deut. 24:16.
ᵇ **14:11** *King Jehoash . . . Judah* Literally, "He and King Amaziah of Judah looked at each other in the face at Beth Shemesh in Judah."
ᶜ **14:13** *almost 200 metres* Literally, "400 *cubits*".

done. [4]But he did not destroy the high places. People still made sacrifices and burned incense in these places of worship.

[5]The LORD caused King Azariah to become sick with leprosy. He was a leper until the day he died. Azariah lived in a separate house. His son Jotham was in charge of the king's palace, and he judged the people.

[6]All the great things that Azariah did are written in the book, *The History of the Kings of Judah*. [7]Azariah died and was buried with his ancestors in the City of David. Azariah's son Jotham became the new king after him.

Zechariah's Short Rule Over Israel

[8]Zechariah son of Jeroboam ruled over Samaria in Israel for six months. This was during the thirty-eighth year that Azariah was king of Judah. [9]Zechariah did what the LORD said was wrong. He did the same things his ancestors did. He did not stop committing the sins of Jeroboam son of Nebat who caused Israel to sin.

[10]Shallum son of Jabesh made plans against Zechariah. Shallum killed Zechariah in Ibleam.[a] Shallum became the new king. [11]All the other things that Zechariah did are written in the book, *The History of the Kings of Israel*. [12]In this way the LORD's word came true. He had told Jehu that four generations of his descendants would be kings of Israel.

Shallum's Short Rule Over Israel

[13]Shallum son of Jabesh became king of Israel during the thirty-ninth year that Uzziah[b] was king of Judah. Shallum ruled for one month in Samaria.

[14]Menahem son of Gadi came up from Tirzah to Samaria and killed Shallum son of Jabesh. Then Menahem became the new king after him.

[15]All the things Shallum did, including his plans against Zechariah, are written in the book, *The History of the Kings of Israel*.

Menahem's Rule Over Israel

[16]Menahem defeated Tiphsah and the area around it. The people refused to open the city gate for him. So Menahem defeated them and ripped open all the pregnant women in that city.

[17]Menahem son of Gadi became king over Israel during the thirty-ninth year that Azariah was king of Judah. Menahem ruled ten years in Samaria. [18]Menahem did what the LORD said was wrong. He did not stop committing the sins of Jeroboam son of Nebat who caused Israel to sin.

[19]King Pul of Assyria came to fight against Israel. Menahem gave Pul 34,000 kilogrammes[c] of silver so that Pul would support him and help him gain complete control of the kingdom. [20]Menahem raised the money by making all the rich and powerful men pay taxes. He taxed each man 50 pieces[d] of silver and gave the money to the king of Assyria. So the king of Assyria left and did not stay there in Israel.

[21]All the great things that Menahem did are written in the book, *The History of the Kings of Israel*. [22]Menahem died and was buried with his ancestors. His son Pekahiah became the new king after him.

Pekahiah's Rule Over Israel

[23]Pekahiah son of Menahem became king over Israel in Samaria during the fiftieth year that Azariah was king of Judah. Pekahiah ruled for two years. [24]He did what the LORD said was wrong. He did not stop committing the sins of Jeroboam son of Nebat that caused Israel to sin.

[25]The commander of Pekahiah's army was Pekah son of Remaliah. Pekah took 50 men from Gilead with him and killed Pekahiah, along with Argob and Arieh,[e] in Samaria at the king's palace. Then Pekah became the new king.

[26]All the great things Pekahiah did are written in the book, *The History of the Kings of Israel*.

Pekah's Rule Over Israel

[27]Pekah son of Remaliah began to rule over Israel in Samaria during the fifty-second year that Azariah was king of Judah. Pekah ruled for 20 years. [28]Pekah did what the LORD said was wrong. He did not stop committing the sins of Jeroboam son of Nebat who caused Israel to sin.

[29]King Tiglath Pileser of Assyria came to fight against Israel while Pekah was king of Israel. Tiglath Pileser captured Ijon, Abel Bethmaacah, Janoah, Kedesh, Hazor, Gilead, Galilee and all the area of Naphtali. He took the people from these places as prisoners to Assyria. [30]Hoshea son of Elah made plans against Pekah son of Remaliah and killed him. Then Hoshea became the new king. This was during the twentieth year that Jotham son of Uzziah was king of Judah.

[31]All the great things that Pekah did are written in the book, *The History of the Kings of Israel*.

Jotham's Rule Over Judah

[32]Jotham son of Uzziah became king of Judah. This was during the second year that Pekah son of

---

[a] **15:10** *in Ibleam* This is found in some copies of the ancient Greek version. The standard Hebrew text has "in public".
[b] **15:13** *Uzziah* Another name for Azariah.
[c] **15:19** *34,000 kilogrammes* Literally, "1,000 *talents*".
[d] **15:20** *50 pieces* Literally, "50 *shekels*".
[e] **15:25** *Argob and Arieh* Some scholars think these two names were not part of the original Hebrew text.

Remaliah was king of Israel. [33]Jotham was 25 years old when he became king. He ruled for 16 years in Jerusalem. His mother was named Jerusha, the daughter of Zadok. [34]Jotham did what the LORD said was right, just as his father Uzziah had done. [35]But he did not destroy the high places. The people still made sacrifices and burned incense at those places of worship. Jotham built the upper gate of the LORD's Temple. [36]All the great things that Jotham did are written in the book, *The History of the Kings of Judah.*

[37]At that time the LORD sent King Rezin of Aram and Pekah son of Remaliah to fight against Judah.

[38]Jotham died and was buried with his ancestors in the City of David, his ancestor. Jotham's son Ahaz became the new king after him.

Ahaz Becomes King Over Judah

16 Ahaz son of Jotham became king of Judah during the seventeenth year that Pekah son of Remaliah was king of Israel. [2]Ahaz was 20 years old when he became king. He ruled for 16 years in Jerusalem. Unlike his ancestor David, Ahaz did not do what the LORD said was right. [3]He did the same bad things the kings of Israel had done. He even burned his son as a sacrifice.[a] He copied the terrible sins of the nations that the LORD had forced to leave the country when the Israelites came. [4]Ahaz made sacrifices and burned incense at the high places and on the hills and under every green tree.

[5]King Rezin of Aram and King Pekah son of Remaliah of Israel came to fight against Jerusalem. Rezin and Pekah surrounded Ahaz, but could not defeat him. [6]At that time King Rezin of Aram took back Elath for Aram. Rezin took all the people of Judah who were living in Elath. The Arameans settled in Elath, and they still live there today.

[7]Ahaz sent messengers to King Tiglath Pileser of Assyria with this message: "I am your servant. I am like a son to you. Come and save me from the king of Aram and the king of Israel. They have come to fight me." [8]Ahaz also took the silver and gold that was in the Temple of the LORD and in the treasuries of the king's palace. Then Ahaz sent a gift to the king of Assyria. [9]The king of Assyria listened to Ahaz and went to fight against Damascus. The king captured that city and took the people from Damascus as prisoners to Kir. He also killed Rezin.

[10]King Ahaz went to Damascus to meet King Tiglath Pileser of Assyria. Ahaz saw the altar at Damascus. He sent a model and plan of this altar to Uriah the priest. [11]Then Uriah the priest built an altar just like the model King Ahaz had sent

him from Damascus. Uriah the priest built the altar this way before King Ahaz returned from Damascus.

[12]When the king arrived from Damascus, he saw the altar. He offered sacrifices on the altar. [13]Ahaz burned his burnt offerings and grain offerings on it. He poured his drink offering and sprinkled the blood of his fellowship offerings on this altar.

[14]Ahaz took the bronze altar that was before the LORD from the front of the Temple. This bronze altar was between Ahaz's altar and the Temple of the LORD. Ahaz put the bronze altar on the north side of his own altar. [15]He commanded Uriah the priest, "Use the large new altar to burn the morning burnt offerings, the evening grain offerings and the drink offerings from all the people of this country. Sprinkle all the blood from the burnt offering and other sacrifices on the large altar. But I will use the bronze altar to get answers from God." [16]Uriah the priest did everything that King Ahaz commanded him to do.

[17]There were stands with bronze panels and bowls for the priests to wash their hands. King Ahaz took apart the panels and removed the bowls from the stands. He also took the large basin off the bronze bulls that stood under it. He put the basin on a stone pavement. [18]Workers had built a covered place inside the Temple area for the Sabbath meetings. But Ahaz removed the covered place and the outside entrance for the king. He removed all these from the LORD's Temple. Ahaz did this because of the king of Assyria.

[19]All the great things that Ahaz did are written in the book, *The History of the Kings of Judah.* [20]Ahaz died and was buried with his ancestors in the City of David. Ahaz's son Hezekiah became the new king after him.

Hoshea Begins His Rule Over Israel

17 Hoshea son of Elah began to rule in Samaria over Israel. This was during the twelfth year that Ahaz was king of Judah. Hoshea ruled for nine years. [2]He did what the LORD said was wrong, but he was not as bad as the kings of Israel who had ruled before him.

[3]King Shalmaneser of Assyria came to fight against Hoshea and defeated him. So Hoshea paid tribute to Shalmaneser.

[4]Later, Hoshea sent messengers to the king of Egypt to ask for help. That king's name was So. That year Hoshea did not pay tribute to the king of Assyria as he did every other year. The king of Assyria learned that Hoshea had made plans against him. So he arrested Hoshea and put him in jail.

---

[a] **16:3** *burned his son as a sacrifice* Literally, "made his son pass through the fire".

⁵The king of Assyria attacked many places in Israel. Then he came to Samaria and fought against it for three years. ⁶The king of Assyria took Samaria during the ninth year that Hoshea was king of Israel. He captured many Israelites and took them as prisoners to Assyria. He made them live in Halah by the Habor River at Gozan and in other cities of the Medes.

⁷These things happened because the Israelites had sinned against the LORD their God. And it was the Lord who brought the Israelites out of the land of Egypt! He saved them from the power of Pharaoh, the king of Egypt. But the Israelites began worshipping other gods. ⁸They began doing the same things that other people did. And the LORD had forced those people to leave their land when the Israelites came. The Israelites also chose to be ruled by kings. ⁹The Israelites secretly did things against the LORD their God, and those things were wrong!

The Israelites built high places in all their cities—from the smallest town to the largest city. ¹⁰They put up memorial stones and Asherah poles on every high hill and under every green tree. ¹¹They burned incense there in all those places for worship.ᵃ They did these things like the nations that the LORD forced out of the land before them. The Israelites did evil things that made the LORD angry. ¹²They served idols, and the LORD had said to them, "You must not do this."

¹³The LORD used every prophet and every seer to warn Israel and Judah. He said, "Turn away from the evil things you do. Obey my commands and laws. Follow all the law that I gave to your ancestors. I used my servants the prophets to give this law to you."

¹⁴But the people would not listen. They were very stubborn like their ancestors. Their ancestors did not believe the LORD their God. ¹⁵They refused to follow his laws and the agreement he made with their ancestors. They would not listen to his warnings. They worshipped idols that were worth nothing and they themselves became worth nothing. The LORD had warned them not to do the evil things that the people in the nations around them did. But they lived the same way those people lived.

¹⁶They stopped following the commands of the LORD their God. They made two gold statues of calves. They made Asherah poles. They worshipped all the stars of heaven and served Baal. ¹⁷They sacrificed their sons and daughters in the fire. They tried to learn the future from fortune-tellers and used magic. They sold themselves to do what the LORD said was evil, trying to make him angry. ¹⁸So

the LORD became very angry with Israel and sent them away. Only the people of Judah were left in the land.

¹⁹But even the people of Judah did not obey the commands of the LORD their God. They lived the same way the Israelites had lived. ²⁰So the LORD rejected all the descendants of Israel. He caused them many troubles. He let their enemies defeat them. Finally, he sent them all away from him.

²¹This all began when the LORD separated the Israelites from David's family. That's when they made Jeroboam son of Nebat their king. Jeroboam led the Israelites away from following the LORD. He caused them to commit great sin. ²²So the Israelites sinned in all the ways Jeroboam did. And they did not stop committing these sins. ²³Finally, the LORD sent them away from his land. Through his prophets he had warned the people that this would happen. So the Israelites were taken out of their country into Assyria. And they are still there today.

Foreigners Settle in Israel

²⁴The king of Assyria took the Israelites out of Samaria and brought in other people from Babylon, Cuthah, Avva, Hamath and Sepharvaim. They took over Samaria and lived in the cities around it. ²⁵When these people began to live in Samaria, they did not honour the LORD, so the LORD sent lions to attack them. The lions killed some of them. ²⁶Some people said to the king of Assyria, "The people who you took away and put in the cities of Samaria don't know the law of the god of that country. So that god sent lions to attack them. The lions killed them because they don't know the law of the god of that country."

²⁷So the king of Assyria gave this command: "You took some priests from Samaria. Send one of them who I captured back to Samaria. Let that priest go and live there. Then he can teach the people the law of the god of that country."

²⁸So one of the priests who the Assyrians had carried away from Samaria came to live in Bethel. He taught the people how they should honour the LORD.

²⁹But all those people made gods of their own. They put them in the temples at the high places that the people of Samaria had made. They did this wherever they lived. ³⁰The people of Babylon made the false god Succoth Benoth. The people of Cuthah made the false god Nergal. The people of Hamath made the false god Ashima. ³¹The people of Avva made the false gods Nibhaz and Tartak. The people from Sepharvaim also burned

---

ᵃ **17:11 places for worship** Or "high places", places for worshipping God or false gods. These places were often on the hills and mountains.

their children in the fire to honour their false gods, Adrammelech and Anammelech.

³²But they also worshipped the LORD. They chose priests for the high places from among the people. These priests made sacrifices for the people in the temples at those places of worship. ³³They respected the LORD but also served their own gods, just as they did in their own countries. ³⁴Even today they live the same way they did in the past. They don't honour the LORD. They don't obey the rules and commands of the Israelites. They don't obey the law or the commands that the LORD gave to the children of Jacob. ³⁵The LORD made an agreement with the Israelites. He commanded them, "You must not honour other gods. You must not worship them or serve them or offer sacrifices to them. ³⁶But you must follow the LORD, who brought you out of Egypt. He used his great power to save you. You must worship him and make sacrifices to him. ³⁷You must obey the rules, laws, teachings and commands that he wrote for you. You must obey these things all the time. You must not respect other gods. ³⁸You must not forget the agreement that I made with you. You must not respect other gods. ³⁹No, you must respect only the LORD your God. Then he will save you from all your enemies."

⁴⁰But the Israelites did not listen. They kept on doing the same things they did before. ⁴¹So now those other nations respected the LORD, but they also served their own idols. Their children and grandchildren did the same thing their ancestors did. They still do these things to this day.

Hezekiah Begins His Rule Over Judah

18 Hezekiah son of Ahaz was king of Judah. Hezekiah began to rule during the third year that Hoshea son of Elah was king of Israel. ²Hezekiah was 25 years old when he began to rule. He ruled for 29 years in Jerusalem. His mother's name was Abi,ᵃ the daughter of Zechariah.

³Hezekiah did what the LORD said was right, just as David his ancestor had done.

⁴Hezekiah destroyed the high places. He broke the memorial stones and cut down the Asherah poles. At that time the Israelites burned incense to the bronze snake made by Moses. This bronze snake was called "Nehushtan".ᵇ Hezekiah broke this bronze snake into pieces.

⁵Hezekiah trusted in the LORD, the God of Israel. There was no one like Hezekiah among all the kings of Judah before him or after him. ⁶He

was very faithful to the LORD and did not stop following him. He obeyed the commands that the LORD had given to Moses. ⁷The LORD was with Hezekiah, so he was successful in everything he did.

Hezekiah broke away from the king of Assyria and stopped serving him. ⁸Hezekiah defeated the Philistines all the way to Gaza and the area around it. He defeated all the Philistine cities— from the smallest town to the largest city.

The Assyrians Capture Samaria

⁹King Shalmaneser of Assyria went to fight against Samaria. His army surrounded the city. This happened during the fourth year that Hezekiah was king of Judah. (This was also the seventh year that Hoshea son of Elah was king of Israel.) ¹⁰At the end of the third year, Shalmaneser captured Samaria. He took Samaria during the sixth year that Hezekiah was king of Judah. (This was also the ninth year that Hoshea was king of Israel.) ¹¹The king of Assyria took the Israelites as prisoners to Assyria. He made them live in Halah, on the Habor (the river of Gozan) and in the cities of the Medes. ¹²This happened because the Israelites did not obey the LORD their God. They broke his agreement and did not obey everything that the LORD's servant Moses had commanded. The Israelites would not listen to the Lord's agreement, or do what it taught them to do.

Assyria Gets Ready to Take Judah

¹³During Hezekiah's fourteenth year as king, King Sennacherib of Assyria went to fight against all the strong cities of Judah. Sennacherib defeated them all. ¹⁴Then King Hezekiah of Judah sent a message to the king of Assyria at Lachish. Hezekiah said, "I have done wrong. Leave me alone, and I will pay whatever you want."

Then the king of Assyria told King Hezekiah of Judah to pay him more than 10,000 kilogrammesᶜ of silver and 1,000 kilogrammesᵈ of gold. ¹⁵Hezekiah gave all the silver that was in the LORD's Temple and in the king's treasuries. ¹⁶That is when Hezekiah cut off the gold that he had put on the doors and doorposts of the LORD's Temple and gave it to the king of Assyria.

The King of Assyria Sends Men to Jerusalem

¹⁷The king of Assyria sent his three most important officers with a large army to King Hezekiah in Jerusalem. They left Lachish and went to Jerusalem. They stood near the aqueduct

---

ᵃ **18:2 Abi** Or "Abijah".
ᵇ **18:4 Nehushtan** This Hebrew name is like the words meaning "bronze" and "snake".
ᶜ **18:14 10,000 kilogrammes** Literally, "300 *talents*".
ᵈ **18:14 1,000 kilogrammes** Literally, "30 *talents*".

by the Upper Pool,[a] on the street that leads up to Laundryman's Field. [18]These men called for the king, but Eliakim son of Hilkiah, Shebna and Joah son of Asaph went out to meet them. Eliakim was the palace manager, Joah was the record keeper and Shebna was the royal secretary.

[19]The commander said to them, "Tell Hezekiah this is what the great king, the king of Assyria says:

"'What are you trusting in to help you? [20]If you say, "I trust in power and great battle plans," then that is useless. Now I ask you, who do you trust so much that you are willing to rebel against me? [21]Are you depending on Egypt to help you? Egypt is like a broken walking stick. If you lean on it for support, it will only hurt you and make a hole in your hand. Pharaoh, the king of Egypt, cannot be trusted by anyone who depends on him for help. [22]Maybe you will say, "We trust the LORD our God to help us." But I know that Hezekiah destroyed the altars and high places where people worshipped the Lord. Hezekiah told the people of Judah and Jerusalem, "You must worship only at this one altar here in Jerusalem."

[23]"'If you still want to fight my master, the king of Assyria, I will make this agreement with you. I promise that I will give you 2,000 horses if you can find enough men to ride them into battle. [24]But even then you couldn't beat one of my master's lowest ranking officers. So why do you still depend on Egypt's chariots and horsemen?

[25]"'Now, do you think I came to this country to destroy it without the LORD's help? No, the LORD said to me, "Go up against this country and destroy it!"'"

[26]Then Eliakim son of Hilkiah, Shebna and Joah said to the commander, "Please speak to us in Aramaic, not Hebrew.[b] We will understand you, but we don't want the people sitting there on the wall to understand what you say."

[27]But the commander said, "My master sent me to speak to everyone, not only to you and your king. I must also speak to those people there on the wall. When we surround your city, they will suffer too. Like you, they will become so hungry they will eat their own waste and drink their own urine!"

[28]Then the commander, shouting loudly in Hebrew, gave this warning to them all:

"Hear this message from the great king, the king of Assyria! [29]This is what the king says: 'Don't let Hezekiah fool you! He cannot save you from my power. [30]Don't listen to him when he tells you to trust in the LORD. Don't believe him when he says, "The LORD will save us. He will not let the king of Assyria defeat the city."

[31]"'Don't listen to Hezekiah! This is what the king of Assyria says: Come out here and show me that you want peace. Then you will all be free to have grapes from your own vines, figs from your own trees and water from your own well. [32]After some time, I will come and take you to a land like your own. In that new land, you will have plenty of grain for making bread and vineyards for producing wine. I am offering you a choice to live instead of dying.

[33]"'Don't believe Hezekiah when he tells you, "The LORD will save us." He is wrong. [33]Did any of the gods of other nations save their land from the king of Assyria? [34]When I destroyed the cities of Hamath and Arpad, where were their gods? What about the gods of Sepharvaim, Hena and Ivvah? Were any gods able to save Samaria from my power? [35]None of the gods of these other places were able to save their land from me! So why do you think the LORD can save Jerusalem from me?'"

[36]But the people were silent. They did not say a word to the commander, because King Hezekiah had commanded them, "Don't say anything to him."

[37]Then the palace manager (Eliakim son of Hilkiah), the royal secretary (Shebna) and the record keeper (Joah son of Asaph) went to Hezekiah. Their clothes were torn to show they were upset. They told Hezekiah everything the Assyrian commander had said.

Hezekiah Talks With Isaiah the Prophet

19 When King Hezekiah heard this, he tore his clothes to show he was upset. Then he put on sackcloth and went to the LORD's Temple.

[2]Hezekiah sent Eliakim the palace manager, Shebna the royal secretary and the leading priests to the prophet Isaiah son of Amoz. They wore the special clothes that showed they were sad and upset. [3]They said to Isaiah, "King Hezekiah has commanded that today will be a special day for sorrow and sadness. It will be a

---

[a] **18:17 Upper Pool** The Pool of Siloam at the southern tip of the City of David (Jerusalem), just above the older pool now called Birket al Hamrah.
[b] **18:26 Hebrew** Literally, "Judean", the language of Judah and Israel.

very sad day, like the time a child should be born, but is not strong enough to come from its mother's womb. [4]The commander's master, the king of Assyria, has sent him to say bad things about the living God. Maybe the LORD your God will hear all those things and answer them. Maybe the LORD your God will show how wrong the enemy is! So pray for the people who are still left alive."

[5]King Hezekiah's officers went to Isaiah. [6]Isaiah said to them, "Give this message to your master, Hezekiah: The LORD says, 'Don't be afraid of what you heard from the commanders. Don't believe what those "boys" from the king of Assyria said to make fun of me. [7]Look, I will send a spirit against the king of Assyria. He will get a report warning him about a danger, so he will return to his own country. And I will cut him down with a sword in his own country.'"

The Assyrian Army Leaves Jerusalem

[8]The commander heard that the king of Assyria had left Lachish. He found him at Libnah, fighting against that city. [9]Then the king of Assyria heard a report that said, "Tirhakah,[a] the king of Ethiopia, has come to fight against you."

So the king of Assyria sent messengers to Hezekiah again. [10]He told them, "Tell King Hezekiah of Judah these things:

'Don't be fooled by the god you trust when he says Jerusalem will not be defeated by the king of Assyria. [11]You have heard what the kings of Assyria did to all the other countries. We completely destroyed them! Will you be saved? No! [12]Did the gods of those nations save their people? No, my ancestors destroyed them all. They destroyed Gozan, Haran, Rezeph and the people of Eden living in Tel Assar. [13]Where is the king of Hamath? The king of Arpad? The king of the city of Sepharvaim? The kings of Hena and Ivvah?'"

Hezekiah Prays to the LORD

[14]Hezekiah received the letters from the messengers and read them. Then he went up to the LORD's Temple and laid the letters out in front of the LORD. [15]Hezekiah prayed before the LORD and said, "LORD, God of Israel, you sit as King above the winged creatures. You alone are the God who rules all the kingdoms on earth. You made heaven and earth. [16]LORD, please listen to me. LORD, open your eyes and look at this message. Hear the words that Sennacherib sent to insult the living God. [17]It is true, LORD. The kings of Assyria did destroy all those nations. [18]They did throw the gods of those nations into the fire. But they were not real gods. They were only wood and stone—statues that people made. That is why the kings of Assyria could destroy them. [19]But you are the LORD our God, so please save us from the king of Assyria. Then all the other nations will know that you, LORD, are the only God."

God Answers Hezekiah

[20]Then Isaiah son of Amoz sent this message to Hezekiah. Isaiah said, "The LORD, the God of Israel, says this: 'You prayed to me about the message that came from King Sennacherib of Assyria. I have heard you.' [21]This is the LORD's message against Sennacherib:

"'The people of Jerusalem[b] hate you,
and they make fun of you.
Jerusalem shakes her head at you
and laughs behind your back.
[22]But you have insulted and made fun of me.
I am the one you have been shouting at
with such a proud look on your face!
You have acted against me, the Holy One of
Israel!
[23]I am the Lord, but your messengers have
insulted me.
They told me your boastful words:
"I climbed the highest mountains with all my
chariots.
I reached the most difficult peaks in
Lebanon.
There I cut down the tallest cedar trees
and the best pines.
I went deep inside the country
and saw its thickest forests.
[24]I have dug wells in faraway lands,
finding water everywhere to drink.
I have dried up the rivers of Egypt
and walked on the land where they flowed."

[25]"'Sennacherib, how can you say such things?
You should know that I planned all this
long ago.
Long ago I decided what you would do,
and now I am making it happen.
I let you tear down those strong cities
and turn them into piles of rocks.
[26]The people there were powerless to stop you.
They were afraid and confused.
They were about to be cut down
like grass and plants in the field.
They were like grass growing on the
housetops,
dying before it grows tall.

27I know all about your battles;
  I know when you rested,
when you went out to war,
  and when you came home.
I also know when you got upset at me.
28Yes, you were upset at me.
  I heard your proud insults.
So I will put my hook in your nose
  and my bit in your mouth.
Then I will turn you around
  and lead you back the way you came.'"

The LORD's Message for Hezekiah

29Then the Lord said, "I will give you a sign to show that these words are true. You were not able to plant seeds this year, so next year you will eat grain that grows wild from the previous year's crop. But in the third year, you will eat grain from seeds that you planted. You will harvest your crops and have plenty to eat. You will plant grapevines and eat their fruit. You will plant vineyards and eat the grapes from them. 30The people from the family of Judah who have escaped and are left alive will be like plants that send their roots deep into the ground and produce fruit above the ground. 31That is because a few people will come out of Jerusalem alive. There will be survivors coming from Mount Zion. The strong love of the LORD All-Powerful will do this.

32So the LORD says this about the king of Assyria:

'He will not come into this city
  or shoot an arrow at this city.
He will not bring his shields up against this
    city
  or build up a hill of dirt to attack its walls.
33He will go back the way he came,
  and he will not come into this city.
  The LORD says this.
34I will protect this city and save it.
  I will do this for myself and for my servant
    David.'"

The Assyrian Army Is Destroyed

35That night the angel of the LORD went out and killed 185,000 people in the Assyrian camp. When the others got up in the morning, they saw all the dead bodies. 36So King Sennacherib of Assyria left and went back to Nineveh where he stayed. 37One day Sennacherib was in the temple of his god Nisroch, worshipping him. His sons Adrammelech and Sharezer killed him with a sword and ran away to Ararat. So his son Esarhaddon became the new king of Assyria.

Hezekiah's Illness

20 At that time Hezekiah became sick and almost died. The prophet Isaiah son of Amoz went to see him and told him, "The LORD says, 'You will die soon, so you should tell your family what they should do when you die. You will not get well.'"

2Hezekiah turned his face to the wall ⌊that faced the Temple⌋ and began praying to the LORD. 3"LORD, remember that I have sincerely served you with all my heart. I have done what you say is good." Then Hezekiah cried very hard.

4Before Isaiah had left the middle courtyard, he received this message from the LORD, 5"Go back and speak to Hezekiah, the leader of my people. Tell him, 'This is what the LORD, the God of your ancestor David, says: I heard your prayer and I saw your tears, so I will heal you. On the third day, you will go up to the Temple of the LORD. 6I will add 15 years to your life. I will save you and this city from the king of Assyria. I will protect this city. I will do this for myself and because of the promise I made to my servant David.'"

7Then Isaiah said, "Crush figs together and put them on your sore; you will get well."

So they took the mixture of figs and put it on Hezekiah's sore place, and he got well.

8Hezekiah asked Isaiah, "What will be the sign that the LORD will heal me, and that I will go up to the Temple of the LORD on the third day?"

9Isaiah said, "Which do you want? Should the shadow go forward ten steps or go back ten steps?ᵃ This is the sign for you from the LORD to show that the LORD will do what he said he would do."

10Hezekiah answered, "It is an easy thing for the shadow to go down ten steps. No, make the shadow go back ten steps."

11Then Isaiah prayed, and the LORD made the shadow move back ten steps. It went back up the steps that it had already been on.

Messengers From Babylon

12At that time Merodach Baladan son of Baladan was king of Babylon. He sent letters and a gift to Hezekiah when he heard that Hezekiah had been sick. 13Hezekiah listened to the messengers and then showed them all the valuable things he owned. He showed them the silver, the gold, the spices, the expensive perfume and the building where he stored the weapons. He showed them everything in his treasuries, in his palace and in his kingdom.

14Then Isaiah the prophet came to King Hezekiah and asked him, "What did these men say? Where did they come from?"

ᵃ 20:9 the shadow . . . steps This may mean the steps of a special building that Hezekiah used like a clock. When the sun shone on the steps, the shadows showed what time of the day it was.

Hezekiah said, "These men came from a faraway country, from Babylon."

¹⁵Isaiah said, "What did they see in your palace?"

Hezekiah answered, "They saw everything I own. I showed them all my wealth."

¹⁶Then Isaiah said to Hezekiah, "Listen to this message from the LORD. ¹⁷The time is coming when everything in your palace and everything your ancestors have saved until today will be carried away to Babylon. Nothing will be left! The LORD said this. ¹⁸The Babylonians will take your sons, and your sons will become officers[a] in the palace of the king of Babylon."

¹⁹Then Hezekiah told Isaiah, "This message from the LORD is good." (Hezekiah said this because he thought, "There will be real peace and security during my lifetime.")

²⁰All the great things that Hezekiah did, including his work on the pool and the aqueduct to bring water into the city, are written in the book, *The History of the Kings of Judah*. ²¹Hezekiah died and was buried with his ancestors. And his son Manasseh became the new king after him.

INSIGHT

Visitors to modern Israel today can still wade through the water in the series of tunnels that Hezekiah dug thousands of years ago. What a great reminder that the Bible isn't a lot of made-up stories – it's historical reality!

2 Kings 20:20

Manasseh Begins His Evil Rule Over Judah

21 Manasseh was twelve years old when he began to rule. He ruled for 55 years in Jerusalem. His mother's name was Hephzibah.

²Manasseh did what the LORD said was wrong. He did the terrible things the other nations did. (And the LORD forced those nations to leave their country when the Israelites came.) ³Manasseh rebuilt the high places that his father Hezekiah had destroyed. He also built altars for Baal and made an Asherah pole, just as King Ahab of Israel had done. Manasseh worshipped and served the stars of heaven. ⁴When the LORD said, "I will put my name in Jerusalem he was talking about the Temple there that was only for him. But Manasseh built altars there for other gods. ⁵He built altars for the stars of heaven in the two courtyards of the LORD's Temple. ⁶He sacrificed his own son and burned him on the altar.[b] He used different ways of trying to know the future. He even tried to contact ghosts and spirits of the dead for advice and secret knowledge.

Manasseh did more and more things that the LORD saw as evil, which made the Lord angry. ⁷Manasseh made a carved statue of Asherah. He put this statue in the Temple. The LORD had said to David and to David's son Solomon about this Temple: "I have chosen Jerusalem from all the cities in Israel. I will put my name in the Temple in Jerusalem forever. ⁸I will not cause the Israelites to leave the land that I gave to their ancestors. I will let the people stay in their land if they obey everything I commanded them and all the teachings that my servant Moses gave them." ⁹But the people did not listen to God. Manasseh did more evil things than all the nations that lived in Canaan before Israel came. And the LORD destroyed those nations when the Israelites came to take their land.

¹⁰The LORD used his servants the prophets to say this: ¹¹"King Manasseh of Judah has done these hated things and has done more evil than the Amorites before him. He also has caused Judah to sin because of his idols. ¹²So the LORD, the God of Israel, says, 'Look! I will bring so much trouble against Jerusalem and Judah that anyone who hears about it will be shocked.[c] ¹³I will stretch the measuring line of Samaria[d] and the plumb line[e] of Ahab's family over Jerusalem. A man wipes a dish, and then he turns it upside down. I will do that to Jerusalem. ¹⁴There will still be a few of my people left, but I will leave them. I will give them to their enemies. Their enemies will take them as prisoners—they will be like the valuable things soldiers take in war. ¹⁵This is because my people did what I said was wrong. They have made me angry with them since the day their ancestors came up out of Egypt. ¹⁶And Manasseh killed many innocent people. He filled Jerusalem from one end to another with blood. And all these sins are in addition to the sins that caused Judah to sin. Manasseh caused Judah to do what the LORD said was wrong.'"

---

a **20:18** *officers* Or "eunuchs". See "EUNUCH" in the Word List.

b **21:6** *sacrificed . . . on the altar* Literally, "made his son pass through the fire".

c **21:12** *will be shocked* Literally, "both his ears will tingle".

d **21:13** *measuring line of Samaria* Workers used a string with a weight to mark a straight line at the end of a stone wall. The pieces of stone that were outside the line were chipped off and thrown away. This shows that God was "throwing away" Samaria and Ahab's family of kings.

e **21:13** *plumb line* A string with a weight on one end used to show that a wall or building was not straight.

17All the things that Manasseh did, including the sins that he committed, are written in the book, *The History of the Kings of Judah.* 18Manasseh died and was buried with his ancestors. He was buried in the garden at his house. It was called the "Garden of Uzza". His son Amon became the new king after him.

Amon's Short Rule

19Amon was 22 years old when he began to rule. He ruled for two years in Jerusalem. His mother's name was Meshullemeth daughter of Haruz from Jotbah.

20Amon did what the LORD said was wrong, just as his father Manasseh had done. 21Amon lived just as his father had lived. He worshipped and served the same idols his father had worshipped. 22Amon left the LORD, the God of his ancestors, and did not live the way the LORD wanted.

23Amon's servants made plans against him and killed him in his palace. 24The common people killed all the officers who made plans against King Amon. Then the people made Amon's son Josiah the new king after him.

25The other things that Amon did are written in the book, *The History of the Kings of Judah.* 26Amon was buried in his grave at the Garden of Uzza. His son Josiah became the new king.

Josiah Begins His Rule Over Judah

22 Josiah was eight years old when he began to rule. He ruled for 31 years in Jerusalem. His mother's name was Jedidah the daughter of Adaiah of Bozkath. 2Josiah did what the LORD said was right. He followed God like his ancestor David. Josiah obeyed God's teachings—he did exactly what God wanted.

Josiah Orders the Repair of the Temple

3During the eighteenth year that Josiah was king, he sent Shaphan son of Azaliah son of Meshullam, the secretary, to the LORD's Temple. Josiah said, 4"Go up to Hilkiah the high priest. Tell him that he must get the money that people brought to the LORD's Temple. The gatekeepers collected that money from the people. 5The priests must use that money to pay the workers to repair the LORD's Temple. They must give that money to the men who supervise the work on the LORD's Temple. 6Use that money for the carpenters, stonemasons and stonecutters. Also use that money to buy the timber and cut stones that are needed to repair the Temple. 7Don't count the money that you give to the workers. They can be trusted."

Book of the Law Found in the Temple

8Hilkiah the high priest said to Shaphan the secretary, "Look, I found the *Book of the Law*a in the LORD's Temple!" Hilkiah gave the book to Shaphan, and Shaphan read it.

9He went to King Josiah and told him what happened. Shaphan said, "Your servants have gathered all the money that was in the Temple. They gave it to the men who supervise the work on the LORD's Temple." 10Then he told the king, "And Hilkiah the priest also gave this book to me." Then Shaphan read the book to the king.

11When the king heard the words of the *Book of the Law*, he tore his clothes to show he was sad and upset. 12Then he gave a command to Hilkiah the priest, Ahikam son of Shaphan, Acbor son of Micaiah, Shaphan the secretary and Asaiah the king's servant. 13King Josiah said, "Go and ask the LORD what we should do. Ask for me, for the people and for all Judah. Ask about the words of this book that was found. The LORD is angry with us, because our ancestors did not listen to the words of this book. They did not obey all the commands that were written for us."

Josiah and Huldah the Prophetess

14So Hilkiah the priest, Ahikam, Acbor, Shaphan and Asaiah went to Huldah the woman prophet. Huldah was the wife of Shallum son of Tikvah, son of Harhas. He took care of the priests' clothes. Huldah was living in the second quarter in Jerusalem. They went and talked with Huldah.

15Then Huldah said to them, "The LORD, the God of Israel, says: Tell the man who sent you to me: 16'The LORD says this: I am bringing trouble on this place and on the people who live here. These are the troubles that are mentioned in the book that the king of Judah read. 17The people of Judah have left me and have burned incense to other gods. They made me very angry. They made many idols. That is why I will show my anger against this place. My anger will be like a fire that cannot be stopped!'

18-19"King Josiah of Judah sent you to ask advice from the LORD. Tell Josiah that this is what the LORD, the God of Israel, says: 'You heard the words I spoke against this place and those who live here. And when you heard those things, your heart was soft, and you showed your sorrow before the LORD. I said that terrible things would happen to this place. So you tore your clothes to show your sadness, and you began to cry. That is why I heard you.' This is what the LORD says. 20'I will bring you to be with your ancestors. You will die and go to your grave in peace. So your eyes

---

a **22:8** *Book of the Law* This is probably the book of Deuteronomy. Also in 23:2.

will not see all the trouble that I am bringing on this place.'"

Then Hilkiah the priest, Ahikam, Acbor, Shaphan and Asaiah gave that message to the king.

The People Hear the Law

23 King Josiah told all the leaders of Judah and Jerusalem to come and meet with him. [2]Then the king went up to the LORD's Temple. All the people of Judah and the people who lived in Jerusalem went with him. The priests, the prophets and all the people—from the least important to the most important—went with him. Then he read the *Book of the Agreement.* This was the *Book of the Law* that was found in the Lord's Temple. Josiah read the book so that all the people could hear it.

[3]The king stood by the column and made an agreement with the LORD. He agreed to follow the LORD and to obey his commands, the agreement and his rules. He agreed to do this with all his heart and soul. He agreed to obey the agreement written in this book. All the people stood to show that they agreed to follow the agreement.

[4]Then the king commanded Hilkiah the high priest, the other priests and the gatekeepers to bring out of the LORD's Temple all the dishes and things that were made to honour Baal, Asherah and the stars of heaven. Then Josiah burned those things outside Jerusalem in the fields in Kidron Valley. Then they carried the ashes to Bethel. [5]The kings of Judah had chosen some ordinary men to serve as priests. These false priests were burning incense at the high places in every city of Judah and all the towns around Jerusalem. They burned incense to honour Baal, the sun, the moon, the constellations and all the stars in the sky. But Josiah stopped those false priests. [6]Josiah removed the Asherah pole from the LORD's Temple. He took the Asherah pole outside the city to the Kidron Valley and burned it there. Then he beat the burned pieces into dust and scattered the dust over the graves of the common people.[a]

[7]Then King Josiah broke down the houses of the male prostitutes who were in the LORD's Temple. Women also used these houses and made little tent covers to honour the false goddess Asherah.

[8-9]At that time the priests did not bring the sacrifices to Jerusalem and offer them on the LORD's altar in the Temple. The priests lived in cities all over Judah. They burned incense and offered sacrifices at the high places in those cities. The high places were everywhere, from Geba to Beersheba. And the priests ate their bread without yeast in those towns with the ordinary people—⌊not at the special place for priests in the Temple in Jerusalem⌋. But King Josiah ruined the high places and brought the priests to Jerusalem. Josiah also destroyed the high places that were on the left side of the city gate, by the Gate of Joshua. (Joshua was the ruler of the city.)

[10]Topheth was a place in the Valley of Hinnom's Son where people killed their children and burned them on an altar to honour the false god Molech.[b] Josiah ruined that place so that no one could use it again. [11]In the past the kings of Judah had put some horses and a chariot near the entrance to the LORD's Temple. This was near the room of an important official named Nathan Melech. The horses and chariot were to honour the sun god.[c] Josiah removed the horses and burned the chariot.

[12]In the past the kings of Judah had built altars on the roof of Ahab's building. King Manasseh had also built altars in the two courtyards of the LORD's Temple. Josiah destroyed all the altars and threw the broken pieces into the Kidron Valley.

[13]In the past King Solomon built some high places on Destroyer Hill near Jerusalem. The high places were on the south side of that hill. King Solomon built one of these places of worship to honour Ashtoreth, that horrible thing the people of Sidon worship. He also built one to honour Chemosh, that horrible thing the Moabites worship. And King Solomon built one high place to honour Milcom, that horrible thing the Ammonites worship. But King Josiah ruined all these places of worship. [14]He broke all the memorial stones and Asherah poles. Then he scattered dead men's bones over that place.[d]

[15]Josiah also broke down the altar and high place at Bethel. Jeroboam son of Nebat had made this altar. Jeroboam caused Israel to sin.[e] Josiah broke down both that altar and the high place. He broke the stones of the altar to pieces. Then he beat it into dust and he burned the Asherah pole. [16]Josiah looked around and saw graves on the mountain. He sent men, and they took the bones from the graves. Then he burned the bones on the altar. In this way Josiah ruined the altar. This

---

[a] **23:6 scattered . . . common people** This was a strong way of showing that the Asherah pole could never be used again.
[b] **23:10 people . . . Molech** Literally, "people made their son or daughter pass through fire to Molech".
[c] **23:11 horses . . . sun god** The people thought the sun was a god who drove his chariot (the sun) across the sky each day.
[d] **23:14 scattered . . . place** This was the way he defiled (ruined) those places so that they could not be used for places of worship.
[e] **23:15 Jeroboam . . . sin** See 1 Kgs 12:26–30.

happened according to the message from the LORD that the man of God had announced.[a] The man of God had announced these things when Jeroboam stood beside the altar at the feast.

Then Josiah looked around and saw the grave of the man of God.[b]

[17]Josiah said, "What is that monument I see?"

The people of the city told him, "It is the grave of the man of God who came from Judah. This man of God told us about the things you have done to the altar at Bethel. He told us a long time ago."

[18]Josiah said, "Leave the man of God alone. Don't move his bones." So they left his bones and the bones of the man of God from Samaria.

[19]Josiah also destroyed all the temples at the high places in the cities of Samaria. The kings of Israel had built those temples, which had made the LORD very angry. Josiah destroyed them, just as he had destroyed the place of worship at Bethel.

[20]Josiah killed all the priests of the high places that were in Samaria. He killed the priests on those altars and burned men's bones on the altars so that they could never be used again. Then he went back to Jerusalem.

The People of Judah Celebrate Passover

[21]Then King Josiah gave a command to all the people. He said, "Celebrate Passover for the LORD your God. Do this just as it is written in the Book of the Agreement."

[22]The people had not celebrated a Passover like this since the days when the judges ruled Israel. None of the kings of Israel or the kings of Judah ever had such a big celebration for Passover. [23]They celebrated this Passover for the LORD in Jerusalem during Josiah's eighteenth year as king.

[24]Josiah made a law against anyone trying to contact ghosts or spirits of the dead. He destroyed the people's household gods, their idols, and all the horrible things people worshipped in Judah and Jerusalem. He did this to follow the teaching written in the book that Hilkiah the priest found in the LORD's Temple.

[25]There had never been a king like Josiah before. Josiah turned to the LORD with all his heart, with all his soul and with all his strength.[c] No king had followed all the Law of Moses like Josiah. And there has never been another king like Josiah since that time.

[26]But the LORD did not stop being angry with the people of Judah. He was still angry with them for everything that Manasseh had done. [27]The LORD said, "I forced the Israelites to leave their land. I will do the same to Judah. I will take Judah out of my sight. I will not accept Jerusalem. Yes, I chose that city. I was talking about Jerusalem when I said, 'My name will be there.' But I will destroy the Temple that is in that place."

[28]All the other things that Josiah did are written in the book, The History of the Kings of Judah.

The Death of Josiah

[29]While Josiah was king, Pharaoh Neco, the king of Egypt, went to fight against the king of Assyria at the Euphrates River. Josiah went out to meet Neco at Megiddo. Pharaoh saw Josiah and killed him. [30]Josiah's officers put his body in a chariot and carried him from Megiddo to Jerusalem. They buried Josiah in his own grave.

Then the common people took Josiah's son Jehoahaz and anointed him. They made Jehoahaz the new king.

Jehoahaz Becomes King of Judah

[31]Jehoahaz was 23 years old when he became king. He ruled for three months in Jerusalem. His mother's name was Hamutal, daughter of Jeremiah from Libnah. [32]Jehoahaz did what the LORD said was wrong. He did all the same things that his ancestors had done.

[33]Pharaoh Neco put Jehoahaz in prison at Riblah in the land of Hamath. So Jehoahaz could not rule in Jerusalem. Pharaoh Neco forced Judah to pay 3,400 kilogrammes[d] of silver and 34 kilogrammes[e] of gold.

[34]Pharaoh Neco made Josiah's son Eliakim the new king. Eliakim took the place of Josiah his father. Pharaoh Neco changed Eliakim's name to Jehoiakim. And Pharaoh Neco took Jehoahaz away to Egypt where he died. [35]Jehoiakim gave the silver and the gold to Pharaoh. But Jehoiakim made the common people pay taxes and used that money to give to Pharaoh Neco. So everyone paid their share of silver and gold, and King Jehoiakim gave the money to Pharaoh Neco.

[36]Jehoiakim was 25 years old when he became king. He ruled for eleven years in Jerusalem. His mother's name was Zebidah daughter of Pedaiah from Rumah. [37]Jehoiakim did what the LORD said was wrong. He did all the same things his ancestors had done.

---

[a] 23:16 announced See 1 Kgs 13:1–3.
[b] 23:16 The man of God . . . the grave of the man of God This is from the ancient Greek version.
[c] 23:25 with all his heart . . . strength See Deut. 6:4–5.
[d] 23:33 3,400 kilogrammes Literally, "100 talents".
[e] 23:33 34 kilogrammes Literally, "one talent".

King Nebuchadnezzar Comes to Judah

24 In the time of Jehoiakim, King Nebuchadnezzar of Babylon came to the country of Judah. Jehoiakim served Nebuchadnezzar for three years. Then Jehoiakim turned against Nebuchadnezzar and broke away from his rule. ²The Lord sent groups of Babylonians, Arameans, Moabites and Ammonites to fight against Jehoiakim. He sent them to destroy Judah. This happened just as the Lord had said through his servants the prophets.

³This happened to Judah because the Lord commanded it. He wanted to send them all away from the land because of the many sins Manasseh had committed. ⁴He did this because Manasseh killed many innocent people and filled Jerusalem with their blood. The Lord would not forgive these sins.

⁵The other things that Jehoiakim did are written in the book, *The History of the Kings of Judah.* ⁶Jehoiakim died and was buried with his ancestors. His son Jehoiachin became the new king after him.

⁷The king of Babylon captured all the land between the brook of Egypt and the Euphrates River. This land had been controlled by Egypt. So the king of Egypt did not leave Egypt any more.

Nebuchadnezzar Captures Jerusalem

⁸Jehoiachin was 18 years old when he began to rule. He ruled for three months in Jerusalem. His mother's name was Nehushta daughter of Elnathan from Jerusalem. ⁹Jehoiachin did what the Lord said was wrong. He did all the same things that his father had done.

¹⁰At that time the officers of King Nebuchadnezzar of Babylon came to Jerusalem and surrounded it. ¹¹Then King Nebuchadnezzar of Babylon came to the city. ¹²King Jehoiachin of Judah went out to meet the king of Babylon. His mother, his officers, leaders and officials also went with him. Then the king of Babylon captured Jehoiachin. This was during the eighth year of Nebuchadnezzar's rule.

¹³Nebuchadnezzar took from Jerusalem all the treasures in the Lord's Temple and all the treasures in the king's palace. He cut up all the gold dishes that King Solomon of Israel had put in the Lord's Temple. This happened just as the Lord had said.

¹⁴Nebuchadnezzar captured all the people of Jerusalem, including the leaders and other wealthy people. He took 10,000 people and made them prisoners. He took all the skilled workers and craftsmen. No one was left, except the poorest of the common people. ¹⁵Nebuchadnezzar took Jehoiachin to Babylon as a prisoner. He also took the king's mother, his wives, officers and the leading men of the land. He took them from Jerusalem to Babylon as prisoners. ¹⁶There were 7,000 soldiers. Nebuchadnezzar took all the soldiers and 1,000 of the skilled workers and craftsmen. All these men were trained soldiers, ready for war. The king of Babylon took them to Babylon as prisoners.

King Zedekiah

¹⁷The king of Babylon made Mattaniah the new king. Mattaniah was Jehoiachin's uncle. He changed his name to Zedekiah. ¹⁸Zedekiah was 21 years old when he began to rule. He ruled for 11 years in Jerusalem. His mother's name was Hamutal daughter of Jeremiah from Libnah. ¹⁹Zedekiah did what the Lord said was wrong. He did all the same things that Jehoiakim had done. ²⁰The Lord became so angry with Jerusalem and Judah that he completely rejected them and sent them all away.

Nebuchadnezzar Ends Zedekiah's Rule

Zedekiah rebelled and refused to obey the king of Babylon.

INSIGHT

Nebuchadnezzar was the powerful king of Babylon (modern-day Iraq). His army destroyed Jerusalem and captured all the people, taking them to live in exile. This was one of many occasions in Israel's history that the people were forced to live away from their homeland.

2 Kings 25

---

25 So King Nebuchadnezzar of Babylon and all his army came to fight against Jerusalem. This happened on the tenth day of the tenth month of Zedekiah's ninth year as king. Nebuchadnezzar put his army around Jerusalem to stop people from going in and out of the city. Then he built a wall of dirt around the city. ²His army stayed around Jerusalem until Zedekiah's eleventh year as king of Judah. ³The famine was getting worse and worse in the city. By the ninth day of the fourth month, there was no more food for the common people in the city.

⁴Nebuchadnezzar's army finally broke through the city wall. That night King Zedekiah and all his soldiers ran away. They used the secret gate that went through the double walls. It was by the

GOD'S ANGER AT SIN

It seems like a very long time since the "glory days" of David and Solomon in the earlier chapters of Kings. Since those days, rebellion had caused a civil war and the northern kingdom, still called Israel, had broken away from the southern kingdom, now known as Judah.

Kings have come and kings have gone; some honoured God but most did not. Overall, the story is one of slow, sad decline. And now, right at the end of the history of the kings of Israel and Judah, we see total disaster.

DIG IN   READ 2 Kings 25:8–21

- How does the invading army treat God's holy city and the Temple?
- What happens to most of the people (vv.11,18–21)?

By now, invading armies have been tearing apart Israel and Judah for years. Jerusalem is left till last. What happens there is particularly heartbreaking to the Jewish people. The Temple is destroyed, and God's people are removed from the land he led them into and taken into exile as prisoners of foreign rulers.

Imagine the grief the people of God must have felt. Everything they owned, everything they'd built and all that it stood for – their whole identity as the people of God – torn to shreds. It seemed that God had left them alone.

- Why had God allowed it to happen?

LOOK back at 2 Kings 17:7–23

- What things did the Israelites do that displeased God?
- How had God tried to warn them (v.13)?

The people sinned against God. In defiance of the law and his covenant with them, they turned to alternative gods and "sold themselves to do what the LORD said was evil" (v.17). As idolatry crept in, God's judgement got nearer and nearer.

This is far from a surprise. The Bible shows us that for decades God had sent prophets to tell God's people in the clearest possible terms that he was unhappy with them and that his judgement would be harsh. We can read some of these powerful prophecies in our Bibles – in the books of Isaiah, Jeremiah and many others.

DIG THROUGH

- Have you ever felt the pain of God taking away something that you had come to rely on to give you identity and meaning? Can you share the anguish of the people of Jerusalem?
- How does God deal differently with the sin of people today? God insisting that sin is punished is a key theme running through the whole of the Bible, ending with Jesus taking the punishment for all the things we have done wrong.

DIG DEEPER

The books of Kings help us see why God acted as he did, allowing the nation to be destroyed and his people sent off into exile. But a large portion of the Old Testament is given over to telling this tragic story. Prophets including Isaiah and Jeremiah warn the people of what was going to happen and the book of Lamentations is a prophecy of how God's people would feel after the invasion.

The Bible is an amazingly unified book. The apostle Paul refers to 2 Kings 17:17 in his letter to the Romans explaining our sinful state (see the idea of being sold out to sinning in Romans 7:14). Who can save us from our sin, Paul asks? "Jesus Christ our Lord!" (Romans 7:25).

king's garden. The enemy soldiers were all around the city, but Zedekiah and his men escaped on the road to the desert. 5The Babylonian army chased King Zedekiah and caught him near Jericho. All of Zedekiah's soldiers left him and ran away.

6The Babylonians took King Zedekiah to the king of Babylon at Riblah. The Babylonians decided to punish Zedekiah. 7They killed Zedekiah's sons in front of him. Then they put out Zedekiah's eyes. They put chains on him and took him to Babylon.

Jerusalem Is Destroyed

8Nebuchadnezzar came to Jerusalem on the seventh day of the fifth month of his nineteenth year as king of Babylon. The captain of Nebuchadnezzar's best soldiers was Nebuzaradan. 9Nebuzaradan burned the LORD's Temple, the king's palace and all the houses in Jerusalem. He destroyed even the largest houses.

10Then the Babylonian army that was with Nebuzaradan pulled down the walls around Jerusalem. 11Nebuzaradan captured all the people who were still left in the city. He took all the people as prisoners, even those who had tried to surrender. 12He let only the poorest of the common people stay there. He let them stay so that they could take care of the grapes and other crops.

13The Babylonian soldiers broke into pieces the bronze columns in the LORD's Temple. They also broke the bronze stands and the large bronze basin that were in the LORD's Temple. They took all the bronze to Babylon. 14They also took the pots, the shovels, the tools for trimming the lamps, the spoons and all the bronze dishes that were used in the Temple. 15Nebuzaradan took all the firepans and bowls. He took all the things made of gold for the gold. And he took everything made of silver for the silver. 16–17So Nebuzaradan took the large bronze basin and the 2 bronze columns. (Each column was about 8 metres[a] tall. The capitals on the columns were about 1.5 metres[b] tall. They were made from bronze and had a design like a net and pomegranates. Both columns had the same kind of design.) He also took the stands that Solomon made for the LORD's Temple. The bronze from these things was too heavy to be weighed.

The People of Judah Taken as Prisoners

18Also from the Temple Nebuzaradan took Seraiah the high priest, Zephaniah the second priest and the three men who guarded the entrance.

19From the city Nebuzaradan took one official who was in charge of the army and five of the king's advisors[c] who were still in the city. He took one secretary of the commander of the army who was in charge of counting the common people and choosing some of them to be soldiers and 60 people who just happened to be in the city. 20–21Then Nebuzaradan took all these people to the king of Babylon at Riblah in the area of Hamath. The king of Babylon killed them there at Riblah. And the people of Judah were led away as prisoners from their land.

Gedaliah, Governor of Judah

22King Nebuchadnezzar of Babylon left some people in the land of Judah. There was a man named Gedaliah son of Ahikam son of Shaphan. Nebuchadnezzar made Gedaliah governor over the people in Judah.

23The army captains were Ishmael son of Nethaniah, Johanan son of Kareah, Seraiah son of Tanhumeth from Netophah and Jaazaniah son of the Maacathite. These army captains and their men heard that the king of Babylon had made Gedaliah governor, so they went to Mizpah to meet with him. 24Gedaliah made promises to these officers and their men. He said to them, "Don't be afraid of the Babylonian officers. Stay here and serve the king of Babylon. Then everything will be all right with you."

25Ishmael son of Nethaniah son of Elishama was from the king's family. In the seventh month, Ishmael and ten of his men attacked Gedaliah and killed all the men of Judah and Babylonians who were with Gedaliah at Mizpah. 26Then the army officers and all the people ran away to Egypt. Everyone, from the least important to the most important, ran away because they were afraid of the Babylonians.

27Later, Evil Merodach became the king of Babylon. He let King Jehoiachin of Judah out of prison. This happened in the thirty-seventh year after Jehoiachin was captured. This was on the twenty-seventh day of the twelfth month from the time that Evil Merodach began to rule. 28Evil Merodach was kind to Jehoiachin. He gave him a more important place to sit than the other kings who were with him in Babylon. 29Evil Merodach let Jehoiachin stop wearing prison clothes. And every day for the rest of his life, he ate at the same table with the king. 30And each day, for as long as Jehoiachin lived, the king gave him enough money to pay for whatever he needed.

---

[a] **25:16–17 8 metres** Literally, "18 *cubits*".
[b] **25:16–17 about 1.5 metres** Literally, "3 *cubits*".
[c] **25:19 king's advisors** Literally, "men who saw the king's face".

Who According to tradition, the writer, known as "the Chronicler", was Ezra, and also wrote Ezra and Nehemiah. It seems likely that the author was a priest, since the theme of the priesthood and Temple runs through these books.

When It was probably written sometime after the Jews had returned to Jerusalem from exile in Babylon.

What Chronicles aims to answer a simple question: "Does God care about Israel any more?" Just as Kings was written to explain their history to the Jews in exile, Chronicles is addressed to those who have returned.

After the shattering experience of exile in Babylon, the concern of Chronicles is to express the continuity of God's relationship with his people, from the time of David through the divided kingdoms and on into the post-exile state. That is why it begins with so many genealogies. Because only by going right back to the beginning can Israel look to the future.

So the argument of the book – and the emphasis it puts on the historical account – is that the Israel which was re-established after the exile was the same nation it had been before. It followed the same practices, worshipped the same God and was led by the same royal line. Thus, the book places a great emphasis on the importance of the Temple and the priesthood. These, too, were part of the continuity. The modern kings were the successors of David. The rebuilt Temple was the successor of Solomon's Temple, and Moses' Holy Tent. The priesthood were the successors of Aaron. The line was continuing.

A lot of 1 Chronicles is found in 1 Samuel. Both books tell the story of King David, although from a slightly different perspective. In 1 Chronicles, David is given the full-on hero treatment. He's the person who made Jerusalem great, who planned the Temple and who brought the Box of the Agreement into the city. He's powerful because he trusted in the Lord.

QUICK TOUR **1 CHRONICLES**

Family history 1:1 – 9:44
The Death of Saul 10:1–14
David becomes king 11:1–9
The return of the Holy Box 15:1–29

David's song 16:7–36
"Your descendants will be kings" 17:1–27
The plans for the Temple 28:1–21
Solomon takes over 29:21–30

"Your son will build a house for me. I will make your son's family rule forever. I will be his father, and he will be my son . . . I will never stop loving your son. I will put him in charge of my house and kingdom forever. His rule will continue forever!"

1 Chronicles 17:12–14

Family History From Adam to Noah

1 The first generations of people were Adam, Seth, Enosh, [2]Kenan, Mahalalel, Jared, [3]Enoch, Methuselah, Lamech and Noah.[a]

[4]The sons of Noah were Shem, Ham and Japheth.

Japheth's Descendants

[5]The sons of Japheth were Gomer, Magog, Madai, Javan, Tubal, Meshech and Tiras.
[6]The sons of Gomer were Ashkenaz, Riphath[b] and Togarmah.
[7]The sons of Javan were Elishah, Tarshish, Kittim and Rodanim.

Ham's Descendants

[8]The sons of Ham were Cush,[c] Mizraim,[d] Put and Canaan.
[9]The sons of Cush were Seba, Havilah, Sabtah, Raamah and Sabteca.
   The sons of Raamah were Sheba and Dedan.
[10]Nimrod, a descendant of Cush, grew up to become the strongest and bravest soldier in the world.
[11]Mizraim was the father of the people of Lud, Anam, Lehab, Naphtuh, [12]Pathrus, Casluh and Caphtor. (The Philistines came from Casluh.)
[13]Canaan was the father of Sidon. Sidon was his first child. Canaan was also the father of the Hittites, [14]Jebusites, Amorites, Girgashites, [15]Hivites, Arkites, Sinites, [16]Arvadites, Zemarites and the people from Hamath.

Shem's Descendants

[17]Shem's sons were Elam, Asshur, Arphaxad, Lud and Aram. Aram's sons were[e] Uz, Hul, Gether and Meshech.[f]
[18]Arphaxad was the father of Shelah. Shelah was the father of Eber.
[19]Eber had two sons. One son was named Peleg,[g] because the people on the earth were divided into different languages during his lifetime. Peleg's brother was named Joktan. [20](Joktan was the father of Almodad, Sheleph, Hazarmaveth, Jerah, [21]Hadoram, Uzal, Diklah, [22]Ebal,[h] Abimael, Sheba, [23]Ophir, Havilah and Jobab. All these men were Joktan's sons.)

[24]Shem's descendants were Arphaxad, Shelah, [25]Eber, Peleg, Reu, [26]Serug, Nahor, Terah [27]and Abram. (Abram is also called Abraham.)

Abraham's Family

[28]Abraham's sons were Isaac and Ishmael. [29]These are their descendants:
   Ishmael's first son was Nebaioth. His other sons were Kedar, Adbeel, Mibsam, [30]Mishma, Dumah, Massa, Hadad, Tema, [31]Jetur, Naphish and Kedemah. These were Ishmael's sons.

[32]Abraham also had sons by Keturah, his slave woman. They were Zimran, Jokshan, Medan, Midian, Ishbak and Shuah.
   Jokshan's sons were Sheba and Dedan.
[33]Midian's sons were Ephah, Epher, Hanoch, Abida and Eldaah.
   These men were the descendants of Keturah.

Isaac's Descendants

[34]Abraham was the father of Isaac. Isaac's sons were Esau and Israel.
[35]Esau's sons were Eliphaz, Reuel, Jeush, Jalam and Korah.
[36]Eliphaz's sons were Teman, Omar, Zepho,[i] Gatam and Kenaz. Also Eliphaz and Timna had a son named Amalek.
[37]Reuel's sons were Nahath, Zerah, Shammah and Mizzah.

The Edomites

[38]Seir's sons were Lotan, Shobal, Zibeon, Anah, Dishon, Ezer and Dishan.
[39]Lotan's sons were Hori and Homam.[j] Lotan had a sister named Timna.
[40]Shobal's sons were Alvan, Manahath, Ebal, Shepho and Onam.
   Zibeon's sons were Aiah and Anah.

---

a **1:1–3** This list of names gives the name of a man, followed by his descendants.
b **1:6** *Riphath* Or "Diphath".
c **1:8** *Cush* That is, Ethiopia.
d **1:8** *Mizraim* That is, Egypt.
e **1:17** *Aram's sons were* This is found in one Hebrew copy and some copies of the ancient Greek version. It is also found in the standard Hebrew text of Gen. 10:23, but not here.
f **1:17** *Meshech* Or "Mash". See Gen. 10:23.
g **1:19** *Peleg* This name means "division".
h **1:22** *Ebal* Or "Obal". See Gen. 10:28.
i **1:36** *Zepho* Or "Zephi".
j **1:39** *Homam* Or "Heman". See Gen. 36:22.

⁴¹Anah's son was Dishon.
Dishon's sons were Hemdan, Eshban, Ithran and Keran.
⁴²Ezer's sons were Bilhan, Zaavan and Akan. Dishan's sons were Uz and Aran.

The Kings of Edom

⁴³There were kings in Edom long before there were kings in Israel. These are the names of the kings of Edom:
Bela was the son of Beor. The name of Bela's city was Dinhabah.
⁴⁴When Bela died, Jobab son of Zerah became the new king. Jobab came from Bozrah.
⁴⁵When Jobab died, Husham became the new king. Husham was from the country of the Temanites.
⁴⁶When Husham died, Hadad son of Bedad became the new king. Hadad defeated Midian in the country of Moab. Hadad's city was named Avith.
⁴⁷When Hadad died, Samlah became the new king. Samlah was from Masrekah.
⁴⁸When Samlah died, Shaul became the new king. Shaul was from Rehoboth by the Euphrates River.
⁴⁹When Shaul died, Baal Hanan son of Acbor became the new king.
⁵⁰When Baal Hanan died, Hadad became the new king. Hadad's city was named Pau.ᵃ Hadad's wife was named Mehetabel. Mehetabel was Matred's daughter. Matred was Mezahab's daughter. ⁵¹Then Hadad died.

The leaders of Edom were Timna, Alvah, Jetheth, ⁵²Oholibamah, Elah, Pinon, ⁵³Kenaz, Teman, Mibzar, ⁵⁴Magdiel and Iram. This is a list of the leaders of Edom.

Israel's Sons

2 Israel's sons were Reuben, Simeon, Levi, Judah, Issachar, Zebulun, ²Dan, Joseph, Benjamin, Naphtali, Gad and Asher.

Judah's Sons

³Judah's sons were Er, Onan and Shelah. Bathshuaᵇ from Canaan was their mother. The LORD killed Er, the first son, because he saw that he was evil. ⁴Judah's daughter-in-law Tamar gave birth to Perez and Zerah.ᶜ So Judah had five sons.

⁵Perez's sons were Hezron and Hamul.
⁶Zerah had five sons. They were Zimri, Ethan, Heman, Calcol and Darda.
⁷Zimri's son was Carmi. Carmi's son was Achar.ᵈ Achar was the man who brought many troubles to Israel. Achar kept the things he took in battle, but he was supposed to give them all to God.
⁸Ethan's son was Azariah.
⁹Hezron's sons were Jerahmeel, Ram and Caleb.ᵉ

Ram's Descendants

¹⁰Ram was Amminadab's father, and Amminadab was Nahshon's father. Nahshon was the leader of the people of Judah.ᶠ ¹¹Nahshon was Salmon's father. Salmon was Boaz's father. ¹²Boaz was Obed's father. Obed was Jesse's father. ¹³Jesse was Eliab's father. Eliab was Jesse's first son. Jesse's second son was Abinadab. His third son was Shimea. ¹⁴Nethanel was Jesse's fourth son. Jesse's fifth son was Raddai. ¹⁵Ozem was Jesse's sixth son, and David was his seventh son. ¹⁶Their sisters were Zeruiah and Abigail. Zeruiah's three sons were Abishai, Joab and Asahel. ¹⁷Abigail was Amasa's mother. Amasa's father was Jether. Jether was from the Ishmaelites.

Caleb's Descendants

¹⁸Caleb was Hezron's son. Caleb had children with his wife Azubah. Azubah was the daughter of Jerioth.ᵍ Azubah's sons were Jesher, Shobab and Ardon. ¹⁹When Azubah died, Caleb married Ephrathah. Caleb and Ephrathah had a son. They named him Hur. ²⁰Hur was Uri's father, and Uri was Bezalel's father.
²¹Later, when Hezron was 60 years old, he married the daughter of Makir, who first settled the land of Gilead. After Hezron married Makir's daughter, she gave birth to Segub. ²²Segub was Jair's father. Jair had 23 cities in the country of Gilead. ²³But Geshur and Aram took Jair's villages. Among them were Kenath and the small towns around it.

ᵃ **1:50 Pau** Or "Pai".
ᵇ **2:3 Bathshua** This name means "the daughter of Shua". See Gen. 38:2.
ᶜ **2:4** Judah had sex with his own daughter-in-law, Tamar, and caused her to be pregnant. See Gen. 38:12–30.
ᵈ **2:7 Achar** Or "Achan". See Josh. 7:11.
ᵉ **2:9 Caleb** Literally, "Kelubai".
ᶠ **2:10 Nahshon . . . Judah** Nahshon was leader of the tribe of Judah at the time the Israelites came out of Egypt. See Num. 1:7; 2:3; 7:12.
ᵍ **2:18** Or "Caleb had children with Azubah his wife and with Jerioth."

There were 60 small towns in all. All these towns belonged to the sons of Makir, who first settled the land of Gilead.

²⁴After Hezron died, his son Caleb married Ephrathah, Hezron's widow. And they had a son named Ashhur, who first settled the town of Tekoa.

Jerahmeel's Descendants

²⁵Jerahmeel was Hezron's first son. Jerahmeel's sons were Ram, Bunah, Oren, Ozem and Ahijah. Ram was Jerahmeel's first son. ²⁶Jerahmeel had another wife named Atarah. Onam's mother was Atarah.

²⁷Jerahmeel's first son, Ram, had sons. They were Maaz, Jamin and Eker.

²⁸Onam's sons were Shammai and Jada. Shammai's sons were Nadab and Abishur. ²⁹Abishur's wife was named Abihail. They had two sons. Their names were Ahban and Molid.

³⁰Nadab's sons were Seled and Appaim. Seled died without having children.

³¹Appaim's son was Ishi. Ishi's son was Sheshan. Sheshan's son was Ahlai.

³²Jada was Shammai's brother. Jada's sons were Jether and Jonathan. Jether died without having children.

³³Jonathan's sons were Peleth and Zaza. This was the list of Jerahmeel's children.

³⁴Sheshan did not have sons. He only had daughters. Sheshan had a servant from Egypt named Jarha. ³⁵Sheshan let his daughter marry Jarha. They had a son. His name was Attai.

³⁶Attai was Nathan's father. Nathan was Zabad's father. ³⁷Zabad was Ephlal's father. Ephlal was Obed's father. ³⁸Obed was Jehu's father. Jehu was Azariah's father. ³⁹Azariah was Helez's father. Helez was Eleasah's father. ⁴⁰Eleasah was Sismai's father. Sismai was Shallum's father. ⁴¹Shallum was Jekamiah's father, and Jekamiah was Elishama's father.

Other Descendants of Caleb

⁴²Jerahmeel's brother Caleb had other descendants. His first son was Mesha, who first settled the town of Ziph. Caleb had another son named Mareshah, the father of Hebron.

⁴³Hebron's sons were Korah, Tappuah, Rekem and Shema. ⁴⁴Shema was the father of Raham, who first settled the town of Jorkeam. Rekem was Shammai's father. ⁴⁵Shammai's son was Maon, who first settled the town of Beth Zur.

⁴⁶Caleb's slave woman was named Ephah. Ephah was the mother of Haran, Moza and Gazez. Haran was Gazez's father.

⁴⁷Jahdai's sons were Regem, Jotham, Geshan, Pelet, Ephah and Shaaph.

⁴⁸Maacah was another slave woman of Caleb. Maacah was the mother of Sheber and Tirhanah. ⁴⁹Maacah was also the mother of Shaaph and Sheva. Shaaph first settled the town of Madmannah. And Sheva settled the towns of Macbenah and Gibea. Caleb's daughter was Acsah.

⁵⁰This is a list of Caleb's descendants: Hur, the first son of Caleb's wife Ephrathah, had three sons: Shobal, who first settled the town of Kiriath Jearim; ⁵¹Salma, who first settled the town of Bethlehem; and Hareph, who settled the town of Beth Gader.

⁵²Shobal, the ancestor of Kiriath Jearim, had these descendants: Haroeh, half the people from Manahti, ⁵³and the tribes from Kiriath Jearim, the Ithrites, Puthites, Shumathites and Mishraites. Shobal's descendants also included the Zorathites and Eshtaolites, who came from the Mishraites.

⁵⁴This is a list of Salma's descendants: the people from Bethlehem, Netophah, Atroth Beth Joab, half the people from Manahti, the Zorites, ⁵⁵and the families of scribes who lived at Jabez, Tirath, Shimeath and Sucah. These scribes are the Kenites who came from the family of Hammath, who was also the ancestor of the Rechabites.

David's Sons

3 These are David's sons who were born in the town of Hebron.

The first was Amnon. Amnon's mother was Ahinoam. She was from the town of Jezreel.

The second son was Daniel. His mother was Abigail from Carmel in Judah.

²The third son was Absalom. His mother was Maacah, daughter of Talmai. Talmai was the king of Geshur.

The fourth son was Adonijah. His mother was Haggith.

³The fifth son was Shephatiah. His mother was Abital.

The sixth son was Ithream. His mother was David's wife Eglah.

⁴These six sons were born to David in Hebron. He ruled as king in Hebron for seven years and six months.

David ruled as king in Jerusalem for 33 years. ⁵And these are his children who were born in Jerusalem:

Shimea, Shobab, Nathan and Solomon. Their mother was Bathsheba,[a] the daughter of Ammiel.

6–8Nine other sons: Ibhar, Elishua, Eliphelet, Nogah, Nepheg, Japhia, Elishama, Eliada and Eliphelet.

9These were all of David's sons, except for the sons of his slave women. Their sister was named Tamar.

Kings of Judah After David's Time

10Solomon's son was Rehoboam. Rehoboam's son was Abijah. Abijah's son was Asa. Asa's son was Jehoshaphat. 11Jehoshaphat's son was Jehoram. Jehoram's son was Ahaziah. Ahaziah's son was Joash. 12Joash's son was Amaziah. Amaziah's son was Azariah. Azariah's son was Jotham. 13Jotham's son was Ahaz. Ahaz's son was Hezekiah. Hezekiah's son was Manasseh. 14Manasseh's son was Amon. Amon's son was Josiah.

15This is a list of Josiah's sons: The first son was Johanan. The second son was Jehoiakim. The third son was Zedekiah. The fourth son was Shallum.

16Jehoiakim's sons were Jehoiachin,[b] his son, and Zedekiah, his son.[c]

David's Family After Babylonian Captivity

17The children of Jehoiachin, who became a prisoner in Babylon, were Shealtiel, 18Malkiram, Pedaiah, Shenazzar, Jekamiah, Hoshama and Nedabiah.

19Pedaiah's sons were Zerubbabel and Shimei. Zerubbabel's sons were Meshullam and Hananiah. Shelomith was their sister. 20Zerubbabel had five other sons also. Their names were Hashubah, Ohel, Berekiah, Hasadiah and Jushab Hesed.

21Hananiah's son was Pelatiah. His son was Jeshaiah.[d] His son was Rephaiah. His son was Arnan. His son was Obadiah. His son was Shecaniah.[e]

22This is a list of Shecaniah's descendants: Shemaiah. Shemaiah had six sons: Shemaiah, Hattush, Igal, Bariah, Neariah and Shaphat.

23Neariah had three sons. They were Elioenai, Hizkiah and Azrikam.

24Elioenai had seven sons. They were Hodaviah, Eliashib, Pelaiah, Akkub, Johanan, Delaiah and Anani.

Other Family Groups of Judah

4 Judah was the ancestor of Perez, Hezron, Carmi, Hur and Shobal.

2Shobal's son was Reaiah, the father of Jahath. Jahath was the father of Ahumai and Lahad, ancestors of the Zorathites.

3–4Hur was the first son of his mother Ephrathah. Some of his descendants settled the town of Bethlehem. Some of his other descendants were Etam, Penuel and Ezer. Etam's sons were Jezreel, Ishma and Idbash, and their sister was named Hazzelelponi. Penuel first settled the town of Gedor, and Ezer settled the town of Hushah.

5Ashhur, who first settled the town of Tekoa, had two wives. Their names were Helah and Naarah. 6Naarah had four sons: Ahuzzam, Hepher, Temeni and Haahashtari. 7The sons of Helah were Zereth, Zohar, Ethnan and Koz. 8Koz was the father of Anub and Hazzobebah. Koz was also the ancestor of the families of Aharhel, the son of Harum.

9Jabez was a very good man, who was better than his brothers. His mother said, "I have named him Jabez[f] because I was in much pain when I had him." 10Jabez prayed to the God of Israel and said, "I pray that you would bless me and give me more land! Be near me and don't let anyone hurt me! Then I will not have any pain." God gave Jabez what he asked for.

11Kelub was Shuhah's brother and Mehir's father. Mehir was Eshton's father. 12Eshton was the father of Beth Rapha, Paseah and Tehinnah, who first settled the town of Nahash. These men were all from Recah.

13The sons of Kenaz were Othniel and Seraiah. Othniel's sons were Hathath and Meonothai. 14Meonothai was Ophrah's father.

And Seraiah was the father of Joab, the ancestor of those who live in the Valley of the Craftsmen.[g] The place was called this because the people there were all skilled workers.

---

a 3:5 *Bathsheba* The standard Hebrew text has "Bathshua".
b 3:16 *Jehoiachin* The Hebrew text has "Jeconiah," another name for King Jehoiachin. Also in verse 17.
c 3:16 This can be interpreted in two ways: "This Zedekiah was the son of Jehoiakim and the brother of Jehoiachin" or "This Zedekiah is the son of Jehoiachin and the grandson of Jehoiakim."
d 3:21 *Jeshaiah* Or "Isaiah".
e 3:21 The Hebrew text is not clear.
f 4:9 *Jabez* This name is like the Hebrew word meaning "pain".
g 4:14 *Valley of the Craftsmen* Literally, "Ge Harashim".

INSIGHT

In Bible times most people worked from home and people of the same profession often lived together. "Ge Harashim" means "valley of craftsmen".

1 Chronicles 4:14

¹⁵Caleb was Jephunneh's son. Caleb's sons were Iru, Elah and Naam. Elah's son was Kenaz.
¹⁶Jehallelel's sons were Ziph, Ziphah, Tiria and Asarel.
¹⁷⁻¹⁸Ezrah's sons were Jether, Mered, Epher and Jalon. Mered married Bithiah, a daughter of the king of Egypt. They had a daughter named Miriam and two sons named Shammai and Ishbah. Ishbah first settled the town of Eshtemoa. Mered also had a wife from the tribe of Judah. She had three sons: Jered, father of Gedor; Heber, father of Soco; and Jekuthiel, father of Zanoah.
¹⁹Hodiah's wife was Naham's sister. Her sons were named Keilah and Eshtemoa. Keilah was from the Garmite family. And Eshtemoa was from the Maacathite family.
²⁰Shimon's sons were Amnon, Rinnah, Ben Hanan, and Tilon.
Ishi's sons were Zoheth and Ben Zoheth.
²¹Shelah was one of Judah's sons. Shelah's descendants were Er, who first settled the town of Lecah; Laadah, who settled the town of Mareshah; the tribes of linen workers, who lived in the town of Beth Ashbea; ²²Jokim and the men who lived in the town of Cozeba; and Joash and Saraph, who married Moabite women and then returned to Bethlehem.ᵃ The writings about this family are very old. ²³They were skilled workers who made things from clay. They lived in Netaim and Gederah and worked for the king.

Simeon's Children

²⁴Simeon's sons were Nemuel, Jamin, Jarib, Zerah and Shaul. ²⁵Shaul's son was Shallum. Shallum's son was Mibsam. Mibsam's son was Mishma.
²⁶Mishma's son was Hammuel. Hammuel's son was Zaccur. Zaccur's son was Shimei.
²⁷Shimei had sixteen sons and six daughters, but Shimei's brothers did not have many children. Shimei's brothers did not have large families. Their families were not as large as the other tribes in Judah.
²⁸Shimei's descendants lived in Beersheba, Moladah, Hazar Shual, ²⁹Bilhah, Ezem, Tolad, ³⁰Bethuel, Hormah, Ziklag, ³¹Beth Marcaboth, Hazar Susim, Beth Biri and Shaaraim. They lived in these towns until David became king. ³²The five villages near these towns were Etam, Ain, Rimmon, Token and Ashan. ³³There were also other villages as far away as Baalath. This is where they lived. And they also wrote the history about their family.

³⁴⁻³⁸These men were leaders of their tribes: Meshobab, Jamlech, Joshah (Amaziah's son), Joel, Jehu son of Joshibiah, Joshibiah son of Seraiah, Seraiah son of Asiel, Elioenai, Jaakobah, Jeshohaiah, Asaiah, Adiel, Jesimiel, Benaiah and Ziza (Shiphi's son). Shiphi was Allon's son, and Allon was Jedaiah's son. Jedaiah was Shimri's son, and Shimri was Shemaiah's son.

These men's families grew to be very large. ³⁹They went to the area outside the town of Gedor to the east side of the valley. They went to that place to look for fields for their sheep and cattle. ⁴⁰They found good fields with plenty of grass. They found plenty of good land there. The land was peaceful and quiet. Ham's descendants lived there in the past. ⁴¹This happened during the time that Hezekiah was king of Judah. These men came to Gedor and fought against the Hamites. They destroyed the tents of the Hamites. They also fought against the Meunites who lived there. These men destroyed all the Meunites. There are no Meunites in this place even today. So these men began to live there. They lived there because the land had grass for their sheep.

⁴²Five hundred people from the tribe of Simeon went to the hill country of Seir. Ishi's sons led these men. The sons were Pelatiah, Neariah, Rephaiah and Uzziel. The Simeonite men fought against the people living in that place. ⁴³There were only a few Amalekites still living, and these Simeonites killed them. Since that time until now, the Simeonites have lived in Seir.

Reuben's Descendants

5 Reuben was Israel's first son. Reuben should have received the special privileges of the oldest son. But he had sex with his father's wife. So those privileges were given to Joseph's sons. In the family history, Reuben's name is not listed as the first son. ²Judah became stronger than his

---

ᵃ 4:21–22 *married . . . Bethlehem* Or "ruled in Moab and Jashubi Lehem".

brothers, so the leaders came from his family. But Joseph's family got the other privileges that belong to the oldest son.

³Reuben's sons were Hanoch, Pallu, Hezron and Carmi. ⁴These are the names of Joel's descendants: Shemaiah was Joel's son. Gog was Shemaiah's son. Shimei was Gog's son. ⁵Micah was Shimei's son. Reaiah was Micah's son. Baal was Reaiah's son. ⁶Beerah was Baal's son. King Tiglath Pileser of Assyria forced Beerah to leave his home. So Beerah became the king's prisoner. Beerah was a leader of the tribe of Reuben. ⁷Joel's brothers and all his tribes are listed just as they are written in the family histories: Jeiel was the first son, then Zechariah ⁸and Bela. Bela was Azaz's son. Azaz was Shema's son. Shema was Joel's son. They lived in the area of Aroer all the way to Nebo and Baal Meon. ⁹Bela's people lived to the east as far as the edge of the desert, near the Euphrates River. They lived there because they had many cattle in the land of Gilead. ¹⁰When Saul was king, Bela's people fought a war against the Hagrites. They defeated the Hagrites. Bela's people lived in the tents that had belonged to the Hagrites. They lived in those tents and travelled throughout the area east of Gilead.

Gad's Descendants

¹¹The people of Gad lived across the river from Reuben, in the area of Bashan. They spread all the way to the town of Salecah. ¹²Joel was the first leader in Bashan. Shapham was the second leader. Then Janai became the leader.ᵃ ¹³The seven brothers in their families were Michael, Meshullam, Sheba, Jorai, Jacan, Zia and Eber. ¹⁴They were the descendants of Abihail. Abihail was Huri's son. Huri was Jaroah's son. Jaroah was Gilead's son. Gilead was Michael's son. Michael was Jeshishai's son. Jeshishai was Jahdo's son. Jahdo was Buz's son. ¹⁵Ahi was Abdiel's son. Abdiel was Guni's son. Ahi was the leader of their family. ¹⁶The people in the tribe of Gad lived in the area of Gilead. They lived in the area of Bashan, in the small towns around Bashan and in all the pastures in the area of Sharon all the way to the borders. ¹⁷During the time of Jotham and Jeroboam, all these people's names were written in the family history of Gad. Jotham was the king of Judah and Jeroboam was the king of Israel.

Some Soldiers Skilled in War

¹⁸From half the tribe of Manasseh and from the tribes of Reuben and Gad there were 44,760 brave men ready for war. They were skilled in war. They carried shields and swords. And they were also good with bows and arrows. ¹⁹They started a war against the Hagrites and the people of Jetur, Naphish and Nodab. ²⁰The men from the tribes of Manasseh, Reuben and Gad prayed to God during the war. They asked God to help them because they trusted him, so God helped them. He allowed them to defeat the Hagrites and those who were with the Hagrites. ²¹They took the animals that belonged to the Hagrites. They took 50,000 camels, 250,000 sheep, 2,000 donkeys and 100,000 people. ²²Many Hagrites were killed because God helped the people of Reuben win the war. Then the tribes of Manasseh, Reuben and Gad settled in the land of the Hagrites. They lived there until the time when the Israelites were taken into captivity.

²³Half the tribe of Manasseh lived in the area of Bashan all the way to Baal Hermon, Senir and Mount Hermon. They became a very large group of people.

²⁴These were the family leaders from half the tribe of Manasseh: Epher, Ishi, Eliel, Azriel, Jeremiah, Hodaviah and Jahdiel. They were all strong, brave and famous men, and they were leaders in their families. ²⁵But they sinned against the God their ancestors had worshipped. They began worshipping the false gods of the people God had destroyed, the people who had lived in the land before them.

²⁶The God of Israel made King Pul of Assyria want to go to war. He was also called Tiglath Pileser. He fought against the tribes of Manasseh, Reuben and Gad. He forced them to leave their homes and made them prisoners. Pul took them to Halah, Habor, Hara and near the Gozan River. Those tribes from Israel have lived in those places since that time until today.

Levi's Descendants

6 Levi's sons were Gershon, Kohath and Merari.

²Kohath's sons were Amram, Izhar, Hebron and Uzziel.

³Amram's children were Aaron, Moses and Miriam.

Aaron's sons were Nadab, Abihu, Eleazar and Ithamar. ⁴Eleazar was Phinehas' father. Phinehas was Abishua's father. ⁵Abishua was Bukki's father. Bukki was Uzzi's father. ⁶Uzzi was Zerahiah's father. Zerahiah was Meraioth's father. ⁷Meraioth was

---

ᵃ **5:12 Then Janai became the leader** Or "Then there was Janai, and then Shaphat was in Bashan."

Amariah's father. Amariah was Ahitub's father. 8Ahitub was Zadok's father. Zadok was Ahimaaz's father. 9Ahimaaz was Azariah's father. Azariah was Johanan's father. 10Johanan was Azariah's father. (Azariah is the one who served as priest in the Temple that Solomon built in Jerusalem.) 11Azariah was Amariah's father. Amariah was Ahitub's father. 12Ahitub was Zadok's father. Zadok was Shallum's father. 13Shallum was Hilkiah's father. Hilkiah was Azariah's father. 14Azariah was Seraiah's father. Seraiah was Jehozadak's father.

15Jehozadak was forced to leave his home when the LORD sent the people of Judah and Jerusalem away. Through Nebuchadnezzar the Lord caused them all to be made prisoners in another country.

Other Descendants of Levi

16Levi's sons were Gershon, Kohath and Merari.

17The names of Gershon's sons were Libni and Shimei.

18Kohath's sons were Amram, Izhar, Hebron and Uzziel.

19Merari's sons were Mahli and Mushi.

This is a list of the families in the tribe of Levi. They are listed with their fathers' names first:

20These were Gershon's descendants: Libni was Gershon's son. Jahath was Libni's son. Zimmah was Jahath's son. 21Joah was Zimmah's son. Iddo was Joah's son. Zerah was Iddo's son. Jeatherai was Zerah's son.

22These were Kohath's descendants: Amminadab was Kohath's son. Korah was Amminadab's son. Assir was Korah's son. 23Elkanah was Assir's son. Ebiasaph was Elkanah's son. Assir was Ebiasaph's son. 24Tahath was Assir's son. Uriel was Tahath's son. Uzziah was Uriel's son. Shaul was Uzziah's son.

25Elkanah's sons were Amasai and Ahimoth. 26Zophai was Elkanah's son. Nahath was Zophai's son. 27Eliab was Nahath's son. Jeroham was Eliab's son. Elkanah was Jeroham's son. Samuel was Elkanah's son. 28Samuel's sons were his oldest son Joel and Abijah.

29These are Merari's sons: Mahli was Merari's son, Libni was Mahli's son, Shimei was Libni's son and Uzzah was Shimei's son. 30Shimea was Uzzah's son. Haggiah was Shimea's son. Asaiah was Haggiah's son.

The Temple Musicians

31These are the men David chose to take care of the music at the tent of the LORD's house after God's Holy Box was put there. 32These men served by singing at the Holy Tent. The Holy Tent is also called the Meeting Tent. These men served until Solomon built the LORD's Temple in Jerusalem. They served by following the rules given to them for their work.

33These are the names of the men and their sons who served with music:

The descendants from the Kohath family were Heman the singer who was Joel's son; Joel was Samuel's son; 34Samuel was Elkanah's son; Elkanah was Jeroham's son; Jeroham was Eliel's son; Eliel was Toah's son; 35Toah was Zuph's son; Zuph was Elkanah's son; Elkanah was Mahath's son; Mahath was Amasai's son; 36Amasai was Elkanah's son; Elkanah was Joel's son; Joel was Azariah's son; Azariah was Zephaniah's son; 37Zephaniah was Tahath's son; Tahath was Assir's son; Assir was Ebiasaph's son; Ebiasaph was Korah's son; 38Korah was Izhar's son; Izhar was Kohath's son; Kohath was Levi's son; Levi was Israel's son.

39Heman's relative was Asaph. Asaph served by Heman's right side. Asaph was Berekiah's son. Berekiah was Shimea's son. 40Shimea was Michael's son. Michael was Baaseiah's son. Baaseiah was Malkijah's son. 41Malkijah was Ethni's son. Ethni was Zerah's son. Zerah was Adaiah's son. 42Adaiah was Ethan's son. Ethan was Zimmah's son. Zimmah was Shimei's son. 43Shimei was Jahath's son. Jahath was Gershon's son. Gershon was Levi's son.

44Merari's descendants were the relatives of Heman and Asaph. They were the singing group on Heman's left side. Ethan was Kishi's son. Kishi was Abdi's son. Abdi was Malluch's son. 45Malluch was Hashabiah's son. Hashabiah was Amaziah's son. Amaziah was Hilkiah's son. 46Hilkiah was Amzi's son. Amzi was Bani's son. Bani was Shemer's son. 47Shemer was Mahli's son. Mahli was Mushi's son. Mushi was Merari's son. Merari was Levi's son.

48Heman and Asaph's brothers were from the tribe of Levi. The tribe of Levi was also called Levites. The Levites were chosen to do the work in the Holy Tent. The Holy Tent was God's house. 49But only Aaron's descendants were permitted to burn incense on the altar of burnt offering and on the altar of incense. Aaron's descendants did all the work in the Most Holy Place in God's house. They also did the ceremonies to make the Israelites pure. They followed all the rules and laws that Moses, God's servant, commanded.

Aaron's Descendants

50These were Aaron's sons: Eleazar was Aaron's son. Phinehas was Eleazar's son. Abishua was Phinehas' son. 51Bukki was Abishua's son. Uzzi was Bukki's son. Zerahiah was Uzzi's son. 52Meraioth was Zerahiah's son. Amariah was Meraioth's son. Ahitub was Amariah's son. 53Zadok was Ahitub's son. Ahimaaz was Zadok's son.

Homes for the Levite Families

54These are the places where Aaron's descendants lived. They lived in their camps in the land that was given to them. The Kohath families got the first share of the land that was given to the Levites. 55They were given the town of Hebron and the fields around it. This was in the area of Judah. 56But the fields farther from town and the villages near the town of Hebron were given to Caleb son of Jephunneh. 57The descendants of Aaron were given the city of Hebron. Hebron was a city of safety.[a] They were also given the cities of Libnah, Jattir, Eshtemoa, 58Hilen, Debir, 59Ashan, Juttah and Beth Shemesh. They got all the cities and the fields around them. 60From the tribe of Benjamin they got the cities of Gibeon, Geba, Alemeth and Anathoth. They got all the cities and the fields around them.

Thirteen cities were given to the Kohath families.

61The rest of Kohath's descendants got ten towns from half the tribe of Manasseh.

62The tribes that were the descendants of Gershon got 13 cities. They got the cities from the tribes of Issachar, Asher, Naphtali and the part of Manasseh living in the area of Bashan.

63The tribes that were the descendants of Merari got 12 cities. They got the cities from the tribes of Reuben, Gad and Zebulun. They got them by throwing lots.

64So the Israelites gave those towns and fields to the Levites. 65All those cities came from the tribes of Judah, Simeon and Benjamin. They decided which Levite family got which city by throwing lots.

66The tribe of Ephraim gave some of the Kohath families some towns. Those towns were chosen by throwing lots. 67They were given the city of Shechem. Shechem is a city of safety. They were also given the towns of Gezer, 68Jokmeam, Beth

Horon, 69Aijalon and Gath Rimmon. They also got fields with those towns. Those towns were in the hill country of Ephraim. 70And from half the tribe of Manasseh, the Israelites gave the towns of Aner and Bileam to the Kohath families. The Kohath families also got fields with those towns.

Other Levite Families Get Homes

71The Gershon families got the towns of Golan in the area of Bashan and Ashtaroth from half the tribe of Manasseh. They also got the fields near those towns.

72-73The Gershon families also got the towns of Kedesh, Daberath, Ramoth and Gannim from the tribe of Issachar. They also got the fields near those towns.

74-75The Gershon families also got the towns of Mashal, Abdon, Hukok and Rehob from the tribe of Asher. They also got the fields near those towns.

76The Gershon families also got the towns of Kedesh in Galilee, Hammon and Kiriathaim from the tribe of Naphtali. They also got the fields near those towns.

77The rest of the Levites, from the Merari families, got the towns of Jokneam, Kartah, Rimmono and Tabor from the tribe of Zebulun. They also got the fields near those towns.

78-79The Merari families also got the towns of Bezer in the desert, Jahzah, Kedemoth and Mephaath from the tribe of Reuben. The tribe of Reuben lived on the east side of the Jordan River, east of the city of Jericho. These Merari families also got the fields near those towns.

80-81And the Merari families got the towns of Ramoth in Gilead, Mahanaim, Heshbon and Jazer from the tribe of Gad. They also got the fields near those towns.

Issachar's Descendants

7 Issachar had four sons. Their names were Tola, Puah, Jashub and Shimron. 2Tola's sons were Uzzi, Rephaiah, Jeriel, Jahmai, Ibsam and Samuel. They were all leaders of their families. Those men and their descendants were strong soldiers. Their families grew. By the time David was king, there were 22,600 men ready for war. 3Uzzi's son was Izrahiah. Izrahiah's sons were Michael, Obadiah, Joel and Isshiah. All five of them were leaders of their families. 4Their family history shows they had 36,000 soldiers ready for war. They had a large family because they had many wives and children. 5The family history shows there were 87,000 strong soldiers in all the tribes of Issachar.

---

[a] **6:57** *city of safety* A special city where an Israelite could run to in order to escape the angry relatives of a person who was accidentally killed by that Israelite. See Num. 35:6–34 and Josh. 20:1–9. Also in verse 67.

Benjamin's Descendants

⁶Benjamin had three sons. Their names were Bela, Beker and Jediael.

⁷Bela had five sons. Their names were Ezbon, Uzzi, Uzziel, Jerimoth and Iri. They were leaders of their families. Their family history shows they had 22,034 soldiers.

⁸Beker's sons were Zemirah, Joash, Eliezer, Elioenai, Omri, Jeremoth, Abijah, Anathoth and Alemeth. They all were Beker's children. ⁹Their family history shows who the family leaders were. And it also shows they had 20,200 soldiers.

¹⁰Jediael's son was Bilhan. Bilhan's sons were Jeush, Benjamin, Ehud, Kenaanah, Zethan, Tarshish and Ahishahar. ¹¹All of Jediael's sons were leaders of their families. They had 17,200 soldiers ready for war.

¹²The Shuppites and Huppites were the descendants of Ir. Hushim was the son of Aher.

Naphtali's Descendants

¹³Naphtali's sons were Jahziel, Guni, Jezer and Shallum.

And these are the descendants of Bilhah.ᵃ

Manasseh's Descendants

¹⁴These are Manasseh's descendants: Manasseh's Aramean slave woman had a son named Asriel. She also bore Makir, the father of Gilead. ¹⁵Makir married a woman from the Huppites and Shuppites. Makir's sister was named Maacah. The name of the second son was Zelophehad, who had only daughters. ¹⁶Makir's wife Maacah had a son. She named this son Peresh. His brother was named Sheresh. The sons of Sheresh were Ulam and Rakem.

¹⁷Ulam's son was Bedan.

These were the descendants of Gilead. Gilead was Makir's son. Makir was Manasseh's son. ¹⁸Makir's sister Hammolekethᵇ had Ishhod, Abiezer and Mahlah.

¹⁹Shemida's sons were Ahian, Shechem, Likhi and Aniam.

Ephraim's Descendants

²⁰These were the names of Ephraim's descendants: Ephraim's son was Shuthelah. Shuthelah's son was Bered. Bered's son was Tahath. ²¹Tahath's son was Eleadah.

Eleadah's son was Tahath. Tahath's son was Zabad. Zabad's son was Shuthelah.

Some men who grew up in the city of Gath killed Ezer and Elead. This happened because Ezer and Elead went there to steal cattle and sheep from those men in Gath. ²²Ephraim was the father of Ezer and Elead. He cried for many days because Ezer and Elead were dead. Ephraim's family came to comfort him. ²³Then Ephraim had sex with his wife. She became pregnant and had a son. Ephraim named this new son Beriahᶜ because something bad had happened to his family. ²⁴Ephraim's daughter was Sheerah. Sheerah built Lower Beth Horon and Upper Beth Horon and Lower Uzzen Sheerah and Upper Uzzen Sheerah.

²⁵Rephah was Ephraim's son. Resheph was Rephah's son. Telah was Resheph's son. Tahan was Telah's son. ²⁶Ladan was Tahan's son. Ammihud was Ladan's son. Elishama was Ammihud's son. ²⁷Nun was Elishama's son. Joshua was Nun's son.

²⁸These are the cities and lands where Ephraim's descendants lived: Bethel and the villages near it, Naaran to the east, Gezer and the villages near it on the west, and Shechem and the villages near it all the way to Ayyah and the villages near it. ²⁹Along the borders of Manasseh's land were the towns of Beth Shan, Taanach, Megiddo and Dor and the small towns near them. The descendants of Joseph lived in these towns. Joseph was the son of Israel.

Asher's Descendants

³⁰Asher's sons were Imnah, Ishvah, Ishvi and Beriah. Their sister was named Serah.

³¹Beriah's sons were Heber and Malkiel. Malkiel was the ancestor of Birzaith.

³²Heber was the father of Japhlet, Shomer, Hotham and of their sister Shua.

³³Japhlet had three sons. They were named Pasach, Bimhal and Ashvath.

³⁴Shomer's sons were Ahi, Rohgah, Jehubbahᵈ and Aram.

³⁵Shomer's brother was Helem. Helem's sons were Zophah, Imna, Shelesh and Amal.

³⁶Zophah's sons were Suah, Harnepher, Shual, Beri, Imrah, ³⁷Bezer, Hod, Shamma, Shilshah, Ithran and Beera.

ᵃ **7:13 Bilhah** Jacob's slave woman and the mother of Dan and Naphtali. See Gen. 30:4–8.
ᵇ **7:18 Hammoleketh** Or "the woman who ruled" or "queen".
ᶜ **7:23 Beriah** This is like the Hebrew word meaning "bad" or "trouble".
ᵈ **7:34 Jehubbah** Or "Hubbah".

³⁸Jether's sons were Jephunneh, Pispah and Ara.

³⁹Ulla's sons were Arah, Hanniel and Rizia.

⁴⁰All these men were descendants of Asher. They were leaders of their families. They were the best men. They were soldiers and great leaders. Their family history shows 26,000 soldiers ready for war.

More About Benjamin's Family

8 Benjamin was Bela's father. Bela was Benjamin's first son. Ashbel was Benjamin's second son. Aharah was Benjamin's third son. ²Nohah was Benjamin's fourth son. And Rapha was Benjamin's fifth son.

³⁻⁵Bela's sons were Addar, Gera, Abihud, Abishua, Naaman, Ahoah, Gera, Shephuphan and Huram.

⁶⁻⁷These were the descendants of Ehud. They were leaders of their families in Geba. They were forced to leave their homes and move to Manahath. Ehud's descendants were Naaman, Ahijah and Gera. Gera forced them to leave their homes. He was the father of Uzza and Ahihud.

⁸Shaharaim divorced his wives Hushim and Baara in Moab. After he did this he had some children with another wife. ⁹⁻¹⁰Shaharaim had Jobab, Zibia, Mesha, Malcam, Jeuz, Sakia and Mirmah with his wife Hodesh. They were leaders of their families. ¹¹Shaharaim and Hushim had two sons named Abitub and Elpaal.

¹²⁻¹³Elpaal's sons were Eber, Misham, Shemed, Beriah and Shema. Shemed built the towns of Ono and Lod and the small towns around Lod. Beriah and Shema were the leaders of the families living in Aijalon. They forced the people who lived in Gath to leave.

¹⁴Beriah's sons were Shashak and Jeremoth, ¹⁵Zebadiah, Arad, Eder, ¹⁶Michael, Ishpah and Joha. ¹⁷Elpaal's sons were Zebadiah, Meshullam, Hizki, Heber, ¹⁸Ishmerai, Izliah and Jobab.

¹⁹Shimei's sons were Jakim, Zicri, Zabdi, ²⁰Elienai, Zillethai, Eliel, ²¹Adaiah, Beraiah and Shimrath.

²²Shashak's sons were Ishpan, Eber, Eliel, ²³Abdon, Zicri, Hanan, ²⁴Hananiah, Elam, Anthothijah, ²⁵Iphdeiah and Penuel.

²⁶Jeroham's sons were Shamsherai, Shehariah, Athaliah, ²⁷Jaareshiah, Elijah and Zicri.

²⁸All these men were leaders of their families. They were listed in their family histories as leaders. They lived in Jerusalem.

²⁹Jeiel was the ancestor of the town of Gibeon, where he lived with his wife Maacah. ³⁰His oldest son was Abdon. Other sons were Zur, Kish, Baal, Ner, Nadab, ³¹Gedor, Ahio, Zeker ˻and Mikloth˼. ³²Mikloth was the father of Shimeah. These sons also lived near their relatives in Jerusalem.

³³Ner was Kish's father. Kish was Saul's father, and Saul was the father of Jonathan, Malki Shua, Abinadab and Esh Baal.

³⁴Jonathan's son was Merib Baal. Merib Baal was Micah's father.

³⁵Micah's sons were Pithon, Melech, Tarea and Ahaz.

³⁶Ahaz was Jehoaddah's father. Jehoaddah was the father of Alemeth, Azmaveth and Zimri. Zimri was Moza's father. ³⁷Moza was Binea's father. Raphah was Binea's son. Eleasah was Raphah's son. And Azel was Eleasah's son.

³⁸Azel had six sons. Their names were Azrikam, Bokeru, Ishmael, Sheariah, Obadiah and Hanan. All these sons were Azel's children.

³⁹Azel's brother was Eshek. Eshek had some sons. These were Eshek's sons: Ulam was Azel's oldest son. Jeush was Eshek's second son. Eliphelet was Eshek's third son. ⁴⁰Ulam's sons were strong soldiers who were very good with bows and arrows. They had many sons and grandsons. In all, there were 150 sons and grandsons.

All these men were descendants of Benjamin.

9 The names of all the Israelites were listed in their family histories. Those family histories were put in the book, *The History of the Kings of Israel.*

The People in Jerusalem

The people of Judah were made prisoners and forced to go to Babylon. They were taken there because they were not faithful to God. ²The first people to come back and live in their own lands and towns were some Israelites, priests, Levites and servants who work in the Temple.

³These are the people from the tribes of Judah, Benjamin, Ephraim and Manasseh who lived in Jerusalem:

⁴Uthai was Ammihud's son. Ammihud was Omri's son. Omri was Imri's son. Imri was Bani's son. Bani was a descendant of Perez. Perez was Judah's son.

⁵The Shilonites who lived in Jerusalem were Asaiah the oldest son and his sons.

YOUR PLACE IN HISTORY

Every year TV shows like *The X Factor* and *American Idol* thrust a new crop of talented people into the limelight. At various points during the mentoring and the knock-out stages, they get to meet music legends – people they've always looked up to. Almost every time they say they are overwhelmed just to be in the same room as these famous performers. It's a great honour to have your name mentioned next to those of your heroes.

DIG IN

READ 1 Chronicles 9:1–34

- What do all the people in this long list have in common (v.1)?
- What groups of people does the writer specifically name?

The first nine chapters of Chronicles attempt to give a full family tree from the first man, Adam, right through to this time in the Old Testament.

It is now seventy years since the exile took place and these are the men, women and families who have survived and come home. Most will be walking streets they've never seen before, living in places where their parents and grandparents lived.

They have questions: "Who am I?" "Is the God that my grandparents worshipped my God too?" "Are the promises of the God my parents trust still relevant to me?"

And they have good reason to ask. After all, the reason their families were forced to leave their land was because God brought armies to attack their nation, with many being killed and the rest being carted off to be servants in exile. (You'll find the history in 2 Kings.) They need to be reminded and reassured that they are still God's people.

That's what's happening here and in the rest of 1 and 2 Chronicles (which are one long book in the Hebrew Bible). The Chronicler is listing all the families who returned from exile alongside the men and women of Israel's history. In effect he's saying, "You're the latest in a long line of God's people. You – yes, you! – are part of God's story."

Over history, some people have looked down on Chronicles because it paints quite a one-sided, rosy view of Israel's history. It doesn't show David and Solomon's faults the way the books of Samuel and Kings do – it's not warts-and-all like those books. But that's not the Chronicler's aim. Chronicles is nothing less than one person's attempt to get a whole nation to lift up their heads and to get them to remember who they are – and who their God is. And to prove to them that the God who has always been with them is nowhere near finished with them yet.

DIG THROUGH

- "You – yes, you! – are part of the story". Have you ever stopped to consider that you are part of this same family of faith that started with Adam? You may not be descended from the Jewish people but the Bible says that non-Jews are now joined to their family tree (Romans 11:17–24).

DIG DEEPER

This lengthy genealogy (family history) is mirrored in the first chapter of the book of Matthew. Chronicles was the last book in the original Hebrew Scriptures. Matthew was always placed first in the New Testament. Clearly Matthew wanted to emphasize continuity in God's story from these times right up to Jesus.

⁶The Zerahites who lived in Jerusalem were Jeuel and their relatives. There were 690 of them in all.

⁷These are the people from the tribe of Benjamin who lived in Jerusalem: Sallu was Meshullam's son. Meshullam was Hodaviah's son. Hodaviah was Hassenuah's son. ⁸Ibneiah was Jeroham's son. Elah was Uzzi's son. Uzzi was Micri's son. And Meshullam was Shephatiah's son. Shephatiah was Reuel's son. Reuel was Ibnijah's son. ⁹The family history of Benjamin shows there were 956 of them living in Jerusalem. All these men were leaders in their families.

¹⁰These are the priests who lived in Jerusalem: Jedaiah, Jehoiarib, Jakin and ¹¹Azariah. Azariah was Hilkiah's son. Hilkiah was Meshullam's son. Meshullam was Zadok's son. Zadok was Meraioth's son. Meraioth was Ahitub's son. Ahitub was the important official responsible for God's Temple. ¹²Also there was Jeroham's son, Adaiah. Jeroham was Pashhur's son. Pashhur was Malkijah's son. And there was Adiel's son, Maasai. Adiel was Jahzerah's son. Jahzerah was Meshullam's son. Meshullam was Meshillemith's son. Meshillemith was Immer's son.

¹³There were 1,760 priests. They were leaders of their families. They were responsible for the work of serving in God's Temple.

¹⁴These are the people from the tribe of Levi who lived in Jerusalem: Hasshub's son, Shemaiah. Hasshub was Azrikam's son. Azrikam was Hashabiah's son. Hashabiah was a descendant of Merari. ¹⁵Also living in Jerusalem were Bakbakkar, Heresh, Galal and Mattaniah. Mattaniah was Mica's son. Mica was Zicri's son. Zicri was Asaph's son. ¹⁶Obadiah was Shemaiah's son. Shemaiah was Galal's son. Galal was Jeduthun's son. Berekiah was Asa's son. Asa was Elkanah's son. Berekiah lived in the small towns near the people of Netophah.

¹⁷These are the gatekeepers who lived in Jerusalem: Shallum, Akkub, Talmon, Ahiman and their relatives. Shallum was their leader. ¹⁸Now these men stand next to the King's Gate on the east side. They were the gatekeepers from the tribe of Levi. ¹⁹Shallum was Kore's son. Kore was Ebiasaph's son. Ebiasaph was Korah's son. Shallum and his brothers were gatekeepers. They were from the family of Korah. They had the job of

guarding the entrance to the Holy Tent. They did this just as their ancestors had done before them. Their ancestors had the job of guarding the entrance to the area where the LORD lived among the people. ²⁰In the past, Phinehas was in charge of the gatekeepers. Phinehas was Eleazar's son. The LORD was with Phinehas. ²¹Zechariah son of Meshelemiah was the gatekeeper at the entrance to the Holy Tent.

²²In all there were 212 men who were chosen to guard the gates of the Holy Tent. Their names were written in their family histories in their small towns. David and Samuel the seer chose these men because they could be trusted. ²³The gatekeepers and their descendants had the responsibility of guarding the gates of the LORD's house, the Holy Tent. ²⁴There were gates on the four sides: east, west, north and south. ²⁵The gatekeepers' relatives who lived in the small towns had to come and help them at certain times. They came and helped the gatekeepers for seven days each time.

INSIGHT

Being a Temple gatekeeper involved much more than merely being a security guard. They also washed dishes, baked bread, mixed spices and kept accounts.

1 Chronicles 9:22–32

---

²⁶There were four gatekeepers who were the leaders of all the gatekeepers. They were Levites. They had the job of caring for the rooms and treasures in God's Temple. ²⁷They stayed up all night guarding God's Temple, and they had the job of opening God's Temple every morning.

²⁸Some of the gatekeepers had the job of caring for the dishes used in the Temple services. They counted them when they were brought in. They also counted these dishes when they were taken out. ²⁹Other gatekeepers were chosen to care for the furniture and the special dishes. They also took care of the flour, wine, oil, incense and special oil.ᵃ ³⁰But it was the priests who had the job of mixing the special oil.

³¹There was a Levite named Mattithiah who had the job of baking the bread used for the offerings. Mattithiah was Shallum's oldest son. Shallum was from the Korah family. ³²Some of the

---

ᵃ **9:29 special oil** Or "perfume". This might be the oil used to anoint priests, prophets and kings. See Exod. 30:22–38.

gatekeepers who were in the Korah family had the job of preparing the bread put on the table every Sabbath.

³³The Levites who were singers and leaders of their families stayed in the rooms at the Temple. They did not have to do other work because they were responsible for the work in the Temple day and night.

³⁴All these Levites were leaders of their families. They were listed as leaders in their family histories. They lived in Jerusalem.

The Family History of King Saul

³⁵Jeiel was the ancestor of the town of Gibeon, where he lived with his wife Maacah. ³⁶Jeiel's oldest son was Abdon. Other sons were Zur, Kish, Baal, Ner, Nadab, ³⁷Gedor, Ahio, Zechariah and Mikloth. ³⁸Mikloth was Shimeam's father. Jeiel's family lived near their relatives in Jerusalem.

³⁹Ner was Kish's father. Kish was Saul's father. And Saul was the father of Jonathan, Malki Shua, Abinadab and Esh Baal.

⁴⁰Jonathan's son was Merib Baal. Merib Baal was Micah's father.

⁴¹Micah's sons were Pithon, Melech, Tahrea and Ahaz. ⁴²Ahaz was the father of Jadah.^a Jadah was the father of Alemeth, Azmaveth and Zimri. Zimri was Moza's father. ⁴³Moza was the father of Binea. Rephaiah was Binea's son. Eleasah was Rephaiah's son. And Azel was Eleasah's son.

⁴⁴Azel had six sons. Their names were Azrikam, Bokeru, Ishmael, Sheariah, Obadiah and Hanan. They were Azel's children.

The Death of King Saul

10 The Philistines fought against the Israelites. The Israelites ran away from the Philistines. Many Israelites were killed on Mount Gilboa. ²The Philistines continued chasing Saul and his sons. They caught them and killed them. The Philistines killed Saul's sons Jonathan, Abinadab and Malki Shua. ³The fighting was heavy around Saul. The archers shot Saul with their arrows and wounded him.

⁴Then Saul said to the helper who carried his armour, "Pull out your sword and use it to kill me. Then these foreigners^b will not hurt me and make fun of me when they come."

But the helper was afraid. He refused to kill Saul. So Saul used his own sword to kill himself by falling on it. ⁵When the helper saw that Saul was dead, he also fell on his own sword and died. ⁶So Saul and three of his sons died. All of Saul's family died together.

⁷When all the Israelites living in the valley saw that their own army had run away and that Saul and his sons were dead, they left their towns and ran away. Then the Philistines came into the towns and lived in them.

⁸The next day, the Philistines came to take valuable things from the dead bodies. They found Saul's body and the bodies of his sons on Mount Gilboa. ⁹The Philistines took things from Saul's body. They took Saul's head and armour. They sent messengers through all their country to tell the news to their false gods and to their people. ¹⁰The Philistines put Saul's armour in the temple of their false gods. They hung Saul's head in the temple of Dagon.

¹¹All the people living in the town of Jabesh Gilead heard everything that the Philistines had done to Saul. ¹²All the brave men from Jabesh Gilead went to get the bodies of Saul and his sons. They brought them back to Jabesh Gilead. They buried the bones of Saul and his sons under the large tree in Jabesh. Then they showed their sadness and fasted for seven days.

¹³Saul died because he was not faithful to the Lord. He did not obey the Lord. He even tried to get advice by contacting a ghost ¹⁴instead of asking the Lord. That is why the Lord killed Saul and gave the kingdom to Jesse's son David.

David Becomes King Over Israel

11 All the Israelites came to David at the town of Hebron. They said to David, "We are your own flesh and blood.^c ²In the past you led us in war. You led us even though Saul was the king. The Lord said to you 'David, you will be the shepherd of my people, the Israelites. You will become the leader over my people.'"

³All the leaders of Israel came to King David at the town of Hebron. David made an agreement with them in Hebron before the Lord. The leaders anointed David. That made him king over Israel. The Lord had promised through Samuel that this would happen.

David Captures Jerusalem

⁴David and all the Israelites went to the city of Jerusalem. Jerusalem was called Jebus at that time. The people living in that city were named Jebusites. They ⁵said to David, "You cannot get

---

^a **9:42 Jadah** This is from the ancient Greek translation and some Hebrew copies. Most Hebrew copies have "Jarah" for "Jadah" in this verse.

^b **10:4 foreigners** Literally, "uncircumcised". This means people who did not share in the agreement God made with Israel. See "CIRCUMCISE, CIRCUMCISION" in the Word List.

^c **11:1 We are . . . blood** A way of saying they were David's relatives.

inside our city." But David did defeat them. He took over the fortress of Zion, and it became the City of David.

⁶David said, "The one who leads the attack on the Jebusites will become the commander over all my army." So Joab led the attack. He was Zeruiah's son. Joab became the commander of the army.

⁷Then David made his home in the fortress. That is why it is named the City of David. ⁸David built the city around the fortress. He built it from the Millo to the wall around the city. Joab repaired the other parts of the city. ⁹David continued to grow greater, and the LORD All-Powerful was with him.

The Three Heroes

¹⁰This is a list of the leaders over David's special soldiers. These heroes became very powerful with David in his kingdom. They and all the Israelites supported David and made him king, just as the LORD had promised.

¹¹This is a list of David's special soldiers:

Jashobeam the Hacmonite*a* was the leader of the king's special forces.*b* Jashobeam used his spear to kill 300 men at one time.

¹²Next there was Eleazar son of Dodai*c* from Ahoah. Eleazar was one of the Three Heroes.*d* ¹³Eleazar was with David at Pasdammim. The Philistines had come to that place to fight a war. There was a field full of barley there. The Israelites ran away from the Philistines. ¹⁴But the Three Heroes stood there in that field and defended it. They defeated the Philistines. The LORD gave the Israelites a great victory.

¹⁵Once David was at the cave of Adullam, and three of the Thirty Heroes*e* went down to meet him by a rock near the cave. At the same time the Philistine army was camped in the Valley of Rephaim.

¹⁶Another time David was in the fortress, and a group of Philistine soldiers was stationed in Bethlehem. ¹⁷David was thirsty for some water from his home town, so he said, "Oh, if only I could have some water from that well by the gate in Bethlehem." ¹⁸So the Three Heroes*f* fought their way through the Philistine army and got some water from the well near the city gate in Bethlehem. They took it to David, but he refused to drink it. He poured it on the ground as an offering to the LORD. ¹⁹David said, "God, I cannot drink this water. It would be like drinking the blood of the men who risked their lives to get this water for me." That is why David refused to drink the water. The Three Heroes did many brave things like that.

Other Brave Soldiers

²⁰Joab's brother, Abishai, was the leader of the Three Heroes. Abishai used his spear against 300 enemies and killed them. He was as famous as the Three Heroes. ²¹Abishai was even more famous than the Three Heroes.*g* He became their leader, even though he was not one of the Three Heroes.

²²Then there was Benaiah son of Jehoiada, from Kabzeel. He was the son of a powerful man.*h* Benaiah did many brave things. He killed two of the best soldiers in Moab. One day when it was snowing, Benaiah went down into a hole in the ground and killed a lion. ²³And Benaiah killed a big Egyptian soldier. That man was over 2 metres*i* tall. The Egyptian had a spear that was very large and heavy. It was as big as the pole on a weaver's loom. Benaiah had only a club. He grabbed the spear in the Egyptian's hands and took it away from him. Then Benaiah killed the Egyptian with his own spear. ²⁴Benaiah son of Jehoiada did many brave things like that. He was as famous as the Three Heroes. ²⁵Benaiah was even more famous than the Thirty Heroes, but he was not one of the Three Heroes. David made Benaiah the leader of his bodyguards.

The Thirty Heroes

²⁶The following men were among the king's special forces:

Asahel, Joab's brother;
Elhanan son of Dodai from Bethlehem;
²⁷Shammoth the Harodite;
Helez the Pelonite;
²⁸Ira son of Ikkesh from Tekoa;
Abiezer from Anathoth;
²⁹Sibbecai the Hushathite;
Ilai from Ahoah;
³⁰Maharai from Netophah;
Heled son of Baanah from Netophah;

---

a **11:11 *Jashobeam the Hacmonite*** This is "Josheb Basshebeth the Tahkemonite" in 2 Sam. 23:8.
b **11:11 *king's special forces*** A special group of soldiers who formed three-man squads and went on special missions for the king.
c **11:12 *Eleazar son of Dodai*** Or "Eleazar his cousin".
d **11:12 *Three Heroes*** These were David's three bravest soldiers. Also in verses 18,20,24.
e **11:15 *Thirty Heroes*** Or "the king's special forces". These men were David's famous group of very brave soldiers. Also in verses 25,42.
f **11:18 *Three Heroes*** These were David's three bravest soldiers. Also in verses 19–21.
g **11:21 *Three Heroes*** Or possibly, "Thirty Heroes".
h **11:22 *powerful man*** That is, a man from the warrior class ready to protect his people in war.
i **11:23 *over 2 metres*** Literally, "5 cubits".

31Ithai son of Ribai from Gibeah in Benjamin;
    Benaiah the Pirathonite;
32Hurai from the Brooks of Gaash;
    Abiel the Arbathite;
33Azmaveth the Baharumite;
    Eliahba the Shaalbonite;
34the sons of Hashem the Gizonite;
    Jonathan son of Shagee the Hararite;
35Ahiam son of Sacar the Hararite;
    Eliphal son of Ur;
36Hepher the Mekerathite;
    Ahijah the Pelonite;
37Hezro the Carmelite;
    Naarai son of Ezbai;
38Joel, Nathan's brother;
    Mibhar son of Hagri;
39Zelek the Ammonite;
    Naharai the officer from Beeroth, who
        carried the armour for Joab son of
        Zeruiah;
40Ira the Ithrite;
    Gareb the Ithrite;
41Uriah the Hittite;
    Zabad son of Ahlai;
42Adina who was the son of Shiza from the tribe
        of Reuben and was the leader of the tribe of
        Reuben, but he was also one of the Thirty
        Heroes;
43Hanan son of Maacah;
    Joshaphat the Mithnite;
44Uzzia the Ashterathite;
    Shama and Jeiel sons of Hotham from Aroer;
45Jediael son of Shimri
    and his brother Joha the Tizite;
46Eliel the Mahavite;
    Jeribai and Joshaviah the sons of Elnaam;
    Ithmah the Moabite;
47Eliel, Obed and Jaasiel the Mezobaite.

The Brave Men Who Joined David

12 This is a list of the men who came to David while he was at Ziklag. This was when David was hiding from Saul son of Kish. These men helped David in battle. 2They could shoot arrows from their bows with either their right or left hand. They could also throw stones from their slings with either their right or left hand. They were Saul's relatives from the tribe of Benjamin:

3Ahiezer, their leader and Joash (sons of
    Shemaah the Gibeathite); Jeziel and Pelet
    (sons of Azmaveth); Beracah and Jehu from
    the town of Anathoth; 4Ishmaiah the
    Gibeonite (a hero and leader of the Thirty

Heroes); Jeremiah, Jahaziel, Johanan and Jozabad from the Gederathites; 5Eluzai, Jerimoth, Bealiah and Shemariah; Shephatiah from Haruph; 6Elkanah, Isshiah, Azarel, Joezer and Jashobeam, all from the tribe of Korah; 7and Joelah and Zebadiah, the sons of Jeroham from the town of Gedor.

The Gadites

8Part of the tribe of Gad joined David at his fortress in the desert. They were brave soldiers trained for war and skilled with the shield and spear. They looked as fierce as lions, and they could run as fast as gazelles through the mountains.

9Ezer was the leader of the army from the tribe of Gad. Obadiah was the second in command. Eliab was the third in command. 10Mishmannah was the fourth in command. Jeremiah was the fifth in command. 11Attai was the sixth in command. Eliel was the seventh in command. 12Johanan was the eighth in command. Elzabad was the ninth in command. 13Jeremiah was the tenth in command. Macbannai was the eleventh in command.

14These men were leaders of the Gadite army. The weakest from that group was worth 100 men, and the strongest was worth 1,000 men.[a] 15They were the soldiers who crossed the Jordan River in the first month of the year, when it was flooded over its banks. They chased away the people in the valley who were on both sides of the river.

Other Soldiers Join David

16Other men from the tribes of Benjamin and Judah also came to David at the fortress. 17David went out to meet them and said, "If you have come in peace to help me, I welcome you. Join me. But if you have come to spy on me when I have done nothing wrong, may the God of our ancestors see what you did and punish you."

18Amasai was the leader of the Thirty Heroes.[b] Then the Spirit came on Amasai, and he said,

"We are yours, David!
    We are with you, son of Jesse.
Peace, peace to you.
    Peace to those who help you,
    because your God helps you."

So David welcomed these men into his group and put them in charge of the troops.

19Some of the men from the tribe of Manasseh also joined David. They joined him when he went with the Philistines to fight Saul. But David and

---

[a] **12:14** *The weakest . . . 1,000 men* Or "The smallest was commander over 100 men, the greatest over 1,000 men."
[b] **12:18** *Thirty Heroes* Or "The Three" or "the chariot officers".

his men did not really help the Philistines. The Philistine leaders talked about David helping them, but then they decided to send him away. They said, "If David goes back to his master Saul, our heads will be cut off!" ²⁰These were the men from Manasseh who joined David when he went to the town of Ziklag: Adnah, Jozabad, Jediael, Michael, Jozabad, Elihu and Zillethai. All of them were generalsᵃ from the tribe of Manasseh. ²¹They helped David fight against bad men who were going around the country and stealing things from people. All these men of Manasseh were brave soldiers. They became leaders in David's army.

²²More and more men came every day to help David. So he had a large and powerful army.

Other Men Join David at Hebron

²³These are the numbers of the men who came to David at the town of Hebron. These men were ready for war. They came to give Saul's kingdom to David. That is what the Lord said would happen. This is their number:

²⁴From the tribe of Judah there were
    6,800 men ready for war. They carried
    shields and spears.
²⁵From the tribe of Simeon there were
    7,100 men. They were brave soldiers ready
    for war.
²⁶From the tribe of Levi there were 4,600 men.
    ²⁷Jehoiada was in that group. He was a
    leader from Aaron's family. There were
    3,700 men with Jehoiada. ²⁸Zadok was also
    in that group. He was a brave young soldier.
    He came with 22 officers from his family.
²⁹From the tribe of Benjamin there were
    3,000 men. They were Saul's relatives.
    Most of them stayed faithful to Saul's family
    until that time.
³⁰From the tribe of Ephraim there were
    20,800 men. They were brave soldiers.
    They were famous men in their own
    families.
³¹From half the tribe of Manasseh there were
    18,000 men. They were called by name to
    come and make David king.
³²From the family of Issachar there were
    200 wise leaders. These men understood
    the right thing for Israel to do at the right
    time. Their relatives were with them and
    under their command.
³³From the tribe of Zebulun there were 50,000
    trained soldiers. They were trained to use
    all kinds of weapons and were very loyal to
    David.

³⁴From the tribe of Naphtali there were 1,000
    officers. They had 37,000 men with them.
    These men carried shields and spears.
³⁵From the tribe of Dan there were
    28,600 men ready for war.
³⁶From the tribe of Asher there were
    40,000 trained soldiers ready for war.
³⁷From the east side of the Jordan River, there
    were 120,000 men from the tribes of
    Reuben, Gad and half of Manasseh. They
    had all kinds of weapons.

³⁸All these men were brave fighters. They came to the town of Hebron for one reason—to make David king of all Israel. All the other Israelites also agreed that David should be king. ³⁹The men spent three days at Hebron with David. They ate and drank, because their relatives had prepared food for them. ⁴⁰Also, their neighbours from the areas where the tribes of Issachar, Zebulun and Naphtali live brought food on donkeys, camels, mules and cattle. They brought much flour, fig cakes, raisins, wine, oil, cattle and sheep. The people in Israel were very happy.

Bringing Back the Box of the Agreement

13 David talked with all the officers of his army. ²Then he called the Israelites together and said, "If you think it is a good idea, and if it is what the Lord our God wants, let us send a message to our brothers in all the areas of Israel. Let's also send the message to the priests and Levites who live with our brothers in their towns and the fields near those towns. Let the message tell them to come and join us. ³Let's bring our God's Holy Box back to us in Jerusalem. We did not pay attention to it while Saul was king." ⁴So all the Israelites agreed with David. They all thought it was the right thing to do.

⁵So David gathered all the Israelites from the Shihor River in Egypt to the town of Lebo Hamath. They came together to bring the Box of the Agreement back from the town of Kiriath Jearim. ⁶David and all the Israelites with him went to Baalah of Judah. (Baalah is another name for Kiriath Jearim.) They went there to bring out the Holy Box of God the Lord, who sits above the winged creatures. It is the Box that is called by his name.

⁷The people moved God's Holy Box from Abinadab's house and put it on a new cart. Uzzah and Ahio were driving the cart.

⁸David and all the Israelites were celebrating before God. They were praising God and singing songs. They were playing harps, lyres, drums, cymbals and trumpets.

ᵃ **12:20** *generals* Literally, "leaders over 1,000 men".

⁹They came to Kidon's threshing floor. The oxen pulling the cart stumbled, and the Holy Box almost fell. Uzzah reached out with his hand to catch it. ¹⁰The LORD became very angry with Uzzah and killed him because he touched the Holy Box. So Uzzah died there before God. ¹¹And David was angry because the LORD had shown his anger in killing Uzzah. So that place has been called "Perez Uzzah"ᵃ ever since then.

¹²That day David began to fear what God might do to him. So he said, "Should I really be the one in charge of God's Holy Box?" ¹³So he did not take the Holy Box with him to the City of David. He left it at Obed Edom's house. Obed Edom was from the city of Gath. ¹⁴God's Holy Box stayed with Obed Edom's family in his house for three months. The LORD blessed Obed Edom's family and everything Obed Edom owned.

David's Kingdom Grows

14 Hiram was king of the city of Tyre. He sent messengers to David. He also sent logs from cedar trees, stonecutters and carpenters to David. Hiram sent them to build a house for David. ²Then David understood that the LORD had really made him king of Israel. And he had made his kingdom large and powerful for the benefit of Israel, his people.

³David married more women in the city of Jerusalem and had more sons and daughters. ⁴These are the names of David's children born in Jerusalem: Shammua, Shobab, Nathan, Solomon, ⁵Ibhar, Elishua, Elpelet, ⁶Nogah, Nepheg, Japhia, ⁷Elishama, Beeliada and Eliphelet.

David Defeats the Philistines

⁸The Philistines heard that David had been chosen to be the king of Israel, so all the Philistines went to look for him. When David heard about it, he went out to fight them. ⁹The Philistines attacked the people living in the Valley of Rephaim and stole their things. ¹⁰David asked God, "Should I go and fight the Philistines? Will you let me defeat them?"

The LORD answered David, "Go. I will let you defeat the Philistines."

¹¹Then David and his men went up to the town of Baal Perazim. There David and his men defeated the Philistines. David said, "Waters break out from a broken dam. In the same way, God has broken through my enemies! God has done this through me." That is why that place is named Baal Perazim.ᵇ ¹²The Philistines had left their idols at Baal Perazim. David ordered his men to burn the idols.

Another Victory Over the Philistines

¹³The Philistines attacked the people living in the Valley of Rephaim again. ¹⁴David prayed to God again, and God answered his prayer. God said, "David, don't follow the Philistines up the hill when you attack. Instead, go around them and hide on the other side of the balsam trees. ¹⁵When you hear the sound of marching in the tops of the balsam trees, go out to battle because that is the sign that God has gone out in front of you to defeat the Philistines." ¹⁶David did what God told him to do. So David and his men defeated the Philistine army. They killed Philistine soldiers all the way from the town of Gibeon to the town of Gezer. ¹⁷So David became famous in all the countries. The LORD made all nations afraid of him.

The Box of the Agreement in Jerusalem

15 David built houses for himself in the City of David. Then he built a place to put God's Holy Box. He set up a tent for it. ²Then he said, "Only the Levites are permitted to carry God's Holy Box. The LORD chose them to carry it and to serve him forever."

³David told all the Israelites to meet together at Jerusalem to see the LORD's Holy Box carried to the place he had made for it. ⁴He called together the descendants of Aaron and the Levites.

⁵There were 120 people from the tribe of Kohath. Uriel was their leader.
⁶There were 220 people from the tribe of Merari. Asaiah was their leader.
⁷There were 130 people from the tribe of Gershon. Joel was their leader.
⁸There were 200 people from the tribe of Elizaphan. Shemaiah was their leader.
⁹There were 80 people from the tribe of Hebron. Eliel was their leader.
¹⁰There were 112 people from the tribe of Uzziel. Amminadab was their leader.

David Talks to the Priests and Levites

¹¹Then David asked the priests, Zadok and Abiathar, to come to him. David also asked these Levites to come to him: Uriel, Asaiah, Joel, Shemaiah, Eliel and Amminadab. ¹²David said to them, "You are the leaders from the tribe of Levi. You and the other Levites must make yourselves holy.ᶜ Then bring the Holy Box of the LORD, the God of Israel, to the place I have made for it. ¹³The first time we tried to bring it, we failed to ask the LORD about the right way to move it. And

---

ᵃ **13:11** *Perez Uzzah* This name means "the outburst at Uzzah".
ᵇ **14:11** *Baal Perazim* This name means "the Lord breaks through".
ᶜ **15:12** *holy* Here, this means "prepared to serve the LORD". Also in verse 14.

he punished us because you Levites did not carry it."

[14]Then the priests and Levites made themselves holy so that they could carry the Holy Box of the LORD, the God of Israel. [15]The Levites used the special poles to carry God's Holy Box on their shoulders, the way Moses commanded. They carried the Holy Box just as the LORD had said.

The Singers

[16]David told the Levite leaders to get their brothers, the singers. The singers were to take their lyres, harps and cymbals and sing happy songs.

[17]Then the Levites got Heman and his brothers, Asaph and Ethan. Heman was Joel's son. Asaph was Berekiah's son. Ethan was Kushaiah's son. These men were from the Merari tribe. [18]There was also a second group of Levites. They were Zechariah, Jaaziel, Shemiramoth, Jehiel, Unni, Eliab, Benaiah, Maaseiah, Mattithiah, Eliphelehu, Mikneiah, Obed Edom and Jeiel. These men were the Levite guards.

[19]The singers Heman, Asaph and Ethan played bronze cymbals. [20]Zechariah, Jaaziel, Shemiramoth, Jehiel, Unni, Eliab, Maaseiah and Benaiah played the alamoth harps. [21]Mattithiah, Eliphelehu, Mikneiah, Obed Edom, Jeiel and Azaziah played the sheminith harps.[a] This was their job forever. [22]The Levite leader Kenaniah was in charge of the singing. Kenaniah had this job because he was very skilled at singing.

[23]Berekiah and Elkanah were two of the guards for the Holy Box. [24]The priests Shebaniah, Joshaphat, Nethanel, Amasai, Zechariah, Benaiah and Eliezer had the job of blowing trumpets as they walked in front of God's Holy Box. Obed Edom and Jehiah were the other guards for the Holy Box.

[25]David, the elders of Israel and the generals[b] went to get the Box of the LORD's Agreement. They brought it out from Obed Edom's house. Everyone was very happy! [26]God had helped the Levites who carried the Box of the LORD's Agreement. So they sacrificed seven bulls and seven rams to him. [27]All the Levites who carried the Holy Box wore robes made from fine linen. Kenaniah, the man in charge of the singing, and all the singers had robes made from fine linen. David also wore a robe made from fine linen. He also wore an ephod made of fine linen.

[28]So all the Israelites joined in bringing up the Box of the LORD's Agreement. They shouted, they blew rams' horns and trumpets, and they played cymbals, lyres and harps.

[29]When the Box of the LORD's Agreement arrived at the City of David, Saul's daughter Michal looked through a window. When she saw King David dancing and playing, she lost her respect for him.

16 The Levites brought God's Holy Box and put it inside the tent David had set up for it. Then they offered burnt offerings and fellowship offerings to God. [2]After David had finished giving the burnt offerings and fellowship offerings, he used the LORD's name to bless the people. [3]Then he gave a loaf of bread, some dates and raisins to every Israelite man and woman.

[4]Then David chose some of the Levites to serve before the LORD's Holy Box. They had the job of celebrating and giving thanks and praise to the LORD, the God of Israel. [5]Asaph was the leader of the first group. His group played the cymbals. Zechariah was the leader of the second group. The other Levites were Uzziel, Shemiramoth, Jehiel, Mattithiah, Eliab, Benaiah, Obed Edom and Jeiel. These men played the lyres and harps. [6]Benaiah and Jahaziel were the priests who always blew the trumpets before the Box of God's Agreement. [7]This was when David first gave Asaph and his brothers the job of singing praises to the LORD.

David's Song of Thanks

[8]Give thanks to the LORD and call out to him!
  Tell the nations what he has done!
[9]Sing to him; sing praises to him.
  Tell about the amazing things he has done.
[10]Be proud of his holy name.
  You followers of the LORD, be happy!
[11]Depend on the LORD for strength.
  Always go to him for help.
[12]Remember the amazing things he has done.
  Remember his miracles and his fair decisions.
[13]The people of Israel are his servants.
  The descendants of Jacob are his chosen people.
[14]The LORD is our God.
  He rules the whole world.
[15]Remember his agreement forever,
  the promise he gave that will never end.
[16]Remember the agreement he made with Abraham.
  Remember his promise to Isaac.
[17]He gave it as a law for Jacob,
  as an agreement with Israel that will last forever.

---

[a] 15:20–21 *alamoth, sheminith* The meaning of these words is uncertain, but they may refer to types of instruments, special ways of tuning an instrument, or two different groups that played harps in the Temple orchestra.
[b] 15:25 *generals* Literally, "leaders over 1,000 men".

A NEW SONG OF WORSHIP

The books of 1 and 2 Chronicles tell the same history of the Hebrew people as the books of Samuel and Kings, but they are written with a different emphasis. The writer has a special purpose – to encourage the Jewish people returning from exile to remember God and that they are his people.

A main theme is seeing how worship develops in Israel and, as we read, we get to see how David and Solomon in particular lead their people in deeper love and obedience to God.

DIG IN

READ 1 Chronicles 16:1–37

- What is the "Holy Box" and why does David bring it into Jerusalem (see chapter 13)?
- How does David tell the people to worship God?
- How often is worship to happen (v.37)?

The "Holy Box" is the main symbol of God's presence with his people during this time. For some time it has been kept elsewhere and when David finally manages to bring the special box to Jerusalem, he gives instructions that are to change the way God's people worship him forever.

Until now the Hebrew people's worship had been offered to God by one man – the high priest from Aaron's family line (check out Leviticus chapter 16). Now David is sharing the job around – naming Levites as the ministers of worship on behalf of the people.

And they will do something else completely new – they will come into the presence of God singing together. This moment is where music and songs are first introduced as acceptable offerings to God.

- What elements does David's first worship song include?
- What does the song say about God?

Lots of the words and phrases recorded from David's song will be familiar from hymns and worship songs that are still sung today. There's thankfulness, praise of God's power and character, and declarations of dependence on him.

One more important point (v.37) – it was to be a regular thing. Little by little, God is revealing more of what he wants from his people's hearts in worship.

DIG THROUGH

- David's song is a good model for a worship song or service. If you're involved with leading others in worship, is this a model you might find helpful?
- Down the ages, God's people have always been a singing people. Ask God to help you sing worship songs to him.

DIG DEEPER

- Exodus 25:10–22 explains the origins of the Holy Box. It was made to contain the stone tablets on which God wrote the Ten Commandments for Israel during the time of Moses.
- Bible commentators agree that the song recorded by the Chronicler is actually a blend of three of the psalms written by David. Check out and compare these passages: Psalm 105:1–15 and 1 Chronicles 16:8–22; Psalm 96:1–13 and 1 Chronicles 16:23–33; Psalm 106:1,47–48 and 1 Chronicles 16:34–36. As you read them, try to spot the differences in theme.

¹⁸He said, "I will give you the land of Canaan. It will be your very own."

¹⁹At the time God said this, there were only a
    few of his people,
    and they were foreigners there.
²⁰They travelled around from nation to nation,
    from one kingdom to another.
²¹But the Lord did not let anyone mistreat
    them.
    He warned kings not to harm them.
²²He said, "Don't hurt my chosen people.
    Don't hurt my prophets."
²³Let the whole world sing to the LORD!
    Tell the good news every day about how he
    saves us.
²⁴Tell all the nations how wonderful he is!
    Tell people everywhere about the amazing
    things he does.
²⁵The LORD is great and worthy of praise.
    He is more awesome than any of the
    "gods".
²⁶All the "gods" in other nations are nothing but
    statues,
    but the LORD made the heavens!
²⁷He lives in the presence of glory and honour.
    His Temple is a place of power and joy.
²⁸Praise the LORD, all people of every nation;
    praise the LORD's glory and power!
²⁹Give the LORD praise worthy of his glory.
    Come into his presence with your
    offerings.
    Worship the LORD in all his holy beauty.
³⁰Everyone on earth should tremble before
    him!
    But the world stands firm and cannot be
    moved.
³¹Let the heavens rejoice and the earth be
    happy!
    Let people everywhere say, "The LORD
    rules!"
³²Let the sea and everything in it shout for joy!
    Let the fields and everything in them be
    happy!
³³The trees of the forest will sing for joy when
    they see the LORD,
    because he is coming to rule the world.
³⁴Give thanks to the LORD because he is good.
    His faithful love will last forever.
³⁵Say to him,
    "Save us, God our Saviour.
  Bring us back
    and save us from the other nations.
  Then we will give thanks to your holy name
    and joyfully praise you."

³⁶Praise the LORD, the God of Israel!
    He always was and will always be worthy of
    praise!

All the people praised the LORD and said "Amen!"

³⁷Then David left Asaph and his brothers there in front of the Box of the LORD's Agreement. David left them there to serve in front of it every day. ³⁸He also left Obed Edom and 68 other Levites to serve with Asaph and his brothers. Obed Edom and Hosah were guards. Obed Edom was Jeduthun's son.

³⁹David left Zadok the priest and the other priests who served with him in front of the LORD's Tent*a* at the high place in Gibeon. ⁴⁰Every morning and evening Zadok and the other priests offered burnt offerings to the LORD on the altar of burnt offerings. They did this to follow the rules written in the Law of the LORD, which he had given Israel. ⁴¹Heman, Jeduthun and all the other Levites were chosen by name to praise the LORD, singing, "His faithful love will last forever." ⁴²Heman and Jeduthun had the job of blowing the trumpets and playing cymbals. They also had the job of playing other musical instruments when songs were sung to God. Jeduthun's sons guarded the gates.

⁴³After the celebration, all the people left and went home. David also went home to bless his family.

God's Promise to David

17 After David had moved into his palace, he said to Nathan the prophet, "Look, I am living in this nice palace made of cedar, but the Box of the LORD's Agreement sits in a tent."

²Nathan answered David, "You may do what you want to do. God is with you."

³But that night the word of God came to Nathan. ⁴God said,

"Go and tell this to my servant David: 'The LORD says, David, you are not the one to build a house for me to live in. ^{5–6}Since the time I brought Israel out of Egypt until now, I have not lived in a house. I have moved around in a tent. I chose people to be special leaders for the Israelites. They were like shepherds for my people. While I was going around in Israel to different places, I never said to any of them: "Why haven't you built a house of cedar wood for me?"'

⁷"Now, tell this to my servant David: 'The LORD All-Powerful says, I took you from the

---

a **16:39** *LORD's Tent* Or "Tabernacle". Also called the "Meeting Tent". The people would go to this tent to meet with God. They used this tent until Solomon built the Temple in Jerusalem.

fields and from taking care of the sheep. I made you king of my people Israel. [8]I have been with you everywhere you went. I went ahead of you and I killed your enemies. Now I will make you one of the most famous men on earth. [9]I am giving this place to my people Israel. They will plant their trees, and they will sit in peace under those trees. They will not be bothered any more. Evil people will not hurt them as they did at first. [10]Those bad things happened, but I chose leaders to care for my people Israel. And I will also defeat all your enemies.

"'I tell you that the LORD will build a house for you.[a] [11]When you die, and you join your ancestors, then I will let your own son be the new king. The new king will be one of your sons, and I will make his kingdom strong. [12]Your son will build a house for me. I will make your son's family rule forever. [13]I will be his father, and he will be my son. Saul was the king before you, and I took away my support from Saul. But I will never stop loving your son. [14]I will put him in charge of my house and kingdom forever. His rule will continue forever!'"

[15]Nathan told David about the vision and everything God had said.

David's Prayer

[16]Then King David went to the Holy Tent and sat before the LORD. David said,

"LORD God, you have done so much for me and my family. And I don't understand why. [17]Besides all these things, God, you let me know what will happen to my family in the future. LORD God, you have treated me like a very important man. [18]What more can I say? You have done so much for me. And I am only your servant. You know that. [19]LORD, you have done this wonderful thing for me and because you wanted to. [20]There is no one like you, LORD. There is no God except you. We have never heard of any god doing wonderful things like those! [21]Is there any other nation like Israel? No, Israel is the only nation on earth that you have done these wonderful things for. You took us out of Egypt and you made us free. You made yourself famous. You went in front of your people, and forced other people to leave their land for us. [22]You took Israel to be your people forever, and you, LORD, became their God!

[23]"LORD, you made this promise to me and my family. Now, keep your promise forever. Do what you said you would. [24]Keep your promise so that people will honour your name forever. Then people will say, 'The LORD All-Powerful is Israel's God!' I am your servant. Please let my family be strong and continue to serve you.

[25]"My God, you spoke to me, your servant. You made it clear that you would make my family a family of kings. That is why I am being so bold—that is why I am asking you to do these things. [26]LORD, you are God, and you yourself promised to do these good things for me. [27]You have been kind enough to bless my family. You were kind enough to promise that my family will serve you forever. LORD, you yourself blessed my family, so my family really will be blessed forever."

David Wins Over Different Nations

18 Later, David attacked the Philistines and defeated them. He took the town of Gath and the other small towns around it from the Philistines.

[2]Then David defeated the country of Moab. The Moabites became David's servants and brought tribute to him.

[3]David also fought against Hadadezer's army. Hadadezer was the king of Zobah. David fought against that army all the way to the town of Hamath. David did this when he went to set up a monument for himself at the Euphrates River.[b] [4]David took 1,000 chariots, 7,000 chariot drivers and 20,000 soldiers from Hadadezer. David also crippled most of Hadadezer's horses that were used for pulling chariots. But David saved enough horses to pull 100 chariots.

[5]The Arameans from the city of Damascus came to help King Hadadezer of Zobah. But David defeated and killed 22,000 Aramean soldiers. [6]Then David put fortresses in the city of Damascus in Aram. The Arameans became David's servants and brought tribute to him. So the LORD gave victory to David everywhere he went.

[7]David took the gold shields from Hadadezer's army leaders and brought them to Jerusalem. [8]David also took much bronze from the towns of Tebah and Cun. These towns belonged to Hadadezer. Later, Solomon used this bronze to make the bronze basin, the bronze columns and other things made from bronze for the Temple.

---

[a] 17:10 **build a house for you** This does not mean a real house. It means the Lord would make men from David's family kings for many years.
[b] 18:3 **David did this . . . the Euphrates River** Or "David did this because Hadadezer tried to spread his kingdom all the way to the Euphrates River."

⁹Tou was king of the city of Hamath. Hadadezer was the king of Zobah. Tou heard that David had defeated all of Hadadezer's army. ¹⁰So Tou sent his son Hadoram to King David to ask for peace and to bless him. He did this because David had fought against Hadadezer and defeated him. Hadadezer had been at war with Tou before. Hadoram gave David all kinds of things made of gold, silver and bronze. ¹¹King David made these things holy and gave them to the LORD. David did the same thing with all the silver and gold he had taken from Edom, Moab, the Ammonites, the Philistines and Amalekites.

¹²Abishai son of Zeruiah killed 18,000 Edomites in the Valley of Salt. ¹³Abishai also put fortresses in Edom and all the Edomites became David's servants. The LORD gave David victory everywhere he went.

David's Important Officials

¹⁴David was king over all Israel. He did what was right and fair for everyone. ¹⁵Joab son of Zeruiah was the commander of David's army. Jehoshaphat son of Ahilud wrote about the things David did. ¹⁶Zadok and Abimelech were the priests. Zadok was Ahitub's son, and Abimelech was Abiathar's son. Shavsha was the scribe. ¹⁷Benaiah was responsible for leading the Kerethites and Pelethites.ᵃ Benaiah was Jehoiada's son. And David's sons were important officials. They served at King David's side.

The Ammonites Shame David's Men

19 Nahash was king of the Ammonites. When Nahash died, his son became the new king. ²Then David said, "Nahash was kind to me, so I will be kind to Hanun, Nahash's son." So David sent messengers to comfort Hanun about the death of his father. David's messengers went to the country of Ammon to comfort Hanun.

³But the Ammonite leaders said to Hanun, "Don't be fooled. David didn't really send these men to comfort you or to honour your dead father! No, David sent his servants to spy on you and your land. He really wants to destroy your country!" ⁴So Hanun arrested David's servants and cut off their beards.ᵇ Hanun also cut their clothes off at the hip and sent them away.

⁵David's men were too embarrassed to go home. Some people went to David and told him what had happened to his men. So King David sent this message to his men: "Stay in the town of Jericho until your beards grow again. Then you can come back home."

⁶The Ammonites saw they had caused themselves to become hated enemies of David. Then Hanun and the Ammonites used 34,000 kilogrammesᶜ of silver to buy chariots and chariot drivers from Mesopotamia.ᵈ They also got chariots and chariot drivers from the towns of Maacah and Zobah in Aram. ⁷The Ammonites bought 32,000 chariots. They also paid the king of Maacah and his army to come and help them. The king of Maacah and his people came and set up a camp near the town of Medeba. The Ammonites themselves came out of their towns and got ready for battle.

⁸David heard that the Ammonites were getting ready for war. So he sent Joab and the whole army of Israel to fight the Ammonites. ⁹The Ammonites came out and got ready for battle. They were near the city gate. The kings who had come to help stayed out in the fields by themselves.

¹⁰Joab saw that there were two army groups ready to fight against him. One group was in front of him and the other group was behind him. So Joab chose some of the best soldiers of Israel and sent them out to fight against the Aramean army. ¹¹He put the rest of the Israelite army under his brother Abishai's command. These soldiers went out to fight against the Ammonite army. ¹²Joab said to Abishai, "If the Arameans are too strong for me, you must help me. But if the Ammonites are too strong for you, I will help you. ¹³Let's be brave and strong while we fight for our people and for the cities of our God! May the LORD do what he thinks is right."

¹⁴Joab and the army with him attacked the Aramean army. The Arameans ran away from Joab and his army. ¹⁵When the Ammonite army saw that the Aramean army was running away, they also ran away. They ran away from Abishai and his army. The Ammonites went back to their city, and Joab went back to Jerusalem.

¹⁶The Aramean leaders saw that Israel had defeated them. So they sent messengers to get help from the Arameans living east of the Euphrates River. Shophach was the commander of Hadadezer's army from Aram. Shophach also led the other Aramean soldiers.

¹⁷David heard the news that the Arameans were gathering for battle, so he gathered all the Israelites. David led them across the Jordan River, and they came face to face with the Arameans. David got his army ready for battle and they

---

ᵃ **18:17** *Kerethites and Pelethites* These were the king's bodyguards.
ᵇ **19:4** *cut off their beards* This was an insult to an Israelite man, who was forbidden to cut the corners of his beard. See Lev. 19:27.
ᶜ **19:6** *34,000 kilogrammes* Literally, "1,000 *talents*".
ᵈ **19:6** *Mesopotamia* Literally, "Aram Naharaim".

attacked the Arameans. ¹⁸The Arameans ran away from the Israelites. David and his army killed 7,000 Aramean chariot drivers and 40,000 Aramean soldiers. David and his army also killed Shophach, the commander of the Aramean army.

¹⁹When Hadadezer's officers saw that Israel had defeated them, they made peace with David. They became his servants. So the Arameans refused to help the Ammonites again.

Joab Destroys the Ammonites

20 In the spring,ᵃ Joab led the army of Israel out to battle. That was the time of year when kings went out to battle, but David stayed in Jerusalem. The army of Israel went to the country of Ammon and destroyed it. Then they went to the city of Rabbah. The army camped around the city—they stayed there to keep people from going in or out of the city. Joab and the army of Israel fought against the city of Rabbah until they destroyed it.

INSIGHT

In Old Testament times springtime was the right time of year for war. This was because once the spring harvest was in there wasn't so much to do on the land and there would be plenty of food for the soldiers to eat.
1 Chronicles 20:1

²David took the crown from their king'sᵇ head. It was made of gold and weighed 34 kilogrammes.ᶜ There were also valuable stones in it. The crown was put on David's head. Then David ordered that anything of value be taken from the city. ³He forced the people who lived there to leave, and he put them to work using saws, iron picks and axes. He did the same thing to all the cities of the Ammonites. Then David and all the army went back to Jerusalem.

Philistine Giants Are Killed

⁴Later, the Israelites went to war against the Philistines at the town of Gezer. At that time Sibbecai from Hushah killed Sippai, who was one of the descendants of the giant Rephaites. So those Philistines became like slaves to the Israelites.

⁵Another time when the Israelites fought against the Philistines, Elhanan son of Jair killed Lahmi. Lahmi was Goliath's brother. Goliath was from the town of Gath. Lahmi's spear was very big and heavy. It was like the large pole on a loom.

⁶Later, the Israelites fought another war with the Philistines at the town of Gath. In this town there was a very large man. He had 24 fingers and toes—six fingers on each hand and six toes on each foot. He was another descendant of the Rephaites. ⁷So when that man made fun of Israel, Jonathan killed him. Jonathan was Shimea's son. Shimea was David's brother.

⁸These Philistine men were descendants of the Rephaites from the town of Gath. David and his servants killed those giants.

David Sins by Counting Israel

21 Satanᵈ was against the Israelites. He encouraged David to count the Israelites. ²So David said to Joab and the leaders of the people, "Go and count all the Israelites. Count everyone in the country—from the town of Beersheba all the way to the town of Dan. Then tell me, so I will know how many people there are."

³But Joab answered, "May the LORD make his nation 100 times as large! Sir, all the Israelites are your servants. Why do you want to do this thing, my lord and king? You will make all the Israelites guilty of sin!"

⁴But King David was stubborn. Joab had to do what the king said. So Joab left and went through the whole country of Israel counting the people. Then he came back to Jerusalem ⁵and told David how many people there were. In Israel there were 1,100,000 men who could use a sword. And there were 470,000 men in Judah who could use a sword. ⁶Joab did not count the tribes of Levi and Benjamin because he did not like King David's order. ⁷David had done a bad thing in God's sight, so God punished Israel.

INSIGHT

David usually placed his trust in God when he went into battle, but here he ordered his men to be counted. He displeased God by putting his security in the number of soldiers in his army rather than in God's deliverance.
1 Chronicles 21:1–7

ᵃ **20:1 In the spring** Literally, "At the return of the year".
ᵇ **20:2 their king's** Or "Milcom", the god of the Ammonite people.
ᶜ **20:2 34 kilogrammes** Literally, "1 *talent*".
ᵈ **21:1 Satan** Or "An adversary", someone who was against the king.

FROM TENT TO TEMPLE

It's been said that the royal family must think the whole world is beautiful. They never see an untidy lawn, a broken window or a grubby carpet. That's because wherever they go, people prepare for weeks, even months, for their arrival. Lawns are neatly trimmed, windows shined spotless, floors immaculately swept.

Preparing for the arrival of such a VIP is a costly venture – and the more important the person, the more costly the preparations.

DIG IN

READ 1 Chronicles 21:18 – 22:19

- Why will David not accept Araunah's land as a gift (v.24)?
- What does this and David's extravagance later in this passage say about his heart (22:2–4,14–16)?

Up to now God's official dwelling place among the nation of Israel has been a tent. David's ambition has been to create for his God something permanent, something glorious, something fitting for a magnificent God. He didn't think it was right that he should have a palace while the Box of the Agreement sat in a tent (17:1).

Only now does God give David the green light. Once the angel of the Lord names the site where David should build the Temple, he gets straight to work.

Araunah wants to donate the land but David is insistent that he will pay full price. His desire to bless God extravagantly with a magnificent Temple is made even clearer as we find out just how much he is willing to invest.

- How does David invest himself in the temple-building project?

By now, David is an old man and knows he will never see the building work finished. God has told him that his son, Solomon, would see the project through to completion instead. Yet he throws himself into God's work, giving his time, his talent and his treasure to the building work. His vision for the Temple is as strong as ever and he is committed to it, even if he never sees it finished (1 Chronicles 22:5). What a powerful example for us!

DIG THROUGH

- David is known as the man "after God's own heart". If David's heart is extravagant towards God, what might that say about God's heart towards us?
- What does extravagant, sacrificial worship look like for you? It could involve your treasure but also perhaps it should make demands on your time or talent?

DIG DEEPER

- God first declares that he wants to live among his people in Exodus 25. At that time he gives the first plans for a special, holy place where he can live (Exodus 25:8). No longer is he just coming to be with certain people at special times. Now he wants to "put down roots" – to stick around.
- The fire falling down from heaven is a sign of God's stamp of approval on David's plans (1 Chronicles 21:26). Fire also fell when the tent was first set up (Leviticus 9:24) and will fall again when the Temple is eventually opened (2 Chronicles 7:1). Can you think of any other times where God causes fire to fall from heaven?

God Punishes Israel

⁸Then David said to God, "I have done something very foolish. I have committed a terrible sin by counting the Israelites. Now, I beg you to take the sin away from me, your servant."

⁹⁻¹⁰Gad was David's seer. The LORD said to Gad, "Go and tell David: 'This is what the LORD says: I am going to give you three choices. You must choose one of them. Then I will punish you the way you choose.'"

¹¹⁻¹²Then Gad went to David. He said to David, "The LORD says, 'David, choose which punishment you want: three years without enough food, or three months of running away from your enemies while they chase you with swords, or three days of punishment from the LORD. Terrible sicknesses will spread through the country, and the angel of the LORD will go through Israel destroying the people.' David, God sent me. Now, you must decide which answer I will give to him."

¹³David said to Gad, "This is very upsetting! But the LORD is very merciful, so let him punish me and not anyone else."

¹⁴So the LORD sent terrible sicknesses to Israel, and 70,000 people died. ¹⁵God sent an angel to destroy Jerusalem. But when the angel started to destroy Jerusalem, the LORD saw it and felt sorry for all the suffering. So he said to the angel who was destroying the people, "Stop! That is enough!" This happened when the angel of the LORD was standing at the threshing floor of Araunahᵃ the Jebusite.ᵇ

¹⁶David looked up and saw the angel of the LORD in the sky. The angel was holding his sword over the city of Jerusalem. Then David and the leaders bowed with their faces touching the ground. They were wearing the special clothes to show their sadness. ¹⁷David said to God, "I am the one who sinned. I gave the order for the people to be counted! I was wrong. The Israelites did not do anything wrong. LORD my God, punish me and my family, but stop the terrible sicknesses that are killing your people."

¹⁸Then the angel of the LORD spoke to Gad. He said, "Tell David to build an altar to worship the LORD. David must build that altar near the threshing floor of Araunah the Jebusite." ¹⁹Gad told David this, and David went to Araunah's threshing floor.

²⁰Araunah was threshing the wheat. He turned around and saw the angel. His four sons ran away to hide. ²¹David walked up the hill to Araunah. Araunah saw him and left the threshing floor. He walked to David and bowed with his face to the ground in front of him.

²²David said to Araunah, "Sell me your threshing floor. I will pay you the full price. Then I can use the area to build an altar to worship the LORD. Then the terrible sicknesses will be stopped."

²³Araunah said to David, "Take this threshing floor. You are my lord and king, so do whatever you want. Look, I will also give you cattle for the burnt offering. You can have the wooden threshing tools to burn for the fire on the altar. And I will give the wheat for the grain offering. I will give all this to you."

²⁴But King David answered Araunah, "No, I will pay you the full price. I will not take anything that is yours and give it to the LORD. I will not give offerings that cost me nothing."

INSIGHT

David refused to offer God something that had cost him nothing. As King of Israel this was a tall order since everything in the kingdom was rightfully his. David understood the true meaning of sacrifice.
1 Chronicles 21:24

²⁵So David gave Araunah 600 gold coinsᶜ for the place. ²⁶David built an altar for worshiping the LORD there. David offered burnt offerings and fellowship offerings. He prayed to the LORD. The LORD answered David by sending fire down from heaven. The fire came down on the altar of burnt offering. ²⁷Then the LORD commanded the angel to put his sword back into its sheath.

²⁸David saw that the LORD had answered him on the threshing floor of Araunah, so David offered sacrifices there. ²⁹(The LORD's Holy Tent and the altar of burnt offerings were at the high place in the town of Gibeon. Moses had made the Holy Tent while the Israelites were in the desert. ³⁰David could not go to the Holy Tent to speak with God because he was afraid. He was afraid of the angel of the LORD and his sword.)

22 David said, "The Temple of the LORD God and the altar for burning offerings for the Israelites will be built here."

David Makes Plans for the Temple

²David gave an order for all foreigners living in Israel to be gathered together. He chose stonecutters from that group of foreigners. Their job was to cut stones ready to be used for building God's Temple.

ᵃ **21:15 Araunah** In Hebrew, "Ornan". Also in verses 18–25,28.
ᵇ **21:15 Jebusite** A person who lived in Jerusalem before the Israelites took the city. "Jebus" was the old name for Jerusalem.
ᶜ **21:25 coins** Literally, "shekels".

³David got iron for making nails and hinges for the gate doors. He also got more bronze than could be weighed ⁴and more cedar logs than could be counted. The people from the cities of Sidon and Tyre brought many cedar logs to David.

⁵David said, "We should build a very great Temple for the LORD, but my son Solomon is young and does not yet have enough experience to know how to do it well. It should be so great and beautiful that it will be famous among all the nations. So I will prepare what is needed to build it." So before David died he prepared everything needed to build a great Temple.

⁶Then David called for his son Solomon and told him to build the Temple for the LORD, the God of Israel. ⁷David said to Solomon, "My son, I wanted to build a temple for the name of the LORD my God. ⁸But the LORD said to me, 'David, you have fought many wars and you have killed many people. So you cannot build a temple for my name. ⁹But you have a son who is a man of peace. I will give your son a time of peace. His enemies around him will not bother him. His name is Solomon.ᵃ And I will give Israel peace and quiet during the time that he is king. ¹⁰Solomon will build a temple for my name. He will be my son, and I will be his Father. I will make his kingdom strong, and someone from his family will rule Israel forever!'"

¹¹David also said, "Now, son, may the LORD be with you. May you be successful and build the Temple for the LORD your God, as he said you would. ¹²He will make you the king of Israel. May the LORD give you wisdom and understanding so that you can lead the people and obey the Law of the LORD your God. ¹³And you will have success, if you are careful to obey the rules and laws that the LORD gave Moses for Israel. Be strong and brave. Don't be afraid.

¹⁴"Solomon, I have worked hard making plans for building the LORD's Temple. I have given 3,400 tonnesᵇ of gold and over 34,000 tonnesᶜ of silver. I have given so much bronze and iron that it cannot be weighed. And I have given wood and stone. Solomon, you can add to them. ¹⁵You have many stonecutters and carpenters. You have men skilled in every kind of work. ¹⁶They are skilled in working with gold, silver, bronze and iron. You have more skilled workers than can be counted. Now begin the work. And may the LORD be with you."

¹⁷Then David ordered all the leaders of Israel to help his son Solomon. ¹⁸David said to these leaders, "The LORD your God is with you. He has given you a time of peace. He helped me defeat the people living around us. The LORD and his people are now in control of this land. ¹⁹Now give your heart and soul to the LORD your God, and do what he says. Build the holy place of the LORD God. Then bring the Box of the LORD's Agreement and all the other holy things into the Temple built for the LORD's name."

The Levites Work in the Temple

23 David became an old man, so he made his son Solomon the new king of Israel. ²David gathered all the leaders of Israel and also the priests and Levites. ³David counted the Levites who were 30 years old and older. All together there were 38,000 Levites. ⁴David said, "24,000 will supervise the work of building the LORD's Temple, 6,000 will be court officers and judges, ⁵4,000 will be gatekeepers and 4,000 will be musicians. I made special musical instruments for them. They will use them to praise the LORD."

⁶David separated the Levites into three groups. They were the tribes of Levi's three sons, Gershon, Kohath and Merari.

The Gershon Family Group

⁷From the tribe of Gershon there were Ladan and Shimei. ⁸Ladan had three sons. His oldest son was Jehiel. His other sons were Zethan and Joel. ⁹Shimei's sons were Shelomoth, Haziel and Haran. These three sons were leaders in Ladan's families. ¹⁰Shimei had four sons. They were Jahath, Ziza, Jeush and Beriah. ¹¹Jahath was the oldest son and Ziza was the second son. But Jeush and Beriah did not have many children. So Jeush and Beriah were counted like one family.

The Kohath Family Group

¹²Kohath had four sons. They were Amram, Izhar, Hebron and Uzziel. ¹³Amram's sons were Aaron and Moses. Aaron was chosen for a special work. He and his descendants were chosen to always be the ones to do this special work—to prepare the holy things for the Temple service. They were the ones to burn the incense before the LORD, to serve him as priests and give blessings to the people in his name forever. ¹⁴Moses was the man of God, and his sons were part of the tribe of Levi. ¹⁵Moses' sons were Gershom and Eliezer. ¹⁶Gershom's oldest son was Shubael. ¹⁷Eliezer's oldest

ᵃ **22:9 Solomon** This name is like the Hebrew word meaning "peace".
ᵇ **22:14 3,400 tonnes** Literally, "100,000 *talents*".
ᶜ **22:14 34,000 tonnes** Literally, "1,000,000 *talents*".

son was Rehabiah. Eliezer had no other sons. But Rehabiah had very many sons. [18]Izhar's oldest son was Shelomith. [19]Hebron's oldest son was Jeriah. Hebron's second son was Amariah. Jahaziel was the third son, and Jekameam was the fourth son. [20]Uzziel's oldest son was Micah, and Isshiah was his second son.

The Merari Family Group

[21]Merari's sons were Mahli and Mushi. Mahli's sons were Eleazar and Kish. [22]Eleazar died without having sons. He only had daughters. Eleazar's daughters married their own relatives. Their relatives were Kish's sons. [23]Mushi's sons were Mahli, Eder and Jeremoth. There were three sons in all.

The Levites' Work

[24]These were Levi's descendants. They were listed by their families. They were the leaders of families. Each person's name was listed. The people who were listed were 20 years old or older. They served in the LORD's Temple. [25]David had said, "The LORD, the God of Israel, has given peace to his people. And he has come to live in Jerusalem forever. [26]So the Levites don't need to carry the Holy Tent or any of the things used in its services any more." [27]David's last instructions for the Israelites were to count the descendants from the tribe of Levi. They counted the Levite men who were 20 years old and older. [28]The Levites had the job of helping Aaron's descendants in the service of the LORD's Temple. They also took care of the Temple courtyard and the side rooms in the Temple. And they made sure all the holy things were kept pure. It was their job to serve in God's Temple. [29]They were responsible for putting the special bread on the table in the Temple and for the flour, the grain offerings and the bread made without yeast. They were also responsible for the baking pans and the mixed offerings. They did all the measuring. [30]The Levites stood every morning and gave thanks and praise to the LORD. They also did this every evening. [31]The Levites prepared all the burnt offerings to the LORD on the Sabbath days, during New Moon celebrations and on the other special meeting days. They served before the LORD every day. There were special rules for how many Levites should serve each time. [32]So the Levites did everything that they were supposed to do. They took care of the Holy Tent and the Holy Place. And they helped their relatives, the priests, Aaron's descendants, with the services at the LORD's Temple.

The Groups of the Priests

24 These were the groups of Aaron's sons: Aaron's sons were Nadab, Abihu, Eleazar and Ithamar. [2]But Nadab and Abihu died before their father did. Nadab and Abihu had no sons, so Eleazar and Ithamar served as the priests. [3]David separated the tribes of Eleazar and Ithamar into two different groups. He did this so that these groups could do the duties of work they were given to do. David did this with the help of Zadok and Ahimelech. Zadok was a descendant of Eleazar and Ahimelech was a descendant of Ithamar. [4]There were more leaders from Eleazar's family than from Ithamar's. There were 16 leaders from Eleazar's family and there were eight leaders from Ithamar's family. [5]Men were chosen from each family. They were chosen by throwing lots. Some of the men were chosen to be in charge of the Holy Place. And other men were chosen to serve as priests. All these men were from the families of Eleazar and Ithamar.

[6]Shemaiah was the secretary.[a] He was Nethanel's son. Shemaiah was from the tribe of Levi. Shemaiah wrote the names of those descendants. He wrote their names in front of King David and these leaders: Zadok the priest, Ahimelech and the leaders from the families of the priests and of the Levites. Ahimelech was Abiathar's son. Each time they threw the lots a man was chosen and Shemaiah wrote down that man's name. So they divided the work among groups of men from the families of Eleazar and Ithamar.

[7]The first was Jehoiarib's group.
The second was Jedaiah's group.
[8]The third was Harim's group.
The fourth was Seorim's group.
[9]The fifth was Malkijah's group.
The sixth was Mijamin's group.
[10]The seventh was Hakkoz's group.
The eighth was Abijah's group.
[11]The ninth was Jeshua's group.
The tenth was Shecaniah's group.
[12]The eleventh was Eliashib's group.
The twelfth was Jakim's group.
[13]The thirteenth was Huppah's group.
The fourteenth was Jeshebeab's group.
[14]The fifteenth was Bilgah's group.
The sixteenth was Immer's group.
[15]The seventeenth was Hezir's group.
The eighteenth was Happizzez's group.

---

[a] **24:6 secretary** A man who wrote down and copied books and letters.

[16]The nineteenth was Pethahiah's group.
The twentieth was Jehezkel's group.
[17]The twenty-first was Jakin's group.
The twenty-second was Gamul's group.
[18]The twenty-third was Delaiah's group.
The twenty-fourth was Maaziah's group.

[19]These were the groups chosen to serve in the LORD's Temple. They obeyed Aaron's rules for serving in the Temple. The LORD, the God of Israel, had given them to Aaron.

The Other Levites

[20]These are the names of the rest of Levi's descendants:

Shubael was a descendant of Amram.
Jehdeiah was a descendant of Shubael.
[21]Isshiah was the oldest son of Rehabiah.
[22]From the Izhar family group there was Shelomoth.
Jahath was a descendant of Shelomoth.
[23]Jeriah was the oldest son of Hebron.
Amariah was Hebron's second son.
Jahaziel was his third son,
and Jekameam was his fourth son.
[24]Uzziel's son was Micah.
Micah's son was Shamir.
[25]Isshiah was Micah's brother.
Isshiah's son was Zechariah.
[26a]Merari's descendants were Mahli, Mushi and Jaaziah his son.
[27]Jaaziah son of Merari had sons named Shoham, Zaccur and Ibri.
[28]Mahli's son was Eleazar, but Eleazar did not have sons.
[29]Kish's son was Jerahmeel.
[30]Mushi's sons were Mahli, Eder and Jerimoth.

These are the leaders of the Levite families. They are listed by their families. [31]They were chosen for special jobs by throwing lots, like their relatives, the priests. The priests were Aaron's descendants. They threw lots in front of King David, Zadok, Ahimelech and the leaders of the priests' and Levite families. The older families and the younger families were treated the same when their jobs were chosen.

The Music Groups

25 David and the leaders of the army separated the sons of Asaph, Heman and Jeduthun for special service. Their special service was to prophesy God's message with harps, lyres and cymbals. Here is a list of the men who served this way:

[2]From Asaph's family: Zaccur, Joseph, Nethaniah and Asarelah. King David chose Asaph to prophesy. And Asaph led his sons. [3]From Jeduthun's family: Gedaliah, Zeri, Jeshaiah, Shimei, Hashabiah and Mattithiah. There were six of them. Jeduthun led his sons. Jeduthun used harps to prophesy and give thanks and praise to the LORD. [4]Heman's sons who served were Bukkiah, Mattaniah, Uzziel, Shubael and Jerimoth; Hananiah, Hanani, Eliathah, Giddalti and Romamti Ezer; Joshbekashah, Mallothi, Hothir and Mahazioth. [5]All these men were Heman's sons. Heman was David's seer. God promised to make Heman strong. So Heman had many sons. God gave Heman fourteen sons and three daughters.

[6]Heman led all his sons in singing in the LORD's temple.[b] His sons used cymbals, lyres and harps. That was their way of serving in God's temple. King David chose these men. [7]These men and their relatives from the tribe of Levi were trained to sing. There were 288 men who learned to sing praises to the LORD. [8]They threw lots to choose the different kinds of work each person was to do. Everyone was treated the same. Young and old were treated the same. And the teacher was treated the same as the student.

[9]The first one chosen was Asaph (Joseph). Second, there were 12 men chosen from Gedaliah's sons and relatives.
[10]Third, there were 12 men chosen from Zaccur's sons and relatives.
[11]Fourth, there were 12 men chosen from Izri's sons and relatives.
[12]Fifth, there were 12 men chosen from Nethaniah's sons and relatives.
[13]Sixth, there were 12 men chosen from Bukkiah's sons and relatives.
[14]Seventh, there were 12 men chosen from Asarelah's sons and relatives.
[15]Eighth, there were 12 men chosen from Jeshaiah's sons and relatives.
[16]Ninth, there were 12 men chosen from Mattaniah's sons and relatives.
[17]Tenth, there were 12 men chosen from Shimei's sons and relatives.
[18]Eleventh, there were 12 men chosen from Azarel's sons and relatives.
[19]Twelfth, there were 12 men chosen from Hashabiah's sons and relatives.
[20]Thirteenth, there were 12 men chosen from Shubael's sons and relatives.

---

[a] **24:26,27** The Hebrew text is not clear.
[b] **25:6 temple** Here, this means the Holy Tent where people went to worship the Lord.

21Fourteenth, there were 12 men chosen from Mattithiah's sons and relatives. 22Fifteenth, there were 12 men chosen from Jeremoth's sons and relatives. 23Sixteenth, there were 12 men chosen from Hananiah's sons and relatives. 24Seventeenth, there were 12 men chosen from Joshbekashah's sons and relatives. 25Eighteenth, there were 12 men chosen from Hanani's sons and relatives. 26Nineteenth, there were 12 men chosen from Mallothi's sons and relatives. 27Twentieth, there were 12 men chosen from Eliathah's sons and relatives. 28Twenty-first, there were 12 men chosen from Hothir's sons and relatives. 29Twenty-second, there were 12 men chosen from Giddalti's sons and relatives. 30Twenty-third, there were 12 men chosen from Mahazioth's sons and relatives. 31Twenty-fourth, there were 12 men chosen from Romamti Ezer's sons and relatives.

The Gatekeepers

26 These are the groups of the gatekeepers from the Korah family:

Meshelemiah was the son of Kore, who was from the family of Asaph. 2These were Meshelemiah's sons: Zechariah was the oldest son, and Jediael was the second. Zebadiah was the third, Jathniel the fourth, 3Elam the fifth, Jehohanan the sixth and Eliehoenai the seventh son.

4These were Obed Edom's sons: His oldest son was Shemaiah. Jehozabad was his second son, Joah his third, Sacar his fourth, Nethanel his fifth, 5Ammiel his sixth, Issachar his seventh and Peullethai his eighth son. God really blessed Obed Edom.[a]

6Obed Edom's son Shemaiah also had sons. His sons were leaders in their father's family because they were brave soldiers. 7Shemaiah's sons were Othni, Rephael, Obed, Elzabad, Elihu and Semakiah. Elzabad's relatives were skilled workers. 8All these men were Obed Edom's descendants. These men and their sons and relatives were powerful men. They were good guards. Obed Edom had 62 descendants.

9Meshelemiah's sons and relatives were also powerful men. In all there were 18 of them. 10These are the gatekeepers from the Merari family: Hosah, son of Merari, chose his son Shimri to be the leader, even though he was not the oldest son. 11Hilkiah was Hosah's second son, Tebaliah his third and Zechariah his fourth son. In all Hosah had 13 sons and relatives who were gatekeepers.

12These were the leaders of the groups of the gatekeepers. The gatekeepers had a special way to serve in the LORD's Temple, just as their relatives did. 13Each family was given a gate to guard. Lots were thrown to choose a gate for a family. Young and old were treated the same.

14Meshelemiah was chosen to guard the East Gate. Then lots were thrown for Meshelemiah's son Zechariah. Zechariah was a wise counsellor. Zechariah was chosen for the North Gate. 15Obed Edom was chosen for the South Gate. And Obed Edom's sons were chosen to guard the house where the valuable things were kept. 16Shuppim and Hosah were chosen for the West Gate and the Shalleketh Gate on the upper road.

Guards stood side by side. 17Six Levites stood guard every day at the East Gate. Four Levites stood guard every day at the North Gate. Four Levites stood guard at the South Gate. And two Levites guarded the house where the valuable things were kept. 18There were four guards at the western court[b] and two guards on the road to the court.

19These were the groups of the gatekeepers from the families of Korah and Merari.

The Treasurers and Other Officials

20Ahijah was from the tribe of Levi. Ahijah was responsible for taking care of the valuable things in God's Temple. Ahijah also was responsible for the places where the holy things were kept.

21Ladan was from Gershon's family. Jehieli was one of the leaders of the tribe of Ladan. 22Jehieli's sons were Zetham and Zetham's brother Joel. They were responsible for the valuable things in the LORD's Temple.

23Other leaders were chosen from the tribes of Amram, Izhar, Hebron and Uzziel.

24Shubael was the leader responsible for the valuable things kept in the Temple. Shubael was Gershom's son. Gershom was Moses' son. 25These were Shubael's relatives: His relatives from Eliezer were Rehabiah, Eliezer's son; Jeshaiah, Rehabiah's son; Joram, Jeshaiah's son; Zicri, Joram's son; and Shelomith, Zicri's son. 26Shelomith and his relatives were responsible for everything that David had collected for the Temple.

---

a 26:5 *Obed Edom* God blessed Obed Edom when the Box of the Agreement stayed at his house. See 1 Chr. 21.
b 26:18 *court* The meaning of this word is uncertain.

The officers of the army also gave things for the Temple. [27]They gave some of the things taken in wars. They gave these things to be used for the LORD's Temple. [28]Shelomith and his relatives took care of all the things that people gave to be used for the Temple. This included the things given by Samuel the seer, Saul son of Kish, Abner son of Ner and Joab son of Zeruiah.

[29]Kenaniah was from the Izhar family. Kenaniah and his sons had work outside the Temple. They worked as court officers and judges in different places in Israel.

[30]Hashabiah was from the Hebron family. Hashabiah and his relatives were responsible for all the LORD's work and for the king's business in Israel west of the Jordan River. There were 1,700 powerful men in Hashabiah's group. [31]The family history of the Hebron family shows that Jeriah was their leader. When David had been king for 40 years, he ordered his people to search through the family histories for strong and skilled men. Some of them were found among the Hebron family living in the town of Jazer in Gilead. [32]Jeriah had 2,700 relatives who were powerful men and leaders of families. King David gave these 2,700 relatives the responsibility of leading the tribes of Reuben, Gad and half of Manasseh in taking care of God's work and the king's business.

Army Groups

27 This is the list of the Israelites who served the king in the army. Each group was on duty one month each year. There were rulers of families, captains, generals and the court officers who served the king. Each army group had 24,000 men.

[2]Jashobeam son of Zabdiel was in charge of the first group for the first month. There were 24,000 men in this group. [3]Jashobeam was a descendant of Perez and was the leader of all the army officers for the first month.

[4]Dodai, from the Ahohites, was in charge of the army group for the second month. Mikloth was a leader in this group, which also had 24,000 men.

[5]The third commander, for the third month, was Benaiah son of Jehoiada, the leading priest. There were 24,000 men in the group Benaiah led. [6]He was the same Benaiah who was a brave soldier from the Thirty Heroes. He was their leader. His son Ammizabad was in charge of his group.

[7]The fourth commander, for the fourth month, was Asahel the brother of Joab. Later, his son Zebadiah took his place as commander. There were 24,000 men in this group.

[8]The fifth commander, for the fifth month, was Shamhuth from Izrah's family. There were 24,000 men in this group.

[9]The sixth commander, for the sixth month, was Ira son of Ikkesh from the town of Tekoa. There were 24,000 men in this group.

[10]The seventh commander, for the seventh month, was Helez from the Pelonites and a descendant of Ephraim. There were 24,000 men in this group.

[11]The eighth commander, for the eighth month, was Sibbecai from Hushah and from Zerah's family. There were 24,000 men in this group.

[12]The ninth commander, for the ninth month, was Abiezer from the town of Anathoth and the tribe of Benjamin. There were 24,000 men in this group.

[13]The tenth commander, for the tenth month, was Maharai from Netophah and from Zerah's family. There were 24,000 men in this group.

[14]The eleventh commander, for the eleventh month, was Benaiah from Pirathon and the tribe of Ephraim. There were 24,000 men in this group.

[15]The twelfth commander, for the twelfth month, was Heldai from Netophah and from Othniel's family. And there were 24,000 men in this group.

Leaders of the Israelite Tribes

[16]These were the leaders of the tribes of Israel:

Eliezer son of Zicri, leader of the tribe of Reuben;

Shephatiah son of Maacah, leader of the tribe of Simeon;

[17]Hashabiah son of Kemuel, leader of the tribe of Levi;

Zadok, leader of the people of Aaron;

[18]Elihu, one of David's brothers, leader of the tribe of Judah;

Omri son of Michael, leader of the tribe of Issachar;

[19]Ishmaiah son of Obadiah, leader of the tribe of Zebulun;

Jeremoth son of Azriel, leader of the tribe of Naphtali;

[20]Hoshea son of Azaziah, leader of the tribe of Ephraim;

Joel son of Pedaiah, leader of West Manasseh;

²¹Iddo son of Zechariah, leader of East Manasseh;

Jaasiel son of Abner, leader of the tribe of Benjamin;

²²Azarel son of Jeroham, leader of the tribe of Dan.

So these were the leaders of the tribes of Israel.

David Counts the Israelites

²³David decided to count the men in Israel. There were very many people because the LORD had promised to make the Israelites as many as the stars in the sky. So David counted only the men who were 20 years old and older. ²⁴Joab son of Zeruiah began to count the people, but he did not finish.ᵃ God became angry with the Israelites. That is why the number of the people was not put in the book, *The History of King David.*

The King's Administrators

²⁵This is the list of men who were responsible for the king's property:

Azmaveth son of Adiel was in charge of the king's storerooms.

Jonathan son of Uzziah was in charge of the storerooms in the small towns, villages, fields and towers.

²⁶Ezri son of Kelub was in charge of the field workers.

²⁷Shimei from Ramah was in charge of the vineyards.

Zabdi from Shepham was in charge of the storage and care of the wine that came from the vineyards.

²⁸Baal Hanan from Geder was in charge of the olive trees and sycamore trees in the western hill country.

Joash was in charge of storing the olive oil.

²⁹Shitrai from Sharon was in charge of the cattle around Sharon.

Shaphat son of Adlai was in charge of the cattle in the valleys.

³⁰Obil the Ishmaelite was in charge of the camels.

Jehdeiah the Meronothite was in charge of the donkeys.

³¹Jaziz the Hagrite was in charge of the sheep.

All these men were the leaders who took care of King David's property.

³²Jonathan was a wise counsellor and a scribe. He was David's uncle. Jehiel son of Hacmoni took care of the king's sons. ³³Ahithophel was the king's counsellor. Hushai was the king's friend. Hushai was from the Arkites. ³⁴Jehoiada and Abiathar later took Ahithophel's place as the king's counsellor. Jehoiada was Benaiah's son. Joab was the commander of the king's army.

David's Plans for the Temple

28 David gathered all the leaders of the Israelites and commanded them to come to Jerusalem. David called all the leaders of the tribes, the commanders of the army groups serving the king, the captains, the generals, the officials taking care of the property and animals that belonged to the king and his sons, the king's important officials, the powerful heroes and all the brave soldiers.

²King David stood up and said, "Listen to me, my brothers and my people. In my heart I wanted to build a place to keep the Box of the LORD's Agreement. I wanted to build a place that would be God's footstool.ᵇ And I made the plans for building that house for God. ³But God said to me, 'No David, you must not build a house for my name. You must not do that because you are a soldier, and you have killed many men.'

⁴"The LORD, the God of Israel, chose the tribe of Judah to lead the twelve tribes of Israel. Then from that tribe he chose my father's family. And from that family he chose me to be the king of Israel forever. Yes, God wanted to make me king of Israel. ⁵The LORD has given me many sons. And from all those sons, he chose Solomon to be the new king of Israel. But really, Israel is the LORD's kingdom. ⁶He said to me, 'David, your son Solomon will build my Temple and the area around it, because I have chosen Solomon to be my son, and I will be his father.ᶜ ⁷Solomon is obeying my laws and commands now. If he continues to obey my laws, I will make Solomon's kingdom strong forever.'"

⁸David said, "Now, in front of all Israel, the LORD's people, and before God, I tell you these things: Be careful to obey all the commands of the LORD your God. Then you can keep this good land and pass it on to your descendants forever.

⁹"And you, my son Solomon, know the God of your father. Serve God with a pure heart. Be happy to serve him, because the LORD knows what is in everyone's heart. He knows what you are thinking. If you go to him for help, you will

---

ᵃ **27:24 Joab . . . did not finish** God stopped him. See 1 Chr. 21:1–30.
ᵇ **28:2 footstool** Usually this was a small stool in front of a chair, but here, it means the Temple. It is as if God were the king sitting in his chair and resting his feet on the building David wanted to build.
ᶜ **28:6 I will be his father** This showed that God was making Solomon the king. See Ps. 2:7.

get an answer. But if you turn away from him, he will leave you forever. [10]Solomon, you must understand that the LORD has chosen you to build his holy place—the Temple. Be strong and finish the job."

INSIGHT

David hands over to Solomon the plans for the Temple and officially hands over the throne. David is paralleled to Moses here. Just as Moses did not make it to the promised land but handed over to Joshua, so David hands over to Solomon. Verse 20 is very similar to Joshua 1:9.

1 Chronicles 28:9–21

[11]Then David gave his son Solomon the plans for building the Temple. They included plans for the porch around the Temple, its buildings, its storerooms, its upper rooms, its inside rooms and the room for the mercy-cover. [12]David had made plans for all parts of the Temple. He gave them to Solomon. David gave him all the plans for the courtyard around the LORD's Temple and for all the rooms around it. He gave him the plans for the Temple storerooms and for the storerooms where they kept the holy things used in the Temple. [13]David told Solomon about the groups of the priests and Levites. He told Solomon about all the work of serving in the LORD's Temple and about all the things to be used in the Temple service. [14]David told Solomon how much gold and silver should be used to make all the things to be used in the Temple. [15]There were plans for gold lamps and lampstands, and there were plans for silver lamps and lampstands. David told Solomon how much gold or silver to use for each lampstand and its lamps. The different lampstands were to be used where needed. [16]David told him how much gold should be used for each table for the holy bread and how much silver should be used for the silver tables. [17]He told Solomon how much pure gold should be used to make the forks, sprinkling bowls and pitchers. He told him how much gold should be used to make each gold dish and how much silver should be used to make each silver dish. [18]He told him how much pure

gold should be used for the altar of incense. David also gave Solomon the plans for ⌊God's⌋ chariot—the mercy-cover with the winged creatures spreading their wings over the Box of the LORD's Agreement. The winged creatures were made of gold.

[19]David said, "All these plans were written with the LORD guiding me. He helped me understand everything in the plans."

[20]David also said to his son Solomon, "Be strong and brave and finish this work. Don't be afraid, because the LORD God, my God, is with you. He will help you until all the work is finished. He will not leave you. You will build the LORD's Temple. [21]The groups of the priests and Levites are ready for all the work on God's Temple. Every skilled worker is ready to help you with all the work. The officials and all the people will do whatever you tell them."

Gifts for Building the Temple

29 King David said to all the Israelites who were gathered together, "God chose my son Solomon. Solomon is young and does not know all that he needs to do this work. But the work is very important. This house is not for people; this house is for the LORD God. [2]I have done my best to provide what is needed for the building of my God's Temple. I have given gold for the things made of gold. I have given silver for the things made of silver. I have given bronze for the things made of bronze. I have given iron for the things made of iron. I have given wood for the things made of wood. I have also given onyx stones for the settings,[a] mosaic tiles,[b] all kinds of valuable stones in many different colours, and white marble stones. [3]I am making a special gift of gold and silver things for my God's Temple. I am doing this because I really want the Temple of my God to be built. I am giving all these things to build this holy Temple. [4]I have given more than 100 tonnes[c] of pure gold from Ophir. I have given almost 240 tonnes[d] of pure silver. The silver is for covering the walls of the buildings in the Temple. [5]I have given gold and silver for all the things made of gold and silver. I have given gold and silver so that skilled men can make all different kinds of things for the Temple. Now, how many of you Israelites are ready to give yourselves to the LORD today?"

[6]The family leaders, the leaders of the tribes of Israel, the generals, the captains and the officials

---

[a] **29:2** *settings* The frames in which stones are mounted.
[b] **29:2** *mosaic tiles* Literally, "stones set in mortar".
[c] **29:4** *more than 100 tonnes* Literally, "3,000 *talents*".
[d] **29:4** *almost 240 tonnes* Literally, "7,000 *talents*".

responsible for the king's work, were all ready and gave their valuable things. [7]These are the things they gave for God's house: 170 tonnes[a] of gold; 340 tonnes[b] of silver; 612 tonnes[c] of bronze; and 3,400 tonnes[d] of iron. [8]People who had valuable stones gave them to the LORD's Temple. Jehiel took care of the valuable stones. He was from the Gershon family. [9]The people were very happy because their leaders were willing to give so much. The leaders had given freely to the LORD from good hearts. King David was also very happy.

David's Beautiful Prayer

[10]Then David praised the LORD in front of all the people who were gathered together. David said,

"LORD, the God of Israel, our Father,
  may you be praised for ever and ever!
[11]Greatness, power, glory, victory and honour
    belong to you,
  because everything in heaven and on earth
    belongs to you!
The kingdom belongs to you, LORD!
  You are the head, the Ruler over
    everything.
[12]Riches and honour come from you.
  You rule everything.
You have the power and strength in your
    hand!
  And in your hand is the power to make
    anyone great and powerful!
[13]Now, our God, we thank you,
  and we praise your glorious name!

[14]"All these things didn't come from me and my
    people.
  All these things come from you.
  We are only giving back to you things that
    came from you.
[15]We are only foreigners travelling through this
    world
  like our ancestors.
Our time on earth is like a passing shadow,
  and we cannot stop it.
[16]LORD our God, we gathered all these things to
    build your Temple.
  We build it to honour your name.
But all these things have come from you.
  Everything belongs to you.
[17]My God, I know that you test people,

and that you are happy when people do
    what is right.
I gladly give you all these things
  with a pure, honest heart.
I see your people gathered here,
  and I see that they are happy about giving
    these things to you.
[18]LORD, you are the God of our ancestors,
    Abraham, Isaac and Jacob.
Please help your people plan the right things.
  Help them be loyal and true to you.
[19]And help my son Solomon be true to you.
  Help him always obey your commands,
    laws and rules.
Help Solomon do these things.
  And help him build this Temple that I have
    planned."

[20]Then David said to all the people gathered together, "Now give praise to the LORD your God." So all the people gave praise to the LORD God, the God their ancestors worshipped. They bowed to the ground to give honour to the LORD and to the king.

Solomon Becomes King

[21]The next day the people offered sacrifices and burnt offerings to the LORD—1,000 bulls, 1,000 rams, 1,000 lambs and the drink offerings that go with them. They offered these and many other sacrifices to the LORD for all the Israelites. [22]That day the people were very happy as they ate and drank there together with the LORD.

And they made David's son Solomon king the second time.[e] They anointed Solomon to be king, and they anointed Zadok to be priest. They did this in the place where the LORD was.

[23]Then Solomon sat on the LORD's throne as king. Solomon took his father's place. He was very successful. All the Israelites obeyed him. [24]All the leaders, soldiers and King David's sons accepted Solomon as king and obeyed him. [25]The LORD made Solomon very great. All the Israelites knew that the Lord was making him great. He gave Solomon the honour that a king should have. No king in Israel before Solomon had such honour.

David's Death

[26-27]David son of Jesse was king over all Israel for 40 years. He was king in the city of Hebron for seven years. Then he was king in the city of Jerusalem for 33 years. [28]David died when he was

---

[a] **29:7 170 tonnes** Literally, "5,000 *talents* and 10,000 *darics*".
[b] **29:7 340 tonnes** Literally, "10,000 *talents*".
[c] **29:7 612 tonnes** Literally, "18,000 *talents*".
[d] **29:7 3,400 tonnes** Literally, "100,000 *talents*".
[e] **29:22 And they made . . . time** Solomon was chosen to be king the first time when his half-brother Adonijah tried to make himself king. See 1 Kgs 1:5–39.

old. He had lived a good, long life and had many riches and honours. His son Solomon became the new king after him.

²⁹The things that King David did, from beginning to end, are in the books written by Samuel the seer, Nathan the prophet and Gad the seer. ³⁰Those writings tell all about what David did as king of Israel. They tell about David's power and what happened to him and to Israel and to all the kingdoms around them.

2 CHRONICLES

Who
According to tradition, Ezra was the author of Chronicles (not to mention Ezra and Nehemiah). Many experts assign the writing of these books to the same writer, who they call "the Chronicler".

When
It was probably written sometime after the Jews had returned to Jerusalem from exile in Babylon.

What
The second book of Chronicles is mainly about the life of Solomon and the building of the Temple. It also gives us accounts of kings like those we get in 1 and 2 Kings.

Primarily, this is a book about the Temple. Indeed, it seems that the writer of Chronicles is almost obsessed with rites and rituals, about who did what and when. Perhaps the reason is that he was probably writing for an audience who had just returned from Babylon and who were, themselves, struggling to rebuild the Temple. By telling them the history of the first Temple he was giving them a model, something to aim at. He saw the Temple as the symbol that God was with Israel and Israel worshipped God.

1 Chronicles builds a picture of David as comparable with Moses. Similar comparisons are drawn here, with the importance of Solomon and the builder Huram-Abi likened to Bezalel and Oholiab in Exodus (Exodus 35:30 – 36:7). (In fact, the only other reference to Bezalel in the Old Testament is found in Chronicles.)

The point here is to establish and reinforce the continuity of the history of Israel. Just as God gave instructions for the building of the Holy Tent, he has also given instructions for the building of the Temple. That's also why we get so many names and tribes. The people who had returned from exile needed to know the role that their ancestors, their tribe, had played. Thus the history was personalized for them. They were urged to continue the work that had been given to their ancestors.

QUICK TOUR ▶ **2 CHRONICLES**

"But if you don't obey my laws and commands that I gave you, and if you worship other gods and serve them, then I will take the Israelites out from my land that I gave them. And I will leave this Temple that I have made holy for my name. I will make this Temple something that all the nations will speak evil about."

2 Chronicles 7:19–20

Solomon Asks for Wisdom

1 Solomon, the son of David, became a very strong king, because the LORD his God was with him and made him very great.

2-3The people of Israel and the captains, generals, judges, leaders and heads of the families were all gathered together. Solomon spoke to them, and then they all went to the high place at Gibeon. They went there because God's Meeting Tent was there. The LORD's servant Moses made this tent when he and the Israelites were in the desert. 4David had carried God's Box of the Agreement from Kiriath Jearim to Jerusalem where he had set up another tent for it. 5But the bronze altar that Bezalel son of Uri, who was the son of Hur, had made was in front of the Holy Tent at Gibeon. So Solomon and the people went there to ask the LORD for advice. 6Solomon went up to the bronze altar before the LORD at the Meeting Tent and offered a thousand burnt offerings on it.

7That night God came to Solomon and said, "Ask for whatever you want me to give you."

8Solomon said to God, "You were very kind to my father David when you allowed me to rule on his throne after him. 9Now, LORD God, continue to keep your promise to my father David. You made me king over so many people that they are like the dust of the earth. 10Now give me wisdom and knowledge so that I can lead these people in the right way. No one could rule this great nation without your help."

11God said to Solomon, "You have the right attitude. You did not ask for long life and riches for yourself. You did not ask for the death of your enemies. You asked for wisdom and knowledge so that you can make the right decisions. 12So I will give you wisdom and knowledge, but I will also give you wealth, riches and honour. No king who lived before you has ever had so much wealth and honour, and no king in the future will have as much wealth and honour."

13Solomon left the Meeting Tent that was at the high place in Gibeon and went back to Jerusalem to rule as the king of Israel.

Solomon Strengthens His Army

14Solomon started gathering horses and chariots for his army. He had 1,400 chariots and 12,000 horses. He kept them in the chariot cities*a* and in Jerusalem where he lived. 15In Jerusalem Solomon gathered so much gold and silver that it was as common as rocks. He gathered so much cedar wood that it was as common as sycamore trees in the western hill country. 16Solomon imported horses from Egypt and Kue.*b* His merchants bought the horses in Kue for a set price. 17They also bought chariots from Egypt for 600 pieces*c* of silver each and horses for 150 pieces of silver each. They then sold the horses and chariots to the kings of the Hittites and Arameans.

Plans for the Temple and Palace

2 Solomon planned to build a temple to give honour to the LORD's name. He also planned to build a palace for himself. 2He got 70,000 labourers and 80,000 stonemasons to cut stones in the mountains. He chose 3,600 foremen to supervise the workers.

3Then Solomon sent this message to King Hiram of Tyre:

"Help me as you helped my father David. You sent him cedar logs so that he could build a palace for himself to live in. 4I will build a temple to honour the name of the LORD my God. At the temple we will burn incense in front of him, and we will always put the holy bread on the special table. We will offer burnt offerings every morning and evening, on the Sabbath days, during New Moon celebrations and on the other special meeting days that the LORD our God has commanded us to celebrate. This is a rule for the people of Israel to obey forever.

5"I will build a great temple because our God is greater than all the other gods. 6No one can really build a house to put our God in. The whole sky and the highest heaven cannot contain our God, so I cannot build a temple to put him in. I can only build a place to burn incense to honour him.

7"Now I would like you to send me a man who is skilled in working with gold, silver, bronze and iron. He must know how to work with purple, red and blue cloth. He will work here in Judah and Jerusalem with the craftsmen my father chose. 8Also send me wood from cedar trees, pine trees and algum trees*d* from the country of Lebanon. I know your servants are experienced at cutting down trees from Lebanon. My servants will help your servants. 9I will need lots of wood because the temple I am building will be very large and beautiful.

---

a **1:14 chariot cities** Cities with special places to keep the horses and chariots.
b **1:16 Kue** Or "Cilicia", a country in what is now southern Turkey.
c **1:17 pieces** Literally, "shekels".
d **2:8 algum trees** Or "Almug", as in 1 Kgs. No one knows exactly what type of wood this was, but it might have been sandalwood.

¹⁰This is what I will pay for your servants to cut down the trees for wood. I will give them 2,000 tonnes[a] of wheat for food, 4,400 tonnes of barley, 440,000 litres[b] of wine and 440,000 litres of oil."

¹¹Then Hiram answered Solomon and sent this message to him:

"Solomon, the LORD loves his people. That is why he chose you to be their king." ¹²Hiram also said, "Praise the LORD, the God of Israel! He made heaven and earth. He gave a wise son to King David. Solomon, you have wisdom and understanding. You are building a temple for the LORD. You are also building a palace for yourself. ¹³I will send you a skilled craftsman named Huram Abi.[c] ¹⁴His mother was from the tribe of Dan, and his father was from the city of Tyre. Huram Abi has skill in working with gold, silver, bronze, iron, stone and wood. He also has skill in working with purple, blue and red cloth and expensive linen. Huram Abi can design and build anything you tell him. He will work with your craftsmen and with the craftsmen of your father King David.

¹⁵"Now, sir, you offered to give us wheat, barley, oil and wine. Give them to my servants, ¹⁶and we will cut as much wood as you need from Lebanon. We will tie the logs together and float them by sea to the town of Joppa. Then you can carry the wood to Jerusalem."

¹⁷So Solomon counted all the foreigners living in Israel. (This was after the time when his father David counted the people.) They found 153,600 foreigners in the country. ¹⁸Solomon chose 70,000 men to carry the stones, 80,000 men to cut the stone in the mountains and 3,600 men to supervise the workers.

Solomon Builds the Temple

3 Solomon built the LORD's Temple in Jerusalem on Mount Moriah, where the LORD had appeared to David, his father. The place David prepared for the Temple had been the threshing floor of Araunah[d] the Jebusite.[e] ²His workers began building on the second day of the second month of Solomon's fourth year as king of Israel.

³The foundation Solomon planned for God's Temple was 27 metres[f] long and 9 metres[g] wide. ⁴The porch across the front of the Temple was 9 metres long and 9 metres[h] high. The inside of the porch was covered with pure gold. ⁵He had panels made of cypress wood put on the walls of the larger room. These panels were covered with pure gold and decorated with designs of palm trees and chains. ⁶He added precious stones as decorations for the Temple and brought gold from Parvaim.[i] ⁷He used the gold to cover the ceiling beams, doorposts, walls and doors. The workers also carved designs of winged creatures on the walls.

⁸The next part of the building was the Most Holy Place. This room was 9 metres long and 9 metres wide, the same width as the Temple. The inside walls were covered with over 20 tonnes[j] of pure gold. ⁹The nails were made of gold and weighed 575 grammes[k] each. He covered the upper rooms with gold. ¹⁰Solomon had the workers make two statues of winged creatures to put in the Most Holy Place. They covered the statues with gold. ¹¹⁻¹³The wings of the statues were spread out to each side and measured over 4 metres[l] across. So the wings of both statues placed side by side reached all the way across the 9-metre room. One wing of each statue touched the wall on each side of the room. And the tips of their other wings touched in the middle of the room. These winged creatures stood facing out towards the main room of the Temple.

¹⁴Across the entrance there was a curtain made from blue, purple and red materials and expensive linen. It was decorated with designs of winged creatures.

¹⁵Two columns were made for the front of the Temple. The columns were 15.5 metres[m] tall. The top part of the two columns was 2.2 metres long. ¹⁶A network of chains decorated the tops of the columns. And a 100 pomegranates[n] decorated the

---

a **2:10** *2,000 tonnes* Literally, "20,000 *cors*".
b **2:10** *440,000 litres* Literally, "20,000 *baths*".
c **2:13** Or "I will send one of the craftsmen of my father Hiram."
d **3:1** *Araunah* In Hebrew, "Ornan".
e **3:1** *Jebusite* A person who lived in Jerusalem before the Israelites took the city. "Jebus" was the old name for Jerusalem.
f **3:3** *27 metres* Literally, "60 *cubits*".
g **3:3** *9 metres* Literally, "20 *cubits*". Also in verses 4,8,11,13 and 4:1.
h **3:4** *9 metres* This is from some copies of the ancient Greek and Syriac versions. The standard Hebrew text has "120 *cubits*".
i **3:6** *Parvaim* This was a place where there was much gold. It was probably in the country of Ophir.
j **3:8** *20 tonnes* Literally, "600 *talents*".
k **3:9** *575 grammes* Literally, "50 *shekels*".
l **3:11** *over 4 metres* Literally, "5 *cubits*" (2.2 m) for each wing. Also in verse 15.
m **3:15** *15.5 metres* Literally, "35 *cubits*".
n **3:16** *pomegranates* Small bells shaped like pomegranates, a red fruit with many tiny seeds covered with a soft, juicy part of the fruit. Also in 4:13.

A HOUSE FIT FOR A KING

Haven't I read this somewhere before? Yes, probably! The writer of the two books of Chronicles doesn't mind repeating history that's been written down before. In fact, he even mentions it and encourages his readers to check it out (2 Chronicles 36:8)!

The parallel account of the reign of David, Solomon and the other kings of Judah that we get in Chronicles is designed to help God's people see something important: how the kings went about worshipping God . . . and what it all points ahead to.

DIG IN

READ 2 Chronicles 2:1–6

- Why does Solomon undertake this project (vv.1,5)?
- What limitation does he recognize (v.6)?

Solomon is continuing the work his father started in building a temple fit for a king. David handed over the baton to his son before he died (1 Chronicles 28:9–10,20–21). But Solomon clearly knows God for himself and this is important to him.

What's this Temple to be for? Certainly not to contain God – Solomon knew that (v.6). But it is a place where God has promised to be. It is the next step in the story of the powerful God of heaven coming to live among his people.

READ 2 Chronicles 3:1–9

- What does the scale of the operation and the materials used say to you?

The Temple is no sideline to Solomon's reign. He knows it's what God has given him to do. So he gets on with the job promptly, after securing the people and the resources he needs. In both cases, these are extravagant and lavish. The number of people involved is huge – as is the amount of gold and other precious materials Solomon orders to be used.

Why so much detail? The level of artistry and creativity on display points to the fact that God is holy. Even the king's own palace next door will look humble in comparison. It will also make the Temple a talking point among the nations. No longer was the almighty God to be worshipped in a tent – now he will be worshipped in a house fit for a king.

DIG THROUGH

- If you've been to a cathedral – or even an ornately decorated parish church – you'll have seen impressive artistry on display, all done for the worship of God. Do you think we approach God with the same level of devotion and reverence today?
- Can we live in a way that honours God extravagantly? How can we do everyday things – working, studying, chatting and caring for each other – in a way that suitably reflects the God we serve and his presence in our lives?

DIG DEEPER

- The story of the powerful God of heaven coming to live among his people started with Moses. After giving his people the Ten Commandments, God said "build a special place for me, and I will live among them" (Exodus 25:8). Look back at the account in Exodus chapters 25 – 40 to see how God first began to live among his people.
- What does this all point ahead to? Check out the Bible Bit entitled "Glory!" to find out.

chains. [17]Solomon had the columns set up in front of the Temple. One column stood on the right side. The other column stood on the left side. He named the column on the right side "Jakin".[a] And he named the column on the left side "Boaz".[b]

Furniture for the Temple

4 Solomon had Huram make[c] a bronze altar that was 9 metres long, 9 metres wide and 4.4 metres[d] tall. [2]Then he melted bronze to make a large round basin called the Sea. It was just over 2 metres tall, 4.5 metres across and about 13.5 metres[e] around. [3]Below the rim of the basin were images of bulls in two rows all the way around. They were moulded in place as part of the basin, six bulls every 44 centimetres. [4]The large basin rested on top of twelve large statues of bulls. Three bulls looked towards the north, three towards the west, three towards the south and three towards the east. The large basin was on top of these bulls, which all faced out from the centre. [5]The side of the basin was 75 millimetres[f] thick. The rim was like the rim of a cup or the flower of a lily. The basin held about 60,000 litres.[g]

[6]He made ten bowls and put five on each side of the large basin. These ten bowls were for washing the things used for the burnt offerings. But the large basin was for holding the water the priests would use for washing.

[7]He made ten lampstands of gold. He followed the plans made for these lampstands. He put the lampstands in the Temple, five on the south side and five on the north side. [8]He made ten tables and put them in the Temple, five on the south side and five on the north side. And he used gold to make 100 bowls. [9]He also made the priests' courtyard, the large courtyard and the doors that open to them. He used bronze to cover these doors. [10]He put the large basin at the south-east corner of the Temple. [11-16]He also made the pots, shovels and bowls.

So Huram finished everything King Solomon wanted him to make for God's Temple:

2 columns;

2 bowl-shaped capitals for the top of the columns;

2 nets made of bronze chains to decorate the capitals;

400 pomegranates to make two rows around each net covering the capitals;

the stands and the bowls on the stands;

the large basin with 12 bulls under it;

the pots, shovels and bowls.

These were all the things King Solomon wanted Huram to make for the LORD's Temple. They were made of polished bronze. [17]King Solomon had the bronze for all these objects poured into clay moulds. The moulds were made in the Jordan Valley between the towns of Succoth and Zeredah. [18]There were so many bronze objects made that no one was ever able to weigh all the bronze used.

[19]Solomon also ordered all these furnishings to be made for God's Temple: the golden altar and the tables that held the special bread offered to God; [20]the lamps and lampstands made of pure gold that were put inside the Holy Place in front of the Most Holy Place; [21]the flowers, lamps and tongs;[h] [22]the pure gold lamp snuffers, bowls, dishes and pans for carrying coals; the doors for the Temple, the inside doors for the Most Holy Place and the doors for the main hall.

5 When all the work was completed on the LORD's Temple, Solomon brought in everything his father David had set aside for the Temple. Solomon put the silver, the gold and all the utensils into the storage rooms in God's Temple.

The Holy Box Carried Into the Temple

[2]Solomon commanded the leaders of Israel, the leaders of the tribes and the heads of families to meet together in Jerusalem. He did this so that they could bring the Box of the LORD's Agreement up to the Temple from the City of David, that is, Zion. [3]All the men of Israel met together before King Solomon during the special festival[i] in the seventh month of the year.

[4]When all the leaders of Israel arrived, the Levites[j] lifted the Box of the Agreement [5]and carried it up to the Temple. The priests and the Levites[k] also brought the Meeting Tent and all the holy things that were in it to the Temple in Jerusalem. [6]Then King Solomon and all the Israelites met in front of the Box of the Agreement

---

[a] 3:17 *Jakin* In Hebrew, Jakin seems to mean "he establishes".
[b] 3:17 *Boaz* In Hebrew, Boaz seems to mean "in him is strength".
[c] 4:1 *Solomon . . . make* Literally, "He made". See verses 11 and 2:13–14.
[d] 4:1 *4.5 metres* Literally, "10 *cubits*".
[e] 4:2 *about 13.5 metres* Literally, "30 *cubits*".
[f] 4:5 *75 millimetres* Literally, "1 *handbreadth*".
[g] 4:5 *60,000 litres* Literally, "3,000 *baths*".
[h] 4:21 *tongs* A tool used to hold hot coals.
[i] 5:3 *the special festival* That is, the Festival of Shelters. See "FESTIVAL OF SHELTERS" in the Word List.
[j] 5:4 *Levites* Or "priests from the tribe of Levi".
[k] 5:5 *The priests and the Levites* Or "The priests from the tribe of Levi".

to offer sheep and bulls as sacrifices. There were so many offerings that no one could count them. 7Then the priests carried the Box of the LORD's Agreement to the place that was prepared for it in the Most Holy Place inside the Temple. They put the Box of the Agreement under the wings of the winged creatures. 8The winged creatures stood with their wings spread over the Box of the Agreement and the poles that were used to carry it. 9The poles are still there today. They were too long for the Most Holy Place, so their ends could be seen by anyone standing in the Holy Place, although no one outside could see them. 10The only things inside the Holy Box are the two tablets that Moses put there at Mount Horeb. This is where the LORD made his agreement with the Israelites after they came out of Egypt.

11The priests who were there from every group had made themselves ready to serve the LORD. As they all came out of the Holy Place, they stood together, but not in their special groups. 12The Levite singers stood at the east side of the altar. All the singing groups of Asaph, Heman and Jeduthun were there. And their sons and relatives were there. The Levite singers were dressed in white linen. They had cymbals, lyres and harps. There were 120 priests there with the Levite singers. The 120 priests blew trumpets. 13Those who blew the trumpets and those who sang were like one person. They made one sound when they praised and thanked the LORD. They made a loud noise with the trumpets, cymbals and musical instruments. They praised the LORD, singing,

"The LORD is good.
His faithful love will last forever."

Then the LORD's Temple was filled with a cloud. 14The priests could not continue to serve because of the cloud, because the Glory of the LORD filled the Temple.

INSIGHT

When the Temple was dedicated and Solomon prayed, God's glory appeared in cloud and in fire. These were the same things God used when he guided the Israelites out of Egypt (see Exodus 13).
2 Chronicles 5:13 and 7:1

6 Then Solomon said, "The LORD chose to live in a dark cloud. 2But, Lord, I have built a beautiful house for you to live in forever."

a 6:12–13 *1.3 metres* Literally, "3 *cubits*".

Solomon's Speech

3King Solomon turned around and blessed all the Israelites gathered in front of him. 4He said,

"Praise the LORD, the God of Israel, who has done what he promised my father David. The Lord said, 5'I led Israel out of Egypt long ago. And in all that time, I have not chosen a city from any tribe of Israel for a place to build a house for my name. I have not chosen a man to lead my people, the people of Israel. 6But now I have chosen Jerusalem as a place for my name, and I have chosen David to lead my people Israel.'

7"My father David wanted to build a temple for the name of the LORD, the God of Israel. 8But the LORD said to my father, 'David, it is good that you want to build a temple for my name, 9but you cannot build the Temple. Your son will build the Temple for my name.' 10Now, the LORD has done what he said he would do. I am the new king in my father's place. David was my father. Now I am Israel's king. That is what the LORD promised, and I have built the Temple for the name of the LORD, the God of Israel. 11I have put the Box of the Agreement in the Temple. The LORD's Agreement with Israel is in that box."

Solomon's Prayer

12–13Solomon had made a bronze platform and placed it in the middle of the outer courtyard. The platform was 2.2 metres long, 2.2 metres wide and 1.3 metresª tall. Solomon stood on the platform and faced the LORD's altar. In front of all the Israelites who were gathered together, Solomon knelt, lifted his hands towards heaven, 14and said,

"LORD, God of Israel, there is no god like you in heaven or on earth. You keep the agreement that you made with your people. You are kind and loyal to those who follow you with all their heart. 15You made a promise to your servant, my father David, and you kept that promise. You made that promise with your own mouth, and with your own hands you made it come true today. 16Now, LORD, God of Israel, keep the other promises you made to your servant David, my father. You said, 'David, if your sons carefully obey me as you did, you will always have someone from your family ruling the people of Israel.' 17Again, LORD, God of Israel, I ask you to keep the promise you made to your servant, my father David.

GLORY!

The Temple that Solomon built took years to build. The planning and the craftsmanship were stunning – we get the sense that every aspect of the work was done to the highest standards.

Now it's time for the owner to take up residence.

DIG IN

READ 2 Chronicles 6:41 – 7:10

- What was the people's reaction to the presence of God (v.3)?

Something big is going on here. Fire from heaven – and the glory of the Lord everywhere! There's no other possible response but to hit the floor, face down. Worship comes very naturally when God reveals himself in great power like this.

The fire is God's seal of approval on the project. He is pleased with the offering – once again, extravagant beyond belief!

READ 2 Chronicles 9:1–12

- What was the queen of Sheba's reaction to Solomon's palace?
- How did Solomon repay the queen's generosity (v.12)?

Word had obviously spread about Solomon's wealth, wisdom and his success in building the Temple and now the great and the good travelled to see him. This is a reminder that God's people are to be a blessing to the nations. Notice how Solomon sends the queen of Sheba away with even more than she came with.

Remember, the Chronicler has a specific purpose in writing Israel's history in this particular way. He wants to remind the people – back from exile but in a discouraged state – that they have fulfilled their calling to be a blessing to the nations. He also wants to draw out that even in the midst of Israel's sinfulness, God still wants to come and live among them.

The Temple, important though it was to Israel, is just a picture of much greater things in store for Israel in the future. Later, Jesus refers to his own body as the new "temple" which would be destroyed and then raised up again in three days (John 2:18–21). The best is yet to come. Today God is present with us because of Jesus; we no longer need to go to a temple.

DIG THROUGH

- Did you notice what the focus of their worship was (5:13; 6:14,42; 7:3,6)? They were overwhelmed with the goodness and love of the Lord. The people returning from exile needed to be reminded that this was unchanged despite their sin. We can also be reminded of this as we take in the reality and depth of his present, and personal, love for us; why not read Romans 5:1–11 and ask the Holy Spirit to reveal the depth of God's love for you?
- In what ways is your church or youth group involved with being a blessing to the nations? Are you playing a part in that yourself? When we have been given so much, surely it's our job to make sure others are blessed too?

DIG DEEPER

The Chronicler wants his readers to notice the similarities between the occasion described here in chapters 6 and 7 and that in Leviticus chapters 8 and 9 where Moses and Aaron consecrate the Meeting Tent. There, as here, the ceremonies last seven days, the glory of the Lord appears, fire falls from heaven and people bowed to the ground (Leviticus 9:23–24).

18"But, God, will you really live here with us on the earth? The whole sky and the highest heaven cannot contain you. Certainly this house that I built cannot contain you either. 19But please listen to my prayer and my request. I am your servant, and you are the LORD my God. Hear this prayer that I am praying to you today. 20In the past you said, 'I will be honoured there.' So please watch over this Temple, night and day. And listen to my prayer as I turn towards this Temple and pray to you. 21And please listen to our prayers in the future when I and your people Israel turn to this place and pray to you. We know that you live in heaven. We ask you to hear our prayer there and forgive us.

22"Whoever does wrong to someone will be brought to this altar. If they are not guilty, they will make an oath and promise that they are innocent. 23Please listen from heaven and judge them. If they are guilty, please show us that they are guilty. And if they are innocent, please show us that they are not guilty.

24"Sometimes your people Israel will sin against you, and their enemies will defeat them. Then the people will come back to you and praise you. They will pray to you in this Temple. 25In heaven, please listen to the prayers of your people Israel. Forgive them for their sins and let them have their land again. You gave this land to their ancestors.

26"Sometimes they will sin against you, and you will stop the rain from falling on their land. Then they will pray towards this place and praise your name. You will make them suffer, and they will be sorry for their sins. 27So please listen in heaven to their prayer. Then forgive us for our sins. Teach the people to do what is right. Then, please send rain to the land you gave them.

28"The land might become very dry so that no food will grow on it. Or maybe a great sickness will spread among the people. Maybe all the food that is growing will be destroyed by insects. Or your people might be attacked in some of their cities by their enemies. Or many of your people might get sick. 29When any of these things happen, people feel the need to spread their hands in prayer towards this Temple. 30Please listen to their prayer while you are in your home in heaven and forgive them and help them. Only you know what people are really thinking, so only you can judge them fairly. 31Do this so that your people will fear and respect you all the time that they live in this land you gave to our ancestors.

32"People from other places will hear about your greatness and your power. They will come from far away to pray at this Temple. 33From your home in heaven, please listen to their prayers. Please do everything those from other places ask you. Then they will fear and respect you the same as your people in Israel. Then all people everywhere will know that I built this Temple to honour you.

34"Sometimes you will command your people to go and fight against their enemies. Then your people will turn towards this city that you have chosen and the Temple that I built in your honour, and they will pray to you. 35Listen to their prayers from your home in heaven, and help them.

36"Your people will sin against you. I know this because everyone sins. And you will be angry with your people. You will let their enemies defeat them. Their enemies will make them prisoners and carry them to some faraway land. 37In that faraway land, your people will think about what happened. They will be sorry for their sins, and they will pray to you. They will say, 'We have sinned and done wrong.' 38They will be in that faraway land of their enemies, but they will turn back to you. They will be sorry for their sins with their whole heart and soul. They will turn towards the land you gave their ancestors. They will look towards the city you chose and towards the Temple I built, and they will pray to you. 39Please listen from your home in heaven. Accept their prayers when they beg for help, and help them. Forgive your people who have sinned against you. 40Now, my God, I ask you, open your eyes and your ears. Listen and pay attention to the prayers we are praying in this place.

41"Now, LORD God, get up and come to your
　　special place,
　the Box of the Agreement that shows
　　your strength.
LORD God, may your priests be dressed with
　　salvation,
　and may your true followers be happy about
　　these good things.
42LORD God, accept your anointed king.
　Remember your loyal servant David."

The Temple Dedicated to the LORD

7 When Solomon finished praying, fire came down from the sky and burned up the burnt offering and the sacrifices. The Glory of the LORD

filled the Temple. ²The priests could not enter the LORD's Temple because the Glory of the LORD filled it. ³When all the Israelites saw the fire come down from heaven and the Glory of the LORD on the Temple, they bowed down on the pavement with their faces low to the ground. They worshipped and thanked the LORD, singing,

"The LORD is good.
His faithful love will last forever."

⁴Then King Solomon and all the Israelites offered sacrifices to the LORD. ⁵King Solomon offered 22,000 bulls and 120,000 sheep. So the king and the people showed that they had dedicated the Temple to God. ⁶The priests stood ready to do their work. The Levites stood with the instruments they would use to play music to the LORD. King David had made these instruments to use when they gave thanks to the LORD and sang, "His faithful love will last forever." The priests blew their trumpets as they stood opposite the Levites. And all the Israelites were standing.

⁷King Solomon also dedicated the middle of the courtyard, the part that is in front of the Temple of the LORD. There he offered burnt offerings, grain offerings and the fat from the animals that were used as fellowship offerings. He did this because the bronze altar he had built was too small to hold all these offerings.

⁸So there at the Temple, King Solomon and all the people of Israel celebrated the festival.ᵃ People came from as far away as Hamath Pass in the north and the border of Egypt in the south. This huge crowd of people enjoyed themselves for seven days. ⁹On the eighth day, they had a holy meeting because they had celebrated for seven days. They made the altar holy and it was to be used only for worshipping the Lord. And they celebrated the festival for seven days. ¹⁰On the twenty-third day of the seventh month, Solomon told the people to go home. All the people thanked the king, said goodbye, and went home. They were happy because of all the good things that the LORD had done for David his servant and for his people Israel.

The LORD Comes to Solomon

¹¹So Solomon finished building the LORD's Temple and the king's palace. Solomon did everything that he had planned to do in building a house for the LORD and for himself. ¹²Then the LORD appeared to Solomon at night and said to him,

"Solomon, I have heard your prayer, and I have chosen this place for myself to be a house for sacrifices. ¹³There may be times

when I will close the sky so that there is no rain, or I may command locusts to destroy the crops, or I may send sicknesses to my people. ¹⁴Then, if my people who are called by my name become humble and pray, and look to me for help, and turn away from their evil ways, I will hear them from heaven. I will forgive their sin and heal their land. ¹⁵Now, my eyes are open, and my ears will pay attention to the prayers prayed in this place. ¹⁶I have chosen this Temple, and I have made it a holy place. So I will be honoured there forever. I will watch over it and think of it always. ¹⁷You must serve me with a pure and honest heart, just as your father David did. You must obey my laws and do everything that I commanded you. If you obey all I have commanded, and if you obey my laws and rules, ¹⁸then I will make you a strong king and your kingdom will be great. That is the agreement I made with David your father when I told him that Israel would always be ruled by one of his descendants.

¹⁹"But if you don't obey my laws and commands that I gave you, and if you worship other gods and serve them, ²⁰then I will take the Israelites out from my land that I gave them. And I will leave this Temple that I have made holy for my name. I will make this Temple something that all the nations will speak evil about. ²¹Everyone who sees it will be amazed. They will ask, 'Why did the LORD do this terrible thing to this land and to this Temple?' ²²People will say, 'This happened because they left the LORD, the God of their ancestors. He brought them out of Egypt, but they decided to follow other gods. They began to worship and to serve those gods. That is why he caused all these bad things to happen to them.'"

The Cities Solomon Built

8 It took 20 years for King Solomon to build the LORD's Temple and the king's palace. ²Then Solomon rebuilt the towns that Hiram gave him and then moved Israelites into those towns to live there. ³After this Solomon went to Hamath of Zobah and captured it. ⁴He also built the town of Tadmor in the desert. He built all the towns in Hamath to store things in. ⁵He rebuilt the towns of Upper Beth Horon and Lower Beth Horon. He made them into strong fortresses with strong walls, gates and bars in the gates. ⁶He also rebuilt the town of Baalath and all the other towns where he stored things. He built all the cities where the chariots were kept and where the

---

ᵃ **7:8** *festival* This was probably Passover.

horse riders lived. Solomon built all he wanted in Jerusalem, Lebanon and in all the country where he was king.

⁷⁻⁸There were many people left in the land who were not Israelites. There were Hittites, Amorites, Perizzites, Hivites and Jebusites. The Israelites had not been able to destroy them, but Solomon forced them to work for him as slaves. They are still slaves today. ⁹Solomon did not force any of the Israelites to be his slaves. They were soldiers, government officials, officers, captains and chariot commanders and drivers. ¹⁰There were 250 supervisors over Solomon's projects. They supervised the men.

¹¹Solomon brought Pharaoh's daughter up from the City of David to the house he had built for her. He said, "My wife must not live in King David's palace because the places where the LORD's Holy Box has been are holy places."

¹²Then Solomon offered burnt offerings to the LORD on the LORD's altar. He built that altar in front of the Temple porch. ¹³Solomon offered sacrifices every day the way Moses commanded. Sacrifices were to be offered on Sabbath days, during New Moon celebrations and at the three yearly festivals. The three yearly festivals were the Festival of Unleavened Bread, the Festival of Harvest and the Festival of Shelters. ¹⁴Solomon followed his father David's instructions. He chose the groups of priests for their service and the Levites for their duties. The Levites were to lead the praise and help the priests from day to day to do what needed to be done in the Temple service. And he chose the gatekeepers by their groups to serve at each gate. This is the way David, the man of God, instructed. ¹⁵The Israelites did not change or disobey any of Solomon's instructions to the priests and Levites. They did not change any of the instructions, even in the way they should keep the valuable things.

¹⁶So Solomon completed his work on the LORD's Temple. Work began the day they laid the foundation and continued without stopping until the day the Temple was finished.

¹⁷King Solomon also built ships at Ezion Geber. This town is near Elath on the shore of the Red Sea, in the land of Edom. ¹⁸Hiram sent ships to Solomon. Hiram's own men sailed the ships. They were skilled at sailing on the sea. His men went with Solomon's servants to Ophir[a] and brought back more than 15,000 kilogrammes[b] of gold to King Solomon.

The Queen of Sheba Visits Solomon

9 The queen of Sheba heard about Solomon, so she came to test him with hard questions. She had a very large group with her. She had camels that carried spices, much gold and valuable stones. She travelled to Jerusalem with a very large group of servants. There were many camels carrying spices, jewels and a lot of gold. She met Solomon and asked him all the questions that she could think of. ²Solomon answered all the questions. None of her questions was too hard for him to explain. ³The queen of Sheba saw that Solomon was very wise. She also saw the beautiful palace he had built. ⁴She saw the food at the king's table. She saw his officials meeting together. She saw the servants in the palace and the good clothes they wore. She saw his parties and the sacrifices that he offered in the LORD's Temple. She was so amazed, she could hardly breathe!

⁵Then she said to King Solomon, "Everything I heard in my country about your great works and your wisdom is true. ⁶I did not believe what people told me until I came and saw it with my own eyes. But you have twice as much wisdom as I had heard. You are much greater than people told me. ⁷Your wives[c] and officers are very fortunate! They can serve you and hear your wisdom every day. ⁸Praise the LORD your God! He was pleased to make you king of Israel. The LORD God loves Israel, so he made you the king. You follow the law and treat people fairly."

⁹Then the queen of Sheba gave King Solomon more than 4,000 kilogrammes[d] of gold, a huge amount of spices and precious stones. She gave Solomon more spices than anyone has ever brought into Israel.

¹⁰Hiram's servants brought gold from Ophir. They also brought in jewels and a special kind of wood.[e] ¹¹King Solomon used this special wood to make steps for the LORD's Temple and the king's palace. Solomon also used the algum wood to make lyres and harps for the singers. No one ever saw such beautiful things like those made from the algum wood in the country of Judah.

¹²King Solomon gave the queen of Sheba everything she asked for. He gave her more than she brought to give him. Then the queen of Sheba and her servants left and went back to their own country.

---

[a] 8:18 *Ophir* A place where there was much gold. Today no one knows where Ophir really was. Also in 9:10.
[b] 8:18 *15,000 kilogrammes* Literally, "450 talents".
[c] 9:7 *wives* This is from the ancient Greek version. The standard Hebrew text has "men".
[d] 9:9 *4,000 kilogrammes* Literally, "120 talents".
[e] 9:10 *special . . . wood* Literally, "algum" or "almug", as in 1 Kgs. No one knows exactly what type of wood this was, but it might have been sandalwood.

Solomon's Great Wealth

¹³Every year Solomon got almost 23,000 kilogrammes*ᵃ* of gold. ¹⁴In addition to the gold brought in by the travelling merchants and traders, all the kings of Arabia and the governors of the land also brought gold and silver to Solomon.

¹⁵King Solomon made 200 large shields of hammered gold. He used about 7 kilogrammes*ᵇ* of gold for each shield. ¹⁶He also made 300 smaller shields of hammered gold. He used about 3.5 kilogrammes*ᶜ* of gold for each shield. The king put them in the Forest-of-Lebanon House.*ᵈ*

¹⁷King Solomon also built a large throne with ivory decorations. It was covered with pure gold. ¹⁸There were six steps leading up to the throne. The back of the throne was round at the top. There were armrests on both sides of the throne, and there were lions in the sides of the throne under the armrests. ¹⁹There were also two lions on each of the six steps, one at each end. There was nothing like it in any other kingdom.

²⁰All of Solomon's cups and glasses were made of gold. And all the dishes*ᵉ* in the Forest-of-Lebanon House were made from pure gold. Nothing in the palace was made from silver. There was so much gold that in Solomon's time people did not think silver was important!

²¹The king also had cargo ships that went to Tarshish to trade with other countries. Hiram's men were on these ships. Every three years the ships would come back with a new load of gold, silver, ivory and apes and baboons.

²²King Solomon became greater in riches and wisdom than any other king on earth. ²³People everywhere wanted to see Solomon and hear the great wisdom that God had given him. ²⁴Every year people came to see the king, and everyone brought a gift. They brought things made from gold and silver, clothes, weapons, spices, horses and mules.

²⁵Solomon had 4,000 stalls for his horses and chariots, and he had 12,000 horses. Solomon built special cities for these chariots. So the chariots were kept in these cities. He also kept some of the chariots with him in Jerusalem. ²⁶Solomon was the king over all the kings from the Euphrates River all the way to the land of the Philistines and to the border of Egypt. ²⁷King Solomon had so much silver that it was as common as rocks in Jerusalem. And he had so much cedar wood that it was as common as sycamore trees in the hill country. ²⁸The people brought horses to Solomon from Egypt and from all the other countries.

Solomon's Death

²⁹Everything else Solomon did, from the beginning to the end, is written in the writings of Nathan the Prophet, in *The Prophecy of Ahijah* from Shiloh and in *The Visions of Iddo the Seer*. Iddo was a seer who wrote about Jeroboam son of Nebat. ³⁰Solomon ruled in Jerusalem over all Israel for 40 years. ³¹Then he died*ᶠ* and was buried in the city of David, his father. Then Solomon's son Rehoboam became the next king.

Rehoboam Acts Foolishly

10 Rehoboam went to Shechem, where all the Israelites had gone to make him king. ²Jeroboam son of Nebat was still in Egypt, where he had gone to escape from Solomon. When he heard about the plans to make Rehoboam king, he returned from Egypt. ³The people of Israel sent for Jeroboam, and together they went and spoke to Rehoboam. They said, ⁴"Your father forced us to work very hard. Now, make it easier for us. Stop the heavy work that your father forced us to do and we will serve you."

⁵Rehoboam answered, "Come back to me in three days, and I will answer you." So the people left.

⁶There were some older men who had helped Solomon make decisions when he was alive. So King Rehoboam asked these men what he should do. He said, "How do you think I should answer the people?"

⁷They answered, "If you do what is good for the people, you will please them. If you speak kindly to them, they will always work for you."

⁸But Rehoboam did not listen to the advice from the older men. He asked the young men who were his friends. ⁹Rehoboam said, "The people said, 'Give us easier work than your father gave us.' How do you think I should answer them? What should I tell them?"

¹⁰Then the young men who grew up with him answered, "Those people came to you and said, 'Your father forced us to work very hard. Now make our work easier.' So you should tell them, 'My little finger is stronger than my father's whole body. ¹¹My father forced you to work hard, but I will make you work much harder! My father punished you with whips, but I will punish you with whips that have sharp metal tips.'"

ᵃ **9:13 23,000 kilogrammes** Literally, "666 *talents*".
ᵇ **9:15 about 7 kilogrammes** Literally, "600 ˌ*shekels*ˌ".
ᶜ **9:16 about 3.5 kilogrammes** Literally, "300 ˌ*shekels*ˌ".
ᵈ **9:16 Forest-of-Lebanon House** The largest of king Solomon's palace buildings. See 1 Kgs 7:2–5.
ᵉ **9:20 dishes** The Hebrew word can mean "dishes", "tools" or "weapons".
ᶠ **9:31 died** Literally, "slept with his ancestors".

¹²Three days later, Jeroboam and all the people came back to Rehoboam, just as he had told them to do. ¹³King Rehoboam did not follow the advice of the older men. Instead, he was rude to the people. ¹⁴He did what his friends told him to do and said, "My father forced you to work hard, but I will make you work much harder! My father punished you with whips, but I will punish you with whips that have sharp metal tips." ¹⁵So the king did not do what the people wanted. The LORD caused this to happen. He did this in order to keep the promise he made to Jeroboam son of Nebat when he sent Ahijah, the prophet from Shiloh, to speak to him.

¹⁶The Israelites saw that the new king refused to listen to them, so they said to him,

"We are not part of David's family are we?
    We don't get any of Jesse's land, do we?
So, people of Israel, let's go home
    and let David's son rule his own people!"

So the Israelites went home. ¹⁷But Rehoboam still ruled over the Israelites who lived in the cities of Judah.

¹⁸A man named Adoniram was one of the men who directed the workers. King Rehoboam sent Adoniram to talk to the people, but the Israelites threw stones at him until he died. King Rehoboam ran to his chariot and escaped to Jerusalem. ¹⁹So Israel rebelled against the family of David, and that is how things are even today.

INSIGHT

Rehoboam tried to prove he was a great leader but he made a classic mistake. By trying to force the people to respect him the harsh treatment dished out by the new king caused the people to rebel instead.

2 Chronicles 10

11 Rehoboam went back to Jerusalem and gathered together an army of 180,000 men from the families of Judah and the tribe of Benjamin. Rehoboam wanted to go and fight against the Israelites and take back his kingdom. ²But the LORD spoke to a man of God named Shemaiah. He said, ³"Talk to Rehoboam, the son of Solomon, king of Judah, and to all the Israelites. ⁴Say to them, 'The LORD says that you must not go to war against your brothers. Everyone, go home!

I made all this happen.'" So all the men in Rehoboam's army obeyed the LORD and went home. They did not attack Jeroboam.

Rehoboam Strengthens Judah

⁵Rehoboam lived in Jerusalem and built strong cities in Judah to defend against attacks. ⁶He repaired the cities of Bethlehem, Etam, Tekoa, ⁷Beth Zur, Soco, Adullam, ⁸Gath, Mareshah, Ziph, ⁹Adoraim, Lachish, Azekah, ¹⁰Zorah, Aijalon and Hebron. These cities in Judah and Benjamin were made strong. ¹¹When Rehoboam made these cities strong, he put commanders in them. He also put supplies of food, oil and wine in them. ¹²Also, he put shields and spears in every city and made the cities very strong. He kept the people and cities of Judah and Benjamin under his control.

¹³The priests and the Levites from all over Israel agreed with Rehoboam and joined him. ¹⁴The Levites left their grasslands and their own fields and came to Judah and Jerusalem. The Levites did this because Jeroboam and his sons refused to let them serve as priests to the LORD. ¹⁵Jeroboam chose his own priests to serve in the high places, where he set up the goat and calf idols he had made. ¹⁶When the Levites left Israel, the people in all the tribes of Israel who were faithful to the LORD, the God of Israel, came to Jerusalem to sacrifice to the LORD, the God of their fathers. ¹⁷These people made the kingdom of Judah strong, and they supported Solomon's son Rehoboam for three years. They did this because during that time they lived the way David and Solomon had lived.

Rehoboam's Family

¹⁸Rehoboam married Mahalath. Her father was Jerimoth. Her mother was Abihail. Jerimoth was David's son. Abihail was Eliab's daughter, and Eliab was Jesse's son. ¹⁹Mahalath gave Rehoboam these sons: Jeush, Shemariah and Zaham. ²⁰Then Rehoboam married Maacah. Maacah was Absalom's granddaughter.ᵃ And Maacah gave Rehoboam these children: Abijah, Attai, Ziza and Shelomith. ²¹Rehoboam loved Maacah more than he loved all his other wives and slave women. Rehoboam had 18 wives and 60 slave women. He was the father of 28 sons and 60 daughters.

²²Rehoboam chose Abijah to be the leader among his own brothers. He did this because he planned to make Abijah king. ²³Rehoboam acted wisely and spread all his sons through all the areas of Judah and Benjamin to every strong city. And Rehoboam gave plenty of supplies to his sons. He also looked for wives for them.

ᵃ **11:20 granddaughter** Literally, "daughter".

King Shishak of Egypt Attacks Jerusalem

12 Rehoboam became a strong king and made his kingdom strong. Then Rehoboam and the whole tribe of Judah[a] refused to obey the Law of the LORD.

²During the fifth year that Rehoboam was king, Shishak king of Egypt came to attack Jerusalem. This happened because Rehoboam and the people of Judah rebelled against the LORD. ³Shishak had 1,200 chariots, 60,000 horsemen and an army that no one could count. In Shishak's large army there were Libyan soldiers, Sukkite soldiers and Ethiopian soldiers. ⁴Shishak defeated the strong cities of Judah. Then Shishak brought his army to Jerusalem.

⁵Then Shemaiah the prophet came to Rehoboam and the leaders of Judah. The leaders of Judah had gathered together in Jerusalem because they all were afraid of Shishak. Shemaiah said to Rehoboam and the leaders of Judah, "This is what the LORD says: 'Rehoboam, you and the people of Judah have left me and refused to obey my law. So now I will leave you to face Shishak without my help.'"

⁶Then the leaders of Judah and King Rehoboam were sorry and humbled themselves. They said, "The LORD is right."

⁷The LORD saw that the king and the leaders of Judah had humbled themselves. Then the message from the Lord came to Shemaiah. The LORD said, "The king and the leaders humbled themselves. So I will not destroy them, but I will save them soon. I will not use Shishak to pour out my anger on Jerusalem. ⁸But the people of Jerusalem will become Shishak's servants. This will happen so that they may learn that serving me is different from serving the kings of other nations."

⁹Shishak took the treasures from the LORD's Temple and from the king's palace. He also took the gold shields that Solomon had made. ¹⁰King Rehoboam made more shields to put in their places, but they were made from bronze. He gave them to the guards on duty at the palace gates. ¹¹Every time the king went to the LORD's Temple, the guards took out the shields and went with him. Afterwards, they put the shields back on the wall in the guardroom.

¹²Rehoboam humbled himself, and the LORD stopped being angry with him. So he did not completely destroy Rehoboam. There was some good in Judah.

¹³King Rehoboam made himself a strong king in Jerusalem. He was 41 years old when he became

king of Judah. Rehoboam ruled for 17 years in Jerusalem, the city the LORD chose for his own. He chose this city from all the other cities of Israel. Rehoboam's mother was Naamah. She was an Ammonite. ¹⁴Rehoboam did evil because he didn't decide in his heart to obey the LORD.

¹⁵All the things Rehoboam did when he was king, from the beginning to the end of his rule, are written in the writings of Shemaiah the prophet and in the writings of Iddo the seer. Those men wrote family histories. And there were wars between Rehoboam and Jeroboam all the time both kings ruled. ¹⁶Rehoboam rested with his ancestors and was buried in the City of David. Then Rehoboam's son Abijah became the next king after him.

Abijah, King of Judah

13 Abijah became the new king of Judah. This was during the eighteenth year that Jeroboam son of Nebat ruled Israel. ²Abijah ruled in Jerusalem for three years. His mother's name was Maacah. She was the daughter of Uriel, from the town of Gibeah. And there was war between Abijah and Jeroboam. ³Abijah's army had 400,000 brave soldiers. Abijah led that army into battle. Jeroboam's army had 800,000 brave soldiers. Jeroboam got ready to have a war with Abijah.

⁴Then Abijah stood on Mount Zemaraim in the hill country of Ephraim and said, "Jeroboam and all Israel, listen to me! ⁵You should know that the LORD, the God of Israel, made a lasting agreement[b] with David and his sons, which gave them the right to rule over Israel forever. ⁶But Jeroboam turned against his master. Jeroboam son of Nebat was one of the servants of David's son Solomon. ⁷Then some good-for-nothing friends joined with Jeroboam, and together they turned against Rehoboam, Solomon's son. Rehoboam was young and did not have enough experience to stop them.

⁸"Now, you people have decided to defeat the LORD's kingdom—the kingdom that is ruled by David's sons. You have so many people with you and you have the gold calves—the 'gods' that Jeroboam made for you. ⁹You threw out the LORD's priests, the descendants of Aaron. And you threw out the Levites. Then you chose your own priests, as every other nation on earth does. And now, anyone who will bring a young bull and seven rams can become a priest to serve these 'no-gods'.

¹⁰"But as for us, the LORD is our God. We people of Judah have not refused to obey God.

---

[a] **12:1** *Judah* Literally, "Israel".
[b] **13:5** *lasting agreement* Literally, "agreement of salt". When people ate salt together, it meant their agreement of friendship would never be broken. Abijah was saying here that God had made an agreement with David that would never be broken.

We have not left him. The priests who serve the LORD are Aaron's sons, and the Levites help the priests in their work. ¹¹They offer burnt offerings and burn incense of spices to the LORD every morning and every evening. They put the bread in rows on the special table in the Temple. And they take care of the lamps on the gold lampstand so that it shines brightly each and every evening. We very carefully serve the LORD our God, but you people have abandoned him. ¹²God himself is with us. He is our ruler, and his priests are with us. God's priests blow his trumpets to wake you up and make you excited about coming to him. Men of Israel, don't fight against the LORD, God of your ancestors, because you will not succeed!"

¹³But Jeroboam sent a group of soldiers to sneak behind Abijah's army. Jeroboam's army was in front of Abijah's army. The hidden soldiers from Jeroboam's army were behind Abijah's army. ¹⁴When the soldiers in Abijah's army from Judah looked around, they saw Jeroboam's army attacking both in front and behind.ᵃ The men of Judah shouted out to the LORD and the priests blew the trumpets. ¹⁵Then the men in Abijah's army shouted. When the men of Judah shouted, God defeated Jeroboam's army. Jeroboam's whole army from Israel was defeated by Abijah's army from Judah. ¹⁶The men of Israel ran away from the men of Judah. God let the army from Judah defeat the army from Israel. ¹⁷Abijah's army greatly defeated the army of Israel, and 500,000 of the best men of Israel were killed. ¹⁸So at that time the Israelites were defeated, and the people of Judah won. The army from Judah won because they depended on the LORD, the God of their ancestors.

¹⁹Abijah's army chased Jeroboam's army, and they captured the towns of Bethel, Jeshanah and Ephron from Jeroboam. They captured the towns and the small villages near them.

²⁰Jeroboam never became strong again while Abijah lived. The LORD killed Jeroboam, ²¹but Abijah became strong. He married 14 women and was the father of 22 sons and 16 daughters. ²²Everything else Abijah did is written in the books of the prophet Iddo.

14 When Abijah died, they buried him in the City of David. Abijah's son Asa became the new king after him. There was peace in the country for ten years in Asa's time.

Asa, King of Judah

²Asa did what the LORD his God said was good and right. ³He took away the altars of the foreigners and the high places. He also smashed the memorial stones and cut down the Asherah poles. ⁴He commanded the people of Judah to follow the LORD, the God their ancestors had worshipped, and to obey his laws and commands. ⁵He also removed all the high places and incense altars from all the towns in Judah. So the kingdom had peace when Asa was king. ⁶Asa built strong cities in Judah while there was peace in Judah. He had no war in these years because the LORD gave him peace.

⁷Asa said to the people of Judah, "Let's build these towns and make walls around them. Let's make towers, gates and bars in the gates. Let's do this while we still live in this country. This country is ours because we have followed the LORD our God. He has given us peace all around us." So they built and had success.

⁸Asa had an army of 300,000 men from the tribe of Judah and 280,000 men from the tribe of Benjamin. The men from Judah carried large shields and spears. The men from Benjamin carried small shields and shot arrows from bows. All of them were strong and brave soldiers.

⁹Then Zerah from Ethiopiaᵇ came out against Asa's army. He had 1,000,000 men and 300 chariots in his army. His army went as far as the town of Mareshah. ¹⁰Asa went out to fight against Zerah. Asa's army got ready for battle in the Valley of Zephathah at Mareshah.

¹¹Asa called out to the LORD his God and said, "LORD, only you can help weak people against those who are strong! Help us, LORD our God! We depend on you. We fight against this large army in your name. LORD, you are our God! Don't let anyone defeat you!"

INSIGHT

Throughout 2 Chronicles we are repeatedly shown how important it is for God's people to place their trust in him. Here we see that Asa's army was half the size of Zerah's army, but Asa won because he prayed and depended on God for his victory.

2 Chronicles 14

¹²Then the LORD used Asa's army from Judah to defeat the Ethiopian army. And the army ran away. ¹³Asa's army chased the Ethiopian army all the way to the town of Gerar. So many Ethiopians were killed that they could not get together as an

---

ᵃ **13:14** *When the soldiers . . . behind* The standard Hebrew text has "The battle was in front and in the back."
ᵇ **14:9** *Ethiopia* Or "Cush".

army to fight again. They were crushed by the LORD and his army. Asa and his army carried many valuable things away from the enemy. [14]Asa and his army defeated all the towns near Gerar. The people living in those towns were afraid of the LORD. Those towns had very many valuable things. Asa's army took those valuable things away from those towns. [15]His army also attacked the camps where the shepherds lived and took many sheep and camels. Then they went back to Jerusalem.

Asa's Changes

15 The Spirit of God came on Azariah, who was Obed's son. [2]Azariah went to meet Asa and said, "Listen to me, Asa and all you people of Judah and Benjamin. The LORD is with you when you are with him. If you look for him, you will find him. But if you leave him, he will leave you. [3]For a long time Israel was without the true God. And they were without a teaching priest, and without the law. [4]But when the Israelites had trouble, they turned again to the LORD, the God of Israel. They looked for him and found him. [5]In those times of trouble, no one could travel safely. There was great trouble in all the nations. [6]One nation would destroy another nation and one city would destroy another city. This was happening because God gave them all kinds of trouble. [7]But Asa, you and the people of Judah and Benjamin, be strong. Don't be weak and don't give up, because you will get a reward for your good work!"

[8]Asa felt encouraged when he heard these words and the message from Obed the prophet. Then he removed the hated idols from the whole area of Judah and Benjamin. He also removed the hated idols from the towns he had captured in the hill country of Ephraim. And he repaired the LORD's altar that was in front of the porch of the LORD's Temple.

[9]Then Asa gathered all the people from Judah and Benjamin and the people from the tribes of Ephraim, Manasseh and Simeon who had moved from the country of Israel to live in the country of Judah. A great many of these people came to Judah because they saw that the LORD, Asa's God, was with him.

[10]Asa and these people gathered together in Jerusalem on the third month in the fifteenth year of Asa's rule. [11]At that time they sacrificed 700 bulls and 7,000 sheep and goats to the LORD. Asa's army had taken the animals and other valuable things from their enemies. [12]Then they made an agreement to serve the LORD God with all their heart and with all their soul. He is the God their

ancestors served. [13]Anyone who refused to serve the LORD God was to be killed. It did not matter if that person was important or not or if that person was a man or woman. [14]Then Asa and the people made an oath to the LORD. They shouted it out loudly and blew their trumpets and horns. [15]All the people of Judah were happy about the oath, because they had promised with all their heart. They followed God with all their heart. They looked for God and found him, so the LORD gave them peace in all the country.

[16]King Asa also removed Maacah, his grandmother, from being queen mother. He did this because she had set up one of those awful poles to honour the goddess Asherah. Asa cut down that Asherah pole, smashed it into small pieces and burned the pieces in the Kidron Valley. [17]Asa did not destroy the high places, even though he was faithful to God all his life.

[18]Asa and his father had given some special gifts to God. Asa put these gifts of gold, silver and other things into the Temple. [19]There was no more war until the thirty-fifth year of Asa's rule.[a]

Asa's Last Years

16 In Asa's thirty-sixth year as king,[b] Baasha attacked Judah and then built up the city of Ramah to keep Asa from leaving Judah on any kind of military campaign. [2]So Asa took gold and silver from the treasuries of the LORD's Temple and the king's palace. He gave it to his officials and sent them to King Ben-Hadad of Aram. Ben-Hadad was the son of Tabrimmon. Tabrimmon was the son of Hezion. Damascus was Ben-Hadad's capital city. [3]Asa sent this message: "My father and your father had a peace agreement. Now I want to make a peace agreement with you. I am sending you this gift of gold and silver. Please break your treaty with King Baasha of Israel and make him leave us alone."

[4]King Ben-Hadad made that agreement with King Asa and sent his army to fight against the Israelite towns of Ijon, Dan, Abel Maim and the storage cities in the area of Naphtali. [5]When Baasha heard about these attacks, he stopped building up Ramah and went back to Tirzah. He stopped all the work he was doing. [6]Then King Asa gave an order for all the men in Judah, with no exceptions. They had to go to Ramah and carry away all the stone and wood that Baasha was using to build up the city. They carried the material to Geba in Benjamin and to Mizpah and used it to strengthen those two cities.

[7]At that time Hanani the seer came to King Asa of Judah and said to him, "Asa, you depended on

[a] 15:19 *thirty-fifth year of Asa's rule* About the year 880 BC.
[b] 16:1 *thirty-sixth year as king* About the year 879 BC.

the king of Aram to help you and not the LORD your God. That's why the king's army has escaped from you. ⁸Did you forget what happened with the Ethiopians and the Libyans who also had a powerful army with many chariots and horsemen? That time you depended on the LORD to help you, and he let you defeat them. ⁹The eyes of the LORD go around looking in all the earth for people who are faithful to him so that he can make them strong. Asa, you did a foolish thing. So from now on you will have wars."

¹⁰Asa was angry with Hanani because of what he said. He was so angry that he put Hanani in prison. At the same time he was also very rough and cruel to some of the people.

INSIGHT

Asa didn't always get things right and he didn't respond very well to correction. In fact, when a seer told Asa he'd made a mistake, Asa had him locked up in prison!
2 Chronicles 16:7–10

¹¹Everything Asa did, from the beginning to the end, is written in the book, *The History of the Kings of Judah and Israel.* ¹²Asa's feet became infected in his thirty-ninth year as king.ᵃ Even though the infection was very serious, Asa did not go to the LORD for help. He went to the doctors instead. ¹³Asa died during his forty-first year as kingᵇ and rested with his ancestors. ¹⁴The people buried Asa in his own tomb that he had made for himself in the City of David. They laid him in a bed that was filled with spices and different kinds of mixed perfumes, and they burned a large fire for him.ᶜ

Jehoshaphat, King of Judah

17 Asa's son Jehoshaphat became the new king after him. Jehoshaphat made Judah strong so that they could fight against Israel. ²He put groups of soldiers in all the towns of Judah that were made into fortresses. He built fortresses in Judah and in the towns of Ephraim that his father Asa had captured.

³The LORD was with Jehoshaphat because in his young life he did the good things his ancestor David did. Jehoshaphat did not follow the Baal idols. ⁴He followed the God that his ancestors had worshipped. He followed God's commands and did not live the same way the Israelites lived. ⁵The LORD made Jehoshaphat a strong king over Judah. All the people of Judah brought gifts to Jehoshaphat. So he had much wealth and honour. ⁶His heart found pleasure in the ways of the LORD. He removed the high places and the Asherah poles from the country of Judah.

⁷During the third year of Jehoshaphat's rule,ᵈ he sent his leaders to teach in the towns of Judah. These leaders were Ben Hail, Obadiah, Zechariah, Nethanel and Micaiah. ⁸Jehoshaphat also sent Levites with these leaders. These Levites were Shemaiah, Nethaniah, Zebadiah, Asahel, Shemiramoth, Jehonathan, Adonijah and Tobijah. He also sent the priests Elishama and Jehoram. ⁹These leaders, Levites and priests taught the people in Judah. They had the *Book of the Law of the LORD* with them. They went through all the towns of Judah and taught the people.

¹⁰The nations near Judah were afraid of the LORD, so they did not start a war against Jehoshaphat. ¹¹Some of the Philistines brought gifts to Jehoshaphat. They also brought silver to him because they knew he was a very powerful king. Some Arabian people brought flocks to Jehoshaphat. They brought 7,700 rams and 7,700 goats to him.

¹²Jehoshaphat became more and more powerful. He built fortresses and storage cities in the country of Judah, ¹³and he kept many supplies in these cities.

Jehoshaphat kept an army of trained soldiers in Jerusalem. ¹⁴These soldiers were from two tribes, and they are listed here by families:

From the tribe of Judah,
Adnah was the commander of 300,000 soldiers.
¹⁵Jehohanan was the commander of 280,000 soldiers.
¹⁶Amasiah son of Zicri was the commander of 200,000 soldiers. He had volunteered to serve the LORD in this way.
¹⁷From the tribe of Benjamin,
Eliada, a war hero, was the commander of 200,000 soldiers who used bows, arrows and shields,
¹⁸and Jehozabad was the commander of 180,000 men armed for battle.

¹⁹All these soldiers served King Jehoshaphat. The king also had other men in the fortresses throughout the country of Judah.

ᵃ 16:12 *thirty-ninth year as king* About the year 875 BC.
ᵇ 16:13 *forty-first year as king* About the year 873 BC.
ᶜ 16:14 This probably means the people burned spices in honour of Asa, but it could also mean they burned his body.
ᵈ 17:7 *third year of Jehoshaphat's rule* About the year 871 BC.

Micaiah Warns King Ahab

18 Jehoshaphat became very rich and famous. He made an agreement with King Ahab through marriage.ᵃ ²A few years later, Jehoshaphat visited Ahab in the town of Samaria. Ahab sacrificed many sheep and cattle for Jehoshaphat and the people with him. Ahab encouraged Jehoshaphat to join in an attack on the city of Ramoth Gilead. ³Ahab said to Jehoshaphat, "Will you go with me to attack Ramoth Gilead?" Ahab was the king of Israel and Jehoshaphat was the king of Judah. Jehoshaphat answered, "Yes, you and I will be as one—my men will be as yours in battle. ⁴But first let's ask the LORD for advice."

⁵So Ahab called a meeting of the prophets. There were about 400 prophets at that time. Ahab asked the prophets, "Should we go and attack Ramoth Gilead or not?"

The prophets answered Ahab, "Yes, because God will let you defeat Ramoth Gilead."

⁶But Jehoshaphat said, "Doesn't the LORD have another prophet here? Let's ask him what God says."

⁷King Ahab answered, "Yes, there is another prophet. His name is Micaiah son of Imlah. But I hate him. He never says anything good about me when he speaks for the LORD. He always says things that I don't like."

Jehoshaphat said, "The king shouldn't say things like that!"

⁸So King Ahab told one of his officers to go and find Micaiah.

⁹At that time the two kings were sitting on their thrones, with their royal robes on, at the judgement place near the gates of Samaria. All the prophets were standing before them, prophesying. ¹⁰One of the prophets was named Zedekiah son of Kenaanah. Zedekiah made some iron hornsᵇ and said to Ahab, "The LORD says, 'You will use these iron horns to fight against the army of Aram. You will defeat them and destroy them.'" ¹¹All the other prophets agreed with Zedekiah and said, "Your army should march now to go and fight against the Arameans at Ramoth Gilead. You will win the battle. The LORD will let you defeat them."

¹²While this was happening, the officer went to find Micaiah. When he found him, the officer told him, "All the other prophets have said that the king will succeed, so you should say the same thing."

¹³But Micaiah answered, "As surely as the LORD lives, I can say only what my God says."

¹⁴Micaiah went and stood before King Ahab. The king asked him, "Micaiah, should we go and attack the Arameans at Ramoth Gilead or not?"

Micaiah answered, "Yes, go and be successful! You will take the city."

¹⁵But Ahab answered, "How many times do I have to tell you? Tell me the truth. What does the LORD say?"

¹⁶So Micaiah answered, "I can see the army of Israel scattered all over the hills, like sheep with no one to lead them. This is what the LORD says, 'These men have no leaders. Let them go home in peace.'"

¹⁷Then Ahab said to Jehoshaphat, "See, I told you! This prophet never says anything good about me. He always says something bad."

¹⁸Micaiah said, "Hear the message from the LORD: I saw the LORD sitting on his throne. All of heaven's army was standing around him, some on his left side and some on his right side. ¹⁹The LORD said, 'Which of you will go and fool Ahab into attacking the Arameans at Ramoth Gilead so that he will be killed?' The angels discussed many different plans. ²⁰Then a spirit went and stood before the LORD. He said, 'I will fool him!' The LORD asked, 'How will you do it?' ²¹He answered, 'I will go out and become a spirit of lies in the mouths of Ahab's prophets—they will all speak lies.' So the Lord said, 'Yes, that will fool Ahab. Go out and do that!'

²²"So that is what has happened here. The LORD made your prophets lie to you. The LORD himself decided to bring this disaster to you."

²³Then the prophet Zedekiah went to Micaiah and hit him on the face. Zedekiah said, "How is it that the Spirit of the LORD left me to speak through you?"

²⁴Micaiah answered, "Look, what I said will happen! And when you see it, you will go into the deepest part of your house to hide!"

²⁵Then King Ahab ordered one of his officers to arrest Micaiah. Ahab said, "Arrest him and take him to Amon the governor of the city and prince Joash. ²⁶Tell them to put Micaiah in prison. Give him nothing but bread and water to eat. Keep him there until I come home from the battle."

²⁷Micaiah said, "Listen to me, everyone! Ahab, if you come back alive from the battle, the LORD has not spoken through me."

The Battle at Ramoth Gilead

²⁸King Ahab of Israel and King Jehoshaphat of Judah went to fight the Arameans at Ramoth Gilead. ²⁹Ahab said to Jehoshaphat, "Disguise yourself when you go into battle, but wear your own clothes. And I will disguise myself." The king of Israel went into battle dressed like an ordinary soldier.

ᵃ **18:1** Jehoshaphat's son, Jehoram, married Athaliah, Ahab's daughter. See 2 Chr. 21:6.
ᵇ **18:10** *iron horns* These were a symbol of great strength.

³⁰The king of Aram had 32 chariot commanders. He gave them this command, "Don't go after anyone except the king of Israel, no matter how important they are!" ³¹During the battle, the commanders saw King Jehoshaphat and thought he was the king of Israel. So they went to kill him. Jehoshaphat started shouting, and the LORD helped him. God made the chariot commanders turn away from Jehoshaphat. ³²When the commanders saw that he was not King Ahab, they stopped chasing him.

³³Then a soldier pulled back on his bow and shot an arrow into the air. By chance it hit the king of Israel between two pieces of his armour. King Ahab said to his chariot driver, "I've been hit! Turn the chariot around and take me off the battlefield!"

³⁴The armies continued fighting all that day. King Ahab leaned against the side of his chariot to hold himself up, facing the Arameans. He watched until evening. Then, just as the sun was setting, he died.

19 King Jehoshaphat of Judah came back safely to his house in Jerusalem. ²The prophet Jehu, son of Hanani, went out to meet the king. Jehu said to him, "Why did you help those who are wicked? Why do you love those who hate the LORD? That's the reason the LORD is angry with you now. ³Fortunately, you did some good things in your life. You did remove the Asherah poles from this country, and you did decide to ask God for his advice."

Jehoshaphat Chooses Judges

⁴Jehoshaphat lived in Jerusalem, but he would go out among the people throughout Judah, from Beersheba to the hill country of Ephraim. He helped the people turn back to the LORD, the God their ancestors worshipped. ⁵Jehoshaphat went from town to town and appointed judges in each of the fortresses of Judah. ⁶He told the judges, "Be careful in what you are doing, because you are not judging for people, but for the LORD. He will be with you when you make decisions. ⁷You must fear the LORD. Protect justice and do what is right because the LORD our God is fair. He does not treat some people as if they are more important than others, and he does not accept bribes to change his judgements."

⁸In Jerusalem, Jehoshaphat chose some of the Levites, priests and heads of the families of Israel to be judges. These men lived in Jerusalem and used the law of the LORD to settle problems among the people. ⁹Jehoshaphat commanded them, "You must serve faithfully with all your heart. You must fear the LORD. ¹⁰People from cities around the country will bring their problems to you. You will listen to cases where people have broken a law or a command or maybe killed someone. In all these cases you must warn the people not to sin against the LORD so that he will not get angry and punish you and your people.

¹¹"Amariah is the high priest, so he will make the final decision about the people's responsibilities to the LORD. Zebadiah son of Ishmael is the leader of the tribe of Judah, so he will make the final decision about the people's responsibilities to the king. The Levites will serve as scribes for you. Be brave and do what is right! May the LORD be with those of you who are good judges."

Jehoshaphat Faces War

20 Later, the Moabites, the Ammonites and some Meunites^a came to start a war with Jehoshaphat. ²Some men came and told Jehoshaphat, "There is a large army coming against you from Edom. They are coming from the other side of the Dead Sea. They are already in Hazazon Tamar!" (Hazazon Tamar is also called En Gedi.) ³Jehoshaphat became afraid, and he decided to ask the LORD what to do. He announced a time of fasting for everyone in Judah. ⁴The people of Judah came together to ask the LORD for help. They came from out of all the towns of Judah to ask for the LORD's help. ⁵Jehoshaphat was in the new courtyard of the LORD's Temple. He stood up in the meeting of the people from Judah and Jerusalem ⁶and said,

"LORD God of our ancestors, you are the God in heaven. You rule over all the kingdoms in all the nations. You have power and strength. No one can stand against you. ⁷You are our God! You forced the people living in this land to leave. You did this in front of your people Israel. You gave this land to the descendants of Abraham forever. Abraham was your friend. ⁸His descendants lived in this land, and built a temple for your name. ⁹They said, 'If trouble comes to us—the sword, punishment, sicknesses or famine— we will stand in front of this Temple and in front of you. Your name is on this Temple. We will shout to you when we are in trouble. Then you will hear and save us.'

¹⁰"But now, here are men from Ammon, Moab and Mount Seir. You would not let the Israelites enter their lands when they came out of Egypt.^b So the Israelites turned away and didn't destroy them. ¹¹But see the kind of reward those people give us for not

---

^a 20:1 *Meunites* This is found in some copies of the ancient Greek version. The standard Hebrew text has "Ammonites".
^b 20:10 *You would not let . . . Egypt* See Deut. 2:4–9,19.

destroying them. They have come to force us out of your land that you gave to us. ¹²Our God, punish those people. We don't have the strength to stop this large army that is coming against us. We don't know what to do! We are looking to you for help."ᵃ

¹³All the men of Judah stood before the LORD with their wives, babies and children. ¹⁴Then the Spirit of the LORD came on Jahaziel son of Zechariah. (Zechariah was the son of Benaiah, the son of Jeiel, the son of Mattaniah.) Jahaziel was a Levite from the family of Asaph. In the middle of the meeting, ¹⁵Jahaziel said, "Listen to me King Jehoshaphat and everyone living in Judah and Jerusalem! The LORD says this to you: 'Don't be afraid or worry about this large army, because the battle is not your battle. It is God's battle! ¹⁶Tomorrow, they will come up through the Ziz Pass. You must go down to them. You will find them at the end of the valley on the other side of the desert of Jeruel. ¹⁷You will not have to fight this battle. Just stand there and watch the LORD save you. Judah and Jerusalem, don't be afraid. Don't worry, because the LORD is with you. So go out to stand against those people tomorrow.'"

¹⁸Jehoshaphat bowed with his face to the ground. And all the people of Judah and Jerusalem bowed down before the LORD and worshipped him. ¹⁹The Levites from the Kohath family groups and the Korah family stood up to praise the LORD, the God of Israel. They sang very loudly.

²⁰Early the next morning, Jehoshaphat's army went out into the desert of Tekoa. As they marched out, Jehoshaphat stood there saying, "Listen to me, men of Judah and Jerusalem. Have faith in the LORD your God, and you will stand strong! Have faith in his prophets, and you will succeed!"

²¹Jehoshaphat encouraged the men and gave them instructions. Then he had the Temple singers stand up in their special clothes to praise the LORD. They marched in front of the army and sang,

"Give thanks to the LORD!
His faithful love will last forever."

²²As they began to sing and to praise God, the LORD set an ambush for the army from Ammon, Moab and Mount Seir who had come to attack Judah. The enemy was defeated! ²³The Ammonites and the Moabites started to fight the men from Mount Seir. After they had killed them, the Ammonites and Moabites turned on themselves and killed each other.

²⁴The men from Judah arrived at the lookout point in the desert. They looked for the enemy's large army, but all they saw were dead bodies lying on the ground. There were no survivors. ²⁵Jehoshaphat and his army came to take things from the bodies. They found many animals, riches, clothes and other valuable things. It was more than Jehoshaphat and his men could carry away. There was so much that they spent three days taking everything from the dead bodies. ²⁶On the fourth day Jehoshaphat and his army met in the Valley of Beracah.ᵇ They praised the LORD. That is why people still call that place, "The Valley of Beracah".

²⁷All the men from Judah and Jerusalem were very happy as they marched back to Jerusalem with Jehoshaphat in the front. The LORD made them very happy when he defeated their enemy. ²⁸They entered Jerusalem with lyres, harps and trumpets and went to the Temple of the LORD.

²⁹People in all the surrounding kingdoms became afraid of God when they heard that the LORD fought against the enemies of Israel. ³⁰That is why there was peace for Jehoshaphat's kingdom—his God brought him rest from the enemies that were all around him.

Summary of Jehoshaphat's Rule

³¹Jehoshaphat ruled over the country of Judah. He was 35 years old when he became king, and he ruled for 25 years in Jerusalem. His mother's name was Azubah, the daughter of Shilhi. ³²⁻³³Like his father Asa, Jehoshaphat was good and did everything that the LORD wanted, except he did not destroy the high places. Also, the people did not turn back to the God that their ancestors worshipped.

³⁴Everything else Jehoshaphat did, from beginning to end, is written in *The Official Records of Jehu Son of Hanani*. It was copied and included in the book, *The History of the Kings of Israel*.

³⁵Later on, King Jehoshaphat of Judah made an agreement with King Ahaziah of Israel. Ahaziah was very evil. ³⁶Jehoshaphat joined with Ahaziah to make ships to go to the city of Tarshish. They built some ships at Ezion Geber. ³⁷There was a man from the town of Mareshah named Eliezer son of Dodavahu. He spoke against Jehoshaphat and said, "Jehoshaphat, since you have joined with Ahaziah, the LORD will destroy what you have built." The ships were wrecked, so Jehoshaphat and Ahaziah were not able to send them to Tarshish.

ᵃ 20:12 **We are . . . help** Literally, "But our eyes are on you!"
ᵇ 20:26 **Beracah** This word means "blessing" or "praise".

21

Then Jehoshaphat died and was buried with his ancestors in the City of David. Then his son, Jehoram became the next king. ²Jehoram's brothers were Azariah, Jehiel, Zechariah, Azariah, Michael and Shephatiah. They were the sons of King Jehoshaphat of Judah.ᵃ ³Jehoshaphat gave his sons many gifts of silver, gold and precious things. He also gave them strong fortresses in Judah. But Jehoshaphat gave the kingdom to Jehoram because he was his oldest son.

Jehoram, King of Judah

⁴Jehoram took over his father's kingdom and made himself strong. Then he used a sword to kill all his brothers. He also killed some of the leaders of Israel. ⁵Jehoram was 32 years old when he began to rule. He ruled for eight years in Jerusalem. ⁶He lived the same way the kings of Israel lived. He lived the same way Ahab's family lived. This was because Jehoram married Ahab's daughter. And Jehoram did evil in the LORD's sight. ⁷But the LORD would not destroy David's family because of the agreement he made with David. He had promised to keep a lamp burning for David and his children forever.ᵇ

⁸In Jehoram's time, Edom broke away from under Judah's authority. The people of Edom chose their own king. ⁹So Jehoram went to Edom with all his commanders and chariots. The Edomite army surrounded Jehoram and his chariot commanders. But Jehoram fought his way out at night. ¹⁰Since that time and until now the country of Edom has been rebellious against Judah. The people from the town of Libnah also turned against Jehoram. This happened because Jehoram left the LORD God. He is the God Jehoram's ancestors followed. ¹¹Jehoram also built high places on the hills in Judah. He caused the people of Jerusalem to start worshipping other gods. He led the people of Judah away from their God.

¹²Jehoram received this message from Elijah the prophet:

"This is what the LORD, the God your father David followed, says, 'Jehoram, you have not lived the way your father Jehoshaphat lived. You have not lived the way King Asa of Judah lived. ¹³But you have lived the way the kings of Israel lived. You have caused the people of Judah and Jerusalem to stop doing what God wants. That is what Ahab and his family did. They were unfaithful to God.

You have killed your brothers, and they were better than you. ¹⁴So now, the LORD will soon punish your people with terrible suffering. He will punish your children, your wives and all your property. ¹⁵You will have a painful sickness in your intestines that will get worse and worse. Your intestines will finally come out.'"

¹⁶The LORD caused the Philistines and the Arabs living near the Ethiopians to be angry with Jehoram. ¹⁷They attacked Judah and carried away all the riches in the king's palace. They also took Jehoram's sons and wives. Only Jehoram's youngest son, Ahaziah,ᶜ was left.

¹⁸After this happened, the LORD made Jehoram sick with a disease in his intestines that could not be cured. ¹⁹His intestines fell out two years later because of his sickness. He died in terrible pain. The people did not make a large fire to honour Jehoram as they had done for his father. ²⁰Jehoram was 32 years old when he became king. He ruled for eight years in Jerusalem. No one was sad when he died. The people buried Jehoram in the City of David, but not in the graves where the kings are buried.

Ahaziah, King of Judah

22

The people of Jerusalem chose Ahaziah to be the new king in Jehoram's place. Ahaziah was Jehoram's youngest son. The people who came with the Arabs to attack Jehoram's camp killed all of Jehoram's older sons. So Ahaziah began to rule in Judah. ²He was 22 years old when he began to rule.ᵈ He ruled for one year in Jerusalem. His mother's name was Athaliah. Her father was Omri. ³Ahaziah also lived the way Ahab's family lived because his mother encouraged him to do wrong. ⁴Ahaziah did what the LORD considered to be evil. That is what Ahab's family did. And Ahab's family gave advice to Ahaziah after his father died. They gave Ahaziah bad advice that led to his death. ⁵⁻⁶Ahaziah followed the advice of Ahab's family and joined King Joram to fight against King Hazael from Aram. They fought near the town of Ramoth in Gilead. Joram, who was the son of King Ahab of Israel, was wounded in the battle. He went back to the town of Jezreel to heal from the wounds he suffered at Ramoth. King Ahaziahᵉ went there later to visit him.

⁷God caused Ahaziah's death when he went to visit Joram. Ahaziah arrived and went out with

---

ᵃ **21:2 Judah** Literally, "Israel".
ᵇ **21:7 He . . . forever** Here, the writer means that one of David's descendants would always rule.
ᶜ **21:17 Ahaziah** Literally, "Jehoahaz".
ᵈ **22:2 He was . . . rule** The standard Hebrew text has "42 years old". 2 Kgs 8:26 says Ahaziah was 22 years old when he began to rule.
ᵉ **22:6 Ahaziah** Literally, "Azariah".

Joram to meet Jehu son of Nimshi. The LORD chose Jehu to destroy Ahab's family. [8]Jehu was punishing Ahab's family. He found the leaders of Judah and Ahaziah's relatives who served Ahaziah. He killed the leaders of Judah and Ahaziah's relatives. [9]Then Jehu looked for Ahaziah. Jehu's men caught him when he tried to hide in the town of Samaria. They brought him to Jehu. They killed Ahaziah and buried him. They said, "Ahaziah is the descendant of Jehoshaphat. Jehoshaphat followed the LORD with all his heart." Ahaziah's family had no power to hold the kingdom of Judah together.

Queen Athaliah

[10]Athaliah was Ahaziah's mother. When she saw that her son was dead, she killed all the king's children in Judah. [11]But Jehosheba took Ahaziah's son Joash and hid him. Jehosheba put Joash and his nurse in the inside bedroom. Jehosheba was King Jehoram's daughter. She was also the wife of Jehoiada the priest, and sister of Ahaziah. Athaliah did not kill Joash, because Jehosheba had hidden him. [12]Joash was hidden with the priests in God's Temple for six years. During that time, Athaliah ruled over the land as queen.

Priest Jehoiada and King Joash

23 After six years, Jehoiada showed his strength and made an agreement with the captains. These captains were Azariah son of Jeroham, Ishmael son of Jehohanan, Azariah son of Obed, Maaseiah son of Adaiah and Elishaphat son of Zicri. [2]They went around and gathered the Levites from all the towns of Judah. They also gathered the leaders of the families of Israel. Then they went to Jerusalem. [3]All the people meeting together made an agreement with the king in God's Temple.

Jehoiada said to the people, "The king's son will rule. That is what the LORD promised about David's descendants. [4]Now, this is what you must do: One-third of you priests and Levites who go on duty on the Sabbath will guard the doors. [5]And one-third of you will be at the king's palace, and one-third of you will be at the Foundation Gate. But all the other people will stay in the courtyards of the LORD's Temple. [6]Only the priests and Levites who serve in the LORD's Temple are permitted to enter it. They are the only ones who have been made holy. Don't let anyone else enter. All the others must do only the work the LORD has given them. [7]The Levites must stay near the king. Every man must have his sword with him. If anyone tries to enter the Temple, kill that person. You must stay with the king everywhere he goes."

[8]The Levites and all the people of Judah obeyed all that Jehoiada the priest commanded. Jehoiada the priest did not excuse anyone from the groups of the priests. So each captain had all his men together. As the men in each group came off duty on the Sabbath, they stayed to join those who were coming on duty. [9]Jehoiada the priest gave the spears and the large and small shields that belonged to King David to the officers. The weapons were kept in God's Temple. [10]Then Jehoiada told the men where to stand. Every man had his weapon in his hand. The men stood all the way from the right side of the Temple to the left side of the Temple. They stood near the altar and the Temple and near the king. [11]They brought out the king's son and put the crown on him. They gave him a copy of the agreement. Then they made Joash king. Jehoiada and his sons anointed Joash and said, "Long live the king!"

[12]Athaliah heard the noise of the people running to the Temple and praising the king. She came into the LORD's Temple to the people. [13]She looked and saw the king standing by his column at the front entrance. The officers and the men who blew trumpets were near the king. The people of the land were happy and blowing trumpets. The singers were playing on musical instruments. They led the people in singing praises. Then Athaliah tore her clothes[a] and said, "Treason! Treason!"[b]

[14]Jehoiada the priest brought out the army captains. He said to them, "Take Athaliah outside among the army. Use your swords to kill anyone who follows her." Then the priest warned the soldiers, "Don't kill Athaliah in the LORD's Temple." [15]So those men grabbed Athaliah when she came to the entrance of the Horse Gate at the king's palace. Then they killed her there.

[16]Then Jehoiada made an agreement with all the people and the king. They all agreed that they would be the LORD's people. [17]All the people went into the temple of the idol Baal and tore it down. They also broke the altars and idols that were in Baal's temple. They killed Mattan the priest of Baal in front of the altars of Baal.

[18]Then Jehoiada put the Levite priests in charge of the LORD's Temple. David had given them the jobs they were supposed to do there. They were to offer the burnt offerings to the LORD, as the Law of Moses commanded. And they were to do this with great joy and singing, just as David had ordered. [19]Jehoiada put guards at the gates of the LORD's Temple to prevent any unclean person from entering the Temple.

[20]Jehoiada took the army captains, the leaders, the rulers of the people and all the people of the

---

[a] **23:13** *tore her clothes* A way to show that she was very upset.
[b] **23:13** *Treason* Turning against the government. Here, Athaliah was blaming the people for turning against her government.

land with him. Then Jehoiada took the king out of the LORD's Temple. They went through the Upper Gate to the king's palace and put the king on the throne. 21All the people of Judah were very happy, and the city of Jerusalem had peace because Athaliah had been killed with a sword.

Joash Rebuilds the Temple

24 Joash was seven years old when he became king. He ruled for 40 years in Jerusalem. His mother Zibiah was from the town of Beersheba. 2During the whole time Jehoiada the priest was living, Joash did what was pleasing to the LORD. 3Jehoiada chose two wives for Joash. Joash had sons and daughters.

4Then later on, Joash decided to rebuild the LORD's Temple. 5Joash called the priests and the Levites together. He said to them, "Go out to the towns of Judah and gather the money all the Israelites pay every year. Use that money to rebuild your God's Temple. Hurry and do this." But the Levites didn't hurry.

6So King Joash called Jehoiada the leading priest. The king said, "Jehoiada, why haven't you made the Levites bring in the tax money from Judah and Jerusalem? The LORD's servant Moses and the Israelites used that tax money for the Tent of the Agreement."

7In the past, Athaliah's sons had broken into God's Temple and used the holy things in the LORD's Temple for their worship of the Baal gods. Athaliah was a very wicked woman.

8King Joash gave a command for a box to be made and put outside the gate at the LORD's Temple. 9Then the Levites made an announcement in Judah and Jerusalem. They told the people to bring in the tax money for the LORD. That tax money is what Moses the servant of God had required the Israelites to give while they were in the desert. 10All the leaders and the people were happy. They brought their money and put it in the box. They continued giving until the box was full. 11Then the Levites would take the box to the king's officials. They saw that the box was full of money. The king's secretary and the leading priest's officer came and took the money out of the box. Then they took the box back to its place again. They did this often and gathered much money. 12Then King Joash and Jehoiada gave the money to the people who worked on the LORD's Temple. And the people who worked on the LORD's Temple hired skilled woodcarvers and carpenters to rebuild the LORD's Temple. They also hired workers who knew how to work with iron and bronze to rebuild the LORD's Temple.

13The men who supervised the work were very faithful, and the work they did went well. They rebuilt God's Temple the way it was before and made it strong. 14When the workers had finished, they brought the money that was left to King Joash and Jehoiada. They used that money to make things for the LORD's Temple. These things were used for the service in the Temple and for offering burnt offerings. They also made bowls and other things from gold and silver. The priests offered burnt offerings in the LORD's Temple every day while Jehoiada was alive.

15Jehoiada became old. He had a very long life, and he died when he was 130 years old. 16The people buried Jehoiada in the City of David where the kings are buried. The people buried Jehoiada there because in his life he had done much good in Israel for God and for God's Temple.

17After Jehoiada died, the leaders of Judah came and bowed to King Joash. The king listened to the leaders. 18They all stopped worshiping at the Temple of the LORD, the God their ancestors worshiped. Instead, they started worshiping Asherah poles and other idols. Because they sinned in this way, God was angry with the people of Judah and Jerusalem. 19God sent prophets to the people to bring them back to the LORD. The prophets warned them, but they refused to listen.

20The Spirit of God filled Zechariah the son of Jehoiada the priest, and he stood in front of the people and said, "This is what God says: 'Why do you people refuse to obey the LORD's commands? You will not be successful. You have left the LORD. So he has also left you!'"

21But the people made plans against Zechariah. The king commanded the people to kill Zechariah, so they threw rocks at him until he died. The people did this in the courtyard of the LORD's Temple. 22Joash the king didn't remember Jehoiada's kindness to him. Jehoiada was Zechariah's father. But Joash killed Zechariah, Jehoiada's son. Before Zechariah died, he said, "May the LORD see what you are doing and punish you!"

23At the end of the year, the Aramean army came against Joash. They attacked Judah and Jerusalem and killed all the leaders of the people. They sent all the valuable things to the king of Damascus. 24The Aramean army came with only a small group of men, but the LORD let them defeat the much larger army of Judah. This was a punishment for Joash because the people of Judah had left the LORD, the God their ancestors worshiped. 25When the Arameans left Joash, he was badly wounded. His own servants made plans against him because he had killed Zechariah the son of Jehoiada the priest. They killed Joash on his own bed. After he died, the people buried him in the City of David, but not in the place where the kings are buried. 26One of the servants who agreed to kill Joash was Zabad, son of

Shimeath, a woman from Ammon. The other was Jehozabad, son of Shimrith, a woman from Moab. ²⁷The story about Joash's sons, the great prophecies against him and how he rebuilt God's Temple are written in the book, *Commentary on the Kings.* Joash's son Amaziah became the new king after him.

Amaziah, King of Judah

25 Amaziah was 25 years old when he became king. He ruled for 29 years in Jerusalem. His mother's name was Jehoaddin. Jehoaddin was from Jerusalem. ²Amaziah did what the LORD wanted him to do, but not with all his heart. ³He became a strong king and killed the officials who had killed his father the king. ⁴But Amaziah obeyed the law written in the *Book of Moses* and did not kill the officials' children. The LORD commanded, "Parents must not be put to death for something their children did, and children must not be put to death for something their parents did. People should be put to death only for what they themselves did."ᵃ

⁵Amaziah gathered the people of Judah together. He grouped them by families and he put generals and captains in charge of these groups. The leaders were in charge of all the soldiers from Judah and Benjamin. All the men who were chosen to be soldiers were 20 years old and older. In all there were 300,000 skilled soldiers ready to fight with spears and shields. ⁶Amaziah also hired 100,000 soldiers from Israel. He paid 3,400 kilogrammesᵇ of silver to hire these soldiers. ⁷But a man of God came to Amaziah and said, "King, don't let the army of Israel go with you. The LORD is not with Israel or the people of Ephraim. ⁸Maybe you will make yourself strong and ready for war, but God can help you win or help you lose." ⁹Amaziah said to the man of God, "But what about the money I already paid to the Israelite army?" The man of God answered, "The LORD has plenty. He can give you much more than that."

¹⁰So Amaziah sent the Israelite army back home to Ephraim. These men were very angry with the king and the people of Judah. They went back home very angry.

¹¹Then Amaziah became very brave and led his army to the Salt Valley in the country of Edom. There his army killed 10,000 men from Seir.ᶜ ¹²They also captured 10,000 men from Seir and took them to the top of a cliff. Then the army of Judah threw them from the top of the cliff while they were still alive and their bodies were broken on the rocks below.

¹³Meanwhile, the Israelite army was attacking towns in Judah. They attacked the towns from Beth Horon all the way to Samaria. They killed 3,000 people and took many valuable things. They were angry because Amaziah didn't let them join him in the war.

¹⁴Amaziah came home after he defeated the Edomites. He brought the idols that the people of Seir worshipped. He started to worship those idols. He bowed down in front of them and burned incense to them. ¹⁵The LORD was very angry with Amaziah, so he sent a prophet to him. The prophet said, "Amaziah, why have you worshipped the gods those people worship? Those gods could not even save their own people from you!"

¹⁶When the prophet spoke, Amaziah said to the prophet, "We never made you an advisor to the king. Be quiet! If you don't be quiet, you will be killed." The prophet became quiet, but then said, "God has decided to destroy you because you did this and didn't listen to my advice."

¹⁷King Amaziah of Judah talked with his advisors. Then he sent a message to King Jehoash of Israel. Amaziah said to Jehoash, "Let's meet face to face." Jehoash was Jehoahaz's son. Jehoahaz was Jehu's son.

¹⁸Then Jehoash sent his answer to Amaziah. Jehoash was the king of Israel and Amaziah was the king of Judah. Jehoash told this story: "A little thornbush of Lebanon sent a message to a big cedar tree of Lebanon. The little thornbush said, 'Let your daughter marry my son.' But a wild animal came and walked over the thornbush and destroyed it. ¹⁹You say to yourself, 'I have defeated Edom!' You are proud and you boast. But you should stay at home. There is no need for you to get into trouble. If you fight me, you and Judah will be destroyed."

²⁰But Amaziah refused to listen. God made this happen. God planned to let Israel defeat Judah, because the people of Judah followed the gods the people of Edom followed. ²¹So King Jehoash of Israel met King Amaziah of Judah face to face at the town of Beth Shemesh in Judah. ²²Israel defeated Judah. Every man of Judah ran away to his home. ²³Jehoash captured Amaziah at Beth Shemesh and took him to Jerusalem. Amaziah was the son of Joash, and Joash was the son of Ahaziah. Jehoash tore down the wall of Jerusalem from the Ephraim Gate to the Corner Gate, a section about 200 metresᵈ long. ²⁴He took the gold and silver and all the other things in God's Temple that Obed Edom was responsible for. Jehoash also took the treasures from the king's

---

ᵃ **25:4** *Parents . . . did* See Deut. 24:16.
ᵇ **25:6** *3,400 kilogrammes* Literally, "100 *talents*".
ᶜ **25:11** *Seir* Or "Edom", a country east of Judah.
ᵈ **25:23** *200 metres* Literally, "400 *cubits*".

palace and some people as hostages. Then he went back to Samaria.

²⁵Amaziah lived for 15 years after Jehoash died. Amaziah's father was King Joash of Judah. ²⁶Everything else Amaziah did, from beginning to end, is written in the book, *The History of the Kings of Judah and Israel.* ²⁷When Amaziah stopped obeying the LORD, the people in Jerusalem made plans against Amaziah. He ran away to the town of Lachish. But the people sent men to Lachish and they killed Amaziah there. ²⁸Then they carried his body on horses and buried him with his ancestors in the City of Judah.

Uzziah, King of Judah

26 Then the people of Judah chose Uzziah to be the new king in place of Amaziah. Amaziah was Uzziah's father. Uzziah was 16 years old when he became king. ²Uzziah rebuilt the town of Elath and gave it back to Judah. He did this after Amaziah died and was buried with his ancestors.

³Uzziah was 16 years old when he became king. He ruled for 52 years in Jerusalem. His mother's name was Jecoliah. Jecoliah was from Jerusalem. ⁴Uzziah did what the LORD wanted him to do. He obeyed God the same as his father Amaziah had done. ⁵Uzziah followed God in the time of Zechariah's life. Zechariah taught Uzziah how to respect and obey God. When Uzziah was obeying the LORD, God gave him success.

⁶Uzziah fought a war against the Philistines. He tore down the walls around the towns of Gath, Jabneh and Ashdod. Uzziah built towns near the town of Ashdod and in other places among the Philistines. ⁷God helped Uzziah fight the Philistines, the Arabs living in the town of Gur Baal and the Meunites. ⁸The Ammonites paid tribute to Uzziah. His name became famous all the way to the border of Egypt. He was famous because he was very powerful.

⁹Uzziah built towers in Jerusalem at the Corner Gate, at the Valley Gate and at the place where the wall turned. He made them strong. ¹⁰He built towers in the desert. He also dug many wells. He had large herds of cattle in the hill country and in the flat lands. He loved farming. So he had workers who took care of his crops and vineyards in the hills and in the fertile valleys.

¹¹Uzziah had an army of trained soldiers. They were put in groups by Jeiel the secretary and Maaseiah the officer. Hananiah was their leader. Jeiel and Maaseiah counted the soldiers and put them into groups. Hananiah was one of the king's officers. ¹²There were 2,600 leaders over the soldiers. ¹³These family leaders were in charge of an army of 307,500 men who fought with great power. These soldiers helped the king against the enemy. ¹⁴Uzziah gave the army shields, spears, helmets, armour, bows and stones for the slings. ¹⁵In Jerusalem, Uzziah had skilled workers who invented weapons that could shoot arrows and throw large stones. He put these weapons on the towers and corners of the city walls. Uzziah became famous. People knew his name in faraway places. He had much help and became a powerful king.

¹⁶But when Uzziah became strong, his pride caused him to be destroyed. He was not faithful to the LORD his God. He went into the LORD's Temple to burn incense on the altar for incense. ¹⁷Azariah the priest and 80 brave priests who served the LORD followed Uzziah into the Temple. ¹⁸They told him to stop what he was doing. They said, "Uzziah, it is not your job to burn incense to the LORD. It is not right. That is only for the priests, Aaron's descendants, to do. They are the ones who have been prepared for the holy work of burning incense. You have done wrong, so you must go out of the Most Holy Place. The LORD God will not honour you for this."

¹⁹Uzziah was still standing beside the incense altar holding the pan for burning the incense. He became very angry at the priests and began shouting at them. Suddenly, there in the LORD's Temple as the priests watched, leprosy began to break out on Uzziah's forehead. ²⁰Azariah the leading priest and all the priests could see the leprosy on his forehead. They immediately forced him to leave the Temple. And Uzziah got out as fast as he could, because the LORD had punished him. ²¹So Uzziah the king was a leper. He could not enter the LORD's Temple. His son Jotham controlled the king's palace and became governor for the people.

²²Everything else Uzziah did, from beginning to end, is written by the prophet Isaiah son of Amoz. ²³Uzziah died and was buried near his ancestors in the field near the king's burial places. This was because the people said, "Uzziah has leprosy." And Uzziah's son Jotham became the new king in his place.

Jotham, King of Judah

27 Jotham was 25 years old when he became king. He ruled for 16 years in Jerusalem. His mother's name was Jerusha. Jerusha was Zadok's daughter. ²Jotham did what was pleasing to the LORD. He followed the example of his father Uzziah, except for one thing. He did not sin as his father had done by entering the LORD's Temple. But the people continued doing wrong. ³Jotham rebuilt the Upper Gate of the LORD's Temple. He did much building on the wall at the place named Ophel. ⁴He also built towns in the hill country of Judah. He built fortresses and towers in the forests. ⁵Jotham also fought against the king of

the Ammonites and his army and defeated them. So each year for three years the Ammonites gave Jotham 3,400 kilogrammes[a] of silver, 1,000 tonnes[b] of wheat and 1,000 tonnes of barley.

⁶Jotham became powerful because he faithfully obeyed the LORD his God. ⁷Everything else Jotham did and all his wars are written in the book, *The History of the Kings of Israel and Judah.* ⁸Jotham was 25 years old when he became king. He ruled for 16 years in Jerusalem. ⁹Then Jotham died and was buried with his ancestors. The people buried him in the City of David. Jotham's son Ahaz became king in his place.

INSIGHT

Ahaz was one of the worst kings of Judah. He didn't even start good and turn bad – he started bad and just got worse, worshipping false gods, sacrificing his own children and closing down the Temple. The Lord punished him (as he did other kings who didn't obey him) with troubles and defeat in battle.

2 Chronicles 28

Ahaz, King of Judah

28 Ahaz was 20 years old when he became king. He ruled for 16 years in Jerusalem. He did not do what is right, as David his ancestor had done. Ahaz did not do what the LORD wanted him to do. ²He followed the bad example of the kings of Israel. He used moulds to make idols to worship the Baal gods. ³He burned incense in the Valley of Ben Hinnom[c] and sacrificed his own sons by burning them in the fire. He did the same terrible sins that the people living in that land did. The LORD had forced them out when the Israelites entered that land. ⁴Ahaz offered sacrifices and burned incense in the high places, on the hills and under every green tree.

⁵⁻⁶Because Ahaz did these things, the LORD his God let the king of Aram defeat him. The king and his army defeated Ahaz and took many people of Judah as prisoners to the city of Damascus. Ahaz also suffered a terrible defeat by the king of Israel, Pekah son of Remaliah. Pekah and his army killed 120,000 of the bravest soldiers in Judah in one day. All this happened because the people of Judah

had turned away from the LORD, the God their ancestors worshipped. ⁷Zicri was a brave soldier from Ephraim. He killed the king's son Maaseiah. He also killed Azrikam, the officer in charge of the king's palace, and Elkanah, who was second in command to the king.

⁸The Israelite army captured 200,000 of their own relatives living in Judah. They took women, children and many valuable things from Judah and carried them back to Samaria. ⁹But one of the LORD's prophets named Oded was there. Oded met the Israelite army that came back to Samaria. He said to the Israelite army, "The LORD, the God your ancestors worshipped, let you defeat the people of Judah because he was angry with them. But now he is angry with you, because he has seen how cruel you were in killing them. ¹⁰And now you plan to keep the people of Judah and Jerusalem as slaves. But you are as guilty as they are for sinning against the LORD your God. ¹¹Now listen to me. Send back all those you captured, your own brothers and sisters, because the LORD's terrible anger is against you."

¹²Then some of the leaders in Ephraim saw the Israelite soldiers coming home from war. They met the Israelite soldiers and warned them. The leaders were Azariah son of Jehohanan, Berekiah son of Meshillemoth, Jehizkiah son of Shallum and Amasa son of Hadlai. ¹³They said to the Israelite soldiers, "Don't bring the prisoners from Judah here. If you do that, it will add to our sin against the LORD. It will make our sin and guilt before him even worse than it is now, and he is already very angry with Israel!"

¹⁴So the soldiers gave the prisoners and valuable things to the leaders and to the people. ¹⁵The leaders (Azariah, Berekiah, Jehizkiah and Amasa) stood up and helped the prisoners. These four men got the clothes that the Israelite army had taken and gave them to the people who were naked. The leaders also gave them sandals. They gave the prisoners from Judah something to eat and drink. They rubbed oil on them to soften and heal their wounds. Then the leaders from Ephraim put the weak prisoners on donkeys and took them back home to their families in Jericho, the city of palm trees. Then the four leaders went back home to Samaria.

¹⁶⁻¹⁷At that same time, the people from Edom came again and defeated the people of Judah. The Edomites captured people and took them away as prisoners. So King Ahaz asked the king of Assyria to help him. ¹⁸The Philistines also attacked the

---

[a] **27:5 3,400 kilogrammes** Literally, "100 *talents*".
[b] **27:5 1,000 tonnes** Literally, "10,000 *cors*".
[c] **28:3 Valley of Ben Hinnom** Later, called "Gehenna". This valley was west and south of Jerusalem. Many babies and young children were sacrificed to false gods in this valley.

towns in the hills and in south Judah. The Philistines captured the towns of Beth Shemesh, Aijalon, Gederoth, Soco, Timnah and Gimzo. They also captured the villages near these towns. Then the Philistines lived in them. ¹⁹The LORD gave troubles to Judah because King Ahaz of Judah encouraged the people of Judah to sin. He was very unfaithful to the LORD. ²⁰King Tiglath Pileser of Assyria came and gave Ahaz trouble instead of helping him. ²¹Ahaz took some valuable things from the LORD's Temple and from the king's palace and from the prince's house. Ahaz gave them to the king of Assyria, but that didn't help him.

²²Even with all these troubles, Ahaz became more and more unfaithful to the LORD. ²³He offered sacrifices to the gods that the people of Damascus worshipped. The people of Damascus had defeated Ahaz. So he thought to himself, "The gods the people of Aram worship helped them. So if I offer sacrifices to them, maybe they will help me also." Ahaz worshipped these gods. In this way he sinned, and he made the people of Israel sin.

²⁴Ahaz gathered the things from God's Temple and broke them to pieces. Then he closed the doors of the LORD's Temple. He made altars and put them on every street corner in Jerusalem. ²⁵In every town in Judah Ahaz made high places for burning incense to worship other gods. Ahaz made the LORD, the God his ancestors obeyed, very angry.

²⁶Everything else Ahaz did, from the beginning to the end, is written in the book, *The History of the Kings of Judah and Israel*. ²⁷Ahaz died and was buried with his ancestors. The people buried him in the city of Jerusalem. But they didn't bury him in the same burial place where the kings of Israel were buried. Ahaz's son Hezekiah became the new king in his place.

Hezekiah, King of Judah

29 Hezekiah became king when he was 25 years old. He ruled for 29 years in Jerusalem. His mother's name was Abijah. Abijah was Zechariah's daughter. ²Hezekiah did what the LORD wanted him to do. He did what was right just as David his ancestor had done.

³Hezekiah repaired the doors of the LORD's Temple and made them strong. He opened the Temple again. He did this in the first month of the first year after he became king. ^{4–5}Hezekiah called the priests and Levites together in one assembly. He had a meeting with them in the courtyard on the east side of the Temple. Hezekiah said to them, "Listen to me, Levites! Make yourselves ready for holy service. Make the Temple of the LORD God ready for holy service. He is the God your ancestors obeyed. Take away the things from the Temple that don't belong in there. These things make the Temple unclean. ⁶Our ancestors were not faithful and did what the LORD says is evil. They stopped following him. They no longer paid any attention to the LORD's house^a and turned their backs on him. ⁷They shut the doors of the porch of the Temple and let the fire go out in the lamps. They stopped burning incense and offering burnt offerings in the Holy Place to the God of Israel. ⁸So the LORD became very angry with the people of Judah and Jerusalem. He punished them so badly that it shocks and scares people to hear about it. But then they just laugh and shout their own insults against Judah. You know this is true. You have seen it happen. ⁹That is why our ancestors were killed in battle. Our sons, daughters and wives were made prisoners. ¹⁰So now I, Hezekiah, have decided to make an agreement with the LORD, the God of Israel. Then he will not be angry with us any more. ¹¹So my sons,^b don't be lazy or waste any more time. The LORD chose you to serve him ⌊in the Temple⌋ and to burn incense."

^{12–14}This is a list of the Levites who started to work:

From the Kohath family there were Mahath son of Amasai and Joel son of Azariah.
From the Merari family there were Kish son of Abdi and Azariah son of Jehallelel.
From the Gershon family there were Joah son of Zimmah and Eden son of Joab.
From Elizaphan's descendants there were Shimri and Jeiel.
From Asaph's descendants there were Zechariah and Mattaniah.
From Heman's descendants there were Jehiel and Shimei.
From Jeduthun's descendants there were Shemaiah and Uzziel.

¹⁵Then these Levites gathered their brothers together and made themselves ready for holy service in the Temple. They obeyed the king's command that came from the LORD. They went into the LORD's Temple to clean it. ¹⁶The priests went into the inside part of the LORD's Temple to clean it. They took out all the unclean things they found there. They brought the unclean things out to the courtyard of the LORD's Temple. Then the Levites took these things out to the Kidron Valley. ¹⁷On the first day of the first month, the Levites began to make the Temple ready for holy service.

---

^a 29:6 LORD's house Another name for the Temple in Jerusalem.
^b 29:11 *my sons* Here, Hezekiah is speaking to the priests like a father to his sons. They are not really his children.

By the eighth day, they had finished cleaning all the area up to the porch of the LORD's Temple. For eight more days they cleaned the LORD's Temple itself to make it ready for holy use. They finished on the sixteenth day of the first month.

18Then they went to King Hezekiah and said to him, "King Hezekiah, we cleaned all of the LORD's Temple and the altar for burning offerings and all the things in the Temple. We cleaned the table for the rows of bread with all the things used for that table. 19During the time that Ahaz was king, he rebelled against God. He threw away many of the things that were in the Temple. But we repaired all those things and made them ready for their special use. They are now in front of the LORD's altar."

20King Hezekiah gathered the city officials and went up to the Temple of the LORD early the next morning. 21They brought seven bulls, seven rams, seven lambs and seven young male goats. These animals were for a sin offering for the kingdom of Judah, for the Holy Place to make it clean, and for the people of Judah. King Hezekiah commanded the priests who were descendants of Aaron to offer these animals on the LORD's altar. 22So the priests killed the bulls and kept the blood. Then they sprinkled the bulls' blood on the altar. Then they killed the rams and sprinkled the rams' blood on the altar. Then they killed the lambs and sprinkled the lambs' blood on the altar. 23-24Then the priests brought the male goats in front of the king, and the people gathered together. The goats were the sin offering. The priests put their hands on the goats and killed the goats. They made a sin offering with the goats' blood on the altar. They did this so that God would forgive the sins of the Israelites. The king said that the burnt offering and the sin offering should be made for all the Israelites.

25King Hezekiah put the Levites in the LORD's Temple with cymbals, harps and lyres as David, Gad, the king's seer, and the prophet Nathan had commanded. This command came from the LORD through his prophets. 26So the Levites stood ready with David's instruments of music, and the priests stood ready with their trumpets. 27Then Hezekiah gave the order to sacrifice the burnt offering on the altar. When the burnt offering began, singing to the LORD also began. The trumpets were blown, and the instruments of David king of Israel were played. 28All the assembly bowed down, the musicians sang and the trumpet players blew their trumpets until the burnt offering was finished.

29After the sacrifices were finished, King Hezekiah and all the people with him bowed down and worshipped. 30King Hezekiah and his officials ordered the Levites to give praise to the LORD. They sang songs that David and Asaph the seer had written. They praised God and became happy. They all bowed and worshipped God. 31Hezekiah said, "Now you people of Judah have given yourselves to the LORD. Come near and bring sacrifices and thank offerings to the LORD's Temple." So the people brought sacrifices and thank offerings and those who wanted to offer more also brought burnt offerings. 32This is how many burnt offerings the assembly brought to the Temple: 70 bulls, 100 rams and 200 lambs. All these animals were sacrificed as burnt offerings to the LORD. 33There were also 600 bulls and 3,000 sheep and goats that were sacrificed as holy offerings. 34But there were not enough priests to skin and cut up all the animals for the burnt offerings. So their relatives, the Levites, helped them until the work was finished and until other priests could make themselves ready for holy service. The Levites had been more serious than the priests about making themselves ready to serve. 35There were many burnt offerings, and the fat of fellowship offerings, and drink offerings. So the service in the LORD's Temple began again. 36Hezekiah and the people were very happy about the things God had prepared for his people. And they were happy he had done it so quickly!

Hezekiah Celebrates Passover

30 King Hezekiah sent messages to all the people of Israel and Judah. He wrote letters to the people of Ephraim and Manassehª also. He invited all these people to come to the LORD's Temple in Jerusalem so that they all could celebrate Passover for the LORD, the God of Israel. 2King Hezekiah agreed with all his officials and all the assembly in Jerusalem to have Passover in the second month. 3They could not celebrate the Passover festival at the regular time, because not enough priests had made themselves ready for holy service and the people had not gathered in Jerusalem. 4The agreement satisfied King Hezekiah and all the assembly. 5So they sent the announcement throughout Israel, from the town of Beersheba all the way to the town of Dan. They told the people to come to Jerusalem to celebrate Passover for the LORD, the God of Israel. Not many people had been celebrating it as it was described in the law. 6So the messengers took the king's letters throughout Israel and Judah. This is what the letters said:

"Children of Israel, turn back to the LORD, the God who Abraham, Isaac and Israel

---

ª 30:1 Ephraim and Manasseh Joseph's sons. Since these were the largest tribes, Ephraim and Manasseh sometimes means the whole northern kingdom of Israel.

obeyed. Then God will come back to you who are still alive and have escaped from the kings of Assyria. [7]Don't be like your fathers or your brothers. The LORD was their God, but they turned against him. So he made people hate them and speak evil about them. You can see with your own eyes that this is true. [8]Don't be stubborn as your ancestors were. But obey the LORD with a willing heart. Come to the Temple that he has made to be holy forever. Serve the LORD your God. Then his fearful anger will turn away from you. [9]If you come back and obey the LORD, your relatives and your children will find mercy from the people who captured them. And your relatives and your children will come back to this land. The LORD your God is kind and merciful. He will not turn away from you if you come back to him."

[10]The messengers went to every town in the area of Ephraim and Manasseh. They went all the way to the area of Zebulun, but the people laughed at the messengers and made fun of them. [11]But, some men from the areas of Asher, Manasseh and Zebulun humbled themselves and went to Jerusalem. [12]Also, in Judah God's power united the people so that they would obey the king and his officials concerning the word of the LORD.

[13]Many people came together in Jerusalem to celebrate the Festival of Unleavened Bread in the second month. It was a very large crowd. [14]The people took away the altars in Jerusalem that were for false gods and all the incense altars that were for false gods. They threw them into the Kidron Valley. [15]Then they killed the Passover lamb on the fourteenth day of the second month. The priests and the Levites felt ashamed. They made themselves ready for holy service. The priests and the Levites brought burnt offerings into the LORD's Temple. [16]They took their regular places in the Temple as described in the Law of Moses, the man of God. The Levites gave the blood to the priests. Then the priests sprinkled the blood on the altar. [17]There were many people in the group who had not made themselves ready for holy service, so they were not permitted to kill the Passover lambs. That is why the Levites were responsible for killing the Passover lambs for everyone who was not clean. The Levites made each lamb holy for the LORD. [18-19]Many people from Ephraim, Manasseh, Issachar and Zebulun had not prepared themselves in the right way for the Passover festival.

They did not celebrate Passover the right way, as the Law of Moses says. But Hezekiah prayed for the people. So he said this prayer, "LORD God, you are good. These people sincerely wanted to worship you in the right way, but they did not make themselves clean as the law says. Please forgive these people. You are the LORD, the God our ancestors worshipped. Forgive them, even if some did not make themselves clean as the rules of the Most Holy Place say." [20]The LORD listened to King Hezekiah's prayer and forgave the people. [21]The people of Israel in Jerusalem celebrated the Festival of Unleavened Bread with great joy for seven days. And the Levites and priests praised the LORD every day with all their strength.[a] [22]King Hezekiah encouraged all the Levites who understood very well how to do the service of the LORD. The people celebrated the festival for seven days and offered fellowship offerings. They gave thanks and praise to the LORD, the God of their ancestors.

[23]All the people agreed to stay seven more days. They were joyful as they celebrated the festival for seven more days. [24]King Hezekiah of Judah gave 1,000 bulls and 7,000 sheep to the assembly to kill and eat. The leaders gave 1,000 bulls and 10,000 sheep to the assembly. Many priests prepared themselves for holy service. [25]All the assembly of Judah, the priests, the Levites, all the assembly who came from Israel and the travellers who came from Israel and moved to Judah—all these people were very happy. [26]So there was much joy in Jerusalem. There had not been a celebration like this since the time of Solomon son of King David of Israel. [27]The priests and the Levites stood up and asked God to bless the people, and he heard them. Their prayer came up to heaven, the holy place where he lives.

King Hezekiah Makes Improvements

31 When the Passover celebration had finished, the Israelites who were in Jerusalem for Passover went out to the towns of Judah. Then they smashed the stone idols that were in the towns. These stone idols were used to worship false gods. They also cut down the Asherah poles. And they destroyed the high places and the altars all through the areas of Judah and Benjamin. They did the same things in the area of Ephraim and Manasseh. They did these things until they destroyed all the things used for worshipping the false gods. Then all the Israelites went back home to their own towns.

[2]The priests and Levites had been divided into groups, and each group had its own special job to

---

[a] **30:21 with all their strength** Or "with mighty instruments of the LORD".

do. So King Hezekiah told these groups to begin doing their jobs again. So the priests and Levites again had the job of offering the burnt offerings and the fellowship offerings. And they had the job of serving in the Temple and singing and praising God by the doors to the LORD's house.[a] [3]Hezekiah gave some of his own animals to be offered as the burnt offerings. These animals were used for the daily burnt offerings that were given each morning and each evening. They were offered on the Sabbath days, during New Moon celebrations and on the other special meeting days, as the Law of the LORD commands.

[4]The people were supposed to give a part of everything they owned to the priests and Levites. So Hezekiah commanded the people living in Jerusalem to give them their share. In that way the priests and Levites could spend all their time doing what the Law of the LORD told them to do. [5]People all around the country heard about this command. So the Israelites gave the first part of their harvest of grain, grapes, oil, honey and all the things they grew in their fields. They brought one-tenth of all these many things. [6]The men of Israel and Judah living in the towns of Judah also brought one-tenth of their cattle and sheep. They also brought one-tenth of the things that were put in a special place that was only for the LORD their God. They brought all these things and put them in piles.

[7]The people began to bring these things in the third month and they finished bringing the collection in the seventh month. [8]When Hezekiah and the leaders came, they saw the piles of things that had been collected. They praised the LORD and his people, the Israelites.

[9]Then Hezekiah asked the priests and the Levites about the piles of things. [10]Azariah the high priest from Zadok's family said to Hezekiah, "From the time that the people started bringing the offerings into the LORD's house, we have had plenty to eat. We have eaten until we are full and there is still plenty left over! The LORD has really blessed his people. That is why we have so much left over."

[11]Then Hezekiah commanded the priests to make storerooms ready in the LORD's Temple. So this was done. [12]Then the priests brought the offerings, tithes[b] and other things that were to be given only to God. All these things were put in the storerooms in the Temple. Conaniah the Levite was in charge of everything that was collected. Shimei was second in charge of these things. Shimei was Conaniah's brother. [13]Conaniah and his brother Shimei were supervisors of these

men: Jehiel, Azaziah, Nahath, Asahel, Jerimoth, Jozabad, Eliel, Ismakiah, Mahath and Benaiah. King Hezekiah and Azariah the official in charge of God's Temple chose these men.

[14]Kore was in charge of the offerings that the people freely gave to God. He was responsible for giving out the collections that were given to the LORD. And he was responsible for giving out the gifts that had been made holy. Kore was the gatekeeper at the East Gate. His father's name was Imnah the Levite. [15]Eden, Miniamin, Jeshua, Shemaiah, Amariah and Shecaniah helped Kore. These men served faithfully in the towns where the priests were living. They divided the gifts among their fellow priests in each of the different groups. They gave the same amount to young and old alike.

[16]These men also gave the collection of things to the males three years old and older who had their names in the Levite family histories. All these males were to enter the LORD's Temple for daily service to do the things they were responsible to do. Each group of Levites had their own responsibility. [17]The priests were given their part of the collection. This was done by families, in the way they were listed in the family histories. The Levites who were 20 years old and older were given their part of the collection, according to their groups and responsibilities. [18]The Levites' babies, wives, sons and daughters also got part of the collection. This was done for all the Levites who were listed in the family histories. This was because the Levites faithfully kept themselves holy and ready for service.

[19]Some of Aaron's descendants, the priests, lived in the towns or on farms near the towns where the Levites were living. Men were chosen by name in each of these towns to give part of the collection to these descendants of Aaron. All the males and those named in the family histories of the Levites got part of the collection.

[20]So King Hezekiah did those good things throughout Judah. He did what was good and right and faithful before the LORD his God. [21]He had success in every work he began—the service of God's Temple and in obeying the law and commands, and in following his God. Hezekiah did all these things with all his heart.

The King of Assyria Attacks Judah

32 After Hezekiah had faithfully done everything the LORD commanded, King Sennacherib of Assyria came to attack the country of Judah. Sennacherib and his army camped outside the fortresses. He did this so that he could make

---

[a] **31:2 LORD's house** Or "LORD's Camp", that is, the courtyard of the Temple in Jerusalem.
[b] **31:12 tithes** One-tenth of a person's crops or animals.

plans to defeat these towns. Sennacherib wanted to win them for himself. ²Hezekiah knew that Sennacherib had come to Jerusalem to attack it. ³Then Hezekiah talked to his officials and army officers. They all agreed to stop the waters of the water springs outside the city. The officials and army officers helped Hezekiah. ⁴Many people came together and stopped all the springs and the stream that flowed through the middle of the country. They said, "The king of Assyria will not find much water when he comes here!" ⁵Hezekiah made Jerusalem stronger. This is how he did it: He rebuilt all the parts of the wall that were broken down. He also built towers on the wall. He also built another wall outside the first wall. He rebuilt the strong places on the east side of the old part of Jerusalem. He made many weapons and shields. ⁶⁻⁷Hezekiah chose officers of war to be in charge of the people. He met with these officers at the open place near the city gate. He talked to the officers and encouraged them. He said, "Be strong and brave. Don't be afraid or worry about the king of Assyria or the large army with him. There is a greater power with us than the king of Assyria has with him! ⁸The king of Assyria only has men. But we have the LORD our God with us! Our God will help us. He will fight our battles!" So King Hezekiah of Judah encouraged the people and made them feel stronger.

⁹King Sennacherib of Assyria and all his army were camped near the town of Lachish so that they could defeat it. Then Sennacherib sent his officers to King Hezekiah of Judah and to all the people of Judah in Jerusalem. His officers had a message for Hezekiah and all the people in Jerusalem:

¹⁰"This is what King Sennacherib of Assyria says: 'What do you trust in that makes you stay under attack in Jerusalem? ¹¹Hezekiah is fooling you. You are being tricked into staying in Jerusalem so that you will die from hunger and thirst. Hezekiah says to you, "The LORD our God will save us from the king of Assyria." ¹²But Hezekiah himself took away the high places and altars that belonged to that god. He told you people of Judah and Jerusalem that you must worship and burn incense on only one altar. ¹³Of course, you know what my ancestors and I have done to all the peoples in other countries. The gods of the other countries could not save their people. Those gods could not stop me from destroying their people. ¹⁴My ancestors destroyed those countries. There is no god

that can stop me from destroying his people. So you think your god can save you from me? ¹⁵Don't let Hezekiah fool you or trick you. Don't believe him because no god of any nation or kingdom has ever been able to keep his people safe from me or my ancestors. Don't think your god can stop me from destroying you.'"

¹⁶The officers of the king of Assyria said worse things against the LORD God and against Hezekiah, God's servant. ¹⁷The king of Assyria also wrote letters that insulted the LORD, the God of Israel. This is what the king of Assyria said in those letters: "The gods of the other nations could not stop me from destroying their people. In the same way, Hezekiah's god will not be able to stop me from destroying his people." ¹⁸Then the Assyrian officers shouted loudly to the people of Jerusalem who were on the city wall. They spoke in the language of Judah so that the people on the wall would understand and be frightened enough that the Assyrians could capture the city of Jerusalem. ¹⁹Then they insulted the God of Jerusalem just as they had insulted all the gods of the people from other nations—even though those gods are only things people made with their hands.

²⁰Hezekiah the king and the prophet Isaiah son of Amoz prayed about this problem. They prayed very loudly to heaven. ²¹Then the LORD sent an angel to the king of Assyria's camp. That angel killed all the soldiers, leaders and officers in the Assyrian army. So the king of Assyria went back home to his own country, and his people were ashamed of him. He went into the temple of his god and some of his own sons killed him there with a sword. ²²So the LORD saved Hezekiah and the people in Jerusalem from King Sennacherib of Assyria and from all other people. He cared for Hezekiah and the people of Jerusalem. ²³Many people brought gifts for the LORD to Jerusalem. They brought valuable things to King Hezekiah of Judah. From that time on, all the nations respected Hezekiah.

²⁴It was in those days that Hezekiah became very sick and near death. He prayed to the LORD, who spoke to Hezekiah and gave him a sign.ᵃ ²⁵But Hezekiah's heart was proud, so he did not give God thanks for his kindness. This is why God was angry with Hezekiah and with the people of Judah and Jerusalem. ²⁶But Hezekiah and the people living in Jerusalem changed their hearts and lives. They became humble and stopped being proud. So the LORD's anger didn't come on them while Hezekiah was alive.

²⁷Hezekiah had many riches and much honour. He made places to keep silver, gold, valuable

---

ᵃ 32:24 he spoke . . . sign See Isa. 38:1–8 for the story about Hezekiah and how the LORD gave him 15 more years to live.

jewels, spices, shields and all kinds of things. [28]Hezekiah had storage buildings for the grain, new wine and oil that people sent to him. He had stalls for all the cattle and pens for the sheep. [29]Hezekiah also built many towns, and he had many flocks of sheep and cattle. God gave him much wealth. [30]It was Hezekiah who stopped up the upper source of the waters of the Gihon Spring in Jerusalem and made the waters flow straight down on the west side of the City of David. And he was successful in everything he did.

[31]One day the leaders of Babylon sent messengers to Hezekiah. The messengers asked him about a strange sign that had happened in the nations.[a] When they came, God left Hezekiah alone to test him and to know everything that was in Hezekiah's heart.[b]

[32]Everything else Hezekiah did as king and the ways he served God faithfully are written in the book, *The Vision of the Prophet Isaiah Son of Amoz* and in the book, *The History of the Kings of Judah and Israel*. [33]Hezekiah died and was buried with his ancestors. The people buried him on the hill where the graves of David's ancestors are. All the people of Judah and those living in Jerusalem gave honour to Hezekiah when he died. Hezekiah's son Manasseh became the new king in his place.

INSIGHT

Manasseh, King of Judah

33 Manasseh was twelve years old when he became king of Judah. He was king for 55 years in Jerusalem. [2]Manasseh did what the LORD said was wrong. He followed the terrible and sinful ways of the nations that the LORD had forced out of the land before the Israelites. [3]Manasseh rebuilt the high places that his father Hezekiah had broken down. Manasseh built altars for the Baal gods and made Asherah poles. He bowed down to the constellations[c] and worshipped those groups of stars. [4]Manasseh built altars for false gods in the LORD's Temple. The LORD said about the Temple, "My name will be in Jerusalem forever." [5]He built altars for all the groups of stars in the two courtyards of the LORD's Temple. [6]He also burned his own children for a sacrifice in the Valley of Ben Hinnom.[d] He also made use of those who try to tell the future, people who reveal hidden knowledge, and those who control evil spirits. He even tried to contact ghosts and spirits of the dead for advice and secret knowledge. He made the LORD angry by doing many things the LORD saw as evil. [7]Manasseh also made a statue of an idol and put it in God's Temple—the very same Temple that God had talked about to David and his son Solomon. God had said, "I will put my name in this house and in Jerusalem—the city that I chose from all the cities in all the tribes—and my name will be there forever! [8]I will not continue to keep the Israelites off the land that I chose to give to their ancestors. But they must obey everything I commanded them. The Israelites must obey all the laws, rules and commands that I gave Moses to give to them."

[9]Manasseh encouraged the people of Judah and the people living in Jerusalem to do wrong. They were worse than the nations that were in the land before the Israelites—and the LORD destroyed those people.

[10]The LORD spoke to Manasseh and to his people, but they refused to listen. [11]So the LORD brought commanders from the king of Assyria's army to attack Judah. These commanders captured Manasseh and made him their prisoner. They put hooks in him and brass chains on his hands and took him to the country of Babylon.

[12]When these troubles came to him, Manasseh begged for help from the LORD his God. He humbled himself before the God of his ancestors. [13]Manasseh prayed to God and begged him for help. God heard his begging and felt sorry for him, so he let Manasseh return to Jerusalem and to his throne. Then Manasseh knew that the LORD was the true God.

[14]After that happened, Manasseh built an outer wall for the City of David. This wall went to the west of Gihon Spring in Kidron Valley, to the entrance of the Fish Gate and around the hill of Ophel.[e] He made the wall very tall. Then he put

---

[a] **32:31** *a strange sign . . . nations* See Isa. 38:1–8.
[b] **32:31** *in Hezekiah's heart* See 2 Kgs 20:12–19.
[c] **33:3** *constellations* Groups of stars. These are probably the twelve "signs of the Zodiac". Some people thought the stars, not God, controlled their life.
[d] **33:6** *Valley of Ben Hinnom* Later, called "Gehenna". This valley was west and south of Jerusalem. Many babies and young children were sacrificed to false gods in this valley.
[e] **33:14** *Ophel* The upper part of the City of David, just south of the Temple area.

officers in all the fortresses in Judah. [15]Manasseh took away the strange idol gods, and he took the idol out of the LORD's Temple. He took away all the altars he had built on the Temple hill and in Jerusalem. Manasseh threw all the altars out of the city of Jerusalem. [16]Then he set up the LORD's altar and offered fellowship offerings and thank offerings on it. He gave a command for all the people of Judah to serve the LORD, the God of Israel. [17]The people continued to offer sacrifices at the high places, but their sacrifices were only to the LORD their God.

[18]Everything else Manasseh did, his prayer to his God and the words of the seers who spoke to him in the name of the LORD, the God of Israel, are all written in the book, *The Official Records of the Kings of Israel*. [19]Manasseh's prayer and how God listened and felt sorry for him are written in *The Book of the Seers*. Also all his sins, the wrongs he did before he humbled himself, and the places where he built high places and set up the Asherah poles are written in *The Book of the Seers*. [20]So Manasseh died and was buried with his ancestors. The people buried Manasseh in his own palace. Manasseh's son Amon became the new king in his place.

Amon, King of Judah

[21]Amon was 22 years old when he became king of Judah. He was king for two years in Jerusalem. [22]Amon did evil before the LORD, just as his father Manasseh had done. Amon offered sacrifices to all the carved idols and statues that Manasseh his father had made. Amon worshipped those idols. [23]Amon did not humble himself in front of the LORD like Manasseh his father humbled himself. But Amon sinned more and more. [24]His own servants made plans to kill him. And they killed Amon in his own house. [25]But the people of Judah killed all those servants who had murdered King Amon. Then they chose Amon's son Josiah to be the new king.

Josiah, King of Judah

34 Josiah was eight years old when he became king. He was king for 31 years in Jerusalem. [2]He lived in a way that pleased the LORD, always doing what was right, as his ancestor David had done. Josiah never changed this way of life. [3]When Josiah was in his eighth year as king, he began to follow the God worshipped by David his ancestor. He was still young when he began to obey God. When he was in his twelfth year as king he began to destroy the high places in Judah and Jerusalem, the Asherah poles, the carved idols and those that had been made from moulds. [4]As Josiah watched, the people broke down the altars for the Baal gods. Then he cut down the incense altars that stood high above the people. He broke the idols that were carved and the idols that were made from moulds. He beat the idols into powder and sprinkled the powder on the graves of the people who had offered sacrifices to the Baal gods. [5]Josiah even burned the bones of the priests who had served the Baal gods on their own altars. This is how he destroyed idols and idol worship from Judah and Jerusalem. [6]Josiah did the same for the towns in the areas of Manasseh, Ephraim, Simeon and all the way to Naphtali. He did the same for the ruins near all these towns.*a* [7]Josiah broke down the altars and the Asherah poles. He beat the idols into powder. He cut down all the incense altars used for Baal worship in all the country of Israel. Then he went back to Jerusalem.

[8]When Josiah was in his eighteenth year as king of Judah, he sent Shaphan, Maaseiah and Joah to rebuild and repair the Temple of the LORD his God. Shaphan was the son of Azaliah. Maaseiah was the city leader. Joah, who was the son of Joahaz, wrote about what happened.

So Josiah commanded that the Temple be repaired so that he could make Judah and the Temple clean. [9]These men came to Hilkiah the high priest. They gave him the money that people gave for God's Temple. The Levite doorkeepers had collected this money from the people of Manasseh, Ephraim and from all the Israelites who were left. They also collected this money from all Judah, Benjamin and all the people living in Jerusalem. [10]Then the Levites paid the men who supervised the work on the LORD's Temple. And the supervisors paid the workers who repaired the LORD's Temple. [11]They gave the money to carpenters and builders to buy large rocks that were already cut, and to buy wood. The wood was used to rebuild the buildings and to make beams for the buildings. In the past, the kings of Judah did not take care of the Temple buildings. The buildings had become old and ruined. [12-13]The men worked faithfully. Their supervisors were Jahath and Obadiah. Jahath and Obadiah were Levites, and they were descendants of Merari. Other supervisors were Zechariah and Meshullam. They were descendants of Kohath. The Levites who were skilled in playing musical instruments also supervised the labourers and all the other workers. Some Levites worked as secretaries, officials and doorkeepers.

The Book of the Law Found

[14]The Levites brought out the money that was in the LORD's Temple. At that time Hilkiah the

---

a **34:6** *ruins near all these towns* The Hebrew text is not clear.

priest found the *Book of the Law of the LORD* that was given through Moses. ¹⁵Hilkiah said to Shaphan the secretary, "I found the *Book of the Law* in the LORD's house."ᵃ Hilkiah gave the book to Shaphan. ¹⁶Shaphan brought the book to King Josiah. Shaphan reported to the king, "Your servants are doing everything you told them to do. ¹⁷They got the money that was in the LORD's Temple and are paying the supervisors and the workers." ¹⁸Then Shaphan said to King Josiah, "Hilkiah the priest gave a book to me." Then Shaphan read from the book in front of the king. ¹⁹When King Josiah heard the words of the law being read, he tore his clothes.ᵇ ²⁰Then the king gave a command to Hilkiah, Ahikam son of Shaphan, Abdon son of Micah, Shaphan the secretary and Asaiah the servant. ²¹The king said, "Go, ask the LORD for me and for the people who are left in Israel and in Judah. Ask about the words in the book that was found. The LORD is very angry with us because our ancestors did not obey the LORD's word. They did not do everything this book says to do."

²²Hilkiah and the king's servantsᶜ went to the newer part of Jerusalem to see Huldah the prophetess. She was the wife of Shallum, the son of Tokhath, whose father was Hasrah. Shallum had the job of taking care of the king's clothes. Hilkiah and the king's servants told Huldah what had happened. ²³Huldah said to them, "This is what the LORD, the God of Israel, says: Tell King Josiah that ²⁴the LORD says, 'I will bring trouble to this place and to the people living here. I will bring all the terrible things that are written in the book that was read in front of the king of Judah. ²⁵I will do this because the people left me and burned incense to other gods. They made me angry because of all the bad things they have done. So I will pour out my anger on this place. Like a hot burning fire, my anger will not be put out!'

²⁶"Go back to King Josiah of Judah, who sent you to ask what the LORD wants. Tell him, 'This is what the LORD, the God of Israel, says about the words you heard being read: ²⁷Josiah, when you heard my words against this city and its people, you were sorry and humbled yourself before me. You even tore your clothes to show your sorrow and cried before me. Because your heart was tender, I the LORD, have heard you.

²⁸"'So I will take you to be with your ancestors. You will go to your grave in peace. You will not have to see any of the trouble that I will bring on this place and on the people living here.'" This

was the message that Hilkiah and the king's servants brought back to King Josiah.

²⁹Then King Josiah called for all the leaders of Judah and Jerusalem to come and meet with him. ³⁰The king went up to the LORD's Temple. All the people from Judah, the people living in Jerusalem, the priests, the Levites and all the people, both important and not important, were with Josiah. He read to them all the words in the *Book of the Agreement.* That book was found in the LORD's Temple. ³¹Then the king stood up in his place. He made an agreement with the LORD. He agreed to follow the LORD and to obey his commands, laws and rules. He agreed to obey with all his heart and soul the words of the agreement written in this book. ³²Then Josiah made all the people in Jerusalem and Benjamin promise to accept the agreement. The people of Jerusalem obeyed the agreement of God, the God their ancestors obeyed. ³³In all the areas that belonged to the Israelites, Josiah removed the awful idols they had worshiped. He led all the people in Israel to serve the LORD their God. And for as long as Josiah lived, the people continued to serve the LORD, the God of their ancestors.

Josiah Celebrates Passover

35 King Josiah celebrated the Passover festival to the LORD in Jerusalem. The Passover lamb was killed on the fourteenth day of the first month. ²Josiah chose the priests to do their duties. He encouraged the priests while they were serving in the LORD's Temple. ³He spoke to the Levites who taught the Israelites and who were made holy for service to the LORD. He said to the Levites, "Put the Holy Box in the Temple that Solomon built. Solomon was David's son. David was king of Israel. Don't carry the Holy Box from place to place on your shoulders again. Now serve the LORD your God and his people, the Israelites. ⁴Make yourselves ready for service in the Temple by your tribes. Do the jobs that King David and his son King Solomon gave you to do. ⁵All the people who come to the Temple will need directions from the Levites who serve their own family group. So take your places all around the Holy Place so that you can help those families you are responsible for. ⁶Kill the Passover lambs and make yourselves holy to the Lord. Get ready to help your fellow Israelites. Do everything the LORD commanded us in the laws he gave to Moses."

⁷Josiah gave the Israelites 30,000 sheep and goats to kill for the Passover sacrifices. He also gave 3,000 cattle to the people. All these animals

---

ᵃ **34:15** *the LORD's house* Another name for the Temple in Jerusalem.
ᵇ **34:19** *tore his clothes* A way of showing that a person was upset. Josiah was upset because his people had not obeyed the Lord's laws. Also in verse 27.
ᶜ **34:22** *the king's servants* Literally, "those . . . of the king".

were from King Josiah's own animals. ⁸Josiah's officials also freely gave animals to the people, to the priests and Levites to use for Passover. Hilkiah the high priest, Zechariah and Jehiel were the officials in charge of the Temple. They gave the priests 2,600 lambs and goats and 300 bulls for Passover sacrifices. ⁹Also Conaniah with Shemaiah and Nethanel, his brothers, and Hashabiah, Jeiel and Jozabad gave 500 sheep and goats and 500 bulls for Passover sacrifices to the Levites. These men were leaders of the Levites.

¹⁰When everything was ready for the Passover service to begin, the priests and Levites went to their places. This is what the king commanded. ¹¹The Passover lambs were killed. Then the Levites skinned the animals and gave the blood to the priests. The priests sprinkled the blood on the altar. ¹²Then they gave the animals to be used for burnt offerings to the different tribes. This was done so that the burnt offerings could be offered to the LORD the way the Law of Moses taught. And they did the same with the bulls. ¹³The Levites roasted the Passover sacrifices over the fire in the way they were commanded. And they boiled the holy offerings in pots, kettles and pans. Then they quickly gave the meat to the people. ¹⁴After this was finished, the Levites got meat for themselves and for the priests who were descendants of Aaron. These priests were kept very busy, working until it got dark. They worked hard burning the burnt offerings and the fat of the sacrifices. ¹⁵The Levite singers were descendants of Asaph. They took their places, following their instructions from King David, Asaph, Heman and Jeduthun the king's prophet. The gatekeepers at each gate did not have to leave their places because their brother Levites made everything ready for them for Passover.

¹⁶So everything was done that day for the worship of the LORD as King Josiah commanded. Passover was celebrated and the burnt offerings were offered on the LORD's altar. ¹⁷The Israelites who were there celebrated Passover and the Festival of Unleavened Bread for seven days. ¹⁸Passover hadn't been celebrated like this since the time of Samuel the prophet! None of the kings of Israel had ever celebrated a Passover like this. King Josiah, the priests, the Levites and the people of Judah and Israel who were there with all the people in Jerusalem celebrated Passover in a very special way. ¹⁹They celebrated this Passover in Josiah's eighteenth year as king.

The Death of Josiah

²⁰Josiah did all these good things for the Temple. Later, King Neco of Egypt led an army to fight against the town of Carchemish on the Euphrates River. King Josiah went out to fight against Neco. ²¹But Neco sent messengers to Josiah. They said,

"King Josiah, this war is not your problem. I didn't come to fight against you. I came to fight my enemies. God told me to hurry. He is on my side, so don't bother me. If you fight against me, God will destroy you!"

INSIGHT

The plain of Megiddo must be one of the bloodiest battlegrounds in the world. Archaeologists have uncovered twenty cities one on top of the other that have been destroyed at this site.

2 Chronicles 35:22

---

²²But Josiah did not go away. He put on different clothes to hide who he was and went to fight the battle. Josiah refused to listen to the warning Neco had received from God and went to fight on the plain of Megiddo. ²³Then King Josiah was shot by arrows while he was in battle. He told his servants, "Take me away, I am wounded badly!"

²⁴So the servants took Josiah out of his chariot and put him in another chariot he had brought with him to the battle. Then they took Josiah to Jerusalem. He died there and was buried in the tombs where his ancestors were buried. All the people of Judah and Jerusalem were very sad because Josiah was dead. ²⁵Jeremiah wrote and sang some funeral songs for Josiah. And the men and women singers still sing these sad songs today. It became something the people of Israel always do—they sing a sad song for Josiah. These songs are written in the book, *Funeral Songs.*

²⁶⁻²⁷Everything else Josiah did while he was king, from the beginning to the end of his rule, is written in the book, *The History of the Kings of Israel and Judah.* The book tells about the way he served God faithfully by obeying the Law of the LORD.

Jehoahaz, King of Judah

36 The people of Judah chose Jehoahaz to be the new king in Jerusalem. Jehoahaz was Josiah's son. ²He was 23 years old when he became king of Judah. He was king in Jerusalem for three months. ³Then King Neco from Egypt made Jehoahaz a prisoner. Neco made the people of Judah pay 3,400 kilogrammes[a] of silver and

---

ᵃ 36:3 *3,400 kilogrammes* Literally, "100 *talents*".

34 kilogrammes[a] of gold for a fine. [4]Neco chose Jehoahaz's brother Eliakim to be the new king of Judah and Jerusalem. Neco gave Eliakim a new name. He named him Jehoiakim. But Neco took Jehoahaz to Egypt.

Jehoiakim, King of Judah

[5]Jehoiakim was 25 years old when he became the new king of Judah. He was king in Jerusalem for eleven years. Jehoiakim did not obey God. He did what the LORD his God considered evil.

[6]King Nebuchadnezzar from Babylon attacked Judah. He made Jehoiakim a prisoner and put bronze chains on him. Then Nebuchadnezzar took King Jehoiakim to Babylon. [7]Nebuchadnezzar took some of the things from the LORD's Temple. He carried them to Babylon and put them in his own house. [8]Everything else Jehoiakim did, the terrible sins he did, and everything he was guilty of doing, are written in the book, *The History of the Kings of Israel and Judah*. Jehoiakim's son Jehoiachin became the new king in his place.

Jehoiachin, King of Judah

[9]Jehoiachin was 18 years old when he became king of Judah. He was king in Jerusalem for three months and ten days. He did not obey God. He did what the LORD considered evil. [10]In the spring, King Nebuchadnezzar sent some servants to get Jehoiachin. They brought Jehoiachin and some valuable treasures from the LORD's Temple to Babylon. Nebuchadnezzar chose Zedekiah to be the new king of Judah and Jerusalem. Zedekiah was one of Jehoiachin's relatives.

Zedekiah, King of Judah

[11]Zedekiah was 21 years old when he became king of Judah. He was king in Jerusalem for eleven years. [12]Zedekiah did what the LORD considered evil. The prophet Jeremiah told him what the LORD had said. But Zedekiah did not humble himself and obey what Jeremiah said.

Jerusalem Is Destroyed

[13]Zedekiah turned against King Nebuchadnezzar. In the past Nebuchadnezzar had forced Zedekiah to make a promise with an oath in God's name to be faithful to him. But Zedekiah was stubborn and would not change his life. He refused to obey the LORD, the God of Israel. [14]Also, all the leaders of the priests and the leaders of the people of Judah became unfaithful to the Lord, sinning more and

more. They followed the evil example of the other nations. They ruined the Temple that the LORD had made holy in Jerusalem. [15]The LORD, the God of their ancestors, sent prophets again and again to warn his people. He did this because he felt sorry for them and for his Temple. He didn't want to destroy them or his Temple. [16]But they made fun of God's prophets and refused to listen to them. They hated God's messages. Finally, the LORD could not hold his anger any longer. He became angry with his people and there was nothing that could be done to stop it. [17]So God brought the king of Babylon to attack the people of Judah and Jerusalem.[b] The king of Babylon killed the young men even when they were in the Temple. He didn't have mercy on the people of Judah and Jerusalem. The king of Babylon killed young and old people. He killed men and women. He killed sick and healthy people. God permitted Nebuchadnezzar to punish the people of Judah and Jerusalem. [18]Nebuchadnezzar carried all the things in God's Temple away to Babylon. He took all the valuable things from the LORD's Temple, from the king and from the king's officials. [19]Nebuchadnezzar and his army burned the Temple. They broke down Jerusalem's wall and burned all the houses that belonged to the king and his officials. They took or destroyed every valuable thing in Jerusalem. [20]Nebuchadnezzar took the people who were still alive back to Babylon and forced them to be slaves. They stayed in Babylon as slaves until the Persian kingdom defeated the kingdom of Babylon. [21]The land of Judah became an empty desert and stayed that way for 70 years. All this time the land rested to make up for the Sabbath rests[c] that the people had not kept. This is just what the LORD said would happen in the warning he gave through the prophet Jeremiah.[d]

[22]In the first year that Cyrus king of Persia began to rule,[e] the LORD caused him to make a special announcement. He did this so that what the LORD had promised through Jeremiah the prophet would really happen. Cyrus sent messengers to every place in his kingdom. They carried this message:

[23]This is what King Cyrus of Persia says:

The LORD, the God of heaven, made me king over the whole earth. He gave me the responsibility of building a temple for him in Jerusalem. Now, all of you who are his people are free to go to Jerusalem. And may the LORD your God be with you.

---

[a] 36:3 *34 kilogrammes* Literally, "1 *talent*".

[b] 36:17 This happened in the year 586 BC, when Jerusalem was finally destroyed by King Nebuchadnezzar from Babylon.

[c] 36:21 *Sabbath rests* The Law said that every seventh year the land was not to be farmed. See Lev. 25:1–7.

[d] 36:21 *warning . . . Jeremiah* See Jer. 25:11; 29:10.

[e] 36:22 *began to rule* Probably meaning when Cyrus, after capturing Babylonia, became ruler of a great empire about 538 BC.

Who It is likely that Ezra is a continuation by "the Chronicler" taking Israel past its exile and into the return. Whether the author of all three books was Ezra, we don't know, although the use of Ezra's memoirs and the first person "I" makes it look likely.

When It would have been written sometime after the return of the exiles to Jerusalem.

What God promised that the land would be restored to his people and Ezra tells how this was achieved, using foreign kings (Cyrus, Darius and Artaxerxes), Jewish leaders (Joshua, Zerubbabel, Ezra and Nehemiah) and prophets (Haggai and Zechariah).

Ezra is really 3 Chronicles. The beginning of Ezra is virtually identical to the end of Chronicles and follows on in time immediately.

The first part tells how the Jews returned to Jerusalem and started rebuilding. Faced with the opposition of some of the people who had settled in the area while the Jews were in captivity in Babylon, their initial enthusiasm wanes.

The second half of the book deals with the return of Ezra. He stops the people from intermarrying with the tribes around them and calls them back to focus on God.

Early manuscripts put both Ezra and Nehemiah together into one book. However, the beginning of Nehemiah (Nehemiah 1:1) indicates that they are two separate documents, although both cover similar ground. Ezra was a really important figure in Judaism: he was the person who brought the "Torah" (the "Book of the Law") back from exile and read it out to the people (Nehemiah chapters 8 – 10).

Ezra is not in chronological order. If you want to read Ezra in chronological order, read it like this:

The return Ezra 1:1 – 4:5
Work stops Ezra 4:24
Work starts again Ezra 4:24 – 6:22
Work stops again Ezra 4:6–23
Ezra returns Ezra 7:1 – 10:44

QUICK TOUR ▶ **EZRA**

Return 1:1–11
Rebuilding and opposition 3:7 – 4:5
Haggai gets them going again 5:1 – 6:5
The Temple and the Passover 6:13–22

Ezra returns 7:1–27
The problem 9:1–15
The solution 10:1–17

"They sang songs of praise and thanksgiving, taking turns in singing each part. They sang, 'The LORD is good. His faithful love will last forever.' Then all the people cheered – they gave a loud shout and praised the LORD because the foundation of the LORD's Temple had been laid."

Ezra 3:11

Cyrus Helps the Prisoners Return

1 In the first year that Cyrus king of Persia began to rule,[a] the LORD caused him to make an announcement. It was written down, and Cyrus ordered that it be read throughout his kingdom. This was done so that what the LORD had told Jeremiah[b] years before would now happen. This was the announcement:

²From King Cyrus of Persia:
The LORD, the God of heaven, gave all the kingdoms on earth to me. And he chose me to build a temple for him at Jerusalem in the country of Judah. ³If any of God's people are living among you, I pray that God will bless them. You must let them go to Jerusalem in the country of Judah. You must let them go and build the Temple of the LORD, the God of Israel, the God who is in Jerusalem. ⁴And so in any place where there might be survivors of Israel, the men in that place must support these survivors. Give them silver, gold, animals and other things. Give them gifts for God's Temple in Jerusalem.

⁵So the family leaders from the tribes of Judah and Benjamin prepared to go up to Jerusalem. They were going to Jerusalem to build the LORD's Temple. Also everyone who God had encouraged prepared to go to Jerusalem. ⁶All their neighbours gave them many gifts. They gave them silver, gold, animals and other expensive things. Their neighbours freely gave them all those things. ⁷Also, King Cyrus brought out the things that belonged in the LORD's Temple that Nebuchadnezzar had taken away from Jerusalem. He had put them in his temple where he kept his false gods. ⁸King Cyrus of Persia told Mithredath, the man who kept his money, to bring those things out. So Mithredath brought them out to Sheshbazzar, the leader of Judah.

⁹This is what Mithredath brought out of the Lord's Temple: 30 gold dishes, 1,000 silver dishes, 29 knives, ¹⁰30 gold bowls, 410 silver bowls similar to the gold bowls and 1,000 other dishes. ¹¹All together, there were 5,400 things made from gold and silver. Sheshbazzar brought them all with him when the prisoners left Babylon and went back to Jerusalem.

The List of the Prisoners Who Returned

2 These are the people of the province who returned from captivity. King Nebuchadnezzar of Babylon had taken these people as prisoners to Babylon. They now returned to Jerusalem and Judah, everyone to their own town. ²These are the people who returned with Zerubbabel: Jeshua, Nehemiah, Seraiah, Reelaiah, Mordecai, Bilshan, Mispar, Bigvai, Rehum and Baanah. This is the list of names and numbers of men from Israel who returned:

INSIGHT

According to Babylonian records not all the Jews returned from exile. Some, who had become prominent business people, bankers and government officials, decided to stay in Babylon.

Ezra 2:1

---

³the descendants of Parosh	2,172
⁴the descendants of Shephatiah	372
⁵the descendants of Arah	775
⁶the descendants of Pahath Moab of the family of Jeshua and Joab	2,812
⁷the descendants of Elam	1,254
⁸the descendants of Zattu	945
⁹the descendants of Zaccai	760
¹⁰the descendants of Bani	642
¹¹the descendants of Bebai	623
¹²the descendants of Azgad	1,222
¹³the descendants of Adonikam	666
¹⁴the descendants of Bigvai	2,056
¹⁵the descendants of Adin	454
¹⁶the descendants of Ater through the family of Hezekiah	98
¹⁷the descendants of Bezai	323
¹⁸the descendants of Jorah	112
¹⁹the descendants of Hashum	223
²⁰the descendants of Gibbar	95
²¹from the town of Bethlehem	123
²²from the town of Netophah	56
²³from the town of Anathoth	128
²⁴from the town of Azmaveth	42
²⁵from the towns of Kiriath Jearim, Kephirah and Beeroth	743
²⁶from the towns of Ramah and Geba	621
²⁷from the town of Micmash	122
²⁸from the towns of Bethel and Ai	223
²⁹from the town of Nebo	52
³⁰from the town of Magbish	156
³¹from the other town named Elam	1,254
³²from the town of Harim	320
³³from the towns of Lod, Hadid and Ono	725
³⁴from the town of Jericho	345
³⁵from the town of Senaah	3,630

---

a 1:1 *began to rule* Probably meaning when Cyrus, after capturing Babylonia, became ruler of a great empire about 538 BC.
b 1:1 *what the LORD had told Jeremiah* See Jer. 25:12–14.

³⁶These are the priests who returned:
the descendants of Jedaiah through
the family of Jeshua   973
³⁷the descendants of Immer   1,052
³⁸the descendants of Pashhur   1,247
³⁹the descendants of Harim   1,017

⁴⁰These are the people from the tribe of Levi:
the descendants of Jeshua and Kadmiel
through the family of Hodaviah   74

⁴¹These are the singers:
the descendants of Asaph   128

⁴²These are the Temple gatekeepers:
the descendants of Shallum, Ater,
Talmon, Akkub, Hatita and Shobai   139

⁴³These are the special Temple servants:
Ziha, Hasupha, Tabbaoth,
⁴⁴Keros, Siaha, Padon,
⁴⁵Lebanah, Hagabah, Akkub,
⁴⁶Hagab, Shalmai, Hanan,
⁴⁷Giddel, Gahar, Reaiah,
⁴⁸Rezin, Nekoda, Gazzam,
⁴⁹Uzza, Paseah, Besai,
⁵⁰Asnah, Meunim, Nephussim,
⁵¹Bakbuk, Hakupha, Harhur,
⁵²Bazluth, Mehida, Harsha,
⁵³Barkos, Sisera, Temah,
⁵⁴Neziah and Hatipha.

⁵⁵These are Solomon's servants whose descendants returned:
Sotai, Hassophereth, Peruda,
⁵⁶Jaalah, Darkon, Giddel,
⁵⁷Shephatiah, Hattil, Pokereth Hazzebaim and
Ami,
⁵⁸The total of the descendants of the
Temple servants and of Solomon's servants   392

⁵⁹These people came to Jerusalem from the towns
of Tel Melah, Tel Harsha, Kerub, Addon and
Immer:
⁶⁰the descendants of Delaiah, Tobiah and
Nekoda   652
But none of these could prove that they were
descendants from the family of Israel.

⁶¹There were also these three families of priests:
the descendants of Hobaiah, Hakkoz and
Barzillai. (If a man married a daughter of
Barzillai from Gilead, he was counted as a
descendant of Barzillai.)

⁶²These three families searched for their family histories, but they could not find them. Their names were not included in the list of priests. They could not prove that their ancestors were priests, so they could not serve as priests. ⁶³The governor ordered them not to eat any of the holy food until a priest could use the Urim and Thummim to ask God what to do.

⁶⁴⁻⁶⁵All together, there were 42,360 people in the group who came back. This is not counting their 7,337 men and women slaves. They also had 200 men and women singers with them. ⁶⁶⁻⁶⁷They had 736 horses, 245 mules, 435 camels and 6,720 donkeys.

⁶⁸When the group arrived at the place in Jerusalem where the Lord's Temple had been, the family leaders gave their gifts for building this house of God again. They wanted to build it in this same place. ⁶⁹They gave as much as they were able. These are the things they gave for building the Temple: 500 kilogrammes^a of gold, 3,000 kilogrammes^b of silver and 100 robes that priests wear.

⁷⁰So the priests, Levites and some of the other people moved to Jerusalem and the area around it. This group included the Temple singers, gatekeepers and the Temple servants. The other Israelites settled in their own home towns.

Rebuilding the Altar

3 So by the seventh month,^c the Israelites had moved back to their own home towns. At that time all the people met together in Jerusalem. They were all united as one people. ²Then Jeshua son of Jozadak and the priests with him, along with Zerubbabel son of Shealtiel and the people with him, built the altar of the God of Israel. They built the altar of the God of Israel so that they could offer sacrifices on it. They built it just as it says in the Law of Moses. Moses was God's special servant.

³They were afraid of the other people living near them, but that didn't stop them. They built the altar on its old foundation and offered burnt offerings on it to the Lord. They offered sacrifices in the morning and in the evening. ⁴Then they celebrated the Festival of Shelters just as the Law of Moses said. They offered the right number of burnt offerings for each day of the festival. ⁵After that, they began offering the continual burnt offerings each day and the offerings for the New Moon and all the other festivals that were commanded by the Lord. The

---

^a **2:69 500 kilogrammes** Literally, "61,000 *drachmas*".
^b **2:69 3,000 kilogrammes** Literally, "5,000 *minas*".
^c **3:1 seventh month** That is, September–October, 538 BC.

people also began giving any other gifts they wanted to give to the LORD. ⁶So on the first day of the seventh month, these Israelites again began offering sacrifices to the LORD. This was done, even though the LORD's Temple had not been rebuilt.

Rebuilding the Temple

⁷Then those who had come back from captivity gave money to the stonecutters and carpenters. They also gave food, wine and olive oil. They used these things to pay the people of Tyre and Sidon to bring cedar logs from Lebanon. They wanted to bring the logs in ships to the coastal town of Joppa as they did for the first Temple. King Cyrus of Persia gave permission for them to do this.

⁸So in the second month*ᵃ* of the second year after they came to the Temple in Jerusalem, Zerubbabel son of Shealtiel and Jeshua son of Jozadak began the work. Their brothers, the priests, Levites and everyone who came back to Jerusalem from captivity began working with them. They chose Levites who were 20 years old and older to be the leaders in the building of the LORD's Temple. ⁹These were the men who supervised the work of building the LORD's Temple: Jeshua and his sons, Kadmiel and his sons (the descendants of Judah), the sons of Henadad and their brothers, the Levites. ¹⁰The builders finished laying the foundation for the LORD's Temple. When the foundation was finished, the priests put on their special clothing. Then they got their trumpets, and the sons of Asaph got their cymbals. They all took their places to praise the LORD. This was done the way King David of Israel had ordered in the past. ¹¹They sang songs of praise and thanksgiving, taking turns in singing each part.*ᵇ* They sang,

"The LORD is good.
His faithful love will last forever."

Then all the people cheered—they gave a loud shout and praised the LORD because the foundation of the LORD's Temple had been laid.

¹²But many of the older priests, Levites and family leaders, who could remember seeing the first Temple, began to cry aloud. They cried while the others there shouted for joy. ¹³The sound could be heard far away. All of them made so much noise that no one could tell the difference between the shouts of joy and the crying.

Enemies Against Rebuilding the Temple

4 Some people living in the area were against the people of Judah and Benjamin. They heard that these people who had returned from captivity were building a temple for the LORD, the God of Israel. ²So they came to Zerubbabel and to the family leaders and said, "Let us help you build. We want to worship your God, the same as you. We have offered sacrifices to him ever since King Esarhaddon of Assyria brought us here."

³But Zerubbabel, Jeshua and the other family leaders of Israel answered, "No, you people cannot help us build a temple for our God. Only we can build the Temple for the LORD. He is the God of Israel. This is what King Cyrus of Persia commanded us to do."

⁴So these people who lived near them tried to discourage them and make them afraid so that they would stop building the Temple. ⁵They paid government officials to work against the people of Judah to keep them from completing their building plans. They did this the whole time Cyrus was the king of Persia and continued up to the time Darius became king.

⁶The year Xerxes*ᶜ* became the king of Persia, these enemies of Judah sent him a letter containing their complaints against the people of Judah and Jerusalem.

INSIGHT

Most of the Old Testament was written in Hebrew, but these letters (4:8 – 6:18; 7:12 – 26) were written in Aramaic, the language Jesus would have spoken centuries later. Three other Old Testament passages were also written in Aramaic (Genesis 31:47; Jeremiah 10:11; Daniel 2:4 – 7:28).

Ezra 4:7

Enemies Against Rebuilding Jerusalem

⁷Later, when Artaxerxes became the new king of Persia, some of these men wrote another letter complaining about the Jews. The men who wrote the letter were Bishlam, Mithredath, Tabeel and

---

ᵃ **3:8 second month** That is, April–May, 536 BC.
ᵇ **3:11 taking turns . . . part** These songs were sung in two parts. One group (the Levites) sang the first part and the other group (the people) responded with the second part. Here, these are probably Ps. 111–118 and Ps. 136.
ᶜ **4:6 Xerxes** Hebrew, "Ahasuerus". He was king of Persia about 485–465 BC.

the other people in their group. The letter was written in Aramaic and translated.[a]

[8b] Then Rehum the commanding officer and Shimshai the secretary wrote a letter against the people of Jerusalem. They wrote the letter to Artaxerxes the king. This is what they wrote:

[9]From Rehum the commanding officer and Shimshai the secretary, and from the judges and important officials over the men from Tripolis, Persia, Erech and Babylon and from the Elamites from Susa, [10]and from the other people who the great and powerful Ashurbanipal moved to the city of Samaria and other places in the country west of the Euphrates River.

[11]This is the copy of the letter sent to King Artaxerxes:

From your servants living in the area west of the Euphrates River.

[12]King Artaxerxes, we wish to inform you that the Jews you sent from there are now in Jerusalem. They are trying to rebuild that terrible city. The people there have always refused to obey other kings. Now they have almost finished repairing the foundations and building the walls.[c]

[13]Also, King Artaxerxes, you should know that if Jerusalem and its walls are rebuilt, the people of Jerusalem will stop paying their taxes. They will stop sending money to honour you. They also will stop paying customs fees, and the king will lose all that money.

[14]We have a responsibility to the king. We don't want to see this happen, so we are sending this letter to inform the king. [15]King Artaxerxes, we suggest that you search the writings of the kings who ruled before you. You will find in the writings that Jerusalem is a city that is difficult to rule. It has always refused to obey other kings and nations who tried to control it. It has a long history as a place where trouble begins. That is why it was destroyed.

[16]King Artaxerxes, we wish to inform you that if this city and its walls are rebuilt, you will lose control of the area west of the Euphrates River.

[17]Then King Artaxerxes sent this answer:

To Rehum the commanding officer, Shimshai the secretary, and all the people with them living in Samaria and other places west of the Euphrates River.

Greetings:

[18]The letter you sent us has been translated and read to me. [19]I gave an order for the writings of the kings before me to be searched. We found that Jerusalem has a long history of refusing to obey their kings. It has been a place where this kind of refusal and revolt has happened often. [20]Jerusalem has had powerful kings ruling over it and over the whole area west of the Euphrates River. Their kings received taxes, customs, fees and tribute. [21]Now, order the people to stop the work of rebuilding the city. I do not want them to rebuild Jerusalem until I myself give the order. [22]Make sure you stop the work right away. The longer that work continues, the more loss it will cause for my kingdom.

[23]So a copy of the letter that King Artaxerxes sent was read to Rehum, Shimshai the secretary and the people with them. They went very quickly to the Jews in Jerusalem and forced them to stop building.

The Work on the Temple Stopped

[24]So the work stopped[d] on God's Temple in Jerusalem. The work did not continue until the second year[e] that Darius was king of Persia.

5 At that time the prophets Haggai[f] and Zechariah son of Iddo[g] began to prophesy in the name of God. They encouraged the Jews in Judah and Jerusalem. [2]So Zerubbabel son of Shealtiel and Jeshua son of Jozadak again started working on the Temple in Jerusalem. All of God's prophets were with them and were supporting

---

[a] **4:7 The letter . . . translated** Or "The letter was written in the local language, but with Aramaic characters, and then translated into Aramaic." This would mean the scribe used the "modern" Aramaic alphabet rather than the older alphabet that was still being used in Judah.

[b] **4:8** Here, the original language changes from Hebrew to Aramaic.

[c] **4:12 building the walls** This was a way of protecting a city. These men wanted the king to think that the Jews were preparing to rebel against the king.

[d] **4:24 the work stopped** Here, this refers to the time of Xerxes, when work on the Temple was stopped, not to the time of Artaxerxes, when work on the walls around Jerusalem was stopped.

[e] **4:24 second year** That is, 520 BC.

[f] **5:1 Haggai** See Hag. 1:1.

[g] **5:1 Zechariah son of Iddo** See Zech. 1:1.

EVERYTHING'S CHANGING

Have you ever been away from where you're used to living for a very long time? What does it feel like to return – do you wonder if you'll belong to the same gang? Will your daily life go on like before? Are you even the same?

Around 597 BC the Babylonians started capturing God's people from Jerusalem. In the years that followed, others were captured or left. Ten years later, as if all they had done wasn't enough, the Babylonians destroyed the Temple in Jerusalem – the symbol of God's presence with the people.

Around fifty years have passed as we start reading Ezra . . .

DIG IN

READ Ezra 1:1–8

- What did Cyrus announce?
- Who was behind Cyrus's announcement?

It must have been such a shock – having lived in Babylon they'd been surrounded by false gods and different ways of doing things. But God had made a promise that Jerusalem and the Temple would be rebuilt (Isaiah 44:24–28) – this was an act of God!

I wonder what the first group of exiles were thinking as they headed "home". Returning to a destroyed Jerusalem and Temple was going to be tough. The first few chapters of Ezra are a mixture of progress and setbacks. It's pretty likely that they wondered if things would ever be the same as before their families had been taken to Babylon. Were they still considered God's special people since they'd lived for so long in a foreign land?

If you read chapter 4 you'll discover that due to opposition, the rebuilding work stops altogether . . .

READ Ezra 5:1–2

- Who comes to help?
- What is the consequence?

Haggai and Zechariah must have said some pretty cool things to get the people to start working again. Like being a fly on the wall, we can read exactly what they said to them . . .

READ Haggai 1:1–15

- How do you think these words made the people feel?
- What's the good news (v.13)?

God wasn't happy with the way the people had stopped building his house and were pretty content just to build their own. But – he is still with them; they are still his people. So they can get off their backsides, get excited and get that Temple finished.

READ Ezra 6:3–5,16–19

- How is the Temple to be built?
- What would the Passover remind them of?

Okay, so it might not mean a lot to us, but it would have done to them. The Temple was to be exactly the same as the first one that Solomon built (1 Kings 6:2) and some of the original items the Babylonians took were to be returned. And . . . the priests are back, the sacrifices are back and the Passover can be celebrated – reminding them of God's rescue from a foreign land. Through their worship, God shows that they still belong to him.

DIG THROUGH

The people needed to know that their faith was the same as their forefathers'. They needn't have worried; God had made a promise and he kept it – they were still his people. In the same way, it doesn't matter what we've been through. Because of Jesus, we remain God's people – that's his promise to us.

- The people gave up building the Temple pretty easily. How often do we do that – start with excitement and then, when the going gets tough . . . ? Ask God for perseverance in the things you do for him.

the work. ³At that time Tattenai was the governor of the area west of the Euphrates River. Tattenai, Shethar Bozenai and the men with them went to Zerubbabel, Jeshua and the others who were building. Tattenai and the people with him asked Zerubbabel and the people with him, "Who gave you permission to rebuild this Temple and repair it like new?" ⁴They also asked Zerubbabel, "What are the names of the men who are working on this building?"

⁵But God was watching over the Jewish leaders. The builders didn't have to stop working until a report could be sent to King Darius. They continued working until the king sent his answer back.

⁶Tattenai the governor of the area west of the Euphrates River, Shethar Bozenai and the important people with them sent a letter to King Darius. ⁷This is a copy of that letter:

To King Darius.

Greetings:

⁸King Darius, you should know that we went to the province of Judah. We went to the Temple of the great God. The people in Judah are building that Temple with large stones. They are putting big wooden timbers in the walls. The work is being done with much care and the people of Judah are working very hard. They are building very fast; it will soon be done.

⁹We asked their leaders some questions about the work they are doing. We asked them, "Who gave you permission to rebuild this Temple and make it like new?" ¹⁰We also asked for their names. We wanted to write down the names of their leaders so that you would know who they are.

¹¹This is the answer they gave us:

"We are the servants of the God of heaven and earth. We are rebuilding the Temple that a great king of Israel built and finished many years ago. ¹²But our ancestors made the God of heaven angry, so God put them under the control of King Nebuchadnezzar of Babylon. Nebuchadnezzar destroyed this Temple, and he forced the people to go to Babylon as prisoners. ¹³But, in the first year that Cyrus was king of Babylon, King Cyrus gave a special order for God's Temple to be rebuilt. ¹⁴And Cyrus brought out from his false god's temple in Babylon the gold and silver things that were taken from God's

Temple in the past. Nebuchadnezzar took them from the Temple in Jerusalem and brought them to his false god's temple in Babylon. Then King Cyrus gave those gold and silver things to Sheshbazzar." Cyrus chose Sheshbazzar to be governor.

¹⁵Then Cyrus said to Sheshbazzar, "Take these gold and silver things and put them back in the Temple in Jerusalem. Rebuild God's Temple in the same place it was in the past."

¹⁶So Sheshbazzar came and built the foundations of God's Temple in Jerusalem. From that day until now, the work has continued, but it is not yet finished.

¹⁷Now, if it pleases the king, please search the official records of the king. See if it is true that King Cyrus gave an order to rebuild God's Temple in Jerusalem. And then, sir, please send us a letter to let us know what you have decided to do about this.

The Order of Darius

6 So King Darius gave an order to search the writings of the kings before him. The writings were kept in Babylon in the same place the money was kept. ²A scroll was found in the fortress of Ecbatana. (Ecbatana is in the province of Media.) This is what was written on that scroll:

Official Note: ³During the first year that Cyrus was king, he gave an order about the Temple of God in Jerusalem. The order said:

Let the Temple of God be rebuilt. It will be a place to offer sacrifices. Let its foundations be built. The Temple must be 27 metres*a* high and 27 metres wide. ⁴Its wall will be in layers that have three rows of large stones*b* and one row of wooden timbers. The cost of building the Temple must be paid for from the king's treasury. ⁵Also, the gold and silver things from God's Temple must be put back in their places. Nebuchadnezzar took them from the Temple in Jerusalem and brought them to Babylon. They must be put back in God's Temple.

⁶So King Darius sent this message to his officials:

To Tattenai, governor of the area west of the Euphrates River, to Shethar Bozenai and to all the officials living in that province.

I order you to stay away from Jerusalem. [7]Don't bother the workers. Don't try to stop the work on this Temple of God. Let the Jewish governor and the Jewish leaders rebuild it. Let them rebuild God's Temple in the same place it was in the past.

[8]Now I give you this order to help the Jewish leaders building God's Temple: Pay the full cost of the building from the king's treasury. The money will come from the taxes collected from the provinces in the area west of the Euphrates River. Do these things quickly so that the work will not stop. [9]Give them anything they need. If they need young bulls, rams or lambs for sacrifices to the God of heaven, give these things to them. If the priests of Jerusalem ask for wheat, salt, wine and oil, give these things to them every day without fail. [10]Give them to the Jewish priests so that they may offer sacrifices that please the God of heaven. Give these things so that the priests may pray for me and my sons.

[11]Also, I give this order: If anyone changes this order, a wooden beam must be pulled from their house and pushed through their body. Then their house must be destroyed until it is only a pile of rocks.

[12]God put his name there in Jerusalem. May God defeat any king or other person who tries to change this order. If anyone tries to destroy this Temple in Jerusalem, may God destroy that person.

I, Darius, have ordered it. This order must be obeyed quickly and completely.

INSIGHT

King Darius was pretty serious in his decree about the rebuilding of the Temple. He ended it by saying if anyone tried to change it they would be impaled on a beam taken from their own house. Ouch!

Ezra 6:11

The Temple Completed and Dedicated

[13]So Tattenai the governor of the area west of the Euphrates River, Shethar Bozenai and the men with them obeyed King Darius' order. They obeyed the order quickly and completely. [14]So the Jewish leaders continued to build. Encouraged by the preaching of Haggai the prophet and Zechariah son of Iddo, they had great success. They finished building the Temple as the God of Israel had commanded and as Cyrus, Darius and Artaxerxes, the kings of Persia, had ordered. [15]The Temple was finished on the third day of the month of Adar.[a] That was in the sixth year of the rule of King Darius.[b]

[16]Then the Israelites celebrated the dedication of God's Temple with much happiness. The priests, the Levites and all the other people who came back from captivity joined in the celebration.

[17]This is the way they dedicated God's Temple: They offered 100 bulls, 200 rams and 400 lambs. And they offered twelve male goats for all Israel for a sin offering. That is one goat for each of the twelve tribes of Israel. [18]Then they chose the priests in their groups and the Levites in their groups to serve in God's Temple in Jerusalem. They did these things as it is written in the *Book of Moses.*

The Passover Festival

[19c] On the fourteenth day of the first month,[d] the Jews who came back from captivity celebrated Passover. [20]The priests and Levites made themselves pure. They all made themselves clean and ready to celebrate Passover. The Levites killed the Passover lamb for all the Jews who came back from captivity. They did that for their brothers the priests and for themselves. [21]So all the Israelites who came back from captivity ate the Passover meal. Other people washed themselves and made themselves pure from the unclean things of the people living in that country. These pure people also shared in the Passover meal. They did this so that they could go to the Lord, the God of Israel, for help. [22]They celebrated the Festival of Unleavened Bread with much joy for seven days. The Lord made them very happy because he had changed the attitude of the king of Assyria.[e] So the king of Assyria had helped them do the work on God's Temple.

Ezra Comes to Jerusalem

7 After these things,[f] during the rule of King Artaxerxes of Persia, Ezra came to Jerusalem from Babylon. Ezra was the son of Seraiah. Seraiah was the son of Azariah. Azariah was the son of

---

[a] **6:15 third . . . Adar** That is, February–March. Some ancient writers have "twenty-third of Adar".
[b] **6:15 the sixth year . . . Darius** That is, 515 BC.
[c] **6:19** Here, the original language changes from Aramaic back to Hebrew.
[d] **6:19 first month** That is, March–April, 515 BC.
[e] **6:22 king of Assyria** This probably means King Darius of Persia.
[f] **7:1 After these things** There is a time period of 58 years between Ezra 6 and Ezra 7. The story of Esther takes place at this time.

Hilkiah. [2]Hilkiah was the son of Shallum. Shallum was the son of Zadok. Zadok was the son of Ahitub. [3]Ahitub was the son of Amariah. Amariah was the son of Azariah. Azariah was the son of Meraioth. [4]Meraioth was the son of Zerahiah. Zerahiah was the son of Uzzi. Uzzi was the son of Bukki. [5]Bukki was the son of Abishua. Abishua was the son of Phinehas. Phinehas was the son of Eleazar. Eleazar was the son of Aaron the high priest.

[6]Ezra came to Jerusalem from Babylon. He was a teacher[a] and knew the Law of Moses very well. The Law of Moses was given by the LORD, the God of Israel. King Artaxerxes gave Ezra everything he asked for because the LORD was with Ezra. [7]Among the people who came with Ezra were Israelites, priests, Levites, singers, gatekeepers and Temple servants. They arrived in Jerusalem during the seventh year of King Artaxerxes. [8]Ezra arrived in Jerusalem in the fifth month[b] of the seventh year that Artaxerxes was king. [9]Ezra left Babylon on the first day of the first month and arrived in Jerusalem on the first day of the fifth month. With God's blessing his journey went well. [10]Ezra had always given his time and attention to studying and obeying the Law of the LORD. He also loved to teach its rules and commandments to others in Israel.

INSIGHT

Ezra's role in preserving the faith earned him the name "Father of Judaism". He is believed to have dictated 94 books (including 24 in the Old Testament) from memory! These might otherwise have been lost or burned during the exile.

Ezra 7:10

King Artaxerxes' Letter to Ezra

[11]Ezra was a priest and teacher. He knew much about the commands and laws the LORD gave Israel. This is a copy of the letter King Artaxerxes gave to Ezra the teacher:

[12c] From King Artaxerxes,
To Ezra the priest, a teacher of the law of the God of heaven:

Greetings.

[13]I give this order: Any of the Israelites living in my kingdom, including priests and Levites, who want to go with you to Jerusalem, may go. [14]I and my seven advisors send you to Judah and Jerusalem. Go and see how your people are doing in obeying the law of your God. You have that law with you. [15]I and my advisors are giving gold and silver to the God of Israel, who lives in Jerusalem. You must take this gold and silver with you. [16]You must also go through all the provinces of Babylonia. Collect the gifts from your people, from the priests and from the Levites. The gifts are for the Temple of their God in Jerusalem. [17]Use this money to buy bulls, rams and lambs. Buy the grain offerings and drink offerings that go with these sacrifices. Then sacrifice them on the altar in the Temple of your God in Jerusalem. [18]Then you and the other Jews may spend the silver and gold left over any way you want to. Use it in a way that is pleasing to your God. [19]Take all these things to the God of Jerusalem. They are for the worship in the Temple of your God. [20]And you may get any other things that you need for the Temple of your God. Use the money in the king's treasury to buy anything you need.

[21]Now I, King Artaxerxes, give this order: I order all the men who keep the king's money in the area west of the Euphrates River to give Ezra anything he wants. Ezra is a priest and a teacher of the Law of the God of heaven. Do this quickly and completely. [22]Give this much to Ezra: 3,400 kilogrammes[d] of silver, 10 tonnes[e] of wheat, 2,200 litres[f] of wine, 2,200 litres of olive oil and as much salt as Ezra wants. [23]Anything that the God of heaven has ordered for Ezra to get, you must give to Ezra quickly and completely. Do this for the Temple of the God of heaven. We don't want God to be angry with my kingdom or my sons.

[24]I want you men to know that it is against the law to make the priests, Levites, singers, gatekeepers, Temple servants and other workers in God's Temple pay taxes. They don't have to pay taxes, money to honour the king or any customs fees. [25]Ezra,

---

[a] **7:6 teacher** Literally, "scribe". This was a person who made copies of books. These men studied those books and became teachers.
[b] **7:8 fifth month** That is, July–August, 458 BC.
[c] **7:12** Here, the text changes from Hebrew to Aramaic.
[d] **7:22 3,400 kilogrammes** Literally, "100 talents".
[e] **7:22 10 tonnes** Literally, "100 cors".
[f] **7:22 2,200 litres** Literally, "100 baths".

I give you the authority to use the wisdom you have from your God and choose civil and religious judges. These men will be judges for all the people living in the area west of the Euphrates River. They will judge all the people who know the laws of your God and they will teach those who don't know those laws. 26Anyone who does not obey the law of your God, or the law of the king, must be punished. Depending on the crime, they must be punished with death, or sent away to another country, or their property taken away, or put into prison.

Ezra Praises God for the King's Letter

27aPraise the LORD, the God of our ancestors. He put the idea into the king's heart to honour the LORD's Temple in Jerusalem. 28God showed his faithful love to me for all to see. And because the king, his advisors and the king's important officials saw this, they were willing to help. The LORD my God was with me, and that gave me courage. So I gathered some leaders from Israel to go back to Jerusalem with me.

List of Leaders Returning With Ezra

8 These are the names of the family leaders and the other people who came with me to Jerusalem from Babylon. We came to Jerusalem during the rule of King Artaxerxes. Here is the list of names:

2from the descendants of Phinehas: Gershom;
  from the descendants of Ithamar: Daniel;
  from the descendants of David: Hattush;
3from the descendants of Shecaniah: the
  descendants of Parosh, Zechariah and
  150 other men;
4from the descendants of Pahath Moab:
  Eliehoenai son of Zerahiah and 200 other
  men;
5from the descendants of Zattu: Shecaniah son
  of Jahaziel and 300 other men;
6from the descendants of Adin: Ebed son of
  Jonathan and 50 other men;
7from the descendants of Elam: Jeshaiah son of
  Athaliah and 70 other men;
8from the descendants of Shephatiah: Zebadiah
  son of Michael and 80 other men;
9from the descendants of Joab: Obadiah son of
  Jehiel and 218 other men;
10from the descendants of Bani: Shelomith son
  of Josiphiah and 160 other men;
11from the descendants of Bebai: Zechariah son
  of Bebai and 28 other men;

12from the descendants of Azgad: Johanan son
  of Hakkatan and 110 other men;
13from the last of the descendants of Adonikam:
  Eliphelet, Jeuel, Shemaiah and 60 other
  men;
14from the descendants of Bigvai: Uthai, Zaccur
  and 70 other men.

The Return to Jerusalem

15I called all these people to meet together at the river that flows towards Ahava. We camped at that place for three days. I learned there were priests in the group, but there were no Levites. 16So I called these leaders: Eliezer, Ariel, Shemaiah, Elnathan, Jarib, Elnathan, Nathan, Zechariah and Meshullam. And I called Joiarib and Elnathan who were teachers. 17I sent the men to Iddo, leader in the town of Casiphia. I told them what to say to Iddo and his relatives, who were Temple workers now living in Casiphia. I told the men to ask Iddo and his relatives to send us workers to serve in God's Temple. 18Because God was with us, they sent Sherebiah, a skilled man from the descendants of Mahli (Mahli was a son of Levi, one of Israel's sons.) They also sent his sons and brothers, 18 men in all. 19They also sent Hashabiah and Jeshaiah from the descendants of Merari, along with their brothers and nephews. In all there were 20 men. 20Besides these, there were 220 Temple workers whose ancestors had been chosen by David and his officials to help the Levites. The names of all these men were written on the list.

21There, near the Ahava River, I announced that we should all fast to humble ourselves before our God. We wanted to ask God to give us a safe journey and protect us, our children and everything we owned. 22I didn't want to ask King Artaxerxes for protection because of what we had told him. We had said, "Our God is with everyone who trusts him, but he is very angry with everyone who turns away from him." So I was embarrassed to ask the king to send soldiers and horsemen to protect us from enemies on our journey. 23So we fasted and prayed to our God about our journey. And he answered our prayers.

24Then I chose twelve of the priests who were leaders. I chose Sherebiah, Hashabiah and ten of their brothers. 25I weighed the silver, gold and the other things that were given for God's Temple. I gave them to the twelve priests I had chosen. King Artaxerxes, his advisors, his important officials and all the Israelites in Babylon gave those things for God's Temple. 26I weighed all these things. There were 22 tonnesb of silver. There were also 3,400 kilogrammesc of silver utensils. There were

---

a **7:27** Here, the text changes from Aramaic back to Hebrew.
b **8:26** *22 tonnes* Literally, "650 *talents*".
c **8:26** *3,400 kilogrammes* Literally, "100 *talents*".

3,400 kilogrammes of gold. [27]And I gave them 20 gold bowls. The bowls weighed more than 8 kilogrammes.[a] And I gave them two beautiful dishes made from polished bronze that were as valuable as gold. [28]Then I said to the twelve priests: "You and these things are holy to the LORD. People gave this silver and gold to the LORD, the God of your ancestors. [29]So guard these things carefully. You are responsible for them until you give them to the Temple leaders in Jerusalem. You will give them to the leading Levites and the family leaders of Israel. They will weigh them and put them in the rooms of the LORD's Temple in Jerusalem."

[30]So the priests and Levites accepted the silver, gold and special things that Ezra had weighed and given to them. They were told to take them to God's Temple in Jerusalem.

[31]On the twelfth day of the first month,[b] we left the Ahava River and started towards Jerusalem. God was with us, and he protected us from enemies and robbers along the way. [32]Then we arrived in Jerusalem. We rested there for three days. [33]On the fourth day, we went to the Temple and weighed the silver, gold and special things. We gave them to Meremoth son of Uriah the priest. Eleazar son of Phinehas was with Meremoth. The Levites, Jozabad son of Jeshua and Noadiah son of Binnui were with them also. [34]We counted and weighed everything and we wrote down the total weight.

[35]Then the Jewish people who came back from captivity offered burnt offerings to the God of Israel. They offered twelve bulls for all Israel, 96 rams, 77 male lambs and twelve male goats for a sin offering. All this was a burnt offering to the LORD.

[36]Then the people gave the letter from King Artaxerxes to the royal satraps and to the governors of the area west of the Euphrates River. Then the leaders gave their support to the Israelites and to the Temple.

Marriages to Non-Jewish People

9 After we finished all these things, the leaders of the Israelites came to me and said, "Ezra, the Israelites have not kept themselves separate from the other people living around us. And the priests and the Levites have not kept themselves separate. The Israelites are being influenced by evil things done by the Canaanites, Hittites, Perizzites, Jebusites, Ammonites, Moabites, Egyptians and Amorites. [2]The Israelites have married the people living around us. The Israelites are supposed to be special, but now they are mixed with the other people living around them. The leaders and important officials of the Israelites have set a bad example in this thing." [3]When I heard about this, I tore my robe and my coat to show I was upset. I pulled hair from my head and beard. I sat down, shocked and upset. [4]Then everyone who respected God's Law shook with fear. They were afraid because the Israelites who came back from captivity were not faithful to God. I was shocked and upset. I sat there until the evening sacrifice, and the people gathered around me.

[5]Then, when it was time for the evening sacrifice, I got up. I had made myself look shameful while I was sitting there. My robe and coat were torn, and I fell on my knees with my hands lifted up to the LORD my God. [6]Then I prayed,

"My God, I am too ashamed and embarrassed to look at you. I am ashamed because our sins are higher than our heads. Our guilt has reached all the way up to the heavens. [7]We have been guilty of many sins from the days of our ancestors until now. We sinned, so our kings and priests were punished. Foreign kings attacked us and took our people away. They took away our wealth and made us ashamed. It is the same even today.

[8]"But now, finally, you have been kind to us. You have let a few of us escape captivity and come to live in this holy place. LORD, you gave us new life and relief from our slavery. [9]Yes, we were slaves, but you would not let us be slaves forever. You were kind to us. You made the kings of Persia be kind to us. Your Temple was ruined, but you gave us new life so that we can rebuild your Temple and repair it like new. God, you helped us build a wall to protect Judah and Jerusalem.

[10]"Now, God, what can we say to you? We have stopped obeying you again. [11]You used your servants the prophets to give these commands to us. You said, 'The land you are going to live in and own is a ruined land. It has been ruined by evil things the people living there have done. They have done very bad things in every place in this land. They have made this land dirty with their sins. [12]So Israelites, don't let your children marry their children. Don't join them. Don't want the things they have. Obey my commands so that you will be strong and enjoy the good things of the land. And then you can keep this land and give it to your children.'

[13]"What has happened to us is our own fault. We have done evil things, and we have much guilt. But you, our God, have punished us much less than we deserve. We have done many terrible sins, and we should have been punished even more. And you have even let some of our people

---

[a] *8:27 8 kilogrammes* Literally, "1,000 *darics*".
[b] *8:31 first month* That is, March–April, 458 BC.

WHO AM I?

If you've been away from home for a long time, perhaps on holiday, there may be certain things you need to do when you get back to feel as though you still belong. Maybe it's sleeping with a specific pillow at night, or hanging out with your mates, or stroking the cat.

But what if you came home to discover your mum or sister had moved out and two random people have moved in? You'd really lose the sense of belonging, of being family.

As you'll discover, the exiles who had returned to Jerusalem had been doing a fair amount of mixing with other nations – it's no wonder they'd lost a sense of family and identity. They needed to be reminded that their identity would be maintained through purity, through obeying God's law. Enter Ezra – he was sent by God to teach God's word to the people (7:6).

DIG IN

READ Ezra 9:1–5

- What appears to be the problem (vv.1–2)?
- What is Ezra's response (v.3)?
- Why do you think Ezra reacted so violently here? (Check out 10:1,6 too.)

Is Ezra being racist? It might seem like it, but that's not what's going on here. Ezra knows that God's law revealed the people's sin and that they are right to be afraid. Many years previously, before the Israelites had even arrived in the land God had promised them, let alone been thrown out of it, God told them they weren't to marry foreigners. This was to make sure they didn't go off the rails and follow foreign gods (Deuteronomy 7:1–4).

READ Ezra 9:6–15

- How does Ezra describe the people and the results of their actions (vv.6–7,10–12)?
- In contrast, how has God treated the people (vv.8–9,13–15)?
- What do these verses tell us about God?

In his distress, Ezra prays to God. He is overwhelmed by the guilt of his people and the sin that they just kept on committing. The consequence of their past sin had been God's punishment – they were taken away by foreigners, ripped out of the land God had given them. Depressingly, nothing much had changed . . .

But did you see the undeserved goodness of the Lord (v.15)? He rescued them (vv.8–9,13), looked after them and enabled them to set up the Temple (v.9).

READ Ezra 10:1–17

- What do the people do in response?

Getting rid of their wives is a pretty drastic measure, but God's law, and obedience to it, had to come first (Ezra 9:12–14). Having just returned from exile, these were risky times for the people and so they needed to keep a strong understanding of who they were – a holy nation for God (Exodus 19:5–6).

DIG THROUGH

- Having married foreigners, the people were disobeying God, diluting their distinctiveness and not living as a holy nation. Check out 1 Peter 2:9 in the New Testament. Do you belong to God? Knowing who we are should make all the difference to the way we live and the choices we make.
- Despite all that God had done for them, the people had started putting more importance on other things than on God. But did you notice God's awesome grace to the people? It's easy to make other things more important than God isn't it – but can they treat you with as much love and kindness as God?

escape captivity. [14]So we know that we must not break your commands. We must not marry those people. They do very bad things. God, if we continue to marry these bad people, we know you will destroy us. Then there would be no one from the Israelites left alive.

[15]"LORD, God of Israel, you are good, and you still have let some of us live. Yes, we are guilty, and because of our guilt, not one of us should be allowed to stand in front of you."

The People Confess Their Sin

10 Ezra was praying and confessing. He was crying and bowing down in front of God's Temple. While Ezra was doing that, a large group of the Israelites—men, women and children—gathered around him. They were crying. [2]Then Shecaniah son of Jehiel, one of the descendants of Elam, spoke to Ezra and said, "We have not been faithful to our God. We have married the people living around us. But, even though we have done this, there is still hope for Israel. [3]Now let us make an agreement before our God to send away all these women and their children. We will do that to follow the advice of Ezra and the people who respect the laws of our God. We will obey God's Law. [4]Get up, Ezra. This is your responsibility, but we will support you. So be brave and do it."

[5]So Ezra got up. He made the leading priests, the Levites and all the Israelites promise to do what he said. [6]Then Ezra went away from the front of God's house. He went to the room of Jehohanan son of Eliashib. While Ezra was there, he didn't eat food or drink water. He did that because he was still very sad. He was very sad about the Israelites who came back to Jerusalem. [7]Then he sent a message to every place in Judah and Jerusalem. The message told all the Jewish people who had come back from captivity to meet together in Jerusalem. [8]Those who did not come to Jerusalem in three days like the officials and leaders said would lose their property and be removed from the group.

[9]So in three days all the men from the families of Judah and Benjamin gathered in Jerusalem. And on the twentieth day of the ninth month,[a] all the people met together in the Temple courtyard. They were very upset because of the reason for the meeting and because of the heavy rain. [10]Then Ezra the priest stood and said to them, "You people have not been faithful to God. You have married foreign women. You have made Israel more guilty by doing that. [11]Now you must confess your sins to the LORD, the God of your ancestors. You must obey his command. Separate yourselves from the people living around you and from your foreign wives."

[12]Then the whole group who met together answered Ezra. They shouted, "Ezra, you are right! We must do what you say. [13]But there are many people here. And it is the rainy time of year, so we cannot stay outside. This problem cannot be solved in a day or two because we have sinned in a very bad way. [14]Let our leaders decide for the whole group meeting here. Then let every man in our towns who married a foreign woman come here to Jerusalem at a planned time. Let them come here with the leaders and judges of their towns. Then God will stop being angry with us."

[15]Only a few men were against this plan. They were Jonathan son of Asahel and Jahzeiah son of Tikvah. Meshullam and Shabbethai the Levite also were against the plan.

[16]So the Israelites who came back to Jerusalem accepted the plan. Ezra the priest chose men who were family leaders. He chose one man from each tribe. Each man was chosen by name. On the first day of the tenth month,[b] the men who were chosen sat down to study each of the cases. [17]And by the first day of the first month,[c] they finished discussing all the men who had married foreign women.

List of Men Who Married Foreign Women

[18]These are the names of the descendants of the priests who married foreign women:

From the descendants of Jeshua son of Jozadak and Jeshua's brothers, these men: Maaseiah, Eliezer, Jarib and Gedaliah. [19]All of them promised to divorce their wives. And then each one of them offered a ram from the flock for a guilt offering. They did that because of their guilt.

[20]From the descendants of Immer, these men: Hanani and Zebadiah.

[21]From the descendants of Harim, these men: Maaseiah, Elijah, Shemaiah, Jehiel and Uzziah.

[22]From the descendants of Pashhur, these men: Elioenai, Maaseiah, Ishmael, Nethanel, Jozabad and Elasah.

[23]Among the Levites:
Jozabad, Shimei, Kelaiah (also called Kelita), Pethahiah, Judah and Eliezer.

[24]Among the singers: Eliashib.

---

[a] **10:9 ninth month** That is, November–December.
[b] **10:16 tenth month** That is, December–January.
[c] **10:17 first month** That is, March–April.

Among the gatekeepers: Shallum, Telem and Uri.

25Among the Israelites:

From the descendants of Parosh, these men: Ramiah, Izziah, Malkijah, Mijamin, Eleazar, Malkijah and Benaiah.

26From the descendants of Elam, these men: Mattaniah, Zechariah, Jehiel, Abdi, Jeremoth and Elijah.

27From the descendants of Zattu, these men: Elioenai, Eliashib, Mattaniah, Jeremoth, Zabad and Aziza.

28From the descendants of Bebai, these men: Jehohanan, Hananiah, Zabbai and Athlai.

29From the descendants of Bani, these men: Meshullam, Malluch, Adaiah, Jashub, Sheal and Jeremoth.

30From the descendants of Pahath Moab, these men: Adna, Kelal, Benaiah, Maaseiah, Mattaniah, Bezalel, Binnui and Manasseh.

31From the descendants of Harim, these men: Eliezer, Ishijah, Malkijah, Shemaiah, Shimeon, 32Benjamin, Malluch and Shemariah.

33From the descendants of Hashum, these men: Mattenai, Mattattah, Zabad, Eliphelet, Jeremai, Manasseh and Shimei.

34From the descendants of Bani, these men: Maadai, Amram, Uel, 35Benaiah, Bedeiah, Keluhi, 36Vaniah, Meremoth, Eliashib, 37Mattaniah, Mattenai and Jaasu.

38From the descendants of Binnui, these men: Shimei, 39Shelemiah, Nathan, Adaiah, 40Macnadebai, Shashai, Sharai, 41Azarel, Shelemiah, Shemariah, 42Shallum, Amariah and Joseph.

43From the descendants of Nebo, these men: Jeiel, Mattithiah, Zabad, Zebina, Jaddai, Joel and Benaiah.

44All these men married foreign women, and some of them had children with these wives.

PEER PRESSURE

ONE of your greatest weapons when people are putting pressure on you to do something is to know what *you* want to do. You are the only person who really has a right to make a decision about your actions because you are the only person who has to live with the consequences. Knowing your own mind and being able to stand up against a crowd who disagrees with you makes you a much stronger person than someone who goes along with whatever anyone else says.

But if knowing your own mind is key, so is the courage to stick with your convictions. The

> **SUPPORT EACH OTHER IN SUCH SITUATIONS AND ASK JESUS TO HELP YOU STAND UP FOR WHAT YOU BELIEVE IN.**

disciples prayed for boldness (Acts 4:29) and sometimes we need to do the same. Are you feeling under pressure to do something? Think through why you do or don't want to do it and ask God to help you explain your decision to

your peers. True friends will respect you for having your own opinions and being strong enough to tell others your views.

And if people don't respect you and continue trying to change your mind, ask them why it's so important to them for you to follow what they do. Perhaps they're not as convinced as they're making out and want to validate their actions by doing the same thing. Spend time chatting and praying with Christian friends about how you can support each other in such situations and ask Jesus to help you stand up for what you believe in. ←

If you would like to, pray this prayer:

Dear Lord, I thank you that I am yours and I belong to you. I bring to you the situations where I feel pressured by others to act in a way that I don't feel is right. Please give me the strength and boldness to say "no" and to be the person you created me to be. Help me to stand out in a way that honours you and glorifies your name. I thank you that I am not alone but that you are with me every step of the way.

Amen

PRAYER

CAN you think of times you've prayed and seen God do amazing things? It feels great, doesn't it! You feel so close to God and you're full of faith when you next come to pray. But what about those times when you've prayed and prayed and felt as if nothing's changed? It can be so discouraging and you start to wonder, "What's the point?" The good news for us is that stories in the Bible show us that it doesn't mean we're doing anything wrong. It's strange to think about it but even Jesus had unanswered prayers. In John 17:20–21, Jesus asked for unity amongst all believers but we know that even to this day, more than 2,000 years later, that desire has not yet been fulfilled. And if Jesus didn't always get a "yes", we shouldn't expect to get one every time we ask for something.

This means it can be confusing trying to work out what prayer is all about and what it achieves. It seems to be much more about our relationship with God than it is about the shopping list of requests that we can sometimes make it. God wants us to be honest with him about what we're thinking and feeling (just look at Psalms like 55 and 77 to see this in the Bible). If we're stressed about school or college, he wants us to talk to him about it. If we're worried about a friendship, he wants us to bring it to him. If we're fed up and angry with the world, he'd rather we come to him and get it off our chest than bottle it up. It's not that he doesn't know what we're thinking and feeling and, indeed, the Bible says God "knows what you need before you ask him" (Matthew 6:8). But if, for example, we're planning what to do with our future, God wants us to ask him. He does this for our benefit because prayer is one of the ways we get to know him better. It's not a one-way street where we just tell our side of the story

either; the best prayer times are when we make space to listen to God and find out what he has to say to us.

Prayer doesn't have to be silent, alone, head bowed and hands clasped together. Find out what works for you and try different things to keep your praying fresh. Go somewhere on your own words. Be totally honest with God, but remember who you're speaking to.

It is such a privilege that God allows us to come to him and that he wants us to chat to him about anything and everything, bringing all our requests to him with an attitude of thanksgiving. When we do, God gives us

> ## IT IS SUCH A PRIVILEGE THAT GOD ALLOWS US TO COME TO HIM AND THAT HE WANTS US TO CHAT TO HIM ABOUT ANYTHING AND EVERYTHING.

your own and pray out loud if that helps you; gather a group of mates if there's an issue that concerns you all; use the words of the Lord's Prayer to help you focus (Matthew 6:5–13); borrow bits from the Psalms if you're stuck for peace about the future which helps us cope with the difficult things life throws our way (Philippians 4:6–7). ←

FOLLOWING JESUS

DO you have a mentor or life coach? Luke Skywalker had Obi-Wan Kenobi; the Karate Kid had Mr Miyagi; Harry Potter had Professor Dumbledore. You're probably thinking, "Yeah, but none of those characters are real, live people!" And you're right. However, these are all pairings that illustrate something the Bible has a lot to say about: discipleship.

Calling yourself a "follower" or "disciple" of Jesus is, arguably, the most significant auto-biographical statement you could ever make. You're basically saying that the most powerful being in the universe is your personal life coach! That's something Luke Skywalker, the Karate Kid and Harry Potter couldn't hold a candle to. But the really tough question is this: does your lifestyle match up with this statement?

Before he ascended into heaven, Jesus didn't tell his followers to go and make pizza. He didn't tell them to go and build houses. He didn't even tell them to go and make converts to Christianity. He told them to go and make "followers" or "disciples" (Matthew 28:19). And that command still stands for us today as followers of Jesus. It's a lifelong commitment for an eternal reward.

So, that leads us to our next question. Who do you mentor or coach? You're never too young to be a role model for someone else (1 Timothy 4:12). In fact, the chances are you're already influencing some of the people around you. Are you a good influence? Always remember that the best life coach *ever* was and is Jesus (Matthew 4:18–20). And the better we know him, the better influence we can have as we seek to make disciples. ←

REMEMBER THAT THE BEST LIFE COACH EVER IS JESUS. AND THE BETTER WE KNOW HIM, THE BETTER INFLUENCE WE CAN HAVE AS WE SEEK TO MAKE DISCIPLES.

If you want to, pray this short prayer:

Lord Jesus, make me a true follower of you. Give me wisdom as I ask for advice from mentors you've already placed in my life, and please give me courage as I seek out others who are willing to pass on their legacy to me. Equally, help me to find just the right people to invest in, as I do my best to be a disciple who makes disciples.

Amen

NEHEMIAH

Who The author is unknown. Probably the book was begun by the same "Chronicler" who compiled Chronicles and Ezra. Parts came from Nehemiah's own writings. Some believe the author was Ezra.

When Nehemiah's story begins during the twentieth year of Artaxerxes's reign (about 444 BC). Some of the writing dates to around 400 BC: the last emperor mentioned is the Persian king Darius II who reigned from 423–405 BC.

What The rebuilding of Jerusalem related in the book of Ezra has ground to a halt. Nehemiah, a high-ranking Jewish official at the palace of the Persian king, Artaxerxes, decides to act.

Nehemiah is the king's wine servant – an important and trusted position in a time when kings faced many assassination attempts. You want someone looking after your wine whom you can trust! While he is in the Persian city of Susa, he hears that Jerusalem is in danger. The city's walls are broken and the defences are useless. The city is under threat.

So Nehemiah takes steps. He approaches the king and gets permission to return. Artaxerxes even gives him some building supplies. Once at Jerusalem, Nehemiah has to overcome opposition from local enemies, but eventually the walls are finished and dedicated.

Nehemiah is about prayer and action. Nehemiah makes plans and puts those plans into action; but he also prays. The first thing he does when he hears the bad news about Jerusalem is to fast and pray. Everything that Nehemiah does is grown out of prayer and dedication to God.

Like Ezra, Nehemiah also calls the people to remain totally dedicated to God. Indeed the book includes the account of Ezra reading out the "Torah" (the "Book of the Law") to the people as they stand and listen (chapters 8 – 10). Ezra is a kind of second Moses in Judaism, reading out the law to the people and reinstituting the Festival of Shelters (or Succoth) – a festival which recalls the Israelites' time in the desert. According to the book, this was the first time it had been celebrated since the time of Joshua (8:13–18).

QUICK TOUR ▶ NEHEMIAH

"But we prayed to our God. And we put guards on the walls to watch day and night so that we could be ready to meet them."

Nehemiah 4:9

Nehemiah's Prayer

1 These are the words of Nehemiah son of Hacaliah: I, Nehemiah, was in the capital city of Susa in the month of Kislev. This was in the twentieth year[a] that Artaxerxes was king. ²While I was in Susa, one of my brothers named Hanani and some other men came from Judah. I asked them about the Jews who had escaped captivity and still lived in Judah. I also asked them about the city of Jerusalem.

³They answered, "Nehemiah, the Jews who escaped captivity and are in the land of Judah are in much trouble. They are having many problems and are full of shame because the wall of Jerusalem is broken down, and its gates have been destroyed by fire."

⁴When I heard this about the people of Jerusalem and about the wall, I sat down and cried. I was very sad. I fasted and prayed to the God of heaven for several days. ⁵Then I prayed this prayer:

"LORD, God of heaven, you are the great and powerful God. You are the God who keeps his agreement of love with people who love you and obey your commands.

⁶"Please open your eyes and ears and listen to the prayer your servant is praying before you day and night. I am praying for your servants, the Israelites. I confess the sins we Israelites have done against you. I am confessing that I have sinned against you and that the other people in my father's family have sinned against you. ⁷We Israelites have been very bad to you. We have not obeyed the commands, rules and laws you gave your servant Moses.

⁸"Please remember the teaching you gave your servant Moses. You said to him, 'If you Israelites are not faithful, I will force you to be scattered among the other nations. ⁹But if you Israelites come back to me and obey my commands, this is what I will do: Even if your people have been forced to leave their homes and go to the ends of the earth, I will gather them from there. And I will bring them back to the place I have chosen to put my name.'

¹⁰"The Israelites are your servants and your people. You used your great power and rescued them. ¹¹So, Lord, please listen to my prayer. And listen to the prayers of all your other servants who are happy to honour you. Help me today as I ask the king for help. Make him pleased with me so that he will be kind and give me what I ask for."

At that time, I was the king's wine servant.[b]

The King Sends Nehemiah to Jerusalem

2 In the month of Nisan in the twentieth year[c] of King Artaxerxes, some wine was brought to the king. I took the wine and gave it to the king. I had never before been sad when I was with him, but now I was sad. ²So the king asked me, "Are you sick? Why do you look sad? I think your heart is full of sadness."

Then I was very afraid. ³But even though I was afraid, I said to the king, "May the king live forever! I am sad because the city where my ancestors are buried lies in ruins, and the gates of that city have been destroyed by fire."

⁴Then the king said to me, "What do you want me to do?"

Before I answered, I prayed to the God of heaven. ⁵Then I answered the king, "If it would please the king, and if I have been good to you, please send me to Jerusalem, the city in Judah where my ancestors are buried. I want to go there and rebuild that city."

INSIGHT

Nehemiah was a man of prayer and action. He sought God and organized the rebuilding of the wall, got the people ready to protect it and reminded them God was on their side.
Nehemiah 1 – 2

⁶The king and the queen who was sitting next to him asked me, "How long will your trip take? When will you get back here?"

The king was happy to send me, so I gave him a certain time. ⁷I also said to the king, "If it would please the king to do something else for me, let me ask. Please give me some letters to show the governors of the area west of the Euphrates River. I need these letters so that the governors will give me permission to pass safely through their lands on my way to Judah. ⁸I also need timber for the heavy wooden beams for the gates, the walls, the walls around the Temple and my house. So I need a letter from you to Asaph, who is in charge of your forests."

The king gave me the letters and everything I asked for. The king did that because my God was kind to me.

---

[a] **1:1** *Kislev . . . twentieth year* This was about December, 444 BC.
[b] **1:11** *wine servant* This important official was always close to the king and tasted his food and wine to make sure they were safe to eat and drink.
[c] **2:1** *twentieth year* That is, 443 BC.

REMEMBER THE LORD, WHO IS GREAT AND POWERFUL!

What do you do when the going gets tough? Get going? Cry? Give up?

If you have read through Ezra you will know that some of the people who had been captured by the Babylonians have returned to Jerusalem to rebuild the Temple. It's been tough – they had been removed from the land as an act of judgement from God and returning was never going to be easy – they've come up against negativity and had a crisis of identity.

DIG IN   READ Nehemiah 1:1 – 2:18

- What kind of man is Nehemiah?
- What is the problem in far-off Jerusalem (1:3)?
- What has God put into Nehemiah's "heart to do for Jerusalem" (2:12)? We can learn tons about Nehemiah here – his understanding of God's law (1:8–9), his love for God (1:5,11; 2:8) and the people (1:4), his great work ethic (1:11; 2:1–2), his awareness of how God uses people (1:11), his faith (2:3–8), his wisdom (1:4; 2:4–8). Don't forget these – Nehemiah's character is going to be essential for the task of rebuilding Jerusalem's walls.

READ Nehemiah 2:19–20; 4:1–23

- What taunts do Sanballat and Tobiah throw at the people (2:19; 4:2–3)?
- How do the words of Sanballat and Tobiah affect the people (2:20; 4:4–5,9)?
- What other discouragements were the people facing (4:10–12)?

It could have been pretty stressful for Nehemiah – he left his probably well paid, high status job as wine servant to the king to move to Jerusalem and do God's work. He's barely got started when these guys begin to kick up a fuss – they were insulting (4:3) and intimidating (4:7–8). To cap it all, the task was huge, the workers got tired and their families put pressure on them to return home (4:10–12). No matter how much passion there is for God's work there's always discouragement to face. It's not looking good.

- What is Nehemiah's response
  - » before God (4:4,9)?
  - » with the people (4:13–14,16–23)?
  - » to Sanballat and Tobiah (4:4–5,9)?
- Who's the real hero (4:14–15)?

I wonder what we would have done – thrown some nasty words back? Sat down and cried? Nehemiah's response to everything that is thrown at him is to pray. He gets on his knees and asks God for help. And then he puts together an action plan to protect the wall and keep the people safe and their spirits up. It's practical and it's spiritual (vv.13–23).

Verse 14 is amazing! It's a motivational speech with the best encouragement for keeping going – the greatness of the Lord. That's what the people need to hear!

DIG THROUGH

- When people make fun of you for doing what God wants you to do – maybe that's telling your friends about Jesus, or not going out with that girl or guy – what is your reaction? Are you discouraged? Or do you pray? What is God teaching you through the example of Nehemiah?
- Everything seemed to be stacked against Nehemiah – the opposition from outside and the tiredness of the people. It could have been so easy to think God had disappeared. In Nehemiah 4 did you notice how his faith stays unshakeable (vv.4,9,14–15,20) and that God was at work all along (v.15)? What can you learn from this about God and trusting him?

⁹So I went to the governors of the area west of the Euphrates River and gave them the letters from the king. The king had also sent army officers and soldiers on horses with me. ¹⁰Sanballat from Horon and Tobiah the Ammonite official heard about what I was doing. They were very upset and angry that someone had come to help the Israelites.

Nehemiah Inspects the Walls of Jerusalem

¹¹⁻¹²I went to Jerusalem and stayed there three days. Then at night I started out with a few men. I had not said anything to anyone about what my God had put on my heart to do for Jerusalem. There were no horses with me except the horse I was riding. ¹³While it was dark I went out through the Valley Gate. I rode towards the Dragon Well and the Gate of the Ash Piles. I was inspecting the walls of Jerusalem that had been broken down and the gates in the wall that had been burned with fire. ¹⁴Then I rode on towards the Fountain Gate and the King's Pool. As I got close, I could see there was not enough room for my horse to get through. ¹⁵So I went up the valley in the dark, inspecting the wall. Finally, I turned back and went back in through the Valley Gate. ¹⁶The officials and important Israelites didn't know where I had gone. They didn't know what I was doing. I had not yet said anything to the Jews, the priests, the king's family, the officials or any of the other people who would be doing the work.

¹⁷Then I said to them, "You can see the trouble we have here: Jerusalem is a pile of ruins, and its gates have been burned with fire. Come, let's rebuild the wall of Jerusalem. Then we will not be ashamed any more."

¹⁸I also told them that my God had been kind to me. I told them what the king had said to me. Then they answered, "Let's start to work, now!" So we began this good work. ¹⁹But Sanballat from Horon, Tobiah the Ammonite official and Geshem the Arab heard that we were building again. They insulted us and laughed at us. They said, "What are you doing? Are you turning against the king?"

²⁰But this is what I said to them: "The God of heaven will help us succeed. We are God's servants and we will rebuild this city. You cannot help us in this work because none of your family lived here in Jerusalem. You don't own any of this land, and you have no right to be in this place."

Builders of the Wall

3 The name of the high priest was Eliashib. He and his brothers, the priests, went to work and built the Sheep Gate. They prayed to make that gate holy to God. They set the gates in place in the wall. The priests worked on the wall of Jerusalem as far as the Tower of the Hundred and the Tower of Hananel. They prayed to make all this work holy to God.

²The men from Jericho built the wall next to the priests. And Zaccur, son of a man named Imri, built the wall next to the men of Jericho.

³The sons of a man named Hassenaah built the Fish Gate. They set the beams and the gates in place on the wall. Then they put the locks and bolts on the gates.

⁴Meremoth son of Uriah repaired the next section of the wall. (Uriah was the son of Hakkoz.)

Meshullam son of Berekiah repaired the next section of the wall. (Berekiah was the son of Meshezabel.)

Zadok son of Baana repaired the next section of the wall.

⁵The men from Tekoa repaired the next section of the wall, but the leaders from Tekoa refused to work for Nehemiah their governor.

⁶Joiada and Meshullam repaired the Old Gate. Joiada is the son of Paseah and Meshullam is the son of Besodeiah. They set the beams in place. They set the gates on the hinges. Then they put the locks and bolts on the gates.

⁷The men from Gibeon and Mizpah repaired the next section of the wall. Melatiah from Gibeon and Jadon from Meronoth did the work. Gibeon and Meronoth are places that are controlled by the governors of the area west of the Euphrates River.

⁸Uzziel son of Harhaiah repaired the next section of the wall. Uzziel was a goldsmith. Hananiah was one of the perfume makers. These men built and repaired Jerusalem as far as the Broad Wall.

⁹Rephaiah son of Hur repaired the next section of the wall. Rephaiah was the governor of half of Jerusalem.

¹⁰Jedaiah son of Harumaph repaired the next section of the wall. Jedaiah repaired the wall next to his own house. Hattush son of Hashabneiah repaired the next section. ¹¹Malkijah son of Harim and Hasshub son of Pahath-Moab repaired the next section. They also repaired Oven Tower.

INSIGHT

The people who rebuilt the walls weren't trained builders. They were goldsmiths, perfumers, governors and others who all put their jobs on hold to help. Even the women helped out. Each one sacrificed their time to rebuild God's city.

Nehemiah 3:12

¹²Shallum son of Hallohesh repaired the next section of the wall. His daughters helped him.

Shallum was the governor of the other half of Jerusalem.

[13]The Valley Gate was repaired by Hanun and the people who live in the town of Zanoah. They built the Valley Gate. They set the gates on their hinges. Then they put the locks and bolts on the gates. They also repaired 440 metres[a] of the wall. They worked on the wall all the way to the Gate of Ash Piles.

[14]Malkijah son of Recab repaired the Gate of Ash Piles. Malkijah was the governor of the district of Beth Hakkerem. He repaired the gate. He set the gates on the hinges. Then he put the locks and bolts on the gates.

[15]Shallun son of Col-Hozeh repaired the Fountain Gate. Shallun was the governor of the district of Mizpah. He repaired the gate and put a roof over it. He set the gates on the hinges. Then he put the locks and bolts on the gates. He also repaired the wall of the Pool of Siloam that is next to the King's Garden. He repaired the wall all the way to the steps that go down from the City of David.

[16]Nehemiah son of Azbuk repaired the next section. This Nehemiah was the governor of half the district of Beth Zur. He made repairs up to a place that is opposite the tombs of David. And he worked as far as the man-made pool and the House of Heroes.

[17]The men from the tribe of Levi repaired the next section. They worked under Rehum son of Bani. Hashabiah repaired the next section. Hashabiah was governor of half the district of Keilah. He made repairs for his own district.

[18]Their brothers repaired the next section. They worked under Binnui son of Henadad. Binnui was the governor of the other half of the district of Keilah.

[19]Ezer son of Jeshua repaired the next section. Ezer was governor of Mizpah. He repaired the section of wall from the room for weapons to the corner of the wall. [20]Baruch son of Zabbai repaired the next section. Baruch worked very hard and repaired the section of wall from the corner to the entrance to the house of Eliashib the high priest. [21]Meremoth son of Uriah, the son of Hakkoz, repaired the next section of wall from the entrance to Eliashib's house to the end of that house. [22]The next section of walls was repaired by the priests who lived in that area.[b]

[23]Benjamin and Hasshub repaired the wall in front of their own house. And Azariah son of Maaseiah, the son of Ananiah, repaired the wall next to his house.

[24]Binnui son of Henadad repaired the section of wall from Azariah's house to the bend in the wall and then to the corner.

[25]Palal son of Uzai worked opposite the bend in the wall near the tower. This is the tower at the king's upper house. That is near the courtyard of the king's guard. Pedaiah son of Parosh worked next to Palal.

[26]The Temple servants lived on Ophel Hill. They repaired the next section all the way to the east side of the Water Gate and the tower near it.

[27]The men from Tekoa repaired the rest of that section from the big tower all the way to the Ophel wall.

[28]The priests repaired the section over the Horse Gate. Each priest repaired the wall in front of his own house. [29]Zadok son of Immer repaired the section in front of his house. Shemaiah son of Shecaniah repaired the next section. Shemaiah was the guard of the East Gate.

[30]Hananiah son of Shelemiah and Hanun son of Zalaph repaired the rest of that section of wall. (Hanun was Zalaph's sixth son.)

Meshullam son of Berekiah repaired the section in front of his house. [31]Malkijah repaired the next section of wall all the way to the houses of the Temple servants and the merchants opposite the Inspection Gate. Malkijah repaired the section all the way to the room over the corner of the wall. Malkijah was a goldsmith. [32]The goldsmiths and the merchants repaired the section of wall from that corner to the Sheep Gate.

Sanballat and Tobiah

4 When Sanballat heard that we were building the wall of Jerusalem, he was very angry and upset. He started making fun of the Jews. [2]Sanballat talked with his friends and the army at Samaria and said, "What are these weak Jews doing? Do they think we will leave them alone? Do they think they will offer sacrifices? Maybe they think that they can finish building in only one day. They cannot bring stones back to life from these piles of rubbish and dirt. These are just piles of ashes and dirt!"

[3]Tobiah the Ammonite was with Sanballat. Tobiah said, "What do these Jews think they are building? If even a small fox climbed up on it, he would break down their wall of stones!"

[4]Nehemiah prayed and said, "Our God, listen to our prayer. These men hate us. Sanballat and Tobiah are insulting us. Make bad things happen to them. Make them ashamed, like people taken away as prisoners. [5]Don't take away their guilt or

---

[a] 3:13 440 metres Literally, "1,000 cubits".
[b] 3:22 that area Or possibly, "the Jordan Valley".

forgive the sins they have done in your sight. They have insulted and discouraged the builders."

6We built the wall of Jerusalem all the way around the city. But it was only half as tall as it should be. We did this much because the people worked with all their heart.

7But Sanballat, Tobiah, the Arabs, the Ammonites and the men from Ashdod were very angry. They heard that the people continued working on the walls of Jerusalem. They heard that the people were repairing the holes in the wall. 8So all these men got together and made plans against Jerusalem. They planned to stir up trouble against Jerusalem. They planned to come and fight against the city. 9But we prayed to our God. And we put guards on the walls to watch day and night so that we could be ready to meet them.

10And so at that time the people of Judah said, "The workers are becoming tired. There is too much dirt and rubbish in the way. We cannot continue to build the wall. 11And our enemies are saying, 'Before the Jews know it or see us, we will be right there among them. We will kill them and that will stop the work.'"

12Then the Jews living among our enemies came and said this to us ten times, "Our enemies are all around us. They are everywhere we turn."

13So I put some of the people behind the lowest places along the wall, and I put them by the holes in the wall. I put families together, with their swords, spears and bows. 14After looking over everything, I stood up and spoke to the important families, the officials and the rest of the people. I said, "Don't be afraid of our enemies. Remember the Lord, who is great and powerful! You must fight for your brothers, your sons and your daughters! You must fight for your wives and your homes!"

15Then our enemies heard that we knew about their plans. They realized that God had ruined their plans. So we all went back to work on the wall. Everyone went back to their own place and did their part. 16From that day on, half of my men worked on the wall. The other half of my men were on guard, ready with spears, shields, bows and armour. The army officers stood behind all the people of Judah who were building the wall. 17The builders and their helpers had their tools in one hand and a weapon in the other hand. 18Each of the builders wore his sword at his side as he worked. The man who blew the trumpet to warn the people stayed next to me. 19Then I spoke to the leading families, the officials and the rest of the people. I said, "This is a very big job and we are spread out along the wall. We are far from each other. 20So if you hear the trumpet, run to that place. We will all meet together there, and our God will fight for us!"

21So we continued to work on the wall of Jerusalem, and half the men held spears. We worked from the first light of the morning until the stars came out at night.

22At that time I also said this to the people, "Every builder and his helper must stay inside Jerusalem at night. Then they can be guards at night and workers during the day." 23So none of us took off our clothes—not me, not my brothers, not my men and not the guards. Each of us had our weapon ready at all times, even when we went to get water.

Nehemiah Helps the Poor

5 Many of the poor people began to complain against their fellow Jews. 2Some of them were saying, "We have many children. We must get some grain if we are going to eat and stay alive."

3Other people were saying, "This is a time of famine. We have to use our fields, vineyards and homes to pay for grain."

4And still other people were saying, "We have to pay the king's tax on our fields and vineyards. But we cannot afford to pay, so we are borrowing money to pay the tax. 5We are as good as the others. Our sons are as good as their sons. But we will have to sell our sons and daughters as slaves. Some of us have already had to sell our daughters as slaves. There is nothing we can do. We have already lost our fields and vineyards. Other people own them now."

6When I heard their complaints, I was very angry. 7I calmed myself down, and then I went to the rich families and the officials. I told them, "You are forcing your own people to pay interest on the money you loan them. You must stop doing that!" Then I called for all the people to meet together 8and said to them, "Our fellow Jews were sold as slaves to people in other countries. We did our best to buy them back and make them free. And now, you are selling them like slaves again!"

The rich people and officials kept quiet. They could not find anything to say. 9So I continued speaking. I said, "What you people are doing is not right! You know that you should fear and respect our God. You should not do the shameful things other people do! 10My men, my brothers and I are also lending money and grain to the people. But let's stop forcing them to pay interest on these loans. 11You must give their fields, vineyards, olive fields and houses back to them, right now! And you must give back the interest you charged them. You charged them one per cent for the money, grain, new wine and oil that you loaned them."

12Then the rich people and the officials said, "We will give it back and not demand anything more from them. Nehemiah, we will do as you say."

Then I called the priests. I made the rich people and the officials promise to God that they would do what they said. [13]Then I shook out the folds of my clothes. I said, "God will do the same thing to everyone who does not keep their promise. God will shake them out of their houses and they will lose everything they worked for. They will lose everything!"

I finished saying these things and all the people agreed. They all said, "Amen" and praised the LORD. So the people did as they had promised.

[14]And also, during the whole time that I was appointed to be governor in the land of Judah, neither my brothers nor I ate the food that was allowed for the governor. I never forced the people to pay taxes to buy my food. I was governor from the twentieth year until the thirty-second year that Artaxerxes was king.[a] I was governor of Judah for twelve years. [15]But the governors who ruled before me had made life hard for the people. The governors had forced everyone to pay 40 coins[b] of silver. They also made the people give them food and wine. The leaders under these governors also ruled over the people and made life even harder. But I respected and feared God, so I didn't do things like that. [16]I worked hard at building the wall of Jerusalem. All my men gathered there to work on the wall. We didn't take any land from anyone.

[17]Also, I regularly fed 150 Jews who were always welcome at my table, and I fed those who came to us from the nations around us. [18]Every day I prepared this much food for the people who ate at my table: one ox, six good sheep and different kinds of birds. Every ten days all kinds of wine were brought to my table. But I never demanded that they give me the food that was allowed for the governor. I knew that the work the people were doing was very hard. [19]My God, remember all the good I have done for these people.

INSIGHT

Nehemiah set a great example of leadership. He wasn't in it for what he could gain (he didn't even take what he was entitled to), instead he was more concerned with being generous and making sure everyone was fed.

Nehemiah 5

More Problems

6 Then Sanballat, Tobiah, Geshem the Arab and our other enemies heard that I had built the wall. We repaired all the holes in the wall, but we had not yet set the gates in place. [2]So Sanballat and Geshem sent me this message: "Come, Nehemiah, let's meet together. We can meet in the town of Kephirim on the plain of Ono." But they were planning to hurt me.

[3]So I sent messengers to them with this answer: "I am doing important work, so I cannot come down. I don't want the work to stop just so I can come down and meet with you."

[4]Sanballat and Geshem sent the same message to me four times, and I sent the same answer back to them each time. [5]Then, the fifth time, Sanballat sent his helper to me with the same message. And he had a letter in his hand that was not sealed. [6]This is what the letter said:

There is a rumour going around. People are talking about it everywhere. And, by the way, Geshem says it is true. People are saying that you and the Jews are planning to turn against the king. This is why you are building the wall of Jerusalem. People are also saying that you will be the new king of the Jews. [7]And the rumour is that you have chosen prophets to announce this about you in Jerusalem: "There is a king in Judah!"

Now I warn you, Nehemiah, King Artaxerxes will hear about this. So come, let's meet and talk about this together.

[8]So I sent this answer back to Sanballat: "Nothing you are saying is happening. You are just making all that up in your own head."

[9]Our enemies were only trying to make us afraid. They were thinking to themselves, "The Jews will be afraid and too weak to keep on working. Then the wall will not be finished."

But I prayed, "God, make me strong."

[10]One day I went to the house of a man named Shemaiah son of Delaiah. Delaiah was the son of Mehetabel. Shemaiah had to stay in his house. He said, "Nehemiah, let's meet in God's Temple. Let's go inside the Holy Place[c] and lock the doors. Men are coming to kill you. Tonight they are coming to kill you."

[11]But I said to Shemaiah, "Should a man like me run away? You know that an ordinary man

---

[a] **5:14** *the twentieth year . . . king* This was from 444–432 BC.
[b] **5:15** *40 coins* Literally, "40 *shekels*".
[c] **6:10** *Holy Place* Literally, "palace". Only priests were allowed to go into this part of the Temple.

like me cannot go into the Holy Place without being put to death. I will not go!"

12I knew that God had not sent Shemaiah. I knew that he had prophesied against me because Tobiah and Sanballat had paid him to do that. 13They hired Shemaiah to scare me and make me sin ⌊by going into that part of the Temple⌋. They were planning those bad things against me so that they could shame me.

14My God, please remember Tobiah and Sanballat and the bad things they have done. Also remember the woman prophet Noadiah and the other prophets who have been trying to scare me.

The Wall Is Finished

15So the wall of Jerusalem was completed on the twenty-fifth day of the month of Elul.*a* It had taken 52 days to finish building the wall. 16Then all our enemies heard that we had completed the wall, and all the nations around us saw that it was finished. So they lost their courage, because they understood that this work had been done with the help of our God.

17Also in those days after the wall had been completed, the rich people of Judah were sending many letters to Tobiah, and he was answering their letters. 18They sent those letters because many people in Judah had promised to be loyal to him. The reason for this is that Tobiah was son-in-law to Shecaniah son of Arah. And Tobiah's son Jehohanan had married the daughter of Meshullam. Meshullam is the son of Berekiah. 19And in the past, those people had made a special promise to Tobiah. So they kept telling me how good Tobiah was. And they kept telling Tobiah what I was doing. Tobiah kept sending me letters to make me afraid.

7 After we finished building the wall and set the gates in place, we chose the men who would guard the gates and the men to sing in the Temple and help the priests. 2Next, I put my brother Hanani in charge of Jerusalem. I chose another man named Hananiah to be the commander of the fortress. I picked Hanani because he was a very honest man and he feared God more than most people do. 3Then I said to Hanani and Hananiah, "Each day you must wait until the sun has been up for several hours before you open the gates of Jerusalem. You must shut and lock the gates before the sun goes down. Also choose people who live in Jerusalem as guards. Put some of them at special places to guard the city, and put the other people near their own houses."

The List of Captives Who Returned

4Now the city was large and there was plenty of room. But there were few people in it, and the houses had not yet been rebuilt. 5So my God put it in my heart to have all the people meet together. I called together all the important people, the officials and the common people. I did this so that I could make a list of all the families. I found the family lists*b* of the people who had been the first to return from captivity. This is what I found written there:

6These are the people of the province who came back from captivity. In the past, King Nebuchadnezzar of Babylon had taken them as prisoners to Babylon. These people came back to Jerusalem and Judah. They all went to their own towns. 7They returned with Zerubbabel, Jeshua, Nehemiah, Azariah, Raamiah, Nahamani, Mordecai, Bilshan, Mispereth, Bigvai, Nehum and Baanah. This is the list of names and numbers of men from Israel who came back:

8the descendants of Parosh	2,172
9the descendants of Shephatiah	372
10the descendants of Arah	652
11the descendants of Pahath Moab of the family of Jeshua and Joab	2,818
12the descendants of Elam	1,254
13the descendants of Zattu	845
14the descendants of Zaccai	760
15the descendants of Binnui	648
16the descendants of Bebai	628
17the descendants of Azgad	2,322
18the descendants of Adonikam	667
19the descendants of Bigvai	2,067
20the descendants of Adin	655
21the descendants of Ater through the family of Hezekiah	98
22the descendants of Hashum	328
23the descendants of Bezai	324
24the descendants of Hariph	112
25the descendants of Gibeon	95
26from the towns of Bethlehem and Netophah	188
27from the town of Anathoth	128
28from the town of Beth Azmaveth	42
29from the town of Kiriath Jearim, Kephirah and Beeroth	743
30from the towns of Ramah and Geba	621
31from the town of Micmash	122
32from the towns of Bethel and Ai	123
33from the other town of Nebo	52
34from the other town of Elam	1,254
35from the town of Harim	320
36from the town of Jericho	345

a **6:15 Elul** That is, August–September, 443 BC.
b **7:5 family lists** See Ezra 2.

³⁷from the towns of Lod, Hadid and Ono   721
³⁸from the town of Senaah   3,930

³⁹These are the priests:
  the descendants of Jedaiah through
    the family of Jeshua   973
⁴⁰the descendants of Immer   1,052
⁴¹the descendants of Pashhur   1,247
⁴²the descendants of Harim   1,017

⁴³These are the people from the tribe of Levi:
  the descendants of Jeshua and Kadmiel
    through the family of Hodeiah^a   74

⁴⁴These are the singers:
  the descendants of Asaph   148

⁴⁵These are the gatekeepers:
  the descendants of Shallum, Ater,
    Talmon, Akkub, Hatita and Shobai   138

⁴⁶These are the special Temple servants:
  the descendants of Ziha, Hasupha,
    Tabbaoth,
⁴⁷Keros, Sia, Padon,
⁴⁸Lebana, Hagaba, Shalmai,
⁴⁹Hanan, Giddel, Gahar,
⁵⁰Reaiah, Rezin, Nekoda,
⁵¹Gazzam, Uzza, Paseah,
⁵²Besai, Meunim, Nephussim,
⁵³Bakbuk, Hakupha, Harhur,
⁵⁴Bazluth, Mehida, Harsha,
⁵⁵Barkos, Sisera, Temah,
⁵⁶Neziah and Hatipha.

⁵⁷These are Solomon's servants whose descendants returned:
  Sotai, Sophereth, Perida,
⁵⁸Jaalah, Darkon, Giddel,
⁵⁹Shephatiah, Hattil, Pokereth Hazzebaim and
    Amon.
⁶⁰The total of the descendants of the
Temple servants and of Solomon's servants   392

⁶¹⁻⁶²These people came to Jerusalem from the towns of Tel Melah, Tel Harsha, Kerub, Addon and Immer:

  the descendants of Delaiah, Tobiah
    and Nekoda   642

But none of these could prove that they were descendants from the family of Israel.

⁶³There were also these three families of priests: the descendants of Hobaiah, Hakkoz and Barzillai, who was given this name because he married a daughter of Barzillai from Gilead.

⁶⁴These three families searched for their family histories, but they could not find them. So they were not considered fit to serve as priests. ⁶⁵The governor ordered them not to eat any of the holy food until a priest could use the Urim and Thummim to ask God what to do.

⁶⁶⁻⁶⁷All together, there were 42,360 people in the group who came back. This is not counting their 7,337 men and women slaves. They also had 245 men and women singers with them. ⁶⁸⁻⁶⁹They had 736 horses, 245 mules, 435 camels and 6,720 donkeys.

⁷⁰Some of the family leaders gave money to support the work. The governor gave 8 kilogrammes^b of gold to the treasury. He also gave 50 bowls and 530 robes for the priests. ⁷¹The family leaders gave 170 kilogrammes^c of gold to the treasury to support the work. They also gave 1,260 kilogrammes^d of silver. ⁷²All together the other people gave 170 kilogrammes of gold, 1,100 kilogrammes^e of silver and 67 robes for the priests. ⁷³So the priests, the people from the tribe of Levi, the gatekeepers, the singers and the Temple servants settled down in their own towns. And all the other Israelites settled down in their own towns. By the seventh month^f of the year, all the Israelites had settled down in their own towns.

Ezra Reads the Law

8 So all the Israelites met together in the seventh month of the year. They were united and in complete agreement. They all met together in the open place in front of the Water Gate. All the people asked Ezra the teacher to bring out the *Book of the Law of Moses*, which the LORD had given to the Israelites. ²So Ezra the priest brought the law before those who had met together. This was on the first day of the month.^g It was the

---

^a **7:43 Hodeiah** Or "Hodaviah".
^b **7:70 8 kilogrammes** Literally, "1,000 *drachmas*".
^c **7:71 170 kilogrammes** Literally, "20,000 *drachmas*".
^d **7:71 1,260 kilogrammes** Literally, "2,200 *minas*".
^e **7:72 1,100 kilogrammes** Literally, "2,000 *minas*".
^f **7:73 seventh month** That is, September–October. Also in 8:1,14–15.
^g **8:2 first day of the month** This was a special day of worship. The people met together and shared a fellowship meal.

seventh month of the year. Men, women and anyone old enough to listen and understand were at the meeting. [3]Ezra read in a loud voice from the *Book of the Law* from early morning until noon. He was facing the open place that was in front of the Water Gate. He read to all the men and women, and to everyone old enough to listen and understand. All the people listened carefully and paid attention to the *Book of the Law*.

[4]Ezra stood on a high wooden stage. It had been built just for this special time. On his right side stood Mattithiah, Shema, Anaiah, Uriah, Hilkiah and Maaseiah. And on his left side stood Pedaiah, Mishael, Malkijah, Hashum, Hashbad-danah, Zechariah and Meshullam.

[5]So Ezra opened the book. All the people could see him because he was standing above them on the high stage. As he opened the *Book of the Law*, all the people stood up. [6]Ezra praised the LORD, the great God, and all the people held up their hands and said, "Amen! Amen!" Then all the people bowed down and put their faces low to the ground and they worshipped the LORD.

[7]These men from the tribe of Levi taught the people about the law as they were all standing there. The Levites were Jeshua, Bani, Sherebiah, Jamin, Akkub, Shabbethai, Hodiah, Maaseiah, Kelita, Azariah, Jozabad, Hanan and Pelaiah. [8]They read the *Book of the Law of God*. They made it easy to understand, and explained what it meant. They did this so that the people could understand what was being read.

[9]Then Nehemiah the governor, Ezra the priest and teacher, and the Levites who were teaching the people spoke. They said, "Today is a special day[a] to the LORD your God. Don't be sad and cry." They said that because all the people had begun to cry as they were listening to the messages of God in the law.

[10]Nehemiah said, "Go and enjoy the good food and sweet drinks. Give some food and drinks to those who didn't prepare any food. Today is a special day to our Lord. Don't be sad, because the joy of the LORD will make you strong."

[11]The Levites helped the people to calm down. They said, "Be quiet, calm down, this is a special day. Don't be sad."

[12]Then all the people went to eat the special meal. They shared their food and drinks. They celebrated that special day. They were happy that they could hear the reading of God's law and *were now able to understand it*.

[13]Then on the second day of the month,[b] the leaders of all the families went to meet with Ezra, the priests and the Levites. They all gathered around Ezra the teacher to study the words of the law.

[14-15]They studied and found these commands in the law. The LORD gave this command to the people through Moses: In the seventh month of the year, the Israelites must go to Jerusalem to celebrate a special festival. They must live in temporary shelters. And the people are supposed to go through all their towns and Jerusalem and say this: "Go out into the hill country and get branches from different kinds of olive trees. Get branches from myrtle trees, palm trees and shade trees. Use the branches to make temporary shelters. Do what the law says."

[16]So the people went out and got tree branches. Then they built temporary shelters for themselves. They built shelters on their own roofs and in their own courtyards. And they built shelters in the Temple courtyard, in the open place near the Water Gate and near Ephraim Gate. [17]The whole group that had come back from captivity built shelters. They lived in the shelters they had built. Since the days of Joshua son of Nun up until that day, the Israelites had not celebrated the Festival of Shelters like this. Everyone was very happy!

[18]Ezra read to them from the *Book of the Law* every day of the festival from the first day of the festival to the last day. The Israelites celebrated the festival for seven days. Then on the eighth day, the people met together for a special meeting, as the law says.

The People of Israel Confess Their Sins

9 Then on the twenty-fourth day of that same month, the Israelites gathered together for a day of fasting. They wore sackcloth and put ashes on their heads to show they were sad and upset. [2]Those people who were true Israelites separated themselves from foreigners. The Israelites stood and confessed their sins and the sins of their ancestors. [3]They stood there for about three hours, and the people read the *Book of the Law* of the LORD their God. Then for three more hours they confessed their sins and bowed down to worship the LORD their God.

[4]Then these Levites stood on the stairs: Jeshua, Bani, Kadmiel, Shebaniah, Bunni, Sherebiah, Bani and Kenani. They called out to the LORD their God with loud voices. [5]And these Levites called out to the people: Jeshua, Bani, Kadmiel, Bani,

---

[a] **8:9 *special day*** The first and second days of each month were special days of worship. The people met together and shared a fellowship meal.

[b] **8:13 *second day of the month*** The first and second days of each month were special days of worship. The people met together and shared a fellowship meal.

WE MAKE A FIRM AGREEMENT

In the past God had made agreements with the Israelites that he would be their God and they his people (see Exodus 19). This is an important moment for the people – having returned to the land that God had given them, they come to say sorry for the past and re-establish their commitment to the relationship agreement. Wherever they might be in the building project, we're supposed to understand that it's not bricks and temples that keep the people in God's place; it's understanding and acting on God's law. (It's suggested that the events in Nehemiah 9 and 10 took place between those of Ezra 8 and 9.)

DIG IN

READ Nehemiah 9:1–3

- Who was included as they got together and who wasn't?
- Did you notice anything special about how God is described?

This was a time just for the people of God – a special moment where they worship the Lord their God. He is their God; they belong to him. Having had the word of God read to them (chapter 8), they would have been reminded of all they and their ancestors had failed to do to keep the agreement with God. Did you notice the word "Lord"? This reminds the people of when God made an agreement with Moses to rescue them (Exodus chapters 3 – 4) and how he'd always stuck to it, unlike them. With all this in mind it was totally apt they confess their sin!

READ Nehemiah 9:5–37

- From these verses can you find
  » how God is described?
  » what God has done for the people?
  » how the people have acted?

Because of the special agreement God had with the people of Israel he always looked after them, rescued them, provided for them. But because of their sin and stubbornness they had frequently messed up. God had been continually faithful and they'd blown it! Did you notice how remembering all God is and has done formed the basis of their confession?

READ Nehemiah 9:38; 10:28–32

- What do the people now want to do (v.38)?
- What do the people promise to do (v.28; v.30 onwards)?
- What are the consequences of not keeping their promises (v.29)?

Ezra and Nehemiah both tell the great story of the restoration of God's people physically and spiritually through the rebuilding of Jerusalem – this agreement is the high point. The people of Israel heard and believed the word of God (ch.8), they said sorry for their sin (ch.9) and they set out to be obedient (ch.10). More than anything they'd done up to this point in the rebuilding project, this was what reminded them of their special relationship with God.

DIG THROUGH

- The people listened to God's word being read to them (chapter 8) and realized how much they had messed up. When you listen to God's word are you ready to say sorry?
- There's a real focus on who God is in the way the people confess – they can see all he's done for them. What can you learn from that?

Hashabneiah, Sherebiah, Hodiah, Shebaniah and Pethahiah. They said,

"Stand up and praise the LORD your God!
    He has always lived and will live forever."

The People Pray

"God, may everyone praise your glorious name,
    which is greater than all our blessing and
        praise.
⁶You alone are the LORD.
    You made the sky, the heavens,
        and all the stars.
You made the earth
    and everything on it.
You made the seas
    and everything in them.
You give life to everything.
    All the heavenly angels bow down and
        worship you.

⁷"You are the LORD,
    the God who chose Abram.
You led him from Ur in Babylonia.
    You changed his name to Abraham.
⁸You saw he was true and loyal to you,
    and you made an agreement with him.
You promised to give him the land
    of the Canaanites, Hittites, Amorites,
        Perizzites, Jebusites and Girgashites.
But you promised to give that land to
    Abraham's descendants.
    And you kept your promise because you
        are good.

⁹"You saw our ancestors suffering in Egypt
    and heard them call for help by the Red Sea.
¹⁰You showed the miracles to Pharaoh.
    You did amazing things to his officials and
        his people.
You knew that the Egyptians thought
    they were better than our ancestors.
But you proved how great you are,
    and they remember that even today.
¹¹You split the Red Sea in front of them,
    and they walked through on dry land.
The Egyptian soldiers were chasing them,
    but you threw that enemy into the sea.
    And they sank like a rock into the sea.
¹²With the tall cloud, you led them by day,
    and at night you used the column of fire.
That is the way you lit their path
    and showed them where to go.
¹³Then you came down to Mount Sinai.
    You spoke to them from heaven.
You gave them good laws and true teachings.
    You gave them laws and commands that
        were very good.

¹⁴You told them about your special day of
    rest—the Sabbath.
    Through your servant Moses,
    you gave them commands, laws and
        teachings.
¹⁵They were hungry,
    so you gave them food from heaven.
They were thirsty,
    so you gave them water from a rock.
You told them,
    'Come, take this land.'
You used your power,
    and took the land for them.

¹⁶"But our ancestors became proud and
    stubborn.
    They refused to obey your commands.
¹⁷They refused to listen.
    They forgot the amazing things you did
        with them.
They became stubborn.
    They decided to return to Egypt and
        become slaves again.

"But you are a forgiving God!
    You are kind and full of mercy.
You are patient and full of love.
    So you didn't leave them!
¹⁸You didn't leave them even when they made
    gold calves and said,
    'These are the gods that led us out of Egypt.'

¹⁹"But because you are so kind,
    you did not leave them in the desert.
You provided the tall cloud every day
    that showed them the way to go.
And you gave them a fire at night
    that never stopped lighting their path.
²⁰You gave them your good Spirit to make them
    wise.
    You gave them manna for food.
    You gave them water for their thirst.
²¹You took care of them for 40 years.
    They had all they needed in the desert.
Their clothes did not wear out,
    and their feet did not swell and hurt.

²²"You gave them kingdoms and nations,
    and you gave them faraway places where
        few people live.
They got the land of King Sihon of Heshbon.
    They got the land of King Og of Bashan.
²³You made their descendants
    as many as the stars in the sky.
You brought them to the land
    you promised to give their ancestors.
    They went in and took that land.
²⁴Their children took the land.

They defeated the Canaanites living there.
You let them defeat those people.
You let them do whatever they wanted
to those nations, people and kings.
²⁵They defeated powerful cities.
They took the fertile land.
They got houses filled with good things.
They got wells that had already been dug.
They got vineyards, olive trees and plenty of
fruit trees.
They ate until they were full and fat.
They enjoyed all the wonderful things you
gave them.

²⁶"And then they turned against you.
They threw away your teachings.
They killed your prophets.
Those prophets warned the people.
They tried to bring them back to you.
But our ancestors said terrible things
against you.
²⁷So you let their enemies have them.
The enemy caused them much trouble.
When trouble came, our ancestors called to
you for help.
And in heaven, you heard them.
You are very kind,
so you sent people to save them.
And they rescued them from their enemies.
²⁸Then as soon as our ancestors were rested,
they started doing terrible things again!
So you let the enemy defeat them
and punish them.
They called to you for help,
and in heaven you heard them and helped
them.
You are so kind.
That happened so many times.
²⁹You warned them to come back,
but they were too proud.
They refused to listen to your commands.
If people obey your laws, they will live.
But our ancestors broke your laws.
They were stubborn.
They turned their backs on you.
They refused to listen.

³⁰"You were very patient with our ancestors.
You let them mistreat you for many years.
You warned them with your Spirit.
You sent the prophets to warn them.
But our ancestors didn't listen.
So you gave them to people in other
countries.
³¹"But you are so kind!
You didn't completely destroy them.
You didn't leave them.
You are such a kind and merciful God!

³²"Our God, you are the great God,
the awesome, powerful soldier!
You are kind and loyal.
You keep your agreement.
We have had many troubles,
and our troubles are important to you.
Bad things happened to all our people,
and to our kings and leaders,
and to our priests and prophets.
Those terrible things have happened
from the days of the king of Assyria until
today!
³³But God, in all that has happened to us, you
have been just.
You have been faithful to us.
We are the ones who have done wrong.
³⁴Our kings, leaders, priests and fathers did not
obey your law.
They didn't listen to your commands.
They ignored your warnings.
³⁵Our ancestors didn't serve you even when
they were living in their own kingdom.
They didn't stop doing evil.
They enjoyed all the wonderful things you
gave them.
They enjoyed the rich land and had plenty
of room,
but they didn't stop their evil ways.

³⁶"And now, we are slaves.
We are slaves in this land,
the land you gave our ancestors so they could
enjoy its fruit
and all the good things that grow here.
³⁷The harvest is big in this land.
But we sinned, so that harvest goes to the
kings you put over us.
They control us and our cattle.
They do anything they want.
We are in a lot of trouble.

³⁸"Because of all these things, we are making
an agreement that cannot be changed. We are
putting this agreement in writing. Our leaders,
Levites and priests are signing their names to this
agreement and sealing it with a seal."

10 These are the names on the sealed agreement:

Nehemiah the governor, son of Hacaliah.
Zedekiah, ²Seraiah, Azariah, Jeremiah,
³Pashhur, Amariah, Malkijah, ⁴Hattush,
Shebaniah, Malluch, ⁵Harim, Meremoth,
Obadiah, ⁶Daniel, Ginnethon, Baruch,
⁷Meshullam, Abijah, Mijamin, ⁸Maaziah,
Bilgai and Shemaiah. These were the priests
who put their names on the sealed
agreement.

9And these are the Levites who put their names on the sealed agreement:

Jeshua son of Azaniah, Binnui from the family of Henadad, Kadmiel, 10and their brothers: Shebaniah, Hodiah, Kelita, Pelaiah, Hanan, 11Mica, Rehob, Hashabiah, 12Zaccur, Sherebiah, Shebaniah, 13Hodiah, Bani and Beninu.

14And these are the names of the leaders who put their names on the sealed agreement:

Parosh, Pahath-Moab, Elam, Zattu, Bani, 15Bunni, Azgad, Bebai, 16Adonijah, Bigvai, Adin, 17Ater, Hezekiah, Azzur, 18Hodiah, Hashum, Bezai, 19Hariph, Anathoth, Nebai, 20Magpiash, Meshullam, Hezir, 21Meshezabel, Zadok, Jaddua, 22Pelatiah, Hanan, Anaiah, 23Hoshea, Hananiah, Hasshub, 24Hallohesh, Pilha, Shobek, 25Rehum, Hashabnah, Maaseiah, 26Ahiah, Hanan, Anan, 27Malluch, Harim and Baanah.

28-29So all these people now make this special promise to God. And they all ask for bad things to happen if they don't keep their promise. All these people promise to follow the law of God. That law of God was given to us through Moses his servant. These people promise with an oath to carefully obey all the commands, rules and teachings of our Lord GOD. Now, these are the people who are making this promise: The rest of the people—the priests, Levites, gatekeepers, singers, Temple servants and all the Israelites who separated themselves from the people living around them. They have separated themselves to obey God's law. Their wives, sons and daughters who are able to listen and understand also did this. All these people joined their brothers and the important people to accept for themselves the promise to obey God's law. And they accepted the curse that asks for bad things to happen to them if they don't obey God's law.

30"We promise not to let our daughters marry the people living around us. And we promise not to let our sons marry their daughters.

31"We promise not to work on the Sabbath day. If the people living around us bring grain or other things to sell on the Sabbath, we will not buy them on that special day or on any other festival. Every seventh year,[a] we will not plant or work the land. And every seventh year, we will cancel every debt that other people owe to us.

32"We will accept the responsibility for obeying the commands to take care of God's Temple. We will give 5 grammes[b] of silver each year to support the Temple service to honour our God. 33This money will pay for the special bread that the priests put on the table in the Temple. It will pay for the daily grain offerings and burnt offerings. It will pay for the offerings on the Sabbaths, New Moon celebrations and other special meeting days. It will pay for the holy offerings and for the sin offerings that make the Israelites pure. It will pay for any work needed on the Temple of our God.

34"We, the priests, the Levites and the people have thrown lots to decide when each of our families is to bring a gift of wood to the Temple of our God at certain times each year. The wood is to burn on the altar of the LORD our God. We must do that just as it is written in the law.

35"We also accept the responsibility of bringing the first part of our harvest, whether from the grain in our fields or the fruit from our trees. We will bring them to the LORD's Temple each year.

36"Just as it is also written in the law, this is what we will do: We will bring our firstborn sons and our firstborn cattle, sheep and goats. We will bring these to the Temple of our God, to the priests who are serving there.

37"And we will also bring the first part of our harvest to priests to put in the storage rooms of our God's Temple. We will bring the first of our ground meal, the first of our grain offerings, the first fruit from our trees and the first of our new wine and oil. And we will bring a tenth of our crops to the Levites, because they are the ones who collect these things in all the towns where we work. 38A priest from the family of Aaron must be with the Levites when they receive the crops. Then the Levites must bring the crops to the Temple of our God and put them in the storerooms of the Temple treasury. 39The Israelites and the Levites must bring their gifts to the storerooms. They are to bring their gifts of grain, new wine and oil. All the things for the Temple are kept in the storerooms, and that is where the priests who are on duty stay. The singers and gatekeepers also stay there.

"We all promise that we will take care of the Temple of our God."

---

a 10:31 *seventh year* See Exod. 23:10–11.
b 10:32 *5 grammes* Literally, "⅓ *shekel*".

New People Move Into Jerusalem

11 Now the leaders of the Israelites moved into the city of Jerusalem. The rest of the people used lots to decide who else should move there with the leaders. They chose a tenth of the people to live in Jerusalem, the holy city. The rest of the people stayed in their own towns. ²The people who stayed asked God to bless those who were willing to move to Jerusalem.

³Some of the Israelites, priests, Levites, Temple servants and descendants of Solomon's servants lived in the various towns throughout Judah. These people all lived on property they owned in these towns. But the area leaders lived in Jerusalem. ⁴And other people from the families of Judah and Benjamin lived in Jerusalem.

These are the descendants of Judah who moved into Jerusalem:

Athaiah son of Uzziah (the son of Zechariah, who was the son of Amariah, who was the son of Shephatiah, who was the son of Mahalalel, who was a descendant of Perez) ⁵and Maaseiah son of Baruch (the son of Col-Hozeh, who was the son of Hazaiah, who was the son of Adaiah, who was the son of Joiarib, who was the son of Zechariah, who was a descendant of Shelah). ⁶The number of Perez's descendants living in Jerusalem was 468. All of them were brave men.

⁷These are the descendants of Benjamin who moved into Jerusalem:

Sallu son of Meshullam (the son of Joed, who was the son of Pedaiah, who was the son of Kolaiah, who was the son of Maaseiah, who was the son of Ithiel, who was the son of Jeshaiah, ⁸and those who followed Jeshaiah were Gabbai and Sallai. All together there were 928 men. ⁹Joel son of Zicri was in charge of them. And Judah son of Hassenuah was in charge of the Second District of the city of Jerusalem.

¹⁰These are the priests who moved into Jerusalem:

Jedaiah son of Joiarib, Jakin, ¹¹and Seraiah son of Hilkiah (the son of Meshullam, who was the son of Zadok, who was the son of Meraioth, who was the son of Ahitub), who was the supervisor in the Temple of God, ¹²and 822 men of their brothers that did the work for the Temple, and Adaiah son of Jeroham (the son of Pelaliah, who was the son of Amzi, who was the son of Zechariah, who was the son of Pashhur, who was the

son of Malkijah), ¹³and 242 men who were Adaiah's brothers (leaders of their families), Amashsai son of Azarel (the son of Ahzai, who was the son of Meshillemoth, who was the son of Immer), ¹⁴and 128 of Amashsai's brothers. (These men were brave soldiers. The officer over them was Zabdiel son of Haggedolim.)

¹⁵These are the Levites who moved into Jerusalem:

Shemaiah son of Hasshub (the son of Azrikam, who was the son of Hashabiah, who was the son of Bunni), ¹⁶Shabbethai and Jozabad (two of the leaders of the Levites in charge of the outside work of God's Temple), ¹⁷Mattaniah (the son of Mica, who was the son of Zabdi, who was the son of Asaph), the director who led the people in singing songs of praise and prayer, Bakbukiah (the second in charge over his brothers) and Abda son of Shammua (the son of Galal, who was the son of Jeduthun). ¹⁸So there were 284 Levites who moved into Jerusalem, the holy city.

¹⁹These are the gatekeepers who moved into Jerusalem:

Akkub, Talmon and 172 of their brothers. They watched and guarded the gates of the city.

²⁰The other Israelites, and the other priests and Levites, lived in all the towns of Judah. Everyone lived on the land that their ancestors had owned. ²¹The Temple servants lived on the hill of Ophel. Ziha and Gishpa were in charge of the Temple servants.

²²The officer over the Levites in Jerusalem was Uzzi. Uzzi was the son of Bani (the son of Hashabiah, who was the son of Mattaniah, who was the son of Mica). Uzzi was a descendant of Asaph. Asaph's descendants were the singers who were responsible for the service in God's Temple. ²³The singers obeyed orders from the king, which told them what to do from day to day. ²⁴Pethahiah son of Meshezabel told the people what the king wanted done. (Meshezabel was one of the descendants of Zerah. Zerah was Judah's son.)

²⁵The people of Judah lived in these towns: in Kiriath Arba and the small towns around it, in Dibon and the small towns around it, in Jekabzeel and the small towns around it, ²⁶in Jeshua, in Moladah, in Beth Pelet, ²⁷in Hazar Shual, in Beersheba and the small towns around it, ²⁸in Ziklag, in Meconah and the small towns around it, ²⁹in En Rimmon, in Zorah, in Jarmuth, ³⁰in Zanoah and Adullam and the small towns

around them, in Lachish and the fields around it, and in Azekah and the small towns around it. So the people of Judah were living all the way from Beersheba to the Valley of Hinnom.

³¹The descendants of the family of Benjamin from Geba lived in Micmash, Aija, Bethel and the small towns around it, ³²in Anathoth, Nob and Ananiah, ³³in Hazor, Ramah and Gittaim, ³⁴in Hadid, Zeboim and Neballat, ³⁵in Lod and Ono and in the Valley of the Craftsmen. ³⁶Some of the groups from the family of Levi moved to the land of Benjamin.

Priests and Levites

12 These are the priests and Levites who came back to the land of Judah. They came back with Zerubbabel son of Shealtiel and Jeshua. This is a list of their names:

Seraiah, Jeremiah, Ezra,
²Amariah, Malluch, Hattush,
³Shecaniah, Rehum, Meremoth,
⁴Iddo, Ginnethon, Abijah,
⁵Mijamin, Maadiah, Bilgah,
⁶Shemaiah, Joiarib, Jedaiah,
⁷Sallu, Amok, Hilkiah and Jedaiah.

These men were the leaders of the priests and their relatives in the days of Jeshua.

⁸The Levites were Jeshua, Binnui, Kadmiel, Sherebiah, Judah and also Mattaniah. These men, with Mattaniah's relatives, were in charge of the songs of praise to God. ⁹Bakbukiah and Unni were the relatives of those Levites. These two men stood opposite them in the services. ¹⁰Jeshua was the father of Joiakim. Joiakim was the father of Eliashib. Eliashib was the father of Joiada. ¹¹Joiada was the father of Jonathan and Jonathan was the father of Jaddua.

¹²In the days of Joiakim, these men were the leaders of the families of priests:

The leader of Seraiah's family was Meraiah.
The leader of Jeremiah's family was Hananiah.
¹³The leader of Ezra's family was Meshullam.
The leader of Amariah's family was Jehohanan.
¹⁴The leader of Malluch's family was Jonathan.
The leader of Shecaniah's family was Joseph.
¹⁵The leader of Harim's family was Adna.
The leader of Meremoth's family was Helkai.
¹⁶The leader of Iddo's family was Zechariah.
The leader of Ginnethon's family was Meshullam.
¹⁷The leader of Abijah's family was Zicri.
The leader of Miniamin and Maadiah's families was Piltai.

¹⁸The leader of Bilgah's family was Shammua.
The leader of Shemaiah's family was Jehonathan.
¹⁹The leader of Joiarib's family was Mattenai.
The leader of Jedaiah's family was Uzzi.
²⁰The leader of Sallu's family was Kallai.
The leader of Amok's family was Eber.
²¹The leader of Hilkiah's family was Hashabiah.
The leader of Jedaiah's family was Nethanel.

²²The names of the leaders of the families of the Levites and the priests in the days of Eliashib, Joiada, Johanan and Jaddua were written down during the rule of Darius the Persian king. ²³The family leaders among the descendants of the Levites and up to the time of Johanan son of Eliashib were written in the history book. ²⁴And these were the leaders of the Levites: Hashabiah, Sherebiah, Jeshua the son of Kadmiel and their brothers. Their brothers stood opposite them to sing praise and honour to God. One group answered the other group. That is what was commanded by David the man of God.

²⁵The gatekeepers who guarded the storerooms next to the gates were Mattaniah, Bakbukiah, Obadiah, Meshullam, Talmon and Akkub. ²⁶They served in the days of Joiakim. Joiakim was the son of Jeshua, who was the son of Jozadak. And the gatekeepers also served in the days of Nehemiah the governor and in the days of Ezra the priest and teacher.

Dedication of the Wall of Jerusalem

²⁷The people dedicated the wall of Jerusalem. They brought all the Levites to Jerusalem. The Levites came from the towns they lived in. They came to Jerusalem to celebrate the dedication of the wall of Jerusalem. They came to sing songs of praise and thanks to God. They played their cymbals, harps and lyres.

²⁸⁻²⁹And all the singers also came to Jerusalem. They came from the towns all around Jerusalem. They came from the town of Netophah, from Beth Gilgal, Geba and Azmaveth. The singers had built small towns for themselves in the area around Jerusalem.

³⁰So the priests and Levites made themselves pure in a ceremony. Then they also made the people, the gates and the wall of Jerusalem pure in a ceremony.

³¹I told the leaders of Judah to go up and stand on top of the wall. I also chose two large singing groups to give thanks to God. One group was to start going up on top of the wall on the right side, towards the Ash Pile Gate. ³²Hoshaiah and half of the leaders of Judah followed the singers. ³³Also following them were Azariah, Ezra, Meshullam, ³⁴Judah, Benjamin, Shemaiah and Jeremiah. ³⁵And

some of the priests with trumpets also followed them up to the wall. Zechariah also followed them. (Zechariah was the son of Jonathan, who was the son of Shemaiah, who was the son of Mattaniah, who was the son of Micaiah, who was the son of Zaccur, who was the son of Asaph.) ³⁶There were also Asaph's brothers, who were Shemaiah, Azarel, Milalai, Gilalai, Maai, Nethanel, Judah and Hanani. They had the musical instruments that David, the man of God, had made. Ezra the teacher led the group of people who were there to dedicate the wall. ³⁷They went to the Fountain Gate and walked up the stairs all the way to the City of David. They were on top of the city wall. They walked past the house of David and went towards the Water Gate.

³⁸The second group of singers started out in the other direction, to the left. I followed them as they went up to the top of the wall. Half of the people also followed them. They went past the Tower of Ovens to the Broad Wall. ³⁹Then they went over these gates: the Gate of Ephraim, the Old Gate and the Fish Gate. And they went over the Tower of Hananel and the Tower of the Hundred. They went as far as the Sheep Gate and stopped at the Guard Gate. ⁴⁰Then the two singing groups went to their places in God's Temple. And I stood in my place. And half of the officials stood in their places in the Temple. ⁴¹Next these priests stood in their places: Eliakim, Maaseiah, Mijamin, Micaiah, Elioenai, Zechariah and Hananiah. These priests had their trumpets with them. ⁴²Then these priests stood in their places in the Temple: Maaseiah, Shemaiah, Eleazar, Uzzi, Jehohanan, Malkijah, Elam and Ezer.

The two singing groups began singing with Jezrahiah leading them. ⁴³So on that special day, the priests offered many sacrifices. Everyone was very happy because God had made them happy. Even the women and children were excited and happy. People far away could hear the happy sounds coming from Jerusalem.

⁴⁴Men were chosen to be in charge of the storerooms on that day. People brought the first part of the harvest and a tenth of their crops. So the men in charge put these things in the storerooms. The Jewish people were very happy about the priests and Levites on duty. So they brought many things to be put in the storerooms. ⁴⁵The priests and Levites did their work for their God. They performed the ceremonies that made people pure, and the singers and gatekeepers did their part. They did everything that David and Solomon had commanded. ⁴⁶(Long ago, in the days of David, Asaph had been the director. And he had many songs of praise and thanks to God.)

⁴⁷So in the days of Zerubbabel and of Nehemiah, all the Israelites gave every day to support the singers and gatekeepers. The people also set aside the money for the other Levites. And the Levites set aside the money for the descendants of Aaron.

Nehemiah's Last Commands

13 On that day the *Book of Moses* was read out loud, so that all the people could hear. They found this law written there: No Ammonite and no Moabite would be permitted to join in the meetings with God. ²That law was written because those people didn't give the Israelites food and water. And they had paid Balaam to put a curse on the Israelites. But our God changed that curse and made it a blessing for us. ³So when the Israelites heard that law, they obeyed it. They separated themselves from the people who were descendants of foreigners.

⁴⁻⁵But, before that happened, Eliashib had given a room in the Temple to Tobiah. Eliashib was the priest in charge of the storerooms in our God's Temple. And he was a close friend of Tobiah. That room had been used for storing the grain offerings, incense and the utensils used in Temple. They also kept the tenth of grain, new wine and oil for the Levites, singers and gatekeepers in that room. And they also kept the gifts for the priests in that room. But Eliashib gave that room to Tobiah.

⁶I was not in Jerusalem while this was happening. I had gone back to the king of Babylon. I went back to Babylon in the thirty-second year that Artaxerxes was king of Babylon.ᵃ Later, I asked the king for permission to go back to Jerusalem. ⁷So I came back to Jerusalem. There I heard about the sad thing that Eliashib had done. He had given Tobiah a room in the Temple of God! ⁸I was very angry about what Eliashib had done, so I threw all of Tobiah's things out of the room. ⁹I gave commands for the rooms to be made pure and clean. Then I put the utensils used in Temple, the grain offerings and the incense back into the rooms.

¹⁰I also heard that the people had not given the Levites their share. So the Levites and singers had gone back to work in their own fields. ¹¹So I told the officials that they were wrong. I asked them, "Why didn't you take care of God's Temple?" Then I called all Levites together and told them to go back to their places and duties in the Temple. ¹²Then everyone in Judah brought their tenth of grain, new wine and oil to the Temple. These things were put into the storerooms.

¹³I put these men in charge of the storerooms: Shelemiah the priest, Zadok the teacher and a Levite named Pedaiah. And I made Hanan son of Zaccur, son of Mattaniah, their helper. I knew

---

ᵃ **13:6** *the thirty-second year . . . Babylon* That is, 432 BC.

I could trust these men. They were responsible for giving the supplies to their relatives.

¹⁴My God, please remember me for these things I have done. Don't forget all I have faithfully done for the Temple of my God and for its services.

¹⁵In those days in Judah, I saw people working on the Sabbath day. I saw people pressing grapes to make wine. I saw people bringing in grain and loading it on donkeys. I saw people carrying grapes, figs and all kinds of things in the city. They were bringing all these things into Jerusalem on the Sabbath day, so I warned them about this. I told them they must not sell food on the Sabbath day.

¹⁶There were some men from the city of Tyre living in Jerusalem. They were bringing fish and all kinds of things into Jerusalem and selling them on the Sabbath day. And the Jews were buying them. ¹⁷I told the important people of Judah that they were wrong. I said, "You are doing a very bad thing. You are ruining the Sabbath day. ¹⁸You know that your ancestors did the same things. That is why our God brought all the troubles and disaster to us and to this city. Now you people are making it so that more of these bad things will happen to Israel. They are doing this because you are breaking the Sabbath by treating it just as if it were any other day."

¹⁹So this is what I did: Every Friday evening, just before dark, I commanded the gatekeepers to shut and lock the gates to Jerusalem. They were not to be opened until the Sabbath day was over. I put some of my own men at the gates. They were commanded to make sure that no load was brought into Jerusalem on the Sabbath day.

²⁰Once or twice, traders and merchants had to stay the night outside Jerusalem. ²¹But I warned them, "Don't stay the night in front of the wall. If you do that again, I will arrest you." So from that time on they didn't come on the Sabbath day to sell their things.

²²Then I commanded the Levites to make themselves pure. After they did that, they were to go and guard the gates. This was done to make sure the Sabbath day was kept a holy day.

My God, please remember me for doing this. Be kind to me and show me your great love!

²³In those days I also noticed that some Jewish men had married women from the countries of Ashdod, Ammon and Moab. ²⁴And half of the children from those marriages didn't know how to speak the Jewish language. They spoke the language of Ashdod, Ammon or Moab. ²⁵This made me so angry that I asked God to curse them. I fought with them. I hit some of them, and I pulled out their hair. I forced them to make a promise in God's name. I said to them, "You must not marry the daughters of these foreigners. Don't let their daughters marry your sons, and don't let your daughters marry the sons of these foreigners. ²⁶You know that marriages like this caused Solomon to sin. In all the many nations, there was not a king as great as Solomon. God loved him and made him king over the whole nation of Israel. But even Solomon was made to sin because of foreign women. ²⁷And now, we hear that you also are doing this terrible sin. You are not being true to our God. You are marrying foreign women."

²⁸Joiada was the son of Eliashib the high priest. One of Joiada's sons was a son-in-law of Sanballat from Horon. I forced him to leave this place. I forced him to run away.

INSIGHT

Among the restoration of Jewish laws and festivals Nehemiah bans all foreigners. This sounds rather drastic but in the past the Israelites had repeatedly been led astray into worshipping false gods by foreigners still living in the land. The restored kingdom was too precious to risk.

Nehemiah 13:30

²⁹My God, punish these people. They made the priesthood unclean. They treated it as if it was not important. They did not obey the agreement that you made with the priests and Levites. ³⁰So I made the priests and Levites clean and pure. I took away all the foreigners and the strange things they taught. And I gave the Levites and priests their own duties and responsibilities. ³¹And I made sure that people would bring gifts of wood and the first part of their harvest at the right times.

My God, remember me for doing these good things.

Who   We don't know who wrote the book, but the evidence suggests a Jew living in a Persian city. Some believe that it may have been Esther's cousin and guardian Mordecai.

When   It was probably written around 460 BC, after the second group of exiles had returned to Jerusalem.

What   Esther is a book about liberation and rescue. It shows how God worked behind the scenes to rescue his people. This rescue is still celebrated today in the Festival of Purim, which is described in the final chapter of the book.

The tale of a Hebrew girl who becomes queen of Persia and who rescues her people, Esther has a certain fairy-tale quality about it. And it has one extremely unusual feature: the book doesn't once mention God – although some scholars argue that the Jewish letters for God YHWH (Yahweh) are hidden in the book in the form of an acrostic, reflecting the way that God's purposes are hidden from us, woven into the strands of history. This – and the fact that Esther marries a non-Jew – led to many rabbis having reservations about including the book in the final list of Hebrew Scriptures.

However, it has become one of the most popular books among Jews, particularly because it is commemorated in the Jewish Festival of Purim, a celebration of national deliverance. Purim is the only biblical festival not mentioned in the "Torah" (the "Book of the Law"), and the celebration has a riotous, frivolous quality to it, very different to the other festivals.

Esther, indeed, has some comedy moments. But it also has a serious side. It is about persecution and deliverance, and its message of perseverance and triumph has given strength to many Jews in similar circumstances down the centuries.

QUICK TOUR   ESTHER

"If you keep quiet now, help and freedom for the Jews will come from another place. But you and your father's family will all die. And who knows, maybe you have been chosen to be the queen for such a time as this."

Esther 4:14

Queen Vashti Disobeys the King

1 This is what happened during the time when Xerxes[a] was king. Xerxes ruled over the 127 provinces from India to Ethiopia. [2]King Xerxes ruled from his throne in the capital city of Susa.

[3]In the third year of Xerxes' rule, he gave a party for his officers and leaders. The army leaders and important leaders from Persia and Media were there. [4]The party continued for 180 days. Throughout this time, King Xerxes was showing the great wealth of his kingdom and the amazing beauty and wealth of his palace. [5]And when the 180 days were over, King Xerxes gave another party that continued for seven days. It was held in the inside garden of the palace. All the people who were in the capital city of Susa were invited, from the most important to the least important. [6]The inside garden had white and blue linen hangings around the room. They were held in place with cords of white linen and purple material on silver rings and marble pillars. There were couches made of gold and silver. They were sitting on mosaic pavement made of porphyry,[b] marble, mother-of-pearl and other expensive stones. [7]Wine was served in gold cups, and every cup was different. There was plenty of the king's wine, because the king was very generous. [8]The king had given a command to his servants. He told them that each guest must be given as much wine as he wanted, and the wine server obeyed the king.

[9]Queen Vashti also gave a party for the women in the king's palace.

[10-11]On the seventh day of the party, King Xerxes was in high spirits from drinking wine. He gave a command to the seven eunuchs who served him. The eunuchs were Mehuman, Biztha, Harbona, Bigtha, Abagtha, Zethar and Carcas. He commanded them to bring Queen Vashti to him wearing her royal crown. She was to come so that she could show her beauty to the leaders and important people. She was very beautiful.

[12]But when the eunuchs told Queen Vashti about the king's command, she refused to come. Then the king was very angry. [13-14]It was the custom for the king to ask the advice of the experts about the law and punishments. So King Xerxes spoke with the wise men who understood the laws. They were very close to the king. Their names were Carshena, Shethar, Admatha, Tarshish, Meres, Marsena and Memucan. They were the seven most important officials of Persia and Media. They had special privileges to see the king. They were the highest officials in the kingdom. [15]The king asked them, "What does the law say must be done to Queen Vashti? She has not obeyed the command of King Xerxes that the eunuchs had taken to her."

[16]Then Memucan answered the king with the other officials listening, "Queen Vashti has done wrong. She has done wrong against the king and also against all the leaders and people of all the provinces of King Xerxes. [17]I say this, because all the other women will hear about what Queen Vashti did. Then they will stop obeying their husbands. They will say to their husbands, 'King Xerxes commanded Queen Vashti to be brought to him, but she refused to come.' [18]Today the wives of the Persian and Median leaders have heard what the queen did, and these women will be influenced by what she did. They will do the same thing to the king's important leaders. And there will be plenty of disrespect and anger.

[19]"So if it pleases the king, here is a suggestion: Let the king give a royal command and let it be written in the laws of Persia and Media. The laws of Persia and Media cannot be changed. The royal command should be that Vashti is never again to enter the presence of King Xerxes. Let the king also give her royal position to someone else who is better than she is. [20]Then when the king's command is announced in all parts of his large kingdom, all the women will respect their husbands. From the most important to the least important, all the women will respect their husbands."

[21]The king and his important officials were happy with this advice, so King Xerxes did as Memucan suggested. [22]King Xerxes sent letters to all parts of the kingdom. He sent them to each province, written in its own language. He sent them to each nation in its own language. These letters announced in each person's language that every man was to be the ruler over his own family.

Esther Made Queen

2 Later, King Xerxes stopped being angry. Then he remembered Vashti and what she had done. He remembered his commands about her. [2]Then the king's personal servants had a suggestion. They said, "Search for beautiful young virgins for the king. [3]Let the king choose leaders in every province of his kingdom. Then let the leaders bring every beautiful young virgin to the capital city of Susa. These young women will be put with the group of the king's women. They will be under the care of Hegai, the king's eunuch, who is in charge of the women. Then give beauty treatments to all of them. [4]Then let the one who is pleasing to the king become the new queen in

---

[a] **1:1 Xerxes** Hebrew, "Ahasuerus". He was king of Persia about 485–465 BC.
[b] **1:6 porphyry** A dark red or purple stone.

GOD: THE DIRECTOR OF YOUR LIFE

How did you find yourself where you are now at your school or college, or in the job you're doing? Was it all a complete accident? Was it all your own doing? Or is there more to it than that? . . .

DIG IN

READ Esther 1:1 – 2:23

The first two chapters of Esther introduce us to her story's four colourful main characters: the king, Xerxes; the two goodies, Esther and Mordecai; and a dastardly baddie, Haman.

Let's start with a whistle-stop tour of what you need to know about each of them and what happens to them in the opening chapters.

Mordecai and Esther were cousins. Mordecai had raised Esther, who was an orphan. They were both very devout Jews, they loved and respected each other, and Esther just happened to be very, very beautiful. King Xerxes was a very powerful, extravagant and generous king who liked to throw enormous parties. At one of these parties, he asked his beautiful wife, Queen Vashti, to come and meet his guests so he could show her off. However, she didn't like the idea of this and she refused. Xerxes wasn't happy, so he permanently and publicly banned her from his presence, and his people began a search for a new beautiful wife to take her place . . .

Esther was beautiful, remember? It turned out that she was beautiful enough to be chosen as the new queen. Imagine that – an ordinary orphaned Jew, being chosen to stand alongside the most powerful man in the land . . .

Mordecai gets honoured by the king too – having overheard a plot to kill the king, he made sure the assassins were stopped, via Esther, the new queen.

All this, in the first two chapters.

READ Esther 3:1 – 4:17

Here we meet the evil Haman, who is quick to take offence.

- What is Haman's plan (3:8–11)?
- How do Mordecai and the other Jews respond to the news (4:1–3)?
- Even in these dire circumstances, what hope does Mordecai give Esther (4:14)?

DIG THROUGH

"And who knows, maybe you have been chosen to be the queen for such a time as this" (4:14).

- God is not mentioned by name anywhere in Esther, but all over the place there are clues that he is in control of events: a complete nobody gets promoted to queen and another complete nobody manages to prevent a royal assassination. What evidence can you see in your own life that God engineered events so that they would turn out for his glory?

- The circumstances of your own life are no accident. Have you ever considered that you are in the situation you are in right now because God has a purpose for you? It's not likely to be as grand as becoming royalty, but whatever your situation, there will be "good things" (Ephesians 2:10) that God has prepared specifically for you to do. What opportunities do you have right now that no one else does? Is there someone in your life you could encourage? A non-Christian you could share Jesus with? A lonely person you could befriend? What might God be asking you to do at "such a time as this"?

DIG DEEPER

- At the end of chapter 4 Esther and Mordecai are still in grave danger. Read on to see how the invisible but active God rescues them from this apparently impossible situation.

Vashti's place." The king liked this suggestion, so he accepted it.

5Now there was a Jew from the tribe of Benjamin named Mordecai. Mordecai was the son of Jair, and Jair was the son of Shimei, and Shimei was the son of Kish. Mordecai was in the capital city, Susa. 6Mordecai had been carried into captivity from Jerusalem by King Nebuchadnezzar of Babylon. He was with the group that was taken into captivity with King Jehoiachin[a] of Judah. 7Mordecai had a cousin named Hadassah. She didn't have a father or a mother, so Mordecai took care of her. Mordecai had adopted her as his own daughter when her father and mother died. Hadassah was also called Esther. She had a very pretty face and a good figure.

8When the king's command had been heard, many young women were brought to the capital city of Susa. They were put under the care of Hegai. Esther was one of these women. She was taken to the king's palace and put into Hegai's care. Hegai was in charge of the king's women. 9He liked Esther. She became his favourite, so he quickly gave Esther beauty treatments and special food. He chose seven slave women from the king's palace and gave them to Esther. Then he moved Esther and her seven women servants into the best place where the king's women lived. 10Esther didn't tell anyone she was a Jew. She didn't tell anyone about her family background, because Mordecai had told her not to. 11Every day Mordecai walked back and forth near the area where the king's women lived. He did this because he wanted to find out how Esther was, and what was happening to her.

INSIGHT

Think we're obsessed with image and beauty in the twenty-first century? Before Esther could meet the king she had to go through a whole year's worth of beauty treatments!

Esther 2:12–13

12Before a young woman could take her turn to go in before King Xerxes, she had to complete twelve months of beauty treatments—six months with oil of myrrh and six months with perfumes and cosmetics. 13When her time came to go in to the king, she could choose to wear or take whatever she wanted from the women's living

area. 14In the evening the young woman would go to the king's palace. And in the morning she would return to another area where the king's women lived. Then she would be placed under the care of a man named Shaashgaz. He was the king's eunuch in charge of the slave women. She would not go back to the king again unless he was pleased with her. Then he would call her by name to come back to him.

15The time came for Esther to go to the king. She was the one Mordecai had adopted, the daughter of his uncle Abihail. All she wanted to take with her was what Hegai, the king's officer in charge of the women, suggested. Everyone who saw Esther liked her. 16So Esther was taken to King Xerxes in the palace. This happened in the tenth month, the month of Tebeth, in the seventh year of his rule.

17The king loved Esther more than any of the other young women, and she became his favourite. He approved of her more than any of the others. So King Xerxes put a crown on Esther's head and made her the new queen in place of Vashti. 18And the king gave a big party for Esther. It was for all his important people and leaders. He announced a festival in all the provinces and sent out gifts to people, because he was a generous king.

Mordecai Learns About an Evil Plan

19Mordecai was sitting next to the king's gate at the time the young women were gathered together the second time. 20Esther had still kept it a secret that she was a Jew. She had not told anyone about her family background. This is what Mordecai had told her to do. She still obeyed Mordecai just as she had done when he was taking care of her.

21During the time Mordecai was sitting next to the king's gate, this happened: Bigthana and Teresh, two of the king's officers who guarded the doorway, became angry with the king. They began to make plans to kill King Xerxes. 22But Mordecai learned about these plans and told Queen Esther. Then she told the king. She also told him that Mordecai was the one who had learned about the evil plan. 23Then the report was checked out. It was learned that Mordecai's report was true. The two guards who had planned to kill the king were hanged on a post. All these things were written down in a book of the king's histories in front of the king.

Haman's Plan to Destroy the Jews

3 After these things happened, King Xerxes honoured Haman son of Hammedatha the Agagite. The king promoted Haman and gave him

---

[a] **2:6 Jehoiachin** The Hebrew text has "Jeconiah", another name for King Jehoiachin, who was taken prisoner in the year 597 BC.

a place of honour higher than any of the other leaders. ²All the king's leaders at the king's gate would bow down and give honour to Haman. This is what the king commanded them to do. But Mordecai refused to bow down or give honour to Haman. ³Then the king's leaders at the gate asked Mordecai, "Why don't you obey the king's command to bow down to Haman?"

⁴Day after day, the king's leaders spoke to Mordecai, but he refused to obey the command to bow down to Haman. So they told Haman about it. They wanted to see what Haman would do about Mordecai. Mordecai had told them that he was a Jew. ⁵When Haman saw that Mordecai refused to bow down to him or give him honour, he was very angry. ⁶Haman had learned that Mordecai was a Jew. But he was not satisfied to kill only Mordecai. He also wanted to find a way to destroy all of Mordecai's people, the Jews, in all of Xerxes' kingdom.

⁷In the twelfth year of King Xerxes' rule, in the first month, the month of Nisan, Haman threw lots to choose a special day and month. And the twelfth month, the month of Adar was chosen. (At that time the lot was called "pur".) ⁸Then Haman came to King Xerxes and said, "King Xerxes, there is a certain group of people scattered among the people in all the provinces of your kingdom. They keep themselves separate from other people. Their customs are different from those of all other people. And they don't obey the king's laws. It is not right for the king to allow them to continue to live in your kingdom.

⁹"If it pleases the king, I have a suggestion: Give a command to destroy these people. And I will put 340,000 kilogrammes*a* of silver into the king's treasury. This money could be used to pay the men who do these things."

¹⁰So the king took the official ring off his finger and gave it to Haman son of Hammedatha the Agagite. Haman was the enemy of the Jews. ¹¹Then the king said to Haman, "Keep the money. Do what you want with the people."

¹²Then on the thirteenth day of the first month, the king's secretaries were called. They wrote out all of Haman's commands in the language of each province. And they wrote them in the language of each group of people. They wrote to the king's satraps, the governors of the different provinces and the leaders of the different groups of people. They wrote with the authority of King Xerxes himself, and sealed the commands with the king's own ring.

¹³Messengers carried the letters to all the king's provinces. The letters were the king's command to ruin, kill and completely destroy all the Jews.

This meant young people and old people, women and little children too. The command was to kill all the Jews on a single day. The day was to be the thirteenth day of the twelfth month, the month of Adar. And the command was to take everything that belonged to the Jews.

¹⁴A copy of the letters with the command was to be given as a law. It was to be a law in every province and announced to the people of every nation living in the kingdom. Then everyone would be ready for that day. ¹⁵At the king's command the messengers hurried off. The command was given in the capital city of Susa. The king and Haman sat down to drink, but the city of Susa was in confusion.

Mordecai Persuades Esther to Help

4 When Mordecai heard about all that had been done, he tore his clothes. Then he put on sackcloth, put ashes on his head and went out into the city crying loudly. ²But Mordecai went only as far as the king's gate. No one was allowed to enter the gate dressed in sackcloth. ³In every province where the king's command had come, there was much crying and sadness among the Jews. They were fasting and crying loudly. Many Jews were lying on the ground dressed in sackcloth with ashes on their heads.

⁴Esther's slave women and eunuchs came to her and told her about Mordecai. This made Queen Esther very sad and upset. She sent clothes for Mordecai to put on instead of the sackcloth, but he would not accept them. ⁵Then Esther called Hathach, one of the king's eunuchs who had been chosen to serve her. She commanded him to find out what was bothering Mordecai, and why. ⁶So Hathach went out to where Mordecai was in the open place of the city in front of the king's gate. ⁷Then Mordecai told Hathach everything that had happened to him. Mordecai told him about the exact amount of money Haman had promised to put into the king's treasury for killing Jews. ⁸Mordecai also gave Hathach a copy of the king's command to kill the Jews. The command had been sent out all over the city of Susa. He wanted Hathach to show it to Esther and tell her everything. And he told him to encourage Esther to go to the king and beg him for mercy for Mordecai and her people.

⁹Hathach went back and told Esther everything Mordecai had said.

¹⁰Then Esther told Hathach to say this to Mordecai: ¹¹"Mordecai, all the king's leaders and all the people of the king's provinces know this: The king has one law for any man or woman who goes to the king without being called. That person

---

a **3:9 340,000 kilogrammes** Literally, "10,000 *talents*".

must be put to death unless the king holds out his gold sceptre to them. If the king does this, that person's life will be saved. And I have not been called to go to see the king for 30 days."

12–13Then Esther's message was given to Mordecai. When he got her message, Mordecai sent his answer back: "Esther, don't think that just because you live in the king's palace you will be the only Jew to escape. 14If you keep quiet now, help and freedom for the Jews will come from another place. But you and your father's family will all die. And who knows, maybe you have been chosen to be the queen for such a time as this."

15–16Then Esther sent this answer to Mordecai: "Mordecai, go and get all the Jews in Susa together, and fast for me. Don't eat or drink for three days and nights. I and my women servants will fast too. After we fast, I will go to the king. I know it is against the law to go to the king if he didn't call me, but I will do it anyway. If I die, I die."

17So Mordecai went away and did everything Esther told him to do.

INSIGHT

Esther used fasting as a way of preparing herself to take action to secure freedom for God's people. Today Christians continue to use a time of fasting to prepare themselves for the things God has asked them to do.

Esther 4:16

Esther Speaks to the King

5 On the third day, Esther put on her special robes. Then she stood in the inside area of the king's palace, in front of the king's hall. The king was sitting on his throne in the hall, facing the place where people enter the throne room. 2When the king saw Queen Esther standing in the court, he was very pleased. He held out to her the gold sceptre that was in his hand. So Esther went into the room and went up to the king. Then she touched the end of the king's gold sceptre.

3Then the king asked, "What is bothering you Queen Esther? What do you want to ask me? I will give you anything you ask for, even half my kingdom."

4Esther said, "I have prepared a party for you and Haman. Will you and Haman please come to the party today?"

5Then the king said, "Bring Haman quickly so that we may do what Esther asks."

So the king and Haman went to the party Esther had prepared for them. 6While they were drinking wine, the king asked her again, "Now Esther, what do you want to ask for? Ask for anything, I will give it to you. So what is it you want? I will give you anything you want, up to half my kingdom."

7Esther answered, "This is what I want to ask for: 8If the king is pleased with me and thinks it good to give me what I ask for, let the king and Haman come tomorrow. I will prepare another party for them. Then I will tell you what I really want."

Haman's Anger at Mordecai

9Haman left the king's palace that day very happy and in a good mood. But when he saw Mordecai at the king's gate, he became very angry. Haman was very angry with him because Mordecai didn't show any respect when Haman walked by. Mordecai was not afraid of Haman, and this made Haman angry. 10But Haman controlled his anger and went home. Then Haman called together his friends and his wife, Zeresh. 11Haman started boasting about how rich he was. He was boasting to his friends about his many sons, and about all the ways the king had honoured him. And he was boasting about how the king had promoted him above all the other leaders. 12"And that's not all," Haman added. "I'm the only one Queen Esther invited to be with the king at the party she gave. And the queen has also invited me to be with the king again tomorrow. 13But all this means nothing to me. I cannot be happy as long as I see that Jew Mordecai sitting at the king's gate."

14Then Haman's wife Zeresh and all his friends had a suggestion. They said, "Tell someone to build a post to hang him on. Make it 22 metres[a] tall. In the morning ask the king to hang Mordecai on it. Then go to the party with the king and you can be happy."

Haman liked this suggestion, so he ordered someone to build the hanging post.

Mordecai Is Honoured

6 That same night, the king could not sleep. So he told a servant to bring the history book and read it to him. (*The Book of History of the Kings* lists everything that happens during a king's rule.) 2The servant read the book to the king. He read about the evil plan to kill King Xerxes. That

---

a **5:14** *22 metres* Literally, "50 *cubits*". Also in 7:9.

was when Mordecai had learned about Bigthana and Teresh. These two men were the king's officers who guarded the doorway. They had planned to kill the king, but Mordecai learned about the plan and told someone about it.

3Then the king asked, "What honour and good things have been given to Mordecai for this?"

The servants answered the king, "Nothing has been done for Mordecai."

4Haman had just entered the outer area of the king's palace. He had come to ask the king to hang Mordecai on the hanging post Haman had commanded to be built. The king said, "Who just came into the courtyard?" 5The king's servants said, "Haman is standing in the courtyard."

So the king said, "Bring him in."

6When Haman came in, the king asked him a question. He said, "Haman, what should be done for a man the king wants to honour?"

Haman thought to himself, "Who is there that the king would want to honour more than me? I'm sure that the king is talking about honouring me."

7So Haman answered the king, "Do this for the man the king loves to honour: 8Have the servants bring a special robe the king himself has worn and a horse the king himself has ridden. Have the servants put the king's special mark on the horse's head. 9Then put one of the king's most important leaders in charge of the robe and the horse, and let the leader put the robe on the man the king wants to honour. Then let him lead him on the horse through the city streets. As he leads him, let him announce, 'This is done for the man the king wants to honour!'"

10"Go quickly," the king commanded Haman. "Get the robe and the horse and do just as you have suggested for Mordecai the Jew. He is sitting near the king's gate. Do everything that you suggested."

11So Haman got the robe and the horse. Then he put the robe on Mordecai and led him on horseback through the city streets. Haman announced ahead of Mordecai, "This is done for the man the king wants to honour!"

12After that, Mordecai went back to the king's gate, but Haman hurried home with his head covered because he was embarrassed and ashamed. 13Then Haman told his wife Zeresh and all his friends everything that had happened to him. His wife and the men who gave him advice said, "If Mordecai is a Jew, you cannot win. You have already started to fall. Surely you will be ruined!"

14While they were still talking to Haman, the king's eunuchs came to Haman's house. They made Haman hurry to the party that Esther had prepared.

Haman Is Hanged

7 So the king and Haman went to eat with Queen Esther. 2Then as they were drinking wine on the second day of the party, the king again asked Esther a question, "Queen Esther, what is it you want to ask for? Ask anything and it will be given to you. What do you want? I will give you anything, even half my kingdom."

3Then Queen Esther answered, "King, if you like me and it pleases you, please let me live. And I ask you to let my people live too. This is what I ask for. 4I ask this because my people and I have been sold to be destroyed—to be killed and wiped out completely. If we had just been sold as slaves, I would have kept quiet, because that would not be enough of a problem to bother the king."

5Then King Xerxes asked Queen Esther, "Who did this to you? Where is the man who dared to do such a thing to your people?"

6Esther said, "The man against us, our enemy, is this wicked Haman."

Then Haman was filled with terror before the king and queen. 7The king was very angry. He got up, left his wine, and went out into the garden. But Haman stayed inside to beg Queen Esther to save his life. He begged for his life because he knew that the king had already decided to kill him. 8Just as the king was coming back in from the garden to the party room, he saw Haman there on the couch where Esther was lying. The king said with anger in his voice, "Will you attack the queen even while I am in the house?"

As soon as the king had said this, servants came in and took Haman away.[a] 9One of the eunuchs who served the king was named Harbona. He said, "A hanging post 22 metres tall has been built near Haman's house. Haman had it made so that he could hang Mordecai on it. Mordecai is the man who helped you when he told us about the evil plans to kill you."

The king said, "Hang Haman on that post!"

10So they hanged Haman on the hanging post he had built for Mordecai. Then the king stopped being angry.

The King's Order to Help the Jews

8 That same day King Xerxes gave Queen Esther everything that belonged to Haman, the enemy of the Jews. Esther told the king that Mordecai was her cousin. Then Mordecai came to see the king. 2The king took off his royal ring that he had taken back from Haman. He gave it to

---

[a] **7:8 took Haman away** Literally, "covered Haman's face", showing that he was to be killed.

YOU ARE NOT ALONE

This Bible Bit will make better sense if you've read the earlier chapters of this book, as Esther is a complete story and, like a blockbuster film or a good book, you don't want to start it in the middle.

Esther, Mordecai and the Jews are in grave danger because of evil Haman's plot. How will God intervene in this apparently impossible situation?

DIG IN

READ Esther 7:1 – 8:17

- There are all kinds of strong emotions in chapter 8. How do you imagine Esther was feeling in verses 1–8? Can you put yourself in her shoes?
- What could potentially have gone wrong as Esther addressed the king (7:3–4; 8:3–6)?
- What could potentially have been the result?

Clearly God's hand has been at work to save his people through Esther's actions. Let's look at how things have changed.

- What are the differences between Esther in these chapters and the orphan Esther we first met in 2:7?
- What are the differences between Mordecai in chapter 8:15, and what we saw of him in 3:2–4 and 4:1?
- What are the differences between the experience of the Jewish people in 4:3, and what we see in 8:16?
- What are some of the many ways that God intervened to bring these massive changes about?

DIG THROUGH

- Think of the humble beginnings of both Esther and Mordecai. They were very ordinary, faithful believers. But they gathered up courage and took risks, and they saw amazing results. Is there a situation in your life where you, an ordinary believer, might be able to take a small risk and make a small difference (or a big risk and a big difference)? Perhaps there's a friend you've not plucked up the courage to talk to about God? Perhaps there's something you could do with your time that would benefit others and you've not yet got around to doing it? Be encouraged – your courageous actions for God could have huge benefits for everyone – not necessarily in this life, but definitely in the one to come.

DIG DEEPER

- Take a look at Isaiah 43:4 and Genesis 12:1–3. The fact that this story has a happy ending fits with the fact that God has promised all along to preserve his people: his people will never be wiped out. This was true back in Abraham's time, it was true for the Jews in Esther's time, and it's true for us as God's people now. The church will never be eliminated in any culture or time.
- This isn't the only time God used one or two powerless people to achieve mighty things against all the odds – the Bible is full of stories like this. If you'd like to read some more, check out Judges 6, 1 Kings 19 and 1 Corinthians 1:18 – 2:5 (and they're just for starters). There's also another important one: how about a backwater carpenter, born in a cowshed, growing up to save the souls of humankind from sin . . . The Bible shows us again and again that with God, one person can make a difference. What difference will you make?

Mordecai. And Esther put Mordecai in charge of everything that Haman had owned.

³Then Esther spoke to the king again. She fell at the king's feet and began crying. She begged the king to cancel the evil plan of Haman the Agagite. Haman had thought up the plan to hurt the Jews.

⁴Then the king held out the gold sceptre to Esther. Esther got up and stood in front of the king. ⁵Then she said, "King, if you like me and if it pleases you, do this for me. Please do this if you think it is a good idea. If the king is happy with me, please write a command that would stop the command Haman sent out. Haman the Agagite thought of a plan to destroy the Jews in all the king's provinces, and he sent out commands for this to happen. ⁶I am begging the king because I could not bear to see these terrible things happen to my people. I could not bear to see my family killed."

⁷King Xerxes answered Queen Esther and Mordecai the Jew, "Because Haman was against the Jews, I have given his property to Esther. And my soldiers have hanged him on the hanging post. ⁸Now write another command by the authority of the king. Write it to help the Jews in a way that seems best to you. Then seal the order with the king's special ring. No official letter written by the authority of the king and sealed with the king's ring can be cancelled."

INSIGHT

Did you know that this is the longest verse in the Bible? (The number of words varies in different translations.) In contrast, John 11:35 is the shortest verse, generally with just two words.

Esther 8:9

⁹Very quickly the king's secretaries were called. This was done on the twenty-third day of the third month, the month of Sivan. They wrote out all of Mordecai's commands to the Jews, and to the satraps, the governors and officials of the 127 provinces. These provinces reached from India to Ethiopia. The commands were written in the language of each province and translated into the language of each group of people. The commands were written to the Jews in their own language and alphabet. ¹⁰Mordecai wrote commands by the authority of King Xerxes. Then he sealed the letters with the king's ring and sent them by messengers on horses. The messengers rode fast horses, which were bred especially for the king.

¹¹The king's commands in the letters said this: The Jews in every city have the right to gather together to protect themselves. They have the right to ruin, kill and completely destroy any army from any group who might attack them and their women and children. And the Jews have the right to take and destroy the property of their enemies. ¹²The day set for the Jews to do this was the thirteenth day of the twelfth month, the month of Adar. They were permitted to do this in all King Xerxes' provinces. ¹³A copy of the letter with the king's command was to be sent out. It became a law in every province. They announced it to all the people of every nation living in the kingdom. They did this so that the Jews would be ready for that special day. They would be allowed to pay their enemies back. ¹⁴The messengers hurried out, riding on the king's horses. The king commanded them to hurry. And the command was also put in the capital city of Susa.

¹⁵Mordecai left the king. He was wearing special clothes from the king. His clothes were blue and white, and he had on a large gold crown. He also had a purple robe made of the best linen. There was a special celebration in Susa. The people were very happy. ¹⁶It was an especially happy day for the Jews, a day of great joy and happiness.

¹⁷Wherever the king's command went in every province and every city, there was joy and gladness among the Jews. They were having parties and celebrating. Many of the common people from other groups became Jews. They did this because they were afraid of the Jews.

Victory for the Jews

9 On the thirteenth day of the twelfth month (Adar), the people were supposed to obey the king's command. This was the day the enemies of the Jews hoped to defeat them, but now things had changed. The Jews were stronger than their enemies who hated them. ²The Jews met together in their cities in all the provinces of King Xerxes so that they would be strong enough to attack the people who wanted to destroy them. No one was strong enough to stand against them. They were afraid of the Jews. ³And all the officials of the provinces, the satraps, the governors and the king's administrators helped the Jews. All the leaders helped them because they were afraid of Mordecai. ⁴Mordecai had become a very important man in the king's palace. Everyone in the provinces knew his name and knew how important he was. And Mordecai became more and more powerful.

⁵The Jews defeated all their enemies. They used swords to kill and destroy them. They did what

they wanted to the people who hated them. ⁶They killed and destroyed 500 men in the capital city of Susa. ⁷They also killed these men: Parshandatha, Dalphon, Aspatha, ⁸Poratha, Adalia, Aridatha, ⁹Parmashta, Arisai, Aridai and Vaizatha. ¹⁰These men were the ten sons of Haman. Haman son of Hammedatha was the enemy of the Jews. The Jews killed all the men, but they didn't take anything that belonged to them.

¹¹That day the king heard how many men had been killed in the capital city of Susa. ¹²So the king said to Queen Esther, "The Jews have killed 500 men in Susa, including Haman's ten sons. Now, what do you want done in the other provinces of the king? Tell me, and I will have it done. Ask, and I will do it."

¹³Esther said, "If it pleases the king, please let the Jews in Susa do the same thing again tomorrow. Also, hang the bodies of Haman's ten sons on posts."

¹⁴So the king gave the command that it should be done. So the law was given in Susa, and they hanged Haman's ten sons. ¹⁵The Jews in Susa met together on the fourteenth day of the month of Adar. They killed 300 men in Susa, but they didn't take the things that belonged to them.

¹⁶At the same time, the Jews living in the other provinces also met together. They met together so that they would be strong enough to protect themselves. And so they got rid of their enemies. They killed 75,000 of their enemies. But the Jews didn't take anything that belonged to them. ¹⁷This happened on the thirteenth day of the month of Adar. On the fourteenth day the Jews rested and made that day a happy day of feasting.

The Festival of Purim

¹⁸The Jews in Susa had met together on the thirteenth and fourteenth days of the month of Adar. And then on the fifteenth day they rested. So they made the fifteenth day a happy day of feasting. ¹⁹So those who live in the country and small villages celebrate Purim on the fourteenth day of Adar. They keep the fourteenth day as a happy day of feasting. On this day they have parties and give presents to each other.

²⁰Mordecai wrote everything down that had happened, and then he sent letters to all the Jews in all of King Xerxes' provinces. He sent letters far and near. ²¹He did this to tell the Jews to celebrate Purim every year on the fourteenth and fifteenth days of the month of Adar. ²²They were to celebrate those days because on those days the Jews got rid of their enemies. And they were also

to celebrate that month as the month when their sadness was turned into joy. It was a month when their crying was changed into a day of celebration. Mordecai wrote letters to all the Jews and told them to celebrate those days as a happy day of feasting. They should have parties, give gifts to each other and give presents to the poor.

²³So the Jews agreed to do what Mordecai had written to them. And they agreed to continue the celebration they had begun.

²⁴Haman son of Hammedatha the Agagite was the enemy of all the Jews. He had made an evil plan against the Jews to destroy them. And Haman had thrown the lot to choose a day to ruin and to destroy the Jews. At that time the lot was called a "pur". ²⁵Haman did this, but Esther went to talk to the king. So he sent out new commands. These commands not only ruined Haman's plans, but these commands caused those bad things to happen to Haman and his family! So Haman and his sons were hanged on the posts.

²⁶⁻²⁷At this time, lots were called "purim" So this festival is called "Purim". Mordecai wrote a letter and told the Jews to celebrate this festival. And so the Jews started the custom of celebrating these two days every year. ²⁸They do this to help them remember what they had seen happen to them. The Jews and all the people who join them celebrate these two days every year at the right time in just the right way. Every generation and every family remembers these two days. They celebrate this festival in each and every province and in each and every town. And the Jews will never stop celebrating the days of Purim. Their descendants will always remember this festival.

²⁹So Queen Esther daughter of Abihail, along with Mordecai the Jew, wrote an official letter about Purim. They wrote with full authority of the king to prove that the second letter was true. ³⁰So Mordecai sent letters to all the Jews in the 127 provinces of King Xerxes' kingdom. He told the people that the festival should bring peace and make people trust[a] each other. ³¹He wrote these letters to tell the people to start celebrating Purim. And he told them when to celebrate this new festival. Mordecai the Jew and Queen Esther had sent out the command for the Jews to establish this two-day festival for themselves and their descendants. They will remember this festival just as they remember the other festivals when they fast and cry about the bad things that had happened. ³²Esther's letter made the rules for Purim official, and these things were written down in a book.

---

[a] **9:30** *peace . . . trust* Or "fellowship and truth". Zech. 8:19 teaches that this is how people should celebrate the festivals and why God gave them.

Mordecai Honoured

10 King Xerxes made people pay taxes. All the people in the kingdom, even the faraway cities on the coast, had to pay taxes. ²And all the great things Xerxes did are written in the *Book of History of the Kings of Media and Persia.* Also written in those history books are all the things Mordecai did. The king made Mordecai a great man. ³Mordecai the Jew was second in importance to King Xerxes. He was the most important man among the Jews. His fellow Jews respected him very much, because he worked hard for the good of his people and brought peace to all the Jews.

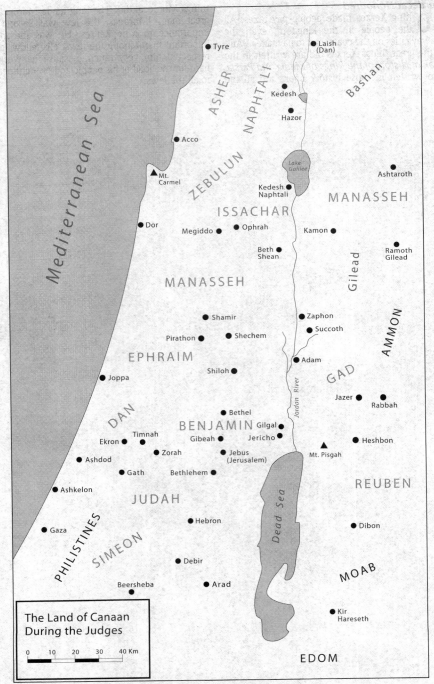

The Land of Canaan
During the Judges

0   10   20   30   40 Km

The Hebrew word for wisdom has a meaning similar to "life skills". So the books which make up this section of the Old Testament are not full of a load of theory, but practical, helpful advice to help you live your life.

These five books of the Bible – Job, Psalms, Proverbs, Ecclesiastes and Song of Songs – are extremely varied in their subject matter. All human life is here. Pain, pleasure, love, hate, sex, anger, cynical boredom, wild jubilation – all the emotions and attitudes which fill our days can be found in these five books. Above all, they are focused on God, on his relationship with humanity and how all wisdom and knowledge is based on a proper respect for him and his works.

Collecting wisdom was very important to the people of ancient times. It was important to listen to people who were considered wise, to collect their observations and learn from their experiences. So some of these books – like Psalms and Proverbs – contain collections of psalms and proverbs by different authors.

In many ways they are the most "human" books of the Bible. They ask difficult questions and reflect bleak and often depressing moods, but just as they talk about the bad things, they also celebrate the good. There is often an almost awestruck appreciation of the physical world and what it means to be human.

Job is one of the most profound books of the Bible: it's a long examination of the problem of suffering. Job is a good man, but he ends up suffering. How can that be right?

Psalms is a collection of 150 poems or songs, written by many different authors. Psalms is a kind of spiritual journal, reflecting on all the ups and downs of a believer's life.

Proverbs is a collection of wise and insightful sayings to help you live your life right.

Ecclesiastes is a dark, almost depressive meditation on the futility of life. The book recognizes God's greatness, but at times the mood is pretty sombre and bleak.

Song of Songs is a love poem, about how good it is to fall in love. It's about men and women and the joys of a physical relationship. Some have also interpreted this book as a metaphor for our relationship with God.

Who

We don't know who wrote this. It is unlikely to have been Job himself. The author was probably an Israelite writing sometime later, bringing this story together from a variety of sources.

When

As to when the book was written, it could have been any time from the reign of Solomon to the exile. But the action is set in the time of the patriarchs, around 2000–1500 BC. Job is a very similar type of character to people like Abraham and Isaac.

What

Job deals with one of the most profound of all human problems – why do good people suffer? The book itself is in the form of a dramatic dialogue or a debate between Job and various friends.

Job lives in the country of Uz which is somewhere in the East. He is a genuinely good man, rich in livestock, living to a great age and blessed with a big family. Then disaster strikes. His family die, his riches are wiped out, he catches a horrible disease and he's reduced to sitting on a rubbish heap.

Yet throughout it all, Job holds on to two facts: God exists and there must be some kind of explanation. Despite the "advice" of his friends, who are certain that Job must have done something to deserve his suffering, Job remains resolute. He hasn't sinned, and he wants an explanation.

Job and his friends want a nice, neat solution to why suffering occurs, but they don't get one. Instead they come face to face with God; and in the light of that they accept that some questions just have to be put aside. The book may be concerned with the problem of suffering, but in the end it doesn't actually answer the question. In the end, God sweeps in, washing away all the arguments and the shallow theories with the reality of his power and presence.

QUICK TOUR ▶ JOB

"I know that there is someone to defend me and that he lives! And in the end, he will stand here on earth and defend me. After I leave my body and my skin has been destroyed, I know I will still see God."

Job 19:25–26

Job, the Good Man

1 There was a man named Job who lived in the country of Uz. He was a good, honest man. He respected God and refused to do evil. [2]Job had seven sons and three daughters. [3]He owned 7,000 sheep, 3,000 camels, 1,000 oxen and 500 female donkeys. He had many servants. He was the richest man in the East.

[4]Job's sons took turns having dinner parties in their homes, and they invited their sisters. [5]The day after each of these parties, Job got up early in the morning, sent for his children and offered a burnt offering for each of them. He thought, "Maybe my children were careless and sinned against God at their party." Job always did this so that his children would be forgiven for their sins.

[6]Then the day came for the angels[a] to meet with the LORD. Even Satan was there with them. [7]The LORD said to Satan, "Where have you been?"

Satan answered the LORD, "I have been roaming around the earth, going from place to place."

[8]Then the LORD said to Satan, "Have you noticed my servant Job? There is no one on earth like him. He is a good, faithful man. He respects God and refuses to do evil."

[9]Satan answered the LORD, "But Job has a good reason to respect you. [10]You always protect him, his family and everything he has. You have blessed him and made him successful in everything he does. He is so wealthy that his herds and flocks are all over the country. [11]But if you were to destroy everything he has, I promise you that he would curse you to your face."

[12]The LORD said to Satan, "All right, do whatever you want with anything that he has, but don't hurt Job himself."

Then Satan left the meeting.

Job Loses Everything

[13]One day Job's sons and daughters were eating and drinking wine at the oldest brother's house. [14]A messenger came to Job and said, "We were ploughing the fields with the oxen and the donkeys were eating grass nearby, [15]when some Sabeans[b] attacked us and took your animals! They killed the other servants. I am the only one who escaped to come and tell you the news!"

[16]That messenger was still speaking when another one came in and said, "A bolt of lightning[c] struck your sheep and servants and burned them up. I am the only one who escaped to come and tell you the news!"

[17]That messenger was still speaking when another one came in and said, "The Chaldeans[d] sent out three raiding parties that attacked us and took the camels! They killed the other servants. I am the only one who escaped to come and tell you the news!"

[18]That messenger was still speaking when another one came in and said, "Your sons and daughters were eating and drinking wine at the oldest brother's house. [19]A strong wind suddenly came in from across the desert and blew the house down. It fell on your sons and daughters, and they are all dead. I am the only one who escaped to come and tell you the news!"

[20]When Job heard this, he got up, tore his clothes and shaved his head to show his sadness. Then he fell to the ground to bow down before God [21]and said,

"When I was born into this world,
   I was naked and had nothing.
When I die and leave this world,
   I will be naked and have nothing.
The LORD gives,
   and the LORD takes away.
Praise the name of the LORD!"

[22]Even after all this, Job did not sin. He did not accuse God of doing anything wrong.

INSIGHT

When catastrophe strikes, many people's response is to blame God, but Job's response was to worship him. Think about how you respond in difficult times? Do you blame God or do you trust him, believing he is still good whatever your circumstances?

Job 1:20–22

Satan Bothers Job Again

2 Then another day came for the angels[e] to meet with the LORD. Satan joined them for this meeting with the LORD. [2]The LORD said to Satan, "Where have you been?"

Satan answered the LORD, "I have been roaming around the earth, going from place to place."

---

[a] **1:6 angels** Literally, "sons of God".
[b] **1:15 Sabeans** People who lived in the southern part of the Arabian Desert.
[c] **1:16 A bolt of lightning** Or "God's fire fell from the sky".
[d] **1:17 Chaldeans** Tribes of people who moved from place to place in the area between the Euphrates and Jordan rivers.
[e] **2:1 angels** Literally, "sons of God".

WHEN SUFFERING COMES

How do you respond to suffering and things that don't make sense in life? What do you do in those "Where is God?" moments? Written in poetic form, the book of Job is an account of a real man in history. Job was a man who loved God but who suffered a great deal and this book travels with him on a journey of anguished questions, sorrow, anger and confusion, as well as flashes of hope, wisdom and clarity. Does any of that journey sound familiar to you? Let's travel with Job as he asks questions and feels emotions that you may recognize from your own times of suffering.

DIG IN → **READ Job 1:1–22**

- Make a list of everything Job has (vv.1–3).
- Now make a list of everything Job loses (vv.13–22). What does he have left?

One of the most difficult things about suffering is trying to make sense of it. What happened to Job appeared to be completely random and unprovoked (remember he didn't know anything about the heavenly conversation described in vv.6–12). It's clear that Job was a righteous man – he didn't deserve what happened to him.

▶ READ Job 3:1–26
- Take a look at Job's initial response to his sufferings. How many times does he "wish" for something? How many times does he ask "Why?"?

Some people suggest that believers ought to keep quiet and keep smiling no matter what problems they face. Though it's true that Christians can have a different perspective to non-believers (we believe that God is in control – Romans 8:28; that he is good and he loves us – John 3:16; and that ultimately there will be no more crying or tears – Revelation 21:4) it's still appropriate for Christians to grieve for their losses and acknowledge their pain. Job shows us here that it's natural to ask why, and human to wish for things to be different.

The next chapters see Job's continued wrestling with his sufferings and unanswered questions. To make matters worse, his only remaining friends give him advice and condolences that, though meant well, fail to make sense of his situation. Indeed, they only serve to confuse and anger poor Job further (check out the Bible Bit "With Friends Like These").

▶ READ Job 19:1–29
Chapter 19 gives us a glimpse of how Job expresses his torment.

- As Job cries out in anger to God, list the images he uses to describe how he experiences God's silence in verses 7–12.
- In verse 20, Job really sounds ready to die. Yet in the next few verses, he somehow seems to seize a scrap of hope. In verse 25 we see who Job believes will defend him in the end. How do verses 25–27 compare with verses 6–19?

When faced with suffering, Job knows that the one hope he has is in God; one day Job will see him and all his suffering will be over. When things are tough for you, can you say, "I will see him with my own eyes . . . And I cannot tell you how excited that makes me feel!" (19:27)? This is the only thing that's really worth living for.

DIG THROUGH →

- Job is not the only person in the Bible who has felt as though God is against them, but who in the end recognizes that God is God, even while the struggles remain (check out Psalm 102, especially verses 1–2 and 9–10).
- Why do Job and the psalmist conclude that God has the last word? Pick almost any group of verses in Job 38 – 41 and you will find it hard to argue.

³Then the LORD said to Satan, "Have you noticed my servant Job? There is no one on earth like him. He is a good, faithful man. He respects God and refuses to do evil. He is still faithful, even though you asked me to let you destroy, without reason, everything he has."

⁴Satan answered, "Skin for skin!ᵃ A man will give everything he has to protect himself. ⁵I swear, if you attack his flesh and bones, he will curse you to your face!"

⁶So the LORD said to Satan, "All right, Job is in your hands, but you are not allowed to kill him."

⁷So Satan left the meeting with the LORD and gave Job painful sores all over his body, from the bottom of his feet to the top of his head. ⁸Job sat on the pile of ashes where he was mourning and used a piece of broken pottery to scrape his sores. ⁹His wife said to him, "Are you still holding on to your faith? Why don't you just curse God and die!"

¹⁰Job answered, "You sound like one of those fools on the street corner! How can we accept all the good things that God gives us and not accept the problems?" So even after all that happened to Job, he did not sin. He did not accuse God of doing anything wrong.

Job's Three Friends Come to See Him

¹¹Job's three friends heard about all the bad things that happened to him, so Eliphaz came from Teman, Bildad from Shuah and Zophar from Naamah. They met together and went to comfort Job and show him their sympathy. ¹²But his friends didn't even recognize him when they first saw him in the distance! They began to cry loudly. They tore their clothes and threw dirt in the air over their heads to show how sad they were. ¹³Then they sat on the ground with Job for seven days and seven nights. They didn't say a word, because they saw he was in so much pain.

Job Curses the Day He Was Born

3 Then Job opened his mouth and cursed the day he was born. ²He said,

³"I wish the day I was born would be lost forever.
  I wish the night they said, 'It's a boy!' had never happened.
⁴I wish that day had remained dark.
  I wish God above had forgotten that day and not let any light shine on it.
⁵I wish that bitter day had remained as dark as death,
  covered with the darkest clouds.

⁶I wish the darkness had carried away that night,
  that it was left off the calendar
  and not included in any of the months.
⁷I wish that night had produced nothing
  and no happy shouts had been heard.
⁸Some magicians think they can wake Leviathan.ᵇ
  So let them say their curses and curse the day I was born.

INSIGHT

Leviathan is mentioned frequently in Job. It was a mythical sea monster that represented the forces of chaos, so when Job refers to this monster he is saying that life is meaningless and makes no sense. Although Leviathan (or chaos) may seem to be in control, the reality is that God is greater and is in ultimate control.

Job 3:8

⁹Let that day's morning star be dark.
  Let that night wait for a morning that never comes.
  I wish it had never seen the first rays of sunlight.
¹⁰I wish it had stopped me from being born
  and kept me from seeing all these troubles.

¹¹"Why didn't I die when I was born?
  Why didn't I die as I came from my mother's womb?
¹²Why did my mother hold me on her knees?
  Why did her breasts feed me?
¹³If I had died when I was born,
  I would be at peace now.
  I wish I were asleep and at rest
¹⁴ with the kings and their advisors
  who built palaces that are now in ruins.
¹⁵I wish I were buried with rulers
  who filled their graves with gold and silver.
¹⁶Why wasn't I a child who died at birth
  and was put in the ground?
  I wish I had been buried like a baby
  who never saw the light of day.
¹⁷There the wicked stop causing trouble,
  and the weary find rest.
¹⁸Even prisoners find relief there;

ᵃ **2:4 Skin for skin** This means a person will do anything to avoid pain.
ᵇ **3:8 Leviathan** Here, this is probably a giant sea monster. Some people thought magicians were able to make it "swallow the sun", that is, cause an eclipse.

they no longer hear their guards shouting at
     them.
¹⁹Everyone—from the greatest to the least
     important—will be there,
     and even the slave is free from his master.

²⁰"Why must a suffering person continue to
     live?
     Why let anyone live such a bitter life?
²¹Such people want to die, but death does not
     come.
     They search for death more than for hidden
     treasure.
²²They would be happy to find their grave.
     They would rejoice to find their tomb.
²³But God keeps their future a secret
     and builds a wall around them to protect
     them.
²⁴When it is time to eat, all I can do is sigh with
     sadness, not joy.
     My groans pour out like water.
²⁵I was afraid something terrible would
     happen,
     and what I feared most has happened.
²⁶I cannot calm down or relax.
     I am too upset to rest!"

Eliphaz Speaks

4 Eliphaz from Teman answered:

²"I must say something.
     Would it upset you if I speak?
³Job, you have taught many people.
     You encouraged those who were ready to
     give up.
⁴Your words helped those who were ready to
     fall.
     You gave strength to those who could not
     stand by themselves.
⁵But now trouble comes to you,
     and you are discouraged.
     Trouble hits you,
     and you are upset.
⁶You worship God.
     You trust him.
     You are a good man,
     so let that be your hope.
⁷Can you think of any innocent person who
     was ever destroyed?
     Do you know of any place where good
     people are punished?
⁸Yes, I have seen people whose lives were
     cut short,
     but they were evil troublemakers.

⁹They lost the breath God gave them.
     They were cut off from his breath of life.
¹⁰They were like roaring lions,
     like growling lions with broken teeth—
¹¹like a lioness that cannot find prey.
     They died, and their cubs starved to
     death.

¹²"I happened to hear a message.
     My ears caught a whisper of it.
¹³Like a bad dreamᵃ in the night,
     it ruined my sleep.
¹⁴It frightened me,
     and I trembled down to my bones.
¹⁵A spirit passed by my face.
     The hair on my body stood up!
¹⁶The spirit stood still,
     but I could not see what it was.
     A shape stood before my eyes,
     and there was silence.
     Then I heard a quiet voice:
¹⁷'A person cannot be more right than God.
     People cannot be more pure than their
     Maker.
¹⁸Look, God cannot even trust his heavenly
     servants.
     He sees faults even in his angels.
¹⁹So surely people are worse!
     They live in houses of clayᵇ built on dust.
     They can be crushed as easily as a moth!
²⁰From dawn to sunset people are destroyed.
     They die—gone forever—and no one even
     notices.
²¹The ropes of their tent are pulled up,
     and they die before gaining wisdom.'

5 "Job, call out if you want, and see if anyone
     answers!
     But to which of the angels will you turn?
²A fool's anger will kill him.
     His jealousy will destroy him.
³I saw a fool who thought he was safe,
     but suddenly he died.ᶜ
⁴There was no one to help his children.
     No one defended them in court.
⁵Hungry people ate all his crops,
     even the grain growing among the thorns,
     and greedy people took all he had.
⁶Bad times don't come up from the dirt.
     Trouble does not grow from the ground.
⁷But people are born to have trouble,
     as surely as sparks rise from a fire.
⁸If I were you, I would turn to God
     and tell him about my problems.

ᵃ **4:13 bad dream** Or "vision of the night". See "VISION" in the Word List.
ᵇ **4:19 houses of clay** This means the human body.
ᶜ **5:3 suddenly he died** Or "suddenly his home was cursed".

WITH FRIENDS LIKE THESE . . .

Having set the scene in Job 1, the author now homes in on Job's friends, Eliphaz, Bildad and Zophar. They all try to comfort Job with their wisdom, but although their intentions are good, each of them misses the mark in some way . . .

DIG IN

READ Job 2:11-13

- What things do Job's friends do when they encounter him for the first time since his suffering began?
- What do you think of their approach? Do you think it was helpful? Unhelpful? Why?

READ Job 4:1-11
- What does Eliphaz think of Job (vv.1–6)?
- By contrast, what kinds of people does Eliphaz believe deserve suffering (vv.7–11)?

Eliphaz believes that suffering is a punishment for those who are sinful. He recognizes that no mortal man can be perfect and assumes Job's suffering must be a form of discipline for his imperfections (v.17). However, he also acknowledges that Job is a righteous man, and so concludes that his suffering should not last long – Job just needs to be patient.

READ Job 11:1-20
- What does Zophar conclude about Job's suffering (v.6b)? What course of action does he suggest in response (vv.13–14)?
- What does he predict will be the consequent result (v.15–19)?

READ Job 25: 1-6
- What does Bildad conclude about God in these verses?
- What does he conclude about humanity?
- What is he therefore implying about Job and the reason for his sufferings?

DIG THROUGH

- So what is Job's response to his friends' counsel? Take a look at the following verses to get an idea: 12:1–3; 19:1–5; 26:1–4. (In case you didn't notice, the verses in chapter 26 are heavily sarcastic!)

It's clear from how Job responds that he was far from comforted by what his friends had to say to him. In fact, their words seemed to make his pain even worse. However, it's important to remember that their intentions were good. They came from a long way to be with their friend (2:11) and there is no mention of anyone local – everyone else had rejected him. The friends' seven days of silence with Job (2:13) showed a genuine sharing of grief for his terrible situation.

There is even some truth in what the friends said, and they did try to appeal to godly wisdom. However, it is equally clear that the friends' words fell short of the truth, as God's own verdict shows in Job 42:7.

DIG DEEPER

Read through the final chapters of Job starting with chapter 38.
- God's reply to Job is perhaps unexpected. Is it what you imagined he would say? Were you looking for an answer to the question of why innocent people suffer? Did you expect God to declare Job innocent? Did you hope to make sense of the way that God deals with his people? If so, you will have been disappointed by these final chapters.
- Why do you think God chooses to answer in the way that he does? How does Job respond to God's answer? How does this help you to respond to your own suffering, or to comfort others?

⁹People cannot understand the wonderful
   things God does.
     His miracles are too many to count.
¹⁰He sends rain all over the earth
   and waters the fields.
¹¹He raises up the humble
   and makes sad people happy.
¹²He spoils the plans of even the smartest
   people
     so that they will not succeed.
¹³He catches those who think they are wise in
   their own clever traps
   and brings to an end their evil plans.
¹⁴Daylight will be like darkness for them.
   Even at noon they will have to feel their
   way as in the dark.
¹⁵God saves the poor from the hurtful words of
   the wicked.
   He saves them from those who are
   powerful.
¹⁶So the poor have hope;
   God shuts the mouths of those who would
   cause them harm.

¹⁷"You are fortunate when God corrects you.
   So don't complain when God All-Powerful
   punishes you.
¹⁸God might injure you, but he will bandage
   those wounds.
   He might hurt you, but his hands also heal.
¹⁹He will save you again and again.
   No evil will harm you.*ᵃ*
²⁰God will save you from death
   when there is famine.
   He will protect you from the sword
   when there is war.
²¹If people say things to hurt you, God will
   protect you.
   Whatever harm you face, you will not be
   afraid.
²²You will laugh at destruction and famine.
   You will not be afraid of wild animals!
²³It is as if you have a peace treaty
   with the wild animals and the rocks in the
   field.
²⁴You will live in peace because your tent is
   safe.
   You will count your property and find
   nothing missing.
²⁵You will have many children.
   They will be as many as the blades of grass
   on the earth.
²⁶You will be like the wheat that grows until
   harvest time.
   Yes, you will live to a ripe old age.

²⁷"We have studied this and know it is true.
   So listen to us, and learn for yourself."

Job Answers Eliphaz

6 Then Job answered:

²"I wish my suffering could be weighed
   and all my trouble be put on the scales.
³They would be heavier than all the sand of the
   sea!
   That is why my words are so crazy.
⁴God All-Powerful has shot me with his arrows.
   My spirit feels their poison!
   God's terrible weapons are lined up
   against me.
⁵Even a wild donkey does not complain when
   it has grass to eat.
   And a cow is quiet when it has food.
⁶Food without salt does not taste good,
   and the white of an egg has no taste.
⁷I refuse to touch that kind of food;
   it makes me sick!

⁸"I wish I could have what I ask for.
   I wish God would give me what I want.
⁹I wish he would crush me—
   just go ahead and kill me!
¹⁰Then I would be comforted by this one
   thing:
   Even through all this pain,
   I never refused to obey the commands of
   the Holy One.

¹¹"With my strength gone, I have no hope to go
   on living.
   With nothing to look forward to, why
   should I be patient?
¹²I am not strong like a rock.
   My body is not made from bronze.
¹³I don't have the power to help myself,
   because all hope of success has been taken
   away from me.

¹⁴"Friends should be loyal to you in times of
   trouble,
   even if you turn away from God
   All-Powerful.*ᵇ*
¹⁵But I cannot trust you, my friends.
   You are like a stream that has no water
   except when it floods.
¹⁶In the winter, the stream runs deep
   with melting ice and snow.
¹⁷But when it is hot and dry, the water stops
   flowing,
   and the stream disappears.

ᵃ **5:19** Literally, "In six troubles, he will rescue you, and in seven, evil will not touch you."
ᵇ **6:14** Or "People who fail to be loyal to their friends have also failed to respect God All-Powerful."

¹⁸It twists and turns along the way
and then disappears into the desert.
¹⁹Traders from Tema search for it.
Travellers from Sheba hope to find it.
²⁰They are sure they can find water,
but they will be disappointed.
²¹Now, you are like those streams.
You see my troubles and are afraid.
²²But have I ever asked you to help me
or to offer a bribe for me from your wealth?
²³No, and I have never said, 'Save me from
my enemies!'
or 'Save me from those who are cruel!'

²⁴"So now, teach me, and I will be quiet.
Show me what I have done wrong.
²⁵Honest words are powerful,
but your arguments prove nothing.
²⁶Do you plan to criticize me?
Will you speak more tiring words?
²⁷Are you the kind of people
who would gamble for orphans
and sell out your own friends?
²⁸Now, look me in the face,
and see that I am telling the truth!
²⁹That's enough! Stop being so
unfair!
Think again, because I am innocent.
³⁰I am not lying.
I know right from wrong.

7 "People have a hard struggle on earth.
Their life is like that of a hired worker.
²They are like a slave looking for cool shade
or a hired worker waiting for pay day.
³Month after frustrating month has gone by.
I have suffered night after night.
⁴When I lie down, I think,
'How long before it's time to get up?'
The night drags on.
I toss and turn until the sun comes up.
⁵My skin is covered with worms and scabs.
It is cracked and covered with sores.

⁶"My days pass by faster than a weaver's
shuttle,ᵃ
and my life will end without hope.
⁷God, remember, my life is like a breath.
I will not get a second chance to enjoy it.
⁸Those who see me now will never see me
again.
You watch me for a while, but then I am
gone.
⁹Just as clouds that come and go,

people are put in the grave, never to rise
again.
¹⁰They don't come back to their old homes.
The people there would not know them.

¹¹"So I will not be quiet!
I will let my suffering spirit speak!
I will let my bitter soul complain!
¹²Am I one of your enemies?
Is that why you put a guard over me?ᵇ
¹³My bed should bring me comfort.
My couch should give me rest and relief.
¹⁴But when I lie down, you scare me with
dreams;
you frighten me with visions.
¹⁵So I would rather be choked to death
than to live like this.
¹⁶I hate my life—I give up.
I don't want to live forever.
Leave me alone!
My life means nothing.
¹⁷God, why are people so important to you?
Why do you even notice them?
¹⁸Why do you visit them every morning
and test them at every moment?
¹⁹You never look away from me
or leave me alone for a second.
²⁰You are always watching us!
If I sinned, would that hurt you?
Why have you made me your target?
Have I become a problem for you?
²¹Why don't you just pardon me for doing
wrong?
Why don't you just forgive me for my sins?
Soon I will die and be in my grave.
You will search for me, but I will be gone."

INSIGHT

*Job's friends believed that pain and
suffering were punishments from God for
his sin. However, we know that wasn't the
case, as God said Job was good, faithful
and refused to do evil (1:8).*

Job 8

Bildad Speaks to Job

8 Then Bildad from Shuah answered:

²"How long will you talk like that?
Your words are nothing but hot air!

ᵃ **7:6 weaver's shuttle** The tool a person who makes cloth uses to pass the thread between the other threads.
ᵇ **7:12** Literally, "Am I Yam or Tannin that you should appoint a guard to watch me?" In ancient Canaanite stories, Yam was the
god of the sea, and Tannin was a sea monster.

³God is always fair.
God All-Powerful does what is right.
⁴If your children sinned against God,
he punished them.
They paid for their sins.
⁵But now, look to God
and pray to the All-Powerful.
⁶If you are pure and good,
he will quickly come to help you.
He will give your family back to you.
⁷Then you will have a lot more
than you had in the beginning!

⁸"Ask those who are now old.
Find out what their ancestors learned.
⁹It seems as though we were born
yesterday.
We are too young to know anything.
Our days on earth are very short, like a
shadow.
¹⁰Maybe the old people can tell you
something.
Maybe they will teach you what they
learned.

¹¹"Can papyrus grow tall on a dry land?
Can reeds grow without water?
¹²No, they will dry up before harvest.
They will be too small to cut and use.
¹³People who forget God are like that.
Those who oppose him have no hope.
¹⁴They have put their trust in something
weak.
It is like a spider's web.
¹⁵When they lean against it,
it will break.
When they reach out for it,
it will not hold them up.
¹⁶Such people are like a vine that gets plenty of
water and sunshine,
and its branches spread throughout the
garden.
¹⁷Its roots spread among the rocks,
searching for good soil.
¹⁸But if you move it, it will die,
and no one can tell it was ever there.
¹⁹Everything might have been going well,
but another vine will take its place.
²⁰God does not support evil people,
and he does not abandon the innocent.
²¹So perhaps you might laugh again.
Maybe shouts of joy will come from your
lips.
²²Maybe your enemies will be humiliated
and the homes of the wicked destroyed."

Job Answers Bildad

9 Then Job answered:

²"Of course, I know that this is true.
But how can a human being win an
argument with God?
³Anyone who chose to argue with him
could not answer one question in a
thousand!
⁴God is so wise and powerful that
no one could oppose him and survive.
⁵When God is angry, he moves mountains
before they know what happened.
⁶He can shake the earth,
and it will tremble down to its foundations.
⁷With one command he can stop the sun from
rising.
He can lock up the stars and keep them
from shining.
⁸He alone made the skies,
and he walks on the ocean waves.

⁹"God made the Bear, Orion and the Pleiades.ᵃ
He made the stars that cross the southern sky.
¹⁰He does things too marvellous for people to
understand.
He does too many miracles to count!
¹¹When he passes by, I cannot see him.
He goes right past me, and I don't notice.
¹²If he takes something away, no one can
stop him.
No one can say to him, 'What are you
doing?'
¹³God will not hold back his anger.
Even Rahab's helpers are afraid of him.
¹⁴So I cannot argue with God.
I would not know what to say to him.
¹⁵I am innocent, but I cannot give him an
answer.
All I can do is beg my Judge for mercy.
¹⁶Even if I called and he answered,
I cannot believe he would listen to me.
¹⁷He would just send storms to crush me.
He would give me more wounds for no
reason.
¹⁸He would not let me catch my breath again.
He would just give me more trouble.
¹⁹I cannot defeat God.
He is too powerful!
I cannot take him to court for justice.
Who could force him to come?
²⁰I am innocent, but anything I say makes me
seem guilty.
I am innocent, but if I speak, my mouth
proves me wrong.

ᵃ **9:9 Bear, Orion and the Pleiades** Names of well-known constellations (groups of stars) in the night sky.

²¹I am innocent, but I don't know what to
think.
I hate my own life.
²²So I say, 'Does it make any difference?
God destroys the innocent as well as the
guilty.'
²³It must be God who laughs when a disaster
kills innocent people.
²⁴It must be God who keeps the leaders from
seeing when an evil person takes control.
If it is not God, then who is it?

²⁵"My days are passing faster than a runner.
They are flying by without any joy.
²⁶They go by as quickly as papyrus boats,
as fast as an eagle swooping down on its
prey.

²⁷"I could say, 'I will not complain.
I will forget my pain and put a smile on my
face.'
²⁸But the suffering still frightens me.
I know that God will not see me as
innocent.
²⁹I will be found guilty,
so why should I even think about it?
³⁰Even if I scrubbed my hands with soap
and washed myself whiter than snow,
³¹God would still push me into the slime pit,ᵃ
and even my clothes would hate to
touch me.
³²God is not a human like me, so I cannot argue
with him.
I cannot take him to court.
³³I wish there were someone who could listen
to both sides,ᵇ
someone to judge both of us in a fair way.
³⁴I wish someone could take away the threat of
God's punishment.
Then he would not frighten me any more.
³⁵Then I could say what I want without being
afraid of him.
But I cannot do that now.

10

"I hate my own life, so I will complain
freely.
I am very bitter, so now I will speak.
²I will say to God, 'Don't just say I am guilty!
Tell me what you have against me.
³Do you enjoy hurting me?
Do you enjoy ignoring me while smiling at
what evil people say?
⁴Do you have human eyes?
Do you see things the way people do?

⁵Is your life as short as ours?
Is your life as short as a man's life?
⁶You look for my wrong
and search for my sin.
⁷You know I am innocent,
but no one can save me from your
power!
⁸Your hands made me and shaped my body.
Will you now destroy me completely?
⁹Remember, you moulded me like clay.
Will you turn me into clay again?
¹⁰You poured me like milk into my mother
and formed me like someone making
cheese.
¹¹You put me together with bones and
muscles,
and then you clothed me with skin and
flesh.
¹²You gave me life and were very kind to me.
You cared for me and watched over my
spirit.
¹³But this is what you hid in your heart.
Now I know what you were planning
for me.
¹⁴If I sinned, you would be watching me
so that you could punish me for doing
wrong.
¹⁵If I sin, I am guilty
and should be cursed.
But even when I am innocent,
I cannot lift up my head.
I am so ashamed
because of all the troubles I have.
¹⁶If I have any success and feel proud,
you hunt me down like a lion
and show your power over me.
¹⁷You bring witness after witness
to prove that I am wrong.
Again and again you show your anger
as you send army after army against me.

¹⁸"So why did you let me be born?
I wish I had died before anyone saw me.
¹⁹I wish I had never lived.
I wish they had carried me from my
mother's womb straight to the grave.
²⁰My life is almost finished.
So leave me alone!
Let me enjoy the little time I have left.
²¹I am going soon to the land of no return,
the place of death and darkness—
²²that land of darkest night, of shadows and
confusion,
where even the light is darkness."

ᵃ 9:31 *slime pit* The grave, a place where bodies rot.
ᵇ 9:33 *someone . . . sides* Literally, "a mediator" or "an umpire".

Zophar Speaks to Job

11 Then Zophar from Naamah answered Job and said,

²"This flood of words should be answered!
Does all this talking make Job right?
³Do you think we don't have
an answer for you?
Do you think no one will warn you
when you laugh at God?
⁴You say to God,
'My arguments are right,
and you can see I am pure.'
⁵I wish God would answer you
and tell you that you are wrong.
⁶He could tell you the secret of wisdom.
He would tell you that every story has two
sides.
You can be sure of this:
God is not punishing you as much as he
should.

⁷"Do you think you really understand
God?
Do you completely understand God
All-Powerful?
⁸That knowledge is higher than the heavens
and deeper than the place of death.
So what can you do?
How can you learn it all?
⁹It is greater than the earth
and bigger than the seas.

¹⁰"If God decides to arrest you and take you to
court,
no one could stop him.
¹¹God knows who is worthless.
When he sees evil, he remembers it.
¹²A wild donkey cannot give birth to a man,
and a stupid person will never become
wise.
¹³Prepare your heart to serve only God.
Lift your arms and pray to him.
¹⁴Put away the sin that you still hold on to.
Don't keep evil in your tent.
¹⁵If you will do that, you can look to God
without shame.
You can stand strong and not be afraid.
¹⁶Then you can forget your troubles,
like water that has already passed by.
¹⁷Your life will be brighter than the sunshine at
noon.
Life's darkest hours will shine like the
morning sun.
¹⁸You will feel safe because there is hope.
God will protect you and give you rest.
¹⁹You will lie down without fear of anyone.
Many people will come to you for help.

²⁰Evil people might look for help,
but they will not escape their troubles.
Their hope leads only to death."

Job Answers His Friends

12 Then Job answered them:

²"I'm sure you think you are
the only wise people left.
You think that when you die,
wisdom will be gone with you.
³But my mind is as good as yours.
You aren't any smarter than I am.
You haven't said anything
that people don't already know.

⁴"My friends laugh at me now.
They say, 'He prayed to God and got his
answer.'
I am a good, innocent man,
but still they laugh at me.
⁵Those who have no troubles make fun of
those who do.
They hit a man when he is down.
⁶But robbers' tents are not bothered.
Those who make God angry live in peace,
even though God has them in his power.

⁷"But ask the animals, and they will teach
you.
Or ask the birds that fly, and they will tell
you.
⁸Or speak to the earth, and it will teach you.
Or let the fish in the sea tell you their
wisdom.
⁹Everyone knows
that the Lord has made these things.
¹⁰Every animal that lives and everyone who
breathes—
they are all under God's power.
¹¹But just as the tongue tastes food,
the ears test the words they hear.
¹²People say, 'Wisdom is to be found in those
who are old.
Long life brings understanding.'

¹³"But wisdom and power belong to God.
Good advice and understanding are his.
¹⁴Anything God tears down cannot be rebuilt.
Anyone he puts in prison cannot be set free.
¹⁵If he holds back the rain, the earth will dry up.
If he lets the rain loose, it will flood the
land.
¹⁶God is strong and always wins.
He controls those who fool others and those
who are fooled.
¹⁷He strips advisors of their wisdom
and makes leaders act like fools.

¹⁸He strips kings of their authority
and makes them slaves.
¹⁹He strips priests of their power
and removes those who feel so secure in
their position.
²⁰He makes trusted advisors be silent.
He takes away the wisdom of the older
leaders.
²¹He brings disgrace to important people.
He takes power away from rulers.
²²He exposes even the darkest secrets.
He sends light into places that are as dark
as death.
²³God makes nations great,
and then he destroys them.
He makes nations grow large,
and then he scatters their people.
²⁴He makes their leaders foolish.
He makes them wander around in the
desert.
²⁵They are like someone feeling their way in the
dark.
They are like drunks who don't know
where they are going.

13 "I have seen all this before.
I have already heard everything you say.
I understand all these things.
²I know as much as you do.
I am as smart as you are.
³But I don't want to argue with you.
I want to speak to God All-Powerful.
I want to argue with God about my
troubles.
⁴But you men try to cover up your ignorance
with lies.
You are like worthless doctors who cannot
heal anyone.
⁵I wish you would just be quiet.
That would be the wisest thing you could do.

⁶"Now, listen to my argument.
Listen to what I have to say.
⁷Will you speak lies for God?
Do you really believe your lies are what
God wants you to say?
⁸Are you trying to defend God against me?
You are not being fair.
You are choosing God's side simply because
he is God.
⁹If God checked you very closely,
would he see that you are right?
Do you really think you can fool God
the same as you fool people?
¹⁰You know that God would criticize you

if you chose someone's side simply because
they were important.
¹¹God's majesty frightens you.
You are afraid of him.
¹²The wise sayings you quote are worthless.
Your arguments are as weak as clay.

¹³"Be quiet and let me talk!
I accept whatever happens to me.
¹⁴I will put myself in danger
and take my life in my own hands.
¹⁵I will continue to trust God even if he kills
me.^a
But I will defend myself to his face.
¹⁶And if he lets me live, it will be because I had
the confidence to speak.
No guilty person would dare meet God face
to face.
¹⁷Listen carefully to what I say.
Let me explain.
¹⁸I am ready now to defend myself.
I will carefully present my arguments.
I know I will be shown to be right.
¹⁹If anyone can prove I am wrong,
I will shut up and wait to die.

²⁰"God, just give me two things,
and then I will not hide from you:
²¹Stop punishing me,
and don't frighten me with your terrors.
²²Then call to me, and I will answer you.
Or let me speak, and you answer me.
²³How many sins have I committed?
What wrongs have I done?
Show me where I went wrong or how I
sinned.
²⁴God, why do you avoid me
and treat me like your enemy?
²⁵Are you trying to scare me?
I am only a leaf blowing in the wind.
You are attacking a piece of straw!
²⁶You have a list of terrible charges against me.
Are you making me suffer for the sins I did
when I was young?
²⁷You have put chains on my feet.
You watch every step I take.
You see every move I make.
²⁸So I am becoming weaker and weaker,
like a piece of wood rotting away,
like a piece of cloth eaten by moths.

14 "We are all human beings.^b
Our life is short and full of trouble.
²Our life is like a flower that grows quickly and
then dies away.

^a **13:15** *I will . . . kills me* Or "If he decides to kill me, I have no hope."
^b **14:1** *human beings* Literally, "born of woman".

Our life is like a shadow that is here for a
short time and then is gone.
3God, do you need to keep an eye on
something so small?
Why bother to bring charges against me?

4"No one can make something clean from
something so dirty.
5The length of our life has been decided.
You alone know how long that is.
You have set the limits for us and nothing
can change them.
6So stop watching us; leave us alone,
and let us enjoy this hard life until we have
put in our time.

7"There is always hope for a tree.
If it is cut down, it can grow again.
It will keep sending out new branches.
8Its roots might grow old in the ground
and its stump die in the dirt,
9but with water, it will grow again.
It will grow branches like a new plant.
10But when a man dies,
he becomes weak and sick, and then he
is gone!
11Like a lake that goes dry
or a river that loses its source,
12so people lose their lives,
never to live again.
The skies will all pass away
before they rise from death.
The skies will all disappear before
anyone wakes up from that sleep!

13"I wish you would hide me in my grave.
I wish you would hide me there, until your
anger is gone.
Then you could pick a time to remember me.
14If a man dies, will he live again?
If so, I would gladly suffer through this time
waiting for my release.a
15God, you would call me,
and I would answer you.
Then I, the one you made,
would be important to you.
16You would still watch every step I take,
but you would not remember my sins.
17It would be as if you had sealed my sins in
a bag.
It would be as if you had covered my guilt
with plaster.

18"Mountains fall and crumble away.
Large rocks break loose and fall.

19Water flowing over stones wears them
down.
Floods wash away the soil on the ground.
In the same way, God, you destroy the hope
people have.
20You defeat them completely
and then they are gone.
You change the way they look
and send them away forever to the place of
death.
21If their sons are honoured, they will never
know it.
If their sons do wrong, they will never
see it.
22They only feel the pain in their bodies,
and they alone cry for themselves."

Eliphaz Answers Job

15 Then Eliphaz from Teman answered Job:
2"If you were really wise,
you would not answer with your worthless
personal opinions!
A wise man would not be so full of hot air.
3Do you think a wise man would use empty
words
and meaningless speeches to win his
arguments?
4If you had your way,
no one would respect God and pray to him.
5What you say clearly shows your sin.
Job, you are trying to hide your sin by using
clever words.
6I don't need to prove to you that you are
wrong.
The words from your own mouth show that
you are wrong.
Your own lips speak against you.

7"Do you think you were the first person ever
to be born?
Were you born before the hills?
8Did you listen to God's secret plans?
Do you think you are the only wise person?
9Do you know something we don't know?
We understand as well as you.
10The old, grey-haired men agree with us.
People older than your father are on our side.
11Why do you reject these comforting words
from God?
We have spoken his message to you in a
gentle way.
12Why will you not understand?
Why can you not see the truth?

---

a **14:14** *I would . . . release* Or "I would wait my whole tour of duty for my replacement to come."

¹³You are expressing your anger against God
when you say these things.

¹⁴"People cannot really be pure.
They*a* cannot be more right than God!
¹⁵God does not even trust his angels.*b*
He does not even think the sky is pure.
¹⁶People are even worse.
They are rotten and full of sin.
They drink up evil like water.

¹⁷"Listen to me, and I will explain it to you.
Let me tell you what I have seen.
¹⁸I will tell you what wise men would say,
things they heard from their fathers and
then freely passed on.
They didn't hide any secrets from me.
¹⁹These are important people in our country!
Everyone knows who they are.
²⁰And they said that an evil man suffers all
his life.
A cruel man suffers all his numbered
years.
²¹Every noise scares him.
His enemy will attack him when he thinks
he is safe.
²²An evil man has no hope of escaping the
darkness.
There is a sword somewhere waiting to
kill him.
²³He wanders from place to place, looking
for food.
But he knows a dark day is coming, which
he brought on himself.
²⁴He lives in fear, with worry and suffering
threatening him
like a king ready to attack.
²⁵That is because that evil man shook his fist at
God, refusing to obey.
He dared to attack God All-Powerful,
²⁶like a soldier with a thick, strong shield
who runs at his enemy to strike him in
the neck.

²⁷"He might be rich and fat,
²⁸but his town will be ruined;
his home will be destroyed;
his house will be empty.
²⁹He will not be rich for long.
His wealth will not last.
His crops will not grow large.
³⁰He will not escape the darkness.
He will be like a tree whose leaves die
from disease
and are blown away by the wind.

³¹That evil man should not fool himself by
trusting in worthless things,
because he will keep nothing.
³²He will die before his time,
like a tree whose top branches have already
begun to die.
³³He will be like a vine that loses its grapes
before they ripen.
He will be like an olive tree that loses its
buds.
³⁴That is because people without God have
nothing.
Those who take bribes will have their
homes destroyed by fire.
³⁵They are always thinking of ways to do evil
and cause trouble.
They are always planning how they might
cheat others."

Job Answers Eliphaz

16 Then Job answered:

²"I have heard all these things before.
You men give me trouble, not comfort.
³Your long speeches never end!
Why do you continue arguing?
⁴I also could say the same things you say,
if you had my troubles.
I could say wise things against you
and shake my head at you.
⁵But I would say things to encourage you
and give you hope.

⁶"Nothing I say makes my pain go away.
But keeping quiet does not help either.
⁷God, you surely took away my strength.
You destroyed my whole family.
⁸You have made me thin and weak,
and people think that means I am guilty.

⁹"God attacks me;
he is angry with me and tears my body
apart.
He grinds his teeth against me.
My enemy looks at me with hate.
¹⁰People have crowded around me.
They make fun of me and slap my face.
¹¹God has given me to evil people.
He let the wicked hurt me.
¹²I was enjoying a quiet, peaceful life,
but then God crushed me.
Yes, he took me by the neck
and broke me into pieces.
He has made me his target.
¹³ With his archers all around me,

---

a **15:14 They** Literally, "a man born of woman".
b **15:15 angels** Literally, "holy ones".

He cuts me open without mercy
and spills my insides on the ground.

¹⁴Again and again he attacks me.
He runs at me like a soldier in battle.

¹⁵"I am very sad, so I wear this sackcloth.
I sit here in dust and ashes, feeling
defeated.

¹⁶My face is red from crying.
There are dark rings around my eyes.

¹⁷I was never cruel to anyone,
and my prayers are pure.

¹⁸"Earth, don't hide the wrong things that were
done to me.ᵃ
Don't let my begging for fairness be
stopped.

¹⁹Even now there is someone in heaven who
will speak for me.
There is someone above who will testify
for me.

²⁰My friend speaks for me,
while my eyes pour out tears to God.

²¹He speaks to God for me,
like someoneᵇ presenting an argument for a
friend.

²²"In only a few years
I will go to that place of no return.

17

My spirit is broken;
I am ready to give up.
My life is almost gone;
the grave is waiting for me.

²People stand around me and laugh at me.
I watch them as they tease and insult me.

³"God, give me some support.
No one else will!

⁴You have closed my friends' minds,
and they don't understand.
Please don't let them win.

⁵You know what people say:
'A man neglects his own children to help
his friends.'ᶜ
But my friends have turned against me.

⁶God has made my name a bad word to
everyone.
People spit in my face.

⁷My eyes are almost blind from my grief.
My whole body is as thin as a shadow.

⁸Good people wonder how this could happen.
The innocent are upset with anyone who is
against God.

⁹But those who do right will continue to do
what is right.
Those who are not guilty grow stronger and
stronger.

¹⁰"But come on, all of you, and try to prove me
wrong.
I don't find any of you to be wise.

¹¹My life is passing away, and my plans are
destroyed.
My hope is gone.

¹²Everything is confused—
night is day, and evening comes when it
should be dawn.

¹³"I might hope for the grave to be my new
home.
I might hope to make my bed in the dark
grave.

¹⁴I might say to the grave, 'You are my father,'
and to the worms, 'my mother' or 'my
sister'.

¹⁵But you can't really call that hope, can you?
Does anyone see any hope for me?

¹⁶Will hope go down with me to the place of
death?
Will we go down into the dirt together?"

Bildad Answers Job

18

Then Bildad from Shuah answered:

²"Will you ever stop talking?
Be reasonable, and let us say something.

³Do you think we are stupid?
You behave as if we are as stupid as cattle.

⁴Your anger is hurting no one but you.
Do you think this world was made for you
alone?
Do you think God should move mountains
just to satisfy you?

⁵"Yes, the light of those who are evil will go
out.
Their fire will stop burning.

⁶The light in their houses will become dark.
The lamps next to them will go out.

⁷Their steps, once strong and fast, become
weak.
Their own evil plans make them fall.

⁸Their own feet lead them into a net.
They fall into its hidden pit and are caught.

⁹A trap catches them by the heel,
and it holds them tight.

ᵃ **16:18 Earth . . . done to me** Literally, "Earth, don't cover my blood." See Gen. 4:10–11.
ᵇ **16:21 someone** Literally, "son of man".
ᶜ **17:5 You know . . . friends** Literally, "He promises a share to his friends and his children's eyes go blind."

¹⁰A rope is hidden on the ground to trip them.
 A trap is waiting in their path.

¹¹"On every side terrors frighten them.
 Fears follow every step they take.
¹²Disaster is hungry for them.
 Ruin stands close by, waiting for them to
 fall.
¹³Diseases will eat away their skin.
 Death itself^a will eat their arms and legs.
¹⁴They will be taken away from the safety of
 their tents
 and be led away to meet death, the king of
 terrors.
¹⁵Nothing will be left in their tents,
 which will be sprinkled with burning
 sulphur.
¹⁶Their roots below will dry up,
 and their branches above will die.
¹⁷People on earth will not remember them.
 Their names will be forgotten.
¹⁸They will be forced from light into
 darkness.
 They will be chased out of this world.
¹⁹They will leave behind no children, no
 descendants.
 None of their people will be left alive.
²⁰People in the west will be shocked at what
 happened to them.
 People in the east will be numb with fear.
²¹This is what will happen to the homes of those
 who are evil.
 This is the place of those who don't know
 God!"

Job Answers

19

Then Job answered:

²"How long will you hurt me
 and crush me with your words?
³You have insulted me ten times now.
 You have attacked me without shame!
⁴Even if I have sinned,
 it is my problem, not yours!
⁵You want me to look bad to make yourselves
 look good.
 You say my troubles are proof that I did
 wrong.
⁶I want you to know it was God who did this.
 He set this trap for me.
⁷I shout, 'He hurt me!' but get no answer.
 No one hears my cry for fairness.
⁸God has blocked my way to keep me from
 getting through.
 He has hidden my path in darkness.

⁹He took away my honour.
 He took the crown from my head.
¹⁰He hits me on every side until I am worn
 out.
 He takes away my hope.
 It is like a tree pulled up by the roots.
¹¹His anger burns against me.
 He treats me like an enemy.
¹²He sends his army to attack me.
 They build attack towers around me.
 They camp around my tent.

¹³"God has made my brothers hate me.
 Those who knew me have become
 strangers.
¹⁴My relatives have left me.
 My friends have forgotten me.
¹⁵My servant girls and visitors in my home
 look at me as if I am a stranger and a
 foreigner.
¹⁶I call for my servant, but he does not
 answer.
 Even if I beg for help, he will not answer.
¹⁷My wife hates the smell of my breath.
 My own brothers hate me.
¹⁸Even little children make fun of me.
 When I get up, they say bad things about
 me.
¹⁹All my close friends hate me.
 Even my loved ones have turned against
 me.

²⁰"I am so thin, my skin hangs loose on my
 bones.
 I have little life left in me.

²¹"Pity me, my friends, pity me,
 because God is against me.
²²Why do you persecute me as God does?
 Don't you get tired of hurting me?

²³"I wish someone would write down
 everything I say.
 I wish my words were written on a scroll.
²⁴I wish they were carved with an iron tool into
 lead
 or scratched on a rock so that they would
 last forever.
²⁵I know that there is someone to defend me
 and that he lives!
 And in the end, he will stand here on earth
 and defend me.
²⁶After I leave my body and my skin has been
 destroyed,
 I know I will still see God.

^a **18:13 Death itself** Literally, "Death's firstborn", a name for a deadly disease, or the worms that eat a dead body.

27I will see him with my own eyes.
  I myself, not someone else, will see God.
  And I cannot tell you how excited that
    makes me feel!a

28"Maybe you will say, 'How can we push Job a
    little harder
  and make him realize that he is the source
    of his problems?'
29But you need to worry about your own
    punishment.
  God might use the sword against you!
  Then you will know there is a time for
    judgement."

Zophar Answers Job

20 Then Zophar from Naamah answered:

2"You upset me, so I must answer you.
  I must tell you what I am thinking.
3You insulted me with your answers!
  But I am wise and know how to answer
    you.

4-5"You know that the joy of the wicked does not
    last long.
  That has been true for a long time, ever
    since Adam wasb put on earth.
  Those who don't know God are happy for
    only a short time.
6Maybe an evil man's pride will reach up to the
    sky,
  and his head will touch the clouds.
7But he will be gone forever like his own body
    waste.
  People who knew him will say, 'Where is
    he?'
8Like a dream, he will fly away, never to be
    found.
  He will be chased away like a bad dream.c
9Those who knew him before will not see him
    again.
  His family will never again get to see him.
10His children will have to give back what he
    took from the poor.
  His own hands will give up his wealth.
11When he was young, his bones were
    strong,
  but, like the rest of his body, they will soon
    lie in the dirt.

12"Evil tastes sweet in his mouth.
  He keeps it under his tongue to enjoy it fully.
13He hates to let it go
  and holds it in his mouth.
14But that evil will turn sour in his stomach.
  It will be like a snake's bitter poison inside
    him.
15The evil man will spit out the riches he has
    swallowed.
  God will make him vomit them up.
16What he drank will be like a snake's poison;
  it will kill him like the bite of a deadly
    snake.
17He will never again enjoy so much wealth—
  rivers flowing with honey and cream.d
18He will be forced to give back his profits.
  He will not be allowed to enjoy what he
    worked for,
19because he hurt the poor and left them with
    nothing.
  He took houses he did not build.

20"The evil man is never satisfied.
  But the things he wants cannot save him.
21After filling himself, there is nothing left.
  His success will not continue.
22Even while he has plenty, he will be pressed
    down with trouble.
  His problems will come down on him!
23If he does get all he wants,
  God will throw his burning anger against
    him.
  God will attack him and rain down
    punishment on him.
24Maybe he will run away from an iron sword,
  but then a bronze arrowe will strike him
    down.
25It will go through his body
  and stick out of his back.
  Its shining point will pierce his liver,
  and he will be shocked with terror.
26All his treasures will be lost in darkness.
  He will be destroyed by a fire, a fire that no
    human started.
  It will destroy everything left in his house.
27Heaven will prove that he is guilty.
  The earth will be a witness against him.
28His house and everything in it will be carried
    away
  in the flood of God's anger.

---

a 19:25–27 Or "And in the end, he will stand here on earth and defend me, even after my skin has been destroyed. But I want to see God while I am still in my body. I want to see him with my own eyes, not through someone else's eyes. And I cannot tell you how much I want this to happen!"
b 20:4–5 Adam was Or "people were".
c 20:8 bad dream Or "vision of the night". See "VISION" in the Word List.
d 20:17 rivers . . . cream A figure meaning a plentiful supply of rich food. The word translated "cream" could mean butter, curds or yogurt.
e 20:24 bronze arrow Literally, "bronze bow". Or "powerful bow", possibly a bow made of sinew, wood and horn.

²⁹That is what God will do to those who
    are evil.
    That is what he plans to give them."

Job Answers

21 Then Job answered:

²"Listen to what I say.
    Let this be your way of comforting me.
³Be patient while I speak.
    Then after I have finished speaking, you
    may make fun of me.

⁴"My complaint is not against people.
    There is a good reason why I am not
    patient.
⁵Look at me and be shocked.
    Put your hand over your mouth, and stare
    at me in shock!
⁶When I think about what happened to me,
    I feel afraid and my body shakes!
⁷Why do evil people live long lives?
    Why do they grow old and successful?
⁸They watch their children grow up
    and live to see their grandchildren.
⁹Their homes are safe and free from fear.
    God does not punish them.
¹⁰Their bulls never fail to mate.
    Their cows have healthy calves.
¹¹They send their children out to play like
    lambs.
    Their children dance around.
¹²They sing and dance to the sound of harps and
    flutes.
¹³Evil people enjoy success during their lives
    and then go to the grave without
    suffering.
¹⁴They say to God, 'Leave us alone!
    We don't care what you want us to do!'
¹⁵And they say, 'Who is God All-Powerful?
    We don't need to serve him!
    It will not help to pray to him!'

¹⁶"Of course, evil people don't make their own
    success.
    I would never follow their advice.
¹⁷But how often does God blow out their
    light?
    How often does trouble come to them?
    How often does God become angry with
    them and punish them?
¹⁸Does God blow them away, as the wind blows
    straw
    or as strong winds blow the grain husks?
¹⁹But you say, 'God is saving their punishment
    for their children.'

No! Let God punish the evil people
    themselves so that they will know what
    they have done!
²⁰Let them see their own punishment.
    Let them feel the anger of God
    All-Powerful.
²¹When their life is finished and they are dead,
    they will not care about the family they
    leave behind.

²²"No one can teach God anything he doesn't
    already know.
    God judges even those in high places.
²³One person dies after living a full and
    successful life,
    a life completely safe and comfortable,
²⁴with a body that was well fed
    and bones that were still strong.
²⁵But another person dies after a hard life that
    has made them bitter,
    never having enjoyed anything good.
²⁶In the end, both of these people will lie
    together in the dirt.
    The worms will cover them both.

²⁷"But I know what you are thinking,
    and I know you want to hurt me.
²⁸You might say, 'Show me a good man's
    house.
    Now, show me where evil people live.'ᵃ

²⁹"Surely you have talked with travellers.
    Surely you will accept their stories.
³⁰Evil people are spared when disaster comes.
    They survive when God shows his anger.
³¹No one criticizes them to their faces for how
    they lived.
    No one punishes them for the evil they
    have done.
³²When they are carried to the grave,
    they will have someone to watch over the
    place they are buried.
³³So even the soil in the valley will be pleasant
    for them,
    and thousands of people will join their
    funeral procession.

³⁴"So your empty words are no comfort to me.
    There is no truth at all in your answers!"

Eliphaz Answers Job

22 Then Eliphaz from Teman answered:

²"Does God need our help?
    Even the wisest of us is not really useful
    to him.

ᵃ **21:28 Show me . . . live** Or "Show me a wicked ruler's house. Show me where evil people live."

³Does your living right benefit him?
    Does God All-Powerful gain anything if you
        follow him?
⁴Why does God blame and punish you?
    Is it because you worship him?
⁵No, it is because you sin so much.
    You never stop sinning.
⁶Maybe to guarantee loans you took things
        from people for no reason.
    Maybe you took a poor man's clothes to
        make sure he paid you back.^a
⁷Maybe you failed to give water or food
    to people who were tired or hungry.
⁸You have a lot of farmland,
    and people respect you.
⁹But maybe you sent widows away without
        giving them anything.
    And maybe you took advantage of
        orphans.
¹⁰That is why traps are all around you,
    and sudden trouble makes you afraid.
¹¹That is why it is so dark that you cannot see,
    and why a flood of water covers you.

¹²"God lives in the highest part of heaven
    and looks down on the highest stars.
¹³But you might say, 'What does God
        know?
    Can he see through the dark clouds to
        judge us?
¹⁴Thick clouds hide us from his eyes,
    so he cannot see us as he walks around the
        edge of the sky.'

¹⁵"Job, you are walking on the old path
    that evil people walked on long ago.
¹⁶They were destroyed before it was their time
        to die.
    They were washed away by the flood.
¹⁷They told God, 'Leave us alone!'
    and said, 'God All-Powerful cannot do
        anything to us!'
¹⁸And it was God who filled their houses with
        good things.
    No, I would never follow the advice of evil
        people.
¹⁹Those who do what is right are happy to see
        them destroyed.
    The innocent laugh at them and say,
²⁰'Surely our enemies are destroyed!
    Their wealth burned up in the fire!'

²¹"Now, Job, give yourself to God and make
        peace with him.
    Do this, and you will get many good things.

²²Accept his teaching.
    Pay attention to what he says.
²³If you return to God All-Powerful, you will be
        restored.
    But remove the evil from your house.
²⁴Think of your gold as nothing but dirt.
    Think of your finest gold as rocks from a
        stream.
²⁵And let God All-Powerful be your gold.
    Let him be your pile of silver.
²⁶Then you will enjoy God All-Powerful,
    and you will look up to him.
²⁷When you pray, he will hear you.
    And you will be able to do all that you
        promised him.
²⁸If you decide to do something, it will be
        successful.
    And your future will be very bright!
²⁹When people are brought down and you ask
        God to help them,
    he will rescue those who have been
        humbled.
³⁰Even those who are guilty will be forgiven.
    They will be saved because you did what
        was right."

Job Answers

23 Then Job answered:

²"I am still complaining today.
    I groan because God is still making me
        suffer.
³I wish I knew where to find him.
    I wish I knew how to go to where he lives.
⁴I would present my case to him.
    I would make my arguments to show that I
        am innocent.
⁵He could give his reply, and I would
        understand.
    I would listen closely to what he says.
⁶Would God use his power against me?
    No, he would listen to me!
⁷Since I am an honest man, he would let me
        tell my story.
    Then my Judge would set me free!

⁸"If I go to the east, God is not there.
    If I go to the west, I still don't see him.
⁹When he is working in the north, I don't see
        him.
    When he turns to the south, I still don't see
        him.
¹⁰But God knows me.
    He is testing me and will see that I am as
        pure as gold.

---

^a **22:6 paid you back** See Deut. 24:12–13 for rules about making loans to the poor.

¹¹I have always lived the way God wants.
  I have never stopped following him.
¹²I always obey his commands.
  I love the words from his mouth more than
    I love my food.

¹³"But God never changes,
  and who can stand against him?
  He does anything he wants.
¹⁴He will do to me what he planned,
  and he has many other plans for me.
¹⁵That is why I am terrified to stand before
    him.
  Just thinking about it makes me afraid.
¹⁶The fear of God has made me lose my
    courage.
  God All-Powerful makes me afraid.
¹⁷What has happened to me is like a dark cloud
    over my face.
  But the darkness will not keep me quiet.

24 "Why doesn't God All-Powerful set times
  for judgement?
  Why must his followers wait so long for
    justice to come?

²"Evil people move property markers to steal
    their neighbour's land.
  They steal livestock and add them to their
    own flocks.
³They steal a donkey that belongs to an orphan.
  They take a widow's cow until she pays
    what she owes.
⁴They force the poor to move out of their
    way.
  The only way any of the poor stay alive is to
    run and hide.

⁵"Like wild donkeys, the poor search for food
    in the desert.
  This is the only way they can feed their
    children.
⁶They pick up grain from fields they don't
    own.
  They take the grapes left on the vines that
    belong to the wicked.
⁷They must sleep all night without clothes.
  They have no covers to protect them from
    the cold.
⁸They are soaked with cold mountain rains.
  They stay close to the large rocks for shelter.

⁹"Evil people take children from the poor to
    pay for what they owe.
  They will even take a nursing baby from its
    mother.
¹⁰The poor have no clothes, so they work
    naked.

They carry bundles of grain for others,
  but they go hungry.
¹¹They press olives to make oil, but not for
    themselves.
  They mash grapes for wine, but they stay
    thirsty.
¹²In the city you can hear the sad sounds of
    dying people.
  Those who are hurt cry out for help,
    but God does not listen.

¹³"Some people rebel against the light.
  They don't know what God wants.
  They don't live the way he wants.
¹⁴A murderer gets up at dawn and kills poor,
    helpless people.
  And at night he becomes a thief.
¹⁵A man who commits adultery waits for the
    night to come.
  He thinks, 'No one will see me,' but still,
    he covers his face.
¹⁶When it is dark, evil people go out and break
    into houses.
  But during the day they lock themselves in
    their homes to avoid the light.
¹⁷The darkest night is their morning.
  They are friends with the terrors of
    darkness.

¹⁸"⌊You say,⌋ 'Evil people are taken away like
    things carried away in a flood.
  The land they own is cursed, so no one
    goes to work in their vineyards.
¹⁹As hot, dry weather melts away the winter
    snows,
  so the grave takes away those who have
    sinned.
²⁰Their own mothers will forget them.
  Only the worms will want them.
  No one will remember them.
  They will be broken like a rotten stick!
²¹These evil people hurt women who have no
    children to protect them,
  and they refuse to help widows.
²²By his power God removes the
    powerful.
  Even if they have a high position, they
    cannot be sure of their lives.
²³They might feel safe and secure,
  but God is watching how they live.
²⁴They might be successful for a while,
  but then they will be gone.
  Like everyone else, they will be cut down
    like grain.'

²⁵"I swear these things are true!
  Who can prove that I lied?
  Who can show that I am wrong?"

Bildad Answers Job

25 Then Bildad from Shuah answered:

2"God is the ruler.
  He makes people fear and respect him.
  He keeps peace in his kingdom above.
3No one can count his stars.*a*
  His sun rises on all people.
4How can anyone claim to be right before
    God?
  No human being*b* can really be pure.
5In God's eyes even the moon is not pure and
    bright;
  even the stars are not pure.
6People are much less pure.
  They are like maggots, as worthless as
    worms!"

Job Answers Bildad

26 Then Job answered:

2"Bildad, what a great help you are to this
    tired, weary man!
  You have really supported me!
3You have given such wonderful advice to this
    foolish man!
  You have provided so much useful
    information!*c*

4Who helped you say these things?
  Whose spirit inspired you to speak?

5"The ghosts and their neighbours
  in the underworld*d* shake with fear.
6But God can see clearly into that place of
    death.
  Death*e* is not hidden from God.
7God stretched the northern sky over empty
    space.
  He hung the earth on nothing.
8He fills the thick clouds with water.
  But he does not let its heavy weight break
    the clouds open.
9He covers the face of the full moon.
  He spreads his clouds over it and hides it.
10He drew the horizon on the ocean,
  like a circle where light and darkness meet.
11The foundations that hold up the sky
  shake with fear when God threatens them.
12With his own power God calmed the sea.
  With his wisdom he destroyed Rahab.

13His breath made the skies clear.
  His hand destroyed the snake that tried to
    get away.*f*
14These are only a few of the amazing things
    God has done.
  We hear only a small whisper of God's
    thundering power."

27 Job continued his answer:

2"God All-Powerful has been unfair to me;
  he has made my life bitter.
3But as long as I have life in me,
  as long as breath from God is in my
    nostrils,
4I will not be a hypocrite.
  I will not lie.
5You will never hear me say you men are
    right!
  To the day I die, I will never be untrue to
    myself.
6I will never stop believing that what I have
    done is right!
  My conscience will always be clear!
7May my enemies be punished like those who
    are evil.
  May those who stood against me end up
    like all who have done wrong.
8What hope do people without God have when
    it is time to die,
  when God takes their life away?
9When they have troubles and cry out for help,
  God will not listen to them!
10It will be too late for them to enjoy talking
    with God All-Powerful.
  They should have prayed to God all the time.

11"I will teach you about God's power.
  I will not hide anything about God
    All-Powerful.
12But you have seen it all with your own eyes.
  So why do you say such useless things?

13*g* "Here is what God has planned for those
    who are evil.
  This is what cruel people will get from God
    All-Powerful.
14They may have many children, but all of them
    will be killed in war.
  Or their children will not have enough to eat.

---

a **25:3** *his stars* Or "his troops". This means God's heavenly army. It could be all the angels or all the stars in the sky.
b **25:4** *No human being* Literally, "No one born from woman".
c **26:2–3** Job is being sarcastic here—showing by the way he speaks that he does not really mean it.
d **26:5** *The ghosts . . . underworld* Literally, "The ghosts under the water". This refers to Sheol, the place of death.
e **26:6** *Death* Or "Abaddon", a Hebrew name meaning "death" or "destruction". See Rev. 9:11.
f **26:13** *snake . . . get away* Or "the escaping monster". This might be another name for Rahab. See Isa. 27:1.
g **27:13** Though Zophar is not mentioned in the text, many scholars think he answers Job in verses 13–23.

¹⁵All those who are left will die,
and the widows will not even cry for
them.
¹⁶Evil people collect silver as easily as dirt.
They may have so many clothes that they
are piled up like clay.
¹⁷But their piles of clothes will be worn by those
who have lived right.
All that silver will be given to those who
have done no wrong.
¹⁸Evil people might build houses, but they will
not last long.
They will be like a spider's web or a
guard's tent.
¹⁹They might be rich when they go to bed,
but when they open their eyes, all their
riches will be gone.
²⁰Terrible fears will come over them like a
flood,
like a storm in the night that blows
everything away.
²¹The east wind will carry them away, and they
will be gone.
The storm will sweep them out of their
homes.
²²They may try to run away from the power of
the storm,
but it will come down on them without
mercy.
²³It will make a sound like clapping hands as
they run away.
It will mock them as they run from their
homes."

The Value of Wisdom

28 "There are mines where people get silver
and places where people melt gold to
make it pure.
²Iron is dug out of the ground,
and copper is melted out of the rocks.
³Miners carry lights deep into caves
to search for these rocks in the deepest
darkness.
⁴Far from where people live, they dig deep into
the ground,
down where no one else has been before.
There they work all alone, hanging from
ropes.
⁵Food grows on the ground above.
But underground it is different,
as if everything were melted by fire.
⁶In the rocks there are sapphires
and grains of pure gold.
⁷Wild birds know nothing about the way to
these places.

No falcon ᵃ has ever seen it.
⁸Wild animals have never been there.
Lions have not travelled that way.
⁹Miners dig the hardest rocks.
They dig away at the mountains and make
them bare.
¹⁰They cut tunnels through the rocks
and see all the treasures they hold.
¹¹They even find places where rivers begin.
They bring to light what once was hidden.

¹²"But where can anyone find wisdom?
Where can we get understanding?
¹³People don't know where wisdom is.
It cannot be found by anyone on earth.
¹⁴The deep ocean says, 'It's not here with me.'
The sea says, 'It's not here with me.'
¹⁵You cannot buy wisdom with even the purest
gold.
There's not enough silver in the world to
pay for it.
¹⁶You cannot buy it with gold from Ophir
or with precious onyx or sapphires.
¹⁷Wisdom is worth more than gold or crystal.
It cannot be bought with expensive jewels
set in gold.
¹⁸It is far more valuable than coral and jasper,
more precious than rubies.
¹⁹The topaz from Ethiopia cannot match its
value,
which is greater than the purest gold.

²⁰"So where does wisdom come from?
Where can we find understanding?
²¹Wisdom is hidden from every living thing on
earth.
Even birds in the sky cannot see it.
²²Death and destruction ᵇ say,
'We have never seen wisdom;
we have only heard rumours about it.'

²³"Only God knows the way to wisdom.
Only he knows where wisdom is.
²⁴He can see to the very ends of the earth.
He sees everything under the sky.
²⁵God gave the wind its power.
He decided how big to make the oceans.
²⁶He decided where to send the rain
and where the thunderstorms should go.
²⁷He looked at wisdom and discussed it.
He examined it and saw how much it is
worth.
²⁸Then he said to humans,
'To fear and respect the Lord is wisdom.
To turn away from evil is understanding.'"

ᵃ **28:7 falcon** A kind of bird, like a hawk.
ᵇ **28:22 Death and destruction** Or "Abaddon", a Hebrew name meaning "death" or "destruction". See Rev. 9:11.

Job Continues His Speech

29 Job continued to speak:

2 "I wish my life could be the same as it was a
  few months ago,
  when God watched over me and cared
  for me.
3 God's light shone above me,
  so I could walk through the darkness.
4 I wish for the days when I was successful,
  when I enjoyed God's friendship and
  blessing in my home.
5 God All-Powerful was still with me then,
  and my children were all around me.
6 Life was so good that I washed my feet in
  cream
  and had plenty of the finest oils.*a*

7 "Those were the days when I went to the
  city gate
  and sat in the public meeting of the leaders.
8 When the young men saw me coming, they
  stepped out of my way.
  And the old men stood up to show they
  respected me.
9 The leaders of the people stopped talking
  and put their hands over their mouths.
10 Even the most important leaders were
  quiet,
  as if their tongues were stuck to the roof of
  their mouths.
11 All who heard me said good things about
  me.
  Those who saw what I did praised me,
12 because I helped the poor when they cried
  out.
  I helped the orphans who had no one to
  care for them.
13 People who were dying asked God to bless
  me.
  My help brought joy to widows in need.
14 Right living was my clothing.
  Fairness was my robe and turban.
15 I was like eyes for the blind,
  like feet for the lame.
16 I was like a father to the poor.
  I helped people I didn't even know win
  their case in court.
17 I stopped evil people from hurting others
  and saved innocent people from their
  attacks.*b*

18 "I always thought I would live a long life,
  growing old with my family around me.
19 I was like a healthy plant with roots that have
  plenty of water
  and branches that are wet with dew.
20 I thought each new day would bring more
  honour
  and be full of new possibilities.*c*

21 "In the past people listened to me.
  They waited quietly for my advice.
22 When I finished speaking, they had nothing
  more to say.
  My words fell gently on their ears.
23 They waited for my words as they would
  for rain.
  They drank them in like rain in the
  springtime.
24 I smiled at them, and they could hardly
  believe it.
  My smile made them feel better.
25 I was their leader and made decisions about
  their future.
  I was like a king among his troops,
  comforting those who were sad.

30 "But now men younger than I make fun
  of me—
  men whose fathers were too worthless to
  put with my sheep dogs.
2 Their fathers are still too weak to be of any
  use to me.
  All their strength has gone.
3 They are starving with nothing to eat,
  so they chew on the dry, ruined land.
4 They pull up salt plants in the desert
  and eat the roots from the broom tree.
5 They are forced away from other people,
  who shout at them as if they were thieves.
6 They must live in the dry riverbeds,
  hillside caves and holes in the ground.
7 They howl in the bushes
  and huddle together under thornbushes.
8 They are a bunch of worthless people without
  names,
  who were forced to leave their country.

9 "Now their sons sing songs to make fun of
  me.
  My name has become a bad word to
  them.

---

a **29:6 had plenty of the finest oils** Literally, "Around the anointed rock near me were streams of oil." This probably means Job had so much olive oil that there were streams of oil running down the altar from the part Job gave as a gift to God.
b **29:17** Literally, "I shattered the teeth of the crooked and snatched the victims from their teeth."
c **29:20** Literally, "My glory is new with me and my bow in my hand renewed." The words "glory" and "bow" might both refer to a rainbow—the promise of good weather after a storm. Or this might be understood as, "My soul feels new every day, my hand always strong enough to shoot a new bow."

¹⁰They hate me and stay far away from me,
  except when they come to spit in my
  face!
¹¹God has taken the string from my bow and
  made me weak,
  so they feel free to do whatever they want
  to me.
¹²They attack me on my right side.
  They knock my feet out from under me.
  They build ramps to attack and destroy me
  like a city.
¹³They guard the road so that I cannot
  escape.
  They succeed in destroying me, without
  help from anyone.
¹⁴They break a hole in the wall and come
  rushing through it,
  and the crashing rocks fall on me.
¹⁵I am shaking with fear.
  They chased my honour away like dust in
  the wind.
  My safety disappears like a cloud.

¹⁶"Now my life is almost over, and soon
  I will die.
  Days of suffering have grabbed me.
¹⁷All my bones ache at night.
  Pain never stops chewing on me.
¹⁸God grabbed the collar of my coat
  and twisted my clothes out of shape.
¹⁹He threw me into the mud,
  and I became like dust and ashes.

²⁰"God, I cry out to you for help, but you don't
  answer.
  I stand here before you, but you pay no
  attention to me.
²¹You have become cruel to me;
  you use your power to hurt me.
²²You let the strong wind blow me away.
  You throw me around in the storm.
²³I know you will lead me to my death,
  to that place where all the living must go.

²⁴"Surely no one would attack a man who is
  already ruined,
  when he is hurt and crying for help.
²⁵God, you know that I cried for those who
  were in trouble.
  You know that I mourned for the poor.
²⁶But when I hoped for good, trouble came
  instead.
  When I looked for light, darkness came.
²⁷I constantly feel upset.
  And my suffering has only just begun.

²⁸I am always depressed, without any
  relief.
  I stand in the public meeting and cry for
  help.
²⁹The sad sounds that come from my mouth
  are like the cries of wild dogs or ostriches.
³⁰My skin is burnt and peeling away.
  My body is hot with fever.
³¹My harp is tuned to play songs of sorrow.
  My flute makes sad sounds like someone
  crying.

31

"I made an agreement with my eyes
not to look at a girl with desire on my
mind.
²What does God above have for us?
  What does God All-Powerful send from
  heaven to repay us?
³He sends trouble to the wicked
  and disaster to those who do wrong.
⁴God is the one who knows what I do
  and sees every step I take.

⁵"I have not lied to anyone.
  I never tried to cheat people.
⁶If God would use accurate scales,ᵃ
  he would know that I am innocent.
⁷If I ever stepped off the right path,
  if my eyes led my heart to do evil,
  or if my hands are dirty with sin,
⁸then let others eat what I planted.
  Let my crops be pulled up by the roots.

⁹"If I have desired another woman
  or waited at my neighbour's door to sin
  with his wife,
¹⁰then let my wife serve someone else,
  and let other men sleep with her.
¹¹To do such a thing would be shameful,
  a sin that must be punished.
¹²Such sin is like a fire that burns until it
  destroys everything.
  It would completely ruin my life's work.

¹³"If I refused to be fair to my slaves
  when they had a complaint against me,
¹⁴then what will I do when I must face God?
  What will I say when he asks me to explain
  what I did?
¹⁵The one who made me in my mother's womb
  also made them.
  God shaped us all inside our mothers.

¹⁶"I have never refused to help the poor.
  I always gave widows what they needed.

ᵃ **31:6** *accurate scales* Literally, "scales of righteousness". As a wordplay, this could mean either "accurate scales" or "scales that show a person is good".

¹⁷I have never been selfish with my food.
I shared what I had with orphans.
¹⁸All my life I have been like a father to
orphans
and have taken care of widows.
¹⁹Whenever I found people suffering because
they didn't have clothes
or saw a poor man with no coat,
²⁰ I always gave them something to wear.
I used the wool from my own sheep to make
them warm.
And they thanked me with all their heart.
²¹I never threatened an orphan,
even when I knew I had support in court.[a]
²²If I have ever done that, may my arm be
pulled from its socket
and fall from my shoulder!
²³But I didn't do any of these bad things.
I fear God's punishment too much.
His majesty scares me.[b]

²⁴"I have never trusted in riches.
I never said even to pure gold, 'You are my
hope.'
²⁵I have been wealthy,
but that didn't make me proud.
I earned a lot of money,
but that is not what made me happy.
²⁶I have never worshipped the bright sun
or the beautiful moon.
²⁷I was never foolish enough
to worship the sun and the moon.
²⁸This is also a sin that must be punished.
If I had worshipped them, I would have
been unfaithful to God All-Powerful.

²⁹"I have never been happy
when my enemies were destroyed.
I have never laughed at my enemies
when bad things happened to them.
³⁰I have never let my mouth sin by cursing my
enemies
and wishing for them to die.
³¹The people in my house know that
I have never let anyone go hungry.
³²I always invited strangers into my home
so that they would not have to sleep in the
streets.
³³I have not tried to hide my sins as some
people do.
I have never hidden my guilt.
³⁴I was never so afraid of what people might say
or of making enemies
that I kept my sins secret and avoided
going out.

³⁵"How I wish someone would listen to me!
I will sign my name to all I have said.
Now let God All-Powerful answer me.
Let him make a list of what he thinks I did
wrong.
³⁶I would wear it around my neck.
I would put it on my head like a crown.
³⁷Then I could explain everything I have done.
I could come to God with my head held
high like a prince.

³⁸"I did not use my land in a wrong way.
I never caused it to suffer.
³⁹I always paid the workers for the food I got
from the land.
I never let any of them starve.
⁴⁰If I ever did any of these bad things,
let thorns and weeds grow in my fields
instead of wheat and barley!"

Job's words are finished.

Elihu Adds to the Argument

32 Then Job's three friends gave up trying to answer him, because he was so sure that he was innocent. ²But there was a young man there named Elihu son of Barakel. He was a descendant of a man named Buz. Elihu was from the family of Ram. He became very angry because Job kept saying he was innocent—that he was right and God was wrong. ³Elihu was also angry with Job's three friends because they could not answer him, and yet they still considered him guilty of doing wrong. ⁴Elihu was the youngest one there, so he had waited until everyone finished talking. ⁵But when he saw that Job's three friends had nothing more to say, his anger forced him to speak. ⁶So here's what Elihu son of Barakel the Buzite said:

"I am only a young man, and you are all older.
That is why I was afraid to tell you what I
think.
⁷I thought to myself, 'Older people should
speak first.
They have lived many years, so they have
learned many things.'
⁸But it is the spirit in people, the breath from
God All-Powerful,
that makes them understand.
⁹Old men are not the only wise people.
They are not the only ones who understand
what is right.

¹⁰"So please listen to me,
and I will tell you what I think.

---

[a] **31:21** Or "I never shook my fist at an orphan who was at the gate asking for help."
[b] **31:23** *His majesty . . . me* Or "I could not stand before his majesty."

¹¹I waited patiently while you men talked.
  I listened to the answers you gave as you
    searched for the right words.
¹²I listened carefully to what you said.
  Not one of you proved Job wrong.
  Not one of you answered his arguments.
¹³You men cannot say that you have found
    wisdom.
  The answer to Job's arguments must come
    from God, not people.
¹⁴Job was arguing with you, not me,
  so I will not use your arguments to answer
    him.

¹⁵"Job, these men lost the argument.
  They don't have anything more to say.
  They don't have any more answers.
¹⁶I waited for them to answer you.
  But now they are quiet.
  They stand there with nothing more to say.
¹⁷So now I will give you my answer.
  Yes, I will tell you what I think.
¹⁸I have so much to say
  that I cannot hold it in.
¹⁹I feel like a jar of wine that has never been
    opened.
  I am like a new wineskin ready to burst.
²⁰I must speak so that I will feel better.
  I must answer your arguments.
²¹I will treat you the same as I would treat
    anyone else.
  I will not praise you to win your favour.
²²I cannot treat one person better than
    another.
  If I did, God my Maker would punish me!

33 "Now, Job, listen to me.
  Listen carefully to what I say.
²Look, my mouth is open.
  You can see I am ready to speak.
³My heart is honest, so my words are sincere.
  I will speak the truth about what I know.
⁴God's Spirit made me.
  My life comes from God All-Powerful.
⁵Listen to me and answer if you can.
  Get your arguments ready to face me.
⁶You and I are the same before God.
  He used clay to make us both.
⁷Don't be afraid of me.
  I will not be hard on you.

⁸"But, Job, I heard what you said.
  These were your very words:
⁹'I am pure and innocent;
  I did nothing wrong; I am not guilty!

¹⁰But God found an excuse to attack me.
  He treats me like an enemy.
¹¹He put chains on my feet
  and watches everything I do.'

¹²"But you are wrong about this, and I will
    prove it to you.
  God knows more than any of us.ᵃ
¹³You are arguing with God!
  Why do you think he should explain
    everything to you?
¹⁴But maybe God does explain what he
    does
  but speaks in ways that people don't
    understand.
¹⁵He may speak in a dream, or in a vision at
    night,
  when people are in a deep sleep lying in
    their beds.
¹⁶He may whisper something in their ear,
  and they are frightened when they hear his
    warnings.
¹⁷God warns people to stop them from doing
    wrong
  and to keep them from becoming proud.
¹⁸He does this to save them from death.ᵇ
  He wants to keep them from being
    destroyed.

¹⁹"Or those who are sick in bed might be
    suffering punishment from God.
  The pain that makes their bones ache might
    be a warning from him.
²⁰They feel so bad they cannot eat.
  Even the best food makes them sick.
²¹Their bodies might waste away until they
    become thin
  and all their bones stick out.
²²They might be close to death,
  their lives about to end.
²³But maybe one of God's thousands of angels
    will speak for them
  and tell about the good things they have
    done.
²⁴Maybe the angel will be kind and say to
    God,
  'Save this one from the place of death!
  I have found a way to pay for his life.'
²⁵Then that person will become young and
    strong again.
  He will be as he was when he was young.
²⁶He will pray and God will answer.
  He will worship God and shout with
    joy.
  He will again stand as right before God.

ᵃ 33:12 *God . . . any of us* Or "God is much greater than anyone."
ᵇ 33:18 *death* Literally, "the Pit", the place where people go when they die. Also in verse 22.

²⁷He will tell everyone, 'I sinned.
I changed good into bad,
but God didn't give me the punishment I
deserved!
²⁸He saved me from going down to death.
Now I can enjoy life again.'

²⁹"God does all these things.
He does them for people again and again.
³⁰He wants them to be saved from death
so that they can enjoy life.

³¹"Job, pay attention and listen to me.
Be quiet and let me talk.
³²But if you have an answer, go ahead and speak.
Tell me your argument.
I would be happy to know that you are
innocent!
³³But if you have nothing to say, then listen
to me.
Be quiet, and I will teach you wisdom."

34

Then Elihu continued his speech:

²"Listen to what I say, you wise men.
Pay attention, you who know so much.
³Your tongue tastes the food it touches,
and your ear tests the words it hears.
⁴So let us test these arguments and decide for
ourselves what is right.
Together we will learn what is good.
⁵Job says, 'I am innocent,
and God is not being fair to me.
⁶I am right, but I am judged to be a liar.
I have done no wrong, but I am badly hurt.'

⁷"Would anyone but Job say such things?
He has more thirst for insulting God than
for water.
⁸He is a friend of evil people.
He likes to spend time with the wicked.
⁹He knows this because he says,
'You will gain nothing if you try to please
God.'

¹⁰"You men can understand, so listen to me.
God would never do what is evil!
God All-Powerful would never do wrong.
¹¹He pays us back for what we have done.
He gives us what we deserve.
¹²The truth is that God does no wrong.
God All-Powerful is always fair.
¹³No one chose God to be in charge of the
earth.
No one gave him responsibility for the
whole world.
¹⁴If God decided to take away his spirit
and the breath of life he gave us,

¹⁵then everything on earth would die.
We would all become dust again.

¹⁶"If you men are wise,
you will listen to what I say.
¹⁷Can someone be a ruler if he hates justice?
Job, God is not only powerful, but he is
fair.
Do you think you can judge him guilty?
¹⁸God is the one who says to kings, 'You are
worthless!'
He says to leaders, 'You are evil!'
¹⁹He does not respect leaders more than other
people.
And he does not respect the rich more than
the poor.
God made everyone.
²⁰Any of us can die suddenly, in the middle of
the night.
Anyone can get sick and pass away.
Even powerful people die for no reason we
can see.

²¹"God watches what people do.
He sees every step they take.
²²There is no place dark enough
for evil people to hide from God.
²³God does not need to set a time
for people to come before him and be
judged.
²⁴He does not have to ask questions when
people do wrong,
even if they are powerful leaders.
He simply destroys them
and chooses others to take their place.
²⁵When he learns what people have done,
he defeats them, and overnight they are
gone.
²⁶He will punish them for the evil they have
done,
and he will do it where everyone can see.
²⁷He will do this because they rebelled against
him
and ignored what he wanted.
²⁸They hurt the poor and made them cry to God
for help.
And he hears their cry!
²⁹But if God decides not to help them,
no one can judge him guilty.
If he hides himself, no one can find him.
But he is the ruler over every person and
nation.
³⁰He keeps the wicked from ruling
so that they will not bring harm to the
people.

³¹"A person should say to God,
'I am guilty; I will not sin any more.

³²Show me the sins I am not able to see.
  If I have done wrong, I will not do it
    again.'
³³Job, you want God to reward you,
  but you refuse to change.
  It is your decision, not mine.
  Tell me what you think.
³⁴A wise person would listen to me.
  A wise person would say,
³⁵'Job talks like an ignorant person.
  What he says doesn't make sense!'
³⁶I think Job should be punished even more
  because he answers us like someone who
    is evil!
³⁷To his other sins he adds refusal to listen.
  He shows no respect for us,
  and he never stops arguing against God!"

35

Elihu continued talking and said,

²"Job, it is not fair for you to say,
  'I am more right than God,'
³because you also ask him,
  'What's the use of trying to please you?
  What good will it do me if I don't sin?'

⁴"Job, I want to answer you and your friends
  here with you.
⁵Look up at the sky.
  Look at the clouds, which are so much
    higher than you.
⁶If you sin, it does not hurt God.
  Even if your sins are too many to count,
    that does nothing to God.
⁷And if you are good, that does not help God.
  He gets nothing from you.
⁸Job, the good and bad things you do
  affect only other people like yourself.

⁹"If people are being hurt, they cry out
  and beg for protection from those who
    hurt them.
¹⁰But they forget to say, 'Where is God,
  the one who made me?
  He is the one who gives us songs to sing in
    the night.
¹¹He is the one who makes us smarter than any
    animal on earth
  and wiser than any bird.'

¹²"Or if evil people ask God for help, he will not
    answer them,
  because they are too proud.
¹³God will not listen to their worthless begging.
  God All-Powerful will not pay attention to
    them.
¹⁴So, Job, God will not listen to you
  when you say that you don't see him.

You say you are waiting for your chance to
    meet with him
  and prove that you are innocent.

¹⁵"Job thinks that God does not punish evil
  and that he pays no attention to sin.
¹⁶So he continues his worthless talking.
  Everything he has said shows he does not
    know what he is talking about."

36

Elihu continued talking and said,

²"Be patient with me a little longer.
  God has a few more words that he wants
    me to say.
³I will share my knowledge with everyone.
  I will prove that my Maker is right.
⁴Job, I am telling the truth.
  I know what I am talking about.

⁵"God is very powerful,
  but he does not hate people.
  He is very powerful,
  but he is also very wise.
⁶He will not let evil people live.
  He brings justice to the poor.
⁷He watches over those who do what is right.
  He lets them rule in high places.
⁸So if people are punished,
  if they are tied with chains and ropes, they
    did something wrong.
⁹And God will tell them what they did,
  that they sinned and were proud.
¹⁰He will force them to listen to his warning.
  He will command them to stop
    sinning.
¹¹If they serve and obey him, he will make them
    successful
  and they will live a happy life.
¹²But if they refuse to obey him, they will be
    destroyed.
  They will die like fools.

¹³"People who don't care about God are always
    bitter.
  Even when he punishes them, they refuse
    to pray to him for help.
¹⁴They will die while they are still young,
  like the male prostitutes.
¹⁵God saves those who suffer by using their
    suffering.
  He uses their troubles to speak in a way
    that makes them listen.

¹⁶"In fact, God wants to help you out of your
    troubles.
  He wants to take away your burdens that
    are crushing you.

He wants to load your table with plenty of
food.
¹⁷But you are full of this talk about guilt,
judgement and justice!
¹⁸Job, don't let your anger fill you with doubt
about God.
And don't let the price of forgiveness turn
you away.
¹⁹Do you think your wealth will keep you out of
trouble?
Will your great strength be of any help to
you now?
²⁰Don't be like those who wish darkness would
come and hide them.
They try to disappear into the night.ᵃ
²¹Job, don't let your suffering cause you to
choose evil.
Be careful not to do wrong.

²²"Look, God's power makes him great!
He is the greatest teacher of all.
²³No one can tell him what to do.
No one can say, 'God, you have done wrong.'
²⁴Remember to praise him for what he has
done,
as many others have done in song.
²⁵Everyone can see what he has done,
even people in faraway countries.
²⁶Yes, God is great, but we cannot understand
his greatness.
We don't know how long he has lived.

²⁷"God takes up water from the earth
and changes it into mist and rain.
²⁸So the clouds pour out the water,
and the rain falls on many people.
²⁹No one can understand how he spreads the
clouds out
or how the thunder rumbles from his home
in the sky.
³⁰Look, he spreads lightning all over the sky
and covers the deepest part of the ocean.
³¹He uses them to control the nations
and to give them plenty of food.
³²He grabs the lightning with his hands,
and commands it to strike where he
wants.
³³The thunder warns that a storm is coming.
So even the cattle know it is near.

37
"The thunder and lightning frighten me;
my heart pounds in my chest.
²Listen to God's thundering voice!
Listen to the sound coming from his
mouth.

³He sends his lightning to flash across the sky.
It lights up the earth from one end to the
other.
⁴Then comes the roaring sound,
the thundering sound of his great voice!
And even as his voice thunders,
the lightning continues to flash.
⁵God's thundering voice is amazing!
He does great things we cannot understand.
⁶He says to the snow,
'Fall on the earth.'
And he says to the rain,
'Pour down on the earth.'
⁷God does this to stop everyone's work
and to show the people he made what he
can do.
⁸The animals run into their dens
and stay where they feel safe.
⁹Whirlwinds come from the south.
The cold winds come from the north.
¹⁰God's breath makes ice
and freezes even large bodies of water.
¹¹He fills the clouds with water
and scatters his lightning through them.
¹²He orders the clouds to be blown all around
the earth.
The clouds do whatever he commands.
¹³He causes the clouds to punish people with
floods
or to water his earth and show his love.

¹⁴"Job, stop for a minute and listen.
Think about the wonderful things God does.
¹⁵Do you know how God controls the clouds?
Do you know how he makes his lightning
flash?
¹⁶Do you know how the clouds hang in the sky?
This is just one of the amazing works of the
one who knows everything.
¹⁷All you know is that you sweat, your clothes
stick to you,
and all is still and quiet when the heatwave
comes from the south.
¹⁸Can you help God spread out the sky
and make it shine like polished brass?

¹⁹"Job, tell us what we should say to God!
We cannot think of what to say because of
our ignorance.ᵇ
²⁰I would not tell God that I wanted to talk to
him.
That would be like asking to be destroyed.
²¹A person cannot look at the sun.
It is too bright as it shines in the sky after
the wind blows the clouds away.

ᵃ 36:19–20 The Hebrew text is not clear.
ᵇ 37:19 *We cannot . . . ignorance* Literally, "We cannot arrange add our thoughts because of the darkness."

²²In the same way, God's golden glory shines
   from the Holy Mountain.ᵃ
   He is surrounded by the brightest light.
²³We have seen that God All-Powerful really is
   all powerful!
   But he is just and never treats anyone
   unfairly.ᵇ
²⁴That is why people fear and respect him.
   He shows no respect for those who think
   they are wise."

INSIGHT

*God's answer to Job reminds us of how
mighty and awesome God is – the God
who created and controls the universe,
the God of the big picture and the
smallest detail. In the face of who God is,
all Job's arguments seem to dissolve.*

Job 38 – 39

God Speaks to Job

38 Then the LORD spoke to Job from a
whirlwind and said,

²"Who is this ignorant person
   saying these foolish things?ᶜ
³Prepare yourself for an attack!
   Get ready to answer the questions I will ask
   you.

⁴"Where were you when I made the earth?
   If you are so smart, answer me.
⁵And who decided how big the earth should
   be?
   Who measured it with a measuring line?
⁶What is the earth resting on?
   Who put the first stone in its place
⁷when the morning stars sang together
   and the angelsᵈ shouted with joy?

⁸"Who closed the flood gates
   as the sea gushed from the womb?
⁹Who covered it with clouds
   and wrapped it in darkness?
¹⁰I set the limits for the sea
   and put it behind locked gates.

¹¹I said to the sea, 'You can come this far, but no
   farther.
   This is where your proud waves will stop.'

¹²"Did you ever in your life command the
   morning to begin
   or the day to dawn?
¹³Did you ever tell the morning light to grab the
   earth
   and shake those who are evil out of their
   hiding places?
¹⁴The morning light makes the hills
   and valleys easy to see.
When the daylight comes to the earth,
   the shapes of these places stand out like the
   folds of a coat.
They take shape like soft clay
   that is pressed with a stamp.
¹⁵Evil people don't like the daylight.
   When it shines brightly, it keeps them from
   doing the bad things they do.

¹⁶"Have you ever gone to the deepest parts of
   the sea?
   Have you ever walked on the ocean
   bottom?
¹⁷Has anyone shown you the gates to the world
   of the dead?
   Have you ever seen those gates that lead to
   the dark place of death?
¹⁸Do you really understand how big the earth is?
   Tell me, if you know all this.

¹⁹"Where does light come from?
   Where does darkness come from?
²⁰Can you take them back to where they
   belong?
   Do you know how to get there?
²¹Surely you know these things, since you are so
   old and wise.
   You were alive when I made them, weren't
   you?ᵉ

²²"Have you ever gone into the storerooms
   where I keep the snow and the hail?
²³I save them there for times of trouble,
   for the times of war and battle.
²⁴Have you ever gone to the place where the
   sun comes up,
   where it makes the east wind blow all over
   the earth?ᶠ

ᵃ **37:22 Holy Mountain** Or "the north" or "Zaphon".
ᵇ **37:23 But he . . . unfairly** Or "He does not answer us when we try to sue him for justice."
ᶜ **38:2** Or "Who is this person darkening advice with ignorant words."
ᵈ **38:7 angels** Literally, "sons of God".
ᵉ **38:19–21** This is sarcasm—saying something in a way that everyone understands is not really true.
ᶠ **38:24** Or "Where is the place that the fog disperses and the place where the east wind scatters it all over the earth?"

²⁵Who dug ditches in the sky for the heavy
rain?
Who made a path for the thunderstorm?
²⁶Who makes it rain even in desert places
where no one lives?
²⁷The rain gives that dry empty land all the
water it needs,
and grass begins to grow.
²⁸Does the rain have a father?
Who produces the drops of dew?
²⁹Does ice have a mother?
Who gives birth to the frost?
³⁰That's when the water freezes as hard as a rock.
Even the deep sea freezes over!

³¹"Can you tie up the Pleiades?ᵃ
Can you unfasten the belt of Orion?ᵇ
³²Can you bring out the other constellationsᶜ at
the right times?
Can you lead out the Bearᵈ with its cubs?
³³Do you know the laws that control the sky?
Can you put each star in its place above the
earth?ᵉ

³⁴"Can you shout at the clouds
and command them to cover you with rain?
³⁵Can you give a command to the lightning?
Will it come to you and say, 'Here we are;
what do you want, sir?'
Will it go wherever you want it to go?

³⁶"Who makes people wise?
Who puts wisdom deep inside them?
³⁷Who is wise enough to count the clouds
and tip them over to pour out their rain?
³⁸The rain makes the dust become mud
and the clumps of dirt stick together.

³⁹"Do you find food for the lions?
Do you feed their hungry babies?
⁴⁰No, they hide in their caves
or wait in the grass, ready to attack their
prey.
⁴¹Who feeds the ravens when their babies cry
out to God
and wander around without food?

39

"Do you know when the mountain goats
are born?
Do you watch when the mother deer gives
birth?

²Do you know how many months they must
carry their babies?
Do you know when it is the right time for
them to be born?
³When these animals feel their birth pains, they
lie down,
and their babies are born.
⁴Their babies grow strong out in the wild.
Then they leave their mothers and never
come back.

⁵"Who let the wild donkeys go free?
Who untied their ropes and let them loose?
⁶I let the wild donkey have the desert for a
home.
I gave the salt lands to them for a place to
live.
⁷They are happy to be away from the noise of
the city.
They never have to listen to their drivers
shouting at them.
⁸They live in the mountains.
That is their pasture.
That is where they look for food to eat.

⁹"Will a wild bull agree to serve you?
Will he stay in your barn at night?
¹⁰Will he let you put ropes on him
to plough your fields?
¹¹A wild bull is very strong,
but can you trust him to do your work?
¹²Can you trust him to gather your grain
and bring it to your threshing floor?

¹³"An ostrich gets excited and flaps its wings,
but it cannot fly.
Its wings and feathers are not like the wings
of a stork.
¹⁴An ostrich lays her eggs on the ground
and lets the sand keep them warm.
¹⁵The ostrich forgets that someone might step
on her eggs
or that a wild animal might break them.
¹⁶An ostrich leaves her little babies.
She treats them as if they were not her
own.
If her babies die, she does not care that all
her work was for nothing.
¹⁷That's because I did not give wisdom to the
ostrich.
She is foolish, and I made her that way.

ᵃ **38:31** *Pleiades* A famous group of stars. It is often called "The Seven Sisters".
ᵇ **38:31** *Orion* A famous group of stars. It looks like a hunter or powerful soldier.
ᶜ **38:32** *constellations* Groups of stars in the night sky. Here, this probably means the twelve constellations of the Zodiac. They
seem to pass through the sky so that a new constellation is in a certain part of the sky each month.
ᵈ **38:32** *Bear* A famous group of stars. It looks like a bear. It is often called "the Big Dipper". Near it is a smaller constellation that
looks like a small bear. It is often called "the Little Dipper".
ᵉ **38:33** *Can you . . . earth* Or "Can you put it in charge over the earth?"

¹⁸But when the ostrich gets up to run, she
    laughs at the horse and its rider,
  because she can run faster than any
    horse.

¹⁹"Did you give the horse its strength?
    Did you put the mane[a] on its neck?
²⁰Did you make it able to jump like a locust
    or snort[b] so loudly that it scares people?
²¹A horse is proud to be so strong.
    Eager to run into battle, it digs at the
      ground with its hooves.
²²It laughs at fear; nothing makes it afraid!
    It does not run away from battle.
²³The soldier's quiver shakes on the horse's
    side.
  The spear and weapons its rider carries
    shine in the sun.[c]
²⁴The horse gets very excited and races over the
    ground.[c]
  When it hears the trumpet blow, it cannot
    stand still.
²⁵When the trumpet sounds, it snorts,
    'Hurray!'
  It can smell the battle from far away
  and hear the shouts of commanders with all
    the other sounds of battle.

²⁶"Did you teach the hawk how to spread its
    wings
  and fly towards the south?
²⁷Did you tell the eagle to fly up in the sky
  and build its nest so high?
²⁸It makes its home on the edge of a cliff.
    A rocky ledge is its fortress.
²⁹From there it watches far away,
    searching for its food.
³⁰You will find eagles where something
    has died.
  Their young ones feast on the blood."

40

Then the LORD said to Job,

²"You wanted to argue with God All-Powerful.
  You wanted to correct me and prove that I
    was wrong.
  So give me your answer!"

³Then Job answered the LORD:

⁴"I am not worthy to speak!
    What can I say to you?
  I cannot answer you!
    I will put my hand over my mouth.

⁵I spoke once, but I will not speak again.
  I spoke twice, but I will not say anything
    more."

⁶Then the LORD spoke to Job again from the
storm:

⁷"Get yourself ready to face me.
  I have some questions for you to answer.

⁸"Are you trying to show that I am unfair?
  Are you trying to look innocent by saying
    that I am guilty?
⁹Are your arms as strong as mine?
  Do you have a voice like mine that is as
    loud as thunder?
¹⁰If so, let me see your glory and majesty.
  Clothe yourself with honour and
    greatness.
¹¹If you are as powerful as God, then show your
    anger!
  Punish those who are proud and humble
    them.
¹²Yes, just look at the proud and make them
    humble.
  Crush those evil people where they stand.
¹³Bury them all in the dirt.
  Wrap their bodies up and put them in their
    graves.
¹⁴If you can do any of these things, then even I
    will praise you.
  And I will admit that you can save yourself
    by your own power.

¹⁵"Look at the behemoth.[d]
  I made the behemoth, and I made you.
  He eats grass like a cow.
¹⁶But he has great strength in his body.
  The muscles in his stomach are
    powerful.
¹⁷His tail stands strong like a cedar tree.
  His leg muscles are very strong.
¹⁸His bones are as strong as bronze.
  His legs are like iron bars.
¹⁹The behemoth is the most amazing animal
    I made,
  but I can defeat him.
²⁰He eats the grass that grows on the hills
  where the wild animals play.
²¹He lies under the lotus plants.
  He hides among the reeds of the swamp.
²²The lotus plants hide him in their shade.
  He lives under the willow trees that grow
    near the river.

---

[a] **39:19 mane** The hair on a horse's neck.
[b] **39:20 snort** The sound a horse makes by blowing air very hard through the nose.
[c] **39:24 races over the ground** Literally, "swallows up the ground".
[d] **40:15 behemoth** This might be a hippopotamus, a rhinoceros or possibly an elephant.

23If the river floods, the behemoth will not run
　　away.
　　He is not afraid if the Jordan River splashes
　　　on his face.
24No one can blind his eyes and capture him.
　　No one can catch him in a trap.

41

"Can you catch Leviathan*a* with a fish
hook?
　　Can you tie his tongue with a rope?
2Can you put a rope through his nose
　　or a hook through his jaw?
3Will he beg you to let him go free?
　　Will he speak to you with gentle words?
4Will he make an agreement with you
　　and promise to serve you forever?
5Will you play with Leviathan as you would
　　　play with a bird?
　　Will you put a rope on him so that your
　　　girls can play with him?
6Will fishermen try to buy him from you?
　　Will they cut him into pieces and sell him
　　　to the merchants?
7Can you throw spears into his skin or head?

8"If you ever lay a hand on Leviathan, you will
　　　never do it again!
　　Just think about the battle that would
　　　be!
9Do you think you can defeat him?
　　Well, forget it! There is no hope.
　　Just looking at him will scare you!
10No one is brave enough to wake him up
　　and make him angry.

　"Well, no one can challenge me either!*b*
11I owe nothing to anyone.
　　Everything under heaven belongs to me.*c*

12"I will tell you about Leviathan's legs,
　　his strength, and his graceful shape.
13No one can pierce his skin.
　　It is like armour!*d*
14No one can force him to open his jaws.
　　The teeth in his mouth scare people.
15His back has rows of shields
　　tightly sealed together.
16They are so close to each other
　　that no air can pass between them.
17The shields are joined to each other.
　　They hold together so tightly that they
　　　cannot be pulled apart.

18When Leviathan sneezes, it is like lightning
　　　flashing out.
　　His eyes shine like the light of dawn.
19Burning torches come from his mouth.
　　Sparks of fire shoot out.
20Smoke pours from his nose
　　like burning weeds under a boiling pot.
21His breath sets coals on fire,
　　and flames shoot from his mouth.
22His neck is very powerful.
　　People are afraid and run away from him.
23There is no soft spot in his skin.
　　It is as hard as iron.
24His heart is like a rock; he has no fear.
　　It is as hard as a millstone.
25When he gets up, even the strongest people*e*
　　　are afraid.
　　They run away when he swings his tail.
26Swords, spears and darts only bounce off
　　　when they hit him.
　　These weapons don't hurt him at all!
27He breaks iron as easily as straw.
　　He breaks bronze like rotten wood.
28Arrows don't make him run away.
　　Rocks thrown at him seem as light as chaff.
29When a wooden club hits him, it feels to him
　　　like a piece of straw.
　　He laughs when anyone throws a spear at
　　　him.
30The skin on his belly is like sharp pieces of
　　　broken pottery.
　　He leaves tracks in the mud like a threshing
　　　board.
31He stirs up the water like a boiling pot.
　　He makes it bubble like a pot of boiling oil.
32When he swims, he leaves a sparkling path
　　　behind him.
　　He stirs up the water and makes it white
　　　with foam.
33No animal on earth is like him.
　　He is an animal made without fear.
34He looks down on the proudest of creatures.
　　He is king over all the wild animals."

Job Answers the LORD

42

Then Job answered the LORD:

2"I know you can do everything.
　　You make plans, and nothing can change or
　　　stop them.
3You asked, 'Who is this ignorant person saying
　　　these foolish things?'*f*

---

a 41:1 *Leviathan* This animal might be a crocodile or a giant sea monster.
b 41:10 *Well, no one . . . either* Or "No one can stand and fight him."
c 41:11 Or "No one has come near to Leviathan and survived—no one under heaven!"
d 41:13 *It is like armour* Or "No one can approach him with a bridle."
e 41:25 *strongest people* Or "gods".
f 42:3 *Who . . . things* Or "Who is this person darkening advice with ignorant words."

I talked about things I did not understand.
I talked about things too amazing for me to
know.

4"You said to me, 'Listen, and I will speak.
I will ask you questions, and you will
answer me.'
5In the past I heard about you,
but now I have seen you with my own
eyes.
6And I am ashamed of myself.[a]
I am so sorry.
As I sit in the dust and ashes,[b]
I promise to change my heart and my life."

INSIGHT

God never tells Job about his
conversation with Satan (see Job 1 and 2)
and the real reason for his suffering, but
Job is more than satisfied. He's had an
audience with God and knows God hasn't
forgotten or abandoned him.

Job 42:1–6

The LORD Gives Job's Wealth Back

7After the LORD had finished talking to Job, he
spoke to Eliphaz from Teman. He said, "I am
angry with you and your two friends, because you
did not tell the truth about me, as my servant Job
did. 8So now, Eliphaz, get seven bulls and seven
rams. Take them to my servant Job. Kill them
and offer them as a burnt offering for yourselves.
My servant Job will pray for you, and I will
answer his prayer. Then I will not give you the
punishment you deserve. You should be punished,
because you were very foolish. You did not say
what is right about me, as my servant Job did."

INSIGHT

Have you ever wondered if it's okay to
question God? Job did this and God didn't
seem to mind. In fact he criticized Job's
friends who thought they were defending
God. In the end God said it was Job who
had done what was right.

Job 42:7–8

9So Eliphaz from Teman, Bildad from Shuah
and Zophar from Naamah obeyed the LORD. Then
the LORD answered Job's prayer.
10Job prayed for his friends, and the LORD
made Job successful again. The LORD gave him
twice as much as he had before. 11Then all his
brothers and sisters and all the people who knew
him before came to his house. They all ate a big
meal with him. They comforted him and were
sorry that the LORD had brought him so much
trouble. Each person gave Job a piece of silver and
a gold ring.
12The LORD blessed Job with even more than
he had in the beginning. Job got 14,000 sheep,
6,000 camels, 2,000 oxen and 1,000 female
donkeys. 13He also had seven sons and three
daughters. 14He named the first daughter Jemimah
and the second daughter Keziah. He named the
third daughter Keren Happuch. 15Job's daughters
were among the most beautiful women in the
whole country. And, like their brothers, they each
got a share of their father's property.[c]
16So Job lived for 140 years more. He lived
to see his children, his grandchildren, his great-
grandchildren and his great-great-grandchildren.
17Job lived to be a very old man who had lived a
good, long life.

---

[a] **42:6 I am ashamed of myself** Or "I take back what I said."
[b] **42:6 dust and ashes** People sat in dust and ashes to show that they were very sad about something.
[c] **42:15 And . . . property** Usually a person's property was divided only among the sons, but here, even Job's daughters got part
of his property.

Who Psalms is a collection of poems or songs by a number of writers. Authorship is as follows: David 73, Asaph 12, the Korah family 11, Solomon 2, Moses 1, Heman 1, Ethan 1, Anonymous 49.

When The collection was brought together over at least 400 years. It was probably finalized in the third century BC, where it served as a prayer book for use in the Temple and synagogues.

What Each "chapter" is a separate poem, composed at a different time, for a different purpose, and even by a different person. "Psalms" is a Greek word which comes from the psalterion, a kind of stringed instrument.

Many psalms are cries for help: direct, passionate, emotional prayers. These often end with renewed faith and confidence that the prayers have been heard. Other psalms thank God for answers to prayers. Although most of the psalms praise God in some way, there are many which specifically focus on his greatness and power. A few psalms are pilgrimage songs or "songs of ascents". They may have been sung by pilgrims going to the city for one of the three annual festivals of Passover, Purim and Shelters. Then there are wisdom psalms, which are closer to the style of Proverbs.

This variety of styles reflects the variety of subject matter. The book of Psalms is like a diary or a spiritual journal, the emotional outpouring of real human beings. Although the Hebrew title is "Praises", not all the psalms praise God. More than perhaps any other part of the Bible, the psalms reflect wishes, hopes, anger, desperation, joy, sadness and much, much more. The questions they ask, the honesty with which the psalmist confronts God, are universal experiences of mankind.

QUICK TOUR **PSALMS**

Praise the creator Psalm 8
David's escape Psalm 18
The glory of God Psalm 19
So alone Psalm 22
The Lord is my shepherd Psalm 23
Trust in God Psalm 27
The hunted deer Psalm 42
God's blessing Psalm 46
Forgiveness and mercy Psalm 51
Saying thanks Psalm 66

God's promise to David Psalm 89
Joyful worship Psalm 95
Intense suffering, intense faith Psalm 102
The glory of creation Psalm 104
The return of the exiles Psalm 107
The great king Psalm 110
The joy of the Law Psalm 119
Pilgrimage song Psalm 121
Song of exile Psalm 137
Praise God Psalm 150

"The LORD God goes up to his throne at the sound of the trumpet and horn. Sing praises to God, sing praises! Sing praises to our King, sing praises! God is the King of the whole world. Sing songs of praise!"

Psalm 47:5–7

BOOK 1
(Psalms 1–41)

1 Great blessings belong to those
who don't listen to evil advice,
who don't live like sinners,
and who don't join those who make fun
of God.*a*

[2] Instead, they love the LORD's teachings
and think about them day and night.
[3] So they grow strong,
like a tree planted by a stream—
a tree that produces fruit when it should
and has leaves that never fall.
Everything they do is successful.

[4] But the wicked are not like that.
They are like chaff that the wind blows
away.
[5] When the time for judgement comes, the
wicked will be found guilty.
Sinners have no place among those who do
what is right.*b*
[6] The LORD shows his people how to live,
but the wicked have lost their way.

2 Why are the nations so angry?
Why are the people making such foolish
plans?
[2] Their kings and leaders join together
to fight against the LORD and his chosen
king.*c*
[3] They say, "Let's rebel against them.
Let's break free from them!"

[4] But the one who rules in heaven laughs
at them.
The Lord makes fun of them.
[5] He speaks to them in anger,
and it fills them with fear.
[6] He says, "I have chosen this man to be king,
and he will rule on Zion, my holy
mountain."

[7] Let me tell you about the LORD's
agreement:
He said to me, "Today I have become
your father,*d*
and you are my son.

[8] If you ask, I will give you the nations.
Everyone on earth will be yours.
[9] You will rule over them with great
power.
You will scatter your enemies like broken
pieces of pottery!"

[10] So, kings and rulers, be smart
and learn this lesson.
[11] Serve the LORD
with fear and trembling.
[12] Show that you are loyal to his son,*e*
or the Lord will be angry and destroy
you.
He is almost angry enough to do that now,
but those who go to him for protection will
be blessed.

*A song of David written during the time he was
running from his son Absalom.*

3 LORD, I have so many enemies.
So many people have turned against me.
[2] They say to themselves,
"God will not rescue him!"   *Selah*

[3] But you, LORD, protect me.
You bring me honour;
you give me hope.

[4] I will pray to the LORD,
and he will answer me from his
holy mountain.   *Selah*

[5] I can lie down to rest and know that I will
wake up,
because the LORD covers and protects
me.
[6] So I will not be afraid of my enemies,
even if thousands of them surround me.

[7] LORD, get up!*f*
My God, come rescue me!
If you hit my enemies on the cheek,
you will break all their teeth.

[8] LORD, the victory*g* is yours!
You are so good to your people.   *Selah*

---

a **1:1** Or "The one who does not follow the advice of the wicked or turn onto Sinners Road or stay at Scoffers' House is blessed."
b **1:5** Or "The wicked will not be allowed to sit as judges nor sinners in the meeting of good people."
c **2:2 *chosen king*** Literally, "anointed one". This might be anyone God chose to serve in a special way, but it is usually the king he has chosen.
d **2:7 *I have become your father*** Literally, "I fathered you." Originally, this probably meant God was "adopting" the king as his son.
e **2:12 *Show . . . his son*** Literally, "Kiss the son."
f **3:7 *LORD, get up*** The people said this when they lifted the Box of the Agreement and took it into battle, showing that God was with them. See Num. 10:35–36. Also in 7:6; 9:19; 10:12; 17:13; 132:8.
g **3:8 *victory*** Or "salvation".

To the director: With stringed instruments.
A song of David.

4 God, you showed that I was innocent.
You gave me relief from all my troubles.
So listen to me now when I call to you for help.
Be kind to me and hear my prayer.

2 Men,[a] how long will you try to dishonour me?
Do you enjoy wasting your time
searching for new lies against me? *Selah*

3 You can be sure that anyone who serves the
LORD faithfully is special to him.
The LORD listens when I pray to him.

4 Tremble with fear, and stop sinning.[b]
Think about this when you go to bed,
and calm down. *Selah*
5 Give the right sacrifices to the LORD,
and put your trust in him!

6 Many people say, "I wish I could enjoy the
good life.
LORD, give us some of those blessings."[c]
7 But you have made me happier than they will
ever be with all their wine and grain.
8 When I go to bed, I sleep in peace,
because, LORD, you keep me safe.

To the director: With flutes.[d]
A song of David.

5 LORD, listen to me
and understand what I am trying to say.
2 My God and King,
listen to my prayer.
3 Every morning, LORD, I lay my gifts before you
and look to you for help.
And every morning you hear my prayers.

4 God, you don't want evil people near you.
They cannot stay in your presence.[e]
5 Fools[f] cannot come near you.
You hate those who do evil.
6 You destroy those who tell lies.
LORD, you hate those who make secret
plans to hurt others.

7 But by your great mercy, I can enter your
house.

I can worship in your holy Temple with fear
and respect for you.
8 LORD, show me your right way of living,
and make it easy for me to follow.
People are looking for my weaknesses,
so show me how you want me to live.

9 My enemies never tell the truth.
They only want to destroy people.
Their words are as dangerous as an open
grave.
They use their tongues for telling lies.
10 Punish them, God!
Let them be caught in their own traps.
They have turned against you,
so punish them for their many crimes.
11 But let those who trust in you be happy forever.
Protect and strengthen those who love your
name.
12 LORD, when you bless good people,
you surround them with your love,
like a large shield that protects them.

To the director: With stringed instruments,
on the sheminith. A song of David.

6 LORD, don't punish me.
Don't correct me when you are so angry.
2 LORD, be kind to me.
I am sick and weak.
Heal me, LORD!
My bones are shaking.
3 I am trembling all over.
LORD, how long until you heal me?[g]

4 LORD, come back and make me strong again.
Save me because you are so loyal and kind.
5 If I am dead, I cannot sing about you.
Those in the grave don't praise you.

6 Lord, I am so weak.
I cried to you all night.
My pillow is soaked;
my bed is dripping wet from my tears.
7 My enemies have caused me such sorrow
that my eyes are worn out from crying.

8 Go away, you wicked people,
because the LORD has heard my cries.
9 The LORD has heard my request for mercy.
The LORD has accepted my prayer.

---

[a] 4:2 *Men* Literally, "Sons of man". This may be a term of respect spoken to the leaders who were judging the writer of this psalm.
[b] 4:4 Or "Be angry, but don't sin." See Eph. 4:26, which is based on the ancient Greek version.
[c] 4:6 *I wish . . . blessings* Or "Who will show us good? Lift up on us the light of your face, LORD."
[d] Psalm 5 *With flutes* This might be the name of a tune instead of a type of instrument.
[e] 5:4 Or "You are not a God who likes evil people, and they don't respect you."
[f] 5:5 *Fools* Here, this means people who do not follow God and his wise teachings.
[g] 6:3 *LORD . . . heal me* Literally, "As for you, LORD, how long?"

¹⁰All my enemies will be filled with fear and
  shame.
  They will be sorry when disgrace suddenly
  comes upon them.

*A song^a of David that he sang to the LORD about
Cush from the tribe of Benjamin.*

7 LORD my God, I come to you for protection.
  Save me from those who are chasing me.
²If you don't help me, I will be torn apart like
    an animal caught by a lion.
  I will be carried away with no one to
    save me.

³LORD my God, what have I done to deserve
    this?
  I am not guilty of any wrong.
⁴I have done nothing to hurt a friend^b
  or to help his wicked enemy.
⁵If that is not the truth, then punish me.
  Let an enemy chase me, catch me and
    kill me.
  Let him grind me into the dirt and put
    me in my grave.   *Selah*

⁶LORD, get up and show your anger!
  My enemy is angry, so stand and fight
    against him.
  Get me the justice that you demand.
⁷Gather the nations around you,
  and take your place as judge.
⁸LORD, judge the people.
  LORD, judge me.
  Prove that I am right and that I am
    innocent.
⁹Stop those who do evil.
  Support those who do good.
  God, you are fair.
  You know what people are thinking.

¹⁰God helps people who want to do right,
  so he will protect me.
¹¹God is a good judge.
  He always condemns evil.
¹²If the wicked will not change,
  then God is ready to punish them.
¹³He has prepared his deadly weapons.
  His sword is sharp.
  His bow is strung, drawn back,
    and ready to shoot its flaming arrow.

¹⁴The minds of the wicked are full of evil;
  they are pregnant with wicked plans,
  which give birth to lies.
¹⁵They dig a pit to trap others,
  but they are the ones who will fall into it.
¹⁶The trouble they cause will come back on them.
  They plan harm for others,
  but they are the ones who will be hurt.

¹⁷I praise the LORD because he is good.
  I praise the name of the LORD Most High.

To the director: With the gittith. A song of David.

8 LORD our Lord, your name is the most
  wonderful in all the earth!
  It brings you praise everywhere in heaven.

²From the mouths of children and babies come
    songs of praise to you.
  They sing of your power to silence your
    enemies who were seeking revenge.

³I look at the heavens you made with your
    hands.
  I see the moon and the stars you created.
⁴And I wonder, "Why are people so important
    to you?
  Why do you even think about them?
  Why do you care so much about humans?^c
  Why do you even notice them?"

⁵But you made them almost like gods
  and crowned them with glory and honour.
⁶You put them in charge of everything you made.
  You put everything under their control.
⁷People rule over the sheep and cattle
  and all the wild animals.
⁸They rule over the birds in the sky
  and the fish that swim in the sea.

⁹LORD our Lord,
  your name is the most wonderful name in
    all the earth!

*^dTo the director: Use the Alamoth of Ben.^e
A song of David.*

9 I will praise you, LORD, with all my heart.
  I will tell about the wonderful things you
    have done.

^a **Psalm 7 song** Hebrew, "*shiggayon*", which may mean a special kind of song, perhaps one that is sad or full of emotion.
^b **7:4 friend** Or "ally".
^c **8:4 people . . . humans** Literally, "man . . . son of man" or "Enosh . . . son of Adam". These are Hebrew ways of saying humans—descendants of Adam and Enosh.
^d **Psalm 9** In many Hebrew copies and in the ancient Greek version, Psalms 9 and 10 are combined as one psalm.
^e **Psalm 9 Alamoth of Ben** This might be the name of a tune, "On the Death of the Son", a music style, or one of the orchestral groups in the Temple. See 1 Chr. 15:20.

²I will sing for joy because you make me
   happy.
   God Most High, I praise your name.
³My enemies turned to run from you,
   but they fell and were destroyed.

⁴You listened to me from your throne like a
   good judge,
   and you decided that I was right.
⁵You told the nations how wrong they were.
   You destroyed those evil people.
   You erased their names from our memory
   for ever and ever.
⁶The enemy is finished!
   You destroyed their cities.
   There is nothing left to remind us of
   them.

⁷The LORD set up his throne to bring justice,
   and he will rule forever.
⁸He judges everyone on earth fairly.
   He judges all nations honestly.
⁹Many people are suffering—
   crushed by the weight of their troubles.
   But the LORD is a refuge for them,
   a safe place they can run to.

¹⁰LORD, those who know your name
   come to you for protection.
   And when they come,
   you do not leave them without help.

¹¹Sing praises to the LORD, who sits as King in
   Zion.ᵃ
   Tell the nations about the great things he
   has done.
¹²He punishes murderers
   and remembers those who are in need.
   When suffering people cry for help,
   he does not ignore them.

¹³I said this prayer: "LORD, be kind to me.
   See how my enemies are hurting me.
   Save me from the 'gates of death'.
¹⁴Then, at the gates of Jerusalem,ᵇ I can sing
   praises to you.
   I will be so happy because you saved me."

¹⁵Those other nations have fallen into the pit
   they dug to catch others.
   They have been caught in their own trap.
¹⁶The LORD showed that he judges fairly.
   The wicked were caught by what they did
   to hurt others.   *Higgayonᶜ Selah*

¹⁷The wicked will go to the place of death,
   as will all the nations that forget God.
¹⁸It may seem that those who are poor and
   needy have been forgotten,
   but God will not forget them.
   He will not leave them without hope.

¹⁹LORD, get up and judge the nations.
   Don't let anyone think they can win against
   you.
²⁰Teach them a lesson, LORD.
   Let them know they are only human.   *Selah*

INSIGHT

*The psalmist is pleading with God to sort
out the injustice he sees around him.
Justice is a major theme in the Bible. The
Hebrew word for righteousness tsedeq is
also sometimes translated "just".*

Psalm 10

10 LORD, why do you stay so far away?
   Why do you hide from people in times of
   trouble?
²The wicked are proud and make evil plans to
   hurt the poor,
   who are caught in their traps and made to
   suffer.
³Those greedy people boast about the things
   they want to get.
   They curse the LORD and show that they
   hate him.
⁴The wicked are too proud to ask God for help.
   He does not fit into their plans.
⁵They succeed in everything they do.
   They don't understand how you can judge
   them.
   They make fun of all their enemies.
⁶They say to themselves, "Nothing bad will
   ever happen to us.
   We will have our fun and never be
   punished."
⁷They are always cursing, lying
   and planning evil things to do.
⁸They hide just outside the villages,
   waiting to kill innocent people,
   always looking for any helpless person they
   can hurt.
⁹They are like lions hiding in the bushes
   to catch weak and helpless animals.

ᵃ **9:11 Sing . . . Zion** Or "Inhabitants of Zion, sing praises to the LORD." See "ZION" in the Word List.
ᵇ **9:14 Jerusalem** Literally, "daughter Zion". See "ZION" in the Word List.
ᶜ **9:16 Higgayon** Or "Meditation". Together with *Selah* this may mean a time to pause and think quietly.

They lay their traps for the poor,
who are caught in their nets.
¹⁰Again and again they hurt people
who are already weak and suffering.
¹¹They say to themselves, "God has forgotten
about us.
He is not watching.
He will never see what we are doing."

¹²LORD, get up and do something.
Punish those who are wicked, God.
Don't forget those who are poor and helpless.
¹³The wicked turn against God
because they think he will not punish them.
¹⁴But, Lord, you do see the pain and suffering
they cause.
You see it, so punish them.
Those who were left helpless put their trust in
you.
After all, you are the one who cares for
orphans.
¹⁵Break the arms of those who are wicked and
evil.
Punish them for the evil they have done,
and stop them from doing any more.

¹⁶LORD, you are King for ever and ever,
so I know you will remove the wicked
nations from your land.
¹⁷LORD, you have heard what the poor want.
Listen to their prayers, and do what they
ask.
¹⁸Protect the orphans and those who have been
hurt.
Don't let powerful people drive us from our
land!

To the director: A song of David.

11 I trust in the LORD, so why did you tell me
to run and hide?
Why did you say, "Fly like a bird to your
mountain?"

²Like hunters, the wicked hide in the dark.
They get their bows ready and aim their
arrows.
They shoot at good, honest people.
³And what can good people do
when the wicked destroy all that is good?

⁴The LORD is in his holy temple.
The LORD sits on his throne in heaven.
He sees everything that happens.
He watches people closely.

⁵The LORD examines those who are good and
those who are wicked;
he hates those who enjoy hurting others.
⁶He will make hot coals and burning sulphur
fall like rain on the wicked.
They will get nothing but a hot, burning
wind.
⁷The LORD always does what is right, and he
loves seeing people do right.
Those who live good lives will be with him.^a

To the director: With the sheminith.
A song of David.

12 Save me, LORD!
We can no longer trust anyone!
All the good, loyal people are gone.
²People lie to their neighbours.
They say whatever they think people want
to hear.

³The LORD should cut off their lying lips
and cut out their boasting tongues.
⁴Those people think they can win any argument.
They say, "We are so good with words,
no one will be our master."

⁵They took advantage of the poor
and stole what little they had.
But the LORD knows what they did, and he says,
"I will rescue those who are poor and
helpless,
and I will punish those who hurt them."^b
⁶The LORD's words are true and pure,
like silver purified by fire,
like silver melted seven times to make it
perfectly pure.

⁷LORD, take care of the helpless.
Protect them forever from the wicked
people in this world.
⁸The wicked are all around us,
and everyone thinks evil is something to be
praised!

To the director: A song of David.

13 How long will you forget me, LORD?
Will you forget me forever?
How long will you refuse to accept me?^c
²How long must I wonder if you have forgotten
me?
How long must I feel this sadness in my
heart?
How long will my enemy win against me?

---

^a **11:7** *Those . . . him* Literally, "They will see his face."
^b **12:5** *I will rescue . . . hurt them* Or "I will rescue poor, helpless people who were hurt and asked me for help."
^c **13:1** *refuse to accept me* Literally, "hide your face from me".

³L ORD my God, look at me and give me an
    answer.
  Make me feel strong again, or I will die.
⁴Then my enemy will say, "I have won!"
  He will be so happy to see me defeated.

⁵But I trust in your faithful love, Lord.
  I will be happy when you save me.
⁶Then I will sing to the L ORD
  because he was so good to me.

To the director: A song of David.

14
Only fools think there is no God.
People like that are evil and do terrible
  things.
They never do what is right.

²The L ORD looks down from heaven
  to see if there is anyone who is wise,
  anyone who looks to him for help.
³But everyone has gone the wrong way.
  Everyone has turned bad.
 No one does anything good.
  No, not one person!

⁴Those who are evil treat my people like bread
  to be eaten.
  And they never ask for the L ORD's help.
  Don't they know what they are doing?
⁵They will have plenty to fear,
  because God is with those who do what is
  right.
⁶You wicked people want to spoil the hopes of
  the poor,
  but the L ORD will protect them.

⁷I wish the one who lives on Mount Zion
  would bring victory to Israel!
When the L ORD makes his people successful
  again,
  the people of Jacob will be happy;
  the people of Israel will be glad.

A song of David.

15
L ORD, who can live in your Holy Tent?ᵃ
Who can live on your holy mountain?

²Only those who live pure lives, do what is right,
  and speak the truth from their hearts.
³Such people don't say bad things about others.
  They don't do things to hurt their
    neighbours.
  They don't tell shameful things about those
    close to them.
⁴They hate those who fail to please God
  and honour those who respect the L ORD.
If they make a promise to their neighbour,
  they do what they promised.ᵇ
⁵If they loan money to someone,
  they do not charge them interest.
And they refuse to testify against an innocent
  person,
  even if someone offers them money to do it.

Whoever lives like this will always stand strong.

A miktam of David.

16
Protect me, God,
because I depend on you.
²Some of youᶜ have said to the L ORD,
  "You are my Lord.
  Every good thing I have comes from you."
³But you have also said about the godsᵈ of this
  land,
  "They are my powerful gods.
  They are the ones who make me happy."
⁴But those who worship other gods will have
  many troubles.
  I will not share in the gifts of blood they
    offer to their idols.
  I will not even say their names.

⁵L ORD, you give me all that I need.
  You support me.
  You give me my share.
⁶My shareᵉ is wonderful.
  My inheritanceᶠ is very beautiful.

⁷I praise the L ORD because he taught me well.
  Even at night he put his instructions deep
    inside my mind.ᵍ
⁸I never forget that the L ORD is with me.ʰ
  He is right here beside me,
  so nothing can harm me.

ᵃ **15:1** *Holy Tent* The special tent where the people of Israel worshipped God. Here, it is probably the Temple on the "holy mountain" (see "Z ION" in the Word List) in Jerusalem.
ᵇ **15:4** *If they . . . promised* Or "They promised not to do bad things, and they do not do bad things."
ᶜ **16:2** *Some of you* Literally, "you" (singular). Most translations assume it should be "I", leading to a different meaning for verses 2 and 3, which are very difficult in the Hebrew text.
ᵈ **16:3** *gods* Literally, "holy ones".
ᵉ **16:6** *share* Or "section of land".
ᶠ **16:6** *inheritance* Here, this probably means the land each Israelite received.
ᵍ **16:7** *mind* Literally, "my kidneys".
ʰ **16:8** Literally, "I set the L ORD before me always."

⁹That is why I feel so happy.
   I am filled with joy!
   Even this weak body of mine is safe,
¹⁰because you, LORD, will not leave me in the
      grave.ᵃ
   You will not let your faithful servantᵇ rot
      there.
¹¹You have shown me the way that leads to life.
   Being together with you will fill me with
      joy.
   Sitting beside you, I will never stop
      celebrating.

A prayer of David.ᶜ

17 LORD, hear my prayer for justice.
   I am calling loudly to you.
I am being honest in what I say,
   so please listen to my prayer.
²You will make the right decision,
   because you can see the truth.
³You were with me all night
   and looked deep into my heart.
You questioned me and found that
   I did not say or do anything wrong.
⁴Unlike most people, I have obeyed your
      commands,
   so I have never been like those who are
      cruel and evil.
⁵I have followed your way.
   My feet never left your path.

⁶Every time I call to you, God, you answer me.
   So listen to me now, and hear what I say.
⁷Show your amazing kindness
   and rescue those who depend on you.
Use your great power
   and protect them from their enemies.
⁸Protect me like the pupilᵈ of your eye.
   Hide me in the shadow of your wings.
⁹Save me from the wicked people who are
      trying to destroy me.
   Protect me from those who come to hurt
      me.
¹⁰They think only of themselves
   and boast about what they will do.
¹¹They have been following me,
   and now they are all around me.
They watch me, waiting to throw me to the
      ground.

¹²Like hungry lions, they want to kill and eat.
   Like young lions, they hide, ready to attack.

¹³LORD, get up and face the enemy.
   Make them surrender.
   Use your sword and save me from these
      wicked people.
¹⁴Use your power, LORD,
   and remove them from this life.
But bless the people you love with the food
      they need.
   Give them plenty for their children and
      grandchildren.

¹⁵I have done only what is right, so I will see
      your face.
   And seeing you,ᵉ I will be fully satisfied.

ᶠ*To the director: A song of David, the LORD's servant.*
   He sang this song to the LORD when the LORD
   saved him from Saul and all his other enemies.

18 I love you, LORD!
   You are my strength.

²The LORD is my Rock, my fortress, my place of
      safety.
   He is my God, the Rock I run to for
      protection.
   He is my shield; by his power I am saved.ᵍ
   He is my hiding place high in the hills.
³I called to the LORD for help,
   and he saved me from my enemies!
   He is worthy of my praise!

⁴Death had its ropes wrapped around me.
   A deadly flood was carrying me away.
⁵The ropes of the grave wrapped around me.
   Death set its trap right there in front of me.
⁶In my trouble I called to the LORD.
   Yes, I cried out to my God for help.
There in his Temple he heard my voice.
   He heard my cry for help.

⁷The earth shook and shivered.
   The foundations of the mountains trembled.
   They shook because he was angry.
⁸Smoke came from his nose.
   Burning flames came from his mouth.
   Red-hot coals fell from him.

ᵃ **16:10 grave** Literally, "Sheol".
ᵇ **16:10 faithful servant** Sometimes translated "Holy One", this word usually means a person who is devoted to God and pleasing
to him.
ᶜ **Psalm 17 A prayer of David** Or "A prayer dedicated to David."
ᵈ **17:8 pupil** The centre of the eye, which everyone wants to protect.
ᵉ **17:15 you** Literally, "your likeness".
ᶠ **Psalm 18** This song is also found in 2 Sam. 22.
ᵍ **18:2 by his power I am saved** Literally, "He is the horn of my salvation."

⁹He tore open the sky and came down!
  He stood on a thick, dark cloud.
¹⁰He flew across the sky, riding on a winged
      creature
    racing on the wings of the wind.
¹¹He wrapped himself in darkness that covered
      him like a tent.
    He was hidden by dark clouds heavy with
      water.
¹²Out of the brightness before him,
    hail broke through the clouds with flashes
      of lightning.
¹³The LORD thundered from the sky;
    God Most High let his voice be heard.^a
¹⁴He scattered his enemies with his arrows—
    the lightning bolts that threw them into
      confusion.
¹⁵LORD, you shouted your command,
    and a powerful wind began to blow.^b
  Then the bottom of the sea could be seen,
    and the earth's foundations were
      uncovered.

¹⁶He reached down from above and grabbed
      me.
    He pulled me from the deep water.
¹⁷He saved me from my powerful enemies, who
      hated me.
    They were too strong for me, so he saved me.
¹⁸They attacked me in my time of trouble,
    but the LORD was there to support me.
¹⁹He was pleased with me, so he rescued me.
    He took me to a safe place.

²⁰The LORD rewarded me for doing what is
      right.
    He was good to me because I am innocent.
²¹The LORD did this because I have obeyed him.
    I have not turned against my God.
²²I always remembered his laws.
    I never rejected his rules.
²³He knows I did nothing that was wrong.
    I have kept myself from sinning.
²⁴So the LORD rewarded me for doing what is
      right.
    He could see that I am innocent.

²⁵Lord, you are faithful to those who are
      faithful.
    You are good to those who are good.
²⁶You never do wrong to those who have done
      no wrong.
    But you outsmart the wicked, no matter
      how clever they are.

²⁷You help those who are humble,
    but you humiliate the proud.
²⁸LORD, you provide the flame for my lamp.
    You, God, turn the darkness around me into
      light.
²⁹With your help I can defeat an army.
    If my God is with me, I can climb over
      enemy walls.

³⁰God's way is perfect.
    The LORD's promise always proves to be true.
    He protects those who trust in him.
³¹There is no God except the LORD.
    There is no Rock except our God.
³²God is the one who gives me strength.
    He clears the path I need to take.
³³He makes my feet as steady as those of a deer.
    Even on steep mountains he keeps me from
      falling.
³⁴He trains me for war
    so that my arms can bend the most
      powerful bow.

³⁵Lord, you have given me your shield to protect
      me.
    You support me with your right hand.
    It is your help that has made me great.
³⁶You cleared a path for my feet
    so that I could walk without stumbling.

³⁷I chased my enemies and caught them.
    I did not stop until they were destroyed.
³⁸I struck them down, and they could not get up
      again.
    They fell under my feet.
³⁹God, you made me strong in battle.
    You made my enemies fall before me.
⁴⁰You made my enemies turn and run away.
    I destroyed those who hated me.
⁴¹They cried out for help,
    but there was no one to save them.
  They cried out to the LORD,
    but he did not answer them.
⁴²I beat them to pieces like dust blown by the
      wind.
    I smashed them like mud in the streets.

⁴³You saved me from those who fought against
      me.
    You made me the ruler over nations.
    People I didn't know now serve me.
⁴⁴As soon as they heard about me, they were
      ready to obey.
    Those foreigners fall helpless before me!

---

^a **18:13** The ancient Greek version and some Hebrew copies add "with hailstones and bolts of lightning".
^b **18:15** *and . . . blow* Or "and a blast of breath came from your nose".

⁴⁵They lose all their courage
 and come out of their hiding places shaking
  with fear.

⁴⁶The LORD lives!
 I praise my Rock, the God who saves me.
 How great he is!
⁴⁷He is the God who punishes my enemies
  for me,
 the one who puts people under my control.
⁴⁸He saves me from my enemies!

You, LORD, help me defeat those who
  attack me.
 You save me from cruel people.
⁴⁹LORD, that is why I praise you among the
  nations.
 That is why I sing songs of praise to your
  name.

⁵⁰The LORD helps his king win battle after battle.
 He shows his faithful love to his chosen
  king,[a]
 to David and his descendants forever.

To the director: A song of David.

19

The heavens tell about the glory of God.
 The skies announce what his hands have
  made.
²Each new day tells more of the story,
 and each night reveals more and more
  about God's power.[b]
³You cannot hear them say anything.
 They don't make any sound we can hear.
⁴But their message goes throughout the world.
 Their teaching reaches the ends of the earth.

The sun's tent is set up in the heavens.
⁵ It comes out like a happy bridegroom from
  his bedroom.
 It begins its path across the sky
 like an athlete eager to run a race.
⁶It starts at one end of the sky
 and runs all the way to the other end.
 Nothing can hide from its heat.

⁷The LORD's teachings are perfect.
 They give strength to his people.
 The LORD's rules can be trusted.
 They help even the foolish become wise.
⁸The LORD's laws teach what is right.
 They bring people joy.

The LORD's commands are full of light.
 They show us the way to be happy.

⁹Learning respect for the LORD is good.
 It will last forever.
 The LORD's judgements are right.
 They are completely fair.
¹⁰His teachings are worth more than pure gold.
 They are sweeter than the best honey
  dripping from the honeycomb.
¹¹His teachings warn his servants,
 and good things come to those who obey
  them.

¹²People cannot know all their own faults.
 So forgive me when I sin without knowing it.
¹³And keep me from doing what I know is
  wrong.
 Don't let sin control me.
 Then I can be free from guilt,
  innocent of sinning on purpose.
¹⁴May my words and thoughts please you.
 LORD, you are my Rock, the one who
  protects me.

To the director: A song of David.

20

May the LORD answer you in times of
 trouble.
 May the God of Jacob protect you.
²May he send you help from his Holy Place.
 May he support you from Zion.
³May he remember all the gifts you have
  offered.
 May he accept all your sacrifices.   *Selah*

⁴May he give you what you really want.
 May he make all your plans successful.
⁵We will celebrate when he helps you.
 We will praise the name of God.
 May the LORD give you everything you ask for.

⁶Now I know the LORD helps his chosen king.
 From his holy heaven he answered.
 With his great power he saved him.
⁷Some give the credit for victory to their
  chariots and soldiers,
 but we honour the LORD our God.
⁸They fall in battle, totally defeated,
 but we survive and stand strong!

⁹LORD, save the king!
 Answer us when we call to you for help.

---

[a] **18:50 chosen king** Literally, "anointed one". This might be anyone God chose to serve in a special way, but it is usually the king he has chosen. Also in 20:6; 28:8.
[b] **19:2** Or "Like the changing of the guards, each day passes the news to the next day and each night passes information to the next night."

21 Lord, your strength makes the king happy.
He is so happy when you give him victory.
²And you gave him what he wanted.
You gave him what he asked for.   *Selah*

³You gave the king such wonderful blessings.
You put a gold crown on his head.
⁴He asked for life, and you gave it.
You gave him life that goes on forever.
⁵You led him to victory that brought him great
glory.
You gave him honour and fame.
⁶You have given him blessings that will last
forever.
You have given him the joy of being near you.
⁷The king trusts in the Lord,
and the faithful love of God Most High will
keep him from falling.
⁸Lord, you will show all your enemies that you
are strong.
Your power will defeat those who hate you.
⁹When you appear,
you will burn them up like a blazing furnace.
In your anger, Lord, you will completely
destroy them;
they will be swallowed by flames of fire.ᵃ
¹⁰Their families will be destroyed.
They will be removed from the earth.
¹¹That is because they made evil plans against
you.
They wanted to do things they could not do.
¹²You will make them turn and run away
when you aim your arrows at their faces.

¹³Lord, we lift you up with our songs of praise.
We sing and play songs about your power!

22 My God, my God, why have you left me?
You seem too far away to save me,
too far to hear my cries for help!
²My God, I cry out to you all day,
but you do not answer.
I cry out to you at night,
but you give me no rest.

³God, you are the Holy One.
You sit as King upon the praises of Israel.

⁴Our ancestors trusted you.
Yes, they trusted you, and you saved them.
⁵They called to you for help and escaped their
enemies.
They trusted you and were not
disappointed!

⁶But I feel like a worm, less than human!
People insult me and look down on me.
⁷Everyone who sees me makes fun of me.
They shake their heads and stick out their
tongues at me.
⁸They say, "Call to the Lord for help.
Maybe he will save you.
If he likes you so much, surely he will
rescue you!"

⁹God, the truth is, you are the one who
brought me into this world.
You made me feel safe while I was still at
my mother's breasts.
¹⁰You have been my God since the day I was
born.
I was thrown into your arms as I came from
my mother's womb.

¹¹So don't leave me!
Trouble is near, and there is no one to help
me.
¹²My enemies surround me like angry bulls.
They are like the powerful bulls of Bashan,
and they are all around me.
¹³Their mouths are opened wide,
like a lion roaring and tearing at its prey.

INSIGHT

*Those travelling through the region of
Bashan needed to beware. The area was
notorious for not only strong bulls and
fierce lions, but giant people.*

Psalm 22:12–13

---

¹⁴My strength is gone,
like water poured out on the ground.
My bones have separated.
My courage is gone.ᶜ
¹⁵My mouthᵈ is as dry as a piece of baked
pottery.

ᵃ **21:9** Or "You will make your king like a burning oven when you come to help him, Lord. And in his anger, he will completely destroy them."
ᵇ **Psalm 22 "The Deer of Dawn"** This is probably the name of the tune for this song, but it might refer to a music style or type of instrument.
ᶜ **22:14 My courage is gone** Literally, "My heart is melted inside me like wax."
ᵈ **22:15 mouth** Or "strength".

My tongue is sticking to the roof of my
   mouth.
You have left me dying in the dust.
¹⁶Evil people are all around me.
They are closing in on me like a pack of dogs.
My hands and feet are shrivelled up.ᵃ
¹⁷I can see each one of my bones.
My enemies are looking at me;
they just keep staring.
¹⁸They divide my clothes among themselves,
and they throw lots for what I am wearing.

¹⁹Lord, don't leave me!
You are my strength—hurry and help me!
²⁰Save me from the sword.
Save my precious life from these dogs.
²¹Rescue me from the lion's mouth.
Protect me from the horns of the bulls.ᵇ

²²I will tell my people about you.
I will praise you in the great assembly.
²³Praise the Lord, all you who worship him!
Honour him, you descendants of Jacob!
Fear and respect him, all you people of Israel!
²⁴He does not ignore those who need help.
He does not hate them.
He does not turn away from them.
He listens when they cry for help.

²⁵Lord, because of you I offer praise in the great
   assembly.
In front of all these worshippers I will do all
   that I promised.
²⁶Poor people, come eat and be satisfied.ᶜ
You who have come looking for the Lord,
   praise him!
May your hearts be happyᵈ forever.
²⁷May all people on earth be thankful to the
   Lord and turn to him.
May all the nations worship him,
²⁸because the Lord is King,
and he rules the nations.
²⁹All who are alive and well here on earth
will enjoy a meal in worship before the Lord.

And all who are on their way to the grave, or
   already there,
will bow down in worship before him.
³⁰Our descendants will serve him.
Those who are not yet born will be told
   about him.
³¹Each generation will tell their children
about the good things the Lord has done.

A song of David.

23 The Lord is my shepherd.
I will always have everything I need.ᵉ
²He gives me green pastures to lie in.
He leads me by calm pools of water.
³He restores my strength.
He leads me on right pathsᶠ to show that he
   is good.
⁴Even if I walk through a valley as dark as the
   grave,ᵍ
I will not be afraid of any danger, because
   you are with me.
Your rod and staffʰ comfort me.

⁵You prepared a meal for me in front of my
   enemies.
You welcomed me as an honoured guest.ⁱ
My cup is full and spilling over.
⁶Your goodness and mercy will be with me all
   my life,
and I will live in the Lord's houseʲ a long,
   long time.ᵏ

A song of David.

24 The earth and everything on it belong to
the Lord.
The world and all its people belong to
   him.
²He built the earth on the water.
He built it over the rivers.

³Who can go up on the Lord's mountain?ˡ
Who can stand in his holy Temple?

ᵃ **22:16** *My . . . shrivelled up* This translation is based on a correction of the difficult Hebrew text, which is literally, "Like a lion my hands and feet".
ᵇ **22:21** *Protect me . . . bulls* Or "You have answered me and protected me from the horns of the bulls." This could be both a prayer for help (like the first half of the psalm) and also a statement that God had answered this prayer (like the second half of the psalm).
ᶜ **22:26** *come eat . . . satisfied* This person was giving a thank offering that would be shared with other people at the Temple. This was how someone shared their happiness when God blessed them. See Lev. 3:1–5 and Deut. 14:22–29.
ᵈ **22:26** *be happy* Literally, "live".
ᵉ **23:1** *I will . . . need* Literally, "I will lack nothing."
ᶠ **23:3** *right paths* Or "paths of goodness".
ᵍ **23:4** *valley . . . grave* Or "death's dark valley" or "a very dark valley".
ʰ **23:4** *rod and staff* The club and walking stick a shepherd uses to protect and guide his sheep.
ⁱ **23:5** *You welcomed . . . guest* Literally, "You anointed my head with oil."
ʲ **23:6** *house* Or "Temple". See Temple in the Word List.
ᵏ **23:6** *I . . . long time* Or "I will return again and again to the Lord's Temple for as long as I live."
ˡ **24:3** *Lord's mountain* Mount Zion, the hill in Jerusalem where the Temple was built.

⁴Only those who have not done evil,
  who have pure hearts,
who have not used my name*ᵃ* to hide their lies,
  and who have not made false promises.

⁵Good people ask the LORD to bless others.
  They ask God, their Saviour, to do good
    things.
⁶They try to follow God.
  They go to the God of Jacob for help.   *Selah*

⁷Gates, proudly lift your heads!
  Open, ancient doors,
  and the glorious King will come in.
⁸Who is the glorious King?
  He is the LORD, the powerful soldier.
  He is the LORD, the war hero.

⁹Gates, proudly lift your heads!
  Open, ancient doors,
  and the glorious King will come in.
¹⁰Who is the glorious King?
  The LORD All-Powerful is the glorious King.

ᵇA song of David.

25 LORD, I put my life in your hands.*ᶜ*
    ²I trust in you, my God.
  Please don't disappoint me.
    Don't let my enemies laugh at my defeat.
³But no one who trusts in you will be
    disappointed.
  Disappointment is for those who try to
    deceive others.

⁴LORD, help me learn your ways.
  Show me how you want me to live.
⁵Guide me and teach me your truths.
  You are my God, my Saviour.
  You are the one I have been waiting for.
⁶Remember to be kind to me, LORD.
  Show me the tender love that you have
    always had.
⁷Don't remember the sinful things I did when I
    was young.
  Because you are good, LORD, remember me
    with your faithful love.

⁸The LORD is good and does what is right.
  He shows sinners the right way to live.
⁹He teaches his ways to humble people.
  He leads them with fairness.
¹⁰The LORD is kind and true to those
  who obey what he said in his agreement.

¹¹LORD, I have done many wrong things.
  But I ask you to forgive them all to show
    your goodness.

¹²When people choose to follow the LORD,
  he shows them the best way to live.
¹³They will enjoy good things,
  and their children will get the land God
    promised.
¹⁴The LORD tells his secrets to his followers.
  He teaches them about his agreement.
¹⁵I always look to the LORD for help.
  Only he can free me from my troubles.*ᵈ*

¹⁶I am hurt and lonely.
  Turn to me, and show me mercy.
¹⁷Free me from my troubles.
  Help me solve my problems.
¹⁸Look at my trials and troubles.
  Forgive me for all the sins I have done.
¹⁹Look at all the enemies I have.
  They hate me and want to hurt me.
²⁰Protect me! Save me from them!
  I come to you for protection, so don't let me
    be disappointed.
²¹You are good and do what is right.
  I trust you to protect me.
²²God, save the people of Israel
  from all their troubles.

A song of David.

26 LORD, you be the judge and prove that
    I have lived a pure life.
  I have depended on you, LORD, to keep me
    from falling.
²Look closely at me, LORD, and test me.
  Judge my deepest thoughts and
    emotions.
³I always remember your faithful love.
  I depend on your faithfulness.
⁴I don't run around with troublemakers.
  I have nothing to do with hypocrites.
⁵I hate being around evil people.
  I refuse to join those gangs of crooks.

⁶LORD, I wash my hands to make myself pure,
  so that I can come to your altar.
⁷I sing a song to give you thanks,
  and I tell about all the wonderful things you
    have done.
⁸LORD, I love the house*ᵉ* where you live,
  the place where your glory is.

ᵃ **24:4 *my name*** Literally, "my soul".
ᵇ **Psalm 25** In Hebrew, each verse in this psalm begins with the next letter of the alphabet.
ᶜ **25:1 *I put . . . hands*** Literally, "I lift my soul to you."
ᵈ **25:15 *Only . . . troubles*** Literally, "For he will remove my feet from the net."
ᵉ **26:8 *house*** Or "Temple". See "TEMPLE" in the Word List.

⁹Lord, don't treat me like one of those sinners.
  Don't kill me with those murderers.
¹⁰They are guilty of cheating people.
  They take bribes to do wrong.
¹¹But I am innocent,
  so be kind to me and save me.
¹²I am safe from all danger
  as I stand here praising you, LORD, in the
    assembly of your people.

A song of David.

27 LORD, you are my Light and my Saviour,
      so why should I be afraid of anyone?
The LORD is where my life is safe,
  so I will be afraid of no one!
²Evil people may surround me
  and try to destroy me.
But when my enemies attack me,
  they will stumble and fall.
³Even if an army surrounds me,
  I will not be afraid.
If my enemies make war against me,
  I will trust in the Lord.

⁴I ask only one thing from the LORD.
  This is what I want most:
Let me live in the LORD's house all my life,
  enjoying the LORD's beauty
  and spending time in his palace.ᵃ

⁵He will protect me when I am in danger.
  He will hide me in his tent.ᵇ
  He will take me up to his place of safety.
⁶If he will help me defeat the enemies around
    me,
  I will offer sacrifices in his tent with shouts
    of joy.
  I will sing and play songs to honour the LORD.

⁷LORD, hear my voice.
  Be kind and answer me.
⁸LORD, I remember you told us to come to you,
  so I am coming to ask for your help.
⁹Don't turn away from me.
  Don't be angry with your servant.
  You are the only one who can help me.
My God, don't leave me all alone.
  You are my Saviour.
¹⁰Even if my mother and father leave me,
  the LORD will take me in.

¹¹I have enemies, LORD, so teach me your ways.
  Show me the right way to live.
¹²Don't let them do to me what they want.
  They have told lies about me and want to
    hurt me.
¹³But I really believe
  that I will see the LORD's goodness before
    I die.ᶜ
¹⁴Wait for the LORD's help.
  Be strong and brave,
  and wait for the LORD's help.

A song of David.

28 LORD, my Rock, I call to you for help.
      Don't close your ears to my prayer.
If you don't answer me,
  I will be the same as those already in the
    grave.
²I lift my hands and pray towards your Most
    Holy Place.
  Hear me when I call to you.
  Show mercy to me.
³Don't punish me the way you punish the
    wicked,
  the people who do evil.
They greet their neighbours like friends
  but secretly plan to hurt them.
⁴They have done bad things to others,
  so make bad things happen to them.
Pay them back for all they have done.
  Give them the punishment they
    deserve.
⁵They pay no attention to what the LORD has
    done
  or to the good things he has made.
So he will destroy them all
  and leave them lying in ruins.

⁶Praise the LORD!
  He has heard my prayer for mercy.
⁷The LORD is my strength and shield.
  I trusted him with all my heart.
He helped me, so I am happy.
  I sing songs of praise to him.
⁸The LORD gives strength to his people.
  He saves and protects his chosen king.

⁹Save your people.
  Bless those who belong to you.
  Lead them and honour themᵈ forever.

ᵃ **27:4** *palace* A large house built for a king. Here, it is the Temple. See "TEMPLE" in the Word List.
ᵇ **27:5** *tent* The place where God lives among his people. Here, it is the Temple in Jerusalem. See "HOLY TENT" and "TEMPLE" in the Word List.
ᶜ **27:13** *before I die* Literally, "in the land of the living".
ᵈ **28:9** *honour them* Or "forgive them". Literally, "lift them up".

A song of David.

29 Praise the LORD, you heavenly angels![a]
Praise the LORD's glory and power.
[2] Praise the LORD and honour his name!
Worship the LORD in all his holy beauty.

[3] The LORD's voice can be heard over the sea.
The voice of our glorious LORD God is like
thunder over the great ocean.
[4] The LORD's voice is powerful.
It shows the LORD's glory.
[5] The LORD's voice shatters great cedar trees.
The LORD breaks the great cedars of
Lebanon.
[6] He makes Lebanon shake like a young calf
dancing.
Sirion[b] trembles like a young bull jumping
up and down.
[7] The LORD's voice causes the lightning to flash.
[8] His voice shakes the desert.
The desert of Kadesh[c] trembles at his voice.
[9] The LORD's voice frightens the deer.[d]
He destroys the forests.
In his temple everyone shouts, "Glory to God!"

[10] The LORD ruled as king at the time of the flood,
and the LORD will rule as king forever.
[11] May the LORD make his people strong.
May the LORD bless his people with peace.

A song of David for the dedication of the Temple.[e]

30 LORD, you lifted me out of my troubles.
You did not give my enemies a reason to
laugh,
so I will praise you.
[2] LORD my God, I prayed to you,
and you healed me.
[3] LORD, you lifted me out of the grave.
I was falling into the place of death, but you
saved my life.

[4] Praise the LORD, you who are loyal to him!
Praise him who alone is holy![f]
[5] His anger lasts for a little while,
but then his kindness brings life.
The night may be filled with tears,
but in the morning we can sing for joy!

[6] When I was safe and secure,
I thought nothing could hurt me.
[7] Yes, LORD, while you were kind to me,
I felt that nothing could defeat me.[g]
But when you turned away from me,
I was filled with fear.

[8] So, LORD, I turned and prayed to you.
I asked you, Lord, to show me mercy.
[9] I said, "What good is it if I die
and go down to the grave?
The dead just lie in the dirt.
They cannot praise you.
They cannot tell anyone how faithful
you are.
[10] LORD, hear my prayer, and be kind to me.
LORD, help me!"

[11] You have changed my sorrow into dancing.
You have taken away my sackcloth
and clothed me with joy.
[12] You wanted me to praise you and not be silent.
LORD my God, I will praise you forever!

To the director: A song of David.

31 LORD, I come to you for protection.
Don't let me be disappointed.
You always do what is right, so save me.
[2] Listen to me.
Come quickly and save me.
Be my Rock, my place of safety.
Be my fortress and protect me!
[3] Yes, you are my Rock and my protection.
For the good of your name, lead me and
guide me.
[4] Save me from the traps my enemy has set.
You are my place of safety.
[5] LORD, you are the God we can trust.
I put my life[h] in your hands.
Save me!

[6] I hate those who worship false gods.
I trust only in the LORD.
[7] Your kindness makes me so happy.
You have seen my suffering.
You know about the troubles I have.
[8] You will not let my enemies take me.
You will free me from their traps.

---

[a] **29:1 heavenly angels** Literally, "sons of gods". This probably means God's angels who are pictured here as priests worshipping
him in heaven.
[b] **29:6 Sirion** Or "Mount Hermon".
[c] **29:8 desert of Kadesh** A desert in Syria. This might also mean "the holy desert".
[d] **29:9 deer** Or "oak trees".
[e] **Psalm 30 A song . . . Temple** Or "A psalm. The song for the dedication of the house. Dedicated to David."
[f] **30:4 him . . . holy** Literally, "his holy remembrance".
[g] **30:7 I felt . . . defeat me** Literally, "You placed me on the strong mountains."
[h] **31:5 life** Literally, "spirit".

⁹LORD, I have many troubles, so be kind to me.
  I have cried until my eyes hurt.
  My throat and stomach are aching.
¹⁰Because of my sin, my life is ending in grief;
  my years are passing away in sighs of pain.
  My life is ending in weakness.
  My strength is draining away.
¹¹My enemies despise me,
  and even my neighbours have turned away.
  When my friends see me in the street,
  they turn the other way.
  They are afraid to be around me.
¹²People want to forget me like someone already
    dead,
  thrown away like a broken dish.
¹³I hear them whispering all around me.
  And everything they say terrifies me.
  They have turned against me
  and plan to kill me.

¹⁴LORD, I trust in you.
  You are my God.
¹⁵My life is in your hands.
  Save me from those who are persecuting
    me.
¹⁶Please welcome and accept your servant.ᵃ
  Be kind to me and save me.
¹⁷LORD, I am praying to you.
  Don't let me be disappointed.
  The wicked are the ones who should be
    disappointed.
  Let them go to the grave in silence.
¹⁸Those evil people boast
  and tell lies about those who do right.
  They are so proud now,
  but their lying lips will be silent.

¹⁹Lord, you have hidden away many wonderful
    things for your followers.
  You have done so many good things for
    those who trust in you.
  You have blessed them so that all the world
    can see.
²⁰Others make plans to hurt them.
  They say such bad things about them.
  But you hide your people in your shelter
    and protect them.
²¹Praise the LORD, because he showed me how
    wonderful his faithful love is
  when the city was surrounded by
    enemies.
²²I was afraid and said, "I am in a place where
    he cannot see me."
  But I prayed to you, and you heard my loud
    cries for help.

²³Love the LORD, all of you who are his loyal
    followers.
  The LORD protects those who are loyal to
    him.
  But he punishes those who boast about their
    own power.
  He gives them all the punishment they
    deserve.
²⁴Be strong and brave,
  all of you who are waiting for the LORD's help.

A maskil of David.

32 It is a great blessing
  when people are forgiven for the
    wrongs they have done,
  when their sins are erased.ᵇ
²It is a great blessing
  when the LORD says they are not guilty,
  when they don't try to hide their sins.

³Lord, I prayed to you again and again,
  but I did not talk about my sins.
  So I only became weaker and more
    miserable.
⁴Every day you made life harder for me.
  I became like a dry land in the hot
    summertime.   *Selah*

⁵But then I decided to confess my sins to the
    LORD.
  I stopped hiding my guilt and told you
    about my sins.
  And you forgave them all!   *Selah*

⁶That is why your loyal followers pray to you
    while there is still time.
  Then when trouble rises like a flood, it will
    not reach them.
⁷You are a hiding place for me.
  You protect me from my troubles.
  You surround me and protect me,
  so I sing about the way you saved me. *Selah*

⁸The Lord says, "I will teach you
  and guide you in the way you should live.
  I will watch over you and be your guide.
⁹Don't be like a stupid horse or mule that will
    not come to you
  unless you put a bit in its mouth and pull it
    with reins."

¹⁰Many pains will come to the wicked,
  but the LORD's faithful love will surround
    those who trust in him.

ᵃ **31:16 Please . . . servant** Literally, "Let your face shine on your servant."
ᵇ **32:1 erased** Or "covered over" or "atoned".

HE HEARD! HE FORGAVE! HOORAY!

Have you ever written a "Christmas list", detailing the things you would like as presents? Often it's the best way for relatives to know what you would like. How does it feel when someone is generous enough to buy you something? Hopefully, we're just as good at saying thanks as we are at asking!

There are many psalms devoted to this sort of thing – saying thanks to God for hearing and answering prayer.

DIG IN   READ Psalm 32:1–11

When you have written an essay at school has the teacher told you to write an introduction? An introduction – like verses 1 and 2 – is a way of summarizing everything you are about to say.
- What is the great blessing (vv.1–2)?
- What is God's part in this and what is the people's part (v.2)?

David has learnt how wonderful it is to have his wrongdoings forgiven! He has experienced the forgiveness of God and the foolishness of trying to keep sin hidden. In these two verses he introduces the subject of the rest of the poem. He is thankful and happy at what he has discovered!
- What had David not done and what was the result (vv.3–4)?
- How did he feel (v.4)?

Has this ever happened to you? You've messed up but you'd rather ignore the issue than ask God to forgive you. It leaves you feeling miserable and, in some cases, life becomes more and more difficult. David remembers the time he was in a similar position and how horrible it was.
- What did David do (v.5)?
- How did God respond (v.5)?
- How do we know if God has forgiven us?
- How do you think David felt now?

When David did ask for forgiveness there was a complete change of events. All David had to do was ask, and he was forgiven. All you need to do is ask.
- How do the images in this section help you to understand David's points (vv.6–9)?

David starts this section with "That is why" because he wants us to remember and follow his example; we too should pray and confess to God. Confessing sins is great because God forgives us and we feel loads better, so pray!
- What happens to those who don't trust in God (v.10)? What about those who do (v.10)?
- What does David say we should do if we know God's forgiveness and love (v.11)?

Hey, if God has forgiven you for your sin, rejoice! Or rather say thanks, be happy and enjoy it! It's great to know that God goes on loving us. His faithful love surrounds us: we're protected by him! It's a massive change from the misery of verses 3 and 4.

DIG THROUGH

- Sometimes we sin and then ask God to forgive us but still feel miserable, as if we're not forgiven. What does this psalm teach us?
- Yet we can go from feeling bad about our sin to saying sorry and forgetting about it. Don't forget to rejoice and enjoy being forgiven.

DIG DEEPER

- For more psalms like this when the psalmist thanks God for answering prayers see: Psalms 18, 30, 34 and 56. As you read, ask yourself what is the psalmist giving thanks for? What has God done?

¹¹Good people, rejoice and be very happy in the
LORD.
  All you who want to do right, rejoice!

INSIGHT

The word "rejoice" here is translated
from the Hebrew word giyl, which means
to spin round. Often when we read
the words "praise" or "rejoice" in the
Psalms, the original language implies
a physical response to God, not just
singing.

Psalm 32:11

33 Sing for joy to the LORD, you who do what
  is right!
  His faithful followers should praise him.
²Play the lyre and praise the LORD.
  Play the ten-stringed harp for him.
³Sing a new song[a] to him.
  Play it well and sing it loud!

⁴The LORD's word is true,
  and he is faithful in everything he
    does.
⁵He loves goodness and justice.
  The LORD's faithful love fills the earth.

⁶The LORD spoke the command, and the world
    was made.
  The breath from his mouth created
    everything in the heavens.
⁷He gathered together the water of the sea.
  He put the ocean in its place.
⁸Everyone on earth should fear and respect the
    LORD.
  All the people in the world should fear
    him,
⁹because when he speaks, things happen.
  And if he says, "Stop!"—then it stops.[b]
¹⁰The LORD can ruin every decision the nations
    make.
  He can spoil all their plans.
¹¹But the LORD's decisions are good forever.
  His plans are good for generation after
    generation.
¹²Great blessings belong to those who have the
    LORD as their God!
  He chose them to be his own special
    people.

¹³The LORD looked down from heaven
  and saw all the people.
¹⁴From his high throne he looked down
  at all the people living on earth.
¹⁵He created every person's mind,
  and he knows what each one is doing.
¹⁶A king is not saved by the power of his army.
  A soldier does not survive by his own great
    strength.
¹⁷Horses don't really bring victory in war.
  Their strength cannot help you escape.
¹⁸The LORD watches over his followers,
  those who wait for him to show his faithful
    love.
¹⁹He saves them from death.
  He gives them strength when they are
    hungry.
²⁰So we will wait for the LORD.
  He helps us and protects us.
²¹He makes us happy
  because we trust him who alone is holy.
²²LORD, we trust in you,
  so continue to show us your faithful love.

[c] A song of David when he pretended to be mad so that
  Abimelech would send him away, which he did.

34 I will praise the LORD at all times.
  I will never stop singing his praises.
²Humble people, listen and be happy,
  while I boast about the LORD.
³Praise the LORD with me.
  Let us honour his name.

⁴I went to the LORD for help, and he listened.
  He saved me from all that I fear.
⁵If you look to him for help,
  he will put a smile on your face.
  You will have no need to be ashamed.
⁶As a poor, helpless man I prayed to the LORD,
  and he heard me.
  He saved me from all my troubles.
⁷The LORD's angel builds a camp around his
    followers,
  and he protects them.

⁸Give the LORD a chance to show you[d] how
    good he is.
  Great blessings belong to those who depend
    on him!
⁹The LORD's holy people should fear and respect
    him.
  Those who respect him will always have
    what they need.

[a] **33:3 new song** Whenever God did a new and wonderful thing for his people, they would write a new song about it.
[b] **33:9 And if . . . stops** Or "He gives the command, and it stands!" The word "stand" can mean "stand forever" or "stop".
[c] **Psalm 34** In Hebrew, each verse in this psalm begins with the next letter of the alphabet.
[d] **34:8 Give . . . show you** Literally, "Taste and see".

¹⁰Even strong lions get weak and hungry,
   but those who go to the Lord for help will
     have every good thing.
¹¹Children, come and listen to me;
   I will teach you to respect the Lord.
¹²Do you want to enjoy life?
   Do you want to have many happy days?
¹³Then avoid saying anything hurtful,
   and never let a lie come out of your mouth.
¹⁴Stop doing anything evil, and do good.
   Look for peace, and do all you can to help
     people live peacefully.

¹⁵The Lord watches over those who do what is
     right,
   and he hears their prayers.
¹⁶But the Lord is against those who do evil,
   so they are forgotten soon after they die.
¹⁷Pray to the Lord, and he will hear you.
   He will save you from all your troubles.
¹⁸The Lord is close to those who have suffered
     disappointment.
   He saves those who are discouraged.

¹⁹Good people might have many problems,
   but the Lord will take them all away.
²⁰He will protect them completely.
   Not one of their bones will be broken.
²¹But troubles will kill the wicked.
   The enemies of those who do what is right
     will all be punished.
²²The Lord saves his servants.
   All who go to him for protection will escape
     punishment.

A song of David.

35 Lord, oppose those who oppose me.
   Fight those who fight me.
²Pick up your shields, large and small.
   Get up and help me!
³Take a spear and javelin
   and fight those who are chasing me.
   Tell me, "I will rescue you."

⁴Some people are trying to kill me.
   Disappoint them and make them ashamed.
   Make them turn and run away.
   They are planning to hurt me.
   Defeat and embarrass them.
⁵Make them like chaff blown by the wind.ᵃ
   Let them be chased by the angel of the Lord.
⁶Make their road dark and slippery.
   Let the angel of the Lord chase them.

⁷I did nothing wrong, but they tried to
     trap me.
   For no reason at all, they dug a pit to
     catch me.
⁸So let them fall into their own traps.
   Let them stumble into their own nets.
   Let some unknown danger catch them.
⁹Then I will sing for joy to the Lord.
   I will be happy when he saves me.
¹⁰With my whole self I will say,
   "Lord, there is no one like you.
   You protect the poor from those who are
     stronger.
   You save the poor and helpless from those
     who try to rob them."

¹¹There are witnessesᵇ trying to harm me.
   They ask me questions that I know nothing
     about.
¹²They pay me back evil for the good I have
     done.
   They make me so very sad.
¹³When they were sick,
   I was sad and wore sackcloth.
   I went without eating to show my sorrow.
   But my prayers for them were not
     answered.
¹⁴So I mourned for them
   the same as for a friend or a brother.
   I bowed my head in sorrow,
   crying as I would for my own mother.
¹⁵But when I had troubles, they came and
     laughed.
   They joined together against me.
   People I don't even know have attacked me.
   And they keep on insulting me.
¹⁶They make fun of me, saying terrible things.
   They grind their teeth to show their anger.

¹⁷My Lord, how long will you watch this
     happen?
   Save me from these people.
   They are attacking me like lions.
   So protect my precious life from them.
¹⁸I will praise you in the great assembly.
   I will praise you there among the crowds.
¹⁹Don't let my lying enemies keep on laughing
     at me.
   They have no reason to hate me.
   Surely they will be punished for their secret
     plans.ᶜ
²⁰They have no friendly words for others,
   but plan ways to hurt those who want to
     live in peace.

ᵃ **35:5 wind** This may be a wordplay, because the Hebrew word also means "spirit."
ᵇ **35:11 witnesses** People who tell what they have seen or heard. Here, these people were probably telling lies.
ᶜ **35:19 Surely . . . plans** Literally, "Will the people who hate me freely wink their eyes?"

21They are telling lies about me.
They say, "Aha! We know what you did!"
22Lord, surely you can see what is happening.
So don't keep quiet.
Lord, don't leave me.
23Wake up! Get up!
My God and my Lord, fight for me, and
bring me justice.
24Lord my God, judge me with your fairness.
Don't let those people laugh at me.
25Don't let them think, "Aha! We got what we
wanted!"
Don't let them say, "We destroyed him!"
26Let my enemies be ashamed and
embarrassed—
all those who were happy about my
troubles.
Proud of themselves, they treated me as
worthless.
So let them be covered with shame and
disgrace.
27To those who want the best for me,
I wish them joy and happiness.
May they always say, "Praise the Lord,
who wants what is best for his servant."

28So, Lord, I will tell people how good you are.
I will praise you all day long.

To the director: A song of David, the Lord's servant.

36 Deep in the hearts of the wicked a voice
tells them to do wrong.
They have no respect for God.
2They lie to themselves.
They don't see their own faults,
so they are not sorry for what they do.
3Their words are wicked lies.
They have stopped doing anything wise or
good.
4They make wicked plans in bed at night.
They choose a way of life that does no good.
And they never say no to anything evil.

5Lord, your faithful love is so great, it reaches
the sky!
Your faithfulness is as high as the clouds.
6Your goodness is higher than the highest
mountains.
Your fairness is deeper than the deepest
ocean.
Lord, you protect people and animals.
7Nothing is more precious than your true
love.

All people can find protection close to you,
like baby birds under their mother's wings.
8They get strength from all the good things in
your house.
You let them drink from your wonderful
river.
9The fountain of life flows from you.
Your light lets us see light.

10Continue to love those who really know you,
and do good to those who are true to you.*a*
11Don't let proud people trap me.
Don't let the wicked force me to run away.

12Put this on their grave markers:
"Here fell the wicked.
They were crushed.
They will never stand up again."

INSIGHT

*Some psalms, such as this one and
Psalms 34, 111 and 146 were written in
the form of an acrostic – each phrase
begins with a successive letter of the
Hebrew alphabet.*

Psalm 37

---

b A song of David.

37 Don't get upset about evil people.
Don't be jealous of those who do wrong.
2They are like grass and other green plants
that dry up quickly and then die.

3So trust in the Lord and do good.
Live on your land and be dependable.*c*
4Enjoy serving the Lord,
and he will give you whatever you ask for.
5Depend on the Lord.
Trust in him, and he will help you.
6He will make it as clear as day that you are
right.
Everyone will see that you are being fair.

7Trust in the Lord and wait quietly for his
help.
Don't be angry when people make evil
plans and succeed.
8Don't become so angry and upset
that you, too, want to do evil.

---

a **36:10** *true to you* Or "honest hearted".
b **Psalm 37** In Hebrew, about every other verse in this psalm begins with the next letter of the alphabet.
c **37:3** *be dependable* Literally, "shepherd faithfulness".

⁹The wicked will be destroyed,
   but those who call to the LORD for help will
      get the land he promised.
¹⁰In a short time there will be no more evil
      people.
   You can look for them all you want, but
      they will be gone.
¹¹Humble people will get the land God promised,
   and they will enjoy peace.

¹²The wicked plan bad things for those who are
      good.
   They show their teeth in anger at them.
¹³But our Lord will laugh at them.
   He will make sure they get what they
      deserve.
¹⁴The wicked draw their swords to kill the poor
      and the helpless.
   They aim their arrows to murder all who do
      what is right.
¹⁵But their bows will break,
   and their swords will pierce their own hearts.

¹⁶A few good people are better
   than a large crowd of those who are evil.
¹⁷The wicked will be destroyed,
   but the LORD cares for those who are good.
¹⁸The LORD protects pure people all their life.
   Their reward will last forever.
¹⁹When trouble comes,
   good people will not be destroyed.
   When times of hunger come,
      good people will have plenty to eat.
²⁰But evil people are the LORD's enemies,
   and they will be destroyed.
   Their valleys will dry up and burn.
   They will be destroyed completely.
²¹The wicked borrow money and never pay it
      back.
   But good people are kind and generous.
²²Everyone the Lord blesses will get the land he
      promised.
   Everyone he curses will be destroyed.

²³The LORD shows us how we should live,
   and he is pleased when he sees people
      living that way.
²⁴If they stumble, they will not fall,
   because the LORD reaches out to steady
      them.

²⁵I was young, and now I am old,
   but I have never seen good people left with
      no one to help them;

I have never seen their children begging for
      food.
²⁶They are kind and generous,
   and their children are a blessing.

²⁷Stop doing anything evil and do good,
   and you will always have a place to live.
²⁸The LORD loves what is right,
   and he will never leave his followers
      without help.
   He will always protect them,
   but he will destroy the families of the
      wicked.
²⁹Good people will get the land God promised
   and will live in it forever.

³⁰Those who do what is right give good
      advice.
   Their decisions are always fair.
³¹They have learned God's teachings,
   and they will never stop living right.ᵃ
³²The wicked are always looking for ways
   to kill good people.
³³But the LORD will not let the wicked defeat
      them.
   He will not let good people be judged
      guilty.

³⁴Do what the LORD says, and wait for his help.
   He will reward you and give you the land
      he promised.
   You will see the wicked being forced to
      leave.

³⁵I once saw a wicked man who was powerful.
   He was like a strong, healthy tree.
³⁶But then he was gone.
   I looked for him, but I could not find him.

³⁷Be pure and honest.
   Peace-loving people will have many
      descendants.
³⁸But those who break the law will be destroyed
      completely.
   And their descendants will be forced to
      leave the land.ᵇ

³⁹The LORD saves those who are good.
   When they have troubles, he is their
      strength.
⁴⁰The LORD helps good people and rescues
      them.
   They depend on him, so he rescues them
      from the wicked.

ᵃ **37:31** *they . . . right* Literally, "his steps will not slip".
ᵇ **37:38** *forced to leave the land* Or "destroyed". Literally, "cut off".

A song of David for the day of remembrance.[a]

38

LORD, don't criticize me when you are angry.
Don't discipline me in anger.
[2]You have hurt me.
You punished me and hurt me deeply.
[3]You punished me severely, so my whole body
is sore.
I sinned, and now all my bones hurt.
[4]My guilt is like a heavy burden.
I am sinking beneath its weight.

[5]I did a foolish thing,
and now I have infected sores that stink.
[6]I am bent and bowed down.
I am depressed all day long.
[7]I am burning with fever,
and my whole body hurts.
[8]I hurt so much I cannot feel anything.
My pounding heart makes me scream!

[9]My Lord, you heard my groaning.
You can hear my sighs.
[10]My heart is pounding.
My strength is gone, and I am going blind.[b]
[11]Because of my sickness,
my friends and neighbours will not visit me;
my family will not come near me.
[12]My enemies say bad things about me.
They are spreading lies and rumours.
They talk about me all the time.

[13]But I am like a deaf man and cannot hear.
I am like someone who cannot speak.
[14]I am like those who cannot hear what people
are saying about them.
I cannot answer to prove my enemies wrong.
[15]LORD, you must defend me.
Lord my God, you must speak for me.
[16]That's why I prayed, "Don't let my enemies
smile at my pain.
Full of pride, they will laugh if I stumble
and fall."
[17]I know I am guilty of doing wrong.
I cannot forget my pain.
[18]Lord, I told you about the evil I have done.
I am sorry for my sin.
[19]But my enemies are alive and healthy,
and they have told many lies.
[20]I did nothing but good,
and they paid me back with evil.

I try to do what is right,
but that only makes them turn against me.
[21]LORD, don't leave me.
My God, stay close to me.
[22]Come quickly and help me.
My Lord, you are the one who saves me.

To the director, Jeduthun.[c] A song of David.

39

I said, "I will be careful about what I say.
I will not let my tongue cause me to sin.
I will keep my mouth closed[d]
when I am around wicked people."
[2]So I didn't say anything.
I didn't even say anything good,
but I became even more upset.
[3]I was very angry,
and the more I thought about it, the angrier
I became.
So I said something.
[4]LORD, tell me, what will happen to me now?
Tell me, how long will I live?
Let me know how short my life really is.
[5]You gave me only a short life.
Compared to you, my whole life is nothing.
The life of every human is like a cloud that
quickly disappears.   *Selah*

[6]Our life is like an image in a mirror.[e]
We rush through life collecting things,
but we don't know who will get them after
we die.

[7]So, Lord, what hope do I have?
I put my trust in you.
[8]Save me from the bad things I did.
Don't let me be treated like a fool.
[9]I will not open my mouth.
I will not say anything.
You did what should have been done.
[10]But please stop punishing me.
You will destroy me if you do not stop.
[11]You punish people for doing wrong to teach
them the right way to live.
As a moth destroys cloth, you destroy what
people love.
Yes, our lives are like a small cloud that
quickly disappears.   *Selah*

[12]LORD, hear my prayer!
Listen to the words I cry to you.
Look at my tears.

---

[a] Psalm 38 *for . . . remembrance* The ancient Greek version has "for the Sabbath".
[b] 38:10 *I am going blind* Or "My eyes have lost their sparkle." Literally, "Even the light of my eyes is no longer with me."
[c] Psalm 39 *Jeduthun* Or "and to Jeduthun", one of the three main temple musicians. See 1 Chr. 9:16; 16:38–42.
[d] 39:1 *will keep . . . closed* Literally, "guard my mouth with a muzzle".
[e] 39:6 *Our life . . . mirror* Or "This life is not real—it is only a shadow" or "People wander around in the dark—not knowing what will happen."

I am only a traveller passing through this life
    with you.
  Like all my ancestors, I will live here only a
    short time.*a*
¹³Leave me alone*b* and let me be happy
  before I am dead and gone.

To the director: A song of David.

40 I called*c* to the Lord, and he heard me.
     He heard my cries.
²He lifted me out of the grave.*d*
  He lifted me from that muddy place.*e*
He picked me up, put me on solid ground,
  and kept my feet from slipping.
³He put a new song*f* in my mouth,
  a song of praise to our God.
Many will see what he did and worship him.
  They will put their trust in the Lord.

⁴Great blessings belong to those who trust in
    the Lord,
  for those who do not turn to demons and
    false gods*g* for help.
⁵Lord my God, you have done many amazing
    things!
  You have made great plans for us—too
    many to list.
I could talk on and on about them,
  because there are too many to count.

⁶Lord, you made me understand this:*h*
  You don't really want sacrifices and grain
    offerings.
  You don't want burnt offerings and sin
    offerings.
⁷So I said, "Here I am,
  ready to do what was written about me in
    the book.
⁸My God, I am happy to do whatever you want.
  I never stop thinking about your teachings."

⁹I told the good news of victory*i* to the people
    in the great assembly.
  And, Lord, you know that I will never stop
    telling that good news.
¹⁰I told about the good things you did.
  I did not hide these things in my heart.

I spoke of how you can be trusted to save us.
  I did not hide your love and loyalty from
    those in the great assembly.

¹¹Lord, do not hide your mercy from me.
  Let your love and loyalty always protect me.
¹²Troubles have surrounded me.
  They are too many to count!
My sins have caught me,
  and I cannot escape them.
They are more than the hairs on my head.
  I have lost my courage.
¹³Please, Lord, rescue me!
  Lord, hurry and help me!
¹⁴People are trying to kill me.
  Please disappoint them.
  Humiliate them completely!
They wanted to hurt me.
  Make them run away in shame!
¹⁵May those who make fun of me
  be too embarrassed to speak!
¹⁶But may those who come to you
  be happy and rejoice.
May those who love being saved by you
  always be able to say, "Praise the Lord!"*j*

¹⁷My Lord, I am only a poor, helpless man,
  but please pay attention to me.
You are my helper, the one who can save me.
  My God, don't be too late.

To the director: A song of David.

41 Those who help the poor succeed will get
     many blessings.*k*
  When trouble comes, the Lord will save
    them.
²The Lord will protect them and save their lives.
  He will bless them in this land.
  He will not let their enemies harm them.
³When they are sick in bed,
  the Lord will give them strength and make
    them well!

⁴I say, "Lord, be kind to me.
  I sinned against you, but forgive me and
    make me well."
⁵My enemies say bad things about me.

---

^a **39:12** *I will live . . . time* Literally, "I am a settler."
^b **39:13** *Leave me alone* Or "Stop looking at me."
^c **40:1** *called* Or "waited patiently".
^d **40:2** *grave* Literally, "pit of destruction". That is, "Sheol", the place of death.
^e **40:2** *muddy place* In many ancient stories, Sheol, the place of death, is a dark place with mud all around, like a grave.
^f **40:3** *new song* Whenever God did a new and wonderful thing for his people, they would write a new song about it.
^g **40:4** *demons and false gods* Or "proud and deceptive people".
^h **40:6** *you made . . . this* Literally, "you have dug my ears". The ancient Greek version has "you prepared a body for me".
ⁱ **40:9** *victory* Or "goodness" or "righteousness".
^j **40:16** *Praise the Lord* Literally, "The Lord is great" or "May the Lord be magnified."
^k **41:1** Or "Those who teach the poor will be very fortunate."

They ask, "When will he die and be
   forgotten?"
[6]If they come to see me,
   they don't say what they are really
      thinking.
They come to gather a little gossip
   and then go to spread their rumours.
[7]Those who hate me whisper about me.
   They think the worst about me.
[8]They say, "He did something wrong.
   That is why he is sick.
   He will never get well."
[9]My best friend, the one I trusted,
   the one who ate with me—even he has
      turned against me.

[10]Lord, please be kind to me.
   Let me get up, and I will pay them back.
[11]Don't let my enemy defeat me.
   Then I will know that you care for me.
[12]I was innocent and you supported me.
   You let me stand and serve you forever.

[13]Praise the Lord, the God of Israel.
   He always was, and he always will be.

Amen and Amen!

BOOK 2
(Psalms 42–72)

To the director: A maskil from the Korah family.

42 Like a deer drinking from a stream,
   I reach out to you, my God.[a]
[2]My soul thirsts for the living God.
   When can I go to meet with him?
[3]Instead of food, I have only tears day and
      night,
   as my enemies laugh at me and say, "Where
      is your God?"

[4]My heart breaks as I remember the pleasant
      times in the past,
   when I walked with the crowds as I led
      them up to God's Temple.
I remember the happy songs of praise
   as they celebrated the festival.

[5–6]Why am I so sad?
   Why am I so upset?
I tell myself, "Wait for God's help!

You will again be able to praise him,
   your God, the one who will save you."
In my sadness I say, "I will remember you
   from here on this small hill,[b]
   where Mount Hermon and the Jordan River
      meet."
[7]I hear the roar of the water coming from deep
      within the earth.
   It shouts to the water below as it tumbles
      down the waterfall.
God, your waves come one after another,
   crashing all around and over me.[c]

[8]By day the Lord shows his faithful love,
   and at night I have a song for him—a
      prayer for the God of my life.[d]
[9]I say to God, my Rock,
   "Why have you forgotten me?
   Why must I suffer this sadness that my
      enemies have brought me?"
[10]Their constant insults are killing me.
   They never stop asking, "Where is your
      God?"

[11]Why am I so sad?
   Why am I so upset?
I tell myself, "Wait for God's help!
   You will again be able to praise him,
   your God, the one who will save you."

43 Bring justice to me, God!
   Defend me against this nation that has
      broken its agreement.
   Save me from these evil liars.
[2]God, you are my place of safety.
   Why have you turned me away?
Why must I suffer this sadness
   that my enemies have brought me?
[3]Send your light and your truth to guide me,
   to lead me to your holy mountain, to your
      home.
[4]I want to go to God's altar,
   to the God who makes me so very happy.
God, my God, I want to play my harp
   and sing praises to you!

[5]Why am I so sad?
   Why am I so upset?
I tell myself, "Wait for God's help!
   You will again have a chance to praise him,
   your God, the one who will save you."

---

[a] **42:1** Or "As a deer stretches out to drink water from a stream, so my soul thirsts for you, God."
[b] **42:5–6** *small hill* Or "Mount Mizar".
[c] **42:7** *God, your waves . . . over me* These word pictures describe the psalmist's feelings about the many troubles the Lord has allowed him to experience.
[d] **42:8** *the God of my life* Or "my living God".

MY TEARS HAVE BEEN MY FOOD

We've all had those times when we feel low or sad or upset. Sometimes these sad times can go on for days, weeks, even months. Often it can feel as though God is far away – we barely feel like eating or meeting friends, let alone praying. When the heartache drags on we can wonder if we'll ever feel good again. Psalms 42 and 43 are for times like that.

DIG IN

READ Psalms 42:1 – 43:5

- Write down all the different ways the psalmist describes his feelings.
- What is the worst of all these things (42:9; 43:2)?
- How do those around him respond to his suffering (42:3,10)?

He is feeling utterly awful. He cannot stop crying; he can't eat he's crying so much, he feels forgotten by God and the people around him look at all his pain and think "If God is supposed to look after you why are you in this mess?!"

- How does the psalmist describe his longing for God?
- What does he remember? And how does it make him feel (42:4–6)?

He's thirsty for God, like a dehydrated deer drinking from a river – gulping, parched, desperate. He longs to go and meet with God and remembers how he used to be really happy worshipping with all the people. We're told he was from the family of Korah, who were the worship leaders at that time. He loved to praise God and help others to do it. And now he can't – he's far away from the people, he misses them and misses being close to God. Have you ever felt like this?

- What does the psalmist do (42:5,8,11; 43:5)?
- What does he tell himself about God (42:5,8,9; 43:2,4)?
- What does he remind himself about the future (42:5; 43:4–5)?

It's really surprising isn't it? Often when we feel miserable we like to remind ourselves how bad everything is. But the psalmist shows us there are better things we can do: he tells himself the truth and he keeps praying. He reminds himself that God is the saving God, that he is faithful, that he is the "rock" (solid and strong), a place of safety. What great things to remember – God is still the same God, he is still there. And he reminds himself that this miserable time won't last forever; he will *praise God again and God* will *rescue him from the pain.*

DIG THROUGH

- Try to listen to what you tell yourself when you're sad. What thoughts discourage you? What do other people say that discourages you? But how does putting your hope in God give you a happier way of seeing things?
- Why not write down all the good things God is and has done for you. Next time you feel sad, have a look at it.

DIG DEEPER

- There are lots more psalms about difficult times. Have a look at Psalms 6, 10, 13, 55, 88, 130 and 137. In each one, see if you can spot the problem, what it says about God and how it changes the psalmists' thinking. You may be surprised by how much the psalmists praise God through bad times!

*To the director: A maskil from the
Korah family.*

44

God, we have heard about you.
Our ancestors told us what you did in
their lifetime.
They told us what you did long ago.
²With your great power you took this land from
other people,
and you gave it to us.
You crushed those foreigners
and forced them to leave this land.
³It was not our fathers' swords that took the
land.
It was not their strong arms that brought
them victory.
It was your power.
It was because you accepted them and
smiled down on them.

⁴God, you are my king.
Give the command and lead Jacob's people
to victory.
⁵We need your help to push our enemies back.
Only in your name can we trample those
who attacked us.
⁶I don't put my trust in my bow.
My sword cannot save me.
⁷You are the one who saved us from our
enemies.
You are the one who put our enemies to
shame.
⁸We have praised you all day long,
and we will praise your name forever.

Selah

⁹But you left us and put us to shame.
You did not go with us into battle.
¹⁰You let our enemies push us back.
You let them take our wealth.
¹¹You gave us away like sheep to be killed
and eaten.
You scattered us among the nations.
¹²You sold your people for nothing.
You did not even argue over the price.
¹³You made us a joke to our neighbours.
They laugh and make fun of us.
¹⁴You made us one of the stories that people
love to tell.
People all over the world laugh at us and
shake their heads.
¹⁵All I can think about is my shame.
Just look at my face, and you will see it.

¹⁶All I can hear are the jokes and insults of the
enemy,
as I watch them take their revenge.

¹⁷We wonder why all this has happened to us.
We have not forgotten you
or broken the agreement you gave us.
¹⁸We have not turned away from you
or stopped following you.
¹⁹But you crushed us in this home of jackals.
You left us in this place as dark as death.

²⁰Did we forget the name of our God?
Did we pray to foreign gods?
²¹If we did, then God knows it,
because he knows our deepest secrets.
²²All day long we died for you.
We are like sheep being led away to be killed.

²³Lord, wake up!
Why are you sleeping?
Get up! Don't ignore us forever!
²⁴Why are you hiding from us?
Have you forgotten our pain and troubles?

²⁵We have been pushed down into the dirt.
We are lying face down in the dust.ᵃ
²⁶Get up and help us!
Rescue us because of your faithful love.

*To the director: To the tune "Shoshanim".ᵇ
A maskil from the Korah family.
A love song.*

45

Beautiful thoughts fill my mind
as I speak these lines for the king.
These words come from my tongue
as from the pen of a skilled writer.

²You are more handsome than anyone,
and you say such pleasant things.
So God will always bless you.
³Put on your sword, mighty warrior,
so impressive in your splendid uniform.
⁴Go out in your greatness to win the victory for
what is true and right.
Let us see the amazing things you can do
with your powerful right arm.ᶜ
⁵Your sharp arrows will go deep into the hearts
of your enemies,
who will fall to the ground in front of you.
⁶God,ᵈ your kingdom will last forever.
You use your authority for justice.

ᵃ **44:25** This shows that the people were being treated like slaves who must bow down to their masters.
ᵇ **Psalm 45** *To the tune "Shoshanim"* Or "On the Shoshanim".
ᶜ **45:4** *right arm* This pictures God as a warrior-king. The right arm is a symbol of his power and authority.
ᵈ **45:6** *God* This might be a song to God as king. Or here, the writer might be using the word "God" as a title for the king.

⁷You love what is right and hate what is wrong.
So God, your God, chose you to be king,
giving you more joy and honour than
anyone like you.ᵃ
⁸From your clothes comes the wonderful smell
of myrrh, aloes and cassia.
In palaces decorated with ivory, you enjoy
the music of stringed instruments.
⁹Here are ladies of honour, daughters of
kings.
Your brideᵇ stands at your right side,
wearing a gown decorated with the finest
gold.

¹⁰My lady,ᶜ listen to me.
Listen carefully and understand me.
Forget your people and your father's family,
¹¹ so that the king will be pleased with your
beauty.
He will be your new husband,ᵈ
so you must honour him.
¹²People from Tyre will bring you gifts.
Their richest people will try to win your
friendship.

¹³The princess is so beautiful in her gown,
like a pearl set in gold.
¹⁴Clothed in beauty, she is led to the king,
followed by her bridesmaids.
¹⁵Filled with joy and excitement,
they enter into the king's palace.

¹⁶Your sons will be kings like their ancestors.
You will make them rulers throughout the
land.
¹⁷You will be famous for generations.
People will praise you for ever and ever.

To the director: A song from the Korah family.
Use the alamoth.ᵉ A song.

46 God is our protection and source of
strength.
He is always ready to help us in times of
trouble.
²So we are not afraid when the earth quakes
and the mountains fall into the sea.
³We are not afraid when the seas become
rough and dark
and the mountains tremble.   *Selah*

⁴There is a river whose streams bring happiness
to God's city,
to the holy city of God Most High.
⁵God is in that city, so it will never be
destroyed.
He is there to help even before sunrise.
⁶Nations will shake with fear and kingdoms
will fall
when God shouts and makes the earth
move.
⁷The LORD All-Powerful is with us.
The God of Jacob is our place of safety.   *Selah*

⁸Look at the powerful things the LORD has
done.
See the awesome things he has done on
earth.
⁹He stops wars all over the world.
He breaks the soldiers' bows, shatters their
spears and burns their shields.ᶠ
¹⁰God says, "Stop fighting and know that I am
God!
I am the one who defeats the nations;
I am the one who controls the world."

¹¹The LORD All-Powerful is with us.
The God of Jacob is our place of safety.   *Selah*

To the director: A song from the Korah family.

47 Everyone, clap your hands.
Shout with joy to God!
²The LORD Most High is awesome.
He is the great King over all the earth.
³He helped us defeat other nations.
He put those people under our control.
⁴He chose our land for us.
He chose that wonderful land for Jacob,
the one he loved.   *Selah*

⁵The LORD God goes up to his throne
at the sound of the trumpet and horn.
⁶Sing praises to God, sing praises!
Sing praises to our King, sing praises!
⁷God is the King of the whole world.
Sing songs of praise!ᵍ
⁸God sits on his holy throne;
he rules all the nations.
⁹The leaders of the nations have come together
with the people of the God of Abraham.

ᵃ **45:7 chose . . . anyone like you** Literally, "anointed you with the oil of gladness above your companions". This refers to the
special oil used in the dedication of a new priest or king.
ᵇ **45:9 bride** Or "queen".
ᶜ **45:10 My lady** Literally, "Daughter".
ᵈ **45:11 husband** Or "master".
ᵉ **Psalm 46 alamoth** This might be a musical instrument, a special way of tuning an instrument, a music style or one of the
groups that played harps in the Temple orchestra. See 1 Chr. 15:21.
ᶠ **46:9 shields** Or "chariots".
ᵍ **47:7 songs of praise** Literally, "*maskil*". See "MASKIL" in the Word List.

All the rulers of the world belong to God.
He is over them all!

A song of praise from the Korah family.

48 The Lord is great!
He is praised throughout the city of our
God, his holy mountain.
[2] His city is such a pleasant place.
It brings joy to people from around the world.
Mount Zion is the true mountain of God.[a]
It is the city of the great King.
[3] In the palaces of that city,
God is known as the fortress.
[4] Once some kings met together
and planned an attack against this city.
They marched towards the city,
[5] but when they saw it, they were amazed.
They all panicked and ran away.
[6] Fear grabbed them;
they trembled like a woman giving birth.
[7] God, with a strong east wind,
you wrecked their big ships.

[8] Yes, we heard the stories about your power.
But we also saw it in the city of our God,
the city of the Lord All-Powerful.
God makes that city strong forever.   *Selah*

[9] God, here we are in your Temple,
remembering the true love you have
shown us.
[10] Your name is known everywhere, God,
and people throughout the earth praise you.
You have shown that you do what is right.
[11] Mount Zion is happy,
and the towns of Judah rejoice
because your decisions are fair.

[12] Walk around Jerusalem,
and count its towers.
[13] Notice its strong walls,
and look at its huge buildings.
Then you can tell your children about them.
[14] These things show us what God is like:
He is our God for ever and ever.
He will always take care of us!

To the director: A song from the Korah family.

49 Listen to this, all you nations.
Pay attention, all you people on earth.
[2] Everyone, rich and poor,
listen to me.

[3] I have some very wise words for you.
My thoughts will give you understanding.
[4] I listened to these sayings.
And now, with my harp, I will sing and
make the hidden meaning clear.

[5] Why should I be afraid when trouble
comes?
There is no need to fear when evil enemies
surround me.
[6] They think their wealth will protect them.
They boast about how rich they are.
[7] But no one has enough to buy back a life,
and you cannot bribe[b] God.
[8] You will never get enough money
to pay for your own life.
[9] You will never have enough
to buy the right to live forever
and keep your body out of the grave.

[10] Look, the wise die the same as fools and
stupid people.[c]
They die and leave their wealth to others.
[11] The grave will be their new home forever.
And how much land they owned will not
make any difference.
[12] People might be wealthy, but they cannot stay
here forever.
They will die like the animals.

[13] That is what happens to all who trust in
themselves
and to anyone who accepts their way
of life.   *Selah*

[14] They are just like sheep, but the grave will be
their pen.
Death will be their shepherd.
When morning comes, the good people will
enjoy victory,
as the bodies of the proud slowly rot in the
grave,
far away from their fancy houses.
[15] But God will pay the price to save me from
the grave.
He will take me to be with him.   *Selah*

[16] Don't be afraid of people just because they are
rich.
Don't be afraid of people just because they
have big, fancy houses.
[17] They will not take anything with them when
they die.
They will not take their wealth with them.

---

[a] **48:2** *true mountain of God* Literally, "the summit of Zaphon". In Canaanite stories, Mount Zaphon was where the gods lived.
[b] **49:7** *bribe* Here, this means offering a gift or sacrifice so that God will not punish a guilty person.
[c] **49:10** *stupid people* Or "animals".

¹⁸A wealthy man might tell himself how well he
has done in life.
And other people might praise him.
¹⁹But the time will come for him to die and go
to his ancestors.
And he will never again see the light of day.
²⁰Wealthy people don't seem to understand
that they will die like the animals.

One of Asaph's songs.

50 The Lord God Most Powerful has spoken.
He calls to everyone on earth,
from where the sun rises to where it sets.
²God shines like a light from Zion,
the city of perfect beauty.
³Our God is coming and will not keep quiet.
Fire burns in front of him.
There is a great storm around him.
⁴He tells the sky and the earth to be witnesses
as he judges his people.
⁵He says, "My followers, gather around me.
Come, my worshippers, who made an
agreement with me."

⁶God is the judge,
and the skies tell how fair he is.   *Selah*

⁷God says, "My people, listen to me!
People of Israel, I will show my evidence
against you.
I am God, your God.
⁸The problem I have with you is not your
sacrifices
or the burnt offerings you bring to me
every day.
⁹Why would I want more bulls from your barns
or goats from your pens?
¹⁰I already own all the animals in the forest.
I own all the animals on a thousand hills.
¹¹I know every bird in the mountains.
Everything that moves in the fields is mine.
¹²If I were hungry, I would not ask you for food.
I already own the world and everything
in it.
¹³I don't eat the meat of bulls or drink the blood
of goats."

¹⁴You made promises to God Most High,
so give him what you promised.
Bring your sacrifices and thank offerings.
¹⁵God says, "Call me when trouble comes.
I will help you, and you will honour me."

¹⁶But God says to the wicked,
"Stop quoting my laws!

Stop talking about my agreement!
¹⁷You hate it when I tell you what to do.
You ignore what I say.
¹⁸You see a thief and run to join him.
You jump into bed with those who commit
adultery.
¹⁹The words that come from your mouth are
evil.
You use your tongue for telling lies.
²⁰You sit around talking about people
and find fault with your own family.
²¹When you did these things, I said nothing.
So you thought that Iᵃ was just like you.
But I will not be quiet any longer.
I will correct you and make clear what
I have against you.

²²"You people who have forgotten God,
understand what I am telling you,
or I will tear you apart,
and no one will be able to save you!
²³Whoever gives a thank offering shows me
honour.
And whoever decides to do what is right
will see my power to save."

INSIGHT

*This psalm was written by David after
Nathan the prophet confronted him about
his adultery with Bathsheba. It is a great
psalm of repentance and mercy.*
Psalm 51

*To the director: A song of David written when Nathan the
prophet came to him after David's sin with Bathsheba.*

51 God, be merciful to me
because of your faithful love.
Because of your great compassion,
erase all the wrongs I have done.
²Scrub away my guilt.
Wash me clean from my sin.

³I know I have done wrong.
I remember my sin all the time.
⁴I did what you said is wrong.
You are the one I have sinned against.
I say this so that people will know
that I am wrong and you are right.
What you decided is fair.
⁵I was born to do wrong,
a sinner before I left my mother's womb.

ᵃ **50:21** *that I* Or "that the 'I ᴀᴍ'".

⁶You want me to be completely loyal,
    so put true wisdom deep inside me.
⁷Remove my sin and make me pure.ᵃ
    Wash me until I am whiter than snow!
⁸Let me hear sounds of joy and happiness
    again.
    Let the bones you crushed be happy again.
⁹Don't look at my sins.
    Erase them all.

¹⁰God, create a pure heart in me,
    and make my spirit strong again.
¹¹Don't push me away
    or take your Holy Spirit from me.
¹²Your help made me so happy.
    Give me that joy again.
    Make my spirit strong and ready to obey you.
¹³I will teach the guilty how you want them to
    live,
    and the sinners will come back to you.

¹⁴God, spare me from the punishment of death.ᵇ
    My God, you are the one who saves me!
    Let me sing about all the good things you
    do for me!
¹⁵My Lord, I will open my mouth
    and sing your praises!
¹⁶You don't really want sacrifices,
    or I would give them to you.
¹⁷The sacrifice that God wants is a humble
    spirit.
    God, you will not reject a person who
    comes to you
    with a broken heart, ready to obey.

¹⁸God, please be good to Zion.
    Rebuild the walls of Jerusalem.
¹⁹Then you can enjoy the kind of sacrifices you
    want.ᶜ
    You will receive whole burnt offerings,
    and people will again offer bulls on your
    altar.

To the director: A maskil of David written when
Doeg the Edomite went to Saul and told him,
"David is in Ahimelech's house."

52 You think you are so great, and all you
have to boast about is evil!
    But God's faithful love protects me all the
    time.

²You make plans to hurt people.
    You use your tongue like a sharp razor,
    always making up lies!
³You love evil more than good.
    You love lies more than truth.   *Selah*

⁴You love to say things that confuse people.
    You are nothing but a liar!
⁵So God will ruin you forever!
    He will grab you and pull you from your
    home,ᵈ
    like someone pulling up a plant by the
    roots!   *Selah*

⁶It will be a shock for good people who see this
    happen.
    But then they will laugh at you and say,
⁷"Look what happened to this man
    who refused to depend on God!
This fool trusted in his great wealth.
    And he thought that hurting others would
    make him stronger."

⁸But I am like a green olive tree growing in
    God's Temple.
    I will trust God's faithful love for ever and
    ever.
⁹God, I praise you forever for what you have
    done.
    I will speak your nameᵉ before your
    followers because it is so good!

To the director: Use the mahalath.ᶠ A maskil of David.

53 Only fools think there is no God.
People like that are evil and do terrible
    things.
    They never do what is right.

²God looks down from heaven to see
    if there is anyone who is wise,
    anyone who looks to him for help.
³But everyone has turned away from him.
    Everyone has become evil.
No one does anything good.
    No, not one person!

⁴Those who are evil treat my people like bread
    to be eaten.
    And they never ask for God's help.
    Don't they understand what they are doing?

ᵃ **51:7** *Remove . . . pure* Literally, "Cleanse me with hyssop." See "ʜʏssop" in the Word List.
ᵇ **51:14** *spare . . . death* Or "don't consider me guilty of murder".
ᶜ **51:19** *the kind . . . you want* Or "the offering of righteousness".
ᵈ **52:5** *home* This means the body. This is like saying, "God will end your life here on earth."
ᵉ **52:9** *speak your name* Or "I will trust your name."
ᶠ **Psalm 53** *mahalath* Probably a musical term. It might be the name of an instrument or a tune, or it might mean a certain
musical style.

5They will be filled with fear—
    a fear like they have never felt before!
People of Israel, you will defeat those who
        attacked you,
    because God has rejected them.
And he will scatter their bones.

6I wish the one who lives on Mount Zion
    would bring victory to Israel!
When God makes Israel successful again,
    the people of Jacob will be very happy;
    the people of Israel will be glad.

*To the director: With instruments. A maskil of
David written when the Ziphites went to Saul and told him,
    "We think David is hiding among our people."*

54

God, use your power and save me.
    Use your great power to set me free.*a*
2God, listen to my prayer.
    Listen to what I say.
3Strangers who don't even think about God
    have turned against me.
    Those powerful men are trying to
        kill me.   *Selah*

4Look, my God will help me.
    My Lord will support me.
5He will punish the people who turned
        against me.
    God, be faithful to me and destroy them.

6LORD, I will give freewill offerings to you.
    I will praise your good name.
7You saved me from all my troubles.
    I saw my enemies defeated.

To the director: With instruments. A maskil of David.

55

God, hear my prayer.
    Don't ignore my cry for help.
2Please listen and answer me.
    Let me speak to you and tell you what
        upsets me.
3My enemies shout at me and threaten me.
    In their anger they attack me.
    They bring troubles crashing down on me.

4My heart is pounding inside me.
    I am afraid to die.
5I am trembling with fear.
    I am terrified!
6Oh, I wish I had wings like a dove.
    I would fly away and find a place to
        rest.

7I would run far away
    and live in the desert.   *Selah*

8I would hurry and find a place to hide.
    I would escape from this storm of trouble.
9My Lord, confuse their words and stop their
        plans.
    I see so much cruelty and fighting in this
        city.
10Day and night, in every neighbourhood,
    the city is filled with evil and trouble.
11There is so much crime in the streets.
    People who hurt and cheat others are
        everywhere.

12If it were an enemy insulting me,
    I could bear it.
If it were my enemies attacking me,
    I could hide.
13But it is you, the one so close to me,
    my companion, my good friend, who does
        this.
14We used to share our secrets with each other,
    as we walked through the crowds together
        in God's Temple.

15I wish death would take my enemies by
        surprise!
    I wish the earth would open up and
        swallow them alive,*b*
    because they plan such terrible things
        together.

16I will call to God for help,
    and the LORD will save me.
17I speak to God morning, noon and night.
    I tell him what upsets me, and he listens to
        me!
18I have fought in many battles,
    but he has always rescued me and brought
        me back safely.
19God, who has always ruled as king,
    will hear me and punish my enemies.
                                    Selah

But they will never change.
    They don't fear and respect God.

20This one who was once my friend now attacks
        his friends.
    He is breaking every promise he made.
21His words about peace are as smooth as butter,
    but he has only war on his mind.
His words are as slick as oil,
    but they cut like a knife.

---

a **54:1** Literally, "God, save me with your name, judge me with your might."
b **55:15** *I wish . . . alive* Literally, "I wish they would go down into Sheol alive." See Num. 16:31–33.

22Give your worries to the LORD,
  and he will care for you.
    He will never let those who are good be
      defeated.
23But, God, you will send those liars and
  murderers to the grave.
    They will die before their life is half
      finished!
As for me, I will put my trust in you.

*To the director: To the tune "The Dove in the
Distant Oak". A miktam of David written when the
Philistines captured him in Gath.*

56 God, people have attacked me, so be
    merciful to me.
    They have been chasing me all day, closing
      in to attack me.
2My enemies come at me constantly.
    There are so many fighting against me.*a*
3When I am afraid,
  I put my trust in you.
4I trust God, so I am not afraid of what people
    can do to me!
  I praise God for his promise to me.

5My enemies are always twisting my words.
  They are always making plans against
    me.
6They hide together and watch every move
  I make,
    hoping for some way to kill me.
7God, send them away because of the bad
    things they did.
  Show your anger and defeat those
    people.
8You know how upset I have been.
  You have kept all my tears in a bottle.
  I am sure you have counted each one.

9When I call for help, my enemies will turn
    and run.
  Yes, I know that God is on my side!
10I praise God for his promise.
  I praise the LORD for his promise to me.
11I trust God, so I am not afraid
  of what people can do to me!

12God, I will keep the special promises I made
    to you.
  I will give you my thank offering.
13You saved me from death.
  You kept me from being defeated.
So I will serve you in the light
  that only the living can see.

*To the director: To the tune "Don't Destroy".
A miktam of David written when he escaped from
Saul and went into the cave.*

57 God, be merciful to me! Have mercy
    because I depend on you to protect me.
I run to you like a bird to its mother,
  waiting for this trouble to pass.

2I pray to God Most High for help,
  and he takes care of me completely!
3From heaven he helps me and saves me.
  He will punish the one who attacks me.
                     Selah

God will remain loyal to me
  and send his love to protect me.

4My life is in danger.
  My enemies are all around me.
They are like man-eating lions,
  with teeth like spears or arrows
  and tongues like sharp swords.

5God, rise above the heavens!
  Let all the world see your glory.
6My enemies set a trap for my feet
  to bring me down.
They dug a deep pit to catch me,
  but they fell into it.   *Selah*

7God, I am ready, heart and soul,
  to sing songs of praise.
8Wake up, my soul!
  Harps and lyres, wake up,
  and let's wake the dawn!
9My Lord, I will praise you before all people.
  I will sing praises about you to every nation.
10Your love is so great, it reaches the sky!
  Your faithfulness is as high as the clouds.
11Rise above the heavens, God.
  Let all the world see your glory.

*To the director: To the tune "Don't Destroy".
A miktam of David.*

58 You judges are not being fair in your
    decisions.
  You are not judging people fairly.
2No, you only think of evil things to do.
  You do violent crimes in this country.
3Those wicked people started doing wrong as
    soon as they were born.
  They have been liars from birth.
4Their anger is as deadly as the poison of a
    snake.*b*
  They shut their ears like a deaf cobra

---

a **56:2 *There are . . . against me*** Or "There are many attacking me from above."
b **58:4 *anger . . . snake*** A wordplay in Hebrew. The word meaning "anger" can also mean "venom" (poison).

[5]that does not listen to the music of the snake
    charmers,
  no matter how well they play.

[6]God, they are like lions.
  So, Lord, break their teeth.
[7]May they disappear like water down a drain.
  May they be crushed like weeds on a path.[a]
[8]May they be like snails melting away as they
    move.
  May they be like a baby born dead, who
    never saw the light of day.
[9]May they be destroyed suddenly,
  like the thorns that are burned to quickly
    heat a pot.

[10]Good people will be happy
  when the wicked get the punishment they
    deserve.
  They will feel like soldiers
  walking through the blood of their enemies![b]
[11]Then people will say, "Good people really are
    rewarded.
  Yes, there is a God judging the world!"[c]

To the director: To the tune "Don't Destroy".
A miktam of David written when Saul sent people
to watch David's house to try to kill him.

59 God, save me from my enemies.
  Protect me from those who stand
    against me.
[2]Save me from those who do wrong.
  Save me from those murderers.

[3]Look, powerful men are waiting for me.
  Lord, they are waiting to kill me,
  even though I did not sin or commit a
    crime.
[4]I have done nothing wrong, but they are
    rushing to attack me.
  Come and see for yourself!
[5]You are the Lord God All-Powerful, the God of
    Israel!
  Wake up and punish those enemy nations.
  Show no mercy to those evil traitors.   *Selah*

[6]Those evil men are like dogs
  that come into town in the evening,
  growling and roaming the streets.
[7]Listen to their threats and insults.
  They say such cruel things,
  and they don't care who hears them.

[8]Lord, laugh at them.
  Make fun of them all.

[9]God, my strength, I look to you for help.[d]
  You are my place of safety, high in the
    mountains.
[10]God loves me, and he will help me win.
  He will help me defeat my enemies.
[11]Do not just kill them, or my people might
    forget.
  My Lord and Protector, scatter and defeat
    them with your strength.
[12]Those evil people curse and tell lies.
  Punish them for what they said.
  Let their pride trap them.
[13]Destroy them in your anger.
  Destroy them completely!
  Then people all over the world will know
    that God rules over the people of Jacob.
                                        Selah

[14]Those evil men are like dogs
  that come into town in the evening,
  growling and roaming the streets.
[15]They roam around looking for food,
  but even if they eat their fill,
  they still growl and complain.
[16]But I will sing about your strength.
  Every morning I will sing about your love.
  You have been my place of safety,
  the place I can run to when troubles come.
[17]I will sing praises to you, my source of strength.
  You, God, are my place of safety.
  You are the God who loves me!

To the director: To the tune "Lily of the Agreement".
A miktam of David for teaching. Written when David fought
Aram Naharaim and Aram Zobah, and Joab came back and
defeated 12,000 Edomite soldiers at Salt Valley.

60 God, you were angry with us.
  You rejected us and destroyed our
    defences.
  Please make us strong again.
[2]You shook the earth and split it open.
  It is falling apart like a broken wall.
  Please put it back together.
[3]You have given your people many troubles.
  We are dizzy and fall down like drunks.
[4]But you have provided a flag to show your
    faithful followers
  where to gather to escape the enemy's
    attack.   *Selah*

---

[a] **58:7** Or "May he shoot his arrows, cutting them down as if they were withering grass."
[b] **58:10** *They . . . enemies* Literally, "They will wash their feet in the blood of the wicked."
[c] **58:11** *Yes . . . world* Or "There really are judges in this land doing their job."
[d] **59:9** *God . . . help* Or "I will sing my songs of praise to you." See Ps. 59:17.

⁵Use your great power and give us victory!
  Answer our prayer and save the people you
  love.

⁶From his Temple*ᵃ* God made this promise:
  "I will enjoy victory and give the land to my
  people!
I will divide up the city of Shechem for them.
I will give them Succoth Valley piece by
  piece.
⁷The lands of Gilead and Manasseh will be mine.
  Ephraim will be my helmet.
  Judah will be my royal sceptre.
⁸Moab will be the bowl for washing my feet.
  Edom will be the slave who carries my
  sandals.
  I will shout in victory over the Philistines."

⁹But, God, it seems that you have left us!
  You do not go out with our army.
¹⁰So who will lead me into the strong, protected
  city?
  Who will lead me into battle against Edom?
¹¹Help us defeat the enemy!
  No one on earth can rescue us.
¹²Only God can make us strong.
  Only God can defeat our enemies!

To the director: With stringed instruments.
A song of David.

61 God, hear my cry for help.
  Listen to my prayer.
²From a faraway land I call to you for help.
  I feel so weak and helpless!
Carry me to a high rock
  where no one can reach me.
³You are my place of safety,
  a strong tower that protects me from my
  enemies.

⁴I want to live in your tent*ᵇ* forever.
  I want to hide where you can protect me.
                                        Selah

⁵God, you heard what I promised to give you,
  but everything your worshippers have
  comes from you.

⁶Give the king a long life.
  Let him live forever!
⁷Let him rule in your presence forever.
  Protect him with your faithful love.

⁸Then I will praise your name forever.
  Every day I will do what I promised.

*To the director, Jeduthun.*ᶜ *A song of David.*

62 I must calm down and turn to God;
  only he can rescue me.
²He is my Rock, the only one who can save
  me.
  He is my high place of safety, where no
  army can defeat me.

³How long will you people attack me?
  Do you all want to kill me?
I am like a leaning wall,
  like a fence ready to fall.
⁴You want only to destroy me,
  to bring me down from my important
  position.
It makes you happy to tell lies about me.
  In public, you say nice things,
  but in private, you curse me.   *Selah*

⁵I must calm down and turn to God;
  he is my only hope.
⁶He is my Rock, the only one who can
  save me.
  He is my high place of safety, where no
  army can defeat me.
⁷My victory and honour come from God.
  He is the mighty Rock, where I am safe.

⁸People, always put your trust in God!
  Tell him all your problems.
  God is our place of safety.   *Selah*

⁹People cannot really help.
  You cannot depend on them.
Compared to God, they are nothing—
  no more than a gentle puff of air!
¹⁰Don't trust in your power to take things by
  force.
  Don't think you will gain anything by
  stealing.
And if you become wealthy,
  don't put your trust in riches.

¹¹God says there is one thing you can really
  depend on,
  and I believe it:
  "Strength comes from God!"
¹²My Lord, your love is real.
  You reward all people for what they do.

ᵃ **60:6** *From his Temple* Or "In his holiness".
ᵇ **61:4** *tent* The place where God lives among his people. Here, it is the Temple in Jerusalem. See "Holy Tent" and "Temple" in
the Word List.
ᶜ **Psalm 62** *Jeduthun* Or "and to Jeduthun", one of the three main temple musicians. See 1 Chr. 9:16; 16:38–42.

63

*A song of David written when he was
in the desert of Judah.*

God, you are my God.
  I am searching so hard to find you.
Body and soul, I thirst for you
  in this dry and weary land without water.
²Yes, I have seen you in your Temple.ª
  I have seen your strength and glory.
³Your faithful love is better than life,
  so my lips praise you.
⁴By my life, I will praise you.
  In your name, I lift my hands in prayer.
⁵When I sit down to satisfy my hunger,
  my joyful lips hunger to praise you!

⁶I remember you while lying on my bed.
  I think about you in the middle of the night.
⁷That is because you are the one who helps me.
  It makes me happy to be under your
    protection!
⁸I stay close to you,
  and you hold me with your powerful arm.

⁹Those who are trying to kill me will be
    destroyed.
  They will go down to their graves.
¹⁰They will be killed with swords.
  Wild dogs will eat their dead bodies.
¹¹But the king will be happy with his God,
  and those who promised to obey him will
    praise him
  when he defeats those liars.

To the director: A song of David.

64

God, listen to my complaint.
  Save me from the terrible threats of my
    enemies!
²Protect me from the secret plans of the
    wicked.
  Hide me from that gang of evil people.
³They sharpen their tongues to use like swords.
  They aim their poisonous words like
    arrows.
⁴Suddenly, from their hiding places, they let
    their arrows fly.
  They shoot to kill innocent people.
⁵They encourage each other to do wrong.
  They talk about how to set their traps,
    and they say, "No one will see them here!"
⁶They make plans to do evil and say,
  "We have the perfect plan!"
  Yes, people are dishonest and hard to
    understand.

⁷But suddenly, God will shoot his arrows
  and strike down those wicked people.
⁸He will use their own words against them,
  and they will be destroyed.
Then everyone who sees them
  will shake their heads in amazement.
⁹People will see what God has done.
  They will tell other people about him.
Then everyone will learn more about God.
  They will learn to fear and respect him.
¹⁰Good people are happy to serve the LORD.
  They depend on him to protect them.
All those who want to do right will praise
    him!

To the director: A praise song of David.

65

God in Zion, we praise you
  and give you what we promised.
²Anyone can come to you,
  and you will listen to their prayers.
³When our sins become too heavy for us,
  you wipe them away.
⁴You have blessed us to be the people you
    chose
  to come and stay in your Temple.
We are so happy to have the wonderful things
  that are in your Temple, your holy palace.

⁵God, you answer our prayers and do what
    is right.
  You do amazing things to save us.
People all over the world look to you for help,
  even those who live across the sea.
⁶You are so strong you made the mountains.
  They show how powerful you are.
⁷You can calm the roughest seas
  or silence the shouts of the nations.
⁸In even the faraway places on earth,
  people are amazed at the things you do.
From where the sun rises to where it sets,
  they sing your praises.

⁹You take care of the land.
  You water it and make it fertile.
Your streams are always filled with water.
  That's how you make the crops grow.
¹⁰You pour rain on the ploughed fields.
  You soak the ground with water.
You soften the soil with showers
  and cause the young plants to grow.
¹¹You bless each year with a plentiful harvest.
  The wonderful crops show you were here.
¹²The desert fields are wet and green.
  Even the hills look happy.

ª 63:2 *your Temple* Or "your holiness".

THIRSTING AFTER GOD

How do problems affect your walk with God? Do you find yourself running towards him – or running away from him? In this psalm, David shows us how sometimes the worst circumstances can make for the most glorious praise.

DIG IN

READ Psalm 63:1–11

- Look at the heading and verse 1. Who wrote this psalm and where was he at the time?
- How does he use his circumstances to focus on God?

David wrote about half of the psalms in our Bibles and this is one of his. It was probably written when he was in the desert fleeing his son, Absalom, who was plotting to overthrow his kingdom (check out the story in 2 Samuel 15).

Imagine that: your son organizes an uprising against you and you are forced to flee for your life. Only yesterday you had everything; now you're miles away, hiding out in the desert.

But David is a true worshipper. Rather than let his circumstances get in the way of him meeting with God, he uses them to lead him into an encounter with God.

He is thirsty (not surprisingly, being in the desert), but he turns this into a thirst for God (v.1). He is a hunted man so he realizes his life may now be very short, but he gives what he has left to God (v.4). He is hungry, but he is hungrier for God (v.5). He's not getting much sleep for fear of attack, so he uses his wakefulness to praise God (v.6).

- Look again at verses 9 to 11. What does David confidently expect will happen?

As a result of his praise, something stirs in David: faith. He becomes newly confident that things are going to be okay. Even though his situation is bleak, he finds new hope that God will rescue him. In the end, he does (see 2 Samuel 18:6–18).

DIG THROUGH

- This psalm is an amazing testimony to how it is possible to turn our situation and circumstances (however bad they get) into a focus for praising God. Do you have the praise habit? Do you find it easy or difficult turning everyday struggles into prayer and praise? Do you tend to crash out every time a little trouble comes your way?
- Praising God puts things back into perspective. David searches for God (v.1), recalls his faithfulness in the past (vv.2–3) and prays to him. How can you use this simple framework to help you next time you find yourself struggling?

DIG DEEPER

Growing in maturity as a Christian means learning to deal with all the ups and downs of life. We all experience "mountain-top" times where everything seems to make sense, and moments "in the valley" when sadness and pain surround us. Paul wrote to the Philippian church that he had learnt "to be satisfied with what I have and with whatever happens . . . Christ is the one who gives me the strength I need to do whatever I must do" (Philippians 4:11–13).

¹³The pastures are covered with flocks.
  The valleys are blanketed with grain.
  They are all singing and shouting for joy.

To the director: A song of praise.

66 Everything on earth, shout with joy to
God!
²Praise his glorious name!
  Honour him with songs of praise!
³Tell God, "Your works are wonderful!
  Your great power makes your enemies bow
    down in fear before you.
⁴Let the whole world worship you.
  Let everyone sing praises to your name."
                                    Selah

⁵Look at what God has done!
  These things amaze us.
⁶He changed the sea to dry land,*a*
  and his people went across the water*b* on foot.
  So let's celebrate because of what he has
    done!
⁷He rules the world with his great power.
  He watches people everywhere.
  No one can rebel against him.   *Selah*

⁸People, praise our God.
  Sing loud songs of praise to him.
⁹He continues to give us life,
  and he keeps us from falling.
¹⁰God, you have tested us
  the way people test silver with fire.
¹¹You let us be trapped.
  You put heavy burdens on us.
¹²You let our enemies run over us.
  We went through fire and water,
  but you brought us to a safe place.
¹³When I was in trouble, I asked for help,
  and I made promises to you.
¹⁴So now I bring sacrifices to your Temple.
  I am giving you what I promised.
¹⁵I bring my best sheep as burnt offerings.
  I offer the smoke from them up to you.
  I give you sacrifices of bulls and goats.
                                    Selah

¹⁶All you people who worship God,
  come and I will tell you what he has done
    for me.
¹⁷⁻¹⁸I cried out to him for help,
  and I praised him.
  If I had been hiding sin in my heart,
  the Lord would not have listened to me.

¹⁹But God did listen to me;
  he heard my prayer.
²⁰Praise God!
  He did not turn away from me—he listened
    to my prayer.
  He continues to show his love to me!

To the director: With instruments. A song of praise.

67 God, show mercy to us and bless us.
Please accept us!   *Selah*

²Let everyone on earth learn about you.
  Let every nation see how you save people.
³May people praise you, God!
  May all people praise you.
⁴May all nations rejoice and be happy
  because you judge people fairly.
  You rule over every nation.

⁵May the people praise you, God!
  May all people praise you.
⁶God, our God, bless us.
  Let our land give us a great harvest.
⁷May God bless us,
  and may all people on earth fear and respect
    him.

To the director: A praise song of David.

68 God, get up and scatter your enemies!
May all your enemies run from you.
²May your enemies be scattered
  like smoke blown away by the wind.
  May your enemies be destroyed
  like wax melting in a fire.
³But let good people be happy.
  Let them gather before God
  and enjoy themselves together.

⁴Sing to God! Sing praises to his name!
  Prepare the way for the one who rides on
    the clouds.
  His name is YAH.*c*
  Worship before him with joy.
⁵God, who lives in his holy palace, is a father to
    orphans,
  and he takes care of widows.
⁶God provides homes for those who are
    lonely.
  He frees people from prison and makes
    them happy.
  But those who turn against him will live in
    the desert.

a **66:6 changed the sea to dry land** This was with Moses at the Red Sea. See Exod. 14.
b **66:6 water** Literally, "river". Although this word is not used for the Jordan River elsewhere, some think this line may refer to the later crossing there. See Josh. 3:14–17.
c **68:4 YAH** This is a Hebrew name for God. It is like the Hebrew name usually translated "LORD".

[7]God, you led your people out of Egypt.
  You marched across the desert.   *Selah*

[8]The ground shook and rain poured from
    the sky
  when God, the God of Israel, came to Sinai.
[9]God, you sent the rain
  to make a tired, old land strong again.
[10]Your people[a] came back to live there,
  and you provided good things for the poor.

[11]My Lord gave the command,
  and many people went to tell the good
    news:
[12]"The armies of powerful kings ran away!
  At home, the women divide the things
    brought from the battle.
[13]Those who stayed at home will share in the
    wealth—
  metal doves with wings covered in silver
    and feathers sparkling with gold."

[14]God All-Powerful scattered the kings
  like snow falling on Mount Zalmon.
[15]Mount Bashan is a great mountain,
  a mountain with many high peaks.
[16]With so many peaks, Bashan, why are you
    jealous of Mount Zion?
  That is where God has chosen to live.
  The LORD will live there forever.
[17]With his millions of chariots,
  the Lord came from Sinai into the holy
    place.
[18]You, LORD, went up to your high place,
  leading a parade of captives.
  You received gifts from people,[b]
    even those who turned against you.
  You, LORD God, went up there to live.

[19]Praise the Lord!
  Every day he helps us with the loads we
    must carry.
  He is the God who saves us.   *Selah*

[20]He is our God, the God who saves us.
  My Lord GOD saves us from death.
[21]God will smash the heads of his enemies.
  He will punish those who fight against
    him.[c]
[22]My Lord said, "If they run up to Bashan or
    down to the depths of the sea,
  I will bring them back.

[23]So you will march through pools of their
    blood,
  and there will be plenty left for your
    dogs."

[24]God, everyone can see your victory
    parade—
  the victory march of my God and King into
    his holy place![d]
[25]Singers come marching in front, followed by
    the musicians;
  they are surrounded by young girls playing
    tambourines.
[26]Praise God in the meeting place.[e]
  Praise the LORD, people of Israel!
[27]There is the smallest tribe, Benjamin, leading
    them.
  And there comes a large group of leaders
    from Judah.
  Following them are the leaders of Zebulun
    and Naphtali.

[28]God, show us your power!
  Show us the power you used for us in the
    past.
[29]Kings will bring their wealth to you,
  to your Temple in Jerusalem.
[30]Punish the people in Egypt.
  They are like cattle in the marshes, like
    bulls among the calves.
You humiliated them.
  You scattered them in war.
Now let them come crawling to you,
  bringing their pieces of silver.
[31]Messengers from Egypt will come bearing
    gifts.
  Ethiopia will offer God their tribute.

[32]Kings on earth, sing to God!
  Sing songs of praise to our Lord!   *Selah*

[33]Sing to him who rides his chariot through the
    ancient skies.
  Listen to his powerful voice!
[34]Tell everyone how powerful he is!
  He rules over Israel.
  His power fills the skies.
[35]God is awesome in his Temple!
  He is the God of Israel.
  He gives strength and power to his people.

Praise God!

---

[a] 68:10 *people* Or "animals" or "living things".
[b] 68:18 *received gifts from people* Or "took people as gifts". Or "gave gifts to people", as in the ancient Syriac and Aramaic
versions and in Eph. 4:8.
[c] 68:21 Literally, "God will smash the heads of his enemies. He will smash the hairy skull walking in guilt."
[d] 68:24 *of my God . . . holy place* Or "led by my holy God and King!"
[e] 68:26 *in the meeting place* Or "with the trumpets that announce the assembly!"

To the director: To the tune "The Lilies". A song of David.

69

God, save me from all my troubles!
    The rising water has reached my neck.
²I have nothing to stand on.
    I am sinking down, down into the mud.
I am in deep water,
    and the waves are about to cover me.
³I am getting weak from calling for help.
    My throat is sore.
I have waited and looked for your help
    until my eyes are hurting.
⁴I have more enemies than the hairs on my head.
    They hate me for no reason.
    They try hard to destroy me.
My enemies tell lies about me.
    They say I stole from them
    and they demand that I pay for things I did
      not steal.

⁵God, you know my faults.
    I cannot hide my sins from you.
⁶My Lord GOD All-Powerful, don't let me
      embarrass your followers.
    God of Israel, don't let me bring disgrace to
      those who worship you.
⁷My face is covered with shame.
    I carry this shame for you.
⁸My own brothers treat me like a stranger.
    They act as if I came from a foreign land.

⁹I am filled with anger when people dishonour
      your Temple!
    When they insult you, I feel they are
      insulting me.
¹⁰When I spend time crying and fasting,
    they make fun of me.
¹¹When I wear sackcloth to show my sorrow,
    they tell jokes about me.
¹²They talk about me in public places.
    The beer drinkers make up songs about me.

¹³As for me, LORD, this is my prayer to you:
    Please accept me!
God, I want you to answer me with love.
    I know I can trust you to save me.
¹⁴Pull me from the mud,
    and don't let me sink down deeper.
Save me from those who hate me.
    Save me from this deep water.
¹⁵Don't let the waves drown me.
    Don't let the deep sea swallow me
    or the grave close its mouth on me.

¹⁶Answer me, LORD, from the goodness of your
      faithful love.
    Out of your great kindness turn to me and
      help me!

¹⁷Don't turn away from your servant.
    I am in trouble, so hurry and help me!

INSIGHT

Many of the psalms were written during very difficult times. That's why they're so full of desperate cries for help and brutally honest declarations of defiance against their enemies.

Psalm 69

¹⁸Come and save me.
    Rescue me from my enemies.

¹⁹You know the insults I have suffered.
    You know all my enemies.
    You saw how they shamed me.
²⁰I feel the pain of their hateful words.
    They make me feel weak and helpless!
I wanted some sympathy,
    but there was none.
I waited for someone to comfort me,
    but no one came.
²¹They gave me poison, not food.
    They gave me vinegar, not wine.

²²Their tables are covered with food.
    Let their fellowship meals destroy them.
²³Let them go blind and their backs become
      weak.
²⁴Show them how angry you are.
    Let them feel what your anger can do.
²⁵Make their homes empty.
    Don't let anyone live there.
²⁶They try to hurt people you have already
      punished.
    They tell everyone about the suffering you
      gave them.
²⁷Punish them for the bad things they have done.
    Don't show them how good you can be.
²⁸Erase their names from the book of life.
    Take them off the list of those who do what
      is right.

²⁹I am sad and hurting.
    God, lift me up and save me!

³⁰I will praise God's name in song.
    I will honour him by giving him thanks.
³¹The LORD will be happier with this
    than with the offering of an ox or a
      full-grown bull as a sacrifice.
³²Poor people, you came to worship God.
    You will be happy to know these things.

33The LORD listens to poor, helpless people.
 He does not turn away from those who are
   in prison.

34Praise him, heaven and earth!
 Sea and everything in it, praise him!
35God will save Zion.
 He will rebuild the cities of Judah.
 The people will settle there again,
   and they will own the land.
36The descendants of his servants will get that
   land.
 Those who love his name will live there.

To the director: A song of David to help people remember.

70
Please, God, rescue me!
 LORD, hurry and help me!
2People are trying to kill me.
 Please disappoint them.
 Humiliate them!
 They want to hurt me.
 Make them run away in shame.
3May those who make fun of me
 be too embarrassed to speak.
4But may those who come to you
 be happy and rejoice.
 May those who love being saved by you
   always be able to say, "God is great!"

5I am only a poor, helpless man.
 God, please hurry to me.
 You are my helper, the one who can save me.
 LORD, don't be too late!

71
LORD, I depend on you for protection.
 Don't let me be disappointed.
2You always do what is right, so come and
   save me.
 Listen to me and save me.
3Be my Rock, my place of safety.
 Be my fortress, and protect me!
 You are my Rock and my protection.
4My God, save me from wicked people.
 Save me from cruel, evil people.
5Lord GOD, you are my hope.
 I have trusted in you since I was a young
   boy.
6I depended on you even before I was born.
 I relied on you even in my mother's womb.
 I have always prayed to you.ᵃ

7People look at my life as an example to follow
 because you have been my source of
   strength,

8I never stop praising you.
 All day long I tell people how wonderful
   you are.
9Don't throw me away just because I am old.
 Don't leave me as I lose my strength.
10My enemies are talking about me.
 They come together and make plans to kill
   me.
11They say, "Go and get him!
 God has left him, so there is no one to help
   him."

12God, don't leave me!
 My God, hurry and help me!
13Defeat my enemies.
 Destroy them completely!
 They are trying to hurt me.
 Let them suffer shame and disgrace.
14Then I will always trust in you
 and praise you more and more.
15I will tell people how good you are.
 I will tell about all the times you saved
   me—
 too many times to count.
16I will tell about your greatness, my Lord
   GOD.
 I will talk only about you and your
   goodness.

17God, you have taught me since I was a young
   boy.
 And to this day I have told people about the
   wonderful things you do.
18Now that I am old and grey,
 don't leave me, God.
 I must tell the next generation
 about your power and greatness.

19God, your goodness reaches far above the
   skies.
 You have done wonderful things.
 God, there is no one like you.
20You have let me see troubles and hard times,
 but you will give me new life;
 you will lift me up from this pit of death!
21You will help me do even greater things.
 You will comfort me again!

22I will sing and honour you with a harp, my
   God,
 because you always do what you promise.
 I will play my lyre and sing praise to you,
   the Holy One of Israel.
23I will shout for joy,
 singing songs of praise to you for saving me.

ᵃ **71:6 prayed to you** Or "praised you".

²⁴My tongue will sing about your goodness all
the time,
because those who wanted to kill me
have been defeated and disgraced.

To Solomon.[a]

72 God, help the king to be like you and
make fair decisions.
Help the king's son know what justice is.
²Help the king judge your people fairly.
Help him make wise decisions for your poor
people.
³Let there be peace and justice throughout the
land,
known on every mountain and hill.
⁴May the king be fair to the poor.
May he help the helpless and punish those
who hurt them.

⁵May people always fear and respect you, God,
as long as the sun shines and the moon is in
the sky.
⁶Help the king be like rain falling on the fields,
like showers falling on the land.
⁷Let goodness grow everywhere while he is
king.
Let peace continue as long as there is a moon.

⁸Let his kingdom grow from sea to sea,
from the Euphrates River to the faraway
places on earth.[b]
⁹May all the people living in the desert bow
down to him.
May all his enemies bow before him with
their faces in the dirt.
¹⁰May the kings of Tarshish and all the faraway
lands by the sea bring gifts to him.
May the kings of Sheba and Seba bring their
tribute to him.
¹¹May all kings bow down to our king.
May all nations serve him.

¹²Our king helps the poor who cry out to
him—
those in need who have no one to help
them.
¹³He feels sorry for all who are weak and poor.
He protects their lives.
¹⁴He saves them from the cruel people who try
to hurt them.
Their lives are important to him.

¹⁵Long live the king!
Let him receive gold from Sheba.
Always pray for the king.
Ask God to bless him every day.
¹⁶May the fields grow plenty of grain
and the hills be covered with crops.
May the fields be as fertile as Lebanon,
and may people fill the cities as grass covers
a field.
¹⁷May the king be famous forever.
May people remember his name as long as
the sun shines.
May all nations be blessed through him,
and may they all bless him.

¹⁸Praise the LORD God, the God of Israel!
Only he can do such amazing things.
¹⁹Praise his glorious name forever!
Let his glory fill the whole world.
Amen and Amen!

²⁰This ends the prayers of David son of Jesse.

BOOK 3
(Psalms 73–89)

Asaph's song of praise.

73 God is so good to Israel,
to those whose hearts are pure.
²But I almost slipped and lost my balance.
I almost fell into sin.
³I saw that wicked people were successful,
and I became jealous of those proud people.

⁴They are healthy.
They don't have to struggle to survive.[c]
⁵They don't suffer like the rest of us.
They don't have troubles like other people.
⁶So they are proud and hateful.
This is as easy to see as the jewels and fancy
clothes they wear.
⁷If they see something they like, they go and
take it.
They do whatever they want.
⁸They make fun of others and say cruel things
about them.
In their pride they make plans to hurt
people.
⁹They think they are gods!
They think they are the rulers of the earth.
¹⁰[d] Even God's people turn to them
and do what they say.

---

a **Psalm 72** *To Solomon* This might mean that this song was written by Solomon or dedicated to him, or that it is from some
special collection of songs.
b **72:8** *faraway places on earth* This usually means the countries around the Mediterranean Sea.
c **73:4** Literally, "They have no bonds to their death."
d **73:10** The Hebrew text is not clear.

WHAT ON EARTH COULD I WANT?

William's parents worked for the church. They didn't have much money and William always felt a little jealous of his friends who had more. When he was seventeen he learnt to drive, but he couldn't afford to buy a car. Loads of his mates had cars and other great gear but William knew they didn't really belong to them. His mates stole and did other things dishonestly to be able to afford the best new gadgets. William was beginning to wonder what the point was of living for Jesus when it meant he could never have new and expensive things.

DIG IN

READ Psalm 73:1–28

- In verse 2 the psalmist says he almost sins, why is this (v.3)?
- What is it about the wicked that makes the psalmist jealous (vv.3–12)?
- Why does this upset him (vv.4,13–14)?

The psalmist, like William, looks at the wicked and sees that they get richer and richer. They do what they want, they're successful and have loads of nice stuff, whilst he tries to do what's good and love God, and yet is suffering and struggling – it's not fair!

- What does the psalmist do and where does he get answers (vv.15–20)?

He didn't want to speak to others about his questions for fear he might discourage them but it all became too hard for him. However, when he went to the Temple (church) he found the wisdom he so desperately needed.

- What is the problem for the wicked (vv.18–19)?
- How awful is the situation for them (v.20)?

There is no security for the wicked. When terrible things happen, they have nowhere to go. And when they die, they are finished, they disappear. They are described like a terrible dream – almost as if they are unreal, they do not count for anything as far as God is concerned.

- In contrast, what does God do for his people (vv.22–24)?
- What does the psalmist realize is most important in life (vv.25–28)?

What a great realization! He sees that whilst the wicked might have everything materially, the psalmist is "held" by God and when he dies he will go to heaven. He doesn't need anything else! It doesn't matter what happens to him in this life: God is his forever. All he needs is God – there is no other place of safety.

DIG THROUGH

- Re-read verse 25. Can you say that? Ask God to help you to treasure him above everything else.
- Ask God to help you remember that those who do not love him will be destroyed – it does not matter how great their lives look now.
- What would you say to William?

DIG DEEPER

- This psalm can be classed as a "wisdom psalm" – it gives guidance about how to feel, think and act in God's world. Have a look at other similar psalms: 37, 49 and 112.

11Those evil people say, "God does not know
    what we are doing!
God Most High does not know!"

12Those proud people are wicked,
    but they are rich and getting richer.
13Clearly, then, I gain nothing by keeping my
        thoughts pure!
    What good is it to keep myself from sin?
14God, I suffer all day long,
    and you punish me every morning.

15I wanted to tell others these things,
    but that would have made me a traitor to
        your people.
16I tried hard to understand all this,
    but it was too hard for me.
17But then, God, I went to your Temple,
    and I understood what will happen to the
        wicked.
18Clearly, you have put them in danger.
    You make it easy for them to fall and be
        destroyed.
19Trouble can come suddenly,
    and they will be ruined.
Terrible things can happen to them,
    and they will be finished.
20Then they will be like a dream
    that we forget when we wake up.
You will make them disappear
    like the monsters in our dreams.

21I let thoughts about such people upset me.
    I was always angry.
22I was so stupid and ignorant.
    I was like an animal in the way I treated
        you.
23But I am always with you.
    You hold my hand.
24You lead me and give me good advice,
    and later you will lead me to glory.[a]
25In heaven, God, I have only you.
    And if I am with you, what on earth could I
        want?
26Maybe my mind[b] and body will become
        weak,
    but God is my source of strength.[c]
He is mine forever!

27God, people who leave you will be lost.
    You will destroy all who are not faithful
        to you.

28As for me, all I need is to be close to God.
    I have made the Lord GOD my place of
        safety.
And, God, I will tell about all that you have
    done.

A maskil of Asaph.

74

God, why have you turned away from us
    for so long?
Why are you still angry with us, your own
    flock?
2Remember the people you bought so long ago.
    You saved us, and we belong to you.
And remember Mount Zion, the place
    where you lived.
3God, come and walk through these ancient
        ruins.
Come back to the Holy Place that the
    enemy destroyed.

4The enemy shouted their war cries in the
        Temple.
    They put up their flags there to show they
        had won the war.
5Their soldiers attacked the doors,
    like workmen chopping down trees.
6Using axes and hatchets,
    they smashed the carved panels inside.
7They burned down your Holy Place.
It was built to honour your name,
    but they pulled it down to the ground.
8The enemy decided to crush us completely.
    They burned every holy place[d] in the
        country.
9We do not see any of our signs.[e]
    There are no more prophets.
And no one knows how long this will last.
10God, how much longer will the enemy make
        fun of us?
    Will you let them insult your name
        forever?
11Why won't you help us?
    Use your power to defeat our enemies!

12God, you have been our King for a long
        time.
    You have saved us many times on this
        earth.
13With your great power you split open
        the sea
    and broke the heads of the sea monster.

---

[a] **73:24 lead me to glory** Or "receive me in honour".
[b] **73:26 mind** Literally, "heart".
[c] **73:26 my . . . strength** Literally, "the Rock of my heart".
[d] **74:8 holy place** Or "El meeting place". This means every place where people went to meet with God.
[e] **74:9 signs** These were probably signal fires that people burned as a way of passing messages from one town to the next. In war, this was a way people showed other towns that the enemy had not yet destroyed their own town.

¹⁴Yes, you smashed the heads of Leviathan^a
    and left his body for animals to eat.
¹⁵You make the springs and rivers flow,
    and you make the rivers dry up.
¹⁶You control the day and the night.
    You made the sun and the moon.
¹⁷You set the limits for everything on earth.
    And you created summer and winter.

¹⁸Lord, remember, the enemy insulted you!
    Those foolish people hate your name!
¹⁹Don't give us like a helpless dove to those wild
        animals.
    Never forget your poor, suffering people.
²⁰Remember the agreement you gave us,
    because violence fills every dark place in
        this land.

²¹Your people were treated badly.
    Don't let them be hurt any more.
    Let your poor, helpless people praise you.

²²God, get up and defend yourself!
    Remember, those fools challenged you.
²³Don't forget the shouts of your enemies.
    They insulted you again and again.

To the director: To the tune "Do Not Destroy".
One of Asaph's songs of praise.

75

We praise you, God!
We praise you because you^b are near
    to us.
We tell about the amazing things you have
    done.

²God says, "I have chosen a time for
        judgement,
    and I will judge fairly.
³The earth and all its people may shake,
    but I am the one who keeps it steady.
                                    Selah

⁴"To those who are proud I say, 'Stop your
        boasting.'
    I warn the wicked, 'Don't boast about how
        strong you are.
⁵Don't be so sure that you will win.
    Don't boast that victory is yours!'"

⁶There is no power on earth
    that can decide what will happen.^c

⁷God is the judge.
    He decides who will be important.
    He lifts one person up and brings another
        down.
⁸The Lord has a cup in his hand.
    It is filled with the poisoned wine of his anger.
    He will pour out this wine,
        and the wicked will drink it to the last drop.

⁹I will always tell people how great God is.
    I will sing praise to the God of Jacob.
¹⁰God says, "I will take away any power the
        wicked have
    and give it to those who are good."

To the director: With instruments.
One of Asaph's songs of praise.

76

People in Judah know God.
People in Israel respect his name.
²His Temple is in Salem.^d
    His house is on Mount Zion.
³There he shattered the arrows,
    shields, swords and other weapons of war.
                                    Selah

⁴God, you are glorious coming back
    from the hills where you defeated your
        enemies.
⁵They thought they were strong, but now they
        lie dead in the fields.
    Their bodies are stripped of all they owned.
    They could not defend themselves.^e
⁶The God of Jacob shouted at them,
    and their army of chariots and horses fell
        dead.
⁷God, you are awesome!
    No one can stand against you when you are
        angry.
⁸You stood as judge and announced your
        decision.
    You saved the humble people of the land.
⁹From heaven you gave the decision,
    and the whole earth was silent and afraid.

¹⁰Even human anger can bring you honour
    when you use it to punish your enemies.^f

¹¹People, you made promises to the Lord your
        God.
    Now give him what you promised.

---

^a **74:13–14** *sea monster . . . Leviathan* These were creatures from ancient stories. People believed that they kept the world
from being a safe, orderly place. So this verse means that God controls every part of the world and everything in it.
^b **75:1** *you* Literally, "your name".
^c **75:6** Literally, "Not from the east or the west and not from the desert mountains."
^d **76:2** *Salem* Another name for Jerusalem. This name means "Peace".
^e **76:5** *They . . . themselves* Literally, "The warriors could not find their hands."
^f **76:7–10** The Hebrew text is not clear.

People everywhere fear and respect God,
and they will bring gifts to him.
¹²God defeats great leaders;
all the kings on earth fear him.

To the director, Jeduthun.ᵃ One of Asaph's songs.

77 I cry out to God for help.
I cry out to you, God; listen to me!
²My Lord, in my time of trouble I came to you.
I reached out for you all night long.
My soul refused to be comforted.
³I thought about you, God,
and tried to tell you how I felt, but
I could not.   *Selah*

⁴You would not let me sleep.
I tried to say something, but I was too
upset.
⁵I kept thinking about the past,
about things that happened long ago.
⁶During the night, I thought about my songs.
I talked to myself, trying to understand
what was happening.
⁷I wondered, "Has our Lord rejected us forever?
Will he ever accept us again?
⁸Has his love gone forever?
Will he never again speak to us?
⁹Has God forgotten what mercy is?
Has his compassion changed to anger?"   *Selah*

¹⁰Then I said, "What bothers me most is the
thought
that the power of God Most High is no
longer there for us."

¹¹Lord, I remember what you have done.
I remember the amazing things you did
long ago.
¹²I think about those things.
I think about them all the time.

¹³God, all that you do is holy.
No god is as great as you are.
¹⁴You are the God who does amazing things.
You showed the nations your great power.
¹⁵By your power you saved your people,
the descendants of Jacob and Joseph.   *Selah*

¹⁶God, the water saw you and became afraid.
The deep water shook with fear.
¹⁷The thick clouds dropped their water.
Thunder roared in the sky above.
Your arrows of lightning flashed through the
clouds.

¹⁸There were loud claps of thunder.
Lightning lit up the world.
The earth shook and trembled.
¹⁹You walked through the water and crossed the
deep sea,
but you left no footprints.
²⁰You led your people like sheep,
using Moses and Aaron to guide them.

A maskil of Asaph.

78 My people, listen to my teachings.
Listen to what I say.
²I will tell you a story.
I will tell you about things from the past
that are hard to understand.
³We have heard the story and know it well.
Our fathers told it to us.
⁴And we will not forget to tell it to our
children.
We will tell those who come after us.
We will all praise the Lord
and tell about the amazing things he did.

⁵He made an agreement with Jacob.
He gave the Law to Israel.
And he commanded our ancestors
to teach it to their children.
⁶Then all the children born to them would
know the law
and teach it to their own children.
⁷This would make them all trust in God,
helping them to never forget what he had
done
and to always obey his commands.
⁸They would not be like their ancestors,
who were stubborn and refused to obey.
Their hearts were not devoted to God,
and they were not faithful to him.

⁹The men from Ephraim had their weapons,
but they ran from the battle.
¹⁰They did not keep their agreement with God.
They refused to obey his teachings.
¹¹They forgot the great things he had done
and the amazing things he had shown
them.
¹²While their ancestors watched,
he showed his great power at Zoan in
Egypt.
¹³He split the Red Sea and led the people across.
The water stood like a solid wall on both
sides of them.
¹⁴Each day God led them with the tall cloud,
and each night he led them with the light
from the column of fire.

ᵃ **Psalm 77** *Jeduthun* Or "and to Jeduthun", one of the three main temple musicians. See 1 Chr. 9:16; 16:38–42.

¹⁵He split the rocks in the desert
  and gave them an ocean of fresh water.
¹⁶He brought a stream of water out of the rock
  and made it flow like a river!

¹⁷But they continued sinning against him.
  They rebelled against God Most High in the
    desert.
¹⁸Then they decided to test God
  by telling him to give them the food they
    wanted.
¹⁹They complained about him and said,
  "Can God give us food in the desert?
²⁰Yes, he struck the rock and a flood of water
    came out.
  But can he give us bread and meat?"
²¹The LORD heard what they said,
  and he became angry with Jacob's people.
  He was angry with Israel
²²because they did not trust in him.
  They did not believe that God could save
    them.
²³But then God commanded the clouds to part
  like doors opening in the sky.
²⁴And he poured down manna for them to eat,
  like grain coming down from heaven.
²⁵So they ate the food of angels.
  God sent them all that they could eat.
²⁶He sent a strong wind from the east,
  and by his power he made the south
    wind blow.
²⁷He made quail fall like rain until they covered
    the ground.
  There were so many birds that they were
    like sand on the seashore.
²⁸The birds fell in the middle of the camp,
  all around their tents.
²⁹The people ate until they were full.
  God had given them what they wanted.
³⁰But before they were fully satisfied,
  while the food was still in their mouths,
³¹God became angry and killed even the
    strongest of them.
  He brought down Israel's best young men.

³²But the people continued to sin!
  They did not trust in the amazing things
    God could do.
³³So he ended their worthless lives;
  he brought their years to a close with
    disaster.
³⁴When he killed some of them, the others
    would turn back to him.
  They would come running back to God.
³⁵They would remember that God was their
    Rock.

They would remember that God Most High
    protected them.
³⁶But they tried to fool him with their words;
  they told him lies.
³⁷Their hearts were not really with him.
  They were not faithful to the agreement he
    gave them.
³⁸But God was merciful.
  He forgave their sins and did not destroy
    them.
  Many times he held back his anger.
  He never let it get out of control.
³⁹He remembered that they were only
    people,
  like a wind that blows and then is gone.

⁴⁰Oh, they caused him so much trouble in the
    desert!
  They made him so sad.
⁴¹Again and again they tested his patience.
  They really hurt the Holy One of Israel.
⁴²They forgot about his power.
  They forgot the many times he saved them
    from the enemy.
⁴³They forgot the miracles in Egypt,
  the miracles in the fields of Zoan.
⁴⁴God turned the rivers into blood,
  and the Egyptians could not drink the
    water.
⁴⁵He sent swarms of flies that bit them.
  He sent the frogs that ruined their lives.
⁴⁶He gave their crops to grasshoppers
  and their other plants to locusts.
⁴⁷He destroyed their vines with hail
  and their trees with sleet.
⁴⁸He killed their animals with hail
  and their cattle with lightning.
⁴⁹He showed the Egyptians his anger.
  He sent his destroying angels against them.
⁵⁰He found a way to show his anger.
  He did not spare their lives.
  He let them die with a deadly disease.
⁵¹He killed all the firstborn sons in Egypt.
  He killed every firstborn in Ham's[a] family.
⁵²Then he led Israel like a shepherd.
  He led his people like sheep into the desert.
⁵³He guided them safely.
  They had nothing to fear.
  He drowned their enemies in the sea.
⁵⁴He led his people to his holy land,
  to the mountain he took with his own
    power.
⁵⁵He forced the other nations out before
    them
  and gave each family its share of the land.
  He gave each tribe of Israel a place to live.

---

[a] **78:51** *Ham* The Egyptians were Ham's descendants. See Gen. 10:6–10.

56But they tested God Most High and made him
　　very sad.
　　They didn't obey his commands.
57They turned against him and were unfaithful
　　just like their ancestors.
　　They changed directions like a boomerang.
58They built high places and made God
　　angry.
　　They built statues of false gods and made
　　him jealous.
59God heard what they were doing and became
　　very angry.
　　So he rejected Israel completely!
60He abandoned his place at Shiloh,ᵃ
　　the Holy Tent where he lived among the
　　people.
61He let foreigners capture the Box of the
　　Agreement,
　　the symbol of his power and glory.
62He showed his anger against his people
　　and let them be killed in war.
63Their young men were burned to death,
　　and there were no wedding songs for their
　　young women.
64Their priests were killed,
　　but the widows had no time to mourn for
　　them.

65Finally, our Lord got up
　　like a man waking from his sleep,
　　like a soldier after drinking too much
　　wine.
66He forced his enemies to turn back
　　defeated.
　　He brought them shame that will last
　　forever.
67Then he rejected Joseph's family.
　　He did not accept Ephraim's family.
68No, he chose the tribe of Judah,
　　and he chose Mount Zion, the place he
　　loves.
69He built his holy Temple high on that
　　mountain.
　　Like the earth, God built his Temple to last
　　forever.
70He chose David to be his special servant
　　and took him from the sheep pens.
71God took him away from the job of caring for
　　sheep.
　　And he gave him the work of leading his
　　people,
　　Israel, the descendants of Jacob.
72And David led them with a pure heart
　　and guided them very wisely.

One of Asaph's songs of praise.

79 God, some people from other nations
　　came to fight your people.
　　They ruined your holy Temple.
　　They left Jerusalem in ruins.
2They left the bodies of your servants for the
　　wild birds to eat.
　　They let wild animals eat the bodies of your
　　followers.
3Blood flowed like water all over Jerusalem.
　　No one is left to bury the bodies.
4The countries around us insult us.
　　The people around us laugh at us and make
　　fun of us.

5LORD, will you be angry with us forever?
　　Will your strong feelingsᵇ continue to burn
　　like a fire?
6Turn your anger against the nations that do
　　not know you,
　　against the people who do not honour you
　　as God.
7Those nations killed Jacob's family
　　and destroyed their land.
8Please don't punish us for the sins of our
　　ancestors.
　　Hurry, show us your mercy!
　　We need you so much!
9Our God and Saviour, help us!
　　That will bring glory to your name.
　　Save us and forgive our sins
　　for the good of your name.
10Don't give the other nations a reason to say,
　　"Where is their God? Can't he help them?"
　　Let us see you punish those people.
　　Punish them for killing your servants.
11Listen to the sad cries of the prisoners!
　　Use your great power to free those who are
　　sentenced to die.

12Punish the nations around us!
　　Pay them back seven times for what they
　　did to us.
　　Punish them for insulting you.
13We are your people, the sheep of your flock.
　　We will praise you forever.
　　We will praise you for ever and ever!

To the director: To the tune "Lilies of the Agreement".
One of Asaph's songs of praise.

80 Shepherd of Israel, listen to us.
　　You lead your peopleᶜ like sheep.

ᵇ **78:60 place at Shiloh** See 1 Sam. 4:4–11; Jer. 7:17.
ᵇ **79:5 strong feelings** The Hebrew word can mean any strong feelings such as zeal, jealousy or love.
ᶜ **80:1 your people** Literally, "Joseph", the father of Ephraim and Manasseh, whose names are often used to mean all the tribes in
northern Israel.

You sit on your throne above the winged
creatures.
Let us see you.
[2]Shepherd of Israel, show your greatness to
the tribes of Ephraim, Benjamin and
Manasseh.
Come and save your people.

[3]God, accept us again.
Smile down on us and save us!

[4]Lord God All-Powerful, when will you listen
to our prayers?
How long will you be angry with us?
[5]Instead of bread and water,
you gave your people tears.
[6]You made us the target of everyone's hatred.
Our enemies make fun of us.

[7]God All-Powerful, accept us again.
Smile down on us and save us!

[8]When you brought us out of Egypt,
we were like your special vine.
You forced other nations to leave this land,
and you planted that vine here.
[9]You prepared the ground for it,
and it sent its roots down deep and spread
throughout the land.
[10]It covered the mountains,
and its leaves shaded even the giant cedar
trees.
[11]Its branches spread to the Mediterranean Sea,
and its shoots spread east to the Euphrates
River.

[12]God, why did you pull down the walls that
protect your vine?
Now everyone who passes by picks its grapes.
[13]Wild pigs come and ruin it.
Wild animals eat the leaves.

[14]God All-Powerful, come back.
Look down from heaven at your vine and
protect it.
[15]Look at the vine you planted with your own
hands.
Look at the young plant[a] you raised.
[16]Our enemies have cut it down and burned it up.
Show them how angry you are and destroy
them.

[17]Reach out and help your chosen one.[b]
Reach out to the people[c] you raised up.
[18]Then we will never leave you.
Let us live, and we will worship you.
[19]Lord God All-Powerful, accept us again.
Smile down on us and save us!

To the director: On the gittith. One of Asaph's songs.

81 Be happy and sing to God, our strength.
Shout with joy to the God of Jacob.
[2]Begin the music.
Play the tambourines.
Play the pleasant harps and lyres.
[3]Blow the ram's horn at the time of the new
moon[d]
and at the time of the full moon,[e] when our
festival begins.
[4]This is the law for the people of Israel.
The God of Jacob gave the command.
[5]God made this agreement with Joseph's people,
when he led them out of Egypt.

In a voice I had never heard before, God said,
[6]"I took the load from your shoulder.
I let you drop the worker's basket.
[7]When you were in trouble, you called for help
and I set you free.
I was hidden in the storm clouds, and I
answered you.
I tested you by the water at Meribah."[f] *Selah*

[8]"My people, I am warning you.
Israel, listen to me!
[9]Don't worship any of the false gods
that the foreigners worship.
[10]I, the Lord, am your God.
I brought you out of Egypt.
Israel, open your mouth,
and I will feed you.

[11]"But my people did not listen to me.
Israel did not obey me.
[12]So I let them go their own stubborn way
and do whatever they wanted.
[13]If my people would listen to me
and live the way I want,
[14]I would defeat their enemies
and punish those who cause them trouble.
[15]Those who hate the Lord would shake with fear.
They would be punished forever.

---

[a] **80:15 young plant** Literally, "son".
[b] **80:17 chosen one** Literally, "the man of your right hand".
[c] **80:17 people** Literally, "son of man".
[d] **81:3 new moon** The first day of the Hebrew month. There were special meetings on these days when the people shared
fellowship offerings as part of their worship to God.
[e] **81:3 full moon** The middle of the Hebrew month. Many of the special meetings and festivals started at the time of a full moon.
[f] **81:7 Meribah** See Exod. 17:1–7.

16I would give the best wheat to my people.
　　I would give them the purest honey, until
　　　they were satisfied."

One of Asaph's songs of praise.

82 God stands in the assembly of the gods.*a*
　　He stands as judge among the judges.
2He says, "How long will you judge unfairly
　　and show special favours to the wicked?"
　　　　　　　　　　　　　　　　Selah

3"Defend the poor and orphans.
　　Protect the rights of the poor.
4Help those who are poor and helpless.
　　Save them from those who are evil.

5"They*b* don't know what is happening.
　　They don't understand!
They don't know what they are doing.
　　Their world is falling down around them!"
6I, God Most High, say,
　　"You are gods,*c* my own sons.
7But you will die as all people must die.
　　Your life will end like that of any ruler."

8Get up, God! You be the judge!
　　You be the leader over all the nations!

One of Asaph's songs of praise.

83 God, don't keep quiet!
　　Don't close your ears!
　　Please say something, God.
2Your enemies are getting ready to do
　　something.
　　Those who hate you will soon attack.
3They are making secret plans against your
　　people.
　　Your enemies are discussing plans against
　　　the people you love.
4They say, "Come, let us destroy them
　　completely.
　　Then no one will ever again remember the
　　　name Israel."
5God, they have all joined together.
　　They have united against you.
6–7Their army includes the Edomites, Ishmaelites,
　　Moabites and Hagar's descendants,
　　the people of Byblos, Ammon and Amalek,
　　the Philistines and the people of Tyre.

8Even the Assyrians have joined them.
　　They have made Lot's descendants very
　　　powerful.   *Selah*

9God, defeat them just as you defeated Midian.
　　Do what you did to Sisera and Jabin at the
　　　Kishon River.
10You destroyed the enemy at Endor,
　　and their bodies rotted on the ground.
11Punish their leaders as you did Oreb and Zeeb.
　　Do what you did to Zebah and Zalmunna.
12They said, "Let's make this land our own—
　　these fields of grass that belong to God!"
13Make them like weeds blown by the wind.
　　Scatter them the way wind scatters straw.
14Be like a fire that destroys a forest
　　or like a flame that sets the hills on fire.
15Chase them away with your blasts of wind;
　　frighten them with your storms.
16LORD, cover them with shame
　　until they come to you for help.
17May they be forever ashamed and afraid.
　　Disgrace and defeat them.
18Then they will know that your name is
　　YAHWEH—
　　that you alone are the LORD.
They will know that you are God Most High,
　　ruler over all the earth!

To the director: On the gittith.
A song of praise from the Korah family.

84 LORD All-Powerful,
　　the place where you live is so beautiful!
2LORD, I cannot wait to enter your Temple.
　　I am so excited!
Every part of me cries out
　　to be with the Living God.
3LORD All-Powerful, my King, my God,
　　even the birds have found a home in your
　　　Temple.
They make their nests near your altar,
　　and there they have their babies.
4Great blessings belong to those who live at
　　your Temple!
　　They continue to praise you.   *Selah*

5Great blessings belong to those who depend
　　on you for strength!
　　Their heart's desire is to make the journey
　　to your Temple.

---

a **82:1 assembly of the gods** Other nations taught that El (God) and the other gods met together to decide what to do with the people on earth. But many times kings and leaders were also called "gods". So this psalm may be God's warning to the leaders of Israel.
b **82:5 They** This might mean that the poor don't understand what is happening. Or it might mean that the "gods" or leaders don't understand that they are ruining the world by not being fair and by not doing what is right.
c **82:6 gods** Or "judges".

⁶They travel through Baca Valley,
  which God has made into a place of
    springs.
  Autumn rains form pools of water there.
⁷The people travel from town to town[a]
  on their way to Zion, where they will meet
    with God.

⁸LORD God All-Powerful, listen to my prayer.
  God of Jacob, listen to me.   *Selah*

⁹God, watch over the king, our protector.[b]
  Be kind to him, your chosen king.[c]

¹⁰One day in your Temple is better
  than a thousand days anywhere else.
  Serving as a guard at the gate of my God's
    house is better
  than living in the homes of the wicked.
¹¹The LORD God is our protector and glorious
    king.[d]
  He blesses us with kindness and honour.
  The LORD freely gives every good thing
  to those who do what is right.
¹²LORD All-Powerful,
  great blessings belong to those who trust
    in you!

To the director: A song of praise from the Korah family.

85 LORD, you have been so kind to your
      land.
  You have brought success again to the
    people of Jacob.
²You have forgiven the bad things your
    people did.
  You have taken away the guilt of their sins!
                                        Selah

³You stopped being angry with them.
  Your terrible anger has gone away.

⁴Our God and Saviour, accept us again.
  Don't be angry with us any more.
⁵Will you be angry with us forever?
  Will your anger reach to our children and to
    their children?
⁶Please, give us new life!
  Make your people happy to be yours.
⁷LORD, save us
  and show us your love.

⁸I heard what the LORD God said.
  He said there would be peace for his people
    and his loyal followers.
  So they must not go back to their foolish
    way of living.
⁹He will soon save his faithful followers.
  His glory will again live in our land.[e]
¹⁰God's love will come together with his faithful
    people.
  Goodness and peace will greet them with
    a kiss.
¹¹People on earth will be loyal to God,
  and God in heaven will be good to them.[f]
¹²The LORD will give us many good things.
  The ground will grow many good crops.
¹³Goodness will go before the Lord
  and prepare the way for him.

A prayer of David.

86 I am a poor, helpless man.
      LORD, please listen to me and answer my
      prayer!
²I am your follower, so please protect me.
  I am your servant, and you are my God.
  I trust in you, so save me.
³My Lord, be kind to me.
  I have been praying to you all day.
⁴My Lord, I put my life in your hands.
  I am your servant, so make me happy.
⁵My Lord, you are good and merciful.
  You love all those who call to you for help.
⁶LORD, hear my prayer.
  Listen to my cry for mercy.
⁷I am praying to you in my time of trouble.
  I know you will answer me.

⁸My Lord, there is no God like you.
  No one can do what you have done.
⁹My Lord, you made everyone.
  I wish they all would come and worship
    you and honour your name.
¹⁰You are great and do amazing things.
  You and you alone are God.

¹¹LORD, teach me your ways,
  and I will live and obey your truths.
  Help me make worshipping your name
    the most important thing in my life.
¹²My Lord God, I praise you with all my heart.
  I will honour your name forever!

---

[a] **84:7** *town to town* Or "wall to wall".
[b] **84:9** *the king, our protector* Literally, "our shield". This line could also mean "God, our Shield, look!"
[c] **84:9** *chosen king* Literally, "anointed one". This might be anyone God chose to serve in a special way, but it is usually the king he has chosen. Also in 89:38,51.
[d] **84:11** *protector and glorious king* Literally, "sun and shield".
[e] **85:9** *His . . . land* Or "We will soon live with honour in our land."
[f] **85:11** Literally, "Loyalty will sprout from the ground, and goodness will look down from the sky."

¹³You have such great love for me.
  You save me from the place of death.

¹⁴Proud people are attacking me, God.
  A gang of cruel men is trying to kill me.
  They don't respect you.
¹⁵My Lord, you are a kind and merciful God.
  You are patient, loyal and full of love.
¹⁶Show that you hear me and be kind to me.
  I am your servant, so give me strength.
  I am your slave, as my mother was, so
    save me!
¹⁷Lord, show me a sign that you care for me.
  My enemies will see it and be disappointed,
  because you helped and comforted me.

A song of praise from the Korah family.

87 The Lord built his city on the holy hills.
  ²He loves the gates of Zion more than
    any other place in Israel.
³City of God,
  We hear such wonderful things about you!
                                                Selah

⁴God says, "Some of my people live in Egypt^a
    and Babylon.
  Some of them were born in Philistia, Tyre
    and even Ethiopia."
⁵But about Zion he says,
  "I know each and every person born there."
  It is the city built by God Most High.
⁶The Lord keeps a list of all his people,
  and he knows where each of them was
    born.   *Selah*

⁷At the festivals, people will dance and sing,
  "All good things come from Zion."

*A song from the Korah family. To the director: About a painful
  sickness. A maskil of Heman the Ezrahite.*

88 Lord God, you are my Saviour.
  I have been praying to you day and night.
²Please pay attention to my prayers.
  Listen to my prayers for mercy.

³My soul has had enough of this pain!
  I am ready to die.
⁴People already treat me like a dead man,
  like someone too weak to live.
⁵Look for me among the dead,
  like a body in the grave.
  I am one of those you have forgotten,
  cut off from you and your care.

⁶You put me in that hole in the ground.
  Yes, you put me in that dark place.
⁷Your anger presses down on me like a heavy
    weight.
  It's like one wave after another pounding
    against me.   *Selah*

⁸You made my friends leave me.
  They all avoid me like someone no one
    wants to touch.
  Like a prisoner in my house, I cannot go out.
    ⁹My eyes hurt from crying.
  Lord, I pray to you constantly!
  I lift my arms in prayer to you.

¹⁰Do you do miracles for the dead?
  Do ghosts rise up and praise you? No!
                                                Selah

¹¹The dead in their graves cannot talk about
    your faithful love.
  People in the world of the dead^b cannot
    talk about your faithfulness.
¹²The dead who lie in darkness cannot see the
    amazing things you do.
  Those in the world of the forgotten cannot
    talk about your goodness.

¹³Lord, I am asking you to help me!
  Early each morning I pray to you.
¹⁴Lord, why have you abandoned me?
  Why do you refuse to listen to me?
¹⁵I have been sick and weak since I was young.
  I have suffered your anger, and I am helpless.
¹⁶Your anger covers me like a flood.
  Your attacks are killing me.
¹⁷They surround me on every side.
  I feel like a drowning man.
¹⁸You caused my friends and loved ones to
    leave me.
  Now darkness is my closest friend.

INSIGHT

*This is the only psalm written by Ethan
the Ezrahite. It speaks of trusting in
the Lord's faithfulness despite difficult
circumstances. Despite the chaos all
about he knows that God is all-powerful
and is in control.*

Psalm 89

---

^a **87:4** *Egypt* Literally, "Rahab". This name means the "Dragon". It became a popular name for Egypt.
^b **88:11** *the world of the dead* Or "Abaddon", a Hebrew name meaning "death" or "destruction". See Rev. 9:11.

89 I will sing forever about the LORD's love.
I will sing about his faithfulness for ever
and ever!
²I will say, "Your faithful love will last forever.
Your loyalty is like the sky—there is no end
to it!"
³You said, "I made an agreement with my
chosen king.
I made this promise to my servant David:
⁴'There will always be someone from your
family to rule.
I will make your kingdom continue for ever
and ever.'" *Selah*

⁵LORD, the heavens praise you for the amazing
things you do.
The assembly of holy ones sings about your
loyalty.
⁶No one in heaven is equal to the LORD.
None of the "gods" can compare to the
LORD.
⁷When God's holy ones—the angels around his
throne—meet together,
they fear and respect him;
he is more awesome than all those around
him.
⁸LORD God All-Powerful, there is no one like
you.
You are strong, LORD, and always faithful.
⁹You rule the stormy sea.
You can calm its angry waves.
¹⁰You defeated Rahab.
You scattered your enemies with your own
powerful arm.

¹¹Everything in heaven and earth belongs
to you.
You made the world and everything in it.
¹²You created everything north and south.
Mount Tabor and Mount Hermon sing
praises to your name.
¹³You have the power!
Your power is great!
Victory is yours!
¹⁴Your kingdom is built on truth and justice.
Love and faithfulness are servants before
your throne.

¹⁵LORD, your loyal followers are happy.
They live in the light of your kindness.
¹⁶Your name always makes them happy.
They praise your goodness.
¹⁷You are their amazing strength.
Their power comes from you.
¹⁸The king, our protector, belongs to the LORD,
who is the Holy One of Israel.

¹⁹Lord, you once spoke in a vision
to your followers:
"I have made a young soldier strong.
From among my people I chose him for an
important position.
²⁰I have found my servant David
and anointed him as king with my special oil.
²¹I will support him with my right hand,
and my arm will make him strong.
²²So no enemy will ever control him.
The wicked will never defeat him.
²³I will destroy his enemies before his eyes.
I will defeat those who hate him.
²⁴I will always love and support him.
I will always make him strong.
²⁵I will put him in charge of the sea.
He will control the rivers.
²⁶He will say to me, 'You are my father.
You are my God, my Rock, my Saviour.'
²⁷And I will make him my firstborn son.
He will be the great king on earth.
²⁸My love will protect him forever.
My agreement with him will never end.
²⁹I will make his family continue forever.
His kingdom will last as long as the skies.

³⁰"If his descendants stop following my law
and stop obeying my commands,
³¹if they break my laws
and ignore my commands,
³²I will punish them severely
for their sins and wrongs.
³³But I will never take my love from him.
I will never stop being loyal to him.
³⁴I will not break my agreement with David.
I will never change what I said.
³⁵By my holiness, I made a promise to him,
and I would not lie to David.
³⁶His family will continue forever.
His kingdom will last as long as the sun.
³⁷Like the moon, it will last forever.
The sky is a witness to the agreement that
can be trusted." *Selah*

³⁸But now, Lord, you have become angry with
your chosen king,
and you have left him all alone.
³⁹You ended the agreement you made with your
servant.
You threw the king's crown into the dirt.
⁴⁰You pulled down the walls of his city.
You destroyed all his fortresses.
⁴¹Everyone passing by steals from him.
His neighbours laugh at him.
⁴²You made all the king's enemies happy
and let his enemies win the war.
⁴³You helped them defend themselves.
You did not help your king win the battle.

44You did not let him win.
  You threw his throne to the ground.
45You cut his life short.
  You shamed him.   *Selah*

46LORD, how long will this continue?
  Will you ignore us forever?
  Will your anger burn like a fire forever?
47Remember how short my life is.
  You created us to live a short life and
    then die.
48Is there anyone alive who will never die?
  Will anyone escape the grave?   *Selah*

49Lord, where is the love you showed in the past?
  You promised David that you would be
    loyal to his family.
50My Lord, remember how people have insulted
    me, your servant.
  The insults of people everywhere have hurt
    me deeply.
51LORD, those hurtful words have come from
    your enemies.
  They insult your chosen king wherever
    he goes.

52Praise the LORD forever!
  Amen and Amen!

BOOK 4
(Psalms 90–106)

The prayer of Moses, the man of God.

90 Lord, you have been our home
  since the time of our first ancestors.
2You were God before the mountains were
    born,
  before the earth and the world were made.
  You have always been and will always be
    God!

3You bring people into this world,
  and you change them into dust again.
4To you, a thousand years is like yesterday,
  like a few hours in the night.
5You end our lives like a passing dream.
  We are like the grass that appears in the
    morning.
6In the morning it looks so fresh and new,
  but by evening it is dry and dying.

7When you are angry, we are terrified.
  We know that your anger can destroy us!
8You know all the wrong things we do.
  You see even the sins we think are secret.
9Your anger can end our life.
  We are here no longer than a brief moan.

10We live for about 70 years
  or, if we are strong, 80 years.
  But most of them are filled with hard work
    and pain.
  Then, suddenly, the years are gone, and we
    fly away.

11No one really knows the full power of your
    anger,
  but our fear and respect for you is as great
    as your anger.
12Teach us how short our lives are
  so that we can become wise.

13LORD, come back to us.
  Be kind to your servants.
14Fill us with your love every morning.
  Let us be happy and enjoy our lives.
15For years you have made life hard for us
  and have given us many troubles.
  Now make us happy for just as long.
16Let your servants see the wonderful things you
    can do for them.
  And let their children see your glory.
17Lord, our God, be kind to us.
  Make everything we do successful.
  Yes, make it all successful.

91 You can go to God Most High to hide.
  You can go to God All-Powerful for
    protection.
2I say to the LORD, "You are my place of safety,
    my fortress.
  My God, I trust in you."

3God will save you from hidden dangers
  and from deadly diseases.
4You can go to him for protection.
  He will cover you like a bird spreading its
    wings over its babies.
  You can trust him to surround and protect
    you like a shield.
5You will have nothing to fear at night
  and no need to be afraid of enemy arrows
    during the day.
6You will have no fear of diseases that come in
    the dark
  or terrible suffering that comes at noon.
7A thousand people may fall dead at your side
  or ten thousand right beside you,
  but nothing bad will happen to you!
8All you will have to do is watch,
  and you will see that the wicked are
    punished.

9You trust in the LORD for protection.
  You have made God Most High your place
    of safety.

¹⁰So nothing bad will happen to you.
   No diseases will come near your home.
¹¹He will command his angels to protect you
      wherever you go.
¹²Their hands will catch you
   so that you will not hit your foot on a rock.
¹³You will have power to trample on lions
   and poisonous snakes.

¹⁴The Lord says, "If someone trusts me, I will
      save them.
   I will protect my followers who call to me
      for help.
¹⁵When my followers call to me, I will answer
      them.
   I will be with them when they are in trouble.
   I will rescue them and honour them.
¹⁶I will give my followers a long life
   and show them my power to save."

A song of praise for the Sabbath.

92 It is good to praise the LORD.
   God Most High, it is good to praise your
      name.
²It is good to sing about your love in the
      morning
   and about your faithfulness at night.
³It is good to play for you on the ten-stringed
      instrument and lyre
   and to add the soft sounds of the harp to
      my praise.

⁴LORD, you make us very happy because of
      what you have done.
   I gladly sing about it.
⁵LORD, you did such great things.
   Your thoughts are too hard for us to
      understand.
⁶Stupid people don't know this.
   Fools don't understand.
⁷The wicked may sprout like grass,
   and those who do evil may blossom like
      flowers.
   But they will be destroyed, never to be seen
      again.
⁸And you, Lord, will be honoured forever.

⁹LORD, all your enemies will be destroyed,
   and all who do evil will be scattered.
¹⁰But you have made me as strong as a wild ox.
   You have given me your blessing.ᵃ

¹¹My eyes will see the defeat of those waiting to
      attack me.
   My ears will hear the cries of my evil
      enemies.

¹²Good people are like budding palm trees.
   They grow strong like the cedar trees of
      Lebanon.
¹³They are planted in the LORD's house.ᵇ
   They grow strong there in the courtyards of
      our God.
¹⁴Even when they are old,
   they will continue producing fruit like
      young, healthy trees.
¹⁵They are there to show everyone that the
      LORD is good.ᶜ
   He is my Rock, and he does no wrong.ᵈ

93 The LORD is King.
   The LORD wears majesty and strength like
      clothes.
He is ready, so the whole world is safe.
   It will not be shaken.
²Your kingdom has continued forever.
   You have lived forever!

³LORD, the ocean roars.
   The mighty ocean sounds like thunder
      as the waves crash on the shore.
⁴The crashing waves of the sea are loud and
      powerful,
   but the LORD above is even more powerful.

⁵LORD, your laws will continue forever.ᵉ
   Your holy Temple will stand for a long time.

94 The LORD is a God who punishes people.
   God, come and punish them.
²You are the judge of the whole earth.
   Give proud people the punishment they
      deserve.
³LORD, how long will the wicked have their
      fun?
   How much longer?

⁴How much longer will those criminals
   boast about the evil they did?
⁵LORD, they hurt your people
   and make them suffer.
⁶They kill widows and foreigners living in our
      country.
   They murder orphans.

ᵃ **92:10** *You . . . blessing* Or "You poured your refreshing oil over me."
ᵇ **92:13** *house* Or "Temple". See "TEMPLE" in the Word List.
ᶜ **92:15** *good* This is a wordplay. The Hebrew word means "straight" (like the trees) and "good" or "honest".
ᵈ **92:15** *he . . . wrong* Or "there is no crookedness in him".
ᵉ **93:5** *your laws . . . forever* Or "your agreement can really be trusted".

7And they say the LORD does not see them
doing these evil things!
They say the God of Jacob does not know
what is happening.

8You evil people are foolish.
When will you learn your lesson?
You are so stupid!
You must try to understand.
9God made our ears,
so surely he can hear what is happening!
He made our eyes,
so surely he can see you!
10The one who disciplines nations will surely
correct you.
He is the one who teaches us everything.
11The LORD knows what people are thinking.
He knows that their thoughts are like a puff
of wind.

12LORD, great blessings belong to those you
discipline,
to those you teach from your law.
13You help them stay calm when trouble
comes.
You will help them until the wicked are put
in their graves.
14The LORD will not leave his people.
He will not leave them without help.
15Justice will return and bring fairness.
And those who want to do right will be
there to see it.

16No one helped me fight against the wicked.
No one stood with me against those who do
evil.
17And if the LORD had not helped me,
I would have been silenced by death.
18I know I was ready to fall,
but, LORD, your faithful love supported me.
19I was very worried and upset,
but you comforted me and made me happy!

20You don't help crooked judges.
They use the law to make life hard for the
people.
21They attack those who do right.
They say innocent people are guilty and put
them to death.
22But the LORD is my place of safety, high on the
mountain.
God, my Rock, is my safe place!
23He will punish those evil judges for the bad
things they did.

He will destroy them because they sinned.
The LORD our God will destroy them.

95 Come, let us sing praise to the LORD!
Let us shout praises to the Rock who
saves us.
2Come and worship him with songs of
thanks.a
Let us sing happy songs of praise to him.
3For the LORD is a great God,
the great King ruling over all the other
"gods".
4The deepest caves are his,
and the highest mountains belong to him.
5The ocean is his because he created it.
He made the dry land with his own hands.

6Come, let us bow down and worship him!
Let us kneel before the LORD who made us.
7He is our God,
and we are the people he cares for,
his sheep that walk by his side.

Listen to his voice today:
8"Don't be stubborn, as you were at
Meribah,
as you were at Massahb in the desert.
9Your ancestors doubted and tested me,
even after they saw what I could do!
10I was angry with them for 40 years.
I said, 'They are not faithful to me.
They refuse to do what I say.'
11So in my anger I made this vow:
'They will never enter my land of rest.'"

96 Sing a new songc to the LORD!
Let the whole world sing to the LORD!
2Sing to the LORD and praise his name!
Tell the good news every day about how he
saves us!
3Tell all the nations how wonderful he is!
Tell people everywhere about the amazing
things he does.

4The LORD is great and worthy of praise.
He is more awesome than any of the
"gods".
5All the "gods" in other nations are nothing but
statues,
but the LORD made the heavens.
6He lives in the presence of glory and
honour.
His Temple is a place of power and
beauty.

a 95:2 *songs of thanks* Or "thank offerings".
b 95:8 *Meribah . . . Massah* See Exod. 17:1–7.
c 96:1 *new song* Whenever God did a new and wonderful thing for his people, they would write a new song about it.

⁷Praise the LORD, all people of every nation;
  praise the LORD's glory and power.
⁸Give the LORD praise worthy of his glory!
  Come, bring your offerings into his
    courtyard.
⁹Worship the LORD in all his holy beauty.
  Everyone on earth should tremble before
    him.
¹⁰Tell the nations that the LORD is King!
  The world stands firm and cannot be
    moved.
  He will judge all people fairly.
¹¹Let the heavens rejoice and the earth be
    happy!
  Let the sea and everything in it shout for
    joy!
¹²Let the fields and everything in them be
    happy!
  Let the trees in the forest sing for joy
¹³when they see the LORD who is coming!
  He is coming to judge^a all people on
    earth.
  He will judge the world with fairness.
  He will judge the nations with truth.

97 The LORD rules, and the earth is happy.
  All the faraway lands are happy.
²Thick, dark clouds surround him.
  Goodness and justice make his kingdom
    strong.
³Fire goes before him
  and destroys his enemies.
⁴His lightning flashes in the sky.
  The earth sees it and trembles with fear.
⁵The mountains melt like wax before the LORD,
  before the Lord of all the earth.
⁶The skies tell about his goodness,
  and the nations see his glory.

⁷People worship their idols.
  They boast about their "gods".
But they will be embarrassed.
  And all their "gods" will bow down before
    the Lord.
⁸Zion, listen and be happy!
  Cities of Judah, be glad!
  Rejoice because the LORD's decisions are
    fair.
⁹LORD Most High, you really are the ruler of the
    earth.
  You are much better than the "gods".

¹⁰Hate evil, you who love the LORD.
  He protects his faithful followers.
  He saves them from being hurt by evil
    people.
¹¹God blesses^b those who do what is right.
  Happiness comes to those who want to do
    good.
¹²You who do what is right, be happy for what
    the LORD has done.
  Praise him who alone is holy!^c

A song of praise.

98 Sing a new song^d to the LORD,
  because he has done amazing things!
His powerful and holy right arm^e
  has brought him another victory.
²The LORD showed the nations his power to save.
  He showed them his goodness.
³He has kept his promise of love and loyalty to
    the people of Israel.
  People everywhere have seen our God's
    power to save.

⁴Everyone on earth, shout with joy to the LORD.
  Start singing happy songs of praise!
⁵Praise the LORD with harps.
  Yes, praise him with music from the harps.
⁶Blow the pipes and horns,
  and shout for joy to the LORD our King!

⁷Let the sea and everything in it,
  the earth and all who live in it shout his
    praise!
⁸Rivers, clap your hands!
  All together now, mountains sing out!
⁹Sing before the LORD
  because he is coming to judge the world.
He will judge the world fairly.
  He will judge the nations in a way that is
    right.

99 The LORD is King,
  so let the nations shake with fear.
He sits as King above the winged creatures,
  so let the whole earth shake.
²The LORD in Zion is great!
  He is the great leader over all people.
³Let all the nations praise your name.
  Your name is great and awesome.
  Your name is holy.

---

^a 96:13 *judge* Or "rule". Also in 98:9.
^b 97:11 *God blesses* Literally, "Light is sown for".
^c 97:12 *him . . . holy* Literally, "his holy remembrance".
^d 98:1 *new song* Whenever God did a new and wonderful thing for his people, they would write a new song about it.
^e 98:1 *holy right arm* This pictures God as a warrior-king. The right arm symbolizes his power and authority. "Holy" may refer to the special cleansing and dedication that Israelites performed before going into battle.

⁴You are the powerful King who loves justice.
    You have made things right.
    You have brought goodness and fairness to
        Jacob.
⁵Praise the LORD our God,
    and bow down before his footstool,ᵃ
    for he is holy.

⁶Moses and Aaron were some of his priests,
    and Samuel was one of the men who called
        on his name.
    They prayed to the LORD,
        and he answered them.
⁷God spoke from the tall cloud,
    and they obeyed the commands
    and law he gave them.

⁸LORD our God, you answered their prayers.
    You showed them that you are a forgiving
        God
    and that you punish people for the evil
        they do.
⁹Praise the LORD our God.
    Bow down towards his holy mountain and
        worship him.
    The LORD our God is holy!

A song of thanks.

100

Earth, sing to the LORD!
²Be happy as you serve the LORD!
    Come before him with happy songs!
³Know that the LORD is God.
    He made us, and we belong to him.
    We are his people, the sheep he takes care of.

⁴Come through the gates to his Temple giving
        thanks to him.
    Enter his courtyards with songs of praise.
    Honour him and bless his name.
⁵The LORD is good!
    There is no end to his faithful love.
    We can trust him for ever and ever!

A song of David.

101

I will sing about love and justice.
    LORD, I will sing to you.
²I will be careful to live a pure life.
    I will live in my house with complete honesty.
    When will you come to me?

³I will not even look at anything shameful.ᵇ
    I hate all wrongdoing.
    I want no part of it!

⁴I will not be involved in anything dishonest.
    I will have nothing to do with evil.
⁵I will stop anyone who secretly
    says bad things about a neighbour.
    I will not allow people to be proud
    and think they are better than others.

⁶I will look throughout the land for those who
        can be trusted.
    Only such people can live with me.
    Only those who live pure lives can be my
        servants.
⁷I will never let a dishonest person live in my
        house.
    I will not let liars stay near me.
⁸My goal each day will be to destroy the
        wicked living in our land.
    I will force all who do evil to leave the city
        of the LORD.

*A prayer for a time of suffering, when anyone feels weak and
wants to tell their complaints to the LORD.*

102

LORD, hear my prayer.
    Listen to my cry for help.
²Don't turn away from me when I have
        troubles.
    Listen to me, and answer me quickly when
        I cry for help.

³My life is passing away like smoke.
    My life is like a fire slowly burning out.
⁴My strength has gone—
    I am like dry, dying grass.
    I even forget to eat.
⁵Because of my sadness, I am losing so much
        weight
    that my skin hangs from my bones.
⁶I am lonely, like an owl living in the desert,
    like an owl living among old ruined buildings.
⁷I cannot sleep.
    I am like a lonely bird on the roof.
⁸My enemies insult me all the time.
    They make fun of me and use me as an
        example in their curses.
⁹My great sadness is my only food.
    My tears fall into my drink.
¹⁰You were angry with me,
    so you picked me up and threw me away.

¹¹My life has almost finished, like the long
        shadows at the end of the day.
    I am like dry and dying grass.
¹²But you, LORD, will rule as king forever!
    Your name will last for ever and ever!

ᵃ 99:5 *footstool* This probably means the Temple. See "TEMPLE" in the Word List.
ᵇ 101:3 *anything shameful* Or "an idol".

I WILL

How good are you at obeying? If you know anything about the Old Testament you will know that the people were not very good at obeying God.

In Exodus 19 God made an agreement with the people that he would be their God and would keep all his promises to them that they would be great, blessed and in a safe land. All they needed to do was love him and obey his laws – which they made a hash of!

When they got to the land, they were jealous of the other nations and wanted a king to rule them instead of God (1 Samuel 8). However, the king was almost a trendsetter and the way he followed God at any given time was usually the model for how the people would follow God too. So things would only work if the king kept God's commands (Deuteronomy 17:14–20) and brought right decisions to the land (1 Kings 3:28 and Jeremiah 33:15). That's just what David's "royal psalm" is about.

DIG IN

READ Psalm 101:1–8

- What things does the psalmist king promise he will do in his own life (vv.1–4)?
- Why?

He wants to sing about the love and justice of God, the God who promises to look after the people. The king wants to keep all his ways pure and honest and good before the Lord. This has to be really important considering his job was to lead the people in following God.

- What sort of thing is he passionate about in others (vv.5–8)?
- What will he do to those who are evil and wicked?

He does not want bad people in the land, let alone in his house. Part of his job would be to rule and make decisions in the law courts. He feels he has to sing about justice – it's his job! Does a lot of this language seem harsh? It shows us how important it was for the people to live rightly in the land and how seriously God takes sin.

- What words can you find repeated throughout the psalm?
- Do you think the king can do all these things?

He says "I will" a lot! He is making promises of the things he will do and the things he will not do. It is possible this was written for his coronation. Either way, they are big asks! Have you ever tried to "not even look at anything shameful"? A typical human king could never keep these promises – either in his own personal life or in the way he brings justice to the land. What hope is there for the people of Israel?

DIG THROUGH

- The people learnt that no king was ever perfect. But they needed a king who could keep the promises of this psalm. Enter King Jesus! He was the only one who could keep everything in Psalm 101. This is good news for us too – God's agreement with us depends not on our obedience but on that of King Jesus. Praise him for that!

- Even though Jesus is the only one who can keep all these promises, this psalm does show us the sort of thing God is passionate about. Ask him to help you live in purity, honesty, justice and love.

DIG DEEPER

- There are more psalms about the king: check out Psalms 18, 20, 45, 72 and 110. Ask yourself what these psalms say about the importance of the king for the people.

¹³You will rise up and comfort Zion.
  The time has come for you to be kind to
    Zion.
¹⁴Your servants love her stones.
  They love even the dust of that city!
¹⁵The nations will worship the LORD's name.
  All the kings on earth will honour you.
¹⁶The LORD will rebuild Zion,
  and people will again see her glory.
¹⁷He will listen to the prayers of those in
    poverty.
  He will not ignore them.

¹⁸Write these things for future generations,
  so that they will praise the LORD.
¹⁹The LORD will look down from his Holy Place
    above.
  He will look down at the earth from
    heaven.
²⁰And he will hear the prisoners' prayers.
  He will free those who were condemned to
    die.
²¹Then people in Zion will tell about the LORD.
  They will praise his name in Jerusalem
²²when nations gather together
  and kingdoms come to serve the LORD.

²³God has made me feel old for my age.
  He has made my life too short.
²⁴So I cry out, "Don't let me die young, my
    God,
  you whose years never end!
²⁵Long ago, you made the world.
  You made the sky with your own hands!
²⁶The earth and sky will end,
  but you will live forever!
  They will wear out like clothes,
    and like clothes, you will change them.
²⁷But you never change.
  You will live forever!
²⁸We are your servants today.
  Our children will live here,
  and their descendants will come here to
    worship you."

A song of David.

103

My soul, praise the LORD!
Every part of me, praise his holy name!
²My soul, praise the LORD
  and never forget how kind he is!
³He forgives all our sins
  and heals all our sicknesses.
⁴He saves us from the grave,
  and he gives us love and compassion.

⁵He gives us plenty of good things.
  He makes us young again,
  like an eagle that grows new feathers.
⁶The LORD does what is fair.
  He brings justice to all who have been hurt
    by others.
⁷He taught his laws to Moses.
  He let Israel see the powerful things he
    can do.
⁸The LORD is kind and merciful.
  He is patient and full of love.
⁹He does not always criticize.
  He does not stay angry with us forever.
¹⁰We sinned against him,
  but he didn't give us the punishment we
    deserved.
¹¹His love for his followers is as great
  as heaven is high above the earth.
¹²And he has taken our sins
  as far away from us as the east is from the
    west.
¹³The LORD is as kind to his followers
  as a father is to his children.
¹⁴He knows all about us.
  He knows we are made from dirt.

¹⁵He knows our lives are like grass,
  like a wild flower that grows so quickly,
¹⁶but when the hot wind blows, it dies.
  Soon, you cannot even see where it was.
¹⁷But the LORD has always loved his
    followers,
  and he will continue to love them
    forever
  and be good to their descendants.
¹⁸He will be good to those who are faithful to
    his agreement
  and who remember to obey his
    commands.

¹⁹The LORD set his throne up in heaven,
  and he rules over everything.
²⁰Angels, praise the LORD!
  You angels are the powerful soldiers who
    obey his commands.
  You listen to him and obey his commands.
²¹Praise the LORD, all his armies.ᵃ
  You are his servants,
  and you do what he wants.
²²Everything the LORD has made should
    praise him
  throughout the world that he rules!

My soul, praise the LORD!

ᵃ **103:21 armies** This word can mean "armies", "angels" or the "stars and planets". This word is part of the name translated "LORD All-Powerful". It shows that God is in control of all the powers in the universe.

104

My soul, praise the LORD!
LORD my God, you are very great!
You are clothed with glory and honour.
2 You wear light like a robe.
You spread out the skies like a curtain.
3 You built your home above them.[a]
You use the thick clouds like a chariot
and ride across the sky on the wings of the
wind.
4You make the winds your messengers
and flames of fire your servants.

5You built the earth on its foundations,
so it can never be moved.
6You covered it with water like a blanket.
The water covered even the mountains.
7But you gave the command, and the water
turned back.
You shouted at the water, and it rushed
away.
8The water flowed down from the mountains
into the valleys,
to the places you made for it.
9You set the limits for the seas,
and the water will never again rise to cover
the earth.

10Lord, you cause water to flow from springs
into the streams
that flow down between the mountains.
11The streams provide water for all the wild
animals.
Even the wild donkeys come there to drink.
12Wild birds come to live by the pools;
they sing in the branches of nearby trees.
13You send rain down on the mountains.
The earth gets everything it needs from
what you have made.
14You make the grass for the animals
and the plants for the crops we grow,
plants that make food from the earth.
15You give us the wine that makes us happy,
the oil that makes our skin soft,[b]
and the food that makes us strong.

16The great cedar trees of Lebanon belong to the
LORD.
He planted them and gives them the water
they need.
17That's where the birds make their nests,
and the storks live in the fir trees.

18The high mountains are a home for wild
goats.
The large rocks are hiding places for rock
badgers.

19Lord, you made the moon to show us when
the festivals begin.
And the sun always knows when to set.
20You made darkness to be the night—
the time when wild animals come out and
roam around.
21Lions roar as they attack,
as if they are asking God for the food he
gives them.
22When the sun rises, they leave
and go back to their dens to rest.
23Then people go out to do their work,
and they work until evening.

24Lord, you created so many things!
With your wisdom you made them all.
The earth is full of the living things you
made.
25Look at the ocean, so big and wide!
It is filled with all kinds of sea life.
There are creatures large and small—too
many to count!
26Ships sail over the ocean,
and playing there is Leviathan,[c]
the great sea creature you made.

27Lord, all living things depend on you.
You give them food at the right time.
28You give it, and they eat it.
They are filled with good food from your
open hands.
29When you turn away from them,
they become frightened.
When you take away their breath,[d]
they die, and their bodies return to the
dust.
30But when you send out your life-giving
breath,[e]
things come alive, and the world is like new
again!

31May the LORD's glory continue forever!
May the LORD enjoy what he made.
32He just looks at the earth and it trembles.
He touches the mountains and smoke rises
from them.

---

a 104:3 **above them** Literally, "on the water above". This is like the picture of the world in Gen. 1. There the sky was like a bowl
turned upside down on the earth. There was water below the bowl and water above it.
b 104:15 **makes our skin soft** Literally, "makes our face shine". This can also mean "makes us happy".
c 104:26 **Leviathan** This might mean any large sea animal, like a whale. But it probably means "the sea monster", the "Dragon"
or "Rahab". This creature represents the great power of the ocean, the power that God controls.
d 104:29 **breath** Or "spirit".
e 104:30 **life-giving breath** Or "Spirit".

³³I will sing to the LORD for the rest of my life.
　　I will sing praises to my God as long as
　　　I live.
³⁴May my words be pleasing to him.
　　The LORD is the one who makes me happy.
³⁵I wish sinners would disappear from the earth.
　　I wish the wicked would be gone forever.

My soul, praise the LORD!
　　Praise the LORD!

105

Give thanks to the LORD and call out to
him!
　Tell the nations what he has done!
²Sing to him; sing praises to him.
　　Tell about the amazing things he has done.
³Be glad you belong to him who alone is holy.
　　You followers of the LORD, be happy!
⁴Depend on the LORD for strength.
　　Always go to him for help.
⁵Remember the amazing things he has done.
　　Remember his miracles and his fair
　　　decisions.
⁶You belong to the family of his servant
　　Abraham.
　　You are descendants of Jacob, the people
　　　God chose.

⁷The LORD is our God.
　　He rules the whole world.

⁸He will remember his agreement forever.
　　He will always keep the promises he made
　　　to his people.
⁹He will keep the agreement he made with
　　Abraham
　　and the promise he made to Isaac.
¹⁰He gave it as a law to Jacob.
　　He gave it to Israel as an agreement that
　　　will last forever!
¹¹He said, "I will give you the land of Canaan.
　　It will be your very own."

¹²At the time God said this, there were only a
　　few of his people,
　　and they were foreigners there.
¹³They travelled around from nation to nation,
　　from one kingdom to another.
¹⁴But the Lord did not let anyone mistreat
　　them.
　　He warned kings not to harm them.
¹⁵He said, "Don't hurt my chosen people.
　　Don't harm my prophets."

¹⁶He caused a famine in that country,
　　and people did not have enough food.

¹⁷But he sent a man named Joseph to go ahead
　　of them.
　　Joseph was sold like a slave.
¹⁸They tied a rope around his feet
　　and put an iron ring around his neck.
¹⁹Joseph was a slave until what he said had
　　really happened.
　　The LORD's message proved that Joseph was
　　　right.
²⁰So the king of Egypt set him free.
　　That nation's leader let him out of jail.
²¹He put Joseph in charge of his house.
　　Joseph took care of everything the king
　　　owned.
²²Joseph gave instructions to the other leaders.
　　He taught the older men.
²³Then Israel came to Egypt.
　　Jacob lived there in Ham's country.ᵃ
²⁴Jacob's family became very large
　　and more powerful than their enemies.
²⁵So the Egyptians began to hate his people.
　　They made plans against his servants.
²⁶So the Lord sent Moses, his servant,
　　and Aaron, his chosen priest.
²⁷He used Moses and Aaron
　　to do many miracles in Ham's country.
²⁸He sent darkness to cover their land,
　　but the Egyptians did not listen to him.
²⁹So he changed the water into blood,
　　and all their fish died.
³⁰Their country was filled with frogs,
　　even in the king's bedroom.
³¹The Lord gave the command,
　　and the flies and gnats came.
　　They were everywhere!
³²He made the rain become hail.
　　Lightning struck throughout their land.
³³He destroyed their vines and fig trees.
　　He destroyed every tree in their country.
³⁴He gave the command, and the locusts and
　　grasshoppers came.
　　There were too many to count!
³⁵They ate all the plants in the country,
　　including all the crops in their fields.
³⁶Then the Lord killed every firstborn in their
　　country.
　　He killed their oldest sons.

³⁷He led his people out of Egypt.
　　They were carrying gold and silver,
　　and none of them stumbled or fell behind.
³⁸Egypt was happy to see his people go,
　　because they were afraid of them.
³⁹The Lord spread out his cloud like a blanket.
　　He used his column of fire to give his
　　people light at night.

ᵃ **105:23** *Ham's country* Or "Egypt". The Egyptians were Ham's descendants. See Gen. 10:6–20.

40They asked for food, and he sent them quail.
　He also gave them plenty of bread from
　　heaven.
41He split the rock, and water came bubbling
　　out.
　A river began flowing in the desert!
42The Lord remembered his holy promise
　that he had made to his servant Abraham.
43Yes, God brought his people out of Egypt.
　They came out rejoicing and singing their
　　happy songs!
44Then he gave his people the lands of other
　　nations.
　His people got what others had worked for.
45He did this so that his people would obey
　his laws
　and follow his teachings.

Praise the LORD!

106 Praise the LORD!

Give thanks to the LORD because he is good!
　His faithful love will last forever!
2No one can describe how great the LORD
　really is.
　No one can praise him enough.
3Those who obey his commands are happy.
　They do good things all the time.

4LORD, remember me when you show kindness
　to your people.
　Remember to save me too!
5Let me share in the good things you do
　for your chosen people.
　Let me rejoice with your nation.
　Let me join with your people in praise.

6We sinned just as our ancestors did.
　We were wrong; we did bad things!
7Lord, our ancestors learned nothing
　from the miracles you did in Egypt.
　They forgot your kindness at the Red Sea
　and rebelled against you.

8But the Lord saved our ancestors for the
　honour of his name.
　He saved them to show his great power.
9He gave the command, and the Red Sea
　became dry.
　He led them through the deep sea on land
　as dry as the desert.
10He saved our ancestors
　and rescued them from their enemies.

11He covered their enemies with the sea.
　Not one of them escaped!
12Then our ancestors believed what he
　had said.
　They sang praises to him.
13But they quickly forgot about what he did.
　They did not listen to his advice.
14They became hungry in the desert,
　and they tested him in the wilderness.
15He gave them what they asked for,
　but he also gave them a terrible
　　disease.

16The people became jealous of Moses.
　They became jealous of Aaron, the LORD's
　　holy priest.
17The ground opened up and swallowed
　　Dathan.
　Then the ground closed up and covered
　　Abiram's group.
18Then a fire burned that mob of people.
　It burned those wicked people.

19The people made a gold calf at Mount
　　Horeb.
　They worshipped a statue!
20They traded their glorious God
　for a statue of a grass-eating bull!
21They forgot all about God, the one who saved
　　them,
　the one who did the miracles in Egypt.
22He did amazing things there in Ham's
　　country!*a*
　He did awesome things at the Red Sea!
23God wanted to destroy those people,
　but Moses, the leader he chose, stood in
　　the way.
　God was very angry, but Moses begged him to
　　stop,
　so God did not destroy the people.*b*

24But then they refused to go into the wonderful
　　land of Canaan.
　They did not believe that God would help
　　them defeat the people there.
25Our ancestors complained in their tents
　and refused to obey the LORD.
26So he gave them a warning and swore
　that they would die in the desert.
27He promised to scatter them among the
　　nations
　and to let other people defeat their
　　descendants.

---

a **106:22** *Ham's country* Or "Egypt". The Egyptians were Ham's descendants. See Gen. 10:6–20.
b **106:23** Or "God said he would destroy them. But Moses, his chosen one, stood in the breach and repelled his anger from destroying." This compares Moses to a soldier standing at a break in a wall defending the city against enemy soldiers.

²⁸At Baal Peor they joined in worshipping Baal
and ate sacrifices to honour the dead.*ᵃ*

²⁹These bad things they did made the LORD
angry,
so a terrible sickness began to spread among
them.

³⁰But Phinehas began punishing those doing
wrong,*ᵇ*
and the sickness stopped.

³¹So Phinehas will always be remembered
for doing what was right.

³²At Meribah the people made the LORD angry
and created trouble for Moses.

³³They upset Moses,
and he spoke without stopping to think.

³⁴The LORD told the people to destroy the other
nations living in Canaan.
But the Israelites did not obey him.

³⁵They mixed with the other people
and did what those people were doing.

³⁶They began worshipping the false gods those
people worshipped.
And their idols became a trap.

³⁷They even offered their own children
as sacrifices to demons.

³⁸They killed their innocent sons and daughters
and offered them to the false gods of Canaan.
So the land was polluted with the sin of
murder.

³⁹They were unfaithful to him,
and they became dirty with the sins of other
nations.

⁴⁰So the LORD became angry with his people.
He rejected those who belonged to him.

⁴¹He gave his people to other nations
and let their enemies rule over them.

⁴²Their enemies controlled them
and made life hard for them.

⁴³He saved his people many times,
but they turned against him and did what
they wanted to do.
His people did many bad things.

⁴⁴But whenever they were in trouble,
he listened to their prayers.

⁴⁵He always remembered his agreement,
and because of his faithful love, he
comforted them.

⁴⁶Other nations took them as prisoners,
but the Lord caused them to be kind to his
people.

⁴⁷LORD our God, save us!
Bring us back together from those
nations.
Then we will give thanks to you, the holy one,
and joyfully praise you.

⁴⁸Praise the LORD, the God of Israel!
He always was and will always be worthy of
praise.
Let all the people say, "Amen!"

Praise the LORD!

BOOK 5
(Psalms 107–150)

107 Praise the LORD, because he is good!
His faithful love will last forever!

²Everyone the LORD has saved should repeat
that word of thanks.
Praise him, all who have been rescued from
the enemy.

³He gathered his people together from many
different countries.
He brought them from east and west, north
and south.*ᶜ*

⁴Some of them wandered in the dry desert.
They were looking for a place to live,
but they could not find a city.

⁵They were hungry and thirsty
and growing weak.

⁶Then they called to the LORD for help,
and he saved them from their troubles.

⁷He led them on a road that led straight
to the city where they would live.

⁸Thank the LORD for his faithful love
and for the amazing things he does for
people.

⁹He satisfies those who are thirsty.
He fills those who are hungry with good
things.

¹⁰Some of God's people were prisoners,
locked behind bars in dark prisons.

¹¹That was because they had fought against
what God said.
They refused to listen to the advice of God
Most High.

¹²God made life hard for those people
because of what they did.
They stumbled and fell,
and there was no one to help them.

¹³They were in trouble, so they called to the
LORD for help,
and he saved them from their troubles.

ᵃ **106:28** *the dead* This might refer to "lifeless gods" or to dead friends or relatives honoured with meals eaten at their graves.
ᵇ **106:30** *began . . . wrong* Literally, "stood and intervened". For the story of what Phinehas did see Num. 25:1–16.
ᶜ **107:3** *south* Literally, "the sea".

SEX *and* RELATIONSHIPS

YOU may be surprised to find this feature in a Bible, but relationships were just as important in both Old and New Testament times as they are now. You may think that where relationships are concerned, the Bible says some things that may have made sense when it was written thousands of years ago, but today seem like absolute madness. Yet, once you dig deeper, you realize these things make a lot of sense, even though they go against much of what our modern culture tells us!

Popular culture says, "If it feels good, do it," suggesting that if we think something will

FORGET ABOUT OTHER PEOPLE'S OPINIONS – FOLLOWING GOD'S WAY IS THE BEST WAY.

make us happy, then we should definitely do it. But this isn't always true; the Bible has set out guidelines for us to live by and these might mean turning down someone you really fancy, or waiting to have sex. Even though giving in to these things may make you happy for a short time, God knows what is best for you long term – he has the bigger picture – so find out what he has to say about sex and relationships.

So what does the Bible say? That sex was created for within the marriage relationship

(1 Corinthians 6:18 – 7:2; 1 Thessalonians 4:3–7; Hebrews 13:4), and that we should respect other people in relationships and not just use them to make ourselves feel good (Philippians 2:4). Some of these verses also imply that we should not rush into sex and relationships even though it might feel good at the time.

If you want to stand out and make a difference as a Christian, just try telling your friends you are going to wait for sex until marriage – it's the most counter-cultural thing you can do! Or try not dating for a while, even though everyone else is. Give yourself time to find out who you are without anyone else attached!

If you think about it, there are an awful lot of people who wish they had waited longer before having sex, but you probably won't meet many who wish they'd done it sooner. Forget about other people's opinions – following God's way is the best way. ←

Pray this prayer if you agree with it:

Lord, thank you that you designed me and know what is best for me. Please help me to live like I'm your child and help me to respect my body and the bodies of other people. Give me wisdom, strength and self-discipline in my relationships and please protect me from bad situations and bad decisions.

Amen

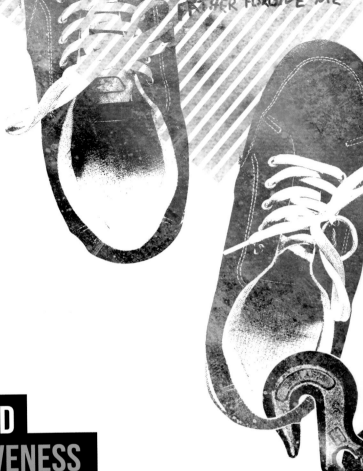

FATHER FORGIVE ME

SIN AND FORGIVENESS

IT'S UGLY, it's hairy, it's probably got one eye and six legs and you're pretty sure it's lurking somewhere just out of sight under your bed. You lie awake at night listening for that telltale creak or groan that will make you run for cover under your favourite duvet. Are those shadows moving on the wall? And that funny shape next to the wardrobe, is it just your dressing-gown, or a monster!

Okay, so maybe you are too old to believe in monsters under the bed or in the back of the wardrobe, but for many of us sin is just as ugly, hairy and scary and it can make us want to hide under the covers and hope it will go away. It's easy to think you are the only one in the world to struggle with sin. You look fine on the outside, but if people knew what you were really like there would be trouble, right? If they really knew what went on in your head or behind closed doors, they would think differently.

Let's get real. Everyone struggles with sin (check out Galatians 5:17). Some sins are obvious, while others are hidden – thoughts and attitudes that are less easily detected. One thing you can be sure of is that you are not alone. No matter how bad you think you are, there are lots of other people struggling with the same things you struggle with. Or maybe you reckon you are actually quite a good person: you've never murdered anyone, you don't steal or get drunk, and you are doing quite nicely. But the Bible makes it clear that we all sin and that by ourselves we are in a fight that we are losing; it is totally impossible for us to live up to God's standard (Romans 3:23).

Most world religions leave it at that, saying that we are responsible for making up for our sins and wrongdoings, either by trying to live a perfect life, or by paying some kind of penance – saying special prayers, going on

take the punishment we deserve so that we can walk free. He "paid the fine", "did the prison sentence", took our place so that we can have access to God's forgiveness. It means that every time we mess up, whatever we have done, God will forgive us if we say we are sorry and ask Jesus to be in charge of our lives (1 John 1:8–10).

Forgiveness is not something that just happens once, on the day of our salvation. The Bible says: "Continue to live in a way that gives meaning to your salvation. Do this with fear and respect for God" (Philippians 2:12). We should come to God regularly and repent of (say sorry

THE BIBLE SAYS THAT BECAUSE JESUS, A PERFECT MAN, DIED, HE WAS ABLE TO TAKE THE PUNISHMENT WE DESERVE THAT SO WE CAN WALK FREE.

pilgrimages or witnessing to a particular number of people. In many other religions people must work their way to God.

Christianity is different. And what makes the difference is grace and forgiveness. As Christians we know that it is crazy to believe that we can be "good enough" for God; it's impossible. The Bible says that because Jesus, a perfect man, died, he was able to

for) the wrong things we have done. We should thank God for his forgiveness and then rejoice that he has thrown our sin far away.

To find out more, check out:
Hebrews 4:16; 1 John 2:1. ←

Take some time now to pray to God and confess any sins that he brings to mind. Ask for his forgiveness, and then thank him for it and leave the burden of that sin behind.

WORRYING

LIFE is full of worries. "How will I do in my exams?" "Does that girl/boy like me in the same way I like them?" "What should I do with my life?" "I can't get a job, how am I going to manage financially?" Sometimes the worries overwhelm us and we can find ourselves feeling pretty miserable and depressed. However, the Bible tells us not to worry – and it's not just an unhelpful and clichéd saying. Jesus tells us we don't have to worry because we have a God who knows us, who knows what we need and who is more than capable of meeting those needs (Philippians 4:19).

So how do we stop? We can't just tell ourselves, "That's it! No more worrying," and expect everything to change. The apostle Paul tells us that we don't need to fight battles in the same way the rest of the world does. Instead we should "capture every thought and make it give up and obey Christ" (2 Corinthians 10:5). That means every time we start worrying about our coursework, we have to take the thoughts to God. Every time we get anxious about our future, we ask God to remind us that

REMEMBER THAT GOD KNOWS WHAT WE NEED AND HE WILL LOOK AFTER US.

he is in control and we don't have anything to fear. And every time we're concerned about needing money, we remember that God knows what we need and he will look after us.

You may also find the following verses helpful: John 14:1,27; Philippians 4:4–7; 1 Peter 5:7. ←

Why not pray this prayer:

Dear Father, thank you that you love me and you care about all the things I am concerned about. Please take all my fears and worries and replace them with your peace and love.

Amen

¹⁴He took them out of their dark prisons.
    He broke the ropes that held them.
¹⁵Thank the LORD for his faithful love
    and for the amazing things he does for
      people.
¹⁶He breaks down their bronze gates.
    He shatters their iron bars.

¹⁷Some people became fools and turned against
      God,
    and they suffered for the evil they did.
¹⁸They became so sick that they refused to eat,
    so they almost died.
¹⁹They were in trouble, so they called to the
      LORD for help,
    and he saved them from their troubles.
²⁰He gave the command and healed them,
    so they were saved from the grave.
²¹Thank the LORD for his faithful love
    and for the amazing things he does for
      people.
²²Offer sacrifices of thanks to him.
    Sing with joy about all that he has done.

²³Some sailed the sea in ships.
    Their work carried them across the water.
²⁴They saw what the LORD can do.
    They saw the amazing things he did at sea.
²⁵He gave the command, and a strong wind
      began to blow.
    The waves became higher and higher.
²⁶The waves lifted them high into the sky
    and dropped them into the deep sea.
    Facing such danger, the men lost their
      courage.
²⁷They were stumbling and falling like
      drunks.
    Their skill as sailors was useless.
²⁸In their trouble they cried out to the LORD,
    and he saved them from the danger.
²⁹He stopped the storm
    and calmed the waves.
³⁰The sailors were happy when the sea became
      calm,
    and he led them safely to where they
      wanted to go.
³¹Thank the LORD for his faithful love
    and for the amazing things he does for
      people.
³²Praise God in the great assembly.
    Praise him when the older leaders meet
      together.

³³He changed rivers into a desert.
    He stopped springs from flowing.
³⁴He made the fertile land become salty,
    because the people living there did such evil
      things.

³⁵He changed the desert into a land with pools
    of water.
    He caused springs to flow from dry ground.
³⁶He led the hungry to that good land,
    and they built a city to live in.
³⁷They planted seeds in their fields and grapes in
      their vineyards,
    and they had a good harvest.
³⁸God blessed them with many children
    and plenty of animals.

³⁹But because of disaster and troubles,
    their families became small and weak.
⁴⁰God shames even great leaders
    and makes them wander through empty
      deserts.
⁴¹But he rescues the poor from their misery.
    He makes their families large like flocks of
      sheep.
⁴²Good people see this and are happy.
    But the wicked see it and don't know what
      to say.

⁴³Whoever is wise will remember these things
    and begin to understand the LORD's faithful
      love.

A praise song of David.

108 God, I am ready, heart and soul,
    to sing songs of praise.
    Wake up, my soul!
²Harps and lyres, wake up,
    and let's wake the dawn!
³LORD, I will praise you before all people.
    I will sing praises about you to every
      nation.
⁴Your love is so great, it reaches above the sky!
    Your faithfulness is as high as the clouds.
⁵Rise above the heavens, God.
    Let all the world see your glory.
⁶Use your great power and help us!
    Answer my prayer and save the people you
      love.

⁷From his Temple God made this promise:
    "I will enjoy victory and give the land to my
      people.
  I will divide up the city of Shechem for them.
    I will give them Succoth Valley piece by
      piece.
⁸Gilead and Manasseh will be mine.
    Ephraim will be my helmet.
    Judah will be my royal sceptre.
⁹Moab will be the bowl for washing my feet.
    Edom will be the slave who carries my
      sandals.
  I will shout in victory over the Philistines."

10–11But, God, it seems that you have left us!
　You do not go out with our army.
So who will lead me into the strong, protected
　　city?
　Who will lead me into battle against Edom?
12Help us defeat the enemy!
　No one on earth can rescue us.
13Only God can make us strong.
　Only God can defeat our enemies!

To the director: A praise song of David.

109

God, I praise you!
Hear my prayer and do something!
2Wicked people are telling lies about me.
　They are saying things that are not true.
3They are saying hateful things about me.
　They are attacking me for no reason.
4I loved them, but they were against me.
　So I said a prayer.
5I did good things to them,
　but they are doing bad things to me.
I loved them,
　but they hated me.

6They said, "Choose someone evil to represent
　　him.
　Let the one at his side really be his accuser.
7Let even his prayer be used as evidence
　　against him,
　and let the court find him guilty.
8Let his life be cut short,
　and let someone else take over his work.
9Let his children become orphans,
　and let his wife be a widow.
10Make his children wander around as beggars,
　forced from homes that lie in ruins.
11Let the people he owes take everything he
　　owns.
　Let strangers get everything he worked for.
12Let no one be kind to him.
　Let no one show mercy to his children.
13May his family come to an end.
　May his name be unknown to future
　　generations.
14May the LORD remember the sins of his
　　father,
　and may his mother's sins never be erased.
15May the LORD never forget those sins,
　and may no one ever remember his family."

16They said about me, "He never did anything
　　good.
　He never loved anyone.
　He made life hard for the poor and the
　　helpless.
17He loved to curse others,
　so let those bad things happen to him.
He never blessed others,
　so don't let good things happen to him.
18Cursing was a daily part of his life,
　like the clothes he wears.
Cursing others became a part of him,
　like the water he drinks and the oil he puts
　　on his body.
19So let curses cover him like the robe he
　　wears
　and always surround him like a belt."

20My enemies said these evil things against me.
　But may those curses be the way the LORD
　　punishes them.
21My Lord GOD, treat me in a way that brings
　　honour to your name.
　Save me because of your faithful love.
22I am only a poor, helpless man.
　I am so sad; my heart is broken.
23I feel my life is over, fading like a shadow at
　　day's end.
　I feel like a bug that someone brushed
　　away.
24My knees are weak from fasting.
　I have lost weight and become thin.
25My enemies insult me.
　They look at me and shake their heads.

26LORD my God, help me!
　Show your faithful love and save me!
27Then they will know that you did it.
　They will know that it was your power,
　　LORD, that helped me.
28They curse me, but you can bless me.
　They attacked me, so defeat them.
　Then I, your servant, will be happy.
29Humiliate my enemies!
　Let them wear their shame like a coat.

30I give thanks to the LORD.
　I praise him in front of everyone.
31He stands by the helpless
　and saves them from those who try to put
　　them to death.

A praise song of David.

110

The LORD said to my lord,[a]
"Sit at my right side, while I put your
enemies under your control."

2The LORD will cause your kingdom to grow,
　beginning at Zion,
　until you rule the lands of your enemies!

---

a 110:1 *my lord* That is, the king.

[3]Your people will gladly join you
  when you gather your army together.
You will wear your special clothes
  and meet together early in the morning.
Your young men will be all around you
  like dew on the ground.[a]

[4]The LORD has made a promise with an oath
  and will not change his mind:
"You are a priest forever—
  the kind of priest Melchizedek was."

[5]My Lord is at your right side.
  He will defeat the other kings when he
    becomes angry.
[6]He will judge the nations.
  The ground will be covered with dead
    bodies.
  He will punish the leaders of powerful
    nations all around the world.

[7]The king will drink from a stream on the
    way.
  Then he will lift his head and become
    strong![b]

111 [c] Praise the LORD!

I thank the LORD with all my heart
  in the assembly of his good people.
[2]The LORD does wonderful things,
  which are always in the thoughts of those
    who delight in them.
[3]The things he does are great and glorious!
  There is no end to his goodness.
[4]He does amazing things so that we will
    remember
  that the LORD is kind and merciful.
[5]He gives food to his followers.
  He remembers his agreement forever.
[6]He has shown his people how powerful
    he is
  by giving them the land of other nations.

[7]Everything he does is good and fair.
  All his commands can be trusted.
[8]His commands will continue forever.
  They must be done with truth and honesty.
[9]He rescued his people and made his
    agreement with them forever.
  His name is awesome and holy.

[10]Wisdom begins with fear and respect for the
    LORD.
  Those who obey him are very wise.
  Praises will be sung to him forever.

112 [d] Praise the LORD!

Great blessings belong to those who fear and
    respect the LORD,
  who are happy to do what he commands.
[2]Their descendants will be given power on
    earth.
  Those who do right will be greatly blessed.
[3]Their family will be very rich,
  and their goodness will last forever.
[4]A light shines in the dark for those who are
    good,
  for those who are merciful, kind and
    fair.
[5]It is good for people to be kind and generous
  and to be fair in business.
[6]Such good people will never fall.
  They will always be remembered.
[7]They will not be afraid of bad news.
  They are confident because they trust in the
    LORD.
[8]They remain confident and without fear,
  so they defeat their enemies.
[9]They were unselfish and gave to the poor.
  The good things they did will last forever.
  They will win great honour.

[10]The wicked become angry when they see this.
  They grind their teeth in anger, but then
    they disappear.
  They will never get what they want most.

113 Praise the LORD!

Servants of the LORD, praise him!
  Praise the LORD's name.
[2]May the LORD's name be praised
  now and forever.
[3]May the LORD's name be praised
  from where the sun rises to where it goes
    down.
[4]The LORD is higher than all nations.
  His glory rises to the skies.

[5]There is no one like the LORD our God.
  He sits on his throne high in heaven.

---

[a] 110:3 The Hebrew text is not clear. Literally, "Your people will be freewill offerings on your day of power. In holy splendour from the womb of dawn your dew of youth will be yours."
[b] 110:7 **lift his head and become strong** Literally, "lift his head". Here, the poet probably means two things: "he will raise his head after drinking the water", and "he will become strong or important".
[c] **Psalm 111** In Hebrew, each line of this psalm begins with the next letter in the alphabet.
[d] **Psalm 112** In Hebrew, each line of this psalm begins with the next letter in the alphabet.

⁶He is so high above us that he must look
　　down
　　to see the sky and the earth.
⁷He lifts the poor out of the dirt
　　and rescues beggars from the rubbish dump.
⁸He puts them in important positions,
　　giving them a place among the leaders of
　　his people.
⁹He gives children to the woman whose home
　　is empty.
　　He makes her a happy mother.

Praise the LORD!

114

The people of Israel escaped from
Egypt.
　　Yes, Jacob's descendants left that foreign
　　country.
²Then Judah became God's special people,
　　and Israel became his kingdom.
³The Red Sea saw this and ran away.
　　The Jordan River turned and ran.
⁴The mountains danced like rams.
　　The hills danced like lambs.

⁵Red Sea, why did you run away?
　　Jordan River, why did you turn and run
　　away?
⁶Mountains, why did you dance like rams?
　　Hills, why did you dance like lambs?

⁷The earth shook in front of the Lord,
　　the God of Jacob.
⁸He is the one who caused water to flow from
　　a rock.
　　He made a spring of water flow from that
　　hard rock.

115

LORD, you should receive the honour,
not us.
　　The honour belongs to you
　　because of your faithful love and loyalty.

²Why should the nations wonder
　　where our God is?
³Our God is in heaven,
　　and he does whatever he wants.
⁴The "gods" of those nations are only statues
　　that some human made from gold and
　　silver.
⁵Those statues have mouths, but cannot talk.
　　They have eyes, but cannot see.
⁶They have ears, but cannot hear.
　　They have noses, but cannot smell.
⁷They have hands, but cannot feel.

They have feet, but cannot walk.
　　No sounds come from their throats.
⁸The people who make and trust in those statues
　　will become like them!

⁹People of Israel, trust in the LORD!
　　He is your strength and shield.
¹⁰Aaron's family, trust in the LORD!
　　He is your strength and shield.
¹¹Followers of the LORD, trust in the LORD!
　　He is your strength and shield.

¹²The LORD remembers us,
　　and he will bless us.
　　He will bless the people of Israel.
　　He will bless Aaron's family.
¹³The LORD will bless all his followers,
　　whether they seem important or not.

¹⁴May the LORD give more and more to you
　　and to your children.
¹⁵May you receive blessings from the LORD,ᵃ
　　who made heaven and earth.

¹⁶Heaven belongs to the LORD,
　　but he gave the earth to people.
¹⁷The dead don't praise him.
　　Those in the grave don't praise the LORD.
¹⁸But we will praise the LORD
　　now and forever!

Praise the LORD!

116

I love the LORD for hearing me,
for listening to my prayers.
²Yes, he paid attention to me,
　　so I will always call to him whenever I need
　　help.
³Death's ropes were around me.
　　The grave was closing in on me.
　　I was worried and afraid.
⁴Then I called on the LORD's name.
　　I said, "LORD, save me!"

⁵The LORD is good and merciful;
　　our God is so kind.
⁶The LORD takes care of helpless people.
　　I was without help, and he saved me.
⁷My soul, relax!
　　The LORD is caring for you.
⁸Lord, you saved my soul from death.
　　You stopped my tears.
　　You kept me from falling.
⁹I will continue to serve the LORD
　　in the land of the living.

ᵃ 115:15 *May . . . the LORD* Or "The LORD welcomes you with a blessing."

10I continued believing even when I said,
 "I am completely ruined!"
11Yes, even when I was upset and said,
 "There is no one I can trust!"

12What can I give the LORD
 for all that he has done for me?
13He saved me,
 so I will give him a drink offering,
 and I will call on the LORD's name.
14I will give the LORD what I promised.
 I will go in front of all his people now.

15Very dear to the LORD are the lives of his
 followers.
 He cares when they face death.
16LORD, I am your servant!
 Yes, I am your slave, as my mother was.
 You set me free from the chains of death.
17I will give you a thank offering.
 I will call on the LORD's name.
18I will stand before the gathering of his people
 and give the LORD what I promised.
19I will do this in Jerusalem,
 in the courtyards of the LORD's Temple.

Praise the LORD!

117

Praise the LORD, all you nations.
 Praise him, all you people.
2He loves us very much!
 The LORD will be faithful to us forever!

Praise the LORD!

118

Praise the LORD because he is good!
 His faithful love will last forever!
2Israel, say it:
 "His faithful love will last forever!"
3Aaron's family,a say it:
 "His faithful love will last forever!"
4You people worshipping the LORD, say it:
 "His faithful love will last forever!"

5I was in trouble, so I called to the LORD for help.
 The LORD answered and made me free.
6The LORD is with me, so I will not be afraid.
 No one on earth can do anything to harm me.
7The LORD is my helper.
 I will see my enemies defeated.
8It is better to trust in the LORD
 than to trust in people.

9It is better to trust in the LORD
 than to trust in great leaders.

10Many enemies surrounded me,
 but with the LORD's power I defeated them.
11They surrounded me again and again,
 but I defeated them with the LORD's power.
12They surrounded me like a swarm of bees,
 but they were quickly destroyed like a
  fast-burning bush.
 I defeated them with the LORD's power.

13My enemy attacked me and almost destroyed
 me,
 but the LORD helped me.
14The LORD is my strength,
 the reason I sing for joy!b
 He is the one who saved me.
15You can hear the victory celebration in the
 homes of those who do what is right.
 The LORD has shown his great power again!
16The LORD's arm is raised in victory.
 The LORD has shown his great power again.

17I will live and not die,
 and I will tell what the LORD has done.
18The LORD punished me,
 but he did not let me die.

19Gates of goodness, open for me,
 and I will come in and worship the LORD.
20Those are the LORD's gates,
 and only good people can go through them.
21Lord, I thank you for answering my prayer.
 I thank you for saving me.

22The stone that the builders rejected
 became the cornerstone.
23The LORD made this happen,
 and we think it is wonderful!
24This is the day the LORD has made.
 Let us rejoice and be happy today!

25⌊The people say,⌋ "Praise the LORD!
 The LORD saved us!c
26Welcome to the one who comes in the name
 of the LORD."
 ⌊The priests answer,⌋ "We welcome you to
  the LORD's house!
27The LORD is God, and he accepts us.
 Tie up the lamb for the sacrifice and carry it
  to the horns of the altar."

---

a 118:3 Aaron's family That is, the priests.
b 118:14 the reason . . . joy Literally, "my song" or possibly, "my power".
c 118:25 Literally, "LORD, please save us. LORD, please make us successful." This was a shout of victory to honour a king returning after winning a war.

28Lord, you are my God, and I thank you.
  My God, I praise you!

29Praise the LORD because he is good.
  His faithful love will last forever.

INSIGHT

This is the longest psalm and the longest chapter in the entire Bible. In the original Hebrew language, it's broken down into twenty-two different sections or mini-psalms – one for each letter of the Hebrew alphabet. It celebrates God's Law.
Psalms 119

Aleph[a]

119 Great blessings belong to those who live pure lives!
  They follow the LORD's teachings.
2Great blessings belong to those who follow his rules!
  They seek him with all their heart.
3They don't do wrong.
  They follow his ways.
4Lord, you gave us your instructions
  and told us to always obey them.
5How I wish I could be more faithful
  in obeying your laws!
6Then I would never feel ashamed
  when I look closely at your commands.
7The more I understand how fair your laws are,
  the more sincerely I will praise you.
8I will obey your laws,
  so please don't leave me!

Beth

9How can a young person live a pure life?
  By obeying your word.
10I try with all my heart to serve you.
  Help me obey your commands.
11I study your teachings very carefully
  so that I will not sin against you.
12LORD, you are worthy of praise!
  Teach me your laws.
13I will repeat the laws we have heard from you.
14I enjoy following your rules
  as much as others enjoy great riches.

15I will study your instructions.
  I will give thought to your way of life.
16I enjoy your laws.
  I will not forget your word.

Gimel

17Be good to me, your servant,
  so that I may live to obey your word.
18Open my eyes so that I can see
  all the wonderful things in your teachings.
19I feel like a stranger visiting here on earth.
  I need to know your commands.
  Don't keep them hidden from me.
20I constantly feel a hunger
  to understand your laws.
21You tell the proud how angry you are with them.
  All those who refuse to obey your word are cursed.
22Don't let me be ashamed and embarrassed.
  I have obeyed your rules.
23Even if rulers say bad things about me,
  I am your servant,
  and I continue to study your laws.
24Your rules make me happy.
  They give me good advice.

Daleth

25I lie here like a dying man.
  Say the word, and I will live again.[b]
26I told you about my life, and you answered me.
  Now, teach me your laws.
27Help me understand your instructions,
  and I will think about your wonderful teachings.[c]
28I am sad and tired.
  Say the word, and make me strong again.
29Don't let me live a lie.
  Guide me with your teachings.
30I have chosen to be loyal to you.
  I respect your laws.
31I follow your rules closely, LORD.
  Don't let me be put to shame.
32I do my best to follow your commands,
  because you are the one who gives me the desire.

He

33LORD, teach me your laws,
  and I will always follow them.
34Help me understand your teachings,
  and I will follow them.

---

[a] **Psalm 119 Aleph** The first letter of the Hebrew alphabet. This psalm has a section for each letter of the Hebrew alphabet, and each of the eight verses in each section begins with the Hebrew letter for its section.
[b] **119:25 Say . . . again** Or "Give me life as you promised."
[c] **119:27 teachings** Or "deeds".

Obeying them will be my greatest desire.
³⁵Help me follow your commands,
  because that makes me happy.
³⁶Give me the desire to follow your rules,
  not the desire to get rich.
³⁷Don't let me look at worthless things.
  Help me live your way.
³⁸Do what you promised me, your servant,
  so that people will respect you.
³⁹Take away the shame I fear.
  Your laws are good.
⁴⁰See how much I want to obey your
    instructions!
  Be good to me, and let me live.

Waw

⁴¹Lord, show me your faithful love.
  Save me, as you promised.
⁴²Then I will have an answer for those who
    make fun of me
  for trusting what you say.
⁴³Let me always say what is true.
  I depend on your judgement to be fair.
⁴⁴I will follow your teachings for ever and ever.
⁴⁵So I will live in freedom,
  because I do my best to know your
    instructions.
⁴⁶I will discuss your rules with kings,
  and no one will embarrass me.
⁴⁷What joy your commands give me!
  How I love them!
⁴⁸Not only do I love your commands, but I also
    honour them.
  I will study your laws.

Zain

⁴⁹Remember your promise to me, your
    servant.
  It gives me hope.
⁵⁰You comfort me in my suffering,
  because your promise gives me new life.
⁵¹People full of pride are always making fun of
    me,
  but I have not stopped following your
    teachings.
⁵²I remember the laws you gave us long ago,
    Lord,
  and they bring me comfort.
⁵³I am overcome with anger when I see wicked
    people,
  who have stopped following your
    teachings.
⁵⁴Your laws are the songs I sing
  wherever I am living.
⁵⁵Lord, in the night I remembered your name,
  and I obeyed your teachings.
⁵⁶This happened because I carefully obey your
    instructions.

Heth

⁵⁷Lord, I decided that my duty is to obey your
    commandments.
⁵⁸I beg you with all my heart,
  be kind to me, as you promised.
⁵⁹I thought very carefully about my life,
  and I decided to follow your rules.
⁶⁰Without wasting any time,
  I hurried back to obey your commands.
⁶¹The wicked tried to trap me,
  but I have not forgotten your teachings.
⁶²In the middle of the night, I get up to thank
    you
  because your laws are so fair.
⁶³I am a friend to everyone who worships you.
  I am a friend to everyone who obeys your
    instructions.
⁶⁴Lord, your faithful love fills the earth.
  Teach me your laws.

Teth

⁶⁵Lord, you did good things for me, your
    servant.
  You did what you promised to do.
⁶⁶Give me the knowledge to make wise
    decisions.
  I trust your commands.
⁶⁷Before I suffered, I did many wrong things.
  But now I carefully obey everything you say.
⁶⁸You are good, and you do good things.
  Teach me your laws.
⁶⁹People full of pride made up lies about me.
  But I keep obeying your instructions with
    all my heart.
⁷⁰Those people are so stupid that they care for
    nothing,
  but I enjoy studying your teachings.
⁷¹Suffering was good for me;
  I learned your laws.
⁷²Your teachings are worth more to me
  than a thousand pieces of silver and gold.

Yod

⁷³With your hands you made me and helped me
    become what I am.
  Now help me learn and understand your
    commands.
⁷⁴Your followers will see me and be happy,
  because I trust in your word.
⁷⁵Lord, I know that your decisions are fair,
  and you were right to punish me.
⁷⁶Now comfort me with your faithful love,
  as you promised.
⁷⁷Comfort me and let me live.
  I enjoy your teachings.
⁷⁸Bring shame on those proud people who lied
    about me.
  All I want to do is study your instructions.

79Let your followers come back to me
  so that they may learn your rules.
80Let me obey your laws perfectly
  so that I will not be ashamed.

Kaph

81I feel weaker and weaker as I wait for you to
  save me.
  But I put my trust in your word.
82I keep looking for what you promised, but my
  eyes are feeling tired.
  When will you comfort me?
83Even when I am like a dried wineskin on the
  rubbish pile,
  I will not forget your laws.
84How long must I wait for you
  to punish those who persecute me?
85Proud people have tried to trap me
  and make me disobey your teachings.
86All your commands can be trusted.
  Those people are wrong to persecute me.
  Help me!
87They have almost destroyed me,
  but I have not stopped obeying your
  instructions.
88Show me your faithful love and let me live.
  I will do whatever you say.

Lamedh

89LORD, your word continues forever in
  heaven.
90You are loyal for ever and ever.
  You made the earth, and it still stands.
91All things continue today because of your
  laws.
  Like slaves, they all obey you.
92If I had not found joy in your teachings,
  my suffering would have destroyed me.
93I will never forget your commands,
  because through them you gave me new
  life.
94I am yours, so save me!
  I have done my best to know your
  instructions.
95The wicked tried to destroy me,
  but your rules made me wise.
96Everything has its limits,
  except your commands.

Mem

97Oh, how I love your teachings!
  I talk about them all the time.
98Your commands are always with me,
  and they make me wiser than my enemies.
99I am wiser than all my teachers,
  because I study your rules.

100I understand more than those who are older,
  because I obey your instructions.
101I have avoided every path that leads to evil
  so that I could obey your word.
102You are my teacher,
  so I will always do whatever you decide.
103Your words are so sweet to me,
  like the taste of honey!
104I gain understanding from your instructions,
  so I hate anything that leads people the
  wrong way.

Nun

105Your word is like a lamp that guides my
  steps,
  a light that shows the path I should take.
106Your laws are good and fair.
  I have promised to obey them, and I will
  keep my promise.
107LORD, I have suffered for a long time.
  Say the word, and I will live again!*d*
108LORD, accept the praise I want to give you,
  and teach me your laws.
109My life is always in danger,
  but I have not forgotten your teachings.
110The wicked try to trap me,
  but I have not disobeyed your instructions.
111The rules you have given me to follow will be
  mine forever.
  They give me great joy.
112More than anything, I want to obey your laws
  always,
  until the end of my life.

Samekh

113Lord, I hate those who are not completely
  loyal to you,
  but I love your teachings.
114Hide me and protect me.
  I trust what you say.
115Don't come near me, you who are evil,
  so that I can obey my God's commands.
116Support me, Lord, as you promised, and I will
  live.
  I trust in you, so don't disappoint me.
117Help me and I will be saved.
  And I will always give attention to your
  laws.
118You reject all who don't obey your laws,
  because they are liars and did not do what
  they said.
119You throw away the wicked of this world like
  rubbish.
  So I love your rules.
120I am shaking with fear before you.
  I fear and respect your judgements.

a 119:107 *Say . . . again* Or "Give me life as you promised."

Ain

121I have done what is right and good.
  Don't let me fall into the hands of those
    who want to hurt me.
122Promise to be good to me, your servant.
  Don't let those proud people do harm to me.
123I have worn out my eyes looking for your
    help,
  waiting for you to save me, as you
    promised.
124Show your faithful love to me, your servant.
  Teach me your laws.
125I am your servant.
  Give me wisdom to understand your rules.
126LORD, it is time for you to do something.
  The people do what is against your
    teachings.
127I love your commands more than gold,
  more than the purest gold.
128I carefully obey all your commands.
  So I hate anything that leads people the
    wrong way.

Pe

129Lord, your rules are wonderful.
  That is why I follow them.
130As people understand your word, it brings
    light to their lives.
  Your word makes even simple people wise.
131My desire to hear your commands is so
    strong
  that I wait with open mouth, gasping for
    breath.
132Look at me, and be kind to me,
  just as you always are to those who love
    your name.
133Guide me, as you promised.
  Don't let evil rule over me.
134Save me from those who want to hurt me,
  and I will obey your instructions.
135Accept your servant,
  and teach me your laws.
136I have cried a river of tears
  because people don't obey your teachings.

Tsadhe

137LORD, you do what is right,
  and your decisions are fair.
138The rules you have given us are right.
  We can trust them completely.
139Something that really upsets me is the
    thought
  that my enemies ignore your commands.
140I love your word.
  Time and again it has been proved true.
141I am young, and people don't respect me.
  But I have not forgotten your instructions.

142Your goodness is forever,
  and your teachings can be trusted.
143Even though I have troubles and hard times,
  your commands give me joy.
144Your rules are always right.
  Help me understand them so that I can live.

Qoph

145LORD, I call to you with all my heart.
  Answer me, and I will obey your laws.
146I call to you.
  Save me, and I will obey your rules.
147I get up early in the morning to pray to you.
  I trust what you say.
148Late into the night I stay awake
  to think about your word.
149I know your love is true, so listen to me.
  LORD, you always do what is right, so let
    me live.
150Here come those who have evil plans to hurt
    me.
  They live far away from your teachings.
151But you are near me, LORD,
  and all your commands can be trusted.
152Long ago I learned from your rules
  that you made them to last forever.

Resh

153Look at my suffering and rescue me.
  I have not forgotten your teachings.
154Argue my case, and set me free.
  Let me live, as you promised.
155The wicked have no hope of being saved,
  because they don't follow your laws.
156LORD, you are very kind.
  You always do what is right, so let me live.
157I have many enemies trying to hurt me,
  but I have not stopped following your rules.
158I look at those traitors and hate what I see,
  because they refuse to do what you say.
159See how much I love your instructions!
  LORD, I know your love is true, so let me live.
160Every word you say can be trusted.
  Your laws are fair and will last forever.

Shin

161Powerful leaders attack me for no reason,
  but the only thing I fear is your command.
162Your word makes me happy,
  like someone who has found a great
    treasure.
163I hate lies; they make me sick!
  But I love your teachings.
164Seven times a day I praise you
  because your laws are fair.
165Those who love your teachings will find true
    peace.
  Nothing can make them fall.

¹⁶⁶Lᴏʀᴅ, I am waiting for you to save me.
  I obey your commands.
¹⁶⁷I follow your rules.
  I love them very much.
¹⁶⁸I obey all your instructions and rules,
  because you know everything I do.

Taw

¹⁶⁹Lᴏʀᴅ, listen to my cry for help.
  Make me wise, as you promised.
¹⁷⁰Listen to my prayer.
  Save me, as you promised.
¹⁷¹I will burst into songs of praise,
  because you have taught me your laws.
¹⁷²Let my voice sing about your word,
  because all your commands are good.
¹⁷³I have chosen to follow your instructions,
  so reach out and help me!
¹⁷⁴Lᴏʀᴅ, I want you to save me.
  Your teachings make me happy.
¹⁷⁵Let me live to praise you.
  Let me find the help I need in your laws.
¹⁷⁶I have wandered away like a lost sheep.
  Come and find me.
 I am your servant,
  and I have not forgotten your commands.

A song for going up to the Temple.

120 I was in trouble.
  I called to the Lᴏʀᴅ for help,
 and he answered me!
²I said, "Lᴏʀᴅ, save me from liars,
  from those who say things that are not true."

³You liars, what will God do to you?
  Do you know how he will punish you?
⁴He will punish you with a soldier's sharp arrows
  and with hot burning coals.

⁵How I hate living here among these people!
  It's like living in Meshech or in the tents of
   Kedar.ᵃ
⁶I have lived too long
  with those who hate peace.
⁷I ask for peace,
  but they want war.

A song for going up to the Temple.

121 I look up to the hills,
  but where will my help really come
   from?
²My help will come from the Lᴏʀᴅ,
  the Creator of heaven and earth.

³He will not let you fall.
  Your Protector will not fall asleep.
⁴Israel's Protector does not get tired.
  He never sleeps.
⁵The Lᴏʀᴅ is your Protector.
  The Lᴏʀᴅ stands by your side, shading and
   protecting you.
⁶The sun cannot harm you during the day,
  and the moon cannot harm you at night.
⁷The Lᴏʀᴅ will protect you from every danger.
  He will protect your soul.
⁸The Lᴏʀᴅ will protect you as you come
  and go,ᵇ
  both now and forever!

A song of David for going up to the Temple.

122 I was happy when the people said,
  "Let us go to the Lᴏʀᴅ's Temple."
²Here we are,
  standing at the gates of Jerusalem.

³This is New Jerusalem!
  The city has been rebuilt as one united city.
⁴This is where the tribes come,
  the people who belong to the Lᴏʀᴅ.
 They come here to praise the Lᴏʀᴅ
  as he commanded the people of Israel to do.
⁵The kings from David's family put their
   thrones here.
  They set up their thrones to judge the people.

⁶Pray for peace in Jerusalem:
  "May those who love you find peace.
⁷May there be peace within your walls.
  May there be safety in your great buildings."
⁸For the good of my family and neighbours,
  I pray that there will be peace here.
⁹For the good of the Temple of the Lᴏʀᴅ our
   God,
  I pray that good things will happen to this
   city.

ᵃ **120:5 Meshech . . . Kedar** Places where the people were known as wild and savage fighters.
ᵇ **121:8 come and go** This may refer to going to war.

A song for going up to the Temple.

123

Lord, I look up and pray to you.
You sit as King in heaven.
²A slave looks to his master to provide what he
needs,
and a servant girl depends on the woman
she serves.
So we depend on the LORD our God,
waiting for him to have mercy on us.

³LORD, be merciful to us,
because we have been insulted for far too
long.
⁴We have had enough of the hateful words of
those proud people
who make fun of us and show us no respect.

A song of David for going up to the Temple.

124

What would have happened to us if
the LORD had not been on our side?
Tell us about it, Israel.
²What would have happened to us if the LORD
had not been on our side
when people attacked us?
³They would have swallowed us alive
when they became angry with us.
⁴Their armies would have been
like a flood washing over us,
like a river drowning us.
⁵Those proud people would have been
like water rising up to our mouth and
drowning us.

⁶Praise the LORD!
He did not let our enemies tear us apart.
⁷We escaped like a bird from the net of a hunter.
The net broke, and we escaped!
⁸Our help came from the LORD,
the one who made heaven and earth!

A song for going up to the Temple.

125

Those who trust in the LORD are like
Mount Zion.
They will never be shaken.
They will continue forever.
²Like the mountains that surround Jerusalem,
the LORD surrounds and protects his people
now and forever.
³The wicked will not always control the land of
those who do right.
If they did, even those who do right might
start doing wrong.

⁴LORD, be good to those who are good,
to those who have pure hearts.
⁵But, LORD, when you punish those who do evil,
also punish those who have stopped
following your way.

Let Israel always enjoy peace!

A song for going up to the Temple.

126

It will be like a dream
when the LORD comes back with the
captives of Zion.ᵃ
²We will laugh and sing happy songs!
Then the other nations will say,
"The LORD did a great thing for Zion!"
³Yes, we will be happy
because the LORD did a great thing for us.
⁴So, LORD, bring back the good times,
like a desert stream filled again with flowing
water.

INSIGHT

*The desert in question was the Negev, a
rocky desert in southern Israel. Finding a
stream there is something very special,
and would be a welcome discovery
for a weary desert traveller seeking
refreshment.*

Psalm 126:4

⁵Then those who were sad when they planted
will be happy when they gather the harvest!
⁶Those who cried as they carried the seedsᵇ
will be happy when they bring in the crops!

A song from Solomon for going up to the Temple.

127

If it is not the LORD who builds a house,
the builders are wasting their time.
If it is not the LORD who watches over the city,
the guards are wasting their time.

²It is a waste of time to get up early and stay
up late,
trying to make a living.
The Lord provides for those he loves,
even while they are sleeping.

³Children are a giftᶜ from the LORD,
a reward from a mother's womb.

ᵃ **126:1** *when . . . Zion* Or "when the LORD restores Zion." See "ZION" in the Word List.
ᵇ **126:6** *carried the seeds* Or "carried all their possessions".
ᶜ **127:3** *gift* Literally, "inheritance". This usually means the land God gave to each family in Israel.

[4]A young man's sons
　are like the arrows in a soldier's hand.
[5]The man who fills his quiver with sons
　enjoys a great blessing.
He will never be defeated
　when he opposes his enemy at the city gates.[a]

A song for going up to the Temple.

128
Great blessings belong to those who
fear and respect the LORD
and live the way he wants.

[2]You will get what you work for.
　You will enjoy the Lord's blessings, and all
　　will go well for you.
[3]At home, your wife will have many children,
　like a vine full of grapes.
The children around your table
　will be like an orchard full of olive trees.
[4]Yes, the LORD will really bless
　those who respect him.
[5]May the LORD bless you from Mount Zion.
　May you enjoy the blessings of Jerusalem all
　　your life.
[6]And may you live to see your grandchildren.

Let Israel always enjoy peace!

A song for going up to the Temple.

129
All my life enemies have attacked me.
Say it again, Israel.
[2]All my life enemies have attacked me,
　but they have never defeated me.
[3]They beat me until I had deep cuts.
　My back looked like a freshly ploughed
　　field.
[4]But the LORD does what is right;
　he cut the ropes and set me free from those
　　wicked people.

[5]May those who hate Zion be put to shame.
　May they be stopped and chased away.
[6]They will be like grass on a flat roof
　that dies before it has time to grow.
[7]The one who goes to harvest it
　will not find enough to cut and stack.
[8]May no one walking by those wicked people
　ever say,
　"May the LORD bless you!
We bless you in the name of the LORD."

A song for going up to the Temple.

130
LORD, I am in deep trouble,
so I am calling to you for help.
[2]My Lord, listen to me.
Listen to my cry for help.
[3]LORD, if you punished people for all their sins,
　no one would be left alive.
[4]But you forgive people
　so that they will respect and honour you.

[5]I am waiting for the LORD to help me.
　My soul waits for him.
　I trust what he says.
[6]I am waiting for my Lord,
　like a guard waiting and waiting for the
　　morning to come.

[7]Israel, trust in the LORD.
　The LORD is the one who is faithful and true.
He saves us again and again,
[8]　and he is the one who will save the people
　　of Israel from all their sins.

A song of David for going up to the Temple.

131
LORD, I don't feel proud.
I don't see myself as better than
others.
I am not thinking about doing great things
　or reaching impossible goals.
[2]No, right now I am calm and quiet,
　like a child after nursing,
　content in its mother's arms.[b]

[3]Israel, trust in the LORD.
　Trust in him now and forever!

A song for going up to the Temple.

132
LORD, remember how David suffered.
[2]He made a promise to you, LORD,
　an oath to the Mighty God of Jacob.
[3]He said, "I will not go into my house
　or lie down on my bed.
[4]I will not sleep
　or let my eyes rest,
[5]until I find a home for the LORD,
　a tent for the Mighty God of Jacob!"

[6]We heard about this in Ephrathah.[c]
　We found the Box of the Agreement at
　　Kiriath Jearim.[d]

---

[b] **127:5** *city gates* This can refer to either a battle to protect the city or to a court case held in this public place.
[a] **131:2** *like a child . . . arms* Or "like a baby on its mother's back, like a baby on my back, so is my soul". The metaphor may refer to the custom of a working mother tying her baby on her back after nursing.
[c] **132:6** *Ephrathah* Bethlehem, the town where David was born.
[d] **132:6** *Kiriath Jearim* Literally, "fields of the forest". The Hebrew word meaning "forest" is like the name of this city.

7Now, let's go to the Lord's house.
Let's worship at his throne.*a*

8Lord, get up and go to your resting place;
go with the Box that shows your power.

9May your priests be clothed in victory
and your loyal followers be filled with
joy.

10For the sake of your servant David,
don't reject your chosen king.*b*

11The Lord made a promise to David, an oath of
loyalty to him:
"I will always put one of your descendants
on your throne.

12If your descendants obey my agreement and
the laws I teach them,
then the king will always be someone from
your family."

13The Lord has chosen Zion
as the place he wants for his home.

14He said, "This will always be my place of
rest.
This is where I want to live.

15I will bless this city with plenty of food.
Even the poor will have enough to eat.

16I will clothe the priests with salvation,
and my followers will be filled with joy.

17"This is where I will make David's family
strong.
I will never let the lamp of my chosen king
stop burning.

18I will cover his enemies with shame,
and on his head will be a shining crown."

A song of David for going up to the Temple.

133 Oh, how wonderful, how pleasing it is
when God's people all come together
as one!*c*

2It is like the sweet-smelling oil that is poured
over the high priest's*d* head,
that runs down his beard flowing over his
robes.

3It is like a gentle rain*e* from Mount Hermon
falling on Mount Zion.
It is there that the Lord has promised his
blessing of eternal life.

A song for going up to the Temple.

134 Praise the Lord, all his servants
who serve in the Temple at night.

2Lift your hands towards the Temple,
and praise the Lord.

3May the Lord, who made heaven and earth,
bless you from Zion.

135 Praise the Lord!

Praise the name of the Lord!
Praise him, you servants of the Lord,

2you who serve in the Lord's Temple,
in the courtyard of the Temple of our God.

3Praise the Lord, because he is good.
Praise his name, because it brings such joy!

4The Lord chose Jacob to be his own.
Yes, he chose Israel to be his own people.

5I know the Lord is great!
Our Lord is greater than all the gods!

6The Lord does whatever he wants,
in heaven and on earth, in the seas and the
deep oceans.

7He brings the clouds from the other side of the
earth.
He sends the lightning and the rain,
and he opens the doors to release the
winds.

8He destroyed the firstborn males
of the people in Egypt and their animals.

9He did great wonders and miracles in Egypt.
He used them against Pharaoh and his
officials.

10He defeated many nations
and killed powerful kings.

11He defeated Sihon, king of the Amorites,
Og, king of Bashan,
and all the kingdoms in Canaan.

12Then he gave their land to Israel, his people.

13Lord, your name will be famous forever!
Lord, people will remember you for ever
and ever.

14The Lord defends his people;
he is kind to his servants.

---

a **132:7 at his throne** Literally, "at his footstool". This can mean the Box of the Agreement, the Holy Tent or the Temple. God is like a king sitting on his throne and resting his feet on the place where people worship him.
b **132:10 chosen king** Literally, "anointed one". This might be anyone God chose to serve in a special way, but it is usually the king he has chosen.
c **133:1 when . . . as one** Or "when brothers live together in peace".
d **133:2 high priest's** Literally, "Aaron's".
e **133:3 gentle rain** Or "mist" or "snow". The Hebrew can mean either "the oil is like the mist . . ." or "Aaron's beard is like the snow . . .".

¹⁵The gods of other nations are only gold and
    silver idols
    that people have made.
¹⁶They have mouths, but cannot speak.
    They have eyes, but cannot see.
¹⁷They have ears, but cannot hear.
    They have mouths, but no breath.
¹⁸Those who make idols and trust in them
    will become just like the idols they have
    made.

¹⁹Family of Israel, praise the LORD!
    Family of Aaron, praise the LORD!
²⁰Family of Levi, praise the LORD!
    All you who worship the LORD, praise the
    LORD!
²¹The LORD should be praised from Zion,
    from Jerusalem, his home.

    Praise the LORD!

136 Praise the LORD because he is good.
    His faithful love will last forever.
²Praise the God of gods!
    His faithful love will last forever.
³Praise the Lord of lords!
    His faithful love will last forever.

⁴Praise him who alone does wonderful
    miracles!
    His faithful love will last forever.
⁵Praise the one who used wisdom to make the
    skies!
    His faithful love will last forever.
⁶He spread the land over the sea.
    His faithful love will last forever.
⁷He made the great lights.
    His faithful love will last forever.
⁸He made the sun to rule the day.
    His faithful love will last forever.
⁹He made the moon and stars to rule the night.
    His faithful love will last forever.

¹⁰He killed the firstborn males in Egypt, both
    men and animals.
    His faithful love will last forever.
¹¹He took Israel out of Egypt.
    His faithful love will last forever.
¹²He used his powerful arms and strong hands.
    His faithful love will last forever.
¹³He split the Red Sea into two parts.
    His faithful love will last forever.
¹⁴He led Israel through the sea.
    His faithful love will last forever.

¹⁵He drowned Pharaoh and his army in the
    Red Sea.
    His faithful love will last forever.

¹⁶He led his people through the desert.
    His faithful love will last forever.
¹⁷He defeated powerful kings.
    His faithful love will last forever.
¹⁸He defeated strong kings.
    His faithful love will last forever.
¹⁹He defeated Sihon king of the Amorites.
    His faithful love will last forever.
²⁰He defeated Og king of Bashan.
    His faithful love will last forever.
²¹He gave their land to Israel.
    His faithful love will last forever.
²²He gave it as a gift to Israel, his servant.
    His faithful love will last forever.

²³He remembered us when we were
    defeated.
    His faithful love will last forever.
²⁴He saved us from our enemies.
    His faithful love will last forever.
²⁵He provides food for all living things.
    His faithful love will last forever.

²⁶Praise the God of heaven!
    His faithful love will last forever.

137 We sat by the rivers in Babylon
    and cried as we remembered Zion.
²We hung our harps nearby,
    there on the willow trees.ᵃ
³There in Babylon, those who captured us told
    us to sing.
    Our enemies told us to entertain them.
    They said, "Sing us one of your songs about
    Zion."

⁴But we cannot sing the LORD's songs
    in a foreign country!
⁵Jerusalem, if I ever forget you,
    may I never play a song again.
⁶If I fail to remember you,
    may I never sing again.
    I will always remember Jerusalem
    as my greatest joy!

⁷LORD, be sure to punish the Edomites for what
    they did
    when Jerusalem was captured.
    They shouted, "Destroy its buildings!
    Pull them down to the ground!"

ᵃ **137:2** These instruments were used to praise God in the Temple in Jerusalem. Since it had been destroyed, the people had no
reason to play the songs.

HIS FAITHFUL LOVE WILL LAST FOREVER!

How does it feel when someone praises you for something? Maybe you're happy to receive your school report, maybe you're not, but isn't it good when the teacher says you've done something well? There are lots of psalms that express how great God is, praising him for the good things that he has done.

DIG IN

READ Psalm 136:1–26

- What does the writer say over and over again?
- Why do you think he keeps saying this?
- What does the writer seem to be feeling?

Everything that the writer remembers that God has done is reinforced with this truth about God – his faithful love will last forever! Everything that he has done in history springs from the fact that he loves his people. The writer particularly focuses on things that happened to God's special people in the first few books of the Bible, things that we too are involved in as they are part of our history too.

- Who's in charge (vv.1–3)?
- What will our response to that be?

God is bigger, better, more powerful and awesome than anyone or anything. Doesn't that make you want to worship and praise him?

- What's the writer talking about (vv.4–9)?
- Read Genesis 1 to share the writer's memories of what God has done.

Creation is awesome and we are safe because we live in his world, under his rule and care.

- Have you read the stories the writer is referring to (vv.10–16)? If not, check out Exodus 1 – 19.
- How do these events show God's faithful love to the people?

In Genesis God promised to Abraham, Isaac and Jacob that they would become a special nation: God's people living in a special land and enjoying everything good God had for them. But at the beginning of Exodus we find his people living in Egypt as slaves. Then God dramatically appears to Moses and tells him that he has seen their suffering and he is about to act in keeping with the promises he had made (Exodus 3:16–17). These verses in Psalm 136 recount some of the things God did to rescue them. His faithful love will last forever!

Verses 17–22 remember the times when God gave his people victory over evil nations and kings. He gave them a land to live in, just as he had promised. And he does the same for us – one day we will go to be with him in heaven where many good things wait for us (Colossians 1:12–14).

- Many times God delivered his people from their enemies. How has he rescued us (vv.24–26)?

Our every need is provided for – he gives us food and he has rescued us from anything that wants to destroy us. We belong to him forever.

DIG THROUGH

- How has God shown his faithful love to you, according to this psalm? Think about both the things you can see and, in particular, the things you can't see in this world. How does Jesus' death demonstrate God's faithful love?
- Why not write your own prayer poem, putting "his faithful love will last forever" after each line?

DIG DEEPER

- For more psalms looking back at God's goodness check out psalms 78, 105 and 135. Look for what God has done for the people so that they want to praise him!

⁸Babylon, you will be destroyed!
   Bless the one who pays you back for what
     you did to us.
⁹Bless the one who grabs your babies
   and smashes them against a rock.

A song of David.

138
LORD, I praise you with all my heart.
   I sing songs of praise to you before the
     gods.
²I bow down towards your holy Temple,
   and I praise your name for your love and
     loyalty.
 You are famous,
   and doing what you promised will make
     you even more famous!
³When I called to you for help,
   you answered me and gave me strength.

⁴LORD, all the kings on earth will praise you
   when they hear what you say.
⁵They will sing about what the LORD has done,
   because the glory of the LORD is very great.

⁶The LORD has the highest place above all
    others,
   but he still cares for the humble.
 Even from there, so high above,
   he knows what the proud do.
⁷If I am in trouble, you keep me alive.
   If my enemies are angry, you save me from
     them.
⁸LORD, I know you will do what you have
    promised.
   Your faithful love will last forever.
 LORD, you made us, so don't leave us!

To the director: A praise song of David.

139
LORD, you have tested me,
   so you know all about me.
²You know when I sit down and when I get up.
   You know my thoughts from far away.
³You know where I go and where I lie down.
   You know everything I do.
⁴LORD, you know what I want to say,
   even before the words leave my mouth.
⁵You are all around me—in front of me and
    behind me.
   I feel your hand on my shoulder.

⁶I am amazed at what you know;
   it is too much for me to understand.
⁷Your Spirit is everywhere I go.
   I cannot escape your presence.
⁸If I go up to heaven, you will be there.
   If I go down to the place of death, you will
     be there.
⁹If I go east where the sun rises
   or go to live in the west beyond the sea,
¹⁰even there you will take my hand and lead me.
   Your strong right hand will protect me.

¹¹Suppose I wanted to hide from you and said,
   "Surely the darkness will hide me.
 The day will change to night and cover
    me."
¹²Even the darkness is not dark to you.
   The night is as bright as the day.
   Darkness and light are the same.

¹³You formed the way I think and feel.ᵃ
   You put me together in my mother's
     womb.
¹⁴I praise you because you made me in such a
    wonderful way.
   I know how amazing that was!
¹⁵You could see my bones grow as my body took
    shape,
   hidden in my mother's womb.ᵇ
¹⁶You could see my body grow each passing
    day.ᶜ
   You listed all my parts, and not one of them
     was missing.

¹⁷Your thoughts are beyond my understanding.ᵈ
   They cannot be measured!
¹⁸If I could count them, they would be more
    than all the grains of sand.
   But when I finished, I would have just
     begun.ᵉ

¹⁹You murderers, get away from me!
   God, kill those wicked people—
²⁰those who say bad things about you.
   Your enemies use your name falsely.ᶠ
²¹LORD, I hate those who hate you.
   I hate those who are against you.
²²I hate them completely!
   Your enemies are also my enemies.
²³God, examine me and know my mind.
   Test me and know all my worries.

ᵃ 139:13 *the way I think and feel* Literally, "my kidneys", which were thought to be the centre of emotions.
ᵇ 139:15 *mother's womb* Literally, "deepest parts of the earth", meaning a place we know nothing about.
ᶜ 139:16 *You . . . day* Or "You watched me every day."
ᵈ 139:17 *beyond my understanding* Or "precious to me".
ᵉ 139:18 *I . . . begun* Or "I would still be with you."
ᶠ 139:20 *Your enemies . . . falsely* The Hebrew text is not clear.

WHO ARE YOU?

How much, how often, do you long to be understood – by your family, by your friends? God sees deep inside you. He knows how you really feel, and still loves you.

DIG IN

READ Psalm 139:1–22

- What does the psalmist mean when he says that God has tested him (v.1)?

The psalmist feels able to express his true feelings to God in the psalms. He doesn't worry about being nice and polite, but just pours out his heart to God. Do you ever do that?

- How do you feel knowing that God can even hear what you think (vv.1–4)?

It's a scary thought, but it's a really good thing. At times we all have strong feelings that we can't put into words. Sometimes we feel as if our prayers are worthless because they don't sound very good. But because God knows what we want to say, we don't have to worry about that! In Romans 8:26–27 we read that God's Holy Spirit prays for us when we just don't know how.

- The psalmist feels overwhelmed by God's knowledge, saying in verse 5 "you are all around me". What do you think he means by that?
- Why might the psalmist want the darkness to surround him (vv.11–12)?

Hiding in the darkness is like Adam and Eve putting on fig leaves (Genesis 3). Did it help when they did that? What would have been better?

READ Psalm 139:23–24

At the beginning of the psalm, the psalmist says that God has looked deep inside him and knows him. At the end of his poem he asks God to keep doing this.

Adam and Eve were cast out of the Garden of Eden because of their sin, but this psalm gives us hope. It offers a beautiful picture of a relationship with God as it was always meant to be: walking with God, not hiding anything from him. This relationship is back on track for anyone who believes in Jesus. One day it will be seen in every part of our lives, and we'll never go the wrong way again.

DIG THROUGH

Ever wonder who you are or who you're going to be? In Psalm 139 the psalmist shows that he is defined by God: by who God is, by where God is, by the fact that God made him and knows him. That can be the same for you too!

- Use Psalm 139 as inspiration to write your own psalm about who God is, and look back at it when you feel unsure of yourself.

DIG DEEPER

- Take a look at Colossians 1 for more about finding your identity in God.
- Why not find out more about why we pray? Use a concordance to look up references to prayer in the Bible, have a look on the Internet or follow some Bible study notes on prayer. Here are some useful passages and verses to get you started: Matthew 6:5–13, 7:7–11, John 14:13, Philippians 4:6 and 1 Peter 5:7.

24Make sure that I am not going the wrong way.*a*
  Lead me on the path that has always been
    right.*b*

To the director: A praise song of David.

140

LORD, save me from people who are
  evil.
  Protect me from those who are cruel,
2from those who plan to do evil
  and always cause trouble.
3Their words are as harmful as the fangs of a
    snake,
  as deadly as its venom.   *Selah*

4LORD, save me from the wicked!
  Protect me from these cruel people who
    plan to hurt me.
5These proud people are trying to trap me.
  They spread nets to catch me;
  they set traps in my path.   *Selah*

6LORD, you are my God.
  LORD, listen to my prayer.
7My Lord GOD, you are the powerful one who
    saves me.
  You protect my head in battle.
8LORD, don't let the wicked have what they
    want.
  Don't let their plans succeed.   *Selah*

9My enemies are planning trouble for me.
  Lord, make that trouble fall on them.
10Pour burning coals on their heads.
  Throw them into the fire.
  Throw them into pits from which they can
    never escape.
11Don't let those cruel liars enjoy success here.
  Let disaster hunt them down.

12I know the LORD will provide justice for the poor
  and will defend the helpless.
13Those who do what is right will praise your
    name;
  those who are honest will live in your
    presence.

A praise song of David.

141

LORD, I call to you for help.
  Listen to me as I pray.
  Please hurry and help me!
2Accept my prayer like a gift of burning incense,
  the words I lift up like an evening sacrifice.

3LORD, help me to control what I say.
  Don't let me say anything bad.
4Take away any desire to do evil.
  Keep me from joining the wicked in doing
    wrong.
  Help me stay away from their feasts.

5If good people correct me,
  I will consider it a good thing.
If they criticize me,
  I will accept it like a warm welcome.*c*
But my prayer will always be against the
    wicked
  and the evil they do.
6Let their judges be put to death.*d*
  Then everyone will know that I told the
    truth.
7Like rocks in a field that a farmer has
    ploughed,
  so our bones will be scattered in the
    grave.

8My Lord GOD, I look to you for help.
  I look to you for protection; don't let me
    die.
9Those evil people are trying to trap me.
  Don't let me fall into their traps.
10Let the wicked fall into their own
    traps,
  while I walk away unharmed.

A maskil of David written when he was in the cave.
A prayer.

142

I cry out to the LORD.
  I beg the LORD to help me.
2I tell him my problems;
  I tell him about my troubles.
3I am ready to give up.
  But you, Lord, know the path I am on,
  and you know that my enemies have set a
    trap for me.
4I look around,
  and I don't see anyone I know.
I have no place to run.
  There is no one to save me.

5LORD, I cry out to you for help:
  "You are my place of safety.
  You are all I need in life."
6Listen to my prayer.
  I am so weak.
Save me from those who are chasing me.
  They are stronger than I am.

---

a **139:24 Make sure . . . way** Or "See that I don't worship idols."
b **139:24 Lead me . . . right** Or "Guide me on the ancient path."
c **141:5 a warm welcome** Or "like oil poured over my head".
d **141:6 Let their judges . . . to death** Or "Let their judges be thrown from the cliffs."

[7]Help me escape this trap,[a]
  so that I can praise your name.
Then good people will celebrate with me,
  because you took care of me.

A praise song of David.

143

LORD, hear my prayer.
  Listen to my call for help and answer
  my prayer.
  Show me how good and loyal you are.
[2]Don't judge me, your servant.
  No one alive could be judged innocent by
  your standards.
[3]My enemies are chasing me.
  They have crushed me into the dirt.
They are pushing me into the dark grave,
  like people who died long ago.
[4]I am ready to give up.
  I am losing my courage.

[5]But I remember what happened long ago.
  I am thinking about all you have
  done.
  I am talking about what you made with
  your hands!
[6]I lift my hands in prayer to you.
  I am waiting for your help, like a dry land
  waiting for rain.   *Selah*

[7]Hurry and answer me, LORD!
  I have lost my courage.
Don't turn away from me.
  Don't let me die and become like the
  people lying in the grave.
[8]Show me your faithful love this
  morning.
  I trust in you.
Show me what I should do.
  I put my life in your hands!
[9]LORD, I come to you for protection.
  Save me from my enemies.
[10]Show me what you want me to do.
  You are my God.
Let your good Spirit
  lead me over level ground.

[11]LORD, let me live
  so that people will praise your name.
Show me how good you are
  and save me from my trouble.
[12]Show me your love
  and defeat my enemies.
Destroy those who are trying to kill me
  because I am your servant.

A song of David.

144

Praise the LORD!
  He is my Rock.
He prepares me for war.
  He trains me for battle.
[2]He loves me and protects me.
  He is my safe place high on the mountain.
He rescues me.
  He is my shield.
I trust in him.
  He helps me rule my people.

[3]LORD, why are people important to you?
  Why do you even notice us?
[4]Our life is like a puff of air.
  It is like a passing shadow.

[5]LORD, tear open the skies and come down.
  Touch the mountains, and smoke will rise
  from them.
[6]Send the lightning and make my enemies run
  away.
  Shoot your "arrows" and make them run
  away.
[7]Reach down from heaven and save me!
  Don't let me drown in this sea of enemies.
  Save me from these foreigners.
[8]They are all liars,
  even when they swear to tell the truth.

[9]God, I will sing a new song[b] for you.
  I will play a ten-stringed harp and sing
  praise to you.
[10]You are the one who gives victory to kings.
  You saved your servant David from the
  sword of his enemy.
[11]Save me from these foreigners.
  They are all liars,
  even when they swear to tell the truth.

[12]May our sons be as strong as trees
  and our daughters as beautiful as the carved
  columns of a palace.
[13]May our barns be filled
  with crops of all kinds.
May our sheep produce so many lambs
  that thousands of sheep will fill our fields.
[14]   And may our cows be heavy with calves.
May no enemy break through our walls
  or carry away any of our people.
  May there be no cries of pain in our streets.

[15]How wonderful to have such blessings!
  Yes, great blessings belong to those who
  have the LORD as their God.

---

[a] **142:7** *trap* Literally, "frame around my soul".
[b] **144:9** *new song* Whenever God did a new and wonderful thing for his people, they would write a new song about it.

A song of David.

145

I will tell of your greatness, my God and King.
I will praise your name for ever and ever.
[2]I will praise you every day.
I will praise your name for ever and ever.
[3]The LORD is great and deserves all our praise!
No one can fully understand his greatness!

[4]Each generation will praise you
and tell the next generation about the great
things you do.
[5]Your majesty and glory are wonderful.
I will tell about your miracles.
[6]People will tell about the amazing things you
do,
and I will tell everyone how great you are.
[7]They will talk about your goodness
and sing about your justice.

[8]The LORD is kind and merciful,
patient and full of love.
[9]The LORD is good to everyone.
He shows his mercy to everything he made.
[10]LORD, all you have made will give thanks to you.
Your loyal followers will praise you.
[11]They will tell how great your kingdom is.
They will tell how great you are.
[12]So others will learn about the mighty things
you do,
about the glory of your kingdom—how
marvellous it is!
[13]Your kingdom will never end,
and you will rule forever.

The LORD can be trusted in all he says.
He is loyal in all that he does.[a]
[14]The LORD lifts up people who have fallen.
He helps those who are in trouble.
[15]All living things look to you for their food,
and you give them their food at the right
time.
[16]You open your hands
and give every living thing all that it needs.

[17]Everything the LORD does is good.
Everything he does shows how loyal he is.
[18]The LORD is near to everyone
who sincerely calls to him for help.
[19]He listens to his followers and does what they
want.
He answers their prayers and saves them.
[20]The LORD protects everyone who loves him,
but he destroys all who do evil.

[21]I will praise the LORD!
Let everyone praise him who alone is holy
for ever and ever!

146

Praise the LORD!
My soul, praise the LORD!
[2]I will praise the LORD all my life.
I will sing praises to him as long as I live.

[3]Don't depend on your leaders for help.
Don't depend on people, because they
cannot save you.
[4]People die and are buried.
Then all their plans to help are gone.
[5]It is a great blessing for people to have the
God of Jacob to help them.
They depend on the LORD their God.
[6]He made heaven and earth.
He made the sea and everything in it.
He can be trusted to do what he says.
[7]He does what is right for those who have been
hurt.
He gives food to the hungry.
The LORD frees people locked up in prison.
[8]The LORD makes the blind see again.
The LORD helps those who are in trouble.
The LORD loves those who do right.
[9]The LORD protects foreigners in our
country.
He cares for widows and orphans,
but he destroys the wicked.

[10]The LORD will rule forever!
Zion, your God will rule for ever and ever!

Praise the LORD!

147

Praise the LORD because he is good.
Sing praises to our God.
It is good and pleasant to praise him.
[2]The LORD rebuilds Jerusalem.
He brings back the Israelites who were
taken as prisoners.
[3]He heals their broken hearts
and bandages their wounds.

[4]He counts the stars
and knows each of them by name.
[5]Our Lord is great and powerful.
There is no limit to what he knows.
[6]The LORD supports the humble,
but he shames the wicked.

[7]Give thanks to the LORD.
Praise our God with harps.

---

[a] **145:13 The LORD . . . he does** This is found in the ancient Greek and Syriac versions and a Hebrew scroll from Qumran, but not in the standard Hebrew text.

⁸He fills the sky with clouds.
   He sends rain to the earth.
   He makes the grass grow on the
     mountains.
⁹He gives food to the animals.
   He feeds the young birds that cry out.

¹⁰War horses and powerful soldiers
   are not what he cares about.
¹¹The Lord enjoys people who worship him
   and trust in his faithful love.

INSIGHT

In the Bible we often find that "Zion" and "Jerusalem" are used almost interchangeably. Mount Zion is in Jerusalem and is important because it's where the Temple stood. Zion is therefore used particularly with reference to the religious significance of the city.

Psalm 147:12

¹²Jerusalem, praise the Lord!
   Zion, praise your God!
¹³He makes your gates strong,
   and he blesses the people in your city.
¹⁴He brought peace to your country,
   so you have plenty of grain for food.

¹⁵He gives a command to the earth,
   and it quickly obeys.
¹⁶He makes the snow fall until the ground is as
     white as wool.
   He makes sleet blow through the air like
     dust.
¹⁷He makes hail fall like rocks from the sky.
   No one can stand the cold he sends.
¹⁸Then he gives another command, and warm
     air begins to blow.
   The ice melts, and water begins to flow.

¹⁹He gave his commands to Jacob.
   He gave his laws and rules to Israel.
²⁰He did not do this for any other nation.
   He did not teach his laws to other people.

Praise the Lord!

148 Praise the Lord!

Angels above,
   praise the Lord from heaven!
²Praise him, all you angels!
   Praise him, all his army!ᵃ
³Sun and moon, praise him!
   Stars and lights in the sky, praise him!
⁴Praise him, highest heaven!
   Waters above the sky, praise him!
⁵Let them praise the Lord's name,
   because he gave the command and created
     them all!
⁶He made all these continue forever.
   He made the laws that will never end.

⁷Everything on earth, praise him!
   Great sea animals and all the oceans, praise
     the Lord!
⁸Praise him, fire and hail, snow and clouds,
   and the stormy winds that obey him.
⁹Praise him, mountains and hills,
   fruit trees and cedar trees.
¹⁰Praise him, wild animals and cattle, reptiles
     and birds.
¹¹Praise him, kings of the earth and all nations,
   princes and all rulers on earth.
¹²Praise him, young men and women,
   old people and children.

¹³Praise the Lord's name!
   Honour his name forever!
His name is greater than any other.
   He is more glorious than heaven and earth.
¹⁴He made his people strong.
   His loyal followers praise him.
Israel, his precious people, praise the Lord!

149 Praise the Lord!

Sing a new songᵇ to the Lord!
   Sing his praise in the assembly of his
     followers.

²Let Israel be happy with their Maker.
   Let the people of Zion rejoice with their King.
³Let them praise him by dancing
   and playing their tambourines and harps.
⁴The Lord is happy with his people.
   He did a wonderful thing for his humble
     people.
   He saved them!

ᵃ **148:2 army** This word can mean "armies," "angels" or the "stars and planets". This word is part of the name translated "Lord All-Powerful". It shows that God is in control of all the powers in the universe.
ᵇ **149:1 new song** Whenever God did a new and wonderful thing for his people, they would write a new song about it.

[5]Let his followers be happy for this
　　victory!
　　Let them sing for joy, even in their
　　　beds!

[6]Let the people shout praise to God.
　　And with a sharp sword in their hand,
[7]let them take revenge on the other
　　nations.
　　Let them go and punish those people.
[8]They will put their kings in chains
　　and their leaders in chains of iron.
[9]They will punish those nations as God
　　commanded.
　　This is an honour for all his followers.

Praise the LORD!

150 Praise the LORD!

Praise God in his Temple!
　　Praise him in heaven, his strong fortress!
[2]Praise him for the great things he does!
　　Praise him for all his greatness!
[3]Praise him with trumpets and horns!
　　Praise him with harps and lyres!
[4]Praise him with tambourines and dancing!
　　Praise him with stringed instruments and
　　　flutes!
[5]Praise him with loud cymbals!
　　Praise him with crashing cymbals!

[6]Everything that breathes, praise the LORD!

Praise the LORD!

PROVERBS

Who These proverb collections are attributed to a number of writers, including Solomon, Agur the son of Jakeh, King Lemuel and others to simply "the wise". The servants of Hezekiah are credited with compiling some of them.

When If we assume that Solomon had a hand in the book, it dates from the tenth century BC. The mention of Hezekiah's men implies it was edited sometime between 715 and 686 BC, which would tie in with Hezekiah's interest in the writings of David and Asaph (2 Chronicles 29:30).

What Proverbs is an anthology of sayings on life, character and conduct. The Hebrew word for "proverb" can also mean "comparison" or even "taunt". In some ways that sums up this book; it's full of provocations and nuggets of wisdom to make us think.

The book does not develop an argument, or narrate a story. It is, rather, a series of collections of practical advice about the way we should live. Proverbs advises us to act justly, to tell the truth, to work hard, to avoid damaging relationships. In the eyes of the writers of Proverbs, behaviour like this is what it means to "fear and respect the Lord".

The first nine chapters introduce the concept of wisdom, and much of it is written as though from a father giving advice to his son.

Among the recurring themes, we are urged to avoid bad influences and choose true, wise friends, to help the poor and fight for justice. The reader is advised to use words carefully, not only giving up gossip, lies and foolish talk, but welcoming the right word of correction from a friend. We are urged to get out of bed and work hard. We are warned against sleeping around, adultery, prostitutes or even associating with people who don't see anything wrong with their actions.

Proverbs urges us to gather up and treasure wisdom. Never mind your CD collection, or your designer labels or books or your gadgets – a personal collection of wisdom is one of the best investments you will ever make.

QUICK TOUR ▶ **PROVERBS**

"Knowledge begins with fear and respect for the Lord, but stubborn fools hate wisdom and refuse to learn."

Proverbs 1:7

Introduction

1 These are the proverbs of Solomon, the son of David and king of Israel. ²They will help you learn to be wise, to accept correction, and to understand wise sayings. ³They will teach you to develop your mind in the right way. You will learn to do what is right and to be honest and fair. ⁴These proverbs will make even those without education smart. They will teach young people what they need to know and how to use what they have learned. ⁵Even the wise could become wiser by listening to these proverbs. They will gain understanding and learn to solve difficult problems. ⁶These sayings will help you understand proverbs, stories with hidden meanings, words of the wise, and other difficult sayings.

⁷Knowledge begins with fear and respect for the LORD, but stubborn fools hate wisdom and refuse to learn.

Advice to a Son

⁸My son,ᵃ listen to your father when he corrects you, and don't ignore what your mother teaches you. ⁹What you learn from your parents will bring you honour and respect, like a crown or a gold medal.ᵇ

¹⁰My son, those who love to do wrong will try to trick you. Don't listen to them. ¹¹They will say, "Come with us. Let's hide and beat to death anyone who happens to walk by. ¹²We will swallow them whole, as the grave swallows the dying. ¹³We will take everything they have and fill our houses with stolen goods. ¹⁴So join us, and you can share everything we get."

¹⁵My son, don't follow them. Don't even take the first step along that path. ¹⁶They run to do something evil, and they cannot wait to kill someone.

¹⁷You cannot trap birds with a net if they see you spreading it out. ¹⁸But evil people cannot see the trap they set for themselves. ¹⁹This is what happens to those who are greedy. Whatever they get destroys them.

The Good Woman—Wisdom

²⁰Listen! Wisdomᶜ is shouting in the streets. She is crying out in the marketplace. ²¹She is calling out where the noisy crowd gathers:

²²"Fools, how long will you love being ignorant? How long will you make fun of wisdom? How long will you hate knowledge? ²³I wanted to tell you everything I knew and give you all my knowledge, but you didn't listen to my advice and teaching.

²⁴"I tried to help, but you refused to listen. I offered my hand, but you turned away from me. ²⁵You ignored my advice and refused to be corrected. ²⁶So I will laugh at your troubles and make fun of you when what you fear happens. ²⁷Disasters will strike you like a storm. Problems will pound you like a strong wind. Trouble and misery will weigh you down.

²⁸"Fools will call for me, but I will not answer. They will look for me, but they will not find me. ²⁹That is because they hated knowledge. They refused to fear and respect the LORD. ³⁰They ignored my advice and refused to be corrected. ³¹They filled their lives with what they wanted. They went their own way, so they will get what they deserve.

³²"Fools die because they refuse to follow wisdom. They are content to follow their foolish ways, and that will destroy them. ³³But those who listen to me will live in safety and comfort. They will have nothing to fear."

Listen to Wisdom

2 My son, pay attention to what I say. Remember my commands. ²Listen to wisdom, and do your best to understand. ³Ask for good judgement. Cry out for understanding. ⁴Look for wisdom like silver. Search for it like hidden treasure. ⁵If you do this, you will understand what it means to respect the LORD, and you will come to know God.

⁶The LORD is the source of wisdom; knowledge and understanding come from his mouth. ⁷He gives good advice to honest people and shields those who do what is right. ⁸He makes sure that people are treated fairly. He watches over his loyal followers.

⁹If you listen to him, you will understand what is just and fair and how to do what is right. ¹⁰You will gain wisdom, and knowledge will bring you joy. ¹¹Planning ahead will protect you, and understanding will guard you. ¹²These will keep you from following the wrong path and will protect you from those who have evil plans. ¹³Such people have left the straight path and now walk in darkness. ¹⁴They enjoy doing evil and are happy with the confusion it brings. ¹⁵Their ways are crooked; they lie and cheat.

¹⁶Wisdom will save you from that other woman, another man's wife, who tempts you with sweet words. ¹⁷She married when she was young, but then she left her husband. She forgot the marriage vows she made before God. ¹⁸Going into her house leads to death. She will lead you to

---

ᵃ **1:8 My son** The proverbs in this section may have been directed originally to a teenage boy, perhaps a prince, who was becoming a young man. They are intended to teach him how to be a responsible person and leader who loves and respects God.
ᵇ **1:9** Literally, "They are like a wreath of favour to your head and a necklace around your neck."
ᶜ **1:20 Wisdom** Wisdom is pictured here as a good woman trying to get the attention of this young man, calling him to be wise and obey God. In a later passage (9:13–18), Foolishness is represented as another woman who is urging him towards a life of sin.

THE RIGHT WAY TO GO

Imagine coming to a fork in the road. Both ways claim to take you to the same destination. Which do you choose?

DIG IN

READ Proverbs 1:1–7

- Whose name is attached to this book (v.1)?
- In what ways does it promise to help the reader (vv.2–6)?
- What is the right starting place for a person who wants to be wise (v.7)?

Proverbs is one of few books of the Bible to give such a clear introduction to what it is and what its purpose is. We're left in no doubt on either count: many of the proverbs were written by Solomon, known as one of the wisest men who ever lived (see "Dig Deeper", below) and it's all about getting the kind of wisdom he was famous for.

What kind of wisdom is that? Well, it's spelled out for us here. It's important to spot that you don't need to be either old or particularly intelligent to be wise (v.4). Pay attention to this book and you'll see the benefits, whoever you are and wherever you are in life.

There are all kinds of wisdom about all kinds of things in Proverbs. But something key is stated here and repeated throughout the book: wisdom always begins with a right fear of and respect for God. Unless you get this bit right, you will never know what it truly means to live wisely.

READ Proverbs 1:20–33

- How is wisdom pictured here?
- What does she say will happen if you don't heed her words (vv.24–31)?

Throughout the early part of Proverbs, Wisdom is pictured as a good woman who invites you to follow her way in order for your life to be "in safety and comfort" (v.33). The consequences of ignoring her invitation are disasters, problems, trouble and misery (later another woman appears, Foolishness, who calls passers-by into her house of death – see Proverbs 9:13–18). It couldn't be much clearer, could it?

DIG THROUGH

- Verses 32 and 33 make it very clear that there are "two ways" we can go – there is a wise and a foolish way to live. Does this mean that only people who believe in God know anything wise? Of course not – there are many people who do not consider themselves Christians who happen to have lots of wise things to say. So what's the difference?

DIG DEEPER

Even though it was probably compiled long after he died, verse 1 makes it very clear who is largely responsible for the book of Proverbs – King Solomon. Solomon stands out as the wisest king in Israel's history. When God came to him in a dream and asked him what he wanted more than anything, he asked for wisdom (see 1 Kings 3).

We have evidence of his wisdom both in his dealings with people (1 Kings 3:16–28) and in his reputation among the nations (1 Kings 10:1–13). However, Solomon's reign does not end as gloriously as that of his father, David, as he turns away from God towards the end of his life.

the grave. [19]All who enter lose their life and never return.

[20]Wisdom will help you follow the example of good people and stay on the right path. [21]Honest people will live in the land, and those who do right will remain there. [22]But the wicked will be forced to leave. Those who lie and cheat will be thrown out of the land.

The Blessing of Wisdom

3 My son, don't forget my teaching. Remember what I tell you to do. [2]What I teach will give you a good, long life, and all will go well for you.

[3]Don't ever let love and loyalty leave you. Tie them around your neck, and write them on your heart. [4]Then God will be pleased and think well of you and so will everyone else.

INSIGHT

People often quote these verses to those seeking guidance from God. The "right way" referred to here isn't so much about someone finding their own individual path, as finding the straight and moral path that all God's people should take in obedience to him.

Proverbs 3:5–6

[5]Trust the LORD completely, and don't depend on your own knowledge. [6]With every step you take, think about what he wants, and he will help you go the right way. [7]Don't trust in your own wisdom, but fear and respect the LORD and stay away from evil. [8]If you do this, it will be like a refreshing drink and medicine for your body.

[9]Honour the LORD with your wealth and the first part of your harvest. [10]Then your barns will be full of grain, and your barrels will be overflowing with wine.

[11]My son, don't reject the LORD's discipline, and don't be angry when he corrects you. [12]The LORD corrects the one he loves, just as a father corrects a child he cares about.

[13]Those who find wisdom are fortunate; they will be blessed when they gain understanding. [14]Profit that comes from wisdom is better than silver and even the finest gold. [15]Wisdom is worth more than fine jewels. Nothing you desire has more value.

[16]With her right hand, Wisdom offers long life—with the other hand, riches and honour.

[17]Wisdom will lead you to a life of joy and peace. [18]Wisdom is like a life-giving tree to those who hold on to her; she is a blessing to those who keep her close.

[19]With wisdom and understanding, the LORD created the earth and sky. [20]With his knowledge, he made the oceans and the clouds that produce rain.

[21]My son, don't ever let wisdom out of your sight. Hold on to wisdom and careful planning. [22]They will bring you a long life filled with honour. [23]As you go through life, you will always be safe and never fall. [24]When you lie down, you will not be afraid. When you rest, your sleep will be peaceful. [25]You have no reason to fear a sudden disaster or the destruction that comes to the wicked. [26]You can trust the LORD to protect you. He will not let you fall into harm.

[27]Do everything you possibly can for those who need help. [28]If your neighbour needs something you have, don't say, "Come back tomorrow." Give it to him immediately.

[29]Don't make plans to harm your neighbour, who lives near you and trusts you.[a]

[30]Don't take people to court without good reason, especially when they have done nothing to harm you.

[31]Don't envy those who are violent. Never choose to be like them. [32]Such crooked people are disgusting to the LORD. But he is a friend to those who are good and honest.

[33]The LORD curses a wicked family, but he blesses the homes of those who are good.

[34]He will humiliate those who make fun of others, but he is kind to those who are humble.

[35]The way the wise live will bring them honour, but the way fools live will bring them shame.

A Father's Advice About Wisdom

4 Children, listen to your father's teaching. Pay attention and you will learn how to learn. [2]The advice I give is good, so don't ever forget what I teach you.

[3]When I was my father's little boy and my mother's dear son,[b] [4]my father taught me this: "Pay attention to what I say. Obey my commands and you will have a good life. [5]Try to get wisdom and understanding. Don't forget my teaching or ignore what I say. [6]Don't turn away from wisdom, and she will protect you. Love her, and she will keep you safe.

[7]"The first step to becoming wise is to look for wisdom, so use everything you have to get understanding. [8]Love wisdom, and she will make you great. Hold on to wisdom, and she will bring

---

[a] **3:29 neighbour . . . trusts you** Or "neighbour. After all, you live near one another for protection."
[b] **4:3 dear son** Or "only son".

THE GOOD LIFE

How can I live a good and happy life? Check out your local bookshop or library and you'll find dozens, if not hundreds, of books claiming to tell you the answer to that question. The world of advertising and product marketing is geared to tell us that "Brand X" has the power to turn your drab existence into the good life!

There is no shortage of possible solutions to how to live life well. What we need though – and what the Bible offers – is the truth that cuts through the hype.

DIG IN
READ Proverbs 3:1–12

• What are the first keys to a good life the writer gives us (vv.1–10)?

The father's advice to the son here covers a few keys that lead to a godly life. Firstly, the "teaching" (v.1) refers to the Torah, the Jewish Scriptures which were taught in every good Jewish home. It's the same for Christians – sticking close to God's word is the first and best way to live wisely.

Relationships come second (vv.3–4). God is looking for us to love each other faithfully.

Next is a determination to trust God completely and not rely on our own wisdom. We all have times in our lives when things are going well. At those moments it is tempting to think we are in control. But the Lord wants to be the one who helps us go the right way.

Our attitude to money is another key area of wise living. We should always give generously of the things God has blessed us with. This is living with gratitude, aware that everything belongs to God.

• How should we feel when God disciplines us (vv.11–12)?

It's awful to be told off and it's easy to get angry when we realize that God is correcting us. But the writer wants us to see that actually love and discipline are two sides of the same coin.

Proverbs reminds us that some things in life never change. Whether you lived in Bible times or live in the twenty-first century AD, these truths have been tried and tested over many centuries. They are observations that the writers proved to be true again and again.

DIG THROUGH

• Who do you most aspire to be like? Why? What is it about their life that attracts you? Can you see how any of these wisdom values operate in their lives?

• We are so easily fooled into thinking that the latest author, TV presenter or style guru has the answer to how to live the good life. And often what they say may have some value. But how will you ensure that God's wisdom is always first in your life?

DIG DEEPER

• "Don't forget my teaching" (v.1). Many of the proverbs were originally written using figures of speech and regular, memorable rhythms in order that people could learn them by heart. Memorizing God's word has a great value in helping us live wisely. Why not try to learn verses 5 and 6 (or 5–8 if you're keen!) by heart?

you honour. [9]Wisdom will reward you with a crown of honour and glory."

[10]Son, listen to me. Do what I say, and you will live a long time. [11]I am teaching you about wisdom and guiding you on the right path. [12]As you walk on it, you will not step into a trap. Even if you run, you will not trip and fall. [13]Always remember this teaching. Don't forget it. It is the key to life, so guard it well.

[14]Don't take the path of the wicked; don't follow those who do evil. [15]Stay away from that path; don't even go near it. Turn around and go another way. [16]The wicked cannot sleep until they have done something evil. They will not rest until they bring someone down. [17]Evil and violence are their food and drink.

[18]The path of those who do what is right is like the early morning light. It gets brighter and brighter until the full light of day. [19]But the path of the wicked is like a dark night. They trip and fall over what they cannot see.

[20]My son, pay attention to what I say. Listen closely to my words. [21]Don't let them out of your sight. Never stop thinking about them. [22]These words are the secret of life and health to all who discover them. [23]Above all, be careful what you think because your thoughts control your life.

[24]Don't bend the truth or say things that you know are not right. [25]Keep your eyes on the path, and look straight ahead. [26]Make sure you are going the right way, and nothing will make you fall. [27]Don't go to the right or to the left, and you will stay away from evil.

The Wisdom of Avoiding Adultery

5 Son, listen to this piece of wisdom from me. Pay attention to what I know to be true. [2]Remember to live wisely, and what you learn will keep your lips from saying the wrong thing. [3]Now, another man's wife might be very charming, and the words from her lips so sweet and inviting. [4]But in the end, she will bring only bitterness and pain. It will be like bitter poison and a sharp sword. [5]She is on a path leading to death, and she will lead you straight to the grave. [6]Don't follow her. She has lost her way and does not even know it. Be careful. Stay on the road that leads to life.

[7]Now, my sons, listen to me. Don't forget the words I say. [8]Stay away from the woman who commits adultery. Don't even go near her house. [9]If you do, others will get the honour you should have had. Some stranger will get everything you worked years to get. [10]People you don't know will take all your wealth. Others will get what you worked for. [11]At the end of your life, you will be sad that you ruined your health and lost everything you had. [12-13]Then you will say, "Why didn't I listen to my parents? Why didn't I pay attention to

my teachers? I didn't want to be disciplined. I refused to be corrected. [14]So now I have suffered through just about every kind of trouble anyone can have, and everyone knows it."

[15]Now, about sex and marriage: Drink only the water that comes from your own well, [16]and don't let your water flow out into the streets. [17]Keep it for yourself, and don't share it with strangers. [18]Be happy with your own wife. Enjoy the woman you married while you were young. [19]She is like a beautiful deer, a lovely fawn. Let her love satisfy you completely. Stay drunk on her love, [20]and don't go stumbling into the arms of another woman.

[21]The LORD clearly sees everything you do. He watches where you go. [22]The sins of the wicked will trap them. Those sins will be like ropes holding them back. [23]Evil people will die because they refuse to be disciplined. They will be trapped by their own desires.

Dangers of Debt

6 My son, don't make yourself responsible for the debts of others. Don't make such deals with friends or strangers. [2]If you do, your words will trap you. [3]You will be under the power of other people, so you must go and free yourself. Beg them to free you from that debt. [4]Don't wait to rest or sleep. [5]Escape from that trap like a deer running from a hunter. Free yourself like a bird flying from a trap.

The Dangers of Being Lazy

[6]You lazy people, you should watch what the ants do and learn from them. [7]Ants have no ruler, no boss and no leader. [8]But in the summer, ants gather all their food and save it. So when winter comes, there is plenty to eat.

[9]You lazy people, how long are you going to lie there? When will you get up? [10]You say, "I need a rest. I think I'll take a short nap." [11]But then you sleep and sleep and become poorer and poorer. Soon you will have nothing. It will be as if a thief came and stole everything you owned.

Troublemakers

[12]Some people are just troublemakers. They are always thinking up some crooked plan and telling lies. [13]They use secret signals to cheat people; they wink their eyes, shuffle their feet and point a finger. [14]They are always planning to do something bad. [15]But they will be punished. Disaster will strike, and they will be destroyed. There will be no one to help them.

What the LORD Hates

[16]The LORD hates these seven things:
[17]   eyes that show pride,
        tongues that tell lies,
        hands that kill innocent people,

18 hearts that plan evil things to do,
   feet that run to do evil,
19 witnesses in court who tell lies,
   and anyone who causes family members to
      fight.

Warning Against Adultery

20My son, remember your father's command, and don't forget your mother's teaching. 21Remember their words always. Tie them around your neck and keep them over your heart. 22Let this teaching lead you wherever you go. It will watch over you while you sleep. And when you wake up, it will give you good advice.

23Your parents give you commands and teachings that are like lights to show you the right way. This teaching corrects you and trains you to follow the path to life. 24It stops you from going to an evil woman, and it protects you from the smooth talk of another man's wife. 25Such a woman might be beautiful, but don't let that beauty tempt you. Don't let her eyes capture you. 26A prostitute might cost a loaf of bread, but the wife of another man could cost you your life. 27If you drop a hot coal in your lap, your clothes will be burned. 28If you step on one, your feet will be burned. 29If you sleep with another man's wife, you will be punished.

30-31A hungry man might steal to fill his stomach. If he is caught, he must pay seven times more than he stole. It might cost him everything he owns, but other people understand. They don't lose all their respect for him. 32But a man who commits adultery is a fool. He brings about his own destruction. 33He will suffer disease and disgrace and never be free from the shame. 34The woman's husband will be jealous and angry and do everything he can to get revenge. 35No payment—no amount of money—will stop him.

Wisdom Will Keep You From Adultery

7 My son, remember my words. Don't forget what I have told you. 2Consider my teaching to be as precious as your own eyes. Obey my commands, and you will have a good life. 3Tie them around your finger. Write them on your heart. 4Treat wisdom like the woman you love and knowledge like the one dearest to you. 5Wisdom will save you from that other woman, the other man's wife, who tempts you with such sweet words.

6One day I was at home, standing by a window. I looked out through the shutters, 7and I saw some foolish teenagers. I noticed one of them had no sense at all. 8Walking along, he came to a corner and followed a path leading to a sinful woman's house. 9The sun had set, and daylight was fading. It was almost dark. 10The woman came out to meet him, dressed like a prostitute. She clearly had plans for him. 11She was a wild and rebellious woman who would not stay at home. 12She walked the streets, always looking for someone to trap. 13She grabbed the young man and kissed him. Without shame, she looked him in the eye and said, 14"I offered a fellowship offering today. I gave what I promised to give, 15and I still have plenty of food left. So I came out to find you, and here you are! 16I have clean sheets on my bed—special ones from Egypt. 17My bed smells wonderful with myrrh, aloes and cinnamon. 18Come, let's enjoy ourselves all night. We can make love until dawn. 19My husband has gone on a business trip. 20He took enough money for a long trip and won't be home for two weeks."a

21This is what the woman said to tempt the young man, and her smooth words tricked him. 22He followed her, like a bull being led to the slaughter. He was like a deer walking into a trap, 23where a hunter waits to shoot an arrow through its heart. The boy was like a bird flying into a net, never seeing the danger he was in.

24Now, sons, listen to me. Pay attention to what I say. 25Don't let your heart lead you to an evil woman like that. Don't go where she wants to lead you. 26She has brought down some of the most powerful men; she has left many dead bodies in her path. 27Her house is the place of death. The road to it leads straight to the grave.

INSIGHT

In a number of proverbs wisdom is personified as "she". Wisdom is pure and wise and is to be sought after. She walks with kings and rulers and brings prosperity and righteousness.

Proverbs 8

Wisdom—the Good Woman

8 Listen! Wisdom is calling.
   Yes, understanding is shouting for us.
2 Wisdom stands at the top of the hill,
   by the road where the paths meet.
3 She is near the entrance to the city,
   calling from the open gates.

---

a 7:20 won't be . . . weeks Literally, "will not come home until the full moon". The fellowship offering (see verse 14) was usually at the time of the new moon, the first day of the Hebrew month, which was two weeks before the full moon.

⁴"I am calling out to all of you.
I am speaking to everyone.
⁵You who are ignorant, learn to be wise.
You who are foolish, get some common
sense.
⁶Listen, I have something important to say,
and I am telling you what is right.
⁷My words are true,
and I will not say anything that is wrong.
⁸Everything I say is right;
there is nothing false or crooked about it.
⁹These things are clear to any intelligent
person.
They are right to anyone with knowledge.
¹⁰Choose discipline over silver
and knowledge over the finest gold.
¹¹Wisdom is better than pearls,
and nothing you desire compares with her.

The Value of Wisdom

¹²"I am wisdom.
I live with good judgement.
I am at home with knowledge and planning.
¹³To respect the LORD means to hate evil.
I hate pride and boasting,
evil lives and hurtful words.
¹⁴I have good advice and common sense to
offer.
I have understanding and power.
¹⁵With my help kings rule,
and governors make good laws.
¹⁶With my help leaders govern,
and important officials make good
decisions.ᵃ
¹⁷I love those who love me,
and those who look for me will find me.
¹⁸With me there are riches and honour.
I have lasting wealth to give to you.
¹⁹What I give is better than fine gold.
What I produce is better than pure silver.
²⁰I lead people the right way—
along the paths of justice.
²¹I give riches to those who love me,
and I fill their houses with treasures.

²²"The LORD made me in the beginning,
long before he did anything else.
²³I was formed a long time ago,
before the world was made.
²⁴I was born before there was an ocean,
before the springs began to flow.
²⁵I was born before the mountains appeared,
before the hills were set into place,

²⁶before the earth and fields were made,
before the dust of this world was formed.
²⁷I was there when he set up the skies,
when he marked where the ocean would
meet the land.
²⁸I was there when he put the clouds in the
sky,
when he made the deep springs flow.
²⁹I was there when he set the limits on the sea
to make it stop where he commanded.
I was there when he laid the foundations of
the earth,
³⁰ learning as a childᵇ by his side.
I made him happy every day,
and I was always happy to be with him.
³¹I was so pleased with the world he made
and enjoyed the people he put there.

³²"Now, children, listen to me.
If you do what I tell you, you will enjoy
blessings.
³³Listen to my teaching and be wise;
don't ignore what I say.
³⁴Those who watch for me at my door,
waiting for a chance to listen to me,
will enjoy great blessings.
³⁵Those who are there to see me find life,
and the LORD will be pleased with them.
³⁶But those who do not look for me are hurting
themselves.
Whoever rejects me chooses death."

Wisdom's Invitation

9 Wisdom has built her house; she has made it
strong with seven columns.ᶜ ²She has cooked
meat, mixed wine and put food on the table.
³She has sent her servant girls to announce from
the highest hill in the city,ᵈ ⁴"Whoever needs
instruction, come." She invites all the simple people
and says, ⁵"Come, eat my food and drink the wine
I have prepared. ⁶Leave your old, foolish ways and
live! Advance along the path of understanding."

⁷Criticize a person who is rude and shows no
respect, and you will only get insults. Correct the
wicked, and you will only get hurt. ⁸Don't correct
such people, or they will hate you. But correct
those who are wise, and they will love you.
⁹Teach the wise, and they will become wiser.
Instruct those who do what is right, and they will
gain more knowledge.

¹⁰Wisdom begins with fear and respect for
the LORD. Knowledge of the Holy One leads
to understanding. ¹¹Wisdom will help you live

ᵃ **8:16 and important . . . decisions** Some Hebrew copies have "as well as important officials, all the judges on earth".
ᵇ **8:30 learning as a child** Or "as a skilled worker".
ᶜ **9:1 seven columns** In ancient Israel, a good house was one that had four main rooms with seven columns to support the roof.
ᵈ **9:3** Or "She has sent out her servant girls and invited people to come to the highest hill in the city to eat with her."

longer; she will add years to your life. [12]If you become wise, it will be for your own good. If you are rude and show no respect, you are the one who will suffer.

Foolishness Also Calls

[13]Foolishness is that other woman, who is loud, stupid and knows nothing. [14]She sits on her chair at the door of her house, up on the highest hill of the city. [15]When people walk by, she calls out to them. They show no interest in her, but still she says, [16]"Whoever needs instruction, come." She invites all the simple people and says, [17]"Stolen water is sweet. Stolen bread tastes good." [18]Those simple people don't realize that her house is full of ghosts and that her guests have entered the world of the dead.

INSIGHT

This large collection of proverbs by Solomon (Proverbs 10 – 22:16) follow the classic proverb format of couplets that contrast one line against each other e.g. "Laziness makes you poor, but working hard makes you rich".

Proverbs 10

Proverbs of Solomon

10
These are the proverbs of Solomon:
A wise son makes his father happy; a foolish son makes his mother sad.

[2]Wealth gained by doing wrong will not really help you, but doing right will save you from death.

[3]The LORD takes care of good people and gives them the food they need, but he keeps the wicked from getting what they want.

[4]Laziness makes you poor, but working hard makes you rich.

[5]A smart son works hard all summer, but the son who sleeps through the harvest is a disgrace.

[6]People say things to bless those who are good, but the things the wicked say hide their violent plans.

[7]Good people leave memories that bless us, but the wicked are soon forgotten.

[8]The wise follow instruction, but the fool who won't stop talking will suffer for it.

[9]Honest people can always feel secure, but lying cheaters will be caught.

[10]Evil secrets[a] lead to pain and suffering, but speaking openly brings peace.[b]

[11]Words that bring life flow from good people, but the words of the wicked hide their violent plans.

[12]Hate stirs up arguments, but love forgives and forgets.

[13]Words of wisdom come from those who are smart; the stupid won't learn without a beating.

[14]Wise people are quiet and learn new things, but fools talk and bring trouble on themselves.

[15]Wealth protects the rich, but poverty destroys the poor.

[16]What good people do brings life, but wicked people produce only sin.

[17]Those who accept correction show others how to live. Those who reject correction lead others the wrong way.

[18]People sometimes lie to hide their hatred, but saying bad things about someone is even more foolish.

[19]A person who talks too much gets into trouble. A wise person learns to be quiet.

[20]Words from good people are like pure silver, but thoughts from the wicked are worthless.

[21]Good people say things that help others, but the wicked die from a lack of understanding.

[22]It is the LORD's blessing that brings wealth, and no hard work can add to it.[c]

[23]Fools enjoy doing wrong, but the wise enjoy wisdom.

[24]The wicked will be defeated by what they fear, but good people will get what they want.

[25]The wicked are destroyed when trouble comes, but good people stand strong forever.

[26]Sending a lazy person to do anything is as irritating as vinegar on your teeth or smoke in your eyes.

[27]Respect for the LORD will add years to your life, but the wicked will have their lives cut short.

[28]What good people hope for brings happiness,[d] but what the wicked hope for brings destruction.

[29]The LORD protects those who do right, but he destroys those who do wrong.

[30]Good people will always be safe, but the wicked will be forced out of the land.

[31]Those who do what is right say wise things, but people stop listening to troublemakers.[e]

[32]Good people know the right things to say, but the wicked say things to make trouble.

---

[a] **10:10** *Evil secrets* Or "secret signals lead to pain and suffering". See 6:12–15.
[b] **10:10** *speaking openly brings peace* This is from the ancient Greek version. The Hebrew text repeats the second half of verse 8.
[c] **10:22** Or "A blessing from the LORD will bring you true wealth—wealth without troubles."
[d] **10:28** *good people . . . happiness* Or "Good people can look forward to happiness."
[e] **10:31** Or "The mouth of a good man speaks wisdom, but the tongue of a troublemaker will be cut off."

11 The LORD hates false scales, but he loves accurate weights.

²Proud and boastful people will be shamed, but wisdom stays with those who are modest and humble.

³Good people are guided by their honesty, but crooks who lie and cheat will ruin themselves.

⁴Money is worthless when you face God's punishment, but living right will save you from death.

⁵Doing right makes life better for those who are good, but the wicked are destroyed by their own wicked ways.

⁶Doing right sets honest people free, but people who can't be trusted are trapped by their greed.

⁷When the wicked die, all their hopes are lost; everything they thought they could do comes to nothing.

⁸Good people escape from trouble, but the wicked come along and are trapped by it.

⁹With their words hypocrites can destroy their neighbours. But with what they know, good people can escape.

¹⁰When good people are successful, the whole city is happy, and they all shout with joy when evil people are destroyed.

¹¹Blessings from the honest people living in a city will make it great, but the things evil people say can destroy it.

¹²Stupid people say bad things about their neighbours.ᵃ Wise people know to be quiet.

¹³People who tell secrets about others cannot be trusted. Those who can be trusted keep quiet.

¹⁴A nation without wise leaders will fall. Many good advisors make a nation safe.

¹⁵You will be sorry if you promise to pay a stranger's debt. Refuse to make such promises and you will be safe.

¹⁶A kind and gentle woman gains respect, but violent men gain only wealth.

¹⁷People who are kind will be rewarded for their kindness, but cruel people will be rewarded with trouble.

¹⁸The work of evil people is all lies, but those who do right will receive a good reward.ᵇ

¹⁹People who do what is right are on their way to life, but those who always want to do wrong are on their way to death.

²⁰The LORD hates those who love to do evil, but he is pleased with those who try to do right.

²¹The truth is, evil people will be punished, and good people will be set free.

²²A beautiful woman without good sense is like a gold ring in a pig's nose.

²³What good people want brings more good. What evil people want brings more trouble.

²⁴Some people give freely and gain more; others refuse to give and end up with less.

²⁵Give freely, and you will profit. Help others, and you will gain more for yourself.

²⁶People curse a greedy man who refuses to sell his grain, but they bless a man who sells his grain to feed others.

²⁷People are pleased with those who try to do good. Those who look for trouble will find it.

²⁸Those who trust in their riches will fall like dead leaves, but good people will blossom.

²⁹Those who cause trouble for their families will inherit nothing but the wind. A foolish person will end up as a servant to one who is wise.

³⁰What good people produce is like a life-giving tree. Those who are wise give new life to others.ᶜ

³¹If good people are rewarded here on earth, then surely those who do evil will also get what they deserve.

12 Whoever loves discipline loves to learn; whoever hates to be corrected is stupid.

²It is good to learn what pleases the LORD, because he condemns those who plan to do wrong.

³Evil people are never safe, but good people remain safe and secure.

⁴A good wife is like a crown to her husband, but a shameful wife is like a cancer.

⁵Good people are honest and fair in all they do, but those who are evil lie and cannot be trusted.

⁶Evil people use their words to hurt others, but the words from good people can save others from danger.

⁷When evil people are destroyed, they are gone and forgotten, but good people are remembered long after they are gone.

⁸You praise people for their intelligence, but no one respects those who are stupid.

⁹It is better to appear unimportant and have a servant than to pretend to be important and have no food.

¹⁰Good people take good care of their animals, but the wicked know only how to be cruel.ᵈ

¹¹Farmers who work their land have plenty of food, but those who waste their time on worthless projects are foolish.

ᵃ **11:12 Stupid people . . . neighbours** Or "The neighbours hate a stupid person."
ᵇ **11:18** This is a wordplay in Hebrew. The word "lies" sounds like the word "reward".
ᶜ **11:30** Or, according to one ancient version, "The fruit of a good man is a tree of life, but a violent man takes lives."
ᵈ **12:10 but the wicked . . . cruel** Or "but even the 'kindness' of the wicked is still cruelty".

¹²The wicked want a share of what an evil man might catch. But like a plant with deep roots, a good man is the one who produces the most.ᵃ

¹³The wicked are trapped by their foolish words, but good people escape from such trouble.

¹⁴People get good things for the words they say, and they are rewarded for the work they do.

¹⁵Fools always think their own way is best, but wise people listen to what others tell them.

¹⁶Fools are easily upset, but wise people avoid insulting others.

¹⁷Good people speak the truth and can be trusted in court, but liars make bad witnesses.

¹⁸Speak without thinking, and your words can cut like a knife. Be wise, and your words can heal.

¹⁹Lies last only a moment, but the truth lasts forever.

²⁰People who work for evil make trouble, but those who plan for peace bring happiness.

²¹The Lord will keep good people safe, but evil people will have many troubles.

²²The LORD hates people who tell lies, but he is pleased with those who tell the truth.

²³Smart people don't tell everything they know, but fools tell everything and show they are fools.

²⁴Those who work hard will be put in charge of others, but lazy people will have to work like slaves.

²⁵Worry takes away your joy, but a kind word makes you happy.

²⁶Good people are careful about choosing their friends, but evil people always choose the wrong ones.

²⁷Lazy people don't get what they want, but riches come to those who work hard.

²⁸Along the path of goodness there is life; that is the way to live forever.ᵇ

13 A wise son listens to his father's advice, but a proud son will not listen to correction.

²People get good things for the words they say, but those who cannot be trusted say only bad things.

³People who are careful about what they say will save their lives, but those who speak without thinking will be destroyed.

⁴Lazy people always want things but never get them. Those who work hard get plenty.

⁵Good people hate lies, but the wicked do evil, shameful things.

⁶Goodness protects honest people, but evil destroys those who love to sin.

⁷Some people pretend they are rich, but they have nothing. Others pretend they are poor, but they are really rich.

⁸The rich might have to pay a ransom to save their lives, but the poor never receive such threats.

⁹The light of those who do right shines brighter and brighter, but the lamp of the wicked becomes darker and darker.ᶜ

¹⁰Pride causes arguments, but those who listen to others are wise.

¹¹Money gained by cheating others will soon be gone. Money earned through hard work will grow and grow.

¹²Hope that is delayed makes you sad, but a wish that comes true fills you with joy.

¹³Those who reject a command hurt themselves; those who respect a command will be rewarded.

¹⁴The teaching of the wise is a source of life; their words will save you from deadly traps.

¹⁵People like a person with good sense, but life is hard for someone who cannot be trusted.

¹⁶Wise people always think before they do anything, but fools show how stupid they are by what they do.

¹⁷An unreliable messenger brings trouble, but one who can be trusted brings peace.

¹⁸If you refuse to learn from your mistakes, you will be poor, and no one will respect you. If you listen when you are criticized, you will be honoured.

¹⁹People are happy when they get what they want. But stupid people want nothing but evil, and they refuse to change.

²⁰Be friends with those who are wise, and you will become wise. Choose fools to be your friends, and you will have trouble.

²¹Trouble chases sinners wherever they go, but good things happen to good people.

²²It is good to have something to pass down to your grandchildren. But wealth hidden away by sinners will be given to those who are good.

²³The poor might have good land that produces plenty of food, but bad decisions can take it away.ᵈ

²⁴If you don't correct your children, you don't love them. If you love them, you will be quick to discipline them.

²⁵Good people will have plenty to eat, but the wicked will go hungry.

ᵃ **12:12** The Hebrew text is not clear.
ᵇ **12:28** *that is . . . forever* Or "but there is a path that leads to death".
ᶜ **13:9** Or "The light of those who do right is happy; the lamp of the wicked goes out."
ᵈ **13:23** Or "The fields of the poor might produce plenty of food, but the unjust often take it away."

14

A wise woman makes her home what it should be, but the home of a foolish woman is destroyed by her own actions.[a]

2Those who do what is right respect the LORD, but dishonest people hate him.

3Foolish words cause you trouble; wise words protect you.

4A barn with no cattle might be clean, but strong bulls are needed for a good harvest.

5A good witness is one who does not lie. A bad witness is a liar who cannot be trusted.

6Anyone who makes fun of wisdom will never find it, but knowledge comes easily to those who understand its value.

7Stay away from fools, there is nothing they can teach you.

8Wisdom lets smart people know what they are doing, but stupid people only think they know.

9Fines are needed to make fools obey the law, but good people are happy to obey it.

10When you are sad, no one else feels the pain; and when you are happy, no one else can really feel the joy.

11An evil person's house will be destroyed, but a good person's family will do well.

12There is a way that people think is right, but it leads only to death.

13Laughter might hide your sadness. But when the laughter is gone, the sadness remains.

14Evil people will be paid back for the wrong they do, and good people will be rewarded for the good they do.

15Fools believe every word they hear, but wise people think carefully about everything.

16Wise people are careful and avoid trouble; fools are too confident and careless.

17A quick-tempered person does stupid things, but it is also true that people don't like anyone who quietly plans evil.

18Fools are rewarded with more foolishness. Smart people are rewarded with knowledge.

19Good people will defeat those who are evil, and the wicked will be forced to show respect to those who are good.

20The poor have no friends, not even their neighbours, but the rich have many friends.

21It is wrong to say bad things about your neighbours. Be kind to the poor, and you will be blessed.

22Whoever works to do good will find love and loyalty. It is a mistake to work at doing evil.

23If you work hard, you will have plenty. If you do nothing but talk, you will not have enough.

24A wise person's reward is wealth, but a fool's reward is foolishness.

25A witness who tells the truth saves lives, but one who tells lies hurts others.

26People who respect the LORD will be safe, and they will make their children feel secure.

27Respect for the LORD gives true life and will save you from death's trap.

28Kings of large nations have great honour. Rulers without a country have nothing.

29A patient person is very smart. A quick-tempered person makes stupid mistakes.

30Peace of mind makes the body healthy, but jealousy is like a cancer.

31Whoever takes advantage of the poor insults their Maker, but whoever is kind to them honours him.

32The wicked will be defeated by their evil, but good people are protected by their honesty.[b]

33A wise person is always thinking wise thoughts, but a fool knows nothing about wisdom.

34Goodness makes a nation great, but sin is a shame to any people.

35Kings are pleased with intelligent officials, but they will punish shameful ones.

15

A gentle answer makes anger disappear, but a rough answer makes it grow.

2Listening to wise people increases your knowledge, but only nonsense comes from the mouths of fools.

3The LORD sees what happens everywhere. He watches everyone, good and evil.

4Kind words are like a life-giving tree, but lying words will crush your spirit.

5Fools refuse to listen to their father's advice, but those who accept discipline are smart.

6Good people are rich in many ways, but those who are evil get nothing but trouble.

7Wise people say things that give you new knowledge, but fools say nothing worth hearing.

8The LORD hates the offerings of the wicked, but he is happy to hear the prayers of those who do what is right.

9The LORD hates the way evil people live, but he loves those who try to do good.

10Whoever stops living right will be punished. Whoever hates to be corrected will be destroyed.

11The LORD knows everything, even what happens in the place of death. So surely he knows what people are thinking.

12Fools hate to be told they are wrong, so they refuse to ask wise people for advice.

13If you are happy, your face shows it. If you are sad, your spirit feels defeated.

14Intelligent people want more knowledge, but fools only want more nonsense.

---

[a] 14:1 Or "Wisdom builds her house, but Foolishness tears hers down with her own hands."
[b] 14:32 Or "The wicked will be crushed by their evil, and those who hope for their destruction are right to do so."

THE POWER OF WORDS

As we read through Proverbs, we find that this book of ancient wisdom has lots to say about our choice of words and the power of speech.

DIG IN   READ Proverbs 15:1–7

- In what circumstance might the advice in verse 1 prove helpful?
- What power do words carry according to verse 4?

This chapter starts with a great example of the intensely practical advice which Proverbs gives to people who seek to apply it (v.1). All of us will have been involved in a confrontation or heated argument where we've raised our voices and allowed our language to become unkind and less than gracious. Those kinds of encounters lead nowhere good – sometimes they can even escalate to violence.

When we get used to giving "gentle answers" to people who try to pick fights with us, we quickly learn that they can diffuse even the tensest situation. It's hard to continue being angry with someone who looks us in the eye, tries to genuinely listen and give a reasonable answer in reply.

The writer also gives us real insight into the power of words to lift up or depress people (v.4). Kind and thoughtful words can bring new life and healing to people, even making a difference to a person's health! But words that turn out to be lies can crush us just as easily.

READ Proverbs 15:23–33

- What other things does the writer tell us about the power of words?

When we make a habit of encouraging others, we quickly realize that it's an enjoyable thing to do. Here we are reminded that not only is it great to hear the "right word at the right time" but it also brings us great joy to speak it (v.23).

A lesson that it's wise to learn early can be found in verses 31 and 32. Words of criticism and correction may not always be pleasant to hear but they can be valuable to us, and if we refuse to listen we can actually do ourselves harm. The goal is to find the kernel of truth in every criticism and act on it, rather than being so offended we refuse to see it.

DIG THROUGH

- When we speak and listen in ways that are kind and humble we show that we respect the Lord. Check out verses 25–26, 29 and 33. Why not ask him to change your words into kind ones that please him?
- Can you think of a recent time when your words may have hurt or upset someone else? Do you need to ask forgiveness and restore your relationship? How will you guard your tongue better in future?
- Think of five people you're going to see or spend time with over the next week. How can you use the power of words to bring new life or healing to them? Think creatively, make notes about what you're going to say to them and follow through on it.

DIG DEEPER

Some of the best teaching on the power of the tongue in the New Testament is in the letter of James. In his short letter James draws on Proverbs as he makes his points. He ends his chapter on controlling the things we say (James 3) with a section on what true wisdom is (James 3:13–18).

¹⁵Life is always hard for the poor, but the right attitude can turn it into a party.

¹⁶It is better to be poor and respect the LORD than to be rich and have many troubles.

¹⁷It is better to eat a little where there is love than to eat a lot where there is hate.

¹⁸A quick temper causes fights, but patience brings peace and calm.

¹⁹For lazy people, life is a path overgrown with thorns and thistles. For those who do what is right, it is a smooth highway.

²⁰Wise children make their parents happy. Foolish children bring them shame.

²¹Doing foolish things makes a fool happy, but a wise person is careful to do what is right.

²²If you don't ask for advice, your plans will fail. With many advisors, they will succeed.

²³People are happy when they give a good answer. And there is nothing better than the right word at the right time.

²⁴What wise people do leads to life here on earth*ᵃ* and stops them from going down to the place of death.

²⁵The LORD destroys a proud man's house but protects a widow's property.

²⁶The LORD hates evil thoughts, but he is pleased with kind words.

²⁷Whoever takes money to do wrong invites disaster. Refuse such gifts, and you will live.

²⁸Good people think before they answer, but the wicked do not, and what they say causes trouble.

²⁹The LORD is far away from the wicked, but he always hears the prayers of those who do what is right.

³⁰A smile*ᵇ* makes people happy. Good news makes them feel better.

³¹To be counted among the wise, you must learn to accept helpful criticism.

³²If you refuse to be corrected, you are only hurting yourself. Listen to criticism, and you will gain understanding.

³³Wisdom teaches you to respect the LORD. You must be humbled before you can be honoured.

16 People might plan what they want to say, but it is the LORD who gives them the right words.

²People think that whatever they do is right, but the LORD judges their reason for doing it.

³Turn to the LORD for help in everything you do, and you will be successful.

⁴The LORD has a plan for everything. In his plan, the wicked will be destroyed.

⁵The LORD hates those who are proud. You can be sure he will punish them all.

⁶Faithful love and loyalty will remove your guilt.*ᶜ* Respect the LORD, and you will stay far away from evil.

⁷When people live to please the LORD, even their enemies will be at peace with them.

⁸It is better to be poor and do right than to be rich and do wrong.

⁹People can plan what they want to do, but it is the LORD who guides their steps.

¹⁰When a king speaks, his words are law. So when he makes a decision, it is never a mistake.

¹¹The LORD wants all scales and balances to be right; he wants all business agreements to be fair.

¹²Kings hate to see anyone doing wrong, because kingdoms grow strong only when everyone is honest and fair.

¹³Kings want to hear the truth. They like those who are honest.

¹⁴When a king gets angry, he can put someone to death. So it is wise to keep the king happy.

¹⁵When the king is happy, life is better for everyone. When he is pleased, it is like a refreshing spring rain.

¹⁶Wisdom is worth much more than gold. Understanding is worth much more than silver.

¹⁷Good people try to avoid evil. They watch what they do and protect themselves.

¹⁸Pride is the first step towards destruction. Proud thoughts will lead you to defeat.

¹⁹It is better to be a humble person living among the poor than to share the wealth among the proud.

²⁰Good things happen to those who learn from their experiences, and the LORD blesses those who trust him.

²¹People will know if someone is wise. Those who choose their words carefully can be very convincing.

²²Good sense is a spring of fresh water to those who have it, but fools can offer only foolishness.

²³Wise people always think before they speak, so what they say is worth listening to.

²⁴Kind words are like honey; they are easy to accept and good for your health.

²⁵There is a way that seems right to people, but that way leads only to death.

²⁶The thought of hunger keeps the workers working so that they can eat.

²⁷Troublemakers create disasters. Their advice destroys like a wildfire.

²⁸Troublemakers are always causing problems. Their gossip breaks up the closest of friends.

ᵃ **15:24** *here on earth* Literally, "above", that is, "above the ground".

ᵇ **15:30** *smile* Literally, "a sparkle in the eyes".

ᶜ **16:6** *remove your guilt* Or "make atonement". The Hebrew word means "to cover" or "to erase" a person's sins.

²⁹Cruel people trick their neighbours and make them do wrong. ³⁰With a wink of the eye, they plan to trick someone. With a grin, they make plans to hurt their friends.

³¹Grey hair is a crown of glory on people who have lived good lives. It is earned by living right.

³²It is better to be patient than to be a strong soldier. It is better to control your anger than to capture a city.

³³People might throw lots to make a decision, but the answer always comes from the LORD.

17

It is better to have nothing but a dry piece of bread to eat in peace than a whole house full of food with everyone arguing.

²A smart servant will gain control over his master's foolish son. He will be treated like a son and get a share of the inheritance.

³Fire is used to make gold and silver pure, but a person's heart is made pure by the LORD.

⁴People who do evil listen to evil ideas. Liars listen to liars.

⁵Whoever makes fun of beggars insults their Maker. Whoever laughs at someone else's trouble will be punished.

⁶Grandchildren are the pride and joy of old age, and children take great pride in their parents.

⁷You wouldn't expect to hear a fine speech from a fool, and you shouldn't expect lies from a ruler.

⁸Some people think a bribe is like a lucky charm—it seems to work wherever they go.

⁹Forgive someone, and you will strengthen your friendship. Keep reminding them, and you will destroy it.

¹⁰Smart people learn more from a single correction than fools learn from a hundred beatings.

¹¹Those who are evil only want to cause trouble. In the end, punishment without mercy will be sent to them.

¹²It is better to meet a bear robbed of her cubs than a fool who is busy doing foolish things.

¹³If you do wrong to those who were good to you, you will have trouble the rest of your life.

¹⁴The start of an argument is like a small leak in a dam. Stop it before a big fight breaks out.

¹⁵The LORD hates these two things: punishing the innocent and letting the guilty go free.

¹⁶Money is wasted on fools. They cannot buy wisdom when they have no sense.

¹⁷A friend loves you all the time, but a brother was born to help in times of trouble.

¹⁸Only a fool would promise to pay for someone else's debts.

¹⁹A troublemaker loves to start arguments. Anyone who likes to boast is asking for trouble.

²⁰Crooks will not profit from their crimes, and those who plan to cause trouble will be trapped when it comes.

²¹A man who has a fool for a son will be disappointed. A fool brings no joy to his father.

²²Happiness is good medicine, but sorrow is a disease.

²³A wicked judge will accept a bribe, and that keeps justice from being done.

²⁴Intelligent people think about what needs to be done here and now. Fools are always dreaming about faraway places.

²⁵Foolish children upset their parents and make them sad.

²⁶It is wrong to punish an innocent person or attack leaders for doing what is right.

²⁷Intelligent people choose their words carefully. Those who know what they are doing remain calm.ᵃ

²⁸Silent fools seem wise. They say nothing and appear to be smart.

18

Some people like to do things their own way, and they get upset when people give them advice.

²Fools don't want to learn from others. They only want to share their own ideas.

³Do something evil, and people will hate you. Do something shameful, and they will have no respect for you.

⁴Words from wise people are like water bubbling up from a deep well—the well of wisdom.

⁵You must be fair in judging others. It is wrong to favour the guilty and rob the innocent of justice.

⁶Fools say things to start arguments. They are just asking for a beating.

⁷Fools hurt themselves when they speak. Their own words trap them.

⁸People love to hear gossip. It is like tasty food on its way to the stomach.

⁹Someone who does careless work is as bad as someone who destroys things.

¹⁰The name of the LORD is like a strong tower. Those who do what is right can run to him for protection.

¹¹The rich think their wealth will protect them. They think it is a strong fortress.

¹²A proud person will soon be ruined, but a humble person will be honoured.

¹³Let people finish speaking before you try to answer them. That way you will not embarrass yourself and look foolish.

ᵃ **17:27 remain calm** Literally, "have a cool spirit".

¹⁴A good attitude will support you when you are sick, but if you give up, nothing can help.*

¹⁵Wise people want to learn more, so they listen closely to gain knowledge.

¹⁶Gifts can open many doors and help you meet important people.

¹⁷The first person to speak always seems right until someone comes and asks the right questions.

¹⁸The best way to settle an argument between two powerful people may be to use lots.

¹⁹An insulted brother is harder to win back than a city with strong walls. Arguments separate people like the strong bars of a palace gate.

²⁰Your words can be as satisfying as fruit, as pleasing as the food that fills your stomach.

²¹The tongue can speak words that bring life or death. Those who love to talk must be ready to accept what it brings.

²²If you find a wife, you have found something good. She shows that the Lord is happy with you.

²³The poor are polite when they beg for help. The rich are rude with their answer.

²⁴Some friends are fun to be with,* but a true friend can be better than a brother.

19 It is better to be poor and honest than to be a liar and a fool.

²Being excited about something is not enough. You must also know what you are doing. Don't rush into something, or you might do it wrong.

³People ruin their lives with the foolish things they do, and then they blame the Lord for it.

⁴Wealth will bring you many friends, but become poor and your friends will leave you.

⁵A witness who lies will be punished; that liar will not escape.

⁶Many people are nice to a generous person. Everyone wants to be friends with someone who gives gifts.

⁷If you are poor, your family will turn against you, and your friends will avoid you even more. You might beg them for help, but no one will come to help you.

⁸Be a friend to yourself; do all you can to be wise. Try hard to understand, and you will be rewarded.

⁹A witness who lies will be punished. That liar will be destroyed.

¹⁰A fool should not be rich, and a slave should not rule over princes.

¹¹Experience makes you more patient, and you are most patient when you ignore insults.

¹²The shouts of an angry king are like a roaring lion, but his kind words are like a gentle rain falling softly on the grass.

¹³A foolish son brings a flood of troubles to his father, and a complaining wife is like the constant dripping of water.

¹⁴People receive houses and money from their parents, but a good wife is a gift from the Lord.

¹⁵Laziness brings on sleep, and an appetite for rest brings on hunger.

¹⁶Obey the law and live; ignore it and die.

¹⁷Giving help to the poor is like loaning money to the Lord. He will pay you back for your kindness.

¹⁸Discipline your children while there is still hope. Avoiding it can be deadly.

¹⁹People who are quick to become angry must pay the price. Protect them from punishment, and they become worse.

²⁰Listen to advice and accept discipline; then you, too, will become wise.

²¹People might make many plans, but what the Lord says is what will happen.

²²People want a friend they can trust. It is better to be poor than to be a liar.

²³Respect the Lord and you will have a good life, one that is satisfying and free from trouble.

²⁴Some people are too lazy to take care of themselves. They will not even lift the food from their plate to their mouth.

²⁵Punish a rude, arrogant person, and even slow learners will become wiser. But just a little correction is enough to teach a person who has understanding.

²⁶Those who would steal from their father and chase away their mother are disgusting, shameful people.

²⁷My son, if you stop listening to instructions, you will keep making stupid mistakes.

²⁸Using a criminal as a witness makes a joke of justice. People like that only want to do wrong.

²⁹People who show no respect for anything must be brought to justice. You must punish such fools.

20 Wine and beer make people lose control; they get loud and stumble around. And that is foolish.

²An angry king is like a roaring lion. If you make him angry, you could lose your life.

³People who refuse to argue deserve respect. Any fool can start an argument.

⁴Some people are too lazy to plant seeds. So at harvest time, they look for food and find nothing.

⁵Getting information from someone can be like getting water from a deep well. If you are smart, you will draw it out.

ᵃ **18:14** *help* Literally, "lift up" or "heal".
ᵇ **18:24** *Some friends . . . with* Or "Some friends can bring disaster."

⁶You might call many people your "friends", but it is hard to find someone who can really be trusted.

⁷When people live good, honest lives, their children are blessed.

⁸When the king sits and judges people, he must look carefully to separate the evil from the good.

⁹Can anyone say their heart is pure? Who can say, "I am free from sin"?

¹⁰The LORD hates it when people use the wrong weights and measures to cheat others.

¹¹Even children show what they are like by the things they do. You can see if their actions are pure and right.

¹²It was the LORD who gave us eyes for seeing and ears for hearing.

¹³If you love to sleep, you will become poor. Use your time working and you will have plenty to eat.

¹⁴When buying something, people always say, "It's no good. It costs too much." Then they go away and tell others what a good deal they got.

¹⁵The right knowledge can bring you gold, pearls and other expensive things.

¹⁶If someone promises to pay the debt of a stranger, get a coat or something from him to keep until the debt is paid.

¹⁷It may seem to be a good thing to get something by cheating, but in the end, it will be worth nothing.

¹⁸Get good advice when you make your plans. Before you start a war, find good advisors.

¹⁹You cannot trust someone who would talk about things told in private. So don't be friends with someone who talks too much.

²⁰Those who would curse their father or mother are like a lamp that goes out on the darkest night.

²¹If your wealth was easy to get, it will not be worth much to you.ᵃ

²²Don't ever say, "I'll pay them back for what they did to me!" Wait for the LORD. He will make things right.

²³The LORD hates it when people use the wrong weights to cheat others. It is wrong to use scales that are not accurate.

²⁴The LORD guides our steps, and we never know where he will lead us.ᵇ

²⁵Think carefully before you promise to give something to God. Later, you might wish you had not made that promise.

²⁶Like a farmer who separates wheat from the chaff, a wise king will decide who is wrong and crush them.

²⁷Your spirit is like a lamp to the LORD. He is able to see into your deepest parts.ᶜ

²⁸A king who is loyal and true will keep his power. Loyalty will keep his kingdom strong.

²⁹We admire a young man for his strength, but we respect an old man for his grey hair.

³⁰A beating can remove evil and make you completely clean.ᵈ

21 To the LORD, a king's mind is like a ditch used to water the fields. He can lead the king wherever he wants him to go.

²People think that whatever they do is right, but the LORD judges the reasons for everything they do.

³Do what is right and fair. The LORD loves that more than sacrifices.

⁴Proud looks and proud thoughts are sins. They show a person is evil.

⁵Careful planning leads to profit. Acting too quickly leads to poverty.

⁶Wealth that comes from telling lies disappears quickly and leads to death.

⁷The bad things that evil people do will destroy them, because they refuse to do what is right.

⁸Criminals cause trouble wherever they go, but good people are honest and fair.

⁹It is better to live in a small corner on the roof than to share the house with a woman who is always arguing.

¹⁰Evil people always want to do more evil, and they show no mercy to people around them.

¹¹When you punish a proud person who laughs at what is right, even fools will learn something.ᵉ But a little instruction is enough for the wise to learn what they should.

¹²God is good. He knows what the wicked are doing, and he will punish them.

¹³Those who refuse to help the poor will not receive help when they need it themselves.

¹⁴If anyone is angry with you, give them a gift in private. A gift given in secret will calm even the strongest anger.

¹⁵A decision that is fair makes good people happy, but it makes those who are evil very afraid.

¹⁶Whoever leaves the path of wisdom will be on their way to an early death.

¹⁷Loving pleasure leads to poverty. Wine and luxury will never make you wealthy.

ᵃ **20:21** Or "An inheritance greedily guarded in the beginning will not be blessed in the end."
ᵇ **20:24** Or "A man's steps are from the LORD, and people don't understand his way."
ᶜ **20:27** Or "The LORD examines your breath and searches your deepest thoughts."
ᵈ **20:30** The Hebrew text here is hard to understand.
ᵉ **21:11** Or "Punish a rude, arrogant person, and the others will become wise."

18The wicked must pay for what happens to good people; the cheaters will be taken in exchange for the honest.

19It is better to live alone in the desert than with a quick-tempered wife who loves to argue.

20Wise people save the nice things they have. Fools use up everything as soon as they get it.

21People who try hard to do good and be faithful will find life, goodness and honour.

22A wise person can defeat a city full of warriors and tear down the defences they trust in.

23People who are careful about what they say will save themselves from trouble.

24Proud people think they are better than others. They show they are evil by what they do.

25Lazy people will cause their own destruction because they refuse to work.

26Some people are greedy and never have enough. Good people are generous and have plenty.

27God hates sacrifices from the wicked, especially when their reason for offering them is evil.

28Witnesses who lie will be caught and punished. A careful listener will always be there to speak up.

29Good people know they are right, but the wicked have to pretend.

30There is no one wise enough to make a plan that can succeed if the LORD is against it.

31You can prepare your horses for battle, but only the LORD can give you the victory.

22 It is better to be respected than to be rich. A good name is worth more than silver or gold.

2The rich and the poor are the same. The LORD made them all.

3Wise people see trouble coming and get out of its way, but fools go straight to it and suffer for it.

4Respect the LORD and be humble. Then you will have wealth, honour and true life.

5Evil people are trapped by many troubles, but those who want to live avoid them.

6Teach children in a way that fits their needs, and even when they are old, they will not leave the right path.

7The rich rule over the poor. The one who borrows is a slave to the one who lends.

8Those who spread trouble will harvest trouble. In the end, they will be destroyed for the trouble they caused.

9Generous people will be blessed, because they share their food with the poor.

10Get rid of the proud who laugh at what is right, and trouble will leave with them. All arguments and insults will end.

11Love a pure heart and kind words, and the king will be your friend.

12The LORD watches over true knowledge, and he opposes those who try to deceive others.

13A person who is lazy and wants to stay at home says, "There is a lion outside, and I might be killed in the streets!"

14The sin of adultery is a trap, and the LORD gets very angry with those who fall into it.

15Children do foolish things, but if you punish them, they will learn not to do them.

16These two things will make you poor: hurting the poor to make yourself rich and giving gifts to the rich.

Thirty Wise Sayings

17Listen carefully to these words from the wise. Pay attention to what I have learned. 18It will be good for you to remember these words and have them ready when they are needed. 19I will teach you these things now. I want you to trust the LORD. 20I have written 30 sayings for you.[a] These are words of advice and wisdom. 21They will teach you things that you can know for sure to be true. Then you can give good answers to the one who sent you.

— 1 —

22It is easy to steal from the poor, but don't do it. And don't take advantage of them in court. 23The LORD is on their side. He supports the poor, and he will take from those who take from them.

— 2 —

24Don't be friends with people who become angry easily. Don't stay around quick-tempered people. 25If you do, you may learn to be like them. Then you will have the same problems they do.

— 3 —

26Don't promise to pay what another person owes. 27If you cannot pay, you will lose everything you have. So why should you lose the bed you sleep on?

— 4 —

28Never move an old property line that was marked long ago by your ancestors.

— 5 —

29Skilled workers will always serve kings. They will never have to work for less important people.

---

a 22:20 *I have . . . for you* Or "I wrote this for you earlier."

MORE WORDS TO THE WISE

Life is a journey of learning – if we choose to make it one! Some people go through life making the same mistakes over and over again. Others seem to sail through, learning all the time.

DIG IN

READ Proverbs 22:1–16

- Would you rather be rich or have a good reputation (v.1)?
- What else does this passage say about money (vv.2,4,7,16)?

According to the Proverbs, it's far better to have the riches of good relationships than physical wealth. Even though the Bible has no problem with money and wealth in itself (verse 2 of this passage says in God's sight rich and poor are the same), we are not to make it the focus of our lives. By comparison, healthy relationships with people are worth so much more.

We are particularly to watch out that we don't oppress other people in our desire for wealth (v.16). This is a serious sin which Jesus also condemns. (Check out Matthew 23:1–7,23–26.)

- Look again at verse 4. What does it claim for believers in God?

Verse 4 is a good example of how Proverbs works. The proverbs contained in this book sometimes sound like promises from God. But they're not meant to be read like that. They are instead wise observations that have stood the test of time – things that many generations of people who have feared God have proved to be true. Respecting the Lord and keeping a humble heart will not necessarily guarantee you "wealth, honour and true life" but generations have discovered that this way of living pleases God.

Another example of this is verse 6, a popular verse quoted by people on the topic of raising children. Parents need to do their best to raise their children according to God's word and to teach them a love and respect for God.

DIG THROUGH

- Proverbs exists because down the generations, people who loved and followed God found certain things to be true. What have you personally discovered in Proverbs that's going to make a difference in your life at home, school or college?
- Have you learnt things from Proverbs that you feel excited about passing on?
- Have you been raised by parents seeking to follow verse 6? If so, give thanks to God for them and think of ways to thank and honour them for their desire to be obedient to God.

DIG DEEPER

- Proverbs offers such a wealth of wisdom to people who are willing to listen and learn from it. It's worth taking the time to read the whole book, perhaps a chapter a day, highlighting the verses that you most want to remember and try to live by.
- Here are some of the headings you might group verses by: Speaking and Listening, Generosity, Friends and Family, Guidance for the Future.

— 6 —

23 When you sit and eat with an important person, remember who you are with. ²Never eat too much, even if you are very hungry. ³Don't eat too much of his fine food. It might be a trick.

— 7 —

⁴Don't ruin your health trying to get rich. If you are smart, you will give it up. ⁵In the blink of an eye, money can disappear, as if it grew wings and flew away like a bird.

— 8 —

⁶Don't eat with selfish people. Control any desire you have for their finest foods. ⁷They might tell you to eat and drink all you want, but they don't really mean it. They are the kind of people who are only thinking about the cost. ⁸And if you eat their food, you will get sick and be embarrassed.

— 9 —

⁹Don't try to teach fools. They will make fun of your wise words.

— 10 —

¹⁰Never move an old property line, and don't take land that belongs to orphans. ¹¹The Lord will be against you. He is powerful and protects orphans.

— 11 —

¹²Listen to your teacher and learn all you can.

— 12 —

¹³Always correct children when they need it. If you spank them, it will not kill them. ¹⁴In fact, you might save their lives.

— 13 —

¹⁵My son, it makes me happy when you make a wise decision. ¹⁶It makes me feel good inside when you say the right things.

— 14 —

¹⁷Never envy evil people, but always respect the Lord. ¹⁸This will give you something to hope for that will not disappoint you.

— 15 —

¹⁹So listen, my son, and be wise. Always be careful to follow the right path. ²⁰Don't make friends with people who drink too much wine and eat too much food. ²¹Those who eat and drink too much become poor. They sleep too much and end up wearing rags.

— 16 —

²²Listen to your father. Without him, you would never have been born. Respect your mother, even when she is old. ²³Truth, wisdom, learning and understanding are worth paying money for. They are worth far too much to ever sell. ²⁴The father of a good person is very happy. A wise child brings him joy. ²⁵Make both of your parents happy. Give your mother that same joy.

— 17 —

²⁶My son, listen closely to what I am saying. Let my life be your example. ²⁷Prostitutes and bad women are a trap. They are like a deep well that you cannot escape. ²⁸A bad woman waits for you like a thief, and she causes many men to be unfaithful to their wives.

— 18 —

^{29–30}Who gets into fights and arguments? Who gets hurt for no reason and has red, bloodshot eyes? People who stay out too late drinking wine, staring into their strong drinks. ³¹So be careful with wine. It is pretty and red as it sparkles in the cup. And it goes down so smoothly when you drink it. ³²But in the end, it will bite like a snake; it will sting you with its poison. ³³Wine will cause you to see strange things and to say things that make no sense. ³⁴When you lie down, you will think you are on a rough sea and feel like you are at the top of the mast. ³⁵You will say, "They hit me, but I never felt it. They beat me, but I don't remember it. Now I can't wake up. I need another drink."

— 19 —

24 Don't be jealous of evil people. Have no desire to be around them. ²In their hearts they plan to do evil. All they talk about is making trouble.

— 20 —

³Good homes are built on wisdom and understanding. ⁴Knowledge fills the rooms with rare and beautiful treasures.

— 21 —

⁵Wisdom makes a man more powerful. Knowledge gives a man strength. ⁶Get good advice before you start a war. To win, you must have many good advisors.

— 22 —

⁷Fools cannot understand wisdom. They have nothing to say when people are discussing important things.

— 23 —

8If you start planning ways to do wrong, people will learn that you are a troublemaker. 9Such foolish plans are wrong, and people have no respect for someone who laughs at what is right.

— 24 —

10If you are weak in times of trouble, that is real weakness.

— 25 —

11If you see someone on their way to death or in danger of being killed, you must do something to save them. 12You cannot say, "It's none of my business." The Lord knows everything, and he knows why you do things. He watches you, and he will pay you back for what you do.

— 26 —

13My son, eat honey; it is good. Honey straight from the honeycomb is the sweetest. 14In the same way, know that wisdom is good for you. Wisdom will give you something to hope for that will not disappoint you.

— 27 —

15Don't be like a criminal who makes plans to rob those who are good or take away their homes. 16Good people might fall again and again, but they always get up. It is the wicked who are defeated by their troubles.

— 28 —

17Don't be happy when your enemy has troubles. Don't be glad when they fall. 18The LORD will see this, and he might be upset with you and decide not to punish your enemy.

— 29 —

19Don't let those who are evil upset you, and don't be jealous of them. 20They have no hope. Their light will burn out.

— 30 —

21Son, respect the LORD and the king, and don't join with those who are against them, 22because people like that can quickly be destroyed. You have no idea how much trouble God and the king can make for their enemies.

More Wise Sayings

23These are also words from the wise:

A judge must be fair. He must not support some people simply because he knows them. 24The people will turn against a judge who lets the guilty go free. Even the people of other nations will curse him. 25But if a judge punishes the guilty, then people will be happy with him, and he will be a blessing to them.

26An honest answer is as pleasing as a kiss on the lips.

27First get your fields ready, next plant your crops and then build your house.

28Don't speak against someone without a good reason, or you will appear foolish.

29Don't say, "You hurt me, so I will do the same to you. I will punish you for what you did to me."

30I walked past a field that belonged to a lazy man. It was a vineyard that belonged to someone who understood nothing. 31Weeds were growing everywhere! Wild vines covered the ground, and the wall around the vineyard was broken and falling down. 32I looked at this and thought about it. This is what I learned: 33a little sleep, a little rest, folding your arms and taking a nap. 34Suddenly, you will be poor, as if a thief had come. You will have nothing but the feeling you were robbed.

More Wise Sayings From Solomon

25 These are some more wise sayings from Solomon. These proverbs were copied by servants of Hezekiah, the king of Judah.

2We honour God for the things he keeps secret. But we honour kings for the things they can discover.

3We cannot discover how high the sky is above us or how deep the earth is below. The same is true with the minds of kings. We cannot understand them.

4Remove the worthless things from silver to make it pure, and a worker can make something beautiful. 5Take the evil advisors away from a king, and goodness will make his kingdom strong.

6Don't boast about yourself before the king and pretend you are someone important. 7It is much better for the king to invite you to take a more important position than to embarrass you in front of his officials.

8Don't be too quick to tell a judge about something you saw. You will be embarrassed if someone else proves you wrong.

9If you want to tell your friends about your own problems, tell them. But don't discuss what someone told you in private. 10Whoever hears it will lose their respect for you and will never trust you again.

11Saying the right thing at the right time is like a golden apple in a silver setting. 12Wise advice to a listening ear is like gold earrings or fine jewellery.

13To his master who sent him, a messenger who can be trusted is as refreshing as a drink of cold water on a hot summer day.*a*

a **25:13 drink . . . day** Literally, "as the cold snow at harvest time". This probably refers to snow or ice brought down from Mount Hermon in Lebanon.

¹⁴People who promise to give gifts but never give them are like clouds and wind that bring no rain.

¹⁵With patience, you can make anyone change their thinking, even a ruler. Gentle speech is very powerful.

¹⁶Honey is good, but don't eat too much of it, or you will be sick. ¹⁷And don't visit your neighbours' homes too often, or they will begin to hate you.

¹⁸A person who gives false testimony against a neighbour is as deadly as a club, a sword or a very sharp arrow. ¹⁹Never depend on a liar in times of trouble. It's like chewing with a bad tooth or walking with an injured foot.

²⁰Singing happy songs to a sad person is as foolish as taking a coat off on a cold day or mixing soda and vinegar.

²¹If your enemies are hungry, give them something to eat. If they are thirsty, give them some water. ²²This will make them feel the burning pain of shame,ª and the Lᴏʀᴅ will reward you for being good to them.

²³Just as wind blowing from the north brings rain, telling secrets brings anger.

²⁴It is better to live in a small corner of the roof than to share the house with a woman who is always arguing.

²⁵Good news from a faraway place is like a cool drink of water when you are hot and thirsty.

²⁶Good people who don't stand strong against evil are like springs that have been polluted or pools that have turned dirty and muddy.

²⁷Just as eating too much honey is not good, it is not good for people to always be looking for honour.

²⁸People who cannot control themselves are like cities without walls to protect them.

Wise Sayings About Fools

26 Just as snow should not fall in summer, nor rain at harvest time, so people should not honour a fool.

²Don't worry when someone curses you for no reason. Nothing bad will happen. Such words are like birds that fly past and never stop.

³You have to whip a horse, you have to put a bridle on a mule, and you have to beat a fool.

⁴⁻⁵There is no good way to answer fools when they say something stupid. If you answer them, then you, too, will look like a fool. If you don't answer them, they will think they are smart.

⁶Never let a fool carry your message. If you do, it will be like cutting off your own feet. You are only asking for trouble.

⁷A fool trying to say something wise is like a paralysed person trying to walk.

⁸Showing honour to a fool is as bad as tying a rock in a sling.

⁹A fool trying to say something wise is like a drunk trying to pick a thorn out of his hand.

¹⁰Hiring a fool or a stranger who is just passing by is dangerous—you don't know who might get hurt.

¹¹Like a dog that returns to its vomit, a fool does the same foolish things again and again.

¹²People who think they are wise when they are not are worse than fools.

¹³A person who is lazy and wants to stay at home says, "What if there is a lion out there? Really, there might be a lion in the street!"

¹⁴Like a door swinging on its hinges, a lazy man turns back and forth on his bed.

¹⁵Lazy people are too lazy to lift the food from their plate to their mouth.

¹⁶Lazy people think they are seven times smarter than the people who really have good sense.

¹⁷To step between two people arguing is as foolish as going out into the street and grabbing a stray dog by the ears.

¹⁸⁻¹⁹Anyone who would trick someone and then say, "I was only joking" is like a fool who shoots flaming arrows into the air and accidentally kills someone.

²⁰Without wood, a fire goes out. Without gossip, arguments stop.

²¹Charcoal keeps the coals glowing, wood keeps the fire burning, and troublemakers keep arguments alive.

²²People love to hear gossip. It is like tasty food on its way to the stomach.

²³Good words that hide an evil heart are like silver paint over a cheap, clay pot. ²⁴Evil people say things to make themselves look good, but they keep their evil plans a secret. ²⁵What they say sounds good, but don't trust them. They are full of evil ideas. ²⁶They hide their evil plans with nice words, but in the end, everyone will see the evil they do.

²⁷Whoever digs a pit can fall into it. Whoever rolls a large stone can be crushed by it.

²⁸Liars hate the people they hurt, and false praise can hurt people.

27 Never boast about what you will do in the future; you have no idea what tomorrow will bring.

²Never praise yourself. Let others do it.

ª **25:22 This . . . shame** Literally, "for you will heap coals of fire on his head".

[3]A stone is heavy, and sand is hard to carry, but the irritation caused by a fool is much harder to bear.

[4]Anger is cruel and can destroy like a flood, but jealousy is much worse.

[5]Open criticism is better than hidden love.

[6]You can trust what your friend says, even when it hurts. But your enemies want to hurt you, even when they greet you like a friend.

[7]When you are full, you will not even eat honey. When you are hungry, even something bitter tastes sweet.

[8]A man away from home is like a bird away from its nest.

[9]Perfume and incense make you feel good, and so does good advice from a friend.

[10]Don't forget your own friends or your father's friends. If you have a problem, go to your neighbour for help. It is better to ask a neighbour who is near than a brother who is far away.

[11]My son, be wise. This will make me happy. Then I will be able to answer those who criticize me.

[12]Wise people see trouble coming and get out of its way, but fools go straight to the trouble and suffer for it.

[13]When you make a deal with a stranger, get something from him and any other foreigners with him to make sure he will pay you.

[14]Don't wake up your neighbours early in the morning with a shout of "Good morning!" They will treat it like a curse, not a blessing.

INSIGHT

In Bible times houses were made of mud and had flat roofs. Leaky roofs were a common problem and the subject of many jokes.

Proverbs 27:15

[15]A complaining wife is like water that never stops dripping on a rainy day. [16]Stopping her is like trying to stop the wind or trying to hold oil in your hand.

[17]As one piece of iron sharpens another, so friends keep each other sharp.

[18]People who take care of fig trees are allowed to eat the fruit. In the same way, people who take care of their masters will be rewarded.

[19]Just as you can see your own face reflected in water, so your heart reflects the kind of person you are.

[20]Just as the place of death and destruction is never full, people always want more and more.

[21]People use fire to purify gold and silver. In the same way, you are tested by the praise people give you.

[22]Even if you pound fools to powder like grain in a bowl, you will never force the foolishness out of them.

[23]Learn all you can about your sheep. Take care of your goats the best you can. [24]Neither wealth nor nations last forever. [25]Cut the hay, and new grass will grow. Then gather the new plants that grow on the hills. [26]Cut the wool from your lambs, and make your clothes. Sell some of your goats, and buy some land. [27]Then there will be plenty of goat's milk for you and your family, with enough to keep the servants healthy.

28

The wicked are afraid of everything, but those who do what is right are as brave as lions.

[2]A lawless nation will have many bad leaders. But a smart leader will rule for a long time in a land where people obey the law.

[3]A leader who takes advantage of the poor is like a hard rain that destroys the crops.[a]

[4]Those who refuse to obey the law promote evil. Those who obey the law oppose evil.

[5]The wicked don't understand justice, but those who love the Lord understand it completely.

[6]It is better to be poor and honest than rich and evil.

[7]A smart son obeys the laws, but a son who spends time with worthless people brings shame to his father.

[8]If you get rich by charging high interest rates, your wealth will go to someone who is kind to the poor.

[9]When people do not listen to God's teachings, he does not listen to their prayers.

[10]Those who plan to hurt good people will fall into their own traps, but good things will happen to those who are good.

[11]The rich always think they are wise, but a poor person who is wise can see the truth.

[12]When good people become leaders, everything is great, but when the wicked rise to power, everyone hides.

[13]Whoever hides their sins will not be successful, but whoever confesses their sins and stops doing wrong will receive mercy.

[14]People who respect others will be blessed, but stubborn people will have plenty of troubles.

[15]An evil ruler over those who are helpless is like an angry lion or a charging bear.

---

[a] **28:3** Or "A poor person who takes advantage of beggars is like a hard rain and no food."

¹⁶A foolish ruler hurts the people under him, but a ruler who hates wrong will rule for a long time.

¹⁷A murderer will never have peace. Don't support such a person.

¹⁸Honest people will be safe, but dishonest people will be ruined.

¹⁹Whoever works hard will have plenty to eat, but whoever wastes their time with dreams will always be poor.

²⁰People who can be trusted will have many blessings, but those who are just trying to get rich in a hurry will be punished.

²¹It is wrong for a judge to support someone simply because he knows them. But some judges will change their decisions for the price of a loaf of bread.

²²Selfish people only want to get rich. They do not realize that they are very close to being poor.

²³Correct someone, and later they will thank you. That is much better than just saying something to be nice.

²⁴Someone might steal from their parents and say, "I did nothing wrong." But that person is as bad as an enemy who smashes everything in the house.

²⁵Greedy people might sue you in court, but those who trust the LORD are rewarded.

²⁶It is foolish to be too confident. Those who ask for advice are wise and will escape disaster.

²⁷Whoever gives to the poor will have plenty. Whoever refuses to help them will get nothing but curses.

²⁸When the wicked rise to power, everyone hides. When they are defeated, good people multiply.

29 Some people refuse to bend when someone corrects them. Eventually they will break, and there will be no one to repair the damage.

²When the rulers are good, the people are happy. When the rulers are evil, the people complain.

³A son who loves wisdom makes his father happy. One who wastes his money on prostitutes will lose his wealth.

⁴A nation will be strong when it has a fair and just king. A nation will be weak when it has a king who is selfish and demands gifts.

⁵If you give false praise to others in order to get what you want, you are only setting a trap for yourself.

⁶Evil people are defeated by their sin, but good people will sing and be happy.

⁷Good people want to do what is right for the poor, but the wicked don't care.

⁸Proud people who laugh at what is right cause problems that divide whole cities, but people who are wise are able to calm those who are angry.

⁹If someone who is wise tries to settle a problem with a fool, the fool will argue and say stupid things, and they will never agree.

¹⁰If you always try to be honest, murderers will hate you, but those who do what is right will want you to be their friend.

¹¹Fools are quick to express their anger, but wise people are patient and control themselves.

¹²If a ruler listens to lies, all his officials will be evil.

¹³In one way the poor and those who steal from them are the same: the LORD made them both.

¹⁴If a king judges the poor fairly, he will rule for a long time.

¹⁵Punishment and discipline can make children wise, but children who are never corrected will bring shame to their mother.

¹⁶If the wicked are ruling the nation, sin will be everywhere, but those who do what is right will win in the end.

¹⁷Correct your children whenever they are wrong. Then you will always be proud of them. They will never make you ashamed.

¹⁸If a nation is not guided by God, the people will lose self-control, but the nation that obeys God's law will be happy.

¹⁹Servants will not learn a lesson if you only talk to them. They might understand you, but they will not obey.

²⁰There is more hope for a fool than for someone who speaks without thinking.

²¹Give your servants everything they want, and they will learn to be wasteful.

²²An angry person causes arguments, and someone who is quick-tempered is guilty of many sins.

²³Your pride can bring you down. Humility will bring you honour.

²⁴You are your own worst enemy if you take part in a crime. You will not be able to tell the truth even when people threaten you.

²⁵Fear can be a trap, but if you trust in the LORD, you will be safe.

²⁶Many people want the friendship of a ruler, but the LORD is the only one who judges people fairly.

²⁷Good people think the wicked are disgusting, and the wicked feel disgust for those who are honest.

Wise Sayings of Agur Son of Jakeh

30 These are the wise sayings of Agur son of Jakeh from Massa. He says, "God, I am tired, so tired. How can I keep going?"ᵃ

²I am stupid. I am not as smart as other people are. ³I have not learned to be wise. I know

---

ᵃ **30:1** *He says, "God, . . . keep going?"* Or "This is his message to Ithiel and Ucal."

nothing about the Holy One.[a] 4Who has ever gone up to heaven and come back down? Who gathered the winds in his hand? Who can gather up all the water in his lap? Who set the limits for the world? What is his name, and what is his son's name? Do you know?

5You can trust this: Every word that God speaks is true. God is a safe place for those who go to him. 6So don't try to change what God says. If you do, he will punish you and prove that you are a liar.

7God, I ask you to do two things for me before I die. 8Don't let me tell lies. And don't make me too rich or too poor—give me only enough food for each day. 9If I have too much, I might deny that I need you, LORD. But if I am too poor, I might steal and bring shame to the name of my God.

10Never say bad things about a slave to his master. If you do, he will curse you, and you will suffer for it.

11Some people curse their fathers and refuse to bless their mothers.

12Some people think they are pure, but they have done nothing to remove the filth of their sin.

13Some people are so proud of themselves, and they look down on everyone else.

14There are people whose teeth are like swords and their jaws like knives. They take everything they can from the poor.

15Greedy people know only two things:[b] "Give me," and "Give me." There are three other things that are never satisfied—really, four things that never have enough: 16the place of death, a woman with no children, dry ground that needs rain and a fire that will never stop by itself.

17People who make fun of their father or refuse to obey their mother should have their eyes plucked out by wild birds and be eaten by vultures.

18There are three things that are hard for me to understand—really, four things that I don't understand: 19an eagle flying in the sky, a snake moving on a rock, a ship moving across the ocean and a man in love with a woman.

20A woman who is not faithful to her husband acts as if she is innocent. She eats, wipes her mouth and says she has done nothing wrong.

21There are three things that make trouble on the earth—really, four that the earth cannot bear: 22a slave who becomes a king, fools who have everything they need, 23a woman whose husband hated her but still married her and a servant girl who becomes ruler over the woman she serves.

24There are four things on the earth that are small but very wise:

25ants are small and weak, but they save their food all summer;

26badgers are small animals, but they make their homes in the rocks;

27locusts have no king, but they are able to work together;

28lizards are small enough to catch with your hands, but you can find them living in kings' palaces.

29There are three things that look proud when they walk—really, there are four:

30a lion—he is the warrior of the animals and runs from nothing,

31a cockerel walking proudly,[c]

a goat

and a king among his people.

32If you have been foolish enough to become proud and make plans against other people, stop and think about what you are doing. 33Stirring milk causes butter to form. Hitting someone's nose causes blood to flow. And making people angry causes trouble.

Wise Words for a King

31 These are the wise sayings that King Lemuel's mother taught him:

2I prayed for a son, and you are the son I gave birth to. 3Don't waste your strength on women. Women destroy kings, so don't waste yourself on them. 4Lemuel, it is not wise for kings to drink wine. It is not wise for rulers to want beer. 5They may drink too much and forget what the law says. Then they might take away the rights of the poor. 6Give beer to people without hope. Give wine to those who are in trouble. 7Let them drink to forget their troubles. Let them forget they are poor.

8Speak up for people who cannot speak for themselves. Help people who are in trouble. 9Stand up for what you know is right, and judge all people fairly. Protect the rights of the poor and those who need help.

The Perfect Wife

10[d] How hard it is to find the perfect wife.[e]
    She is worth far more than jewels.

---

[a] **30:3 Holy One** Literally, "the holy ones".
[b] **30:15** Literally, "A leech has two daughters".
[c] **30:31 a cockerel walking proudly** Or possibly, "a greyhound" or "a war horse".
[d] **31:10–31** In Hebrew, each verse of this poem starts with the next letter of the alphabet, so this poem shows all the good qualities of a woman "from A to Z".
[e] **31:10 the perfect wife** Or "a noble woman".

¹¹Her husband depends on her.
  He will never be poor.
¹²She does good for her husband all her life.
  She never causes him trouble.

¹³She is always gathering wool and flax[a]
  and enjoys making things with her hands.

INSIGHT

This woman is the Alpha Betty of the Bible! She's described in an acrostic, with each line beginning with the next letter of the Hebrew alphabet. This passage is traditionally recited by Jewish men to their wives on the evening of the Sabbath.

Proverbs 31:10–31

¹⁴She is like a ship from a faraway place.
  She brings home food from everywhere.
¹⁵She wakes up early in the morning,
  cooks food for her family, and gives the
  servants their share.
¹⁶She looks at land and buys it.
  She uses the money she has earned and
  plants a vineyard.
¹⁷She works very hard.
  She is strong and able to do all her
  work.

¹⁸She works late into the night
  to make sure her business earns a profit.
¹⁹She makes her own thread
  and weaves her own cloth.
²⁰She always gives to the poor
  and helps those who need it.
²¹She does not worry about her family when it
  snows.
  She has given them all good, warm clothes.
²²She makes sheets and covers for the beds,
  and she wears clothes of fine linen.

²³Her husband is a respected member of the city
  council,
  where he meets with the other leaders.
²⁴She makes clothes and belts
  and sells them to the merchants.
²⁵She is a strong person,[b] and people respect her.
  She looks to the future with confidence.
²⁶She speaks with wisdom
  and teaches others to be loving and kind.
²⁷She oversees the care of her house.
  She is never lazy.
²⁸Her children say good things about her.
  Her husband boasts about her and says,
²⁹"There are many good women,
  but you are the best."

³⁰Grace and beauty can fool you,
  but a woman who respects the LORD should
  be praised.
³¹Give her the reward she deserves.
  Praise her in public for what she has done.

---

a 31:13 *flax* A plant used to make linen cloth.
b 31:25 *She is a strong person* Or "She is praised."

Who
The author – the Teacher (*Qoheleth*) – is identified as "a son of David and king of Jerusalem", which is usually taken to mean Solomon. However, it could mean a king from the line of Solomon, or even an ideal, archetypal king.

When
It was probably written around 400 BC, but if the author was Solomon, then it dates from the tenth century BC.

What
Ecclesiastes is one of the most surprising books of the Bible – a cynical, weary summary of the apparent pointlessness of life. Its repeated refrain is this: everything is futile, pointless, a waste of time.

It covers subjects such as the cycles of nature, the accumulation of wealth, the joys of friendship, the fears of old age.

Given this type of content, you might think that this is a very surprising book to find in the Bible. Admittedly, despite this apparent cynicism, Ecclesiastes does have moments of humour and lightness, not to mention passages of startling and moving beauty. But still, the overriding feeling is one of weariness. This is why there have been many disputes as to what Ecclesiastes is doing in the Bible. Many Christians feel uncomfortable with its corrosive cynicism, its penetrating rejection of superficial optimism and cheerful platitudes.

Others argue that that is exactly what gives Ecclesiastes its unique strength. It represents the thoughts of many, many people: people who are close to despair, who believe life to be without purpose – the kind of people we pass every day in our modern towns and cities.

Whether this book is the genuine record of one man's anguish, or a more artificial, measured attempt to portray a way of thinking, is difficult to judge. Either way this book calls us to do all we can to help people who are trapped in the worldview of Ecclesiastes. Life is not meaningless; life is purposeful even if, sometimes, it really doesn't feel that way.

QUICK TOUR ▶ **ECCLESIASTES**

"Everything is so meaningless. The teacher says that it is all a waste of time!"

Ecclesiastes 1:2

1

These are the words from the Teacher, a son of David and king of Jerusalem.

²Everything is so meaningless. The Teacher says that it is all a waste of time!ᵃ ³Do people really gain anything from all the hard work they do in this life?ᵇ

INSIGHT

The meaning of the original Hebrew here is "vapour" or "breath". The Teacher is trying to say that life is as fleeting as breath: nothing lasts. It's all a load of hot air.

Ecclesiastes 1:2

Things Never Change

⁴People live and people die, but the earth continues forever. ⁵The sun rises and the sun goes down, and then it hurries to rise again in the same place.

⁶The wind blows to the south, and the wind blows to the north. The wind blows around and around. Then it turns and blows back to the place it began.

⁷All rivers flow again and again to the same place. They all flow to the sea, but the sea never becomes full.

⁸Words cannot fully explain things,ᶜ but people continue speaking.ᵈ Words come again and again to our ears, but our ears don't become full. And our eyes don't become full of what we see.

Nothing Is New

⁹All things continue the way they have been since the beginning. The same things will be done that have always been done. There is nothing new in this life.

¹⁰Someone might say, "Look, this is new," but that thing has always been here. It was here before we were.

¹¹People don't remember what happened long ago. In the future they will not remember what is happening now. And later, other people will not remember what the people before them did.

Does Wisdom Bring Happiness?

¹²I, the Teacher, was king over Israel in Jerusalem. ¹³I decided to study and to use my wisdom to learn about everything that is done in this life. I learned that it is a very hard thing that God has given us to do. ¹⁴I looked at everything done on earth, and I saw that it is all a waste of time. It is like trying to catch the wind.ᵉ ¹⁵If something is crooked, you cannot say it is straight. And if something is missing, you cannot say it is there.

¹⁶I said to myself, "I am very wise. I am wiser than all the kings who ruled Jerusalem before me. I know what wisdom and knowledge really are."

¹⁷I decided to learn how wisdom and knowledge are better than thinking foolish thoughts. But I learned that trying to become wise is like trying to catch the wind. ¹⁸With much wisdom comes frustration. The one who gains more wisdom also gains more sorrow.

Does "Having Fun" Bring Happiness?

2

I said to myself, "I should have fun—I should enjoy everything as much as I can." But I learned that this is also useless. ²It is foolish to laugh all the time. Having fun does not do any good.

³So I decided to fill my body with wine while I filled my mind with wisdom. I tried this foolishness because I wanted to find a way to be happy. I wanted to see what was good for people to do during their few days of life.

Does Hard Work Bring Happiness?

⁴Then I began doing great things. I built houses, and I planted vineyards for myself. ⁵I planted gardens, and I made parks. I planted all kinds of fruit trees. ⁶I made pools of water for myself, and I used them to water my growing trees. ⁷I bought men and women slaves, and there were slaves born in my house. I owned many great things. I had herds of cattle and flocks of sheep. I owned more things than any other person in Jerusalem did.

⁸I also gathered silver and gold for myself. I took treasures from kings and their nations. I had men and women singing for me. I had everything any man could want.

⁹I became very rich and famous. I was greater than anyone who lived in Jerusalem before me. My wisdom was always there to help me. ¹⁰Anything my eyes saw and wanted, I got for myself. My

---

ᵃ **1:2 meaningless . . . a waste of time** The Hebrew word means "vapour" or "breath" or "something that is useless, meaningless, empty, wrong or a waste of time".

ᵇ **1:3 in this life** Literally, "under the sun". Also in verses 9,13.

ᶜ **1:8 Words cannot fully explain things** Literally, "All words are weak."

ᵈ **1:8 but people continue speaking** The Hebrew could also be translated, "People cannot speak."

ᵉ **1:14 trying to catch the wind** Or "It is very troubling to the spirit." The word for "troubling" can also mean "craving", and the word for "spirit" can also mean "wind". Also in verse 17 and 2:11,17,26.

WHAT ARE YOU LIVING FOR?

Think of someone who has it all – maybe an actor, a footballer, a pop star. Celebrities like this have cars, clothes, houses, holidays; they go to the best clubs, wear the most fashionable clothes, date the most attractive people. That's what our culture says a good life should look like.

But does it make them happy? You only have to look at how out of control some of their lives are to see that fame and money by themselves don't bring happiness.

Ecclesiastes is written from the perspective of someone who had it all – traditionally it is believed to be King Solomon, the richest king of Israel. He had land, palaces, gold, silver, servants, hundreds of wives, and he was so wise that the Queen of Sheba came to hear him speak. But some of the first words in Ecclesiastes are "Everything is so meaningless" (v.2) – so what's going on?

DIG IN

READ Ecclesiastes 1:1 – 2:26

The Teacher in Ecclesiastes is searching for meaning and for happiness. He tries enjoying himself, he tries working hard, he tries success and he tries gaining wisdom, but in the end it's as useless as "trying to catch the wind" (2:26).

- Look at the adverts in a magazine or newspaper. What do they tell you about what our society thinks are the important things in life?
- The Teacher in Ecclesiastes says "there is nothing new in this life" (1:9). Compare the things the Teacher tries out in chapters 1 and 2 with what you found in the magazines. What are the similarities?
- Is it a good idea to try everything?

READ Ecclesiastes 5:10–20

It's easy to think that if we just had a bit more money then everything would be all right. But the Teacher says, "those who love money will never be satisfied with the money they have" (5:10). The Teacher advises that an honest day's work is more likely to lead to a peaceful night's sleep.

DIG THROUGH

- Do you think you have enough money? Do you tend to think, "If only I had some more money, I could buy . . . and then I'd be happier?" The Teacher tells you this simply won't happen! Can you believe that?
- Read Ecclesiastes 5:10–20 again and write down the things the Teacher says make a good attitude to work and to money.
- How would you explain to a friend that money is not the most important thing in life?

DIG DEEPER

- Solomon's wealth and marriages actually distracted him from wholeheartedly following the Lord. You can read about some of the trouble he got into in 1 Kings 11:1–13.
- In Philippians 4:10–20, one of the apostle Paul's letters, he says that he has learnt "to be satisfied with what I have and with whatever happens" (v.11). What do you think he means by that? How can you learn to be content?
- Jesus talks about the really important things in life in his "Sermon on the Mount" in Matthew chapters 5 – 7. He even mentions Solomon when he talks about wealth in Matthew 6:19–34.

mind was pleased with everything I did. And this happiness was the reward for all my hard work. ¹¹But then I looked at everything I had done and the wealth I had gained. I decided it was all a waste of time! It was like trying to catch the wind. There is nothing to gain from anything we do in this life.[a]

Maybe Wisdom Is the Answer

¹²Then I decided to think about what it means to be wise or to be foolish or to do crazy things. And I thought about the one who will be the next king. The new king will do the same as the kings before him.[b] ¹³I saw that wisdom is better than foolishness in the same way that light is better than darkness. ¹⁴Wise people use their minds like eyes to see where they are going. But for fools, it is as if they are walking in the dark.

I also saw that fools and wise people both end the same way. ¹⁵I thought to myself, "The same thing that happens to a fool will also happen to me. So why have I tried so hard to become wise?" I said to myself, "Being wise is also meaningless." ¹⁶Whether people are wise or foolish, they will still die, and no one will remember either one of them forever. In the future people will forget everything both of them did. So the two are really the same.

Is There Real Happiness in Life?

¹⁷This made me hate life. It was depressing to think that everything in this life is useless, like trying to catch the wind. ¹⁸I began to hate all the hard work I had done, because I saw that I would not be the one to enjoy all that I had worked for. Someone else will get it. ¹⁹And I don't know if they will be wise or foolish. But they will control everything I earned by all my hard work and wisdom. This doesn't make any sense.

²⁰So I began to feel sad about all the work I had done. ²¹People can work hard using all their wisdom and knowledge and skill. But they will die and other people will get the things they worked for. They did not do the work, but they will get everything. That makes me very sad. It is also not fair and is senseless.

²²What do people really have after all their work and struggling in this life? ²³Throughout their life they have pain, frustrations and hard work. Even at night, a person's mind does not rest. This is also senseless.

²⁴⁻²⁵There is no one who has tried to enjoy life more than I have. And this is what I learned: the best thing people can do is eat, drink and enjoy the work they must do. I also saw that this comes from God.[c] ²⁶If people do good and please God, he will give them wisdom, knowledge and joy. But those who sin will get only the work of gathering and carrying things. God takes from the bad person and gives to the good person. But all this work is useless. It is like trying to catch the wind.

A Time for Everything

3 There is a right time for everything, and everything on earth will happen at the right time.

²There is a time to be born
and a time to die.
There is a time to plant
and a time to pull up plants.
³There is a time to kill
and a time to heal.
There is a time to destroy
and a time to build.
⁴There is a time to cry
and a time to laugh.
There is a time to be sad
and a time to dance with joy.
⁵There is a time to throw weapons down
and a time to pick them up.[d]
There is a time to hug someone
and a time to stop holding so tightly.
⁶There is a time to look for something
and a time to consider it lost.
There is a time to keep things
and a time to throw things away.
⁷There is a time to tear cloth
and a time to sew it.
There is a time to be silent
and a time to speak.
⁸There is a time to love
and a time to hate.
There is a time for war
and a time for peace.

God Controls His World

⁹Do people really gain anything from their hard work? ¹⁰I saw all the hard work God gave us to do. ¹¹God gave us the ability to think about his world,[e] but we can never completely understand everything he does. And yet, he does everything at just the right time.

---

[a] **2:11** *in this life* Literally, "under the sun". Also in verses 17,22.
[b] **2:12** *And I thought . . . before him* The Hebrew text is not clear.
[c] **2:24–25** Or "The best people can do is eat, drink and enjoy their work. I also saw that this comes from God. No one can eat or enjoy life without God."
[d] **3:5** Literally, "There is a time to throw stones away and a time to gather stones."
[e] **3:11** *the ability . . . world* Or "a desire to know the future".

WHY IS IT LIKE THIS?

Have you ever heard an adult talking to a child who has just learnt to ask "Why?"? Maybe it went something like this:

> *Adult:* It's time to go home now.
> *Child:* Why?
> *Adult:* Because it's nearly dinner time.
> *Child:* Why?
> *Adult:* Because we need to eat.
> *Child:* Why?
> *Adult:* Because that's how our bodies work.
> *Child:* But why?
> *Adult:* I don't know. It just is!

That's a fairly trivial example, but there are much more serious things in life that make you want to ask "Why?" and sometimes the answers still seem to be "I don't know. It just is!"

> Why do we have to work all our lives?
>
> Why is there suffering?
>
> Why are some people rich and others poor?
>
> Why do people we love die?

The Teacher in Ecclesiastes asks all these questions. He doesn't find all the answers. In fact, he ends up exactly where he started, reflecting on how meaningless everything is (Ecclesiastes 1:2; 12:8). But on the way he finds a peace in recognizing that God is above everything, even the things we don't understand.

DIG IN

READ Ecclesiastes 3:1-17

The first part of this passage is beautiful poetry, but it can seem a bit confusing. Is there really a time for hate, a time to destroy and a time for war?

Perhaps the Teacher isn't saying that these things should happen, just that they do happen. But that still leaves the question: "Why?"

READ Ecclesiastes 7:15 – 8:17

The Teacher talks about lots of strange, sad and unjust things he has seen in his life. There are no easy answers to explain how God works or why these things happen, but the Teacher gives us hope that we can be wise in how we deal with them.

READ Ecclesiastes 12:9-14

We may not be able to find answers to every question about life, but Ecclesiastes does reassure us of this: God sees everything that happens and will one day judge it all.

That may sound scary (it probably should!) but it's also reassuring. In the end, all the injustice and evil in the world will be called to account. God won't leave us without answers forever.

DIG THROUGH

- Is it always good to ask the question "Why?"
- Read Ecclesiastes 3:1–8 again. Think about times you've experienced some of these things. Talk to God about anything in this passage you don't understand.
- How does it change your perspective to know that in the end God will judge everything that goes on? How about: hard times you've gone through; how you act at school or at work; what you hope for in life; how you feel about injustice?

[12]I learned that the best thing for people to do is to be happy and enjoy themselves as long as they live. [13]God wants everyone to eat, drink and enjoy their work. These are gifts from God.

[14]I learned that anything God does will continue forever. People cannot add anything to the work of God, and they cannot take anything away from it. God did this so that people would respect him. [15]What happened in the past has happened, and what will happen in the future will happen. But God wants to help those who have been treated badly.[a]

[16]I also saw these things in this life:[b] I saw that the courts should be filled with goodness and fairness, but there is evil there now. [17]So I said to myself, "God has planned a time for everything, and he has planned a time to judge everything people do. He will judge good people and bad people."

Are People Like Animals?

[18]I thought about what people do to each other. And I said to myself, "God wants people to see that they are like animals. [19]The same thing happens to animals and to people—they die. People and animals have the same 'breath'.[c] Is a dead animal different from a dead person? It is all so senseless! [20]The bodies of people and animals end the same way. They came from the earth, and, in the end, they will go back to the earth. [21]Who knows what happens to a person's spirit? Who knows if a human's spirit goes up to God while an animal's spirit goes down into the ground?"

[22]So I saw that the best thing people can do is to enjoy what they do, because that is all they have. Besides, no one can help another person see what will happen in the future.

Is It Better to Be Dead?

4 Again I saw that many people are treated badly. I saw their tears, and I saw that there was no one to comfort them. I saw that cruel people had all the power, and I saw that there was no one to comfort the people they hurt. [2]I decided that it is better for those who have died than for those who are still alive. [3]And it is even better for those who died at birth, because they never saw the evil that is done in this world.[d]

Why Work So Hard?

[4]Then I thought, "Why do people work so hard?" I saw people try to succeed and be better than other people. They do this because they are jealous. They don't want other people to have more than they have. This is senseless. It is like trying to catch the wind.[e]

[5]Some people say, "It is foolish to fold your hands and do nothing. If you don't work, you will starve to death." [6]Maybe that is true. But I say it is better to be satisfied with the few things you have than to always be struggling to get more.

[7]Again I saw something else that didn't make sense: [8]I saw a man who has no family, not a son or even a brother. But he continues to work very hard. He is never satisfied with what he has. And he works so hard that he never stops and asks himself, "Why am I working so hard? Why don't I let myself enjoy my life?" This is also a very bad and senseless thing.

Friends and Family Give Strength

[9]Two people are better than one. When two people work together, they get more work done. [10]If one person falls, the other person can reach out to help. But those who are alone when they fall have no one to help them.

[11]If two people sleep together, they will be warm. But a person sleeping alone will not be warm.

[12]An enemy might be able to defeat one person, but two people can stand back-to-back to defend each other. And three people are even stronger. They are like a rope that has three parts wrapped together—it is very hard to break.

People, Politics and Popularity

[13]A young leader who is poor but wise is better than a king who is old but foolish. That old king does not listen to warnings. [14]Maybe the young ruler was born a poor man in the kingdom. And maybe he came from prison to rule the country. [15]But I have watched people in this life, and I know this: people will follow that young man. He will become the new king. [16]Many people will follow this young man. But later, those same people will not like him. This is also senseless. It is like trying to catch the wind.

Be Careful About Making Promises

5 Be very careful when you go to worship God. It is better to listen to God than to give sacrifices like fools. Fools often do bad things, and they don't even know it. [2]Be careful when you make promises to God. Be careful about what you

---

[a] **3:15** Or "What happens now also happened in the past. What happens in the future has also happened before. God makes things happen again and again."

[b] **3:16** *in this life* Literally, "under the sun". Also in 4:15; 5:13; 6:1.

[c] **3:19** *breath* Or "spirit".

[d] **4:3** *in this world* Literally, "under the sun".

[e] **4:4** *trying to catch the wind* Or "It is very troubling to the spirit." The word for "troubling" can also mean "craving", and the word for "spirit" can also mean "wind". Also in verse 16.

say to him. Don't let your feelings cause you to speak too soon. God is in heaven, and you are on the earth. So you need to say only a few things to him. This saying is true:

³Bad dreams come from too many worries,
　　and too many words come from the mouth
　　　　of a fool.

⁴If you make a vow to God, keep your vow. Don't be slow to do what you promised. God is not happy with fools. Give God what you promised to give him. ⁵It is better to promise nothing than to promise something and not be able to do it. ⁶So don't let your words cause you to sin. Don't say to the priest,ᵃ "I didn't mean what I said." If you do this, God might become angry with your words and destroy everything you have worked for. ⁷You should not let your useless dreams and boasting bring you trouble. You should respect God.

INSIGHT

In Bible times promises were taken very seriously. Making a promise was like signing a legal contract. Once you'd made it you couldn't back out.
Ecclesiastes 5:4–7

The Poor and the Rich

⁸You may be in a place where the poor people are made to suffer by those in power. You may see their rights taken away unfairly. But don't be surprised! The official who is making life hard for them is under orders from another one in a higher position. And they are both under even higher officials. ⁹It is best for a country to have a king in charge who will make sure the fields are prepared to produce good crops.ᵇ

Wealth Cannot Buy Happiness

¹⁰Those who love money will never be satisfied with the money they have. Those who love wealth will not be satisfied when they get more and more. This is also senseless.

¹¹The more wealth people have, the more "friends" they have to help spend it. So the rich really gain nothing. They can only look at their wealth.

¹²Those who work hard all day come home and sleep in peace. It is not important if they have little or much to eat. But the rich worry about their wealth and are not able to sleep.

¹³There is a very sad thing that I have seen happen in this life. People save their money for the future.ᶜ ¹⁴Then something bad happens and they lose everything. So they have nothing to give to their children.

¹⁵People come into the world with nothing. And when they die, they leave with nothing. They might work hard to get things, but they cannot take anything with them when they die. ¹⁶It is very sad that people leave the world just as they came. So what does a person gain from "trying to catch the wind"? ¹⁷They only get days that are filled with sadness and sorrow. In the end, they are troubled, sick and angry.

Enjoy Your Life's Work

¹⁸I have seen what is best for people to do on earth. They should eat, drink and enjoy the work they have during their short time here. God has given them these few days, and that is all they have.

¹⁹If God gives some people wealth, property and the power to enjoy those things, they should enjoy them. They should accept the things they have and enjoy their work—that is a gift from God. ²⁰People don't have many years to live, so they must remember these things all their life. God will keep them busy with the work they love to do.ᵈ

Wealth Does Not Bring Happiness

6 I have seen another thing in this life that is not fair and is very hard to understand. ²God gives some people great wealth, riches and honour. They have everything they need and everything they could ever want. But then God does not let them enjoy those things. Some stranger comes and takes everything. This is a very bad and senseless thing.

³A man might live a long time and have 100 children. But if he is not satisfied with those good things, and if no one remembers him after his death, I say that a baby who dies at birth is better off than that man. ⁴It is senseless when a baby is born dead. The baby is quickly buried in a dark grave, without even a name. ⁵The baby never saw the sun and never knew anything. But the baby finds more rest than the man who never enjoyed what God gave him. ⁶He might

---

ᵃ **5:6 priest** Or "angel" or "messenger". This might be an angel, a priest or a prophet.
ᵇ **5:9 It is best . . . crops** Or "Even the king gets his share of the profit. The wealth of the country is divided among them."
ᶜ **5:13 for the future** Or "to their harm".
ᵈ **5:20 God . . . to do** Or "God will do whatever he wants to them."

live 2,000 years. But if he does not enjoy life, then the baby who was born dead has found the easiest way to the same end.[a]

7People work and work to feed themselves, but they are never satisfied. 8In the same way, a wise person is no better than a fool is. It is better to be a poor person who knows how to accept life as it is. 9It is better to be happy with what you have than to always want more and more. Always wanting more and more is useless. It is like trying to catch the wind.[b]

10-11You are only what you were created to be—a human—and it is useless to argue about it. People cannot argue with God about this because he is more powerful than they are, and a long argument will not change that fact.

12Who knows what is best for people during their short life on earth? Their life passes like a shadow. No one can tell them what will happen later.

A Collection of Wise Teachings

7 A good reputation is better than expensive pleasures.[c]
  The day someone dies is better than the day they were born.

2It is better to go to a funeral than to a party.
  Yes, because everyone must die, and the living need to remember this.

3Sorrow is even better than laughter, because when our face is sad, our heart becomes good.

4A wise person thinks about death, but a fool thinks only about having a good time.

5It is better to be criticized by the wise than praised by the foolish.

6The laughter of fools is such a waste.
  It is like thorns burning under a pot.
  The thorns burn so quickly that the pot does not get hot.[d]

7Power over people makes even a wise person a fool,
  and a bribe can cause anyone to be dishonest.

8Finishing something is better than starting it.
  Being patient is better than being proud.

9Don't become angry quickly, because getting angry is foolish.

10Don't ask, "Why was life so much better in the 'good old days'?"
  That is not a wise question to ask.

11Wisdom is better if you also have property. Wise people[e] will get more than enough wealth. 12Wisdom and money can protect you. But knowledge gained through wisdom is even better—it can save your life.

13Look at what God has made. You cannot change a thing, even if you think it is wrong. 14When life is good, enjoy it. But when life is hard, remember that God gives us good times and hard times. And no one knows what will happen in the future.

People Cannot Really Be Good

15In my short life, I have seen everything. I have seen good people die young, and I have seen evil people live long lives. 16-17So why ruin your life? Don't be too good or too bad, and don't be too wise or too foolish. Why should you die before your time?

18Try to be a little of this and a little of that.[f] Even God's followers will do some good things and some bad things. 19-20Surely there is no one on earth who always does good and never sins. But wisdom can make one person stronger than ten leaders in a city.

21Don't listen to everything people say. You might hear your own servant saying bad things about you. 22And you know that many times you too have said bad things about other people.

23I used my wisdom and thought about all these things. I wanted to be wise, but I couldn't do it. 24I cannot understand why things are as they are. It is too hard for anyone to understand. 25I studied and I tried very hard to find true wisdom. I tried to find a reason for everything.

I did learn that it is foolish to be evil, and it is crazy to act like a fool. 26I also found that some women are dangerous like traps. Their hearts are like nets, and their arms are like chains. It is worse than death to be caught by these women. God's followers should run away from them. Let the sinners be caught by them.

27-28The Teacher says, "I added all this together to see what answer I could find. I am still looking for answers, but I did find this: I found one good

---

[a] 6:6 **then the baby . . . the same end** Or "Isn't it true that all go to the same place?"
[b] 6:9 Or "Having what you can see is better than chasing after the things you want. This is also like trying to catch the wind."
[c] 7:1 **A good reputation . . . pleasures** Literally, "better a name than good perfume". This is a wordplay in Hebrew. The word for "name" and the word for "perfume" sound alike.
[d] 7:6 Or "The cackling of fools, like the crackling of thorns under a pot, is senseless."
[e] 7:11 **Wise people** Literally, "People who see the sun". This means wise people can see and plan what they should do.
[f] 7:18 **Try . . . of that** Or "Hold onto this, but don't let go of that."

man in a thousand. But I did not find even one good woman.

29"There is one other thing I have learned. God made people good, but they have found many ways to be bad."

Wisdom and Power

8 No one can understand and explain things the way wise people can. Their wisdom makes them happy. It changes a sad face into a happy one.

2I say you should always obey the king's command. Do this because you made a promise to God. 3Don't be afraid to give suggestions to the king, and don't support something that is wrong. But remember, the king gives the commands that please him. 4He has the authority to give commands, and no one can tell him what to do. 5People will be safe if they obey his command. But wise people know the right time to do this, and they also know when to do the right thing.

6There is a right time and a right way to do everything. You must decide what you should do, even when it might cause problems 7and you are not sure what will happen. No one can tell you what will happen in the future.

8No one has the power to keep their spirit from leaving or to stop their death. During war, no soldier has the freedom to go wherever he wants. In the same way, evil does not allow anyone who does wrong to go free.

9I saw all this. I thought very hard about the things that happen in this world. I saw that people always struggle for the power to rule others, and this is bad for them.

10I also saw great and beautiful funerals for evil people. While the people were going home after the funeral services, they said good things about the evil people who had died. This happened even in the towns where the evil people had done many bad things. This is senseless.

Justice, Rewards and Punishment

11Sometimes people are not immediately punished for the bad things they do. Their punishment is slow to come, and that makes other people want to do bad things too.

12A sinner might do a hundred evil things and still live a long time. But I know that it is still better to obey and respect God. 13Evil people don't respect God, so they will not get good things or live long lives. Their lives will not be like the shadows that become longer and longer as the sun goes down.

14There is something else that happens on earth that does not seem fair. Bad things should happen to bad people, and good things should happen to good people. But sometimes bad things happen to good people, and good things happen to bad people. This is not fair. 15So I decided it was more important to enjoy life because the best thing people can do in this life*a* is to eat, drink and enjoy life. At least that will help people enjoy the hard work God gave them to do during their life on earth.

We Cannot Understand All God Does

16I carefully studied the things people do in this life. I saw how busy people are. They work day and night, and they almost never sleep. 17I also saw that no one can understand all that God does. People can try and try to understand the things that happen here on earth, but they cannot. There may be wise people who claim to understand the meaning of these things, but they are wrong. No one can understand it all.

Is Death Fair?

9 I thought about all this very carefully. I saw that God controls what happens to the good and wise people and what they do. People don't know if they will be loved or hated, and they don't know what will happen in the future.

2But, there is one thing that happens to everyone—we all die! Death comes to good people and bad people. Death comes to those who are pure and to those who are not pure. Death comes to those who give sacrifices and to those who don't give sacrifices. Good people will die just as sinners do. Those who make promises to God will die just as those who are afraid to make those promises do.

3Of all the things that happen in this life, the worst thing is that all people end life the same way. But it is also very bad that people always think evil and foolish thoughts. And those thoughts lead to death. 4There is hope for those who are still alive— it does not matter who they are. But this saying is true:

A living dog is better than a dead lion.

5The living know that they will die, but the dead don't know anything. They have no more reward. People will soon forget them. 6After people are dead, their love, hate and jealousy are all gone. And they will never again share in what happens on earth.

Enjoy Life While You Can

7So go and eat your food now and enjoy it. Drink your wine and be happy. It is all right with God if you do these things. 8Wear nice clothes and make yourself look good. 9Enjoy life with the wife you love. Enjoy every day of your short life. God has given you this short life on earth—and it is all you have. So enjoy the work you have to do in this life. [10]Every time you find work to do, do it the best you can. In the grave there is no work. There is no thinking, no knowledge and there is no wisdom. And we are all going to the place of death.

INSIGHT

Sometimes life can seem really random and death the only certainty. It's a mystery, says the Teacher, but we are all in God's hands – and he will always be a God of justice.

Ecclesiastes 9:11–12

Life Is Not Fair

[11]I also saw other things in this life that were not fair. The fastest runner does not always win the race; the strongest soldier does not always win the battle; wise people don't always get the food; smart people don't always get the wealth; educated people don't always get the praise they deserve. When the time comes, bad things can happen to anyone! [12]You never know when hard times will come. Like fish in a net or birds in a snare, people are often trapped by some disaster that suddenly falls on them.

The Power of Wisdom

[13]I also saw a person doing a wise thing in this life, and it seemed very important to me. [14]There was a small town with a few people in it. A great king fought against that town and put his armies all around it. [15]But there was a wise man in that town. He was poor, but he used his wisdom to save his town. After everything was finished, the people forgot about the poor man. [16]But I still say that wisdom is better than strength. They forgot about the poor man's wisdom, and the people stopped listening to what he said. But I still believe that wisdom is better.

[17]Words spoken by the wise are heard more clearly
than those shouted by a leader among fools.

[18]Wisdom is better than weapons of war,
but one fool[a] can destroy much good.

10 A few dead flies will make even the best perfume stink. In the same way, a little foolishness can ruin much wisdom and honour.

[2]The thoughts of the wise lead them the right way, but the thoughts of the foolish lead them the wrong way. [3]Fools show how foolish they are, just walking down the road. Their minds are empty, and everyone knows it.

[4]Don't leave your job simply because the boss is angry with you. If you remain calm and helpful, you can correct even great mistakes.[b]

[5]Here is something else that I have seen in this life[c] that isn't fair. It is the kind of mistake that rulers make. [6]Fools are given important positions, while the rich get jobs that are not important. [7]I have seen servants riding on horses, while rulers were walking beside them like slaves.

Every Job Has Its Dangers

[8]If you dig a hole, you might fall into it. If you break down a wall, you might be bitten by a snake. [9]If you are moving large stones, you might be hurt by them. If you cut down a tree, you are in danger of it falling on you.

[10]But wisdom will make any job easier. It is very hard to cut with a dull knife. But if you sharpen the knife, the job is easier.

[11]Someone might know how to control snakes. But that skill is useless if a snake bites when that person is not around.

[12]Words from the wise bring praise,
but words from a fool bring destruction.

[13]Fools begin by saying something foolish. But in the end, they speak nonsense. [14]Fools are always talking about what they will do, but you never know what will happen. People cannot tell what will happen in the future.

[15]Fools aren't smart enough to find their way home,
so they must work hard all their lives.

The Value of Work

[16]It is very bad for a country if the king is like a child. And it is very bad for a country if its rulers spend all their time eating. [17]But it is very good for a country if the king comes from a good family.[d]

---

[a] **9:18 fool** Literally, "sinner".
[b] **10:4 If you . . . great mistakes** Literally, "A healer can put to rest great sins." The word "healer" means a person who is forgiving and tries to help other people.
[c] **10:5 in this life** Literally, "under the sun".
[d] **10:17 comes from a good family** Literally, "is a son of freedmen". This is a person who was never a slave and whose parents were not slaves.

And it is very good for a country if the rulers control their eating and drinking. They eat and drink to become strong, not to become drunk.

¹⁸If someone is too lazy to work,
>   their house will begin to leak, and the roof will fall in.

¹⁹People enjoy eating, and wine makes life happier. But money solves a lot of problems.

Gossip

²⁰Don't say bad things about the king. Don't even think bad things about him. And don't say bad things about rich people, even if you are alone in your home. A little bird might fly and tell them everything you said.

Boldly Face the Future

11 Do good wherever you go.ᵃ
After a while, the good you do will come back to you.
²Invest what you have in several different things.ᵇ
>   You don't know what bad things might happen on earth.

³There are some things you can be sure of.
If clouds are full of rain,
>   they will pour water on the earth.
If a tree falls—to the south or to the north—
>   then it will stay where it falls.
⁴But there are some things that you cannot be sure of.
>   You must take a chance.
If you wait for perfect weather,
>   you will never plant your seeds.
If you are afraid that every cloud will bring rain,
>   you will never harvest your crops.

⁵You don't know where the wind blows.
And you don't know how a baby grows in its mother's womb.
In the same way, you don't know what God will do
>   —and he makes everything happen.
⁶So begin planting early in the morning,
>   and don't stop working until evening.
You don't know what might make you rich.
>   Maybe everything you do will be successful.

⁷It is good to be alive.
>   It is nice to see the light from the sun.
⁸You should enjoy every day of your life,
>   no matter how long you live.
But remember that you will die,
>   and you will be dead much longer than you were alive.
And after you are dead,
>   you cannot do anything.

Serve God While You Are Young

⁹So young people, enjoy yourselves while you are young.
Be happy.
>   Do whatever your heart leads you to do.
Do whatever you want,
>   but remember that God will judge you for everything you do.
¹⁰Don't let your anger control you,
>   and don't let your body lead you to sin.ᶜ
People do foolish things in the dawn of life
>   while they are young.

The Problems of Old Age

12 Remember your Creator while you are young, before the bad times come— before the years come when you say, "I have wasted my life."ᵈ

²Remember your Creator while you are young, before the time comes when the sun and the moon and the stars become dark to you—before problems come again and again like one storm after another.

³At that time your arms will lose their strength. Your legs will become weak and bent. Your teeth will fall out, and you will not be able to chew your food. Your eyes will not see clearly. ⁴You will become hard of hearing. You will not hear the noise in the streets. Even the stone grinding your grain will seem quiet to you. You will not be able to hear the women singing. But even the sound of a bird singing will wake you early in the morning because you will not be able to sleep.

⁵You will be afraid of high places. You will be afraid of tripping over every small thing in your path. Your hair will become white like the flowers on an almond tree. You will drag yourself along like a grasshopper when you walk. You will lose your desire,ᵉ and then you will go to your eternal home. The mourners will gather in the streets as they carry your body to the grave.

ᵃ **11:1** *Do good . . . go* Or "Throw your bread on the water."
ᵇ **11:2** *Invest . . . different things* Or "Give a part to seven, or even eight."
ᶜ **11:10** *Don't let . . . sin* Or "Don't worry about things. Protect yourself from troubles."
ᵈ **12:1** *I have wasted my life* Literally, "I take no pleasure in them." This might mean "I don't like the things I did when I was young" or "I don't enjoy life now that I am old."
ᵉ **12:5** *desire* Or "appetite" or "sexual desire". The Hebrew text is not clear.

Death

⁶Remember your Creator while you are young,
  before the silver rope snaps and the gold
    bowl is crushed
like a jar broken at the well,
  like a stone cover on a well that breaks and
    falls in.
⁷Your body came from the earth.
  And when you die, it will return to the
    earth.
But your spirit came from God,
  and when you die, it will return to him.

⁸Everything is so meaningless. The Teacher
says that it is all a waste of time!^a

Final Words of Advice

⁹The Teacher was very wise. He used his
wisdom to teach the people. He very carefully
studied and arranged^b many wise teachings.
¹⁰The Teacher tried very hard to find the right
words, and he wrote the teachings that are true
and dependable.

¹¹Words from the wise are like sharp goads.
When these sayings are written down and saved,
they can be used to guide people, just as a
shepherd uses a sharp stick to make his sheep go
the right way. ¹²So, son, study these sayings, but
be careful about other teachings. People are
always writing books, and too much study will
make you very tired.

^{13–14}Now, what should we learn from every-
thing that is written in this book?^c The most
important thing a person can do is to respect God
and obey his commands, because he knows about
everything people do—even the secret things. He
knows about all the good and all the bad, and he
will judge people for everything they do.

---

^a **12:8 *meaningless . . . a waste of time*** The Hebrew word means "vapour", "breath" or "something that is useless,
meaningless, empty, wrong or a waste of time".
^b **12:9 *arranged*** This Hebrew word means "to make straight", "arrange", "correct" or "edit".
^c **12:13–14 *Now . . . book*** Literally, "The sum of the matter, when all is heard, is . . .".

Who Traditionally ascribed to King Solomon, but there is a lot of debate about that. The full title of the book is "The Song of Songs which is Solomon's", which could mean that it was written in honour of Solomon.

When Again, there has been a lot of debate about this. Some believe that the book was written during the reign of Solomon. Others argue that the language of the book is more typical of a later period than Solomon's, probably the third century BC.

What Song of Songs is a celebration of spontaneous and natural love. Not surprisingly, many commentators have found this difficult to come to terms with and have sought alternative explanations.

Many Jewish rabbis saw the song as an allegory of the love between God and his people, while Christian teachers saw it as an allegory of the love between Christ and his Church, or even between Christ and the believer's soul. The problem with these theories is that there is no hint of them in the book itself, nor is a similar allegory or image found in the rest of the Bible.

The Bible has a lot to say about the bad side of love, about degradation, lust, perversion and even rape. Song of Songs celebrates what is good about physical love. The most powerful voice in the poem is, perhaps, that of the woman – who is not a royal queen, but a young girl from the village of Shunem (Joshua 19:18; 2 Kings 4:8). It is she who speaks most profoundly of love, who affirms its spontaneity, power and mystery.

Talking of mystery, one of the features of the book which modern readers struggle with is the comparisons: the woman is compared to one of Pharaoh's horses (1:9), she's got hair like little goats dancing (4:1) and a nose like Mount Lebanon (7:4). But in ancient poetry of this type the comparison is not visual, but qualitative: the subject is compared to a certain quality – usually the absolute "best of". To be a horse in Pharaoh's court was to be the best you could be.

QUICK TOUR **SONG OF SONGS**

Love is better than wine 1:1 – 2:7
The wedding 3:6 – 5:1
Dream lover 5:2–16

Wedding dance 7:1–13
If only . . . 8:1–14

"Keep me near you like a seal you wear over your heart, like a signet ring you wear on your hand. Love is as strong as death. Passion is as strong as the grave. Its sparks become a flame, and it grows to become a great fire! A flood cannot put out love. Rivers cannot drown love. Would people despise a man for giving everything he owns for love?"

Song of Songs 8:6–7

1 Solomon's Most Wonderful Song.

The Woman to the Man She Loves

²Cover me with kisses,
   for your love is better than wine.
³The sweet-smelling oil you have on is so
      pleasing,
   but the person you are[a] is even more
      wonderful.
   That is why all the young women love you.
⁴Take me with you.
   Let's run away.

The king took me into his room.

The Women of Jerusalem to the Man

We will rejoice and be happy for you.
   Remember, your love is better than wine.
   With good reason, the young women love
      you.

She Speaks to the Women

⁵Women of Jerusalem,
   I am dark and beautiful,
   as black as the tents of Kedar and Salmah.[b]

⁶Don't look at how dark I am,
   at how dark the sun has made me.
   My brothers were angry with me.
   They forced me to take care of their
      vineyards,
   so I could not take care of myself.[c]

She Speaks to Him

⁷I love you with all my heart!
   Tell me, where do you feed your sheep?
   Where do you take them to rest at noon?
   I want to be able to find you
      without losing my way
      among the flocks of your friends.

He Speaks to Her

⁸You are such a beautiful woman.
   Surely you know what to do.
   Go, follow the sheep.
   Feed your young goats near the shepherds'
      tents.

⁹My love, you are more exciting to me
   than any mare among the stallions[d] pulling
      Pharaoh's chariots.[e]
¹⁰Your cheeks are so beautiful
   with those ornaments hanging beside them.

Your neck is so lovely
   under that beautiful string of jewels.
¹¹Let's make you some more gold jewellery
   and decorate it with silver.

She Speaks

¹²The smell of my perfume reaches out
   to the king lying on his couch.
¹³My love is like the small bag of myrrh
   ⌊around my neck⌋,
   lying all night between my breasts.
¹⁴My love is like a bunch of henna flowers
   near the vineyards of En Gedi.

He Speaks

¹⁵Oh, my love, you are beautiful!
   You are so beautiful!
   Your eyes are as pretty as doves.

She Speaks

¹⁶And you, my love, are so handsome!
   You are a delight to my heart!
   Our bed here on the grass is so pleasant.
¹⁷   Cedar and fir trees surround us
   and make a house over our heads.

2 I feel like a small flower in the fields of Sharon
   or like a lily of the valley.

He Speaks

²My love, when I compare you to other women,
   you are like a lily among thorns!

She Speaks

³My love, compared to other men,
   you are an apple tree in the middle of the
      woods!
   I love sitting here in its shade
   and enjoying the delicious fruit.
⁴I am like a guest at your banquet,
   and you have shown me your love.
⁵My desire for you makes me feel weak.
   So give me raisins for strength.
   Refresh me with apples.
⁶Let my head rest in your left hand,
   while you hold me close with your right arm.

⁷Promise me, women of Jerusalem,
   by the gazelles and wild deer,
   that you will not interfere with our love.
   Let it continue until it is finished.

---

[a] **1:3 the person you are** Literally, "your name", which is often used to mean the person. "Name" is probably used here because in Hebrew it sounds like the word translated "sweet-smelling oil".
[b] **1:5 Kedar and Salmah** Arabian tribes. For "Salmah" the standard Hebrew text has "Solomon".
[c] **1:6 myself** Literally, "my own vineyard".
[d] **1:9 mare . . . stallions** Female and male horses. Only male horses were used to pull chariots.
[e] **1:9** Literally, "To a mare among Pharaoh's chariots I compare you, my love."

WHAT LOVE FEELS LIKE

This is different! Tucked away amidst all this Old Testament history and prophecy is a little love poem which, on the face of it, looks very much as though it's about sex.

For that reason, it's a poem that Jews and Christians down the ages have struggled to know what to do with. It doesn't seem to "fit". It doesn't seem to have an obvious storyline (or at least people disagree about what it is). It doesn't even seem to teach anything about God.

So how should we read it? Well, first, don't make the mistake many do and pretend it's not there. Let's read it and see what God has for us.

DIG IN

READ Song of Songs 2:8–17

- What sort of approach is the woman's lover ("He") making in this passage?
- What does he compare their love to (vv.11–13)?

The male lover ("He") is wooing her with all he's got – racing towards her with tender words, comparing their love for each other like springtime after a long winter. Notice how sensual the poetry is – the lovers hear, touch and smell. The world is waking up; everything is alive with possibility. This is what love feels like!

Desire, expectation, running away together: Song of Songs conveys the excitement of being in love . . . and the anticipation and ecstasy of that love expressed in sex.

The Bible says, "All Scripture is given by God. And all Scripture is useful . . ." (2 Timothy 3:16). So what is Song of Songs useful for? Is it to tell us about love and sex? Down the centuries people have wondered whether it might mean other things too.

Some people firmly believe that it's a picture of God's love for his people and a prophetic picture of how Christ loves the church, frequently described in the Bible as "his bride" (see especially Revelation 19:7–8). Song of Songs may well be pointing towards this, helping us to understand Jesus' passion for his people.

But others think it's just as likely to simply be a picture of what God intends love and sex to look like. Nowhere else in the Bible is sex celebrated so much and the intimacy and innocence of pure love-making within marriage given such a high value.

Without it, we might struggle to know what God actually thinks about sex. Reading it, we can be sure: God loves it!

DIG THROUGH

- Does Song of Songs awaken anything in you? You may not have been in love yourself yet, but can you catch the poet's excitement about it? Turn your feelings to prayer – for a future partner perhaps, or for a special person already in your life. (It's worth remembering that singleness is also important and great – see Bible Bit "Love Always Protects" on Song of Songs chapter 8.)
- Why do you think that Song of Songs has been included in the Bible for us today? How do you think the book can help us today?

DIG DEEPER

The picture of the lovers reminds us of the two first lovers in the Garden of Eden (Genesis 2:18–25). Innocent and unashamed before sin crept in, this is the ideal for a man and a woman enjoying each other in marriage: a man "is joined to his wife. In this way two people become one" (Genesis 2:24).

She Speaks Again

8I hear the voice of the one I love.
Here he comes, jumping across the
  mountains,
skipping over the hills.
9My love is like a gazelle
or a young deer.
Look, there he is behind our wall.
He is trying to see in through the window,
looking through the screen.
10My love speaks to me,
"Get up, my love, my beautiful one.
Let's go away!
11Look, winter is past,
the rains have come and gone.
12The flowers are blooming in the fields.
It's time to sing!a
Listen, the doves have returned.
13Young figs are growing on the fig trees.
Smell the vines in bloom.
Get up, my love, my beautiful one.
Let's go away!"

He Speaks

14My dove, hiding in the caves high on the cliff,
hidden here on the mountain,
let me see you,
let me hear your voice.
Your voice is so pleasant,
and you are so beautiful!

She Speaks to the Women

15Catch the foxes for us—
the little foxes that spoil the vineyard.
Our vineyard is now in bloom.

16My love is mine,
and I am his!
My love feeds among the lilies,
17   while the day breathes its last breath
and the shadows run away.
Turn, my love,
be like a gazelle or a young deer on the cleft
  mountains!b

She Speaks

3 At night on my bed,
I look for the man I love.
I looked for him,
but I could not find him.
2I will get up now!
I will go around the city.

In the streets and squares,
I will look for the man I love.

I looked for him,
but I could not find him.
3The guards patrolling the city found me.
I asked them, "Have you seen the man I
  love?"

4As soon as I passed them,
I found the man I love!
I held him and would not let him go,
until I took him to my mother's house,
to the place my life began.

She Speaks to the Women

5Promise me, women of Jerusalem,
by the gazelles and wild deer,
that you will not interfere with our love.
Let it continue until it is finished.

The Women of Jerusalem Speak

6What is this coming out of the desert?
It looks like a big cloud of smoke.
And it smells like myrrh and frankincense
and the other spices traders sell.

7Look, Solomon's travelling chair.c
There are 60 soldiers guarding it,
strong soldiers of Israel.
8All of them are trained fighting men
with their swords at their side,
ready for any danger of the night.

9King Solomon made a travelling chair for
  himself.
The wood came from Lebanon.
10The poles were made from silver,
and the supports were made from gold.
The seat was covered with purple cloth.
It was inlaid with love by the women of
  Jerusalem.

11Women of Zion, come out
and see King Solomon.
See the crownd his mother put on him
the day he was married,
the day he was so happy!

He Speaks to Her

4 My love, you are so beautiful!
Oh, you are beautiful!

---

a 2:12 *sing* Or "prune".
b 2:17 *the cleft mountains* Or "the mountains of Bether" or "the mountains of spice".
c 3:7 *travelling chair* A kind of chair that the rich travelled in. These chairs were covered and had poles that slaves used to carry them. Also in verse 9.
d 3:11 *crown* This might be a wreath of flowers he wore on his head at his wedding.

KEEP SEX SPECIAL

Some people get very embarrassed by Song of Songs, and passages like this are the ones they're particularly afraid of! But Song of Songs reassures us that there's no need to be embarrassed. God created men and women to enjoy sex, and to delight in each other's bodies.

Sadly, our enemy the devil does everything in his power to corrupt this wonderful gift so that we misuse it or start to fear it. When the precious gift of sex is used for wrong motives – such as to make money, or for entertainment – rather than being enjoyed as a very special, intimate part of the marriage relationship, it actually does us harm.

DIG IN

READ Song of Songs 4:1–15

- In what ways does the lover express his love for his wife?
- Does this passage make you feel uncomfortable? Why is that?

Don't be surprised or ashamed if this passage makes you uncomfortable. Our culture has corrupted sex and the effects can be seen everywhere. One is our culture's massive problem with pornography. Porn does not value the human body and sex the way our two lovers are doing in Song of Songs. It devalues and exploits them and leaves us feeling dirty and ashamed.

For this reason, we need Song of Songs, perhaps more than any generation in history. Song of Songs helps us to correct wrong thinking about sex by showing us how these two lovers express their love in a pure and beautiful way.

Let's look at some of the ways he expresses his love:

He repays beauty with beauty (vv.1–5). The lover takes his time to appreciate this gorgeous woman with carefully chosen words that are sure to delight her and make her feel amazing. You know what it feels like when someone you like compliments you on how you look? Between two lovers, this is even better.

He sees every part of her as beautiful (v.7). Truth is, we've all got bits we're not all that proud of and sometimes we fixate on them, allowing that to change how others see us. But in a secure, intimate relationship these things don't matter.

He appreciates the fact that he is hers alone (v.9) and that she is his alone (v.12). They are captivated by each other! God designed sex to be between one man and one woman only: they find their pleasure is intensified by the knowledge that they are each other's one-and-only.

DIG THROUGH

- Do you think this picture of sex is most people's experience today? God longs that it might be. No matter where you are in the dating game ask God to use Song of Songs to help you get a right understanding of sex and where it fits into a loving marriage relationship.
- There's no escaping sex in our culture. Pray for wisdom in dealing with films and TV shows that present a corrupted version of the beauty of sex, and for wise words when you are talking about these things with friends (check out Ephesians 4:29).

Your eyes are as lovely as doves
    under your veil.
Your hair is long and flowing,
    like little goats dancing down the slopes of
    Mount Gilead.
²Your teeth are white like ewes[a]
    just coming from their bath.
They all give birth to twins;
    not one of them has lost a baby.
³Your lips are like a red silk thread.
    Your mouth is beautiful.
Your cheeks under your veil
    are like two slices of pomegranate.
⁴Your neck is as beautiful as the tower of
    David,
    decorated with its rows of stones.[b]
It has a thousand shields on its walls,
    the shields of powerful soldiers.
⁵Your breasts are as lovely as twin fawns,
    like twins of a gazelle,
    feeding among the lilies.
⁶I cannot wait to be on those lovely hills
    that smell of myrrh and frankincense.
I will go now, before the day dawns,
    before the darkness goes away.
⁷My love, you are beautiful all over.
    Every part of you is perfect.
⁸Come away with me from Lebanon,
    my bride.
    Let us leave Lebanon behind.
Come down from its high mountains,
    from the peaks of Mount Amana,
    from the peaks of Senir and Hermon.
Come away from the lion's caves,
    from the mountains where leopards live.
⁹My bride, my dearest, you have stolen my
    heart
    with just one look from your eyes.
A single sparkle from your necklace
    has put me under your control.
¹⁰Your love is a delight, my bride, my dearest!
    Your love is better than wine.
And the smell of your perfume
    is more pleasing than any spice!
¹¹My bride, your lips are as sweet as honey,
    your kisses are a delight, like honey and milk.
Your clothes smell wonderful,
    like the cedars of Lebanon.
¹²My bride, my dearest, you are so lovely,
    like a private garden or a hidden spring,
    a fountain protected from strangers.

¹³You are a royal garden
    filled with pomegranates and other choice
    fruits,
with all kinds of spices
    like henna[c] and nard.
¹⁴Besides nard there is saffron,[d] calamus[e] and
    cinnamon,[f]
    and trees that produce the best spices,
    like frankincense, myrrh and aloes.
¹⁵You are a garden fountain,
    a spring of fresh water
    that flows down from the mountains of
    Lebanon.

She Speaks

¹⁶Wake up, north wind.
    Come, south wind.
Blow on my garden.
    Spread its sweet smell.
Let my love enter his garden
    and eat its pleasant fruit.

He Speaks

5 My bride, my dearest, I have entered my
    garden.
    I have gathered my myrrh and spice.
I have eaten my honey and honeycomb.
    I have drunk my wine and milk.

The Women Speak to the Lovers

Dearest friends, eat, drink!
    Be drunk with love!

She Speaks

²I was asleep,
    but my mind was awake.
I thought I heard my love knocking and
    saying,
    "Open up for me, my dearest, my love,
    my dove, my perfect one!
My head is all wet with dew.
    My hair is soaked from the evening mist."

³But I said, "I have taken off my robe.
    I don't want to put it on again.
I have washed my feet.
    I don't want to get them dirty again."

⁴My love put his hand through the latch
    opening,
    and I began to feel excited.

---

[a] **4:2 ewes** Female goats.
[b] **4:4 Your neck . . . stones** This would mean she wore many necklaces, one above the other, which looked like rows of stones in a tower.
[c] **4:13 henna** A plant with sweet-smelling, blue-yellow flowers that grows in clusters (groups) like grapes.
[d] **4:14 saffron** A kind of yellow flower used in making perfume.
[e] **4:14 calamus** A kind of reed plant used in making perfume.
[f] **4:14 cinnamon** A kind of plant used as a spice and in making perfume.

[5]I got up to let my love come in,
  myrrh dripping from my hands.
Myrrh-scented lotion dripped from my fingers
  onto the handles of the door.
[6]I opened the door for my love,
  but he was already gone!
I was so sad,
  I thought I would die.
I looked for him,
  but I could not find him.
I called out for him,
  but he did not answer.
[7]The guards patrolling the city found me.
  They hit me and hurt me.
The guards on the wall
  took away my robe.

[8]I tell you, women of Jerusalem,
  if you find my love,
  tell him I am weak with love.

The Women of Jerusalem Answer Her

[9]Most beautiful woman,
  how is the one you love different from
    other men?
Is he better than all others?
  Is that why you ask us to make this
    promise?

INSIGHT

The woman sings of her lover, detailing his appeal from head to toe. This is a wasf, a classic Arabic poetic device, and the effect is to build a fantastic mix of images.

Song of Songs 5:10–16

She Answers

[10]My love is tanned and radiant.
  He would stand out among 10,000 men.
[11]His head is like the purest gold.
  His hair is curly and as black as a raven.
[12]His eyes are like doves by a stream,
  like doves in a pool of milk,
  like a jewel in its setting.
[13]His cheeks are like a garden of spices,
  like flowers used for perfume.
His lips are like lilies,[a]
  dripping with liquid myrrh.

[14]His arms are like gold rods,
  filled with jewels.
His body is like smooth ivory
  with sapphires set in it.
[15]His legs are like marble pillars
  on bases of fine gold.
He stands tall
  like the finest cedar tree in Lebanon!
[16]His kisses are so sweet.
  He is everything I desire.
Yes, women of Jerusalem,
  this is my love, my friend.

The Women of Jerusalem Speak to Her

6 Most beautiful woman,
  where is the one you love?
Which way did he go?
  Tell us so that we can help you look for him.

She Answers the Women of Jerusalem

[2]My love has gone down to his garden,
  where sweet-smelling spices grow.
There, like a sheep, he will eat the grass,
  and he will enjoy the lilies.
[3]I belong to my love, and he belongs to me.
  He is the one feeding among the lilies.

He Speaks to Her

[4]My love, you are as beautiful as Tirzah,[b]
  as pleasant as Jerusalem,
  as awesome as the stars in the sky.[c]
[5]Don't look at me!
  Your eyes excite me too much!
And your hair ⌊is long and flowing⌋,
  like little goats dancing down the slopes of
    Mount Gilead.
[6]Your teeth are white like ewes[d]
  just coming from their bath.
They all give birth to twins.
  Not one of them has lost a baby.
[7]Your cheeks under your veil
  are like slices of pomegranate.

[8]There might be 60 queens
  and 80 slave women,
  and young women too many to count,
[9]but there is only one ⌊woman for me⌋,
  my dove, my perfect one.
She is the favourite of her mother,
  her mother's favourite child.
The young women see her and praise her.
  Even the queens and slave women
    praise her.

---

[a] **5:13** *lilies* A kind of flower. Here, it is probably a red flower.
[b] **6:4** *Tirzah* One of the capital cities of northern Israel.
[c] **6:4** *the stars in the sky* Or "an army ready for war". The meaning of the Hebrew word here and in verse 10 is uncertain.
[d] **6:6** *ewes* Female goats.

The Women Praise Her

10Who is that young woman?
 She shines like the dawn.
She is as pretty as the moon,
 as bright as the sun.
She is as amazing
 as all the stars across the sky.

He Speaks to Her

11I went down to the grove of walnut trees.
 I wanted to see the new spring growth in
  the valley,
to see if the vines were budding yet,
 to see if the pomegranate trees were in
  bloom.
12I was so excited
 when she put me in the royal chariot.*a*

The Women of Jerusalem Call to Her

13Come back, come back, Shulamith!*b*
 Come back, come back, so we may look
  at you.

Why are you staring at Shulamith,
 as she dances the Mahanaim dance?*c*

He Praises Her Beauty

7 Princess,*d* your feet are beautiful in those
  sandals.
 The curves of your thighs are like jewellery
  made by an artist.
2Your navel is like a round cup;*e*
 may it never be without wine.
Your belly is like a pile of wheat
 surrounded by lilies.
3Your breasts are like twin fawns
 of a young gazelle.
4Your neck is as graceful as an ivory tower.
 Your eyes sparkle like the pools in Heshbon
  near the gate of Bath Rabbim.
Your nose has such a beautiful shape,
 like Mount Lebanon seen from Damascus.
5Your head is held high, like Mount Carmel.
 Your hair is like silk.
Its waves look so attractive,
 it could capture even a king.
6You are so beautiful and so pleasant,
 a lovely, delightful young woman!

7You are tall—
 as tall as a palm tree.
And your breasts are like
 the clusters of fruit on that tree.
8I would love to climb that tree
 and take hold of its branches.

May your breasts be like clusters of grapes,
 your breath like the sweet smell of
  apples,
9 and your lips like the best wine.

She Speaks to Him

So let this wine flow straight to my love,
 flowing gently over lips and teeth.*f*
10I belong to the one I love,
 and he desires only me.
11Come, my love,
 let's go out into the field;
 let's spend the night in the villages.
12Let's get up early and go to the vineyards.
 Let's see if the vines are budding yet.
Let's see if the blossoms have opened
 and the pomegranate trees are in bloom.
 There I will give you my love.

13Smell the mandrakes*g*
 and all the pleasant flowers by our door.
I have saved many pleasant things for you,
 my love,
 pleasant things, new and old.

INSIGHT

In the culture of the time only a brother
and sister could kiss openly. Even a
husband and wife could not express their
love publicly. Here the woman is wishing
she could show their love to the world.
  Song of Songs 8:1

8 If only you were my brother
 who nursed at my mother's breasts.
Then, if I met you outside, I could kiss you,
 and no one would say I did wrong.

---

a **6:12** *the royal chariot* Or "the chariots of my noble people". See "CHARIOT" in the Word List.
b **6:13** *Shulamith* Or "Shulamite". The word might be the feminine form of the name "Solomon". This could mean she was or would become the bride of Solomon. This name might also mean "perfect", "at peace" or "woman from Shunem".
c **6:13** *Mahanaim dance* Or "the victory dance" or "the dance of the two camps".
d **7:1** *Princess* Literally, "Daughter of a prince".
e **7:2** *round cup* Or "turned bowl", a stone bowl made on a lathe and used for mixing wine before it is poured into cups. This might also mean a bowl shaped like a crescent or half-moon.
f **7:9** *over lips and teeth* This follows the Greek, Syriac and Latin versions. The Hebrew text has "over lips of sleepers".
g **7:13** *mandrakes* Plants with roots that look like people. People thought these plants had the power to make people fall in love.

LOVE ALWAYS PROTECTS

Song of Songs is a joyful celebration of love and a fearless, innocent celebration of sex as its purest expression.

DIG IN

READ Song of Songs 8:3–9

- How do the pictures in verses 3 and 4 relate to each other?
- How do verses 6 and 7 help to explain why?

The female lover feels safe in the embrace of her husband (v.3) and craves the security of having him near her (v.6).

Sex is a wonderful gift and it's a gift to be enjoyed. But the Bible is always absolutely clear that God designed it only for men and women who have made a commitment to one another in marriage. That's not because God is a spoilsport – not at all. It's entirely for our own good.

Sexual passion is incredibly powerful – it can be like a wildfire, starting with a small spark and quickly becoming a fire which even rivers can't put out (vv.6–7). That's why God insists that it is safely contained within a committed marriage relationship – with him at the centre.

- Why does the poet include the brothers' voices in verses 8 and 9?

In every culture, brothers want to make sure that their sisters are treated well by men – these brothers have a role to play in protecting their sister's purity and honour. (Big brothers always think their little sister isn't quite ready, as in verse 8.)

There's something important here for us in our churches and youth groups too. We need to treat one another like brothers and sisters – guarding each other from unhelpful temptations and encouraging each other to stay pure.

DIG THROUGH

- When will you know you are "ready" for love? Do you think this might be at a time when you are also "ready" for marriage? Are you praying that God would be preparing your heart for your future, whilst protecting you from awakening love too soon?
- How will you respond when a boy or a girl wants to start a relationship with you? Do you have a wise person you trust who you can talk honestly with about it?
- Hey, just because we've spent some time looking at the goodness of love, marriage and sex it doesn't mean that that's the only thing that's "normal". Singleness is great! Check out 1 Corinthians 7:38 if you want reassurance that it's good, wise and normal to be or to stay single.
- In what practical ways can we help our "brothers and sisters" at church or in our youth group stay pure? Think about what you wear and how you look; what movies or TV shows you watch together or talk about; and how you encourage each other to relate to non-Christians.

DIG DEEPER

A passage that shows the kind of love God desires for husbands and wives is Ephesians 5:22–33. It shows how God intends marriage to be and gives a picture of Christ's love for his bride, the church.

²I would lead you into my mother's house,
to the place where my life began.
I would give you spiced wine
squeezed from my pomegranates.

She Speaks to the Women

³His left arm is under my head,
and his right hand holds me.

⁴Promise me, women of Jerusalem,
that you will not interfere with our love.
Let it continue until it is finished.

The Women of Jerusalem Speak

⁵Who is this woman coming out of the desert,
leaning on the arm of the one she loves?

She Speaks to Him

There under the apple tree, I woke you up.
That was where your life began,
where your mother gave birth to you.
⁶Keep me near you like a seal you wear over
your heart,
like a signet ring you wear on your
hand.
Love is as strong as death.
Passion is as strong as the grave.ᵃ
Its sparks become a flame,
and it grows to become a great fire!ᵇ
⁷A flood cannot put out love.
Rivers cannot drown love.
Would people despise a man for giving
everything he owns for love?

Her Brothers Speak

⁸We have a little sister,
and her breasts are not yet grown.
What should we do to help our sister
if someone wants to marry her?
⁹If she were a flat wall,
we would build silver towers on it.
If she were a door,

we would use cedar to make it more
attractive.

She Answers Her Brothers

¹⁰True, I was like a wall,
but now my breasts are like towers.
So when he sees me,
he is very pleased.

¹¹Solomon had a vineyard at Baal Hamon.
He put men in charge of the vineyard.
Each man brought in grapes
worth 1,000 piecesᶜ of silver.

¹²Solomon, you can keep your silver.
Give 200 pieces to each man for the grapes
he brought.
But I will keep my own vineyard.

INSIGHT

*In this book, the vineyard represents
both a physical place and the sexuality
of the lovers. In real life Solomon's
vineyards had many keepers. The
woman's "vineyard", her body, is for
one person only.*

Song of Songs 8:12

He Speaks to Her

¹³There you are, sitting in the garden.
Friends are listening to your voice.
Let me hear it too!

She Speaks to Him

¹⁴Hurry, my love!
Run like a gazelle
or like a young deer
on the mountains covered with spices.

ᵃ **8:6 the grave** Or "Sheol", the place where dead people go.
ᵇ **8:6 great fire** Or "the flame of the LORD".
ᶜ **8:11 1,000 pieces** Literally, "1,000 *shekels*". Also in verse 12.

There are seventeen books of the Bible which are known as "The Prophets" but commonly separated into "Major" and "Minor Prophets". The distinction refers not to their importance, but to their length. Some of the Minor Prophets are only one chapter long, whereas the majority of the Major Prophets are lengthy books: the longest of them, Isaiah, contains sixty-six chapters.

Prophets played a significant part in the life of Israel. It was through them that God spoke. In a time when the monarchy was often corrupt and evil, it was up to the prophets to give people the truth. Although many were abused and ignored, they were accorded respect and allowed to exercise their gifts, even if that made for uncomfortable listening. It was also a risky business. If a prophet's words were not proved to be true, they could be taken and stoned.

Prophecy is often confused with prediction, with the ability to see the future. Prophets certainly did predict the future – a major theme of the prophets is the impending destruction of Israel and Judah and the salvation that was to come through the Messiah – but if they looked to the future, they also challenged the present. They challenged injustice and oppression and idolatry that was going on. They argued with kings, berated the people and tried to pass on what they knew to be true.

Biblical prophecy is fundamentally about passing on a message from God. Descriptions of the prophetic experience in the Bible are often physical. Prophets shake, their message burns inside them, they cannot help but speak. Their message bursts out in outrageous language and actions, shocking people into listening, and reflecting a passionate God who will do anything to make his people turn around.

Isaiah is a long book warning of the judgement of God, but also looking to the Messiah and the world that is to come.

Jeremiah prophesied during the final days of the doomed country of Judah.

Lamentations is a short, sad poem about the fall of Jerusalem.

Ezekiel contains a series of powerful (and even bizarre) visions warning the people in Jerusalem to change their ways and urging them to stay faithful in exile.

Daniel is part prophecy, part the story of a Jew exiled in Babylon who refused to compromise his faith.

Who The prophet Isaiah, son of Amoz. We know that he was married with two sons, Shear Jashub (7:3) and Maher Shalal Hash Baz (8:3). He lived mainly in Jerusalem and reportedly wrote a biography of King Uzziah (2 Chronicles 26:22).

When He began his ministry in "the year that King Uzziah died" i.e. 740 BC (6:1) and lived at least until 681 BC, when the Assyrians were defeated. According to Jewish tradition, he died a gruesome death during the reign of King Manasseh: he was sawn in half.

What Isaiah's core themes are judgement and redemption. God would judge his people for their sins, but he would also rescue them from captivity. Isaiah's name means "the Lord saves".

It contains some of the most inspiring, moving and powerful pictures of God's reign in all its glory, when the exiles are brought back home, and when the Lord will create a new world, free of suffering, sadness and pain.

The book of Isaiah is not chronologically arranged. We are constantly thrown forward and backward in time. Political observations and historical accounts jostle with visions of the far future and calls to repentance. Signs of the near future mingle with announcements of the Messiah. The Messiah – the anointed one who would rescue Israel and usher in a new age of peace and wholeness – is a major feature of Isaiah's visions. Isaiah constantly emphasizes God's power and might – he is a "fire" that will scorch the earth. But if he is a fire in judgement, he is also a stream in the desert, and a road back from exile.

Many experts believe the book is the work of three different "Isaiahs" rather than just one, basing their claims on the differences in style and emphasis between different sections. But if there are differences, there are also many similarities as well, and phrases that crop up throughout the book, which are not found elsewhere in Scripture.

QUICK TOUR ➤ **ISAIAH**

"I am creating a new heaven and a new earth. The troubles of the past will be forgotten. No one will remember them. My people will be happy and rejoice for ever and ever because of what I will make. I will make a Jerusalem that is full of joy, and I will make her people happy. Then I will rejoice with Jerusalem. I will be happy with my people. There will never again be crying and sadness in that city."

Isaiah 65:17–19

1

This is the vision of Isaiah son of Amoz. God showed Isaiah what would happen to Judah and Jerusalem. Isaiah saw this during the time when Uzziah, Jotham, Ahaz and Hezekiah were kings of Judah.

God's Case Against Israel

²Heaven and earth, listen! This is what the LORD says:

"I raised my children and helped them
    grow up,
but they have turned against me.
³A bull knows its master,
    and a donkey knows where its owner
      feeds it.
But Israel does not know me.
My people do not understand."

⁴Oh, what a sinful nation! Their guilt is like a heavy weight that they must carry. They are evil, destructive children.*ᵃ* They left the LORD and insulted the Holy One of Israel. They turned away and treated him like a stranger. ⁵What good will it do to keep punishing you? You will continue to rebel. Your whole head and heart are already sick and aching.*ᵇ* ⁶From the bottom of your feet to the top of your head, every part of your body has wounds, cuts and open sores. You have not taken care of them. Your wounds have not been cleaned and bandaged. ⁷Your land is in ruins, and your cities are in flames. Your enemies have taken your land, and foreigners are taking what it produces. It looks like some foreigners destroyed it.*ᶜ*

Warnings for Jerusalem

⁸The city of Jerusalem*ᵈ* is now empty, like a shelter left in a vineyard or like an old straw hut in a field of melons. It is a city under attack. ⁹If the LORD All-Powerful had not allowed a few people to live, we would have been destroyed completely like the cities of Sodom and Gomorrah.

¹⁰You officers of Sodom, listen to the LORD's message. You people of Gomorrah,*ᵉ* listen to God's message. ¹¹He says, "Why do you offer me all these sacrifices? They mean nothing to me. I have had enough of your offerings of rams and the fat from well-fed cattle. The blood of the bulls, sheep and goats you bring gives me no pleasure at all. ¹²When you people come to meet with me, you trample everything in my courtyard. Who told you to do this?

¹³"Stop bringing me these worthless sacrifices. I hate the incense you give me. I cannot stand your festivals for the New Moon, the Sabbath and other special meeting days. I hate the evil you do during those holy times together. ¹⁴I hate your monthly meetings and councils. They have become like heavy weights to me, and I am tired of carrying them.

¹⁵"When you raise your arms to pray to me, I will refuse to look at you. You will say more and more prayers, but I will refuse to listen because your hands are covered with blood.

¹⁶"Wash yourselves and make yourselves clean. Get rid of the evil I see you doing. Stop doing wrong. ¹⁷Learn to do good. Work for justice. Help those who suffer under the control of others. Speak up for the widows and orphans. Argue for their rights.

¹⁸"I, the LORD, am the one speaking to you. Come, let's discuss this. Even if your sins are as dark as red dye, that stain can be removed and you will be as pure as wool that is as white as snow.

¹⁹"If you listen to what I say, you will get the good things from this land. ²⁰But if you refuse to listen and rebel against me, your enemies will destroy you."

The LORD himself said this.

Unfaithful Jerusalem

²¹Look at Jerusalem. She was a faithful city. What made her become like a prostitute? In the past, Jerusalem was filled with justice, and goodness should live there now. Instead, there are murderers.

²²Once you were like pure silver, but now you are like the useless part people throw away. You are like good wine that has been weakened with water. ²³Your rulers are rebels and friends of thieves. They demand bribes and accept money for doing wrong. They take money to cheat people, and they don't speak up for widows and orphans. They will not even listen to their cries for help.

²⁴Because of this, the Lord GOD All-Powerful, the Mighty One of Israel, says, "Look, I will get relief from my enemies. You will not cause me any more trouble. ²⁵In the same way people use lye to clean silver, I will clean away all your wrongs. I will remove all the impurities from you. ²⁶I will bring back the kind of judges you had in

---

ᵃ **1:4** *They . . . children* Or "They are destructive children of evil parents."
ᵇ **1:5** *Your whole . . . aching* Or "Every head and heart is already sick and aching."
ᶜ **1:7** *It looks . . . destroyed it* Or "It looks like the land of the foreigners that was destroyed." This might refer to civil war in Israel or to some time when God destroyed foreign nations, such as Sodom and Gomorrah.
ᵈ **1:8** *city of Jerusalem* Literally, "daughter Zion". See "ZION" in the Word List.
ᵉ **1:10** *officers of Sodom . . . Gomorrah* Here, this refers to leaders and people from Judah.

the beginning. Your counsellors will be like those you had long ago. Then you will be called 'The Good and Faithful City'."

²⁷God is good and does what is right, so he will rescue Zion and the people who come back to him. ²⁸But all the criminals and sinners will be destroyed. Those who stopped following the LORD will be removed.

²⁹In the future you will be ashamed of the oak trees and special gardens*a* you chose to worship. ³⁰You will be like an oak tree whose leaves are dying. You will be like a garden dying without water. ³¹Powerful people will be like small, dry pieces of wood, and what they did will be like the sparks that start a fire. These people and their works will both burn up, and no one will be able to put out that fire.

God's Message to Judah and Jerusalem

2 Isaiah son of Amoz saw this message about Judah and Jerusalem:

²In the last days the mountain of the LORD's
     Temple
   will be the highest of all mountains.
It will be raised higher than the hills.
   There will be a steady stream of people
     from all nations going there.
³People from many places will go there
     and say,
   "Come, let's go up to the mountain of the
     LORD,
   to the Temple of the God of Jacob.
Then God will teach us his way of living,
   and we will follow him."

His teaching, the LORD's message, will begin in
     Jerusalem on Mount Zion
   and will go out to all the world.
⁴Then God will act as judge to end arguments
     between nations.
   He will decide what is right for people from
     many lands.
They will stop using their weapons for war.
   They will hammer their swords into
     ploughs
   and use their spears to make tools for
     harvesting.
All fighting between nations will end.
   They will never again train for war.
⁵Family of Jacob, let us follow the LORD.

⁶Family of Jacob, you have abandoned your people. This is clear because they have been filled with bad influences from the East,*b* and now your people try to tell the future like the Philistines. They have completely accepted those strange ideas. ⁷Jacob's land is filled with silver and gold, with all kinds of treasures. His land is filled with horses and too many chariots to count. ⁸His land is full of gods that the people bow down to worship. They made those idols themselves. ⁹The people have become worse and worse. They have become very low, and you leaders did nothing to lift them up!*c*

¹⁰Find a place behind the rocks to hide from the LORD's anger! Or dig a hole in the ground to hide from his glorious power!

¹¹Proud people will stop being proud. They will bow down to the ground with shame, and only the LORD will still stand high.

¹²The LORD All-Powerful has set a day to punish the proud and boastful people. He will bring them down. ¹³They may be as tall as the cedar trees of Lebanon or the great oak trees of Bashan, but the LORD will cut them down. ¹⁴They may be as tall as the mountains or as high as the hills, but he will bring them down. ¹⁵They may be as tall as the city's towers or as strong as its high walls, but he will pull them down. ¹⁶They may be as fast as the ships from Tarshish and carry as much treasure, but he will destroy them all.

¹⁷On that day the proud people will fall. They will bow low to the ground, and only the LORD will stand high. ¹⁸The idols will all be gone. ¹⁹When the LORD rises up to terrify the earth, people will crawl into holes in the ground or find caves in the rocks to hide in. The LORD's coming will terrify them. They will run from his great glory.

²⁰At that time people will throw away the idols they made from gold and silver. They will take those statues they made to worship and throw them into holes in the ground where bats and moles live. ²¹They will go down into cracks in the rocks and boulders because the LORD's coming will terrify them, and they will run from his great glory, when he rises up to terrify the earth.

²²Stop trusting other people to save you. Do not think too highly of them; they are only humans who have not stopped breathing yet.

3 Understand what I am telling you: the Lord GOD All-Powerful will take away everything Judah and Jerusalem depend on. He will take away all the food and water. ²He will take away all the heroes and soldiers, all their judges, prophets, fortune-tellers, leaders, ³army officers and important officials, counsellors, magicians and those who claim they can control the future.

---

a **1:29 special gardens** Gardens where people worshipped false gods.
b **2:6 East** This usually refers to the area around Babylon.
c **2:9 They ... up** Or "The people have become very low. Surely you will not forgive them!"

[4]He says, "I will put young boys in charge of you. They will be your leaders. [5]The people will turn against each other. Young people will not respect those who are older. The common people will not respect important leaders."

[6]Looking for someone to be in charge a man will say to his own brother, "You still have a coat, so you will be our leader. You will be in charge of all these ruins!"

[7]But the brother will refuse and say, "I cannot help you. I don't have enough food or clothes for my own family. I cannot be your leader!"

[8]This will happen because Jerusalem has stumbled, and Judah has fallen. They turned against the LORD. They said and did things against him, right in front of his glorious eyes.

[9]The look on their faces shows they are guilty. They are like the people of Sodom; they don't care who sees their sin. But it will be very bad for them. They will get what they deserve.

[10]Tell the good people who do what is right that good things will happen to them. They will receive a reward for what they do. [11]But it will be very bad for wicked people, because they, too, will get what they deserve. They will get what they did to others. [12]Even children will defeat my people, and women will rule over them.

My people, your guides lead you the wrong way, and they destroy the path you should follow.

God's Decision About His People

[13]Look, the LORD is standing to judge his people. [14]The LORD is ready to present his case against the officials who lead his people.

He says, "You people have burned the vineyard,[a] and what you stole from the poor is still in your houses. [15]What gives you the right to hurt my people? What gives you the right to push the faces of the poor into the dirt?" The Lord GOD All-Powerful said this.

[16]The LORD says, "The women in Zion have become very proud. They walk around with their heads in the air, acting as if they are better than other people. They flirt with their eyes and make tinkling sounds with their ankle bracelets as they take their quick little steps."

[17]The Lord will put sores on the heads of those women in Zion. The LORD will make their heads bald. [18]Then the Lord will take away everything they are proud of: the beautiful ankle bracelets, the necklaces that look like the sun and the moon, [19]the earrings, bracelets and veils, [20]the scarves, the ankle chains, the cloth belts worn around their waists, the bottles of perfume, the charms,[b] [21]the signet rings and the nose rings, [22]the fine dresses, robes, cloaks and purses, [23]the mirrors, linen dresses, turbans and long shawls.

[24]Those women now have sweet-smelling perfume, but it will get mouldy and stink. Now they wear belts, but then they will have only ropes to wear. Now they have their hair fixed in fancy ways, but then their heads will be shaved—they will have no hair.[c] Now they have party dresses, but then they will have only mourning clothes. They have beauty marks on their faces now, but then they will have another mark. It will be a mark burned into their skin to show that they are slaves.

[25]Your men will be killed with swords. Your heroes will die in war. [26]There will be crying and sadness in the meeting places by the city gates. Jerusalem will sit there empty, like a woman who has lost everything to thieves and robbers and now just sits on the ground and cries.

4 At that time seven women will grab one man and say, "Please marry us! We will supply our own food and make our own clothes. You won't have to do anything else if you let us wear your name and take away our shame."

[2]At that time the LORD's plant[d] will be very beautiful and glorious. The people in Israel who survived will be very proud of what the land grows. [3]And all those who are left in Zion and Jerusalem will be called holy. Their names were on the list of people in Jerusalem who were allowed to live.

[4]The Lord will wash away the filth[e] from the daughters of Zion.[f] He will wash away the blood from Jerusalem. With a spirit of judgement that burns like fire, he will make everything pure. [5]Then the LORD will create a cloud of smoke in the day and a bright flame of fire[g] at night over every building and over every meeting of the people on the mountain of Zion. And there will be a covering over everyone[h] for protection. [6]It will be a shelter to protect the people from the heat of the sun and from all kinds of storms and rain.

---

[a] 3:14 vineyard A garden for growing grapes. Here, this probably means Judah.

[b] 3:20 charms Things people wore on bracelets and necklaces. People thought these things would protect them from evil or danger.

[c] 3:24 they will have no hair This means that they will become slaves.

[d] 4:2 the LORD's plant This might refer to the country of Judah or to the future king or Messiah. See Isa. 5:7.

[e] 4:4 wash away the filth This is like a special ceremony for washing away the blood after a menstrual period. After this a man and wife could have sex.

[f] 4:4 daughters of Zion This can refer either to the small towns around Jerusalem or to the women living there.

[g] 4:5 cloud of smoke . . . fire The signs God used to show that he was with his people.

[h] 4:5 everyone Literally, "glory", but this can also mean "soul" or "person".

Judah, God's Vineyard

5 Now I will sing a song for my friend, my love song about his vineyard.

My friend had a vineyard
  on a very fertile hill.
[2]He dug and cleared the field
  and planted the best grapevines there.
He built a tower in the middle
  and cut a winepress into the stone.
He expected good grapes to grow there,
  but there were only rotten ones.

[3]My friend said, "You people living in
  Jerusalem and you people of Judah,[a]
  think about me and my vineyard.
[4]What more could I do for my vineyard?
  I did everything I could.
I hoped for good grapes to grow,
  but there were only rotten ones.
  Why did that happen?

[5]"Now I will tell you
  what I will do to my vineyard:
I will pull up the thornbushes that protect it,
  and I will burn them.
I will break down the stone wall
  and use the stones as a path.
[6]I will turn my vineyard into useless land.
  No one will care for the plants or work in
  the field.
  Weeds and thorns will grow there.
I will command the clouds
  not to rain on it."

[7]The vineyard that belongs to the LORD All-Powerful is the house of Israel. The grapevine, the plant he loves, is the man of Judah.[b]

The Lord hoped for justice,
  but there was only killing.
He hoped for fairness,
  but there were only cries from people being
  treated badly.

[8]Look at you people! You join houses to houses and fields to fields until there is no room for anyone else. But ⌊when the punishment comes,⌋ you will be forced to live alone. You will be the only people in the whole land. [9]I heard the LORD All-Powerful make this oath: "I swear, all these houses will be destroyed. These big, fancy houses will be empty. [10]A four-hectare vineyard will make only a little wine,[c] and many sacks of seed will grow only a little grain."[d]

[11]How terrible it will be for you people who rise early in the morning and go looking for beer to drink. You stay awake late at night, getting drunk on wine. [12]At your parties with your wine, and harps, drums, flutes and other musical instruments, you don't see what the LORD has done. You don't notice what his hands have made.

[13]My people don't really know God. So they will be captured and taken away. Everyone, the respected leaders and the common people as well, will be hungry and thirsty. [14]They will die, and the place of death will open its mouth wide and swallow many of them. Then the noisy crowds and all the beautiful, happy people who are now so comfortable will go down into the grave.

[15]Everyone, common people and leaders alike, will be humbled. Those who are now so proud will bow their heads in shame. [16]The LORD All-Powerful will judge fairly, and people will honour him. They will respect the Holy God when he brings justice. [17]Their cities will become fields where lambs can graze. Young goats will eat grass where rich people once lived.

[18]Look at those people! They pull their guilt and sins behind them like people pulling carts with ropes.[e] [19]They say, "We wish God would hurry and do what he plans to do so that we can see it. Let the plan of the Holy One of Israel happen soon so that we can know what it is."

[20]Look at those people! They say good is bad and bad is good. They think light is dark and dark is light. They think sour is sweet and sweet is sour. [21]They think they are so smart. They think they are very intelligent. [22]They are famous for drinking wine and are heroes known for mixing drinks. [23]And if you pay them enough money, they will forgive a criminal. But they will not let good people be judged fairly. [24]So bad things will happen to them. Their descendants will be destroyed completely, just as fire burns straw and leaves. Their descendants will be like plants with rotten roots, whose flowers have all blown away like dust in the wind.

Those people refused to obey the teachings[f] of the LORD All-Powerful. They hated the message from the Holy One of Israel. [25]So the LORD became angry with his people, and he raised his hand to

---

[a] **5:3 You people . . . Judah** Or "Rulers of Jerusalem and leader of Judah . . .".

[b] **5:7 man of Judah** This could mean either "the king of Judah" or simply, "people of Judah".

[c] **5:10 only a little wine** Literally, "one *bath*", a measure that equals about 22 litres.

[d] **5:10 only a little grain** Literally, "A *homer* of seed will grow only an *ephah* of grain." A *homer* equals about 220 litres. An *ephah* equals about 22 litres.

[e] **5:18 ropes** Literally, "useless ropes". The Hebrew words here are like those meaning "useless things", that is, idols.

[f] **5:24 teachings** This can also mean "laws". Sometimes this means the laws God gave Moses to teach to the people of Israel.

punish them. Even the mountains shook with fear. Dead bodies were left in the streets like rubbish. And he is not finished yet. He is still angry, and his arm is raised to continue punishing his people.

God Will Bring Armies to Punish Israel

26Look! God is giving a sign to the nations far away. He is raising a flag and whistling for them to come.

Now the enemy is coming from a faraway land and will soon enter the country. They are moving very quickly. 27The enemy soldiers never get tired and stumble. They never get sleepy and fall asleep. Their weapon belts are always ready. Their sandal straps never break. 28Their arrows are sharp. Their bows are strung and ready to shoot. The horses' hooves are as hard as flint. Clouds of dust rise from behind their chariots.

29The shouts of the enemy sound like the roar of lions. Like strong, young lions, they growl and grab their prey. The captives struggle and try to escape, but there is no one to save them. 30Then there is a roar as loud as the ocean waves, and the captives turn their faces to the ground. And there is only darkness closing in as the light fades away in a black cloud.

God Calls Isaiah to Be a Prophet

6 In the year that King Uzziah died,[a] I saw the Lord sitting on a very high and wonderful throne. His long robe filled the Temple. 2Seraph angels stood around him. Each angel had six wings. They used two wings to cover their faces, two wings to cover their bodies and two wings to fly. 3The angels were calling to each other,

"Holy, holy, holy is the LORD All-Powerful. His glory fills the whole earth."

4The sound was so loud that it caused the frame around the door to shake, and the Temple was filled with smoke.[b]

5I was frightened and said, "Oh, no! I will be destroyed. I am not pure enough to speak to God, and I live among people who are not pure enough to speak to him.[c] But I have seen the King, the LORD All-Powerful."

6There was a fire on the altar. One of the Seraph angels used a pair of tongs to take a hot coal from the fire. Then the angel flew to me with it in his hand. 7Then he touched my mouth with the hot coal and said, "When this hot coal touched your lips, your guilt was taken away, and your sins were erased."[d]

8Then I heard the Lord's voice, saying, "Who can I send? Who will go for us?"

So I said, "Here I am. Send me!"

9Then the Lord said, "Go and tell the people, 'Listen closely, but don't understand. Look closely, but don't learn.' 10Confuse them. Make them unable to understand what they hear and see. If you don't do this, they might really look with their eyes, hear with their ears and understand with their minds. Then they might come back to me and be healed!"

11Then I asked, "Lord, for how long should I do this?"

He answered, "Do this until the cities are destroyed and all the people are gone. Do this until there is no one left living in the houses and the land is destroyed and empty."

12The LORD will make the people go far away, and there will be large areas of empty land in the country. 13A tenth of the people will be allowed to stay in the land, but it will be destroyed again. They will be like an oak tree. When the tree is chopped down, a stump is left. This stump will be a very special seed that will grow again.

Trouble With Aram

7 Ahaz was the son of Jotham, who was the son of Uzziah. Rezin was the king of Aram, Pekah son of Remaliah[e] was the king of Israel. When Ahaz was king of Judah, Rezin and Pekah went up to Jerusalem to attack it, but they were not able to defeat the city.[f]

2The family of David received a message that said, "The armies of Aram and Ephraim have joined together in one camp." When King Ahaz heard this message, he and the people became frightened. They shook with fear like trees of the forest blowing in the wind.

3Then the LORD told Isaiah, "You and your son Shear Jashub[g] should go out and talk to Ahaz. Go to the place where the water flows into the Upper Pool,[h] on the street that leads up to Laundryman's Field.

a 6:1 *year . . . died* This was probably 740 BC.
b 6:4 *smoke* This showed that God was in the Temple. See Exod. 40:34–35.
c 6:5 *I am not pure . . . him* Literally, "I am a man of unclean lips and live among people of unclean lips."
d 6:7 *erased* Or "atoned" or "covered over".
e 7:1 *Pekah son of Remaliah* A king of northern Israel. He ruled about 740–731 BC.
f 7:1 *Rezin and Pekah . . . the city* Or "Rezin and Pekah went up to attack Jerusalem, but they were not able to fight."
g 7:3 *Shear Jashub* This is a name that means "a few people will come back".
h 7:3 *Upper Pool* Probably the Pool of Siloam at the southern tip of the City of David, just above the older pool now called the Red Pool.

PROPHET OF DOOM

You've been called to see the head teacher and you don't know why. You approach with fear and trembling, enter the hushed office and nervously take a seat. Heart racing, palms sweating, short of breath — you feel about ten centimetres tall.

But, relief! It's good news: the head's being really kind towards you and she's not going to bring up any of your misdemeanours. Instead she's got a special assignment for you to do for her.

DIG IN   READ Isaiah 6:1–13

- What is Isaiah's first response (v.5)? Why?
- What is the significance of the angel touching Isaiah's mouth with the burning coal (v.7)?

Here, just as Isaiah's prophecy is getting going, he breaks off to tell of his first face-to-face encounter with God himself. Naturally, Isaiah is terrified.

Something important needs to happen before Isaiah is allowed to go any further. That's because God is holy (v.3) – a state of purity and perfection that humans cannot reach. Isaiah senses rightly that he is not pure enough to speak to God in his present state (v.5). The hot coal touching Isaiah's lips is an act of "atonement" that God declares is good enough to remove his sins.

- What is God calling Isaiah to do?
- Why do you think Isaiah volunteers to go (v.8)?

Perhaps because he feels the weight of sin lifted off him and perhaps because he is so caught up in the glorious presence of God, Isaiah steps forward and says "Send me" (v.8). God commissions him to serve him in bringing a harsh message to the people.

READ Isaiah 1:2–31

Here we find a summary of what Isaiah's message will be.

- What does God accuse the people of (vv.2–4,21–23)?
- How will his righteous judgement come (vv.7,9,20,28,30–31)?
- Where can you see glimmers of hope in the passage?

In this "flashforward" prophecy, Isaiah makes it clear that God's judgement is coming and it won't be pretty. The land his people know and love will be attacked by foreign armies and laid waste. Many will be killed in the attacks and only a few will survive.

DIG THROUGH

- Look again at Isaiah's vision of God in Isaiah 6:1–4. What feelings does it stir up inside you? Do you ever forget how holy and majestic God is?
- Do you think God would be happy about the way you speak when you're with others? Do you ever feel guilty about things you've said? (From time to time at least, you ought to! Check out James 3:1–12.) But what hope do we get from Isaiah's encounter with God (Isaiah 6:7)?
- "I'm probably saying the wrong thing." "No one ever takes any notice." Do you ever get down like that when you've tried to tell people about Jesus? Don't give up! Isaiah probably didn't always say what he should in his everyday life (though he certainly did in his Bible prophecies!), and even when he did say the right thing people didn't take any notice! Yet God still wanted Isaiah to act as his mouthpiece. Isn't that awesome?!

4"Tell Ahaz, 'Be careful, but be calm. Don't be afraid. Don't let those two men, Rezin and Remaliah's son,*a* frighten you! They are like two burning sticks. They might be hot now, but soon they will be nothing but smoke. Rezin, Aram and Remaliah's son became angry 5and made plans against you. They said, 6"Let's go and fight against Judah and divide it among ourselves. Then we will make Tabeel's son the new king of Judah."

7"But the Lord GOD says: Their plan will not succeed. It will not happen 8because Aram depends on its capital Damascus, and Damascus is led by its weak king Rezin. And don't worry about Ephraim. Within 65 years it will be crushed, no longer a nation. 9Ephraim depends on its capital Samaria, and Samaria is led by Remaliah's son. So you have no reason to fear. Believe this, or you will not survive.'"

Immanuel—God Is With Us

10Then the LORD spoke to Ahaz again 11and said, "Ask for a sign from the LORD your God to prove that this is true. You can ask for any sign you want. The sign can come from a place as deep as Sheol*b* or as high as the skies."*c*

12But Ahaz said, "I will not ask for a sign as proof. I will not test the LORD."

13Then Isaiah said, "Family of David, listen very carefully! Is it not enough that you would test the patience of humans? Will you now test the patience of my God? 14But the Lord will still show you this sign:

"The young woman is pregnant*d*
    and will give birth to a son.
    She will name him Immanuel.*e*
15He will eat milk curds and honey*f*
    as he learns to choose good and refuse evil.
16But before he is old enough to make that choice,
    the land of the two kings you fear will be empty.

17"But the LORD will bring troubled times to you. These troubles will be worse than anything that has happened since the time Israel separated from Judah. This will happen to your people and to your father's family when God brings the king of Assyria to fight against you.

18"At that time the LORD will call for the 'Fly' that is now near the streams of Egypt, and he will call for the 'Bee' that is now in the country of Assyria. Those enemies will come to your country. 19They will settle in the deep valleys and in the caves, by the thornbushes and watering holes. 20The Lord will use Assyria to punish Judah. Assyria will be hired and used like a razor to shave off Judah's beard and to remove the hair from his head and body.*g*

21"At that time someone might keep only one young cow and two sheep alive. 22But there will be enough milk for them to eat milk curds. In fact, everyone left in the country will eat milk curds and honey. 23There are now fields that have 1,000 grapevines, and each grapevine is worth 1,000 pieces of silver. But those fields will be covered with weeds and thorns. 24That land will be wild and used only as a hunting ground where people go with bows and arrows. 25People once worked the soil and grew food on these hills, but at that time they will not go there, because the fields will be covered with weeds and thorns. It will be a place where cattle graze and sheep wander."

Assyria Is Coming Soon

8 The LORD told me, "Get a large scroll,*h* and use an ordinary pen*i* to write these words: 'This is for Maher Shalal Hash Baz.'"*j*

---

a **7:4 Remaliah's son** Pekah, the king of northern Israel. He ruled about 740–731 BC.
b **7:11 The sign . . . Sheol** Or "Make your request deep." The Hebrew word for "request" is like the word for Sheol.
c **7:11 The sign . . . skies** Literally, "Make your request very high."
d **7:14 The young woman is pregnant** Or "Look at this young woman. She is pregnant." The ancient Greek version (quoted in Matt. 1:23) translates "young woman" here with a word meaning "virgin" and has "Look! The virgin will become pregnant."
e **7:14 Immanuel** This name means "God is with us."
f **7:15 milk curds and honey** This refers to some of the first solid foods, something like yogurt, that were fed to a baby. This is also the food that even the poor can find to eat. Also in verse 22.
g **7:20 shave . . . body** This means that the people of Judah would be humiliated and treated like slaves.
h **8:1 scroll** This Hebrew word might also mean a clay or stone tablet.
i **8:1 ordinary pen** Literally, "stylus of a man". This might be a pen for writing on clay.
j **8:1 Maher Shalal Hash Baz** This means "There will soon be looting and stealing."

[2]I found some men who could be trusted to serve as witnesses: Uriah the priest and Zechariah son of Jeberekiah. They watched me write those words. [3]Then I went to my wife, the woman prophet. She became pregnant and had a son. The Lord told me, "Name the boy Maher Shalal Hash Baz." [4]He said that because before the boy learns to say "Mummy" and "Daddy", God will take all the wealth and riches from Damascus[a] and Samaria and give them to the king of Assyria.

[5]The Lord spoke to me again. [6]He said, "These people[b] refuse to accept the slow-moving waters of Shiloah.[c] They prefer Rezin and Remaliah's son." [7]But the Lord will bring the king of Assyria and all his power against them. The Assyrians will come like their swift moving river, like water that rises and spills over its banks. [8]This water will be like a flash flood as it passes through Judah. It will rise to Judah's throat and almost drown him.

But he will spread his wings over your whole country, Immanuel.[d]

[9]All you nations, prepare for war.
    You will be defeated.
Listen, all you faraway countries!
    Prepare for battle.
    You will be defeated.
[10]Make your plans for the fight.
    Your plans will be defeated.
Give orders to your armies,
    but your orders will be useless,
    because God is with us![e]

Warnings to Isaiah

[11]The Lord spoke to me with his great power and warned[f] me not to be like these people. He said, [12]"Don't think there is a plan against you just because the people say there is. Don't be afraid of what they fear. Don't let them frighten you!"

[13]The Lord All-Powerful is the one you should fear. He is the one you should respect.[g] He is the one who should frighten you. [14]If you people would respect him, he would be a safe place[h] for you. But you don't respect him, so he is like a stone that you stumble over. He is a rock that makes both families of Israel fall. He has become

a trap that all the people of Jerusalem will fall into. [15](Many people will trip over this rock. They will fall and be broken. They will be caught in the trap.)

[16]The Lord said, "Write this agreement.[i] Tie it up and seal it so that it cannot be changed. Give these teachings to my followers for safekeeping."

[17]The Lord has turned away from the family
    of Jacob,
    but I will wait for him.
    I trust that he will come to save us.

[18]Here I am with the children the Lord has given me. We are here as signs from the Lord All-Powerful, who lives on Mount Zion. He is using us to show his plans for the people of Israel.

[19]People will say to you, "Go to those who know how to get advice from ghosts and spirits of the dead and who mumble and chirp like birds. Ask them what to do. Shouldn't people go to their gods, the spirits of their ancestors, for help? By contacting the dead, those still living [20]can get advice or some message to help them know what to do." But I tell you for sure, there is no future for those who talk like that. [21]They will lose everything and wander through the land tired and hungry. And when they become hungry, they will become angry. And looking up, they will curse their king and their gods. [22]And looking down at the earth, they will see only trouble and depressing darkness closing in—terrifying darkness and gloom.

A New Day Is Coming

9 But there will be an end to the gloom those people suffered. In the past, people thought the land of Zebulun and Naphtali was not important. But later, that land will be honoured— the land along the sea, the land east of the Jordan River and Galilee where the people from other nations live. [2]Those people lived in darkness, but they will see a great light. They lived in a place as dark as death, but a great light will shine on them.

[3]God, you will make the nation grow, and you will make the people happy. They will rejoice in your presence as they do at harvest time. It will

---

[a] **8:4 Damascus** A city in the country of Aram (Syria).
[b] **8:6 These people** Probably Judeans who wanted to join Rezin and Pekah. Also in verse 11.
[c] **8:6 Shiloah** A channel that carried water from Gihon Spring to a pool at the south end of the City of David (Jerusalem). Men from David's family were anointed to be kings there.
[d] **8:8 But he . . . Immanuel** Or "Immanuel, it will spread throughout your whole country." This might be a promise of God's protection, or it might be a warning about Assyria's power.
[e] **8:10 God is with us** In Hebrew this is like the name Immanuel.
[f] **8:11 warned** Or "prevented".
[g] **8:13 respect** Literally, "consider holy".
[h] **8:14 safe place** Or "holy place".
[i] **8:16 Write this agreement** Or "Take a document." This could refer to the large scroll in verse 1 or to the promise that follows in verse 17.

be like the joy when people take their share of things they have won in war. [4]That will happen because you will lift the heavy yoke off their shoulders and take away their heavy burden. You will take away the rod that the enemy used to punish your people, as you did when you defeated Midian.[a]

[5]Every boot that marched in battle and every uniform stained with blood will be destroyed and thrown into the fire. [6]This will happen when a special child is born. God will give us a son who will be responsible for leading the people. His name will be "Wonderful Counsellor, Powerful God, Father Who Lives Forever, Prince of Peace." [7]His power will continue to grow, and there will be peace without end. This will establish him as the king sitting on David's throne and ruling his kingdom. He will rule with goodness and justice for ever and ever. The strong love that the LORD All-Powerful has for his people will make this happen!

God Will Punish Israel

[8]The Lord gave a command against Jacob and someone in Israel fell.[b] [9]So all the people in Ephraim, including the ruler in Samaria, learned their lesson.

Those people are very proud and boastful now. They say, [10]"Yes, those bricks fell, but we will rebuild with strong stone. Yes, those little trees were chopped down, but we will plant new trees. And they will be large, strong trees."

[11]The LORD found people to go up and fight against Rezin. He stirred up Rezin's enemies. [12]As for Israel, the Arameans are in front of him and the Philistines are behind him. And they are both eating away at him. But the Lord is not finished yet. He is still angry, and his arm is raised to continue punishing Israel.

[13]The people did not stop sinning. They did not come to the LORD All-Powerful for help. [14]So the LORD cut off Israel's head and tail. He took away the branch and the stalk in one day. [15](Israel's leaders and those in power are the "head". And their lying prophets are the "tail".)

[16]Their guides are leading them the wrong way, so those who follow them will be destroyed. [17]All of them are evil. So the Lord is not happy with the young men, and he will not show mercy to their widows and orphans. That is because they are evil hypocrites. They tell lies.

The Lord has punished them, but he has not finished yet. He is still angry, and his arm is raised to continue punishing his people.

[18]That evil was like a small fire that started among the weeds and thorns and then spread to the larger bushes in the forest. Finally, it became a giant fire, and everything went up in smoke.

[19]The LORD All-Powerful was angry, so the land was burned. The people were fuel for the fire. No one showed any compassion to anyone else. [20]People looked to the right and grabbed whatever they could, but they were still hungry. They grabbed whatever was on their left, but still they were not satisfied. So they turned on themselves and began to eat the bodies of their own children. [21]Manasseh fought against Ephraim, and Ephraim fought against Manasseh. Then both of them turned on Judah.

But the Lord has not finished punishing his people. He is still angry, and his arm is raised to continue punishing them.

10 Just look at those lawmakers who write evil laws and make life hard for the people. [2]They are not fair to the poor. They take away the rights of the poor and allow people to steal from widows and orphans.

[3]Lawmakers, you will have to explain what you have done. What will you do then? Your destruction is coming from a faraway country. Where will you run for help? Your money and your riches will not help you. [4]You will have to bow down like a prisoner. You will fall down like a dead man, but that will not help you. God will still be angry and ready to punish you.

God Will Punish Assyria's Pride

[5]The Lord says, "I will use Assyria like a stick. In my anger I will use Assyria to punish Israel. [6]I will send Assyria to fight against the people who do evil. I am angry with them, and I will command Assyria to fight against them. Assyria will defeat them and take their wealth. Israel will be like mud for Assyria to walk on in the streets.

[7]"But Assyria does not understand that I will use him. He does not think of himself as my tool. He only wants to destroy other people. He only plans to destroy many nations. [8]Assyria says to himself, 'All of my officers are like kings! [9]The city of Calno is no better than the city of Carchemish. Arpad is like Hamath, and Samaria is like Damascus. [10]I defeated those evil kingdoms and now I control them. The idols those people worship are better than the idols of Jerusalem and Samaria. [11]I defeated Samaria and her gods. I will also defeat Jerusalem and the idols her people have made.'"

[12]When the Lord finishes doing what he planned to Jerusalem and Mount Zion, he will punish Assyria. The king of Assyria is very proud. His pride made him do many bad things, so God will punish him.

---

[a] 9:4 *as you . . . Midian* See Judg. 7:15–25.
[b] 9:8 Or "The Lord sent a command to Jacob and it happened to Israel."

[13]The king of Assyria said, "I am very wise. By my own wisdom and power I have done many great things. I have defeated many nations. I have taken their wealth and their people as slaves. I am a very powerful man. [14]With my own hands I have taken the riches of all these people—like someone taking eggs from a bird's nest. A bird often leaves its nest and eggs, and there is nothing to protect the nest. There is no bird to chirp and fight with its wings and beak, so anyone can come and take the eggs. And there is no one to stop me from taking all the people on earth."

[15]An axe is not better than the one who cuts with it. A saw is not better than the one who uses it. Is a stick stronger than the one who picks it up? It can't do anything to the person who is using it to punish someone! [16]But Assyria doesn't understand this. So the Lord GOD All-Powerful will send a terrible disease against him. He will lose his wealth and power like a sick man losing weight. Then Assyria's glory will be destroyed. It will be like a fire burning until everything is gone. [17]The Light of Israel[a] will be like a fire. The Holy One will be like a flame. He will be like a fire that first begins to burn the weeds and thorns [18]and then spreads to burn up the tall trees and vineyards. Finally, everything will be destroyed— even the people. Assyria will be like a rotting log. [19]There will be a few trees left standing in the forest, so few that even a child could count them.

[20]Then the people from Jacob's family who are left living in Israel will stop depending on the one who beat them. They will learn to depend on the LORD, the Holy One of Israel. [21]Those who are left in Jacob's family will again follow the Powerful God.[b]

[22]Israel, your people are as many as the sands of the sea, but only a few of them will be left to come back to God. But before that happens, your country will be destroyed. God has announced that he will destroy the land. And then justice will come into the land like a river flowing full. [23]The Lord GOD All-Powerful really will destroy this land.

[24]The Lord GOD All-Powerful says, "My people living in Zion, don't be afraid of Assyria! Yes, he will beat you, and it will be just as the time when Egypt beat you with a stick. [25]But after a short time, my anger will stop. I will be satisfied that Assyria has punished you enough."

[26]Then the LORD All-Powerful will beat Assyria with a whip, just as he defeated Midian at Raven Rock.[c] He will punish his enemies, as he did when he raised his stick over the sea[d] and led his people from Egypt.

[27]He will take away the troubles Assyria brought you, troubles that are like heavy weights carried with a yoke on your neck. But that yoke will be taken off your neck. The burden will be lifted from your shoulders.

The Army of Assyria Invades Israel

[28e]The army of Assyria will enter near Aiath. The army will walk through Migron. They will keep their food in Micmash. [29]The army will cross over the mountains and sleep at Geba. Ramah will be afraid. The people at Gibeah of Saul[f] will run away.

[30]Cry out, Bath Gallim![g] Laishah, listen! Anathoth, answer me! [31]The people of Madmenah are running away. The people of Gebim[h] are hiding. [32]This day the army will stop at Nob and prepare to fight against Mount Zion, the hill of Jerusalem.

[33]Look, the Lord GOD All-Powerful will use his great power and chop down that great tree. Their highest officials will be brought down. Their most important leaders will be humbled. [34]God will cut down his enemies. Like the tall trees of Lebanon he will cut them down with an axe.

The King of Peace Is Coming

11 A small tree[i] will begin to grow from the stump of Jesse.[j] That branch will grow from Jesse's roots. [2]The LORD's Spirit will always be with that new king to give him wisdom, understanding, guidance and power. The Spirit will help him know and respect the LORD. [3]He will find joy in obeying the LORD.

This king will not judge people by the way things look. He will not judge by listening to rumours. [4-5]He will judge the poor fairly and honestly. He will be fair when he decides what to do for the poor of the land. If he decides people should be beaten, he will give the command, and

---

[a] **10:17 The Light of Israel** This is a name for God, like "The Holy One" in the next sentence. See "ISRAEL" in the Word List.
[b] **10:21 Powerful God** See Isa. 9:6.
[c] **10:26 Midian at Raven Rock** Or "Midian at the Rock of Oreb". See Judg. 7:25.
[d] **10:26 he raised . . . sea** See Exod. 14:1 – 15:21.
[e] **10:28–32** Isaiah uses names with double meanings to describe the different ways the Assyrian army would fight against Judah.
[f] **10:29 Geba, Ramah, Gibeah of Saul** Towns north of Jerusalem.
[g] **10:30 Bath Gallim** Gallim, a city south of Jerusalem. This name means "daughter of the waves", and might refer to birds that make loud noises by the shore.
[h] **10:31 Gebim** An unknown city. This name is like the Hebrew word for "pit" or "cistern", a hole in the ground for storing water.
[i] **11:1 small tree** That is, a new king will come from the family of David.
[j] **11:1 Jesse** King David's father.

SINGING TO THE SAVING GOD

Isaiah's name gives away the central message of his book of prophecy: it means "the Lord saves". As we've already discovered, his words will strike fear into the hearts of God's people because they predict a time of chaos and upheaval. Their kings have been faithless and the people have followed suit, so God's punishment is coming.

But all the way through – amongst words of doom and gloom – there are bright, hopeful promises about a new day coming for Israel. This is the salvation Isaiah's name refers to. God has an amazing plan for his people to be restored in ways that they couldn't begin to imagine.

DIG IN

READ Isaiah 11:1–16

- Can you guess who the new king is from the clues in verses 1–5?
- What will be the hallmarks of this new king's reign (vv.6–9)?
- What will happen to God's people at that time (v.12 especially)?

Jesse was King David's father and many years later a baby was born whose family tree would run right back to David: Jesus (Matthew 1:1). He would be filled with the Holy Spirit (Matthew 3:16) and he would live perfectly before God his whole life.

This passage also looks ahead to a future even beyond us – when Jesus will judge the world fairly (Revelation 20:11–15) and perfect peace will reign on earth. God's people are to be scattered throughout the world, but when Jesus comes all will be gathered up again in one glorious family of believers.

READ Isaiah 12:1–6

- How will the people respond to all the promises in the previous chapter?

It's a wonderful song of praise to God. Singing is an appropriate response to God's saving work in our lives. In our world where attention and fame are lavished on only the very best singers, it can be easy to think we should leave the singing to the professionals. But singing unites us and celebrates God's presence among us (v.6). We need to sing!

DIG THROUGH

- Look at the second part of 11:9: "The world will be full of knowledge about him, like the sea is full of water." Imagine what the world would be like if everyone knew God. What might this look like in your school, in your local area or in your nation?
- Have you ever written a song? Even a simple song that expresses your heart to God? The Bible is full of encouragement to "sing a new song" to God (check out Psalms 33:3, 96:1 and 98:1). Why not take this short passage, add your own tune and sing it out in worship? The Lord loves to hear us sing from our hearts.

DIG DEEPER

- God's people are a singing people. This is clear from the fact that a whole book of the Bible (Psalms) is given over to songs people have sung to God throughout Israel's history. Songs are also interspersed throughout the book of Revelation, making it clear there is going to be a lot of singing in heaven! Look up Revelation 5:9–10 or 15:3–4.

they will be beaten. If he decides people must die, he will give the command, and those evil people will be killed. Goodness and fairness will be like a belt he wears around his waist.

⁶Then wolves will live at peace with lambs, and leopards will lie down with young goats. An ox and a lion will eat together. And a little child will be able to lead them. ⁷Bears and cattle will graze in the same field, and their young will lie down together in peace. Lions will eat hay like cattle. ⁸Even snakes will not hurt people. Babies will be able to play near a cobra's*ᵃ* hole and reach into the nest of a poisonous snake.

⁹People will stop hurting each other. People on my holy mountain will not want to destroy things because they will know the LORD. The world will be full of knowledge about him, like the sea is full of water.

¹⁰At that time there will be someone special from Jesse's family. He will be like a flag that all the nations gather around. The nations will come to him and ask him what they should do. And the place where he is will be filled with glory.

¹¹At that time the Lord will again reach out and gather his people who are left in countries like Assyria, North Egypt, South Egypt, Ethiopia, Elam, Babylonia,*ᵇ* Hamath and other faraway countries around the world. ¹²He will gather the people of Israel and Judah who were forced to leave their country. They were scattered to all the faraway places on earth. But he will raise the flag as a sign for the other nations, and he will gather his people together again.

¹³Then Ephraim will not be jealous of Judah, and Judah will have no enemies left. And Judah will not cause trouble for Ephraim. ¹⁴But Ephraim and Judah will attack the Philistines. These two nations will be like birds flying down to catch a small animal. Together, they will take the riches from the people in the East.*ᶜ* Ephraim and Judah will control Edom, Moab and the people in Ammon.*ᵈ*

¹⁵Just as the LORD divided the Red Sea near Egypt,*ᵉ* he will raise his arm in anger over the Euphrates River and hit it. It will divide into seven small rivers. They will be so small that the people can walk across with their sandals on. ¹⁶Then God's people who are left in Assyria will have a way to leave, just like the time God took the people out of Egypt.

A Song of Praise to God

12 At that time you will say,

"I praise you, LORD!
　You have been angry with me,
but don't be angry with me now.
　Show your love to me.
²God is the one who saves me.
　I trust him and will not be afraid.
The LORD GOD*ᶠ* is my strength,
　the reason I sing for joy!*ᵍ*
He is the one who saved me."

³You people will get your water from the spring
　of salvation.
Then you will be happy.
⁴At that time you will say,
　"Praise the LORD and call out his name!
Tell everyone what he has done
　and how wonderful he is."
⁵Sing songs of praise about the LORD,
　because he has done great things.
Spread this news about God throughout the
　whole world.
Let all people know these things.
⁶People of Zion, shout about these things!
　The Holy One of Israel is with you in a
　powerful way.
So sing and be happy!

God's Message to Babylon

13 God gave Isaiah son of Amoz this message*ʰ*
　about Babylon:

²"Raise a flag on that mountain*ⁱ* where nothing
　grows.
　Call out to the men.
Wave your arms to let them know
　they should enter through the gates for
　important leaders.

³"I have separated these men from the people,
　and I myself will command them.
I have gathered these proud, happy soldiers
　of mine
　to show how angry I am.

⁴"Listen to that loud noise in the mountains.
　It sounds like crowds of people.

ᵃ **11:8 cobra** A very poisonous snake.
ᵇ **11:11 Babylonia** Literally, "Shinar", which may be a form of the name Sumer.
ᶜ **11:14 East** This usually refers to the area around Babylon.
ᵈ **11:14 Edom, Moab . . . Ammon** Three countries east of Israel. They were Israel's enemies for many years.
ᵉ **11:15 the LORD . . . Egypt** Or "the LORD will dry up the tongue of the Sea of Egypt".
ᶠ **12:2 The LORD GOD** Literally, "YAH YAHWEH", two forms of a Hebrew name for God. See "YAHWEH" in the Word List.
ᵍ **12:2 the reason . . . joy** Literally, "my song" or possibly, "my power".
ʰ **13:1 message** Or "burden".
ⁱ **13:2 mountain** This probably means Babylon.

People from many kingdoms are gathering
     together.
The LORD All-Powerful is calling his army
     together.
⁵They are coming from a faraway land.
They are coming from beyond the horizon.
The LORD will use this army as a weapon to
     show his anger.
They will destroy the whole country."

⁶The LORD's special day is near. So cry and be
sad for yourselves. A time is coming when the
enemy will steal your wealth. God All-Powerful
will make that happen.ᵃ ⁷People will lose their
courage. Fear will make them weak. ⁸Everyone
will be afraid. They will stare at each other with
shock on their faces. Fear will grip them like the
pains of a woman in childbirth.

God's Judgement Against Babylon

⁹Look, the LORD's special day is coming! It will
be a terrible day. God will be very angry. He will
destroy the country and wipe out the sinful
people who live there. ¹⁰The skies will be dark.
The sun, the moon and the stars will not shine.
¹¹The Lord says, "I will cause bad things to
happen to the world. I will punish the evil people
for their sin. I will make proud people lose their
pride. I will stop the boasting of cruel people.
¹²There will be only a few people left. They will be
as rare as pure gold. ¹³In my anger I will shake the
sky, and the earth will be moved from its place."
That will happen on the day the LORD All-
Powerful shows his anger. ¹⁴Then the people from
Babylon will run away like wounded deer or sheep
that have no shepherd. Everyone will turn and run
back to their own country and people. ¹⁵Anyone
caught by the enemy will be killed with a sword.
¹⁶Everything in their houses will be stolen. Their
wives will be raped, and their little children will
be beaten to death while they watch.

¹⁷The Lord says, "Look, I will cause the armies
of Media to attack Babylon. No one can stop
them even with offers of gold and silver. ¹⁸With
their bows and arrows they will kill the young
men. They will not show any kindness or mercy
even to the babies and young children. ¹⁹Babylon
will be destroyed like the time God destroyed
Sodom and Gomorrah.

"Babylon is the most beautiful of all kingdoms,
and the Babyloniansᵇ are very proud of their city.

²⁰But no one will ever live in Babylon again.
People will stay away from there. Not even those
who move from place to place will ever set up
their tents there. And shepherds will not let their
sheep rest there. ²¹The only animals living there
will be wild animals from the desert. People will
not be living in their houses in Babylon. The
houses will be full of owls and large birds. Wild
goatsᶜ will play in the houses. ²²Wild dogs and
wolves will howl in the great and beautiful
buildings. Babylon will be finished. The end is
near, and it will not be delayed."

Israel Will Return Home

14 The LORD will again show his love to
Jacob. He will again choose the people of
Israel. He will give them their land. Then the
non-Israelitesᵈ will join the Israelites, and both
will become one family—Jacob's family. ²Those
nations will bring the Israelites back to their land.
The men and women from the other nations will
become slaves to Israel. In the past, those people
forced the Israelites to become their slaves. But in
the future the Israelites will defeat those nations,
and Israel will then rule over them in the LORD's
land. ³In the past, you were slaves. People forced
you to work hard. But the LORD will take away
the hard work you were forced to do.

A Song About the King of Babylon

⁴At that time you will begin to sing this song
about the king of Babylon:

The king was cruel when he ruled us,
     but now his rule is finished.
⁵The LORD breaks the sceptre of evil rulers;
     he takes away their power.
⁶In anger, the king of Babylon beat the people.
     He never stopped beating them.
He was an evil ruler who ruled in anger.
     He never stopped hurting people.
⁷But now, the whole country rests and is
     quiet.
Now the people begin to celebrate.
⁸You were an evil king,
     and now you are finished.
Even the pine trees are happy.
     The cedar trees of Lebanon rejoice.
They say, "The king chopped us down,
     but now the king has fallen,
     and he will never stand again."

ᵃ 13:6 *A time . . . happen* This is a wordplay in Hebrew. The word meaning "stealing things in war" sounds like the word
meaning "God All-Powerful".
ᵇ 13:19 *Babylonians* Literally, "Chaldeans".
ᶜ 13:21 *Wild goats* The Hebrew word means "hairy", "goat" or "goat-demon".
ᵈ 14:1 *non-Israelites* This usually means those who live in a country but are not yet citizens of that country. Here, it is the
non-Israelites who decided to follow God.

⁹The place of death is excited
    that you are coming.
Sheol is waking the spirits
    of all the leaders of the earth for you.
Sheol is making the kings stand up
    from their thrones to meet you.
¹⁰They will make fun of you, saying,
    "Now you are as dead as we are.
    Now you are just like us."
¹¹Your pride has been sent down to Sheol.
    The music from your harps announces the
        coming of your proud spirit.
Maggots will be the bed you lie on,
    and other worms will cover your body like
        a blanket.
¹²You were like the morning star,
    but you have fallen from the sky.
In the past, all the nations on earth bowed
        down before you,
    but now you have been cut down.
¹³You always told yourself,
    "I will go to the skies above.
I will put my throne above God's stars.
    I will sit on Zaphon,ᵃ the holy mountain
        where the gods meet.
¹⁴I will go up to the altar above the tops of the
        clouds.
    I will be like God Most High."

¹⁵But that did not happen.
    You were brought down to the deep
        pit—Sheol, the place of death.
¹⁶People will come to look at your dead body.
    They will think about you and say,
"Is this the same man
    who caused great fear in all the kingdoms
        on earth,
¹⁷who destroyed cities
    and turned the land into a desert,
who captured people in war
    and would not let them go home?"
¹⁸The kings of other nations lie buried with
        honour,
    each king with his own grave.
¹⁹But you were thrown out, far from your
        grave,
    like a rotting branch cut from a tree.
You are like a dead man who fell in battle,
    trampled under the feet of other soldiers.
Now you look like any other dead man
    wrapped in burial clothes.
²⁰Other kings have their own graves,
    but you will not join them,

because you ruined your own country
    and killed your own people.
So your wicked descendants will be stopped.

²¹Prepare to kill his children,
    because their father is guilty.
His children will never take control of the
        land.
    They will never fill the world with their
        cities.

²²The LORD All-Powerful said, "I will stand and
fight against those people. I will destroy the famous
city, Babylon. I will destroy all the people there.
I will destroy their children, their grandchildren
and their great-grandchildren." The LORD himself
said this. ²³"I will change Babylon. It will be a place
for animals,ᵇ not people. It will be a swamp. I will
use the 'broom of destruction' to sweep Babylon
away." The LORD All-Powerful said this.

God Will Also Punish Assyria

²⁴The LORD All-Powerful made this promise:
"This will happen exactly as I meant for it to
happen. It will happen just the way I planned.
²⁵I will destroy the king of Assyria in my country.
I will walk on him on my mountains. He forced
my people to be his slaves; he put a yoke on their
necks. But that pole will be taken off Judah's
neck, and that burden will be removed. ²⁶This
is what I plan to do for this land. I will use my
power to punish all those nations."
²⁷When the LORD All-Powerful makes a plan,
no one can change it. When he raises his arm to
punish, no one can stop him.

God's Message to Philistia

²⁸This messageᶜ was given to me the year King
Ahaz died:ᵈ
²⁹Country of Philistia, don't be happy that the
king who beat you is now dead. It is true that his
rule has ended, but his son will come and rule.
It will be like one snake giving birth to a more
dangerous one. The new king will be like a quick
and dangerous snake to you. ³⁰But even the
poorest of my people will be able to eat safely. And
their children will be able to lie down and feel
safe. But I will make your family die from hunger,
and your enemy will kill anyone who survives.

³¹People near the city gates, cry!
    People in the city, cry out!

ᵃ **14:13** *Zaphon* This Hebrew word means "north", "hidden".
ᵇ **14:23** *animals* Literally, "porcupines".
ᶜ **14:28** *message* Or "burden". Also in 15:1.
ᵈ **14:28** *year King Ahaz died* About 727 BC.

Everyone in Philistia,
    your courage will melt like hot wax.

Look to the north!
    There is a cloud of dust.
An army is coming,
    and everyone in that army is strong.[a]
32But what will the messengers from that nation
    report about us?
They will say, "The LORD made Zion
    strong,
and his poor people went there for safety."

INSIGHT

The Moabites were relatives of the Israelites but they had been enemies since the king of Moab refused to let the Israelites pass through Moab to get to Canaan about 700 years earlier (Judges 11:17).

Isaiah 15:1

God's Message to Moab

15 This is a message about Moab:

One night armies took the wealth from Ar
    in Moab,
    and the city was destroyed.
One night armies took the wealth from Kir in
    Moab,
    and the city was destroyed.
2The king's family and the people of Dibon[b] go
    to the places of worship[c] to cry.
The people of Moab are crying for Nebo[d]
    and Medeba.[e]
They have shaved their heads and beards to
    show their sadness.
3Everywhere in Moab, on the housetops and in
    the streets,
    people are wearing sackcloth.
    Everyone is crying.
4In Heshbon and Elealeh they are crying
    loudly.
You can hear their voices as far away as
    Jahaz.
Even the soldiers are frightened.
    They are shaking with fear.

5My heart cries, full of sorrow for Moab.
    Its people run away to Zoar for safety.
    They run to Eglath Shelishiyah.
The people are crying
    as they go up the road to Luhith.
You can hear their cries of sorrow
    as they follow the road to Horonaim.
6But Nimrim Brook is as dry as a desert.
    The grass has dried up,
and the plants are all dead.
    Nothing is green.
7So the people gather up everything they
    own
    and carry it across the Valley of
    Willows.

8You can hear crying everywhere in Moab—
    as far away as Eglaim and Beer Elim.
9The water of Dimon[f] is full of blood,
    and I will bring even more troubles to
    Dimon.
A few people living in Moab have escaped
    the enemy,
    but I will send lions to eat them.

16 You people should send a gift to the king of the land. You should send a lamb from Sela, through the desert, to the mountain in the city of Jerusalem.[g]

2The women of Moab try to cross the River
    Arnon.
They run around looking for help,
    like little birds that have fallen from their
    nest.
3They say, "Help us!
    Tell us what to do.
Protect us from our enemies
    as shade protects us from the noon sun.
We are running from our enemies.
    Hide us!
Don't give us to our enemies.
4People from Moab were forced to leave their
    homes.
So let them live in your land.
    Hide them from their enemies."

The robbing will stop.
    The enemy will be defeated.
The men who hurt the people will be gone
    from the land.

---

[a] **14:31** *everyone . . . strong* Or "there are no stragglers in that group".
[b] **15:2** *Dibon* A city in the country of Moab. This name is like a Hebrew word meaning "to be very sad".
[c] **15:2** *places of worship* Or "high places". See "HIGH PLACE" in the Word List.
[d] **15:2** *Nebo* A city in the country of Moab and the name of a false god.
[e] **15:2** *Medeba* A city in the country of Moab. This name is like a Hebrew word meaning "to be very sad".
[f] **15:9** *Dimon* This is probably the city of Dibon. Dimon is like the Hebrew word meaning "blood".
[g] **16:1** *city of Jerusalem* Literally, "daughter Zion". See "ZION" in the Word List.

[5]Then a new king will come.
He will be from David's family.[a]
He will be loyal, loving and kind.
He will be a king who judges fairly.
He will do what is right and good.

[6]We have heard that the people of Moab
are proud and conceited.
They are hot-tempered boasters,
but their boasts are only empty words.
[7]Because of their pride, everyone in Moab
will mourn.
They will wish for the way things used
to be.
They will wish for the raisin cakes from Kir
Hareseth.[b]
[8]The fields of Heshbon and the vines of Sibmah
no longer grow grapes.
Foreign rulers have destroyed the vines.
The enemy has reached Jazer
and has spread into the desert and down to
the sea.[c]
[9]I will cry with the people of Jazer and Sibmah
because the grapes have been destroyed.
I will cry with the people of Heshbon and
Elealeh
because there will be no harvest.
There will be no summer fruit,
and there will be no shouts of joy for the
harvest.
[10]There will be no joy and happiness in the
orchard.
I will end the happy singing and shouting in
the vineyard.
The grapes are ready to make wine,
but they will all be ruined.
[11]So I will hum a sad song for Moab and
Kir Heres,[d]
like a harp playing a funeral song.
[12]The people of Moab will go to their high
places
and make a great effort to worship.
They will go to their temple to pray,
but it will not help them.

[13]The LORD said these things about Moab many
times. [14]And now the LORD says, "In three years

(counting as exactly as a hired helper would) all
those people and the things they are proud of
will be gone. Only a few of their weakest people
will be left."

God's Message to Aram

17 This is a message[e] about Damascus:[f]

"Damascus is now a city, but it will be
destroyed.
Only ruined buildings will be left there.
[2]People will leave the cities of Aroer.[g]
Flocks of sheep will wander freely in those
empty towns;
there will be no one to bother them.
[3]The fortresses of Ephraim will be destroyed.
The government in Damascus will be
finished.
Those left in Aram will lose everything,
just like the people of Israel," says the LORD
All-Powerful.

[4]"At that time Jacob's wealth will all be gone.
Yes, Israel will be like a sick man who has
become weak and thin.

[5]"That time will be like the grain harvest in
Rephaim Valley.[h] The workers gather the plants
that grow in the field. Then they cut the heads of
grain from the plants and collect the grain.
[6]"That time will also be like the olive harvest.
People knock olives from the trees, but a few
olives are usually left at the top of each tree. Four
or five olives are left on some of the top branches.
It will be the same for those cities," says the LORD
All-Powerful.

[7]Then the people will look up to the one who
made them. Their eyes will see the Holy One
of Israel. [8]They will not trust the great things
they have made. They will not go to the special
gardens[i] and altars[j] they made for false gods. [9]At
that time all the walled cities will be empty. They
will be like the mountains and the forests[k] in the
land before the Israelites came. In the past, all
the people ran away because the Israelites were
coming. In the future the country will be empty
again. [10]This will happen because you have

---

[a] **16:5** *David's family* The royal family of Judah. God promised that men from David's family would be kings in Judah.
[b] **16:7** *Kir Hareseth* A city in the country of Moab.
[c] **16:8** *Foreign rulers . . . the sea* Or "These grapes made many foreign rulers drunk. The vines spread far to the city of Jazer, then into the desert and down to the sea."
[d] **16:11** *Kir Heres* Kir Hareseth, a city in the country of Moab. Kir Heres means "a city chosen to be destroyed".
[e] **17:1** *message* Or "burden".
[f] **17:1** *Damascus* A city in the country of Aram (Syria).
[g] **17:2** *Aroer* A place in the country of Aram (Syria).
[h] **17:5** *Rephaim Valley* A valley south-west of Jerusalem.
[i] **17:8** *special gardens* Gardens where people worshipped false gods.
[j] **17:8** *altars* These might be altars for burning incense, or they might be altars for worshipping a special false god.
[k] **17:9** *mountains and the forests* With a minor change in the Hebrew, this could be "the Horites and Amorites".

forgotten the God who saves you. You have not remembered that God is your place of safety.

You brought some very good grapevines from faraway places. You might plant those grapevines, but they will not grow. [11]You will plant your grapevines one day and try to make them grow, and the next day they will blossom. But at harvest time, you will go to gather the fruit from the plants, and you will see that everything is dead. A sickness will kill all the plants.

[12]Listen to all these people!
> Their loud crying sounds like the noise from
> > the sea.
> Listen, it is like the crashing of waves in
> > the sea.
[13]And like the waves,
> they will rush away when God speaks
> > harshly to them.
> They will be like chaff blown away by the wind.
> They will be like weeds chased by a storm.
[14]That night, the people will be frightened.
> By morning, nothing will be left.
So our enemies will get nothing.
> They will come to our land, but nothing
> > will be there.

God's Message to Ethiopia

18 Look at the land along the rivers of Ethiopia where you can hear the buzzing of insect wings. [2]That land sends people down the Nile River in reed boats.[a]

> Fast messengers, go to the people
> > who are tall and smooth,
> > who are feared far and wide.
> Their powerful nation defeats all its enemies.
> > It is the land divided by rivers.
> > Go and warn them!
[3]Like a flag on a hill,
> > everyone on earth will see what happens.
> Like a trumpet call,
> > everyone in the country will hear it.

[4]The LORD said, "I will be in the place prepared for me.[b] I will quietly watch these things happen. On a beautiful summer day, at noon, people will be resting. (It will be during the hot harvest time when there is no rain, but only early morning dew.) [5]Then something terrible will happen.

Earlier in the year, the flowers bloomed and the new grapes formed buds and began to grow. But before the crop is harvested, the enemy will come and cut the plants. They will break the vines and throw them away. [6]The vines will be left for the birds from the mountains and the wild animals to eat. The birds will feed on them throughout the summer, and that winter the wild animals will eat the vines."

[7]At that time a special offering will be brought to the LORD All-Powerful from the people who are tall and smooth, from those who are feared far and wide, from that powerful nation that defeats other countries and whose land is divided by rivers.[c] This offering will be brought to the LORD's place on Mount Zion.

God's Message to Egypt

19 A message[d] about Egypt: Look, the LORD is coming on a fast cloud. He will enter Egypt, and all the false gods of Egypt will shake with fear. Egypt's courage will melt away like hot wax.

[2]The Lord says, "I will cause the Egyptians to fight against themselves. Men will fight their brothers. Neighbours will be against neighbours. Cities will be against cities. Kingdoms will be against kingdoms.[e] [3]The Egyptians will be afraid and confused. They will ask their false gods and spirits of the dead what they should do. They will seek advice from ghosts and spirits of their dead ancestors, but I will ruin their plans." [4]The Lord GOD All-Powerful says, "I will give Egypt to a hard master. A powerful king will rule over the people."

[5]The water in the Nile River will dry up and disappear. [6]All the rivers will smell very bad.[f] The canals in Egypt will be dry, and the water will be gone. All the water plants will rot. [7]All the plants along the riverbanks will die and blow away. Even the plants at the widest part of the river will dry up, blow away and disappear.

[8]The fishermen, all those who catch fish from the Nile River, will become sad and they will cry. They depend on the Nile River for their food, but it will be dry. [9]Those who make cloth from flax, who weave it into linen, will all be sad. [10]Those who weave cloth will be broken, and those who work for money will be depressed.

[11]The leaders of the city of Zoan[g] are fools. Pharaoh's "wise advisors" give bad advice. They say they are wise. They say they are from the old

---

[a] **18:2 *reed boats*** These boats were made by tying many reeds (a type of water plant) together.
[b] **18:4 *the place prepared for me*** Probably the Temple in Jerusalem.
[c] **18:7** Or "At that time the people who are tall and smooth, who are feared far and wide, that powerful nation who defeats other countries and whose land is divided by rivers, those people will be brought to the LORD All-Powerful as a special gift."
[d] **19:1 *message*** Or "burden".
[e] **19:2 *Kingdoms will be against kingdoms*** Or "States will be against states." This means Egyptians will fight other Egyptians.
[f] **19:6 *smell very bad*** In Hebrew this is like a name for the Nile River.
[g] **19:11 *Zoan*** A city in Egypt. Also in verse 13.

family of the kings, but they are not as smart as they think. ¹²Egypt, where are your wise men? They should learn what the Lord All-Powerful has planned for Egypt. They should be the ones to tell you what will happen.

¹³The leaders of Zoan have been fooled. The leaders of Noph*a* have believed lies, so they lead Egypt the wrong way. ¹⁴The Lord confused them, so they wander around and lead Egypt the wrong way. Everything they do is wrong. They are like drunks rolling in their vomit. ¹⁵There is nothing the leaders can do. (They are "the heads and the tails". They are "the tops and the stalks of plants".*b*)

¹⁶At that time the Egyptians will be like frightened women. They will be afraid of the Lord All-Powerful, because he will raise his arm to punish the people. ¹⁷The land of Judah brings fear to everyone in Egypt. Anyone in Egypt who hears the name Judah will be afraid. This will happen because the Lord All-Powerful has planned terrible things to happen to Egypt. ¹⁸At that time there will be five cities in Egypt where people speak Hebrew.*c* One of these cities will be named "Destruction City".*d* The people in these cities will promise to follow the Lord All-Powerful.

¹⁹At that time there will be an altar for the Lord in the middle of Egypt. At the border of Egypt there will be a monument to show honour to the Lord. ²⁰This will be a sign to show that the Lord All-Powerful does amazing things. Any time the people cry for help from the Lord, he will send help. He will send someone to save and defend the people—to rescue the people from those who hurt them.

²¹At that time the Lord will make himself known to the Egyptians, and they really will know the Lord. They will serve him and give him many sacrifices. They will make promises*e* to the Lord, and they will do what they promise. ²²The Lord will punish the Egyptians, but then he will heal them, and they will come back to him. The Lord will listen to their prayers and heal them.

²³At that time there will be a highway from Egypt to Assyria. Then the Assyrians will go to Egypt, and the Egyptians will go to Assyria. Egypt will work with Assyria.*f* ²⁴Then Israel, Assyria and Egypt will join together and control the land. This will be a blessing for the land. ²⁵The Lord All-Powerful will bless these countries. He will

say, "Egypt, you are my people. Assyria, I made you. Israel, I own you. You are all blessed!"

Assyria Will Defeat Egypt and Ethiopia

20 Sargon*g* was the king of Assyria. He sent his military commander to fight against Ashdod. The commander went there and captured the city. ²At that time the Lord spoke through Isaiah son of Amoz. He said, "Go, take the sackcloth off your waist and the sandals off your feet." So Isaiah obeyed the Lord and went without clothes or sandals.

³Then the Lord said, "My servant Isaiah has gone without clothes or sandals for three years. This is a sign for Egypt and Ethiopia. ⁴The king of Assyria will defeat Egypt and Ethiopia. Assyria will take prisoners and lead them away from their countries. The people, young and old, will be led away without clothes or sandals. They will be completely naked. ⁵Those who looked to Ethiopia for help will be shattered. Those who were amazed by Egypt's glory will be ashamed."

⁶People living along the coast will say, "We trusted those countries to help us. We ran to them so that they would rescue us from the king of Assyria. But look at them. They have been captured, so how can we escape?"

INSIGHT

Three years is a long while to go naked! But Isaiah may not have gone without clothing the whole time – he may just have done it from time to time to press the message home. He was dressing like a captive to illustrate the fate of Egypt and Ethiopia at the hands of the Assyrians.

Isaiah 20:1–6

God's Message About Babylon

21 This is a message*h* about the "desert by the sea":*i*

It is coming like a storm blowing through the Negev.

a **19:13 Noph** Or "Memphis", a city in Egypt.
b **19:15 the heads and . . . stalks of plants** See Isa. 9:14–15.
c **19:18 Hebrew** Literally, "the language of Canaan".
d **19:18 Destruction City** This is a wordplay on the name meaning "Sun City", which is also called On or Heliopolis.
e **19:21 promises** A special kind of promise to God. See Lev. 22:18–24.
f **19:23 Egypt will work with Assyria** Or "Egypt will serve Assyria."
g **20:1 Sargon** A king of Assyria. He was king about 721–705 BC.
h **21:1 message** Or "burden". Also in verses 11,13.
i **21:1 the "desert by the sea"** Probably Babylon.

It is coming in from the desert, from a
frightening nation.
²I was given a vision of the hard times to
come.
I see traitors turning against you.
I see people taking your wealth.

Elam, go against them!
Media, surround the city!
I will put an end to all their moaning.

³I saw those terrible things, and now I am
afraid.
My fear makes my stomach hurt like the
pain of giving birth.
What I hear frightens me.
What I see makes me shake with fear.
⁴I am worried and shaking with fear.
My pleasant evening has become a
nightmare.

⁵People are rushing around shouting their
orders:
"Set the table!
Post the guard!
Get something to eat and drink!
Officers, get up!
Polish your shields!"

⁶The Lord said to me, "Go and find someone to
guard this city. He must report whatever he sees.
⁷Whether he sees a chariot and a team of horses
or men riding donkeys or camels, he must listen
carefully."ᵃ
⁸Then one day the watchmanᵇ called out,

"My master, every day I have been in the
watchtowerᶜ watching.
Every night I have been standing on duty.
⁹Look! I see a man in a chariot
with a team of horses."ᵈ

The messenger said,
"Babylon has been defeated!
It has fallen to the ground!
All the statues of her false gods
were thrown to the ground and broken to
pieces."

¹⁰My people, you will be like the grain crushed
on my threshing floor. I have told you everything
I heard from the Lord All-Powerful, the God of
Israel.

God's Message About Dumah

¹¹This is a message about Dumah:ᵉ

There is someone calling to me from Seir,ᶠ
"Guard, how much of the night is left?
How much longer will it be night?"

¹²The guard answered,
"Morning is coming, but then night will
come again.
If you have something else to ask,
then come backᵍ later and ask."

God's Message About Arabia

¹³This is a message about Arabia:

A caravan from Dedan spent the night
near some trees in the Arabian Desert.
¹⁴They gave water to some thirsty travellers.
The people of Tema gave them food.
¹⁵They were running from swords
that were ready to kill.
They were running from bows
that were ready to shoot.
They were running from a hard battle.

¹⁶The Lord told me this would happen. He said,
"In one year, the way a hired helper counts time,
all Kedar's glory will be gone. ¹⁷Only a few of the
archers, the great soldiers of Kedar, will be left
alive." The Lord, the God of Israel, told me this.

God's Message About Jerusalem

22 This is a messageʰ about the Valley of
Vision:ⁱ

Jerusalem, what is wrong?
Why has everyone gone up to hide in their
upper rooms?
²This city was so happy,
but now there is a terrible uproar.
There are bodies lying everywhere,
but they were not killed with swords.

ᵃ **21:7** Or "Whether he sees a column of teams of horsemen, columns of donkeys or columns of camels, he must listen carefully."
ᵇ **21:8** *the watchman* Or "the seer", an ancient title for a prophet. The standard Hebrew text has "a lion".
ᶜ **21:8** *watchtower* A tall building where guards stood and watched to see if anyone was coming near their city.
ᵈ **21:9** *a man . . . horses* Or "a column of teams of horsemen". This might be a team of horses pulling a war chariot or mounted archers in the Assyrian army who often worked in pairs.
ᵉ **21:11** *Dumah* This Hebrew word means "silence". It may refer to Edom or to a city in Arabia.
ᶠ **21:11** *Seir* A mountain in Edom or a city in Arabia.
ᵍ **21:12** *come back* This can also mean "change your heart" or "repent".
ʰ **22:1** *message* Or "burden".
ⁱ **22:1** *Valley of Vision* This probably means one of the valleys near Jerusalem. Also in verse 5.

The people died,
    but not while fighting.
[3]All your officers ran away together,
    but they have all been captured without
        bows.[a]
All the leaders ran away together,
    but they were found and captured.

[4]So I say, "Don't look at me!
    Let me cry!
Don't rush to comfort me
    about the destruction of Jerusalem."

[5]The Lord GOD All-Powerful chose a special day for there to be riots and confusion. People trampled on each other in the Valley of Vision. The city walls were pulled down. People in the valley shouted up at those on the mountain. [6]Horsemen from Elam took their bags of arrows and rode into battle. Soldiers from Kir rattled their shields. [7]Your favourite valley was filled with chariots. Horsemen were stationed in front of the city gates. [8]Then the cover protecting Judah[b] was removed, and the people turned to the weapons they kept at the Forest Palace.[c]

[9–11]Then you noticed how many cracks there were in the walls around the City of David, so you began collecting water from the Lower Pool.[d] You counted the houses and used stones from them to repair the walls. Then you built a pool between the double walls[e] for storing water from the Old Pool.[f]

You did all this to protect yourselves, but you did not trust the God who made all these things. You did not even notice the one who made all these things so long ago. [12]So the Lord GOD All-Powerful told the people to cry and mourn for their dead friends. He told them to shave their heads and wear mourning clothes. [13]But look, everyone was happy. The people rejoiced, saying,

"Kill the cattle and sheep,
    and let's celebrate.
Let's eat meat and drink wine.
    Eat and drink, for tomorrow we die."

[14]The LORD All-Powerful said this to me and I heard it with my own ears: "You are guilty of doing wrong, and I promise that you will die before this guilt is forgiven." The Lord GOD All-Powerful said these things.

God's Message to Shebna

[15]The Lord GOD All-Powerful told me to go to Shebna, the palace manager, [16]and say this: "What are you doing here? None of your relatives are buried here, are they? Then what right do you have to prepare a tomb for yourself in this high place? Why are you cutting a tomb out of this rock?

[17-18]"What a big man you are! But the LORD will crush you. He will roll you into a small ball and throw you far away into the open arms of another country, and there you will die.

"You are very proud of your chariots. But in that faraway land, your new ruler will have better chariots. And your chariots will not look important in his palace. [19]I will force you out of your position here. Your new leader will take you away from your important job. [20]At that time I will call for my servant Eliakim son of Hilkiah. [21]I will take your robe and put it on him. I will give him your sceptre. I will give him the important job you have, and he will be like a father to the people of Jerusalem and Judah's family.[g]

[22]"I will put the key to David's house around his neck. If he opens a door, no one will be able to close it. If he closes a door, no one will be able to open it. [23]He will be like a favourite chair in his father's house. I will make him like a strong peg in a solid board. [24]All the honoured and important things of his father's house will hang on him. All the adults and little children will depend on him. They will be like little dishes and big water bottles hanging on him."

[25]The LORD All-Powerful said, "At that time the peg that is now in the solid board will get weak and break. It will fall to the ground, and everything hanging on it will be destroyed. Then everything I said in this message will happen. It will happen because I, the LORD, said it would."

God's Message About Tyre

23

This is a message[h] about Tyre:

Ships travelling from Cyprus heard this
        message:
    "Cry, you ships from Tarshish!
    Your harbour has been destroyed."

---

[a] **22:3 but they have . . . bows** Or "but the archers captured them".
[b] **22:8 cover protecting Judah** This might be the wall around Jerusalem, but see Isa. 4:5–6.
[c] **22:8 Forest Palace** A part of Solomon's palace where his weapons and wealth were stored.
[d] **22:9–11 Lower Pool** The pool at the southern tip of the City of David, just below the Upper Pool (the Pool of Siloam).
[e] **22:9–11 pool between the double walls** This is probably the Upper Pool (Pool of Siloam).
[f] **22:9–11 Old Pool** Probably the pool at Gihon Spring on the eastern slopes of the city.
[g] **22:21 people of Jerusalem and Judah's family** Or "The king sitting on the throne in Jerusalem, the royal family of Judah".
[h] **23:1 message** Or "burden".

INSIGHT

Tyre was famous for its ships – and rich because of its trade with colonies in the Mediterranean, including Cyprus and possibly parts of Spain (then known as Tarshish). But God is not impressed by beautiful landscapes or the wealth of a nation.

Isaiah 23:1

²You people living near the sea, mourn in silence.
The merchants of Sidon sent traders across the sea
and filled the city with riches.
³They travelled the seas looking for grain.
The men from Tyre bought grain that grows near the Nile River
and sold it to other nations.

⁴Sidon, you should be very sad,
because now the Sea and the Fortress of the Sea*a* say,
"I have no children.
I have never felt the pain of birth;
I have never given birth to children.
I have never raised young men and women."

⁵When Egypt hears the news about Tyre,
it will feel the pain of sorrow.
⁶You ships, try to escape to Tarshish!
Cry out, you people living near the sea!
⁷Can this be that happy city that was founded so long ago?
Is it that same city whose people travelled so far to settle in other lands?*b*
⁸Who made these plans against Tyre?
This city produced so many leaders.
Its merchants were like princes.
Its traders had the whole world's respect.
⁹It was the LORD All-Powerful.
He decided to destroy the great things they were so proud of.
He wanted to disgrace those who were so highly respected.
¹⁰Ships from Tarshish, go back home.
Cross the sea as if it were a river.
No one will stop you now.

¹¹The LORD raised his arm over the sea
to make the kingdoms angry enough to fight against Tyre.
He commanded Canaan
to destroy her place of safety.*c*
¹²He said, "City of Sidon,*d* you have been hurt badly,
so you will no longer rejoice like a bride.
Go ahead, go to Cyprus for help,
but you will not find a place to rest there either."
¹³As for Babylon, look at the land of the Chaldeans!
It is not even a country now.
Assyria built war towers to attack it.
The soldiers took everything from the beautiful houses.
Assyria destroyed Babylon.
They turned it into a pile of ruins
and made it a place for wild animals.
¹⁴So be sad, you ships from Tarshish.
Your place of safety has been destroyed.

¹⁵People will forget about Tyre for 70 years—that is, about the length of a king's rule. After 70 years, Tyre will be like the prostitute in this song:

¹⁶"Oh, woman who men forgot,
take your harp and walk through the city.
Play your song well and sing it often.
Maybe someone will remember you."

¹⁷After 70 years, the LORD will review Tyre's case, and he will give her a decision. Tyre will again have trade. She will be like a prostitute for all the nations on earth. ¹⁸But Tyre will not keep the money she earns. The profit from her trade will be saved for the LORD. Tyre will give that money to the people who serve the LORD to buy good food and nice clothes.

God Will Punish Israel

24 Look, the LORD is destroying this land.*e* He will clean out the land completely and force all the people to go far away. ²At that time whatever happens to the common people will also happen to the priests. Slaves and masters will be the same. Women slaves and their women masters will be the same. Buyers and sellers will be the same. Those who borrow and those who lend will be the same. Bankers and those who owe the bank will be the same. ³Everyone will be forced

---

a **23:4 Fortress of the Sea** Another name for the city of Tyre.
b **23:7 travelled . . . other lands?** Or "came from so far to live here?"
c **23:11** Or "He raised his arm over the sea and shook nations. He gave a command about Canaan to destroy its fortresses."
d **23:12 City of Sidon** Literally, "Daughter Sidon".
e **24:1 land** Or "earth".

out of the land. All the wealth will be taken. This will happen because the Lord commanded it. ⁴The country will be empty and sad. The world will be empty and weak. The great leaders of the people in this land will become weak.

⁵The people have ruined the land. They did what God said was wrong. They did not obey God's laws. They made an agreement with God a long time ago, but they broke their agreement with God. ⁶The people living in this land are guilty of doing wrong, so God promised to destroy the land. The people will be punished, and only a few of them will survive.

⁷The grapevines are dying. The new wine is bad. People who were happy are now sad. ⁸They have stopped showing their joy. The happy music from the drums and harps has ended. ⁹They no longer sing as they drink their wine. The beer now tastes bitter to those who drink it.

¹⁰"Total Confusion" is a good name for this city. The city has been destroyed. People cannot enter the houses. The doors are blocked. ¹¹People still ask for wine in the marketplaces, but all the joy is gone. It was carried off with everything else. ¹²All that is left is destruction. Even the gates are crushed.

¹³At harvest time, people knock olives from
 the trees.
 But a few olives are left in the trees.
 It will be like that in this land and among
 the nations.
¹⁴Those who are left will begin shouting louder
 than the ocean.
 They will rejoice about the Lord's greatness.
¹⁵They will say, "People in the east, praise the
 Lord!
 People in faraway lands,
 praise the name of the Lord, the God of
 Israel."
¹⁶We hear songs from every place on earth
 praising God, who does what is right.
 But I say, "Enough!
 I have had enough.
 What I see is terrible.
 Traitors are turning against people and
 hurting them."

¹⁷I see troubles for all you people on earth.
 I see death traps and pits waiting for
 everyone.
¹⁸People will hear about the danger,
 and they will be afraid.
 Some of them will run away,
 but they will fall into a pit and be trapped.
 And those who climb out of the pit
 will be caught in another trap.

The floodgates in the sky above will open,
 and the floods will begin.
 The foundations of the earth will shake.
¹⁹There will be earthquakes,
 and the earth will split open.
²⁰The sins of the world are very heavy,
 so the earth will fall under the weight.
 It will shake like an old house.
 It will fall like a drunk.
 It will not be able to stand.

²¹At that time the Lord will judge
 the heavenly armies in heaven
 and the earthly kings on earth.
²²Many people will be gathered together.
 They have been locked in the Pit.
 They have been in prison.ᵃ
 But finally, after a long time, they will be
 judged.
²³The Lord will rule as king on Mount Zion in
 Jerusalem.
 His glory will be shown to the city leaders
 with such brightness that
 the moon will be embarrassed
 and the sun will be ashamed.

A Song of Praise to God

25 Lord, you are my God.
 I honour you and praise your name,
 because you have done amazing things.
 The words you said long ago are completely
 true;
 everything happened exactly as you said it
 would.
²And you destroyed the city that was protected
 by strong walls.
 Now it is only a pile of rocks.
 The foreign palace has been destroyed.
 It will never be rebuilt.
³That is why powerful nations will honour
 you.
 Powerful people from strong cities will
 fear you.
⁴You have been a safe place for poor people in
 trouble.
 You are like a shelter from floods and shade
 from the heat
 when powerful men attack.
 They are like rain streaming down the walls
 that protect us from the storm.
⁵Like the heat of summer in a dry land,
 the angry shouts of those foreigners brought
 us to our knees.
 But like a thick cloud that blocks the summer
 heat,
 you answered their challenge.

ᵃ **24:22 Pit . . . prison** This is probably "Sheol", the grave.

God's Banquet for His Servants

⁶The LORD All-Powerful will give a feast for all the people on this mountain. At the feast, there will be the best foods and wines. The meat will be good and tender, the wine pure and clear. ⁷But now there is a veil covering all nations and people. This veil is called "death". ⁸But death will be destroyed forever.ᵃ And the Lord GOD will wipe away every tear from every face. In the past, all his people were sad, but God will take away that sadness from the earth. All of this will happen because the LORD said it would.

⁹At that time people will say,
    "Here is our God!
He is the one we have been waiting for.
    He has come to save us.
We have been waiting for our LORD.
    So we will rejoice and be happy when he
        saves us."
¹⁰The LORD's power is on this mountain,
    and Moabᵇ will be defeated.
The Lord will trample the enemy
    like someone walking on straw in a pile of
        waste.
¹¹They will reach out their arms to escape
    like someone trying to swim.
But their pride will sink
    with each stroke they take.
¹²He will destroy their high walls and safe
        places.
    He will throw them down into the dust on
        the ground.

A Song of Praise to God

26 At that time people will sing this song in Judah:

We have a strong city with strong walls and
        defences.
    But God gives us our salvation.ᶜ
²Open the gates for those who do what is right.
    They are the God's faithful followers.

³God, you give true peace
    to people who depend on you,
    to those who trust in you.

⁴So trust the LORD always,
    because in the LORD GODᵈ you have a place
        of safety forever.

⁵But he will destroy the proud city
    and punish those who live there.
He will throw that high city down to the
        ground.
    It will fall into the dust.
⁶And those who were hurt by that city will
    walk all over its ruins.
Those who lost everything will trample it
    under their feet.

⁷Honesty is the path good people follow.
    They follow the path that is straight and
        true.
And God, you make that way smooth
    and easy to follow.
⁸But, LORD, we are waiting for your way of
        justice.
    We want to honour you and your name.
⁹At night my soul longs to be with you,
    and the spirit in me wants to be with you at
        the dawn of every new day.
When your way of justice comes to the
        world,
    people will learn the right way of living.
¹⁰Evil people will not learn to do good,
    even if you show them only kindness.
They will still do wrong, even if they live in a
        good world.
    They never see the LORD's greatness.
¹¹LORD, your arm is raised to punish them,
    but they don't see it.
Show them how strong your loveᵉ is for your
        people.
    Then those who are evil will be
        ashamed.
Yes, your fire will destroy your enemies.
¹²LORD, you are the one who will bring us
        peace.
    All our success has come from you.

God Will Give New Life to His People

¹³LORD, you are our God,
    but in the past, we followed other lords.
We belonged to other masters,ᶠ
    but now we want people to remember only
        one name—yours.
¹⁴Those dead lords will not come to life.
    Those ghosts will not rise from death.
You decided to destroy them,
    and you destroyed everything that makes us
        think about them.

ᵃ 25:8 **But death . . . forever** Some Greek versions have "But death will be swallowed in victory."
ᵇ 25:10 **Moab** Or "the enemy". This name is like a Hebrew word meaning "enemy".
ᶜ 26:1 Or "We have a strong city that provides us with salvation. It has strong walls and defences."
ᵈ 26:4 **the LORD GOD** Literally, "YAH YAWEH", two forms of a Hebrew name for God. See YAHWEH in the Word List.
ᵉ 26:11 **strong . . . love** The Hebrew word means strong feelings like love, hate, anger, zeal or jealousy.
ᶠ 26:13 **we followed . . . masters** This is a wordplay. It could also be translated, "Husbands other than you married us." One word sounds like "Baal", the other like a title for God.

¹⁵LORD, you have helped the nation you love.
  You made our nation grow
  and brought honour to yourself.^a
¹⁶LORD, people remember you
  when they are in trouble.
 So because of your punishment,
  we called out to you.
¹⁷LORD, because of you we were in pain,
  like a woman giving birth,
  who struggles and cries out when it is
  time.
¹⁸But we struggled in pain for nothing.
 We gave birth only to wind.
 We did nothing to save the land.
  No one was born to live in the world.
¹⁹⌊But the Lord says,⌋
 "Your people have died,
  but they will live again.
 The bodies of my people
  will rise from death.
 Dead people in the ground,
  stand and be happy!
 The dew covering you is like
  the dew sparkling in the light of a new day.
 It shows that a new time is coming,
  when the earth will give birth to the dead
  who are in it."

Judgement: Reward or Punishment

²⁰My people, go into your rooms
  and lock your doors.
 Hide in there for a short time
  until God's anger is finished.
²¹Look! The LORD is coming out from his place^b
  to judge the people of the world for the bad
  things they have done.
 The earth will reveal the blood that has been
  spilled on it.
 It will no longer hide the proof of those
  murders.

27 At that time the LORD will judge
  Leviathan,^c
  that fast-moving giant snake.
 With his great sword, his sharp and powerful
  sword,
  he will punish Leviathan, that twisting,
  giant snake.
 He will kill the monster of the sea.

²At that time people will sing
  about the pleasant vineyard.
³"I, the LORD, will care for the vineyard.
  I will water it at the right time.
 I will guard it day and night.
  No one will hurt it.
⁴I am not angry.
 But if there is war and someone builds a wall
  of thornbushes,^d
  then I will march to it and burn it.
⁵But if anyone comes to me for safety
  and wants to make peace with me,
  then let them come and make peace.
⁶In the future Jacob will take root firmly on
  his soil.
 Then Israel will sprout and bloom,
  and the world will be filled with his fruit."

God Will Send Israel Away

⁷Israel was not hurt as badly as the enemy who tried to hurt it. Not as many of its people were killed as those who tried to kill them.

⁸The Lord will settle his argument with Israel by sending the people far away. He will speak harshly to Israel. His words will burn like the hot desert wind.

⁹How will Jacob's guilt be forgiven? What will happen so his sins can be taken away? The rocks of the altar will be crushed to dust; the statues^e and altars for worshipping false gods will all be destroyed.

¹⁰The great city will be empty; it will be like a desert. All the people will be gone—they will run away. The city will be like an open pasture. Young cattle will eat grass there. The cattle will eat leaves from the branches of the vines. ¹¹The vines will become dry, and the branches will break off. Women will use them for firewood.

 The people refuse to understand. So God, their Maker, will not comfort them or be kind to them.

¹²At that time the LORD will begin separating his people from others. He will begin at the Euphrates River and will gather his people from there^f to the river of Egypt.^g

 You people of Israel will be gathered together one by one. ¹³Many of my people are now lost in Assyria. Some of my people have run away to Egypt. But at that time a great trumpet will be blown, and all those people will come back to

---

^a **26:15** Or "You gathered together the nation you love, the nation you drove into faraway lands."
^b **26:21** *his place* Probably the Temple in Jerusalem.
^c **27:1** *Leviathan* A dragon, giant snake or sea monster. Some ancient stories say the Dragon was an enemy of God.
^d **27:4** *a wall of thornbushes* Literally, "thorns and thistles". Farmers planted walls of thornbushes around vineyards to protect them from animals. See Isa. 5:5.
^e **27:9** *statues* Or "idols". See "IDOL" in the Word List.
^f **27:12** *He will begin . . . from there* Literally, "He will begin threshing at the stream of the river." This Hebrew word for stream is like the word meaning "head of grain".
^g **27:12** *Euphrates River . . . river of Egypt* These are the borders of the land God promised to give Israel.

Jerusalem. They will bow down before the Lord on that holy mountain.

Warnings to Northern Israel

28 Look at Samaria!
The drunks of Ephraim are proud of that city.
It sits on a hill with a rich valley around it.
    They think their city is a beautiful crown of flowers.
But they are drunk with wine,
    and this "beautiful crown" is just a dying plant.

²Look, the Lord has someone who is strong and brave.
    He will come into the country like a storm of hail and rain.
Like a powerful river of water flooding the country,
    he will throw that crownᵃ down to the ground.
³The drunks of Ephraim are proud of their beautiful crown,
    but that city will be trampled down.
⁴That city sits on a hill with a rich valley around it.
    But that beautiful crown of flowers is just a dying plant.
It will be like the first figs of summer.
    As soon as someone sees a ripe one, they pick it and eat it.

⁵At that time the Lord All-Powerful will become the "Beautiful Crown". He will be the "Wonderful Crown of Flowers" for his people who are left. ⁶Then he will give wisdom to the judges who rule his people. He will give strength to the people who are in battles at the city gates. ⁷But now those leaders are drunk. The priests and prophets are all drunk with wine and beer. They stumble and fall down. The prophets are drunk when they see their dreams. The judges are drunk when they make their decisions. ⁸Every table is covered with vomit. There is not a clean place anywhere.

God Wants to Help His People

⁹⌊The people say,⌋ "Who does he think he is trying to teach and explain his message to? Does he think we are babies who were at their mother's breast only a very short time ago? ¹⁰⌊He speaks to us as though we were babies:⌋

    "Saw lasaw saw lasaw
    Qaw laqaw qaw laqaw
    Ze'er sham ze'er sham."ᵇ

¹¹So God will use this strange way of talking, and he will use other languages to speak to these people. ¹²In the past he spoke to them and said, "Here is a resting place. Let those who are tired come and rest. This is the place of peace."

But they would not listen to him. ¹³So the Lord's words will be senseless soundsᶜ to them:

    "Saw lasaw saw lasaw.
    Qaw laqaw qaw laqaw.
    Ze'er sham ze'er sham."

When the people try to walk, they will fall backwards. They will be defeated, trapped and captured.

No One Escapes God's Judgement

¹⁴You leaders in Jerusalem should listen to the Lord's message, but now you refuse to listen to him. ¹⁵You have said, "We have made an agreement with death. We have a contract with death. So we will not be punished. Punishment will pass us without hurting us. We will hide behind our tricks and lies."

¹⁶Because of these things, the Lord God says, "Look, I am putting a foundation stone on the ground in Zion, a stone that has been tested. It is a cornerstone of great value that will make a strong foundation to build on. Anyone who trusts in that rock will never be put to shame.ᵈ

¹⁷"If what you build on that foundation is not right, I will know it. I will use justice and goodness like a measuring lineᵉ to test it." You cannot hide behind a wall built on lies. It will be destroyed by hailstorms and washed away by floods. ¹⁸Your agreement with death will be erased. Your contract with Sheol will not help you.

"Disaster will come to you, and it will beat you down to the ground. ¹⁹It will come against you day after day. Your punishment will be terrible. It will come early in the morning, and it will continue day and night.

ᵃ **28:2 that crown** That is, Samaria.
ᵇ **28:10 Saw lasaw . . . ze'er sham** This is probably a Hebrew song to teach little children how to write. It sounds like baby talk or a foreign language, but it can also be translated, "A command here, a command there. A rule here, a rule there. A lesson here, a lesson there." Also in verse 13.
ᶜ **28:13 senseless sounds** Or "gibberish" or "baby talk".
ᵈ **28:16 Anyone . . . shame** This is from the ancient Greek version. The standard Hebrew text has, "Whoever trusts will not panic."
ᵉ **28:17 measuring line** A string made straight by a weight hanging on it.

"Then you will understand what the LORD is telling you. You will be filled with fear, as helpless [20]as a man trying to sleep on a bed that is too short, with a blanket that is too small."

[21]The LORD will fight as he did at Mount Perazim. He will be angry as he was in Gibeon Valley.[a] He will do what he must do. It will be what some stranger should do, but he will finish his work. Yes, this is a stranger's job. [22]Now don't complain about these things. If you fight against them, you will only tighten the ropes around you.

The words I heard will not change. They came from the Lord GOD All-Powerful, the ruler of all the earth, and these things will be done.

The LORD Punishes Fairly

[23]Listen closely to the message I am telling you. [24]Does a farmer plough his field all the time? No, he doesn't work the soil all the time. [25]He prepares the ground, and then he plants the seed. He plants different kinds of seeds in different ways. He scatters dill seeds, he throws cumin seeds on the ground and he plants wheat in rows. A farmer plants barley in its special place, and he plants spelt seeds at the edge of his field. [26]Our God is using this to teach you a lesson. This example shows us that God is fair when he punishes his people. [27]Does a farmer use large boards with sharp teeth to crush dill seeds? No, and he doesn't use a cart to crush cumin seeds. A farmer uses a small stick to break the husks from these seeds of grain. [28]People grind grain to make flour, but they don't grind it forever. As God does in punishing people, a worker might drive his cart over the grain to remove the husks, but he does not allow the horses[b] to crush it. [29]This lesson comes from the LORD All-Powerful, who gives wonderful advice. He is very wise.

God Punishes Jerusalem

29 God says, "Look at Ariel,[c] the city where David settled. You continue to have your festivals, year after year. [2]But I will punish you, Jerusalem. The city will be filled with sadness and crying. I will use it like an altar. [3]"I will put armies all around you, and I will raise war towers against you. [4]You will find yourself speaking from the ground. Your voice will come from deep in the earth like the voice of a ghost from under the ground, rising like a whisper from the dust.

[5]"But then your enemies will be blown away like dust. Those cruel men will be like chaff blowing in the wind. It will happen suddenly, in the blink of an eye. [6]I, the LORD All-Powerful, will come to your rescue with earthquakes, thunder and loud noises, with storms, winds and fire that destroys. [7]And all those nations fighting against Jerusalem will fade away like a nightmare. The armies that surround and attack the city will vanish like a dream at the end of the night. [8]Those armies will be disappointed, like a hungry man dreaming about food. When he wakes up, he is still hungry. They will be like a thirsty man dreaming about water. When he wakes up, he is still thirsty. So also for those nations fighting against Zion. The victory they want is only a dream."

[9]People of Jerusalem, you will be surprised
      and amazed!
   You are completely blind to the truth.
   So now you act like drunk, but not from wine.
   Now you stumble, but not from beer.
[10]The LORD has put you to sleep.
   He has closed your eyes to the truth.
   And he has blindfolded your prophets and
      leaders.

[11]To you my words are like the words in a book that is closed and sealed.[d] You can give the book to someone who can read and tell that person to read it. But that person will say, "I cannot read the book. It is closed and I cannot open it." [12]Or you can give the book to someone who cannot read and tell that person to read it. That person will say, "I cannot read the book because I don't know how to read."

[13]The Lord says, "These people come to honour me with words, but I am not really important to them. The worship they give me is nothing but human rules they have memorized. [14]So I will continue to amaze them by doing powerful and amazing things. Their wise men will lose their wisdom. Even the most intelligent among them will not be able to understand."

[15]Look at them! They try to hide things from the LORD. They think he will not understand. They do their evil things in darkness. They tell themselves: "No one can see us. No one will know who we are."

[16]You turn things upside down. You think the clay is equal to the potter. You think that something that is made can tell the one who made it, "You did not make me!" This is like a pot telling its maker, "You know nothing."

---

[a] **28:21 *Mount Perazim . . . Gibeon Valley*** See 1 Chr. 14:8–17.
[b] **28:28 *horses*** This word also means "horsemen".
[c] **29:1 *Ariel*** A name used here for Jerusalem. It may mean "altar hearth" or "Lion of God". Also in verses 2 and 7, translated "Jerusalem".
[d] **29:11 *sealed*** A piece of clay or wax was put on the closed book to show that the book should not be opened.

A Better Time Is Coming

¹⁷This is the truth: after a very short time, Lebanon will become rich farmland, and the farmland will be like thick forests. ¹⁸The deaf will hear the words in the book. The blind will see through the darkness and fog. ¹⁹The LORD will make poor people happy. The poorest people will rejoice in the Holy One of Israel.

²⁰This will happen when the people who are mean and cruel have come to an end. It will happen when those who enjoy doing bad things are gone. ²¹(They lie about good people. They try to trap people in court. They try to destroy innocent people.)

²²So the LORD, who made Abraham free, speaks to Jacob's people. He says, "Now the people of Jacob will not feel ashamed. Their faces will no longer look embarrassed. ²³Yes, when they see all their children, the children I myself have made for them, they will honour my name as holy. They will honourᵃ the Holy One of Jacob. They will respect the God of Israel. ²⁴Many of these people did not understand, so they did what was wrong. They complained, but now they will learn their lesson."

Israel Should Trust in God, Not Egypt

30 The LORD said, "Look at these children. They don't obey me. They make plans, but they don't ask me to help them. They make agreements with other nations, but my Spirit does not want those agreements. These people are adding more and more sins to the ones they have already done. ²They are going down to Egypt for help, but they did not ask me if that was the right thing to do. They hope they will be saved by the Pharaoh. They want Egypt to protect them.

³"But I tell you, hiding in Egypt will not help you. Pharaoh will not be able to protect you. ⁴Your leaders have gone to Zoan, and your representatives have gone to Hanes.ᵇ ⁵But they will be disappointed. They are depending on a nation that cannot help them. Egypt is useless—it will not help. Egypt will bring nothing but shame and embarrassment."

God's Message to Judah

⁶This is a messageᶜ about the Negev animals:ᵈ

There is a dangerous place full of lions, adders,ᵉ deadly snakesᶠ and useless people. And there are people who load their wealth onto donkeys and their treasures on the backs of camels. They carry them to a people who cannot help. ⁷That useless nation is Egypt. Egypt's help is worth nothing, so I call Egypt the "Do-Nothing Dragon".ᵍ

⁸Now write this on a sign so that all people can see it, and write this in a book. Write these things for a future time. This will be far, far in the future:ʰ

⁹These people are like children who refuse to obey. They lie and refuse to listen to the LORD's teachings. ¹⁰They tell the prophets, "Don't see dreamsⁱ about things we should do. Don't tell us the truth. Say nice things to us and make us feel good. See only good things for us. ¹¹Stop seeing things that will really happen. Get out of our way. Stop telling us about the Holy One of Israel."

Judah's Help Comes Only From God

¹²The Holy One of Israel says, "You people have refused to accept my message. You depend on fighting and lies to help you. ¹³You are guilty of these things. So you are like a tall wall with cracks in it. That wall will fall and break into small pieces. ¹⁴You will be like a large clay jar that breaks into many small, useless pieces. You cannot use them to get a hot coal from the fire or to get water from a pool in the ground."

¹⁵The Lord GOD, the Holy One of Israel, says, "If you come back to me you will be saved. Only by remaining calm and trusting in me can you be strong."

But you don't want to do that. ¹⁶You say, "No, we need fast horses for battle." That is true—you will need fast horses, but only to run away because your enemy will be faster than your horses. ¹⁷One enemy soldier will make threats, and a thousand of your men will run away. And when five of them make threats, all of you will run away. The only thing that will be left of your army will be a flagpole on a hill.

God Will Help His People

¹⁸So the LORD is waiting to show his mercy to you. He wants to rise and comfort you. The LORD is the God who does the right thing, so he will bless everyone who waits for his help.

ᵃ **29:23 honour** Or "treat as holy".

ᵇ **30:4 Zoan, Hanes** Cities in Egypt.

ᶜ **30:6 message** Or "burden".

ᵈ **30:6 Negev animals** Or "Creatures of the South", a phrase that can refer to Egypt.

ᵉ **30:6 adders** Very poisonous snakes.

ᶠ **30:6 deadly snakes** Literally, "flying snakes".

ᵍ **30:7 Do-Nothing Dragon** Or "Resting Rahab", the great sea monster. Some ancient stories tell about Rahab fighting with God.

ʰ **30:8 Write . . . future** Or "Write this for the future as a witness forever."

ⁱ **30:10 dreams** Or "visions". Special kinds of dreams God used to speak to his prophets.

¹⁹You people who live in Jerusalem on Mount Zion will not continue crying. The Lord will hear your crying, and he will comfort you. When he hears you, he will help you.

²⁰The Lord might give you sorrow and pain like the bread and water you eat every day. But God is your teacher, and he will not continue to hide from you. You will see your teacher with your own eyes. ²¹If you wander from the right path, either to the right or to the left, you will hear a voice behind you saying, "You should go this way. Here is the right way."

²²Then you will take your idols covered with gold and silver and make them unfit to be used again. You will throw them away like filthy rags*ᵃ* and say, "Go away!"

²³At that time the Lord will send you rain. You will plant seeds, and the ground will grow food for you. You will have a very large harvest. You will have plenty of food in the fields for your animals. There will be large fields for your sheep. ²⁴Even the oxen and donkeys you use to plough your fields will eat the very best food,*ᵇ* not just straw. ²⁵Every mountain and hill will have streams filled with water. These things will happen after many people are killed and the enemy's towers are pulled down.

²⁶At that time the light from the moon will be as bright as the sun, and the light from the sun will be seven times brighter than it is now. One day of sunlight will be like a whole week's worth. This will happen when the LORD bandages his broken people and heals the hurts from their beatings.

²⁷Look! The LORD is coming from far away. His anger is like a fire with thick clouds of smoke. His mouth is filled with anger, and his tongue is like a burning fire. ²⁸His breath is like a great river that rises until it reaches the throat. He will judge the nations as if putting them through a strainer that separates the ones fit for destruction. He will put a bit in their mouths to lead them to the place they don't want to go.

²⁹You will sing happy songs, like the nights when you begin a festival. You will be very happy walking to the LORD's mountain and listening to the flute on the way to worship the Rock of Israel.

³⁰The LORD will cause all people to hear his great voice and to see his powerful arm come down in anger. That arm will be like a great fire that burns everything. His power will be like a great storm with much rain and hail. ³¹Assyria

will be frightened by the LORD's voice and the stick that will beat him. ³²And as the LORD beats Assyria, his people will keep the rhythm with their drums and harps.

³³Topheth*ᶜ* has been made ready for a long time. It is ready for the king.*ᵈ* It was made very deep and wide. There is a very big pile of wood and fire there, and the LORD's breath will come like a stream of burning sulphur to start the fire.

Israel Should Depend on God's Power

31 Look at the people going down to Egypt for help. They think the horses they get will save them. They hope the many chariots and powerful soldiers will protect them. But the people don't trust the Holy One of Israel. They didn't ask the LORD for help. ²But he is the wise one who is bringing the disaster. And they will not be able to stop what he commanded. The Lord will attack those who are evil and all who try to help them.

³The Egyptians are only human, not God. The horses from Egypt are only animals, not spirit. The LORD will stretch out his arm, and the helper will be defeated. And those who wanted help will fall. They will all be destroyed together.

⁴The LORD told me: "When a lion or its cub catches an animal to eat, the lion stands over the dead animal and roars, and nothing can frighten it away. If men come and yell at the lion, the lion will not be afraid. They might make a lot of noise, but the lion will not run away."

In the same way, the LORD All-Powerful will come down to Mount Zion. He will fight on that hill. ⁵Just as birds fly over their nest to protect it, so the LORD All-Powerful will defend*ᵉ* Jerusalem. He will save her. He will "pass over" and save Jerusalem.

⁶People of Israel, you should come back to the God you turned away from. ⁷That is because when those things happen, people will reject the gold and silver idols you made when you sinned against me.

⁸It is true that Assyria will be defeated with a sword, but it will not be a human sword that defeats him. Assyria will be destroyed, but that destruction will not come from a man's sword. Assyria will run away from God's sword, but the young men will be caught and made slaves. ⁹Their place of safety will be destroyed. Their leaders will be defeated, and they will abandon their flag.

ᵃ **30:22 You . . . rags** Or "You will throw those gods away like menstrual cloths."
ᵇ **30:24 best food** This may mean grain that has been separated from the husks, or it may mean fodder—a mixture of grain, straw and leaves that has been allowed to ferment.
ᶜ **30:33 Topheth** Gehenna, the Valley of Hinnom. In this valley people killed their children to honour the false god, "Molech".
ᵈ **30:33 king** This is like the name of the false god, "Molech".
ᵉ **31:5 defend** Literally, "fight on" or "fight against".

The LORD, whose fireplace is on Zion and whose oven[a] is in Jerusalem, is the one who said this.

Leaders Should Be Good and Fair

32 Listen to what I say! A king should rule in a way that brings justice. Leaders should make fair decisions when they lead the people. [2]If this would happen, the king[b] would be like a shelter to hide from the wind and rain, like streams of water in a dry land and like the cool shadow of a large rock in a hot land. [3]Then people would actually see what they look at. They would actually listen to what they hear. [4]People who are now confused would be able to understand. Those who cannot speak clearly now would be able to speak clearly and quickly. [5]Fools[c] would not be called great men. People would not respect men who make secret plans.

[6]Fools say foolish things, and in their minds they plan evil things to do. They want to do what is wrong. They say bad things about the LORD. They don't let hungry people eat their food. They don't let thirsty people drink the water. [7]They use evil like a tool and plan ways to steal from the poor. They tell lies about the poor and keep them from being judged fairly.

[8]But a good leader plans good things to do, and that will make him a leader over other leaders.

Hard Times Are Coming

[9]Some of you women are calm now; you feel safe. But you should stand and listen to the words I say. [10]You feel safe now, but after one year you will be troubled. That is because you will not gather grapes next year—there will be no grapes to gather. [11]Women, you are calm now, but you should be afraid. You feel safe now, but you should be worried. Take off your nice clothes and put on sackcloth. Wrap it around your waist. [12]Beat your breasts in sorrow. Cry because your fields are empty. Your vineyards once gave grapes, but now they are empty. [13]Cry for the land of my people. Cry because only thorns and weeds will grow there. Cry for the city and for all the houses that were once filled with joy.

[14]People will leave the capital city. The palace and towers will be left empty. People will not live in houses—they will live in caves. Wild donkeys and sheep will live in the city—animals will go there to eat grass.

[15]This will continue until God gives us his Spirit from above. Then the desert will become rich farmland and the farmland will be like thick forests. [16]That is, what is now a desert will be filled with right decisions, and what is now farmland will be filled with justice. [17]That justice will bring peace and safety forever. [18]My people will be safe in their homes and in their calm, peaceful fields.

[19]But before this happens, the forest must fall and the city must be torn down. [20]Some of you live away from the cities. You plant seeds by every stream and let your cattle and donkeys roam free. You will be very blessed.

The LORD Will Show His Power

33 Look at you. You attack others when you have not been attacked. You turn against others when no one has turned against you. So when you stop your attacks, you will be attacked. When you stop turning against others, they will turn against you.

[2]LORD, be kind to us.
  We have waited for your help.
  Give us strength every morning.
    Save us when we are in trouble.
[3]Your powerful voice makes people run away in fear.
  Your greatness causes the nations to run away.

[4]You people stole things in war. Those things will be taken from you. Many will come and take your wealth. It will be like the times when locusts come and eat all your crops.

[5]The LORD is very great. He lives in a very high place. He fills Zion with justice and goodness.

[6]Jerusalem, you are rich with wisdom and knowledge of God. You are rich with salvation. You respect the LORD, and that makes you rich.

[7]But listen! The messengers are crying outside. The messengers[d] who bring peace are crying very hard. [8]The roads are empty; there is no one walking along the paths. People don't respect each other. They have broken the agreements they made, and they refuse to believe what witnesses[e] tell them. [9]The land is sick and dying. Lebanon is dying and Sharon Valley is dry and empty. Bashan and Carmel once grew beautiful plants, but now those plants have stopped growing.

[10]The LORD says, "Now, I will stand and show people how great and powerful I am. [11]You people have done useless things. These things are like

---

[a] **31:9 fireplace . . . oven** That is, the altar in the Temple.
[b] **32:2 king** Literally, "man".
[c] **32:5 Fools** Here, this means people who don't follow God and his wise teachings.
[d] **33:7 messengers . . . messengers** The Hebrew text has two different words that can also mean "angels".
[e] **33:8 witnesses** Literally, "cities".

hay and straw. They are worth nothing! Your breath will be like a fire and burn you. ¹²People will be burned until their bones become lime.ª They will burn quickly like thorns and dry bushes.

¹³"You people in faraway lands, listen to what I have done. You people who are near me, learn about my power."

¹⁴The sinners in Zion are afraid. Those who do wrong shake with fear. They say, "Can any of us live through this fire that destroys? Who can live near this fire that burns forever?"ᵇ

¹⁵Good, honest people who refuse to hurt others for money ⌊will live through that fire⌋. They refuse to take bribes or listen to plans to murder other people. They refuse to look at plans for doing bad things. ¹⁶They will live safely in high places. They will be protected in high rock fortresses. They will always have food and water.

¹⁷Your eyes will see the King in his beauty. You will see the great land. ¹⁸⁻¹⁹When you think about the troubles you had in the past, you will wonder, "Where are those foreigners who spoke languages we could not understand. Where are the officials and tax collectors from other lands? Where are the spies who counted our defence towers?"

God Will Protect Jerusalem

²⁰Look at Zion, the city of our religious festivals. Look at Jerusalem—that beautiful place of rest. Jerusalem is like a tent that will never be moved. The pegs that hold her in place will never be pulled up. Her ropes will never be broken, ²¹⁻²³because the Lᴏʀᴅ is our powerful leader there. That land is a place with streams and wide rivers, but there will be no enemy boats or powerful ships on those rivers. You men who work on such boats can stop your work with the ropes. You cannot make the mast strong enough. You will not be able to open your sails, because the Lᴏʀᴅ is our judge. He makes our laws. He is our king. He saves us. The Lᴏʀᴅ will give us our wealth. Even lame people will get their share. ²⁴No one living there will say, "I am sick," because everyone living there has had their guilt removed.

God Will Punish His Enemies

34 All you nations, come near and listen! Listen, all you people. The earth and everyone on it should listen to these things. Everything in this world should hear this. ²The

Lᴏʀᴅ is angry with all the nations and their armies. He will destroy them all and put them to death. ³Their bodies will be thrown outside. The stink will rise from the bodies, and the blood will flow down the mountains. ⁴Every star in the sky will disappear, and the skies will be rolled shut like a scroll.ᶜ ⁵The Lord says, "When my sword is finished with everything in the sky, it will come down on Edom. I have judged them guilty, and they must die."

⁶The Lᴏʀᴅ decided on a time for sacrifice in Bozrah, and a time for killing in all of Edom. So the sword of the Lᴏʀᴅ is covered with blood and fat—blood from the "goats" and fat from the kidneys of the "rams".ᵈ ⁷So the rams, the cattle and even the strong bulls will be killed. The land will be wet with their blood. The soil will be soaked with their fat.

⁸Yes, the Lᴏʀᴅ has chosen a time for punishment. He has chosen a year when people must pay for the wrong they did to Zion. ⁹Edom's rivers will be like hot tar. Edom's ground will be like burning sulphur. ¹⁰The fires will burn day and night, and the smoke will rise forever. Year after year Edom will lie empty. No one will ever travel through that land again. ¹¹Birds and small animals will own the land. It will be a home for owls and ravens. God will look carefully at Edom and decide to make it empty and useless.ᵉ ¹²People will call Edom the Kingdom of Nothing. The leaders there will have nothing left to rule.

¹³Thorns and wild bushes will cover the palaces and walls that protected the cities. It will be a place where jackals roam, a place for owls to live. ¹⁴Wildcats and wild dogs will gather there. Wild goatsᶠ will call out to each other. Night creaturesᵍ will spend some time there and find a place to rest. ¹⁵Snakes will make their homes there and lay their eggs. The eggs will open, and small snakes will crawl from the dark places. Birds that eat dead things will gather there like women visiting their friends.

¹⁶Look in the Lᴏʀᴅ's scroll and read what it says: Not one of these will be missing. Not one will be without its mate. God said he would make this happen, so his Spirit will bring them together. ¹⁷God decided what he should do with them, and then he chose a place for them. He drew a line and showed them their land. So the animals will own that land forever. They will live there year after year.

ª **33:12** *lime* A white powder that is often used to make mortar or cement. It can be made by burning bones, shells or limestone.
ᵇ **33:14** *fire that . . . burns forever* This might mean God, the Fire (Light) of Israel.
ᶜ **34:4** *rolled shut like a scroll* This is like someone closing a book when they have finished reading it. Everything in the sky will wither and fall like dead leaves from the tree, like figs dried up on the tree.
ᵈ **34:6** *goats . . . rams* This probably refers to the people and leaders of Edom.
ᵉ **34:11** *God . . . useless* Literally, "He will stretch over it the measuring string of 'emptiness' and the plumb line of 'uselessness'." These two words described the empty earth in Gen. 1:2.
ᶠ **34:14** *Wild goats* The Hebrew word means "hairy", "goat" or "goat-demon".
ᵍ **34:14** *Night creatures* Or "Lilith, the night demon".

God Will Comfort His People

35 The dry desert will rejoice. The desert will be glad and blossom. ²It will be covered with flowers and dance with joy. It will be as beautiful as the forest of Lebanon, the hill of Carmel and the Sharon Valley. This will happen because all people will see the Glory of the LORD. They will see the beauty of our God.

³Make the weak arms strong again. Strengthen the weak knees. ⁴People are afraid and confused. Say to them, "Be strong! Don't be afraid!" Look, your God will come and punish your enemies. He will come and give you your reward. He will save you. ⁵Then the eyes of the blind will be opened so that they can see, and the ears of the deaf will be opened so that they can hear. ⁶Those who are lame will dance like deer, and those who cannot speak now will use their voices to sing happy songs. This will happen when springs of water begin to flow in the dry desert. ⁷Now people see mirages[a] that look like water, but then there will be real pools of water. There will be wells in the dry land where water flows from the ground. Tall water plants will grow where wild animals once ruled.

⁸There will be a great road there, a highway called "The Holy Road". Evil people will not be allowed to walk on that road. It will be only for those who follow the right way, never for those who live foolishly. ⁹There will be no dangers on that road—no lions or other animals that attack people. The only people to travel that road will be the people God saves.

¹⁰The LORD will make his people free, and they will come back to him. They will come into Zion rejoicing. They will be happy forever. Their happiness will be like a crown on their heads. Gladness and joy will fill them completely. Sorrow and sadness will be far, far away.

The Assyrians Invade Judah

36 During Hezekiah's fourteenth year as king, Sennacherib king of Assyria went to fight against all the strong cities of Judah. Sennacherib defeated those cities. ²He sent his commander with a large army to King Hezekiah in Jerusalem. The commander and his army left Lachish and went to Jerusalem. They stopped near the aqueduct[b] by the Upper Pool,[c] on the street that leads up to Laundryman's Field.

³Three men from Jerusalem went out to talk with the commander. These men were Eliakim son of Hilkiah, Joah son of Asaph and Shebna.

Eliakim was the palace manager, Joah was the record keeper and Shebna was the royal secretary.

⁴The commander told them, "Tell Hezekiah this is what the great king, the king of Assyria says:

"'What are you trusting in to help you? ⁵I tell you, if you are trusting in power and great battle plans, that is useless. Those are nothing but empty words. Now I ask you, who do you trust so much that you are willing to rebel against me? ⁶Are you depending on Egypt to help you? Egypt is like a broken walking stick. If you lean on it for support, it will only stab you and hurt you. Pharaoh, the king of Egypt, cannot be trusted by anyone who depends on him for help.

⁷"'So maybe you will say, "We trust the LORD our God to help us." But Hezekiah destroyed the altars and high places where people worshipped your God. Hezekiah told the people of Judah and Jerusalem, "You must worship only at this one altar here in Jerusalem."

⁸"'If you still want to fight, my master, the king of Assyria, will make this agreement with you. I promise that I will give you 2,000 horses if you can find enough men to ride them into battle. ⁹But even then, you couldn't beat even one of my master's lowest ranking officers. So why do you still depend on Egypt's chariots and horsemen?

¹⁰"'Now, do you think I came to this country to destroy it without the LORD's help. No, it was the LORD who said to me, "Go up against this country and destroy it!"'"

¹¹Then Eliakim, Shebna and Joah said to the commander, "Please, speak to us in Aramaic, not Hebrew.[d] We will understand you, but we don't want the people there on the wall to understand what you say."

¹²But the commander said, "My master sent me to speak to everyone, not just you and your king. I must also speak to those people sitting there on the wall. When we surround your city, they will suffer too. Like you, they will become so hungry they will eat their own waste and drink their own urine!"

¹³Then the commander, shouting loudly in Hebrew, gave this warning to them all:

---

[a] **35:7 mirages** In the desert, heat rising from the ground looks like water from far away. This is a mirage.

[b] **36:2 aqueduct** A ditch or pipe that carries water from one place to another. Here, this is the Shiloah, a channel that carried water from Gihon Spring to the Old Pool and the Pool of Siloam.

[c] **36:2 Upper Pool** The Pool of Siloam at the southern tip of the City of David (Jerusalem), just above the older pool.

[d] **36:11 Hebrew** Literally, "Judean", the language of Judah and Israel.

"Hear this message from the great king, the king of Assyria! [14]This is what the king says: 'Don't let Hezekiah fool you! He cannot save you from my power. [15]Don't listen to him when he tells you to trust in the LORD. Don't believe him when he says, "The LORD will save us. He will not let the king of Assyria defeat the city."

[16]"'Don't listen to Hezekiah! This is what the king of Assyria says: Come out here and show me that you want peace. Then you will all be free to have grapes from your own vines, figs from your own trees and water from your own well. [17]After some time, I will come and take you to a land like your own. In that new land, you will have plenty of grain for making bread and vineyards for producing wine.

[18]"'Don't believe Hezekiah when he tells you, "The LORD will save us." He is wrong. Did any of the gods of other nations save their land from the king of Assyria? [19]When I destroyed the cities of Hamath and Arpad, where were their gods? What about the gods of Sepharvaim? Were any gods able to save Samaria from my power? [20]None of the gods of these other places were able to save their land from me! So why do you think the LORD can save Jerusalem from me?'"

[21]But the people were silent. They did not say a word to the commander, because King Hezekiah had commanded them, "Don't say anything to him."

[22]Then the palace manager (Eliakim son of Hilkiah), the royal secretary (Shebna) and the record keeper (Joah son of Asaph) went to Hezekiah. Their clothes were torn to show they were upset. They told Hezekiah everything the Assyrian commander had said.

Hezekiah Asks God to Help

37 When King Hezekiah listened to their message, he tore his clothes to show he was upset. Then he put on sackcloth and went to the LORD's Temple.

[2]Hezekiah sent Eliakim, the palace manager, Shebna, the royal secretary and the leading priests to the prophet Isaiah son of Amoz. They wore the special clothes that showed they were sad and upset. [3]They said to Isaiah, "King Hezekiah has commanded that today will be a special day for sorrow and sadness. It will be a very sad day—as sad as when a baby should be born, but there is not enough strength for the birth. [4]The commander's master, the king of Assyria, has sent him to say bad things about the living God.

Maybe the LORD your God will hear it and prove the enemy is wrong. So pray for those who are still left alive."

[5]When King Hezekiah's officers came to Isaiah, [6]he said to them, "Give this message to your master, Hezekiah: The LORD says, 'Don't be afraid of what you heard from the commanders! Don't believe what those "boys" from the king of Assyria said to make fun of me. [7]Look, I will send a spirit against the king of Assyria. He will get a report that will make him return to his own country. And I will cut him down with a sword in his own country.'"

The Assyrian Army Leaves Jerusalem

[8]The commander heard that the king of Assyria had left Lachish. He found him at Libnah, fighting against that city. [9]Then the king of Assyria got a report that said, "King Tirhakah[a] of Ethiopia is coming to fight you."

So the king of Assyria sent messengers to Hezekiah again. [10]He told them, "Tell King Hezekiah of Judah these things:

"'Don't be fooled by the god you trust when he says, "Jerusalem will not be defeated by the king of Assyria." [11]You have heard what the kings of Assyria did to all the other countries. We destroyed them completely. Will you be saved? No! [12]Did the gods of those people save them? No, my ancestors destroyed them all. They destroyed the cities of Gozan, Haran, Rezeph and the people of Eden living in Tel Assar. [13]Where is the king of Hamath? The king of Arpad? The king of the city of Sepharvaim? The kings of Hena and Ivvah?'"

Hezekiah Prays to the LORD

[14]Hezekiah received the letters from the messengers and read them. Then he went up to the LORD's Temple and laid the letters out in front of the LORD. [15]He prayed to the LORD: [16]"LORD All-Powerful, God of Israel, you sit as King above the winged creatures. You alone are the God who rules all the kingdoms on earth. You made heaven and earth. [17]LORD, please pay attention and hear this. Open your eyes, LORD, and see what is happening. Listen to all the insults against the living God in the message Sennacherib sent! [18]It is true, LORD. The kings of Assyria did destroy all those nations. [19]They did throw the gods of those nations into the fire, but they were not real gods. They were only wood and stone—statues that people made. That is why the kings of Assyria could destroy them. [20]But you are the LORD our

---

[a] **37:9 Tirhakah** This is probably Taharqa, the Pharaoh of Egypt about 690–664 BC.

God, so please save us from the king of Assyria. Then all the other nations will know that you are the Lord, the only God."

God Answers Hezekiah

[21]Then Isaiah son of Amoz sent this message to Hezekiah: "The Lord, the God of Israel, says, 'You prayed to me about the message that came from King Sennacherib of Assyria. I have heard you.[a] [22]So this is the Lord's message against Sennacherib:

"'The virgin daughter Zion[b] does not think
   you are important.
She makes fun of you.
Daughter Jerusalem shakes her head at you
   and laughs behind your back.
[23]But who is the one you have insulted and
   made fun of?
Who is the one you have been shouting at
   with such a proud look on your face?
All this you have done against the Holy One
   of Israel!
[24]You sent your officers to insult the Lord.
   This is what you said:
"I took my many chariots up the high
   mountains
   deep inside Lebanon.
I cut down its tallest cedars
   and its best fir trees.
I have been on its highest mountain
   and deep inside its forests.
[25]I dug wells and drank water from new
   places.
   I dried up the rivers of Egypt
   and walked where the water was."

[26]"'How could you say this, Sennacherib?
   Did no one ever tell you that I, the Lord,
   planned these things long ago?
From ancient times I decided what would
   happen.
   And now I have made it happen.
I let you tear down strong cities
   and change them into piles of rocks.
[27]The people living there had no power.
   They were afraid and confused.
They were about to be cut down
   like grass and plants in the field.
They were like grass growing on the
   housetops,
   dying before it grows tall.
[28]I know all about your battles;
   I know when you rested,

when you went out to war,
   and when you came home.
I also know when you got upset at me.
[29]Yes, you were upset at me.
   I heard your proud insults.
So I will put my hook in your nose
   and my bit in your mouth.
Then I will turn you around
   and lead you back the way you came.'"

The Lord's Message for Hezekiah

[30]Then the Lord said, "I will give you a sign to show you that these words are true. You will not be able to plant seeds this year, so next year you will eat grain that grew wild from the previous year's crop. But in the third year, you will eat grain from seeds that you planted. You will harvest your crops, and you will have plenty to eat. You will plant vineyards and eat grapes from them. [31]"The people from the family of Judah who have escaped and are left alive will be like plants that send their roots deep into the ground and produce fruit above the ground. [32]That is because a few people will come out of Jerusalem alive. There will be survivors coming from Mount Zion." The strong love of the Lord All-Powerful will do this.

[33]So the Lord says this about the king of Assyria:

"He will not come into this city
   or shoot an arrow here.
He will not bring his shields up against this city
   or build up a ramp of soil to attack its walls.
[34]He will go back the way he came.
   He will not come into this city.
   The Lord says this!
[35]I will protect this city and save it.
   I will do this for myself and for my servant
   David."

INSIGHT

What a miraculous moment! Hezekiah has prayed (37:14–20) and 185,000 Assyrians are struck dead by the angel of the Lord. Now that's judgement!
Isaiah 37:36–37

The Assyrian Army Is Destroyed

[36]That night the angel of the Lord went out and killed 185,000 men in the Assyrian camp.

---

[a] *37:21 I have heard you* This is from the ancient Greek version and 2 Kgs 19:20.
[b] *37:22 The virgin daughter Zion* The city of Jerusalem, which is in danger of attack by the Assyrians. See "Zion" in the Word List.

When the people got up in the morning, they saw all the dead bodies. 37So King Sennacherib of Assyria went back to Nineveh and stayed there.

38One day Sennacherib was in the temple of his god Nisroch, worshipping him. His sons Adrammelech and Sharezer killed him with a sword and ran away to Ararat. So Sennacherib's son Esarhaddon became the new king of Assyria.

Hezekiah's Illness

38 At that time Hezekiah became sick and almost died. The prophet Isaiah son of Amoz went to see him and told him, "The LORD told me to tell you this: 'You will die soon. So you should tell your family what they should do when you die. You will not get well.'"

2Hezekiah turned towards the wall that faced the Temple and began praying to the LORD. 3"LORD, remember that I have faithfully served you with all my heart. I have done what you say is good." Then Hezekiah cried very hard.

4Then Isaiah received this message from the LORD: 5"Go to Hezekiah and tell him that the LORD, the God of your ancestor David, says, 'I heard your prayer, and I saw your tears. I will add 15 years to your life. 6I will save you and this city from the king of Assyria. I will protect this city.'"

21a Then Isaiah told Hezekiah, "Crush figs together and put them on your sore. Then you will get well."

22Hezekiah asked Isaiah, "What is the sign that proves I will get well and go to the LORD's Temple?"

7This is the sign from the LORD to show you that he will do what he says: 8"Look, I am causing the shadow that is on the steps of Ahaz*b* to move back ten steps. The sun's shadow will go back up the ten steps that it has already been on."

Hezekiah's Song

9This is the letter from Hezekiah when he became well:

10I thought I would live a full life.
    But now, in the middle of my life, the time
        has come for me to die.
11So I said, "I will not see the LORD GOD*c* in the
        land of the living again.
    I will not see the people living on earth.
12My life has been taken away,
    like a shepherd's tent that he pulls up and
        moves.

I am like a cloth that a weaver finishes,
    then cuts and removes from the loom.
    You ended my life in such a short time.
13All night I cried as loud as a lion,
    but my hopes were crushed like a lion
        eating bones.
    You finished my life in such a short time.
14I cried like a bird
    and moaned like a dove.
My eyes became tired,
    but I continued looking to the heavens.
Lord, I am so depressed.
    Promise to help me."
15What can I say?
    He told me what would happen,
        and he will make it happen.
I have had these troubles in my soul,
    so now I will be humble all my life.
16Lord, use this hard time to make my spirit
        live again.
    Help my spirit become strong and healthy.
Help me become well!
    Help me live again!

17Look, my troubles are gone!
    I now have peace.
You love me very much.
    You did not let me rot in the grave.
You took my sins
    and threw them away.
18The dead cannot praise you.
    People in Sheol cannot sing praises to you.
Those who have died and gone below
    are not trusting in your faithfulness.
19People who are alive, people like me,
    are the ones who will praise you.
Fathers should tell their children about how
        faithful you are.
20So I say, "The LORD saved me.
    So we will sing and play songs in the LORD's
        Temple all our lives."*d*

Messengers From Babylon

39 At that time Merodach Baladan son of Baladan was king of Babylon. He sent some men with letters and a gift to Hezekiah when he heard that Hezekiah had been sick. 2This made Hezekiah very happy, so he showed them all the valuable things in his storehouses. He showed them the silver, the gold, the spices and the expensive perfumes. He showed them the building where he stored the weapons. He

---

a **38:21,22** These verses fit better here than at the end of the chapter, where they appear in the standard Hebrew text. See 2 Kgs 20:6–9.
b **38:8 steps of Ahaz** The steps of a special building that Hezekiah used like a clock. When the sun shone on the steps, the shadows showed what time of the day it was.
c **38:11 the LORD GOD** Literally, "YAH YAWEH", two forms of a Hebrew name for God. See "YAHWEH" in the Word List.
d **38:20** Verses 21–22 have been placed after verse 6, see*a*.

showed them everything in his treasuries and everything in his house and throughout his kingdom.

³Then Isaiah the prophet went to King Hezekiah and asked him, "What did these men say? Where did they come from?"

Hezekiah said, "These men came all the way from Babylon just to see me."

⁴So Isaiah asked him, "What did they see in your house?"

Hezekiah said, "They saw everything in my palace. I showed them all my wealth."

⁵Then Isaiah said to Hezekiah, "Listen to this message from the LORD All-Powerful: ⁶'The time is coming when everything in your house and everything your ancestors have saved until today will be carried away to Babylon. Nothing will be left!' The LORD All-Powerful said this. ⁷The Babylonians will take your own sons, and your sons will become officers*ª* in the palace of the king of Babylon."

⁸Then Hezekiah told Isaiah, "This message from the LORD is good." (Hezekiah said this because he thought, "There will be real peace and security during my lifetime.")

Israel's Punishment Will End

40

Your God says,
"Comfort, comfort my people.
²Speak kindly to Jerusalem and tell her,
'Your time of service is finished.
You have paid the price for your sins.'
I, the LORD, have punished you twice
for every sin you committed."

³Listen, there is someone shouting:
"Prepare a way in the desert for the LORD.
Make a straight road there for our God.
⁴Every valley must be filled.
Every mountain and hill should be made flat.
The crooked roads should be made straight,
and the rough ground made smooth.
⁵Then the Glory of the LORD will be shown to
everyone.
Together, all people will see it.
Yes, this is what the LORD himself said!"

⁶A voice said, "Speak!"
So the man said, "What should I say?"
The voice said, "People are like grass.
Any glory they enjoy is like a wild flower.
⁷When a wind from the LORD blows on them,
the grass dies and the flower falls.
Yes, all people are like grass.
⁸Grass dies and flowers fall,
but the word of our God lasts forever."

Salvation: God's Good News

⁹Zion, you have good news to tell.
Go up on a high mountain and shout the
good news.
Jerusalem, you have good news to tell.
Don't be afraid; speak loudly.
Tell this news to all the cities of Judah:
"Look, here is your God!"
¹⁰The Lord GOD is coming with power.
He will use his power to rule all the people.
He will bring rewards for his people.
He will have their payment with him.
¹¹Like a good shepherd, he takes care of his
people.
He gathers them like lambs in his arms.
He holds them close, while their mothers
walk beside him.

God Made the World; He Rules It

¹²Who measured the oceans in the palm of his
hand?
Who used his hand to measure the sky?
Who used a bowl to measure all the dust of
the earth?
Who used scales to measure the mountains
and hills?
¹³Who could know the LORD's mind?
Who could be his teacher or give him
advice?
¹⁴Did the Lord ask for anyone's help?
Did anyone teach him to be fair?
Did anyone teach him knowledge?
Did anyone teach him to be wise?
¹⁵Look, all the nations in the world are like one
small drop in the bucket.
If the Lord took all the faraway nations and
put them on his scales,
they would be like small pieces of dust.
¹⁶All the trees in Lebanon are not enough
to burn on the altar for the Lord.
And all the animals in Lebanon
are not enough to kill for a sacrifice.
¹⁷Compared to God, all the nations of the world
are nothing.
Compared to him, they are worth nothing
at all.

People Cannot Imagine What God Is Like

¹⁸Can you compare God to anything?
Can you make a picture of God?
¹⁹No, but some people make statues from rock
or wood,
and they call them gods.
One worker makes a statue.
Then another worker covers it with gold
and makes silver chains for it.

ª **39:7 officers** Or "eunuchs". See "EUNUCH" in the Word List.

THE COMFORTING GREATNESS OF GOD

"What's going to happen to me when I leave home? Will I get a job? Will I meet someone and fall in love? Will the mistakes I've made in the past affect my future? What if I mess up again?"

If this sounds like you, don't panic – you're not alone! Life is full of these kinds of worries and "what-ifs". The good news is, God knows exactly how you're feeling.

DIG IN

READ Isaiah 40:1–31

- What's different in this chapter from what's gone before? (See the Bible Bit "Prophet of Doom" on Isaiah chapter 6 for help.)
- What is the main emphasis of Isaiah's message now?

This chapter marks a turning point in Isaiah's prophecy. He shifts gear from a tough message of God's judgement, to a tender promise of his comfort.

Time shifts as well: Isaiah is no longer writing for people in his own present day. Over the next twenty-seven chapters, Isaiah prophesies the word of God to the exiles in Babylon (as they will be two hundred years later) – a bit like you writing a letter for your great-great-grandchildren. They will be downtrodden and oppressed, he prophesies, but through all this coming persecution, they need to remember one thing – it's the one thing we need to remember too, as we face worries of all kinds – God is good and he has a wonderful plan for his people.

- List all the aspects of God's character Isaiah draws their attention to (vv.11–31).
- How does God bring the comfort his people so desperately need to hear? He does it by enlarging their vision of who he is. He shows them he is greater than anything or anyone on earth or in the heavens. Take time to meditate on the God pictured here: the one who measured out the oceans (v.12); who is infinitely fair, all-knowing and wise (v.14); who is in full control of the earth and the heavens (vv.23,26). When we get a clear picture of just how big God is everything else shrinks in comparison.

DIG THROUGH

- Ever feel like this: "If God is as big as he says, why would he be interested in me?" or "Surely, God's too busy to deal with me and my worries?" Actually, this passage turns that idea on its head. God may be bigger than the earth and the heavens – but he cares deeply about people too (vv.1–2). He knows every star by name (v.26) and he knows your name too (John 10:3).
- God comforts his people here by revealing himself to them and inviting them to trust him (vv.29–31). Sadly, we can seek ways of finding reassurance other than God himself. Where and to what things do people turn for comfort instead of God? What is it about God (according to this passage) that means it makes much more sense to trust him than anyone or anything else? Does that comfort you?

DIG DEEPER

How could Isaiah's prophecy give both judgement to God's people in his present day and comfort for their children's children in the future? That's one of the amazing things about God: as well as being greater than anything on earth or in heaven, he is also greater than time. Isaiah's inspired prophecies did come true – in a way that builds our faith and certainty that God is much bigger than us, and fully in control of time and eternity.

²⁰For the base he chooses special wood,
 a kind of wood that will not rot.
Then he finds a good wood worker,
 and the worker makes a "god" that will not
 fall over.
²¹Surely you know the truth, don't you?
 Surely you have heard.
 Surely someone told you long ago.
 Surely you understand who made the earth.
²²It is the Lord who sits above the circle of the
 earth.
 And compared to him, people are like
 grasshoppers.
He rolled open the skies like a piece of cloth.
 He stretched out the skies like a tent to sit
 under.
²³He takes away the power of rulers.
 He makes the world's leaders completely
 worthless.
²⁴They are like plants that are planted in the
 ground.
 But before they can send their roots into the
 ground,
God blows on the "plants";
 they become dead and dry,
 and the wind blows them away like straw.
²⁵The Holy One says, "Can you compare me to
 anyone?
 No one is equal to me."

²⁶Look up to the skies.
 Who created all those stars?
Who created all those "armies" in the sky?
 Who knows every star by name?
He is very strong and powerful,
 so not one of these stars is lost.

²⁷People of Jacob, this is true.
 Israel, you should believe it.
So why do you say, "The Lord cannot see the
 way I live;
 he will not find me and punish me"?ᵃ

²⁸Surely you know the truth.
 Surely you have heard.
The Lord is the God who lives forever!
 He created all the faraway places on earth.
He does not get tired and weary.
 You cannot learn all he knows.
²⁹He helps tired people be strong.
 He gives power to those without it.
³⁰Young men get tired and need to rest.

Even young boys stumble and fall.
³¹But those who trust in the Lord will become
 strong again.
 They will be like eagles that grow new
 feathers.ᵇ
They will run and not get weak.
 They will walk and not get tired.

The Lord Is the Eternal Creator

41 The Lord says,
 "Faraway countries, be quiet and listen
 to me!
 Nations be brave.ᶜ
Come to me and speak.
 We will meet together
 and decide who is right.
²Who woke up the man who is coming from
 the east?
 He called Justice to march with him.
He uses his sword to crush nations.
 He uses his bow and conquers kings—
 they run away like straw blown by the
 wind.
³He chases armies and is never hurt.
 He goes places he has never been before.
⁴Who was able to make all this happen?
 Who controlled the lives of everyone from
 the beginning?
I, the Lord, am the one.
 I was here at the beginning,
 and I will be here when all things are
 finished.
⁵People along the coast saw this,
 and they were frightened.
Nations at the ends of the earth
 shook with fear.
They have come near.
 They have arrived.

⁶"Workers help each other. They encourage
each other to be strong. ⁷One worker cuts wood
to make a statue. He encourages the man who
works with gold. Another worker uses a hammer
and makes the metal smooth. Then he encourages
the man at the anvil.ᵈ This last worker says, 'This
work is good; the metal will not come off.' Then
he nails the statue to a base so that it will not fall
over. And it never moves!"

Only the Lord Can Save Us

⁸The Lord says, "You, Israel, are my servant.
 Jacob, I chose you.

ᵃ **40:27 The Lord . . . punish me** Or "My way is hidden from the Lord; he ignores my case."
ᵇ **40:31 like . . . feathers** This probably refers to the ancient belief that eagles regain their youth when they moult (lose and grow
back their feathers). See Ps. 103:5. This line could also be translated, "They will rise up like eagles on their wings."
ᶜ **41:1 be brave** Or "be strong again", as in Isa. 40:31.
ᵈ **41:7 anvil** A heavy metal block. A worker puts hot metal on an anvil and beats the hot metal to change its shape.

You are from the family of my friend,
   Abraham.
9You were in a faraway country,
   but I reached out to you.
I called you from that faraway place.
   I said, 'You are my servant.'
I chose you,
   and I have not rejected you.
10Don't worry—I am with you.
   Don't be afraid—I am your God.
I will make you strong and help you.
   I will support you with my right hand that
      brings victory.
11Look, some people are angry with you,
   but they will be ashamed and disgraced.
   Your enemies will be lost and disappear.
12You will look for the people who were
      against you,
   but you will not be able to find them.
Those who fought against you
   will disappear completely.
13I am the LORD your God,
   who holds your right hand.
And I tell you, 'Don't be afraid!
   I will help you.'
14People of Israel, descendants of Jacob, you
      may be weak and worthless,*a*
   but do not be afraid.
   I myself will help you."

This is what the LORD himself says.

"I am the Holy One of Israel,
   the one who saves you.
15Look, I have made you like a new threshing
      board with many sharp teeth.
   You will trample mountains and crush them.
   You will make the hills*b* like chaff.
16You will throw them into the air,
   and the wind will blow them away and
      scatter them.
Then you will be happy in the LORD.
   You will be proud of the Holy One of Israel.

17"The poor and needy look for water,
   but they cannot find any.
   Their tongues are dry with thirst.
I, the LORD, will answer their prayers.
   I, the God of Israel, will not leave them to die.
18I will make rivers flow on dry hills.
   I will make springs of water flow through
      the valleys.
I will change the desert into a lake filled with
   water.

There will be springs of water in that dry
   land.
19I will make trees grow in the desert.
   There will be cedar, acacia, olive, cypress,
      fir and pine trees.
20I will do this so that people will see it and
      know who did it.
   They will notice what happened.
Then they will understand that the LORD made
   it happen,
   that the Holy One of Israel created it all."

The LORD Challenges the False Gods

21The LORD, the king of Jacob, says, "Come,
present your arguments. Show me your proof. 22Let
your idols come in and tell us what will happen.
Idols, tell us what happened in the beginning. We
will listen closely so that we can make a decision.
Tell us what will happen in the future. 23What signs
did you give in the past to prove that you really are
gods? Do something! Do anything, good or bad, so
that we can see that you are alive. Then we might
fear and respect you.
   24"Look, you false gods are worthless. You
cannot do anything. Only some horrible fool*c*
would want to worship you.

The LORD Proves He Is the Only God

25"I called someone in the north*d* to come.
   He is coming from the east where the sun
      rises,
   and he honours my name.
He tramples kings
   the way a potter softens clay with his
      feet.

26"Who told us about this before it happened
   so that we could say he was right?
None of your idols told us anything.
   They didn't say a word,
   and they cannot hear anything you say.
27I, the Lord, was the first one to tell Zion about
      these things.
   I sent a messenger to Jerusalem to say,
   'Look, your people are coming back!'

28"I looked at those false gods.
   Not one of them said anything.
   They had no advice to offer.
I asked them questions,
   but they didn't say a word.
29Those gods are all less than nothing.
   They cannot do anything.
   They are worthless.

---

a **41:14 Jacob . . . worthless** Literally, "Worm of Jacob, men of Israel".
b **41:15 mountains . . . hills** Symbols of the power of Israel's enemies.
c **41:24 fool** Literally, "horrible thing". The Hebrew word usually describes idols and other wicked things that God hates.
d **41:25 someone in the north** This probably means Cyrus, a king of Persia. He ruled about 550–530 BC.

The Lord's Special Servant

42 "Here is my servant,
the one I support.
He is the one I have chosen,
and I am very pleased with him.
I have filled him with my Spirit,
and he will bring justice to the nations.
[2]He will not cry out or shout
or try to make himself heard in the streets.
[3]He will not break even a crushed reed.[a]
He will not put out even the weakest
flame.
He will bring true justice.
[4]He will not grow weak or give up
until he has brought justice to the world.
And people in faraway places will hope to
receive his teachings."

The Lord Is Ruler and Creator of the World

[5]The Lord, the true God, said these things.
He is the one who created the sky and spread
it out over the earth.
He formed the earth and everything it
produced.
He breathes life into all the people on earth.
He gives a spirit to everyone who walks on
the earth.

[6]"I, the Lord, was right to call you.
I will hold your hand and protect you.
You will be the sign of my agreement with the
people.
You will be a light for the other nations.
[7]You will make the blind able to see.
You will free those who are held as
captives.
You will lead those who live in darkness out
of their prison.

[8]"I am Yahweh.
That is my name.
I will not give my glory to another.
I will not let statues take the praise that
should be mine.
[9]In the past, I told you what would happen,
and it happened!
Now I am telling you something new,
and I am telling you now, before it
happens."

A Song of Praise to the Lord

[10]Sing a new song[b] to the Lord;
praise him everywhere on earth—

all you who sail on the seas,
everything in the sea,
and all you people in faraway places!
[11]Deserts and cities, villages of Kedar,
praise the Lord!
People living in Sela, sing for joy!
Sing from the top of your mountain.
[12]Give glory to the Lord.
Praise him, all you people in faraway lands!
[13]The Lord will go out like a strong soldier.
Like a man going into battle, he will be full
of excitement.
He will shout with a loud cry,
and he will defeat his enemies.

God Is Very Patient

[14]"For a long time I have said nothing.
I have controlled myself and kept quiet.
But now I will cry out like a woman giving
birth.
My breathing is getting faster and louder.
[15]I will destroy the hills and mountains.
I will dry up all the plants that grow there.
I will change rivers to dry land
and dry up pools of water.
[16]Then I will lead the blind along a path they
never knew
to places where they have never been
before.
I will change darkness into light for them.
I will make the rough ground smooth.
I will do these things for them;
I will not abandon my people.
[17]But some of them have left me.
They say to their gold statues, 'You are
my gods.'
They trust their false gods,
but they will be disappointed and shamed.

Israel Refused to Listen to God

[18]"Deaf people, listen to me!
Blind people, look and see!
[19]In all the world, no one is more blind than my
servant.[c]
No one is more deaf than my messenger.
No one is more blind than my chosen people,
the servant of the Lord.
[20]My people see what they should do,
but they do not obey me.
They can hear with their ears,
but they refuse to listen to me."
[21]The Lord wants them to do what is right.
He wants them to honour his wonderful
teachings.[d]

---

[a] **42:3 reed** A plant that grows near water.
[b] **42:10 new song** Whenever God did a new and wonderful thing for his people, they would write a new song about it.
[c] **42:19 my servant** Here, this probably means the people of Israel.
[d] **42:21** Or "The Lord will make his teachings very wonderful. He will do this because he is good."

²²But look at his people.
> Others have defeated them and have stolen
> from them.

The young men are afraid.
> They are locked in prisons.

People have taken advantage of them,
> and there is no one to protect them.

Others take their money,
> and there is no one to say, "Give it back!"

²³Will any of you pay attention to this warning? Will you ever learn to listen? ²⁴Who let Jacob be defeated? Who let others take what belonged to Israel? The LORD allowed them to do this. We sinned against him, so he let people take away our wealth. The people did not want to live the way he wanted. They refused to listen to his teaching. ²⁵So he poured out his anger on them and brought wars against them. It was as if there were fires all around them, but they didn't know what was happening. It was as if they were burning, but they didn't try to understand.

God Is Always With His People

43 Jacob, the LORD created you. Israel, he made you, and now he says, "Don't be afraid. I saved you. I named you. You are mine. ²When you have troubles, I am with you. When you cross rivers, you will not be hurt. When you walk through fire, you will not be burned; the flames will not hurt you. ³That's because I, the LORD, am your God. I, the Holy One of Israel, am your Saviour. I gave Egypt to pay for you. I gave Ethiopia and Seba to make you mine. ⁴You are precious to me, and I have given you a special place of honour. I love you. That's why I am willing to trade others, to give up whole nations, to save your life.

⁵"So don't be afraid, because I am with you. I will gather your children and bring them to you. I will gather them from the east and from the west. ⁶I will tell the north: give my people to me. I will tell the south: don't keep my people in prison. Bring my sons and daughters to me from the faraway places. ⁷Bring to me all the people who are mine—the people who have my name. I made them for myself. I made them, and they are mine.

⁸"Bring out the people who have eyes but are blind. Bring out the people who have ears but are deaf.[a] ⁹All people and all nations should also be gathered together. Which of their gods said this would happen? Which of their gods would tell what happened in the beginning? They should bring their witnesses. The witnesses should speak the truth. This will show they are right."

¹⁰The LORD says, "You people are my witnesses and the servant I chose. I chose you so that you would help people believe me. I chose you so that you would understand that 'I Am He'—⌐I am the true God⌐. There was no God before me, and there will be no God after me. ¹¹I myself am the LORD, and there is no other Saviour. ¹²I am the one who spoke to you, saved you and told you those things. It was not some stranger who was with you. You are my witnesses, and I am God." (This is what the LORD himself said.) ¹³"I have always been God. When I do something, no one can change what I have done. And no one can save people from my power."

¹⁴The LORD, the Holy One of Israel, saves you, and he says, "I will send armies to Babylon for you. Many people will be captured. Those Chaldeans will be taken away in their own boats. (They are so proud of those boats.)[b] ¹⁵I am the LORD your Holy One. I made Israel. I am your King."

God Will Save His People Again

¹⁶The Lord is making roads through the sea. He is making a path for his people, even through rough waters. The LORD says, ¹⁷"Those who fight against me with their chariots, horses and armies will be defeated. They will never rise again. They will be destroyed. They will be put out like the flame in a lamp. ¹⁸So don't remember what happened in earlier times. Don't think about what happened a long time ago, ¹⁹because I am doing something new! Now you will grow like a new plant. Surely you know this is true. I will even make a road in the desert, and rivers will flow through that dry land. ²⁰The wild animals will thank me. The large animals and birds will honour me when I put water in the desert and make rivers flow through that dry land. I will do this to give water to my chosen people. ²¹I made them, and they will sing songs of praise to me.

²²"Jacob, you did not pray to me. Israel, you became tired of me. ²³You have not brought your sheep as sacrifices to me. You have not honoured me with your sacrifices. I did not force you to give gifts to me like slaves. I did not force you to burn incense until you became tired. ²⁴So you did not use your money to buy things to honour me. But you did force me to be like your slave. You sinned until the bad things you did made me very tired.

²⁵"I, I am the one who wipes away all your sins. I do this to please myself. I will not remember your sins. ²⁶But you should remember me. Let's meet together and decide what is right. Tell your story

---

a **43:8 blind . . . deaf** This probably means the Israelites who would not believe God. See Isa. 6:9–10.
b **43:14 I will send . . . boats** Or with minor changes to the Hebrew, "I will send someone against Babylon to break open the gates, and the shouts of victory from the Chaldeans will be changed to crying."

and prove that you are innocent. [27]Your first father sinned, and your lawyers[a] committed crimes against me. [28]I will make your Temple leaders unfit to serve there. I will destroy Jacob.[b] Bad things will happen to Israel.

The LORD Is the Only God

44 "Jacob, you are my servant. Israel, I chose you. Listen to me! [2]I am the LORD, and I made you. I am the one who created you. I have helped you since you were in your mother's womb. Jacob, my servant, don't be afraid. Jeshurun,[c] I chose you.

[3]"I will pour water for thirsty people, and streams will flow through the desert. I will pour my Spirit on your children, and I will bless[d] your family. [4]They will sprout like grass in the spring and grow like trees by streams of water.

[5]"One man will call himself, 'I am the LORD's'. Another will use the name, 'Jacob'. Another man will sign his name as 'The LORD's Hand'. And another will use the name, 'Israel'."

[6]The LORD is the king of Israel. The LORD All-Powerful is the one who will free Israel. And he says, "I am the only God. There are no other gods. I am the Beginning and the End. [7]There is no other God like me. If there is, that god should speak now. Let him lay out everything he has done since the time I made these ancient people. Let him show me the signs he gave long ago that prove he knew what would happen in the future.

[8]"Don't be afraid! Don't worry. I am the one who always told you what would happen. You are my proof.[e] There is no other God; I am the only one. There is no other 'Rock'; I know I am the only one."

False Gods Are Useless

[9]Some people make idols, but they are worthless. They love their statues, which are useless. Those who serve as witnesses for these statues cannot even see. They don't know enough to be ashamed.

[10]Who made these false gods? Who covered these useless statues? [11]Workers made them, and the workers are only human. If they all would come together before me, we could discuss this. Then they would all be ashamed and afraid.

[12]One worker uses his tools to heat iron over hot coals. Then he uses his hammer to beat the metal to shape it into a statue. He uses his own powerful arms, but when he gets hungry, he loses his strength. If he does not drink water, he becomes weak.

[13]Another worker uses his string line[f] and compass[g] to draw lines on the wood to show where he should cut. Then he uses his chisels[h] and cuts a statue from the wood. He uses his callipers[i] to measure the statue. In this way the worker makes the wood look exactly like a man, and this statue of a man does nothing but sit in the house.

[14]To split the cedar tree, the worker took some oak or cypress ⌊wedges⌋. To make sure he had plenty of wood, he planted some pines. But it was the rain that made them grow.

[15]When the man wanted a fire, he took some of the wood to keep him warm. He also used some of it to bake his bread. But then he used that same wood to make a statue to worship as a god! That god is only a statue that he made, but he bows down to it! [16]He burns half of the wood in the fire. He uses the fire to cook his meat, and he eats the meat until he is full. He burns the wood to keep himself warm. He says, "Good! Now I am warm, and I can see by the light of the fire." [17]There is a little of the wood left, so he makes a statue and calls it his god. He bows down before it and worships it. He prays to it and says, "You are my god, save me!"

[18]People like that don't know what they are doing! They don't understand. It is as if they have mud in their eyes so they cannot see. Their minds cannot understand. [19]They don't realize what they are doing. They aren't smart enough to think, "I burned half of the wood in the fire. I used the hot coals to bake my bread and cook the meat I ate. And I used the wood that was left to make this terrible thing. I am worshipping a block of wood!"

[20]Someone like that is deceived. They don't know what they are doing.[j] They cannot save themselves, and they will not admit, "This statue I am holding is a lie!"

---

[a] **43:27 lawyers** Or "speakers", people who argue a person's case in court. This might refer to priests or prophets.

[b] **43:28 destroy Jacob** Or "I will make Jacob completely mine."

[c] **44:2 Jeshurun** Another name for Israel. It means "good" or "honest".

[d] **44:3 bless** This is a wordplay. This Hebrew word sounds like the word meaning "pool".

[e] **44:8 proof** Or "witnesses".

[f] **44:13 string line** In ancient times, this was a piece of string with wet paint on it. It was used to make straight lines on wood or stone.

[g] **44:13 compass** A tool used to draw circles and copy measurements.

[h] **44:13 chisels** Sharp tools used to carve wood or stone.

[i] **44:13 callipers** A special measuring tool, like a compass.

[j] **44:20 They . . . doing** Literally, "They eat ashes."

The Lord, the True God, Helps Israel

21"Jacob, remember these things!
    Israel, remember, you are my servant.
I made you, and you are my servant.
    So, Israel, don't forget me.
22Your sins were like a big cloud,
    but I wiped them all away.
Your sins are gone,
    like a cloud that disappeared into thin air.
I rescued and protected you,
    so come back to me."

23Skies, rejoice for what the LORD has done.
    Earth, shout for joy down to your deepest
        parts!
Start singing, you mountains
    and all you trees in the forest!
Yes, the LORD has saved Jacob.
    He has shown his glory by rescuing Israel.
24The one who rescued you is the LORD,
    the one who formed you in your mother's
        womb.
He says, "I, the LORD, made everything.
    I put the skies there myself.
    I spread out the earth before me."

25False prophets tell lies, but the Lord shows that their lies are false. He makes fools of those who do magic. He confuses even the wise. They think they know a lot, but he makes them look foolish. 26The Lord sends his servants to tell his messages to the people, and he makes those messages come true. He sends messengers to tell the people what they should do, and he proves that the advice is good.

God Chooses Cyrus to Rebuild Judah

The Lord says to Jerusalem, "People will live
    in you again."
He says to the cities of Judah, "You will be
    rebuilt."
He says to them, "I will repair your ruins."
27He tells the deep waters, "Become dry!
    I will make your streams dry too."
28He says to Cyrus, "You are my shepherd.
    You will do what I want.
You will say to Jerusalem, 'You will be rebuilt!'
    You will tell the Temple, 'Your foundations
        will be put in place!'"

God Chooses Cyrus to Make Israel Free

45
This is what the LORD said to Cyrus, his
chosen king:[a]

INSIGHT

Surprisingly, Isaiah predicts that Cyrus, a Persian king, will be God's appointed servant — allowing the Israelite exiles to return to Jerusalem. Josephus, a first-century historian, says that Cyrus was so impressed with Isaiah's divine prediction that it made him want to do what it said.

Isaiah 44:28 – 45:1

"I took you by your right hand to help you
    defeat nations,
to strip other kings of their power,
    and to open city gates that will not be
        closed again.
2I will go in front of you
    and make the mountains flat.
I will break the city gates of bronze
    and cut the iron bars on the gates.
3I will give you the wealth that is stored in
    secret places.
    I will give you those hidden treasures.
Then you will know that I am the LORD,
    the God of Israel, who calls you by
        name.
4I do this for my servant, Jacob.
    I do it for my chosen people, Israel.
Cyrus, I am calling you by name.
    You don't know me, but I know you.[b]
5I am the LORD, the only God.
    There is no other God except me.
I put your clothes on you,[c]
    but still you don't know me.
6I am doing this so that everyone will know
    that I am the only God.
From the east to the west, people will know
    that I am the LORD
    and that there is no other God.
7I made the light and the darkness.
    I bring peace, and I cause trouble.
    I, the LORD, do all these things.

8"May the clouds in the skies above
    pour goodness on the earth like rain.
May the earth open up
    to let salvation grow.
And may goodness grow with that salvation,
    which I, the LORD, created.

---

[a] **45:1 chosen king** Literally, "the anointed one".
[b] **45:4 I know you** Or "I will give you a title."
[c] **45:5 I put . . . you** This also means "I made you strong."

God Controls His Creation

⁹"Look at these people! They are arguing with the one who made them. Look at them argue with me. They are like pieces of clay from a broken pot. Clay does not say to the one moulding it, 'Man, what are you doing?' Things that are made don't have the power to question the one who makes them. ¹⁰A father gives life to his children, and they cannot ask, 'Why are you giving me life?' They cannot question their mother and ask, 'Why are you giving birth to me?'"

¹¹The Lord God is the Holy One of Israel. He created Israel, and he says,

"My children, you asked me to show you
    a sign.
  You told me to show you what I have done.ᵃ
¹²I made the earth,
  and I created the people on it.
I used my own hands to make the skies.
  And I command all the armies in the sky.ᵇ
¹³I was right to give power to Cyrus,ᶜ
  and I will make his work easy.
He will rebuild my city,
  and he will set my people free without
    bribes or payment."
The Lord All-Powerful says this.

¹⁴The Lord says, "Egypt and Ethiopia are rich,
  but, Israel, you will get those riches.
The tall people from Seba will be yours.
  They will walk behind you with chains
    around their necks.
They will bow down before you
  and ask you to pray for them and say,
'The true God really is with you,
  and there is no other God.'"

¹⁵You are the God people cannot see.
  You are the God who saves Israel.
¹⁶Many people make false gods,
  but they will be disappointed.
All of them will go away ashamed.
¹⁷But Israel will be saved by the Lord.
  That salvation will continue forever.
Never again will Israel be shamed.
¹⁸The Lord is God.
  He made the skies and the earth.
  He put the earth in its place.
He did not want the earth to be empty when
    he made it.
  He created it to be lived on.

"I am the Lord.
  There is no other God.
¹⁹I have spoken openly, not in secret.
  I did not hide my words in a dark and
    secret place.
I did not tell the people of Jacob
  to look for me in empty places.
I am the Lord, and I speak the truth.
  I say only what is right.

The Lord Proves He Is the Only God

²⁰"You people who escaped from other nations, gather together before me. (These people carry statues of false gods. They pray to useless gods, but they don't know what they are doing. ²¹Tell them to come to me. Let them present their case and discuss these things.)

"Who told you about this before it happened? Who told you this so long ago? I, the Lord, am the one who said these things. I am the only God, the one who does what is right. I am the one who saves, and there is no other! ²²So all you people in faraway places, turn to me and be saved, because I am God, and there is no other.

²³"When I make a promise, that promise is true. It will happen. And I swear by my own power that everyone will bow before me and will take an oath to obey me. ²⁴They will say, 'Goodness and strength come only from the Lord.'"

And all who show their anger against him will be humiliated. ²⁵The Lord will help the people of Israel do what is rightᵈ and praise their God.

False Gods Are Useless

46 The Lord says, "Bel has fallen to the ground. Neboᵉ is kneeling before me.

"Men put those idols on the backs of animals. They are only heavy burdens that must be carried. They do nothing but make people tired. ²But they all bowed down and fell to the ground. They couldn't escape; they were all carried away like prisoners.

³"Family of Jacob, listen to me! You who are left from the family of Israel, listen! I have carried you since you left your mother's womb. I carried you when you were born, ⁴and I will still be carrying you when you are old. Your hair will turn grey, and I will still carry you. I made you, and I will carry you to safety.

⁵"Can you compare me to anyone? No one is equal to me. You cannot understand everything about me. There is nothing like me. ⁶Some people

---

ᵃ **45:11** *My children . . . done* Or "Those who are coming asked for my children. They commanded me to give them the people I made with my own hands."
ᵇ **45:12** *armies in the sky* Sometimes this means the angels, and sometimes it means the stars.
ᶜ **45:13** *I was right . . . Cyrus* Or "I gave Cyrus power to do something good."
ᵈ **45:25** *do what is right* Or "find justice".
ᵉ **46:1** *Nebo* A false god of Babylon.

are rich with gold and silver. Gold falls from their purses, and they weigh their silver on scales. They pay an artist to make a false god from wood. Then they bow down and worship that false god. [7]They put their false god on their shoulders and carry it. That false god is useless; people have to carry it! People set the statue on the ground, and it cannot move. That false god never walks away from its place. People can yell at it, but it will not answer. That false god is only a statue; it cannot save people from their troubles.

[8]"Sinners, change your heart and mind. Think about this again. Remember it and be strong. [9]Remember what happened long ago. Remember, I am God and there is no other God. There is no other like me.

[10]"In the beginning, I told you what would happen in the end. A long time ago, I told you things that have not happened yet. When I plan something, it happens. I do whatever I want to do. [11]I am calling a man from the east to do what I want. He will come like an eagle from a faraway country. He will do all that I have planned. Everything I said will happen just as I said it would.

[12]"Listen to me, you stubborn[a] people! You are far from doing what is right. [13]But I am close to making things right. Salvation will not be delayed much longer. I will bring salvation to Zion and to my wonderful Israel."

God's Message to Babylon

47 "Fall down and sit in the dirt, city of Babylon.
　　You have no throne, so sit on the ground, people of Babylon.[b]
You are not the ruler now.
　　You are no longer the beautiful young princess that people said you were.
[2]Get the millstones ready
　　and grind the grain into flour.
Take off your veil and fancy clothes.
　　Lift your skirt and get ready to cross the rivers.[c]
[3]Men will see your naked body
　　and use you for sex.
I will make you pay for the bad things you did,
　　and I will not let anyone help you.

[4]"My people say, 'God saves us.
　　His name is the LORD All-Powerful, the Holy One of Israel.'

[5]"So Babylon, sit down and shut up.
　　Daughter of the Chaldeans, go into the dark prison.
　　You will no longer be 'The Queen of the Kingdoms'.

[6]"I was angry with my people.
　　They were mine, but I turned against them.
I let you punish them,
　　but you showed them no mercy.
Even for those who were old
　　you made the work hard.
[7]You said, 'I will live forever.
　　I will always be the queen.'
You didn't care what you did to my people.
　　You didn't think about what might happen later.
[8]So now listen, you who love only pleasure!
　　Feeling so safe, you tell yourself,
'I alone am important, and no one else matters.
　　I will never be a widow or lose my children.'
[9]These two things will happen to you:
　　First, you will lose your children and then your husband.
　　And none of your magic spells will help you.
[10]You do bad things but still feel safe.[d]
　　You say to yourself, 'No one sees the wrong I do.'
You thought your wisdom and knowledge
　　would save you.
You tell yourself, 'I alone am important,
　　and no one else matters.'

[11]"But disaster is coming your way.
　　You don't know when it will happen, but disaster is coming.
　　And there is nothing you can do to stop it.

INSIGHT

Someone once called sarcasm "the lowest form of wit", however, it can be very effective. You can occasionally find it used in the Bible, especially in the prophets' writings, as they tried to shake people from their godless stupor.

Isaiah 47:12

---

[a] **46:12** *stubborn* Literally, "mighty of heart".
[b] **47:1** *city of Babylon, people of Babylon* Literally, "virgin daughter of Babylon", "daughter of the Chaldeans".
[c] **47:2** *rivers* The Tigris and Euphrates rivers. Babylon was between these two rivers.
[d] **47:10** *You . . . safe* Or "You put your trust in your evil."

¹²You worked hard all your life
    learning magic and spells.
So start using that magic.
    Maybe those spells will help you.
    Maybe you will be able to frighten someone.
¹³You have many advisors.
    Are you tired of the advice they give?
Then send out your men who read the stars.
    They can tell when the month starts,
    so maybe they can tell you when your
        troubles will come.
¹⁴But they cannot even save themselves.
    They will burn like straw.
They will burn so fast that there will be no
    coals left to cook bread.
    There will be no fire left to sit by.
¹⁵That's what will happen to those you have
    worked with,
    the people you have done business with all
        your life.
They will all go their own way.
    There will be no one left to save you."

God's Message to Israel

48 "Family of Jacob, listen to me!
    You people call yourself 'Israel',
    but you are from Judah's family.
When you take an oath, I, the LORD, the God
    of Israel,
    am the one whose name you use,
    but you are not honest and sincere.

²"Yes, you call yourselves citizens of the holy
    city,ᵃ
    those who depend on the God of Israel.
The LORD All-Powerful is his name.

³"Long ago I told you what would happen.
    I told you about these things.
    And suddenly I made them happen.
⁴I did that because I knew you were stubborn.
    You were like iron that will not bend,
    with heads as hard as bronze.
⁵So long ago I told you what would happen.
    I told you about those things long before
        they happened.
I did this so that you could not say,
    'The gods we made did this.
    Our idols, our statues, made this happen.'

God Promises to Make Israel Pure

⁶"You heard what I said would happen.
    And you can see it has all been done.
    Shouldn't you tell this to others?
Now I will tell you about new things,
    secrets you have not known before.

⁷This is something that is happening now,
    not long ago.
    You have not heard about it before today.
    So you cannot say, 'We already knew that.'
⁸But even in the past you didn't listen.
    You didn't learn anything.
    You never listen to what I say.
I have always known that you would turn
    against me.
    You have rebelled against me from the time
        you were born.

⁹"But I will be patient.
    I will do this for myself.
People will praise me for not becoming angry
    and destroying you.
    You will praise me for waiting.

¹⁰"Look, I will make you pure,
    but not in the way you make silver pure.
    I will make you pure by giving you
        troubles.
¹¹I will do this for myself—for me!
    I will not let you treat me as if I am not
        important.
    I will not let some false god take my glory
        and praise.

¹²"Jacob, listen to me!
    Israel, I called you to be my people.
    So listen to me!
I am the Beginning,
    and I am the End.
¹³I made the earth with my own hands.
    My right hand made the sky.
And if I call them,
    they will come to stand before me.

¹⁴"All of you, come here and listen to me.
    Did any of the false gods say these things
        would happen?
Cyrus, the LORD's chosen one,ᵇ will do what
    God wants.
    He will attack Babylon and the Chaldeans.

¹⁵"I told you that I would call him.
    I will lead him and make him succeed.
¹⁶Come here and listen to me!
    I was there when Babylon began as a
        nation.
And from the beginning, I spoke clearly
    so that people could know what I said."

Now, the Lord GOD sends me and his Spirit
to tell you these things. ¹⁷The LORD, the Saviour,
the Holy One of Israel, says,

"I am the LORD your God.
I teach you for your own good.
I lead you in the way you should go.
18If you had obeyed me,
then peace would have come to you
like a full flowing river.
Good things would have come to you again
and again,
like the waves of the sea.
19If you had obeyed me,
you would have had as many children as
there are grains of sand.
And they would always have been mine
and would never have been destroyed."

20My people, leave Babylon!
My people, run from the Chaldeans!
Tell the news with joy.
Spread the news around the world.
Tell them,
"The LORD rescued his servant Jacob."
21They never got thirsty as he led them through
the desert,
because he made water flow from a rock.
He split the rock,
and water flowed out.

22But the LORD also said,
"There is no peace for evil people."

God Calls His Special Servant

49 Hear me, people by the sea.
Listen to me, you faraway nations.
The LORD called me before I was born.
He called my name while I was still in my
mother's womb.
2He used me to speak for him.
He used me like a sharp sword,
but he also held me in his hand to protect me.
He used me like a sharp arrow,
but he also kept me safe in his arrow bag.

3He told me, "Israel, you are my servant.
I will do wonderful things with you."

4I said, "I worked hard for nothing.
I wore myself out, but I did nothing useful.
I used all my power,
but I did not really do anything.
So the LORD must decide what to do with me.
He must decide my reward."
5The LORD is the one who made me in my
mother's womb,
so that I could be his servant.
He wanted me to lead Jacob and Israel back
to him.
The LORD gives me honour.
I get my strength from my God.

6And now he says, "You are a very important
servant to me.
You must bring back to me the tribes of
Jacob.
You must bring back the people of Israel
who are still alive.
But I have something else for you to do that is
even more important:
I will make you a light for the other nations.
You will show people all over the world the
way to be saved."

7The LORD, the Saviour and Holy One of Israel,
speaks to his servant.
People hate that servant.
Nations despise him.
He is now a slave to rulers.
The Lord says to him,
"Kings will see you and stand to honour you.
Great leaders will bow down to you."

This will happen for the LORD. The Holy One of
Israel is the one who chose you, and he can be
trusted.

The Day of Salvation

8This is what the LORD says:
"There will be a special time when I show my
kindness.
Then I will answer your prayers.
There will be a special day when I will save
you.
Then I will help you and protect you.
And you will be the proof of my agreement
with the people.
The country is destroyed now,
but you will give the land back to the
people who own it.
9You will tell the prisoners,
'Come out of your prison!'
You will tell those who are in darkness,
'Come out of the dark!'
The people will eat along the road,
and they will have food even on empty hills.
10They will not be hungry or thirsty.
The hot sun and wind will not hurt them.
Their Comforter will lead them.
He will lead them by springs of water.
11I will make a road for my people.
The mountains will be made flat,
and the low roads will be raised.

12"Look! People are coming to me from faraway
places.
They are coming to me from the north and
from the west.
They are coming to me from Aswan in
Egypt."

¹³Heavens and earth, be happy!
  Mountains, shout with joy!
The Lord comforts his people.
  He is good to his poor people.

¹⁴But now Zion says, "The Lord has left me;
  the Lord has forgotten me."

¹⁵But the Lord says,
  "Can a woman forget her baby?
    Can she forget the child who came from
      her body?
  Even if she can forget her children,
    I cannot forget you.
¹⁶I drew a picture of you on my hand.
  You are always before my eyes.ᵃ
¹⁷Your children will come back to you,
  and those who destroyed you will leave.
¹⁸Look up! Look all around you!
  All your children are gathering together and
    coming to you."
The Lord says, "On my life, I promise you
  this:
  Your children will be like jewels that you tie
    around your neck.
  Your children will be like the necklace that
    a bride wears.

¹⁹"You are destroyed and defeated now.
  Your land is useless.
But after a short time, you will have many
  people in your land.
  And those who destroyed you will be far,
    far away.
²⁰You were sad for the children you lost,
  but they will tell you,
  'This place is too small!
  Give us a bigger place to live!'
²¹Then you will say to yourself,
  'Who gave me all these children?
I was sad and lonely.
  My children were taken away.
They were gone.
  So who gave me these children?
Look, I was the only one left.
  Where did all these children come from?'"

²²This is what the Lord God says:
  "Look, I will wave my hand to the nations.
  I will raise my flag for everyone to see.
Then they will bring your children to you.
  They will carry your children on their
    shoulders,
  and they will hold them in their arms.
²³Kings will be their teachers.
  The daughters of kings will care for them.

The kings and their daughters will bow down
  to you.
  They will kiss the ground at your feet.
Then you will know that I am the Lord,
  and anyone who trusts in me will not be
    disappointed."

²⁴If a strong soldier takes a prisoner,
  can you set him free?
If a powerful soldier guards someone,
  can the prisoner escape?
²⁵Here is the Lord's answer:
  "The prisoners will escape.
    Those captured by the strong soldier will be
      set free.
That's because I will fight your battles,
  and I will save your children.
²⁶Those people hurt you,
  but I will force them to eat their own
    bodies.
  Their own blood will be the wine that
    makes them drunk.
Then everyone will know that the Lord
  saved you.
  Everyone will know that the Powerful One
    of Jacob saved you."

Israel Punished Because of Their Sin

50 This is what the Lord says:
  "People of Israel, do you think I divorced
    your mother?
  Then where is the paper that proves it?
My children, do you think I sold you to pay
  a debt?
  Did I owe money to someone?
No, you were sold because of the bad things
  you did.
  Your mother was sent away because of
    your sins.
²I came home and found no one there.
  I called and called, but no one answered.
Do you think I cannot get you back?
  Do you think I cannot save you?
Look, if I gave the command, the ocean would
  dry up!
  I can turn rivers into a desert.
The fish would die without water,
  and their bodies would rot.
³I can make the skies dark.
  I can cover the skies in darkness as black as
    sackcloth."

God's Servant Depends on God

⁴The Lord God gave me the ability to teach, so
now I teach these sad people. Every morning he
wakes me and teaches me like a student. ⁵The Lord

ᵃ **49:16** *I . . . eyes* Or "I see your figure before me always." This is a wordplay. The Hebrew word "figure" also means "walls".

GOD helps me learn, and I have not turned against him. I will not stop following him. 6I will let those people beat me and pull the hair from my beard. I will not hide my face when they say bad things to me and spit at me. 7The Lord GOD will help me, so the bad things they say will not hurt me. I will be strong. I know I will not be disappointed.

8God is with me, and he is the one who shows that I am innocent. So no one can say I am guilty. If anyone wants to try to prove me wrong, they should come here, and we will have a trial. 9But look, the Lord GOD helps me, so no one can prove me guilty. As for them, they will all be like worthless old clothes, eaten by moths.

10People who respect the LORD also listen to his servant. That servant lives completely trusting in God without knowing what will happen. He really trusts in the LORD's name and depends on his God. 11The Lord says, "Look, you people want to do whatever you want. So light your own fires and torches, but you will be punished. You will fall into your fires and torches and be burned. I will make that happen."

Israel Should Be Like Abraham

51 "Some of you people try hard to live good lives. You go to the LORD for help. Listen to me. You should look at Abraham your father. He is the rock you were cut from. 2Abraham is your father, so look at him. Look at Sarah, who gave birth to you. Abraham was alone when I called him. Then I blessed him, and he began a great family with many descendants."

3In the same way, the LORD will bless Zion. He will feel sorry for her and her people, and he will do something great for her. He will turn the desert into a garden. It will be like the Garden of Eden. The land was empty, but it will become like the LORD's garden. People there will be very happy. They will sing victory songs to thank God for what he did.

4"My people, listen to me!
My decisions will be like lights showing
people how to live.
5I will soon save you and show that I am fair.
I will use my power and judge all nations.
All the faraway places are waiting for me.
They wait for my power to help them.
6Look up to the heavens!
Look around you at the earth below!
The skies will disappear like clouds of smoke.
The earth will become like worthless old
clothes.
The people on earth will die,

but my salvation will continue forever.
My goodness will never end.
7You people who understand goodness should
listen to me.
You people who follow my teachings should
hear the things I say.
Don't be afraid of evil people.
Don't let their insults upset you.
8They will be like old clothes eaten by moths.
They will be like wool eaten by worms.
But my goodness will last forever.
My salvation will continue for ever and ever."

God's Own Power Will Save His People

9Wake up! Wake up!
Arm of the LORD, clothe yourself with
strength.
Show your power the way you did long ago,
as you have from ancient times.
You are the one who destroyed Rahab.
You defeated the Dragon.*a*
10You dried up the water that was in the
deep sea.
You made a road through the deepest parts
of the sea.
Your people crossed over and were saved.
11The LORD will save his people.
They will return to Zion with joy.
They will be very happy.
Their happiness will be like a crown on
their heads forever.
They will be singing with joy.
All sadness will be gone far away.

12The Lord says, "I am the one who comforts
you.
So why should you be afraid of people?
They are only humans who live and die like
the grass.
13I, the LORD, am the one who made you.
With my power I made the earth
and spread the sky over the earth.
But you have forgotten me,
so you are always afraid that angry men will
hurt you.
Those men planned to destroy you,
but where are they now?

14"People in prison will soon be made free.
They will not die and rot in prison.
They will have plenty of food.
15"I am the LORD your God,
the one who stirs up the sea and makes the
waves roar."
The LORD All-Powerful is his name.

---

a 51:9 Rahab . . . Dragon This is Rahab the great sea monster. Some ancient stories tell about Rahab fighting with God.

[16]"My servant, I gave you the words I want you to say, and I covered you with my hands to protect you. I did this to make a new heaven and earth and so that you would say to Israel, 'You are my people.'"

God Punished Israel

[17]Wake up! Wake up!
  Jerusalem, get up!
The LORD was very angry with you.
  So you were punished.
It was like a cup of poison you had to drink,
  and you drank it all.

[18]Jerusalem had many people, but none of them became leaders for her. None of the children she raised became guides to lead her. [19]Troubles came to you, Jerusalem, in pairs: Your land was destroyed and lies in ruins, and your people suffered from famine and war.

But no one felt sorry for you or showed you mercy. [20]Your people became weak. They fell on the ground and lay there. They were lying on every street corner, like animals caught in a net. They were punished by the LORD's anger until they could not accept any more punishment. When God said he would give them more punishment, they became very weak.

[21]Listen to me, poor Jerusalem. You are weak like a drunk, but you are not drunk from wine. You are weak ⌊from that "cup of poison"⌋.

[22]Your God is the one who fights for his people. He is your Lord GOD, and he says to you, "Look, I am taking this 'cup of poison' away from you. It is full of my anger, and I am taking it out of your hand. You will not be punished by my anger again. [23]I will now use my anger to punish the people who hurt you. They tried to kill you. They told you, 'Bow down before us, and we will walk on you.' They forced you to bow down before them, and then they walked on your back. You were like a road for them to walk on."

Israel Will Be Saved

52 Wake up! Wake up!
  Zion, clothe yourself with strength.
Holy city of Jerusalem, stand up
  and put on your beautiful clothes!
  Those filthy foreigners[a] will not enter you
    again.

[2]Jerusalem, get up and shake off the dust!
  City of Zion,[b] you were a prisoner,
    but take the chains off your neck.
[3]The LORD says,
  "You were not sold for money.
  So I will not use money to set you free."

[4]The Lord GOD says, "First, my people went down to Egypt and became slaves. Then Assyria made them slaves. [5]Now look what has happened. Another nation has taken my people," says the LORD. "That country did not pay to take my people, but they rule over them and laugh at them, and they say bad things about me all the time." The LORD is the one saying these things.

[6]"This happened so that my people will learn about me. My people will know who I am. My people will know my name, and they will know that I Am He[c] is speaking to them."

[7]How wonderful it is to see someone coming over the hills to tell good news. How wonderful to hear him announce, "There is peace! We have been saved!" and to hear him say to Zion, "Your God is the king!"

[8]The city guards[d] are shouting.
  They are all rejoicing together.
  They can all see the LORD returning to Zion.

[9]Ruins of Jerusalem, be happy again!
  Rejoice because the LORD
    comforted his people and set Jerusalem free.
[10]The LORD showed his holy strength to all the
    nations.
  All the faraway countries saw how God
    saved his people.

[11]So leave Babylon!
  Leave that place!
Priests, you carry the things that belong to
    the LORD.
  So make yourselves pure.
  Don't touch anything that is not pure.
[12]You will leave Babylon,
  but they will not force you to leave in a
    hurry.
  You will not be forced to run away.
The LORD will be in front of you.
  The God of Israel will be behind you.[e]

---

[a] **52:1** *filthy foreigners* Or "unclean men that have not been circumcised".

[b] **52:2** *City of Zion* Literally, "Daughter Zion". See "ZION" in the Word List.

[c] **52:6** *I Am He* This is like YAHWEH, the Hebrew name for God. It shows that God lives forever, and that he is always with his people. See Exod. 3:13–17.

[d] **52:8** *guards* Men who stand on the city walls and watch for messengers or trouble coming to the city. Here, this probably means the prophets.

[e] **52:12** *The LORD . . . behind you* This shows that God will protect his people. Compare Exod. 14:19,20.

A SNEAK PREVIEW OF JESUS

"Wait a minute . . . I thought I was reading the Old Testament! This sounds a lot like the Gospels to me!"

What you have to understand about the Bible is its unity. Who but God could have created such a flawlessly constructed book, over such a long period of time, which fits together so perfectly? Jesus is the hero of the whole Bible so it's not surprising he should show up in Isaiah.

DIG IN

READ Isaiah 52:13 – 53:12

- What is this servant from God being sent to do (53:4–5)?
- What did the people think of him (53:2–3)?
- How was he treated (53:7–9)?

Isaiah gives us a picture of a man who would come and suffer greatly for the sake of others. He would be badly treated, mocked and misunderstood. Eventually he would die, taking punishment which was not meant for him, but for others.

But he was also going to be honoured and people would be amazed by him. God would be pleased with him.

This is clearly a "sneak preview" of Jesus, foretelling with remarkable accuracy what Jesus would go through in the last days of his life on earth. It's amazing to think that, writing more than 500 years before Jesus was born, Isaiah would get such a clear and detailed picture of Jesus.

- What details from Jesus' life do you recognize in this prophecy?
- What is given as the reason for the servant's suffering (v.5)?

In Isaiah, God is going public with the news that he is going to save his people. But despite what they might have thought, this was not going to come by force.

The saving they needed was of a different kind. Their sin, shame and guilt needed to be dealt with by a holy God; all the punishment that was in store for Israel for their repeated sin still had to be poured out. But it was going to be poured out on this man instead – he would be "put to death for the sins of his people" (53:8).

DIG THROUGH

- How many aspects of Jesus did you spot in Isaiah's description of him? You will be amazed to read how many of the details of this prophecy are fulfilled in Jesus' life, such as Matthew 8:14–17 (healing others) and even quite minor details like Matthew 26:63 (staying silent) and Matthew 27:57–60 (his grave).
- How do you cope with criticism? For most of us, serious persecution for our faith is unlikely but open criticism can be common. Peter refers to this part of Isaiah to encourage Christians to be patient under persecution (1 Peter 2). How can we learn from it?

DIG DEEPER

- Isaiah is probably the most quoted of all the prophets in the New Testament. Dramatically, Jesus starts his own ministry with a public reading of Isaiah 61:1–2. Check out Luke 4:16–21.

God's Suffering Servant

¹³The Lord says, "Look, my servant will succeed in what he has to do, and he will be raised to a position of high honour. ¹⁴Many people were shocked when they saw him. He was beaten so badly that they could hardly recognize him as a man. ¹⁵But it is also true that many nations will be amazed at him. Kings will look at him and be unable to speak. They will see what they had never been told. They will understand what they had never heard."ᵃ

53 Who really believed what we heard? Who saw in it the LORD's great power?ᵇ ²He was always close to the Lord. He grew up like a young plant, like a root growing in dry ground. There was nothing special or impressive about the way he looked, nothing we could see that would cause us to like him. ³People made fun of him, and even his friends left him. He was a man who suffered a lot of pain and sickness. We treated him like someone of no importance, like someone people will not even look at but turn away from in disgust.

⁴The fact is, it was our suffering he took on himself; he bore our pain. But we thought that God was punishing him, that God was beating him for something he did. ⁵But he was being punished for what we did. He was crushed because of our guilt. He took the punishment we deserved, and this brought us peace. We were healed because of his pain. ⁶We had all wandered away like sheep. We had gone our own way. And yet the LORD put all our guilt on him.

⁷He was treated badly, but he never protested. He said nothing, like a lamb being led away to be killed. He was like a sheep that makes no sound as its wool is being cut off. He never opened his mouth to defend himself. ⁸He was taken away by force and judged unfairly. The people of his time did not even notice that he was killed.ᶜ But he was put to deathᵈ for the sins of hisᵉ people. ⁹He had done no wrong to anyone. He had never even told a lie. But he was buried among the wicked. His tomb was with the rich.

¹⁰But the LORD was pleased with this humble servant who suffered such pain.ᶠ Even after giving himself as an offering for sin, he will see his descendants and enjoy a long life. He will succeed in doing what the LORD wanted. ¹¹After his suffering he will see the light,ᵍ and he will be satisfied with what he experienced.

The Lord says, "My servant, who always does what is right, will make his people right with me; he will take away their sins. ¹²For this reason, I will treat him as one of my great people. I will give him the rewards of one who wins in battle, and he will share them with his powerful ones. I will do this because he gave his life for the people. He was considered a criminal, but the truth is, he carried away the sins of many. Now he will stand before me and speak for those who have sinned."

God Brings His People Home

54 "Woman without children, be happy! You never gave birth to a child, but you should sing and shout for joy.

"Yes, the woman who is aloneʰ
    will have more children than the woman
        with a husband."
This is what the LORD says.

²"Make your tent bigger.
    Open your doors wide.
    Don't think small!
Make your tent large and strong,
³   because you will grow in all directions.
Your children will take over many nations
    and live in the cities that were destroyed.
⁴Don't be afraid!
    You will not be disappointed.
People will not say bad things against you.
    You will not be embarrassed.
When you were young, you felt shame.
    But you will forget that shame now.
You will not remember the shame you felt
    when you lost your husband.ⁱ
⁵Your real husband is the one who made you.
    His name is the LORD All-Powerful.

ᵃ **52:15 They will see . . . heard** Or "Those who were not told the message saw what happened. Those who did not hear understood."

ᵇ **53:1 Who . . . power** Or "Upon whom was the arm of the Lord revealed?" This could mean, "Who received the punishment from the Lord?"

ᶜ **53:8 The people . . . killed** Or "There is no story about his descendants, because he was taken from the land of the living."

ᵈ **53:8 put to death** Or "punished".

ᵉ **53:8 his** This is the reading in a Hebrew copy among the Dead Sea Scrolls. The standard Hebrew text has "my".

ᶠ **53:10 But the LORD . . . such pain** Or "The LORD decided to crush him. He decided that he must suffer."

ᵍ **53:11 the light** This is found in some Hebrew scrolls from Qumran and the ancient Greek version. Light is often used as a symbol for life.

ʰ **54:1 Yes, the woman . . . alone** This Hebrew word is like the word "destroyed". This probably means "Jerusalem, the city that is destroyed."

ⁱ **54:4 husband** In Hebrew this word is like the name Baal. This means that the LORD is Jerusalem's true God, not the false god Baal.

The Holy One of Israel is your Saviour,[a]
and he is the God of all the earth!

6"Like a woman whose husband has left her,
you were very sad,
like a young wife left all alone.
But the LORD has called you back to him."
This is what your God says.

7"For a short time I turned away from you,
but with all my love I will welcome you
again.

8I was so angry that for a while I did not want
to see you.
But now I want to comfort you with
kindness forever."
The LORD your Saviour said this.

9"Remember, in Noah's time I punished the
world with the flood.
But I made a promise to Noah that I would
never again destroy the world with water.
In the same way, I promise that I will never
again be angry with you
and say bad things to you.

10"The mountains may disappear,
and the hills may become dust,
but my faithful love will never leave you.
I will make peace with you,
and it will never end."
The LORD who loves you said this.

11"You poor city!
Enemies came against you like storms,
and no one comforted you.
But I will rebuild you.
I will use a beautiful mortar to lay the
stones of your walls.
I will use sapphire stones when I lay the
foundation.

12The stones on top of the wall will be made
from rubies.
I will use shiny jewels for the gates.
I will use precious stones to build the walls
around you.

13I, the LORD, will teach your children,
and they will have real peace.

14You will be built on goodness.
You will be safe from cruelty and fear.
So you will have nothing to fear.
Nothing will come to hurt you.

15I will never send anyone to attack you.
And if any army tries to attack you, you will
defeat them.

16"Look, I made the blacksmith. He blows on the
fire to make it hotter. Then he takes the hot iron and
makes the kind of tool he wants to make. In the
same way, I made the 'destroyer' to destroy things.

17"People will make weapons to fight against
you, but their weapons will not defeat you. Some
people will say things against you, but anyone
who speaks against you will be proved wrong.
This is how I will defend my servants! They have
this blessing[b] from me, their LORD." The LORD
himself said this.

God Gives "Food" That Really Satisfies

55 "All you people who are thirsty, come!
Here is water for you to drink.
Don't worry if you have no money.
Come, eat and drink until you are full!
You don't need money.
The milk and wine are free.

2Why waste your money on something that is
not real food?
Why should you work for something that
does not really satisfy you?
Listen closely to me and you will eat what is
good.
You will enjoy the food that satisfies your
soul.

3Listen closely to what I say.
Listen to me so that you will live.
I will make an agreement with you that will
last forever.
It will be an agreement you can trust,
like the one I made with David:
a promise to love him and be loyal to him
forever.

4I made David a witness of my power for all
nations.
I promised him that he would become a
ruler and commander of many nations."

5There are nations in places you don't know,
but you will call for them to come.
They don't know you,
but they will run to you.
This will happen because the LORD, your God,
wants it.
It will happen because the Holy One of
Israel honours you.

6So you should look for the LORD
before it is too late.
You should call to him now,
while he is near.

7Evil people should stop living evil lives.
They should stop thinking bad thoughts.

---

[a] **54:5** *Saviour* Or "Protector", someone who cared for and protected the family of a dead relative. Often this person bought back
(redeemed) the poor relatives from slavery, making them free again.
[b] **54:17** *blessing* Or "victory".

They should come to the LORD again,
and he will comfort them.
They should come to our God
because he will freely forgive them.

People Cannot Understand God

8The LORD says, "My thoughts are not like yours.
Your ways are not like mine.
9Just as the heavens are higher than the earth,
so my ways are higher than your ways,
and my thoughts are higher than your
thoughts.

10"Rain and snow fall from the sky
and don't return until they have watered
the ground.
Then the ground causes the plants to sprout
and grow,
and they produce seeds for the farmer and
food for people to eat.
11In the same way, my words leave my mouth,
and they don't come back without results.
My words make the things happen that I want
to happen.
They succeed in doing what I send them
to do.

12"So you will go out from there with joy.
You will be led out in peace.
When you come to the mountains and hills,
they will begin singing.
All the trees in the fields will clap their hands.
13Large cypress trees will grow where there
were thornbushes.
Myrtle trees will grow where there were
weeds.
All this will happen to make the LORD known,
to be a permanent reminder of his goodness
and power."

All Nations Will Follow the LORD

56 This is what the LORD says: "Be fair to all
people. Do what is right, because soon my
salvation will come to you. My goodness will
soon be shown to the whole world. 2I will bless
those who refuse to do wrong and who obey the
law about the Sabbath."

3Foreigners who follow the LORD should not
say, "The LORD will not accept me like the rest of
his people." A eunuch should not say, "Without
children I am like a dead tree."

4To these people the LORD says, "Some eunuchs
choose to do what I want. They obey the laws

about the Sabbath, and they follow my agreement.*a*
5So I will put a memorial in my Temple with their
names on it so that they will be remembered in
my city! Yes, I will give them something better
than sons and daughters. I will give them a name
that will last forever! They will not be cut off*b* from
my people.

6"And some foreigners choose to follow me,
the LORD. They love me and want to serve me.
They keep the Sabbath as a special day, and they
follow my agreement carefully. 7So I will bring
them to my holy mountain and make them happy
in my house of prayer. The offerings and sacrifices
they give me will please me. And my Temple will
be called a house of prayer for all nations. 8I am the
Lord GOD who brought my people Israel back
home after they were taken away. And there are
others I will gather to join with my people!"

9Wild animals in the forest,
come and eat.
10The watchmen*c* are all blind.
They don't know what they are doing.
They are like dogs that will not bark.
They lie on the ground and sleep.
Oh, they love to sleep.
11They are like hungry dogs.
They are never satisfied.
The shepherds don't know what they are doing.
Like their sheep, they have all wandered
away.
They are greedy.
All they want is to satisfy themselves.
12They say, "I will drink some wine.
I will drink some beer.
I will do the same thing tomorrow,
but I will drink even more."

Israel Does Not Follow God

57 All the good people are gone,
and no one even noticed.
The loyal followers were gathered up,
but no one knows why.

The reason they were gathered up
is that trouble is coming.
2But peace will come too,
and those who trust him will get to rest in
their own beds.

3"Come here, you children of witches.
Your father committed adultery,
and your mother was unfaithful.

---

a **56:4** *agreement* This usually means the agreement God made with Israel through Moses. (See "AGREEMENT" in the Word List.)
Here, it might mean the agreement of Isa. 55:3.
b **56:5** *cut off* To be removed from the list of the people of Israel. This included a person's being forced to leave family, land and
the people of Israel.
c **56:10** *The watchmen* Literally, "The seers," an ancient title for prophets.

⁴You are children out of control, full of lies.
  You make fun of me.
You make faces
  and stick out your tongue at me.ᵃ
⁵All you want is to worship false gods
  under every green tree.
You kill children by every stream
  and sacrifice them in the rocky places.
⁶You have chosen the smooth rocks in the
    rivers to be your gods.
  You offer them wine and grain to worship
    them.
And those rocks are all you will ever have.
  You give me no choice but to punish you!
⁷You make your bed on every hill and high
    mountain.ᵇ
  You go up to those places and offer
    sacrifices.
⁸You hide the things that help you remember
    me
  behind the doors and doorframes.ᶜ
You were with me,
  but you got up to go to them.
You spread out your bed
  and gave yourself to them.ᵈ
You love their beds
  and enjoy looking at their naked bodies.ᵉ
⁹You use your oils and perfumes
  to look nice for Molech.
You sent your messengers to faraway lands,
  and this will bring you down to the place of
    death.ᶠ
¹⁰All of them made you tired,
  but you never gave up.
You found new strength,
  because you enjoyed them.
¹¹You did not remember me.
  You did not even notice me!
So who were you worrying about?
  Who were you afraid of?
  Why did you lie?
Look, I have been quiet for a long time.
  Is that why you didn't honour me?
¹²I could tell about your 'good works' and all
    the 'religious' things you do,
  but that will not help you.
¹³When you need help,
  you cry to those false gods that you have
    gathered around you.

Let them help you!
But I tell you, the wind will blow them all
    away.
  A puff of wind will blow them all away.
But the one who depends on me
  will get the land I promised
  and enjoy my holy mountain."ᵍ

The LORD Will Save His People

¹⁴Clear the road! Clear the road!
  Make the way clear for my people!

¹⁵God is high and lifted up.
  He lives forever.
  His name is holy.
He says, "I live in a high and holy place,
  but I also live with people who are humble
    and sorry for their sins.
I will give new life to those who are humble
    in spirit.
I will give new life to those who are sorry
    for their sins.
¹⁶I will not accuse my people forever.
  I will not always be angry.
If I continued to show my anger,
  then the human spirit, the life I gave them,
    would die before me.
¹⁷Israel's evil greed made me angry,
  so I punished them.
I turned away from them
  because I was angry.
But they continued to do wrong.
  They did whatever they wanted.
¹⁸I have seen their way of life, but I will heal
    them.
  I will guide and comfort them and those
    who mourn for them.
¹⁹I will teach them a new word: peace.
  I will give peace to those who are near and
    to those who are far away.
I will heal them."
  The LORD himself said this.

²⁰But evil people are like the angry ocean.
  They cannot be quiet and peaceful.
They are angry, and like the ocean,
  they stir up mud.
²¹My God says,
  "There is no peace for evil people."

ᵃ **57:4 make faces . . . at me** This probably refers to the god Bel, which is usually shown making a face and sticking out his tongue.
ᵇ **57:7 every hill and high mountain** The people worshipped false gods in these places. The people thought these false gods would give them good crops and more children.
ᶜ **57:8 doorframes** The Israelites were supposed to put special things on their doorframes to help them remember God. See Deut. 6:9.
ᵈ **57:8 gave yourself to them** Or "and made agreements with them".
ᵉ **57:8 naked bodies** This is a wordplay. The Hebrew word also means "memorial", as in Isa. 56:5.
ᶠ **57:9 this will . . . death** Or "You even send them down to Sheol."
ᵍ **57:13 holy mountain** Mount Zion, one of the mountains Jerusalem was built on.

People Must Be Told to Follow God

58 "Shout as loud as you can and don't stop. Shout like a trumpet!
Tell the people what they did wrong.
  Tell the family of Jacob about their sins.
²They still come every day to worship me,
  acting as if they want to learn my ways.
They pretend to be a nation that does what is right
  and obeys the commands of their God.
They ask me to judge them fairly.
  They want their God to be near them.

³"They say, 'We fast to show honour to you. Why don't you see us? We starve our bodies to show honour to you. Why don't you notice us?'"
But God says, "You do things to please yourselves on those special days of fasting. And you punish your servants, not your own bodies. ⁴You are hungry, but not for food. You are hungry for arguing and fighting, not for bread. You are hungry to hit people with your evil hands. This is not the way to fast if you want your prayers to be heard in heaven! ⁵Do you think I want to see people punish their bodies on those days of fasting? Do you think I want people to look sad and bow their heads like dead plants? Do you think I want people to wear mourning clothes and sit in ashes to show their sadness? That is what you do on your days of fasting. Do you think that is what the LORD wants?

⁶"I will tell you the kind of day I want: a day to set people free. I want a day when you take the burdens from others. I want a day when you set troubled people free and you take the burdens from their shoulders. ⁷I want you to share your food with the hungry. I want you to find the poor who don't have homes and bring them into your own homes. When you see people who have no clothes, give them your clothes! Don't hide from your relatives when they need help."

⁸If you do these things, your light will begin to shine like the light of dawn. Then your wounds will heal. Your "Goodness" will walk in front of you, and the Glory of the LORD will come following behind you. ⁹Then you will call to the LORD, and he will answer you. You will cry out to him, and he will say, "Here I am."

Stop saying things to hurt people or accusing them of doing things they didn't do. ¹⁰Feel sorry for hungry people and give them food. Help those who are troubled and satisfy their needs. Then your light will shine in the darkness. You will be like the bright sunshine at noon.

¹¹The LORD will always lead you and satisfy your needs in dry lands. He will give strength to your bones. You will be like a garden that has plenty of water, like a spring that never goes dry.

¹²You will rebuild the cities that have been in ruins for so long. You will build on their ancient foundations. You will be famous for repairing the walls, for furnishing the empty streets with houses.

¹³"But you must stop breaking God's law about the Sabbath. Stop doing things to please yourself on that special day. It should be a day you honour as special to the LORD, a day that you enjoy. You can honour it by not going your own way, by not doing or saying whatever you please. ¹⁴Then you will find joy in knowing your LORD. I will give you the highest honour and let you enjoy the land I promised your ancestor Jacob. I, the LORD, am the one telling you this."

Evil People Should Change Their Lives

59 Look, the LORD's power is enough to save you. He can hear you when you ask him for help. ²It is your sins that separate you from your God. He turns away from you when he sees them. ³That's because your hands are covered with blood from the people you murdered. You tell lies and say evil things. ⁴You can't be trusted, even in court. You lie about each other and depend on false arguments to win your cases. You create pain and produce wickedness. ⁵You hatch evil, like eggs from a poisonous snake. Anyone who eats the eggs will die. And if you break one of them open, a poisonous snake will come out.

Your lies are like spiders' webs. ⁶They cannot be used for clothes, and you cannot cover yourself with them.

Your hands are always busy sinning and hurting others. ⁷Your feet run towards evil. You are always ready to kill innocent people. You think of nothing but evil. Everywhere you go you cause trouble and ruin. ⁸You don't know how to live in peace. You don't do what is right and fair. You are crooked, and anyone who lives like that will never know true peace.

Israel's Sin Brings Trouble

⁹All fairness and goodness has gone.
  There is only darkness around us,
    so we must wait for the light.
  We hope for a bright light,
    but all we have is darkness.
¹⁰We are like people without eyes.
    We walk into walls like blind people.
  We stumble and fall as if it was night.
    Even in the daylight, we cannot see.
    At noontime, we fall like dead men.
¹¹We are always complaining;
    we growl like bears and moan like doves.
  We are waiting for justice,
    but there is none.
  We are waiting to be saved,
    but salvation is still far away.

¹²That's because we committed crimes against
    our God.
    Our own sins speak out against us.
We know we are guilty.
    We know we have sinned.
¹³We rebelled against the LORD
    and lied to him.
We turned away from our God
    and left him.
We planned to hurt others
    and to rebel against God.
From hearts filled with lies,
    we talked about it and made our plans.
¹⁴We pushed Justice away.
    Fairness stands off in the distance.
Truth has fallen in the streets.
    Goodness is not allowed in the city.
¹⁵Loyalty has gone,
    and people who try to do good are robbed.

The LORD looked and saw there was no
    justice.
    He did not like what he saw.
¹⁶He did not see anyone speak up for the
    people.
    He was shocked to see that no one stood up
    for them.
So with his own power he saved them.
    His desire to do what is right gave him
    strength.
¹⁷He put on the armour of goodness,
    the helmet of salvation,
the uniform of punishment,
    and the coat of strong love.
¹⁸He will give his enemies the punishment they
    deserve.
    They will feel his anger.
He will punish all his enemies.
    People along the coast will get the
    punishment they deserve.
¹⁹People from the west to the east will fear
    the LORD
    and respect his Glory.
He will come quickly, like a fast-flowing river
    driven by a wind from the LORD.

²⁰This is what the LORD has decided:
    "A saviour[a] will come to Zion
    to save the people of Jacob who have
    turned away from sin."

²¹The LORD says, "As for me, this is the agreement that I will make with these people. I promise
that my Spirit which that I put on you and my
words that I put in your mouth will never leave

you. They will be with you and your children and
your children's children, for now and forever.

God Is Coming

60 "Jerusalem, get up and shine![b]
    Your Light is coming!
    The Glory of the LORD will shine on you.
²Darkness now covers the earth,
    and the people are in darkness.
But the LORD will shine on you,
    and his Glory will appear over you.
³Then the nations will come to your light.
    Kings will come to your bright sunrise.
⁴Look around you!
    See all the people gathering around.
Those are your sons coming from far away,
    and your daughters are there beside them.

⁵"At that time you will see your people,
    and your faces will shine with happiness.
First, you will be afraid,
    but then you will be excited.
All the riches from across the seas will be set
    before you.
    The riches of the nations will come to you.
⁶Herds of camels from Midian and Ephah
    will cross your land.
Long lines of camels will come from Sheba.
    They will bring gold and incense.
    People will sing praises to the LORD.
⁷People will collect all the sheep from Kedar
    and give them to you.
    They will bring you rams from Nebaioth.
You will offer those animals on my altar,
    and I will accept them.
I will make my wonderful Temple
    even more beautiful.
⁸Look at the people.
    They are rushing towards you like clouds
    quickly crossing the sky.
    They are like doves flying to their nests.
⁹The faraway lands are waiting for me.
    The great cargo ships are ready to sail.
They are ready to bring your children from
    faraway lands.
    They will bring silver and gold with them
to honour the LORD your God, the Holy One
    of Israel.
    He has done wonderful things for you.
¹⁰Children from other lands will rebuild your
    walls.
    Their kings will serve you.

"When I was angry, I hurt you,
    but now I want to be kind to you.

---

[a] **59:20 saviour** Literally "redeemer", someone who frees prisoners or slaves by paying the price for their freedom.
[b] **60:1 Jerusalem . . . shine** Or "Jerusalem, my light, get up!"

SPIRITUAL GIFTS

WHEN the Holy Spirit came, in Acts 2, the new believers discovered that they had been given some amazing supernatural gifts to help them convince people Jesus was alive. We can read about some of these spiritual gifts in Acts and in Paul's letters. Take a look at 1 Corinthians 12:8–11:

Wisdom (v.8): Solomon asked God for the gift of wisdom in Old Testament times (1 Kings 3:9) and we get to see how God answered his prayer soon after (vv.16–28). The Holy Spirit gave the early Church similar gifts of wisdom – indeed James encourages his readers to ask for them (James 1:5).

Knowledge (v.8): In the Gospels, Jesus frequently had supernatural insight into people's lives – the woman at the well for example (John 4:16–19). He didn't do it to show off; he did it to prove who he was and to show his compassion. In Acts 5:3, Peter has a similar amazing insight through the Holy Spirit.

Faith (v.9): This is a special gift of faith to believe that God can change otherwise

> ## THE HOLY SPIRIT IS STILL AT WORK IN US TODAY AND THE BIBLE SAYS WE SHOULD USE THE MANY DIFFERENT GIFTS WE HAVE BEEN GIVEN.

impossible situations. Jesus demonstrated this powerfully when he raised Lazarus from the dead (John 11:38–44). The book of Acts is a long list of amazing acts of faith in the power of the Spirit.

Healing and Miracles (vv.9–10): The disciples continued Jesus' ministry of healing the sick

and performing miracles in the power of the Holy Spirit. At one point in the book of Acts, Peter and the disciples are seeing all those that are brought to them healed (Acts 5:16).

Prophecy and Discernment (v.10): Much of the Bible is a work of prophecy – people speaking and writing down what God has revealed to them. So it's no surprise that the Holy Spirit continued to reveal God's heart to individuals to encourage and build up the Church as it grew.

Languages and Interpretation (v.10): God gave the Church a new gift at Pentecost (Acts 2) – the ability to pray and praise God in languages other than their own. Sometimes this was in recognizable earthly languages (2:6–11), sometimes it was in unique heavenly languages. When spoken in public, God also gave the gift of an interpretation so people could understand what was being prayed.

The Holy Spirit is still at work in us today and the Bible says we should use the many different gifts we have been given to serve each other and bring glory to Jesus (1 Peter 4:10–11). That means you too! ←

THE CHURCH

"CHURCH" is just a little word, but it's one that conjures up many different images in people's minds . . . a historical old building, the Salvation Army singing hymns on the streets, a family fun day in the park, old ladies having a coffee morning, people singing and jumping . . . and that's just in the UK. What about applying that amazing word to the rest of the world? Then you've got to add images of American evangelists preaching on TV; African congregations singing and dancing in villages; giant prayer gatherings in Korea; persecuted Christians meeting secretly in the Middle East . . . the list goes on. There are literally millions of expressions of "church" across the globe, each as different as the Christians that make them up.

We can read a lot about the Church in the New Testament. Jesus said, "'I will build my church on this rock. The power of death will not be able to defeat my church'" (Matthew 16:18). Later we read that "Christ loved the church and gave his life for it" (Ephesians 5:25) – that's how much it matters. God's plan for the world is the Church. You might hear stuff in the media about how the Church is on the decline or saying that the new religion is shopping or football or whatever, but don't believe a word of it. A quick search on the Internet will show you that today there are more Christians in the world than ever before; the Church is growing, thousands become Christians every day and, even now, people are prepared to die for their faith. You are part of that!

It might not always feel that dynamic and your local church might seem insignificant or full of people in dodgy jumpers with funny teeth. But God is as excited about the Church solution for the earth; *you* are seeing thousands saved; *you* are feeding the poor and protecting the persecuted; *you* are standing up for the marginalized; *you* are praying without ceasing; *you* are caring for orphans; *you* are presenting your case before politicians; *you* are calling business leaders to account; *you* are creating new songs of heaven; *you* are persecuted but not crushed; *you* are in prison and yet still free; *you* are worshipping with your whole being; *you* are

STEP UP AND TAKE YOUR PLACE IN THIS AMAZING, GLOBAL, REVOLUTIONARY, GROWING MOVEMENT THAT WE CALL THE CHURCH.

as a husband is about his new bride! So get thinking about how you can make your church the most beautiful bride ever! Read the book of Acts and find out about the kinds of things the Church did when it was starting out, just after Jesus walked on the earth . . . perhaps you can help your church become more like that. The world around us is desperate for the Church to be everything it is supposed to be; desperate for our worship to be more than just songs, but also to be loving and serving the people around us.

So next time you are sitting in church, remember that church is not just *your* church, it's the global Church and that church is not just an organization, it's *you: you* are God's

"Jesus with skin on" to your community, your family, your school, your city, your world. Step up and take your place in this amazing, global, revolutionary, growing movement that we call the Church. ←

Pray this prayer if you agree:

Lord Jesus, help me to be an incredible, useful, passionate member of your bride, the Church. Help me to see the Church through your eyes and to serve, give, love and participate as if you were physically there as part of my church. Help me make your Church look more like you.

Amen

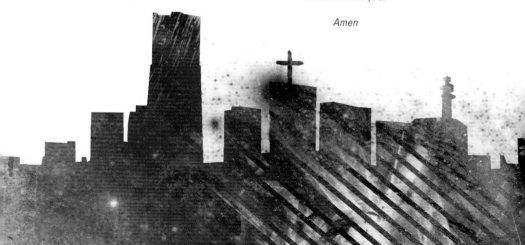

FOLLOWING JESUS

THE GAME of cricket is a mystery to some and an absolute passion to others. What on earth is the strangely named "silly mid-wicket", a "square leg" or a "googly"? These and lots of other secrets are only made known to those who love the game of cricket and are keen enough to find out. Even football, which may seem a far simpler game than cricket, has its hidden depths. How many of the millions who sit in the stadiums understand the "offside rule" or know what a "flat back 4" or the "spine" of a team is? Anyone, of course, can play the games, but if you want to be exceptional, you need to know this stuff.

Jesus spent a lot of time teaching his followers (a very ordinary bunch of guys) by example about the things of God. He tells them, in Matthew 13, that they have been chosen to "know the secret truths about God's kingdom" – not about some game or other, but about the very "kingdom of heaven". Those words of course were not just for his followers back

WE'LL FIND THAT WE BECOME MORE AND MORE IN TUNE WITH HIM AND THAT HE GIVES US EYES TO SEE AND EARS TO HEAR WHAT FOLLOWING JESUS IS ALL ABOUT.

then but are for us as well, more than two thousand years later. As we follow Jesus and put in the effort required in terms of prayer, Bible study, spending time with other Christians and telling our friends about Jesus, we'll find that we become more and more in tune with him and that he gives us eyes to see and ears to hear what following Jesus is all about.

To find out more read Matthew 28:16–20; Romans 12:1–16; Colossians 3:1–10. ←

So I will comfort you.
[11]Your gates will always be open.
They will not be closed, day or night.
They will welcome the nations bringing their
wealth,
with their kings being led in a victory
parade.
[12]Any nation or kingdom that does not serve
you will die.
It will be completely destroyed.
[13]All the great things of Lebanon will be given
to you.
People will bring pine, fir and cypress trees
to you.
These trees will be used for timber
to make my Holy Place[a] more beautiful.
This place is like a stool in front of my throne,
and I will honour it.[b]
[14]In the past, people hurt you,
but they will bow down before you.
In the past, people hated you,
but they will bow down at your feet.
They will call you 'The City of the LORD',
'Zion of the Holy One of Israel'.

[15]"People hated you.
You were left all alone with no one passing
through.
But I will make you great from now on.
You will be happy for ever and ever.
[16]Nations will give you what you need,
like a child drinking milk from its mother.
But you will 'drink' riches from kings.
Then you will know that I, the LORD, am
the one who saves you.
I, the Mighty God of Israel, am the one who
protects you.

[17]"I will replace your copper with gold
and your iron with silver.
I will replace your wood with copper
and your rocks with iron.
Your new ruler will be peace.
Your new leader will be justice.
[18]There will be no more news of violence in
your country.
People will never again attack your country
and steal from you.
You will name your walls, 'Salvation'
and your gates, 'Praise'.

[19]"The sun will no longer be your light during
the day.

The light from the moon will no longer be
your light at night.
The LORD will be your light forever.
Your God will be your glory.
[20]Your sun will never go down again.
Your moon will never again be dark.
That's because the LORD will be your light
forever,
and the dark days of mourning will end.

[21]"All your people will be good.
They will get the land forever.
They are the young plant in my garden[c]
that will grow to be a wonderful tree.
I made them with my own hands.[d]
[22]The smallest family will become a large family
group.
The smallest tribe will become a powerful
nation.
When the time is right,
I, the LORD, will come quickly.
I will make these things happen."

The LORD's Message of Freedom

61 The Spirit of the Lord GOD is on me. The
LORD has chosen me to tell good news to
the poor and to comfort those who are sad. He
sent me to tell the captives and prisoners that
they have been set free. [2]He sent me to announce
that the time has come for the LORD to show his
kindness, when our God will also punish evil
people. He has sent me to comfort those who are
sad, [3]those in Zion who mourn. I will take away
the ashes on their head, and I will give them a
crown. I will take away their sadness, and I will
give them the oil of happiness. I will take away
their sorrow, and I will give them celebration
clothes. He sent me to name them "Good Trees"
and "The LORD's Wonderful Plant".

[4]Then the old cities that were destroyed will
be rebuilt. Those ancient ruins will be made new,
as they were in the beginning.

[5]Then your enemies will come to care for your
sheep, and their children will work in your fields
and in your gardens. [6]You will be called, "The
LORD's Priests", "The Servants of our God". You
will be proud of all the riches that have come to
you from all the nations on earth.

[7]In the past, other people shamed you and
said bad things to you. You were shamed much
more than any other people. So in your land you
will get twice as much as other people. You will
get the joy that continues forever.

---

[a] **60:13** *my Holy Place* This probably means the Temple in Jerusalem.
[b] **60:13** *I will honour it* Or "I will give it glory."
[c] **60:21** *young plant . . . garden* See Isa. 4:1 and 5:7.
[d] **60:21** *They are . . . hands* Or "They are the plant I planted, which I made with my own hands, to show how wonderful I am."

8"I am the LORD and I love justice. I hate stealing and everything that is wrong. So I will give the people what they deserve. I will make an agreement with my people forever. 9Their descendants will be known throughout the earth, and everyone will know their children. Whoever sees them will know that the LORD has blessed them."

God's Servant Brings Salvation

10The LORD makes me very happy.
    I am completely happy with my God.
He dressed me in the clothes of salvation.
    He put the victory coat on me.
I look like a man dressed for his wedding,
    like a bride covered with jewels.
11The earth causes plants to grow,
    and a garden makes the seeds planted there
        rise up.
In the same way, the Lord GOD will make
        goodness and praise
    grow throughout the nations.

New Jerusalem: A City Full of Goodness

62 I love Zion,
    so I will continue to speak for her.
I love Jerusalem,
    so I will not stop speaking.
I will speak until goodness*a* shines like a
        bright light,
    until salvation burns bright like a flame.
2Then all nations will see your goodness.
    All kings will see your honour.
Then you will have a new name
    that the LORD himself will give you.
3You will be like a beautiful crown that the
    LORD holds up,
    like a king's crown in the hand of your
        God.
4You will never again be called "The People
    God Left".
    Your land will never again be called
        "The Land God Destroyed".
You will be called "The People God Loves".
    Your land will be called "God's Bride",
because the LORD loves you,
    and your land will be his.*b*
5As a young man takes a bride and she belongs
        to him,
    so your land will belong to your
        children.*c*
As a man is happy with his new wife,
    so your God will be happy with you.

6Jerusalem, I put guards on your walls.
    They will not be silent.
    They will keep praying day and
        night.

Guards, keep praying to the LORD.
    Remind him of his promise.
    Don't ever stop praying.
7Don't give him any rest until he rebuilds
    Jerusalem
    and makes it a place that everyone on earth
        will praise.

8The LORD made a promise and guaranteed it
    by his own power.
    And he will use that power to keep his
        promise.
The Lord said, "I promise that I will never
    again give your food to your enemies.
    I promise that they will never again take the
        wine you make.
9Whoever gathers the food will eat it and praise
    the LORD.
    Whoever gathers the grape will drink the
        wine in the courtyards of my Temple."

10Come through the gates!
    Clear the way for the people!
Prepare the road!
    Move all the stones off the road!
Raise a flag as a sign for the nations!

11Listen, the LORD is speaking
    to all the faraway lands:
"Tell the people of Zion,
    'Look, your Saviour is coming.
He is bringing your reward to you.
    He is bringing it with him.'"
12His people will be called "The Holy
        People",
    "The Saved People of the LORD".
And you, Jerusalem, will be called "The City
        God Wants",
    "The City God Is With".

The LORD Punishes the Nations

63 Who is this coming from Edom,
    from the city of Bozrah?
His clothes are stained bright red.
    He is glorious in his clothes.
He is walking tall with his great power.
    He says, "I have the power to save you,
    and I speak the truth."

---

a **62:1 goodness** Or "victory".
b **62:4 your land . . . his** Or "He will marry your land." This is a wordplay. The Hebrew word also means "He will be the lord of the land."
c **62:5 your land . . . children** Or "Your builders will marry you."

²"Why are your clothes bright red?
They are like the clothes of someone who
tramples grapes to make wine."

³He answers, "I walked in the winepress by
myself.
No one helped me.
I was angry, and I trampled the grapes.
The juiceᵃ splashed on my clothes, so now
they are stained.
⁴I chose a time to punish people.
Now the time has come for me to save and
protect my people.
⁵I looked around, but I saw no one to help me.
I was surprised that no one supported me.
So I used my own power to save my people.
My own anger supported me.
⁶Because I was angry, I trampled down the
nations.
In my anger I punished them
and spilled their bloodᵇ on the ground."

The LORD Has Been Kind to His People

⁷I will remember the kind things the LORD has
done,
and I will remember to praise him.
The LORD has given many good things
to the family of Israel.
He has been very kind to us.
He has shown us mercy.
⁸He said, "These are my people.
These are my real children."
So he saved them.
⁹The people had many troubles,
but he was not against them.
He loved them and felt sorry for them,
so he saved them.
He sent his special angel to save them.
He picked them up and carried them, just
as he did long ago.
¹⁰But they turned against him
and made his Holy Spirit very sad.
So the Lord became their enemy
and fought against them.

¹¹Then they remembered what happened
long ago.
They remembered Moses and those with
him.
So where is the one who brought them
through the sea
along with the shepherds who led his flock?
Where is the one
who sent his Holy Spirit to live among them?
¹²He was by Moses' side

and led him with his wonderful hand.
He divided the water,
so that the people could walk through the sea.
He made his name famous
by doing those great things.
¹³He led the people through the deep sea.
Like a horse running through the desert,
they walked without falling.
¹⁴Like cattle going down to the valley,
The Spirit of the LORD led them.
This is how you led your people
and made your name wonderful.

A Prayer for God to Help His People

¹⁵Look down from heaven and see what is
happening.
Look at us from your great and holy home
in heaven.
Where is the anger and power you once
showed in defending us?
Please don't keep your kind love from us!
¹⁶Look, you are our father!
Abraham does not know us.
Israel does not recognize us.
LORD, you are our father!
You are the one who has always saved us!
¹⁷LORD, why are you pushing us away from you?
Why are you making it hard for us to
follow you?
Come back to us!
We are your servants.
Come to us and help us!
Our tribes belong to you.
¹⁸Your holy people had their land only a short
time.
Then our enemies trampled down your holy
Temple.
¹⁹Some people don't follow you.
They don't wear your name.
And we have been like them
for a very long time.

64

If you would tear open the skies
and come down to earth, then everything
would change.
Mountains would melt before you.
²The mountains would burst into flames like
burning bushes.
The mountains would boil like water on
the fire.
Then your enemies would learn about you.
And all nations would shake with fear when
they see you.
³But you have done awesome things that we
did not expect.

ᵃ **63:3 juice** Or "strong drink" or "blood".
ᵇ **63:6 blood** Or "strong drink" or "strength".

You came down, and mountains shook in
  fear before you.
⁴No one has ever heard of such a God.
  No one has ever heard such a story.
No one has ever seen any God except you,
  who does such great things for those who
    trust him.

⁵You welcome people who enjoy doing good
  and who remember you
  by living the way you want them to.
But we sinned against you,
  and you became angry with us.ᵃ
  But you always saved us!
⁶We are all dirty with sin.
  Even our good works are not pure.
  They are like bloodstained rags.
We are all like dead leaves.
  Our sins have carried us away like
    wind.
⁷We don't call to you for help.
  We aren't excited about following you,
    so you have turned away from us.
We are helpless before you,
  because we are full of sin.
⁸But, LORD, you are our father.
  We are like clay, and you are the potter.
  Your hands made us all.
⁹LORD, don't continue to be angry with us!
  Don't remember our sins forever!
Please, look at us!
  We are all your people.
¹⁰Your holy cities are as empty as the desert.
  Zion has become a desert.
  Jerusalem is destroyed.
¹¹Our ancestors worshipped you in our holy
  Temple.
  That wonderful Temple has now been
    burned.
  All our precious possessions have been
    destroyed.
¹²LORD, will these things always keep you from
  helping?
  Will you continue to say nothing?
  Will you punish us forever?

The LORD Answers

65 "The people who found me were not
  looking for me. I made myself known to
people who were not asking for me. I spoke to a
nation that does not use my name. I said, 'Here
I am! Here I am!'

²"All day long I stood ready to accept those
who turned against me. But they kept doing
whatever they wanted to do, and all they did was
wrong. ³They keep doing things, right in front of
me, that make me angry. They offer sacrifices and
burn incense in their special gardens.ᵇ ⁴They sit
among the graves, waiting to get messages from
the dead. They eat the meat of pigs, and their pots
are full of soup made from unclean meat. ⁵But
they tell others, 'Don't come near me! Don't
touch me because I am holy!' They are like smoke
in my eyes, and their fire burns all the time.

Israel Must Be Punished

⁶"Look, here is a letter that lists all your sins.
I will not be quiet until I pay you back for these
sins. I will do it by punishing you. ⁷I, the LORD,
am doing this because of your sins and the sins of
your ancestors. They did these sins when they
burned incense in the mountains. They shamed
me on those hills, and I punished them first."

⁸The LORD says, "When there is new wine in
the grapes, people squeeze out the wine. But they
don't completely destroy the grapes because the
grapes can still be used. I will do the same thing
to my servants. I will not destroy them completely.
⁹I will keep some of the people of Jacob. Some
of the people of Judah will get my mountains.
I will choose the people who will get the land.
My servants will live there. ¹⁰Then Sharon Valley
will be a field for sheep. The Valley of Achorᶜ will
be a place for cattle to rest. All this will be for my
people—for the people who come to me for help.

¹¹"But you people left the LORD, so you will be
punished. You forgot about my holy mountain.ᵈ
You began to worship Luck. You held feasts for
the false god Fate.ᵉ ¹²But I decided what would
happen to you: you will be killed with a sword.
You will all be killed because I called to you, but
you refused to answer me. I spoke to you, but you
would not listen. You did what I said is evil and
chose to do what I did not like.

¹³"So this is what the Lord GOD says:
  My servants will eat,
    but you evil people will be hungry.
  My servants will drink,
    but you will be thirsty.
  My servants will be happy,
    but you will suffer shame.
¹⁴My servants will shout for joy,
    but you will cry out in pain.ᶠ

ᵃ **64:5 we sinned . . . us** Or "But you became angry with us and we sinned."
ᵇ **65:3 special gardens** Gardens where people worshipped false gods.
ᶜ **65:10 Valley of Achor** A valley about ten miles north of Jerusalem.
ᵈ **65:11 my holy mountain** Mount Zion, the mountain Jerusalem is built on.
ᵉ **65:11 Luck . . . Fate** Two false gods. The people thought these gods controlled their futures.
ᶠ **65:14 My servants . . . pain** Literally, "My servants will rejoice with good hearts, and you will scream with painful hearts."

Your spirits will be broken,
  and you will be very sad.
15Your names will be like curses to my chosen
    servants.
  The Lord GOD will kill you,
    and then he will call his servants by a new
      name.
16People now ask blessings from the earth.
  But in the future they will ask blessings
    from the faithful God.
People now trust in the power of the earth
    when they make a promise.
  But in the future they will trust in the God
    who is faithful.
That's because the troubles in the past will all
    be forgotten.
  They will be hidden from my sight.

INSIGHT

Isaiah is a bit like a mini-Bible. It has
66 chapters and the Bible has 66 books
and both end with a new heaven and
new earth, free of pain, sickness,
sadness and death. Nature and
humanity will live in harmony and God
will be amongst his people.

Isaiah 65:17–25

A New Time Is Coming

17"I am creating a new heaven and a new
    earth.
  The troubles of the past will be forgotten.
    No one will remember them.
18My people will be happy and rejoice for ever
    and ever
  because of what I will make.
I will make a Jerusalem that is full of joy,
  and I will make her people happy.

19"Then I will rejoice with Jerusalem.
  I will be happy with my people.
There will never again be crying
  and sadness in that city.
20In that city there will never be a baby who
    lives only a few days,
  and every older person will live for a long,
    long time.
A person who lives for 100 years will be called
    young.
  And whoever doesn't live that long will be
    considered cursed.

21"In that city whoever builds a house will
    live there;
  whoever plants a vineyard will eat the
    grapes from that garden.
22Never again will one person build a house
  and another person live there.
Never again will one person plant a garden
  and another eat the fruit from it.
My people will live as long as the trees.
  My chosen people will get full use of
    whatever they make.
23The work they do will not be wasted,
  and they will not have children whose lives
    end in disaster.
I, the LORD, will bless them as my own,
  and I will bless their descendants as well.
24I will answer them before they call for help.
  I will help them before they finish asking.
25Wolves and little lambs will eat together.
  Lions will eat hay like cattle,
    and snakes will eat only dust.
They will not hurt or destroy each other on
    my holy mountain."
  This is what the LORD said.

God Will Judge All Nations

66 This is what the LORD says:
  "Heaven is my throne,
  and the earth is where I rest my feet.
So do you think you can build a house
    for me?
  Do I need a place to rest?
2I am the one who made all things.
  They are all here because I made them,"
    says the LORD.
  "These are the people I care for:
  the poor, humble people who obey my
    commands.
3Some people kill bulls as a sacrifice,
  but they also beat people.
They kill sheep as a sacrifice,
  but they also break the necks of dogs.
They offer up grain offerings,
  but they also offer the blood of pigs.a
They burn incense,
  but they also love their worthless idols.
They choose their own ways,
  and they love their terrible idols.
4So I decided to use their own tricks.
  I will punish them using what they are most
    afraid of.
I will do this because I called to them,
  but they did not answer.
I spoke to them,
  but they did not listen.

---

a 66:3 dogs . . . pigs God did not want his people to offer dogs and pigs as sacrifices.

They did what I said is evil.
   They chose to do what I did not like."

5You who obey the LORD's commands,
   listen to what he says:
"Your brothers hated you.
   They turned against you because you
      followed me.
Your brothers said, 'When the LORD shows his
      glory,
   then we will rejoice with you.'
But they will be punished."

Punishment and a New Nation

6Listen! There is a loud noise coming from the
city and from the Temple. It is the LORD punishing
his enemies. He is giving them the punishment
they deserve.
7-8"A woman does not give birth before she
feels the pain. A woman must feel the pain of
childbirth before she can see the boy she gives
birth to. Who ever heard of such a thing? In the
same way, no one ever saw a new world begin in
one day. No one has ever heard of a new nation
that began in one day. But when Zion feels the
pain, she will give birth to her children. 9In the
same way, I will not cause pain without allowing
something new to be born."
   The LORD says this: "I promise that if I cause
you the pain of birth, I will not stop you from
having your new nation." Your God said this.

10"Jerusalem and all her friends, be happy!
   All of you who were sad for her, be happy
      and rejoice with her!
11Be happy that you will receive mercy
   like milk coming from her breast.
Jerusalem's 'milk' will satisfy you!
   You will drink it and enjoy her glory."

12This is what the LORD says:
"Look, I will give Jerusalem peace that will
      flow in like a river.
   Wealth from all the nations will come
      flowing into her like a flood.
And like little babies, you will drink that 'milk'.
   I will hold you in my arms,
      and bounce you on my knees.
13I will comfort you like a mother comforting
      her child.
   You will be comforted in Jerusalem."

14When you see these things, you will be happy.
   You will be free and grow like grass.
The LORD's servants will see his power,
   but his enemies will see his anger.
15Look, the LORD is coming with fire.
   His armies are coming with clouds of dust.
He is angry,
   and he will punish his enemies with flames.
16The LORD will judge the people
   and will punish them with fire and his sword.
There will be many people killed by the LORD.

17The LORD says, "These are the people who
wash themselves and make themselves pure so
that they can go into their special gardensa to
worship their idols. They follow each other into
the gardens to eat meat from pigs, rats and other
dirty things. But they will all be destroyed together.
18"They have evil thoughts and do evil things,
so I am coming to punish them. I will gather all
nations and all people. Everyone will be gathered
together to see my glory.b 19I will put a mark on
some of the people. I will send some of these
saved people to Tarshish, Libya,c Ludd (the land of
archers), Tubal,e Greece and all the faraway lands.
Those people have never heard my teachings.
They have never seen my glory. So the saved
people will tell the nations about my glory. 20And
they will bring all your brothers and sisters from
those other nations to my holy mountainf Jerusalem as an offering to the LORD. Your brothers and
sisters will ride on horses, mules, camels and in
chariots and carts. They will be like the gifts that
the Israelites bring on clean plates to the Temple
of the LORD. 21I will also choose some of these
people to be priests and Levites." The LORD himself
said this.

The New Heavens and the New Earth

22The LORD says, "I will make a new world—
new heavens and a new earth—that will last
forever. In the same way, your names and your
children will always be with me. 23Everyone will
come to worship me on every worship day; they
will come every Sabbath and every first day of
the month.g This is what I, the LORD, have said.
24"Whoever goes out of the city will see the
dead bodies of those who sinned against me. The
worms eating those bodies will never die, and
the fires burning them will never go out. It will be
horrible to anyone who sees it."

---

a 66:17 special gardens Gardens where people worshipped false gods.
b 66:18 my glory See "GLORY" in the Word List.
c 66:19 Libya A country in North Africa, west of Egypt.
d 66:19 Lud This country was probably in the country that is now western Turkey.
e 66:19 Tubal This country was probably in what is now eastern Turkey.
f 66:20 my holy mountain This is probably Mount Zion, the mountain Jerusalem is built on.
g 66:23 first day of the month Literally, "new moon". See "NEW MOON" in the Word List.

Who

Jeremiah, son of Hilkiah the Priest, lived in Anathoth, about three miles north of Jerusalem. He was a prophet who worked in the southern kingdom of Judah.

When

He began his career in the reign of Josiah and his work breaks into three periods:

- 627–605 BC Prophesied while Judah was threatened by Assyria and Egypt.
- 605–586 BC Proclaimed God's judgement against Babylon.
- 586–580 BC Prophesied in Jerusalem while the city was captured.

What

God was going to punish the people of Judah for their evil. And Jeremiah had the difficult job of telling them about it. He had to tell them that, unless they changed their ways, the kingdom of Judah would be destroyed.

Jeremiah lived through terrible times. A succession of increasingly ineffective and appalling monarchs took the kingdom of Judah down a road which led to the destruction of Jerusalem and the Temple of Solomon, and the beginning of the people's exile in Babylon. Few people in the Bible have led lives of such conflict; he was forever being thrown into jail, or tried for his life, or forced to flee. He was publicly humiliated by false prophets and even thrown into a cistern (a place where water was stored – though at the time it held only mud). The reason for this harsh treatment is simple: those in power did not want to hear his message.

Time and time again, Jeremiah calls the people to repent; time and time again he is ignored, reviled or abused. He is repaid with beatings, exclusion and imprisonment. And all the time the forces of destruction are gathering and waiting to pounce.

Jeremiah is a very honest book. The prophet was originally a timid figure and, despite promises that he would receive strength from God, he often struggled with his calling (not surprising when you see what happened to him). He often calls for vengeance on his enemies and he often breaks down in tears. Yet he does remain strong. At one of the lowest points he is instructed to buy a field: it is a metaphor, a sign that one day the people will return to their land. He keeps the memory of his first calling close to his heart and he keeps going. While all around him collapses, Jeremiah's foundations remain firm.

QUICK TOUR   JEREMIAH

"In the future I will make this agreement with the people of Israel . . . I will put my teachings in their minds, and I will write them on their hearts. I will be their God, and they will be my people."

Jeremiah 31:33

1 These are the messages of Jeremiah, the son of Hilkiah. Jeremiah belonged to the family of priests who lived in the town of Anathoth.*ᵃ* That town is in the land that belongs to the tribe of Benjamin. ²The LORD began to speak to Jeremiah in the thirteenth yearᵇ that Josiah, son of Amon, was king of the nation of Judah. ³He continued to speak to Jeremiah during the time that Jehoiakim, son of Josiah, was king of Judah and during the eleven years and five months that Zedekiah, also a son of Josiah, was king of Judah. In the fifth month of Zedekiah's eleventh year as king, the people who lived in Jerusalem were taken away into exile.

God Calls Jeremiah

⁴The LORD's message came to me:

⁵"Before I made you in your mother's womb,
    I knew you.
Before you were born,
    I chose you for a special work.
    I chose you to be a prophet to the nations."

⁶Then I said, "But, Lord GOD, I don't know how to speak. I am only a boy."
⁷But the LORD said to me,

"Don't say, 'I am only a boy.'
    You must go everywhere I send you
    and say everything I tell you to say.
⁸Don't be afraid of anyone.
    I am with you, and I will protect you."
This message is from the LORD.

⁹Then the LORD reached out with his hand and touched my mouth. He said to me,

"Jeremiah, I am putting my words in your
    mouth.
¹⁰Today I have put you in charge of nations and
    kingdoms.
    You will pull up and tear down.
You will destroy and overthrow.
    You will build up and plant."

Two Visions

¹¹The LORD's message came to me: "Jeremiah, what do you see?"
I answered, "I see a stick made from almond wood."
¹²The LORD said to me, "You have seen very well, and I am watchingᶜ to make sure that my message to you comes true."

¹³The LORD's message came to me again: "Jeremiah, what do you see?"
I answered, "I see a pot of boiling water. That pot is tipping over from the north."

¹⁴The LORD said to me, "Something terrible will
    come from the north.
    It will happen to all the people who live in
    this country.
¹⁵In a short time I will call all the people in the
    northern kingdoms."
    This is what the LORD says.

"The kings of those countries will come
    and set up their thrones near the gates of
    Jerusalem.
They will attack the city walls of Jerusalem.
    They will attack all the cities in Judah.
¹⁶And I will announce judgement against my
    people,
    because they are evil and have turned away
    from me.
They offered sacrifices to other gods
    and worshipped idols they made with their
    own hands.

¹⁷"As for you, Jeremiah, get ready.
    Stand up and speak to the people.
Tell them everything that I tell you to say.
    Don't be afraid of the people.
If you are afraid of them,
    I will give you good reason to be afraid of
    them.
¹⁸As for me, today I will make you like a strong
    city,
    an iron column, a bronze wall.
You will be able to stand against everyone in
    the land,
    against the kings of the land of Judah,
    the leaders of Judah, the priests of
    Judah,
    and against the people of the land of
    Judah.
¹⁹All those people will fight against you,
    but they will not defeat you,
because I am with you,
    and I will save you."
This message is from the LORD.

Judah Was Not Faithful

2 The LORD's message came to me: ²"Jeremiah, go and speak to the people of Jerusalem. Tell them that this is what the LORD says:

ᵃ **1:1 priests . . . of Anathoth** These priests probably belonged to the family of the priest Abiathar. Abiathar was a high priest in Jerusalem during the time David was king. He was sent away to Anathoth by King Solomon. See 1 Kgs 2:26.
ᵇ **1:2 the thirteenth year** That is, 627 BC.
ᶜ **1:12 watching** This is a wordplay. *Shaqed* is the Hebrew word for "almond wood", and *shoqed* means "watching".

"'At the time you were a young nation, you
were faithful to me.
You followed me like a young bride.
You followed me through the desert,
through a land that had never been used for
farmland.
3The people of Israel were a holy gift to the
LORD.
They were the first fruit he gathered.
Anyone who tried to hurt them was judged
guilty
and was punished severely.'"
This message is from the LORD.

4Family of Jacob, hear the LORD's message.
Tribes of Israel, listen.

5This is what the LORD says:
"Do you think that I was not fair to your
ancestors?
Is that why they turned away from me?
Your ancestors worshipped worthless
idols,
and they became worthless themselves.
6Your ancestors did not say,
'The LORD brought us out of Egypt.
He led us through the desert,
through a dry and rocky land.
He led us through a dark and dangerous
land.
No one lives there;
people don't even travel through that
land.
But the Lord led us through that land.
So where is he now?'

7"I brought you into a good land,
a land filled with many good things.
I did this so that you could eat the fruit and
crops that grow there.
But you only made my land 'dirty'.
I gave that land to you,
but you made it a bad place.

8"The priests did not ask,
'Where is the LORD?'
The people who know the law did not want to
know me.
The leaders of the people of Israel turned
against me.
The prophets spoke in the name of the false
god Baal.
They worshipped worthless idols."

9The LORD says, "So now I will accuse you
again,
and I will also accuse your grandchildren.
10Go across the sea to the island of Cyprus.
Send someone to the land of Kedar.
Look very carefully.
See if anyone has ever done anything like
this.
11Has any nation ever stopped worshipping their
old gods
so that they could worship new gods?
No! And their gods are not really gods
at all!
But my people stopped worshipping their
glorious God
and started worshipping idols that are
worth nothing.

12"Skies, be shocked at what happened!
Shake with great fear!"
This message is from the LORD.
13"My people have done two evil things:
they have turned away from me,
the only one who can give them life;[a]
and they have made gods for themselves
that can give them nothing.[b]

14"Israel is not a slave, is he?
He was not born a slave, was he?
Then why did the enemy carry him away
as a captive?
15Like a lion the enemy has roared at
Israel.
They have destroyed Israel's land.
The cities have been burned,
and no one is left in them.
16People of Israel, armies from Memphis and
Tahpanhes[c]
have smashed the top of your head.
17This trouble is your own fault.
The LORD your God was leading you the
right way,[d]
but you turned away from him.
18People of Judah, think about this.
How did it help you to go to Egypt and
drink from the Nile River?
How did it help you to go to Assyria and
drink from the Euphrates River?
19You have done wrong,
and that will only bring punishment
to you.
Trouble will come to you,
and it will teach you a lesson.

---

[a] 2:13 *the only one . . . life* Literally, "the spring of living water".
[b] 2:13 *and they . . . nothing* Literally, "and they have dug their own wells that are cracked and cannot hold water".
[c] 2:16 *Memphis and Tahpanhes* Two cities in Egypt.
[d] 2:17 *was leading . . . way* This is not in the ancient Greek version.

Think about it and understand how bad it is to
turn away from the LORD your God.
It is wrong not to fear and respect me."
This message is from Lord GOD All-Powerful.

20"Judah, long ago you broke free from me,
like an ox that breaks its yoke and the ropes
holding it.
You said to me, 'I will not serve you!'
On every high hill and under every green tree
you offered your body in the worship of
false gods.
21Judah, I planted you like a special vine.
You were all from good seed.
How did you turn into a different vine that
grows bad fruit?
22Even if you wash yourself with lye,
even if you use much soap,
I can still see your guilt."
This message is from the Lord GOD.

23"Judah, how can you say to me,
'I am not guilty because I have not
worshipped the Baal idols'?
Think about what you did in the valley.
Think about what you have done.
You are like a fast she-camel
that runs from place to place.
24You are like a wild donkey that lives in the
desert.
At mating time, she sniffs the wind.
No one can control her when she is in heat.
At mating time, every male that wants her will
get her.
She is easy to find.
25Judah, stop chasing after idols!
Stop wanting those other gods.
But you say, 'It is no use! I cannot stop!
I love those other gods.
I can't stop chasing them.'

26"A thief is ashamed
when people catch him stealing.
The people of Israel should be ashamed too
and so should their kings and leaders,
priests and prophets.
27They say to pieces of wood,
'You are my father.'
They say to a rock,
'You gave birth to me.'
All these people will be ashamed.
They don't look to me for help.
They have turned their backs on me.
But when the people of Judah get into trouble,
they say to me,
'Come and save us!'
28But where are the idols you made for
yourselves?

Let's see if they come and save you when
you are in trouble!
People of Judah, you have as many idols as
you have cities!

29"Why do you argue with me?
You have all turned against me."
This message is from the LORD.
30"I punished you people of Judah,
but it did not help.
You did not come back
when you were punished.
With your swords you killed the prophets who
came to you.
Like a dangerous lion, you killed the
prophets.
31People of this generation,
pay attention to the LORD's message.

"Have I been like a desert to the people of
Israel?
Have I been like a dark and dangerous land
to them?
My people say, 'We are free to go our own
way.
We will not come back to you!'
Why do they say these things?
32A young woman does not forget her
jewellery.
A bride does not forget to wear her
wedding dress.
But my people have forgotten me
too many times to count.

33"Judah, you have become so good at finding
lovers.
Even the worst women could learn some
evil ways from you.
34You have blood on your hands!
It is the blood of poor, innocent people.
You did not catch them breaking into your
house.
You killed them for no reason!
35But still, you say, 'I am innocent.
God is not angry with me.'
So I will also judge you guilty of lying,
because you say,
'I have done nothing wrong.'
36You go from one place to another looking
for help,
always changing your mind.
But Egypt will also disappoint you,
just as Assyria did.
37So you will eventually leave Egypt too,
and you will hide your face in shame.
You trusted these countries,
but the LORD rejected them,
so they cannot help you win.

3 "If a man divorces his wife and she goes and
marries someone else,
the first husband cannot take her back.
If he did,[a] it would make the land unclean.
Judah, you and all your false gods are like a
prostitute with many lovers!
So why do you think you can come back
to me?"
This message is from the LORD.
[2]"Look up to the bare hilltops, Judah.
Is there anywhere that you have not had
sex with your lovers?
You sat by the road waiting for lovers,
like an Arab in the desert.
You made the land 'dirty'
with all the evil sins you did
when you were unfaithful to me.
[3]You sinned, so the rain has not come.
There has not been any springtime rains.
But still you refuse to be ashamed.
The look on your face is like that of a
prostitute who refuses to be ashamed.
[4]But didn't you just call me 'Father'?
Didn't you say, 'You have been my friend
since I was a child'?
[5]You also said, 'God will not always be angry
with me.
His anger will not continue forever.'

"Judah, you say that,
but you do as much evil as you can."

The Two Bad Sisters: Israel and Judah

[6]The LORD spoke to me during the time King
Josiah was ruling the nation of Judah. He said,
"Jeremiah, you saw the bad things Israel[b] did!
You saw how she was unfaithful to me. She was
unfaithful to me with every idol on every hill and
under every green tree. [7]I said to myself, 'Israel
will come back to me after she has finished doing
these evil things.' But she did not come back to
me. And Israel's unfaithful sister, Judah, saw what
she did. [8]Judah knew why I sent Israel away. I
divorced her because she committed the sin of
adultery. But that did not make her unfaithful
sister Judah afraid. She also went out and acted
like a prostitute. [9]And that did not bother her at
all. Like a prostitute she committed adultery by
worshipping idols made from stone and wood.
She polluted the whole country with her sin.
[10]Israel's unfaithful sister did not come back to
me with her whole heart. She only pretended
to come back." This message is from the LORD.

[11]The LORD said to me, "Israel was not faithful
to me, but she had a better excuse than unfaithful
Judah. [12]So go and speak to my people in the
north. This is what I want you to say:

"'Come back to me, you faithless people of
Israel.'
This is what the LORD says.
'Come, and I will stop frowning at you.
I am full of mercy,' says the LORD.
'I will not be angry with you forever.'
[13]But you must confess your sin.
You turned against the LORD your God.
You worshipped the idols of other nations.
You worshipped them under every green tree.
You did not obey me.'"
This is what the LORD says.

[14]The LORD says, "You people are unfaithful, but
come back to me because I am your master. I will
take one person from every city and two people
from every family and bring you to Zion. [15]Then
I will give you new rulers who will be faithful
to me. They will lead you with knowledge and
understanding. [16]In those days there will be many
of you in the land." This message is from the LORD.
"At that time people will never again say,
'I remember the days when we had the Box of
the LORD's Agreement.' They will not even think
about the Holy Box any more. They will not even
remember or miss it. They will never make another
Holy Box. [17]At that time the city of Jerusalem will
be called The LORD's Throne. All nations will come
together in the city of Jerusalem to give honour to
the name of the LORD. They will not follow their
stubborn, evil hearts any more. [18]In those days the
family of Judah will join the family of Israel. They
will come together from a land in the north to
the land I gave to their ancestors."
[19-20]This message is from the LORD:

"I want to treat you like my own children.
I want to give you a pleasant land,
a land more beautiful than any other nation.
I thought you would call me 'Father'.
I thought you would always follow me.
But you have been unfaithful to me, family
of Israel!
You have been like an unfaithful wife who
leaves her husband.
[21]You can hear crying on the bare hills.
The people of Israel are crying and praying
for mercy.

---

[a] **3:1** *If he did* It was against the Law of Moses for a man to marry a woman he had divorced if that woman had become another
man's wife. See Deut. 24:1–4.
[b] **3:6** *Israel* Here, the name Israel means the northern kingdom of Israel. Israel was destroyed by the Assyrians about 100 years
before Jeremiah's time.

When agreeing to do something they don't really want to do, people often say that they're doing it "with a heavy heart". It's picture language which we understand instantly.

Most of Jeremiah's prophetic writing is pretty gloomy stuff. He has a harsh message for God's people and the unenviable task of delivering it, in spite of ridicule and even persecution. No wonder he has a heavy heart.

DIG IN

READ Jeremiah 3:6 – 4:4

- What have the people of Israel and Judah done to displease God (vv.6–11,20–21)?
- What is it that has offended him so much?

Israel and Judah separated in roughly 930 BC as a result of a minor dispute. Ten of the twelve tribes grouped to become the northern kingdom, and continued to be called Israel. The remaining two joined forces in the south, as Judah. But neither stayed faithful to God.

God persevered with them, in the hope that they would learn their lesson and return to him. But they never did. Israel got pulled to bits by the Assyrians in 722 BC. Then Jeremiah – like Isaiah, a young man when he was called to be a prophet – had the tough job of telling Judah that their time was up. God's judgement was coming.

We'll see later in Jeremiah how God allows Jerusalem to be attacked and destroyed and all of the people scattered into exile (see the Bible Bit "Enemy at the Gates" on Jeremiah chapter 21).

- But what does God promise in 3:12,18,22?
- What conditions does he attach (4:1–4)?

Even though a difficult time is coming for Judah as it did for Israel, God is promising to be merciful to the people and to turn his anger away. His offer is for a new era of blessing through a new agreement which is coming. Destruction will eventually result in a glorious new beginning as the people are brought back together.

But there is a condition: real repentance is required. They need to turn away from the idols they have been worshipping and begin trusting God as their Saviour.

DIG THROUGH

- Do you think it's a bit unfair that God is bringing his judgement on everyone in Judah? Surely there are some people who love God and want to serve him? (Later in Jeremiah, God points to a time when he would look at all people individually and judge them for their own sin – see the Bible Bit on Jeremiah, chapter 31.)

It's clear that God can see how corruption and sin can have an effect on whole nations and generations. And things don't change. A parent with an alcohol or gambling problem can have obvious consequences on the future of their children. More subtle, perhaps, is when a parent is addicted to work or puts making money ahead of time with the family.

- Can you see how your sin might have consequences for other people?

DIG DEEPER

- Look at how seriously God takes his relationship with his people, comparing them to women who have been unfaithful to their husbands. This is quite a common picture in the Bible. God is an intensely personal God who feels things deeply. For instance, Exodus 34:14 says he is "the jealous LORD". Check out Hosea 2 for more insights.

They have taken the wrong path.
They have forgotten me, the LORD their God.

22"My children, you have been unfaithful,
but I want you to come back to me.
Come back and I will show you the way to be faithful.

"Just say, 'Yes, we will come back,
because you are the LORD our God.
23It was useless for us to worship idols on the hills.
The wild celebrations we had there were foolish.
Surely the salvation of Israel
comes only from the LORD our God.
24For as long as we can remember, that shameful god Baal
has eaten everything our fathers owned.
He took their sheep and cattle,
their sons and daughters.
25Let us lie down in our shame.
Let disgrace cover us like a blanket.
We have sinned against the LORD our God.
We and our fathers have sinned.
We have not obeyed the LORD our God
from the time we were children.'"

4 This message is from the LORD.
"Israel, if you want to come back,
then come back to me.
Throw away your idols.
Don't wander farther away from me.
2If you do these things,
then you will be able to use my name to make a promise.
You will be able to say,
'As the LORD lives.'
You will be able to use these words
in a truthful, honest and right way.
If you do these things,
the nations will be blessed by the Lord.
They will boast about what
the Lord has done."

3This is what the LORD says to the people of Judah and to Jerusalem:

"Your fields have not been ploughed.
Plough those fields!
Don't plant seeds among the thorns.

4Become the LORD's people.
Change your hearts.a
Men of Judah and people of Jerusalem, if you don't change,
then I will become very angry.
My anger will spread fast like a fire,
and it will burn you up.
No one will be able to put out that fire
because of the evil you have done.

Disaster From the North

5"Give this message to the people of Judah:

"Tell everyone in the city of Jerusalem:
'Blow the trumpet all over the country.'
Shout out loud and say,
'Come together!
Let us all escape to the strong cities for protection.'
6Raise the signal flag towards Zion.
Run for your lives! Don't wait!
Do this because I am bringing disaster from the north.b
I am bringing terrible destruction."
7A lion has come out of his cave.
A destroyer of nations has begun to march.
He has left his home to destroy your land.
Your towns will be destroyed.
There will be no one left to live in them.
8The LORD is angry with us,
so put on sackcloth and cry out loud!
9The LORD says, "When this happens,
the king and his officers will lose their courage.
The priests will be filled with fear,
and the prophets will be shocked."

10Then I, Jeremiah, said, "Lord GOD, you have tricked the people of Judah and Jerusalem. You said to them, 'You will have peace.' But now the sword is pointing at their throats!"

11At that time this message will be given
to the people of Judah and Jerusalem:
"A hot wind blows from the bare hills.
It comes from the desert to my people.
It is not like the gentle wind that is used
to separate the grain from the chaff.
12It is a stronger wind than that,
and it comes from me.
Now I will announce my judgement
against the people of Judah."

---

a 4:4 Become . . . hearts Literally, "Be circumcised to the LORD. Cut away the foreskin of your hearts." See "CIRCUMCISE" in the Word List. Jeremiah is saying that real circumcision must be from inside a person's heart (mind).
b 4:6 north The Babylonian army came from this direction to attack Judah. Armies from countries north and east of Israel often came this way to attack Judah and Israel.

¹³Look! The enemy rises up like a cloud.
    His chariots look like a windstorm.
    His horses are faster than eagles.
  It will be very bad for us!
    We are ruined!

¹⁴People of Jerusalem,
    wash the evil from your hearts.
  Make your hearts pure so that you can be saved.
    Don't continue making evil plans.
¹⁵Listen! The voice of a messenger
    from the land of Dan*a* is speaking.
  Someone is bringing bad news
    from the hill country of Ephraim:*b*
¹⁶"Report it to this nation.*c*
    Spread the news to the people in Jerusalem.
  Enemies are coming from a faraway country.
    They are shouting words of war against the
      cities of Judah.
¹⁷The enemy has surrounded Jerusalem
    like men guarding a field.
  Judah, you turned against me,
    so the enemy is coming against you."
  This message is from the LORD.

¹⁸"The way you have lived and the things you
      have done
    have brought this trouble to you.
  It is your evil that made your life so hard.
    Your evil life brought the pain that hurts
      deep in your heart."

Jeremiah's Cry

¹⁹My sadness and worry is making my stomach
      hurt.
    I am bent over in pain.
  I am so afraid.
    My heart is pounding inside me.
  I cannot keep quiet, because I have heard the
      trumpet.
    The trumpet is calling the army to war.
²⁰Disaster follows disaster.
    The whole country has been destroyed!
  Suddenly my tents are destroyed.
    My curtains are torn down.
²¹How long must I see the war flags
    and hear the trumpet's call to battle?

²²The Lord said, "My people are foolish.
    They don't know me.
  They are stupid children.

They don't understand.
  They are skilful at doing evil,
    but they don't know how to do good."

Disaster Is Coming

²³I looked at the earth.
    It was empty; there was nothing on it.
  I looked at the sky,
    and its light was gone.*d*
²⁴I looked at the mountains,
    and they were shaking.
  All the hills were trembling.
²⁵I looked, but there were no people.
    All the birds of the sky had flown away.
²⁶I looked, and the good land had become a
      desert.
    All the cities in that land had been destroyed
    by the LORD and his great anger.

²⁷This is what the LORD says:
  "The whole country will be ruined,
    but I will not completely destroy the land.
²⁸So the people in the land will cry for the dead.
    The sky will grow dark.
  I have spoken and will not change.
    I have made a decision, and I will not
      change my mind."

²⁹The people of Judah will hear the sound
    of the horsemen and the archers,
    and the people will run away!
  Some of them will hide in caves;*e*
    some will hide in the bushes;
    some will climb up into the rocks.
  All the cities of Judah will be empty.
    No one will live in them.

³⁰Judah, you have been destroyed.
    So what are you doing now?
  Why are you putting on your best red dress?
    Why are you putting on your gold
      jewellery?
  Why are you putting on your eye make-up?
    You make yourself beautiful,
    but it is a waste of time.
  Your lovers hate you.
    They are trying to kill you.
³¹I hear a cry like a woman in labour,
    a scream like a woman giving birth to her
      first baby.
    It is the cry of daughter Zion.*f*

---

a **4:15** *land of Dan* The people from the tribe of Dan lived near the border in the northern part of Israel. They would be the first
to be attacked by an enemy from the north.
b **4:15** *hill country of Ephraim* This was the central part of the land that had been the northern kingdom of Israel.
c **4:16** *Report . . . nation* The Hebrew text is not clear.
d **4:23** *the earth . . . gone* Jeremiah is comparing his country to the time before people were put on the earth. See Gen. 1:1.
e **4:29** *hide in caves* This is from the ancient Greek version.
f **4:31** *daughter Zion* Another name for Jerusalem. See "ZION" in the Word List.

She is lifting her hands in prayer, saying,
"Oh! I am about to faint!
Murderers are all around me!"

The Evil of the People of Judah

5 The Lord says, "Walk the streets of Jerusalem. Look around and think about these things. Search the public squares of the city. See if you can find one good person, one who does honest things and who searches for the truth. If you find one good person, I will forgive Jerusalem. ²The people make promises and say, 'As the LORD lives.' But they don't really mean it!"

³LORD, I know that you want people
to be loyal to you.
You hit the people of Judah,
but they did not feel any pain.
You destroyed them,
but they refused to learn their lesson.
They became very stubborn.
They refused to be sorry for the bad things
they had done.

⁴But I said to myself,
"It must be only the poor who are so
foolish.
They have not learned the way of the LORD.
They don't know the teachings of their
God.
⁵So I will go to the leaders of Judah.
I will talk to them.
Surely the leaders know the way of the
LORD.
Surely they know the law of their God."
But the leaders had all joined together
to break away from serving God.
⁶So a lion from the forest will attack them.
A wolf from the desert will kill them.
A leopard is hiding near their cities,
to tear to pieces anyone who comes out.
That's because the people have sinned again
and again.
Many times they have wandered away
from God.

⁷God says, "People of Judah, why should I
forgive you?
Your children have abandoned me.
They made promises to idols that are not
really gods!
I gave your children everything they
needed,
but they were still unfaithful to me!
They spent their time with prostitutes.

⁸Like stallions, they ate and were ready to
mate,
eager for sex with their neighbour's wife.
⁹Should I not punish the people of Judah for
doing these things?"
This message is from the LORD.
"You know I should punish a nation such
as this.
I should give it the punishment it deserves.

¹⁰"Go along the rows of Judah's grapevines.
Cut down the vines. (But don't completely
destroy them.)
Cut off all their branches, because they
don't belong to the LORD.
¹¹The family of Israel and the family of Judah
have been unfaithful to me in every way."
This message is from the LORD.

¹²Those people lied about the LORD.
They said, "He will not do anything to us.
Nothing bad will happen to us.
We will never see an army attack us.
We will never starve.
¹³The prophets are only empty wind.ᵃ
The word of God is not in them.ᵇ
Bad things will happen to them."

¹⁴The LORD God All-Powerful said these things:
"The people said I would not punish
them.
So, Jeremiah, the words I give you will be
like fire,
and these people will be like wood.
That fire will burn them up completely."
¹⁵Family of Israel, this message is from the
LORD.
"I will soon bring a nation from far away to
attack you.
It is an old nation;
it is an ancient nation.
The people of that nation speak a language
that you do not know.
You cannot understand what they say.
¹⁶Their arrow bags are like open graves.
All their men are strong soldiers.
¹⁷They will eat all the crops that you gathered.
They will eat all your food.
They will destroy your sons and daughters.
They will eat your flocks and your herds.
They will eat your grapes and your figs.
They will destroy your strong cities with their
swords.
They will destroy the strong cities that you
trust in."

ᵃ **5:13 wind** This is a wordplay. The Hebrew word for wind is like the word for spirit.
ᵇ **5:13 The word . . . them** Literally, "And the 'He said' is not in them."

18This message is from the LORD: "But, Judah, when these terrible days come, I will not fully destroy you. 19The people will ask, 'Why has the LORD our God done all these things to us?' Give them this answer from me: 'You people of Judah left me, and you served foreign idols in your own land. Because you did this, you will now serve foreigners in a land that does not belong to you.'

20"Tell this message to the family of Jacob,
   and tell it in the nation of Judah.
21Hear this message,
   you foolish people who have no sense.
You have eyes, but you don't see!
   You have ears, but you don't listen!
22Surely you are afraid of me."
   This message is from the LORD.
   "You should shake with fear in front of me.
I am the one who made the sandy shores to
   hold back the sea.
   I made it that way to keep the water in its
      place forever.
The waves may pound the beach, but they
   will not destroy it.
The waves may roar as they come in, but
   they cannot go beyond the beach.
23But the people of Judah are stubborn.
   They are always planning ways to turn
      against me.
   They turned away from me and left me.
24The people of Judah never say to themselves,
   'Let's fear and respect the LORD our God.
He gives us autumn and spring rains at just
   the right time.
He makes sure that we have a good harvest
   time.'
25You don't have these blessings because you
   have done wrong.
   Your sins have kept these good things away
      from you.
26Among my people are those who are evil.
   They are like men who make nets for
      catching birds.a
They set their traps,
   but they catch people instead of birds.
27Like a cage full of birds,
   their lives are full of evil lies.
Their cheating has made them rich and
   powerful.
28   They are well fed and well dressed.

There is no end to the evil they do.
   They don't care what happens to orphans,
   and they don't help the poor get what they
      need.
29Should I punish the people of Judah for these
   things?"
   This is what the LORD is asking you, and he
      says,
"A nation like this should get the punishment
   it deserves.

30"A terrible and shocking thing
   has happened in the land of Judah.
31The prophets tell lies.
   The priests will not do what they were
      chosen to do,b
and my people love it this way!
   But what will you people do when your
      punishment comes?

The Enemy Surrounds Jerusalem

6 "Run for your lives, people of Benjamin!
   Run away from the city of Jerusalem!
Blow the war trumpet in the city of Tekoa!
   Put up the warning flag in the city of Beth
      Hakkerem!
Do these things because disaster is coming
   from the north.c
   Terrible destruction is coming to you.
2Jerusalem,d you are like a beautiful meadow.e
   But I will destroy you!
3Enemy shepherds will surround you
   with all their flocks.
They will set up their tents all around you,
   and each one will let his sheep eat the grass.

4"Get ready to fight against Jerusalem.
   Get up! We will attack the city at noon.
But it is already getting late.
   The evening shadows are growing long.
5So get up! We will attack the city at night!
   Let's destroy the strong walls that are
      around Jerusalem."

6This is what the LORD All-Powerful says:
   "Cut down the trees around Jerusalem,
   and build a siege moundf against it.
This city should be punished
   because inside there is no justice—only
      slavery.

---

a 5:26 *men . . . birds* The Hebrew text is not clear.
b 5:31 *priests . . . were chosen to do* The Hebrew text is not clear.
c 6:1 *north* The Babylonian army came from this direction to attack Judah. Armies from countries north and east of Israel often came this way to attack Judah and Israel.
d 6:2 *Jerusalem* Literally, "daughter Zion". Also in verse 23. See "ZION" in the Word List.
e 6:2 *you are like a beautiful meadow* The Hebrew text is not clear.
f 6:6 *siege mound* A large pile of soil and rock that an army put against the wall of a city they were attacking. This made it easier for the enemy soldiers to climb over the wall into the city.

⁷As a well keeps its water fresh,
  so Jerusalem keeps its wickedness fresh.
I hear about the robbing and violence in this
  city all the time.
I see nothing but pain and sickness there all
  the time.
⁸Listen to this warning, Jerusalem,
  or I will turn my back on you.
I will make your land an empty desert.
  No one will be able to live there."

⁹This is what the LORD All-Powerful says:
"Gatherᵃ the people of Israel who were left on
  their land.
  Gather them the way you would gather the
    last grapes on a grapevine.
Check each vine,
  like the workers check each vine when they
    pick the grapes."
¹⁰Who can I speak to?
  Who can I warn?
  Who will listen to me?
The people of Israel have closed their ears,
  so they cannot hear my warnings.
They don't like the LORD's teachings.
  They don't want to hear his message.
¹¹But I am full of the LORD's anger,
  and I am tired of holding it in!
"Pour out my anger on the children playing in
  the streets
  and on the young soldiers gathered there as
    well.
A man and his wife will both be captured
  as well as all the old people.
¹²Their houses will be given to others.
  Their fields and their wives will be given to
    other people.
I will raise my hand and punish the people of
  Judah."
  This message is from the LORD.

¹³"All the people of Israel want more and more
  money.
  All of them, from the least important to the
    most important, are like that.
  Even the prophets and priests tell lies.
¹⁴They should bandage the wounds my people
  have suffered,
  but they treat their wounds like small
    scratches.
They say, 'It's all right, everything is all right.'

But it is not all right!
¹⁵They should be ashamed of the evil things
  they do,
  but they are not ashamed at all.
They don't know enough to be embarrassed
  by their sins.
So they will be punished with everyone else.
They will be thrown to the ground when I
  punish the people."
This is what the LORD says.

¹⁶And the LORD says this:
"Stand at the crossroads and look.
  Ask where the old road is.
Ask for the road that will lead the right way,
  and walk on that road.
If you do, you will find rest for yourselves.
  But you said, 'We will not walk on the good
    road.'
¹⁷I chose watchmen to watch over you.
  I told them, 'Listen for the sound of the war
    trumpet.'
  But they said, 'We will not listen!'
¹⁸So listen, all you nations,
  and pay attention, you people in those
    countries.ᵇ
¹⁹Hear this, people of the earth:
  I am going to bring disaster to the people of
    Judah
  because of all the evil they planned,
and because they ignored my messages.
  They refused to obey my law.

²⁰"Why do you bring me incense from the
  country of Sheba?ᶜ
  Why do you bring me sweet-smelling cane
    from a faraway country?
Your burnt offerings don't make me happy.
  Your sacrifices don't please me."

²¹So this is what the LORD says:
"I will give the people of Judah problems.
  They will be like stones that make people
    fall.
Fathers and sons will stumble over them.
  Friends and neighbours will die."

²²This is what the LORD says:
"An army is coming from the north.ᵈ
  A great nation is coming from faraway
    places on earth.

ᵃ 6:9 **Gather** Or "glean". There was a law that a farmer must leave some grain in his field during harvest, so that poor people and
travellers could find something to eat. See Lev. 19:9; 23:22.
ᵇ 6:18 **pay . . . countries** The Hebrew text is not clear.
ᶜ 6:20 **Sheba** A land south of Israel, located where part of Saudi Arabia is today. Sheba controlled the spice trade in the time of
Jeremiah.
ᵈ 6:22 **north** The Babylonian army came from this direction to attack Judah. Armies from countries north and east of Israel often
came this way to attack Judah and Israel.

23The soldiers carry bows and spears.
  They are cruel; they have no mercy.
They are so powerful.
  They sound like the roaring ocean as they
    ride their horses.
That army is coming, ready for battle.
  It is coming to attack you, Jerusalem."
24We have heard the news about that army,
  and we are paralysed with fear.
We feel trapped by our troubles,
  in pain like a woman giving birth.
25Don't go out into the fields.
  Don't go on the roads
because the enemy has swords,
  and there is danger everywhere.
26My people, put on sackcloth
  and roll in the ashes.*a*
Cry loudly for the dead.
  Cry as if you had lost an only son.
Do this because the destroyer
  will come against us very quickly.

27"Jeremiah, I want you to be
  like a worker who tests metals.
You will test my people
  and watch how they live.
28My people have turned against me,
  and they are very stubborn.
They say bad things about people.
They are like bronze and iron
  that are covered with rust and tarnish.
29⌊They are like a worker who tried to make
    silver pure.⌋
The bellows*b* blew strongly, and the fire
    became hotter,
  but only lead came from the fire.*c*
The worker wasted his time
  trying to make that silver pure.
  In the same way, the evil was not removed
    from my people.
30My people will be called 'Rejected Silver'.
  They will be given that name because the
    LORD did not accept them."

Jeremiah's Temple Sermon

7 This is the LORD's message to Jeremiah:
  2"Jeremiah, stand at the gate of the LORD's
house. Teach this message at the gate:

"'Hear the message from the LORD, all you
people of the nation of Judah. All you who come
through these gates to worship the LORD, hear
this message. 3The LORD All-Powerful, the God
of Israel, says: Change your lives and do what is
right. Then I will let you live in this place.*d* 4Don't
trust the lies that some people say. They say, "This
is the Temple of the LORD, the Temple of the
LORD, the Temple of the LORD!"*e* 5If you change
your lives and do what is right, I will let you live
in this place. You must be fair to each other. 6You
must not take advantage of widows or orphans or
people visiting in your land. Don't kill innocent
people! And don't follow other gods, because
they will only ruin your lives. 7If you obey me,
I will let you live in this place. I gave this land to
your ancestors for them to keep forever.

8"'But you are trusting lies that are worthless.
9Will you steal and murder? Will you commit
adultery? Will you falsely accuse other people?
Will you worship the false god Baal and follow
other gods that you have not known? 10If you
commit these sins, do you think that you can
stand before me in this house that is called by my
name? Do you think you can stand before me
and say, "We are safe," just so you can do all
these terrible things? 11This Temple is called by
my name. Is this Temple nothing more to you
than a hideout for robbers? I have been watching
you.'" This message is from the LORD.

12"'You people of Judah, go now to the town of
Shiloh. Go to the place where I first made a house
for my name. The people of Israel also did evil
things. Go and see what I did to that place because
of the evil they did.*f* 13You people of Judah were
doing all these evil things too. This message is
from the LORD! I spoke to you again and again,
but you refused to listen to me. I called to you, but
you did not answer. 14So I will destroy the house
called by my name in Jerusalem. I will destroy that
Temple as I destroyed Shiloh. And that house in
Jerusalem that is called by my name is the Temple
you trust in. I gave that place to you and to your
ancestors. 15I will throw you away from me just as
I threw away all your brothers from Ephraim.'

16"As for you, Jeremiah, don't pray for these
people of Judah. Don't beg for them or pray for
them. Don't beg me to help them. I will not listen

---

a 6:26 *roll in the ashes* This is one way people showed that they were sad or crying for a dead person.
b 6:29 *bellows* A tool for blowing air on a fire to make the fire hotter.
c 6:29 *lead came from the fire* Workers melted metals like silver to make the metals pure. Lead was the first metal to melt, so
the workers poured the lead out, leaving the other metal pure. Here, Jeremiah is saying the people are all bad—they are all lead
and no silver!
d 7:3 *I will . . . place* This can also mean "I will live with you."
e 7:4 *This is . . . LORD* Many people in Jerusalem thought the Lord would always protect the city where his Temple was, so it
didn't matter how evil they were.
f 7:12 *Go . . . they did* Shiloh was probably destroyed by the Philistines in the time of Eli and Samuel. See 1 Sam. 4.

to your prayer for them. [17]I know you see what they are doing in the towns of Judah. You can see what they are doing in the streets of the city of Jerusalem. [18]This is what the people of Judah are doing. The children gather wood. The fathers use the wood to make a fire. The women make the dough and then make cakes of bread to offer to the Queen of Heaven. The people of Judah pour out drink offerings to worship other gods. They do this to make me angry. [19]But I am not the one they are really hurting." This message is from the LORD. "They are only hurting themselves. They are bringing shame on themselves."

[20]So this is what the Lord GOD says: "I will show my anger against this place. I will punish people and animals. I will punish the trees in the field and the crops that grow in the ground. My anger will be like a hot fire—no one will be able to stop it."

Obedience Is Better Than Sacrifice

[21]This is what the LORD All-Powerful, the God of Israel, says: "Go and offer as many burnt offerings and sacrifices as you want. Eat the meat of those sacrifices yourselves. [22]When I brought your ancestors out of Egypt I spoke to them, but I did not give them any commands about burnt offerings and sacrifices. [23]I only gave them this command: 'Obey me and I will be your God, and you will be my people. Do all that I command, and good things will happen to you.'

[24]"But your ancestors did not listen to me. They did not pay attention to me. They were stubborn and did what they wanted to do. They did not become good. They became even more evil—they went backwards, not forwards. [25]From the day that your ancestors left Egypt to this day, I have sent my servants to you. My servants are the prophets. I sent them to you again and again. [26]But your ancestors did not listen to me. They did not pay attention to me. They were very stubborn and did even more evil than their fathers did.

[27]"Jeremiah, you will tell these things to the people of Judah. But they will not listen to you. You will call to them, but they will not answer you. [28]So you must tell them these things: 'This is the nation that did not obey the LORD its God. These people did not listen to God's teachings. They don't know the true teachings.'

The Valley of Slaughter

[29]"Jeremiah, cut off your hair and throw it away.[a] Go up to the bare hilltop and cry, because the LORD has rejected this generation of people. He has turned his back on these people. And in anger he will punish them. [30]Do this because I

have seen the people of Judah doing evil things." This message is from the LORD. "They have set up their idols, and I hate those idols. They have set up idols in the Temple that is called by my name. They have made my house 'dirty'! [31]The people of Judah built the high places of Topheth in the Valley of Ben Hinnom where they killed their own sons and daughters and burned them as sacrifices. This is something I never commanded. Something like this never even entered my mind! [32]So I warn you. The days are coming," says the LORD, "when people will not call this place Topheth or the Valley of Ben Hinnom any more. No, they will call it the Valley of Slaughter. They will give it this name because they will bury the dead people in Topheth until there is no more room to bury anyone else. [33]Then the bodies of the dead people will become food for the birds of the sky. Wild animals will eat the bodies of those people. There will be no one left alive to chase the birds or animals away. [34]I will bring an end to the sounds of joy and happiness in the towns of Judah and in the streets of Jerusalem. There will be no more sounds of the bride and bridegroom in Judah or Jerusalem. The land will become an empty desert."

INSIGHT

For a time the Judeans copied their Phoenician neighbours and burned children alive as sacrifices to false gods. They did this in the Hinnom Valley, which was later known as Gehenna. Jesus used it as a synonym for hell.

Jeremiah 7:31–32

8 This message is from the LORD: "At that time men will take the bones of the kings and important rulers of Judah from their tombs. They will take the bones of the priests and prophets from their tombs. They will take the bones of all the people of Jerusalem from their tombs. [2]They will spread the bones on the ground under the sun, the moon and the stars. The people of Jerusalem love to worship the sun, the moon and the stars. No one will gather the bones and bury them again. So the bones of those people will be like dung thrown on the ground.

[3]"I will force the people of Judah to leave their homes and their land. They will be taken away to foreign lands. Some of the people of Judah who were not killed in the war will wish

---

[a] **7:29 cut . . . away** This showed that Jeremiah was sad.

that they had been killed." This message is from the LORD All-Powerful.

Sin and Punishment

⁴"Jeremiah, say this to the people of Judah: 'This is what the LORD says:

"'You know if a man falls down,
  he gets up again.
And if a man goes the wrong way,
  he turns around and comes back.
⁵The people of Judah went the wrong way.
  But why do the people of Jerusalem
    continue going the wrong way?
They believe their own lies.
  They refuse to turn around and come back.
⁶I have listened to them very carefully,
  but they don't say what is right.
They are not sorry for their sins.
  They don't think about the evil they have
    done.
They do things without thinking.
  They are like horses running into a battle.
⁷Even the birds in the sky
  know the right time to do things.
The storks, doves, swifts and thrushes
  know when it is time to fly to a new home.
But my people don't know
  what the LORD wants them to do.

⁸"'You keep saying, "We are wise because we
    have the LORD's teachings!"
  But this is not true, because the scribes
    have lied with their pens.
⁹These "wise people" refused to listen to the
    LORD's teachings.
  So they are not really wise at all.
These "wise people" were trapped.
  They became shocked and ashamed.
¹⁰So I will give their wives to other men.
  I will give their fields to new owners.
All the people of Israel want more and more
    money.
  All of them, from the least important to the
    most important, are like that.
  Even the prophets and priests tell lies.
¹¹They should bandage the wounds my people
    have suffered,
  but they treat their wounds like small
    scratches.
They say, "It's all right, everything is all right."
  But it is not all right!
¹²They should be ashamed of the evil things
    they do,

but they are not ashamed at all.
They don't know enough to be embarrassed
    by their sins.
So they will be punished with everyone else.
  They will be thrown to the ground when I
    punish the people.'"
This is what the LORD says.

¹³"'I will take away their fruit and crops
  so that there will be no harvest, says the LORD.
There will be no grapes on the vine and no
  figs on the fig tree.
  Even the leaves will become dry and die.
I will take away the things I gave them.'"*ᵃ*

¹⁴"They will say, 'Why are we just sitting here?
  Come, let's run to the strong cities.
If the LORD our God is going to make us die,
  then let's die there.
We have sinned against the LORD,
  so he has given us poisoned water to drink.
¹⁵We hoped to have peace,
  but nothing good has come.
We hoped that he would forgive us,
  but only disaster has come.
¹⁶From the land of the tribe of Dan,
  we hear the snorting*ᵇ* of the enemy's
    horses.
  The ground shakes from the pounding of
    their hooves.
They have come to destroy the land
  and everything in it.
They have come to destroy the city
  and all the people who live there.'"

¹⁷"People of Judah, I am sending poisonous
    snakes*ᶜ* to attack you.
  These snakes cannot be controlled.
They will bite you."
  This message is from the LORD.

Jeremiah Cries Out to God

¹⁸There is no relief for my sadness.
  I am sick with sorrow.
¹⁹Listen to my poor people.
  Everywhere in this land they are crying for
    help.
They say, "Is the LORD still at Zion?
  Is Zion's King still there?"

And God says, "Why did my people make me
    angry
  by worshipping idols,
    their useless false gods?"

ᵃ **8:13** *I will take away . . . gave them* The Hebrew text is not clear.
ᵇ **8:16** *snorting* The sound caused by forcing breath very hard through the nose.
ᶜ **8:17** *poisonous snakes* This probably means one of Judah's enemies.

²⁰The people cry out,
  "Summer is over.
The time for harvest is past.
  And still no one has come to save us."

²¹I hurt because my people are hurting.
  I am filled with sorrow, too sad to speak.
²²There must be some medicine in the land of
    Gilead.
  There must be a doctor there.
So why are my people still hurting?
  Why has no one healed them?

9 If my head were filled with water,
  and if my eyes were a fountain of tears,
I would cry day and night for my people
  who have been destroyed.

²If only I had a place in the desert—
  a house where travellers spend the
    night—
so I could leave my people.
  I could go away from them,
because they are all unfaithful to God.
  They have all turned against him.

³"They use their tongues like a bow;
  lies fly from their mouths like arrows.
Lies, not truth,
  have grown strong in this land.
They go from one sin to another.
  They don't know me."
This is what the LORD says.

⁴"Watch your neighbours!
  Don't trust your own brothers,
because every brother is a cheat.
  Every neighbour talks behind your back.
⁵Everyone lies to their neighbour.
  No one speaks the truth.
The people of Judah have taught
  their tongues to lie.
They sinned until they were too tired
  to come back.
⁶One bad thing followed another,
  and lies followed lies.
The people refused to know me."
  This is what the LORD says.

⁷So the LORD All-Powerful says,
  "A worker heats metal in a fire to test it and
    see if it is pure.
  I will test the people of Judah like that.
I have no other choice.
  My people have sinned.
⁸The people of Judah have tongues as sharp as
    arrows.
  Their mouths speak lies.
They all speak kindly to their neighbours,

but they are secretly planning ways to
  attack them.
⁹Should I punish the people of Judah for doing
  these things?"
This message is from the LORD.
  "You know I should punish a nation such as this.
  I should give it the punishment it deserves."

¹⁰I, Jeremiah, will cry for the mountains.
  I will sing a funeral song for the empty fields,
  because all the animals have been taken away.
No one goes there any more.
  The sounds of cattle cannot be heard.
The birds have flown away,
  and the animals are gone.

¹¹The Lord says, "I will make the city of
  Jerusalem a pile of ruins.
  It will be a home for jackals.
I will destroy the cities in the land of Judah,
  so no one will live there."

¹²Is anyone wise enough to understand this
picture of our land? Why is it ruined and as empty
as an endless desert? Has the LORD told anyone
who can explain to us why this has happened?
¹³The LORD answered, "This has happened
because the people of Judah stopped following the
teachings I gave them. They refused to listen to me,
and they have not done what I told them to do.
¹⁴They were stubborn and decided to worship the
false god Baal, as their ancestors had taught them."
¹⁵So the LORD All-Powerful, the God of Israel, says,
"I will soon make the people of Judah eat bitter
food and drink poisoned water. ¹⁶I will scatter them
through other nations that they and their ancestors
knew nothing about. I will send an army with
swords to chase them down until they have all
been killed."

¹⁷This is what the LORD All-Powerful says:
  "Now think about these things!
Call for the women who get paid to cry at
    funerals.
  Send for the people who are good at that job.
¹⁸The people say,
  'Let those women come quickly
    and cry for us.
Then our eyes will fill with tears
  that flow over our eyelids like streams of
    water.'

¹⁹"The sound of loud crying is heard from Zion:
  'We are really ruined!
    We are so ashamed!
We must leave our land,
  because our houses have been destroyed.
  Now our houses are only piles of rock.'"

²⁰Now, women of Judah, listen to the message
from the LORD.
Listen to the words from his mouth.
Teach your daughters how to cry loudly.
Each of them must learn to sing this funeral
song:
²¹"Death has climbed in through our windows
and has come into our palaces.
Death has come to our children who play in
the streets
and to the young men who meet in the
public places."

²²This is what you should say: "The LORD says,
'Dead bodies will lie
in the fields like dung.
Their bodies will lie on the ground like grain a
farmer has cut.
But there will be no one to gather them.'"

²³This is what the LORD says:
"The wise must not boast about their wisdom.
The strong men must not boast about their
strength.
The rich must not boast about their money.
²⁴But if someone wants to boast, then let them
boast about this:
Let them boast that they learned to know me.
Let them boast that they understand that I am
the LORD,
that I am kind and fair,
and that I do good things on earth.
I love this kind of boasting."
This message is from the LORD.

INSIGHT

For Jews, circumcision is an outward
symbol of being "set apart" as God's
people. Here, God is saying that he
wants his people to be circumcised in
their hearts not merely in the flesh. They
should be truly committed to him and set
apart deep in their hearts.

Jeremiah 9:25–26

²⁵This is what the LORD says: "The time is
coming when I will punish all those who are
circumcised only in the body. ²⁶I am talking about
the people of the nations of Egypt, Judah, Edom,
Ammon, Moab and all those who live in the
desert. The circumcision they do is not the kind
the Lord wants. But the people of Israel are not
really circumcised either. They are not circumcised
in their hearts."^a

The LORD and the Idols

10 Family of Israel, listen to the LORD! He is
speaking to you. ²This is what the LORD
says:

"Don't live like people from other nations.
Don't be afraid of special signs in the sky.^b
The other nations are afraid of what they see
in the sky.
But you must not be afraid of them.
³The customs of other people are worth
nothing.
Their idols are nothing but wood from the
forest.
Their idols are made by workers with their
chisels.^c
⁴They make their idols beautiful with silver and
gold.
They use hammers and nails to fasten their
idols down
so they will not fall over.
⁵The idols of the other nations are like
a scarecrow in a cucumber field.
They cannot walk.
They cannot talk, and the people must carry
them.
So don't be afraid of their idols.
They cannot hurt you.
And they cannot help you either."

⁶LORD, there is no one like you.
You are great!
Your name is great and powerful!
⁷Everyone should respect you, King of all the
nations.
You deserve their respect.
There are many wise men among the
nations,
but not one of them is as wise as you.

⁸They are all stupid and foolish.
The only teaching they get is from the
useless wooden idols they worship!
⁹These idols are covered with silver from
Tarshish
and gold from the city of Uphaz.
They are the work of craftsmen and
goldsmiths.

---

^a **9:26 circumcised in their hearts** See the note at Jer. 4:4.
^b **10:2 special signs in the sky** People believed that such things as comets, meteors or eclipses of the sun and moon could be
used to learn what was going to happen in the future.
^c **10:3 chisels** Sharp tools used to carve wood or stone.

They are dressed in royal blue and purple
robes,
all made by skilled workers.
¹⁰But the LORD is the only true God.
He is the only God who is alive.
He is the King who rules forever.
The earth shakes when he is angry.
The people of the nations cannot stop his
anger.

¹¹The Lord says, "Tell them this message:
'These false gods did not make heaven and
earth.
They will be destroyed and disappear from
heaven and earth.'"ᵃ

¹²God is the one who used his power and made
the earth.
He used his wisdom and built the world.
With his understanding he stretched the sky
over the earth.
¹³God causes the loud thunder,
and he causes great floods of water to fall
from the sky.
He makes clouds rise in the sky everywhere
on earth.
He sends lightning with the rain.
He brings out the wind from his
storehouses.

¹⁴People are so stupid!
Metalworkers are fooled by the idols that
they themselves made.
These statues are nothing but lies.
They are stupid.ᵇ
¹⁵These idols are worth nothing.
They are something to make fun of.
In the time of judgement they will be
destroyed.
¹⁶But Jacob's Godᶜ is not like the idols.
He made everything,
and Israel is the family that God chose to be
his own people.
His name is LORD All-Powerful.

Destruction Is Coming

¹⁷Get everything you own and prepare to
leave.
People of Judah, you are trapped in the city,
and the enemy is all around it.

¹⁸This is what the LORD says:
"This time, I will throw the people of Judah
out of this country.
I will bring pain and trouble to them.
I will do this so that they will learn their
lesson."ᵈ

¹⁹I am hurt badly.
I am injured and I cannot be healed.
But I told myself, "This is my sickness;
I must suffer through it."
²⁰My tent is ruined.
All its ropes are broken.
My children have left me.
They are gone.
No one is left to put up my tent.
No one is left to set up a shelter for me.
²¹The shepherds are stupid.
They don't try to find the LORD.
They are not wise,
so their flocks are scattered and lost.
²²Listen! A loud noise!
The noise is coming from the north.ᵉ
It will destroy the cities of Judah.
Judah will become an empty desert.
It will be a home for jackals.

²³LORD, I know that our lives do not belong
to us.
We have no control over what happens.
²⁴So correct us, LORD!
But please be fair.
Don't punish us in anger,
or you will destroy us!
²⁵If you are angry, then punish the other
nations.
They don't know or respect you.
They don't worship you.
Those nations destroyed Jacob's family.
They destroyed Israel completely.
They destroyed Israel's homeland.

The Agreement Is Broken

11 This is the message from the LORD:
²"Jeremiah, listen to the words of this
agreement and tell them to the people living in
Jerusalem and the rest of Judah. ³Tell them that this
is what the LORD, the God of Israel, says: 'Bad
things will happen to anyone who does not obey
this agreement. ⁴I am talking about the agreement

ᵃ 10:11 **Tell them this message . . . earth** This part was written in Aramaic, not Hebrew. This was the language people used
often when writing to people in other countries. It was also the language spoken in Babylon.
ᵇ 10:14 **They are stupid** Literally, "They have no spirit." This might also mean "They are not alive."
ᶜ 10:16 **Jacob's God** Literally, "Jacob's share". This means that God and Jacob (the people of Israel) had a special relationship—God
belonged to Israel, and Israel belonged to God.
ᵈ 10:18 **they will learn their lesson** The Hebrew text is not clear.
ᵉ 10:22 **north** The Babylonian army came from this direction to attack Judah. Armies from countries north and east of Israel often
came this way to attack Judah and Israel.

I made with your ancestors when I brought them out of that furnace[a] called Egypt.' At that time I told them, 'Listen to me and obey all the commands I give you. Then you will be my people and I will be your God.'

⁵"I did this to keep the promise that I had made to your ancestors. I promised to give them a very fertile land—a land flowing with milk and honey. And you are living in that country today."

I answered, "Amen, Lord."

⁶The Lord said to me, "Jeremiah, tell this message in the towns of Judah and in the streets of Jerusalem: 'Listen to the words of this agreement, and then obey these laws. ⁷I gave a warning to your ancestors at the time I brought them out of the land of Egypt. I have warned them again and again to this day. I told them to obey me. ⁸But your ancestors did not listen to me. They were stubborn and did what their own evil hearts wanted. The agreement says that bad things will happen to them if they don't obey. So I made all the bad things happen to them. I commanded them to obey the agreement, but they did not.'"

⁹The Lord said to me, "Jeremiah, I know that the people of Judah and the people living in Jerusalem have made secret plans. ¹⁰They are committing the same sins that their ancestors did. Their ancestors refused to listen to my message. They followed and worshiped other gods. The family of Israel and the family of Judah have broken the agreement I made with their ancestors."

¹¹So this is what the Lord says: "I will soon make something terrible happen to the people of Judah. They will not be able to escape. They will be sorry and cry to me for help, but I will not listen to them. ¹²The people in the towns of Judah and in the city of Jerusalem will go and pray to their idols for help. They burn incense to those idols. But their idols will not be able to help the people of Judah when that terrible disaster comes.

¹³"People of Judah, you have many idols—there are as many idols as there are towns in Judah. You have built many altars for worshiping that shameful god Baal—there are as many altars as there are streets in Jerusalem.

¹⁴"As for you, Jeremiah, don't pray for these people of Judah. Don't beg for them. Don't say prayers for them. I will not listen. They will suffer and then call to me for help, but I will not listen.

¹⁵"Judah is the one I love, but why is she in my temple?
    She has done too many evil things.

Judah, do you think vows and sacrifices will
    keep you from being destroyed?
Will I then allow you to enjoy your evil
    ways?"

¹⁶The Lord gave you a name.
    He called you, "A green olive tree, beautiful
      to look at."
But with a powerful storm, he will set that
    tree on fire,
    and its branches will be burned up.[b]
¹⁷The Lord All-Powerful planted you,
    and he said that disaster will come to you.
That is because the family of Israel
    and the family of Judah have done evil
      things.
They offered sacrifices to Baal,
    and that made him angry!

Evil Plans Against Jeremiah

¹⁸The Lord showed me that the men of Anathoth[c] were making plans against me. He showed me what they were doing, so I knew they were against me. ¹⁹Before he showed me this, I was like a gentle lamb waiting to be butchered. I did not understand that they were against me. They were saying this about me: "Let us destroy the tree and its fruit! Let us kill him! Then people will forget him." ²⁰So I prayed, "Lord All-Powerful, you are a fair judge. You know how to test people's hearts and minds. I trust you to defend me, so I want to see you give them the punishment they deserve."

²¹The Lord said to me: "Those people from Anathoth are planning to take your life. They are telling you not to prophesy in the name of the Lord or they will kill you. This is what I have to say about them: ²²I, the Lord All-Powerful, promise that I will soon punish those people. Their young men will die in war. Their sons and daughters will die from hunger. ²³No one from the city of Anathoth will be left. No one will survive. I will punish them and cause something bad to happen to them."

Jeremiah Complains to God

12 Lord, if I argue with you,
    you are always right.
But I want to ask you about some things that
    don't seem right.
Why are wicked people successful?
Why do people you cannot trust have such
    easy lives?

---

[a] **11:4 furnace** Literally, "iron furnace". That is, an oven hot enough to soften iron so that it can be hammered into something useful.

[b] **11:15–16** The meaning of these verses is uncertain.

[c] **11:18 men of Anathoth** Anathoth was Jeremiah's home town. The people who were plotting against him there included his own relatives. See Jer. 12:6.

2You have put these wicked people here like
   plants with strong roots.
   They grow and produce fruit.
With their mouths they say that you are near
   and dear to them,
   but in their hearts they are really far away
    from you.
3But you know my heart, LORD.
   You see me and test my mind.
Drag the evil people away like sheep to be killed.
   Choose them for the day of slaughter.
4How much longer will the land be dry?
   How long will the grass be dry and dead?
The birds and the animals of this land have all
   died,
   and it is the fault of the wicked.
But they are saying,
   "Jeremiah will not live long enough to see
    what happens to us."

INSIGHT

*God speaks to people in many different
ways. This is a great reminder that when
someone prays honestly to God, he may
actually talk back! In Jeremiah's case,
it was not very good news for him and
his people, but God stayed true to his
promises for them.*

Jeremiah 12:5–17

God's Answer to Jeremiah

5"Jeremiah, if running a race against men
   makes you tired,
   how will you race against horses?
If you trip and fall in an open field,
   what will you do in the thornbushes by the
    Jordan River?
6These men are your own brothers.
   Members of your own family are making
    plans against you.
   People from your own family are shouting
    at you.
Don't trust them,
   even when they speak to you like friends.

The LORD Rejects Judah

7"I have abandoned my house.
   I have left my own property.*a*
I have given Judah, the one I love,
   to her enemies.

8My own people turned against me like a wild
   lion.
   They roared at me, so I turned away from
    them.
9My own people have become like
   a dying animal surrounded by vultures.
These birds are circling around her.
   Come on, wild animals.
   Come get something to eat.
10Many shepherds have ruined my vineyard.
   They have trampled the plants in my field.
   They have made my beautiful field a
    desert.
11They have turned it into an empty desert.
   It is dry and dead.
The whole land has been ruined,
   and no one is left to care for it.
12The empty hills are covered with soldiers
   who have come to destroy everything.
The LORD is using them to punish that land
   from one end to the other.
   No one is safe.
13The people will plant wheat,
   but they will harvest only thorns.
They will work hard until they are very
   tired,
   but they will get nothing for all their work.
They will be ashamed of their crop.
   The LORD's anger caused this."

The LORD's Promise to Israel's Neighbours

14This is what the LORD says: "I will tell you
what I will do for all those who live around the
land of Israel. They are very wicked. They have
destroyed the land I gave to the people of Israel. I
will pull the evil people up and throw them out of
their land, and I will pull the people of Judah up
with them. 15But after I pull them up out of their
land, I will feel sorry for them. I will bring each
family home to their own land. 16I want them to
learn the ways of my people. They once taught
my people to use Baal's name to make promises.
Now I want them to begin their promises by
saying, 'As the LORD lives.' Then I will make them
successful as a part of my people. 17But if a nation
does not listen to my message, I will completely
destroy it. I will pull it up like a dead plant." This
message is from the LORD.

The Sign of the Loincloth

13 This is what the LORD said to me: "Jeremiah, go and buy a linen loincloth.*b*
Then put it around your waist. Don't let it get
wet."

---

a **12:7 house . . . my own property** That is, the people of Judah.
b **13:1 loincloth** A common undergarment in ancient Judah. It was a short skirt that was wrapped around the hips. It reached
about halfway down the thighs.

²So I bought a linen loincloth, just as the LORD told me to do, and I put it around my waist. ³Then the message from the LORD came to me a second time. ⁴This was the message: "Jeremiah, take the loincloth you bought and are wearing, and go to Perath.ᵃ Hide the loincloth there in a crack in the rocks."

⁵So I went to Perath and hid the loincloth there, just as the LORD told me to do. ⁶Many days later the LORD said to me, "Now, Jeremiah, go to Perath. Get the loincloth that I told you to hide there."

⁷So I went to Perath and dug up the loincloth. I took it out of the crack in the rocks where I had hidden it. But now I could not wear the loincloth, because it was ruined. It was not good for anything.

⁸Then the message from the LORD came to me. ⁹This is what the LORD said: "The loincloth is ruined and not good for anything. In the same way, I will ruin the proud people of Judah and Jerusalem. ¹⁰I will ruin them because they refuse to listen to my messages. They are stubborn and do only what they want to do. They follow and worship other gods. They will be like this linen loincloth. They will be ruined and not good for anything. ¹¹A loincloth is wrapped tightly around a man's waist. In the same way, I wrapped the family of Israel and the family of Judah around me." This message is from the LORD. "I did that so that they would be my people and bring me fame, praise and honour. But my people did not listen to me."

Warnings to Judah

¹²"Jeremiah, say to the people of Judah: 'This is what the LORD, the God of Israel, says: Every wineskin should be filled with wine.' They will laugh and say to you, 'Of course, we know that every wineskin should be filled with wine.' ¹³Then you will say to them, 'This is what the LORD says: I will make everyone who lives in this land as helpless as a drunk. I am talking about the kings who sit on David's throne. I am also talking about the priests, the prophets and all the people who live in Jerusalem. ¹⁴I will make them stumble and fall against each other, even the fathers and sons.' This message is from the LORD. 'I will not feel sorry for them or have mercy on them. I will not allow my pity for them to stop me from destroying the people of Judah.'"

¹⁵Listen and pay attention.
  The LORD has spoken to you.
  Do not be proud.
¹⁶Honour the LORD your God.
  Praise him or he will bring darkness.
  Praise him before you fall on the dark
    hills.
You people of Judah are hoping for light,
  but the Lord will turn the light into thick
    darkness.
  He will change it into the deepest gloom.
¹⁷If you people of Judah don't listen to him,
  I will hide and cry.
Your pride will cause me to cry.
  I will cry very hard.
My eyes will overflow with tears,
  because the LORD's flockᵇ will be captured.
¹⁸Tell these things to the king and his wife,
  "Come down from your thrones.
  Your beautiful crowns have fallen from your
    heads."
¹⁹The cities in the Negev are locked.
  No one can open them.
All the people of Judah have been taken away
    as captives.
  They were carried away as prisoners.

²⁰Jerusalem, look!
  The enemy is coming from the north!ᶜ
Where is the flockᵈ you were once in
    charge of?
  That beautiful flock has gone now.
²¹I will let your enemies become your
    rulers—
  people you once trusted with your secrets.
  What will you say then?
Surely you will feel great pain,
  like a woman giving birth.
²²You might ask yourself,
  "Why has this bad thing happened to me?"
It happened because of your many sins.
  That's why they were allowed to tear off
    your clothes
  and take advantage of you.
²³A black man cannot change the colour of his
    skin,
  and a leopard cannot change its spots.
In the same way, Jerusalem, you cannot
    change and do good.
  You always do bad things.

ᵃ **13:4 Perath** Probably a village near Jerusalem. This town is called Parah in the list of the cities of the land of Benjamin in Josh. 18:23. But this name also means the Euphrates River.
ᵇ **13:17 LORD's flock** This is a figurative name for the people of Judah. The Lord is thought of as a shepherd, while his people are seen as his flock of sheep.
ᶜ **13:20 north** The Babylonian army came from this direction to attack Judah. Armies from countries north and east of Israel often came this way to attack Judah and Israel.
ᵈ **13:20 flock** Here, the word "flock" refers to all the towns around Jerusalem, as if Jerusalem were the shepherd and the towns of Judah were her flock.

²⁴"I will force you to leave your homes.
   You will run in all directions.
   You will be like chaff blown away by the
      desert wind.
²⁵This is what will happen to you.
   This is your part in my plans."
   This message is from the LORD.
"Why will this happen?
   Because you forgot me.
   You trusted false gods.
²⁶Jerusalem, I will pull your skirt up over
      your face.
   Everyone will see you,
   and you will be ashamed.
²⁷I have seen the terrible things you have
      done.ᵃ
   I have seen you laughing and having sex
      with your lovers.
   I know all about your sickening worship of
      other gods.
   I have seen you on the hills and in the
      fields.
   It will be very bad for you, Jerusalem.
   How long will you continue your filthy
      sins?"

Drought and False Prophets

14 This is the LORD's message to Jeremiah
about the time of no rain:

²"The nation of Judah cries for people who
      have died.
   The people in the cities of Judah grow
      weaker and weaker.
   They lie on the ground.
   People in Jerusalem, cry to God for help.
³The leaders of the people send their servants
      to get water.
   The servants go to the water storage places,
   but they don't find any water.
   The servants come back with empty jars,
   so they are ashamed and embarrassed.
   They cover their heads in shame.
⁴No one prepares the ground for crops.ᵇ
   No rain falls on the land.
   The farmers are depressed.
   So they cover their heads in shame.
⁵Even the mother deer in the field leaves her
      newborn baby alone,
   because there is no grass.
⁶Wild donkeys stand on the bare hills.
   They sniff the wind like jackals.
   But their eyes cannot find any food,
   because there are no plants to eat."

⁷We know that this is our fault.
   We are now suffering because of our sins.
   LORD, do something to help us for the good
      of your name.
   We admit that we have left you many times.
   We have sinned against you.
⁸God, you are the hope of Israel!
   You save Israel in times of trouble.
   But now you are like a stranger in the land,
   like a traveller who only stays one
      night.
⁹You are like a man who has been taken by
      surprise,
   like a soldier who does not have the power
      to save anyone.
   But, LORD, you are with us.
   We are called by your name, so don't leave
      us without help!

¹⁰This is what the LORD says about the people
of Judah: "The people of Judah love nothing more
than to wander away from me. They don't
hesitate to leave me. So now the LORD will not
accept them. Now he will remember the evil they
do. He will punish them for their sins."

¹¹Then the LORD said to me, "Jeremiah, don't
pray for good things to happen to the people of
Judah. ¹²They might begin to fast and pray to me,
but I will not listen to their prayers. Even if they
offer burnt offerings and grain offerings to me,
I will not accept them. I will destroy the people of
Judah with war. I will take away their food, and
they will starve. And I will destroy them with
terrible diseases."

¹³But I said, "Lord GOD, the prophets were
telling the people something different. They were
telling the people of Judah, 'You will not suffer
from war or from hunger. The Lord will give you
peace in this land.'"

¹⁴Then the LORD said to me, "Jeremiah, those
prophets are telling lies in my name. I did not send
them or command them or speak to them. Their
prophecies came from false visions, worthless
magic and their own wishful thinking. ¹⁵So this is
what I, the LORD, say about the prophets who are
speaking in my name. I did not send them. They
said, 'No enemy will ever attack this country.
There will never be hunger in this land.' So those
prophets will die from hunger or by an enemy's
sword. ¹⁶And the people they spoke to will be
thrown into the streets. The people will die from
hunger and from an enemy's sword. I will punish
them, and no one will be there to bury them, their
wives, their sons or their daughters.

ᵃ **13:27** *I have seen . . . done* Probably the worship of false gods. Part of that worship was having sex with temple prostitutes.
ᵇ **14:4** *No one . . . crops* This follows the ancient Greek version. The Hebrew text is not clear.

[17]"Jeremiah, speak this message to the people of Judah:

'My eyes fill with tears
    night and day without stopping.
I will cry for my dear people,[a]
    because someone hit them and crushed
      them.
They have been hurt very badly.
[18]If I go into the country,
    I see the bodies of those killed in war.
If I go into the city,
    I see people sick from hunger.
The priests and prophets continue their work,
    but they don't understand what is
      happening.'"

[19]Lord, have you completely rejected the nation
    of Judah?
    Do you hate Zion?
You hurt us so badly that we cannot be made
    well again.
    Why did you do that?
We were hoping for peace,
    but nothing good has come.
We were hoping for a time of healing,
    but only terror came.
[20]Lord, we know that we are wicked.
    We know that our ancestors did evil
      things.
    Yes, we sinned against you.
[21]For the good of your name, don't push us
    away.
    Don't take away the honour from your
      glorious throne.
Remember your agreement with us
    and do not break it.
[22]Foreign idols don't have the power to bring
    rain.
    The sky does not have the power to send
      down showers of rain.
You, the Lord our God, are our only hope.
    You are the one who made all these things.

15 The Lord said to me, "Jeremiah, even if Moses and Samuel were here to pray for the people of Judah, I would not feel sorry for them. Send the people of Judah away from me! Tell them to go! [2]They might ask you, 'Where will we go?' Tell them this is what the Lord says:

"'I have chosen some people to die.
    They will die.
I have chosen some to be killed with swords.
    They will be killed with swords.

I have chosen some to die from hunger.
    They will die from hunger.
I have chosen some to be taken away to a
    foreign country.
    They will be prisoners there.
[3]I will send four kinds of destroyers against
    them.'
This message is from the Lord:
'I will send the enemy with a sword to kill.
I will send the dogs to drag their bodies
    away.
I will send birds of the air and wild animals
    to eat and destroy their bodies.
[4]I will make the people of Judah
    an example of something terrible for all the
      people on earth.
I will do this to the people of Judah
    because of what Manasseh[b] did in Jerusalem.
Manasseh was the son of King Hezekiah.
    Manasseh was a king of Judah.

[5]"'No one will feel sorry for you, city of
    Jerusalem.
No one will be sad and cry for you.
No one will go out of their way to even ask
    how you are.
[6]Jerusalem, you left me.'
    This message is from the Lord.
'Again and again you left me!
    So I will punish and destroy you.
    I am tired of being patient with you.

INSIGHT

Wind winnowing is an agricultural method developed by ancient cultures for separating grain from useless chaff. The harvester would throw the grain mixed with chaff into the air with a winnowing fork (like a pitchfork) and allow the wind to blow away the lighter chaff, so only the grain remained.

Jeremiah 15:7

[7]In every city throughout the land
    I will scatter my people like chaff in the
      wind.
They have not changed the way they live,
    so I will destroy them.
I will take away their children.
[8]There will be more widows in Judah
    than grains of sand by the sea.

---

[a] **14:17** *my dear people* Literally, "virgin daughter, my people".
[b] **15:4** *Manasseh* Manasseh was the most evil king of Judah according to 2 Kgs 21:1–16. He worshipped many gods.

In full daylight an attack will come against the
young men
and cause their mothers to suffer.
I will bring pain and fear on the people of
Judah.
It will come upon them suddenly.
⁹The enemy will attack with swords and kill
the people.
They will kill the survivors from Judah.
A woman with seven children will lose them.
She will cry until she becomes weak and
struggles to breathe.
She will be upset and confused,
because her bright day has become dark.'"
This message is from the LORD.

Jeremiah Complains to God Again

¹⁰Mother, I am sorry
that you gave birth to me.
I am the one who must accuse
and criticize the whole land.
I have not loaned or borrowed anything,
but everyone curses me.
¹¹Surely, LORD, I have served you well.
In times of disaster and trouble,
I prayed to you about my enemies.

God Answers Jeremiah

¹²"Jeremiah, you know that no one can shatter a
piece of iron.
I mean the iron mixed with bronze that is
from the north.ᵃ
¹³The people of Judah have many treasures.
I will give these riches to other people.
They will not have to buy them,
because Judah has many sins.
The people sinned in every part of Judah.
¹⁴People of Judah, I will make you slaves of your
enemies.
You will be slaves in a land that you never
knew.
I am very angry.
My anger is like a hot fire,
and you will be burned."

¹⁵LORD, you understand me.
Remember me and take care of me.
People are hurting me.
Give them the punishment they deserve.
You are being patient with them.
But don't destroy me while you remain
patient with them.
Think about me.
Think about the pain I suffer for you.
¹⁶Your words came to me, and I ate them up.

They made me very happy.
I was glad to be called by your name,
LORD God All-Powerful.
¹⁷I never sat with the crowd
as they laughed and had fun.
I sat by myself because of your influence
on me.
You filled me with anger at the evil around
me.
¹⁸I don't understand why I still hurt.
I don't understand why my wound is not
cured and cannot be healed.
I think you have changed.
You are like a spring of water that became
dry.
You are like a spring whose water has
stopped flowing.

¹⁹Then the LORD said, "Jeremiah, if you change
and come back to me,
I will not punish you.
If you change and come back to me,
then you may serve me.
If you speak important things, not worthless
words,
then you may speak for me.
The people of Judah should change and come
back to you.
But don't you change and be like them.
²⁰I will make you strong.
The people will think you are strong,
like a wall made of bronze.
The people of Judah will fight against you,
but they will not defeat you.
They will not defeat you,
because I am with you.
I will help you, and I will save you."
This message is from the LORD.
²¹"I will save you from these evil people.
They frighten you, but I will save you from
them."

The Day of Disaster

16 The LORD's message came to me: ²"Jeremiah, you must not get married. You must
not have sons or daughters in this place."
³This is what the LORD says about the sons and
daughters who are born in the land of Judah and
about their mothers and fathers: ⁴"They will die
from terrible diseases. And no one will cry for
them or bury them. Their bodies will lie on the
ground like dung, or they will die in war, or they
will starve to death. Their dead bodies will be
food for the birds of the sky and the wild animals
of the earth."

ᵃ **15:12 *north*** This may refer to the direction from which the Babylonian army came to attack Judah and Israel.

⁵So the LORD says, "Jeremiah, don't go into a house where people are eating a funeral meal. Don't go there to cry for the dead or to show your sorrow. Don't do these things, because I have taken back my blessing. I will not be kind to the people of Judah. I will not feel sorry for them." This message is from the LORD.

⁶"Important people and common people will die in the land of Judah. No one will bury them or cry for them. No one will cut himself or shave his head to show sorrow for them. ⁷No one will bring food to those who are crying for the dead. No one will comfort those whose mother or father has died. No one will offer a drink to comfort those who are crying for the dead.

⁸"Jeremiah, don't go into a house where the people are having a party. Don't go into that house and sit down to eat and drink. ⁹This is what the LORD All-Powerful, the God of Israel says: I will soon stop the sounds of people having fun. I will stop the happy sounds of people enjoying a wedding party. This will happen during your lifetime. I will do these things very soon.

¹⁰"Jeremiah, you will tell the people of Judah these things, and the people will ask you, 'Why has the LORD said these terrible things to us? What have we done wrong? What sin have we done against the LORD our God?' ¹¹You must tell them: 'Terrible things will happen to you because your ancestors stopped following me.' This message is from the LORD. 'They stopped following me and began to follow and serve other gods. They worshipped those other gods. Your ancestors left me and stopped obeying my law. ¹²But you people have sinned more than your ancestors. You are very stubborn, and you are doing only what you want to do. You are not obeying me. Because you do only what you want to do, ¹³so I will throw you out of this country. I will force you to go to a foreign land. You will go to a land that you and your ancestors never knew. There you can serve false gods all you want to. I will not help you or show you any favours.'

¹⁴"The LORD says that the time is coming when people will not begin their promises by saying, 'As surely as the LORD lives, the Lord who brought the Israelites out of the land of Egypt.' ¹⁵Instead, they will say, 'As surely as the LORD lives, the Lord who brought the Israelites out of the northern land, who brought them out of all the countries where he had sent them.' They will say that because I will bring the Israelites back to the land I gave to their ancestors.

¹⁶"I will soon send for many fishermen to come to this land." This message is from the LORD. "They will catch the people of Judah. After that happens, I will send for many hunters[a] to come to this land. They will hunt the people of Judah on every mountain and hill and in the cracks of the rocks. ¹⁷I see everything they do. The people of Judah cannot hide the things they do. Their sin is not hidden from me. ¹⁸I will pay the people of Judah back for the evil things they did—I will punish them two times for every sin. I will do this because they have made my land 'dirty'. They made my land 'dirty' with their terrible idols. I hate those idols, but they have filled my country with their idols."

¹⁹LORD, you are my strength and my protection.
    You are a safe place to run to in times of trouble.
The nations will come to you from all around the world.
    They will say, "Our fathers had false gods.
They worshipped those worthless idols,
    but the idols did not help them.
²⁰Can people make real gods for themselves?
    No, they can only make statues that are not really gods."

²¹"So I will teach those who make idols.
    Right now I will teach them about my power and my strength.
Then they will know that I am God.
    They will know that I am the LORD.

Guilt Written on the Heart

17 "The sins of Judah are written where they cannot be erased—
    cut into stone with an iron pen,
cut deep with a hard tip into the stone that is the hearts of the people.
    Their sins are carved into the horns of their altars.[b]
²Even their children remember the altars
    that were dedicated to false gods.
They remember the wooden poles
    that were dedicated to Asherah.
Those objects of worship were everywhere,
    under the green trees and on the hills
³and on the mountains and in the fields.
So, because of this sin throughout your land,
    I will let your enemies take your wealth and treasures
    and the altars to false gods throughout your land.
⁴Because of what you have done,
    you will lose the land I gave you.
And I will let your enemies take you to be slaves
    in a land you do not know.

---

a **16:16** *fishermen . . . hunters* This means the enemy soldiers from Babylon.
b **17:1** *horns of their altars* The corners of altars were shaped like horns, and the blood of sacrifices was smeared on them. So Jeremiah may mean that the people's sins have made their altars unfit for sacrifices.

DEPENDING ON GOD ALONE

What was God's problem with the people of Judah at the time of Jeremiah? The easy answer to give is "their sin". But what does that really mean?

At the heart of all sin is the desire to trust in something – anything – other than God himself. God's desire for his people then and now is that they trust him and him alone.

DIG IN
READ Jeremiah 17:1–13

- What things does God count as sinful about Judah's behaviour (vv.1–3)?
- How does God know whether we are trusting in him or not (vv.9–10)?

Time and time again, God's people were seduced by the idols and the false gods of the nations that surrounded them. They would go to "high places" and built altars and monuments to false gods and goddesses; their attention was distracted and divided. They made excuses for themselves and lost sight of how God felt about it: perhaps they thought that God didn't mind a little bit of idolatry – or that he couldn't see it? But God knew what was going on because he can see inside people's hearts (v.10). Because this is a serious matter to God, there had to be a consequence. This is the central reason for the coming judgement.

- What is the promise for those who do trust in God (vv.7–8)?
- And what will become of those who don't (vv.3–6)?

Blessing for those who trust in God includes provision even when things get tough (v.8). A tree with deep roots can get the moisture it needs from way underground, so even in a time of drought it stays green and keeps producing fruit.

But people who don't trust in God are more like a bush in a desert – withered and dried out because no rain is falling. This is a picture of what will soon happen in Jeremiah's time.

DIG THROUGH

- Do you tend to phone a friend before bringing your worries to God? "Bad things will happen to those who put their trust in people" (v.5) is a warning against relying on people in place of God. Does this mean we should refuse help from people when we're in trouble and instead wait for God to help us?
- An old saying goes, "At the heart of every problem is the problem of the heart." Our minds are "sick" (v.9) and lead us into sin – our wills and emotions place other things above God. Here are some you might recognize: your ambitions, hopes and dreams; your friends, family and those you want to impress; your position or status; your own happiness, comfort and well-being; your things and the things you want; your skills and abilities. Do you think you need to change any priorities?

DIG DEEPER

- Paul warns the Colossians not to be "led away by the teaching of those who have nothing worth saying and only plan to deceive you" (Colossians 2:8). He tells them, "You must depend on Christ only" (2:7). See also the wise words from Proverbs 3:5–8.

This is because you have made me angry.
    And my anger is like a hot fire that will
        burn forever."

Trusting in People and Trusting in God

⁵This is what the LORD says:
"Bad things will happen to those who put
        their trust in people.
    Bad things will happen to those who
        depend on human strength.
    That is because they have stopped trusting
        the LORD.
⁶They are like a bush in a desert where no one
        lives.
    It is in a hot and dry land.
    It is in bad soil.
    That bush does not know about the good
        things that God can give.

⁷"But those who trust in the LORD will be
        blessed.
    They know that the LORD will do what
        he says.
⁸They will be strong like trees planted near a
        stream
    that send out roots to the water.
    They have nothing to fear when the days
        get hot.
    Their leaves are always green.
    They never worry, even in a year that has
        no rain.
    They always produce fruit.

⁹"Nothing can hide its evil as well as the
        human mind.
    It can be very sick,
    and no one really understands it.
¹⁰But I am the LORD,
    and I can look into a person's heart.
    I can test a person's mind and decide what
        each one should have.
    I can give each person the right payment for
        what they do.
¹¹Sometimes a bird will hatch an egg that it did
        not lay.
    Those who cheat to get money are like that
        bird.
    But when their lives are half finished,
        they will lose the money.
    At the end of their lives,
        it will be clear that they were fools."

¹²From the very beginning, our Temple
    has been a glorious throne for God.
    It is a very important place.
¹³LORD, you are the hope of Israel.
    You are like a spring of living water.
    Those who stop following the LORD
    will have a very short life.ᵃ

Jeremiah's Third Complaint

¹⁴LORD, if you heal me, I surely will be healed.
    Save me, and I surely will be saved.
    Lord, I praise you!
¹⁵The people of Judah continue to ask me
        questions.
    They say, "Jeremiah, what about the
        message from the LORD?
    Let's see that message come true."

¹⁶Lord, I did not run away from you.
    I followed you.
    I became the shepherdᵇ you wanted.
    I did not want the terrible day to come.
    You know what I said.
    You see all that is happening.
¹⁷Please don't make me afraid of you.
    I depend on you in times of trouble.
¹⁸People are hurting me.
    Make them ashamed,
        but don't disappoint me.
    Let them be filled with fear,
        but don't give me any reason to fear.
    Bring the terrible day of disaster to my enemies.
    Break them, and break them again.

Keeping the Sabbath Day Holy

¹⁹This is what the LORD said to me: "Jeremiah,
go and stand at the People's Gate,ᶜ where the
kings of Judah go in and out. Tell the people my
message, and then go to all the other gates of
Jerusalem and do the same.

²⁰"Say to the people, 'Listen to this message
from the LORD. Listen, kings of Judah. Listen, all
you people of Judah. All you who come through
these gates into Jerusalem, listen to me! ²¹This is
what the LORD says: be careful that you don't carry
a load on the Sabbath day. And don't bring a load
through the gates of Jerusalem on the Sabbath day.
²²Don't bring a load out of your houses on the
Sabbath day. Don't do any work on that day. You
must make the Sabbath day a holy day. I gave this
same command to your ancestors, ²³but they did

ᵃ **17:13 will have a very short life** Literally, "he will be written in the dirt". This might mean that a person's name was written
on a list of people who would soon die, or that a person's life will soon be gone—like a name written in the sand.
ᵇ **17:16 shepherd** God's people are sometimes called his "sheep", and the person who takes care of them is called the
"shepherd".
ᶜ **17:19 People's Gate** This might be one of the gates into Jerusalem or perhaps one of the southern gates into the Temple area
used by those who were not priests.

not obey me. They did not pay attention to me. Your ancestors were very stubborn. I punished them, but it did not do any good. They did not listen to me. 24But you must be careful to obey me, says the LORD. You must not bring a load through the gates of Jerusalem on the Sabbath. You must make the Sabbath day a holy day. You will do this by not doing any work on that day.

25"'If you obey this command, the kings and leaders will be from David's family. It will be the kings who sit on David's throne and the leaders from Judah and Jerusalem who come through the gates of Jerusalem riding on chariots and on horses. And Jerusalem will have people living in it forever. 26People will come to Jerusalem from the towns and villages of Judah, from the land where the tribe of Benjamin lives,ª from the western foothills, from the hill country and from the Negev. All these people will bring burnt offerings, sacrifices, grain offerings, incense and thank offerings to the Temple of the LORD in Jerusalem.

27"'But if you don't listen to me and obey me, bad things will happen. If you carry loads into Jerusalem on the Sabbath day, you are not keeping it as a holy day. So I will start a fire that cannot be put out. That fire will start at the gates of Jerusalem, and it will burn until it burns even the palaces.'"

The Potter and the Clay

18 This is the message that came to Jeremiah from the LORD: 2"Jeremiah, go down to the potter's house. I will give you my message there."

3So I went down to the potter's house and saw him working with clay on a potter's wheel. 4He was shaping the clay into a pot. But something went wrong with this pot. So he used the same clay to make another pot. With his hands he shaped the pot the way he wanted it to be.

5Then this message from the LORD came to me: 6"Family of Israel, you know that I can do the same thing with you. You are like the clay in the potter's hands, and I am the potter." This message is from the LORD. 7"There may be times when I will announce my plans to completely destroy a nation or a kingdom. I may say that I am going to pull it up by its roots. 8But if the people of that nation change their hearts and lives and stop doing evil things, I will change my mind. I will not bring on them the disaster I planned. 9There may be other times when I will announce my plans to build up a nation or a kingdom and make it strong. 10But if I see that nation doing evil things and refusing to obey me, I will change my mind about the good I had planned to do for them.

11"So, Jeremiah, say to the people of Judah and those who live in Jerusalem, 'This is what the LORD says: I am the potter preparing troubles for you and making plans against you. So stop doing the evil things you are doing. Every person must change and start doing good.' 12But the people of Judah will answer, 'We don't care what you say. We will continue to live as we like. We would rather be stubborn and do the evil things we want to do.'

13"Listen to what the LORD says:

"Ask the other nations this question:
  'Have you ever heard of anything so
    bad?'
Israel, a nation as dear to me as a young
    daughter,
  has done this terrible thing!
14It is as strange as finding no snow on
    Lebanon's mountains
  or seeing the cool streams that come from
    there stop flowing.
  That just does not happen!
15But my people have forgotten me.
  They burn offerings to worthless idols.
They have left the right way that their
    ancestors followed,
  and they stumble on the path they have
    chosen.
Instead of staying on the good road I showed
    them,
  they prefer to walk on bumpy paths.
16So their land will become an empty desert,
  a place for people from now on to make
    fun of.
All who pass by there will be shocked by what
    has happened.
  They will just shake their heads at what
    they see.
17Like a strong east wind, I will scatter my
    people.
  I will use their enemies to scatter them like
    dust.
When disaster comes upon them,
  they will see me leaving, not coming to
    help."

The People Plan Evil and Jeremiah Prays

18Then the enemies of Jeremiah said, "Come, let us make plans against Jeremiah. We will always have a priest to tell us what the law says. We will still have wise men to advise us and prophets to tell us a message from God. So who needs Jeremiah? Let's tell lies to ruin him. And let's stop listening to what he says."

19LORD, listen to me!
  Listen to what my enemies are saying.

ª 17:26 **the land where . . . Benjamin lives** The land of Benjamin was just north of the land of Judah.

20I have done only good to them.
It is not right for them to pay me back with
    evil.
But they are preparing a death trap for me!
Remember that I prayed to you for them.
I asked only good for them.
I tried to keep you from punishing them in
    anger.
21So now make their children starve to death!
Let their enemies kill them with swords.
Let their wives lose their children and
    husbands.
Let their men die from disease,
and let their young men be killed in battle.
22They dug a pit for me to fall into.
They hid traps for me to step in.
So let them cry out in their houses
    when you suddenly bring an enemy against
    them.
23LORD, you know about their plans to kill me.
So don't forgive their crimes or erase their
    sins.
Make them fall down in defeat.
Punish them in your anger!

The Broken Jar

19 The LORD said to me, "Jeremiah, go and buy a clay jar from a potter. Take some of the leaders of the people and some of the leading priests with you. 2Go out to the Valley of Ben Hinnom, near the front of the Potsherd Gate.a I have a message I want to announce there. 3Say to those who are with you, 'King of Judah and people of Jerusalem, listen to this message from the LORD! This is what the LORD All-Powerful, the God of Israel, says: I will soon make a terrible thing happen to this place! Everyone who hears about it will be amazed and full of fear. 4I will do these things because the people of Judah have stopped following me. They have made this a place for foreign gods. The people of Judah have burned sacrifices in this place to other gods. The people long ago did not worship those gods. Their ancestors did not worship them. These are new gods from other countries. The kings of Judah filled this place with the blood of innocent children. 5The kings of Judah built high places for the god Baal. They use those places to burn their sons in the fire. They burned their sons as burnt offerings to the god Baal. I did not tell them to do that. I did not ask them to offer their sons as sacrifices. I never even thought of such a thing. 6Now people call this place Topheth and the Valley of Hinnom. But I give you this warning. This message is from the LORD: The days are coming, when people will

call this place the Valley of Slaughter. 7At this place, I will ruin the plans of the people of Judah and Jerusalem. The enemy will chase them, and I will let the people of Judah be killed with swords in this place. I will make their dead bodies food for the birds and wild animals. 8I will completely destroy this city. People will whistle and shake their heads when they pass by Jerusalem. They will be shocked when they see how the city was destroyed. 9The enemy will bring its army around the city. That army will not let people go out to get food, so the people in the city will begin to starve. They will become so hungry that they will eat the bodies of their own sons and daughters, and then they will begin to eat each other.'

10"Jeremiah, tell this to the people, and while they are watching, break the jar. 11Then say this: 'The LORD All-Powerful says, I will break the nation of Judah and the city of Jerusalem, just as someone breaking a clay jar! And like a broken jar, the nation of Judah cannot be put back together again. The dead people will be buried here in Topheth until there is no more room. 12I will do this to these people and to this place. I will make this city like Topheth.' This message is from the LORD. 13'The houses in Jerusalem will become as "dirty" as this place, Topheth. The kings' palaces will be ruined like this place, Topheth, because the people worshipped false gods on the roofs of their houses.b They worshipped the stars and burned sacrifices to honour them. They gave drink offerings to false gods.'"

14Then Jeremiah left Topheth where the LORD had told him to speak. Jeremiah went to the LORD's Temple and stood in the courtyard of the Temple. Jeremiah said to all the people: 15"This is what the LORD All-Powerful, the God of Israel says: 'I said I would bring many disasters to Jerusalem and the villages around it. I will soon make this happen because the people are very stubborn. They refuse to listen and obey me.'"

Jeremiah and Pashhur

20 Pashhur son of Immer was a priest. He was the highest officer in the Temple of the LORD. When he heard Jeremiah say those things in the Temple courtyard, 2he had Jeremiah the prophet beaten. And he had his hands and feet locked between large blocks of wood. This was at the Upper Gate of Benjamin of the LORD's Temple. 3The next day Pashhur took Jeremiah out from between the blocks of wood. Then Jeremiah said to him, "The LORD's name for you is not Pashhur. Now his name for you is 'Surrounded by Terror'. 4That is your name because of what the LORD says:

---

a 19:2 **Potsherd Gate** The exact location of this gate is not known, though it was probably at the south-western part of the city.
b 19:13 **roofs of their houses** People built their houses with flat roofs that were used as an extra room.

'I will soon make you a terror to yourself and to all your friends. You will watch enemies killing your friends with swords. I will give all the people of Judah to the king of Babylon. He will take them away to the country of Babylon, and his army will kill the people of Judah with their swords. 5The people of Jerusalem worked hard to build things and become wealthy, but I will give all these things to their enemies. The king in Jerusalem has many treasures, but I will give all the treasures to the enemy. The enemy will take them and carry them away to the country of Babylon. 6And Pashhur, you and all the people living in your house will be taken away. You will be forced to go and live in the country of Babylon. You will die in Babylon, and you will be buried in that foreign country. You told lies to your friends. You said these things would not happen. But all your friends will also die and be buried in Babylon.'"

Jeremiah's Fifth Complaint

7LORD, you tricked me, and I certainly was
     fooled.
 You are stronger than I am, so you won.
I have become a joke.
 People laugh at me and make fun of me all
     day long.
8Every time I speak, I shout.
 I am always shouting about violence and
     destruction.
I tell the people about the message that I
     received from the LORD.
 But they only insult me and make fun of me.
9Sometimes I say to myself, "I will forget about
     him.
 I will not speak any more in his name."
But when I say that, his message is like a fire
     burning inside me!
 It feels like it is burning deep in my bones!
I get tired of trying to hold his message inside.
 And finally, I am not able to hold it in.
10I hear people whispering against me.
 Everywhere, I hear things that frighten me.
 Even my friends are speaking against me.
People are just waiting for me to make a
     mistake.
 They are saying, "Let us lie and say that he
     did something bad.
Maybe we can trick Jeremiah.
 Then we will have him.
 We will finally be rid of him.
Then we will grab him
 and take our revenge on him."
11But the LORD is with me.
 He is like a strong soldier.

So those who are chasing me will fall.
 They will not defeat me.
They will fail.
 They will be disappointed.
They will be ashamed,
 and they will never forget that shame.

12LORD All-Powerful, you test good people.
 You look deeply into a person's mind.
I told you my arguments against these
     people.
 So let me see you give them the
     punishment they deserve.
13Sing to the LORD!
 Praise the LORD!
He saves the lives of the poor!
 He saves them from the wicked!

Jeremiah's Sixth Complaint

14Curse the day that I was born!
 Don't bless the day my mother had me.
15Curse the man who told my father the news
     that I was born.
 "It's a boy!" he said.
 "You have a son."
He made my father very happy
 when he told him the news.
16Let that man be like the cities the LORD
     destroyed.[a]
 He had no pity on them.
Let him hear shouts of war in the morning;
 let him hear battle cries at noontime,
17because he did not kill me
 while I was in my mother's womb.
If he had killed me then,
 my mother would have been my grave,
 and I would not have been born.
18Why did I have to come out of her body?
 All I have seen is trouble and sorrow,
 and my life will end in shame.

God Rejects King Zedekiah's Request

21 This is the message that came to Jeremiah from the LORD. This was when King Zedekiah of Judah sent Pashhur[b] son of Malkijah and the priest Zephaniah son of Maaseiah to Jeremiah. They brought a message for Jeremiah. 2They said to Jeremiah, "Pray to the LORD for us. Ask him what will happen. We want to know, because King Nebuchadnezzar of Babylon is attacking us. Maybe the LORD will do great things for us, as he did in the past. Maybe he will make Nebuchadnezzar stop attacking us and leave."

3Then Jeremiah answered Pashhur and Zephaniah. He said, "Tell King Zedekiah, 4'This is what

---

[a] **20:16 cities the LORD destroyed** That is, Sodom and Gomorrah. See Gen. 19.
[b] **21:1 Pashhur** This is not the same Pashhur as the man in Jer. 20:1.

ENEMY AT THE GATES

The scene could come straight out of a Hollywood screenplay. The attractive heroine is bound and gagged, tied to a chair in a dark room as the villain towers over her with a knife, ready to slit her throat. Beads of sweat drip off her terrified brow as the music swells to a crescendo.

Suddenly, a door bursts open and there's a shaft of light. The suave hero steps into the room and . . . sits down and does nothing.

DIG IN
READ Jeremiah 21:1–14

- Why is Jeremiah called upon by the king (v.2)?
- What does God tell Jeremiah is going to happen (verse 3 onwards)?

Now, as predicted earlier in Jeremiah, the enemy armies of Babylon are at the gates of Jerusalem, the holy city of the people of God. Jeremiah is asked to pray for help. But the news that comes back from God is not what the people want to hear. The God they're all looking to for help says he will not help them defend their city.

- Why not? Why is God suddenly on the side of the enemy?
- Yet what mercy does God show his people (v.9)?

It looks very bleak for Jerusalem as King Zedekiah learns of his fate. Can you imagine how the people must have felt as they heard the armies from the north getting closer? Totally abandoned.

Until now God has always fought for his people – not against them! Their whole understanding of God is about to be shaken. But it's true – Nebuchadnezzar will be used by God to bring judgement on his people.

We mustn't read this section out of context, but see it as part of the whole. This judgement is for a specific purpose – so that the people's hearts can be turned around. God has their best interests at heart. And despite the impending judgement, there is still mercy from God in view. The city will be destroyed by fire, but the people can escape with their lives – into exile.

DIG THROUGH

What does God's judgement on an ancient people have to do with us today? He punished them with an end goal of salvation in mind. The Good News message contains both punishment and salvation. The reason it's such good news is that Jesus gets all the punishment, we get all the salvation.

DIG DEEPER

- This passage vividly shows that God will use any circumstances he chooses to get people to turn their hearts towards him. It may not be comfortable. We may not expect it. It might even put our understanding of God to the test. But for God our character is much more important than our comfort. He's looking at our long-term good. Check out 1 Peter 1:3–9, which illustrates this brilliantly for us.

the LORD, the God of Israel, says: You have weapons of war in your hands that you are using to defend yourselves from the Babylonians and their king. But I will make those weapons worthless.

"'The army from Babylon is outside the wall all around the city. Soon I will bring that army into Jerusalem. 5I myself will fight against you people of Judah. I will fight against you with my own powerful hand. I am very angry with you, so I will fight against you with my own powerful arm. I will fight very hard against you and show how angry I am. 6I will kill everything living in Jerusalem, both people and animals. They will die from a terrible disease that will spread all through the city. 7After that happens, says the LORD, I will give King Zedekiah of Judah and all his officials to King Nebuchadnezzar of Babylon. And I will give to Nebuchadnezzar the people who remain alive in Jerusalem—those who did not die from the terrible disease and the people who did not die in war or from hunger. I will give them all to King Nebuchadnezzar. The people of Judah will be captured by their enemies who want to kill them. Nebuchadnezzar's army will use their swords to kill the people of Judah and Jerusalem. Nebuchadnezzar will not show any mercy. He will not feel sorry for them.'

8"Also tell the people of Jerusalem, 'This is what the LORD says: Understand that I will let you choose to live or die. 9Anyone who stays in Jerusalem will die in war or from hunger or from a terrible disease. But anyone who goes out of Jerusalem and surrenders to the Babylonians attacking you will live. Only those who leave the city will win anything in this war—their lives! 10I have decided to make trouble for the city of Jerusalem. I will not help this city! I will give it to the king of Babylon, who will burn it with fire.'" This message is from the LORD.

11"Say this to Judah's royal family: 'Listen to the message from the LORD. 12Family of David, this is what the LORD says:

"'You must judge people fairly every day.
    Save people from those who rob them.
If you don't do that, I will be angry.
    My anger will be like a fire that no one can
        put out.
    This will happen because you have done
        evil things.

13"'Jerusalem, I am against you.
    You sit on top of the mountain.
    You sit like a queen over this valley.
You people of Jerusalem say,
    "No one can attack us.
    No one can come into our strong city."
This message is from the LORD.

14You will get the punishment you deserve.
    I will start a fire in your forests
    that will completely burn everything around
        you.'"
This message is from the LORD.

Judgement Against Evil Kings

22 The LORD said, "Jeremiah, go down to the king's palace. Go to the king of Judah and tell this message there: 2'Listen to this message from the LORD, King of Judah. You rule from David's throne, so listen. King, you and your officials must listen well. Your people who come through the gates of Jerusalem must listen to the message from the Lord. 3This is what the LORD says: Do what is right and fair. Protect those who have been robbed from the ones who robbed them. Don't take advantage of orphans or widows. Don't kill innocent people. 4If you obey these commands, kings who sit on David's throne will continue to come through the gates into the city of Jerusalem. They will come through the gates with their officials. The kings, their officials and their people will come riding in chariots and on horses. 5But I, the LORD, tell you that if you don't obey these commands, then I promise with an oath in my own name that this king's palace will be destroyed—it will become a pile of rocks.'"

INSIGHT

Both Gilead and Lebanon were mountainous regions to which merchants would travel in order to buy goods and then trade them across the known world. Here, God is warning the house of Judah that he's about to change them from being fruitful to being desolate.

Jeremiah 22:6–7

6This is what the LORD says about the palace where the king of Judah lives:

"The palace is tall like the forests of Gilead,
    like the mountains of Lebanon.
But I will make it like a desert,
    as empty as a city where no one lives.
7I will send men to destroy the palace,
    each armed with weapons.
They will cut up your strong, beautiful cedar
        beams
    and throw them into the fire.

8"People from many nations will pass by this city. They will ask each other, 'Why has the LORD done such a terrible thing to Jerusalem? Jerusalem was such a great city.' ⁹This will be the answer to that question: 'God destroyed Jerusalem because the people of Judah stopped following the agreement of the Lord their God. They worshipped and served other gods.'"

Judgement Against King Jehoahaz

¹⁰Don't cry for the king who has died.ᵃ
  Don't cry for him.
But cry very hard for the king
  who must leave this place.ᵇ
Cry for him because he will never return
  or see his homeland again.

¹¹This is what the Lord says about Jehoahazᶜ son of Josiah, who became king of Judah after his father Josiah died: "Jehoahaz has gone away from Jerusalem. He will never return. ¹²He will die in the place where the Egyptians have taken him, and he will not see this land again."

Judgement Against King Jehoiakim

¹³"It will be very bad for King Jehoiakim.
  He is doing wrong so that he can build his
    palace.
He is cheating people so that he can build
    rooms upstairs.
He is not paying his own people.
  He is making them work for nothing.

¹⁴"Jehoiakim says,
  'I will build myself a great palace, with huge
    rooms upstairs.'
So he built it with large windows.
  He used cedar wood for panelling, and he
    painted it red.

¹⁵"Jehoiakim, having a lot of cedar in your house
    does not make you a great king.
Your father Josiah was satisfied to have food
    and drink.
  He did what was right and fair,
    so everything went well for him.
¹⁶Josiah helped poor and needy people,
    so everything went well for him.
Jehoiakim, what does it mean "to know God"?
    It means doing what is right and being fair.
That is what it means to know me.
    This message is from the Lord.

¹⁷"Jehoiakim, your eyes look only for what
    benefits you.

You are always thinking about getting more
    for yourself.
You are willing to kill innocent people.
  You are willing to steal things from other
    people."

¹⁸So this is what the Lord says to King
    Jehoiakim son of Josiah:
"The people of Judah will not cry for
    Jehoiakim.
  They will not say to each other, 'Brother,
    I am so sad!
  Sister, I am so sad!'
They will not cry for Jehoiakim.
  They will not say about him, 'Master, I am
    so sad!
  King, I am so sad!'
¹⁹The people of Jerusalem will bury Jehoiakim
    like a donkey.
  They will drag his body away and throw it
    outside the gates of Jerusalem.

²⁰"Judah, go up to the mountains of Lebanon
    and cry out.
  Let your voice be heard in the mountains of
    Bashan.
Cry out in the mountains of Abarim,
  because all your 'lovers' will be destroyed.

²¹"Judah, you felt safe, but I warned you.
  I warned you, but you refused to listen.
You have lived like this from the time you
    were young.
  And from the time you were young,
    you have not obeyed me.
²²Judah, the punishment I give will come like a
    storm,
  and it will blow all your shepherds away.
You thought some of the other nations would
    help you.
  But these nations will also be defeated.
Then you will really be disappointed.
  You will be ashamed of all the evil things
    you did.

²³"King, you seem so safe in your palace of
    cedar.
  It's as if you live in Lebanon!ᵈ
But when your punishment comes, you will
    groan.
  You will be in pain like a woman giving
    birth!"

ᵃ **22:10** *the king who has died* That is, King Josiah who was killed in battle against the Egyptians in 609 BC.
ᵇ **22:10** *the king . . . place* This means Josiah's son, Jehoahaz. He became king after Josiah died. He is also called Shallum. King Neco of Egypt defeated Josiah. And Neco took Jehoahaz off the throne of Judah and made him a prisoner in Egypt.
ᶜ **22:11** *Jehoahaz* The Hebrew text has "Shallum", another name for Jehoahaz.
ᵈ **22:23** *It's as if . . . Lebanon* The king's palace in Jerusalem was built with wood from the mountains of Lebanon, which was famous for its cedar trees.

Judgement Against King Jehoiachin

24"As surely as I live," says the LORD, "I will do this to you, Jehoiachin[a] son of Jehoiakim, king of Judah. Even if you were a signet ring on my right hand, I would still pull you off. 25Jehoiachin, I will give you to King Nebuchadnezzar of Babylon and the Babylonians. Those are the people you are afraid of. They want to kill you. 26I will throw you and your mother into another country where neither of you was born. You and your mother will die in that country. 27Jehoiachin, you will want to come back to your land, but you will never be allowed to come back."

28Jehoiachin is like a broken pot that someone
  threw away.
He is like a pot that no one wants.
Why will Jehoiachin and his children be
  thrown out
and sent away into a foreign land?
29Land, land, land of Judah!
  Listen to this message from the LORD!
30The LORD says, "Write this down about
  Jehoiachin:
'He does not have children any more!
Jehoiachin will not be successful
  because none of his children will sit on the
  throne of David.
None of his children will rule in Judah.'"

23 "It will be very bad for the shepherds of the people of Judah. They are destroying the sheep. They are making the sheep run from my pasture in all directions." This message is from the LORD.

2They are responsible for my people. And this is what the LORD, the God of Israel, says to them: "You shepherds have made my sheep run away in all directions. You have forced them to go away, and you have not taken care of them. But I will take care of you—I will punish you for the evil things you did." This message is from the LORD: 3"I sent my sheep to other countries. But I will gather together my sheep that are left, and I will bring them back to their pasture. When my sheep are back in their pasture, they will have many children and grow in number. 4I will place new shepherds over my sheep. They will take care of my sheep, and my sheep will never again feel afraid. None of my sheep will be lost." This message is from the LORD.

The Good "Branch"

5This message is from the LORD:

"The time is coming,
  when I will raise up a good 'branch' from
    David's family.
He will be a king who will rule in a wise way.
  He will do what is fair and right in the land.
6When he rules, Judah will be safe,
  and Israel will live in safety.
This will be the king's name:
  The LORD Is Our Victory.[b]

7"So the time is coming," says the LORD, "when people will not begin their promises by saying, 'As surely as the LORD lives, the one who brought the Israelites out of the land of Egypt.' 8Instead, they will say, 'As surely as the LORD lives, the one who brought the Israelites out of the land of the north and out of all the countries where he had sent them.' At that time, the people of Israel will live in their own land."

Judgements Against False Prophets

9A message to the prophets:
I am very sad—my heart is broken.
  All my bones are shaking.
Because of the LORD and his holy words,
  I am like a man who is drunk.
10The land of Judah is full of people who
    commit adultery.
  They are unfaithful in many ways.
So God cursed the land,
  and it became very dry.
The plants are dried and dying in the pastures.
  The fields have become like the desert.
The prophets are evil.
  They use their influence and power in the
    wrong way.
11This message is from the LORD:
"The prophets and even the priests are evil.
  I have seen them doing evil things in my
    own Temple.
12So I will make their path dark and slippery,
  and they will fall in the darkness.
I will bring disaster on them;
  I will punish them."
This message is from the LORD.

13"I saw the prophets of Samaria doing
    something very wrong.
  I saw them prophesy in the name of the
    false god Baal.
They led the people of Israel away from me.
14I have even seen the prophets of Jerusalem
    doing sinful things.

---

[a] 22:24 Jehoiachin The Hebrew text has "Coniah", a short form for "Jeconiah", another name for King Jehoiachin. Also in verse 28 and 37:1.
[b] 23:6 The LORD Is Our Victory This is a wordplay. In Hebrew this is like the name Zedekiah, the king of Judah at the time this prophecy was probably given. But Jeremiah is talking about another king.

They are committing adultery and living a
life of lies.
They support their fellow prophets
and never stop doing evil.
They have become like Sodom;
they are all like Gomorrah."

¹⁵So this is what the LORD All-Powerful says
about those Jerusalem prophets:
"I will make them suffer.
Their food will be bitter, their water like
poison.
I will punish them because they started a
spiritual sickness
that spread through the whole country."

¹⁶This is what the LORD All-Powerful says:
"Don't pay attention to what those prophets
are saying to you.
They are trying to fool you.
They talk about visions,
but they did not get their visions from me.
Their visions come from their own minds.
¹⁷Some of the people hate the real messages
from the LORD,
so the prophets give them a different
message.
They say, 'You will have peace.'
Some of the people are very stubborn.
They do only what they want to do.
So the prophets say,
'Nothing bad will happen to you!'
¹⁸But none of these prophets has stood in the
heavenly council.ᵃ
None of them has seen or heard the
message from the LORD.
None of them has paid close attention to his
message.
¹⁹Now the punishment from the LORD will come
like a storm.
His anger will be like a tornado,
crashing down on the heads of all who are
wicked.
²⁰The LORD's anger will not stop
until he finishes what he plans to do.
When that day is over,
you will understand this clearly.
²¹I did not send those prophets,
but they ran to tell their messages.
I did not speak to them,
but they spoke in my name.
²²If they had stood in my heavenly council,
then they would have told my messages to
the people of Judah.

They would have stopped the people from
doing bad things.
They would have stopped them from
doing evil."

²³This message is from the LORD.
"I am God, and I am always near.
I am not far away.
²⁴Someone might try to hide from me in some
hiding place.
But it is easy for me to see that person, says
the LORD,
because I am everywhere in heaven and
earth."

This message is from the LORD: ²⁵"There are
prophets who tell lies in my name. They say, 'I have
had a dream! I have had a dream!' I heard them say
those things. ²⁶How long will this continue? They
think up lies and then they teach them to the
people. ²⁷They are trying to make the people of
Judah forget my name by telling each other these
false dreams. They are trying to make my people
forget me, just as their ancestors forgot me and
worshipped the false god Baal. ²⁸Straw is not the
same as wheat! In the same way, the dreams of
those prophets are not messages from me. If people
want to tell about their dreams, let them. But those
who hear my message must speak it truthfully."
This is what the LORD says. ²⁹Yes, the LORD says,
"You must treat my message carefully, like a fire or
like a hammer that can smash a rock."

³⁰This message is from the LORD: "So I am
against the false prophets. They keep stealing my
words from each other." ³¹Yes, the LORD says,
"I am against the false prophets. They use their
own words and pretend that it is a message
from me. ³²I am against the false prophets who
tell false dreams." This message is from the LORD.
"They mislead my people with their lies and
false teachings. I did not send them to teach the
people. I never commanded them to do anything
for me. They cannot help the people of Judah at
all." This message is from the LORD.

The Sad Message From the LORD

³³"The people of Judah, or a prophet or a
priest, may ask you, 'Jeremiah, what is the LORD's
announcement?' You will answer them and say,
'You are his burden,ᵇ and I will throw this burden
down.' This message is from the LORD.

³⁴"A prophet or a priest, or maybe one of the
people, might say, 'This is the LORD's announcement
. . .' Because of that lie, I will punish that person

ᵃ 23:18 *heavenly council* The people in the Old Testament often talk about God as the leader of a council of heavenly beings
(angels). Compare 1 Kgs 22:19–23; Isa. 6:1–8 and Job 1 and 2.
ᵇ 23:33 *burden* This is a wordplay. The Hebrew word translated "burden" here is like the word for "announcement".

and their whole family. ³⁵This is what you will say to each other: 'What was the LORD's answer?' or 'What did the LORD say?' ³⁶But you will never again use the expression, 'The LORD's announcement.' That is because his message should not be a burden for anyone. But you changed the words of our God. He is the living God, the LORD All-Powerful!

³⁷"If you want to learn about God's message, ask a prophet, 'What answer did the LORD give you?' or 'What did the LORD say?' ³⁸But don't say, 'What was the LORD's announcement?' If you use those words, the LORD will say this to you: 'You should not have called my message "the LORD's announcement". I told you not to use those words. ³⁹But you called my message a burden, so I will pick you up like a burden and throw you away from me. I gave the city of Jerusalem to your ancestors. But I will throw you and that city away from me, ⁴⁰and I will make you a disgrace forever. You will never forget your shame.'"

The Good Figs and the Bad Figs

24 The LORD showed me these things: I saw two baskets of figs arranged in front of the Temple of the LORD. (I saw this vision after King Nebuchadnezzar of Babylon took Jehoiachin*ᵃ* as a prisoner. Jehoiachin, the son of King Jehoiakim and all his important officials were taken away from Jerusalem. They were taken to Babylon. Nebuchadnezzar also took away all the carpenters and metalworkers of Judah.) ²One basket had very good figs in it, the kind that ripen early in the season. But the other basket had rotten figs. They were too rotten to eat.

³The LORD said to me, "What do you see, Jeremiah?"

I answered, "I see figs. The good figs are very good, and the rotten figs are very rotten. They are too rotten to eat."

⁴Then the message from the LORD came to me. ⁵The LORD, the God of Israel, said: "The people of Judah were taken from their country. Their enemy brought them to Babylon. Those people will be like these good figs. I will be kind to them. ⁶I will protect them. I will bring them back to the land of Judah. I will not tear them down—I will build them up. I will not pull them up—I will plant them so that they can grow. ⁷I will make them want to know me. They will know that I am the LORD. They will be my people, and I will be their God. I will do this because the prisoners

in Babylon will turn to me with their whole hearts."

⁸But the LORD also says, "I will treat King Zedekiah of Judah like those figs that are too rotten to eat. Zedekiah, his high officials, all those who are left in Jerusalem and those people of Judah who are living in Egypt will be like those rotten figs. ⁹I will punish them. Their punishment will shock all the people on earth. People will make fun of those people from Judah. People will tell jokes about them and curse them in all the places where I scatter them. ¹⁰I will bring war, famine and disease against them. I will attack them until they have all been killed. Then they will no longer be on the land that I gave to them and to their ancestors."

A Summary of Jeremiah's Message

25 This is the message that came to Jeremiah concerning all the people of Judah. This message came in the fourth year that Jehoiakim*ᵇ* son of Josiah was king of Judah. The fourth year of his time as king was the first year that Nebuchadnezzar was king of Babylon. ²This is the message that Jeremiah the prophet spoke to all the people of Judah and all the people of Jerusalem:

³I have been a prophet for these past 23 years, from the thirteenth year that Josiah son of Amon was the king of Judah. And from that time until today, I have spoken messages to you from the LORD again and again. But you have not listened. ⁴The LORD has sent his servants, the prophets, to you over and over again. But you have not listened to them. You have not paid any attention to them.

⁵Those prophets said, "Change your lives and stop doing evil! If you change, you can return to the land that the LORD gave you and your ancestors long ago. He gave you this land to live in forever. ⁶Don't follow other gods. Don't serve or worship them. Don't worship idols that someone has made. That only makes me angry with you. By doing this you only hurt yourselves."*ᶜ*

⁷"But you did not listen to me." This message is from the LORD. "You worshiped idols that someone made, and that made me angry. And it only hurt you."

⁸So this is what the LORD All-Powerful says, "You have not listened to my messages. ⁹I will soon send for all the tribes of the north."*ᵈ* This message is from the LORD. "I will soon send for King

---

ᵃ **24:1** *Jehoiachin* The Hebrew text has "Jeconiah", another name for King Jehoiachin, who was taken prisoner in the year 597 BC. Also in 27:20; 28:4; 29:2.

ᵇ **25:1** *the fourth year . . . Jehoiakim* This was about 605 BC.

ᶜ **25:6** *By doing this you only hurt yourselves* This is from the ancient Greek version. The standard Hebrew text has "Then I will not hurt you."

ᵈ **25:9** *north* The Babylonian army came from this direction to attack Judah. Armies from countries north and east of Israel often came this way to attack Judah and Israel.

Nebuchadnezzar of Babylon. He is my servant. I will bring those people against the land of Judah and against the people of Judah. I will bring them against all the nations around you too. I will destroy all those countries. I will make those lands like an empty desert forever. People will see those countries and wonder at how badly they were destroyed. ¹⁰I will bring an end to the sounds of joy and happiness in those places. There will be no more happy sounds of the brides and bridegrooms. I will take away the sound of people grinding meal. I will take away the light of the lamp. ¹¹That whole area will be an empty desert. All these people will be slaves of the king of Babylon for 70 years.

¹²"But when the 70 years have passed, I will punish the king of Babylon. I will punish the nation of Babylon." This message is from the LORD. "I will punish the land of the Babylonians for their sins. I will make that land a desert forever. ¹³I said that many bad things will happen to Babylon, and all of them will happen. Jeremiah spoke about those foreign nations. And all the warnings are written in this book. ¹⁴Yes, the people of Babylon will have to serve many nations and many great kings. I will give them the punishment they deserve for all the things they have done."

Judgement on the Nations of the World

¹⁵The LORD, the God of Israel, said this to me: "Jeremiah, take this cup of wine from my hand. It is the wine of my anger. I am sending you to different nations. Make all the nations drink from this cup. ¹⁶They will drink this wine. Then they will vomit and act like crazy people. They will do this because of the war that I will soon bring against them."

¹⁷So I took the cup of wine from the LORD's hand. I went to those nations and I made them drink from the cup. ¹⁸I poured this wine for the people of Jerusalem and Judah. I made the kings and leaders of Judah drink from the cup. I did this so that they would become an empty desert. I did this so that place would be destroyed so badly that people would mock and say curses about it. And it happened—Judah is like that now.

¹⁹I also made Pharaoh, the king of Egypt, drink from that cup. I made his officials, his important leaders and all his people drink from it.

²⁰I also made all the Arabs and all the kings of the land of Uz drink from the cup.

I made all the kings of the land of the Philistines drink from it too. These were the kings of the cities of Ashkelon, Gaza, Ekron and what remains of the city Ashdod.

²¹Then I made the people of Edom, Moab and Ammon drink from the cup.

²²I made all the kings of Tyre and Sidon and all the kings of the faraway countries drink from that cup. ²³I made the people of Dedan, Tema and Buz and all those who cut their hair at their temples drink from it. ²⁴I made all the kings of Arabia drink from the cup. These kings live in the desert. ²⁵I made all the kings from Zimri, Elam and Media drink from the cup. ²⁶I made all the kings of the north, those who were near and far, drink from the cup. I made them drink one after the other. I made all the kingdoms that are on earth drink from that cup. Finally, after all these other nations, the king of Babylon will drink from it too.

²⁷"Jeremiah, say to those nations, this is what the LORD All-Powerful, the God of Israel, says: 'Drink this cup of my anger. Get drunk from it and vomit. Fall down and don't get up. Don't get up because I am bringing wars against you.'

²⁸"They will refuse to take the cup from your hand. They will refuse to drink it, but you will tell them, 'This is what the LORD All-Powerful says: You will surely drink from this cup! ²⁹I am already making these bad things happen to Jerusalem, the city that is called by my name. Maybe you people think that you will not be punished, but you are wrong. You will be punished! I am giving the command for war to come against all the people of the earth.'" This message is from the LORD.

³⁰"Jeremiah, tell these people what I have said. This is what I want you to say:
'The LORD will shout from heaven.
He will roar like thunder from his holy Temple.
He will give a shout against his people
like the shouts of workers trampling grapes.
He will shout against all people on earth.
³¹The sound will echo throughout the earth,
announcing that the LORD is accusing the nations.
He will judge all people on earth,
and he will kill the wicked with his sword.'"
This message is from the LORD.

³²This is what the LORD All-Powerful says:
"Disasters will soon spread
from country to country.
They will come like a powerful storm
to all the faraway places on earth!"

³³The dead bodies of those killed by the LORD will reach from one end of the earth to the other. No one will cry for them. No one will gather up their bodies and bury them. They will be left lying on the ground like dung.

³⁴Shepherds, you should be leading the sheep.
Start crying, you great leaders!
Roll around on the ground in pain, you leaders of the sheep.

It is now time for your slaughter.
    You will be scattered everywhere, like
        pieces flying from a broken jar.
35There will be no place for the shepherds
        to hide.
    They will not escape.
36I hear the shepherds shouting.
    I hear the leaders of the sheep crying,
        because the LORD is destroying their
            pastures.
37Those peaceful pastures will be ruined
    because of the LORD's anger.
38He is like an angry lion that has left his cave.
    And because of his terrible anger
and by the attacks of the enemy army,
    their land will become an empty desert.

Jeremiah's Lesson at the Temple

26 This message came from the LORD during the first year that Jehoiakim*a* son of Josiah was king of Judah. 2The LORD said, "Jeremiah, stand in the Temple courtyard of the LORD. Give this message to all the people of Judah who are coming to worship at the Temple of the LORD. Tell them everything that I tell you to speak. Don't leave out any part of my message. 3Maybe they will listen and obey my message. Maybe they will stop living such evil lives. If they change, I will change my mind about my plans to punish them. I am planning this punishment because of the many evil things they have done. 4You will say to them, 'This is what the LORD says: I gave my teachings to you. You must obey me and follow my teachings. 5You must listen to what my servants say to you. The prophets are my servants. I have sent my prophets to you again and again, but you did not listen to them. 6If you don't obey me, I will make my Temple in Jerusalem just like my Holy Tent at Shiloh.*b* People all over the world will think of Jerusalem when they ask for bad things to happen to other cities.'"

7The priests, the prophets and all the people heard Jeremiah say all these words at the LORD's Temple. 8Jeremiah finished speaking everything the LORD had commanded him to say to the people. Then the priests, the prophets and all the people grabbed Jeremiah. They said, "You will die for saying such terrible things! 9How dare you say such a thing in the name of the LORD! How dare you say that this Temple will be destroyed like the one at Shiloh! How dare you say that Jerusalem will become a desert with no one living in it!" All the people gathered around Jeremiah in the Temple of the LORD.

10Now the rulers of Judah heard about everything that was happening. So they came out of the king's palace. They went up to the LORD's Temple. They took their places at the entrance of the New Gate. The New Gate is a gate leading to the LORD's Temple. 11Then the priests and the prophets spoke to the rulers and all the other people. They said, "Jeremiah should be killed. He said bad things about Jerusalem. You heard him say those things."

12Then Jeremiah spoke to all the rulers of Judah and all the other people. He said, "The LORD sent me to say these things about this Temple and this city. Everything that you have heard is from the Lord. 13You people, change your lives! You must start doing good! You must obey the LORD your God. If you do that, he will change his mind. He will not do the bad things he told you about. 14As for me, I am in your power. Do to me what you think is good and right. 15But if you kill me, be sure of one thing. You will be guilty of killing an innocent person. You will make this city and everyone living in it guilty too. The LORD really did send me to you. The message you heard really is from the Lord."

16Then the rulers and all the people spoke. They said to the priests and the prophets, "Jeremiah must not be killed. What he told us comes from the LORD our God."

17Then some of the leaders stood up and spoke to all the people. 18They said, "Micah the prophet was from the city of Moresheth. He was a prophet during the time that Hezekiah was king of Judah. Micah said this to all the people of Judah: 'This is what the LORD All-Powerful says:

"'Zion will be destroyed.
    It will become a ploughed field.
Jerusalem will become a pile of rocks.
    Temple Mount will be an empty hill*c*
        overgrown with bushes.'

Micah 3:12

19"King Hezekiah of Judah and the people of Judah did not kill Micah. You know that Hezekiah respected the LORD and wanted to please him. So the LORD changed his mind and didn't do the bad things to Judah that he said he would do. If we hurt Jeremiah, we will bring many troubles on ourselves. And those troubles will be our own fault."

20In the past there was another man who spoke the LORD's message. His name was Uriah son of

---

a **26:1 the first year . . . Jehoiakim** This was 609 BC.
b **26:6 my Holy Tent at Shiloh** The Holy Place at Shiloh was probably destroyed during the time of Samuel. See Jer. 7 and 1 Sam. 4.
c **26:18 empty hill** Or "high place", a term usually used for local shrines (places for worship) where people often worshipped idols.

Shemaiah from the city of Kiriath Jearim. Uriah said the same things against this city and this land as Jeremiah did. ²¹King Jehoiakim, his army officers and the leaders of Judah heard Uriah and became angry. King Jehoiakim wanted to kill Uriah, but Uriah heard about it. Uriah was afraid, so he escaped to the land of Egypt. ²²But King Jehoiakim sent Elnathan son of Acbor and some other men to Egypt. ²³They brought Uriah from Egypt and took him to King Jehoiakim. Jehoiakim gave an order for Uriah to be killed with a sword. Uriah's body was thrown into the burial place where the poor are buried.

²⁴There was an important man named Ahikam son of Shaphan who supported Jeremiah. He kept Jeremiah from being killed by the priests and prophets.

The LORD Made Nebuchadnezzar Ruler

27 A message from the LORD came to Jeremiah. It came during the fourth year that Zedekiah*ᵃ* son of Josiah was king of Judah. ²This is what the LORD said to me: "Jeremiah, make a yoke out of straps and poles. Put that yoke on the back of your neck. ³Then send a message to the kings of Edom, Moab, Ammon, Tyre and Sidon. Send the message with the messengers of these kings who have come to Jerusalem to see King Zedekiah of Judah. ⁴Tell them to give the message to their masters. Tell them that this is what the LORD All-Powerful, the God of Israel, says: 'Tell your masters that ⁵I made the earth and all the people on it. I made all the animals on the earth. I did this with my great power and my strong arm. I can give the earth to anyone I want. ⁶Now I have given all your countries to King Nebuchadnezzar of Babylon. He is my servant. I will make even the wild animals obey him. ⁷All nations will serve Nebuchadnezzar and his son and his grandson. Then the time will come for Babylon to be defeated. Many nations and great kings will make Babylon their servant.

⁸"'But if some nations or kingdoms refuse to serve King Nebuchadnezzar of Babylon and refuse to be put under his control, I will punish them, says the LORD. I will destroy them with war, hunger and disease. I will use Nebuchadnezzar to destroy any nation that fights against him. ⁹So don't listen to your prophets. Don't listen to those who use magic to tell what will happen in the future. Don't listen to those who say they can interpret dreams. Don't listen to those who talk to the dead or to people who practise magic. All of them tell you, "You will not be slaves to the king

of Babylon." ¹⁰But they are telling you lies. They will only cause you to be taken far from your homeland. I will force you to leave your homes, and you will die in another land.

¹¹"'But the nations that put their necks under the yoke of the king of Babylon and obey him will live. I will let them stay in their own country and serve the king of Babylon,' says the LORD. 'The people from those nations will live in their own land and farm it.'"

¹²I gave the same message to King Zedekiah of Judah. I said, "Zedekiah, you must place your neck under the yoke of the king of Babylon and obey him. If you serve the king of Babylon and his people, you will live. ¹³If you don't agree to serve the king of Babylon, you and your people will die from war, hunger and disease. This is what the LORD said would happen. ¹⁴But the false prophets are saying, 'You will never be slaves to the king of Babylon.'

"Don't listen to those prophets, because they are telling you lies. ¹⁵I didn't send them,' says the LORD. 'They are telling lies and saying that the message is from me. So I will send you people of Judah away. You will die, and the prophets who spoke to you will die also.'"

¹⁶Then I told the priests and all the people that this is what the LORD says: "Those false prophets are saying, 'The Babylonians took many things from the LORD's Temple. These things will be brought back soon.' Don't listen to them because they are telling you lies. ¹⁷Don't listen to those prophets. Serve the king of Babylon. Accept your punishment, and you will live. There is no reason for you to cause this city of Jerusalem to be destroyed. ¹⁸If they are prophets and their message is from the LORD, let them pray. Let them pray to the LORD about the things that are still in the LORD's Temple, in the king's palace and in Jerusalem. Let them pray that all those things will not be taken away to Babylon.

¹⁹"This is what the LORD All-Powerful says about the things that are still left in Jerusalem. In the Temple, there are the pillars, the bronze sea, the moveable stands and other things.*ᵇ* King Nebuchadnezzar of Babylon left those things in Jerusalem. ²⁰He didn't take them away when he took Jehoiachin son of Jehoiakim king of Judah away as a prisoner. Nebuchadnezzar also took other important people away from Judah and Jerusalem. ²¹This is what the LORD All-Powerful, the God of Israel, says about the things still left in the LORD's Temple and in the king's palace and in Jerusalem: ²²'All those things will also be taken to

---

ᵃ **27:1 the fourth year . . . Zedekiah** The standard Hebrew text has "At the beginning of the kingship of Jehoiakim". This is probably a scribal error. Verse 3 talks about Zedekiah, and 28:1 says "that same year" was the fourth year of Zedekiah's reign (594–593 BC).
ᵇ **27:19 pillars . . . other things** For a description of these things, see 1 Kgs 7:23–37.

Babylon. They will be brought to Babylon until the day comes when I go to get them,' says the LORD. 'Then I will bring those things back. I will put them back in this place.'"

The False Prophet Hananiah

28 That same year, in the fifth month of the fourth year that Zedekiah*a* was king of Judah, the prophet Hananiah son of Azzur spoke to me. Hananiah was from the town of Gibeon. He was in the LORD's Temple when he spoke to me. The priests and all the people were there also. This is what Hananiah said: ²"The LORD All-Powerful, the God of Israel, says: 'I will break the yoke that the king of Babylon has put on the people of Judah. ³Before two years are over, I will bring back all the things that King Nebuchadnezzar of Babylon took from the LORD's Temple. Nebuchadnezzar has carried those things to Babylon. But I will bring them back here to Jerusalem. ⁴I will also bring the king of Judah, Jehoiachin son of Jehoiakim, back to this place. And I will bring back all the people of Judah that Nebuchadnezzar forced to leave their homes and go to Babylon,' says the LORD. 'So I will break the yoke that the king of Babylon put on the people of Judah.'"

⁵Then the prophet Jeremiah answered the prophet Hananiah. They were standing in the Temple of the LORD. The priests and all the people there could hear Jeremiah's answer. ⁶Jeremiah said to Hananiah, "Amen! May the LORD do that. May the LORD make the message you say come true. May he bring the things of the LORD's Temple back to this place from Babylon. And may he bring all those who were forced to leave their homes back to this place.

⁷"But listen to what I have to say to you and to all the people. ⁸There were prophets long before you and I became prophets, Hananiah. They spoke against many countries and great kingdoms and always warned that war, hunger and disease would come to them. ⁹But the prophet who says that we will have peace must be tested. If his message comes true, people can know that he really was sent by the LORD."

¹⁰Jeremiah was wearing a yoke around his neck. The prophet Hananiah took the yoke from Jeremiah's neck and broke it. ¹¹Then Hananiah spoke loudly so that all the people could hear him. He said, "This is what the LORD says: 'In the same way, I will break the yoke of King Nebuchadnezzar of Babylon. He put that yoke on all the nations of the world, but I will break it before two years are over.'"

After Hananiah said that, Jeremiah left the Temple.

¹²After Hananiah had taken the yoke off Jeremiah's neck and had broken it, this message from the LORD came to Jeremiah: ¹³The LORD said to Jeremiah, "Go and tell Hananiah that this is what the LORD says: 'You have broken a wooden yoke, but I will make a yoke of iron in the place of the wooden yoke. ¹⁴The LORD All-Powerful, the God of Israel, is the one saying this. I will put a yoke of iron on the necks of all these nations. I will do that to make them serve King Nebuchadnezzar of Babylon, and they will be slaves to him. I will even give Nebuchadnezzar control over the wild animals.'"

¹⁵Then the prophet Jeremiah said to the prophet Hananiah, "Listen, Hananiah! The LORD did not send you. But you have made the people of Judah trust in lies. ¹⁶So this is what the LORD says: 'Soon I will take you from this world, Hananiah. You will die this year, because you taught the people to turn against the LORD.'"

¹⁷Hananiah died in the seventh month of that same year.

A Letter to the Captives in Babylon

29 Jeremiah sent a letter to the captives in Babylon. He sent it to the leaders, the priests, the prophets and all the other people who Nebuchadnezzar had taken from Jerusalem to Babylon. ²(This letter was sent after King Jehoiachin, the queen mother, the officials and the leaders of Judah and Jerusalem, the carpenters and the metalworkers had been taken from Jerusalem.) ³King Zedekiah of Judah sent Elasah son of Shaphan and Gemariah son of Hilkiah to King Nebuchadnezzar. Jeremiah gave them the letter to take to Babylon. This is what the letter said:

⁴This is what the LORD All-Powerful, the God of Israel, says to all the people he sent into captivity from Jerusalem to Babylon:

⁵"Build houses and live in them. Settle in the land. Plant gardens and eat the food you grow. ⁶Get married and have sons and daughters. Find wives for your sons, and let your daughters be married. Do this so that they also may have sons and daughters. Have many children and grow in number in Babylon. Don't become fewer in number. ⁷Also, do good things for the city I sent you to. Pray to the LORD for the city you are living in, because if there is peace in that city, you will have peace also." ⁸The LORD All-Powerful, the God of Israel, says, "Don't let your prophets and those who practise magic fool you. Don't listen to the dreams they have. ⁹They are telling lies, and they are saying that their

---

a 28:1 the fourth year . . . Zedekiah This was about 594–593 BC.

message is from me. But I didn't send it." This message is from the LORD.

¹⁰This is what the LORD says: "Babylon will be powerful for 70 years. After that time, I will come to you people who are living in Babylon. I will keep my good promise to bring you back to Jerusalem. ¹¹I say this because I know the plans that I have for you." This message is from the LORD. "I have good plans for you. I don't plan to hurt you. I plan to give you hope and a good future. ¹²Then you will call my name. You will come to me and pray to me, and I will listen to you. ¹³You will search for me, and when you search for me with all your heart, you will find me. ¹⁴I will let you find me." This message is from the LORD. "And I will bring you back from your captivity. I forced you to leave this place. But I will gather you from all the nations and places where I have sent you," says the LORD, "and I will bring you back to this place."

¹⁵You people might say, "But the LORD has given us prophets here in Babylon." ¹⁶But this is what the LORD says about your relatives who were not carried away to Babylon. I am talking about the king who is sitting on David's throne now and all the other people who are still in the city of Jerusalem. ¹⁷The LORD All-Powerful says, "I will soon bring war, hunger and disease against those who are still in Jerusalem. And I will make them just like bad figs that are too rotten to eat. ¹⁸I will attack those who are still in Jerusalem with war, hunger and disease. I will cause such pain that all the kingdoms of the earth will be frightened at what has happened to those people. They will be destroyed. People will be amazed when they hear what happened. And people will use them as an example when they ask for bad things to happen to people. People will insult them wherever I force them to go. ¹⁹I will make all these things happen because the people of Jerusalem have not listened to my message." This message is from the LORD. "I sent my message to them again and again. I used my servants, the prophets, to give my messages to them, but they didn't listen." This message is from the LORD. ²⁰"You people are captives. I forced you to leave Jerusalem and go to Babylon. So listen to the message from the LORD."

²¹This is what the LORD All-Powerful, the God of Israel, says about Ahab son of Kolaiah and Zedekiah son of Maaseiah: "These two men have been telling you lies. They have said that their message is from me. I will give these two prophets to King Nebuchadnezzar of Babylon. And he will kill them in front of all you who are captives in Babylon. ²²They will be an example of a terrible way to die. Yes, in the future, when the Jewish captives want something bad to happen to someone, they will say this curse: 'May the LORD treat you like Zedekiah and Ahab, those men the king of Babylon burned in the fire!' ²³They did very bad things among the people of Israel. They committed the sin of adultery with their neighbours' wives. They also spoke lies and said those lies were a message from me. I did not tell them to do that. I know what they have done. I am a witness." This message is from the LORD.

God's Message to Shemaiah

²⁴Also give a message to Shemaiah from the Nehelam family. ²⁵This is what the LORD All-Powerful, the God of Israel, says: "Shemaiah, you sent letters to all the people in Jerusalem and to the priest Zephaniah son of Maaseiah. You also sent letters to all the priests. You sent those letters in your own name, not by my authority. Your letter to Zephaniah said, ²⁶'The LORD has made you priest in place of Jehoiada. You are to be in charge of the LORD's Temple. You know you should arrest any madman who pretends to be a prophet. Anyone like that should have chains put around his feet and neck. ²⁷You have Jeremiah from Anathoth there, who is pretending to be a prophet. So why have you not stopped him? ²⁸He has sent this message to us in Babylon: You people in Babylon will be there for a long time, so build houses and settle down. Plant gardens and eat what they produce.'"

²⁹Zephaniah the priest read the letter to Jeremiah the prophet. ³⁰Then this message from the LORD came to Jeremiah: ³¹"Jeremiah, send this message to all the captives in Babylon: 'This is what the LORD says about Shemaiah, the man from the Nehelam family. Shemaiah has spoken to you, but I didn't send him. He has made you believe a lie. ³²Because Shemaiah has done that, says the LORD, I will soon punish Shemaiah, the man from the Nehelam family. I will completely destroy his family, and he will not share in the good things I will do for my people.'" This message is from the LORD. "'I will punish Shemaiah because he has taught the people to turn against the LORD.'"

Promises of Hope

30 This is the message that came to Jeremiah from the LORD. ²The LORD, the God of the people of Israel, said, "Jeremiah, write in a book the words I have spoken to you. Write this book for yourself. ³Do this because the days will come, says the LORD, when I will bring my people, Israel and Judah, back from exile." This message is from the LORD. "I will put the people back in the land that I gave to their ancestors. Then my people will own that land again."

⁴The LORD spoke to me about the people of Israel and Judah. ⁵This is what the LORD said:

"We hear people crying from fear.
    There is fear, not peace.

⁶"Ask this question and consider it:
    Can a man have a baby? Of course not!
Then why do I see every strong man holding
        his stomach
like a woman having labour pains?
Why is everyone's face turning white
    like a dead man?

⁷"This is a very important time for Jacob.
    This is a time of great trouble.
There will never be another time like this,
    but Jacob will be saved.

⁸"At that time," says the LORD All-Powerful, "I will break the yoke from the necks of the people of Israel and Judah, and I will break the ropes holding you. People from foreign countries will never again force my people to be slaves. ⁹The people of Israel and Judah will not serve foreign countries. No, they will serve the LORD their God. I will send them David their king,ᵃ and they will serve him.

¹⁰"So Jacob, my servant, don't be afraid!"
    This message is from the LORD.
"Israel, don't be afraid.
    I will save you from that faraway place.
You are captivesᵇ in that faraway land,
    but I will save your descendants.
I will bring them back from that land.
Jacob will have peace again.
    People will not bother Jacob.
    There will be no enemy to frighten my
        people.
¹¹People of Israel and Judah, I am with you."
    This message is from the LORD.
"I will save you.
    I sent you to those nations,
    but I will completely destroy all of them.
It is true; I will destroy those nations,
    but I will not destroy you.
You must be punished for the bad things you
        did,
    but I will discipline you fairly."

¹²This is what the LORD says:
"You people of Israel and Judah have a wound
        that cannot be cured.
You have an injury that will not heal.
¹³There is no one to care for your sores,
    so you will not be healed.
¹⁴You became friends with many nations,
    but those nations don't care about you.
Your 'friends' have forgotten you.
I hurt you like an enemy.
    I punished you very hard.
I did this because of your great guilt.
    I did this because of your many sins.
¹⁵Israel and Judah, why are you still crying
        about your wound?
    There is no cure for it.
I did this to you because of your great guilt.
    I did this because of your many sins.
¹⁶Those nations destroyed you,
    but now they have been destroyed.
    Israel and Judah, your enemies will become
        captives.
They stole things from you,
    but others will steal from them.
They took things from you in war,
    but others will take things from them in
        war.
¹⁷And I will bring your health back
    and heal your wounds," says the LORD,
"because other people said you were outcasts.ᶜ
    They said, 'No one cares about Zion.'"

¹⁸This is what the LORD says:
"Jacob's people are now in captivity,
    but they will come back.
And I will have pity on Jacob's houses.
The cityᵈ is now only an empty hill covered
        with ruined buildings,
    but the city will be rebuilt on its hill.
And the king's palace will be rebuilt where
        it should be.
¹⁹People in those places will sing songs of
        praise,
    and there will be the sound of laughter.
I will give them many children.
    Israel and Judah will not be small.
I will bring honour to them.
    No one will look down on them.
²⁰Jacob's family will be like the family of Israel
        long ago.
I will make Israel and Judah strong,
    and I will punish those who hurt them."
²¹The LORD says,

ᵃ **30:9 David their king** This means another king of Israel who will be great like King David.
ᵇ **30:10 captives** Here, it means the Jewish people who were taken away as prisoners to Babylon.
ᶜ **30:17 outcasts** People who are thrown out of a group by others who don't like or respect them.
ᵈ **30:18 city** This probably refers to Jerusalem. But it might also mean all the cities of Israel and Judah.

"One of their own people will lead them.
　　That ruler will come from my people.
People can come close to me only if I ask
　　them to.
　　So I will ask that leader to come near,
　　and he will be close to me.
²²You will be my people,
　　and I will be your God."

²³The LORD was very angry!
　　He punished the people.
The punishment came like a storm.
　　It came like a tornado against those wicked
　　people.
²⁴The LORD will be angry until he finishes
　　punishing them.
He will be angry until he finishes the
　　punishment he planned.
When that day comes,
　　you people of Judah will understand.

The New Israel

31 This is what the LORD said, "At that time
I will be the God of all the tribes of Israel.
And they will be my people."

²This is what the LORD says:
"Those who escaped the enemy's sword will
　　find comfort in the desert.
　　Israel will go there looking for rest."
³From far away, the LORD
　　will appear to his people.

The Lord says, "I love you people with a love
　　that continues forever.
　　That is why I have continued showing you
　　kindness.
⁴Israel, my bride, I will rebuild you.
　　You will be a country again.
You will pick up your tambourines again.
　　You will dance with all the other people
　　who are having fun.
⁵You farmers of Israel will plant vineyards again.
　　You will plant the vineyards on the hills
　　around the city of Samaria.
　　The farmers will enjoy the fruit from the
　　vineyards.
⁶There will be a time when watchmenᵃ shout
　　this message:
　　'Come, let's go up to Zion to worship the
　　LORD our God!'
Even the watchmen in the hill country of
　　Ephraimᵇ will shout that message."

⁷This is what the LORD says:
"Be happy and sing for Jacob!
　　Shout for Israel, the greatest of the nations!
Sing your praises and shout:
　　'LORD, save your people!ᶜ
　　Save those of Israel who are still living.'
⁸Remember, I will bring Israel
　　from that country in the north.
I will gather the people of Israel
　　from the faraway places on earth.
Some of the people will be blind and lame.
　　Some of the women will be pregnant and
　　ready to give birth.
　　But many people will come back.
⁹They will come back crying,
　　but I will lead them and comfort them.
I will lead them by streams of water.
　　I will lead them on an easy road,
　　where they will not stumble.
I will lead them in that way because I am
　　Israel's father.
　　And Ephraim is my firstborn son.

¹⁰"Nations, listen to this message from the
　　LORD!
　　Tell this message in the faraway lands by
　　the sea:
'God scattered the people of Israel,
　　but he will bring them back together.
　　And he will watch over his flock like a
　　shepherd.'
¹¹The LORD will bring Jacob back.
　　He will save his people from those who are
　　stronger.
¹²The people of Israel will come to the top of
　　Zion,
　　and they will shout with joy.
Their faces will shine with happiness about
　　the good things the LORD gives them.
He will give them grain, new wine, olive
　　oil, young sheep and cattle.
They will be like a garden that has plenty of
　　water.
　　And the people of Israel will not be troubled
　　any more.
¹³Then the young women of Israel will be happy
　　and dance.
　　And the men, young and old, will join in
　　the dancing.
I will change their sadness into happiness.
　　I will comfort my people, making them
　　happy instead of sad.
¹⁴I will give the priests plenty of food.

ᵃ **31:6 watchmen** This usually means a guard who stands on the city walls watching for people coming to the city. Here, it
probably means the prophets.
ᵇ **31:6 hill country of Ephraim** This was the central part of the land that had been the northern kingdom of Israel.
ᶜ **31:7 LORD, save your people** Or "The LORD has saved his people!" This is often a shout of victory.

THE NEW AGREEMENT

Ever made a promise that you know you'll never keep? It's not just you. We all have, and sadly some of them are promises we have solemnly made to God.

God is the perfect promise-keeper, always remembering the agreements he makes with his people. He never goes back on what he's said. Unfortunately, we've never been able to say the same about ourselves.

DIG IN

READ Jeremiah 31:27–40

- Which agreement is God talking about in verse 32?
- Why were God's people unable to keep up their side of the agreement?
- What will the new solution be, according to Jeremiah (vv.33–34)?

Throughout history, God's relationship with his people has all been on the basis of his promises to them. Remember the story of Noah (Genesis 6 – 9)? After the devastating flood, God brings a beautiful rainbow – a visible promise that he will never wipe people out in that way again. Or how about Abram – sent off to a new place with a promise that God would write history through him and his family (Genesis 12:1–3)?

The roots of God's relationship with his people in Jeremiah's time were the laws given to Moses – an agreement written on stones on Mount Sinai (Exodus 34:10–28) and passed down through generations. But this was an imperfect agreement – like an unfaithful wife, Israel always let God down, because of the power of sin.

Now, God is showing Jeremiah a day when this will be different, pointing ahead to a time when God's people will no longer be defined by their Jewish ancestry but because they are in Christ and their sin is forgiven (v.34). Those people are us!

DIG THROUGH

- Go through verses 30–37 and discover the terms of this new agreement. It's going to be personal: people will be responsible for their own sin – not the sin of their ancestors (v.30). God will teach people's minds and hearts directly, not through cold commandments or exclusive priesthoods (v.33). God will be accessible to everyone from the greatest to the least and he will grant them total forgiveness of their sin (v.34). And this agreement will be everlasting (vv.35–37).
- How do these new promises apply to us as Christian believers today? And what (or who) makes them possible? (Clue: Titus 3:4–7.) Why not spend some time thanking God for his kindness and love to us in this amazing new agreement?

DIG DEEPER

The "new agreement" which Jeremiah prophesies here is the way God relates to us today, made possible by Christ's death and resurrection. Jesus described it as "the new agreement . . . it will begin when my blood is poured out for you" (Luke 22:20).

Verses 31–34 are quoted by the author of the letter to the Hebrews, helping us to understand it better. He writes that "the new agreement that Jesus brought from God to his people is much greater than the old one. And the new agreement is based on better promises" (Hebrews 8:6).

And my people will be filled and satisfied
 with the good things I give them."
This message is from the LORD.

15This is what the LORD says:
"A sound is heard in Ramah—
 bitter crying and great sadness.
Rachel[a] cries for her children,
 and she refuses to be comforted,
 because her children are gone."

16But the LORD says, "Stop crying.
 Don't fill your eyes with tears.
You will be rewarded for your work."
 This message is from the LORD.
 "The people of Israel will come back from
  their enemy's land.
17Israel, there is hope for you."
 This message is from the LORD.
 "Your children will come back to their own
  land.
18I have heard Ephraim crying:
 'Lord, you punished me, and I have learned
  my lesson.
I was like a calf that was never trained.
Please stop punishing me,
 and I will come back to you.
You really are the LORD my God.
19I wandered away from you.
But I finally realized how wrong I was.
So I changed my heart and life.
I am ashamed and embarrassed
 about the foolish things I did when I was
  young.'"
20The LORD says,
"You know that Ephraim is my dear son.
 I love that child.
Yes, I often criticized Ephraim,
 but I still think about him.
I love him very much,
 and I really do want to comfort him.

21"People of Israel, repair the road signs.
 Put up markers that show the way home.
Look carefully at the road you are on.
 Remember the way you went.
Israel, my bride, come home.
 Come back to your towns.
22You have been an unfaithful woman.
 How long before you find your way
  back?

But I, the LORD, will cause something new and
 different:
 the woman will start courting the man."[b]

23This is what the LORD All-Powerful, the God
of Israel, says: "I will again do good things for the
people of Judah. I will bring back those who were
taken away as prisoners. At that time the people
in the land of Judah and in its towns will once
again use these words: 'May the LORD bless you,
good home and holy mountain!'[c]
24"People in all the towns of Judah will live
together in peace. Farmers and those who move
around with their flocks will live peacefully
together in Judah. 25I will give rest and strength
to those who are weak and tired."
26After hearing that, I, Jeremiah, woke up and
looked around. My sleep was very pleasant.
27"The days are coming," says the LORD, "when
I will help the family of Israel and Judah to grow.
I will help their children and animals to grow too.
It will be like planting and caring for a plant. 28In
the past I watched over Israel and Judah, but I
watched for the time to pull them up. I tore them
down. I destroyed them. I gave them many troubles
to them. But now I will watch over them to build
them up and make them strong." This message is
from the LORD.
29"People will not use this saying any more:

'The parents ate the sour grapes,
 but the children got the sour taste.'[d]

30No, people will die for their own sins. Those
who eat sour grapes will get the sour taste."

The New Agreement

31This is what the LORD said, "The time is
coming when I will make a new agreement with
the family of Israel and with the family of Judah.
32It will not be like the agreement I made with
their ancestors. I made that agreement when
I took them by the hand and brought them out
of Egypt. I was their master, but they broke that
agreement." This message is from the LORD.
33"In the future I will make this agreement
with the people of Israel." This message is from
the LORD. "I will put my teachings in their minds,
and I will write them on their hearts. I will be
their God, and they will be my people. 34People
will not have to teach their neighbours and

---

[a] **31:15 Rachel** Jacob's wife. Here, this means all the women who are crying for their husbands and children who have died in
the war with Babylon.
[b] **31:22 the woman . . . man** One possible meaning of the Hebrew phrase. The meaning would be that Israel will change and
seek to be near the LORD instead of rejecting his love for them.
[c] **31:23 good home and holy mountain** This was a blessing for the Temple and for Mount Zion, the mountain the Temple was
built on.
[d] **31:29 The parents . . . sour taste** This means the children were suffering for things their parents did.

relatives to know the LORD, because all people, from the least important to the most important, will know me." This message is from the LORD. "I will forgive them for the evil things they did. I will not remember their sins."

The LORD Will Never Leave Israel

35He makes the sun shine in the day,
    and he makes the moon and the stars shine
      at night.
He stirs up the sea so that its waves crash on
    the shore.
The LORD All-Powerful is his name.

This is what the LORD says:
36"The descendants of Israel will never stop
    being a nation.
That would happen only if I lost control of
    the sun, moon, stars and sea."

37The LORD says, "I will never reject the
    descendants of Israel.
That would happen only if people could
    measure the sky above,
and learn all the secrets of the earth below.
Only then would I reject them for the bad
    things they have done."
This message is from the LORD.

The New Jerusalem

38This message is from the LORD, "The days are coming when the city of Jerusalem will be rebuilt for the LORD. The whole city will be rebuilt— from the Tower of Hananel to the Corner Gate. 39The measuring line*a* will stretch from the Corner Gate straight to the hill of Gareb and then turn to the place named Goah. 40The whole valley where dead bodies and ashes are thrown and all the terraces down to the bottom of Kidron Valley all the way to the corner of Horse Gate will be holy to the LORD. The city of Jerusalem will never again be torn down or destroyed."

Jeremiah Buys a Field

32 This is the message from the LORD that came to Jeremiah during the tenth year that Zedekiah was king of Judah.*b* The tenth year of Zedekiah was the eighteenth year of Nebuchadnezzar. 2At that time the army of the king of Babylon was surrounding the city of Jerusalem, and Jeremiah was under arrest in the courtyard of the guardhouse. This courtyard was at the palace of the king of Judah. 3King Zedekiah

of Judah had put Jeremiah in prison in that place. Zedekiah didn't like the things Jeremiah prophesied. Jeremiah had said, "This is what the LORD says: 'I will soon give the city of Jerusalem to the king of Babylon. Nebuchadnezzar will capture this city. 4King Zedekiah of Judah will not escape from the army of the Babylonians. But he will surely be given to the king of Babylon. And Zedekiah will speak to the king of Babylon face to face. He will see him with his own eyes. 5The king of Babylon will take Zedekiah to Babylon. Zedekiah will stay there until I have punished him.' This message is from the LORD. 'If you fight against the army of the Babylonians, you will not succeed.'"

INSIGHT

It's about 588–87 BC and Jeremiah is in prison. His home town is under foreign occupation and God tells him to buy a plot of land there. It might seem stupid paying for a field you may never see, but for Jeremiah it was an act of faith that God would one day bring him and his fellow Jews home.

Jeremiah 32:7–15

6While Jeremiah was a prisoner, he said, "This message from the LORD came to me. This was the message: 7'Jeremiah, your cousin, Hanamel, will come to you soon. He is the son of your uncle Shallum. Hanamel will say to you, "Jeremiah, buy my field near the town of Anathoth. Buy it because you are my nearest relative. It is your right and your responsibility to buy that field."'

8"Then it happened just as the LORD said. My cousin Hanamel came to me in the courtyard of the guardhouse. Hanamel said to me, 'Jeremiah, buy my field near the town of Anathoth, in the land of the tribe of Benjamin. Buy that land for yourself because it is your right to buy it and own it.'"

So I knew that this was a message from the LORD. 9I bought the field at Anathoth from my cousin Hanamel. I weighed out 17 pieces of silver for him. 10I signed the deed and had a copy of the deed sealed up.*c* I got some men to witness what I had done, and I weighed out the silver on the scales. 11Then I took the sealed copy of the deed,

---

a **31:39 measuring line** A rope or chain for measuring property lines.
b **32:1 the tenth year . . . Judah** This was the year Jerusalem was destroyed by Nebuchadnezzar.
c **32:10 sealed up** Important documents were rolled up and tied with a string. Then a piece of clay or wax was put on the string. Then a person's mark was put in that clay or wax. This way, people could prove nothing in the document had been changed.

which contained the demands and limits of my purchase, and the copy that was not sealed. ¹²I gave the deed to Baruch son of Neriah, the son of Mahseiah. I did this while my cousin Hanamel and the other witnesses were there. They also signed the deed. And many other people of Judah saw this as they were sitting there in the courtyard of the guardhouse.

¹³With all the people watching, I said to Baruch, ¹⁴"This is what the LORD All-Powerful, the God of Israel, says: 'Take both copies of the deed—the sealed copy and the copy that was not sealed—and put them in a clay jar. Do this so that these deeds will last a long time.' ¹⁵The LORD All-Powerful, the God of Israel, says, 'In the future my people will once again buy houses, fields and vineyards in the land of Israel.'"

¹⁶After I gave the deed to Baruch son of Neriah, I prayed to the LORD:

¹⁷"Lord GOD, with your great power you made the earth and the sky. There is nothing too hard for you to do. ¹⁸You are loyal and kind to thousands of people, but you also bring punishment to children for their fathers' sins. Great and powerful God, your name is the LORD All-Powerful. ¹⁹You plan and do great things. You see everything that people do. You give a reward to those who do good things, and you punish those who do bad things—you give them what they deserve. ²⁰You have been doing powerful miracles in the land of Egypt until now, in Israel and elsewhere. You are the one who made yourself as famous as you are today. ²¹You used powerful miracles and brought your people Israel out of Egypt. You used your own powerful hand to do this. Your power was amazing!

²²"You gave the Israelites this land that you promised to give to their ancestors long ago. It is a very good land filled with many good things. ²³They came into this land and took it for their own. But they didn't obey you. They didn't follow your teachings or do what you commanded. So you made all these terrible things happen to them.

²⁴"And now the enemy has surrounded the city. They are building ramps so that they can get over the walls of Jerusalem and capture it. Because of war, hunger and disease, the city of Jerusalem will fall to the Babylonian army. The Babylonians are attacking the city now. You said this would happen, and now you see it is happening.

²⁵"Lord GOD, all those bad things are happening. But now you are telling me, 'Jeremiah, buy the field with silver and choose some men to witness the purchase.' You are telling me this while the Babylonian army is ready to capture the city. Why should I waste my money like that?"

²⁶Then this message from the LORD came to Jeremiah: ²⁷"I am the LORD. I am the God of every person on the earth. You know that nothing is impossible for me." ²⁸The LORD also said, "I will soon give the city of Jerusalem to the Babylonian army and to King Nebuchadnezzar of Babylon. The army will capture the city. ²⁹The Babylonian army is already attacking the city of Jerusalem. They will soon enter the city and start a fire. They will burn down this city. There are houses in this city where the people of Jerusalem made me angry by offering sacrifices to the false god Baal on the housetops. And they poured out drink offerings to other idol gods. The Babylonian army will burn down those houses. ³⁰I have watched the people of Israel and the people of Judah. Everything they do is evil. They have done evil things since they were young. The people of Israel have made me very angry because they worship idols that they made with their own hands." This message is from the LORD. ³¹"From the time that Jerusalem was built until now, the people of this city have made me angry. This city has made me very angry, so I must remove it from my sight. ³²I will destroy Jerusalem because of all the evil things the people of Israel and Judah have done. The people, their kings, leaders, their priests and prophets, the men of Judah and the people of Jerusalem have all made me angry.

³³"They should have come to me for help, but they turned their backs on me. I tried to teach them again and again, but they would not listen to me. I tried to correct them, but they would not listen. ³⁴They have made their idols, and I hate those idols. They put their idols in the Temple that is called by my name, so they made my Temple 'dirty'. ³⁵In the Valley of Ben Hinnom,ᵃ they built high places to the false god Baal. They built those worship places so that they could burn their sons and daughters as sacrifices. I never commanded them to do such a terrible thing. I never even thought the people of Judah would do such a terrible thing.

³⁶"You people are saying, 'The king of Babylon will capture Jerusalem. He will use war, hunger and disease to defeat this city.' But this is what

---

ᵃ **32:35** *Valley of Ben Hinnom* This valley is also called "Gehenna". This name comes from the Hebrew name "Ge Hinnom—Hinnom's Valley". This place became an example of how God punishes wicked people.

the LORD, the God of the people of Israel, says: [37]I have forced the people of Israel and Judah to leave their land. I was very angry with them, but I will bring them back to this place. I will gather them from the land where I forced them to go. I will bring them back to this place. I will let them live in peace and safety. [38]The people of Israel and Judah will be my people, and I will be their God. [39]I will give them the desire to be one united people. They will have one goal—to worship me all their lives. They and their children will want to do this.

[40]"I will make an agreement with the people of Israel and Judah that will last forever. In this agreement I will never turn away from them. I will always be good to them. I will make them want to respect me. Then they will never turn away from me. [41]They will make me happy. I will enjoy doing good to them. And I will surely plant them in this land and make them grow. I will do this with all my heart and soul."

[42]This is what the LORD says: "I have brought this great disaster to the people of Israel and Judah. In the same way, I will bring good things to them. I promise to do good things for them. [43]You people are saying, 'This land is an empty desert. There are no people or animals here. The Babylonian army defeated this country.' But in the future people will once again buy fields in this land. [44]They will use their money and buy fields. They will sign and seal their agreements. They will witness the people signing their deeds. They will again buy fields in the land where the tribe of Benjamin lives, in the area around Jerusalem, in the towns of the land of Judah, in the hill country, in the western foothills and in the area of the southern desert. This will happen because I will bring them back home." This message is from the LORD.

The Promise of God

33 While Jeremiah was still locked up in the courtyard of the guardhouse, the message from the LORD came to him a second time: [2]"The LORD, made the earth, and it continues the way he made it. The LORD is his name. He says, [3]'Judah, pray to me, and I will answer you. I will tell you important secrets. You have never heard these things before.' [4]The LORD is the God of Israel. This is what he says about the houses in Jerusalem and about the palaces of the kings of Judah: 'The enemy will pull these houses down. They will build ramps up to the top of the city walls. They will use swords and fight the people in these cities.

[5]"'The people in Jerusalem have done many bad things. I am angry with them. I have turned against them, so I will kill many people there. The Babylonian army will come to fight against

Jerusalem. There will be many dead bodies in the houses in Jerusalem.

[6]"'But then I will heal the people in that city. I will let them enjoy peace and safety. [7]I will make good things happen to Judah and Israel again and make them strong as in the past. [8]They sinned against me, but I will wash away that sin. They fought against me, but I will forgive them. [9]Then Jerusalem will be a wonderful place. The people will be happy. People from other nations will praise it when they hear about the good things happening there. They will hear about the good things I am doing for Jerusalem.'

[10]"This is what the LORD says: 'You people say that your country is an empty desert, with no people or animals living there.' Yes, the streets of Jerusalem and the towns of Judah are empty. Nothing lives there now, people or animals. But someday the sounds of life will return— [11]sounds of joy and happiness. There will be the happy sounds of a bride and groom. There will be the sounds of people bringing their gifts to the LORD's Temple. They will say, 'Praise the LORD All-Powerful! The LORD is good! His faithful love will last forever!' They will say this because I will again do good things to Judah. It will be as it was in the beginning.' This is what the LORD says.

[12]The LORD All-Powerful says, "This place is empty now. There are no people or animals living here. But there will be people in all the towns of Judah. There will be shepherds, and there will be pastures where they will let their flocks rest. [13]Shepherds will count their sheep as the sheep walk in front of them. They will be counting their sheep all around the country—in the hill country, in the western foothills, in the Negev and in all the other towns of Judah."

The Good Branch

[14]This message is from the LORD: "I made a special promise to the people of Israel and Judah. The time is coming when I will do what I promised. [15]At that time I will make a good 'branch' grow from David's family. That branch will do what is good and right for the country. [16]During the time that he rules, the people of Judah will be safe. The people in Jerusalem will live in safety. And the city will be called, 'The LORD Is Our Victory'."

[17]The LORD says, "Someone from David's family will always sit on the throne and rule the family of Israel. [18]And there will always be Levite priests to stand before me. They will always be there to offer burnt offerings, grain offerings and sacrifices to me."

[19]This message from the LORD came to Jeremiah. [20]The LORD says, "I have an agreement with day and night. I agreed that they would continue forever. You cannot change that agreement. Day

and night will always come at the right time. If you could change that agreement, 21then you could change my agreement with David and Levi. Then descendants from David would not be the kings, and the family of Levi would not be priests. 22But I will give many descendants to my servant David and to the tribe of Levi. They will be as many as the stars in the sky—no one can count all the stars. And they will be as many as the grains of sand on the seashore—no one can count the grains of sand."

23Jeremiah received this message from the LORD: 24"Jeremiah, have you heard what the people are saying? They are saying, 'The LORD turned away from the two families of Israel and Judah. He chose those people, but now he does not even accept them as a nation.'"

25The LORD says, "If my agreement with day and night does not continue, and if I had not made the laws for the sky and earth, maybe I would leave those people. 26Then maybe I would turn away from Jacob's descendants. And then maybe I would not let David's descendants rule over the descendants of Abraham, Isaac and Jacob. But David is my servant, and I will be kind to those people. I will again cause good things to happen to them."

A Warning to Zedekiah

34 The LORD spoke his message to Jeremiah at the time when King Nebuchadnezzar of Babylon was fighting against Jerusalem and all the towns around it. Nebuchadnezzar had with him all his army and the armies of all the kingdoms and peoples in the empire he ruled.

2This is what the LORD, the God of the people of Israel, said: "Jeremiah, go to King Zedekiah of Judah and give him this message: 'Zedekiah, this is what the LORD says: I will give the city of Jerusalem to the king of Babylon very soon, and he will burn it down. 3You will not escape from the king of Babylon. You will surely be caught and given to him. You will see the king of Babylon with your own eyes. He will talk to you face to face, and you will go to Babylon. 4But listen to the promise of the LORD, King Zedekiah of Judah. This is what the LORD says about you: You will not be killed with a sword. 5You will die in a peaceful way. People made funeral fires to honour your ancestors, the kings who ruled before you. In the same way, people will make a funeral fire to honour you. They will cry for you and sadly say, "Oh, my master!" I myself make this promise to you.'" This message is from the LORD.

6So Jeremiah told all this message to Zedekiah in Jerusalem. 7This was while the army of the king of Babylon was fighting against Jerusalem. The army of Babylon was also fighting against the cities of Judah that had not been captured. These cities were Lachish and Azekah. These were the only fortified cities left in the land of Judah.

The People Break an Agreement

8King Zedekiah had made an agreement with all the people in Jerusalem to give freedom to all the Hebrew slaves. A message from the LORD came to Jeremiah after Zedekiah had made that agreement. 9Everyone was supposed to free their Hebrew slaves. All male and female Hebrew slaves were to be set free. No one was supposed to keep another person from the tribe of Judah in slavery. 10So all the leaders of Judah and all the people accepted this agreement. They would free their male and female slaves so that they would no longer serve them. Everyone agreed, and so all the slaves were set free. 11But after that,a the people who had slaves changed their minds. So they took the people they had set free and made them slaves again.

12Then this message from the LORD came to Jeremiah: 13"This is what the LORD, the God of the people of Israel, says: I brought your ancestors out of the land of Egypt, where they were slaves. When I did that, I made an agreement with them. 14I said to your ancestors, 'At the end of every seven years, everyone must set their Hebrew slaves free. If you have fellow Hebrews who have sold themselves to you, you must let them go free after they have served you for six years.' But your ancestors did not listen to me or pay attention to me. 15A short time ago you changed your hearts to do what is right. Everyone set free their fellow Hebrews who were slaves. And you even made an agreement before me in the Temple that is called by my name. 16But now you have changed your minds. You have shown that you do not honour my name, because each of you has taken back the male and female slaves that you had set free. You have forced them to become slaves again.

17"So this is what the LORD says: You people have not obeyed me. You have not given freedom to your fellow Hebrews. So, because you have not given them freedom, I will give you a special kind of freedom—freedom to die in war or by disease or by hunger! This message is from the LORD. When the other nations see what I have done to you, they will all be shocked. 18I will hand over

---

a **34:11** *after that* In the summer of 588 BC, the Egyptian army came to help the people of Jerusalem. So the Babylonian army had to leave Jerusalem for a short time to fight the Egyptians. The people of Jerusalem thought God had helped them, and things were back to normal, so they didn't keep their promise. They took the slaves they had set free back into slavery.

those who broke my agreement and have not kept the promises they made before me. They cut a calf in half before me and made a vow by walking between the two pieces.*a* 19These are the people who made that agreement before me by walking between the pieces of the calf: the leaders of Judah and Jerusalem, the important officials of the court, the priests and the people of the land. 20So I will give them to their enemies and to everyone who wants to kill them. Their bodies will become food for the birds of the air and for the wild animals of the earth. 21I will give King Zedekiah of Judah and his leaders to their enemies and to everyone who wants to kill them. I will give Zedekiah and his people to the army of the king of Babylon, even though that army has left Jerusalem.*b* 22But I will give the order, says the LORD, to bring the Babylonian army back to Jerusalem. That army will fight against Jerusalem. They will capture it, set it on fire and burn it down. And I will destroy the towns in the land of Judah. They will become empty deserts. No one will live there."

The Recabite Family's Good Example

35 During the time when Jehoiakim, son of King Josiah, was king of Judah, the LORD spoke this message to Jeremiah: 2"Go to the Recabite family*c* and invite them to come to one of the side rooms of the LORD's Temple. Offer them wine to drink."

3So I went to get Jaazaniah*d* son of Jeremiah,*e* who was the son of Habazziniah. And I got all of Jaazaniah's brothers and sons and the whole family of the Recabites together. 4Then I brought them into the Temple of the LORD. We went into the room of the sons of Hanan, the son of Igdaliah. Hanan was a man of God.*f* The room was next to the room where the princes of Judah stay. It was over the room of Maaseiah son of Shallum. Maaseiah was the doorkeeper in the Temple. 5Then I put some bowls full of wine and some cups in front of the Recabite family. And I said to them, "Drink some wine."

6But the Recabite family answered, "We never drink wine. We never drink it because our ancestor Jonadab son of Recab gave us this command: 'You and your descendants must never drink wine. 7Also you must never build houses, plant seeds or plant vineyards. You must never do any of those things. You must live only in tents. If you do that, you will live a long time in the land where you move from place to place.' 8So we have obeyed everything our ancestor Jonadab commanded us. None of us ever drinks wine, and neither do our wives, sons or daughters. 9We never build houses to live in, we never own vineyards or fields, and we never plant crops. 10We have lived in tents and have obeyed everything our ancestor Jonadab commanded us. 11But when King Nebuchadnezzar of Babylon attacked the country of Judah, we did go into Jerusalem. We said to each other, 'Come, we must enter the city of Jerusalem so that we can escape the Babylonian army and the Aramean army.' So we have stayed in Jerusalem."

12Then this message from the LORD came to Jeremiah: 13"The LORD All-Powerful, the God of Israel, says to go to the people of Judah and Jerusalem and tell them this: 'Why is obeying me such a difficult lesson for you to learn?' This message is from the LORD. 14'Jonadab son of Recab ordered his sons not to drink wine, and they have obeyed that command. To this day the descendants of Jonadab have obeyed their ancestor's command. They do not drink wine. But I have given commands to you people of Judah again and again, and you have not obeyed me. 15Time after time I have sent my servants the prophets to you. They said, "You must each stop doing evil things and do what is right. Don't follow other gods. Don't worship or serve them. If you obey me, you will live in the land I have given to you and your ancestors." But you have not paid attention to my message. 16The descendants of Jonadab obeyed the commands that their ancestor gave them, but the people of Judah have not obeyed me.'

17"So this is what the LORD God All-Powerful, the God of Israel, says: 'I said that many bad things would happen to Judah and Jerusalem. I will soon make all those bad things happen. I spoke to the people, but they refused to listen. I called out to them, but they didn't answer me.'"

18Then Jeremiah said to the Recabite family, "This is what the LORD All-Powerful, the God of Israel, says: 'You have obeyed the commands of your ancestor Jonadab. You have followed all his teachings. You have done everything he

---

a **34:18 They . . . two pieces** This is part of a ceremony people used when they made an important agreement. An animal was cut into two pieces. Those who were making the agreement would walk between the pieces. Then they would make a vow, saying something like, "May this same thing happen to me if I don't keep the agreement." See Gen. 15.
b **34:21 left Jerusalem** In the summer of 588 BC, the Egyptian army came to help the people of Jerusalem. So the Babylonian army had to leave Jerusalem for a short time to fight the Egyptians. See Jer. 37:5. See also the footnote to Jer. 34:11.
c **35:2 Recabite family** A group of people descended from Jonadab son of Recab. The family was very loyal to the Lord. See 2 Kgs 10:15–28 for the story about Jonadab. Also in verses 6,18.
d **35:3 Jaazaniah** He was the head of the Recabite family at that time.
e **35:3 Jeremiah** This is not the prophet Jeremiah but a different man with the same name.
f **35:4 man of God** This is usually an honourable title for a prophet. We know nothing else about Hanan.

commanded.' ¹⁹So the LORD All-Powerful, the God of Israel, says: 'There will always be a descendant of Jonadab son of Recab to serve me.'"

King Jehoiakim Burns Jeremiah's Scroll

36 The LORD spoke his message to Jeremiah during the fourth year that Jehoiakim[a] son of Josiah was king of Judah. This was the message from the Lord: ²"Jeremiah, get a scroll and write on it all the messages I have spoken to you. I have spoken to you about the nations of Israel and Judah and all the other nations. Write down all the words that I have spoken to you from the time that Josiah was king, until now. ³Maybe the people of Judah will hear what I am planning to do to them and will stop doing bad things. If they will do that, I will forgive them for the terrible sins they have committed."

⁴So Jeremiah called a man named Baruch son of Neriah. Jeremiah spoke the messages the LORD had given him. While he spoke, Baruch wrote the messages on the scroll. ⁵Then Jeremiah said to Baruch, "I cannot go to the LORD's Temple. I am not allowed to go there. ⁶So I want you to go to the Temple of the LORD. Go there on a day of fasting and read to the people from the scroll. Read to the people the messages from the LORD that you wrote on the scroll as I spoke them to you. Read them to all the people of Judah who come into Jerusalem from the towns where they live. ⁷Perhaps they will ask the LORD to help them. Perhaps each person will stop doing bad things. The LORD has announced that he is very angry with them." ⁸So Baruch son of Neriah did everything Jeremiah the prophet told him to do. Baruch read aloud from the scroll that had the LORD's messages written on it. He read it in the LORD's Temple.

⁹In the ninth month of the fifth year that Jehoiakim was king, a time of fasting was announced. All those who lived in the city of Jerusalem and everyone who had come into Jerusalem from the towns of Judah were supposed to go without eating as they prayed to the LORD. ¹⁰At that time Baruch read the scroll that contained Jeremiah's words. He read the scroll in the Temple of the LORD to all the people who were there. Baruch was in the room of Gemariah in the upper courtyard when he read from the scroll. That room was located at the entrance of the New Gate of the Temple. Gemariah was the son of Shaphan. Gemariah was a scribe in the Temple.

¹¹A man named Micaiah heard all the messages from the LORD that Baruch read from the scroll. Micaiah was the son of Gemariah, the son of Shaphan. ¹²When Micaiah heard the messages from the scroll, he went down to the secretary's room in the king's palace. All the royal officials were sitting there in the king's palace. These are the names of the officials: Elishama the secretary, Delaiah son of Shemaiah, Elnathan son of Acbor, Gemariah son of Shaphan, Zedekiah son of Hananiah; all the other royal officials were there too. ¹³Micaiah told them everything he had heard Baruch read from the scroll.

¹⁴Then all the officials sent a man named Jehudi to Baruch. (Jehudi was the son of Nethaniah, son of Shelemiah. Shelemiah was the son of Cushi.) Jehudi said to Baruch, "Bring the scroll that you read from and come with me."

Baruch son of Neriah took the scroll and went with Jehudi to the officials.

¹⁵Then the officials said to Baruch, "Sit down and read the scroll to us."

So Baruch read the scroll to them.

¹⁶When the royal officials heard all the messages from the scroll, they were afraid and looked at each other. They said to Baruch, "We must tell King Jehoiakim about these messages on the scroll." ¹⁷Then the officials asked Baruch, "Tell us, Baruch, where did you get these messages that you wrote on the scroll? Did you write down what Jeremiah said to you?"

¹⁸"Yes," Baruch answered. "Jeremiah spoke, and I wrote down all the messages with ink on this scroll."

¹⁹Then the royal officials said to Baruch, "You and Jeremiah must go and hide. Don't tell anyone where you are hiding."

²⁰Then the royal officials put the scroll in the room of Elishama the scribe. They went to King Jehoiakim and told him all about the scroll.

²¹So King Jehoiakim sent Jehudi to get the scroll. Jehudi brought the scroll from the room of Elishama the scribe. Then Jehudi read the scroll to the king and all the servants who stood around the king. ²²This happened in the ninth month,[b] so King Jehoiakim was sitting in the part of the palace used for winter. There was a fire burning in a small fireplace in front of the king. ²³Jehudi began to read from the scroll. But each time he read two or three sections, King Jehoiakim grabbed the scroll and used a knife to cut off that part of the scroll and throw it into the fire. Finally, the whole scroll was burned up. ²⁴When King Jehoiakim and his servants heard the message from the scroll, they were not afraid. They did not tear their clothes to show sorrow for doing wrong.

---

[a] **36:1** *the fourth year . . . Jehoiakim* This was about 605 BC.
[b] **36:22** *ninth month* That is, November–December.

²⁵Elnathan, Delaiah and Gemariah tried to talk King Jehoiakim out of burning the scroll, but he would not listen to them. ²⁶Instead King Jehoiakim commanded some men to arrest Baruch the scribe and Jeremiah the prophet. These men were Jerahmeel, a son of the king, Seraiah son of Azriel and Shelemiah son of Abdeel. But they could not find Baruch and Jeremiah, because the LORD had hidden them.

²⁷King Jehoiakim burned the scroll on which Baruch had written all the words that Jeremiah had spoken to him. Then this message from the LORD came to Jeremiah:

²⁸"Get another scroll. Write all the messages on it that were on the first scroll that King Jehoiakim of Judah burned. ²⁹Also tell King Jehoiakim of Judah that this is what the LORD says: 'Jehoiakim, you burned that scroll. You said, "Why did Jeremiah write that the king of Babylon will surely come and destroy this land and kill all the people and animals in it?" ³⁰So this is what the LORD says about King Jehoiakim of Judah: Jehoiakim's descendants will not sit on David's throne. When Jehoiakim dies, he will not get a king's funeral, but his body will be thrown out on the ground. His body will be left out in the heat of the day and the cold frost of the night. ³¹I will punish Jehoiakim and his children, and I will punish his officials. I will do this because they are wicked. I will bring terrible disasters on them and on all those who live in Jerusalem and on the people from Judah. I will bring all these bad things on them, just as I warned them, because they have not listened to me.'"

³²Then Jeremiah took another scroll and gave it to Baruch son of Neriah, the scribe. As Jeremiah spoke, Baruch wrote on the scroll the same messages that were on the scroll that King Jehoiakim had burned in the fire. And many other words like those messages were added to the second scroll.

Jeremiah Is Put Into Prison

37 Nebuchadnezzar was the king of Babylon. He appointed Zedekiah son of Josiah to be the king of Judah in the place of Jehoiachin son of Jehoiakim. ²But Zedekiah, his servants and the people of Judah did not pay attention to the messages the LORD had given to Jeremiah the prophet.

³King Zedekiah sent Jehucal son of Shelemiah and the priest Zephaniah son of Maaseiah to Jeremiah the prophet with a message. This was the message they brought to Jeremiah: "Jeremiah, pray to the LORD our God for us."

⁴At that time Jeremiah had not yet been put into prison, so he was free to go anywhere he wanted. ⁵Also at that time Pharaoh's army had marched from Egypt towards Judah. The Babylonian army had surrounded the city of Jerusalem in order to defeat it. Then they had heard about the army from Egypt marching towards them. So the army from Babylon left Jerusalem to fight with the army from Egypt.

⁶This message from the LORD came to Jeremiah the prophet: ⁷"This is what the LORD, the God of the people of Israel, says: Jehucal and Zephaniah, I know that King Zedekiah of Judah sent you to me to ask questions. Tell King Zedekiah this: 'Pharaoh's army marched out of Egypt to come here to help you against the army of Babylon. But Pharaoh's army will go back to Egypt. ⁸After that, the army from Babylon will come back here and attack Jerusalem. Then they will capture and burn it.' ⁹This is what the LORD says: 'People of Jerusalem, don't fool yourselves. Don't say to yourselves, "The army of Babylon will surely leave us alone." They will not. ¹⁰People of Jerusalem, even if you could defeat all the Babylonian army that is attacking you, there would still be a few wounded men left in their tents. Even those few wounded men would come out of their tents and burn Jerusalem down.'"

¹¹When the Babylonian army left Jerusalem to fight the army of the Pharaoh of Egypt, ¹²Jeremiah wanted to travel from Jerusalem to the land of Benjamin.ᵃ He wanted to be there for a division of some property that belonged to his family. ¹³But when Jeremiah got to the Benjamin Gate of Jerusalem,ᵇ the captain in charge of the guards arrested him. The captain's name was Irijah son of Shelemiah. Shelemiah was the son of Hananiah. So Irijah the captain arrested Jeremiah and said, "Jeremiah, you are leaving us to join the Babylonian side."

¹⁴Jeremiah said to Irijah, "That is not true! I am not leaving to join the Babylonians." But Irijah refused to listen to Jeremiah. And Irijah arrested Jeremiah and took him to the royal officials of Jerusalem. ¹⁵Those officials were very angry with Jeremiah. They gave an order for Jeremiah to be beaten. Then they put him in a prison. The prison was in the house of Jonathan, a scribe for the king of Judah. His house had been made into a prison. ¹⁶They put Jeremiah into a cell under the house of Jonathan. The cell was in a dungeon under the ground. Jeremiah was there for a long time.

¹⁷Then King Zedekiah sent for Jeremiah and had him brought to the palace. Zedekiah talked to Jeremiah in private. He asked Jeremiah, "Is there any message from the LORD?"

ᵃ **37:12** *the land of Benjamin* Jeremiah was going to his home town, Anathoth, which was in the land of Benjamin.
ᵇ **37:13** *Benjamin Gate of Jerusalem* This gate led out of Jerusalem to the road which went north to the land of Benjamin.

Jeremiah answered, "Yes, he said that you will be given to the king of Babylon." [18]Then Jeremiah said to King Zedekiah, "What have I done wrong? What crime have I committed against you or your officials or the people of Jerusalem? Why have you thrown me into prison? [19]King Zedekiah, where are your prophets now? They told you a false message. They said, 'The king of Babylon will not attack you or this land of Judah.' [20]But now, my lord, king of Judah, please listen to me. Please let me bring my request to you. This is what I ask: Don't send me back to the house of Jonathan the scribe. If you send me back, I will die there."

[21]So King Zedekiah gave orders for Jeremiah to be kept in the courtyard of the guardhouse. And he ordered that Jeremiah should be given bread from the street bakers. He was given bread until there was no more bread in the city. So Jeremiah stayed under guard in the courtyard.

Jeremiah Is Thrown Into a Well

38 Some of the royal officials heard what Jeremiah was saying. They were Shephatiah son of Mattan, Gedaliah son of Pashhur, Jehucal son of Shelemiah and Pashhur son of Malkijah. Jeremiah was telling the people, [2]"This is what the LORD says: 'Everyone who stays in Jerusalem will die from war, hunger or disease. But everyone who surrenders to the army of Babylon will live and escape with their lives.' [3]And this is what the LORD says: 'This city of Jerusalem will surely be given to the army of the king of Babylon. He will capture this city.'"

[4]When those officials heard Jeremiah say these things, they went to King Zedekiah. They said to him, "Jeremiah should be put to death. He is discouraging the soldiers who are still in the city and everyone else by what he is saying. He is not looking for peace; he is just trying to cause trouble."

[5]So King Zedekiah said to the officials, "Jeremiah is in your control. I cannot do anything to stop you."

[6]So they took Jeremiah and put him in a well that belonged to the king's son Malkijah. This well was in the courtyard of the guardhouse. They used ropes to lower Jeremiah down into it. The well did not have any water in it, only mud. And Jeremiah sank down into the mud.

[7]But a man named Ebed Melech heard that the officials had put Jeremiah into the well. Ebed Melech was from Ethiopia, and he was a eunuch in the king's palace. King Zedekiah was sitting at the Benjamin Gate, so Ebed Melech left the

king's palace and went to talk to the king at the gate. [8-9]Ebed Melech said, "My lord and king, these officials have done evil. They have treated Jeremiah the prophet badly. They have thrown him into a well and left him there to die."[a]

[10]Then King Zedekiah gave a command to Ebed Melech, the Ethiopian: "Ebed Melech, take three[b] men from the palace with you, and go and get Jeremiah out of the well before he dies."

[11]So Ebed Melech took the men with him. But first he went to a room under the storeroom in the king's palace. He took some old rags and worn-out clothes from that room. Then he let the rags down with some ropes to Jeremiah in the well. [12]Ebed Melech, the Ethiopian, said to Jeremiah, "Put these old rags and worn-out clothes under your arms. When we pull you out, these rags will pad your underarms. Then the ropes will not hurt you." So Jeremiah did as Ebed Melech said. [13]The men pulled Jeremiah up with the ropes and lifted him out of the well. And Jeremiah was kept there in the courtyard of the guardhouse.

INSIGHT

Zedekiah the king of Judah was a weak leader — just see how he keeps changing his mind about what to do with Jeremiah. He puts him in prison, then upgrades his cell. He throws him in a well of mud, then he rescues him. He knows what is right but can never quite bring himself to do it wholeheartedly.

Jeremiah 37:16 – 38:28

Zedekiah Asks Jeremiah Some Questions

[14]Then King Zedekiah sent someone to get Jeremiah the prophet. He had Jeremiah brought to the third entrance to the Temple of the LORD. Then the king said, "Jeremiah, I am going to ask you something. Don't hide anything from me, but tell me everything honestly."

[15]Jeremiah said to Zedekiah, "If I give you an answer, you will probably kill me. And even if I give you advice, you will not listen to me."

[16]But King Zedekiah secretly swore an oath to Jeremiah. Zedekiah said, "As surely as the LORD lives, who gives us breath and life, I will not kill you, Jeremiah. And I promise not to give you to the officials who want to kill you."

---

[a] **38:8–9** *left him there to die* Literally, "he will starve to death because there is no more bread in the city."
[b] **38:10** *three* This is found in one ancient Hebrew copy. Most Hebrew copies have "30".

¹⁷Then Jeremiah said to King Zedekiah, "The LORD God All-Powerful is the God of Israel. This is what he says, 'If you surrender to the officials of the king of Babylon, your life will be saved, and Jerusalem will not be burned down. And you and your family will live. ¹⁸But if you refuse to surrender, Jerusalem will be given to the Babylonian army. They will burn Jerusalem down, and you will not escape from them.'"

¹⁹But King Zedekiah said to Jeremiah, "But I am afraid of the men of Judah who have already gone over to the side of the Babylonian army. I am afraid that the soldiers will give me to those men, and they will treat me badly."

²⁰But Jeremiah answered, "The soldiers will not give you to the men of Judah. King Zedekiah, obey the LORD by doing what I tell you. Then things will go well for you, and your life will be saved. ²¹But if you refuse to surrender to the army of Babylon, the LORD has shown me what will happen. This is what he has told me: ²²All the women who are left in the house of the king of Judah will be brought out. They will be brought to the important officials of the king of Babylon. Your women will make fun of you with a song. This is what they will say:

'Your friends were stronger than you,
 and they led you the wrong way.
You trusted them,
 but now your feet are stuck in the mud,
 and your friends have left you.'

²³"All your wives and children will be brought out. They will be given to the Babylonian army. You yourself will not escape from the army of Babylon. You will be captured by the king of Babylon, and Jerusalem will be burned down."

²⁴Then Zedekiah said to Jeremiah, "Don't tell anyone that I have been talking to you. If you do, you might die. ²⁵If the officials find out that I talked to you, they will come to you and say, 'Jeremiah, tell us what you said to King Zedekiah and what he said to you. Be honest with us, and tell us everything, or we will kill you.' ²⁶If they say this to you, tell them, 'I was begging the king not to send me back to the cell in the dungeon under Jonathan's house. If I were to go back there, I would die.'"

²⁷It happened that the royal officials of the king did come to Jeremiah to question him. So Jeremiah told them everything the king had ordered him to say. Then they left Jeremiah alone. No one had heard what Jeremiah and the king had talked about.

²⁸So Jeremiah was kept there in the courtyard of the guardhouse until the day Jerusalem was captured.

The Fall of Jerusalem

39 This is how Jerusalem was captured: during the tenth month of the ninth year that Zedekiah was king of Judah, King Nebuchadnezzar of Babylon marched against Jerusalem with his whole army. He surrounded the city to defeat it. ²And on the ninth day of the fourth month in Zedekiah's eleventh year, the wall of Jerusalem was broken through. ³Then all the royal officials of the king of Babylon came into the city of Jerusalem. They came in and sat down at the Middle Gate. These are the names of the officials: Nergal-Sharezer, the governor of the district of Samgar, a very high official; Nebo Sarsekim, another very high official; and various other important officials were there also.

⁴King Zedekiah of Judah saw the officials from Babylon, so he and the soldiers with him ran away. They left Jerusalem at night. They went out through the king's garden and out through the gate that was between the two walls. Then they went towards the desert. ⁵The Babylonian army chased Zedekiah and the soldiers with him. They caught up with Zedekiah in the plains of Jericho. They captured Zedekiah and took him to King Nebuchadnezzar of Babylon. Nebuchadnezzar was at the town of Riblah in the land of Hamath. At that place, Nebuchadnezzar decided what to do to Zedekiah. ⁶There at the town of Riblah, the king of Babylon killed Zedekiah's sons and he killed all the royal officials of Judah while Zedekiah watched. ⁷Then Nebuchadnezzar tore out Zedekiah's eyes. He put bronze chains on Zedekiah and took him to Babylon.

⁸The army of Babylon set fire to the king's palace and the houses of the people of Jerusalem. And they broke down the walls of Jerusalem. ⁹Nebuzaradan was the commander of the king of Babylon's special guards. He took all the people who had surrendered to him and all the people still in Jerusalem and made them captives. He carried them away to Babylon. ¹⁰But commander Nebuzaradan left behind some of the poor people of Judah who owned nothing. Nebuzaradan gave them vineyards and farmland in Judah.

¹¹Nebuchadnezzar also gave an order about Jeremiah to commander Nebuzaradan: ¹²"Find Jeremiah and take care of him. Don't hurt him. Give him whatever he asks for."

¹³So Nebuzaradan, the commander of the king's special guards, Nebushazban, a chief officer in the army of Babylon, Nergal-Sharezer, a high official and all the other officers of the army of Babylon sent for Jeremiah. ¹⁴They had him brought from the courtyard of the guardhouse

and turned him over to Gedaliah[a] son of Ahikam, the son of Shaphan. Gedaliah did as he was told and took Jeremiah back home. So Jeremiah was able to stay in Judah among his own people.

The LORD's Message to Ebed Melech

[15]Earlier, when Jeremiah was still being held in the courtyard of the guardhouse, he had received this message from the LORD: [16]Jeremiah, go and tell Ebed Melech[b] the Ethiopian that this is what the LORD All-Powerful, the God of Israel says: 'Very soon I will make everything I said about this city of Jerusalem come true. My words will come true through disaster, not through something good. You will see everything happen with your own eyes. [17]But I will save you on that day, Ebed Melech. This is the message from the LORD. You will not be given to the people you are afraid of. [18]I will save you, Ebed Melech. You will not die from a sword, but you will escape and live. That will happen because you have trusted in me.'" This message is from the LORD.

Jeremiah Is Set Free

40 The LORD spoke his message to Jeremiah after he was set free at the city of Ramah. Nebuzaradan, the commander of the king of Babylon's special guards, found Jeremiah in Ramah. Jeremiah was bound with chains. He was with all the captives from Jerusalem and Judah. They were being taken away in captivity to Babylon. [2]When commander Nebuzaradan found Jeremiah, he spoke to him. He said, "Jeremiah, the LORD, your God, announced that this disaster would come to this place. [3]And now the LORD has done everything just as he said he would do. This disaster happened because you people of Judah sinned against the LORD. You did not obey him. [4]But now, Jeremiah, I will set you free. I am taking the chains off your wrists. If you want to, come with me to Babylon, and I will take good care of you. But if you don't want to come with me, then don't come. Look, the whole country is open to you. Go anywhere you want. [5]Or go back to Gedaliah[c] son of Ahikam, the son of Shaphan. The king of Babylon has chosen Gedaliah to be governor over the towns of Judah. Go and live with Gedaliah among the people. Or you can go anywhere you want."

Then Nebuzaradan gave Jeremiah some food and a present and let him go. [6]So Jeremiah went to Gedaliah son of Ahikam at Mizpah. He stayed with Gedaliah among those who were left behind in the land of Judah.

The Short Rule of Gedaliah

[7]There were some soldiers from the army of Judah, officers and their men, still out in the open country when Jerusalem was destroyed. They heard that the king of Babylon had put Gedaliah son of Ahikam in charge of those who were left in the land. Those who were left were men, women and children who were very poor. They were not carried off to Babylon as captives. [8]So the soldiers came to Gedaliah at Mizpah. They were Ishmael son of Nethaniah, Johanan and his brother Jonathan, sons of Kareah, Seraiah son of Tanhumeth, sons of Ephai from Netophah and Jaazaniah son of the Maacathite and the men who were with them.

[9]Gedaliah son of Ahikam, son of Shaphan, made an oath to make the soldiers and their men feel more secure. This is what he said: "You soldiers, don't be afraid to serve the Babylonian people. Settle down in the land and serve the king of Babylon. If you do this, things will go well for you. [10]I myself will live in Mizpah. I will speak for you before the Chaldeans who come here. You leave that work to me. You should harvest the wine, the summer fruit and the oil. Put what you harvest in your storage jars. Live in the towns that you control."

[11]All the people of Judah who were in the countries of Moab, Ammon, Edom and all the other countries heard that the king of Babylon had left some people of Judah in the land. And they heard that the king of Babylon had chosen Gedaliah son of Ahikam, son of Shaphan, to be governor over them. [12]When the people of Judah heard this news, they came back to the land of Judah. They came back to Gedaliah at Mizpah from all the countries where they had been scattered. So they came back and gathered a large harvest of wine and summer fruit.

[13]Johanan son of Kareah and all the officers of the army of Judah who were still in the open country came to Gedaliah. Gedaliah was at the town of Mizpah. [14]Johanan and the officers with him said to Gedaliah, "Do you know that Baalis, the king of the Ammonites, wants to kill you? He has sent Ishmael son of Nethaniah to kill you." But Gedaliah son of Ahikam didn't believe them.

[15]Then Johanan son of Kareah spoke to Gedaliah in private at Mizpah. Johanan said to Gedaliah, "Let me go and kill Ishmael son of Nethaniah. No one will know anything about it. We should not let Ishmael kill you. That would cause all the people of Judah who are gathered around you to be scattered to different countries again. And that

---

[a] **39:14 Gedaliah** Gedaliah was the man who Nebuchadnezzar appointed as his governor for the land of Judah.
[b] **39:16 Ebed Melech** See Jer. 38:7–13.
[c] **40:5 Or . . . Gedaliah** Or "Before Gedaliah goes back, return to him . . .".

would mean that the few survivors of Judah would be lost."

¹⁶But Gedaliah son of Ahikam said to Johanan son of Kareah, "Don't kill Ishmael. The things you are saying about Ishmael are not true."

41

In the seventh month, Ishmael son of Nethaniah (the son of Elishama) came to Gedaliah son of Ahikam. Ishmael came with ten of his men. They came to the town of Mizpah. Ishmael was a member of the king's family. He had been one of the officers of the king of Judah. Ishmael and his men ate a meal with Gedaliah. ²While they were eating together, Ishmael and his ten men got up and killed Gedaliah son of Ahikam with a sword. Gedaliah was the man the king of Babylon had chosen to be governor of Judah. ³Ishmael also killed all the men of Judah who were with Gedaliah at the town of Mizpah. He also killed the Babylonian soldiers who were there with Gedaliah.

⁴⁻⁵The day after Gedaliah was murdered, 80 men came to Mizpah. They were bringing grain offerings and incense to the LORD's Temple. They had shaved off their beards, torn their clothes and cut themselves.*ᵃ* They came from Shechem, Shiloh and Samaria. None of these men knew that Gedaliah had been murdered. ⁶Ishmael left Mizpah and went to meet the 80 men. He cried*ᵇ* while he walked out to meet them. Ishmael met them and said, "Come with me to meet with Gedaliah son of Ahikam." ⁷⁻⁸As soon as they were in the city, Ishmael and the men with him began to kill the 80 men and throw them into a deep well! But ten of the men said to Ishmael, "Don't kill us! We can give you wheat, barley, olive oil and honey. We can show you the field where we hid it." So Ishmael did not kill them with the others. ⁹Ishmael and his men filled the well with the bodies of the men they had killed. The well was a large one that King Asa had dug long ago. Asa expected a long attack against his city from King Baasha of Israel. So he dug this well to store the water they would need during the attack.

¹⁰Ishmael captured all the other people in the town of Mizpah and started to cross over to the country of the Ammonites. They included the king's daughters, and all those who were left there. Nebuzaradan, the commander of the king of Babylon's special guards, had chosen Gedaliah to watch over those people.

¹¹Johanan son of Kareah and all the army officers who were with him heard about all the evil things Ishmael had done. ¹²So Johanan and the army officers with him took their men and went to fight

Ishmael son of Nethaniah. They caught Ishmael near the big pool of water that is at the town of Gibeon. ¹³When the captives that Ishmael had taken saw Johanan and the army officers, they were very happy. ¹⁴Then all the captives who Ishmael had taken from the town of Mizpah ran to Johanan son of Kareah. ¹⁵But Ishmael and eight of his men escaped from Johanan and ran away to the Ammonites.

¹⁶So Johanan son of Kareah and all his army officers rescued the captives. Ishmael had murdered Gedaliah and then he had taken those people from Mizpah. Among the survivors were soldiers, women, children and court officials. Johanan brought them back from the town of Gibeon.

The Escape to Egypt

¹⁷⁻¹⁸Johanan and the other army officers were afraid of the Chaldeans. The king of Babylon had chosen Gedaliah to be governor of Judah. But Ishmael had murdered Gedaliah, and Johanan was afraid that the Chaldeans would be angry. So they decided to run away to Egypt. On the way to Egypt, they stayed at Geruth Kimham, near the town of Bethlehem.

42

While they were at Geruth Kimham, Johanan son of Kareah and Jezaniah son of Hoshaiah went to Jeremiah the prophet. All the army officers went with Johanan and Jezaniah. All the people, from the least important to the most important, went to Jeremiah. ²They said to him, "Jeremiah, please listen to what we ask. Pray to the LORD your God for all those who are survivors from the family of Judah. Jeremiah, you can see that there are not many of us left. At one time there were many of us. ³Jeremiah, pray that the LORD your God will tell us where we should go and what we should do."

⁴Then Jeremiah the prophet answered, "I understand what you want me to do. I will pray to the LORD your God, as you have asked. I will tell you everything the LORD says. I will not hide anything from you."

⁵Then the people said to Jeremiah, "If we don't do everything the LORD your God tells us, then we hope the LORD will be a true and faithful witness against us. We know he will send you to tell us what to do. ⁶It doesn't matter whether we like the message or not. We will obey the LORD our God. We are sending you to the Lord for a message from him. We will obey what he says. Then good things will happen to us. Yes, we will obey the LORD our God."

ᵃ **41:4–5 shaved . . . cut themselves** The men did this to show that they were sad about the destruction of the Lord's Temple in Jerusalem.
ᵇ **41:6 He cried** Ishmael was acting as though he was sad about the destruction of the Temple.

[7]At the end of ten days, the message from the Lord came to Jeremiah. [8]Then Jeremiah called together Johanan son of Kareah and the army officers who were with him. He also called all the other people together, from the least important to the most important. [9]Then Jeremiah said to them, "You sent me to the Lord, the God of Israel, and I asked him what you wanted me to ask. This is what he says: [10]'If you will stay in Judah, I will make you strong—I will not destroy you. I will plant you, and I will not pull you up. I will do this because I am sad about the terrible things that I made happen to you. [11]Now you are afraid of the king of Babylon. But don't be afraid of him. Don't be afraid of the king of Babylon,' says the Lord, 'because I am with you. I will save you. I will rescue you. He will not get his hands on you. [12]I will be kind to you, and the king of Babylon will also treat you with mercy. He will bring you back to your land.' [13]But you might say, 'We will not stay in Judah.' If you say that, you will disobey the Lord your God. [14]And you might say, 'No, we will go and live in Egypt. We will not be bothered with war there. We will not hear the trumpets of war, and in Egypt we will not be hungry.' [15]If you say that, listen to this message from the Lord, you survivors from Judah. This is what the Lord All-Powerful, the God of Israel, says: 'If you decide to go and live in Egypt, this will happen: [16]You are afraid of the sword of war, but it will defeat you there. And you are worried about hunger, but you will be hungry in Egypt. You will die there. [17]Everyone who decides to go and live in Egypt will die by war, hunger or disease. Not one person who goes to Egypt will survive. Not one of them will escape the terrible things that I will bring to them.'

[18]"This is what the Lord All-Powerful, the God of Israel, says: 'I showed my anger against Jerusalem. I punished the people who lived there. In the same way, I will show my anger against everyone who goes to Egypt. People will use you as an example when they ask for bad things to happen to other people. You will become like a curse word. People will be ashamed of you, and they will insult you. And you will never see Judah again.'

[19]"Survivors of Judah, the Lord told you: 'Don't go to Egypt.' I warn you right now, [20]you are making a mistake that will cause your deaths. You sent me to the Lord your God. You said to me, 'Pray to the Lord our God for us. Tell us everything the Lord our God says to do. We will obey him.' [21]So today, I have told you the message from the Lord. But you have not obeyed the Lord your God. You have not done all that

he sent me to tell you to do. [22]So now be sure you understand this. You want to go and live in Egypt. But these things will happen to you in Egypt: you will die by the sword or hunger or terrible sickness."

INSIGHT

This passage is reminiscent of the time of the judges where "everyone did whatever they thought was right". The remaining residents of Judah make a terrible situation even worse by fighting among themselves, struggling for power, and fleeing to Egypt – which God had told them not to do.

Jeremiah 39:15 – 42:22

43 So Jeremiah finished telling the people the message from the Lord their God. He told them everything that the Lord their God had sent him to tell them.

[2]Azariah son of Hoshaiah, Johanan son of Kareah and some other men were proud and stubborn. They became angry with Jeremiah. They said to him, "Jeremiah, you are lying! The Lord our God didn't send you to say to us, 'You must not go to Egypt to live there.' [3]Jeremiah, we think that Baruch son of Neriah is encouraging you to be against us. He wants you to give us to the Babylonians. He wants you to do this so they can kill us. Or he wants you to do this so that they can make us captives and take us to Babylon."

[4]So Johanan, the army officers and all the people disobeyed the Lord's command. The Lord had commanded them to stay in Judah. [5]But Johanan, son of Kareah, and the army officers did not obey this command. Instead, they took the survivors from Judah to Egypt. In the past the enemy had taken the survivors to other countries, but they had come back to Judah. [6]Now Johanan and all the army officers took all the men, women and children and led them to Egypt. Among those people were the king's daughters. (Nebuzaradan had put Gedaliah in charge of those people. Nebuzaradan was the commander of the king of Babylon's special guards.) Johanan also took Jeremiah the prophet and Baruch son of Neriah. [7]These people didn't listen to the Lord. So they all went to Egypt to the town of Tahpanhes.[a]

[8]In the town of Tahpanhes, Jeremiah received this message from the Lord: [9]"Jeremiah, get some

---

[a] **43:7 Tahpanhes** A town in north-eastern Egypt.

large stones. Take them and bury them in the clay and brick pavement in front of Pharaoh's official building in Tahpanhes. Do this while the people of Judah are watching you. ¹⁰Then say to those who are watching you: 'This is what the LORD All-Powerful, the God of Israel, says: I will send for King Nebuchadnezzar of Babylon to come here. He is my servant, and I will set his throne over these stones I have buried here. Nebuchadnezzar will spread his canopy*ᵃ* above these stones. ¹¹He will come here and attack Egypt. He will bring death to those who are to die. He will bring captivity to those who are to be taken captive. And he will bring the sword to those who are to be killed with a sword. ¹²Nebuchadnezzar will start a fire in the temples of the false gods of Egypt. He will burn the temples and he will take the idols away. Shepherds pick the bugs and thorns off their clothes to make them clean. In the same way, Nebuchadnezzar will pick Egypt clean. Then he will safely leave Egypt. ¹³He will destroy the memorial stones that are in the temple of the sun god*ᵇ* in Egypt, and he will burn down the temples of the false gods of Egypt.'"

The LORD Warns the People of Judah

44 Jeremiah received a message from the Lord for all the people of Judah living in the Egyptian towns of Migdol, Tahpanhes, Memphis and in southern Egypt. This was the message: ²"This is what the LORD All-Powerful, the God of Israel, says: You people saw the disasters that I brought on the city of Jerusalem and on all the towns of Judah. The towns are empty piles of stones today. ³They were destroyed because the people living in them did evil. They gave sacrifices to other gods, and that made me angry! Your people and your ancestors did not worship those gods in the past. ⁴I sent my servants, the prophets, to those people again and again. They spoke my message and said to the people, 'Don't do this terrible thing. I hate it when you worship idols.' ⁵But they didn't listen to the prophets or pay attention to them. They didn't stop doing wicked things. They didn't stop making sacrifices to other gods. ⁶So I showed my anger against them. I punished the towns of Judah and the streets of Jerusalem. My anger made Jerusalem and the towns of Judah the empty piles of stone they are today.

⁷"So this is what the LORD God All-Powerful, the God of Israel, says: Why are you hurting yourselves by continuing to worship idols? You are separating the men and women, the children and babies from the family of Judah. And so you leave yourselves without anyone left from the family of Judah. ⁸Why do you people want to make me angry by making idols? Now you are living in Egypt. And now you are making me angry by offering sacrifices to the false gods of Egypt. You will destroy yourselves, and it will be your own fault. The people of all the other nations on the earth will say bad things about you and make fun of you. ⁹Have you forgotten about the wicked things your ancestors did? And have you forgotten about the wicked things the kings and queens of Judah did? Have you forgotten about the wicked things you and your wives did in Judah and in the streets of Jerusalem? ¹⁰Even to this day the people of Judah have not made themselves humble. They have not shown any respect for me, and they have not followed my teachings. They have not obeyed the laws I gave you and your ancestors.

¹¹"So this is what the LORD All-Powerful, the God of Israel, says: I have decided to make terrible things happen to you. I will destroy the whole family of Judah. ¹²There were a few survivors from Judah. They came here to Egypt. But I will destroy the few survivors from the family of Judah. They will be killed with swords or die from hunger. The people of other nations will point at them and wish evil for them. People will be shocked and frightened by what has happened to them. The name Judah will become a curse word and an insult. ¹³I will punish those who have gone to live in Egypt. I will use war, hunger and disease to punish them. I will punish them just as I punished the city of Jerusalem. ¹⁴Not one of the few survivors of Judah who have gone to live in Egypt will escape my punishment. None of them will survive to come back to Judah. They want to come back to Judah and live there. But not one of them will go back to Judah, except a few people who escape."

¹⁵There were many people from Judah living in southern Egypt. Many of the women from Judah were meeting together in a large group and making sacrifices to other gods, and their husbands knew what they were doing. Those men said to Jeremiah, ¹⁶"We will not listen to the message from the LORD that you spoke to us. ¹⁷We promised to make sacrifices to the Queen of Heaven, and we will do everything we promised. We will offer sacrifices and pour out drink offerings in worship to her. We did that in the past. Our ancestors, our kings and our officials did that in the past. All of us did those things in the towns of Judah and in the streets of Jerusalem. When we worshipped the Queen of Heaven, we had plenty of food. We were

---

ᵃ **43:10 canopy** A temporary covering used for shade. It is like a tent without sides.
ᵇ **43:13 sun god** This was the most important god in Egypt.

successful. Nothing bad happened to us. [18]But then we stopped making sacrifices to the Queen of Heaven, and we stopped pouring out drink offerings to her. And we have had problems ever since we stopped worshipping her. Our people have been killed by war and hunger."

[19]Then the women spoke up[a] and said to Jeremiah, "Our husbands knew what we were doing. We had their permission to make sacrifices to the Queen of Heaven. We had their permission to pour out drink offerings to her. Our husbands also knew that we were making cakes that looked like her."

[20]Then Jeremiah spoke to all the men and women who told him these things. [21]He said, "The LORD remembered that you made sacrifices in the towns of Judah and in the streets of Jerusalem. You and your ancestors, your kings, your officials and the people of the land did that. He remembered what you had done and thought about it. [22]The LORD hated the terrible things you did, and he could not be patient with you any longer. So he made your country an empty desert. No one lives there now. Other people say bad things about that country. [23]The reason all those bad things happened to you is that you made sacrifices to other gods. You sinned against the LORD. You didn't obey him or follow his teachings or the laws he gave you. You didn't keep your part of the agreement."[b]

[24]Then Jeremiah spoke to all the men and women. He said, "All you people of Judah who are now in Egypt, listen to this message from the LORD. [25]This is what the LORD All-Powerful, the God of Israel, says: 'You women did what you said you would do. You said, "We will keep the promises we made. We promised to make sacrifices and pour out drink offerings to the Queen of Heaven." So go ahead. Do what you promised you would do. Keep your promises.' [26]But listen to this message from the LORD, all you people of Judah who are living in Egypt: 'I, the LORD, use my own great name to make this promise: none of the people of Judah who are now living in Egypt will ever again use my name to make promises. They will never again say, "As surely as the Lord GOD lives." [27]I am watching over the people of Judah, but I am not watching over them to take care of them. I am watching over them to bring them harm. The people of Judah who live in Egypt will die from hunger or be killed in war until they are completely destroyed. [28]Some people of Judah

will escape being killed by the sword. They will come back to Judah from Egypt. But only a few people of Judah will escape. Then the survivors of Judah who came to live in Egypt will know whose word proves to be true. They will know whether my word or their word came true. [29]I will give you people proof,' says the LORD, 'that I will punish you here in Egypt. Then you will know for sure that my promises to harm you will really happen. [30]This will be your proof that I will do what I say.' This is what the LORD says: 'Pharaoh Hophra is the king of Egypt. His enemies want to kill him. I will give Pharaoh Hophra to his enemies. Just as I gave Zedekiah king of Judah to his enemy Nebuchadnezzar, in the same way I will give Pharaoh Hophra to his enemies.'"

A Message to Baruch

45 In the fourth year that Jehoiakim[c] son of Josiah was king of Judah, Jeremiah the prophet spoke to Baruch son of Neriah. Baruch wrote down on a scroll everything Jeremiah said: [2]"Baruch, this is what the LORD, the God of Israel, says to you: [3]'You have been complaining about how bad things are for you. You say that I, the LORD, have given you pain and sorrow. You say you are worn out from your suffering and can't get any rest.' [4]Baruch, this is what the LORD told me to say to you: 'Throughout Judah I will tear down everything I have built, and I will pull up all that I have planted. [5]I will cause everyone to suffer terrible things. So if you are making any great plans for yourself, Baruch, forget about them. You will be running for your life. But I promise that wherever you go, I will protect you from death.' This is what the LORD says."

The LORD's Messages About the Nations

46 Jeremiah received the following messages from the LORD about many different nations.

A Message About Egypt

[2]This message is about the nation of Egypt when King Nebuchadnezzar of Babylon defeated the Egyptian army of Pharaoh Neco. This happened at Carchemish, a city by the Euphrates River, in the fourth year that Jehoiakim[d] son of Josiah was king of Judah. The Lord said,

[3]"Get your large and small shields ready.
    March out for battle.
[4]Get the horses ready.
    Soldiers, get on your horses.

---

[a] **44:19 Then the women spoke up** This is from some ancient versions—the Syriac and some copies of the Greek.
[b] **44:23 agreement** This probably means the Law of Moses, the commands and agreement God made with the Israelites.
[c] **45:1 the fourth year . . . Jehoiakim** This was about 605 BC.
[d] **46:2 the fourth year . . . Jehoiakim** This was about 605 BC.

Go to your places for battle.
Put your helmets on.
Sharpen your spears.
Put your armour on.
[5]What do I see?
That army is afraid.
The soldiers are running away.
Their brave soldiers are defeated.
They run away in a hurry.
They don't look back.
There is danger all around."
This is what the LORD says.

[6]"Fast men cannot run away.
Strong soldiers cannot escape.
They will all stumble and fall.
This will happen in the north, by the
Euphrates River.
[7]Who is coming like the Nile River?
Who is coming like that strong, fast river?
[8]It is Egypt that comes like the rising Nile
River.
It is Egypt that comes like that strong,
fast river.
Egypt says, 'I will come and cover the earth.
I will destroy the cities and the people in
them.'
[9]Horsemen, charge into battle.
Chariot drivers, drive fast.
March on, brave soldiers.
Soldiers from Cush and Put, carry your
shields.
Soldiers from Lydia, use your bows.

[10]"But on that day, the Lord GOD All-Powerful
will win.
He will give his enemies the punishment
they deserve.
His sword will kill until it is finished,
until it has satisfied its thirst for blood.
Yes, the Lord GOD All-Powerful will kill them
as a sacrifice
in the land of the north by the Euphrates
River.

[11]"Egypt, go to Gilead and get some medicine.
You will make up many medicines, but they
will not help.
You will not be healed.
[12]The nations will hear you crying.
Your cries will be heard all over the earth.
One 'brave soldier' will run into another
'brave soldier'.
And both 'brave soldiers' will fall down
together."

[13]This is the message the LORD spoke to Jeremiah
the prophet about Nebuchadnezzar coming to
attack Egypt.

[14]"Announce this message in Egypt.
Tell it in the city of Migdol.
Tell it in Memphis and Tahpanhes.
'Get ready for war,
because people all around you are being
killed with swords.'
[15]Egypt, your strong soldiers will be killed.
They will not be able to stand
because the LORD will push them down.
[16]They will stumble again and again.
They will fall over each other.
They will say, 'Get up; let's go back to our
own people.
Let us go back to our homeland.
Our enemy is defeating us.
We must get away.'
[17]In their homelands, those soldiers will
say,
'Pharaoh, the king of Egypt, is only a lot of
noise.
His time of glory is over.'"
[18]This message is from the King.
The King is the LORD All-Powerful.
"I promise, as surely as I live, a powerful
leader will come.
He will be like Mount Tabor or Mount
Carmel among smaller mountains.
[19]People of Egypt, pack your things.
Get ready for captivity,
because Memphis will be a ruined, empty
land.
Those cities will be destroyed,
and no one will live there.

[20]"Egypt is like a beautiful cow.
But a stinging fly is coming from the north[a]
to attack her.
[21]The hired soldiers in Egypt's army are like fat
calves.
They will all turn and run away.
They will not stand strong against the
attack.
Their time of destruction is coming.
They will soon be punished.
[22]Egypt is like a snake hissing
and trying to escape.
The enemy comes closer and closer,
and the Egyptian army is trying to slither
away.
The enemy will attack Egypt with axes,
like men cutting down trees."

---

[a] **46:20** *north* The Babylonian army came from this direction to attack Judah. Armies from countries north and east of Israel often came this way to attack Judah and Israel. Also in 47:2.

²³This is what the LORD says:
"They will chop down Egypt's forest.
There are many trees in that forest,
but they will all be cut down.
There are more enemy soldiers than locusts.
There are so many soldiers that no one can
count them.
²⁴Egypt will be ashamed.
The enemy from the north will defeat her."

²⁵The LORD All-Powerful, the God of Israel, says,
"Very soon I will punish Amon,^a the god of Thebes,
and I will punish Pharaoh, Egypt and her gods.
I will punish the kings of Egypt, and I will punish
the people who depend on Pharaoh. ²⁶I will let
all of them be defeated by their enemies—their
enemies want to kill them. I will give the people to
King Nebuchadnezzar of Babylon and his servants.

"Long ago, Egypt lived in peace. And after all
these times of trouble, Egypt will live in peace
again." This is what the LORD says.

A Message for Northern Israel

²⁷"Jacob, my servant, do not be afraid.
Do not be frightened, Israel.
I will save you from those faraway places.
I will save your children from the countries
where they are captives.
Jacob will have peace and safety again,
and no one will make him afraid."
²⁸This is what the LORD says.
"Jacob, my servant, do not be afraid.
I am with you.
I sent you away to many different places.
I will not destroy you completely.
But I will destroy all those nations.
You must be punished for the bad things
you did.
So I will not let you escape your
punishment.
I will discipline you, but I will be fair."

A Message About the Philistines

47 This is the message from the LORD that
came to Jeremiah the prophet about the
Philistines. This message came before Pharaoh
attacked the city of Gaza.

²This is what the LORD says:
"Look, the enemy is gathering in the north
like rising water.

They will come like a river spilling over its
banks.
They will cover the whole country like a flood.
They will cover the towns and the people
living in them.
Everyone in the country will cry for help.
Everyone will cry out in pain.
³They will hear the sound of running horses,
the noisy chariots, the rumbling wheels.
Fathers will not be able to protect their
children.
They will be too weak to help,
⁴because the time has come to destroy all the
Philistines.
The time has come to destroy all who help
Tyre and Sidon.
The LORD will destroy the Philistines,
those who came from the island of Crete.
⁵The people from Gaza will be sad and shave
their heads.
The people from Ashkelon will be
silenced.
Survivors from the valley, how long will you
cut yourselves?^b

⁶"Sword of the LORD, you have not stopped.
How long will you keep fighting?
Go back into your scabbard!^c
Stop! Be still!
⁷But how can the sword of the Lord rest?
The LORD gave it a command.
He commanded it to attack
the city of Ashkelon and the coast."

A Message About Moab

48 This message is about the country of
Moab. This is what the LORD All-Powerful,
the God of Israel, says:^d

"It will be bad for Mount Nebo.^e
Mount Nebo will be ruined.
The town of Kiriathaim will be humbled.
It will be captured.
The strong place will be humbled.
It will be shattered.
²No one will ever honour Moab again.
Men in Heshbon will plan Moab's defeat,
saying, 'Come, let us put an end to that
nation!'
Town of Madmen, you will also be destroyed.
The enemy is coming to attack you.

---

^a **46:25 Amon** For many centuries Amon was the most important god of Egypt. At the time of this prophecy, he was not
worshipped as much in northern Egypt. But he was still the most important god in southern Egypt, especially around the old
Egyptian capital city of Thebes.
^b **47:5 sad . . . cut yourselves** The people did these things to show their sadness.
^c **47:6 scabbard** A holder for a sword.
^d **48:1 This message . . . says** See Isa. 15 for a similar message.
^e **48:1 Mount Nebo** A mountain in Moab, a country east of Israel.

3Listen to the cries from Horonaim.
They are cries of much confusion and
destruction.
4Moab will be destroyed.
Her little children will cry for help.
5Moab's people go up the path to Luhith.
They are crying bitterly as they go.
On the road down to the town of Horonaim,
cries of pain and suffering can be heard.
6Run away! Run for your lives!
Run away like a weed*a* blowing through the
desert.

7"You trust in the things you made and in your
wealth,
so you will be captured.
The god Chemosh will be taken into captivity,
and his priests and officials will be taken
with him.
8The destroyer will come against every town.
Not one town will escape.
The valley will be ruined.
The high plain will be destroyed.
The Lord said this would happen,
so it will happen.
9Spread salt over the fields in Moab.
The country will be an empty desert.*b*
Moab's towns will become empty.
No one will live in them.
10Bad things will happen to those who
don't obey the Lord and don't use their
swords to kill those people.

11"Moab has never known trouble.
Moab is like wine left to settle.
Moab has never been poured from one jar to
another.
He has not been taken into captivity.
So he tastes as he did before,
and his smell has not changed."
12This is what the Lord says:
"But I will soon send men
to pour you from your jars.*c*
Then they will empty the jars
and smash them to pieces.

13"Then the people of Moab will be ashamed of
their false god, Chemosh. They will be like the
people of Israel who trusted that god in Bethel*d*
but were ashamed when he did not help them.

14"You cannot say, 'We are good soldiers.
We are brave men in battle.'
15The enemy will attack Moab.
The enemy will enter its towns and destroy
them.
Its best young men will be killed in the
slaughter."
This message is from the King.
The King's name is the Lord All-Powerful.
16"The end of Moab is near.
Moab will soon be destroyed.
17All you who live around Moab should cry for
that country.
You know how famous Moab is.
So cry for it.
Say, 'The ruler's power is broken.
Moab's power and glory are gone.'

18"You people living in Dibon,*e*
come down from your place of honour.
Sit on the ground in the dust,
because the destroyer is coming.
And he will destroy your strong cities.

19"You people living in Aroer,
stand next to the road and watch.
See the man running away.
See that woman running away.
Ask them what happened.

20"Moab will be ruined and filled with
shame.
Moab will cry and cry.
Announce at the Arnon River*f*
that Moab is destroyed.
21People on the high plain have been
punished.
Judgement has come to the towns of Holon,
Jahzah and Mephaath.
22Judgement has come to the towns
of Dibon, Nebo and Beth Diblathaim.
23Judgement has come to the towns
of Kiriathaim, Beth Gamul and Beth Meon.
24Judgement has come to the towns
of Kerioth and Bozrah.
Judgement has come to all the towns
of Moab, far and near.
25Moab's strength has been cut off.
Its arm has been broken."
This is what the Lord says.

---

a 48:6 *weed* In Hebrew this word is like the name "Aroer", an important city in Moab.
b 48:9 The Hebrew text is not clear.
c 48:12 *jars* This probably means the cities in Moab.
d 48:13 *in Bethel* This means the temple that King Jeroboam built in the town of Bethel (see 1 Kgs 12:28–33). It is not clear if this means the people still worshipped the Lord there, but in a wrong way, or if they worshipped a false god, perhaps the Canaanite god El or Baal.
e 48:18 *Dibon* A city in the country of Moab.
f 48:20 *Arnon River* An important river in Moab.

26"The people of Moab thought they were
greater than the LORD.
So punish them until they act like a drunk,
falling and rolling around in his vomit.
Then people will make fun of them.

27"Moab, you made fun of Israel.
Israel was caught by a gang of thieves.
Every time you spoke about Israel,
you shook your head and acted as if you
were better than Israel.
28People in Moab, leave your towns.
Go and live among the rocks;
be like a dove that makes its nest
at the opening of a cave.

29"We have heard about Moab's pride.
He was very proud.
He thought he was important.
He was always boasting.
He was very, very proud."

30The LORD says, "I know Moab gets angry
quickly and boasts about himself,
but his boasts are lies.
He cannot do what he says.
31So I cry for Moab.
I cry for everyone in Moab.
I cry for the men from Kir Hareseth.
32I cry with the people of Jazer for Jazer.
Sibmah, in the past your vines spread all the
way to the sea.
They reached as far as the town of Jazer.
But the destroyer has taken your fruit and
grapes.
33Joy and happiness are gone from the large
vineyards of Moab.
I stopped the flow of wine from the
winepresses.
There is no singing and dancing from people
walking on the grapes to make wine.
There are no shouts of joy.

34"The people of the towns of Heshbon and
Elealeh are crying. Their cry is heard even as far
away as the town of Jahaz. Their cry is heard
from the town of Zoar, as far away as the towns
of Horonaim and Eglath Shelishiyah. Even the
waters of Nimrim are dried up. 35I will stop Moab
from making burnt offerings on the high places.
I will stop them from making sacrifices to their
gods." This is what the LORD says.
36"I am very sad for Moab. My heart cries like
the sad sound of a flute playing a funeral song.

I am sad for the people from Kir Hareseth. Their
money and riches have all been taken away.
37Everyone has a shaved head. Everyone's
beard is cut off. Everyone's hands are cut and
bleeding.*a* Everyone is wearing sackcloth around
their waists. 38People are crying for the dead
everywhere in Moab—on every housetop and in
every public square. There is sadness because
I have broken Moab like an empty jar." This is
what the LORD says.
39"Moab is shattered. The people are crying.
Moab has surrendered. Now Moab is ashamed.
People make fun of Moab, but what happened
fills them with fear."

40The LORD says, "Look! An eagle is diving down
from the sky.
It is spreading its wings over Moab.
41The towns of Moab will be captured.
The strong hiding places will be defeated.
At that time Moab's soldiers will be filled
with fear,
like a woman giving birth.
42The nation of Moab will be destroyed,
because they thought that they were more
important than the LORD."

43This is what the LORD says:
"People of Moab, fear, deep holes and traps*b*
wait for you.
44People will be afraid and run away,
and they will fall into the deep holes.
Anyone who climbs out of the deep holes
will be caught in the traps.
I will bring the year of punishment to Moab."
This is what the LORD says.

45"People have run from the powerful enemy.
They ran to safety in the town of Heshbon.
But a fire started in Heshbon.
That fire started in Sihon's town,*c*
and it is destroying the leaders of Moab.
It is destroying those proud people.
46It will be bad for you, Moab.
Chemosh's people are being destroyed.
Your sons and daughters are being taken
away
as prisoners and captives.
47Moab's people will be taken away as captives.
But in days to come, I will bring them
back."
This message is from the LORD.

This ends the judgement on Moab.

---

a 48:37 *Everyone . . . cut and bleeding* The people did these things to show their sadness for people who had died.
b 48:43 *fear, deep holes and traps* This is a wordplay in Hebrew. The Hebrew words are "Pahad, Pahat and Pah".
c 48:45 *Sihon's town* This was Heshbon. See Num. 21:25–30.

A Message About Ammon

49 This message is about the Ammonites. This is what the Lord says:

"Ammonites, do you think that
   the people of Israel don't have children?
Do you think there are no children
   to take the land when the parents die?
Maybe that is why Milcom took Gad's[a] land?"

[2]The Lord says, "The time will come in Rabbah
   of Ammon[b]
when people hear the sounds of battle.
Rabbah of Ammon will be destroyed.
   It will be an empty hill covered with ruined
      buildings,
   and the towns around it will be burned.
Those people forced the people of Israel to
      leave their own land.
   But later, Israel will force them to leave."
This is what the Lord says.

[3]"People in Heshbon, cry because the town of
      Ai is destroyed!
   Women in Rabbah of Ammon, cry!
Put on sackcloth and cry.
Run to the city for safety,
because the enemy will take away the god
      Milcom,
   with his priests and officials.
[4]You boast about your strength,
   but you are losing your strength.
You trust in your wealth to save you.
   You think no one would even think of
      attacking you."
[5]But this is what the Lord God All-Powerful
      says:
   "I will bring troubles to you from every
      side.
You will all run away,
   and no one will be able to bring you
      together again."

[6]"The Ammonites will be taken away as captives.
But the time will come when I will bring the
Ammonites back." This message is from the Lord.

A Message About Edom

[7]This message is about Edom. This is what the
Lord All-Powerful says:

"Is there no more wisdom in Teman?
   Are the wise men of Edom not able to give
      good advice?
   Have they lost their wisdom?

[8]You people living in Dedan, run away and
      hide,
   because I will punish Esau for the bad
      things he did.

[9]"Workers pick grapes from grapevines,
   but they leave a few grapes on the plants.
If thieves come at night,
   they don't take everything.
[10]But I will take everything from Esau.
   I will find all his hiding places.
He will not be able to hide from me.
   His children, relatives and neighbours will
      all die.
[11]No one will be left to care for his children.
   His wives will have no one to depend on."

[12]This is what the Lord says: "Some people don't
deserve to be punished, but they suffer. But, Edom,
you deserve to be punished, so you will really be
punished. You will not escape the punishment you
deserve. You will be punished." [13]The Lord says,
"By my own power, I make this promise: I promise
that Bozrah will be destroyed. It will become a
ruined pile of rocks. People will use it as an example
when they ask for bad things to happen to other
cities. People will insult that city, and all the towns
around Bozrah will become ruins forever."

[14]I heard a message from the Lord:
   He sent this messenger to the nations.
   This is the message:
      "Gather your armies together!
Get ready for battle!
   March against the nation of Edom!
[15]Edom, I will make you become unimportant.
   Everyone will hate you.
[16]Edom, you made other nations afraid,
   so you thought you were important.
But your pride has fooled you.
   You live in caves, high on the cliff.
   Your home is high in the hills.
But even if you build your home as high as an
      eagle's nest,
   I will bring you down from there."
This is what the Lord says.

[17]"Edom will be destroyed.
   People will be shocked to see the destroyed
      cities.
   They will be amazed at the destroyed cities.
[18]Edom will be destroyed like Sodom and
      Gomorrah and the towns around them.
   No one will live there."
This is what the Lord says.

---

[a] **49:1** *Gad's* One of the tribes of Israel. Their land was on the east side of the Jordan River, near the country of Ammon.
[b] **49:2** *Rabbah of Ammon* The capital city of the Ammonites.

19"Sometimes a lion will come from the thick bushes near the Jordan River. And it will go into the fields where people put their sheep and cattle. I am like that lion. I will go to Edom. And I will frighten the people and make them run away. None of their young men will stop me. No one is like me. No one will challenge me. None of their leaders will stand up against me."

20So listen to what the LORD has planned to do
    to the people of Edom.
  Listen to what he has decided to do to the
    people in Teman.
  The enemy will drag away the young kids of
    Edom's flock.
  Edom's pastures will be empty because of
    what they did.
21At the sound of Edom's fall, the earth will
    shake.
  Their cry will be heard all the way to the
    Red Sea.

22Just as an eagle flies high to see the animal it
    will attack,
  so the Lord will spread his wings over
    Bozrah.
  And Edom's soldiers will be filled with fear
    like a woman giving birth.

A Message About Damascus

23This message is about the city of Damascus:

"The towns of Hamath and Arpad are afraid.
  They are afraid because they heard the bad
    news.
They are discouraged.
  They are worried and afraid.
24The city of Damascus has become weak.
  The people want to run away.
  They are ready to panic.
They are overcome with fear and pain,
  like a woman giving birth.

25"Damascus is a happy city.
  The people have not left that 'fun city'
    yet.
26So the young men will die in the public
    squares of that city.
  All her soldiers will be killed at that
    time."
  This is what the LORD All-Powerful says.
27"I will set the walls of Damascus on fire.
  The fire will completely burn up the strong
    cities of Ben-Hadad."a

A Message About Kedar and Hazor

28This message is about the tribe of Kedar and the rulers of Hazor. King Nebuchadnezzar of Babylon defeated them. This is what the LORD says:

"Go and attack the tribe of Kedar.
  Destroy the people of the East.
29Their tents and flocks will be taken away.
  Their tents and all their riches will be
    carried off.
  Their enemy will take away the camels.
Men will shout this to them:
  'Terrible things are happening all around
    us.'
30Run away quickly!
  People in Hazor, find a good place to hide."
  This message is from the LORD.
"Nebuchadnezzar has made plans against
    you.
  He thought of a smart plan to defeat you.

31"There is a nation that feels so safe and
    secure
  that it does not have gates or fences to
    protect it.
And no one lives near enough to help them.
  So attack that nation!" says the LORD.
32"Their camels are there to be taken in battle.
  Their large herds of cattle will be yours.
I will scatter them throughout the earth—
  those people who cut their hair short.b
I will bring disaster on them from every
    direction."
  This message is from the LORD.
33"Hazor will become a home for wild dogs, an
    empty desert forever.
No one will live there.
  No one will stay in that place."

A Message About Elam

34Early in the time when Zedekiah was king of Judah, Jeremiah the prophet received a message from the LORD about the nation of Elam.c

35The LORD All-Powerful says,
"I will break Elam's bow very soon.
  It is Elam's strongest weapon.
36I will bring the four winds against Elam.
  I will bring them from the four corners of
    the skies.
I will send the people of Elam to every place
  on the earth where the four winds blow.
Elam's captives will be carried away to
  every nation.

a 49:27 Ben-Hadad This was the name of several of the kings of Aram-Damascus.
b 49:32 cut their hair short Literally, "cut on the side of their heads", a custom different from that of Israelite men.
c 49:34 Elam A nation east of Babylon.

³⁷I will break Elam to pieces while their enemies
    are watching.
I will break Elam in front of the people who
    want to kill them.
I will bring terrible troubles to them.
I will show them how angry I am."
    This message is from the LORD.
"I will send a sword to chase Elam.
    The sword will chase them until I have
    killed them all.
³⁸I will show Elam that I am in control,
    and I will destroy their king and his officials."
    This message is from the LORD.
³⁹"But in the future I will make good things
    happen to Elam."
    This message is from the LORD.

A Message About Babylon

50 This is the message the LORD spoke through
the prophet Jeremiah about Babylon and its
people.

²"Announce this to all nations!
    Lift up a flag and announce the message!
Speak the whole message and say,
    'The nation of Babylon will be captured.
The god Bel will be put to shame.
    The god Marduk will be very afraid.
Babylon's idols will be put to shame.
    Her gods will be filled with terror.'
³A nation from the north will attack Babylon.
    That nation will make Babylon like an
    empty desert.
No one will live there.
    All the people and animals will run away."
⁴The LORD says, "At that time
    the people of Israel and Judah will come
    together.
Together they will cry,
    and they will look for the LORD their God.
⁵They will ask how to go to Zion.
    They will start in that direction,
And they will say, 'Come, let us join ourselves
    to the LORD.
Let's make an agreement that will last
    forever.
Let's make an agreement that we will never
    forget.'

⁶"My people have been like lost sheep.
    Their shepherds led them the wrong way
and caused them to wander into the
    mountains and hills.
They forgot where their resting place was.
⁷They were attacked by all who saw them.
    And their attackers said,
'We were not wrong to attack them
    because they sinned against the LORD.

They should have stayed close to him, their
    true resting place.
The LORD is the one their fathers trusted in.'

⁸"Run away from Babylon.
    Leave the land of the Babylonians.
Be like the goats that lead the flock.
⁹I will bring many nations together from the
    north.
This group of nations will get ready for war
    against Babylon.
Babylon will be captured by people from the
    north.
Those nations will shoot many arrows at
    Babylon.
Their arrows will be like soldiers
    who don't come back from war with their
    hands empty.
¹⁰The enemy will take all the wealth from the
    Chaldeans.
The soldiers will take all they want."
This is what the LORD says.

¹¹"Babylon, you are excited and happy.
    You took my land.
You dance around like a young cow
    that got into the grain.
Your laughter is like the happy sounds
    that horses make.
¹²Now your mother will be very ashamed.
    The woman who gave you birth will be
    embarrassed.
Babylon will be the least important of all the
    nations.
She will be an empty, dry desert.
¹³The LORD will show his anger,
    so no one will live there.
Babylon will be completely empty.
Everyone who passes by Babylon will be afraid.
    They will shake their heads when they see
    all the destruction.

¹⁴"Prepare for war against Babylon.
    All you soldiers with bows, shoot your
    arrows at Babylon.
Don't save any of your arrows.
    Babylon has sinned against the LORD.
¹⁵Soldiers around Babylon, shout the cry of
    victory!
Babylon has surrendered!
Her walls and towers have been pulled
    down!
The LORD is giving her people the punishment
    they deserve.
You nations should give Babylon the
    punishment she deserves.
Do to her what she has done to other
    nations.

¹⁶Don't let the people from Babylon plant their
        crops.
    Don't let them gather the harvest.
The soldiers of Babylon brought many
        prisoners to their city.
    Now the enemy soldiers have come,
    so the prisoners are going back home.
    They are running back to their own countries.

¹⁷"The people of Israel are like sheep that have
        been scattered,
    chased away by lions.
The first lion to attack them was the king of
        Assyria.
    Now King Nebuchadnezzar of Babylon has
        crushed their bones."
¹⁸So this is what the LORD All-Powerful, the God
        of Israel, says:
    "I will soon punish the king of Babylon and
        his country,
    as I punished the king of Assyria.

¹⁹"I will bring the people of Israel back to their
        own fields,
    where they will have all they want.
They will be like sheep grazing on Mount
        Carmel and in Bashan
    and on the hills in the lands of Ephraim and
        Gilead."
²⁰The LORD says, "If anyone looks for guilt in
        Israel,
    there will be no guilt there.
    If anyone looks for sin in Judah,
    there will be no sin there.
    That's because the only people left alive will
        be the few I save,
    and I will forgive them for all their sins."

²¹The LORD says, "Attack the country of
        Merathaim!
    Attack the people living in Pekod!
Attack them!
    Kill them and destroy them completely!
    Do everything I commanded you!

²²"The noise of battle can be heard all over the
        country.
    It is the noise of much destruction.
²³Babylon was called
    'The Hammer of the Whole Earth'.
    But now the 'Hammer' is shattered.
    Babylon is the most ruined of the nations.
²⁴Babylon, I set a trap for you,
    and you were caught before you knew it.
You fought against the LORD,
    so you were found and captured.
²⁵The LORD has opened up his storeroom
    and brought out the weapons of his anger.

The Lord GOD All-Powerful brought out those
        weapons
    because he has work to do in the land of
        the Chaldeans.

²⁶"Come against Babylon from far away.
    Break open the storehouses where she
        keeps her grain.
Destroy Babylon completely.
    Don't leave anyone alive.
    Pile up her dead bodies like big piles of
        grain.
²⁷Kill all the young men in Babylon.
    Let them be slaughtered like bulls.
How terrible for them that their day of defeat
        has come!
    It is time for them to be punished.
²⁸People are escaping from Babylon
    and coming to Zion.
They are telling everyone the good news
    about what the Lord is doing.
The LORD our God is taking revenge
    against those who destroyed his Temple!

²⁹"Call for the archers.
    Tell them to attack Babylon.
Tell them to surround the city.
    Don't let anyone escape.
Pay her back for the bad things she has done.
    Do to her what she has done to other
        nations.
Babylon did not respect the LORD.
    Babylon was very rude to the Holy One of
        Israel.
    So punish Babylon.
³⁰Babylon's young men will be killed in the
        streets.
    All her soldiers will die on that day."
    This is what the LORD says.

³¹"Babylon, you are too proud,
    and I am against you,"
    says the Lord GOD All-Powerful.
"I am against you,
    and the time has come for you to be
        punished.
³²Proud Babylon will stumble and fall,
    and no one will help her get up.
I will start a fire in her towns.
    That fire will completely burn up everyone
        around her."

³³This is what the LORD All-Powerful says:
    "The people of Israel and Judah are slaves.
    The enemy took them, and the enemy will
        not let Israel go.
³⁴But God will get them back.
    His name is the LORD God All-Powerful.

He will defend them very strongly.
He will argue their case so he can let
their land rest.
But there will be no rest for those living in
Babylon."

35The LORD says,
"Sword, kill the people living in Babylon.
Sword, kill the king's officials
and the wise men of Babylon.
36Sword, kill the priests of Babylon.
They will be like fools.
Sword, kill the soldiers of Babylon.
They will be full of fear.
37Sword, kill the horses and chariots of
Babylon.
Sword, kill all the soldiers hired from other
countries.
They will be like frightened women.
Sword, destroy the treasures of Babylon.
Those treasures will be taken away.
38Sword, strike the waters of Babylon.
Those waters will be dried up.
Babylon has many, many idols.
These idols show that the people of Babylon
are foolish.
So bad things will happen to them.
39Babylon will never again be filled with people.
Wild dogs, ostriches and other desert
animals will live there.
But no one will live there ever again.
40God completely destroyed Sodom and
Gomorrah
and the towns around them.
In the same way, no one will live in Babylon,
and no one will ever go to live there."
This is what the LORD says.

41"Look! There are people coming from the
north.
They come from a powerful nation.
Many kings are coming together from all
around the world.
42Their armies have bows and spears.
The soldiers are cruel.
They have no mercy.
The soldiers come riding on their horses;
the sound is as loud as the roaring sea.
They stand in their places, ready for battle.
They are ready to attack you, city of
Babylon.
43The king of Babylon heard about those
armies,
and he is paralysed with fear.
He is overcome with fear and pain,
like a woman giving birth.

44"Sometimes a lion will come
from the thick bushes near the Jordan
River.
It will walk into the fields
where people have their animals.
I will be like that lion;
I will chase the Babylonians from their land.
Who should I choose to do this?
There is no one like me.
There is no one who can challenge me.
No shepherd will come to chase me away.
I will chase away the Babylonians."

45Listen to what the LORD has planned to do to
Babylon.
Listen to what he has decided to do to the
Babylonians.
"I promise that an enemy will drag away the
young kids of Babylon's flock,
and Babylon will become an empty
pasture.
46Babylon will fall, and that fall will shake the
earth.
People in all nations will hear about the
destruction of Babylon."

51

This is what the LORD says:

"I will cause a powerful, destructive
wind to blow against Babylon and the
Babylonians.*
2I will send foreigners to destroy Babylon like a
wind that blows away chaff.
They will strip everything from the land.
Armies will surround the city,
and there will be terrible destruction.
3The Babylonian soldiers will not get to use
their bows and arrows.
They will not even put on their armour.
Don't feel sorry for the soldiers of Babylon.
Destroy her army completely!
4Babylon's soldiers will be killed in the land of
the Chaldeans.
They will be badly wounded in the streets
of Babylon."

5The LORD All-Powerful did not leave Israel and
Judah alone, like a widow.
No, they are guilty of leaving the Holy One
of Israel.
Their God did not leave them.
They left him!

6Run away from Babylon.
Run to save your lives!
Don't stay and be killed because of
Babylon's sins!

---

a 51:1 **Babylonians** Literally, "Leb Kamai". In Hebrew this was a secret way of writing "Chaldeans".

It is time for the Lord to punish the
    Babylonians for the bad things they have
    done.
Babylon will get the punishment that she
    deserves.
⁷Babylon was like a gold cup in the Lord's
    hand.
She made the whole world drunk.
The nations drank Babylon's wine,
    so they went crazy.
⁸But Babylon will suddenly fall and be broken.
    Cry for her!
Get medicine for her pain,
    and maybe she can be healed.

⁹We tried to heal Babylon,
    but she cannot be healed.
So let us leave her,
    and let each of us go to our own country.
God in heaven will decide Babylon's
    punishment.
    He will decide what will happen to
    Babylon.
¹⁰The Lord got even for us.
    Come, let's tell about that in Zion.
    Let's tell what the Lord our God has done.

¹¹Sharpen the arrows!
    Get your shields!
The Lord has stirred up the kings of the
    Medes
    because he wants to destroy Babylon.
The army from Babylon destroyed his Temple
    in Jerusalem,
    so he will give them the punishment they
    deserve.
¹²Lift up a flag against the walls of Babylon.
    Bring more guards.
Put the watchmen in their places.
    Get ready for a secret attack.
The Lord will do what he has planned.
    He will do what he said he would do
    against the people of Babylon.
¹³Babylon, you live near much water.
    You are rich with treasures, but your end as
    a nation has come.
It is time for you to be destroyed.
¹⁴The Lord All-Powerful used his name to make
    this promise:
"Babylon, I will fill you with enemy soldiers.
    They will cover you like a swarm of locusts.
    They will celebrate their victory over you."

¹⁵God used his great power and made the
    earth.
He used his wisdom to build the world
    and his understanding to stretch out the
    skies.

¹⁶When he thunders, the waters in the skies
    roar.
He sends clouds all over the earth.
He sends lightning with the rain.
    He brings out the wind from his
    storehouses.
¹⁷But people are so stupid.
    They don't understand what God has
    done.
Skilled workers make statues of false gods.
    Those statues are only false gods.
They show how foolish those workers are.
    Those statues are not alive.
¹⁸Those idols are worthless.
    People made them, and they are nothing
    but a joke.
Their time of judgement will come,
    and those idols will be destroyed.
¹⁹But God, who is Jacob's Portion, is not like
    those worthless statues.
    People didn't make God;
God made his people.
    He made everything.
    His name is the Lord All-Powerful.

²⁰The Lord says, "Babylon, you are my club.
    I used you to smash nations.
    I used you to destroy kingdoms.
²¹I used you to smash horse and rider.
    I used you to smash chariot and driver.
²²I used you to smash men and women.
    I used you to smash men, old and young.
    I used you to smash young men and young
    women.
²³I used you to smash shepherds and flocks.
    I used you to smash farmers and oxen.
    I used you to smash governors and
    important officials.
²⁴But I will repay Babylonia and all the
    Babylonians for all the evil things they
    did to Zion.
I will pay them back so that you can see it,
    Judah."
This is what the Lord says.

²⁵And the Lord says,
"Babylon, you are like a volcano
    that destroys the whole country.
But I have turned against you,
    and I will turn you into a burnt-out
    mountain.
²⁶People will not take stones from Babylon to
    use as the foundation of a building.
That is because they will not find any stones
    big enough for cornerstones.
Your city will be a pile of broken rocks
    forever."
This is what the Lord says.

27"Lift up the war flag in the land!
  Blow the trumpet in all the nations!
Prepare the nations for war against Babylon.
  Call these kingdoms to come and fight
    against Babylon:
  Ararat, Minni and Ashkenaz.
  Choose a commander to lead the army against
    her.
  Send so many horses that they are like a
    swarm of locusts.
28Get the nations ready for battle against her.
  Get the kings of the Medes ready.
  Get their governors and all their important
    officials ready.
  Get all the countries they rule ready for
    battle against Babylon.
29The land shakes and moves as if it is in pain.
  It will shake when the LORD does to
    Babylon what he plans—
  to make the land of Babylon an empty desert,
    a place where no one will live.
30Babylon's soldiers have stopped fighting.
  They stay in their fortresses.
  Their strength has gone.
  They have become like frightened women.
  Babylon's houses are burning.
  The bars of her gates are broken.
31One messenger follows another.
  Messenger follows messenger.
  They announce to the king of Babylon
    that his whole city has been captured.
32The places where people cross the rivers have
    been captured.
  The marshlands are burning.
  All of Babylon's soldiers are afraid."

33This is what the LORD All-Powerful, the God of
    Israel, says:
  "Babylon is like a threshing floor,
    where people beat the grain at harvest time.
  And the time to beat Babylon is coming
    soon."

34"King Nebuchadnezzar of Babylon destroyed
    us in the past.
  In the past he hurt us.
  In the past he took our people away,
    and we became like an empty jar.
  He took the best we had.
  He was like a giant monster that ate
    everything until it was full.
  He took the best we had
    and then threw us away.
35Babylon did terrible things to hurt us.
  Now I want those things to happen to
    Babylon," say the people living in Zion.

"The people of Babylon are guilty of killing our
    people.
  Now they are being punished for the bad
    things they did."
  The people of Jerusalem said those things.

36So this is what the LORD says:
  "I will defend you, Judah.
  I will make sure that Babylon is
    punished.
  I will dry up Babylon's sea.
  And I will make her water springs become
    dry.
37Babylon will become a pile of ruined
    buildings,
  a place fit only for wild dogs.
  People will be shocked and shake their heads
    at what is left there.
  It will be a place where no one lives.

38"The people of Babylon are like roaring young
    lions.
  They growl like baby lions.
39They are acting like powerful lions.
  I will give a party for them.
  I will make them drunk.
  They will laugh and have a good time,
    and then they will sleep forever.
  They will never wake up."

This is what the LORD says:
40"Babylon will be like sheep, rams and goats
    waiting to be killed.
  I will lead them to the slaughter.

41"Sheshacha will be defeated.
  The country that the whole earth praised
    will be captured.
  The other nations will look at Babylon,
    and what they see will shock them.
42The sea will rise over Babylon.
  Its roaring waves will cover her.
43Babylon will be like a dry, desert land.
  Its cities will be empty ruins.
  No one will live in those cities.
  No one will even travel through them.
44I will punish the false god Bel in Babylon.
  I will make him vomit out the people he
    swallowed.
  The wall around Babylon will fall,
    and other nations will stop coming to
    Babylon.
45Come out of the city of Babylon, my
    people.
  Run to save your lives.
  Run from the LORD's great anger.

a **51:41 Sheshach** Jeremiah used a special code to create this secret name for Babylon.

46"Don't be sad, my people.
  Rumours will spread, but don't be afraid.
One rumour comes this year.
  Another rumour will come next year.
There will be rumours about terrible fighting
    in the country.
There will be rumours about rulers fighting
  against other rulers.
47The time will surely come when I will punish
  the false gods of Babylon,
and the whole land of Babylon will be put
  to shame.
There will be many dead people,
  lying in the streets of that city.
48Then heaven and earth and all that is in
  them
  will shout with joy about Babylon.
They will shout because an army came from
  the north
  and fought against Babylon."
This is what the LORD says.

49"Babylon killed people from Israel.
  Babylon killed people from every place on
  earth.
  So Babylon must fall!
50You people escaped the swords.
  You must hurry and leave Babylon.
  Don't wait!
You are in a faraway land,
  but remember the LORD where you are and
  remember Jerusalem."

51"We people of Judah are ashamed.
  We have been insulted,
because unfit foreigners have gone into
  the holy places of the LORD's Temple."

52The LORD says, "The time is coming,
  when I will punish the idols of Babylon.
At that time wounded people will cry
  with pain everywhere in that country.
53Babylon might grow until she touches the
  sky.
  Babylon might make her fortresses strong,
but I will send people to fight against that
  city.
  And they will destroy her."
This is what the LORD says.

54"We can hear people crying in Babylon.
  We hear the sound of people destroying
  things in the land of Babylon.
55The LORD will destroy Babylon very soon.
  He will stop the loud noises in that city.

Enemies will come roaring in like ocean
  waves.
  People all around will hear that roar.
56The army will come and destroy Babylon.
  Its soldiers will be captured, and their bows
  will be broken,
This will happen because the LORD punishes
  people for the bad things they do.
He gives them the full punishment they
  deserve.
57I will make Babylon's wise men
  and important officials drunk.
I will make the governors, officers
  and soldiers drunk too.
Then they will sleep forever.
  They will never wake up."
This is what the King says.
  His name is the LORD All-Powerful.

58This is what the LORD All-Powerful says:
"Babylon's thick, strong wall will be pulled
  down.
  Her high gates will be burned.
The people of Babylon will work hard,
  but it will not help.
They will get very tired trying to save the city.
  But they will only be fuel for the flames."

Jeremiah Sends a Message to Babylon

59This is the message that Jeremiah gave to the officer Seraiah[a] son of Neriah. Neriah was the son of Mahseiah. Seraiah went to Babylon with King Zedekiah of Judah. This happened in the fourth year that Zedekiah[b] was king of Judah. At that time Jeremiah gave this message to Seraiah, the officer. 60Jeremiah had written on a scroll all the terrible things that would happen to Babylon. He had written all these things about Babylon. 61Jeremiah said to Seraiah, "Seraiah, go to Babylon. Be sure to read this message so that all the people can hear you. 62Then say, 'LORD, you have said that you will destroy this place, Babylon. You will destroy it so that no people or animals will live in it. This place will be an empty ruin forever.' 63After you finish reading this scroll, tie a stone to it and throw it into the Euphrates River. 64Then say, 'In the same way, Babylon will sink. Babylon will rise no more. It will sink because of the terrible things that I will make happen here.'"
  The words of Jeremiah end here.

The Fall of Jerusalem

52 Zedekiah was 21 years old when he became king of Judah. He ruled in Jerusalem for eleven years. His mother's name

---

a **51:59** *Seraiah* Seraiah was a brother of Baruch, Jeremiah's secretary.
b **51:59** *the fourth year . . . Zedekiah* That is, 594–593 BC.

was Hamutal daughter of Jeremiah.[a] Hamutal's family was from the town of Libnah. [2]Zedekiah did evil things, just as King Jehoiakim had done. The LORD did not like Zedekiah doing those evil things. [3]Terrible things happened to the people of Jerusalem and Judah because the LORD was angry with them. Finally, he threw them out of his presence.

Zedekiah rebelled against the king of Babylon. [4]So in the ninth year of Zedekiah's rule, on the tenth day of the tenth month,[b] King Nebuchadnezzar of Babylon marched against Jerusalem with his whole army. The army of Babylon set up their camp outside Jerusalem. Then they built ramps all around the city walls so that they could get over the walls. [5]The city of Jerusalem was surrounded by the army of Babylon until the eleventh year that Zedekiah[c] was king. [6]By the ninth day of the fourth month of that year, the hunger in the city was very bad. There was no food left for the people in the city to eat. [7]On that day the army of Babylon broke into Jerusalem. The soldiers of Jerusalem ran away. They left the city at night. They went through the gate between the two walls. That gate was near the king's garden. Even though the army of Babylon had surrounded the city, the soldiers of Jerusalem still ran away towards the desert.

[8]But the Babylonian army chased King Zedekiah and caught him on the plains of Jericho. All of Zedekiah's soldiers ran away. [9]The army of Babylon captured King Zedekiah and took him to the king of Babylon who was at the city of Riblah, in the land of Hamath. At Riblah the king of Babylon announced his judgement on King Zedekiah. [10]There, at the town of Riblah, the king of Babylon killed Zedekiah's sons while Zedekiah watched. The king of Babylon also killed all the royal officials of Judah. [11]Then the king of Babylon tore out Zedekiah's eyes. He put bronze chains on him and took him to Babylon. In Babylon he put Zedekiah into prison. He stayed in prison until the day he died.

[12]Nebuzaradan was the commander of the king of Babylon's special guard. He was one of the king's most important officials while at Jerusalem. He came to Jerusalem on the tenth day of the fifth month, in the nineteenth year that Nebuchadnezzar[d] was king. [13]Nebuzaradan burned the LORD's Temple, the king's palace and every important building in Jerusalem, as well as all the houses. [14]All the Babylonian soldiers that were with the commander broke down the walls around Jerusalem. [15]Commander Nebuzaradan took the people who were still in Jerusalem[e] and those who had surrendered earlier and made them captives. He took them and the skilled craftsmen who were left in Jerusalem as captives to Babylon. [16]But Nebuzaradan left some of the poorest people behind in the land. He left them to work in the vineyards and the fields.

[17]The Babylonian army broke up the bronze columns of the LORD's Temple. They also broke up the stands and the bronze basin that were in the LORD's Temple. They carried all that bronze to Babylon. [18]The army of Babylon also took these things from the Temple: pots, shovels, lamp snuffers, bowls, pans and all the bronze utensils that were used in the Temple service. [19]The commander of the king's special guards took these things away: basins, firepans, bowls, pots, lampstands, pans and bowls used for drink offerings. He took everything that was made of gold or silver. [20]The two pillars, the Sea and the twelve bronze bulls under it and the moveable stands were very heavy. King Solomon had made those things for the LORD's Temple. The bronze that those things were made from was so heavy it could not be weighed.

[21]Each of the bronze pillars was 8 metres[f] tall. Each pillar was over 5 metres[g] around. Each pillar was hollow. The wall of each pillar was 75 millimetres[h] thick. [22]The bronze capital on top of the first pillar was over 2 metres[i] tall. It was decorated with a net design and bronze pomegranates all around it. The other pillar had pomegranates too. It was like the first pillar. [23]There were 96 pomegranates on the sides of the pillars. All together, there were 100 pomegranates above the net design that went around the pillars.

[24]The commander of the king's special guards took Seraiah the chief priest and Zephaniah the priest next in rank as prisoners. The three doorkeepers were also taken as prisoners. [25]The commander of the king's special guards also took the officer in charge of the fighting men. He also took seven of the king's advisors as prisoners. They were still there in Jerusalem. He also took the scribe who was in charge of putting people in the army. And he took 60 of the ordinary people

---

[a] **52:1 Jeremiah** This is not the prophet Jeremiah, but a different man with the same name.
[b] **52:4 ninth year . . . tenth month** That is, January of 588 BC.
[c] **52:5 the eleventh year . . . Zedekiah** That is, 587 BC.
[d] **52:12 the nineteenth year . . . Nebuchadnezzar** That is, 587 BC.
[e] **52:15 the people . . . Jerusalem** This is from the ancient Greek version. The phrase, "some of the poorest people", which appears in the standard Hebrew text, seems to have been accidentally copied from the next verse.
[f] **52:21 8 metres** Literally, "18 cubits".
[g] **52:21 over 5 metres** Literally, "12 cubits".
[h] **52:21 75 millimetres** Literally, "4 fingers".
[i] **52:22 2 metres** Literally, "5 cubits".

who were there in the city. [26-27]Nebuzaradan, the commander, took all these officials and brought them to the king of Babylon. The king was at the city of Riblah in the country of Hamath. There at Riblah the king ordered all of them to be killed.

So the people of Judah were taken from their country. [28]This is how many people Nebuchadnezzar carried into captivity:

> In Nebuchadnezzar's seventh year[a] as king of Babylon, 3,023 people were taken from Judah.
> [29]In Nebuchadnezzar's eighteenth year[b] as king of Babylon, 832 people were taken from Jerusalem.
> [30]In Nebuchadnezzar's twenty-third year[c] as king, Nebuzaradan took 745 people of Judah into captivity. Nebuzaradan was the commander of the king's special guards.

In all, 4,600 people were taken captive.

Jehoiachin Is Set Free

[31]King Jehoiachin of Judah was in prison in Babylon for 37 years. In the thirty-seventh year of his imprisonment,[d] King Evil Merodach of Babylon was very kind to Jehoiachin. He let Jehoiachin out of prison in that year. This was the same year that Evil Merodach became king of Babylon. He set Jehoiachin free from prison on the twenty-fifth day of the twelfth month. [32]Evil Merodach spoke kindly to Jehoiachin. He gave Jehoiachin a place of honour higher than the other kings who were with him in Babylon. [33]So Jehoiachin took his prison clothes off. For the rest of his life, he ate regularly at the king's table. [34]Every day the king of Babylon paid Jehoiachin enough to take care of his needs until the day Jehoiachin died.

---

[a] **52:28** *Nebuchadnezzar's seventh year* That is, from the middle of 598 BC to the middle of 597 BC.
[b] **52:29** *Nebuchadnezzar's eighteenth year* That is, from the middle of 588 BC to the middle of 587 BC.
[c] **52:30** *Nebuchadnezzar's twenty-third year* That is, from the middle of 582 BC to the middle of 581 BC.
[d] **52:31** *thirty-seventh year of his imprisonment* That is, 561 BC.

Who The traditional view is that the prophet Jeremiah wrote this book, as it is recorded that he wrote funeral songs for King Josiah (2 Chronicles 35:25). However, no authorship is mentioned in the book.

When It was probably written shortly after the destruction of Jerusalem by the Babylonian army. In 586 BC they destroyed the city of Jerusalem and took the people away into exile in Babylon.

What Lamentations consists of five poems, written by Jeremiah as the city of Jerusalem was descending into chaos and defeat. The Hebrew name for the book is simply "Alas", which sums it up perfectly.

While the prophet understands that Jerusalem's suffering is deserved, he questions whether they really deserved this much. The Babylonians who wrought the destruction are never mentioned by name: this is God's doing. There is an awful feeling that God has deserted them, that he is on the side of their enemies, that he and his people are no longer even on speaking terms. It is not merely that Jerusalem is crushed, not merely that their own sins have brought them to this – it is that feeling that the Lord has turned his back on them.

The language is bleak. Jerusalem is pictured as an abandoned woman, lonely and shamed, mocked by those who pass by, grieving for her lost people.

Yet despite this depth of emotion, this raw grief, the prophet knows that this will not last. If there are questions about God's judgement, there are also statements about his mercy. The Lord will build up his city and his people again. There is hope among the rubble.

The first four chapters of Lamentations are written as acrostics. In Hebrew, each verse of each chapter begins with successive letters of the Hebrew alphabet (chapter 3 has three verses for each letter). It's as if you wrote a poem in which the first sentence begins with "A", the second with "B", the third with "C" and so on. Perhaps the prophet is indicating that the suffering of the people has gone from A–Z, across the complete range of experience.

QUICK TOUR **LAMENTATIONS**

"We are still alive because the LORD's faithful love never ends. Every morning he shows it in new ways! You are so very true and loyal!"

Lamentations 3:22–23

Jerusalem Cries Over Her Destruction

1 Jerusalem once was a city full of people,
    but now the city is so empty.
She[a] was one of the greatest cities in the
    world,
    but now she is like a poor widow.
She was once a princess among cities,
    but now she has been made a slave.

²She cries bitterly in the night.
    Her tears are on her cheeks.
    She has no one to comfort her.
Many nations were friendly to her,
    but not one of them comforts her now.
All her friends have turned their backs on her
    and have become her enemies.

³Judah suffered very much,
    and then she was taken into captivity.
She lives among other nations
    but has found no rest.
The people who chased her caught her
    where there was no way out.[b]

⁴The roads to Zion are very sad,
    because no one comes to Zion for the
    festivals any more.
All of Zion's gates have been destroyed;
    all her priests groan in sorrow.
Zion's young women have been taken away,[c]
    and all this made Zion sad.

⁵Jerusalem's enemies have won.
    Her enemies have been successful.
This happened because the LORD punished her.
    He punished Jerusalem for her many sins.
Her children have gone away.
    Their enemies captured them and took
    them away.

⁶Daughter Zion[d] has lost her beauty.
    Her princes are like starving deer looking
    for grass.
They are too weak to run away from those
    who chase them.

⁷Now that Jerusalem is suffering and homeless,
    she thinks about her past.
She remembers all the nice things she had
    long ago.
But her people were captured by the enemy,
    and there was no one to help her.

When her enemies saw her, they laughed,
    because she had been destroyed.

⁸Jerusalem sinned very badly.
    Because Jerusalem sinned,
    she became a ruined city that people shake
    their heads about.
In the past people respected her.
    But now they hate her,
    because they abused her.
Jerusalem groaned
    and turned away.

⁹Jerusalem's skirts were dirty.
    She gave no thought to what would become
    of her.
Her fall was amazing.
    She had no one to comfort her.
She says, "LORD, see how I am hurt!
    See how my enemy thinks he is so great!"

¹⁰The enemy stretched out his hand.
    He took all her nice things.
In fact, she saw the foreign nations go inside
    her Temple.
And you said those people could not join in
    our assembly!

¹¹All the people of Jerusalem are groaning.
    All of her people are looking for food.
They are giving away all their nice things
    for food to stay alive.
Jerusalem says, "Look, LORD. Look at me!
    See how people hate me.

¹²"All you who pass by on the road, you don't
    seem to care.
    But look at me and see.
Is there any pain like my pain?
    Is there any pain like the pain that has come
    to me?
Is there any pain like the pain that the LORD
    has punished me with?
    He has punished me on the day of his great
    anger.

¹³"The Lord sent fire from above
    that went down into my bones.
He stretched out a net for my feet.
    He turned me all the way around.
He made me into a wasteland.
    I am sick all day.

---

[a] **1:1 She** Throughout this poem, Jerusalem is represented as a woman.
[b] **1:3 where . . . way out** Or "in the narrow valleys".
[c] **1:4 have been taken away** This is from the ancient Greek version. The standard Hebrew text has "are upset".
[d] **1:6 Daughter Zion** The city of Jerusalem pictured as a young woman. Also in 2:1. In chapters 1 and 2, Jerusalem is referred to as "she" and "her". See "ZION" in the Word List.

IS THERE ANY PAIN LIKE MY PAIN?

Funerals are hard, but they're incredibly important. Grieving together with others who knew and loved the deceased does us good. Usually they don't involve long, detailed histories of that person's life. Sure, family and friends might share one or two treasured memories, but these things are often too hard to express in words, so instead we write poems and choose songs to help us.

Lamentations has that feel about it. The greatest pain is the pain of loneliness when we lose someone we love dearly. Here Jerusalem is the weeping widow – saddened at the loss of everything she had. The key to understanding the purpose and significance of the book is to realize that, like a mourner at a funeral, the writer is feeling loss very deeply.

DIG IN

READ Lamentations 1:1-11a

- What's the reason for Jerusalem's tears?
- What has this city lost?
- Why has it happened (vv.5,8)?

A city crying (v.2)? Roads feeling sad (v.4)? Huh? Remember, this is deeply felt poetry, so we should read it slowly and give it time to sink in so we can understand the meaning and the emotion.

Jerusalem, here representing the whole people of God, has been ruined because of her sin. God's judgement, promised by Isaiah, Jeremiah and others, came in the form of the Babylonian army invading (see 2 Kings 25:1–21 and Deuteronomy 28:15–68). As we read here, the city was left in ruins and the people scattered among other nations (v.3).

The emotions on display here would have been those of the remainder of the Jewish people after the massacre. They would have felt totally abandoned by the God they thought they knew.

READ Lamentations 1:11b-22

- Who is speaking now?
- Apart from loss, what other emotions come through?

Halfway through this chapter, we get closer to the emotion as the author of Lamentations (probably Jeremiah) writes as if Jerusalem herself were speaking. Then he writes that Jerusalem now knows the reason for the pain: her sin (vv.18,20,22). She feels remorse and regret.

DIG THROUGH

- "There is no one near to comfort me" (v.16) is a theme also repeated in verses 2, 9, 17 and 21. What's the greatest loss you've ever had to face? Or what's the hardest thing you've ever walked through with someone else? Why not use Lamentations 1 to help you understand their pain, or to help you express your own feelings? Read it knowing that God knows what that kind of pain feels like – Jesus experienced it himself, on the cross.

- Jerusalem's suffering is a direct consequence of her repeated sin against God, in spite of clear warnings given by the prophets. Jesus took the full, just punishment for our sin – so our right standing before God is unchanged, even when we sin repeatedly. Spend some time thanking God for giving us such a secure relationship with him through Jesus.

- Yet our sin always grieves God and very often has bad consequences for our lives. And God will sometimes use all kinds of circumstances – including suffering – to discipline those he loves (check out Hebrews 12:4–11).

DIG DEEPER

- Notice that in the midst of all this pain and suffering, Jerusalem continues to call out to the Lord (vv.20–22). The Psalms are helpful to show us that we must continue to pray during suffering. Read, for instance, David's words in Psalm 69.

¹⁴"My sins were tied up like a yoke.
My sins were tied up in the Lord's hands.
His yoke is on my neck.
He has made me weak.
He has given me to those
who I cannot stand up against.

¹⁵"The Lord rejected all my powerful men
who were inside the city.
Then he brought a group of people against me.
He brought them to kill my young
soldiers.
The Lord has trampled his dearest city*ᵃ*
like grapes in a winepress.

¹⁶"I cry about all these things.
Tears are flowing down my cheeks.
There is no one near to comfort me.
There is no one who can make me feel
better.
My children are like a wasteland,
because the enemy has won."

¹⁷Zion spread out her hands.
There was no one to comfort her.
The LORD had given orders to Jacob's
enemies.
He ordered them to surround the city.
Jerusalem has become a dirty rag
that her enemies threw away.

¹⁸Now Jerusalem says, "I refused to listen to
the LORD,
so he is right for doing these things.
So listen, all you people!
Look at my pain!
My young women and men
have gone into captivity.

¹⁹"I called out to my lovers,
but they tricked me.
My priests and my leaders
have died in the city.
They were looking for food for themselves.
They wanted to keep themselves alive.

²⁰"Look at me, LORD. I am in distress!
I am upset, as if my heart turned upside
down inside me.
I feel this way because
I have been so stubborn.
Out in the streets,
I lost my children to the swords.
Inside, it is like death.

²¹"Listen to me, I am groaning.
I have no one to comfort me.
All my enemies have heard of my trouble.
They are happy that you did this to me.
You said there would be a time of punishment.
You said you would punish my enemies.
Now do what you promised.
Let my enemies be like I am now.

²²"Look how evil my enemies are!
Then you can treat them the same way you
have treated me
because of all my sins.
Do this because I am groaning again and again.
Do this because my heart is sick."

The Lord Destroyed Jerusalem

2 Look how the Lord has covered Daughter
Zion
with the cloud of his anger.
He has thrown her, the glory of Israel,
from the sky to the ground.
In his anger he showed no care even for the
Temple
where he rests his feet.*ᵇ*

²The Lord destroyed the houses of Jacob's
people without mercy.
In his anger he tore down the strong walls
of Judah.*ᶜ*
He threw that kingdom and its rulers
down to the ground in shame.

³He was so angry that he took away the
strength of Israel.
He refused to help them when the enemy
came.
He came against the people of Jacob like a
flaming fire
that burns everything around it.

⁴He bent his bow like an enemy.
With his right hand he pulled back the
arrow.
He killed all our finest young men.
He poured out his anger like fire on the
tents of Zion.

⁵Like an enemy the Lord has swallowed up
Israel.
He has destroyed her palaces and strong
walls.
He has caused great sadness and crying
for the dead in Judah.

ᵃ **1:15** *dearest city* Literally, "virgin daughter Judah", a name for the city of Jerusalem.
ᵇ **2:1** *Temple . . . feet* Literally, "the footstool of his feet", meaning the place God lived among his people.
ᶜ **2:2** *Judah* Literally, "daughter Judah". Also in verse 5. See "JUDAH" in the Word List.

⁶He tore up the place where he lived*ᵃ*
  like someone ploughing up a garden.
He ruined the place where the people
  came together to worship him.
The Lᴏʀᴅ has made people forget
  the special assemblies and special days of
    rest*ᵇ* in Zion.
He rejected the king and the priests.
  He was angry and rejected them.

⁷He rejected his altar,
  and he left his holy place of worship.
He let the enemy pull down the walls
  of the palaces of Jerusalem.
The enemy shouted with joy in the Lᴏʀᴅ's
  Temple.
  They made noise as though it were a festival.

⁸The Lᴏʀᴅ planned to destroy
  the wall of Jerusalem.
He marked it with a measuring line.
  He didn't stop himself from destroying it.
He made all the walls cry out in sadness.
  Together they wasted away.

⁹Jerusalem's gates have sunk into the ground.
  The bars on her gates are completely
    destroyed.
Her king and princes have been taken to other
    nations.
  The teaching of the law has stopped.
And her prophets no longer receive
  visions from the Lᴏʀᴅ.

¹⁰The leaders of Zion sit on the ground.
  They sit on the ground and are quiet.
They pour dust on their heads.
  They put on sackcloth.
The young women of Jerusalem
  bow their heads to the ground in sorrow.

¹¹My eyes are worn out with tears,
  and my insides are upset.
My heart feels like it has been poured on the
    ground,
  because of the destruction of my people.
Children and babies are fainting
  in the public squares of the city.

¹²They ask their mothers,
  "Don't we have something to eat or drink?"
They get weaker and weaker,
  like a soldier wounded in the street,

and they finally die
  in their mothers' arms.

¹³My dear Jerusalem, what can I say about
    you?
  What can I compare you to?
What can I say you are like?
  How can I comfort you, city of Zion?
You have been hurt much too badly
  for anyone to heal.

¹⁴Your prophets saw visions for you,
  but their visions were only worthless lies.
They didn't speak against your sins.
  They didn't try to make things better.
They spoke messages for you,
  but they were false messages that fooled
    you.

¹⁵Those who pass by on the road
  clap their hands and laugh at you.
They make fun of Jerusalem,
  shaking their heads at the sight of her.
They ask, "Is this the city that people called
  'The Most Beautiful City'
  and 'The Joy of all the Earth'?"

¹⁶All your enemies laugh at you.
  They make fun of you and grind their teeth
    in anger.
They say, "We have swallowed them up!
  This is the day we were hoping for.
  We have finally seen this happen!"

¹⁷The Lᴏʀᴅ did what he planned to do.
  He did what he said he would do.
  He did what he commanded a long time ago.
He destroyed, and he had no pity.
  He made your enemies happy because of
    what happened to you.
  He made your enemies strong.

¹⁸Cry out with all your heart*ᶜ* to the Lord!
  Jerusalem, let tears roll down your walls.
  Let your tears flow like a stream day and
    night.
Don't stop crying
  or let your eyes dry.

¹⁹Get up throughout the night and cry for
    help.
  Let your sorrow pour out before the Lord
  like water.

ᵃ **2:6 the place where he lived** Literally, "his own tent", meaning the Temple in Jerusalem.
ᵇ **2:6 special days of rest** Or "Sabbaths". This might mean Saturday (see "Sᴀʙʙᴀᴛʜ" in the Word List) or all the special days when
the people were not supposed to work.
ᶜ **2:18 Cry out . . . heart** Or "Their hearts cried out."

Lift up your hands in prayer to him.
 Ask him to let your children live.
They are starving to death on every street
 corner.

20Look at us, Lord!
 Have you ever treated anyone else so badly?
Is it right for women to eat their own babies,
 the children they have cared for?
Should priests and prophets be killed
 in the Temple of the Lord?

21Young men and old men
 lie on the ground in the streets of the city.
My young women and young men
 have been killed by the sword.
You killed them on the day of your anger.
 You killed them without mercy!

22You invited terror to come to me from all
 around.
 You invited terror as though you were
 inviting it to a festival.
No one escaped on the day of the Lord's
 anger.
 My enemy killed the people who I raised
 and brought up.

The Meaning of Suffering

3 I am a man who has seen much trouble.
 God beat us with a stick, and I saw it
 happen.
2He led and brought me
 into darkness, not light.
3He turned his hand against me.
 He did this again and again, all day.

4He wore out my flesh and skin.
 He broke my bones.
5He built up bitterness and trouble against me.
 He surrounded me with bitterness and
 trouble.
6He put me in the dark,
 like someone who died long ago.

7He shut me in, so I could not get out.
 He put heavy chains on me.
8Even when I cry out and ask for help,
 he does not listen to my prayer.
9He has blocked up my path with stones.
 He has made my path crooked.

10He is like a bear about to attack me,
 like a lion that is in a hiding place.
11He led me off my path.
 He tore me to pieces and ruined me.

12He made his bow ready.
 He made me the target for his arrows.

13He shot me in the stomach
 with his arrows.
14I have become a joke to all my people.
 All day long they sing songs about me and
 make fun of me.
15He gave me this poison to drink.
 He filled me with this bitter drink.

16He pushed my teeth into rocky ground.
 He pushed me into the dirt.
17I thought I would never have peace again.
 I forgot about good things.
18I said to myself, "I no longer have any hope
 that the Lord will help me."

19Remember, I am very sad,
 and I have no home.
 Remember the bitter poison that you
 gave me.
20I remember well all my troubles,
 and I am very sad.
21But then I think about this,
 and I have hope:

22We are still alive because
 the Lord's faithful love never ends.
23Every morning he shows it in new ways!
 You are so very true and loyal!
24I say to myself, "The Lord is my God,
 and I trust him."a

25The Lord is good to those who wait for him.
 He is good to those who look for him.
26It is good to wait quietly
 for the Lord to save.
27It is good for a man to wear his yoke
 from the time he is young.
28He should sit alone and be quiet
 when the Lord puts his yoke on him.
29He should bow down to the Lord.
 Maybe there is still hope.
30He should turn his cheek to the one who
 hits him
 and let people insult him.

31He should remember that
 the Lord does not reject people forever.
32When he punishes, he also has mercy.
 He has mercy because of his great love and
 kindness.

33He does not enjoy causing people pain.
 He does not like to make anyone unhappy.

a 3:24 **The Lord . . . him** Or "The Lord is my portion and I trust him."

DON'T GIVE IN TO THE GLOOM

"In the pits" or "down in the dumps". Ever feel like that? You're not the only one!

DIG IN

READ Lamentations 3:1-42

- "I am a man who has seen much trouble" (v.1). Who's speaking here?
- Can you sympathize with any of his feelings?

In the third chapter, the focus of Lamentations shifts from the voice of the prophet (probably Jeremiah) to the first person. The narrator now refers to himself as "I".

- Who is this person and what's the point of the shift?

When you read what this character is thinking and feeling, it's easy to tell that the writer intends for us to assume that this is Jerusalem (God's people) speaking. This man explains exactly how he is feeling about the way God is treating him. The reason for giving us this "first person" viewpoint is probably because the writer wants to encourage us to empathize with him.

He feels left in the dark (vv.2,6), trapped (v.7), like no one's listening (v.8), lost (v.9), under threat of imminent attack (v.10), wounded (v.13), humiliated (v.14), ground down (v.16), fearful (v.17) and sorrowful (v.20). Truth is, these are feelings that – at one time or another – we will all feel. As human beings, we need to learn how to deal with them.

- What gives this person new hope (vv.21–24)?
- What does he choose to remember about God (vv.25–36)?
- What is his conclusion?

There's a massive turning point in verse 21. The speaker chooses to lift his eyes up from his grief and pain and turn them towards God. The act of remembering the nature and character of God gives him a new hope.

It comes as a bolt out of the blue. How can a guy who is so oppressed and so demoralized suddenly change his outlook so radically?

Answer: he stops thinking about his pain and he starts thinking about God. It really is as simple as that. When we take our eyes off our problems and instead fix them on God, things instantly start to look more hopeful.

DIG THROUGH

- Emotions like these – and the sadness they bring with them – are an inescapable part of life. What matters is how we deal with them.
- Do you think it's possible to learn how to respond to problems better?
- How might you learn to lift up your eyes and look at God sooner?

DIG DEEPER

- Psalm 121 has given encouragement to people through the ages to "look up" to the Lord. With just eight verses, this is a great psalm to memorize that might help you next time you feel down.

34He does not like any prisoner on earth
to be trampled down.
35He does not like anyone to be unfair to
another person.
Some people will do such things right in
front of God Most High.
36The Lord does not like anyone to cheat
another person.
He does not like any of these things.

37No one can say something and make it
happen,
unless the Lord orders it.
38God Most High commands
both good and bad things to happen.
39No one alive can complain
when he punishes them for their sins.

40We should examine the way we are living
and turn back to the LORD.
41Let us offer our hearts to God in heaven.
Let us lift up our hands in prayer to him
and say,
42"We have sinned and refused to listen to
you.
So you have not forgiven us.
43Filled with anger, you chased us
and killed us without mercy!
44You have hidden yourself in a cloud
that keeps our prayers from reaching you.
45You have made us seem like filthy rubbish
to the rest of the world.

46"Our enemies shout insults against us.
47We are filled with fear,
like we have fallen into a pit.
We have fallen into a pit.
We have been broken
and are lying here in ruins."
48Tears stream from my eyes
as I see my people destroyed.

49I cannot stop the tears.
They will keep on flowing
50until the LORD looks down from heaven
and sees our suffering.
51When I see what happened to the women of
my city,
it makes my heart ache.

52For no reason,
my enemies hunted me like a bird.
53They threw me alive into a pit
and then threw stones at me.
54Water came up over my head.
I said to myself, "I am finished."

55LORD, I called your name
from the bottom of the pit.
56You heard my voice.
You didn't close your ears.
You didn't refuse to rescue me.
57You came to me on the day that I called out to
you.
You said to me, "Don't be afraid."

58You defended me
and brought me back to life.
59LORD, you have seen my trouble.
Now judge my case for me.
60You have seen how my enemies have hurt me
and made evil plans against me.

61You heard their insults, LORD,
and all their harmful plans.
62The words and the thoughts of my enemies
are against me all the time—
63when they sit down and when they stand
up.
Look how they make fun of me!

64Give them back what they deserve, LORD.
Pay them back for what they have done.
65Make them stubborn
and then curse them.
66Chase them in anger and destroy them.
Wipe them off the face of the earth, LORD!

INSIGHT

To the devout Jew the devastation of the
Temple was even more tragic than the
destruction of Jerusalem. Having the
Babylonians trampling through the holy
places, where usually only priests were
allowed, was heartbreaking.
Lamentations 4:1

The Horrors of the Attack on Jerusalem

4 See how the gold has turned dark,
how the pure gold has changed.
There are jewels[a] scattered all around
at every street corner.

2The precious people of Zion
were once worth more than gold.
But now they are treated like something
worthless,
like the cheap clay jars a potter makes.

---

[a] 4:1 *jewels* The meaning of the Hebrew word here is uncertain.

³Even a wild dog feeds her babies.
  Even the jackal lets her pups suck at her
    breast.
But my peopleᵃ neglect their young,
  like ostriches in the desert.

⁴Babies are so thirsty
  their tongues stick to the roof of their
    mouths.
Young children ask for bread,
  but no one gives them any.

⁵Those who ate rich food
  are now dying in the streets.
Those who grew up wearing nice red
    clothes
  now pick through rubbish piles.

⁶The sin of my people was very great—
  greater than the sins of Sodom and
    Gomorrah.
Those cities were destroyed suddenly,
  but not by any human hand.ᵇ

⁷Some of the men of Judah were dedicated to
    God in a special way.
  They were purer than snow, whiter than
    milk.
Their skin glowed with colour like coral,
  and their beards shone like sapphire.

⁸But now their faces are blacker than
    soot.
  No one even recognizes them in the
    streets.
The skin on their bones has shrivelled up; it is
  as dry as wood.

⁹It was better for those who were killed by the
    sword
  than for those who died of hunger.
Those starving people were sad and hurt.
  They died because they got no food from
    the field.

¹⁰Then even nice women
  cooked their own children.
The children were food for their mothers.
  This happened when my people were
    destroyed.

¹¹The Lord used all his anger.
  He poured out all his anger.
He made a fire in Zion
  that burned it down to the foundations.

¹²The kings of the earth and the people of the
    world
  could not believe what had happened.
They could not believe that enemies
  would be able to come through the city
    gates of Jerusalem.

¹³This happened because the prophets of
    Jerusalem sinned.
  This happened because the priests of
    Jerusalem did evil things.
They were shedding the blood of good people
  in the city of Jerusalem.

¹⁴The prophets and priests walked around
  like blind men in the streets.
They had become dirty with blood.
  No one could even touch their clothes
    because they were dirty.

¹⁵People shouted, "Go away!
  Go away! Don't touch us."
They wandered around and had no home.
  People in other nations said,
    "We don't want them to live with us."

¹⁶The Lord himself destroyed them.
  He didn't look after them any more.
He didn't respect the priests.
  He was not friendly to the leaders of Judah.

¹⁷We have worn out our eyes looking for
    help,
  but no help comes.
We kept on looking for a nation to save us.
  We kept watch from our watchtower,
    but no nation came to us.

¹⁸Our enemies hunted us all the time.
  We could not even go out into the streets.
Our end came near. Our time was up.
  Our end came!

¹⁹The men who chased us
  were faster than eagles in the sky.
They chased us into the mountains.
  They hid in the desert to catch us.

²⁰The king was very important to us.
He was like the breath we breathe,
  but he was trapped by them.
The Lord himself chose the king,
  and we said this about the king,
    "We will live in his shadow.
      He protects us from the nations."

ᵃ **4:3 my people** Literally, "the daughter of my people".
ᵇ **4:6 not by any human hand** The Hebrew text is not clear.

²¹Be happy, people of Edom.
  Be happy, you who live in the land of Uz.
But remember, the cup of the Lord's anger will
    come around to you too.
  When you drink from that cup,
  you will get drunk and strip off all your
    clothes.

²²Your punishment is complete, Zion.
  You will not go into captivity again.
But the Lord will punish your sins, people of
    Edom.
  He will uncover your sins.

A Prayer to the LORD

5 Remember, LORD, what happened to us.
  Look and see our shame.
²Our land has been turned over to strangers.
  Our houses have been given to
    foreigners.
³We have become orphans with no father.
  Our mothers have become like widows.
⁴We have to buy the water that we drink.
  We have to pay for the wood that we
    use.
⁵We are forced to wear a yoke on our necks.
  We get tired, and we have no rest.
⁶We made an agreement with Egypt.
  We also made an agreement with Assyria to
    get enough bread.
⁷Our ancestors sinned against you, and now
    they are dead.
  And we are suffering because of their sins.
⁸Slaves have become our rulers.
  No one can save us from them.
⁹We risk our lives to get food.
  There are men in the desert with swords.
¹⁰Our skin is hot like an oven.
  We have a high fever because of our
    hunger.
¹¹The enemy raped the women of Zion.
  They raped the women in the cities of
    Judah.

¹²The enemy hanged our princes.
  They didn't honour our leaders.
¹³The enemy made our young men grind
    grain at the mill.
  Our young men stumbled under loads
    of wood.
¹⁴The leaders no longer sit at the gates of the city.
  The young men no longer make music.
¹⁵We have no more joy in our hearts.
  Our dancing has changed to crying for the
    dead.

INSIGHT

*Think Remembrance Day. Think funeral.
Think slow processions. In the original
Hebrew, each line has three words
followed by two words, which makes the
poem seem to "limp" – as if the reader is
walking haltingly along behind a coffin.*
Lamentations 5:15

¹⁶The crown has fallen from our head.
  Things have gone bad for us because we
    sinned.
¹⁷For this reason our hearts have become sick,
    and our eyes cannot see clearly.
¹⁸Mount Zion is a wasteland.
  Foxes run around on Mount Zion.

¹⁹But you rule forever, LORD.
  Your kingly chair lasts for ever and ever.
²⁰You seem to have forgotten us forever.
  You seem to have left us alone for such a
    long time.
²¹Bring us back to you, LORD.
  We will gladly come back to you.
  Make our lives as they were before.
²²You were very angry with us.
  Have you completely rejected us?

Who
A younger contemporary of Jeremiah, Ezekiel, son of Buzi, was a prophet and priest (1:3). He was among the first group of people from Judah to be deported to Babylon in 597 BC (2 Kings 24:8–17).

When
His ministry lasted for at least twenty-three years. The general opinion among experts is that the book was edited soon after the prophet's death – sometime around 570 BC.

What
Ezekiel has been deported to Babylon, along with many others from Jerusalem. While there he sees a series of powerful visions of what is going to happen: the capture of Jerusalem and the destruction of the Temple.

Ezekiel is one of the Old Testament's most bizarre, outrageous figures. He ate a scroll. He lay for 390 days on his left side, and then lay for only 40 days on his right side. He knocked a hole in the wall of his house and climbed through. Not what you'd call well-balanced behaviour.

But Ezekiel was a shock-tactic prophet, bringing people messages from God in a way which they couldn't fail to notice. Indeed, at times his message is contained in language that is quite extreme. Why does he speak this way? Ezekiel is passionate, because God is passionate. He shocks people because God wants to shock people out of their apathy; to get them to open their eyes.

Ezekiel warns the people remaining in Jerusalem to change their ways; he calls on his fellow exiles to recognize the faults that led to their captivity and he urges them to keep faith in the Lord. He will bring them through this.

Ezekiel doesn't only see visions of doom; he also sees visions of glory. His career as a prophet begins with a dazzling vision of God and in the final section of the book – after the final fall of Jerusalem – God gives Ezekiel a vision of a future Jerusalem, with an ideal Temple where God will once again be worshipped in peace and security. The people will return; God will bring his people back to him.

QUICK TOUR **EZEKIEL**

"I will put my Spirit in you, and you will come to life again. Then I will lead you back to your own land. Then you will know that I am the LORD. You will know that I said this and that I made it happen."
Ezekiel 37:14

Introduction

1 I am the priest, Ezekiel son of Buzi. I was in exile by the Kebar Canal in Babylonia when the skies opened up, and I saw visions of God. ²This was on the fifth day of the fourth month of the thirtieth year.ᵃ (This was the fifth year of King Jehoiachin's exile. ³The word of the LORD came to Ezekiel. The power of the LORD came over him at that place.)

The Chariot of the LORD—God's Throne

⁴I was watching a big storm come in from the north. It was a big cloud with a strong wind, and there was fire flashing from it. Light was shining out all around it. It looked like hot metalᵇ glowing in a fire. ⁵Inside the cloud, there were four living beings that looked like people. ⁶But each one of them had four faces and four wings. ⁷Their legs were straight. Their feet looked like calves' feet, and they sparkled like polished brass. ⁸Under their wings were human arms. There were four living beings. Each living being had four faces and four wings. ⁹The wings touched each other. The living beings did not turn when they moved. They went in the direction they were looking.

¹⁰Each living being had four faces. In the front they each had a man's face. There was a lion's face on the right side and a bull's face on the left side. There was an eagle's face on the back. ¹¹Their wings were spread out over them. With two of the wings each living being reached out to touch the one near it, and with the other two wings it covered its body. ¹²Each living being went in the direction it was looking. They went wherever the spiritᶜ caused them to go, but they did not turn when they moved. ¹³That is what the living beings looked like.

Inside the area between the living beings, there was something that looked like burning coals of fire. This fire was like small torches that kept moving around among the living beings. The fire glowed brightly and lightning flashed from it. ¹⁴The living beings ran back and forth—as fast as lightning.ᵈ

¹⁵⁻¹⁶I was looking at the living beings when I noticed four wheels that touched the ground. There was one wheel by each living being. All the wheels looked the same. The wheels looked as if they were made from a clear, yellow jewel. It looked as if there was a wheel inside a wheel. ¹⁷They could turn to move in any direction. ⌊But the living beings⌋ did not turn when they moved.ᵉ

¹⁸The rims of the wheels were tall and frightening. There were eyes all over the rims of all four wheels.

¹⁹The wheels always moved with the living beings. If the living beings went up into the air, the wheels went with them. ²⁰They went wherever the spirit wanted them to go, and the wheels went with them, because the power that moved the living being was in the wheels. ²¹So if the living beings moved, the wheels moved. If the living beings stopped, the wheels stopped. If the wheels went into the air, the living beings went with them, because the spirit was in the wheels.

²²There was an amazing thing over the heads of the living beings. It was like a bowlᶠ turned upside down, and the bowl was clear like crystal. ²³Under this bowl, each living being had wings reaching out to the one next to it. Two wings spread out one way and two wings spread out the other way, covering its body.

²⁴Then I heard the wings. Every time the living beings moved, their wings made a very loud noise like a lot of water rushing by. They were loud like ⌊the Lord⌋ All-Powerful. They were as loud as an army or a crowd of people. When the living beings stopped moving, they put their wings down by their side.

²⁵The living beings stopped moving and lowered their wings. Then there was another loud sound that came from above the bowl over their heads. ²⁶There was something that looked like a throne on top of the bowl. It was blue like sapphire. There was also something that looked like a man sitting on the throne. ²⁷I looked at him from his waist up. He looked like hot metal with fire all around him. I looked at him from his waist down. It looked like fire with a glow that was

---

ᵃ **1:2 fifth day . . . year** If the year refers to Ezekiel's age, this is the same as the fifth year of exile, that is, 31 July 593 BC.
ᵇ **1:4 hot metal** The Hebrew word might mean "melted copper", "an alloy of gold and silver" or "amber". Also in verse 27.
ᶜ **1:12 spirit** Or "wind". Also in verse 20.
ᵈ **1:14** Or "And there was something like lightning shooting back and forth among the living beings."
ᵉ **1:17 The wheels . . . moved** Or "The wheels could move in any four directions, but they did not turn when they moved."
ᶠ **1:22 bowl** This Hebrew word is the same word used in Gen. 1:6–7 to describe the dome of the sky.

shining all around him. ²⁸The light shining around him was like a rainbow in a cloud. It was the Glory of the LORD. As soon as I saw that, I fell to the ground. I bowed with my face to the ground, and then I heard a voice speaking to me.

The LORD Speaks to Ezekiel

2 The voice said, "Son of man, stand up and I will speak with you."

²Then the Spirit came into me^a and lifted me up on my feet, and I listened to the one who spoke to me. ³He said, "Son of man, I am sending you to speak to the family of Israel. Those people and their ancestors turned against me many times. They have sinned against me many times—and they are still sinning against me today. ⁴I am sending you to speak to them, but they are very stubborn. They are very headstrong, but you must speak to them. You must say, 'This is what the Lord GOD says.' ⁵They are people who refuse to obey, so they may not listen to you. But even if they don't stop sinning, at least they will know that there is a prophet living among them.

⁶"Son of man, don't be afraid of the people or what they say. It is true that they will turn against you and try to hurt you. Their words will be sharp like thorns and will sting like scorpions. But don't be afraid of what they say. They are people who refuse to obey, but don't be afraid of them. ⁷You must tell them what I say, whether they listen or not. They are people who usually refuse to listen!

⁸"Son of man, listen to what I am telling you. Don't turn against me like those people who refuse to obey. Now open your mouth to receive the words I will give you to speak."

⁹Then I saw a hand reach out towards me. It was holding a scroll with words written on it. ¹⁰The hand unrolled the scroll in front of me. Words were on the front and on the back of the scroll. There were all kinds of sad songs, sad stories and warnings.

3 God said to me, "Son of man, eat what you see. Eat this scroll, and then go and tell these things to the family of Israel."

²So I opened my mouth and he put the scroll into my mouth. ³Then God said, "Son of man, I am giving you this scroll. Swallow it! Let that scroll fill your body."

So I ate the scroll. It was as sweet as honey in my mouth.

⁴Then God said to me, "Son of man, go to the family of Israel. Speak my words to them. ⁵I am not sending you to foreigners whose language you cannot understand or speak. I am sending

you to the family of Israel. ⁶I am not sending you to many different countries where people speak languages you cannot understand. If you went to those people and spoke to them, they would listen to you. But you will not have to learn those hard languages. ⁷No, I am sending you to the family of Israel. Only these people are headstrong—they are very stubborn! And the people of Israel will refuse to listen to you. They don't want to listen to me. ⁸But I will make you just as stubborn as they are, and just as hardened. ⁹A diamond is harder than flint rock. In the same way, you will be more stubborn than they are. Then you will not be afraid of them or those who always turn against me."

¹⁰Then God said to me, "Son of man, listen to every word I say to you and remember them. ¹¹Then go to all your people in exile and tell them, 'This is what the Lord GOD says.' Even if they will not listen and will not stop sinning, you still must tell them my message."

¹²Then the Spirit^b lifted me up, and I heard a voice behind me. It was very loud, like thunder. It said, "Blessed is the Glory of the LORD!" ¹³Then the wings of the living beings began moving. The wings made a very loud noise as they touched each other, and the wheels in front of them began making a noise as loud as thunder. ¹⁴The Spirit lifted me and took me away. I was very sad and upset in my spirit, but I felt the LORD's power in me. ¹⁵I went to the people of Israel who were forced to live in Tel Aviv^c by the Kebar Canal. I sat there among them for seven days, shocked and silent.

The Watchman of Israel

¹⁶After seven days, the LORD spoke to me and said, ¹⁷"Son of man, I am making you a watchman for Israel. I will tell you about bad things that will happen to them, and you must warn Israel. ¹⁸If I say, 'These evil people will die!' Then you must warn them. You must tell them to change their lives and stop doing evil. If you don't warn them, they will die because they sinned. But I will also make you responsible for their death, because you did not go to them and save their lives.

¹⁹"If you warn them and tell them to change their lives and stop doing evil, but they refuse to listen, they will die because they sinned. But since you warned them, you will have saved your own life.

²⁰"If good people stop being good and begin to do evil, and I send something that makes them

---

^a **2:2 the Spirit came into me** Or "a wind came".
^b **3:12 Spirit** Or "wind". Also in verse 24.
^c **3:15 Tel Aviv** This was a place outside of Israel. The name means "Spring Hill".

stumble and sin, they will die because they sinned. But since you did not warn them and remind them of the good things they had done, I will make you responsible for their death.

21"But if you warn good people and tell them to stop sinning, and they listen to your warning and stop sinning, they will not die. In that way you will have saved your own life."

22The LORD's power came to me. He said to me, "Get up and go to the valley.ᵃ I will speak to you in that place."

23So I got up and went out to the valley. The Glory of the LORD was there—as I had seen it by the Kebar Canal. So I bowed with my face to the ground. 24But the Spirit came into me and lifted me up onto my feet. He said to me, "Go home and lock yourself in your house. 25Son of man, people will come with ropes and tie you up. They will not let you go out among the people. 26I will make your tongue stick to the roof of your mouth—you will not be able to talk. So they will not have anyone to teach them that they are doing wrong, because they are always turning against me. 27But I will talk to you, and then I will allow you to speak. But you must say to them, 'This is what the Lord GOD says.' If a person wants to listen, fine. If a person refuses to listen, fine. But those people always turn against me.

INSIGHT

Reality TV has nothing on Ezekiel. I'm a Prophet, Get Me Out of Here! *would keep the whole nation hooked. But he's not behaving strangely in order to become a celebrity – he's just being obedient. Sometimes obeying God means you have to swallow your pride and look a fool for him.*

Ezekiel 4

Warnings About the Attack of Jerusalem

4 "Son of man, take a brick and scratch a picture on it. Draw a picture of a city—the city of Jerusalem. 2And then pretend you are an army surrounding the city. Build a wall around the city to help you attack it. Build a ramp leading up to the city wall. Bring battering ramsᵇ and set up army camps around the city. 3And then take an iron pan and put it between you and the city. It will be like an iron wall separating you and the city. In this way you will show that you are against it. You will surround the city and attack it. This is an example for the family of Israel to show that I will destroy Jerusalem.

4"Then you must lie down on your left side. You must do this thing that shows that you are taking the sins of the people of Israel on yourself. You will carry the guilt for as many days as you lie on your left side. 5You must bear the guilt of Israel for 390 days.ᶜ In this way I am telling you how long Israel will be punished; one day equals one year.

6"After that time, you will lie on your right side for 40 days. This time you will bear the guilt of Judah for 40 days. One day equals one year. I am telling you how long Judah must be punished.

7"Now, roll up your sleeve and raise your arm over the brick. Act as if you are attacking the city of Jerusalem. Do this to show that you are speaking as my messenger to the people. 8Now look, I am tying ropes on you. You will not be able to roll over from one side to another until your attack against the cityᵈ is finished.

9"You must get some grain to make bread. Get some wheat, barley, beans, lentils, millet and spelt. Mix all these things together in one bowl and grind them to make flour. You will use this flour to make bread. You will eat only this bread during the 390 days that you lie on your side. 10You will be allowed to use only 230 grammesᵉ of that flour each day to make bread. You will eat that bread from time to time throughout the day. 11You can drink half a litreᶠ of water each day. You can drink it from time to time throughout the day. 12You must make your bread each day. You must get dry human dung and burn it. Then you must cook the bread over this burning dung. You must eat this bread in front of the people." 13Then the LORD said, "This will show that the family of Israel will eat unclean bread in foreign countries and that I am the one who forced them to leave Israel and go to there!"

14Then I said, "Oh, but Lord GOD, I have never eaten any unclean food. I have never eaten meat from an animal that died from a disease or from an animal that was killed by a wild animal. I have never eaten unclean meat—not from the time that I was a little baby until now. None of that bad meat ever entered my mouth."

ᵃ 3:22 *the valley* Possibly, Jezreel Valley, a fertile area where many battles were fought. It is often called simply "The Valley".
ᵇ 4:2 *battering rams* Heavy logs that soldiers used to break holes into the gates or walls around a city.
ᶜ 4:5 *390 days* The ancient Greek version has "190 days".
ᵈ 4:8 *your attack against the city* This is a wordplay. The Hebrew word can mean "famine", "time of trouble" or "attack against a city".
ᵉ 4:10 *230 grammes* Literally, "20 *shekels*".
ᶠ 4:11 *half a litre* Literally, "⅙ *hin*".

Martin is a highly successful lawyer who earns a six-figure salary advising some of the world's biggest companies. Sandra is a research scientist working on a cure for cancer. Andrew counsels people who are struggling with debt.

Together they spend most Saturday afternoons on the streets of their town offering to pray with people and share their faith. All of them have family and friends who love them but think they are out of their minds.

DIG IN

READ Ezekiel 4:1–8

- Who is speaking here, and who is the "son of man" being addressed? (See 1:1–3 and 3:22–25 to get the picture.)
- Why is God planning to destroy Jerusalem (vv.3–6)?

Ezekiel is one of a long line of prophets God uses to speak to his people throughout the Old Testament. In Ezekiel 3, God commissions him for this important service (v.4) and Ezekiel uses a certain phrase that confirms it: "God said to me". These same words are spoken by, or about, Samuel, Elijah, Isaiah and other key prophets in the Bible.

Being a prophet wasn't an easy gig. Often they were instructed by God to say things that were hard for people to hear – just like Ezekiel.

Later in this book, Ezekiel's message from God will turn into comfort and hope for God's people, but for now the picture is bleak: God is planning to allow enemies to attack and overthrow Israel (read 2 Kings for the history).

- What bizarre acts does God make Ezekiel perform?
- Why?

One of the things that makes Ezekiel stand out among the prophets of the Old Testament is how often God asks him to act out scenes to get his point across.

The number of days Ezekiel is told to lie on his side is thought to be a reference to Israel's long rebellion against God. Although Israel and Judah have at times repented and come back to God, the overall picture is one of wickedness and disobedience. God can no longer stand it and judgement is coming soon.

Surely he would have looked odd and been criticized for his odd behaviour – lying on his side, cooking bread over a fire of dung! But although it may have looked funny, the message is deadly serious. There will be a severe punishment for the long-standing sin of the people.

DIG THROUGH

- Martin, Sandra and Andrew are all admired and respected people but they feel called by God to do something out of the ordinary for him that their friends and family do not understand. What aspects of being a follower of Jesus look odd to people who don't believe in him? In what ways do we need to be obedient to God that may not look cool or "normal"?
- Like Ezekiel, we have a responsibility to warn other people of the danger of sin. In what ways are we called to do that? How can we do that in a way that is both gracious and truthful? Whose example should we follow (check out John 1:16–17)?

DIG DEEPER

God calls Ezekiel "son of man" throughout this book, perhaps to help Ezekiel remember his humble position before a mighty God. No matter what he is asked to do, his job is not to ask why, but to get on with it. "Son of man" is also a phrase that Jesus uses to describe himself to communicate that he is fully human and willing to be fully obedient to his heavenly Father (e.g. Matthew 20:28).

¹⁵Then God said to me, "Very well, I will let you use dry cow dung to cook your bread. You don't have to use dry human dung."

¹⁶Then God said to me, "Son of man, I am destroying Jerusalem's supply of bread. People will have only a little bread to eat. They will be very worried about their food supply, and they will have only a little water to drink. Every time they take a drink, they will feel more afraid. ¹⁷That is because there will not be enough food and water for everyone. They will be terrified as they watch each other wasting away because of their sins.

People of Jerusalem Scattered

5 "Son of man, after your famine*ᵃ* you must do this: Take a sharp sword and use it like a barber's razor. Shave off your hair and beard. Put the hair on a scale and weigh it. Separate it into three equal parts. ²Put a third of your hair on the brick that has the picture of the city on it. Burn that hair in that 'city'. Then use the sword and cut a third of your hair into small pieces all around the outside of the 'city'. Next, throw a third of your hair into the air and let the wind blow it away. This will show that I will pull out my sword and chase some of the people into faraway countries. ³But then you must get a few of those hairs and wrap them up in your robe. ⁴Take some of those hairs and throw them into the fire. This will show that a fire will start there and burn throughout the whole house of Israel."*ᵇ*

⁵Then the Lord GOD said to me, "The brick is a picture of Jerusalem. I put Jerusalem in the middle of other nations with countries all around her. ⁶The people refused to obey my commands. They were worse than any of the other nations! They broke more of my laws than any of the people in the countries around them. They refused to listen to my commands. They did not obey my laws."

⁷So the Lord GOD says, "I will do this because you did not obey my laws and commands. You broke more of my laws than the people who lived around you, and you did what even they know is wrong!" ⁸The Lord GOD says, "So now, even I am against you! I will punish you while those other people watch. ⁹I will do things to you that I have never done before, and I will never do them again, because you did so many terrible things. ¹⁰People in Jerusalem will be so hungry that parents will eat their own children, and children will eat their own parents. I will punish you in many ways, and those who are left alive I will scatter to the winds."

¹¹The Lord GOD says, "Jerusalem, I promise by my life that I punish you! I promise that I will punish you, because you did terrible things to my Holy Place. You did horrible things that made it dirty. I will punish you. I will not show any mercy or feel sorry for you. ¹²A third of your people will die inside the city from diseases and hunger. Another third will die in battle outside the city. And then I will pull out my sword and chase the last third of your people into faraway countries. ¹³Only then will I stop being angry with your people. I will know that they have been punished for the bad things they did to me. They will know that I am the LORD and that I spoke to them because of my strong love for them!"

¹⁴God said, "Jerusalem, I will destroy you—you will be nothing but a pile of rocks. The people around you will make fun of you. Everyone who walks by will make fun of you. ¹⁵People around you will make fun of you, but you will also be a lesson for them. They will see that I was angry and punished you. I was very angry and I warned you. I, the LORD, told you what I would do. ¹⁶I told you I would send you terrible times of hunger. I told you I would send you things that would destroy you. I told you that I would take away your supply of food and that those times of hunger would come again and again. ¹⁷I told you I would send hunger and wild animals against you that would kill your children. I told you there would be disease and death everywhere in the city. I told you I would bring enemy soldiers to fight against you. I, the LORD, told you all these things would happen!"

Prophecies Against Israel

6 Then the word of the LORD came to me again. ²He said, "Son of man, turn towards the mountains of Israel and speak against them for me. ³Tell them this: 'Mountains of Israel, listen to this message from the Lord GOD! This is what the Lord GOD says to the hills and mountains and to the ravines and valleys: Look! I am bringing the enemy to fight against you. I will destroy your high places. ⁴Your altars will be broken into pieces. Your incense altars will be smashed, and I will throw down your dead bodies in front of your filthy idols. ⁵I will put the dead bodies of the people of Israel in front of their filthy idols. I will scatter your bones around your altars. ⁶Bad things will happen wherever your people live. Their cities will become piles of rock. Their high places will be destroyed so that those places of worship will never be used again. The altars will all be destroyed. People will never worship those filthy idols again. The incense altars will be smashed. Everything you made will be destroyed completely. ⁷Your people will be killed, and then you will know that I am the LORD!

ᵃ **5:1–2 your famine** Or "your attack on the city". See Ezek. 4:8.
ᵇ **5:4 house of Israel** This probably means the people of the northern ten tribes of Israel.

8"But I will let a few of your people escape. They will live in other countries for a short time. I will scatter them and force them to live in other countries. 9Then the survivors will be taken as prisoners. They will be forced to live in other countries, but they will remember me. I broke their spirit.*a* They will hate themselves for the evil things they did. In the past, they turned away from me and left me. They chased after their filthy idols. They were like a woman leaving her husband and running off with another man. They did many terrible things, 10but they will learn that I am the LORD. Then they will know that if I say that I will do something, I will do it! They will know that I caused all these things to happen to them.'"

11Then the Lord GOD said to me, "Clap your hands and stamp your feet. Speak against all the terrible things that the people of Israel have done. Warn them that they will be killed by disease and hunger. Tell them they will be killed in war. 12People far away will die from disease. People near this place will be killed with swords, and those who are left in the city will starve to death. Only then will I stop being angry. 13Only then will you know that I am the LORD. You will know this when you see your dead bodies in front of your filthy idols and around their altars. Those bodies will be near every one of your places for worship,*b* on every high hill and mountain, under every green tree and every oak tree with leaves. You offered your sacrifices everywhere. They were a sweet smell for your filthy idols. 14But I will raise my arm over you and punish you and your people, wherever they live! I will destroy your country! It will be completely empty from the desert in the south to Riblah*c* in the north. Then they will know that I am the LORD!"

Disaster Is Coming to Jerusalem

7 Then the word of the LORD came to me. 2He said, "Now, son of man, here is a message from the Lord GOD. This message is for the land of Israel:

"'The end!
The end is coming.
The whole country will be destroyed.
3Your end is coming now!
I will show how angry I am with you.
I will punish you for the evil things you have done.
I will make you pay for all the terrible things you have done.

4I will not show you any mercy or feel sorry for you.
I am punishing you for the evil things you have done.
You have done such terrible things.
Now, you will know that I am the LORD.'

5"This is what the Lord GOD says: 'There will be one disaster after another! 6The end is coming, and it will come quickly! 7You people living in Israel, disaster is coming. It is time for punishment. Those are not shouts of joy in the mountains. Those are cries of panic. 8Very soon now, I will show you how angry I am. I will show all my anger against you. I will punish you for the evil things you have done. I will make you pay for all the terrible things you have done. 9I will not show you any mercy or feel sorry for you. I am punishing you for the evil things you have done. You have done such terrible things. Now, you will know that I am the LORD.

10"'That time of punishment has come like a plant sprouting, budding and flowering. God has given the signal, the enemy is prepared, and their proud king is ready. 11This violent man is ready to punish the evil people. There are many people in Israel—but he is not one of them. He is not a person in that crowd. He is not some important leader from them.

12"'The time of punishment has come. The day is here. Those who buy things will not be happy, and those who sell things will not feel bad about selling them because that terrible punishment will happen to everyone. 13The people who sold their property*d* will never go back to it. Even if some people escape alive, they will never go back to their property, because this vision is for the whole crowd. So even if some people escape alive, it will not make everyone feel better.

14"'They will blow the trumpet to warn the people. The people will get ready for battle, but they will not go out to fight because I will show the whole crowd how angry I am. 15The enemy with his sword is outside the city. Disease and hunger is inside the city. If some people go out into the fields, enemy soldiers will kill them. If they stay in the city, hunger and disease will destroy them. 16"'But some people will escape. The survivors will run to the mountains, but they will not be happy. They will be sad for all their sins. They will cry and make sad noises like doves. 17They will be too tired and sad to raise their arms. Their legs will be like water. 18They will wear sackcloth and be covered with fear. You will see the shame on

---

a 6:9 *spirit* Literally, "heart".

b 6:13 *places for worship* Or "high places". See "HIGH PLACE" in the Word List.

c 6:14 *Riblah* Most Hebrew copies have "Diblah".

d 7:13 *sold their property* In ancient Israel property did not belong to a person, it belonged to a family. People might sell their property, but at the time of Jubilee their family would get the land back. Here, Ezekiel says the people will never get their property again.

every face. They will shave their heads to show their sadness. [19]They will throw their silver idols into the streets. They will treat their gold statues like dirty rags, because those things will not be able to save them when the LORD shows his anger. Those things were nothing but a trap that caused the people to fall. They will not give food to the people or put food in their bellies.

[20]"'They used their beautiful jewellery and made an idol. They were proud of that statue. They made their terrible statues. They made those filthy things, so I will throw them away like a dirty rag. [21]I will let foreigners take them. Those foreigners will make fun of them. They will kill some of the people and take others away as prisoners. [22]I will turn my head away from them—I will not look at them. The foreigners will ruin my Temple—they will go into the secret parts of that holy building and make it unfit for worship.

[23]"'Make chains for the prisoners, because many people will be punished for killing other people. There will be violence everywhere in the city. [24]I will bring evil people from other nations, and they will get all the houses of the people of Israel. I will stop all you powerful people from being so proud. Those people from other nations will get all your places of worship.

[25]"'You will shake with fear. You will look for peace, but there will be none. [26]You will hear one sad story after another. You will hear nothing but bad news. You will look for a prophet and ask him for a vision. The priests will have nothing to teach you, and the leaders will not have any good advice to give you. [27]Your king will be crying for the people who died. The leaders will wear sackcloth. The common people will be very frightened, because I will pay them back for what they did. I will decide their punishment, and I will punish them. Then they will know that I am the LORD.'"

INSIGHT

Thousands of years ago, God didn't need CCTV. He supernaturally took his prophet Ezekiel right into the inner chambers of the Temple to see the horrible things going on there. Talk about one amazing fly-on-the-wall documentary!

Ezekiel 8

Sinful Things Done at the Temple

8 One day I, Ezekiel, was sitting in my house, and the leaders of Judah were sitting there in front of me. This was on the fifth day of the sixth month of the sixth year of exile.[a] Suddenly, the power of the Lord GOD came on me. [2]I saw something that looked like fire, like a man's body. From the waist down, he was like fire. From the waist up, he was bright and shining like hot metal[b] in a fire. [3]Then I saw something that looked like an arm. The arm reached out and grabbed me by the hair on my head. Then the Spirit[c] lifted me into the air, and in a vision from God he took me to Jerusalem. He took me to the inner gate—the gate that is on the north side. The statue that makes God jealous is by that gate. [4]But the Glory of the God of Israel was there. The Glory looked just like the vision I saw in the valley ⌊by the Kebar Canal⌋.

[5]God spoke to me. He said, "Son of man, look towards the north." So I looked, and there, north of the Altar Gate by the entrance, was that statue that made God jealous.

[6]Then God said to me, "Son of man, do you see what terrible things the people of Israel are doing? They built that thing here, right next to my Temple! And if you come with me, you will see even more terrible things!"

[7]So I went to the entrance to the courtyard, and I saw a hole in the wall. [8]God said to me, "Son of man, make a hole in the wall." So I made a hole in the wall, and there I saw a door.

[9]Then God said to me, "Go in and look at the terrible, evil things that the people are doing here." [10]So I went in and looked. I saw statues of all kinds of reptiles[d] and animals that you hate to think about. The statues were the filthy idols that the people of Israel worshipped. There were pictures of those animals carved all around, on every wall!

[11]Then I noticed that Jaazaniah son of Shaphan and the 70 leaders of Israel were there with the people worshipping in that place. There they were, right at the front of the people, and each leader had his own incense dish in his hand. The smoke from the burning incense was rising into the air. [12]Then God said to me, "Son of man, do you see what the leaders of Israel do in the dark? Each man has a special room for his own false god. They say to themselves, 'The LORD cannot see us. The LORD has left this country.'" [13]Then he said to me, "If you come with me, you will see these men doing even more terrible things!"

---

[a] **8:1 sixth year of exile** This is the autumn of 592 BC.
[b] **8:2 hot metal** The Hebrew word might mean "melted copper", "an alloy of gold and silver" or "amber".
[c] **8:3 Spirit** Or "wind".
[d] **8:10 reptiles** The Hebrew word can mean "lizards", "snakes" and "all kinds of bugs and insects".

¹⁴Then God led me to the entrance to the LORD's Temple. This gate was on the north side. I saw women sitting there and crying. They were sad about the false god Tammuz!*ᵃ*

¹⁵God said to me, "Son of man, do you see these terrible things? Come with me and you will see things that are even worse than this!" ¹⁶Then he led me to the inner courtyard of the LORD's Temple area. There I saw 25 men bowing down and worshipping. They were at the entrance to the LORD's Temple between the porch and the altar—but they were facing the wrong way. Their backs were to the Holy Place. They were bowing down to worship the sun!

¹⁷Then God said, "Son of man, do you see this? The people of Judah think my Temple is so unimportant that they will do these terrible things here in my Temple! This country is filled with violence, and they constantly do things to make me angry. Look, they are wearing rings in their noses to honour the moon as a false god!*ᵇ* ¹⁸I will show them my anger! I will not show them any mercy or feel sorry for them! They will shout to me—but I refuse to listen to them!"

God's Messengers Punish Jerusalem

9 Then God shouted to the leaders in charge of punishing the city. Each leader had his own destructive weapon in his hand.*ᶜ* ²Then I saw six men walking on the road from the upper gate. This gate is on the north side. Each man had his own deadly weapon in his hand. One of the men wore linen clothes.*ᵈ* He wore a scribe's pen and ink set*ᵉ* at his waist. Those men went to the bronze altar in the Temple and stood there. ³Then the Glory of the God of Israel rose from above the winged creatures where he had been. Then the Glory went to the door of the Temple and stopped when he was over the threshold. Then he called to the man wearing the linen clothes and the scribe's pen and ink set.

⁴Then the LORD said to him, "Go through the city of Jerusalem. Put a mark on the forehead of everyone who feels sad and upset about all the terrible things people are doing in this city."

⁵⁻⁶Then I heard God say to the other men, "I want you to follow the first man. You must kill all those who do not have the mark on their foreheads. It doesn't matter if they are old men, young men or young women, children or mothers—you must use your weapon and kill everyone who does not have the mark on their forehead. Don't show any mercy. Don't feel sorry for anyone. Start here at my Temple." So they started with the leaders in front of the Temple.

⁷He said to them, "Make this Temple unclean—fill this courtyard with dead bodies! Now go!" So they went and killed the people in the city.

⁸I stayed there while the men went to kill the people. I bowed with my face to the ground and said, "Oh, Lord GOD, in showing your anger against Jerusalem, are you killing all the survivors in Israel?"

⁹He said, "The family of Israel and Judah has committed many terrible sins! People are being murdered everywhere in this country, and the city is filled with crime. That is because the people say to themselves, 'The LORD has left this country. The LORD cannot see what we are doing.' ¹⁰So I will not show any mercy or feel sorry for them. They have brought it on themselves. I am only giving them the punishment they deserve!"

¹¹Then the man wearing linen clothes and a scribe's pen and ink set spoke up. He said, "I have done what you commanded."

The Glory of the LORD Leaves the Temple

10 Then I looked up at the bowl*ᶠ* over the heads of the winged creatures. The bowl looked clear blue like sapphire, and there was something that looked like a throne over it. ²Then the one sitting on the throne said to the man dressed in linen clothes,*ᵍ* "Step into the area between the wheels*ʰ* under the winged creatures. Take a handful of the burning coals from between the winged creatures and go and throw them over the city of Jerusalem."

The man walked past me. ³The winged creatures were standing in the area south*ⁱ* of the Temple as the man walked to them. The cloud filled the inner courtyard. ⁴Then the Glory of the LORD rose up from the winged creatures near the threshold of the door of the Temple. Then the

---

ᵃ **8:14** *Tammuz* People thought this false god died and his wife Ishtar asked everyone to be sad and cry with her. Ishtar hoped this would bring him back to life. This ceremony was on the second day of the fourth month (June/July). This month was named Tammuz because of this ceremony.

ᵇ **8:17** *Look . . . god* Or "Look at them putting that cut branch in their noses."

ᶜ **9:1** *Each . . . hand* In Hebrew this is like Ezek. 8:11.

ᵈ **9:2** *linen clothes* Priests usually wore these clothes.

ᵉ **9:2** *scribe's pen and ink set* A scribe was a person who copied official documents and counted supplies and things. Scribes often carried a small board with dry ink in it and a pen. They could put water on the ink and then write with it. Also in verse 11.

ᶠ **10:1** *bowl* This Hebrew word is the same word used in Gen. 1:6–7 to describe the dome of the sky.

ᵍ **10:2** *linen clothes* Priests usually wore these clothes.

ʰ **10:2** *area between the wheels* The Hebrew word can mean "chariot wheel", "whirling (spinning) wheel" or "tumbling weed". See chapter 1 for Ezekiel's full description. Also in verse 6.

ⁱ **10:3** *south* Literally, "right".

cloud filled the Temple, and the bright light from the Glory of the LORD filled the whole courtyard. [5]The noise from the wings of the creatures could be heard all the way out into the outer courtyard. The sound was very loud—like the thundering voice when God All-Powerful speaks.

[6]God had given the man dressed in linen clothes a command. He had told him to go into the area between the wheels among the winged creatures and get some hot coals. So the man went there and stood by the wheel. [7]One of the winged creatures reached out his hand and took some of the hot coals from the area between the creatures. He poured the coals into the man's hands, and the man left. [8](The winged creatures had what looked like human arms under their wings.)

[9]Then I noticed that there were four wheels, one by each winged creature. The wheels were shining like a clear yellow jewel. [10]All four wheels looked the same. Each wheel had another wheel inside it. [11]When the creatures moved, they could go in any direction without turning. They went straight in the direction their head was facing. [12]There were eyes all over the bodies of the creatures, on their backs, arms, wings and all over the wheels. [13]I heard someone describe these wheels as "the wheels that spin".

[14-15]Each winged creature had four faces. The first was the face of a bull,[a] the second was the face of a man, the third was a lion's face and the fourth was an eagle's face. (These winged creatures were the living beings I saw in the vision by the Kebar Canal.[b])

Then the winged creatures rose into the air, [16]and the wheels rose with them. When they raised their wings and flew into the air, not even the wheels turned around. [17]If they flew into the air, the wheels went with them. If they stood still, so did the wheels, because the spirit[c] of the living being was in them.

[18]Then the Glory of the LORD rose from the threshold of the Temple, moved to the place over the winged beings, and stopped there. [19]Then the winged creatures raised their wings and flew into the air. I saw them leave. The wheels went with them. Then they stopped at the East Gate of the LORD's Temple. The Glory of the God of Israel was in the air above them.

[20]These were the living beings under the Glory of the God of Israel in the vision at the Kebar Canal. And now I realized that they were the winged creatures. [21]Each living being had four faces, four wings and something that looked like human arms under their wings. [22]The faces of the winged creatures were the same as the four faces on the living beings in the vision by the Kebar Canal. They all looked straight ahead in the direction they were going.

Prophecies Against the Leaders

11 Then the Spirit[d] carried me to the East Gate of the LORD's Temple. This gate faces the east, ₗwhere the sun comes up₎. I saw 25 men there at the entrance of this gate. Some of the leaders were among them, including Jaazaniah son of Azzur and Pelatiah son of Benaiah.

[2]Then God spoke to me and said, "Son of man, these are the men who make evil plans for this city. They always tell the people to do evil things. [3]These men say, 'We will be building our houses again very soon. We are as safe in this city as meat in a pot!' [4]So you must speak to the people for me. Son of man, prophesy against the people."

[5]Then the Spirit of the LORD came on me. He said to me, "Tell them that this is what the LORD says: 'House of Israel, you are planning big things. But I know what you are thinking. [6]You have killed many people in this city. You have filled the streets with dead bodies. [7]Now, the Lord GOD says this: The dead bodies are the meat, and the city is the pot. But someone will come and take you out of this safe pot. [8]You are afraid of the sword, but I am bringing the sword against you! This is what the Lord GOD says.

[9]"'He also says: I will take you out of this city and give you to foreigners. I will punish you. [10]You will die by the sword. I will punish you here in Israel, so you will know that I am the LORD. [11]Yes, this place will be the cooking pot, and you will be the meat cooking in it. I will punish you here in Israel. [12]Then you will know that I am the LORD. It was my law that you broke. You did not obey my commands. You decided to live like the nations around you.'"

[13]As soon as I finished speaking for God, Pelatiah son of Benaiah died! I fell to the ground. I bowed with my face touching the ground and said, "Oh, Lord GOD, you are going to completely destroy all the survivors of Israel!"

Prophecies Against Survivors in Jerusalem

[14]But then the LORD spoke to me and said, [15]"Son of man, remember your brothers, the family of Israel. They were forced to leave their country, but I will bring them back.[e] But now, the

---

[a] **10:14–15** *face of a bull* See Ezek. 1:10.

[b] **10:14–15** *vision by the Kebar Canal* See Ezek. 1.

[c] **10:17** *spirit* Or "wind".

[d] **11:1** *Spirit* Or "wind".

[e] **11:15** *They were . . . back* This is a wordplay. The word meaning "redeemed" sounds like the word meaning "exiled".

people living in Jerusalem are saying, 'Stay far away from the LORD. This land was given to us —it is ours!'

¹⁶"So tell them that this is what the Lord GOD says: 'It is true, I forced my people to go far away to other nations. I did scatter them among many countries. But I will be their temple for a short time while they are in those other countries.' ¹⁷But you must tell those people that the Lord GOD will bring them back. 'I have scattered you among many nations, but I will gather you together and bring you back from those nations. I will give the land of Israel back to you.' ¹⁸When my people come back, they will destroy all the terrible, filthy idols that are here now. ¹⁹I will bring them together and make them like one person. I will put a new spirit*ᵃ in them. I will take away that heart of stone, and I will put a real heart in its place. ²⁰Then they will obey my laws and my commands. They will do the things I tell them. They will be my people, and I will be their God. ²¹But now, their hearts belong to those terrible, filthy idols, and I must punish those people for the bad things they have done. This is what the Lord GOD says."

The Glory of the LORD Leaves Jerusalem

²²Then the winged creatures raised their wings and flew into the air. The wheels went with them. The Glory of the God of Israel was above them. ²³The Glory of the LORD rose into the air and left the city and stopped on the hill east of Jerusalem.*ᵇ ²⁴Then the Spirit*ᶜ lifted me into the air and brought me back to Babylonia. It brought me back to the people who were forced to leave Israel. I saw all this in the vision from God. Then the one I saw in the vision rose into the air and left me. ²⁵Then I spoke to the people in exile. I told them about everything the LORD had shown me.

Ezekiel Leaves Like a Captive

12 Then the LORD spoke to me and said, ²"Son of man, you live among people who refuse to obey me. They have eyes to see what I have done for them, but they don't see those things. They have ears to hear what I told them to do, but they will not listen. They are people who refuse to obey. ³So, son of man, pack some things as if you are leaving on a journey. Pretend you are a prisoner being taken far away. Do this during the day so that everyone can see you. Even though these people refuse to listen to me, maybe when they see you going away, they will understand what I have been trying to tell them.

⁴"During the day, take your bags outside so that the people can see you. Then in the evening, pretend you are going away. Act as if you are a prisoner going to a faraway country. ⁵While the people are watching, make a hole in the wall and go out through that hole in the wall. ⁶At night, put your bag on your shoulder and leave. Cover your face so that you cannot see where you are going. You must do these things so that the people can see you, because I am using you as an example to the family of Israel."

⁷So I did as I was commanded. During the day, I took my bags and acted as if I were going to a faraway country. That evening, I used my hands and made a hole in the wall. During the night, I put my bag on my shoulder and left. I did this so that all the people could see me.

⁸The next morning, the LORD spoke to me and said, ⁹"Son of man, did the people of Israel—those people who always refuse to obey—ask you what you were doing? ¹⁰Tell them that this is what the Lord GOD says: 'This sad message is about the leader of Jerusalem and all the people of Israel who live there.' ¹¹Tell them, 'I am an example for all of you. What I have done will happen to you.' You will be forced to go to a faraway country as prisoners. ¹²And your leader will make a hole in the wall and sneak out at night. He will cover his face so that people will not recognize him. His eyes will not be able to see where he is going. ¹³He will try to escape, but I will catch him! He will be caught in my trap. Then I will bring him to Babylonia—the land of the Chaldeans. But he will not be able to see where he is going.*ᵈ ¹⁴I will force the king's people to live in the foreign countries around Israel, and I will scatter his army to the winds. The enemy soldiers will chase after them. ¹⁵Then they will know that I am the LORD. They will know that I scattered them among the nations. They will know that I forced them to go to other countries.

¹⁶"But I will let a few of the people live. They will not die from the disease, hunger and war. I will let them live so that they can tell other people about the terrible things they did against me. Then they will know that I am the LORD."

Shake With Fear

¹⁷Then the LORD spoke to me and said, ¹⁸"Son of man, you must act as if you are very frightened. You must shake when you eat your food. You must look worried and afraid when you drink your water. ¹⁹You must say this to the common people: 'This is what the Lord GOD says to the people living in Jerusalem and in the other parts

---

*ᵃ 11:19 spirit Or "wind".
*ᵇ 11:23 hill east of Jerusalem This is the Mount of Olives.
*ᶜ 11:24 Spirit Or "wind".
*ᵈ 12:13 But he . . . is going The enemy will poke out his eyes and make him blind.

of Israel. You will be very worried while you eat your food. You will be terrified while you drink your water, because everything in your country will be destroyed! This will happen because the people living there are so violent. [20]Many people live in your cities now, but those cities will be ruined. Your whole country will be destroyed! Then you will know that I am the LORD.'"

Disaster Will Come

[21]Then the LORD spoke to me and said, [22]"Son of man, why do people quote this saying about the land of Israel:

'Trouble will not come soon;
    what is seen in visions will not come'?

[23]"Tell the people that the Lord GOD will end that saying. They will not say that about Israel any more. Now they will quote this saying:

'Trouble will come soon;
    what is seen in visions will happen.'

[24]"There will not be any more false visions in Israel. There will not be any more magicians telling things that don't come true. [25]That's because I am the LORD, and if I say something will happen, it will happen! I will not wait any longer. Those troubles are coming soon—in your own lifetime. Hear me, you people who always refuse to obey! When I say something, I make it happen. This is what the Lord GOD says.'"

[26]Then the LORD spoke to me and said, [27]"Son of man, the people of Israel think that the visions I give you are for a time far in the future. They think you are talking about things that will happen many years from now. [28]So you must tell them this, 'The Lord GOD says: I will not delay any longer. If I say something will happen, it will happen! This is what the Lord GOD says.'"

Warnings Against False Prophets

13 Then the LORD spoke to me and said, [2]"Son of man, you must speak to the prophets of Israel for me. They are only saying what they want to say. You must speak to them. Tell them, 'Listen to this message from the LORD! [3]This is what the Lord GOD says. Bad things will happen to you foolish prophets. You are following your own spirits. You are not telling people what you really see in visions.

[4]"Israel, your prophets are false prophets. They are like jackals hunting for food among the ruins of a city. [5]You have not put guards where the city walls are broken. And you have not

repaired the walls to protect the family of Israel. So when the day comes for the LORD to punish you, you will lose the war!

[6]"Your prophets say they have seen visions. They did their magic to see what will happen next. But everything they said would happen is a lie. They claim to speak for the LORD, but the LORD did not send them. And they still think that what they said is what will happen.

[7]"If you prophets saw visions, they were not true. And all you got from your magic was lies! So how can you say that the LORD told you those things? I did not speak to you!

[8]"So now, the Lord GOD really will speak. He says: You told lies. You saw visions that were not true. So now I am against you! This is what the Lord GOD says. [9]I will punish those prophets who tell their false visions and lie about the future. I will remove them from my people. Their names will not be in the list of the family of Israel. They will never again come to the land of Israel. Then you will know that I am the Lord GOD!

[10]"Again and again those false prophets lied to my people. They said there would be peace, but there is no peace. The people need to repair the walls and prepare for war. But they only slap a thin coat of plaster[a] over the broken walls. [11]Tell them that I will send hail and a strong rain. The wind will blow hard, and a tornado will come. Then the wall will fall down. [12]When the wall falls down, the people will ask the prophets, "What happened to the plaster you put on the wall?" [13]The Lord GOD says, I am angry and I will send a storm against you. I am angry and I will send a strong rain. I am angry and I will make hail fall from the sky and completely destroy you! [14]You put plaster on the wall, but I will destroy the whole wall. I will pull it to the ground. The wall will fall on you, and then you will know that I am the LORD. [15]I will finish showing my anger against the wall and those who put plaster on it. Then I will say, "There is no wall, and there are no workers to put plaster on it. [16]All these things will happen to the false prophets of Israel. They speak to the people of Jerusalem and say there will be peace, but there is no peace. This is what the Lord GOD says.'"

[17]"Son of man, look at the women prophets in Israel. They say the things they want to say, so you must speak against them for me. You must say this to them: [18]'This is what the Lord GOD says: Bad things will happen to you women. You sew cloth bracelets for people to wear on their arms. You make special scarves for people to wear on their heads. ⌊You say those things have magic powers⌋ to control people's lives. You trap the

---

[a] **13:10** *plaster* A type of mud or cement that people used to cover a wall and make it smooth. This is also a wordplay. The Hebrew word is like the word meaning "It will fall". Also in verse 14.

people only to keep yourselves alive! [19]You make them think I am not important. You turn them against me for a few handfuls of barley and a few scraps of bread. You tell lies to my people. They love to listen to lies. You kill those who should live, and you let people live who should die. [20]So this is what the Lord GOD says to you: You make those cloth bracelets to trap people, but I will set them free. I will tear those bracelets off your arms, and the people will be free from you. They will be like birds flying from a trap. [21]And I will tear up those scarves and save my people from your power. They will escape from your trap, and you will know that I am the LORD.

[22]"You prophets tell lies. Your lies hurt good people—I did not want to hurt them! You support the wicked and encourage them. You don't tell them to change their lives. You don't try to save their lives! [23]So you will not see any more useless visions or do any more magic. I will save my people from your power, and you will know that I am the LORD.'"

Warnings Against Idol Worship

14 Some of the leaders of Israel came to me. They sat down to talk with me. [2]The LORD spoke to me and said, [3]"Son of man, these men came to talk to you. But they still have their filthy idols. They kept the things that made them sin. They still worship those statues, so why do they come to me for advice? Should I answer their questions? [4]But I will give them an answer. You must tell them this: 'This is what the Lord GOD says: If any Israelites come to a prophet and ask me for advice, I myself will answer their questions. I, the LORD, will answer them even if they still have their filthy idols, even if they have kept the things that made them sin, and even if they still worship those statues. I will speak to them in spite of all their filthy idols. [5]This is because I want to touch their hearts. I want to show them that I love them, even though they left me for their filthy idols.'

[6]"So tell the family of Israel, 'This is what the Lord GOD says: Come back to me and leave your filthy idols. Turn away from those terrible, false gods. [7]If any Israelites or foreigners who live in Israel come to me for advice, I will give them an answer. I, the LORD, will answer them even if they still have their filthy idols, even if they have kept the things that made them sin, and even if they worship those statues. This is the answer I will give them: [8]I will turn against them and destroy them. They will be an example to others. People will laugh at them. I will remove them from my people. Then you will know that I am the LORD!

[9]And if a prophet is foolish enough to give his own answer, I, the LORD, will show him how foolish he is! I will use my power against him. I will destroy him and remove him from among my people, Israel. [10]So both the one who came for advice and the prophet who gave an answer will get the same punishment. [11]Why? So that those prophets will stop leading my people away from me, and my people will stop being filthy with sin. Then they will be my special people, and I will be their God. This is what the Lord GOD says.'"

Jerusalem Will Be Punished

[12]Then the LORD spoke to me and said, [13]"Son of man, I will punish any nation that leaves me and sins against me. I will stop their food supply. I might cause a famine and remove the people and animals from that country. [14]I would punish that country even if Noah, Daniel and Job[a] lived there. They could save their own lives by their goodness, ˻but they could not save the whole country˼. This is what the Lord GOD says.

[15]"Or I might send wild animals through that country to kill all the people. Then no one would travel through that country because of the wild animals. [16]If Noah, Daniel and Job lived there, those three men could save their own lives. But I promise by my own life that they could not save the lives of other people—not even their own sons and daughters! That evil country would be destroyed. This is what the Lord GOD says.

[17]"Or I might send an enemy army to fight against that country. The soldiers would destroy that country—I would remove all the people and animals from that country. [18]If Noah, Daniel and Job lived there, those three men could save their own lives. But I promise by my own life that they could not save the lives of other people—not even their own sons and daughters! That evil country would be destroyed. This is what the Lord GOD says.

[19]"Or I might send a disease against that country. I will pour my anger down on the people. I will remove all the people and animals from that country. [20]If Noah, Daniel and Job lived there, those three men could save their own lives because they are good men. But I promise by my own life that they could not save the lives of other people—not even their own sons and daughters!

[21]"Yes, this is what the Lord GOD says: So think how bad it will be for Jerusalem. I will send all four of those punishments against that city! I will send enemy soldiers, hunger, disease and wild animals against that city. I will remove all the

---

[a] **14:14 Noah, Daniel and Job** Three men from ancient times. They were famous for being very good and wise men. Here, Daniel might be the Danel in the writings from Ras Shamra. Also in verses 16,18,20.

people and animals from that country. ²²Some of the people will escape from that country. They will bring their sons and daughters and come to you for help. Then you will see how bad those people really are, and you will feel better about all the troubles that I am bringing to Jerusalem. ²³You will see how they live and all the bad things they do. Then you will know that I had a good reason for punishing them. This is what the Lord GOD says."

Jerusalem, the Vine, Will Be Burned

15 Then the LORD spoke to me and said, ²"Son of man, are the pieces of wood from a grapevine*a* any better than the little branches cut from trees in the forest? ³You can't use its wood to make anything, can you? It's not even good for pegs to hang dishes on! ⁴It can be used to make a fire. But after the ends burn and the middle is scorched, what then? ⁵If you can't make anything from that wood before it is burned, you surely can't make anything after it has been burned! ⁶The people of Jerusalem are as useless as the wood from the grapevines growing among the trees of the forest. So I will throw them into the fire to burn like that wood! This is what the Lord GOD says. ⁷I will punish those people. But some of them will be like the sticks that don't burn completely. They will be punished, but they will not be destroyed completely. You will see that I punished them, and you will know that I am the LORD! ⁸I will destroy that country because the people left me ⌊to worship false gods⌋. This is what the Lord GOD says."

INSIGHT

Oh, how rude! The shocking, uncompromising language in much of this chapter shows how outraged God was with Jerusalem's unfaithfulness. But it ends with God promising that Jerusalem will be restored.

Ezekiel 16

God's Love for Jerusalem

16 Then the LORD spoke to me and said, ²"Son of man, tell the people of Jerusalem about the terrible things they have done. ³You must say, 'This is what the Lord GOD says to Jerusalem: Look at your history. You were born in Canaan. Your father was an Amorite. Your mother was a Hittite. ⁴Jerusalem, on the day you were born, there was no one to cut your navel cord. No one put salt on you and washed you to make you clean. No one wrapped you in cloth. ⁵No one felt sorry for you or took care of you. On the day you were born, your parents threw you out into the field, because no one wanted you.

⁶"Then I passed by. I saw you lying there, kicking in the blood. You were covered with blood, but I said, "Please live!" Yes, you were covered with blood, but I said, "Please live!" ⁷I helped you grow like a plant in the field. You grew and grew. You became a young woman: your periods began, your breasts grew, and your hair began to grow. But you were still bare and naked. ⁸I looked you over. I saw you were ready for love, so I spread my clothes over you*b* and covered your nakedness. I promised to marry you. I made the agreement*c* with you, and you became mine. This is what the Lord GOD says.

⁹"I washed you in water. I poured water over you to wash away the blood that was on you, and then I put oil on your skin. ¹⁰*d* I gave you a nice dress and soft leather sandals, a linen headband and a silk scarf. ¹¹I also gave you some jewellery. I put bracelets on your arms and a necklace around your neck. ¹²I gave you a nose ring, earrings and a beautiful crown to wear. ¹³You were beautiful in your gold and silver jewellery, and your linen, silk and embroidered material. You ate the best foods. You were very, very beautiful, and you became the queen! ¹⁴You became famous for your beauty, all because I made you so lovely! This is what the Lord GOD says.

Jerusalem, the Unfaithful Bride

¹⁵"But you began to trust in your beauty. Being well known, you became a prostitute and gave yourself to every man who passed by. Your beauty became theirs to enjoy! ¹⁶You took your beautiful clothes and used them to decorate your places for worship.*e* And you offered yourself as a prostitute there. You gave yourself to every man who came by! ¹⁷Then you took your beautiful jewellery that I gave you, and you used the gold and silver to make statues of men, and you had sex with them too! ¹⁸Then you took the beautiful cloth and made clothes for those statues. You took the perfume and incense I gave you and put it in front of those idols. ¹⁹I gave you bread, honey and oil, but you gave that food to your idols. You offered

---

a **15:2 grapevine** The prophets often compared Israel to a vineyard or grapevine. See verse 6.

b **16:8 spread my clothes over you** This showed that he was agreeing to protect her and care for her. See Ruth 3:1–15.

c **16:8 agreement** Here, this means the marriage agreement. But it also refers to the agreement God made with the people of Israel. See "AGREEMENT" in the Word List.

d **16:10 Verses 10–13** All the materials in this list are the things used in building the Holy Tent. See Exod. 25–40.

e **16:16 places for worship** Or "high places". See "HIGH PLACE" in the Word List. Also in verses 31,39.

them as a sweet smell to please your false gods. This actually happened! This is what the Lord God says.

²⁰"'You and I had children together, but you took our children. You killed them and gave them to those false gods! But that is only some of the evil things you did when you were unfaithful to me and went to those false gods. ²¹You slaughtered^a my sons and then passed them through the fire to those false gods. ²²You left me and did all those terrible things. You never remembered what happened when you were young. You did not remember that you were naked and kicking in blood when I found you.

²³"'After all these evil things, it will be very bad for you! This is what the Lord God says. ²⁴After all those things, you made a mound for worshipping that false god. You built places for worshipping those gods on every street corner. ²⁵There you made your beauty a disgrace. You used it to catch every man who walked by. You raised your skirt so that they could see your legs, and you offered yourself as a prostitute to them. ²⁶Then you went to Egypt, your neighbour that is always ready for sex. With more and more sexual sin, you made me angry. ²⁷So I punished you! I took away part of your land. I let your enemies, the daughters of the Philistines, do what they wanted to you. Even they were shocked at the evil things you did. ²⁸Then you went to have sex with Assyria. You could not get enough. You were never satisfied. ²⁹So you turned to Canaan, and then to Babylonia, and still you were not satisfied. ³⁰You are so weak. You let all those men cause you to sin. You acted just like a prostitute who wants to be the one in control. This is what the Lord God says.

³¹"'But you were not exactly like a prostitute. You built your mounds at the head of every road, and you built your places for worship at every street corner. You had sex with all those men, but you did not ask them to pay you the way a prostitute does. ³²You are a woman guilty of adultery. You would rather have sex with strangers than with your own husband. ³³Most prostitutes force men to pay them for sex, but you gave money to your many lovers. You paid all the men around to come in to have sex with you. ³⁴You are just the opposite of most prostitutes who force men to pay them, because you pay the men to have sex with you.

³⁵"'Prostitute, listen to the message from the Lord. ³⁶This is what the Lord God says: You have spent your money^b and let your lovers and filthy gods see your naked body and have sex with you. You have killed your children and poured out their blood. This was your gift to those false gods. ³⁷So I am bringing all of your lovers together. I will bring all the men you loved and all the men you hated. I will bring them all together and let them see you naked.^c They will see you completely naked. ³⁸Then I will punish you. I will punish you as a murderer and a woman who committed the sin of adultery. You will be punished as if by an angry and jealous husband. ³⁹I will let those lovers have you. They will destroy your mounds. They will burn your places for worship. They will tear off your clothes and take your beautiful jewellery. They will leave you bare and naked ⌊as you were when I found you⌋. ⁴⁰They will bring a crowd of people and throw rocks at you to kill you. Then they will cut you into pieces with their swords. ⁴¹They will burn your house. They will punish you so that all the other women can see. I will stop you from living like a prostitute. I will stop you from paying money to your lovers. ⁴²Then I will stop being angry and jealous. I will calm down. I will not be angry any more. ⁴³Why will all these things happen? Because you did not remember what happened when you were young. You did all those bad things and made me angry. So I had to punish you for doing them, but you planned even more terrible things. This is what the Lord God says.

⁴⁴"'All the people who talk about you will now have one more thing to say. They will say, "Like mother, like daughter." ⁴⁵You are your mother's daughter. You don't care about your husband or your children. You are like your sister. Both of you hated your husband and your children. ⌊You are like your parents.⌋ Your mother was a Hittite and your father was an Amorite. ⁴⁶Your older sister was Samaria. She lived to the north of you with her daughters. Your younger sister was Sodom.^d She lived to the south of you with her daughters. ⁴⁷You did all the terrible things they did, but you also did much worse! ⁴⁸I am the Lord God. As I live, I swear that your sister Sodom and her daughters never did as many bad things as you and your daughters.

⁴⁹"'Your sister Sodom and her daughters were proud. They had too much to eat and too much

---

^a **16:21 slaughtered** This usually means to kill an animal and cut it into pieces for meat, but it often means to kill people as if they were animals.

^b **16:36 spent your money** Literally, "poured out your copper". This might also mean "you have done the things that stain you with sin".

^c **16:37 let them see you naked** The Hebrew words are like the words meaning "to be carried away as a prisoner to a foreign country".

^d **16:46 Samaria . . . Sodom** Ezekiel is saying the people in Judah are just as evil as the people who lived in Samaria and Sodom—and those people were so evil that God completely destroyed those cities.

time on their hands, and they did not help poor, helpless people. [50]Sodom and her daughters became too proud and began to do terrible things in front of me. So I punished them!

[51]"And Samaria did only half as many bad things as you did. You did many more terrible things than Samaria! You have done so many more terrible things than your sisters have done. Sodom and Samaria seem good compared to you. [52]So you must bear your shame. You have made your sisters look good compared to you. You have done terrible things, so you should be ashamed.

[53]"I destroyed Sodom and the towns around it, and I destroyed Samaria and the towns around it. And I will destroy you too, Jerusalem. But I will build those cities again, and I will rebuild you too. [54]I will comfort you. Then you will remember the terrible things you have done, and you will be ashamed. [55]So you and your sisters will be rebuilt. Sodom and the towns around her, Samaria and the towns around her, and you and the towns around you will all be rebuilt.

[56]"In the past, you were proud and made fun of your sister Sodom. But you will not do that again. [57]You did that before you were punished, before your neighbours started making fun of you. The daughters of Edom[a] and Philistia are making fun of you now. [58]Now you must suffer for the terrible things you have done.'" This message is from the LORD.

God Remains Faithful

[59]"This is what the Lord GOD says: I will treat you like you treated me! You broke your marriage promise. You did not respect our agreement. [60]But I will remember the agreement we made when you were young. I made an agreement with you that will continue forever! [61]I will bring your sisters to you, and I will make them your daughters. That was not in our agreement, but I will do that for you. Then you will remember the terrible things you have done, and you will be ashamed. [62]So I will make my agreement with you, and you will know that I am the LORD. [63]You will remember me, and you will be so ashamed of the evil things you did that you will not be able to say anything. But I will make you pure, and you will never be ashamed again! This is what the Lord GOD says.'"

The Eagle and the Vine

17 Then the LORD spoke to me and said, [2]"Son of man, I have a story with a hidden meaning for you to tell the family of Israel. [3]Tell them that this is what the Lord GOD says:

"'A large eagle with big wings came to Lebanon.
He had feathers covered with spots.
[4]He broke the top off that big cedar tree and brought it to Canaan.
He set the branch down in a city of merchants.
[5]Then the eagle took some of the seeds from Canaan.
He planted them in good soil by a good river.
[6]The seeds grew and became a grapevine.
It was a good vine.
The vine was not tall,
but it spread to cover a large area.
The vine grew stems,
and smaller vines grew very long.
[7]Then another eagle with big wings saw the grapevine.
The eagle had many feathers.
The grapevine wanted this new eagle to care for it.
So it stretched its roots and branches towards the eagle.
Its branches stretched towards this eagle.
The branches grew away from the field where it was planted.
The grapevine wanted the new eagle to water it.
[8]The grapevine was planted in a good field near plenty of water.
It could have grown branches and fruit.
It could have become a very good grapevine.

[9]"This is what the Lord GOD says:
Do you think that plant will succeed?
No, the new eagle will pull the plant from the ground,
and the bird will break the plant's roots.
It will eat up all the grapes.
Then the new leaves will wilt.
That plant will be very weak.
It will not take strong arms
or a powerful nation to pull that plant up by the roots.
[10]Will the plant grow where it is planted?
No, the hot east wind will blow, and the plant will become dry and die.
It will die there where it was planted.'"

King Zedekiah Punished

[11]The LORD spoke to me and said, [12]"Explain this story to the people of Israel who always turn against me. Tell them this: 'The first eagle is the king of

---

a **16:57** *Edom* Or "Aram".

Babylonia. He came to Jerusalem and took away the king and other leaders. He brought them to Babylonia. ¹³Then Nebuchadnezzar made an agreement with a man from the king's family. Nebuchadnezzar forced that man to make a promise. So this man promised to be loyal to Nebuchadnezzar. Nebuchadnezzar made this man the new king of Judah. Then he took all the powerful men away from Judah. ¹⁴So Judah became a weak kingdom that could not turn against King Nebuchadnezzar. The people were forced to keep the agreement Nebuchadnezzar made with the new king of Judah. ¹⁵But this new king tried to rebel against Nebuchadnezzar anyway! He sent messengers to Egypt to ask for help. The new king asked for many horses and soldiers. Now, do you think the new king of Judah will succeed? Do you think the new king will have enough power to break the agreement and escape punishment?

¹⁶"The Lord GOD says: By my life, I swear that this new king will die in Babylonia! Nebuchadnezzar made this man the new king of Judah, but he broke his promise with Nebuchadnezzar. This new king ignored that agreement. ¹⁷The king of Egypt will not be able to save the king of Judah. He might send many soldiers, but Egypt's great power will not save Judah. Nebuchadnezzar's army will build dirt roads and dirt walls to capture the city. Many people will die. ¹⁸But the king of Judah will not escape, because he ignored his agreement. He broke his promise to Nebuchadnezzar. ¹⁹The Lord GOD makes this promise: By my life, I swear that I will punish the king of Judah, because he ignored my warnings and broke our agreement. ²⁰I will set my trap, and he will be caught in it. Then I will bring him to Babylon, and I will punish him there. I will punish him because he turned against me, ²¹and I will destroy his army. I will destroy his best soldiers and scatter them to the wind. Then you will know that I am the LORD and that I told you these things.

²²"This is what the Lord GOD says:

"'I will take a branch from a tall cedar tree.
I will take a small branch from the top of
the tree,
and I myself will plant it on a very high
mountain.
²³I myself will plant it on a high mountain in
Israel.
That branch will grow into a tree.
It will grow branches and make fruit
and become a beautiful cedar tree.
Many birds will sit on its branches
and live in the shadows under its branches.

²⁴"Then the other trees will know that
I, the LORD, make tall trees fall to the
ground,
and I make small trees grow tall.
I make green trees become dry,
and I make dry trees become green.
I am the LORD.
If I say that I will do something, then I will
do it!'"

True Justice

18 The LORD spoke to me and said, ²"Why do you people say this proverb:

'The parents ate the sour grapes,
but the children got the sour taste'?ᵃ

³"The Lord GOD says: By my life, I swear that people in Israel will not think this proverb is true any more! ⁴I will treat everyone, child and parent, just the same. The one who sins is the one who will die!

⁵"A person who is good will live! He is fair and does what is right. ⁶He doesn't go to the mountains to share food offered to idols. He doesn't pray to those filthy idols in Israel. He doesn't commit adultery with his neighbour's wife or have sex with a woman during her period. ⁷He doesn't take advantage of others. If someone borrows money from him, he might take something of value before he lends the money. But when that person pays him back, he returns what he took. He lends food to the hungry and clothes to people who need them. ⁸If someone wants to borrow money from him, he lends the money and doesn't charge interest on the loan. He refuses to be crooked. He is always fair with everyone. People can trust him. ⁹He obeys my laws and studies my rules so that he can learn to be fair and dependable. He is good, so he will live. This is what the Lord GOD says.

¹⁰"But someone like that might have a son who does not do any of these good things. The son steals things and kills people. ¹¹He does things his father never did. He goes to the mountains and eats foods offered to false gods. He commits the sin of adultery with his neighbour's wife. ¹²He mistreats poor, helpless people. He takes advantage of them. When a debt is paid,ᵇ he does not give back what he took from them. He prays to filthy idols and does other terrible things. ¹³He lends money to people who need it, but he forces them to pay interest on the loan. The evil son will not be allowed to live. He will be put to death because he did such terrible things, and he will be responsible for his own death.

ᵃ **18:2** *The parents . . . sour taste* This means the children were suffering for things their parents did.
ᵇ **18:12** *When a debt is paid* See Deut. 24:12–13 for the rules about making loans to the poor.

WHAT'S YOUR EXCUSE?

"It's easier for him to live a Christian life, because he has Christian parents."

"If you'd been through the things I've been through, you would understand."

"Everybody else is doing it – why shouldn't I?"

Recognize any of these excuses? The human heart developed a habit for pushing blame away from ourselves and towards someone else from day one: when God asked Adam why he'd eaten the forbidden fruit, he blamed his wife. When God asked his wife, she blamed the snake (Genesis 3:12–13).

For centuries before Ezekiel's time, God's people had been blaming their sinful ways upon the generations that went before (see Ezekiel 18:1–4). In fact it was such a popular excuse, it had become a proverb in their culture. But now God wants to rewrite the story.

DIG IN   READ Ezekiel 18:1–32

- What lifestyle does God approve of as good (vv.5–9,14–17)?
- What lifestyle does God consider sinful and worthy of death (vv.10–13)?
- How does he say he judges people (v.20)?

The story God shows Ezekiel concerns three generations of men – two who live upright lives and please God and one who lives wickedly and receives God's punishment. Notice how all three show that God is interested both in how we treat him and how we treat other people.

It's all designed to show that "A good man's goodness belongs to him alone, and a bad man's evil belongs to him alone" (v.20). In God's eyes, we are responsible for our own sin. There's no excuse good enough – we can't blame it on our upbringing, our brainpower, or our lack of people skills!

- What's God's attitude to change (vv.21–23)?

God doesn't just give us the option to change, he longs for us to change. He loves it when we come to our senses and turn around.

All this looks forward to what God has done through Jesus. We were all, at one time, heading in a direction against God and against his rules, living as evil people. But as soon as we turn to God he sees us as good – he takes no account of the way we used to live, or all the wrong things we've done. God doesn't remember all the bad things we did (v.22) because of Jesus' sacrificial death (Ephesians 1:7). (And amazingly, once we've turned to Jesus, we can know that his death has paid for all the sins we do now and in the future too!)

DIG THROUGH

- Search your heart: what things do you struggle with and what things about yourself do you blame on other people? Own up to them and ask for God's power to help you change.
- "The Lord GOD says, 'I don't want evil people to die. I want them to change their lives so that they can live!'" (v.23). How can we make this hopeful message loud and clear to people we know who don't yet know Jesus?

DIG DEEPER

The apostle Peter echoes verses 23 and 31 in 1 Peter 3:10–12 where he is quoting from Psalm 34:12–16. God wants everyone to have the chance to hear the Good News and respond. Real repentance means we first stop making excuses and own up to our sin.

¹⁴"Now, that evil son might also have a son. But this son sees the bad things his father has done, and he refuses to live as his father did. He treats people fairly. ¹⁵He does not go to the mountains and eat foods offered to false gods. He does not pray to filthy idols in Israel. He does not commit the sin of adultery with his neighbour's wife. ¹⁶He does not take advantage of people. If someone borrows money from him, the good son takes something of value and then gives the other person the money. When that person pays him back, the good son gives back what he took. The good son gives food to hungry people, and he gives clothes to those who need them. ¹⁷He helps the poor. If people want to borrow money, the good son lends them the money, and he does not charge interest on the loan. He obeys my laws and follows them. He will not be put to death for his father's sins. The good son will live. ¹⁸The father hurts people and steals things. He never does anything good for my people! He will die because of his own sins.

¹⁹"You might ask, 'Why will the son not be punished for his father's sins?' The reason is that the son was fair and did good things. He very carefully obeyed my laws, so he will live. ²⁰The one who sins is the one who will be put to death. A son will not be punished for his father's sins, and a father will not be punished for his son's sins. A good man's goodness belongs to him alone, and a bad man's evil belongs to him alone.

²¹"Now, if evil people change their lives, they will live and not die. They might stop doing all the bad things they did and begin to carefully obey all my laws. They might become fair and good. ²²God will not remember all the bad things they did. He will remember only their goodness, so they will live! ²³The Lord GOD says, I don't want evil people to die. I want them to change their lives so that they can live!

²⁴"Now, maybe good people might stop being good. They might change their lives and begin to do all the terrible things that evil people have done in the past. (The evil people changed, so they can live.) So if those good people change and become bad, God will not remember all the good things they did. He will remember that they turned against him and began to sin. So they will die because of their sin.

²⁵"You people might say, 'The Lord isn't fair!' But listen, family of Israel. I am fair. You are the ones who are not fair! ²⁶If good people change and become evil, they must die for the bad things they do. ²⁷And if evil people change and become good and fair, they will save their lives. They will live! ²⁸They saw how wicked they were and came back to me. They stopped doing the evil things they did in the past. So they will live! They will not die!

²⁹The people of Israel said, 'That's not fair! The Lord isn't fair!'

"I am fair! You are the ones who are not fair! ³⁰Why? Because, family of Israel, I will judge each of you only for what you do! This is what the Lord GOD says. So come back to me! Stop committing those crimes and do away with those things that cause you to sin! ³¹Throw away all the terrible idols with which you committed your crimes! Change your heart and spirit. People of Israel, why should you do things that will cost you your life? ³²I don't want to kill you! Please come back and live! This is what the Lord GOD says.

A Sad Song About Israel

19 "You must sing this sad song about the leaders of Israel:

²"'Your mother is like a female lion,
  lying there with the male lions.
She went to lie down with
  the young male lions and had many babies.
³One of her cubs gets up.
  He has grown to be a strong young lion.
He has learned to catch his food.
  He killed and ate a man.

⁴"'The people heard him roar,
  and they caught him in their trap.
They put hooks in his mouth
  and carried the young lion to Egypt.

⁵"'The mother lion had hoped that cub would
    become the leader,
  but now she has lost all hope.
So she took another of her cubs
  and trained him to be a lion.
⁶He hunted with the adult lions
  and became a strong young lion.
He learned to catch his food.
  He killed and ate a man.
⁷He attacked the palaces and destroyed the
    cities.
  Everyone in that country was too afraid to
    speak when hearing his growl.
⁸Then the people who lived around him set a
    trap for him,
  and they caught him in their trap.
⁹They put hooks on him and locked him up.
  They had him in their trap,
  so they took him to the king of Babylon.
And now, you cannot hear his roar
  on the mountains of Israel.

¹⁰"'Your mother is like a grapevine
  planted near the water.
She had plenty of water,
  so she grew many strong vines.

¹¹Then she grew large branches.
    They were like a strong walking stick.
    They were like a king's sceptre.
The vine grew taller and taller.
    It had many branches and reached to the
       clouds.
¹²But the vine was pulled up by the roots,
    and thrown down to the ground.
The hot east wind blew and dried its fruit.
    The strong branches broke, and they were
       thrown into the fire.

¹³"'Now that grapevine is planted in the desert.
    It is a very dry and thirsty land.
¹⁴A fire started in the large branch
    and spread to destroy all its vines and fruit.
So there was no strong walking stick.
    There was no king's sceptre.'

"This was a sad song about death, and it was sung as a sad song about death."

Israel Turned Away From God

20 One day, some of the leaders of Israel came to me to ask the LORD for advice. This was on the tenth day of the fifth month of the seventh year of exile.ᵃ The leaders sat down in front of me.

²Then the LORD spoke to me and said, ³"Son of man, speak to the leaders of Israel. Tell them, 'This is what the Lord GOD says: Have you come to ask me what you should do? I, the Lord GOD, tell you that, as surely as I live, I will not listen to you.' ⁴Should you judge them? Will you judge them, son of man? You must tell them about the terrible things their fathers have done. ⁵You must tell them, 'This is what the Lord GOD says: On the day I chose Israel, I raised my hand to Jacob's family and made a promise to them in Egypt. When I let them know who I was, I raised my hand and said: "I am the LORD your God." ⁶On that day, I promised to take you out of Egypt and lead you to the land I was giving to you. That was a good land filled with many good things.ᵇ It was the most beautiful of all countries!

⁷"'I told the family of Israel to throw away their horrible idols. I told them not to become filthy with those filthy statues from Egypt. I said, "I am the LORD your God." ⁸But they turned against me and refused to listen to me. They did not throw away their horrible idols. They did not leave their filthy statues in Egypt. So I decided to destroy them in Egypt—to let them feel the full force of my anger. ⁹But I did not destroy them. I had already told the Egyptians that I would bring my people out of Egypt. I did not want to ruin my good name,

so I did not destroy Israel in front of those other people. ¹⁰I brought the family of Israel out of Egypt. I led them into the desert. ¹¹Then I gave them my laws and told them all my rules. All those who obey them will live. ¹²I also told them about all the special days of rest, which were a special sign between us. They showed that I am the LORD and that I was making them special to me.

¹³"'But the family of Israel turned against me in the desert. They did not follow my laws. They refused to obey my rules—even though people who obey my laws live because of them. They treated my special days of rest as if they were not important. They worked on those days many times. I decided to destroy them in the desert—to let them feel the full force of my anger. ¹⁴But I did not destroy them. The other nations saw me bring Israel out of Egypt. I did not want to ruin my good name, so I did not destroy Israel in front of those other people. ¹⁵I made another promise to those people in the desert. I promised that I would not bring them into the land I was giving them. That was a good land filled with many good things. It was the most beautiful of all countries!

¹⁶"'The people of Israel refused to obey my rules or to follow my laws. They treated my days of rest as if they were not important. They did all these things because their hearts belonged to their filthy idols. ¹⁷But I felt sorry for them, so I did not destroy them. I did not completely destroy them in the desert. ¹⁸I spoke to their children and told them, "Don't be like your parents. Don't make yourselves filthy with their filthy idols. Don't follow their laws or obey their commands. ¹⁹I am the LORD. I am your God. Obey my laws and keep my commands. Do the things I tell you. ²⁰Show that my days of rest are important to you. Remember, they are a special sign between us. I am the LORD, and these days show you that I am your God."

²¹"'But the children turned against me and did not obey my laws. They did not keep my commands—even though people who obey my laws live because of them. They treated my special days of rest as though they were not important. So I decided to destroy them completely in the desert—to let them feel the full force of my anger. ²²But I stopped myself. The other nations saw me bring Israel out of Egypt. I did not want to ruin my good name, so I did not destroy Israel in front of those other people. ²³So I made a vow against those people in the desert. I vowed to scatter them among the nations, to send them to many different countries.

²⁴"'The people of Israel did not obey my commands. They refused to obey my laws. They

---

ᵃ **20:1** *seventh year of exile* This was the summer of 591 BC.
ᵇ **20:6** *land . . . things* Literally, "land flowing with milk and honey". Also in verse 15.

treated my special days of rest as though they were not important, and they worshipped the filthy idols of their fathers. 25So I gave them laws that were not good. I gave them commands that would not bring life. 26I let them make themselves filthy with their gifts. They even began to sacrifice their own firstborn children. In this way I would destroy them. Then they would know that I am the LORD.' 27So now, son of man, speak to the family of Israel. Tell them, 'This is what the Lord GOD says: The people of Israel said bad things about me and made evil plans against me. 28But I still brought them to the land I promised to give them. They saw all the hills and green trees, so they went to all those places to worship. They took their sacrifices and anger offerings*a* to all those places. They offered their sacrifices that made a sweet smell, and they offered their drink offerings at those places. 29I asked the people of Israel why they were going to the high places. But that high place is still there today.'*b*

30"Since Israel did those things, speak to them and tell them, 'This is what the Lord GOD says: You people are polluting yourselves by doing the things your ancestors did. By offering yourselves as prostitutes to their sickening idols, you make yourselves unfaithful to me. Is that what you want? 31You offer to those idols the same gifts your ancestors did. You are putting your children in the fire as an offering to your false gods. You are still polluting yourselves with these filthy idols today! Do you really think that I should let you come to me and ask me for advice? I am the Lord GOD. By my life, I swear that I will not answer your questions or give you advice! 32You keep saying you want to be like the other nations. You live like the people in other nations. You serve pieces of wood and stone idols!

33"'By my life, says the Lord GOD, I swear that I will rule over you as king. But I will raise my powerful arm and punish you. I will show my anger against you! 34I will bring you out of these other nations. I scattered you among these nations, but I will gather you together and bring you back from these countries. But I will raise my powerful arm and punish you. I will show my anger against you! 35I will lead you into a desert as I did before, but this will be a place where other nations live. We will stand face to face, and I will judge you. 36I will judge you as I judged your ancestors in the desert near Egypt. This is what the Lord GOD says.

37"I will judge you guilty and punish you according to the agreement. 38I will remove all those who turned against me and sinned against me. I will remove them from your homeland. They will never again come to the land of Israel. Then you will know that I am the LORD.

39"'Now, family of Israel, this is what the Lord GOD says: Whoever wants to worship their filthy idols, let them go and worship them. But later, don't think you will get any advice from me. You will not ruin my name any more—not when you continue to give your gifts to your filthy idols! 40The Lord GOD says: People must come to my holy mountain—the high mountain in Israel—to serve me! The whole family of Israel will be on their land; they will be there in their country. There you can come to ask me for advice, and you must come there to bring me your offerings. You must bring the first part of your crops to me there. You must bring all your holy gifts to me in that place. 41Then I will be pleased with the sweet smell of your sacrifices. That will happen when I bring you back. I scattered you among many nations, but I will gather you together and make you my special people again. And all the nations will see it. 42Then you will know that I am the LORD. You will know this when I bring you back to the land of Israel, the land I promised to give to your ancestors. 43In that country you will remember all the evil things you did that made you filthy, and you will be ashamed. 44Family of Israel, you did many evil things, and you should be destroyed because of them. But to protect my good name, I will not give you the punishment you really deserve. Then you will know that I am the LORD. This is what the Lord GOD says.'"

45Then the LORD spoke to me and said, 46"Son of man, look towards the Negev. Speak against the southern part of Judah. Tell them what will happen to the Negev Forest.*c* 47Say to the Negev Forest, 'Listen to the word of the LORD. This is what the Lord GOD says: Look, I am ready to start a fire in your forest. The fire will destroy every green tree and every dry tree. The flame that burns will not be put out. All the land from south to north will be burned by the fire. 48Then all people will see that I, the LORD, have started the fire. The fire will not be put out!'"

49Then I said, "Oh, Lord GOD! If I say this, the people will say that I am only telling them stories."

---

a 20:28 *anger offerings* The people called these meals "fellowship offerings", but Ezekiel is making fun of them and saying that those meals only made God angry.
b 20:29 *But that . . . today* Literally, "And its name is still called Bamah (high place) to this day."
c 20:46 *Negev Forest* God is probably making fun of the people. The Negev is a desert area. There are no forests in the Negev.

Babylon, the Sword

21 So the word of the LORD came to me again: [2]"Son of man, look towards Jerusalem and speak against their holy places. Speak against the land of Israel for me. [3]Say to the land of Israel, 'This is what the LORD says: I am against you! I will pull my sword from its sheath. I will remove all people from you—the good and the evil. [4]I will cut off both good people and evil people from you. I will pull my sword from its sheath and use it against all people from south to north. [5]Then everyone will know that I am the LORD. They will know that I have pulled my sword from its sheath. My sword will not go back into its sheath again until it is finished.'

[6]"Son of man, make sad sounds like a sad person with a broken heart. Make these sad sounds in front of the people. [7]Then they will ask you, 'Why are you making these sad sounds?' Then you must say, 'Because of the sad news that is coming. Every heart will melt with fear. All hands will become weak. Every spirit will become weak. All knees will be like water.' Look, that bad news is coming. These things will happen! This is what the Lord GOD says."

The Sword Is Ready

[8]The LORD spoke to me and said, [9]"Son of man, speak for me and say, 'This is what the Lord says:

"'Look, a sword, a sharp sword,
    and it has been polished.
[10]The sword was made sharp for killing.
    It was polished to flash like lightning.
My son, you ran away from the stick I used to
        punish you.
    You refused to be punished with that
        wooden stick.
[11]So the sword has been made ready.
    Now it can be used.
The sword is sharpened and polished,
    ready for the hand of the killer.

[12]"'Son of man, shout and scream,
    beat your chest to show your sorrow,
because that sword will be used against my
        people
    and against all the rulers of Israel.
When the enemy comes,
    the rulers will be killed with the rest of my
        people.
[13]I will put them all to the test,
    because my punishment did not make them
        change.
This is what the Lord GOD says.'

[14]"Son of man, speak to the people for me.
    Strike your hands together!
Let the sword come down twice, no, three
        times!
    This is a sword for killing.
It is a sword for killing many, many people.
    It will cut into them from every side.
[15]Their hearts will melt with fear,
    and many people will fall.
The sword is ready at their city gates.
    It has been polished for killing and will flash
        like lightning.
[16]Sword, be sharp!
    Cut on the right side.
    Cut straight ahead.
    Cut on the left side.
Go wherever your edge was chosen to go.

[17]"Then I, too, will clap my hands
    and stop showing my anger.
I, the LORD, have spoken!"

Jerusalem Punished

[18]The LORD spoke to me and said, [19]"Son of man, draw a map showing two roads that the king of Babylon can follow with his sword in hand. Both roads will begin at the same place, but then they will separate and go in different directions. At that place you should put up a sign. [20]The sign should show where each road goes. One road leads to the Ammonite city of Rabbah. The other road leads to Judah, to the protected city, Jerusalem. [21]The king of Babylon will come to where the two roads separate. He will decide which way to go by using different kinds of magic—shaking his arrows, asking his family idols, and looking at the liver[a] from an animal he has killed.

INSIGHT

Liver (often from a sheep) was used for divination (a bit like fortune-telling) by those who believed in false gods, because it was considered to be the source of blood and the basis of life itself. It was divided into sections with each one representing a particular god. Specially trained priests were used to interpret the "signs".

Ezekiel 21:21

---

[a] 21:21 *arrows, idols, liver* People who believed in false gods used these things to try to learn the future.

²²"These things will point to the road on his right, the road leading to Jerusalem. They will tell him to attack it with battering rams[a] and command his soldiers to begin the killing. They will shout the battle cry and set the battering rams against the gates. They will build a wall of dirt around the city and a road leading up to the walls. They will build wooden towers to attack the city. ²³But the people in Jerusalem will think this is all a big mistake. They will not believe that this could happen, because they had made a peace agreement with Babylon's king. But the king will remind them that they are guilty of breaking that agreement, and he will take them captive.

²⁴"This is what the Lord GOD says: 'You have done many evil things. Your sins are very clear. You forced me to remember that you are guilty, so the enemy will catch you in his hand. ²⁵And you, evil leader of Israel, you will be killed. Your time of punishment has come! The end is here!

²⁶"This is what the Lord GOD says: Take off the turban! Take off the crown! The time has come to change. The important leaders will be brought low, and those who are not important now will become important leaders. ²⁷I will completely destroy that city! But this will not happen until the right man becomes the new king. Then I will let him have this city.'

The Ammonites Punished

²⁸"Son of man, speak to the people for me. Say, 'This is what the Lord GOD says to the people of Ammon and their shameful god:

"'Look, a sword!
    The sword is out of its sheath.
    It has been polished.
The sword is ready to kill.
    It was polished to flash like lightning!

²⁹"'Your visions are useless.
    Your magic will not help you.
    It is only a bunch of lies.
The sword is now at the throats of evil men.
    They will soon be only dead bodies.
Their time has come.
    The time has come for their evil to end.

Prophecy Against Babylon

³⁰"'Put the sword back in its sheath. Babylon, I will judge you in the place where you were created, in the land where you were born. ³¹I will pour out my anger against you. My anger will burn you like a hot wind. I will hand you over to cruel men.[b] Those men are skilled at killing

people. ³²You will be like fuel for the fire. Your blood will flow deep into the earth—people will never remember you again. I, the LORD, have spoken!'"

Ezekiel Speaks Against Jerusalem

22 The LORD spoke to me and said, ²"Son of man, will you judge the city of murderers? Will you tell her about all the terrible things she has done? ³You must say, 'This is what the Lord GOD says: The city is full of murderers, so her time of punishment will come. She made filthy idols for herself, and those idols made her filthy!

⁴"'People of Jerusalem, you killed many people. You made filthy idols. You are guilty, and the time has come to punish you. Your end has come. Other nations will make fun of you and laugh at you. ⁵People far and near will make fun of you. You have ruined your name. You are filled with confusion.

⁶"'Look, all the leaders in Israel are using their strength just to kill other people. ⁷And the people in Jerusalem don't respect their parents. There in the city, they mistreat the foreigners. They cheat orphans and widows in that place. ⁸You hate all that I consider holy. You treat my special days of rest as if they are not important. ⁹In Jerusalem, people tell lies in order to kill innocent people. They go to the mountains to worship false gods and then come back to Jerusalem to eat their fellowship meals.

"'In Jerusalem, people commit many sexual sins. ¹⁰There men commit sexual sins with their father's wife. There the men rape women—even during their monthly period of bleeding. ¹¹One man commits a terrible sin against his own neighbour's wife. Another man has sex with his daughter-in-law and makes her unclean. Another man rapes his father's daughter—his very own sister. ¹²There men accept bribes to kill people. You lend money and charge interest on the loans. You cheat your neighbours just to make a little money. You have even forgotten me. This is what the Lord GOD says.

¹³"'Now look! I will slam my hand down and stop you! I will punish you for cheating and killing people. ¹⁴Will you be brave then? Will you be strong at the time I come to punish you? I am the LORD. I have spoken, and I will do what I said! ¹⁵I will scatter you among the nations. I will force you to go to many countries. I will completely destroy the filthy things in this city. ¹⁶But Jerusalem, you will become unclean. And the other nations will see all these things happen. Then you will know that I am the LORD.'"

---

[a] 21:22 **battering rams** Heavy logs that soldiers used to break holes into the gates or walls around a city.
[b] 21:31 **cruel men** This is a wordplay. The Hebrew word is like the word meaning "to burn".

Israel Is Like Worthless Waste

[17]The LORD spoke to me and said, [18]"Son of man, bronze, iron, lead and tin are important metals, but when a worker melts silver to make it pure, those metals are poured off as waste. Israel has become like that waste to me. [19]So this is what the Lord GOD says: 'All of you have become like worthless waste. So I will gather you into Jerusalem. [20]Workers put silver, bronze, iron, lead and tin into a fire. They blow on the fire to make it hotter. Then the metals begin to melt. In the same way, I will put you in my fire and melt you. That fire is my hot anger. [21]I will put you in my fire of anger and blow on it, and you will begin to melt. [22]In that city, you will be like silver melting in a fire. Then you will know that I am the LORD, and that I poured out my anger on you.'"

Ezekiel Speaks Against Jerusalem

[23]The LORD spoke to me and said, [24]"Son of man, speak to Israel. Tell her that she is not pure.[a] I am angry at that country, so that country has not received its rain. [25]The prophets in Jerusalem are making evil plans. They are like a lion—it roars when it begins to eat the animal it caught. They have destroyed many lives. They have taken many valuable things and made widows of many of the women in Jerusalem.

[26]"The priests have really hurt my teachings. They don't respect my holy things—they don't show that they are important. They treat holy things the same as things that are not holy. They treat clean things like things that are unclean. They don't teach the people about these things. They refuse to respect my special days of rest. They treat me as though I am not important.

[27]"The leaders in Jerusalem are like a wolf eating the animal it has caught. They attack people and kill them just to get rich.

[28]"The prophets don't warn the people—they cover up the truth. They are like workers who don't really repair a wall—they only put plaster over the holes. They only see lies. They do their magic to learn the future, but they only tell lies. They say, 'This is what the Lord GOD said.' But they are only lying—the LORD did not speak to them!

[29]"The common people take advantage of each other. They cheat and steal from each other. They get rich by taking advantage of poor, helpless beggars and they really cheat the foreigners. They are not fair to them at all!

[30]"I asked the people to ⌊change their lives and⌋ protect their country. I asked people to repair the walls. I wanted them to stand by those holes in the wall and fight to protect their city. But no one came to help! [31]So I will show them my anger—I will completely destroy them. I will punish them for the evil things they have done. It is all their fault. This is what the Lord GOD says."

23

The LORD spoke to me and said, [2]"Son of man, listen to this story about Samaria and Jerusalem. There were two sisters, daughters of the same mother. [3]They became prostitutes in Egypt while they were still young girls. That's where they first let men touch and handle their young breasts. [4]The older daughter was named Oholah,[b] and her sister was named Oholibah.[c] They became my wives, and we had children. I am using the name Oholah to mean Samaria and the name Oholibah to mean Jerusalem.

[5]"Then Oholah became unfaithful to me—she began to live like a prostitute. She began to want her lovers. She saw the Assyrian soldiers [6]in their blue uniforms. They were all handsome young men riding horses. They were leaders and officers, [7]and Oholah gave herself to them. They were handpicked soldiers in the Assyrian army, and she wanted them all! She polluted herself with their filthy idols. [8]She continued the prostitution she began in Egypt. There men made love to her when she was a young girl. They touched her young breasts and used her as a prostitute. [9]So I let her lovers have her. She wanted Assyria, so I gave her to them! [10]They raped[d] her. They took her children and killed her. They punished her, and women still talk about her.

[11]"Her younger sister Oholibah saw all these things happen. But Oholibah sinned more than her sister did! She was more unfaithful than Oholah. [12]She wanted the Assyrian leaders and officers. She wanted those soldiers in blue uniforms riding their horses. They were all handsome young men. [13]I saw that both women were going to ruin their lives with the same mistakes.

[14]"Oholibah continued to be unfaithful to me. In Babylon, she saw pictures of men carved on the walls. These were pictures of Chaldean men wearing their red uniforms. [15]They wore belts around their waists and long turbans on their heads. All those men looked like chariot officers. They all looked like native-born Babylonian men, [16]and Oholibah wanted them. [17]So the Babylonian

---

[a] **22:24** *not pure* This is a wordplay. The Hebrew word also means "not rained on".

[b] **23:4** *Oholah* This name means "Tent". It probably refers to the Holy Tent where the people of Israel went to worship God.

[c] **23:4** *Oholibah* This name means "My Tent is in her".

[d] **23:10** *raped* Literally, "revealed her nakedness". The Hebrew word meaning "revealed" is like the word meaning "carried away as a prisoner to a faraway country".

men came to her bed to have sex with her, using her to satisfy themselves. When they finished with her, she turned away from them with nothing but bad feelings.

18"Oholibah[a] let everyone see that she was unfaithful. She let so many men enjoy her naked body that I turned away from her with the same kind of bad feelings I had before towards her sister. 19But Oholibah thought about her time as a prostitute in Egypt when she was young, and she turned to even more prostitution. 20She remembered the lovers who excited her there, who were like animals in their sexual desires and abilities.

21"Oholibah, you dreamed of those times when you were young, when your lovers touched and handled your young breasts. 22So, Oholibah, this is what the Lord GOD says: You grew tired of your lovers, but I will bring them here to attack you from all sides. 23I will bring all the men from Babylon, especially the Chaldeans. I will bring the men from Pekod, Shoa and Koa and all the men from Assyria. I will bring all the leaders and officers, all those handsome young men, chariot officers and handpicked soldiers riding their horses. 24That crowd of men will come to you in large groups, riding on their horses and in their chariots. They will have their spears, shields and helmets. They will gather around you, and I will tell them what you have done to me. Then they will punish you their own way. 25I will show you how jealous I am. They will become angry and hurt you. They will cut off your nose and ears. They will kill you with a sword. Then they will take your children and burn whatever is left of you. 26They will take your nice clothes and jewellery. 27This is how I will stop your shameful acts and your love affair with Egypt. You will stop wishing you could go back there. You will never remember Egypt again!

28"This is what the Lord GOD says: I am giving you to those you hate, to those you thought were sickening. 29And they will show how much they hate you! They will take everything you worked for, and they will leave you bare and naked! Everyone will see that you are nothing but a prostitute. Your own shameful sins 30are the reason I am punishing you. You acted like a prostitute with other nations, polluting yourself by worshipping their idols. 31You followed the example of your sister Oholah.[b] So I will punish you the same way. I will give you the same cup I gave her to drink.

32"This is what the Lord GOD says:

"You will drink from your sister's cup,
    a big cup, tall and wide.
It holds so much that after you drink it all,
    everyone will laugh and make fun of you.
33You will be drunk and miserable,
    because that cup is full of fear and ruin.
    It is the same cup your sister Samaria drank.
34You will drink until the cup is empty.
    Then you will break it to pieces
    and use them to tear at your breasts.
This will happen because I, the Lord GOD,
    have said so.

35"So this is what the Lord GOD says: Jerusalem, you forgot me. You threw me away and left me behind. So now you must suffer for leaving me and living like a prostitute. You must suffer for your wicked dreams."

Judgement Against Oholah and Oholibah

36The LORD said to me, "Son of man, will you judge Oholah and Oholibah? Then tell them about the terrible things they have done. 37They committed the sin of adultery. They are guilty of murder. They acted like prostitutes—they left me to be with their filthy idols. They had my children, but they forced them to pass through fire. They did this to give food to their filthy idols. 38They also treated my special days of rest and my holy place as though they were not important. 39They killed their children for their idols, and then they went into my holy place and made it filthy too! They did this inside my Temple!

40"They even sent messengers to invite men to come from faraway places. And when the men came, the two sisters bathed themselves, painted their eyes, and put on jewellery. 41They sat on a fine bed with a table set before it, where they had put my incense[c] and my oil.[d]

42"The noise coming from the room sounded like a crowd of people having a party. A lot of rowdy drunkards had come in from the desert. They put bracelets and beautiful crowns on both sisters. 43One of the sisters was worn out from her sexual sins. And I wondered, 'Do they really want to have more sex with her?' 44But they kept

---

[a] **23:18 Oholibah** That is, the city of Jerusalem. See verse 4.

[b] **23:31 Oholah** Samaria. See 23:4.

[c] **23:41 my incense** A special blend of spices that were burned as a gift to God. This special incense was to be burned only in the Temple. See Exod. 30:34–38.

[d] **23:41 my oil** The special oil that was used for anointing priests and things in the Temple to make them holy (special). See Exod. 30:22–33.

going to her as they would go to a prostitute. Yes, they went again and again to Oholah and Oholibah, those wicked women.

⁴⁵"But honest judges will find them guilty of adultery and murder, because they have been unfaithful, and their hands are covered with blood! ⁴⁶"This is what the Lord GOD says: Bring an army against them to attack them and fill them with terror. ⁴⁷The soldiers will throw stones on these women and cut them to pieces with their swords. They will kill their children and burn their houses.

⁴⁸"To Oholah and Oholibah I say: 'This is how I will remove such indecent behaviour from the land. And this will be a warning to all the other women not to do the shameful things you have done. ⁴⁹You will get what you deserve for your indecent acts. You will be punished for your sinful worship of idols. Then you will know that I am the Lord GOD.'"

The Pot and the Meat

24 The word of the LORD came to me. This was on the tenth day of the tenth month in the ninth year of exile.ᵃ He said, ²"Son of man, write today's date and this note: 'On this day the army of the king of Babylon surrounded Jerusalem.' ³The people there refuse to obey me. I have a story with a message for them. Tell them, 'This is what the Lord GOD says:

"'Put the pot on the fire.
    Put on the pot and pour in the water.
⁴Put in the pieces of meat.
    Put in every good piece, the thighs and the
        shoulders.
Fill the pot with the best bones.
⁵   Use the best animals in the flock.
Pile the wood under the pot,
    and boil the pieces of meat.
    Boil the soup until even the bones are cooked.

⁶"'So this is what the Lord GOD says:
It will be bad for Jerusalem.
    It will be bad for that city of murderers.
Jerusalem is like a pot with rust on it,
    and those spots of rust cannot be removed!
That pot is not clean, and the rust cannot be
        removed,
    so the meat must be thrown out and not
        divided among the priests.
⁷Jerusalem is like a pot with rust on it.

This is because the blood from the murders
    is still there!
She put the blood on the bare rock.
    She did not pour the blood on the ground
        and cover it with dirt.ᵇ
⁸I put her blood on the bare rock
    so it would not be covered.
I did this so that people would become angry
    and punish her for killing innocent people.

⁹"'So this is what the Lord GOD says:
It will be bad for that city of murderers!
    I will pile up plenty of wood for the fire.
¹⁰Put plenty of wood under the pot.
    Light the fire.
Cook the meat until it is well done.
    Mix in the spices,ᶜ
    and let the bones be burned up.
¹¹Then let the pot stand empty on the coals.
    Let it become so hot that its stainsᵈ begin
        to glow.
Those stains will be melted away.
    The rust will be destroyed.

¹²"'Jerusalem might work hard
    to scrub away her stains.
But that "rust" will not go away!
    Only the fire of punishment will remove it.

¹³"'You sinned against me
    and became stained with sin.
I wanted to wash you and make you clean,
    but the stains would not come out.
I will not try washing you again
    until my hot anger is finished with you!

¹⁴"I am the LORD. I said your punishment would come, and I will make it happen. I will not hold back the punishment or feel sorry for you. I will punish you for the evil things you did. This is what the Lord GOD says.'"

The Death of Ezekiel's Wife

¹⁵Then the LORD spoke to me and said, ¹⁶"Son of man, you love your wife very much, but I am going to take her away from you. Your wife will die suddenly, but you must not show your sadness. You must not cry loudly. You will cry and your tears will fall, ¹⁷but you must mourn quietly. Dress as you normally do; wear your turban and sandals; don't cover your moustache, and don't eat the food people normally eat when someone dies."

ᵃ **24:1 ninth year of exile** This was 15 January 588 BC.
ᵇ **24:7 blood . . . dirt** The Law of Moses teaches that whoever killed an animal for food must pour the blood on the ground and cover it with dirt. This showed that they were giving the life of that animal back to God. See Lev. 17:1–16 and Deut. 12:1–25. If the blood was not covered with dirt, it was a witness against the killer. See Gen. 4:10, Job 15:18 and Isa. 26:21.
ᶜ **24:10 Mix in the spices** The meaning of this sentence is uncertain.
ᵈ **24:11 stains** Or "bronze".

[18]The next morning I told the people what God had said. That evening, my wife died. The next morning I did what God commanded. [19]Then the people said to me, "Why are you doing this? What does it mean?"

[20]Then I told them that the LORD had spoken to me, [21]telling me to give a message to the family of Israel. "This is what the Lord GOD says: 'Look, I will destroy my holy place. You are proud of that place and sing songs of praise about it. You love to see it. You really love that place. But I will destroy it, and your children that you left behind will be killed in battle. [22]But you will do the same things as Ezekiel has done. You will not cover your moustache or eat the food people normally eat when someone dies. [23]You will wear your turbans and your sandals. You will not show your sadness publicly or cry publicly, but you will waste away with guilt and talk to each other quietly about your grief. [24]So Ezekiel is an example for you. You will do the same things he has done. That time of punishment will come, and then you will know that I am the Lord GOD.'"

[25-26]The Lord said, "Son of man, I will take away the place that makes the people feel safe—Jerusalem, that beautiful city that makes them so happy. They really love that place. They love to look at it. But I will take it away from them, and I will also take their children. On that day one of the survivors will come to you with the bad news about Jerusalem. [27]That same day you will get your voice back. You will be able to talk to the messenger. You will not be silent any more. This will be a sign to the people, and they will know that I am the LORD."

Prophecy Against Ammon

25 The LORD spoke to me and said, [2]"Son of man, look towards the people of Ammon and speak against them for me. [3]Give them this message from the Lord GOD: 'You people shouted for joy when my holy place was destroyed. You were against the land of Israel when it was polluted. You were against the family of Judah when the people were carried away as prisoners. [4]So I will give you to the people from the east. They will get your land. Their armies will set up their camps in your country and will live among you. They will eat your fruit and drink your milk.

[5]"'I will make the city Rabbah a pasture for camels and the country of Ammon a sheep pen. Then you will know that I am the LORD. [6]This is what I, the Lord GOD, say to you. You were happy that Jerusalem was destroyed. You clapped your

hands and stamped your feet. You had fun insulting the land of Israel, [7]so I will punish you. You will be like the valuable things soldiers take in war. You will lose your inheritance and die in faraway lands. I will destroy your country! Then you will know that I am the LORD.'

Prophecy Against Moab and Seir

[8]"This is what the Lord GOD says: 'Moab and Seir[a] say, "The family of Judah is just like any other nation." [9]I will cut into Moab's shoulder—I will take away its cities that are on its borders—the glory of the land, Beth Jeshimoth, Baal Meon and Kiriathaim. [10]Then I will give these cities to the people of the east. They will get your land. I will also let those people from the east destroy the Ammonites, and people will forget they were ever a nation. [11]So I will punish Moab, and then they will know that I am the LORD.'

Prophecy Against Edom

[12]"This is what the Lord GOD says: 'The people of Edom turned against the family of Judah and tried to get even. The people of Edom are guilty. [13]So the Lord GOD says: I will punish Edom. I will destroy the people and the animals there. I will destroy the whole country, all the way from Teman to Dedan. The Edomites will be killed in battle. [14]I will use my people Israel and get even with Edom. In this way the people of Israel will show my anger against Edom. Then the people of Edom will know that I punished them. This is what the Lord GOD says.'

Prophecy Against the Philistines

[15]"This is what the Lord GOD says: 'The Philistines tried to get even. They were very cruel. They let their anger burn inside them too long. [16]So the Lord GOD says, I will punish the Philistines. Yes, I will destroy those people from Crete. I will completely destroy those people who live on the coast. [17]I will punish them—I will get even. I will let my anger teach them a lesson. Then they will know that I am the LORD!'"

The Sad Message About Tyre

26 In the eleventh year of exile,[b] on the first day of the month, the LORD spoke to me. He said, [2]"Son of man, Tyre said bad things about Jerusalem: 'Hurray! The city gate protecting the people is destroyed! The city gate is open for me. The city of Jerusalem is ruined, so I can get plenty of valuable things out of it!'

[3]"So the Lord GOD says: I am against you, Tyre! I will bring many nations to fight against

---

[a] *25:8 Seir* Or "Edom".
[b] *26:1 eleventh year of exile* This was probably the summer of 587 BC. See 2 Kgs 25:3.

you. They will come again and again, like waves on the beach. [4]The enemy soldiers will destroy the walls of Tyre and pull down her towers. I will also scrape the topsoil from her land. I will make Tyre a bare rock. [5]Tyre will become a place by the sea for spreading fishing nets. I have spoken! The Lord GOD says, Tyre will be like the valuable things soldiers take in war. [6]Her daughters on the mainland will be killed in battle. Then they will know that I am the LORD.

Nebuchadnezzar Will Attack Tyre

[7]"This is what the Lord GOD says: I will bring an enemy from the north against Tyre. That enemy is Nebuchadnezzar, the great king of Babylon! He will bring a very large army. There will be horses, chariots, horsemen and many other soldiers. They will be from many different nations. [8]Nebuchadnezzar will kill your daughters on the mainland. He will build towers to attack your city. He will build a dirt road around your city and a dirt road leading up to the walls. [9]He will bring the logs to break down your walls. He will use picks and break down your towers. [10]There will be so many of his horses that the dust from them will cover you. Your walls will shake at the noise of horsemen, carts and chariots when the king of Babylon enters the city through your city gates. Yes, they will come into your city because its walls will be pulled down. [11]The king of Babylon will come riding through your city. His horses' hoofs[a] will come pounding over your streets. He will kill your people with swords. The strong columns in your city will fall to the ground. [12]Nebuchadnezzar's men will take away your riches. They will take the things you wanted to sell. They will break down your walls and destroy your pleasant houses. They will throw the wood and stones into the sea like rubbish. [13]So I will stop the sound of your happy songs. People will not hear your harps any more. [14]I will make you a bare rock. You will be a place by the sea for spreading fishing nets! You will not be rebuilt, because I, the LORD, have spoken! This is what the Lord GOD says.

Other Nations Will Cry for Tyre

[15]"This is what the Lord GOD says to Tyre: The people who live along the coast will tremble at the sound of your fall, when they hear the groans of your people being wounded and killed. [16]Then all the leaders of the countries by the sea will step down from their thrones and show their sadness. They will take off their special robes and their beautiful clothes. They will sit on the ground,

shaking with fear. They will be shocked at how quickly you were destroyed. [17]They will sing this sad song about you:

"'Tyre, you were a famous city,
    but now you are gone!
You were once powerful on the sea,
    you and all your people.
You sailed from coast to coast,
    making all who lived there afraid.
[18]Now the people in those lands are shaken by
    your fall.
Those living by the sea are shocked that you
    are gone!'

[19]"This is what the Lord GOD says: Tyre, you will become an old, empty city. No one will live there. I will cause the sea to flow over you. The great sea will cover you. [20]I will send you down into that deep hole—to the place of death. You will join those who died long ago. I will send you to the world below, like all the other old, empty cities. You will be with all the others who go down to the grave. No one will live in you then. You will never again be in the land of the living! [21]Other people will be afraid about what happened to you. You will be finished. People will look for you, but they will never find you again. That is what the Lord GOD says."

Tyre, the Door to the Seas

27 The word of the LORD came to me again. He said, [2]"Son of man, sing this sad song about Tyre. [3]Tyre is the city by the sea that is the merchant for many nations. Its ships sail to many countries along the coast. "This is what the Lord GOD says:

"'Tyre, you think that you are so beautiful.
    You think you are perfectly beautiful!
[4]The seas are your home.
    Your builders made you perfectly
        beautiful,
    like the ships that sail from you.
[5]Your builders used cypress trees
    from the mountains of Senir to make your
        planks.
They used cedar trees from Lebanon
    to make your mast.
[6]They used oak trees from Bashan to make
    your oars.
They used pine trees from Cyprus to make
    the cabin on your deck.[b]
They decorated that shelter with ivory.

---

[a] **26:11 hoofs** The hard part of a horse's foot.
[b] **27:6 deck** The floor of a ship.

[7]For your sail they used colourful linen made in
Egypt.
That sail was your flag.
The coverings over your cabin were blue and
purple.
They came from the island of Cyprus.
[8]Men from Sidon and Arvad rowed your boats
for you.
Tyre, your wise men were the pilots on
your ships.
[9]Skilled workers from Byblos[a]
were on board to help put caulking[b]
between the boards on your ship.
All the ships of the sea and their sailors
came to trade and do business with you.

[10]"Men from Persia, Lud and Put were in your
army. They were your men of war who hung
their shields and helmets on your walls. They
brought honour and glory to your city. [11]Men
from Arvad and Cilicia were guards standing on
the wall around your city. Men from Gammad
were in your towers. They hung their shields on
the walls around your city and made your beauty
complete.

[12]"Tarshish was one of your best customers.
They traded silver, iron, tin and lead for all the
wonderful things you sold. [13]People in Greece,
Turkey and the area around the Black Sea traded
with you. They traded slaves and bronze for
the things you sold. [14]People from the nation[c] of
Togarmah traded horses, war horses and mules for
the things you sold. [15]The people of Rhodes[d] traded
with you. You sold your things in many places.
People brought ivory tusks and ebony wood to pay
you. [16]Aram traded with you because you had so
many good things. They traded emeralds, purple
cloth, fine needlework, fine linen, coral and rubies
for the things you sold.

[17]"The people in Judah and Israel traded with
you. They paid for the things you sold with the
wheat, olives, early figs, honey, oil and balm.[e]
[18]Damascus was a good customer. They traded
with you for the many wonderful things you had.
They traded wine from Helbon and white wool for
those things. [19]Damascus traded wine from Uzal
for the things you sold. They paid with wrought
iron, cassia and sugar cane. [20]Dedan provided
good business and traded with you for saddle
blankets and riding horses. [21]Arabia and all the
leaders of Kedar traded lambs, rams and goats for
your goods. [22]The merchants of Sheba and Raamah
traded with you. They traded all the best spices
and every kind of precious stone and gold for your
goods. [23]Haran, Canneh, Eden, the merchants of
Sheba, Asshur and Kilmad traded with you. [24]They
paid with the finest clothing, blue cloth, cloth with
fine needlework, rugs of many colours and the
strongest ropes. These were the things they traded
with you. [25]⌊The ships from Tarshish carried the
things you sold.⌋

"Tyre, you are like one of those cargo ships.
You are on the sea, loaded with many
riches.
[26]Your oarsmen rowed you far out to sea.
But a powerful east wind will destroy your
ship at sea.
[27]All your wealth will spill into the sea.
Your wealth—the things you buy and
sell—will spill into the sea.
Your whole crew—sailors, pilots and the men
who put caulking between the boards on
your ship—
will spill into the sea.
The merchants and soldiers in your city
will all sink into the sea.
That will happen on the day
that you are destroyed!

[28]"You send your merchants to faraway places.
Those places will shake with fear when
they hear your pilots' cry!
[29]Your whole crew will jump ship.
The sailors and pilots will jump ship and
swim to the shore.
[30]They will be very sad about you.
They will cry, throw dust on their heads
and roll in ashes.
[31]They will shave their heads for you.
They will put on sackcloth.
They will cry for you like someone crying for
someone who died.

[32]"And in their loud crying they will sing this
sad song about you:

"No one is like Tyre!
Tyre is destroyed, in the middle of the sea!
[33]Your merchants sailed across the seas,
and your goods filled the needs of many
nations.

---

[a] 27:9 Byblos Literally, "Gebal".
[b] 27:9 caulking Often a mixture of tar and rope that was put between the boards to make a ship watertight so that it would not
leak. Also in verse 27.
[c] 27:14 nation Literally, "house". This might mean the royal family of that country.
[d] 27:15 Rhodes Or "Dedan". See verse 20.
[e] 27:17 balm An ointment from some kinds of trees and plants. It is used as medicine.

You made kings rich all over the world
   with your great wealth and the things you
     sold.
34But now you are broken by the seas
   and by the deep waters.
All the things you sell
   and all your people have fallen.
35All the people living on the coast
   are shocked to hear about you.
Their kings are terrified.
   Their faces show their shock.
36The merchants in other nations
   show their surprise at the news.
You have come to a terrible end.
   You are gone forever.'"

Tyre Thinks It Is Like a God

28 The LORD spoke to me and said, 2"Son of
man, say to the ruler of Tyre, 'This is what
the Lord GOD says:

"'You are very proud!
   And you say, "I am a god!
I sit on the seat of gods
   in the middle of the seas."

"'But you are a man and not God!
   You only think you are a god.
3You think you are wiser than Daniel[a]
   and no secret is hidden from you.
4Through your wisdom and understanding
   you have gained riches for yourself.
And you have put gold and silver
   in your treasuries.
5Through your great wisdom and trade,
   you have made your riches grow.
And now, because of those riches
   you have become proud.

6"'So this is what the Lord GOD says:
Tyre, you thought you were like a god.
7I will bring foreigners to fight against you.
   They are most terrible among the nations!
They will pull out their swords
   and use them against the beautiful things
     your wisdom brought you.
They will ruin your glory.
8They will bring you down to the grave.
   You will be like a sailor who died at sea.
9That person will kill you.
   Will you still say, "I am a god"?
No, he will have you in his power.
   You will see that you are a man, not
     God!

10Strangers will treat you like a foreigner[b] and
   kill you,
   because I gave the command!
This is what the Lord GOD says.'"

11The LORD spoke to me and said, 12"Son of
man, sing this sad song about the king of Tyre.
Say to him, 'This is what the Lord GOD says:

"'You were the perfect man—
   so full of wisdom and perfectly handsome.
13You were in Eden,
   the garden of God.
You had every precious stone—
   rubies, topaz and diamonds,
   beryls, onyx and jasper,
   sapphires, turquoise and emeralds.
And each of these stones was set in gold.
   You were given this beauty on the day you
     were created.
God made you strong.
14You were one of the chosen winged
    creatures
   who spread your wings over my throne.
I put you on the holy mountain of God.
   You walked among the jewels that sparkled
     like fire.
15You were good and honest when I created
   you,
   but then you became evil.
16Your business brought you many riches.
   But they also put cruelty inside you,
     and you sinned.
So I treated you like something unclean
   and threw you off the mountain of God.
You were one of the chosen winged creatures
   who spread your wings over my throne.
But I forced you to leave the jewels
   that sparkled like fire.
17Your beauty made you proud.
   Your glory ruined your wisdom.
So I threw you down to the ground,
   and now other kings stare at you.
18With your many sins and dishonest trade
   you made your places of worship unclean.
So I set a fire that spread from inside your city
   and completely destroyed you!
You became a pile of ashes on the ground
   for everyone around you to see.

19"'The nations who knew you before
   were shocked to see what happened to you.
You suffered a terrible punishment,
   and now you are gone forever!'"

---

[a] **28:3 Daniel** A wise man from ancient times. This might be Daniel from the Bible or the Danel mentioned in the writings from Ras Shamra.

[b] **28:10 foreigner** Literally, "uncircumcised". This means a person who did not share in the agreement God made with Israel. See "CIRCUMCISE, CIRCUMCISION" in the Word List.

The Message Against Sidon

20The LORD spoke to me and said, 21"Son of man, look towards Sidon and speak for me against that place. 22Say, 'This is what the Lord GOD says:

"'I am against you, Sidon!
    Your people will learn to respect me.
I will punish Sidon.
    Then people will know that I am the LORD.
Then they will learn that I am holy,
    and they will treat me that way.
23I will send disease and death to Sidon,
    and many people inside the city will die.
Soldiers outside the city will kill many people.
    Then people will know that I am the LORD!

The Nations Will Stop Laughing at Israel

24"'Then the surrounding nations that hate Israel will no longer be like stinging nettles[a] and painful thorns. And they will know that I am the Lord GOD.

25"'This is what the Lord GOD says: I scattered the people of Israel among other nations, but I will gather the family of Israel together again. Then the nations will know that I am holy, and they will treat me that way. At that time the people of Israel will live in their land—I gave that land to my servant Jacob. 26They will live safely in the land. They will build houses and plant vineyards. I will punish the nations around them that hated them. Then the people of Israel will live in safety, and they will know that I am the LORD their God.'"

The Message Against Egypt

29 On the twelfth day of the tenth month of the tenth year of exile,[b] the LORD spoke to me. He said, 2"Son of man, look towards Pharaoh, king of Egypt. Speak for me against him and Egypt. 3Say, 'This is what the Lord GOD says:

"'I am against you, Pharaoh, king of Egypt.
    You are the great monster[c] lying beside the Nile River.
You say, "This is my river!
    I made this river!"

4-5"'But I will put hooks in your jaws.
    The fish in the Nile River will stick to your scales.
I will pull you and your fish up
    out of your rivers and onto the dry land.
You will fall on the ground,
    and no one will pick you up or bury you.

I will give you to the wild animals and birds.
    You will be their food.
6Then all the people living in Egypt
    will know that I am the LORD!

"'Why will I do these things?
Because the people of Israel leaned on Egypt for support,
    but Egypt was only a weak blade of grass.
7The people of Israel leaned on Egypt for support,
    but Egypt only pierced their hands and shoulder.
They leaned on you for support,
    but you broke and twisted their back.

8"'So this is what the Lord GOD says:
I will bring a sword against you.
    I will destroy all your people and animals.
9Egypt will be empty and destroyed.
    Then they will know that I am the LORD.

"'Why will I do these things? Because you said, "This is my river. I made this river." 10So I am against you. I am against the many branches of your Nile River. I will destroy Egypt completely. The cities will be empty from Migdol to Aswan and as far as the border of Ethiopia. 11No person or animal will pass through Egypt. Nothing will pass through or settle there for 40 years. 12I will destroy Egypt. The cities will be in ruins for 40 years! I will scatter the Egyptians among the nations. I will send them away to foreign lands.

13"'But the Lord GOD also says this: After 40 years, I will gather the people of Egypt from those nations where I sent them. I will gather them together again. 14I will bring back the Egyptian captives. I will bring them back to the land of Pathros, to the land where they were born. But their kingdom will not be important. 15It will be the least important kingdom. It will never again lift itself above the other nations. I will make them so small that they will not rule over the nations. 16And the family of Israel will never again depend on Egypt. The Israelites will remember their sin—they will remember that they turned to Egypt for help and not to God, and they will know that I am the Lord GOD.'"

Babylon Will Get Egypt

17On the first day of the first month in the twenty-seventh year of exile,[d] the LORD spoke to me. He said, 18"Son of man, King Nebuchadnezzar

[a] **28:24 nettles** Plants covered with stinging hairs.
[b] **29:1 tenth year of exile** This was the winter of 587 BC.
[c] **29:3 great monster** There were ancient stories about a sea monster that fought against God. The prophets called Egypt that sea monster many times. But here, this might mean the crocodiles that rest on the banks of the Nile River.
[d] **29:17 twenty-seventh year of exile** This was in the spring of 571 BC.

of Babylon made his army fight hard against Tyre. He forced his soldiers to carry such heavy loads that their heads were rubbed bald and their shoulders rubbed raw. But the king and his army got nothing for all their effort. 19So this is what the Lord GOD says: I will give Egypt to King Nebuchadnezzar of Babylon, and he will carry away the people. He will take the many valuable things in Egypt to pay his army. 20I will give Egypt to Nebuchadnezzar as a reward for the hard work he did for me. This is what the Lord GOD says!

21"On that day I will make the family of Israel strong. So Ezekiel, I will let you speak to them. Then they will know that I am the LORD."

The Army of Babylon Will Attack Egypt

30 The word of the LORD came to me again. He said, 2"Son of man, speak for me. Say, 'This is what the Lord GOD says:

"'Cry and say,
    "A terrible day is coming."
3That day is near!
    Yes, the LORD's day for judging is near.
It will be a cloudy day,
    the time for judging the nations.
4A sword will come against Egypt!
    People in Ethiopia will shake with fear,
        when Egypt falls.
The army of Babylon will take the Egyptians as
        prisoners.
    Egypt's foundations will be torn down.

5"'Many people made peace agreements with Egypt. But all those people from Ethiopia, Put, Lud, all Arabia, Libya and the people of Israel*a* will be destroyed!

6"'This is what the LORD says:
    Those who support Egypt will fall!
        The pride in her power will end.
    The people in Egypt will be killed in battle,
        all the way from Migdol to Aswan.
    This is what the Lord GOD says!
7Egypt will join the other countries that were
        destroyed.
    Its cities will be among those that are in ruins.
8I will start a fire in Egypt,
    and all her helpers will be destroyed.
Then they will know that I am the LORD!

9"'At that time I will send out messengers. They will go in ships to carry the bad news to Ethiopia. Ethiopia now feels safe, but the people of Ethiopia will shake with fear when Egypt is punished. That time is coming!

10"'This is what the Lord GOD says:
    I will use the king of Babylon.
    I will use Nebuchadnezzar to destroy the
        people of Egypt.
11Nebuchadnezzar and his people
    are the most terrible of the nations,
    and I will bring them to destroy Egypt.
They will pull out their swords against Egypt.
    They will fill the land with dead bodies.
12I will make the Nile River become dry land.
    Then I will sell the dry land to evil people.
    I will use foreigners to make that land empty.
    I, the LORD, have spoken!"

The Idols of Egypt Will Be Destroyed

13"'This is what the Lord GOD says:
    I will also destroy the idols in Egypt.
    I will take the statues away from Memphis.
    There will no longer be a leader in the land
        of Egypt.
    I will put fear there instead.
14I will make Pathros empty.
    I will start a fire in Zoan.
    I will punish Thebes.
15I will pour out my anger against Pelusium, the
        fortress of Egypt!
    I will destroy the people of Thebes.
16I will start a fire in Egypt;
    the city of Pelusium will ache with fear.
    The soldiers will break into the city of Thebes,
    and Memphis will have new troubles every
        day.
17The young men of Heliopolis and Bubastis*b*
    will die in battle,
    and the women will be taken away as
        prisoners.
18It will be a dark day in Tahpanhes when I
    break Egypt's control.*c*
    Her proud power will be finished!
A cloud will cover Egypt,
    and her daughters will be taken away as
        prisoners.
19So I will punish Egypt.
    Then they will know that I am the LORD!'"

Egypt Will Become Weak Forever

20On the seventh day of the first month of the eleventh year of exile,*d* the LORD spoke to me. He said, 21"Son of man, I have broken the arm of

---

a **30:5 people of Israel** Literally, "sons of the agreement". This might mean "all the people who made peace agreements with Egypt" or it might mean "Israel, the people who made the agreement with God".
b **30:17 Heliopolis and Bubastis** Hebrew, "On and Pi Beseth", cities in Egypt.
c **30:18 control** Literally, "yoke".
d **30:20 eleventh year of exile** This was the summer of 587 BC. Also in 31:1.

Pharaoh, king of Egypt. No one will wrap his arm with a bandage. It will not heal, so his arm will not be strong enough to hold a sword.

22"This is what the Lord GOD says: I am against Pharaoh, king of Egypt. I will break both his arms, the strong arm and the arm that is already broken. I will make the sword fall from his hand. 23I will scatter the Egyptians among the nations. 24I will make the arms of the king of Babylon strong. I will put my sword in his hand, but I will break the arms of Pharaoh. Then Pharaoh will cry out in pain, the kind of cry that a dying man makes. 25So I will make the arms of the king of Babylon strong, but the arms of Pharaoh will fall. Then they will know that I am the LORD.

"I will put my sword in the hand of the king of Babylon. Then he will stretch the sword out against the land of Egypt. 26I will scatter the Egyptians among the nations. Then they will know that I am the LORD!"

Egypt, Like Assyria, Will Be Destroyed

31 On the first day of the third month in the eleventh year of exile, the LORD spoke to me. He said, 2"Son of man, say this to Pharaoh, king of Egypt and to his people:

"'You are so great!
    What can I compare you to?
3You are like Assyria, a nation that once grew
        strong
    like a cedar tree in Lebanon
with beautiful branches that gave the forest
        shade.
    It grew so tall, its top reached the clouds!
4It got all the water it needed
    from deep springs that made it grow tall.
Water flowed all around it like a river
    that sent its streams to the other trees
        there.
5So this cedar grew very tall,
    taller than all those other trees.
And its branches were long and thick
    because it had so much water.
6The birds made their nests in its branches,
    and it was a shelter for animals giving birth.
It provided shelter
    for many other nations.
7It was a great and beautiful tree
    with branches that spread far and wide.
Its roots went down deep
    where there was plenty of water.
8Not even the cedar trees in God's garden
    were as big as this tree.

No cypress tree or plane tree
    had branches so large.
None of the trees in God's garden
    were as beautiful as this tree.
9I gave it so many branches
    and made it so beautiful
that all the trees in Eden, God's garden,
    wished they could be like it!

10"'So this is what the Lord GOD says: That tree grew tall. Its top reached up to the clouds. It grew so big that it became proud! 11So I let a powerful king have that tree. He punished it because it was so evil, and I took that tree out of my garden. 12A foreign army, the most violent in the world, cut it down and scattered its branches on the mountains and in the valleys. Its broken limbs drifted down the rivers flowing through that land. There was no more shade under that tree, so all the people left. 13Now birds live in that fallen tree. Wild animals walk over its fallen branches. 14Now, none of the trees by that water will be proud. They will not try to reach the clouds. None of the strong trees that drink that water will boast about being tall, because all of them must die. They will all go down into the world below, to Sheol, the place of death. They will join the other people who died and went down into that deep hole.

15"'This is what the Lord GOD says: I made the people cry on the day that tree went down to Sheol. I covered it with the deep ocean. I stopped its rivers and all the water stopped flowing. I made Lebanon mourn for it. All the trees of the field became sick with sadness for that big tree. 16I made the tree fall—and the nations shook with fear at the sound of the falling tree. I sent the tree down to the place of death to join the others who had gone down into that deep hole. In the past, all the trees of Eden, the best of Lebanon, drank that water. The trees were comforted in the world below. 17Yes, those trees also went down with the big tree to the place of death. They joined those who were killed in battle. That big tree made the other trees strong. Those trees had lived under the big tree's shadow among the nations.

18"'Egypt, there were many big and powerful trees in Eden. Which of those trees should I compare you to? They all went down into the world below! And you, too, will join those foreigners*a* in that place of death. You will lie there among those killed in battle.

"'Yes, that will happen to Pharaoh and to the crowds of people with him! This is what the Lord GOD says.'"

---

a **31:18** *foreigners* Literally, "uncircumcised". This means people who did not share in the agreement God made with Israel. See "CIRCUMCISE, CIRCUMCISION" in the Word List.

Pharaoh: a Lion or a Dragon?

32 On the first day of the twelfth month in the twelfth year of exile,[a] the LORD spoke to me. He said, 2"Son of man, sing this funeral song for Pharaoh, king of Egypt:

"'You think you are a lion among the nations.
    But you are more like a sea monster.
You splash around in your rivers
    and make the water muddy with your feet.

3"'This is what the Lord GOD says:

"'I have gathered many people together.
    Now I will throw my net over you.
    Then those people will pull you in.
4Then I will drop you on the dry ground.
    I will throw you down in the field.
I will let all the birds come and eat you.
    I will let wild animals from every place
        come and eat you until they are full.
5I will scatter your body on the mountains.
    I will fill the valleys with your dead body.
6I will pour your blood on the mountains,
    and it will soak down into the ground.
    The rivers will be full of you.
7I will make you disappear.
    I will cover the sky and make the stars dark.
    I will cover the sun with a cloud, and the
        moon will not shine.
8I will darken the lights in the sky over you.
    I will make your whole country dark.
    This is what the Lord GOD says.

9"'I will make many people sad and upset when I bring an enemy to destroy you. Nations you don't even know will be upset. 10I will make many people shocked about you. Their kings will be terrified of you, when I swing my sword before them. They will shake with fear on the day you fall. Each king will be afraid for his own life.

11"'That will happen because of what the Lord GOD says: The sword of the king of Babylon will come to fight against you. 12I will use those soldiers to kill your people in battle. They come from the most terrible of the nations. They will destroy the things Egypt is proud of. The people of Egypt will be destroyed. 13There are many animals by the rivers in Egypt. I will also destroy all those animals. People will not make the waters muddy with their feet any more. The hoofs of cattle will not make the water muddy any more. 14So I will make the water in Egypt calm. I will cause their rivers to run slowly—they will be slick like oil.

This is what the Lord GOD says. 15I will make the land of Egypt empty. That land will lose everything. I will punish all the people living in Egypt. Then they will know that I am the LORD!'

16"This is a sad song that people will sing for Egypt. The daughters in other nations will sing this sad song. They will sing it as a sad song about Egypt and all its people. This is what the Lord GOD says."

Egypt to Be Destroyed

17On the fifteenth day of that month in the twelfth year of exile, the LORD spoke to me. He said, 18"Son of man, cry for the people of Egypt. Lead Egypt and the daughters from powerful nations to the grave. Lead them to the world below where they will be with the other people who went down into that deep hole.

19"Egypt, you are no better than anyone else! Go down to the place of death. Go and lie down with those foreigners.[b]

20"Egypt will go to be with all the other men who were killed in battle. The enemy has pulled her and all her people away.

21"Strong and powerful men were killed in battle. Those foreigners went down to the place of death. And from that place, those who were killed will speak to Egypt and his helpers.

22–23"Assyria and all its army are there in the place of death. Their graves are deep down in that deep hole. All the Assyrian soldiers were killed in battle, and their graves are all around its grave. When they were alive, they made people afraid, but they were all killed in battle.

24"Elam is there and all its army is around its grave. All of them were killed in battle. Those foreigners went deep down into the ground. When they were alive, they made people afraid. But they carried their shame with them down to that deep hole. 25They have made a bed for Elam and all its soldiers who were killed in battle. Elam's army is all around its grave. All those foreigners were killed in battle. When they were alive, they scared people. But they carried their shame with them down into that deep hole. They were put with all the other people who were killed.

26"Meshech, Tubal and all their armies are there. Their graves are around it. All those foreigners were killed in battle. When they were alive, they made people afraid. 27But now they are lying down by the powerful men who died long, long ago! They were buried with their weapons of war. Their swords will be laid under their heads. But their sins are on their bones, because when they were alive, they scared people.

---

[a] 32:1 *twelfth year of exile* This was early spring, 585 BC. Also in verse 17.
[b] 32:19 *foreigners* Literally, "uncircumcised". This means people who did not share in the agreement God made with Israel. See "CIRCUMCISE, CIRCUMCISION" in the Word List.

²⁸"Egypt, you also will be destroyed, and you will lie down by those foreigners. You will lie with the other soldiers who were killed in battle.

²⁹"Edom is there also. Its kings and other leaders are there too. They were powerful soldiers, but now they lie with the other men who were killed in battle. They are lying there with those foreigners. They are there with the other people who went down into that deep hole.

³⁰"The rulers from the north are there, all of them, and so are all the soldiers from Sidon. Their strength scared people, but they are embarrassed. Those foreigners lie there with the other men who were killed in battle. They carried their shame with them down into that deep hole.

³¹"Yes, Pharaoh and all his army will be killed in battle. Pharaoh will be comforted when he sees his many men and all the others who went down into the place of death. This is what the Lord GOD says.

³²"People were afraid of Pharaoh when he was alive, but he will lie down next to those foreigners. Pharaoh and his army will lie down with all the other soldiers who were killed in battle. This is what the Lord GOD says."

God Chooses Ezekiel to Be a Watchman

33 The LORD spoke to me and said, ²"Son of man, speak to your people. Say to them, 'Whenever I bring enemy soldiers to fight against a country, the people choose someone to be a watchman. ³If this guard sees enemy soldiers coming, he blows the trumpet and warns the people. ⁴If people hear the warning but ignore it, the enemy will capture them and take them away as prisoners. They will be responsible for their own death. ⁵They heard the trumpet, but they ignored the warning. So they are responsible for their own deaths. If they had paid attention to the warning, they could have saved their own lives. ⁶But what if the guard sees the enemy soldiers coming, but does not blow the trumpet? Since he doesn't warn the people, the enemy will capture them and take them away as prisoners. They will be taken away because they sinned, but the guard will also be responsible for their deaths.'

⁷"Now, son of man, I am choosing you to be a watchman for the family of Israel. If you hear a message from my mouth, you must warn the people for me. ⁸I might say to you, 'These evil people will die.' Then you must go and warn them for me. If you don't warn them and tell them to change their lives, those evil people will die because they sinned. And I will make you responsible for their deaths. ⁹But if you do warn the evil people to change their lives and stop sinning, and if they refuse to stop, they will die because they sinned. But you have saved your life.

God Does Not Want to Destroy People

¹⁰"So, son of man, speak to the family of Israel for me. They might say, 'We have sinned and broken the law. Our sins are too heavy to bear. We rot away because of them. What can we do to live?'

¹¹"You must say to them, 'The Lord GOD says: By my life, I swear that I don't enjoy seeing people die—not even evil people! I don't want them to die. I want them to come back to me. I want them to change their lives so that they can really live. So come back to me! Stop doing bad things! Why must you die, family of Israel?'

¹²"Son of man, tell your people: 'The good things people did in the past will not save them if they become bad and begin to sin. In the same way, the bad things people did in the past will not destroy them if they turn from their evil. So remember, the good things people did in the past will not save them if they begin to sin.'

¹³"Maybe I will tell good people that they will live. But maybe those good people will begin to think that the good things they did in the past will save them. So they might begin to do bad things, but I will not remember the good things they did in the past! No, they will die because of the bad things they begin to do.

¹⁴"Or maybe I will tell some evil people that they will die. But they might change their lives, stop sinning and begin to do what is right. They might become good and fair. ¹⁵They might give back the things they took when they lent money. They might pay for the things they stole. They might begin to follow the laws that give life and stop doing bad things. Then they will surely live. They will not die. ¹⁶I will not remember the bad things they did in the past, because now they do what is right and are fair. So they will live!

¹⁷"But your people say, 'That's not fair! The Lord cannot be like that!'

"But they are the people who are not fair! They are the people who must change! ¹⁸If good people stop doing good and begin to sin, they will die because of their sins. ¹⁹And if evil people stop doing wrong and start living right and being fair, they will live. ²⁰You still say that I am not fair, but I am telling you the truth. Family of Israel, everyone will be judged for what they do!"

Jerusalem Has Been Taken

²¹On the fifth day of the tenth month in the twelfth year of exile,^a a person who had escaped from the battle in Jerusalem came to me and said, "The city has been taken!"

---

^a **33:21** *twelfth year of exile* This was the winter of 586 BC.

²²The evening before that person came to me, the power of the LORD came on me. The Lord opened my mouth. So when that person came, I could speak again. ²³Then the LORD spoke to me and said, ²⁴"Son of man, there are Israelites who live in the ruined cities in Israel. They are saying, 'Abraham was only one man, and God gave him all this land. Now, we are many people, so surely this land belongs to us! It is our land!'

²⁵"You must tell them that this is what the Lord GOD says: 'You eat meat with the blood still in it. You look to your idols for help. You murder people, so why should I give you this land? ²⁶You depend on your own sword. Each of you does terrible things. Each of you commits sexual sins with his neighbour's wife, so you cannot have the land!'

²⁷"You must tell them that this is what the Lord GOD says: 'By my life, I promise that the people living in the ruined cities will be killed with a sword! If any people are out in the country, I will let animals kill and eat them. If people are hiding in the fortresses and the caves, they will die from disease. ²⁸I will make that place an empty wasteland. That country will lose all the things it was proud of. The mountains of Israel will become empty. No one will pass through that place. ²⁹The people have done many terrible things, so I will make that place an empty wasteland. Then they will know that I am the LORD.'

³⁰"And now about you, son of man. Your people lean against the walls and stand in their doorways talking about you. They tell each other, 'Come on, let's go and hear what the LORD says.' ³¹So they come to you as if they were my people. They sit in front of you as if they were my people. They hear your words, but they will not do the things you say. They only want to do what feels good. They only want to cheat people and make more money.

³²"You are nothing to these people but a singer singing love songs. You have a good voice. You play your instrument well. They listen to your words, but they will not do what you say. ³³But the things you sing about really will happen, and then the people will know that there was a prophet living among them."

Israel Is Like a Flock of Sheep

34 The LORD spoke to me and said, ²"Son of man, speak against the shepherds of Israel for me. Speak to them for me. Tell them that this is what the Lord GOD says: 'You shepherds of Israel have only been feeding yourselves. It will be very bad for you! Why don't you shepherds feed the flock? ³You eat the fat sheep and use their wool to make clothes for yourselves. You kill the fat sheep, but you don't feed the flock. ⁴You have not made the weak strong. You have not cared for the sick sheep. You have not put bandages on the sheep that were hurt. Some of the sheep wandered away, and you did not go and get them and bring them back. You did not go to look for the lost sheep. No, you were cruel and severe—that's the way you tried to lead the sheep!

⁵"'And now the sheep are scattered because there was no shepherd. They became food for every wild animal, so they were scattered. ⁶My flock wandered over all the mountains and on every high hill. My flock was scattered all over the face of the earth. There was no one to search or to look for them.

⁷"'So, you shepherds, listen to the word of the LORD. ⁸This is what the Lord GOD says: I swear that wild animals will catch my sheep, and my people will become food for all those animals because they did not have any real shepherds. My shepherds did not look out for my flock. They did not feed my flock. No, they only killed the sheep and fed themselves!

⁹"'So, you shepherds, listen to the word of the LORD! ¹⁰This is what the Lord GOD says: I am against the shepherds. I will demand my sheep from them. I will fire them. They will not be my shepherds any more. Then the shepherds will not be able to feed themselves, and I will save my flock from their mouths. Then my sheep will not be food for them.

¹¹"'This is what the Lord GOD says: I myself will be their Shepherd. I will search for my sheep and take care of them. ¹²If a shepherd is with his sheep when they begin to wander away, he will go searching for them. In the same way, I will search for my sheep. I will save them and bring them back from all the places where they were scattered on that dark and cloudy day. ¹³I will bring them back from those nations. I will gather them from those countries and bring them back to their own land. I will feed them on the mountains of Israel, by the streams, and in all the places where people live. ¹⁴I will lead them to grassy fields. They will go to the place high on the mountains of Israel and lie down on good ground and eat the grass. They will eat in rich grassland on the mountains of Israel. ¹⁵Yes, I will feed my flock, and I will lead them to a place of rest. This is what the Lord GOD says.

¹⁶"'I will search for the lost sheep. I will bring back the sheep that were scattered and put bandages on the sheep that were hurt. I will make the weak sheep strong, but I will destroy the fat and powerful shepherds. I will feed them the punishment they deserve.

¹⁷"'This is what the Lord GOD says: And you, my flock, I will judge between one sheep and another. I will judge between the male sheep and

THE SHEPHERD AND HIS SHEEP

Pastor Phil seemed to be the best thing that had ever happened to Grace Community Church. He came in like a whirlwind – shaking up the sleepy people, inspiring the youth group, starting fresh initiatives that attracted new families and saw many discovering Christ.

But after only a few years, everything crashed down. News broke of a scandal involving Pastor Phil and a woman who was not his wife. He'd let everyone down and the church was left in tatters.

DIG IN

READ Ezekiel 34:1–16

- Who is God referring to when he talks about "shepherds"?
- How have the sheep suffered because of their lack of care and attention (vv.4–6)?

The shepherds here are the leaders God has put over his people. They have failed to care for the people and misused power for their own gain. As a result, they have been scattered, left hungry and put at risk.

This has angered God, who trusted them with his people. Leadership of God's people comes with a high degree of responsibility and God will hold leaders he chooses to account.

- What will happen to the shepherds (vv.9–10)?
- What does God propose instead (v.11 onwards)?

The shepherds who have let the people down so badly will be dismissed (v.10) and a better Shepherd will step in to care for the people.

He will go looking for the scattered sheep (v.12), gather them back together, feed them (v.14) and find a safe place for them to rest (v.15). He will be everything that the human shepherds have failed to be.

God hasn't finished with human leaders though – he still puts leaders over us for our own good. But sometimes we can put too much trust in them and expect them to deliver what only God is capable of giving us.

The truth is that human leaders will always disappoint – even if not as dramatically as Pastor Phil (above). Leaders are not perfect and though they may be very gifted, they all have weaknesses too.

DIG THROUGH

- "Human leaders will always disappoint." In what ways do we put our trust in human leaders rather than in God himself, our Good Shepherd?
- God wants you to let him be your Shepherd. Putting your name in place of every reference to sheep, read verses 11 to 15 again. Or think of someone you know who really needs to know God right now, and pray those verses substituting their name instead.

DIG DEEPER

The most famous place where God is described as our Shepherd is Psalm 23. It was written by David, who was a shepherd before his rise to becoming king so he really understood how a shepherd leads and cares for his sheep.

- Jesus talks of himself as the good shepherd and is the ultimate living fulfilment of Ezekiel's prophecy. Check out John 10:1–16.
- Look at 1 Peter 2:25 which links the idea of Jesus gathering up his sheep who had wandered off: "You were like sheep that went the wrong way. But now you have come back to the Shepherd and Protector of your lives."

the male goats. 18You can eat the grass growing on the good land. So why do you also crush the grass that other sheep want to eat? You can drink plenty of clear water. So why do you also stir the water that other sheep want to drink? 19My flock must eat the grass you crushed with your feet, and they must drink the water you stir with your feet!

20"So the Lord GOD says to them: I myself will judge between the fat sheep and the thin sheep! 21You push with your side and shoulder. You knock down all the weak sheep with your horns. You push until you have forced them away, 22so I will save my flock. They will not be caught by wild animals any more. I will judge between one sheep and another. 23Then I will put one shepherd over them, my servant David. He will feed them and be their shepherd. 24Then I, the LORD, will be their God, and my servant David will be the ruler living among them. I, the LORD, have spoken.

25"And I will make a peace agreement with my sheep. I will take harmful animals away from the land. Then the sheep can be safe in the desert and sleep in the woods. 26I will bless the sheep and the places around my hill. I will cause the rains to fall at the right time and will shower them with blessings. 27And the trees growing in the field will produce their fruit. The earth will give its harvest, so the sheep will be safe on their land. I will break the yokes on them and save them from the power of the people who made them slaves. Then they will know that I am the LORD. 28They will not be caught like an animal by the nations any more. Those animals will not eat them any more. No, they will live safely. No one will make them afraid. 29I will give them some land that will make a good garden. Then they will not suffer from hunger in that land or suffer the insults from the nations any more. 30Then they will know that I am the LORD their God. The family of Israel will know that I am with them and that they are my people. This is what the Lord GOD says! 31"You are my sheep, the sheep of my grassland. You are only human beings, and I am your God. This is what the Lord GOD says.'"

The Message Against Edom

35 The LORD spoke to me and said, 2"Son of man, look towards Mount Seir and speak against it for me. 3Say to it, 'This is what the Lord GOD says:

"'I am against you, Mount Seir!
    I will punish you and make you an empty wasteland.

4I will destroy your cities,
    and you will become empty.
Then you will know that I am the LORD.

5"Why? Because you have always been against my people. You used your sword against Israel at the time of their trouble, at the time of their final punishment. 6So the Lord GOD says: But I promise by my own life that I will let death have you. Death will chase you. You did not hate killing people, so death will chase you. 7I will make Mount Seir an empty ruin. I will kill everyone who enters or leaves that city. 8I will cover its mountains with those who are killed. There will be dead bodies all over your hills, in your valleys and in all your ravines. 9I will make you empty forever. No one will live in your cities. Then you will know that I am the LORD.

10"You said, "These two nations and countries, Israel and Judah, will be ours. We will take them for our own." But the LORD was there! 11And the Lord GOD says: You were jealous of my people. You were angry and hateful to them. So by my life, I swear that I will punish you the same way you hurt them! I will punish you and let my people know that I am with them. 12And then you, too, will know that I am the LORD.

"'I have heard you making fun of Israel's hill country. You said, "It is in ruins, just waiting for us to swallow it up." 13Your proud boasting is really against me. Time after time you have insulted me, and I have heard every word.

14"This is what the Lord GOD says: All the earth will be happy when I destroy you. 15You were happy when the country of Israel was destroyed. I will treat you the same way. Mount Seir and the whole country of Edom will be destroyed. Then you will know that I am the LORD.'"

The Land of Israel Will Be Rebuilt

36 "Son of man, speak to the mountains of Israel for me. Tell them to listen to the word of the LORD! 2Tell them that this is what the Lord GOD says: 'The enemy said bad things about you. They said: "Hurray! Now the ancient mountainsᵃ will be ours!"' 3So speak to the mountains of Israel for me. Tell them that this is what the Lord GOD says: 'The enemy attacked you from every direction. They tore you down and made you so weak that other nations were able to capture you. That made people say bad things about you and make fun of you.

4"So, mountains of Israel, listen to the word of the Lord GOD! This is what the Lord GOD says to the mountains, hills, streams, valleys, empty

---

ᵃ **36:2 mountains** Literally, "high places", usually a reference to places of worship. See "HIGH PLACE" in the Word List.

ruins and abandoned cities that have been looted and laughed at by the other nations around them. ⁵This is what the Lord God says: I swear, I will let my strong feelings speak for me! I will let Edom and the other nations feel my anger. They took my land for themselves. They really had a good time when they showed how much they hated this land. They took the land for themselves, just so they could destroy it.' ⁶So say these things about the land of Israel. Speak to the mountains and to the hills, to the streams and to the valleys. Tell them that this is what the Lord God says: 'I will let my strong feelings and anger speak for me, because you had to suffer the insults from those nations. ⁷So this is what the Lord God says: I am the one making this promise! I swear that the nations around you will have to suffer for those insults.

⁸"'But mountains of Israel, you will grow new trees and produce fruit for my people Israel. My people will soon come back. ⁹I am with you, and I will help you. People will plough your soil and plant seeds in you. ¹⁰There will be many people living on you. The whole family of Israel—all of them—will live there. The cities will have people living in them. The destroyed places will be rebuilt. ¹¹I will give you many people and animals, and they will grow and have many children. I will bring people to live on you as in the past. I will make it better for you than before. Then you will know that I am the Lord. ¹²Yes, I will lead many people—my people, Israel—to your land. You will be their property, and you will not take away their children again.

¹³"'This is what the Lord God says: Land of Israel, people say bad things to you. They say you destroyed your people. They say you took the children away from your people. ¹⁴But you will not destroy people any more or take away their children again. This is what the Lord God says. ¹⁵I will not let those other nations insult you any more. You will not be hurt by them any more. You will not take the children away from your people again. This is what the Lord God says.'"

The Lord Will Protect His Name

¹⁶Then the Lord spoke to me and said, ¹⁷"Son of man, the family of Israel lived in their own country, but they made that land filthy by the bad things they did. To me, they were like a woman who becomes unclean because of her monthly period of bleeding. ¹⁸They spilled blood on the ground when they murdered people in the land. They made the land filthy with their idols, so I showed them how angry I was. ¹⁹I scattered them

among the nations and spread them through all the lands. I gave them the punishment they deserved for the bad things they did. ²⁰But even in those other nations, they ruined my good name. How? Those nations said, 'These are the Lord's people, but they left his land.'

²¹"The people of Israel ruined my holy name wherever they went, and I felt sorry for my name. ²²So tell the family of Israel that this is what the Lord God says: 'Family of Israel, you ruined my holy name in the places where you went. I am going to do something to stop this. I will not do it for your sake, Israel. I will do it for my holy name. ²³I will show the nations how holy my great name really is. You ruined my good name in those nations! But I will show you that I am holy. I will make you respect my name, and then those nations will know that I am the Lord. This is what the Lord God says.

²⁴"'I will take you out of those nations, gather you together, and bring you back to your own land. ²⁵Then I will sprinkle pure water on you and make you pure. I will wash away all your filth, the filth from those nasty idols and I will make you pure. ²⁶I will also put a new spirit in you to change your way of thinking. I will take out the heart of stone from your body and give you a tender, human heart. ²⁷I will put my Spirit inside youᵃ and change you so that you will obey my laws. You will carefully obey my commands. ²⁸Then you will live in the land that I gave to your ancestors. You will be my people, and I will be your God. ²⁹Also, I will save you and keep you from becoming unclean. I will command the grain to grow. I will not bring a famine against you. ³⁰I will give you large crops of fruit from your trees and the harvest from your fields so that you will never again feel the shame of being hungry in a foreign country. ³¹You will remember the bad things you did. You will remember that those things were not good. Then you will hate yourselves because of your sins and the terrible things you did. ³²The Lord God says, I want you to remember this: I am not doing these things for your good! ⌐I am doing them for my good name.⌐ Family of Israel, you should be ashamed and embarrassed about the way you lived!

³³"'This is what the Lord God says: On the day that I wash away your sins, I will bring people back to your cities. The ruined cities will be rebuilt. ³⁴People will begin again to work the land, so when other people pass by they will not see ruins any more. ³⁵They will say, "In the past, this land was ruined, but now it is like the Garden of Eden. The cities were destroyed. They were

---

ᵃ **36:27** *I will put my Spirit inside you* Or "I will make my Spirit live among you."

ruined and empty, but now they are protected, and there are people living in them." ³⁶Then the nations that are still around you will know I am the LORD and that I rebuilt those places. I planted things in this land that was empty. I am the LORD. I said this, and I will make them happen!'

³⁷"This is what the Lord GOD says: I will also let the family of Israel come to me and ask me to do these things for them. I will make them grow and become many people. They will be like flocks of sheep. ³⁸During the special festivals, Jerusalem was filled with flocks of sheep and goats that had been made holy. In the same way, the cities and ruined places will be filled with flocks of people. Then they will know that I am the LORD."

The Vision of the Dry Bones

37 The LORD's power came on me. The Spirit*ᵃ* of the LORD carried me out of the city and put me down in the middle of the valley.*ᵇ* The valley was full of dead men's bones. ²There were many bones lying on the ground in the valley. The Lord made me walk all around among the bones. I saw the bones were very dry.

³Then the Lord said to me, "Son of man, can these bones come to life?"

I answered, "Lord GOD, only you know the answer to that question."

⁴Then he said to me, "Speak to these bones for me. Tell them, 'Dry bones, listen to the word of the LORD! ⁵This is what the Lord GOD says to you: I will cause breath*ᶜ* to come into you, and you will come to life! ⁶I will put sinew and muscles on you, and I will cover you with skin. Then I will put breath in you, and you will come back to life! Then you will know that I am the LORD.'"

⁷So I spoke to the bones for the LORD, as he said. I was still speaking, when I heard the loud noise. The bones began to rattle, and bone joined together with bone! ⁸There before my eyes, I saw sinew and muscles begin to cover the bones. Skin began to cover them, but there was no breath in them.

⁹Then the Lord said to me, "Speak to the wind*ᵈ* for me. Son of man, speak to the wind for me. Tell the wind that this is what the Lord GOD says: 'Wind, come from every direction and breathe air into these dead bodies! Breathe into them and they will come to life again!'"

¹⁰So I spoke to the wind for the LORD, as he said, and the breath came into the dead bodies.

They came to life and stood up. There were many of them—a large army!

¹¹Then he said to me, "Son of man, these bones are like the whole family of Israel. The people of Israel say, 'Our bones have dried up;*ᵉ* our hope has gone. We have been completely destroyed!' ¹²So speak to them for me. Tell them this is what the Lord GOD says: 'My people, I will open your graves and bring you up out of them! Then I will bring you to the land of Israel. ¹³My people, I will open your graves and bring you up out of your graves, and then you will know that I am the LORD. ¹⁴I will put my Spirit*ᶠ* in you, and you will come to life again. Then I will lead you back to your own land. Then you will know that I am the LORD. You will know that I said this and that I made it happen.'" This message is from the LORD.

Judah and Israel to Become One Again

¹⁵The word of the LORD came to me again. He said, ¹⁶"Son of man, get one stick and write this message on it: 'This stick belongs to Judah and his friends,*ᵍ* the people of Israel.' Then take another stick and write on it, 'This stick of Ephraim belongs to Joseph and his friends, the people of Israel.' ¹⁷Then join the two sticks together. In your hand, they will be one stick.

¹⁸"Your people will ask you to explain what that means. ¹⁹Tell them that this is what the Lord GOD says: 'I will take the stick of Joseph, which is in the hand of Ephraim and his friends, the people of Israel. Then I will put that stick with the stick of Judah, and make them one stick. In my hand, they will become one stick!'

²⁰"Take the sticks that you wrote on and hold them in front of you. ²¹Tell the people that this is what the Lord GOD says: 'I will gather the people of Israel from among the nations. I will gather them from all around and bring them back to their own land. ²²I will make them one nation in their land among the mountains of Israel. There will be one king over them all. They will no longer be two nations. They will not be split into two kingdoms any more. ²³And they will no longer continue to make themselves filthy with their idols and horrible statues or with any of their other crimes. Instead, I will save them from all the places where they have sinned, and I will wash them and make them pure. They will be my people, and I will be their God.

²⁴"'And my servant David will be the king over them. There will be only one shepherd over all of

---

ᵃ **37:1 Spirit** Or "wind".
ᵇ **37:1 the valley** Possibly, Jezreel Valley, a fertile area where many battles were fought. It is often called simply "The Valley".
ᶜ **37:5 breath** Or "wind" or "a spirit".
ᵈ **37:9 wind** Or "breath" or "spirit". Also in verse 10.
ᵉ **37:11 bones . . . dried up** This is a way of saying, "We have lost our strength."
ᶠ **37:14 Spirit** Or "spirit" or "wind".
ᵍ **37:16 friends** This is a wordplay. The Hebrew word is like the word meaning "joined together".

GOD'S RESTORATION PROCESS

A graveyard would not be most people's number one choice for a day out. But God has an important message for Ezekiel to hear.

The third of Ezekiel's visions given by God comes at a time of utter hopelessness for God's people. God takes him to an open graveyard, a place where a great army fell a very long time ago.

DIG IN   READ Ezekiel 37:1-14

- Why does God take him to this valley of bones?
- What does God mean by asking, "Son of man, can these bones come to life?" (v.3)?

There's a reason for this day trip. God has another important message for his people. God asks Ezekiel: could life ever return to the people of God?

Imagine what must be going through Ezekiel's mind as he works out how to answer that question! A nation lies in ruins. A people who once believed they were the chosen ones of God, now feel utterly abandoned by him. They had been judged and punished for their sin. Pride has given way to despair, hope to hopelessness. You might reasonably expect him to reply, "Are you having a laugh?"

- What happens when Ezekiel does as God commands (v.7-10)?
- What is the promise for God's people (vv.11-14)?

As Ezekiel steps out in obedience to God's voice, a dramatic thing happens. Even before he's finished speaking (v.7), God shows him a miracle.

The first step is to recreate the bodies. But even though their bodies are restored, they're still dead – they need the breath of life in them. Only when Ezekiel speaks "to the wind" do they come alive and stand up (v.10).

God explains the vision – this was a clear promise that God would restore and recreate the nation of Israel. It also points to another miraculous rebirth in the future (see Dig Deeper, below).

DIG THROUGH

- What's the significance of asking Ezekiel to do the speaking (vv.4,9)? Why didn't God just let him watch?

The answer is that God chooses to involve humanity in his work to restore and recreate the world. As Christians, we are not mere spectators, watching God at work from the sidelines. He calls us to be involved with him (see, for example, 1 Corinthians 3:5–9).

- What should the outcome be of God's restoration process – whether in our personal lives or in our communities?

That people will know that he is the Lord (v.14). Because we've been involved in the process, we might be tempted to take some of the glory. But that's not to happen, God says.

DIG DEEPER

As well as being tremendous comfort to God's people in Ezekiel's time, this story looks ahead to the future and a more glorious resurrection. Jesus' resurrection from the dead on the third day is a central fact of the Christian Good News and was used as eyewitness proof of the claims that Jesus was Lord. In 1 Corinthians 15 the apostle Paul explains how we too will be raised from the dead and what kind of body we will have.

Ezekiel's third vision (there are four in total) ends here, but the bright pictures of the future continue. Read on to the end of the chapter to hear God's promise that Judah and Israel will again be reunited under one king after many years of division.

them. They will live by my rules and obey my laws. They will do the things I tell them. 25They will live on the land that I gave to my servant Jacob. Your ancestors lived in that place, and my people will live there. They and their children and their grandchildren will live there forever. My servant David will be their leader forever. 26And I will make a peace agreement with them. This agreement will continue forever. I agree to give them their land. I agree to make them numerous and to put my holy place among them forever. 27My Holy Tent will be with them. Yes, I will be their God and they will be my people. 28The other nations will know that I am the LORD, and they will know that I make Israel my special people by putting my holy place there among them forever.'"

The Message Against Gog

38 The LORD spoke to me and said, 2"Son of man, look towards Gog in the land of Magog. He is the most important leader of the nations of Meshech and Tubal. Speak for me against Gog. 3Tell him that this is what the Lord GOD says: 'Gog, you are the most important leader of the nations of Meshech and Tubal, but I am against you. 4I will capture you and bring you back. I will bring back all the men in your army, all the horses and horsemen. I will put hooks in your mouths, and I will bring all of you back. All the soldiers will be wearing their uniforms with all their shields and swords. 5Soldiers from Persia, Ethiopia and Put will be with them. They will all be wearing their shields and helmets. 6There will also be Gomer with all its groups of soldiers, and there will be the nation of Togarmah*a* from the far north with all its groups of soldiers. There will be many people in that parade of prisoners.

7"'Be prepared. Yes, prepare yourself and the armies that have joined with you. You must watch and be ready. 8After a long time you will be called for duty. In the later years you will come into the land that has been healed from war. The people in that land were gathered from many nations and brought back to the mountains of Israel. In the past, the mountains of Israel had been destroyed again and again. These people will have come back from those other nations. They all will have lived in safety. 9But you will come to attack them. You will come like a storm. You will come like a thundercloud covering the land. You and all your groups of soldiers from many nations will come to attack them.

10"'This is what the Lord GOD says: At that time an idea will come into your mind. You will

begin to make an evil plan. 11You will say, "I will go and attack the country that has towns without walls. The people there live in peace and think they are safe. There are no walls around the cities to protect them. They don't have any locks on their gates—they don't even have gates! 12I will defeat them and take all their valuable things away from them. I will fight against the places that were destroyed but now have people living in them. I will fight against the people who were gathered from the nations. Now they have cattle and property. They live at the crossroads of the world."*b*

13"'Sheba, Dedan and merchants of Tarshish and all the cities they trade with will ask you, "Did you come to capture valuable things? Did you bring your groups of soldiers together to grab the good things and to carry away silver, gold, cattle and property? Did you come to take all those valuable things?"'

14"Son of man, speak to Gog for me. Tell him that this is what the Lord GOD says: 'You will come to attack my people while they are living in peace and safety. 15You will come from your place out of the far north, and you will bring many people with you. All of them will ride on horses. You will be a large and a powerful army. 16You will come to fight against my people Israel. You will be like a thundercloud covering the land. When that time comes, I will bring you to fight against my land. Then, Gog, the nations will learn how powerful I am! They will learn to respect me and know that I am holy. They will see what I will do to you!

17"'This is what the Lord GOD says: At that time people will remember that I spoke about you in the past. They will remember that I used my servants, the prophets of Israel. They will remember that the prophets of Israel spoke for me in the past and said that I would bring you to fight against them. 18At that time Gog will come to fight against the land of Israel. I will show my anger. This is what the Lord GOD says. 19In my jealousy and fierce anger, I make this promise: there will be a strong earthquake in the land of Israel. 20At that time all living things will shake with fear. The fish in the sea, the birds in the air, the wild animals in the fields and all the little creatures crawling on the ground will shake with fear. The mountains will fall down and the cliffs will break apart. Every wall will fall to the ground! 21On the mountains of Israel, says the Lord GOD, I will call for every kind of terror against*c* Gog. His soldiers will be so afraid that they will attack each other and kill each other with their swords. 22I will punish

---

a **38:6 nation of Togarmah** Or "Beth Togarmah".
b **38:12 They live . . . the world** The powerful countries must travel through there to get to all the other powerful countries.
c **38:21 every kind of terror against** This is from the ancient Greek version. The standard Hebrew text has "a sword against".

Gog with diseases and death. I will cause hailstones, fire and sulphur to rain down on Gog and his groups of soldiers from many nations. ²³Then I will show how great I am. I will prove that I am holy. Many nations will see me do these things, and they will learn who I am. Then they will know that I am the LORD.'

The Death of Gog and His Army

39 "Son of man, speak against Gog for me. Tell him that this is what the Lord GOD says: 'Gog, you are the most important leader of the countries Meshech and Tubal, but I am against you. ²I will capture you and bring you back. I will bring you from the far north. I will bring you to fight against the mountains of Israel. ³But I will knock your bow from your left hand and your arrows from your right hand. ⁴You will be killed on the mountains of Israel. You, your groups of soldiers and all the other nations with you will be killed in the battle. I will give you as food to every kind of bird that eats meat and to all the wild animals. ⁵You will not enter the city. You will be killed out in the open fields. I have spoken! This is what the Lord GOD says.

⁶"I will send fire against Magog and those people living along the coast. They think they are safe, but they will know that I am the LORD. ⁷And I will make my holy name known among my people Israel. I will not let people ruin my holy name any more. The nations will know that I am the LORD. They will know that I am the Holy One in Israel. ⁸That time is coming! It will happen! This is what the Lord GOD says. That is the day I am talking about.

⁹"At that time people living in the cities of Israel will go out to the fields. They will collect the enemy's weapons and burn them. They will burn all the shields, bows and arrows, clubs and spears. They will use the weapons as firewood for seven years. ¹⁰They will not have to gather wood from the fields or chop firewood from the forests because they will use the weapons as firewood. They will take the valuable things from the soldiers who wanted to steal from them. They will take the good things from the soldiers who took good things from them. This is what the Lord GOD says.

¹¹"At that time I will choose a place in Israel to bury Gog. He will be buried in the Valley of the Travellers, east of the Dead Sea. It will block the road for travellers, because Gog and all his army will be buried in that place. So people will then call it "The Valley of Gog's Army". ¹²It will take seven months for the family of Israel to bury them. They must do this to make the land pure. ¹³The common people will bury the enemy soldiers, and the people will become famous on the day that I bring honour to myself. This is what the Lord GOD says.

¹⁴"Workers will be given a full-time job burying the dead soldiers to make the land pure. The workers will work for seven months. They will go around looking for dead bodies. ¹⁵They will go around looking, and if anyone sees a bone, a marker will be put up by it. The sign will stay there until the gravediggers come and bury the bone in the Valley of Gog's Army, ¹⁶near a city named "Army".ᵃ In this way they will make the country pure.'

¹⁷"This is what the Lord GOD says: Son of man, speak to all the birds and wild animals for me. Tell them, 'Come here! Come here! Gather around. Come and eat this sacrifice I am preparing for you. There will be a very big sacrifice on the mountains of Israel. Come, eat the meat and drink the blood. ¹⁸You will eat the meat from the bodies of powerful soldiers and drink the blood from world leaders. They will be like rams, lambs, goats and fat bulls from Bashan. ¹⁹You can eat all the fat you want and drink blood until you are full. You will eat and drink from my sacrifice, which I will kill for you. ²⁰You will have plenty of meat to eat at my table. There will be horses and chariot drivers, powerful soldiers and all the other fighting men.' This is what the Lord GOD says.

²¹"I will let the other nations see what I have done, and they will begin to respect me! They will see my power that I used against the enemy. ²²Then from that day on, the family of Israel will know that I am the LORD their God. ²³And the nations will know why the family of Israel were carried away as prisoners to other countries. They will learn that my people turned against me, so I turned away from them. I let their enemies defeat them, so my people were killed in battle. ²⁴They sinned and made themselves filthy, so I punished them for the things they did. I turned away from them and refused to help them.

²⁵"So this is what the Lord GOD says: Now I will bring the family of Jacob back from captivity. I will have mercy on the whole family of Israel. I will show my strong feelings for my holy name. ²⁶The people will forget their shame and all the times they turned against me. They will live in safety on their own land. No one will make them afraid. ²⁷I will bring my people back from other countries. I will gather them from the lands of their enemies. Then many nations will see how holy I am. ²⁸They will know that I am the LORD their God. That is because I made them leave their homes and go as prisoners to other countries. But then I gathered them together again and brought them back to their own land. ²⁹I will

---

ᵃ **39:16 Army** That is, "Hamonah", a Hebrew word that means "horde" or "crowd".

pour out my Spirit on the family of Israel, and I will never turn away from my people again. This is what the Lord GOD says."

The New Temple

40 In the twenty-fifth year after we were taken away into captivity, at the beginning of the year, on the tenth day of the month,[a] the LORD's power came on me. This was fourteen years after the Babylonians took Jerusalem. On that day, the Lord took me there in a vision.

[2]In the vision, God carried me to the land of Israel. He put me down near a very high mountain. On the mountain in front of me was a building that looked like a city.[b] [3]He took me to that place. There was a man there who looked like polished bronze. He had a cloth tape measure and a measuring stick in his hand. He was standing by the gate. [4]The man said to me, "Son of man, use your eyes and ears. Look at these things and listen to me. Pay attention to everything that I show you, because you have been brought here so that I can show you these things. You must tell the family of Israel all that you see."

[5]I saw a wall that went all the way around the outside of the Temple. In the man's hand there was a stick for measuring things. It was three metres[c] long, so the man measured the thickness of the wall. It was three metres thick. He measured the height of the wall. It was three metres tall.

[6]Then the man went to the east gate. He walked up its steps and measured the opening for the gate. It was three metres wide. [7]The guardrooms were three metres long and three metres wide. The walls between the rooms were two and a half metres[d] thick. The opening by the porch at the end of the gateway that faced the Temple was also three metres wide. [8]Then he measured the porch. [9]It was four metres[e] long. He measured the walls on either side of the gate. Each side wall was one metre[f] wide. The porch was at the end of the gateway that faced the Temple. [10]There were three little guardrooms on each side of the gateway. All these rooms and their side walls measured the same. [11]The man measured the entrance to the gateway. It was five metres[g] wide and six and a half metres[h] long. [12]There was a low wall in front of each room. That wall was 50 centimetres[i] tall and 50 centimetres thick. The rooms were square. Each wall was three metres long.

[13]The man measured the gateway from the outside edge of the roof of one room to the outside edge of the roof of the opposite room. It was twelve and a half metres.[j] Each door was directly opposite the other door. [14k]He measured the faces of all the side walls, including the side walls on either side of the porch at the courtyard. The total was 30 metres.[l] [15]From the inside edge of the outer gate to the far end of the porch was 25 metres.[m] [16]There were small windows[n] above all the guardrooms, the side walls and the porch. The wide part of the windows faced into the gateway. There were carvings of palm trees on the walls that were on either side of the gateway.

The Outer Courtyard

[17]Then the man led me into the outer courtyard. I saw thirty rooms and a pavement that went all the way around the courtyard. The rooms were along the wall and faced in towards the pavement. [18]The pavement was as wide as the gates were long. The pavement reached to the inside end of the gateway. This was the lower pavement. [19]The man measured the distance from the inside of the lower gateway to the outside of the ⌊inner⌋ courtyard. It was 50 metres[o] on the east side as well as on the north side.

[20]Then the man measured the length and width of the north gate that was in the wall surrounding the outer courtyard. [21]This gateway, its three rooms on each side and its porch all measured the same as the first gate. The gateway was 25 metres long and twelve and a half metres wide. [22]Its windows, its porch and its carvings of palm trees measured the same as the east gate. ⌊On the outside,⌋ there were seven steps leading up to the gate. Its porch was at the inside end of the gateway. [23]Across the courtyard from the north gate, there

---

[a] **40:1** *tenth day of the month* This was the Day of Atonement, 573 BC. See Lev. 23:26; 25:9.

[b] **40:2** *On the mountain . . . city* Or "On the mountain, there was a building that looked like a city with a city south of it."

[c] **40:5** *three metres* Literally, "6 *cubits*, each a *cubit* and a *handbreadth*". Also in verse 12.

[d] **40:7** *two and a half metres* Literally, "5 *cubits*". Also in verses 30,48.

[e] **40:9** *four metres* Literally, "8 *cubits*".

[f] **40:9** *one metre* Literally, "2 *cubits*".

[g] **40:11** *five metres* Literally, "10 *cubits*".

[h] **40:11** *six and a half metres* Literally, "13 *cubits*".

[i] **40:12** *50 centimetres* Literally, "1 *cubit*". Also in verse 42.

[j] **40:13** *twelve and a half metres* Literally, "25 *cubits*". Also in verses 21,25,29,30,33,36.

[k] **40:14** The meaning of this verse in the Hebrew text is uncertain.

[l] **40:14** *30 metres* Literally, "60 *cubits*".

[m] **40:15** *25 metres* Literally, "50 *cubits*". Also in verses 21,25,29,33,36.

[n] **40:16** *small windows* These let the soldiers defending the city shoot arrows out at the enemy. The narrow part of the window was on the enemy's side of the wall to give the smallest target.

[o] **40:19** *50 metres* Literally, "100 *cubits*". Also in verse 23,27,47.

was a gate to the inner courtyard. It was like the gate on the east. The man measured from the gate ⌊on the inner wall⌋ to the gate ⌊on the outer wall⌋. It was 50 metres from gate to gate.

24Then the man led me to the south wall. I saw a gate in the south wall. He measured its side walls and its porch. They measured the same as the other gates. 25The gateway and its porch had windows all around like the other gates. The gateway was 25 metres long and twelve and a half metres wide. 26There were seven steps going up to this gate. Its porch was at the inside end of the gateway. It had carvings of palm trees on the walls that were on either side of the gateway. 27A gate was on the south side of the inner courtyard. The man measured from the gate ⌊on the inner wall⌋ to the gate ⌊on the outer wall⌋. It was 50 metres from gate to gate.

The Inner Courtyard

28Then the man led me through the south gate into the inner courtyard. He measured this gate. This gateway measured the same as the other gates to the inner courtyard. 29Its rooms, side walls and porch also measured the same as the other gates. There were windows all around the gateway and its porch. The gateway was 25 metres long and twelve and a half metres wide. 30The porch was twelve and a half metres wide and two and a half metres long. 31And its porch was at the end of the gateway next to the outer courtyard. Carvings of palm trees were on the walls ⌊on either side of the gateway⌋. There were eight steps leading up to the gate.

32Then the man led me into the inner courtyard on the east side. He measured the gate. It measured the same as the other gates. 33Its rooms, side walls and porch also measured the same as the other gates. There were windows all around the gateway and its porch. The gateway was 25 metres long and twelve and a half metres wide. 34And its porch was at the end of the gateway next to the outer courtyard. Carvings of palm trees were on the walls on either side of the gateway. There were eight steps leading up to the gate.

35Then the man led me to the north gate. He measured it, and it measured the same as the other gates. 36Its rooms, side walls and porch also measured the same as the other gates. There were windows all around the gateway and its

porch. The gateway was 25 metres long and twelve and a half metres wide. 37And its porch[a] was at the end of the gateway next to the outer courtyard. Carvings of palm trees were on the walls on either side of the gateway. There were eight steps leading up to the gate.

The Rooms for Preparing Sacrifices

38There was also a doorway in the side walls of the gates. That doorway led into a room where the priests washed the sacrifices. 39There were two tables on each side of the door of this porch. The animals for the burnt offerings, the sin offerings and the guilt offerings were killed on these tables. 40There were also two tables on each side of the door on the outside wall of this porch. 41So there were four tables on the inside wall and four tables on the outside wall—eight tables that the priests used when they killed the animals for sacrifices. 42There were also four tables made from cut stone for the burnt offerings. These tables were 75 centimetres[b] long, 75 centimetres wide and 50 centimetres high. On these tables, the priests put their tools that they used to kill the animals for the burnt offerings and other sacrifices. 43There were meat hooks 75 millimetres long[c] on all the walls in this area. The meat of the offerings was put on the tables.

The Priests' Rooms

44There were two rooms[d] in the inner courtyard. One was by the north gate facing south. The other room was by the south[e] gate facing north. 45The man said to me, "The room that faces south is for the priests who have guard duty for the Temple area. 46And the room that faces north is for the priests who have guard duty for the altar. These men are all from the tribe of Levi. They are descendants of Zadok and have the right to serve in the presence of the LORD.

47The man measured the ⌊inner⌋ courtyard. The courtyard was a perfect square. It was 50 metres long and 50 metres wide. The altar was in front of the Temple.

The Porch of the Temple

48Then the man led me to the porch of the Temple and measured the walls on either side of the porch. Each side wall was two and a half metres thick and one and a half metres[f] wide. The opening between them was seven metres.[g]

a 40:37 porch The Hebrew text has "side walls".
b 40:42 75 centimetres Literally, "1½ cubits".
c 40:43 meat hooks . . . long Or "double shelves 75 millimetres wide . . .".
d 40:44 two rooms Or "rooms for the singers".
e 40:44 south This is from the ancient Greek version. The Hebrew text has "east".
f 40:48 one and a half metres Literally, "3 cubits".
g 40:48 seven metres Literally, "14 cubits".

[49]The porch was ten metres[a] wide and six metres[b] long. Ten steps went up to the porch. There were two columns for the walls on either side of the porch—one at each wall.

The Holy Place of the Temple

41 Then the man led me into the Holy Place. He measured the walls on either side of the room. The side walls were three metres[c] thick on each side. [2]The door was five metres[d] wide. The sides of the doorway were two and a half metres[e] on each side. He measured that room. It was 20 metres[f] long and ten metres wide.

The Most Holy Place in the Temple

[3]Then the man went into the last room. He measured the walls on either side of the doorway. Each side wall was one metre[g] thick and three and a half metres[h] wide. The doorway was three metres wide. [4]Then he measured the length of the room. It was ten metres long and ten metres wide. He said to me, "This is the Most Holy Place."

Other Rooms Around the Temple

[5]Then the man measured the wall of the Temple. It was three metres thick. There were side rooms all around the Temple. They were two metres[i] wide. [6]The side rooms were on three different floors, one above the other. There were 30 rooms on each floor. The wall of the Temple was built with ledges. The side rooms rested on these ledges but were not connected to the Temple wall itself. [7]Each floor of the side rooms around the Temple was wider than the floor below. The walls of the rooms around the Temple became narrower the higher they went so that the rooms on the top floors were wider. A stairway went up from the lowest floor to the highest floor through the middle floor.

[8]I also saw that the Temple had a raised base all the way around it. It was the foundation for the side rooms, and it was three metres high. [9]The outer wall of the side rooms was two and a half metres thick. There was an open area between the side rooms of the Temple [10]and the priests' rooms. It was ten metres[j] wide and went all the way around the Temple. [11]The doors of the side rooms opened onto the raised base. There was one entrance on the north side and one entrance on the south side. The raised base was two and a half metres wide all around.

[12]There was a building in this restricted area west of the Temple. The building was 35 metres[k] wide and 45 metres[l] long. The wall of the building was two and a half metres thick all around. [13]Then the man measured the Temple. The Temple was 50 metres[m] long. The restricted area, including the building and its walls, was also 50 metres long. [14]The restricted area on the east side, in front of the Temple, was 50 metres long.

[15]The man measured the length of the building in the restricted area at the rear of the Temple. It was 50 metres from one wall to the other wall.

The Most Holy Place, the Holy Place and the porch by the courtyard [16]had wood panelling on all the walls. All the windows and doors had wood trim around them. By the doorway, the Temple had wood panelling from the floor up to the windows and up to the part of the wall [17]over the doorway.

On all the walls in the inner room and the outer room of the Temple were carvings [18]of winged creatures and palm trees. A palm tree was between each winged creature, and each one had two faces. [19]One face was a man's face looking towards the palm tree on one side. The other face was a lion's face looking towards the palm tree on the other side. They were carved all around on the Temple. [20]From the floor to the area above the door, winged creatures and palm trees were carved on all walls of the Holy Place.

[21]The walls on either side of the Holy Place were square. In front of the Most Holy Place, there was something that looked like [22]an altar made from wood. It was one and a half metres[n] high and one metre long. Its corners, its base and its sides were wood. The man said to me, "This is the table that is before the LORD."

[23]Both the Holy Place and the Most Holy Place had a double door. [24]Each of the doors was made

---

[a] **40:49** *ten metres* Literally, "20 *cubits*". Also in 41:2,4.
[b] **40:49** *six metres* Literally, "12 *cubits*".
[c] **41:1** *three metres* Literally, "6 *cubits*". Also in verses 3,5.
[d] **41:2** *five metres* Literally, "10 *cubits*".
[e] **41:2** *two and a half metres* Literally, "5 *cubits*". Also in verses 9,12.
[f] **41:2** *20 metres* Literally, "40 *cubits*".
[g] **41:3** *one metre* Literally, "2 *cubits*". Also in verse 22.
[h] **41:3** *three and a half metres* Literally, "7 *cubits*".
[i] **41:5** *two metres* Literally, "4 *cubits*".
[j] **41:10** *ten metres* Literally, "20 *cubits*".
[k] **41:12** *35 metres* Literally, "70 *cubits*".
[l] **41:12** *45 metres* Literally, "90 *cubits*".
[m] **41:13** *50 metres* Literally, "100 *cubits*". Also in verses 14,15.
[n] **41:22** *one and a half metres* Literally, "3 *cubits*".

from two smaller doors. Each door was really two swinging doors. 25Also, winged creatures and palm trees were carved on the doors of the Holy Place. They were like those carved on the walls. There was a wooden roof over the front of the porch. 26There were windows with frames around them and palm trees on the walls on both sides of the porch, on the roof over the porch and on the rooms around the Temple.

The Priests' Room

42 Then the man led me through the north gate out into the outer courtyard. He led me to a building with many rooms that was west of the restricted area and the building on the north side. 2This building was 50 metres*a* long and 25 metres*b* wide. People entered it from the courtyard on the north side. 3The building was three storeys tall and had balconies. The ten-metre*c* inner courtyard was between the building and the Temple. On the other side, the rooms faced the pavement of the outer courtyard. 4There was a path five metres*d* wide and 50 metres long running along the south side of the building, even though the entrance was on the north side. 5-6Since this building was three storeys tall and did not have columns like those columns of the outer courtyards, the top rooms were farther back than the rooms on the middle and bottom floors. The top floor was narrower than the middle floor, which was narrower than the bottom floor because the balconies used this space. 7There was a wall outside that was parallel to the rooms and ran along the outer courtyard. It ran in front of the rooms for 25 metres. 8The row of rooms that ran along the outer courtyard was 25 metres long, although the total length of the building, as on the Temple side, was 50 metres long. 9The entrance was below these rooms at the east end of the building so that people could enter from the outer courtyard. 10The entrance was at the start of the wall beside the courtyard.

There were rooms on the south side, by the restricted area and the other building. These rooms had a 11path in front of them. They were like the rooms on the north side. They had the same length and width and the same kind of doors. 12The entrance to the lower rooms was at the east end of the building so that people could enter from the open end of the path by the wall.

13The man said to me, "The north rooms and south rooms opposite the restricted area are holy. These rooms are for the priests who offer the sacrifices to the LORD. That is where the priests will put the most holy offerings and eat them. That is because that place is holy. The most holy offerings are the grain offerings, the sin offerings and the guilt offerings. 14The priests who enter the holy area must leave their serving clothes in that holy place before they go out into the outer courtyard, because these clothes are holy. If a priest wants to go to the part of the Temple where the other people are, he must go to those rooms and put on other clothes."

The Outer Courtyard

15The man had finished measuring inside the Temple area. Then he brought me out through the east gate and measured all around that area. 16He measured the east side with the measuring stick. It was 250 metres*e* long. 17He measured the north side. It was 250 metres long. 18He measured the south side. It was 250 metres long. 19He went around to the west side and measured it. It was 250 metres long. 20He measured the four sides of the wall that went all the way around the Temple. The wall was 250 metres long and 250 metres wide. It separated the holy area from the area that is not holy.

The LORD Will Live Among His People

43 The man led me to the east gate. 2There the Glory of the God of Israel came from the east. God's voice was loud like the sound of the sea. The ground was bright with the light from the Glory of God. 3The vision that I saw was like the vision I saw by the Kebar Canal. I bowed with my face to the ground. 4The Glory of the LORD came into the Temple through the east gate.

5Then the Spirit*f* picked me up and brought me into the inner courtyard. The Glory of the LORD filled the Temple. 6I heard someone speaking to me from inside the Temple. The man was still standing beside me. 7The voice from the Temple said to me, "Son of man, this is the place with my throne and footstool. I will live in this place among the people of Israel forever. The family of Israel will not ruin my holy name again. The kings and their people will not bring shame to my name by committing sexual sins*g* or by burying

---

a **42:2 50 metres** Literally, "100 *cubits*".
b **42:2 25 metres** Literally, "50 *cubits*".
c **42:3 ten-metre** Literally, "20 *cubits*".
d **42:4 five metres** Literally, "10 *cubits*".
e **42:16 250 metres** Literally, "500 *cubits*".
f **43:5 Spirit** Or "spirit" or "wind".
g **43:7 sexual sins** This might also mean "turning away from God and being unfaithful to him".

the dead bodies of their kings in this place. [8]They will not bring shame to my name by putting their threshold next to my threshold, and their doorposts next to my doorposts. In the past, only a wall separated them from me. So they brought shame to my name every time they sinned and did those terrible things. That is why I became angry and destroyed them. [9]Now let them take their sexual sins and the dead bodies of their kings far away from me. Then I will live among them forever.

[10]"Now, son of man, tell the family of Israel about the Temple. Then, when they learn about the plans for the Temple, they will be ashamed of their sins. [11]And they will be ashamed of all the bad things they have done. Let them know the design of the Temple. Let them know how it should be built, where the entrances and exits are and all the designs on it. Teach them about all its rules and all its laws. Write these things for everyone to see so that they can obey all the laws and rules for the Temple. [12]This is the law of the Temple: the whole area surrounding it on the top of the mountain is most holy. This is the law of the Temple.

The Altar

[13]"These are the measurements of the altar[a] using the long measurements: There was a gutter all the way around the base of the altar. It was 50 centimetres[b] deep and 50 centimetres wide. There was a rim 25 centimetres[c] high around the edge of the gutter. This is how tall the altar was: [14]From the bottom of the gutter to the top of the lower ledge, the base measured one metre.[d] The lower ledge was 50 centimetres wide. The lower ledge to the upper ledge measured two metres[e]. The upper ledge was 50 centimetres wide. [15]The place for the fire on the altar was two metres high. The four corners were shaped like horns. [16]The place for the fire on the altar was six metres[f] long by six metres wide. It was perfectly square. [17]The upper ledge was also square, seven metres[g] long by seven metres wide. The rim around it was 25 centimetres[h] high. (The rim, together with its gutter, was 50 centimetres wide around the top edge of the altar.) The steps going up to the altar were on the east side."

[18]Then the man said to me, "Son of man, this is what the Lord God says: These are the rules for the altar. At the time you build the altar, use these rules to offer burnt offerings and to sprinkle blood on it. [19]You will give a young bull as a sin offering to the priests, the Levites from Zadok's family. They are the men who serve me by bringing the offerings to me. This is what the Lord God says. [20]You will take some of the bull's blood and put it on the altar's four horns, on the four corners of the ledge, and on the rim around it. In this way you will make the altar pure. [21]Then take the bull for the sin offering and burn it in the proper place in the Temple area, outside the Temple building.

[22]"On the second day you will offer a male goat that has nothing wrong with it. It will be for a sin offering. The priests will make the altar pure the same way they made it pure with the bull. [23]When you have finished making the altar pure, you will offer a young bull that has nothing wrong with it and a ram from the flock that has nothing wrong with it. [24]Then you will offer them before the Lord. The priests will sprinkle salt on them. Then they will offer the bull and ram up as a burnt offering to the Lord. [25]You will prepare a goat every day for seven days for a sin offering. Also, you will prepare a young bull and a ram from the flock. These animals must have nothing wrong with them. [26]For seven days the priests will make the altar pure and ready for use in worshipping God. [27]On the eighth day, and every day after that, the priests must offer your burnt offerings and fellowship offerings on the altar. Then I will accept you. This is what the Lord God says."

The Outer Gate

44 Then the man brought me back to the east gate of the Temple area. We were outside the gate and the gate was shut. [2]The Lord said to me, "This gate will stay shut. It will not be opened. No one will enter through it, because the Lord of Israel has entered through it. So it must stay shut. [3]Only the ruler of the people may sit at this gate when he eats a meal with the Lord. He must enter through the porch of the gateway and go out the same way."

The Holiness of the Temple

[4]Then the man led me through the north gate to the front of the Temple. I looked and saw the Glory of the Lord filling the Lord's Temple. I bowed with my face touching the ground. [5]The

---

[a] **43:13 These are . . . altar** Literally, "These are the measurements of the altar in *cubits*, each a *cubit* and a *handbreadth*".
[b] **43:13 50 centimetres** Literally, "1 *cubit*".
[c] **43:13 25 centimetres** Literally, "1 *span*". The distance from the tip of the thumb to the tip of the little finger.
[d] **43:14 one metre** Literally, "2 *cubits*".
[e] **43:14 two metres** Literally, "4 *cubits*".
[f] **43:16 six metres** Literally, "12 *cubits*".
[g] **43:17 seven metres** Literally, "14 *cubits*".
[h] **43:17 25 centimetres** Literally, "½ *cubit*".

LORD said to me, "Son of man, look very carefully! Use your eyes and ears. Look at these things, and listen very carefully to everything that I tell you about all the rules and laws about the LORD's Temple. Look carefully at the entrances to the Temple and at all the exits from the holy place. ⁶Then give this message to all the people of Israel who refused to obey me. Tell them, 'This is what the Lord GOD says: Family of Israel, I have had enough of the terrible things you have done! ⁷You brought foreigners into my Temple who are not circumcised and have not given themselves to me.ᵃ In this way you made my Temple unclean. You broke our agreement and did terrible things, and then you gave me the offerings of bread, the fat and the blood. But this only made my Temple unclean. ⁸You did not take care of my holy things. No, you put foreigners in charge of my holy place!

⁹"'This is what the Lord GOD says: A foreigner who is not truly circumcised must not come into my Temple—not even a foreigner living permanently among the people of Israel. He must be circumcised, and he must give himself completely to me before he can come into my Temple. ¹⁰In the past, the Levites left me when Israel turned away from me. Israel left me to follow their idols. The Levites will be punished for their sin. ¹¹The Levites were chosen to serve in my holy place. They guarded the gates of the Temple. They served in the Temple. They killed the animals for the sacrifices and burnt offerings for the people. They were chosen to help the people and to serve them. ¹²But the Levites helped the people sin against me! They helped the people worship their idols! So I am making this promise against them: They will be punished for their sin. This is what the Lord GOD says.

¹³"'So the Levites will not bring offerings to me like the priests. They will not come near any of my holy things or the things that are most holy. They must carry their shame because of the terrible things that they did. ¹⁴But I will let them take care of the Temple. They will work in the Temple and do the things that must be done in it.

¹⁵"'But the priests, the Levites from Zadok's family, are to stand before me. They took care of my holy place when the people of Israel turned away from me. So they are the ones who will bring the offerings to me. They will offer me the fat and the blood from the animals they sacrifice. This is what the Lord GOD says! ¹⁶They will enter my holy place and come near my table to serve me. They will take care of the things I gave them. ¹⁷When they enter the gates of the inner courtyard, they will wear linen clothes. They will not wear wool while they serve at the gates of the inner courtyard and in the Temple. ¹⁸They will wear linen turbans on their heads, and they will wear linen underwear. They will not wear anything that makes them sweat. ¹⁹Before they go out into the outer courtyard to the people, they will take off the clothes they wear while serving me. They will put these clothes away in the holy rooms. Then they will put on other clothes. In this way they will not let people touch those holy clothes.

²⁰"'These priests will not shave their heads or let their hair grow long.ᵇ The priests may only trim the hair of their heads. ²¹None of the priests may drink wine when they go into the inner courtyard. ²²The priests must not marry a widow or a divorced woman. No, they must only marry a virgin from the family of Israel or a woman whose dead husband was a priest.

²³"'Also, the priests must teach my people the difference between things that are holy and things that are not holy. They must help my people know what is clean and what is unclean. ²⁴The priests will be the judges in court. They will follow my laws when they judge people. They will obey my laws and my rules at all my special feasts. They will respect my special days of rest and keep them holy. ²⁵They will not go near a dead person to make themselves unclean. But they may make themselves unclean if the dead person is their father, mother, son, daughter, brother or a sister who is not married. ²⁶After the priest has been made clean, he must wait seven days. ²⁷Then he can go back into the holy place. But on the day he goes into the inner courtyard to serve in the holy place, he must offer a sin offering for himself. This is what the Lord GOD says.

²⁸"'About the land that will belong to the Levites: I am their property. You will not give the Levites any land in Israel. I am their share in Israel. ²⁹They will have the right to eat the grain offerings, the sin offerings and the guilt offerings. Also, anything in Israel that is a special gift to Godᶜ will belong to them. ³⁰And the first part of the harvest from every kind of crop will be for the priests. You will also give the priests the first part of your flour. This will bring blessings to your house. ³¹The priests must not eat any bird or animal that has died a natural death or has been torn to pieces by a wild animal.

ᵃ **44:7 not circumcised . . . to me** Literally, "not circumcised in their heart or in their body". See "CIRCUMCISE, CIRCUMCISION" in the Word List. Also in verse 9.
ᵇ **44:20 These priests . . . grow long** This would show that they are sad, and the priests must be happy about serving the Lord.
ᶜ **44:29 special gift to God** Anything offered to God that could not be bought back. See Lev. 27:28–29.

The Division of the Land for Holy Use

45 ¹"'You will divide the land for the Israelite tribes by throwing lots. At that time you will separate out a part of the land. It will be a holy part for the LORD. The land will be twelve and a half kilometres[a] long and ten kilometres[b] wide. All this land will be holy. ²A square area that is 250 metres[c] long on each side will be for the Temple. There will be an open space around the Temple that is 25 metres[d] wide. ³In the holy area you will measure twelve and a half kilometres long and five kilometres[e] wide. The Temple will be in this area. The Temple area will be the Most Holy Place.

⁴"'This holy part of the land will be for the priests, the servants of the Temple. This is where they approach the LORD to serve him. It will be a place for the priests' houses and a place for the Temple. ⁵Another area, twelve and a half kilometres long and five kilometres wide, will be for the Levites who serve in the Temple. This land will also become cities for the Levites.

⁶"'And you will give the city an area that is two and a half kilometres[f] wide and twelve and a half kilometres long. It will be along the side of the holy area. It will be for all the family of Israel. ⁷The ruler will have land on both sides of the holy area and the land belonging to the city. It will be next to the holy area and the area belonging to the city. It will be the same width as the land that belongs to a tribe. It will go all the way from the west border to the east border. ⁸This land will be the ruler's property in Israel. So he will not need to make life hard for my people any more. But they will give the land to the Israelites for their tribes.

⁹"'This is what the Lord GOD says: Enough, you rulers of Israel! Stop being cruel and stealing things from people! Be fair and do what is right! Stop forcing my people out from their homes! This is what the Lord GOD says.

¹⁰"'Stop cheating people. Use accurate scales and measurements! ¹¹The *ephah* and the *bath* must be the same size: a *bath* and an *ephah* must both equal 1/10 *homer*.[g] Those measures will be based on the *homer*. ¹²A *shekel*[h] must equal 20 *gerahs*. A *mina* must equal 60 *shekels*. It must be equal to 20 *shekels* plus 25 *shekels* plus 15 *shekels*.

¹³"'This is a special offering that you must give:

1/6 *ephah*[i] of wheat for every *homer* of wheat;
1/6 *ephah* of barley for every *homer* of barley;
¹⁴1/10 *bath*[j] of olive oil for every *cor*[k] of olive oil;
(Remember: Ten *baths* make a *homer*, and ten *baths* make a *cor*.)
¹⁵and one sheep for every 200 sheep from every watering hole in Israel.

"'Those special offerings are for the grain offerings, for the burnt offerings and for the fellowship offerings. These offerings are to remove the sins of the people. This is what the Lord GOD says.

¹⁶"'Everyone in the country will give to this offering for the ruler of Israel. ¹⁷But the ruler must give the things needed for the special holy days. The ruler must provide the burnt offerings, the grain offerings and the drink offerings for the feast days, for the New Moon, for the Sabbaths and for all the other special meeting days of the family of Israel. He must give all the sin offerings, grain offerings, burnt offerings and fellowship offerings that are used to make the family of Israel pure.

¹⁸"'This is what the Lord GOD says: In the first month, on the first day of the month, you will take a young bull that has nothing wrong with it. You must use that bull to make the Temple pure. ¹⁹The priest will take some of the blood from the sin offering and put it on the doorposts of the Temple and on the four corners of the ledge of the altar and on the posts of the gate to the inner courtyard. ²⁰You will do the same thing on the seventh day of that month for anyone who has sinned by mistake or without knowing it. So you will make the Temple pure.

Offerings During the Passover Festival

²¹"'On the fourteenth day of the first month, you must celebrate Passover. The Festival of Unleavened Bread begins at this time. It continues for seven days. ²²At that time the ruler will offer a bull for himself and for all the people of Israel. The bull will be for a sin offering. ²³During the seven days of the festival, the ruler will offer seven bulls

---

[a] **45:1 twelve and a half kilometres** Literally, "25,000 *cubits*". Also in verses 4,6.
[b] **45:1 ten kilometres** Literally, "20,000 *cubits*". This is from the ancient Greek version. The standard Hebrew text has "10,000 *cubits*".
[c] **45:2 250 metres** Literally, "500 *cubits*".
[d] **45:2 25 metres** Literally, "50 *cubits*".
[e] **45:3 five kilometres** Literally, "10,000 *cubits*". Also in verse 5.
[f] **45:6 two and a half kilometres** Literally, "5,000 *cubits*".
[g] **45:11 homer** A measure equal to about 220 litres. Also in verse 13.
[h] **45:12 shekel** A weight equal to 11.5 grammes. This also became an amount of money.
[i] **45:13 1/6 ephah** 3.67 litres.
[j] **45:14 1/10 bath** 2.2 litres.
[k] **45:14 cor** 220 litres.

and seven rams that have nothing wrong with them. They will be burnt offerings to the LORD. The ruler will offer one bull on every day of the seven days of the festival, and he will offer a male goat every day for a sin offering. ²⁴The ruler will give 10 kilogrammes[a] of barley as a grain offering with each bull, and 10 kilogrammes of barley with each ram. He must give 4 litres[b] of oil for each 10 kilogrammes of grain. ²⁵He must do the same thing for the seven days of the Festival ⌊of Shelters⌋. This festival begins on the fifteenth day of the seventh month. These offerings will be the sin offering, the burnt offering, the grain offering and the oil offering.

The Ruler and the Festivals

46 ¹"'This is what the Lord GOD says: The east gate of the inner courtyard will be closed on the six working days. But it will be opened on the Sabbath day and on the day of the New Moon. ²The ruler will go into the porch of that gate and stand by the gatepost. Then the priests will offer the ruler's burnt offering and fellowship offerings. The ruler will worship at the opening of that gate and then go out. But the gate will not be shut until evening. ³On the Sabbath day and on the day of the New Moon, the common people will also worship the LORD at that gate.

⁴"'The ruler will offer burnt offerings to the LORD on the Sabbath. He must provide six lambs that have nothing wrong with them and a ram that has nothing wrong with it. ⁵He must give 10 kilogrammes of grain offering with the ram. As for the grain offering with the lambs, the ruler can give as much as he wants. But he must give 4 litres of olive oil for every 10 kilogrammes of grain.

⁶"'On the day of the New Moon he must offer a young bull that has nothing wrong with it. He will also offer six lambs and a ram that have nothing wrong with them. ⁷The ruler must give 10 kilogrammes of grain as an offering with the bull and 10 kilogrammes of grain as an offering with the ram. As for the grain offering with the lambs, he can give as much as he wants. But he must give 4 litres of olive oil for each offering of grain.

⁸"'When the ruler goes in, he must enter at the porch of the east gate—and he must leave that same way.

⁹"'When the common people come to meet with the LORD at the special festivals, whoever enters through the north gate to worship will go out through the south gate, and whoever enters through the south gate will go out through the north gate. People must not return the same way they entered. Each person must go out straight ahead. ¹⁰The ruler should be there among the people. When the people go in, the ruler will go in with them, and when they go out, the ruler will too.

¹¹"'At the festivals and other special meetings, 10 kilogrammes of grain must be offered with each young bull, and 10 kilogrammes of grain must be offered with each ram. As for the grain offering with the lambs, the ruler can give as much as he wants. But he must give 4 litres of olive oil for each offering of grain.

¹²"'When the ruler gives a freewill offering to the LORD—it might be a burnt offering, a fellowship offering or a freewill offering—the east gate will be opened for him. Then he will offer his burnt offering and his fellowship offerings as he does on the Sabbath day. After he leaves, the gate will be shut.

The Daily Offering

¹³"'Every day you will provide a year-old lamb that has nothing wrong with it. It will be for a burnt offering to the LORD. You will provide it every morning. ¹⁴Also, you will offer a grain offering with the lamb every morning. You will give two kilogrammes[c] of flour and one litre[d] of oil to make the fine flour moist. It will be the daily grain offering to the LORD. ¹⁵So they will give the lamb, the grain offering and the oil every morning for a burnt offering forever.

Laws of Inheritance for the Ruler

¹⁶"'This is what the Lord GOD says: If the ruler gives a gift from part of his land to any of his sons, it will belong to his sons. It is their property. ¹⁷But if the ruler gives a gift from part of his land to one of his slaves, the gift will belong to the slave only until the year of freedom.[e] Then the gift will go back to the ruler. Only the ruler's sons will keep a gift of land from the ruler. ¹⁸And the ruler will not take any of the people's land or force them to leave their land. He must give some of his own land to his sons. In that way my people will not be forced to lose their land.'"

The Special Kitchens

¹⁹The man led me through the entrance at the side of the gate. He led me to the holy rooms for

---

^a 45:24 **10 kilogrammes** Literally, "1 *ephah*". Also in 46:5,7,11.
^b 45:24 **4 litres** Literally, "1 *hin*".
^c 46:14 **two kilogrammes** Literally, "⅙ *ephah*".
^d 46:14 **one litre** Literally, "⅓ *hin*".
^e 46:17 **year of freedom** Or "Jubilee". See "JUBILEE" in the Word List.

the priests on the north side. There I saw a place at the west end of the path. 20The man said to me, "This is where the priests will boil the guilt offering and the sin offering and will bake the grain offering. Why? So they will not need to bring these offerings out into the outer courtyard. So they will not bring those holy things out where the common people are."

21Then the man led me out to the outer courtyard. He led me to the four corners of the courtyard. I saw smaller courtyards in each corner of the large courtyard. 22There was a small, enclosed area in the four corners of the courtyard. Each small courtyard was 20 metres[a] long and 15 metres[b] wide. The four areas measured the same. 23There was a brick wall around each of the four small courtyards, and there were places built into the brick walls for cooking. 24The man said to me, "These are the kitchens where those who serve at the Temple cook the sacrifices for the people."

The Water Flowing From the Temple

47 The man led me back to the entrance of the Temple. I saw water coming out from under the east gate of the Temple. (The front of the Temple is on the east side.) The water flowed down from under the south end of the Temple and ran south of the altar. 2The man led me out through the north gate and then around the outside to the outer gate on the east side. The water was flowing out on the south side of the gate.

3The man walked east with a tape measure in his hand. He measured 500 metres.[c] Then he told me to walk through the water at that place. The water was only ankle deep. 4He measured another 500 metres. Then he told me to walk through the water at that place. There the water came up to my knees. Then he measured another 500 metres and told me to walk through the water at that place. There the water was waist deep. 5He measured another 500 metres, but there the water was too deep to cross. It had become a river. The water was deep enough to swim in. It was a river that was too deep to cross. 6Then the man said to me, "Son of man, did you pay close attention to the things you saw?"

Then the man led me back along the side of the river. 7As I walked back along the side of the water, I saw many trees on both sides of the water. 8He said to me, "This water flows east, down into the valley of the Jordan River. When it flows into the Dead Sea, the salt water there will become fresh water. 9There will be all kinds of living things where this river flows. Even the Dead Sea will be full of fish because this river will make the water fresh. Wherever this river flows, there will be life. 10You will see fishermen standing by the Dead Sea all the way from En Gedi to En Eglaim. You will see them throwing their fishing nets and catching all kinds of fish, as many kinds as are in the Great Sea. 11But the swamps and small marshes will not become fresh. They will be left for salt. 12All kinds of fruit trees will grow on both sides of the river. Their leaves will never become dry and fall. The fruit will never stop growing on those trees. The trees will produce fruit every month, because the water for the trees comes from the Temple. The fruit from the trees will be for food, and their leaves will be for healing."

Division of the Land for the Tribes

13This is what the Lord God says: "These are the borders for dividing the land among the twelve tribes of Israel. Joseph will have two parts. 14You will divide the land equally. I promised to give this land to your ancestors, so I am giving this land to you.

15"Here are the borders of the land: On the north side, it goes from the Mediterranean Sea by way of Hethlon where the road turns towards Hamath and on to Zedad, 16Berothah, Sibraim (which is on the border between Damascus and Hamath) and Hazer Hatticon, which is on the border of Hauran. 17So the border will go from the sea to Hazar Enan on the northern border of Damascus and Hamath. This will be on the north side.

18"On the east side, the border will go from Hazar Enan between Hauran and Damascus and continue along the Jordan River between Gilead and the land of Israel, to the eastern sea and all the way to Tamar. This will be the eastern border.

19"On the south side, the border will go from Tamar all the way to the oasis at Meribah-kadesh. Then it will follow the Brook of Egypt to the Mediterranean Sea. This will be the southern border.

20"On the west side, the Mediterranean Sea will be the border all the way to the area in front of Lebo Hamath. This will be your western border.

21"So you will divide this land among you for the tribes of Israel. 22You will divide it as a property for yourselves and for the foreigners who live among you and who have had children among you. You must treat these foreigners the

---

[a] **46:22 20 metres** Literally, "40 cubits".
[b] **46:22 15 metres** Literally, "30 cubits".
[c] **47:3 500 metres** Literally, "1,000 cubits".

same as people born in Israel. They will get a share of the land given to the tribes of Israel. [23]The tribe where the foreigner lives must give him some land." This is what the Lord God says!

The Land for the Tribes of Israel

48 "The northern border goes east from the coast to Hethlon to Hamath Pass and then all the way to Hazar Enan. This is on the border between Damascus and Hamath. The land for the tribes in this group will go from the east of these borders to the west. [2-7]From north to south, the tribes in this area are Dan, Asher, Naphtali, Manasseh, Ephraim, Reuben and Judah.

The Special Section of Land

[8]"The next area of land will be for a special use. This land is south of Judah's land. This area is twelve and a half kilometres[a] long from north to south. From east to west, it will be as wide as the land that belongs to the other tribes. The Temple will be in the middle of this section of land. [9]You will dedicate this land to the Lord. It will be twelve and a half kilometres long and ten kilometres[b] wide. [10]This special area of land will be divided among the priests and Levites.

"The priests will get one part of this area. The land will be twelve and a half kilometres long on the north side, five kilometres[c] wide on the west side, five kilometres wide on the east side and twelve and a half kilometres long on the south side. The Lord's Temple will be in the middle of this area of land. [11]This land is for Zadok's descendants. These men were chosen to be my holy priests, because they continued to serve me when the other people of Israel left me. Zadok's family did not leave me like the other people from the tribe of Levi. [12]This share from this holy part of the land will be especially for these priests. It will be next to the land of the Levites.

[13]"Next to the land for the priests, the Levites will have a share of the land. It will be twelve and a half kilometres long and five kilometres wide. Together the land of the priests and Levites will be twelve and a half kilometres long and ten kilometres wide. [14]The Levites will not be able to sell or trade any of this land. They will not be able to sell any of it. They must not cut up this part of the country, because this land belongs to the Lord—it is very special. It is the best part of the land.

The Shares for the City Property

[15]"There will be an area of land two and a half kilometres[d] wide by twelve and a half kilometres long that is left over from the land given to the priests and Levites. This land can be for the city, for grasslands for animals and for building houses. The common people may use this land. The city will be in the middle of it. [16]These are the city's measurements: the north side will be 2,250 metres.[e] The south side will be 2,250 metres. The east side will be 2,250 metres. The west side will be 2,250 metres. [17]The city will have grasslands. These grasslands will be 125 metres[f] on the north and 125 metres on the south. They will be 125 metres on the east and 125 metres on the west. [18]What is left of the length along the side of the holy area will be five kilometres on the east and five kilometres on the west. This land will be along the side of the holy area. This land will grow food for the city workers. [19]The city workers from all the tribes of Israel will farm this land.

[20]"This special area of land will be square. It will be twelve and a half kilometres long by twelve and a half kilometres wide. You must set apart this area for its special purposes. One part is for the priests, one part is for the Levites and one part is for the city.

[21-22]"Part of that special land will be for the ruler of the country. That special area of land is square. It is twelve and a half kilometres long by twelve and a half kilometres wide. Part of this special land is for the priests, part of it is for the Levites and part of it is for the Temple. The Temple is in the middle of this area of land. The rest of the land belongs to the ruler of the country. The ruler will get the area between the land of Benjamin and the land of Judah.

[23-27]"South of this special area will be the land for the tribes that lived east of the Jordan River. Each tribe will get a section of land that goes from the eastern border to the western coast. From north to south, these tribes are Benjamin, Simeon, Issachar, Zebulun and Gad.

[28]"The southern border of Gad's land will go from Tamar to the oasis at Meribah-Kadesh, then follow the brook of Egypt to the Mediterranean Sea. [29]This is the land that you will divide among the tribes of Israel. This is what each group will get." This is what the Lord God says!

---

[a] **48:8 twelve and a half kilometres** Literally, "25,000 cubits". Also in verses 9,10,13,15,20,21–22.
[b] **48:9 ten kilometres** Literally, "20,000 cubits", following one Greek copy. Most Greek copies have 25,000 cubits, and the standard Hebrew text has 10,000 cubits. But see Ezek. 45:1, which also has 20,000 cubits. Also in verse 13.
[c] **48:10 five kilometres** Literally, "10,000 cubits". Also in verses 13,18.
[d] **48:15 two and a half kilometres** Literally, "5,000 cubits".
[e] **48:16 2,250 metres** Literally, "4,500 cubits". Also in verses 30,32–34.
[f] **48:17 125 metres** Literally, "250 cubits".

The Gates of the City

³⁰"These are the gates of the city. The gates will be named for the tribes of Israel.

"The north side of the city will be 2,250 metres long. ³¹There will be three gates: Reuben's Gate, Judah's Gate and Levi's Gate.

³²"The east side of the city will be 2,250 metres long. There will be three gates: Joseph's Gate, Benjamin's Gate and Dan's Gate.

³³"The south side of the city will be 2,250 metres long. There will be three gates: Simeon's Gate, Issachar's Gate and Zebulun's Gate.

³⁴"The west side of the city will be 2,250 metres long. There will be three gates: Gad's Gate, Asher's Gate and Naphtali's Gate.

³⁵"The distance around the city will be nine kilometres.ᵃ From now on, the name of the city will be THE LORD IS THERE."ᵇ

ᵃ **48:35** *nine kilometres* Literally, "18,000 *cubits*".
ᵇ **48:35** *THE LORD IS THERE* In Hebrew this name sounds like Jerusalem.

Who
The hero of the book is Daniel – a Jew taken into exile in Babylon in 605 BC. He was one of several young men chosen to serve in King Nebuchadnezzar's court. The traditional view is that Daniel is both the hero and the author of the book.

When
The action of Daniel is set in the time of the Babylonian exile in the sixth century BC. However, some experts argue that the book was actually written much later, around 165 BC.

What
Daniel is an unusual book. For a start, a major chunk of it was written in Aramaic rather than in Hebrew (2:4 – 7:28). It tells the tale of a group of Jews in exile in Babylon, but also recounts prophecies that point to future times.

The first half of the book is a narrative set in the reigns of the Babylonian emperors Nebuchadnezzar and Belshazzar. They feature Daniel and his friends and their struggle to keep their integrity under pressure. Daniel is a kind of Joseph, rising to power and influence in a foreign court through his God-given wisdom and insight and prophetic visions of future empires.

The second part of the book details Daniel's own prophecies of the future and is a series of visions. This is an example of apocalyptic writing. The word "apocalypse" is from the Greek meaning "revelation". An apocalyptic work is one which reveals what will happen and what is really going on. It doesn't mean "the end of the world" although apocalyptic writings are often about some kind of cataclysmic transformation.

The overall theme of the book is that God is in charge of history and in charge of the world. All those kings who think they rule? They don't know the real truth.

One central theme of the book is the pressure to conform, to change our customs and practices. Babylon was a multicultural empire that had absorbed knowledge and customs from those it had conquered. But Daniel is all about integrity – retaining a purity of worship in the face of enormous pressure to conform and to change. In today's multi-faith, relativistic world, Daniel has an important message about the struggle to stay faithful, and the way that God will support us in that struggle.

QUICK TOUR ▶ DANIEL

A vegetarian diet 1:1–21
Nebuchadnezzar's dream 2:1–49
The fiery furnace 3:1–30
The writing on the wall 5:1–31

The lion's den 6:1–28
The four beasts 7:1–28
Seventy years 9:1–19

"King Darius was very happy. He told his servants to lift Daniel out of the lions' den. And when Daniel was lifted out of the den, they did not find any injury on his body. The lions did not hurt Daniel because he trusted in his God."

Daniel 6:23

Daniel Taken to Babylon

1 King Nebuchadnezzar of Babylon came to Jerusalem and surrounded it with his army. This happened during the third year that Jehoiakim*a* was king of Judah. ²The Lord allowed Nebuchadnezzar to defeat Jehoiakim king of Judah. Nebuchadnezzar took all the dishes and other things from God's Temple and carried them to Babylonia.*b* He put those things in the temple of his gods.

³Then King Nebuchadnezzar ordered Ashpenaz, the man in charge of his officials, to bring some of the boys into the palace to train them. He was to include boys from among the Israelites,*c* from important Judean families and from the royal family of Judah. ⁴King Nebuchadnezzar wanted only healthy boys who did not have any bruises, scars or anything wrong with their bodies. He wanted handsome, smart young men who were able to learn things quickly and easily to serve in his palace. He told Ashpenaz to teach these young men the language and writings of the Chaldeans.

⁵King Nebuchadnezzar gave the young men a certain amount of food and wine every day. This was the same kind of food that he ate. He wanted them to be trained for three years. After that, they would become servants of the king of Babylon. ⁶Among those young men were Daniel, Hananiah, Mishael and Azariah from the tribe of Judah. ⁷Ashpenaz gave them Babylonian names. Daniel's new name was Belteshazzar, Hananiah's was Shadrach, Mishael's was Meshach and Azariah's was Abednego.

⁸Daniel did not want to eat the king's rich food and wine because it would make him unclean. So he asked Ashpenaz for permission not to make himself unclean in this way.

⁹God caused Ashpenaz, the man in charge of the officials, to be kind and loyal to Daniel. ¹⁰But Ashpenaz told Daniel, "I am afraid of my master, the king. He ordered me to give you this food and drink. If you don't eat this food, you will begin to look weak and sick. You will look worse than other young men your age. The king will see this, and he will become angry with me. He might cut off my head. And it would be your fault."

¹¹Then Daniel talked to the guard who had been put in charge of Daniel, Hananiah, Mishael and Azariah by Ashpenaz. ¹²He said, "Please give us this test for ten days: don't give us anything but vegetables to eat and water to drink. ¹³Then after ten days, compare us with the other young men who eat the king's food. See for yourself who looks healthier, and then decide how you want to treat us, your servants."

¹⁴So the guard agreed to test Daniel, Hananiah, Mishael and Azariah for ten days. ¹⁵After ten days, Daniel and his friends looked healthier than all the young men who ate the king's food. ¹⁶So the guard continued to take away the king's special food and wine and to give only vegetables to Daniel, Hananiah, Mishael and Azariah.

¹⁷God gave these four young men the wisdom and ability to learn many different kinds of writing and science. Daniel could also understand all kinds of visions and dreams.

¹⁸At the end of the three years of training, Ashpenaz brought all the young men to King Nebuchadnezzar. ¹⁹The king talked to them and found that none of the young men were as good as Daniel, Hananiah, Mishael and Azariah. So these four young men became the king's servants. ²⁰Every time the king asked them about something important, they showed great wisdom and understanding. The king found they were ten times better than all the magicians and wise men in his kingdom. ²¹So Daniel served the king until the first year that Cyrus*d* was king.

Nebuchadnezzar's Dream

2 During Nebuchadnezzar's second year as king, he had dreams. They bothered him, and he could not sleep. ²So the king called his wise men to come to him. They used magic and watched the stars. They did this to try to interpret dreams and to learn what would happen in the future. The king wanted them to tell him what he had dreamed, so they came in and stood in front of him.

³Then the king said to them, "I had a dream that bothers me. I want to know what it means."

INSIGHT

Nebuchadnezzar had a "dream team" to see him through the night and the Chaldeans were a part of it. "Chaldean" was another word for "Babylonian", but it was also used to describe a group of magicians and interpreters of dreams.

Daniel 2:4

---

a **1:1** *the third year . . . Jehoiakim* This was about 605 BC.
b **1:2** *Babylonia* Literally, "Shinar", which may be a form of the name Sumer.
c **1:3** *Israelites* Here, this probably means "ordinary citizens of Judah and Israel". But it could mean "people from the northern tribes of Israel".
d **1:21** *the first year . . . Cyrus* This was about 539–538 BC.

LIVING DISTINCTIVELY

Where do you stand on standing out? Are you very much "one of a kind" or do you tend to be a little more "one of the crowd"? Maybe it depends who you are with . . . ?

DIG IN

READ Daniel 1:1–21

- Why was Daniel chosen to serve at the king's palace (vv.4–5)?
- Why do you think the young men were given new names?

Daniel, Hananiah, Mischael and Azariah were undoubtedly four fine young men – A*s all the way, and good-looking too. Back in Judah they would certainly have been the next generation of leaders in business and politics. So why was Nebuchadnezzar so interested in them? The answer lies in their potential.

If you're trying to conquer a nation (as Nebuchadnezzar was) it's one thing to attack your enemy and weaken them temporarily by brute force – Nebuchadnezzar could have simply killed off all future rivals, like Herod would do in Jesus' day (Matthew 2:16–17) – but how do you know that in a few years' time a new band of leaders won't rise up and take revenge? How do you permanently remove the threat?

Nebuchadnezzar had in mind a specific goal in stealing away the brightest and the best young men of Israel and Judah. By treating them well and educating them in his language and culture, he hoped to influence, change and absorb the Hebrew people – and their strange religion – and stop them forever from being a threat.

That's what's behind their new names. It was a sign to them that their identity and their roots were being rewritten. Or so Nebuchadnezzar hoped!

- Why did Daniel and his friends choose a vegetarian diet?
- How did God honour Daniel and his friends' obedience?

Perhaps Daniel had a sense of what Nebuchadnezzar was trying to do to him and the other Hebrews, or perhaps he simply wanted to be faithful to God in not eating food that may have been sacrificed to idols. Either way, he and his friends found a way they could live distinctively in this foreign culture. They couldn't do anything about their captivity or their names – but they were still able to keep their special identity as God's people.

God gave Daniel and his friends better health than their classmates, and honoured their obedience with special wisdom and discernment.

DIG THROUGH

- "Don't change yourselves to be like the people of this world, but let God change you inside with a new way of thinking" (Romans 12:2). How can we stop ourselves being changed by and absorbed into this world's patterns and habits, and consequently being robbed of our potential for God?
- Living faithfully in a land that's not your own is a main theme of the book of Daniel. Do you think it's possible to show your faith by living in a way that's distinctive and stands out? What might that look like for you?

DIG DEEPER

- God is seen to be involved every step of the way – "The Lord allowed . . ." (v.2); "God caused . . ." (vv.9–17). The Bible teaches that even the circumstances that led the Hebrew people into exile were all by God's design. Why not read through 1 and 2 Kings for the background to what's happening here? The history of Nebuchadnezzar's conquest in Daniel 1:1–2 can be found in 2 Kings 24 and 25.

[4]Then the Chaldeans answered the king in the Aramaic language.[a] They said, "King, live forever! Please tell your dream to us, your servants, and then we will tell you what it means."

[5]Then King Nebuchadnezzar said to them, "No, you must tell me the dream, and then you must tell me what it means. If you don't, I will give an order for you to be cut into pieces. And I will order your houses to be destroyed until they are nothing but piles of dust and ashes. [6]But if you tell me my dream and explain its meaning, I will give me gifts, rewards and great honour. So tell me about my dream and what it means."

[7]Again the wise men said to the king, "O king, tell us about the dream, and we will tell you what it means."

[8]Then King Nebuchadnezzar answered, "I know that you are trying to get more time. You know that I meant what I said. [9]You know that you will be punished if you don't tell me about my dream. So you have all agreed to lie to me. You are hoping for more time so that I will forget what I want you to do. Now tell me the dream. If you can tell me the dream, I will know that you can tell me what it really means."

[10]The Chaldeans answered the king. They said, "There is not a man on earth who can do what the king is asking! No king has ever asked the wise men, the men who do magic or the Chaldeans to do something like this. Not even the greatest and most powerful king has ever asked his wise men to do such a thing. [11]The king is asking something that is too hard to do. Only the gods could tell the king his dream and what it means. But the gods don't live with people."

[12]When the king heard that, he became very angry. So he gave an order for all the wise men of Babylon to be killed. [13]King Nebuchadnezzar's order to kill all the wise men was announced. The king's men were sent to look for Daniel and his friends to kill them.

[14]Arioch was the commander of the king's guards. He was going to kill the wise men of Babylon, but Daniel talked to him. Daniel spoke politely to Arioch [15]and said, "Why did the king order such a severe punishment?"

Then Arioch explained the whole story about the king's dreams to Daniel. [16]When Daniel heard the story, he went to King Nebuchadnezzar. He asked the king to give him some more time. Then he would tell the king what the dream meant.

[17]So Daniel went to his house. He explained the whole story to his friends Hananiah, Mishael and Azariah. [18]Daniel asked his friends to pray to the God of heaven and ask that he would be kind to them and help them understand this secret. Then Daniel and his friends would not be killed with the other wise men of Babylon.

[19]During the night, God explained the secret to Daniel in a vision. Then Daniel praised the God of heaven. [20]He said,

"Praise God's name for ever and ever!
    Power and wisdom belong to him.
[21]He changes the times and seasons.
    He gives power to kings,
    and he takes their power away.
    He gives wisdom to people, so they become
        wise.
    He lets people learn things and become wise.
[22]He knows hidden secrets that are hard to
        understand.
    Light lives with him,
    so he knows what is in the dark and secret
        places.
[23]God of my ancestors, I thank you and praise
        you.
    You gave me wisdom and power.
    You told us what we asked for.
    You told us about the king's dream."

Daniel Explains What the Dream Means

[24]Then Daniel went to Arioch, the man who King Nebuchadnezzar had chosen to kill the wise men of Babylon. Daniel said to Arioch, "Don't kill the wise men of Babylon. Take me to the king. I will tell him what his dream means."

[25]So very quickly, Arioch took Daniel to the king. Arioch said to the king, "I have found a man among the captives[b] from Judah who can tell the king what his dream means."

[26]The king asked Daniel (Belteshazzar) a question. He said, "Are you able to tell me about my dream, and what it means?"

[27]Daniel answered, "King Nebuchadnezzar, no wise man, no man who does magic and no Chaldean could tell the king the secret things he has asked about. [28]But there is a God in heaven who explains secret things. God has given King Nebuchadnezzar dreams to show him what will happen later. This was your dream, and this is what you saw while lying on your bed. [29]King, as you were lying there on your bed, you began thinking about what might happen in the future. God can tell people about secret things—he has shown you what will happen in the future. [30]God also told this secret to me, not because I have greater wisdom than other men, but so that you, king, may know what it means. In that way you will understand what went through your mind.

---

[a] **2:4 Aramaic language** The text of Daniel from here to 7:28 is written in Aramaic. See "ARAMAIC" in the Word List.
[b] **2:25 captives** People taken away as prisoners. Here, it means the Jewish people who were taken to Babylon.

³¹"King, in your dream you saw a large statue in front of you that was very large and shiny. It was very impressive. ³²The head of the statue was made from pure gold. Its chest and the arms were made from silver. The belly and upper part of the legs were made from bronze. ³³The lower part of the legs was made from iron. Its feet were made partly of iron and partly of clay. ³⁴While you were looking at the statue, you saw a rock that was cut loose, but not by human hands. Then the rock hit the statue on its feet of iron and clay and smashed them. ³⁵Then the iron, the clay, the bronze, the silver and the gold broke to pieces all at the same time. And all the pieces became like chaff on a threshing floor in the summertime. The wind blew them away, and there was nothing left. No one could tell that a statue had ever been there. Then the rock that hit the statue became a very large mountain and filled up the whole earth.

INSIGHT

The head of gold in Nebuchadnezzar's dream represented his own Babylonian empire (626–539 BC); the chest and arms of silver, the Medeo–Persian Empire (539–330 BC); the belly and thighs of bronze, the Greek empire (330–63 BC); and the lower legs and the feet of iron and clay, the Roman Empire (63 BC onwards).

Daniel 2:32–33

---

³⁶"That was your dream. Now we will tell the king what it means. ³⁷King, you are the most important king. The God of heaven has given you a kingdom, power, strength and glory. ³⁸He has given you control, and you rule over people and the wild animals and the birds. Wherever they live, God has made you ruler over them all. King Nebuchadnezzar, you are that head of gold on the statue.

³⁹"Another kingdom will come after you, but it will not be as great as your kingdom. Next, a third kingdom will rule over the earth—that is the bronze part. ⁴⁰Then there will be a fourth kingdom. That kingdom will be strong like iron. Just as iron breaks things and smashes them to pieces, that fourth kingdom will break all the other kingdoms and smash them to pieces.

⁴¹"You saw that the feet and toes of the statue were partly clay and partly iron. That means the fourth kingdom will be a divided kingdom. It will have some of the strength of iron in it just as you saw the iron mixed with clay. ⁴²The toes of the statue were partly iron and partly clay. So the fourth kingdom will be partly strong like iron and partly weak like clay. ⁴³You saw the iron mixed with clay, but iron and clay don't completely mix together. In the same way, the people of the fourth kingdom will be a mixture. They will not be united as one people.

⁴⁴"During the time of the kings of the fourth kingdom, the God of heaven will set up another kingdom that will last forever. It will never be destroyed. And it will be the kind of kingdom that cannot be passed on to another group of people. This kingdom will crush all the other kingdoms. It will bring them to an end, but that kingdom itself will last forever.

⁴⁵"King Nebuchadnezzar, you saw a rock cut from a mountain, but no one cut that rock. The rock broke the iron, the bronze, the clay, the silver and the gold to pieces. In this way God showed you what will happen in the future. The dream is true, and you can trust that this is what it means."

⁴⁶Then King Nebuchadnezzar bowed down in front of Daniel to honour him. The king praised him. He gave an order that an offering and incense be given to honour Daniel. ⁴⁷Then the king said to Daniel, "I know for sure your God is the God over all gods and the Lord over all kings. He tells people about things they cannot know. I know this is true because you were able to tell these secret things to me."

⁴⁸Then the king gave Daniel a very important job in his kingdom and gave him many expensive gifts. Nebuchadnezzar made Daniel ruler over the whole province of Babylon and put him in charge of all the wise men of Babylon. ⁴⁹Daniel asked the king to make Shadrach, Meshach and Abednego important officials over the province of Babylon. The king did as Daniel asked. Daniel himself became one of the important officials who was always near the king.

The Idol of Gold and the Hot Furnace

3 King Nebuchadnezzar had a gold idol made that was 27 metres[a] high and almost 3 metres[b] wide. Then he set the idol up on the plain of Dura in the province of Babylon. ²Then he called the satraps, prefects, governors, advisors, treasurers, judges, rulers and all the other officials in his kingdom to come together. He wanted all of them to come to the dedication ceremony for the idol.

---

[a] **3:1** *27 metres* Literally, "60 *cubits*".
[b] **3:1** *almost 3 metres* Literally, "6 *cubits*".

INSIGHT

A cubit is the earliest recorded unit of length, shown in Egyptian hieroglyphs as the length of a forearm (elbow to fingertips). It represented about 44 centimetres, so Nebuchadnezzar's statue would have been 27 metres high × 2.7 metres wide. It just shows how this king liked to big himself up!

Daniel 3:1

³So all the men came and stood in front of the idol that King Nebuchadnezzar had set up. ⁴Then the man who makes announcements for the king spoke in a loud voice, "All you people from many nations and language groups, listen to me. This is what you are commanded to do: ⁵You must bow down as soon as you hear the sound of all the musical instruments. When you hear the horns, flutes, lyres, sambucas,ᵃ harps, bagpipesᵇ and all the other musical instruments, you must worship the gold idol. King Nebuchadnezzar has set this idol up. ⁶Whoever does not bow down and worship this gold idol will immediately be thrown into a very hot furnace."

⁷So as soon as they heard the sound of the horns, flutes, lyres, sambucas, bagpipes and all the other musical instruments, they bowed down and worshipped the gold idol. All the peoples, nations and different language groups there worshipped the gold idol that King Nebuchadnezzar had set up.

⁸Then some of the Chaldeans came up to the king and began speaking against the people from Judah. ⁹They said, "King, may you live forever! ¹⁰King, you gave a command. You said that everyone who hears the sound of the horns, flutes, lyres, sambucas, harps, bagpipes and all the other musical instruments must bow down and worship the gold idol. ¹¹And you also said that whoever does not bow down and worship the gold idol will be thrown into a very hot furnace. ¹²There are some Judeans who you made important officials in the province of Babylon that ignored your order, King. Their names are Shadrach, Meshach and Abednego. They don't worship your gods, and they didn't bow down to worship the gold idol you set up."

¹³Nebuchadnezzar became very angry. He called for Shadrach, Meshach and Abednego. So they were brought to him. ¹⁴And Nebuchadnezzar said to them, "Shadrach, Meshach and Abednego, is it true that you don't worship my gods? And is it true that you didn't bow down and worship the gold idol I have set up? ¹⁵Now when you hear the sound of the horns, flutes, lyres, sambucas, harps, bagpipes and all the other musical instruments, you must bow down and worship the gold idol. If you are ready to worship the idol I have made, that is good. But if you don't worship it, you will be thrown very quickly into the hot furnace. Then no god will be able to save you from my power!"

¹⁶Shadrach, Meshach and Abednego answered the king, "Nebuchadnezzar, we don't need to explain these things to you. ¹⁷If you throw us into the hot furnace, the God we serve can save us. And if he wants to, he can save us from your power. ¹⁸But even if God does not save us, we want you to know, King, that we refuse to serve your gods. We will not worship the gold idol you have set up."

¹⁹Then Nebuchadnezzar became very angry with Shadrach, Meshach and Abednego. He gave an order for the furnace to be heated seven times hotter than it usually was. ²⁰Then he commanded some of the strongest soldiers in his army to tie up Shadrach, Meshach and Abednego. He told the soldiers to throw them into the hot furnace.

²¹So Shadrach, Meshach and Abednego were tied up and thrown into the hot furnace. They were wearing their robes, trousers, turbans and other clothes. ²²The king was very angry when he gave the command, so the soldiers quickly made the furnace very hot. The fire was so hot that the flames killed the strong soldiers. They were killed when they went close to the fire to throw in Shadrach, Meshach and Abednego. ²³Shadrach, Meshach and Abednego fell into the fire. They were tied up very tightly.

²⁴Then King Nebuchadnezzar jumped to his feet. He was very surprised and he asked his advisors, "We tied only three men, and we threw only three men into the fire. Is that right?"

His advisors said, "Yes, King."

²⁵The king said, "Look! I see four men walking around in the fire. They are not tied up and they are not burned. The fourth man looks like an angel."ᶜ

²⁶Then Nebuchadnezzar went to the opening of the hot furnace. He shouted, "Shadrach, Meshach and Abednego, come out! Servants of the Most High God, come here!"

ᵃ **3:5 sambucas** A musical instrument, possibly a seven stringed instrument like a harp. The name in Hebrew comes from some other language, possibly Greek.

ᵇ **3:5 bagpipes** A musical instrument with a bag and several horns or pipes. The name in Hebrew comes from some other language, possibly from the Greek word "symphony".

ᶜ **3:25 angel** Literally, "son of the god".

INSIGHT

Who was the stranger? King Nebuchadnezzar saw a mysterious fourth man, who looked like an angel in the fiery furnace. Many Christians believe it was Jesus and that this is an image of how he is always with us in our troubles.

Daniel 3:25

So Shadrach, Meshach and Abednego came out of the fire. 27When they came out, the satraps, prefects, governors and royal advisors crowded around them. They could see that the fire had not burned Shadrach, Meshach and Abednego. Their bodies were not burned at all. Their hair was not burned, and their robes were not burned. They didn't even smell as if they had been near fire.

28Then Nebuchadnezzar said, "Praise the God of Shadrach, Meshach and Abednego. Their God has sent his angel and saved his servants from the fire! These three men trusted their God and refused to obey my command. They were willing to die instead of serving or worshipping any other god. 29So I now make this law: Anyone from any nation or language group who says anything against the God of Shadrach, Meshach and Abednego will be cut into pieces, and their house will be destroyed until it is a pile of dirt and ashes. No other god can save his people like this." 30Then the king gave Shadrach, Meshach and Abednego more important jobs in the province of Babylon.

Nebuchadnezzar's Dream About a Tree

4 King Nebuchadnezzar sent this letter to the many nations and language groups living around the world.

Greetings:

2I am very happy to tell you about the miracles and wonderful things that the Most High God did for me.

3God has done amazing miracles!
    He has done powerful miracles!
His kingdom continues forever;
    his rule will continue for all generations.

4I, Nebuchadnezzar, was at my palace. I was happy and successful. 5I had a dream that made me afraid. I was lying on my bed, and I saw pictures and visions in my mind. These things made me very frightened. 6So I gave an order that all the wise men of Babylon be brought to me to tell me what my dream meant. 7When the men of magic and the Chaldeans came, I told them about the dream, but they could not tell me what it meant. 8Finally, Daniel came to me, and I told him about my dream. He is the one who was given the name Belteshazzar to honour my god. The spirit of the holy gods is in him. 9I said, "Belteshazzar, you are the most important of all the men of magic. I know that the spirit of the holy gods is in you. So I am sure you can solve any mystery. I will tell you what I dreamed, and you tell me what it means. 10These are the visions I saw while I was lying in my bed: I looked, and there in front of me was a tree standing in the middle of the earth. The tree was very tall. 11The tree grew large and strong. The top of the tree touched the sky.a It could be seen from anywhere on earth. 12The leaves of the tree were beautiful. It had much good fruit on it. And on the tree was plenty of food for everyone. The wild animals found shelter under the tree, and the birds lived in its branches. Every animal ate from the tree.

13"I was looking at those things in the vision while lying on my bed. And then I saw a holy angel coming down from heaven. 14He spoke very loudly and said, 'Cut down the tree, and cut off its branches. Strip off its leaves. Scatter its fruit around. The animals that are under the tree will run away. The birds that are in its branches will fly away. 15But let the stump and roots stay in the ground. Put a band of iron and bronze around it. The stump and roots will stay in the field with the grass all around it. It will live among the wild animals and plants in the fields. It will become wet with dew. 16He will not think like a man any longer. He will have the mind of an animal. Seven seasons will pass while he is like this.'

17"Holy angels announced this punishment so that all the people on earth may know that God Most High rules over human kingdoms. God gives those kingdoms to whoever he wants, and he chooses humble people to rule them.

18"That is what I, King Nebuchadnezzar, dreamed. Now, Belteshazzar,b tell me what it means. None of the wise men in my

---

a 4:10–11 *middle of the earth . . . sky* The Babylonians thought the earth was flat and round like a plate or a wheel. And they thought the sky was like a glass bowl turned upside down on the earth.
b 4:18 *Belteshazzar* Another name for Daniel.

kingdom can tell me what that dream means. But Belteshazzar, you can interpret the dream because the spirit of the holy gods is in you."

¹⁹Then Daniel (also called Belteshazzar) became very quiet for a while. What he was thinking bothered him. So the king said, "Belteshazzar, don't let the dream or its meaning make you afraid."

Then Belteshazzar answered the king, "My lord, I wish the dream were about your enemies, and I wish the meaning of the dream were about those against you. ²⁰⁻²¹You saw a tree in your dream. The tree grew large and strong. Its top touched the sky, and it could be seen from all over the earth. Its leaves were beautiful, and it had plenty of fruit. The fruit gave plenty of food for everyone. It was a home for the wild animals, and its branches were nesting places for the birds. You saw that tree. ²²King, you are that tree! You have become great and powerful. You are like the tall tree that touched the sky—your power reaches to the far parts of the earth.

²³"King, you saw a holy angel coming down from heaven. He said, 'Cut the tree down and destroy it. Put a band of iron and bronze around the stump and leave the stump and its roots in the ground. Leave it in the grass in the field. It will become wet with dew. He will live like a wild animal. Seven seasons will pass while he is like this.'

²⁴"King, this is the meaning of the dream. God Most High has commanded these things to happen to my lord the king: ²⁵King Nebuchadnezzar, you will be forced to go away from people. You will live among the wild animals. You will eat grass like cattle, and you will become wet with dew. Seven seasons will pass, and then you will learn this lesson. You will learn that God Most High rules over human kingdoms and gives them to whoever he wants.

²⁶"The command to leave the stump of the tree and its roots in the ground means this: Your kingdom will be given back to you. This will happen when you learn that Most High God rules your kingdom. ²⁷So, King, please accept my advice. Stop sinning and do what is right. Stop doing bad things and be kind to poor people. Then you might continue to be successful."

²⁸All these things happened to King Nebuchadnezzar. ²⁹⁻³⁰Twelve months after the dream, King Nebuchadnezzar was walking on the roof*ᵃ* of his palace in Babylon. While on the roof, the king said, "Look at Babylon! I built this great city.

It is my palace. I built this great place by my power. I built this place to show how great I am."

³¹The words were still in his mouth when a voice came from heaven. The voice said, "King Nebuchadnezzar, these things will happen to you: your power as king has been taken away from you. ³²You will be forced to go away from people. You will live with the wild animals and eat grass like an ox. Seven seasons will pass before you learn your lesson. Then you will learn that God Most High rules over human kingdoms and gives them to whoever he wants."

³³These things happened immediately. Nebuchadnezzar was forced to go away from people. He began eating grass like an ox. He became wet from dew. His hair grew long like the feathers of an eagle, and his nails grew long like the claws of a bird.

³⁴Then at the end of that time, I, Nebuchadnezzar, looked up towards heaven, and I was in my right mind again. Then I gave praise to God Most High. I gave honour and glory to him who lives forever.

God rules forever!
   His kingdom continues for all generations.
³⁵People on earth
   are not really important.
God does what he wants
   with the powers of heaven
   and the people on earth.
No one can stop his powerful hand
   or question what he does.

³⁶At that time God gave me my right mind again, and he gave back my great honour and power as king. My advisors and the royal people began to ask my advice again. I became the king again—even greater and more powerful than before. ³⁷Now I, Nebuchadnezzar, give praise, honour and glory to the King of Heaven. Everything he does is right. He is always fair, and he is able to make proud people humble!

The Writing on the Wall

5 King Belshazzar gave a big party for 1,000 of his officials. The king was drinking wine with them. ²As Belshazzar was drinking his wine, he ordered his servants to bring the gold and silver cups. His father*ᵇ* Nebuchadnezzar had taken these cups from the Temple in Jerusalem. King Belshazzar wanted his royal people, his wives and

---

ᵃ **4:29–30** *roof* In ancient Israel, houses had flat roofs that were used as an extra room.
ᵇ **5:2** *father* It is uncertain that Belshazzar was related to Nebuchadnezzar. The word "father" here might mean "the previous king". Also in verses 11,13,18.

his slave women to drink from those cups. ³So they brought the gold cups that had been taken from the Temple of God in Jerusalem, and the king and his officials, his wives and his women slaves drank from them. ⁴As they were drinking, they gave praise to their idol gods, which were only statues made from gold, silver, bronze, iron, wood and stone.

⁵Suddenly, a person's hand appeared and began writing on the wall. The fingers scratched words into the plaster on the wall, near the lampstand in the king's palace. The king was watching the hand as it wrote.

⁶King Belshazzar was very afraid. His face became white from fear, and his knees were shaking and knocking together. He could not stand up because his legs were too weak. ⁷The king called for the men of magic and the Chaldeans to be brought to him. He said to these wise men, "I will give a reward to anyone who can read this writing and explain to me what it means. I will give him purple robes[a] to wear and will put a gold chain around his neck. I will make him the third highest ruler in the kingdom."

⁸So all the king's wise men came in, but they could not read the writing or understand what it meant. ⁹King Belshazzar's officials were confused, and the king became even more afraid and worried. His face was white from fear.

¹⁰Then the king's mother came into the place where the party was. She had heard the voices of the king and his royal officials. She said, "King, may you live forever! Don't be afraid! Don't let your face be so white with fear! ¹¹There is a man in your kingdom who has the spirit of the holy gods in him. In the days of your father, this man showed that he could understand secrets. He showed that he was very smart and very wise. He showed that he was like the gods in these things. Your father, King Nebuchadnezzar, put this man in charge of all the wise men. He ruled over all the men of magic and the Chaldeans. ¹²The man I am talking about is named Daniel. The king gave him the name Belteshazzar. He is very clever and he knows many things. He could interpret dreams, explain secrets, and find the answer to very hard problems. Call for Daniel, he will tell you what the writing on the wall means."

¹³So they brought Daniel to the king and he asked, "Is your name Daniel, one of the captives my father the king brought here from Judah? ¹⁴I have heard that the spirit of the gods is in you and that you understand secrets and are very smart and very wise. ¹⁵The wise men and the men of magic were brought to me to read this writing on the wall. I wanted them to explain to me what it means, but they could not explain it. ¹⁶I have heard that you are able to explain what things mean, and that you can find the answer to very hard problems. If you can read this writing on the wall and explain to me what it means, this is what I will do for you: I will give you purple robes to wear and will put a gold chain around your neck. Then you will become the third highest ruler in the kingdom."

¹⁷Then Daniel answered the king, "King Belshazzar, you can keep your gifts for yourself, or you can give them to someone else. But I will still read the writing on the wall for you and explain what it means.

¹⁸"King, God Most High made your father Nebuchadnezzar a very great and powerful king and gave him great wealth. ¹⁹People from many nations and language groups were very frightened of Nebuchadnezzar because God made him a very powerful king. Nebuchadnezzar killed whoever he wanted and let those who pleased him live. If he wanted to make people important, he made them important. If he wanted to bring them down, he brought them down.

²⁰"But Nebuchadnezzar became proud and stubborn, so his power was taken away from him. He was taken off his royal throne and stripped of his glory. ²¹Then Nebuchadnezzar was forced to go away from people. His mind became like the mind of an animal. He lived with the wild donkeys and ate grass like an ox. He became wet with dew. These things happened to him until he learned his lesson. He learned that God Most High rules over human kingdoms, and he gives them to whoever he wants.

²²"But Belshazzar, you already knew this. You are Nebuchadnezzar's son,[b] but still you have not made yourself humble. ²³No, you did not become humble. Instead, you have turned against the Lord of heaven. You ordered the drinking cups from his Temple to be brought to you. Then you and your royal officials, your wives and your slave women drank wine from those cups. You gave praise to the gods of silver and gold, of bronze, iron, wood and stone. They are not really gods; they cannot see or hear or understand anything. But you did not give honour to the God who has the power over your life and everything you do. ²⁴So because of that, God sent the hand that wrote on the wall. ²⁵These are the words that were written on the wall:

---

[a] **5:7 purple robes** These clothes showed that a person was rich and powerful, like a king. Also in verses 16,29.
[b] **5:22 son** This does not necessarily mean they were from the same family. It might only mean that Belshazzar was one of the kings of Babylon after Nebuchadnezzar was king.

THE WRITING'S ON THE WALL

You may have heard this phrase before – it means judgement is coming or disaster is just about to strike. Well, as with many other sayings in modern English, the phrase started life here in the Bible. This is the story behind it.

DIG IN
READ Daniel 5:1–12

- Compare this passage with the last few verses of Daniel 4. What's changed?
- What does the king order to be brought to the feast (5:2)? Why do you think he does this?

It's many years since Daniel and his three friends were taken away from their homeland and made to serve in the palace of the king of Babylon. Things have moved on and Nebuchadnezzar's son (or grandson – it's not quite clear which) is now on the throne. And it seems he has forgotten God altogether.

Whether he was drunk on the wine or just drunk on power, Belshazzar blasphemes against God by demanding that his guests drink from the sacred cups taken out of the Temple in Jerusalem. To make things worse, he then leads them in giving praise to idols too.

Divine judgement comes in the form of a ghostly message – but no one has a clue what the writing means. Until the king's mum suddenly remembers a young man who could interpret dreams . . .

READ Daniel 5:13–30

- What's Daniel's interpretation of events (vv.17–28)?
- What does his explanation say about Daniel's character?

Now well into his life, and probably quite well-off too, Daniel is drafted in to help. Even though he was close to the former king (Daniel 2:49), it seems this one hasn't even heard of him.

The message is bleak for Belshazzar and the prophecy proves true within twenty-four hours. God has revealed himself time and time again to this royal family but they have not listened and stayed humble. Instead they have taken God's blessing for granted.

It may be years later, but Daniel is still fiercely faithful to his God. Once again Daniel's obedience in speaking about God in the face of a powerful king is rewarded.

DIG THROUGH

- Some people would argue that modern life is a bit like this "idolatrous feast". That's a pretty negative description – but does it stand up? Do you agree with it?
- Handwritten messages on the wall may be rare, but in what way do signs come to our world that act as a warning that judgement will come? What's our role as God's people in helping to explain them? Check out Luke 13:1–5 and hear what Jesus would say.

DIG DEEPER

- This book was written to encourage God's people to continue to be faithful to him, even when far from home and the land he promised to them. Peter, when encouraging the New Testament church about their new identity in Christ, urges them to consider themselves as "foreigners and strangers" in this world (check out 1 Peter 2:9–12).
- Daniel says that the king knew all he needed to know (v.22) but chose to deliberately disobey God. God doesn't judge us on how much we know, but how we choose to act on that knowledge. Paul shows in Romans 1:21–25 how God feels towards people who know what's right and then still do what's wrong.

MENE, MENE, TEKEL, UPARSIN.

26"This is what these words mean:

Mene:a
>God has counted the days until your
>kingdom will end.

27Tekel:b
>You have been weighed on the scales and
>found not good enough.

28Uparsin:c
>Your kingdom is being taken from you.
>It will be divided among the Medes and
>Persians."

29Then Belshazzar gave an order for Daniel to be dressed in purple clothes. A gold chain was put around his neck, and he was appointed the third highest ruler in the kingdom. 30That very same night, Belshazzar, king of the Babylonians, was killed. 31A man named Darius the Mede became the new king. Darius was about 62 years old.

Daniel and the Lions

6 Darius thought it would be a good idea to choose 120 satraps to rule throughout his kingdom. 2He chose three men to rule over the 120 satraps. Daniel was one of the three supervisors. The king put these men in this position to keep anyone from cheating him. 3Daniel proved himself to be a better supervisor than any of the others. He did this by his good character and great ability. The king was so impressed with Daniel that he planned to make him ruler over the whole kingdom. 4But when the other supervisors and the satraps heard about this, they were very jealous. They tried to find reasons to accuse Daniel. So they watched what Daniel did as he went about doing the business of the government. But they could not find anything wrong with him, so they could not accuse him of doing anything wrong. Daniel was a man people could trust. He did not cheat the king, and he worked very hard.

5Finally they said, "We will never find any reason to accuse Daniel of doing something wrong. So we must find something to complain about that is connected to the law of his God."

6So the two supervisors and the satraps went as a group to the king. They said, "King Darius, live forever! 7The supervisors, prefects, satraps, advisors and governors have all agreed on something. We think that the king should make

this law and that everyone must obey it: for the next 30 days, whoever prays to any god or man except you, King, will be thrown into the lions' den. 8Now, King, make the law and sign the paper it is written on so that it cannot be changed, because the laws of the Medes and Persians cannot be cancelled or changed." 9So King Darius made the law and signed it.

10Daniel always prayed to God three times every day. Three times every day, he bowed down on his knees to pray and praise God. Even though Daniel heard about the new law, he still went to his house to pray. He went up to the upper room of his house and opened the windows that faced towards Jerusalem. Then Daniel bowed down on his knees and prayed just as he always had done.

11Then the supervisors and satraps went as a group and found Daniel praying and asking God for help. 12So they went to the king and talked to him about the law he had made. They said, "King Darius, you signed a law that says, for the next 30 days anyone who prays to any god or man except you, the king, would be thrown into the lions' den. You did sign that law, didn't you?"

The king answered, "Yes, I signed that law, and the laws of the Medes and Persians cannot be cancelled or changed."

13Then they said to the king, "That man Daniel is not paying any attention to you. He is one of the captivesd from Judah, and he is not paying attention to the law you signed. Daniel still prays to his God three times every day."

14The king became very sad and upset when he heard this. He decided to save Daniel. He worked until sunset trying to think of a way to save him. 15Then the men went as a group to the king and said to him, "Remember, O king, that the law of the Medes and Persians says that no law or command signed by the king can ever be cancelled or changed."

16So King Darius gave the order. They brought Daniel and threw him into the lions' den. The king said to Daniel, "May the God you serve save you!" 17A big rock was brought and put over the opening of the lions' den. Then the king used his ring and put his seal on the rock. He also used the rings of his officials and put their seals on the rock. This showed that no one could move that rock and bring Daniel out of the lion's den. 18Then King Darius went back to his house. He did not eat that night. He did not want anyone to come and entertain him. He could not sleep all night.

---

a 5:26 **Mene** A weight, like the Hebrew word "*mina*". This is like the word "to count".
b 5:27 **Tekel** A weight, like the Hebrew word "*shekel*". This word is like the word meaning "to weigh".
c 5:28 **Uparsin** Literally, "*peres*", a weight. This word is like the word meaning "to divide" or "to split". It is also like the name of the country of Persia.
d 6:13 **captives** People taken away as prisoners. Here, it means the Jewish people who were taken to Babylon.

¹⁹The next morning, King Darius got up just as it was getting light and ran to the lions' den. ²⁰He was very worried. When he got to the lions' den, he called to Daniel. He said, "Daniel, servant of the living God, has your God been able to save you from the lions? You always serve your God."

²¹Daniel answered, "King, live forever! ²²My God sent his angel to save me. The angel closed the lions' mouths. The lions have not hurt me because my God knows I am innocent. I never did anything wrong to you, King."

²³King Darius was very happy. He told his servants to lift Daniel out of the lions' den. And when Daniel was lifted out of the den, they did not find any injury on his body. The lions did not hurt Daniel because he trusted in his God.

²⁴Then the king gave a command to bring the men who had accused Daniel to the lions' den. The men and their wives and children were thrown into the lions' den. The lions grabbed them before they hit the floor. The lions ate their bodies and then chewed on their bones.

²⁵Then King Darius wrote this letter to all the people from other nations and language groups all around the world:

Greetings:

²⁶I am making a new law. This law is for people in every part of my kingdom. All of you must fear and respect the God of Daniel.

Daniel's God is the living God;
    he lives forever.
His kingdom will never be destroyed.
    His rule will never end.
²⁷God helps and saves people.
    He does amazing miracles in heaven and
      on earth.
He saved Daniel
    from the lions.

²⁸So Daniel was successful during the time Darius was king and when Cyrus the Persian was king.

Daniel's Dream About Four Animals

7 During the first year that Belshazzar[a] was king of Babylon, Daniel had a dream. He saw these visions while he was lying on his bed, and he wrote down what he had dreamed. ²Daniel said: "In my vision that night I saw the wind blowing from all four directions. These winds made the sea rough. ³I saw four big animals and each one was different from the others. These four animals came up out of the sea.

⁴"The first animal looked like a lion, but it had wings like an eagle. As I watched, its wings were torn off. It was helped up from the ground, and it stood up on two feet like a human. Then it was given a human mind.

⁵"Then I saw another animal there in front of me that looked like a bear. It was raised up on one of its sides, and it had three ribs in its mouth between its teeth. It was told, 'Get up and eat all the meat you want!'

⁶"Then I noticed another animal in front of me. It looked like a leopard, but it had four wings on its back, and it had four heads. It was given authority to rule.

⁷"After that, in my vision that night, I looked, and there in front of me was a fourth animal. It was terrifying, mean and powerful. It had huge iron teeth and crushed in its teeth whatever it killed. And it smashed with its feet whatever was left. This fourth animal was different from all the other animals I saw. This one had ten horns.

⁸"While I was looking at the horns and thinking about them, another horn grew up among them. This was a little horn with eyes like a human. It also had a mouth that was boasting. Then the little horn pulled out three of the other horns.

Judgement of the Fourth Animal

⁹"As I was looking, thrones were put in their places,
    and the Ancient King[b] sat on his throne.
His clothes were as white as snow.
    His hair was as white as wool.
His throne was made from fire,[c]
    and its wheels were made from flames.
¹⁰A river of fire flowed out
    from in front of the Ancient King.
Millions of people were serving him.
    Hundreds of millions of people stood in
      front of him.
Court was ready to begin,
    and the books were opened.

¹¹"I kept on looking because the little horn was boasting. I kept watching until finally the fourth animal was killed. Its body was destroyed, and it was thrown into the burning fire. ¹²The authority and rule of the other animals had been taken from them. But they were permitted to live for a certain period of time.

---

a **7:1** *the first year . . . Belshazzar* This was about 553 BC.
b **7:9** *Ancient King* Literally, "Ancient of Days". This name pictures God as a great king who has ruled since ancient times. Also in verses 10,13,22.
c **7:9** *fire* Or "light".

SEEING THINGS

We live in a single moment in time. The past is gone, the future is uncertain, now is all we have.

But God is not like that. He created time, so time is his servant. He is outside time altogether, which means, as the Bible says, "To the Lord a day is like a thousand years, and a thousand years is like a day" (2 Peter 3:8). That means he can give his people special insights into the future – he can "pull back the curtain" on what lies ahead. But why does he do that for them?

DIG IN

READ Daniel 7:1–14

- Spend a moment visualizing what Daniel saw. How does it make you feel?
- Who does the character described in verses 9 and 10 remind you of? (Clue: Revelation 20:11–15.)
- And how about the person described in verses 13 and 14?

Daniel's vision of the four animals, each having authority and ruling for a certain amount of time will sound either cool or weird depending on how much you enjoy fantasy stories! But they all pale in comparison to the majestic throne which appears, and the "Ancient King". This is surely God himself – in existence before time began and ruling and reigning over it all.

The one "like a human being" (v.13) is clearly referring to Jesus. Here, tucked away in this short Old Testament book, is an early vision of Jesus and a prophecy about his eternal kingdom, one that will be greater than any kingdom that's come before it.

READ Daniel 7:15–18

- How does the mysterious bystander explain what Daniel has seen?

Confirming what the bystander says, Bible scholars have identified details of this passage and believe that what Daniel saw was four kingdoms that would rise and fall in history – Babylon (which tumbled in Daniel's own lifetime), Persia, Greece and Rome. But he also looks much further ahead to an everlasting kingdom – Jesus'.

Many more of the visions contained here and in the next few chapters have also been fulfilled in history since Daniel wrote them, scholars say. Others have still to come true.

God gave people like Daniel glimpses into the future. And he even gives visions to people like us (Joel 2:28)! Sometimes that might confuse or worry us (v.15), but we don't need to be afraid, because God loves us very much (check out Daniel 10:8–19). Difficult times may come to us – sometimes God's people will be under threat, sometimes it will seem like God isn't in control. But he is. Always.

DIG THROUGH

Does God know the future? That's the question passages like this one force us to ask. Although chapters 1 to 6 of Daniel give a more or less historical account, the Bible is not just a history book, or a self-help book telling us how to live better. It's also a supernatural book, giving glimpses into God's mysterious and cosmic plans.

- What gives you hope for the future? Which Bible passages can you memorize to help you face uncertainty ahead? Try Romans 8:28 for starters.

DIG DEEPER

- Daniel's vision is similar in style to John's long vision in Revelation. Compare the language and the portrayal of the end times here with that in Revelation 5:11–14.

13"As my vision that night continued, I looked, and there in front of me was someone who looked like a human being.*a* He was coming on the clouds in the sky. He came up to the Ancient King, and the King's servants brought him before the King.

14"The one who looked like a human being was given authority, glory and complete ruling power. People from every nation and language group will serve him. His rule will last forever. His kingdom will last forever. It will never be destroyed.

The Meaning of Daniel's Dream

15"I, Daniel, was confused and worried. The visions that went through my mind bothered me. 16I went to someone who was standing there and asked him what all this meant. So he explained it to me. 17He said, 'The four great animals are four kingdoms that will come from the earth. 18But God's holy people will receive the kingdom, and they will have the kingdom for ever and ever.'

19"Then I wanted to know what the fourth animal was and what it meant. The fourth animal was different from all the others. It was more terrifying with its iron teeth and bronze claws. It was the animal that crushed in its teeth whatever it killed and smashed with its feet whatever was left. 20I wanted to know about the ten horns that were on the fourth animal's head and about the little horn that grew there. That little horn pulled out three of the other ten horns. That little horn looked more important than the other horns, and it continued to boast. 21As I was watching, this little horn began attacking and making war against God's holy people and killing them. 22The little horn kept killing God's holy people until the Ancient King came and judged him. The Ancient King announced his decision about the little horn. This judgement helped God's holy people, and they received the kingdom.

23"And he explained this to me: 'The fourth animal is a fourth kingdom that will come on the earth. It will be different from all the other kingdoms. That fourth kingdom will destroy the whole world. It will crush everything under its feet. 24The ten horns are ten kings that will come from this fourth kingdom. After those ten kings are gone, another king will come. He will be different from the kings who ruled before him. He will defeat three of the other kings. 25This special

king will say things against God Most High, and he will hurt and kill God's special people. That king will try to change the times and laws that have already been set. God's holy people will be under that king's power for three and a half years.*b*

26"But the court will decide what should happen, and that king's power will be taken away. His kingdom will end completely. 27Then God's holy people will rule over the kingdom and all the people from all the kingdoms of earth.*c* This kingdom will last forever, and people from all the other kingdoms will respect and serve them.'

28"And that was the end of the dream. I, Daniel, was very afraid. My face became very white from fear, and I did not tell the other people what I saw and heard."

INSIGHT

Animals that use their horns to fight and defend are frequently found in the Bible to symbolize the military might of a nation.

Daniel 8:3

Daniel's Vision of a Ram and a Goat

8 *d*In the third year*e* that Belshazzar was king, I, Daniel, saw another vision, different from the one I saw before. 2In this vision I saw myself in Susa,*f* the king's capital city in the province of Elam. I was standing by the Ulai River. 3I looked up and saw a ram standing at the side of the river. The ram had two long horns. The horns were both long, but one horn was longer than the other horn. The long horn was farther back than the other horn. 4I watched the ram run into things with its horns. I watched the ram run to the west, to the north and to the south. No animal could stop the ram, and no one could save the other animals. That ram did whatever it wanted, and it became very powerful.

5I thought about the ram. While I was watching, I saw a male goat come from the west. It had one large horn that was easy to see. It ran so fast its feet barely touched the ground.

6The goat came to the ram with the two horns. (This was the ram I had seen standing by the Ulai

---

a 7:13 someone . . . human being Or "a person, a real human being". Literally, "like a son of man". This means he looked like a normal person, not an angel or an animal.

b 7:25 three and a half years Literally, "time, times and half time".

c 7:27 God's holy people . . . earth Literally, "The rule and kingdom and greatness of the kingdoms under heaven will be given to the saints."

d 8:1 Here, the original language changes from Aramaic (see "ARAMAIC" in the Word List) back to Hebrew.

e 8:1 third year This was about 551 BC.

f 8:2 Susa The capital city of Persia.

River.) The goat was very angry and ran at the ram. [7]As I watched, the goat ran at the ram and broke both of the ram's horns. The ram could not stop the goat. The goat knocked it to the ground and walked all over it. There was no one to save the ram from the goat.

[8]So the goat became very powerful. But after he became strong, his big horn broke off. Then four horns grew in place of the one big horn. Those four horns were easy to see. They pointed in four different directions.

[9]Then a little horn grew from one of those four horns. It grew and became very big. It grew towards the south-east, towards the Beautiful Land. [10]The little horn became very big. It grew until it reached the sky. It even threw some of heaven's army[a] to the ground and trampled them. [11]That little horn became very strong, and it turned against God, the Ruler of heaven's army. It stopped the daily sacrifices that were offered to the Ruler. And the holy place where people worshipped the Ruler was pulled down. [12]Because of this sin, the daily sacrifices were stopped. Truth was thrown down to the ground. The little horn did these things and was very successful.

[13]Then I heard two holy ones[b] talking with each other. One of them asked the other one, who had been speaking, "How long will the things in this vision last—the stopping of the daily sacrifices, the sin that destroys and the trampling down of the holy place and heaven's army?"

[14]The other holy one said, "This will last for 2,300 days. Then the holy place will be repaired."

The Vision Is Explained to Daniel

[15]I, Daniel, saw this vision and tried to understand what it meant. While I was thinking about the vision, someone who looked like a man suddenly stood in front of me. [16]Then I heard a man's voice. This voice came from above the Ulai River. The voice called out, "Gabriel, explain the vision to this man."

[17]So Gabriel, the angel who looked like a man, came to me. I was very afraid and fell down to the ground. But Gabriel said to me, "Human,[c] understand that this vision is about the time of the end."

[18]While Gabriel was speaking, I fell to the ground and went to sleep. It was a very deep sleep. Then Gabriel touched me and lifted me to

my feet. [19]He said, "Now, I will explain the vision to you. I will tell you what will happen in the future. Your vision was about the end times.

[20]"You saw a ram with two horns. The horns are the countries of Media and Persia. [21]The goat is the king of Greece. The big horn between its eyes is the first king. [22]That horn broke off and four horns grew in its place. The four horns are four kingdoms. Those four kingdoms will come from the nation of the first king, but they will not be as strong as the first king.

[23]"When the end is near for those kingdoms, there will be a very bold and cruel king who will be very dishonest. This will happen when many people have turned against God. [24]This king will be very powerful, but his power does not come from himself.[d] This king will cause terrible destruction. He will be successful in everything he does. He will destroy powerful people—even God's holy people.

[25]"This king will be very clever and will use lies to be successful. He will think that he is very important and will destroy many people, when they least expect it. He will try to fight even the Prince of princes. But that cruel king's power will be destroyed, and it will not be any human power that destroys him.

[26]"What I said and the vision about those times are true. But don't tell anyone what you saw, because those things will not happen for a long, long time."

[27]I, Daniel, became very weak. I was sick for several days after that vision. Then I got up and went back to work for the king, but I was very upset about the vision. I did not understand what it meant.

Daniel's Prayer

9 These things happened during the first year that Darius son of Ahasuerus[e] was king. Darius was a Mede by birth, but he was appointed to be the king of Babylon. [2]During his first year as king, I was studying the Scriptures[f] and noticed in the LORD's message to Jeremiah that 70 years would pass before Jerusalem would be rebuilt.

[3]Then I turned to the Lord God. I prayed to him and asked him for help. I did not eat any food. I put ashes on my head and put on the clothes that showed I was sad. [4]I prayed to the LORD my God and told him about all my sins. I said,

---

[a] **8:10 heaven's army** Or "the stars". Also in verses 11,13.

[b] **8:13 holy ones** Here, these are probably angels.

[c] **8:17 Human** Literally, "Son of man".

[d] **8:24 but his power . . . himself** Some ancient versions don't have these words, so they may have been accidentally copied from verse 22.

[e] **9:1 Ahasuerus** Or "Xerxes".

[f] **9:2 Scriptures** Literally, "scrolls".

"Lord, you are a great and awesome God. You keep your agreement of love and kindness with people who love you. You keep your agreement with the people who obey your commands.

5"But we have sinned. We have done wrong. We have done evil things. We turned against you. We turned away from your commands and good decisions. 6The prophets were your servants. They spoke for you to our kings, to our leaders, to our fathers and to the common people in our country. But we did not listen to them.

7"Lord, you are innocent, and the shame belongs to us, even now. Shame belongs to the people from Judah and Jerusalem, and to all the people of Israel, to those who are near and to those you scattered among many nations. They should be ashamed of all the evil things they did against you.

8"LORD, we should all be ashamed. All our kings and leaders should be ashamed. Our ancestors should be ashamed, because we sinned against you.

9"But, Lord our God, you are kind and forgiving, even though we turned against you. 10We have not obeyed the LORD our God. He used his servants, the prophets and gave us laws, but we have not obeyed his laws. 11All the people of Israel disobeyed your teachings and turned away from you. They did not listen to you. We sinned, so you did what you promised to do. All the curses and promises[a] in the Law of Moses, your servant, happened to us.

12"God said those things would happen to us and our leaders, and he made them happen. He made terrible things happen to us. No other city suffered the way Jerusalem suffered. 13All those terrible things happened to us. This happened just as it is written in the Law of Moses, but we still have not asked the LORD our God for help. We still have not stopped sinning. We still do not pay attention to your truth, Lord. 14The LORD kept the terrible things ready for us—he made them happen to us. The LORD our God did this because he is fair in everything he does. But we still have not listened to him.

15"Lord our God, you used your power and brought us out of Egypt. We are your people. You are famous because of that, even today. We have sinned and done terrible things.

16Lord, we and our ancestors sinned against you, so your people and your city became a disgrace to everyone around us. You do so many good things, so stop being angry at Jerusalem, your city, your holy mountain.

17"Now, our God, hear your servant's prayer. Listen to my prayer for mercy. For your own sake, do good things for your holy place.[b] 18My God, listen to me! Open your eyes and see all the terrible things that have happened to us. See what has happened to the city that is called by your name. I am not saying we are good people. That is not why I am asking these things. I am asking these things because I know you are kind. 19Lord, listen to me! Forgive us! Lord, pay attention, and then do something! Don't wait! Do something now! Do it for your own good! My God, do something now, for your city and your people who are called by your name."

The Vision About the 70 Weeks

20I was praying to the LORD my God about his holy mountain and telling him about my sins and the sins of the people of Israel. 21That was the time of the evening sacrifices. While I was still praying, Gabriel, the one I saw in the first vision, flew quickly to me and touched me. He came at the time of the evening sacrifice. 22Gabriel helped me understand the things I wanted to know. He said, "Daniel, I have come to give you wisdom and to help you understand. 23When you first started praying, the command was given to come speak to you. God loves you very much! You will understand this command, and you will understand the vision.

24"God has allowed 70 weeks[c] for your people and your holy city, Daniel. The 70 weeks are ordered for these reasons: to stop doing bad things, to stop sinning, to make people pure, to bring the goodness that continues forever, to put a seal on visions and prophets, and to dedicate a very holy place.

25"Learn and understand these things, Daniel. From the time that the message went out to go back and rebuild Jerusalem until the time for the chosen leader[d] to come will be seven weeks. Then Jerusalem will be rebuilt. There will again be places for people to meet together in Jerusalem, and there will be a ditch around the city to protect it. Jerusalem will be built for 62 weeks, but there will be many troubles during that time. 26After the 62 weeks, the chosen leader will be killed. He will end up with nothing. Then the armies of the

---

a 9:11 **curses and promises** Part of the agreement that God made with the people of Israel. See, for example, Deut. 27–30.
b 9:17 **do . . . holy place** Literally, "let your face shine on your holy place".
c 9:24 **week** Or "unit of seven". The Hebrew word could mean "week" or "a period of seven years". Also in verses 25,27.
d 9:25 **chosen leader** Literally, "anointed one".

future ruler will destroy the city and the holy place. That end will come like a flood. War will continue until the end. God has ordered that place to be completely destroyed.

27"Then the future ruler will make an agreement with many people. That agreement will continue for one week. The offerings and sacrifices will stop for a half of a week. And a destroyer will come. He will do terrible, destructive things,[a] but God has ordered that destroyer to be completely destroyed."

Daniel's Vision by the Tigris River

10 During the third year that Cyrus was the king of Persia, these things were shown to Daniel. (Daniel's other name is Belteshazzar.) They are true, but very hard to understand. Daniel understood them because they were explained to him in a vision.

2At that time I, Daniel, was very sad for three weeks. 3During those three weeks, I didn't eat any fancy food; I didn't eat any meat or drink any wine. I didn't put any oil on my head. I didn't do any of these things for three weeks.

> **INSIGHT**
>
> Daniel's vision is very similar to John's awesome encounter with Christ (Revelation 1:13–16) several hundred years later.
>
> **Daniel 10:5–6**

4On the twenty-fourth day of the first month of the year, I was standing beside the great Tigris River. 5While I was standing there, I looked up and I saw a man standing in front of me. He was wearing linen clothes. He wore a belt made of pure gold[b] around his waist. 6His body was like a smooth, shiny stone. His face was bright like lightning. His eyes were like flames of fire. His arms and feet were shiny like polished brass. His voice was loud like a crowd of people.

7I, Daniel, was the only one who saw the vision. The men with me didn't see the vision, but they were still afraid. They were so afraid that they ran away and hid. 8So I was left alone. I was watching this vision, and it made me afraid. I lost my strength. My face turned white like a dead person's face, and I was helpless. 9Then I heard the man in

the vision talking. As I listened to his voice, I fell into a deep sleep, with my face on the ground.

10Then a hand touched me. When that happened, I got on my hands and knees. I was so afraid that I was shaking. 11The man in the vision said to me, "Daniel, God loves you very much. Think very carefully about the words I will speak to you. Stand up; I have been sent to you." And when he said this, I stood up. I was still shaking because I was afraid. 12Then the man in the vision started talking again. He said, "Daniel, do not be afraid. From the very first day you decided to get wisdom and to be humble in front of God, he has been listening to your prayers. I came to you because you have been praying. 13But the prince[c] of Persia has been fighting against me for 21 days. Then Michael, one of the most important princes, came to help me because I was stuck there with the king of Persia. 14Now I have come to you, Daniel, to explain to you what will happen to your people in the future. The vision is about a time in the future."

15While the man was talking to me, I bowed low with my face towards the ground. I could not speak. 16Then the one who looked like a man touched my lips. I opened my mouth and started to speak. I said to the one standing in front of me, "Sir, I am upset and afraid because of what I saw in the vision. I feel helpless. 17Sir, I am Daniel your servant. How can I talk with you? My strength is gone and it is hard for me to breathe."

18The one who looked like a man touched me again. When he touched me, I felt better. 19Then he said, "Daniel, don't be afraid. God loves you very much. Peace be with you. Be strong now, be strong."

When he spoke to me, I became stronger. Then I said, "Sir, you have given me strength. Now you can speak."

20So then he said, "Daniel, do you know why I have come to you? Soon I must go back to fight against the prince of Persia. When I go, the prince of Greece will come. 21But Daniel, before I go, I must first tell you what is written in the *Book of Truth*. No one stands with me against those evil angels except Michael, the prince over your people.

11 "During the first year that Darius the Mede was king, I stood up to support Michael[d] in his fight against the prince of Persia.

2"Now then, Daniel, I tell you the truth: three more kings will rule in Persia. Then a fourth king will come who will be much richer than all the other kings of Persia before him. He will use his

---

a 9:27 *He will do . . . things* Or "He will come on the wings of terrible destruction."
b 10:5 *pure gold* Literally, "gold from Uphaz".
c 10:13 *prince* This probably means an angel assigned to a country to protect it. Also in 10:20,21; 11:1; 12:1.
d 11:1 *Michael* See Dan. 10:13.

riches to get power and turn everyone against the kingdom of Greece. ³Then a very strong and powerful king will come who will rule with much power. He will do anything he wants. ⁴Just as he comes to power, his kingdom will be broken up and scattered in all directions. It will not be divided among his descendants. And it will not be ruled in the same way because that kingdom will be pulled up and given to other people.

⁵"The southern king will become strong, but then one of his commanders will defeat him. The commander will begin to rule, and he will be very powerful.

⁶"Then after a few years, the southern king and that commander will make an agreement. The daughter of the southern king will marry the northern king. She will do this to bring peace, but she and the southern king will not be strong enough. People will turn against her and against the one who brought her to that country. And they will turn against her child and against the one who helped her.

⁷"But someone from her family will come to take the southern king's place. He will attack the armies of the northern king. He will go into that king's strong fortress. He will fight and win. ⁸He will take their gods and their metal idols and their expensive things made from silver and gold. He will take those things away to Egypt. Then he will not bother the northern king for a few years. ⁹The northern king will attack the southern kingdom. But he will lose, and then he will go back to his own country.

¹⁰"The northern king's sons will prepare for war. They will get a large army together. It will move through the land very quickly, like a powerful flood. That army will fight all the way to the strong fortress of the southern king. ¹¹Then the southern king will become very angry and march out to fight against the northern king. The northern king will have a large army, but he will lose the war. ¹²The northern army will be defeated, and those soldiers will be carried away. The southern king will be very proud, and he will kill thousands of soldiers from the northern army. But he will not continue to be successful. ¹³The northern king will get another army that will be larger than the first one. After several years he will attack. His army will be ready for war. It will be very large and it will have many weapons.

¹⁴"In those times many people will be against the southern king. Some of your own people who love to fight will rebel against the southern king. They will not win, but they will make this vision come true. ¹⁵Then the northern king will come. He will build ramps against the walls and will capture a strong city. The southern army will not have the power to fight back. Even the best soldiers from the southern army will not be strong enough to stop the northern army.

¹⁶"The northern king will do whatever he wants. No one will be able to stop him. He will gain power and control in the Beautiful Land, and he will have the power to destroy it. ¹⁷The northern king will decide to use all his power to fight against the southern king, and he will make an agreement with the southern king. The king of the north will let one of his daughters marry the southern king so that he can defeat the southern king. But those plans will not succeed. His plans will not help him.

¹⁸"Then the northern king will turn his attention to the cities along the coast and will defeat many of them. But then a commander will put an end to the pride of that northern king. He will turn his pride into shame.

¹⁹"After that happens, the northern king will go back to the strong fortresses of his own country. But he will be weak and will fall. He will be finished.

²⁰"After the northern king, there will be a new ruler who sends out tax collectors so that he can live like a king. But after a few years, he will be destroyed, although he will not die in battle.

²¹"That ruler will be followed by a very cruel and hated man, who will not have the honour of being from a king's family.ᵃ He will become a ruler by being dishonest. He will attack the kingdom when the people feel safe. ²²He will defeat large and powerful armies. He will even defeat the leader with the agreement. ²³Many nations will make agreements with that cruel and hated ruler, but he will lie and trick them. He will gain much power, but only a few people will support him.

²⁴"When the richest countries feel safe, that cruel and hated ruler will attack them. He will attack at just the right time and will be successful where his ancestors were not successful. He will take things from the countries he defeated, and he will give them to his followers. He will plan to defeat and destroy strong cities. He will be successful—but only for a short time.

²⁵"That very cruel and hated ruler will have a very large army. He will use that army to show his strength and courage and attack the southern king. The southern king will get a very large and powerful army and go to war. But the people who are against him will make secret plans, and the southern king will be defeated. ²⁶People who were supposed to be good friends of the southern king will try to destroy him. His army will be defeated. Many of his soldiers will be killed in battle. ²⁷Those two kings will want to make trouble. They will sit

---

ᵃ 11:21 *who . . . king's family* Or "who will not have the good qualities a king should have".

around the table planning their lies, but it will not do either one of them any good because God has set a time for their end to come.

28"The northern king will go back to his own country with much wealth. Then he will decide to do bad things against the holy agreement.[a] He will do the things he planned, and then he will go back to his own country.

29"At the right time, the northern king will attack the southern king again. But this time he will not be successful as he was before. 30Ships from Cyprus will come and fight against the northern king. He will see those ships coming and be afraid. Then he will turn back and take out his anger on the holy agreement. He will turn back and help those who stopped following the holy agreement. 31The northern king will send his army to do terrible things to the Temple in Jerusalem. They will stop the people from offering the daily sacrifice. Then they will do something really terrible. They will set up that terrible thing that causes destruction.

32"The northern king will use lies and smooth talking to trick those who stop following the holy agreement, so they will sin even more. But those who know God and obey him will be strong. They will fight back.

33"Those wise teachers will help the other people understand what is happening. But even they will have to suffer persecution. Some of them will be killed with swords. Some of them will be burned or taken prisoner. Some of them will have their homes and possessions taken away. 34When those wise people are punished, they will receive some help, but many people who join them will be hypocrites. 35Some of the wise people will stumble and make mistakes. But the persecution must come so that they can be made stronger and purer until the time of the end. Then, at the right time, that time of the end will come.

The King Who Praises Himself

36"The northern king will do whatever he wants. He will boast about himself. He will praise himself and think that he is even better than a god. He will say things that no one has ever heard. He will say those things against the God of gods. He will be successful until all the evil things have happened. Then what God has planned to happen will happen.

37"That northern king will not care about the gods his ancestors worshipped. He will not care

about the gods women worship. He will not care about any god. Instead, he will praise himself and make himself more important than any god. 38The northern king will not worship any god, but he will worship power. Power and strength will be his god. His ancestors didn't love power as he does. He will honour the god of power with gold and silver, expensive jewels and gifts.

39"That northern king will attack strong fortresses with the help of this foreign god. He will give much honour to the foreign rulers who join him. He will put many people under their rule. He will make the rulers pay him for the land they rule over.

40"At the time of the end, the southern king will fight a battle against the northern king. The northern king will attack him with chariots and soldiers on horses and many large ships. The northern king will rush through the land like a flood. 41The northern king will attack the Beautiful Land. He will defeat many countries. But Edom, Moab and the leaders of Ammon will be saved from him. 42The northern king will show his power in many countries. Egypt will also learn how powerful he is. 43He will get treasures of gold and silver and all the riches of Egypt. The Libyans and Ethiopians will obey him. 44But that northern king will hear news from the east and the north that will make him afraid and angry. He will go to completely destroy many nations. 45He will set up his king's tents between the sea and the beautiful holy mountain.[b] But finally, that bad king will die. There will be no one to help him when his end comes.

12 "Daniel, at that time the great prince Michael will stand up. Michael is in charge of your people. There will be a time of much trouble, the worst time since nations have been on earth. But Daniel, at that time every one of your people whose name is found written in the book ⌊of life⌋ will be saved. 2There are many who are dead and buried.[c] Some of them will wake up and live forever, but others will wake up to shame and disgrace forever. 3The wise people will shine as bright as the sky. Those who teach others to do what is right will shine like stars for ever and ever.[d]

4"But you, Daniel, keep this message a secret. You must close the book and keep this secret until the time of the end. Many people will go here and there looking for true knowledge, and the true knowledge will increase."

---

⁵Then I, Daniel, noticed two other men. One man was standing on my side of the river, and the other was standing on the other side. ⁶The man who was dressed in linen was standing over the water in the river. One of the two men said to him, "How long will it be before these amazing things come true?"

⁷The man dressed in linen and standing over the water lifted his right and left hands towards heaven. And I heard him make a promise using the name of God who lives forever. He said, "It will be for three and a half years.ᵃ The power of the holy people will be broken, and then all these things will finally come true."

⁸I heard the answer, but I really didn't understand. So I asked, "Sir, what will happen after all this comes true?"

⁹He answered, "Go on about your life Daniel. The message is hidden. It will be a secret until the time of the end. ¹⁰Many people will be made pure—they will make themselves clean. But evil people will continue to be evil. And those wicked people will not understand these things, but the wise people will understand them.

¹¹"The daily sacrifice will be stopped. There will be 1,290 days from that time until the time that the terrible thing that destroys is set up. ¹²The one who waits for and comes to the end of the 1,335 days will be very happy.

¹³"As for you, Daniel, go and live your life until the end. You will get your rest. At the end you will rise from death and receive your share of the promise."

ᵃ **12:7** *three and a half years* Literally, "a time, times and half a time".

This section consists of twelve books. The phrase "Minor Prophets" refers not to the contents of these books, but to their length; some of these books are only one chapter long. In the Hebrew Scriptures they were collectively known as "The Twelve" and they were probably collected together onto one scroll. But they are all separate, distinct books.

Most of these men prophesied during the decline of the kingdoms of Israel and Judah. The themes they deal with are similar to those of the Major Prophets – themes such as the unfaithfulness of the people, social injustice and oppression, the future redemption of God's people, and the coming of a Messiah, a person chosen by God who would rescue his people from their foes. A Jewish work called *Ben Sirach*, written in the early second century BC, talks about the twelve prophets and describes them as offering hope and comfort to the people of Jacob. Despite the frequent mention in these books of divine judgement, there is always comfort and there is always hope.

Hosea is a tale of one man's love for his unfaithful wife, a love which mirrors the merciful, forgiving love of God.

Joel is a short book that tries to explain why Judah has been laid waste by a huge plague of locusts.

Amos is a powerful book that condemns the hypocrisy, idolatry, corruption and injustice of Israel.

Obadiah is only one chapter long and deals with the destruction of Edom.

Jonah is more a story about a prophet than a book of prophecy. It deals with God's offer of forgiveness to the hated, evil Assyrians.

Micah moves between condemnation of Israel's unjust conduct and prophecies of a great, future hope.

Nahum talks about the destruction of Nineveh, the capital of the Assyrian empire.

Habakkuk is a kind of mini book of Job, and asks why God is allowing bad things to happen to his people.

Zephaniah warns that those who follow false gods will face the judgement of God.

Haggai and **Zechariah** are associated with the return to Jerusalem after the exile, and aim to encourage the people to continue working on restoring the Temple. Zechariah talks of a king who will one day return to Jerusalem.

Malachi is the last book of the Old Testament. Malachi reminds people of their obligations to God and their purpose in his plan.

Who Hosea, son of Beeri, lived in the northern kingdom of Israel. After the death of Solomon the united kingdom of Israel split into two: Israel in the north and Judah in the south.

When He prophesied around 750–715 BC, in the troubled, final years of Israel, before it fell to the Assyrians. He prophesied for around forty years. This was a time of massive political disruption.

What In the early part of Hosea's ministry, Israel was strong under its king, Jeroboam II, who captured much of Syria for Israel. But within a couple of decades all that had changed.

In 722 BC the Assyrians captured the capital city, Samaria, and started deporting the inhabitants.

Hosea is a dramatic tale. The prophet is told to marry Gomer, a prostitute. Her unfaithfulness to him and his love for her is a powerful image of God's enduring love for Israel despite its unfaithfulness.

Hosea loves his unfaithful wife; God loves his unfaithful people. He doesn't want to punish them, but the way they have "slept" with other gods gives him little choice. The people are dishonest; the priests are idol worshippers; the kings are corrupt. Hosea condemns social injustice and the false gods and fake worship that bring it forth.

Other prophets performed dramatic acts to get their message across to the people, but Hosea's whole life is a prophetic act: marrying an unfaithful prostitute, naming his children "God Scatters", "No Mercy" and "Not My People", this is a man who truly lives his message.

But despite all this, despite the grim and sordid pictures of Israel's adulterous behaviour, the book is full of hope. God has never stopped loving his people. If Israel will repent and turn back to God, then all will be well. It ends with a series of moving appeals to the wayward kingdom and a picture of what could be: Israel in full bloom, as it were. "I will forgive them for leaving me. I will show them my love without limits, because I have stopped being angry," says God. "I will be like the dew to Israel. Israel will blossom like the lily. He will grow like the cedar trees of Lebanon" (14:4–5).

QUICK TOUR **HOSEA**

"I want faithful love more than I want sacrifice; I want people to know God, not just to bring burnt offerings."

Hosea 6:6

The LORD's Message Through Hosea

1 This is the LORD's message that came to Hosea son of Beeri during the time that Uzziah, Jotham, Ahaz and Hezekiah were kings of Judah, and Jeroboam son of Jehoash was king of Israel.

²This was the LORD's first message to Hosea. The LORD said, "Go, marry a prostitute and have children who will be just like her. Do this to show how the people in this country have acted like prostitutes. They have been unfaithful to the LORD."

The Birth of Jezreel

³So Hosea married Gomer daughter of Diblaim. She became pregnant and gave birth to a son for Hosea. ⁴The LORD said to Hosea, "Name him Jezreel,ᵃ because soon I will punish the family of Jehu for the people he killed at Jezreel Valley.ᵇ Then I will put an end to the kingdom of the nationᶜ of Israel. ⁵And at that time I will break Israel's bow at Jezreel Valley."

INSIGHT

What does your name make people think of? The Israelites associated the name "Jezreel" with Baal worship and bloodshed. Hosea's whole life was dedicated to showing them how worshipping idols was a slap in the face to God.

Hosea 1:4

The Birth of Lo-Ruhamah

⁶Then Gomer became pregnant again and gave birth to a daughter. The LORD said to Hosea, "Name her Lo-Ruhamah,ᵈ because I will not show mercy to the nation of Israel any more, nor will I forgive them. ⁷But I will show mercy to the nation of Judah. I will save them, but I will not use bows or swords or war horses and soldiers to save them. I will save them by my own power."ᵉ

The Birth of Lo-Ammi

⁸After Gomer had finished nursing Lo-Ruhamah, she became pregnant again and gave birth to a son. ⁹Then the Lord said, "Name him Lo-Ammi,ᶠ because you are not my people, and I am not your God."

God's Promise to the Nation of Israel

¹⁰"In the future the number of the people of Israel will be like the sand of the sea, which you cannot measure or count. In the same place that God told them, 'You are not my people,' he will call them 'children of the Living God'.

¹¹"Then the people of Judah and the people of Israel will be gathered together. They will choose one ruler for themselves, and their nation will be too large for the land.ᵍ Jezreel's day will be great!

2 "Then you will say to your brothers, 'You are my people,' and you will say to your sisters, 'He has shown mercy to you.'"ʰ

²"Tell your motherⁱ she has done wrong and is no longer my wife! I cannot be a husband to a woman like this. She must stop acting like a prostitute and get rid of her lovers.ʲ ³If she refuses to change, I will strip off her clothes, and leave her naked like the day she was born. I will take away her people, and she will be like an empty, dry desert. I will cause her to die of thirst. ⁴I will have no pity on her children because they are the children of prostitution. ⁵Their mother has acted like a prostitute. She should be ashamed of what she has done. She said, 'I will go to my lovers,ᵏ who give me food and water, wool and linen, wine and olive oil.'

⁶"So I, the Lord, will block Israel's road with thorns; I will build a wall so that she will not be able to find her path. ⁷She will run after her lovers, but she will not be able to catch up with them. She will look for her lovers, but she will not be able to find them. Then she will say, 'I will go back to my husband, because life was better for me when I was with him.'

⁸"Israel didn't know that I, the Lord, was the one who gave her grain, wine and oil. I kept giving her more and more silver and gold, but she used this silver and gold to make statues of Baal. ⁹So

---

ᵃ **1:4** *Jezreel* This name in Hebrew means "God will plant seeds".
ᵇ **1:4** *people . . . at Jezreel Valley* See 2 Kgs 9 – 10 for the story about Jehu's revolt at Jezreel Valley.
ᶜ **1:4** *nation* Literally, "house". This might mean the royal family of that country. Also in verse 6.
ᵈ **1:6** *Lo-Ruhamah* This name in Hebrew means "She receives no mercy". Also in verse 8 and 2:23.
ᵉ **1:7** *by my own power* Literally, "by the LORD their God".
ᶠ **1:9** *Lo-Ammi* This name in Hebrew means "not my people". Also in 2:23.
ᵍ **1:11** *their nation . . . land* Literally, "they will go up from the land".
ʰ **2:1** Or "Then say to your brothers, 'My people,' and to your sisters, 'You have been shown mercy.'"
ⁱ **2:2** *mother* This means the nation of Israel.
ʲ **2:2** *her lovers* Or "her adulteries". Israel's worship of other gods was like spiritual adultery.
ᵏ **2:5** *lovers* This means Israel's false gods. Also in verses 7,10,13.

AN UNFAITHFUL WIFE, A FAITHFUL HUSBAND

Love is probably the most common topic of all writing and songs, hopes and dreams. Yet our concept of love is often distorted by selfishness and lust. God, who *is* love, teaches his people about real love in a shocking way . . .

DIG IN
READ Hosea 1:1–9; 3:1–5

These verses summarize Hosea's life story, a life which God used powerfully to speak to his people.

- Try to put yourself in Hosea's shoes (1:2). Write an imaginary diary entry detailing all the things you might be feeling if you had such a wife.
- Look at the names God told Hosea to give to his children. (Note that Jezreel literally means "God will sow", pointing to the scattering of his people so that they are no longer a united nation.) What kind of picture do these names paint of God's attitude towards Israel?
- Look at chapter 3 and continue Hosea's diary entry about how these actions will have made him feel.
- How is Gomer's behaviour a picture of Israel's unfaithfulness?
- What does your diary entry tell us about how Hosea's feelings might reflect God's in light of his people's unfaithfulness to him?

God's people had taken to worshipping false gods. Though they still acknowledged the true God, they thought they'd better hedge their bets and worship other gods too – gods who they thought would bring them food and water, wool, linen, oil and wine (2:5). There was no faithfulness. As far as God is concerned, worshipping many gods is like having several lovers as well as a husband. The most powerful way that God could communicate his heart's pain was by using Hosea as a living parable or illustration of what they were doing.

READ Hosea 2:2–13

Here we see that Hosea has a message of judgement for Israel.

- Where did Israel's blessings really come from – even while they were being unfaithful to God (2:8)?
- What did Israel choose to do with these gifts?
- Make a list of the ways that God says he will punish Israel.

READ Hosea 1:10 – 2:1,14–23

Yet Hosea's message is not without hope:

- How do the promises in these verses reverse the curses illustrated by the names of Gomer's children?
- Hosea's relationship with Gomer is a picture of God's relationship with Israel. What is surprising about chapter 2:14–15?

The book of Hosea is quite difficult to understand, so to simplify things we've looked at Hosea's life story, followed by the messages of judgement and then hope. This book helps to illustrate that God didn't so much "change his mind" about judgement, but rather his mercy was always part of the plan, interwoven throughout Hosea's own life's narrative and the story of Israel's history.

DIG THROUGH

- Have you ever thought about your sin as being like a wife who is unfaithful to her husband? It's pretty shocking isn't it?! In what specific ways are you unfaithful to God? What things do you love more than him? You may not think you love something more than God but if God asked you to give up your favourite things, could you? What really is most important in your life?
- When you're with your non-Christian friends, do you ever think, "I'll swap God for the things they're doing for a while"? Do you join in with the gossip or rude jokes? What about smutty magazines? Girls, do you constantly find yourself wanting more clothes? Or guys, are you after the latest gadget, or wanting to play footy rather than going to church?

I will return and take back my grain at the time it is ready to be harvested. I will take back my wine at the time the grapes are ready. I will take back my wool and linen. I gave those things to her so that she could cover her naked body. ¹⁰Now I will strip her. She will be naked, so all her lovers can see her. No one will be able to save her from my power.ᵃ ¹¹I will take away all her fun. I will stop her festivals, her New Moon celebrations, and her days of rest. I will stop all her special feasts. ¹²I will destroy her vines and fig trees. She said, 'My lovers gave these things to me.' But I will change her gardens—they will become like a wild forest. Wild animals will come and eat from those plants.

¹³"Israel served false gods,ᵇ so I will punish her. She burned incense to those false gods. She dressed up—she put on her jewellery and nose ring. Then she went to her lovers and forgot me." This is what the LORD has said.

¹⁴"So I, the Lord, will speak romantic words to her. I will lead her into the desert and speak tender words. ¹⁵There I will give her vineyards. I will give her Achor Valley as a doorway of hope. Then she will answer as she did when she came out of the land of Egypt." ¹⁶This is what the LORD says.

"At that time you will call me 'My husband'. You will not call me 'My Baal'.ᶜ ¹⁷I will take the names of those false gods out of her mouth. Then people will not use those names again.

¹⁸"At that time I will make an agreement for the Israelites with the animals of the field, the birds of the sky and the crawling things on the ground. I will break the bow, the sword and the weapons of war in that land. I will make the land safe, so the people of Israel can lie down in peace. ¹⁹And I will make you my bride forever. I will make you my bride with goodness and justice and with love and mercy. ²⁰I will make you my faithful bride. Then you will really know the LORD. ²¹And at that time I will answer." This is what the LORD says.

"I will speak to the skies,
and they will give rain to the earth.
²²The earth will produce grain, wine and oil,
and they will meet Jezreel's needs.
²³I will sow her many seedsᵈ on her land.
To Lo-Ruhamah, I will show mercy.

To Lo-Ammi, I will say, 'You are my people.'
And they will say to me, 'You are our God.'"

Hosea Buys Gomer Back From Slavery

3 Then the LORD said to me again, "Your wife has many lovers. But you must continue to love her, because it is an example of the LORD's love for Israel. He continues to love them, but they continue to turn to other gods, and they love to share in the offering of raisin cakesᵉ to them."

²So I bought her back for 15 piecesᶠ of silver and 150 kilogrammesᵍ of barley. ³Then I told her, "You must stay at home with me for many days. You will not be like a prostitute. You will not have sex with another man. I will be your husband."

⁴In the same way, the people of Israel will continue many days without a king or a leader. They will be without a sacrifice or a memorial stone. They will be without an ephod or a household god. ⁵After this the people of Israel will come back and look for the LORD their God and for David their king. In the last days they will come to honour the LORD and his goodness.

The LORD Is Angry Against Israel

4 People of Israel, listen to the LORD's message. The LORD has something to say against those who live in this land: "The people in this land are not honest or loyal. They don't really know God. ²They are always cursing, lying, killing, stealing and committing adultery. They murder one person after another. ³So the country is like someone crying for the dead, and all its people are weak. Even the animals of the field, the birds of the sky and the fish in the sea are dying.ʰ ⁴No one should argue or blame another person. Priests, my argument is with you!ⁱ ⁵You priests will fall in the daytime. And at night the prophet will also fall with you. I will also destroy your mother.

⁶"My people are destroyed because they have no knowledge. You priests have refused to learn, so I will refuse to let you be priests for me. You have forgotten the law of your God, so I will forget your children. ⁷They became proud. They sinned more and more against me, so I will change their honour to shame.

ᵃ **2:10 power** Literally, "hand".

ᵇ **2:13 false gods** Literally, "Baals".

ᶜ **2:16 My Baal** This is a wordplay. Baal was a Canaanite god, but the name also means "lord or husband".

ᵈ **2:23 I will sow her many seeds** Jezreel, Lo-Ruhamah and Lo-Ammi are Hosea's children. But the names also have special meanings. The name Jezreel means "God will plant seeds". But Jezreel is also the name of a large valley in Israel. This probably shows that God will bring his people back to Israel.

ᵉ **3:1 raisin cakes** This food was used in the feasts that honoured false gods such as the "Queen of Heaven".

ᶠ **3:2 15 pieces** Literally, "15 ₁shekels₁".

ᵍ **3:2 150 kilogrammes** Literally, "½ homer and 1 letek".

ʰ **4:3 dying** Literally, "being taken away".

ⁱ **4:4** Or "The people cannot complain or blame someone else. The people are helpless, like arguing with a priest." Often the priests and Levites served as judges, and their decisions were final.

[8]"The priests fed on the people's sins. They wanted more and more of their sin offerings.[a] [9]So the priests are no different from the people. I will punish them for the things they did. I will pay them back for the wrong things they did. [10]They will eat, but they will not be satisfied. They will have sex with prostitutes, but they will still have no children.[b] That's because they have left the LORD and have given themselves to other gods.

[11]"Sexual sins, strong drink and new wine ruin a person's ability to think straight. [12]My people are asking pieces of wood for advice. They think those sticks will answer them! They have chased after those false gods like prostitutes and have left their own God. [13]They make sacrifices on the tops of the mountains and burn incense on the hills under oak trees, poplar trees and elm trees.[c] The shade under those trees looks nice. So your daughters lie under those trees like prostitutes, and your daughters-in-law commit sexual sins.

[14]"I cannot blame your daughters or your daughters-in-law for doing this, because your men go and have sex with the temple prostitutes[d] and offer sacrifices with them. This is how foolish people destroy themselves.

The Shameful Sins of Israel

[15]"Israel, you are as unfaithful as a prostitute! May Judah never be guilty of doing what you have done. My people, don't go to Gilgal, and stay away from Beth Aven.[e] Don't make promises there using the LORD's name! [16]The LORD has given many things to Israel. He is like a shepherd who takes his sheep to a large field with plenty of grass. But Israel is stubborn like a young cow that runs away again and again.

[17]"Ephraim has joined his idols, so leave him alone. [18]Ephraim has joined their drunkenness. Let them continue to be prostitutes. Let them be with their lovers.[f] [19]They went to those gods for safety, and they have lost their ability to think.[g] Their altars will bring them shame.

The Leaders Cause Israel and Judah to Sin

5 "Priests, nation[h] of Israel, and people in the king's family, listen to me. You have been judged guilty!

"You were like a trap at Mizpah[i] and like a net spread on the ground at Tabor.[j] [2]You have done many evil things,[k] so I will punish you all. [3]I know Ephraim. I know what Israel has done. Ephraim, right now you act like a prostitute. Israel is dirty with sin. [4]The people of Israel have done many evil things, and these evil things keep them from coming back to their God. They are always thinking of ways to chase after other gods. They don't know the LORD. [5]Israel's pride is a witness against them,[l] so Israel and Ephraim will stumble in their sin. But Judah will also stumble with them.

[6]"The leaders of the people went to look for the LORD. They took their sheep and cattle with them, but they did not find the LORD because he refused to accept them. [7]They have not been faithful to the LORD. Their children are from some stranger. And now, he will destroy them and their land again.[m]

[a] **4:8** This is a wordplay. The word "sins" also means "sin offerings". So instead of eating sacrifices, the priests became hungry for sin itself.

[b] **4:10** *They . . . children* A part of worshipping the false gods was having sex with temple prostitutes. The people thought this would make the gods happy so that they would give the people large families and good crops.

[c] **4:13** *under . . . trees* Trees and groves were an important part of worshipping false gods.

[d] **4:14** *temple prostitutes* Women who were prostitutes at the temples of the false gods. Their sexual sins were part of worshipping those false gods.

[e] **4:15** *Beth Aven* A name meaning "House of Evil". It is a wordplay on the name "Bethel", a name meaning "House of God". There was a temple in this town. Also in 5:8.

[f] **4:18** *lovers* This means Israel's false gods.

[g] **4:19** *They . . . think* Or "The wind has carried them away on its wings" or "The spirit held them tight in its wings." The Hebrew text here is not clear.

[h] **5:1** *nation* Literally, "house." This might mean the royal family of that country. Also in verse 14.

[i] **5:1** *Mizpah* A mountain in Israel. The people worshipped the false gods on many of the hills and mountains.

[j] **5:1** *Tabor* A mountain in Israel.

[k] **5:2** *You . . . evil things* The Hebrew text here is not clear. It seems to be a wordplay of some kind.

[l] **5:5** *them* Literally, "his face".

[m] **5:7** *And now . . . again* The Hebrew text here is not clear.

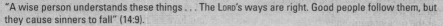

A TENDER FATHER

"A wise person understands these things . . . The LORD's ways are right. Good people follow them, but they cause sinners to fall" (14:9).

These are the final words of Hosea. He indicates that the words that came before them are very important, so read on to find out more . . .

Chapters 4 – 13 of Hosea contain various prophesies of judgement as well as promises of restoration. Here, we are just going to dip into a few of these to get a flavour of what God wants to say to us through his prophet Hosea. By the way, Ephraim (4:17 and elsewhere) was the leading tribe of Israel.

DIG IN

READ Hosea 5:1–15

- List some of the sins of which Israel is guilty (vv.1–7).
- List the ways in which God says he will deal with this sin.

READ Hosea 7:8–16

- What were some of the results of Israel's sin?

Things are bad. God's people have consistently lived in a way that demonstrates that God is far from being their first priority. They are reaping the fruits of this behaviour, one of which is the fact that God is very, very angry. Their situation appears deservedly hopeless. However, chapter 11 shows that this is not the case.

READ Hosea 11:1–12

This is one of the most beautiful passages describing God's love towards his people in the whole Bible.

- List the tender, fatherly images conjured up by these verses.
- How does Israel respond to this tenderness?
- A good and kind father will not allow his children to continuously misbehave and ignore his wise advice. How does God therefore have to respond in 11:5–7?
- Yet, read on for a glimpse into God's mind when considering judgement (11:8–11).
- How have the images of God as lion (5:14) and Israel (Ephraim) as dove (7:11) now been turned around?

READ Hosea 14:1–9

- Hosea has been pleading with Israel to come back to God, her husband, and be faithful to him (Hosea 2:2; 6:1; 12:6; 14:1). Now he even gives the people "words of confession" to use when they come back to God. What things should they say to him (14:2–3)?
- In the verses that follow, what promises does God give to those who come back to him?

DIG THROUGH

- As Christians we can sometimes be guilty of taking grace for granted. The judgement prophecies in books like Hosea remind us of the consequences that our sin truly deserves. Why not come to God now with some words of confession like those in 14:2–3? How about asking God to take away your sin and tell him you don't want to put your hope in anything or anyone but Jesus.

DIG DEEPER

- How did you respond to the imagery of God as a tender Father? Does it come naturally to you to think of him in this way? Or perhaps this is alien or painful for you because your earthly father has been far from tender or kind. Spend some time in prayer to your "Abba" (check out Romans 8:15 and Galatians 4:6 – the word comes closest to the English word "Daddy"). Ask him to heal any barriers that may prevent you from fully embracing this tender aspect of God's character.

A Prophecy of Israel's Destruction

⁸"Blow the horn in Gibeah.
  Blow the trumpet in Ramah.ᵃ
Give the warning at Beth Aven.
  The enemy is behind you, Benjamin.
⁹Ephraim will become empty
  at the time of punishment.
I, God, warn the families of Israel
  that this really will happen.
¹⁰The leaders of Judah are like thieves trying to
    steal someone's property,
  so I will pour out my anger on them like
    water.
¹¹Ephraim will be punished.
  He will be crushed and pressed like grapes,
    because he decided to follow filth.
¹²I will destroy Ephraim as a moth eats a piece
    of cloth.
  I will ruin Judah, like rot on a piece of
    wood.
¹³Ephraim saw his sickness, and Judah saw his
    wound,
  so they went to Assyria for help.
They told their problems to the great king.
  But he cannot heal you or cure your
    wound.
¹⁴I will be like a lion to Ephraim,
  like a young lion to the nation of Judah.
I—yes, I myself—will rip them to pieces.
I will carry them away,
  and no one can save them.
¹⁵I will go back to my place,
  until the people admit they are guilty,
  until they come looking for me.
Yes, in their trouble they will try very hard to
  find me."

The Rewards of Coming Back to the LORD

6 "Come, let's go back to the LORD.
  He hurt us, but he will heal us.
  He wounded us, but he will put bandages
    on us.
²After two days he will bring us back to life.
  He will raise us up on the third day.
  Then we can live near him.
³Let's learn about the LORD.
  Let's try very hard to know him.
We know he is coming,
  just as we know the dawn is coming.

He will come to us like the rain,
  like the spring rain that waters the ground."

The People Are Not Faithful

⁴"Ephraim, what should I do with you?
  Judah, what should I do with you?
Your love for me is like a morning mist,
  like the dew that is gone as soon as the day
    begins.
⁵That's why I sent my prophets to cut you
    down,
  to speak my message that warned you of
    death.
And everyone can see that my judgement
    is fair.
  That is as clear as the morning sun.ᵇ
⁶I want faithful love
  more than I want sacrifice;
I want people to know God,
  not just to bring burnt offerings.
⁷But the people broke the agreement as
    Adam did.ᶜ
  They were unfaithful to me in their country.
⁸Gilead is a city of people who do evil—
  people who have tricked and killed others.
⁹The priests are like gangs of robbers
  hiding and waiting on the road to attack
    someone.
They murder people before they reach safety
    in Shechem.
  They do such evil things.
¹⁰I have seen a terrible thing happen
    in the nationᵈ of Israel.
My peopleᵉ have been unfaithful.
  Israel is too unclean to serve me.

¹¹"Judah, there is also a time of harvest for
    you.
  It will happen when I bring my people back
    from captivity.ᶠ

7 "I will heal Israel!
  Then people will know that Ephraim
    sinned.
They will know about Samaria'sᵍ lies.
  They will know about the thieves who
    come and go in that town.
²They don't believe that I will remember their
    crimes.

ᵃ **5:8** *Gibeah, Ramah* Cities on Judah's border with Israel.
ᵇ **6:5** *And everyone . . . sun* This follows the ancient Greek, Syriac and Aramaic versions. The traditional Hebrew text may be understood to mean "Surely you don't believe that anyone would think you are innocent!" or more literally, "And is your innocence a shining light?"
ᶜ **6:7** *as Adam did* See Gen. 3.
ᵈ **6:10** *nation* Literally, "house". This might mean the royal family of that country.
ᵉ **6:10** *My people* Literally, "Ephraim". See "EPHRAIM" in the Word List.
ᶠ **6:11** *It will . . . captivity* Or "It will happen when I restore my people's fortune."
ᵍ **7:1** *Samaria* The capital city of the northern kingdom of Israel.

The bad things they did are all around.
I can see their sins clearly.
³Their evil makes their king happy.
Their false gods please their leaders.
⁴They are all unfaithful traitors,
just waiting to cause trouble.
They are like an oven that quietly heats up
while the baker prepares the dough.
⁵On holidays for their king,
the leaders get drunk with wine
and join with people who laugh at God.
⁶They burn with anger like fire in an oven,
and they make their secret plans.
All through the night their anger heats up
and by morning becomes a blazing fire.
⁷They are all like hot ovens.
They destroyed their rulers.
All their kings fell.
Not one of them called to me for help.

Israel and the Nations

⁸"Ephraim mixes with the nations.
Ephraim is like a cake that was not cooked
on both sides.
⁹Strangers destroy Ephraim's strength,
but Ephraim does not know it.
Grey hairsᵃ are also sprinkled on Ephraim,
but Ephraim does not know it.
¹⁰Ephraim's pride speaks against him.
The people had many troubles,
but they still didn't go back to the LORD
their God.
They didn't look to him for help.
¹¹So Ephraim has become like a silly dove
without understanding.
The people called to Egypt for help.
They went to Assyria for help.
¹²They go to those countries for help,
but I will trap them.
I will throw my net over them,
and I will bring them down like the birds of
the sky.
I will punish them for their agreements.ᵇ
¹³It will be very bad for those who left me.
They refused to obey me, so they will be
destroyed.
I saved them,
but they speak lies against me.
¹⁴They never call to me from their hearts.

Yes, they cry on their beds.
And they cut themselves when they ask for
grain and new wine.
But in their hearts, they have turned away
from me.
¹⁵I trained them and made their arms strong,
but they made evil plans against me.
¹⁶Like a boomerang, they changed directions,
but they did not come back to me.ᶜ
Their leaders boasted about their strength,
but they will be killed with swords.
And the people in Egypt
will laugh at them.

Idol Worship Leads to Destruction

8 "Give the warning with your trumpet! Like
an eagle the enemy circles over the LORD's
people. They have broken my agreement and
refused to obey my law. ²They yell out at me, 'My
God, we in Israel know you!' ³But Israel refused
the good things, so the enemy chases him.
⁴The Israelites chose their kings, but they didn't
come to me for advice. They chose leaders, but
they didn't choose men I knew. The Israelites
used their silver and gold to make idols for
themselves, so they will be destroyed. ⁵⁻⁶He has
refused your calf, Samaria.ᵈ God says, 'I am very
angry with the Israelites.' The people of Israel will
be punished for their sin. Some worker made
those statues. They are not God. Samaria's calf
will be broken into pieces. ⁷The Israelites did a
foolish thing—it was like trying to plant the wind.
But they will get only troubles—they will harvest
a whirlwind. The grain in the fields will grow, but
it will give no food. Even if it grew something,
strangers would eat it.

⁸"Israel was destroyed;
its people are scattered among the nations,
like some dish that was thrown away
because no one wanted it.
⁹Ephraim went to his 'lovers'.ᵉ
Like a stubborn donkey, they led him off to
Assyria.
¹⁰Yes, Israel was taken to the nations,
but I will bring them back.
But first, they must suffer a little
by carrying the burden of that mighty
king.

ᵃ **7:9 Grey hairs** This word might describe something that was put on the food when people cooked, something that looked like
grey hairs.
ᵇ **7:12 for their agreements** Or "for the report of their treaties".
ᶜ **7:16 they changed . . . to me** Or "They turned, but not upward" or "They turned to the 'no-gods'." That is, the statues people
worshipped as gods.
ᵈ **8:5–6 calf, Samaria** Samaria was the capital city of Israel. The people of Israel made statues of calves and put them in the
temples at Dan and Bethel. It is not clear if these statues represented the Lord or some false god. But God didn't want them to use
these statues. See 1 Kgs 12:26–30.
ᵉ **8:9 lovers** This means Israel's false gods.

Israel Forgets God and Worships Idols

¹¹"Ephraim built more and more altars,
   and that was a sin.
   They have been altars of sin for
      Ephraim.
¹²Even if I wrote 10,000 laws for Ephraim,
   he would treat them as if they were for
      some stranger.
¹³The Israelites love sacrifices.^a
   They offer the meat and eat it.
The LORD does not accept their sacrifices.
   He remembers their sins,
and he will punish them.
   They will be carried away as prisoners to
      Egypt.
¹⁴Israel has built palaces for its kings,
   and now Judah builds fortresses.
But they have forgotten their Maker!
   So I will send a fire to destroy their cities
      and fortresses!"

The Sadness of Exile

9 Israel, don't celebrate like the nations do.
   Don't be happy. You acted like a prostitute
and left your God. You committed your sexual
sin^b on every threshing floor. ²But the grain from
those threshing floors will not provide enough
food for the people. And there will not be
enough wine.

³Your people will not stay in the LORD's land.
Israel^c will return to slavery in Egypt. And some
will go to Assyria, where the food is wrong for
them to eat. ⁴They will have no wine offerings
for the LORD. None of their sacrifices will please
him. What they offer will be like food eaten at a
funeral, and whoever eats it will become unclean.
They can eat that food for their own hunger,
but it cannot be taken into the Lord's Temple.
⁵They will not be able to celebrate the LORD's
feasts or festivals.^d

⁶Even if they escape this disaster, Egypt will
capture them. Memphis^e will bury them. Weeds
will grow over their silver treasures, and thorns
will grow where the Israelites lived.

Israel Rejected the True Prophets

⁷The prophet says, "Israel, learn this: The time
of punishment has come. The time has come for
you to pay for the evil things you did." But the
people of Israel say, "The prophet is a fool. This

man with ⌊God's⌋ Spirit is crazy." The prophet
says, "You will be punished for your terrible
sins. You will be punished for your hate." ⁸God
and the prophet are like guards watching over
Ephraim, but there are many traps along his way.
And people hate the prophet, even in the house
of his God.

⁹The Israelites have gone deep into ruin as
in the time of Gibeah. God will remember the
Israelites' sins, and he will punish them.

Israel Is Ruined by Its Worship of Idols

¹⁰The Lord says, "When I found Israel, it was
like finding fresh grapes in the desert. It was like
seeing the first fruit on a fig tree at the beginning
of the season. But then they came to Baal Peor^f
and offered themselves to that shameful idol.
They became as sickening as that idol they loved.

The Israelites Will Have No Children

¹¹"Like a bird, Ephraim's glory will fly away.
There will be no more pregnancies, no more births
and no more babies. ¹²But even if the Israelites do
raise their children, it will not help, because I will
take the children away from them. I will leave
them, and they will have nothing but troubles.
¹³"I can see that Ephraim is leading his children
into a trap. Ephraim will lead his children out to
the killer." ¹⁴LORD, give them what you will. Give
them a womb that loses babies and breasts that
cannot give milk.

¹⁵"All their evil is in Gilgal;
   I began hating them there.
I will force them to leave my house
   because of the evil things they do.
I will not love them any more.
   Their leaders are rebels who turned
      against me.
¹⁶Ephraim will be punished.
   Their root is dying.
   They will not have any more babies.
They might give birth to babies,
   but I will kill the precious babies who come
      from their bodies."

¹⁷Those people will not listen to my God,
   so he will refuse to listen to them.
And they will wander among the nations
   without a home.

---

^a **8:13 *The Israelites love sacrifices*** The meaning of the Hebrew text here is uncertain.
^b **9:1 *You committed your sexual sin*** This means the people were not faithful to God. But it also means the people had sex
with temple prostitutes. They believed their false gods would give them many children and good crops.
^c **9:3 *Israel*** Literally, "Ephraim". See "EPHRAIM" in the Word List.
^d **9:5** Literally, "What will you do for a day of solemn assembly, for the LORD's festival day?"
^e **9:6 *Memphis*** An important city in Egypt.
^f **9:10 *Baal Peor*** See Num. 25:1–5.

Israel's Riches Led to Its Worship of Idols

10 Israel is like a vine
　　that grows plenty of fruit.
But as Israel got more and more things,
　　he built more and more altars to honour
　　　　false gods.
His land became better and better,
　　so he put up better and better stones to
　　　　honour false gods.
²The people of Israel tried to trick God,
　　but now they must accept their guilt.
He will break down their altars
　　and destroy their memorial stones.

The Evil Decisions of the Israelites

³Now the Israelites say, "We have no king.
We don't honour the Lord. And his king cannot
do anything to us."

⁴They make promises, but they are only telling
lies. They don't keep their promises. They make
agreements ⌊with other countries. God does
not like those agreements⌋. The judges are like
poisonous weeds growing in a ploughed field.

⁵The people in Samaria tremble in fear of losing
the calf-idol they worship at Beth Aven.ᵃ They
were so proud of its beauty! But it will be taken
away, and the people will be sad; the priests who
worshipped it will cry. ⁶It will be carried away as
a gift to the great king of Assyria. This will bring
shame to Israel. They will be shamed for trusting
a wooden idol. ⁷Samaria's false godᵇ will be
destroyed. It will be like a piece of wood floating
away on the water's surface.

⁸Israel sinned and built many high places. The
high places of Avenᶜ will be destroyed. Thorns
and weeds will grow on their altars. Then they
will say to the mountains, "Cover us!" and to the
hills, "Fall on us!"

Israel Will Pay for Sin

⁹"Israel, you have sinned since the time of
Gibeah. And the people have continued to sin
there. Those evil people at Gibeah will be trapped
by war. ¹⁰I will come to punish them. Armies will
come together against them and punish the
Israelites for their double sin.ᵈ

¹¹"Ephraim is like a trained young cow that
loves to walk on grain on the threshing floor.
I will put a good yoke on her neck. I will put
the ropes on Ephraim. Then Judah will begin
ploughing. Jacob will break the ground himself."

¹²If you plant goodness, you will harvest
faithful love. Plough your ground, and you will
harvest with the Lord. He will come, and he
will make goodness fall on you like rain.

¹³But you planted evil, and you harvested
trouble. You have eaten fruit produced by lies,
putting your trust in your own power and in your
great army. ¹⁴So the noise of battle will surround
your people, and the enemy will destroy all
your fortresses. They will do what Shalmanᵉ did
when he destroyed Beth Arbel. They will kill even
mothers and their children by beating them against
rocks. ¹⁵And this will happen to you at Bethel,
because you did so many evil things. When that
day begins, the king of Israel will be fully destroyed.

Israel Has Forgotten the Lord

11 The Lord said, "I loved Israel when he
　　was a child,
　　and I called my son out of Egypt.
²But the more Iᶠ called the Israelites,
　　the more they left me.
The Israelites gave sacrifices to the false godsᵍ
　　and burned incense to the idols.

³"But I was the one who taught Ephraim to
　　walk.
　　I took the Israelites in my arms.
I healed them,
　　but they don't know that.
⁴I led them with ropes,ʰ
　　but they were ropes of love.
I was like a person who set them free.ⁱ
　　I bent down and fed them.

⁵"The Israelites will be captives again, as in
Egypt. Assyria will rule over them, because they
refuse to turn back to God. ⁶The sword will swing
against their cities and completely destroy their
villages. They will all be killed because of their
own evil plans.

ᵃ **10:5 Beth Aven** A name meaning "House of Evil". It is a wordplay on the name "Bethel", a name meaning "House of God".
There was a temple in this town.
ᵇ **10:7 false god** Or "king".
ᶜ **10:8 high places of Aven** Aven means "evil" or "wickedness". This probably means the temple and other places of worship at
Bethel.
ᵈ **10:10** This probably refers to worship at Gibeah and Beth Aven.
ᵉ **10:14 Shalman** This is probably Shalmaneser, king of Assyria.
ᶠ **11:2 I** This is from the ancient Greek version. The standard Hebrew text has "they".
ᵍ **11:2 false gods** Literally, "Baals".
ʰ **11:4 ropes** The Hebrew says, "ropes of a man".
ⁱ **11:4 set them free** Literally, "lifted the yoke from their jaws".

7"My people expect me to come back. They will call to God above, but he will not help them."[a]

The Lord Will Not Destroy Israel

8"Ephraim, I don't want to give you up.
Israel, I want to protect you.
I don't want to destroy you,
as I did the cities of Admah and Zeboiim.[b]
I am changing my mind.
My love for you is too strong.
9I will not let my terrible anger win.
I will not destroy Ephraim again.
I am God and not a human.
I am the Holy One.
I am with you.
I will not show my anger.
10I, the Lord, will roar like a lion,
and my children will come and follow me.
They will come from the west,
shaking with fear.
11They will come from Egypt,
shaking like birds.
They will come shaking like doves from the
land of Assyria,
and I will take them back home."
This is what the Lord said.
12"Ephraim surrounded me with false
gods.
The people of Israel turned against me.[c]
But Judah still walks with God[d]
and is true to the Holy One."[e]

The Lord Is Against Israel

12 Ephraim is wasting its time; Israel "chases the wind" all day long. The people tell more and more lies and steal more and more. They have made agreements with Assyria, and they are carrying their olive oil to Egypt.

2The Lord says, "I have a complaint against Israel.[f] Jacob must be punished for the bad things he did. 3While Jacob was still in his mother's womb, he began to trick his brother.[g] Jacob was a

strong young man, and at that time he fought with God. 4Jacob wrestled with God's angel and won.[h] He cried and asked for a favour. That happened at Bethel. There he spoke to us. 5Yes, Yahweh is the God of the armies.[i] His name is Yahweh. 6So come back to your God. Be loyal to him. Do the right thing, and always trust in your God!

7"Jacob is a dishonest merchant. He even cheats his friend! Even his scales[j] lie. 8Ephraim said, 'I am rich! I have found true riches! No one will learn about my crimes. No one will learn about my sins.'

9"But I am still the Lord your God, as I was when you left the land of Egypt. I will make you live in tents, as you do during the Festival of Shelters.[k] 10I spoke to the prophets and gave them many visions. I gave the prophets many ways to teach my lessons to you. 11But the people in Gilead have sinned. There are many terrible idols in that place. They offer sacrifices to bulls at Gilgal. They have many altars. There are rows and rows of altars—like the rows of dirt in a ploughed field.

12"Jacob ran away to the land of Aram. There he[l] worked to get a wife. He took care of sheep to pay for her. 13Then the Lord used a prophet to bring Jacob's descendants out of Egypt. He used a prophet to keep these people of Israel safe. 14But the people of Israel have made the Lord very angry, and he will punish them for the murders they have committed. They will get what they deserve for insulting their Lord."

Israel Has Ruined Itself

13 "The tribe of Ephraim made themselves very important in Israel. Ephraim spoke and people shook with fear. But Ephraim sinned by worshipping Baal, so they must die. 2Now the Israelites sin more and more. They make idols for themselves. Workers make those fancy statues from silver, and then they talk to their statues. They offer sacrifices to them, and they kiss those

---

a **11:7** Or "My people are hanging on poles around my dwelling place. They called up to him, but he didn't lift them up."

b **11:8** *Admah and Zeboiim* Two cities that were destroyed when God destroyed Sodom and Gomorrah. See Gen. 19; Deut. 29:23.

c **11:12** *Ephraim . . . me* Or "Ephraim surrounded me with lies. The house of Israel surrounded me with deception."

d **11:12** *God* Literally, "El". This might be one of the names of God or it might be El, the most important god of the Canaanites. It is not clear whether this means Judah was being faithful to God or if Judah was worshipping the false gods.

e **11:12** *Holy One* This is a plural form in the Hebrew text and may refer to God or to Canaanite false gods.

f **12:2** *Israel* Literally, "Judah".

g **12:3** *he . . . his brother* Or "he grabbed his brother's heel". This is a wordplay. The Hebrew word is like the name "Jacob". Read Gen. 25:26.

h **12:4** *Jacob wrestled . . . and won* Read Gen. 32:22–28.

i **12:5** *Yahweh is the God of the armies* This is like one of the names for God. It is usually translated "Lord All-Powerful".

j **12:7** *scales* Or "balances", a tool for weighing things.

k **12:9** *as . . . Shelters* Literally, "as in the days of meeting". This might also refer to the meeting of God with his people in the Holy Tent (see "Holy Tent" in the Word List) during their wandering in the desert.

l **12:12** *he* Literally, "Israel", another name for Jacob. See "Israel" in the Word List.

calf idols. ³That is why those people will soon disappear. They will be like a fog that comes early in the morning and then quickly disappears. The Israelites will be like chaff that is blown from the threshing floor. The Israelites will be like smoke that goes out of a window and disappears.

INSIGHT

Holy cow! Excavations at Ashkelon on the coast of Israel have uncovered a small solid bronze calf dating back to Old Testament times. Found in a temple, it is an idol that people would have kissed out of devotion. Calf worship was a problem throughout the history of Israel (see Exodus 32:4; 1 Kings 12:28).
Hosea 13:2

⁴"I have been the LORD your God since the time you were in the land of Egypt. You did not know any other god except me. I am the one who saved you. ⁵I knew you in the desert—I knew you in that dry land. ⁶I gave food to the Israelites, and they ate it. They became full and satisfied. They became proud, and then they forgot me.

⁷"That is why I will be like a lion to them. I will be like a leopard waiting by the road. ⁸I will attack them like a bear whose cubs were robbed from her. I will attack them and rip open their chests. I will be like a lion or other wild animal tearing and eating its prey.

Israel Cannot Be Saved From God's Anger

⁹"Israel, I helped you, but you turned against me. So now I will destroy you. ¹⁰Where is your king? Can he save you in any of your cities? Where are your judges? You asked for them, saying, 'Give me a king and leaders.'ᵃ ¹¹I was angry, and I gave you a king. And when I became very angry, I took him away.

¹²"Israel cannot erase their guilt.
     A list of their sins has been kept to accuse
          them.
¹³The pain of birth will come for them,
     but they are like a baby that doesn't know
          what to do.
When it is time for him to be born,
     he refuses to come out of the womb.

¹⁴"I will save them from the grave.
     I will rescue them from death.
Death, where are your diseases?
     Grave, where is your power?
     I am not looking for revenge.
¹⁵Israel grows among his brothers,
     but a powerful east wind will come—
          the LORD's wind will blow from the
               desert.
Then his well will dry up.
     His spring of water will be dry.
     The wind will take away anything of
          value.
¹⁶Samaria must be punished
     because she turned against her God.
The Israelites will be killed with swords.
     Their children will be torn to pieces,
     and their pregnant women will be ripped
          open."

Return to the LORD

14 Israel, you fell and sinned against God. So come back to the LORD your God. ²Think about what you will say, and come back to the LORD. Say to him,

"Take away our sin,
     and accept these words as our sacrifice.
     We offer you the praise from our lips.ᵇ
³Assyria will not save us.
     We will not ride on war horses.
We will never again say, 'Our God'
     to something we made with our hands.
This is because you are the one who
     shows mercy to orphans."

The LORD Will Forgive Israel

⁴The Lord says,
"I will forgive them for leaving me.
     I will show them my love without
          limits,
     because I have stopped being angry.
⁵I will be like the dew to Israel.
     Israel will blossom like the lily.
     He will grow like the cedar trees of
          Lebanon.
⁶His branches will grow,
     and he will be like a beautiful olive tree.
He will be like the sweet smell
     from the cedar trees of Lebanon.
⁷The people of Israel will again live under my
          protection.
     They will grow like grain.
They will bloom like a vine.
     They will be like the wine of Lebanon.

ᵃ **13:10 You asked for . . . leaders** See 1 Sam. 8:4–9.
ᵇ **14:2 praise from our lips** Literally, "the fruit of our lips".

The LORD Warns Israel About Idols

8"Ephraim, there is no need for idols.
   I am the one who answers your prayers and
      watches over you.
I am like a fir tree that is always green.
   All your blessings come from me."

Final Advice

9A wise person understands these things,
   and a smart person should learn them.
The LORD's ways are right.
   Good people follow them,
   but they cause sinners to fall.

JOEL

Who   Joel, son of Pethuel. We don't know much else about him. He seems to know about the workings of the Temple, so he may have been from Jerusalem or the surrounding region.

When   Any time from the ninth century to the fourth century BC. It does seem to contain references to the fall of Jerusalem, which would put it after the exile in 586 BC. But really, these references could be to any enemy of Judah.

What   The country of Judah has been ravaged by a plague of locusts. Joel sees this as foreshadowing the "day of the Lord" – a time greatly anticipated by the Israelites, who believed that God would then Judge the nations and restore Israel.

Locusts were a sad feature of life in the ancient Middle East. One swarm sweeps through Judah, devastating Jerusalem and Joel asks "Why?" He interprets it as a warning from God, a forerunner of the day of judgement. Joel uses the locusts as a picture of a real army; an army that would be far more devastating. And the only insect repellent that will work against this army is for the people to return to their God.

The dominant theme in Joel is the arrival of the "day of the Lord". This is a day of judgement, but that doesn't necessarily mean "punishment". In the day of the Lord, God will put things right. He will restore his people (2:12–14), bring abundance and safety to them (2:23–26; 3:1) and dwell with them (2:27; 3:17,21).

For the New Testament followers of Jesus, this was a significant prophecy. After the outpouring of the Holy Spirit at Pentecost, Peter preached in Jerusalem that Joel's prophecy had come true: that the Spirit had indeed been poured out on young and old, men and women, servants and free (Joel 2:28–32; Acts 2:17–21).

QUICK TOUR   JOEL

The locusts 1:1–20	God will give his Spirit 2:28–32
The army 2:1–11	Judgement Valley 3:1–17
Turn around 2:12–27	Promise of a new life 3:18–21

"This is the LORD's message: 'Now come back to me with all your heart. Cry and mourn, and don't eat anything! Show that you are sad for doing wrong. Tear your hearts, not your clothes.' Come back to the LORD your God. He is kind and merciful. He does not become angry quickly. He has great love. Maybe he will change his mind about the bad punishment he planned."

Joel 2:12–13

Locusts Will Destroy the Crops

1 Joel son of Pethuel received this message from the LORD:

²Leaders, listen to this message!
    Listen to me, all you people who live in
        the land.
Has anything like this ever happened in your
        life?
    Did anything like this happen during your
        fathers' lifetimes?
³You will tell these things to your children,
    and your children will tell their children,
    and your grandchildren will tell the people
        of the next generation.
⁴What the cutting locust*ᵃ* has left,
    the swarming locust has eaten.
And what the swarming locust has left,
    the hopping locust has eaten.
And what the hopping locust has left,
    the destroying locust has eaten!

INSIGHT

*Can you eat the equivalent of your own
body weight in 24 hours? Locusts can.
They were a problem for farmers in Joel's
time – and they're still around today.
When locusts swept through eastern
Australia in 2004, they damaged an area
twice the size of England.*

Joel 1:4

The Locusts—A Powerful Army

⁵Drunks, wake up and cry!
    All of you who drink wine, cry
because your sweet wine is finished.
    You will not taste it again.
⁶A powerful nation came to attack my
        land.
    Its soldiers were too many to count.
Its weapons were as sharp as a lion's teeth
    and as powerful as a lion's jaw.

⁷It destroyed my grapevine.
    Its good vines withered and died.
It destroyed my fig tree,
    stripped off the bark and threw it away.

The People Cry

⁸Cry like a young woman crying
    because the man she was ready to marry
        has died.
⁹Priests, servants of the LORD, cry
    because there will be no more grain and
        drink offerings in the LORD's Temple.
¹⁰The fields are ruined.
    Even the ground is crying
    because the grain is destroyed;
the new wine is dried up,
    and the olive oil is gone.
¹¹Be sad, farmers!
    Cry loudly for the grapes,
for the wheat and for the barley,
    because the harvest in the field is ruined.
¹²The vines have become dry,
    and the fig tree is dying.
All the trees in the field—
    the pomegranate, the palm and the
        apple—have withered.
    And happiness among the people has
        died.
¹³Priests, put on sackcloth and cry loudly.
    Servants of the altar, cry loudly.
Servants of my God, you will sleep in
        sackcloth,
    because there will be no more grain and
        drink offerings in God's Temple.

The Terrible Destruction of the Locusts

¹⁴Tell the people that there will be a special
time of fasting. Call them together for a special
meeting. Bring the leaders and everyone living in
the land together at the Temple of the LORD your
God, and pray to the LORD.

¹⁵Be sad because the LORD's special day is near.
At that time punishment will come like an attack
from God All-Powerful. ¹⁶Our food is gone. Joy
and happiness are gone from the Temple of our
God. ¹⁷We planted seeds, but the seeds became
dry and dead lying in the soil. Our plants are dry
and dead. Our barns are empty and falling down.

¹⁸The animals are hungry and groaning. The
herds of cattle wander around confused because
they have no grass to eat. The sheep are dying.*ᵇ*
¹⁹LORD, I am calling to you for help. Fire has
changed our green fields into a desert. Flames
have burned all the trees in the field. ²⁰Wild
animals also need your help. The streams are
dry—there is no water! Fire has changed our
green fields into a desert.

ᵃ **1:4** *locust* See "LOCUST" in the Word List. Here, Joel might be talking about an enemy army.
ᵇ **1:18** *dying* Literally, "being punished".

IT'S GOING TO BE SO MUCH WORSE

If your mum's tomato plants get eaten by insects, I imagine she would just pop to the supermarket – no big deal. For God's people living in Judah there were no supermarkets – they relied on everything they could grow themselves and a massive plague of hungry locusts has absolutely ravaged their land.

DIG IN
READ Joel 1:1–13

- Write an article or script for the daily news reporting on the events in these verses. Why not include an eyewitness – one of the farmers, perhaps?

READ Joel 1:14–20

- What does Joel point the people to as a possible cause of this disaster?
- Read Deuteronomy 28:15,38 – what were locusts a sign of?

The land had been given to the people by God but they knew if they started disobeying him things would not go so well. So the locusts were possibly a punishment for the people's rebellion.

Did you also notice Joel says, "the LORD's special day is near" (v.15) as if it hasn't happened yet? What could he mean by this – could there be worse to come?!

READ Joel 2:1–11

- What will the Lord's special day be like? What images does Joel use to describe it?
- How widespread will the devastation be?
- Read Revelation 6:12–17 – on the Lord's special day what will be worse than being punished by God?

Joel is shaking the people awake, saying, "You think the locusts are bad? You wait until the Lord's special day." It's a description of a dark and terrible day – nothing will escape the complete destruction . . .

Joel is warning of the day in the future when Jesus comes again – for those who don't know him it will be a terrible day of judgement and devastation: it will be better for rocks to fall and crush you than to face God's punishment. It's a warning, a wake-up call.

DIG THROUGH

- Does the idea of a day of complete judgement seem real to you? God promises it will happen, so it will. Are you ready? Are you telling others? (Joel says to do this, 1:2–3!)
- For the people of Israel, natural disasters and other problems were the way God woke the people up to their sin and disciplined them. How does God discipline us today? Check out Hebrews 12:4–11. Sometimes God does strip stuff away from us, disciplining us in a good way that always results in us loving him more.

DIG DEEPER

- In the New Testament the Lord's special day is reinterpreted as the second coming of Jesus. This would be both a day of judgement and a day of victory. Check out Romans 2:1–16.

FORGET YOUR HONEYMOON, COME PRAY!

Kristy and Matthew were overjoyed and excited; having just got married they were enjoying a week-long honeymoon in France – something they'd been anticipating and preparing for for a long time. Halfway through the week they got a phone call from their minister asking them to rush back for a prayer meeting that evening at church! Can you imagine their reaction?!

It might seem strange, but Joel did exactly the same as that minister – he called an emergency prayer meeting summoning everybody to drop whatever they were doing – honeymoon or not – and come to pray. What could have been so important?

DIG IN

READ Joel 2:12-20

- What is it about the Lord's character that should draw the people back (v.13)?
- What were the people to pray for (v.17)?
- What was the Lord's response (v.18)?
- What will the Lord do for the people and their enemies (vv.19–20)?

A terrible thing had happened in Judah – because of the people's sin the land had been utterly destroyed by millions of locusts. The people need to get down on their knees and ask God to have mercy on them. As they do this, the Lord meets them with forgiveness, blessing for the land and punishment for their enemies ("the northerners").

READ Joel 2:21-27

- What are all the things the Lord will do for the people and the land?
- What should their response be?

It couldn't be a more different scenario from Joel 1, where everything had been destroyed and stripped away. God is going to send the rain and grow the grass, fruit and grain – there's going to be so much to eat and drink that everyone will be rolling around stuffed full. It's a picture of a land where there has previously been death and suffering, only now the land is fertile and the people are healthy and overjoyed. There no longer needs to be any fear or sadness, just lots of worshipping God.

- Contrast verse 17 with verse 27 – how will the people be comforted by verse 27?

They must have been relieved – God is still with them. While the other nations questioned where God was, his blessing shows that he has not deserted his people. He has done wonderful things for his people and everyone will see it.

DIG THROUGH

- Just as Joel shows us that there will be terrible judgement for those who do not know God, this passage shows us that there are amazing things for those who return to the Lord, both then and in the future. Read Joel 2:26 again and also check out John 14:1–4 and Revelation 21.
- The people were in such a bad way that praying for forgiveness was more important than a honeymoon (2:16)! Do you think of sin as requiring such drastic action? Every day we sin and so every day we need to "come back" to the Lord (v.12). He is kind and merciful – don't forget that!

DIG DEEPER

- Read Joel 2:28–32. The words "After this" indicate that the Lord is talking about a time after the people of Judah were alive. Check out Acts 2 when the Holy Spirit is given, Peter quotes these verses from Joel! He is showing that the times Joel prophesied about were coming true. The Spirit is now poured out on everyone (it wasn't in the Old Testament times) and everyone (not only the Jews) can know God.

The Coming Day of the Lord

2 Blow the trumpet on Zion.
  Shout a warning on my holy mountain.
Let all the people who live in the land shake
  with fear.
  The LORD's special day is coming;
  it is near.

INSIGHT

Sounds awesome! When prophets
like Joel mention "the LORD's special
day", they're talking about a time of
judgement that will come upon the
people of Israel if they are unfaithful to
God. When New Testament authors use
the phrase, they are often referring to
the return of Christ.

Joel 2:1

²It will be a dark, gloomy day.
  It will be a dark and cloudy day.
At sunrise you will see the army spread over
  the mountains.
  It will be a great and powerful army.
There has never been anything like it before,
  and there will never be anything like it again.
³The army will destroy the land like a
  burning fire.
  In front of them the land will be like the
  Garden of Eden.
Behind them the land will be like an empty
  desert.
  Nothing will escape them.
⁴They look like horses.
  They run like war horses.
⁵Listen to them.
It is like the noise of chariots
  riding over the mountains.
It is like the noise of flames
  burning the chaff.
They are a powerful people,
  who are ready for war.
⁶Before this army, people shake with fear.
  Their faces become pale from fear.

⁷The soldiers run fast.
  They climb over the walls.
Each soldier marches straight ahead.
  They don't move from their path.

⁸They don't trip each other.
  Each soldier walks in his own path.
If one of the soldiers is hit and falls down,
  the others keep right on marching.
⁹They run to the city.
  They quickly climb over the wall.
They climb into the houses.
  They climb through the windows like
  thieves.
¹⁰Before them, earth and sky shake.
  The sun and the moon become dark, and
  the stars stop shining.
¹¹The LORD calls loudly to his army.
  His camp is very large.
The army obeys his commands.
  His army is very powerful.
The LORD's special day is a great and terrible
  day.
  No one can stop it.

The LORD Tells the People to Change

¹²This is the LORD's message:
  "Now come back to me with all your heart.
Cry and mourn, and don't eat anything!
  Show that you are sad for doing wrong.
¹³Tear your hearts,
  not your clothes."ᵃ
Come back to the LORD your God.
  He is kind and merciful.
He does not become angry quickly.
  He has great love.
Maybe he will change his mind
  about the bad punishment he planned.
¹⁴Who knows, maybe he will change his mind
  and leave behind a blessing for you.
Then you can give grain and drink offerings
  to the LORD your God.

Pray to the LORD

¹⁵Blow the trumpet at Zion.
  Call for a special meeting.
  Tell everyone to prepare for a time of
  fasting.
¹⁶Bring the people together.
  Call for a special meeting.
Bring together the old men,
  the children and the small babies still at
  their mothers' breasts.
Let the bride and her new husband
  come from their bedroom.
¹⁷Let the priests, the LORD's servants, stand
  between the porchᵇ and the altar and cry.
Let them say, "LORD, have mercy on your
  people.

ᵃ **2:13 Tear your hearts, not your clothes** People tore their clothes to show sadness. Here, God wants the people to feel sad for
the bad things they had done.
ᵇ **2:17 porch** An open area in front of the Temple.

Don't let us be put to shame.
Don't let the other nations make fun of us.
Don't let them laugh at us and say,
  'Where is their God?'"

The LORD Will Help His People

18 Then the LORD showed his care for his land.
  He felt sorry for his people.
19 He answered their prayers and said,
  "I will send you grain, wine and oil.
  You will have plenty to eat.
I will no longer give the other nations any reason
  to make fun of you.
20 I will force the army from the north[a] to leave your land
  and chase them into the dry, empty desert.
The soldiers in front will go east into the Dead Sea,
  and those at the back will drown in the western sea.[b]
An awful smell will rise from their rotting bodies
  because they have done such terrible things!"

The Land Will Be Made New Again

21 Land, don't be afraid.
  Be happy and full of joy.
  The LORD will do great things.
22 Animals of the field, don't be afraid.
  The desert pastures will grow grass.
The trees will grow fruit.
  The fig trees and the vines will grow plenty of fruit.

23 So be happy, people of Zion.
  Be joyful in the LORD your God.
He is good and will give you rain.
  He will send the early rains and the late rains as before.
24 The threshing floors will be filled with wheat,
  and the barrels will overflow with wine and olive oil.

25 "I, the Lord, sent my army against you.
  The swarming locusts and the hopping locusts
  and the destroying locusts and the cutting locusts[c] ate everything you had.
But I will pay you back

for those years of trouble.
26 Then you will have plenty to eat.
  You will be full.
You will praise the name of the LORD your God.
  He has done wonderful things for you.
My people will never again be ashamed.
27 You will know that I am with Israel.
  You will know that I am the LORD your God.
  There is no other God.
My people will never be ashamed again.

INSIGHT

Still to come . . . ? Many of these things happened when the Holy Spirit was poured out on the disciples at Pentecost (see Acts 2). The unnatural events of verses 30 and 31, however, did not take place at Pentecost. Some scholars think that these will happen in the future, when Jesus returns.

Joel 2:28–31

God Will Give His Spirit to All People

28 "After this,
  I will pour out my Spirit on all kinds of people.
Your sons and daughters will prophesy,
  your old men will have special dreams,
  and your young men will see visions.
29 In those days I will pour out my Spirit
  on servants, both men and women.
30 I will work wonders in the sky and on the earth.
  There will be blood, fire and thick smoke.
31 The sun will become dark,
  and the moon as red as blood,
  just before the great and terrible day that the LORD comes!
32 And the LORD will save everyone who looks to him for help.[d]
There will be survivors on Mount Zion and in Jerusalem,
  just as the LORD said.
Yes, those left alive will be the ones
  the LORD has called.

---

[a] **2:20 north** The Babylonian army came from this direction to attack Judah. Armies from countries north and east of Israel often came this way to attack Judah and Israel.

[b] **2:20 the western sea** That is, the Mediterranean Sea.

[c] **2:25 swarming locusts . . . cutting locusts** See Joel 1:4.

[d] **2:32 who looks to him for help** Literally, "who calls on the name of the LORD", meaning to show faith in him by worshipping him or praying to him for help.

Judah's Enemies Will Be Punished

3 "Yes, at that time I will bring back the people of Judah and Jerusalem from captivity. ²I will also gather all the nations together. I will bring all these nations down into Jehoshaphat Valley.ᵃ There I will judge them. Those nations scattered my people, Israel. They forced them to live in other nations, so I will punish those nations. They divided up my land. ³They threw lots for my people. They sold boys to buy a prostitute, and they sold girls to buy wine to drink.

⁴"Tyre! Sidon! All of you areas of Philistia! You are not important to me!ᵇ Are you punishing me for something I did? You might think that you are punishing me, but I will soon punish you. ⁵You took my silver and gold. You took my precious treasures and put them in your temples.ᶜ

⁶"You sold the people of Judah and Jerusalem to the Greeks. That way you could take them far from their land. ⁷You sent my people to that faraway place, but I will bring them back. And I will punish you for what you did. ⁸I will sell your sons and daughters to the people of Judah. Then they will sell them to the faraway Sabeans."ᵈ This is what the LORD said.

INSIGHT

Israel had enemies on every side: to the north, Phoenicia; to the south, Egypt; to the west, Philistia; and to the east, Edom. Not to mention the Assyrians and Babylonians from further afield. They might have been top dog at this time, but they too were to get their comeuppance from God.

Joel 3

Prepare for War

⁹Announce this among the nations:
  Prepare for war!
Wake up the strong men!
  Let all the men of war come near.
  Let them come up!
¹⁰Beat your ploughs into swords.
  Make spears from your pruning hooks.ᵉ

Let the weak man say,
  "I am a strong soldier."
¹¹All you nations, hurry!
  Come together in that place.
  LORD, bring your strong soldiers.

¹²"Wake up, nations!
  Come to Jehoshaphat Valley.
There I will sit to judge
  all the surrounding nations.
¹³Bring the sickle,
  because the harvest is ripe.ᶠ
Come, trample the grapes,
  because the winepress is full.
The barrels will be full and spilling over,
  because their evil is great."

¹⁴There are many, many people in the Valley of
    Decision.ᵍ
  The LORD's special day is near in the Valley
    of Decision.
¹⁵The sun and the moon will become dark.
  The stars will stop shining.
¹⁶The LORD God will shout from Zion.
  He will shout from Jerusalem,
    and the sky and the earth will shake.
But the LORD God will be a safe place for his
    people.
  He will be a place of safety for the people
    of Israel.

¹⁷"Then you will know that I am the LORD your
    God.
  I live on Zion, my holy mountain.
Jerusalem will become holy.
  Strangers will never pass through that city
    again.

A New Life for Judah Promised

¹⁸"On that day, the mountains will drip with
    sweet wine.
  The hills will flow with milk,
    and water will flow through all the empty
    rivers of Judah.
A fountain will come from the LORD's Temple.
  It will give water to Acacia Valley.
¹⁹Egypt will be empty.
  Edom will be an empty wilderness,
because they were cruel to the people of
    Judah.

ᵃ **3:2 Jehoshaphat Valley** This name means "The LORD judges".
ᵇ **3:4 You are not important to me** Literally, "What are you to me?"
ᶜ **3:5 temples** Here, the temples were used to worship idols.
ᵈ **3:8 Sabeans** A group of people from the Arabian Desert.
ᵉ **3:10 pruning hooks** These tools were used to prune (cut) branches of trees. Read Isa. 2:4.
ᶠ **3:13 harvest is ripe** This time of judgement is compared to harvest time.
ᵍ **3:14 Valley of Decision** This is like the name "Jehoshaphat Valley".

They killed innocent people[a] in their country.
20But there will always be people living in Judah.
People will live in Jerusalem through many
generations.

21Those nations killed my people,
so I really will punish them!"

The LORD God will live in Zion!

---

[a] **3:19 killed innocent people** Literally, "shed innocent blood".

Who Amos was a shepherd and fig-grower from Tekoa. His name meant "burden". Although his home was in Judah, he went to preach in Bethel, which was in the northern kingdom of Israel.

When He preached in the northern kingdom during the reigns of King Uzziah in the south and Jeroboam II in the north, a little earlier than Hosea. Probably sometime around 760–750 BC.

What Amos was a farmer from Judah who went north into Israel to condemn the behaviour of the leaders and people. He was not a prophet by profession but he had been given a special task.

The Israelites expected a "day of the Lord" when the other nations would be judged. What they didn't expect was that God would judge them as well – and not very favourably at that.

Amos starts by attacking other nations but then narrows the focus of his attack to deliver a stinging attack on Israel and their skin-deep religion. They pretended to be holy, but their society was crawling with idolatry, corruption and injustice.

This was a time of comparative wealth and comfort – a golden age for the northern kingdom of Israel. But Amos claims that their wealth is just a facade: that it has nothing to do with divine favour. In fact, it is the result of abusing the poor and cheating the oppressed. And it is fitting that he points out the truth about this golden age in Bethel where, in 930 BC, right at the birth of the northern kingdom, its first ruler, Jeroboam I, had set up a golden calf for Israel to worship.

Amos has a true prophet's passionate commitment to the truth, a deep respect for God and an understanding of the significance of all that God has done for his people. He has seen God at work and heard him speak. Now he must pass that message on – an ordinary person who has been suddenly promoted to the rank of a prophet. As he says, everyone is terrified when a lion roars, and ordinary people become prophets when the Lord God speaks (3:8).

QUICK TOUR **AMOS**

"Take your noisy songs away from here. I will not listen to the music from your harps. But let justice flow like a river, and let goodness flow like a stream that never becomes dry."

Amos 5:23–24

Introduction

1 This is the message of Amos, one of the shepherds from the city Tekoa. He saw visions about Israel during the time that Uzziah was king of Judah and Jeroboam son of Joash was king of Israel. This was two years before the earthquake.

INSIGHT

This earthquake is also mentioned by Zechariah the prophet (see Zechariah 14:5) and archaeologists have found evidence of it in an eighth-century site at Hazor, showing tilted walls. All of this helps to date Amos's message and show that it is historically correct.

Amos 1:1

Punishment for Aram

²Amos said,

"The LORD will roar like a lion in Zion.
 His loud voice will shout from Jerusalem.
The green pastures of the shepherds will turn
 brown and die.
 Even Mount Carmel*ᵃ* will become dry."

³This is what the LORD says: "I will definitely punish the people of Damascus for their many crimes.*ᵇ* They crushed the people of Gilead with iron threshing tools. ⁴So I will start a fire at Hazael's*ᶜ* house that will destroy the great palaces of Ben-Hadad.*ᵈ*

⁵"I will also break open the gates of Damascus*ᵉ* and remove the one who sits on the throne in the Valley of Aven.*ᶠ* I will remove the symbol of power from Beth Eden,*ᵍ* and the Arameans will be defeated and taken back to Kir."*ʰ* This is what the LORD said.

Punishment for the Philistines

⁶This is what the LORD says: "I will definitely punish the people of Gaza*ⁱ* for their many crimes. They took an entire nation of people and sent them as slaves to Edom. ⁷So I will start a fire at the wall of Gaza that will destroy the high towers in Gaza. ⁸And I will destroy the one who sits on the throne in Ashdod. I will destroy the king who holds the sceptre in Ashkelon. I will punish the people of Ekron.*ʲ* Then the Philistines who are still left alive will die." This is what the Lord GOD said.

Punishment for Phoenicia

⁹This is what the LORD says: "I will definitely punish the people of Tyre*ᵏ* for their many crimes. They took an entire nation and sent them as slaves to Edom. They did not remember the agreement they had made with their brothers.*ˡ* ¹⁰So I will start a fire at the walls of Tyre that will destroy the high towers in Tyre."

Punishment for the Edomites

¹¹This is what the LORD says: "I will definitely punish the people of Edom for their many crimes. Edom chased his brother with the sword, and he showed no mercy. His anger never stopped. He kept tearing and tearing at Israel like a wild animal. ¹²So I will start a fire at Teman that will destroy the high towers of Bozrah."

Punishment for the Ammonites

¹³This is what the LORD says: "I will definitely punish the Ammonites*ᵐ* for their many crimes. They killed the pregnant women in Gilead. The Ammonites did this so that they could take that land and make their country larger. ¹⁴So I will start a fire at the wall of Rabbah*ⁿ* that will destroy the high towers of Rabbah. Troubles will come to them like a whirlwind*ᵒ* into their country. ¹⁵Then their kings and leaders will be captured. They will all be taken together." This is what the LORD said.

ᵃ **1:2 Mount Carmel** A mountain in northern Israel. The name means "God's vineyard". This shows that it was a very fertile hill.
ᵇ **1:3 for their many crimes** Literally, "for three crimes . . . and for four . . .". This shows that these people were very sinful—and it was time to punish them. Also in verses 6,9,11,13; 2:1,4,6.
ᶜ **1:4 Hazael** Hazael was the king of Aram (Syria). He murdered Ben-Hadad I so that he could become king. See 2 Kgs 8:7.
ᵈ **1:4 Ben-Hadad** Ben-Hadad II, the son of Hazael, king of Aram (Syria). See 2 Kgs 13:3.
ᵉ **1:5 Damascus** The capital city of Aram (Syria).
ᶠ **1:5 the Valley of Aven** A name that can mean "Restful Valley" or "Empty Valley of Misfortune".
ᵍ **1:5 Beth Eden** The royal city of Aram (Syria) on Mount Lebanon. This name means "House of Pleasure" or "Paradise".
ʰ **1:5 Kir** Or "Kur", an area controlled by the Assyrians. See Amos 9:7.
ⁱ **1:6 Gaza** An important city of the Philistines.
ʲ **1:8 Ashdod, Ashkelon, Ekron** Important cities of the Philistines.
ᵏ **1:9 Tyre** The capital city of Phoenicia.
ˡ **1:9 brothers** The people of Israel.
ᵐ **1:13 Ammonites** The Ammonites were the descendants of Ben-Ammi, son of Lot. Read Gen. 19:38.
ⁿ **1:14 Rabbah** The capital city of the Ammonites.
ᵒ **1:14 whirlwind** A strong wind that blows in a circle.

Punishment for Moab

2 This is what the LORD says: "I will definitely punish the people of Moab for their many crimes. Moab burned the bones of the king of Edom into lime. [2]So I will start a fire in Moab that will destroy the high towers of Kerioth.[a] There will be terrible shouting and the sounds of a trumpet, and Moab will die. [3]So I will bring an end to the kings[b] of Moab, and I will kill all the leaders of Moab." This is what the LORD said.

Punishment for Judah

[4]This is what the LORD says: "I will definitely punish Judah for their many crimes. They refused to obey the LORD's teachings and they did not keep his commands. Their ancestors believed lies, and those same lies caused the people of Judah to stop following God. [5]So I will start a fire in Judah that will destroy the high towers of Jerusalem."

INSIGHT

From the beginning of his book Amos pronounces judgement on the surrounding nations, starting with the furthest away: Syria. Perhaps his Israelite audience would have felt safe at this point, but gradually he gets closer and closer, until he launches into God's judgement against them, too.

Amos 2:6

Punishment for Israel

[6]This is what the LORD says: "I will definitely punish Israel for their many crimes. They sold honest people for a little silver. They sold the poor for the price of a pair of sandals. [7]They pushed their faces into the ground and walked on them. They stopped listening to suffering people. Fathers and sons had sex with the same woman. They ruined my holy name. [8]They took clothes from the poor, and then they sat on those clothes while worshipping at their altars. They loaned money to the poor, and then they took their clothes as a promise for payment.[c] They made people pay fines and used the money to buy wine for themselves to drink in the temple of their god.

[9]"But it was I who destroyed the Amorites[d] before them. They were as tall as cedar trees and as strong as oaks, but I destroyed their fruit above and their roots below.[e]

[10]"I was the one who brought you from the land of Egypt. For 40 years I led you through the desert. I helped you take the Amorites' land. [11]I made some of your sons to be prophets and some of your young men to be Nazirites. People of Israel, it is true." This is what the LORD said. [12]"But you made the Nazirites drink wine. You told my prophets not to prophesy. [13]You have become more than I can bear. I am bent low like a cart loaded with grain. [14]No one will escape, not even the fastest runner. Strong men will not be strong enough. Soldiers will not be able to save themselves. [15]People with bows and arrows will not survive. Fast runners will not escape. People on horses will not escape alive. [16]At that time even very brave soldiers will run away. They will not take the time to put their clothes on." This is what the LORD said.

Warning to Israel

3 People of Israel, listen to this message! This is what the LORD said about you, Israel. This message is about all the families that I brought from the land of Egypt. [2]"There are many families on earth, but you are the only family I chose to know in a special way. And you turned against me, so I will punish you for all your sins."

The Cause of Israel's Punishment

[3]Two people will not walk together
    unless they have agreed to do so.
[4]A lion will roar in the forest
    only if it catches its prey.
A young lion roaring in his cave
    means he has caught something to eat.
[5]A bird doesn't fly into a trap
    unless there is food in it.
If a trap closes,
    it will catch the bird.
[6]If people hear the warning blast of a trumpet,
    they shake with fear.
If trouble comes to a city,
    the LORD caused it to happen.

[7]When the Lord GOD decides to do something, he will first tell his servants, the prophets. [8]When a lion roars, people are frightened. When the Lord GOD speaks, a prophet must prophesy.

---

[a] **2:2 Kerioth** A city in Moab. This might be Ar, the capital city of Moab.
[b] **2:3 kings** Literally, "judges".
[c] **2:8 as a promise for payment.** See Deut. 24:12–13 for the rules about making loans to the poor.
[d] **2:9 Amorites** One of the nations who lived in Canaan before the Israelites came. They were the people who scared the Israelites while Moses was leading them in the desert. See Num. 13:33.
[e] **2:9 fruit above . . . below** This means the parents and their children.

PREPARE TO MEET YOUR GOD

I wonder what images you have in your head when you think of God. Is he like a faithful, loving old granddad who likes to give out sweets to his grandchildren? Or is he a gentle giant who smiles when people do good things and turns a blind eye to evil?

We are right to think of God as loving and kind but he is not weak and he certainly doesn't turn a blind eye to evil, as the people in Amos's day are about to find out . . .

DIG IN

READ Amos 2:6–16

- Why is God angry with his people?
- How many of God's laws can you spot – and what have the people done with them?

God has promised judgement on the other nations, before turning his attention to his people, Judah and Israel (check out Amos 1). God's people would be pretty used to this – other nations being bad, them being good, so feel the shock and weight of discovering just how angry God is with them. They have utterly trashed his laws, showing complete disregard to their relationship with God and with others. It hasn't gone unnoticed . . .

READ Amos 9:1–6

- What do these verses say about God's power and control?
- What do these verses tell us about the judgement of God?
- What does God promise (vv.3–4)?

Have you ever had a nightmare where you're desperately trying to run away from something horrid, yet everywhere you turn the horrid thing is there waiting for you – there's nowhere to hide? This is what God's judgement is going to be like for the people. There is no escaping it. God is described as being the all powerful Lord over everything – the earth, heavens and people. He initiates the punishment (vv.1,4) and is in control over everything that will take place – both in causing created things (vv.1,5) and other nations (4:2–3) to bring disaster.

- Check out Amos 5:16–20 for more on how miserable the judgement was going to be.

READ Amos 9:7–15

- What relief is promised (v.8)?
- What does God promise in verses 11–15?

It's like one of those disaster films where the whole of New York City is wiped out except for a few people who then go on to renew the city and repopulate it! Despite the complete rebellion of his people, God won't break his promise to keep them as his special people – they won't be wiped out totally. We can breathe a sigh of relief at the last few verses of Amos – with the hope that this wonderful God will make things good again.

DIG THROUGH

- Has it struck you how all-powerful God is? Why not read Psalm 91 and allow this to sink in?
- Has it struck you how seriously God takes sin? Check out Psalm 51?

DIG DEEPER

- In Amos 5:18,20 the coming judgement is described as "the LORD's special day". This judgement was intended for God's special people then and all people in the future. Check out Bible Bits on Joel "It's Goin' to be So Much Worse" and "Forget Your Honeymoon, Come Pray!" and 1 Thessalonians "Surprise!" for more of this.

⁹⁻¹⁰Go to the high towers in Ashdod*ᵃ* and in Egypt and announce this message from the LORD: "Come together on the mountains of Samaria. See the great confusion there because the people don't know how to do what is right. See how cruel they are to others. They take things from people to hide in their high towers. Their treasuries are filled with the things they have taken in war."

¹¹So the Lord GOD says, "An enemy will surround your land. They will break down your strong walls and take the things you have hidden in your high towers."

¹²The LORD says,

"A lion might attack a lamb,
   and a shepherd might try to save the lamb.
But the shepherd will save
   only a part of that lamb.
He might pull two legs
   or a part of an ear from the lion's mouth.
In the same way, most of the people of Israel
   will not be saved.
Those who live in Samaria will save only a
   corner from a bed,
   or a piece of cloth from a couch."

¹³This is what the Lord GOD All-Powerful says: "Warn the family of Jacob about these things. ¹⁴Israel sinned, and I will punish them for their sins. And when I do, I will also destroy the altars at Bethel.*ᵇ* The horns of the altar will be cut off and fall to the ground. ¹⁵I will destroy the winter house with the summer house. The houses of ivory will be destroyed. Many houses will be destroyed." This is what the LORD said.

The Women Who Love Pleasure

4 Listen to me, you cows of Bashan*ᶜ* on Samaria's mountain. You hurt the poor and crush those in need. You tell your husbands,*ᵈ* "Bring us something to drink!"

²The Lord GOD made a promise. He promised by his holiness that troubles will come to you. People will use hooks and take you away as prisoners. They will use fish hooks to take away your children. ³Your city will be destroyed. The women will rush out through cracks in the wall

and throw themselves onto the pile of dead bodies.*ᵉ*

This is what the LORD says: ⁴"Go to Bethel and sin. Go to Gilgal*ᶠ* and sin even more. Offer your sacrifices in the morning. Bring a tenth of your crops for the three-day festival. ⁵And offer a thank offering made with yeast. Tell everyone about the freewill offerings.*ᵍ* Israel, you love to do those things. So go and do them." This is what the Lord GOD said.

INSIGHT

Amos was basically saying, "We are here, dearly beloved, to sin and boast . . ." He mocks the priests' usual call to worship with bitter sarcasm. Living through a time of affluence and relative stability, Israel continued to go through the motions of worship, while oppressing and abusing the poor, little knowing that within 60 years, their nation would cease to exist.

Amos 4:4

⁶"I didn't give you any food to eat.*ʰ* There was no food in any of your cities, but you didn't come back to me." This is what the LORD said.

⁷"I also stopped the rain, and it was three months before harvest time. So no crops grew. Then I let it rain on one city, but not on another city. Rain fell on one part of the country, but on the other part of the country, the land became very dry. ⁸So the people from two or three cities staggered to another city to get water, but there was not enough water for everyone. Still you didn't come to me for help." This is what the LORD said.

⁹"I made your crops die from heat and disease. I destroyed your gardens and your vineyards. Locusts ate your fig trees and olive trees. But you still didn't come to me for help." This is what the LORD said.

¹⁰"I sent diseases against you, as I did to Egypt. I killed your young men with swords. I took away your horses. I made your camp smell very bad

---

ᵃ **3:9–10** *Ashdod* An important city of the Philistines.
ᵇ **3:14** *Bethel* A town in Israel. This name means "God's house".
ᶜ **4:1** *cows of Bashan* This means the wealthy women in Samaria. Bashan, an area east of the Jordan River, was famous for its big bulls and cows.
ᵈ **4:1** *your husbands* Literally, "their masters".
ᵉ **4:3** *throw . . . dead bodies* Or "You will be thrown away. People will take you to Mount Hermon." The Hebrew text is not clear. It is not clear if the women will be "thrown away" or if the women will be "throwing something away".
ᶠ **4:4** *Bethel . . . Gilgal* Places of worship for the people of Israel. God wanted the people of Israel and the people of Judah to worship him only in the Temple at Jerusalem.
ᵍ **4:4–5** *Offer your sacrifices . . . freewill offerings* All these things were against the Law of Moses. The leaders and false priests started these new festivals and different ways of worshipping God.
ʰ **4:6** *I didn't give you any food to eat* Literally, "I gave you clean teeth."

from all the dead bodies, but still you didn't come back to me for help." This is what the LORD said.

[11]"I destroyed you as I destroyed Sodom and Gomorrah. And those cities were completely destroyed. You were like a burnt stick pulled from a fire, but still you didn't come back to me for help." This is what the LORD says.

[12]"So, Israel, this is what I will do to you. You people of Israel, prepare to meet your God."

[13]He is the one who made the mountains
and created the wind.[a]
He lets people know his thoughts.
He changes the darkness into dawn.
He walks over the mountains of the earth.
His name is YAHWEH, LORD God
All-Powerful.

A Sad Song for Israel

5 People of Israel, listen to this song. This funeral song is about you.

[2]The virgin[b] of Israel has fallen.
She will not get up any more.
She was left alone, lying in the dirt.
There is no one to lift her up.

[3]This is what the Lord GOD says:

"Officers leaving the city with 1,000 men
will return with only 100 men.
Officers leaving the city with 100 men
will return with only ten men."

The LORD Encourages Israel to Come Back

[4]The LORD says this to the nation[c] of Israel:
"Come looking for me and live.
[5] But don't look in Bethel.
Don't go to Gilgal.
Don't cross the border and go down to
Beersheba.[d]
The people of Gilgal will be taken away as
prisoners,[e]
and Bethel will be destroyed.[f]

[6]Come to the LORD and live.
If you don't go to him, a fire will start at
Joseph's house,[g]
and no one in Bethel[h] can stop it.
[7–9]You should go to the Lord for help.
He is the one who made the Pleiades and
Orion.[i]
He changes darkness into the morning light.
He changes the day into the dark night.
He calls for the waters of the sea and pours
them out on the earth.
His name is YAHWEH!
He keeps one strong city safe,
and he lets another strong city be
destroyed."

The Evil Things That the Israelites Did

You change justice to poison.[j]
You throw away fairness like rubbish.
[10]You hate those prophets, who go to public
places and speak against evil,
even though they teach good, simple truths.
[11]You take unfair taxes[k] from the poor,
making them pay for the crops they grow.
You build fancy houses with cut stone,
but you will not live in them.
You plant beautiful vineyards,
but you will not drink the wine from them.
[12]This is because I know about your many
sins.
You have done some very bad things:
You hurt people who do right,
you accept money to do wrong,
and you keep the poor from receiving
justice in court.
[13]At that time wise teachers will be quiet,
because it is a bad time.
[14]You say that God is with you,
so you should do good things, not evil.
Then you will live,
and the LORD God All-Powerful will be with
you.
[15]Hate evil and love goodness.
Bring justice back into the courts.

---

[a] **4:13 the wind** Or "your minds".
[b] **5:2 virgin** The Hebrew word can mean "a woman who has not had sex with anyone", but here, it means the city of Samaria.
[c] **5:4 nation** Literally, "house". This might mean the royal family of that country.
[d] **5:5 Bethel, Gilgal, Beersheba** Ancient places of worship. Abraham and Jacob built altars in these places, but God had told the Israelites that they should go to the Temple in Jerusalem to worship him.
[e] **5:5 taken away as prisoners** In Hebrew this sounds like the name "Gilgal".
[f] **5:5 destroyed** The Hebrew word is like the name "Beth Aven". This name means "House of Wickedness". The prophets often used this name for Bethel.
[g] **5:6 Joseph's house** Here, this means the ten-tribe nation of Israel. Joseph was the ancestor of the tribes of Ephraim and Manasseh in Israel.
[h] **5:6 Bethel** This name means "El's house" or "the house of God". There was a temple here where the people from the northern tribes worshipped.
[i] **5:7–9 Pleiades and Orion** Two well-known groups of stars (constellations).
[j] **5:7–9 poison** Literally, "wormwood", a type of plant with bitter leaves. It could be used as a medicine, or if strong enough, as a poison.
[k] **5:11 take unfair taxes** The meaning of the Hebrew word here is uncertain.

I HATE YOUR RELIGIOUS MEETINGS!

Amos, a wealthy sheep farmer, had a difficult job to do – not unlike most of the Old Testament prophets! In a time when God's people were enjoying peace, and those who were fortunate enough to be born in the right family were helping themselves to as much stuff as they wanted, Amos came with bad news – the good times were about to end.

It doesn't matter how good the times are, if you're not following God judgement is coming . . .

DIG IN
READ Amos 5:21–26

- What is God rejecting (v.21–23)?
- How does this make you feel?

Doesn't God ask his people to remember certain festivals, worship him in song and offer sacrifices for sin? (Check all this out in Leviticus.) So why is he rejecting these things?

- Who had the people begun to worship (v.26)?

Talk about an insult! God had rescued them, made them his people (check out chapter 2:9–13) and they'd chosen to make up their own religion, worshipping random gods. How ridiculous to worship the god of the stars rather than the God who actually made the stars?! Then to add insult to injury, they still perform acts of worship even though they don't care about God at all! For example, sacrifices were meant for the people to perform when they knew they had disobeyed God but were committed to loving him with their whole heart. But their hearts were far from God – and he was angry.

READ Amos 2:6–8; 5:11–15; 8:4–6

- Make a list of the things the people were doing.

We should be shocked by these things. The people of God were oppressing the poor, cheating people out of money and disregarding justice. The king, Jeroboam II had been really successful in making Israel secure, which had created a rich, powerful upper class of people who had way too much time on their hands and had way too much money, gained unjustly. Things weren't so good for the poor – but did the people care?

This is all so far from the way God had set up their beautiful society to be – one with loads of laws that protected the poor and made sure everyone was treated fairly (Leviticus 27:1–8).

READ Amos 6:1–8

Here are God's people, lounging around, stuffing their faces, while the poor are oppressed. They think they are okay . . . but judgement is coming . . . You see, when the people treat others badly, they are also treating God badly.

DIG THROUGH

- God was angry with his people for going to religious meetings, singing songs and celebrating festivals but disobeying him. They were selfish, looked down on others, exploited the poor – what about you? Does your life back up your faith? Check out James 2:14–26 for more on this.
- There is so much need around us. Just like God's people then, our first priority is to our "brothers and sisters" – those in the family of God. Maybe you'd like to consider giving some money to help missionaries in poorer countries, or maybe there's someone in your church who could do with some support financially or emotionally – are you being greedy with either your money or your time?

Maybe then the LORD God All-Powerful
will be kind to the survivors from Joseph's
family.

A Time of Great Sadness Is Coming

[16]The Lord, the LORD God All-Powerful says,
"People will be crying in the public places.
They will be crying in the streets.
They will hire the professional criers.[a]
[17]People will be crying in the vineyards,
because I will pass through and punish
you."
This is what the LORD said.
[18]Some of you want to see
the LORD's special day of judgement.
Why do you want to see that day of the LORD?
His special day will bring darkness, not
light.
[19]You will be like someone who escapes from
a lion
only to be attacked by a bear,
or like someone who goes into the safety of
his house,
leans against the wall,
and is bitten by a snake.
[20]The LORD's special day will be
a day of darkness, not light—a day of
gloom, without a ray of light.

The LORD Rejects Israel's Worship

[21]"I hate your festivals;
I will not accept them.
I don't enjoy your religious meetings.
[22]Even if you offer me burnt offerings and grain
offerings,
I will not accept them.
I will not even look at the fat animals
you give as fellowship offerings.
[23]Take your noisy songs away from here.
I will not listen to the music from your
harps.
[24]But let justice flow like a river,
and let goodness flow like a stream that
never becomes dry.
[25]Israel, you offered me sacrifices
and offerings in the desert for 40 years.[b]
[26]But you also carried statues of Sakkuth, your
king and Kaiwan.[c]

There was also that star god[d] that you made
for yourselves.
[27]So I will send you as captives, far beyond
Damascus."
This is what the LORD says.
His name is God All-Powerful.

Israel's Good Times Will Be Taken Away

6 Oh, look at the people enjoying life in Zion,
and those on Mount Samaria who feel so
safe.
They are such important leaders of a most
important nation.
The family of Israel comes to you for advice.
[2]Go and look at Calneh.
From there, go to the large city Hamath.
Go to the Philistine city of Gath.[e]
Are you better than these kingdoms?
Their countries are larger than yours.
[3]You people are rushing towards the day of
punishment.
You bring near the rule of violence.
[4]But now you lie on ivory beds
and stretch out on your couches.
You eat tender young lambs from the flock
and young calves from the stable.
[5]You play your harps,
and like David, you practise on[f] your
musical instruments.
[6]Instead of showing your sorrow
for the ruin of Israel,
you put on the best perfumes for a celebration
and drink bowls full of wine.
[7]You people are stretched out on your couches
now,
but your good times will end.
You will be taken away as prisoners to a
foreign country,
and you will be some of the first people
taken.

[8]The Lord GOD used his own name and made
an oath. The LORD God All-Powerful said:

"I hate what Jacob is proud of.
I hate his strong towers.
So I will let an enemy take the city
and everything in it."

---

[a] **5:16 professional criers** People who went to funerals and cried loudly for the dead. Families and friends of the dead person often gave food or money to these people.
[b] **5:25** Or "Israel, did you offer me sacrifices and offerings in the desert for 40 years?"
[c] **5:26 Sakkuth, your king and Kaiwan** Or "Sakkuth, Moloch and Kaiwan", names of Assyrian gods.
[d] **5:26 star god** This might be to honour a special god or all the stars in the sky. Many people thought the sun, moon, stars and planets were gods or angels. This verse might also be translated, "You carried the shelter for your king and the footstool for your idols—the star of your gods that you made for yourselves." The ancient Greek version adds the names of these gods: Moloch and Raphan.
[e] **6:2 Calneh, Hamath, Gath** Powerful Babylonian, Syrian and Philistine cities that were all captured by the Assyrians.
[f] **6:5 practise on** Or "invent". The Hebrew word means to "think", "become skilled" or "design".

WORRYING

SARAH'S mum had just had another baby. She'd spent the whole pregnancy worrying. "Will the nursery be ready in time?" "Will I be able to cope with another baby?" "Will we have enough money?"

Sarah could see that her mum was excited about this new addition but at the same time was scared about the responsibility, about the worry that this new life would bring. She needn't have worried. Grace was perfect. Unlike her mum, Grace simply didn't have the capacity to worry about anything. When she needed feeding, Sarah's mum fed her. When

JESUS INVITES US TO COME TO HIM AND GIVE HIM ALL OUR WEARY FRUSTRATIONS.

she was cold, Sarah put a blanket on her. When times were busy, people from church offered to baby-sit. Everything Grace needed was provided for her by those who loved her.

Even though Sarah and her mum are grown up, both need God in a similar way. Just as they provided for Grace, as his children, God provides for their every need too. There was no need for Sarah's mum to have worried because God has promised to look after them.

Somebody once said, "Worry is like a rocking chair. It gives you something to do but doesn't get you anywhere."

It is inevitable that at some point in our lives each of us will face tough times. Often this can lead to feelings of anxiety, worry and even depression. But it's important to remember that even in our toughest struggles, Jesus invites us to come to him and give him all our weary frustrations (Matthew 11:28). For those of us who worry, Jesus gives some sound advice in Matthew 6:25–34. Verse 33 sums up how we should handle worry: "Your first concern should always be God's kingdom and whatever he considers good and right. Then he will give you all these other things you need." ←

Why not take a minute to pray and put your trust in him once again:

Father God, help me to see the bigger picture when I face tough times. I thank you that your word says that "in everything God works for the good of those who love him" (Romans 8:28). Please teach me to be sensitive to your Holy Spirit so that I can always find peace in the middle of my storms.

Amen

GOD, JESUS AND THE HOLY SPIRIT – THE TRINITY

YOU'VE probably heard people talk about the Trinity but did you know that the word "trinity" isn't in the Bible? However, there are many passages where God clearly reveals himself as three persons: the loving Father, the obedient Son (Jesus Christ) and the powerful, yet gentle Holy Spirit.

Right at the start of the Bible, God says, "Now let's make humans who will be like *us*" (Genesis 1:26, emphasis added). But throughout the Bible we are reminded that "The Lord is our God. The Lord is the only God" (Deuteronomy 6:4). So what's going on? Which is it? Is God one or more than one? Well, amazingly, he's both! This is one of the great mysteries of God: three individual persons working together and relating to each other in perfect unity. So instead of "trinity" maybe a better word to describe what's going on here would be "tri-unity".

If you think about it, it does sort of make sense. After all, we read that when a husband and wife are joined in marriage they become "one". That doesn't mean that they're literally joined at the hip on their wedding day but, nevertheless, the Bible does describe them as "one". We also read that "God is love" (1 John 4:8). Surely, by definition, genuine "love" involves more than one person. One person loves, another is loved, and hopefully the feeling is mutual. When we understand God as a tri-unity we see this love relationship in its purest and most perfect form. God is one.

Let's look more closely at the persons of the Trinity, starting with God the *Father*. We read of him as a loving father in both the Old and the New Testaments. For example, "He will say to me, 'You are my Father. You are my God, my Rock, my Saviour'" (Psalm 89:26), and "The Father has loved us so much! This shows how much he loved us: we are called children of God. And we really are his children" (1 John 3:1). When Jesus taught us to pray he started by saying "Our Father . . ." When Jesus was baptized by his cousin, John, it was the Father who spoke from heaven saying, "'This is my Son, the one I love. I am very pleased with him'" (Matthew 3:17). By revealing himself as a father, God shows that he is both compassionate and just. He demands our respect but demonstrates his mercy when his children return to him.

Christians believe that Jesus is the *Son* of God, yet equal to the Father himself. The first chapter of John's Gospel begins by saying this about Jesus: "Before the world began, the Word was there. The Word was with God, and the Word was God." Jesus is 100% human and 100% God – another great mystery. As the

> **" BEFORE THE WORLD BEGAN, THE WORD WAS THERE. THE WORD WAS WITH GOD, AND THE WORD WAS GOD." JESUS IS 100% HUMAN AND 100% GOD – ANOTHER GREAT MYSTERY.**

long-awaited Jewish Messiah, Jesus fulfilled all that was expected of him in the Hebrew Scriptures (what we call the Old Testament). When he was 33 years old he laid down his life for the sins of all humankind, and three days later rose from the dead, proving that he had conquered the power of death. And the Bible promises that he's coming again!

Shortly before his arrest and crucifixion, Jesus promised his followers (which includes us) that he would send a Helper – *the Holy Spirit* – to help them understand the Scriptures and point them to him (John 14:16–17). This happened after Jesus ascended into heaven, when the apostles were filled with the Holy Spirit at Pentecost (Acts 2). But the Holy Spirit is present throughout the Bible – even right at the beginning when we find him "moving over the water" (Genesis 1:2). You can read about the effects of the Holy Spirit in our lives ("the fruit of the Spirit") in Galatians 5:22–23 and how the Spirit enables us to be witnesses and serve his Church ("the gifts of the Spirit") in Romans 12:4–8, 1 Corinthians 12 and Ephesians 4. ←

IMAGE AND SELF-ESTEEM

MOST of the time when people ask who we are, we tell them what we do: "I'm a scientist" or "I'm a student studying for my exams" or "I'm a guitarist". We might go on to say, "I'm a Geordie" or "I'm an American" or "I'm a Manchester City supporter" or "I'm John and Mary's son". But even these answers are about what we do or where we're from.

"Who are you?" Not, "What do you do?" or "Where are you from?" or "Who is your family?" or "What do you like doing?" or "What do you look like?" but *"Who are you?"*

Our identity, the essence of who we are, is something much deeper. It's the thing that you would continue to be even if everything else was stripped away. Think about it. If you were locked up in prison in a remote jungle and no longer had contact with anyone or anything you currently know, what would be left, who would you be? What remains is your identity, the thing that's left after you set aside everything you do, think and relate to. It's the *you* God made.

ONLY BY BEING SECURE IN OUR OWN IDENTITY CAN WE BRING HOPE TO A WORLD THAT HAS LOST ITS IDENTITY.

Many people who aren't Christians spend years trying to "find themselves", working out who they really are. Why? Because they've realized that there must be more to them than what they do or who they are related to. However, without knowing their identity in Christ they wander around unable to find answers to their deepest questions. Yet, as Christians, we can know our identity in God; we need to learn what he says about us and believe it. Check out some of these verses: Psalm 139:14; Jeremiah 1:4–5; Romans 8:38–39; 2 Corinthians 5:17; Ephesians 1:3–8; 2:10.

Only by being secure in our own identity can we bring hope to a world that has lost its identity and is desperately trying to find it through looks, possessions and activities.

If you want, you can pray this prayer:

Father God, thank you for making me just the way you did. Help me to know just who you want me to be and then to live confidently in my own skin, being the person that only I can be for you.

Amen

There Will Be Few Israelites Left Alive

⁹At that time ten people in one house might survive, but they too will die. ¹⁰And when someone dies, a relative will come to get the body so that it can be taken out and burned.ᵃ Relatives will come to take away the bones. They will call to anyone who might be hiding back in the house, "Are there any other dead bodies in there with you?"

That person will answer, "No."

But the relative will interrupt and say, "Hush! We must not mention the name of the LORD."

¹¹Look, the LORD will give the command,
    and the large houses will be broken to
        pieces,
    and the small houses will be broken to
        small pieces.
¹²Do horses run over loose rocks?
    No, and people don't use cows for
        ploughing.
But you turned everything upside down.
    You changed justice and goodness to bitter
        poison.
¹³You are so excited about defeating Lo
    Debar.ᵇ
    And you boast, "We have taken Karnaimᶜ
        by our own strength."

¹⁴"But Israel, I will bring a nation against you that will bring troubles to your whole country from Lebo Hamath to Arabah Brook." This is what the LORD God All-Powerful said.

A Vision of Locusts

7 This is what the Lord GOD showed me: he was making locusts. This was at the time the second crop began to grow, after the king's people had cut the first crop. ²Before the locusts could eat all the grass in the country, I said, "Lord GOD, I beg you, forgive us! Jacob cannot survive! He is too small!"

³Then the LORD changed his mind about this. The LORD said, "It will not happen."

A Vision of Fire

⁴This is what the Lord GOD showed me: I saw the Lord GOD calling for judgement by fire. The fire destroyed the ocean and was beginning to eat up the land. ⁵But I said, "Lord GOD, stop, I beg you! Jacob cannot survive! He is too small!"

⁶Then the LORD changed his mind about this. The Lord GOD said, "It will not happen either."

A Vision of a Plumb Line

⁷This is what the Lord showed me: he stood by a wall with a plumb lineᵈ in his hand. (The wall had been marked with a plumb line.) ⁸The LORD said to me, "Amos, what do you see?"

I said, "A plumb line."

Then the Lord said to me, "See, I will put a plumb line among my people Israel. I will not let their 'crooked ways' pass inspection any more. ⁹Isaac's high places will be destroyed. Israel's holy places will be made into a pile of rocks. I will attack and kill Jeroboam'sᵉ family with swords."

Amaziah Tries to Stop Amos

¹⁰Amaziah, a priest at Bethel,ᶠ sent this message to Jeroboam, the king of Israel: "Amos is making plans against you. He is trying to make the people of Israel fight against you. He has been speaking so much that this country cannot hold all his words. ¹¹Amos has said, 'Jeroboam will die by the sword, and the people of Israel will be taken as prisoners out of their country.'"

¹²Amaziah also said to Amos, "You seer, go down to Judah and eat there.ᵍ Do your prophesying there. ¹³But don't prophesy any more here at Bethel. This is Jeroboam's holy place. This is Israel's temple."

¹⁴Then Amos answered Amaziah, "I am not a professional prophet, and I am not from a prophet's family. I raise cattle and take care of sycamore trees. ¹⁵I was a shepherd and the LORD took me from following the sheep. The LORD said to me, 'Go, prophesy to my people Israel.' ¹⁶So listen to the LORD's message. You tell me, 'Don't prophesy against Israel. Don't speak against Isaac's family.' ¹⁷But the LORD says, 'Your wife will become a prostitute in the city. Your sons and daughters will be killed with swords. Other people will take your land and divide it among themselves, and you will die in a foreignʰ country. The people of Israel will definitely be taken from this country as prisoners.'"

ᵃ **6:10 And when . . . burned** The meaning of the Hebrew text here is uncertain.

ᵇ **6:13 Lo Debar** This name means "nothing".

ᶜ **6:13 Karnaim** This name means "horns". Horns were a symbol of strength.

ᵈ **7:7 plumb line** A string with a weight on one end used to show how straight the walls of a building were. Sometimes the line was coated with paint or chalk to mark a straight line.

ᵉ **7:9 Jeroboam** The king of Israel. See verse 10.

ᶠ **7:10 Bethel** A town in Israel. This name means "God's house".

ᵍ **7:12 eat there** This shows that Amaziah thought that Amos was a professional prophet who prophesied to receive food or money.

ʰ **7:17 foreign** Literally, "unclean". See "UNCLEAN" in the Word List.

A Vision of Ripe Fruit

8 This is what the Lord God showed me: I saw a basket of summer fruit. [2]He said to me, "Amos, what do you see?"

I said, "A basket of summer fruit."

Then the Lord said to me, "The end[a] has come to my people Israel. I will not ignore their sins any more. [3]Their temple songs will become funeral songs." This is what the Lord God said. "There will be dead bodies everywhere. In silence people will take out the dead bodies and throw them onto the pile."[b]

Merchants Only Want to Make Money

[4]Listen to me, you who trample on helpless people.
   You are trying to destroy the poor of this country.
[5]You merchants say,
   "When will the New Moon be over so that we can sell grain?
When will the Sabbath be over
   so that we can bring out more wheat to sell?
We can raise the price
   and make the measure smaller.
We can change the scales
   and cheat the people.
[6]The poor cannot pay their loans,
   so we will buy them as slaves.
We will buy those helpless people
   for the price of a pair of sandals.
Oh, and we can sell the wheat
   that was spilled on the floor."

[7]The Lord made a promise. He used his name, "Pride of Jacob", and made this promise:

"I will never forget what those people did.
[8]There will be an earthquake
   that will shake the whole land because of what they did.
Everyone living there will cry for those who died.
   The land will be tossed around.
The whole land will rise and fall
   like the Nile River in Egypt."

[9]The Lord God also said,
"At that time I will make the sun set at noon
   and make the land dark on a clear day.

[10]I will change your festivals into days of crying for the dead.
All your songs will be songs of sadness for those who are dead.
I will put mourning clothes on every body
   and baldness on every head.[c]
I will cause mourning everywhere,
   like that for an only son who has died.
It will be a very bitter end."

A Famine of God's Word

[11]The Lord God says,

"Look, the days are coming
   when I will cause a famine in the land.
The people will not be hungry for bread.
   They will not be thirsty for water.
No, they will be hungry for words from the Lord.
[12]The people will wander around the country,
   from the Dead Sea to the western coast,
   then through the north around to the east.
They will go back and forth looking for a message from the Lord,
   but they will not find it.
[13]At that time the beautiful young men and women
   will become weak from thirst.
[14]They made promises by the false god[d] of Samaria.
   They took oaths in the name of the god of Dan,[e]
and made vows in the name of the god of Beersheba.[f]
But they will fall
   and never get up again."

A Vision of God Commanding Punishment

9 I saw the Lord standing by the altar, and he said,

"Hit the top of the columns,
   and shake them to the ground.
Push them down on everyone's head.
   Those who survive I will kill with a sword.
None of them will run away.
   None of them will escape.
[2]If they dig deep into the ground,[g]
   I will pull them from there.
If they go up into the skies,[h]

---

[a] **8:2 end** This Hebrew word sounds like the word for "summer fruit".
[b] **8:3 In silence . . . the pile** Or "People will be saying, 'Hush!'" See Amos 6:10.
[c] **8:10 baldness . . . head** People shaved their heads to show that they were very sad or upset.
[d] **8:14 false god** Literally, "sin", referring to the calf god in Samaria.
[e] **8:14 Dan** One of Israel's holy places was in this city.
[f] **8:14 Beersheba** A town in Judah. This name means "well of the oath".
[g] **9:2 ground** Literally, "Sheol, the place of the dead".
[h] **9:2 skies** Or "heaven".

I will bring them down from there.
[3]If they hide at the top of Mount Carmel,[a]
I will find them there and take them from
that place.
If they try to hide from me at the bottom of
the sea,
I will command the snake, and it will bite
them.
[4]If they are captured and taken away by their
enemies,
I will command the sword,
and it will kill them there.
Yes, I will watch over them,
but I will watch for ways to give them
troubles,
not for ways to do good things."

Punishment Will Destroy the People

[5]The Lord GOD All-Powerful will touch the land,
and the land will melt.
Then all the people who live in the land
will cry for the dead.
The land will rise and fall
like the Nile River in Egypt.
[6]He built his upper rooms above the skies.
He put his skies[b] over the earth.
He calls for the waters of the sea
and pours them out as rain on the land.
YAHWEH is his name.

The LORD Promises Destruction for Israel

[7]This is what the LORD says:

"Israel, you are like the Ethiopians to me.
I brought Israel out of the land of Egypt,
the Philistines from Caphtor[c]
and the Arameans from Kir."[d]

[8]The Lord GOD is watching this sinful
kingdom.
The LORD says,
"I will wipe Israel off the face of the
earth,
but I will never completely destroy Jacob's
family.
[9]I am giving the command
to scatter the people of Israel among all
nations.
But it will be like someone sifting flour.
A person shakes flour through a sifter.[e]

The good flour falls through,
but the bad lumps are caught.
[10]"Sinners among my people say,
'Nothing bad will happen to us.'
But all of them will be killed with swords."

INSIGHT

*Who needs kings and queens? The
Israelites had given up on their royal family,
who had become like a fragile, torn tent.
But Amos says that through the line of
David, Israel's fortunes will be restored.
Jesus was from the family line of David.*
Amos 9:11

God Promises to Restore the Kingdom

[11]"David's house[f] has fallen,
but at that time I will set it up again.
I will fix its holes and repair its ruined parts.
I will set it up as it was before.
[12]Then the people left alive in Edom,
and all the people called by my name, will
look to me for help."
This is what the LORD said,
and he will make it happen.
[13]The LORD says, "A time of great blessing is
coming.
Workers will still be harvesting
when it is time to plough the fields again.
They will still be trampling the grapes
when it is time for a new crop.
Sweet wine will drip from the mountains
and pour from the hills.
[14]I will bring my people, Israel,
back from captivity.
They will rebuild the ruined cities,
and they will live in them.
They will plant vineyards
and drink the wine they produce.
They will plant gardens
and eat the crops they produce.
[15]I will plant my people on their land,
and never again will they be pulled up out
of the land that I gave them."
This is what the LORD your God said.

---

[a] 9:3 **Mount Carmel** A mountain in northern Israel. This name means "God's vineyard". This shows that it was a very fertile hill.
[b] 9:6 **skies** Literally, "dome" or "vault".
[c] 9:7 **Caphtor** An island west of Israel, probably Crete or Cyprus.
[d] 9:7 **Kir** Where the Arameans came from and where the Assyrians sent them in exile. There are several places with this name.
[e] 9:9 **sifter** Something like a cup with a screen on its bottom. A sifter is used for removing large lumps from the good flour.
[f] 9:11 **David's house** This probably means his kingdom.

Who
Obadiah was a prophet. His name means "servant of the Lord" or "worshipper of the Lord", and that's all we know about him. He may have been a contemporary of Ezekiel.

When
We're not sure. If verses 11–14 refer to a Philistine invasion, that means Obadiah was writing in the ninth century BC. It is more likely that it refers to the Babylonian destruction of Jerusalem in 586 BC.

What
Only one chapter long, Obadiah is the shortest book in the Old Testament. It deals with the destruction of Edom, a nation south of the Dead Sea. It stands not just for the specific country of Edom, but for all of the "other" nations who have opposed God's will.

The Edomites were descendants of Esau and thus related to the Israelites, yet they were longstanding enemies. Rather than helping them, Edom had stood by while Judah suffered. High in its rocky, mountainous territory, secure and safe, it stood by and even exulted in the shame of Judah. "You stood there and watched," says Obadiah, "as foreigners entered Jerusalem and took what they wanted. In fact, you were no better than those foreigners" (see v.11).

However, the "day of the Lord" is coming, when the Edomites will get their just deserts, along with all the nations who have mistreated God's people. Obadiah prophesies, "You will be finished. It will be as if you never existed" (v.16b).

In the end, the captives will return to take possession of the land and God's people will be restored.

The book declares, in its final lines, that the kingdom will belong to the Lord. And, in a way, it is a warning not just to Edom, but to all of those who stand passively by while evil is committed. They will pay the price for their callous disinterest and for their enjoyment in the suffering of others.

QUICK TOUR ▶ **OBADIAH**

Edom's pride verses 1–9
Edom's cruelty verses 10–14

Israel's victory verses 15–21

"The day of the Lord is coming soon to all the nations. And the evil you did to others will happen to you. The same bad things will fall down on your own head."

Obadiah verse 15

Edom Will Be Punished

¹This is the vision of Obadiah. This is what the Lord God says about Edom:

We heard a report from the LORD.
A messenger was sent to the nations.
He said, "Let's go and fight against Edom."

The LORD Speaks to Edom

²"Edom, I will make you the smallest nation.
Everyone will hate you very much.
³Your pride has fooled you.
You live in those caves high on the cliff.
Your home is high in the hills.
So you say to yourself,
'No one can bring me to the ground.'"

INSIGHT

*The people of Edom were cocky and
thought they were safe from attack as
they lived high up on a hill and hoarded
their wealth in the red cliffs. Yet they
were clearly no match for God, who
promised to destroy them (v.15).*

Obadiah verse 3

Edom Will Be Brought Low

⁴This is what the LORD says:
"Even though you fly high like the eagle
and put your nest among the stars,
I will bring you down from there.
⁵You really will be ruined!
Thieves will come to you.
Robbers will come in the night,
and they will take all they want.
When workers gather grapes in your
vineyards,
they will leave a few grapes behind.
⁶But the enemy will search hard for Esau's
hidden treasures,
and they will find them all.
⁷All those who are your friends
will force you out of the land.
Those who were at peace with you will trick
you,
and they will defeat you.
The soldiers who fought by your side
are planning a trap for you.
They say, 'He doesn't expect a thing!'"

⁸The LORD says, "On that day,
I will destroy the wise people throughout
Edom.
I will destroy all the clever people from the
mountain of Esau.ᵃ
⁹Teman, your brave soldiers will be afraid.
Everyone will be destroyed from the
mountain of Esau.
Many people will be killed.

INSIGHT

*The two sides fighting were actually
related. The people of Judah were
descendants of Jacob and the Edomites
were descendants of Esau, Jacob's
brother. You can read about how Jacob
and Esau fell out in Genesis from
chapter 25 onwards.*

Obadiah verse 10

---

¹⁰You will be covered with shame
because you were very cruel to your
brother Jacob.
So you will be destroyed completely.
¹¹You joined the enemies of Israel.
Strangers carried Israel's treasures away.
Foreigners entered Israel's city gate.
They threw lots to decide what part of
Jerusalem they would get.
And you were right there with them,
waiting to get your share.
¹²You should not have laughedᵇ
at your brother's trouble.
You should not have been happy
when they destroyed Judah.
You should not have boastedᶜ
at the time of their trouble.
¹³You should not have entered the city gate of
my people
and laughed at their problems.
You should not have taken their treasures
in the time of their trouble.
¹⁴You should have not stood where the roads
cross
and destroyed those who were trying to
escape.
You should not have captured those who
escaped alive.
¹⁵The day of the LORD is coming soon
to all the nations.

ᵃ **8 mountain of Esau** That is, Mount Seir in Edom.
ᵇ **12 laughed** Literally, "looked". Also in verse 13.
ᶜ **12 boasted** Literally, "made your mouth big".

OH BROTHER, WHERE ART THOU?

There were once two brothers, Jacob and Esau. Their story, told in Genesis chapters 25 – 36, is crucial to understanding Obadiah's prophecy. The family line of Jacob, later known as Israel, would become God's chosen people. Esau's family line would become known as Edom, living nearby but separately.

DIG IN

READ Obadiah verses 1–21

- What do verses 2–4 tell us about how God saw Edom?
- What had Edom done to Jacob (Israel) (vv.10–14)?
- What punishment are they to receive from God for their behaviour?

To set the scene: in 587 BC, a few years before Obadiah wrote this short prophecy, Babylon had waged a terrible war on God's people – an attack that God had allowed and that prophets like Isaiah and Jeremiah had warned about. (You can read the history in 2 Kings 25:1–21.)

As a consequence, those that survived were in exile – scattered in Babylon and elsewhere, no longer in the promised land that God had given them.

While Jerusalem was getting pummelled, their neighbour to the east, Edom, did not defend or help Israel. In fact, they joined in, despite their shared history (God reminds them they are brothers in v.12).

So Obadiah prophesies God's vengeance against Edom (which happened some years later, in 553 BC). He says it's going to be a particularly nasty time for this proud nation. They will get what's coming to them.

- What do we learn about the kind of justice God is interested in (v.15)?
- What is going to happen to the scattered people of Israel (vv.19–21)?

In his short prophecy, Obadiah reminds us of God's love of justice. Edom's punishment will be fair, according to what they did wrong (v.15).

At the same time as prophesying Edom's doom, Obadiah has a vision of a bright future for Israel. The broken nation would be reunited and their kingdom would stretch further north, south, east and west than it ever had before (vv.19–21).

DIG THROUGH

- Have you ever felt completely deserted by God? Imagine how it must have felt for Israel at this time. Over the last few years, their land and wealth had been raided; friends and relatives had been killed; their whole way of life had been reduced to smouldering rubble.
- When we feel this way, we need encouragement straight from God. Obadiah's prophecy would have come at just the right time for Israel's scattered people. It reminded them that even in the midst of severe trial, God had a perfect plan that he would bring to completion. If you need this kind of encouragement, ask God to speak to you today as you mull over the words of Obadiah.

DIG DEEPER

- Right at the end, Obadiah looks far ahead to a kingdom greater than any of God's people could imagine. This is not to do with a new nation for Israel, but the kingdom that Jesus speaks of in Matthew 12:28 and 25:34.
- Obadiah's prophecy fits snugly into Jeremiah's prophetic writings in Jeremiah 49:7–22 and Lamentations 4:21–22. Check them out and compare them. This is another example of how the Bible fits together despite being written by dozens of authors writing decades, often centuries, apart.

And the evil you did to others will happen
to you.
The same bad things will fall down on your
own head.
[16]You spilled[a] blood on my holy
mountain,[b]
so other nations will spill your blood.[c]
You will be finished.
It will be as if you never existed.
[17]But there will be survivors on Mount
Zion.
They will be my special people.
The nation of Jacob[d] will take back
what belongs to it.
[18]The people of Jacob will be like a fire,
The people of Joseph will be like a flame.
But the nation of Esau[e] will be like ashes.
The people of Judah will burn Edom, and
they will destroy it.
Then there will be no survivors in the nation
of Esau."

This will happen because the LORD said it
would.
[19]Then people from the Negev will live on the
mountain of Esau.
And people from the foothills will take the
Philistine lands.
They will live in the land of Ephraim and
Samaria.
Gilead will belong to Benjamin.
[20]People from Israel were forced to leave their
homes,
but they will take back the land of Canaan,
all the way to Zarephath.
People from Judah were forced to leave
Jerusalem and live in Sepharad.[f]
But they will take back the cities of the
Negev.
[21]The winners[g] will go up on Mount Zion
to rule the people who live on Esau's
mountain.
And the kingdom will belong to the LORD.

---

[a] **16** *spilled* Literally, "drank".
[b] **16** *holy mountain* One of the mountains Jerusalem was built on. Sometimes Zion is used to mean Jerusalem itself. Also in
verses 17,21.
[c] **16** *spill your blood* Literally, "drink and swallow".
[d] **17** *nation of Jacob* Literally, "the house of Jacob". This could mean the people of Israel or only its leaders.
[e] **18** *nation of Esau* Literally, "the house of Esau".
[f] **20** *Sepharad* This is probably Spain.
[g] **21** *winners* Or "saviours". Those who led their people to victory in war.

Who Traditionally the book is believed to have been written by Jonah himself, but it may come from the same source as the tales of Elisha and Elijah. Though who else but Jonah could have known all the facts it records?

When The action takes place around 800–750 BC, as Jonah was living during the time of Jeroboam II. Some, however, think the book was written later, after the exile, or at least after the fall of Nineveh, the capital of Assyria, in 612 BC.

What This little book contains one of the most famous stories of the Bible. It's a favourite with children for its all-action adventure style, not to mention that enormous fish. But this book is not a fairy story; it's a profound statement about God's love.

Unlike the rest of the Prophets, it is a narrative about a prophet, rather than the contents of his message. Indeed, we only have one line of prophecy from Jonah in the whole book and that consists of one simple message: "Forty days from now, Nineveh will be destroyed!"

Jonah features elsewhere in the Bible (2 Kings 14:25), where he predicts success to Jeroboam II and the restoration of the land of Israel to its ancient boundaries. These prophecies must have made Jonah very popular in Israel. However, one of the key factors in Israel's military success was the fact that Damascus – the city with which Israel had been at war – was only quietened because it had been attacked by the Assyrians.

And it is to the Assyrians that Jonah is sent. The startling fact about Jonah is not that he ran away; it's that God wanted to forgive the Assyrians. They were a frightening, brutal people who destroyed countries and deported people. No one in their right mind would go to Nineveh, their capital, and then tell them to repent. And no pious Jew would believe that God would even offer repentance to such people.

Israel believed that the truth was theirs alone and they wrapped it in ritual and rite and sanctimonious piety. But God says that the hated, feared Assyrians were his children as well. And when they repented and listened to his message, he forgave them. This is what is shocking in this book, and why Jonah reacts so angrily. It was not just his courage that was being tested – it was his entire view of God.

 QUICK TOUR **JONAH**

Jonah prophesies for Jeroboam 2 Kings 14:25	In the belly of the fish 2:1–10
Jonah runs away 1:1–17	The Assyrians repent 3:1–10
	All people matter 4:1–11

"He complained to the LORD and said, 'LORD, I knew this would happen! I was in my own country, and you told me to come here. At that time I knew that you would forgive the people of this evil city, so I decided to run away to Tarshish. I knew that you are a kind God. I knew that you show mercy and don't want to punish people. I knew that you are kind, and if these people stopped sinning, you would change your plans to destroy them.'"

Jonah 4:2

God Calls and Jonah Runs

1 The LORD spoke to Jonah[a] son of Amittai: 2"Nineveh[b] is a big city. I have heard about the many evil things the people there are doing. So go and tell them I am ready to punish them."

3But Jonah tried to run away from the LORD. He went to Joppa[c] and found a boat that was going to the faraway city of Tarshish. Jonah paid money for the trip and went on the boat. He wanted to travel with the people on this boat to Tarshish and run away from the LORD.

The Great Storm

4But the LORD brought a great storm on the sea. The wind made the sea very rough. The storm was very strong, and the boat was ready to break apart. 5The men wanted to make the boat lighter to stop it from sinking, so they began throwing the cargo[d] into the sea. The sailors were very frightened. Each man began praying to his god.

Jonah had gone down into the boat to lie down, and he went to sleep. 6The captain of the boat saw Jonah and said, "Wake up! Why are you sleeping? Pray to your god! Maybe your god will hear your prayer and save us!"

What Caused This Storm?

7Then the men said to each other, "We should throw lots to find out why this is happening to us."

So the men threw lots. The lots showed that the troubles came to them because of Jonah. 8Then the men said to Jonah, "It is your fault that this terrible thing is happening to us. Tell us, what have you done? What is your job? Where do you come from? What is your country? Who are your people?"

9Jonah said to them, "I am a Hebrew. I worship the LORD, the God of heaven, who made the land and the sea."

10Jonah told the men he was running away from the LORD. The men became very afraid when they learned this. They asked Jonah, "What terrible thing did you do against your God?"

11The wind and the waves of the sea were becoming stronger and stronger. So the men said to Jonah, "What should we do to save ourselves? What should we do to you to make the sea calm?"

12Jonah said to the men, "I know I did wrong—that is why the storm came on the sea. So throw me into the sea, and the sea will become calm."

13Instead, the men tried to row the ship back to the shore, but they couldn't do it. The wind and the waves of the sea were too strong—and they were becoming stronger and stronger.

Jonah's Punishment

14So the men cried to the LORD, "LORD, please don't say we are guilty of killing an innocent man. Please don't make us die for killing him. We know you are the LORD, and you will do whatever you want."

15So the men threw Jonah into the sea. The storm stopped, and the sea became calm. 16When the men saw this, they began to fear and respect the LORD. They offered a sacrifice and made special promises to the LORD.

> # INSIGHT
>
> In biblical times the phrase "three days and three nights" would have been understood to mean a period long enough for Jonah to be dead. Jesus refers to Jonah and uses the same phrase about himself when alluding to his resurrection (see Matthew 12:40).
>
> **Jonah 1:17**

17When Jonah fell into the sea, the LORD chose a very big fish to swallow Jonah. He was in the stomach of the fish for three days and three nights.

Jonah's Prayer

2 While Jonah was in the stomach of the fish, he prayed to the LORD his God. He said,

2"I was in very bad trouble.
    I called to the LORD for help,
        and he answered me.
I was deep in the grave.
    I cried to you,
        and you heard my voice.

3"You threw me into the sea.
    Your powerful waves splashed over me.
I went down, down into the deep sea.
    The water was all around me.

---

[a] 1:1 **Jonah** This is probably the same prophet mentioned in 2 Kgs 14:25.
[b] 1:2 **Nineveh** The capital city of the country of Assyria. Assyria destroyed Israel in 722–721 BC.
[c] 1:3 **Joppa** A town on the coast of Israel by the Mediterranean Sea.
[d] 1:5 **cargo** The Hebrew word can mean "dishes", "jars" or "tools". Here, this could mean all the jars and boxes the boat carried on its way to Tarshish or the rigging and other heavy tools on the boat.

RUNAWAY PROPHET

If you ever went to Sunday school, you'll know the story of Jonah and the whale! It's one of the classic "picture book" Bible stories. And it's a remarkable adventure as it is: God shows he is in control of all nature by using a big fish to save a man's life. But as with the rest of the Bible, the closer we look, the more we see. Jonah wasn't just an ordinary man who fell into the sea. There's a lot more to discover – about God, and about ourselves.

DIG IN

READ Jonah 1:1-17

- What lengths does Jonah go to in his attempt to avoid obeying God (v.3)?
- He goes off for a nap (v.5). What might this say about his state of mind?

Jonah's on the run. He's heard clearly what God wants him to do but rather than set off for Nineveh, he's heading in exactly the opposite direction, towards Tarshish. To get his attention – and get him back on course – the Lord sends a nasty storm.

Jonah's attitude towards God stinks. He knows full well that he's disobeying God and that the storm is meant for him – but he shuts himself off from God, and goes for a kip. We don't find out what his problem is until later in the book (read on to chapter 4).

- How do the sailors respond when Jonah reveals his true identity (vv.9–17)?

At sea, storms are common and we can assume that these are experienced sailors who are used to a few choppy waves. But something about this storm makes them suspect something is up.

Maybe the men fear worse things will follow if they take Jonah's advice to throw him overboard, and they seem to try everything before eventually they do as he suggests. They seem to fear God a lot more than Jonah, God's servant, does.

DIG THROUGH

We've all been in Jonah's position – asked to do something that we just don't want to do! But when it's God doing the asking, we can only run for so long. Like he did with Jonah, when God puts a call on our lives, he'll see it through, even if we are disobedient on the way there.

The striking contrast between Jonah's cocky reaction to God's hand at work and that of the sailors reminds us that sometimes we can forget to properly respect God and listen to his commands. We can become almost immune to him and try and shut him out (v.5).

DIG DEEPER

- Do any of the details in this chapter ring bells with you? Jonah sleeping peacefully on the boat while the storm rages ... Jonah's captivity in the fish's stomach for three days ... These details are not a coincidence. The runaway prophet who was sent to preach repentance is a faint glimmer of Jesus who, in contrast, will faithfully obey God. You'll find where Jesus talks about Jonah in relation to himself in Matthew 12:38–41.

⁴Then I thought, 'Now I must go where you
cannot see me,'
   but I continued looking to your holy Temple
      for help.

⁵"The seawater closed over me.
   The water covered my mouth,
      and I could not breathe.ᵃ
I went down, down into the deep sea.
   Seaweed wrapped around my head.
⁶I was at the bottom of the sea,
   the place where mountains begin.
I thought I was locked in this prison
      forever,
   but the Lᴏʀᴅ my God took me out of my
      grave.
God, you gave me life again!

⁷"My soul gave up all hope,
   but then I remembered the Lᴏʀᴅ.
I prayed to you,
   and you heard my prayers in your holy
      Temple.

⁸"Some people worship useless idols,
   but those statues never help them.ᵇ
⁹I will give sacrifices to you,
   and I will praise and thank you.
I will make special promises to you,
   and I will do what I promise."
Salvation only comes from the Lᴏʀᴅ!

¹⁰Then the Lᴏʀᴅ spoke to the fish, and it
vomited Jonah out of its stomach onto the dry
land.

God Calls and Jonah Obeys

3 Then the Lᴏʀᴅ spoke to Jonah again and said,
²"Go to that big city Nineveh, and say what
I tell you to say."

³So Jonah obeyed the Lᴏʀᴅ and went to
Nineveh. It was a very large city. A person had
to walk for three days to travel through it.

⁴Jonah went to the centre of the city and began
speaking to the people. He said, "After 40 days,
Nineveh will be destroyed!"

⁵The people of Nineveh believed God. They
decided to stop eating for a time to think
about their sins. They put on special clothes to
show they were sorry. All the people in the city
did this, from the most important to the least
important.

INSIGHT

*The special clothes the king put on would
have been what is known as "sackcloth".
It was probably made of scratchy goat
hair and very uncomfortable. People
would put on sackcloth and sit in ashes
as a sign that they were deeply sorry for
something they had done or as a sign of
mourning.*

Jonah 3:6

---

⁶When the king of Nineveh heard about
this, he left his throne, removed his robe, put on
special clothes to show that he was sorry, and sat
in ashes.ᶜ ⁷The king wrote a special message and
sent it throughout the city:

A command from the king and his great
rulers:

For a short time no person or animal should
eat anything. No herd or flock will be allowed
in the fields. Nothing living in Nineveh will
eat or drink water. ⁸But every person and
every animal must be covered with a special
cloth to show they are sad. People must cry
loudly to God. Everyone must change their
life and stop doing bad things. ⁹Who knows?
Maybe God will stop being angry and change
his mind, and we will not be punished.

¹⁰God saw what the people did. He saw that
they stopped doing evil. So God changed his
mind and did not do what he had planned. He did
not punish the people.

God's Mercy Makes Jonah Angry

4 Jonah was not happy that God had saved the
city. Jonah became angry. ²He complained to
the Lᴏʀᴅ and said, "Lᴏʀᴅ, I knew this would
happen! I was in my own country, and you told
me to come here. At that time I knew that you
would forgive the people of this evil city, so I
decided to run away to Tarshish. I knew that you
are a kind God. I knew that you show mercy and
don't want to punish people. I knew that you
are kind, and if these people stopped sinning,
you would change your plans to destroy them.

ᵃ **2:5 mouth, and I could not breathe** Or "The water surrounded me to my soul." The Hebrew word for soul also means "life",
"self" or "appetite", and "throat" or "mouth."
ᵇ **2:8** Or "People who worship useless things have left the one who is kind to them."
ᶜ **3:6 sat in ashes** People did this to show that they were sad.

GOD'S HEART – IT'S BIGGER THAN YOURS

Jonah's mission to Nineveh has been amazingly successful. Any evangelist would be pretty chuffed if his seven-word sermon (Jonah 3:4) caused an entire city to repent and change their ways!

Seeing the Ninevites's response (Jonah 3:6–9), God, showing his incredible compassion, decides to save them from punishment. Mission accomplished, Jonah! That feels pretty good, right? Er, no . . .

DIG IN

READ Jonah 3:10 – 4:11

- Why is Jonah angry with God (4:1–2)?
- What does verse 3 suggest to you about Jonah's state of mind?

Here we finally get to see the reasons for Jonah's disobedience to God in chapter 1. He is really bitter that God should give Nineveh a second chance. But why?

Some background is needed here. Nineveh is the capital city of the Assyrians – long-sworn enemies of God's people. They were famous for ruthlessly invading and destroying other countries to increase their empire (Jonah 1:2). Jonah is angry that they haven't finally got their comeuppance from God.

Maybe we shouldn't blame Jonah for being angry. After all, God's meant to be on his people's side, right?

- How does God explain his actions to Jonah (4:11)?
- How does God use the plant as a picture to help Jonah understand how he feels?

Clearly Jonah is in a huff and doesn't answer God when he addresses him. His actions suggest that he might even be secretly hoping that Nineveh will start sinning again and God will soon change his mind.

So God uses a physical demonstration, causing a plant to grow up quickly to provide shelter. But just as quickly, he takes the plant away. Having got Jonah's attention, God is able to gently explain that if Jonah pitied the plant which he hadn't planted or caused to grow, how much more should God pity the city of 120,000 people.

DIG THROUGH

Do you have any sympathy with Jonah? It's okay if you do! Jonah's heart is in the right place – wanting only God's glory. But it's based on a limited understanding of God's plans and purposes, and his big heart for people. The bigger picture is that God doesn't want anyone to die without knowing him (2 Peter 3:9) – whoever they are and wherever they're from. God's heart is for the whole world.

- We might find ourselves feeling that some people haven't done enough to deserve God's forgiveness, or that their relationship with God is shallow and won't last. But it's not our call. God will show mercy to whomever he chooses (check out Exodus 33:19; Romans 9:15).

DIG DEEPER

Jonah's story shows us a God who has infinite patience towards us. He is a God who is "kind and merciful. He does not become angry quickly. He has great love" (Joel 2:13). He is patient towards us (2 Peter 3:15) and forgives us our sins over and over again (1 John 1:8–9). Whilst God has infinite patience towards those who say sorry, the unrepentant are punished. The book of Nahum, found later in the Old Testament, prophesies Nineveh's destruction as God's patience runs out with the unrepentant people 150 years later.

Today God is using his church in the same way as Jonah, to call people in the world to "change and turn to him. He has decided on a day when he will judge all the people in the world" (Acts 17:30–31).

³So now, LORD, just kill me. It is better for me to die than to live."

⁴Then the LORD said, "Do you think it is right for you to be angry?"

⁵Jonah went out of the city to a place near the city on the east side. He made a shelter for himself and sat there in the shade, waiting to see what would happen to the city.

The Gourd Plant and the Worm

⁶The LORD made a gourd plant grow quickly over Jonah. This made a cool place for Jonah to sit and helped him to be more comfortable. He was very happy because of this plant.

⁷The next morning, God sent a worm to eat part of the plant. The worm began eating the plant, and the plant died.

⁸After the sun was high in the sky, God caused a hot east wind to blow. The sun became very hot on Jonah's head, and he became very weak. He asked God to let him die. He said, "It is better for me to die than to live."

⁹But God said to Jonah, "Do you think it is right for you to be angry just because this plant died?"

Jonah answered, "Yes, it is right for me to be angry! I am angry enough to die!"

¹⁰And the LORD said, "You did nothing for that plant. You did not make it grow. It grew up in the night, and the next day it died. And now you are sad about it. ¹¹If you can get upset over a plant, surely I can feel sorry for a big city like Nineveh. There are many people and animals in that city. There are more than 120,000 people there who did not know they were doing wrong."ᵃ

ᵃ **4:11 people . . . wrong** Literally, "people who do not know their right from their left". This might mean "innocent children".

Who
Micah was a resident of Moresheth, a small town in southern Judah, about 22 miles (35 km) south-west of Jerusalem. He worked in the southern kingdom during a time of prosperity.

 When
He prophesied between 750 and 686 BC, during the reigns of three kings of Judah: Jotham (750–735 BC), Ahaz (735–715 BC) and Hezekiah (715–687 BC). He was a contemporary of Isaiah, working a little later than Hosea and Amos.

 What
Crying out against injustice and trying to get the people to change their ways, the seven chapters of Micah move between condemnation of Israel's conduct and great prophecies of a future hope.

The big theme is judgement and forgiveness. Micah 6:6–8 seems to sum up Micah's message and those of other prophets of this time. Micah, like Amos, condemns the corruption and selfish greed of the ruling classes. They worship false idols (1:7; 5:12–14); they seize the property of their victims (2:2,9); they indulge in fraud and violence (6:10–12).

He brings a kind of lawsuit against the people (3:8). The kingdom of Israel, with its capital at Samaria, and the kingdom of Judah, with its capital at Jerusalem, are both called to account for their sins (1:2–7). Micah was prophesying during a time of relative peace, stability and wealth.

He uses strong, vivid language: people would shave their heads "bald like an eagle" (1:16) and mountains will melt like wax (1:4). There are images of people sitting at peace under their own grapevine (4:4) and leaders who are "as crooked as a tangled thornbush" (7:4).

In one of his most famous passages Micah looks to a different kind of ruler, a future King who will shepherd his people into a time of great peace: he says that though Bethlehem Ephrathah is one of the smallest towns in the nation of Judah, the Lord will choose one of its people to rule the nation – someone whose family goes back to ancient times (5:2).

QUICK TOUR ▶ **MICAH**

"Human, the LORD has told you what goodness is. This is what he wants from you: be fair to other people, love kindness and loyalty, and humbly obey your God."

Micah 6:8

Samaria and Israel to Be Punished

1 During the time that Jotham, Ahaz and Hezekiah were kings of Judah, the word of the LORD came to Micah. Micah was from Moresheth. He saw these visions about Samaria and Jerusalem.

2Listen, all you people!
Earth and everyone on it,[a] listen!
The Lord GOD will be a witness against you.
The Lord will come from his holy temple.
3See, the LORD is leaving his place
to come down and walk on the high places[b]
of the earth.
4The mountains will melt under him
like wax in a fire.
The valleys will break apart
and slide like water rushing down a hill.
5This will happen because of Jacob's sin,
because of the sins of the nation[c] of Israel.

Samaria, the Cause of Sin

What caused Jacob to sin?
It was Samaria.
Where is the high place in Judah?
It is Jerusalem.
6So I will change Samaria into a pile of rocks in
the field,
a place ready for planting grapes.
I will push Samaria's stones down into the
valley,
leaving nothing but the foundations.
7All her idols will be broken into pieces.
She got them as pay for being a prostitute.
They will be burned in fire.
I will destroy all her statues of false gods,
because Samaria got her riches by being
unfaithful to me.
So those things will be taken by other people
who are not faithful to me.

Micah's Great Sadness

8I will be very sad about what will
happen.
I will go without sandals and clothes.
I will cry like a wild dog.
I will mourn like an ostrich.
9Samaria's[d] wound cannot be healed.
Her disease has spread to Judah.
It has reached the city gate of my people;
it has spread all the way to Jerusalem.
10Don't tell it in Gath.[e]
Don't cry in Acco.[f]
Roll yourself in the dust
at Beth Ophrah.[g]
11You people living in Shaphir,[h]
pass on your way, naked and ashamed.
The people living in Zaanan[i]
will not come out.
The people in Beth Ezel[j] will cry
and take their support from you.
12The people living in Maroth[k]
wait for something good to happen,
even though trouble has come down from the
LORD
and has reached the city gate of
Jerusalem.
13You people living in Lachish,[l]
get the horses ready for your chariots.
You are guilty of the same sins Israel[m]
committed,
and you brought those sins to Jerusalem.[n]
14So you must give goodbye gifts
to Moresheth[o] in Gath.
The houses in Aczib[p] will trick
the kings of Israel.
15You people who live in Mareshah,[q]
I will bring someone against you who will
take the things you own.
The Glory of Israel
will come into Adullam.[r]

[a] 1:2 ***everyone on it*** Literally, "its fullness".
[b] 1:3 ***high places*** Here, this might mean simply "hills" or it might mean places of worship (see "HIGH PLACE" in the Word List).
[c] 1:5 ***nation*** Literally, "house". This might mean the royal family of that country.
[d] 1:9 ***Samaria*** The capital city of the northern kingdom of Israel.
[e] 1:10 ***Gath*** This is a wordplay. This name means "tell".
[f] 1:10 ***Acco*** This name means "cry".
[g] 1:10 ***Beth Ophrah*** This name means "house of dust".
[h] 1:11 ***Shaphir*** This name means "beautiful".
[i] 1:11 ***Zaanan*** This name means "come out".
[j] 1:11 ***Beth Ezel*** This name means "house of support".
[k] 1:12 ***Maroth*** This name means "bitter", "angry" or "sad".
[l] 1:13 ***Lachish*** This name is like the Hebrew word meaning "horse".
[m] 1:13 ***Israel*** Here, probably the northern kingdom of Israel centred in Samaria.
[n] 1:13 ***Jerusalem*** Literally, "Daughter Zion". See "ZION" in the Word List.
[o] 1:14 ***Moresheth*** Micah's home town.
[p] 1:14 ***Aczib*** This name means "lie" or "trick".
[q] 1:15 ***Mareshah*** The name means "a person who takes things".
[r] 1:15 ***Adullam*** A cave that David hid in when he ran away from Saul. See 1 Sam. 22:1.

[16]So cut off your hair, make yourself bald,[a]
    because you will cry for the children you
        love.
Make yourself bald like an eagle[b] and show
        your sadness,
    because your children will be taken away
        from you.

The Evil Plans of People

2 Trouble will come to those who make plans
    to sin.
    They lie on their beds making their evil
        plans.
Then when the morning light comes, they do
        what they planned,
    because they have the power to do what
        they want.
[2]They want fields, so they take them.
    They want houses, so they take them.
They cheat a man
    and take his house and his land.

The Lord's Plans to Punish the People

[3]That is why the Lord says:

"Look, I am planning trouble against this
    family.
    You will not be able to save yourselves.[c]
You will stop being proud,
    because bad times are coming.
[4]Then people will sing songs about you.
    They will sing this sad song:
'We are ruined!
    The Lord took away our land and gave it to
        other people.
Yes, he took my land away from me.
    He has divided our fields among our enemies.
[5]So we will not be able to measure the land
    and divide it among the Lord's people.'"

Micah Is Asked Not to Prophesy

[6]The people say, "Don't prophesy to us.
    Don't say those bad things about us.
    Nothing bad will happen to us."

[7]But people of Jacob,
    I must say these things.
The Lord is losing his patience
    because of the bad things you have done.
If you did what is right,
    I could say nice words to you.

[8]But you attack my people like enemies.
    You steal the clothes off the backs of people
        walking by.
They think they are safe,
    but you are there to treat them like
        prisoners of war.[d]
[9]You have taken nice houses
    away from the women of my people.
You have taken my wealth
    away from their small children forever.
[10]Get-up and leave!
    This will not be your place of rest, because
        you ruined it.
You made it unclean, so it will be destroyed!
    It will be a terrible destruction!

[11]These people don't want to listen to me.
    But if a man comes telling lies, they will
        accept him.
They would accept a false prophet if he comes
        and says,
    "There will be good times in the future,
        with plenty of wine and beer."

The Lord Will Bring His People Together

[12]"Yes, people of Jacob, I will bring all of you
    together.
I will bring together all those in Israel who
    are still living.
I will put them together like sheep in the
    sheep pen,
    like a flock in its pasture.
Then the place will be filled
    with the noise of many people.
[13]The 'One Who Breaks Through Walls' will
    push through and walk to the front of his
    people.
They will break through the gates and leave
    that city.
They will leave with their king marching
    before them—
    with the Lord at the front of his people."

The Leaders of Israel Are Guilty of Evil

3 Then I said, "Listen, leaders of Jacob and
    officers of the nation[e] of Israel!
    You should know what justice is.
[2]But you hate good and love evil.
    You tear the skin off the people
    and tear the flesh off their bones.
[3]You are destroying my people.[f]

---

[a] **1:16 cut . . . bald** This showed that a person made a special agreement with God or that a person was very sad.
[b] **1:16 eagle** Or "vulture". See "VULTURE" in the Word List.
[c] **2:3 save yourselves** Literally, "take your necks off it".
[d] **2:8 They think . . . war** Or "Returning from war, they think they are safe."
[e] **3:1 nation** Literally, "house". This might mean the royal family of that country.
[f] **3:3 You are destroying my people** Literally, "You who eat the flesh of my people."

JUDGEMENT AND DELIVERANCE

A white lie here. A little sin there. God doesn't really mind us sinning a little bit does he?

The bad news is the answer is "yes", God takes all our wrongdoing very seriously. But the good news is that God takes our sin so seriously that he did something about it through his Son, Jesus.

In Micah's day God's people, the Israelites, thought they were doing okay and ignored the warnings God sent them through the prophets. The nation was split between a northern and southern kingdom but they were united in one thing: like us today, the Israelite people kept on sinning against God.

DIG IN

READ Micah 2:1–13

- What was the particular sin of the people in verses 1–2? Why was God angry with them?
- Look at God's judgement of them in verses 3–5. How does the punishment fit the crime?

Pinching other people's land and homes was only the tip of the iceberg and God was very angry at the sin of the Israelites. Their religious leaders and prophets weren't helping the situation either.

- Take a close look at the language of verses 6–11. Why were the Israelite prophets so useless? What had they been saying about the people's sin and how God felt about it?
- How does the uselessness of the prophets match the godlessness of the people?

The split nation of Israel was about to be invaded by foreign armies. God would show them just how far they had wandered away from him and that he wouldn't tolerate their sin any more. He would also show them just how much he loved them with a promise of a rescue.

- Look at verse 12. How does the image of sheep in a pasture work as a picture of what God had planned for his people?
- Verse 13 is the clincher! Who is the "One Who Breaks Through Walls"? How would he be their king and the one who will save them?

DIG THROUGH

- The God of Micah and the Israelites is the same God of you and me today. How seriously do you think God takes sin in your life? How does our sin separate us from God?
- How did Jesus break open a way for you to know God again? How can you thank him for doing this?
- How does the story of Micah and the Israelites change the way you think about sin? If another Christian talks about sin and judgement, and it makes you feel uncomfortable, are you ever tempted to tell them to stop? If people at church never said anything challenging to you, would you ever wonder whether something was missing (2:6–7,11)?

DIG DEEPER

- Find out more about how seriously God takes our sin by checking out Romans 1:18–25, 3:23 and 6:23.
- To think more about the brilliant news of Jesus saving us from sin take a look at 1 Peter 3:18, Colossians 1:21–23 and Ephesians 2:1–10.

You take their skin off them and break their
bones.
You chop their bones up like meat to put in
the pot!
[4] Then you will pray to the LORD,
but he will not answer you.
No, he will hide his face from you,
because what you do is evil."

False Prophets

[5] Some false prophets are telling lies to the
Lord's people. This is what the LORD says about
them:

"These prophets are led by their stomachs.
They promise peace for those who give
them food,
but they promise war to those who do not
give them food.

[6] "This is why it is like night for you
and you don't have visions.
You cannot see what will happen in the
future,
so it is like darkness to you.
The sun has gone down on the prophets.
They cannot see what will happen in the
future,
so it is like darkness to them.
[7] The seers are ashamed;
the fortune-tellers are embarrassed.
None of them will say anything,
because God will not speak to them."

Micah Is an Honest Prophet of God

[8] But the LORD's Spirit has filled me
with power, goodness and strength.
So now I can tell Jacob what they have done
wrong.
I can tell Israel how they have sinned!

The Leaders of Israel Are to Blame

[9] Leaders of Jacob and rulers of Israel, listen
to me!
You hate the right way of living!
If something is straight,
then you make it crooked!
[10] You build Zion by murdering people.[a]
You build Jerusalem by cheating people!
[11] The judges in Jerusalem accept bribes
to help them decide who wins in court.
The priests in Jerusalem must be paid
before they will teach the people.

People must pay the prophets
before they will look into the future.
Then those leaders expect the LORD to help
them.
They say, "The LORD lives here with us,
so nothing bad will happen to us."

[12] Leaders, because of you, Zion will be
destroyed.
It will become a ploughed field.
Jerusalem will become a pile of rocks.
Temple Mount will be an empty hill[b]
overgrown with bushes.

The Law Will Come From Jerusalem

4 In the last days the mountain of the LORD's
Temple
will be on the highest of all mountains.
It will be raised higher than the hills.
There will be a steady stream of people
going there.
[2] People from many nations will go there
and say,
"Come, let's go up to the mountain of the
LORD,
to the Temple of the God of Jacob.
Then God will teach us his way of living,
and we will follow him."

His teaching, the LORD's message, will begin in
Jerusalem on Mount Zion
and will go out to all the world.
[3] Then God will act as judge to end arguments
between people in many places.
He will decide what is right for great
nations far and near.
They will stop using their weapons for war.
They will hammer their swords into
ploughs
and use their spears to make tools for
harvesting.
All fighting between nations will end.
They will never again train for war.
[4] They will sit under their own
grapevine and fig tree.
No one will make them afraid.
That is because the LORD All-Powerful said
it would happen like that.

[5] All the people from other nations follow their
own gods,
but we will follow the LORD our God for
ever and ever![c]

---

[a] 3:10 *murdering people* Literally, "bloodshed".
[b] 3:12 *empty hill* Or "high place", a term usually used for local shrines (places for worship) where people often worshipped idols.
[c] 4:5 Or "All the nations will walk in the name of their gods, but we will walk in the name of the LORD our God, for ever and ever!"

The Kingdom to Be Brought Back

⁶The LORD says, "At that time,
I will gather my people,
    the people I have punished.
I made them suffer far away from home.
    Like scattered sheep, they are hurt and lame.
    but I will bring them back.

⁷"Those left alive are hurt,
    but I will give them a new start.
They were forced to leave home,
    but I will make them a strong nation.
And I, the LORD, will be their king.
    and rule from Mount Zion forever.
⁸And you, Tower of Flocks,^a
    your time will come.
Ophel, hill of Zion,
    you will again have the right to rule.
Yes, the kingdom will be in Jerusalem
    as it was in the past."

Why Must the Israelites Go to Babylon?

⁹Now, why are you crying so loudly?
    Is your king gone?
Have you lost your wise leader?
    Is that why you are suffering like a woman
        in labour?
¹⁰Cry out, you people of Jerusalem,^b and feel
        the pain,
    as if you were giving birth.
You must go out of the city
    and live in the fields.
You will go away to Babylon,
    but you will also be saved from that place.
The LORD will come and rescue you there.
    He will take you away from your enemies.

The LORD Will Destroy the Other Nations

¹¹Many nations have come to fight against you.
    They say, "Look, there is Zion!
    Let's attack her!"

¹²They have their plans,
    but they don't know what the LORD is
        planning.
He brought them here for a special purpose.
    They will be crushed like grain on a
        threshing floor.

Israel Will Defeat Its Enemies

¹³"People of Jerusalem, get up and crush
        them!

I will make you very strong.
It will be as if you have horns of iron and
        hooves of bronze.
    You will beat many people into small pieces.
You will give their wealth to the LORD.
    You will give their treasure to the Lord of all
        the earth."

5 Now, strong city,^c gather your soldiers!
    Our enemies are attacking us!
They will strike Israel's ruler
    in the face with a stick.

> # INSIGHT
>
> *Micah prophesied that the Messiah
> would be born in Bethlehem. This would
> have been a surprise to God's people
> as Bethlehem was such a small town.
> They were expecting a powerful ruler to
> come to them from somewhere of more
> significance.*
>
> **Micah 5:2**

The Messiah to Be Born in Bethlehem

²You, Bethlehem Ephrathah, are the smallest
        town in Judah.
    But from you will come the one who will
        rule Israel for me.
His family began in ancient times.
    He is from days long ago.
³The Lord will let his people be defeated
    until the woman gives birth to her child,
        the promised king.
Then the rest of his brothers will come back
    to join the people of Israel.
⁴He will begin to rule Israel in the power of
        the LORD.
    Like a shepherd, he will lead his people in
        the wonderful name of the LORD his God.
And they will live in safety
    because then his greatness will be known
        all over the world.
⁵   He will bring a time of peace.

Yes, the Assyrian army will come into our
        country
    and march through our land.^d

---

^a **4:8 Tower of Flocks** Or "Migdal Eder". This probably means a part of Jerusalem. The leaders would be like shepherds in a tower watching their sheep.
^b **4:10 people of Jerusalem** Literally, "Daughter Zion", a name for Jerusalem. Also in verse 13. See "ZION" in the Word List.
^c **5:1 strong city** Literally, "daughter of troops", meaning Jerusalem.
^d **5:5 march . . . land** Or "trample our palaces".

But we have plenty of leaders[a]
    we can send against them.
[6]With swords in hand our leaders will defeat
    the Assyrians
    and rule the land of Nimrod.[b]
They[c] will save us from the Assyrians
    when they come into our land and march
    through our territory.
[7]But those from Jacob who are still living and
    scattered among the nations
    will be like dew from the LORD that does
    not depend on anyone.
They will be like rain on the grass
    that does not wait for anyone.
[8]Those from Jacob who are still living
    are scattered among the nations.
But they will be like a lion among the animals
    in the forest.
    They will be like a young lion among flocks
    of sheep.
If the lion passes through,
    he goes where he wants to go.
If he attacks an animal,
    no one can save it.
    The survivors will be like that.
[9]You will lift your hand against your enemies,
    and you will destroy them.

God Will Force His People to Depend on Him

[10]The LORD says, "At that time
    I will take away your horses,
    and I will destroy your chariots.
[11]I will destroy the cities in your country.
    I will pull down all your fortresses.
[12]You will no longer try to do magic.
    You will have no more fortune-tellers.
[13]I will destroy your statues of false gods.
    I will pull down your memorial stones.
    You will not worship what your hands have
    made.
[14]I will destroy the Asherah poles
    and your false gods.[d]
[15]In my anger I will take revenge
    on the nations that refuse to obey me."

The LORD's Complaint

6 Now hear what the LORD says:

"Present your argument to the mountains.
    Let the hills hear your story.[e]

[2]The LORD has a complaint against his people.
    Mountains, listen to the LORD's complaint.
Foundations of the earth, hear the Lord.
    He will prove that Israel is wrong!"

[3]He says, "My people, tell me what I did!
    Did I do something wrong against you?
    Did I make life too hard for you?
[4]I will tell you what I did.
    I sent Moses, Aaron and Miriam to you.
I brought you from the land of Egypt.
    I freed you from slavery.
[5]My people, remember the evil plans of Balak
    king of Moab.
    Remember what Balaam son of Beor said to
    Balak.
Remember what happened from Acacia to
    Gilgal,[f]
    and you will know the LORD is right!"

What Does God Want From Us?

[6]What must I bring when I come to meet with
    the LORD?
    What must I do when I bow down to God
    above?
Should I come to him with burnt offerings
    and a year-old calf?
[7]Will the LORD be pleased with a thousand
    rams
    or with ten thousand rivers of oil?
Should I offer him my first child to pay for my
    wrongs?
    Should I sacrifice my very own child for
    my sins?

INSIGHT

Ever wondered what God wants from his people? The Bible makes it clear through verses like this that God wants those who follow him to stand for justice, mercy and to follow him humbly and obediently.

Micah 6:8

[8]Human, the LORD has told you what
    goodness is.
    This is what he wants from you:

---

[a] **5:5 *plenty of leaders*** Literally, "seven shepherds, no eight leaders".
[b] **5:6 *land of Nimrod*** Another name for Assyria.
[c] **5:6 *They*** Literally, "He".
[d] **5:14 *false gods*** Or "cities".
[e] **6:1** This is like a court case. The mountains and hills are the judge and jury.
[f] **6:5 *Acacia to Gilgal*** This story is found in Num. 22 – 25.

When was the last time you got such an amazing present that you had no idea how you could say thank you properly? As Christians we are given the amazing gift of a brand new start and eternal life with Jesus. The incredible thing is that God doesn't need us to do anything about it other than to know him and enjoy him.

So is there any way we can say thank you to God?

The book of Micah is all about how the Israelites deserved God's judgement for rebelling against him. It's about how God will deliver them from the consequences of their sin. It's also about how they can say thank you to God for what he has done for them.

DIG IN

READ Micah 6:1–8

- Check out verses 1–5. How serious is the case against Israel? What is their crime? (Clue: look back to 2:1–2; 3:1–2,9–11 for extra help.)
- What had the people forgotten? Why was that so serious?
- When are you most tempted to forget what God has done for you?

Sometimes we forget exactly what God has done for us. In the busyness of life, school and everything else we can lose track of just how amazing Jesus' death and resurrection was. Sometimes our sin can make us forget how awesome God really is. Why not take five minutes to pray right now and thank God for what he has done for you through Jesus?

- In verses 6 and 7, Micah has his tongue firmly in his cheek! What kind of offerings does he suggest the Israelites could make to give thanks to God? Why won't they work?
- Check out verse 8. What do you think is an appropriate way to say thank you to God for what he has done?
- What does it mean to be fair to other people, love kindness and loyalty, and humbly obey your God? Take one at a time and think them through.

DIG THROUGH

The way we say thank you to God is to live as though our life really has been changed!

- How would your life look different this week if you acted fairly, loved kindness and loyalty and humbly obeyed God?
- What needs to change in your life? What needs to grow? Ask God to help you live in a way that pleases him this week.

DIG DEEPER

- If you want to get serious about living a godly life, 2 Timothy and Titus are really great books to read. You might also want to check out Isaiah 66:2 and Romans 12:1–2.

be fair to other people,
    love kindness and loyalty,
    and humbly obey your God.

What Were the Israelites Doing?

9The LORD shouts to the city:
"A wise person respects the Lord's name.a
    So pay attention to the punishing rod and to
    the one who uses it!b
10Do the wicked still hide treasures
    that they have stolen?
Do they still cheat people
    with baskets that are too small?
    Yes, all of this is still happening!
11Some people carry special weights
    that they use to cheat people when they
    weigh their goods.
    Should I pardon them?
12The rich in that city are still cruel.
    The people there still tell lies.
    Yes, they tell their lies.
13So I have begun to punish you.
    I will destroy you because of your sins.
14You will eat, but you will not become full.
    You will still be hungry and empty.c
You will try to bring people to safety,
    but people with swords will kill the people
    you rescued.
15You will plant your seeds,
    but you will not gather food.
You will try to squeeze oil from your olives,
    but you will not get any oil.
You will crush your grapes,
    but you will not get enough juice to have
    wine to drink.
16This is because you obey the laws of
    Omri.d
    You do all the evil things that Ahab's family
    does.
You follow their teachings,
    so I will let you be destroyed.
People will be amazed
    when they see your destroyed city.
Then you will bear the shame
    that the other nations bring to you."e

Micah Is Upset at the Evil People Do

7 I am upset because I am like fruit that has
    been gathered,
    like grapes that have already been picked.

There are no grapes left to eat.
    There are none of the early figs that I
    love.
2By this I mean that all the faithful people
    are gone.
There are no good people left.
Everyone is planning to kill someone.
    Everyone is trying to trap their brother.
3People are good at doing bad things with both
    hands.
    Officials ask for bribes.
Judges take money to change their decisions
    in court.
    "Important leaders" do whatever they want
    to do.
4Even the best of them is as crooked
    as a tangled thornbush.

The Day of Punishment Is Coming

Your prophets said this day would come,
    and the day of your watchmenf has
    come.
Now you will be punished.
    Now you will be confused!
5Don't trust your neighbour
    or trust a friend!
Don't even speak freely
    with your wife.
6Your enemies will be the people in your own
    house.
    A son will not honour his father.
A daughter will turn against her mother.
A daughter-in-law will turn against her
    mother-in-law.

The LORD Is the Saviour

7So I will look to the LORD for help.
    I will wait for God to save me.
    My God will hear me.
8I have fallen, but enemy, don't laugh
    at me!
    I will get up again.
I sit in darkness now,
    but the LORD will be a light for me.

The LORD Forgives

9I sinned against the LORD,
    so he was angry with me.
But he will argue my case for me in court.
    He will do what is right for me.

---

a 6:9 *the Lord's name* Literally, "your name".
b 6:9 *So pay attention . . . uses it* The Hebrew text is not clear.
c 6:14 *You . . . empty* The Hebrew text is not clear.
d 6:16 *Omri* A king of Israel who led his nation to worship false gods. See 1 Kgs 16:21–26.
e 6:16 *Then . . . you* Or "My people's shame will be taken away."
f 7:4 *watchmen* Another name for prophets. This shows that the prophets were like guards who stood on a city's wall and watched for trouble coming from far away.

Then he will bring me out into the light,
and I will see that he is right.
¹⁰My enemy said to me,
"Where is the LORD your God?"
But my enemy will see this,
and she will be ashamed.
At that time I will laugh at her.*ᵃ*
People will walk over her,*ᵇ* like mud in the
streets.

The Jews to Return

¹¹The time will come when your walls will be
rebuilt.
At that time the country will grow.
¹²Your people will come back to your land.
They will come back from Assyria and from
the cities of Egypt.
They will come from Egypt
and from the other side of the Euphrates
River.
They will come from the sea in the west
and from the mountains in the east.

¹³The land was ruined by the people
who lived there and by what they did.
¹⁴So rule your people with your rod.
Rule the flock of people who belong to you.
They live in the woods
and up on Mount Carmel.
They live in Bashan and Gilead
as they did in the past.

Israel Will Defeat Its Enemies

¹⁵I did many miracles when I took you out
of Egypt.
I will let you see more miracles like that.
¹⁶The nations will see those miracles,
and they will be ashamed.
They will see that their "power"
is nothing compared to mine.
They will be amazed
and put their hands over their mouths.
They will cover their ears
and refuse to listen.
¹⁷They will crawl in the dust like a snake.
They will shake with fear.
They will be like insects crawling
from their holes in the ground
and coming to the LORD our God.
God, they will fear
and respect you!

Praise for the LORD

¹⁸There is no God like you.
You take away people's guilt.
God will forgive his people who survive.
He will not stay angry with them forever,
because he enjoys being kind.
¹⁹He will come back and comfort us again.
He will throw all our sins into the deep sea.
²⁰God, please be true to Jacob.
Be kind and loyal to Abraham,*ᶜ*
as you promised our ancestors long ago.

ᵃ **7:10** *laugh at her* Literally, "my eyes will stare at her".
ᵇ **7:10** *enemy, laugh at her, walk over her* This probably refers to an enemy city, such as the capital of Edom.
ᶜ **7:20** *Abraham* Here, Abraham is used to mean all the people of Israel. See "ABRAHAM" in the Word List.

Who
"This book is the vision of Nahum from Elkosh," begins the book. (But we don't really know where Elkosh was.) His name means "comforter" and he was a contemporary of Zephaniah and a young Jeremiah.

 When
The book refers to the destruction of the Egyptian city of Thebes (3:8–10) which happened around 663 BC. And it points to the destruction of Nineveh which was to happen in 612 BC. So it must have been written between those times.

 What
The theme of the book is the destruction of Nineveh – and by Nineveh, Nahum means the entire Assyrian empire – an empire which was established through bloodshed, cruelty and widespread massacre.

When Jonah called the people of Nineveh to repentance a century earlier, the people responded and God spared them, but this time Nineveh would not repent.

The great emperor Sennacherib had transformed the city of Nineveh into the capital of his kingdom, with a magnificent palace, and surrounded by redirected rivers and a huge wall. But Nahum warns that soon the river gates will be flung open and panic will flood the palace (2:6).

Much of Nahum's prophecy is bringing "good news" to Judah, who could rejoice in the destruction of "those worthless troublemakers" (1:15).

God is depicted in Nahum as slow but sure. He is "patient" but he will not leave the guilty unpunished. Evil will not triumph. This cruel, oppressive empire will be destroyed; the city which had more merchants than "the stars in the sky" (3:16) will be blown away. The words of Nahum in 3:15, "the fire will destroy you", came to pass in 612 BC when the besieged emperor Sinshariskun set fire to his palace, while in it, rather than be captured.

 **NAHUM**

When God gets angry 1:1–6
The messenger is coming 1:7–15

Time's up! 2:1–13
Doom to the crime capital! 3:1–19

"The LORD is patient, but he is also very powerful! The LORD will punish the guilty; he will not let them go free. He will use whirlwinds and storms to show his power. People walk on the dusty ground, but he walks on the clouds."

Nahum 1:3

INSIGHT

Nineveh was the capital of Assyria but Nineveh here represents the whole Assyrian empire. The fall of this evil empire, so long predicted by the prophets, is now imminent.

Nahum 1:1

1 This book is the vision of Nahum from Elkosh. This is the sad message about the city of Nineveh.[a]

The LORD Is Angry at Nineveh

2The LORD is a jealous God.
    The LORD punishes the guilty,
        and he is very angry.
The LORD punishes his enemies,
    and he stays angry with them.
3The LORD is patient,
    but he is also very powerful!
The LORD will punish the guilty;
    he will not let them go free.
He will use whirlwinds and storms to show
        his power.
    People walk on the dusty ground, but he
        walks on the clouds.
4He will speak harshly to the sea, and it will
        become dry.
    He will dry up all the rivers.
The rich lands of Bashan and Carmel become
        dry and dead.
    The flowers in Lebanon fade away.
5The Lord will come,
    and the mountains will shake
        and the hills will melt away.
He will come,
    and the earth will shake with fear.
The earth and everyone on it
    will shake with fear.
6No one can stand against his great anger.
    No one can endure his terrible anger.
His anger will burn like fire.
    The rocks will shatter when he comes.
7The LORD is good.
    He is a safe place to go to in times of
        trouble.
    He takes care of those who trust him.
8But he will completely destroy his
        enemies.
    He will wash them away like a flood
        and chase them into the darkness.

9Why are you making plans against the
        LORD?
    He will bring complete destruction,
        so you will not cause trouble again.
10You will be destroyed completely
    like thornbushes burning under a pot.
You will be destroyed
    like dry weeds that burn quickly.
11Someone from Nineveh is making evil plans
        against the LORD.
    That advisor is a worthless troublemaker.

12This is what the LORD said:

"The people of Assyria are at full strength.
    They have many soldiers, but they will all
        be cut down.
    They will all be finished.
My people, I made you suffer,
    but I will make you suffer no more.
13Now I will set you free from the power of
        Assyria.
    I will take the yoke off your neck
        and tear away the chains holding you."

14King of Assyria, the LORD gave this command
        about you:
    "You will not have any descendants to wear
        your name.
I will destroy your carved idols
    and metal statues that are in the temple of
        your gods.
I am preparing your grave,
    because your end is coming soon!"[b]

15Judah, look!
    There, coming over the mountains, is a
        messenger bringing good news!
    He says there is peace.
Judah, celebrate your special festivals
    and do what you promised.
Those worthless troublemakers will not come
        through and attack you again.
    They have all been destroyed.

Nineveh Will Be Destroyed

2 An enemy is coming to attack you,
    so guard the strong places of your city.
    Watch the road.
Get ready for war.
    Prepare for battle!
2Yes, the LORD changed Jacob's pride.
    He made it like Israel's pride.
The enemy destroyed them
    and ruined their grapevines.

---

a 1:1 **Nineveh** The capital city of the country of Assyria. Assyria destroyed Israel in 722–721 BC.
b 1:14 **because your end is coming soon** Or "you are not important" or "you are so hated".

JUSTICE, AT LAST

"The LORD is good. He is a safe place to go in times of trouble. He takes care of those who trust him. But he will completely destroy his enemies. He will wash them away like a flood and chase them into the darkness" (Nahum 1:7–8).

These two verses capture the whole purpose of the short book of Nahum. It is a book written to bring comfort to God's beloved people and, at the same time, confront their enemies with God's fearsome judgement against them.

DIG IN
READ Nahum 1:1–15 and 3:1–4

- Why is the Lord angry with Nineveh (1:12–14; 3:1–4)?
- What judgement does he promise?

Around 150 years earlier, God had sent a message to Nineveh via his reluctant prophet Jonah (you can read his story in the book of the same name).

Nineveh was the capital of the Assyrian people, who were feared throughout the region as ruthless invaders and cruel oppressors. They were the global superpower and they liked showing their teeth. Through Jonah's mission, the city repented and changed its wicked ways and God mercifully chose to spare them. But the change of heart didn't last and over generations the city continued with its wickedness. Although the God we see in the Bible "does not become angry quickly" (Joel 2:13), time has run out for Nineveh and God must show judgement.

- Why do you think this would be good news for God's people?

God's people Israel have been watching, waiting and wondering when God was going to do something about this empire of terror. Those like Jonah, who were confused as to why God protected Nineveh last time, will finally see wickedness crushed and peace breaking out (Nahum 1:15).

More than that, they will again be comforted in the secure knowledge that God is in full control of history.

DIG THROUGH

- In what ways do we or other Christians around the world feel under oppressive regimes? Praise God that Christians don't need to take revenge to put things right – we can trust God that he will crush wickedness and bring peace (1:15). Why not read Psalm 9 and use it to praise God that he brings justice.
- Read Psalm 9:7–10, Isaiah 1:16–17, Jeremiah 7:5–6 and Micah 6:6–8. In what ways can our lifestyles demonstrate true justice? How can we keep from oppressing others, deliberately or accidentally? Here are some things to think about: is what we buy (especially food and clothes) helping or exploiting people in developing countries? What is our attitude towards immigrants living in our country? Are we using our influence positively to speak out for those in need?

DIG DEEPER

- Through Nahum we get to see how God is sovereign over all of history. He alone chooses which nations rise and which ones fall – and he can even make them do his bidding. So what's his overall purpose for our world? It's to prepare a people who belong to him, who bring him glory and will be united with his Son. Check out Ephesians 1:3–14.

³The shields of his soldiers are red.
   Their uniforms are bright red.
Their chariots are shining like flames of fire
   and are lined up for battle.
   Their horses are ready to go.
⁴The chariots race wildly through the streets
   and rush back and forth through the
      square.
They look like burning torches,
   like lightning flashing from place to place!

⁵The enemy calls for his best soldiers.
   They stumble as they rush ahead.
They run to the wall
   and set up their shield over the battering
      ram.
⁶But the gates by the rivers are open,
   and the enemy comes flooding in and
      destroys the king's palace.
⁷The enemy takes away the queen,
   and her slave girls moan sadly like doves.
   They beat their breasts to show their
      sadness.

⁸Nineveh is like a pool whose water
   is draining away.
People yell, "Stop! Stop running away!"
   But it does not do any good.

⁹Take the silver!
   Take the gold!
There are many things to take.
   There are many treasures.
¹⁰Now Nineveh is empty.
   Everything has been stolen.
   The city is ruined.
Its people have lost their courage.
   Their hearts melt with fear.
Their knees knock together,
   their bodies shake,
   and their faces turn pale.

¹¹Where is that great city now?
   It was like a den where the lions feed their
      young.
It was a place where people felt safe,
   like lions in a cave with no one there to
      harm them.
¹²The lion was able to catch plenty of food
   to feed his cubs and his mate.
He filled his cave with the animals he killed.
   He filled his den with the meat he gathered.

¹³The Lord All-Powerful says,
   "I am against you, Nineveh.

I will burn your chariots
   and kill your 'young lions' in battle.
   You will not hunt anyone on earth again.
People will never again hear bad news
   from your messengers."

Bad News for Nineveh

3 It will be very bad for that city of murderers.
   Nineveh is a city full of lies.
It is filled with things taken from other
      countries.
   It is filled with plenty of people that it
      hunted and killed.
²You can hear the sounds of whips
   and the noise of wheels.
You can hear horses galloping
   and chariots bouncing along!
³Soldiers on horses are attacking,
   their swords are shining,
   their spears are gleaming!
There are many dead people.
   Dead bodies are piled up—too many bodies
      to count.
   People are tripping over the dead bodies.
⁴All this happened because of Nineveh.
   Nineveh is like a prostitute who could
      never get enough.
   She wanted more and more.
She sold herself to many nations,
   and she used her magic to make them her
      slaves.

⁵The Lord All-Powerful says,
   "I am against you, Nineveh.
   I will pull your dress[a] up over your face.
I will let the nations see your naked body.
   The kingdoms will see your shame.
⁶I will throw dirty things on you
   and treat you in a hateful way.
   People will look at you and laugh.

INSIGHT

*When God said he would lift Nineveh's
dress up over her face and throw filth
at her he was referring to a punishment
that was used at that time to shame
prostitutes and adulteresses, showing
how angry he was at the evil the
Ninevites had done and that their time of
punishment was coming.*

Nahum 3:5–6

ᵃ **3:5 *pull your dress*** This is a wordplay in Hebrew. The Hebrew word also means "to destroy a country and take its people away as prisoners to other nations".

[7]Everyone who sees you will be shocked
and say,
'Nineveh is destroyed. Who will cry for her?'
I know I cannot find anyone to comfort
you, Nineveh."

[8]Nineveh, you are no better than Thebes[a] on the Nile River. Thebes also had water all around her to protect herself from enemies. She used that water like a wall too. [9]Ethiopia and Egypt made Thebes strong. Libya and the Sudan supported her, [10]but Thebes was defeated. Her people were taken away as prisoners to a foreign country. Soldiers beat her small children to death at every street corner. They threw lots to see who got to keep the important people as slaves. They put chains on all the important men of Thebes.

[11]So, Nineveh, you will also fall like a drunk. You will try to hide. You will look for a safe place away from the enemy. [12]But Nineveh, all your strong places will be like fig trees. When new figs become ripe, people come and shake the tree. The figs fall into their mouths. They eat them, and the figs are gone.

[13]Nineveh, your people are all like women, and the enemy soldiers are ready to take them. The gates of your land are open wide for your enemies to come in. Fire has destroyed the wooden bars across the gates.

[14]Get water and store it inside your city, because the enemy soldiers will surround your city. Make your defences strong! Get clay to make more bricks and mix the mortar. Get the moulds for making bricks. [15]You can do all these things, but the fire will still destroy you completely. And the sword will kill you. Your land will look as if a swarm of locusts came and ate everything.

Nineveh, you grew and grew. You became like a swarm of grasshoppers. You were like a swarm of locusts. [16]You have many traders who go to places and buy things. They are as many as the stars in the sky. They are like locusts that come and eat until everything is gone and then leave. [17]And your government officials are also like locusts that settle on a stone wall on a cold day. But when the sun comes up, the rocks become warm, and the locusts all fly away. And no one knows where.

[18]King of Assyria, your shepherds fell asleep. These powerful men are sleeping. And now your sheep have wandered away on the mountains. There is no one to bring them back. [19]Nineveh, you have been hurt badly, and nothing can heal your wound. Everyone who hears the news of your destruction claps their hands. They are all happy, because they all felt the pain you caused again and again.

---

[a] **3:8** *Thebes* A great city in Egypt. It was destroyed in 663 BC by the Assyrian army.

HABAKKUK

 Who
We don't know much about Habakkuk. It is thought that he was a contemporary of Jeremiah – maybe even of Ezekiel and Daniel – but he is not mentioned in any of their books.

 When
Habakkuk probably prophesied at the end of the seventh century BC – around the same time as Jeremiah. He predicts the Babylonian invasion of Judah and the attack on Jerusalem.

 What
Habakkuk lived in troubled times. Judah was in turmoil and everything was falling apart. So Habakkuk's question to God is simple: "Why are you allowing this to happen?"

The book is carefully structured. There are two "dialogues" between the prophet and God, where Habakkuk complains and the Lord responds. And then the book concludes with a prayer or psalm (chapter 3).

Habakkuk raises the same questions as Job, but from a slightly different perspective. Whereas Job asks, "How could you let this happen to me?" Habakkuk asks, "How could you let this happen to us?"

God replies that the Babylonians are coming to punish Judah – which isn't very comforting.

"That's not fair!" Habakkuk responds. "How can you use a wicked nation such as Babylon to punish those who are better than them?" Habakkuk tries to understand God's actions, which seem to him meaningless and mysterious.

God tells Habakkuk that Babylon too will fall; they will get their just deserts. He promises that one day he will punish all oppression and injustice.

The prophet responds with a moving and passionate declaration of faith. God is mighty and powerful – therefore the forces of darkness cannot succeed. God is just – therefore justice will be done in the end. Even though hard times are ahead, Habakkuk will trust in the Lord who will give him strength.

QUICK TOUR ▶ **HABAKKUK**

Habakkuk complains to God 1:1–4
God responds 1:5–11
The second complaint 1:12 – 2:1

God answers 2:2–20
Habakkuk's prayer 3:1–16
Always rejoice in the Lord 3:17–19

"The Lord GOD gives me my strength. He helps me run fast like a deer. He leads me safely on the mountains."

Habakkuk 3:19

Habakkuk Complains to God

1 This is the message that was given to Habakkuk the prophet.

²LORD, I continue to ask for help. When will you listen to me? I cried to you about the violence, but you did nothing! ³People are stealing things and hurting others. They are arguing and fighting. Why do you make me look at these terrible things? ⁴The law is weak and not fair to people. Evil people win their fights against good people. So the law is no longer fair, and justice does not win any more.

The LORD Answers Habakkuk

⁵"Look at the other nations! Watch them, and you will be amazed. I will do something in your lifetime that will amaze you. You would not believe it even if you were told about it. ⁶I will make the Babylonians*ᵃ* a strong nation. They are cruel and powerful fighters. They will march across the earth. They will take houses and cities that don't belong to them. ⁷The Babylonians will scare the other people. They will do what they want to do and go where they want to go. ⁸Their horses will be faster than leopards and more dangerous than wolves at sunset. Their horsemen will come from faraway places. They will attack their enemies quickly, like a hungry eagle swooping down from the sky. ⁹The one thing they want to do is fight. Their armies will march fast like the wind in the desert. And the Babylonian soldiers will take many prisoners—as many as the grains of sand.

¹⁰"The Babylonian soldiers will laugh at the kings of other nations. Foreign rulers will be like jokes to them. The Babylonian soldiers will laugh at the cities with tall, strong walls. They will simply build dirt roads up to the top of the walls and easily defeat the cities. ¹¹Then they will leave like the wind and go on to fight against other places. The only thing the Babylonians worship is their own strength."

Habakkuk's Second Complaint

¹²LORD, you are the one who lives forever!
    You are my holy God who never dies!*ᵇ*
LORD, you created the Babylonians to do what
    must be done.
Our Rock, you created them to punish
    people.
¹³Your eyes are too good to look at evil.

You cannot stand to see people doing wrong.
So why do you permit such evil?
    How can you watch while the wicked
        destroy people who are so much better?

¹⁴You made people like fish in the sea.
    They are like little sea animals without a
        leader.
¹⁵The enemy catches all of them with hooks
    and nets.
    The enemy catches them in his net and
        drags them in,
    and the enemy is very happy with what he
        has caught.
¹⁶His net helps him live like the rich
    and enjoy the best food.
So the enemy worships his net.
    He makes sacrifices and burns incense to
        honour his net.
¹⁷Will he continue to take riches with his net?
    Will he continue destroying people without
        showing mercy?

2 I will stand like a guard and watch.
    I will wait to see what the LORD will say
        to me.
I will wait and learn how he answers my
        questions.

INSIGHT

God told the Israelites to be patient and wait for the fall of Babylon. They had to wait 66 years until it happened – that puts some of the things we have to wait for into perspective doesn't it!

Habakkuk 2:3

God Answers Habakkuk

²The LORD answered me, "Write down what I show you. Write it clearly on a sign so that the message will be easy to read.*ᶜ* ³This message is about a special time in the future. This message is about the end, and it will come true. Just be patient and wait for it. That time will come; it will not be late. ⁴This message cannot help those who refuse to listen to it, but those who are good will live because they believe it.

ᵃ **1:6 Babylonians** Literally, "Chaldeans", a tribe of Arameans who gained control in Babylon. King Nebuchadnezzar was from this tribe.
ᵇ **1:12 LORD, you are . . . never dies** Or "LORD, you have been my holy God forever! Surely we will not die."
ᶜ **2:2 Write down . . . easy to read** Or "Write the vision clearly on tablets so that the person who reads it can run and tell other people."

A GOD WHO DOESN'T MAKE SENSE?

Have you ever found that things didn't go how you wanted them to? If not, I guarantee you it'll happen soon . . . Have you ever wanted to say to God, "God, sometimes you just don't make any sense!"?

DIG IN   READ Habakkuk 1:1–4

This whole book is a conversation between Habakkuk and God. Since the book is written as dialogue, why not try reading these verses out loud, as if you're asking God these questions as Habakkuk was? The book opens with a complaint.

- How do you think Habakkuk was feeling as he asked these questions?
- Make a list of each thing that Habakkuk was complaining about.
- Habakkuk was describing the people around him in Israel, thousands of years ago. How many of his complaints could you also make about people around the world today? Did you realize that you had so much in common with this strangely named man from so many years ago?

READ Habakkuk 1:5–11
In verse 6, we see God's response to Habakkuk: "I will make the Babylonians a strong nation." God is saying he is not going to leave the sin described in the first few verses unpunished – he is going to raise up a group of people to do the punishing. But . . .

- What kind of people are the Babylonians? Look again at verses 5–11 and write down all the words used to describe them.

READ Habakkuk 1:12 – 2:1
- Zoom in on verse 13. What does Habakkuk think of God's answer to his first complaint?
- In verses 14–17 how do you think Habakkuk is feeling as he addresses God?
- How does Habakkuk choose to deal with all of this (2:1)?

So, although Habakkuk cannot make any sense of what God is doing, he has still made the choice to trust him, even though he doesn't understand (or like) what's going on.

DIG THROUGH

I wonder if it surprised you how open Habakkuk was with God – he wasn't ashamed to say, more or less "God, do you really know what you're doing? Do you really care for us any more than you care about fish?" (vv.14–17). Lots of people think it's wrong to question God, but just like with any other relationship, it's easier to resolve things if everything is out in the open – God knows it all anyway.

- Is there something you need to talk to God about right now that you've never admitted to him? Something that makes you angry or bitter or just plain confused? Be honest with the compassionate God who loves you.
- Even in the midst of his confusion, Habakkuk chose to trust God and wait (2:1). He knows that God is trustworthy (take a look at how he describes him in 1:12). If you're finding trusting God hard right now, make a list of all the things you know about God that are good and make him trustworthy. If you can, add the relevant Bible verses. If you're stuck, start with the cross.

DIG DEEPER

- Habakkuk wasn't the only one to question God. Take a look at the book of Job to see another man who was bold enough to say, "God, sometimes you just don't make any sense!"

⁵"Wine can trick a person. In the same way a strong man's pride can fool him, but he will not find peace. He is like death—he always wants more and more. And, like death, he will never be satisfied. He will continue to defeat other nations and to make those people his prisoners. ⁶But soon enough, all those people will laugh at him and tell stories about his defeat. They will laugh and say, 'It's too bad that the man who took so many things will not get to keep them! He made himself rich by collecting debts.'

⁷"Strong man, you have taken money from people. One day they will wake up and realize what is happening, and they will stand against you. Then they will take things from you, and you will be very afraid. ⁸You have stolen things from many nations, so they will take much from you. You have killed many people and destroyed lands and cities. You have killed all the people there.

⁹"Look at you people! You get rich by cheating people, and it hurts your own family! You build your houses high on the cliffs to protect yourself from danger. ¹⁰You planned shameful things, and that will bring shame to your own family. You have done wrong, and it will cost you your life. ¹¹The stones of the walls will cry out against you. Even the wooden rafters*a* in your own house will prove that you are wrong.

¹²"Look at them! They kill people to build their city and do wicked things to make their walled city strong. ¹³But the LORD All-Powerful has decided that a fire will destroy everything that those people worked to build. All their work will be for nothing. ¹⁴Then people everywhere will know about the Glory of the LORD. This news will spread just as water spreads out into the sea. ¹⁵It will be very bad for those who become angry and make other people suffer. Like an angry drunk, they knock others to the ground and strip them naked, just to see their naked bodies.*b*

¹⁶"But they will know the Lord's anger. It will be like a cup of poison in the LORD's right hand. They will taste that anger, and then they will fall to the ground like drunks.

"Evil ruler, you will drink from that cup. You will get shame, not honour. ¹⁷You hurt many people in Lebanon and stole many animals there. So you will be afraid because of the people who died and because of the bad things you did to that country. You will be afraid because of what you did to those cities and to the people who lived there."

The Message About Idols

¹⁸Their false god will not help them, because it is only a statue that someone covered with metal. It is only a statue, so whoever made it cannot expect it to help. That statue cannot even speak! ¹⁹Look at them! They speak to a wooden statue and tell it, "Get up! Rescue me." They talk to a stone that cannot speak and say, "Wake up!" Don't you know those things cannot help you? That statue may be covered with gold and silver, but there is no life in it.

²⁰But the LORD is in his holy temple, so the whole earth should be silent in his presence and show him respect.

INSIGHT

There is a striking contrast between false idols and the living God here. False gods cannot be roused, though the people try desperately. It is reminiscent of Elijah's run in with the prophets of Baal (1 Kings 18).

Habakkuk 2:18–20

Habakkuk's Prayer

3 The prayer of Habakkuk the prophet.*c*

²LORD, I have heard the news about you.
   I am amazed, LORD, at the powerful things
      you did in the past.
Now I pray that you will do great things in
   our time.
   Please make these things happen in our
      own days.
But in your anger,
   remember to show mercy to us.   *Selah*

³God is coming from Teman.
   The Holy One is coming from Mount Paran.
       Selah

His glory covers the heavens,
   and his praise fills the earth!
⁴Rays of light shine from his hand, a bright,
   shining light.
   There is such power hiding in that hand.
⁵The sickness went before him,
   and the destroyer followed behind him.*d*

---

a **2:11 rafters** Boards that support the roof.

b **2:15 Like an angry drunk . . . bodies** The Hebrew text here is hard to understand.

c **3:1** The Hebrew text adds "according to *shigyonoth*", which may be an instruction for a special style of music.

d **3:5** This probably refers to the diseases and the angel of death that God sent against the Egyptians when God freed Israel from slavery.

⁶He stood and judged the earth.
>He looked at the people of all the nations,
>>and they shook with fear.
>For many years the mountains stood strong,
>>but those mountains fell to pieces.
>Those old, old hills fell down.
>>God has always been able to do that.

⁷I saw that the cities of Cushan were in
>>trouble
>>and that the houses of Midian trembled
>>with fear.
⁸LORD, were you angry at the rivers?
>Were you angry at the streams?
>Were you angry at the sea?
>>Were you angry when you rode your horses
>>and chariots to victory?

⁹Even then you showed your rainbow.
>It was proof of your agreement with the
>>families of the earth.ᵃ   *Selah*

And the dry land split the rivers.
¹⁰   The mountains saw you and shook.
>The water flowed off the land.
>The water from the sea made a loud noise
>>as it lost its power over the land.
¹¹The sun and the moon lost their brightness.
>They stopped shining when they saw your
>>bright flashes of lightning.
>That lightning was like spears and arrows
>>shooting through the air.
¹²In anger you walked on the earth
>and punished the nations.
¹³You came to save your people
>and to lead your chosen kingᵇ to victory.
>You killed the leader in every evil family,
>>from the least important person
>>to the most important in the land.ᶜ   *Selah*

¹⁴You used Moses' walking stick
>to stop the enemy soldiers.
>Those soldiers came

like a powerful storm to fight against us.
>They thought they could defeat us as easily
>>as robbing the poor in secret.
¹⁵But you marched your horses
>through the deep water, stirring up the
>>mud.
¹⁶My whole body shook when I heard the
>>story.
>My lips trembled.
>I felt weak deep down in my bones
>>and stood there shaking.
>But I will wait patiently for destruction to
>>come
>>to those who attack us.

INSIGHT

Habakkuk teaches something vital about worship. No matter what the circumstances, God is always worthy of praise.

Habakkuk 3:17–18

Always Trust in the LORD

¹⁷Figs might not grow on the fig trees,
>and grapes might not grow on the vines.
>Olives might not grow on the olive trees,
>>and food might not grow in the fields.
>There might not be any sheep in the pens
>>or cattle in the barns.
¹⁸But I will still be glad because I have the LORD;
>I will rejoice because I have God to protect
>>me.

¹⁹The Lord GOD gives me my strength.
>He helps me run fast like a deer.
>He leads me safely on the mountains.

To the music director. On my stringed
instruments.

ᵃ **3:9 rainbow . . . earth** See Gen. 9.
ᵇ **3:13 chosen king** Literally, "anointed one".
ᶜ **3:13 You killed . . . in the land** Literally, "You struck the head from the wicked house. From the foundation to the neck they were laid bare."

ZEPHANIAH

Who
Zephaniah, son of Cushi, was a distant member of the royal family; his great-great-grandfather was King Hezekiah. He would have been of considerable social standing, which makes his message all the more shocking.

When
Zephaniah worked just before Jeremiah. He prophesied during the reign of King Josiah (640–609 BC), who bought spiritual revival to Judah, probably in the early part of his reign.

What
The theme of the book is universal judgement. Judah was to be judged. And those who were following false gods would face the judgement of the one, true God if they did not repent. It also foretells the judgement of many of their neighbours.

The northern kingdom of Israel had already been swept away in 722 BC by the Assyrian empire. When Zephaniah talks about "Israel" therefore, he is talking about what is left of the once-great nation of Solomon and David: the state of Judah, clustering around the city of Jerusalem.

Zephaniah talks about "the LORD's special day". The people of Judah believed that this would be their moment, the day when the Lord would wipe out all their enemies. But Zephaniah tells them that Judah too will get what it deserves; there will be blessing for those who follow him, but punishment for those who have followed other paths.

Zephaniah prophesied during the reign of King Josiah, who was the last great king of Judah – a good king and a reformer (2 Kings 22:1 – 23:30; 2 Chronicles 34 – 35). This raises the possibility that Zephaniah himself might have been that even rarer thing – a prophet who was listened to.

QUICK TOUR ▶ **ZEPHANIAH**

Judgement on Judah 1:1–7
The day of the Lord is near 1:8–18
Change your lives 2:1–3

Judgement on Judah's enemies 2:4–15
Turn to the Lord 3:1–8
Joy and restoration 3:9–20

"All you humble people, come to the LORD! Obey his laws. Learn to do good things. Learn to be humble. Maybe then you will be safe when the LORD shows his anger."

Zephaniah 2:3

1

This is the message that the LORD gave to Zephaniah. He received this message during the time that Josiah son of Amon was king of Judah. Zephaniah was the son of Cushi, who was the son of Gedaliah. Gedaliah was the son of Amariah, who was the son of Hezekiah.

The LORD's Day for Judging the People

²The LORD says, "I will destroy everything on earth.ᵃ ³I will destroy all the people and all the animals. I will destroy the birds in the air and the fish in the sea. I will destroy the evil people and everything that makes them sin. I will remove all people from the earth." This is what the LORD said.

⁴"I will punish Judah and the people living in Jerusalem. I will remove from this place any signs of Baal worship. No one will remember the priests who serve the idols there. ⁵And those who go up on their roofs to worship the starsᵇ will be forgotten. They worship me, the LORD, but they also use the name of the false god Milcom to make promises. ⁶They have turned away from me, the LORD. They have stopped following me. They no longer ask me, the LORD, for help."

⁷Be silent before the Lord GOD, because the LORD's day for judging the people is coming soon. The LORD has prepared his sacrifice, and he has told his invited guests to get ready.ᶜ

⁸The Lord said, "On the LORD's day of sacrifice, I will punish the king's sons and other leaders. I will punish all the people wearing clothes from other countries. ⁹At that time I will punish all the people who jump over the thresholdᵈ and those who fill their master's houseᵉ with lies and violence."

¹⁰The LORD also said, "At that time people will be calling for help at Fish Gate in Jerusalem and mourning in the new part of town. They will hear the sound of destruction in the hills around the city. ¹¹You people living in the lower part of town will cry, because all the traders and rich merchants will be destroyed.

¹²"At that time I will take a lamp and search through Jerusalem. I will find all those who are satisfied to live their own way. They say, 'The LORD does nothing. He does not help, and he does not hurt!' I will find them, and I will punish them. ¹³Then others will take their wealth and destroy their houses. Those who built houses will not live in them, and those who planted vineyards will not drink the wine from the grapes."

¹⁴The LORD's special day for judging is coming soon! It is near and coming fast. People will hear very sad sounds on the LORD's special day of judgement. Even strong soldiers will cry. ¹⁵The Lord will show his anger at that time. It will be a time of terrible troubles and a time of destruction. It will be a time of darkness—a black, cloudy and stormy day. ¹⁶It will be like a time of war when people hear horns and trumpets in the defence towers and protected cities.

INSIGHT

It's easy to put our trust in money and think it makes us safe and secure, but Zephaniah warns the sinful people that no amount of silver or gold can save them from God's wrath.

Zephaniah 1:18

¹⁷The Lord said, "I will make life very hard on the people. They will walk around like the blind who don't know where they are going. That will happen because they sinned against the LORD. Their blood will be spilled on the ground. Their dead bodies will lie like dung on the ground. ¹⁸Their gold and silver will not help them! At that time the Lord will become very upset and angry. The LORD will destroy the whole world!ᶠ He will completely destroy everyone on earth!"

God Asks People to Change Their Lives

2

Shameless people, change your lives ²before you become like a dry and dying flower. In the heat of day, a flower will wilt and die. You will be like that when the LORD shows his terrible anger. So change your lives before the LORD shows his anger against you! ³All you humble people, come to the LORD! Obey his laws. Learn to do good things. Learn to be humble. Maybe then you will be safe when the LORD shows his anger.

ᵃ **1:2 earth** Or "the land" or "the country". Also in verse 18.
ᵇ **1:5 stars** Literally, "army of heaven". This might mean the stars and planets or the angels.
ᶜ **1:7 prepared . . . get ready** Literally, "prepared his sacrifice. He has made his called ones holy." Here, this time of judgement is compared to a fellowship meal when priests offered a sacrifice to God and had the guests get ready for this special meal with God.
ᵈ **1:9 people wearing . . . threshold** This probably means the priests and people who worshipped foreign gods, such as Dagon or people who copied their ways of worshipping. See 1 Sam. 5:5.
ᵉ **1:9 master's house** This means the temple where the people worshipped God or their false gods.
ᶠ **1:18 world** Or "land" or "country".

JUDGEMENT AND HOPE

Many people flippantly talk about "the end of the world" as if it's something that will never really happen. Far from a science fiction fantasy, the Bible tells us that there will be a day when this world will come to an end. This book is about that day.

DIG IN

READ Zephaniah 1:1 - 3:7

- What are some of the things that God is angry about? Take a look in particular at 1:4–6,12–13; 2:3,15; 3:1–7.

Nowadays we don't hear about people worshipping Baal or the stars so much (1:4–6) but idol worship is something that we all do every day. An idol is anything which is given more importance than God in our lives, and we are all guilty of putting more energy, time and emotion into other things. People might pursue popularity, money, that perfect relationship or a dream career. The possibilities are endless. The theologian John Calvin went as far as to say "our hearts are idol factories".

- In today's terms, which people do you think God would be angry with? Would you be one of them? It's perhaps easy to think that this is about "them back then" and not "me now". If you're in any doubt, take a look at Romans 3:10–18.
- What positive qualities is God looking for in his people (2:3)?
- List a few of the ways that God says he will express his anger.

This is a scary book to read – God is very explicit about the fact that he takes sin very seriously, and that one day he will show his anger and judge all of humanity. Read on, however, as that's not the whole story.

READ Zephaniah 3:8–20

- What reason and purpose does God give for punishing his people? What is a consequence of this (v.9)?

God's anger has been shown very clearly so far, but that's not the only aspect of his character. Here we get a glimpse of the fact that even in his anger he has a loving purpose – to bring people to repentance. Even when he's punishing sin, he manages to do something loving: he brings people back into a relationship with him. The result is the wonderful relief expressed in the final 7 verses. "The LORD stopped your punishment" (v.15) not because of the people's merit (as chapters 1 and 2 show) but because God's character is merciful and kind even in the face of such rebellion.

DIG THROUGH

- The cross of Jesus is the place where we ultimately see God's anger and God's mercy shown in equal measure. Let the book of Zephaniah help you to meditate on how strongly God feels about our rebellion, and how shockingly undeserved and wonderful is the mercy that he shows us.
- Do you believe that because of Christ, God feels like this about you: "He will show how much he loves you and how happy he is with you" (3:17)? Remember these verses in chapter 3 are about the rebellious people in chapters 1 and 2, so you can be confident that, however good or bad you've been, God is happy with you.

DIG DEEPER

- The book of Revelation gives an account of the vision God gave to John of the final judgement. You can find it in Revelation 20 – 21.

The LORD Will Punish Israel's Neighbours

⁴No one will be left in Gaza. Ashkelon will be destroyed. By noon, the people will be forced to leave Ashdod. Ekron*ᵃ* will be empty.*ᵇ* ⁵You people living by the sea, who came from Crete,*ᶜ* this message from the LORD is about you. Canaan, land of the Philistines, you will be destroyed—no one will live there! ⁶Your land by the sea will become empty fields for shepherds and their sheep. ⁷Then the land will belong to the survivors from Judah. The LORD their God will remember the people from Judah and restore their fortunes. Then they will let their sheep eat the grass in those fields. In the evenings they will lie down in the empty houses of Ashkelon.

⁸The Lord says, "I know what the people of Moab and Ammon did. They embarrassed my people. They took their land to make their own countries larger. ⁹So, as surely as I am alive, Moab and the people of Ammon will be destroyed like Sodom and Gomorrah. I am the LORD All-Powerful, the God of Israel, and I promise that those countries will be destroyed completely forever. Their land will be overgrown with weeds. It will be like the land covered with salt by the Dead Sea. The survivors of my people will take that land and everything left in it."

INSIGHT

Ever felt alone when someone has insulted you? God reacts pretty strongly when his people are mocked – in fact he threatens to destroy those who are arrogant enough to criticize them.
Zephaniah 2:8–9

¹⁰This will happen to the people of Moab and Ammon because they were so proud and cruel and humiliated the people of the LORD All-Powerful. ¹¹They will be afraid of the LORD, because he will destroy their gods. Then everyone in all the faraway lands will worship the Lord. ¹²People of Ethiopia, this even means you! The Lord's sword will kill your people. ¹³Then the Lord will turn north and punish Assyria. He will destroy Nineveh—that city will be like an empty, dry desert. ¹⁴Only sheep and wild animals will live in those ruins. Owls and crows will sit on the columns that are left standing. Their calls will be heard coming through the windows. Crows will sit on the doorsteps. Black birds*ᵈ* will make their homes in those empty houses. ¹⁵Nineveh is so proud now. It is such a happy city. The people think they are safe. They think Nineveh is the greatest place in the world, but it will be destroyed! It will be an empty place where only wild animals go to rest. People who pass by will whistle and shake their heads when they see how badly the city was destroyed.

INSIGHT

Ethiopia and Assyria were at the extreme north and south of the known world at that time. It illustrates the breadth of God's judgement.
Zephaniah 2:12–14

The Future of Jerusalem

3 O Jerusalem, city full of sin! You have turned against God and mistreated your own people. ²Your people don't listen to me or accept my teaching. They don't trust the LORD. They don't show any need for God. ³The leaders are as frightening as roaring lions. The judges are like hungry wolves that hunt at night and by dawn have eaten everything. ⁴The prophets there are always making secret plans to get more and more. The priests don't show respect for what is holy. They disobey God's teachings. ⁵But the LORD is still in that city, and he does what is right. He does not mistreat anyone. Every day he makes good decisions for them. Not a day passes without his justice. But those who are wicked keep on sinning without feeling any shame. Now the Lord says to his people,

⁶"I have destroyed nations, tearing down their defence towers. Their streets are in ruins, and no one goes there any more. Their cities are empty; no one lives there. ⁷I thought this would make you respect me. I thought you would change and do what I wanted. Then I would not destroy your city. I would not punish you the way I planned. But you wanted only one thing: to continue doing nothing but evil!"

⁸The LORD said, "So just wait! Wait for me to stand and judge you. I have the right to bring

---

ᵃ **2:4** *Gaza, Ashkelon, Ashdod, Ekron* Philistine cities. In Hebrew, Zephaniah is making wordplays on the names of these cities.
ᵇ **2:4** *empty* In Hebrew this word is like the word meaning "Philistines". Also in verse 6.
ᶜ **2:5** *people . . . from Crete* Probably the Philistines, who came from the island of Crete.
ᵈ **2:14** *Black birds* Or "cedar beams".

people from many nations and use them to punish you. I will use them to show my anger against you. I will use them to show how upset I am, and the whole country will be destroyed. ⁹Then I will change people from other nations so that they can speak the language clearly and call out the name of the LORD. They will all worship me together, shoulder to shoulder, as one people. ¹⁰People will come all the way from the other side of the river in Ethiopia. My scattered people will come to me. My worshippers will come and bring their gifts to me.

¹¹"Then, Jerusalem, you will no longer be ashamed of the wrong things your people do against me. That is because I will remove all the bad people from Jerusalem. I will take away all the proud people. There will not be any of them on my holy mountain.ᵃ ¹²I will let only meek and humble people stay in my city, and they will trust the LORD's name. ¹³The survivors of Israel will not do bad things or tell lies. They will not try to trick people with lies. They will be like sheep that eat and lie down in peace—and no one will bother them."

A Happy Song

¹⁴Jerusalem, sing and be happy!
    Israel, shout for joy!
    Jerusalem, be happy and have fun!
¹⁵The LORD stopped your punishment.
    He destroyed your enemies' strong towers.

King of Israel, the LORD is with you.
    You don't need to worry about anything bad
      happening.
¹⁶At that time Jerusalem will be told,
    "Be strong, don't be afraid!
¹⁷The LORD your God is with you.
    He is like a powerful soldier.
    He will save you.
He will show how much he loves you
    and how happy he is with you.
He will laugh and be happy about you,
¹⁸   like people at a party.
I will take away your shame.
    I will make them stop hurting you.ᵇ
¹⁹At that time I will punish those who hurt
      you.
    I will save my hurt people
    and bring back those who were forced to
      leave.
I will give them praise and honour
    everywhere,
    even in places where they suffered shame.
²⁰At that time I will lead you back home.
    I will bring your people back together.
I will cause people everywhere to honour and
    praise you.
    You will see me bring back all the blessings
    you once had."

This is what the LORD said.

ᵃ **3:11** *holy mountain* Mount Zion, one of the mountains Jerusalem was built on.
ᵇ **3:18** The Hebrew text is not clear.

Who
We don't know anything about Haggai other than that he was an exile in Babylon and returned to Jerusalem in the second wave of returnees, and that he was a contemporary of Zechariah.

When
We can date the book of Haggai with amazing precision. Haggai had four visions, all in the second year of the reign of King Darius (520 BC). He says they were on the first day of the sixth month, the twenty-first day of the seventh month, and the twenty-fourth day of the ninth month (when he had two visions).

What
It's 520 BC. The Jews who had been in exile in Babylon have been allowed to return home to Jerusalem. But life is hard. They started to rebuild the Temple but soon gave up; the Temple is still in ruins.

When Babylon was captured by Cyrus the Great (559–530 BC), the excited exiles were allowed to return to Jerusalem and re-inhabit the land. Then reality set in. Weariness and hardship, combined with local opposition, had led to the abandonment of the Temple rebuilding project. Haggai's job is to encourage the people of God to renew their efforts.

In his first message he warns Israel to reconsider its priorities; to lay aside economic concerns and to focus on the worship of the Lord. The Temple is more than a building project; it is a sign that the land will be dedicated to God.

A month later, when the people's initial enthusiasm has worn off and they are discouraged that this Temple won't be as magnificent as Solomon's Temple, Haggai encourages them to dream and imagine what it could be like. He promises that God will help them.

Two months after that he gives two prophecies: one urging the priests to keep holy and free from sin and the other for Zerubbabel, telling him of his special status and that the Lord would bless him.

QUICK TOUR ➤ **HAGGAI**

Rebuild the Temple 1:1–11
Work begins 1:12–15
Promises of glory 2:1–9

Promises of blessing 2:10–19
The Lord's signet ring 2:20–23

"But the LORD says, 'Zerubbabel, don't be discouraged!' And the LORD says, 'Joshua son of Jehozadak, you are the high priest. Don't be discouraged! And all you people who live in the land, don't be discouraged! Continue this work, because I am with you.' This is what the LORD All-Powerful said. 'I made an agreement with you when you left Egypt, and I have kept my promise. My Spirit is with you, so don't be afraid!'"

Haggai 2:4–5

It Is Time to Build the Temple

1 On the first day of the sixth month of the second year that Darius was king of Persia, Haggai received a message from the LORD. This message was for Zerubbabel son of Shealtiel and Joshua son of Jehozadak. Zerubbabel was the governor of Judah and Joshua was the high priest. This is the message: ²This is what the LORD All-Powerful said, "The people say it is not yet the right time to build the LORD's Temple."

³Again Haggai received a message from the LORD. Haggai spoke this message: ⁴"You people think the right time has come for you to live in nice houses. You live in houses with beautiful wooden panelling on the walls, but the Lord's house is still in ruins. ⁵Now the LORD All-Powerful says, 'Think about what is happening. ⁶You have planted many seeds, but you have gathered only a few crops. You have food to eat, but not enough to get full. You have something to drink, but not enough to get drunk. You have some clothes to wear, but not enough to keep warm. You earn a little money, but you don't know where it all goes. It's as though there is a hole in your pocket!'"*ᵃ*

⁷The LORD All-Powerful said, "Think about what you are doing. ⁸Go up to the mountains, get the wood, and build the Temple. Then I will be pleased with the Temple, and I will be honoured." This is what the LORD said.

INSIGHT

The Israelites had got their priorities wrong. They put their own needs ahead of God's and so didn't reap any rewards for their work. In the New Testament Jesus tells his followers to put God's kingdom first, and then all their needs will be looked after (see Matthew 6).

Haggai 1:9

---

⁹The LORD All-Powerful said, "You people look for a big harvest, but when you go to gather the crop, there is only a little grain. So you bring that grain home, and then I send a wind that blows it all away. Why is this happening? Because my house is still in ruins while each of you runs home to take care of your own house. ¹⁰That is why the sky holds back its dew and why the earth holds back its crops.

¹¹"I gave the command for the land and the mountains to be dry. The grain, the new wine, the olive oil and everything the earth produces will be ruined.*ᵇ* All the people and all the animals will become weak."

Work Begins on the New Temple

¹²The LORD God had sent Haggai to speak to Zerubbabel son of Shealtiel and to the high priest, Joshua son of Jehozadak. So these men and all the people listened to the voice of the LORD their God and to the words of Haggai the prophet. And the people showed their fear and respect for the LORD their God.

¹³Then Haggai, the LORD's messenger, delivered this message to the people: "The LORD says, 'I am with you!'"

¹⁴Zerubbabel son of Shealtiel was the governor of Judah. Joshua son of Jehozadak was the high priest. The LORD made them and the rest of the people excited about working on the Temple of their God, the LORD All-Powerful. ¹⁵So they began this work on the twenty-fourth day of the sixth month in the second year Darius was the king.

The LORD Encourages the People

2 On the twenty-first day of the seventh month, this message from the LORD came to Haggai: ²"Speak to Zerubbabel son of Shealtiel, the governor of Judah, and to Joshua son of Jehozadak, the high priest, and to all the people. Say this: ³'How many of you people look at this Temple and try to compare it to the beautiful Temple that was destroyed? What do you think? Does this Temple seem like nothing when you compare it with the first Temple? ⁴But the LORD says, "Zerubbabel, don't be discouraged!" And the LORD says, "Joshua son of Jehozadak, you are the high priest. Don't be discouraged! And all you people who live in the land, don't be discouraged! Continue this work, because I am with you!" This is what the LORD All-Powerful said!

⁵"'I made an agreement with you when you left Egypt, and I have kept my promise. My Spirit is with you, so don't be afraid!' ⁶This is what the LORD All-Powerful said, 'In just a little while, I will once again shake things up. I will shake heaven and earth, and I will shake the sea and the dry land. ⁷I will shake up the nations, and they will come to you with wealth from every nation. And then I will fill this Temple with glory.' That is what the LORD All-Powerful said! ⁸'All their silver really belongs to me! And all the gold is mine!' This is what the LORD All-Powerful said. ⁹And the

---

ᵃ 1:6 You . . . pocket Or "The one who saves money is putting it into a purse full of holes."
ᵇ 1:11 dry . . . ruined The Hebrew word "dry" is like the Hebrew word "ruined".

THE LORD'S HOUSE

What would you think of someone who bought a ticket at a railway station and then started assembling Ikea flat-pack furniture and nailing paintings to the walls as if they were moving in? You'd probably think they'd lost their mind – why invest so much in a place where you're staying for such a short time, when you have a ticket for a completely different destination? It's a bit like this when we invest all our energy in earthly things, and not in the things of God and heaven. Haggai's contemporaries fell into a similar trap . . .

DIG IN

READ Haggai 1:1–11

Before we go on, we need to understand the significance of the Temple. In Old Testament times, the Temple symbolized God living with his people, and its existence also symbolized a commitment to him – they would have to put time, energy and resources into building it – all of which they could easily have been tempted to use on themselves.

"The people say it is not yet the right time to build the LORD's Temple" (v.2).

- What does this statement about what "the people say" tell us about their commitment to their relationship with God?
- What do verses 3 and 4 add to this picture?
- What are the consequences of this (vv.5–6)?
- Why is this the consequence (v.7–11)?

God tells his people through Haggai that there is a direct correlation between their behaviour and their blessings – if they give him the honour he's due, he'll bless them and give them everything they need and more.

READ Haggai 1:12–15
- What was the people's response to God's message (v.12)?
- How does God respond to their response?

In their fear and in light of their behaviour, the people might have expected God to say "I am against you". However, God has responded to their repentance. He had withheld his blessings only to bring them closer to him. So even this demonstration of his anger is ultimately a demonstration of his love.

READ Haggai 2:1–9
Many of the people rebuilding or witnessing the rebuilding of the Temple would still be able to remember the last time such a Temple was built (Ezra 3:12). In addition to this discouragement, the Temple builders also met with a lot of local opposition that eventually caused the building work to stop (Ezra 4:1–5).

- What is God's response to their discouragement and fear of opposition (Haggai 2:4)?
- How do they know that God means it (v.5)?
- God's word is really powerful – if you check out Ezra 5:1–2 you will see how!

DIG THROUGH

- "You live in houses with beautiful wooden panelling on the walls, but the LORD's house is still in ruins" (1:4). In what ways might your own life be described in this way – have you gradually slipped into investing more time, money and energy in selfish ways at the cost of getting closer to God? God longs to be in a relationship with you and that will get richer and richer the more you invest in him.

L ORD All-Powerful said, 'This last Temple will be more beautiful than the first one, and I will bring peace to this place.' Remember, this is what the L ORD All-Powerful said."

Today Begins a Time of Blessing

¹⁰On the twenty-fourth day of the ninth month in the second year Darius was king of Persia, this message from the L ORD came to Haggai the prophet: ¹¹"The L ORD All-Powerful commands you to ask the priests what the law says about these things: ¹²'Suppose a man carries some meat in the fold of his clothes. This meat is part of a sacrifice, so it is holy. If his clothes touch some bread, cooked food, wine, oil or some other food, will the thing the clothes touch become holy?'"

The priests answered, "No."

¹³Then Haggai said, "Whoever touches a dead body will become unclean. Now if they touch anything else, will it also become unclean?"

The priests answered, "Yes, it will become unclean."

¹⁴Then Haggai said, "This is what the L ORD God said: 'This is also true about the people of this nation. They were not pure and holy before me. So anything they did with their hands and anything they offered at the altar became unclean. ¹⁵'Think about what has happened to you. Think about how things were before you began working on the L ORD's Temple. ¹⁶People wanted 200 kilogrammes of grain, but there were only 100 in the pile. People wanted to get 100 litres of wine from the vat, but there were only 40. ¹⁷That was because I punished you. I sent the diseases that killed your plants and the hail that destroyed the things you made with your hands. I did this, but still you did not come to me.' This is what the L ORD said.

¹⁸"The Lord said, 'Today is the twenty-fourth day of the ninth month. You have finished laying the foundation of the L ORD's Temple. So notice what happens from this day forward. ¹⁹Your seed for planting is still in the barn. And look at the vines, the fig trees, and the pomegranate and olive trees. They have not yet produced any fruit. But beginning today, I will bless you.'"

INSIGHT

A signet ring was engraved with the king's seal and used to stamp official documents. It was a symbol of authority. Zerubbabel had been given authority by God; God's stamp of approval.

Haggai 2:23

²⁰Another message from the L ORD came to Haggai on the twenty-fourth day of the month. This is the message: ²¹"Go to Zerubbabel, the governor of Judah and tell him that I will shake heaven and earth. ²²And I will overthrow many kings and kingdoms and destroy the power of the kingdoms of those other people. I will destroy their chariots and their riders. I will defeat their war horses and riders. These armies are friends now, but they will turn against each other and kill each other with swords." ²³This is what the L ORD All-Powerful says: "Zerubbabel son of Shealtiel, my servant, I have chosen you. I, the L ORD, tell you that at that time I will use you like a signet ring to represent my authority!"

This is what the L ORD All-Powerful said.

ZECHARIAH

Who
Zechariah was the son of Berekiah and grandson of Iddo – possibly the Iddo who returned from exile in 538 BC (Nehemiah 12:4). He was probably a priest and was a contemporary of Haggai.

When
Zechariah's first vision occurred about mid-October, 520 BC, right around the time that Haggai was prophesying. His work continued for at least two years until 518 BC (7:1).

What
Faced with demoralized people in a damaged city, Zechariah inspires the people to see the Temple through to completion. Like Haggai, he urges the people to rebuild the Temple and to live in accordance with God's commands.

Much of the city of Jerusalem is still in ruins; to its inhabitants it is an insignificant place. Far from seeing the day of the Lord, they appear to be witnessing only the "small beginnings" (4:10). God seems very far away – as far away as the glory days of Solomon and David. Zechariah reminds his listeners that there is more going on. When the time is right, God will step in. If people do what is right, Jerusalem will once again be a place of pilgrimage and faith (Zechariah 1:14–17).

Few books of the Bible are as difficult to interpret as Zechariah – it's right up there with Revelation. The first part contains eight strange visions. The second section consists of a series of messages to Israel and its leaders as well as a final, awe-inspiring vision of the far-future.

Ultimately the Lord's commitment to his people will be demonstrated by the arrival of a special person, a ruler for Jerusalem who will not be like any of the other rulers, but will bring peace and salvation. He will be a good shepherd; he will look after his flock. He will cleanse them of their sins. And yet, strangely, the flock will turn on him and reject him and the sheep will be scattered. No prophet has more to say about the Messiah, or points more clearly to Jesus. Zechariah saw a wounded king, a shepherd for whom all creation was waiting. He saw what was coming and his excitement and awe is found on virtually every line.

No wonder the New Testament authors saw in Zechariah many prophecies about Jesus. According to one estimate the New Testament refers to 54 passages from Zechariah. Much of the imagery in Zechariah reappears in Revelation.

QUICK TOUR  **ZECHARIAH**

Back to God 1:1–17
Plumb line 2:1–13
Ruling branch 6:9–15
Did you do it for me? 7:1–14

Enemies punished 8:1–23
Wounded shepherd 13:7–9
Streams of life 14:1–21

"This is what the LORD All-Powerful said: 'You must do what is right and fair. You must be kind and show mercy to each other. Don't hurt widows and orphans, foreigners or poor people. Don't even think of doing bad things to each other!'"

Zechariah 7:8–10

The LORD Wants His People to Return

1 Zechariah son of Berekiah received a message from the LORD. This was in the eighth month of the second year that Darius[a] was king in Persia. (Zechariah was the son of Berekiah, who was the son of Iddo the prophet.) This is that message:

²The LORD became very angry with your ancestors. ³So you must tell the people what the LORD All-Powerful says, "Come back to me, says the LORD All-Powerful, and I will come back to you." This is what the LORD All-Powerful said.

⁴"Don't be like your ancestors. In the past the prophets spoke to them and said, 'The LORD All-Powerful wants you to change your evil way of living. Stop doing evil things!' But your ancestors did not listen to me." This is what the LORD said.

⁵"Your ancestors are gone, and those prophets did not live forever. ⁶The prophets were my servants. I used them to tell your ancestors about my laws and teachings. Your ancestors finally learned their lesson and said, 'The LORD All-Powerful did what he said he would do. He punished us for the way we lived and for all the evil things we did.' So they came back to God."

The Four Horses

⁷On the twenty-fourth day of the eleventh month (Shebat) of the second year that Darius was king of Persia, Zechariah received another message from the LORD. (This was Zechariah son of Berekiah, son of Iddo.) This is the message:

⁸At night I saw a man riding a red horse. He was standing among some myrtle bushes in the valley. Behind him, there were red, brown and white horses. ⁹I said, "Sir, what are these horses for?"

Then the angel speaking to me said, "I will show you what these horses are for."

¹⁰Then the man standing among the myrtle bushes said, "The LORD sent these horses to go here and there on earth."

¹¹Then the horses spoke to the LORD's angel standing among the myrtle bushes and said, "We have gone all over the earth, and everything is calm and quiet."

¹²Then the LORD's angel said, "LORD All-Powerful, how long before you comfort Jerusalem and the cities of Judah? You have shown your anger at these cities for 70 years now."

¹³Then the LORD answered the angel who was talking with me. He spoke good, comforting words.

¹⁴Then the angel told me to tell the people this: The Lord All-Powerful says:

"I have a strong love for Jerusalem and Zion.
¹⁵ And I am very angry at the nations that feel
    so safe.
I was only a little angry,
    and I used them to punish my people.
    But they caused too much damage."
¹⁶So the LORD says, "I will come back to
    Jerusalem and comfort her."
The LORD All-Powerful says, "Jerusalem will
    be rebuilt,
    and my house will be built there."

¹⁷The angel also said, "The LORD All-Powerful
    says,
'My towns will be rich again.
I will comfort Zion.
I will again choose Jerusalem to be my
    special city.'"

The Four Horns and Four Workers

¹⁸Then I looked up and I saw four horns. ¹⁹So I asked the angel who was talking with me, "What do these horns mean?"

He said, "These are the horns that forced the people of Israel, Judah and Jerusalem to go to foreign countries."

²⁰The LORD showed me four workers. ²¹I asked the angel, "What are these four workers coming to do?"

He said, "The horns represent the nations that attacked the people of Judah and forced them to go to foreign countries. The horns 'threw' the people of Judah to the foreign countries. The horns didn't show mercy to anyone. But these four workers have come to frighten the horns and throw them away."

INSIGHT

Though the wall around Jerusalem had been destroyed, God promised his people that they didn't need it. He would live right there with them and would be their protection instead.

Zechariah 2:1–13

Measuring Jerusalem

2 Then I looked up and saw a man holding a rope for measuring things. ²I asked him, "Where are you going?"

---

[a] **1:1 *the second year . . . Darius*** That is, about 520 BC. Also in verse 7.

GOD'S ANGER, COMPASSION AND PROMISE

Imagine how you'd feel if you saw your boyfriend or girlfriend kissing someone else, or your best mate sharing secrets they'd promised only ever to share with you. This is a tiny bit like how God feels when we're not faithful to him: "I have a very strong love for Mount Zion. I love her so much that I became angry when she was not faithful to me" (Zechariah 8:2).

DIG IN   READ Zechariah 1:2–6; 7:7–14

Zechariah's first prophecy tells of God's anger. But all is not lost.

- What did God ask his people to do? Make a list.
- Why does he ask them to do these things (1:3)?
- How did they respond?
- What were the consequences?

"The LORD All-Powerful did what he said he would do. He punished us for the way we lived" (1:6). The people had been removed from the land (the exile) as a result of God's punishment for disobeying him. We can be sure that all of God's promises, whether they be threats or future blessings, will be carried out.

READ Zechariah 3:1–5

The people are now back from exile, yet things in the land are pretty depressing and uninspiring. The Temple is in ruins and the people are probably anxious that they're still under God's judgement.

Zechariah is full of visions – let's zoom in on the vision in chapter 3 about Joshua, the high priest, as it has something encouraging to say to the people with these anxieties. The role of the high priest in Old Testament times was to represent all of the people. When the people sinned, the high priest would come to offer sacrifices on behalf of everyone. When God forgave the high priest because of the sacrifices, it meant that all the people were also forgiven.

- In light of all this, what does verse 1 mean for the people?
- How does the Lord respond to Satan in verse 2?
- What was the result of the Lord's verdict in verses 3–5?
- What does Joshua do to cleanse and purify himself?

All Joshua did was turn up wearing filthy clothes representing his (and the people's) impurity. He could do absolutely nothing to cleanse and purify himself. God's treatment of Joshua shows the people they don't need to feel under God's wrath. The people can be encouraged – there is a bright future and they should get on with rebuilding the Temple (6:9–15).

READ Zechariah 9:9–12

- What words are used to describe the future king?
- What do these verses say he will do? Where will he do these things?

You might have heard these words at Christmas time – this is because the future king is Jesus, and he fulfilled this prophecy hundreds of years later. You can read about it in Matthew 21, Mark 11, Luke 19 or John 12. How amazing that Jesus' actions were being talked about so many years before he was even born! The future promise of Jesus and his death on the cross is how God's anger will be finally spent and God's compassion proved once and for all.

DIG THROUGH

- Like Joshua, all we can ever bring to God is our dirty clothes – our sin. Satan doesn't have to look very hard to find reasons to accuse us of doing wrong. It is only God who can give us new, clean clothes to wear. Take a look at Romans 8:31–34. Why can there be no charge made against the Christian?

He said to me, "I am going to measure Jerusalem, to see how wide and how long it is."
³Then the angel who was speaking to me left, and another angel went out to talk to him. ⁴He said to him, "Run and tell that young man this:

'Jerusalem will be a city without walls,
     because there will be too many people and
     animals living there.'
⁵The LORD says,
'I will be a wall of fire around her, to protect
     her,
     and to bring glory to that city, I will live
     there.'"

God Calls His People Home

The LORD says,

⁶"Hurry! Leave the land in the North in a
     hurry.
     Yes, it is true that I scattered your people in
     every direction."
     This is what the LORD said.
⁷"You people from Zion now live in Babylon.
     Escape! Run away from that city!"
⁸The Lord sent me to the nations that took
     away your wealth.
     He sent me to bring you honour.
     And this is what the LORD All-Powerful says:
"If anyone even touches you,
     it will be the same as poking me in the eye.
⁹Watch and see how I will punish them.
     Their own slaves will become their masters
     and take all their wealth."
Then you will know it was the LORD
     All-Powerful
     who sent me to tell you these things.

¹⁰The LORD says,

"Zion, be happy, because I am coming,
     and I will live in your city.
¹¹At that time people from many nations
     will come to me.
They will become my people,
     and I will live in your city."
Then you will know it was the LORD
     All-Powerful
     who sent me to tell you these things.

¹²The LORD will again choose Jerusalem to be his
     special city.
     Judah will be his share of the holy land.
¹³Everyone, be quiet!
     The LORD is coming out of his holy house.

The High Priest

3 The angel showed me Joshua the high priest, standing in front of the angel of the LORD and Satan was standing by Joshua's right side. Satan was there to accuse Joshua of doing wrong. ²Then the angel of the LORD said to Satan, "The LORD says no to you! The LORD has chosen Jerusalem to be his special city, and he says that you are wrong. He saved this man like a burning stick that someone pulls out of the fire."
³Joshua was wearing a dirty robe as he stood in front of the angel. ⁴Then the angel said to the other angels standing near him, "Take those dirty clothes off Joshua." Then the angel spoke to Joshua. He said, "Now, I have taken away your guilt, and I am giving you a new change of clothes."
⁵Then I said, "Put a clean turban on his head." So they put the clean turban on him and also put clean clothes on him while the angel of the LORD stood there. ⁶Then the angel of the LORD said this to Joshua:

⁷This is what the LORD All-Powerful said:
"Live the way I tell you,
     and do everything I say.
And you will be in charge of my Temple.
     You will take care of its courtyard.
You will be free to go anywhere in my
     Temple,
     just as these angels standing here.
⁸Listen, Joshua, you who are the high priest,
     and listen, you fellow priests seated
     before him.
You are all examples to show what will
     happen when I bring my special
     servant.
     He is called, the Branch.

⁹Look, I put a special stone in front of Joshua.
     There are seven sides[a] on that stone.
I will carve a special message on it.

ᵃ **3:9** *sides* Literally, "eyes".

This will show that in one day, I will
remove the guilt from this land."
This is what the LORD All-Powerful says.

10The LORD All-Powerful says,
"At that time people will sit and talk
with their friends and neighbours.
They will invite each other to sit
under the fig trees and grapevines."

The Lampstand and the Two Olive Trees

4 Then the angel who was talking to me
returned and woke me up. I was like a person
waking up from sleep. 2Then the angel asked me,
"What do you see?"

I said, "I see a solid gold lampstand. There are
seven lamps[a] on the lampstand, and there is a
bowl on top of it. There are seven tubes coming
from the bowl. One tube goes to each lamp. ⌊The
tubes bring the oil in the bowl to each of the
lamps.⌋ 3There are two olive trees by the bowl,
one on the right side and one on the left side.
⌊These trees produce the oil for the lamps.⌋"
4Then I asked the angel who was speaking with
me, "Sir, what do these things mean?"

5The angel speaking with me said, "Don't you
know what these things are?"

"No, sir," I said.

6He said, "This is the message from the LORD
to Zerubbabel: 'Your help will not come from
your own strength and power. No, your help will
come from my Spirit.' This is what the LORD
All-Powerful says. 7That tall mountain will be like
a flat place for Zerubbabel. He will build the
Temple, and when the most important stone is
put in place, the people will shout, 'Beautiful!
Beautiful!'"

8The LORD's message to me also said, 9"Zerubbabel will lay the foundations for my Temple, and
he will finish building it. Then you will know that
the LORD All-Powerful sent me to you people.
10People will not be ashamed of the small
beginnings, and they will be very happy when
they see Zerubbabel with the plumb line,[b]
measuring and checking the finished building.
Now the seven sides[c] of the stone you saw
represent the eyes of the LORD looking in every
direction. They see everything on earth."

11Then I said to him, "I saw one olive tree
on the right side of the lampstand and one on
the left side. What do those two olive trees
mean?" 12I also said to him, "I saw two olive
branches by the gold tubes with gold coloured
oil flowing from them. What do these things
mean?"

13Then the angel said to me, "Don't you know
what these things mean?"

I said, "No, sir."

14So he said, "They represent the two men
chosen[d] to serve the Lord of the whole world."

The Flying Scroll

5 I looked up again, and I saw a flying scroll.
2The angel asked me, "What do you see?"

I said, "I see a flying scroll that is nine metres[e]
long and four and a half metres[f] wide."

3Then the angel told me, "There is a curse
written on that scroll. On one side of the scroll,
there is a curse against thieves and on the other
side is a curse against people who lie when they
make promises. 4The LORD All-Powerful says,
'I will send that scroll to the houses of thieves
and people who lie when they use my name to
make promises. That scroll will settle there and
destroy even the stones and wooden posts of
their houses.'"

The Woman and the Bucket

5The angel who was talking to me went
outside and said, "Look! What do you see
coming?"

6I said, "I don't know. What is it?"

He said, "That is a measuring bucket." He also
said, "That bucket is for measuring the sins[g] of
the people in this country."

7A lid made of lead was lifted off the bucket,
and there was a woman in the bucket. 8The angel
said, "The woman represents evil." Then the
angel pushed the woman down into the bucket
and put the lead lid back on it. 9Then I looked
up and saw two women with wings like a stork.
They flew out, and with the wind in their wings,
they picked up the bucket. They flew through the
air carrying the bucket. 10Then I asked the angel
who was speaking with me, "Where are they
carrying the bucket?"

---

[a] 4:2 *lamps* These lamps made light by burning olive oil.

[b] 4:10 *plumb line* A string with a weight on one end used to show how straight the walls of a building were. Sometimes the line
was coated with paint or chalk to mark a straight line.

[c] 4:10 *sides* This is a wordplay. The Hebrew word also means "eyes".

[d] 4:14 *men chosen* Literally, "sons of extra pure olive oil". Often a special oil was poured over new kings, priests and prophets.
This showed that these people were chosen by God.

[e] 5:2 *nine metres* Literally, "20 cubits".

[f] 5:2 *four and a half metres* Literally, "10 cubits".

[g] 5:6 *sins* The Hebrew text has "their eye", but with a minor change of one character it becomes "their guilt".

[11]The angel told me, "They are going to build a house for it in Babylonia.[a] After they build that house, they will put the bucket there."

The Four Chariots

6 I looked up again, and I saw four chariots coming out from between two bronze mountains. [2]Red horses were pulling the first chariot. Black horses were pulling the second chariot. [3]White horses were pulling the third chariot, and spotted horses were pulling the fourth chariot. [4]I asked the angel who was talking with me, "Sir, what do these mean?"

[5]The angel said, "These are the four winds.[b] They have just come from the Lord of the whole world. [6]The black horses will go north, the white horses will go west[c] and the spotted horses will go south."

[7]These horses wanted to leave and go all over the earth. So the angel told them, "Go throughout the earth." And so they went on their way.

[8]Then the angel called to me and said, "Look, those horses that were going north finished their job ⌊in Babylon⌋. They have calmed the Lord's spirit; he is no longer angry."

Joshua the Priest Gets a Crown

[9]Then I received another message from the Lord. He said, [10]"Heldai, Tobijah and Jedaiah have come from the captives[d] in Babylon. Get silver and gold from these men and go the same day to the house of Josiah son of Zephaniah. [11]Use the silver and gold to make a crown. Put it on the head of the high priest, Joshua son of Jehozadak. [12]Then tell him this is what the Lord All-Powerful says:

'There is a man called the Branch.
    He will grow strong,
        and he will build the Lord's Temple.
[13]Yes, he will build the Lord's Temple,
    and he will receive honour.
He will sit on his throne and be the ruler,
    and a priest will stand by his throne.[e]
    These two will work together in peace.'

[14]The crown will be kept in my Temple,[f] so that when people see it, they will remember Heldai, Tobijah, Jedaiah and the kindness of Zephaniah's son Josiah."

[15]People living far away will come and build the Lord's Temple. Then you will know for sure that the Lord All-Powerful sent me to you people. All these things will happen if you do what the Lord your God says.

The Lord Wants Kindness and Mercy

7 Zechariah received a message from the Lord in the fourth year that Darius[g] was the king of Persia. This was on the fourth day of the ninth month (Kislev). [2]The people of Bethel sent Sharezer, Regem-Melech and his men to ask the Lord a question. [3]They went to the prophets and to the priests at the Temple of the Lord All-Powerful. They said, "For many years we have shown our sadness for the destruction of the Temple. In the fifth month of each year, we have had a special time of crying and fasting. Should we continue to do this?"

[4]I received this message from the Lord All-Powerful: [5]"Tell the priests and the other people in this country, 'For seventy years you fasted and showed your sadness in the fifth month and in the seventh month. But was that fasting really for me? [6]And when you ate and drank, was that for me? No, it was for your own good. [7]The Lord used the earlier prophets to say the same thing long ago. That was when Jerusalem was still a rich city filled with people and there were still people living in the surrounding towns, in the Negev, and in the western foothills.'"

[8]This is the Lord's message to Zechariah:

[9]"This is what the Lord All-Powerful said:
'You must do what is right and fair.
    You must be kind and
        show mercy to each other.
[10]Don't hurt widows and orphans,
    foreigners or poor people.
    Don't even think of doing bad things to
        each other!'"

[11]But they refused to listen
    and refused to do what he wanted.
They closed their ears so that they
    could not hear what God said.
[12]They were very stubborn
    and would not obey the law.
The Lord All-Powerful used his Spirit
    and sent messages to his people through the
        prophets.
But the people would not listen,
    so the Lord All-Powerful became very angry.
[13]The Lord All-Powerful said,

---

[a] **5:11 Babylonia** Literally, "Shinar", which may be a form of the name Sumer.
[b] **6:5 four winds** Or "four spirits". Four winds often means "winds that blow from every direction: north, south, east and west".
[c] **6:6 west** Literally, "behind them".
[d] **6:10 captives** People taken away as prisoners. Here, it means the Jewish people who were taken to Babylon.
[e] **6:13 stand by his throne** Or "be on another throne."
[f] **6:14 my Temple** Literally, "the Temple of the Lord".
[g] **7:1 the fourth year . . . Darius** This was about 518 BC.

"I called to them,
and they did not answer.
So now, if they call to me,
I will not answer.
¹⁴I will bring the other nations against them like
a storm.
They didn't know those nations,
but the country will be destroyed
after those nations pass through.
This pleasant country will be destroyed."

INSIGHT

God gave the people an answer as to why
their prayers had been ignored. He said
they had not been fasting for him but for
themselves and hadn't loved and cared
for the people around them.

Zechariah 7:4–14

The LORD Promises to Bless Jerusalem

8 This is a message from the LORD All-Powerful. ²The LORD All-Powerful says, "I have a very strong love for Mount Zion. I love her so much that I became angry when she was not faithful to me." ³The LORD says, "I have come back to Zion, and I am living in Jerusalem. Jerusalem will be called Faithful City. The mountain of the LORD All-Powerful will be called Holy Mountain."

⁴The LORD All-Powerful says, "Old men and women will again be seen in the public places in Jerusalem. People will live for so long that they will need their walking sticks. ⁵And the city will be filled with children playing in the streets." ⁶The LORD All-Powerful says, "The survivors will think it is wonderful, and so will I!"

⁷The LORD All-Powerful says, "Look, I am rescuing my people from countries in the east and west. ⁸I will bring them back here, and they will live in Jerusalem. They will be my people, and I will be their good and faithful God."

⁹The LORD All-Powerful says, "Be strong! You people are hearing the same message today that the prophets gave when the LORD All-Powerful first laid the foundations to rebuild his Temple. ¹⁰Before that time, people didn't have the money to hire workers or to rent animals. And it was not safe for people to come and go. There was no relief from all the troubles. I had turned everyone against their neighbour. ¹¹But it is not like that now. It will not be like that for the

survivors." This is what the LORD All-Powerful said.

¹²"These people will plant in peace. Their grapevines will produce grapes. The land will give good crops, and the skies will give rain. I will give all these things to my people. ¹³People began using the names Israel and Judah in their curses. But I will save Israel and Judah, and their names will become a blessing. So don't be afraid. Be strong!"

¹⁴The LORD All-Powerful says, "Your ancestors made me angry, so I decided to destroy them. I decided not to change my mind." This is what the LORD All-Powerful said. ¹⁵"But now I have changed my mind. And in the same way I have decided to be good to Jerusalem and to the people of Judah. So don't be afraid! ¹⁶But you must do this: tell the truth to your neighbours. When you make decisions in your cities, be fair and do what is right. Do what brings peace. ¹⁷Don't make secret plans to hurt your neighbours. Don't make false promises. You must not enjoy doing these things, because I hate them!" This is what the LORD said.

¹⁸I received this message from the LORD All-Powerful. ¹⁹The LORD All-Powerful says, "You have special days of sadness and fasting in the fourth month, the fifth month, the seventh month and the tenth month.ᵃ These days of sadness must be changed into days of happiness. They will be good and happy festivals. And you must love truth and peace."

²⁰The LORD All-Powerful says,
"In the future people from many cities will
come to Jerusalem.
²¹People from different cities will greet each
other and say,
'We are going to worship the LORD
All-Powerful.'
⌊And the other person will say,⌋
'I would like to go with you!'"

²²Many people and many powerful nations will come to Jerusalem to find the LORD All-Powerful and to worship him. ²³The LORD All-Powerful says, "At that time many foreigners speaking different languages will come to a Jewish man, take hold of the hem of his robe, and ask, 'We heard that God is with you. Can we come with you to worship him?'"

Judgement Against Other Nations

9 This is the LORD's message against the land of Hadrach and against the city of Damascus. Everyone looks to him for help.ᵇ ²This message is

---

ᵃ **8:19** days... month These were days when the people remembered the destruction of Jerusalem and the Temple. See 2 Kgs 25:1–25 and Jer. 41:1–17; 52:1–12.
ᵇ **9:1** The Hebrew text is not clear.

also against the city of Hamath near Damascus. And this message is against Tyre and Sidon, even though those people have been so wise and skilful. ³Tyre is built like a fortress. The people there have collected so much silver that it is like dust, and gold is as common as clay. ⁴But the Lord will take it all. He will destroy her powerful navy and that city will be destroyed by fire!

⁵The people in Ashkelon will see this and they will be afraid. The people of Gaza will shake with fear, and the people of Ekron will lose all hope when they see this happen. There will be no king left in Gaza. No one will live in Ashkelon any more. ⁶The people in Ashdod will not even know who their real fathers are. The Lord says, "I will completely destroy the proud Philistines. ⁷They will no longer eat meat with the blood still in it or any other forbidden food. Any Philistine left alive will become a part of my people; they will be just one more tribe in Judah. The people of Ekron will become a part of my people, as the Jebusites did. ⁸I will protect my country. I will not let enemy armies pass through it. I will not let them hurt my people any more. With my own eyes I have seen how much my people have suffered."

The Future King

⁹People of Zion,ᵃ rejoice!
   People of Jerusalem, shout with joy!
Look, your king is coming to you!
   He is the good king who won the victory,
      but he is humble.
   He is riding on a donkey, on a young
      donkey born from a work animal.
¹⁰I will take the war chariots away from
      Ephraim
   and the horsemen from Jerusalem.
I will destroy the bows used in war.

Your king will bring news of peace to the
      nations.
   He will rule from sea to sea,
   from the Euphrates River to the ends of the
      earth.

The Lord Will Save His People

¹¹Jerusalem, we used blood to seal your
      agreement,
   so I am setting your people free from that
      empty hole in the ground.ᵇ
¹²Prisoners, go home!
   Now you have something to hope for.
I am telling you now,
I am coming back to you.

¹³Judah, I will use you like a bow.
   Ephraim, I will use you like arrows.
Israel, I will use you like a sword
   to fight against the men of Greece.
¹⁴The Lord will appear to them,
   and he will shoot his arrows like lightning.
The Lord God will blow the trumpet,
   and the army will rush forward like a desert
      dust storm.
¹⁵The Lord All-Powerful will protect them.
   The soldiers will use rocks and slings to
      defeat the enemy.
They will spill the blood of their enemies.
   It will flow like wine.
   It will be like the blood that is thrown on
      the corners of the altar!
¹⁶At that time the Lord their God
   will save his people
   like a shepherd saves his sheep.
They will be very precious to him.
   They will be like sparkling jewels in his land.
¹⁷Everything will be good and beautiful!
   There will be a wonderful crop,
but it will not be just the food and wine.
   It will be all the young men and women!

The Lord's Promises

10 Pray to the Lord for rain in the springtime. The Lord will send the lightning and the rain will fall, and he will make the plants grow in each person's field.

²People use their little statues and magic to learn what will happen in the future, but that is useless. They see visions and tell about their dreams, but it is nothing but worthless lies. So the people are like sheep wandering here and there crying for help, but there is no shepherd to lead them.

³The Lord says, "I am very angry with the shepherds. I made them responsible for what happens to my sheep." (The people of Judah are his flock, and the Lord All-Powerful really does take care of his flock. He cares for them as a soldier cares for his beautiful war horse.)

⁴"The cornerstone, the tent peg, the war bow and the advancing soldiers will all come from Judah together. ⁵They will be like soldiers marching through mud in the streets. They will fight, and since the Lord is with them, they will defeat even the enemy soldiers riding horses. ⁶I will make Judah's family strong. I will help Joseph's family win the war. I will bring them back safely and comfort them. It will be as if I had never left them. I am the Lord their God, and I will help them. ⁷The people of Ephraim will be as

---

ᵃ **9:9 People of Zion** Literally, "Daughter Zion", meaning the city of Jerusalem. See "Zion" in the Word List.
ᵇ **9:11 empty hole in the ground** People stored water in large holes in the ground. People sometimes used those holes as prisons.

happy as soldiers who have too much to drink. Their children will be rejoicing and they, too, will be happy. They will all have a happy time together with the LORD.

⁸"I will give them a signal and call them all together. I really will save them. There will be many people. ⁹Yes, I have been scattering my people throughout the nations. But in those faraway places, they will remember me. They and their children will survive, and they will come back. ¹⁰I will bring them back from Egypt and Assyria. I will bring them to the area of Gilead. And since there will not be enough room, I will also let them live in nearby Lebanon. ¹¹They will go through a sea of troubles, but the waves will be stopped. Even the deepest waters of the Nile River will dry up. I will destroy Assyria's pride and take away Egypt's power. ¹²I, the LORD, will make my people strong, and they will live for me." This is what the LORD said.

God Will Punish the Other Nations

11 Lebanon, open your gates so that the fire will come
and burn your cedar trees.ᵃ
²The cypress trees will cry because the cedar
trees have fallen.
Those powerful trees will be taken away.
Oak trees in Bashan will cry
for the forest that was cut down.
³Listen to the crying shepherds.
Their powerful leaders were taken away.
Listen to the roaring of the young lions.
Their thick bushes near the Jordan River
have all been taken away.

⁴The LORD my God says, "Care for the sheep that have been reared to be killed. ⁵Buyers kill their sheep and are not punished. Those who sell the sheep say, 'Praise the LORD, I am rich!' The shepherds don't feel sorry for their sheep. ⁶And I don't feel sorry for the people who live in this country." The LORD says, "Look, I will let everyone be under the control of their neighbour and king. I will let them destroy the country. I will not stop them!"

⁷So I took care of the sheep that had been reared to be killed—those poor sheep. I found two sticks. I called one stick Favour, and I called the other stick Union. Then I began caring for the sheep. ⁸I fired the three shepherds all in one month. I got angry at the sheep, and they began to hate me. ⁹Then I said, "I will no longer take care of you! I will let those who want to die, die.

I will let those who want to be destroyed, be destroyed and those who are left will destroy each other." ¹⁰Then I took the stick named Favour and I broke it. I did this to show that God's agreement with his people was broken. ¹¹So that day the agreement was finished, and those poor sheep watching me knew that this message was from the LORD.

¹²Then I said, "If you want to pay me, pay me. If not, don't!" So they paid me 30 pieces of silver. ¹³Then the LORD said, "So that's how much money they think I'm worth—such a large amount!ᵇ Take it and throw it into the Temple treasury." So I took the 30 pieces of silver and threw them into the treasury at the LORD's Temple. ¹⁴Then I cut the stick named Union into two pieces. I did this to show that the union between Judah and Israel had been broken.

¹⁵Then the LORD said to me, "Now, get the things a foolish shepherd might use. ¹⁶This will show that I will get a new shepherd for this country. But this young man will not take care of the sheep that are being destroyed. He will not heal the hurt sheep or feed those that are left alive. And the healthy ones will be eaten completely—only their hoofs will be left."

¹⁷Too bad for you, you worthless shepherd!
You abandoned my sheep.
Punish him!
Strike his arm and right eye with a sword.
His arm will be useless.
His right eye will be blind.

Visions About the Nations Around Judah

12 This is a message from the LORD about Israel. The Lord is the one who made the earth and the sky, and he put the human spirit in people. And this is what the LORD said: ²"Look, I will make Jerusalem like a cup of poison to the nations around her. The nations will come and attack that city, and all of Judah will be caught in the trap. ³But I will make Jerusalem like a heavy rock—those who try to take it will hurt themselves. They will be cut and scratched. All the nations on earth will come together to fight against Jerusalem. ⁴But at that time I will scare the horse, and the soldier riding it will panic. I will make all the enemy horses blind, but my eyes will be open—and I will be watching over Judah's family. ⁵The leaders of Judah will encourage the people and say, 'The LORD All-Powerful is your God. He makes us strong.' ⁶At that time I will make the leaders of Judah like a fire burning in a

---

ᵃ **11:1** *cedar trees* In this poem, the trees, bushes and animals are symbols for the leaders of the countries around Judah.
ᵇ **11:13** *such a large amount* 30 pieces of silver was not really a large amount. It was the usual price for a slave. So the Lord was making fun of the people.

forest. They will destroy their enemies like fire burning straw. They will destroy the enemy all around them, and the people in Jerusalem will again be able to sit back and relax."

7The LORD will save the people of Judah first, so the people in Jerusalem will not be able to boast too much. David's family and the other people who live in Jerusalem will not be able to boast that they are better than the other people in Judah. 8But the LORD will protect the people in Jerusalem. Even the man who trips and falls will become a great soldier like David. And the men from David's family will be like gods—like the LORD's own angel leading the people.

9The Lord says, "At that time I will destroy the nations that came to fight against Jerusalem. 10I will fill David's family and the people living in Jerusalem with a spirit of kindness and mercy. They will look to me, the one they stabbed and they will be very sad. They will be as sad as someone crying over the death of their only son, as sad as someone crying over the death of their firstborn son. 11There will be a time of great sadness and crying in Jerusalem. It will be like what happens in Megiddo Valley when people cry over the death of Hadad Rimmon.ª 12Each and every family will cry by itself. The men in David's family will cry by themselves, and their wives will cry by themselves. The men in Nathan's family will cry by themselves, and their wives will cry by themselves. 13The men in Levi's family will cry by themselves, and their wives will cry by themselves. The men in Simeon's family will cry by themselves, and their wives will cry by themselves. 14And the same thing will happen in all the other tribes. The men and women will cry by themselves."

13 But at that time a new spring of water will be opened for David's family and for the other people living in Jerusalem. That fountain will be to wash away their sins and to make the people pure.

No More False Prophets

2The LORD All-Powerful says, "At that time I will remove all the idols from the earth. People will not even remember their names, and I will remove the false prophets and unclean spirits from the earth. 3Whoever continues to prophesy will be punished. Even their parents, their own mother and father, will say to them, 'You have spoken lies in the name of the LORD, so you must

die!' Their own mother and father will stab them for prophesying. 4At that time the prophets will be ashamed of their visions and prophecies. They will not wear the rough cloth that shows a person is a prophet. They will not wear those clothes to trick people with the lies they call prophecies. 5They will say, 'I am not a prophet. I am a farmer. I have worked as a farmer since I was a little child.' 6But other people will say, 'Then what are these wounds in your hands?' He will say, 'I was beaten in the house of my friends.'"

7The LORD All-Powerful says, "Sword, wake up and strike the shepherd, my friend! Strike the shepherd, and the sheep will run away. And I will punish those little ones. 8Two-thirds of the people in the land will be struck down and die," says the LORD, "but one-third will survive. 9Then I will test those survivors by giving them many troubles. The troubles will be like the fire a person uses to prove silver is pure. I will test them the way a person tests gold. Then they will call to me for help, and I will answer them. I will say, 'You are my people.' And they will say, 'The LORD is my God.'"

The Day of Judgement

14 Look, the LORD has a special day of judgement coming, when the riches you have taken will be divided in your city. 2I will bring all the nations together to fight against Jerusalem. They will capture the city and destroy the houses. The women will be raped, and half of the people will be taken away as prisoners. But the rest of the people will not be taken from the city. 3Then the LORD will go to war with those nations. It will be a real battle. 4At that time he will stand on the Mount of Olives, the hill east of Jerusalem. The Mount of Olives will split in half. Part of the mountain will move to the north, and part to the south. A deep valley will open up, from the east to the west. 5You will try to run away as that mountain valley comes closer and closer to you. You will run away like the time you ran from the earthquake during the time of King Uzziah of Judah. But the LORD my God will come, and all his holy onesᵇ will be with him.

6-7That will be a very special day. There will not be any light, cold or frost. Only the LORD knows how, but there will not be any day or night. Then, when darkness usually comes, there will still be light. 8At that time fresh water will flow continuously from Jerusalem.ᶜ That stream will split into two parts; one part will flow east

---

ª 12:11 **Hadad Rimmon** Possibly a name for the Syrian fertility god.
ᵇ 14:5 **holy ones** Here, this probably means angels.
ᶜ 14:8 **water . . . Jerusalem** Literally, "living water will flow from Jerusalem". Jerusalem's main water supply, the Gihon spring, did not flow continuously.

towards the Dead Sea, and the other part will flow west to the coast. It will flow all year long, in the summer as well as in the winter. ⁹And the LORD will be the King of the whole world. At that time all people will worship him as the only LORD with only one name. ¹⁰And the whole land from Geba in the north to Rimmon in the south past Jerusalem will become a flat plain. The city of Jerusalem will stay in the same place, but it will be built high above the land around it. It will reach from the Benjamin Gate to the First Gate (that is, the Corner Gate) and from the Tower of Hananel to the king's winepresses. ¹¹People will move to Jerusalem because it will be a safe place to live. It will never again be destroyed.

¹²But the LORD will punish the nations that fought against Jerusalem. He will send a terrible disease against them. Their skin will begin to rot while they are still alive. Their eyes will rot in their heads, and their tongues will rot in their mouths. ¹³And on that day the LORD will confuse them with panic. Everyone will grab his neighbour, and they will fight each other. ¹⁴Even Judah will fight against Jerusalem. And a great amount of gold, silver and clothing will be taken from the nations surrounding the city. ¹⁵The same kind of terrible disease will strike the animals in the enemy camps, including all their horses, mules, camels and donkeys.

¹⁶Some of the people who came to fight Jerusalem will survive. And every year they will come to worship the king, the LORD All-Powerful. They will come to celebrate the Festival of Shelters. ¹⁷And if people from any of the families on earth don't go to Jerusalem to worship the King, the LORD All-Powerful, no rain will fall on their land. ¹⁸If any of the families in Egypt don't come to celebrate the Festival of Shelters, they will get that terrible disease that the LORD caused the enemy nations to get. ¹⁹That will be the punishment for Egypt, and for any other nation that does not come to celebrate the Festival of Shelters.

²⁰At that time, even the harnesses on the horses will have the label, ONLY FOR THE LORD. And all the pots used in the LORD's Temple will be just as important as the bowls used at the altar. ²¹In fact, every dish in Jerusalem and Judah will be only for the LORD All-Powerful. All the people offering sacrifices will come, take those dishes and cook their special meals in them.

At that time there will not be any merchants buying and selling things*a* in the Temple of the LORD All-Powerful.

---

a **14:21 merchants . . . selling things** Literally, "Canaanites".

Who
Since his name literally means "messenger", Malachi could be a name, but equally could be simply a title. He was probably the last prophet of Old Testament times.

When
This prophecy probably comes from Jerusalem after the exiles have returned in 433 BC. That would make him a contemporary of Ezra and Nehemiah. The situation he describes fits with what Nehemiah found on returning for his second visit.

What
The Temple has been rebuilt, sacrifices are being offered again, but the old sins of Israel are creeping back. God's laws are being disobeyed, his instructions ignored, the ordinary people are once again on the receiving end of injustice and greed.

The exiles may have returned, but Judah is an insignificant backwater, with perhaps 150,000 people at most. And they are still under the control of a foreign power – Persia.

The glory prophesied by Zechariah and Haggai some ninety years before had not come about. There was just economic hardship, drought, crop failure and disease. And as for the Temple – it was like a wood shack compared to the glory of Solomon's day (or the one foreseen by Ezekiel). The Temple, far from being a spiritual powerhouse, was a place where people simply went through the ritual.

Malachi was an intense, sometimes severe patriot. Faced with a disheartened and disobedient people, he reminds them that religious ritual is no good on its own. It only has value if it is a true expression of sincere belief. The law is important. The priests should guard it carefully. But more than that, they should obey it. God has a purpose for these people – a particular role for them to play. By weakening their culture they are hindering that purpose.

Malachi was a messenger. And, as the last prophet in the Old Testament he points, perhaps, to another messenger, still to come. "I am sending my messenger to prepare the way for me," he writes. "Then suddenly, the Lord you are looking for will come to his temple. Yes, the messenger you are waiting for, the one who will tell about my agreement, is really coming!" (3:1). Someone will come. And before him, a messenger to prepare the way. I wonder who?

QUICK TOUR ▶ **MALACHI**

"But for you, my followers, goodness will shine on you like the rising sun. And it will bring healing power like the sun's rays. You will be free and happy, like calves set free from their pens."
Malachi 4:2

1 This is a message from the LORD to Israel. God used Malachi to tell this message to the people.

God Loves Israel

²The LORD said, "I love you people."

But you said, "What shows you love us?"

The LORD said, "Esau was Jacob's brother, but I chose^a Jacob. ³And I did not accept^b Esau. I destroyed his hill country.^c His country was destroyed, and now only jackals live there."

⁴The people of Edom might say, "We were destroyed, but we will go back and rebuild our cities."

But the LORD All-Powerful says, "If they rebuild their cities, I will destroy them again." That is why people say Edom is an evil country—a nation the LORD hates forever.

⁵You people saw these things, and you said, "The LORD is great, even outside Israel!"

The People Don't Respect God

⁶The LORD All-Powerful said, "Children honour their fathers. Servants honour their masters. I am your Father, so why don't you honour me? I am your master, so why don't you respect me? You priests don't respect my name.

"But you say, 'What have we done that shows we don't respect your name?'

⁷"You bring unclean bread to my altar.

"But you ask, 'What makes that bread unclean?'

"It is unclean because you show no respect for the altar of the LORD. ⁸You bring blind animals as sacrifices, and that is wrong. You bring sick and lame animals for sacrifices, and that is wrong. Try giving those sick animals as a gift to your governor. Would he accept those sick animals? No, he would not accept them." This is what the LORD All-Powerful said.

⁹"Now try asking God to be good to you. But he will not listen to you, and it is all your fault." This is what the LORD All-Powerful said.

¹⁰"I wish one of you would close the Temple doors to stop the lighting of useless fires on my altar. I am not pleased with you. I will not accept your gifts." This is what the LORD All-Powerful said.

¹¹"People all around the world respect my name. All around the world they bring good gifts to me and burn good incense as a gift to me, because my name is important to all of them." This is what the LORD All-Powerful said.

¹²"But you people show that you don't respect my name. You say that the Lord's altar is unclean.

And you don't like the food from that altar. ¹³You smell the food and refuse to eat it. You say it is bad. Then you bring sick, lame and hurt animals to me. You try to give sick animals to me as sacrifices, but I will not accept them." This is what the LORD All-Powerful said. ¹⁴"Some people have good, male animals that they could give as sacrifices, but don't. Some people bring good animals and promise to give those healthy animals to me. But then they secretly exchange those good animals and give me sick animals instead. Bad things will happen to those people. I am the Great King and people all around the world respect me!" This is what the LORD All-Powerful said.

INSIGHT

Animals that had defects were not acceptable as sacrifices (see Deuteronomy 15:19–21). God isn't looking for the "leftovers" in the lives of those who love him – he wants to be central and have only the best. They were being disrespectful to God and he was not happy.

Malachi 1:14

Rules for Priests

2 "Priests, this rule is for you. ²Listen to me! Pay attention to what I say. Show honour to my name. If you don't respect my name, bad things will happen to you. You will say blessings,^d but they will become curses. I will make bad things happen because you don't show respect for my name." This is what the LORD All-Powerful said.

³"Look, I will punish your descendants. During the festivals, you priests offer sacrifices to me. You take the dung and inside parts from the dead animals and throw them away. But I will smear the dung on your faces, and you will be thrown away with it! ⁴Then you will learn why I am giving you this command. I am telling you these things so that my agreement with Levi will continue." This is what the LORD All-Powerful said.

⁵⌊The Lord said,⌋ "I made that agreement with Levi. I promised to give him life and peace—and

---

^a **1:2** *chose* Or "loved".
^b **1:3** *did not accept* Or "hated".
^c **1:3** *his hill country* This means the country of Edom. Edom was another name for Esau.
^d **2:2** *blessings* Words asking for good things to happen to a person who tries to obey God's law.

WHOLEHEARTED WORSHIP

Imagine you asked a friend to spend time with you and they turned up late and then spent most of the time on their mobile phone. How would that make you feel? Yes, they turned up, but their heart wasn't really in it was it? This might give us a very tiny glimpse into the fiery message God gives to his prophet Malachi . . .

The book of Malachi is only four chapters long. For the best impact, try to sit down and read the whole thing in one sitting. The study will zoom in on the beginning and the end . . .

DIG IN
READ Malachi 1:1–14

- How does God answer Israel's question, "What shows you love us?" (vv.2–5)?
- How have his people shown a response that is not worthy of that love (vv.7–8,12–14)?

We don't bring animal sacrifices to God today but one of the purposes of the sacrifices back then was for God's people to show God their commitment to him. That's why he was so angry that they were bringing "sick, lame and hurt animals" to the altar. God's people would have known that an animal to be sacrificed must have nothing wrong with it (check out Leviticus 1:1–3).

- In what kinds of ways do you think God's people might be accused of trying to short-change God in modern times? Try to think of examples like time and money being used for God's purposes.
- What is God's response to his people's behaviour and why (1:14)?

READ Malachi 3:13 – 4:5

- What is the first group complaining about (vv.13–15)?
- How are the people in the contrasting group described (v.16)?
- How does God view and treat each group (vv.13,17 – 4:5)?

It seems that some people don't really see the point of serving God or following him because the evil people are having a better time of it than the godly. The problem is that they have their hearts fixed on the now – rather than believing that God will judge the wicked in the future (4:1).

These were depressing times in Jerusalem – the people had returned after being exiled but the Temple doesn't have the same spark to it as it used to – there's no miraculous sign of God's presence (3:1), unlike in Solomon's time (1 Kings 8:10). This may also have affected their worship.

DIG THROUGH

- Do you really love God above anything and everything else in your life? Has your relationship with God become a bit of a part-time hobby? This book is like God's wake-up call to us, reminding us that he is King all of the time, so how we respond to him matters all of the time. Can you think of one or two things you can change today to help move God back into the centre of your life?
- Do you see other people getting stuff that you want even though they don't follow God? Is it tempting to choose to follow the crowd rather than believe God will judge everyone and only those who belong to God will truly be happy and free in the end (4:2)?

DIG DEEPER

- Some of these verses are pretty scary. God is never indifferent to the way that we treat him, but that doesn't make him an angry bully. He's like a loving husband who wants his wife to be faithful. Reading the amazing story of Hosea, a few books back in the Bible, would be a great way to help you understand this (see Bible Bit "An Unfaithful Wife, a Faithful Husband").

I gave him those things. Levi respected me and showed honour to my name. ⁶He taught the true teachings and didn't teach lies. Levi was honest, and he loved peace. He followed me and saved many people from being punished for the evil things they did. ⁷A priest should know God's teachings. People should be able to go to a priest and learn God's teachings. A priest should be the LORD's messenger to the people.

⁸"But you priests stopped following me! You used the teachings to make people do wrong. You ruined the agreement with Levi." This is what the LORD All-Powerful said. ⁹"You don't live the way I told you. You have not accepted my teachings. So I will cause people to hate you and think you are worth nothing."

Judah Was Not True to God

¹⁰We all have the same father. The same God made every one of us. So why do people cheat each other? They show that they don't respect the agreement. They don't respect the agreement that our ancestors made with God. ¹¹The people of Judah cheated other people. People in Jerusalem and Israel did terrible things. God loves the Temple, but the people in Judah didn't respect the LORD's holy Temple. The people of Judah began to worship a foreign goddess. ¹²The LORD will remove them from Judah's family. They might bring gifts to the LORD All-Powerful—but it will not help. ¹³You can cry and cover the LORD's altar with tears, but the Lord will not accept your gifts. He will not be pleased with the things you bring to him.

¹⁴You ask, "Why are our gifts not accepted?" It is because the LORD saw the evil things you did— he is a witness against you. He saw you cheat on your wife. You have been married to her since you were young. She was your girlfriend. Then you made your vows to each other—and she became your wife. ¹⁵God wants husbands and wives to become one body and one spirit. Why? So that they would have holy children and protect that spiritual unity. Don't cheat on your wife. She has been your wife from the time you were young.

¹⁶The LORD, the God of Israel, says, "I hate divorce, and I hate the cruel things that men do. So protect your spiritual unity. Don't cheat on your wife."

The Time of Judgement

¹⁷You have taught wrong things, and it makes the LORD very sad. People were doing evil things, but you said that this pleased the LORD and that he accepted those things. And you taught that God does not punish people for the evil they do.

3 The LORD All-Powerful says, "I am sending my messenger to prepare the way for me. Then suddenly, the Lord you are looking for will come to his temple.ᵃ Yes, the messenger you are waiting for, the one who will tell about my agreement, is really coming!

²"No one can prepare for that time or stand against him when he comes. He will be like a burning fire. He will be like the strong soap people use to make things clean. ³He will make the Levites clean. He will make them pure, like silver is made pure with fire! He will make them pure like gold and silver. Then they will bring gifts to the LORD, and they will do things the right way. ⁴Then the LORD will accept the gifts from Judah and Jerusalem. It will be as it was in the past—as the time long ago. ⁵Then I will bring you to justice. I will be an expert witness and testify about the evil things people do. I will speak out against those who do evil magic or commit adultery. I will speak out against those who make false promises and cheat their workers and don't pay them the money they promised. I will speak out against those who don't help foreigners, or widows and orphans. And I will speak out against those who don't respect me." This is what the LORD All-Powerful said.

Stealing From God

⁶"I am the LORD, and I don't change. You are Jacob's children, and you have not been completely destroyed. ⁷But you never obeyed my laws. Even your ancestors stopped following me. Come back to me, and I will come back to you." This is what the LORD All-Powerful said.

"You say, 'How can we come back?'

⁸"People should not steal things from God, but you stole things from me.

"You say, 'What did we steal from you?'

"You should have given me one-tenth of your things. You should have given me special gifts. ⁹In this way your whole nation has stolen things from me, so bad things are happening to you."

ᵃ **3:1** *temple* Or "palace".

¹⁰The LORD All-Powerful says, "Try this test. Bring one-tenth of your things to me. Put them in the treasury. Bring food to my house. Test me! If you do these things, I will surely bless you. Good things will come to you like rain falling from the sky. You will have more than enough of everything. ¹¹I will not let pests destroy your crops. All your grapevines will produce grapes." This is what the LORD All-Powerful said.

¹²"People from other nations will be good to you. You will have a wonderful country." This is what the LORD All-Powerful said.

The Special Time of Judgement

¹³The LORD says, "You said cruel things to me." But you ask, "What did we say about you?"

¹⁴You said, "It is useless to worship God. We did what the LORD All-Powerful told us, but we didn't gain anything. We cried like people at a funeral to show we were sorry for our sins, but it didn't help. ¹⁵We think proud people are happy. Evil people succeed. They do evil things to test God's patience, and God does not punish them."

¹⁶Then the LORD's followers spoke with each other, and the LORD listened to them. There is a book in front of him. In that book are the names of his followers. They are the people who honour the LORD's name.

¹⁷The LORD said, "They belong to me. I will be kind to them. Parents are very kind to their children who obey them. In the same way, I will be kind to my followers. ¹⁸You people will come back to me, and you will learn the difference between good and evil. You will learn the difference between someone who follows God and someone who does not.

4 "That time of judgement is coming. It will be like a hot furnace. All the proud people will be punished. All the evil people will burn like straw. At that time they will be like a bush burning in the fire, and there will not be a branch or root left." This is what the LORD All-Powerful said.

²"But for you, my followers, goodness will shine on you like the rising sun. And it will bring healing power like the sun's rays. You will be free and happy, like calves set free from their pens. ³When the time comes for me to do these things, you will trample down the wicked. They will be like ashes under your feet." This is what the LORD All-Powerful said.

⁴"Remember and obey the law of my servant Moses. I gave those laws and rules to him at Mount Horeb. They are for all the people of Israel.

⁵"Look, I will send Elijah the prophet to you. He will come before that great and terrible time of judgement from the LORD. ⁶Elijah will help the parents become close to their children, and he will help the children become close to their parents. This must happen, or I will come and completely destroy your country."

BETWEEN THE TESTAMENTS

By the final pages of the Old Testament the Israelites have re-established the kingdom of Israel after exile in Babylon. But between the last book of the Old Testament and the first book of the New, there is a gap of about four hundred years.

So what happened in between?

Although people like Nehemiah and Ezra rebuilt Israel it was always a weak country, and for the next few centuries the country was owned by a number of different empires. First there were the Greeks under their leader Alexander the Great, one of the greatest leaders in history. Alexander invented a policy known as Hellenization, which meant he tried to impose the Greek culture on all the lands he conquered. He established many Greek-style cities throughout the Middle East.

When he died, his massive empire was split between his generals. Two of them, Ptolemy and Seleucis, founded families which each had turns in ruling Israel. The Ptolemies went to Egypt and ruled Israel for about one hundred years. Then the Seleucids had their turn . . . and here's where Hellenization really started to kick in. A Seleucid ruler called Antiochus IV tried to wipe out the Jewish faith. He tried to destroy every copy of the Hebrew Scriptures and he forced people to make offerings to Zeus. He even marched into the Temple, set up a statue of Zeus and sacrificed a pig – an unclean animal.

The Israelites revolted. An uprising, led by a family called the Maccabees, drove out the Seleucids and led to one hundred years of Jewish independence.

And then the Romans came along. In 63 BC a Roman general called Pompey took Jerusalem after besieging Temple Mount for three months. He massacred priests and even marched into the Most Holy Place in the Temple (which he was baffled to find completely empty). The Romans ousted the kings descended from the Maccabean line and installed their own king – a young ruler called Herod. Herod was not actually a native Jew, even though he obeyed – to some extent – the Jewish religion. He was actually an Idumaean, from the territory that in Old Testament times had been called Edom.

After a civil war Herod finally took control of the kingdom in around 37 BC. He began to redevelop Jerusalem. In particular, he massively redeveloped the Temple, building a huge temple platform and making the Temple into one of the richest and most awe-inspiring buildings in the Roman world. It was really thanks to Herod that Jerusalem became a place of pilgrimage, not just for Jews within Palestine but for Jews throughout the Roman world. Indeed, at the time of Jesus there were probably more Jews living in cities around the Mediterranean than there were in Palestine itself.

So, at the beginning of the New Testament the country that was once the Israel of David and Solomon is under the control of the Roman Governor of Syria. And, far from being from the line of David, its king is an Idumaean.

The glory days had never felt further away.

THE NEW TESTAMENT

The New Testament is about Jesus. His words and deeds are the subject of this part of the Bible and, although there are strong personalities and individuals among his early followers, their writings are all concerned with trying to understand the life and teaching of this one man. He was the one towards whom the Old Testament had pointed: the Messiah, the chosen one, the fulfilment of prophecy.

The New Testament falls into two main sections: the Gospels and Acts, and the Letters.

The four Gospels are biographies of Jesus and tell the story of his life, death and resurrection. The book of Acts continues the story: it's a history of the early Church up to about AD 60. At first, sayings of Jesus and stories about him were simply passed from person to person – you can find a reference to this in Paul's first letter to the church at Corinth, where he says, "I gave you the message that I received . . ." (1 Corinthians 15:3). But gradually they were collected and written down.

The Letters are attributed to some of the most important leaders of the early Church: people like Paul and Peter and Jesus' brother, James. They were written to answer questions, explain Jesus' teaching and remind the followers of what Jesus had said. Churches would pass copies of these letters around until, in the end, the most important were collected together. This section also includes the book of Revelation which includes seven messages to churches in Asia Minor, but which is also a vision of the future seen by someone called John while he is a prisoner on the island of Patmos. It's not really like anything else in the New Testament (or the rest of the Bible for that matter).

The New Testament writings all date from the second half of the first century AD. The earliest complete writings are some of Paul's letters – Galatians and 1 and 2 Thessalonians, which date from the late 40s and early 50s AD. But both the Gospels and Paul's letters include sayings and stories about Jesus which go back much earlier.

The process of deciding what writings were to be the Christian Scriptures took a long time: the final version of the New Testament wasn't decided until around AD 390.

We should remember that the first followers of Jesus did not have all that we have today. They did not have Bibles as we have them. There were no church buildings – the first followers met in houses. And they did not realize that they were founding a new religion. That is why the New Testament is so full of references to the Old Testament: they weren't starting a new book, they were finishing the old one.

QUICK TOUR ▶ NEW TESTAMENT

Sermon on the mount Matthew 5:1–16
The ideal prayer Matthew 6:5–15
Good news for the poor Luke 4:16–30
Born again John 3:1–18
Loving your enemies Luke 6:27–36
The servant king John 13:1–20
The risen Saviour Matthew 28:1–20

The Holy Spirit Acts 2:1–47
Conversion of Saul Acts 9:1–31
Faith makes us right Romans 5:1–11
The Lord's Supper 1 Corinthians 11:23–34
Many people, one body Romans 12:1–8
Love 1 Corinthians 13:1–13
Christ sets us free Galatians 5:1–26

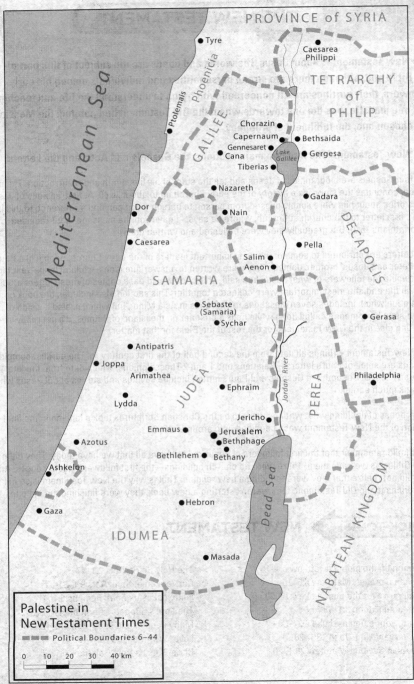

PROVINCE of SYRIA

Mediterranean Sea

● Tyre

Ptolemais ●

Phoenicia

● Caesarea Philippi

TETRARCHY
of
PHILIP

GALILEE

Chorazin ●
Capernaum ●
Gennesaret ●
Cana ● ● Bethsaida
Lake Galilee
Tiberias ● ● Gergesa

Nazareth ●

● Gadara

● Dor

● Nain

DECAPOLIS

● Caesarea

Salim ● ● Pella
Aenon ●

SAMARIA

Sebaste (Samaria) ●
● Sychar

● Gerasa

Antipatris ●

● Joppa

Arimathea ●

JUDEA

● Ephraim

Jordan River

PEREA

● Philadelphia

Lydda ●

● Jericho

Emmaus ● ● Jerusalem
● Bethphage
Bethlehem ● ● Bethany

● Azotus

Ashkelon ●

Dead Sea

● Hebron

● Gaza

IDUMEA

● Masada

NABATEAN KINGDOM

Palestine in
New Testament Times
▰▰▰▰ Political Boundaries 6–44

0   10   20   30   40 km

The Family History of Jesus the Messiah

(Luke 3:23b–38)

1 This is the family history of Jesus the Messiah. He came from the family of David, who was from the family of Abraham.

2 Abraham was the father of Isaac.
Isaac was the father of Jacob.
Jacob was the father of Judah and his brothers.
3 Judah was the father of Perez and Zerah. (Their mother was Tamar.)
Perez was the father of Hezron.
Hezron was the father of Ram.
4 Ram was the father of Amminadab.
Amminadab was the father of Nahshon.
Nahshon was the father of Salmon.
5 Salmon was the father of Boaz. (His mother was Rahab.)
Boaz was the father of Obed. (His mother was Ruth.)
Obed was the father of Jesse.
6 Jesse was the father of King David.
David was the father of Solomon. (His mother had been Uriah's wife.)

7 Solomon was the father of Rehoboam.
Rehoboam was the father of Abijah.
Abijah was the father of Asa.
8 Asa was the father of Jehoshaphat.
Jehoshaphat was the father of Jehoram.
Jehoram was the father of Uzziah.
9 Uzziah was the father of Jotham.
Jotham was the father of Ahaz.
Ahaz was the father of Hezekiah.
10 Hezekiah was the father of Manasseh.
Manasseh was the father of Amon.
Amon was the father of Josiah.
11 Josiah was the grandfather of Jehoiachin*a* and his brothers, who lived during the time that the people were taken away to Babylonia.

12 After they were taken to Babylonia:
Jehoiachin was the father of Shealtiel.
Shealtiel was the grandfather of Zerubbabel.
13 Zerubbabel was the father of Abiud.
Abiud was the father of Eliakim.
Eliakim was the father of Azor.
14 Azor was the father of Zadok.
Zadok was the father of Achim.
Achim was the father of Eliud.
15 Eliud was the father of Eleazar.
Eleazar was the father of Matthan.
Matthan was the father of Jacob.

16 Jacob was the father of Joseph.
Joseph was the husband of Mary,
and Mary was the mother of Jesus, who is called the Messiah.

17 So there were fourteen generations from Abraham to David. There were also fourteen generations from David until the people were taken away to Babylonia. And there were fourteen more from the time the people were taken to Babylonia until the Messiah was born.

INSIGHT

Throughout the Bible God speaks to his people through dreams, and here we read about four significant ones. He speaks to Joseph three times (chapters 1 and 2) and also warns the wise men they are in danger (chapter 2).

Matthew 1:18 – 2:23

The Birth of Jesus the Messiah

(Luke 2:1–7)

18 This is how the birth of Jesus the Messiah happened. His mother Mary was engaged to marry Joseph. But before they married, he learned that she was expecting a baby. (She was pregnant by the power of the Holy Spirit.) 19 Mary's husband, Joseph, was a good man. He did not want to cause her public disgrace, so he planned to divorce her secretly.

20 But after Joseph had thought about this, an angel from the Lord came to him in a dream. The angel said, "Joseph, son of David, don't be afraid to accept Mary as your wife. The baby inside her is from the Holy Spirit. 21 She will give birth to a son. You will name him Jesus.*b* Give him that name because he will save his people from their sins."

22 All this happened to make clear the full meaning of what the Lord said through the prophet:

23 "The virgin will be pregnant and will give birth to a son.
They will name him Immanuel."*c*

(Immanuel means "God with us".)
24 When Joseph woke up, he did what the Lord's angel had told him to do. He married Mary. 25 But Joseph did not have sex with her until her son was born. And he named him Jesus.

---

a **1:11** *Jehoiachin* Literally, "Jechoniah", another name for Jehoiachin.
b **1:21** *Jesus* The name Jesus means "the LORD (YAHWEH) saves".
c **1:23** Quote from Isa. 7:14.

THE ROYAL FAMILY TREE

Have you ever spent any time tracing your family tree? You probably did a simple one in school going back one or two generations. Or maybe someone in your family has researched it and gone back hundreds of years.

This kind of study, known as genealogy, can turn up all sorts of interesting facts and stories. Some people find they are related to key historical figures; some even to royalty.

DIG IN

READ Matthew 1:1–17

- Lots of names – some you may not be able to pronounce! Which do you recognize?
- How has Matthew divided the family line up (v.17)?

Where you come from may not seem to matter so much these days. But for Matthew – a Jew writing to an audience mainly of Jewish people – it mattered a lot. That's why, although it might not seem like a very gripping way to start a book, Matthew begins with a long list of names.

By tracing his family history back, Matthew builds a case for who Jesus is. He is a direct descendant of Abraham, the father of the Jewish race, and also of David, the great King of Israel. He shows that Jesus has both Jewish and royal blood.

- Look more closely at verses 3, 5 and 6. What details does Matthew include here?
- How is that pattern picked up at verse 16?

Jewish family lines are organized by the fathers' names and mothers are not often mentioned. But here, Matthew inserts the names of a few of the mums. And when you dig into their histories you realize that they're scandalous (see below)!

Matthew is preparing the stage for another event that will be seen as scandalous – Jesus being born to a virgin girl. God is a God of surprises, and we're about to get another big surprise. Read verses 18–25.

DIG THROUGH

- It's a huge mistake to think of Jesus as no more than a lone teacher who started making big claims about himself. What assurance does Matthew give us that he's the "real deal"? Have you accepted who Jesus really is yet?
- Matthew doesn't brush over the "blips" in Jesus' family line. Has God used mistakes you have made for good in your life? Do you believe he can?
- Has faith in Jesus been in your family line for a long time? Do you know where it began? Could you find out?

DIG DEEPER

Genealogies are common in the Old Testament. Genesis 5:1–32 and 11:10–32 set up who Abraham was, and 1 Chronicles 1 – 10 establish David. As the first book in the New Testament, Matthew provides a bridge from the past to the present, giving continuity for his Jewish audience and basically saying, "This is the one we've been waiting for."

- Take the time to investigate the women Matthew lists in this family line. Tamar is treated as a prostitute by her father-in-law (Genesis 38:6–26), Rahab actually is a prostitute (Joshua 2:1–21), and Uriah's wife is Bathsheba, with whom David had an affair (2 Samuel 11).

Wise Men Come to Visit Jesus

2 Jesus was born in the town of Bethlehem in Judea during the time when Herod was king. After Jesus was born, some wise men from the east came to Jerusalem. 2They asked people, "Where is the child who has been born to be the king of the Jews? We saw the star that shows he was born. We saw it when it came up, and we have come to worship him."

3When King Herod heard about this, it upset him as well as everyone else in Jerusalem. 4Herod called a meeting of all the leading Jewish priests and teachers of the law. He asked them where the Messiah would be born. 5They answered, "In the town of Bethlehem in Judea, just as the prophet wrote:

6'Bethlehem, in the land of Judah,
    you are important among the rulers of
        Judah.
Yes, a ruler will come from you,
    and that ruler will lead Israel, my people.'"

Micah 5:2

7Then Herod had a private meeting with the wise men from the east. He learned from them the exact time they first saw the star. 8Then he sent them to Bethlehem. He said, "Go and look carefully for the child. When you find him, come tell me. Then I can go and worship him too."

9After the wise men heard the king, they left. They saw the same star they had seen when it first came up, and they followed it. The star went before them until it stopped above the place where the child was. 10They were very happy and excited to see the star.

11The wise men came to the house where the child was with his mother Mary. They bowed down and worshipped him. Then they opened the boxes of gifts they had brought for him. They gave him treasures of gold, frankincense and myrrh. 12But God warned the wise men in a dream not to go back to Herod. So they went home to their own country a different way.

Jesus' Parents Take Him to Egypt

13After the wise men left, an angel from the Lord came to Joseph in a dream. The angel said, "Get up! Take the child with his mother and escape to Egypt. Herod wants to kill the child and will soon start looking for him. Stay in Egypt until I tell you to come back."

14So Joseph got ready and left for Egypt with the child and the mother. They left during the night. 15Joseph stayed in Egypt until Herod died. This gave full meaning to what the Lord said through the prophet: "I called my son to come out of Egypt."a

Herod Kills the Baby Boys in Bethlehem

16Herod saw that the wise men had fooled him, and he was very angry. So he gave an order to kill all the baby boys in Bethlehem and the whole area around Bethlehem. Herod had learned from the wise men the time the baby was born. It was now two years from that time. So he gave the order to kill all the boys who were two years old and younger. 17This gave full meaning to what God said through the prophet Jeremiah:

18"A sound was heard in Ramah—
    bitter crying and great sadness.
It was Rachel crying for her children,
    and she refused to be comforted,
    because her children are gone."

Jeremiah 31:15

Joseph and Mary Return From Egypt

19While Joseph was in Egypt, Herod died. An angel from the Lord came to Joseph in a dream 20and said, "Get up! Take the child with his mother and go to Israel. Those who were trying to kill the child are now dead."

21So Joseph took the child and his mother and went to Israel. 22But he heard that Archelaus was now king in Judea. Archelaus became king when his father Herod died. So Joseph was afraid to go there. Then, after being warned in a dream, he went away to the area of Galilee. 23He went to a town called Nazareth and lived there. This gave full meaning to what God said through the prophets. God said the Messiahb would be called a Nazarene.c

John Prepares the Way for Jesus

(Mark 1:1–8; Luke 3:1–9,15–17; John 1:19–28)

3 When it was the right time, John the Baptizer began telling people a message from God. This was out in the desert area of Judea. 2John said, "Change your hearts and lives, because God's kingdom is now very near."d 3John is the one Isaiah the prophet was talking about when he said,

"There is someone shouting in the desert:
'Prepare the way for the Lord.
    Make the road straight for him.'"

Isaiah 40:3

---

a **2:15** Quote from Hos. 11:1.
b **2:23** *the Messiah* Literally, "he". See MESSIAH in the Word List.
c **2:23** *Nazarene* A person from the town of Nazareth. This name sounds like the Hebrew word for "branch". So Matthew may be referring to the promise of a "branch" of David's family. See Isa. 11:1.
d **3:2** *is now very near* Or "is coming soon" or "has come".

[4]John's clothes were made from camel's hair, and he had a leather belt around his waist. For food, he ate locusts and wild honey. [5]People came out to John from Jerusalem and the rest of Judea and from all the areas along the Jordan River. [6]They confessed the bad things they had done, and John baptized them in the Jordan.

[7]Many Pharisees and Sadducees came to be baptized by John. When he saw them, he said, "You are all snakes! Who warned you to run from God's judgement that is coming? [8]Change your hearts! And show by the way you live that you have changed. [9]I know what you are thinking. You want to say, 'But Abraham is our father!' That means nothing. I tell you, God could make children for Abraham from these rocks. [10]The axe is now ready to cut down the trees.[a] Every tree that does not produce good fruit will be cut down and thrown into the fire.

[11]"I baptize you with water to show that you have changed your hearts and lives. But there is someone coming later who is able to do more than I can. I am not good enough even to be the slave who takes off his sandals. He will baptize you with the Holy Spirit and with fire. [12]He will come ready to clean the grain.[b] He will separate the good grain from the chaff, and he will put the good part into his barn. Then he will burn the useless part with a fire that cannot be stopped."

Jesus Is Baptized by John

(Mark 1:9–11; Luke 3:21–22)

[13]Then Jesus came from Galilee to the Jordan River. He came to John, wanting John to baptize him. [14]But John tried to stop him. John said, "Why do you come to me to be baptized? I should be baptized by you!"

[15]Jesus answered, "Let it be this way for now. We should do whatever God says is right." Then John agreed.

[16]So Jesus was baptized. As soon as he came up out of the water, the sky opened, and he saw God's Spirit coming down on him like a dove. [17]A voice from heaven said, "This is my Son, the one I love. I am very pleased with him."

The Temptation of Jesus

(Mark 1:12–13; Luke 4:1–13)

4 Then the Spirit led Jesus into the desert. He was taken there to be tempted by the devil. [2]Jesus ate nothing for 40 days and nights. After this, he was very hungry. [3]The devil[c] came to

tempt him and said, "If you are the Son of God, tell these rocks to become bread."

[4]Jesus answered, "The Scriptures say,

'It is not just bread that keeps people alive. Their lives depend on what God says.'"
Deuteronomy 8:3

[5]Then the devil led Jesus to the holy city of Jerusalem and put him on a high place at the edge of the Temple area. [6]He said to Jesus, "If you are the Son of God, jump off, because the Scriptures say,

'God will command his angels to help you, and their hands will catch you, so that you will not hit your foot on a rock.'"
Psalm 91:11–12

[7]Jesus answered, "The Scriptures also say, 'You must not test the Lord your God.'"[d] [8]Then the devil led Jesus to the top of a very high mountain and showed him all the kingdoms of the world and all the wonderful things in them. [9]The devil said, "If you will bow down and worship me, I will give you all these things." [10]Jesus said to him, "Get away from me, Satan! The Scriptures say,

'You must worship the Lord your God. Serve only him!'"
Deuteronomy 6:13

[11]So the devil left him. Then some angels came to Jesus and helped him.

Jesus Begins His Work in Galilee

(Mark 1:14–15; Luke 4:14–15)

[12]When Jesus heard that John had been put in prison, he went back to Galilee. [13]But he did not stay in Nazareth. He went to live in Capernaum, a town near Lake Galilee in the area near Zebulun and Naphtali. [14]He did this to give full meaning to what the prophet Isaiah said:

[15]"Listen, land of Zebulun and land of Naphtali,
    lands by the road that goes to the sea, the area past the Jordan River—
    Galilee, where those from other nations live.
[16]The people who live in spiritual darkness have seen a great light.

---

[a] **3:10** *trees* The people who don't obey God. They are like "trees" that will be cut down.
[b] **3:12** *clean the grain* Meaning that Jesus will separate the good people from those who are bad.
[c] **4:3** *The devil* Literally, "The tempter."
[d] **4:7** Quote from Deuteronomy 6:16.

The light has shone for those
who live in the land that is as dark as a
grave."

Isaiah 9:1–2

[17]From that time Jesus began to tell people his message: "Change your hearts and lives, because God's kingdom is now very near."[a]

Jesus Chooses Some Followers

(Mark 1:16–20; Luke 5:1–11)

[18]As Jesus was walking by Lake Galilee, he saw two brothers, Simon (called Peter) and Simon's brother Andrew. These brothers were fishermen, and they were fishing in the lake with a net. [19]Jesus said to them, "Come, follow me and I will make you a different kind of fishermen. You will bring in people, not fish." [20]Simon and Andrew immediately left their nets and followed him.

[21]Jesus continued walking by Lake Galilee. He saw two other brothers, James and John, the sons of Zebedee. They were in a boat with their father Zebedee. They were preparing their nets to catch fish. Jesus told the brothers to come with him. [22]So they immediately left the boat and their father, and they followed Jesus.

Jesus Teaches and Heals the People

(Luke 6:17–19)

[23]Jesus went everywhere in the country of Galilee. He taught in the synagogues and told the Good News about God's kingdom. And he healed all the people's diseases and sicknesses. [24]The news about Jesus spread all over Syria, and people brought to him all those who were sick. They were suffering from different kinds of diseases and pain. Some had demons inside them, some suffered from seizures and some were paralysed. Jesus healed them all. [25]Large crowds followed him— people from Galilee, the Ten Towns, Jerusalem, Judea and the area across the Jordan River.

Jesus Teaches the People

(Luke 6:20–23)

5 When Jesus saw the crowds of people there, he went up on a hill and sat down. His followers came and sat next to him. [2]Then Jesus began teaching the people. He said,

[3]"Great blessings belong to those who know
they are spiritually in need.[b]
God's kingdom belongs to them.

[4]Great blessings belong to those who are
sad now.
God will comfort them.

[5]Great blessings belong to those who are
humble.
They will be given the land God
promised.[c]

[6]Great blessings belong to those who want to
do right more than anything else.[d]
God will fully satisfy them.

[7]Great blessings belong to those who show
mercy to others.
Mercy will be given to them.

[8]Great blessings belong to those whose
thoughts are pure.
They will be with God.

[9]Great blessings belong to those who work to
bring peace.
God will call them his sons and
daughters.

[10]Great blessings belong to those who suffer
persecution for doing what is right.
God's kingdom belongs to them.

[11]"People will insult you and hurt you. They will lie and say all kinds of evil things about you because you follow me. But when they do that, know that great blessings belong to you. [12]Be happy about it. Be very glad because you have a great reward waiting for you in heaven. Be glad that you are like the prophets who lived long ago. People did these same bad things to them.

You Are Like Salt and Light

(Mark 9:50; 4:21; Luke 14:34–35; 8:16)

[13]"You are as needed as salt for those on earth. But if the salt loses its taste, it cannot be made salty again. And then it is good for nothing except to be thrown out for people to walk on.

[14]"You are the light that shines for the world to see. You are like a city built on a hill that cannot be hidden. [15]People don't hide a lamp under a bowl. They put it on a lampstand. Then the light shines for everyone in the house. [16]In the same way, you should be a light for other people. Live so that they will see the good things you do and praise your Father in heaven.

Jesus and the Old Testament Writings

[17]"Don't think that I have come to destroy the Law of Moses or the teaching of the prophets. I have come not to destroy their teachings but to give full meaning to them. [18]I assure you that

---

[a] **4:17** *is now very near* Or "is coming soon" or "has come".

[b] **5:3** *those . . . in need* Literally, "the poor in spirit".

[c] **5:5** *They will . . . promised* This is the meaning of these words in Ps. 37:11. Here, they probably refer to a spiritual "promised land", but they can also mean "The earth will belong to them."

[d] **5:6** *want . . . more than anything else* Literally, "hunger and thirst for righteousness".

SHOCKING STANDARDS

Jesus is sitting on a hill, teaching his disciples and the crowds who had come to him there. His theme is what it means to be the people of God – not just how they should *behave* but how they should *be*.

Suddenly, in the middle of his sermon, he starts talking about himself and answers a question many must have been thinking: "Jesus, we love what you're saying but what are we meant to do with the Jewish law we've grown up with?"

DIG IN   READ Matthew 5:17–20

- What is Jesus' claim about himself?
- What does Jesus mean in verse 19? Is it possible to do what he says?

It's a perfectly good question. Jesus' followers are not used to hearing such a radical message. Does this mean they should throw away all they've learnt of the Jewish law?

Jesus answers them: nothing of the "Law of Moses or the teaching of the prophets" (he means the Old Testament) should be lost. Jesus comes to complete those teachings, not to replace them (v.17).

He explains that the way the Pharisees keep the law is not pleasing to God because it's all about actions. Jesus says life in the kingdom of God is about more than outward rule-keeping – it's about obedience from the heart. And then he goes on to give some concrete examples to help the disciples understand what this might look like in practice.

READ Matthew 5:21–30

- What's different about the standards described here, compared to what they've been taught in the past?
- Does any of it surprise you?

It would certainly have surprised those who heard Jesus.

Shock: murder is a horrific act, but anger is just an emotion, right? However, Jesus says both are as bad as each other in that they both bring God's judgement (vv.21–22). It's exactly the same with adultery and lust (vv.27–28).

Shock: God would rather have you miss a Sunday meeting than have you worship him with a heart full of bitterness towards another person (vv.23–24).

What Jesus is teaching here goes much further than before, much deeper than the standard they've grown up with. It looks into our hearts and minds – the deepest part of our beings. Jesus is asking, "Forget the 'religious' you – the way you behave. Do I have the whole you? Do I have your heart?"

Jesus is not rewriting the rulebook. The old rules still make sense and they still stand. But in Jesus, and enabled by his power, we can be changed from the inside out.

DIG THROUGH

- In what areas can you see you're doing the bare minimum, rather than gladly giving your whole heart? Praying for your friends? Obeying your parents?
- "The Old Testament's so difficult! Can't we just stick to the New?" Whether we admit it or not, this is often the way we think. But this is not Jesus' attitude. Do you need to repent of a bad attitude towards the Bible?
- Jesus came to complete the law for us (vv.17–18) and to bring forgiveness for all the times we fail God (check out Matthew 26:26–28). Chew that over and think about the sense of relief it brings. God wants to change you from the inside out, giving you a heart like his, making you more like Jesus, more fully human. Then you won't just behave in a loving way, you'll increasingly be a loving person.

DIG DEEPER

- The Pharisees embody that part of all of us which automatically defers to rule-keeping, doing the bare minimum, obedience of the head without touching the heart. In Jesus' time they showed how it's possible to keep the rules perfectly but be far away from God. Read Luke 18:9–14 to see how.

nothing will disappear from the law until heaven and earth are gone. The law will not lose even the smallest letter or the smallest part of a letter until it has all been done.

¹⁹"A person should obey every command in the law, even one that does not seem important. Whoever refuses to obey any command and teaches others not to obey it will be the least important in God's kingdom. But whoever obeys the law and teaches others to obey it will be great in God's kingdom. ²⁰I tell you that you must do better than the teachers of the law and the Pharisees. If you are not more pleasing to God than they are, you will never enter God's kingdom.

Jesus Teaches About Anger

²¹"You have heard that it was said to our people long ago, 'You must not murder anyone.ᵃ Any person who commits murder will be judged.' ²²But I tell you, don't be angry with anyone. If you are angry with others, you will be judged. And if you insult someone, you will be judged by the high court. And if you call someone a fool, you will be in danger of the fire of hell.

²³"So, what if you are offering your gift at the altar and remember that someone has something against you? ²⁴Leave your gift there and go and make peace with that person. Then come and offer your gift.

²⁵"If anyone wants to take you to court, make friends with them quickly. Try to do that before you get to the court. If you don't, they might hand you over to the judge. And the judge will hand you over to a guard, who will throw you into jail. ²⁶I assure you that you will not leave there until you have paid everything you owe.

Jesus Teaches About Sexual Sin

²⁷"You have heard that it was said, 'You must not commit adultery.'ᵇ ²⁸But I tell you that if a man looks at a woman and wants to sin sexually with her, he has already committed that sin with her in his mind. ²⁹If your right eye makes you sin, take it out and throw it away. It is better to lose one part of your body than to have your whole body thrown into hell. ³⁰If your right hand makes you sin, cut it off and throw it away. It is better to lose one part of your body than for your whole body to go into hell.

Jesus Teaches About Divorce

(Matt. 19:9; Mark 10:11–12; Luke 16:18)

³¹"It was also said, 'Any man who divorces his wife must give her a written notice of divorce.'ᶜ ³²But I tell you that any man who divorces his wife, except for the problem of sexual sin, is causing his wife to be guilty of adultery. And whoever marries a divorced woman is guilty of adultery.

Jesus Teaches About Making Promises

³³"You have heard that it was said to our people long ago, 'When you make a vow, you must not break your promise. Keep the vows that you make to the Lord.'ᵈ ³⁴But I tell you, when you make a promise, don't try to make it stronger with a vow. Don't make a vow using the name of heaven, because heaven is God's throne. ³⁵Don't make a vow using the name of the earth, because the earth belongs to him.ᵉ Don't make a vow using the name of Jerusalem, because it also belongs to him, the great King. ³⁶And don't even say that your own head is proof that you will keep your promise. You cannot make one hair on your head white or black. ³⁷Say only 'yes' if you mean 'yes', and say only 'no' if you mean 'no'. If you say more than that, it is from the Evil One.

Jesus Teaches About Fighting Back

(Luke 6:29–30)

³⁸"You have heard that it was said, 'An eye for an eye, and a tooth for a tooth.'ᶠ ³⁹But I tell you, don't fight back against someone who wants to do harm to you. If they hit you on the right cheek, let them hit the other cheek too. ⁴⁰If anyone wants to sue you in court and take your shirt, let them have your coat too. ⁴¹If a soldier forces you to walk with him one kilometre,ᵍ go with him two. ⁴²Give to anyone who asks you for something. Don't refuse to give to anyone who wants to borrow from you.

Love Your Enemies

(Luke 6:27–28,32–36)

⁴³"You have heard that it was said, 'Love your neighbourʰ and hate your enemy.' ⁴⁴But I tell you, love your enemies. Pray for those who treat you badly. ⁴⁵If you do this, you will be children who are truly like your Father in heaven. He lets

---

ᵃ **5:21** Quote from Exod. 20:13; Deut. 5:17.
ᵇ **5:27** Quote from Exod. 20:14; Deut. 5:18.
ᶜ **5:31** Quote from Deut. 24:1.
ᵈ **5:33** See Lev. 19:12; Num. 30:2; Deut. 23:21.
ᵉ **5:35** *the earth . . . him* Literally, "it is the footstool of his feet".
ᶠ **5:38** Quote from Exod. 21:24; Lev. 24:20.
ᵍ **5:41** *one kilometre* Literally, "one *milion*".
ʰ **5:43** Quote from Lev. 19:18.

the sun rise for all people, whether they are good or bad. He sends rain to those who do right and to those who do wrong. ⁴⁶If you love only those who love you, why should you get a reward for that? Even the tax collectors do that. ⁴⁷And if you are nice only to your friends, you are no better than anyone else. Even the people who don't know God are nice to their friends. ⁴⁸What I am saying is that you must be perfect, just as your Father in heaven is perfect.

Jesus Teaches About Giving

6 "Be careful! When you do something good, don't do it in front of others so that they will see you. If you do that, you will have no reward from your Father in heaven.

²"When you give to those who are poor, don't announce that you are giving. Don't be like the hypocrites. When they are in the synagogues and on the streets, they blow trumpets before they give so that people will see them. They want everyone to praise them. The truth is, that's all the reward they will get. ³So when you give to the poor, don't let anyone know what you are doing.ᵃ ⁴Your giving should be done in private. Your Father can see what is done in private, and he will reward you.

Jesus Teaches About Prayer

(Luke 11:2–4)

⁵"When you pray, don't be like the hypocrites. They love to stand in the synagogues and on the street corners and pray loudly. They want people to see them. The truth is, that's all the reward they will get. ⁶But when you pray, you should go into your room and close the door. Then pray to your Father. He is there in that private place. He can see what is done in private, and he will reward you.

⁷"And when you pray, don't be like the people who don't know God. They say the same things again and again. They think that if they say it enough, their god will hear them. ⁸Don't be like them. Your Father knows what you need before you ask him. ⁹So this is how you should pray:

'Our Father in heaven,
　　we pray that your name will always be kept
　　　　holy.
¹⁰We pray that your kingdom will come—
　　that what you want will be done here on
　　　　earth, the same as in heaven.

¹¹Give us the food we need for today.
¹²Forgive our sins,
　　just as we have forgiven those who did
　　　　wrong to us.
¹³Don't let us be tempted,
　　but save us from the Evil One.'ᵇ

¹⁴Yes, if you forgive others for the wrongs they do to you, your Father in heaven will also forgive your wrongs. ¹⁵But if you don't forgive others, then your Father in heaven will not forgive the wrongs you do.

Jesus Teaches About Fasting

¹⁶"When you fast, don't make yourselves look sad like the hypocrites. They put a look of suffering on their faces so that people will see they are fasting. The truth is, that's all the reward they will get. ¹⁷So when you fast, wash your face and make yourself look nice. ¹⁸Then no one will know you are fasting, except your Father, who is with you even in private. He can see what is done in private, and he will reward you.

You Cannot Serve Two Masters

(Luke 12:33–34; 11:34–36; 16:13)

¹⁹"Don't save treasures for yourselves here on earth. Moths and rust will destroy them. And thieves can break into your house and steal them. ²⁰Instead, save your treasures in heaven, where they cannot be destroyed by moths or rust and where thieves cannot break in and steal them. ²¹Your heart will be where your treasure is.

²²"People can see who you really are by the way you look at them. If you look at them in a generous way, they will see you as full of light. ²³But if you look at people in a selfish way, they will see you as full of darkness. And if the only light you have is really darkness, you have the worst kind of darkness.ᶜ

²⁴"You cannot serve two masters at the same time. You will hate one and love the other, or you will be loyal to one and not care about the other. You cannot serve God and Moneyᵈ at the same time.

Put God's Kingdom First

(Luke 12:22–34)

²⁵"So I tell you, don't worry about the things you need to live—what you will eat, drink or wear. Life is more than what you eat, and you are more than what you wear. ²⁶Look at the birds.

ᵃ **6:3 don't . . . doing** Literally, "don't let your left hand know what your right hand is doing."
ᵇ **6:13** Some Greek copies add: "For the kingdom and the power and the glory belong to you forever. Amen."
ᶜ **6:22–23** Literally, "The lamp of the body is the eye. So, if your eye is generous, your whole body will be full of light. But if your eye is evil, your whole body will be dark. So, if the light in you is darkness, how much is the darkness."
ᵈ **6:24 Money** Or "*mamona*", an Aramaic word meaning "wealth".

They don't plant, harvest or save food in barns, but your heavenly Father feeds them. Don't you know you are worth much more than they are? 27You cannot add any time to your life by worrying about it.

28"And why do you worry about clothes? Look at the wild flowers in the field. See how they grow. They don't work or make clothes for themselves. 29But I tell you that even Solomon, the great and rich king, was not dressed as beautifully as one of these flowers. 30If God makes what grows in the field so beautiful, what do you think he will do for you? It's just grass—one day it's alive, and the next day someone throws it into a fire. But God cares enough to make it beautiful. Surely he will do much more for you. Your faith is so small!

31"Don't worry and say, 'What will we eat?' or 'What will we drink?' or 'What will we wear?' 32That's what those people who don't know God are always thinking about. Don't worry, because your Father in heaven knows that you need all these things. 33Your first concern should always be God's kingdom and whatever he considers good and right. Then he will give you all these other things you need. 34So don't worry about tomorrow. Tomorrow will take care of itself. Each day has enough trouble of its own.

Be Careful About Criticizing Others

(Luke 6:37–38,41–42)

7 "Don't judge others, and God will not judge you. 2If you judge others, you will be judged the same way you judge them. God will treat you the same way you treat others.

3"Why do you see the small piece of dust that is in your friend's eye, but you don't notice the big piece of wood that is in your own? 4Why do you say to your friend, 'Let me get that piece of dust out of your eye'? Look at yourself first! You still have that big piece of wood in your own eye. 5You are a hypocrite! First, take the wood out of your own eye. Then you will see clearly to get the dust out of your friend's eye.

6"Don't give something that is holy to dogs. They will only turn and hurt you. And don't throw your pearls to pigs. They will only step on them.

Ask God for What You Need

(Luke 11:9–13)

7"Continue to ask, and God will give to you. Continue to search, and you will find. Continue to knock, and the door will open for you. 8Yes, whoever continues to ask will receive. Whoever continues to look will find. And whoever continues to knock will have the door opened for them.

9"Do any of you have a son? If he asked for bread, would you give him a rock? 10Or if he asked for a fish, would you give him a snake? Of course not! 11You people are so bad, but you still know how to give good things to your children. So surely your heavenly Father will give good things to those who ask him.

A Very Important Rule

12"Do for others what you would want them to do for you. This is the meaning of the Law of Moses and the teaching of the prophets.

Only a Few Find the Way to Life

(Luke 13:24)

13"You can enter true life only through the narrow gate. The gate to ruin is very wide, and there is plenty of room on the road that leads there. Many people go that way. 14But the gate that opens the way to true life is narrow. And the road that leads there is hard to follow. Only a few people find it.

What People Do Shows What They Are

(Luke 6:43–44; 13:25–27)

15"Be careful of false prophets. They come to you looking gentle like sheep. But they are really dangerous like wolves. 16You will know these people because of what they do. Good things don't come from people who are bad, just as grapes don't come from thornbushes, and figs don't come from thorny weeds. 17In the same way, every good tree produces good fruit, and bad trees produce bad fruit. 18A good tree cannot produce bad fruit, and a bad tree cannot produce good fruit. 19Every tree that does not produce good fruit is cut down and thrown into the fire. 20You will know these false people by what they do.[a]

21"Not everyone who calls me Lord will enter God's kingdom. The only people who will enter are those who do what my Father in heaven wants. 22On that last Day many will call me Lord. They will say, 'Lord, by the power of your name we spoke for God. And by your name we forced out demons and did many miracles.' 23Then I will tell those people clearly, 'Get away from me, you people who do wrong. I never knew you.'

Two Kinds of People

(Luke 6:47–49)

24"Whoever hears these teachings of mine and obeys them is like a wise man who built his house on rock. 25It rained hard, the floods came and the winds blew and beat against that house. But it did not fall because it was built on rock.

---

a **7:20 by what they do** Literally, "by their fruit".

26"Whoever hears these teachings of mine and does not obey them is like a foolish man who built his house on sand. 27It rained hard, the floods came and the winds blew and beat against that house. And it fell with a loud crash."

28When Jesus finished speaking, the people were amazed at his teaching. 29He did not teach like their teachers of the law. He taught like someone who has authority.

INSIGHT

The healings Matthew writes about in this chapter tell us something important about Jesus. First he healed a leper and a non-Jew (Gentile) – both of whom would usually have been excluded from Jewish society. Then he healed a woman, someone whose status and freedom would have been severely limited at the time. This shows us that he cares about everyone.

Matthew 8:1–17

Jesus Heals a Sick Man

(Mark 1:40–45; Luke 5:12–16)

8 Jesus came down from the hill, and a large crowd followed him. 2Then a man sick with leprosy came to him. The man bowed down before Jesus and said, "Lord, you have the power to heal me if you want."

3Jesus touched the man. He said, "I want to heal you. Be healed!" Immediately the man was healed from his leprosy. 4Then Jesus said to him, "Don't tell anyone about what happened. But go and let the priest look at you.ᵃ And offer the gift that Moses commanded for people who are made well. This will show everyone that you are healed."

Jesus Heals an Officer's Servant

(Luke 7:1–10; John 4:43–54)

5Jesus went to the town of Capernaum. When he entered the city, an army officer came to him and begged for help. 6The officer said, "Lord, my servant is very sick at home in bed. He can't move his body and has much pain."

7Jesus said to the officer, "I will go and heal him."

8The officer answered, "Lord, I am not good enough for you to come into my house. You need only to give the order, and my servant will be healed. 9I know this, because I understand authority. There are people who have authority over me, and I have soldiers under my authority. I tell one soldier, 'Go,' and he goes. I tell another soldier, 'Come,' and he comes. I say to my servant, 'Do this,' and my servant obeys me."

10When Jesus heard this, he was amazed. He said to those who were with him, "The truth is, this man has more faith than anyone I have found, even in Israel. 11Many people will come from the east and from the west. These people will sit and eat with Abraham, Isaac and Jacob in God's kingdom. 12And those who should have the kingdom will be thrown out. They will be thrown outside into the darkness, where people will cry and grind their teeth in pain."

13Then Jesus said to the officer, "Go home. Your servant will be healed just as you believed he would." Right then his servant was healed.

Jesus Heals Many People

(Mark 1:29–34; Luke 4:38–41)

14Jesus went to Peter's house. He saw that Peter's mother-in-law was in bed with a high fever. 15He touched her hand, and the fever left her. Then she stood up and began to serve him.

16That evening people brought to Jesus many people who had demons inside them. He spoke and the demons left the people. He healed all those who were sick. 17So Jesus made clear the full meaning of what Isaiah the prophet said:

"He took away our diseases
    and carried away our sicknesses."

Isaiah 53:4

Following Jesus

(Luke 9:57–62)

18When Jesus saw the crowd around him, he told his followers to go to the other side of the lake. 19Then a teacher of the law came to him and said, "Teacher, I will follow you anywhere you go."

20Jesus said to him, "The foxes have holes to live in. The birds have nests. But the Son of Man has no place to rest."

21Another of Jesus' followers said to him, "Lord, I will follow you too, but first let me go and bury my father."

22But Jesus said to him, "Follow me, and let those who are dead bury their own dead."

Jesus' Followers See His Power

(Mark 4:35–41; Luke 8:22–25)

23Jesus got into a boat, and his followers went with him. 24After the boat left the shore, a very

---

ᵃ **8:4 let the priest look at you** The Law of Moses said a priest must decide when a person with leprosy was well.

bad storm began on the lake. The waves covered the boat. But Jesus was sleeping. 25The followers went to him and woke him. They said, "Lord, save us! We will drown!"

26Jesus answered, "Why are you afraid? You don't have enough faith." Then he stood up and gave a command to the wind and the water. The wind stopped, and the lake became very calm.

27The men were amazed. They said, "What kind of man is this? Even the wind and the water obey him!"

Jesus Sends Demons Out of Two Men

(Mark 5:1–20; Luke 8:26–39)

28Jesus arrived at the other side of the lake in the area where the Gadarene people*a* lived. There, two men who had demons inside them came to him. They lived in the burial caves and were so dangerous that no one could use the road by those caves. 29They came to Jesus and shouted, "What do you want with us, Son of God? Did you come here to punish us before the right time?"

30Near that place there was a large herd of pigs feeding. 31The demons begged Jesus, "If you make us leave these men, please send us into that herd of pigs."

32Jesus said to them, "Go!" So the demons left the men and went into the pigs. Then the whole herd of pigs ran down the hill into the lake, and all were drowned. 33The men who had the work of caring for the pigs ran away. They went into town and told the people everything that happened, especially about the men who had the demons. 34Then the whole town went out to see Jesus. When the people saw him, they begged him to leave their area.

Jesus Heals a Paralysed Man

(Mark 2:1–12; Luke 5:17–26)

9 Jesus got into a boat and went back across the lake to his own town. 2Some people brought to him a man who was paralysed and was lying on a mat. Jesus saw that these people had much faith. So he said to the paralysed man, "Young man, you will be glad to hear this. Your sins are forgiven."

3Some of the teachers of the law heard what Jesus said. They said to themselves, "It is an insult to God for this man to say that!"

4Jesus knew what they were thinking. So he said, "Why are you thinking such evil thoughts? 5-6The Son of Man has power on earth to forgive sins. But how can I prove this to you? Maybe you are thinking it was easy for me to say, 'Your sins are forgiven.' There's no proof that it really happened.

But what if I say to the man, 'Stand up and walk'? Then you will be able to see that I really have this power." So Jesus said to the paralysed man, "Stand up. Take your mat and go home."

7The man stood up and went home. 8The people saw this and they were amazed. They praised God for letting someone have such power.

Matthew (Levi) Follows Jesus

(Mark 2:13–17; Luke 5:27–32)

9When Jesus was leaving, he saw a man named Matthew sitting at the place for collecting taxes. Jesus said to him, "Follow me." So he got up and followed Jesus.

10Jesus ate dinner at Matthew's house. Many tax collectors and others with bad reputations came and ate with him and his followers. 11The Pharisees saw that Jesus was eating with these people. They asked his followers, "Why does your teacher eat with tax collectors and other sinners?"

12Jesus heard them say this. So he said to them, "Sick people are the ones who need a doctor, not those who are healthy. 13You need to go and learn what this Scripture means: 'I don't want animal sacrifices; I want you to show kindness to people.'*b* I came to ask sinners to join me, not those who do everything right."

Jesus Is Not Like Other Religious Leaders

(Mark 2:18–22; Luke 5:33–39)

14Then the followers of John came to Jesus and said, "We and the Pharisees fast often, but your followers don't ever fast. Why?"

15Jesus answered, "At a wedding the friends of the bridegroom are not sad while he is with them. They cannot fast then. But the time will come when the bridegroom will be taken from them. Then they will be sad and fast.

16"When someone sews a patch over a hole in an old coat, they never use a piece of cloth that has not already been shrunk. If they do, the patch will shrink and pull away from the coat. Then the hole will be worse. 17Also, people never pour new wine into old wineskins. They would break, the wine would spill out and the wineskins would be ruined. People always put new wine into new wineskins, which won't break, and the wine stays good."

Jesus Gives Life to a Dead Girl and Heals a Sick Woman

(Mark 5:21–43; Luke 8:40–56)

18While Jesus was still talking, a leader of the synagogue came to him. The leader bowed down

---

a **8:28 Gadarene people** Some Greek copies have "Garasenes" and others have "Gergesenes".
b **9:13** Quote from Hos. 6:6.

before him and said, "My daughter has just died. But if you will come and touch her with your hand, she will live again."

19So Jesus and his followers went with the man.

20On the way, there was a woman who had been bleeding for twelve years. She came close behind Jesus and touched the bottom of his coat. 21She was thinking, "If I can touch his coat, I will be healed."

22Jesus turned and saw the woman. He said, "Be happy, dear woman. You are made well because you believed." Then the woman was healed.

23Jesus continued going with the Jewish leader and went into the leader's house. He saw people there who make music for funerals. And he saw a crowd of people crying loudly. 24Jesus said, "Go away. The girl is not dead. She is only sleeping." But the people laughed at him. 25After the people had been sent out of the house, Jesus went into the girl's room. He held the girl's hand, and she stood up. 26The news about this spread all around the area.

Jesus Heals Three Men

27As Jesus was going away from there, two blind men followed him. They said loudly, "Show kindness to us, Son of David."

28Jesus went inside, and the blind men went with him. He asked them, "Do you believe that I am able to make you see again?" They answered, "Yes, Lord, we believe."

29Then Jesus touched their eyes and said, "You believe that I can make you see again, so it will happen." 30Then the men were able to see. Jesus gave them a strong warning. He said, "Don't tell anyone how this happened." 31But they left and spread the news about Jesus all around that area.

32As these two men were leaving, some people brought another man to Jesus. This man could not talk because he had a demon inside him. 33Jesus forced the demon out, and the man was able to talk. The people were amazed and said, "We have never seen anything like this in Israel."

34But the Pharisees said, "The ruler of demons is the one that gives him power to force demons out."

Jesus Feels Sorry for the People

35Jesus travelled through all the towns and villages. He taught in their synagogues and told people the Good News about God's kingdom. He healed all kinds of diseases and sicknesses. 36Jesus saw the many people and felt sorry for them because they were worried and helpless—like sheep without a shepherd to lead them. 37Jesus

said to his followers, "There is such a big harvest of people to bring in. But there are only a few workers to help harvest them. 38God owns the harvest. Ask him to send more workers to help gather his harvest."

Jesus Sends His Apostles on a Mission

(Mark 3:13–19; 6:7–13; Luke 6:12–16; 9:1–6)

10 Jesus called his twelve followers together. He gave them power over evil spirits and power to heal every kind of disease and sickness. 2These are the names of the twelve apostles:

Simon (also called Peter),
Andrew the brother of Peter,
James the son of Zebedee,
John the brother of James,
3Philip,
Bartholomew,
Thomas,
Matthew the tax collector,
James the son of Alphaeus,
Thaddaeus,
4Simon the Zealot,
Judas Iscariot (the one who handed Jesus over to his enemies).

5Jesus sent the twelve men out with these instructions: "Don't go to the non-Jewish people. And don't go into any town where the Samaritans live. 6But go to the people of Israel. They are like sheep that are lost. 7When you go, tell them this: 'God's kingdom is now very near.'a 8Heal the sick. Bring the dead back to life. Heal the people who have leprosy. And force demons out of people. I give you these powers freely, so help others freely. 9Don't carry any money with you—gold or silver or copper. 10Don't carry a bag. Take only the clothes and sandals you are wearing. And don't take a walking stick. A worker should be given what he needs.

11"When you enter a city or town, find some worthy person there and stay in his home until you leave. 12When you enter that home, say, 'Peace be with you.' 13If the people in that home welcome you, they are worthy of your peace. May they have the peace you wished for them. But if they don't welcome you, they are not worthy of your peace. Take back the peace you wished for them. 14And if the people in a home or a town refuse to welcome you or listen to you, then leave that place and shake the dust off your feet.b 15I can assure you that on the judgement day it will be worse for that town than for the people of Sodom and Gomorrah.

a **10:7** *is now very near* Or "is coming soon" or "has come".
b **10:14** *shake the dust off your feet* A warning. It would show that they were finished talking to these people.

Jesus Warns About Troubles

(Mark 13:9–13; Luke 21:12–17)

16"Listen carefully! I am sending you out, and you will be in danger, like sheep among wolves. So you must be as smart as snakes. But also be like doves that don't hurt anyone. 17Be prepared for trouble, because there are people who will arrest you and take you to be judged. They will whip you in their synagogues. 18Because you follow me, they will make you defend yourselves before governors and kings. But this will happen so that you can tell about me to those kings and governors and to the non-Jewish people. 19When you are arrested, don't worry about what to say or how you should say it. At that time you will be given the words to say. 20It will not really be you speaking; the Spirit of your Father will be speaking through you.

21"Brothers will turn against their own brothers and hand them over to be killed. Fathers will hand over their own children to be killed. Children will fight against their own parents and will have them killed. 22Everyone will hate you because you follow me. But the one who remains faithful to the end will be saved. 23When you are treated badly in one town, go to another town. I promise you that you will not finish going to all the towns of Israel before I come to rule as the Son of Man.

24"Students are not better than their teacher. Servants are not better than their master. 25Students should be happy to be treated the same as their teacher. And servants should be happy to be treated the same as their master. If those people call me 'the ruler of demons', and I am the head of the family,*a* then it is even more certain that they will insult you, the members of the family!

Fear God, Not People

(Luke 12:2–7)

26"So don't be afraid of those people. Everything that is hidden will be shown. Everything that is secret will be made known. 27I tell you all this privately, but I want you to tell it publicly. I whisper secrets in your ear, but I want you to announce them openly where everyone can hear. 28"Don't be afraid of people. They can kill the body, but they cannot kill the soul. The only one you should fear is God, the one who can send the body and the soul to be destroyed in hell. 29When birds are sold, two small birds cost only a penny. But not even one of those little birds can die without your Father knowing it. 30God even knows how many hairs are on your head. 31So don't be afraid. You are worth more than a whole flock of birds.

Don't Be Ashamed of Your Faith

(Luke 12:8–9)

32"If you stand before others and are willing to say you believe in me, then I will tell my Father in heaven that you belong to me. 33But if you stand before others and say you do not believe in me, then I will tell my Father in heaven that you do not belong to me.

Following Jesus May Bring You Trouble

(Luke 12:51–53; 14:26–27)

34"Do not think that I have come to bring peace to the earth. I did not come to bring peace. I came to bring trouble.*b* 35I have come to make this happen:

'A son will turn against his father.
    A daughter will turn against her mother.
A daughter-in-law will turn against her
    mother-in-law.
36   Even members of your own family will be
    your enemies.'

Micah 7:6

37"Those who love their father or mother more than they love me are not worthy of me. And those who love their son or daughter more than they love me are not worthy of me. 38Those who will not accept the cross that is given to them when they follow me are not worthy of me. 39Those who try to keep the life they have will lose it. But those who give up their life for me will find true life.

God Will Bless Those Who Welcome You

(Mark 9:41)

40"Whoever accepts you also accepts me. And whoever accepts me accepts the one who sent me. 41Whoever accepts a prophet because he is a prophet will get the same reward a prophet gets. And whoever accepts a godly person just because that person is godly will get the same reward a godly person gets. 42Whoever helps any of these little ones because they are my followers will definitely get a reward, even if they only give them a cup of cold water."

John Sends Men to Ask Jesus a Question

(Luke 7:18–35)

11 When Jesus finished these instructions for his twelve followers, he left there. He went to the towns in Galilee to teach the people and tell them God's message.

2When John was in prison, he heard about the things that were happening—things the Messiah

---

a **10:25** *call me . . . family* Literally, "call the head of the household Beelzebul". See verse 9:34.
b **10:34** *trouble* Literally, "a sword".

would do. So he sent some of his followers to Jesus. [3]They asked him, "Are you the one we have been expecting, or should we wait for someone else?"

[4]Jesus answered, "Go and tell John what you have heard and seen. [5]The blind can see. The lame can walk. People with leprosy are healed. The deaf can hear. The dead are brought back to life. And the Good News is being told to the poor. [6]Great blessings belong to those who don't have a problem accepting me."

[7]When John's followers left, Jesus began talking to the people about John. He said, "What did you people go out to the desert to see? Someone who is weak, like a stem of grass*a* blowing in the wind? [8]Really, what did you expect to see? Someone dressed in fine clothes? Of course not. People who wear fine clothes are all in kings' palaces. [9]So what did you go out to see? A prophet? Yes, John is a prophet. But I tell you, he is more than that. [10]This Scripture was written about him:

'Listen! I will send my messenger ahead of
　　you.
He will prepare the way for you.'

Malachi 3:1

[11]"The truth is that John the Baptizer is greater than anyone who has ever come into this world. But even the least important person in God's kingdom is greater than John. [12]Since the time John the Baptizer came until now, God's kingdom has been going forward strongly.*b* And people have been trying to take control of it by force. [13]Before John came, the Law of Moses and all the prophets told about the things that would happen. [14]And if you believe what they said, then John is Elijah.*c* He is the one they said would come. [15]You people who hear me, listen!

[16]"What can I say about the people who live today? What are they like? The people today are like children sitting in the marketplace. One group of children calls to the other group,

[17]'We played flute music for you,
　　but you did not dance;
we sang a funeral song,
　　but you were not sad.'

[18]Why do I say people are like that? Because John came and did not eat the usual food or drink wine, and people say, 'He has a demon inside

him.' [19]The Son of Man came eating and drinking, and people say, 'Look at him! He eats too much and drinks too much wine. He's a friend of tax collectors and other sinners.' But wisdom is shown to be right by what it does."

Jesus Warns People Who Refuse to Believe

(Luke 10:13–15)

[20]Then Jesus criticized the cities where he did most of his miracles. He criticized these cities because the people there did not change their lives and stop sinning. [21]Jesus said, "It will be bad for you Chorazin! It will be bad for you Bethsaida!*d* I did many miracles in you. If these same miracles had happened in Tyre and Sidon, the people there would have changed their lives a long time ago. They would have worn sackcloth and put ashes on themselves to show that they were sorry for their sins. [22]But I tell you, on the day of judgement it will be worse for you than for Tyre and Sidon.

[23]"And you, Capernaum, will you be lifted up to heaven? No! You will be thrown down to the place of death. I did many miracles in you. If these same miracles had happened in Sodom, the people there would have stopped sinning, and it would still be a city today. [24]But I tell you, it will be worse for you on the day of judgement than for Sodom."

Jesus Offers Rest to His People

(Luke 10:21–22)

[25]Then Jesus said, "I praise you, Father, Lord of heaven and earth. I am thankful that you have hidden these things from those who are so wise and so smart. But you have shown them to people who are like little children. [26]Yes, Father, you did this because it's what you really wanted to do.

[27]"My Father has given me everything. No one knows the Son—only the Father knows the Son. And no one knows the Father—only the Son knows the Father. And the only people who will know about the Father are those the Son chooses to tell.

[28]"Come to me all of you who are tired from the heavy burden you have been forced to carry. I will give you rest. [29]Accept my teaching.*e* Learn from me. I am gentle and humble in spirit. And you will be able to get some rest. [30]Yes, the teaching that I ask you to accept is easy. The load I give you to carry is light."

---

a **11:7 stem of grass** Literally, "reed".

b **11:12 has been . . . strongly** Or "has suffered violence".

c **11:14 Elijah** See Mal. 4:5–6.

d **11:21 Chorazin, Bethsaida** Jewish towns by Lake Galilee where Jesus performed many miracles to show his authority from God. In spite of this, the people refused to change their godless way of living.

e **11:29 Accept my teaching** Literally, "Take my yoke upon you." A yoke was put on the neck of a work animal for pulling a load. It was a Jewish symbol for the law. See Acts 15:10; Gal. 5:1.

Jesus Is Lord Over the Sabbath Day

(Mark 2:23–28; Luke 6:1–5)

12 About that same time, Jesus was walking through the fields of grain on a Sabbath day. His followers were with him, and they were hungry. So they began to pick the grain and eat it. ²The Pharisees saw this. They said to Jesus, "Look! Your followers are doing something that is against our law to do on the Sabbath day."

³Jesus said to them, "You have read what David did when he and those with him were hungry. ⁴David went into God's house. He and those with him ate the bread that was offered to God. It was against the law for David or those with him to eat that bread. Only the priests were allowed to eat it. ⁵And you have read in the Law of Moses that on every Sabbath day the priests at the Temple break the law about the Sabbath day. But they are not wrong for doing that. ⁶I tell you that there is something here that is greater than the Temple. ⁷The Scriptures say, 'I don't want animal sacrifices; I want you to show kindness to people.'ᵃ You don't really know what that means. If you understood it, you would not judge those who have done nothing wrong.

⁸"The Son of Man is Lord over the Sabbath day."

Jesus Heals a Man on the Sabbath Day

(Mark 3:1–6; Luke 6:6–11)

⁹Jesus went from there to their synagogue. ¹⁰In the synagogue there was a man with a paralysed hand. Some Jews there were looking for a reason to accuse Jesus of doing wrong. So they asked him, "Is it right to heal on the Sabbath day?"ᵇ

¹¹Jesus answered, "If any of you has a sheep and it falls into a ditch on the Sabbath day, you will take the sheep and help it out of the ditch. ¹²Surely a man is more important than a sheep. So it is right to do good on the Sabbath day."

¹³Then Jesus said to the man with the paralysed hand, "Hold out your hand." The man held out his hand, and it became well again, the same as the other hand. ¹⁴But the Pharisees left and made plans to kill Jesus.

Jesus Is God's Chosen Servant

¹⁵Jesus knew what the Pharisees were planning. So he left that place, and many people followed him. He healed all who were sick, ¹⁶but he warned them not to tell others who he was. ¹⁷This was to give full meaning to what Isaiah the prophet said when he spoke for God:

¹⁸"Here is my servant,
  the one I have chosen.
He is the one I love,
  and I am very pleased with him.
I will fill him with my Spirit,
  and he will bring justice to the nations.
¹⁹He will not argue or shout;
  no one will hear his voice in the streets.
²⁰He will not break off even a bent stem of
    grass.ᶜ
  He will not put out even the weakest flame.
  He will not give up until he has made justice
    victorious.
²¹ All people will hope in him."

Isaiah 42:1–4

Jesus' Power Is From God

(Mark 3:20–30; Luke 11:14–23; 12:10)

²²Then some people brought a man to Jesus. This man was blind and could not talk, because he had a demon inside him. Jesus healed the man, and he could talk and see. ²³All the people were amazed at what Jesus did. They said, "Maybe he is the promised Son of David!"

²⁴When the Pharisees heard this, they said, "This man uses the power of Satanᵈ to force demons out of people. Satan is the ruler of demons."

²⁵Jesus knew what the Pharisees were thinking. So he said to them, "Every kingdom that fights against itself will be destroyed. And every city or family that is divided against itself will not survive. ²⁶So if Satan forces out his own demons,ᵉ then he is fighting against himself, and his kingdom will not survive. ²⁷You say that I use the power of Satan to force out demons. If that is true, then what power do your people use when they force out demons? So your own people will prove that you are wrong. ²⁸But I use the power of God's Spirit to force out demons, and this shows that God's kingdom has already come to you. ²⁹Whoever wants to enter a strong man's house and steal his things must first tie him up. Then they can steal the things from his house. ³⁰Whoever is not with me is against me. And anyone who does not work with me is working against me.

³¹"So I tell you, people can be forgiven for every sinful thing they do and for every bad thing they say against God. But anyone who speaks against the Holy Spirit will not be forgiven. ³²You can even speak against the Son of Man and be forgiven. But anyone who speaks against the Holy

---

ᵃ **12:7** Quote from Hos. 6:6.
ᵇ **12:10** *"Is it right . . . day?"* It was against Jewish law to work on the Sabbath day.
ᶜ **12:20** *stem of grass* Literally, "reed".
ᵈ **12:24** *Satan* Literally, "Beelzebul" (the devil). Also in verse 27.
ᵉ **12:26** *if Satan . . . demons* Literally, "if Satan forces out Satan".

Spirit will never be forgiven—not now or in the future.

What You Do Shows What You Are

(Luke 6:43–45)

33"If you want good fruit, you must make the tree good. If your tree is not good, it will have bad fruit. A tree is known by the kind of fruit it produces. 34You snakes! You are so evil. How can you say anything good? What people say with their mouths comes from what fills their hearts. 35Those who are good have good things saved in their hearts. That's why they say good things. But those who are evil have hearts full of evil, and that's why they say things that are evil. 36I tell you that everyone will have to answer for all the careless things they have said. This will happen on the day of judgement. 37Your words will be used to judge you. What you have said will show whether you are right or whether you are guilty."

Some People Doubt Jesus' Authority

(Mark 8:11–12; Luke 11:29–32)

38Then some of the Pharisees and teachers of the law answered Jesus. They said, "Teacher, we want to see you do a miracle as a sign from God."

39Jesus answered, "Evil and sinful people are the ones who want to see a miracle as a sign from God. But no miracle will be done to prove anything to them. The only sign will be the miracle that happened to the prophet Jonah.*a* 40Jonah was in the stomach of the big fish for three days and three nights. In the same way, the Son of Man will be in the grave three days and three nights. 41On the judgement day, you people who live now will be compared with the people from Nineveh,*b* and they will be witnesses who show how guilty you are. Why do I say this? Because when Jonah preached to those people, they changed their lives. And you are listening to someone greater than Jonah, but you refuse to change!

42"On the judgement day, you people who live now will also be compared with the queen of the South,*c* and she will be a witness who shows how guilty you are. I say this because she travelled from far, far away to listen to Solomon's wise teaching. And I tell you that someone greater than Solomon is right here, but you won't listen to me!

The Danger of Emptiness

(Luke 11:24–26)

43"When an evil spirit comes out of a person, it travels through dry places looking for a place to rest, but it finds none. 44So it says, 'I will go back to the home I left.' When it comes back, it finds that home still empty. It is all neat and clean. 45Then the evil spirit goes out and brings seven other spirits more evil than itself. They all go and live there, and that person has even more trouble than before. It is the same way with the evil people who live today."

Jesus' Followers Are His True Family

(Mark 3:31–35; Luke 8:19–21)

46While Jesus was talking to the people, his mother and brothers stood outside. They wanted to talk to him. 47Someone told him, "Your mother and brothers are waiting for you outside. They want to talk to you."

48Jesus answered, "Who is my mother? Who are my brothers?" 49Then he pointed to his followers and said, "See! These people are my mother and my brothers. 50Yes, anyone who does what my Father in heaven wants is my true brother and sister and mother."

A Story About a Farmer Sowing Seed

(Mark 4:1–9; Luke 8:4–8)

13 Later that day, Jesus went outside. He was sitting by the lake, 2and a large crowd gathered around him. So he got into a boat and sat down. All the people stayed on the shore. 3Then Jesus used stories to teach them many things. He told them this story:

"A farmer went out to sow seed. 4While he was scattering the seed, some of it fell by the road. The birds came and ate all that seed. 5Other seed fell on rocky ground, where there was not enough soil. It grew very fast there, because the soil was not deep. 6But when the sun rose, it burned the plants. The plants died because they did not have deep roots. 7Some other seed fell among thorny weeds. The weeds grew and stopped the good plants from growing. 8But some of the seed fell on good ground. There it grew and made grain. Some plants made 100 times more grain, some 60 times more and some 30 times more. 9You people who hear me, listen!"

Why Jesus Used Stories to Teach

(Mark 4:10–12; Luke 8:9–10)

10The followers came to Jesus and asked, "Why do you use these stories to teach the people?"

11Jesus answered, "Only you can know the secret truths about God's kingdom. Those other people cannot know these secret truths. 12The

---

a **12:39 Jonah** The story about Jonah is found in the Old Testament book of Jonah.
b **12:41 Nineveh** City where Jonah preached. See Jonah 3.
c **12:42 queen of the South** Or "queen of Sheba". She travelled about 1,600 kilometres to learn God's wisdom from Solomon. See 1 Kgs 10:1–13.

people who have some understanding will be given more. And they will have even more than they need. But those who do not have much understanding will lose even the little understanding that they have. ¹³This is why I use these stories to teach the people: they see, but they don't really see. They hear, but they don't really hear or understand. ¹⁴So they give full meaning to what God told Isaiah to say to his people:

'"You people will listen and listen,
  but you will not understand.
You will look and look,
  but you will not really see."
¹⁵These people are not able to understand.
  Their ears are stopped up,
  and their eyes are closed.
So they cannot see with their eyes,
  or hear with their ears,
  or understand with their minds.
If they understood, they might turn to me,
  and I would heal them!'

Isaiah 6:9–10

¹⁶But God has blessed you. You understand what you see with your eyes. And you understand what you hear with your ears. ¹⁷I can assure you, many prophets and godly people wanted to see what you now see. But they did not see it. And many prophets and godly people wanted to hear what you now hear. But they did not hear it.

Jesus Explains the Story About Seed

(Mark 4:13–20; Luke 8:11–15)

¹⁸"So listen to the meaning of that story about the farmer:

¹⁹"What about the seed that fell by the path? That is like the people who hear the teaching about God's kingdom but do not understand it. The Evil One comes and takes away what was planted in their hearts.

²⁰"And what about the seed that fell on rocky ground? That is like the people who hear the teaching and quickly and gladly accept it. ²¹But they do not let the teaching go deep into their lives. They keep it only a short time. As soon as trouble or *persecution* comes because of the teaching they accepted, they give up.

²²"And what about the seed that fell among the thorny weeds? That is like the people who hear the teaching but let worries about this life and love for money stop it from growing. So it does not produce good results in their lives.ᵃ

²³"But what about the seed that fell on the good ground? That is like the people who hear the teaching and understand it. They grow and produce a good crop, sometimes 100 times more, sometimes 60 times more and sometimes 30 times more."

A Story About Wheat and Weeds

²⁴Then Jesus used another story to teach them. Jesus said, "God's kingdom is like a man who planted good seed in his field. ²⁵That night, while everyone was asleep, the man's enemy came and planted weeds among the wheat and then left. ²⁶Later, the wheat grew, and heads of grain grew on the plants. But at the same time the weeds also grew. ²⁷Then the man's servants came to him and said, 'You planted good seed in your field. Where did the weeds come from?'

²⁸"The man answered, 'An enemy planted weeds.'

"The servants asked, 'Do you want us to go and pull up the weeds?'

²⁹"He answered, 'No, because when you pull up the weeds, you might also pull up the wheat. ³⁰Let the weeds and the wheat grow together until the harvest time. At the harvest time I will tell the workers this: "First, gather the weeds and tie them together to be burned. Then gather the wheat and bring it to my barn."'"

What Is God's Kingdom Like?

(Mark 4:30–34; Luke 13:18–21)

³¹Then Jesus told the people another story: "God's kingdom is like a mustard seed that a man plants in his field. ³²It is the smallest of all seeds. But when it grows, it is the largest of all garden plants. It becomes a tree big enough for the birds to come and make nests in its branches."

³³Then Jesus told them another story: "God's kingdom is like yeast that a woman mixes into a big bowl of flour to make bread. The yeast makes all the dough rise."

³⁴Jesus used stories to tell all these things to the people. He always used stories to teach them. ³⁵This was to make clear the full meaning of what the prophet said:

"I will speak using stories;
  I will tell things that have been secrets since
    the world was made."

Psalm 78:2

Jesus Explains a Hard Story

³⁶Then Jesus left the people and went into the house. His followers came to him and said,

---

ᵃ **13:22 does not produce . . . lives** Literally, "becomes unfruitful", meaning that these people do not do the good things God wants his people to do.

"Explain to us the meaning of the story about the weeds in the field."

37He answered, "The man who planted the good seed in the field is the Son of Man. 38The field is the world. The good seeds are the people in God's kingdom. The weeds are the people who belong to the Evil One. 39And the enemy who planted the bad seed is the devil. The harvest is the end of time. And the workers who gather are God's angels.

40"The weeds are pulled up and burned in the fire. It will be the same at the end of time. 41The Son of Man will send his angels, and they will find the people who cause sin and all those who do evil. The angels will take those people out of his kingdom. 42They will throw them into the place of fire. There the people will be crying and grinding their teeth in pain. 43Then the godly people will shine like the sun. They will be in the kingdom of their Father. You people who hear me, listen!

Stories About a Treasure and a Pearl

44"God's kingdom is like a treasure hidden in a field. One day a man found the treasure. He hid it again and was so happy that he went and sold everything he owned and bought the field.

45"Also, God's kingdom is like a merchant looking for fine pearls. 46One day he found a very fine pearl. He went and sold everything he had to buy it.

A Story About a Fishing Net

47"Also, God's kingdom is like a net that was put into the lake. The net caught many different kinds of fish. 48It was full, so the fishermen pulled it to the shore. They sat down and put all the good fish in baskets. Then they threw away the bad fish. 49It will be the same at the end of time. The angels will come and separate the evil people from the godly people. 50They will throw the evil people into the place of fire. There the people will cry and grind their teeth in pain."

51Then Jesus asked his followers, "Do you understand all these things?"

They said, "Yes, we understand."

52Then Jesus said to the followers, "So every teacher of the law who has learned about God's kingdom has some new things to teach. He is like the owner of a house. He has new things and old things saved in that house. And he brings out the new with the old."

Jesus Goes to His Home Town

(Mark 6:1–6; Luke 4:16–30)

53When Jesus finished teaching with these stories, he left there. 54He went to the town where he grew up. He taught the people in the synagogue, and they were amazed. They said, "Where did this man get such wisdom and this power to do miracles? 55Isn't he just the son of the carpenter we know? Isn't his mother's name Mary and aren't his brothers James, Joseph, Simon and Judas? 56And don't all his sisters still live here in town? How is he able to do these things?" 57So they had a problem accepting him.

But Jesus said to them, "People everywhere give honour to a prophet, but in his own town or in his own home a prophet does not get any honour." 58Jesus did not do many miracles there, because the people did not believe in him.

Herod Thinks Jesus Is John the Baptizer

(Mark 6:14–29; Luke 9:7–9)

14 About that time, Herod, the ruler of Galilee, heard what the people were saying about Jesus. 2So he said to his servants, "I think this man is really John the Baptizer. He must have risen from death, and that is why he can do these miracles."

How John the Baptizer Was Killed

3Before this time, Herod had arrested John. He had him chained and put in prison. He arrested John because of Herodias, the wife of Philip, Herod's brother. 4John had told him, "It is not right for you to be married to Herodias." 5Herod wanted to kill him, but he was afraid of the people. They believed that John was a prophet.

6On Herod's birthday, the daughter of Herodias danced for him and his group. Herod was very pleased with her. 7So he promised that he would give her anything she wanted. 8Herodias told her daughter what to ask for. So she said to Herod, "Give me the head of John the Baptizer here on this plate."

9King Herod was very sad. But he had promised to give the daughter anything she wanted. And the people eating with Herod had heard his promise. So he gave orders for it to be done. 10He sent men to the prison, where they cut off John's head. 11And the men brought John's head on a plate and gave it to the girl. Then she took the head to her mother, Herodias. 12John's followers came and got his body and buried it. Then they went and told Jesus what had happened.

Jesus Feeds More Than 5,000

(Mark 6:30–44; Luke 9:10–17; John 6:1–14)

13When Jesus heard what had happened to John, he left in a boat. He went alone to a place where no one lived. But the people heard that Jesus had left. So they left their towns and followed him. They went by land to the same place. 14When Jesus got out of the boat, he saw a large crowd of people. He felt sorry for them, and he healed the ones who were sick.

15Late that afternoon, the followers came to Jesus and said, "No one lives in this place. And it is already late. Send the people away so they can go to the towns and buy food for themselves."

16Jesus said, "The people don't need to go away. You give them some food to eat."

17The followers answered, "But we have only five loaves of bread and two fish."

18Jesus said, "Bring the bread and the fish to me." 19Then he told the people to sit down on the grass. He took the five loaves of bread and the two fish. He looked into the sky and thanked God for the food. Then he broke the bread into pieces, which he gave to the followers, and they gave the food to the people. 20Everyone ate until they were full. When they had finished eating, the followers filled twelve baskets with the pieces of food that were not eaten. 21There were about 5,000 men there who ate. There were also women and children who ate.

Jesus Walks on Water

(Mark 6:45–52; John 6:16–21)

22Then Jesus made the followers get into the boat. He told them to go to the other side of the lake. He said he would come later. He stayed there to tell everyone they could go home. 23After Jesus said goodbye to the people, he went up into the hills by himself to pray. It was late, and he was there alone. 24By this time the boat was already a long way from shore. Since the wind was blowing against it, the boat was having trouble because of the waves.

25Between three and six o'clock in the morning, Jesus' followers were still in the boat. Jesus came to them. He was walking on the water. 26When they saw him walking on the water, it scared them. "It's a ghost!" they said, screaming in fear. 27But Jesus quickly spoke to them. He said, "Don't worry! It's me! Don't be afraid."

28Peter said, "Lord, if that is really you, tell me to come to you on the water."

29Jesus said, "Come, Peter."

Then Peter left the boat and walked on the water to Jesus. 30But while Peter was walking on the water, he saw the wind and the waves. He was afraid and began sinking into the water. He shouted, "Lord, save me!"

31Then Jesus caught Peter with his hand. He said, "Your faith is small. Why did you doubt?"

32After Peter and Jesus had got into the boat, the wind stopped. 33Then the followers in the boat worshipped Jesus and said, "You really are the Son of God."

Jesus Heals Many Sick People

(Mark 6:53–56)

34After they had crossed the lake, they came to the shore at Gennesaret. 35Some men there saw Jesus and knew who he was. So they sent word to the other people throughout that area that Jesus had come. The people brought all their sick people to him. 36They begged Jesus to let them only touch the edge of his coat to be healed. And all the sick people who touched his coat were healed.

God's Law and Human Traditions

(Mark 7:1–23)

15 Then some Pharisees and teachers of the law came to Jesus. They came from Jerusalem and asked him, 2"Why do your followers not obey the traditions we have from our great leaders who lived long ago? Your followers don't wash their hands before they eat!"

3Jesus answered, "And why do you refuse to obey God's command so that you can follow your own traditions? 4God said, 'You must respect your father and mother.'*a* And God also said, 'Whoever says anything bad to their father or mother must be killed.'*b* 5But you teach that a person can say to their father or mother, 'I have something I could use to help you. But I will not use it for you. I will give it to God.' 6You are teaching them not to respect their father or mother. So you are teaching that it is not important to do what God said. You think it is more important to follow your own traditions. 7You are hypocrites! Isaiah was right when he spoke for God about you:

8'These people honour me with their words,
   but I am not really important to them.
9Their worship of me is useless.
   The things they teach are only human
       rules.'"

Isaiah 29:13

10Jesus called the people to him. He said, "Listen and understand what I am saying. 11It is not what people put in their mouth that makes them wrong.*c* It is what comes out of their mouth that makes them wrong."

12Then the followers came to Jesus and asked, "Do you know that the Pharisees are upset about what you said?"

---

a **15:4** Quote from Exod. 20:12; Deut. 5:16.
b **15:4** Quote from Exod. 21:17.
c **15:11** *wrong* Literally, "unclean" or "not pure", meaning unacceptable to God. Also in verse 18.

¹³Jesus answered, "Every plant that my Father in heaven has not planted will be pulled up by the roots. ¹⁴Stay away from the Pharisees. They lead the people, but they are like blind men leading other blind men. And if a blind man leads another blind man, both of them will fall into a ditch."

¹⁵Peter said, "Explain to us what you said earlier to the people."

¹⁶Jesus said, "Do you still have trouble understanding? ¹⁷Surely you know that all the food that enters the mouth goes into the stomach. Then it goes out of the body. ¹⁸But the bad things people say with their mouth come from the way they think. And that's what can make people wrong. ¹⁹All these bad things begin in the mind: evil thoughts, murder, adultery, sexual sins, stealing, lying and insulting people. ²⁰These are the things that make people wrong. Eating without washing their hands will never make people unacceptable to God."

Jesus Helps a Non-Jewish Woman

(Mark 7:24–30)

²¹Jesus went from there to the area of Tyre and Sidon. ²²A Canaanite woman from that area came out and began shouting, "Lord, Son of David, please help me! My daughter has a demon inside her, and she is suffering very much."

²³But Jesus did not answer her. So the followers came to him and said, "Tell her to go away. She keeps crying out and will not leave us alone."

²⁴Jesus answered, "God sent me only to the lost people^a of Israel."

²⁵Then the woman came over to Jesus and bowed before him. She said, "Lord, help me!"

²⁶He answered her with the saying, "It is not right to take the children's bread and give it to the dogs."

²⁷The woman said, "Yes, Lord, but even the dogs eat the pieces of food that fall from their master's table."

²⁸Then Jesus answered, "Woman, you have great faith! You will get what you asked for." And right then the woman's daughter was healed.

Jesus Heals Many People

²⁹Then Jesus went from there to the shore of Lake Galilee. He went up into the hills and sat down.

³⁰A large crowd of people came to him. They brought many other sick people and put them before him. There were people who could not walk, people who were blind, paralysed or deaf and many others. Jesus healed them all. ³¹People were amazed when they saw that those who could not speak were now able to speak. Paralysed people were made strong. Those who could not walk were now able to walk. The blind were able to see. Everyone thanked the God of Israel for this.

Jesus Feeds More Than 4,000

(Mark 8:1–10)

³²Jesus called his followers to him and said, "I feel sorry for these people. They have been with me for three days, and now they have nothing to eat. I don't want to send them away hungry. They might faint while going home."

³³The followers asked Jesus, "Where can we get enough bread to feed all these people? We are a long way from any town."

³⁴Jesus asked, "How many loaves of bread do you have?"

They answered, "We have seven loaves of bread and a few small fish."

³⁵Jesus told the people to sit on the ground. ³⁶He took the seven loaves of bread and the fish. Then he gave thanks to God for the food. He broke the bread into pieces, which he gave to the followers, and they gave the food to the people. ³⁷All the people ate until they were full. After this, the followers filled seven baskets with the pieces of food that were not eaten. ³⁸There were about 4,000 men there who ate. There were also some women and children. ³⁹After they had all eaten, Jesus told the people they could go home. He got into the boat and went to the area of Magadan.

Some People Doubt Jesus' Authority

(Mark 8:11–13; Luke 12:54–56)

16 The Pharisees and Sadducees came to Jesus. They wanted to test him. So they asked him to show them a miracle as a sign from God.

²Jesus answered, "When you people see the sunset, you know what the weather will be. If the sky is red, you say we will have good weather. ³And in the morning, if the sky is dark and red, you say that it will be a rainy day. These are signs of the weather. You see these signs in the sky and know what they mean. In the same way, you see the things that are happening now. These are also signs, but you don't know their meaning. ⁴It is the evil and sinful people who want to see a miracle as a sign from God. But no miracle will be done to prove anything to them. The only sign will be the miracle that happened to Jonah."^b Then Jesus went away from there.

---

^a **15:24 people** Literally, "sheep".

^b **16:4 Jonah** A prophet in the Old Testament. After three days in a big fish he came out alive, just as Jesus would come out from the tomb on the third day.

Jesus' Followers Misunderstand Him

(Mark 8:14–21)

⁵Jesus and his followers went across the lake. But the followers forgot to bring bread. ⁶Jesus said to the followers, "Be careful! Guard against the yeast of the Pharisees and the Sadducees."

⁷The followers discussed the meaning of this. They said, "Did Jesus say this because we forgot to bring bread?"

⁸Jesus knew that they were talking about this. So he asked them, "Why are you talking about not having bread? Your faith is small. ⁹Do you still not understand? Remember the five loaves of bread that fed the 5,000 people and the many baskets you filled with the bread that was left? ¹⁰And remember the seven loaves of bread that fed the 4,000 people and the many baskets you filled that time? ¹¹So how could you think that I am concerned about bread? I am telling you to be careful and guard against the yeast of the Pharisees and the Sadducees."

¹²Then the followers understood what Jesus meant. He was not telling them to guard against the yeast used in bread. He was telling them to guard against the teaching of the Pharisees and the Sadducees.

Peter Says Jesus Is the Messiah

(Mark 8:27–30; Luke 9:18–21)

¹³Jesus went to the area of Caesarea Philippi. He said to his followers, "Who do people say I am?"[a]

¹⁴They answered, "Some people say you are John the Baptizer. Others say you are Elijah. And some say you are Jeremiah or one of the prophets."

¹⁵Then Jesus said to his followers, "And who do you say I am?"

¹⁶Simon Peter answered, "You are the Messiah, the Son of the living God."

¹⁷Jesus answered, "You are blessed, Simon son of Jonah. No one taught you that. My Father in heaven showed you who I am. ¹⁸So I tell you, you are Peter. And I will build my church on this rock.[b] The power of death[c] will not be able to defeat my church. ¹⁹I will give you the keys to God's kingdom. When you speak judgement here on earth, that judgement will be *God's judgement.* When you promise forgiveness here on earth, that forgiveness will be God's forgiveness."[d]

²⁰Then Jesus warned his followers not to tell anyone he was the Messiah.

Jesus Says He Must Die

(Mark 8:31 – 9:1; Luke 9:22–27)

²¹From that time Jesus began telling his followers that he must go to Jerusalem. He explained that the older Jewish leaders, the leading priests and the teachers of the law would make him suffer many things. And he told his followers that he must be killed. Then, on the third day, he would be raised from death.

²²Peter took Jesus away from the other followers to talk to him alone. He began to criticize him. He said, "God save you from those sufferings, Lord! That will never happen to you!"

²³Then Jesus said to Peter, "Get away from me, Satan![e] You are not helping me! You don't care about the same things God does. You care only about things that people think are important."

²⁴Then Jesus said to his followers, "If any of you want to be my follower, you must stop thinking about yourself and what you want. You must be willing to carry the cross that is given to you for following me. ²⁵Any of you who try to save the life you have will lose it. But you who give up your life for me will find true life. ²⁶It is worth nothing for you to have the whole world if you yourself are lost. You could never pay enough to buy back your life. ²⁷I, the Son of Man, will come again with my Father's glory and with his angels. And I will reward everyone for what they have done. ²⁸Believe me when I say that there are some people standing here who will live to see me coming as the Son of Man to rule as king."

Jesus Is Seen With Moses and Elijah

(Mark 9:2–13; Luke 9:28–36)

17 Six days later, Jesus took Peter, James and John the brother of James and went up on a high mountain. They were all alone there. ²While these followers watched him, Jesus was changed. His face became bright like the sun, and his clothes became white as light. ³Then two men were there, talking with him. They were Moses and Elijah.

⁴Peter said to Jesus, "Lord, it is good that we are here. If you want, I will make three shelters here— one for you, one for Moses and one for Elijah."

---

[a] **16:13** *I am* Literally, "the Son of Man is".

[b] **16:18** *Peter . . . rock* "Peter", the Greek form of the Aramaic name "Cephas", means "rock". In the Scriptures (Isa. 51:1–2), as well as in Jewish tradition, Abraham was compared to a rock that God could use to "build" his people. So Jesus may imply that Peter is like Abraham. God gave new names to Abraham and Sarah and honoured them as fitting examples of faith for their descendants. In a similar way, Jesus renamed Peter (see Mark 3:16) and honours him here for his bold expression of faith.

[c] **16:18** *power of death* Literally, "gates of Hades".

[d] **16:19** *When you speak . . . God's forgiveness* Literally, "Whatever you bind on earth will have been bound in heaven, and whatever you loose on earth will have been loosed in heaven."

[e] **16:23** *Satan* Name for the devil meaning "the enemy". Jesus means that Peter was talking like Satan.

5While Peter was talking, a bright cloud came over them. A voice came from the cloud and said, "This is my Son, the one I love. I am very pleased with him. Obey him!"

6The followers with Jesus heard this voice. They were very afraid, so they fell to the ground. 7But Jesus came to them and touched them. He said, "Stand up. Don't be afraid." 8The followers looked up, and they saw that Jesus was now alone.

9As Jesus and the followers were coming down the mountain, he gave them this command: "Don't tell anyone about what you saw on the mountain. Wait until the Son of Man has been raised from death. Then you can tell people about what you saw."

10The followers asked Jesus, "Why do the teachers of the law say that Elijah must come[a] before the Messiah comes?"

11Jesus answered, "They are right to say Elijah is coming. And it is true that Elijah will make all things the way they should be. 12But I tell you, Elijah has already come. People did not know who he was, and they treated him badly, doing whatever they wanted to do. It is the same with the Son of Man. Those same people will make the Son of Man suffer." 13Then the followers understood that when Jesus said Elijah, he was really talking about John the Baptizer.

Jesus Frees a Boy From an Evil Spirit

(Mark 9:14–29; Luke 9:37–43a)

14Jesus and the followers went back to the people. A man came to Jesus and bowed before him. 15The man said, "Lord, be kind to my son. He suffers so much from the seizures he has. He often falls into the fire or into the water. 16I brought him to your followers, but they could not heal him."

17Jesus answered, "You people today have no faith. Your lives are so wrong! How long must I stay with you? How long must I continue to be patient with you? Bring the boy here." 18Jesus gave a strong command to the demon inside the boy. The demon came out of the boy, and the boy was healed.

19Then the followers came to Jesus alone. They said, "We tried to force the demon out of the boy, but we could not. Why were we not able to make the demon go out?"

20Jesus answered, "You were not able to make the demon go out, because your faith is too small. Believe me when I tell you, if your faith is only as big as a mustard seed you can say to this mountain, 'Move from here to there,' and it will move. You will be able to do anything." 21b

Jesus Talks About His Death

(Mark 9:30–32; Luke 9:43b–45)

22Later, the followers met together in Galilee. Jesus said to them, "The Son of Man will be handed over to the control of other men, 23who will kill him. But on the third day he will be raised from death." The followers were very sad to hear that Jesus would be killed.

Jesus Teaches About Paying Taxes

24Jesus and his followers went to Capernaum. There the men who collect the two-drachma Temple tax came to Peter and asked, "Does your teacher pay the Temple tax?"

25Peter answered, "Yes, he does."

Peter went into the house where Jesus was. Before Peter could speak, Jesus said to him, "The kings on the earth get different kinds of taxes from people. But who are those who pay the taxes? Are they the king's own people? Or do other people pay the taxes? What do you think?"

26Peter answered, "The other people pay the taxes."

Jesus said, "Then the king's people don't have to pay taxes. 27But we don't want to upset these tax collectors. So do this: Go to the lake and fish. When you catch the first fish, open its mouth. Inside its mouth you will find a four-drachma coin. Take that coin and give it to the tax collectors. That will pay the tax for you and me."

Who Is the Greatest?

(Mark 9:33–37; Luke 9:46–48)

18 About that time the followers came to Jesus and asked, "Who is the greatest in God's kingdom?"

2Jesus called a little child to come to him. He stood the child in front of the followers. 3Then he said, "The truth is, you must change your thinking and become like little children. If you don't do this, you will never enter God's kingdom. 4The greatest person in God's kingdom is the one who makes himself humble like this child.

5"Whoever accepts a little child like this in my name is accepting me.

Jesus Warns About Causes of Sin

(Mark 9:42–48; Luke 17:1–2)

6"If one of these little children believes in me, and someone causes that child to sin, it will be very bad for that person. It would be better for them to have a millstone tied around their neck and be drowned in the deep sea. 7I feel sorry for the people in the world because of the things that

---

a **17:10 Elijah must come** See Mal. 4:5–6.
b **17:21** Some Greek copies add verse 21: "But that kind of spirit comes out only with prayer and fasting."

make people sin. These things must happen, but it will be very bad for anyone who causes them to happen.

8"If your hand or your foot makes you sin, cut it off and throw it away. It is better for you to lose part of your body and have eternal life than to have two hands and two feet and be thrown into the fire that burns forever. 9If your eye makes you sin, take it out and throw it away. It is better for you to have only one eye and have eternal life than to have two eyes and be thrown into the fire of hell.

Jesus Uses a Story About a Lost Sheep

(Luke 15:3–7)

10"Be careful. Don't think these little children are not important. I tell you that these children have angels in heaven. And those angels are always with my Father in heaven. 11a

12"If a man has 100 sheep, but one of the sheep is lost, what will he do? He will leave the other 99 sheep on the hill and go to look for the lost sheep. 13And if he finds the lost sheep, he is happier about that one sheep than about the 99 sheep that were never lost. I can assure you, 14in the same way, your Father in heaven does not want any of these little children to be lost.

Correct Anyone Who Does Wrong

(Luke 17:3)

15"If one of your brothers or sisters in God's family does wrong to you,b go and tell them what they did wrong. Do this when the two of you are alone. If that person listens to you, then you have helped them to be a true brother or sister again. 16But if that person refuses to listen, go to them again and take one or two other believers with you. Then there will be two or three witnesses to prove the truth of everything you say.c 17If the person who sinned refuses to listen to them, then tell the church. And if they refuse to listen to the church, treat them as you would treat someone who does not know God or who is a tax collector.

18"I can assure you that when you speak judgement here on earth, it will be God's judgement. And when you promise forgiveness here on earth, it will be God's forgiveness.d 19To say it another way, if two of you on earth agree on anything you pray for, my Father in heaven will

do what you ask. 20Yes, if two or three people are together believing in me, I am there with them."

A Story About Forgiveness

21Then Peter came to Jesus and asked, "Lord, when someonee won't stop doing wrong to me, how many times must I forgive them? Seven times?"

22Jesus answered, "I tell you, you must forgive them more than seven times. You must continue to forgive them even if they do wrong to you seventy-seven times.f

23"So God's kingdom is like a king who decided to collect the money his servants owed him. 24The king began to collect his money. One servant owed him more than 300 tonnes of silver.g 25He was not able to pay the money to his master, the king. So the master ordered that he and everything he owned be sold, even his wife and children. The money would be used to pay the king what the servant owed.

26"But the servant fell on his knees and begged, 'Be patient with me. I will pay you everything I owe.' 27The master felt sorry for him. So he told the servant he did not have to pay. He let him go free.

28"Later, that same servant found another servant who owed him a hundred silver coins. He grabbed him around the neck and said, 'Pay me the money you owe me!'

29"The other servant fell on his knees and begged him, 'Be patient with me. I will pay you everything I owe.'

30"But the first servant refused to be patient. He told the judge that the other servant owed him money, and that servant was put in jail until he could pay everything he owed. 31All the other servants saw what happened. They felt very sorry for the man. So they went and told their master everything that had happened.

32"Then the master called his servant in and said, 'You evil servant. You begged me to forgive your debt, and I said you did not have to pay anything! 33So you should have given that other man who serves with you the same mercy I gave you.' 34The master was very angry, so he put the servant in jail to be punished. And he had to stay in jail until he could pay everything he owed.

35"This king did the same as my heavenly Father will do to you. You must forgive your

---

a **18:11** Some Greek copies add verse 11: "The Son of Man came to save lost people." See Luke 19:10.
b **18:15** *to you* The best ancient Greek copies do not have these words.
c **18:16** *Then . . . say* See Deut. 19:15.
d **18:18** *when you speak . . . God's forgiveness* Literally, "whatever you bind on earth will have been bound in heaven, and whatever you loose on earth will have been loosed in heaven".
e **18:21** *someone* Literally, "my brother".
f **18:22** *seventy-seven times* Or "seventy times seven", a very large number, meaning there should be no limit to forgiveness.
g **18:24** *more than 300 tonnes of silver* Literally, "10,000 *talanta*" or "*talents*". A *talent* was about 27 to 36 kilogrammes of gold, silver or copper coins.

brother or sister with all your heart, or my heavenly Father will not forgive you."

Jesus Teaches About Divorce

(Mark 10:1–12)

19 After Jesus said all these things, he left Galilee. He went into the area of Judea on the other side of the Jordan River. ²Many people followed him. Jesus healed the sick people there.

³Some Pharisees came to Jesus. They tried to make him say something wrong. They asked him, "Is it right for a man to divorce his wife for any reason he chooses?"

⁴Jesus answered, "Surely you have read this in the Scriptures: when God made the world, 'he made people male and female'.*ᵃ* ⁵And God said, 'That is why a man will leave his father and mother and be joined to his wife. And the two people will become one.'*ᵇ* ⁶So they are no longer two, but one. God has joined them together, so no one should separate them."

⁷The Pharisees asked, "Then why did Moses give a command allowing a man to divorce his wife by writing a certificate of divorce?"*ᶜ*

⁸Jesus answered, "Moses allowed you to divorce your wives because you refused to accept God's teaching. But divorce was not allowed in the beginning. ⁹I tell you that whoever divorces his wife, except for the problem of sexual sin, and marries another woman is guilty of adultery."

¹⁰The followers said to Jesus, "If that is the only reason a man can divorce his wife, it is better not to marry."

¹¹He answered, "This statement is true for some, but not for everyone—only for those who have been given this gift. ¹²There are different reasons why some men don't marry.*ᵈ* Some were born without the ability to produce children. Others were made that way later in life. And others have given up marriage because of God's kingdom. This is for anyone who is able to accept it."

Jesus Welcomes Children

(Mark 10:13–16; Luke 18:15–17)

¹³Then the people brought their little children to Jesus so that he could lay his hands on them to bless them and pray for them. When the followers saw this, they told the people to stop bringing their children to him. ¹⁴But Jesus said, "Let the little children come to me. Don't stop them, because God's kingdom belongs to people who are like these children." ¹⁵After Jesus blessed the children, he left there.

A Rich Man Refuses to Follow Jesus

(Mark 10:17–31; Luke 18:18–30)

¹⁶A man came to Jesus and asked, "Teacher, what good thing must I do to have eternal life?"

¹⁷Jesus answered, "Why do you ask me about what is good? Only God is good. But if you want to have eternal life, obey the law's commands."

¹⁸The man asked, "Which ones?"

Jesus answered, "'You must not murder anyone, you must not commit adultery, you must not steal, you must not tell lies about others, ¹⁹you must respect your father and mother,'*ᵉ* and 'love your neighbour*ᶠ* the same as you love yourself.'"*ᵍ*

²⁰The young man said, "I have obeyed all these commands. What else do I need?"

²¹Jesus answered, "If you want to be perfect, then go and sell all that you own. Give the money to the poor, and you will have riches in heaven. Then come and follow me!"

²²But when the young man heard Jesus tell him to give away his money, he was sad. He didn't want to do this, because he was very rich. So he left.

²³Then Jesus said to his followers, "The truth is, it will be very hard for a rich person to enter God's kingdom. ²⁴Yes, I tell you, it is easier for a camel to go through the eye of a needle than for a rich person to enter God's kingdom."

²⁵The followers were amazed to hear this. They asked, "Then who can be saved?"

²⁶Jesus looked at them and said, "For people it is impossible. But God can do anything."

²⁷Peter said to him, "We left everything we had and followed you. So what will we have?"

²⁸Jesus said to them, "When the time of the new world comes, the Son of Man will sit on his great and glorious throne. And I can promise that you who followed me will sit on twelve thrones, and you will judge the twelve tribes of Israel. ²⁹Everyone who has left houses, brothers, sisters, father, mother, children or farms to follow me will get much more than they left. And they will have eternal life. ³⁰Many people who are first now will be last in the future. And many who are last now will be first in the future.

ᵃ **19:4** Quote from Gen. 1:27; 5:2.
ᵇ **19:5** Quote from Gen. 2:24.
ᶜ **19:7** *a command . . . certificate of divorce* See Deut. 24:1.
ᵈ **19:12** *some men don't marry* Literally, "there are eunuchs". See "EUNUCH" in the Word List.
ᵉ **19:19** Quote from Exod. 20:12–16; Deut. 5:16–20.
ᶠ **19:19** *your neighbour* Or "others". Jesus' teaching in Luke 10:25–37 makes clear that this includes anyone in need.
ᵍ **19:19** Quote from Lev. 19:18.

Jesus Uses a Story About Farm Workers

20 "God's kingdom is like a man who owned some land. One morning, the man went out very early to hire some people to work in his vineyard. ²He agreed to pay the workers one silver coin for working that day. Then he sent them into the vineyard to work.

³"About nine o'clock the man went to the marketplace and saw some other people standing there. They were doing nothing. ⁴So he said to them, 'If you go and work in my field, I will pay you what your work is worth.' ⁵So they went to work in the vineyard.

"The man went out again about twelve o'clock and again at three o'clock. Both times he hired some others to work in his vineyard. ⁶About five o'clock the man went to the marketplace again. He saw some other people standing there. He asked them, 'Why did you stand here all day doing nothing?'

⁷"They said, 'No one gave us a job.'

"The man said to them, 'Then you can go and work in my vineyard.'

⁸"At the end of the day, the owner of the field said to the man in charge of all the workers, 'Call the workers and pay them all. Start by paying the last people I hired. Then pay all of them, ending with the ones I hired first.'

⁹"The workers who were hired at five o'clock came to get their pay. Each worker got one silver coin. ¹⁰Then the workers who were hired first came to get their pay. They thought they would be paid more than the others. But each one of them also received one silver coin. ¹¹When they got their silver coin, they complained to the man who owned the land. ¹²They said, 'Those people were hired last and worked only one hour. But you paid them the same as us. And we worked hard all day in the hot sun.'

¹³"But the man who owned the field said to one of them, 'Friend, I am being fair with you. You agreed to work for one silver coin. ¹⁴So take your pay and go. I want to give the man who was hired last the same pay I gave you. ¹⁵I can do what I want with my own money. Why would you be jealous because I am generous?'

¹⁶"So those who are last now will be first in the future. And those who are first now will be last in the future."

Jesus Talks Again About His Death

(Mark 10:32–34; Luke 18:31–34)

¹⁷Jesus was going to Jerusalem. His twelve followers were with him. While they were walking, he gathered the followers together and spoke to them privately. He said to them, ¹⁸"We are going to Jerusalem. The Son of Man will be handed over to the leading priests and the teachers of the law, and they will say he must die. ¹⁹They will hand him over to the foreigners, who will laugh at him and beat him with whips, and then they will kill him on a cross. But on the third day after his death, he will be raised to life again."

A Mother Asks a Special Favour

(Mark 10:35–45)

²⁰Then Zebedee's wife came to Jesus and brought her sons. She bowed before Jesus and asked him to do something for her.

²¹Jesus said, "What do you want?"

She said, "Promise that one of my sons will sit at your right side in your kingdom and the other at your left."

²²So Jesus said to the sons, "You don't understand what you are asking. Can you drink from the cup*ᵃ* that I must drink from?"

The sons answered, "Yes, we can!"

²³Jesus said to them, "It is true that you will drink from the cup that I drink from. But it is not for me to say who will sit at my right or my left. My Father has decided who will do that. He has prepared those places for them."

²⁴The other ten followers heard this and were angry with the two brothers. ²⁵So Jesus called the followers together. He said, "You know that the rulers of the non-Jewish people love to show their power over the people. And their important leaders love to use all their authority over the people. ²⁶But it should not be that way with you. Whoever wants to be your leader must be your servant. ²⁷Whoever wants to be first must serve the rest of you like a slave. ²⁸Do as I did: the Son of Man did not come for people to serve him. He came to serve others and to give his life to save many people."

Jesus Heals Two Blind Men

(Mark 10:46–52; Luke 18:35–43)

²⁹When Jesus and his followers were leaving Jericho, a large crowd followed him. ³⁰There were two blind men sitting by the road. They heard that Jesus was coming by. So they shouted, "Lord, Son of David, please help us!"

³¹The people there criticized the blind men and told them to be quiet. But they shouted more and more, "Lord, Son of David, please help us!"

³²Jesus stopped and said to them, "What do you want me to do for you?"

³³They answered, "Lord, we want to be able to see."

ᵃ **20:22** *cup* A symbol of suffering. Jesus used the idea of drinking from a cup to mean accepting the suffering he would face in the terrible events that were soon to come. Also in verse 23.

GETTING WHAT WE DON'T DESERVE

Karen had been in the Christian Union since her first day at college. She sought it out when she arrived, made herself available to serve, and made it a big part of her life.

So when elections came round for the leadership team, she was sure she would be on the shortlist. And she certainly never expected to be defeated by Tracy – a new girl who had been there for only a term. How unfair!

DIG IN
READ Matthew 20:1–16

- What do you think drove the landowner to keep on hiring throughout the day?
- Why do some of the workers complain (v.12)?

Imagine the celebration among the workers who got paid first – for doing relatively little work. A whole day's pay for one hour's work! Fantastic!

One by one, the groups got more than they deserved until finally the first group received only what they had been promised – no more than the rest, but still a full day's wages. They'd been treated absolutely fairly and in fact the landowner had done them a favour by giving them a job in the first place. But they were spitting mad.

- What human emotion does this passage expose?
- How does the landowner explain his actions (v.15)?

Jealousy – we don't like it when we feel we are being treated unfairly. But Jesus says we'd better get this reaction out of our system, because in God's kingdom the order of things is going to change completely (v.16). The kingdom Jesus preaches is an upside-down kingdom.

All too often, just like the complaining workmen, we have no grounds for jealousy. We've been treated more than fairly already.

The antidote to jealousy is a proper understanding of God's grace, and this parable reminds us of our complete dependence on it. Jealousy starts because secretly we think we're better than other people or that we deserve more than them. But that's a lie.

When we see ourselves clearly – utterly lost without the free gift of God's grace – we can't possibly be jealous. We can only be grateful.

DIG THROUGH

- How do you respond to other people's success? With envy? Or do you find you can be happy for them? We must learn to rejoice in each other's successes because as God's family we belong to one another (check out Romans 12:5).
- "Why would you be jealous because I am generous?" Have you forgotten how generous our God is? In what ways can we develop a greater level of thankfulness in our lives?

DIG DEEPER

- Another of Jesus' stories – perhaps the most famous of all – tackles the issue of God's fairness towards us. Read the story of the two sons in Luke 15:11–32.

Luke 23:40–43 sees Jesus promising salvation to one of the criminals being crucified beside him. The criminal has no time to "earn" his place in paradise – it's a free gift given in the last few seconds of his life. It's just like that for us. Our salvation comes purely out of God's generosity, so we're never "too late", "too bad" or "too insignificant" to be received into his kingdom.

34Jesus felt sorry for the blind men. He touched their eyes, and immediately they were able to see. Then they became followers of Jesus.

Jesus Enters Jerusalem Like a King

(Mark 11:1–11; Luke 19:28–38; John 12:12–19)

21 Jesus and his followers were coming closer to Jerusalem. But first they stopped at Bethphage at the hill called the Mount of Olives. From there Jesus sent two of his followers into town. 2He said to them, "Go to the town you can see there. When you enter it, you will find a donkey with her colt. Untie them both, and bring them to me. 3If anyone asks you why you are taking the donkeys, tell them, 'The Master needs them. He will send them back soon.'"

4This showed the full meaning of what the prophet said:

5"Tell the people of Zion,*a*
　'Now your king is coming to you.
He is humble and riding on a donkey.
　He is riding on a young donkey, born from a
　　work animal.'"

Zechariah 9:9

6The followers went and did what Jesus told them to do. 7They brought the mother donkey and the young donkey to him. They covered the donkeys with their coats, and Jesus sat on them. 8On the way to Jerusalem, many people spread their coats on the road for Jesus. Others cut branches from the trees and spread them on the road. 9Some of the people were walking ahead of Jesus. Others were walking behind him. They all shouted,

"Praise*b* to the Son of David!
　'Welcome! God bless the one who comes in
　　the name of the Lord!'

Psalm 118:25–26

"Praise to God in heaven!"

10Then Jesus went into Jerusalem. All the people in the city were confused. They asked, "Who is this man?"

11The crowds following Jesus answered, "This is Jesus. He is the prophet from the town of Nazareth in Galilee."

> ## INSIGHT
>
> *Jesus rode into Jerusalem like a king and the people acknowledged this by laying down their cloaks. By choosing to ride on a donkey rather than a warhorse he showed the type of king he was – one who came in humility and peace.*
>
> **Matthew 21:1–11**

Jesus Goes to the Temple

(Mark 11:15–19; Luke 19:45–48; John 2:13–22)

12Jesus went into the Temple area. He threw out all those who were selling and buying things there. He turned over the tables that belonged to those who were exchanging different kinds of money. And he turned over the benches of those who were selling doves. 13Jesus said to them, "The Scriptures say, 'My Temple will be called a house of prayer.'*c* But you are changing it into a 'hiding place for thieves'."*d*

14Some blind and lame people came to Jesus in the Temple area, and he healed them. 15The leading priests and the teachers of the law saw the wonderful things he was doing. And they saw the children praising him in the Temple area. The children were shouting, "Praise to the Son of David." All this made the priests and the teachers of the law angry.

16They asked Jesus, "Do you hear what these children are saying?"

He answered, "Yes. The Scriptures say,

'You have taught children and babies
　to give praise.'*e*

Have you not read that Scripture?"

17Then Jesus left them and went out of the city to Bethany, where he spent the night.

Jesus Shows the Power of Faith

(Mark 11:12–14,20–24)

18Early the next morning, Jesus was going back to the city. He was very hungry. 19He saw a fig tree beside the road and went to get a fig from it. But there were no figs on the tree. There were only leaves. So Jesus said to the tree, "You will

---

a **21:5** *people of Zion* Literally, "daughter Zion", meaning the city of Jerusalem. See "ZION" in the Word List.
b **21:9** *Praise* Literally, "Hosanna", a Hebrew word used in praying to God for help. Here, it was probably a shout of celebration used in praising God or his Messiah. Also in the last line of this verse and in verse 15.
c **21:13** Quote from Isa. 56:7.
d **21:13** Quote from Jer. 7:11.
e **21:16** Quote from Ps. 8:2 (Greek version).

never again produce fruit!" The tree immediately dried up and died.

20When the followers saw this, they were very surprised. They asked, "How did the fig tree dry up and die so quickly?"

21Jesus answered, "The truth is, if you have faith and no doubts, you will be able to do the same as I did to this tree. And you will be able to do more. You will be able to say to this mountain, 'Go, mountain, fall into the sea.' And if you have faith, it will happen. 22If you believe, you will get anything you ask for in prayer."

Jewish Leaders Doubt Jesus' Authority

(Mark 11:27–33; Luke 20:1–8)

23Jesus went into the Temple area. While Jesus was teaching there, the leading priests and the older leaders of the people came to him. They said, "Tell us! What authority do you have to do these things you are doing? Who gave you this authority?"

24Jesus answered, "I will ask you a question too. If you answer me, then I will tell you what authority I have to do these things. 25Tell me: when John baptized people, did his authority come from God, or was it only from other people?"

The priests and the Jewish leaders talked about Jesus' question. They said to each other, "If we answer, 'John's baptism was from God,' then he will say, 'Then why didn't you believe John?' 26But we can't say John's baptism was from someone else. We are afraid of the people, because they all believe John was a prophet."

27So they told Jesus, "We don't know the answer."

Jesus said, "Then I will not tell you who gave me the authority to do these things.

Jesus Uses a Story About Two Sons

28"Tell me what you think about this: There was a man who had two sons. He went to the first son and said, 'Son, go and work today in the vineyard.'

29"The son answered, 'I will not go.' But later he decided he should go, and he went.

30"Then the father went to the other son and said, 'Son, go and work today in the vineyard.' He answered, 'Yes, sir, I will go and work.' But he did not go.

31"Which of the two sons obeyed his father?"

The Jewish leaders answered, "The first son."

Jesus said to them, "The truth is, you are worse than the tax collectors and the prostitutes. In fact, they will enter God's kingdom before you enter.

32John came showing you the right way to live, and you did not believe him. But the tax collectors and prostitutes believed John. You saw that happening, but you would not change. You still refused to believe him.

God Sends His Son

(Mark 12:1–12; Luke 20:9–19)

33"Listen to this story: There was a man who owned a vineyard. He put a wall around the field and dug a hole for a winepress. Then he built a tower. He leased the land to some farmers and then left on a trip. 34Later, it was time for the grapes to be picked. So the man sent his servants to the farmers to get his share of the grapes.

35"But the farmers grabbed the servants and beat one. They killed another one and then stoned to death a third servant. 36So the man sent some other servants to the farmers. He sent more servants than he sent the first time. But the farmers did the same thing to them that they did the first time. 37So the man decided to send his son to the farmers. He said, 'The farmers will respect my son.'

38"But when the farmers saw the son, they said to each other, 'This is the owner's son. This vineyard will be his. If we kill him, it will be ours.' 39So the farmers took the son, threw him out of the vineyard and killed him.

40"So what will the owner of the vineyard do to these farmers when he comes?"

41The Jewish priests and leaders said, "He will surely kill those evil men. Then he will lease the land to other farmers, who will give him his share of the crop at harvest time."

42Jesus said to them, "Surely you have read this in the Scriptures:

'The stone that the builders refused to accept
    became the cornerstone.
The Lord did this,
    and it is wonderful to us.'

Psalm 118:22–23

43"So I tell you that God's kingdom will be taken away from you. It will be given to people who do what God wants in his kingdom. 44Whoever falls on this stone will be broken. And it will crush anyone it falls on."[a]

45When the leading priests and the Pharisees heard these stories, they knew that Jesus was talking about them. 46They wanted to find a way to arrest Jesus. But they were afraid to do anything, because the people believed that Jesus was a prophet.

---

[a] **21:44** Some Greek copies do not have verse 44.

A Story About People Invited to a Dinner

(Luke 14:15–24)

22 Jesus used some more stories to teach the people. He said, [2]"God's kingdom is like a king who prepared a wedding feast for his son. [3]He invited some people to the feast. When it was ready, the king sent his servants to tell the people to come. But they refused to come to the king's feast.

[4]"Then the king sent some more servants. He said to them, 'I have already invited the people. So tell them that my feast is ready. I have killed my best bulls and calves to be eaten. Everything is ready. Come to the wedding feast.'

[5]"But when the servants told the people to come, they refused to listen. They all went to do other things. One went to work in his field, and another went to his business. [6]Some of the other people grabbed the servants, beat them and killed them. [7]The king was very angry. He sent his army to kill those who murdered his servants. And the army burned their city.

[8]"After that, the king said to his servants, 'The wedding feast is ready. I invited those people, but they were not good enough to come to my feast. [9]So go to the street corners and invite everyone you see. Tell them to come to my feast.' [10]So the servants went into the streets. They gathered all the people they could find, good and bad alike, and brought them to where the wedding feast was ready. And the place was filled with guests.

[11]"When the king came in to meet the guests, he saw a man there who was not dressed in the right clothes for a wedding. [12]The king said, 'Friend, how were you allowed to come in here? You are not wearing the right clothes.' But the man said nothing. [13]So the king told some servants, 'Tie this man's hands and feet. Throw him out into the darkness, where people are crying and grinding their teeth in pain.'

[14]"Yes, many people are invited. But only a few are chosen."

The Jewish Leaders Try to Trick Jesus

(Mark 12:13–17; Luke 20:20–26)

[15]Then the Pharisees left the place where Jesus was teaching. They made plans to catch him saying something they could use against him. [16]They sent to Jesus some of their own followers and some from the group called Herodians. They said, "Teacher, we know you are an honest man. We know you always teach the truth about God's way. It doesn't matter to you who is listening. You don't worry about what others might say. [17]So tell us what you think. Is it right to pay taxes to Caesar or not?"

[18]But Jesus knew that these men were trying to trick him. So he said, "You hypocrites! Why are you trying to catch me saying something wrong? [19]Show me a coin used for paying the tax." They showed Jesus a silver coin. [20]Then he asked, "Whose picture is on the coin? And whose name is written on the coin?"

[21]They answered, "It is Caesar's picture and Caesar's name."

Then Jesus said to them, "Give to Caesar what belongs to Caesar, and give to God what belongs to God."

[22]When they heard what Jesus said, they were amazed. They left him and went away.

Some Sadducees Try to Trick Jesus

(Mark 12:18–27; Luke 20:27–40)

[23]That same day some Sadducees came to Jesus. (Sadducees believe that no one will rise from death.) The Sadducees asked Jesus a question. [24]They said, "Teacher, Moses told us that if a married man dies and had no children, his brother must marry the woman. Then they will have children for the dead brother.[a] [25]There were seven brothers among us. The first brother married but died. He had no children. So his brother married the woman. [26]Then the second brother also died. The same thing happened to the third brother and all the other brothers. [27]The woman was the last to die. [28]But all seven men had married her. So when people rise from death, whose wife will she be?"

[29]Jesus answered, "You are so wrong! You don't know what the Scriptures say. And you don't know anything about God's power. [30]At the time when people rise from death, there will be no marriage. People will not be married to each other. Everyone will be like the angels in heaven. [31]Surely you have read what God said to you about people rising from death. [32]God said, 'I am the God of Abraham, the God of Isaac and the God of Jacob.'[b] He is the God only of people who are living. So these men were not really dead."

[33]When the people heard this, they were amazed at Jesus' teaching.

Which Command Is the Most Important?

(Mark 12:28–34; Luke 10:25–28)

[34]The Pharisees learned that Jesus had made the Sadducees look so foolish that they stopped trying to argue with him. So the Pharisees had a

---

[a] **22:24** *if . . . dead brother* See Deut. 25:5–6.
[b] **22:32** Quote from Exod. 3:6.

meeting. 35Then one of them, an expert in the Law of Moses, asked Jesus a question to test him. 36He said, "Teacher, which command in the law is the most important?"

37Jesus answered, "'Love the Lord your God with all your heart, all your soul and all your mind.'*a* 38This is the first and most important command. 39And the second command is like the first: 'Love your neighbour*b* the same as you love yourself.'*c* 40All of the law and the writings of the prophets take their meaning from these two commands."

Is the Messiah David's Son or David's Lord?

(Mark 12:35–37; Luke 20:41–44)

41So while the Pharisees were together, Jesus asked them a question. 42He said, "What do you think about the Messiah? Whose son is he?"

The Pharisees answered, "The Messiah is the Son of David."

43Jesus said to them, "Then why did David call him 'Lord'? David was speaking by the power of the Spirit. He said,

44'The Lord God said to my Lord:
  Sit by me at my right side,
    and I will put your enemies under your
      control.'*d*

Psalm 110:1

45David calls the Messiah 'Lord'. So how can he be David's son?"

46None of the Pharisees could answer Jesus' question. And after that day, no one was brave enough to ask him any more questions.

Jesus Criticizes the Religious Leaders

(Mark 12:38–40; Luke 11:37–52; 20:45–47)

23 Then Jesus spoke to the people and to his followers. He said, 2"The teachers of the law and the Pharisees have the authority to tell you what the Law of Moses says. 3So you should obey them. Do everything they tell you. But their lives are not good examples for you to follow. They don't do what they teach. 4They make long

lists of difficult rules and try to force people to follow them all. But these rules are like heavy loads that are hard for people to carry, and these leaders will not do anything to make it easier for the people.

5"Any good things they do are only for other people to see. They make the little Scripture boxes*e* they wear bigger and bigger. And they make the tassels*f* on their prayer clothes long enough for people to notice them. 6These men love to have the places of honour at banquets and the most important seats in the synagogues. 7They love it when people show respect to them in the marketplaces and call them 'Teacher'.

8"But you must not be called 'Teacher'. You are all equal as brothers and sisters. You have only one Teacher. 9And don't call anyone on earth 'Father'. You have one Father. He is in heaven. 10And you should not be called 'Master'. You have only one Master, the Messiah. 11Whoever serves you like a servant is the greatest among you. 12People who think they are better than others will be made humble. But people who humble themselves will be made great.

13"It will be bad for you teachers of the law and you Pharisees! You are hypocrites! You close the way for people to enter God's kingdom. You yourselves don't enter, and you stop those who are trying to enter. 14*g*

15"It will be bad for you teachers of the law and you Pharisees! You are hypocrites. You travel across the seas and across different countries to find one person who will follow your ways. When you find that person, you make him worse than you are. And you are so bad that you belong in hell!

16"It will be bad for you teachers of the law and you Pharisees! You guide the people, but you are blind. You say, 'If anyone uses the name of the Temple to make a promise, that means nothing. But anyone who uses the gold that is in the Temple to make a promise must keep that promise.' 17You are blind fools! Can't you see that the Temple is greater than the gold in it? It's the Temple that makes the gold holy!

18"And you say, 'If anyone uses the altar to make a promise, that means nothing. But anyone

---

a **22:37** Quote from Deut. 6:5.

b **22:39** *your neighbour* Or "others". Jesus' teaching in Luke 10:25–37 makes clear that this includes anyone in need.

c **22:39** Quote from Lev. 19:18.

d **22:44** *control* Literally, "feet".

e **23:5** *Scripture boxes* Small leather boxes containing four important Scriptures. Some Jews tied these to the forehead and left arm to show their devotion to God and his word. Many Pharisees made these bigger to show that they were more religious than others.

f **23:5** *tassels* Decorations made from wool threads that hung down from the four corners of the clothing or prayer shawls worn by Jews. They were supposed to be reminders of God's commands (see Num. 15:38–41).

g **23:14** Some Greek copies add verse 14: "It will be bad for you, teachers of the law and you Pharisees. You are hypocrites. You cheat widows and take their homes. Then you make long prayers so that people can see you. So you will have a worse punishment." See Mark 12:40; Luke 20:47.

who uses the gift on the altar to make a promise must keep that promise.' ¹⁹You are blind! Can't you see that the altar is greater than any gift on it? It's the altar that makes the gift holy! ²⁰Whoever uses the altar to make a promise is really using the altar and everything on the altar. ²¹And anyone who uses the Temple to make a promise is really using the Temple and God, who lives in it. ²²Whoever uses heaven to make a promise is using God's throne and the one who is seated on it.

²³"It will be bad for you teachers of the law and you Pharisees! You are hypocrites! You give God a tenth of the food you get, even your mint, dill and cumin.ᵃ But you don't obey the really important teachings of the law—being fair, showing mercy and being faithful. These are the things you should do. And you should also continue to do those other things. ²⁴You guide the people, but you are blind! Think about a man picking a little fly out of his drink and then swallowing a camel! You are like that.ᵇ

²⁵"It will be bad for you teachers of the law and you Pharisees! You are hypocrites! You wash clean the outside of your cups and dishes. But inside they are full of what you got by cheating others and pleasing yourselves. ²⁶Pharisees, you are blind! First make the inside of the cup clean and good. Then the outside of the cup will also be clean.

²⁷"It will be bad for you teachers of the law and you Pharisees! You are hypocrites! You are like tombs that are painted white. Outside they look fine, but inside they are full of dead people's bones and all kinds of filth. ²⁸It is the same with you.

People look at you and think you are godly. But on the inside you are full of hypocrisy and evil.

²⁹"It will be bad for you teachers of the law and you Pharisees! You are hypocrites! You build tombs for the prophets. And you show honour to the graves of the godly people who were killed. ³⁰And you say, 'If we had lived during the time of our ancestors, we would not have helped them kill these prophets.' ³¹So you give proof that you are descendants of those who killed the prophets. ³²And you will finish the sin that your ancestors started!

³³"You snakes! You are from a family of poisonous snakes! You will not escape God. You will all be judged guilty and go to hell! ³⁴So I tell you this: I send to you prophets and teachers who are wise and know the Scriptures. You will kill some of them. You will hang some of them on crosses. You will beat some of them in your synagogues. You will chase them from town to town.

³⁵"So you will be guilty for the death of all the good people who have been killed on earth. You will be guilty for the killing of that godly man Abel. And you will be guilty for the killing of Zechariahᶜ son of Berachiah. He was killed between the Temple and the altar. You will be guilty for the killing of all the good people who lived between the time of Abel and the time of Zechariah. ³⁶Believe me when I say that all these things will happen to you people who are living now.

Jesus Warns the People of Jerusalem
(Luke 13:34–35)

³⁷"O Jerusalem, Jerusalem! You kill the prophets. You stone to death those that God has sent to you. Many, many times I wanted to help your people. I wanted to gather them together as a hen gathers her chicks under her wings. But you did not let me. ³⁸Now your house will be left completely empty. ³⁹I tell you, you will not see me again until that time when you will say, 'Welcome! God bless the one who comes in the name of the Lord.'"ᵈ

Jesus Warns About the Future
(Mark 13:1–31; Luke 21:5–33)

24 Jesus left the Temple area and was walking away. But his followers came to him to show him the Temple's buildings. ²He asked them, "Are you looking at these buildings?

ᵃ **23:23 You give . . . cumin** Literally, "You tithe mint, dill and cumin." The Law of Moses required Israelites to share their food supply by dedicating a tenth of their field crops and livestock to God (see Lev. 27:30–32; Deut. 26:12). This did not include such small garden plants as those mentioned here. So these Pharisees were giving more than required to be sure they were not breaking the law.
ᵇ **23:24 You are like that** Meaning "You worry about the smallest mistakes but commit the biggest sin."
ᶜ **23:35 Abel, Zechariah** In the Hebrew Old Testament, these are the first and last persons murdered.
ᵈ **23:39** Quote from Ps. 118:26.

The fact is, they will be destroyed. Every stone will be thrown down to the ground. Not one stone will be left on another."

[3]Later, Jesus was sitting at a place on the Mount of Olives. The followers came to be alone with him. They said, "Tell us when these things will happen. And what will happen to prepare us for your coming and the end of time?"

[4]Jesus answered, "Be careful! Don't let anyone fool you. [5]Many people will come and use my name. They will say, 'I am the Messiah.' And they will fool many people. [6]You will hear about wars that are being fought. And you will hear stories about other wars beginning. But don't be afraid. These things must happen before the end comes. [7]Nations will fight against other nations. Kingdoms will fight against other kingdoms. There will be times when there is no food for people to eat. And there will be earthquakes in different places. [8]These things are only the beginning of troubles, like the first pains of a woman giving birth.

[9]"Then you will be arrested and handed over to be punished and killed. People all over the world will hate you because you believe in me. [10]During that time many believers will lose their faith. They will turn against each other and hate each other. [11]Many false prophets will come and cause many people to believe things that are wrong. [12]There will be so much more evil in the world that the love of most believers will grow cold. [13]But the one who remains faithful to the end will be saved. [14]And the Good News I have shared about God's kingdom will be told throughout the world. It will be spread to every nation. Then the end will come.

[15]"Daniel the prophet spoke about 'the terrible thing that causes destruction'.[a] You will see this terrible thing standing in the holy place." (You who read this should understand what it means.) [16]"The people in Judea at that time should run away to the mountains. [17]They should run away without wasting time to stop for anything. If they are on the roof of their house, they must not go down to get anything out of the house. [18]If they are in the field, they must not go back to get a coat.

[19]"During that time it will be hard for women who are pregnant or have small babies! [20]Pray that it will not be winter or a Sabbath day when these things happen and you have to run away, [21]because it will be a time of great trouble. There will be more trouble than has ever happened since the beginning of the world. And nothing as bad as that will ever happen again.

[22]"But God has decided to make that terrible time short. If it were not made short, no one would continue living. But God will make that time short to help the people he has chosen.

[23]"Someone might say to you at that time, 'Look, there is the Messiah!' Or someone else might say, 'There he is!' But don't believe them. [24]False messiahs and false prophets will come and do great miracles and wonders,[b] trying to fool the people God has chosen, if that is possible. [25]Now I have warned you about this before it happens.

When Jesus, the Son of Man, Comes Again

(Mark 13:24–31; Luke 17:24–37)

[26]"Someone might tell you, 'The Messiah is there in the desert!' But don't go into the desert to look for him. Someone else might say, 'There is the Messiah in that room!' But don't believe it. [27]When the Son of Man comes, everyone will see him. It will be like lightning flashing in the sky that can be seen everywhere. [28]It's like looking for a dead body: you will find it where the vultures are gathering above.

[29]"Right after the trouble of those days, this will happen:

'The sun will become dark,
  and the moon will not give light.
The stars will fall from the sky,
  and everything in the sky will be changed.'[c]

[30]"Then there will be something in the sky that shows the Son of Man is coming. All the people of the world will cry. Everyone will see the Son of Man coming on the clouds in the sky. He will come with power and great glory. [31]He will use a loud trumpet to send his angels all around the earth. They will gather his chosen people from every part of the earth.

[32]"The fig tree teaches us a lesson: when its branches become green and soft and new leaves begin to grow, you know that summer is very near. [33]In the same way, when you see all these things happening, you will know that the time[d] is very near, already present. [34]I assure you that all these things will happen while some of the people of this time are still living. [35]The whole world, earth and sky, will be destroyed, but my words will last forever.

---

[a] **24:15** *'the terrible thing . . . destruction'* See Dan. 9:27; 12:11 (also Dan. 11:31).
[b] **24:24** *miracles and wonders* Here, amazing acts done by Satan's power.
[c] **24:29** See Isa. 13:10; 34:4.
[d] **24:33** *time* The time Jesus has been talking about when something important will happen. See Luke 21:31, where Jesus says that this is the time for God's kingdom to come.

Only God Knows When the Lord Will Come

(Mark 13:32–37; Luke 17:26–30,34–36)

[36]"No one knows when that day or time will be. The Son and the angels in heaven don't know when it will be. Only the Father knows.

[37]"When the Son of Man comes, it will be the same as what happened during Noah's time. [38]In those days before the flood, people were eating and drinking, marrying and giving their children to be married right up to the day Noah entered the boat. [39]They knew nothing about what was happening until the flood came and destroyed them all.

"It will be the same when the Son of Man comes. [40]Two men will be working together in the field. One will be taken and the other will be left. [41]Two women will be grinding grain with a mill. One will be taken and the other will be left.

[42]"So always be ready. You don't know the day your Lord will come. [43]What would a home owner do if he knew when a thief was coming? You know he would be ready and not let the thief break in. [44]So you also must be ready. The Son of Man will come at a time when you don't expect him.

Good Servants and Bad Servants

(Luke 12:41–48)

[45]"Who is the wise and trusted servant? The master trusts one servant to give the other servants their food at the right time. Who is the one the master trusts to do that work? [46]When the master comes and finds that servant doing the work he gave him, it will be a day of blessing for that servant. [47]I can tell you without a doubt, the master will choose that servant to take care of everything he owns.

[48]"But what will happen if that servant is evil and thinks his master will not come back soon? [49]He will begin to beat the other servants. He will eat and drink with others who are drunk. [50]Then the master will come when the servant is not ready, at a time when the servant is not expecting him. [51]Then the master will give that servant a terrible punishment.[a] The master will send him where he belongs, with the other people who only pretend to be good. There people will cry and grind their teeth in pain.

A Story About Ten Girls

25 "At that time God's kingdom will be like ten girls who went to wait for the bridegroom. They took their lamps with them. [2]Five of the girls were foolish, and five were wise. [3]The foolish girls took their lamps with them, but they did not take extra oil for the lamps. [4]The wise girls took their lamps and more oil in jars. [5]When the bridegroom was very late, the girls could not keep their eyes open, and they all fell asleep.

[6]"At midnight someone announced, 'The bridegroom is coming! Come and meet him!'

[7]"Then all the girls woke up. They made their lamps ready. [8]But the foolish girls said to the wise girls, 'Give us some of your oil. The oil in our lamps has all gone.'

[9]"The wise girls answered, 'No! The oil we have might not be enough for all of us. But go to those who sell oil and buy some for yourselves.'

[10]"So the foolish girls went to buy oil. While they were gone, the bridegroom came. The girls who were ready went in with the bridegroom to the wedding feast. Then the door was closed and locked.

[11]"Later, the other girls came. They said, 'Sir, sir! Open the door to let us in.'

[12]"But the bridegroom answered, 'Certainly not! I don't even know you.'

[13]"So always be ready. You don't know the day or the time when the Son of Man will come.

A Story About Three Servants

(Luke 19:11–27)

[14]"At that time God's kingdom will also be like a man leaving home to travel to another place for a visit. Before he left, he talked with his servants. He told his servants to take care of his things while he was gone. [15]He decided how much each servant would be able to care for. The man gave one servant five bags of money.[b] He gave another servant two bags. And he gave a third servant one bag. Then he left. [16]The servant who was given five bags went quickly to invest the money. Those five bags of money earned five more. [17]It was the same with the servant who had two bags. That servant invested the money and earned two more. [18]But the servant who was given one bag of money went away and dug a hole in the ground. Then he hid his master's money in the hole.

[19]"After a long time the master came home. He asked the servants what they had done with his money. [20]The servant who was given five bags brought that amount and five more bags of money to the master. The servant said, 'Master, you trusted me to care for five bags of money. So I used them to earn five more.'

[21]"The master answered, 'You did right. You are a good servant who can be trusted. You did well with that small amount of money. So I will

---

[a] **24:51 give . . . punishment** Literally, "cut him in half".
[b] **25:15 bags of money** Literally, "*talanta*" or "*talents*". A *talent* was about 34 kilogrammes of gold, silver or copper coins. Also in verses 20,22,24,28.

PUTTING OUR GIFTS TO GOOD USE

What are you really good at? Think about it – and make a mental list. Is it a sport? Is it talking to people? Is it singing, dancing or acting? Is it an artistic skill? Is it maths, science or another academic subject?

Perhaps it feels too soon to tell what you're really good at – that's okay. But try to list a few things which you consider your special talents.

DIG IN   READ Matthew 25:14–30

- Who is telling this story? (Clue: Matthew 24:4.)
- Why do the three servants get different amounts to take away (v.15)?
- How do they all respond and use the gifts (vv.16–18)?

It's coming towards the end of his life and Jesus is talking about the future. His disciples want to know what to expect – what will it be like at the end of time? What will be expected of them? And Jesus answers, as he often did, in short, memorable stories (parables).

In this story, Jesus wants to teach his friends an important truth – that God is watching carefully what we do with the gifts he has given us. The three servants receive gifts of differing amounts according to what the man judges they can each handle (v.15). Two of the men do well, by investing the money. But the third does not.

- Why does the third servant hide his money (vv.24–25)?
- How does the man treat the first two servants? And what about the third?

Even though they got different amounts in the first place, servants one and two are both commended for taking the initiative and investing the money. Because they were faithful in this task, they are promised much more in the future (v.23).

It's clear that fear is what stops the third servant using his gift wisely. But there's no sympathy for him when he returns without any profit (vv.26–30).

It is said that there are three main things that we can give to God to show him how much we love him – time, talents and treasure. We are all given different amounts of all three. But how ever much or little we are given, God expects the same – that we put what he gives us to good use.

DIG THROUGH

- Think again about what you're best at in life. How can you make the most of those special talents for God's glory so he will be pleased with you at the end of your life? Will you need to overcome any fear to accomplish it? Don't allow yourself to think of God as a hard taskmaster – remember that he loves you enough to send Jesus to die for you!
- How about the other two things: time and treasure? Do you make good use of your time or are you actually rather lazy (v.26)? What about money? You may not have a lot right now, but do you still find ways to honour God with it?

DIG DEEPER

- It's important we don't read this story and begin to think we have to earn or deserve God's love, or that we need to do anything to be saved. We don't – it's a free gift of grace. But God gives us life to use for his glory. Check out Ephesians 2:8–10, which makes this distinction brilliantly clear.

let you care for much greater things. Come and celebrate with me.'

²²"Then the servant who was given two bags of money came to the master. The servant said, 'Master, you gave me two bags of money to care for. So I used your two bags to earn two more.'

²³"The master answered, 'You did right. You are a good servant who can be trusted. You did well with a small amount of money. So I will let you care for much greater things. Come and celebrate with me.'

²⁴"Then the servant who was given one bag of money came to the master. The servant said, 'Master, I knew you were a very hard man. You harvest what you did not plant. You gather crops where you did not put any seed. ²⁵So I was afraid. I went and hid your money in the ground. Here is the one bag of money you gave me.'

²⁶"The master answered, 'You are a bad and lazy servant! You say you knew that I harvest what I did not plant and that I gather crops where I did not put any seed. ²⁷So you should have put my money in the bank. Then, when I came home, I would get my money back. And I would also get the interest that my money had earned.'

²⁸"So the master told his other servants, 'Take the one bag of money from that servant and give it to the servant who has ten bags. ²⁹Everyone who uses what they have will get more. They will have much more than they need. But people who do not use what they have will have everything taken away from them.' ³⁰Then the master said, 'Throw that useless servant outside into the darkness, where people will cry and grind their teeth in pain.'

Jesus, the Son of Man, Will Judge All People

³¹"The Son of Man will come again in his glory, together with all the angels. He will sit as king on his royal throne. ³²All the people of the world will be gathered before him. Then he will separate everyone into two groups. It will be like a shepherd separating his sheep from his goats. ³³He will put the sheep on his right and the goats on his left.

³⁴"Then the king will say to the godly people on his right, 'Come, my Father has great blessings for you. The kingdom he promised is now yours. It has been prepared for you since the world was made. ³⁵It is yours because when I was hungry, you gave me food to eat. When I was thirsty, you gave me something to drink. When I had no place to stay, you welcomed me into your home. ³⁶When I was without clothes, you gave me something to wear. When I was sick, you cared for me. When I was in prison, you came to visit me.'

³⁷"Then the godly people will answer, 'Lord, when did we see you hungry and give you food? When did we see you thirsty and give you

something to drink? ³⁸When did we see you with no place to stay and welcome you into our home? When did we see you without clothes and give you something to wear? ³⁹When did we see you sick or in prison and care for you?'

⁴⁰"Then the king will answer, 'The truth is, anything you did for any of my people here,^a you also did for me.'

⁴¹"Then the king will say to the evil people on his left, 'Get away from me. God has already decided that you will be punished. Go into the fire that burns forever—the fire that was prepared for the devil and his angels. ⁴²You must go away because when I was hungry, you gave me nothing to eat. When I was thirsty, you gave me nothing to drink. ⁴³When I had no place to stay, you did not welcome me into your home. When I was without clothes, you gave me nothing to wear. When I was sick and in prison, you did not care for me.'

⁴⁴"Then those people will answer, 'Lord, when did we see you hungry or thirsty? When did we see you without a place to stay? When did we see you without clothes or sick or in prison? When did we see any of this and not help you?'

⁴⁵"The king will answer, 'The truth is, anything you refused to do for any of my people here, you refused to do for me.'

⁴⁶"Then these evil people will go away to be punished forever. But the godly people will go and enjoy eternal life."

The Jewish Leaders Plan to Kill Jesus

(Mark 14:1–2; Luke 22:1–2; John 11:45–53)

26 After Jesus finished saying all these things, he said to his followers, ²"You know that the day after tomorrow is Passover. On that day the Son of Man will be handed over to his enemies to be killed on a cross."

³Then the leading priests and the older Jewish leaders had a meeting at the palace where the high priest lived. The high priest's name was Caiaphas. ⁴In the meeting they tried to find a way to arrest and kill Jesus without anyone knowing what they were doing. They planned to arrest Jesus and kill him. ⁵They said, "We cannot arrest Jesus during Passover. We don't want the people to become angry and cause a riot."

A Woman Honours Jesus

(Mark 14:3–9; John 12:1–8)

⁶Jesus was in Bethany at the house of Simon the leper. ⁷While he was there, a woman came to him. She had an alabaster jar filled with expensive perfume. She poured the perfume on Jesus' head while he was eating.

---

^a **25:40 any of my people here** Literally, "one of the least of these brothers of mine". Also in verse 45.

8The followers saw the woman do this and were upset at her. They said, "Why waste that perfume? 9It could be sold for a lot of money, and the money could be given to those who are poor."

10But Jesus knew what had happened. He said, "Why are you bothering this woman? She did a very good thing for me. 11You will always have the poor with you.[a] But you will not always have me. 12This woman poured perfume on my body. She did this to prepare me for burial after I die. 13The Good News will be told to people all over the world. And I can assure you that everywhere the Good News is told, the story of what this woman did will also be told, and people will remember her."

Judas Agrees to Help Jesus' Enemies

(Mark 14:10–11; Luke 22:3–6)

14Then one of the twelve followers went to talk to the leading priests. This was the follower named Judas Iscariot. 15He said, "I will hand Jesus over to you. What will you pay me for doing this?" The priests gave him 30 silver coins. 16After that, Judas waited for the best time to hand Jesus over to them.

The Passover Meal

(Mark 14:12–21; Luke 22:7–14,21–23; John 13:21–30)

17On the first day of the Festival of Unleavened Bread, the followers came to Jesus. They said, "We will prepare everything for you to eat the Passover meal. Where do you want us to have the meal?"

18Jesus answered, "Go into the city. Go to a man I know. Tell him that the Teacher says, 'The chosen time is now very near. I will have the Passover meal with my followers at your house.'" 19They obeyed and did what Jesus told them to do. They prepared the Passover meal.

20In the evening Jesus was at the table with the twelve followers. 21They were all eating. Then Jesus said, "Believe me when I say that one of you twelve here will hand me over to my enemies."

22The followers were very sad to hear this. Each one said, "Lord, surely I am not the one!"

23Jesus answered, "One who has dipped his bread in the same bowl with me will be the one to hand me over. 24The Son of Man will leave this world, just as the Scriptures say. But it will be terrible for the one who hands over the Son of Man to be killed. It would be better for him if he had never been born."

25Then Judas, the very one who would hand him over, said to Jesus, "Teacher, surely I am not the one you are talking about, am I?"

Jesus answered, "Yes, it is you."

The Lord's Supper

(Mark 14:22–26; Luke 22:15–20; 1 Cor. 11:23–25)

26While they were eating, Jesus took some bread and thanked God for it. He broke off some pieces, gave them to his followers and said, "Take this bread and eat it. It is my body."

27Then he took a cup of wine, thanked God for it, and gave it to them. He said, "Each one of you drink some of it. 28This wine is my blood, which will be poured out to forgive the sins of many and begin the new agreement that God makes with his people. 29I want you to know, I will not drink this wine again until that day when we are together in my Father's kingdom and the wine is new. Then I will drink it again with you."

30They all sang a song and then went out to the Mount of Olives.

Jesus Says His Followers Will Leave Him

(Mark 14:27–31; Luke 22:31–34; John 13:36–38)

31Jesus told the followers, "Tonight you will all lose your faith in me. The Scriptures say,

> 'I will kill the shepherd,
>   and the sheep will run away.'
>
> *Zechariah 13:7*

32But after I am killed, I will rise from death. Then I will go into Galilee. I will be there before you get there."

33Peter answered, "All the other followers may lose their faith in you. But my faith will never be shaken."

34Jesus answered, "The truth is, tonight you will say you don't know me. You will deny me three times before the cockerel crows."

35But Peter answered, "I will never say I don't know you! I will even die with you!" And all the other followers said the same thing.

Jesus Prays Alone

(Mark 14:32–42; Luke 22:39–46)

36Then Jesus went with his followers to a place called Gethsemane. He said to them, "Sit here while I go there and pray." 37He told Peter and the two sons of Zebedee to come with him. Then he began to be very sad and troubled. 38Jesus said to Peter and the two sons of Zebedee, "My heart is so heavy with grief, I feel as if I am dying. Wait here and stay awake with me."

39Then Jesus went on a little farther away from them. He fell to the ground and prayed, "My Father, if it is possible, don't make me drink from

---

[a] **26:11 You will . . . with you** See Deut. 15:11.

this cup.*a* But do what you want, not what I want." ⁴⁰Then he went back to his followers and found them sleeping. He said to Peter, "Could you men not stay awake with me for one hour? ⁴¹Stay awake and pray for strength against temptation. Your spirit wants to do what is right, but your body is weak."

⁴²Then Jesus went away a second time and prayed, "My Father, if I must do this*b* and it is not possible for me to escape it, I pray that what you want will be done."

⁴³Then he went back to the followers. Again he found them sleeping. They could not stay awake. ⁴⁴So he left them and went away one more time and prayed. This third time he prayed, he said the same thing.

⁴⁵Then Jesus went back to the followers and said, "Are you still sleeping and resting? The time has come for the Son of Man to be handed over to the control of sinful men. ⁴⁶Stand up! We must go. Here comes the one who will hand me over."

INSIGHT

In his hour of need Jesus' friends fell asleep, despite his requests for them to watch with him. In the end they abandoned him completely. This fulfilled a scripture that had been written many years before (see Zechariah 13:7).

Matthew 26:30–46

Jesus Is Arrested

(Mark 14:43–50; Luke 22:47–53; John 18:3–12)

⁴⁷While Jesus was still speaking, Judas, one of the twelve apostles came up to them. He had a big crowd of people with him, all carrying swords and clubs. They had been sent from the leading priests and the older leaders of the people. ⁴⁸Judas*c* planned to do something to show them which one was Jesus. He said, "The one I kiss will be Jesus. Arrest him." ⁴⁹So he went to Jesus and said, "Hello, Teacher!" Then Judas kissed him.

⁵⁰Jesus answered, "Friend, do the thing you came to do."

Then the men came and grabbed Jesus and arrested him. ⁵¹When that happened, one of the followers with Jesus grabbed his sword and pulled it out. He swung it at the servant of the high priest and cut off his ear.

⁵²Jesus said to the man, "Put your sword back in its place. People who use swords will be killed with swords. ⁵³Surely you know I could ask my Father and he would give me more than twelve armies of angels. ⁵⁴But it must happen this way to show the truth of what the Scriptures said."

⁵⁵Then Jesus said to the crowd, "Why do you come to get me with swords and clubs as if I were a criminal. Every day I sat in the Temple area teaching. You did not arrest me there. ⁵⁶But all these things have happened to show the full meaning of what the prophets wrote." Then all of Jesus' followers left him and ran away.

Jesus Before the Jewish Leaders

(Mark 14:53–65; Luke 22:54–55,63–71; John 18:13–14,19–24)

⁵⁷The men who arrested Jesus led him to the house of Caiaphas the high priest. The teachers of the law and the older Jewish leaders were gathered there. ⁵⁸Peter followed Jesus but stayed back at a distance. He followed him to the courtyard of the high priest's house. Peter went in and sat with the guards. He wanted to see what would happen to Jesus.

⁵⁹The leading priests and the high council tried to find something against Jesus so that they could kill him. They tried to find people to lie and say that Jesus had done wrong. ⁶⁰Many people came and told lies about him. But the council could find no real reason to kill him. Then two people came ⁶¹and said, "This man*d* said, 'I can destroy the Temple of God and build it again in three days.'"

⁶²Then the high priest stood up and said to Jesus, "Don't you have anything to say about these charges against you? Are they telling the truth?" ⁶³But Jesus said nothing.

Again the high priest said to Jesus, "You are now under oath. I command you by the power of the living God to tell us the truth. Are you the Messiah, the Son of God?"

⁶⁴Jesus answered, "Yes, that's right. But I tell you, in the future you will see the Son of Man sitting at the right side of God, the Powerful One. And you will see the Son of Man coming on the clouds of heaven."

⁶⁵When the high priest heard this, he tore his clothes in anger. He said, "This man has said things that insult God! We don't need any more witnesses. You all heard his insulting words. ⁶⁶What do you think?"

---

a **26:39 cup** A symbol of suffering. Jesus used the idea of drinking from a cup to mean accepting the suffering he would face in the terrible events that were soon to come.

b **26:42 do this** Literally, "drink this", referring to the "cup", the symbol of suffering in verse 39.

c **26:48 Judas** Literally, "the one who handed him over".

d **26:61 This man** That is, Jesus. His enemies avoided saying his name.

The Jewish leaders answered, "He is guilty, and he must die."

⁶⁷Then some there spat in Jesus' face, and they hit him with their fists. Others slapped him. ⁶⁸They said, "Show us that you are a prophet, Messiah! Tell us who hit you!"

Peter Is Afraid to Say He Knows Jesus

(Mark 14:66–72; Luke 22:56–62; John 18:15–18,25–27)

⁶⁹While Peter was sitting outside in the courtyard, a servant girl came up to him. She said, "You were with Jesus, that man from Galilee."

⁷⁰But Peter told everyone there that this was not true. "I don't know what you are talking about," he said.

INSIGHT

It was a common Jewish practice to identify a person by the name of the town they came from. Jesus was often referred to by others and he even referred to himself as Jesus of Nazareth (see Mark 1:23–24; Luke 4:16; Luke 24:19; John 18:5; 19:19; Acts 2:22; 22:8).

Matthew 26:71

⁷¹Then he left the courtyard. At the gate another girl saw him and said to the people there, "This man was with Jesus of Nazareth."

⁷²Again, Peter said he was never with Jesus. He said, "I swear to God I don't know the man!"

⁷³A short time later those standing there went to Peter and said, "We know you are one of them. It's clear from the way you talk."

⁷⁴Then Peter began to curse. He said, "I swear to God, I don't know the man!" As soon as he said this, a cockerel crowed. ⁷⁵Then he remembered what Jesus had told him: "Before the cockerel crows, you will say three times that you don't know me." Then Peter went outside and cried bitterly.

Jesus Is Taken to Governor Pilate

(Mark 15:1; Luke 23:1–2; John 18:28–32)

27 Early the next morning, all the leading priests and older leaders of the people met and decided to kill Jesus. ²They tied him, led him away and handed him over to Pilate, the governor.

Judas Kills Himself

(Acts 1:18–19)

³Judas saw that they had decided to kill Jesus. He was the one who had handed him over. When he saw what happened, he was very sorry for what he had done. So he took the 30 silver coins back to the priests and the older leaders. ⁴Judas said, "I sinned. I handed over to you an innocent man to be killed."

The Jewish leaders answered, "We don't care! That's a problem for you, not us."

⁵So Judas threw the money into the Temple. Then he went out from there and hanged himself.

⁶The leading priests picked up the silver coins in the Temple. They said, "Our law does not allow us to keep this money with the Temple money, because this money has paid for a man's death." ⁷So they decided to use the money to buy a field called Potter's Field. This field would be a place to bury people who died while visiting in Jerusalem. ⁸That is why that field is still called the Field of Blood. ⁹This showed the full meaning of what Jeremiah the prophet said:

"They took 30 silver coins. That was how much the people of Israel decided to pay for his life. ¹⁰They used those 30 silver coins to buy the potter's field, as the Lord commanded me."ᵃ

Governor Pilate Questions Jesus

(Mark 15:2–5; Luke 23:3–5; John 18:33–38)

¹¹Jesus stood before Pilate, the governor, who asked him, "Are you the king of the Jews?"

Jesus answered, "Yes, that's right."

¹²Then, when the leading priests and the older Jewish leaders made their accusations against Jesus, he said nothing.

¹³So Pilate said to him, "Don't you hear all these charges they are making against you? Why don't you answer?"

¹⁴But Jesus did not say anything, and this really surprised the governor.

Pilate Tries but Fails to Free Jesus

(Mark 15:6–15; Luke 23:13–25; John 18:39 – 19:16)

¹⁵Every year at Passover time the governor would free one prisoner—whichever one the people wanted him to free. ¹⁶At that time there was a man in prison who was known to be very bad. His name was Barabbas.ᵇ

¹⁷When a crowd gathered, Pilate said to them, "I will free one man for you. Which one do you want me to free: Barabbas or Jesus who is called

---

ᵃ **27:9–10 "They took . . . me"** See Jer. 32:6–9; Zech. 11:12–13.
ᵇ **27:16 Barabbas** In some Greek copies the name is Jesus Barabbas.

the Messiah?" [18]Pilate knew that they had handed Jesus over to him because they were jealous of him.

[19]While Pilate was sitting there in the place for judging, his wife sent a message to him. It said, "Don't do anything with that man. He is not guilty. Last night I had a dream about him, and it troubled me very much."

[20]But the leading priests and older Jewish leaders told the people to ask for Barabbas to be set free and for Jesus to be killed.

[21]Pilate said, "I have Barabbas and Jesus. Which one do you want me to set free for you?"

The people answered, "Barabbas!"

[22]Pilate asked, "So what should I do with Jesus, the one called the Messiah?"

All the people said, "Kill him on a cross!"

[23]Pilate asked, "Why do you want me to kill him? What wrong has he done?"

But they shouted louder, "Kill him on a cross!"

[24]Pilate saw that there was nothing he could do to make the people change. In fact, it looked as if there would be a riot. So he took some water and washed his hands[a] in front of them all. He said, "I am not guilty of this man's death. You are the ones who are doing it!"

[25]The people answered, "We will take full responsibility for his death. You can blame us and even our children!"

[26]Then Pilate set Barabbas free. And he told some soldiers to beat Jesus with whips. Then he handed him over to the soldiers to be killed on a cross.

Pilate's Soldiers Make Fun of Jesus

(Mark 15:16–20; John 19:2–3)

[27]Then Pilate's soldiers took Jesus into the governor's palace, and they gathered the whole company of soldiers around him. [28]They took off Jesus' clothes and put a scarlet robe[b] on him. [29]Then they made a crown from thorny branches and put it on his head, and they put a stick in his right hand. Then they bowed before him, making fun of him. They said, "We salute you, king of the Jews!" [30]They spat on him. Then they took his stick and kept hitting him on the head with it. [31]After they finished making fun of him, the soldiers took off the robe and put his own clothes on him again. Then they led him away to be killed on a cross.

Jesus Is Nailed to a Cross

(Mark 15:21–32; Luke 23:26–39; John 19:17–19)

[32]The soldiers were going out of the city with Jesus. They saw a man from Cyrene named Simon, and they forced him to carry Jesus' cross. [33]They came to the place called Golgotha. (Golgotha means "The Place of the Skull".) [34]There the soldiers gave Jesus some wine mixed with gall.[c] But when he tasted it, he refused to drink it.

[35]The soldiers nailed Jesus to a cross. Then they threw dice to divide his clothes between them. [36]The soldiers stayed there to guard him. [37]They put a sign above his head with the charge against him written on it: "THIS IS JESUS, THE KING OF THE JEWS."

[38]Two criminals were nailed to crosses beside Jesus—one on the right and the other on the left. [39]People walked by and shouted insults at Jesus. They shook their heads [40]and said, "You said you could destroy the Temple and build it again in three days. So save yourself! Come down from that cross if you really are the Son of God!"

[41]The leading priests, the teachers of the law and the older Jewish leaders were also there. They also made fun of Jesus. [42]They said, "He saved others, but he can't save himself! People say he is the king of Israel. If he is the king, he should come down now from the cross. Then we will believe in him. [43]He trusted God. So let God save him now, if God really wants him. He himself said, 'I am the Son of God.'" [44]And in the same way, the criminals on the crosses beside Jesus also insulted him.

Jesus Dies

(Mark 15:33–41; Luke 23:44–49; John 19:28–30)

[45]At noon the whole country became dark. The darkness continued for three hours. [46]About three o'clock Jesus cried out loudly, *"Eli, Eli, lema sabachthani?"* This means "My God, my God, why have you left me alone?"[d]

[47]Some of the people standing there heard this. They said, "He is calling Elijah."[e]

[48]Quickly, one of them ran and got a sponge. He filled the sponge with sour wine and tied the sponge to a stick. Then he used the stick to give the sponge to Jesus to get a drink from it. [49]But the others said, "Don't bother him. We want to see if Elijah will come to save him."

---

[a] **27:24 washed his hands** Pilate did this as a sign to show that he wanted no part in what the people did.

[b] **27:28 scarlet robe** Probably a soldier's robe that looked like the purple robes worn by kings. They put this on Jesus to make fun of him for claiming to be a king.

[c] **27:34 gall** Probably used as a drug to relieve pain.

[d] **27:46** Quote from Ps. 22:1.

[e] **27:47 "He is calling Elijah"** The word for "My God" (*Eli* in Hebrew or *Eloi* in Aramaic) sounded to the people like the name of Elijah, a famous man who spoke for God about 850 BC.

[50]Again Jesus cried out loudly and then died.[a]

[51]When Jesus died, the curtain in the Temple was torn into two pieces. The tear started at the top and tore all the way to the bottom. Also, the earth shook and rocks were broken. [52]The graves opened, and many of God's people who had died were raised from death. [53]They came out of the graves. And after Jesus was raised from death, they went into the holy city of Jerusalem, and many people saw them.

[54]The army officer and the soldiers guarding Jesus saw this earthquake and everything that happened. They were very afraid and said, "He really was the Son of God!"

[55]Many women were standing away from the cross, watching. These were the women who had followed Jesus from Galilee to care for him. [56]Mary Magdalene, Mary the mother of James and Joseph and the mother of James and John[b] were there.

INSIGHT

If you ever wonder whether God really loves you, read these verses again. Jesus said there is no greater love than someone laying down their life for their friends (John 15:13) and that's exactly what he did for humankind on the cross.
Matthew 27:11–54

Jesus Is Buried

(Mark 15:42–47; Luke 23:50–56; John 19:38–42)

[57]That evening a rich man named Joseph came to Jerusalem. He was a follower of Jesus from the town of Arimathea. [58]He went to Pilate and asked to have Jesus' body. Pilate gave orders for the soldiers to give Jesus' body to him. [59]Then Joseph took the body and wrapped it in a new linen cloth. [60]He put Jesus' body in a new tomb that he had dug out of a wall of rock. Then he closed the tomb by rolling a very large stone to cover the entrance. After he did this, he went away. [61]Mary Magdalene and the other woman named Mary were sitting near the tomb.

The Tomb of Jesus Is Guarded

[62]That day was the day called Preparation Day. The next day, the leading priests and the Pharisees went to Pilate. [63]They said, "Sir, we remember that while that liar was still alive he said, 'I will rise from death in three days.' [64]So give the order for the tomb to be guarded well for three days. His followers might come and try to steal the body. Then they could tell everyone that he has risen from death. That lie will be even worse than what they said about him before."

[65]Pilate said, "Take some soldiers, go to the tomb and guard it the best way you know." [66]So they all went to the tomb and made it safe from thieves. They did this by sealing the stone in the entrance and putting soldiers there to guard it.

News That Jesus Has Risen From Death

(Mark 16:1–8; Luke 24:1–12; John 20:1–10)

28 The day after the Sabbath day was the first day of the week. That day at dawn Mary Magdalene and the other woman named Mary went to look at the tomb.

[2]Suddenly an angel of the Lord came from the sky, and there was a huge earthquake. The angel went to the tomb and rolled the stone away from the entrance. Then he sat on top of the stone. [3]The angel was shining as bright as lightning. His clothes were as white as snow. [4]The soldiers guarding the tomb were very afraid of the angel. They shook with fear and then became like dead men.

[5]The angel said to the women, "Don't be afraid. I know you are looking for Jesus, the one who was killed on the cross. [6]But he is not here. He has risen from death, as he said he would. Come and see the place where his body was. [7]And go quickly and tell his followers, 'Jesus has risen from death. He is going into Galilee and will be there before you. You will see him there.'" Then the angel said, "Now I have told you."

[8]So the women left the tomb quickly. They were afraid, but they were also very happy. They ran to tell his followers what had happened. [9]Suddenly, Jesus was there in front of them. He said, "Hello!" The women went to him and, holding on to his feet, worshipped him. [10]Then Jesus said to them, "Don't be afraid. Go and tell my followers[c] to go to Galilee. They will see me there."

Report to the Jewish Leaders

[11]The women went to tell the followers. At the same time, some of the soldiers who had been guarding the tomb went into the city. They went to tell the leading priests everything that had happened. [12]Then the priests met with the older Jewish leaders and made a plan. They paid the soldiers a lot of money [13]and said to them, "Tell the people that Jesus' followers came during the night and stole the body while you were sleeping. [14]If

---

[a] 27:50 *died* Literally, "let his spirit leave".
[b] 27:56 *James and John* Literally, "the sons of Zebedee".
[c] 28:10 *followers* Literally, "brothers".

the governor hears about this, we will talk to him and keep you out of trouble." 15So the soldiers kept the money and obeyed the priests. And that story is still spread among the Jews even today.

Jesus Talks to His Followers

(Mark 16:14–18; Luke 24:36–49; John 20:19–23; Acts 1:6–8)

16The eleven followers went to Galilee, to the mountain where Jesus had told them to go. 17On the mountain the followers saw Jesus. They worshipped him. But some of the followers did not believe that it was really Jesus. 18So he came to them and said, "All authority in heaven and on earth has been given to me. 19So go and make followers of all people in the world. Baptize them in the name of the Father and the Son and the Holy Spirit. 20Teach them to obey everything that I have told you to do. You can be sure that I will be with you always. I will continue with you until the end of time."

Who
Although the Gospel is anonymous, it is traditionally attributed to John Mark, the friend of Paul and Peter, who lived in Jerusalem with his mother Mary during the early Church times (Acts 12:12).

When
A man called Papias of Hierapolis, writing in AD 130, records that an old man told him that Mark wrote down Peter's recollections in Rome while Mark was working alongside Peter (1 Peter 5:13). This would have been between AD 58–65.

What
Mark was probably the first Gospel written. It's the shortest and a lot of it is used by both Matthew and Luke. Jesus is pictured as a man of action and authority and Mark emphasizes what Jesus did rather than what he said and taught.

It's an action-packed Gospel: the blind, the sick and the lame crowd round Jesus in huge numbers; the religious authorities and political leadership fear his popularity and plot his downfall; thousands of people are fed.

Mark's aim is to get across the simple facts. So there is nothing in his Gospel about Jesus' birth and upbringing, and no details about his age or the length of his ministry. The Gospel opens with a bang – "The Good News about Jesus the Messiah, the Son of God" (1:1) and then launches into an account of John the Baptist and Jesus' baptism. If it starts abruptly, it also ends rather quickly, with no resurrection appearance, just two women, an empty tomb and an angel with a message from God. However, many versions of Mark include a longer ending (16:9–20) which was added early in the second century AD.

The simple facts then: Jesus Christ is the Son of God. Mark was probably writing for a mainly non-Jewish, Roman audience. He writes in a very simple type of Greek – one which would have been understood by a wide audience, even those who didn't know much Greek. So he is careful to explain Jewish customs and translate Aramaic words and phrases and he includes testimonies from people such as the Roman army officer who was present when Christ was on the cross. There are also many accounts of healing and miracles – sure signs, according to Mark, that Jesus' power came from God. But he also emphasizes the difficulties, the way that Jesus suffered. The new life that we get through Jesus isn't easy – it's a life of service and suffering.

 QUICK TOUR ▶ **MARK**

"But the man said, 'Don't be afraid. You are looking for Jesus from Nazareth, the one who was killed on a cross. He has risen from death! He is not here. Look, here is the place they put him when he was dead.'"

Mark 16:6

John Prepares the Way for Jesus

(Matt. 3:1–12; Luke 3:1–9,15–17; John 1:19–28)

1 The Good News about Jesus the Messiah, the Son of God,[a] begins [2]with what Isaiah the prophet said would happen. He wrote:

> "Listen! I will send my messenger ahead
>   of you.
> He will prepare the way for you."
>
> *Malachi 3:1*

[3]"There is someone shouting in the
    desert:
'Prepare the way for the Lord.
    Make the road straight for him.'"

Isaiah 40:3

[4]So John the Baptizer came and was baptizing people in the desert area. He told them to be baptized to show that they wanted to change their lives, and then their sins would be forgiven. [5]All the people from Judea, including everyone from Jerusalem, came out to John. They confessed the bad things they had done, and he baptized them in the Jordan River. [6]John wore clothes made from camel's hair and a leather belt around his waist. He ate locusts and wild honey. [7]This is what John told the people: "There is someone coming later who is able to do more than I can. I am not good enough to be the slave who stoops down to untie his sandals. [8]I baptize you with water, but the one who is coming will baptize you with the Holy Spirit."

Jesus Is Baptized by John

(Matt. 3:13–17; Luke 3:21–22)

[9]About that time Jesus came there from the town of Nazareth in Galilee, and John baptized him in the Jordan River. [10]Just as Jesus was coming up out of the water, he saw the sky torn open. And he saw the Spirit coming down on him like a dove. [11]A voice came from heaven and said, "You are my Son, the one I love. I am very pleased with you."

Jesus Goes Away to Be Tempted

(Matt. 4:1–11; Luke 4:1–13)

[12]Then the Spirit sent Jesus into the desert. [13]He was there for 40 days and was tempted by Satan. During this time he was out among the wild animals. Then angels came and helped him.

INSIGHT

The Bible often talks about things happening for forty days (like Jesus being in the desert here, the rains sent in the time of Noah, Moses on Mount Sinai and Elijah travelling to Mount Horeb). Forty days is symbolic of a long period of time and usually refers to a time of seclusion, testing or suffering.

Mark 1:12–13

Jesus Begins His Work in Galilee

(Matt. 4:12–17; Luke 4:14–15)

[14]After John was put in prison, Jesus went into Galilee and told people the Good News from God. [15]He said, "The right time is now here. God's kingdom is very near.[b] Change your hearts and lives, and believe the Good News!"

Jesus Chooses Some Followers

(Matt. 4:18–22; Luke 5:1–11)

[16]Jesus was walking by Lake Galilee. He saw Simon[c] and his brother Andrew. These two men were fishermen, and they were throwing a net into the lake to catch fish. [17]Jesus said to them, "Come, follow me, and I will make you a different kind of fishermen. You will bring in people, not fish." [18]So they immediately left their nets and followed Jesus.

[19]Jesus continued walking by Lake Galilee. He saw two more brothers, James and John, the sons of Zebedee. They were in their boat, preparing their nets to catch fish. [20]Their father Zebedee and the men who worked for him were in the boat with the brothers. When Jesus saw the brothers, he told them to come. They left their father and followed Jesus.

Jesus Frees a Man From an Evil Spirit

(Luke 4:31–37)

[21]Jesus and his followers went to Capernaum. On the Sabbath day, Jesus went into the synagogue and taught the people. [22]They were amazed at his teaching. He did not teach like their teachers of the law. He taught like someone with authority. [23]While Jesus was in the synagogue, a man was there who had an evil spirit inside him. The man shouted, [24]"Jesus of Nazareth! What do you want with us? Did you come to destroy us? I know who you are—God's Holy One!"

---

[a] **1:1** *the Son of God* Some Greek copies do not have these words.
[b] **1:15** *is very near* Or "is coming soon" or "has come".
[c] **1:16** *Simon* Simon's other name was Peter. Also in verses 29,30,36.

25Jesus, his voice full of warning, said, "Be quiet, and come out of him!" 26The evil spirit made the man shake. Then the spirit, screaming loudly, came out of the man.

27The people were amazed. They asked each other, "What is happening here? This man is teaching something new, and he teaches with authority! He even commands evil spirits, and they obey him." 28So the news about Jesus spread quickly everywhere in the area of Galilee.

Jesus Heals Many People

(Matt. 8:14–17; Luke 4:38–41)

29Jesus and the followers left the synagogue. They all went with James and John to the home of Simon and Andrew. 30As soon as they arrived, Jesus was told that Simon's mother-in-law was very sick. She was in bed with a fever. 31So he went in to see her. He held her hand and helped her stand up. The fever left her, and she was healed. Then she began serving them.

32That night, after the sun went down, the people brought to Jesus all those who were sick. They also brought those who had demons inside them. 33Everyone in the town gathered at the door of that house. 34Jesus healed many of those who had different kinds of sicknesses. He also forced many demons out of people. But he would not allow the demons to speak, because they knew who he was.*a*

Jesus Goes to Other Towns

(Luke 4:42–44)

35The next morning Jesus woke up very early. He left the house while it was still dark and went to a place where he could be alone and pray. 36Later, Simon and his friends went to look for Jesus. 37They found him and said, "Everyone is looking for you!"

38Jesus answered, "We should go to another place. We can go to other towns around here, and I can tell God's message to those people too. That is why I came." 39So Jesus travelled everywhere in Galilee. He spoke in the synagogues, and he forced demons out of people.

Jesus Heals a Sick Man

(Matt. 8:1–4; Luke 5:12–16)

40A man who had leprosy came to Jesus. The man bowed on his knees and begged him, "You have the power to heal me if you want."

41These last words made Jesus angry.*b* But he touched him and said, "I want to heal you. Be healed!" 42Immediately the leprosy disappeared, and the man was healed.

43Jesus told the man to go, but he gave him a strong warning: 44"Don't tell anyone about what I did for you. But go and let the priest look at you.*c* And offer a gift to God because you have been healed. Offer the gift that Moses commanded.*d* This will show everyone that you are healed." 45The man left there and told everyone he saw that Jesus had healed him. So the news about Jesus spread. And that is why he could not enter a town if people saw him. He stayed in places where people did not live. But people came from all the towns to the places where he was.

Jesus Heals a Paralysed Man

(Matt. 9:1–8; Luke 5:17–26)

2 A few days later, Jesus came back to Capernaum. The news spread that he was back home. 2A large crowd gathered to hear him speak. The house was so full that there was no place to stand, not even outside the door. While Jesus was teaching, 3some people brought a paralysed man to see him. He was being carried by four of them. 4But they could not get the man inside to Jesus because the house was so full of people. So they went to the roof above Jesus and made a hole in it. Then they lowered the mat with the paralysed man on it. 5When Jesus saw how much faith they had, he said to the paralysed man, "Young man, your sins are forgiven."

6Some of the teachers of the law were sitting there. They saw what Jesus did, and they said to themselves, 7"Why does this man say things like that? What an insult to God! No one but God can forgive sins."

8Jesus knew immediately what these teachers of the law were thinking. So he said to them, "Why do you have these questions in your minds? 9–10The Son of Man has power on earth to forgive sins. But how can I prove this to you? Maybe you are thinking it was easy for me to say to the paralysed man, 'Your sins are forgiven,' because there's no proof it really happened. But what if I say to the man, 'Stand up. Take your mat and walk'? Then you will be able to see if I really have this power or not." So Jesus said to the paralysed man, 11"I tell you, stand up. Take your mat and go home."

12The paralysed man stood up. He picked up his mat and went straight out of the door with

---

a **1:34** *who he was* Meaning that the demons knew that Jesus was the Messiah, the Son of God.
b **1:41** *These . . . angry* Most Greek copies have "Moved with pity . . .". But it is hard to explain why some good Greek copies and Latin versions now consider it to be the original reading.
c **1:44** *let the priest look at you* The Law of Moses said a priest must decide when a person with leprosy was well.
d **1:44** *Moses commanded* See Lev. 14:1–32.

JESUS PROVOKES A RESPONSE

Have you ever been part of a crowd gathered to see a famous celebrity? How easy was it to catch a glimpse? What was it like to be so close to someone so special? Read this section of Mark, where Jesus is the one everyone wants to see.

DIG IN   READ Mark 2:1-12

Can you imagine the scene? A house so full there wasn't even space for one more person and the crowd spilled out into the streets. This was a time without Twitter, mobile phones or any mass communication, so the word about Jesus must have spread powerfully considering it would've been through word of mouth.

Then imagine the desperation of the people who wanted to see Jesus so badly that they actually made a hole in someone's roof and lowered their friend through the ceiling – all in the hope that he might be healed!

- What's surprising about the first thing that Jesus says to the paralysed man (v.5)? Remember why his friends had brought him to Jesus. What would you expect Jesus to have said to him?
- What does the fact that Jesus said this first tell you about the importance of dealing with sin?
- How did the religious people respond (vv.6–7)?

Although the religious people thought they were insulting Jesus, they were actually highlighting something very true and exciting about him: no one but God can forgive sins, and yet Jesus did so. Jesus was demonstrating that he is God.

- How does Jesus further demonstrate this in verse 8?
- How did he finally prove it for everyone to see (vv.9–12)?

What an electrifying snapshot of Jesus' ministry. Heaving crowds, miraculous healing and Jesus doing the one thing that only God can do – forgiving sins. In verse 12 everyone seems delighted with him. Or were they . . . ?

READ Mark 3:1-6

In Old Testament law, the "Sabbath" was given as a day of rest – a "chill-out" day, a time when the people of Israel could remember God and his goodness to them. But later on the Pharisees started twisting things. They started adding their own rules to the law saying, for instance, that you could only heal on the Sabbath if it was a life or death situation. And they often treated this kind of rule-keeping as the only thing that mattered. They turned what was good into nit-picking nastiness.

- In light of verse 4 and Jesus' ability to heal, what would have been the "lawful" thing to do on the Sabbath? To heal or not to heal? Which was more in line with God's intentions for the Sabbath?
- How do verses 2 and 6 show that the Pharisees, for all their proud nit-picking, thought of the Sabbath as a day to do harm?

In verse 6 we see that in contrast to the elation of the crowds in Matthew 2:12, there is also extreme opposition to Jesus from some quarters. The Pharisees (the religious fundamentalists of the day) and the Herodians (a Jewish political group) wanted to kill him.

DIG THROUGH

- In Mark 2 we saw that Jesus is the God who heals and the God who forgives. How might you pray in response to that for your life right now? Do you or a friend need healing? Do you need forgiveness or help to forgive someone else?
- Jesus surprised everyone in Mark 2 by telling a man who was unable to move any part of his body, that his sins were forgiven. He clearly knew that getting right with God is a more pressing need than anything physical ever can be. Who do you know that is in this desperate need? Pray for them now.

everyone watching. They were amazed and praised God. They said, "This is the most amazing thing we have ever seen!"

Levi (Matthew) Follows Jesus

(Matt. 9:9–13; Luke 5:27–32)

¹³Jesus went out to the lake again. A large crowd gathered around him, so he began teaching them. ¹⁴As he walked along the shore, he saw a man named Levi, son of Alphaeus. Levi was sitting at his place for collecting taxes. Jesus said to him, "Follow me." Then Levi stood up and followed Jesus.

¹⁵Later that day, Jesus and his close followers were eating at Levi's house. Many tax collectors and others with bad reputations had also become followers of Jesus. So many of these people were there eating with them. ¹⁶When some teachers of the law who were Pharisees saw Jesus eating with such bad people, they asked his followers, "Why does he eat with tax collectors and sinners?"

¹⁷When Jesus heard this, he said to them, "Sick people are the ones who need a doctor, not those who are healthy. I came to ask sinners to join me, not those who do everything right."

Jesus Is Not Like Other Religious Leaders

(Matt. 9:14–17; Luke 5:33–39)

¹⁸The followers of John and the Pharisees were fasting. Some people came to Jesus and said, "John's followers fast, and the followers of the Pharisees fast. But your followers don't fast. Why?"

¹⁹Jesus answered, "At a wedding the friends of the bridegroom are not sad while he is with them. They cannot fast while the bridegroom is still there. ²⁰But the time will come when the bridegroom will be taken from them. Then they will be sad and fast.

²¹"When someone sews a patch over a hole in an old coat, they never use a piece of cloth that is not yet shrunk. If they do, the patch will shrink and pull away from the coat. Then the hole will be worse. ²²Also, no one ever pours new wine into old wineskins. The wine would break them, and the wine would be ruined along with the wineskins. You always put new wine into new wineskins."

Jesus Is Lord Over the Sabbath Day

(Matt. 12:1–8; Luke 6:1–5)

²³On the Sabbath day, Jesus and his followers were walking through some grain fields. The followers picked some grain to eat. ²⁴Some Pharisees said to Jesus, "Why are your followers doing this? It is against our law to pick grain on the Sabbath."

INSIGHT

Jesus was pointing out that the Pharisees were following the letter of the law instead of the spirit of the law. By focusing on rules rather than people, they were missing the point of the law. Relationship comes before instruction every time.

Mark 2:23–28

²⁵Jesus answered, "You have read what David did when he and the people with him were hungry and needed food. ²⁶It was during the time of Abiathar the high priest. David went into God's house and ate the bread that was offered to God. And the Law of Moses says that only priests can eat that bread. David also gave some of the bread to the people with him."

²⁷Then Jesus said to the Pharisees, "The Sabbath day was made to help people. People were not made to be ruled by the Sabbath. ²⁸So the Son of Man is Lord of every day, even the Sabbath."

Jesus Heals a Man on the Sabbath Day

(Matt. 12:9–14; Luke 6:6–11)

3 Another time Jesus went into the synagogue. In the synagogue there was a man with a paralysed hand. ²Some Jews there were watching Jesus closely. They were waiting to see if he would heal the man on a Sabbath day. They wanted to see Jesus do something wrong so that they could accuse him. ³Jesus said to the man with the paralysed hand, "Stand up here so that everyone can see you."

⁴Then Jesus asked the people, "Which is the right thing to do on the Sabbath day: to do good or to do evil? Is it right to save a life or to destroy one?" The people said nothing to answer him.

⁵Jesus looked at the people. He was angry, but he felt very sad because they were so stubborn. He said to the man, "Hold out your hand." The man held out his hand, and it was healed. ⁶Then the Pharisees left and made plans with the Herodians about a way to kill Jesus.

Many Follow Jesus

⁷Jesus went away with his followers to the lake. A large crowd of people from Galilee followed them. Many also came from Judea, ⁸from Jerusalem, from Idumea, from the area across the Jordan River and from the area around Tyre and Sidon. These people came because they heard about all that Jesus was doing.

⁹Jesus saw how many people there were, so he told his followers to get a small boat and make it ready for him. He wanted the boat so that the crowds of people could not push against him. ¹⁰He had healed many of them, so all the sick people were pushing towards him to touch him. ¹¹Some people had evil spirits inside them. When the evil spirits saw Jesus, they fell to the ground before him and shouted, "You are the Son of God!" ¹²But Jesus gave the spirits a strong warning not to tell anyone who he was.

INSIGHT

The word "apostle" comes from the Greek apostolos which means "messenger". Jesus had chosen and was training the twelve men who would get his message out across the world.

Mark 3:13–15

Jesus Chooses His Twelve Apostles

(Matt. 10:1–4; Luke 6:12–16)

¹³Jesus went up into the hills. He told some of his followers, those he wanted, to join him there. So they went to meet with him. ¹⁴He chose twelve men and called them apostles. He wanted these twelve men to be with him, and he wanted to send them to other places to tell people God's message. ¹⁵He also wanted them to have the power to force demons out of people. ¹⁶These are the names of the twelve men Jesus chose:

Simon (the one Jesus named Peter),
¹⁷James and his brother John, the sons of
    Zebedee (the ones Jesus named Boanerges,
    which means "Sons of Thunder"),
¹⁸Andrew,
Philip,
Bartholomew,
Matthew,
Thomas,
James the son of Alphaeus,
Thaddaeus,
Simon the Zealot,
¹⁹Judas Iscariot (the one who handed Jesus over
    to his enemies).

Jesus' Power Is From God

(Matt. 12:22–32; Luke 11:14–23; 12:10)

²⁰Then Jesus went home, but again a large crowd gathered there. There were so many people that he and his followers could not even eat. ²¹His family heard about all these things. They went to get him because people said he was crazy.

²²And the teachers of the law from Jerusalem said, "Satan[a] is living inside him! He uses power from the ruler of demons to force demons out of people."

²³So Jesus called them together and talked to them using some stories. He said, "Satan will not force his own demons out of people. ²⁴A kingdom that fights against itself will not survive. ²⁵And a family that is divided will not survive. ²⁶If Satan is against himself and is fighting against his own people, he will not survive. That would be the end of Satan.

²⁷"Whoever wants to enter a strong man's house and steal his things must first tie him up. Then they can steal the things from his house.

²⁸"I want you to know that people can be forgiven for all the sinful things they do. They can even be forgiven for the bad things they say against God. ²⁹But anyone who speaks against the Holy Spirit will never be forgiven. They will always be guilty of that sin."

³⁰Jesus said this because the teachers of the law had accused him of having an evil spirit inside him.

Jesus' Followers Are His True Family

(Matt. 12:46–50; Luke 8:19–21)

³¹Then Jesus' mother and brothers came. They stood outside and sent someone in to tell him to come out. ³²Many people were sitting around Jesus. They said to him, "Your mother, your brothers and your sisters[b] are waiting for you outside."

³³Jesus asked, "Who is my mother? Who are my brothers?" ³⁴Then he looked at the people sitting around him and said, "These people are my mother and my brothers! ³⁵My true brother and sister and mother are those who do what God wants."

A Story About a Farmer Sowing Seed

(Matt. 13:1–9; Luke 8:4–8)

4 Another time Jesus began teaching by the lake, and a large crowd gathered around him. He got into a boat so that he could sit and teach from the lake. All the people stayed on the shore near the water. ²Jesus used stories to teach them many things. One of his lessons included this story:

³"Listen! A farmer went out to sow seed. ⁴While he was scattering the seed, some of it fell by the road. The birds came and ate all that seed. ⁵Other seed fell on rocky ground, where there

---

[a] **3:22 Satan** Literally, "Beelzebul" (the devil).
[b] **3:32 and your sisters** Some Greek copies do not have these words.

was not enough soil. It grew quickly there because the soil was not deep. [6]But then the sun rose and the plants were burned. They died because they did not have deep roots. [7]Some other seed fell among thorny weeds. The weeds grew and stopped the good plants from growing. So they did not make grain. [8]But some of the seed fell on good ground. There it began to grow, and it made grain. Some plants made 30 times more grain, some 60 times more and some 100 times more."

[9]Then Jesus said, "You people who hear me, listen!"

Why Jesus Used Stories to Teach

(Matt. 13:10–17; Luke 8:9–10)

[10]Later, when Jesus was away from all the people, the twelve apostles and his other followers asked him about the stories. [11]Jesus said, "Only you can know the secret truth about God's kingdom. But to those other people I tell everything by using stories. [12]I do this so that,

'They will look and look but not really see;
    they will listen and listen but not
        understand.
If they understood, they might turn to me,
    and I would forgive them.'"

Isaiah 6:9–10

Jesus Explains the Story About Seed

(Matt. 13:18–23; Luke 8:11–15)

[13]Then Jesus said to the followers, "Do you understand this story? If you don't, how will you understand any story? [14]The farmer is like someone who plants God's teaching in people. [15]Sometimes the teaching falls on the path. That is like some people who hear the teaching of God. As soon as they hear it, Satan comes and takes away the teaching that was planted in them.

[16]"Other people are like the seed planted on rocky ground. They hear the teaching, and they quickly and gladly accept it. [17]But they don't allow it to go deep into their lives. They keep it only a short time. As soon as trouble or persecution comes because of the teaching they accepted, they give up.

[18]"Others are like the seed planted among the thorny weeds. They hear the teaching, [19]but their lives become full of other things: the worries of this life, the love of money and everything else they want. This keeps the teaching from growing, and it does not produce good results in their lives.[a]

[20]"And others are like the seed planted on the good ground. They hear the teaching and accept it. Then they grow and produce a good crop—sometimes 30 times more, sometimes 60 times more and sometimes 100 times more."

Use the Understanding You Have

(Luke 8:16–18)

[21]Then Jesus said to them, "You don't take a lamp and hide it under a bowl or a bed, do you? Of course not. You put it on a lampstand. [22]Everything that is hidden will be made clear. Every secret thing will be made known. [23]You people who hear me, listen! [24]Think carefully about what you are hearing. The more attention you give, the more understanding you will get. And you will be given even more. [25]The people who have some understanding will receive more. But those who do not have much will lose even the small amount they have."

Jesus Uses a Story About Seed

[26]Then Jesus said, "God's kingdom is like a man who plants seed in the ground. [27]The seed begins to grow. It grows night and day. It doesn't matter whether the man is sleeping or awake, the seed still grows. He doesn't know how it happens. [28]Without any help the ground produces grain. First the plant grows, then the head and then all the grain in the head. [29]When the grain is ready, the man cuts it. This is the harvest time."

What Is God's Kingdom Like?

(Matt. 13:31–32,34–35; Luke 13:18–19)

[30]Then Jesus said, "What can I use to show you what God's kingdom is like? What story can I use to explain it? [31]God's kingdom is like a mustard seed, which is smaller than any other seed on earth that you can plant. [32]But when you plant it, it grows and becomes the largest of all the plants in your garden. It has branches that are very big. The wild birds can come and make nests there and be protected from the sun."

[33]Jesus used many stories like these to teach the people. He taught them all they could understand. [34]He always used stories to teach them. But when he was alone with his followers, Jesus explained everything to them.

Jesus' Followers See His Power

(Matt. 8:23–27; Luke 8:22–25)

[35]That day, at evening, Jesus said to his followers, "Come with me across the lake." [36]So they left the crowd behind and went with Jesus in the boat he was already in. There were also other boats there with him. [37]A very bad wind came up on the lake. The waves were coming over the

---

[a] **4:19 does not produce . . . lives** Literally, "becomes unfruitful", meaning that these people do not do the good things God wants his people to do.

sides and into the boat, and it was almost full of water. ³⁸Jesus was inside the boat, sleeping with his head on a pillow. The followers went and woke him. They said, "Teacher, don't you care about us? We are going to drown!"

³⁹Jesus stood up and gave a command to the wind and the water. He said, "Quiet! Be still!" Then the wind stopped, and the lake became calm.

⁴⁰He said to his followers, "Why are you afraid? Do you still have no faith?"

⁴¹They were very afraid and asked each other, "What kind of man is this? Even the wind and the water obey him!"

Jesus Frees a Man From Evil Spirits

(Matt. 8:28–34; Luke 8:26–39)

5 Jesus and his followers went across the lake to the area where the Gerasene people[a] lived. ²When Jesus got out of the boat, a man came to him from the caves where the dead are buried. This man had an evil spirit living inside him. ³He lived in the burial caves. No one could keep him tied up, even with chains. ⁴Many times people had put chains on his hands and feet, but he broke the chains. No one was strong enough to control him. ⁵Day and night he stayed around the burial caves and on the hills. He would scream and cut himself with rocks.

⁶While Jesus was still far away, the man saw him. He ran to Jesus and bowed down before him. ^{7–8}As Jesus was saying, "You evil spirit, come out of this man," the man shouted loudly, "What do you want with me, Jesus, Son of the Most High God? Promise in God's name not to punish me!"

⁹Then Jesus asked the man, "What is your name?"

The man answered, "My name is Legion,[b] because there are many spirits inside me." ¹⁰The spirits inside the man begged Jesus again and again not to send them out of that area.

¹¹A large herd of pigs was eating on a hill near there. ¹²The evil spirits begged Jesus, "Send us to the pigs. Let us go into them." ¹³So Jesus allowed them to do this. The evil spirits left the man and went into the pigs. Then the herd of pigs ran down the hill and into the lake. They were all drowned. There were about 2,000 pigs in that herd.

¹⁴The men who had the work of caring for the pigs ran away. They ran to the town and to the farms and told everyone what had happened. The people went out to see. ¹⁵They came to Jesus, and they saw the man who had the many evil spirits. He was sitting down and was wearing clothes. He was in his right mind again. When they saw this, they were afraid. ¹⁶Those who had seen

what Jesus did told the others what had happened to the man who had the demons living in him. And they also told them about the pigs. ¹⁷Then the people began to beg Jesus to leave their area.

¹⁸Jesus was preparing to leave in the boat. The man who was now free from the demons begged to go with him. ¹⁹But Jesus did not allow the man to go. He said, "Go home to your family and friends. Tell them about all that the Lord did for you. Tell them how the Lord was good to you."

²⁰So the man left and told the people in the Ten Towns about the great things Jesus had done for him. Everyone was amazed.

Jesus Gives Life to a Dead Girl and Heals a Sick Woman

(Matt. 9:18–26; Luke 8:40–56)

²¹Jesus went back to the other side of the lake in the boat. There, a large crowd of people gathered around him on the shore. ²²A leader of the synagogue came. His name was Jairus. He saw Jesus and bowed down before him. ²³He begged Jesus again and again, saying, "My little daughter is dying. Please come and lay your hands on her. Then she will be healed and will live."

²⁴So Jesus went with Jairus. Many people followed Jesus. They were pushing very close around him.

²⁵There among the people was a woman who had been bleeding for the past twelve years. ²⁶She had suffered very much. Many doctors had tried to help her, and she had spent all the money she had, but she was not improving. In fact, her sickness was getting worse.

²⁷The woman heard about Jesus, so she followed him with the other people and touched his coat. ²⁸She thought, "If I can just touch his clothes, that will be enough to heal me." ²⁹As soon as she touched his coat, her bleeding stopped. She felt that her body was healed from all the suffering. ³⁰Jesus immediately felt power go out from him, so he stopped and turned around. "Who touched my clothes?" he asked.

³¹The followers said to Jesus, "There are so many people pushing against you, but you ask, 'Who touched me?'"

³²But Jesus continued looking for the one who touched him. ³³The woman knew that she was healed, so she came and bowed at Jesus' feet. She was shaking with fear. She told Jesus the whole story. ³⁴He said to her, "Dear woman, you are made well because you believed. Go in peace. You will not suffer any more."

³⁵While Jesus was still there speaking, some men came from the house of Jairus, the synagogue

---

^a **5:1 Gerasene people** Some Greek copies have "Gadarenes" and others have "Gergesenes".
^b **5:9 Legion** This name means very many. A legion was about 6,000 men in the Roman army.

leader. They said, "Your daughter is dead. There is no need to bother the Teacher."

³⁶But Jesus did not care what the men said. He said to the synagogue leader, "Don't be afraid; just believe."

³⁷Jesus let only Peter, James and John the brother of James go with him. ³⁸They went to the synagogue leader's house, where Jesus saw many people crying loudly. There was a lot of confusion. ³⁹He entered the house and said, "Why are you people crying and making so much noise? This child is not dead. She is only sleeping." ⁴⁰But everyone laughed at him.

Jesus told the people to leave the house. Then he went into the room where the child was. He brought the child's father and mother and his three followers into the room with him. ⁴¹Then Jesus held the girl's hand and said to her, *"Talitha, koum!"* (This means "Little girl, I tell you to stand up!") ⁴²The girl immediately stood up and began walking. (She was twelve years old.) The father and mother and the followers were amazed. ⁴³Jesus gave the father and mother very strict orders not to tell people about this. Then he told them to give the girl some food to eat.

Jesus Goes to His Home Town

(Matt. 13:53–58; Luke 4:16–30)

6 Jesus left and went back to his home town. His followers went with him. ²On the Sabbath day Jesus taught in the synagogue, and many people heard him. They were amazed and said, "Where did this man get this teaching? How did he get such wisdom? Who gave it to him? And where did he get the power to do miracles? ³Isn't he just the carpenter we know—Mary's son, the brother of James, Joses, Judas and Simon? And don't his sisters still live here in town?" So they had a problem accepting him.

INSIGHT

Jesus spent at least 15 years in Nazareth, where he learnt to be a carpenter and craftsman in his father's business.
Many of his stories feature men for hire, building terms and references to wood and stone.

Mark 6:3

---

⁴Then Jesus said to them, "People everywhere give honour to a prophet, except in his own town, with his own people or in his home." ⁵Jesus was not able to do any miracles there except the healing of some sick people by laying his hands on them. ⁶He was surprised that the people there had no faith. Then he went to other villages in that area and taught.

Jesus Sends His Apostles on a Mission

(Matt. 10:1,5–15; Luke 9:1–6)

⁷Jesus called his twelve apostles together. He sent them out in groups of two and gave them power over evil spirits. ⁸This is what he told them: "Take nothing for your trip except a stick for walking. Take no bread, no bag and no money. ⁹You can wear sandals, but don't take extra clothes. ¹⁰When you enter a house, stay there until you leave that town. ¹¹If any town refuses to accept you or refuses to listen to you, then leave that town and shake the dust off your feet[a] as a warning to them."

¹²The apostles left and went to other places. They talked to the people and told them to change their hearts and lives. ¹³They forced many demons out of people and put olive oil on[b] many who were sick and healed them.

Herod Thinks Jesus Is John the Baptizer

(Matt. 14:1–12; Luke 9:7–9)

¹⁴King Herod heard about Jesus, because Jesus was now famous. Some people said, "He is John the Baptizer. He must have risen from death, and that is why he can do these miracles."

¹⁵Other people said, "He is Elijah."

And others said, "He is a prophet. He is like the prophets who lived long ago."

¹⁶Herod heard these things about Jesus. He said, "I killed John by cutting off his head. Now he has been raised from death!"

How John the Baptizer Was Killed

¹⁷Herod himself had ordered his soldiers to arrest John and put him in prison. Herod did this to please his wife Herodias. She had been married to Herod's brother Philip, but then Herod married her. ¹⁸John told Herod, "It is not right for you to be married to your brother's wife." ¹⁹So Herodias hated John. She wanted him dead, but she was not able to persuade Herod to kill him. ²⁰Herod was afraid to kill John, because he knew that he was a good and holy man. So he protected him. He liked listening to John, although what John said left him with so many questions.

---

[a] **6:11** *shake the dust off your feet* A warning. It would show that they were finished talking to these people.
[b] **6:13** *put olive oil on* Olive oil was used like a medicine. It also became a symbol of the healing power of God that was given to Jesus and then to his followers by the Holy Spirit.

[21]Then the right time came for Herodias to cause John's death. It happened on Herod's birthday. Herod gave a dinner party for the most important government leaders, the commanders of his army and the most important people in Galilee. [22]The daughter of Herodias came to the party and danced. When she danced, Herod and the people eating with him were very pleased.

So King Herod said to the girl, "I will give you anything you want." [23]He promised her, "Anything you ask for I will give to you—even half of my kingdom."

[24]The girl went to her mother and asked, "What should I ask King Herod to give me?"

Her mother answered, "Ask for the head of John the Baptizer."

[25]So right then the girl went back in to the king. She said to him, "Please give me the head of John the Baptizer. Bring it to me now on a plate."

[26]King Herod was very sad, but he didn't want to break the promise he had made to her in front of his guests. [27]So he sent a soldier to cut off John's head and bring it to him. The soldier went and cut off John's head in the prison. [28]He brought the head back on a plate and gave it to the girl, and the girl gave it to her mother. [29]John's followers heard about what happened, so they came and got John's body and put it in a tomb.

Jesus Feeds More Than 5,000

(Matt. 14:13–21; Luke 9:10–17; John 6:1–14)

[30]The apostles Jesus had sent out came back to him. They gathered around him and told him about all they had done and taught. [31]Jesus and his followers were in a very busy place. There were so many people that he and his followers did not even have time to eat. He said to them, "Come with me. We will go to a quiet place to be alone. There we will get some rest."

[32]So Jesus and his followers went away alone. They went in a boat to a place where no one lived. [33]But many people saw them leave and knew who they were. So people from every town ran to the place where they were going and got there before Jesus and his followers. [34]As Jesus stepped out of the boat, he saw a large crowd waiting. He felt sorry for them, because they were like sheep without a *shepherd* to care for them. So he taught the people many things.

[35]It was now very late in the day. Jesus' followers came to him and said, "No one lives around here, and it is already very late. [36]So send the people away. They need to go to the farms and towns around here to buy some food to eat."

[37]But Jesus answered, "You give them some food to eat."

They said to Jesus, "We can't buy enough bread to feed all these people. We would all have to work for a month to earn enough to buy that much bread!"

[38]Jesus asked them, "How many loaves of bread do you have now? Go and see."

They counted their loaves of bread. They came to Jesus and said, "We have five loaves of bread and two fish."

[39]Then Jesus said to them, "Tell everyone to sit in groups on the green grass." [40]So all the people sat in groups. There were about 50 or 100 people in each group.

[41]Jesus took the five loaves and two fish. He looked up to the sky and thanked God for the food. Then he broke the bread into pieces, which he gave to his followers to distribute to the people. Then he divided the two fish among everyone there.

[42]They all ate until they were full. [43]After they finished eating, the followers filled twelve baskets with the pieces of bread and fish that were left. [44]There were about 5,000 men there who ate.

Jesus Walks on Water

(Matt. 14:22–33; John 6:16–21)

[45]Then Jesus told the followers to get into the boat. He told them to go to the other side of the lake to Bethsaida. He said he would come later. He stayed there to tell everyone they could go home. [46]After saying goodbye to them, he went up into the hills to pray.

[47]That night, the boat was still in the middle of the lake. Jesus was alone on the land. [48]He saw the boat far away on the lake. And he saw the followers working hard to row the boat. The wind was blowing against them. Sometime between three and six o'clock in the morning, Jesus went out to the boat, walking on the water. He continued walking until he was almost past the boat. [49]But the followers saw Jesus walking on the water. They thought he was a ghost, and they started screaming. [50]It scared them all to see him. But he spoke to them and said, "Don't worry! It's me! Don't be afraid." [51]When he got into the boat with the followers, the wind stopped. The followers were completely amazed. [52]They could not believe what had happened. It was like the miracle he had done with the bread. They still didn't understand what that meant.

Jesus Heals Many Sick People

(Matt. 14:34–36)

[53]Jesus and his followers went across the lake and came to shore at Gennesaret. They tied the boat there. [54]When they got out of the boat, the people there saw Jesus. They knew who he was, [55]so they ran to tell others throughout that area. As Jesus went from place to place, the people found out where he was and brought their sick

ones to him on mats. ⁵⁶Jesus went into towns, cities and farms around that area. And everywhere he went, the people brought those who were sick to the marketplaces. They begged him to let them touch any part of his coat. And all those who touched him were healed.

God's Law and Human Traditions

(Matt. 15:1–20)

7 Some Pharisees and some teachers of the law came from Jerusalem and gathered around Jesus. ²They saw that some of his followers ate food with hands that were not clean, meaning that they did not wash their hands in a certain way. ³The Pharisees and all the other Jews never eat before washing their hands in this special way. They do this to follow the traditions they have from their great leaders who lived long ago. ⁴And when these Jews return from the market, they never eat without first washing themselves. And they follow many other rules they have been taught. They follow rules like the washing of cups, pitchers and pots.ª

⁵The Pharisees and teachers of the law said to Jesus, "Your followers don't follow the traditions we have from our great leaders who lived long ago. They eat their food with hands that are not clean. Why do they do this?"

⁶Jesus answered, "You are all hypocrites. Isaiah was right when he wrote these words from God about you:

'These people honour me with their words,
    but I am not really important to them.
⁷Their worship of me is useless
    because the things they teach are only
        human rules.'
                                                    Isaiah 29:13

⁸You have stopped following God's commands, preferring instead the man-made rules you got from others."

⁹Then he said, "You show great skill in avoiding something that God has commanded so that you can follow your own teachings! ¹⁰Moses said, 'You must respect your father and mother.'ᵇ He also said, 'Whoever says anything bad to their father or mother must be killed.'ᶜ ¹¹But you teach that people can say to their father or mother, 'I have something I could use to help you, but I will not use it for you. I will give it to God.' ¹²You are telling people that they do not have to do anything

for their father or mother. ¹³So you are teaching that it is not important to do what God said. You think it is more important to follow those traditions you have, which you pass on to others. And you do many things like that."

¹⁴Jesus called the people to him again. He said, "Everyone should listen to me and understand what I am saying. ¹⁵There is nothing people can put in their mouth that will make them wrong.ᵈ People are made wrong by what comes from inside them." ¹⁶ᵉ

¹⁷Then Jesus left the people and went into the house. The followers asked Jesus about what he had told the people. ¹⁸He said, "Do you still have trouble understanding? Surely you know that nothing that enters the mouth from the outside can make people unacceptable to God. ¹⁹Food does not go into a person's mind. It goes into the stomach. Then it goes out of the body." (When Jesus said this, he meant there is no food that is wrong for people to eat.)

²⁰And Jesus said, "The things that make people wrong are the things that come from the inside. ²¹All these bad things begin inside a person, in the mind: bad thoughts, sexual sins, stealing, murder, ²²adultery, greed, doing bad things to people, lying, doing things that are morally wrong, jealousy, insulting people, proud talking and foolish living. ²³These evil things come from inside a person. And these are the things that make people unacceptable to God."

Jesus Helps a Non-Jewish Woman

(Matt. 15:21–28)

²⁴Jesus went from there to the area around Tyre. He did not want the people in that area to know he was there, so he went into a house. But he could not stay hidden. ²⁵A woman heard that he was there. Her little daughter had an evil spirit inside her. So the woman came to Jesus and bowed down near his feet. ²⁶She was not a Jew. She was born in Phoenicia, an area in Syria. She begged Jesus to force the demon out of her daughter.

²⁷Jesus told the woman, "It is not right to take the children's bread and give it to the dogs. First let the children eat all they want."

²⁸She answered, "That is true, Lord. But the dogs under the table can eat the pieces of food that the children don't eat."

²⁹Then he told her, "That is a very good answer. You may go. The demon has left your daughter."

ª **7:4** *pots* Some Greek copies add "and couches".
ᵇ **7:10** Quote from Exod. 20:12; Deut. 5:16.
ᶜ **7:10** Quote from Exod. 21:17.
ᵈ **7:15** *wrong* Literally, "unclean" or "not pure", meaning unacceptable to God. Also in verse 20.
ᵉ **7:16** Some Greek copies add verse 16: "You people who hear me, listen!"

30The woman went home and found her daughter lying on the bed. The demon was gone.

Jesus Heals a Deaf Man

31Then Jesus left the area around Tyre and went through Sidon. On his way to Lake Galilee he went through the area of the Ten Towns. 32While he was there, some people brought a man to him who was deaf and could not talk clearly. The people begged Jesus to put his hand on the man to heal him.

33Jesus led the man away from the people to be alone with him. He put his fingers in the man's ears. Then he spat on a finger and put it on the man's tongue. 34Jesus looked up to the sky and with a loud sigh he said, *"Ephphatha!"* (This means "Open!") 35As soon as Jesus did this, the man was able to hear. He was able to use his tongue, and he began to speak clearly.

36Jesus told the people not to tell anyone about this. But the more he told them not to say anything, the more people they told. 37They were all completely amazed. They said, "Everything he has done is good. He makes deaf people able to hear and gives a new voice to people who could not talk."

Jesus Feeds More Than 4,000

(Matt. 15:32–39)

8 Another time there was again a large crowd of people with Jesus. The people had nothing to eat, so he called his followers to him and said, 2"I feel sorry for these people. They have been with me for three days, and now they have nothing to eat. 3I should not send them home hungry. If they leave without eating, they will faint on the way home. Some of them live a long way from here."

4Jesus' followers answered, "But we are far away from any towns. Where can we get enough bread to feed all these people?"

5Then Jesus asked them, "How many loaves of bread do you have?"

They answered, "We have seven loaves of bread."

6Jesus told the people to sit on the ground. Then he took the seven loaves and gave thanks to God. He broke the bread into pieces and gave them to his followers. He told them to give the bread to the people, and they did as he said. 7The followers also had a few small fish. Jesus gave thanks for the fish and told them to give the fish to the people.

8They all ate until they were full. Then the followers filled seven baskets with the pieces of food that were left. 9There were about 4,000 men who ate. After they had eaten, Jesus told them to go home. 10Then he went in a boat with his followers to the area of Dalmanutha.

Some People Doubt Jesus' Authority

(Matt. 16:1–4; Luke 11:16,29)

11The Pharisees came to Jesus and asked him questions. They wanted to test him. So they asked him to do a miracle as a sign from God. 12Jesus sighed deeply and said, "Why do you people ask to see a miracle as a sign? I want you to know that no miracle will be done to prove anything to you." 13Then Jesus left them and went in the boat to the other side of the lake.

Jesus' Followers Misunderstand Him

(Matt. 16:5–12)

14The followers had only one loaf of bread with them in the boat. They had forgotten to bring more. 15Jesus warned them, "Be careful! Guard against the yeast of the Pharisees and the yeast of Herod."

16The followers discussed the meaning of this. They said, "Maybe he said this because we have no bread."

17Jesus knew that the followers were talking about this. So he asked them, "Why are you talking about having no bread? Do you still not see or understand? Are you not able to understand? 18Do you have eyes that can't see? Do you have ears that can't hear? Remember what I did before, when we did not have enough bread? 19I divided five loaves of bread for 5,000 people. Remember how many baskets you filled with pieces of food that were not eaten?"

The followers answered, "We filled twelve baskets."

20"And when I divided seven loaves of bread for 4,000 people, how many baskets did you fill with the leftover pieces?"

They answered, "We filled seven baskets."

21Then he said to them, "You remember these things I did, but you still don't understand?"

INSIGHT

This is the only place in the Bible where Jesus prays twice for someone to be healed. Some people think Jesus healed the man's blindness in stages to teach the disciples about the difference between spiritual sight and natural sight.

Mark 8:22–26

Jesus Heals a Blind Man in Bethsaida

22Jesus and his followers came to Bethsaida. Some people brought a blind man to him and begged him to touch the man. 23So Jesus held the blind man's hand and led him out of the village.

GETTING LOST

How do you react when you encounter any kind of suffering in your life? Are you ever tempted to think that because you belong to God, you ought to be spared from going through difficult stuff? You try to do the right thing, and you believe in a good God who can do anything – how does suffering fit into that picture? Read on to see how Jesus helps his disciples, who struggled with the same sort of questions . . .

DIG IN

READ Mark 8:31–38

Bearing in mind that "the Son of Man" was a title that Jesus gave himself . . .

- What does Jesus say will happen to him, according to verses 31–32?
- What do you imagine might have been going through Peter's mind to lead him to do what he did in verse 32? Try to put yourself in his place – it's easy for us to understand what Jesus meant, but how would it have sounded to one of Jesus' best friends, when he had no understanding of what the cross would achieve?
- Why was Jesus' response so extreme?

Jesus knew that going to the cross was to be the turning point of all history. The cross is the only way that sinful men and women can be reconciled with God. In order to show his love for mankind in the ultimate way, Jesus knew that he would have to suffer and die. The only one who would really want to stop Jesus from doing the one thing that could save humanity is Satan. Jesus had to make it clear to his disciples that the cross was the right way, and opposition to it was the wrong way, even if they couldn't fully understand why at this point.

- What two alternatives does Jesus give in verses 34–38?
- What are the benefits and drawbacks of each?

DIG THROUGH

- What is the "cross to carry" for following Jesus (v.34) and what is the cost for you?
- Do you always choose the costly path if it's the right one? Ask God to help you with those times when you're tempted not to, particularly if there's something you have in mind in your life right now.
- Take a look at 1 Peter 2:18–25. Suffering is an expected part of the Christian life because we follow a suffering king. Are you prepared to talk about this as well as the easier parts of Christianity when you talk to your friends about Jesus or give your testimony?

DIG DEEPER

- Read Isaiah, chapter 53. This was written about Jesus as part of a prophecy given by God hundreds of years (700 BC-ish!) before Jesus was born. It's amazing how clearly it corresponds to Jesus' life, and how clear it is that suffering was to be such an important part of his mission on earth.

Then he spat on the man's eyes. He laid his hands on him and asked, "Can you see now?"

²⁴The man looked up and said, "Yes, I see people. They look like trees walking around."

²⁵Again Jesus laid his hands on the man's eyes, and the man opened them wide. His eyes were healed, and he was able to see everything clearly. ²⁶Jesus told him to go home. He said, "Don't go into the town."

Peter Says Jesus Is the Messiah

(Matt. 16:13–20; Luke 9:18–21)

²⁷Jesus and his followers went to the towns in the area of Caesarea Philippi. While they were travelling, Jesus asked the followers, "Who do people say I am?"

²⁸They answered, "Some people say you are John the Baptizer. Others say you are Elijah. And others say you are one of the prophets."

²⁹Then Jesus asked, "Who do you say I am?"

Peter answered, "You are the Messiah."

³⁰Jesus told the followers, "Don't tell anyone who I am."

Jesus Says He Must Die

(Matt. 16:21–28; Luke 9:22–27)

³¹Then Jesus began to teach his followers that he, as the Son of Man, must suffer many things. He told them that he would not be accepted by the older Jewish leaders, the leading priests and the teachers of the law. He said that he must be killed and then rise from death three days later. ³²Jesus told them everything that would happen. He did not keep anything secret.

Peter took Jesus away from the other followers to talk to him alone. Peter criticized him for saying these things. ³³But Jesus turned and looked at his followers. Then he criticized Peter. He said to Peter, "Get away from me, Satan!ᵃ You don't care about the same things God does. You care only about things that people think are important."

³⁴Then Jesus called the crowd and his followers to him. He said, "Any of you who want to be my follower must stop thinking about yourself and what you want. You must be willing to carry the cross that is given to you for following me. ³⁵Any of you who try to save the life you have will lose it. But you who give up your life for me and for the Good News will save it. ³⁶It is worth nothing for you to have the whole world if you yourself are lost. ³⁷You could never pay enough to buy back your life. ³⁸People today are so sinful. They have not been faithful to God. As you live among them, don't be ashamed of me and my teaching.

If that happens, then I, the Son of Man, will be ashamed of you when I come with the glory of my Father and the holy angels."

9 Then Jesus said, "Believe me when I say that some of you people standing here will see God's kingdom come with power before you die."

Jesus Is Seen With Moses and Elijah

(Matt. 17:1–13; Luke 9:28–36)

²Six days later, Jesus took Peter, James and John and went up on a high mountain. They were all alone there. While these followers watched him, Jesus was changed. ³His clothes became shining white—whiter than anyone on earth could make them. ⁴Then they saw two men there talking with Jesus. They were Elijah and Moses.

⁵Peter said to Jesus, "Teacher, it is good that we are here. We will make three shelters here—one for you, one for Moses and one for Elijah." ⁶Peter did not know what to say, because he and the other two followers were so afraid.

⁷Then a cloud came and covered them. A voice came from the cloud and said, "This is my Son, the one I love. Obey him!"

⁸The followers looked, but they saw only Jesus there alone with them.

⁹As Jesus and the followers were walking back down the mountain, he gave them these instructions: "Don't tell anyone about what you saw on the mountain. Wait until after the Son of Man rises from death. Then you can tell people what you saw."

¹⁰So the followers did not talk to anyone else about what they had seen. But they discussed among themselves what Jesus meant about rising from death. ¹¹They asked him, "Why do the teachers of the law say that Elijah must comeᵇ first?"

¹²Jesus answered, "They are right to say that Elijah must come first. Elijah makes all things the way they should be. But why do the Scriptures say that the Son of Man will suffer much and that people will think he is worth nothing? ¹³I tell you that Elijah has already come. And people did to him all the bad things they wanted to do. The Scriptures said this would happen to him."

Jesus Frees a Boy From an Evil Spirit

(Matt. 17:14–20; Luke 9:37–43a)

¹⁴Then Jesus, Peter, James and John went to the other followers. They saw many people around them. The teachers of the law were arguing with the followers. ¹⁵When the people saw Jesus, they were very surprised and ran to welcome him.

ᵃ **8:33** *Satan* Name for the devil meaning "the enemy". Jesus means that Peter was talking like Satan.
ᵇ **9:11** *Elijah must come* See Mal. 4:5–6.

[16]Jesus asked, "What are you arguing about with the teachers of the law?"

[17]A man answered, "Teacher, I brought my son to you. He is controlled by an evil spirit that keeps him from talking. [18]The spirit attacks him and throws him on the ground. He foams at the mouth, grinds his teeth and becomes very stiff. I asked your followers to force the evil spirit out, but they could not."

[19]Jesus answered, "You people today don't believe! How long must I stay with you? How long must I be patient with you? Bring the boy to me!"

[20]So the followers brought the boy to Jesus. When the evil spirit saw Jesus, it attacked the boy. The boy fell down and rolled on the ground. He was foaming at the mouth.

[21]Jesus asked the boy's father, "How long has this been happening to him?"

The father answered, "Since he was very young. [22]The spirit often throws him into a fire or into water to kill him. If you can do anything, please have pity on us and help us."

[23]Jesus said to the father, "Why did you say 'if you can'? All things are possible for the one who believes."

[24]Immediately the father shouted, "I do believe. Help me to believe more!"

[25]Jesus saw that all the people were running there to see what was happening. So he spoke to the evil spirit. He said, "You evil spirit that makes this boy deaf and stops him from talking—I command you to come out of him and never enter him again!"

[26]The evil spirit screamed. It caused the boy to fall on the ground again, and then it came out. The boy looked as if he was dead. Many people said, "He is dead!" [27]But Jesus took hold of his hand and helped him stand up.

[28]Then Jesus went into the house. His followers were alone with him there. They said, "Why weren't we able to force that evil spirit out?"

[29]Jesus answered, "That kind of spirit can be forced out only with prayer."[a]

Jesus Talks About His Death

(Matt. 17:22–23; Luke 9:43b–45)

[30]Then Jesus and his followers left there and went through Galilee. Jesus did not want the people to know where they were. [31]He wanted to teach his followers alone. He said to them, "The Son of Man will be handed over to the control of other men, and they will kill him. But then, after three days, he will rise from death." [32]The followers did not understand what he meant, and they were afraid to ask him.

Who Is the Greatest?

(Matt. 18:1–5; Luke 9:46–48)

[33]Jesus and his followers went to Capernaum. They went into a house, and Jesus said to them, "I heard you arguing on the way here today. What were you arguing about?" [34]But the followers did not answer, because their argument on the road was about which one of them was the greatest.

[35]Jesus sat down and called the twelve apostles to him. He said, "Whoever wants to be the most important must make others more important than themselves. They must serve everyone else."

[36]Then Jesus took a small child and stood the child in front of the followers. He held the child in his arms and said, [37]"Whoever accepts children like these in my name is accepting me. And anyone who accepts me is also accepting the one who sent me."

Whoever Is Not Against Us Is For Us

(Luke 9:49–50)

[38]Then John said, "Teacher, we saw a man using your name to force demons out of someone. He is not one of us. So we told him to stop, because he does not belong to our group."

[39]Jesus said, "Don't stop him. Whoever uses my name to do powerful things will not soon say bad things about me. [40]Whoever is not against us is with us. [41]I can assure you that anyone who helps you by giving you a drink of water because you belong to the Messiah will definitely get a reward.

Jesus Warns About Causes of Sin

(Matt. 18:6–9; Luke 17:1–2)

[42]"If one of these little children believes in me, and someone causes that child to sin, it will be very bad for that person. It would be better for them to have a millstone tied around their neck and be drowned in the sea. [43]If your hand makes you sin, cut it off. It is better for you to lose part of your body and have eternal life than to have two hands and go to hell. There the fire never stops. [44b] [45]If your foot makes you sin, cut it off. It is better for you to lose part of your body and have eternal life than to have two feet and be thrown into hell. [46c] [47]If your eye makes you sin, take it out. It is better for you to have only one eye and enter God's kingdom than to have two eyes

---

[a] **9:29** *prayer* Some Greek copies have "prayer and fasting".
[b] **9:44** Some Greek copies add verse 44, which is the same as verse 48.
[c] **9:46** Some Greek copies add verse 46, which is the same as verse 48.

and be thrown into hell. [48]The worms that eat the people in hell never die. The fire there is never stopped.

[49]"Everyone will be salted with fire.[a]

[50]"Salt is good. But if it loses its salty taste, you can't make it good again. So, don't lose the good quality of salt you have. And live in peace with each other."

Jesus Teaches About Divorce

(Matt. 19:1–12)

10 Then Jesus left there and went into the area of Judea and across the Jordan River. Again, many people came to him, and Jesus taught them as he always did.

[2]Some Pharisees came to Jesus and tried to make him say something wrong. They asked him, "Is it right for a man to divorce his wife?"

[3]Jesus answered, "What did Moses command you to do?"

[4]The Pharisees said, "Moses allowed a man to divorce his wife by writing a certificate of divorce."[b]

[5]Jesus said, "Moses wrote that command for you because you refused to accept God's teaching. [6]But when God made the world, 'he made people male and female'.[c] [7]That is why a man will leave his father and mother and be joined to his wife. [8]And the two people will become one.'[d] So they are no longer two, but one. [9]God has joined them together, so no one should separate them."

[10]Later, when the followers and Jesus were in the house, they asked him again about the question of divorce. [11]He said, "Whoever divorces his wife and marries another woman has sinned against his wife. He is guilty of adultery. [12]And the woman who divorces her husband and marries another man is also guilty of adultery."

Jesus Welcomes Children

(Matt. 19:13–15; Luke 18:15–17)

[13]People brought their small children to Jesus so that he could lay his hands on them to bless them. But the followers told the people to stop. [14]When Jesus saw this, it made him angry. So he said to the followers, "Let the little children come to me. Don't stop them, because they are just the *kind of people* who are part of God's kingdom. [15]The truth is, you must accept God's kingdom like a little child accepts things, or you will never enter it." [16]Then Jesus held the children

in his arms. He laid his hands on them and blessed them.

A Rich Man Refuses to Follow Jesus

(Matt. 19:16–30; Luke 18:18–30)

[17]Jesus started to leave, but a man ran to him and bowed down on his knees before him. The man asked, "Good Teacher, what must I do to get the life that never ends?"

[18]Jesus answered, "Why do you call me good? Only God is good. [19]And you know his commands: 'You must not murder anyone, you must not commit adultery, you must not steal, you must not lie, you must not cheat anyone, you must respect your father and mother.'"[e]

[20]The man said, "Teacher, I have obeyed all these commands since I was a boy."

[21]Jesus looked at the man in a way that showed how much he cared for him. He said, "There is still one thing you need to do. Go and sell everything you have. Give the money to those who are poor, and you will have riches in heaven. Then come and follow me."

[22]The man was very upset when Jesus told him to give away his money, because he was very rich. So he went away sad.

[23]Then Jesus looked at his followers and said to them, "It will be very hard for a rich person to enter God's kingdom!"

[24]The followers were amazed at what Jesus said. But he said again, "My children, it is very hard[f] to enter God's kingdom! [25]It is easier for a camel to go through the eye of a needle than for a rich person to enter God's kingdom!"

[26]The followers were even more amazed and said to each other, "Then who can be saved?"

[27]Jesus looked at them and said, "That is something people cannot do, but God can. He can do anything."

[28]Peter said to Jesus, "We left everything to follow you!"

[29]Jesus said, "I can promise that everyone who has left their home, brothers, sisters, mother, father, children or farm for me and for the Good News about me [30]will get a hundred times more than they left. Here in this world they will get more homes, brothers, sisters, mothers, children and farms. And with these things they will have persecutions. But in the world that is coming they will also get the reward of eternal life. [31]Many people who have the highest place now will have

---

[a] **9:49** Some Greek copies add, "and every sacrifice will be salted with salt". In the Old Testament salt was put on sacrifices. This verse could mean that Jesus' followers will be tested by suffering and that they must offer themselves to God as sacrifices.

[b] **10:4** *"Moses . . . certificate of divorce"* See Deut. 24:1.

[c] **10:6** Quote from Gen. 1:27; 5:2.

[d] **10:8** Quote from Gen. 2:24.

[e] **10:19** Quote from Exod. 20:12–16; Deut. 5:16–20.

[f] **10:24** *hard* Some ancient Greek copies have "hard for those who trust in riches".

the lowest place in the future. And the people who have the lowest place now will have the highest place then."

Jesus Talks Again About His Death

(Matt. 20:17–19; Luke 18:31–34)

32Jesus and those with him were on their way to Jerusalem. He was at the front of the group. His followers were wondering what was happening, and the people who followed behind them were feeling afraid. Jesus gathered the twelve apostles again and talked with them alone. He told them what would happen in Jerusalem. 33He said, "We are going to Jerusalem. The Son of Man will be handed over to the leading priests and teachers of the law. They will say that he must die and will hand him over to the foreigners, 34who will laugh at him and spit on him. They will beat him with whips and kill him. But three days later, he will rise to life again."

James and John Ask for a Favour

(Matt. 20:20–28)

35Then James and John, sons of Zebedee, came to Jesus and said, "Teacher, we want to ask you to do something for us."

36Jesus asked, "What do you want me to do for you?"

37The sons answered, "Let us share the great honour you will have as king. Let one of us sit at your right side and the other at your left."

38Jesus said, "You don't understand what you are asking. Can you drink from the cup*a* that I must drink from? Can you be baptized with the same baptism*b* that I must go through?"

39The sons answered, "Yes, we can!"

Jesus said to the sons, "It is true that you will drink from the cup that I drink from. And you will be baptized with the same baptism that I must go through. 40But it is not for me to say who will sit at my right or my left. God has prepared those places for the ones he chooses."

41When the other ten followers heard this, they were angry with James and John. 42Jesus called all the followers together. He said, "The non-Jewish people have men they call rulers. You know that those rulers love to show their power over the people. And their important leaders love to use all their authority over the people. 43But it should not be that way with you. Whoever wants to be your leader must be willing to serve the rest of you. 44Whoever wants to be first must serve the

others like a slave. 45When the Son of Man came to earth, he did not come for people to serve him. He came to serve others and to give his life to save many people."

Jesus Heals a Blind Man

(Matt. 20:29–34; Luke 18:35–43)

46Then they came to the town of Jericho. When Jesus left there with his followers, a large crowd was with them. A blind man named Bartimaeus (meaning "son of Timaeus") was sitting by the road. He was always begging for money. 47He heard that Jesus from Nazareth was walking by. So he began shouting, "Jesus, Son of David, please help me!"

48Many people criticized the blind man and told him to be quiet. But he shouted more and more, "Son of David, please help me!"

49Jesus stopped and said, "Tell him to come here."

So they called the blind man and said, "You can be happy now. Stand up! Jesus is calling you." 50The blind man stood up quickly. He left his coat there and went to Jesus.

51Jesus asked the man, "What do you want me to do for you?"

He answered, "Teacher, I want to see again."

52Jesus said, "Go. You are healed because you believed." Immediately the man was able to see again. He followed Jesus down the road.

Jesus Enters Jerusalem Like a King

(Matt. 21:1–11; Luke 19:28–40; John 12:12–19)

11 Jesus and his followers were coming closer to Jerusalem. They came to the towns of Bethphage and Bethany at the Mount of Olives. There Jesus sent two of his followers to do something. 2He said to them, "Go to the town you can see there. When you enter it, you will find a young donkey that no one has ever ridden. Untie it and bring it here to me. 3If anyone asks you why you are taking the donkey, tell them, 'The Master needs it. He will send it back soon.'"

4The followers went into the town. They found a young donkey tied in the street near the door of a house, and they untied it. 5Some people were standing there and saw this. They asked, "What are you doing? Why are you untying that donkey?" 6The followers answered the way Jesus told them to, and the people let them take the donkey.

a **10:38 *cup*** A symbol of suffering. Jesus used the idea of drinking from a cup to mean accepting the suffering he would face in the terrible events that were soon to come. Also in verse 39.

b **10:38 *baptized with the same baptism*** Baptism, which usually means to be immersed in water, has a special meaning here—being covered or "buried" in troubles. Also in verse 39.

7The followers brought the donkey to Jesus. They put their coats on it, and Jesus sat on it. 8Many people spread their coats on the road for Jesus. Others cut branches in the fields and spread the branches on the road. 9Some of them were walking ahead of Jesus. Others were walking behind him. Everyone shouted,

"Praise*a* Him!
    Welcome! God bless the one who comes in
    the name of the Lord!

Psalm 118:25–26

10"God bless the kingdom of our father David.
    That kingdom is coming!
Praise to God in heaven!"

11Jesus entered Jerusalem and went to the Temple. He looked at everything in the Temple area, but it was already late. So he went to Bethany with the twelve apostles.

Jesus Says a Fig Tree Will Die

(Matt. 21:18–19)

12The next day, Jesus was leaving Bethany. He was hungry. 13Looking ahead, he saw a fig tree with leaves. So he went closer to see if it had any figs growing on it. But he found nothing but leaves, because it was not the right time for figs to grow. 14So Jesus said to the tree, "People will never eat fruit from you again." His followers heard him say this.

Jesus Goes to the Temple

(Matt. 21:12–17; Luke 19:45–48; John 2:13–22)

15When Jesus and his followers came back to Jerusalem, they entered the Temple area. Jesus began driving out the people who were buying and selling things there. He turned over the tables that belonged to those who were exchanging different kinds of money. And he turned over the benches of those who were selling doves. 16He refused to allow anyone to carry things through the Temple area. 17Then Jesus began teaching the people and said, "It is written in the Scriptures, 'My Temple will be called a house of prayer for all nations.'*b* But you have changed it into a 'hiding place for thieves'."*c*

18When the leading priests and the teachers of the law heard what Jesus said, they began trying to find a way to kill him. They were afraid of him because all the people were amazed at his teaching. 19That night Jesus and his followers left the city.

The Fig Tree and Faith, Prayer and Forgiveness

(Matt. 21:20–22)

20The next morning Jesus was walking with his followers. They saw the fig tree that he had spoken to the day before. The tree was dry and dead, even the roots. 21Peter remembered the tree and said to Jesus, "Teacher, look! Yesterday, you told that fig tree to die. Now it is dry and dead!"

22Jesus answered, "Have faith in God. 23The truth is, you can say to this mountain, 'Go, mountain, fall into the sea.' And if you have no doubts in your mind and believe that what you say will happen, then God will do it for you. 24So I tell you to ask for what you want in prayer. And if you believe that you have received those things, then they will be yours. 25When you are praying and you remember that you are angry with another person about something, forgive that person. Forgive them so that your Father in heaven will also forgive your sins." 26*d*

Jewish Leaders Reject Jesus' Authority

(Matt. 21:23–27; Luke 20:1–8)

27Jesus and his followers went again to Jerusalem. Jesus was walking in the Temple area. The leading priests, the teachers of the law and the older Jewish leaders came to him. 28They said, "Tell us! What authority do you have to do these things? Who gave you this authority?"

29Jesus answered, "I will ask you a question. You answer my question. Then I will tell you whose authority I use to do these things. 30Tell me: when John baptized people, did his authority come from God or was it only from other people? Answer me."

31These Jewish leaders talked about Jesus' question. They said to each other, "If we answer, 'John's baptism was from God,' then he will say, 'Then why didn't you believe John?' 32But we can't say that John's baptism was from someone else." (These leaders were afraid of the people, because they all believed that John was a prophet.)

33So the leaders answered Jesus, "We don't know the answer."

Jesus said, "Then I will not tell you who gave me the authority to do these things."

---

a **11:9** *Praise* Literally, "Hosanna", a Hebrew word used in praying to God for help. Here, it was probably a shout of celebration used in praising God or his Messiah. Also in verse 10.
b **11:17** Quote from Isa. 56:7.
c **11:17** Quote from Jer. 7:11.
d **11:26** Some early Greek copies add verse 26: "But if you don't forgive others, then your Father in heaven will not forgive your sins."

God Sends His Son

(Matt. 21:33–46; Luke 20:9–19)

12 Jesus used stories to teach the people. He said, "A man planted a vineyard. He put a wall around the field and dug a hole for a winepress. Then he built a tower. He leased the land to some farmers and left for a trip.

²"Later, it was time for the grapes to be picked. So the man sent a servant to the farmers to get his share of the grapes. ³But the farmers grabbed the servant and beat him. They sent him away with nothing. ⁴Then the man sent another servant to the farmers. They hit this servant on the head, showing no respect for him. ⁵So the man sent another servant. The farmers killed this servant. The man sent many other servants to the farmers. The farmers beat some of them and killed the others.

⁶"The man had only one person left to send to the farmers. It was his son. He loved his son, but he decided to send him. He said, 'The farmers will respect my son.'

⁷"But the farmers said to each other, 'This is the owner's son, and this vineyard will be his. If we kill him, it will be ours.' ⁸So they took the son, threw him out of the vineyard and killed him.

⁹"So what will the man who owns the vineyard do? He will go and kill those farmers. Then he will lease the land to others. ¹⁰Surely you have read this in the Scriptures:

'The stone that the builders refused to accept
    became the cornerstone.
¹¹The Lord did this,
    and it is wonderful to us.'"

Psalm 118:22–23

¹²When these Jewish leaders heard this story, they knew it was about them. They wanted to find a way to arrest Jesus, but they were afraid of what the crowd would do. So they left him and went away.

The Jewish Leaders Try to Trick Jesus

(Matt. 22:15–22; Luke 20:20–26)

¹³Later, the Jewish leaders sent some Pharisees and some men from the group called Herodians to Jesus. They wanted to catch him saying something they could use against him. ¹⁴They went to Jesus and said, "Teacher, we know that you are an honest man. When you speak, you don't worry about what others might think. It doesn't matter to you who is listening, you always teach the truth about God's way. Tell us, is it right to pay taxes to Caesar? Should we pay them or not?"

¹⁵But Jesus knew that these men were really trying to trick him. He said, "Why are you trying to catch me saying something wrong? Bring me a silver coin. Let me see it." ¹⁶They gave Jesus a coin and he asked, "Whose picture is on the coin? And whose name is written on it?" They answered, "It is Caesar's picture and Caesar's name."

¹⁷Then Jesus said to them, "Give to Caesar what belongs to Caesar, and give to God what belongs to God." The men were amazed at what Jesus said.

Some Sadducees Try to Trick Jesus

(Matt. 22:23–33; Luke 20:27–40)

¹⁸Then some Sadducees came to Jesus. (Sadducees believe that no one will rise from death.) They asked him a question: ¹⁹"Teacher, Moses wrote that if a married man dies and had no children, his brother must marry the woman. Then they will have children for the dead brother.ᵃ ²⁰There were seven brothers. The first brother married but died. He had no children. ²¹So the second brother married the woman. But he also died and had no children. The same thing happened with the third brother. ²²All seven brothers married the woman and died. None of the brothers had children with her. And she was the last to die. ²³But all seven brothers had married her. So at the time when people rise from death, whose wife will she be?"

²⁴Jesus answered, "How could you be so wrong? It's because you don't know what the Scriptures say. And you don't know anything about God's power. ²⁵When people rise from death, there will be no marriage. People will not be married to each other. All people will be like angels in heaven. ²⁶Surely you have read what God said about people rising from death. In the book where Moses wrote about the burning bush,ᵇ it says that God told Moses this: 'I am the God of Abraham, the God of Isaac and the God of Jacob.'ᶜ ²⁷He is the God only of people who are living. So these men were not really dead. You Sadducees are so wrong!"

Which Command Is the Most Important?

(Matt. 22:34–40; Luke 10:25–28)

²⁸One of the teachers of the law came to Jesus. He heard Jesus arguing with the Sadducees and the Pharisees. He saw that Jesus gave good answers to their questions. So he asked him, "Which of God's commands is the most important?"

ᵃ **12:19 if . . . dead brother** See Deut. 25:5–6.
ᵇ **12:26 burning bush** See Exod. 3:1–12.
ᶜ **12:26** Quote from Exod. 3:6.

²⁹Jesus answered, "The most important command is this: 'People of Israel, listen! The Lord our God is the only Lord. ³⁰Love the Lord your God with all your heart, all your soul, all your mind and all your strength.'ᵃ ³¹The second most important command is this: 'Love your neighbourᵇ the same as you love yourself.'ᶜ These two commands are the most important."

³²The man answered, "That was a good answer, Teacher. You are right in saying that God is the only Lord and that there is no other God. ³³And you must love God with all your heart, all your mind and all your strength. And you must love others the same as you love yourself. These commands are more important than all the burnt offerings and sacrifices we give to God."

³⁴Jesus saw that the man answered him wisely. So he said to him, "You are close to God's kingdom." And after that time, no one was brave enough to ask Jesus any more questions.

Is the Messiah David's Son or David's Lord?

(Matt. 22:41–46; Luke 20:41–44)

³⁵Jesus was teaching in the Temple area. He asked, "Why do the teachers of the law say that the Messiah is the son of David? ³⁶With the help of the Holy Spirit, David himself says,

'The Lord God said to my Lord:
Sit by me at my right side,
    and I will put your enemies under your
        control.'ᵈ

Psalm 110:1

³⁷David himself calls the Messiah 'Lord'. So how can the Messiah be David's son?" Many people listened to Jesus and were very pleased.

Jesus Criticizes the Teachers of the Law

(Matt. 23:1–36; Luke 20:45–47)

³⁸Jesus continued teaching. He said, "Be careful of the teachers of the law. They like to walk around wearing clothes that look important. And they love people to greet them with respect in the marketplaces. ³⁹They love to have the most important seats in the synagogues and the places of honour at banquets. ⁴⁰But they cheat widows and take their homes. Then they try to make themselves look good by saying long prayers. God will punish them greatly."

True Giving

(Luke 21:1–4)

⁴¹Jesus sat near the Temple collection boxᵉ and watched as people put money into it. Many rich people put in a lot of money. ⁴²Then a poor widow came and put in two very small copper coins, worth less than a penny.

⁴³Jesus called his followers to him and said, "This poor widow put in only two small coins. But the truth is, she gave more than all those rich people. ⁴⁴They have plenty, and they gave only what they did not need. This woman is very poor, but she gave all she had. It was money she needed to live on."

Jesus Warns About the Future

(Matt. 24:1–25; Luke 21:5–24)

13 Jesus was leaving the Temple area. One of his followers said to him, "Teacher, look how big those stones are! What beautiful buildings!"

²Jesus said, "Do you see these great buildings? They will all be destroyed. Every stone will be thrown down to the ground. Not one stone will be left on another."

³Later, Jesus was sitting at a place on the Mount of Olives. He was alone with Peter, James, John and Andrew. They could all see the Temple, and they said to Jesus, ⁴"Tell us when these things will happen. And what will show us it is time for them to happen?"

⁵Jesus said to them, "Be careful! Don't let anyone fool you. ⁶Many people will come and use my name, saying, 'I am the Messiah.'ᶠ And they will fool many people. ⁷You will hear about wars that are being fought. And you will hear stories about other wars beginning. But don't be afraid. These things must happen before the end comes. ⁸Nations will fight against other nations. Kingdoms will fight against other kingdoms. There will be times when there is no food for people to eat. And there will be earthquakes in different places. These things are only the beginning of troubles, like the first pains of a woman giving birth.

⁹"You must be careful! There are people who will arrest you and take you to be judged for being my followers. They will beat you in their synagogues. You will be forced to stand before kings and governors. You will tell them about me. ¹⁰Before the end comes, the Good News must be told to all nations. ¹¹Even when you are arrested

---

ᵃ **12:29–30** Quote from Deut. 6:4–5.
ᵇ **12:31** *your neighbour* Or "others". Jesus' teaching in Luke 10:25–37 makes clear that this includes anyone in need.
ᶜ **12:31** Quote from Lev. 19:18.
ᵈ **12:36** *control* Literally, "feet".
ᵉ **12:41** *collection box* A special box in the Jewish place for worship where people put their gifts to God.
ᶠ **13:6** *the Messiah* Literally "the one", meaning the chosen one sent by God. See Matt. 24:5 and "MESSIAH" in the Word List.

and put on trial, don't worry about what you will say. Say whatever God tells you at the time. It will not really be you speaking. It will be the Holy Spirit.

¹²"Brothers will turn against their own brothers and hand them over to be killed. Fathers will hand over their own children to be killed. Children will fight against their own parents and have them killed. ¹³All people will hate you because you follow me. But those who remain faithful to the end will be saved.

¹⁴"You will see 'the terrible thing that causes destruction'.ᵃ You will see this thing standing in the place where it should not be." (Reader, I trust you understand what this means.) "Everyone in Judea at that time should run away to the mountains. ¹⁵They should run away without wasting time to stop for anything. If someone is on the roof of their house, they must not go inside to get things out of the house. ¹⁶If someone is in the field, they must not go back to get a coat.

¹⁷"During that time it will be hard for women who are pregnant or have small babies. ¹⁸Pray that these things will not happen in winter, ¹⁹because those days will be full of trouble. There will be more trouble than there has ever been since the beginning, when God made the world. And nothing that bad will ever happen again. ²⁰But the Lord has decided to make that terrible time short. If it were not made short, no one could survive. But the Lord will make that time short to help the special people he has chosen.

²¹"Someone might say to you at that time, 'Look, there is the Messiah!' Or another person might say, 'There he is!' But don't believe them. ²²False messiahs and false prophets will come and do miracles and wonders,ᵇ trying to fool the people God has chosen, if that is possible. ²³So be careful. Now I have warned you about all this before it happens.

When Jesus, the Son of Man, Comes Again

(Matt. 24:29–51; Luke 21:25–36)

²⁴"During the days following that time of trouble,

'The sun will become dark,
    and the moon will not give light.
²⁵The stars will fall from the sky,
    and everything in the sky will be changed.'ᶜ

²⁶"Then people will see the Son of Man coming in the clouds with great power and glory. ²⁷He will send his angels all around the earth. They will gather his chosen people from every part of the earth.

²⁸"The fig tree teaches us a lesson: when its branches become green and soft, and new leaves begin to grow, then you know that summer is very near. ²⁹In the same way, when you see all these things happening, you will know that the timeᵈ is very near, already present. ³⁰I assure you that all these things will happen while some of the people of this time are still living. ³¹The whole world, earth and sky, will be destroyed, but my words will last forever.

³²"No one knows when that day or time will be. The Son and the angels in heaven don't know when that day or time will be. Only the Father knows. ³³Be careful! Always be ready. You don't know when that time will be.

³⁴"It's like a man who goes on a trip and leaves his house in the care of his servants. He gives each one a special job to do. He tells the servant guarding the door to always be ready. And this is what I am telling you now. ³⁵You must always be ready. You don't know when the owner of the house will come back. He might come in the afternoon, or at midnight or when the cockerel crows or when the sun rises. ³⁶If you are always ready, he will not find you sleeping, even if he comes back earlier than expected. ³⁷I tell you this, and I say it to everyone: 'Be ready!'"

The Jewish Leaders Plan to Kill Jesus

(Matt. 26:1–5; Luke 22:1–2; John 11:45–53)

14 It was now only two days before Passover and the Festival of Unleavened Bread. The leading priests and teachers of the law were trying to find a way to arrest Jesus without the people seeing it. Then they could kill him. ²They said, "But we cannot arrest Jesus during the festival. We don't want the people to be angry and cause a riot."

A Woman Honours Jesus

(Matt. 26:6–13; John 12:1–8)

³Jesus was in Bethany at the house of Simon the leper. While he was eating there, a woman came to him. She had an alabaster jar filled with expensive perfume made of pure nard. She opened the jar and poured the perfume on Jesus' head.

ᵃ **13:14 *the terrible thing . . . destruction'*** See Dan. 9:27; 11:31; 12:11.
ᵇ **13:22 *miracles and wonders*** Here, amazing acts done by Satan's power.
ᶜ **13:24–25** See Isa. 13:10; 34:4.
ᵈ **13:29 *time*** The time Jesus has been talking about when something important will happen. See Luke 21:31, where Jesus says that this is the time for God's kingdom to come.

THE ULTIMATE SACRIFICE

How do all 66 books of the Bible fit together? What do the laws of Leviticus have to do with the pastoral pleadings of Paul's letters? Here you'll see just one glimpse of the beautiful thread that runs through the whole Bible.

DIG IN
READ Exodus 12:1–14 and Mark 14:12–25

The meal that Jesus and his disciples eat in Mark 14 is part of the Jewish tradition remembering what happened in Exodus 12. So let's start with the Exodus passage:

- What is the most important ingredient of this special meal?
- What does God say he will do that night?
- What special sign will save his people from the same fate (v.7)?

So, the Passover meal that Jesus is eating reminds them of the time when God "passed over" his people, and saved them from death. Remember, the thing that kept them safe was the blood of the lamb that they had sacrificed. Bear this in mind as we focus in on Mark 14 . . .

- What important ingredient is not mentioned in this traditional meal (remember they are replicating the meal from Exodus 12)?
- In Mark 14:24, Jesus says, "This wine is my blood, which will be poured out for many to begin the new agreement". What purpose did blood serve at the original meal in Exodus 12?

In Exodus, the lamb was killed as a sacrifice to prevent the Israelites from facing the death punishment God was bringing on his enemies. The lamb's blood was used as a sign that the Israelites were God's own people, and that their lives were paid for by the sacrifice. In Mark, there is no mention of lamb on the table even though it's the most important ingredient of the Passover meal.

- In light of all this, what (or who) is the lamb? If you're stuck, skip ahead to John 1:29.

This momentous meal was a breathtaking turning point in history. For centuries the Jews had sacrificed a lamb to pay for their sins – something they had to do again and again. Now, Jesus was offering himself as the sacrificial lamb. His body would be given as a sacrifice to pay for sin to save God's people. His blood was a symbol that this had happened, just like the lamb's blood on the doorframes keeping God's people safe.

DIG THROUGH

- Take a few moments to let what Jesus was offering here sink in. What do you imagine this meal was like for the disciples who were there at the time, and who'd grown up following the meticulous details of Exodus 12? What does it mean to you now that you are living as if there is "blood on the doorframe" keeping you safe from God's anger?

DIG DEEPER

- Take a look at Hebrews 9:25–27. Here the author of Hebrews is marvelling at how amazing and final and awesomely generous was God's sacrifice of his Son for our sakes. With the snapshots of passages in this Bible Bit, we get a glimpse of the fact that the whole Bible fits together as one long story. Exodus tells us about an event that foretold what we saw in Mark, and what is described in Mark is the foundation of everything that follows in the New Testament. In one way or another, the whole Bible points towards Jesus and his amazing sacrifice for us.

[4]Some of the followers there saw this. They were upset and complained to each other. They said, "Why waste that perfume? [5]It was worth a full year's pay.[a] It could have been sold and the money given to those who are poor." And they told the woman what a bad thing she had done.

[6]Jesus said, "Leave her alone. Why are you giving her such trouble? She did a very good thing for me. [7]You will always have the poor with you,[b] and you can help them any time you want. But you will not always have me. [8]This woman did the only thing she could do for me. She poured perfume on my body before I die to prepare it for burial. [9]The Good News will be told to people all over the world. And I can assure you that everywhere the Good News is told, the story of what this woman did will also be told, and people will remember her."

Judas Agrees to Help Jesus' Enemies

(Matt. 26:14–16; Luke 22:3–6)

[10]Then Judas Iscariot, one of the twelve apostles, went to talk to the leading priests about handing Jesus over to them. [11]They were very happy about this, and they promised to pay him. So he waited for the best time to hand Jesus over to them.

The Passover Meal

(Matt. 26:17–25; Luke 22:7–14,21–23; John 13:21–30)

[12]It was now the first day of the Festival of Unleavened Bread—the day the lambs were killed for Passover. Jesus' followers came to him and said, "We will go and prepare everything for you to eat the Passover meal. Where do you want us to have the meal?"

[13]Jesus sent two of his followers into the city. He said to them, "Go into the city. You will see a man carrying a jar of water. He will come to you. Follow him. [14]He will go into a house. Tell the owner of the house, 'The Teacher asks that you show us the room where he and his followers can eat the Passover meal.' [15]The owner will show you a large room upstairs that is ready for us. Prepare the meal for us there."

[16]So the followers left and went into the city. Everything happened the way Jesus said it would. So the followers prepared the Passover meal.

[17]In the evening Jesus went to that house with the twelve apostles. [18]While they were all at the table eating, he said, "Believe me when I say that one of you will hand me over to my enemies— one of you eating with me now."

[19]The followers were very sad to hear this. Each one said to Jesus, "Surely I am not the one!"

[20]Jesus answered, "It is one of you twelve—the one who is dipping his bread into the bowl with me. [21]The Son of Man will suffer what the Scriptures say will happen to him. But it will be terrible for the one who hands over the Son of Man to be killed. It would be better for him if he had never been born."

The Lord's Supper

(Matt. 26:26–30; Luke 22:15–20; 1 Cor. 11:23–25)

[22]While they were eating, Jesus took some bread and thanked God for it. He broke off some pieces, gave them to his followers and said, "Take and eat this bread. It is my body."

[23]Then he took a cup of wine, thanked God for it, and gave it to them. They all drank from the cup. [24]Then he said, "This wine is my blood, which will be poured out for many to begin the new agreement that God makes with his people. [25]I want you to know, I will not drink this wine again until that day when I drink it in God's kingdom and the wine is new."

[26]They all sang a song and then went out to the Mount of Olives.

Jesus Says His Followers Will Leave Him

(Matt. 26:31–35; Luke 22:31–34; John 13:36–38)

[27]Then Jesus told the followers, "You will all lose your faith. The Scriptures say,

> 'I will kill the shepherd,
>   and the sheep will run away.'
>
> *Zechariah 13:7*

[28]But after I am killed, I will rise from death. Then I will go to Galilee. I will be there before you come."

[29]Peter said, "All the other followers may lose their faith. But that will never happen to me."

[30]Jesus answered, "The truth is, tonight you will say you don't know me. You will say it three times before the cockerel crows twice."

[31]But Peter strongly protested, "I will never say I don't know you! I will even die with you!" And all the other followers said the same thing.

Jesus Prays Alone

(Matt. 26:36–46; Luke 22:39–46)

[32]Jesus and his followers went to a place named Gethsemane. He said to them, "Sit here while I pray." [33]But he told Peter, James and John to come with him. He began to be very distressed and troubled, [34]and he said to them, "My heart is

---

[a] **14:5** *a full year's pay* Literally, "300 *denarii*". One Roman *denarius*, a silver coin, was the average pay for one day's work.
[b] **14:7** *You will . . . with you* See Deut. 15:11.

HARD TIMES AND SUFFERING

WHEN life is difficult we often ask why bad things are happening to us and those we love. The underlying question is "Does God care?" We can wonder if he's forgotten us and left us just at the moment we feel we need him the most. As we look in the Bible we read his promises that he will never leave us or turn his back on us (for example, Joshua 1:5 or Hebrews 13:5). But, more than that, the whole of the Bible is the story of God's love for us. From when he created humankind in the Garden of Eden to have a relationship with

GOD IS THE ONE WHO CAN STRENGTHEN AND SUSTAIN US THROUGH ANYTHING; WE JUST NEED TO TURN TO HIM.

him, to the way, time and time again, he urged his people to turn back to him, right through to sending Jesus to the cross to die for us – God proves how much he loves us.

Not only that, but we have a God who can relate to us in our pain. When Jesus walked on earth he suffered physically and emotionally. He was criticized and judged by the religious leaders, he was betrayed and deserted by his friends, he was publicly humiliated, tortured on the cross in the most excruciating way, and he felt abandoned by his Father on the cross. So whatever we're going through, we can talk to a God who knows us, loves us and understands what we're feeling. He is the one who can strengthen and sustain us through anything. We just need to turn to him.

If you're having a difficult time, focus on these words from Isaiah 43:1–4:

"Don't be afraid. I saved you. I named you. You are mine. When you have troubles, I am with you. When you cross rivers, you will not be hurt. When you walk through fire, you will not be burned; the flames will not hurt you . . . You are precious to me, and I have given you a special place of honour. I love you." ←

If you want to, pray this prayer:

Lord God, I thank you that you love me and care for me. I thank you that you understand the pain in my life at the moment and that you are close by me through it all. Please give me the strength to deal with the difficult things in my life and to help me to find strength in you, my loving Father.

Amen

GIVING AND SERVING

IMAGINE if you had been born in a different country, to different parents. How might your life have turned out? You could have been forced to work from the time you were only a child, slaving away in dangerous conditions for fourteen hours a day and still not having enough money to put food in your empty stomach. You might have walked for hours just to get water, and slept in a small room with your parents and siblings. You might have been orphaned, having watched your parents die from diseases that simple healthcare could easily have treated. And there might have been no opportunity for you to go to school. Perhaps you think that "no school" sounds good, but the reality is that this lack of education would mean there'd be no chance of changing your future or that of your family and being able to break out of the cycle of

poverty. All of this could have been your life, just because you were born in a less privileged country.

Poverty and injustice don't exist only in other countries of course. Every town and city has people who are hungry, living on the streets, abused, uncared for or lonely. Seeing this kind of pain and injustice in the world causes many people to ask if God really exists. Christians know that he not only exists but that he is heartbroken about the pain in our world. The Bible is full of references to how passionate God is about justice being done and suffering being relieved.

His plan? To send us. He wants us to be his hands, feet, ears, eyes and mouth, doing what we can to relieve poverty, pain and oppression. Sometimes that will mean getting our hands dirty – getting stuck in and feeding the hungry (Isaiah 58:7). Your church might be running a project you can get involved in or there may be a local charity that would appreciate you giving some time to help. Often we will need to give our money generously to support brilliant charities that are right at the

can do this is by buying fairly traded goods. This tells the world we don't think it's okay to deny someone enough money to live on just so we can buy things cheaply. We can also sign petitions, and share issues with our friends on Facebook and Twitter to make our voice heard and show the world that God exists and he cares.

God doesn't consider us getting involved in helping the poor to be an optional extra. If we

> **GOD DOESN'T CONSIDER US GETTING INVOLVED IN HELPING THE POOR TO BE AN OPTIONAL EXTRA. IF WE WANT TO FOLLOW HIM, WE MUST LOVE OUR NEIGHBOUR THE SAME AS WE LOVE OURSELVES.**

heart of the action, helping, serving and loving people. At other times we need to use our privileged position to speak up for those who have no voice (Proverbs 31:8–9). One way we

want to follow him, we must love our neighbour the same as we love ourselves (Matthew 22:39) and must make sure our faith isn't just words but is backed up with actions (James 2:14–26). He promises to go with us and to be on our side as we fight with him to see his kingdom come on earth.

Read these verses to find out more: Isaiah 61:1–9; Amos 5:4,11–12,21–24; Micah 6:6–8. ←

GUIDANCE

THERE was once a young prince whose father, the king, sent him on a very important quest. As the prince set out on his journey, he quickly discovered that as long as he could still clearly discern the instructing voice of his father, "Cross this bridge, avoid that forest, take a rest at this particular time . . ." he kept making right choices. However, the true tests came once other voices began to distract him, almost completely drowning out the voice of the king: dragons roaring, trolls laughing, enemies taunting, fair maidens crying for help, even other princes mocking his efforts. In the end, the success of his quest rested entirely on his ability to clearly recognize the voice of his father.

It's the same with us, really. Life is full of voices and choices. At times it can be difficult to discern which is the right path to be following, and we all wish it was as simple as that young prince recognizing his own father's voice. Even though it may at times seem downright impossible, according to John 10:27 God wants us to learn to recognize his voice and obey what he's telling us to do. The point is that God wants us to get the best out of life. Psalm 139 tells us that he designed us and he knows what makes us tick. He knows the pitfalls we'll face and the pleasures that wait just around the corner. Decide right now to recognize and follow the voice of your heavenly Father and King.

To find out more, check out: Psalm 37:4,7; Proverbs 2:6–9; Proverbs 3:5–6; Matthew 16:24; Ephesians 5:1–2. ←

Pray this prayer if you agree with it:

Father in heaven, I choose to listen to your voice, follow your plan for my life and obey your instructions. When distractions come, teach me to listen more closely to what you are saying to me and not allow the other voices to drown yours out completely. Help me to better understand what the Bible has to say about following you and your precious guidance.

Amen

so heavy with grief, I feel as if I am dying. Wait here and stay awake."

[35]Jesus went on a little farther away from them, fell to the ground and prayed. He asked that, if possible, he would not have this time of suffering. [36]He said, "*Abba,*[a] Father! You can do all things. Don't make me drink from this cup.[b] But do what you want, not what I want."

[37]Then he went back to his followers and found them sleeping. He said to Peter, "Simon, why are you sleeping? Could you not stay awake with me for one hour? [38]Stay awake and pray for strength against temptation. Your spirit wants to do what is right, but your body is weak."

[39]Again Jesus went away and prayed the same thing. [40]Then he went back to the followers and again found them sleeping. They could not stay awake. They did not know what they should say to him.

[41]After Jesus prayed a third time, he went back to his followers. He said to them, "Are you still sleeping and resting? That's enough! The time has come for the Son of Man to be handed over to the control of sinful men. [42]Stand up! We must go. Here comes the man who is handing me over to them."

Jesus Is Arrested

(Matt. 26:47–56; Luke 22:47–53; John 18:3–12)

[43]While Jesus was still speaking, Judas, one of the twelve apostles, came there. He had a big crowd of people with him, all carrying swords and clubs. They had been sent from the leading priests, the teachers of the law and the older Jewish leaders.

[44]Judas[c] planned to do something to show them which one was Jesus. He said, "The one I kiss will be Jesus. Arrest him and guard him while you lead him away." [45]So Judas went over to Jesus and said, "Teacher!" Then he kissed him. [46]The men grabbed Jesus and arrested him. [47]One of the followers standing near Jesus grabbed his sword and pulled it out. He swung it at the servant of the high priest and cut off his ear.

[48]Then Jesus said, "Why do you come to get me with swords and clubs as if I were a criminal? [49]Every day I was with you teaching in the *Temple area.* You did not arrest me there. But all these things have happened to show the full meaning of what the Scriptures said." [50]Then all of Jesus' followers left him and ran away.

[51]One of those following Jesus was a young man wearing only a linen cloth. When the people tried to grab him, [52]he left the cloth in their hands and ran away naked.

Jesus Before the Jewish Leaders

(Matt. 26:57–68; Luke 22:54–55,63–71; John 18:13–14,19–24)

[53]Those who arrested Jesus led him to the house of the high priest. All the leading priests, the older Jewish leaders and the teachers of the law were gathered there. [54]Peter followed Jesus but stayed back at a distance. He followed him to the courtyard of the high priest's house. He went into the courtyard and sat there with the guards, warming himself by their fire.

[55]The leading priests and the whole high council tried to find something that Jesus had done wrong so they could kill him. But the council could find no proof that would allow them to kill Jesus. [56]Many people came and told lies against Jesus, but they all said different things. None of them agreed.

[57]Then some others stood up and told more lies against Jesus. They said, [58]"We heard this man[d] say, 'I will destroy this Temple built by human hands. And three days later, I will build another Temple not made by human hands.'" [59]But even what these people said did not agree.

[60]Then the high priest stood up before everyone and said to Jesus, "These people said things against you. Do you have something to say about their charges? Are they telling the truth?" [61]But Jesus said nothing to answer him.

The high priest asked Jesus another question: "Are you the Messiah, the Son of the blessed God?"

[62]Jesus answered, "Yes, I am the Son of God. And in the future you will see the Son of Man sitting at the right side of God All-Powerful. And you will see the Son of Man coming on the clouds of heaven."

[63]When the high priest heard this, he tore his clothes in anger. He said, "We don't need any more witnesses! [64]You all heard these insults to God. What do you think?"

Everyone agreed that Jesus was guilty and must be killed. [65]Some of the people there spat at him. They covered his eyes and hit him with their fists. They said, "Be a prophet[e] and tell us who hit you!" Then the guards led Jesus away and beat him.

---

[a] **14:36 Abba** An Aramaic word that was used by Jewish children as a name for their fathers.
[b] **14:36 cup** A symbol of suffering. Jesus used the idea of drinking from a cup to mean accepting the suffering he would face in the terrible events that were soon to come.
[c] **14:44 Judas** Literally, "the one who handed him over".
[d] **14:58 this man** That is, Jesus. His enemies avoided saying his name.
[e] **14:65 prophet** A prophet often knows things that are hidden to other people.

Peter Is Afraid to Say He Knows Jesus

(Matt. 26:69–75; Luke 22:56–62; John 18:15–18,25–27)

⁶⁶While Peter was still in the courtyard, a servant girl of the high priest came there. ⁶⁷She saw him warming himself by the fire. She looked closely at him and said, "You were with Jesus, that man from Nazareth."

⁶⁸But Peter said this was not true. "That makes no sense," he said. "I don't know what you are talking about!" Then he left and went to the entrance of the courtyard, and a cockerel crowed.ᵃ

⁶⁹When the servant girl saw him there, she began saying again to the people standing around, "This man is one of them." ⁷⁰Again Peter said it was not true.

A short time later, the people standing there said, "We know you are one of them, because you are from Galilee."

⁷¹Then Peter began to curse. He said, "I swear to God, I don't know this man you are talking about!"

⁷²As soon as Peter said this, the cockerel crowed the second time. Then he remembered what Jesus had told him: "Before the cockerel crows twice, you will say three times that you don't know me." Then Peter began to cry.

Governor Pilate Questions Jesus

(Matt. 27:1–2,11–14; Luke 23:1–5; John 18:28–38)

15 Very early in the morning, the leading priests, the older Jewish leaders, the teachers of the law and the whole high council decided what to do with Jesus. They tied him, led him away and handed him over to Governor Pilate.

²Pilate asked Jesus, "Are you the king of the Jews?"

Jesus answered, "Yes, that is right."

³The leading priests accused Jesus of many things. ⁴So Pilate asked Jesus another question. He said, "You can see that these people are accusing you of many things. Why don't you answer?"

⁵But Jesus still did not answer, and this really surprised Pilate.

Pilate Tries but Fails to Free Jesus

(Matt. 27:15–31; Luke 23:13–25; John 18:39 – 19:16)

⁶Every year at the Passover time the governor would free one prisoner—whichever one the people wanted. ⁷There was a man in prison at that time named Barabbas. He and the rebels with him had been put in prison for committing murder during a riot.

⁸The people came to Pilate and asked him to free a prisoner as he always did. ⁹Pilate asked them, "Do you want me to free the king of the Jews?" ¹⁰Pilate knew that the leading priests had handed Jesus over to him because they were jealous of him. ¹¹But the leading priests persuaded the people to ask Pilate to free Barabbas, not Jesus.

¹²Pilate asked the people again, "So what should I do with this man you call the king of the Jews?"

¹³The people shouted, "Kill him on a cross!"

¹⁴Pilate asked, "Why? What wrong has he done?"

But the people shouted louder and louder, "Kill him on a cross!"

¹⁵Pilate wanted to please the people, so he set Barabbas free for them. And he told the soldiers to beat Jesus with whips. Then he handed him over to the soldiers to be killed on a cross.

¹⁶Pilate's soldiers took Jesus into the governor's palace (called the Praetorium). They called the whole company of soldiers together. ¹⁷They put a purple robeᵇ on Jesus, made a crown from thorny branches and put it on his head. ¹⁸Then they began greeting him, "We salute you, king of the Jews!" ¹⁹They kept on beating his head with a stick and spitting on him. Then they bowed down on their knees and pretended to honour him as a king. ²⁰After they finished making fun of him, they took off the purple robe and put his own clothes on him again. Then they led him out of the palace to be killed on a cross.

Jesus Is Nailed to a Cross

(Matt. 27:32–44; Luke 23:26–39; John 19:17–19)

²¹There was a man from Cyrene named Simon walking into the city from the fields. He was the father of Alexander and Rufus. The soldiers forced him to carry Jesus' cross. ²²They led Jesus to the place called Golgotha. (Golgotha means "The Place of the Skull".) ²³There they gave him some wine mixed with myrrh, but he refused to drink it. ²⁴The soldiers nailed Jesus to a cross. Then they divided his clothes among themselves, throwing dice to see who would get what.

²⁵It was nine o'clock in the morning when they nailed Jesus to the cross. ²⁶There was a sign with the charge against him written on it. It said, "THE KING OF THE JEWS". ²⁷They also nailed two criminals

---

ᵃ **14:68** Some Greek copies do not have "and a cockerel crowed".

ᵇ **15:17** *purple robe* Probably a soldier's robe that looked like the purple robes worn by kings. They put this on Jesus to make fun of him for claiming to be a king.

to crosses beside Jesus—one on the right and the other on the left. [28a]

[29]People walked by and said bad things to Jesus. They shook their heads and said, "You said you could destroy the Temple and build it again in three days. [30]So save yourself! Come down from that cross!"

[31]The leading priests and the teachers of the law were also there. They made fun of Jesus the same as the other people did. They said to each other, "He saved others, but he can't save himself! [32]If he is really the Messiah, the king of Israel, he should come down from the cross now. When we see this, then we will believe in him." The criminals on the crosses beside Jesus also said bad things to him.

Jesus Dies

(Matt. 27:45–56; Luke 23:44–49; John 19:28–30)

[33]At noon the whole country became dark. This darkness continued until three o'clock. [34]At three o'clock Jesus cried out loudly, *"Eloi, Eloi, lama sabachthani."* This means "My God, my God, why have you left me alone?"[b]

[35]Some of the people standing there heard this. They said, "Listen! He is calling Elijah."[c]

[36]One man there ran and got a sponge. He filled the sponge with sour wine and tied it to a stick. Then he used the stick to give the sponge to Jesus to get a drink from it. The man said, "We should wait now and see if Elijah will come to take him down from the cross."

[37]Then Jesus cried out loudly and died.

INSIGHT

The tearing of the curtain is very significant. Only the high priest could go behind the curtain into the Most Holy Place – the innermost part of the Temple – and only once a year. Because of what Jesus did on the cross, everyone is now welcome in God's presence, all the time.

Mark 15:38

[38]When Jesus died, the curtain in the Temple was torn into two pieces. The tear started at the top and tore all the way to the bottom. [39]The army officer who was standing there in front of the cross saw what happened when Jesus died. The officer said, "This man really was the Son of God!"

[40]Some women were standing away from the cross, watching. Among these women were Mary Magdalene, Salome and Mary the mother of James and Joses. (James was her youngest son.) [41]These were the women who had followed Jesus in Galilee and cared for him. Many other women who had come with Jesus to Jerusalem were also there.

Jesus Is Buried

(Matt. 27:57–61; Luke 23:50–56; John 19:38–42)

[42]This day was called Preparation Day. (That means the day before the Sabbath day.) It was becoming dark. [43]A man named Joseph from Arimathea was brave enough to go to Pilate and ask for Jesus' body. Joseph was an important member of the high council. He was one of the people who wanted God's kingdom to come. [44]Pilate was surprised to hear that Jesus was already dead. So he called for the army officer in charge and asked him if Jesus was already dead. [45]When Pilate heard it from the officer, he told Joseph he could have the body. [46]Joseph bought some linen cloth. He took the body from the cross, wrapped it in the linen and put the body in a tomb that had been dug out of a wall of rock. Then he closed the tomb by rolling a large stone to cover the entrance. [47]Mary Magdalene and Mary the mother of Joses saw the place where Jesus was put.

News That Jesus Has Risen From Death

(Matt. 28:1–8; Luke 24:1–12; John 20:1–10)

16 The next day after the Sabbath day, Mary Magdalene, Salome and Mary the mother of James bought some sweet-smelling spices to put on Jesus' body. [2]Very early on that day, the first day of the week, the women were going to the tomb. It was just after sunrise. [3]The women said to each other, "There is a large stone covering the entrance of the tomb. Who will move the stone for us?"

[4]Then the women looked and saw that the stone had been moved. The stone was very large, but it had been moved away from the entrance. [5]The women walked into the tomb and saw a young man there wearing a white robe. He was sitting on the right side of the tomb. The women were afraid.

---

[a] **15:28** Some Greek copies add verse 28: "And this showed the full meaning of the Scripture that says, 'They put him with criminals.'"
[b] **15:34** Quote from Ps. 22:1.
[c] **15:35** *He is calling Elijah* The word for "My God" (*Eli* in Hebrew or *Eloi* in Aramaic) sounded to the people like the name of Elijah, a famous man who spoke for God about 850 BC.

[6]But the man said, "Don't be afraid. You are looking for Jesus from Nazareth, the one who was killed on a cross. He has risen from death! He is not here. Look, here is the place they put him when he was dead. [7]Now go and tell his followers. And be sure to tell Peter. Tell them, 'Jesus is going into Galilee and will be there before you. You will see him there, as he told you before.'"

[8]The women were very frightened and confused. They left the tomb and ran away. They did not tell anyone about what happened, because they were afraid.[a]

Some Followers See Jesus

(Matt. 28:9–10; John 20:11–18; Luke 24:13–35)

[9]Jesus rose from death early on the first day of the week. He appeared first to Mary Magdalene. Once in the past Jesus had forced seven demons out of Mary. [10]After Mary saw Jesus, she went and told his followers. They were very sad and were crying. [11]But Mary told them that Jesus was alive. She said that she had seen Jesus, but they did not believe her.

[12]Later, Jesus appeared to two followers while they were walking in the country. But Jesus did not look the same as before he was killed. [13]These followers went back to the other followers and told them what happened. Again, the followers did not believe them.

Jesus Talks to His Followers

(Matt. 28:16–20; Luke 24:36–49; John 20:19–23; Acts 1:6–8)

[14]Later, Jesus appeared to the eleven followers while they were eating. He criticized them because they had so little faith. They were stubborn and refused to believe the people who said Jesus had risen from death.

[15]He said to them, "Go everywhere in the world and tell the Good News to everyone. [16]Whoever believes and is baptized will be saved. But those who do not believe will be judged guilty. [17]And the people who believe will be able to do these things as proof: they will use my name to force demons out of people. They will speak in languages they have never learned. [18]If they pick up snakes or drink any poison, they will not be hurt. They will lay their hands on sick people, and they will get well."

Jesus Goes Back to Heaven

(Luke 24:50–53; Acts 1:9–11)

[19]After the Lord Jesus said these things to his followers, he was carried up into heaven. There, Jesus sat at the right side of God. [20]The followers went everywhere in the world telling people the Good News, and the Lord helped them. By giving them power to do miracles the Lord proved that their message was true.

---

[a] **16:8** Some of the oldest Greek copies end the book here. A few later copies have this shorter ending: "But they soon gave all the instructions to Peter and those with him. After that, Jesus himself sent them out from east to west with the holy message that will never change—that people can be saved forever."

LUKE

Who
As with all of the Gospels, the author's name does not appear in the book, but it is certain that the same author wrote Acts. Traditionally, this book has been ascribed to Luke, a doctor and companion to Paul.

When
It was probably written around AD 65–70. It is thought that the "Theophilus" to whom the book is addressed was a high-ranking Roman official, so the book was probably written in Rome.

What
Luke's aim is to write a proper history. An educated man, a doctor and historian, he based his account of Jesus' life on a careful investigation of all the sources (1:3). He is making the case for Christ. He's examined all the evidence and this is his report.

Luke includes stories and songs that had been handed down among the early Church, such as the songs of Mary (1:46–55), Zechariah (1:68–79) and Simeon (2:29–32).

The result is not some dry, stuffy history, but a joyful, optimistic account. In Luke's account, the poor and the marginalized get the full blast of the Good News. "He brought down rulers from their thrones and raised up the humble people," sings Mary. "He filled the hungry with good things, but he sent the rich away with nothing" (1:52–53). Luke's Gospel is packed with tax collectors, prostitutes, lepers and thieves – all "outsiders" in one way or another. The news of Jesus' birth comes to humble, despised shepherds. The Gospel also emphasizes the key role played by Jesus' female followers.

Luke is writing for a non-Jewish audience. (He himself was not a Jew – he probably came from Philippi.) So his Gospel also features non-Jewish "heroes" such as centurions and Samaritans. Like Matthew, he includes a genealogy, but his goes back to Adam, the father of all.

Luke's Gospel is the first part of a two-part work. He also wrote the book of Acts, which takes the story forward from the resurrection of Jesus through the spread of the early Church.

QUICK TOUR → **LUKE**

"I studied it all carefully from the beginning. Then I decided to write it down for you in an organized way. I did this so that you can be sure that what you have been taught is true."

Luke 1:3–4

Luke Writes About the Life of Jesus

1 Most Honourable Theophilus:
Many others have tried to give a report of the things that happened among us to complete God's plan. ²What they have written agrees with what we learned from the people who saw those events from the beginning. They also served God by telling people his message. ³I studied it all carefully from the beginning. Then I decided to write it down for you in an organized way. ⁴I did this so that you can be sure that what you have been taught is true.

An Angel Announces an Important Birth

⁵During the time when Herod ruled Judea, there was a priest named Zechariah. He belonged to Abijah's group.ᵃ His wife came from the family of Aaron. Her name was Elizabeth. ⁶Zechariah and Elizabeth were both good people who pleased God. They did everything the Lord commanded, always following his instructions completely. ⁷But they had no children. Elizabeth could not have a baby, and both of them were very old.

⁸Zechariah was serving as a priest before God for his group. It was his group's time to serve. ⁹The priests always used lots to choose one priest to offer the incense, and Zechariah was the one chosen this time. So he went into the Temple of the Lord to offer the incense. ¹⁰There was a large crowd outside praying at the time the incense was offered.

¹¹Then, on the right side of the incense table, an angel of the Lord came and stood before Zechariah. ¹²When he saw the angel, Zechariah was filled with fear. ¹³But the angel said to him, "Zechariah, don't be afraid. Your prayer has been heard by God. Your wife Elizabeth will give birth to a baby boy, and you will name him John. ¹⁴You will be very happy, and many others will share your joy over his birth. ¹⁵He will be a great man for the Lord. He must never drink wine or anything else that could make him drunk. Even before he is born, he will be filled with the Holy Spirit.

¹⁶"John will help many people of Israel return to the Lord their God. ¹⁷John himself will go ahead of the Lord and make people ready for his coming. He will be powerful like Elijah and will have the same spirit. He will make peace between parents and their children. He will cause people who are not obeying God to change and start thinking the way they should."

¹⁸Zechariah said to the angel, "How can I know that what you say is true? I am an old man, and my wife is also old."

¹⁹The angel answered him, "I am Gabriel, the one who always stands ready before God. He sent me to talk to you and to tell you this good news. ²⁰Now, listen! You will not be able to talk until the day when these things happen. You will lose your speech because you did not believe what I told you. But everything I said will really happen."

²¹Outside, the people were still waiting for Zechariah. They were surprised that he was staying so long in the Temple. ²²Then Zechariah came outside, but he could not speak to them. So the people knew that he had seen a vision inside the Temple. He was not able to speak, so he could only make signs to the people. ²³When his time of service was finished, he went home.

²⁴Later, Zechariah's wife Elizabeth became pregnant. So she did not go out of her house for five months. She said, ²⁵"Look what the Lord has done for me! He decided to help me. Now people will stop thinking there is something wrong with me."

An Angel Announces the Birth of Jesus

²⁶⁻²⁷During Elizabeth's sixth month of pregnancy, God sent the angel Gabriel to a virgin girl who lived in Nazareth, a town in Galilee. She was engaged to marry a man named Joseph from the family of David. Her name was Mary. ²⁸The angel came to her and said, "Greetings! The Lord is with you; you are very special to him."

²⁹But Mary was very confused about what the angel said. She wondered, "What does this mean?"

³⁰The angel said to her, "Don't be afraid, Mary, because God is very pleased with you. ³¹Listen! You will become pregnant and have a baby boy. You will name him Jesus. ³²He will be great. People will call him the Son of the Most High God, and the Lord God will make him king like his ancestor David. ³³He will rule over the people of Jacob forever; his kingdom will never end."

³⁴Mary said to the angel, "How will this happen? I am still a virgin."

³⁵The angel said to Mary, "The Holy Spirit will come to you, and the power of the Most High God will cover you. The baby will be holy and will be called the Son of God. ³⁶And here's something else: your relative Elizabeth is pregnant. She is very old, but she is going to have a son. Everyone thought she could not have a baby, but she has been pregnant now for six months. ³⁷God can do anything!"

³⁸Mary said, "I am the Lord's servant. Let this thing you have said happen to me!" Then the angel went away.

ᵃ **1:5 Abijah's group** Jewish priests were divided into 24 groups. See 1 Chr. 24.

80And so the little boy John grew up and became stronger in spirit. Then he lived in the desert until he appeared in public to tell God's message to the people of Israel.

The Birth of Jesus Christ

(Matt. 1:18–25)

2 It was about that same time that Augustus Caesar sent out an order to all people in the countries that were under Roman rule. The order said that everyone's name must be put on a list. 2This was the first counting of all the people while Quirinius was governor of Syria. 3Everyone travelled to their own home towns to have their name put on the list.

4So Joseph left Nazareth, a town in Galilee, and went to the town of Bethlehem in Judea. It was known as the town of David. Joseph went there because he was from the family of David. 5Joseph registered with Mary because she was engaged to marry him. (She was now pregnant.) 6While Joseph and Mary were in Bethlehem, the time came for her to have the baby. 7She gave birth to her first son. She wrapped him up well and laid him in a box where cattle are fed. She put him there because the guest room was full.

Some Shepherds Hear About Jesus

8That night, some shepherds were out in the fields near Bethlehem watching their sheep. 9An angel of the Lord appeared to them, and the glory of the Lord was shining around them. The shepherds were very frightened. 10The angel said to them, "Don't be afraid. I have some very good news for you—news that will make everyone happy. 11Today your Saviour was born in David's town. He is the Messiah, the Lord. 12This is how you will know him: you will find a baby wrapped in pieces of cloth and lying in a feeding box."

13Then a huge army of angels from heaven joined the first angel, and they were all praising God, saying,

14"Praise God in heaven,
     and on earth let there be peace to the
         people who please him."

15The angels left the shepherds and went back to heaven. The shepherds said to each other, "Let's go to Bethlehem and see this great event the Lord has told us about."

16So they went running and found Mary and Joseph. And there was the baby, lying in the feeding box. 17When they saw the baby, they told them what the angels had said about this child. 18Everyone was surprised when they heard what the shepherds told them. 19Mary continued to think about these things, trying to understand them. 20The shepherds went back to their sheep, praising God and thanking him for everything they had seen and heard. It was just as the angel had told them.

21When the baby was eight days old, he was circumcised, and he was named Jesus. This name was given by the angel before the baby began to grow inside Mary.

Jesus Is Presented in the Temple

22The time came for Mary and Joseph to do the things the Law of Moses taught about being made pure.*a* They brought Jesus to Jerusalem so that they could present him to the Lord. 23It is written in the Law of the Lord: "When a mother's first baby is a boy, he shall be called 'special for the Lord'."*b* 24The Law of the Lord also says that people must give a sacrifice: "You must sacrifice two doves or two young pigeons."*c* So Joseph and Mary went to Jerusalem to do this.

Simeon Sees Jesus

25A man named Simeon lived in Jerusalem. He was a good man who was devoted to God. He was waiting for the time when God would come to help Israel. The Holy Spirit was with him. 26The Holy Spirit told him that he would not die before he saw the Messiah from the Lord. 27The Spirit led Simeon to the Temple. So he was there when Mary and Joseph brought the baby Jesus to do what the Jewish law said they must do. 28Simeon took the baby in his arms and thanked God:

29"Lord, you have kept your promise to me,
     so now you can let me, your servant, die in
         peace.
30I have seen with my own eyes how you will
     save your people.
31   Now all people can see your plan.
32He is a light to show your way to the other
     nations.
     And he will bring honour to your people
         Israel."

33Jesus' father and mother were amazed at what Simeon said about him. 34Then Simeon blessed them and said to Mary, "Many Jews will

---

a **2:22** *pure* The Law of Moses said that 40 days after a Jewish woman gave birth to a baby, she must be made ritually clean by a ceremony at the Temple. See Lev. 12:2–8.
b **2:23** *"When . . . 'special for the Lord'"* See Exod. 13:2,12.
c **2:24** Quote from Lev. 12:8.

Mary Visits Zechariah and Elizabeth

39Mary got up and went quickly to a town in the hill country of Judea. 40She went into Zechariah's house and greeted Elizabeth. 41When Elizabeth heard Mary's greeting, the unborn baby inside her jumped, and she was filled with the Holy Spirit.

42In a loud voice she said to Mary, "God has blessed you more than any other woman. And God has blessed the baby you will have. 43You are the mother of my Lord, and you have come to me! Why has something so good happened to me? 44When I heard your voice, the baby inside me jumped with joy. 45Great blessings are yours because you believed what the Lord said to you! You believed this would happen."

Mary Praises God

46Then Mary said,

"I praise the Lord with all my heart.
47   I am very happy because God is my
        Saviour.
48He has shown his care for me, his servant,
        a person who is so unimportant.
And from now on, people will think of me
        as a person God blessed in a special way.
49Yes, the Powerful One has done great things
        for me.
        His name is very holy.
50He always gives mercy
        to those who worship him.
51He reached out his arm and showed his
        power.
        He scattered those who think they are
        better than anyone else.
52He brought down rulers from their thrones
        and raised up the humble people.
53He filled the hungry with good things,
        but he sent the rich away with nothing.
54God has helped Israel—the people he chose to
        serve him.
        He has never forgotten to give us his mercy.
55This is what he promised our ancestors,
        Abraham and his descendants."

56Mary stayed with Elizabeth for about three months and then went home.

The Birth of John the Baptizer

57When it was time for Elizabeth to give birth, she had a boy. 58Her neighbours and relatives heard that the Lord was very good to her, and they were happy for her.

59When the baby was eight days old, they came to circumcise him. They wanted to name him Zechariah because this was his father's name. 60But his mother said, "No, he will be named John."

61The people said to Elizabeth, "But no one in your family has that name." 62Then they made signs to his father, "What would you like to name him?"

63Zechariah asked for something to write on. Then he wrote, "His name is John." Everyone was surprised. 64Then Zechariah could talk again, and he began praising God. 65And all their neighbours were afraid. In all the hill country of Judea, people continued talking about these things. 66Everyone who heard about these things wondered about them. They thought, "What will this child be?" They could see that the Lord was with him.

Zechariah Praises God

67Then Zechariah, John's father, was filled with the Holy Spirit and told the people a message from God:

68"Praise to the Lord God of Israel.
        He has come to help his people
        and has given them freedom.
69He has given us a powerful Saviour
        from the family of his servant David.
70This is what he promised
        through his holy prophets long ago.
71He promised to save us from our enemies
        and from the power of all those who
        hate us.
72God said he would show mercy to our
        fathers
        and remember his holy agreement.
73This was the promise he made to our father
        Abraham,
74   a promise to free us from the power of our
        enemies,
        so that we could serve him without fear
75   in a way that is holy and right for as long as
        we live.

76"Now you, little boy, will be called a prophet
        of the Most High God.
        You will go first before the Lord to prepare
        the way for him.
77You will make his people understand that they
        will be saved
        by having their sins forgiven.

78"With the loving mercy of our God,
        a new daya from heaven will shine on us.
79It will bring light to those who live in
        darkness, in the fear of death.
        It will guide us into the way that brings
        peace."

a 1:78 new day Literally, "dawn", used here as a symbol, probably meaning the Lord's Messiah.

fall and many will rise because of this boy. He will be a sign from God that some will not accept. ³⁵So the secret thoughts of many will be made known. And the things that happen will be painful for you—like a sword cutting through your heart."

Anna Sees Jesus

³⁶Anna, a prophet, was there at the Temple. She was from the family of Phanuel in the tribe of Asher. She was now very old. She had lived with her husband for seven years ³⁷before he died and left her alone. She was now 84 years old. Anna was always at the Temple; she never left. She worshipped God by fasting and praying day and night. ³⁸Anna was there when Joseph and Mary came to the Temple. She praised God and talked about Jesus to all those who were waiting for God to free Jerusalem.

Joseph and Mary Return Home

³⁹Joseph and Mary finished doing all the things that the Law of the Lord commanded. Then they went home to Nazareth, their own town in Galilee. ⁴⁰The little boy Jesus was developing into a mature young man, full of wisdom. God was blessing him.

Jesus as a Boy

⁴¹Every year Jesus' parents went to Jerusalem for the Passover festival. ⁴²When Jesus was twelve years old, they went to the festival as usual. ⁴³When the festival was over, they went home, but Jesus stayed in Jerusalem. His parents did not know this. ⁴⁴They travelled for a whole day thinking that Jesus was with them in the group. They began looking for him among their family and close friends, ⁴⁵but they did not find him. So they went back to Jerusalem to look for him there. ⁴⁶After three days they found him. Jesus was sitting in the Temple area with the religious teachers, listening and asking them questions. ⁴⁷Everyone who heard him was amazed at his understanding and wise answers. ⁴⁸When his parents saw him, they wondered how this was possible. And his mother said, "Son, why did you do this to us? Your father and I were very worried about you. We have been looking for you." ⁴⁹Jesus said to them, "Why did you have to look for me? You should have known that I must be where my Father's work is."ᵃ ⁵⁰But they did not understand the meaning of what he said to them. ⁵¹Jesus went with them to Nazareth and obeyed them. His mother was still thinking about

all these things. ⁵²As Jesus grew taller, he continued to grow in wisdom. God was pleased with him and so were the people who knew him.

John Prepares the Way for Jesus

(Matt. 3:1–12; Mark 1:1–8; John 1:19–28)

3 It was the fifteenth year of the rule of Tiberius Caesar. These men had been chosen by Caesar to rule four areas that were once under Israel:

Pontius Pilate, the governor of Judea;
Herod, the ruler of Galilee;
Philip, Herod's brother, the ruler of Iturea and Trachonitis;
Lysanias, the ruler of Abilene.

INSIGHT

John might have been expected to become a priest like his father. Instead, he became an itinerant preacher, working in the wilderness, away from the Temple. He was still bringing people to God, but in a new way.

Luke 3:2–3

²Annas and Caiaphas were the high priests. During this time, John, the son of Zechariah, was living in the desert, and he received a message from God. ³So he went through the whole area around the Jordan River and told the people God's message. He told them to be baptized to show that they wanted to change their lives, and then their sins would be forgiven. ⁴This is like the words written in the book of Isaiah the prophet:

"There is someone shouting in the desert:
'Prepare the way for the Lord.
  Make the road straight for him.
⁵Every valley will be filled,
  and every mountain and hill will be made flat.
Crooked roads will be made straight,
  and rough roads will be made smooth.
⁶Then everyone will see
  how God will save his people!'"

Isaiah 40:3–5

⁷Crowds of people came to be baptized by John. But he said to them, "You are all snakes! Who warned you to run from God's judgement that is coming? ⁸Change your hearts! And show

---

ᵃ **2:49 where . . . work is** Or "in my Father's house".

by the way you live that you have changed. I know what you are about to say—'but Abraham is our father!' That means nothing. I tell you, God could make children for Abraham from these rocks! 9The axe is now ready to cut down the trees.*a* Every tree that does not produce good fruit will be cut down and thrown into the fire."

10The people asked John, "What should we do?"

11He answered, "If you have two shirts, share with someone who does not have one. If you have food, share that too."

12Even the tax collectors came to John. They wanted to be baptized. They said to him, "Teacher, what should we do?"

13He told them, "Don't take more taxes from people than you have been ordered to collect."

14The soldiers asked him, "What about us? What should we do?"

He said to them, "Don't use force or lies to make people give you money. Be happy with the pay you get."

15Everyone was hoping for the Messiah to come, and they wondered about John. They thought, "Maybe he is the Messiah."

16John's answer to this was, "I baptize you with water, but there is someone coming later who is able to do more than I can. I am not good enough to be the slave who unties his sandals. He will baptize you with the Holy Spirit and with fire. 17He will come ready to clean the grain.*b* He will separate the good grain from the chaff, and he will put the good part into his barn. Then he will burn the useless part with a fire that cannot be stopped." 18John said many other things like this to encourage the people to change, and he told them the Good News.

How John's Work Later Ended

19John criticized Herod the ruler for what he had done with Herodias, the wife of Herod's brother, as well as for all the other bad things he had done. 20So Herod added another bad thing to all his other wrongs: he put John in jail.

Jesus Is Baptized by John

(Matt. 3:13–17; Mark 1:9–11)

21When all the people were being baptized, Jesus came and was baptized too. And while he was praying, the sky opened, 22and the Holy Spirit came down on him. The Spirit looked like a real dove. Then a voice came from heaven and said, "You are my Son, the one I love. I am very pleased with you."

The Family History of Joseph

(Matt. 1:1–17)

23When Jesus began to teach, he was about 30 years old. People thought that Jesus was Joseph's son.

Joseph was the son of Heli.
24Heli was the son of Matthat.
Matthat was the son of Levi.
Levi was the son of Melchi.
Melchi was the son of Jannai.
Jannai was the son of Joseph.
25Joseph was the son of Mattathias.
Mattathias was the son of Amos.
Amos was the son of Nahum.
Nahum was the son of Esli.
Esli was the son of Naggai.
26Naggai was the son of Maath.
Maath was the son of Mattathias.
Mattathias was the son of Semein.
Semein was the son of Josech.
Josech was the son of Joda.
27Joda was the son of Joanan.
Joanan was the son of Rhesa.
Rhesa was the son of Zerubbabel.
Zerubbabel was the son of Shealtiel.
Shealtiel was the son of Neri.
28Neri was the son of Melchi.
Melchi was the son of Addi.
Addi was the son of Cosam.
Cosam was the son of Elmadam.
Elmadam was the son of Er.
29Er was the son of Joshua.
Joshua was the son of Eliezer.
Eliezer was the son of Jorim.
Jorim was the son of Matthat.
Matthat was the son of Levi.
30Levi was the son of Simeon.
Simeon was the son of Judah.
Judah was the son of Joseph.
Joseph was the son of Jonam.
Jonam was the son of Eliakim.
31Eliakim was the son of Melea.
Melea was the son of Menna.
Menna was the son of Mattatha.
Mattatha was the son of Nathan.
Nathan was the son of David.
32David was the son of Jesse.
Jesse was the son of Obed.
Obed was the son of Boaz.
Boaz was the son of Salmon.
Salmon was the son of Nahshon.
33Nahshon was the son of Amminadab.
Amminadab was the son of Admin.
Admin was the son of Arni.

---

a 3:9 *trees* Meaning the people who don't obey God. They are like "trees" that will be cut down.
b 3:17 *clean the grain* Meaning that Jesus will separate the good people from those who are bad.

Arni was the son of Hezron.
Hezron was the son of Perez.
Perez was the son of Judah.
34Judah was the son of Jacob.
Jacob was the son of Isaac.
Isaac was the son of Abraham.
Abraham was the son of Terah.
Terah was the son of Nahor.
35Nahor was the son of Serug.
Serug was the son of Reu.
Reu was the son of Peleg.
Peleg was the son of Eber.
Eber was the son of Shelah.
36Shelah was the son of Cainan.
Cainan was the son of Arphaxad.
Arphaxad was the son of Shem.
Shem was the son of Noah.
Noah was the son of Lamech.
37Lamech was the son of Methuselah.
Methuselah was the son of Enoch.
Enoch was the son of Jared.
Jared was the son of Mahalaleel.
Mahalaleel was the son of Cainan.
38Cainan was the son of Enos.
Enos was the son of Seth.
Seth was the son of Adam.
Adam was the son of God.

Jesus Is Tempted by the Devil

(Matt. 4:1–11; Mark 1:12–13)

4 Now filled with the Holy Spirit, Jesus returned from the Jordan River. And then the Spirit led him into the desert. 2He was there for 40 days and was tempted by the devil. Jesus ate nothing during this time, and when it was finished, he was very hungry.
3The devil said to him, "If you are the Son of God, tell this rock to become bread."
4Jesus answered him, "The Scriptures say,

'It is not just bread that keeps people alive.'"

Deuteronomy 8:3

5Then the devil took Jesus and in a moment of time showed him all the kingdoms of the world. 6The devil said to him, "I will make you king over all these places. You will have power over them, and you will get all the glory. It has all been given to me. I can give it to anyone I want. 7I will give it all to you, if you will only worship me."
8Jesus answered, "The Scriptures say,

'You must worship the Lord your God.
Serve only him.'"

Deuteronomy 6:13

9Then the devil led Jesus to Jerusalem and put him on a high place at the edge of the Temple area. He said to him, "If you are the Son of God, jump off, 10because the Scriptures say,

'God will command his angels
to take care of you.'

Psalm 91:11

11It is also written,

'Their hands will catch you
so that you will not hit your foot on a
rock.'"

Psalm 91:12

12Jesus answered, "But the Scriptures also say, 'You must not test the Lord your God.'"*a*
13The devil finished tempting Jesus in every way and went away to wait until a better time.

Jesus Begins His Work in Galilee

(Matt. 4:12–17; Mark 1:14–15)

14Jesus went back to Galilee with the power of the Spirit. Stories about him spread all over the area around Galilee. 15He began to teach in the synagogues, and everyone praised him.

Jesus Goes to His Home Town

(Matt. 13:53–58; Mark 6:1–6)

16Jesus travelled to Nazareth, the town where he grew up. On the Sabbath day he went to the synagogue as he always did. He stood up to read. 17The book of Isaiah the prophet was given to him. He opened the book and found the place where this is written:

18"The Spirit of the Lord is on me.
He has chosen me to tell good news to the
poor.
He sent me to tell prisoners that they are free
and to tell the blind that they can see again.
He sent me to free those who have been
treated badly
19   and to announce that the time has come for
the Lord to show his kindness."

Isaiah 61:1–2; 58:6

20Jesus closed the book, gave it back to the helper, and sat down. As everyone in the synagogue watched him closely, 21he began to speak to them. He said, "While you heard me reading these words just now, they were coming true!"
22Everyone there said they liked what Jesus said. They were surprised to hear him speak such

---

a **4:12** Quote from Deut. 6:16.

wonderful words. They said, "How is this possible? Isn't he Joseph's son?"

²³Jesus said to them, "I know you will tell me the old saying: 'Doctor, heal yourself.' You want to say, 'We heard about the things you did in Capernaum. Do those same things here in your own home town!'" ²⁴Then he said, "The truth is, a prophet is not accepted in his own home town.

²⁵⁻²⁶"During the time of Elijah it did not rain in Israel for three and a half years. There was no food anywhere in the whole country. There were many widows in Israel during that time. But the fact is, Elijah was sent to none of those widows in Israel. He was sent only to a widow in Zarephath, a town in Sidon.

²⁷"And there were many people with leprosy living in Israel during the time of the prophet Elisha. But none of them were healed; the only one was Naaman. And he was from the country of Syria, not Israel."

²⁸When the people in the synagogue heard this, they were very angry. ²⁹They got up and forced Jesus out of town. Their town was built on a hill. They took Jesus to the edge of the hill to throw him off. ³⁰But he walked through the middle of the crowd and went away.

INSIGHT

Stoning was considered a legitimate death penalty for sins like blasphemy, Sabbath-breaking and persistent rebellion against parents. The proper way to do it, according to the rabbis' records (the Mishnah*), was to throw the accused off a cliff, then throw rocks at them until they died.*

Luke 4:29

Jesus Frees a Man From an Evil Spirit

(Mark 1:21–28)

³¹Jesus went to Capernaum, a city in Galilee. On the Sabbath day he taught the people. ³²They were amazed at his teaching because he spoke with authority.

³³In the synagogue there was a man who had an evil spirit from the devil inside him. The man shouted loudly, ³⁴"Jesus of Nazareth! What do you want with us? Did you come here to destroy us? I know who you are—God's Holy One!"

³⁵But Jesus warned the evil spirit to stop. He said, "Be quiet! Come out of the man!" The evil spirit threw the man down on the ground in front of everyone. Then the evil spirit left the man and did not hurt him.

³⁶The people were amazed. They said to each other, "What does this mean? With authority and power he commands evil spirits and they come out." ³⁷And so the news about Jesus spread to every place in the whole area.

Jesus Heals Peter's Mother-in-Law

(Matt. 8:14–17; Mark 1:29–34)

³⁸Jesus left the synagogue and went to Simon's[a] house. Simon's mother-in-law was very sick. She had a high fever. They asked Jesus to do something to help her. ³⁹He stood very close to her and ordered the sickness to go away. The sickness left her, and she got up and began serving them.

Jesus Heals Many Others

⁴⁰When the sun went down, the people brought their sick friends to Jesus. They had many different kinds of sicknesses. Jesus laid his hands on each sick person and healed them all. ⁴¹Demons came out of many people. The demons shouted, "You are the Son of God." But Jesus warned the demons not to speak, because they knew he was the Messiah.

Jesus Goes to Other Towns

(Mark 1:35–39)

⁴²The next day Jesus went to a place to be alone. The people looked for him. When they found him, they tried to stop him from leaving. ⁴³But he said to them, "I must tell the Good News about God's kingdom to other towns too. This is why I was sent."

⁴⁴Then Jesus told the Good News in the synagogues in Judea.

Jesus Chooses Some Followers

(Matt. 4:18–22; Mark 1:16–20)

5 As Jesus stood beside Lake Galilee,[b] a crowd of people pushed to get closer to him and to hear the teachings of God. ²Jesus saw two boats at the shore of the lake. The fishermen were washing their nets. ³Jesus got into the boat that belonged to Simon. He asked Simon to push off a little from the shore. Then he sat down in the boat and taught the people on the shore.

⁴When Jesus had finished speaking, he said to Simon, "Take the boat into the deep water. If all

---

[a] **4:38** *Simon* Simon's other name was Peter. Also in 5:3,4,5,10.
[b] **5:1** *Galilee* Literally, "Gennesaret".

of you will put your nets into the water, you will catch some fish."

⁵Simon answered, "Master, we worked hard all night trying to catch fish and caught nothing. But you say I should put the nets into the water, so I will." ⁶The fishermen put their nets into the water. Their nets were filled with so many fish that they began to break. ⁷They called to their friends in the other boat to come and help them. The friends came, and both boats were filled so full of fish that they were almost sinking.

⁸⁻⁹The fishermen were all amazed at the many fish they caught. When Simon Peter saw this, he bowed down before Jesus and said, "Go away from me, Lord. I am a sinful man!" ¹⁰James and John, the sons of Zebedee, were amazed too. (James and John worked together with Simon.)

Jesus said to Simon, "Don't be afraid. From now on your work will be to bring in people, not fish!"

¹¹The men brought their boats to the shore. They left everything and followed Jesus.

Jesus Heals a Sick Man

(Matt. 8:1–4; Mark 1:40–45)

¹²Once Jesus was in a town where a very sick man lived. This man was covered with leprosy. When the man saw Jesus, he bowed before Jesus and begged him, "Lord, you have the power to heal me if you want."

¹³Jesus said, "I want to heal you. Be healed!" Then he touched the man, and immediately the leprosy disappeared. ¹⁴Then Jesus said, "Don't tell anyone about what happened. But go and let the priest look at you.ᵃ And offer a gift to God for your healing as Moses commanded. This will show people that you are healed."

¹⁵But the news about Jesus spread more and more. Many people came to hear him and to be healed of their sicknesses. ¹⁶Jesus often went away to other places to be alone so that he could pray.

Jesus Heals a Paralysed Man

(Matt. 9:1–8; Mark 2:1–12)

¹⁷One day Jesus was teaching the people. The Pharisees and teachers of the law were sitting there too. They had come from every town in Galilee and Judea and from Jerusalem. The Lord was giving Jesus the power to heal people. ¹⁸There was a man who was paralysed, and some other men were carrying him on a mat. They tried to bring him and put him down before Jesus. ¹⁹But there were so many people that they could not find a way to Jesus. So they went up on the roof and lowered the paralysed man down through a hole in the ceiling. They lowered the mat into the room so that the paralysed man was lying in front of Jesus. ²⁰Jesus saw how much faith they had and said to the sick man, "Friend, your sins are forgiven."

²¹The Jewish teachers of the law and the Pharisees thought to themselves, "Who is this man who dares to say such things? What an insult to God! No one but God can forgive sins."

²²But Jesus knew what they were thinking and said, "Why do you have these questions in your minds? ²³⁻²⁴The Son of Man has power on earth to forgive sins. But how can I prove this to you? Maybe you are thinking it was easy for me to say, 'Your sins are forgiven.' There's no proof that it really happened. But what if I say to the man, 'Stand up and walk'? Then you will be able to see that I really have this power." So Jesus said to the paralysed man, "I tell you, stand up! Take your mat and go home!"

²⁵The man immediately stood up in front of everyone. He picked up his mat and walked home, praising God. ²⁶Everyone was completely amazed and began to praise God. They were filled with great respect for God's power. They said, "Today we saw amazing things!"

INSIGHT

Tax collectors weren't popular. As well as running a tax-collecting business for the Romans, they exploited the people by adding a percentage on top of the various taxes for themselves.

Luke 5:27–32

Levi (Matthew) Follows Jesus

(Matt. 9:9–13; Mark 2:13–17)

²⁷After this Jesus went out and saw a tax collector sitting at his place for collecting taxes. His name was Levi. Jesus said to him, "Follow me!" ²⁸Levi got up, left everything and followed Jesus.

²⁹Then Levi gave a big dinner at his house for Jesus. At the table there were many tax collectors and some other people too. ³⁰But the Pharisees and those who taught the law for the Pharisees began to complain to the followers of Jesus, "Why do you eat and drink with tax collectors and other sinners?"

³¹Jesus answered them, "Sick people are the ones who need a doctor, not those who are healthy. ³²I have come to ask sinners to change the way they live, not those who do everything right."

ᵃ **5:14** *let the priest look at you* The Law of Moses said a priest must decide when a person with leprosy was well.

Jesus Is Not Like Other Religious Leaders

(Matt. 9:14–17; Mark 2:18–22)

³³They said to Jesus, "John's followers often fast and pray, the same as the followers of the Pharisees. But your followers eat and drink all the time."

³⁴Jesus said to them, "At a wedding you cannot ask the friends of the bridegroom to fast while he is still with them. ³⁵But the time will come when the groom will be taken away from them. Then his friends will be sad and fast."

³⁶Jesus told them this story: "No one takes cloth off a new coat to cover a hole in an old coat. That would ruin the new coat, and the cloth from the new coat would not be the same as the old cloth. ³⁷Also, no one ever pours new wine*a* into old wineskins. The new wine would break them. The wine would spill out, and the wineskins would be ruined. ³⁸You always put new wine into new wineskins. ³⁹No one who drinks old wine wants new wine. They say, 'The old wine is better.'"

Jesus Is Lord Over the Sabbath Day

(Matt. 12:1–8; Mark 2:23–28)

6 One Sabbath day, Jesus was walking through some grain fields. His followers picked the grain, rubbed it in their hands and ate it. ²Some Pharisees said, "Why are you doing that? It is against the Law of Moses to do that on the Sabbath day."

³Jesus answered, "You have read about what David did when he and the people with him were hungry. ⁴David went into God's house. He took the bread that was offered to God and ate it. And he gave some of the bread to the people with him. This was against the Law of Moses, which says that only the priests can eat that bread." ⁵Then Jesus said to the Pharisees, "The Son of Man is Lord over the Sabbath day."

Jesus Heals a Man on the Sabbath Day

(Matt. 12:9–14; Mark 3:1–6)

⁶On another Sabbath day Jesus went into the synagogue and taught the people. A man with a paralysed right hand was there. ⁷The teachers of the law and the Pharisees were watching Jesus closely. They were waiting to see if he would heal on the Sabbath day. They wanted to see him do something wrong so that they could accuse him. ⁸But Jesus knew what they were thinking. He said to the man with the paralysed hand, "Get up and stand here where everyone can see." The man got up and stood there. ⁹Then Jesus said to them, "I ask you, which is the right thing to do on the Sabbath day: to do good or to do evil? Is it right to save a life or to destroy one?"

¹⁰Jesus looked around at all of them and then said to the man, "Hold out your hand." The man held out his hand, and it was healed. ¹¹The Pharisees and the teachers of the law got so angry they couldn't think straight. They talked to each other about what they could do to Jesus.

Jesus Chooses His Twelve Apostles

(Matt. 10:1–4; Mark 3:13–19)

¹²A few days later, Jesus went out to the hills to pray. He stayed there all night praying to God. ¹³The next morning he called his followers. He chose these twelve and called them apostles:

¹⁴Simon (Jesus named him Peter),
Andrew brother of Peter,
James,
John,
Philip,
Bartholomew,
¹⁵Matthew,
Thomas,
James the son of Alphaeus,
Simon called the Zealot,
¹⁶Judas the son of James,
Judas Iscariot (the one who turned against Jesus).

Jesus Teaches and Heals the People

(Matt. 4:23–25; 5:1–12)

¹⁷Jesus and the apostles came down from the mountain. Jesus stood on a flat place. A large crowd of his followers were there. Also, there were many people from all around Judea, Jerusalem and the coastal cities of Tyre and Sidon. ¹⁸They all came to hear Jesus teach and to be healed of their sicknesses. He healed the people who were troubled by evil spirits. ¹⁹Everyone was trying to touch him, because power was coming out from him. Jesus healed them all.

²⁰Jesus looked at his followers and said,

"Great blessings belong to you who are poor.
    God's kingdom belongs to you.
²¹Great blessings belong to you who are hungry now.
    You will be filled.
Great blessings belong to you who are crying now.
    You will be happy and laughing.

²²"People will hate you because you belong to the Son of Man. They will make you leave their group. They will insult you. They will think it is wrong even to say your name. When these things

---

a **5:37 *new wine*** Grape juice that is just beginning to ferment.

happen, know that great blessings belong to you. 23You can be happy then and jump for joy, because you have a great reward in heaven. The ancestors of those people did the same things to the prophets.

24"But how bad it will be for you rich people,
  because you had your easy life.
25How bad it will be for you people who are full now,
  because you will be hungry.
How bad it will be for you people who are laughing now,
  because you will be sad and cry.

26"How bad it is when everyone says nothing but good about you. Just look at the false prophets. Their ancestors always said good things about them.

Love Your Enemies

(Matt. 5:38–48; 7:12a)

27"But I say to you people who are listening to me, love your enemies. Do good to those who hate you. 28Ask God to bless the people who ask for bad things to happen to you. Pray for the people who are mean to you. 29If someone hits you on the side of your face, let them hit the other side too. If someone takes your coat, don't stop them from taking your shirt too. 30Give to everyone who asks you for something. When someone takes something that is yours, don't ask for it back. 31Do for others what you want them to do for you.

32"If you love only those who love you, should you get any special praise for doing that? No, even sinners love those who love them! 33If you do good only to those who do good to you, should you get any special praise for doing that? No, even sinners do that! 34If you lend things to people, always expecting to get something back, should you get any special praise for that? No, even sinners lend to other sinners so that they can get back the same amount!

35"I'm telling you to love your enemies and do good to them. Lend to people without expecting to get anything back. If you do this, you will have a great reward. You will be children of the Most High God. Yes, because God is good even to the people who are full of sin and not thankful. 36Give love and mercy the same as your Father gives love and mercy.

Be Careful About Criticizing Others

(Matt. 7:1–5)

37"Don't judge others, and God will not judge you. Don't condemn others, and you will not be condemned. Forgive others, and you will be forgiven. 38Give to others, and you will receive. You will be given much. It will be poured into your hands—more than you can hold. You will be given so much that it will spill into your lap. The way you give to others is the way God will give to you."

39Jesus told them this story: "Can a blind man lead another blind man? No. Both of them will fall into a ditch. 40Students are not better than their teacher. But when they have been fully taught, they will be like their teacher.

41"Why do you see the small piece of dust that is in your friend's eye, but you don't notice the big piece of wood that is in your own? 42How can you say to your friend, 'Let me get that piece of dust out of your eye'? Can you not see that big piece of wood in your own eye? You are a hypocrite. First, take the wood out of your own eye. Then you will see clearly to get the dust out of your friend's eye.

Only Good Trees Produce Good Fruit

(Matt. 7:17–20; 12:34b–35)

43"A good tree does not produce bad fruit. And a bad tree does not produce good fruit. 44Every tree is known by the kind of fruit it produces. You won't find figs on thorny weeds. And you can't pick grapes from thornbushes! 45Good people have good things saved in their hearts. That's why they say good things. But those who are evil have hearts full of evil, and that's why they say things that are evil. What people say with their mouths comes from what fills their hearts.

Two Kinds of People

(Matt. 7:24–27)

46"Why do you call me, 'Lord, Lord,' but you don't do what I say? 47The people who come to me, who listen to my teachings and obey them—I will show you what they are like. 48They are like a man building a house. He digs deep and builds his house on rock. The floods come, and the water crashes against the house. But the flood cannot move the house, because it was built well.

49"But the people who hear my words and do not obey are like a man who builds a house without preparing a foundation. When the floods come, the house falls down easily and is completely destroyed."

Jesus Heals an Officer's Servant

(Matt. 8:5–13; John 4:43–54)

7 Jesus finished saying all these things to the people. Then he went into Capernaum. 2In Capernaum there was an army officer. He had a servant who was very sick; he was near death. The officer loved the servant very much. 3When he

heard about Jesus, he sent some older Jewish leaders to him. He wanted the men to ask Jesus to come and save the life of his servant. ⁴The men went to Jesus. They begged Jesus to help the officer. They said, "This man is worthy of your help. ⁵He loves our people and he built the synagogue for us."

⁶So Jesus went with them. Just before they reached the officer's house, the officer sent friends to say, "Lord, you don't need to do anything special for me. I am not good enough for you to come into my house. ⁷That is why I did not come to you myself. You need only to give the order, and my servant will be healed. ⁸I know this because I am a man under the authority of other men. And I have soldiers under my authority. I tell one soldier, 'Go,' and he goes. And I tell another soldier, 'Come,' and he comes. And I say to my servant, 'Do this,' and my servant obeys me."

⁹When Jesus heard this, he was amazed. He turned to the people following him and said, "I tell you, this is the most faith I have seen anywhere, even in Israel."

¹⁰The group that had been sent to Jesus went back to the house. There they found that the servant was healed.

Jesus Brings a Woman's Son Back to Life

¹¹The next day Jesus and his followers went to a town called Nain. A big crowd was travelling with them. ¹²When Jesus came near the town gate, he saw some people carrying a dead body. It was the only son of a woman who was a widow. Walking with her were many other people from the town. ¹³When the Lord saw the woman, he felt very sorry for her and said, "Don't cry." ¹⁴He walked to the open coffin and touched it. The men who were carrying the coffin stopped. Jesus spoke to the dead son: "Young man, I tell you, get up!" ¹⁵Then the boy sat up and began to talk, and Jesus gave him back to his mother.

¹⁶Everyone was filled with fear. They began praising God and said, "A great prophet is here with us!" and "God is taking care of his people."

¹⁷This news about Jesus spread all over Judea and to all the other places around there.

John Sends Men to Ask Jesus a Question

(Matt. 11:2–19)

¹⁸John's followers told him about all these things. John called for two of his followers. ¹⁹He sent them to the Lord to ask, "Are you the one we heard was coming, or should we wait for someone else?"

²⁰So the men came to Jesus. They said, "John the Baptizer sent us to you with this question:

'Are you the one who is coming, or should we wait for someone else?'"

²¹Right then Jesus healed many people of their sicknesses and diseases. He healed those who had evil spirits and made many who were blind able to see again. ²²Then he said to John's followers, "Go and tell John what you have seen and heard. The blind can see. The lame can walk. People with leprosy are healed. The deaf can hear. The dead are brought back to life. And the Good News is being told to the poor. ²³Great blessings belong to those who don't have a problem accepting me."

²⁴When John's followers left, Jesus began talking to the people about John: "What did you people go out into the desert to see? Someone who is weak, like a stem of grassᵃ blowing in the wind? ²⁵Really, what did you expect to see? Someone dressed in fine clothes? Of course not. People who wear fancy clothes and live in luxury are all in kings' palaces. ²⁶So what did you go out to see? A prophet? Yes, John is a prophet. But I tell you, he is more than that. ²⁷This Scripture was written about him:

'Listen! I will send my messenger ahead of
    you.
He will prepare the way for you.'
                                    Malachi 3:1

²⁸I tell you, no one ever born is greater than John. But even the least important person in God's kingdom is greater than John."

²⁹(When the people heard this, they all agreed that God's teaching was good. Even the tax collectors agreed. These were the people who were baptized by John. ³⁰But the Pharisees and experts in the law refused to accept God's plan for themselves; they did not let John baptize them.)

³¹"What shall I say about the people of this time? What can I compare them to? What are they like? ³²They are like a group of children sitting in the marketplace and shouting to another group,

'We played flute music for you,
    but you did not dance;
we sang a sad song,
    but you did not cry.'

³³John the Baptizer came and did not eat the usual food or drink wine. And you say, 'He has a demon inside him.' ³⁴The Son of Man came eating and drinking. And you say, 'Look at him! He eats too much and drinks too much wine! He

---

ᵃ **7:24** *stem of grass* Literally, "reed".

is a friend of tax collectors and other sinners!'
[35]But wisdom is shown to be right by those who accept it."

Simon the Pharisee

[36]One of the Pharisees asked Jesus to eat with him. Jesus went into the Pharisee's house and took a place at the table.

[37]There was a sinful woman in that town. She knew that Jesus was eating at the Pharisee's house. So the woman brought some expensive perfume in an alabaster jar. [38]She stood at Jesus' feet, crying. Then she began to wash his feet with her tears. She dried his feet with her hair. She kissed his feet many times and rubbed them with the perfume.

[39]When the Pharisee who asked Jesus to come to his house saw this, he said to himself, "If this man were a prophet,[a] he would know that the woman who is touching him is a sinner!"

[40]In reply to what the Pharisee was thinking, Jesus said, "Simon, I have something to say to you."

Simon said, "Let me hear it, Teacher."

[41]Jesus said, "There were two men. Both men owed money to the same banker. One man owed him 500 silver coins. The other man owed him 50 silver coins. [42]The men had no money, so they could not pay their debt. But the banker told the men that they did not have to pay him. Which one of those two men will love him more?"

[43]Simon answered, "I think it would be the one who owed him the most money."

Jesus said to him, "You are right." [44]Then he turned to the woman and said to Simon, "Do you see this woman? When I came into your house, you gave me no water for my feet. But she washed my feet with her tears and dried my feet with her hair. [45]You did not greet me with a kiss, but she has been kissing my feet since I came in. [46]You did not honour me with oil for my head, but she rubbed my feet with her sweet-smelling oil. [47]I tell you that her many sins are forgiven. This is clear, because she showed great love. People who are forgiven only a little will love only a little."

[48]Then Jesus said to her, "Your sins are forgiven."

[49]The people sitting at the table began to think to themselves, "Who does this man think he is? How can he forgive sins?"

[50]Jesus said to the woman, "Because you believed, you are saved from your sins. Go in peace."

INSIGHT

The word "disciple" in Jesus' time could only be used for men, but he also had female followers who accompanied him on his journeys. Some were rich, some were poor, and some, such as prostitutes, were women that no "respectable" Jewish man would normally have mixed with.

Luke 8:2–3

The Group With Jesus

8 The next day, Jesus travelled through some cities and small towns. Jesus told the people a message from God, the Good News about God's kingdom. The twelve apostles were with him. [2]There were also some women with him. Jesus had healed these women of sicknesses and evil spirits. One of them was Mary, who was called Magdalene. Seven demons had come out of her. [3]Also with these women were Joanna, the wife of Chuza (the manager of Herod's property), Susanna and many other women. These women used their own money to help Jesus and his apostles.

A Story About a Farmer Sowing Seed

(Matt. 13:1–17; Mark 4:1–12)

[4]A large crowd came together. People came to Jesus from every town, and he told them this story:

[5]"A farmer went out to sow seed. While he was scattering the seed, some of it fell beside the road. People walked on the seed, and the birds ate it all. [6]Other seed fell on rock. It began to grow but then died because it had no water. [7]Some other seed fell among thorny weeds. This seed grew, but later the weeds stopped the plants from growing. [8]The rest of the seed fell on good ground. This seed grew and made 100 times more grain."

Jesus finished the story. Then he called out, "You people who hear me, listen!"

[9]Jesus' followers asked him, "What does this story mean?"

[10]He said, "You have been chosen to know the secret truths about God's kingdom. But I use stories to speak to other people. I do this so that,

'They will look,
    but they will not see.
They will listen,
    but they will not understand.'

Isaiah 6:9

---

[a] **7:39 prophet** A prophet often knows things that are hidden to other people.

Jesus Explains the Story About Seed

(Matt. 13:18–23; Mark 4:13–20)

[11]"This is what the story means: the seed is God's teaching. [12]Some people are like the seed that fell beside the path. They hear God's teaching, but then the devil comes and causes them to stop thinking about it. This keeps them from believing it and being saved. [13]Others are like the seed that fell on rock. That is like the people who hear God's teaching and gladly accept it. But they don't have deep roots. They believe for a while. But when trouble comes, they turn away from God.

[14]"What about the seed that fell among the thorny weeds? That is like the people who hear God's teaching, but they let the worries, riches and pleasures of this life stop them from growing. So the teaching does not produce good results in their lives.[a] [15]And what about the seed that fell on the good ground? That is like the people who hear God's teaching with a good, honest heart. They obey it and patiently produce a good crop.

Use the Understanding You Have

(Mark 4:21–25)

[16]"No one lights a lamp and then covers it with a bowl or hides it under a bed. Instead, they put the lamp on a lampstand so that the people who come in will have enough light to see. [17]Everything that is hidden will become clear. Every secret thing will be made known, and everyone will see it. [18]So think carefully about what you are hearing. The people who have some understanding will receive more. But those who do not have understanding will lose even what they think they have."

Jesus' Followers Are His True Family

(Matt. 12:46–50; Mark 3:31–35)

[19]Jesus' mother and brothers came to visit him. But they could not get close to him, because there were so many people. [20]Someone said to Jesus, "Your mother and your brothers are standing outside. They want to see you."

[21]Jesus answered them, "My mother and my brothers are those who listen to God's teaching and obey it."

Jesus' Followers See His Power

(Matt. 8:23–27; Mark 4:35–41)

[22]One day Jesus and his followers got into a boat. He said to them, "Come with me across the lake." And so they started across. [23]While they were sailing, Jesus slept. A big storm blew across the lake, and the boat began to fill with water. They were in danger. [24]The followers went to Jesus and woke him. They said, "Master! Master! We will drown!"

INSIGHT

Lake Galilee – also known as the Lake of Gennesaret and the Sea of Tiberias – is Israel's largest freshwater lake. It is almost 13 kilometres wide and 21 kilometres long and is well known for sudden and violent storms when the wind sweeps down from the surrounding hills.

Luke 8:22–25

Jesus got up. He gave a command to the wind and the waves. The wind stopped, and the lake became calm. [25]He said to his followers, "Where is your faith?"

They were afraid and amazed. They said to each other, "What kind of man is this? He commands the wind and the water, and they obey him."

Jesus Frees a Man From Evil Spirits

(Matt. 8:28–34; Mark 5:1–20)

[26]Jesus and his followers sailed on across the lake. They sailed to the area where the Gerasene people[b] live, across from Galilee. [27]When Jesus got out of the boat, a man from that town came to him. This man had demons inside him. For a long time he had worn no clothes. He did not live in a house but in the caves where the dead are buried.

[28–29]The demon inside the man had often seized him, and he had been put in jail with his hands and feet in chains. But he would always break the chains. The demon inside him would force him to go out to the places where no one lived. Jesus commanded the evil spirit to come out of the man. When the man saw Jesus, he fell down before him, shouting loudly, "What do you want with me, Jesus, Son of the Most High God? Please, don't punish me!"

[30]Jesus asked him, "What is your name?"

The man answered, "Legion."[c] (He said his name was "Legion" because many demons had

---

[a] **8:14 produce . . . lives** Literally, "bear a crop to maturity", meaning that these people do not do the good things God wants his people to do.
[b] **8:26 Gerasene people** Some Greek copies have "Gadarenes" and others have "Gergesenes".
[c] **8:30 "Legion"** This name means very many. A legion was about 6,000 men in the Roman army.

gone into him.) 31The demons begged Jesus not to send them into the bottomless pit.*a* 32On that hill there was a big herd of pigs eating. The demons begged Jesus to allow them to go into the pigs. So he allowed them to do this. 33Then the demons came out of the man and went into the pigs. The herd of pigs ran down the hill into the lake, and all were drowned.

34The men who were caring for the pigs ran away and told the story in the fields and in the town. 35People went out to see what had happened. They came to Jesus and found the man sitting there at the feet of Jesus. The man had clothes on and was in his right mind again; the demons were gone. This made the people afraid. 36The men who saw these things happen told the others all about how Jesus had made the man well. 37All those who lived in the area around Gerasa asked Jesus to go away because they were afraid.

So Jesus got into the boat to go back to Galilee. 38The man he had healed begged to go with him. But Jesus sent him away, saying, 39"Go back home and tell people what God has done for you."

So the man went all over town telling what Jesus had done for him.

Jesus Gives Life to a Dead Girl and Heals a Sick Woman

(Matt. 9:18–26; Mark 5:21–43)

40When Jesus went back to Galilee, the people welcomed him. Everyone was waiting for him. 41–42A man named Jairus came to him. He was a leader of the synagogue. He had only one daughter. She was twelve years old, and she was dying. So Jairus bowed down at the feet of Jesus and begged him to come to his house.

While Jesus was going to Jairus' house, the people crowded all around him. 43A woman was there who had been bleeding for twelve years. She had spent all her money on doctors,*b* but no doctor was able to heal her. 44The woman came behind Jesus and touched the bottom of his coat. At that moment, her bleeding stopped. 45Then Jesus said, "Who touched me?"

They all said they had not touched him. And Peter said, "Master, people are all around you, pushing against you."

46But Jesus said, "Someone touched me. I felt power go out from me." 47When the woman saw that she could not hide, she came forward, shaking. She bowed down before Jesus. While everyone listened, she explained why she had touched him. Then she said that she had been

healed immediately when she touched him. 48Jesus said to her, "My daughter, you are made well because you believed. Go in peace."

49While Jesus was still speaking, someone came from the house of the synagogue leader and said, "Your daughter has died! There is no need to bother the Teacher any more."

50Jesus heard this and said to Jairus, "Don't be afraid! Just believe and your daughter will be well."

51Jesus went to the house. He let only Peter, John, James and the girl's father and mother go inside with him. 52Everyone was crying and feeling sad because the girl was dead. But Jesus said, "Don't cry. She is not dead. She is only sleeping."

53The people laughed at him, because they knew that the girl was dead. 54But Jesus held her hand and called to her, "Little girl, stand up!" 55Her spirit came back into her, and she stood up immediately. Jesus said, "Give her something to eat." 56The girl's parents were amazed. He told them not to tell anyone about what had happened.

Jesus Sends His Apostles on a Mission

(Matt. 10:5–15; Mark 6:7–13)

9 Jesus called his twelve apostles together. He gave them power to heal sicknesses and power to force demons out of people. 2He sent them to tell about God's kingdom and to heal the sick. 3He said to them, "When you travel, don't take a walking stick. Also, don't carry a bag, food or money. Take for your trip only the clothes you are wearing. 4When you go into a house, stay there until it is time to leave. 5If the people in the town will not welcome you, go outside the town and shake the dust off your feet as a warning to them."

6So the apostles went out. They travelled through all the towns. They told the Good News and healed people everywhere.

Herod Is Confused About Jesus

(Matt. 14:1–12; Mark 6:14–29)

7Herod the ruler heard about all these things that were happening. He was confused because some people said, "John the Baptizer has risen from death." 8Others said, "Elijah has come to us." And some others said, "One of the prophets from long ago has risen from death." 9Herod said, "I cut off John's head. So who is this man I hear these things about?" Herod continued trying to see Jesus.

---

a **8:31 bottomless pit** Literally, "the abyss", something like a deep hole where evil spirits are kept.
b **8:43 She had spent . . . doctors** Some Greek copies do not have these words.

WHAT FOLLOWING JESUS
REALLY MEANS

Jesus is the ultimate "man on a mission". Even when he was getting celebrity status – earning fame for miraculous healings and insightful teaching – Jesus never lost sight of who he was and why he'd come. But it's clear the disciples did not feel quite the same. Can you imagine being part of "Team Jesus"? You were with the entourage – you had an "Access All Areas" pass. Some of the stardust would have rubbed off on you too. You'd hope it would never end.

DIG IN

READ Luke 9:18–27

- Take a quick look back at what had just happened (Luke 9:10–17). How many people had come out to see Jesus recently?
- What does Jesus want to know (vv.18–20)?
- Why does he tell them to keep the answer a secret (v.21)?

Well over 5,000 people (we only hear about the number of men) were routinely coming to hear Jesus. The crowds were massive, but you know how fame works – many, many more people would have heard about this "ordinary" man who was saying and doing extraordinary things. Word was spreading and people were wondering who this guy was.

Jesus wanted to know what people were saying – but he was far more interested to hear his closest friends' opinion. Peter nails it. But Jesus asks them not to blab – in case people misunderstand his real purpose . . .

- What does Jesus say will happen to him (v.22)?
- What must the disciples do if they want to carry on following him?

Think of all those crowds going back home, spreading the word about Jesus and getting people's hopes up that here, at last, was a leader who would free the people of God from the Roman occupation of their land. This was the wrong message. Jesus would indeed bring freedom – but not in the way people might have expected. He didn't want to scupper the perfect plan of God.

And then, Jesus really bursts their bubble. Far from the celebrity lifestyle they might have been getting used to, Jesus promises a tough road ahead.

DIG THROUGH

- Look at verses 23–27 again and imagine the force they must have hit the disciples with. How hard do they hit you today? Can you get your head around what they are asking of you?
- Is your faith in any way related to being part of a gang or a group like the disciples? Would you continue on with God if all of that was stripped away? Do you, as an individual, have faith in Jesus? Here there's a big challenge to keep following Jesus even when you're away from the fun of your church youth group or when a Christian summer camp ends and it feels like "the party is over". That's the way of his kingdom.

DIG DEEPER

- What does it mean to "carry the cross that is given to you every day" (v.23)? The disciples would have seen the public spectacle of condemned men dragging crosses, being led to their deaths by Roman soldiers. Jesus is talking about it symbolically.
- Following Jesus is a very serious matter. It's not something you do because everyone else is. It's something you do once you've thought hard about it and "counted the cost". Luke 14:25–33 gives two helpful examples of what this might mean in practice.

Jesus Feeds More Than 5,000

(Matt. 14:13–21; Mark 6:30–44; John 6:1–14)

10When the apostles came back, they told Jesus what they had done on their trip. Then he took them away to a town called Bethsaida. There, he and his apostles could be alone together. 11But the people learned where Jesus went and followed him. He welcomed them and talked with them about God's kingdom. He healed the people who were sick.

12Late in the afternoon, the twelve apostles came to Jesus and said, "No one lives in this place. Send the people away. They need to find food and places to sleep in the farms and towns around here."

13But Jesus said to the apostles, "You give them something to eat."

They said, "We have only five loaves of bread and two fish. Do you want us to go and buy food for all these people?" 14(There were about 5,000 men there.)

Jesus said to his followers, "Tell the people to sit in groups of about 50 people."

15So the followers did this and everyone sat down. 16Then Jesus took the five loaves of bread and two fish. He looked up into the sky and thanked God for the food. Then he broke it into pieces, which he gave to the followers to give to the people. 17They all ate until they were full. And there was a lot of food left. Twelve baskets were filled with the pieces of food that were not eaten.

Peter Says Jesus Is the Messiah

(Matt. 16:13–19; Mark 8:27–29)

18One day Jesus was praying alone. His followers came together there, and he asked them, "Who do the people say I am?"

19They answered, "Some people say you are John the Baptizer. Others say you are Elijah. And some people say you are one of the prophets from long ago that has come back to life."

20Then Jesus said to his followers, "And who do you say I am?"

Peter answered, "You are the Messiah from God."

21Jesus warned them not to tell anyone.

Jesus Says He Must Die

(Matt. 16:21–28; Mark 8:31 – 9:1)

22Then Jesus said, "I, the Son of Man, must suffer many things. I will be rejected by the older Jewish leaders, the leading priests and teachers of the law. And I will be killed. But after three days, I will be raised from death."

23Jesus continued to say to all of them, "Any of you who want to be my follower must stop thinking about yourself and what you want. You must be willing to carry the cross that is given to you every day for following me. 24Any of you who try to save the life you have will lose it. But you who give up your life for me will save it. 25It is worth nothing for you to have the whole world if you yourself are destroyed or lost. 26Don't be ashamed of me and my teaching. If that happens, then I, the Son of Man, will be ashamed of you when I come with my glory and the glory of the Father and the holy angels. 27Believe me when I say that some of you people standing here will see God's kingdom before you die."

Jesus Is Seen With Moses and Elijah

(Matt. 17:1–8; Mark 9:2–8)

28About eight days after Jesus said these things, he took Peter, John and James and went up into the hills to pray. 29While Jesus was praying, his face began to change. His clothes became shining white. 30Then two men were there, talking with him. They were Moses and Elijah. 31They also looked bright and glorious. They were talking with Jesus about his death that would take place in Jerusalem. 32Peter and the others were asleep. But they woke up and saw the glory of Jesus. They also saw the two men who were standing with him. 33When Moses and Elijah were leaving, Peter said, "Master, it is good that we are here. We will make three shelters[a] here—one to honour you, one to honour Moses and one to honour Elijah." Peter did not know what he was saying.

34While Peter was still talking, a cloud came all around them. Peter, John and James were afraid when the cloud covered them. 35A voice came from the cloud and said, "This is my Son. He is the one I have chosen. Obey him."

36When the voice stopped, only Jesus was there. Peter, John and James said nothing. And for a long time after that, they told no one about what they had seen.

Jesus Frees a Boy From an Evil Spirit

(Matt. 17:14–18; Mark 9:14–27)

37The next day, Jesus, Peter, John and James came down from the mountain. A large group of people met Jesus. 38A man in the group shouted to him, "Teacher, please come and look at my son. He is the only child I have. 39An evil spirit comes into him, and then he shouts. He loses control of himself and foams at the mouth. The evil spirit continues to hurt him and almost never

---

[a] **9:33 shelters** Or "tents". The same word is translated "holy tent" in the Old Testament, so it may be used here to mean a place for worship.

leaves him. 40I begged your followers to make the evil spirit leave my son, but they could not do it."

41Jesus answered, "You people today have no faith. Your lives are all wrong. How long must I be with you and be patient with you?" Then Jesus said to the man, "Bring your son here."

42While the boy was coming, the demon threw the boy to the ground. The boy lost control of himself. But Jesus gave a strong command to the evil spirit. Then the boy was healed, and Jesus gave him back to his father. 43All the people were amazed at the great power of God.

Jesus Talks About His Death

(Matt. 17:22–23; Mark 9:30–32)

The people were still amazed about all the things Jesus did. He said to his followers, 44"Don't forget what I will tell you now: the Son of Man will soon be handed over to the control of other men." 45But the followers did not understand what he meant. The meaning was hidden from them so that they could not understand it. But they were afraid to ask Jesus about what he said.

Who Is the Greatest?

(Matt. 18:1–5; Mark 9:33–37)

46Jesus' followers began to have an argument about which one of them was the greatest. 47Jesus knew what they were thinking, so he took a little child and stood the child beside him. 48Then he said to the followers, "When you accept a little child like this as one who belongs to me, you accept me. And anyone who accepts me also accepts the one who sent me. The one among you who is the most humble—this is the one who is great."

Whoever Is Not Against You Is for You

(Mark 9:38–40)

49John answered, "Master, we saw someone using your name to force demons out of people. We told him to stop because he does not belong to our group."

50Jesus said to him, "Don't stop him. Whoever is not against you is for you."

A Samaritan Town

51The time was coming near when Jesus would leave and go back to heaven. He decided to go to Jerusalem. 52He sent some men ahead of him. They went into a town in Samaria to make everything ready for him. 53But the people there would not welcome Jesus because he was going towards Jerusalem. 54James and John, the followers of Jesus, saw this. They said, "Lord, do you want us to call fire down from heaven and destroy those people?"*a*

55But Jesus turned and criticized them for saying this.*b* 56Then he and his followers went to another town.

INSIGHT

Samaria lay in the centre of Israel, between Judea in the south and Galilee in the north. The Samaritans were descended from people who'd been "drafted in" to replace the thousands of Jews deported to Assyria in the eighth century BC. The newcomers adopted the Israelite religion but tweaked it a bit. As a result, the people of Judah looked down on them and never considered them to be real Jews.

Luke 9:51–56

Following Jesus

(Matt. 8:19–22)

57They were all travelling along the road. Someone said to Jesus, "I will follow you anywhere you go."

58He answered, "The foxes have holes to live in. The birds have nests. But the Son of Man has no place where he can rest his head."

59Jesus said to another man, "Follow me!"

But the man said, "Lord, let me go and bury my father first."

60But Jesus said to him, "Let the people who are dead bury their own dead. You must go and tell about God's kingdom."

61Another man said, "I will follow you, Lord, but first let me go and say goodbye to my family."

62Jesus said, "Anyone who begins to plough a field but looks back is not prepared for God's kingdom."

Jesus Sends Out 72 of His Followers

10 After this, the Lord chose 72*c* more followers. He sent them out in groups of two. He sent them ahead of him into every town

---

a **9:54** Some Greek copies add "as Elijah did?"
b **9:55–56** Some Greek copies add "And he said, 'You don't know what kind of spirit you belong to. The Son of Man did not come to destroy people's lives but to save them.'"
c **10:1** *72* Some Greek copies say 70. Also in verse 17.

and place where he planned to go. ²He said to them, "There is such a big harvest of people to bring in. But there are only a few workers to help bring them in. God owns the harvest. Ask him to send more workers to help bring in his harvest.

³"You can go now. But listen! I am sending you, and you will be like sheep among wolves. ⁴Don't carry any money, a bag or sandals. Don't stop to talk with people on the road. ⁵Before you go into a house, say, 'Peace be with this home.' ⁶If the people living there love peace, your blessing of peace will stay with them. But if not, your blessing of peace will come back to you. ⁷Stay in the peace-loving house. Eat and drink what the people there give you. A worker should be given his pay. Don't leave that house to stay in another house.

⁸"If you go into a town and the people welcome you, eat the food they give you. ⁹Heal the sick people who live there, and tell them, 'God's kingdom is now very near you!'ᵃ

¹⁰"But if you go into a town and the people don't welcome you, then go out into the streets of that town and say, ¹¹'Even the dirt from your town that sticks to our feet we wipe off against you. But remember this: God's kingdom has now come very near.' ¹²I tell you, on the judgement day it will be worse for the people of that town than for the people of Sodom.

Warning for Those Who Reject Jesus

(Matt. 11:20–24)

¹³"It will be bad for you, Chorazin! It will be bad for you, Bethsaida!ᵇ You people saw me do many miracles, but you refused to change. If those same miracles had happened in Tyre and Sidon,ᶜ even those people would have changed their hearts and lives long ago. They would have worn sackcloth and sat in ashes to show that they were sorry for their sins. ¹⁴But on the judgement day it will be worse for you than for Tyre and Sidon. ¹⁵And you, Capernaum, will you be lifted up to heaven? No, you will be thrown down to the place of death!

¹⁶"When anyone listens to you my followers, they are really listening to me. But when anyone refuses to accept you, they are really refusing to accept me. And when anyone refuses to accept me, they are refusing to accept the one who sent me."

Satan Falls

¹⁷When the 72 followers came back from their trip, they were very happy. They said, "Lord, even the demons obeyed us when we used your name!"

¹⁸Jesus said to them, "I saw Satan falling like lightning from the sky. ¹⁹He is the enemy, but know that I have given you more power than he has. I have given you power to crush his snakes and scorpions under your feet. Nothing will hurt you. ²⁰Yes, even the spirits obey you. And you can be happy, but not because you have this power. Be happy because your names are written in heaven."

Jesus Prays to the Father

(Matt. 11:25–27; 13:16–17)

²¹Then the Holy Spirit made Jesus feel very happy. Jesus said, "I praise you, Father, Lord of heaven and earth. I am thankful that you have hidden these things from those who are so wise and so smart. But you have shown them to people who are like little children. Yes, Father, you did this because it's what you really wanted to do.

²²"My Father has given me all things. No one knows who the Son is—only the Father knows. And only the Son knows who the Father is. The only people who will know about the Father are those the Son chooses to tell."

²³Then Jesus turned to his followers. They were there alone with him. He said, "It is a great blessing for you to see what you now see! ²⁴I tell you, many prophets and kings wanted to see what you now see, but they could not. And they wanted to hear what you now hear, but they could not."

Story About the Good Samaritan

²⁵Then an expert in the law stood up to test Jesus. He said, "Teacher, what must I do to get eternal life?"

²⁶Jesus said to him, "What is written in the law? What do you understand from it?"

²⁷The man answered, "'Love the Lord your God with all your heart, all your soul, all your strength and all your mind.'ᵈ Also, 'Love your neighbour the same as you love yourself.'"ᵉ

²⁸Jesus said, "Your answer is right. Do this and you will have eternal life."

²⁹But the man wanted to show that the way he was living was right. So he said to Jesus, "But who is my neighbour?"

ᵃ **10:9 is now very near you** Or "is coming to you soon" or "has come to you".
ᵇ **10:13 Chorazin, Bethsaida** Jewish towns by Lake Galilee where Jesus performed many miracles to show his authority from God. In spite of this, the people refused to change their godless way of living.
ᶜ **10:13 Tyre and Sidon** Pagan cities that were famous for how evil they were.
ᵈ **10:27** Quote from Deut. 6:5.
ᵉ **10:27** Quote from Lev. 19:18.

BEING A GOOD NEIGHBOUR

Jesus was a very public figure. But unlike today's celebrities, hustled by bodyguards straight into the back of a limo, Jesus made himself incredibly accessible. The Gospels show that he loved to be among people teaching, talking and answering their questions. What's more, Jesus made a point of talking to and teaching *everyone* – not just his own people, the Jews.

DIG IN
READ Luke 10:25–37

- What is Jesus being asked here, and who is doing the asking (vv.25,29)?
- What motives were behind the questions?
- How does Jesus respond?

The interrogator is a clever man – a religious lawyer – and he clearly has an agenda (he wants to test Jesus, v.25). He asks a question he has no real interest in knowing the answer to, just to see if he can catch Jesus out.

Jesus forces the listeners – and us – to look deeper. Rather than giving a direct "legal" answer, Jesus tells a story.

- Of the three men who passed by the dying man, which was the least likely to help?
- What words would you use to describe the actions of the Samaritan (vv.33–35)?
- How do you think this story was meant to make Jesus' audience think differently about God's people and those who were not Jews?

Jerusalem to Jericho was seventeen miles of rough terrain – exactly the sort of place where robbers and bandits could hide out and attack passing travellers. The man, who we assume to be a Jew, is brutally attacked and left for dead. A Jewish priest and then a worker at the Temple pass by, refusing to get involved. Although this sounds callous, Jesus' audience may not have been surprised. To intervene would have made the men "unclean". But his listeners would have been shocked by the next bit.

A Samaritan would not normally go near a Jew – he wouldn't have been welcome. His people were second-class citizens, or worse. Yet this Samaritan decides that the injured man is his neighbour. He not only rescues him, but makes unlimited provision for his needs at the inn (v.35).

The question has been turned on its head. No longer is it "Who do I have to be nice to, because of my religion or my cultural identity?" Now it's "Who are you going to be nice to, because of your compassion?"

DIG THROUGH

- Do you see, too, that none of us ever loves "enough"? There's no point us trying to "big ourselves up" in front of Jesus because of the way we live, the way the lawyer did – that would be really arrogant and proud. Jesus himself is the only perfectly loving person and we've all got a long way to go before we'll be much like him!
- Can you think of any examples in your neighbourhood where people – even Christians – have a tendency to prefer "their own kind of people"? What does this story say about that?
- What's the application of Jesus' story for you? Perhaps you struggle with questions like "How much love and kindness is too much?" or "How far do I have to go?" or "How little can I get away with?" In light of this story, do you think those are the right kinds of question?

DIG DEEPER

- By making the hero of this story a Samaritan, Jesus is making a very powerful statement which Luke picks up on here and elsewhere in his book. God's love and his plan to save people is now no longer just for the Jews. It's for foreigners, strangers, even the Jews' enemies. Is this really something new? Read Jesus' speech right at the beginning of his ministry (Luke 4:16–30) where he points out two examples from Israel's history of God's compassion for the outsider.

30To answer this question, Jesus said, "A man was going down the road from Jerusalem to Jericho. Some robbers surrounded him, tore off his clothes and beat him. Then they left him lying there on the ground almost dead. 31"It happened that a Jewish priest was going down that road. When he saw the man, he did not stop to help him. He walked away. 32Next, a Levite came near. He saw the hurt man, but he went around him. He would not stop to help him either. He just walked away.

33"Then a Samaritan man travelled down that road. He came to the place where the hurt man was lying. He saw the man and felt very sorry for him. 34The Samaritan went to him and poured olive oil and wine*a* on his wounds. Then he covered the man's wounds with cloth. The Samaritan had a donkey. He put the hurt man on his donkey, and he took him to an inn. There he cared for him. 35The next day, the Samaritan took out two silver coins and gave them to the man who worked at the inn. He said, 'Take care of this hurt man. If you spend more money on him, I will pay it back to you when I come again.'"

36Then Jesus said, "Which one of these three men do you think was really a neighbour to the man who was hurt by the robbers?"

37The law expert answered, "The one who helped him."

Jesus said, "Then you go and do the same."

Mary and Martha

38While Jesus and his followers were travelling, he went into a town, and a woman named Martha let him stay at her house. 39She had a sister named Mary. Mary was sitting at Jesus' feet and listening to him teach. 40But her sister Martha was busy doing all the work that had to be done. Martha went in and said, "Lord, don't you care that my sister has left me to do all the work by myself? Tell her to help me!"

41But the Lord answered her, "Martha, Martha, you are getting worried and upset about too many things. 42Only one thing is important. Mary has made the right choice, and it will never be taken away from her."

Jesus Teaches About Prayer

(Matt. 6:9–15)

11 One day Jesus was out praying, and when he finished, one of his followers said to him, "John taught his followers how to pray. Lord, teach us how to pray too."

2Jesus said to the followers, "This is how you should pray:

'Father, we pray that your name will always be kept holy.
We pray that your kingdom will come.
3Give us the food we need for each day.
4Forgive our sins,
just as we forgive everyone who has done wrong to us.
And don't let us be tempted.'"

Ask God for What You Need

(Matt. 7:7–11)

5–6Then Jesus said to them, "Suppose one of you went to your friend's house very late at night and said to him, 'A friend of mine has come into town to visit me. But I have nothing for him to eat. Please give me three loaves of bread.' 7Your friend inside the house answers, 'Go away! Don't bother me! The door is already locked. My children and I are in bed. I cannot get up and give you the bread now.' 8I tell you, maybe friendship is not enough to make him get up to give you the bread. But he will surely get up to give you what you need if you continue to ask. 9So I tell you, continue to ask, and God will give to you. Continue to search, and you will find. Continue to knock, and the door will open for you. 10Yes, whoever continues to ask will receive. Whoever continues to look will find. And whoever continues to knock will have the door opened for them. 11Do any of you have a son? What would you do if your son asked you for a fish? Would any father give him a snake? 12Or, if he asked for an egg, would you give him a scorpion? Of course not! 13Even you who are bad know how to give good things to your children. So surely your heavenly Father knows how to give the Holy Spirit to the people who ask him."

Jesus' Power Is From God

(Matt. 12:22–30; Mark 3:20–27)

14Once Jesus was sending a demon out of a man who could not talk. When the demon came out, the man was able to speak. The crowds were amazed. 15But some of the people said, "He uses the power of Satan*b* to force demons out of people. Satan is the ruler of demons."

16Some others there wanted to test Jesus. They asked him to do a miracle as a sign from God. 17But he knew what they were thinking. So he said to them, "Every kingdom that fights against itself will be destroyed. And a family that fights against itself will break apart. 18So if Satan is

---

a **10:34** *olive oil and wine* These were used like medicine to soften and clean wounds.
b **11:15** *Satan* Literally, "Beelzebul" (the devil). Also in verses 18–19.

fighting against himself, how will his kingdom survive? You say that I use the power of Satan to force out demons. [19]But if I use Satan's power to force out demons, then what power do your people use when they force out demons? So your own people will prove that you are wrong. [20]But I use the power of God to force out demons. This shows that God's kingdom has now come to you.

[21]"When a strong man with many weapons guards his own house, the things in his house are safe. [22]But suppose a stronger man comes and defeats him. The stronger man will take away the weapons that the first man trusted to keep his house safe. Then the stronger man will do what he wants with the other man's things.

[23]"Whoever is not with me is against me. And anyone who does not work with me is working against me.

The Danger of Emptiness

(Matt. 12:43–45)

[24]"When an evil spirit comes out of a person, it travels through dry places, looking for a place to rest. But it finds no place to rest. So it says, 'I will go back to the home I left.' [25]When it comes back, it finds that home all neat and clean. [26]Then the evil spirit goes out and brings back seven other spirits more evil than itself. They all go and live there, and that person has even more trouble than before."

The People God Blesses

[27]As Jesus was saying these things, a woman with the people there called out to him, "Blessings from God belong to the woman who gave birth to you and fed you!"

[28]But Jesus said, "The people who hear the teaching of God and obey it—they are the ones who have God's blessing."

Some People Doubt Jesus' Authority

(Matt. 12:38–42; Mark 8:12)

[29]The crowd grew larger and larger. Jesus said, "The people who live today are evil. They ask for a miracle as a sign from God. But no miracle will be done to prove anything to them. The only sign will be the miracle that happened to Jonah.[a] [30]Jonah was a sign for those who lived in Nineveh.[b] It is the same with the Son of Man. He will be a sign for the people of this time.

[31]"On the judgement day, you people who live now will be compared with the queen of the South,[c] and she will be a witness who shows how guilty you are. Why do I say this? Because she travelled from far, far away to listen to Solomon's wise teaching. And I tell you that someone[d] greater than Solomon is right here, but you won't listen to me!

[32]"On the judgement day, you people who live now will also be compared with the people from Nineveh, and they will be witnesses who show how guilty you are. I say this because when Jonah preached to those people, they changed their hearts and lives. And you are listening to someone greater than Jonah, but you refuse to change!

Be a Light for the World

(Matt. 5:15; 6:22–23)

[33]"No one takes a light and puts it under a bowl or hides it. Instead, they put it on a lampstand so that the people who come in can see. [34]The only source of light for the body is the eye. When you look at people and want to help them, you are full of light. But when you look at people in a selfish way, you are full of darkness.[e] [35]So be careful! Don't let the light in you become darkness. [36]If you are full of light, and there is no part of you that is dark, then you will shine brightly, as though you have the light of a lamp shining on you."

Jesus Criticizes the Religious Leaders

(Matt. 23:1–36; Mark 12:38–40; Luke 20:45–47)

[37]After Jesus had finished speaking, a Pharisee asked Jesus to eat with him. So he went and took a place at the table. [38]But the Pharisee was surprised when he saw that Jesus did not wash his hands[f] first before the meal. [39]The Lord said to him, "The washing you Pharisees do is like cleaning only the outside of a cup or a dish. But what is inside you? You want only to cheat and hurt people. [40]You are foolish! The same one who made what is outside also made what is inside. [41]So pay attention to what is inside. Give to the people who need help. Then you will be fully clean.

[42]"But it will be bad for you Pharisees! You give God a tenth of the food you get, even your mint, your rue and every other little plant in

---

[a] **11:29 Jonah** A prophet in the Old Testament. After three days in a big fish he came out alive, just as Jesus would come out from the tomb on the third day.

[b] **11:30 Nineveh** City where Jonah preached. See Jonah 3.

[c] **11:31 queen of the South** Or "queen of Sheba". She travelled about 1,600 kilometres to learn God's wisdom from Solomon. See 1 Kgs 10:1–13.

[d] **11:31 someone** Literally, "something". Also in verse 32.

[e] **11:34** Literally, "The lamp of the body is your eye. When your eye is pure, your whole body is full of light. But if it is evil, your body is dark."

[f] **11:38 wash his hands** Washing the hands was a Jewish religious custom that the Pharisees thought was very important.

your garden.ᵃ But you forget to be fair to others and to love God. These are the things you should do. And you should continue to do those other things.

⁴³"It will be bad for you Pharisees because you love to have the most important seats in the synagogues. And you love it when people show respect to you in the marketplaces. ⁴⁴It will be bad for you, because you are like hidden graves that people walk on without realizing it."

⁴⁵One of the experts in the law said to Jesus, "Teacher, when you say these things about the Pharisees, you are criticizing our group too."

⁴⁶Jesus answered, "It will be bad for you, you experts in the law! You make strict rules that are very hard for people to obey.ᵇ You try to force others to obey your rules. But you yourselves don't even try to follow any of those rules. ⁴⁷It will be bad for you, because you build tombs for the prophets. But these are the same prophets your ancestors killed! ⁴⁸And now you show all people that you agree with what your ancestors did. They killed the prophets, and you build tombs for the prophets! ⁴⁹This is why God in his wisdom said, 'I will send prophets and apostlesᶜ to them. Some of my prophets and apostles will be killed by evil men. Others will be treated badly.'

⁵⁰"So you people who live now will be punished for the deaths of all the prophets who have been killed since the beginning of the world. ⁵¹You will be considered guilty for all those deaths, from the killing of Abel to the killing of Zechariah,ᵈ who was killed between the altar and the Temple. Yes, I tell you that you people will be punished for them all.

⁵²"It will be bad for you, you experts in the law! You have taken away the key to learning about God. You yourselves would not learn, and you stopped others from learning too."

⁵³When Jesus went out, the teachers of the law and the Pharisees began to give him much trouble. They tried to make him answer questions about many things. ⁵⁴They were trying to find a way to catch Jesus saying something wrong.

Don't Be Like the Pharisees

12 Many thousands of people came together. There were so many people that they were stepping on each other. Before Jesus spoke to the people, he said to his followers, "Be careful

of the yeast of the Pharisees. I mean that they are hypocrites. ²Everything that is hidden will be shown, and everything that is secret will be made known. ³Whatever you say privately will be made public. And whatever you whisper in a closed room will be announced openly where everyone can hear."

Fear Only God

(Matt. 10:28–31)

⁴Then Jesus said to the people, "I tell you, my friends, don't be afraid of people. They can kill the body, but after that they can do nothing more to hurt you. ⁵I will show you the one to fear. You should fear God, who has the power to kill you and also to throw you into hell. Yes, he is the one you should fear.

⁶"When birds are sold, five small birds cost only two pennies. But God does not forget any of them. ⁷Yes, God even knows how many hairs you have on your head. Don't be afraid. You are worth much more than many birds.

Don't Be Ashamed of Your Faith

(Matt. 10:32–33; 12:32; 10:19–20)

⁸"I tell you, if you stand before others and are willing to say you believe in me, then Iᵉ will say that you belong to me. I will say this in the presence of God's angels. ⁹But if you stand before others and say you do not believe in me, then I will say that you do not belong to me. I will say this in the presence of God's angels.

¹⁰"Whoever says something against the Son of Man can be forgiven. But whoever speaks against the Holy Spirit will not be forgiven.

¹¹"When men bring you into the synagogues before the leaders and other important men, don't worry about what you will say. ¹²The Holy Spirit will teach you at that time what you should say."

Jesus Warns Against Selfishness

¹³One of the men in the crowd said to Jesus, "Teacher, our father just died and left some things for us. Tell my brother to share them with me."

¹⁴But Jesus said to him, "Who said I should be your judge or decide how to divide your father's things between you and your brother?" ¹⁵Then Jesus said to them, "Be careful and guard against

---

ᵃ **11:42 You give . . . garden** Literally, "You tithe mint, rue and every herb." The Law of Moses required Israelites to share their food supply by dedicating a tenth of their field crops and livestock to God (see Lev. 27:30–32; Deut. 26:12). This did not include such small garden plants as those mentioned here. So these Pharisees were giving more than required to be sure they were not breaking the law.

ᵇ **11:46 You make . . . obey** Literally, "You put heavy burdens on people that are hard for them to carry."

ᶜ **11:49 prophets and apostles** People chosen by God to tell his Good News to the world.

ᵈ **11:51 Abel, Zechariah** In the Hebrew Old Testament, these are the first and last persons murdered.

ᵉ **12:8 I** Literally, "the Son of Man" (Jesus).

all kinds of greed. People do not get life from the many things they own."

[16]Then Jesus used this story: "There was a rich man who had some land. His land grew a very good crop of food. [17]He thought to himself, 'What will I do? I have no place to keep all my crops.'

[18]"Then he said, 'I know what I will do. I will tear down my barns and build bigger barns! I will put all my wheat and good things together in my new barns. [19]Then I can say to myself, I have many good things stored. I have saved enough for many years. Rest, eat, drink and enjoy life!'

[20]"But God said to that man, 'Foolish man! Tonight you will die. So what about the things you prepared for yourself? Who will get those things now?'

[21]"This is how it will be for anyone who saves things only for himself. To God that person is not rich."

Put God's Kingdom First

(Matt. 6:25–34; 19–21)

[22]Jesus said to his followers, "So I tell you, don't worry about the things you need to live— what you will eat or what you will wear. [23]Life is more important than food, and the body is more important than what you put on it. [24]Look at the birds. They don't plant, harvest or save food in houses or barns, but God feeds them. And you are worth much more than crows. [25]None of you can add any time to your life by worrying about it. [26]And if you can't do the little things, why worry about the big things?

[27]"Think about how the wild flowers grow. They don't work or make clothes for themselves. But I tell you that even Solomon, the great and rich king, was not dressed as beautifully as one of these flowers. [28]If God makes what grows in the field so beautiful, what do you think he will do for you? That's just grass—one day it's alive, and the next day someone throws it into a fire. But God cares enough to make it beautiful. Surely he will do much more for you. Your faith is so small!

[29]"So don't always think about what you will eat or what you will drink. Don't worry about it. [30]That's what all those people who don't know God are always thinking about. But your Father knows that you need these things. [31]What you should be thinking about is God's kingdom. Then he will give you all these other things you need.

Don't Trust in Money

[32]"Don't fear, little flock. Your Father wants to share his kingdom with you. [33]Sell the things you have and give that money to those who need it.

This is the only way you can keep your riches from being lost. You will be storing treasure in heaven that lasts forever. Thieves can't steal that treasure, and moths can't destroy it. [34]Your heart will be where your treasure is.

Always Be Ready

(Matt. 24:42–44)

[35]"Be ready! Be fully dressed and have your lights shining. [36]Be like servants who are waiting for their master to come home from a wedding party. The master comes and knocks, and the servants immediately open the door for him. [37]When their master sees that they are ready and waiting for him, it will be a great day for those servants. I can tell you without a doubt, the master will get himself ready to serve a meal and tell the servants to sit down. Then he will serve them. [38]Those servants might have to wait until midnight or later for their master. But they will be glad they did when he comes in and finds them still waiting.

[39]"What would a home owner do if he knew when a thief was coming? You know he would not let the thief break in. [40]So you also must be ready, because the Son of Man will come at a time when you don't expect him!"

Who Is the Trusted Servant?

(Matt. 24:45–51)

[41]Peter said, "Lord, did you tell this story for us or for all people?"

[42]The Lord said, "Who is the wise and trusted servant? The master trusts one servant to give the other servants their food at the right time. Who is the servant that the master trusts to do that work? [43]When the master comes and finds him doing the work he gave him, it will be a great day for that servant! [44]I can tell you without a doubt, the master will choose that servant to take care of everything he owns.

[45]"But what will happen if that servant is evil and thinks his master will not come back soon? He will begin to beat the other servants, men and women. He will eat and drink until he has had too much. [46]Then the master will come when the servant is not ready, at a time when the servant is not expecting him. The master will give that servant a terrible punishment.[a] The master will send him where he belongs, with the other people who don't obey.

[47]"That servant knew what his master wanted him to do. But he did not make himself ready or try to do what his master wanted. So that servant will be punished very much! [48]But what about the

---

[a] **12:46 give . . . punishment** Literally, "cut him in half".

servant who does not know what his master wants? He also does things that deserve punishment. But he will get less punishment than the servant who knew what he should do. Whoever has been given much will be responsible for much. Much more will be expected from the one who has been given more."

Following Jesus May Bring You Trouble

(Matt. 10:34–36)

⁴⁹Jesus continued speaking: "I came to bring fire to the world. I wish it were already burning! ⁵⁰There is a kind of baptism*ᵃ* that I must go through. I will feel very troubled until it is finished. ⁵¹Do you think I came to give peace to the world? No, I came to divide the world! ⁵²From now on, a family of five will be divided, three against two and two against three.

⁵³A father and son will be divided.
  The son will turn against his father.
  The father will turn against his son.
A mother and her daughter will be divided.
  The daughter will turn against her mother.
  The mother will turn against her daughter.
A mother-in-law and her daughter-in-law will
  be divided.
  The daughter-in-law will turn against her
    mother-in-law.
  The mother-in-law will turn against her
    daughter-in-law."

Understanding the Times

(Matt. 16:2–3)

⁵⁴Then Jesus said to the people, "When you see clouds growing bigger in the west, you say, 'A storm is coming.' And soon it begins to rain. ⁵⁵When you feel the wind begin to blow from the south, you say, 'It will be a hot day.' And you are right. ⁵⁶You hypocrites! You can understand the weather. Why don't you understand what is happening now?

Settle Your Problems

(Matt. 5:25–26)

⁵⁷"Why can't you decide for yourselves what is right? ⁵⁸Suppose someone is suing you, and you are both going to court. Try hard to settle it on the way. If you don't settle it, you may have to go before the judge. And the judge will hand you over to the officer, who will throw you into jail. ⁵⁹I tell you, you will not get out of there until you have paid every penny you owe."

Change Your Hearts

13 Some people there with Jesus at that time told him about what had happened to some worshippers from Galilee. Pilate had given orders for them to be killed. Their blood was mixed with the blood of the animals they had brought for sacrificing. ²Jesus answered, "Do you think this happened to those people because they were more sinful than all other people from Galilee? ³No, they were not. But if you don't decide now to change your lives, you will all be destroyed like those people! ⁴And what about those 18 people who died when the tower of Siloam fell on them? Do you think they were more sinful than everyone else in Jerusalem? ⁵They were not. But I tell you if you don't decide now to change your lives, you will all be destroyed too!"

The Useless Tree

⁶Jesus told this story: "A man had a fig tree. He planted it in his garden. He came looking for some fruit on it, but he found none. ⁷He had a servant who took care of his garden. So he said to his servant, 'I have been looking for fruit on this tree for three years, but I never find any. Cut it down! Why should it waste the ground?' ⁸But the servant answered, 'Master, let the tree have one more year to produce fruit. Let me dig up the dirt around it and fertilize it. ⁹Maybe the tree will have fruit on it next year. If it still does not produce, then you can cut it down.'"

Jesus Heals a Woman on the Sabbath

¹⁰Jesus taught in one of the synagogues on the Sabbath day. ¹¹A woman was there who had an evil spirit inside her that had caused her a physical problem for 18 years. Her back was always bent so that she could not stand up straight. ¹²When Jesus saw her, he told her to come closer and said, "My dear woman, you are now free from the problem that has troubled you." ¹³He laid his hands on her, and immediately she was able to stand up straight. She began praising God.

¹⁴The synagogue leader was angry because Jesus healed on the Sabbath day. He said to the people, "There are six days for work. So come to be healed on one of those days. Don't come for healing on the Sabbath day."

¹⁵The Lord answered, "You people are hypocrites! All of you untie your work animals and lead them to drink water every day—even on the Sabbath day. ¹⁶This woman that I healed is a true descendant of Abraham.*ᵇ* But Satan has held her for 18 years. Surely it is not wrong for her to be

---

ᵃ **12:50 baptism** This word, which usually means to be immersed in water, has a special meaning here—being covered or "buried" in troubles.
ᵇ **13:16 true descendant of Abraham** Literally, "daughter of Abraham".

made free from her physical problem on a Sabbath day!" [17]When Jesus said this, all those who were criticizing him felt ashamed of themselves. And all the people were happy because of the wonderful things he was doing.

What Is God's Kingdom Like?

(Matt. 13:31–33; Mark 4:30–32)

[18]Then Jesus said, "What is God's kingdom like? What can I compare it with? [19]God's kingdom is like the seed of the mustard plant. Someone plants this seed in their garden. The seed grows and becomes a tree, and the birds build nests on its branches."

[20]Jesus said again, "What can I compare God's kingdom with? [21]It is like yeast that a woman mixes into a big bowl of flour to make bread. The yeast makes all the dough rise."

The Narrow Door

(Matt. 7:13–14,21–23)

[22]Jesus was teaching in every town and village. He continued to travel towards Jerusalem. [23]Someone said to him, "Lord, how many people will be saved? Only a few?"

Jesus said, [24]"The door to heaven is narrow. Try hard to enter it. Many people will want to enter there, but they will not be able to go in. [25]If a man locks the door of his house, you can stand outside and knock on the door, but he won't open it. You can say, 'Sir, open the door for us.' But he will answer, 'I don't know you. Where did you come from?' [26]Then you will say, 'We ate and drank with you. You taught in the streets of our town.' [27]Then he will say to you, 'I don't know you. Where did you come from? Get away from me! You are all people who do wrong!'

[28]"You will see Abraham, Isaac, Jacob and all the prophets in God's kingdom. But you will be left outside. There you will cry and grind your teeth in pain. [29]People will come from the east, west, north and south. They will sit down at the table in God's kingdom. [30]People who have the lowest place in life now will have the highest place in God's kingdom. And people who have the highest place now will have the lowest place in God's kingdom."

Jesus Will Die in Jerusalem

(Matt. 23:37–39)

[31]Just then some Pharisees came to Jesus and said, "Go away from here and hide. Herod wants to kill you!"

[32]Jesus said to them, "Go and tell that fox,[a] 'Today and tomorrow I am forcing demons out of people and finishing my work of healing. Then, the next day, the work will be finished.' [33]After that, I must go, because all prophets should die in Jerusalem.

[34]"Jerusalem, Jerusalem! You kill the prophets. You stone to death the people God has sent to you. How many times I wanted to help your people. I wanted to gather them together as a hen gathers her chicks under her wings. But you did not let me. [35]Now your home will be left completely empty. I tell you, you will not see me again until that time when you will say, 'Welcome! God bless the one who comes in the name of the Lord.'"[b]

Is It Right to Heal on the Sabbath Day?

14 On a Sabbath day, Jesus went to the home of a leading Pharisee to eat with him. The people there were all watching him very closely. [2]A man with badly swollen arms and legs was there in front of him. [3]Jesus said to the Pharisees and experts in the law, "Is it right or wrong to heal on the Sabbath day?" [4]But they would not answer his question. So he took the man and healed him. Then he sent the man away. [5]Jesus said to the Pharisees and experts in the law, "If your son or work animal falls into a well on the Sabbath day, you know you would pull him out immediately." [6]They could say nothing against what Jesus said.

Don't Make Yourself Important

[7]Then Jesus noticed that some of the guests were choosing the best places to sit. So he told this story: [8]"When someone invites you to a wedding, don't sit in the most important seat. They may have invited someone more important than you. [9]And if you are sitting in the most important seat, they will come to you and say, 'Give this man your seat!' Then you will have to move down to the last place and be embarrassed. [10]"So when someone invites you, go and sit in the seat that is not important. Then they will come to you and say, 'Friend, move up here to this better place!' What an honour this will be for you in front of all the other guests. [11]Everyone who makes themselves important will be made humble. But everyone who makes themselves humble will be made important."

You Will Be Rewarded

[12]Then Jesus said to the Pharisee who had invited him, "When you give a lunch or a dinner, don't invite only your friends, brothers, relatives and rich neighbours. At another time they will

---

[a] **13:32 fox** Jesus means that Herod is clever and sly like a fox.
[b] **13:35** Quote from Ps. 118:26.

pay you back by inviting you to eat with them. ¹³Instead, when you give a feast, invite the poor, the lame and the blind. ¹⁴Then you will have great blessings, because these people cannot pay you back. They have nothing. But God will reward you at the time when all godly people rise from death."

A Story About People Invited to a Dinner

(Matt. 22:1–10)

¹⁵One of the men sitting at the table with Jesus heard these things. The man said to him, "It will be a great blessing for anyone to eat a meal in God's kingdom!"

¹⁶Jesus said to him, "A man gave a big dinner. He invited many people. ¹⁷When it was time to eat, he sent his servant to tell the guests, 'Come. The food is ready.' ¹⁸But all the guests said they could not come. Each one made an excuse. The first one said, 'I have just bought a field, so I must go and look at it. Please excuse me.' ¹⁹Another man said, 'I have just bought five pairs of work animals; I must go and try them out. Please excuse me.' ²⁰A third man said, 'I just got married; I can't come.'

²¹"So the servant returned and told his master what had happened. The master was angry. He said, 'Hurry! Go into the streets and alleys of the town. Bring me the poor, the paralysed, the blind and the lame.'

²²"Later, the servant said to him, 'Master, I did what you told me to do, but we still have places for more people.' ²³The master said to the servant, 'Go out to the main roads and country lanes. Tell the people there to come. I want my house to be full! ²⁴None of those people I invited first will get to eat any of this food.'"

Decide if You Can Follow Me

(Matt. 10:37–38)

²⁵Many people were travelling with Jesus. He said to them, ²⁶"If you come to me but will not leave your family, you cannot be my follower. You must love me more than your father, mother, wife, children, brothers and sisters—even more than your own life! ²⁷Whoever will not carry the cross that is given to them when they follow me cannot be my follower.

²⁸"If you wanted to build a building, you would first sit down and decide how much it would cost. You must see if you have enough money to finish the job. ²⁹If you don't do that, you might begin the work, but you would not be able to finish. And if you could not finish it, everyone

would laugh at you. ³⁰They would say, 'This man began to build, but he was not able to finish.'

³¹"If a king is going to fight against another king, first he will sit down and plan. If he has only 10,000 men, he will try to decide if he is able to defeat the other king who has 20,000 men. ³²If he thinks he cannot defeat the other king, he will send some men to ask for peace while that king's army is still far away.

³³"It is the same for each of you. You must leave everything you have to follow me. If not, you cannot be my follower.

Don't Lose Your Influence

(Matt. 5:13; Mark 9:50)

³⁴"Salt is a good thing. But if the salt loses its salty taste, you can't make it salty again. ³⁵It is worth nothing. You can't even use it for the soil or for manure. People just throw it away.

"You people who hear me, listen!"

Joy in Heaven

(Matt. 18:12–14)

15 Many tax collectors and sinners came to listen to Jesus. ²Then the Pharisees and the teachers of the law began to complain, "Look, this man[a] welcomes sinners and even eats with them!"

³Then Jesus told them this story: ⁴"Suppose one of you has 100 sheep, but one of them gets lost. What will you do? You will leave the other 99 sheep there in the field and go out and look for the lost sheep. You will continue to search for it until you find it. ⁵And when you find it, you will be very happy. You will carry it ⁶home, go to your friends and neighbours and say to them, 'Be happy with me because I found my lost sheep!' ⁷In the same way, I tell you, heaven is a happy place when one sinner decides to change. There is more joy for that one sinner than for 99 good people who don't need to change.

⁸"Suppose a woman has ten silver coins,[b] but she loses one of them. She will take a light and clean the house. She will look carefully for the coin until she finds it. ⁹And when she finds it, she will call her friends and neighbours and say to them, 'Be happy with me because I have found the coin that I lost!' ¹⁰In the same way, it's a happy time for the angels of God when one sinner decides to change."

Story About Two Sons

¹¹Then Jesus said, "There was a man who had two sons. ¹²The younger son said to his father,

---

[a] **15:2 this man** That is, Jesus. His enemies avoided saying his name.
[b] **15:8 silver coins** Each coin, a Greek drachma, was worth the average pay for one day's work.

THE WANDERER RETURNS

You are about to hear one of the best-loved and most powerful stories in the whole Bible. But at the end, Jesus needs an answer from you. So listen carefully . . .

DIG IN

READ Luke 15:1-2,11-32

- Which two broad groups of people does Luke say Jesus is talking to (vv.1-2)?
- In the story, what is the younger son saying to his father by moving out (v.12)?
- So why does the father receive him back?

Luke makes a point of saying who was in the crowd around Jesus that day because it has a direct bearing on how we should understand the story. There were two groups of people – "tax collectors and sinners" and "Pharisees and the teachers of the law". The first were the social outsiders, the ones who saw themselves as "unclean" and far from God. The others were the religious elite – the ones who thought they had God's approval.

By leaving, the son isn't just saying "see you later". He's actually wishing his father dead by taking off with the inheritance that he really should only be entitled to after his father's death! But his father generously gives it to him anyway.

The young son had no claim whatsoever to come back, so when everything went pear-shaped he expected that he wouldn't be welcomed home. But he had no one else to turn to. His father takes him back for one reason alone – compassion (v.20).

- Why does the older son complain? What's his problem?
- What point is Jesus trying to make about the older son?

The older son is horrified because the situation doesn't seem fair. He has been the "good" son, working hard and never letting his father down. But clearly, his heart is just as messed up as his little brother's – it's full of bitterness, resentment and envy. And it all comes out when he sees his father's forgiveness for his selfish brother, his kindness towards someone who really doesn't deserve it. He might work for his father, but sadly it seems as though he hardly knows him at all.

Two brothers, two groups of people listening: the sinner who repents and finds mercy, and the "righteous" person who hardens his heart.

DIG THROUGH

- Here's the question Jesus is asking you: which brother are you? It's a serious question. Do you see yourself as the foolish younger son – a sinner who walked away from God and has been received back through no goodness of your own? Or do you feel like the older brother – as if you're working away for God and you deserve to be treated more fairly?
- This story is sometimes known as "The Prodigal Son" but a better name is "The Lost Sons". In what ways are they both as lost as each other?

DIG DEEPER

This simple story (or "parable") is a great example of how Jesus could communicate powerful truths in a way that was both easy to grasp and yet full of wisdom. There are so many layers of meaning in his parables that we can study them for a lifetime and continue to find God speaking fresh things to us by the power of the Holy Spirit. This is true of the whole Bible – it's truly a book for life.

'Give me now the part of your property that I am supposed to receive some day.' So the father divided his wealth between his two sons.

¹³"A few days later the younger son gathered up all that he had and left. He travelled far away to another country, and there he wasted his money living like a fool. ¹⁴After he had spent everything he had, there was a terrible famine throughout the country. He was hungry and needed money. ¹⁵So he went and got a job with one of the people who lived there. The man sent him into the fields to feed pigs. ¹⁶He was so hungry that he wanted to eat the food the pigs were eating. But no one gave him anything.

¹⁷"The son realized that he had been very foolish. He thought, 'All my father's hired workers have plenty of food. But here I am, almost dead because I have nothing to eat. ¹⁸I will leave and go to my father. I will say to him: Father, I have sinned against God and have done wrong to you. ¹⁹I am no longer worthy to be called your son. But let me be like one of your hired workers.' ²⁰So he left and went to his father.

The Younger Son Returns

"While the son was still a long way off, his father saw him coming and felt sorry for him. So he ran to him and hugged and kissed him. ²¹The son said, 'Father, I have sinned against God and have done wrong to you. I am no longer worthy to be called your son.'

²²"But the father said to his servants, 'Hurry! Bring the best clothes and put them on him. Also, put a ring on his finger and good sandals on his feet. ²³And bring our best calf and kill it so that we can celebrate with plenty to eat. ²⁴My son was dead, but now he is alive again! He was lost, but now he is found!' So they began to have a party.

The Older Son Complains

²⁵"The older son had been out in the field. When he came near the house, he heard the sound of music and dancing. ²⁶So he called to one of the servant boys and asked, 'What does all this mean?' ²⁷The boy said, 'Your brother has come back, and your father killed the best calf to eat. He is happy because he has his son back safe and sound.'

²⁸"The older son was angry and would not go in to the party. So his father went out and begged him to come in. ²⁹But he said to his father, 'Look, for all these years I have worked like a slave for you. I have always done what you told me to do, and you never gave me even a young goat for a party with my friends. ³⁰But then this son of yours comes home after wasting your money on prostitutes, and you kill the best calf for him!'

³¹"His father said to him, 'Oh, my son, you are always with me, and everything I have is yours. ³²But this was a day to be happy and celebrate. Your brother was dead, but now he is alive. He was lost, but now he is found.'"

True Wealth

16 Jesus said to his followers, "Once there was a rich man. He hired a manager to take care of his business. Later, he learned that his manager was cheating him. ²So he called the manager in and said to him, 'I have heard bad things about you. Give me a report of what you have done with my money. You can't be my manager any more.'

³"So, the manager thought to himself, 'What will I do? My master is taking my job away from me. I am not strong enough to dig ditches. I am too proud to beg. ⁴I know what I will do! I will do something to make friends, so that when I lose my job, they will welcome me into their homes.'

⁵"So the manager called in each person who owed the master some money. He asked the first one, 'How much do you owe my master?' ⁶He answered, 'I owe him 100 large jars*ᵃ* of olive oil.' The manager said to him, 'Here is your bill. Hurry! Sit down and make the bill less. Write 50 jars.'

⁷"Then the manager asked another one, 'How much do you owe my master?' He answered, 'I owe him 100 measures*ᵇ* of wheat.' Then the manager said to him, 'Here is your bill; you can make it less. Write 80 measures.'

⁸"Later, the master told the dishonest manager that he had done a smart thing. Yes, worldly people are smarter in their business with each other than spiritual people are.

⁹"I tell you, use the worldly things you have now to make 'friends' for later. Then, when those things are gone, you will be welcomed into a home that lasts forever. ¹⁰Whoever can be trusted with small things can also be trusted with big things. Whoever is dishonest in little things will be dishonest in big things too. ¹¹If you cannot be trusted with worldly riches, you will not be trusted with the true riches. ¹²And if you cannot be trusted with the things that belong to someone else, you will not be given anything of your own.

¹³"You cannot serve two masters at the same time. You will hate one master and love the other. Or you will be loyal to one and not care about the other. You cannot serve God and Money*ᶜ* at the same time."

ᵃ **16:6 jars** Greek *batous*, from the Hebrew *bath*, a measure equalling about 22 litres.
ᵇ **16:7 measures** Greek *korous*, from the Hebrew *cor*, a measure equalling about 220 litres.
ᶜ **16:13 Money** Or "*mamona*", an Aramaic word meaning "wealth".

God's Law Cannot Be Changed

(Matt. 11:12–13)

[14]The Pharisees were listening to all these things. They criticized Jesus because they all loved money. [15]Jesus said to them, "You make yourselves look good in front of people. But God knows what is really in your hearts. What people think is important is worth nothing to God.

[16]"Before John the Baptizer came, people were taught the Law of Moses and the writings of the prophets. But ever since the time of John, the Good News about God's kingdom has been told. And everyone is trying hard to get into it. [17]But not even the smallest part of a letter in the law can be changed. It would be easier for heaven and earth to pass away.

Divorce and Remarriage

[18]"Any man who divorces his wife and marries another woman is guilty of adultery. And the man who marries a divorced woman is also guilty of adultery."

INSIGHT

The Gospels include a lot of stories, known as "parables", that Jesus told. These stories have a deeper meaning to help people understand more about God. Like this parable, many of the stories in Luke favour the poor over the rich.

Luke 16:19–31

The Rich Man and Lazarus

[19]Jesus said, "There was a rich man who always dressed in the finest clothes. He was so rich that he was able to enjoy all the best things every day. [20]There was also a very poor man named Lazarus. Lazarus' body was covered with sores. He was often put by the rich man's gate. [21]Lazarus wanted only to eat the scraps of food left on the floor under the rich man's table. And the dogs came and licked his sores.

[22]"Later, Lazarus died. The angels took him and placed him in the arms of Abraham. The rich man also died and was buried. [23]He was sent to the place of death[a] and was in great pain. He saw Abraham far away with Lazarus in his arms. [24]He called, 'Father Abraham, have mercy on me! Send Lazarus to me so that he can dip his finger in water and cool my tongue. I am suffering in this fire!'

[25]"But Abraham said, 'My child, remember when you lived? You had all the good things in life. But Lazarus had nothing but problems. Now he is comforted here, and you are suffering. [26]Also, there is a big pit between you and us. No one can cross over to help you, and no one can come here from there.'

[27]"The rich man said, 'Then please, father Abraham, send Lazarus to my father's house on earth. [28]I have five brothers. He could warn my brothers so that they will not come to this place of pain.'

[29]"But Abraham said, 'They have the Law of Moses and the writings of the prophets to read; let them learn from that.'

[30]"The rich man said, 'No, father Abraham! But if someone came to them from the dead, then they would decide to change their lives.'

[31]"But Abraham said to him, 'If your brothers won't listen to Moses and the prophets, they won't listen to someone who comes back from the dead.'"

Sin and Forgiveness

(Matt. 18:6–7,21–22; Mark 9:42)

17 Jesus said to his followers, "Things will surely happen that will make people sin. But it will be very bad for anyone who makes this happen. [2]It will be very bad for anyone who makes one of these little children sin. It would be better for them to have a millstone tied around their neck and be drowned in the sea. [3]So be careful!

"If your brother or sister in God's family does something wrong, warn them. If they are sorry for what they did, forgive them. [4]Even if they do something wrong to you seven times in one day, but they say they are sorry each time, you should forgive them."

How Big Is Your Faith?

[5]The apostles said to the Lord, "Give us more faith!"

[6]The Lord said, "If your faith is as big as a mustard seed, you can say to this mulberry tree, 'Dig yourself up and plant yourself in the ocean!' And the tree will obey you.

Be Good Servants

[7]"Suppose one of you has a servant who has been working in the field, ploughing or caring for the sheep. When he comes in from work, what would you say to him? Would you say, 'Come in, sit down and eat'? [8]Of course not! You would say to your servant, 'Prepare something for me to eat. Then get ready and serve me. When I finish eating

---

[a] **16:23 place of death** Literally, "Hades".

and drinking, then you can eat.' ⁹The servant should not get any special thanks for doing his job. He is only doing what his master told him to do. ¹⁰It is the same with you. When you finish doing all that you are told to do, you should say, 'We are not worthy of any special thanks. We have only done the work we should do.'"

Be Thankful

¹¹Jesus was travelling to Jerusalem. He went from Galilee to Samaria. ¹²He came into a small town, and ten men met him there. They did not come close to him, because they all had leprosy. ¹³But the men shouted, "Jesus! Master! Please help us!"

¹⁴When Jesus saw the men, he said, "Go and show yourselves to the priests."ᵃ

While the ten men were going to the priests, they were healed. ¹⁵When one of them saw that he was healed, he went back to Jesus. He praised God loudly. ¹⁶He bowed down at Jesus' feet and thanked him. (He was a Samaritan.) ¹⁷Jesus said, "Ten men were healed; where are the other nine? ¹⁸This man is not even one of our people. Is he the only one who came back to give praise to God?" ¹⁹Then Jesus said to the man, "Stand up! You can go. You were healed because you believed."

The Coming of God's Kingdom

(Matt. 24:23–28,37–41)

²⁰Some of the Pharisees asked Jesus, "When will God's kingdom come?"

Jesus answered, "God's kingdom is coming, but not in a way that you can see it. ²¹People will not say, 'Look, God's kingdom is here!' or 'There it is!' No, God's kingdom is here with you."ᵇ

²²Then Jesus said to his followers, "The time will come when you will want very much to see one of the days of the Son of Man, but you will not be able to. ²³People will say to you, 'Look, there it is!' or 'Look, here it is!' Stay where you are; don't go away and search. ²⁴When the Son of Man comes again, you will know it. On that day he will shine like lightning flashes across the sky. ²⁵But first, the Son of Man must suffer many things. The people of today will refuse to accept him.

²⁶"When the Son of Man comes again, it will be the same as it was when Noah lived. ²⁷People were eating, drinking and getting married even on the day when Noah entered the boat. Then the flood came and killed them all.

²⁸"It will be the same as during the time of Lot, when God destroyed Sodom. Those people were eating, drinking, buying, selling, planting and building houses for themselves. ²⁹They were doing these things even on the day when Lot left town. Then fire and sulphur rained down from the sky and killed them all. ³⁰This is exactly how it will be when the Son of Man comes again.

³¹"On that day if a man is on his roof, he will not have time to go inside and get his things. If a man is in the field, he cannot go back home. ³²Remember what happened to Lot's wife!ᶜ

³³"Whoever tries to keep the life they have will lose it. But whoever gives up their life will save it. ³⁴That night there may be two people sleeping in one room. One will be taken and the other will be left. ³⁵Two women will be grinding grain together. One will be taken and the other will be left." ³⁶ᵈ

³⁷The followers asked Jesus, "Where will this be, Lord?"

Jesus answered, "It's like looking for a dead body—you will find it where the vultures are gathering above."

God Will Answer His People

18 Then Jesus taught the followers that they should always pray and never lose hope. He used this story to teach them: ²"Once there was a judge in a town. He did not care about God. He also did not care what people thought about him. ³In that same town there was a woman whose husband had died. She came many times to this judge and said, 'There is a man who is doing bad things to me. Give me my rights!' ⁴But the judge did not want to help the woman. After a long time, the judge thought to himself, 'I don't care about God. And I don't care about what people think. ⁵But this woman is bothering me. If I give her what she wants, then she will leave me alone. But if I don't give her what she wants, she will bother me until I am sick.'"

⁶The Lord said, "Listen, there is meaning in what the bad judge said. ⁷God's people shout to him night and day, and he will always give them what is right. He will not be slow to answer them. ⁸I tell you, God will help his people quickly. But when the Son of Man comes again, will he find people on earth who believe in him?"

Being Right With God

⁹There were some people who thought they were very good and looked down on everyone

---

ᵃ **17:14** *show yourselves to the priests* The Law of Moses said a priest must decide when a person with leprosy was well.
ᵇ **17:21** *here with you* Or "inside you."
ᶜ **17:32** *Lot's wife* The story about Lot's wife is found in Gen. 19:15–17,26.
ᵈ **17:36** A few Greek copies add verse 36: "Two men will be in the same field. One man will be taken, but the other man will be left behind."

else. Jesus used this story to teach them: [10]"Once there was a Pharisee and a tax collector. One day they both went to the Temple to pray. [11]The Pharisee stood alone, away from the tax collector. When the Pharisee prayed, he said, 'God, I thank you that I am not as bad as other people. I am not like men who steal, cheat or commit adultery. I thank you that I am better than this tax collector. [12]Yes, I fast twice a week, and I give a tenth of all I get!'

[13]"The tax collector stood alone too. But when he prayed, he would not even look up to heaven. He felt very humble before God. He said, 'God, have mercy on me. I am a sinner!' [14]I tell you, when this man finished his prayer and went home, he was right with God. But the Pharisee, who felt that he was better than others, was not right with God. People who make themselves important will be made humble. But those who make themselves humble will be made important."

Jesus Welcomes Children

(Matt. 19:13–15; Mark 10:13–16)

[15]Some people brought their small children to Jesus so that he could lay his hands on them to bless them. When the followers saw this, they told the people not to do this. [16]But Jesus called the little children to him and said to his followers, "Let the little children come to me. Don't stop them, because God's kingdom belongs to people who are like these little children. [17]The truth is, you must accept God's kingdom like a little child accepts things, or you will never enter it."

A Rich Man Refuses to Follow Jesus

(Matt. 19:16–30; Mark 10:17–31)

[18]A religious leader asked Jesus, "Good Teacher, what must I do to get eternal life?"

[19]Jesus said to him, "Why do you call me good? Only God is good. [20]And you know his commands: 'You must not commit adultery, you must not murder anyone, you must not steal, you must not tell lies about others, you must respect your father and mother.'"[a]

[21]But the leader said, "I have obeyed all these commands since I was a boy."

[22]When Jesus heard this, he said to the leader, "But there is still one thing you need to do. Sell everything you have and give the money to those who are poor. You will have riches in heaven. Then come and follow me." [23]But when the man heard Jesus tell him to give away his money, he was sad. He didn't want to do this, because he was very rich.

[24]When Jesus saw that the man was sad, he said, "It will be very hard for rich people to enter God's kingdom. [25]It is easier for a camel to go through the eye of a needle than for a rich person to enter God's kingdom."

Who Can Be Saved?

[26]When the people heard this, they said, "Then who can be saved?"

[27]Jesus answered, "God can do things that are not possible for people to do."

[28]Peter said, "Look, we left everything we had and followed you."

[29]Jesus said, "I can promise that everyone who has left their home, wife, brothers, parents or children for God's kingdom [30]will get much more than they left. They will get many times more in this life. And in the world that is coming they will get the reward of eternal life."

Jesus Talks Again About His Death

(Matt. 20:17–19; Mark 10:32–34)

[31]Then Jesus talked to the twelve apostles alone. He said to them, "Listen, we are going to Jerusalem. Everything that God told the prophets to write about the Son of Man will happen. [32]He will be handed over to the foreigners, who will laugh at him, insult him and spit on him. [33]They will beat him with whips and then kill him. But on the third day after his death, he will rise to life again." [34]The apostles tried to understand this, but they could not; the meaning was hidden from them.

Jesus Heals a Blind Man

(Matt. 20:29–34; Mark 10:46–52)

[35]Jesus came near to the city of Jericho. There was a blind man sitting beside the road. He was begging people for money. [36]When he heard the people coming down the road, he asked, "What is happening?"

[37]They told him, "Jesus, the one from Nazareth, is coming here."

[38]The blind man was excited and said, "Jesus, Son of David, please help me!"

[39]The people who were in front leading the group criticized the blind man. They told him to be quiet. But he shouted more and more, "Son of David, please help me!"

[40]Jesus stopped there and said, "Bring that man to me!" When he came close, Jesus asked him, [41]"What do you want me to do for you?"

He said, "Lord, I want to see again."

[42]Jesus said to him, "You can see now. You are healed because you believed."

[43]Then the man was able to see. He followed Jesus, thanking God. Everyone who saw this praised God for what happened.

---

[a] **18:20** Quote from Exod. 20:12–16; Deut. 5:16–20.

FRIEND OF SINNERS

When Jesus comes to town, where does he stay?

Elsewhere he's shown that he's not concerned about who he hangs out with: workers, tax collectors, prostitutes, rich and poor. The common denominator was not economic, political or cultural. This story makes it crystal clear that the place Jesus wanted to be was among the lost. And the lost loved him.

DIG IN   READ Luke 19:1–10

- What's Zacchaeus's position in society (v.2)?
- Why did he find it so hard to get a good view of Jesus (v.3)?

If you'd stopped someone on the streets of Jericho and asked them to define the word "sinner" for you, they would probably walk you to the door of Zacchaeus's office. Not only was this man a tax collector, he was a senior one. He probably had a team of heavies to do the actual dirty work of collecting taxes (and there would have been plenty of it, as Jericho was on a major trading route). He probably spent most of his day with his feet up, creaming off his share.

So the fact that Zacchaeus couldn't get a glimpse of Jesus wasn't just because he was short. We can safely assume that he would have been bumped out of the way by the crowds of ordinary people who knew exactly who he was – and hated him for it.

- What is it that prompts Zacchaeus's statement in verse 8?
- How does Jesus respond (v.9)?

Imagine the shock, the horror, when Jesus stops, looks up, and demands to stay at Zacchaeus's home! But this is the thing about Jesus. He knew his purpose: to find lost people and save them. He found Zacchaeus halfway up a tree, called him by name and saved his life.

Zacchaeus's response (v.8) may sound over the top, but there's every reason for it to be genuine. Receiving the acceptance of Jesus prompts a natural overflow of grace in him. This is what grace looks like.

It turned out that everyone was wrong. This money-grabbing sinner could come to have a good heart. He wasn't beyond hope. Even he could be saved – it just took someone to show him some God-shaped grace. And that's something where Jesus always takes the lead.

DIG THROUGH

- This is a story as much about the people's reactions as about Zacchaeus himself. Look at the way they behave in verse 7. If you'd been in the crowd, who do you think you'd have identified with – Zacchaeus or the people?
- Do you feel like Zacchaeus, intrigued by Jesus but never quite able to make a response to him? Pray that he would show you his grace in a way that refreshes your faith and helps you become the person he's made you to be. Remember, no one's too lost to be saved by Jesus.

DIG DEEPER

- Tax collectors, prostitutes, the sick and the disabled: they were all considered outcasts in Jesus' time. But they were not off-limits to Jesus. In fact, he makes it very clear in Luke 19:10 that his purpose is to go to "the lost". Who do you think these people are today? Luke 15 contains three stories of lost things. Read them to glimpse more of Jesus' heart for the lost.

Here, just before Jesus enters Jerusalem for the final days before his trial and execution, Luke makes it crystal clear who this Jesus is. Not just a miracle maker. Not just an impressive teacher. Jesus is the saving hope of the world.

Zacchaeus

19 Jesus was going through the city of Jericho. [2]In Jericho there was a man named Zacchaeus. He was a wealthy, very important tax collector. [3]He wanted to see who Jesus was. There were many others who wanted to see Jesus too. Zacchaeus was too short to see above the people. [4]So he ran to a place where he knew Jesus would pass. Then he climbed a sycamore tree so he could see him.

[5]When Jesus came to where Zacchaeus was, he looked up and saw him in the tree. Jesus said, "Zacchaeus, hurry! Come down! I must stay at your house today."

[6]Zacchaeus hurried and came down. He was happy to have Jesus in his house. [7]Everyone saw this. They began to complain, "Look at the kind of man Jesus is staying with. Zacchaeus is a sinner!"

[8]Zacchaeus said to the Lord, "I want to do good. I will give half of my money to the poor. If I have cheated anyone, I will pay them back four times more."

[9]Jesus said, "Today is the day for this family to be saved from sin. Yes, even this tax collector is one of God's chosen people.[a] [10]The Son of Man came to find lost people and save them."

Use What God Gives You

(Matt. 25:14–30)

[11]As the crowd listened to what he was saying, Jesus went on to tell a story. He was now near Jerusalem and knew that the people thought it was almost time for God's kingdom to come. [12]So he said, "A very important man was preparing to go to a country far away to be made a king. Then he planned to return home and rule his people. [13]So he called ten of his servants together. He gave a bag of money[b] to each servant. He said, 'Do business with this money until I come back.' [14]But the people in the kingdom hated the man. They sent a group to follow him to the other country. There they said, 'We don't want this man to be our king.'

[15]"But the man was made king. When he came home, he said, 'Call those servants who have my money. I want to know how much more money they earned with it.' [16]The first servant came and said, 'Sir, I earned ten bags of money with the one bag you gave me.' [17]The king said to him, 'That's great! You are a good servant. I see that I can trust you with small things. So now I will let you rule over ten of my cities.'

[18]"The second servant said, 'Sir, with your one bag of money I earned five bags.' [19]The king said to this servant, 'You can rule over five cities.'

[20]"Then another servant came in and said to the king, 'Sir, here is your bag of money. I wrapped it in a piece of cloth and hid it. [21]I was afraid of you because you are a hard man. You even take money that you didn't earn and gather food that you didn't grow.'

[22]"Then the king said to him, 'What a bad servant you are! I will use your own words to condemn you. You said that I am a hard man. You said that I even take money that I didn't earn and gather food that I didn't grow. [23]If that is true, you should have put my money in the bank. Then, when I came back, my money would have earned some interest.' [24]Then the king said to the men who were watching, 'Take the bag of money away from this servant and give it to the servant who earned ten bags of money.'

[25]"The men said to the king, 'But sir, that servant already has ten bags of money.'

[26]"The king said, 'People who use what they have will get more. But those who do not use what they have will have everything taken away from them. [27]Now where are my enemies? Where are the people who did not want me to be king? Bring my enemies here and kill them. I will watch them die.'"

INSIGHT

Jesus wasn't the only one to make a triumphal entry into Jerusalem. Pilate, the Roman governor, visited Jerusalem each year for the Passover. He normally lived in Caesarea but came to keep order during the festival and to hand over the high priest's ceremonial robes which were kept under Roman custody.

Luke 19:28–38

Jesus Enters Jerusalem Like a King

(Matt. 21:1–11; Mark 11:1–11; John 12:12–19)

[28]After Jesus said these things, he continued travelling towards Jerusalem. [29]He came near Bethphage and Bethany, towns near the hill called the Mount of Olives. He sent out two of his followers. [30]He said, "Go into the town you can see there. When you enter the town, you will find a young donkey tied there that no one has ever ridden. Untie it, and bring it here to me. [31]If anyone asks you why you are taking the donkey, you should say, 'The Master needs it.'"

---

[a] **19:9 one of God's chosen people** Literally, "a son of Abraham".
[b] **19:13 bag of money** One bag of money was a Greek *mina*, enough to pay a person for working three months. Also in verses 16,18,20,24,25.

³²The two followers went into town. They found the donkey exactly as Jesus had told them. ³³They untied it, but its owners came out. They said to the followers, "Why are you untying our donkey?"

³⁴The followers answered, "The Master needs it." ³⁵So the followers brought the donkey to Jesus. They put their coats on its back. Then they put Jesus on the donkey. ³⁶He rode along the road towards Jerusalem. The followers spread their coats on the road before him.

³⁷Jesus was coming close to Jerusalem. He was already near the bottom of the Mount of Olives. The whole group of followers were happy. They were very excited and praised God. They thanked God for all the powerful things they had seen. ³⁸They said,

"Welcome! God bless the king who comes in the name of the Lord.

Psalm 118:26

"Peace begins in heaven,
   and glory belongs to God!"

³⁹Some of the Pharisees said to Jesus, "Teacher, tell your followers not to say these things."

⁴⁰But Jesus answered, "I tell you, if my followers didn't say them, these stones would shout them."

Jesus Cries for Jerusalem

⁴¹Jesus came near to Jerusalem. Looking at the city, he began to cry for it ⁴²and said, "I wish you knew today what would bring you peace. But it is hidden from you now. ⁴³A time is coming when your enemies will build a wall around you and hold you in on all sides. ⁴⁴They will destroy you and all your people. Not one stone of your buildings will stay on top of another. All this will happen because you missed the opportunity for God to save you."

INSIGHT

In Jesus' day the Temple was not just a place of worship: it operated as a central bank, the seat of local government, a meeting place, the home of the local guard (police), and was the city's major employer. In the Antonia Fortress, attached to the Temple, there were 500 Roman soldiers.

Luke 19:45

Jesus Goes to the Temple

(Matt. 21:12–17; Mark 11:15–19; John 2:13–22)

⁴⁵Jesus went into the Temple area. He began to throw out the people who were selling things there. ⁴⁶He said, "The Scriptures say, 'My Temple will be a house of prayer.'ᵃ But you have changed it into a 'hiding place for thieves'."ᵇ

⁴⁷Jesus taught the people in the Temple area every day. The leading priests, the teachers of the law and some of the leaders of the people wanted to kill him. ⁴⁸But they did not know how they could do it, because everyone was listening to him. The people were very interested in what Jesus said.

Jewish Leaders Doubt Jesus' Authority

(Matt. 21:23–27; Mark 11:27–33)

20 One day Jesus was in the Temple area teaching the people. He was telling them the Good News. The leading priests, teachers of the law and older Jewish leaders came to talk to Jesus. ²They said, "Tell us what authority you have to do these things. Who gave you this authority?"

³Jesus answered, "I will ask you a question too. Tell me: ⁴when John baptized people, did his authority come from God or was it only from other people?"

⁵The priests, the teachers of the law and the Jewish leaders all talked about this. They said to each other, "If we answer, 'John's baptism was from God,' then he will say, 'Then why did you not believe John?' ⁶But if we say that John's baptism was from someone else, the people will stone us to death. They all believe that John was a prophet." ⁷So they answered, "We don't know the answer."

⁸So Jesus said to them, "Then I will not tell you who gave me the authority to do these things."

God Sends His Son

(Matt. 21:33–46; Mark 12:1–12)

⁹Then Jesus told the people this story: "A man planted a vineyard. Then he leased the land to some farmers and went away for a long time. ¹⁰Later, it was time for the grapes to be picked. So the man sent a servant to those farmers to get his share of the grapes. But they beat the servant and sent him away with nothing. ¹¹So the man sent another servant. They beat this servant too, showing no respect for him. They sent the servant away with nothing. ¹²So the man sent a third servant to the farmers. They hurt this servant badly and threw him out.

ᵃ **19:46** Quote from Isa. 56:7.
ᵇ **19:46** Quote from Jer. 7:11.

¹³"The owner of the vineyard said, 'What shall I do now? I will send my son. I love my son very much. Maybe the farmers will respect my son.' ¹⁴When the farmers saw the son, they said to each other, 'This is the owner's son. This vineyard will be his. If we kill him, it will be ours.' ¹⁵So the farmers threw the son out of the vineyard and killed him.

"What will the owner of the vineyard do? ¹⁶He will come and kill those farmers. Then he will lease the land to some other farmers."

When the people heard this story, they said, "This should never happen!" ¹⁷But Jesus looked into their eyes and said, "Then what does this verse mean:

'The stone that the builders refused to accept became the cornerstone'?

Psalm 118:22

¹⁸Everyone who falls on that stone will be broken. If that stone falls on you, it will crush you!"

¹⁹When the teachers of the law and the leading priests heard this story, they knew it was about them. So they wanted to arrest Jesus right then, but they were afraid of what the people would do.

The Jewish Leaders Try to Trick Jesus

(Matt. 22:15–22; Mark 12:13–17)

²⁰So the Jewish leaders looked for a way to trap Jesus. They sent some men to him, who pretended to be sincere. They wanted to catch him saying something they could use against him. If he said something wrong, they could hand him over to the governor, who had the authority to arrest him. ²¹So the men said to Jesus, "Teacher, we know that what you say and teach is true. It doesn't matter who is listening—you teach the same to all people. You always teach the truth about God's way. ²²Tell us, is it right for us to pay taxes to Caesar or not?"

²³But Jesus knew that these men were trying to trick him. He said to them, ²⁴"Show me a silver coin. Whose name and picture are on it?"

They said, "Caesar's."

²⁵He said to them, "Then give to Caesar what belongs to Caesar, and give to God what belongs to God."

²⁶The men were amazed at his wise answer. They had nothing to say. They were not able to use against Jesus anything he said there in front of the people.

Some Sadducees Try to Trick Jesus

(Matt. 22:23–33; Mark 12:18–27)

²⁷Some Sadducees came to Jesus. (Sadducees believe that people will not rise from death.) They asked him, ²⁸"Teacher, Moses wrote that if a married man dies and had no children, his brother must marry his widow. Then they will have children for the dead brother.ᵃ ²⁹Once there were seven brothers. The first brother married a woman but died. He had no children. ³⁰Then the second brother married the woman, and he died. ³¹And the third brother married the woman, and he died. The same thing happened with all the other brothers. They all died and had no children. ³²The woman was the last to die. ³³But all seven brothers married her. So when people rise from death, whose wife will this woman be?"

³⁴Jesus said to the Sadducees, "On earth, people marry each other. ³⁵Some people will be worthy to be raised from death and live again after this life. In that life they will not marry. ³⁶In that life people are like angels and cannot die. They are children of God, because they have been raised from death. ³⁷Moses clearly showed that people are raised from death. When Moses wrote about the burning bush,ᵇ he said that the Lord is 'the God of Abraham, the God of Isaac and the God of Jacob.'ᶜ ³⁸He is the God only of people who are living. So these men were not really dead. Yes, to God all people are still living."

³⁹Some of the teachers of the law said, "Teacher, your answer was very good." ⁴⁰No one was brave enough to ask him another question.

ᵃ **20:28** *if . . . dead brother* See Deut. 25:5–6.
ᵇ **20:37** *burning bush* See Exod. 3:1–12.
ᶜ **20:37** *'the God of . . . Jacob'* Words taken from Exod. 3:6.

Is the Messiah David's Son or David's Lord?

(Matt. 22:41–46; Mark 12:35–37)

⁴¹Then Jesus said, "Why do people say that the Messiah is the Son of David? ⁴²In the book of Psalms, David himself says,

'The Lord God said to my Lord:
Sit by me at my right side,
⁴³ and I will put your enemies under your power.'ᵃ

Psalm 110:1

⁴⁴David calls the Messiah 'Lord'. So how can the Messiah also be David's son?"

Warning Against the Teachers of the Law

(Matt. 23:1–36; Mark 12:38–40; Luke 11:37–54)

⁴⁵While all the people were listening to Jesus, he said to his followers, ⁴⁶"Be careful of the teachers of the law. They like to walk around wearing clothes that look important. And they love it when people show respect to them in the marketplaces. They love to have the most important seats in the synagogues and the places of honour at banquets. ⁴⁷But they cheat widows and take their homes. Then they try to make themselves look good by saying long prayers. God will punish them severely."

True Giving

(Mark 12:41–44)

21 Jesus looked up and saw some rich people putting their gifts to God into the Temple collection box. ²Then he saw a poor widow put two small copper coins into the box. ³He said, "This poor widow gave only two small coins. But the truth is, she gave more than all those rich people. ⁴They have plenty, and they gave only what they did not need. This woman is very poor, but she gave all she had to live on."

Jesus Warns About the Future

(Matt. 24:1–14; Mark 13:1–13)

⁵Some of the followers were talking about the Temple. They said, "This is a beautiful Temple, built with the best stones. Look at the many good gifts that have been offered to God."

⁶But Jesus said, "The time will come when all that you see here will be destroyed. Every stone of these buildings will be thrown down to the ground. Not one stone will be left on another."

INSIGHT

The beautiful stones that the disciples admired were faced in white marble and decorated with gold. Each one was huge, measuring 13.7 metres × 3.2 metres × 4 metres. Nevertheless, not many years after the completion of the building, Jesus' words came true: the Romans smashed the Temple to pieces after the Jews rebelled.

Luke 21:5–6

⁷Some followers asked Jesus, "Teacher, when will these things happen? What will show us that it is time for these things to happen?"

⁸Jesus said, "Be careful! Don't be fooled. Many people will come using my name. They will say, 'I am the Messiah'ᵇ and 'The right time has come!' But don't follow them. ⁹When you hear about wars and riots, don't be afraid. These things must happen first. Then the end will come later."

¹⁰Then Jesus said to them, "Nations will fight against other nations. Kingdoms will fight against other kingdoms. ¹¹There will be great earthquakes, sicknesses and other bad things in many places. In some places there will be no food for the people to eat. Terrible things will happen, and amazing things will come from heaven to warn people.

¹²"But before all these things happen, people will arrest you and do bad things to you. They will judge you in their synagogues and put you in jail. You will be forced to stand before kings and governors. They will do all these things to you because you follow me. ¹³But this will give you an opportunity to tell about me. ¹⁴Decide now not to worry about what you will say. ¹⁵I will give you the wisdom to say things that none of your enemies can answer. ¹⁶Even your parents, brothers, relatives and friends will turn against you. They will have some of you killed. ¹⁷Everyone will hate you because you follow me. ¹⁸But none of these things can really harm you. ¹⁹You will save yourselves by continuing to be strong in your faith through all these things.

The Destruction of Jerusalem

(Matt. 24:15–21; Mark 13:14–19)

²⁰"You will see armies all around Jerusalem. Then you will know that the time for its

---

ᵃ **20:43 and I . . . power** Literally, "until I make your enemies a footstool for your feet".
ᵇ **21:8 the Messiah** Literally "the one", meaning the chosen one sent by God. See Matt. 24:5 and "MESSIAH" in the Word List.

destruction has come. 21The people in Judea at that time should run away to the mountains. The people in Jerusalem must leave quickly. If you are near the city, don't go in! 22The prophets wrote many things about the time when God will punish his people. The time I am talking about is when all these things must happen. 23During that time, it will be hard for women who are pregnant or have small babies, because very bad times will come to this land. God will be angry with these people. 24Some of the people will be killed by soldiers. Others will be made prisoners and taken to all the different countries. The holy city of Jerusalem will be under the control of foreigners until their time is completed.

Don't Fear

(Matt. 24:29–31; Mark 13:24–27)

25"Amazing things will happen to the sun, moon and stars. And people all over the earth will be upset and confused by the noise of the sea and its crashing waves. 26They will be afraid and worried about what will happen to the world. Everything in the sky will be changed. 27Then people will see the Son of Man coming in a cloud with power and great glory. 28When these things begin to happen, stand up tall and don't be afraid. Know that it is almost time for God to free you!"

My Words Will Live Forever

(Matt. 24:32–35; Mark 13:28–31)

29Then Jesus told this story: "Look at all the trees. The fig tree is a good example. 30When it turns green, you know that summer is very near. 31In the same way, when you see all these things happening, you will know that God's kingdom is very near.

32"I assure you that all these things will happen while some of the people of this time are still living. 33The whole world, earth and sky, will be destroyed, but my words will last forever.

Be Ready All the Time

34"Be careful not to spend your time having parties and getting drunk or worrying about this life. If you do that, you won't be able to think straight, and the end might come when you are not ready. 35It will come as a surprise to everyone on earth. 36So be ready all the time. Pray that you will be able to get through all these things that will happen and stand safe before the Son of Man."

37During the day Jesus taught the people in the Temple area. At night he went out of the city and stayed all night on the hill called Mount of Olives. 38Every morning all the people got up early to go and listen to Jesus at the Temple.

The Jewish Leaders Plan to Kill Jesus

(Matt. 26:1–5,14–16; Mark 14:1–2,10–11; John 11:45–53)

22 It was almost time for the Festival of Unleavened Bread, called Passover. 2The leading priests and teachers of the law wanted to kill Jesus. But they were trying to find a quiet way to do it, because they were afraid of what the people would do.

Judas Agrees to Help Jesus' Enemies

(Matt. 26:14–16; Mark 14:10–11)

3One of Jesus' twelve apostles was named Judas Iscariot. Satan entered him, 4and he went and talked with the leading priests and some of the soldiers who guarded the Temple. He talked to them about a way to hand Jesus over to them. 5The priests were very happy about this. They promised to give Judas money for doing this. 6He agreed. Then he waited for the best time to hand him over to them. He wanted to do it when no one was around to see it.

The Passover Meal

(Matt. 26:17–25; Mark 14:12–21; John 13:21–30)

7The Day of Unleavened Bread*a* came. This was the day when the Jews always killed the lambs for Passover. 8Jesus said to Peter and John, "Go and prepare the Passover meal for us to eat."

9They said to him, "Where do you want us to prepare the meal?"

He said to them, 10"When you go into the city, you will see a man carrying a jar of water. Follow him. He will go into a house. 11Tell the owner of the house, 'The Teacher asks that you please show us the room where he and his followers can eat the Passover meal.' 12Then the owner will show you a large room upstairs that is ready for us. Prepare the meal there."

13So Peter and John left. Everything happened the way Jesus had said. So they prepared the Passover meal.

The Lord's Supper

(Matt. 26:26–30; Mark 14:22–26; 1 Cor. 11:23–25)

14The time came for them to eat the Passover meal. Jesus and the apostles were together at the table. 15Jesus said to them, "I wanted very much to eat this Passover meal with you before I die.

---

a **22:7 Day of Unleavened Bread** Same as Passover.

[16]I will never eat another Passover meal until it is given its full meaning in God's kingdom."

[17]Then Jesus took a cup of wine. He gave thanks to God for it and said, "Take this cup and give it to everyone here. [18]I will not drink wine again until God's kingdom comes."

[19]Then he took some bread and thanked God for it. He broke off some pieces, gave them to the apostles and said, "This bread is my body that I am giving for you. Eat this to remember me." [20]In the same way, after supper, Jesus took the cup of wine and said, "This wine represents the new agreement that God makes with his people. It will begin when my blood is poured out for you."[a]

Who Will Turn Against Jesus?

[21]Jesus said, "But here on this table is the hand of the one who will hand me over to my enemies. [22]The Son of Man will do what God has planned. But it will be very bad for the one who hands over the Son of Man to be killed."

[23]Then the apostles asked each other, "Which one of us would do that?"

Be Like a Servant

[24]Later, the apostles began to argue about which one of them was the most important. [25]But Jesus said to them, "The kings of the world rule over their people, and those who have authority over others want to be called 'the great providers for the people'. [26]But you must not be like that. The one with the most authority among you should act as if he is the least important. The one who leads should be like one who serves. [27]Who is more important: the one serving or the one sitting at the table being served? Everyone thinks it's the one being served. But I have been with you as the one who serves.

[28]"You men have stayed with me through many struggles. [29]So I give you authority to rule with me in the kingdom the Father has given me. [30]You will eat and drink at my table in that kingdom. You will sit on thrones and judge the twelve tribes of Israel.

Peter Will Be Tested and Fail

(Matt. 26:31–35; Mark 14:27–31; John 13:36–38)

[31]"Satan has asked to test you men like a farmer tests his wheat. O Simon, Simon,[b] [32]I have prayed that you will not lose your faith! Help your brothers be stronger when you come back to me."

[33]But Peter said to Jesus, "Lord, I am ready to go to jail with you. I will even die with you!"

[34]But Jesus said, "Peter, before the cockerel crows tomorrow morning, you will say you don't know me. You will say this three times."

Be Ready for Trouble

[35]Then Jesus said to the apostles, "Remember when I sent you out without money, a bag or sandals? Did you need anything?"

The apostles said, "No."

[36]Jesus said to them, "But now if you have money or a bag, carry that with you. If you don't have a sword, sell your coat and buy one. [37]The Scriptures say,

'He was considered a criminal.'

Isaiah 53:12

This Scripture must come true. It was written about me, and it is happening now."

[38]The followers said, "Look, Lord, here are two swords."

Jesus said to them, "That's enough."[c]

Jesus Prays Alone

(Matt. 26:36–46; Mark 14:32–42)

[39-40]Jesus left the city and went to the Mount of Olives. His followers went with him. (He went there often.) He said to his followers, "Pray for strength against temptation."

[41]Then Jesus went about 50 steps away from them. He knelt down and prayed, [42]"Father, if you are willing, please don't make me drink from this cup.[d] But do what you want, not what I want." [43]Then an angel from heaven came to help him. [44]Jesus was full of pain; he struggled hard in prayer. Sweat dripped from his face like drops of blood falling to the ground.[e] [45]When he finished praying, he went to his followers. He found them asleep, worn out from their grieving. [46]Jesus said to them, "Why are you sleeping? Get up and pray for strength against temptation."

Jesus Is Arrested

(Matt. 26:47–56; Mark 14:43–50; John 18:3–11)

[47]While Jesus was speaking, a crowd came up. It was led by Judas, one of the twelve apostles. He came over to Jesus to kiss him.

[48]But Jesus said to him, "Judas, are you using the kiss of friendship to hand over the Son of Man to his enemies?" [49]The followers of Jesus were

---

[a] **22:20** A few Greek copies do not have Jesus' words in the last part of verse 19 and all of verse 20.

[b] **22:31** *Simon* Simon's other name was Peter.

[c] **22:38** *"That's enough"* Or "Enough of that!" meaning "Don't talk any more about such things."

[d] **22:42** *cup* A symbol of suffering. Jesus used the idea of drinking from a cup to mean accepting the suffering he would face in the terrible events that were soon to come.

[e] **22:44** Some Greek copies do not have verses 43 and 44.

standing there too. They saw what was happening and said to Jesus, "Lord, should we use our swords?" 50And one of them did use his sword. He cut off the right ear of the servant of the high priest.

51Jesus said, "Stop!" Then he touched the servant's ear and healed him.

52Jesus spoke to the group that came to arrest him. They were the leading priests, the older Jewish leaders and the Jewish soldiers. He said to them, "Why did you come out here with swords and clubs? Do you think I am a criminal? 53I was with you every day in the Temple area. Why didn't you try to arrest me there? But this is your time—the time when darkness rules."

Peter Is Afraid to Say He Knows Jesus

(Matt. 26:57–58,69–75; Mark 14:53–54,66–72; John 18:12–18,25–27)

54They arrested Jesus and took him away to the house of the high priest. Peter followed Jesus but stayed back at a distance. 55The soldiers started a fire in the middle of the courtyard and sat together. Peter sat with them. 56A servant girl saw him sitting there. She could see because of the light from the fire. She looked closely at Peter's face. Then she said, "This one was also with that man."

57But Peter said this was not true. He said, "Woman, I don't know him." 58A short time later, someone else saw Peter and said, "You are also one of that group."

But Peter said, "Man, I am not!"

59About an hour later, another man said, "It's true. I'm sure this man was with him, because he is from Galilee."

60But Peter said, "Man, I don't know what you are talking about!"

Immediately, while he was still speaking, a cockerel crowed. 61Then the Lord turned and looked into Peter's eyes. And Peter remembered what the Lord had said, "Before the cockerel crows in the morning, you will say three times that you don't know me." 62Then Peter went outside and cried bitterly.

The Guards Treat Jesus Badly

(Matt. 26:67–68; Mark 14:65)

63The men guarding Jesus made fun of him and beat him. 64They covered his eyes so that he could not see them. Then they hit him and said, "Be a prophet and tell us who hit you!" 65And they shouted all kinds of insults at him.

Jesus Before the Jewish Leaders

(Matt. 26:59–66; Mark 14:55–64; John 18:19–24)

66The next morning, the older leaders of the people, the leading priests and the teachers of the law came together. They led Jesus away to their high council. 67They said, "If you are the Messiah, then tell us that you are."

Jesus said to them, "If I tell you I am the Messiah, you will not believe me. 68And if I ask you, you will not answer. 69But beginning now, the Son of Man will sit at the right side of God All-Powerful."

70They all said, "Then are you the Son of God?"

Jesus said to them, "You are right in saying that I am."

71They said, "Why do we need witnesses now? We all heard what he said!"

Governor Pilate Questions Jesus

(Matt. 27:1–2,11–14; Mark 15:1–5; John 18:28–38)

23 Then the whole group stood up and led Jesus away to Pilate. 2They began to accuse Jesus and said to Pilate, "We caught this man trying to change the thinking of our people. He says we should not pay taxes to Caesar. He calls himself the Messiah, a king."

3Pilate asked Jesus, "Are you the king of the Jews?"

Jesus answered, "Yes, what you say is true."

4Pilate said to the leading priests and the people, "I find nothing wrong with this man."

5But they kept on saying, "His teaching is causing trouble all over Judea. He began in Galilee, and now he is here!"

Pilate Sends Jesus to Herod

6Pilate heard this and asked if Jesus was from Galilee. 7He learned that Jesus was under Herod's authority. Herod was in Jerusalem at that time, so Pilate sent Jesus to him.

8When Herod saw Jesus, he was very happy. He had heard all about him and had wanted to meet him for a long time. Herod wanted to see a miracle, so he was hoping that Jesus would do one. 9He asked him many questions, but Jesus said nothing. 10The leading priests and teachers of the law were standing there shouting things against Jesus. 11Then Herod and his soldiers laughed at him. They made fun of him by dressing him in clothes like kings wear. Then Herod sent him back to Pilate. 12In the past Pilate and Herod had always been enemies. But on that day they became friends.

Pilate Tries but Fails to Free Jesus

(Matt. 27:15–26; Mark 15:6–15; John 18:39 – 19:16)

13Pilate called all the people together with the leading priests and the Jewish leaders. 14He said to them, "You brought this man to me. You said he was trying to change the people. But I judged him before you all and have not found him guilty of the things you say he has done. [15]Herod didn't find him guilty either. He sent him back to us. Look, he has done nothing bad enough for the death penalty. [16]So, after I punish him a little, I will let him go free." [17a]

[18]But they all shouted, "Kill him! Let Barabbas go free!" [19](Barabbas was a man who was in jail for starting a riot in the city and for murder.)

[20]Pilate wanted to let Jesus go free. So again Pilate told them that he would let him go. [21]But they shouted again, "Kill him! Kill him on a cross!"

[22]A third time Pilate said to the people, "Why? What wrong has he done? He is not guilty. I can find no reason to kill him. So I will let him go free after I punish him a little."

[23]But the people continued to shout. They demanded that Jesus be killed on a cross. Their shouting got so loud that [24]Pilate decided to give them what they wanted. [25]They wanted Barabbas to go free—the one who was in jail for starting a riot and for murder. Pilate let Barabbas go free. And he handed Jesus over to be killed. This is what the people wanted.

Jesus Is Nailed to a Cross

(Matt. 27:32–44; Mark 15:21–32; John 19:17–19)

[26]The soldiers led Jesus away. At that same time there was a man from Cyrene named Simon coming into the city from the fields. The soldiers forced him to carry Jesus' cross and walk behind him.

[27]A large crowd followed Jesus. Some of the women were sad and crying. They felt sorry for him. [28]But Jesus turned and said to them, "Women of Jerusalem, don't cry for me. Cry for yourselves and for your children too. [29]The time is coming when people will say, 'The women who cannot have babies are the ones God has blessed. It's really a blessing that they have no children to care for.' [30]Then the people will say to the mountains, 'Fall on us!' They will say to the hills, 'Cover us!'[b] [31]If this can happen to someone who is good, what will happen to those who are guilty?"[c]

[32]There were also two criminals led out with Jesus to be killed. [33]They were led to a place called "The Skull". There the soldiers nailed Jesus to the cross. They also nailed the criminals to crosses beside Jesus—one on the right and the other on the left.

[34]And Jesus was saying, "Father, forgive these people, because they do not know what they are doing."[d]

The soldiers threw dice to divide Jesus' clothes between them. [35]The people stood there watching everything. The Jewish leaders laughed at Jesus. They said, "If he is God's Chosen One, the Messiah, then let him save himself. He saved others, didn't he?"

[36]Even the soldiers laughed at Jesus and made fun of him. They came and offered him some sour wine. [37]They said, "If you are the king of the Jews, save yourself!" [38](At the top of the cross these words were written: "THIS IS THE KING OF THE JEWS.")

[39]One of the criminals hanging there began to shout insults at Jesus: "Aren't you the Messiah? Then save yourself, and save us too!"

[40]But the other criminal stopped him. He said, "You should fear God. All of us will die soon. [41]You and I are guilty. We deserve to die because we did wrong. But this man has done nothing wrong." [42]Then he said, "Jesus, remember me when you begin ruling as king!"

[43]Then Jesus said to him, "I tell you for sure, today you will be with me in paradise."

Jesus Dies

(Matt. 27:45–56; Mark 15:33–41; John 19:28–30)

[44]It was about noon, but it turned dark throughout the land until three o'clock in the afternoon, [45]because the sun stopped shining. The curtain in the Temple was torn into two pieces. [46]Jesus shouted, "Father, I put my life in your hands!"[e] After Jesus said this, he died.

[47]The army officer there saw what happened. He praised God, saying, "I know this man was a good man!"

[48]Many people had come out of the city to see all this. When they saw it, they felt very sorry and left. [49]The people who were close friends of Jesus were there. Also, there were some women who had followed Jesus from Galilee. They all stood far away from the cross and watched these things.

Jesus Is Buried

(Matt. 27:57–61; Mark 15:42–47; John 19:38–42)

[50-51]A man named Joseph was there from the Jewish town of Arimathea. He was a good man, who lived the way God wanted. He was waiting

---

a **23:17** A few Greek copies add verse 17: "Every year at the Passover festival, Pilate had to release one prisoner to the people."
b **23:30** Quote from Hos. 10:8.
c **23:31** *If this can happen . . . guilty* Literally, "If they do these things in the green tree, what will happen in the dry?"
d **23:34** *And Jesus . . . they are doing* Some early copies of Luke do not have these words.
e **23:46** *I put . . . hands!* Literally, "I put my spirit in your hands." Quote from Ps. 31:5.

for God's kingdom to come. Joseph was a member of the Jewish council. But he did not agree when the other Jewish leaders decided to kill Jesus. [52]He went to Pilate and asked for the body of Jesus. [53]He took the body down from the cross and wrapped it in cloth. Then he put it in a tomb that had been dug out of a wall of rock. This tomb had never been used before. [54]It was late on Preparation Day. When the sun went down, the Sabbath day would begin.

[55]The women who had come from Galilee with Jesus followed Joseph. They saw the tomb. Inside they saw where he put Jesus' body. [56]Then they left to prepare some sweet-smelling spices to put on the body.

On the Sabbath day they rested, as commanded in the Law of Moses.

News That Jesus Has Risen From Death

(Matt. 28:1–10; Mark 16:1–8; John 20:1–10)

24 Very early Sunday morning, the women came to the tomb where Jesus' body had been laid. They brought the sweet-smelling spices they had prepared. [2]They saw that the heavy stone that covered the entrance had been rolled away. [3]They went in, but they did not find the body of the Lord Jesus. [4]They did not understand this. While they were wondering about it, two men in shining clothes stood beside them. [5]The women were very frightened. They bowed down with their faces to the ground. The men said to them, "Why are you looking for a living person here? This is a place for dead people. [6]Jesus is not here. He has risen from death. Do you remember what he said in Galilee? [7]He said that the Son of Man must be handed over to the control of sinful men, be killed on a cross and rise from death on the third day." [8]Then the women remembered what Jesus had said.

[9]The women left the tomb and went to find the eleven apostles and the other followers. They told them everything that happened at the tomb. [10]These women were Mary Magdalene, Joanna, Mary the mother of James and some others. They told the apostles everything that had happened. [11]But the apostles did not believe what they said. It sounded like nonsense. [12]But Peter got up and ran to the tomb to see. He looked in, but he saw only the cloth that Jesus' body had been wrapped in. It was just lying there. Peter went away to be alone, wondering what had happened.[a]

On The Road to Emmaus

(Mark 16:12–13)

[13]That same day two of Jesus' followers[b] were going to a town named Emmaus. It is about 11 kilometres[c] from Jerusalem. [14]They were talking about everything that had happened. [15]While they were talking, discussing these things, Jesus himself came near and walked with them. [16](But the two followers were not allowed to recognize Jesus.) [17]He asked them, "What's this I hear you discussing with each other as you walk?"

They both stopped, their faces looking very sad. [18]And then one of them, named Cleopas, said, "You must be the only person in Jerusalem who doesn't know what has just happened there."

[19]Jesus said, "What are you talking about?"

They said, "It's about Jesus, the one from Nazareth. To God and to all the people he was a great prophet. He said and did many powerful things. [20]But our leaders and the leading priests handed him over to be judged and killed. They nailed him to a cross. [21]We were hoping that he would be the one to free Israel. But then all this happened.

"And now something else: it has been three days since he was killed, [22]but today some of our women told us an amazing thing. Early this morning they went to the tomb where the body of Jesus was laid. [23]But they did not find his body there. They came and told us they had seen some angels in a vision. The angels told them Jesus was alive! [24]So some of our group went to the tomb too. It was just as the women said. They saw the tomb, but they did not see Jesus."

[25]Then Jesus said to them, "You are foolish and slow to realize what is true. You should believe everything the prophets said. [26]The prophets said that the Messiah must suffer these things before he begins his time of glory." [27]Then he began to explain everything that had been written about himself in the Scriptures. He started with the books of Moses and then talked about what the prophets had said about him.

[28]They came near the town of Emmaus, and Jesus acted as if he did not plan to stop there. [29]But they wanted him to stay. They begged him, "Stay with us. It's almost night. There's hardly any daylight left." So he went in to stay with them.

[30]Joining them at the supper table, Jesus took some bread and gave thanks. He broke some off

---

[a] **24:12** A few Greek copies do not have this verse.
[b] **24:13** *two . . . followers* Literally, "two of them". It is clear from the story that they are both followers of Jesus, but only one of them is named (verse 18). He may be the same as the man named Clopas, described in John 19:25 as the husband of one of the women there named Mary. If so, the other follower in this story may be that Mary.
[c] **24:13** *11 kilometres* Literally, "60 *stadious*".

and gave it to them. 31Then both of them were allowed to recognize him. But when they saw who he was, he disappeared. 32They said to each other, "When he talked to us on the road, it felt like a fire burning in us. How exciting it was when he explained to us the true meaning of the Scriptures!"

33So right then they got up and went back to Jerusalem. There they found the eleven apostles meeting together with the other followers of Jesus. 34The group told them, "The Lord really has risen from death! He appeared to Simon."

35Then the two followers told them what had happened on the road. They talked about how they recognized Jesus when he shared the bread with them.

Jesus Appears to His Followers

(Matt. 28:16–20; Mark 16:14–18; John 20:19–23; Acts 1:6–8)

36While the two followers were telling these things to the others, Jesus himself came and stood among them. He said to them, "Peace be with you."

37This surprised the followers. They were afraid. They thought they were seeing a ghost. 38But Jesus said, "Why are you troubled? Why do you doubt what you see? 39Look at my hands and my feet. It's really me. Touch me. You can see that I have a living body; a ghost does not have a body like this."

40As soon as Jesus said this, he showed them his hands and his feet. 41The followers were amazed and very, very happy to see that Jesus was alive. They still could not believe what they saw. He said to them, "Do you have any food here?" 42They gave him a piece of cooked fish. 43While the followers watched, he took the fish and ate it.

44Jesus said to them, "Remember when I was with you before? I said that everything written about me must happen—everything written in the Law of Moses, the books of the prophets and the Psalms."

45Then Jesus helped the followers understand these Scriptures about him. 46Jesus said to them, "It is written that the Messiah would be killed and rise from death on the third day. 47–48You saw these things happen—you are witnesses. You must go and tell people that they must change and turn to God, which will bring them his forgiveness. You must start from Jerusalem and tell this message in my name to the people of all nations. 49Remember that I will send you the one my Father promised. Stay in the city until you are given that power from heaven."

Jesus Goes Back to Heaven

(Mark 16:19–20; Acts 1:9–11)

50Jesus led his followers out of Jerusalem almost to Bethany. He raised his hands and blessed his followers. 51While he was blessing them, he was separated from them and carried into heaven. 52They worshipped him and went back to Jerusalem very happy. 53They stayed at the Temple all the time, praising God.

Who
Tradition has it that this book is the work of the apostle John. However, he is not named in this Gospel, but referred to as the follower whom "Jesus loved very much". Some experts suggest that it was someone called John the Elder, who lived in Jerusalem. Whoever it was, he clearly knew Jesus intimately.

 When
Tradition says this was the last of the four Gospels to be written. It probably dates from between AD 70 and 100. It refers to Peter's death, which probably occurred in AD 65 or 66.

 What
John's Gospel is very different to the other three. There is more interpretation and more reflection than the other Gospels. John sees things from a different perspective. His big theme is who Jesus is. He calls Jesus "the Word", the power by which God created everything there is.

Mark, Matthew and Luke tell us of Jesus' authority to forgive sins; John tells us where this authority came from. In the other Gospels Jesus' claim to be God in human form is shown through his actions. In John it is right there at the start. "The Word became a man and lived among us. We saw his divine greatness – the greatness that belongs to the only Son of the Father," he writes (John 1:14).

In proof of his divine origins, Jesus performs seven miraculous signs in John, each of which tells us more about his nature and origins. There are also seven key speeches where Jesus begins by saying "I AM . . ." Indeed, in one crucial incident he says "before Abraham was born, I AM" (8:58). The phrase "I AM" would have been recognized by most Jews as a clear reference to the most sacred name of God.

John's Gospel is the work of someone who, prayerfully and over many years, asked God what it all meant. And what it meant was life: life in all its fullness, life in all its power, life everlasting.

QUICK TOUR ▶ JOHN

In the beginning 1:1–18	Blind man sees 9:1–41
The wedding 2:1–12	The gate and the good shepherd 10:1–42
Born again 3:1–21	The raising of Lazarus 11:1–44
At the well 4:1–42	Washing feet 13:1–20
The healing of the son 4:43–54	A new rule 13:31–35
Feeding 5,000 6:1–15	The way, the truth and the life 14:1–31
Water walking 6:16–21	The true vine 15:1–17
Bread of life 6:22–59	Jesus and Pilate 18:28 – 19:16
Light of the world 8:12–20	Crucifixion 19:17–42
"I AM" 8:21–59	Resurrection 20:1–29

"This is how God showed his great love for the world: he gave his only Son, so that everyone who believes in him would not be lost but have eternal life. God sent his Son into the world. He did not send him to judge the world guilty, but to save the world through him."

John 3:16–17

Christ Comes to the World

1 Before the world began, the Word[a] was there. The Word was with God, and the Word was God. [2]He was there with God in the beginning. [3]Everything was made through him, and nothing was made without him. [4]In him there was life, and that life was a light for the people of the world. [5]The light[b] shines in the darkness, and the darkness has not defeated[c] it.

[6]There was a man named John, who was sent by God. [7]He came to tell people about the light. Through him all people could hear about the light and believe. [8]John was not the light. But he came to tell people about the light. [9]The true light was coming into the world. This is the true light that gives light to all people.

[10]The Word was already in the world. The world was made through him, but the world did not know him. [11]He came to the world that was his own. And his own people did not accept him. [12]But some people did accept him. They believed in him, and he gave them the right to become children of God. [13]They became God's children, but not in the way babies are usually born. It was not because of any human desire or plan. They were born from God himself.

[14]The Word became a man and lived among us. We saw his divine greatness—the greatness that belongs to the only Son of the Father. The Word was full of grace and truth. [15]John told people about him. He said loudly, "This is the one I was talking about when I said, 'The one who is coming after me is greater than I am, because he was living before I was even born.'"

[16]Yes, the Word was full of grace and truth, and from him we all received one blessing after another.[d] [17]That is, the law was given to us through Moses, but grace and truth came through Jesus Christ. [18]No one has ever seen God. The only Son is the one who has shown us what God is like. He is himself God and is very close to the Father.[e]

John Tells About the Messiah

(Matt. 3:1–12; Mark 1:1–8; Luke 3:1–9,15–17)

[19]The Jewish leaders in Jerusalem sent some priests and Levites to John to ask him, "Who are you?" He told them the truth. [20]Without any hesitation he said openly and plainly, "I am not the Messiah."

[21]They asked him, "Then who are you? Are you Elijah?"

He answered, "No, I am not Elijah."

They asked, "Are you the Prophet?"[f]

He answered, "No, I am not the Prophet."

[22]Then they said, "Who are you? Tell us about yourself. Give us an answer to tell the people who sent us. What do you say about yourself?"

[23]John told them in the words of the prophet Isaiah:

"I am the voice of someone shouting in the desert:
    'Make a straight road ready for the Lord.'"
                                    Isaiah 40:3

[24]These Jews were sent from the Pharisees. [25]They said to John, "You say you are not the Messiah. You say you are not Elijah or the Prophet. Then why do you baptize people?"

[26]John answered, "I baptize people with water. But there is someone here with you that you don't know. [27]He is the one who is coming later. I am not good enough to be the slave who unties the strings on his sandals."

[28]These things all happened at Bethany on the other side of the Jordan River. This is where John was baptizing people.

Jesus, the Lamb of God

[29]The next day John saw Jesus coming towards him and said, "Look, the Lamb of God. He takes away the sins of the world! [30]This is the one I was talking about when I said, 'There is a man coming after me who is greater than I am, because he was living even before I was born.' [31]I did not know who he was. But I came baptizing people with water so that Israel could know that he is the Messiah."[g]

[32–34]Then John said this for everyone to hear: "I also did not know who the Messiah was. But the one who sent me to baptize with water told me, 'You will see the Spirit come down and rest on a man. He is the one who will baptize with the Holy Spirit.' I have seen this happen. I saw the Spirit come down from heaven like a dove and

---

[a] 1:1 **Word** The Greek word is "*logos*", meaning any kind of communication. It could be translated "message". Here, it describes Jesus Christ before he was sent to earth as a human being, which is the way God chose to tell the world about himself. Also in verses 10,14,16.

[b] 1:5 **light** Meaning Christ, the Word, who brought to the world understanding about God. Also in verse 7.

[c] 1:5 **defeated** Or "understood".

[d] 1:16 **one blessing after another** Literally, "grace in place of grace".

[e] 1:18 **The only Son . . . Father** Or more literally, "The only God, who is very close to the Father, has shown us what he is like." Some other Greek copies say, "The only Son is very close to the Father and has shown us what he is like."

[f] 1:21 **Prophet** They probably meant the prophet that God told Moses he would send. See Deut. 18:15–19. Also in verse 25.

[g] 1:31 **so that . . . the Messiah** Literally, "so that he might be revealed as the Messiah to Israel". See "MESSIAH" in the Word List.

A BIG INTRODUCTION

Whenever a VIP (very important person) steps up to a podium – maybe to receive an award or to make an important speech – it's good manners for the host to take the time to introduce them properly.

The host might give a brief account of the special guest's life and maybe list some of their major achievements. These few words would help everyone understand and properly appreciate what makes the special guest special.

DIG IN

READ John 1:1–18

- Take pen and paper and, as you read the passage, list everything John says about "the Word".
- How does the writer contrast "the Word" with John the Baptist (vv.6–8,15)?
- Who is "the Word"? If you haven't guessed yet, verse 17 confirms it.

The Gospel of John opens quite differently to the other three Gospels. Matthew starts with a family tree going back to Abraham. Mark opens with a quote from Isaiah and gets straight to the story of John the Baptizer preparing the way for Jesus' ministry. After a brief personal introduction, Luke jumps straight to John's birth.

But John the Gospel writer takes us back way, way further. He goes right back to before the world began. Even before the world existed, writes John, the Word existed with God and was himself God.

Why does he use this strange term "Word" to describe Jesus? Why not just use his name? Perhaps because in the Greek logos or "word" was used by some to mean "the reason why". John is making some big claims about Jesus. Above all, he wants to make it crystal clear that Jesus is not just sent by God (like John the Baptizer was, v.6) he actually is God. This fact should colour everything else we read in the fourth Gospel from this point onwards.

- What is so unique about Jesus that John points out in verse 14?

John says that even though Jesus was involved in the creation process, he chose to become part of creation himself, taking on flesh and blood and living alongside us – part of a family, part of a community. This is the story we're about to read.

DIG THROUGH

- What do verses 10–13 say about how people responded to Jesus? What happened to the ones who did believe in him? (This is closely connected to verse 14, because many people simply could not accept that God would become a human being to save his people.)
- Look over your notes from above. Keep them in your Bible so that as you read John you keep in mind this special introduction that the author wants you to remember at all times.

DIG DEEPER

- Check out Colossians 1:15–20 where Paul writes further about the mystery of Christ who existed with God and as God before the world was made.
- Nobody had ever seen the face of God and Judaism taught that just to see God would result in instant death. Moses asked to see him, but got to see only what you might call a "reflection" (Exodus 33 – 34). We read that Isaiah caught a glimpse from a distance (Isaiah 6). But in Jesus, writes John, the world got to see God "in the flesh" for the first time ever. How about that for a special guest!

rest on this man. So this is what I tell people: 'He is the Son of God.'"[a]

The First Followers of Jesus

[35]The next day John was there again and had two of his followers with him. [36]He saw Jesus walking by and said, "Look, the Lamb of God!"

[37]The two followers heard him say this, so they followed Jesus. [38]Jesus turned and saw the two men following him. He asked, "What do you want?"

They said, "Rabbi, where are you staying?" ("Rabbi" means "Teacher".)

[39]He answered, "Come with me and you will see." So the two men went with him. They saw the place where he was staying, and they stayed there with him that day. It was about four o'clock.

[40]These men followed Jesus after they had heard about him from John. One of them was Andrew, the brother of Simon Peter. [41]The first thing Andrew did was to go and find his brother Simon. Andrew said to him, "We have found the Messiah." ("Messiah" means "Christ".)

[42]Then Andrew brought Simon to Jesus. Jesus looked at him and said, "You are Simon, the son of John. You will be called Cephas." ("Cephas" means "Peter".[b])

[43]The next day Jesus decided to go to Galilee. He met Philip and said to him, "Follow me." [44]Philip was from the town of Bethsaida, the same as Andrew and Peter. [45]Philip found Nathanael and told him, "We have found the man that Moses wrote about in the law. The prophets wrote about him too. He is Jesus, the son of Joseph. He is from Nazareth."

[46]But Nathanael said to Philip, "Nazareth! Can anything good come from Nazareth?"

Philip answered, "Come and see."

[47]Jesus saw Nathanael coming towards him and said, "This man coming is a true Israelite, one you can trust."[c]

[48]Nathanael asked, "How do you know me?"

Jesus answered, "I saw you when you were under the fig tree, before Philip told you about me."

[49]Then Nathanael said, "Teacher, you are the Son of God. You are the King of Israel."

[50]Jesus said to him, "Do you believe this just because I said I saw you under the fig tree? You will see much greater things than that!" [51]Then he said, "Believe me when I say that you will all see heaven open. You will see 'angels of God going up and coming down'[d] on the Son of Man."

The Wedding at Cana

2 Two days later there was a wedding in the town of Cana in Galilee, and Jesus' mother was there. [2]Jesus and his followers were also invited. [3]At the wedding there was not enough wine, so Jesus' mother said to him, "They have no more wine."

[4]Jesus answered, "Dear woman, why are you telling me this? The right time for me has not yet come."

[5]His mother said to the servants, "Do what he tells you."

[6]There were six large stone water jars there that were used by the Jews in their washing ceremonies.[e] Each one held about 80 to 120 litres.[f]

[7]Jesus said to the servants, "Fill the jars with water." So they filled them to the top.

[8]Then he said to them, "Now take out some water and take it to the man in charge of the feast."

So they did what he said. [9]Then the man in charge tasted it, but the water had become wine. He did not know where the wine had come from, but the servants who brought the water knew. He called the bridegroom [10]and said to him, "People always serve the best wine first. Later, when the guests are drunk, they serve the cheaper wine. But you have saved the best wine until now."

[11]This was the first of all the miraculous signs Jesus did. He did it in the town of Cana in Galilee. By this he showed his divine greatness, and his followers believed in him.

[12]Then Jesus went to the town of Capernaum. His mother and brothers and his followers went with him. They all stayed there for a few days.

Jesus at the Temple

(Matt. 21:12–13; Mark 11:15–17; Luke 19:45–46)

[13]It was almost time for the Jewish Passover, so Jesus went to Jerusalem. [14]There in the Temple area he saw men selling cattle, sheep and doves. He saw others sitting at tables, exchanging and trading people's money. [15]Jesus made a whip with some pieces of rope and forced all the sheep and cattle out of the Temple area. He turned over the

---

[a] **1:32–34 He is the Son of God** Some very early Greek copies have "He is the chosen one of God."

[b] **1:42 Peter** The Greek name "Peter", like the Aramaic name "Cephas", means "rock".

[c] **1:47 one you can trust** Literally, "in whom is no deceit". In the Old Testament, Israel's other name, Jacob, is explained with words that mean "deceit" or "trickery", for which he was well known. See Gen. 27:35,36.

[d] **1:51** Quote from Gen. 28:12, which is part of the story about Jacob's dream of a ladder with angels going up and coming down on it between heaven and earth. See Gen. 28:10–17.

[e] **2:6 washing ceremonies** The Jews had religious rules about washing in special ways before eating, before worshipping in the Temple and at other special times. Also in 3:25.

[f] **2:6 80 to 120 litres** Literally, "2 or 3 metretas".

tables of the money traders and scattered their money. [16]Then he said to those who were selling pigeons, "Take these things out of here! Don't make my Father's house a place for buying and selling!"

[17]This caused his followers to remember these words written in the Scriptures:

"I am filled with anger when people dishonour your Temple!"

Psalm 69:9

[18]Some Jews said to Jesus, "Show us a miracle as a sign from God. Prove that you have the right to do these things."

[19]Jesus answered, "Destroy this temple and I will build it again in three days."

[20]They answered, "People worked 46 years to build this Temple! Do you really believe you can build it again in three days?"

[21]But the temple Jesus meant was his own body. [22]After he was raised from death, his followers remembered that he had said this. So they believed the Scriptures, and they believed what Jesus said.

[23]Jesus was in Jerusalem for the Passover festival. Many people believed in him because they saw the miraculous signs he did. [24]But Jesus did not trust them, because he knew how all people think. [25]He did not need anyone to tell him what a person was like. He already knew.

Jesus and Nicodemus

3 There was a man named Nicodemus, one of the Pharisees. He was an important Jewish leader. [2]One night he came to Jesus and said, "Teacher, we know that you are a teacher sent from God. No one can do these miraculous signs that you do unless they have God's help."

[3]Jesus answered, "I assure you, everyone must be born again.[a] Anyone who is not born again cannot be in God's kingdom."

[4]Nicodemus said, "How can a man who is already old be born again? Can he go back into his mother's womb and be born a second time?"

[5]Jesus answered, "Believe me when I say that everyone must be born from water and the Spirit. Anyone who is not born from water and the Spirit cannot enter God's kingdom. [6]The only life people get from their human parents is physical. But the new life that the Spirit gives a person is spiritual. [7]Don't be surprised that I told you, 'You must be born again.' [8]The wind blows wherever it wants to. You hear it, but you don't know where it is coming from or where it is going. It is the same with everyone who is born from the Spirit."

[9]Nicodemus asked, "How is all this possible?"

[10]Jesus said, "You are an important teacher of Israel, and you still don't understand these things? [11]The truth is, we talk about what we know. We tell about what we have seen. But you people don't accept what we tell you. [12]I have told you about things here on earth, but you do not believe me. So I'm sure you will not believe me if I tell you about heavenly things! [13]The only one who has ever gone up to heaven is the one who came down from heaven—the Son of Man.

[14]"Moses lifted up the snake in the desert.[b] It is the same with the Son of Man. He must be lifted up too. [15]Then everyone who believes in him can have eternal life."[c]

[16]This is how God showed his great love for the world: he gave his only Son, so that everyone who believes in him would not be lost but have eternal life. [17]God sent his Son into the world. He did not send him to judge the world guilty, but to save the world through him. [18]People who believe in God's Son are not judged guilty. But people who do not believe are already judged, because they have not believed in God's only Son. [19]They are judged by this fact: the light[d] has come into the world. But they did not want light. They wanted darkness, because they were doing evil things. [20]Everyone who does evil hates the light. They will not come to the light, because the light will show all the bad things they have done. [21]But anyone who follows the true way comes to the light. Then the light will show that whatever they have done was done through God.

Jesus and John the Baptizer

[22]After this, Jesus and his followers went into the area of Judea. There he stayed with his followers and baptized people. [23]John was also baptizing people in Aenon, a place near Salim with plenty of water. People were going there to be baptized. [24]This was before John was put in prison.

[25]Some of John's followers had an argument with another Jew about religious washing.[e] [26]Then they came to John and said, "Teacher, remember the man who was with you on the

---

[a] **3:3 born again** In this verse and in verse 7 this phrase could be translated "born from above".

[b] **3:14 Moses lifted . . . desert** When God's people were dying from snake bites, God told Moses to put a brass snake on a pole for them to look at and be healed. See Num. 21:4–9.

[c] **3:15** Some scholars think that Jesus' words to Nicodemus continue to verse 21.

[d] **3:19 light** This means Christ, the Word, who brought to the world understanding about God.

[e] **3:25 religious washing** The Jews had religious rules about washing in special ways before eating, before worshipping in the Temple and at other special times.

other side of the Jordan River? He is the one you were telling everyone about. He is also baptizing people, and many are going to him."

27John answered, "A person can receive only what God gives. 28You yourselves heard me say, 'I am not the Messiah. I am only the one God sent to prepare the way for him.' 29I am like the friend of the bridegroom at a wedding. The bride is for the bridegroom, not for the friend. The friend just waits for instructions from the bridegroom. And he is happy to do whatever the bridegroom wants. That's how I feel now. I could not be happier. 30He must become more and more important, and I must become less important.

The One Who Comes From Heaven

31"The one who comes from above is greater than all others. The one who is from the earth belongs to the earth. He talks about things that are on the earth. But the one who comes from heaven is greater than all others. 32He tells what he has seen and heard, but people don't accept what he says. 33Whoever accepts what he says has given proof that God speaks the truth. 34God sent him, and he tells people what God says. God gives him the Spirit fully. 35The Father loves the Son and has given him power over everything. 36Whoever believes in the Son has eternal life. But those who do not obey the Son will never have that life. They cannot get away from God's anger."

Jesus Talks to a Woman in Samaria

4 Jesus learned that the Pharisees had heard the report that he was making and baptizing more followers than John. 2(But really, Jesus himself did not baptize anyone; his followers baptized people for him.) 3So he left Judea and went back to Galilee. 4On the way to Galilee, he had to go through the country of Samaria.

5In Samaria Jesus came to the town called Sychar, which is near the field that Jacob gave to his son Joseph. 6Jacob's well was there. Jesus was tired from his long journey, so he was sitting beside the well. It was about noon. 7A Samaritan woman came to the well to get some water, and Jesus said to her, "Please give me a drink." 8This happened while his followers were in town buying some food.

9The woman answered, "I am surprised that you ask me for a drink! You are a Jew and I am a Samaritan woman!" (Jews have nothing to do with Samaritans.a)

10Jesus answered, "You don't know what God can give you. And you don't know who I am, the one who asked you for a drink. If you knew, you would have asked me, and I would have given you living water."

11The woman said, "Sir, where will you get that living water? The well is very deep, and you have nothing to get water with. 12Are you greater than our ancestor Jacob? He is the one who gave us this well. He drank from it himself, and his sons and all his animals drank from it too."

13Jesus answered, "Everyone who drinks this water will be thirsty again. 14But anyone who drinks the water I give will never be thirsty again. The water I give people will be like a spring flowing inside them. It will bring them eternal life."

15The woman said to Jesus, "Sir, give me this water. Then I will never be thirsty again and won't have to come back here to get more water."

16Jesus told her, "Go and get your husband and come back."

17The woman answered, "But I have no husband."

Jesus said to her, "You are right to say you have no husband. 18That's because, although you have had five husbands, the man you live with now is not your husband. That much was the truth."

19The woman said, "Sir, I can see that you are a prophet.b 20Our fathers worshipped on this mountain. But you Jews say that Jerusalem is the place where people must worship."

21Jesus said, "Believe me, woman! The time is coming when you will not have to be in Jerusalem or on this mountain to worship the Father. 22You Samaritans worship something you don't understand. We Jews understand what we worship, since salvation comes from the Jews. 23But the time is coming when the true worshippers will worship the Father in spirit and truth. In fact, that time is now here. And these are the kind of people the Father wants to be his worshippers. 24God is spirit. So the people who worship him must worship in spirit and truth."

25The woman said, "I know that the Messiah is coming. When he comes, he will explain everything to us." (Messiah is the one we call Christ.)

26Then Jesus said, "He is talking to you now—I am the Messiah."

27Just then Jesus' followers came back from town. They were surprised because they saw Jesus talking with a woman. But none of them asked, "What do you want?" or "Why are you talking with her?"

28Then the woman left her water jar and went back to town. She told the people there, 29"A man told me everything I have ever done. Come and see him. Maybe he is the Messiah." 30So the people left the town and went to see Jesus.

---

a 4:9 *Jews have nothing to do with Samaritans* Or "Jews don't use things that Samaritans have used."
b 4:19 *prophet* A prophet often knows things that are hidden to other people.

31While the woman was in town, Jesus' followers were begging him, "Teacher, eat something!"

32But Jesus answered, "I have food to eat that you know nothing about."

33So the followers asked each other, "Has someone already brought him some food?"

34Jesus said, "My food is to do what the one who sent me wants me to do. My food is to finish the work that he gave me to do. 35When you plant, you always say, 'Four more months to wait before we gather the grain.' But I tell you, open your eyes and look at the fields. They are ready for harvesting now. 36Even now, the people who harvest the crop are being paid. They are bringing in those who will have eternal life. So now the people who plant can be happy together with those who harvest. 37It is true when we say, 'One person plants, but another person harvests the crop.' 38I sent you to harvest a crop that you did not work for. Others did the work, and you get the profit from their work."

39Many of the Samaritans in that town believed in Jesus. They believed because of what the woman had told them about him. She had told them, "He told me everything I have ever done." 40The Samaritans went to Jesus. They begged him to stay with them. So he stayed there two days. 41Many more people became believers because of the things he said.

42The people said to the woman, "First we believed in Jesus because of what you told us. But now we believe because we have heard him ourselves. We know now that he really is the one who will save the world."

Jesus Heals an Official's Son

(Matt. 8:5–13; Luke 7:1–10)

43Two days later Jesus left and went to Galilee. 44Jesus had said before that a prophet is not respected in his own country. 45So when he arrived in Galilee, the people there welcomed him, but only because they had seen everything he had done at the Passover festival in Jerusalem.

46Jesus went to visit Cana in Galilee again. Cana is where he had changed the water into wine. One of the king's important officials lived in the town of Capernaum. This man's son was sick. 47The man heard that Jesus had come from Judea and was now in Galilee. So he went to Jesus and begged him to come to Capernaum and heal his son, who was almost dead. 48Jesus said to him, "You people must see miraculous signs and wonders before you will believe in me."

49The king's official said, "Sir, come before my little son dies."

50Jesus answered, "Go. Your son will live."

The man believed what Jesus told him and went home. 51On the way home, the man's servants came and met him. They said, "Your son is well."

52The man asked, "What time did my son begin to get well?"

They answered, "It was about one o'clock yesterday when the fever left him."

53The father knew that one o'clock was the same time that Jesus had said, "Your son will live." So the man and everyone in his house believed in Jesus.

54That was the second miraculous sign that Jesus did after coming from Judea to Galilee.

Jesus Heals a Man at a Pool

5 Later, Jesus went to Jerusalem for a special Jewish festival. 2In Jerusalem there is a pool with five covered porches. In Aramaic it is called Bethzatha.*a* This pool is near the Sheep Gate. 3Many sick people were lying on the porches beside the pool. Some of them were blind, some were lame and some were paralysed.*b 4c* 5One of the men lying there had been sick for 38 years. 6Jesus saw him lying there and knew that he had been sick for a very long time. So he asked him, "Do you want to be well?"

7The sick man answered, "Sir, there is no one to help me get into the water when it starts moving. I try to be the first one into the water. But when I try, someone else always goes in before I can."

8Then Jesus said, "Stand up! Pick up your mat and walk." 9Immediately the man was well. He picked up his mat and started walking.

---

a **5:2** *Bethzatha* Also called Bethsaida or Bethesda, a pool of water north of the Temple in Jerusalem.
b **5:3** At the end of verse 3, some Greek copies add "and they waited for the water to move".
c **5:4** A few later copies add verse 4: "Sometimes an angel of the Lord came down to the pool and shook the water. After this, the first person to go into the pool was healed from any sickness he had."

can we buy enough bread for all these people to eat?" [6]He asked Philip this question to test him. Jesus already knew what he planned to do.

[7]Philip answered, "We would all have to work a month to buy enough bread for each person here to have only a little piece!"

[8]Another follower there was Andrew, the brother of Simon Peter. Andrew said, [9]"Here is a boy with five loaves of barley bread and two little fish. But that is not enough for so many people."

[10]Jesus said, "Tell everyone to sit down." This was a place with a lot of grass, and about 5,000 men sat down there. [11]Jesus took the loaves of bread and gave thanks for them. Then he gave them to the people who were waiting to eat. He did the same with the fish. He gave them as much as they wanted.

[12]They all had plenty to eat. When they had finished, Jesus said to his followers, "Gather up the pieces of fish and bread that were not eaten. Don't waste anything." [13]So they gathered up the pieces that were left. The people had started eating with only five loaves of barley bread. But the followers filled twelve large baskets with the pieces of food that were left.

[14]The people saw this miraculous sign that Jesus did and said, "He must be the Prophet[a] who is coming into the world."

[15]Jesus knew that the people planned to come and get him and make him their king. So he left and went back into the hills alone.

Jesus Walks on Water

(Matt. 14:22–27; Mark 6:45–52)

[16]That evening Jesus' followers went down to the lake. [17]It was dark now, and Jesus had not yet come back to them. They got into a boat and started going across the lake to Capernaum. [18]The wind was blowing very hard, and the waves on the lake were becoming bigger. [19]They rowed the boat for about five or six kilometres.[b] Then they saw Jesus. He was walking on the water, coming towards the boat. They were afraid. [20]But he said to them, "Don't be afraid. It's me." [21]When he said this, they were glad to take him into the boat. And then the boat reached the shore at the place where they wanted to go.

The People Look for Jesus

[22]The next day came. Some people had stayed on the other side of the lake. They knew that Jesus had not gone with his followers in the boat. They knew that the followers had left in the boat

without him. And they knew it was the only boat that was there. [23]But then some boats from Tiberias came and landed near the place where the people had eaten the day before. This was where they had eaten the bread after the Lord gave thanks. [24]The people saw that Jesus and his followers were not there now. So they got into the boats and went to Capernaum to find Jesus.

Jesus, the Bread of Life

[25]The people found Jesus on the other side of the lake. They asked him, "Teacher, when did you get here?"

[26]He answered, "Why are you looking for me? Is it because you saw miraculous signs? The truth is, you are looking for me because you ate the bread and were satisfied. [27]But earthly food spoils and ruins. So don't work to get that kind of food. But work to get the food that stays good and gives you eternal life. The Son of Man will give you that food. He is the only one qualified by God the Father to give it to you."

[28]The people asked Jesus, "What does God want us to do?"

[29]Jesus answered, "The work God wants you to do is this: to believe in the one he sent."

[30]So the people asked, "What miraculous sign will you do for us? If we can see you do a miracle, then we will believe you. What will you do? [31]Our ancestors were given manna to eat in the desert. As the Scriptures say, 'He gave them bread from heaven to eat.'"[c]

[32]Jesus said, "I can assure you that Moses was not the one who gave your people bread from heaven. But my Father gives you the true bread from heaven. [33]God's bread is the one who comes down from heaven and gives life to the world."

[34]The people said, "Sir, from now on give us bread like that."

[35]Then Jesus said, "I am the bread that gives life. No one who comes to me will ever be hungry. No one who believes in me will ever be thirsty. [36]I told you before that you have seen me, and still you don't believe. [37]The Father gives me my people. Every one of them will come to me. I will always accept them. [38]I came down from heaven to do what God wants, not what I want. [39]I must not lose anyone God has given me. But I must raise them up on the last day. This is what the one who sent me wants me to do. [40]Everyone who sees the Son and believes in him has eternal life. I will raise them up on the last day. This is what my Father wants."

---

[a] **6:14** *Prophet* They probably meant the prophet that God told Moses he would send. See Deut. 18:15–19.
[b] **6:19** *five or six kilometres* Literally, "25 or 30 *stadia*".
[c] **6:31** Quote from Ps. 78:24.

⁴¹Some Jews began to complain about Jesus because he said, "I am the bread that comes down from heaven." ⁴²They said, "This is Jesus. We know his father and mother. He is only Joseph's son. How can he say, 'I came down from heaven'?"

⁴³But Jesus said, "Stop complaining to each other. ⁴⁴The Father is the one who sent me, and he is the one who brings people to me. I will raise them up on the last day. Anyone the Father does not bring to me cannot come to me. ⁴⁵It is written in the prophets: 'God will teach them all.'ᵃ People listen to the Father and learn from him. They are the ones who come to me. ⁴⁶I don't mean that there is anyone who has seen the Father. The only one who has ever seen the Father is the one who came from God.

⁴⁷"I can assure you that anyone who believes has eternal life. ⁴⁸I am the bread that gives life. ⁴⁹Your ancestors ate the manna God gave them in the desert, but it didn't keep them from dying. ⁵⁰Here is the bread that comes down from heaven. Whoever eats this bread will never die. ⁵¹I am the living bread that came down from heaven. Whoever eats this bread will live forever. This bread is my body. I will give my body so that the people in the world can have life."

⁵²Then the Jews began to argue among themselves. They said, "How can this man give us his body to eat?"

⁵³Jesus said, "Believe me when I say that you must eat the body of the Son of Man, and you must drink his blood. If you don't do this, you have no real life. ⁵⁴Those who eat my body and drink my blood have eternal life. I will raise them up on the last day. ⁵⁵My body is true food, and my blood is true drink. ⁵⁶Those who eat my body and drink my blood live in me, and I live in them.

⁵⁷"The Father sent me. He lives, and I live because of him. So everyone who eats my body will live because of me. ⁵⁸I am not like the bread that your ancestors ate. They ate that bread, but they still died. I am the bread that came down from heaven. Whoever eats this bread will live forever."

⁵⁹Jesus said all this while he was teaching in the synagogue in the town of Capernaum.

Many Followers Leave Jesus

⁶⁰When Jesus' followers heard this, many of them said, "This teaching is too hard. Who can accept it?"

⁶¹Jesus already knew that his followers were complaining about this. So he said, "Is this teaching a problem for you? ⁶²Then what would you think if you saw the Son of Man going up to where he came from? ⁶³It is the Spirit that gives life. The body is of no value for that. But the things I have told you are from the Spirit, so they give life. ⁶⁴But some of you don't believe." (Jesus knew the people who did not believe. He knew this from the beginning. And he knew the one who would hand him over to his enemies.) ⁶⁵Jesus said, "That is why I said, 'Anyone the Father does not help to come to me cannot come.'"

⁶⁶After Jesus had said these things, many of his followers left and stopped following him.

⁶⁷Jesus asked the twelve apostles, "Do you want to leave too?"

⁶⁸Simon Peter answered him, "Lord, where would we go? You have the words that give eternal life. ⁶⁹We believe in you. We know that you are the Holy One from God."

⁷⁰Then Jesus answered, "I chose all twelve of you. But one of you is a devil." ⁷¹He was talking about Judas, the son of Simon Iscariot. Judas was one of the twelve apostles, but later he would hand Jesus over to his enemies.

INSIGHT

If you like camping, you'd enjoy the Festival of Shelters, a Jewish holiday that is still celebrated today. For one week in the autumn, people live in shelters outside their homes as a reminder of God's faithfulness to his people during the wilderness years on the way to the promised land.

John 7:2

Jesus and His Brothers

7 After this, Jesus travelled around the country of Galilee. He did not want to travel in Judea, because the Jewish leaders there wanted to kill him. ²It was time for the Jewish Festival of Shelters. ³So his brothers said to him, "You should leave here and go to the festival in Judea. Then your followers there can see the miracles you do. ⁴If you want to be well known, you must not hide what you do. If you can do such amazing things, let the whole world see." ⁵Jesus' brothers said this because even they did not believe in him.

⁶Jesus said to them, "The right time for me has not yet come, but any time is right for you to go. ⁷The world cannot hate you. But the world hates me, because I tell the people in the world that they do evil things. ⁸So you go to the festival. I will not go now, because the right time for me

has not yet come." ⁹After Jesus said this, he stayed in Galilee.

¹⁰So his brothers left to go to the festival. After they left, Jesus went too, but he did not let people see him. ¹¹At the festival the Jewish leaders were looking for him. They said, "Where is that man?" ¹²There was a large group of people there. Many of them were talking secretly to each other about Jesus. Some people said, "He is a good man." But others said, "No, he fools the people." ¹³But no one was brave enough to talk about him openly. They were afraid of the Jewish leaders.

Jesus Teaches in Jerusalem

¹⁴When the festival was about half finished, Jesus went to the Temple area and began to teach. ¹⁵The Jewish leaders were amazed and said, "How did this man learn so much? He never had the kind of teaching we had!"

¹⁶Jesus answered, "What I teach is not my own. My teaching comes from the one who sent me. ¹⁷People who really want to do what God wants will know that my teaching comes from God. They will know that this teaching is not my own. ¹⁸If I taught my own ideas, I would just be trying to get honour for myself. But if I am trying to bring honour to the one who sent me, I can be trusted. Anyone doing that is not going to lie. ¹⁹Didn't Moses give you the law? But you don't obey that law. If you do, then why are you trying to kill me?"

²⁰The people answered, "A demon is making you crazy! We are not trying to kill you."

²¹Jesus said to them, "I did one miracle on a Sabbath day, and you were all surprised. ²²But you obey the law Moses gave you about circumcision—and sometimes you do it on a Sabbath day. (But really, Moses is not the one who gave you circumcision. It came from our ancestors who lived before Moses.) Yes, you often circumcise baby boys on a Sabbath day. ²³This shows that someone can be circumcised on a Sabbath day to obey the Law of Moses. So why are you angry with me for healing a person's whole body on the Sabbath day? ²⁴Stop judging by the way things look. Be fair and judge by what is really right."

People Wonder if Jesus Is the Messiah

²⁵Then some of the people who lived in Jerusalem said, "This is the man they are trying to kill. ²⁶But he is teaching where everyone can see and hear him. And no one is trying to stop him from teaching. Maybe the leaders have decided that he really is the Messiah. ²⁷But when the real Messiah comes, no one will know where he comes from. And we know where this man's home is."

²⁸So, as Jesus continued to teach in the Temple area, he said loudly, "Do you really know me and where I am from? I am here, but not by my own decision. I was sent by one who is very real. But you don't know him. ²⁹I know him because I am from him. He is the one who sent me."

³⁰When Jesus said this, the people tried to grab him. But no one was able even to touch him, because the right time for him had not yet come. ³¹But many of the people believed in Jesus. They said, "We are waiting for the Messiah to come. When he comes, will he do more miraculous signs than this man has done?"

INSIGHT

The chief priests and Pharisees sent some of the many Temple police to arrest Jesus. They were drawn from the thousands of Levites who, along with many other practical roles, were charged with maintaining order in the Temple precincts.

John 7:32

The Jewish Leaders Try to Arrest Jesus

³²The Pharisees heard what the people were saying about Jesus. So the leading priests and the Pharisees sent some Temple police to arrest him. ³³Then Jesus said, "I will be with you a little while longer. Then I will go back to the one who sent me. ³⁴You will look for me, but you will not find me. And you cannot come where I am."

³⁵These Jews said to each other, "Where will this man go that we cannot find him? Will he go to the Greek cities where our people live? Will he teach the Greek people there? ³⁶He says, 'You will look for me, but you will not find me.' He also says, 'You cannot come where I am.' What does this mean?"

Jesus Talks About the Holy Spirit

³⁷The last day of the festival came. It was the most important day. On that day Jesus stood up and said loudly, "Whoever is thirsty may come to me and drink. ³⁸If anyone believes in me, rivers of living water will flow out from their heart. That is what the Scriptures say." ³⁹Jesus was talking about the Spirit. The Spirit had not yet been given to people, because Jesus had not yet been raised to glory. But later, those who believed in Jesus would receive the Spirit.

The People Argue About Jesus

[40]When the people heard the things that Jesus said, some of them said, "This man really is the Prophet."[a]

[41]Other people said, "He is the Messiah."

And others said, "The Messiah will not come from Galilee. [42]The Scriptures say that the Messiah will come from the family of David. And they say that he will come from Bethlehem, the town where David lived." [43]So the people did not agree with each other about Jesus. [44]Some of the people wanted to arrest him. But no one tried to do it.

Some Jewish Leaders Refuse to Believe

[45]The Temple police went back to the leading priests and the Pharisees. The priests and the Pharisees asked, "Why didn't you bring Jesus?"

[46]The Temple police answered, "We have never heard anyone say such amazing things!"

[47]The Pharisees answered, "So he has fooled you too! [48]You don't see any of the leaders or any of us Pharisees believing in him, do you? [49]But those people out there know nothing about the law. They are under God's curse!"

[50]But Nicodemus was there in that group. He was the one who had gone to see Jesus before.[b] He said, [51]"Our law will not let us judge anyone without first hearing them and finding out what they have done."

[52]The Jewish leaders answered, "You must be from Galilee too! Study the Scriptures. You will find nothing about a prophet[c] coming from Galilee."

A Woman Caught in Adultery

[53]Then they all left and went home.

8 But Jesus went to the Mount of Olives. [2]Early in the morning he went back to the Temple area. The people all came to him, and he sat and taught them.

[3]The teachers of the law and the Pharisees brought a woman they had caught in bed with a man who was not her husband. They forced her to stand in front of the people. [4]They said to Jesus, "Teacher, this woman was caught in the act of adultery. [5]The Law of Moses commands us to stone to death any such woman. What do you say we should do?"

[6]They were saying this to trick Jesus. They wanted to catch him saying something wrong that they could use as a charge against him. But Jesus stooped down and started writing on the ground with his finger. [7]The Jewish leaders continued to ask him their question. So he stood up and said, "Anyone here who has never sinned should throw the first stone at her." [8]Then Jesus stooped down again and wrote on the ground.

[9]When they heard this, they began to leave one by one. The older men left first, and then the others. Jesus was left alone with the woman standing there in front of him. [10]He looked up again and said to her, "Where did they all go? Did no one judge you guilty?"

[11]She answered, "No one, sir."

Then Jesus said, "I don't judge you either. You can go now, but don't sin again."[d]

Jesus Is the Light of the World

[12]Later, Jesus talked to the people again. He said, "I am the light of the world. Whoever follows me will never live in darkness. They will have the light that gives life."

[13]But the Pharisees said to Jesus, "When you talk about yourself, you are the only one to say that these things are true. So we cannot accept what you say."

[14]Jesus answered, "Yes, I am saying these things about myself. But people can believe what I say, because I know where I came from. And I know where I am going. But you don't know where I came from or where I am going. [15]You judge me the way people judge other people. I don't judge anyone. [16]But if I judge, my judging is true, because when I judge I am not alone. The Father who sent me is with me. [17]Your own law says that when two witnesses say the same thing, you must accept what they say. [18]I am one of the witnesses who speaks about myself. And the Father who sent me is my other witness."

[19]The people asked, "Where is your father?"

Jesus answered, "You don't know me or my Father. But if you knew me, you would know my Father too." [20]Jesus said these things while he was teaching in the Temple area, near the place where the Temple offerings were collected. But no one arrested him, because the right time for him had not yet come.

Some Jews Don't Understand Jesus

[21]Again, Jesus said to the people, "I will leave you. You will look for me, but you will die without forgiveness for your sin. You cannot come where I am going."

---

[a] **7:40** *Prophet* They probably meant the prophet that God told Moses he would send. See Deut. 18:15–19.

[b] **7:50** *He was the one . . . before* The story about Nicodemus going and talking to Jesus is in John 3:1–21.

[c] **7:52** *a prophet* Two early Greek copies have "the Prophet", which would mean the "prophet like Moses" mentioned in Deut. 18:15. In Acts 3:22 and 7:37 this is understood to be the Messiah, as in verse 40 above.

[d] **8:11** The oldest and best Greek copies do not have verses 7:53 – 8:11. Other copies have this section in different places.

[22]So the Jewish leaders asked themselves, "Will he kill himself? Is that why he said, 'You cannot come where I am going'?"

[23]But Jesus said to them, "You people are from here below, but I am from above. You belong to this world, but I don't belong to this world. [24]I told you that you would die without forgiveness for your sins. Yes, if you don't believe that I AM,[a] you will die without forgiveness for your sins."

[25]They asked, "Then who are you?"

Jesus answered, "I am what I have told you from the beginning. [26]I have much more I could say to judge you. But I tell people only what I have heard from the one who sent me, and he speaks the truth."

[27]They did not understand who he was talking about. He was telling them about the Father. [28]So he said to them, "You will lift up[b] the Son of Man. Then you will know that I AM. You will know that whatever I do is not by my own authority. You will know that I say only what the Father has taught me. [29]The one who sent me is with me. I always do what pleases him. So he has not left me alone." [30]While he was saying these things, many people believed in him.

Jesus Talks About Freedom From Sin

[31]So Jesus said to the Jews who believed in him, "If you continue to accept and obey my teaching, you are really my followers. [32]You will know the truth, and the truth will make you free."

[33]They answered, "We are Abraham's descendants. And we have never been slaves. So why do you say that we will be free?"

[34]Jesus said, "The truth is, everyone living a sinful life is a slave—a slave to sin. [35]A slave does not stay with a family forever. But a son belongs to the family forever. [36]So if the Son makes you free, you are really free. [37]I know you are Abraham's descendants. But you want to kill me, because you don't want to accept my teaching. [38]I am telling you what my Father has shown me. But you do what your father has told you."

[39]They said, "Our father is Abraham."

Jesus said, "If you were really Abraham's descendants, you would do what Abraham did. [40]I am someone who has told you the truth I heard from God. But you are trying to kill me. Abraham did nothing like that. [41]So you are doing what your own father did."

But they said, "We are not like children who never knew who their father was. God is our Father. He is the only Father we have."

[42]Jesus said to them, "If God were really your Father, you would love me. I came from God, and now I am here. I did not come by my own authority. God sent me. [43]You don't understand the things I say, because you cannot accept my teaching. [44]Your father is the devil. You belong to him. You want to do what he wants. He was a murderer from the beginning. He was always against the truth. There is no truth in him. He is like the lies he tells. Yes, the devil is a liar. He is the father of lies.

[45]"I am telling you the truth, and that is why you don't believe me. [46]Can any of you prove that I am guilty of sin? If I tell the truth, why don't you believe me? [47]Whoever belongs to God accepts what he says. But you don't accept what God says, because you don't belong to God."

Jesus Talks About Himself and Abraham

[48]The Jews there answered, "We say you are a Samaritan. We say a demon is making you crazy! Are we not right when we say this?"

[49]Jesus answered, "I have no demon in me. I give honour to my Father, but you give no honour to me. [50]I am not trying to get honour for myself. There is one who wants this honour for me. He is the judge. [51]I promise you, whoever continues to obey my teaching will never die."

[52]The Jews said to Jesus, "Now we know that you have a demon in you! Even Abraham and the prophets died. But you say, 'Whoever obeys my teaching will never die.' [53]Do you think you are greater than our father Abraham? He died, and so did the prophets. Who do you think you are?"

[54]Jesus answered, "If I give honour to myself, that honour is worth nothing. The one who gives me honour is my Father. And you say that he is your God. [55]But you don't really know him. I know him. If I said I did not know him, I would be a liar like you. But I do know him, and I obey what he says. [56]Your father Abraham was very happy that he would see the day when I came. He saw that day and was happy."

[57]The Jews said to Jesus, "What? How can you say you have seen Abraham? You are not even 50 years old!"

[58]Jesus answered, "The fact is, before Abraham was born, I AM." [59]When he said this, they picked up stones to throw at him. But Jesus hid, and then he left the Temple area.

---

[a] **8:24 *I AM*** This is like the name of God used in the Old Testament. See Exod. 3:14. However, it can also mean "I am he", meaning "I am the Messiah". Also in verses 28,58.

[b] **8:28 *lift up*** Meaning to be nailed to a cross and "lifted up" on it to die. It may also have a second meaning: to be "lifted up" from death to heaven.

Jesus Heals a Man Born Blind

9 While Jesus was walking, he saw a man who had been blind since the time he was born. [2]Jesus' followers asked him, "Teacher, why was this man born blind? Whose sin made it happen? Was it his own sin or that of his parents?"

[3]Jesus answered, "It was not any sin of this man or his parents that caused him to be blind. He was born blind so that he could be used to show what great things God can do. [4]While it is daytime, we must continue doing the work of the one who sent me. The night is coming, and no one can work at night. [5]While I am in the world, I am the light of the world."

[6]After Jesus said this, he spat on the dirt, made some mud and put it on the man's eyes. [7]Jesus told him, "Go and wash in Siloam Pool." (Siloam means "Sent".) So the man went to the pool, washed and came back. He was now able to see.

[8]His neighbours and some others who had seen him begging said, "Look! Is this the same man who always sits and begs?"

[9]Some people said, "Yes! He is the one." But others said, "No, he can't be the same man. He only looks like him."

So the man himself said, "I am that same man."

[10]They asked, "What happened? How did you get your sight?"

[11]He answered, "The man they call Jesus made some mud and put it on my eyes. Then he told me to go to Siloam and wash. So I went there and washed. And then I could see."

[12]They asked him, "Where is this man?"

He answered, "I don't know."

Some Pharisees Have Questions

[13]Then the people brought the man to the Pharisees. [14]The day Jesus had made mud and healed the man's eyes was a Sabbath day. [15]So the Pharisees asked the man, "How did you get your sight?"

He answered, "He put mud on my eyes. I washed, and now I can see."

[16]Some of the Pharisees said, "That man does not obey the law about the Sabbath day. So he is not from God."

Others said, "But someone who is a sinner cannot do these miraculous signs." So they could not agree with each other.

[17]They asked the man again, "Since it was your eyes he healed, what do you say about him?"

He answered, "He is a prophet."

[18]The Jewish leaders still did not believe that this really happened to the man—that he was blind and was now healed. But later they sent for his parents. [19]They asked them, "Is this your son? You say he was born blind. So how can he see?"

[20]His parents answered, "We know that this man is our son. And we know that he was born blind. [21]But we don't know why he can see now. We don't know who healed his eyes. Ask him. He is old enough to answer for himself." [22]They said this because they were afraid of the Jewish leaders. The leaders had already decided that they would punish anyone who said Jesus was the Messiah. They would stop them from coming to the synagogue. [23]That is why his parents said, "He is old enough. Ask him."

[24]So the Jewish leaders called the man who had been blind. They told him to come in again. They said, "You should honour God and tell us the truth. We know that this man is a sinner."

[25]The man answered, "I don't know if he is a sinner. But I do know this: I was blind, and now I can see."

[26]They asked, "What did he do to you? How did he heal your eyes?"

[27]He answered, "I have already told you that. But you would not listen to me. Why do you want to hear it again? Do you want to be his followers too?"

[28]At this they shouted insults at him and said, "You are his follower, not us! We are followers of Moses. [29]We know that God spoke to Moses. But we don't even know where this man comes from!"

[30]The man answered, "This is really strange! You don't know where he comes from, but he healed my eyes. [31]We all know that God does not listen to sinners, but he will listen to anyone who worships and obeys him. [32]This is the first time we have ever heard of anyone healing the eyes of someone born blind. [33]So he must be from God. If he were not from God, he could not do anything like this."

[34]The Jewish leaders answered, "You were born full of sin! Are you trying to teach us?" And they told the man to get out of the synagogue and to stay out.

Spiritual Blindness

[35]When Jesus heard that they had forced the man to leave, he found him and asked him, "Do you believe in the Son of Man?"

[36]The man said, "Tell me who he is, sir, so I can believe in him."

[37]Jesus said to him, "You have already seen him. The Son of Man is the one talking with you now."

[38]The man answered, "Yes, I believe, Lord!" Then he bowed and worshipped Jesus.

[39]Jesus said, "I came into this world so that the world could be judged. I came so that people who are blind[a] could see. And I came so that people who think they see would become blind."

---

[a] **9:39** *people who are blind* Jesus is talking about people who are spiritually blind (without understanding), not physically blind.

[40]Some of the Pharisees were near Jesus. They heard him say this. They asked, "What? Are you saying that we are blind too?"

[41]Jesus said, "If you were really blind, you would not be guilty of sin. But you say that you see, so you are still guilty."

INSIGHT

A sheepfold was an area surrounded by a rough stone wall, where one or more families kept their sheep. There was no proper door, so the shepherd or a hired "gatekeeper" guarded the entrance when the sheep were inside the fold at night. Jesus says that he is the gate, protecting us from those who would harm us and opening the way to God.

John 10:1–18

The Shepherd and His Sheep

10 Jesus said, "It is certainly true that when a man enters the sheep pen, he should use the gate. If he climbs in some other way, he is a robber. He is trying to steal the sheep. [2]But the man who takes care of the sheep enters through the gate. He is the shepherd. [3]The man who guards the gate opens the gate for the shepherd. And the sheep listen to the voice of the shepherd. He calls his own sheep by name and leads them out. [4]When he has all his own sheep together, he walks ahead of them. The sheep follow him, because they know his voice. [5]But sheep will never follow someone they don't know. They will run away, because they don't know that person's voice."

[6]Jesus told the people this story, but they did not understand what it meant.

Jesus Is the Good Shepherd

[7]So Jesus said again, "I assure you, I am the gate for the sheep. [8]All those who came before me were thieves and robbers. The sheep did not listen to them. [9]I am the gate. Whoever enters through me will be saved. They will be able to come in and go out. They will find everything they need. [10]A thief comes to steal, kill and destroy. But I came to give life—life that is more than you can imagine now.

[11]"I am the good shepherd, and the good shepherd gives his life for the sheep. [12]The worker who is paid to keep the sheep is different from the shepherd. The paid worker does not own the sheep. So when he sees a wolf coming, he runs away and leaves the sheep alone. Then the wolf attacks the sheep and scatters them. [13]The man runs away because he is only a paid worker. He does not really care for the sheep.

[14-15]"I am the shepherd who cares for the sheep. I know my sheep just as the Father knows me. And my sheep know me just as I know the Father. I give my life for these sheep. [16]I have other sheep too. They are not in this flock here. I must lead them also. They will listen to my voice. In the future there will be one flock and one shepherd.[a] [17]The Father loves me because I give my life. I give my life so that I can get it back again. [18]No one takes my life away from me. I give my own life freely. I have the right to give my life, and I have the right to get it back again. This is what the Father told me."

[19]Again the Jews were divided over what Jesus was saying. [20]Many of them said, "A demon has come into him and made him crazy. Why listen to him?"

[21]But others said, "These aren't the words of someone controlled by a demon. A demon cannot heal the eyes of a blind man."

The Jewish Leaders Against Jesus

[22]It was winter, and the time came for the Festival of Dedication[b] at Jerusalem. [23]Jesus was in the Temple area at Solomon's Porch. [24]The Jewish leaders gathered around him. They said, "How long will you make us wonder about you? If you are the Messiah, then tell us clearly."

[25]Jesus answered, "I have told you already, but you did not believe. I do miracles in my Father's name. These miracles show who I am. [26]But you do not believe, because you are not my sheep. [27]My sheep listen to my voice. I know them, and they follow me. [28]I give my sheep eternal life. They will never die. And while they are under my care, no one can take them from me. [29]The power my Father has given me is the greatest of all powers.[c] No one can take anything from the Father. [30]And I am the same as the Father."

[31]Again the Jews there picked up stones to kill Jesus. [32]But he said to them, "The many wonderful things you have seen me do are from

---

[a] **10:16 I have other sheep . . . shepherd** Jesus means he has followers who are not Jews. See John 11:52.

[b] **10:22 Festival of Dedication** Hanukkah, or "Festival of Lights", a special week in December celebrating the time in 165 BC when the Jerusalem Temple was made pure and ready again for Jewish worship. Before then it had been under the control of a foreign (Greek) army and used for pagan worship.

[c] **10:29 The power . . . powers** Literally, "What my Father has given me is greater than all." There are many variations in the early Greek copies. Some later copies have "My Father, who has given [them] to me, is greater than all."

the Father. Which of these good things are you killing me for?"

[33]They answered, "We are not killing you for any good thing you did. But you say things that insult God. You are only a man, but you say you are the same as God! That is why we are trying to kill you!"

[34]Jesus answered, "It is written in your law that God said, 'I said you are gods.'[a] [35]This Scripture called those people gods—the people who received God's message. And Scripture is always true. [36]So why do you accuse me of insulting God for saying, 'I am God's Son'? I am the one God chose and sent into the world. [37]If I don't do what my Father does, then don't believe what I say. [38]But if I do what my Father does, you should believe in what I do. You might not believe in me, but you should believe in the things I do. Then you will know and understand that the Father is in me and I am in the Father."

[39]They tried again to arrest Jesus, but he escaped from them.

[40]Then he went back across the Jordan River to the place where John began his work of baptizing people. Jesus stayed there, [41]and many people came to him. They said, "John never did any miraculous signs, but everything John said about this man is true." [42]And many people there believed in Jesus.

The Death of Lazarus

11 There was a man named Lazarus who was sick. He lived in the town of Bethany, where Mary and her sister Martha lived. [2](Mary is the same woman who put perfume on the Lord and wiped his feet with her hair.) Mary's brother was Lazarus, the man who was now sick. [3]So Mary and Martha sent someone to tell Jesus, "Lord, your dear friend Lazarus is sick."

[4]When Jesus heard this he said, "The end of this sickness will not be death. No, this sickness is for the glory of God. This has happened to bring glory to the Son of God." [5]Jesus loved Martha and her sister and Lazarus. [6]So when he heard that Lazarus was sick, he stayed where he was for two more days [7]and then said to his followers, "We should go back to Judea."

[8]They answered, "But Teacher, those Jews there tried to stone you to death. That was only a short time ago. Now you want to go back there?"

[9]Jesus answered, "We have only twelve hours of light in the day, don't you agree? If you walk in the day, you will not stumble and fall because you have the light of this world.[b] [10]But if you wait until night, you will stumble because you are walking without light."

[11]Then Jesus said, "Our friend Lazarus is now sleeping, but I am going there to wake him."

[12]The followers answered, "But, Lord, if he can sleep, he will get well." [13]They thought Jesus meant that Lazarus was literally sleeping, but he really meant that Lazarus was dead.

[14]So then Jesus said plainly, "Lazarus is dead. [15]And I am glad I was not there. I am happy for you because now you will believe in me. We will go to him now."

[16]Then Thomas, the one called "Twin", said to the other followers, "We will go too. We will die there with Jesus."

INSIGHT

For Jews, burial usually followed soon after death because of the hot climate. After being wrapped in strips of cloth, Lazarus's body would have been buried in a tomb that was probably in a cave. A large piece of rock or stone would have been placed across the entrance to make it impassable.

John 11:17

Jesus in Bethany

[17]When Jesus came to Bethany, he heard that Lazarus had already been dead and in the tomb for four days. [18]Bethany was about three kilometres[c] from Jerusalem. [19]Many Jews had come to see Martha and Mary. They came to comfort them about their brother Lazarus.

[20]When Martha heard that Jesus was coming, she went out to greet him. But Mary stayed at home. [21]Martha said to Jesus, "Lord, if you had been here, my brother would not have died. [22]But I know that even now God will give you anything you ask."

[23]Jesus said, "Your brother will rise to live again."

[24]Martha answered, "I know that he will rise to live again at the time of the resurrection on the last day."

[25]Jesus said to her, "I am the resurrection. I am life. Everyone who believes in me will have life, even if they die. [26]And everyone who lives and

---

[a] **10:34** Quote from Ps. 82:6.
[b] **11:9** *the light of this world* This could simply refer to the sun, but see John 8:12, where Jesus says, "I am the light of the world." See also 9:4–5 and 12:35.
[c] **11:18** *three kilometres* Literally, "15 *stadia*".

FRIENDS IN NEED

Jesus loved being around friends and his friends loved being around him. Three people who were special to Jesus were Mary, Martha and Lazarus – two sisters and a brother – who we meet in Luke 10:38–42, later in John 12, and here.

DIG IN

READ John 11:1–57

- Why do Mary and Martha send for Jesus?
- Why does Jesus hang back?

Some days earlier, Lazarus had been taken sick and it looked as though it was going to be fatal. His sisters sent urgent word to Jesus – because they knew he was "Lord" (v.3) and had the power to heal him. Mary and Martha had effectively dialled 999 – and they were after an emergency response. But they didn't get one.

"Jesus loved Martha and her sister and Lazarus . . . so . . . he stayed" (vv.5–6). There's a massive lesson God wants us to learn here: God's timing is perfect. Though it can be hard to understand why, sometimes he makes us wait – because he loves us.

There was a greater purpose at stake here. Jesus was going to use these circumstances to reveal God's glory and prove something about himself – that he has the authority to raise people from death back to life.

- What does Martha think Jesus meant by "Your brother will rise to live again" (vv.23–24)?
- Verse 35 is the shortest verse in the Bible yet one of the most powerful. What does it tell you about Jesus?

Although she has not lost her confidence in Jesus (vv.21–22,27), Martha interprets Jesus' words as a promise about a future resurrection. She has no idea what's about to happen next.

Jesus, on the other hand, knows exactly what's coming. He knows how happy the family will be, how amazed the watching crowd will be at the miracle, and how powerfully the miracle will prove Jesus' power to raise the dead to life. And yet, it doesn't stop him feeling deeply for his friends. God shares their suffering, so deeply that he sheds tears.

DIG THROUGH

- Imagine how Mary and Martha must have felt after sending for Jesus, eagerly expecting his arrival and then watching their brother die before Jesus got there. Have you felt like that too – praying and trusting God to show up (or intervene) in the nick of time – and then he hasn't?
- Think about what Jesus has just demonstrated and look at the immediate effects in verse 45. Jesus used his friends' heartbreak and disappointment for a glorious purpose. In what ways does God use such moments in our lives for his greater glory?

DIG DEEPER

- Jesus' statement "I am the resurrection. I am the life" (v.25) is one of seven "I am" statements which John records Jesus saying during his life. Each was said in the context of a story or miracle proving who Jesus was. Look them all up, examining the stories and events which prompt them: "I am the bread that gives life" (John 6:35); "I am the light of the world" (John 8:12); "I am the gate for the sheep" (John 10:7); "I am the good shepherd" (John 10:11); "I am the way, the truth and the life" (John 14:6) and "I am the true vine" (John 15:1).
- The Old Testament tells of a powerful vision given to the prophet Ezekiel about the future resurrection of God's people. Read Ezekiel 37 and check out the Bible Bit about that chapter.

believes in me will never really die. Martha, do you believe this?"

27Martha answered, "Yes, Lord. I believe that you are the Messiah, the Son of God. You are the one who was coming to the world."

Jesus Cries

28After Martha said these things, she went back to her sister Mary. She spoke to Mary alone and said, "The Teacher is here. He is asking for you." 29When Mary heard this, she immediately left to go to where he was. 30He had not yet come into the village. He was still at the place where Martha had met him. 31The Jews who were in the house comforting Mary saw her get up and leave quickly. They thought she was going to the tomb to cry there. So they followed her. 32Mary went to the place where Jesus was. When she saw him, she bowed at his feet and said, "Lord, if you had been here, my brother would not have died."

33When Jesus saw Mary crying and the people with her crying too, he was very upset and deeply troubled. 34He asked, "Where did you put him?"

They said, "Lord, come and see."

35Jesus cried.

36And the Jews said, "Look! He loved Lazarus very much!"

37But some of them said, "Jesus healed the eyes of the blind man. Why didn't he help Lazarus and stop him from dying?"

Jesus Raises Lazarus From Death

38Again feeling very upset, Jesus came to the tomb. It was a cave with a large stone covering the entrance. 39He said, "Move the stone away."

Martha said, "But, Lord, it has been four days since Lazarus died. There will be a bad smell." Martha was the sister of the dead man.

40Then Jesus said to her, "Remember what I told you? I said that if you believed, you would see God's divine greatness."

41So they moved the stone away from the entrance. Then Jesus looked up and said, "Father, I thank you that you have heard me. 42I know that you always hear me. But I said these things because of the people here around me. I want them to believe that you sent me." 43After Jesus said this, he called in a loud voice, "Lazarus, come out!" 44The dead man came out. His hands and feet were wrapped with pieces of cloth. He also had a cloth wrapped around his face.

Jesus said to the people, "Take off the cloth and let him go."

The Jewish Leaders Plan to Kill Jesus

(Matt. 26:1–5; Mark 14:1–2; Luke 22:1–2)

45There were many Jews who had come to visit Mary. When they saw what Jesus did, many of them believed in him. 46But some of them went to the Pharisees and told them what Jesus had done. 47Then the leading priests and Pharisees called a meeting of the high council. They said, "What should we do? This man is doing many miraculous signs. 48If we let him continue doing these things, everyone will believe in him. Then the Romans will come and take control of our Temple and our nation."

49One of the men there was Caiaphas. He was the high priest that year. He said, "You people know nothing! 50It is better for one man to die for the people than for the whole nation to be destroyed. But you don't realize this."

51Caiaphas did not think of this himself. As that year's high priest, he was really prophesying that Jesus would die for the Jewish people. 52Yes, he would die for the Jewish people. But he would also die for God's other children scattered all over the world. He would die to bring them all together and make them one people.

53That day the Jewish leaders began planning to kill Jesus. 54So Jesus stopped travelling around openly among the Jews. He went away to a town called Ephraim in an area near the desert. He stayed there with his followers.

55It was almost time for the Jewish Passover festival and many people from the country went to Jerusalem. They went to do all that was necessary to make themselves pure for the festival. 56The people were looking for Jesus. They stood in the Temple area asking each other, "Is he coming to the festival? What do you think?" 57But the leading priests and the Pharisees had given a special order about Jesus. They said that anyone who knew where he was must tell them so that they could arrest him.

A Woman Honours Jesus

(Matt. 26:6–13; Mark 14:3–9)

12 Six days before the Passover festival began, Jesus went to Bethany. That is where Lazarus lived, the man Jesus raised from death. 2There they had a dinner for Jesus. Martha served the food, and Lazarus was one of the people eating with Jesus. 3Mary brought in half a litre*a* of expensive perfume made of pure nard. She poured the perfume on Jesus' feet. Then she wiped his feet with her hair. And the sweet smell from the perfume filled the whole house.

---

a **12:3 half a litre** Literally, "*litra*" (327 grammes).

[4]Judas Iscariot, one of Jesus' followers, was there—the one who would later hand Jesus over to his enemies. Judas said, [5]"That perfume was worth a full year's pay.[a] It should have been sold, and the money should have been given to the poor people." [6]But Judas did not really care about the poor. He said this because he was a thief. He was the one who kept the money bag for the group of followers, and he often stole money from it.

[7]Jesus answered, "Don't stop her. It was right for her to save this perfume for today—the day for me to be prepared for burial. [8]You will always have those who are poor with you.[b] But you will not always have me."

Some Priests Plan to Kill Lazarus

[9]Many of the Jews heard that Jesus was in Bethany, so they went there to see him. They also went there to see Lazarus, the one Jesus had raised from death. [10]So the leading priests made plans to kill Lazarus too. [11]They wanted to kill him because he was the reason many Jews were leaving them and believing in Jesus.

Jesus Enters Jerusalem Like a King

(Matt. 21:1–11; Mark 11:1–11; Luke 19:28–40)

[12]The next day the people in Jerusalem heard that Jesus was coming there. These were the crowds of people who had come to the Passover festival. [13]They took branches of palm trees and went out to meet Jesus. They shouted,

"Praise[c] Him!
　　Welcome! God bless the one who comes in
　　　the name of the Lord!

Psalm 118:25–26

"God bless the King of Israel!"

[14]Jesus found a donkey and rode on it, as the Scriptures say,

[15]"Do not be afraid, people of Zion![d]
　Look! Your king is coming.
　He is riding on a young donkey."

Zechariah 9:9

[16]The followers of Jesus did not understand at that time what was happening. But after he was raised to glory, they understood that this was written about him. Then they remembered that they had done these things for him.

[17]There were many people with Jesus when he raised Lazarus from death and told him to come out of the tomb. Now they were telling others about what Jesus had done. [18]That's why so many people went out to meet him—because they had heard about this miraculous sign. [19]So the Pharisees said to each other, "Look! Our plan is not working. The people are all following him!"

Jesus Talks About Life and Death

[20]There were some Greeks there too. These were some of the people who went to Jerusalem to worship at the Passover festival. [21]They went to Philip, who was from Bethsaida in Galilee. They said, "Sir, we want to meet Jesus." [22]Philip went and told Andrew. Then Andrew and Philip went and told Jesus.

[23]Jesus said to them, "The time has come for the Son of Man to receive his glory. [24]It is a fact that a grain of wheat must fall to the ground and die before it can grow and produce much more wheat. If it doesn't die, it will never be more than a single seed. [25]Those who love the life they have now will lose it. But whoever is willing to give up their life in this world will keep it. They will have eternal life. [26]Whoever wants to serve me must follow me. Yes, my servants must be with me everywhere I am. My Father will give honour to anyone who serves me.

Jesus Talks About His Death

[27]"Now I am very troubled. What should I say? Should I say, 'Father save me from this time of suffering'? No, I came to this time so that I could suffer. [28]Father, do what will bring you glory!"

Then a voice came from heaven, "I have already brought glory to myself. I will do it again."

[29]The people standing there heard the voice. They said it was thunder.

But others said, "An angel spoke to him!"

[30]Jesus said, "That voice was for you and not for me. [31]Now is the time for the world to be judged. Now the ruler of this world[e] will be thrown out. [32]I will be lifted up[f] from the earth. When that happens, I will draw all people to myself." [33]Jesus said this to show how he would die.

[34]The people said, "But our law says that the Messiah will live forever. So why do you say, 'The Son of Man must be lifted up'? Who is this 'Son of Man'?"

---

[a] **12:5 a full year's pay** Literally, "300 *denarii*". One Roman *denarius*, a silver coin, was the average pay for one day's work.
[b] **12:8 You will . . . with you** See Deut. 15:11.
[c] **12:13 Praise** Literally, "Hosanna", a Hebrew word used in praying to God for help. Here, it was probably a shout of celebration used in praising God or his Messiah.
[d] **12:15 people of Zion** Literally, "daughter Zion", meaning the city of Jerusalem. See "Zion" in the Word List.
[e] **12:31 ruler of this world** See "Satan" in the Word List.
[f] **12:32 lifted up** Meaning to be nailed to a cross and "lifted up" on it to die. It may also have a second meaning: to be "lifted up" from death to heaven. Also in verse 34.

[35]Then Jesus said, "The light[a] will be with you for only a short time more. So walk while you have the light. Then the darkness will not catch you. People who walk in the darkness don't know where they are going. [36]So put your trust in the light while you still have it. Then you will be children of light." When Jesus finished saying these things, he went away to a place where the people could not find him.

Some Jews Refuse to Believe in Jesus

[37]The people saw all these miraculous signs Jesus did, but they still did not believe in him. [38]This was to give full meaning to what Isaiah the prophet said:

"Lord, who believed what we told them?
    Who has seen the Lord's power?"

Isaiah 53:1

[39]This is why the people could not believe. Because Isaiah also said,

[40]"God made the people blind.
    He closed their minds.
He did this so that they would not see with
    their eyes
    and understand with their minds.
'If they understood,' he said, 'they might turn
    to me,
    and I would heal them.'"

Isaiah 6:10

[41]Isaiah said this because he saw Jesus' divine greatness. So he spoke about him.

[42]But many people believed in Jesus. Even many of the Jewish leaders believed in him, but they were afraid of the Pharisees, so they did not say openly that they believed. They were afraid they would be ordered to stay out of the synagogue. [43]They loved praise from people more than praise from God.

Jesus' Teaching Will Judge People

[44]Then Jesus said loudly, "Everyone who believes in me is really believing in the one who sent me. [45]Everyone who sees me is really seeing the one who sent me. [46]I came into this world as a light. I came so that everyone who believes in me will not stay in darkness.

[47]"I did not come into the world to judge people. I came to save the people in the world. So I am not the one who judges those who hear my teaching and do not obey. [48]But there is a judge for all those who refuse to believe in me and do not accept what I say. The message I have spoken will judge them on the last day. [49]That is because what I taught was not from myself. The Father who sent me told me what to say. Every word I speak is from him. [50]And I know that whatever he tells me to do will bring eternal life. So the things I say are exactly what the Father has told me to say."

Jesus Washes His Followers' Feet

13 It was almost time for the Jewish Passover festival. Jesus knew that the time had come for him to leave this world and go back to the Father. Jesus had always loved the people in the world who were his. Now was the time he showed them his love the most.

[2]Jesus and his followers were at the evening meal. The devil had already persuaded Judas Iscariot to hand Jesus over to his enemies. (Judas was the son of Simon.) [3]The Father had given Jesus power over everything. Jesus knew this. He also knew that he had come from God. And he knew that he was going back to God. [4]So while they were eating, Jesus stood up and took off his robe. He got a towel and wrapped it around his waist. [5]Then he poured water into a bowl and began to wash the followers' feet.[b] He dried their feet with the towel that was wrapped around his waist.

> ## INSIGHT
>
> *Washing people's feet was a task reserved for servants. People walked long distances on dusty roads in sandals, so normally the host would arrange for their feet to be washed upon arrival – not during the middle of a meal. But Jesus did this to illustrate for his disciples what God's love is like.*
>
> **John 13:3–16**

[6]He came to Simon Peter. But Peter said to him, "Lord, why would you wash my feet?"

[7]Jesus answered, "You don't know what I am doing now. But later you will understand."

[8]Peter said, "No! You will never wash my feet." Jesus answered, "If I don't wash your feet, you are not one of my people."

---

[a] **12:35** *light* This means Christ, as in John 1:5–9. Also, it is a symbol of goodness and truth, qualities associated with Christ and his kingdom.

[b] **13:5** *wash . . . feet* A social custom of the first century, because people wore open sandals on very dusty roads. It was a humble duty, usually done by a servant. Also in verses 6–14.

⁹Simon Peter said, "Lord, after you wash my feet, wash my hands and my head too!"

¹⁰Jesus said, "After a person has had a bath, his whole body is clean. He needs only to wash his feet. And you are clean, but not all of you." ¹¹Jesus knew who would hand him over to his enemies. That is why he said, "Not all of you are clean."

¹²When Jesus had finished washing their feet, he put on his clothes and went back to the table. He asked, "Do you understand what I have just done for you? ¹³You call me 'Teacher'. And you call me 'Lord'. And this is right, because that is what I am. ¹⁴I am your Lord and Teacher. But I washed your feet like a servant. So you also should wash each other's feet. ¹⁵I did this as an example for you. So you should serve each other just as I served you. ¹⁶Believe me, servants are not greater than their master. Those who are sent to do something are not greater than the one who sent them. ¹⁷If you know these things, great blessings will be yours if you do them.

¹⁸"I am not talking about all of you. I know the people I have chosen. But what the Scriptures say must happen: 'The man who shared my food has turned against me.'ᵃ ¹⁹I am telling you this now before it happens. Then when it happens, you will believe that I AM.ᵇ ²⁰I assure you, whoever accepts the person I send also accepts me. And whoever accepts me also accepts the one who sent me."

Who Will Turn Against Jesus?

(Matt. 26:20–25; Mark 14:17–21; Luke 22:21–23)

²¹After Jesus said these things, he felt very troubled. He said openly, "Believe me when I say that one of you will hand me over to my enemies."

²²His followers all looked at each other. They did not understand who Jesus was talking about. ²³One of the followers was next to Jesus and was leaning close to him. This was the one Jesus loved very much. ²⁴Simon Peter made signs to this follower to ask Jesus who he was talking about. ²⁵That follower leaned closer to Jesus and asked, "Lord, who is it?"

²⁶Jesus answered him, "I will dip this bread into the dish. The man I give it to is the one." So Jesus took a piece of bread, dipped it and gave it to Judas Iscariot, the son of Simon. ²⁷When Judas took the bread, Satan entered him. Jesus said to Judas, "What you will do—do it quickly!" ²⁸No one at the table understood why Jesus said this to Judas. ²⁹Since Judas was the one in charge of the money, some of them thought that Jesus meant for him to go and buy some things they needed for the feast. Or they thought that Jesus wanted him to go and give something to the poor.

³⁰Judas ate the bread Jesus gave him. Then he immediately went out. It was night.

Jesus Talks About His Death

³¹When Judas was gone, Jesus said, "Now is the time for the Son of Man to receive his glory. And God will receive glory through him. ³²If God receives glory through him, he will give glory to the Son through himself. And that will happen very soon."

³³Jesus said, "My children, I will be with you only a short time more. You will look for me, but I tell you now what I told the Jewish leaders: where I am going you cannot come.

³⁴"I give you a new command: love each other. You must love each other just as I loved you. ³⁵All people will know that you are my followers if you love each other."

Jesus Says Peter Will Deny Him

(Matt. 26:31–35; Mark 14:27–31; Luke 22:31–34)

³⁶Simon Peter asked Jesus, "Lord, where are you going?"

Jesus answered, "Where I am going you cannot follow now. But you will follow later."

³⁷Peter asked, "Lord, why can't I follow you now? I am ready to die for you!"

³⁸Jesus answered, "Will you really give your life for me? The truth is, before the cockerel crows, you will say three times that you don't know me."

Jesus Comforts His Followers

14 Jesus said, "Don't be troubled. Trust in God, and trust in me. ²There are many rooms in my Father's house. I would not tell you this if it were not true. I am going there to prepare a place for you. ³After I go and prepare a place for you, I will come back. Then I will take you with me, so that you can be where I am. ⁴You know the way to the place where I am going."

⁵Thomas said, "Lord, we don't know where you are going, so how can we know the way?"

⁶Jesus answered, "I am the way, the truth and the life. The only way to the Father is through me. ⁷If you really knew me, you would know my Father too. But now you know the Father. You have seen him."

⁸Philip said to him, "Lord, show us the Father. That is all we need."

ᵃ **13:18 has turned against me** Literally, "has lifted up his heel against me". Quote from Ps. 41:9.
ᵇ **13:19 I AM** This is like the name of God used in the Old Testament. See Exod. 3:14. However, it can also mean "I am he", meaning "I am the Messiah".

⁹Jesus answered, "Philip, I have been with you for a long time. So you should know me. Anyone who has seen me has seen the Father too. So why do you say, 'Show us the Father'? ¹⁰Don't you believe that I am in the Father and the Father is in me? The things I have told you don't come from me. The Father lives in me, and he is doing his own work. ¹¹Believe me when I say that I am in the Father and the Father is in me. Or believe because of the miracles I have done.

¹²"I can assure you that whoever believes in me will do the same things I have done. And they will do even greater things than I have done, because I am going to the Father. ¹³And if you ask for anything in my name, I will do it for you. Then the Father's glory will be shown through the Son. ¹⁴If you ask me for anything in my name, I will do it.

The Promise of the Holy Spirit

¹⁵"If you love me, you will do what I command. ¹⁶I will ask the Father, and he will give you another Helper[a] to be with you forever. ¹⁷The Helper is the Spirit of truth.[b] The people of the world cannot accept him, because they don't see him or know him. But you know him. He lives with you, and he will be in you.

¹⁸"I will not leave you all alone like orphans. I will come back to you. ¹⁹In a very short time the people in the world will not see me any more. But you will see me. You will live because I live. ²⁰On that day you will know that I am in the Father. You will know that you are in me and I am in you. ²¹Those who really love me are the ones who not only know my commands but also obey them. My Father will love such people, and I will love them. I will make myself known to them."

²²Then Judas (not Judas Iscariot) said, "Lord, how will you make yourself known to us, but not to the world?"

²³Jesus answered, "All who love me will obey my teaching. My Father will love them. My Father and I will come to them and live with them. ²⁴But anyone who does not love me does not obey my teaching. This teaching that you hear is not really mine. It is from my Father who sent me.

²⁵"I have told you all these things while I am with you. ²⁶But the Helper will teach you everything and cause you to remember all that I told you. This Helper is the Holy Spirit that the Father will send in my name.

²⁷"I leave you peace. It is my own peace I give you. I give you peace in a different way than the world does. So don't be troubled. Don't be afraid. ²⁸You heard me say to you, 'I am leaving, but I will come back to you.' If you loved me, you would be happy that I am going back to the Father, because the Father is greater than I am. ²⁹I have told you this now, before it happens. Then when it happens, you will believe.

³⁰"I will not talk with you much longer. The ruler of this world[c] is coming. He has no power over me. ³¹But the world must know that I love the Father. So I do exactly what the Father told me to do.

"Come now, let's go."

Jesus Is Like a Vine

15 Jesus said, "I am the true vine, and my Father is the gardener. ²He cuts off every branch[d] of mine that does not produce fruit.[e] He also trims every branch that produces fruit to prepare it to produce even more. ³You have already been prepared to produce more fruit by the teaching I have given you. ⁴Stay joined to me and I will stay joined to you. No branch can produce fruit alone. It must stay connected to the vine. It is the same with you. You cannot produce fruit alone. You must stay joined to me.

⁵"I am the vine, and you are the branches. If you stay joined to me, and I to you, you will produce plenty of fruit. But separated from me you won't be able to do anything. ⁶If you don't stay joined to me, you will be like a branch that has been thrown out and has dried up. All the dead branches like that are gathered up, thrown into the fire and burned. ⁷Stay joined together with me, and follow my teachings. If you do this, you can ask for anything you want, and it will be given to you. ⁸Show that you are my followers by producing much fruit. This will bring honour[f] to my Father.

⁹"I have loved you as the Father has loved me. Now continue in my love. ¹⁰I have obeyed my Father's commands, and he continues to love me. In the same way, if you obey my commands, I will continue to love you. ¹¹I have told you these things so that you can have the true happiness that I have. I want you to be completely happy. ¹²This is what I command you: love each other as I have loved you. ¹³The greatest love people can show is to die for their friends. ¹⁴You are my

---

[a] **14:16 Helper** Or "Comforter", the Holy Spirit (see "Holy Spirit" in the Word List). Also in verse 26.
[b] **14:17 Spirit of truth** The Holy Spirit (see "Holy Spirit" in the Word List). It was his work to help Jesus' followers understand God's truth. See John 16:13.
[c] **14:30 ruler of this world** See "Satan" in the Word List.
[d] **15:2 branch** The "branches" are Jesus' followers. See verse 5.
[e] **15:2 produce fruit** Meaning the way Jesus' followers must live to show they belong to him. See verses 7–10.
[f] **15:8 honour** Or "glory". See "Glory" in the Word List.

friends if you do what I tell you to do. ¹⁵I no longer call you servants, because servants don't know what their master is doing. But now I call you friends, because I have told you everything that my Father told me.

¹⁶"You did not choose me. I chose you. And I gave you this work: to go and produce fruit— fruit that will last. Then the Father will give you anything you ask for in my name. ¹⁷This is my command: love each other.

Jesus Warns His Followers

¹⁸"If the world hates you, remember that they hated me first. ¹⁹If you belonged to the world, the world would love you as it loves its own people. But I have chosen you to be different from those in the world. So you don't belong to the world, and that is why the world hates you.

²⁰"Remember the lesson I told you: servants are not greater than their master. If people treated me badly, they will treat you badly too. And if they obeyed my teaching, they will obey yours too. ²¹They will do to you whatever they did to me, because you belong to me. They don't know the one who sent me. ²²If I had not come and spoken to the people of the world, they would not be guilty of sin. But now I have spoken to them. So they have no excuse for their sin.

²³"Whoever hates me also hates my Father. ²⁴I did things among the people of the world that no one else has ever done. If I had not done those things, they would not be guilty of sin. But they have seen what I did, and still they hate me and my Father. ²⁵But this happened to make clear the full meaning of what is written in their law: 'They hated me for no reason.'ᵃ

²⁶"I will send you the Helperᵇ from the Father. The Helper is the Spirit of truthᶜ who comes from the Father. When he comes, he will tell people about me. ²⁷And you will tell people about me too, because you have been with me from the beginning.

16 "I have told you all this so that you won't lose your faith when you face troubles. ²People will tell you to leave their synagogues and never come back. In fact, the time will come when they will think that killing you would be doing a service for God. ³They will do this because they have not known the Father, and they have not known me. ⁴I have told you all this now to prepare you. So when the time comes for these things to happen, you will remember that I warned you.

The Work of the Holy Spirit

"I did not tell you these things at the beginning, because I was with you then. ⁵Now I am going back to the one who sent me. And none of you asks me, 'Where are you going?' ⁶But you are filled with sadness because I have told you all this. ⁷Let me assure you, it is better for you that I go away. I say this because when I go away I will send the Helper to you. But if I did not go, the Helper would not come.

⁸"When the Helper comes, he will show the people of the world how wrong they are about sin, about being right with God and about judgement. ⁹He will prove that they are guilty of sin, because they don't believe in me. ¹⁰He will show them how wrong they are about how to be right with God. The Helper is the one who will do this, because I am going to the Father. You will not see me then. ¹¹And he will show them how wrong their judgement is, because their leaderᵈ has already been condemned.

¹²"I have so much more to tell you, but it is too much for you to accept now. ¹³But when the Spirit of truth comes, he will lead you into all truth. He will not speak his own words. He will speak only what he hears and will tell you what will happen in the future. ¹⁴The Spirit of truth will bring glory to me by telling you what he receives from me. ¹⁵All that the Father has is mine. That is why I said that the Spirit will tell you what he receives from me.

Sadness Will Turn Into Happiness

¹⁶"After a short time you won't see me. Then after another short time you will see me again."

¹⁷Some of the followers said to each other, "What does he mean when he says, 'After a short time you won't see me. Then after another short time you will see me again'? And what does he mean when he says, 'Because I am going to the Father'?" ¹⁸They also asked, "What does he mean by 'a short time'? We don't understand what he is saying."

¹⁹Jesus saw that the followers wanted to ask him about this. So he said to them, "Are you asking each other what I meant when I said, 'After a short time you won't see me. Then after another short time you will see me again'? ²⁰The truth is, you will cry and be sad, but the world will be happy. You will be sad, but then your sadness will change to happiness.

²¹"When a woman gives birth to a baby, she has pain, because her time has come. But when her baby is born, she forgets the pain. She forgets

---

ᵃ **15:25** *'They hated me for no reason'* These words could be from Ps. 35:19 or Ps. 69:4.
ᵇ **15:26** *Helper* Or "Comforter". Also in 16:7–8.
ᶜ **15:26** *Spirit of truth* The Holy Spirit (see "HOLY SPIRIT" in the Word List). It was his work to help Jesus' followers understand God's truth. See John 16:13.
ᵈ **16:11** *their leader* Literally, "the ruler of this world", meaning Satan. See "SATAN" in the Word List.

HELP IS ON THE WAY

Jesus is heard talking about the Holy Spirit and the Helper throughout John's Gospel. And through Jesus' teaching and example the disciples gradually get to learn who he is and what he does. The promise of the Helper is fulfilled after Jesus' ascension – when they finally experience the Holy Spirit for themselves and the Spirit fills the believers (Acts 2).

In this passage Jesus explains more about the Holy Spirit and what they should expect – very soon.

DIG IN

READ John 16:4–15

- "I am going back to the one who sent me" (v.5). What does Jesus mean?
- Why are the disciples filled with sadness about this?

"We're moving on" are such sad words to hear when a close friend or a teacher you trust breaks the news that soon they'll be leaving. You can't help but feel abandoned. Imagine, then, when the twelve disciples first realized that Jesus was soon to leave them. Jesus is approaching the end of his life on earth and his time with his closest friends.

But this was all God's plan. In the end this would be better for everyone – for the whole world. And the disciples' personal despair would turn into great joy.

READ John 16:16–24

- Who is the "Helper" and what is his job?

Jesus calls the Holy Spirit "the Helper" here because we need help! People who don't yet believe in Jesus need help from God to understand how wrong they are (v.8). It's sinful not to believe in Jesus (v.9) – he's God's Son, completely good, far better than us (v.10). So if our opinion is that he's bad, or irrelevant, then we're seriously wrong (v.11). But everyone needs the Spirit's help to see that.

We also need help to understand God's word. You've probably noticed by now that Jesus' teaching is not always easy to understand. Even seemingly simple lessons can sometimes carry a deeper meaning than what we see at first glance. The Spirit helped the disciples, and helps us to grasp the full meaning of Jesus' words and apply them to our world (vv.12–15).

DIG THROUGH

- Consider how remarkable Jesus' words are in verse 7. It is better, he says, for us to be alive now – in the day of the Holy Spirit – than to have been alive in Jesus time. On earth, Jesus could only be in one place at one time. Now, the blessing of God is available to the whole world all of the time.
- Help is available now! The Holy Spirit is with us and, if we believe the words of Jesus, that means we have access to all the promises in verses 8–11 and 12–15. Think carefully about what that means for you and others today and ask him for his help. Think of some non-Christians you know. Pray that the Spirit would help them to see that it's wrong to reject Jesus. And pray that he would help you to understand Jesus' words and to live by them.

DIG DEEPER

- Read the first two chapters of Acts to find out how the Holy Spirit fell upon the believers for the first time. Notice particularly how Peter talks about the Holy Spirit in his preaching in Acts 2:33–41, confirming and fulfilling what Jesus is saying here in John 16.

because she is so happy that a child has been born into the world. ²²It is the same with you. Now you are sad, but I will see you again, and you will be happy. You will have a joy that no one can take away. ²³In that day you will not have to ask me about anything. And I assure you, my Father will give you anything you ask him for in my name. ²⁴You have never asked for anything in this way before. But ask in my name, and you will receive. And you will have the fullest joy possible.

Victory Over the World

²⁵"I have told you these things, using words that hide the meaning. But the time will come when I will not use words like that to tell you things. I will speak to you in plain words about the Father. ²⁶Then you will be able to ask the Father for things in my name. I am not saying that I will have to ask the Father for you. ²⁷The Father himself loves you because you have loved me. And he loves you because you have believed that I came from God. ²⁸I came from the Father into the world. Now I am leaving the world and going back to the Father."

²⁹Then his followers said, "You are already speaking plainly to us. You are not using words that hide the meaning. ³⁰We can see now that you know all things. You answer our questions even before we ask them. This makes us believe that you came from God."

³¹Jesus said, "So now you believe? ³²Listen to me. A time is coming when you will be scattered, each to his own home. In fact, that time is already here. You will leave me, and I will be alone. But I am never really alone, because the Father is with me.

³³"I have told you these things so that you can have peace in me. In this world you will have troubles. But be brave! I have defeated the world!"

Jesus Prays for Himself and His Followers

17 After Jesus said these things, he looked towards heaven and prayed, "Father, the time has come. Give glory to your Son so that the Son can give glory to you. ²You gave the Son power over all people so that he could give eternal life to all those you have given to him. ³And this is eternal life: that people can know you, the only true God, and that they can know Jesus Christ, the one you sent. ⁴I finished the work you gave me to do. I brought you glory on earth. ⁵And now, Father, give me glory with you. Give me the glory I had with you before the world was made.

⁶"You gave me some people from the world. I have shown them what you are like. They belonged to you, and you gave them to me. They

have obeyed your teaching. ⁷Now they know that everything I have came from you. ⁸I told them the words you gave me, and they accepted them. They knew that I came from you and believed that you sent me. ⁹I pray for them now. I am not praying for the people in the world. But I am praying for these people you gave me, because they are yours. ¹⁰All I have is yours, and all you have is mine. And my glory is seen in them.

¹¹"Now I am coming to you. I will not stay in the world, but these followers of mine are still in the world. Holy Father, keep them safe by the power of your name—the name you gave me. Then they will be one, just as you and I are one. ¹²While I was with them, I kept them safe by the power of your name—the name you gave me. I protected them. And only one of them was lost—the one who was sure to be lost. This was to show the truth of what the Scriptures said would happen.

¹³"I am coming to you now. But I pray these things while I am still in the world. I say all this so that these followers can have the true happiness that I have. I want them to be completely happy. ¹⁴I have given them your teaching. And the world has hated them, because they don't belong to the world, just as I don't belong to the world.

¹⁵"I am not asking you to take them out of the world. But I am asking that you keep them safe from the Evil One. ¹⁶They don't belong to the world, just as I don't belong to the world. ¹⁷Make them ready for your service through your truth. Your teaching is truth. ¹⁸I have sent them into the world, just as you sent me into the world. ¹⁹I am making myself completely ready to serve you. I do this for them, so that they also might be fully qualified for your service.

²⁰"I pray not only for these followers but also for those who will believe in me because of their teaching. ²¹Father, I pray that all who believe in me can be one. You are in me and I am in you. I pray that they can also be one in us. Then the world will believe that you sent me. ²²I have given them the glory that you gave me. I gave them this glory so that they can be one, just as you and I are one. ²³I will be in them, and you will be in me. So they will be completely one. Then the world will know that you sent me and that you loved them just as you loved me.

²⁴"Father, I want these people you have given me to be with me where I will be. I want them to see my glory—the glory you gave me because you loved me before the world was made. ²⁵Father, you are the one who always does what is right. The world does not know you, but I know you, and these followers of mine know that you sent me. ²⁶I showed them what you are like, and I will show them again. Then they will have

the same love that you have for me, and I will live in them."

Jesus Is Arrested

(Matt. 26:47–56; Mark 14:43–50; Luke 22:47–53)

18 When Jesus finished praying, he left with his followers and went across the Kidron Valley. He went into a garden there, his followers still with him.

²Judas, the one responsible for handing Jesus over, knew where this place was. He knew because Jesus often met there with his followers. ³So Judas led a group of soldiers to the garden, along with some guards from the leading priests and the Pharisees. The soldiers and guards were carrying torches, lanterns and weapons.

⁴Jesus already knew everything that would happen to him. So he went out and asked them, "Who are you looking for?"

⁵They answered, "Jesus from Nazareth."

He said, "I am Jesus."ᵃ (Judas, the one responsible for handing Jesus over, was standing there with them.) ⁶When Jesus said, "I am Jesus," the men moved back and fell to the ground.

⁷He asked them again, "Who are you looking for?"

They said, "Jesus from Nazareth."

⁸Jesus said, "I told you that I am Jesus. So if you are looking for me, let these other men go free." ⁹This was to show the truth of what Jesus said earlier: "I have not lost anyone you gave me."

¹⁰Simon Peter had a sword, which he pulled out. He struck the servant of the high priest and cut off his right ear. (The servant's name was Malchus.) ¹¹Jesus said to Peter, "Put your sword back in its place! I must drink from the cupᵇ the Father has given me."

Jesus Is Brought Before Annas

(Matt. 26:57–58; Mark 14:53–54; Luke 22:54)

¹²Then the soldiers with their commander and the Jewish guards arrested Jesus. They tied him ¹³and brought him first to Annas, the father-in-law of Caiaphas. Caiaphas was the high priest that year. ¹⁴He was also the one who had told the other Jewish leaders that it would be better if one man died for all the people.

Peter Lies About Knowing Jesus

(Matt. 26:69–70; Mark 14:66–68; Luke 22:55–57)

¹⁵Simon Peter and another one of Jesus' followers went with Jesus. This follower knew the high priest. So he went with Jesus into the courtyard of the high priest's house. ¹⁶But Peter waited outside near the door. The follower who knew the high priest came back outside and spoke to the girl in charge of the gate. Then he brought Peter inside. ¹⁷The girl at the gate said to Peter, "Are you also one of the followers of that man?"

Peter answered, "No, I am not!"

¹⁸It was cold, so the servants and guards had built a fire. They were standing around it, warming themselves and Peter was standing with them.

The High Priest Questions Jesus

(Matt. 26:59–66; Mark 14:55–64; Luke 22:66–71)

¹⁹The high priest asked Jesus questions about his followers and what he taught them. ²⁰Jesus answered, "I have always spoken openly to all people. I always taught in the synagogues and in the Temple area. All the Jews come together there. I never said anything in secret. ²¹So why do you question me? Ask the people who heard my teaching. They know what I said."

²²When Jesus said this, one of the guards standing there hit him. The guard said, "You should not talk to the high priest like that!"

²³Jesus answered, "If I said something wrong, tell everyone here what was wrong. But if what I said is right, then why do you hit me?"

²⁴So Annas sent Jesus to Caiaphas the high priest. He was still tied.

Peter Lies Again

(Matt. 26:71–75; Mark 14:69–72; Luke 22:58–62)

²⁵Simon Peter was standing by the fire, keeping himself warm. The other people said to Peter, "Aren't you one of the followers of that man?"

Peter denied it. He said, "No, I am not."

²⁶One of the servants of the high priest was there. He was a relative of the man whose ear Peter had cut off. The servant said, "I think I saw you with him in the garden!"

²⁷But again Peter said, "No, I was not with him!" As soon as he said this, a cockerel crowed.

Jesus Is Brought Before Pilate

(Matt. 27:1–2,11–31; Mark 15:1–20; Luke 23:1–25)

²⁸Then the guards took Jesus from Caiaphas' house to the Roman governor's palace. It was early in the morning. The Jews there would not go inside the palace. They did not want to make

---

ᵃ **18:5** *"I am Jesus"* Literally, "I am", which could have the same meaning here that it has in 8:24,28,58; 13:19. Also in verse 8.
ᵇ **18:11** *cup* A symbol of suffering. Jesus used the idea of drinking from a cup to mean accepting the suffering he would face in the terrible events that were soon to come.

themselves unclean,[a] because they wanted to eat the Passover meal. 29So Pilate went outside to them and asked, "What do you say this man has done wrong?"

30They answered, "He is a bad man. That is why we brought him to you."

31Pilate said to them, "You take him yourselves and judge him by your own law."

The Jewish leaders answered, "But your law does not allow us to punish anyone by killing them." 32(This was to show the truth of what Jesus said about how he would die.)

33Then Pilate went back inside the palace. He called for Jesus and asked him, "Are you the king of the Jews?"

34Jesus said, "Is that your own question, or did other people tell you about me?"

35Pilate said, "I am not a Jew! It was your own people and their leading priests who handed you over to me. What have you done wrong?"

36Jesus said, "My kingdom does not belong to this world. If it did, my servants would fight so that I would not be handed over to the Jewish leaders. No, my kingdom is not an earthly one."

37Pilate said, "So you are a king."

Jesus answered, "You are right to say that I am a king. I was born for this: to tell people about the truth. That is why I came into the world. And everyone who belongs to the truth listens to me."

38Pilate said, "What is truth?" Then he went out to the Jewish leaders again and said to them, "I can find nothing against this man. 39But it is one of your customs for me to free one prisoner to you at the time of Passover. Do you want me to free this 'king of the Jews'?"

40They shouted back, "No, not him! Let Barabbas go free!" (Barabbas was a rebel.)

19 Then Pilate ordered that Jesus be taken away and whipped. 2The soldiers did what Pilate ordered. And they made a crown from thorny branches and put it on his head. Then they put a purple robe[b] around him. 3They kept coming up to him and saying, "We salute you, king of the Jews!" And they kept hitting him in the face.

4Again Pilate came out and said to the Jewish leaders, "Look! I am bringing Jesus out to you. I want you to know that I find nothing I can charge him with." 5Then Jesus came out wearing the crown of thorns and the purple robe. Pilate said to the Jews, "Here is the man!"

6When the leading priests and the Jewish guards saw Jesus they shouted, "Kill him on a cross! Kill him on a cross!"

But Pilate answered, "You take him and nail him to a cross yourselves. I find nothing I can charge him with."

7The Jewish leaders answered, "We have a law that says he must die, because he said he is the Son of God."

8When Pilate heard this, he was more afraid. 9So he went back inside the palace and asked Jesus, "Where are you from?" But Jesus did not answer him. 10Pilate said, "You refuse to speak to me? Remember, I have the power to make you free or to kill you on a cross."

11Jesus answered, "The only power you have over me is the power given to you by God. So the one who handed me over to you is guilty of a greater sin."

12After this, Pilate tried to let Jesus go free. But the Jewish leaders shouted, "Anyone who makes himself a king is against Caesar. So if you let this man go free, that means you are not Caesar's friend."

13When Pilate heard this, he brought Jesus out to the place called "The Stone Pavement". (In Aramaic the name is *Gabbatha.*) Pilate sat down on the judge's seat there. 14It was now almost noon on Preparation Day of Passover week. Pilate said to the Jews, "Here is your king!"

15They shouted, "Take him away! Take him away! Kill him on a cross!"

Pilate asked them, "Do you want me to kill your king on a cross?"

The leading priests answered, "The only king we have is Caesar!"

---

[a] **18:28** *unclean* Going into a non-Jewish place would ruin the special cleansing the Jews did to make themselves fit for worship. See John 11:55.

[b] **19:2** *purple robe* Probably a soldier's robe that looked like the purple robes worn by kings. They put this on Jesus to make fun of him for claiming to be a king.

16Then Pilate handed Jesus over to the soldiers with orders for him to be killed on a cross. So they took him away.

INSIGHT

Crosses for crucifixions were probably T-shaped and not as tall as you see in films. The victim's outstretched arms were nailed to the crosspiece, which was then lifted onto the vertical beam (already fixed in the ground). His legs would have been pushed up beneath him and a nail driven through the foot or ankle. The victim could bear some weight by balancing on a small peg on the upright beam, but in the end he would die from suffocation, blood loss or sheer exhaustion.

John 19:17–18

Jesus Is Nailed to a Cross

(Matt. 27:32–44; Mark 15:21–32; Luke 23:26–39)

17Jesus carried his own cross to a place called "The Place of the Skull". (In Aramaic the name of this place is "Golgotha".) 18There they nailed Jesus to the cross. They also nailed two other men to crosses. They put them on each side of Jesus with him in the middle.

19Pilate told them to write a sign and put it on the cross. The sign said, "JESUS OF NAZARETH, THE KING OF THE JEWS." 20The sign was written in Aramaic, in Latin and in Greek. Many of the Jews read this sign, because the place where Jesus was nailed to the cross was near the city.

21The leading Jewish priests said to Pilate, "Don't write, 'The King of the Jews.' But write, 'This man said, I am the King of the Jews.'"

22Pilate answered, "I will not change what I have written."

23After the soldiers nailed Jesus to the cross, they took his clothes and divided them into four parts. Each soldier got one part. They also took his tunic. It was all one piece of cloth woven from top to bottom. 24So the soldiers said to each other, "We should not tear this into pieces. Let's throw lots to see who will get it." This happened to make clear the full meaning of what the Scriptures say:

"They divided my clothes among them,
  and they threw lots for what I was
    wearing."

Psalm 22:18

So the soldiers did this.

25Jesus' mother stood near his cross. Her sister was also standing there, with Mary the wife of Clopas and Mary Magdalene. 26Jesus saw his mother. He also saw the follower he loved very much standing there. He said to his mother, "Dear woman, here is your son." 27Then he said to the follower, "Here is your mother." So after that, this follower took Jesus' mother to live in his home.

Jesus Dies

(Matt. 27:45–56; Mark 15:33–41; Luke 23:44–49)

28Later, Jesus knew that everything had been done. To make the Scriptures come true he said, "I am thirsty."a 29There was a jar full of sour wine there, so the soldiers soaked a sponge in it. They put the sponge on a branch of a hyssop plant and lifted it to Jesus' mouth. 30When he tasted the wine, he said, "It is finished." Then he bowed his head and died.

31This day was Preparation Day. The next day was a special Sabbath day. The Jewish leaders did not want the bodies to stay on the cross on the Sabbath day. So they asked Pilate to order that the legs of the men be broken. And they asked that the bodies be taken down from the crosses. 32So the soldiers came and broke the legsb of the two men on the crosses beside Jesus. 33But when the soldiers came close to Jesus, they saw that he was already dead. So they did not break his legs.

34But one of the soldiers stuck his spear into Jesus' side. Immediately blood and water came out. 35(The one who saw this happen has told you about it. He told you about it so that you also can believe. The things he says are true. He knows that he tells the truth.) 36These things happened to give full meaning to the Scriptures that said, "None of his bones will be broken"c 37and "People will look at the one they stabbed."d

Jesus Is Buried

(Matt. 27:57–61; Mark 15:42–47; Luke 23:50–56)

38Later, a man named Joseph from Arimathea asked Pilate for the body of Jesus. (Joseph was a follower of Jesus, but he did not tell anyone, because he was afraid of the Jewish leaders.)

---

a **19:28** *"I am thirsty"* See Ps. 22:15; 69:21.
b **19:32** *broke the legs* The legs were broken to make those on the crosses die more quickly.
c **19:36** Quote from Ps. 34:20. The idea is from Exod. 12:46; Num. 9:12.
d **19:37** Quote from Zech. 12:10.

Pilate said Joseph could take Jesus' body, so he came and took it away.

39Nicodemus went with Joseph. He was the man who had come to Jesus before and talked to him at night. He brought about 30 kilogrammes[a] of spices—a mixture of myrrh and aloes. 40These two men took Jesus' body and wrapped it in pieces of linen cloth with the spices. (This is how the Jews bury people.) 41In the place where Jesus was killed on the cross, there was a garden. In the garden there was a new tomb. No one had ever been buried there before. 42The men put Jesus in that tomb because it was nearby, and the Jews were preparing to start their Sabbath day.

News That Jesus Has Risen From Death

(Matt. 28:1–10; Mark 16:1–8; Luke 24:1–12)

20 Early on Sunday morning, while it was still dark, Mary Magdalene went to the tomb. She saw that the large stone had been moved away from the entrance. 2So she ran to Simon Peter and the other follower (the one Jesus loved very much). She said, "They have taken the Lord out of the tomb, and we don't know where they have put him."

3So Peter and the other follower started going to the tomb. 4They were both running, but the other follower ran faster than Peter and reached the tomb first. 5He bent down and looked in. He saw the pieces of linen cloth lying there, but he did not go in.

6When Simon Peter finally reached the tomb, he went in and saw the pieces of linen lying there. 7He also saw the cloth that had been around Jesus' head. It was rolled up and laid in a different place from the pieces of linen. 8Then the other follower went in—the one who had reached the tomb first. He saw what had happened and believed. 9(These followers did not yet understand from the Scriptures that Jesus must rise from death.)

Jesus Appears to Mary Magdalene

(Mark 16:9–11)

10Then the followers went back home. 11But Mary stood outside the tomb, crying. While she was crying, she bent down and looked inside the tomb. 12She saw two angels dressed in white sitting where Jesus' body had been. One was sitting where the head had been; the other was sitting where the feet had been.

13The angels asked Mary, "Woman, why are you crying?"

Mary answered, "They have taken away the body of my Lord, and I don't know where they

have put him." 14When Mary said this, she turned around and saw Jesus standing there. But she did not know it was Jesus.

15He asked her, "Woman, why are you crying? Who are you looking for?"

She thought he was the man in charge of the garden. So she said to him, "Did you take him away, sir? Tell me where you have put him. I will go and get him."

16Jesus said to her, "Mary."

She turned towards him and said in Aramaic, *"Rabboni"*, which means "Teacher".

17Jesus said to her, "You don't need to hold on to me! I have not yet gone back up to the Father. But go to my followers[b] and tell them this: 'I am going back to my Father and your Father. I am going back to my God and your God.'"

18Mary Magdalene went to the followers and told them, "I saw the Lord!" And she told them what he had said to her.

Jesus Appears to His Followers

(Matt. 28:16–20; Mark 16:14–18; Luke 24:36–49)

19The day was Sunday, and that same evening the followers were together. They had the doors locked because they were afraid of the Jewish leaders. Suddenly, Jesus was standing there among them. He said, "Peace be with you!" 20As soon as he said this, he showed them his hands and his side. When the followers saw the Lord, they were very happy.

21Then Jesus said again, "Peace be with you. It was the Father who sent me, and I am now sending you in the same way." 22Then he breathed on them and said, "Receive the Holy Spirit. 23If you forgive the sins of anyone, their sins are forgiven. If there is anyone whose sins you don't forgive, their sins are not forgiven."

Jesus Appears to Thomas

24Thomas (called "the twin") was one of the twelve, but he was not with the other followers when Jesus came. 25They told him, "We saw the Lord." Thomas said, "That's hard to believe. I will have to see the nail holes in his hands, put my finger where the nails were and put my hand into his side. Only then will I believe it."

26A week later the followers were in the house again, and Thomas was with them. The doors were locked, but Jesus came and stood among them. He said, "Peace be with you!" 27Then he said to Thomas, "Put your finger here. Look at my hands. Put your hand here in my side. Stop doubting and believe."

---

[a] **19:39** *about 30 kilogrammes* Literally, "100 *litras*".
[b] **20:17** *followers* Literally, "brothers".

28Thomas said to Jesus, "My Lord and my God!"

29Jesus said to him, "You believe because you see me. Great blessings belong to the people who believe without seeing me!"

Why John Wrote This Book

30Jesus did many other miraculous signs that his followers saw, which are not written in this book. 31But these are written so that you can believe that Jesus is the Messiah, the Son of God. Then, by believing, you can have life through his name.

Jesus Appears to Seven Followers

21 Later, Jesus appeared again to his followers by Lake Galilee.[a] This is how it happened: 2Some of the followers were together—Simon Peter, Thomas (called Didymus), Nathanael from Cana in Galilee, the two sons of Zebedee and two other followers. 3Simon Peter said, "I am going out to fish."

The other followers said, "We will go with you." So all of them went out and got into the boat. They fished that night but caught nothing.

4Early the next morning Jesus stood on the shore. But the followers did not know it was Jesus. 5Then he said to them, "Friends, have you caught any fish?"

They answered, "No."

6He said, "Throw your net into the water on the right side of your boat. You will find some fish there." So they did this. They caught so many fish that they could not pull the net back into the boat.

7The follower Jesus loved very much said to Peter, "That man is the Lord!" When Peter heard him say it was the Lord, he wrapped his coat around himself. (He had taken his clothes off to work.) Then he jumped into the water. 8The other followers went to shore in the boat. They pulled the net full of fish. They were not very far from shore, only about 100 metres.[b] 9When they stepped out of the boat and onto the shore, they saw a fire of hot coals. There were fish cooking on the fire and there was also some bread to eat. 10Then Jesus said, "Bring some of the fish that you caught."

11Simon Peter got into the boat and pulled the net to the shore. It was full of big fish—153 of them! But even with that many fish, the net did not tear. 12Jesus said to them, "Come and eat." None of the followers would ask him, "Who are you?" They knew he was the Lord. 13Jesus walked over to get the bread and gave it to them. He also gave them the fish.

14This was now the third time Jesus appeared to his followers after he was raised from death.

Jesus Talks to Peter

15When they had finished eating, Jesus said to Simon Peter, "Simon, son of John, do you love me more than these other men love me?"

Peter answered, "Yes, Lord, you know that I love you."

Then Jesus said to him, "Take care of my lambs."[c]

16Again Jesus said to him, "Simon, son of John, do you love me?"

Peter answered, "Yes, Lord, you know that I love you."

Then Jesus said, "Take care of my sheep."

17A third time Jesus said, "Simon, son of John, do you love me?"

Peter was sad because Jesus asked him three times, "Do you love me?" He said, "Lord, you know everything. You know that I love you!"

Jesus said to him, "Take care of my sheep. 18The truth is, when you were young, you tied your own belt and went where you wanted. But when you are old, you will put out your hands, and someone else will tie your belt. They will lead you where you don't want to go." 19(Jesus said this to show how Peter would die to give glory to God.) Then he said to Peter, "Follow me!"

20Peter turned and saw the follower Jesus loved very much walking behind them. (This was the follower who had leaned against Jesus at the supper and said, "Lord, who is it that will hand you over?") 21When Peter saw him behind them, he asked Jesus, "Lord, what about him?"

22Jesus answered, "Maybe I want him to live until I come. That should not matter to you. You follow me!"

23So a story spread among the followers of Jesus. They were saying that this follower would not die. But Jesus did not say he would not die. He only said, "Maybe I want him to live until I come. That should not matter to you."

24That follower is the one who is telling these things. He is the one who has now written them all down. We know that what he says is true.

25There are many other things that Jesus did. If every one of them were written down, I think the whole world would not be big enough for all the books that would be written.

---

[a] **21:1 Lake Galilee** Literally, "Lake of Tiberias", another name for Lake Galilee. See John 6:1.

[b] **21:8 100 metres** Literally, "200 cubits".

[c] **21:15 lambs** Jesus uses this word and the word "sheep" in verses 16 and 17 to mean his followers, as in John 10.

Who

Written by Luke, the doctor, who also wrote the Gospel of Luke. Clearly it is the work of a companion of Paul – there are large chunks of the book where the writer uses "us" and "we", indicating that he was part of what was going on.

When

It was probably written about AD 65–70. It ends a little after Paul's imprisonment in Rome but does not give any result of his trial, which it surely would have done had the result been known.

What

Jesus had promised his followers that he would send them the Holy Spirit. This book tells that story and what happens next. Luke had written an account of Jesus' life; now he tells the story of the early Church, from the resurrection of Jesus in Jerusalem to the imprisonment of Paul in Rome.

The early Church grew at lightning speed. And this incredible growth quickly brought it into conflict with the Jewish and Roman authorities, so Acts features several episodes where followers of Jesus are martyred for their beliefs.

Christianity was dangerous. But it was a life-changing faith, and nothing illustrates that better than the conversion of Saul, who went from being Christianity's greatest enemy to its staunchest follower.

Saul, who became Paul, played a crucial role in some of the key issues facing Christianity. Acts shows us a group of people trying to work out what had happened and what it all meant. Understandably, there were disagreements within the Church itself as to what the Church should be like. Was the Church a part of the Jewish faith, or was it something new? Should they try to recruit non-Jews to the cause? And how should the Church organize itself?

So Acts is the history of the first decades of the Church. But it is also a kind of biography of the Holy Spirit, who is a constant figure in the background, inspiring, protecting, punishing, informing and pushing the first Christians to ever greater lengths as they spread the Good News of Jesus Christ.

QUICK TOUR ACTS

"So Jesus is the one God raised from death. We are all witnesses of this. We saw him. Jesus was lifted up to heaven. Now he is with God, at God's right side. The Father has given the Holy Spirit to him, as he promised. So Jesus has now poured out that Spirit. This is what you see and hear."

Acts 2:32–33

Luke Writes Another Book

1 Dear Theophilus,
The first book I wrote was about everything Jesus did and taught from the beginning ²until the day he was carried up into heaven. Before he went, he talked to the apostles he had chosen. With the help of the Holy Spirit, he told them what they should do. ³This was after his death, but he showed them that he was alive, proving it to them in many ways. The apostles saw Jesus many times during the 40 days after he was raised from death. He spoke to them about God's kingdom. ⁴Once when Jesus was eating with them, he told them not to leave Jerusalem. He said, "Wait here until you receive what the Father promised to send. Remember, I told you about it before. ⁵John baptized people with water, but in a few days you will be baptized with the Holy Spirit."

Jesus Is Carried Up Into Heaven

⁶The apostles were all together. They asked Jesus, "Lord, is this the time for you to give the people of Israel their kingdom again?"

⁷Jesus said to them, "The Father is the only one who has the authority to decide dates and times. They are not for you to know. ⁸But the Holy Spirit will come on you and give you power. You will be my witnesses. You will tell people everywhere about me—in Jerusalem, in the rest of Judea, in Samaria and in every part of the world."

⁹After Jesus said this, he was lifted up into the sky. While they were watching, he went into a cloud, and they could not see him. ¹⁰They were staring into the sky where he had gone. Suddenly two men wearing white clothes were standing beside them. ¹¹They said, "Men from Galilee, why are you standing here looking into the sky? You saw Jesus carried away from you into heaven. He will come back in the same way you saw him go."

A New Apostle Is Chosen

¹²Then the apostles went back to Jerusalem from the Mount of Olives, which is about a kilometre*ᵃ* from Jerusalem. ¹³When they entered the city, they went to the upstairs room where they were staying. These are the ones who were there: Peter, John, James, Andrew, Philip, Thomas, Bartholomew, Matthew, James (the son of Alphaeus), Simon the Zealot and Judas (the son of James).

¹⁴The apostles were all together. They were constantly praying with the same purpose. Some women, Mary the mother of Jesus and his brothers were there with the apostles.

¹⁵After a few days there was a meeting of the believers. There were about 120 of them. Peter stood up and said, ¹⁶⁻¹⁷"Brothers and sisters, in the Scriptures the Holy Spirit said through David that something must happen. He was talking about Judas, one of our own group. Judas served together with us. The Spirit said that Judas would lead men to arrest Jesus."

¹⁸(Judas was paid for doing this. He used the money to buy a field. But he fell on his head, his body broke open and all his intestines poured out. ¹⁹And all the people of Jerusalem learned about this. That is why they named that field Akeldama, which in their language means "field of blood".)

²⁰Peter said, "In the book of Psalms, this is written about Judas:

'People should not go near his land;
no one should live there.'
Psalm 69:25

And it is also written:

'Let another man have his work.'
Psalm 109:8

²¹⁻²²"So now another man must join us and be a witness of Jesus' resurrection. He must be one of those men who were part of our group during all the time the Lord Jesus was with us. He must have been with us from the time John was baptizing people until the day when Jesus was carried up from us into heaven."

²³They put two men before the group. One was Joseph Barsabbas. He was also called Justus. The other man was Matthias. ²⁴⁻²⁵They prayed, "Lord, you know the minds of all people. Show us which one of these two men you choose to do this work. Judas turned away from it and went where he belongs. Lord, show us which man should take his place as an apostle!" ²⁶Then they used lots to choose one of the two men. The lots showed that Matthias was the one the Lord wanted. So he became an apostle with the other eleven.

The Coming of the Holy Spirit

2 When the day of Pentecost came, they were all together in one place. ²Suddenly a noise came from heaven. It sounded like a strong wind blowing. This noise filled the whole house where they were sitting. ³They saw something that looked like flames of fire. The flames were separated and stood over each person there. ⁴They were all filled with the Holy Spirit, and

---

*ᵃ **1:12** about a kilometre Literally, "a Sabbath day's journey".*

THE OUTPOURING

The book of Acts is also known as "The Acts of the Apostles" – a title which promises drama and excitement. But Jesus' crew don't look up to much in the first chapter of the book – sitting around waiting, asking dumb questions and trying to decide who to replace Judas with!

So how does this bunch of ordinary people – not highly educated, not powerful in the world's eyes – go on to change their city and country, the surrounding nations and, ultimately, the whole world? The answer is right before us, here in Acts 2.

DIG IN   READ Acts 2:1–41

- What is the first thing the church is empowered by the Holy Spirit to do?
- How does Peter challenge his listeners (vv.38–40)?
- What's the end result (v.41)?

Throughout the book of Acts, we're going to see how God the Holy Spirit brings the new church to life – guiding, speaking through dreams and visions, performing miracles, working salvation and bringing people to God. But the first thing we see the Spirit doing is enabling the Good News to be heard.

Peter calls the people listening to salvation. He invites them to understand what God has been saying and doing through history and to respond to that. They do – en masse! The new church grows rapidly.

READ ON to verse 47

- What were the main features of the new church's life together?

A church that's devoted, that loves hearing the word preached, that shares life together. A church that sees God doing miraculous things, that takes care of one another's needs and that grows. That sounds like a great church!

Much of the book of Acts describes a church that is trying to be obedient to God, working in the specific context of the first-century world. Not everything from that time will apply to us today. But these features in verses 42 to 47 are universal – and should be true of all our churches wherever and whenever they are.

DIG THROUGH

The first gift of the Holy Spirit to the new church was to help the believers to communicate the Good News of God in languages that everyone could understand. This gives us some idea of how important sharing the Good News is to God and how central it is to the story of Acts.
- How does what happens in verses 42 to 47 compare to your experience of church? What's attractive about it to you? Can you see how outsiders might be attracted to that way of life?
- What can you do to help build this kind of church?

DIG DEEPER

- Acts 2:1–11 is a powerful reversal of the story of the Tower of Babel in Genesis, where languages became a barrier between people – now, by the Spirit, they are a bridge. It's also a very powerful sign that God's intention was (and is) to reach people from all over the world with the Good News. (You can find out more in the Bible Bit on Acts 8, "The Ripple Effect".)

they began to speak different languages. The Holy Spirit was giving them the power to do this.

5There were some godly Jews in Jerusalem at this time. They were from every country in the world. 6A large crowd came together because they heard the noise. They were surprised because, as the apostles were speaking, everyone heard in their own language.

7They were all amazed at this. They did not understand how the apostles could do this. They said, "Look! These men we hear speaking are all from Galilee.*a* 8But we hear them in our own languages. How is this possible? We are from all these different places: 9Parthia, Media, Elam, Mesopotamia, Judea, Cappadocia, Pontus, Asia, 10Phrygia, Pamphylia, Egypt, the areas of Libya near the city of Cyrene, Rome, 11Crete and Arabia. Some of us were born Jews, and others have changed their religion to worship God like Jews. We are from these different countries, but we can hear these men in our own languages! We can all understand the great things they are saying about God."

12The people were all amazed and confused. They asked each other, "What is happening?" 13But others were laughing at the apostles, saying they were drunk from too much wine.

Peter Speaks to the People

14Then Peter stood up with the other eleven apostles. He spoke loudly so that all the people could hear. He said, "My Jewish brothers and all of you who live in Jerusalem, listen to me. I will tell you something you need to know. Listen carefully. 15These men are not drunk as you think; it's only nine o'clock in the morning. 16But Joel the prophet wrote about what you see happening here today. This is what he wrote:

17'God says: In the last days
   I will pour out my Spirit on all people.
Your sons and daughters will prophesy.
   Your young men will see visions,
      and your old men will have special dreams.
18In those days I will pour out my Spirit
   on my servants, men and women,
   and they will prophesy.
19I will work wonders in the sky above
   and cause miraculous signs on the earth
      below.
   There will be blood, fire and thick smoke.

20The sun will become dark,
   and the moon as red as blood,
      just before the great and glorious day that
      the Lord comes.
21And the Lord will save everyone
   who looks to him for help.'*b*

Joel 2:28–32

22"My fellow Israelites, listen to these words: Jesus from Nazareth was a very special man. God clearly showed this to you. He proved it by the miracles, wonders and miraculous signs he did through Jesus. You all saw these things, so you know this is true. 23Jesus was handed over to you, and you killed him. With the help of evil men, you nailed him to a cross. But God knew all this would happen. It was his plan—a plan he made long ago. 24Jesus suffered the pain of death, but God made him free. He raised him from death. There was no way for death to hold him. 25David said this about him:

'I never forget that the Lord is with me.
   He is right here beside me,
      so nothing can harm me.
26That is why I feel so happy
   and sing for joy!
   There is hope even for this weak body of
      mine,
27because you, Lord, will not leave me in the
      grave.*c*
   You will not let the body of your faithful
      servant*d* rot there.
28You have shown me the way that leads to
      life.
   Being together with you will fill me with
      joy.'

Psalm 16:8–11

29"My brothers, I can tell you for sure about David, our great ancestor. He died, was buried and his tomb is still here with us today. 30He was a prophet and knew something that God had said. God had promised David that someone from his own family would sit on David's throne as king.*e* 31David knew this before it happened. That is why he said this about that future king:

'He was not left in the grave.
   His body did not rot there.'

---

a **2:7 from Galilee** The people thought men from Galilee could speak only their own language.
b **2:21 who looks to him for help** Literally, "who calls on the name of the Lord", meaning to show faith in him by worshipping him or praying to him for help.
c **2:27 grave** Literally, "Hades". Also in verse 31.
d **2:27 faithful servant** Sometimes translated "Holy One", this word usually means a person who is devoted to God and pleasing to him.
e **2:30 God had promised . . . as king** See 2 Sam. 7:12–13 and Ps. 132:11.

David was talking about the Messiah rising from death. [32]So Jesus is the one God raised from death. We are all witnesses of this. We saw him. [33]Jesus was lifted up to heaven. Now he is with God, at God's right side. The Father has given the Holy Spirit to him, as he promised. So Jesus has now poured out that Spirit. This is what you see and hear. [34]David was not the one who was lifted up to heaven. David himself said,

'The Lord God said to my Lord:
Sit at my right side,
[35]   until I put your enemies under your
            power.'[a]

                                        Psalm 110:1

[36]"So, all the people of Israel should know this for certain: God has made Jesus to be Lord and Messiah. He is the one you nailed to the cross!"

[37]When the people heard this, they felt very, very sorry. They asked Peter and the other apostles, "Brothers, what should we do?"

[38]Peter said to them, "Change your hearts and lives and be baptized, each one of you, in the name of Jesus Christ. Then God will forgive your sins, and you will receive the gift of the Holy Spirit. [39]This promise is for you. It is also for your children and for the people who are far away. It is for everyone the Lord our God calls to himself."

[40]Peter warned them with many other words; he begged them, "Save yourselves from the evil of the people who live now!" [41]Then those who accepted what Peter said were baptized. On that day about 3,000 people were added to the group of believers.

The Believers Share

[42]The believers spent their time listening to the teaching of the apostles. They shared everything with each other. They ate[b] together and prayed together. [43]Many wonders and miraculous signs were happening through the apostles, and everyone felt great respect for God. [44]All the believers stayed together and shared everything. [45]They sold their land and the things they owned. Then they divided the money and gave it to those who needed it. [46]The believers shared a common purpose, and every day they spent much of their time together in the Temple area. They also ate together in their homes. They were happy to share their food and ate with joyful hearts. [47]The believers praised God and were respected by all

the people. More and more people were being saved every day, and the Lord was adding them to their group.

Peter Heals a Lame Man

3 One day Peter and John went to the Temple area. It was three o'clock in the afternoon, which was the time for the daily Temple prayer service. [2]As they were entering the Temple area, a man was there who had been lame all his life. He was being carried by some friends who brought him to the Temple every day. They put him by one of the gates outside the Temple. It was called Beautiful Gate. There he begged for money from the people going to the Temple. [3]That day he saw Peter and John going into the Temple area. He asked them for money.

[4]Peter and John looked at the lame man and said, "Look at us!" [5]He looked at them; he thought they would give him some money. [6]But Peter said, "I don't have any silver or gold, but I do have something else I can give you. By the power of Jesus Christ from Nazareth—stand up and walk!"

[7]Then Peter took the man's right hand and lifted him up. Immediately his feet and legs became strong. [8]He jumped up, stood on his feet and began to walk. He went into the Temple area with them. He was walking and jumping and praising God. [9-10]All the people recognized him. They knew he was the lame man who always sat by the Beautiful Gate to beg for money. Now they saw this same man walking and praising God. They were amazed. They did not understand how this could happen.

Peter Speaks to the People

[11]The man was holding on to Peter and John. All the people were amazed. They ran to Peter and John at Solomon's Porch.

[12]When Peter saw this, he said to the people, "My Jewish brothers, why are you surprised at this? You are looking at us as if it was our power that made this man walk. Do you think this was done because we are good? [13]No, God did it! He is the God of Abraham, the God of Isaac and the God of Jacob. He is the God of all our fathers. He gave glory to Jesus, his special servant. But you handed him over to be killed. Pilate decided to let him go free. But you told Pilate you did not want him. [14]Jesus was holy and good, but you said you did not want him. You told Pilate to give you a murderer[c] instead of Jesus. [15]And so you killed

---

[a] **2:35 until I put . . . power** Literally, "until I make your enemies a footstool for your feet".
[b] **2:42 ate** Literally, "broke bread". This may mean a meal or the Lord's Supper, the special meal Jesus told his followers to eat to remember him. Also in verse 46. See Luke 22:14-20.
[c] **3:14 murderer** Barabbas, the man the Jews chose to let go free instead of Jesus. See Luke 23:18.

the one who gives life! But God raised him from death. We are witnesses of this—we saw it with our own eyes.

¹⁶"This lame man was healed because we trusted in Jesus. It was Jesus' power that made him well. You can see this man, and you know him. He was made completely well because of faith in Jesus. You all saw it happen!

¹⁷"My brothers, I know that what you did to Jesus was done because you did not understand what you were doing. And your leaders did not understand any more than you did. ¹⁸But God said these things would happen. Through the prophets he said that his Messiah would suffer and die. I have told you how God made this happen. ¹⁹So you must change your hearts and lives. Come back to God, and he will forgive your sins. ²⁰Then the Lord will give you times of spiritual rest. He will send you Jesus, the one he chose to be the Messiah.

²¹"But Jesus must stay in heaven until the time when all things will be made right again. God spoke about this time long ago through his holy prophets. ²²Moses said, 'The Lord your God will give you a prophet. That prophet will come from among your own people. He will be like me. You must obey everything he tells you. ²³And anyone who refuses to obey that prophet will die, separated from God's people.'*ᵃ*

²⁴"Samuel, and all the other prophets who spoke for God after Samuel, said that this time would come. ²⁵And what those prophets talked about is for you, their descendants. You have received the agreement that God made with your fathers. God said to your father Abraham, 'Every nation on earth will be blessed through your descendants.'*ᵇ* ²⁶God has sent his special servant Jesus. He sent him to you first. He sent him to bless you by causing each of you to turn away from your evil ways."

The Apostles and the Jewish High Council

4 While Peter and John were speaking to the people, some Jewish leaders came up to them. There were some priests, the captain of the soldiers that guarded the Temple and some Sadducees. ²They were upset because of what Peter and John were teaching the people. By telling people about Jesus, the apostles were teaching that people will rise from death. ³The Jewish leaders arrested Peter and John and put them in jail. It was already night, so they kept them in jail until the next day. ⁴But many of the

people who heard the apostles believed what they said. There were now about 5,000 men in the group of believers.

⁵The next day the Jewish rulers, the older Jewish leaders and the teachers of the law met in Jerusalem. ⁶Annas the high priest, Caiaphas, John and Alexander were there. Everyone from the high priest's family was there. ⁷They made Peter and John stand before all the people. They kept asking them, "How did you make this man well? What power did you use? By whose authority did you do this?"

⁸Then Peter was filled with the Holy Spirit and said to them, "Rulers of the people and you older leaders, ⁹are you questioning us today about what we did to help this man? Are you asking us what made him well? ¹⁰We want all of you and all the people of Israel to know that this man was made well by the power of Jesus Christ from Nazareth. You nailed Jesus to a cross, but God raised him from death. This man was lame, but he is now well. He is able to stand here before you because of the power of Jesus! ¹¹Jesus is

'the stoneᶜ that you builders thought was not
    important.
  But this stone has become the cornerstone.'
                Psalm 118:22

¹²Jesus is the only one who can save people. His name is the only power in the world that has been given to save anyone. We must be saved through him!"

¹³The Jewish leaders understood that Peter and John had no special training or education. But they also saw that they were not afraid to speak. So the leaders were amazed. They also realized that Peter and John had been with Jesus. ¹⁴And they saw the man who had been healed standing there with the apostles. So there was nothing they could say in reply.

¹⁵The Jewish leaders told them to leave the council meeting. Then the leaders talked to each other about what they should do. ¹⁶They said, "What shall we do with these men? Everyone in Jerusalem knows about the miracle they did as a sign from God. It's too obvious. We can't say it didn't happen. ¹⁷But we must make them afraid to talk to anyone again using that name.ᵈ Then this problem will not spread among the people."

¹⁸So the Jewish leaders called Peter and John in again. They told the apostles not to say anything or to teach anything in the name of Jesus. ¹⁹But

---

ᵃ **3:22–23** Quote from Deut. 18:15,19.
ᵇ **3:25** Quote from Gen. 22:18; 26:24.
ᶜ **4:11** *stone* A picture or symbol meaning Jesus.
ᵈ **4:17** *that name* That is, Jesus' name. The Jewish leaders avoided saying his name. See Luke 15:2.

Peter and John answered them, "What do you think is right? What would God want? Should we obey you or God? [20]We cannot be quiet. We must tell people about what we have seen and heard."

[21-22]The Jewish leaders could not find a way to punish the apostles, because all the people were praising God for what had been done. This miracle was a sign from God. The man who was healed was more than 40 years old. So the Jewish leaders warned the apostles again and let them go free.

Peter and John Return to the Believers

[23]Peter and John left the meeting of Jewish leaders and went to their own group. They told the group everything that the leading priests and the older Jewish leaders had said to them. [24]When the believers heard this, they all prayed to God with one purpose. They said, "Master, you are the one who made the sky, the earth, the sea and everything in the world. [25]Our ancestor David was your servant. With the help of the Holy Spirit he wrote these words:

'Why are the nations shouting?
    Why are the people planning such useless
        things?

[26]'The kings of the earth prepare themselves to
        fight,
    and the rulers all come together against the
        Lord and against his Messiah.'
                                Psalm 2:1–2

[27]That's what actually happened when Herod, Pontius Pilate, the other nations and the people of Israel all came together against Jesus here in Jerusalem. He is your holy Servant, the one you made to be the Messiah. [28]These people who came together against Jesus made your plan happen. It was done because of your power and your will. [29]And now, Lord, listen to what they are saying. They are trying to make us afraid. We are your servants. Help us to say what you want us to say without fear. [30]Help us to be brave by showing us your power. Make sick people well. Cause miraculous signs and wonders to happen by the authority[a] of Jesus, your holy servant."

[31]After the believers had prayed, the place where they were meeting shook. They were all filled with the Holy Spirit, and they continued to speak God's message without fear.

The Believers Share

[32]The whole group of believers were united in their thinking and in what they wanted. None of them said that the things they had were their own. Instead, they shared everything. [33]With great power the apostles were making it known to everyone that the Lord Jesus was raised from death. And God blessed all the believers very much. [34]None of them could say they needed anything. Everyone who owned fields or houses sold them. They brought the money they got [35]and gave it to the apostles. Then everyone was given whatever they needed.

[36]One of the believers was named Joseph. The apostles called him Barnabas, a name that means "one who encourages others". He was a Levite born in Cyprus. [37]Joseph sold a field he owned. He brought the money and gave it to the apostles.

Ananias and Sapphira

5 There was a man named Ananias. His wife's name was Sapphira. Ananias sold some land he had, [2]but he gave only part of the money to the apostles. He secretly kept some of the money for himself. His wife knew this, and she agreed to it.

[3]Peter said, "Ananias, why did you let Satan fill your mind with such an idea? You kept part of the money for yourself and lied about it to the Holy Spirit! [4]Before you sold the field, it belonged to you. And even after you sold it, you could have used the money any way you wanted. How could you even think of doing such a thing? You lied to God, not to us!"

[5-6]When Ananias heard this, he fell down and died. Some young men came and wrapped up his body. They carried it out and buried it. And everyone who heard about this was filled with fear.

[7]About three hours later his wife came in. Sapphira did not know about what had happened to her husband. [8]Peter said to her, "Tell me how much money you got for your field. Was it this much?"

Sapphira answered, "Yes, that was all we got for the field."

[9]Peter said to her, "Why did you and your husband agree to test the Spirit of the Lord? Listen! Do you hear those footsteps? The men who buried your husband are at the door. They will carry you out in the same way." [10]At that moment Sapphira fell down by his feet and died. The young men came in and saw that she was dead. They carried her out and buried her beside her husband. [11]The whole church and all the other people who heard about this were filled with fear.

---

[a] 4:30 *authority* Literally, "name".

Proofs From God

¹²The apostles were given the power to do many miraculous signs and wonders among the people. They were together in Solomon's Porch, and they all had the same purpose. ¹³None of the other people dared to stand with the apostles, but everyone was saying wonderful things about them. ¹⁴More and more people believed in the Lord, and many men and women were added to the group of believers. ¹⁵So the people brought those who were sick into the streets and put them on little beds and mats. They were hoping that Peter's shadow might fall on them as he walked by. ¹⁶People came from all the towns around Jerusalem. They brought those who were sick or troubled by evil spirits. All of them were healed.

The Apostles Are Arrested

¹⁷The high priest and all his friends, a group called the Sadducees, became very jealous. ¹⁸They grabbed the apostles and put them in jail. ¹⁹But during the night, an angel of the Lord opened the doors of the jail. The angel led the apostles outside and said, ²⁰"Go and stand in the Temple area. Tell the people everything about this new life." ²¹When the apostles heard this, they did what they were told. They went into the Temple area about sunrise and began to teach the people.

The high priest and his friends came together and called a meeting of the high council and all the older Jewish leaders. They sent some men to the jail to bring the apostles to them. ²²When the men went to the jail, they could not find the apostles there. So they went back and told the Jewish leaders about this. ²³They said, "The jail was closed and locked. The guards were standing at the doors. But when we opened the doors, the jail was empty!" ²⁴The captain of the Temple guards and the leading priests heard this. They were confused and wondered what it all meant.

²⁵Then another man came and told them, "Listen! The men you put in jail are standing in the Temple area teaching the people." ²⁶The captain and his men went out and brought the apostles back. But the soldiers did not use force, because they were afraid of the people. They were afraid the people would stone them to death.

²⁷The soldiers brought the apostles in and made them stand before the council. The high priest questioned them. ²⁸He said, "We told you never again to teach using that name.ᵃ But look at what you have done! You have filled Jerusalem

with your teaching. And you are trying to blame us for his death."

²⁹Peter and the other apostles answered, "We must obey God, not you! ³⁰You killed Jesus by nailing him to a cross. But God, the same God our fathers had, raised Jesus from death. ³¹Jesus is the one God honoured by giving him a place at his right side. He made him our Leader and Saviour. God did this to give all the people of Israel the opportunity to change and turn to God to have their sins forgiven. ³²We saw all these things happen, and we can say that they are true. The Holy Spirit also shows that these things are true. God has given this Spirit to all those who obey him."

³³When the council members heard this, they became very angry. They began to plan a way to kill the apostles. ³⁴But one member of the council, a Pharisee named Gamaliel, stood up. He was a teacher of the law, and all the people respected him. He told the men to make the apostles leave the meeting for a few minutes. ³⁵Then he said to them, "Men of Israel, be careful of what you are planning to do to these men. ³⁶Remember when Theudas appeared? He said he was an important man, and about 400 men joined him. But he was killed, and all who followed him were scattered and ran away. They were not able to do anything. ³⁷Later, during the time of the census, a man named Judas came from Galilee. Many people joined his group, but he was also killed, and all his followers were scattered. ³⁸And so now I tell you, stay away from these men. Leave them alone. If their plan is something they thought up, it will fail. ³⁹But if it is from God, you will not be able to stop them. You might even be fighting against God himself!"

INSIGHT

You may know that Jesus was whipped, but the apostles were beaten, too – at the hands of the religious council! First-century Jewish law prescribed a maximum of 39 lashes with a tripled strip of calf's hide: two blows to the back, then one to the chest.

Acts 5:40

The Jewish leaders agreed with what Gamaliel said. ⁴⁰They called the apostles in again. They beat them and told them not to speak any more

---

ᵃ **5:28 *that name*** That is, Jesus' name. The Jewish leaders avoided saying his name. See Acts 4:17–18.

using the name of Jesus. Then they let them go free. ⁴¹The apostles left the council meeting. They were happy because they were given the honour of suffering dishonour for Jesus. ⁴²The apostles did not stop teaching the people. They continued to tell the Good News—that Jesus is the Messiah. They did this every day in the Temple area and in people's homes.

Seven Men Chosen for a Special Work

6 More and more people were becoming followers of Jesus. But during this same time, the Greek-speaking followers began to complain against the other Jewish followers. They said that their widows were not getting their share of what the followers received every day. ²The twelve apostles called the whole group of followers together.

The apostles said to them, "It would not be right for us to give up our work of teaching God's word in order to be in charge of getting food to people. ³So, brothers and sisters, choose seven of your men who have a good reputation. They must be full of wisdom and the Spirit. We will give them this work to do. ⁴Then we can use all our time to pray and to teach the word of God."

⁵The whole group liked the idea. So they chose these seven men: Stephen (a man with great faith and full of the Holy Spirit), Philip,*ᵃ* Prochorus, Nicanor, Timon, Parmenas and Nicolaus (a man from Antioch who had become a Jew). ⁶Then they put these men before the apostles, who prayed and laid their hands on them.*ᵇ*

⁷The word of God was reaching more and more people. The group of followers in Jerusalem became larger and larger. Even a big group of Jewish priests believed and obeyed.

Some Jews Against Stephen

⁸Stephen received a great blessing. God gave him power to do great wonders and miraculous signs among the people. ⁹But some of the Jews there were from the synagogue of Free Men,*ᶜ* as it was called. The group included Jews from Cyrene, Alexandria, Cilicia and Asia. They started arguing with Stephen. ¹⁰But the Spirit was helping him speak with wisdom. His words were so strong that these Jews could not argue with him.

¹¹So they told some men to say, "We heard Stephen say bad things against Moses and against God!" ¹²By doing this, these Jews upset the people, the older Jewish leaders and the teachers of the law. They became so angry that they came and grabbed Stephen and took him to a meeting of the high council.

¹³The Jews brought some men into the meeting to tell lies about Stephen. These men said, "This man is always saying things against this holy place and against the Law of Moses. ¹⁴We heard him say that Jesus from Nazareth will destroy this place and change what Moses told us to do." ¹⁵Everyone there in the council meeting was staring at Stephen. They saw that his face looked like the face of an angel.

Stephen's Speech

7 The high priest said to Stephen, "Is all this true?" ²Stephen answered, "My Jewish fathers and brothers, listen to me. Our great and glorious God appeared to Abraham, our ancestor, when he was in Mesopotamia. This was before he lived in Haran. ³God said to him, 'Leave your country and your people, and go to the country I will show you.'*ᵈ*

⁴"So Abraham left the country of Chaldea.*ᵉ* He went to live in Haran. After his father died, God sent him to this place, where you live now. ⁵But God did not give Abraham any of this land, not even a foot of it. But God promised that in the future he would give Abraham this land for himself and for his children. This was before Abraham had any children.

⁶"This is what God said to him: 'Your descendants will live in another country. They will be foreigners. The people there will make them slaves and mistreat them for 400 years. ⁷But I will punish the nation that made them slaves.'*ᶠ* And God also said, 'After those things happen, your people will come out of that country. Then they will worship me here in this place.'*ᵍ*

⁸"God made an agreement with Abraham; the sign for this agreement was circumcision. And so when Abraham had a son, he circumcised him when he was eight days old. His son's name was Isaac. Isaac also circumcised his son Jacob. And Jacob did the same for his sons, who became the twelve great ancestors of our people.

⁹"These ancestors of ours became jealous of their brother Joseph and sold him to be a slave in

---

ᵃ **6:5** *Philip* Not the apostle named Philip.
ᵇ **6:6** *laid their hands on them* This act was a way of asking God to bless people in a special way—to heal them, to cause the Holy Spirit to come into them or to give them power for a special work.
ᶜ **6:9** *Free Men* Jews who had been slaves or whose fathers had been slaves, but were now free.
ᵈ **7:3** Quote from Gen. 12:1.
ᵉ **7:4** *Chaldea* Or "Babylonia", a land in the southern part of Mesopotamia. See verse 2.
ᶠ **7:7** Quote from Gen. 15:13–14.
ᵍ **7:7** Quote from Gen. 15:14; Exod. 3:12.

Egypt. But God was with him [10]and saved him from all his troubles. Pharaoh was the king of Egypt then. He liked Joseph and respected him because of the wisdom God gave him. Pharaoh gave Joseph the job of being a governor of Egypt. He even let him rule over all the people in Pharaoh's house. [11]But all the land of Egypt and of Canaan became dry. It became so dry that food could not grow, and the people suffered very much. Our people could not find anything to eat.

[12]"But Jacob heard that there was food in Egypt. So he sent our people there. This was their first trip to Egypt. [13]Then they went there a second time. This time Joseph told his brothers who he was. And Pharaoh learned about Joseph's family. [14]Then Joseph sent some men to tell Jacob, his father, to come to Egypt. He also invited all his relatives, a total of 75 people. [15]So Jacob went down to Egypt. He and our other ancestors lived there until they died. [16]Later, their bodies were moved to Shechem, where they were put in a tomb. It was the same tomb that Abraham had bought in Shechem from the sons of Hamor. He paid them with silver.

[17]"The number of our people in Egypt grew. There were more and more of our people there. The promise that God made to Abraham was soon to come true. [18]Then a different king began to rule Egypt, one who knew nothing about Joseph. [19]This king tricked our people. He treated them badly, making them leave their children outside to die.

[20]"This was the time when Moses was born. He was a very beautiful child, and for three months his parents took care of him at home. [21]When they put him outside, Pharaoh's daughter took him. She raised him as her own son. [22]The Egyptians taught Moses everything they knew. He was powerful in all he said and did.

[23]"When Moses was about 40 years old, he decided to visit his own people, the people of Israel. [24]He saw one of them being mistreated by an Egyptian, so he defended him. Moses hit the Egyptian to pay him back for hurting the man. He hit him so hard that it killed him. [25]Moses thought that his people would understand that God was using him to save them. But they did not understand.

[26]"The next day, Moses saw two of his own people fighting. He tried to make peace between them. He said, 'Men, you are brothers! Why are you trying to hurt each other?' [27]The man who was hurting the other one pushed Moses away and said to him, 'Did anyone say you could be our ruler and judge? [28]Will you kill me just as you killed that Egyptian yesterday?'[a] [29]When Moses heard him say this, he left Egypt. He went to live in the land of Midian, where he was a stranger. During the time he lived there, he had two sons.

[30]"Forty years later Moses was in the desert near Mount Sinai. An angel appeared to him in the flame of a burning bush. [31]When Moses saw this, he was amazed. He went near to look closer at it. He heard a voice; it was the Lord's. [32]The Lord said, 'I am the same God your ancestors had—the God of Abraham, the God of Isaac and the God of Jacob.'[b] Moses began to shake with fear. He was afraid to look at the bush.

[33]"The Lord said to him, 'Take off your sandals, because the place where you are now standing is holy ground. [34]I have seen my people suffer much in Egypt. I have heard my people crying and have come down to save them. Come now, Moses, I am sending you back to Egypt.'[c]

[35]"This Moses was the one his people said they did not want. They said, 'Did anyone say you could be our ruler and judge?'[d] But he is the one God sent to be a ruler and saviour. God sent him with the help of an angel, the one Moses saw in the burning bush. [36]So Moses led the people out of Egypt. He worked wonders and miraculous signs in Egypt, at the Red Sea and then in the desert for 40 years.

[37]"This is the same Moses who said these words to the people of Israel: 'God will give you a prophet. That prophet will come from among your own people. He will be like me.'[e] [38]This same Moses was with the gathering of God's people in the desert. He was with the angel who spoke to him at Mount Sinai, and he was with our ancestors. He received life-giving words from God to give to us.

[39]"But our ancestors did not want to obey Moses. They rejected him. They wanted to go back to Egypt again. [40]They said to Aaron, 'Moses led us out of the country of Egypt. But we don't know what has happened to him. So make some gods to go before us and lead us.'[f] [41]So the people made an idol that looked like a calf. Then they brought sacrifices to it. They were very happy with what they had made with their own hands. [42]But God turned against them and let them

a **7:28** Quote from Exod. 2:14.
b **7:32** Quote from Exod. 3:6.
c **7:34** Quote from Exod. 3:5–10.
d **7:35** Quote from Exod. 2:14.
e **7:37** Quote from Deut. 18:15.
f **7:40** Quote from Exod. 32:1.

continue worshipping the army of false gods in the sky. This is what God says in the book that contains what the prophets wrote:

'People of Israel, you did not bring me blood
     offerings and sacrifices
   in the desert for 40 years;
[43]You carried with you the tent for worshipping
     Moloch
   and the image of the star of your god
     Rephan.
These were the idols you made to worship.
   So I will send you away beyond Babylon.'
                                    Amos 5:25–27

[44]"The Holy Tent[a] was with our ancestors in the desert. God told Moses how to make this tent. He made it like the plan that God showed him. [45]Later, Joshua led our ancestors to capture the lands of the other nations. Our people went in and God made the other people leave. When our people went into this new land, they took with them this same tent. Our people received this tent from their fathers, and our people kept it until the time of David. [46]God was very pleased with David. He asked God to let him build a temple for the people of Israel.[b] [47]But Solomon was the one who built the Temple for God.

[48]"But the Most High God does not need buildings made by human hands to live in. This is what the prophet writes:

[49]'The Lord says, Heaven is my throne,
   and the earth is where I rest my feet.
So do you think you can build a house for me?
   Do I need a place to rest?
[50]Remember, I made all these things!'"
                                    Isaiah 66:1–2

[51]Then Stephen said, "You stubborn Jewish leaders! You refuse to give your hearts to God or even listen to him. You are always against what the Holy Spirit wants you to do. That's how your ancestors were, and you are just like them! [52]They persecuted every prophet who ever lived. They even killed those who long ago said that the Righteous One would come. And now you have turned against that Righteous One and killed him. [53]You are the people who received God's law, which he gave you through his angels. But you don't obey it!"

Stephen Is Killed

[54]When those in the council meeting heard this, they became very angry. They were so angry they were grinding their teeth at him. [55]But Stephen was full of the Holy Spirit. He looked up into heaven and saw the glory of God. And he saw Jesus standing at God's right side. [56]Stephen said, "Look! I see heaven open. And I see the Son of Man standing at God's right side."

[57]Everyone there started shouting loudly, covering their ears with their hands. Together they all ran at Stephen. [58]They took him out of the city and began throwing stones at him. The men who told lies against Stephen gave their coats to a young man named Saul. [59]As they were throwing the stones at him, Stephen was praying. He said, "Lord Jesus, receive my spirit!" [60]He fell on his knees and shouted, "Lord, don't blame them for this sin!" These were his last words before he died.

8 Saul agreed that the killing of Stephen was a good thing. [2]Some godly men buried Stephen and cried loudly for him.

Trouble for the Believers

On that day the Jews began to persecute the church in Jerusalem, making them suffer very much. [3]Saul was also trying to destroy the group. He went into their houses, dragged out men and women and put them in jail. All the believers left Jerusalem. Only the apostles stayed. The believers went to different places in Judea and Samaria. [4]They were scattered everywhere. And everywhere they went, they told people the Good News.

Philip Tells the Good News in Samaria

[5]Philip[c] went to the city of Samaria and told people about the Messiah. [6]The people there heard Philip and saw the miraculous signs he was doing. They all listened carefully to what he said. [7]Many of these people had evil spirits inside them, but Philip made the evil spirits leave them. The spirits made a lot of noise as they came out. There were also many weak and lame people there. Philip made these people well too. [8]What a happy day this was for that city!

[9]Now there was a man named Simon who lived in that city. Before Philip went there, Simon had been doing magic and amazing all the people of Samaria. He boasted and called himself a great man. [10]All the people—the least important and the most important—believed what he said. They said, "This man has the power of God that is called 'the Great Power'." [11]Simon amazed the people with his magic for so long that the people became his followers. [12]But Philip told the people the Good News about God's kingdom and the

---

[a] **7:44 Holy Tent** Literally, "Tent of the Testimony". See "HOLY TENT" in the Word List.
[b] **7:46 the people of Israel** Literally, "the house of Jacob". Some Greek copies have "the God of Jacob".
[c] **8:5 Philip** Not the apostle named Philip.

THE RIPPLE EFFECT

Acts is the story of how the Good News of Jesus spread – from a tiny number of witnesses of Jesus' resurrection in Jerusalem to the creation of new churches all around the Mediterranean. It's a bit like what happens when you drop a stone in a pool of water – the impact spreads ripples a long way.

Hardly any time has passed since the believers received the Holy Spirit in Acts 2. But already the Good News has spread to neighbouring Judea and Samaria – and it's about to go a whole lot further . . .

DIG IN

READ Acts 8:26–39

- What can we find out about the eunuch Philip is sent to meet (vv.27–28)?
- How does Philip take the opportunity to witness about Jesus?

Here's a man who is both wealthy and powerful. Perhaps he'd been in Jerusalem on business for the queen of Ethiopia. But, no, verse 27 tells us he was actually there to worship – he's hungry for God – and he's reading his own copy of Isaiah (almost unheard of in those days). He's not a Jew but he's seeking the true God.

Philip, who we first met in Acts 6 was a leader in the church who God was already using powerfully as a travelling evangelist. Check out Acts 8:5–13 to see how he shared the Good News with the Samaritans. Now God is sending him to meet another person even further out on the fringe of Jewish life.

- In what ways was Philip obedient to God's leading (vv.26,29)?
- What was the role of the Holy Spirit in this encounter?

Certainly none of this encounter would have happened if Philip had not been obedient to the leading of the angel and the Holy Spirit. But most of all, we can see that the Holy Spirit was in charge all the way through, both in miraculous ways and quite "ordinary" ones. He lined everything up for Philip – and even helped him make a sharp exit afterwards (v.39)!

The ripple effect started with Jesus' promise in Acts 1:8: "You will be my witnesses . . . in every part of the world" and as we read through Acts we are watching the impact of this grow wider and wider.

DIG THROUGH

- Philip was willing to go when and where God told him – even out into the desert on what might have seemed like a "wild goose chase". And he was willing to speak out, not intimidated by this high-powered official. How can we expect to see the Holy Spirit leading us in our witness to Jesus?
- Did you notice how Philip was able to explain God's word to the eunuch? Throughout Acts you'll see that as the Good News of Jesus is shared with people they believe! Who might you be able to share the Good News of Jesus with today? Don't worry about saying the wrong thing – God's Spirit will help you!

DIG DEEPER

- Philip shows how the text the eunuch was reading – from Isaiah 53 – refers specifically to Jesus: he is the "servant" who came to take away the sins of the world. Jesus is the key to unlocking the full meaning of the Old Testament. Without him, it doesn't make sense. Spend more time in Isaiah looking out for glimpses of Jesus.

power of Jesus Christ. Men and women believed Philip and were baptized. [13]Simon himself also believed, and after he was baptized, he stayed close to Philip. When he saw the miraculous signs and powerful things Philip did, he was amazed.

[14]The apostles in Jerusalem heard that the people of Samaria had accepted the word of God. So they sent Peter and John to the people in Samaria. [15]When Peter and John arrived, they prayed for the Samaritan believers to receive the Holy Spirit. [16]These people had been baptized in the name of the Lord Jesus, but the Holy Spirit had not yet come down on any of them. This is why Peter and John prayed. [17]When the two apostles laid their hands on the people, they received the Holy Spirit.

[18]Simon saw that the Spirit was given to people when the apostles laid their hands on them. So he offered the apostles money. [19]He said, "Give me this power so that when I lay my hands on someone, they will receive the Holy Spirit."

[20]Peter said to Simon, "You and your money should both be destroyed because you thought you could buy God's gift with money. [21]You cannot share with us in this work. Your heart is not right before God. [22]Change your heart! Turn away from these evil thoughts and pray to the Lord. Maybe he will forgive you. [23]I see that you are full of bitter jealousy and cannot stop yourself from doing wrong."

[24]Simon answered, "Both of you pray to the Lord for me, so that what you have said will not happen to me."

[25]Then the two apostles told the people what they had seen Jesus do. They told them the message of the Lord. Then they went back to Jerusalem. On the way, they went through many Samaritan towns and told people the Good News.

Philip Teaches a Man From Ethiopia

[26]An angel of the Lord spoke to Philip. The angel said, "Get ready and go south on the road that leads down to Gaza from Jerusalem—the road that goes through the desert."

[27]So Philip got ready and went. On the road he saw a man from Ethiopia. He was a eunuch and an important official in the service of Candace, the queen of the Ethiopians. He was responsible for taking care of all her money. This man had gone to Jerusalem to worship. [28]Now he was on his way home. He was sitting in his chariot reading from the book of Isaiah the prophet.

[29]The Spirit said to Philip, "Go to that chariot and stay near it." [30]So he went towards the chariot, and he heard the man reading from Isaiah the prophet. Philip asked him, "Do you understand what you are reading?"

[31]The man answered, "How can I understand? I need someone to explain it to me." Then he invited Philip to climb in and sit with him. [32]The part of the Scriptures that he was reading was this:

"He was like a sheep being led to the butcher,
    like a lamb that makes no sound as its wool
        is cut off.
    He said nothing.
[33]He was shamed, and all his rights were taken
        away.
    His life on earth has ended.
    So there will be no story about his
        descendants."

Isaiah 53:7–8

[34]The official[a] said to Philip, "Please, tell me, who is the prophet talking about? Is he talking about himself or about someone else?" [35]Philip began to speak. He started with this same Scripture and told the man the Good News about Jesus.

[36]While they were travelling down the road, they came to some water. The official said, "Look, here is water! What is stopping me from being baptized?" [37b] [38]Then he ordered his chariot to stop. Both Philip and the official went down into the water, and Philip baptized him. [39]When they came up out of the water, the Spirit of the Lord took Philip away; the official never saw him again, but he was very happy as he continued on his way home. [40]Later, Philip appeared in a city called Azotus and went from there towards the city of Caesarea. He told people the Good News in all the towns on the way from Azotus to Caesarea.

Saul Becomes a Follower of Jesus

9 In Jerusalem Saul was still trying to scare the followers of the Lord, even saying he would kill them. He went to the high priest [2]and asked him to write letters to the synagogues in the city of Damascus. Saul wanted the high priest to give him the authority to find people in Damascus who were followers of the Way. If he found any believers there, men or women, he would arrest them and bring them back to Jerusalem.

---

[a] **8:34** *official* Literally, "eunuch". Also in verses 36,38,39.
[b] **8:37** Some late copies of Acts add verse 37: "Philip answered, 'If you believe with all your heart, you can.' The official said, 'I believe that Jesus Christ is the Son of God.'"

³So Saul went to Damascus. When he came near the city, a very bright light from heaven suddenly flashed around him. ⁴He fell to the ground and heard a voice saying to him, "Saul, Saul! Why are you persecuting me?"

⁵Saul said, "Who are you, Lord?"

The voice answered, "I am Jesus, the one you are persecuting. ⁶Get up now and go into the city. Someone there will tell you what you must do."

⁷The men travelling with Saul just stood there, unable to speak. They heard the voice, but they saw no one. ⁸Saul got up from the ground and opened his eyes, but he could not see. So the men with him held his hand and led him into Damascus. ⁹For three days, Saul could not see; he did not eat or drink.

¹⁰There was a follower of Jesus in Damascus named Ananias. In a vision the Lord said to him, "Ananias!"

Ananias answered, "Here I am, Lord."

¹¹The Lord said to him, "Get up and go to the street called Straight Street. Find the house of Judas*ᵃ* and ask for a man named Saul from the city of Tarsus. He is there now, praying. ¹²He has seen a vision in which a man named Ananias came and laid his hands on him so that he could see again."

¹³But Ananias answered, "Lord, many people have told me about this man. They told me about the many bad things he did to your holy people in Jerusalem. ¹⁴Now he has come here to Damascus. The leading priests have given him the power to arrest all people who trust in you."*ᵇ*

¹⁵But the Lord Jesus said to Ananias, "Go! I have chosen Saul for an important work. I want him to tell other nations, their rulers and the people of Israel about me. ¹⁶I will show him all that he must suffer for me."

¹⁷So Ananias left and went to the house of Judas. He laid his hands on Saul and said, "Saul, my brother, the Lord Jesus sent me. He is the one you saw on the road on your way here. He sent me so that you can see again and also be filled with the Holy Spirit." ¹⁸Immediately, something that looked like fish scales fell off Saul's eyes. He was able to see! Then he got up and was baptized. ¹⁹After eating some food, he began to feel strong again.

Saul Begins to Tell People About Jesus

Saul stayed with the followers of Jesus in Damascus for a few days. ²⁰Soon he began to go to the synagogues and tell people about Jesus. He told the people, "Jesus is the Son of God!"

²¹All the people who heard Saul were amazed. They said, "This is the same man who was in Jerusalem trying to destroy the people who trust in Jesus!*ᶜ* And that's why he has come here—to arrest the followers of Jesus and take them back to the leading priests."

²²But Saul became more and more powerful in proving that Jesus is the Messiah. His proofs were so strong that the Jews who lived in Damascus could not argue with him.

Saul Escapes From Some Jews

²³After many days, some Jews made plans to kill Saul. ²⁴They were watching the city gates day and night. They wanted to kill Saul, but he learned about their plan. ²⁵One night some followers that Saul had taught helped him leave the city. They put him in a basket and lowered it down through a hole in the city wall.

Saul in Jerusalem

²⁶Then Saul went to Jerusalem. He tried to join the group of followers, but they were all afraid of him. They did not believe that he was really a follower of Jesus. ²⁷But Barnabas accepted Saul and took him to the apostles. He told them how Saul had seen the Lord on the road and how the Lord had spoken to Saul. Then he told them how boldly Saul had spoken for the Lord in Damascus.

²⁸And so Saul stayed with the followers and went all around Jerusalem speaking boldly for the Lord. ²⁹He often had arguments with the Greek-speaking Jews, who began making plans to kill him. ³⁰When the believers learned about this, they took Saul to Caesarea, and from there they sent him to the city of Tarsus.

³¹The church in Judea, Galilee and Samaria had a time of peace. And with the help of the Holy Spirit, these groups of believers became stronger in faith and showed their respect for the Lord by the way they lived. So the church everywhere grew in numbers.

Peter in Lydda and Joppa

³²Peter was travelling through all the areas around Jerusalem, and he stopped to visit the believers*ᵈ* who lived in Lydda. ³³There he met a man named Aeneas, who was paralysed and had not been able to get out of bed for the past eight

---

ᵃ **9:11 Judas** This is not either of the apostles named Judas.
ᵇ **9:14 who trust in you** Literally, "who call on your name", meaning to show faith in Jesus by worshipping him or praying to him for help.
ᶜ **9:21 who trust in Jesus** Literally, "who call on this name".
ᵈ **9:32 believers** Literally, "holy ones", a name for people who believe in Jesus. Also in verse 41.

years. ³⁴Peter said to him, "Aeneas, Jesus Christ heals you. Get up and make your bed!" He stood up immediately. ³⁵All the people living in Lydda and on the plain of Sharon saw him, and they decided to follow the Lord.

³⁶In the city of Joppa there was a follower of Jesus named Tabitha. Her Greek name, Dorcas, means "a deer". She was always doing good things for people and giving money to those in need. ³⁷While Peter was in Lydda, Tabitha became sick and died. They washed her body and put it in an upstairs room. ³⁸The followers in Joppa heard that Peter was in Lydda, which was not far away. So they sent two men, who begged him, "Hurry, please come quickly!"

³⁹Peter got ready and went with them. When he arrived, they took him to the upstairs room. All the widows stood around him. They were crying and showing him the coats and other clothes that Tabitha had made during her time with them. ⁴⁰Peter sent all the people out of the room. He knelt down and prayed. Then he turned to Tabitha's body and said, "Tabitha, stand up!" She opened her eyes. When she saw Peter, she sat up. ⁴¹He gave her his hand and helped her stand up. Then he called the believers and the widows into the room. He showed them Tabitha; she was alive!

⁴²People everywhere in Joppa learned about this, and many believed in the Lord. ⁴³Peter stayed in Joppa for many days at the home of a man named Simon, who was a leatherworker.

INSIGHT

Tanning was a smelly job, using a combination of urine and animal faeces to turn the animal hides into finished leather. Still, at least the sea breeze at Joppa could whisk away some of the stench of the drying hides!

Acts 9:43

Peter and Cornelius

10 In the city of Caesarea there was a man named Cornelius, a Roman army officer in what was called the Italian Unit. ²He was a religious man. He and all the others who lived in his house were worshippers of the true God. He gave much of his money to help the poor among the Jewish people and always prayed to God. ³One afternoon about three o'clock, Cornelius had a vision. He clearly saw an angel from God coming to him and saying, "Cornelius!"

⁴Staring at the angel in fear, Cornelius said, "What do you want, sir?"

The angel said to him, "God has heard your prayers and has seen your gifts to the poor. He remembers you and all you have done. ⁵Send some men now to the city of Joppa to get a man named Simon, who is also called Peter. ⁶He is staying with someone also named Simon, a leatherworker who has a house beside the sea."

⁷The angel who spoke to Cornelius left. Then Cornelius called two of his servants and a soldier. The soldier was a religious man, one of his close helpers. ⁸Cornelius explained everything to these three men and sent them to Joppa.

⁹The next day about noon, as they got near to Joppa, Peter was going up to the roof to pray. ¹⁰He was hungry and wanted to eat. But while the food was being prepared, he had a vision. ¹¹He saw something coming down through the open sky. It looked like a big sheet being lowered to the ground by its four corners. ¹²In it were all kinds of animals, reptiles and birds. ¹³Then a voice said to him, "Get up, Peter; kill anything here and eat it."

¹⁴But Peter said, "I can't do that, Lord! I have never eaten anything that is not pure or fit to be used for food."

¹⁵But the voice said to him again, "God has made these things pure. Don't say they are unfit to eat." ¹⁶This happened three times. Then the whole thing was taken back up into heaven. ¹⁷Peter wondered what this vision meant.

The men Cornelius sent had found Simon's house. They were standing at the door. ¹⁸They asked, "Is Simon Peter staying here?"

¹⁹While Peter was still thinking about the vision, the Spirit said to him, "Listen, three men are looking for you. ²⁰Get up and go downstairs. Go with these men without wondering if it's all right, because I sent them." ²¹So Peter went downstairs and said to them, "I think I'm the man you are looking for. Why did you come here?"

²²The men said, "A holy angel told Cornelius to invite you to his house. He is an army officer. He is a good man who worships God, and all the Jewish people respect him. The angel told him to invite you to his house so that he can listen to what you have to say." ²³Peter asked the men to come in and stay for the night.

The next day Peter got ready and went away with the three men. Some of the believers from Joppa went with him. ²⁴The next day they came to the city of Caesarea. Cornelius was waiting for them and had already gathered his relatives and close friends at his house.

²⁵When Peter entered the house, Cornelius met him. He fell down at Peter's feet and

WAKING UP TO GOD'S PLAN

"So go and make followers of all people in the world" (Matthew 28:19). Jesus' words to his disciples made it pretty clear that the Good News was for people everywhere. So did his words to the apostles in Acts 1:8: "You will be my witnesses . . . in Jerusalem, in the rest of Judea, in Samaria and in every part of the world."

But up till now, almost everybody who had believed in Jesus had been a Jew. It probably seemed to men like Peter that anyone who wanted to follow him would have to become a Jew first. That was all about to change!

DIG IN

READ Acts 10:9-29

- What is God showing to Peter (vv.11–16) and what is his reaction?
- How did the vision help Peter see what he should do next (v.28)?

It had been a long time since breakfast, so perhaps it's no surprise that Peter had visions of food! But this is no ordinary vision and God's request "Get up, Peter; kill anything here and eat it" sounds plain wrong. Peter – raised a good Jewish boy – would know that his religion's strict food laws would allow him to do no such thing.

But God shows this vision to him three times and reassures him that what Peter thought was off-limits God actually approved of. So when Cornelius's servants show up – something starts to dawn on him.

By the time he gets to Cornelius's house Peter is ready to do something else no good Jewish boy would ever do – enter his house and receive his hospitality. Peter is waking up to the fact that God's promise is for non-Jews – also known as "Gentiles" – too.

READ Acts 10:34-48

- How does Peter's new understanding affect what he does next (vv.34–35)?
- How does God confirm it (vv.44–46)?

Peter wastes no time in preaching the Good News – and even before he's finished, the Holy Spirit is sent to confirm his words. The non-Jews are filled with the Spirit and speak in tongues in exactly the same way as the Jews in Acts 2:1–11. This was proof that the promise was for Jews and non-Jews alike.

DIG THROUGH

- Sometimes God can turn our understanding of his ways totally on its head. Can you remember a time when God showed you something in his word that radically changed the way you think?
- Read Paul's words to the church in Ephesus in Ephesians 2:11–16. In what ways can we demonstrate the unity between us that God calls for among his people? How can we take down barriers that culture, the media and peer pressure might try to put up between us today?

DIG DEEPER

- For thousands of years, the Jewish people had understood themselves to be the people of God – the only people of God. To find out this was not true was such a shock to the early church leaders that some took a long time to be convinced. Read Acts 11:1–18 to see how Peter explained it to them. Even after this, some parts of the church struggled with the implications for years afterwards: check out Acts 15 and the book of Galatians for more about this.

worshipped him. 26But Peter told him to get up. Peter said, "Stand up! I am only a man like you." 27Peter continued talking with Cornelius. Then Peter went inside and saw a large group of people gathered there.

28Peter said to the people, "You understand that it is against our law for a Jew to associate with or visit anyone who is not a Jew. But God has shown me that I should not consider anyone unfit or say they are not pure. 29That's why I didn't argue when your men asked me to come here. Now, please tell me why you sent for me."

30Cornelius said, "Four days ago, I was praying in my house. It was at this same time—three o'clock in the afternoon. Suddenly there was someone standing before me wearing bright, shiny clothes. 31He said, 'Cornelius, God has heard your prayer and has seen your gifts to the poor. He remembers you and all you have done. 32So send some men to the city of Joppa and tell Simon Peter to come. He is staying with another man named Simon, a leatherworker who has a house beside the sea.' 33So I sent for you immediately. It was very good of you to come here. Now we are all here before God to hear everything the Lord has commanded you to tell us."

Peter Speaks in the House of Cornelius

34Peter began to speak: "Now I understand that God does not consider some people to be better than others. 35He accepts anyone who worships him and does what is right. It is not important what nation they come from. 36God has spoken to the people of Israel. He sent them the Good News that peace has come through Jesus Christ. Jesus is the one who is Lord over all people.

37"You know what has happened all over Judea. It began in Galilee after John told the people they needed to be baptized. 38You know about Jesus from Nazareth. God made him the Messiah by giving him the Holy Spirit and power. Jesus went everywhere doing good for people. He healed those who were ruled by the devil, showing that God was with him.

39"We saw all that Jesus did in Judea and in Jerusalem. But he was killed. They put him on a cross made of wood. 40But on the third day after his death, God raised him to life and let him be seen openly. 41He was not seen by everyone, but only by us, the ones God had already chosen to be witnesses. We ate and drank with him after he was raised from death.

42"Jesus told us to go and speak to the people. He told us to tell them that he is the one God chose to be the Judge of all who are living and all who have died. 43Everyone who believes in Jesus will have their sins forgiven through his name. All the prophets agree that this is true."

God Shows That He Accepts All People

44While Peter was still speaking these words, the Holy Spirit came down on all those who were listening to his speech. 45The Jewish believers who came with Peter were amazed that the Holy Spirit had been poured out as a gift also to people who were not Jews. 46They heard them speaking different languages and praising God. Then Peter said, 47"How can anyone object to these people being baptized in water? They have received the Holy Spirit just as we did!" 48So Peter told them to baptize Cornelius and his relatives and friends in the name of Jesus Christ. Then they asked Peter to stay with them for a few days.

Peter Returns to Jerusalem

11 The apostles and the believers in Judea heard that non-Jewish people had accepted God's teaching too. 2But when Peter came to Jerusalem, some Jewish believers*a* argued with him. 3They said, "You went into the homes of people who are not Jews and are not circumcised, and you even ate with them!"

4So Peter explained the whole story to them. 5He said, "I was in the city of Joppa. While I was praying, I had a vision. I saw something coming down from heaven. It looked like a big sheet being lowered to the ground by its four corners. It came down close to me, 6and I looked inside. I saw all kinds of animals, including wild ones, as well as reptiles and birds. 7I heard a voice say to me, 'Get up, Peter. Kill anything here and eat it!'

8"But I said, 'I can't do that, Lord! I have never eaten anything that is not pure or fit to be used for food.'

9"But the voice from heaven answered again, 'God has made these things pure. Don't say they are unfit to eat!'

10"This happened three times. Then the whole thing was taken back into heaven. 11Suddenly there were three men standing outside the house where I was staying. They had been sent from Caesarea to get me. 12The Spirit told me to go with them without wondering if it was all right. These six brothers here also went with me, and we went to the house of Cornelius. 13He told us about the angel who had appeared to him in his house. The angel had said, 'Send some men to Joppa to get Simon,

---

a **11:2** *Jewish believers* Literally, "those of circumcision". This may mean Jews who thought all followers of Christ must be circumcised and obey the Law of Moses. See Gal. 2:12.

the one who is also called Peter. [14]He will speak to you, and what he tells you will save you and everyone living in your house.'

[15]"After I began speaking, the Holy Spirit came on them just as he came on us at the beginning.[a] [16]Then I remembered the words of the Lord Jesus: 'John baptized people in water, but you will be baptized in the Holy Spirit.' [17]God gave these people the same gift he gave us who believed in the Lord Jesus Christ. So how could I object to what God wanted to do?"

[18]When the Jewish believers heard this, they stopped arguing. They praised God and said, "So God is allowing even those who are not Jews to change their hearts so that they can have the life he gives!"

The Good News Comes to Antioch

[19]The believers had been scattered by the persecution[b] that began when Stephen was killed. Some of them went as far as Phoenicia, Cyprus and Antioch. They told the Good News in these places, but only to Jews. [20]Some of these believers were men from Cyprus and Cyrene. When these men came to Antioch, they began speaking to people who were not Jews.[c] They told them the Good News about the Lord Jesus. [21]The Lord was helping these men, and a large number of people believed and decided to follow the Lord.

[22]When the church in Jerusalem heard about this, they sent Barnabas to Antioch. [23-24]Barnabas was a good man, full of the Holy Spirit and faith. When he arrived in Antioch and saw how God had blessed the believers there, he was very happy. He encouraged them all, saying, "Always be faithful to the Lord. Serve him with all your heart." Many more people became followers of the Lord.

[25]Then Barnabas went to the city of Tarsus to look for Saul. [26]When he found him, he brought him to Antioch. They stayed there a whole year. Every time the church came together, Barnabas and Saul met with them and taught many people. It was in Antioch that people began calling the followers of the Lord Jesus "Christians".

[27]About that same time some prophets went from Jerusalem to Antioch. [28]One of them, named Agabus, stood up and spoke with the help of the Spirit. He said, "A very bad time is coming to the whole world. There will be no food for people to eat." (This time of famine happened when Claudius was emperor.) [29]The Lord's followers decided that they would each send as much as they could to help their brothers and sisters who lived in Judea. [30]They gathered the money and gave it to Barnabas and Saul, who took it to the elders in Judea.

More Trouble for the Believers

12 During this same time, King Herod began to do harm to some of those who were part of the church. [2]He ordered James, the brother of John, to be killed with a sword. [3]Herod saw that the Jews liked this, so he decided to arrest Peter too. This happened during the Festival of Unleavened Bread. [4]He arrested Peter and put him in jail, where he was guarded by a group of 16 soldiers. Herod planned to bring Peter before the people, but he wanted to wait until after the Passover festival. [5]So Peter was kept in jail, but the church was constantly praying to God for him.

Peter Is Led Out of the Jail

[6]One night, Peter, bound with two chains, was sleeping between two of the soldiers. More soldiers were guarding the door of the jail. Herod was planning to bring Peter out before the people the next day. [7]Suddenly an angel of the Lord was standing there, and the room was filled with light. The angel tapped Peter on the side and woke him up. The angel said, "Hurry, get up!" The chains fell off Peter's hands. [8]The angel said, "Get dressed and put on your sandals." Peter did as he was told. Then the angel said, "Put on your coat and follow me."

[9]So the angel went out and Peter followed. He did not know if the angel was really doing this. He thought he might be seeing a vision. [10]Peter and the angel went past the first guard and the second guard. Then they came to the iron gate that separated them from the city. The gate opened for them by itself. After they had gone through the gate and walked down the street, the angel suddenly left.

[11]Peter realized then what had happened. He thought, "Now I know that the Lord really sent his angel to me. He has rescued me from Herod and from all the bad things the Jews thought would happen to me."

[12]When Peter realized this, he went to the home of Mary, the mother of John Mark. Many people were gathered there and were praying. [13]Peter knocked on the outside door. A servant

---

[a] **11:15 beginning** The day of Pentecost described in Acts 2, when the Holy Spirit came on Jesus' first followers to give them power to begin their work of telling the world the Good News of salvation through Jesus.
[b] **11:19 persecution** A time when the Jewish leaders in Jerusalem were punishing people who believed in Christ. See Acts 8:1–4.
[c] **11:20 people who were not Jews** Literally, "Hellenists", meaning people who have been influenced by Greek culture. Some Greek copies have "Greeks".

girl named Rhoda came to answer it. ¹⁴She recognized Peter's voice, and she was very happy. She even forgot to open the door. She ran inside and told the group, "Peter is at the door!" ¹⁵The believers said to her, "You are crazy!" But she continued to say that it was true. So they said, "It must be Peter's angel."

¹⁶But Peter continued to knock. When the believers opened the door, they saw him. They were amazed. ¹⁷Peter made a sign with his hand to tell them to be quiet. He explained to them how the Lord had led him out of the jail. He said, "Tell James and the other brothers what happened." Then he left and went to another place.

INSIGHT

There are so many men called James in the New Testament! This James is the brother of Jesus (who wrote the book of James) not the disciple James, the brother of John, or another disciple often known as James the younger! By the time of Jesus' ascension this James had turned from unbelief to faith and, although he wasn't one of the original twelve apostles, at this time James seems to have been the leader of the Jerusalem Church.

Acts 12:17

¹⁸The next day the soldiers were very upset. They wondered what had happened to Peter. ¹⁹Herod looked everywhere for him but could not find him. So he questioned the guards and then ordered that they be killed.

The Death of Herod Agrippa

Later, Herod moved from Judea. He went to the city of Caesarea and stayed there a while. ²⁰Herod was very angry with the people from the cities of Tyre and Sidon. But these cities needed food from his country, so a group of them came to ask him for peace. They were able to get Blastus, the king's personal servant, on their side.

²¹Herod decided on a day to meet with them. On that day he was wearing a beautiful royal robe. He sat on his throne and made a speech to the people. ²²The people shouted, "This is the voice of a god, not a man!" ²³Herod did not give the glory to God. So an angel of the Lord caused

him to get sick. He was eaten by worms and he died.

²⁴The message of God was spreading, reaching more and more people.

²⁵After Barnabas and Saul finished their work in Jerusalem, they returned to Antioch, taking John Mark with them.

Barnabas and Saul Given a Special Work

13 In the church at Antioch there were some prophets and teachers. They were Barnabas, Simeon (also called Niger), Lucius (from the city of Cyrene), Manaen (who had grown up with King Herod[a]) and Saul. ²These men were all serving the Lord and fasting when the Holy Spirit said to them, "Appoint Barnabas and Saul to do a special work for me. They are the ones I have chosen to do it."

³So the church fasted and prayed. They laid their hands on Barnabas and Saul and sent them out.

Barnabas and Saul in Cyprus

⁴Barnabas and Saul were sent out by the Holy Spirit. They went to the city of Seleucia. Then they sailed from there to the island of Cyprus. ⁵When Barnabas and Saul came to the city of Salamis, they told the message of God in the Jewish synagogues. John Mark was with them to help.

⁶They went across the whole island to the city of Paphos. There they met a Jewish man named Barjesus who did magic. He was a false prophet. ⁷He always stayed close to Sergius Paulus, who was the governor and a very smart man. He invited Barnabas and Saul to come and visit him, because he wanted to hear the message of God. ⁸But the magician Elymas (as Barjesus was called in Greek) spoke against them, trying to stop the governor from believing in Jesus. ⁹But Saul (also known as Paul), filled with the Holy Spirit, looked hard at Elymas ¹⁰and said, "You son of the devil, full of lies and all kinds of evil tricks! You are an enemy of everything that is right. Will you never stop trying to change the Lord's truths into lies? ¹¹Now the Lord will touch you and you will be blind. For a time you will not be able to see anything—not even the light from the sun."

Then everything became dark for Elymas. He walked around lost. He was trying to find someone to lead him by the hand. ¹²When the governor saw this, he believed. He was amazed at the teaching about the Lord.

Paul and Barnabas Go to Antioch in Pisidia

¹³Paul and the people with him sailed away from Paphos. They came to Perga, a city in

---

ᵃ **13:1** *King Herod* Literally, "Herod the tetrarch". See "HEROD AGRIPPA I" in the Word List.

Pamphylia. There John Mark left them and returned to Jerusalem. [14]They continued their trip from Perga and went to Antioch, a city near Pisidia.

On the Sabbath day they went into the Jewish synagogue and sat down. [15]The Law of Moses and the writings of the prophets were read. Then the leaders of the synagogue sent a message to Paul and Barnabas: "Brothers, if you have something to say that will help the people here, please speak."

[16]Paul stood up, raised his hand to get their attention, and said, "People of Israel and all you others who worship the true God, please listen to me! [17]The God of Israel chose our ancestors. And during the time our people lived in Egypt as foreigners, he made them great. Then he brought them out of that country with great power. [18]And he was patient with them for 40 years in the desert. [19]God destroyed seven nations in the land of Canaan and gave their land to his people. [20]All this happened in about 450 years.

"After this, God gave our people judges to lead them until the time of Samuel the prophet. [21]Then the people asked for a king. God gave them Saul, the son of Kish. Saul was from the tribe of Benjamin. He was king for 40 years. [22]After God took Saul away, God made David their king. This is what God said about David: 'David, the son of Jesse, is the kind of person who does what pleases me. He will do everything I want him to do.'

[23]"As he promised, God has brought one of David's descendants to Israel to be their Saviour. That descendant is Jesus. [24]Before he came, John told all the people of Israel what they should do. He told them to be baptized to show they wanted to change their lives. [25]When John was finishing his work, he said, 'Who do you think I am? I am not the Messiah.[a] He is coming later, and I am not worthy to be the slave who unties his sandals.'

[26]"My brothers, sons in the family of Abraham, and you other people who also worship the true God, listen! The news about this salvation has been sent to us. [27]The Jews living in Jerusalem and their leaders did not realize that Jesus was the Saviour. The words the prophets wrote about him were read every Sabbath day, but they did not understand. They condemned Jesus. When they did this, they made the words of the prophets come true. [28]They could not find any real reason why Jesus should die, but they asked Pilate to kill him.

[29]"These Jews did all the bad things that the Scriptures said would be done to Jesus. Then they took Jesus down from the cross and put him in a tomb. [30]But God raised him up from death! [31]After this, for many days, those who had gone with Jesus from Galilee to Jerusalem saw him. They are now his witnesses to our people.

[32]"We tell you the Good News about the promise God made to our ancestors. [33]We are their descendants, and God has made this promise come true for us. God did this by raising Jesus from death. We also read about this in Psalm 2:

'You are my Son.
    Today I have become your Father.'

Psalm 2:7

[34]God raised Jesus from death. Jesus will never go back to the grave and become dust. So God said,

'I will give you the true and holy promises
    that I made to David.'

Isaiah 55:3

[35]But in another Psalm it says,

'You will not let your Holy One rot in the
    grave.'

Psalm 16:10

[36]David did God's will during the time he lived. Then he died and was buried like all his ancestors. And his body did rot in the grave! [37]But the one God raised from death did not rot in the grave. [38–39]Brothers, understand what we are telling you. You can have forgiveness of your sins through this Jesus. The Law of Moses could not free you from your sins. But you can be free from all guilt and made right with God if you believe in Jesus. [40]So be careful! Don't let what the prophets said happen to you:

[41]'Listen, you people who doubt!
    You can wonder, but then go away and die;
because during your time,
    I will do something you will not believe.
You will not believe it,
    even if someone explains it to you!'"

Habakkuk 1:5

[42]As Paul and Barnabas were leaving the synagogue, the people asked them to come again on the next Sabbath day and tell them more about these things. [43]After the meeting, many of the people followed Paul and Barnabas, including many Jews and people who had changed their religion to be like Jews and worship the true God.

---

[a] **13:25 the Messiah** Literally, "I" (that is, "he" or "the one"), meaning the chosen one sent by God. Compare John 1:20. See "Messiah" in the Word List.

Paul and Barnabas encouraged them to continue trusting in God's grace.

⁴⁴On the next Sabbath day, almost all the people in the city came together to hear the word of the Lord. ⁴⁵When the Jews there saw all these people, they became very jealous. Shouting insults, they argued against everything Paul said. ⁴⁶But Paul and Barnabas spoke very boldly. They said, "We had to tell God's message to you Jews first, but you refuse to listen. You have made it clear that you are not worthy of having eternal life. So we will now go to those who are not Jews. ⁴⁷This is what the Lord told us to do:

'I have made you a light for the other nations,
    to show people all over the world the way
        to be saved.'"

Isaiah 49:6

⁴⁸When the non-Jewish people heard Paul say this, they were happy. They gave honour to the message of the Lord, and many of them believed it. These were the ones chosen to have eternal life.

⁴⁹And so the message of the Lord was being told throughout the whole country. ⁵⁰But the Jews there caused some of the important religious women and the leaders of the city to be angry and turn against Paul and Barnabas and throw them out of town. ⁵¹So Paul and Barnabas shook the dust off their feet.ᵃ Then they went to the city of Iconium. ⁵²But the Lord's followers in Antioch were happy and filled with the Holy Spirit.

Paul and Barnabas in Iconium

14 Paul and Barnabas went to the city of Iconium. As they did in Antioch, they entered the Jewish synagogue. They spoke to the people there. They spoke so well that many Jews and Greeks believed what they said. ²But some of the Jews did not believe. They said things that caused the non-Jewish people to be angry and turn against the believers.

³So Paul and Barnabas stayed in Iconium a long time, and they spoke bravely for the Lord. They told the people about God's grace. The Lord proved that what they said was true by causing miraculous signs and wonders to be done through them. ⁴But some of the people in the city agreed with the Jews who did not believe Paul and Barnabas. Others followed the apostles. So the city was divided.

⁵Some of the Jews there, as well as their leaders and some of the non-Jewish people, planned to hurt Paul and Barnabas. They wanted to stone them to death. ⁶When Paul and Barnabas learned about this, they left the city. They went to Lystra and Derbe, cities in Lycaonia and to the surrounding areas. ⁷They told people the Good News there too.

Paul in Lystra and Derbe

⁸In Lystra there was a man who had something wrong with his feet. He had been born lame and had never walked. ⁹He was sitting and listening to Paul speak. Paul looked straight at him and saw that the man believed God could heal him. ¹⁰So Paul shouted, "Stand up on your feet!" The man jumped up and began walking around.

¹¹When the people saw what Paul did, they shouted in their own Lycaonian language. They said, "The gods have come down to us in the form of humans!" ¹²The people began to call Barnabas "Zeus", and they called Paul "Hermes", because he was the main speaker. ¹³The temple of Zeus was near the city. The priest of this temple brought some bulls and flowers to the city gates. The priest and the people wanted to offer a sacrifice to Paul and Barnabas.

¹⁴But when the apostles, Barnabas and Paul, understood what the people were doing, they tore their own clothes.ᵇ Then they ran in among the people and shouted to them: ¹⁵"Men, why are you doing this? We are not gods. We are human just like you. We came to tell you the Good News. We are telling you to turn away from these worthless things. Turn to the true living God, the one who made the sky, the earth, the sea and everything that is in them. ¹⁶"In the past God let all the nations do what they wanted. ¹⁷But God was always there doing the good things that prove he is real. He gives you rain from heaven and good harvests at the right times. He gives you plenty of food and fills your hearts with joy." ¹⁸Even after saying all this, Paul and Barnabas still could hardly stop the people from offering sacrifices to them.

¹⁹Then some Jews came from Antioch and Iconium and persuaded the people to turn against Paul. So they threw stones at him and dragged him out of the town. They thought they had killed him. ²⁰But when the followers of Jesus gathered around him, he got up and went back into the town. The next day he and Barnabas left and went to the city of Derbe.

The Return to Antioch in Syria

²¹They also told people the Good News in the city of Derbe, and many people became followers

---

ᵃ **13:51 shook the dust off their feet** A warning. It showed they were finished talking to these people.
ᵇ **14:14 tore . . . clothes** This showed they were very upset.

of Jesus. Then Paul and Barnabas returned to the cities of Lystra, Iconium and Antioch. ²²In those cities they helped the followers grow stronger in their faith and encouraged them to continue to trust in God. They told them, "We must suffer many things on our way into God's kingdom." ²³They also chose elders for each church and stopped eating for a period of time to pray for them. These elders were men who had put their trust in the Lord Jesus, so Paul and Barnabas put them in his care.

²⁴Paul and Barnabas went through the country of Pisidia. Then they came to the country of Pamphylia. ²⁵They told people the message of God in the city of Perga, and then they went down to the city of Attalia. ²⁶And from there they sailed away to Antioch in Syria. This is the city where the believers had put them into God's care and sent them to do this work. Now they had finished it.

²⁷When Paul and Barnabas arrived in Antioch, they gathered the church together. They told the believers about everything God had used them to do. They said, "God opened a door for the non-Jewish people to believe!" ²⁸And they stayed there a long time with the Lord's followers.

INSIGHT

Some people just love rules. The hot topic in the early Church meetings was whether non-Jews had to conform to Jewish customs before they could become full "church members". The agreement they came to tried to reflect what they all believed about forgiveness and grace in the new family of God.

Acts 15:1–21

The Meeting at Jerusalem

15 Then some men from Judea came to Antioch and began teaching the family of believers there: "You cannot be saved if you are not circumcised as Moses taught us."ᵃ ²Paul and Barnabas were against this teaching and argued with these men about it. So the group decided to send Paul, Barnabas and some others to Jerusalem to talk more about this with the apostles and elders.

³The church helped them get ready to leave on their trip. The men went through the countries of Phoenicia and Samaria, where they told all about how the non-Jewish people had turned to the true God. This made all the believers very happy. ⁴When the men arrived in Jerusalem, the apostles, the elders and the whole church welcomed them. Paul, Barnabas and the others told the church all that God had done with them. ⁵Some of the believers in Jerusalem had belonged to the Pharisees. They stood up and said, "The non-Jewish believers must be circumcised. We must tell them to obey the Law of Moses!"

⁶Then the apostles and the elders gathered to study this problem. ⁷After a long debate, Peter stood up and said to them, "My brothers, I am sure you remember what happened in the early days. God chose me from among you to tell the Good News to those who are not Jewish. It was from me that they heard the Good News and believed. ⁸God knows everyone, even their thoughts, and he accepted these non-Jewish people. He showed this to us by giving them the Holy Spirit the same as he did to us. ⁹To God, those people are not different from us. When they believed, God made their hearts pure. ¹⁰So now, why are you putting a heavy burdenᵇ around the necks of the non-Jewish followers of Jesus? Are you trying to make God angry? We and our fathers were not able to carry that burden. ¹¹No, we believe that we and these people will be saved the same way—by the grace of the Lord Jesus."

¹²Then the whole group became quiet. They listened while Paul and Barnabas told them about all the miraculous signs and wonders that God had done through them among the non-Jewish people. ¹³When they had finished speaking, James said, "My brothers, listen to me. ¹⁴Simon Peter has told us how God showed his love for the non-Jewish people. For the first time, God accepted them and made them his people. ¹⁵The words of the prophets agree with this too:

¹⁶'I will return after this.
    I will build David's house again.
    It has fallen down.
I will build again the parts of his house that
    have been pulled down.
    I will make his house new.
¹⁷Then the rest of the world will look for the
    Lord God—
    all those of other nations who are my
    people too.

ᵃ **15:1 circumcised as Moses taught us** The men from Judea were Jewish believers who thought the church in Antioch was wrong because they did not require non-Jewish believers to be physically circumcised (see "CIRCUMCISE" in the Word List) in keeping with Jewish law.
ᵇ **15:10 burden** The Jewish law. Some of the Jews tried to make the non-Jewish believers follow this law.

The Lord said this.
And he is the one who does all these
things.'

Amos 9:11–12

[18]'All this has been known from the beginning of time.'[a]

[19]"So I think we should not make things hard for those who have turned to God from among the non-Jewish people. [20]Instead, we should send a letter telling them only the things they should not do:

Don't eat food that has been given to idols. This makes the food unclean.
Don't be involved in sexual sin.
Don't eat meat from animals that have been strangled or any meat that still has the blood in it.

[21]They should not do any of these things, because there are still men in every city who teach the Law of Moses. The words of Moses have been read in the synagogue every Sabbath day for many years."

The Letter to the Non-Jewish Believers

[22]The apostles, the elders and the whole church wanted to send some men with Paul and Barnabas to Antioch. The group decided to choose some of their own men. They chose Judas (also called Barsabbas) and Silas, men who were respected by the believers. [23]The group sent the letter with these men. The letter said:

From the apostles and elders, your brothers,

To all the non-Jewish brothers in the city of Antioch and in the countries of Syria and Cilicia.

Dear Brothers:
[24]We have heard that some men have come to you from our group. What they said troubled and upset you. But we did not tell them to do this. [25]We have all agreed to choose some men and send them to you. They will be with our dear friends, Barnabas and Paul. [26]Barnabas and Paul have given their lives to serve our Lord Jesus Christ. [27]So we have sent Judas and Silas with them. They will tell you the same things. [28]We agree with the Holy Spirit that you should have no more burdens, except for these necessary things:

[29]Don't eat food that has been given to idols. Don't eat meat from animals that have been strangled or any meat that still has the blood in it.
Don't be involved in sexual sin.

If you stay away from these, you will do well.

We say goodbye now.

[30]So Paul, Barnabas, Judas and Silas left Jerusalem and went to Antioch. There they gathered the group of believers together and gave them the letter. [31]When the believers read it, they were happy. The letter comforted them. [32]Judas and Silas, who were also prophets, said many things to encourage the believers and make them stronger in their faith. [33]Judas and Silas stayed there for a while, then they left. They received a blessing of peace from the believers. Then they went back to those who had sent them. [34][b]

[35]But Paul and Barnabas stayed in Antioch. They and many others taught the believers and told other people the Good News about the Lord.

Paul and Barnabas Separate

[36]A few days later, Paul said to Barnabas, "We should go back to all the towns where we told people the message of the Lord. We should visit the believers to see how they are doing." [37]Barnabas wanted to bring John Mark with them too. [38]But on their first trip John Mark did not continue with them in the work. He had left them at Pamphylia. So Paul did not think it was a good idea to take him this time. [39]Paul and Barnabas had a big argument about this. It was so bad that they separated and went different ways. Barnabas sailed to Cyprus and took Mark with him. [40]Paul chose Silas to go with him. The believers in Antioch put Paul into the Lord's care and sent him out. [41]Paul and Silas went through the countries of Syria and Cilicia, helping the churches grow stronger.

Timothy Goes With Paul and Silas

16 Paul went to the city of Derbe and then to Lystra, where a follower of Jesus named Timothy lived. Timothy's mother was a Jewish believer, but his father was a Greek. [2]The believers in the cities of Lystra and Iconium had only good things to say about him. [3]Paul wanted Timothy to travel with him, but all the Jews living in that area knew that his father was a Greek. So Paul circumcised Timothy to please the Jews.

---

[a] **15:18** See Isa. 45:21.
[b] **15:34** Some Greek copies add verse 34: "But Silas decided to remain there."

⁴Then Paul and those with him travelled through other cities. They gave the believers the rules and decisions from the apostles and elders in Jerusalem. They told them to obey these rules. ⁵So the churches were becoming stronger in their faith, and the number of believers was growing every day.

Paul Is Called to Macedonia

⁶Paul and those with him went through the areas of Phrygia and Galatia because the Holy Spirit did not allow them to tell the Good News in the province of Asia. ⁷When they reached the border of Mysia, they tried to go on into Bithynia, but the Spirit of Jesus did not let them go there. ⁸So they passed by Mysia and went to the city of Troas.

⁹That night Paul saw a vision. In it, a man from Macedonia came to Paul. The man stood there and begged, "Come across to Macedonia and help us." ¹⁰After Paul had seen the vision, we*ᵃ* immediately prepared to leave for Macedonia. We understood that God had called us to tell the Good News to those people.

The Conversion of Lydia

¹¹We left Troas in a ship and sailed to the island of Samothrace. The next day we sailed to the city of Neapolis. ¹²Then we went to Philippi, a Roman colony and the leading city in that part of Macedonia. We stayed there for a few days.

¹³On the Sabbath day we went out through the city gate to the river. There we thought we might find a special place for prayer. Some women had gathered there, so we sat down and talked with them. ¹⁴There was a woman there named Lydia from the city of Thyatira. Her job was selling purple cloth. She was a worshipper of the true God. Lydia was listening to Paul, and the Lord opened her heart to accept what Paul was saying. ¹⁵She and all the people living in her house were baptized. Then she invited us into her home. She said, "If you think I am a true believer in the Lord Jesus, come and stay in my house." She persuaded us to stay with her.

Paul and Silas in Jail

¹⁶One day we were going to the place for prayer, and a servant girl met us. She had a spirit*ᵇ* in her that gave her the power to tell what would happen in the future. By doing this she earned a lot of money for the men who owned her. ¹⁷She

started following Paul and the rest of us around. She kept shouting, "These men are servants of the Most High God! They are telling you how you can be saved!" ¹⁸She continued doing this for many days. This bothered Paul, so he turned and said to the spirit, "By the power of Jesus Christ, I command you to come out of her!" Immediately, the spirit came out.

¹⁹When the men who owned the servant girl saw this, they realized that they could no longer use her to make money. So they grabbed Paul and Silas and dragged them to the public square to meet with the authorities. ²⁰They brought Paul and Silas before the Roman officials and said, "These men are Jews, and they are making trouble in our city. ²¹They are telling people to do things that are not right for us as Romans to do."

²²The whole crowd turned against Paul and Silas. The officials tore the clothes off both men and ordered that they be beaten with rods. ²³They were beaten severely and thrown into jail. The officials told the jailer, "Guard them very carefully!" ²⁴When the jailer heard this special order, he put Paul and Silas far inside the jail and bound their feet between large blocks of wood.

²⁵About midnight Paul and Silas were praying and singing songs to God. The other prisoners were listening to them. ²⁶Suddenly there was an earthquake so strong that it shook the foundation of the jail. All the doors of the jail opened, and the chains on all the prisoners fell off. ²⁷The jailer woke up and saw that the jail doors were open. He thought that the prisoners had already escaped, so he got his sword and was ready to kill himself.*ᶜ* ²⁸But Paul shouted, "Don't hurt yourself! We are all here!"

²⁹The jailer told someone to bring a light. Then he ran inside and, shaking with fear, fell down in front of Paul and Silas. ³⁰Then he brought them outside and said, "Men, what must I do to be saved?"

³¹They said to him, "Believe in the Lord Jesus, and you will be saved—you and all who live in your house." ³²So Paul and Silas told the message of the Lord to the jailer and all the people who lived in his house. ³³It was late at night, but the jailer took Paul and Silas and washed their wounds. Then the jailer and all his people were baptized. ³⁴After this the jailer took Paul and Silas home and gave them some food. All the people were very happy because they now believed in God.

ᵃ **16:10 we** Luke, the writer, apparently went with Paul to Macedonia but stayed in Philippi when Paul left. (See verse 40.) The first person pronoun occurs again in 20:5 – 21:18 and 27:1–28.
ᵇ **16:16 spirit** A spirit from the devil that gave special knowledge.
ᶜ **16:27 kill himself** He thought the leaders would kill him for letting the prisoners escape.

35The next morning the Roman officials sent some soldiers to tell the jailer, "Let these men go free."

36The jailer said to Paul, "The officials have sent these soldiers to let you go free. You can leave now. Go in peace."

37But Paul said to the soldiers, "Those officials did not prove that we did anything wrong, but they beat us in public and put us in jail. And we are Roman citizens.a Now they want us to go away quietly. No, they must come here themselves and lead us out!"

38The soldiers told the officials what Paul said. When they heard that Paul and Silas were Roman citizens, they were afraid. 39So they came and told them they were sorry. They led them out of the jail and asked them to leave the city. 40But when Paul and Silas came out of the jail, they went to Lydia's house. They saw some of the believers there and encouraged them. Then they left.

Paul and Silas in Thessalonica

17 Paul and Silas travelled through the cities of Amphipolis and Apollonia. They came to the city of Thessalonica, where there was a Jewish synagogue. 2Paul went into the synagogue to see the Jews as he always did. For the next three weeks, on each Sabbath day, he discussed the Scriptures with them. 3He explained the Scriptures to show them that the Messiah had to die and then rise from death. He said, "This Jesus that I am telling you about is the Messiah." 4Some of the Jews there believed Paul and Silas and decided to join them. Also, a large number of Greeks who were worshippers of the true God and many important women joined them.

5But the Jews who did not believe became jealous, so they got some bad men from around the marketplace to make trouble. They formed a mob and caused a riot in the city. They went to Jason's house, looking for Paul and Silas. They wanted to bring them out before the people. 6When they did not find them, they dragged Jason and some of the other believers to the city leaders. The people shouted, "These men have made trouble everywhere in the world, and now they have come here too! 7Jason is looking after them in his house. They all do things against the laws of Caesar. They say there is another king called Jesus."

8When the city leaders and the other people heard this, they became very upset. 9They made Jason and the other believers deposit money to guarantee that there would be no more trouble. Then they let them go.

Paul and Silas Go to Berea

10That same night the believers sent Paul and Silas to another city named Berea. When they arrived there, they went to the Jewish synagogue. 11The people in Berea were more open-minded than those in Thessalonica. They were so glad to hear the message Paul told them. They studied the Scriptures every day to make sure that what they heard was really true. 12The result was that many of them believed, including many important Greek women and men.

13But when the Jews in Thessalonica learned that Paul was telling people God's message in Berea, they went there too. They upset the people and made trouble. 14So the believers immediately sent Paul away to the coast, but Silas and Timothy stayed in Berea. 15Those who went with Paul took him to the city of Athens. They returned with a message for Silas and Timothy to come and join him as soon as they could.

Paul in Athens

16While Paul was waiting for Silas and Timothy in Athens, he was upset because he saw that the city was full of idols. 17In the synagogue he talked with the Jews and with the Greeks who were worshippers of the true God. He also went to the public square every day and talked with everyone who came by. 18Some of the Epicurean and some of the Stoic philosophers argued with him.

Some of them said, "This man doesn't really know what he is talking about. What is he trying to say?" Paul was telling them the Good News about Jesus and the resurrection. So they said, "He seems to be telling us about some other gods."

19They took Paul to a meeting of the Areopagus council. They said, "Please explain to us this new idea that you have been teaching. 20The things you are saying are new to us. We have never heard this teaching before, and we want to know what it means." 21(The people of Athens and the foreigners who lived there spent all their time either telling or listening to all the latest ideas.)

22Then Paul stood up before the meeting of the Areopagus council and said, "Men of Athens, everything I see here tells me you are very religious. 23I was going through your city and I saw the things you worship. I found an altar that had these words written on it: 'TO AN UNKNOWN GOD.' You worship a god that you don't know. This is the God I want to tell you about.

24"He is the God who made the whole world and everything in it. He is the Lord of the land and the sky. He does not live in temples built by human hands. 25He is the one who gives people

---

a 16:37 **Roman citizens** Roman law said that Roman citizens must not be beaten before their trial.

life, breath and everything else they need. He does not need any help from them. He has everything he needs. 26God began by making one man, and from him he made all the different people who live everywhere in the world. He decided exactly when and where they would live.

INSIGHT

Paul was always reasonable and patient, even when being attacked or imprisoned. He was also well-informed, quoting philosophy and literature. Here he is also shown to be a skilful public speaker, attracting the interest of those around him by picking on a topic that's clearly of popular interest: the many gods the Athenians worshipped.

Acts 17:22–34

27"God wanted people to look for him, and perhaps in searching all around for him, they would find him. But he is not far from any of us. 28It is through him that we are able to live, to do what we do and to be who we are. As your own poets have said, 'We all come from him.'

29"That's right. We all come from God. So you must not think that he is like something people imagine or make. He is not made of gold, silver or stone. 30In the past people did not understand God, and he overlooked this. But now he is telling everyone in the world to change and turn to him. 31He has decided on a day when he will judge all the people in the world in a way that is fair. To do this he will use a man he chose long ago. And he has proved to everyone that this is the man to do it. He proved it by raising him from death!"

32When the people heard about a person being raised from death, some of them laughed. But others said, "We will hear more about this from you later." 33So Paul left the council meeting. 34But some of the people joined with Paul and became believers. Among these were Dionysius, a member of the Areopagus council, a woman named Damaris and some others.

Paul in Corinth

18 Later, Paul left Athens and went to the city of Corinth. 2There he met a Jewish man named Aquila, who was born in the country of Pontus. But he and his wife, Priscilla, had

recently moved to Corinth from Italy. They left Italy because Claudius had given an order for all Jews to leave Rome. Paul went to visit Aquila and Priscilla. 3They were tentmakers, just as Paul was, so he stayed with them and worked with them.

4Every Sabbath day Paul went to the synagogue and talked with both Jews and Greeks, trying to persuade them to believe in Jesus. 5But after Silas and Timothy came from Macedonia, Paul spent all his time telling God's message to the Jews, trying to convince them that Jesus is the Messiah. 6But they disagreed with what Paul was teaching and started insulting him. So Paul shook the dust from his clothes.*a* He said to them, "If you are not saved, it will be your own fault! I have done all I can do. After this I will go only to the non-Jewish people."

7Paul left the synagogue and moved into the home of Titius Justus, a man who was a worshipper of the true God. His house was next to the synagogue. 8Crispus was the leader of that synagogue. He and all the people living in his house believed in the Lord Jesus. Many other people in Corinth also listened to Paul. They, too, believed and were baptized.

9During the night, Paul had a vision. The Lord said to him, "Don't be afraid, and don't stop talking to people. 10I am with you, and no one will be able to hurt you. Many of my people are in this city." 11Paul stayed there for a year and a half teaching God's message to the people.

Paul Is Brought Before Gallio

12During the time that Gallio was the governor of Achaia, some of the Jews came together against Paul. They took him to court. 13They said to Gallio, "This man is teaching people to worship God in a way that is against our law!"

14Paul was ready to say something, but Gallio spoke to the Jews. He said, "I would listen to you if your complaint was about a crime or other wrong. 15But it is only about words and names—arguments about your own law. So you must solve this problem yourselves. I don't want to be a judge of these matters." 16So Gallio made them leave the court.

17Then they all grabbed Sosthenes, the leader of the synagogue. They beat him before the court. But this did not bother Gallio.

Paul Returns to Antioch

18Paul stayed with the believers for many days. Then he left and sailed for Syria. Priscilla and Aquila were also with him. At Cenchrea Paul had

---

a **18:6 shook the dust from his clothes** A warning. It showed Paul was finished talking to these Jews.

cut off his hair,[a] because he had made a vow[b] to God. [19]Then they went to the city of Ephesus, where Paul left Priscilla and Aquila. While Paul was in Ephesus, he went into the synagogue and talked with the Jews. [20]They asked him to stay longer, but he refused. [21]He left them and said, "I will come back to you again if God wants me to." And so he sailed away from Ephesus.

[22]When Paul arrived at Caesarea, he went to Jerusalem and visited the church there. After that, he went to Antioch. [23]Paul stayed in Antioch for a while. Then he left there and went through the countries of Galatia and Phrygia. He travelled from town to town in these countries, helping all the followers of Jesus grow stronger in their faith.

Apollos in Ephesus and Corinth

[24]A Jew named Apollos came to Ephesus. Born in the city of Alexandria, he was an educated man who knew the Scriptures well. [25]He had been taught about the Lord and was always excited[c] to talk to people about Jesus. What he taught was right, but the only baptism he knew about was the baptism that John taught. [26]Apollos began to speak very boldly in the synagogue. When Priscilla and Aquila heard him speak, they took him to their home and helped him understand the way of God better.

[27]Apollos wanted to go to Achaia. So the believers in Ephesus helped him. They wrote a letter to the Lord's followers in Achaia and asked them to accept Apollos. When he arrived there, he was a great help to those who had believed in Jesus because of God's grace. [28]He argued very strongly against the Jews before all the people. He clearly proved that the Jews were wrong. He used the Scriptures and showed that Jesus is the Messiah.

Paul in Ephesus

19 While Apollos was in the city of Corinth, Paul was visiting some places on his way to Ephesus. In Ephesus he found some other followers of the Lord. [2]He asked them, "Did you receive the Holy Spirit when you believed?"

These followers said to him, "We have never even heard of a Holy Spirit!"

[3]Paul asked them, "So what kind of baptism did you have?"

They said, "It was the baptism that John taught."

[4]Paul said, "John told people to be baptized to show they wanted to change their lives. He told

people to believe in the one who would come after him, and that one is Jesus."

[5]When these followers heard this, they were baptized in the name of the Lord Jesus. [6]Then Paul laid his hands on them, and the Holy Spirit came on them. They began speaking different languages and prophesying. [7]There were about twelve men in this group.

[8]Paul went into the synagogue and spoke very boldly. He continued doing this for three months. He talked with the Jews, trying to persuade them to accept what he was telling them about God's kingdom. [9]But some of them became stubborn and refused to believe. In front of everyone, they said bad things about the Way. So Paul left these Jews and took the Lord's followers with him. He went to a place where a man named Tyrannus had a school. There Paul talked with people every day. [10]He did this for two years. Because of this work, everyone in Asia, Jews and Greeks, heard the word of the Lord.

The Sons of Sceva

[11]God used Paul to do some very special miracles. [12]Some people carried away handkerchiefs and clothes that Paul had used and put them on those who were sick. The sick people were healed, and evil spirits left them.

[13–14]Some Jews also were travelling around forcing evil spirits out of people. The seven sons of Sceva, one of the leading priests, were doing this. These Jews tried to use the name of the Lord Jesus to make the evil spirits go out of people. They all said, "By the same Jesus that Paul talks about, I order you to come out!"

[15]But one day an evil spirit said to them, "I know Jesus, and I know about Paul, but who are you?"

[16]Then the man who had the evil spirit inside him jumped on these Jews. He was much stronger than all of them. He beat them up and tore their clothes off. They all ran away from that house.

[17]All the people in Ephesus, Jews and Greeks, learned about this. They were all filled with fear and gave great honour to the Lord Jesus. [18]Many of the believers began to confess, telling about all the evil things they had done. [19]Some of them had used magic. These believers brought their magic books and burned them before everyone. These books were worth about 50,000 silver coins.[d] [20]This is how the word of the Lord was spreading in a powerful way, causing more and more people to believe.

---

[a] **18:18 cut off his hair** This may show that Paul was ending a Nazirite vow, a time of special dedication and service promised to God. See "Nazirite" in the Word List.

[b] **18:18 vow** Probably a Nazirite vow, a time of special dedication and service promised to God. See "Nazirite" in the Word List.

[c] **18:25 excited** Or "on fire with the Spirit".

[d] **19:19 silver coins** Probably Greek drachmas. One coin was worth the average pay for one day's work.

Paul Plans a Trip

²¹After this, Paul made plans to go to Jerusalem. He planned to go through the regions of Macedonia and Achaia, and then go to Jerusalem. He thought, "After I visit Jerusalem, I must also visit Rome." ²²Timothy and Erastus were two of his helpers. Paul sent them ahead to Macedonia. But he stayed in Asia for a while.

Trouble in Ephesus

²³But during that time there was some trouble in Ephesus about the Way. This is how it all happened: ²⁴There was a man named Demetrius who worked with silver. He made little silver models that looked like the temple of the goddess Artemis. The men who did this work made a lot of money.

²⁵Demetrius had a meeting with these men and some others who did the same kind of work. He told them, "Men, you know that we make a lot of money from our business. ²⁶But look at what this man Paul is doing. Listen to what he is saying. He has convinced many people in Ephesus and all over Asia to change their religion. He says the gods that people make by hand are not real. ²⁷I'm afraid this is going to turn people against our business. But there is also another problem. People will begin to think that the temple of the great goddess Artemis is not important. Her greatness will be destroyed. And Artemis is the goddess that everyone in Asia and the whole world worships."

²⁸When the men heard this, they became very angry. They shouted, "Great is Artemis, the goddess of Ephesus!" ²⁹The whole city was thrown into confusion. The people grabbed Gaius and Aristarchus, two men from Macedonia who were travelling with Paul, and rushed all together into the stadium. ³⁰Paul wanted to go in and talk to the people, but the Lord's followers did not let him go. ³¹Also, some leaders of the country who were friends of Paul sent him a message telling him not to go into the stadium.

³²Some people were shouting one thing and others were shouting something else. The meeting was very confused. Most of the people did not know why they had come there. ³³Some Jews made a man named Alexander stand before the crowd, and they told him what to say. Alexander waved his hand, trying to explain things to the people. ³⁴But when the people saw that Alexander was a Jew, they all began shouting the same thing. For two hours they continued shouting, "Great is Artemis of Ephesus!"

³⁵Then the city clerk persuaded the people to be quiet. He said, "Men of Ephesus, everyone knows that Ephesus is the city that keeps the temple of the great goddess Artemis. Everyone knows that we also keep her holy rock.ᵃ ³⁶No one can deny this, so you should be quiet. You must stop and think before you do anything else. ³⁷"You brought these menᵇ here, but they have not said anything bad against our goddess. They have not stolen anything from her temple. ³⁸We have courts of law and there are judges. Do Demetrius and those men who work with him have a charge against anyone? If so, they should go to the courts. Let them argue with each other there. ³⁹"Is there something else you want to talk about? Then come to the regular town meeting of the people. It can be decided there. ⁴⁰I say this because someone might see this trouble today and accuse us of starting a riot. We could not explain all this trouble, because there is no real reason for this meeting." ⁴¹After the city clerk said this, he told the people to go home.

Paul Goes to Macedonia and Greece

20 When the trouble stopped, Paul invited the Lord's followers to come and visit him. After encouraging them, he said goodbye and left for Macedonia. ²On his way through Macedonia he had many words of encouragement for the followers in various places. Then he went to Greece ³and stayed there for three months.

Paul was ready to sail for Syria, but some Jews were planning something against him. So he decided to go back through Macedonia to Syria. ⁴These men were travelling with him: Sopater, the son of Pyrrhus, from the city of Berea; Aristarchus and Secundus, from the city of Thessalonica; Gaius, from the city of Derbe; Timothy; and two men from Asia, Tychicus and Trophimus. ⁵These men went first, ahead of Paul. They waited for us in the city of Troas. ⁶We sailed from the city of Philippi after the Festival of Unleavened Bread. We met these men in Troas five days later and stayed there for seven days.

Paul's Last Visit to Troas

⁷On Sundayᶜ we all met together to eat the Lord's Supper.ᵈ Paul talked to the group. Because

---

ᵃ **19:35** *holy rock* Probably a meteorite or rock that the people thought looked like Artemis and worshipped.
ᵇ **19:37** *men* Gaius and Aristarchus, the men travelling with Paul.
ᶜ **20:7** *Sunday* Literally, "first day of the week", which for the Jews began at sunset on Saturday. But if Luke is using Greek time here, then the meeting was Sunday night.
ᵈ **20:7** *to eat the Lord's Supper* Literally, "to break bread". This may mean a meal or the Lord's Supper, the special meal Jesus told his followers to eat to remember him. See Luke 22:14–20.

he was planning to leave the next day, he continued talking until midnight. 8We were all together in a room upstairs, and there were many lights in the room. 9There was a young man named Eutychus sitting in the window. Paul continued talking, and Eutychus became very, very sleepy. Finally, he went to sleep and fell out of the window. He fell to the ground from the third floor. When the people went down and lifted him up, he was dead.

10Paul went down to where Eutychus was, knelt down beside him and put his arms around him. He said to the other believers, "Don't worry. He is alive now." 11Then Paul went upstairs again, broke off some pieces of bread and ate. He spoke to them for a long time. It was early morning when he finished, and then he left. 12The Lord's followers took Eutychus home alive, and they were all greatly comforted.

The Trip From Troas to Miletus

13We went on ahead of Paul and sailed for the city of Assos, planning to meet him there. This is what he told us to do because he wanted to go by land. 14When he caught up with us at Assos, we took him on board, and we all sailed to Mitylene. 15The next day, we sailed away from there and came to a place near the island of Chios. Then the next day, we sailed to the island of Samos. A day later, we came to the city of Miletus. 16Paul had already decided not to stop at Ephesus. He did not want to stay too long in Asia. He was hurrying because he wanted to be in Jerusalem on the day of Pentecost if possible.

Paul Speaks to the Elders From Ephesus

17In Miletus Paul sent a message back to Ephesus, telling the elders of the church in Ephesus to come to him.

18When they came, Paul said to them, "You know about my life from the first day I came to Asia. You know the way I lived all the time I was with you. 19The Jews planned things against me, and this gave me much trouble. But you know that I always served the Lord, sometimes with tears. I never thought about myself first. 20I always did what was best for you. I told you the Good News about Jesus in public before the people and also taught in your homes. 21I told everyone, Jews and Greeks, to change and turn to God. I told them all to believe in our Lord Jesus.

22"But now I must obey the Spirit and go to Jerusalem. I don't know what will happen to me

there. 23I know only that in every city the Holy Spirit tells me that troubles and even jail wait for me. 24I don't care about my own life. The most important thing is that I finish my work. I want to finish the work that the Lord Jesus gave me to do—to tell people the Good News about God's grace.

25"And now listen to me. I know that none of you will ever see me again. All the time I was with you, I told you the Good News about God's kingdom. 26So today I can tell you one thing that I am sure of: God will not blame me if some of you are not saved. 27I can say this because I know that I told you everything that God wants you to know. 28Be careful for yourselves and for all the people God has given you. The Holy Spirit gave you the work of caring for*a* this flock.*b* You must be shepherds to the church of God,*c* the people he bought with his own blood.*d* 29I know that after I leave, some men will come into your group. They will be like wild wolves and will try to destroy the flock. 30Also, men from your own group will begin to teach things that are wrong. They will lead some of the Lord's followers away from the truth to follow them. 31So be careful! And always remember what I did during the three years I was with you. I never stopped reminding each one of you how you should live, counselling you day and night and crying over you.

32"Now I am putting you in God's care. I am depending on the message about his grace to make you strong. That message is able to give you the blessings that God gives to all his holy people. 33When I was with you, I never wanted anyone's money or fine clothes. 34You know that I always worked to take care of my own needs and the needs of the people who were with me. 35I always showed you that you should work just as I did and help people who are weak. I taught you to remember the words of the Lord Jesus: 'It is a greater blessing to give than to receive.'"

36When Paul had finished speaking, he knelt down, and they all prayed together. 37–38They cried and cried. They were especially sad because Paul had said they would never see him again. They hugged him and kissed him. Then they went with him to the ship to say goodbye.

Paul Goes to Jerusalem

21 After we said goodbye to the elders, we sailed away straight to the island of Cos. The next day we went to the island of Rhodes,

a **20:28 gave . . . caring for** Literally, "made you overseers of".
b **20:28 flock** A flock is many sheep. Here, it means a group of God's people who follow their leaders (elders) like sheep following a shepherd.
c **20:28 of God** Some Greek copies say, "of the Lord".
d **20:28 his own blood** Or "the blood of his own Son".

and from there we went to Patara. ²There we found a ship that was going to the area of Phoenicia. We got on the ship and sailed away.

³We sailed near the island of Cyprus. We could see it on the north side, but we did not stop. We sailed to the country of Syria. We stopped at Tyre because the ship needed to unload its cargo there. ⁴We found the Lord's followers there and stayed with them for seven days. They warned Paul not to go to Jerusalem because of what the Spirit had told them. ⁵But when our time there was up, we returned to the ship to continue our trip. All the followers, even the women and children, came with us to the seashore. We all knelt down on the beach, prayed, ⁶and said goodbye. Then we got on the ship, and the followers went home.

⁷We continued our trip from Tyre and went to the city of Ptolemais. We greeted the believers there and stayed with them for one day. ⁸The next day we left Ptolemais and went to the city of Caesarea. We went into the home of Philip and stayed with him. He had the work of telling the Good News. He was one of the seven helpers.ᵃ ⁹He had four unmarried daughters who had the gift of prophesying.

¹⁰After we had been there for several days, a prophet named Agabus came from Judea. ¹¹He came to us and borrowed Paul's belt. He used it to tie his own hands and feet. He said, "The Holy Spirit tells me, 'This is how the Jews in Jerusalem will tie up the man who wears this belt.ᵇ Then they will hand him over to people who don't know God.'"

¹²When we heard this, we and the other followers there begged Paul not to go to Jerusalem. ¹³But he said, "Why are you crying and making me feel so sad? I am willing to be put in jail in Jerusalem. I am even ready to die for the name of the Lord Jesus!"

¹⁴We could not persuade him to stay away from Jerusalem. So we stopped begging him and said, "We pray that what the Lord wants will be done."

¹⁵After this, we got ready and left for Jerusalem. ¹⁶Some of the followers of Jesus from Caesarea went with us. These followers took us to the home of Mnason, a man from Cyprus, who was one of the first people to be a follower of Jesus. They took us to his home so that we could stay with him.

Paul Visits James

¹⁷The brothers and sisters in Jerusalem were very happy to see us. ¹⁸The next day Paul went with us to visit James, and all the elders were there. ¹⁹After greeting them, Paul told them point by point all that God had used him to do among the non-Jewish people.

²⁰When the leaders heard this, they praised God. Then they said to Paul, "Brother, you can see that thousands of Jews have become believers, but they think it is very important to obey the Law of Moses. ²¹They have been told that you teach the Jews who live in non-Jewish regions to stop following the Law of Moses. They have heard that you tell them not to circumcise their sons or follow our other customs.

²²"What should we do? The Jewish believers here will find out that you have come. ²³So we will tell you what to do: Four of our men have made a vowᶜ to God. ²⁴Take these men with you and share in their cleansing ceremony.ᵈ Pay their expenses so that they can shave their heads.ᵉ This will prove to everyone that the things they have heard about you are not true. They will see that you obey the Law of Moses in your own life.

²⁵"In regard to the non-Jewish believers, we have already sent a letter to them saying what we think they should do:

'Don't eat food that has been given to idols.
Don't eat meat from animals that have been strangled or any meat that still has the blood in it.
Don't be involved in sexual sin.'"

Paul Is Arrested

²⁶So Paul took the four men with him. The next day he shared in their cleansing ceremony. Then he went to the Temple area and announced the time when the days of the cleansing ceremony would be finished. On the last day an offering would be given for each of the men.

²⁷When the seven-day period was almost finished, some Jews from Asia saw Paul in the Temple area. They stirred up everyone into an angry mob. They grabbed Paul ²⁸and shouted, "Men of Israel, help us! This is the man who is teaching things that are against the Law of Moses, against our people and against this Temple of ours. This is what he teaches people everywhere. And now he has brought some Greeks into the Temple area and has made this holy place unclean!" ²⁹(The Jews said this because they had seen Trophimus with Paul in Jerusalem. Trophimus was a man from Ephesus. The Jews

---

ᵃ **21:8 seven helpers** Men chosen for a special work. See Acts 6:1–6.
ᵇ **21:11 belt** Paul's belt; so Agabus means that the Jews in Jerusalem will tie Paul up (arrest him).
ᶜ **21:23 vow** Probably a Nazirite vow, a time of special dedication and service promised to God. See "NAZIRITE" in the Word List.
ᵈ **21:24 cleansing ceremony** The special things Jews did to end the Nazirite vow. Also in verse 26.
ᵉ **21:24 shave their heads** This showed that their vow was completed.

thought that Paul had taken him into the holy area of the Temple.)

³⁰An angry reaction spread throughout the city, and everyone came running to the Temple. They grabbed Paul and dragged him out of the holy area, and the gates were closed immediately. ³¹While they were trying to kill Paul, the commander of the Roman army in Jerusalem got word that the whole city was in a state of riot. ³²Immediately the commander ran to where the crowd had gathered, taking with him some army officers and soldiers. When the people saw the commander and his soldiers, they stopped beating Paul.

³³The commander went over to Paul and arrested him. He told his soldiers to tie him up with two chains. Then he asked, "Who is this man? What has he done wrong?" ³⁴Some people there were shouting one thing, and others were shouting something else. Because of all this confusion and shouting, the commander could not learn the truth about what had happened. So he told the soldiers to take Paul to the army building. ³⁵⁻³⁶The whole crowd was following them. When the soldiers came to the steps, they had to carry Paul. They did this to protect him, because the people were ready to hurt him. The people were shouting, "Kill him!"

³⁷When the soldiers were ready to take Paul into the army building, he asked the commander, "Can I say something to you?"

The commander said, "Oh, you speak Greek? ³⁸Then you are not the man I thought you were. I thought you were the Egyptian who started some trouble against the government not long ago and led four thousand terrorists out to the desert."

³⁹Paul said, "No, I am a Jew from Tarsus in the country of Cilicia. I am a citizen of that important city. Please, let me speak to the people."

⁴⁰The commander told Paul he could speak. So he stood on the steps and waved his hand so that the people would be quiet. The people became quiet and Paul spoke to them in Aramaic.

Paul Speaks to the People

22 Paul said, "My brothers and fathers, listen to me! I will make my defence to you."

²When the Jews heard Paul speaking Aramaic, they became very quiet. Then Paul said,

³"I am a Jew, born in Tarsus in the country of Cilicia. I grew up here in this city. I was a student of Gamaliel,ᵃ who carefully taught me everything about the law of our fathers. I was very serious about serving God, the same as all of you here today. ⁴I persecuted the people who followed the Way. Some of them were killed because of me. I arrested men and women and put them in jail.

⁵"The high priest and the whole council of older Jewish leaders can tell you that this is true. At one time these leaders gave me some letters. The letters were to the Jewish brothers in the city of Damascus. I was going there to arrest the followers of Jesus and bring them back to Jerusalem for punishment.

Paul Tells About His Conversion

⁶"But something happened to me on my way to Damascus. It was about noon when I came close to Damascus. Suddenly a bright light from heaven flashed all around me. ⁷I fell to the ground and heard a voice saying to me, 'Saul, Saul, why are you persecuting me?'

⁸"I asked, 'Who are you, Lord?' The voice said, 'I am Jesus from Nazareth, the one you are persecuting.' ⁹The men who were with me did not understand the voice, but they saw the light.

¹⁰"I said, 'What shall I do, Lord?' The Lord answered, 'Get up and go into Damascus. There you will be told all that I have planned for you to do.' ¹¹I could not see, because the bright light had made me blind. So the men led me into Damascus.

¹²"In Damascus a man named Ananiasᵇ came to me. He was a man who was devoted to God and obeyed the Law of Moses. All the Jews who lived there respected him. ¹³He came to me and said, 'Saul, my brother, look up and see again!' Immediately I was able to see him.

¹⁴"Ananias told me, 'The God of our fathers chose you long ago to know his plan. He chose you to see the Righteous One and to hear words from him. ¹⁵You will be his witness to all people. You will tell them what you have seen and heard. ¹⁶Now, don't wait any longer. Get up, be baptized and wash away your sins, trusting in Jesus to save you.'ᶜ

¹⁷"Later, I came back to Jerusalem. I was praying in the Temple area, and I saw a vision. ¹⁸I saw Jesus, and he said to me, 'Hurry and leave Jerusalem now! The people here will not accept the truth you tell them about me.'

¹⁹"I said, 'But, Lord, the people know that I was the one who put the believers in jail and beat them. I went through all the synagogues to find and arrest the people who believe in you. ²⁰The people also know that I was there when Stephen,

---

ᵃ **22:3 Gamaliel** A very important teacher of the Pharisees, a Jewish religious group. See Acts 5:34.

ᵇ **22:12 Ananias** In Acts there are three men with this name. See Acts 5:1 and 23:2 for the other two.

ᶜ **22:16 trusting in Jesus to save you** Literally, "calling on his name", meaning to show faith in Jesus by worshipping him or praying to him for help.

your witness, was killed. I stood there and agreed that they should kill him. I even held the coats of the men who were killing him!'

21"But Jesus said to me, 'Leave now. I will send you far away to the non-Jewish people.'"

22The people stopped listening when Paul said this last thing. They all shouted, "Get rid of this man! He doesn't deserve to live in this world any more." 23They kept on shouting, ripping off their clothes and throwing dust into the air.*a* 24Then the commander told the soldiers to take Paul into the army building and beat him to make him talk. He wanted to find out why the people were shouting against him like this. 25So the soldiers were tying Paul, preparing to beat him. But he said to an army officer there, "Do you have the right to beat a Roman citizen*b* who has not been proved guilty?"

26When the officer heard this, he went to the commander and told him about it. The officer said, "Do you know what you are doing? This man is a Roman citizen!"

27The commander came to Paul and said, "Tell me, are you really a Roman citizen?"

He answered, "Yes."

28The commander said, "I paid a lot of money to become a Roman citizen."

But Paul said, "I was born a citizen."

29The men who were preparing to question Paul moved away from him immediately. The commander was afraid because he had already put Paul in chains, and he was a Roman citizen.

Paul Speaks to the Jewish Leaders

30The next day the commander decided to learn why the Jews were accusing Paul. So he ordered the leading priests and the whole high council to meet together. He had Paul's chains taken off and had him brought in to face the council.

23 Paul looked at the council members and said, "Brothers, I have lived my life in a good way before God. I have always done what I thought was right." 2Ananias,*c* the high priest, was there. When he heard this, he told the men who were standing near Paul to hit him in the mouth. 3Paul said to Ananias, "God will hit you too! You are like a dirty wall that has been painted white. You sit there and judge me, using the Law of Moses. But you are telling them to hit me, and that is against the law."

4The men standing near Paul said to him, "Are you sure you want to insult God's high priest like that?"

5Paul said, "Brothers, I did not know this man was the high priest. The Scriptures say, 'You must not say bad things about a leader of your people.'"*d*

6Paul knew that some of the men in the council meeting were Sadducees and some were Pharisees. So he shouted, "My brothers, I am a Pharisee and my father was a Pharisee! I am on trial here because I believe that people will rise from death."

7When Paul said this, a big argument started between the Pharisees and the Sadducees. The group was divided. 8(The Sadducees believe that after people die, they will not live again as an angel or as a spirit. But the Pharisees believe in both.) 9All these Jews began shouting louder and louder. Some of the teachers of the law, who were Pharisees, stood up and argued, "We find nothing wrong with this man. Maybe an angel or a spirit really did speak to him."

10The argument turned into a fight, and the commander was afraid that the Jews would tear Paul to pieces. So he told the soldiers to go down and take Paul away from these Jews and put him in the army building.

11The next night the Lord Jesus came and stood by Paul. He said, "Be brave! You have told people in Jerusalem about me. You must do the same in Rome."

Some Jews Plan to Kill Paul

12The next morning some of the Jews made a plan to kill Paul. They made a promise to God that they would not eat or drink anything until they had killed him. 13There were more than 40 of them who made this plan. 14They went and talked to the leading priests and the older Jewish leaders. They said, "We have promised ourselves that we will not eat or drink until we have killed Paul. 15So this is what we want you to do: Send a message to the commander from you and the high council. Tell him you want him to bring Paul out to you. Say that you want to ask him more questions. We will be waiting to kill him while he is on the way here."

16But Paul's nephew heard about this plan. He went to the army building and told Paul. 17Then Paul called one of the army officers and said to him, "Take this young man to the commander. He has a message for him." 18So the army officer brought Paul's nephew to the commander. The officer said, "The prisoner Paul asked me to bring

---

a **22:23** *ripping . . . air* These actions were signs of very strong anger.
b **22:25** *Roman citizen* Roman law said that Roman citizens must not be beaten before their trial. Also at 23:27.
c **23:2** *Ananias* Not the same man named Ananias in Acts 22:12.
d **23:5** Quote from Exod. 22:28.

this young man to you. He has something to tell you."

¹⁹The commander led the young man to a place where they could be alone. The commander asked, "What do you want to tell me?"

²⁰The young man said, "Some Jews have decided to ask you to bring Paul down to their council meeting tomorrow. They want you to think that they plan to ask Paul more questions. ²¹But don't believe them! More than 40 of them are hiding and waiting to kill him. They have all promised to God not to eat or drink until they have killed him. Now they are waiting for you to say yes."

²²The commander sent the young man away, telling him, "Don't tell anyone that you have told me about their plan."

Paul Is Sent to Caesarea

²³Then the commander called two army officers. He said to them, "I need some men to go to Caesarea. Get 200 soldiers ready. Also, get 70 horsemen and 200 men to carry spears. Be ready to leave at nine o'clock tonight. ²⁴Get some horses for Paul to ride so that he can be taken to Governor Felix safely." ²⁵The commander wrote a letter about Paul. This is what it said:

²⁶From Claudius Lysias,

To the Most Honourable Governor Felix.

Greetings:

²⁷Some Jews had taken this man and planned to kill him. But I learned that he is a Roman citizen, so I went with my soldiers and saved him. ²⁸I wanted to know why they were accusing him. So I brought him before their council meeting. ²⁹This is what I learned: The Jews said this man did some things that were wrong. But these charges were about their own Jewish laws, and there was nothing worthy of jail or death. ³⁰I was told that some of the Jews were making a plan to kill him. So I decided to send him to you. I also told those Jews to tell you what they have against him.

³¹The soldiers did what they were told. They got Paul and took him to the city of Antipatris that night. ³²The next day the horsemen went with Paul to Caesarea, but the other soldiers went back to the army building in Jerusalem. ³³The horsemen entered Caesarea, gave the letter to Governor Felix and then turned Paul over to him.

³⁴The governor read the letter and asked Paul, "What country are you from?" The governor learned that Paul was from Cilicia. ³⁵The governor said, "I will hear your case when the Jews who are accusing you come here too." Then the governor gave orders for Paul to be kept in the palace. (This building had been built by Herod.)

Some Jews Accuse Paul

24 Five days later Ananias, the high priest, went to the city of Caesarea. He brought with him some of the older Jewish leaders and a lawyer named Tertullus. They went to Caesarea to make charges against Paul before the governor. ²⁻³Paul was called into the meeting, and Tertullus began to make his accusations.

Tertullus said, "Most Honourable Felix, our people enjoy much peace because of you, and many wrong things in our country are being made right through your wise help. For this we all continue to be very thankful. ⁴But I don't want to take any more of your time. So I will say only a few words. Please be patient. ⁵This man is a troublemaker. He causes trouble with the Jews everywhere in the world. He is a leader of the Nazarene group. ⁶⁻⁸Also, he was trying to make the Temple unclean, but we stopped him.ᵃ You can decide if all this is true. Ask him some questions yourself." ⁹The other Jews agreed and said it was all true.

Paul Defends Himself Before Felix

¹⁰The governor made a sign for Paul to speak. So Paul answered, "Governor Felix, I know that you have been a judge over this nation for a long time. So I am happy to defend myself before you. ¹¹I went to worship in Jerusalem only twelve days ago. You can learn for yourself that this is true. ¹²These Jews who are accusing me did not find me arguing with anyone at the Temple or making trouble with the people. And I was not making trouble or arguing in the synagogues or anywhere else in the city. ¹³These men cannot prove the things they are saying against me now.

¹⁴"But I will tell you this: I worship the God of our fathers as a follower of the Way, which these Jews say is not the right way, and I believe everything that is taught in the Law of Moses and all that is written in the books of the prophets. ¹⁵I have the same hope in God that these Jews have—the hope that all people, good and bad, will be raised from death. ¹⁶This is why I always try to do what I believe is right before God and before everyone.

ᵃ **24:6–8** Some Greek copies add 6b–8a: "And we wanted to judge him by our own law. But the officer Lysias came and used great force to take him from us. And Lysias ordered those who wanted to accuse him to come to you."

17-18"I was away from Jerusalem for many years. I went back there to take money to help my people. I also had some gifts to offer at the Temple. I was doing this when some Jews saw me there. I had finished the cleansing ceremony.[a] I had not made any trouble, and no one was gathering around me. 19But some Jews from Asia were there. They should be here, standing before you. If I have really done anything wrong, they are the ones who should accuse me. They were there! 20Ask these men here if they found any wrong in me when I stood before the high council meeting in Jerusalem. 21I did say one thing when I stood before them and shouted, 'You are judging me today because I believe that people will rise from death!'"

22Felix already understood a lot about the Way. He stopped the trial and said, "When commander Lysias comes here, I will decide what to do with you." 23Felix told the army officer to keep Paul guarded but to give him some freedom and to let his friends bring whatever he needed.

Paul Speaks to Felix and His Wife

24After a few days Felix came with his wife Drusilla, who was a Jew. Felix asked for Paul to be brought to him. He listened to Paul talk about believing in Christ Jesus. 25But Felix became afraid when Paul spoke about things like doing right, self-control and the judgement that will come in the future. He said, "Go away now. When I have more time, I will call for you." 26But Felix had another reason for talking with Paul. He hoped Paul would pay him a bribe, so he sent for Paul often and talked with him.

27But after two years, Porcius Festus became governor. So Felix was no longer governor. But he had left Paul in prison to please the Jews.

Paul Asks to See Caesar

25 Festus became governor, and three days later he went from Caesarea to Jerusalem. 2The leading priests and the important Jewish leaders made charges against Paul before Festus. 3They asked Festus to do them a favour. They wanted him to send Paul back to Jerusalem because they had a plan to kill Paul on the way. 4But Festus answered, "No, Paul will be kept in Caesarea. I will be going there soon myself, 5and your leaders can go with me. If this man has really done anything wrong, they can accuse him there."

6Festus stayed in Jerusalem another eight or ten days and then went back to Caesarea. The next day Festus told the soldiers to bring Paul before him. Festus was seated on the judgement seat. 7Paul came into the room, and the Jews who had come from Jerusalem stood around him. They made many serious charges against him, but they could not prove anything. 8Paul defended himself, saying, "I have done nothing wrong against the Jewish law, against the Temple or against Caesar."

9But Festus wanted to please the Jews. So he asked Paul, "Do you want to go to Jerusalem for me to judge you there on these charges?"

10Paul said, "I am standing at Caesar's judgement seat now. This is where I should be judged. I have done nothing wrong to the Jews, and you know it. 11If I have done something wrong and the law says I must die, then I agree that I should die. I don't ask to be saved from death. But if these charges are not true, then no one can hand me over to these people. No, I want Caesar to hear my case!"

12Festus talked about this with his advisors. Then he said, "You have asked to see Caesar, so you will go to Caesar!"

Festus Asks King Agrippa About Paul

13A few days later King Agrippa and Bernice came to Caesarea to visit Festus. 14They stayed there many days, and Festus told the king about Paul's case. Festus said, "There is a man that Felix left in prison. 15When I went to Jerusalem, the leading priests and the older Jewish leaders there made charges against him. They wanted me to order his death. 16But I told them, 'When a man is accused of doing something wrong, Romans don't hand him over for others to judge. First, he must face the people accusing him. And then he must be allowed to defend himself against their charges.'

17"So when these Jews came here for the trial, I did not waste time. The next day I sat on the judgement seat and ordered Paul to be brought in. 18The Jews stood up and accused him. But they did not accuse him of the kind of crimes I thought they would. 19Their charges were all about their own religion and about a man named Jesus. Jesus died, but Paul said that he is still alive. 20I did not have any idea about how to judge these matters. So I asked Paul, 'Do you want to go to Jerusalem and be judged there?' 21But Paul asked to be kept in Caesarea. He wants a decision from the emperor. So I ordered that he be held until I could send him to Caesar in Rome."

22Agrippa said to Festus, "I would like to hear this man too."

---

a 24:17–18 *cleansing ceremony* The special things Jews did to end the Nazirite vow. See "NAZIRITE" in the Word List.

Festus said, "Tomorrow you can hear him."

²³The next day Agrippa and Bernice came to the meeting with great show, acting like very important people. They entered the room with military leaders and important men of the city. Festus ordered the soldiers to bring Paul in.

²⁴Festus said, "King Agrippa and all of you gathered here with us, you see this man. All the Jewish people, here and in Jerusalem, have complained to me about him. When they complain about him, they shout that he should be killed. ²⁵When I judged him, I did not find him guilty of any crime worthy of death. But he asked to be judged by Caesar, so I decided to send him to Rome. ²⁶However, I don't really know what to tell Caesar that this man has done wrong. So I have brought him before all of you—especially you, King Agrippa. I hope that you can question him and give me something to write to Caesar. ²⁷I think it is foolish to send a prisoner to Caesar without making some charges against him."

Paul Before King Agrippa

26 Agrippa said to Paul, "You may now speak to defend yourself." Paul raised his hand to get their attention and began to speak. ²He said, "King Agrippa, I feel it is a blessing for me to stand here before you today and answer all the charges these Jews have made against me. ³I am very happy to talk to you, because you know so much about all the Jewish customs and the things the Jews argue about. Please listen to me patiently.

⁴"All the Jews know about my whole life. They know the way I lived from the beginning in my own country and later in Jerusalem. ⁵These Jews have known me for a long time. If they want to, they can tell you that I was a good Pharisee. And the Pharisees obey the laws of the Jewish religion more carefully than any other group. ⁶Now I am on trial because I hope for the promise that God made to our fathers. ⁷This is the promise that all the twelve tribes of our people hope to receive. For this hope the Jews serve God day and night. My king, the Jews have accused me because I hope for this same promise. ⁸Why do you people think it is impossible for God to raise people from death?

⁹"I used to think that I should do everything I could against Jesus from Nazareth. ¹⁰And that's what I did, beginning in Jerusalem. The leading priests gave me the authority to put many of God's people in jail. And when they were being killed, I agreed that it was a good thing. ¹¹I visited all the synagogues and punished them, trying to make them curse*ᵃ* Jesus. My anger against these people was so strong that I went to other cities to find them and punish them.

Paul Tells About Seeing Jesus

¹²"Once the leading priests gave me permission and the authority to go to the city of Damascus. ¹³On the way there, at noon, I saw a light from heaven, brighter than the sun. It flashed all around me and those travelling with me. ¹⁴We all fell to the ground. Then I heard a voice talking to me in Aramaic. The voice said, 'Saul, Saul, why are you persecuting me? You are only hurting yourself by fighting me.'

¹⁵"I said, 'Who are you, Lord?'

"The Lord said, 'I am Jesus. I am the one you are persecuting. ¹⁶Stand up! I have chosen you to be my servant. You will tell people about me—what you have seen today and what I will show you. This is why I have come to you. ¹⁷I will keep you safe from your own people and from the non-Jewish people, the ones I am sending you to. ¹⁸You will make them able to understand the truth. They will turn away from darkness to the light. They will turn away from the power of Satan, and turn to God. Then their sins can be forgiven, and they can be given a place among God's people—those who have been made holy by believing in me.'"

Paul Tells About His Work

¹⁹Paul continued speaking: "King Agrippa, after I had this vision from heaven, I obeyed it. ²⁰I began telling people to change their hearts and lives and turn back to God. And I told them to do things that showed that they had really changed. I went first to people in Damascus. Then I went to Jerusalem and to every part of Judea and told the people there. I also went to the non-Jewish people.

²¹"This is why the Jews grabbed me and were trying to kill me at the Temple. ²²But God helped me, and he is still helping me today. With God's help I am standing here today and telling all people what I have seen. But I am saying nothing new. I am saying only what Moses and the prophets said would happen. ²³They said that the Messiah would die and be the first to rise from death. They said that he would bring the light of God's saving truth*ᵇ* to the Jewish people and to the non-Jewish people."

Paul Tries to Persuade Agrippa

²⁴While Paul was still defending himself, Festus shouted, "Paul, you are out of your mind! Too much study has made you crazy."

ᵃ **26:11** *curse* Literally, "blaspheme", the same as saying they did not believe in Jesus.
ᵇ **26:23** *bring . . . truth* Literally, "proclaim light".

25Paul said, "Most Honourable Festus, I am not crazy. What I am saying is true. It all makes perfect sense. 26King Agrippa knows about all this, and I can speak freely to him. I know that he has heard about these things, because they happened where everyone could see them. 27King Agrippa, do you believe what the prophets wrote? I know you believe!"

28King Agrippa said to Paul, "Do you think you can persuade me so easily to become a 'Christ-follower'?"

29Paul said, "It makes no difference to me if it is easy or hard. I just pray to God that not only you but everyone listening to me today could be saved and be just like me—except for these chains!"

30King Agrippa, Governor Festus, Bernice and all the people sitting with them stood up 31and left the room. They were talking to each other. They said, "This man has done nothing worthy of being put to death or even put in jail." 32And Agrippa said to Festus, "We could let him go free, but he has asked to see Caesar."

Paul Sails for Rome

27 It was decided that we would sail for Italy. An army officer named Julius, who served in the emperor's special army, was put in charge of guarding Paul and some other prisoners on the journey. 2We got on a ship from the city of Adramyttium that was ready to sail to different places in Asia. Aristarchus, a man from Thessalonica in Macedonia, went with us.

3The next day we came to the city of Sidon. Julius was very good to Paul and gave him freedom to go and visit his friends there, who gave him whatever he needed. 4We left that city and sailed close to the island of Cyprus because the wind was blowing against us. 5We went across the sea by Cilicia and Pamphylia. Then we came to the city of Myra in Lycia. 6There the army officer found a ship from the city of Alexandria that was going to Italy. So he put us on it.

7We sailed slowly for many days. It was hard for us to reach the city of Cnidus because the wind was blowing against us. We could not go any farther that way, so we sailed by the south side of the island of Crete near Salmone. 8We sailed along the coast, but the sailing was hard. Then we came to a place called Safe Harbours, near the city of Lasea.

9We had lost much time, and it was now dangerous to sail, because it was already after the Jewish day of fasting.[a] So Paul warned them,

10"Men, I can see that there will be a lot of trouble on this journey. The ship, everything in it and even our lives may be lost!" 11But the captain and the owner of the ship did not agree with Paul. So the army officer accepted what they said instead of believing Paul. 12Also, that harbour was not a good place for the ship to stay for the winter, so most of the men decided that we should leave there. They hoped we could reach Phoenix, where the ship could stay for the winter. Phoenix was a city on the island of Crete. It had a harbour that faced south-west and north-west.

The Storm

13Then a good wind began to blow from the south. The men on the ship thought, "This is the wind we wanted, and now we have it!" So they pulled up the anchor. We sailed very close to the island of Crete. 14But then a very strong wind called the "North-easter" came from across the island. 15This wind took the ship and carried it away. The ship could not sail against the wind, so we stopped trying and let the wind blow us.

16We went below a small island named Cauda. With the island protecting us from the wind, we were able to bring in the lifeboat, but it was very hard to do. 17After the men brought the lifeboat in, they tied ropes around the ship to hold it together. The men were afraid that the ship would hit the sandbanks of Syrtis. So they lowered the sail and let the wind carry the ship.

18The next day the storm was blowing against us so hard that the men threw some things out of the ship.[b] 19A day later they threw out the ship's equipment. 20For many days we could not see the sun or the stars. The storm was very bad. We lost all hope of staying alive—we thought we would die.

21The men did not eat for a long time. Then one day Paul stood up before them and said, "Men, I told you not to leave Crete. You should have listened to me. Then you would not have had all this trouble and loss. 22But now I tell you to be happy. None of you will die, but the ship will be lost. 23Last night an angel came to me from God—the God I worship and belong to. 24The angel said, 'Paul, don't be afraid! You must stand before Caesar. And God has given you this promise: he will save the lives of all those sailing with you.' 25So men, there is nothing to worry about. I trust God, and I am sure everything will happen just as his angel told me. 26But we will crash on an island."

---

[a] **27:9** *day of fasting* The Day of Atonement, an important Jewish holy day in the autumn of the year. This was the time of year that bad storms happened on the sea.
[b] **27:18** *threw some things . . . ship* The men did this to make the ship lighter so that it would not sink easily.

27On the fourteenth night we were still being blown around in the Adriatic Sea. The sailors thought we were close to land. 28They threw a rope into the water with a weight on the end of it. They found that the water was 40 metres*a* deep. They went a little farther and threw the rope in again. It was 30 metres*b* deep. 29The sailors were afraid that we would hit the rocks, so they threw four anchors into the water. Then they prayed for daylight to come. 30Some of the sailors wanted to leave the ship, and they lowered the lifeboat to the water. They wanted the other men to think that they were throwing more anchors from the front of the ship. 31But Paul told the army officer and the other soldiers, "If these men do not stay in the ship, you will lose all hope of survival." 32So the soldiers cut the ropes and let the lifeboat fall into the water.

33Just before dawn Paul began persuading all the people to eat something. He said, "For the past two weeks you have been waiting and watching. You have not eaten for 14 days. 34Now I beg you to eat something. You need it to stay alive. None of you will lose even one hair from your heads." 35After he said this, Paul took some bread and thanked God for it before all of them. He broke off a piece and began eating. 36All the men felt better and started eating too. 37(There were 276 people on the ship.) 38We ate all we wanted. Then we began making the ship lighter by throwing the grain into the sea.

The Ship Is Destroyed

39When daylight came, the sailors saw land, but they did not know what land it was. They saw a bay with a beach and wanted to sail the ship to the beach if they could. 40So they cut the ropes to the anchors and left the anchors in the sea. At the same time, they untied the ropes that were holding the rudders. Then they raised the front sail into the wind and sailed towards the beach. 41But the ship hit a sandbank. The front of the ship stuck there and could not move. Then the big waves began to break the back of the ship to pieces.

42The soldiers decided to kill the prisoners so that none of the prisoners could swim away and escape. 43But Julius the army officer wanted to let Paul live. So he did not allow the soldiers to kill the prisoners. He told the people who could swim to jump into the water and swim to land. 44The others used wooden boards or pieces of the ship. And this is how all the people went safely to land.

Paul on the Island of Malta

28 When we were safely on land, we learned that the island was called Malta. 2The people who lived there were very good to us. It was raining and very cold, so they built a fire and welcomed all of us. 3Paul gathered a pile of sticks for the fire. He was putting the sticks on the fire, and a poisonous snake came out because of the heat and bit him on the hand. 4When the people living on the island saw the snake hanging from his hand, they said, "This man must be a murderer! He did not die in the sea, but Justice*c* does not want him to live."

5But Paul shook the snake off into the fire and was not hurt. 6The people thought he would swell up or fall down dead. They waited and watched him for a long time, but nothing bad happened to him. So they changed their opinion. They said, "He is a god!"

7There were some fields around that same area. They were owned by a man named Publius, the most important Roman official on the island. He welcomed us into his home and was very good to us. We stayed in his house for three days. 8Publius' father was very sick. He had a fever and dysentery, but Paul went to him and prayed for him. He laid his hands on the man and healed him. 9After this happened, all the other sick people on the island came to Paul, and he healed them too.

10–11The people on the island gave us many honours. And after we had been there three months and were ready to leave, they provided us with everything we needed for our trip.

Paul Goes to Rome

We got on a ship from Alexandria that had stayed on the island of Malta during the winter. On the front of the ship was the sign for the twin gods.*d* 12We stopped at the city of Syracuse. We stayed there for three days and then left. 13We came to the city of Rhegium. The next day a wind began to blow from the south-west, so we were able to leave. A day later we came to the city of Puteoli. 14We found some believers there, who asked us to stay with them for a week. Finally, we came to Rome. 15The brothers and sisters in Rome heard about us and came out to meet us at the Market of Appius*e* and at the Three Inns.*f* When Paul saw these believers, he thanked God and felt encouraged.

---

a **27:28** *40 metres* Literally, "20 fathoms".
b **27:28** *30 metres* Literally, "15 fathoms".
c **28:4** *Justice* The people thought there was a goddess named Justice who would punish bad people.
d **28:10–11** *twin gods* Statues of Castor and Pollux, Greek gods.
e **28:15** *Market of Appius* A town about 69 kilometres from Rome.
f **28:15** *Three Inns* A town about 48 kilometres from Rome.

Paul in Rome

[16]When we came to Rome, Paul was allowed to live alone. But a soldier stayed with him to guard him.

[17]Three days later Paul sent for some of the most important Jews. When they came together, he said, "My brothers, I have done nothing against our people or against the customs of our fathers. But I was arrested in Jerusalem and handed over to the Romans. [18]They asked me many questions, but they could not find any reason why I should be put to death. So they wanted to let me go free. [19]But the Jews there did not want that. So I had to ask to come to Rome to have my trial before Caesar. That doesn't mean I am accusing my people of doing anything wrong. [20]That is why I wanted to see you and talk with you. I am bound with this chain because I believe in the hope of Israel."

[21]The Jews answered Paul, "We have received no letters from Judea about you. None of our Jewish brothers who have travelled from there brought news about you or told us anything bad about you. [22]We want to hear your ideas. We know that people everywhere are speaking against this new group."

[23]Paul and the Jews chose a day for a meeting. On that day many more of these Jews met with Paul at his house. He spoke to them all day long, explaining God's kingdom to them. He used the Law of Moses and the writings of the prophets to persuade them to believe in Jesus. [24]Some of the Jews believed what he said, but others did not believe. [25]They had an argument among themselves and were ready to leave. But Paul said one more thing to them: "The Holy Spirit spoke the truth to your fathers through Isaiah the prophet. He said,

[26]'Go to this people and tell them:
"You will listen and listen,

but you will not understand.
You will look and you will see,
but you will not understand what you see."
[27]These people are not able to understand.
Their ears are stopped up,
and their eyes are closed.
So they cannot see with their eyes,
or hear with their ears,
or understand with their minds.
If they understood, they might turn to me,
and I would heal them.'

Isaiah 6:9–10

[28]"I want you Jews to know that God has sent his salvation to the non-Jewish people. They will listen!" [29a]

INSIGHT

It wasn't fair. Paul was held in Caesarea for two years – for something that he didn't do – and lived under house arrest in Rome for another two years. But he didn't let that stop him. Instead of moaning, he wrote many encouraging letters to the churches he had helped establish during his travels. We don't know exactly what happened to him after this point, but it is thought that he was martyred.

Acts 28:30

[30]Paul stayed two full years in his own rented house. He welcomed all the people who came and visited him. [31]He told them about God's kingdom and taught them about the Lord Jesus Christ. He was very bold, and no one tried to stop him from speaking.

---

[a] **28:29** Some late copies of Acts add verse 29: "After Paul said this, the Jews left, still having a big argument with each other."

This section contains letters written to churches and individuals in the very early years of Christianity. Most of these letters were written by Paul, the great evangelist and teacher. The rest were written by other apostles and one by an unnamed writer.

PAUL'S LETTERS

Romans was written by Paul to introduce himself to the church at Rome and to share some of his core beliefs.

1 and 2 Corinthians were written to challenge and correct the sinful behaviour of the church at Corinth.

Galatians was written to a group of churches planted by Paul on his first missionary journey.

Ephesians emphasizes the need for unity and summarizes Paul's ideas and beliefs.

Philippians is a thank-you letter from Paul. He encourages the church at Philippi to keep going.

Colossians was written to a church that Paul had heard about from a friend. He encourages the church to focus on Jesus.

1 and 2 Thessalonians are early letters written to encourage new converts to Christianity.

1 and 2 Timothy are letters written to Paul's helper Timothy, dealing with practical issues of running a church.

Titus was written to one of Paul's most trusted associates and deals with practical church matters, holiness and honesty.

Philemon is a short letter written on behalf of a runaway slave.

GENERAL LETTERS

Hebrews deals with the relationship of Christianity to the Old Testament law.

James is a practical guide on how to live as a Christian.

1 and 2 Peter challenge false teachers and encourage those facing persecution.

1, 2 and 3 John deal with false teaching and the need for Christians to live the right way.

Jude rejects false teaching.

Revelation is a massive, powerful vision of the future, filled with mystical imagery and symbolic numbers.

Who Written by Paul to the church in Rome. Paul had never been to Rome at the time he wrote this letter, but he knew many people there. He dictated the letter to Tertius (16:22).

 When Around AD 57. It was probably written in Corinth, since there are references in the letter to people living there.

What How Christianity came to Rome we don't know. It was probably taken back to the city by some of those Jews who became Christians at Pentecost (Acts 2:10–11). Rome was the biggest, most important city in the known world.

Although Paul is writing to introduce himself, he uses the letter to set out his core beliefs, his understanding of what the basis of Christianity is. And the message that Paul has been given – the message he's already spent more than twenty years spreading around – is that all who put their faith in Jesus are saved.

Faith in Jesus Christ. That's the golden thread that runs right through Romans. His big argument in this letter is that we are all – Jew and non-Jew – "guilty of sin" (3:9): we've all fallen short of what is required and there's nothing we can do for ourselves to gain salvation. It is God's gift to us through the blood sacrifice of Jesus (3:21–31). He states his core message right at the beginning of his letter: the Good News is the power of God for the salvation of everyone (1:16–17).

Romans addresses some deep and complicated questions. Can we be saved through obeying the Jewish law? If not, what's the point of the law in the first place? What is the purpose of Israel in God's plan for the world? Because of stuff like this it may be that the letter was written because of tensions between Jewish and non-Jewish Christians. Whatever the case, Paul reminds them (and us) that we are all "one body" in Christ (12:5).

The last four chapters are full of practical stuff that Christians are supposed to do. "Don't change yourselves to be like the people of this world," Paul writes, "but let God change you inside with a new way of thinking" (12:2). As followers of Jesus we're the original transformers: living Christ-shaped lives of love, peace and hope. But, Paul argues, we do this as a response to salvation, not in order to obtain it.

 ROMANS

Paul the apostle 1:1–15
Good news 1:16–17
No one good 3:1–20
Great news 3:21–31
New life 5:1–11

In Christ 6:1–14
Live the Spirit 8:1–17
The future 8:18–39
Chosen 11:1–36
Basic rules 12:9–21

"I am proud of the Good News, because it is the power God uses to save everyone who believes – to save the Jews first, and now to save those who are not Jews. The Good News shows how God makes people right with himself. God's way of making people right begins and ends with faith. As the Scriptures say, 'The one who is right with God by faith will live forever.'"

Romans 1:16–17

1

Greetings from Paul, a servant of Christ Jesus. God chose me to be an apostle and gave me the work of telling his Good News. ²God promised long ago through his prophets in the Holy Scriptures to give this Good News to his people. ³⁻⁴The Good News is about God's Son, Jesus Christ our Lord. As a human, he was born from the family of David, but through the Holy Spirit*a* he was shown to be God's powerful Son when he was raised from death.

⁵Through Christ, God gave me the special work of an apostle—to lead people of all nations to believe and obey him. I do all this to honour Christ. ⁶You are some of those who have been chosen to belong to Jesus Christ.

⁷This letter is to all of you in Rome. God loves you, and he has chosen you to be his holy people.

Grace and peace to you from God our Father and from the Lord Jesus Christ.

A Prayer of Thanks

⁸First I want to say that I thank my God through Jesus Christ for all of you. I thank him because people everywhere in the world are talking about your great faith. ⁹⁻¹⁰Every time I pray, I remember you. God knows this is true. He is the one I serve with all my heart by telling people the Good News about his Son. I pray that I will be allowed to come to you. It will happen if God wants it. ¹¹I want very much to see you and give you some spiritual gift to make your faith stronger. ¹²I mean that I want us to help each other with the faith that we have. Your faith will help me, and my faith will help you.

¹³Brothers and sisters, I want you to know that I have planned many times to come to you, but something always happens to change my plans. I would like to see the same good result among you that I have had from my work among the other non-Jewish people.

¹⁴I must serve all people—those who share in Greek culture and those who are less civilized,*b* the educated as well as the ignorant. ¹⁵That is why I want so much to tell the Good News to you there in Rome.

¹⁶I am proud of the Good News, because it is the power God uses to save everyone who believes—to save the Jews first, and now to save those who are not Jews. ¹⁷The Good News shows how God makes people right with himself. God's way of making people right begins and ends with faith. As the Scriptures say, "The one who is right with God by faith will live forever."*c*

All People Have Done Wrong

¹⁸God shows his anger from heaven against all the evil and wrong things that people do. Their evil lives hide the truth they have. ¹⁹This makes God angry because they have been shown what he is like. Yes, God has made it clear to them.

²⁰There are things about God that people cannot see—his eternal power and all that makes him God. But since the beginning of the world, those things have been easy for people to understand. They are made clear in what God has made. So people have no excuse for the evil they do.

²¹People knew God, but they did not honour him as God, and they did not thank him. Their ideas were all useless. There was not one good thought left in their foolish minds. ²²They said they were wise, but they became fools. ²³Instead of honouring the divine greatness of God, who lives forever, they traded it for the worship of idols—things made to look like humans, who get sick and die, or like birds, animals and snakes.

²⁴People wanted only to do evil. So God left them and let them go their sinful way. And so they became completely immoral and used their bodies in shameful ways with each other. ²⁵They traded the truth of God for a lie. They bowed down and worshipped the things God made instead of worshipping the God who made those things. He is the one who should be praised forever. Amen.

²⁶Because people did those things, God left them and let them do the shameful things they wanted to do. Women stopped having natural sex with men and started having sex with other women. ²⁷In the same way, men stopped having natural sex with women and began wanting each other all the time. Men did shameful things with other men, and in their bodies they received the punishment for those wrongs.

²⁸People did not think it was important to have a true knowledge of God. So God left them and allowed them to have their own worthless thinking. And so they do what they should not do. ²⁹They are filled with every kind of sin, evil, greed and hatred. They are full of jealousy, murder, fighting, lying and thinking the worst about each other. They gossip ³⁰and say evil things about each other. They hate God. They are rude, proud and boast about themselves. They invent ways of doing evil. They don't obey their parents, ³¹they are foolish, they don't keep their promises and they show no kindness or mercy to others.

---

a **1:3–4 Holy Spirit** Literally, "spirit of holiness".
b **1:14 those who share . . . civilized** Literally, "Greeks and barbarians". See "GREEK" in the Word List.
c **1:17** Quote from Hab. 2:4.

SIN CITIES

Big cities tend to attract the extremes of human behaviour and world capitals, like London and New York, even more so. You can be anonymous in a big city; there're a lot more people there, so there's more freedom for alternative lifestyle choices – and more tolerance for the questionable ones.

This was particularly true of Rome, the capital city of the dominant Roman Empire at the time of Paul's letter to the Romans. Rome was a hotbed of wrongdoing, and the practices Paul lists in the first chapter were typical of the city. By all accounts, the emperors themselves led the way in living selfish, morally wrong, pleasure-seeking lives.

DIG IN
READ Romans 1:16–32

- What sinful lifestyles is Paul condemning here?
- What is the root sin behind them all (v.25)?

All the sinful acts Paul lists – sexual perversion, practising homosexuality, greed, murder, jealousy, hatred, and more – are bad but they're not the heart of the matter. They are just symptoms of a deeper disease. According to Paul, all these evils stem from one decision, people have "traded the truth of God for a lie" (v.25) and chosen to worship created things rather than the Creator.

- How does he describe the Good News (vv.16–17)?
- Who is it for and how does it work?

Paul wades right in and the first thing he says hits those who were proud of their sinful lifestyles right between the eyes: "I am proud of the Good News" (v.16). The Good News, says Paul, is not a code to live by, or a rulebook; it's not even a particular lifestyle. It's actually the power of God to save.

The way it works begins and ends with faith (v.17), and this is the heart of his argument that he unpacks through the rest of the letter.

DIG THROUGH

- Look carefully at the list of sins in verses 29–31. Be honest: how many apply to you personally? Some? Most?
- We can see God's hard line on what people who do these things deserve in verse 32. So what are we going to do with our sin?
- How do you think this letter might have been received if it fell into the hands of a non-believing Roman citizen?
- How would it go down with one of your non-Christian friends if they read it today? Would they be able to handle the idea of "sin"?

DIG DEEPER

- It would be wrong to imagine that sin is a "modern" invention, or even that it started with the Romans. If you look through the early chapters of the Bible, you'll see human beings reaching the depths of sin within the first generations (Genesis 2 – 11).
- Paul doesn't skirt around the issue in Romans. His opening gambit is "I am proud of the Good News" (Romans 1:16). Do you see any evidence of the church today being a little embarrassed about certain parts of the Bible or biblical views on, say, sexuality? How about you?

³²They know God's law says that anyone who lives like that should die. But they not only continue to do these things themselves, they also encourage others who do them.

Let God Be the Judge

2 So do you think that you can judge those other people? You are wrong. You too are guilty of sin. You judge them, but you do the same things they do. So when you judge them, you are really condemning yourself. ²God judges all who do such things, and we know his judgement is right. ³And since you do the same things as those people you judge, surely you understand that God will punish you too. How could you think you would be able to escape his judgement? ⁴God has been kind to you. He has been very patient, waiting for you to change. But you think nothing of his kindness. Maybe you don't understand that God is kind to you so that you will decide to change your lives.

⁵But you are so stubborn! You refuse to change. So you are making your own punishment greater and greater. You will be punished on the day when God will show his anger. On that day everyone will see how right God is to judge people. ⁶He will reward or punish everyone for what they have done. ⁷Some people live for God's glory, for honour and for life that cannot be destroyed. They live for those things by always continuing to do good. God will give eternal life to them. ⁸But others are selfish and refuse to follow truth. They follow evil. God will show his anger and punish them. ⁹He will give trouble and suffering to everyone who does evil—to the Jews first and also to those who are not Jews. ¹⁰But he will give glory, honour and peace to everyone who does good—to the Jews first and also to those who are not Jews. ¹¹God judges everyone the same. It doesn't matter who they are.

¹²People who have the law and those who have never heard of the law are all the same when they sin. People who don't have the law and are sinners will be lost. And, in the same way, those who have the law and are sinners will be judged by the law. ¹³Hearing the law does not make people right with God. They will be right before him only if they always do what the law says.

¹⁴Those who are not Jews don't have the law. But when they naturally do what the law commands without even knowing the law, then they are their own law. This is true even though they don't have the written law. ¹⁵They show that in their hearts they know what is right and wrong, the same as the law commands, and their consciences agree. Sometimes their thoughts tell them that they have done wrong, and this makes them guilty. And sometimes their thoughts tell them that they have done right, and this makes them not guilty.

¹⁶All this will happen on the day when God will judge people's secret thoughts through Jesus Christ. This is part of the Good News that I tell everyone.

The Jews and the Law

¹⁷What about you? You say you are a Jew. You trust in the law and proudly claim to be close to God. ¹⁸You know what God wants you to do. And you know what is important, because you have learned the law. ¹⁹You think you are a guide for people who don't know the right way, a light for those who are in the dark. ²⁰You think you can show foolish people what is right. And you think you are a teacher for those who are just beginning to learn. You have the law, and so you think you know everything and have all truth. ²¹You teach others, so why don't you teach yourself? You tell them not to steal, but you yourself steal. ²²You say they must not commit adultery, but you yourself are guilty of that sin. You hate idols, but you steal them from their temples. ²³You are so proud that you have God's law, but you bring shame to God by breaking his law. ²⁴As the Scriptures say, "People in other nations insult God because of you."*ᵃ*

²⁵If you follow the law, then your circumcision has meaning. But if you break the law, then it is as if you were never circumcised. ²⁶Those who are not Jews are not circumcised. But if they do what the law says, it is as if they were circumcised. ²⁷You have the written law and circumcision, but you break the law. So those who are not circumcised in their bodies, but still obey the law, will show that you are guilty.

²⁸You are not a true Jew if you are only a Jew in your physical body. True circumcision is not only on the outside of the body. ²⁹A true Jew is one who is a Jew inside. True circumcision is done in the heart. It is done by the Spirit, not by the written law. And anyone who is circumcised in the heart by the Spirit gets praise from God, not from people.

3 So, do Jews have anything that others don't have? Do they get any benefit from being circumcised? ²Yes, the Jews have many benefits. The most important one is this: God trusted them with his promises. ³It is true that some Jews were not faithful to God. But will that stop God

ᵃ **2:24** Quote from Isa. 52:5. See also Ezek. 36:20–23.

FREE GIFT FROM GOD

How many times have you bought a magazine offering a "free gift" on the cover, only to find there's a catch and you need to collect tokens or buy something else in order to qualify? Unsurprisingly, people are naturally suspicious of getting something for nothing. "There's no such thing as a free lunch," the saying goes: there are almost always strings attached. Almost.

DIG IN
READ Romans 3:21–31

- How does God deal with the problem of sin (vv.24–26)?
- Who's taking the initiative here – God or us?
- How was God going to make people right with himself again?

The history of the people of God is told in story after story of people failing to make the grade with him. People could never keep God's law properly and time and time again they turned away from him. Neither judgement nor comfort from the prophets could keep the hearts of human beings on track. Their own efforts failed time and time again. Something altogether different was required . . .

"But God has a way to make people right . . . He has now shown us that new way" (v.21). Jesus, who we glimpsed all through the Old Testament and saw in flesh in the Gospels, has made a way to keep us on track by taking the punishment for us through his death and resurrection. All we have to do to benefit from what he has done for us is simply put our faith in Jesus.

There's no way whatsoever we could earn that. It's a free gift.

- Who is this promise for (v.29)?
- Is anyone excluded from it?

The Jews knew that historically they were God's chosen people. They felt a sense of entitlement, a superiority complex even, about their relationship with God. So it would have come as a huge shock to hear Paul, who had been raised a Jew and trained by the Jewish elite, say that this new "way of faith" (v.27) would be for non-Jews too.

Jews who thought that the promise was for them alone were wrong. You no longer need to be, or do, anything to qualify for the grace of God, except place your faith in the Saviour, Jesus.

DIG THROUGH

- Do you have any trouble accepting things for free? Do you feel guilty receiving things you haven't worked for? Is there a part of you that feels you need to do something to earn them?
- There was a feeling among early Jewish believers that the promises of God were for them alone – that they had a right to something special because of their religious heritage and what they'd done in the past. Can this feeling creep into believers and churches today?

DIG DEEPER

"But God has a way to make people right, and it has nothing to do with the law. He has now shown us that new way, which the law and the prophets told us about" (Romans 3:21). What Paul lays out here is the completion of everything that the Bible has pointed to up until now. It's important to see that this is not a "replacement" for the law but a fulfilment of it (v.31). This is God's amazing, eternal wisdom working itself out over thousands of years.

from doing what he promised? ⁴No, even if everyone else fails to keep their promises, God will always do what he says. As the Scriptures say about him,

> "You will be proved right in what you say,
>   and you will win when people accuse you."
> *Psalm 51:4*

⁵When we do wrong, that shows more clearly that God is right. So can we say that God does wrong when he punishes us? (That's the way some people think.) ⁶Of course not. If God could not punish us, how could he judge the world? ⁷Someone might say, "When I lie, it really gives God glory, because my lie makes his truth easier to see. So why am I judged a sinner?" ⁸It would be the same to say, "We should do evil so that good will come." Many people criticize us, saying that's what we teach. They are wrong, and they should be condemned for saying that.

All People Are Guilty

⁹So are we Jews better than other people? No, we have already said that those who are Jews, as well as those who are not Jews, are the same. They are all guilty of sin. ¹⁰As the Scriptures say,

> "There is no one doing what is right,
>   not even one.
> ¹¹There is no one who understands.
>   There is no one who is trying to be with
>   God.
> ¹²They have all turned away from him,
>   and now they are of no use to anyone.
> There is no one who does good,
>   not even one."
> *Psalm 14:1–3*

> ¹³"Their words are as dangerous as an open
>   grave.
>   They use their tongues for telling lies."
> *Psalm 5:9*

> "Their words are like the poison of snakes."
> *Psalm 140:3*

> ¹⁴"Their mouths are full of cursing and angry
>   words."
> *Psalm 10:7*

> ¹⁵"They are always ready to kill someone.
> ¹⁶   Everywhere they go they cause trouble and
>   ruin.

> ¹⁷They don't know how to live in peace."
> *Isaiah 59:7–8*

> ¹⁸"They have no fear or respect for God."
> *Psalm 36:1*

¹⁹What the law says is for those who are under the law. It stops anyone from making excuses. And it brings the whole world under God's judgement, ²⁰because no one can be made right with God by following the law. The law only shows us our sin.

How God Makes People Right

²¹But God has a way to make people right, and it has nothing to do with the law. He has now shown us that new way, which the law and the prophets told us about. ²²God makes people right through their faith in*ᵃ* Jesus Christ. He does this for all who believe in Christ. Everyone is the same. ²³All have sinned and are not good enough to share God's divine greatness. ²⁴They are made right with God by his grace. This is a free gift. They are made right with God by being made free from sin through Jesus Christ. ²⁵⁻²⁶God gave Jesus as a way to forgive people's sins through their faith in him. God can forgive them because the blood sacrifice of Jesus pays for their sins. God gave Jesus to show that he always does what is right and fair. He was right in the past when he was patient and did not punish people for their sins. And in our own time he still does what is right. God worked all this out in a way that allows him to judge people fairly and still make right any person who has faith in Jesus.

²⁷So do we have any reason to boast about ourselves? No reason at all. And why not? Because we are depending on the way of faith, not on what we have done in following the law. ²⁸I mean we are made right with God through faith, not through what we have done to follow the law. This is what we believe. ²⁹God is not only the God of the Jews. He is also the God of those who are not Jews. ³⁰There is only one God. He will make Jews*ᵇ* right with him by their faith, and he will also make non-Jews*ᶜ* right with him through their faith. ³¹So do we destroy the law by following the way of faith? Not at all! In fact, faith causes us to be what the law actually wants.

The Example of Abraham

4 So what can we say about Abraham, the father of our people? What did he learn about faith? ²If Abraham was made right by the things he

---

ᵃ **3:22 *their faith in*** Or "the faithfulness of".
ᵇ **3:30 *Jews*** Literally, "circumcision".
ᶜ **3:30 *non-Jews*** Literally, "uncircumcision".

did, he would have had a reason to boast about himself. But God knew that he had no reason to boast. [3]That's why the Scriptures say, "Abraham believed God. And because he believed, God accepted him as one who has done what is right."[a]

[4]When people work, their pay is not given to them as a gift. They earn the pay they get. [5]But people cannot do any work that will make them right with God. So they must trust in him. Then he accepts their faith, and that makes them right with him. He is the one who makes even evil people right. [6]David said the same thing when he was talking about the blessing people have when God accepts them as good without looking at what they have done:

[7]"It is a great blessing
 when people are forgiven for the wrongs
 they have done,
 when their sins are erased!
[8]It is a great blessing when the Lord accepts
 people
 as if they are without sin!"

Psalm 32:1–2

[9]Is this blessing only for those who are circumcised? Or is it also for those who are not circumcised? We have already said that it was because of Abraham's faith that he was accepted as one who is right with God. [10]So how did this happen? Did God accept Abraham before or after he was circumcised? God accepted him before his circumcision. [11]Abraham was circumcised later to show that God accepted him. His circumcision was proof that he was right with God through faith before he was circumcised. So Abraham is the father of all those who believe but are not circumcised. They believe and are accepted as people who are right with God. [12]And Abraham is also the father of those who have been circumcised. But it is not their circumcision that makes him their father. He is their father only if they live following the faith that our father Abraham had before he was circumcised.

God's Promise Received Through Faith

[13]Abraham and his descendants received the promise that they would get the whole world. But Abraham did not receive that promise because he followed the law. He received that promise because he was right with God through his faith. [14]If people could get God's promise by following the law, then faith is worthless. And God's promise to Abraham is worthless, [15]because the law can only bring God's anger on those who disobey it. But if there is no law, then there is nothing to disobey.

[16]So people get what God promised by having faith. This happens so that the promise can be a free gift. And if the promise is a free gift, then all of Abraham's people will get that promise. The promise is not just for those who live under the Law of Moses. It is for all who live with faith as Abraham did. He is the father of us all. [17]As the Scriptures say, "I have made you a father of many nations."[b] This is true before God, the one Abraham believed—the God who gives life to the dead and speaks of things that don't yet exist as if they are real.

[18]There was no hope that Abraham would have children, but Abraham believed God and continued to hope. And that is why he became the father of many nations. As God told him, "You will have many descendants."[c] [19]Abraham was almost a hundred years old, so he was past the age for having children. Also, Sarah could not have children. Abraham was well aware of this, but his faith in God never became weak. [20]He never doubted that God would do what he promised. He never stopped believing. In fact, he grew stronger in his faith and just praised God. [21]Abraham felt sure that God was able to do what he promised. [22]So that's why "he was accepted as one who is right with God".[d] [23]These words ("he was accepted") were written not only for Abraham. [24]They were also written for us. God will also accept us because we believe. We believe in the one who raised Jesus our Lord from death. [25]Jesus was handed over to die for our sins, and he was raised from death to make us right with God.

Right With God

5 We have been made right with God because of our faith. So we have[e] peace with God through our Lord Jesus Christ. [2]Through our faith, Christ has brought us into that blessing of God's grace that we now enjoy. And we are very happy because of the hope we have of sharing God's glory. [3]And we are also happy with the troubles we have. Why are we happy with troubles? Because we know that these troubles make us more patient. [4]And this patience is proof that we are strong. And this proof gives us hope. [5]And this hope will never disappoint us. We know this because God has poured out his love to fill our hearts through the Holy Spirit he gave us.

---

[a] **4:3** Quote from Gen. 15:6.
[b] **4:17** Quote from Gen. 17:5 of God speaking to Abraham.
[c] **4:18** Quote from Gen. 15:5.
[d] **4:22** Quote from Gen. 15:6.
[e] **5:1** *we have* Some important Greek copies have "let us have".

⁶Christ died for us when we were unable to help ourselves. We were living against God, but at just the right time Christ died for us. ⁷Very few people will die to save the life of someone else, even if it is for a good person. Someone might be willing to die for an especially good person. ⁸But Christ died for us while we were still sinners, and by this God showed how much he loves us.

⁹We have been made right with God by the blood sacrifice of Christ. So through Christ we will surely be saved from God's anger. ¹⁰I mean that while we were God's enemies, he made friends with us through his Son's death. And the fact that we are now God's friends makes it even more certain that he will save us through his Son's life. ¹¹And not only will we be saved, but we also rejoice right now in what God has done for us through our Lord Jesus Christ. It is because of Jesus that we are now God's friends.

Adam and Christ

¹²Sin came into the world because of what one man did. And with sin came death. So this is why all people must die—because all people have sinned. ¹³Sin was in the world before the Law of Moses. But God does not consider people guilty of sin if there is no law. ¹⁴But from the time of Adam to the time of Moses, everyone had to die. Adam died because he sinned by not obeying God's command. But even those who did not sin that same way had to die.

That one man, Adam, can be compared to Christ, the one who was coming in the future. ¹⁵But God's free gift is not like Adam's sin. Many people died because of the sin of that one man. But the grace that people received from God was much greater. Many received God's gift of life by the grace of this other man, Jesus Christ. ¹⁶After Adam sinned once, he was judged guilty. But the gift of God is different. His free gift came after many sins, and it makes people right with him. ¹⁷One man sinned, and so death ruled all people because of that one man. But now some people accept God's full grace and his great gift of being made right. Surely they will have true life and rule through the one man, Jesus Christ.

¹⁸So that one sin of Adam brought the punishment of death to all people. But in the same way, Christ did something so good that it makes all people right with God. And that brings them true life. ¹⁹One man disobeyed God and many became sinners. But in the same way, one man obeyed God and many will be made right. ²⁰The law was brought in so that more people would sin the way Adam did. But where sin increased, there was even more of God's grace. ²¹Sin once used death to rule us. But God gave us more of his grace so that grace could rule by

making us right with him. And this brings us eternal life through Jesus Christ our Lord.

Dead to Sin but Alive in Christ

6 So do you think we should continue sinning so that God will give us more and more grace? ²Of course not! Our old sinful life ended. It's dead. So how can we continue living in sin? ³Did you forget that all of us became part of Christ Jesus when we were baptized? In our baptism we shared in his death. ⁴So when we were baptized, we were buried with Christ and took part in his death. And just as Christ was raised from death by the wonderful power of the Father, so we can now live a new life.

⁵Christ died, and we have been joined with him by dying too. So we will also be joined with him by rising from death as he did. ⁶We know that our old life was put to death on the cross with Christ. This happened so that our sinful selves would have no power over us. Then we would not be slaves to sin. ⁷Anyone who has died is made free from sin's control.

⁸If we died with Christ, we know that we will also live with him. ⁹Christ was raised from death. And we know that he cannot die again. Death has no power over him now. ¹⁰Yes, when Christ died, he died to defeat the power of sin once—enough for all time. He now has a new life, and his new life is with God. ¹¹In the same way, you should see yourselves as being dead to the power of sin and alive for God through Christ Jesus.

INSIGHT

Paul has been saying that we only gain a right standing before God through faith in Jesus, not through our own works, but that doesn't mean we should take advantage of God's kindness. Rather, out of thankfulness, we should throw ourselves into serving him with even greater abandon!

Romans 6:14–15

¹²But don't let sin control your life here on earth. You must not be ruled by the things your sinful self makes you want to do. ¹³Don't offer the parts of your body to serve sin. Don't use your bodies to do evil, but offer yourselves to God, as people who have died and now live. Offer the parts of your body to God to be used for doing good. ¹⁴Sin will not be your master, because you are not under law. You now live under God's grace.

Slaves of Goodness

¹⁵So what should we do? Should we sin because we are under grace and not under law? Certainly not! ¹⁶Surely you know that you become the slaves of whatever you give yourselves to. Anything or anyone you follow will be your master. You can follow sin, or you can obey God. Following sin brings spiritual death, but obeying God makes you right with him. ¹⁷In the past you were slaves to sin—sin controlled you. But thank God, you fully obeyed what you were taught. ¹⁸You were made free from sin, and now you are slaves to what is right. ¹⁹I use this example from everyday life because you need help in understanding spiritual truths. In the past you offered the parts of your body to be slaves to your immoral and sinful thoughts. The result was that you lived only for sin. In the same way, you must now offer yourselves as slaves to what is right. Then you will live only for God.

²⁰In the past you were slaves to sin, and you did not even think about doing right. ²¹You did evil things, and now you are ashamed of what you did. Did those things help you? No, they only brought death. ²²But now you are free from sin. You have become slaves of God, and the result is that you live only for God. This will bring you eternal life. ²³When people sin, they earn what sin pays—death. But God gives his people a free gift—eternal life in Christ Jesus our Lord.

INSIGHT

Paul uses the example of Jewish widows to help the new Christians understand their new freedom from the law. They may have previously been "married" to the idea of being obedient to the law, but now it is as if they have a new husband, "Christ", and a new understanding of what marriage (i.e. a relationship with God) can be.

Romans 7:1–6

An Example From Marriage

7 Brothers and sisters, you all understand the Law of Moses. So surely you know that the law rules over people only while they are alive. ²It's like what the law says about marriage. A woman must stay married to her husband as long as he is alive. But if her husband dies, she is made free from the law of marriage. ³If she marries another man while her husband is still alive, the law says she is guilty of adultery. But if her husband dies, she is made free from the law of marriage. So if she marries another man after her husband dies, she is not guilty of adultery.

⁴In the same way, my brothers and sisters, your old selves died and you became free from the law through the body of Christ. Now you belong to someone else. You belong to the one who was raised from death. We belong to Christ so that we can be used in service to God. ⁵In the past we were ruled by our sinful selves. The law made us want to do sinful things. And those sinful desires controlled our bodies, so that what we did only brought us spiritual death. ⁶In the past the law held us as prisoners, but our old selves died, and we were made free from the law. So now we serve God in a new way, not in the old way, with the written rules. Now we serve God in the new way, with the Spirit.

Our Fight Against Sin

⁷You might think I am saying that sin and the law are the same. That is not true. But the law was the only way I could learn what sin means. I would never have known that it is wrong to want something that is not mine. But the law said, "You must not want what belongs to someone else."ᵃ ⁸And sin found a way to use that command and make me want all kinds of things that weren't mine. So sin came to me because of the command. But without the law, sin has no power. ⁹Before I knew the law, I was alive. But when I heard the law's command, sin began to live, ¹⁰and I died spiritually. The command was meant to bring life, but for me it brought death. ¹¹Sin found a way to fool me by using the command to make me die.

¹²Now the law is holy, and the command is holy and right and good. ¹³Does this mean that something that is good brought death to me? No, it was sin that used the good command to bring me death. This shows how terrible sin really is. It can use a good command to produce a result that shows sin at its very worst.

The War Inside Us

¹⁴We know that the law is spiritual, but I am not. I am so human. Sin rules me as if I were its slave. ¹⁵I don't understand why I act the way I do. I don't do the good I want to do, and I do the evil I hate. ¹⁶And if I don't want to do what I do, that means I agree that the law is good. ¹⁷But I am not really the one doing the evil. It is sin living in me that does it. ¹⁸Yes, I know that nothing good lives in me—I mean nothing good lives in the part of me that is not spiritual. I want to do what is good, but I don't

---

ᵃ **7:7** Quote from Exod. 20:17; Deut. 5:21.

do it. ¹⁹I don't do the good that I want to do. I do the evil that I don't want to do. ²⁰So if I do what I don't want to do, then I am not really the one doing it. It is the sin living in me that does it.

²¹So I have learned this rule: when I want to do good, evil is there with me. ²²In my mind I am happy with God's law. ²³But I see another law working in my body. That law makes war against the law that my mind accepts. That other law working in my body is the law of sin, and that law makes me its prisoner. ²⁴What a miserable person I am! Who will save me from this body that brings me death? ²⁵I thank God for his salvation through Jesus Christ our Lord!

So in my mind I am a slave to God's law, but in my sinful self I am a slave to the law of sin.

Life in the Spirit

8 So now anyone who is in Christ Jesus is not judged guilty. ²That is because in Christ Jesus the law of the Spirit that brings life made you*a* free. It made you free from the law that brings sin and death. ³The law was without power because it was made weak by our sinful selves. But God did what the law could not do: he sent his own Son to earth with the same human life that everyone else uses for sin. God sent him to be an offering to pay for sin. So God used a human life to destroy sin. ⁴He did this so that we could be right just as the law said we must be. Now we don't live following our sinful selves. We live following the Spirit.

⁵People who live following their sinful selves think only about what they want. But those who live following the Spirit are thinking about what the Spirit wants them to do. ⁶If your thinking is controlled by your sinful self, there is spiritual death. But if your thinking is controlled by the Spirit, there is life and peace. ⁷Why is this true? Because anyone whose thinking is controlled by their sinful self is against God. They refuse to obey God's law. And really they are not able to obey it. ⁸Those who are ruled by their sinful selves cannot please God.

⁹But you are not ruled by your sinful selves. You are ruled by the Spirit, if that Spirit of God really lives in you. Whoever does not have the Spirit of Christ does not belong to Christ. ¹⁰Your body will always be dead because of sin. But if Christ is in you, then the Spirit gives you life, because Christ made you right with God. ¹¹God raised Jesus from death. And if God's Spirit lives in you, he will also give life to your bodies that die. Yes, God is the one who raised Christ from death, and he will raise you to life through his Spirit living in you.

¹²So, my brothers and sisters, we must not be ruled by our sinful selves. We must not live the way our sinful selves want. ¹³If you use your lives to do what your sinful selves want, you will die spiritually. But if you use the Spirit's help to stop doing the wrong things you do with your body, you will have true life.

¹⁴The true children of God are those who let God's Spirit lead them. ¹⁵The Spirit that we received is not a spirit that makes us slaves again and causes us to fear. The Spirit that we have makes us God's chosen children. And with that Spirit we cry out, "*Abba*,*b* Father." ¹⁶And the Spirit himself speaks to our spirits and makes us sure that we are God's children. ¹⁷If we are God's children, we will get the blessings God has for his people. He will give us all that he has given Christ. But we must suffer like Christ suffered. Then we will be able to share his glory.

We Will Have Glory in the Future

¹⁸We have sufferings now, but these are nothing compared to the great glory that will be given to us. ¹⁹Everything that God made is waiting with excitement for the time when he will show the world who his children are. The whole world wants very much for that to happen. ²⁰Everything God made was allowed to become like something that cannot fulfil its purpose. That was not its choice, but God made it happen with this hope in view: ²¹that the creation would be made free from ruin—that everything God made would have the same freedom and glory that belong to God's children.

²²We know that everything God made has been waiting until now in pain like a woman ready to give birth to a child. ²³Not only the world, but we also have been waiting with pain inside us. We have the Spirit as the first part of God's promise. So we are waiting for God to finish making us his own children. I mean we are waiting for our bodies to be made free. ²⁴We were saved to have this hope. If we can see what we are waiting for, that is not really hope. People don't hope for something they already have. ²⁵But we are hoping for something we don't have yet, and we are waiting for it patiently.

²⁶Also, the Spirit helps us. We are very weak, but the Spirit helps us with our weakness. We don't know how to pray as we should, but the Spirit himself speaks to God for us. He begs God for us, speaking to him with feelings too deep for words. ²⁷God already knows our deepest thoughts. And he understands what the Spirit is saying, because the Spirit speaks for his people in the way that agrees with what God wants.

---

a **8:2 *you*** Some Greek copies have "me". Also in the next sentence.
b **8:15 *Abba*** An Aramaic word that was used by Jewish children as a name for their father.

FOLLOWING THE SPIRIT

Every civilized nation operates under the rule of law. If you want to live there, you must follow the "law of the land". Laws differ from place to place: you can't drive above 70 mph in the UK, for instance, but in some parts of Europe no limit is enforced. Christians are, of course, under the same human laws as everyone else but the Bible talks about another kind of law too.

DIG IN

READ Romans 8:1–17

- What does Paul mean by "the law" in verse 3?
- How did Jesus accomplish what the law could not (v.3)?
- What should God's people now follow instead of "our sinful selves" (v.4)?

The "law" that Paul is talking about here is the law given to Moses – the code God's people were meant to live by. In previous chapters Paul has described how this law has always been powerless in helping people to overcome sin. But now its true purpose has finally been revealed: to show us our sin and our need to be saved (Romans 3:19–20).

Jesus, by his death on the cross, has achieved a full and final victory over sin and accomplished what the law by itself never could. The power of sin has been broken in our lives and a new era has begun for God's people.

Whereas before, God's people tried to obey God as best they could by following the law (they always failed because of their sinfulness), now God gives us his Spirit who enables us to live as God wants without needing the law to guide us.

- How is life different for people who follow the Spirit?
- What's the long-term outcome of following the Spirit instead of our sinful selves?

Following the Spirit brings freedom, life and peace (vv.2,6). It gets us in line with God and his purposes; allows us to please him (v.8); helps us to fight the temptation to sin and brings true life (v.13).

When we become Christians, it's as if we travel from one country with its old rules, where we were slaves, to a new country where we're free! Sadly, the opposite is true when we choose to live for ourselves. Following our sinful selves might feel like freedom – but it's actually like returning to the old country and its laws where we were slaves. Living by the Spirit makes us children, not slaves.

DIG THROUGH

- The signs of physical death are obvious! But what about spiritual death (v.6)? Use the passage to help you identify some of the signs of spiritual death?
- Paul says that when we go back to following our sinful selves, we basically go back to being slaves. In what ways can we knowingly do this, returning ourselves to slavery?
- In what ways can we open ourselves up to let the Spirit of God lead us?

DIG DEEPER

- Look at verse 17: "If we are God's children, we will get the blessings God has for his people." During his time on earth Jesus addressed God in a shocking new way, calling him *"Abba"*, the Aramaic word for "Daddy". This suggested a greater level of intimacy with God than anyone had presumed to have before and a greater level of rights and privileges. Here, Paul reminds us that as sons and daughters of God, we now have access to them too. Check out Galatians 3:26 for confirmation.

PEER PRESSURE

HAVE you ever heard the phrase "under the influence"? It's usually applied to people who've been attempting to do something when they're high or drunk. All of us are under the influence of *something* or *someone* and it might not be alcohol or cannabis. Maybe it's the buzz we get from doing stuff that really impresses our friends. Maybe it's the depression we feel as a result of failing an exam and not measuring up to other people's expectations. Maybe it's the rush that comes along with

EVERYONE EXPERIENCES PEER PRESSURE. ALL OF US ARE VICTIMS — IT'S JUST PART OF GROWING UP.

catching the eye of someone we really fancy, and then wondering if they felt it too. Other people have a massive influence over us, which is why we are vulnerable to a little thing called "peer pressure".

Everyone experiences peer pressure. All of us are victims — it's just part of growing up. Sooner or later we discover that the people around us are into stuff that we know is bad for us but, nevertheless, we still want to be in on the action! After all, we don't want to

end up feeling lonely, right? So in order to be part of the "in" crowd, we can find ourselves compromising little by little until, eventually, we've changed into someone we don't even recognize any more.

The Bible is full of amazing stories of young men and women who battled with peer pressure. People like Shadrach, Meshach and Abednego who stood up to the evil king (Daniel 3), Joseph with his over-the-top coat and jealous brothers (Genesis 37:3–11), and even Peter — one of Jesus' closest friends — who had trouble standing up for Jesus when he needed him most (Matthew 26:69–75). When the pressure was on, they either stood their ground or caved in miserably. Either way, their lives are examples for us of how we should (or shouldn't) deal with peer pressure today. ←

Pray this prayer if you mean it:

Lord, help me not to give in to peer pressure, but to stand up for what I believe in. Help me remember that what you think about me is much more important than what anyone else thinks.

Amen

WITNESSING AND EVANGELISM

TOM had never been so nervous before in his life. For weeks he'd been planning to throw a party for all of his school friends where he could show them photos and videos from his youth group's summer mission trip, and then take a few minutes to talk about his faith in God and invite them to begin a journey of faith themselves. Well tonight was the night. The party was already in full swing, and Tom knew his little speech was minutes away, so he popped into the kitchen to gather his thoughts. Thankfully his mother was there to offer some much needed encouragement.

"Tom, this is your big night!" she began. "How are you feeling? You look pretty nervous."

Tom took a deep breath and sighed. "I think I'm just afraid that once some of my friends find out that I'm a Christian, they'll . . . I dunno . . . treat me differently."

His mother paused, looked him in the eye, and then gave him a hug. "You know, that's perfectly normal. Talking to someone about your faith in Jesus isn't always the easiest thing to do. Jesus himself said that if the world hated him back in his day, we shouldn't expect it to be any different for us today. But let me ask you something that might help. Would you say that you're someone who is *passionate* about God?"

Tom didn't need to think very hard about that one. "Of course!"

"Well, I was once told that the word 'passion' comes from the Latin word meaning 'to suffer'. That's why people refer to Jesus' *suffering* on the cross and the torture that he went through as 'the *passion* of Christ'. So you might say that the way to know how *passionate* you really are about something is to ask yourself how much you'd be willing to *suffer* for it. And if Jesus endured all that for us, then surely we can respond by making a stand for him, despite what others may say about us, or the way they might treat us."

Tom was stunned. "Wow. That really makes sense. I mean, there's no way any of the people in that room are going to crucify me or

torture me! But, more importantly, I guess that if I say I'm passionate for Christ, then I'd better be willing to back that up with my actions."

A smile spread across his mother's face as she said, "Exactly. And that's what you're about to do right now. I'm with you all the way."

Tom felt loads better. He thanked his mum, then quietly bowed his head and said a quick prayer before leaving the kitchen. ←

Lord Jesus, thank you for being passionate enough about me to die on the cross for my sins. Would you help me now as I shine my light brighter than I ever have before in front of my friends. Please send your Holy Spirit to show them that you are real.

Amen

If this is your prayer, why not pray it too?

"GO AND MAKE FOLLWERS OF ALL PEOPLE IN THE WORLD. BAPTIZE THEM IN THE NAME OF THE FATHER AND THE SON AND THE HOLY SPIRIT"
MATTHEW 28:19

SPIRITUAL GIFTS

HAVE you ever looked at someone else and thought they had an amazing gift that you wish you had? It can be easy to think other people's gifts are better than ours, but we're really missing the point if we do. God has given special gifts to all Christians, and they are *all* of value – otherwise he wouldn't have given them to us!

The important thing isn't to be concerned about which gift we think seems the best, but to know that all gifts are given to be used for the benefit of others (1 Corinthians 12:7). They are not gifts for us to use selfishly, just to enjoy and get credit for; they are there to build the Church and God's kingdom. We're told that we all make up the "body" of Christ and we really can't do without any part. For the whole body to be able to work at its best, everyone needs to bring their gift. God didn't design any of us to work alone; he spread his gifts out among us so we could work as a team, rather than giving them to a couple of "super-Christians" to do all the work! (See 1 Corinthians 12.)

KEEP OFFERING YOUR GIFTS BACK TO GOD AND TO HIS CHURCH TO PLAY YOUR PART IN SEEING HIS KINGDOM COME ON EARTH.

So make sure you know what your gifts are then use them. Keep offering your gifts back to God and to his Church to play your part in seeing his kingdom come on earth. ←

If you agree, pray this prayer:

Lord, thank you for the gifts you have given me. Please help me to see the value in them and to understand how you would like me to use these gifts to bless the Church and to build your kingdom. I offer myself and my gifts to you, and ask that you would use me to bring you glory.

Amen

²⁸We know that in everything God works for the good of those who love him. These are the people God chose, because that was his plan. ²⁹God knew them before he made the world. And he decided that they would be like his Son. Then Jesus would be the firstborn of many brothers and sisters. ³⁰God planned for them to be like his Son. He chose them and made them right with him. And after he made them right, he gave them his glory.

God's Love in Christ Jesus

³¹So what should we say about this? If God is for us, no one can stand against us. And God is with us. ³²He even let his own Son suffer for us. God gave his Son for all of us. So now with Jesus, God will surely give us all things. ³³Who can accuse the people God has chosen? No one! God is the one who makes them right. ³⁴Who can say that God's people are guilty? No one! Christ Jesus died for us, but that is not all. He was also raised from death. And now he is at God's right side, speaking to him for us. ³⁵Can anything separate us from Christ's love? Can trouble or problems or persecution separate us from his love? If we have no food or clothes or face danger or even death, will that separate us from his love? ³⁶As the Scriptures say,

> "For you we are in danger of death all the
>   time.
> People think we are worth no more than
>   sheep to be killed."
>
> *Psalm 44:22*

³⁷But in all these troubles we have complete victory through God, who has shown his love for us. ³⁸⁻³⁹Yes, I am sure that nothing can separate us from God's love—not death or life, not angels or ruling spirits. I am sure that nothing now, nothing in the future, no powers, nothing above us or below us—nothing in the whole created world—will ever be able to separate us from the love God has shown us in Christ Jesus our Lord.

God and the Jewish People

9 I am in Christ and I am telling you the truth. I am not lying. And my conscience, ruled by the Holy Spirit, agrees that what I say now is true. ²I have great sorrow and always feel much

sadness ³for my own people. They are my brothers and sisters, my earthly family. I wish I could help them. I would even have a curse on me and cut myself off from Christ if that would help them. ⁴They are the people of Israel, God's chosen children. They have the glory of God and the agreements he made between himself and his people. God gave them the Law of Moses, the Temple worship and his promises. ⁵They are the descendants of our great fathers, and they are the earthly family of the Messiah, who is God over all things. Praise him forever!ᵃ Amen.

⁶I don't mean that God failed to keep his promise to the Jewish people. But only some of the people of Israel are really God's people.ᵇ ⁷And only some of Abraham's descendants are true children of Abraham. This is what God said to Abraham: "Your true descendants will be those who come through Isaac."ᶜ ⁸This means that not all of Abraham's descendants are God's true children. Abraham's true children are those who become God's children because of the promise he made to Abraham. ⁹Here is what God said in that promise: "About this time next year I will come back, and Sarah will have a son."ᵈ

¹⁰And that is not all. Rebecca also had sons, and they had the same father. He is our father Isaac. ¹¹⁻¹²But before the two sons were born, God told Rebecca, "The older son will serve the younger."ᵉ This was before the boys had done anything good or bad. God said this before they were born so that the boy he wanted would be chosen because of God's own plan. He was chosen because he was the one God wanted to call, not because of anything the boys did. ¹³As the Scriptures say, "I loved Jacob, but I hated Esau."ᶠ

¹⁴So what does this mean? That God is not fair? We cannot say that. ¹⁵God said to Moses, "I will show mercy to anyone I want to show mercy to. I will show pity to anyone I choose."ᵍ ¹⁶So God will choose to show mercy to whoever he wants, and his choice does not depend on what people want or try to do. ¹⁷In the Scriptures God says to Pharaoh: "I made you king so that you could do this for me. I wanted to show my power through you. I wanted my name to be announced throughout the world."ʰ ¹⁸So God shows mercy to whoever he wants to show mercy to and makes stubborn those he wants to make stubborn.

ᵃ **9:5** *Messiah, who is . . . forever!* Or "Messiah. May God, who rules over all things, be praised forever!"
ᵇ **9:6** *God's people* Literally, "Israel", the people God chose to bring his blessings to the world.
ᶜ **9:7** Quote from Gen. 21:12.
ᵈ **9:9** Quote from Gen. 18:10,14.
ᵉ **9:11–12** Quote from Gen. 25:23.
ᶠ **9:13** Quote from Mal. 1:2–3.
ᵍ **9:15** Quote from Exod. 33:19.
ʰ **9:17** Quote from Exod. 9:16.

¹⁹So one of you will ask me, "If God controls what we do, why does he blame us for our sins?" ²⁰Don't ask that. You are only human and have no right to question God. A clay jar does not question the one who made it. It does not say, "Why did you make me like this?" ²¹The one who makes the jar can make anything he wants. He uses the same clay to make different things. He might make one thing for special purposes and another for daily use.

²²It is the same way with what God has done. He wanted to show his anger and to let people see his power. But he patiently endured those he was angry with—people who were ready to be destroyed. ²³He waited with patience so that he could make known the riches of his glory to the people he has chosen to receive his mercy. God has already prepared them to share his glory. ²⁴We are those people, the ones God chose not only from the Jews but also from those who are not Jews. ²⁵As the Scriptures say in the book of Hosea,

> "The people who are not mine—
>   I will say they are my people.
> And the people I did not love—
>   I will say they are the people I love."
>
> *Hosea 2:23*

²⁶And,

> "Where God said in the past,
>   'You are not my people'—
>   there they will be called children of the
>   living God."
>
> *Hosea 1:10*

²⁷And Isaiah cries out about Israel:

> "There are so many people of Israel,
>   they are like the grains of sand by the sea.
> But only a few of them will be saved.
> ²⁸ Yes, the Lord will quickly finish judging the
>   people on the earth."
>
> *Isaiah 10:22–23*

²⁹It is just as Isaiah said:

> "The Lord All-Powerful
>   allowed some of our people to live.
> If he had not done that,
>   we would now be like Sodom,
>   and we would be like Gomorrah."
>
> *Isaiah 1:9*

³⁰So what does all this mean? It means that people who are not Jews were made right with God because of their faith, even though they were not trying to make themselves right. ³¹And the people of Israel, who tried to make themselves right with God by following the law, did not succeed. ³²They failed because they tried to make themselves right by the things they did. They did not trust in God to make them right. They fell over the stone that makes people fall. ³³The Scriptures talk about that stone:

> "Look, I put in Zion a stone that will make
>   people stumble.
> It is a rock that will make people fall.
> But anyone who trusts in him
>   will never be disappointed."
>
> *Isaiah 8:14; 28:16*

10 Brothers and sisters, what I want most is for all the people of Israel to be saved. That is my prayer to God. ²I can say this about them: they really try hard to follow God, but they don't know the right way. ³They did not know the way that God makes people right with him. And they tried to make themselves right in their own way. So they did not accept God's way of making people right. ⁴Christ ended the law so that everyone who believes in him is made right with God.

⁵Moses writes about being made right by following the law. He says, "The person who obeys these laws is the one who will have life through them."ᵃ ⁶But this is what the Scriptures say about being made right through faith: "Don't say to yourself, 'Who will go up into heaven?'" (This means "Who will go up to heaven to get Christ and bring him down to earth?") ⁷"And don't say, 'Who will go down into the world below?'" (This means "Who will go down to get Christ and bring him up from death?")

⁸This is what the Scripture says: "God's teaching is near you; it is in your mouth and in your heart."ᵇ It is the teaching of faith that we tell people. ⁹If you openly say, "Jesus is Lord" and

ᵃ **10:5** Quote from Lev. 18:5.
ᵇ **10:6–8** Quotes from Deut. 30:12–14.

believe in your heart that God raised him from death, you will be saved. [10]Yes, we believe in Jesus deep in our hearts, and so we are made right with God. And we openly say that we believe in him, and so we are saved.

[11]Yes, the Scriptures say, "Anyone who trusts in him will never be disappointed."[a] [12]It says this because there is no difference between those who are Jews and those who are not. The same Lord is the Lord of all people. And he richly blesses everyone who looks to him for help. [13]Yes, "everyone who trusts in the Lord[b] will be saved".[c]

[14]But before people can pray to the Lord for help, they must believe in him. And before they can believe in the Lord, they must hear about him. And for anyone to hear about the Lord, someone must tell them. [15]And before anyone can go and tell them, they must be sent. As the Scriptures say, "How wonderful it is to see someone coming to tell good news!"[d]

[16]But not all the people accepted that good news. Isaiah said, "Lord, who believed what we told them?"[e] [17]So faith comes from hearing the Good News. And people hear the Good News when someone tells them about Christ.

[18]But I ask, "Did those people not hear the Good News?" Yes, they heard—as the Scriptures say,

> "Their voices went out all around the world.
> Their words went everywhere in the
>   world."
>
> *Psalm 19:4*

[19]Again I ask, "Did the people of Israel not understand?" Yes, they did understand. First, Moses says this for God:

> "I will use those who are not really a nation to
>   make you jealous.
> I will use a nation that does not understand
>   to make you angry."
>
> *Deuteronomy 32:21*

[20]Then Isaiah is bold enough to say this for God:

> "The people who found me were not looking
>   for me.
> I made myself known to people who were
>   not asking for me."
>
> *Isaiah 65:1*

[21]But about the people of Israel God says,

> "All day long I stood ready to accept those
>   people,
> but they are stubborn and refuse to obey me."
>
> *Isaiah 65:2*

God Has Not Forgotten His People

11 So I ask, "Did God decide that he does not want his people?" That cannot be true. I myself am an Israelite. I am from the family of Abraham, from the tribe of Benjamin. [2]God chose the Israelites to be his people before they were born. And he has never said that he doesn't want them. Surely you know what the Scriptures say about Elijah. The Scriptures tell about Elijah praying to God against the people of Israel. He said, [3]"Lord, they have killed your prophets and destroyed your altars. I am the only prophet still living, and they are trying to kill me now."[f] [4]But what answer did God give to Elijah? God said, "I have kept for myself seven thousand men who have never given worship to Baal."[g]

[5]It is the same now. God has chosen a few people by his grace. [6]And if he chose them by grace, then it is not what they have done that made them his people. If they could be made his people by what they did, his gift of grace would not really be a gift.

[7]So this is what has happened: the people of Israel wanted God's blessing, but they did not all get it. The people he chose did get his blessing, but the others became hard and refused to listen to him. [8]As the Scriptures say,

> "God caused the people to fall asleep."
>
> *Isaiah 29:10*

> "God closed their eyes so that they could not
>   see,
> and he closed their ears so that they could
>   not hear.
> This continues until now."
>
> *Deuteronomy 29:4*

[9]And David says,

> "Let those people be caught and trapped at
>   their own feasts.
> Let them fall and be punished.

---

[a] **10:11** Quote from Isa. 28:16.
[b] **10:13** *who trusts in the Lord* Literally, "who calls on the name of the Lord", meaning to show faith in him by worshipping him or praying to him for help.
[c] **10:13** Quote from Joel 2:32.
[d] **10:15** Quote from Isa. 52:7.
[e] **10:16** Quote from Isa. 53:1.
[f] **11:3** Quote from 1 Kgs 19:10,14.
[g] **11:4** Quote from 1 Kgs 19:18.

[10]Let their eyes be closed so that they cannot
see.
And let them be troubled forever."

Psalm 69:22–23

[11]So I ask: when the Jews fell, did that fall
destroy them? No! But their mistake brought
salvation to those who are not Jews. The purpose
of this was to make the Jews jealous. [12]Their
mistake brought rich blessings to the world. And
what they lost brought rich blessings to the non-
Jewish people. So surely the world will get much
richer blessings when enough Jews become the
kind of people God wants.

[13]Now I am speaking to you people who are not
Jews. I am an apostle to the non-Jewish people.
So while I have that work, I will do the best I can.
[14]I hope I can make my own people jealous.
That way, maybe I can help some of them to be
saved. [15]God turned away from the Jews. When
that happened, he became friends with the other
people in the world. So when he accepts the Jews,
it will be like bringing people to life after death.
[16]If the first piece of bread is offered to God, then
the whole loaf is made holy. If the roots of a tree
are holy, the tree's branches are holy too.

INSIGHT

*If you've got brothers or sisters, there are
probably times when you think they get
better treatment than you. Paul tries to
make both Jews and non-Jews see that
they are part of the same family tree –
God has no favourites.*

Romans 11:17–21

[17]It is as if some of the branches from an olive
tree have been broken off, and the branch of a wild
olive tree has been joined to that first tree. If you are
not a Jew, you are the same as that wild branch,
and you now share the strength and life of the first
tree. [18]But don't act as if you are better than those
branches that were broken off. You have no reason
to be proud of yourself, because you don't give life
to the root. The root gives life to you. [19]You might
say, "Branches were broken off so that I could
be joined to their tree." [20]That is true. But those
branches were broken off because they did not
believe. And you continue to be part of the tree only
because you believe. Don't be proud, but be afraid.
[21]If God did not let the natural branches of that tree
stay, he will not let you stay if you stop believing.

[22]So you see that God is kind, but he can
also be very strict. He punishes those who stop

following him. But he is kind to you, if you
continue trusting in his kindness. If you don't
continue depending on him, you will be cut off
from the tree. [23]And if the Jews will believe in
God again, he will accept them back. He is able to
put them back where they were. [24]It is not natural
for a wild branch to become part of a good tree.
But you non-Jewish people are like a branch cut
from a wild olive tree. And you were joined to a
good olive tree. But those Jews are like a branch
that grew from the good tree. So surely they can
be joined to their own tree again.

[25]I want you to understand this secret truth,
brothers and sisters. This truth will help you
understand that you don't know everything. The
truth is this: part of Israel has been made stubborn,
but that will change when enough non-Jewish
people have come to God. [26]And that is how all
Israel will be saved. The Scriptures say,

"The Saviour will come from Zion;
he will take away all evil from the family of
Jacob.
[27]And I will make this agreement with those
people
when I take away their sins."

Isaiah 59:20–21; 27:9

[28]The Jews refuse to accept the Good News,
so they are God's enemies. This has happened to
help you who are not Jews. But they are still
God's chosen people, and he loves them because
of the promises he made to their ancestors. [29]God
never changes his mind about the people he calls.
He never decides to take back the blessings he
has given them. [30]At one time you refused to
obey God. But now you have received mercy,
because the Jews refused to obey. [31]And now they
are the ones who refuse to obey, because God
showed mercy to you. But this happened so that
they can also receive mercy from him. [32]All
people have refused to obey God. And he has put
them all together as people who don't obey him
so that he can show mercy to everyone.

Praise to God

[33]Yes, God's riches are very great! His wisdom
and knowledge have no end! No one can explain
what God decides. No one can understand his
ways. [34]As the Scriptures say,

"Who can know what is on the Lord's mind?
Who is able to give him advice?"

Isaiah 40:13

[35]"Who has ever given God anything?
God owes nothing to anyone."

Job 41:11

A WHOLE LIFE OF WORSHIP

Say the word "worship" and most of us think immediately of singing together in church or a type of Christian music we might have on our iPods. This is like saying parenthood is remembering your child's birthday. It's important, but it's only one piece of a much bigger thing . . .

DIG IN

READ Romans 11:33 – 12:21

- How do these last verses of chapter 11 link to what's in chapter 12?
- Why does Paul use this word "sacrifice" (12:1)? What does it suggest?

Even though the chapter break splits this section up, it's good to read this passage as one piece (chapter and verse divisions were all added many years after the Bible was written). Praise and worship to God and living our lives are not two separate things. They are the same thing. Giving God glory (11:36) is all about living well for him.

Sacrifice points back to the Old Testament ritual of offering valuable livestock to God as a way of worshipping him. As the name suggests, these sacrifices were a costly offering for the person to make. By saying we should be "living sacrifices", Paul is saying we need to give ourselves fully to God. More than that, he's suggesting that we should see ourselves as "dead" before him – that we have laid down our rights to our lives in order that he can use them as he wishes.

- What gifts does he list, and what's important about how he says they should be used (12:6–8)?
- What happens from verse 9 onwards and how does it connect with the earlier verses?

From verses 3 to 8, Paul is addressing the church specifically, reminding them how the Spirit has distributed gifts. What's important here is not so much what gift you have been given, but that you use it – and that you use it as well as you can.

From verse 9 onwards, the focus shifts to how Christians should live. This is crucial. God will have things for you to do with your life – specific things he's got planned out for you to achieve. But worshipping God is not just about what you achieve for God, it's about how you do it.

DIG THROUGH

- We need to understand that worship is more than just singing. What we do with our gifts and how we live speak volumes of our love for God and our faith in him. Look at verses 9–21 and then ask yourself some tough questions:
  - » Will my life be marked by genuine love?
  - » Will people know me as a generous person?
  - » Will I keep a humble heart?

DIG DEEPER

- Sacrifice is a big theme through the pages of God's word. But it was never designed to be an automatic way of getting God's approval. Even when in the past God demanded a blood sacrifice, he drew a distinction between outward ritual and the attitude of a person's heart. Check out Psalm 40:6–8 and Isaiah 1:11–17 for insight into this.
- Paul's letters to the early church address the question of how the church uses its gifts together. It's a pattern for us as "the body of Christ" as we meet together from week to week. Check out 1 Corinthians 12 – 14 and Ephesians 4 for more helpful teaching on this subject.

[36]Yes, God made all things. And everything continues through him and for him. To God be the glory forever! Amen.

Give Your Lives to God

12 So I beg you, brothers and sisters, because of the great mercy God has shown us, offer your lives[a] as a living sacrifice to him—an offering that is only for God and pleasing to him. Considering what he has done, it is only right that you should worship him in this way. [2]Don't change yourselves to be like the people of this world, but let God change you inside with a new way of thinking. Then you will be able to understand and accept what God wants for you. You will be able to know what is good and pleasing to him and what is perfect.

[3]God has given me a special gift, and that is why I have something to say to each one of you. Don't think that you are better than you really are. You must see yourself just as you are. Decide what you are by the faith God has given each of us. [4]Each one of us has one body, and that body has many parts. These parts don't all do the same thing. [5]In the same way, we are many people, but in Christ we are all one body. We are the parts of that body, and each part belongs to all the others.

[6]We all have different gifts. Each gift came because of the grace God gave us. Whoever has the gift of prophecy should use that gift in a way that fits the kind of faith they have. [7]Whoever has the gift of serving should serve. Whoever has the gift of teaching should teach. [8]Whoever has the gift of comforting others should do that. Whoever has the gift of giving to help others should give generously. Whoever has the gift of leading should work hard at it. Whoever has the gift of showing kindness to others should do it gladly.

[9]Your love must be real. Hate what is evil. Do only what is good. [10]Love each other as your own family. And try to be first in giving honour to each other. [11]As you serve the Lord, work hard and don't be lazy. Be excited about serving him! [12]Be happy because of the hope you have. Be patient when you have troubles. Pray all the time. [13]Share with God's people who need help. Look for people who need help and welcome them into your homes.

[14]Wish only good for those who treat you badly. Ask God to bless them, not curse them. [15]When others are happy, you should be happy with them. And when others are sad, you should be sad too.

[16]Live together in peace with each other. Don't be proud, but be willing to be friends with people who are not important to others. Don't think of yourself as smarter than everyone else.

[17]If someone does you wrong, don't try to pay them back by hurting them. Try to do what everyone thinks is right. [18]Do the best you can to live in peace with everyone. [19]My friends, don't try to punish anyone who does wrong to you. Wait for God in his anger to punish them. In the Scriptures the Lord says, "I will punish them for what they have done."[b] [20]Instead,

"If you have enemies who are hungry,
    give them something to eat.
If they are thirsty,
    give them something to drink.
In doing this you will make them feel
    ashamed."[c]

Proverbs 25:21–22

[21]Don't let evil defeat you, but defeat evil by doing good.

Obey Your Government Rulers

13 All of you must obey the government rulers. Everyone who rules was given the power to rule by God. And all those who rule now were given that power by God. [2]So anyone who is against the government is really against something God has commanded. Those who are against the government bring punishment on themselves. [3]People who do right don't have to fear the rulers. But those who do wrong must fear them. Do you want to be free from fearing them? Then do only what is right, and they will praise you.

---

[a] **12:1** *lives* Literally, "bodies". Paul is using the language of Old Testament animal sacrifice to express the idea of a complete giving of oneself to God.
[b] **12:19** Quote from Deut. 32:35.
[c] **12:20** *you will make them feel ashamed* Literally, "you will pour burning coals on their head". People in Old Testament times often put ashes on their heads to show that they were sad or sorry.

⁴Rulers are God's servants to help you. But if you do wrong, you have reason to be afraid. They have the power to punish, and they will use it. They are God's servants to punish those who do wrong. ⁵So you must obey the government, not just because you might be punished, but because you know it is the right thing to do.

⁶And this is why you pay taxes too. Those rulers are working for God, and they give all their time to the work of ruling. ⁷Give everyone what you owe them. If you owe them any kind of tax, then pay it. Show respect to those you should respect. And show honour to those you should honour.

Loving Others Is the Only Law

⁸You should owe nothing to anyone, except that you will always owe love to each other. The person who loves others has done all that the law commands. ⁹The law says, "You must not commit adultery, you must not murder anyone, you must not steal, you must not want what belongs to someone else."ᵃ All these commands and all other commands are really only one rule: "Love your neighbourᵇ the same as you love yourself."ᶜ ¹⁰Love doesn't hurt others. So loving is the same as obeying all the law.

¹¹I say this because you know that we live in an important time. Yes, it is now time for you to wake up from your sleep. Our salvation is nearer now than when we first believed. ¹²The night is almost finished. The day is almost here. So we should stop doing whatever belongs to darkness. We should prepare ourselves to fight evil with the weapons that belong to the light. ¹³We should live in a right way, like people who belong to the day. We should not have wild parties or be drunk. We should not be involved in sexual sin or any kind of immoral behaviour. We should not cause arguments and trouble or be jealous. ¹⁴But be so much like the Lord Jesus Christ that when people look at you, they will see him.ᵈ Don't think about how to satisfy the desires of your sinful self.

Don't Criticize Others

14 Be willing to accept those who still have doubts about what believers can do. And don't argue with them about their different ideas. ²Some people believe they can eat any kind of food,ᵉ but those who have doubts eat only vegetables. ³Those who know they can eat any kind of food must not feel that they are better than those who eat only vegetables. And those who eat only vegetables must not decide that those who eat all foods are wrong. God has accepted them. ⁴You cannot judge the servants of someone else. Their own master decides if they are doing right or wrong. And the Lord's servants will be right, because the Lord is able to make them right.

⁵Some people might believe that one day is more important than another. And others might believe that every day is the same. Everyone should be sure about their beliefs in their own mind. ⁶Those who think one day is more important than other days are doing that for the Lord. And those who eat all kinds of food are doing that for the Lord. Yes, they give thanks to God for that food. And those who refuse to eat some foods do that for the Lord. They also give thanks to God.

⁷We don't live or die just for ourselves. ⁸If we live, we are living for the Lord. And if we die, we are dying for the Lord. So living or dying, we belong to the Lord. ⁹That is why Christ died and rose from death to live again—so that he could be Lord over those who have died and those who are living.

¹⁰So why do you judge your brother or sister in Christ? Or why do you think you are better than they are? We will all stand before God, and he will judge us all. ¹¹Yes, the Scriptures say,

"'As surely as I live,' says the Lord,
  'Everyone will bow before me;
    everyone will say that I am God.'"

                        Isaiah 45:23

¹²So each of us will have to explain to God about the things we do.

Don't Cause Others to Sin

¹³So we should stop judging each other. Let's decide not to do anything that will cause a problem for a brother or sister or hurt their faith. ¹⁴I know that there is no food that is wrong to eat. The Lord Jesus is the one who convinced me of that. But if someone believes that something is wrong, then it is wrong for that person. ¹⁵If you hurt the faith of your brother or sister because of something you eat, you are not really following the way of love. Don't destroy anyone's faith by eating something they think is wrong. Christ died for them. ¹⁶Don't allow what is good for you to become something they say is evil.

ᵃ **13:9** Quote from Exod. 20:13–15,17.
ᵇ **13:9** *your neighbour* Or "others". Jesus' teaching in Luke 10:25–37 makes clear that this includes anyone in need.
ᶜ **13:9** Quote from Lev. 19:18.
ᵈ **13:14** *But be . . . see him* Literally, "But clothe yourselves with the Lord Jesus Christ."
ᵉ **14:2** *any kind of food* The Jewish law said there were some foods that Jews could not eat. When they became followers of Christ, some of them did not understand that they could now eat all foods.

WHAT SEEMS RIDICULOUS TO YOU . . .

Here's a scenario that may be familiar to you. Charlie and Anya's families belonged to the same church but their backgrounds were quite different. Anya's parents were from another country and her family life seemed stricter, with different traditions and habits.

A big youth group party was approaching but Anya kept making excuses and saying she had other plans. Eventually Charlie persuaded her to tell him why she wasn't coming. "My dad doesn't like me dancing with boys around," she said.

"What?!" exclaimed Charlie, bursting into laughter. "That's just ridiculous! You shouldn't be so uptight!" Anya's eyes welled up and she ran out. She was clearly very upset.

DIG IN

READ Romans 14:1–21

- What point is Paul trying to make by talking about food and special days (vv.2–3,5–6)?
- Reading between the lines, what do you think might be happening in this church?
- What does he say is the most important thing (vv.17–21)?

The church in Rome was made up of people from different backgrounds, and many of them believed slightly different things about how they should work out their faith. This is a common problem today too.

The truth is, Christians who agree on the big things – like the life, death and resurrection of Jesus – sometimes don't agree on finer points of theology or what happens in church services. And sometimes it's hard for us, like Charlie above, to believe people could get so "uptight" about them.

We read that there is freedom in the life of the Spirit (2 Corinthians 3:17). But loving one another means we must always put one another first. If what we're planning to do will cause our brother or sister in Christ to question their faith, then we should be sensitive to that and not offend them, even if it is not in itself wrong.

DIG THROUGH

- Brainstorm the kinds of thing that might fall into the category of causing your friend to sin – things which seem okay to you but which other people might have trouble with. And perhaps there are things that your friends enjoy but which you are unsure about?
- Do you belong to a church or group involving people from different countries and cultures? Often a clash of cultures may occur and offence can easily be taken. How should we treat each other, according to Paul?

DIG DEEPER

Paul uses food laws as his example because they were a part of Israel's history; he knew that the believers in Rome with a Jewish upbringing would understand exactly what he was talking about. Under the Law of Moses, food laws were given to God's people as a way of setting them apart from the other nations around them (check out Deuteronomy 14:1–21). The laws were a part of their identity and meant a lot to them. But now God wants one family made of all sorts of different people, where these differences don't exclude anyone or make others do things they aren't happy with. God's new family should be one of loving brothers and sisters, not bickering ones!

[17]In God's kingdom what we eat and drink is not important. Here is what is important: a right way of life, peace and joy—all from the Holy Spirit. [18]Whoever serves Christ by living this way is pleasing God, and they will be accepted by others.

[19]So let's try as hard as we can to do what will bring peace. Let's do whatever will help each other grow stronger in faith. [20]Don't let the eating of food destroy the work of God. All food is right to eat, but it is wrong for anyone to eat something that hurts the faith of another person. [21]It is better not to eat meat or drink wine or do anything else that hurts the faith of your brother or sister.

[22]You should keep your beliefs about these things a secret between yourself and God. It is a blessing to be able to do what you think is right without feeling guilty. [23]But anyone who eats something without being sure it is right is doing wrong. That is because they did not believe it was right. And if you do anything that you believe is not right, it is sin.

15 Some of us have no problem with these things. So we should be patient with those who are not so strong and have doubts. We should not do what pleases us. [2]but do what pleases them and is for their good. We should do whatever helps everyone grow stronger in faith. [3]Even Christ did not live trying to please himself. As the Scriptures say, "When people insult you, I feel they are insulting me."[a] [4]Everything that was written in the past was written to teach us. Those things were written so that we could have hope. That hope comes from the patience and encouragement that the Scriptures give us. [5]All patience and encouragement come from God. And I pray that God will help you all agree with each other, as Christ Jesus wants. [6]Then you will all be joined together. And all together you will give glory to the God and Father of our Lord Jesus Christ. [7]Christ accepted you, so you should accept each other. This will bring honour[b] to God. [8]I tell you that Christ became a servant of the Jews to show that God has done what he promised their great ancestors. [9]Christ also did this so that the non-Jewish people could praise God for the mercy he gives to them. The Scriptures say,

"So I will give thanks to you among the people
    of other nations;
  I will sing praise to your name."
                                    Psalm 18:49

[10]And the Scriptures say,

"You people of other nations should be happy
    together with God's people."
                                    Deuteronomy 32:43

[11]The Scriptures also say,

"Praise the Lord all you people of other
    nations;
  all people should praise the Lord."
                                    Psalm 117:1

[12]And Isaiah says,

"Someone will come from Jesse's family.[c]
  He will come to rule over the nations,
and they will put their hope in him."
                                    Isaiah 11:10

[13]I pray that the God who gives hope will fill you with much joy and peace as you trust in him. Then you will have more and more hope, and it will flow out of you by the power of the Holy Spirit.

Paul Talks About His Work

[14]My brothers and sisters, I know without a doubt that you are full of goodness and have all the knowledge you need. So you are certainly able to counsel each other. [15]But I have written to you very openly about some things that I wanted you to remember. I did this because God gave me this special gift: [16]to be a servant of Christ Jesus for those who are not Jews. I serve like a priest whose duty it is to tell God's Good News. He gave me this work so that you non-Jewish people could be an offering that he will accept—an offering made holy by the Holy Spirit.

[17]That is why I feel so good about what I have done for God in my service to Christ Jesus. [18]I will not talk about anything I did myself. I will talk only about what Christ has done with me in leading the non-Jewish people to obey God. They have obeyed him because of what I have said and done. [19]And they obeyed him because of the power of the miraculous signs and wonders that happened—all because of the power of God's Spirit. I have told people the Good News about Christ in every place from Jerusalem to Illyricum. And so I have finished that part of my work. [20]I always want to tell the Good News in places where people have never heard of Christ. I do this because I don't want to build on the work

---

[a] **15:3** Quote from Ps. 69:9.
[b] **15:7** *honour* Or "glory". See "GLORY" in the Word List.
[c] **15:12** *Jesse's family* Jesse was the father of David, king of Israel. Jesus was from their family.

that someone else has already started. ²¹But as the Scriptures say,

> "Those who were not told about him will see,
>   and those who have not heard about him
>   will understand."

Isaiah 52:15

Paul's Plan to Visit Rome

²²That's what has kept me so busy and prevented my coming to see you even though I have wanted to come many times.

²³Now I have finished my work in these areas. And for many years I have wanted to visit you. ²⁴So I will visit you when I go to Spain. Yes, I hope to visit you while I am travelling to Spain, and I will stay and enjoy being with you. Then you can help me continue on my trip.

²⁵Now I am going to Jerusalem to help God's people there. ²⁶Some of them are poor, and the believers in Macedonia and Achaia wanted to help them. So they gathered some money to send them. ²⁷They were happy to do this. And it was like paying something they owed them, because as non-Jews they have been blessed spiritually by the Jews. So now they should use the material blessings they have to help the Jews. ²⁸I am going to Jerusalem to make sure the poor get this money that has been given for them.

After I finish that, I will leave for Spain and stop to visit you on the way. ²⁹And I know that when I visit you, I will bring you Christ's full blessing.

³⁰Brothers and sisters, I beg you to help me in my work by praying to God for me. Do this because of our Lord Jesus and the love that the Spirit gives us. ³¹Pray that I will be saved from those in Judea who refuse to accept our message. And pray that this help I am bringing to Jerusalem will please God's people there. ³²Then, if God wants me to, I will come to you. I will come with joy, and together you and I will have a time of rest. ³³The God who gives peace be with you all. Amen.

Paul Has Some Final Things to Say

16 I want you to know that you can trust our sister in Christ, Phoebe. She is a special servant of the church in Cenchrea. ²I ask you to accept her in the Lord. Accept her the way God's people should. Help her with anything she needs from you. She has helped me very much, and she has helped many others too.

INSIGHT

---

³Give my greetings to Priscilla and Aquila, who have worked together with me for Christ Jesus. ⁴They risked their own lives to save mine. I am thankful to them, and all the non-Jewish churches are thankful to them. ⁵Also, give greetings to the church that meets in their house.

Give greetings to my dear friend Epaenetus. He was the first person to follow Christ in Asia. ⁶Greetings also to Mary. She worked very hard for you.

⁷And greet Andronicus and Junia. They are my relatives, and they were in prison with me. They were followers of Christ before I was. And they are some of the most important of the ones Christ sent out to do his work.[a]

⁸Give my greetings to Ampliatus, my dear friend in the Lord, ⁹and to Urbanus. He has worked together with me for Christ.

Give greetings also to my dear friend Stachys ¹⁰and to Apelles, who has proved himself to be a true follower of Christ.

Give greetings to everyone in the family of Aristobulus ¹¹and to Herodion, my relative.

Greetings to all those in the family of Narcissus who belong to the Lord ¹²and to Tryphaena and Tryphosa, women who work very hard for the Lord.

Greetings to my dear friend Persis. She has also worked very hard for the Lord.

¹³Greetings also to Rufus, one of the Lord's chosen people and to his mother, who has been a mother to me too.

¹⁴Give my greetings to Asyncritus, Phlegon, Hermes, Patrobas, Hermas and all the believers who are with them.

¹⁵Give greetings to Philologus and Julia, to Nereus and his sister, to Olympas and to all of God's people with them.

¹⁶Give each other the special greeting of God's people.[b]

---

[a] **16:7** *most important . . . work* Literally, "important among (or to) the apostles".
[b] **16:16** *the special greeting of God's people* Literally, "a holy kiss".

All the churches that belong to Christ send their greetings to you.

17Brothers and sisters, I want you to be very careful of those who cause arguments and hurt people's faith by teaching things that are against what you learned. Stay away from them. 18People like that are not serving our Lord Christ. They are only pleasing themselves. They use fancy talk and say nice things to fool those who don't know about evil. 19Everyone has heard that you do what you were taught, and I am very happy about that. But I want you to be wise about what is good and to know nothing about what is evil.

20The God who brings peace will soon defeat Satan and give you power over him.

The grace of our Lord Jesus be with you.

21Timothy, a worker together with me, sends you his greetings. Also Lucius, Jason and Sosipater (these are my relatives) send their greetings.

22I am Tertius, the one writing this letter for Paul. I send you my own greetings as one who belongs to the Lord.

23Gaius is letting me and the whole church here use his home. He sends his greetings to you. Erastus and our brother Quartus also send their greetings. Erastus is the city treasurer here. 24a

25Praise God! He is the one who can make you strong in faith. He can use the Good News that I teach to make you strong. It is the message about Jesus Christ that I tell people. That message is the secret truth that was hidden for ages and ages but has been made known. 26It has now been shown to us. It was made known by what the prophets wrote, as God commanded. And it has now been made known to all people so that they can believe and obey God, who lives forever. 27Glory forever to the only wise God through Jesus Christ. Amen.

---

a **16:24** Some Greek copies add verse 24: "The grace of our Lord Jesus Christ be with you all. Amen."

1 CORINTHIANS

Who Written by Paul, to the Christians in the Greek city of Corinth, a cosmopolitan city-port about 40 miles (65 km) south-west of Athens, who he had visited previously.

When Around AD 55, towards the end of Paul's time in Ephesus. By that time Paul had known the Corinthian church for about 3 years.

What Paul challenges the behaviour of the Corinthian church, which is no better than the society around them. He calls on them to stop arguing and urges them to value the only thing that really counts – love.

Paul's relationship with the followers in Corinth was not an easy one. Partly this was due to the atmosphere of the city itself. Corinth was a wealthy sea port with a reputation for sexual immorality. This atmosphere of immoral behaviour infected the Christian community. Paul paints a picture of a group of followers infected by wealth and sex. The Corinthian church had many of the signs of a true church, but they were behaving like spoilt brats, rather than children of God.

Although this is called "1 Corinthians" Paul is following up a previous letter, which we no longer have (5:9). Perhaps Paul's meaning in the first letter had not been clear, but there were still arguments in the church and accusations of sexual immorality. So he wrote from Ephesus and dispatched Timothy to try to deal with the situation.

Paul was especially concerned with the amount of arguments and splits in the church. They treated each other differently according to wealth and position; they split into factions. Some of them were puffed up with their own social status and wealth. So Paul encourages them to change their ways, to worship God as he should be worshipped.

Above all, he talks about love. In one of the greatest passages ever written he argues that love is the most important thing (chapter 13). If they only loved one another, then the splits and the arguments would disappear.

QUICK TOUR **1 CORINTHIANS**

Gang warfare 1:10–31	One body 12:1–31
Grow up! 3:1–23	Love 13:1–13
Sexual immorality 5:1–13	Help each other 14:26–40
A slave for everyone 9:1–27	We will be raised 15:1–34
Rules for worship 11:1–34	Death is dead 15:35–58

"So these three things continue: faith, hope and love. And the greatest of these is love."

1 Corinthians 13:13

1 Greetings from Paul. I am an apostle because Christ Jesus chose me. He chose me because that is what God wanted. Greetings also from Sosthenes, our brother in Christ.

²To God's church in Corinth, you who have been made holy because you belong to Christ Jesus. You were chosen to be God's holy people together with all people everywhere who trust in the Lord*a* Jesus Christ—their Lord and ours.

³Grace and peace to you from God our Father and the Lord Jesus Christ.

Paul Gives Thanks to God

⁴I always thank my God for you because of the grace that he has given you through Christ Jesus. ⁵In him you have been blessed in every way. You have been blessed in all your speaking and all your knowledge. ⁶This proves that what we told you about Christ is true. ⁷Now you have every gift from God while you wait for our Lord Jesus Christ to come again. ⁸He will keep you strong until the end so that on the day when our Lord Jesus Christ comes, you will be free from all blame. ⁹God is faithful. He is the one who has chosen you to share life with his Son, Jesus Christ our Lord.

Stop Arguing With Each Other

¹⁰Brothers and sisters, by the authority of our Lord Jesus Christ, I beg all of you to agree with each other. You should not be divided into different groups. Be completely joined together again with the same kind of thinking and the same purpose. ¹¹My brothers and sisters, some members of Chloe's family told me that there are arguments among you. ¹²This is what I mean: one of you says, "I follow Paul," and someone else says, "I follow Apollos." Another says, "I follow Peter,"*b* and someone else says, "I follow Christ." ¹³Christ cannot be divided into different groups. It wasn't Paul who died on the cross for you, was it? Were you baptized in Paul's name? ¹⁴I am thankful that I did not baptize any of you except Crispus and Gaius. ¹⁵I am thankful because now no one can say that you were baptized in my name. ¹⁶(I also baptized the family of Stephanas, but I don't remember that I myself baptized any others.) ¹⁷Christ did not give me the work of baptizing people. He gave me the work of telling the Good News. But he sent me to tell the Good News without using clever speech, which would take away the power that is in the cross*c* of Christ.

God's Power and Wisdom in Christ Jesus

¹⁸The teaching about the cross seems foolish to those who are lost. But to us who are being saved it is the power of God. ¹⁹As the Scriptures say,

> "I will destroy the wisdom of the wise.
> I will confuse the understanding of the
>   intelligent."
>
> *Isaiah 29:14*

²⁰So what does this say about the philosopher, the law expert or anyone in this world who is skilled at making clever arguments? God has made the wisdom of the world look foolish. ²¹Yes, God in his wisdom decided that the world would never find him through its own wisdom. So he used the message that sounds foolish to save those who believe it. ²²The Jews ask for miraculous signs, and the Greeks want wisdom. ²³But this is the message we tell everyone: Christ was killed on a cross. This message is a problem for Jews, and to other people it is nonsense. ²⁴But Christ is God's power and wisdom to the people God has chosen, both Jews and Greeks. ²⁵Even the foolishness of God is wiser than human wisdom. Even the weakness of God is stronger than human strength.

²⁶Brothers and sisters, God chose you to be his. Think about that! Not many of you were wise in the way the world judges wisdom. Not many of you had great influence, and not many of you came from important families. ²⁷But God chose the foolish things of the world to shame the wise. He chose the weak things of the world to shame the strong. ²⁸And God chose what the world thinks is not important—what the world hates and thinks is nothing. He chose these to destroy what the world thinks is important. ²⁹God did this so that no one can stand before him and boast about anything. ³⁰It is God who has made you part of Christ Jesus. And Christ has become for us wisdom from God. He is the reason we are right with God and have been made holy. Christ is the one who set us free from sin. ³¹So, as the Scriptures say, "Whoever boasts should boast only about the Lord."*d*

---

a **1:2** *who trust in the Lord* Literally, "who call on the name of the Lord", meaning to show faith in him by worshipping or praying to him for help.
b **1:12** *Peter* Literally, "Cephas", the Aramaic name for Peter, one of Jesus' twelve apostles. Both names mean "rock". Also in 3:22; 9:6; 15:5.
c **1:17** *cross* Paul uses the cross as a picture of the Good News, the story of Christ's death to pay for people's sins. The cross (Christ's death) was God's way to save people.
d **1:31** Quote from Jer. 9:24.

My Message: Jesus Christ on the Cross

2 Dear brothers and sisters, when I came to you, I told you the secret truth of God. But I did not use fancy words or great wisdom. ²I decided that while I was with you I would forget about everything except Jesus Christ and his death on the cross. ³When I came to you, I was weak and shook with fear. ⁴My teaching and my speaking were not with wise words that persuade people. But the proof of my teaching was the power that the Spirit gives. ⁵I did this so that your faith would be in God's power, not in human wisdom.

God's Wisdom

⁶We teach wisdom to people who are mature, but the wisdom we teach is not from this world. It is not the wisdom of the rulers of this world, who are losing their power. ⁷But we speak God's secret wisdom that has been hidden from everyone until now. God planned this wisdom for our glory. He planned it before the world began. ⁸None of the rulers of this world understood this wisdom. If they had understood it, they would not have killed our great and glorious Lord on a cross. ⁹But as the Scriptures say,

"No one has ever seen,
  no one has ever heard,
no one has ever imagined
    what God has prepared for those who
      love him."

Isaiah 64:4

¹⁰But God has shown us these things through the Spirit.

The Spirit knows all things. The Spirit even knows the deep secrets of God. ¹¹It is like this: No one knows the thoughts that another person has. Only the person's spirit that lives inside knows those thoughts. It is the same with God. No one knows God's thoughts except God's Spirit. ¹²We received the Spirit that is from God, not the spirit of the world. We received God's Spirit so that we can know all that God has given us.

¹³When we say this, we don't use words taught to us by human wisdom. We use words taught to us by the Spirit. We use the Spirit's words to explain spiritual truths. ¹⁴People who do not have God's Spirit do not accept the things that come from his Spirit. They think these things are foolish. They cannot understand them, because they can only be understood with the Spirit's help. ¹⁵We who have the Spirit are able to make judgements about all these things. But anyone without the Spirit is not able to make proper judgements about us. ¹⁶As the Scriptures say,

"Who can know what is on the Lord's mind?
  Who is able to give him advice?"

Isaiah 40:13

But we have been given Christ's way of thinking.

INSIGHT

Paul is warning the Corinthians about getting caught up in church and Christian "celebrity culture", following whoever the biggest new preacher is. Christian leaders are just servants of God. Ultimately God is always the most important.

1 Corinthians 3:1–9

Teachers Are Only God's Servants

3 Brothers and sisters, when I was there, I could not talk to you the way I talk to people who are led by the Spirit. I had to talk to you like ordinary people of the world. You were like babies in Christ. ²And the teaching I gave you was like milk, not solid food. I did this because you were not ready for solid food. And even now you are not ready. ³You are still not following the Spirit. You are jealous of each other, and you are always arguing with each other. This shows that you are still following your own selfish desires. You are acting like ordinary people of the world. ⁴One of you says, "I follow Paul," and someone else says, "I follow Apollos." When you say things like that, you are acting like people of the world.

⁵Is Apollos so important? Is Paul so important? We are only servants of God who helped you believe. Each one of us did the work God gave us to do. ⁶I planted the seed and Apollos watered it. But God is the one who made the seed grow. ⁷So the one who plants is not important, and the one who waters is not important. Only God is important, because he is the one who makes things grow. ⁸The one who plants and the one who waters have the same purpose. And each one will be rewarded for his own work. ⁹We are workers together for God, and you are like a farm that belongs to God.

And you are a house that belongs to God. ¹⁰Like an expert builder I built the foundation of that house. I used the gift that God gave me to do this. Other people are building on that foundation. But everyone should be careful how they build. ¹¹The foundation that has already been built is Jesus Christ, and no one can build any other foundation. ¹²People can build on that foundation using gold, silver, jewels, wood, grass or straw. [13]But the work that each person does will be clearly seen, because the Day will make it plain. That Day will appear with fire, and the fire will test everyone's work. [14]If the building they put on the foundation still stands, they will get their reward. [15]But if their building is burned up, they will suffer loss. They will be saved, but it will be like someone escaping from a fire.

[16]You should know that you yourselves are God's temple.[a] God's Spirit lives in you. [17]If you destroy God's temple, God will destroy you, because God's temple is holy. You yourselves are God's temple.

[18]Don't fool yourselves. Whoever thinks they are wise in this world should become a fool. That's the only way they can be wise. [19]I say this because the wisdom of this world is foolishness to God. As the Scriptures say, "He catches those who think they are wise in their own clever traps."[b] [20]The Scriptures also say, "The Lord knows the thoughts of the wise. He knows that their thoughts are worth nothing."[c] [21]So there is not a person on earth that any of you should be boasting about. Everything is yours: [22]Paul, Apollos, Peter, the world, life, death, the present and the future—all these are yours. [23]And you belong to Christ, and Christ belongs to God.

Apostles of Christ Jesus

4 You should think of us as servants of Christ, the ones God has trusted to do the work of making known his secret truths. [2]Those who are trusted with such an important work must show that they are worthy of that trust. [3]But I don't consider your judgement on this point to be worth anything. Even an opinion from a court of law would mean nothing. I don't even trust my own judgement. [4]I don't know of any wrong I have done, but that does not make me right. The Lord is the one who must decide if I have done well or not. [5]So don't judge anyone now. The time for judging will be when the Lord comes. He will shine light on everything that is now hidden in darkness. He will make known the secret purposes of our hearts. Then the praise each person should get will come from God.

[6]Brothers and sisters, I have used Apollos and myself as examples for you. I did this so that you could learn from us the meaning of the words, "Follow only what the Scriptures say." Then you will not boast about one person and say he is better than another person. [7]Who do you think

you are? Everything you have was given to you. So, if everything you have was given to you, why do you act as if you got it all by your own power?

[8]You think you have everything you need. You think you are rich. You think you have become kings without us. I wish you really were kings. Then we could rule together with you. [9]But it seems to me that God has given me and the other apostles the last place. We are like prisoners condemned to die, led in a parade for the whole world to see—not just people but angels too. [10]We are fools for Christ, but you think you are so wise in Christ. We are weak, but you think you are so strong. People give you honour, but they don't honour us. [11]Even now we still don't have enough to eat or drink, and we don't have enough clothes. We often get beatings. We have no homes. [12]We work hard with our own hands to feed ourselves. When people insult us, we ask God to bless them. When people treat us badly, we accept it. [13]When people say bad things about us, we try to say something that will help them. But people still treat us like the world's rubbish—everyone's rubbish.

[14]I am not trying to make you feel ashamed, but I am writing this to counsel you as my own dear children. [15]You may have ten thousand teachers in Christ, but you don't have many fathers. Through the Good News I became your father in Christ Jesus. [16]So I beg you to be like me. [17]That is why I am sending Timothy to you. He is my son in the Lord. I love him and trust him. He will help you remember the way I live in Christ Jesus—a way of life that I teach in every meeting of the church wherever I am.

[18]Some of you have become so proud, it seems as though you think I won't be coming there again. [19]But I will come to you very soon, the Lord willing. Then I will see if these proud talkers have the power to do anything more than talk. [20]God's kingdom is not seen in talk but in power. [21]Which do you want: that I come to you with punishment or that I come with love and gentleness?

Don't Let Your People Live in Sin

5 I don't want to believe what I am hearing—that there is sexual sin among you. And it is such a bad kind of sexual sin that even those who have never known God don't allow it. People say that a man there has his father's wife. [2]And still you are proud of yourselves! You should have been filled with sadness. And the man who committed that sin should be put out of your

---

[a] **3:16** *temple* God's house—the place where God's people worship him. Here, it means that believers are the spiritual temple where God lives.
[b] **3:19** Quote from Job 5:13.
[c] **3:20** Quote from Ps. 94:11.

group. ³I cannot be there with you in person, but I am with you in spirit. And I have already judged the man who did this. I judged him the same as I would if I were really there. ⁴Come together in the name of our Lord Jesus. I will be with you in spirit, and you will have the power of our Lord Jesus with you. ⁵Then turn this man over to Satan. His sinful self ͣ has to be destroyed so that his spirit will be saved on the day when the Lord comes again.

⁶Your proud talk is not good. You know the saying, "Just a little yeast makes the whole batch of dough rise." ⁷Take out all the old yeast, so that you will be a new batch of dough. You really are bread without yeast—Passover bread.ᵇ Yes, Christ our Passover Lambᶜ has already been killed. ⁸So let us eat our Passover meal, but not with the bread that has the old yeast, the yeast of sin and wrongdoing. But let us eat the bread that has no yeast. This is the bread of goodness and truth.

⁹I wrote to you in my letter that you should not associate with people who sin sexually. ¹⁰But I did not mean the people of this world. You would have to leave the world to get away from all the people who sin sexually, or who are greedy and cheat each other or who worship idols. ¹¹I meant you must not associate with people who claim to be believers but continue to live in sin. Don't even eat with a brother or sister who sins sexually, is greedy, worships idols, hurts others with insults, gets drunk or cheats people.

¹²⁻¹³It is not my business to judge those who are not part of the group of believers. God will judge them, but you must judge those who are part of your group. The Scriptures say, "Make the evil person leave your group."ᵈ

Judging Problems Between Believers

6 When one of you has something against someone else in your group, why do you go to the judges in the law courts? The way they think and live is wrong. So why do you let them decide who is right? Why don't you let God's holy people decide who is right? ²Don't you know that God's people will judge the world? So if you will judge the world, then surely you can judge small arguments like this. ³You know that in the future we will judge angels. So surely we can judge life's ordinary problems. ⁴So if you have such matters to be judged, why do you take them to those who are not part of the church? They mean nothing to you. ⁵I say this to shame you. Surely there is someone in your group wise enough to judge a complaint between two believers. ⁶But now one believer goes to court against another, and you let people who are not believers judge their case!

⁷The lawsuits that you have against each other show that you are already defeated. It would be better for you to let someone wrong you. It would be better to let someone cheat you. ⁸But you are the ones doing wrong and cheating. And you do this to your own brothers and sisters in Christ!

⁹⁻¹⁰Surely you know that people who do wrong will not get to enjoy God's kingdom. Don't be fooled. These are the people who will not get to enjoy his kingdom: those who sin sexually, those who worship idols, those who commit adultery, men who let other men use them for sex or who have sex with other men, those who steal, those who are greedy, those who drink too much, those who abuse others with insults and those who cheat. ¹¹In the past some of you were like that. But you were washed clean, you were made holy, and you were made right with God in the name of the Lord Jesus Christ and by the Spirit of our God.

INSIGHT

Lawsuits were very common in Corinth. Trials were seen as social events and to sit on a jury was considered a privilege. Trials took place in the heart of the marketplace.

1 Corinthians 6:1–11

Use Your Bodies for God's Glory

¹²"I am allowed to do anything," you say. My answer to this is that not all things are good. Even if it is true that "I am allowed to do anything", I will not let anything control me like a slave. ¹³Someone else says, "Food is for the stomach, and the stomach for food." Yes, and God will destroy them both. But the body is not for sexual sin. The body is for the Lord,ᵉ and the Lord is for the body. ¹⁴And God will raise our bodies from death with the same power he used to raise the Lord Jesus. ¹⁵Surely you know that your bodies are parts of Christ himself. So I must never take what is part of Christ and join it to a prostitute!

ͣ **5:5 sinful self** Or "body". Literally, "flesh".
ᵇ **5:7 Passover bread** The special bread without yeast that the Jews ate at their Passover meal. Paul means that believers are free from sin, just as the Passover bread was free from yeast.
ᶜ **5:7 Passover Lamb** Jesus was a sacrifice for his people, like a lamb killed for the Jewish Passover Feast.
ᵈ **5:12–13** Quote from Deut. 22:21,24.
ᵉ **6:13 The body is for the Lord** See Exod. 28:36.

X-RATED CORINTH

It's the big question everyone wants to know the answer to. What about sex . . . ? How far can you go? When is too far, too far?

In first-century Corinth, the Christians were asking the same kind of questions we ask today and Corinth was obsessed with sex. They had a temple to the goddess of love and the word "Corinthianize" became slang for sleeping around.

Then Paul comes on the scene and revolutionizes their attitude to sex and relationships.

DIG IN

READ 1 Corinthians 6:12–13

- Paul quotes the Corinthian phrase, "I am allowed to do anything". What do you think the Corinthians meant by that?
- How does he reply? What did that mean?

"Food is for the stomach, and the stomach for food" (v.13) means that what you put in your body has no effect on the stuff going on in your head. Whoops. I don't think so! But that's what they thought about sex too: that it was just for fun, nothing serious.

- According to Paul, why is sex more than just a physical act?

READ 1 Corinthians 6:14–17

God is for sex. He invented it for marriage and loves it when married couples enjoy it. Paul argues that sex is like glue that binds a marriage together.

- Why should Christians keep their bodies pure?
- Why is sex more than just a cheap thrill?
- Look closely at Paul's argument in these verses. What makes sex so special?

READ 1 Corinthians 6:18–20

- What does it mean to "run away from sexual sin"?
- How is sexual sin different from other sin?

So it's not a case of how far you go. Paul says "run away!" Don't push the boundaries – run away before there's any chance you could commit sexual sin – your body belongs to God.

DIG THROUGH

- How is God's attitude to sex radically different from the world's? What would your non-Christian mates think if they read Paul's words?
- If you are a Christian your body belongs to God. How does that change the way you think about sex, lust and relationships?
- Perhaps you have been hurt by someone or someone has hurt you. Who do you need to talk to? How can you bring about change?
- It might be that you've already gone too far. The Good News is that God gives forgiveness to all who ask and there's always a fresh start with Jesus. It's important to ask God for help. It will also help to find an older Christian you trust to chat about it.

DIG DEEPER

- For more help and advice on God's intentions for sex check out Genesis 2:23–25, Galatians 5:16–21, Ephesians 5:1–3, Colossians 3:5 and 1 Thessalonians 4:3–5.

[16]The Scriptures say, "The two people will become one."[a] So you should know that anyone who is joined with a prostitute becomes one with her in body. [17]But anyone who is joined with the Lord is one with him in spirit.

[18]So run away from sexual sin. It involves the body in a way that no other sin does. So if you commit sexual sin, you are sinning against your own body. [19]You should know that your body is a temple[b] for the Holy Spirit who you received from God and who lives in you. You don't own yourselves. [20]God paid a high price to make you his. So honour God with your body.

About Marriage

7 Now I will discuss the things you wrote to me about. You asked if it is better for a man not to have any sex at all. [2]But sexual sin is a danger, so each man should enjoy his own wife, and each woman should enjoy her own husband. [3]The husband should give his wife what he deserves as his wife. And the wife should give her husband what he deserves as her husband. [4]The wife does not have power over her own body. Her husband has the power over her body. And the husband does not have power over his own body. His wife has the power over his body. [5]Don't refuse to give your bodies to each other. But you might both agree to stay away from sex for a while so that you can give your time to prayer. Then come together again so that Satan will not be able to tempt you in your weakness. [6]I say this only to give you permission to be separated for a time. It is not a rule. [7]I wish everyone could be like me. But God has given each person a different ability. He makes some able to live one way, others to live a different way.

[8]Now for those who are not married and for the widows I say this: it is good for you to stay single like me. [9]But if you cannot control your body, then you should marry. It is better to marry than to burn with sexual desire.

[10]Now, I have a command for those who are married. Actually, it is not from me; it is what the Lord commanded. A wife should not leave her husband. [11]But if a wife does leave, she should remain single or get back together with her husband. And a husband should not divorce his wife.

[12]The advice I have for the others is from me. The Lord did not give us any teaching about this. If you have a wife who is not a believer, you should not divorce her if she will continue to live with you. [13]And if you have a husband who is not a believer, you should not divorce him if he will continue to live with you. [14]The husband who is not a believer is set apart for God through his believing wife. And the wife who is not a believer is set apart for God through her believing husband. If this were not true, your children would be unfit for God's use. But now they are set apart for him.

[15]But if the husband or wife who is not a believer decides to leave, let them leave. When this happens, the brother or sister in Christ is free. God chose you to have a life of peace. [16]Wives, maybe you will save your husband; and husbands, maybe you will save your wife. You don't know now what might happen later.

Live as God Called You

[17]But each one of you should continue to live the way the Lord God has given you to live—the way you were when God chose you. I tell people in all the churches to follow this rule. [18]If a man was already circumcised when he was chosen, he should not change his circumcision. If a man was without circumcision when he was chosen, he should not be circumcised. [19]It is not important if anyone is circumcised or not. What is important is obeying God's commands. [20]Each one of you should stay the way you were when God chose you. [21]If you were a slave when God chose you, don't let that bother you. But if you can be free, then do it. [22]If you were a slave when the Lord chose you, you are now free in the Lord. You belong to the Lord. In the same way, if you were free when you were chosen, you are now Christ's slave. [23]God paid a high price for you, so don't be slaves to anyone else. [24]Brothers and sisters, in your new life with God, each one of you should continue the way you were when God chose you.

Questions About Getting Married

[25]Now I write about people who are not married.[c] I have no command from the Lord about this, but I give my opinion. And I can be trusted, because the Lord has given me mercy. [26]This is a time of trouble. So I think it is good for you to stay the way you are. [27]If you have a wife, don't try to get free from her. If you are not married, don't try to find a wife. [28]But if you decide to marry, that is not a sin. And it is not a sin for a girl who has never married to get married. But those who marry will have trouble in this life, and I want you to be free from this trouble.

[29]Brothers and sisters, this is what I mean: we don't have much time left. So starting now, those

---

[a] **6:16** Quote from Gen. 2:24.
[b] **6:19** *temple* God's house—the place where God's people worship him. Here, it means that believers are the spiritual temple where God lives.
[c] **7:25** *people who are not married* Literally, "virgins".

who have wives should be the same as those who don't. ³⁰It should not be important whether you are sad or whether you are happy. If you buy something, it should not matter to you that you own it. ³¹You should use the things of the world without letting them become important to you. This is how you should live, because this world, the way it is now, will soon be gone.

³²I want you to be free from worry. A man who is not married is busy with the Lord's work. He is trying to please the Lord. ³³But a man who is married is busy with things of the world. He is trying to please his wife. ³⁴He must think about two things—pleasing his wife and pleasing the Lord. A woman who is not married or a girl who has never married is busy with the Lord's work. She wants to give herself fully—body and spirit—to the Lord. But a married woman is busy with things of the world. She is trying to please her husband. ³⁵I am saying this to help you. I am not trying to limit you, but I want you to live in the right way. And I want you to give yourselves fully to the Lord without giving your time to other things.

³⁶A man might think that he is not doing the right thing with his fiancée. She might be almost past the best age to marry.*ᵃ* So he might feel that he should marry her. He should do what he wants. It is no sin for them to get married. ³⁷But another man might be more sure in his mind. There may be no need for marriage, so he is free to do what he wants. If he has decided in his own heart not to marry his fiancée, he is doing the right thing. ³⁸So the man who marries his fiancée does right, and the man who does not marry does better.

³⁹A woman should stay with her husband as long as he lives. But if the husband dies, the woman is free to marry any man she wants, but he should belong to the Lord. ⁴⁰The woman is happier if she does not marry again. This is my opinion, and I believe that I have God's Spirit.

About Food Offered to Idols

8 Now I will write about meat that is sacrificed*ᵇ* to idols. It is certainly true that "we all have knowledge", as you say. But this knowledge only fills people with pride. It is love that helps the church grow stronger. ²Those who think they know something do not yet know anything as they should. ³But God knows the person who loves him.

⁴So this is what I say about eating meat: we know that an idol is really nothing in the world, and we know that there is only one God. ⁵It's

really not important if there are things called gods in heaven or on earth—and there are many of these "gods" and "lords" out there. ⁶For us there is only one God, and he is our Father. All things came from him, and we live for him. And there is only one Lord, Jesus Christ. All things were made through him, and we also have life through him.

⁷But not all people know this. Some have had the habit of worshipping idols. So now when they eat meat, they still feel as if it belongs to an idol. They are not sure that it is right to eat this meat. So when they eat it, they feel guilty. ⁸But food will not bring us closer to God. Refusing to eat does not make us less pleasing to God, and eating does not make us closer to him.

⁹But be careful with your freedom. Your freedom to eat anything may make those who have doubts about what they can eat fall into sin. ¹⁰You understand that it's all right to eat anything, so you can eat even in an idol's temple. But someone who has doubts might see you eating there, and this might encourage them to eat meat sacrificed to idols too. But they really think it is wrong. ¹¹So this weak brother or sister—someone Christ died for—is lost because of your better understanding. ¹²When you sin against your brothers and sisters in Christ in this way and you hurt them by causing them to do things they feel are wrong, you are also sinning against Christ. ¹³So if the food I eat makes another believer fall into sin, I will never eat meat again. I will stop eating meat, so that I will not make my brother or sister sin.

Rights That Paul Has Not Used

9 I am a free man. I am an apostle. I have seen Jesus our Lord. You people are an example of my work in the Lord. ²Others may not accept me as an apostle, but surely you do. You are proof that I am an apostle in the Lord.

³Some people want to judge me. So this is the answer I give them: ⁴we have the right to eat and drink, don't we? ⁵We have the right to bring a believing wife with us when we travel, don't we? The other apostles and the Lord's brothers and Peter all do this. ⁶And are Barnabas and I the only ones who must work to earn our living? ⁷No soldier ever serves in the army and pays his own salary. No one ever plants a vineyard without eating some of the grapes himself. No one takes care of a flock of sheep without drinking some of the milk.

⁸These aren't just my own thoughts. God's law says the same thing. ⁹Yes, it is written in the Law

---

ᵃ **7:36 She . . . to marry** Or "He may have trouble controlling his desires."
ᵇ **8:1 sacrificed** Killed and offered as a gift to show worship. Also in verse 10.

of Moses: "When a work animal is being used to separate grain, don't keep it from eating the grain."[a] When God said this, was he thinking only about work animals? No. [10]He was really talking about us. Yes, that was written for us. The one who ploughs and the one who separates the grain should both expect to get some of the grain for their work. [11]We planted spiritual seed among you, so we should be able to harvest from you some things for this life. Surely that is not asking too much. [12]Others have this right to get things from you. So surely we have this right too. But we don't use this right. No, we endure everything ourselves so that we will not stop anyone from obeying the Good News of Christ. [13]Surely you know that those who work at the Temple get their food from the Temple. And those who serve at the altar get part of what is offered at the altar. [14]It is the same with those who have the work of telling the Good News. The Lord has commanded that those who tell the Good News should get their living from this work.

[15]But I have not used any of these rights, and I am not trying to get anything from you. That is not my purpose for writing this. I would rather die than to have someone take away what for me is a great source of pride. [16]It's not my work of telling the Good News that gives me any reason to boast. That is my duty—something I must do. If I don't tell people the Good News, I am in real trouble. [17]If I did it because it was my own choice, I would deserve to be paid. But I have no choice. I must tell the Good News. So I am only doing the duty that was given to me. [18]So what do I get for doing it? My reward is that when I tell people the Good News I can offer it to them for free and not use the rights that come with doing this work.

[19]I am free. I belong to no other person, but I make myself a slave to everyone. I do this to help save as many people as I can. [20]To the Jews I became like a Jew so that I could help save Jews. I myself am not ruled by the law, but to those who are ruled by the law I became like someone who is ruled by the law. I did this to help save those who are ruled by the law. [21]To those who are without the law I became like someone who is without the law. I did this to help save those who are without the law. (But really, I am not without God's law—I am ruled by the law of Christ.) [22]To those who are weak, I became weak so that I could help save them. I became all things

to all people. I did this so that I could save people in any way possible. [23]I do all this to make the Good News known. I do it so that I can share in the blessings of the Good News.

[24]You know that in a race all the runners run, but only one runner gets the prize. So run like that. Run to win! [25]All who compete in the games use strict training. They do this so that they can win a prize—one that doesn't last. But our prize is one that will last forever. [26]So I run like someone who has a goal. I fight like a boxer who is hitting something, not just the air. [27]It is my own body I fight to make it do what I want. I do this so that I won't miss getting the prize myself after telling others about it.

Warning From History

10 Brothers and sisters, I want you to know what happened to our ancestors who were with Moses. They were all under the cloud,[b] and they all walked through the sea. [2]They were all baptized[c] into Moses in the cloud and in the sea. [3]They all ate the same spiritual food, [4]and they all drank the same spiritual drink. They drank from that spiritual rock that was with them, and that rock was Christ. [5]But God was not pleased with most of those people, so they were killed in the desert.

[6]And these things that happened are examples for us. These examples should stop us from wanting evil things like those people did. [7]Don't worship idols as some of them did. As the Scriptures say, "The people sat down to eat and drink and then got up to have a wild party."[d] [8]We should not commit sexual sins as some of them did. In one day 23,000 of them died because of their sin. [9]We should not test Christ[e] as some of them did. Because of that, they were killed by snakes. [10]And don't complain as some of them did. Because they complained, they were killed by the angel that destroys.

[11]The things that happened to those people are examples. They were written to be warnings for us. We live in the time that all those past histories were pointing to. [12]So anyone who thinks they are standing strong should be careful that they don't fall. [13]The only temptations that you have are the same temptations that all people have. But you can trust God. He will not let you be tempted more than you can bear. But when you are tempted, God will also give you a way to escape that temptation. Then you will be able to endure it.

---

[a] **9:9** Quote from Deut. 25:4.

[b] **10:1** *cloud* The cloud that led and protected the people of Israel on their journey out of Egypt, across the Red Sea and through the wilderness. See Exod. 13:20–22; 14:19–20.

[c] **10:2** *baptized* See "BAPTIZE" in the Word List. Here, Paul seems to mean that what happened to the Jews with Moses can be compared to the baptism of a believer into Christ.

[d] **10:7** Quote from Exod. 32:6.

[e] **10:9** *Christ* Some Greek copies say, "the Lord".

[14]So, my dear friends, stay away from worshipping idols. [15]You are intelligent people. Judge for yourselves the truth of what I say now. [16]The cup of blessing*a* that we give thanks for is a sharing in the blood sacrifice of Christ, isn't it? And the bread that we break is a sharing in the body of Christ, isn't it? [17]There is one loaf of bread, so we who are many are one body, because we all share in that one loaf.

[18]And think about what the people of Israel do. When they eat the sacrifices, they are united by sharing what was offered on the altar. [19]So, am I saying that sacrifices to idols are the same as those Jewish sacrifices? No, because an idol is nothing, and the things offered to idols are worth nothing. [20]But I am saying that when food is sacrificed to idols, it is an offering to demons, not to God. And I don't want you to share anything with demons. [21]You cannot drink the cup of the Lord and then go and drink a cup that honours demons. You cannot share a meal at the Lord's table and then go and share a meal that honours demons. [22]Doing that would make the Lord jealous.*b* Do you really want to do that? Do you think we are stronger than he is?

Use Your Freedom for God's Glory

[23]"All things are allowed," you say. But not all things are good. "All things are allowed." But some things don't help anyone. [24]Try to do what is good for others, not just what is good for yourselves.

[25]Eat any meat that is sold in the meat market. Don't ask questions about it to see if it is something you think is wrong to eat. [26]You can eat it, "because the earth and everything in it belong to the Lord".*c*

[27]Someone who is not a believer might invite you to eat with them. If you want to go, then eat anything that is put before you. Don't ask questions to see if it is something you think is wrong to eat. [28]But if someone tells you, "That food was offered to idols," then don't eat it. That's because some people think it is wrong, and it might cause a problem for the person who told you that. [29]I don't mean that you think it is wrong. But the other person might think it is wrong. That's the only reason not to eat it. My own freedom should not be judged by what another person thinks. [30]I eat the meal with thankfulness. So I don't want to be criticized because of something I thank God for.

[31]So if you eat, or if you drink or if you do anything, do it for the glory of God. [32]Never do anything that might make other people do wrong—Jews, non-Jews or anyone in God's church. [33]I do the same thing. I try to please everyone in every way. I am not trying to do what is good for me. I am trying to do what is good for the most people so that they can be saved.

11 Follow my example, just as I follow the example of Christ.

Being Under Authority

[2]I praise you because you remember me in all things. You follow closely the teachings I gave you. [3]But I want you to understand this: the head of every man is Christ. And the head of a woman is the man.*d* And the head of Christ is God.

[4]Every man who prophesies or prays with his head covered brings shame to his head. [5]But every woman who prays or prophesies should have her head covered. If her head is not covered, she brings shame to her head. Then she is the same as a woman who has her head shaved. [6]If a woman does not cover her head, it is the same as cutting off all her hair. But it is shameful for a woman to cut off her hair or to shave her head. So she should cover her head.

[7]But a man should not cover his head, because he is made like God and is God's glory. But woman is man's glory. [8]Man did not come from woman. Woman came from man. [9]And man was not made for woman. Woman was made for man. [10]So that is why a woman should have her head covered with something that shows she is under authority.*e* Also, she should do this because of the angels.

[11]But in the Lord the woman needs the man, and the man needs the woman. [12]This is true because woman came from man, but also man is born from woman. Really, everything comes from God.

[13]Decide this for yourselves: is it right for a woman to pray to God without something on her head? [14]Even nature itself teaches you that wearing long hair is shameful for a man. [15]But wearing long hair is a woman's honour. Long hair is given to the woman to cover her head. [16]Some people may still want to argue about this. But we and the churches of God don't accept what those people are doing.

---

a **10:16 cup of blessing** The cup of wine that believers in Christ thank God for and drink at the Lord's Supper.
b **10:22 make the Lord jealous** See Deut. 32:16–17.
c **10:26** Quote from Ps. 24:1; 50:12; 89:11.
d **11:3 the man** This could also mean "her husband".
e **11:10 have her head . . . authority** Literally, "have authority on her head". This could also be translated, "keep control of her head", meaning "do what will keep people from misunderstanding her uncovered head".

The Lord's Supper

¹⁷In the things I tell you now I don't praise you. Your meetings hurt you more than they help you. ¹⁸First, I hear that when you meet together as a church you are divided. And this is not hard to believe ¹⁹because of your idea that you must have separate groups to show who the real believers are!

²⁰When you all come together, it is not really the Lord's Supper*a* you are eating. ²¹I say this because when you eat, each one eats without waiting for the others. Some people don't get enough to eat or drink, while others have too much.*b* ²²You can eat and drink in your own homes. It seems that you think God's church is not important. You embarrass those who are poor. What can I say? Should I praise you? No, I cannot praise you for this.

²³The teaching I gave you is the same that I received from the Lord: on the night when the Lord Jesus was handed over to be killed, he took bread ²⁴and gave thanks for it. Then he divided the bread and said, "This is my body; it is for you. Eat this to remember me." ²⁵In the same way, after they had eaten, Jesus took the cup of wine and said, "This wine represents the new agreement that God makes with his people, which begins with my blood sacrifice. When you drink this, do it to remember me." ²⁶This means that every time you eat this bread and drink this cup, you are telling others about the Lord's death until he comes again.

²⁷So if you eat the bread or drink the cup of the Lord in a way that does not fit its meaning, you are sinning against the body and the blood of the Lord. ²⁸Before you eat the bread and drink the cup, you should examine your own attitude. ²⁹If you eat and drink without paying attention to those who are the Lord's body, your eating and drinking will cause you to be judged guilty. ³⁰That is why many in your group are sick and weak, and many have died. ³¹But if we judged ourselves in the right way, then God would not judge us. ³²But when the Lord judges us, he punishes us to show us the right way. He does this so that we will not be condemned with the world.

³³So, my brothers and sisters, when you come together to eat, wait for each other. ³⁴If some are too hungry to wait, they should eat at home. Do this so that your meeting together will not bring God's judgement on you. I will tell you what to do about the other things when I come.

Gifts From the Holy Spirit

12 Now, brothers and sisters, I want you to understand about spiritual gifts. ²You remember the lives you lived before you were believers. You let yourselves be influenced and led away to worship idols—things that have no life. ³So I tell you that no one who is speaking with the help of God's Spirit says, "Jesus be cursed." And no one can say, "Jesus is Lord," without the help of the Holy Spirit.

⁴There are different kinds of spiritual gifts, but they are all from the same Spirit. ⁵There are different ways to serve, but we all serve the same Lord. ⁶And there are different ways that God works in people, but it is the same God who works in all of us to do everything.

⁷Something from the Spirit can be seen in each person. The Spirit gives this to each one to help others. ⁸The Spirit gives one person the ability to speak with wisdom. And the same Spirit gives another person the ability to speak with knowledge. ⁹The same Spirit gives faith to one person and to another he gives gifts of healing. ¹⁰The Spirit gives to one person the power to do miracles, to another the ability to prophesy, and to another the ability to judge what is from the Spirit and what is not. The Spirit gives one person the ability to speak in different kinds of languages, and to another the ability to interpret those languages. ¹¹One Spirit, the same Spirit, does all these things. The Spirit decides what to give each one.

The Body of Christ

¹²A person has only one body, but it has many parts. Yes, there are many parts, but all those parts are still just one body. Christ is like that too. ¹³Some of us are Jews and some of us are not; some of us are slaves and some of us are free. But we were all baptized to become one body through one Spirit. And we were all given*c* the one Spirit.

¹⁴And a person's body has more than one part. It has many parts. ¹⁵The foot might say, "I am not a hand, so I don't belong to the body." But saying this would not stop the foot from being a part of the body. ¹⁶The ear might say, "I am not an eye, so I don't belong to the body." But saying this would not make the ear stop being a part of the body. ¹⁷If the whole body were an eye, it would not be able to hear. If the whole body were an ear, it would not be able to smell anything. ¹⁸⁻¹⁹If each part of the body were the same part, there would be no body. But as it is, God put the parts in the

---

a **11:20** *Lord's Supper* The special meal Jesus told his followers to eat to remember him. See Luke 22:14–20.
b **11:21** *have too much* Literally, "get drunk".
c **12:13** *given* Literally, "given to drink".

SPIRIT LEVEL

Back in Corinth, God was doing exciting stuff with those baby Christians. Some were getting weirdly wise, some were happily healed and others were becoming know-it-alls. What was going on and what was God up to?

DIG IN

READ 1 Corinthians 12:1–11

This was a special time in church history. God was building his church and his people were experiencing spiritual gifts they'd never seen before. Let's dig into the passage and see if we can work out what was happening.

- Where do spiritual gifts come from (vv.4–6)?
- What is the purpose of spiritual gifts (vv.5–7)?

Look at me! Look at me! Some of the Corinthian Christians thought the gifts made them look extra cool but Paul was very clear that God gave them these gifts to help other people. They were to build up and strengthen the church.

- Who decided which gifts were given (v.11)?

READ 1 Corinthians 12:12–31

- Make a list of the gifts Paul talks about. What was each gift for?
- Why doesn't everybody have the same gifts?
- What does Paul liken the church to?
- How did these gifts help build up the Corinthian church?

DIG THROUGH

- Today God still gives his people unique gifts by his Spirit. Not everyone will experience the same gifts and they might not be as public or obvious as the Corinthians. (Check out v.28. There's something to suit everyone.) What gifts has God given you? How can you use your gifts to help others in your church?
- Paul tells the Corinthians they should give "attention to the spiritual gifts" (1 Corinthians 12:31), especially those that build up the church (1 Corinthians 14:12). Spiritual gifts help us love God more and serve him better. Which gifts would you like to have? Why not ask God to show you how you can use them well?

DIG DEEPER

- We read about spiritual gifts in various places in the New Testament. For more information on spiritual gifts in general see Acts 2, Romans 12:1–8 and 1 Corinthians 14:1–25.
- For more specific information on some of the gifts Paul lists here check out these passages: prophecy (1 Corinthians 14:26–32; Ephesians 4:10–12); discerning spirits (1 Thessalonians 5:21; 1 John 4:1); speaking in or interpreting different languages (Acts 2; 1 Corinthians 13:1; 1 Corinthians 14:1–25).

ALL YOU NEED IS LOVE

Think about the films and TV shows you've seen over the past month or the magazines and books you've read recently. What do they say about love and do you agree?

DIG IN
READ 1 Corinthians 13:1–3

- Paul picks out four gifts of the Spirit as examples. What are they and what point is he making?
- What is shocking about Paul's main point?
- What sort of love is he talking about?

Tongues, prophecy, faith and giving were pretty high-profile gifts to have. If you had them back in Paul's day, you would have looked super-duper spiritual. But Paul says they count for nothing unless motivated by love.

READ 1 Corinthians 13:4–7
- So what is love? List all the characteristics Paul talks about. What do they say about God's view of true love?
- Remember what you said about how films and magazines portray love. How does God's view compare?

READ 1 Corinthians 13:8–13
Paul writes "when perfection comes" (v.10). In the original Greek this means completeness and fulfilment.
- What do you think he means?

Paul could be talking about a few things here. Some people say he means life after Jesus returns. Others think he means when the church grows up or in heaven. One thing's for sure – when everything else has gone: LOVE remains.

- How can love last forever? What kind of love is Paul talking about? (Clue: check out 1 John 4:7–8.)
- Look at verses 11 and 12. How does love mature? What does that mean for your life today?
- After all is said and done, why is love "the greatest" (v.13)?

DIG THROUGH

- How does God's view of love make you think about the way you see friends and family? What needs to change? What do you need to do?
- And what about the people you don't like? How does God's view of love shape the way you see them? What needs to change? What do you need to do?
- So gifts count for nothing unless motivated by love. How are you tempted to use your gifts just to make you look good? What about to make others feel bad? Are there better ways you could use your gifts to benefit those around you?

DIG DEEPER

- The Bible has so much to say about love. It's like a chorus that repeats again and again. To find out more about God's love for us look up: Exodus 34:6, Numbers 14:18, John 3:16 and 1 John 4:7–21.
- To find out more about how we should love God and one another see Luke 10:27, John 13:34–35, Galatians 5:13, Ephesians 4:2, 1 Peter 1:22 and 2 John 1:5.

body as he wanted them. He made a place for each one. ²⁰So there are many parts, but only one body.

²¹The eye cannot say to the hand, "I don't need you!" And the head cannot say to the foot, "I don't need you!" ²²No, those parts of the body that seem to be weaker are actually very important. ²³And the parts that we think are not worth very much are the parts we give the most care to. And we give special care to the parts of the body that we don't want to show. ²⁴The more beautiful parts don't need this special care. But God put the body together and gave more honour to the parts that need it. ²⁵God did this so that our body would not be divided. God wanted the different parts to care the same for each other. ²⁶If one part of the body suffers, then all the other parts suffer with it. Or if one part is honoured, then all the other parts share its honour.

²⁷All of you together are the body of Christ. Each one of you is a part of that body. ²⁸And in the church God has given a place first to apostles, second to prophets and third to teachers. Then God has given a place to those who do miracles, those who have gifts of healing, those who can help others, those who are able to lead and those who can speak in different kinds of languages. ²⁹Not all are apostles. Not all are prophets. Not all are teachers. Not all do miracles. ³⁰Not all have gifts of healing. Not all speak in different kinds of languages. Not all interpret those languages. ³¹Continue to give your attention to the spiritual gifts you consider to be the greatest. But now I want to point out a way of life that is even greater.

Let Love Be Your Guide

13 I may speak in different languages, whether human or even of angels. But if I don't have love, I am only a noisy bell or a ringing cymbal. ²I may have the gift of prophecy, I may understand all secrets and know everything there is to know, and I may have faith so great that I can move mountains. But even with all this, if I don't have love, I am nothing. ³I may give away everything I have to help others, and I may even give my body as an offering to be burned. But I gain nothing by doing all this if I don't have love.

⁴Love is patient and kind. Love is not jealous, it does not boast and it is not proud. ⁵Love is not rude, it is not selfish and it cannot be made angry easily. Love does not remember wrongs done against it. ⁶Love is never happy when others do wrong, but it is always happy with the truth. ⁷Love never gives up on people. It never stops trusting, never loses hope and never gives up.

⁸Love will never end. But all those gifts will come to an end—even the gift of prophecy, the gift of speaking in different kinds of languages and

the gift of knowledge. ⁹These will all end because this knowledge and these prophecies we have now are not complete. ¹⁰But when perfection comes, the things that are not complete will end.

> ## INSIGHT
>
> *Mirrors in Paul's day were made of polished metal, rather than mirrored glass. So, if the metal was dull, the image was blurred and poor.*
>
> **1 Corinthians 13:12**

¹¹When I was a child, I talked like a child, I thought like a child and I made plans like a child. When I became a man, I stopped those childish ways. ¹²It is the same with us. Now we see God as if we are looking at a reflection in a mirror. But then, in the future, we will see him right before our eyes. Now I know only a part, but at that time I will know fully, as God has known me. ¹³So these three things continue: faith, hope and love. And the greatest of these is love.

Use Spiritual Gifts to Help the Church

14 Love should be the goal of your life, but you should also want to have the gifts that come from the Spirit. And the gift you should want most is to be able to prophesy. ²I will explain why. Those who have the gift of speaking in a different language are not speaking to people. They are speaking to God. No one understands them—they are speaking secret things through the Spirit. ³But those who prophesy are speaking to people. They help people grow stronger in faith, and they give encouragement and comfort. ⁴Those who speak in a different language are helping only themselves. But those who prophesy are helping the whole church.

⁵I would like all of you to have the gift of speaking in different languages. But what I want more is for you to prophesy. Anyone who prophesies is more important than those who can only speak in different languages. However, if they can also interpret those languages, they are as important as the one who prophesies. If they can interpret, then the church can be helped by what they say.

⁶Brothers and sisters, will it help you if I come to you speaking in different languages? No, it will help you only if I bring you a new truth or some knowledge, prophecy or teaching. ⁷This is true even with lifeless things that make sounds—like a flute or a harp. If the different musical notes are not made clear, you can't understand what song is

being played. Each note must be played clearly for you to be able to understand the tune. [8]And in a war, if the trumpet does not sound clearly, the soldiers will not know it is time to prepare for fighting.

[9]It is the same with you. If you don't speak clearly in a language people know, they cannot understand what you are saying. You will be talking to the air! [10]It is true that there are many different languages in the world, and they all have meaning. [11]But if I don't understand the meaning of what someone is saying, it will just be strange sounds to me, and I will sound just as strange to them. [12]That's why you who want spiritual gifts so much should prefer those gifts that help the church grow stronger.

[13]So those who have the gift of speaking in a different language should pray that they can also interpret what they say. [14]If I pray in a different language, my spirit is praying, but my mind does nothing. [15]So what should I do? I will pray with my spirit, but I will also pray with my mind. I will sing with my spirit, but I will also sing with my mind. [16]You might be praising God with your spirit. But someone there without understanding cannot say "Amen" to your prayer of thanks, because they don't know what you are saying. [17]You may be thanking God in a good way, but others are not helped.

[18]I thank God that my gift of speaking in different kinds of languages is greater than any of yours. [19]But in the church meetings I would rather speak five words that I understand than thousands of words in a different language. I would rather speak with my understanding, so that I can teach others.

[20]Brothers and sisters, don't think like children. In evil things be like babies, but in your thinking you should be like full-grown adults. [21]As the Scriptures[a] say,

"Using those who speak a different language
 and using the lips of foreigners,
 I will speak to these people.
 But even then, they will not obey me."
 Isaiah 28:11–12

This is what the Lord says.

[22]And from this we see that the use of different languages shows how God deals with those who don't believe, not with those who believe. And prophecy shows how God works through those who believe, not through unbelievers. [23]Suppose the whole church meets together and you all speak in different languages. If some people come in who

are without understanding or don't believe, they will say you are crazy. [24]But suppose you are all prophesying and someone comes in who does not believe or who is without understanding. Their sin will be shown to them, and they will be judged by everything you say. [25]The secret things in their heart will be made known. So they will bow down and worship God. They will say, "Without a doubt, God is here with you."[b]

Your Meetings Should Be Helpful to All

[26]So, brothers and sisters, what should you do? When you meet together, one person has a song, another has a teaching and another has a new truth from God. One person speaks in a different language, and another interprets that language. The purpose of whatever you do should be to help everyone grow stronger in faith. [27]When you meet together, if anyone speaks to the group in a different language, it should be only two or no more than three people who do this. And they should speak one after the other. And someone else should interpret what they say. [28]But if there is no interpreter, then anyone who speaks in a different language should be quiet in the church meeting. They should speak only to themselves and to God.

[29]And only two or three prophets should speak. The others should judge what they say. [30]And if a message from God comes to someone who is sitting, the first speaker should be quiet. [31]You can all prophesy one after the other. This way everyone can be taught and encouraged. [32]The spirits of prophets are under the control of the prophets themselves. [33]God is not a God of confusion but a God of peace. This is the rule for all the meetings of God's people.

[34]The women should keep quiet in these church meetings. They are not allowed to speak out but should be under authority, as the Law of Moses says. [35]If there is something they want to know, they should ask their own husbands at home. It is shameful for a woman to speak up like that in the church meeting.

[36]God's teaching did not come from you, and you are not the only ones who have received it. [37]If you think you are a prophet or that you have a spiritual gift, you should understand that what I am writing to you is the Lord's command. [38]If you do not accept this, you will not be accepted.

[39]So my brothers and sisters, continue to give your attention to prophesying. And don't stop anyone from using the gift of speaking in different languages. [40]But everything should be done in a way that is right and orderly.

---

[a] **14:21 Scriptures** Literally, "law", which sometimes means the Old Testament.
[b] **14:25** See Isa. 45:14 and Zech. 8:23.

The Good News About Jesus Christ

15 Now, brothers and sisters, I want you to remember the Good News I told you. You received that Good News message, and you continue to base your life on it. ²That Good News, the message you heard from me, is God's way to save you. But you must continue believing it. If you don't, you believed for nothing.

³I gave you the message that I received. I told you the most important truths: that Christ died for our sins, as the Scriptures say; ⁴that he was buried and was raised to life on the third day, as the Scriptures say; ⁵and that he appeared to Peter and then to the twelve apostles. ⁶After that, Christ appeared to more than 500 other believers at the same time. Most of them are still living today, but some have died. ⁷Then he appeared to James and later to all the apostles. ⁸Last of all, he appeared to me. I was different, like a baby born before the normal time.

⁹All the other apostles are greater than I am. I say this because I persecuted the church of God. That is why I am not even good enough to be called an apostle. ¹⁰But, because of God's grace, that is what I am. And his grace that he gave me was not wasted. I worked harder than all the other apostles. (But I was not really the one working. It was God's grace that was with me.) ¹¹So then it is not important whether I told you God's message or whether it was the other apostles who told you—we all tell people the same message, and this is what you believed.

We Will Be Raised From Death

¹²We tell everyone that Christ was raised from death. So why do some of you say that people will not be raised from death? ¹³If no one will ever be raised from death, then Christ has never been raised. ¹⁴And if Christ has never been raised, then the message we tell is worth nothing. And your faith is worth nothing. ¹⁵And we will also be guilty of lying about God, because we have told people about him, saying that he raised Christ from death. And if no one is raised from death, then God never raised Christ from death. ¹⁶If those who have died are not raised, then Christ has not been raised either. ¹⁷And if Christ has not been raised from death, then your faith is for nothing; you are still guilty of your sins. ¹⁸And those in Christ who have already died are lost. ¹⁹If our hope in Christ is only for this life here on earth, then people should feel more sorry for us than for anyone else.

²⁰But Christ really has been raised from death —the first one of all those who will be raised.

²¹Death comes to people because of what one man did. But now there is resurrection from death because of another man. ²²I mean that in Adam all of us die. And in the same way, in Christ all of us will be made alive again. ²³But everyone will be raised to life in the right order. Christ was first to be raised. Then, when Christ comes again, those who belong to him will be raised to life. ²⁴Then the end will come. Christ will destroy all rulers, authorities and powers. Then he will give the kingdom to God the Father.

²⁵Christ must rule until God puts all enemies under his control.ᵃ ²⁶The last enemy to be destroyed will be death. ²⁷As the Scriptures say, "God put everything under his control."ᵇ When it says that "everything" is put under him, it is clear that this does not include God himself. God is the one putting everything under Christ's control. ²⁸After everything has been put under Christ, then the Son himself will be put under God. God is the one who put everything under Christ. And Christ will be put under God so that God will be the complete ruler over everything.

²⁹If no one will ever be raised from death, then what will the people do who are baptized for those who have died? If the dead are never raised, then why are people baptized for them?

INSIGHT

We don't know exactly what Paul means when he says he fought wild animals, but he may be referring to the Roman practice of putting prisoners (and about a decade later this often included Christians) into an arena with wild animals, where they were mauled in front of huge crowds for sport.

1 Corinthians 15:32

³⁰And what about us? Why do we put ourselves in danger every hour? ³¹I face death every day. That is true, brothers and sisters, just as it is true that I am proud of what you are because of Christ Jesus our Lord. ³²I fought wild animals in Ephesus. If I did that only for human reasons, then I have gained nothing. If we are not raised from death, "Let us eat and drink, because tomorrow we die."ᶜ

³³Don't be fooled: "Bad friends will ruin good habits." ³⁴Come back to your right way of

---

ᵃ **15:25 control** Literally, "feet".
ᵇ **15:27** Quote from Ps. 8:6.
ᶜ **15:32** Quote from Isa. 22:13; 56:12.

thinking and stop sinning. Some of you don't know God. I say this to shame you.

What Kind of Body Will We Have?

35But someone may ask, "How are the dead raised? What kind of body will they have?" 36These are stupid questions. When you plant something, it must die in the ground before it can live and grow. 37And when you plant something, what you plant does not have the same "body" that it will have later. What you plant is only a seed, maybe wheat or something else. 38But God gives it the body that he has planned for it, and he gives each kind of seed its own body. 39All things made of flesh are not the same: people have one kind of flesh, animals have another, birds have another and fish have yet another kind. 40Also there are heavenly bodies and earthly bodies. But the beauty of the heavenly bodies is one kind, and the beauty of the earthly bodies is another. 41The sun has one kind of beauty, the moon has another kind and the stars have another. And each star is different in its beauty.

42It will be the same when those who have died are raised to life. The body that is "planted" in the grave will ruin and decay, but it will be raised to a life that cannot be destroyed. 43When the body is "planted", it is without honour. But when it is raised, it will be great and glorious. When the body is "planted", it is weak. But when it is raised, it will be full of power. 44The body that is "planted" is a physical body. When it is raised, it will be a spiritual body.

There is a physical body. So there is also a spiritual body. 45As the Scriptures say, "The first man, Adam, became a living person."*ab* But the last Adam*c* is a life-giving spirit. 46The spiritual man did not come first. It was the physical man that came first; then came the spiritual. 47The first man came from the dust of the earth. The second man came from heaven. 48All people belong to the earth. They are like that first man of earth. But those who belong to heaven are like that man of heaven. 49We were made like that man of earth, so we will also be made like that man of heaven.

50I tell you this, brothers and sisters: our bodies of flesh and blood cannot have a part in God's kingdom. Something that will ruin cannot have a part in something that never ruins. 51But listen, I tell you this secret: we will not all die, but we will all be changed. 52It will only take the time of a second. We will be changed as quickly as an eye blinks. This will happen when the last trumpet blows. The trumpet will blow and those who

have died will be raised to live forever. And we will all be changed. 53This body that ruins must clothe itself with something that will never ruin. And this body that dies must clothe itself with something that will never die. 54So this body that ruins will clothe itself with that which never ruins. And this body that dies will clothe itself with that which never dies. When this happens, the Scriptures will be made true:

"Death is swallowed in victory."

Isaiah 25:8

55"O death, where is your victory?
  Where is your power to hurt?"

Hosea 13:14

56Death's power to hurt is sin, and the power of sin is the law. 57But we thank God who gives us the victory through our Lord Jesus Christ!

58So, my dear brothers and sisters, stand strong. Don't let anything change you. Always give yourselves fully to the work of the Lord. You know that your work in the Lord is never wasted.

The Collection for Believers in Judea

16 Now, about the collection of money for God's people: do the same as I told the Galatian churches to do. 2On the first day of every week, each of you should take some of your money and put it in a special place. Save up as much as you can from what you are blessed with. Then you will not have to gather it all after I come. 3When I arrive, I will send some men to take your gift to Jerusalem. These will be the ones you all agree should go. I will send them with letters of introduction. 4If it seems good for me to go too, we can all travel together.

Paul's Plans

5I plan to go through Macedonia, so I will come to you after that. 6Maybe I will stay with you for a time. I might even stay all winter. Then you can help me on my trip, wherever I go. 7I don't want to come and see you now, because I would have to leave and go to other places. I hope to stay a longer time with you, if the Lord allows it. 8But I will stay in Ephesus until Pentecost. 9I will stay here, because a good opportunity for a great and growing work has been given to me now. And there are many people working against it.

10Timothy might come to you. Try to make him feel comfortable with you. He is working for the Lord just as I am. 11So none of you should refuse

---

a **15:45** *person* Literally, "soul".
b **15:45** Quote from Gen. 2:7.
c **15:45** *Adam* The name Adam means "man". Here, "the last Adam" refers to Christ, the "man of heaven".

to accept Timothy. Help him continue on his trip in peace so that he can come back to me. I am expecting him to come back with the other brothers.

¹²Now about our brother Apollos: I strongly encouraged him to visit you with the other brothers. He prefers not to come now, but he will come when he has the opportunity.

Paul Ends His Letter

¹³Be careful. Hold firmly to your faith. Have courage and be strong. ¹⁴Do everything in love.

¹⁵You know that Stephanas and his family were the first believers in Achaia. They have given themselves to the service of God's people. I ask you, brothers and sisters, ¹⁶to follow the leading of people like these and others who work hard and serve together with them.

¹⁷I am happy that Stephanas, Fortunatus and Achaicus have come. You are not here, but they have filled your place. ¹⁸They have been a great encouragement to me and to you as well. You should recognize the value of such people.

¹⁹The churches in Asia send you their greetings. Aquila and Priscilla greet you in the Lord. Also the church that meets in their house sends greetings. ²⁰All the brothers and sisters here send their greetings. Give each other the special greeting of God's people.ᵃ

²¹Here's my greeting in my own handwriting— PAUL.

²²If anyone does not love the Lord, let that person be separated from God—lost forever! Come, O Lord!ᵇ

²³The grace of the Lord Jesus be with you.

²⁴My love be with all of you in Christ Jesus.

ᵃ **16:20** *the special greeting of God's people* Literally, "a holy kiss".
ᵇ **16:22** *Come, O Lord* This is a translation of the Aramaic "*marana tha*".

Who

The apostle Paul. Writing once again to the Christian community at Corinth, after a brief, painful visit to the church. Paul is probably writing from northern Macedonia.

When

Paul wrote this letter around AD 55–56, less than a year after writing 1 Corinthians. He writes to correct rumours about himself and to encourage the church to deal with troublemakers.

What

Paul had only been able to visit Corinth for a short time, not the long stay he'd promised (1 Corinthians 16:6), and instead returned to Asia. His opponents seized on this, claiming that Paul didn't keep his promises.

The result is one of Paul's most personal letters. He argues that he stayed away because he wanted to see if his instructions were being followed. He defends his work of spreading the Good News message and he promises to visit the Corinthians again. He defends his own conduct and points to his own incredible track record. And he inspires Jesus' followers not to lose heart (4:16–17).

Reading this letter it's impossible not to feel the weight of Paul's anxiety for the Corinthian church and the depth of his concern for them. We can also see at times a more vulnerable side of Paul – a side that feels the need to assert his own integrity and honesty. Finally, we begin to understand just how much his work has cost him – the hardship and suffering that he has had to endure. This letter shows us what it was like to be an apostle in the early Church. Paul talks of imprisonment, beatings, shipwrecks, unrelenting danger (11:23–27). No mega-churches and big worship bands here!

But in all this, it is God's strength which shines through. "My grace is all you need. Only when you are weak can everything be done completely by my power," God says to Paul (12:9). It's a message he passes on through this letter – and one he lived out in his life.

QUICK TOUR ▶ 2 CORINTHIANS

Non-arrival 1:1 – 2:17	Eager giving 9:1–15
New agreement 3:1–18	A true apostle 10:1–18
Jars of clay 4:1–18	Suffering 11:16 – 12:10
Light and dark 6:14 – 7:16	

"That is why we never give up. Our physical body is becoming older and weaker, but our spirit inside us is made new every day. We have small troubles for a while now, but these troubles are helping us gain an eternal glory. That eternal glory is much greater than our troubles. So we think about what we cannot see, not what we see. What we see lasts only a short time, and what we cannot see will last forever."

2 Corinthians 4:16–18

1 Greetings from Paul, an apostle of Christ Jesus. I am an apostle because that is what God wanted. Greetings also from Timothy our brother in Christ.

To God's church in Corinth and to all of God's holy people throughout Achaia.

²Grace and peace to you from God our Father and the Lord Jesus Christ.

INSIGHT

Corinth was very multi-cultural. Many came to this major city, the commercial hub of Greece, from around the world. Paul's greeting here reflects this as he uses a Greek greeting "grace" and also a Hebrew one "peace".

2 Corinthians 1:2

Paul Gives Thanks to God

³Praise be to the God and Father of our Lord Jesus Christ. He is the Father who is full of mercy, the God of all comfort. ⁴He comforts us every time we have trouble so that when others have trouble, we can comfort them with the same comfort God gives us. ⁵We share in the many sufferings of Christ. In the same way, much comfort comes to us through Christ. ⁶If we have troubles, it is for your comfort and salvation. If we are comforted, it is so that we can comfort you. And this helps you patiently accept the same sufferings we have. ⁷Our hope for you is strong. We know that you share in our sufferings. So we know that you also share in our comfort.

⁸Brothers and sisters, we want you to know about the trouble we suffered in Asia. We had great burdens there, which were greater than our own strength. We even gave up hope for life. ⁹In fact, it seems like God has been telling us we are going to die. But this is so that we will not trust in ourselves but in God, who raises people from death. ¹⁰He saved us from these great dangers of death, and he will continue to save us. We feel sure he will always save us. ¹¹And you can help us with your prayers. Then many people will give thanks for us—that God blessed us because of their many prayers.

The Change in Paul's Plans

¹²This is what we are proud of, and I can say with a clear conscience that it is true: in every-

thing we have done in the world, we have done it with an honest and pure heart from God. And this is even truer in what we have done with you. We did this by God's grace, not by the kind of wisdom the world has. ¹³We write to you only what you can read and understand. And I hope you will fully understand, ¹⁴just as you already understand many things about us. I hope you will understand that you can be proud of us, just as we will be proud of you on the day when our Lord Jesus Christ comes again.

¹⁵I was very sure of all this. That is why I made plans to visit you first. Then you could be blessed twice. ¹⁶I planned to visit you on my way to Macedonia and again on my way back. I wanted to get help from you for my trip to Judea. ¹⁷Do you think that I made these plans without really thinking? Or maybe you think I make plans as the world does, saying yes and no at the same time.

¹⁸But if you can believe God, then you can believe that what we tell you is never both yes and no. ¹⁹The Son of God, Jesus Christ, the one that Silas, Timothy and I told you about, was not yes and no. In Christ it has always been yes. ²⁰The yes to all of God's promises is in Christ. And that is why we say "Amen" through Christ to the glory of God. ²¹And God is the one who makes you and us strong in Christ. God is also the one who chose us for his work.ᵃ ²²He put his mark on us to show that we are his. Yes, he put his Spirit in our hearts as the first payment that guarantees all that he will give us.

²³I tell you this, and I ask God to be my witness that this is true: the reason I did not come back to Corinth was that I did not want to punish or hurt you. ²⁴I don't mean that we are trying to control your faith. You are strong in faith. But we are workers with you for your own happiness.

2 So I decided that my next visit to you would not be another visit to make you sad. ²If I make you sad, then who will make me happy? Only you can make me happy—you, the ones I made sad. ³I wrote you a letter so that when I came to you I would not be made sad by those who should make me happy. I felt sure that all of you would share my joy. ⁴When I wrote to you before, I was very troubled and my heart was full of sadness. I wrote with many tears. I did not write to make you sad, but to let you know how much I love you.

Forgive the Person Who Did Wrong

⁵Someone in your group has caused sadness—not to me, but to all of you. I mean he has caused

---

ᵃ **1:21 chose us for his work** Literally, "anointed us". In Greek this word is related to the title "Christ", which means "anointed one". See "ANOINT" and "CHRIST" in the Word List.

YOU CAN SEE IT IN MY FACE

Say Paul put out an ad on Corinth TV: "Does your acne get your down? Are you ashamed of that pizza face? Try new zit-away gospel cream for a spot-free face that really shines."

DIG IN

READ 2 Corinthians 3:1–11

First up, there's a bit of Old Testament history here. Hundreds of years previously, Moses climbed Mount Sinai and met with God. It was such a holy experience that it made his face glow, giving him a face that shone, reflecting the brilliance of God. It was so radiant, in fact, that the Israelites had to look away (Exodus 34:29–35). Here Paul describes how Moses carved the words of the Ten Commandments onto stone tablets and as Moses came down the mountain the people knew 'the law' was coming to them with the glory of God (v.7).

- Think about the symbolism of what was happening. What did Moses' shining face say about God and his laws?
- What "new agreement" (see v.6) do you think Paul is hinting at in verses 10 and 11? What new agreement would surpass the old one?

READ 2 Corinthians 3:12–15

Paul says we have a hope that will last forever. So we should speak very openly!

- Speak openly about what? What is the hope we have?
- Who is Paul writing about in verse 14?
- Who takes the covering away? (Check out verse 16.)

The old agreement told you how bad you were, and none of the sacrifices could deal with your sin permanently. Only Jesus lifts the covering. Only Jesus removes sin forever, bringing us back to God.

READ 2 Corinthians 3:16–18

- What happens when we turn to the Lord? What does this mean for Christians?
- What effect does the Spirit have in our lives (v.17)?
- Who or what makes the change?

DIG THROUGH

- The Spirit changes us to become more like Jesus every day – in what areas of your life would you like to "shine" more like Jesus? Ask the Holy Spirit to help you change.
- God is in the business of making us new day by day. What areas of wrongdoing challenge you most? How does this passage encourage you to keep fighting sin?

DIG DEEPER

- The light of the Good News is a common theme throughout the Bible. You might also want to check out Isaiah 60:1, Matthew 5:14–16, John 1:9, John 3:19–21 and John 9:5.
- For more about the old and new agreements read Romans 5:20–21, Romans 6:14–23, Romans 7, Romans 8:1–4 and Galatians 5:1–6.

sadness to all in some way. (I don't want to make it sound worse than it really is.) ⁶The punishment that most of your group gave him is enough for him. ⁷But now you should forgive him and encourage him. This will keep him from having too much sadness and giving up completely. ⁸So I beg you to show him that you love him. ⁹This is why I wrote to you. I wanted to test you and see if you obey in everything. ¹⁰If you forgive someone, then I also forgive them. And if I had anything to forgive I forgave it for you with the agreement of Christ. ¹¹I did this so that Satan would not win anything from us. We know very well what his plans are.

God Gives Us Victory Over Troubles

¹²I went to Troas to tell people the Good News about Christ. The Lord gave me a good opportunity there. ¹³But I had no peace because I did not find my brother Titus. So I said goodbye and went to Macedonia.

¹⁴But thanks be to God, who always leads us in victory through Christ. God uses us to spread his knowledge everywhere like a sweet-smelling perfume. ¹⁵Our offering to God is to be the perfume of Christ that goes out to those who are being saved and to those who are being lost. ¹⁶To those who are being lost, this perfume smells like death, and it brings them death. But to those who are being saved, it has the sweet smell of life, and it brings them life. So who is good enough to do this work? ¹⁷Certainly not those who are out there selling God's message for a profit! But we don't do that. With Christ's help we speak God's truth honestly, knowing that we must answer to him.

Servants of God's New Agreement

3 Why are we starting again to tell you all these good things about ourselves? Do we need letters of introduction to you or from you, like some other people? ²No, you yourselves are our letter, written on our hearts. It is known and read by all people. ³You show that you are a letter from Christ that he sent through us. This letter is not written with ink but with the Spirit of the living God. It is not written on stone tablets*a* but on human hearts.

⁴Christ is the one who makes us sure of this before God. ⁵I don't mean that we are able to do anything good ourselves. It is God who makes us able to do all that we do. ⁶He made us able to be servants of a new agreement from himself to his

people. It is not an agreement of written laws, but it is of the Spirit. The written law brings death, but the Spirit gives life.

An Agreement With Greater Glory

⁷The old agreement*b* that brought death, written with words on stone, came with God's glory. In fact, the face of Moses was so bright with glory (a glory that was ending) that the people of Israel could not continue looking at his face. ⁸So surely the new agreement that comes from the life-giving Spirit has even more glory. ⁹This is what I mean: that old agreement judged people guilty of sin, but it had glory. So surely the new agreement that makes people right with God has much greater glory. ¹⁰That old agreement had glory. But it really loses its glory when it is compared to the much greater glory of the new agreement. ¹¹If the agreement that was brought to an end came with glory, then the agreement that never ends has much greater glory.

¹²We are so sure of this hope that we can speak very openly. ¹³We are not like Moses, who put a covering over his face so that the people of Israel would not see it. The glory was disappearing, and Moses did not want them to watch it end. ¹⁴But their minds were closed. And even today, when those people read the writings of the old agreement,*c* that same covering hides the meaning. That covering has not been removed for them. It is taken away only through Christ. ¹⁵Yes, even today, when they read the Law of Moses, there is a covering over their minds. ¹⁶But when someone changes and follows the Lord, that covering is taken away. ¹⁷The Lord is the Spirit, and where the Spirit of the Lord is, there is freedom. ¹⁸And our faces are not covered. We all show the Lord's glory, and we are being changed to be like him. This change in us brings more and more glory, which comes from the Lord, who is the Spirit.

Spiritual Treasure in Clay Jars

4 God, with his mercy, gave us this work to do, so we don't give up. ²But we have turned away from secret and shameful ways. We don't use trickery, and we don't change the teaching of God. We teach the truth plainly. This is how we show people who we are. And this is how they can know in their hearts what kind of people we are before God. ³The Good News that we tell people may be hidden, but it is hidden only to

---

a **3:3 stone tablets** Meaning the law that God gave to Moses, which was written on stone tablets. Also in verse 7. See Exod. 24:12; 25:16.
b **3:7 agreement** In verses 7–11 literally, "service" or "ministry".
c **3:14 old agreement** See "AGREEMENT" in the Word List. Here, "old agreement" is used to mean the Law of Moses on which that agreement was based.

SHAKEN NOT STIRRED

What encourages you to tell people about Jesus? Sometimes it can be tough. Mates take the mickey and people can give you a hard time because you're a Christian. So why keep going? Is it really worth the hassle?

Paul and his friends were often under attack from people who taught things that weren't the true message. There were people like this in Corinth threatening the confidence of those who followed Jesus. But Paul had some words of encouragement for the Corinthian church that are just as true today as they were back then.

DIG IN

READ 2 Corinthians 4:1–12

- What is the "treasure" Paul talks about in verse 7?
- Why don't people always see the Good News Christians have? What does Paul's picture about the jars of clay mean?

The Good News is the most precious treasure anyone can have. Sometimes people give Christians a hard time because they don't see this treasure hidden in us (just like money in a piggy bank). Yet Paul says we're the toughest nuts in the universe. Tough times might come but nothing can shake us.

- What sorts of hard times could we face (vv.11–12)?
- What can we be confident of as we face death for Jesus' sake?

READ 2 Corinthians 4:13–15

- What effect should faith in Jesus have on our lives (v.13)?
- Who benefits most from us telling people about Jesus? Why is that such Good News for everyone?

It's great that God gets the glory when we tell people about him.

READ 2 Corinthians 4:16–18

- If we have faith in Christ, what can we look forward to in the future?
- How does that encourage you to live for Jesus today?

DIG THROUGH

Paul writes in 2 Timothy 3:12 "every believer in Christ Jesus who wants to live in a way that honours God will be persecuted". That's tough news for all Christians.

- What situations make it hard for us to tell people about Jesus today?
- What tough situations do you face? How does this passage in 2 Corinthians encourage you to keep going?
- Who can you talk to about Jesus this week and how will this passage encourage you as you do that?

DIG DEEPER

- The hope of the Good News is like fuel that keeps Christians going. You might also find encouragement by reading Galatians 5:5, Ephesians 1:11–14 and Colossians 1:3–7.
- Want to think more about evangelism? Check out Matthew 5:16, Matthew 28:19–20, 2 Timothy 4:2 and 1 Peter 3:15.

those who are lost. [4]The ruler[a] of this world has blinded the minds of those who don't believe. They cannot see the light of the Good News—the message about the divine greatness of Christ. Christ is the one who is exactly like God. [5]We don't tell people about ourselves. But we tell people that Jesus Christ is Lord, and we tell them that we are your servants for Jesus. [6]God once said, "Let light shine out of the darkness!"[b] And this is the same God who made his light shine in our hearts to let us know that his own divine greatness is seen in the face of Christ.

INSIGHT

It was common in Bible times for people to hide their treasures in clay jars. It's a bit like hiding money under the mattress or in a biscuit tin. However, the jars were very fragile, and easily broken.

2 Corinthians 4:7

[7]We have this treasure from God, but we are only like clay jars that hold the treasure. This is to show that the amazing power we have is from God, not from us. [8]We have troubles all around us, but we are not defeated. We often don't know what to do, but we don't give up. [9]We are persecuted, but God does not leave us. We are hurt sometimes, but we are not destroyed. [10]So we constantly experience the death of Jesus in our own bodies, but this is so that the life of Jesus can also be seen in our bodies. [11]We are alive, but for Jesus we are always in danger of death, so that the life of Jesus can be seen in our bodies that die. [12]So death is working in us, but the result is that life is working in you.

[13]The Scriptures say, "I believed, so I spoke."[c] Our faith is like that too. We believe, and so we speak. [14]God raised the Lord Jesus from death, and we know that he will also raise us with Jesus. God will bring us together with you, and we will stand before him. [15]All these things are for you. And so the grace of God is being given to more and more people. This will bring more and more thanks to God for his glory.

Living by Faith

[16]That is why we never give up. Our physical body is becoming older and weaker, but our spirit inside us is made new every day. [17]We have small troubles for a while now, but these troubles are helping us gain an eternal glory. That eternal glory is much greater than our troubles. [18]So we think about what we cannot see, not what we see. What we see lasts only a short time, and what we cannot see will last forever.

5 We know that our body—the tent we live in here on earth—will be destroyed. But when that happens, God will have a home for us to live in. It will not be the kind of home people build here. It will be a home in heaven that will last forever. [2]But now we are tired of this body. We want God to give us our heavenly home. [3]It will clothe us and we will not be naked. [4]While we live in this tent, we have burdens and so we complain. I don't mean that we want to remove this tent, but we want to be clothed with our heavenly home. Then this body that dies will be covered with life. [5]This is what God himself made us for. And he has given us the Spirit as the first payment to guarantee the life to come.

[6]So we always have confidence. We know that while we live in this body, we are away from the Lord. [7]We live by what we believe will happen, not by what we can see. [8]So I say that we have confidence. And we really want to be away from this body and be at home with the Lord. [9]Our only goal is to always please the Lord, whether we are living here in this body or there with him. [10]We must all stand before Christ to be judged. Everyone will get what they should. They will be paid for whatever they did—good or bad—when they lived in this earthly body.

Helping People Become God's Friends

[11]We know what it means to fear the Lord, so we try to help people accept the truth. God knows what we really are, and I hope that in your hearts you know us too. [12]We are not trying to prove ourselves to you again. But we are telling you about ourselves. We are giving you reasons to be proud of us. Then you will have an answer for those who are proud about what can be seen. They don't care about what is in a person's heart. [13]If we are crazy, it is for God. If we are in our right mind, it is for you. [14]The love of Christ controls us, because we know that one person died for everyone. So all have died. [15]He died for all so that those who live would not continue to live for themselves. He died for them and was raised from death so that they would live for him.

[16]From this time on we don't think of anyone as the world thinks of people. It is true that in the

---

[a] **4:4 The ruler** Literally, "The god".
[b] **4:6 Let . . . darkness** See Gen. 1:3.
[c] **4:13** Quote from Ps. 116:10.

WALK BY FAITH, NOT BY SIGHT

Anyone for a spot of camping?

DIG IN

READ 2 Corinthians 5:1–5

- What is Paul talking about in verse 1? What is our earthly tent and heavenly home?

Paul compares our earthly existence to being in a tent. Think about that for a minute. Tents are good for a while but they're not meant to last forever. You take them down and move on. In contrast, our heavenly home is a solid "building" made to last by God. That means it's a sure bet.

- How does life in our earthly tent compare to our heavenly house?
- What purpose has God made us for (vv.4–5)? How does that make you feel about the future? How does it make you feel about today?
- Check out verse 5. What guarantee do Christians have? How do we know we're saved?

READ 2 Corinthians 5:6–10

Christians have the amazing promise that they will be with God forever. That's confidence that will change the way you live.

- What does it mean to "live by what we believe will happen, not by what we can see" (v.7)?

Sometimes people say "seeing is believing". Erm, no. Paul says we live by faith in God who we can't see.

- What is our goal (v.9)? How will you aim for that goal this week?
- What warning and encouragement does Paul give us about the future (v.10)? Compare verses 5 and 10. Why can Christians be confident on judgement day?

DIG THROUGH

- It's not easy to walk by faith. It's natural to want to trust what we see instead. When do you find it hardest to not just go along with what everybody else is doing?
- When do you find it hard to trust that God is working even though you can't see what he's doing?
- How does the certainty of a heavenly dwelling affect the way you relate to the world, your family and your friends?

DIG DEEPER

- We can learn some more about what will happen to Christians in the future. Check out Matthew 24:42–44, 1 Thessalonians 4:13 – 5:11 and Revelation 21.
- Want to read more about faith? Check out Luke 17:6, John 14:12, Romans 4:5 and Hebrews 11.
- To read about people in the Bible who had faith, take a look at the Bible Bit on Hebrews 11 entitled "Have Faith".

past we thought of Christ as the world thinks. But we don't think that way now. [17]When anyone is in Christ, it is a whole new world.[a] The old things are gone; suddenly, everything is new! [18]All this is from God. Through Christ, God made peace between himself and us. And God gave us the work of bringing people into peace with him. [19]I mean that God was in Christ, making peace between the world and himself. In Christ, God did not hold people guilty for their sins. And he gave us this message of peace to tell people. [20]So we have been sent to speak for Christ. It is like God is calling to people through us. We speak for Christ when we beg you to be at peace with God. [21]Christ had no sin, but God made him become sin[b] so that in Christ we could be right with God.

6 We are workers together with God. So we beg you: don't let the grace that you received from God be for nothing. [2]God says,

> "I heard you at the right time,
>   and I gave you help on the day of
>   salvation."
>
> Isaiah 49:8

I tell you that the "right time" is now. The "day of salvation" is now.

[3]We don't want people to find anything wrong with our work. So we do nothing that will be a problem to others. [4]But in every way we show that we are servants of God. We never give up, even though we face troubles, difficulties and problems of every kind. [5]We are beaten and thrown into prison. People get upset with us and fight against us. We work hard, and sometimes we get no sleep or food. [6]We show that we are God's servants by our pure lives, by our understanding, by our patience and by our kindness. We show it by the Holy Spirit, by genuine love, [7]by speaking the truth and by depending on God's power. This right way of living has prepared us to defend ourselves against every kind of attack. [8]Some people honour us, but others shame us. Some people say good things about us, but others say bad things. Some people say we are liars, but we speak the truth. [9]To some people we are not known, but we are well known. We seem to be dying. But look—we continue to live! We are punished, but we are not killed. [10]We have much sadness, but we are always rejoicing. We are poor, but we are making many people rich in faith. We have nothing, but really we have everything.

[11]We have spoken freely to you people in Corinth. We have opened our hearts to you. [12]Our feelings of love for you have not stopped. It is you who have stopped your feelings of love for us. [13]I speak to you as if you were my children. Do the same as we have done—open your hearts also.

We Are God's Temple

[14]You are not the same as those who don't believe. So don't join yourselves to them. Good and evil don't belong together. Light and darkness cannot share the same room. [15]How can there be any unity between Christ and the devil?[c] What does a believer have in common with an unbeliever? [16]God's temple[d] cannot have anything to do with idols, and we are the temple of the living God. As God said,

> "I will live with them
>   and walk with them;
> I will be their God,
>   and they will be my people."
>
> Leviticus 26:11–12

[17]"So come away from those people
    and separate yourselves from them, says
        the Lord.
Don't touch anything that is not clean,
    and I will accept you."

Isaiah 52:11

---

[a] **5:17** *When anyone . . . world* Or "Anyone who is in Christ is a new creation."
[b] **5:21** *sin* Or "an offering for sin".
[c] **6:15** *the devil* Literally, "*beliar*", one form of the Hebrew word "*belial*", which means "worthlessness" and was used to refer to the devil or the enemy of Christ.
[d] **6:16** *God's temple* God's house—the place where God's people worship him. Here, it means that believers are the spiritual temple where God lives.

18"I will be your father,
    and you will be my sons and daughters,
    says the Lord All-Powerful."

2 Samuel 7:14; 7:8

7 Dear friends, we have these promises from God. So we should make ourselves pure—free from anything that makes our body or our soul unclean. Our respect for God should make us try to be completely holy in the way we live.

Paul's Joy

2Open your hearts to us. We have not done wrong to anyone or caused harm to anyone. And we have not cheated anyone. 3I do not say this to blame you. I told you before that we love you so much we would live or die with you. 4I feel that I can tell you anything. I am very proud of you. Even with all the troubles we have had, I am greatly encouraged and feel very happy.

5When we came into Macedonia, we had no rest. We found trouble all around us. We had fighting on the outside and fear on the inside. 6But God encourages those who are troubled, and he certainly encouraged us by bringing Titus to us. 7It was so good to see him, but we were encouraged even more to hear about the encouragement you gave him. He told us that you really want to see me and that you are very sorry for what you did. And he told us how ready and willing you are to help me. When I heard this, I was so much happier.

8Even if the letter I wrote to you made you sad, I am not sorry I wrote it. I know that letter made you sad, and I was sorry for that. But it made you sad only for a short time. 9Now I am happy, not because you were made sad, but because your sorrow made you decide to change. That is what God wanted, so you were not hurt by us in any way. 10The kind of sorrow God wants makes people decide to change their lives. This leads them to salvation, and we cannot be sorry for that. But the kind of sorrow the world has will bring death. 11You had the kind of sorrow God wanted you to have. Now see what that sorrow has brought you: it has made you very serious. It made you want to prove that you were not wrong. It made you angry and afraid. It made you want to see me. It made you care. It made you want the right thing to be done. You proved that you were not guilty in any part of that problem. 12The main reason I wrote that letter was not because of the one who did the wrong or the one who was hurt. I wrote so that you would realize, before God, how very much you care for us. 13And that is what was so encouraging to us.

We were greatly encouraged, but we were especially pleased to see how happy Titus was.

You all made him feel so much better. 14I had boasted about you to Titus, and you didn't embarrass me. We have always told you the truth, and now what we told Titus about you has been shown to be true. 15And his love for you is stronger when he remembers that you were all ready to obey. You welcomed him with respect and fear. 16I am so happy that I can trust you fully.

Help for God's People in Judea

8 And now, brothers and sisters, we want to tell you what God's grace has done in the churches in Macedonia. 2These believers have been tested by great troubles, and they are very poor. But their great joy caused them to be very generous in their giving. 3I can tell you that they gave as much as they were able and even more than they could afford. No one told them to do this. It was their idea. 4But they asked us again and again—they begged us to let them share in this service for God's people. 5And they gave in a way that we did not expect: they gave themselves to the Lord and to us before they gave their money. This is what God wants.

6So we asked Titus to help you finish this special work of giving. He is the one who started this work. 7You are rich in everything—in faith, in speaking ability, in knowledge, in the willingness to help and in the love you learned from us. So now we want you to be rich in this work of giving too.

8I am not ordering you to give, but I want to see how real your love is by comparing you with others who have been so ready and willing to help. 9You know the grace of our Lord Jesus Christ. You know that he gave up his heavenly riches and became poor for you. He gave up everything so that you could be richly blessed.

10This is what I think you should do: last year you were the first to want to give, and you were the first who gave. 11So now finish the work you started. Then your "doing" will be equal to your "wanting to do". Give from what you have. 12If you want to give, your gift will be accepted. Your gift will be judged by what you have, not by what you don't have. 13We don't want you to have troubles while others are comforted. We want everything to be equal. 14At this time you have plenty and can provide what they need. Then later, when they have plenty, they can provide what you need. Then everyone will have an equal share. 15As the Scriptures say,

"Those who gathered much did not have
    too much,
and those who gathered little did not have
    too little."

Exodus 16:18

Titus and His Companions

[16]I thank God because he gave Titus the same love for you that I have. [17]Titus agreed to do what we asked. In fact, he himself wanted very much to visit you. [18]We are sending with Titus the brother who is praised by all the churches. He is praised because of his service to the Good News. [19]Also, he was chosen by the churches to go with us when we take this gift. We are doing this service to bring honour[a] to the Lord and to show that we really want to help.

[20]We are being careful so that no one will criticize us about the way we are caring for this large gift. [21]We are trying to do what is right. We want to do what the Lord accepts as right and also what people think is right.

[22]Also, we are sending with them our brother who is always ready to help. He has proved this to us in many ways. And he wants to help even more now because he has much faith in you. [23]Now about Titus—he is my partner. He is working together with me to help you. And about the other brothers—they are sent from the churches, and they bring honour to Christ. [24]So show these men that you really have love. Show them why we are proud of you. Then all the churches can see it.

Your Giving Is a Blessing

9 I really don't need to write to you about this help for God's people. [2]I know that you want to help. I have been boasting about you to the people in Macedonia. I told them that you people in Achaia have been ready to give since last year. And your desire to give has made most of the people here ready to give also. [3]But I am sending these brothers to you. I don't want our boasting about you in this to be for nothing. I want you to be ready just as I said you would be. [4]If any of those from Macedonia come with me, and they find that you are not ready, we will be ashamed. We will be ashamed that we were so sure of you. And you will be ashamed too! [5]So I thought that I should ask these brothers to go to you before we do. They will help in getting together the generous gift you promised. Then it will be ready when we come, and it will be seen as a blessing you are giving, not as something you were forced to do.

[6]Remember this: the one who plants few seeds will have a small harvest. But the one who plants a lot will have a big harvest. [7]Each one of you should give what you have decided in your heart to give. You should not give if it makes you unhappy or if you feel forced to give. God loves those who are happy to give. [8]And God can give you more blessings than you need, and you will always have plenty of everything. You will have enough to give to every good work. [9]As the Scriptures say,

> "They were unselfish and gave to the poor.
> The good things they did will last forever."
>
> *Psalm 112:9*

[10]God is the one who gives seed to those who plant, and he gives bread for food. And God will give you spiritual seed and make that seed grow. He will produce a great harvest from your goodness. [11]God will make you rich in every way so that you can always give freely. And your giving through us will make people give thanks to God.

INSIGHT

Giving willingly and generously is one way that we can really stand out from the crowd. Most of the time our culture tells us to hoard stuff for ourselves and look after "number one". God's economy is the opposite – he says the more you give, the more you will be blessed.

2 Corinthians 9:6–7

[12]The service you are offering helps God's people with their needs, but that is not all it does. It is also bringing more and more thanks to God. [13]This service is a proof of your faith, and people will praise God because of it. They will praise God that you freely share what you have with them and with all people. They will praise him because they see you following the Good News about Christ that you openly accepted. [14]And when they pray, they will wish they could be with you. They will feel this way because of the great grace that God gave you. [15]Thanks be to God for his gift that is too wonderful to describe.

Paul Defends His Ministry

10 I, Paul, am begging you with the gentleness and the kindness of Christ. Some say that I am bold when I am writing to you from a distance, but not when I am there with you. [2]They think the reasons for what we do are the same as those of the world. I plan to be very bold against those people when I come. I hope I will not need to use that same boldness with you. [3]We live in this world, but we don't fight our battles in the same way the world does. [4]The weapons we

[a] **8:19 honour** Or "glory". See "GLORY" in the Word List.

use are not human ones. Our weapons have power from God and can destroy the enemy's strong places. We destroy people's arguments, [5]and we tear down every proud idea that raises itself against the knowledge of God. We also capture every thought and make it give up and obey Christ. [6]We are ready to punish anyone there who does not obey, but first we want you to be fully obedient.

[7]You must look at the facts before you. If you feel sure you belong to Christ, you must remember that we belong to Christ the same as you do. [8]It may seem as though we boast too much about the authority the Lord gave us. But he gave us this authority to strengthen you, not to hurt you. So I will not be ashamed of whatever boasting we do. [9]I don't want you to think that I am trying to scare you with my letters. [10]Some people say, "Paul's letters are powerful and sound important, but when he is with us, he is weak and the worst speaker you have ever heard." [11]Those people should know this: when we are there with you, we will show the same power that we show now in our letters.

[12]We don't dare put ourselves in the same class with those who think they are so important. We don't compare ourselves to them. They use themselves to measure themselves, and they judge themselves by what they themselves are. This shows that they know nothing.

[13]But we will not boast about anything outside the work that was given us to do. We will limit our boasting to the work God gave us, but this work includes our work with you. [14]We would be boasting too much only if we had not already come to you. But we have come to you with the Good News about Christ. [15]We limit our boasting to the work that is ours. We don't boast about the work other people have done. We hope that your faith will continue to grow. We hope that you will help our work to grow much larger. [16]We want to tell the Good News in the areas beyond your city. We don't want to boast about work that has already been done in someone else's area. [17]"Whoever boasts should boast only about the Lord."[a] [18]What people say about themselves means nothing. What counts is whether the Lord says they have done well.

Paul and the False Apostles

11 I wish you would be patient with me even when I am a little foolish. But you are already patient with me. [2]I am jealous for you with a jealousy that comes from God. I promised

to give you to Christ. He must be your only husband. I want to give you to Christ to be his pure bride.[b] [3]But I am afraid that your minds will be led away from your true and pure following of Christ. This could happen just as Eve was tricked by that snake with his clever lies. [4]You seem to be quite patient with anyone who comes to you and tells you about a Jesus that is different from the Jesus we told you about. You seem very willing to accept a spirit or a message that is different from the Spirit and message that you received from us.

[5]I don't think that those "super apostles" are any better than I am. [6]It is true that I am not a trained speaker, but I do have knowledge. We have shown this to you clearly in every way.

[7]I did the work of telling God's Good News to you without pay. I humbled myself to make you important. Do you think that was wrong? [8]I accepted pay from other churches. I took their money so that I could serve you. [9]If I needed something when I was with you, I did not trouble any of you. The brothers who came from Macedonia gave me all that I needed. I did not allow myself to be a burden to you in any way. And I will never be a burden to you. [10]No one there in Achaia will stop me from boasting about that. I say this with the truth of Christ in me. [11]And why do I not burden you? Do you think it is because I don't love you? God knows that I love you.

[12]And I will continue doing what I am doing now, because I want to stop those people from having a reason to boast. They would like to say that the work they boast about is the same as ours. [13]They are false apostles, lying workers. They only pretend to be apostles of Christ. [14]That does not surprise us, because even Satan changes himself to look like an angel of light.[c] [15]So it does not surprise us if Satan's servants make themselves look like servants who work for what is right. But in the end those people will get the punishment they deserve.

Paul Tells About His Sufferings

[16]I tell you again: no one should think that I am a fool. But if you think I am a fool, then accept me as you would accept a fool. Then I can boast a little too. [17]But I am not talking the way the Lord would talk. I am boasting like a fool. [18]Others are boasting about their lives in the world. So I will boast too. [19]You are wise, so you will gladly be patient with fools! [20]I say this because you are even patient with someone who forces you to do things and uses you. You are patient with those

---

[a] **10:17** Quote from Jer. 9:24.
[b] **11:2** *bride* Literally, "virgin".
[c] **11:14** *angel of light* Messenger from God. The devil fools people so that they think he is from God.

who trick you, or think they are better than you or hit you in the face! [21]I am ashamed to say it, but we were too "weak" to do such things to you.

But if anyone dares to boast, I will too. (I am talking like a fool.) [22]Are those people Hebrews? So am I. Are they Israelites?[a] So am I. Are they from Abraham's family? So am I. [23]Are they serving Christ? I am serving him more. (I am crazy to talk like this.) I have worked much harder than they have. I have been in prison more often. I have been hurt more in beatings. I have been near death many times.

[24]Five times the Jews have given me their punishment of 39 lashes with a whip. [25]Three different times I was beaten with rods. Once I was almost killed with rocks. Three times I was in ships that were wrecked, and one of those times I spent the night and the next day in the sea. [26]In my constant travelling I have been in danger from rivers, from thieves, from my own people and from people who are not Jews. I have been in danger in cities, in places where no one lives and on the sea. And I have been in danger from people who pretend to be believers but are not.

[27]I have done hard and tiring work, and many times I did not sleep. I have been hungry and thirsty. Many times I have been without food. I have been cold and without clothes. [28]And there are many other problems. One of these is the care I have for all the churches. I worry about each group of believers every day. [29]I feel weak every time another person is weak. I feel deeply upset every time another person is led into sin.

[30]If I must boast, I will boast about the things that show I am weak. [31]God knows that I am not lying. He is the God and Father of the Lord Jesus, and he is to be praised forever. [32]When I was in Damascus, the governor under King Aretas wanted to arrest me, so he put guards around the city. [33]But some friends put me in a basket. Then they put the basket through a hole in the wall and lowered me down. So I escaped from the governor.

A Special Blessing in Paul's Life

12 There is more that I have to say about myself. It won't help, but I will talk now about visions and revelations from the Lord. [2]I know a man[b] in Christ who was taken up to the third heaven. This happened 14 years ago. I don't know if the man was in his body or out of his body, but God knows. [3-4]And I know that this man was taken up to paradise. I don't know if he was in his body or away from his body, but he heard things that he is not able to explain. He heard things that no one is allowed to tell. [5]I will boast about a man like that, but I will not boast about myself. I will boast only about my weaknesses.

[6]But if I wanted to say more about myself, I would not be a fool, because I would be telling the truth. But I won't say any more, because I don't want people to think more of me than what they see me do or hear me say.

[7]But I must not be too proud of the wonderful things that were shown to me. So a painful problem[c] was given to me—an angel from Satan, sent to make me suffer, so that I would not think that I am better than anyone else. [8]I begged the Lord three times to take this problem away from me. [9]But the Lord said, "My grace is all you need. Only when you are weak can everything be done completely by my power." So I will gladly boast about my weaknesses. Then Christ's power can stay in me. [10]Yes, I am glad to have weaknesses if they are for Christ. I am glad to be insulted and have hard times. I am glad when I am persecuted and have problems, because it is when I am weak that I am really strong.

Paul's Love for the Believers in Corinth

[11]I have been talking like a fool, but you made me do it. You people are the ones who should say good things about me. I am worth nothing, but those "super apostles" are not worth any more than I am! [12]When I was with you, I patiently did the things that prove I am an apostle— signs, wonders and miracles. [13]So you received everything that the other churches have received. Only one thing was different: I was not a burden to you. Forgive me for this!

[14]I am now ready to visit you for the third time, and I will not be a burden to you. I don't want any of the things you own. I only want you. Children should not have to save up to give to their parents. Parents should save to give to their children. [15]So I am happy to give everything I have for you. I will even give myself for you. If I love you more, will you love me less?

[16]It is clear that I was not a burden to you, but you think that I tricked you and used lies to catch you. [17]Did I cheat you by using any of the men I sent to you? You know I didn't. [18]I asked Titus to go to you, and I sent our brother with him. Titus did not cheat you, did he? No, you know that his actions and his attitude were the same as ours.

[19]Do you think that we have been defending ourselves to you all this time? No, we say these things in Christ and before God. You are our dear friends, and everything we do is to make you

---

[a] **11:22 Hebrews . . . Israelites** Other names for the Jewish people.
[b] **12:2 a man** In 12:2–5 Paul is probably talking about himself.
[c] **12:7 painful problem** Literally, "thorn in the flesh".

stronger. ²⁰I do this because I am afraid that when I come, you will not be what I want you to be. And I am afraid that I will not be what you want me to be. I am afraid that I will find arguing, jealousy, anger, selfish fighting, evil talk, gossip, pride and confusion there. ²¹I am afraid that when I come to you again, my God will make me humble before you. I may have to cry over the loss of some who sinned before. Many of them have still not changed their hearts to be sorry for their evil lives, their sexual sins and the shameful things they have done.

Final Warnings and Greetings

13 This will be my third time to visit you. And remember, "For every complaint there must be two or three people to say that they know it is true."ᵃ ²When I was with you the second time, I gave a warning to those who had sinned. I am not there now, but I am giving another warning to them and to anyone else who has sinned. When I come to you again, I will punish you. ³You want proof that Christ is speaking through me. My proof is that he is not weak in dealing with you but is showing his power among you. ⁴It is true that Christ was weak when he was killed on the cross, but he lives now by God's power. It is also true that we share his weakness, but in dealing with you, we will be alive in him by God's power.

⁵Look closely at yourselves. Test yourselves to see if you are living in the faith. Don't you realize that Christ Jesus is in you? Of course, if you fail the test—if you are not living in the faith—then Christ is not living in you. ⁶But I hope you will see that we have not failed the test. ⁷We pray to God that you will not do anything wrong. Our concern here is not for people to see that we have passed the test in our work with you. Our main concern is that you do what is right, even if it looks as if we have failed the test. ⁸We cannot do anything that is against the truth but only what promotes the truth. ⁹We are happy to be weak if you are strong. And this is what we pray—that your lives will be made completely right again. ¹⁰I'm writing this before I come so that when I am there I will not have to use my authority to punish you. The Lord gave me that authority to make you stronger, not to destroy you.

¹¹Now, brothers and sisters, be filled with joy. Try to make everything right, and do what I have asked you to do. Agree with each other, and live in peace. Then the God of love and peace will be with you.

¹²Give each other the special greeting of God's people.ᵇ All of God's holy people here send you their greetings.ᶜ

¹³I pray that you will enjoy the grace of the Lord Jesus Christ, the love of God and the fellowshipᵈ of the Holy Spirit.

ᵃ **13:1** Quote from Deut. 19:15.
ᵇ **13:12** *the special greeting of God's people* Literally, "a holy kiss".
ᶜ **13:12** Some translations number this verse as two verses, which makes the last verse 14.
ᵈ **13:13** *fellowship* This can mean a sharing or participation in the Holy Spirit or the loving association and unity among believers that is created by the Spirit.

Who

Written by Paul. He is writing to a group of churches in the region of Galatia, a region of present-day Turkey – probably the churches he set up during his first missionary journey (Acts 13:13 – 14:28).

When

It was probably written around AD 48, making it the first of Paul's letters and one of the earliest of the New Testament writings.

What

The theme is similar to that of Romans. It is apparent that many Jews felt that non-Jews becoming Christians should follow Jewish religious laws. Paul writes to combat these ideas. They need faith in Jesus, not outward ceremonies.

Galatia is a region. Paul is writing here to the churches in south Galatia that he had established on his first missionary journey – churches in Derbe, Lystra and Iconium.

Something has happened to these churches. In the short space of time since Paul left them they have been infiltrated by people who believe that all Christian men should follow Jewish religious laws and get circumcised. And the activities of this pressure group are not being felt just in Galatia – back in Antioch prominent "pillars" of the church like Peter are giving in to their pressure.

These people were also claiming that Paul was not a "proper" apostle, and that he was toning down the requirements of the Jewish law in order to make the Good News acceptable to non-Jews. Eventually there was to be a major council meeting which decided the issue in Paul's favour (Acts 15).

Paul's anger at what these people are saying is evident for all to see. For Paul, this isn't some side-issue – it's crucial to his message of grace. So he writes in very strong, passionate terms, asserting his right to be called an apostle and arguing that the Good News is a message of love and grace, not of rules and regulations. In what is his most strongly worded letter, Paul criticizes the Galatians for being foolish (3:1). He makes the case for freedom – not to do what we want, but to serve Christ (5:1–15).

QUICK TOUR ▷ GALATIANS

Only one Good News message 1:1–10
Authority from God 1:11–24
A bit of biography 2:1–21

Foolish people! 3:1–14
The purpose of the law 3:15 – 4:8
True freedom 5:1 – 6:10

"When someone belongs to Christ Jesus, it is not important if they are circumcised or not. The important thing is faith – the kind of faith that works through love."

Galatians 5:6

1 Greetings from Paul, an apostle. I was chosen to be an apostle, but not by any group or person here on earth. My authority came from none other than Jesus Christ and God the Father, who raised Jesus from death. ²Greetings also from all those in God's family who are with me.

To the churches in Galatia:*ᵃ*

³I pray that God our Father and the Lord Jesus Christ will be good to you and give you peace. ⁴Jesus gave himself for our sins to free us from this evil world we live in. This is what God our Father wanted. ⁵The glory belongs to God for ever and ever. Amen.

There Is Only One Good News Message

⁶A short time ago God chose you to follow him. He chose you through his grace that came through Christ. But now I am amazed that you are already turning away and believing something different from the Good News we told you. ⁷There is no other message that is the Good News, but some people are confusing you. They want to change the Good News about Christ. ⁸We told you the true Good News message. So anyone who tells you a different message should be condemned—even if it's one of us or even an angel from heaven! ⁹I said this before. Now I say it again: you have already accepted the Good News. Anyone who tells you another way to be saved should be condemned!

¹⁰Now do you think I am trying to make people accept me? No, God is the one I am trying to please. Am I trying to please people? If I wanted to please people, I would not be a servant of Christ.

Paul's Authority Is From God

¹¹Brothers and sisters, I want you to know that the Good News message I told you was not made up by anyone. ¹²I did not get my message from any other human. The Good News is not something I learned from other people. Jesus Christ himself gave it to me. He showed me the Good News that I should tell people.

¹³You have heard about my past life in the Jewish religion. I persecuted the church of God very much. I tried to destroy his people. ¹⁴I was becoming a leader in the Jewish religion. I did better than most other Jews my own age. I tried harder than anyone else to follow the traditions we got from our ancestors.

¹⁵But God had special plans for me even before I was born. So he chose me through his grace. It pleased him ¹⁶to let me see and know his Son so that I could tell the Good News about him to the non-Jewish people. I immediately prepared to do this work without asking for advice or help from anyone. ¹⁷I did not go to Jerusalem to see those who were apostles before I was. Instead, I went away to Arabia. Later, I went back to the city of Damascus.

INSIGHT

The word "Gentile" is often used to refer to anyone who is not ethnically Jewish. It would have been incredible in Paul's day to think that God had any plan at all for non-Jews but Paul is saying here that salvation is now available to everyone (both Jews and Gentiles) through Jesus.
Galatians 1:15–16

---

¹⁸Three years later I went to Jerusalem to meet Peter.*ᵇ* I stayed with him for 15 days. ¹⁹I met no other apostles—only James, the brother of the Lord. ²⁰God knows there is nothing untrue in any of this. ²¹Later, I went to the areas of Syria and Cilicia.

²²No one in any of Christ's churches in Judea had ever met me before. ²³They had only heard this about me: "This man was persecuting us. But now he is telling people about the same faith that he once tried to destroy." ²⁴These believers praised God because of me.

INSIGHT

Paul often travelled with Barnabas, a Jewish Christian, and Titus, a non-Jewish Christian. This pattern of spiritual mentors/disciples and spiritual parents/children is seen throughout the Bible.
Galatians 2:1

The Other Apostles Accepted Paul

2 After 14 years I went back to Jerusalem with Barnabas and took Titus with me. ²I went there because God showed me that I should go. I explained to them the message that I tell the non-Jewish people. I also met alone with those who were considered to be the leaders. I wanted to be

---

ᵃ **1:2** *Galatia* Probably the area where Paul began churches on his first missionary trip. Read Acts 13 and 14.
ᵇ **1:18** *Peter* Literally, "Cephas", the Aramaic name for Peter, one of Jesus' twelve apostles. Both names mean "rock". Also in 2:9,11,14.

TRUTH ACHE

Those giddy Galatians were in a muddle. They'd heard the Good News about Jesus but their hazy heads were in a spin over wacky teaching from preachers who said there were rules to being a follower of Christ. Don't do this. Don't do that. It didn't sound like freedom at all.

As if that wasn't enough, these dodgy teachers called Paul a fraud. So Paul gets straight down to sorting out truth from lies. The heat was on in southern Galatia.

DIG IN
READ Galatians 1:1–5

- How does Paul start the letter? Why do you think he's so keen to get straight down to talking about Jesus?
- What core truths about Jesus does Paul want to get across? What has Jesus done for us and why is this such Good News?

Hear all about it! Hear all about it! It's the best news you'll ever hear. Jesus has saved us from sin. He's our Lord and our Saviour forever. That's the Good News. That's the truth. No more and no less. But some of these wacky teachers were saying the Galatians still had to obey the old law to be saved. So Paul says: No! That's a dodgy truth extraction!

READ Galatians 1:6–10

- What is Paul astonished about in verse 6?
- What does he mean when he says they've turned to a different Good News message? There's only one, isn't there?
- Look ahead to Galatians 3:2–4 and 4:8–10. What kind of teaching were the Galatians hearing that just wasn't true? If they believed it, how would it change the way they thought about themselves and what Jesus had done for them?

Paul gets tough on those dodgy truth extractors. He twice says they should be "condemned" (Galatians 1:8–9). It's clear he wants the churches in Galatia to believe the real truth about Jesus. Only the truth would set them free.

- Why is Paul so harsh on those who preach a dodgy Good News message (v.8)?
- How do we know Paul's message is the right one (v.10)?

DIG THROUGH

- How can you tell if someone is teaching you a misleading or dodgy Good News message today?
- What rules are there today that people try to add in to the message?
- How would it affect your friendships, confidence and identity as a Christian if you turned to anything other than the real Good News message?
- How can you keep yourself (and other Christian friends) from believing stuff that doesn't bring the real freedom of the true Good News message?

DIG DEEPER

- For more info on how to know the truth when you hear it check out 1 Corinthians 15:1–4 and 1 Thessalonians 5:21.
- Paul also goes into more detail about the real Good News message in Galatians 1:11 – 2:10. See if you can spot
  » who the message is from.
  » what the message is about and what it isn't.

THE BIG DEAL

Our man Paul is back on the case. Having proved the point that he's preaching the real Good News message he gets right back to arguing why the Good News is big big news. Now it's time to talk technical. It's like the science bit in a TV ad for shampoo only this is a rinse and shine that keeps the "ming" out forever.

DIG IN
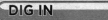

READ Galatians 2:15–16

The Jews thought they could be declared right with God by obeying the rules and regulations of the law.

- What *doesn't* make a person right in God's eyes? Why can't simply obeying laws make you right in God's eyes?
- What might "following the law" look like today? Why can't we be saved by following the law?

We may not often memorize Old Testament laws in church today, but that doesn't mean we don't often trust in law instead of Jesus. Whenever we're tempted to think that spending time with God, Bible studies or evangelism save us we're putting our faith in following the law. All these things are good, but just doing them – however regularly – can't save us.

- When are you most tempted to trust in things you do rather than trusting in Jesus?
- Read verse 16 again. What *does* make a person right in God's eyes?

Faith in Jesus is believing in his power to save us from sin and give us new life. Jesus took the punishment for our sin on the cross and rose again from death into new life. He said whoever believes in him will not be lost but have eternal life (John 3:16), which is the awesome promise for all who have faith in him.

READ Galatians 2:17–21

DIG THROUGH
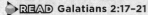

- With most deals you don't get something for nothing, but Jesus has already done everything required for you to know God. All you need to do is have faith in him. How does that make you feel? Take a moment to thank God.
- The false teachers took issue with the idea of "faith alone" because they thought it would mean people could just sin more (v.17). Does all this mean God doesn't care about how we live now? What does Paul say is sin (v.18)? What motivates you now to love others and take care of God's world?
- Knowing God has given us new life changes everything. How can you tell people about this Good News this week?

DIG DEEPER

- Want to read more about the best deal in the universe? See John 14:6, Galatians 5:1, Ephesians 2:1–10, Colossians 1:21–23 and 1 Peter 3:18.
- In many other religions you have to earn your salvation. Take a look at some of the things that believers of other religions are required to do and thank God that all he requires of you is faith.

sure we were in agreement so that my past work and the work I do now would not be wasted.

[3]Titus, who was with me, is a Greek. But these leaders still did not force him to be circumcised. [4]We needed to talk about these problems, because some who pretended to be our brothers had come into our group secretly. They came in like spies to find out about the freedom we have in Christ Jesus. They wanted to make us slaves, [5]but we did not agree with anything those false brothers wanted. We wanted the truth of the Good News to continue for you.

[6]Those men who were considered to be important did not change the Good News message I tell people. (It doesn't matter to me if they were "important" or not. To God everyone is the same.) [7]But these leaders saw that God had given me a special work, the same as Peter. God gave Peter the work of telling the Good News to the Jews. But God gave me the work of telling the Good News to the non-Jewish people. [8]God gave Peter the power to work as an apostle for the Jewish people. God gave me the power to work as an apostle too, but for those who are not Jews. [9]James, Peter and John seemed to be the leaders. And they saw that God had given me this special gift of ministry, so they accepted Barnabas and me. They said to us, "We agree that you should go to those who are not Jews, and we will go to the Jews." [10]They asked us to do only one thing—to remember to help those who are poor. And this was something that I really wanted to do.

Paul Shows That Peter Was Wrong

[11]When Peter came to Antioch, he did something that was not right. I stood against him, because he was wrong. [12]This is what happened: When Peter first came to Antioch, he ate and associated with the non-Jewish people. But when some Jewish men came from James, Peter separated himself from the non-Jews. He stopped eating with them because he was afraid of those Jews who say that even non-Jewish believers must be circumcised. [13]So Peter was a hypocrite. The other Jewish believers joined with him, so they were hypocrites too. Even Barnabas was influenced by what these Jewish believers did. [14]They were not following the truth of the Good News. When I saw this, I spoke to Peter in front of everyone. I said, "Peter, you are a Jew, but you don't live like one. You live like someone who is not a Jew. So why are you trying to force those who are not Jewish to live like Jews?"

[15]We are Jews by birth. We were not born "sinners", as we call those who are not Jews. [16]But we know that no one is made right with God by following the law. It is trusting in[a] Jesus Christ that makes a person right with God. So we have put our faith in Christ Jesus, because we wanted to be made right with God. And we are right with him because we trusted in[b] Christ—not because we followed the law. I can say this because no one can be made right with God by following the law.

[17]We Jews came to Christ to be made right with God, so it is clear that we were sinners too. Does this mean that Christ makes us sinners? Of course not. [18]But I would be wrong to begin teaching again those things that I gave up. [19]It was the law itself that caused me to end my life under the law. I died to the law so that I could live for God. I have been nailed to the cross with Christ. [20]So I am not the one living now—it is Christ living in me. I still live in my body, but I live by faith in[c] the Son of God. He is the one who loved me and gave himself to save me. [21]I am not the one destroying the meaning of God's grace. If following the law is how people are made right with God, then Christ did not have to die.

God's Blessing Comes Through Faith

3 You people in Galatia are so foolish! Why do I say this? Because I told you very clearly about the death of Jesus Christ on the cross. But now it seems as though you have let someone use their magical powers to make you forget. [2]Tell me this one thing: how did you receive the Spirit? Did you receive the Spirit by following the law? No, you received the Spirit because you heard the message about Jesus and believed it. [3]You began your life in Christ with the Spirit. Now do you try to complete it by your own power? That is foolish. [4]You have experienced many things. Were all those experiences wasted? I hope they were not wasted! [5]Does God give you the Spirit because you follow the law? Does God work miracles among you because you follow the law? No, God gives you his Spirit and works miracles among you because you heard the message about Jesus and believed it.

[6]The Scriptures say the same thing about Abraham. "Abraham believed God, and because of this faith he was accepted as one who is right with God."[d] [7]So you should know that the true children of Abraham are those who have faith.

---

[a] **2:16** *trusting in* Or "the faithfulness of".
[b] **2:16** *because we trusted in* Or "through the faithfulness of".
[c] **2:20** *faith in* Or "the faithfulness of".
[d] **3:6** Quote from Gen. 15:6.

8The Scriptures explained what would happen in the future. These writings said that God would make the non-Jewish people right through their faith. God told this Good News to Abraham before it happened. God said to Abraham, "By blessing you, I will bless all people on earth."[a] 9Abraham believed this, and because he believed, he was blessed. All people who believe are blessed the same way Abraham was.

10But people who depend on following the law to make them right are under a curse. As the Scriptures say, "They must do everything that is written in the law. If they do not always obey, they are under a curse."[b] 11So it is clear that no one can be made right with God by the law. The Scriptures say, "The people God approves because of their faith will live forever."[c]

12The law does not depend on faith. No, it says that the only way a person will find life by the law is to obey its commands.[d] 13The law says we are under a curse for not always obeying it. But Christ took away that curse. He changed places with us and put himself under that curse. The Scriptures say, "Anyone who is hung on a tree[e] is under a curse."[f] 14Because of what Christ Jesus did, the blessing God promised to Abraham was given to all people. Christ died so that by believing in him we could have the Spirit that God promised.

The Law and the Promise

15Brothers and sisters, let me give you an example from everyday life. Think about an agreement that one person makes with another. After that agreement is made official, no one can stop it or add anything to it and no one can ignore it. 16God made promises to Abraham and his Descendant.[g] The Scripture does not say, "and to your descendants". That would mean many people. But it says, "and to your Descendant". That means only one, and that one is Christ. 17This is what I mean: The agreement that God gave to Abraham was made official long before the law came. The law came 430 years later. So the law could not take away the agreement and change God's promise.

18Can following the law give us the blessing God promised? If we could receive it by following the law, then it would not be God's promise that

brings it to us. But God freely gave his blessings to Abraham through the promise God made.

19So what was the law for? The law was given to show the wrong things people do. The law would continue until the special Descendant of Abraham came. This is the Descendant mentioned in the promise, which came directly from God. But the law was given through angels, and the angels used Moses as a mediator to give the law to the people. 20But when God gave the promise, there was no mediator, because a mediator is not needed when there is only one side, and God is one.[h]

The Purpose of the Law of Moses

21Does this mean that the law works against God's promises? Of course not. The law was never God's way of giving new life to people. If it were, then we could be made right with God by following the law. 22But this is not possible. The Scriptures put the whole world in prison under the control of sin, so that the only way for people to get what God promised would be through faith in[i] Jesus Christ. It is given to those who believe in him.

23Before this faith came, the law held us as prisoners. We had no freedom until God showed us the way of faith that was coming. 24I mean the law was the guardian in charge of us until Christ came. After he came, we could be made right with God through faith. 25Now that the way of faith has come, we no longer need the law to be our guardian.

26–27You were all baptized into Christ, and so you were all clothed with Christ. This shows that you are all children of God through faith in Christ Jesus. 28Now, in Christ, it doesn't matter if you are a Jew or a Greek, a slave or free, male or female. You are all the same in Christ Jesus. 29You belong to Christ, so you are Abraham's descendants. You get all of God's blessings because of the promise that God made to Abraham.

4 This is what I am saying: When young children inherit all that their father owned, they are still no different from his slaves. It doesn't matter that they own everything. 2While they are children, they must obey those who are chosen to care for them. But when they reach the age the

---

[a] **3:8** Quote from Gen. 12:3.
[b] **3:10** Quote from Deut. 27:26.
[c] **3:11** Quote from Hab. 2:4.
[d] **3:12** *the only way . . . commands* See Lev. 18:5.
[e] **3:13** *hung on a tree* Deut. 21:22–23 says that when a person was killed for doing wrong, his body was hung on a tree to show shame. Paul means that the cross of Jesus was like that.
[f] **3:13** Quote from Deut. 21:23.
[g] **3:16** *Descendant* Literally, "seed", which could also mean "family". In that case, it would refer to the one family of God in Christ.
[h] **3:20** Literally, "But the mediator is not of one, but God is one."
[i] **3:22** *faith in* Or "the faithfulness of".

father set, they are free. ³It is the same for us. We were once like children, slaves to the useless rules*ᵃ* of this world. ⁴But when the right time came, God sent his Son, who was born from a woman and lived under the law. ⁵God did this so that he could buy the freedom of those who were under the law. God's purpose was to make us his children.

⁶Since you are now God's children, he has sent the Spirit of his Son into your hearts. The Spirit cries out, "Abba,*ᵇ* Father." ⁷Now you are not slaves like before. You are God's children, and you will receive everything he promised his children.

Paul's Love for the Galatian Believers

⁸In the past you did not know God. You were slaves to gods that were not real. ⁹But now you know the true God. Really, though, it is God who knows you. So why do you turn back to the same kind of weak and useless rules you followed before? Do you want to be slaves to those things again? ¹⁰⁻¹¹It worries me that you follow teachings about special days, months, seasons and years. I fear that my work for you has been wasted.

¹²Brothers and sisters, I became like you. So please become like me. You were very good to me before. ¹³You know that I came to you the first time because I was sick. That was when I told the Good News to you. ¹⁴My sickness was a burden to you, but you did not stop showing me respect or make me leave. Instead, you welcomed me as if I were an angel from God. You accepted me as if I were Jesus Christ himself! ¹⁵You were very happy then. Where is that joy now? I can say without a doubt that you would have done anything to help me. If it had been possible, you would have taken out your own eyes and given them to me. ¹⁶Am I now your enemy because I tell you the truth?

¹⁷Those people*ᶜ* are working hard to persuade you, but this is not good for you. They want to persuade you to turn against us and work hard for them. ¹⁸It is good for you to work hard, of course, if it is for something good. That's something you should do whether I am there or not. ¹⁹My little children, I am in pain again over you, like a mother giving birth. I will feel this pain until people can look at you and see Christ. ²⁰I wish I could be with you now. Then maybe I could change the way I am talking to you. Now I don't know what to do about you.

The Example of Hagar and Sarah

²¹Some of you people want to be under the law. Tell me, do you know what the law says? ²²The Scriptures say that Abraham had two sons. The mother of one son was a slave woman, and the mother of the other son was a free woman. ²³Abraham's son from the slave woman was born in the normal human way. But the son from the free woman was born because of the promise God made to Abraham.

²⁴This true story makes a picture for us. The two women are like the two agreements between God and his people. One agreement is the law that God made on Mount Sinai. The people who are under this agreement are like slaves. The mother named Hagar is like that agreement. ²⁵So Hagar is like Mount Sinai in Arabia. She is a picture of the earthly Jewish city of Jerusalem. This city is a slave, and all its people are slaves to the law. ²⁶But the heavenly Jerusalem that is above is like the free woman, who is our mother. ²⁷The Scriptures say,

"Be happy, woman—you who cannot have
        children.
    Be glad you never gave birth.
Shout and cry with joy!
    You never felt those labour pains.
The woman who is alone*ᵈ* will have more
        children
    than the woman who has a husband."
                                                    Isaiah 54:1

²⁸My brothers and sisters, you are children who were born because of God's promise, just as Isaac was. ²⁹But the other son of Abraham, who was born in the normal way, caused trouble for the one who was born by the power of the Spirit. It is the same today. ³⁰But what do the Scriptures say? "Throw out the slave woman and her son! The son of the free woman will receive everything his father has, but the son of the slave woman will receive nothing."*ᵉ* ³¹So, my brothers and sisters, we are not children of the slave woman. We are children of the free woman.

Keep Your Freedom

5 We have freedom now, because Christ made us free. So stand strong in that freedom. Don't go back into slavery again. ²Listen! I, Paul, tell you that if you start following the law by being circumcised, then Christ cannot help you. ³Again, I warn everyone: if you allow yourselves

---

ᵃ **4:3 rules** Or "powers". Also in verse 9.
ᵇ **4:6 Abba** An Aramaic word that was used by Jewish children as a name for their father.
ᶜ **4:17 Those people** The false teachers who were bothering the believers in Galatia. See Gal. 1:7.
ᵈ **4:27 woman . . . alone** This means her husband has left her.
ᵉ **4:30** Quote from Gen. 21:10.

FRUITS YOU, SIR

Paul's standing in the fruit and veg shop in Galatia. "Roll up! Roll up! Brand new fruit straight off the vine. It'll change your life. Lasts forever. Never mouldy. Nine for the price of none!"

In this passage we'll see how life with God's Spirit totally changes everything. Start smacking those lips, it's the fruit of the Spirit.

DIG IN
READ Galatians 5:16–18

You can't mix oil with water. Everybody knows that. But you can't mix the Spirit with the sinful self either ("sinful self" is Paul's way of saying "sinful human nature").

- How is life different when you walk by the Spirit?
- How does the Spirit help you to battle sin?

Think about it: if you are a Christian, everything changes when you have God working in your life. So why do most of us still struggle with sin?

READ Galatians 5:19–21
- What does it look like to live a life controlled by the sinful self?

It's not all wild orgies and drug-fuelled binges. Check out Paul's list in detail. Paul also talks about envy, anger, selfishness and hatred. If we're honest, isn't that stuff we're all tempted to dabble in from time to time?

- What things on this list challenge you the most?
- How can you change your attitudes and behaviour? We can only change by the Spirit's power, so why not ask God to help you live this new life, a life centred on godly things?
- Sometimes God gives us Christian friends to help us change and live as he wants. If you're struggling with something in particular, it's important to talk about it with someone you trust. Maybe you could chat to your youth leader or an older Christian friend.

READ Galatians 5:22–26
- What are the changes the Spirit brings into the lives of Christians?
- What makes fruit so good? Why is fruit such a good picture for the way God's Spirit works in people's lives?
- Which of these fruits do you want more of in your life? Ask God for his help.

DIG THROUGH

- When we walk by the Spirit, God is making us more like Jesus. How cool is that?
- How might God's Spirit bear fruit in your life this week? What difference should it make to those around you?
- In what ways can the Spirit working through Christians bring change to society?

DIG DEEPER

- Christians still struggle with sin. Check out Romans 8:1–17 to learn more about how God's Spirit helps us fight sin and temptation.
- For most of us changes in attitude and behaviour take time. To see more about the changes God's Spirit makes and the new life in the Spirit, check out 2 Corinthians 3:4–6 and Colossians 3:1–17.

to be circumcised, then you must follow the whole law. [4]If you try to be made right with God through the law, your life with Christ is finished—you have left God's grace. [5]I say this because our hope of being right with God comes through faith. And the Spirit helps us feel sure as we wait for that hope. [6]When someone belongs to Christ Jesus, it is not important if they are circumcised or not. The important thing is faith—the kind of faith that works through love.

[7]You were doing so well. Who caused you to stop following the truth? [8]It certainly wasn't the one who chose you. [9]Be careful! "Just a little yeast makes the whole batch of dough rise."[a] [10]I trust in the Lord that you will not believe those different ideas. Someone is trying to confuse you. Whoever it is will be punished.

[11]My brothers and sisters, I don't teach that a man must be circumcised. If I do teach circumcision, then why am I still being persecuted? If I still taught circumcision, then my message about the cross would not be a problem. [12]I wish those people who are bothering you would add castration[b] to their circumcision.

[13]My brothers and sisters, God chose you to be free. But don't use your freedom as an excuse to do what pleases your sinful selves. Instead, serve each other with love. [14]The whole law is made complete in this one command: "Love your neighbour[c] the same as you love yourself."[d] [15]If you continue hurting each other and tearing each other apart, be careful, or you will completely destroy each other.

The Spirit and Human Nature

[16]So I tell you, live the way the Spirit leads you. Then you will not do the evil things your sinful self wants. [17]The sinful self wants what is against the Spirit, and the Spirit wants what is against the sinful self. They are always fighting against each other, so that you don't do what you really want to do. [18]But if you let the Spirit lead you, you are not under law.[e]

[19]The wrong things the sinful self does are clear: committing sexual sin, being morally bad, doing all kinds of shameful things, [20]worshipping false gods, taking part in witchcraft, hating people, causing trouble, being jealous, angry or selfish, causing people to argue and divide into separate groups, [21]being filled with envy, getting drunk, having wild parties and doing other things like this. I warn you now as I warned you before: the people who do these things will not have a part in God's kingdom. [22]But the fruit that the Spirit produces in a person's life is love, joy, peace, patience, kindness, goodness, faithfulness, [23]gentleness and self-control. There is no law against these kinds of things. [24]Those who belong to Christ Jesus have crucified their sinful self. They have given up their old selfish feelings and the evil things they wanted to do. [25]We get our new life from the Spirit, so we should follow the Spirit. [26]We must not feel proud and boast about ourselves. We must not cause trouble for each other or be jealous of each other.

Help Each Other

6 Brothers and sisters, someone in your group might do something wrong. You who are following the Spirit should go to the one who is sinning. Help make that person right again, and do it in a gentle way. But be careful, because you might be tempted to sin too. [2]Help each other with your troubles. When you do this, you are obeying the law of Christ. [3]If you think you are too important to do this, you are only fooling yourself. [4]Don't compare yourself with others. Just look at your own work to see if you have done anything to be proud of. [5]You must each accept the responsibilities that are yours.

Never Stop Doing Good

[6]Whoever is being taught God's word should share the good things they have with the one who is teaching them.

---

[a] **5:9** *"Just . . . rise"* A proverb meaning that a small thing (like a little wrong teaching) can make a big problem or that just one person can have a bad influence on the whole group.
[b] **5:12** *castration* Paul uses a word that means "to cut off" in place of "circumcision", which means "to cut around", to show how angry he is at the false teachers for forcing non-Jewish men to be circumcised.
[c] **5:14** *your neighbour* Or "others". Jesus' teaching in Luke 10:25–37 makes clear that this includes anyone in need.
[d] **5:14** Quote from Lev. 19:18.
[e] **5:18** *law* Here, a law system, like the Law of Moses.

[7]If you think you can fool God, you are only fooling yourselves. You will harvest what you plant. [8]If you live to satisfy your sinful self, the harvest you will get from that will be eternal death. But if you live to please the Spirit, your harvest from the Spirit will be eternal life. [9]We must not get tired of doing good. We will receive our harvest of eternal life at the right time. We must not give up. [10]When we have the opportunity to do good to anyone, we should do it. But we should give special attention to those who are in the family of believers.

INSIGHT

Paul usually dictated his letters to a friend, but here he says that he is writing in his own hand in large letters. Some think that this was because he had poor eyesight but it was probably because he wanted to emphasize some of his main points in summary.

Galatians 6:11

Paul Ends His Letter

[11]This is my own handwriting. You can see how big the letters are. [12]Those men who are trying to force you to be circumcised are only doing it so that their people will accept them. They are afraid they will be persecuted if they follow only the cross[a] of Christ. [13]They are circumcised, but they don't obey the law themselves. They want you to be circumcised so that they can boast about what they did to you.

[14]I hope I will never boast about things like that. The cross of our Lord Jesus Christ is my only reason for boasting. Through Jesus' death on the cross the world is dead[b] to me, and I am dead to the world. [15]It doesn't matter if anyone is circumcised or not. The only thing that matters is this new life we have from God.[c] [16]Peace and mercy to those who follow this rule—to all God's people.[d]

[17]So don't give me any more trouble. I have scars on my body that show[e] I belong to Jesus.

[18]My brothers and sisters, I pray that the grace of our Lord Jesus Christ will be with each one of you. Amen.

---

[a] **6:12** *cross* Paul uses the cross as a picture of the Good News, the story of Christ's death to pay for people's sins. The cross (Christ's death) was God's way to save people. Also in verse 14.

[b] **6:14** *is dead* Literally, "has been crucified".

[c] **6:15** *this new life . . . God* Or "being the new people God has made".

[d] **6:16** *all God's people* Literally, "the Israel of God".

[e] **6:17** *scars . . . show* Many times Paul was beaten by people who tried to stop him from teaching about Christ. The scars were from these beatings.

Who Paul, writing to the churches in and around Ephesus, which was a wealthy port city in the Roman province of Asia (modern-day Turkey). They were founded on his third missionary journey.

When Paul was probably writing this letter from prison in Rome in the early 60s AD (Acts 28). He wrote it at about the same time as Colossians and Philemon.

What The letter to the churches at Ephesus brings together some of the major themes of Paul's teaching, as a kind of summary of his thoughts. The letter seems to have been intended as a general letter to several churches.

Ephesians emphasizes especially the need for unity. Christ has brought us all back from the dead. He is our peace. Followers of Jesus need to recognize that we are all joined together and that we should all work for and support one another. Christ has brought together Jew and non-Jew, we all have our role to play and no one is more important than another.

The overriding theme in this letter is the way in which God has planned all this from the start. Christ has died to give us freedom (1:7–8), and the same Christ now sits with God and rules over all things. Christ has given us life and he has given us a future (2:4–6). This is God's gift to us. There is nothing we can do to earn it.

Ephesus was home to the temple of Artemis – one of the seven wonders of the ancient world. It was a city fascinated with pagan magic and the occult (Acts 19:19). This helps to explain Paul's emphasis on the need for followers of Jesus to live light-filled lives and to "Have no part in the things that people in darkness do" (5:11).

Paul has an almost breathless tone of wonder at God's kindness, wisdom and love. He talks of "how wide, how long, how high and how deep" the love of Christ is, a love which is "greater than anyone can ever know" (3:18–19). It is his power that is at work in us.

QUICK TOUR ▶ **EPHESIANS**

"There is one body and one Spirit, and God chose you to have one hope. There is one Lord, one faith and one baptism. There is one God and Father of us all, who rules over everyone. He works through all of us and in all of us."

Ephesians 4:4–6

1 Greetings from Paul, an apostle for Christ Jesus. I am an apostle because that is what God wanted.

To God's holy people in Ephesus,[a] believers who belong to Christ Jesus.

²Grace and peace to you from God our Father and the Lord Jesus Christ.

Spiritual Blessings in Christ

³Praise be to the God and Father of our Lord Jesus Christ. In Christ, God has given us every spiritual blessing in heaven. ⁴In Christ, he chose us before the world was made. He chose us in love to be his holy people—people who could stand before him without any fault. ⁵And before the world was made, God decided to make us his own children through Jesus Christ. This was what God wanted, and it pleased him to do it. ⁶And this brings praise to God because of his wonderful grace. God gave that grace to us freely. He gave us that grace in Christ, the one he loves.

⁷In Christ we are made free by his blood sacrifice. We have forgiveness of sins because of God's rich grace. ⁸God gave us that grace fully and freely. With full wisdom and understanding, ⁹he let us know his secret plan. This was what God wanted, and he planned to do it through Christ. ¹⁰God's goal was to finish his plan when the right time came. He planned that all things in heaven and on earth be joined together with Christ as the head.

¹¹In Christ we were chosen to be God's people. God had already planned for us to be his people, because that is what he wanted. And he is the one who makes everything agree with what he decides and wants. ¹²We Jews were the first to hope in Christ. And we were chosen so that we would bring praise to God in all his glory. ¹³It is the same with you. You heard the true message, the Good News about the way God saves you. When you heard that Good News, you believed in Christ. And in Christ, God put his special mark on you by giving you the Holy Spirit that he promised. ¹⁴The Spirit is the first payment that guarantees we will get all that God has for us. Then we will enjoy complete freedom as people who belong to him. The goal for all of us is the praise of God in all his glory.

Paul's Prayer

¹⁵⁻¹⁶That is why I always remember you in my prayers and thank God for you. I have done this ever since I heard about your faith in the Lord Jesus and your love for all of God's people. ¹⁷I always pray to the great and glorious Father, the God of our Lord Jesus Christ. I pray that he will give you the Spirit, who will let you know truths about God and help you understand them, so that you will know him better.

¹⁸I pray that God will open your minds to see his truth. Then you will know the hope that he has chosen us to have. You will know that the blessings God has promised his holy people are rich and glorious. ¹⁹And you will know that God's power is very great for us who believe. It is the same as the mighty power ²⁰he used to raise Christ from death and put him at his right side in the heavenly places. ²¹He put Christ over all rulers, authorities, powers and kings. He gave him authority over everything that has power in this world or in the next world. ²²God put everything under Christ's power and made him head over everything for the church. ²³The church is Christ's body. It is filled with him. He makes everything complete in every way.

From Death to Life

2 In the past you were spiritually dead because of your sins and the things you did against God. ²Yes, in the past your lives were full of those sins. You lived the way the world lives, following the ruler of the evil powers[b] that are above the earth. That same spirit is now working in those who refuse to obey God. ³In the past all of us lived like that, trying to please our sinful selves. We did all the things our bodies and minds wanted. Like everyone else in the world, we deserved to suffer God's anger just because of the way we were.

⁴But God is rich in mercy, and he loved us very much. ⁵We were spiritually dead because of all we had done against him. But he gave us new life together with Christ. (You have been saved by God's grace.) ⁶Yes, it is because we are a part of Christ Jesus that God raised us from death and seated us together with him in the heavenly places. ⁷God did this so that his kindness to us who belong to Christ Jesus would clearly show for all time to come the amazing richness of his grace.

⁸I mean that you have been saved by grace because you believed. You did not save yourselves; it was a gift from God. ⁹You are not saved by the things you have done, so there is nothing to boast about. ¹⁰God has made us what we are. In Christ Jesus, God made us new people so that we would spend our lives doing the good things he had already planned for us to do.

---

[a] **1:1 in Ephesus** Some Greek copies do not have the words "in Ephesus".
[b] **2:2 ruler of the evil powers** See "SATAN" in the Word List.

WHAT'S THE POINT?

What do you think the purpose of the universe is? What is the purpose of your life? Would it be good to know that God has an unstoppable plan for his people and for this world?

DIG IN

READ Ephesians 1:1–23

- Look at verses 1–11. Whose name keeps coming up? Why?
- Why not get out a pen and paper and jot down all the "spiritual blessings" that Paul says we have in Jesus Christ.

Did you notice how often "Christ" came up and that we have all these spiritual blessings because of him? There is no spiritual blessing or good thing outside of Christ.

- Read verses 9–11. What is God's plan? (Clue: there are two main things.)
- How do you think Jesus' death and resurrection shows that God is accomplishing his plan?

If you've read other Bible passages, you may know that in the beginning God made a perfect world. But God's people going their own way with disastrous consequences spoilt it – humanity was made distant from God and distant from one another.

Paul tells us that since before the beginning God had planned to bring everything and everyone back together as one in Jesus, with him as head of everything. This is the purpose of life and the universe – to join everything together in Jesus Christ! How does that make you feel?

- Look at verses 21–23. What has God done for Christ?
- What is Christ ruler over?

Does it seem hard to believe that Christ rules over everything and everyone? That means he's in charge of everyone from your teachers to politicians, presidents and kings. And you! Isn't it good to know that despite what it might look like right now, Christ is in charge and God's plan is that one day everyone will know it?

- What image does Paul use to describe the relationship of Christ with the church?

It may seem a complicated idea but it comes up a lot in Ephesians – Jesus Christ is the head and the church is the body. Think how close that makes our relationship with him – he's as attached to us as your head is to your body! When Paul talks about the church, he is not just talking about the building at the end of your street, but about everyone that follows Jesus. Jesus is in charge of the church and if you love Jesus you are part of this amazing plan for the church, and you belong to him, along with everyone else.

DIG THROUGH

- How exciting that God has got this plan to join everything together through Jesus. And nothing will stop him. Thank him for that!
- Do you ever act as if life revolves around you? What about when things don't go your way? Why not ask God to help you remember that life and the universe is about Jesus?
- Think about those spiritual blessings – which one excites you the most? Thank God that his plans for the universe include blessing you!

DIG DEEPER

- The idea that God's plan is for everyone and everything to come together as one under Christ is a central theme of Ephesians. Look out for it as you read on.
- A key part of God's plan to bring about unity under Christ is to get people who wouldn't normally hang out together to be as one in church. Check out Ephesians 2:11–22.

One in Christ

[11]You were not born as Jews. You are the people the Jews call "uncircumcised".[a] Those Jews who call you "uncircumcised" call themselves "circumcised". (Their circumcision is only something they themselves do to their bodies.) [12]Remember that in the past you were without Christ. You were not citizens of Israel, and you did not know about the agreements[b] with the promises that God made to his people. You had no hope, and you did not know God. [13]Yes, at one time you were far away from God, but now you are united with Christ Jesus and you have been brought near to God through the blood sacrifice of Christ.

[14]Christ is the reason we are now at peace. He made us Jews and you who are not Jews one people. We were separated by a wall of hate that stood between us, but Christ broke down that wall. By giving his own body, [15]Christ ended the law with its many commands and rules. His purpose was to make the two groups become one in him. By doing this he would make peace. [16]Through the cross Christ ended the hate between the two groups. And after they became one body, he wanted to bring them both back to God. He did this with his death on the cross. [17]Christ came and brought the message of peace to you non-Jews who were far away from God. And he brought that message of peace to those who were near to God. [18]Yes, through Christ we all have the right to come to the Father in one Spirit.

[19]So now you non-Jewish people are not strangers or foreigners, but you are citizens together with God's holy people. You belong to God's family. [20]You believers are like a building that God owns. That building was built on the foundation that the apostles and prophets prepared. Christ Jesus himself is the most important stone[c] in that building. [21]The whole building is joined together in Christ, and he makes it grow and become a holy temple[d] in the Lord. [22]And in Christ you are being built together with his other people. You are being made into a place where God lives through the Spirit.

Paul's Work for the Non-Jewish People

3 So I, Paul, am a prisoner because I serve Christ Jesus for you who are not Jews. [2]Surely you know that God gave me this work through his grace to help you. [3]God let me know his secret plan by showing it to me. I have already written a little about this. [4]And if you read what I wrote, you can see that I understand the secret truth about Christ. [5]People who lived in other times were not told that secret truth. But now, through the Spirit, God has made it known to his holy apostles and prophets. [6]And this is the secret truth: that by accepting the Good News, those who are not Jews will share with the Jews in the blessings God has for his people. They are part of the same body, and they share in the promise God made through Christ Jesus.

[7]By God's special gift of grace, I became a servant to tell that Good News. He gave me that grace by using his power. [8]I am the least important of all God's people. But he gave me this gift—to tell the non-Jewish people the Good News about the riches Christ has. These riches are too great to understand fully. [9]And God gave me the work of telling all people about the plan for his secret truth. That secret truth has been hidden in him since the beginning of time. He is the one who created everything. [10]His purpose was that all the rulers and powers in the heavenly places will now know the many different ways he shows his wisdom. They will know this because of the church. [11]This agrees with the plan God had since the beginning of time. He did what he planned, and he did it through Christ Jesus our Lord. [12]In Christ we come before God with freedom and without fear. We can do this because of our faith in Christ. [13]So I ask you not to be discouraged because of what is happening to me. My sufferings are for your benefit—for your honour and glory.

---

[a] **2:11 uncircumcised** People not having the mark of circumcision like the Jews have.

[b] **2:12 agreements** The agreements with special promises that God gave at various times to people in the Old Testament. See "AGREEMENT" in the Word List.

[c] **2:20 most important stone** Literally, "cornerstone". The first and most important stone in a building.

[d] **2:21 temple** God's house—the place where God's people worship him. Here, it means that believers are the spiritual temple where God lives.

The Love of Christ

[14]So I bow in prayer before the Father. [15]Every family in heaven and on earth gets its true name from him. [16]I ask the Father with his great glory to give you the power to be strong in your spirits. He will give you that strength through his Spirit. [17]I pray that Christ will live in your hearts because of your faith. I pray that your life will be strong in love and be built on love. [18]And I pray that you and all God's holy people will have the power to understand the greatness of Christ's love—how wide, how long, how high and how deep that love is. [19]Christ's love is greater than anyone can ever know, but I pray that you will be able to know that love. Then you can be filled with everything God has for you.

[20]With God's power working in us, he can do much, much more than anything we can ask or think of. [21]To him be glory in the church and in Christ Jesus for all time, for ever and ever. Amen.

The Unity of the Body

4 So, as a prisoner for the Lord, I beg you to live the way God's people should live, because he chose you to be his. [2]Always be humble and gentle. Be patient and accept each other with love. [3]You are joined together with peace through the Spirit. Do all you can to continue as you are, letting peace hold you together. [4]There is one body and one Spirit, and God chose you to have one hope. [5]There is one Lord, one faith and one baptism. [6]There is one God and Father of us all, who rules over everyone. He works through all of us and in all of us.

[7]Christ gave each one of us a special gift. Everyone received what he wanted to give them. [8]That is why the Scriptures say,

> "He went up high into the sky;
>   he took prisoners with him,
>   and he gave gifts to people."
>
> *Psalm 68:18*

[9]When it says, "He went up," what does it mean? It means that he first came down low to earth. [10]So Christ came down, and he is the same one who went up. He went up above the highest heaven in order to fill everything with himself. [11]And that same Christ gave these gifts to people: he made some to be apostles, some to be prophets, some to go and tell the Good News, and some to care for and teach God's people.[a] [12]Christ gave these gifts to prepare God's holy people for the work of serving, to make the body of Christ

stronger. [13]This work must continue until we are all joined together in what we believe and in what we know about the Son of God. Our goal is to become like a full-grown man—to look just like Christ and have all his perfection.

[14]Then we will no longer be like babies. We will not be people who are always changing like a ship that the waves carry one way and then another. We will not be influenced by every new teaching we hear from people who are trying to deceive us—those who make clever plans and use every kind of trick to fool others into following the wrong way. [15]No, we will speak the truth with love. We will grow to be like Christ in every way. He is the head, [16]and the whole body depends on him. All the parts of the body are joined and held together, with each part doing its own work. This causes the whole body to grow and to be stronger in love.

The Way You Should Live

[17]I have something from the Lord to tell you. I warn you: don't continue living like those who don't believe. Their thoughts are worth nothing. [18]They have no understanding, and they know nothing because they refuse to listen. So they cannot have the life that God gives. [19]They have lost their feeling of shame and use their lives to do what is morally wrong. More and more they want to do all kinds of evil. [20]But that way of life is nothing like what you learned when you came to know Christ. [21]I know that you heard about him, and in him you were taught the truth. Yes, the truth is in Jesus. [22]You were taught to leave your old self. This means that you must stop living the evil way you lived before. That old self gets worse and worse, because people are fooled by the evil they want to do. [23]You must be made new in your hearts and in your thinking. [24]Be that new person who was made to be like God, truly good and pleasing to him.

[25]So you must stop telling lies. "You must always speak the truth to each other,"[b] because we all belong to each other in the same body. [26]"When you are angry, don't let that anger make you sin,"[c] and don't stay angry all day. [27]Don't give the devil a way to defeat you. [28]Whoever has been stealing must stop it and start working. They must use their hands for doing something useful. Then they will have something to share with those who are poor.

[29]When you talk, don't say anything bad. But say the good things that people need—whatever will help them grow stronger. Then what you say

---

[a] **4:11 to care for . . . people** Literally, "to be shepherds and teachers".
[b] **4:25** Quote from Zech. 8:16.
[c] **4:26** Quote from Ps. 4:4 (Greek version).

STAYING TOGETHER

Krystal enjoys going to church. She likes being able to sing to God and she likes listening to the preacher explain bits of the Bible. It excites her that when she goes to church she knows more of what it means to follow Jesus. But she doesn't like the chatting at the end. It's okay hanging out with her mates, but sometimes the younger kids are there and she finds them annoying. The grown-ups often speak with her, although she's not really sure they have much in common. Recently Krystal has been reading Ephesians and it's been making her think . . .

DIG IN   READ Ephesians 1:1 – 2:22

Let's remind ourselves of some exciting things we've discovered in Ephesians so far.

- God's grand plan is to bring everything together to worship Christ. This is the purpose of the universe and life (1:10) and we get blessed (1:1–11).
- We become God's people by his grace – we can't boast that we're good (2:5,7–9).
- Even people who wouldn't normally hang out together do now, because Jesus' death meant that all those barriers were destroyed (ch.2).

READ Ephesians 4:1–6

- What are the reasons for living life the way God wants (vv.1,3–6)?
- What four things does God want in our lives (v.2)? Do you find this easy to do with everyone?

Tricky stuff! It's really not easy to be humble, gentle, patient and loving – especially with people we find difficult. Krystal was certainly finding it hard to accept others at her church. But because we are joined together, these are the things we are to learn to be in order to keep that togetherness that Jesus has made.

READ Ephesians 4:7–16

- God has given all sorts of people to the church. Can you name some (v.11)?
- Why did Christ give people those jobs (vv.12,16)?

It's not just that God gave "gifts" but that people too are the gifts! He gave us to one another and to the church. If you love Jesus you have a part to play in the church to which you've been given. You may still need to discover your place in the church, or what talents you can share, but God wants you there, learning to serve him so that the church stays joined together and gets stronger. (In the same way, it also means the people Krystal doesn't get on with are important and vice versa.)

DIG THROUGH

- Is there someone at your church who you find it difficult to be humble, patient, gentle or loving towards? Why not ask God to help you remember that you are joined to them and help you change.
- Is it time to start finding out how God has gifted you? Why not ask your church leader if there is some way he thinks you can help out at church?
- How might you encourage and help someone like Krystal?

DIG DEEPER

- Read Ephesians 5:2 – 6:9. Think about the ways that Jesus as head of the church is mirrored in these relationships.

will be a blessing to those who hear you. [30]And don't make the Holy Spirit sad. God gave you his Spirit as proof that you belong to him and that he will keep you safe until the day he makes you free. [31]Don't be bitter or angry. Don't lose your temper. Never shout angrily or say things to hurt others. Never do anything evil. [32]Be kind and loving to each other. Forgive each other just as God forgave you through Christ.

5 You are God's dear children, so try to be like him. [2]Live a life of love. Love others just as Christ loved us. He gave himself for us—a sweet-smelling offering and sacrifice to God.

[3]But there must be no sexual sin among you. There must not be any kind of evil or selfishly wanting more and more, because such things are not right for God's holy people. [4]Also, there must be no evil talk among you. Don't say things that are foolish or filthy. These are not for you. But you should be giving thanks to God. [5]You can be sure of this: no one will have a place in the kingdom of Christ and of God if that person commits sexual sins, or does evil things or is a person who selfishly wants more and more. A greedy person like that is serving a false god.

[6]Don't let anyone fool you with words that are not true. God gets very angry when people who don't obey him talk like that. [7]So don't have anything to do with them. [8]In the past you were full of darkness, but now you are full of light in the Lord. So live like children who belong to the light. [9]This light produces every kind of goodness, right living and truth. [10]Try to learn what pleases the Lord. [11]Have no part in the things that people in darkness do, which produce nothing good. Instead, tell everyone how wrong those things are. [12]Actually, it is shameful to even talk about the things those people do in secret. [13]But the light makes clear how wrong those things are. [14]Yes, everything is made clear by the light. This is why we say,

"Wake up, you who are sleeping!
    Rise from death,
and Christ will shine on you."

[15]So be very careful how you live. Live wisely, not like fools. [16]I mean that you should use every opportunity you have for doing good, because these are evil times. [17]So don't be foolish with your lives, but learn what the Lord wants you to do. [18]Don't be drunk with wine, which will ruin your life, but be filled with the Spirit. [19]Encourage each other with psalms, hymns and spiritual songs. Sing and make music in your hearts to the Lord. [20]Always give thanks to God the Father for everything in the name of our Lord Jesus Christ.

Wives and Husbands

[21]Be willing to serve each other out of respect for Christ.

INSIGHT

The word "serve" has quite a negative connotation in our culture, but this verse isn't anti-women. Husbands are told to love their wives as much as Christ loved the Church and as much as they love themselves.

Ephesians 5:22

[22]Wives, be willing to serve your husbands the same as the Lord. [23]A husband is the head of his wife, just as Christ is the head of the church. Christ is the Saviour of the church, which is his body. [24]The church serves under Christ, so it is the same with you wives. You should be willing to serve your husbands in everything.

[25]Husbands, love your wives the same as Christ loved the church and gave his life for it. [26]He died to make the church holy. He used the telling of the Good News to make the church clean by washing it with water. [27]Christ died so that he could give the church to himself like a bride in all her beauty. He died so that the church could be holy and without fault, with no evil or sin or any other thing wrong in it.

[28]And husbands should love their wives like that. They should love their wives as they love their own bodies. The man who loves his wife loves himself, [29]because no one ever hates his own body, but feeds and takes care of it. And that is what Christ does for the church [30]because we are parts of his body. [31]The Scriptures say, "That is why a man will leave his father and mother and join his wife, and the two people will become one."[a] [32]That secret truth is very important—I am talking about Christ and the church. [33]But each one of you must love his wife as he loves himself. And a wife must respect her husband.

Children and Parents

6 Children, obey your parents the way the Lord wants, because this is the right thing to do. [2]The command says, "You must respect your father and mother."[b] This is the first command that has a promise with it. [3]And this is the

---

[a] **5:31** Quote from Gen. 2:24.
[b] **6:2** Quote from Exod. 20:12; Deut. 5:16.

promise: "Then all will go well with you, and you will have a long life on the earth."[a]

4Fathers, don't make your children angry, but raise them with the kind of teaching and training you learn from the Lord.

Slaves and Masters

5Slaves, obey your masters here on earth with fear and respect. And do this with a heart that is true, just as you obey Christ. 6You must do this not just to please your masters while they are watching, but all the time. Since you are really slaves of Christ, you must do with all your heart what God wants. 7Do your work, and be happy to do it. Work as though it is the Lord you are serving, not just an earthly master. 8Remember that the Lord will give everyone a reward for doing good. Everyone, slave or free, will get a reward for the good things they do.

9Masters, in the same way, be good to your slaves. Don't say things to scare them. You know that the one who is your Master and their Master is in heaven, and he treats everyone the same.

Wear the Full Armour of God

10Here is one last word of advice. Depend on the Lord for your strength. Put your trust in his great power. 11Wear the full armour of God. Wear God's armour so that you can fight against the devil's clever tricks. 12Our fight is not against people on earth. We are fighting against the rulers and authorities and the powers of this world's darkness. We are fighting against the spiritual powers of evil in the heavenly places. 13That is why you need to put on God's full armour. Then on the day of evil, you will be able to stand strong. And when you have finished the whole fight, you will still be standing.

14So stand strong with the belt of truth tied around your waist, and on your chest wear the protection of right living. 15On your feet wear the Good News of peace to help you stand strong. 16And also use the shield of faith with which you can stop all the burning arrows that come from the Evil One. 17Accept God's salvation as your helmet. And take the sword of the Spirit—that sword is the teaching of God. 18Pray in the Spirit at all times. Pray with all kinds of prayers, and ask for everything you need. To do this you must always be ready. Never give up. Always pray for all of God's people.

19Also pray for me—that when I speak, God will give me words so that I can tell the secret truth about the Good News without fear. 20I have the work of speaking for that Good News, and that is what I am doing now, here in prison. Pray that when I tell people the Good News, I will speak without fear as I should.

INSIGHT

The "shield of faith" here is a comparison to Roman battle shields. The shield was designed to protect against burning darts, one of the most dangerous weapons of the time. During combat the soldiers would line their shields up together forming a wall and roof that was practically impossible to break through. Standing with others always helps protect from temptation and attack.

Ephesians 6:16

Final Greetings

21I am sending you Tychicus, our dear brother and faithful helper in the Lord's work. He will tell you everything that is happening with me. Then you will know how I am and what I am doing. 22That's why I am sending him—to let you know how we are and to encourage you.

23I pray that God the Father and the Lord Jesus Christ will give peace and love with faith to all the brothers and sisters there. 24I pray that God's grace will be with all of you who love our Lord Jesus Christ with love that never ends.

---

[a] **6:3** Quote from Exod. 20:12; Deut. 5:16.

Who

Paul, writing to the Christian community in the Roman colony of Philippi (northern Greece). He established this church during his second missionary journey (Acts 16:6–40).

When

Paul was writing from imprisonment in Rome, probably sometime around AD 61. His warnings about his imminent death (e.g. 1:20) suggest that he wrote it while he was under house arrest in Rome.

What

The Philippians, hearing of Paul's imprisonment, had sent him a gift. Paul is writing to thank them. He takes the opportunity to encourage them to keep on running, because the race is not yet won, and warns them of possible pitfalls.

The letter also includes what seems to be a very early Christian hymn or poem (2:6–11). This is a wonderful summary of what Jesus did for us and how his followers should follow his example.

The Philippian church was very special to Paul. He founded it around AD 50 during his second missionary journey (Acts 16). It was the first church he founded on European soil. Luke stayed in Philippi after Paul left, which may be because it was Luke's home town.

The first convert was a woman called Lydia, and women continued to play a significant role in the church: Paul encourages two of them – Euodia and Syntyche – to be reconciled to each other (4:2).

In return, the Philippian church had always taken an active interest in Paul's work. This is reflected in their support for him while he is in prison. This, perhaps, is why his prayer for them is so full of joy (1:3–11). This church doesn't need correcting or rebuking; Paul encourages them to continue in their faith, despite the persecution they face.

Paul had faced opposition in the city – he had even been imprisoned there (Acts 16:23) – and clearly the Philippian church also faced enemies (3:2). But Paul reminds them that whatever hardships they face, Jesus is the only prize that matters.

QUICK TOUR ▷ PHILIPPIANS

Paul's prayer 1:1–11
Prison life 1:12–30
True humility 2:1–18
Timothy and Epaphroditus 2:19–30

Run the race 3:1–21
Remain faithful 4:1–9
How to be satisfied 4:10–23

"Brothers and sisters, I know that I still have a long way to go. But there is one thing I do: I forget what is in the past and try as hard as I can to reach the goal before me. I keep running hard towards the finish line to get the prize that is mine because God has called me through Christ Jesus to life up there in heaven."

Philippians 3:13–14

1 Greetings from Paul and Timothy, servants of Jesus Christ.

To all of you in Philippi who are God's holy people in Christ Jesus, including your elders[a] and special servants.

²Grace and peace to you from God our Father and the Lord Jesus Christ.

Paul's Prayer

³I thank God every time I remember you. ⁴And I always pray for all of you with joy. ⁵I thank God for the help you gave me while I told people the Good News. You helped from the first day you believed until now. ⁶I am sure that the good work God began in you will continue until he completes it on the day when Jesus Christ comes again.

⁷I know I am right to think like this about all of you because you are so close to my heart. This is because you have all played such an important part in God's grace to me—now, during this time that I am in prison, and whenever I am defending and proving the truth of the Good News. ⁸God knows that I want very much to see you. I love all of you with the love of Christ Jesus.

⁹This is my prayer for you:

that your love will grow more and more; that you will have knowledge and understanding with your love; ¹⁰that you will see the difference between what is important and what is not and choose what is important; that you will be pure and free from blame, ready for the coming of Christ; ¹¹that your life will be full of the many good works that are produced by Jesus Christ to bring glory and praise to God.

INSIGHT

Even though the apostle Paul is in prison, he isn't moaning about what a hard time he's having; he is rejoicing that God's work is still being done, through his hardship.

Philippians 1:12–18

Paul's Troubles Help the Lord's Work

¹²Brothers and sisters, I want you to know that all that has happened to me has helped to spread the Good News. ¹³All the Roman guards and all the others here know that I am in prison for serving Christ. ¹⁴My being in prison has caused most of the believers to put their trust in the Lord and to show more courage in telling people God's message.

¹⁵Some people are telling the message about Christ because they are jealous and bitter. Others do it because they want to help. ¹⁶They are doing it out of love. They know that God gave me the work of defending the Good News. ¹⁷But those others tell about Christ because of their selfish ambition. Their reason for doing it is wrong. They only do it because they think it will make trouble for me in prison. ¹⁸But that doesn't matter. What is important is that they are telling people about Christ, whether they are sincere or not. So I am glad they are doing it.

I will continue to be glad, ¹⁹because I know that your prayers and the help the Spirit of Jesus Christ gives me will cause this trouble to result in my freedom.[b] ²⁰I am full of hope and feel sure I will not have any reason to be ashamed. I am certain I will continue to have the same boldness to speak freely that I always have. I will let God use my life to bring more honour to Christ. It doesn't matter whether I live or die. ²¹To me, the only important thing about living is Christ. And even death would be for my benefit.[c] ²²If I continue living here on earth, I will be able to work for the Lord. But what would I choose—to live or to die? I don't know. ²³It would be a hard choice. Sometimes I want to leave this life and be with Christ. That would be much better for me; ²⁴however, you people need me here alive. ²⁵I am sure of this, so I know that I will stay here and be with you to help you grow and have joy in your faith. ²⁶When I am there with you again, you will be bursting with pride over what Christ Jesus did to help me.

²⁷Just be sure you live as God's people in a way that honours the Good News about Christ. Then whether I come and visit you or am away from you, I will hear good things about you. I will know that you stand together with the same purpose and that you work together like a team to help others believe the Good News. ²⁸And you will not be afraid of those who are against you. All of this is proof from God that you are being saved and that your enemies will be lost. ²⁹God has blessed you in ways that serve Christ. He allowed you to believe in Christ. But that is not all. He has also given you the honour of suffering for him. ³⁰You saw the difficulties I had to face, and you hear that I am still having troubles. Now you must face them too.

---

[a] **1:1 elders** Here, literally, "overseers". See "ELDERS (NEW TESTAMENT)" in the Word List.
[b] **1:19 freedom** Or "salvation".
[c] **1:21 death . . . benefit** Paul says that death would be better, because death would bring him nearer to Christ.

REAL JOY

"Always be filled with joy in the Lord. I will say it again. Be filled with joy" (Philippians 4:4).

What's the worst situation you've found yourself in so far in your life? How did you respond to it? What kinds of feelings did you have? What words would you use to describe what it was like for you? Take a look at this letter that Paul wrote to the Christians in Philippi when he was in a very dire situation.

DIG IN

READ Philippians 1:1 – 4:23

You may be surprised by Paul's attitude to the suffering he is experiencing.

- According to 1:7, what situation was Paul in when he was writing this letter?

How do you think you would feel if you were put in prison for telling people about Jesus? There are all kinds of emotions that you might be going through and most of them would be pretty negative. Let's take a look at how Paul responded to his situation:

- For each of the following verses, write down the word that Paul uses to describe how he's feeling about various matters as he writes this letter in prison: 1:4,18; 2:2,17; 4:1,10.
- What are the various things that are making Paul feel this way (use the same verses)?
- How else does Paul put a different spin on his situation (1:14)?

This is not just an exercise in positive thinking or pretending that a difficult situation is okay. Paul was simply so focused on the Good News that even being in prison could not dampen his passion for it. In fact he goes even further than that. Check out chapter 1:19–26.

- According to these verses, what is Paul's attitude to life? What is his attitude to death?

DIG THROUGH

- "To me, the only important thing about living is Christ. And even death would be for my benefit" (1:21). How close are you to being able to agree with Paul's words? Ask God to show you more and more the importance and beauty of his Good News, so that it can become the most important thing about being alive for you too.

- Paul is able to find joy even in the most depressing of situations because his joy is in Christ and in the sharing of the Good News rather than in circumstances. At the beginning of chapter 2 Paul says, "Think about what we have in Christ: the encouragement he has brought us," before listing some of the riches that come from being a Christian. Try taking his advice and list all the blessings that you have because of Jesus. If you're in a difficult situation, it won't change things; but it will give you a bigger, more eternal perspective and might just change how you view it.

DIG DEEPER

- Look back at John 3:22–30 where John the Baptist talks about his attitude to Jesus (that's who he means when he talks about "the bridegroom"). What further insight does this give you about how to find joy as a Christian?

REAL UNITY

Think of a time when you had an argument with a friend or family member. What caused the argument? What helped you to sort it out again?

DIG IN

READ Philippians 1:1 – 4:23

Paul's big priority for the church at Philippi becomes clear as you read through this letter.

- What does Paul want to hear about the believers (1:27)?
- What does he say would "make my joy complete" (2:2)?
- What does Paul ask for in chapter 4:2?

Paul wants to hear that the believers are living "as God's people in a way that honours the Good News about Christ". He knows that God wants his people to be united in their purposes and passions, and one reason for this is that it makes evangelism more effective (most people are more likely to want to join a team that agrees on things than one that is always arguing). You can see from Paul's language that he feels really strongly about this.

- What is Paul grateful for (1:5)?

Paul is not a lone operator – he can only carry out his ministry with the help of other Christians. He himself is part of the team that he wants to stay united.

So we can see that Paul wants the Philippians (and us) to know that being united is really, really important. But how do we do it? Sometimes, especially when we have different opinions, agreeing with each other can be really difficult. But after Paul talks about making his joy complete (2:2), he shows us how. Check out Philippians 2:3–5.

- What does Paul describe here as the really important key that makes unity possible?

So exercising "humility" like Jesus is what helps us to be united.

- What might it look like to think in a really humble way? How do we do it? Check out chapter 2:6–8 for a mind-blowing example for us to follow.

DIG THROUGH

- "Be humble, and honour others more than yourselves" (2:3). This can be a real challenge, but Paul makes it clear that it's really important and we have Jesus as our example. What will it mean in practice for you to think of others as more significant than yourself? What kind of difference do you imagine it could make for sorting out arguments?
- What one thing could you do today to live out this kind of change? Ultimately we need God to change our hearts – ask him to give you humility.

DIG DEEPER

- Take a look at Ephesians 4:1–6. This is part of a letter by the same author, Paul, but to a different church. So you can see that this issue of humble unity is very important for everyone, not just the Philippians!
- *And just in case you're still not convinced,* read John 17:22–23. Here Jesus is praying to God about Christians in the future (you and me). It's clear that Jesus is saying that our unity will help others recognize his reality.

Be United and Care for Each Other

2 Think about what we have in Christ: the encouragement he has brought us, the comfort of his love, our sharing in his Spirit, and the mercy and kindness he has shown us. If you enjoy these blessings, ²then do what will make my joy complete: agree with each other, and show your love for each other. Be united in your goals and in the way you think. ³In whatever you do, don't let selfishness or pride be your guide. Be humble, and honour others more than yourselves. ⁴Don't be interested only in your own life, but care about the lives of others too.

Learn From Christ to Be Unselfish

⁵In your life together, think the way Christ Jesus thought.

⁶He was like God in every way,
  but he did not think that his being equal
    with God was something to use for his
    own benefit.
⁷Instead, he gave up everything, even his place
    with God.
  He accepted the role of a servant, appearing
    in human form.
  During his life as a man,
⁸ he humbled himself by being fully obedient
    to God,
  even when that caused his death—death on
    a cross.
⁹So God gave Jesus the place of highest honour.
  And he gave him the name that is greater
    than any other.
¹⁰So every person will bow down before Jesus to
    honour the name God gave him.
  Everyone in heaven, on earth and under the
    earth will bow.
¹¹They will all confess, "Jesus Christ is Lord,"
  and this will bring glory to God the Father.

INSIGHT

It was because Jesus was willing to become the lowest of the low that God decided to raise him up to the heights of heaven. Humility will always be honoured. If not in this world, then by God in the world to come.

Philippians 2:5–11

Be the People God Wants You to Be

¹²My dear friends, you always obeyed what you were taught. Just as you obeyed when I was with you, it is even more important for you to obey now that I am not there. So you must continue to live in a way that gives meaning to your salvation. Do this with fear and respect for God. ¹³Yes, it is God who is working in you. He helps you want to do what pleases him, and he gives you the power to do it.

¹⁴Do everything without complaining or arguing. ¹⁵Then you will be free from blame and pure, children of God without any fault. But you are living with evil people all around you, who have lost their sense of what is right. Among those people you shine like lights in a dark world, ¹⁶and you offer them the teaching that gives life. So I can be proud of you when Christ comes again. You will show that my work was not wasted— that I ran in the race and won.

¹⁷Your faith makes you give your lives as a sacrifice in serving God. Maybe I will have to offer my own life with your sacrifice. But if that happens, I will be glad, and I will share my joy with all of you. ¹⁸You also should be glad and share your joy with me.

News About Timothy and Epaphroditus

¹⁹With the blessing of the Lord Jesus, I hope I will be able to send Timothy to you soon. I will be glad to learn how you are. ²⁰I have no one else like Timothy, who genuinely cares for you. ²¹Others are interested only in their own lives. They don't care about the work of Christ Jesus. ²²You know the kind of person Timothy is. He has served with me in telling the Good News like a son with his father. ²³I plan to send him to you quickly, as soon as I know what will happen to me. ²⁴I am sure the Lord will help me come to you soon.

²⁵For now, I think I must send Epaphroditus back to you. He is my brother in God's family, who works and serves with me in the Lord's army. When I needed help, you sent him to me, ²⁶but now he wants very much to see all of you again. He is worried because you heard that he was sick. ²⁷He was sick and near death. But God helped him and me too, so that I would not have even more grief. ²⁸So I want very much to send him to you. When you see him, you can be happy. And I can stop worrying about you. ²⁹Welcome him in the Lord with much joy. Give honour to people like Epaphroditus. ³⁰He should be honoured because he almost died for the work of Christ. He put his life in danger so that he could help me. This was help that you could not give me.

Christ Is More Important Than Anything

3 And now, my brothers and sisters, be filled with joy in the Lord. It is no trouble for me to write the same things to you again. I want to be sure that you are prepared.

INSIGHT

Circumcision is a Jewish tradition, set in place in the Old Testament laws. Paul is saying that for the Christian "circumcision" is spiritual, not physical. Those cleansed from sin by Jesus Christ are the true people of God.

Philippians 3:1–11

[2]Be careful of the dogs—those men whose work does only harm. They want to cut everyone who isn't circumcised.[a] [3]But we are the ones who have the true circumcision[b] we who worship God through his Spirit. We don't trust in ourselves or anything we can do. We take pride only in Christ Jesus. [4]Even if I am able to trust in myself, still I don't do it. If anyone else thinks they have a reason to trust in themselves, they should know that I have a greater reason for doing so. [5]I was circumcised on the eighth day after my birth. I am from the people of Israel and the tribe of Benjamin. I am a true Jew, and so were my parents. The law was very important to me. That is why I became a Pharisee. [6]I was so eager to defend my religion[c] that I persecuted the church. And no one could find fault with the way I obeyed the Law of Moses.

[7]At one time all these things were important to me. But because of Christ, I decided that they are worth nothing. [8]Not only these things, but now I think that all things are worth nothing compared with the greatness of knowing Christ Jesus my Lord. Because of Christ, I lost these things, and now I know that they are all worthless rubbish. All I want now is Christ. [9]I want to belong to him. In Christ I am right with God, but my being right does not come from following the law. It comes from God through faith. God uses my faith in[d] Christ to make me right with him. [10]All I want is to know Christ and the power that raised him from death. I want to share in his sufferings and be like him even in his death. [11]Then there is hope that I myself will somehow be raised from death.

Trying to Reach the Goal

[12]I don't mean that I am exactly what God wants me to be. I have not yet reached that goal. But I continue trying to reach it and make it mine. That's what Christ Jesus wants me to do. It is the reason he made me his. [13]Brothers and sisters, I know that I still have a long way to go. But there is one thing I do: I forget what is in the past and try as hard as I can to reach the goal before me. [14]I keep running hard towards the finish line to get the prize that is mine because God has called me through Christ Jesus to life up there in heaven.

[15]All of us who have grown to be spiritually mature should think this way too. And if there is any of this that you don't agree with, God will make it clear to you. [16]But we should continue following the truth we already have.

[17]Brothers and sisters, join together in following my example. Also, learn by watching those who are living the way we showed you. [18]There are many who live like enemies of the cross of Christ. I have often told you about them. And it makes me cry to tell you about them now. [19]The way they live is leading them to destruction. They have replaced God with their own desires. They do shameful things, and they are proud of what they do. They think only about earthly things. [20]But the government that rules us is in heaven. We are waiting for our Saviour, the Lord Jesus Christ, to come from there. [21]He will change our humble bodies and make them like his own glorious body. Christ can do this by his power, with which he is able to rule everything.

Some Things to Do

4 My dear brothers and sisters, I love you and want to see you. You bring me joy and make me proud of you. Continue following the Lord as I have told you.

[2]Euodia and Syntyche, you both belong to the Lord, so please agree with each other. [3]For this I make a special request to my friend who has served with me so faithfully: help these women. They worked hard with me in telling people the Good News, together with Clement and others who worked with me. Their names are written in the book of life.[e]

---

[a] **3:2 want to cut . . . circumcised** There is a play on words here in Greek. The key word is like "circumcision" (see "CIRCUMCISION" in the Word List), but it means "mutilation" or "cutting to pieces".

[b] **3:3 we are . . . circumcision** Literally, "we are the circumcision". The word is used here in a spiritual sense. See "CIRCUMCISION" in the Word List.

[c] **3:6 eager to defend my religion** Before Paul became a believer in Jesus as the Messiah, he thought it was his duty as a good Jew to oppose the Jews who had become Christ-followers.

[d] **3:9 my faith in** Or "the faithfulness of".

[e] **4:3 book of life** God's book that contains the names of his chosen people. See Rev. 3:5; 21:27.

[4]Always be filled with joy in the Lord. I will say it again. Be filled with joy.

[5]Let everyone see that you are gentle and kind. The Lord is coming soon. [6]Don't worry about anything, but pray and ask God for everything you need, always giving thanks for what you have. [7]And because you belong to Christ Jesus, God's peace will stand guard over all your thoughts and feelings. His peace can do this far better than our human minds.[a]

INSIGHT

The apostle Paul was speaking from experience here. If anyone had cause to worry and stress, it was him! (See 2 Corinthians 11:23–27.) But he'd found the secret to attaining true peace.

Philippians 4:6–7

---

[8]Brothers and sisters, continue to think about what is good and worthy of praise. Think about what is true and honourable and right and pure and beautiful and respected. [9]And do what you learned and received from me—what I told you and what you saw me do. And the God who gives peace will be with you.

Paul Thanks the Philippian Believers

[10]I am so happy, and I thank the Lord that you have again shown your care for me. You continued to care about me, but there was no way for you to show it. [11]I am telling you this, but not because I need something. I have learned to be satisfied with what I have and with whatever happens. [12]I know how to live when I am poor and when I have plenty. I have learned the secret of how to live through any kind of situation—when I have enough to eat or when I am hungry, when I have everything I need or when I have nothing. [13]Christ is the one who gives me the strength I need to do whatever I must do.

[14]But it was good that you helped me when I needed help. [15]You people in Philippi remember when I first came to tell people in Macedonia the Good News. When I left there, you were the only church that gave me help. [16]Several times you sent me things I needed when I was in Thessalonica. [17]Really, it is not that I want to get gifts from you. But I want you to have the benefit that comes from giving. [18]I have everything I need. I have even more than I need. I have all I need because Epaphroditus brought your gift to me. Your gift is like a sweet-smelling sacrifice offered to God. God accepts that sacrifice and it pleases him. [19]My God will use his glorious riches to give you everything you need. He will do this through Christ Jesus. [20]Glory to our God and Father for ever and ever. Amen.

[21]Give our greetings to God's people there—to each one who belongs to Christ Jesus. Those in God's family who are with me send you their greetings. [22]And greetings to you from all of God's people here, especially those who work in the service of the emperor.

[23]The grace of the Lord Jesus Christ be with each one of you.

---

[a] **4:7 can do . . . minds** Literally, "surpasses (is better than) every mind", which could also mean "is beyond all understanding".

Who Paul, writing to the Christian community at Colossae. Although he never visited Colossae, Paul heard of the church's faith from Epaphras, who had founded and led the church.

When Paul was writing from Rome where he was awaiting trial in around AD 62. Timothy was in Rome with him and was probably acting as his secretary for this letter.

What Paul introduces himself to the church at Colossae. Although he has never been there he has heard all about the faith of the Colossian church from one of their leaders, Epaphras, who is in prison with him.

Around this time Paul also met Onesimus the runaway slave, also from Colossae (4:9; Philemon v.10).

Paul probably wrote Colossians about the same time as he wrote Philemon and Ephesians. All three letters were sent with Paul's helpers Tychicus and Onesimus (4:7–9; Ephesians 6:21; Philemon v.10).

As well as founding the church at Colossae, Epaphras had probably founded the churches in Laodicea and Hierapolis (4:12–13). He was concerned for his Colossian flock – they were confused. They seem to have been lured into some kind of Judaism mixed with mystical pagan festivals, a pick 'n' mix menu of Jewish dietary laws, angel worship and new moon festivals. The Colossians had been mixing ideas from Christianity with ideas from other philosophies and religions which they viewed as equally true. Perhaps a false leader within the church had been acting like some spiritual guru and advising the Colossians to use rites and rituals to protect themselves from evil influences.

Paul tells them to forget false ideas and practices and focus on Jesus. Christ is the supreme power over all powers. Paul urges the Colossian followers to stick to what they know and not get lured down theological blind alleys. He urges the Colossians to trust in the strength of God, who "made us free from the power of darkness. And he brought us into the kingdom of his dear Son. The Son paid the price to make us free. In him we have the forgiveness of our sins" (1:13–14).

QUICK TOUR ▶ COLOSSIANS

Hello Colossae 1:1–8
All about Jesus 1:9–23
Suffering for the truth 1:24 – 2:5

Don't let them tell you what to do 2:6–19
New life in Christ 2:20 – 4:2

"Don't lie to each other. You have taken off those old clothes – the person you once were and the bad things you did then. Now you are wearing a new life, a life that is new every day. You are growing in your understanding of the one who made you. You are becoming more and more like him. In this new life it doesn't matter if you are a Greek or a Jew, circumcised or not. It doesn't matter if you speak a different language or even if you are a Scythian. It doesn't matter if you are a slave or free. Christ is all that matters, and he is in all of you."

Colossians 3:9–11

1 Greetings from Paul, an apostle for Christ Jesus. I am an apostle because that is what God wanted. Greetings also from Timothy, our brother in Christ.

²To the holy and faithful brothers and sisters in Christ who live in Colossae.

Grace and peace to you from God our Father.

³In our prayers we always thank God for you. He is the Father of our Lord Jesus Christ. ⁴We thank him because we have heard about the faith you have in Christ Jesus and the love you have for all of God's people. ⁵Your faith and love continue because you know what is waiting for you in heaven—the hope you have had since you first heard the true message, the Good News ⁶that was told to you. Throughout the world, this Good News is bringing blessings and is spreading. And that's what has been happening among you since the first time you heard it and understood the truth about God's grace. ⁷You heard it from Epaphras, our dear friend and co-worker. He is a faithful servant of Christ for us.ᵃ ⁸He also told us about the love you have from the Spirit.

⁹Since the day we heard these things about you, we have continued praying for you. This is what we pray:

that God will make you completely sure of what he wants by giving you all the wisdom and spiritual understanding you need; ¹⁰that this will help you live in a way that brings honour to the Lord and pleases him in every way; that your life will produce good works of every kind and that you will grow in your knowledge of God;ᵇ ¹¹that God will strengthen you with his own great power, so that you will be patient and not give up when troubles come.

Then you will be happy ¹²and give thanks to the Father. He has made you able to have what he has promised to give all his holy people, who live in the light. ¹³God made us free from the power of darkness. And he brought us into the kingdom of his dear Son. ¹⁴The Son paid the price to make us free. In him we have forgiveness for our sins.

The Son of God Is the Same as God

¹⁵No one can see God,
   but the Son is exactly like God.
   He rules over everything that has been made.ᶜ
¹⁶Through his power all things were made:
   things in heaven and on earth, seen and not seen—
all spiritual rulers, lords, powers and authorities.
   Everything was made through him and for him.

¹⁷The Son was there before anything was made.
   And all things continue because of him.
¹⁸He is the head of the body, which is the church.
   He is the beginning of everything else.
And he is the first among all who will be raised from death.ᵈ
   So in everything he is most important.

¹⁹God was pleased for all of himself to live in the Son.
²⁰   And through him, God was happy to bring all things back to himself again—
   things on earth and things in heaven.

ᵃ **1:7 us** Many ancient Greek copies have "you".
ᵇ **1:10 that your life . . . God** Or "that your knowledge of God will produce more and more good works of every kind in your life".
ᶜ **1:15 He . . . made** Literally, "He is the firstborn of all creation." See "FIRSTBORN" in the Word List.
ᵈ **1:18 first . . . death** Literally, "firstborn from the dead".

JESUS' IDENTITY, OUR IDENTITY

Our identity is shaped by the people we look up to. Maybe for you that's a musician, a sports star, a celebrity or someone in your family. Who they are and what they do influences who we are and what we do. Our identity is connected to theirs.

That's even more of a reality for followers of Jesus. Paul's letter to the Colossians explains that who Jesus is and what he's done has a huge impact on our identity and our lives as believers.

DIG IN

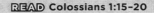 **READ** Colossians 1:15–20

People have all kinds of ideas about Jesus: that he was a prophet, that he was a wise teacher, that he was a holy man, and many others. The New Testament teaches us that he was much more than any of those as Paul's words about Jesus' identity explain. These verses are beautiful and contain some of the most amazing truths in the Bible.

- What does the passage say about Jesus' identity?

Read the passage again and see if you can follow the themes as you read the verses:

- The first part is about Jesus' role in creation – he helped make everything in the first place and he holds it all together.
- The second part is about Jesus' role in God's new creation – he is making everything new, starting with his death and resurrection.

From before the beginning to after the end and all the way in between, there is nothing and no one in the universe that's more important than Jesus. That's an incredible claim. But perhaps not so far-fetched when you read that "God was pleased for all of himself to live in the Son" (v.19). Yes, Jesus is God!

READ Colossians 1:21 – 2:15

Our identity is also a key theme in Colossians. Paul often talks about our new life. But what does that mean?

Paul tells us that "God gave you new life together with Christ" (Colossians 2:13). Our new identity is completely connected to Jesus' identity. We're like a sheet of paper placed between the pages of a book: whatever happens to the book also happens to the piece of paper.

And, what's more, Paul says that Christ lives among us (Colossians 1:27)! Everything that Jesus is and everything that he has done is now part of us.

DIG THROUGH

- Paul's words about the identity of Christ were written almost 2,000 years ago yet are still true today. How would you explain to someone else what you believe about who Jesus is?
- Would the Good News still make sense if Jesus were just a teacher or a prophet as some people claim? Why not?
- Look through the second passage again and write down:
  » everything it says about Jesus.
  » everything it says about us, particularly the ways in which we're now connected to Jesus.
  Use these truths to help you worship.

DIG DEEPER

- John 1 is another famous chapter about Jesus' identity. Read John 1:1–18 together with Colossians 1:15–20. Can you see the similarities?
- If you want an even deeper understanding of how our identity and Jesus' identity are connected together read Romans chapters 6 – 8.

God made peace by using the blood sacrifice
of his Son on the cross.

²¹At one time you were separated from God.
You were his enemies in your minds, because the
evil you did was against him. ²²But now he has
made you his friends again. He did this by the
death Christ suffered while he was in his body.
He did it so that he could present you to himself
as people who are holy, free from blame and
without anything that would make you guilty
before him. ²³And that is what will happen if you
continue to believe in the Good News you heard.
You must remain strong and sure in your faith.
You must not let anything cause you to give up
the hope that became yours when you heard the
Good News. That same Good News has been told
to everyone on earth, and that's the work that I,
Paul, was given to do.

Paul's Work for the Church

²⁴I am happy in my sufferings for you. There
is much that Christ must still suffer. And I
gladly accept my part of those sufferings in my
body for the good of his body, the church. ²⁵I
became a servant of the church because God gave
me a special work to do. This work helps you.
My work is to tell the complete message of
God. ²⁶This message is the secret truth that
was hidden since the beginning of time. It was
hidden from everyone for ages, but now it has
been made known to God's holy people. ²⁷God
decided to let his people know just how rich and
glorious that truth is. That secret truth, which is
for all people, is that Christ lives among you. He is
our hope for glory. ²⁸So we continue to tell people
about Christ. We use all wisdom to counsel every
person and teach every person. We are trying to
bring everyone before God as people who have
grown to be spiritually mature in Christ. ²⁹To do
this, I work and struggle using the great strength
that Christ gives me. That strength is working in
my life.

2 I want you to know that I am trying very hard
to help you. And I am trying to help those in
Laodicea and others who have never seen me. ²I
want them to be strengthened and joined together
with love and to have the full confidence that
comes from understanding. I want them to know
completely the secret truth that God has made
known. That truth is Christ himself. ³In him all
the treasures of wisdom and knowledge are kept
safe.

⁴I tell you this so that no one can fool you by
telling you ideas that seem good, but are false.
⁵Even though I am far away, my thoughts are
always with you. I am happy to see your good
lives and your strong faith in Christ.

Continue to Follow Christ Jesus

⁶You accepted Christ Jesus as Lord, so continue
to live following him. ⁷You must depend on Christ
only, drawing life and strength from him. Just
as you were taught the truth, continue to grow
stronger in your understanding of it. And never
stop giving thanks to God.

⁸Be sure you are not led away by the teaching
of those who have nothing worth saying and only
plan to deceive you. That teaching is not from
Christ. It is only human tradition and comes from
the powers that influence*ᵃ* this world. ⁹I say this
because all of God lives in Christ fully, even in his
life on earth. ¹⁰And because you belong to Christ
you are complete, having everything you need.
Christ is ruler over every other power and
authority.

¹¹In Christ you had a different kind of circumcision, one that was not done by human hands.
That is, you were made free from the power of
your sinful self. That is the kind of circumcision
Christ does. ¹²When you were baptized, you
were buried with Christ, and you were raised up
with him because of your faith in God's power.
God's power was shown when he raised Christ
from death.

¹³You were spiritually dead because of your
sins and because you were not free from the
power of your sinful self.*ᵇ* But God gave you new
life together with Christ. He forgave all our sins.
¹⁴Because we broke God's laws, we owed a
debt—a debt that listed all the rules we failed to
follow. But God forgave us of that debt. He took it
away and nailed it to the cross. ¹⁵He defeated the
rulers and powers of the spiritual world. With the
cross he won the victory over them and led them
away, as defeated and powerless prisoners for the
whole world to see.

Don't Follow Rules That People Make

¹⁶So don't let anyone make rules for you about
eating and drinking or about Jewish customs
(festivals, New Moon celebrations or Sabbath
days). ¹⁷In the past these things were like a
shadow that showed what was coming. But the
new things that were coming are found in Christ.
¹⁸Some people enjoy acting as if they are humble

ᵃ **2:8 powers that influence** Or "elementary rules of". Also in verse 20.
ᵇ **2:13 and because . . . sinful self** Literally, "because of the uncircumcision of your flesh". See "CIRCUMCISION" in the Word List.

WHAT DIFFERENCE DOES IT MAKE?

Imagine you receive a phone call saying that you've inherited millions of pounds. Would that knowledge make a difference to how you live?

Paul tells us in Colossians that Christ is among us (1:27). Think about that for a moment . . . it's the most amazing thing that we could know – something that makes a huge difference for our lives!

DIG IN
READ Colossians 2:6 – 3:4

Christ living among us means that we don't have to try to live a godly life by ourselves – God has already provided everything we need for our Christian life.

In this passage Paul tells believers about everything they have in Christ, and criticizes those who suggest they need other rules or ideas or experiences. What he writes is just as relevant to us today.

- Make a note of everything that Paul says about what we have because of Christ.
- What are the other ideas Paul criticizes? Why does he criticize them?

It's worth remembering how Paul introduces the passage: "You accepted Christ Jesus as Lord, so continue to live following him. You must depend on Christ only, drawing life and strength from him" (2:6–7).

- Do you feel inferior to other Christians because of things you do or don't do, or because of spiritual experiences you haven't had? What do you think Paul would say about that?

READ Colossians 3:5 – 4:6

Throughout this letter Paul switches back and forth from meaty theology to really practical teaching about how we should live as Christians. He wants each of us to have integrity and be of good character.

As you read the passage, think about how each of Paul's instructions relates to our new life in Christ.

- What are some of the things we should "take off" that don't have integrity and don't belong in our new life (3:5–9)?
- What kinds of thing do have integrity and do we "wear" when we become Christians (3:10–17)?

The heart of this passage is Colossians 3:17: "Everything you say and everything you do should be done for Jesus your Lord." Now that's a true life of integrity!

DIG THROUGH

How different would your life be if you weren't a Christian? Would others notice any differences?

- Are there things you feel challenged either to do or not to do as you read the passage from Colossians 3 and 4? Pray about those things.

Think again about Paul's encouragement that whatever you do should be done "for Jesus your Lord".

- What would it mean for you to do this
  - » at school or work?
  - » in how you use your money?
  - » in how you use your time?
  - » in your hobbies?
  - » with your friends?
  - » with your family?
  - » whenever you find yourself thinking about relationships?

Don't forget that with Christ living among us we already have everything we need to live godly lives!

DIG DEEPER

- Does some of Paul's teaching sound familiar? Jesus also taught about the difference that following him should make in our lives. Check out Matthew chapters 5 – 7.
- If you struggle with living a life of integrity you're not alone! Paul knew what he was talking about from personal experience. Check out Romans 7:14–25.

and love to worship angels.[a] They always talk about the visions they have seen. Don't listen to them when they say you are wrong because you don't do these things. It is so foolish for them to feel such pride, because it is all based on their own human ideas. [19]They don't keep themselves under the control of the head. Christ is the head, and the whole body depends on him. Because of Christ all the parts of the body care for each other and help each other. So the body is made stronger and held together as God causes it to grow.

[20]You died with Christ and were made free from the powers that influence this world. So why do you act as if you still belong to the world? I mean, why do you follow rules like these: [21]"Don't eat this", "Don't taste that", "Don't touch that"? [22]These rules are talking about earthly things that are gone after they are used. They are only human commands and teachings. [23]These rules may seem to be wise as part of a made-up religion in which people pretend to be humble and punish their bodies. But they don't help people stop doing the evil that the sinful self wants to do.

INSIGHT

Colossae had a population made up of many different nationalities and because of this some very strange ideas had crept in, and ideas from many faiths became mixed together. This is known as "syncretism".

Colossians 2:8–23

Your New Life

3 You were raised from death with Christ. So live for what is in heaven, where Christ is sitting at the right hand of God. [2]Think only about what is up there, not what is here on earth. [3]Your old self has died, and your new life is kept with Christ in God. [4]Yes, Christ is now your life, and when he comes again, you will share in his glory.

[5]So put everything evil out of your life: sexual sin, doing anything immoral, letting sinful thoughts control you and wanting things that are wrong. And don't keep wanting more and more for yourself, which is the same as worshipping a false god. [6]God will show his anger against those

who don't obey him,[b] because they do these evil things. [7]You also did these things in the past, when you lived like them.

[8]But now put these things out of your life: anger, losing your temper, doing or saying things to hurt others and saying shameful things. [9]Don't lie to each other. You have taken off those old clothes—the person you once were and the bad things you did then. [10]Now you are wearing a new life, a life that is new every day. You are growing in your understanding of the one who made you. You are becoming more and more like him. [11]In this new life it doesn't matter if you are a Greek or a Jew, circumcised or not. It doesn't matter if you speak a different language or even if you are a Scythian.[c] It doesn't matter if you are a slave or free. Christ is all that matters, and he is in all of you.

Your New Life With Each Other

[12]God has chosen you and made you his holy people. He loves you. So your new life should be like this: Show mercy to others. Be kind, humble, gentle and patient. [13]Don't be angry with each other, but forgive each other. If you feel someone has wronged you, forgive them. Forgive others because the Lord forgave you. [14]Together with these things, the most important part of your new life is to love each other. Love is what holds everything together in perfect unity. [15]Let the peace that Christ gives control your thinking. It is for peace that you were chosen to be together in one body.[d] And always be thankful.

[16]Let the teaching of Christ live inside you richly. Use all wisdom to teach and counsel each other. Sing psalms, hymns and spiritual songs with thankfulness in your hearts to God. [17]Everything you say and everything you do should be done for Jesus your Lord. And in all you do, give thanks to God the Father through Jesus.

Your New Life at Home

[18]Wives, be willing to serve your husbands. This is the right thing to do in following the Lord.

[19]Husbands, love your wives and be gentle to them.

[20]Children, obey your parents in everything. This pleases the Lord.

[21]Fathers, don't upset your children. If you are too hard to please, they might want to stop trying.

[22]Servants, obey your masters in everything. Obey all the time, even when they can't see you. Don't just pretend to work hard so that they will

---

[a] **2:18 worship angels** Or "worship with angels" (that they see in visions).
[b] **3:6 against . . . him** Some Greek copies do not have these words.
[c] **3:11 Scythians** Known as wild and uncivilized people.
[d] **3:15 body** Christ's spiritual body, meaning the church—his people.

treat you well. No, you must serve your masters honestly because you respect the Lord. [23]In all the work you are given, do the best you can. Work as though you are working for the Lord, not any earthly master. [24]Remember that you will receive your reward from the Lord, who will give you what he promised his people. Yes, you are serving Christ. He is your real Master.[a] [25]Remember that anyone who does wrong will be punished for that wrong. And the Lord treats everyone the same.

4 Masters, give what is good and fair to your servants. Remember that you have a Master in heaven.

Some Things to Do

[2]Never stop praying. Be ready for anything by praying and being thankful. [3]Also pray for us. Pray that God will give us an opportunity to tell people his message. I am in prison for doing this. But pray that we can continue to tell people the secret truth that God has made known about Christ. [4]Pray that I will say what is necessary to make this truth clear to everyone.

[5]Be wise in the way you act with those who are not believers. Use your time in the best way you can. [6]When you talk, you should always be kind and wise. Then you will be able to answer everyone in the way you should.

News About Those With Paul

[7]Tychicus is my dear brother in Christ. He is a faithful helper and he serves the Lord with me. He will tell you everything that is happening with me. [8]That is why I am sending him. I want you to know how we are, and I am sending him to encourage you. [9]I am sending him with Onesimus, the faithful and dear brother from your group. They will tell you everything that has happened here.

[10]Aristarchus, the one here in prison with me, sends you his greetings. Mark, the cousin of Barnabas, also sends his greetings. (I have already told you what to do about Mark. If he comes, welcome him.) [11]And greetings from Jesus, the one who is also called Justus. These are the only Jewish believers who work with me for God's kingdom. They have been a great comfort to me.

[12]Epaphras, another servant of Jesus Christ from your group, sends his greetings. He constantly struggles for you in prayer. He prays that you will grow to be spiritually mature and have everything that God wants for you. [13]I know that he has worked hard for you and the people in Laodicea and in Hierapolis. [14]Greetings also from Demas and our dear friend Luke, the doctor.

[15]Give our greetings to the brothers and sisters in Laodicea. Greetings also to Nympha and to the church that meets in her house. [16]After this letter is read to you, be sure it is also read to the church in Laodicea. And you read the letter that I wrote to them. [17]Tell Archippus, "Be sure to do the work the Lord gave you."

[18]Here's my greeting in my own handwriting— PAUL. Remember me in prison. I pray that God's grace will be with you all.

---

[a] **3:24 Yes, you . . . Master** Or "Serve the Lord Christ." The Greek word translated "Lord" is the same as the word for "master" in verses 22 and 23.

Who Paul, writing to the Christian community at Thessalonica (now Thessaloniki, Greece), the capital of Roman Macedonia. He founded the church during his second missionary journey.

When This is one of Paul's earliest letters. He wrote the letter from Corinth, towards the end of his second missionary journey (Acts 18:1–18). This would put the letter around AD 50–51.

What Paul had visited Thessalonica in the winter of AD 49. He only stayed for a short while, because of the fierce opposition (Acts 17:5–10), but in the short time he was with them, Paul obviously developed a deep affection for them.

He writes this letter to encourage the new believers in their faith and explains some key issues – especially those concerning the future.

The letter is full of Paul's delight in the church. He's like a nursing mother (2:7) or a father (2:11) watching their child take their first, faltering steps. He's full of joy at their efforts, while still concerned that they don't fall over. So, this is a letter of support, dealing with some issues that had arisen and repeating some of his teaching.

Paul is writing to address two main issues: when the Lord will return and what to do while waiting. The second coming of Jesus is the big theme which runs through this letter. The followers in Thessalonica were worried because some of their number had died (4:13) and it may be that this was a result of persecution.

Paul says that they are not lost or gone forever. The Lord is coming again and he will bring them with him (4:14). We don't know when it will happen. Paul describes Jesus' return as being like a thief in the night and says that when Christ comes again, the dead in Christ will rise and will be gathered up along with the living to meet the Lord (4:15–17). In the meantime, followers are urged to live lives which are holy and blameless (3:11 – 4:8; 5:23).

QUICK TOUR **1 THESSALONIANS**

Their faith 1:1–10
Paul's work 2:1–20
The good life 4:1–12

The Lord's return 4:13 – 5:11
Final instructions 5:12–28

"God did not choose us to suffer his anger. God chose us to have salvation through our Lord Jesus Christ. Jesus died for us so that we can live together with him. It is not important if we are alive or dead when he comes."

1 Thessalonians 5:9–10

1

Greetings from Paul, Silas and Timothy. To the church in Thessalonica that belongs to God the Father and the Lord Jesus Christ.

Grace and peace be yours.

The Life and Faith of the Thessalonians

²We always remember you when we pray, and we thank God for all of you. ³Every time we pray to God our Father, we thank him for all that you have done because of your faith. We thank him for the work you have done because of your love. And we thank him that you continue to be strong because of your hope in our Lord Jesus Christ.

⁴Brothers and sisters, God loves you. And we know that he has chosen you to be his people. ⁵When we brought the Good News to you, we came with more than words. We brought that Good News with power, with the Holy Spirit and with the sure knowledge that it was true. Also you know how we lived when we were with you. We lived that way to help you. ⁶And you became like us and like the Lord. You suffered much, but still you accepted the teaching with joy. The Holy Spirit gave you that joy.

INSIGHT

The way Christians live is the best way of showing anyone that the Good News of Jesus is true. Paul, Silas and Timothy exemplified this when they lived among the Thessalonians.

1 Thessalonians 1:5

---

⁷You became an example to all the believers in Macedonia and Achaia. ⁸The Lord's teaching has spread from you throughout Greece and beyond. In fact, your faith in God has become known everywhere, so we never have to tell anyone about it. ⁹People everywhere are already telling the story about the good way you accepted us when we were there with you. They tell about how you stopped worshipping idols and changed to serve the living and true God. ¹⁰And you began waiting for God's Son to come from heaven—the Son God raised from death. He is Jesus, who saves us from God's angry judgement that is coming.

Paul's Work in Thessalonica

2

Brothers and sisters, you know that our visit to you was not a failure. ²But before we came to you, people in Philippi had abused us with insults and made us suffer. You know all about that. And then, when we came to you, many people there caused us trouble. We told you God's Good News but only because he gave us the courage we needed. ³We had nothing to gain by asking you to believe the Good News. We were not trying to trick or fool anyone. ⁴No, we did it because God is the one who gave us this work. And this was only after he tested us and saw that we could be trusted to do it. So when we speak, we are only trying to please God, not anyone else. He is the one who can see what is in our hearts.

⁵You know that we never tried to influence you by saying nice things about you. We were not trying to get your money. We had no greed to hide from you. God knows that this is true. ⁶We were not looking for praise from people—not from you or anyone else.

⁷When we were with you, as apostles of Christ we could have used our authority to make you help us. But we were very gentleᵃ with you. We were like a mother caring for her little children. ⁸It was our deep love for you that made us happy to share God's Good News with you. But not only that—we were also happy to share even our own lives with you. That's how much we had come to love you. ⁹Brothers and sisters, I know that you remember how hard we worked. We worked night and day to support ourselves, so that we would not be a burden to anyone while we did the work of telling you God's Good News.

INSIGHT

Rather than taking money from the churches he was working with, Paul supported himself by working as a tentmaker (Acts 18:3).

1 Thessalonians 2:5–9

---

¹⁰When we were there with you believers, we were pure, honest and without fault in the way we lived. You know, just as God does, that this is true. ¹¹You know that we treated each one of you the way a father treats his own children. ¹²We encouraged you, we comforted you and we told you to live good lives for God. He calls you to be part of his glorious kingdom.

¹³Also, we always thank God because of the way you accepted his message. You heard it and accepted it as God's message, not our own. And it

---

ᵃ **2:7 But . . . gentle** Several Greek copies have "But we became babies".

GROW, GROW, GROW!

What do we do when things get hard? Do we moan and complain? Do we give up when the going gets tough?

DIG IN

READ 1 Thessalonians 1:2–6

- Who does Paul thank God for (v.2)?
- What three things does he particularly thank God for (v.3)?
- What is surprising about verse 6?

It had been a tough time for these believers – you can read all about it in Acts 17 – yet, despite the suffering, they believed the message about Jesus that Paul brought to them. On one occasion Paul had to leave Thessalonica because other people made trouble for them but the new believers had to stay – that's where they lived!

Despite things being hard, Paul can give thanks for the faith, love and hope of the church at Thessalonica.

- What do faith, love and hope look like in action (v.3)?

Faith causes us to be drawn to God: remembering all he has done, trusting him to go on loving and providing for us and obeying him in good works. Love means we reach out to others, caring and serving even when we're hurt! And hope isn't wishful thinking but knowing that Jesus will come back and take us to be with him – this keeps us going.

- Check out:
  » The effect of their faith.
  » What a true response to the Good News message looks like (v.6).

JUMP TO 2 Thessalonians 1:1–4

A short time has passed and things aren't getting any better.

- What is happening to their faith, love and hope?
- What is happening to their troubles?

READ 2 Thessalonians 1:5–12

- What will happen to those who are causing the believers to suffer (v.6,8–9)?
- What will happen to the believers (v.7)?
- What does he pray for the believers (v.11)?

Paul says a lot in 1 and 2 Thessalonians about what will happen when Jesus comes again. Here he's encouraging the believers, telling them that suffering will end and that God will punish those who are causing it. The believers need to know that if they stick with their faith and keep going they will enter God's kingdom. Meanwhile, Paul prays that God will give them the grace to keep on growing in their faith and doing good works so that Jesus will get the glory.

DIG THROUGH

- Does it surprise you that the believers' faith, love and hope grew even though they suffered? Ask God to help you grow in these things even when the going is tough.
- So how did the believers grow? Check out 2 Thessalonians 1:11–12.

It was only through God's power and grace. Sometimes we might think or be made to think that spiritual growth depends on us, but it doesn't! It is God's work that brings us to faith (1 Thessalonians 1:4–6; 2:13) and because of God's work that our faith grows so that we can do good things for him.

really is God's message. And it works in you who believe. [14]Brothers and sisters, you are just like God's churches in Judea[a] that belong to Christ Jesus. I mean that you were treated badly by your own people, just as those believers were treated badly by other Jews—[15]the same Jews who killed the Lord Jesus and the prophets. And they forced us to leave their country. They are not pleasing to God, and they are against everyone else. [16]And they are trying to stop us from teaching those who are not Jews. They don't want them to be saved. But they are just adding more and more sins to the ones they already have. Now the time has come for them to suffer God's anger.

Paul's Desire to Visit Them Again

[17]Brothers and sisters, we were separated from you for a short time. But even though we were not there, our thoughts were still with you. We wanted very much to see you, and we tried very hard to do this. [18]Yes, we wanted to come to you. I, Paul, tried more than once to come, but Satan stopped us. [19]You are our hope, our joy and the crown we will be proud of when our Lord Jesus Christ comes. [20]You bring us honour and joy.

3 We could not come to you, but it was very hard to wait any longer. [2]So we decided to send Timothy to you and stay in Athens alone. Timothy is our brother. He works with us for God to tell people the Good News about Christ. We sent Timothy to strengthen and encourage you in your faith. [3]We sent him so that none of you would be upset by the troubles we have now. You yourselves know that we must have these troubles. [4]Even when we were with you, we told you that we would all have to suffer. And you know that it happened just as we said. [5]This is why I sent Timothy to you, so that I could know about your faith. I sent him when I could not wait any more. I was afraid that the devil might have defeated you with his temptations. Then our hard work would have been wasted.

[6]But now Timothy has come back from his visit with you and told us good news about your faith and love. He told us that you always remember us in a good way. He told us that you want very much to see us again. And it is the same with us—we want very much to see you. [7]So, brothers and sisters, we are encouraged about you because of your faith. We have much trouble and suffering, but still we are encouraged. [8]Our life is really full if you stand strong in the Lord. [9]We have so much joy before our God because of you! So we thank God for you. But we cannot thank him enough for

all the joy we feel. [10]Night and day we continue praying with all our heart that we can come there and see you again. We want to give you everything you need to make your faith strong.

[11]We pray that our God and Father and our Lord Jesus will prepare the way for us to come to you. [12]We pray that the Lord will make your love grow. We pray that he will give you more and more love for each other and for all people. We pray that you will love everyone in the same way we love you. [13]This will strengthen your desire to do what is right, and you will be holy and without fault before our God and Father when our Lord Jesus comes with all his holy people.

A Life That Pleases God

4 Brothers and sisters, now I have some other things to tell you. We taught you how to live in a way that will please God. And you are living that way. Now we ask and encourage you in the Lord Jesus to live that way more and more. [2]You know all that we told you to do by the authority of the Lord Jesus. [3]God wants you to be holy. He wants you to stay away from sexual sins. [4]God wants each one of you to learn to control your own body. Use your body in a way that is holy and that gives honour to God.[b] [5]Don't let your sexual desires control you like the people who don't know God. [6]Never wrong any of your fellow believers or cheat them in this way. The Lord will punish those who do that. We have already told you this and warned you about it. [7]God chose us to be holy. He does not want us to live in sin. [8]So anyone who refuses to obey this teaching is refusing to obey God, not us. And God is the one who gives you his Holy Spirit.

[9]We don't need to write to you about having love for your brothers and sisters in Christ. God has already taught you to love each other. [10]In fact, you love all the believers in Macedonia. We encourage you now, brothers and sisters, to show your love more and more.

[11]Do all you can to live a peaceful life. Mind your own business, and earn your own living, as we told you before. [12]If you do these things, then those who are not believers will respect the way you live. And you will not have to depend on others for what you need.

The Lord's Coming

[13]Brothers and sisters, we want you to know about those who have died. We don't want you to be sad like other people—those who have no hope. [14]We believe that Jesus died, but we also believe that he rose again. So we believe that God

---

[a] **2:14 Judea** The Jewish land where Jesus lived and taught and where the church first began.
[b] **4:4** Or "God wants each of you to learn to live with your wife in a way that is holy and that gives honour to God."

HE'S COMING BACK - HAVE HOPE!

It was a really sad time for Jayden. His gran, who was a Christian, had just died and at the end of the week there would be a celebration to thank God for her life. But Jayden was confused – the last thing he felt like doing was celebrating, he just wanted to cry. Gran was gone and he couldn't get her back.

The new believers in Thessalonica would have been able to sympathize with Jayden. Here Paul has some encouraging words for them, for Jayden and for us.

DIG IN   READ 1 Thessalonians 4:13-14

- Something in verse 13 might seem shocking. What is it?
- Who should the believers be different from when someone dies?

Paul isn't saying here that it is wrong to be sad when someone dies. When we lose someone we love it's hard – we miss them and feel sad. That's okay, but Paul is saying that we don't need to feel like people "who have no hope". Often when we use the word "hope" it is in terms of wishful thinking, "I hope I get a bike for my birthday." But in the Bible "hope" means something that is great, that we know will happen and be ours.

- What is the "hope" Paul is talking about (v.14)?
- How can this change a Christian's view of death?

Coping with death can be an awful thing for those who don't know Jesus. If someone close to them dies, they have no hope of seeing them again and it's very distressing. But among Christians it's different. If our Christian friend or relative dies, we can be sure (because of Jesus' death and resurrection) that they are with Jesus and will be with him when he comes back again. The Christian hope looks forward to the wonderful things that will happen when Jesus returns, but Christians who die before then won't lose out in any way whatsoever. That's something that the believers in Thessalonica, like Jayden, hadn't quite grasped.

- What reassuring thing could you say to Jayden to help him understand his gran's death?

READ 1 Thessalonians 4:15-18

Paul says that when Jesus comes back, people's bodies will be raised from the dead – it's pretty dramatic stuff!

- Why not draw a picture or graphic strip to illustrate the events Paul talks about?

What an exciting message from God! The whole world will see and experience Jesus coming back to earth. First those who have already died will have their bodies raised and will physically meet Jesus, and then those who are still alive will follow. No one will miss out on the thrilling event of meeting Jesus. There'll be no more separation from each other or Jesus. It will be the best reunion ever!

- The believers in Thessalonica were anxious about Jesus' return. What would happen to all their friends who had already died? Would they see Jesus, or would they miss out? What would you say to them?
- Why does Paul write all these things (v.10,18)?

DIG THROUGH

- Has someone you know who loved Jesus died? Through your tears have hope that they are with Jesus and that we will all meet up together when Jesus comes back.
- What do you feel about the idea you will meet Jesus? How does this change your priorities?

DIG DEEPER

- Check out Philippians 1:21–23. If you've read this before, what Paul says might have struck you as rather surprising. How does this passage from Thessalonians shed light on how he's able to say this?

SURPRISE!

Have you ever come home from holiday to find that someone's broken into your house and taken everything? Was it a shock? A nasty surprise? What would you have done differently if you'd known the thief was coming?

DIG IN

READ 1 Thessalonians 5:1–5

- Who are the two kinds of people Paul describes?
- What will the day of the Lord be like for each group?

The Bible often uses light to illustrate being with God and darkness to represent not being with God. The people who live in darkness think they're safe. They don't believe Jesus will come again and think they're okay. Do you know people like that? Then there are those who live in light, believing God.

For each of them the return of Jesus will be very different. See how terrible it will be for those in darkness – it will be sudden, unexpected, unavoidable and as painful as giving birth (ask your mum about this!). The believers wanted to know the exact date because they were afraid they wouldn't be ready. However, Paul's words show that for those in the light, Jesus' return won't be a nasty surprise, for being ready is not about knowing when.

READ 1 Thessalonians 5:6–7

- What does not being ready look like?

Paul says that those who live in darkness, without God, are like those asleep or drunk when a thief comes – they are lazy and lacking in control – and for them, Jesus' return will be a nasty surprise. God wants his people to be spiritually alert, remembering that Jesus is coming back and living as though we belong to the light!

READ 1 Thessalonians 5:8–11

- How can we get ready?
- Why might we need to put on armour?

Christians are in a battle against the devil and our sin. The devil wants us to doubt Jesus is coming back so that we start living like those in darkness and give in to sin. However, Paul reminds us that we have God's "armour" to help us. We need to strap on faith (remembering what God has done and acting on it with good works) and love (for God and others). And we need to grab the helmet of the hope of salvation, which reminds us what is true: that Jesus died for us so that we can live with him when he comes again (vv.9–10). So we don't need to be afraid: God has already done everything we need to secure a life with Jesus. But we need to stay alert, reminding ourselves of these things.

DIG THROUGH

- Why not draw a picture of a helmet and write verses 9–10 in it. Every time you are tempted to disbelieve that God has forgiven you, or you are tempted to do wrong, have a look at it.
- In verse 11 Paul wants the believers to encourage each other – to remind each other that Jesus is coming again and to live in light of that. Why not speak to a Christian friend this week and encourage them with these verses?

DIG DEEPER

- Paul wrote to the Thessalonians for a second time because some people were spreading rumours that Jesus had already come back. Of course, this wasn't true. Read about it in 2 Thessalonians 2:1–12.

will raise to life through Jesus any who have died and bring them together with him when he comes. [15]What we tell you now is the Lord's own message. Those of us who are still living when the Lord comes again will join him, but not before those who have already died. [16]The Lord himself will come down from heaven with a loud command, with the voice of the archangel and with the trumpet call of God. And the people who have died and were in Christ will rise first. [17]After that, we who are still alive at that time will be gathered up with those who have died. We will be taken up in the clouds and meet the Lord in the air. And we will be with the Lord forever. [18]So encourage each other with these words.

INSIGHT

Many people falsely claim that they know when the world is going to end or when Jesus will return. But Jesus says in Matthew 24:36–44 that no one knows the exact day or hour. Paul reiterates this but adds that as we know it is coming we should be ready.

1 Thessalonians 5:1–11

Be Ready for the Lord's Coming

5 Now, brothers and sisters, we don't need to write to you about times and dates. [2]You know very well that the day when the Lord comes again will be a surprise, like a thief who comes at night. [3]People will say, "We have peace and we are safe." At that time destruction will come to them quickly, like the pains of a woman giving birth. And those people will not escape.

[4]But you, brothers and sisters, are not living in darkness. And so that day will not surprise you like a thief. [5]You are all people who belong to the light. You belong to the day. We don't belong to the night or to darkness. [6]So we should not be like other people. We should not be sleeping. We should be awake and have self-control. [7]People

who sleep, sleep at night. People who drink too much, drink at night. [8]But we belong to the day, so we should control ourselves. We should wear faith and love to protect us. And the hope of salvation should be our helmet.

[9]God did not choose us to suffer his anger. God chose us to have salvation through our Lord Jesus Christ. [10]Jesus died for us so that we can live together with him. It is not important if we are alive or dead when he comes. [11]So encourage each other and help each other grow stronger in faith, just as you are already doing.

Final Instructions and Greetings

[12]Now brothers and sisters, we ask you to recognize the value of those who work hard among you—those who, as followers of the Lord, serve as your leaders and tell you how to live. [13]Show them the highest respect and love because of the work they do.

Live in peace with each other. [14]We ask you, brothers and sisters, to warn those who will not work. Encourage those who are afraid. Help those who are weak. Be patient with everyone. [15]No one should ever try to pay back wrong for wrong. But always try to do what is good for each other and for all people.

[16]Always be full of joy. [17]Never stop praying. [18]Whatever happens, always be thankful. This is how God wants you to live in Christ Jesus.

[19]Don't stop the work of the Holy Spirit. [20]Don't treat prophecy like something that is not important. [21]But test everything. Keep what is good, [22]and stay away from everything that is evil.

[23]We pray that God himself, the God of peace, will make you pure—belonging only to him. We pray that your whole self—spirit, soul and body— will be kept safe and be free from blame when our Lord Jesus Christ comes. [24]The one who calls you will do that for you. You can trust him.

[25]Brothers and sisters, please pray for us. [26]Give all the brothers and sisters the special greeting of God's people.[a] [27]I tell you by the authority of the Lord to read this letter to all the believers there. [28]The grace of our Lord Jesus Christ be with you.

---

[a] **5:26 the special greeting of God's people** Literally, "a holy kiss".

Who Paul, writing again to the Christian community at Thessalonica. He is following up his previous letter to them. Apparently he had received news from the city that some strange rumours had been circulating ...

When Paul's second letter to the Thessalonians was written shortly after his first letter to them, probably around AD 51, to encourage them and clarify some misunderstandings.

What Paul reiterates his pride in the Thessalonians and his thankfulness for their faith. They need some encouragement, for they are encountering suffering. He reminds them that God is a God of judgement and that those who are causing the suffering will be judged and punished.

He goes on to clear up a misunderstanding. Someone in Thessalonica claims to have a letter from Paul saying that "the day of the Lord has already come" (2:1–2). It may be that they thought that the persecution and hardships they were experiencing were part of that event. Or it may be that they thought the day had already come and that they had missed it. Paul writes to reassure them and explain in more detail about the second coming of Jesus.

Paul first reassures those who believe that the day of the Lord had already come that it hasn't (2:1 – 3:5). He encourages the church to keep going in the face of persecution. He assures them that the trials they are going through are not punishments but tests of their faith.

He also addresses a specific problem: there were some in the community who were refusing to work (3:6–15). Either they thought that they would just hang around and wait for the second coming or, more likely, they were sponging off the richer Christians in their city.

This explains the sharper tone of this letter compared to his first. It includes some pretty blunt commands to keep away from anyone who doesn't obey the contents of the letter. They are not enemies, but their behaviour has consequences and they need to be warned (3:14–15).

QUICK TOUR ▶ **2 THESSALONIANS**

The Lord will bring justice 1:1–12
He hasn't returned yet 2:1–12
Be faithful 2:13–17

Keep praying 3:1–5
Don't be lazy 3:6–15

"We pray that the Lord Jesus Christ himself and God our Father will comfort you and strengthen you in every good thing you do and say. God loved us and gave us through his grace a wonderful hope and comfort that has no end."

2 Thessalonians 2:16–17

1 Greetings from Paul, Silas and Timothy. To the church of those in Thessalonica, who are in God our Father and the Lord Jesus Christ.

²Grace and peace to you from God the Father and the Lord Jesus Christ.

³We thank God for you always. And that's what we should do, because you give us good reason to be thankful: your faith is growing more and more. And the love that every one of you has for each other is also growing. ⁴So we tell the other churches of God how proud we are of you. We tell them how you patiently continue to be strong and have faith, even though you are being persecuted and are suffering many troubles.

INSIGHT

Christians in the early Church often faced persecution for their faith. Early on this came mainly from the Jews, and many Christians were imprisoned or martyred. Later on the Romans, too, decided that Christians were a threat and they often tortured them as a form of public entertainment.

2 Thessalonians 1:4–7

Paul Talks About God's Judgement

⁵This is proof that God is right in his judgement. He wants you to be worthy of his kingdom. Your suffering is for that kingdom. ⁶God will do what is right. He will punish those who are causing you trouble. ⁷And he will bring relief to you who are troubled. He will bring it to you and to us when the Lord Jesus comes from heaven for all to see, together with his powerful angels. ⁸He will come with burning fire to punish those who don't know God—those who refuse to accept the Good News about our Lord Jesus. ⁹They will be punished with a destruction that never ends. They will not be allowed to be with the Lord but will be kept away from his great power. ¹⁰This will happen on the day when the Lord Jesus comes to receive honour with his holy people. He will be admired among all who have believed. And this includes you because you believed what we told you.

¹¹That is why we always pray for you. We ask our God to help you live the good way he wanted when he chose you. The goodness you have makes you want to do good. And the faith you have makes you work. We pray that with his power God will help you do these things more and more. ¹²Then the name of our Lord Jesus will be honoured because of you, and you will be honoured because of him. This can happen only by the grace of our God and the Lord Jesus Christ.

Evil Things Will Happen

2 Brothers and sisters, we have something to say about the coming of our Lord Jesus Christ. We want to talk to you about that time when we will meet together with him. ²Don't let yourselves be easily upset or worried if you hear that the day of the Lord has already come. Someone might say that this idea came from us—in something the Spirit told us, or in something we said or in a letter we wrote. ³Don't be fooled by anything they might say. That day of the Lord will not come until the turning away from God happens. And that day will not come until the Man of Evil appears, the one who belongs to hell.ᵃ ⁴He will stand against and put himself above everything that people worship or think is worthy of worship. He will even go into God's Templeᵇ and sit there, claiming that he is God.

⁵I told you before that all these things would happen. Remember? ⁶And you know what is stopping that Man of Evil now. He is being stopped now so that he will appear at the right time. ⁷The secret power of evil is already working in the world now. But there is one who is stopping that secret power of evil. And he will continue to stop it until he is taken out of the way. ⁸Then that Man of Evil will appear. But the Lord Jesus will kill him with the breath that comes from his mouth. The Lord will come in a way that everyone will see, and that will be the end of the Man of Evil.

⁹When that Man of Evil comes, it will be the work of Satan. He will come with great power, and he will do all kinds of false miracles, signs and wonders. ¹⁰The Man of Evil will use every kind of evil to fool those who are lost. They are lost because they refused to love the truth and be saved. ¹¹So God will send them something powerful that leads them away from the truth and causes them to believe a lie. ¹²They will all be condemned because they did not believe the truth and because they enjoyed doing evil.

You Are Chosen for Salvation

¹³Brothers and sisters, you are people the Lord loves. And we always thank God for you. That's what we should do, because God chose you to be some of the first peopleᶜ to be saved. You are saved by the Spirit making you holy and by your

---

ᵃ **2:3 belongs to hell** Literally, "is the son of destruction".
ᵇ **2:4 Temple** Probably the Temple in Jerusalem. See "Tᴇᴍᴘʟᴇ" in the Word List.
ᶜ **2:13 to be . . . people** Some Greek copies say, "from the beginning".

FOLLOW MY EXAMPLE – DO SOME WORK!

Heidi started to believe in Jesus when she was very young, but recently she had begun to wonder if it was all worth it. There were lots of things she wanted to do that she knew God did not want her to do. She began to question whether it was *really* that important to follow God's word *all* the time.

DIG IN   READ 2 Thessalonians 3:1–5

- What does Paul want to happen (vv.1–2)?
- What should the church keep doing (vv.4–5)?

Paul had been specially commissioned by God to bring his words to the early church – so when he wants the believers to obey him, it's because it is God's words they will be obeying.

Paul wants the word of God to be spread quickly across the world – for everyone to hear the Good News of Jesus. And he wants the church to believe and obey God's teaching. The believers need to pray about this because there are many others who will distract them from this, people who don't believe in God or obey his word. Paul even points to some in the church at Thessalonica who can be like this . . .

READ 2 Thessalonians 3:6–15

Paul wants everyone to be joined together on a mission to spread the word of God, yet there seem to be some who aren't exactly going great guns.

- What were those who were being lazy not doing (v.6)?
- How were Paul and his friends different from those refusing to work (vv.7,9)?
- Why did they not ask for money (v.9)?
- Under whose authority does Paul command them to start working (v.12)?
- What should the believers do if anyone refuses to obey (vv.14–15)?

Some believers were refusing to obey the teaching of Paul and the other apostles – they weren't doing any work. It is possible this is because they thought Jesus was coming back in their lifetime and didn't see the point of keeping busy any more. Either way they weren't following the example of Paul and they weren't obeying the words of God. Paul has a strong message for them – start working, or risk being chucked out of church!

DIG THROUGH

- The problem was that the believers were not following the example or the teaching of Paul. Here he says that spreading the word of God across the world and obedience in the church is the most important thing. How are you getting on with this? Would you rather other people did all the work of sharing the Good News?

DIG DEEPER

- The writers of Proverbs have some words of warning for those who are lazy. Why not take a look at Proverbs 6:6–11, Proverbs 10:4–5, Proverbs 14:23 and Proverbs 19:15.

faith in the truth. [14]God chose you to have that salvation. He chose you by using the Good News that we told you. You were chosen so that you can share in the glory of our Lord Jesus Christ. [15]So, brothers and sisters, stand strong and continue to believe the teachings we gave you when we were there and by letter.

[16-17]We pray that the Lord Jesus Christ himself and God our Father will comfort you and strengthen you in every good thing you do and say. God loved us and gave us through his grace a wonderful hope and comfort that has no end.

Pray for Us

3 And now, brothers and sisters, pray for us. Pray that the Lord's teaching will continue to spread quickly. And pray that people will give honour to that teaching, the same as happened with you. [2]And pray that we will be protected from crooked and evil people. Not everyone believes in the Lord, you know.

[3]But the Lord is faithful. He will give you strength and protect you from the Evil One. [4]The Lord gives us confidence that you are doing what we told you and that you will continue to do it. [5]We pray that the Lord will cause you to feel God's love and remember Christ's patient endurance.

The Obligation to Work

[6]Brothers and sisters, by the authority of our Lord Jesus Christ we tell you to stay away from any believer who refuses to work. People who refuse to work are not following the teaching that we gave them. [7]You yourselves know that you should live like we do. We were not lazy when we were with you. [8]We never accepted food from anyone without paying for it. We worked and worked so that we would not be a burden to any of you. We worked night and day. [9]We had the right to ask you to help us. But we worked to take care of ourselves so that we would be an example

for you to follow. [10]When we were with you, we gave you this rule: "Whoever will not work should not be allowed to eat."

INSIGHT

Hard work is a Christian virtue. No laziness allowed! Paul's warning here echoes Proverbs 19:15 which says that if someone is not willing to work when they are capable of it, then they shouldn't eat either. The early followers of Jesus worked hard to spread the Good News and we should follow their example.
2 Thessalonians 3:6–12

[11]We hear that some people in your group refuse to work. They are doing nothing except being busy in the lives of others. [12]Our instruction to them is to stop bothering others, to start working and earn their own food. It is by the authority of the Lord Jesus Christ that we are urging them to do this. [13]Brothers and sisters, never get tired of doing good.

[14]If there are some there who refuse to do what we tell you in this letter, remember who they are. Don't associate with them. Then maybe they will feel ashamed. [15]But don't treat them as enemies. Counsel them as fellow believers.

Final Words

[16]We pray that the Lord of peace will give you peace at all times and in every way. The Lord be with you all.

[17]Here's my greeting in my own handwriting— PAUL. I do this in all my letters to show they are from me. This is the way I write.

[18]The grace of our Lord Jesus Christ be with you all.

1 TIMOTHY

Who
Paul, writing to his apprentice, Timothy. This is one of three pastoral letters that Paul sent to those who would continue his work. He first met Timothy on his second missionary journey (Acts 16:1–3).

When
Probably around AD 65–66. Some have suggested that Paul may have been released from Rome and then wrote 1 Timothy later. But there isn't any evidence for this, so we just don't know.

What
Paul had known Timothy for years and regarded him as a kind of son. Timothy was now at Ephesus, helping to lead the church there. Paul writes to him giving guidelines on how to choose church leaders and how to combat false teaching.

It is a letter full of the practicalities of leading a group of Christians in a first-century city like Ephesus.

In particular, Timothy is facing some kind of conflict with false teaching. He has to instruct some people – his "elders and betters" in some ways – not to spread false teaching or to involve themselves in a load of old superstition (1:3–7; 4:11–12).

We don't know what kind of thing they were saying – it seems to have involved some strange ideas about the law (1:7–11; 4:3–5). But there were also people in the church who spent too much time listening to myths and superstitions (4:7).

We should remember when reading this that Paul was addressing a specific community. There are important principles behind what Paul was saying but the specific advice he gives is to do with the culture and society of first-century Ephesus.

Paul's overriding point is that Christians – and especially those in any position of leadership – have to demonstrate lifestyles which reflect, rather than contradict, the Good News.

QUICK TOUR ➤ **1 TIMOTHY**

False and true teaching 1:1–20	Be a good servant 4:6 – 5:2
How to pray 2:1–15	Special instructions 5:3 – 6:2
Church leaders 3:1–13	True wealth 6:3–21
False teachers 4:1–5	

"Be careful in your life and in your teaching. Continue to live and teach rightly. Then you will save yourself and those who listen to your teaching."

1 Timothy 4:16

1 Greetings from Paul, an apostle for Christ Jesus. I am an apostle by the command of God our Saviour and Christ Jesus our hope.

²I write to you, Timothy. You are like a true son to me because of our faith.

Grace, mercy and peace from God the Father and Christ Jesus our Lord.

Warnings Against False Teachings

³When I went to Macedonia, I asked you to stay in Ephesus. Some people there are teaching things that are not true, and I want you to tell them to stop. ⁴Tell them not to give their time to meaningless stories and to long lists of ancestors to prove their ideas. Such things only cause arguments. They don't help God's work, which is done only by faith. ⁵My purpose in telling you to do this is to promote love—the kind of love shown by those whose thoughts are pure, who do what they know is right and whose faith in God is real. ⁶But some have missed this key point in their teaching and have gone off in another direction. Now they talk about things that help no one. ⁷They want people to respect them as teachers of the law*a* but they don't know what they are talking about. They don't even understand the things they say they are sure of.

⁸We know that the law is good if someone uses it in the right way. ⁹We also know that the law is not made for those who do what is right. It is made for those who are against the law and refuse to follow it. The law is for sinners who are against God and all that is pleasing to him. It is for those who have no interest in spiritual things and for those who kill their fathers or mothers or anyone else. ¹⁰It is for those who commit sexual sins, homosexuals, those who sell slaves, those who tell lies, those who don't tell the truth under oath and those who are against the true teaching of God. ¹¹That teaching is part of the Good News that our blessed God gave me to tell. In it we see his glory.

Thanks for God's Mercy

¹²I thank Christ Jesus our Lord because he trusted me and gave me this work of serving him. He gives me strength. ¹³In the past I insulted Christ. As a proud and violent man, I persecuted his people. But God gave me mercy because I did not know what I was doing. I did that before I became a believer. ¹⁴But our Lord gave me a full measure of his grace. And with that grace came the faith and love that are in Christ Jesus.

¹⁵Here is a true statement that should be accepted without question: Christ Jesus came into the world to save sinners, and I am the worst of them. ¹⁶But I was given mercy so that in me Christ Jesus could show that he has patience without limit. Christ showed his patience with me, the worst of all sinners. He wanted me to be an example for those who would believe in him and have eternal life. ¹⁷Honour and glory to the King who rules forever. He cannot be destroyed and cannot be seen. Honour and glory for ever and ever to the only God. Amen.

¹⁸Timothy, you are like a son to me. What I am telling you to do agrees with the prophecies*b* that were told about you in the past. I want you to remember those prophecies and fight the good fight of faith. ¹⁹Continue to trust in God and do what you know is right. Some people have not done this, and their faith is now in ruins. ²⁰Hymenaeus and Alexander are men like that. I have given them to Satan so that they will learn not to speak against God.

God Wants Us to Pray for Everyone

2 First of all, I ask that you pray for all people. Ask God to bless them and give them what they need. And give thanks. ²You should pray for rulers and for all who have authority. Pray for these leaders so that we can live quiet and peaceful lives—lives full of honour and respect for God. ³This is good and pleases God our Saviour.

⁴God wants everyone to be saved and to fully understand the truth. ⁵There is only one God, and there is only one way that people can reach God. That way is through Christ Jesus, who as a man ⁶gave himself to pay for everyone to be free. This is the message that was given to us at just the right time. ⁷And I was chosen as an apostle to tell people that message. (I am telling the truth; I am not lying.) I was chosen to teach those who are not Jews to believe and understand the truth.

Special Instructions for Men and Women

⁸I want the men everywhere to pray. Those who lift their hands in prayer must be men who live to please God. They must be men who keep themselves from getting angry and having arguments.

⁹And I want the women to make themselves attractive in the right way. Their clothes should be sensible and appropriate. They should not draw attention to themselves with fancy hairstyles or gold jewellery or pearls or expensive clothes. ¹⁰But they should make themselves attractive by the good things they do. That is more appropriate for women who say they are devoted to God.

---

a **1:7 the law** Probably the law God gave to Moses for his people. See "LAW" in the Word List. Also in verse 8.
b **1:18 prophecies** Things that prophets said about Timothy's life before those things happened.

THE TRUTH, THE WHOLE TRUTH AND NOTHING BUT . . .

. . . the Truth. When you know the truth it radically changes your life forever.

It's clear from the start of Paul's first letter to Timothy that he doesn't want Christians just to *know* the truth about Jesus but to *live* by the truth, the whole truth and nothing but the truth.

DIG IN

READ 1 Timothy 1:1-11

This book is an intimate letter from Paul to his young apprentice, Timothy, who he calls a "true son to me because of our faith". It's also a practical letter to a church leader whose congregation was under threat from some seriously dodgy teaching. There were men in Timothy's town who claimed to be Christians but preached stuff that just wasn't true (1:3–7; 4:1–5).

- What effect was false teaching having on the church (v.4,6)?
- How did Paul know they weren't teaching the truth? Check out 1 Timothy 4:1–7 and 1 Timothy 6:3–5 too.

READ 1 Timothy 1:12-17

- What example does Paul give of trustworthy teaching (v.15)?
- What effect has knowing the truth made on Paul's life (vv.13–14)?
- How does what we believe influence the way we live (v.16)? How does the way we live our lives influence what we believe?

READ 1 Timothy 2:1-7

Paul isn't just concerned for the church but also for political leaders.

- Why should we pray for those in authority (vv.2–3)?
- What does Paul say about the things that please God and what he wants? How can all people be saved (vv.4–7)?

DIG THROUGH

In 1 Timothy 2:4 Paul states that God wants "everyone to be saved and to fully understand the truth". It's in hearing the truth about Jesus that people are saved (2:7).

- Imagine you are telling your mates about Jesus. What are the most important things you would want to share with them about him? Clue: look especially at verses 5 and 6. Check out Ephesians 2:4–7 as well.
- Paul was radically changed by the Good News. How does the truth about Jesus change the way you view the world and yourself?
- Take a moment to thank God for the truth about Jesus and pray for opportunities to share this Good News with others.

DIG DEEPER

- Jesus said that he was "the truth" and that when we know him (the truth) it will make us free. For a closer look, check out John 8:32 and John 14:6.

INSIGHT

[11]A woman should learn while listening quietly and being completely willing to obey. [12]I don't allow a woman to teach a man or tell him what to do. She must listen quietly, [13]because Adam was made first. Eve was made later. [14]Also, Adam was not the one who was tricked.[a] It was the woman who was tricked and became a sinner. [15]But women will be saved in their work of having children. They will be saved if they continue to live in faith, love and holiness with sensible behaviour.

Leaders in the Church

3 It is a true statement that anyone whose goal is to serve as an elder[b] has his heart set on a good work. [2]An elder[c] must be such a good man that no one can rightly criticize him. He must be faithful to his wife.[d] He must have self-control and think carefully about the way he lives. He must be respected by others. He must be ready to help people by welcoming them into his home. He must be a good teacher. [3]He must not get drunk or like to fight. He must be gentle and peaceful. He must not be someone who loves money. [4]He must be a good leader of his own family. This means that his children obey him with full respect. [5]If a man does not know how to lead his own family, he will not be able to take care of God's church.

[6]An elder must not be a new believer. It might make him too proud of himself. Then he would be condemned for his pride the same as the devil was. [7]An elder must also have the respect of people who are not part of the church. Then he will not be criticized by others and be caught in the devil's trap.

Special Servants

[8]In the same way, the men who are chosen to be special servants must be worthy of respect. They must not be men who say things they don't mean or who spend their time drinking too much. They must not be men who are willing to cheat people for money. [9]They must follow the true faith that God has now made known to us and always do what they know is right. [10]You should test them first. Then, if you find that they have done nothing wrong, they can be special servants.

[11]In the same way, the women[e] must be worthy of respect. They must not be women who speak evil about other people. They must have self-control. They must be women who can be trusted in everything.

[12]The men who are special servants must be faithful in marriage.[f] They must be good leaders of children and their own families. [13]Those who do well as special servants are making an honourable place for themselves. And they will feel very sure of their faith in Christ Jesus.

The Secret of Our Life

[14]I hope I can come to you soon. But I am writing this to you now, [15]so that, even if I cannot come soon, you will know how people should live in the family[g] of God. That family is the church of the living God. And God's church is the support and foundation of the truth. [16]Yes, God has shown us the secret of lives that honour and please him. That amazing secret is the truth we can all agree on:

Christ[h] was made known to us in human form;
he was shown by the Spirit[i] to be all he claimed;
he was seen by angels.
The message about him was told to the nations;
people in the world believed in him;
he was taken up to heaven in glory.

---

[a] **2:14 Adam was not . . . tricked** The devil tricked Eve, and Eve caused Adam to sin. See Gen. 3:1–13.
[b] **3:1 whose . . . elder** Literally, "who aspires to supervision".
[c] **3:2 elder** Here, literally, "overseer". See "ELDERS (NEW TESTAMENT)" in the Word List.
[d] **3:2 faithful to his wife** Literally, "a man of one woman".
[e] **3:11 women** Probably the women who serve as special servants (See Rom. 16:1). It could be translated, "their wives", meaning the wives of the special servants, although there is no word for "their" in the Greek text.
[f] **3:12 faithful in marriage** Literally, "a man of one woman".
[g] **3:15 family** Literally, "house". This could mean that God's people are like God's temple.
[h] **3:16 Christ** Literally, "who". Some Greek copies have "God".
[i] **3:16 by the Spirit** Or "in his spiritual form".

A Warning About False Teachers

4 The Spirit clearly says that in the last times some will turn away from what we believe. They will obey spirits that tell lies. And they will follow the teachings of demons. ²Those teachings come through people who tell lies and trick others. These evil people cannot see what is right and what is wrong. It is like their conscience has been destroyed with a hot iron. ³They say that it is wrong to marry. And they say that there are some foods that people must not eat. But God made these foods, and those who believe and who understand the truth can eat them with thanks. ⁴Everything that God made is good. Nothing he made should be refused if it is accepted with thanks to him. ⁵Everything he created is made holy by what he has said and by prayer.

Be a Good Servant of Christ Jesus

⁶Tell this to the brothers and sisters there. This will show that you are a good servant of Christ Jesus. You will show that you are made strong by the words of faith and good teaching you have followed. ⁷Do not spend any time on all the silly stories that don't agree with God's truth. Instead, train yourself to live in a way that honours and pleases God. ⁸Training your body helps you in some ways. But trying to please God helps you in every way. It brings you blessings in this life and in the future life too. ⁹Here is a true statement that should be accepted without question: ¹⁰We hope in the living God, the Saviour of all people. In particular, he is the Saviour of all those who believe in him. This is why we work and struggle.

INSIGHT

Look at the apostle Paul's instructions to Timothy. Even those who are young can lead the way in their church if they follow these guidelines and set a positive example.

1 Timothy 4:11–16

---

¹¹Command and teach these things. ¹²You are young, but don't let anyone treat you as if you are not important. Be an example to show the believers how they should live. Show them by what you say, by the way you live, by your love, by your faith and by your pure life.

¹³Continue to read the Scriptures to the people, encourage them and teach them. Do this until I come. ¹⁴Remember to use the gift you have, which was given to you through a prophecy[a] when the group of elders laid their hands on you. ¹⁵Continue to do these things. Give your life to doing them. Then everyone can see how well you are doing. ¹⁶Be careful in your life and in your teaching. Continue to live and teach rightly. Then you will save yourself and those who listen to your teaching.

5 Don't speak angrily to an older man. But talk to him as if he were your father. Treat the younger men like brothers. ²Treat the older women like mothers. And treat the younger women with respect like sisters.

Taking Care of Widows

³Take care of widows who really need help. ⁴But if a widow has children or grandchildren, the first thing they need to learn is this: to honour God by taking care of their own family. In doing this, they will be repaying their parents and grandparents, and this pleases God. ⁵A widow who really needs help is one who has been left all alone. She trusts God to take care of her. She prays all the time, night and day and asks God for help. ⁶But the widow who uses her life to please herself is really dead while she is still living. ⁷Tell the believers there to take care of their family so that no one can say they are doing wrong. ⁸Everyone should take care of all their own people. Most importantly, they should take care of their own family. If they do not do that, then they do not accept what we believe. They are worse than someone who does not even believe in God.

⁹To be added to your list of widows, a woman must be 60 years old or older. She must have been faithful to her husband.[b] ¹⁰She must be known for the good she has done: raising children, welcoming travellers into her home, serving the needs[c] of God's people, helping those in trouble and using her life to do all kinds of good.

¹¹But don't put younger widows on that list. When their strong physical needs pull them away from their commitment to Christ, they will want to marry again. ¹²Then they will be guilty of not doing what they first promised to do. ¹³Also, these younger widows begin to waste their time going from house to house. They also begin to gossip and try to run other people's lives. They

---

[a] **4:14 prophecy** Something said about Timothy's life before that thing happened.
[b] **5:9 faithful to her husband** Literally, "a woman of one man".
[c] **5:10 serving the needs** Literally, "washing the feet", a social custom of the first century, because people wore open sandals on very dusty roads.

FIGHT THE GOOD FIGHT

Have you heard the one about the church youth leader, the boxer and a big fight? No, neither have I! Funny that, you hardly ever hear about Christians getting into fights, but that's exactly what Paul encourages us to do in this passage.

Okay, so the fight might not be against flesh and blood but it's no less intense a struggle against sin and the lies of the devil. Paul talks about fighting the good fight of faith twice in his first letter (1 Timothy 1:18; 6:12). What do you think he means?

DIG IN   READ 1 Timothy 4:11–16

Here are some really encouraging words for a young person who is a Christian. Poor timid Timothy, he does seem to be having a hard time of it!

- Why do you think people looked down on Timothy (v.12)? How does Paul encourage him to respond?
- What did the Christian fight look like for Timothy? What does it look like for you today?
- How does Paul encourage Timothy to fight the fight? What instructions does he give him?

READ 1 Timothy 6:11–16

It's all about the Good News. The only real power for change in our lives is the Good News that Jesus is Lord over everything, even our sin. That's why we need to ask for his help in fighting sin in our lives.

- What does Paul say Timothy must stay away from and what should he pursue in the Christian fight? (Clue: look back at 6:3–10.) What do Paul's words "Always try to do what is right, to honour God and to have faith, love, patience and gentleness" (v.11) mean for you today?

DIG THROUGH

- How is your Christian fight going at the moment? What areas of the battle do you especially need God's help with? How can you get help from other Christian friends and older Christians?
- In what ways does the fact that the Christian life is a fight change the way you see the world and prepare you for the future?
- Take a moment to pray about specific things in your life, asking God to help you stay away from temptation and do what is right, honour God and to have faith, love, patience and gentleness.

DIG DEEPER

- Want to read more on fighting the fight? Check out 1 Corinthians 9:24–27 and 2 Timothy 2:1–7.
- Take a look at Ephesians 6:10–18 to see how you can prepare yourself daily for the good fight of faith.

say things they should not say. ¹⁴So I want the younger widows to marry, have children and take care of their homes. If they do this, our enemy will not have any reason to criticize them. ¹⁵But some of the younger widows have already turned away to follow Satan.

¹⁶If any woman who is a believer has widows in her family, she^a should take care of them herself. Then the church will not have that burden and will be able to care for the widows who have no one else to help them.

More About Elders and Other Matters

¹⁷The elders who lead the church in a good way should receive double honour^b—in particular, those who do the work of counselling and teaching. ¹⁸As the Scriptures say, "When a work animal is being used to separate grain, don't keep it from eating the grain."^c And the Scriptures also say, "A worker should be given his pay."^d

¹⁹Don't listen to someone who accuses an elder. You should listen to them only if there are two or three others who can say what the elder did wrong. ²⁰Tell those who sin that they are wrong. Do this in front of the whole church so that the others will have a warning.

²¹Before God and Christ Jesus and the chosen angels, I tell you to make these judgements without any prejudice. Treat every person the same.

²²Think carefully before you lay your hands on anyone to make him an elder. Don't share in the sins of others. Keep yourself pure.

²³Timothy, stop drinking only water and drink a little wine. This will help your stomach, and you will not be sick so often.

²⁴The sins of some people are easy to see. Their sins show that they will be judged. But the sins of some others are seen only later. ²⁵It is the same with the good things people do. Some are easy to see. But even if they are not obvious now, none of them will stay hidden forever.

Special Instructions for Slaves

6 All those who are slaves should show full respect to their masters. Then God's name and our teaching will not be criticized. ²Some slaves have masters who are believers, so they are brothers. Does this mean they should show their masters any less respect? No, they should serve them even better, because they are helping believers, people they should love.

These are the things you must teach and tell everyone to do.

False Teaching and True Riches

³Some people teach what is false and do not agree with the true teaching that comes from our Lord Jesus Christ. They do not accept the teaching that leads us to honour and please God. ⁴They are proud of what they know, but they understand nothing. They are sick with a love for arguing and fighting about words. And that brings jealousy, quarrels, insults and evil mistrust. ⁵They are always making trouble, because they are people whose thinking has been confused. They have lost their understanding of the truth. They think that pretending to honour God is a way to get rich.

⁶Living in a way that honours God is, in fact, a way for people to be very rich, because it means being satisfied with what they have. ⁷When we came into the world, we brought nothing. And when we die, we can take nothing out. ⁸So, if we have food and clothes, we will be satisfied with that. ⁹People who want to be rich bring temptations to themselves. They are caught in a trap. They begin to want many foolish things that will hurt them. These things ruin and destroy people. ¹⁰The love of money causes all kinds of evil. Some people have turned away from what we believe because they want to get more and more money. But they have caused themselves a lot of pain and sorrow.

Some Things to Remember

¹¹But you belong to God. So you should stay away from all those things. Always try to do what is right, to honour God and to have faith, love, patience and gentleness. ¹²We have to fight to keep our faith. Try as hard as you can to win that worthy fight. Take hold of eternal life. It is the life you were chosen to have when you confessed your faith in Jesus—that wonderful truth you spoke so openly for all to hear. ¹³Before God and Christ Jesus I give you a command. Jesus is the one who confessed that same wonderful truth when he stood before Pontius Pilate. And God is the one who gives life to everything. Now I tell you this: ¹⁴do what you were commanded to do without fault or blame until the time when our Lord Jesus Christ comes again. ¹⁵God will make that happen at the right time. God is the blessed and only Ruler. He is the King of all kings and the Lord of all lords. ¹⁶God is the only one who never dies. He lives in light so bright that people cannot go near it. No one has ever seen him; no one is able to see him. All honour and power belong to him forever. Amen.

---

^a **5:16 woman . . . she** Some Greek copies have "man or woman . . . he/she".
^b **5:17 double honour** Or "double pay".
^c **5:18** Quote from Deut. 25:4.
^d **5:18** Quote from Luke 10:7.

17Give this command to those who are rich with the things of this world. Tell them not to be proud. Tell them to hope in God, not their money. Money cannot be trusted, but God takes care of us richly. He gives us everything to enjoy. 18Tell those who are rich to do good—to be rich in good works. And tell them they should be happy to give and ready to share. 19By doing this, they will be saving up a treasure for themselves. And that treasure will be a strong foundation on which their future life will be built. They will be able to have the life that is true life.

20Timothy, God has trusted you with many things. Keep these things safe. Stay away from people who talk about useless things that are not from God and who argue against you with a "knowledge" that is not knowledge at all. 21Some people who claim to have that "knowledge" have gone completely away from what we believe.

I pray that God's grace will be with you all.

Who Paul, writing to Timothy, his "dear son". Paul had known Timothy since he was young and knew his mother and grandmother well. He regarded him as a kind of son. Timothy was now in Ephesus helping to lead the church there.

 When Around AD 67–68. Sent from Rome during the last years of Paul's imprisonment, he sends a final letter of encouragement and direction to his "son".

 What Paul was writing to Timothy from prison in Rome. This seems to be his final imprisonment and he had no illusions about the future – he realized that his race was almost run.

This, Paul's final letter, is intensely personal. Paul was lonely. In jail in Rome, Paul's friends have either left him for other duties or deserted him for the world (4:9–12). Only Luke remains with him. Paul has had some kind of hearing which did not go well.

At this time, perhaps more than any other, Paul is missing his "dear son". Along with some important books and parchments, Timothy is asked to bring Paul a cloak which he left in Troas. Everything is wintry. Cold.

In the middle of all this suffering, Paul is reminded of an early Christian saying or hymn: "If we died with him, we will also live with him. If we remain faithful even in suffering, we will also rule with him . . ." (2:11–12). Paul endures all this so that people can obtain salvation. There is a bigger picture.

Paul reminds Timothy of how he had been specially commissioned for the work he was to do and how he prays constantly for him. And he urges Timothy to hold on to sound teaching and to the inspired Scriptures – which for Timothy would have been the Jewish Scriptures (our Old Testament). Above all, he encourages Timothy to be bold, have courage and continue in his work. Keep running, he says, right until the point you reach the finishing line.

QUICK TOUR ▶ 2 TIMOTHY

No shame 1:1–18
A loyal soldier of Christ 2:1–13
A worker who pleases God 2:14–26
The last days 3:1–9

Keep running 3:10 – 4:8
Personal instructions 4:9–18
Final greetings 4:19–22

"But I am not ashamed. I know the one I have put my trust in, and I am sure that he is able to protect what I have put into his care until that Day."

2 Timothy 1:12

1 Greetings from Paul, an apostle for Christ Jesus. I am an apostle because that is what God wanted. God wanted me to tell people about the promise of life that is in Christ Jesus.

²To Timothy, a dear son to me.

Grace, mercy and peace to you from God the Father and from Christ Jesus our Lord.

Thanksgiving and Encouragement

³I always remember you in my prayers day and night. And in these prayers I thank God for you. He is the God my ancestors served, and I have always served him with a clear conscience. ⁴I remember that you cried for me. I want very much to see you so that I can be filled with joy. ⁵I remember your true faith. That kind of faith first belonged to your grandmother Lois and to your mother Eunice. I know you now have that same faith. ⁶That is why I want you to remember the gift God gave you. God gave you that gift when I laid my hands on you. Now I want you to use that gift and let it grow more and more, like a small flame grows into a fire. ⁷The Spirit God gave us does not make us afraid. His Spirit is a source of power and love and self-control.

⁸So don't be ashamed to tell people about our Lord Jesus. And don't be ashamed of me—I am in prison for the Lord. But suffer with me for the Good News. God gives us the strength to do that.

⁹God saved us and chose us to be his holy people, but not because of anything we ourselves did. God saved us and made us his people because that was what he wanted and because of his grace. That grace was given to us through Christ Jesus before time began. ¹⁰And now it has been shown to us in the coming of our Saviour Christ Jesus. He destroyed death and showed us the way to have life. Yes, through the Good News Jesus showed us the way to have life that cannot be destroyed.

¹¹I was chosen to tell people that message as an apostle and teacher. ¹²And I suffer now because of that work. But I am not ashamed. I know the one I have put my trust in, and I am sure that he is able to protect what I have put into his care[a] until that Day.

¹³What you heard me teach is an example of what you should teach. Follow that model of true teaching with the faith and love we have in Christ Jesus. ¹⁴This teaching is a treasure that you have been trusted with. Protect it with the help of the Holy Spirit, who lives inside us.

¹⁵You know that everyone in Asia has left me. Even Phygelus and Hermogenes have left me. ¹⁶I pray that the Lord will show mercy to the family of Onesiphorus. Many times Onesiphorus encouraged me. He was not ashamed that I was in prison. ¹⁷No, he was not ashamed. When he came to Rome, he looked and looked for me until he found me. ¹⁸I pray that the Lord Jesus will make sure Onesiphorus receives mercy from the Lord God on that Day. You know how many ways this brother helped me in Ephesus.

A Loyal Soldier of Christ Jesus

2 Timothy, you are a son to me. Be strong in the grace that we have because we belong to Christ Jesus. ²What you have heard me teach publicly you should teach to others. Share these teachings with people you can trust. Then they will be able to teach others these same things. ³As a good soldier of Christ Jesus, accept your share of the troubles we have. ⁴A soldier wants to please his commanding officer, so he does not spend any time on activities that are not a part of his duty. ⁵Athletes in a race must obey all the rules to win. ⁶The farmer who works hard deserves the first part of the harvest. ⁷Think about what I am saying. The Lord will help you understand it all.

⁸Remember Jesus Christ. He is from the family of David. After Jesus died, he was raised from death. This is the Good News that I tell people. ⁹And because I tell that message, I am suffering. I am even bound with chains like someone who has really done wrong. But God's message is not bound. ¹⁰So I patiently accept all these troubles. I do this to help the people God has chosen so that they can have the salvation that is in Christ Jesus. With this salvation comes glory that never ends. ¹¹Here is a true statement:

If we died with him,
we will also live with him.
¹²If we remain faithful even in suffering,
we will also rule with him.
If we refuse to say we know him,
he will refuse to say he knows us.
¹³If we are not faithful,
he will still be faithful
because he cannot be false to himself.

A Worker Who Pleases God

¹⁴Keep on telling everyone these truths. And warn them before God not to argue about words. Such arguments don't help anyone, and they ruin those who listen to them. ¹⁵Do your best to be the kind of person God will accept, and give yourself to him. Be a worker who has no reason to be ashamed of his work, one who applies the true teaching in the right way.

---

[a] 1:12 **what . . . care** Or "what he has trusted me with".

INTEGRITY MATTERS

This was the last letter Paul ever wrote. If you were to write a letter for the last time, what would you want to say? You'd write about the stuff that mattered most to you and the things you really wanted the reader to know. Let's sit up, pay attention and listen in to Paul's final words.

DIG IN

READ 2 Timothy 1:1–7

- What do these verses tell us about Timothy's character and friendship with Paul?
- What kind of spirit does God give to Christians (v.7)?

READ 2 Timothy 1:8–18

Paul had suffered a lot for the sake of the Good News message. He was in prison as he wrote these words and many of his friends had abandoned him. If nothing else, he is a real life example of how Christians can expect to be given a hard time for what they believe.

- Paul tells Timothy not to be ashamed of the message of Jesus and to join with him in suffering for the sake of the Good News. What encouragements are there from:
  - » what God is like (vv.8,12)?
  - » the way God saves people (v.9)?
  - » what the Good News is about (v.10)?

READ 2 Timothy 2:1–26

Since life as a Christian will be tough, it's no surprise Paul encourages Timothy to "be strong" and get into training.

- Paul talks about passing on the baton of faith to others (v.2). What does he mean by "what you have heard me teach publicly you should teach to others. Share these teachings with people you can trust"? How should these important things be passed on?
- In what ways is the Christian life like being a soldier, an athlete and a farmer? How can you get into training in practical ways this week?
- Once again, Paul says there is stuff we should stay away from and other things we should pursue instead. List everything Paul warns against in verses 22–26. What does he encourage us to be like? Why?

DIG THROUGH

- Why do we sometimes feel ashamed of being a Christian? When are you most tempted to feel ashamed of the Good News? What should motivate us to stick up for faith in Jesus at school, college or with our mates?
- How can you stay away from what Paul says are things young people want to do? What has to go and what has to grow in your life? How might that help others to accept the Good News when we share it?
- How do we react when our mates disagree with our Christian beliefs? Do we argue (vv.14,16,23–24), or do we try to be faithful to the Bible (v.15) and speak kindly (vv.22,24–25)? Ask God to help you speak kindly and faithfully.

DIG DEEPER

- See Colossians 3:1–17 and 1 Peter 2:12 for more advice on integrity.
- Suffering for the sake of the Good News is a major theme in the New Testament. Check out Luke 9:26, Romans 1:16 and Revelation 21:1–4 for extra encouragement about not being ashamed of the Good News message. The book of 1 Peter has a lot to say about suffering, see 1:5–7, 2:19–23 and 3:14.

[16]Stay away from people who talk about useless things that are not from God. That kind of talk will lead a person further and further away from God. [17]Their evil teaching will spread like a sickness inside the body. Hymenaeus and Philetus are men like that. [18]They have left the true teaching. They say that the day when people will be raised from death has already come and gone. And they are destroying the faith of some people.

[19]But God's strong foundation never moves, and these words are written on it: "The Lord knows those who belong to him."[a] Also, these words are written there: "Everyone who says they believe in the Lord must stop doing wrong."

[20]In a large house there are things made of gold and silver. But there are also things made of wood and clay. Some of these are used for special purposes, others for ordinary jobs. [21]The Lord wants to use you for special purposes, so make yourself clean from all evil. Then you will be holy, and the Master can use you. You will be ready for any good work.

[22]Stay away from the evil things a young person like you typically wants to do. Always try to do what is right and to have faith, love and peace, together with others who trust in the Lord with pure hearts. [23]Stay away from foolish and stupid arguments. You know that these arguments grow into bigger arguments. [24]As a servant of the Lord, you must not argue. You must be kind to everyone. You must be a good teacher, and you must be patient. [25]You must gently teach those who don't agree with you. Maybe God will let them change their hearts so that they can accept the truth. [26]The devil has trapped them and now makes them do what he wants. But maybe they can wake up to see what is happening and free themselves from the devil's trap.

INSIGHT

Many People Will Stop Loving God

3 Remember this: there are some terrible times coming in the last days. [2]People will love only themselves and money. They will be proud and boast about themselves. They will abuse others with insults. They will not obey their parents. They will be ungrateful and against all that is pleasing to God. [3]They will have no love for others and will refuse to forgive anyone. They will talk about others to hurt them and will have no self-control. They will be cruel and hate what is good. [4]People will turn against their friends. They will do foolish things without thinking and will be so proud of themselves. Instead of loving God, they will love pleasure. [5]They will pretend to honour God, but they will refuse the power that helps us truly honour and please him. Stay away from these people!

[6]Some of them go into homes and get control over weak women, whose lives are full of sin—women who are led into sin by all the things they want. [7]These women always want to learn something new, but they are never able to fully understand the truth. [8]Just as Jannes and Jambres[b] fought against Moses, these people fight against the truth. Their thinking has been confused. The faith they have and teach is worthless. [9]But they will not succeed in what they are trying to do. Everyone will see how foolish they are. That is what happened to Jannes and Jambres.

Last Instructions

[10]But you know all about me. You know what I teach and the way I live. You know my goal in life. You know my faith, my patience and my love. You know that I never stop trying. [11]You know about my persecutions and my sufferings. You know all the things that happened to me in Antioch, Iconium and Lystra—the persecution I suffered in those places. But the Lord saved me from all of it. [12]In fact, every believer in Christ Jesus who wants to live in a way that honours God will be persecuted. [13]People who are evil and cheat others will become worse and worse. They will fool others, but they will also be fooling themselves.

[14]But you should continue following the teaching you learned. You know it is true, because you know you can trust those who taught you. [15]You have known the Holy Scriptures[c] since you were a child. These Scriptures are able to make you wise. And that wisdom leads to salvation through faith in Christ Jesus. [16]All Scripture is given by God. And all Scripture is useful for teaching and for showing people what is wrong in their lives. It is useful for correcting faults and teaching the right way to live. [17]Using the Scriptures, those who serve God will be prepared and will have everything they need to do every good work.

---

[a] **2:19** Quote from Num. 16:5.
[b] **3:8** *Jannes and Jambres* Probably the magicians who opposed Moses in Pharaoh's court. See Exod. 7:11–12,22.
[c] **3:15** *Holy Scriptures* Writings that Jews and followers of Christ accepted to be from God—the Old Testament.

PREACH THE WORD

Telling people about Jesus can be pretty scary at times, especially when they take the mickey or make life hard for you. It shouldn't come as a surprise to us when people reject the message of Jesus because many who heard him rejected Jesus himself.

DIG IN

READ 2 Timothy 3:1-9

Paul writes about how life will be hard before Jesus comes back again.

- What does Paul warn people will be like in the "last days"? Why should Timothy have nothing to do with them?

READ 2 Timothy 3:10-17

- What warnings does Paul give about how Christians will be treated? How do you feel about Paul's warning, in verse 12 especially?
- In such difficult times, what does Paul say Christians should continue doing? Why? What encouragements can we have?

READ 2 Timothy 4:1-22

Now we get to the nitty-gritty as Paul writes his last recorded words and talks about the stuff that really matters. He reminds Timothy that God is with him and one day will judge everyone.

- What instruction does Paul give Timothy in verse 2? What is God's message that Timothy must preach? (Clue: 2 Timothy 3:14–17.) When should Timothy be ready to do this?
- What other results should we sometimes expect from people when the Bible is taught (vv.3–5)? Why does this happen? How should Timothy respond?
- What are Paul's reflections on his life in verses 6 to 8? What is he looking forward to?

In his final words from verse 9 onwards, Paul is pretty blunt about those who have left him or fought against his teaching. He also has lots of good words to say about those who have kept the faith and kept on telling the Good News even when life got tough.

- What reassurances and encouragements does Paul have in verse 18? What can we learn from them?

DIG THROUGH

- What opportunities have you had to tell people about Jesus and how have these experiences encouraged you to keep going?
- What's the worst thing that could happen to you when telling people about Jesus? How does the sure thing of life with Jesus in the future make a difference to the way you share him with friends today?
- Take a moment to pray for opportunities to share the Good News with your mates. Ask for God to be with you and give you strength (2 Timothy 4:17) in knowing what to say and to see the opportunities when they come.
- Are you ever tempted to change the Good News message to make it sound a bit better to your friends? It's sometimes really tempting to do this. Ask God to help you stay faithful to the Bible even when it's tough.

DIG DEEPER

- Want to see exactly what tough times Paul faced for telling people about Jesus? Check out Acts 13:14 – 14:23.
- Evangelism can be tough. For more encouragement about telling people about Jesus see 1 Corinthians 1:18, 2 Corinthians 3:12–16, 2 Corinthians 4:1–6 and 1 Peter 3:15–16.

4 Before God and Christ Jesus, I give you a command. Christ is the one who will judge all people—those who are living and those who have died. He is coming again to rule in his kingdom. So I give you this command: ²tell everyone God's message. Be ready at all times to do whatever is needed. Tell people what they need to do, tell them when they are doing wrong, and encourage them. Do this with great patience and careful teaching.

³The time will come when people will not listen to the true teaching. But people will find more and more teachers who please them. They will find teachers who say what they want to hear. ⁴People will stop listening to the truth. They will begin to follow the teaching in false stories. ⁵But you should control yourself at all times. When troubles come, accept them. Do the work of telling the Good News. Do all the duties of a servant of God.

⁶My life is being given as an offering for God. The time has come for me to leave this life here. ⁷I have fought the good fight. I have finished the race. I have served the Lord faithfully. ⁸Now, a prize is waiting for me—the crown that will show I am right with God. The Lord, the judge who judges rightly, will give it to me on that Day. Yes, he will give it to me and to everyone else who is eagerly looking forward to his coming.

Personal Notes

⁹Do your best to come to me as soon as you can. ¹⁰Demas loved this world too much. That is why he left me. He went to Thessalonica. Crescens went to Galatia. And Titus went to Dalmatia. ¹¹Luke is the only one still with me. Get Mark and bring him with you when you come. He can help me in my work here. ¹²I sent Tychicus to Ephesus. ¹³When I was in Troas, I left my coat there with Carpus. So when you come, bring it to me. Also, bring my books. The books written on parchment are the ones I need.

¹⁴Alexander the metalworker caused me so much harm. The Lord will punish him for what he did. ¹⁵He fought against everything we teach.

You should be careful that he doesn't hurt you too.

¹⁶The first time I defended myself, no one helped me. Everyone left me. I pray that God will forgive them. ¹⁷But the Lord stayed with me. The Lord gave me strength so that I could tell the Good News everywhere. He wanted all those who are not Jews to hear that Good News. So I was saved from the lion's mouth. ¹⁸The Lord will save me when anyone tries to hurt me. He will bring me safely to his heavenly kingdom. Glory for ever and ever be the Lord's. Amen.

INSIGHT

Paul asks Timothy to bring him his books and parchments. Parchments were writings on animal skin – usually goat or sheepskin. This indicates that they were important documents. Books consisted of sheets of parchment or papyrus sewn together, and this is what would have been used in the early Church. We don't know what was written on them but they could have been important documents relating to his trial or his letters.

2 Timothy 4:13

Final Greetings

¹⁹Give my greetings to Priscilla and Aquila and to the family of Onesiphorus. ²⁰Erastus stayed in Corinth. And I left Trophimus in Miletus—he was sick. ²¹Try as hard as you can to come to me before winter.

Greetings to you from Eubulus, Pudens, Linus, Claudia and all the brothers and sisters here.

²²Timothy, I pray that the Lord will be with your spirit. And may his grace be with you all.

Who
Paul, writing to his trusted co-worker, Titus. This is another of the pastoral letters Paul sent to encourage church leaders facing difficult times. Titus was a leader in the church in Crete (1:5).

When
We're not sure, but probably sometime during the 60s AD. According to the letter, Titus is on the island of Crete, where Paul left him to continue the work he founded when he spent time there during his journey to Rome.

What
Titus worked with Paul on several of his journeys. He played a key role in the conflict with the Corinthian church, and spent time working in Dalmatia (modern-day Croatia). At the time of this letter, Titus is in Crete.

Paul is writing to encourage him and advise him, in a similar way to his letters to Timothy. He advises Titus on leadership, holiness and honesty. Church leaders should be people of good reputation and personal behaviour. Arguments and disputes should be avoided.

As with his letter to Timothy, Paul writes to Titus because there are false teachers sniffing around for personal gain (1:10–11). And, as in 1 Timothy, we don't know exactly what they were teaching but Paul contrasts them with "proper" leaders – elders who are examples of the right kind of Christian life (1:5–9). But upright lives are not just the work of leaders: all Christians have a duty; young and old, slave and free (2:1–10; 3:1–3).

It's quite a toughly-worded letter. Paul is very harsh about the inhabitants of the island: "Even one of their own prophets said, 'Cretans are always liars. They are evil animals and lazy people who do nothing but eat.' The words that prophet said are true" (1:12–13). He doesn't pull his punches! But Paul understood that a lot was at stake. Above all, it matters how we conduct ourselves. We used to be evil and stupid and disobedient but that behaviour should have gone now. We have been given new life through Jesus and that means new ways of behaving.

QUICK TOUR ▶ TITUS

Greetings 1:1–4
Church leaders 1:5–16
Good examples 2:1–15

Doing good 3:1–11
Final instructions and greetings 3:12–15

"But then the kindness and love of God our Saviour was made known. He saved us because of his mercy, not because of any good things we did."

Titus 3:4–5

1 Greetings from Paul, a servant of God and an apostle of Jesus Christ. I was sent to help God's chosen people have faith and understand the truth that produces a life of devotion to God. ²This faith and knowledge make us sure that we have eternal life. God promised that life to us before time began—and God does not lie. ³At the right time, God let the world know about that life. He did this through the telling of the Good News message, and he trusted me with that work. I told people that message because God our Saviour commanded me to.

⁴To Titus, a true son to me in the faith we share together.

Grace and peace to you from God the Father and Christ Jesus our Saviour.

Titus' Work in Crete

⁵I left you in Crete so that you could finish doing what still needed to be done. And I also left you there so that you could choose men to be elders in every town. ⁶To be an elder, a man must not be guilty of living in a wrong way. He must be faithful to his wife,ᵃ and his children must be faithful to God.ᵇ They must not be known as children who are wild or don't obey. ⁷An elderᶜ has the job of taking care of God's work. So people should not be able to say that he lives in a wrong way. He must not be someone who is proud and selfish or who gets angry quickly. He must not drink too much, and he must not be someone who likes to fight. He must not be a man who will do almost anything for money. ⁸An elder must be ready to help people by welcoming them into his home. He must love what is good. He must be wise. He must do what is right. He must be devoted to God and pleasing to him. And he must be able to control himself. ⁹An elder must be faithful to the same true message we teach. Then he will be able to encourage others with teaching that is true and right. And he will be able to show those who are against this teaching that they are wrong.

¹⁰This is important, because there are many people who refuse to obey—people who talk about worthless things and mislead others. I am talking especially about those who say that men who are not Jews must be circumcised to please God. ¹¹These people must be stopped, because they are destroying whole families by teaching what they should not teach. They teach only to cheat people and make money. ¹²Even one of their own prophets said, "Cretans are always liars. They are evil animals and lazy people who do nothing but eat." ¹³The words that prophet

said are true. So tell those people that they are wrong. You must be strict with them. Then they will become strong in the faith, ¹⁴and they will stop paying attention to the stories told by those Jews. They will stop following the commands of those who have turned away from the truth.

¹⁵To people who are pure, everything is pure. But to those who are full of sin and don't believe, nothing is pure. Really, their thinking has become evil and their consciences have been ruined. ¹⁶They say they know God, but the evil things they do show that they don't accept him. They are disgusting. They refuse to obey God and are not capable of doing anything good.

Following the True Teaching

2 You, however, must tell everyone how to live in a way that agrees with the true teaching. ²Teach the older men to have self-control, to be serious and to be wise. They must be strong in faith, in love and in patience.

³Also, teach the older women to live the way those who serve the Lord should live. They should not go around saying bad things about others or be in the habit of drinking too much. They should teach what is good. ⁴By doing this they will teach the younger women to love their husbands and children. ⁵They will teach them to be wise and pure, to take care of their homes, to be kind and to be willing to serve their husbands. Then no one will be able to criticize the teaching God gave us.

⁶In the same way, tell the young men to be wise. ⁷You should be an example for them in every way by the good things you do. When you teach, be honest and serious. ⁸And your teaching should be clearly right so that you cannot be criticized. Then anyone who is against you will be ashamed. There will not be anything bad they can say about us.

INSIGHT

In Bible times, slavery was an accepted part of everyday life and there would have been Christians among their number. Slavery has been outlawed today but most of us have someone they are subservient to, perhaps a teacher, tutor or boss. How do you behave towards them?

Titus 2:9–10

ᵃ **1:6 faithful to his wife** Literally, "a man of one woman".
ᵇ **1:6 faithful to God** This word can mean "trustworthy" or "believers". Here, both meanings may be included. Compare this verse with 1 Tim. 3:4.
ᶜ **1:7 elder** Here, literally, "overseer". See "ELDERS (NEW TESTAMENT)" in the Word List.

BELIEF AND BEHAVIOUR

Laura and Lisa responded to the Good News message on the same night at a church youth camp. They both started out as "on-fire" Christians – telling their friends about Jesus, getting to know their Bibles better and praying together most days.

But as the weeks turned into months, they drifted apart. While Laura grew in her faith, Lisa got distracted. They both still call themselves Christians but their lives – what they get up to and how they think – are now totally different. Laura's friends know why she chooses not to drink and sleep around. Lisa's friends don't think of her as different at all.

DIG IN   READ Titus 2:1–14

- What can you tell about Titus, the recipient of this letter?
- What about the people Paul is referring to?

The apostle Paul is writing here to Titus, an old friend. Together they planted a church in Crete, and Paul left Titus in charge.

It sounds as if in this church there are some people like Laura and some like Lisa. All have heard the Good News of Jesus and what it means to trust in him, but they're not all living as they should. Some are getting distracted and falling into bad habits. Some are teaching wrong things and causing others to go astray.

Belief in Jesus, Paul reminds Titus, must result in different behaviour. If people's lives aren't being changed, there is something wrong with their faith. Understanding the truth should lead to "devotion to God" (Titus 1:1).

- What groups of people is Paul giving Titus guidance on?
- What practical suggestions are there for young men and women (vv.4–7)?
- How are older people particularly instructed (v.2–3)?

Paul thinks there are specific ways in which the lives of believing men and women of all ages should look different to the world. At different stages in our lives there are unique ways we can show that our faith makes a difference to how we live.

Nobody is excluded. Paul covers everyone: men and women; young and old. He even specifically addresses the other big divide in society at this time – those who were slaves and those who were free (vv.9–10). In short, this message applies to everyone – the whole family of God. It was a message for believers then and it's a message for us today. Our lives should be an example to others.

DIG THROUGH

- Look again at Titus 2:11. What is the main reason the church should live differently to the world? Paul is absolutely clear that we should live well because of the grace God has shown us.
- But there's another dimension too, of which Paul is keen to remind Titus. Look carefully at verses 5, 8 and 10. What is the common theme? Paul highlights the fact that the way we live has an impact on other people. When people say they're Christians, their lives are on trial. We need to live well so that people can see that the Good News really is good.

DIG DEEPER

On either side of these key verses in Titus 2, Paul draws attention to people who are drawing others away from the true teaching. They are misleading them and this is having a destructive impact on the family of God (Titus 1:10–11). False teaching was common in the early church, and is still visible today. But being able to put up a defence against false teaching results from having good doctrine (a set of beliefs), stemming from a firm grasp of the Good News. The book of 2 Peter has much more to say on this.

9And tell this to those who are slaves: they should be willing to serve their masters at all times; they should try to please them, not argue with them; 10they should not steal from them; and they should show their masters that they can be trusted. Then, in everything they do, they will show that the teaching of God our Saviour is good.

11That is the way we should live, because God's grace has come. That grace can save everyone. 12It teaches us not to live against God and not to do the bad things the world wants to do. It teaches us to live on earth now in a wise and right way—a way that shows true devotion to God. 13We should live like that while we are waiting for the coming of our great God and Saviour Jesus Christ. He is our great hope, and he will come with glory. 14He gave himself for us. He died to free us from all evil. He died to make us pure—people who belong only to him and who always want to do good.

15These are the things you should tell people. Encourage them, and when they are wrong, correct them. You have full authority to do this, so don't let anyone think they can ignore you.

The Right Way to Live

3 Remind your people that they should always be under the authority of rulers and government leaders. They should obey these leaders and be ready to do good. 2Tell them not to speak evil of anyone but to live in peace with others. They should be gentle and polite to everyone.

3In the past we were foolish too. We did not obey, we were wrong and we were slaves to the many things our bodies wanted and enjoyed. We spent our lives doing evil and being jealous. People hated us and we hated each other. 4But then the kindness and love of God our Saviour was made known. 5He saved us because of his mercy, not because of any good things we did. He saved us through the washing that made us new people. He saved us by making us new through the Holy Spirit. 6God poured out to us that Holy Spirit fully through Jesus Christ our Saviour. 7We were made right with God by his grace. God saved us so that we could be his children and look forward to receiving life that never ends. 8This is a true statement.

And I want you to be sure that the people understand these things. Then those who believe in God will be careful to use their lives for doing good. These things are good and will help everyone.

9Stay away from those who have foolish arguments, who talk about useless family histories, or who make trouble and fight about what the Law of Moses teaches. These things are useless and will not help anyone. 10Give a warning to all those who cause arguments. If they continue to cause trouble after a second warning, then don't associate with them. 11You know that people like that are evil and sinful. Their sins prove they are wrong.

INSIGHT

Paul would have had to stay in Nicopolis over the winter, as ships wouldn't have sailed during the stormy winter months.
Titus 3:12

Final Instructions and Greetings

12I will send Artemas and Tychicus to you. When I send them, try hard to come to me at Nicopolis. I have decided to stay there this winter. 13Zenas the lawyer and Apollos will be travelling from there. Do all that you can to help them prepare for their trip. Be sure that they have everything they need. 14Our people must learn to use their lives for doing good and helping anyone who has a need. Then they will not have empty lives.

15All the people with me here send you their greetings. Give my greetings to those who love us in the faith.

Grace be with you all.

Who
Paul, writing to Philemon, probably a convert of Paul's. Philemon lived in Colossae where, along with a woman called Apphia and a fellow worker called Archippus, he was a leader of a group of Christians who met in his house.

When
AD 60–61. Paul was in Rome, where he was under arrest. The letter was probably written around the same time as his letter to the Colossians and Ephesians. All three letters were sent with Tychicus and Onesimus.

What
Paul is writing to Philemon, a rich Christian, to ask for mercy on behalf of one of Philemon's slaves, Onesimus. He sends the letter back with Onesimus, accompanied by Tychicus.

It is usually suggested that Onesimus is a runaway slave, but it doesn't explicitly say this in the letter. Of course, it is quite possible that Onesimus had run away – many slaves did. Often they joined groups of robbers and bandits, or they attempted to disappear in the large cities. But Onesimus has become a believer and seems to have chosen to serve Paul. In Colossians, where he is mentioned, Paul calls him "the faithful and dear brother from your group" (Colossians 4:9).

Whatever the case, it seems that there was a problem between Onesimus and his master. Some money or expense seems to have been involved. Something had caused Philemon to believe Onesimus (whose name means "useful") was "useless" (v.11). But Paul writes pleading that the two should be reconciled. More, that Onesimus should be welcomed back "not to be just a slave, but better than a slave, to be a dear brother. That's what he is to me. And I know he will mean even more to you, both as your slave and as one who shares your faith in the Lord" (vv.15–16).

In the world of the New Testament such a request would have been utterly radical. Slaves and masters were not "brothers", they were not on the same level. But Onesimus is different now. He has joined the kingdom of God, where everyone is equal.

QUICK TOUR ▶ **PHILEMON**

Philemon's love and faith verses 4–7
Plea for Onesimus verses 8–22

Final greetings verses 23–25

"Onesimus was separated from you for a short time. Maybe that happened so that you could have him back forever, not to be just a slave, but better than a slave, to be a dear brother. That's what he is to me. And I know he will mean even more to you, both as your slave and as one who shares your faith in the Lord."

Philemon verses 15–16

¹Greetings from Paul, a prisoner for Christ Jesus, and from Timothy, our brother.

To Philemon, our dear friend and worker with us. ²Also to our sister Apphia, to Archippus, who serves with us in the Lord's army and to the church that meets in your home.

³Grace and peace to you from God our Father and the Lord Jesus Christ.

Philemon's Love and Faith

⁴I remember you in my prayers. And I always thank my God for you. ⁵I thank God because I hear about the love you have for all of God's holy people and the faith you have in the Lord Jesus. ⁶I pray that the faith you share will make you understand every blessing we have in Christ. ⁷My brother, you have shown love to God's people, and your help has greatly encouraged them. And this has been a great joy and encouragement to me.

INSIGHT

Onesimus was not, as this verse might suggest, Paul's actual son, but a "spiritual son". He had probably become a Christian under Paul's guidance while Paul was imprisoned in Rome.

Philemon verse 10

Accept Onesimus as a Brother

⁸There is something that you should do. And because of the authority I have in Christ, I feel free to command you to do it. ⁹But I am not commanding you; I am asking you to do it out of love. I, Paul, am an old man now, and I am a prisoner for Christ Jesus. ¹⁰I am asking you for my son Onesimus. He became my son while I was in prison. ¹¹In the past he was useless to you. But now he has become useful*ᵃ* for both you and me.

¹²I am sending him back to you, but it's as hard as losing part of myself. ¹³I would like to keep him here to help me while I am still in prison for telling the Good News. By helping me here, he would be representing you. ¹⁴But I did not want to do anything without asking you first. Then whatever you do for me will be what you want to do, not what I forced you to do.

¹⁵Onesimus was separated from you for a short time. Maybe that happened so that you could have him back forever, ¹⁶not to be just a slave, but better than a slave, to be a dear brother. That's what he is to me. And I know he will mean even more to you, both as your slave and as one who shares your faith in the Lord.

¹⁷If you accept me as your friend, then accept Onesimus back. Welcome him like you would welcome me. ¹⁸If he has done any wrong to you or owes you anything, charge that to me. ¹⁹I, Paul, am writing this in my own handwriting: I will pay back anything Onesimus owes. And I will say nothing about what you owe me for your own life. ²⁰So, my brother, as a follower of the Lord please do this favour*ᵇ* for me. It would be such a great encouragement to me as your brother in Christ. ²¹I write this letter knowing that you will do what I ask, and even more than I ask.

²²Also, please prepare a room for me. I hope that God will answer your prayers and that I will be able to come and see you.

Final Greetings

²³Epaphras is a prisoner with me for Christ Jesus. He sends you his greetings. ²⁴Also Mark, Aristarchus, Demas and Luke send their greetings. They are workers together with me.

²⁵The grace of our Lord Jesus Christ be with each one of you.

ᵃ **11 useless . . . useful** Paul here makes a play on words with the name Onesimus, which means "useful".
ᵇ **20 please do this favour** Paul here makes another wordplay on the name Onesimus, using a verb related to it.

THE GOOD NEWS IN ACTION

Paul's letters make up a large chunk of the New Testament and you'll probably know by now that a particular issue or problem always prompts them. Although Philemon is addressed to an individual rather than a whole church, this letter from Paul is the same. There's a situation going on here – and we get to read Paul's response to it.

DIG IN

READ Philemon verses 1–25

- How does Paul feel about the runaway slave, Onesimus (vv.10–13)?
- So why do you think Paul sends him back home to Philemon?

Paul obviously really likes Onesimus and could easily have kept hold of him and never mentioned it to Philemon. But he chooses to get involved. He sends Onesimus back home with this short letter.

Paul has learnt that loving God means loving people. And he knows that the relationship between these two men has been damaged and must be repaired, even if that comes at a cost. He doesn't know for sure how Philemon will respond – he'd be within his rights to have Onesimus punished, maybe even killed. But Paul appeals to Philemon's head and his heart.

- How does Paul get personally involved (vv.17–21)?
- What lesson does he teach by doing this?

Paul is so committed to seeing forgiveness and reconciliation worked out in this situation, that he puts himself on the line. He asks Philemon to treat Onesimus as if it were Paul himself showing up on his doorstep. Any debts that Philemon still considers are owed should be charged to Paul, not Onesimus.

Forgiveness between brothers and sisters in Christ is so important that we should go to any length to promote it – even if it costs us something to get involved.

This little story is a powerful demonstration of the Good News. We are like the slaves who ran away from God. But Jesus pays our debts and recommends that God takes us back, no longer as slaves but as sons and daughters.

DIG THROUGH

- This story has three characters: Philemon (the one who needs to forgive), Onesimus (the one who needs to ask for forgiveness) and Paul (the one who brings the two together). Put yourself in the story. How do you think each felt?
- Paul sees correcting and protecting this relationship between two Christians as really important. How can we get better at handling conflict, and resolving it?
- Does this story encourage you to play the role of peacemaker? It should. Sadly, disagreements between Christian brothers and sisters are common. But God loves people who are peacemakers (Matthew 5:9).

DIG DEEPER

- Read Jesus' story of the unforgiving servant (Matthew 18:21–35), which has a powerful message about forgiveness. Why should forgiveness be our response to those who have wronged us?
- Do you think the story had a happy ending? Did Philemon take Onesimus back as a brother? (Almost certainly, he did. Otherwise we wouldn't have evidence of the letter.)

Who
The author is not known. Some people have suggested Barnabas, Luke or even Apollos. Whoever he was, he knew Timothy (13:23). We don't even know who he was sending it to, but it seems to be aimed at Jewish Christians.

When
It was probably written in the late 60s AD. It was certainly written before the destruction of the Jerusalem Temple by the Romans in AD 70, because when the writer refers to the Temple, he uses the present tense.

What
Hebrews is a letter aimed at Jewish Christians. It is drenched in references to the Jewish Scriptures. It is full of Jewish imagery – of priests and sacrifices and the Temple and the law.

Some Jewish Christians were wavering. The Jews had history, a Temple and a high priest. What did Christianity have? They were, it seems, thinking of leaving, and throughout the book there are encouragements and warnings not to turn away (e.g. 3:12 – 4:13).

You can see why. This is a group of people who had suffered. The author urges his readers, "don't forget those who are in prison" or "who are suffering" (13:3). And he is writing to people who had suffered and been abused – who had even had their possessions taken away. He reminds them of their track record of faithful obedience when suffering (10:32–34). "But we are not those who turn back and are lost," he says, "we are the people who have faith and are saved" (10:39).

Above all he points to Jesus. The writer of Hebrews argues that Christianity is the fulfilment of Judaism. The old system is completed by the new. The rules and regulations have been superseded, the barriers torn down.

It's all about faith. Faith makes us sure of what we hope for and gives proof of things that we can't see. To prove this, the writer scrolls through centuries of Jewish history, looking at all the heroes and showing how they were characterized by faith. But even heroes like Aaron, Moses, Abraham and Joshua must bow to their superior, the one true high priest, Jesus Christ. He is our once-for-all sacrifice, offering salvation for all. All you need is faith.

QUICK TOUR **HEBREWS**

Tempted as we are 2:5–18
Greater than Moses 3:1–19
Great high priest 4:14 – 5:10
The better agreement 8:1–13

No more sacrifice 10:1–18
Faith makes us sure 11:1–40
Eyes on Jesus 12:1–13

"Faith is what makes real the things we hope for. It is proof of what we cannot see."
Hebrews 11:1

God Has Spoken Through His Son

1 In the past God spoke to our people through the prophets. He spoke to them many times and in many different ways. ²And now in these last days, God has spoken to us again through his Son. He made the whole world through his Son. And he has chosen his Son to have all things. ³The Son shows the glory of God. He is a perfect copy of God's nature, and he holds everything together by his powerful command. The Son made people clean from their sins. Then he sat down at the right side*a* of God, the Great One in heaven. ⁴The Son became much greater than the angels, and God gave him a name that is much greater than any of their names.

INSIGHT

The writer of Hebrews obviously knew the Old Testament very well as he quotes from it more than eighty times. His aim is to show how the new agreement through Jesus is superior to the old law.

Hebrews 1:1–4

---

⁵God never said this to any of the angels:

"You are my Son.
  Today I have become your Father."

Psalm 2:7

God also never said about an angel,

"I will be his Father,
  and he will be my son."

2 Samuel 7:14

⁶And then, when God presents his firstborn Son to the world,*b* he says,

"Let all God's angels worship him."*c*

⁷This is what God said about the angels:

"He changes his angels into winds*d*
  and his servants into flaming fire."

Psalm 104:4

⁸But this is what he said about his Son:

"God, your kingdom will last for ever and ever.
  You use your authority for justice.
⁹You love what is right and hate what is wrong.
  So God, your God, has chosen you,
    giving you more honour and joy than
      anyone like you."

Psalm 45:6–7

¹⁰God also said,

"O Lord, in the beginning you made the earth,
  and your hands made the sky.
¹¹These things will disappear, but you will stay.
  They will all wear out like old clothes.
¹²You will fold them up like a coat,
  and they will be changed like clothes.
But you never change,
  and your life will never end."

Psalm 102:25–27

¹³And God never said this to an angel:

"Sit at my right side
  until I put your enemies under your power."*e*

Psalm 110:1

¹⁴All the angels are spirits who serve God and are sent to help those who will receive salvation.

Our Salvation Is Greater Than the Law

2 So we must be more careful to follow what we were taught. We must be careful so that we will not be pulled away from the true way. ²The teaching that God spoke through angels was shown to be true. And every time his people did something against that teaching, they were punished for what they did. They were punished when they did not obey that teaching. ³So surely we also will be punished if we don't pay attention to the salvation we have that is so great. It was the Lord Jesus who first told people about it. And those who heard him proved to us that it is true. ⁴God also proved it by using miraculous signs, wonders and all kinds of miracles. And he proved it by giving people various gifts through the Holy Spirit in just the way he wanted.

Christ Became Like People to Save Them

⁵God did not choose angels to be the rulers over the new world that was coming. That future world is the world we have been talking about. ⁶It is written somewhere in the Scriptures,

---

a **1:3 right side** The place of honour and authority (power).
b **1:6 world** This may mean the world into which Jesus was born (see Luke 2:1–14) or it may have the same meaning as in 2:5—the world to come, to which Christ is presented as king after his resurrection (see Phil. 2:9–11).
c **1:6 "Let . . . him"** These words are found in Deut. 32:43 in the ancient Greek version and in a Hebrew scroll from Qumran.
d **1:7 winds** This can also mean "spirits".
e **1:13 until I put . . . power** Literally, "until I make your enemies a footstool for your feet".

JESUS: GOD AND HUMAN, OUR SAVIOUR

"Before the world began, the Word was there . . . Everything was made through him" (John 1:1,3). This is John's way of saying before the world began God was there and he created everything. John is talking about Jesus. He wants to make it clear that Jesus is God. Hebrews also starts by talking about Jesus and who he is . . .

DIG IN
READ Hebrews 1:1–4

In verses 1 and 2 the writer of this letter compares two periods of time: "in the past" and "in these last days".
- How did God speak in the past? What's changed?

The writer to the Hebrews wants to point out how things have changed because of Jesus and goes on to give a vivid description of him.

Look again at verses 1–4 and then read John 1:1–18.
- Are there similarities or differences between what John says and what the writer to the Hebrews says?
- What do the writers say about Jesus' relationship with God? And what do they say about what he has done for us? You might find it helpful to note your answers on two lists: one with the heading "Jesus and God" and the other with the heading "Jesus and us".

READ Hebrews 2:9–18
- Why is Jesus crowned with glory and honour (v.9)?
- What benefits are there for us in what Jesus did (vv.10,14–15,17–18)?
- Why did Jesus have to suffer and die in order to rescue us (vv.9–11,14–18)?

It's complicated but amazing! Jesus has received glory, but in order to become our Saviour he had to suffer, be tempted and die just as we do (vv.10,17). He needed to keep going, trusting God, right up to death so we could be rescued. And because of all that we are free from the grip of Satan and death (vv.14–15), forgiven for our sins and can be helped when tempted (vv.17–18). Jesus knows what it's like – he's been there!

READ Hebrews 2:1–4
- Verse 3 says, "It was the Lord Jesus who first told people about it." What is "it"?
- What is the warning (vv.1,3)?
- What do we need to make sure we do (v.1)?
- Why did God give the Holy Spirit (v.4)?

DIG THROUGH

- As you read the rest of Hebrews, you will find many references to the salvation and new life that Jesus won for us. Make note of them and thank God for each one. As believers in Jesus, we already have this life, but it is good to keep remembering it. You could make this a part of your daily prayers.
- Are you creative? Write a poem about who Jesus is or what he has done. Are you musical? Write a tune to go with the poem and turn it into a song! Use your creativity to worship God and thank him for what he's done in Jesus.

DIG DEEPER

- Hebrews 1 quotes several passages from the Old Testament indicating that the promises to and about kings (in particular King David) may also be read as prophecies about Jesus. Read Psalms 2, 45, 102 and 110. What might they be prophesying about Jesus?

"Why are people so important to you?
Why do you even think about them?
Why do you care about the son of man?[a]
Is he so important?
[7]For a short time you made him lower than the
angels.
You crowned him with glory and honour.
[8]You put everything under his control."[b]

Psalm 8:4–6

If God put everything under his control, then
there was nothing left that he did not rule. But
we don't yet see him ruling over everything. [9]For
a short time Jesus was made lower than the
angels, but now we see him wearing a crown of
glory and honour because he suffered and died.
Because of God's grace, Jesus died for everyone.
[10]God—the one who made all things and for
whose glory all things exist—wanted many
people to be his children and share his glory. So
he did what he needed to do. He made perfect
the one who leads those people to salvation. He
made Jesus a perfect Saviour through his suffering.
[11]Jesus, the one who makes people holy, and
those who are made holy are from the same
family. So he is not ashamed to call them his
brothers and sisters. [12]He says,

"God, I will tell my brothers and sisters about
you.
Before all your people I will sing your
praises."

Psalm 22:22

[13]He also says,

"I will trust in God."

Isaiah 8:17

And he says,

"I am here, and with me are the children God
has given me."

Isaiah 8:18

[14]These children are people with physical
bodies. So Jesus himself became like them and
had the same experiences they have. Jesus did
this so that, by dying, he could destroy the one
who has the power of death—the devil. [15]Jesus
became like these people and died so that he
could free them. They were like slaves all their
lives because of their fear of death. [16]Clearly, it is
not angels that Jesus helps. He helps the people
who are from Abraham. [17]For this reason, Jesus
had to be made like us, his brothers and sisters,
in every way. He became like people so that he
could be their merciful and faithful high priest in
service to God. Then he could bring forgiveness
for the people's sins. [18]And now he can help those
who are tempted. He is able to help because he
himself suffered and was tempted.

Jesus Is Greater Than Moses

3 So, my brothers and sisters, you who are
chosen by God to be his holy people, think
about Jesus. He is the one we believe God sent to
save us and to be our high priest. [2]God made him
our high priest, and he was faithful to God just as
Moses was. He did everything God wanted him to
do in God's house. [3]When someone builds a house,
people will honour the builder more than the
house. It is the same with Jesus. He should have
more honour than Moses. [4]Every house is built by
someone, but God built everything. [5]Moses was
faithful as a servant in God's whole house. He told
people what God would say in the future. [6]But
Christ is faithful in ruling God's house as the Son.
And we are God's house, if we remain confident of
the great hope we are glad to say we have.

We Must Continue to Follow God

[7]So it is just as the Holy Spirit says:

"If you hear God's voice today,
[8]   don't be stubborn as in the past,
when you turned against God.
That was the day you tested God in the
desert.
[9]For 40 years in the desert, your people saw
what I did.
But they tested me and my patience.
[10]So I was angry with them.
I said, 'Their thoughts are always wrong.
They have never understood my ways.'
[11]So I was angry and made a promise:
'They will never enter my place of rest.'"

Psalm 95:7–11

[12]So, brothers and sisters, be careful that none
of you has the evil thoughts that cause so much
doubt that you stop following the living God.
[13]But encourage each other every day, while you
still have something called "today".[c] Help each
other so that none of you will be fooled by sin
and become too hard to change. [14]We have

---

[a] **2:6 son of man** This can mean any human, but the name "Son of Man" (see "Son of Man" in the Word List) is often used to
mean Jesus, who showed what God planned for all people to be.
[b] **2:8 control** Literally, "feet".
[c] **3:13 today** This word is taken from verse 7. It means it is important to do this now, while there is still opportunity.

the honour of sharing in all that Christ has if we continue until the end to have the sure faith we had in the beginning. [15]That's why the Spirit said,

> "If you hear God's voice today,
>   don't be stubborn as in the past,
>   when you turned against God."
>
> *Psalm 95:7–8*

[16]Who were those who heard God's voice and turned against him? It was all the people Moses led out of Egypt. [17]And who was God angry with for 40 years? He was angry with those who sinned. And their dead bodies were left in the desert. [18]And which people was God talking to when he promised that they would never enter his place of rest? He was talking to those who did not obey him. [19]So we see that they were not allowed to enter and have God's rest, because they did not believe.

4 And we still have the promise that God gave those people. That promise is that we can enter his place of rest. So we should be very careful that none of you fails to get that promise. [2]Yes, the good news about it was told to us just as it was to them. But the message they heard did not help them. They heard it but did not accept it with faith. [3]Only we who believe it are able to enter God's place of rest. As God said,

> "I was angry and made a promise:
> 'They will never enter my place of rest.'"
>
> *Psalm 95:11*

But God's work was finished from the time he made the world. [4]Yes, somewhere in the Scriptures he talked about the seventh day of the week. He said, "So on the seventh day, God rested from all his work."[a] [5]But in the Scripture above God said, "They will never enter my place of rest."

[6]So the opportunity is still there for some to enter and enjoy God's rest. But those who first heard the good news about it did not enter, because they did not obey. [7]So God planned another special day. It is called "today". He spoke about that day through David a long time later using the words we quoted before:

> "If you hear God's voice today,
>   don't be stubborn."
>
> *Psalm 95:7–8*

[8]We know that Joshua did not lead the people into the place of rest that God promised. We know this because God spoke later about another day for rest. [9]This shows that the seventh-day rest[b] for God's people is still to come. [10]God rested after he finished his work. So everyone who enters God's place of rest will also have rest from their own work just as God did. [11]So let us try as hard as we can to enter God's place of rest. We must try hard so that none of us will be lost by following the example of those who refused to obey God.

[12]God's word[c] is alive and working. It is sharper than the sharpest sword and cuts all the way into us. It cuts deep to the place where the soul and the spirit are joined. God's word cuts to the centre of our joints and our bones. It judges the thoughts and feelings in our hearts. [13]Nothing in all the world can be hidden from God. He can clearly see all things. Everything is open before him. And to him we must explain the way we have lived.

Jesus Christ Is Our High Priest

[14]We have a great high priest who has gone to live with God in heaven. He is Jesus the Son of God. So let us continue to express our faith in him. [15]Jesus, our high priest, is able to understand our weaknesses. When Jesus lived on earth, he was tempted in every way. He was tempted in the same ways we are tempted, but he never sinned. [16]With Jesus as our high priest, we can feel free to come before God's throne where there is grace. There we receive mercy and kindness to help us when we need it.

5 Every Jewish high priest is chosen from among men. That priest is given the work of helping people with the things they must do for God. He must offer to God gifts and sacrifices for sins. [2]The high priest has his own weaknesses. So he is able to be gentle with those who do wrong out of ignorance. [3]He offers sacrifices for their sins, but he must also offer sacrifices for his own sins.

[4]To be a high priest is an honour. But no one chooses himself for this work. That person must be chosen by God just as Aaron was. [5]It is the same with Christ. He did not choose himself to have the honour of becoming a high priest. But God chose him. God said to him,

> "You are my Son.
>   Today I have become your Father."
>
> *Psalm 2:7*

---

[a] **4:4** Quote from Gen. 2:2.
[b] **4:9** *seventh-day rest* Literally, "Sabbath rest", meaning a sharing in the rest God began after he created the world.
[c] **4:12** *God's word* God's teachings and commands.

[6]And in another part of the Scriptures God says,

"You are a priest forever—
    the kind of priest Melchizedek was."
                                        Psalm 110:4

[7]While Jesus lived on earth he prayed to God, asking for help from the one who could save him from death. He prayed to God with loud cries and tears. And his prayers were answered because of his great respect for God. [8]Jesus was the Son of God, but he still suffered, and through his sufferings he learned to obey whatever God says. [9]This made him the perfect high priest, who provides the way for everyone who obeys him to be saved forever. [10]God made him high priest, just like Melchizedek.

Warning Against Falling Away

[11]We have many things to tell you about this. But it is hard to explain because you have stopped trying to understand. [12]You have had enough time that by now you should be teachers. But you need someone to teach you again the first lessons of God's teaching. You still need the teaching that is like milk. You are not ready for solid food. [13]Anyone who lives on milk is still a baby and is not able to understand much about living right. [14]But solid food is for people who have grown up. From their experience they have learned to see the difference between good and evil.

6 So we should have finished with the basic lessons about Christ. We should not have to keep going back to where we started. [2]We began our new life by turning away from the evil we did in the past and by believing in God. That's when we were taught about baptisms,[a] laying hands on people,[b] the resurrection of those who have died, and the final judgement. Now we need to go forward to more mature teaching. [3]And that's what we will do if God allows.

[4-6]After people have left the way of Christ, can you make them change their lives again? I am talking about people who once learned the truth, received God's gift and shared in the Holy Spirit. They were blessed to hear God's good message and see the great power of his new world. But then they left it all behind, and it is not possible to make them change again. That's because those

who leave Christ are nailing him to the cross again, shaming him before everyone.

[7]Some people are like land that gets plenty of rain and produces a good crop for those who farm it. That kind of land has God's blessing. [8]But other people are like land that grows only thorns and weeds. It is useless and in danger of being cursed by God. It will be destroyed by fire.

[9]Dear friends, I am not saying this because I think it is happening to you. We really expect that you will do better—that you will do the good things that will result in your salvation. [10]God is fair, and he will remember all the work you have done. He will remember that you showed your love to him by helping his people and that you continue to help them. [11]We want each of you to be willing and eager to show your love like that the rest of your life. Then you will be sure to get what you hope for. [12]We don't want you to be lazy. We want you to be like those who, because of their faith and patience, will get what God has promised.

[13]God made a promise to Abraham. And there is no one greater than God, so he made the promise with an oath in his own name—an oath that he would do what he promised. [14]He said, "I will surely bless you. I will give you many descendants."[c] [15]Abraham waited patiently for this to happen, and later he received what God promised.

[16]People always use the name of someone greater than themselves to make a promise with an oath. The oath proves that what they say is true, and there is no more arguing about it. [17]God wanted to prove that his promise was true. He wanted to prove this to those who would get what he promised. He wanted them to understand clearly that his purposes never change. So God said something would happen, and he proved what he said by adding an oath. [18]These two things cannot change: God cannot lie when he says something, and he cannot lie when he makes an oath.

So both of these things are a great help to us who have come to God for safety. They encourage us to hold on to the hope that is ours. [19]This hope we have is like an anchor for us. It is strong and sure and keeps us safe. It goes behind the curtain[d] in God's temple. [20]Jesus has already entered there and opened the way for us. He has become the high priest forever, just like Melchizedek.

---

[a] **6:1-2 baptisms** The word here may mean the baptism (brief "burial" in water) of believers in Christ, or it may mean Jewish ceremonial washings.
[b] **6:1-2 laying hands on people** This act was a way of asking God to bless people in a special way—to heal them, to cause the Holy Spirit to come into them, or to give them power for a special work.
[c] **6:14** Quote from Gen. 22:17.
[d] **6:19 curtain** The spiritual curtain in the heavenly temple, which was symbolized by the physical one that separated the inner sanctuary (and God's presence) from the other room in the Holy Tent and in the Jerusalem Temple. See "CURTAIN" in the Word List. Also in 10:20.

The Priest Melchizedek

7 Melchizedek was the king of Salem and a priest for God the Most High. He met Abraham when Abraham was coming back after defeating the kings. That day Melchizedek blessed him. ²Then Abraham gave him a tenth of everything he had.

The name Melchizedek, king of Salem, has two meanings. First, Melchizedek means "king of justice". And "king of Salem" means "king of peace". ³No one knows who his father or mother was or where he came from.ᵃ And no one knows when he was born or when he died. Melchizedek is like the Son of God in that he will always be a priest.

⁴You can see that Melchizedek was very great. Abraham, our great ancestor, gave him a tenth of everything he won in battle. ⁵Now the law says that those from the tribe of Levi who become priests must get a tenth from their own people, even though they and their people are both from the family of Abraham. ⁶Melchizedek was not even from the tribe of Levi, but Abraham gave him a tenth of what he had. And Melchizedek blessed Abraham—the one who had God's promises. ⁷And everyone knows that the more important person always blesses the less important person.

⁸Those priests get a tenth, but they are only men who live and then die. But Melchizedek, who got a tenth from Abraham, continues to live, as the Scriptures say. ⁹Now those from the family of Levi are the ones who get a tenth from the people. But we can say that when Abraham paid Melchizedek a tenth, then Levi also paid it. ¹⁰Levi was not yet born, but he already existed in his ancestor Abraham when Melchizedek met him.

¹¹The people were given the law under the system of priests from the tribe of Levi. But no one could be made spiritually perfect through that system of priests. So there was a need for another priest to come. I mean a priest like Melchizedek, not Aaron. ¹²And when a different kind of priest comes, then the law must be changed too. ¹³⁻¹⁴We are talking about our Lord Christ, who belonged to a different tribe. No one from that tribe ever served as a priest at the altar. It is clear that our Lord Jesus came from the tribe of Judah. And Moses said nothing about priests belonging to that tribe.

Jesus Is a Priest Like Melchizedek

¹⁵And these things become even clearer when we see that another priest has come who is like Melchizedek. ¹⁶He was made a priest, but not because he met the requirement of being born into the right family. He became a priest by the power of a life that will never end. ¹⁷This is what the Scriptures say about him: "You are a priest forever—the kind of priest Melchizedek was."ᵇ

¹⁸The old rule is now ended because it was weak and unable to help us. ¹⁹The Law of Moses could not make anything perfect. But now a better hope has been given to us. And with that hope we can come near to God.

²⁰Also, it is important that God made a promise with an oath when he made Jesus high priest. When those other men became priests, there was no oath. ²¹But Christ became a priest with God's oath. God said to him,

> "The Lord has made a promise with an oath
> and will not change his mind:
> 'You are a priest forever.'"
>
> *Psalm 110:4*

²²So this means that Jesus is the guarantee of a better agreement from God to his people.

²³Also, when one of those other priests died, he could not continue being a priest. So there were many of those priests. ²⁴But Jesus lives forever. He will never stop serving as a priest. ²⁵So Christ can save those who come to God through him. Christ can do this forever, because he always lives and is ready to help people when they come before God.

²⁶So Jesus is the kind of high priest we need. He is holy. He has no sin in him. He is pure and not influenced by sinners. And he is raised above the heavens. ²⁷He is not like those other priests. They had to offer sacrifices every day, first for their own sins and then for the sins of the people. But Jesus doesn't need to do that. He offered only one sacrifice for all time. He offered himself. ²⁸The law chooses high priests who are men and have the same weaknesses that all people have. But after the law, God spoke the oath that made his Son high priest. And that Son, made perfect through suffering, will serve forever.

Jesus Our High Priest

8 Here is the point of what we are saying: we have a high priest like that, who sits on the right sideᶜ of God's throne in heaven. ²Our high priest serves in the Most Holy Place. He serves in the true place of worshipᵈ that was made by God, not by anyone here on earth.

³Every high priest has the work of offering gifts and sacrifices to God. So our high priest must also

---

ᵃ **7:3 No one . . . came from** Literally, "Melchizedek was without father, without mother, without genealogy."
ᵇ **7:17** Quote from Ps. 110:4.
ᶜ **8:1 right side** The place of honour and authority (power).
ᵈ **8:2 place of worship** Literally, "Tabernacle" or "tent".

offer something to God. ⁴If our high priest were now living on earth, he would not be a priest. I say this because there are already priests here who follow the law by offering gifts to God. ⁵The work that these priests do is really only a copy and a shadow of what is in heaven. That is why God warned Moses when he was ready to build the Holy Tent: "Be sure to make everything exactly like the pattern I showed you on the mountain."*ᵃ* ⁶But the work that has been given to Jesus is much greater than the work that was given to those priests. In the same way, the new agreement that Jesus brought from God to his people is much greater than the old one. And the new agreement is based on better promises.

⁷If there was nothing wrong with the first agreement, then there would be no need for a second agreement. ⁸But God found something wrong with the people. He said,

"The time is coming, says the Lord,
　when I will make a new agreement with
　　the people of Israel and the people of
　　Judah.
⁹It will not be like the agreement that I made
　with their ancestors.
　That is the agreement I gave when I took
　　them by the hand and led them out of
　　Egypt.
They did not continue following the
　　agreement I made with them,
　and I turned away from them, says the
　　Lord.
¹⁰This is the new agreement I will make
　with the people of Israel in the future, says
　　the Lord:
I will put my laws in their minds,
　and I will write my laws on their hearts.
I will be their God,
　and they will be my people.
¹¹Never again will anyone have to teach their
　neighbours
　or their family to know the Lord.
　All people—the greatest and the least
　　important—will know me.
¹²And I will forgive the wrongs they have
　done,
　and I will not remember their sins."
　　　　　　　　　　　Jeremiah 31:31–34

¹³God called this a new agreement, so he has made the first agreement old. And anything that is old and useless is ready to disappear.

Worship Under the Old Agreement

9 The first agreement had rules for worship and a place for worship here on earth. ²This place was inside a tent. The first area in the tent was called the Holy Place. In the Holy Place were the lamp and the table with the special bread offered to God. ³Behind the second curtain was a room called the Most Holy Place. ⁴In the Most Holy Place was a golden altar for burning incense. And also there was the Box of the Agreement. The Box was covered with gold. Inside this Box was a gold jar of manna and Aaron's staff—the staff that once grew leaves. Also in the Box were the flat stones with the Ten Commandments of the old agreement on them. ⁵Above the Box were the winged creatures that showed God's glory. These winged creatures were over the place of mercy.*ᵇ* But we cannot say everything about this now.

⁶Everything in the tent was made ready in the way I have explained. Then the priests went into the first room every day to perform their worship duties. ⁷But only the high priest could go into the second room, and he went in only once a year. Also, he could never enter that room without taking blood with him. He offered that blood to God for himself and for the sins the people committed without knowing they were sinning. ⁸The Holy Spirit uses those two separate rooms to teach us that the way into the Most Holy Place was not open while the first room was still there. ⁹This is an example for us today. It shows that the gifts and sacrifices the priests offer to God are not able to make the consciences of the worshippers completely clear. ¹⁰These gifts and sacrifices are only about food and drink and special washings. They are only rules about the body. God gave them for his people to follow until the time of his new way.

Worship Under the New Agreement

¹¹But Christ has already come to be the high priest. He is the high priest of the good things we now have. But Christ does not serve in a place like the tent that those other priests served in. He serves in a better place. Unlike that tent, this one is perfect. It was not made by anyone here on earth. It does not belong to this world. ¹²Christ entered the Most Holy Place only once—enough for all time. He entered the Most Holy Place by using his own blood, not the blood of goats or young bulls. He entered there and made us free from sin forever.

ᵃ **8:5** Quote from Exod. 25:40.
ᵇ **9:5** *place of mercy* Or "mercy seat", a place on top of the "Box of the Agreement", where the high priest put the blood of an animal once a year to pay for the sins of the people.

THE OLD AND THE NEW

Lots of the things that happened or were said in the Old Testament were not only relevant to the people at the time but also to God's people in the future.

DIG IN

READ Hebrews 9:1–10 and take a look at Leviticus

- Where is the Most Holy Place? What was inside the Most Holy Place?
- Who could go into the Most Holy Place and how often?
- Why did they go there? What did they have to do in order to enter?

READ Hebrews 9:23–24

The writer describes the Holy Tent and sacrifices as "copies of the true things". Jesus, our high priest, showed us the real thing when he made the sacrifice to end all sacrifices. He went into heaven, the God-made Holy Place, to purify us from our sins, and he is still there.

- How does it make you feel to think that by being with God, Jesus is making it possible for you to have access to God now and forever?

READ Hebrews 10:19–25

Matthew 27:51 tells us that the curtain separating man from God was torn when Jesus was on the cross. Here we read that Jesus became the curtain!

- Because of Jesus – the sin that separated you from God is gone! Why not thank Jesus for this.

DIG THROUGH

- What does the writer to the Hebrews encourage us to do, in the light of Jesus' once-for-all sacrifice?
- Do we still offer sacrifices today? Check out Hebrews 13:15–16. What kind of sacrifices should we offer to God?
- Think of ways in which you can offer sacrifices to God on a daily basis.

DIG DEEPER

We have seen that the Holy Tent and the sacrificial system were copies of the things in heaven, of Jesus' sacrifice and of his position as high priest. The old things – Old Testament rituals and traditions – prefigured the new things, meaning that they were similar to, or gave clues about, what was to come.

- Can you think of any other things in the Bible that prefigure what God has done and will do through Jesus? Are there any people in the Old Testament who are similar in some way to Jesus? Does anything happen that hints at what God would do through Jesus?
- Read the stories of Abram, Sarah and Isaac, Joseph, Moses, Joshua, Esther and King David. Can you find elements in their stories that prefigure what God would do?

[13]The blood of goats and bulls and the ashes of a cow were sprinkled on those who were no longer pure enough to enter the place of worship. The blood and ashes made them pure again—but only their bodies. [14]So surely the blood sacrifice of Christ can do much more. Christ offered himself through the eternal Spirit[a] as a perfect sacrifice to God. His blood will make us completely clean from the evil we have done. It will give us clear consciences so that we can worship the living God.

[15]So Christ brings a new agreement from God to his people. He brings this agreement so that those who are chosen by God can have the blessings God promised, blessings that last forever. This can happen only because Christ died to free people from sins committed against the commands of the first agreement.

[16]When someone dies and leaves a will, there must be proof that the one who wrote the will is dead. [17]A will means nothing while the one who wrote it is still living. It can be used only after that person's death. [18]That is why blood to prove death was needed to begin the first agreement between God and his people. [19]First, Moses told the people every command in the law. Then he took the blood of young bulls and mixed it with water. He used red wool and a branch of hyssop to sprinkle the blood and water on the book of the law and on all the people. [20]Then he said, "This is the blood that makes the agreement good—the agreement that God commanded you to follow."[b] [21]In the same way, Moses sprinkled the blood on the Holy Tent. He sprinkled the blood over everything used in worship. [22]The law says that almost everything must be made clean by blood. Sins cannot be forgiven without a blood sacrifice.

Jesus Christ Is Our Sacrifice for Sin

[23]These things are copies of the real things that are in heaven. These copies had to be made clean by animal sacrifices. But the real things in heaven must have much better sacrifices. [24]Christ went into the Most Holy Place. But it was not the man-made one, which is only a copy of the real one. He went into heaven, and he is there now before God to help us.

[25]The high priest enters the Most Holy Place once every year. He takes with him blood to offer. But he does not offer his own blood like Christ did. Christ went into heaven, but not to offer himself many times like the high priest offers blood again and again. [26]If Christ had offered himself many times, he would have needed to suffer many times since the world was made. But he came to offer himself only once. And that once is enough for all time. He came at a time when the world is nearing an end. He came to take away all sin by offering himself as a sacrifice.

[27]Everyone must die once. Then they are judged. [28]So Christ was offered as a sacrifice once to take away the sins of many people. And he will come a second time, but not to offer himself for sin. He will come the second time to bring salvation to those who are waiting for him.

Jesus Christ—the Only Sacrifice We Need

10 The law gave us only an unclear picture of the good things coming in the future. The law is not a perfect picture of the real things. The law tells people to offer the same sacrifices every year. Those who come to worship God continue to offer those sacrifices. But the law can never make them perfect. [2]If the law could make people perfect, those sacrifices would have already stopped. They would already be clean from their sins, and they would not still feel guilty. [3]But that's not what happens. Their sacrifices make them remember their sins every year, [4]because it is not possible for the blood of bulls and goats to take away sins.

[5]So when Christ came into the world he said,

"You did not really want sacrifices and
    offerings,
  but you have prepared a body for me.
[6]You were not satisfied with burnt offerings
    and sacrifices to take away sins.
[7]Then I said, 'Here I am, God.
  It is written about me in the book of the law.
  I have come to do what you want.'"

Psalm 40:6–8

[8]First Christ said, "You did not really want sacrifices and offerings. You were not satisfied with burnt offerings and sacrifices to take away sin." (These are all sacrifices that the law commands.) [9]Then he said, "Here I am, God. I have come to do what you want." So God ends that first system of sacrifices and starts his new way. [10]Jesus Christ did the things God wanted him to do. And because of that, we are made holy through the sacrifice of Christ's body. Christ made that sacrifice once—enough for all time.

[11]Every day the priests stand and do their religious service. Again and again they offer the same sacrifices, which can never take away sins. [12]But Christ offered only one sacrifice for sins, and that sacrifice is good for all time. Then he sat down at the right side of God. [13]And now Christ

---

[a] **9:14** *Spirit* Probably the Holy Spirit. See "Holy Spirit" in the Word List.
[b] **9:20** Quote from Exod. 24:8.

waits there for his enemies to be put under his power.[a] [14]With one sacrifice Christ made his people perfect forever. They are the ones who are being made holy.

[15]The Holy Spirit also tells us about this. First he says,

[16]"This is the agreement[b] I will make
  with my people in the future, says the Lord.
I will put my laws in their hearts.
  I will write my laws in their minds."
Jeremiah 31:33

[17]Then he says,

"I will forget their sins
  and never again remember the evil they
    have done."
Jeremiah 31:34

[18]And after everything is forgiven, there is no more need for a sacrifice to pay for sins.

INSIGHT

When the writer talks about making the same sacrifices every year he is referring to the annual Jewish holiday of Yom Kippur (Day of Atonement). On this day the high priest would take a goat known as a "scapegoat" and symbolically transfer the sins of Israel onto it. It would then be carried out to the desert where it, along with the sins of Israel, would be lost or forgotten (Leviticus 16:7–10).
Hebrews 10:1–18

Come Near to God

[19]And so, brothers and sisters, we are completely free to enter the Most Holy Place. We can do this without fear because of the blood sacrifice of Jesus. [20]We enter through a new way that Jesus opened for us. It is a living way that leads through the curtain—Christ's body. [21]And we have a great priest who rules the house of God. [22]Sprinkled with the blood of Christ, our hearts have been made free from a guilty conscience, and our bodies have been washed with pure water. So come near to God with a sincere heart, full of confidence because of our faith in Christ. [23]We must hold on to the hope we have, never hesitating to tell people about it. We can trust God to do what he promised.

Help Each Other to Be Strong

[24]We should think about each other to see how we can encourage each other to show love and do good works. [25]We must not stop meeting together, as some are doing. No, we need to keep on encouraging each other. This becomes more and more important as you see the Day getting closer.

Don't Turn Away From God's Son

[26]If we decide to continue sinning after we have learned the truth, then there is no other sacrifice that will take away sins. [27]If we continue sinning, all that is left for us is a fearful time of waiting for the judgement and the angry fire that will destroy those who live against God. [28]Whoever refused to obey the Law of Moses was found guilty from the testimony given by two or three witnesses. Such people were not forgiven. They were killed. [29]So think how much more punishment people deserve who show their hate for the Son of God—people who show they have no respect for the blood sacrifice that began the new agreement and once made them holy or who insult the Spirit of God's grace. [30]We know that God said, "I will punish people for the wrongs they do; I will repay them."[c] And he also said, "The Lord will judge his people."[d] [31]It is a terrible thing to face punishment from the living God.

Keep the Courage and Patience You Had

[32]Remember the days when you first learned the truth. You had a hard struggle with much suffering, but you remained strong. [33]Sometimes people said hateful things to you and mistreated you in public. And sometimes you helped others who were being treated the same way. [34]Yes, you helped them in prison and shared in their suffering. And you were still happy when everything you owned was taken away from you. You continued to be happy, because you knew that you had something much better—something that would continue forever.

[35]So don't lose the courage that you had in the past. Your courage will be rewarded richly. [36]You must be patient. After you have done what God wants, you will get what he promised you. [37]He says,

---

[a] **10:13 to be put under his power** Literally, "to be made a footstool for his feet".
[b] **10:16 agreement** The new and better agreement that God has given to his people through Jesus. See "AGREEMENT" in the Word List.
[c] **10:30** Quote from Deut. 32:35.
[d] **10:30** Quote from Deut. 32:36 or Ps. 135:14.

"Very soon now, the one who is coming
　　will come and will not be late.
38The person who is right with me
　　will live by trusting in me.
　But I will not be pleased with the one
　　who turns back in fear."

Habakkuk 2:3–4 (Greek version)

39But we are not those who turn back and are lost. No, we are the people who have faith and are saved.

INSIGHT

This incredible chapter gives not only one of the best definitions of "faith" in the Bible, but also a sort of "hall of fame" when it comes to having faith and trusting in God. These people weren't perfect, but at some time each one displayed incredible faith.

Hebrews 11

Faith

11 Faith is what makes real the things we hope for. It is proof of what we cannot see. 2God was pleased with the people who lived a long time ago because they had faith like this.

3Faith helps us understand that God created the whole world by his command. This means that the things we see were made by something that cannot be seen.

4Cain and Abel both offered sacrifices to God. But Abel offered a better sacrifice to God because he had faith. God said he was pleased with what Abel offered. And so God called him a good man because he had faith. Abel died, but through his faith he is still speaking.

5Enoch was carried away from this earth, so he never died. The Scriptures tell us that before he was carried off, he was a man who pleased God. Later, no one knew where he was, because God had taken Enoch to be with him. This all happened because he had faith. 6Without faith no one can please God. Whoever comes to God must believe that he is real and that he rewards those who sincerely try to find him.

7Noah was warned by God about things that he could not yet see. But he had faith and respect for God, so he built a large boat to save his family. With his faith, Noah showed that the world was wrong. And he became one of those who are made right with God through faith.

8God called Abraham to travel to another place that he promised to give him. Abraham did not know where that other place was. But he obeyed God and started travelling because he had faith. 9Abraham lived in the country that God promised to give him. He lived there like a visitor who did not belong. He did this because he had faith. He lived in tents with Isaac and Jacob, who also received the same promise from God. 10Abraham was waiting for the city*a* that has real foundations. He was waiting for the city that is planned and built by God.

11Sarah was not able to have children, and Abraham was too old. But he had faith in God, trusting him to do what he promised. And so God made them able to have children. 12Abraham was so old he was almost dead. But from that one man came as many descendants as there are stars in the sky. So many people came from him that they are like grains of sand on the seashore.

13All these great people continued living with faith until they died. They did not get the things God promised his people. But they were happy just to see those promises coming far in the future. They accepted the fact that they were like strangers and foreigners here on earth. 14When people accept something like that, they show they are waiting for a country that will be their own. 15If they were thinking about the country they had left, they could have gone back. 16But they were waiting for a better country—a heavenly country. So God is not ashamed to be called their God. And he has prepared a city for them.

17–18God tested Abraham's faith. God told him to offer Isaac as a sacrifice. Abraham obeyed because he had faith. He already had the promises from God. And God had already said to him, "It is through Isaac that your descendants will come."*b* But Abraham was ready to offer his only son. He did this because he had faith. 19He believed that God could raise people from death. And really, when God stopped Abraham from killing Isaac, it was as if he got him back from death.

20Isaac blessed the future of Jacob and Esau. He did that because he had faith. 21And Jacob, also because he had faith, blessed each one of Joseph's sons. He did this while he was dying, leaning on his rod and worshipping God.

22And when Joseph was almost dead, he spoke about the people of Israel leaving Egypt. And he told them what they should do with his body. He did this because he had faith.

---

a **11:10** *city* The spiritual "city" where God's people live with him. Also called "the heavenly Jerusalem". See Heb. 12:22.
b **11:17–18** Quote from Gen. 21:12.

HAVE FAITH

"But we are not those who turn back and are lost. No, we are the people who have faith and are saved" (Hebrews 10:39). The writer of Hebrews wants his readers to look more closely at what it means to have faith in God and what they can learn from Old Testament people of faith.

DIG IN

READ Hebrews 3:7-11

These verses look back at some who didn't have faith or whose faith was weak.

- Who are the people that are spoken about here?
- What did they do wrong?

READ Hebrews 3:16-19

The writer says that the Israelites couldn't enter God's place of rest because they didn't obey, and then says it was because they didn't believe.

- Is the writer saying that believing and obeying are the same thing?
- Do you think you can believe without obeying? Can you obey without believing?

READ Hebrews 11:1-31

- What did these people do right?

These people obeyed God because they had faith, and their faith pleased God.

- What is faith? Look closely at these verses to see how faith might be connected with the following:
  - » Obedience
  - » Being right with God
  - » Pleasing God
  - » God's promises
  - » Suffering
  - » Courage
  - » Perseverance
  - » Miracles
  - » Salvation
- Where does faith come from? Check out Romans 10:17 and 12:3.

READ Hebrews 12:1-3

Here, the writer encourages us to follow the example of Noah, Abraham and others whose faith in God made them able to "run the race that is before us and never give up" (v.1).

If we think of the Christian life as a race, then it's faith that gets us from the here and now to the finishing line. We've got our hope in the finishing line, the place we want to aim towards. Think of any sport – cycling, go-carting, horse riding, running – the direction you look in is the direction you take! In the same way, faith directs our lives to the same finishing line as all other believers, because we have all put our hope in Jesus.

DIG THROUGH

- It's really easy to put our faith in things other than Jesus – our friends, our family, our own abilities. Who or what do you put your faith in? God wants us to put our faith first and foremost in Jesus, to trust his promises and keep going.
- In Hebrews 11 we read about some of the heroes of the faith: people who obeyed God because they had faith in his promises. Is there a modern-day hero of the faith in your family or church? Try to spend time with them: ask them questions about their Christian life; ask if they will give you advice or pray with you. Such people can inspire and support us in our own Christian life.

DIG DEEPER

- Look at the list of some of the other heroes of the faith in Hebrews 11:32-38.
- Find the stories of Gideon, Samson and the others mentioned in verse 32 and write summaries of their stories to continue the hall of fame.

²³And the mother and father of Moses hid him for three months after he was born. They did this because they had faith. They saw that Moses was a beautiful baby. And they were not afraid to disobey the king's order.

²⁴⁻²⁵Moses grew up and became a man. He refused to be called the son of Pharaoh's daughter. He chose not to enjoy the pleasures of sin that last such a short time. Instead, he chose to suffer with God's people. He did this because he had faith. ²⁶He thought it was better to suffer for the Messiah than to have all the treasures of Egypt. He was waiting for the reward that God would give him.

²⁷Moses left Egypt because he had faith. He was not afraid of the king's anger. He remained strong as if he could see the God no one can see. ²⁸Moses prepared the Passover meal and spread the blood on the doorways of his people, so that the angel of death*ᵃ* would not kill their firstborn sons. Moses did this because he had faith.

²⁹And God's people all walked through the Red Sea as if it were dry land. They were able to do this because they had faith. But when the Egyptians tried to follow them, they were drowned.

³⁰And the walls of Jericho fell because of the faith of God's people. They marched around the walls for seven days, and then the walls fell.

³¹And Rahab, the prostitute, welcomed the Israelite spies like friends. And because of her faith, she was not killed with the ones who refused to obey.

INSIGHT

Throughout the Bible there are stories of many who suffered greatly for their faith. When the writer talks about being "cut in half" he is probably referring to the prophet Isaiah as it is thought that he met this fate.

Hebrews 11:37

³²Do I need to give you more examples? I don't have enough time to tell you about Gideon, Barak, Samson, Jephthah, David, Samuel and the prophets. ³³All of them had great faith. And with that faith they defeated kingdoms. They did what was right, and God helped them in the ways he promised. With their faith some people closed the mouths of lions. ³⁴And some were able to stop blazing fires. Others escaped from being killed with swords. Some who were weak were made strong. They became powerful in battle and defeated other armies. ³⁵There were women who lost loved ones but got them back when they were raised from death. Others were tortured but refused to accept their freedom. They did this so that they could be raised from death to a better life. ³⁶Some were laughed at and beaten. Others were tied up and put in prison. ³⁷They were killed with stones. They were cut in half. They were killed with swords. The only clothes some of them had were sheepskins or goatskins. They were poor, persecuted and treated badly by others. ³⁸The world was not good enough for these great people. They had to wander in deserts and mountains, living in caves and holes in the ground.

³⁹God was pleased with all of them because of their faith. But not one of them received God's great promise. ⁴⁰God planned something better for us. He wanted to make us perfect. Of course, he wanted those great people to be made perfect too, but not before we could all enjoy that blessing together.

We Also Should Follow Jesus' Example

12 We have all these great people around us as examples. Their lives tell us what faith means. So we, too, should run the race that is before us and never give up. We should remove from our lives anything that would slow us down and the sin that so often makes us fall. ²We must never stop looking to Jesus. He is the leader of our faith, and he is the one who makes our faith complete. He suffered death on a cross. But he accepted the shame of the cross as if it were nothing because of the joy he could see waiting for him. And now he is sitting at the right side of God's throne. ³Think about Jesus. He patiently endured the angry insults that sinful people were shouting at him. Think about him so that you won't get discouraged and stop trying.

God Is Like a Father

⁴You are struggling against sin, but you have not had to give up your life for the cause. ⁵You are children of God, and he speaks words of comfort to you. You have forgotten these words:

"My child, don't think the Lord's discipline is worth nothing,
    and don't stop trying when he corrects you.

ᵃ **11:28 *angel of death*** Literally, "the destroyer". To punish the Egyptians, God sent an angel to kill the oldest son in each home. See Exod. 12:29–32.

⁶The Lord disciplines everyone he loves;
  he punishes everyone he accepts as a
  child."

Proverbs 3:11–12

⁷So accept sufferings like a father's discipline. God does these things to you like a father correcting his children. You know that all children are disciplined by their fathers. ⁸So, if you never receive the discipline that every child must have, you are not true children and don't really belong to God. ⁹We have all had fathers here on earth who corrected us with discipline. And we respected them. So it is even more important that we accept discipline from the Father of our spirits. If we do this, we will have life. ¹⁰Our fathers on earth disciplined us for a short time in the way they thought was best. But God disciplines us to help us so that we can be holy like him. ¹¹We don't enjoy discipline when we get it. It is painful. But later, after we have learned our lesson from it, we will enjoy the peace that comes from doing what is right.

Be Careful How You Live

¹²You have become weak, so make yourselves strong again. ¹³Live in the right way so that you will be saved and your weakness will not cause you to be lost.

¹⁴Try to live in peace with everyone. And try to keep your lives free from sin. Anyone whose life is not holy will never see the Lord. ¹⁵Be careful that no one fails to receive God's grace. Be careful that no one loses their faith and becomes like a bitter weed growing among you. Someone like that can ruin your whole group. ¹⁶Be careful that no one commits sexual sin. And be careful that no one is like Esau and never thinks about God. As the oldest son, Esau would have inherited everything from his father. But he sold all that for a single meal. ¹⁷You remember that after Esau did this, he wanted to get his father's blessing. He wanted that blessing so much that he cried. But his father refused to give him the blessing, because Esau could find no way to change what he had done.

¹⁸You have not come to a place that can be seen and touched, like the mountain the people of Israel saw, which was burning with fire and covered with darkness, gloom and storms. ¹⁹There

is no sound of a trumpet or a voice speaking words like those they heard. When they heard the voice, they begged never to hear another word. ²⁰They did not want to hear the command: "If anything, even an animal, touches the mountain, it must be killed with stones."ᵃ ²¹What they saw was so terrible that Moses said, "I am shaking with fear."ᵇᶜ

²²But you have come to Mount Zion, to the city of the living God, the heavenly Jerusalem.ᵈ You have come to a place where thousands of angels have gathered to celebrate. ²³You have come to the meeting of God's firstbornᵉ children. Their names are written in heaven. You have come to God, the judge of all people. And you have come to the spirits of good people who have been made perfect. ²⁴You have come to Jesus— the one who brought the new agreement from God to his people. You have come to the sprinkled bloodᶠ that tells us about better things than the blood of Abel.

²⁵Be careful and don't refuse to listen when God speaks. Those people refused to listen to him when he warned them on earth. And they did not escape. Now God is speaking from heaven. So now it will be worse for those who refuse to listen to him. ²⁶When he spoke before, his voice shook the earth. But now he has promised, "Once again I will shake the earth, but I will also shake heaven."ᵍ ²⁷The words "once again" clearly show us that everything that was created will be destroyed— that is, the things that can be shaken. And only what cannot be shaken will remain.

²⁸So we should be thankful because we have a kingdom that cannot be shaken. And because we are thankful, we should worship God in a way that will please him. We should do this with respect and fear, ²⁹because our God is like a fire that can destroy us.

Worship That Pleases God

13 Continue loving each other as brothers and sisters in Christ. ²Always remember to help people by welcoming them into your home. Some people have done that and have helped angels without knowing it. ³Don't forget those who are in prison. Remember them as though you were in prison with them. And don't forget those who are suffering. Remember them as though you were suffering with them.

ᵃ **12:20** Quote from Exod. 19:12–13.
ᵇ **12:21** Quote from Deut. 9:19.
ᶜ **12:18–21** These verses refer to things that happened to the people of Israel in the time of Moses as described in Exod. 19.
ᵈ **12:22** *Jerusalem* Here, the spiritual city of God's people.
ᵉ **12:23** *firstborn* The first son born in a Jewish family had the most important place in the family and received special blessings. All God's children are like that.
ᶠ **12:24** *sprinkled blood* The blood (death) of Jesus.
ᵍ **12:26** Quote from Hag. 2:6.

[4]Marriage should be honoured by everyone. And every marriage should be kept pure between husband and wife. God will judge guilty those who commit sexual sins and adultery. [5]Keep your lives free from the love of money. And be satisfied with what you have. God has said,

"I will never leave you;
I will never run away from you."

Deuteronomy 31:6

[6]So we can feel sure and say,

"The Lord is my helper;
I will not be afraid.
People can do nothing to me."

Psalm 118:6

[7]Remember your leaders. They taught God's message to you. Remember how they lived and died, and copy their faith. [8]Jesus Christ is the same yesterday, today and forever. [9]Don't let all kinds of strange teachings lead you into the wrong way. Depend only on God's grace for spiritual strength, not on rules about foods. Obeying those rules doesn't help anyone.

[10]We have a sacrifice. And those priests who serve in the Holy Tent cannot eat from the sacrifice we have. [11]The high priest carries the blood of animals into the Most Holy Place and offers that blood for sins. But the bodies of those animals are burned outside the camp. [12]So Jesus also suffered outside the city. He died to make his people holy with his own blood. [13]So we should go to Jesus outside the camp and accept the same shame that he had. [14]Here on earth we don't have a city that lasts forever. But we are waiting for the city that we will have in the future. [15]So through Jesus we should never stop offering our sacrifice to God. That sacrifice is our praise, coming from lips that speak his name. [16]And don't forget to do good and to share what you have with others, because sacrifices like these are very pleasing to God.

[17]Obey your leaders. Be willing to do what they say. They are responsible for your spiritual welfare, so they are always watching to protect you. Obey them so that their work will give them joy, not grief. It won't help you to make it hard for them.

[18]Continue praying for us. We feel right about what we do, because we always try to do what is best. [19]And I beg you to pray that God will send me back to you soon. I want this more than anything else.

[20–21]I pray that the God of peace will give you every good thing you need so that you can do what he wants. God is the one who raised from death our Lord Jesus, the Great Shepherd of his sheep. He raised him because Jesus sacrificed his blood to begin the new agreement that never ends. I pray that God will work through Jesus Christ to do the things in us that please him. To him be glory forever. Amen.

[22]My brothers and sisters, I beg you to listen patiently to what I have said. I wrote this letter to strengthen you. And it is not very long. [23]I want you to know that our brother Timothy is out of prison. If he comes to me soon, we will both come to see you.

[24]Give my greetings to all your leaders and to all God's people. All those from Italy send you their greetings.

[25]I pray that God's grace will be with you all.

Who James, the brother of Jesus. He is writing to Jewish Christians: "God's people [literally the twelve tribes] who are scattered all over the world" (1:1), which probably means those living in cities outside of Palestine.

When Probably one of the earliest New Testament writings. Since James died in AD 62 the letter has to date from earlier than that. It was probably written in the mid-40s.

What His name was actually Yaakov (Jacob). Jacob – or James as he became in English – challenges us to express our faith in practical and loving ways. The big theme of James is that faith has to be lived out: it cannot just be a set of nice spiritual thoughts.

"Greetings from James, a servant of God and of the Lord Jesus Christ," he begins this letter. An amazing way to start considering who he really was: the brother of Jesus; someone who had grown up with Jesus, in the same family (Matthew 13:55). Now he is the leader of the Jerusalem church (Acts 15), and yet he describes himself as a servant.

His emphasis on actions has led some writers to criticize James for not being "Christian" enough. However, the spiritual fruit he talks about demonstrates the reality of the believer's faith.

The letter contains more quotes from Christ than all the other New Testament letters put together. And like his brother, Jesus, James shows a concern for the poor and the low-status. He paints a picture of a Christian community where there was still a gulf between rich and poor. There is in-fighting and backbiting. People live lives that are more like the world than the kingdom of God (1:27; 4:4).

In a strongly worded rebuke, James champions the rights of the poor, criticizes snobs and bigots, and urges us to control our tongues. It doesn't say that actions are a substitute for faith; it says that if our faith doesn't result in practical, loving deeds then it's not real.

QUICK TOUR ➤ **JAMES**

Trials 1:1–18
Hearing and doing 1:19–27
Look after the poor 2:1–13
Faith and works 2:14–26

Control your tongue 3:1–18
Why do you fight? 4:1 – 5:6
Be patient 5:7–11
The power of prayer 5:13–20

"My brothers and sisters, if a person claims to have faith but does nothing, that faith is worth nothing. Faith like that cannot save anyone."

James 2:14

1 Greetings from James, a servant of God and of the Lord Jesus Christ.

To God's people[a] who are scattered all over the world.

Faith and Wisdom

2My brothers and sisters, you will have many kinds of trouble. But this gives you a reason to be very happy. 3You know that when your faith is tested, you learn to be patient in suffering. 4If you let that patience work in you, the end result will be good. You will be mature and complete. You will be all that God wants you to be.

5Do any of you need wisdom? Ask God for it. He is generous and enjoys giving to everyone. So he will give you wisdom. 6But when you ask God, you must believe. Don't doubt him. Whoever doubts is like a wave in the sea that is blown up and down by the wind. 7-8People like that are thinking two different things at the same time. They can never decide what to do. So they should not think they will receive anything from the Lord.

True Riches

9Believers who are poor should be glad that God considers them so important. 10Believers who are rich should be glad when bad things happen that humble them. Their riches won't keep them from disappearing as quickly as wild flowers. 11As the sun rises and gets hotter, its heat dries up the plants and the flowers fall off. The flowers that were so beautiful are now dead. That's how it is with the rich. While they are still making plans for their business, they will die.

Temptation Does Not Come From God

12Great blessings belong to those who are tempted and remain faithful! After they have proved their faith, God will give them the reward[b] of eternal life. God promised this to all people who love him. 13Whenever you feel tempted to do something bad, you should not say, "God is tempting me." Evil cannot tempt God, and God himself does not tempt anyone. 14You are tempted by the evil things you want. Your own desire leads you away and traps you. 15Your desire grows inside you until it results in sin. Then the sin grows bigger and bigger and finally ends in death.

16My dear brothers and sisters, don't be fooled about this. 17Everything good comes from God.

Every perfect gift is from him. These good gifts come down from the Father who made all the lights in the sky. But God never changes like the shadows from those lights. He is always the same. 18God decided to give us life through the true message he sent to us. He wanted us to be the most important of all that he created.

Listening and Obeying

19My dear brothers and sisters, always be more willing to listen than to speak. Keep control of your anger. 20Anger does not help you live the way God wants. 21So get rid of everything evil in your lives—every kind of wrong you do. Be humble and accept God's teaching that is planted in your hearts. This teaching can save you.

INSIGHT

James makes a connection between listening and obeying here, and makes it clear that simply hearing is not enough. The Hebrew word sh'mah means both "listen" and "obey". It is the first word of the divine instructions given by God to man in the book of Exodus.

James 1:22

22Do what God's teaching says; don't just listen and do nothing. When you only sit and listen, you are fooling yourselves. 23Hearing God's teaching and doing nothing is like looking at your face in the mirror 24and doing nothing about what you saw. You go away and immediately forget how bad you looked. 25But when you look into God's perfect law that sets people free, pay attention to it. If you do what it says, you will have God's blessing. Never just listen to his teaching and forget what you heard.

The True Way to Worship God

26You might think you are a very religious person. But if your tongue is out of control, you are fooling yourself. Your careless talk makes your offerings to God useless. 27The worship that God wants is this: caring for orphans or widows who need help and keeping yourself free from the world's evil influence. This is the kind of worship that God accepts as pure and good.

---

[a] 1:1 **God's people** Literally, "the twelve tribes". Believers in Christ are like the tribes of Israel, God's chosen people in the Old Testament.
[b] 1:12 **reward** Literally, "wreath", a ring of leaves or branches that was placed on the head of the winners of athletic contests to honour them. It is a symbol of victory and reward.

TESTING, TESTING

Unfortunately, no one has a 100% easy life. We will all have downs as well as ups and these will lead to choices. For all of us, the choices that we make and the way that we respond to their consequences will contribute to the kind of people that we become. Take a look at the following verses in James to see why he feels able to say something as crazy as "you will have many kinds of trouble. But this gives you reason to be very happy" (James 1:2).

DIG IN

READ James 1:2-4

- Why does James suggest that the troubles of the Christian life should make us happy?
- When you're in the midst of troubles, they often make no sense at all and happiness is the last thing that you feel. Take a moment to think back over your Christian life so far . . . How has God changed and matured you when you've gone through tough times? Or how has he better equipped you to help other Christians who may be suffering in similar ways?
- Sometimes it's hard to see changes in ourselves: they're more visible to others. Can you think of Christians you know or whose testimonies you've read whose suffering has produced "patience" (v.3)?

It's not always possible to see God's handiwork in us as he shapes and refines us through our suffering – we may not see the full picture until we are in heaven with him. However, whether it's visible to us or not we can be sure of the promise that if we are his we "will be mature and complete . . . all that God wants [us] to be" (v.4). Take a look at verse 12 to see what lies in store for those who remain faithful . . .

READ James 1:13-18

Now James addresses a question that may have been planted in your mind by all that talk of trials and tests: where does temptation come from?

- Where does temptation definitely not come from (v.13)?
- Where does temptation definitely come from (v.14)?
- How does this happen, according to verse 15?

DIG THROUGH

- It's quite shocking to see that James tells us that temptation comes from within ourselves – from our "own desires". We may like to imagine that our temptations come from circumstances and things beyond our control. But think back over times in your own life when you have given in to temptation. Can you see that although circumstances may have made things more difficult for you, it was ultimately your own sinful desires that led you to that place?
- Have you been tempted to blame other people or other things for the choices that you made? You may feel that you want to ask God for forgiveness for blaming others or for making excuses. Ask God to show you the true state of your heart, and give thanks that Jesus has made a way for you to know and be loved by God no matter what you may have done.

DIG DEEPER

- How can we avoid temptation? What does Paul suggest in 2 Timothy 2:16,22–23?
- Look back to when Adam and Eve were first tempted, in Genesis 3. What can we learn from their mistakes?

GENUINE CHRISTIANITY

If I told you I was an international rock star, would you believe me? You would be wise to want to see some evidence for my claim – does my lifestyle match up? Saying that something is true is one thing. Behaving in a way that matches up with your words is something else entirely . . .

DIG IN
READ James 1:22–27

- To what does James compare ignoring God's teaching?

Imagine you're getting ready for a date or a job interview. You check the mirror before you leave and see a massive piece of spinach between your front teeth. Would you just walk out and leave it there? Of course not! James says that hearing a sermon or reading a Bible passage and leaving unchanged is just as ludicrous. Simply listening is not enough.

- What does James say will be the result if you pay attention to what God says (v.25)?

Freedom is often the last thing people think of as a direct result of following God's "rules".

- In your Christian life so far, how many examples can you think of where freedom has been the result of obedience? If you're stuck, think about your non-Christian friends and some of their problems. Would they have been free from them if they'd followed the teaching of the Bible?
- Praise God that his teaching is there because he wants the best for us and to give us freedom from things that could trap and hurt us.

READ James 2:14–26

- What is the difference between a demon's belief in God (the demons knew who Jesus was, Mark 5:7–10) and the faith of a genuine Christian (James 2:18–20)?
- How does the example given in verses 15–17 help to illustrate this?
- What meant that Abraham could be called "God's friend" (v.23)?
- What did Abraham do to prove that he had faith in God (v.21)?
- How do verses 18–26 show why it is not accurate to say, "Some people have faith, and others have good works" (v.18)?

DIG THROUGH

- Compare James 2:24 with Ephesians 2:8–9. Confused?

James says, "people are made right with God by what they do. They cannot be made right by faith alone", while Ephesians says, "you have been saved by grace because you believed. You did not save yourselves; it was a gift from God. You are not saved by the things you have done".

- How can both these things be true?

James is talking about two inseparable things – faith and good deeds. We can see how inseparable they are by taking either out of the equation. If a person does endless good deeds but rejects Jesus (has no faith), they can't be called a Christian (John 14:6). So good deeds without faith cannot save you and make you a Christian. That's what the Ephesians verse means. Equally, as James illustrates, if someone says they follow Jesus and yet there is no evidence that this is true, we must question whether this faith is genuine.

Like the rock star illustration at the beginning, anyone can make a statement, but only actions and lifestyle can prove it to be true. This is what James wants to teach us – it is only when faith and good deeds are present that we can be sure that faith is genuine.

Love All People

2 My dear brothers and sisters, you are believers in our glorious Lord Jesus Christ. So don't treat some people better than others. ²Suppose someone comes into your meeting wearing very nice clothes and a gold ring. At the same time a poor person comes in wearing old, dirty clothes. ³You show special attention to the person wearing nice clothes. You say, "Sit here in this good seat." But you say to the poor person, "Stand there!" or "Sit on the floor by our feet!" ⁴Doesn't this show that you think some people are more important than others? You set yourselves up as judges— judges who make bad decisions.

⁵Listen, my dear brothers and sisters. God chose the poor people in the world to be rich in faith. He chose them to receive the kingdom God promised to those who love him. ⁶But you show no respect to those who are poor. And you know that the rich are the ones who always try to control your lives. They are the ones who take you to court. ⁷And the rich are the ones who insult the good name of your Lord, the one you belong to.

⁸One law rules over all other laws. This royal law is found in the Scriptures: "Love your neighbour*ᵃ* the same as you love yourself."*ᵇ* If you obey this law, you are doing right. ⁹But if you are treating one person as more important than another, you are sinning. You are guilty of breaking God's law.

¹⁰You might follow all of God's law. But if you fail to obey only one command, you are guilty of breaking all the commands in that law. ¹¹God said, "Don't commit adultery."*ᶜ* The same God also said, "Don't kill."*ᵈ* So if you don't commit adultery, but you kill someone, you are guilty of breaking all of God's law.

¹²You will be judged by the law that makes people free. You should remember this in everything you say and do. ¹³Yes, you must show mercy to others. If you do not show mercy, then God will not show mercy to you when he judges you. But the one who shows mercy can stand without fear before the Judge.

Faith and Good Works

¹⁴My brothers and sisters, if a person claims to have faith but does nothing, that faith is worth nothing. Faith like that cannot save anyone. ¹⁵Suppose a brother or sister in Christ comes to you in need of clothes or something to eat. ¹⁶And you say to them, "God be with you! I hope you stay warm and get plenty to eat," but you don't give them the things they need. If you don't help them, your words are worthless. ¹⁷It is the same with faith. If it is just faith and nothing more—if it doesn't do anything—it is dead.

¹⁸But someone might argue, "Some people have faith, and others have good works." My answer would be that you can't show me your faith if you don't do anything. But I will show you my faith by the good I do. ¹⁹You believe there is one God. That's good, but even the demons believe that! And they shake with fear.

²⁰You fool! Faith that does nothing is worth nothing. Do you want me to prove this to you? ²¹Our father Abraham was made right with God by what he did. He offered his son Isaac to God on the altar. ²²So you see that Abraham's faith and what he did worked together. His faith was made perfect by what he did. ²³This shows the full meaning of the Scriptures that say, "Abraham believed God, and because of this faith he was accepted as one who is right with God."*ᵉ* Abraham was called "God's friend".*ᶠ* ²⁴So you see that people are made right with God by what they do. They cannot be made right by faith alone.

²⁵Another example is Rahab. She was a prostitute, but she was made right with God by something she did. She helped those who were spying for God's people. She welcomed them into her home and helped them escape by a different road.*ᵍ*

²⁶A person's body that does not have a spirit is dead. It is the same with faith—faith that does nothing is dead!

Controlling the Things We Say

3 My brothers and sisters, not many of you should be teachers. I say this because, as you know, we who teach will be judged more strictly than others.

²We all make many mistakes. A person who never said anything wrong would be perfect. Someone like that would be able to control their whole body too. ³We put bits into the mouths of horses to make them obey us. With these bits we can control their whole body. ⁴It is the same with ships. A ship is very big, and it is pushed by strong winds. But a very small rudder controls that big ship. And the one who controls the rudder decides where the ship will go. It goes where he

---

ᵃ **2:8 your neighbour** Or "others". Jesus' teaching in Luke 10:25–37 makes clear that this includes anyone in need.
ᵇ **2:8** Quote from Lev. 19:18.
ᶜ **2:11** Quote from Exod. 20:14; Deut. 5:18.
ᵈ **2:11** Quote from Exod. 20:13; Deut. 5:17.
ᵉ **2:23** Quote from Gen. 15:6.
ᶠ **2:23** Quote from 2 Chr. 20:7; Isa. 41:8.
ᵍ **2:25 She helped . . . road** The story about Rahab is found in Josh. 2:1–21.

TAMING THE TONGUE

Have you ever said something and then wished straight away that you could take it back? Have you ever spoken words in anger that you wouldn't usually even dream of saying? Here are examples of some battles of the tongue that we face as Christians and which James shows us are more serious than we might have thought.

DIG IN
READ James 3:2–12

- What is the tongue likened to, and how is it similar to these things (vv.2–6)?
- Can you think of times when these examples seem to vividly describe ways you've used your tongue?
- List the words used to describe the tongue in verses 7–9. Why do you think James uses such strong language?

READ James 3:13–18

If we can do so much damage with such a small part of our bodies, what kind of help is there available for us? What is the antidote to the evil we can do with our tongues? James tells us about the good weapon of wisdom.

- The tongue can also be guilty of boasting. Who should avoid doing this according to verses 13–18? Have you ever been guilty of the things described in verse 14? What does that tell you about how appropriate boasting is for you?
- What clues are given here about how to tell the difference between wisdom that comes from God and "wisdom" that does not?
- Imagine how different things might be if your tongue was used following the principles of verse 17. Do you speak in this way when you are in discussions (or arguments) with others? Check out James 1:19 which shows how this might be achieved?

READ James 4:11–12

- For what reason does James say we should not say anything against (criticize) one another?
- Who has the right to judge, and why?
- Can you imagine what changes there would be in the church if all believers lived in this way? In what ways can you influence this kind of change in your own church? Pause to ask God to help you to do this.

DIG THROUGH

- As always, Jesus is the supreme example of godly behaviour, and this includes the way that he uses his tongue. Read through chapter 18 of John's Gospel and look at the way that Jesus conducts himself during a grossly unfair trial where he, the Son of God, stands to be brutally put to death with no evidence of any crime.
- How do you react when you are wrongly accused of something? What can you learn from Jesus' example here?
- Can you think of any other examples in the Gospel accounts where the way Jesus speaks (or listens) to others teaches us something about how we could conduct ourselves?

wants it to go. [5]It is the same with our tongue. It is a small part of the body, but it can boast about doing great things.

A big forest fire can be started with only a little flame. [6]The tongue is like a fire. It is a world of evil among the parts of our body. It spreads its evil through our whole body and starts a fire that influences all of life. It gets this fire from hell.

[7]Humans have control over every kind of wild animal, bird, reptile and fish, and they have controlled all these things. [8]But no one can control the tongue. It is wild and evil, full of deadly poison. [9]We use our tongues to praise our Lord and Father, but then we curse people who were created in God's likeness. [10]These praises and curses come from the same mouth. My brothers and sisters, this should not happen. [11]Do good water and bad water flow from the same spring? Of course not. [12]My brothers and sisters, can a fig tree make olives? Or can a grapevine make figs? No, and a well full of salty water cannot give good water.

True Wisdom

[13]Are there any among you who are really wise and understanding? Then you should show your wisdom by living right. You should do what is good with humility. A wise person does not boast. [14]If you are selfish and have bitter jealousy in your hearts, you have no reason to boast. Your boasting is a lie that hides the truth. [15]If you live that way, you do not have the wisdom that comes from God. No, you are thinking the way the world thinks. And that kind of thinking is not from the Spirit. It is from the devil. [16]Where there is jealousy and selfishness, there will be confusion and every kind of evil. [17]But the wisdom that comes from God is like this: First, it is pure. It is also peaceful, gentle and easy to please. This wisdom is always ready to help people who have trouble and to do good for others. This wisdom is always fair and honest. [18]People who work for peace in a peaceful way get the blessings that come from right living.

Give Yourselves to God

4 Do you know where your fights and arguments come from? They come from the selfish desires that make war inside you. [2]You want things, but you don't get them. So you kill and are jealous of others. But you still cannot get what you want. So you argue and fight. You don't get what you want because you don't ask God.

[3]Or when you ask, you don't receive anything, because the reason you ask is wrong. You only want to use it for your own pleasure.

[4]You people are not faithful to God! You should know that loving what the world has is the same as hating God. So anyone who wants to be friends with this evil world becomes God's enemy. [5]Do you think the Scriptures mean nothing? The Scriptures say, "The Spirit God made to live in us wants us only for himself."[a] [6]But the kindness God shows us is greater. As the Scripture says, "God is against the proud, but he is kind to the humble."[b]

[7]So give yourselves to God. Stand against the devil, and he will run away from you. [8]Come near to God and he will come near to you. You are sinners, so clean sin out of your lives.[c] You are trying to follow God and the world at the same time. Make your thinking pure. [9]Be sad, be sorry and cry! Change your laughter into crying. Change your joy into sadness. [10]Be humble before the Lord, and he will make you great.

You Are Not the Judge

[11]Brothers and sisters, don't say anything against each other. If you criticize your brother or sister in Christ or judge them, you are criticizing and judging the law they follow. And when you are judging the law, you are not a follower of the law. You have become a judge. [12]God is the one who gave us the law, and he is the Judge. He is the only one who can save and destroy. So it is not right for you to judge anyone.

Let God Plan Your Life

[13]Some of you say, "Today or tomorrow we will go to some city. We will stay there for a year, do business and make money." Listen, think about this: [14]you don't know what will happen tomorrow. Your life is like a fog. You can see it for a short time, but then it goes away. [15]So you should say, "If the Lord wants, we will live and do this or that." [16]But now you are proud and boast about yourself. All such boasting is wrong. [17]If you fail to do what you know is right, you are sinning.

A Warning to Rich and Selfish People

5 You rich people, listen! Cry and be very sad because much trouble will come to you. [2]Your riches will rot and be worth nothing. Your clothes will be eaten by moths. [3]Your gold and silver will rust, and that rust will be proof that you were

---

[a] **4:5 "The Spirit . . . himself"** Other possible translations: "God strongly desires the spirit that he made to live in us." Or "The spirit that he made to live in us is full of envious desires." See Exod. 20:5.
[b] **4:6** Quote from Prov. 3:34.
[c] **4:8 so clean sin out of your lives** Literally, "so wash your hands".

wrong. That rust will eat your bodies, like fire. You saved your treasure in the last days. ⁴People worked in your fields, but you did not pay them. They are crying out against you. They harvested your crops. Now the Lord All-Powerful has heard their cries.

⁵Your life on earth was full of rich living. You pleased yourselves with everything you wanted. You made yourselves fat, like an animal ready for the day of slaughter.ᵃ ⁶You showed no mercy to good people. They were not against you, but you killed them.

Be Patient

⁷Brothers and sisters, be patient; the Lord will come. So be patient until that time. Look at the farmers. They have to be patient. They have to wait for their valuable crop to grow and produce a harvest. They wait patiently for the first rain and the last rain.ᵇ ⁸You must be patient too. Never stop hoping. The Lord will soon be here. ⁹Brothers and sisters, don't complain against each other. If you don't stop complaining, you will be judged guilty. And the Judge is ready to come!

¹⁰Brothers and sisters, follow the example of the prophets who spoke for the Lord. They suffered many bad things, but they were patient. ¹¹And we say that those who accepted their troubles with patience now have God's blessing. You have heard about Job's patience.ᶜ You know that after all his troubles, the Lord helped him. This shows that the Lord is full of mercy and is kind.

Be Careful What You Say

¹²My brothers and sisters, it is very important that you do not use an oath when you make a promise. Don't use the name of heaven, earth or anything else to prove what you say. When you mean yes, say only "yes". When you mean no, say only "no". Do this so that you will not be judged guilty.

The Power of Prayer

¹³Are you having troubles? You should pray. Are you happy? You should sing. ¹⁴Are you sick? Ask the elders of the church to come and put oil on youᵈ in the name of the Lord and pray for you. ¹⁵If such a prayer is offered in faith, it will heal anyone who is sick. The Lord will heal them. And if they have sinned, he will forgive them.

¹⁶So always confess to each other the wrong things you have done. Then pray for each other. Then God can heal you. Anyone who lives the way God wants can pray, and great things will happen. ¹⁷Elijah was a person just like us. He prayed that it would not rain. And it did not rain on the land for three and a half years! ¹⁸Then Elijah prayed that it would rain. And the rain came down from the sky, and the land grew crops again.

Helping People When They Sin

¹⁹My brothers and sisters, if anyone wanders away from the truth and someone helps that person come back, ²⁰remember this: anyone who brings a sinner back from the wrong way will save that person from eternal death and cause many sins to be forgiven.

ᵃ 5:5 **You made yourselves fat . . . slaughter** Literally, "You fattened your hearts for the day of slaughter."
ᵇ 5:7 **first rain . . . last rain** The "first rain" came in the autumn, and the "last rain" came in the spring.
ᶜ 5:11 **Job's patience** See the book of Job in the Old Testament.
ᵈ 5:14 **put oil on you** Oil was used like medicine.

Who Peter, the fisherman, brother of Andrew and friend of Jesus. He was writing to Christian communities in the Black Sea coastal area, the northern half of what was formerly Asia Minor (modern-day Turkey).

When Probably sometime between AD 62 and 64. The reference to Babylon (5:13) is almost certainly a Christian code word for Rome, so he probably wrote this letter from Rome, before the great persecution of Christians under Emperor Nero.

What Peter writes to encourage those who are suffering persecution. This is a not a letter to a person, or even to one church. It is a circular letter written to people who were facing or about to face suffering.

It was tough being a Christian in the days of the early Church. Follow Jesus and you were very often ostracized, mocked, expelled from your family or work, sometimes even killed. Even today there are many societies where to be a Christian is to face danger and isolation.

Peter is realistic. Suffering, mockery, abuse: it comes with the territory; it's part and parcel of being a Christian. The big issue is how we respond to it. Peter points to Christ's example: Christ suffered and then entered into glory, and the same will be true of his followers. Our suffering is a prelude to the glory that is awaiting us.

So Peter urges people not to lose faith, but to remember they are a special, holy people. They are God's people now. And that means living in a way that will honour God. They are to show love to one another – real love, love which comes from a pure heart (1:22) – and to use their God-given gifts wisely.

A few years after Peter wrote this letter a great fire broke out in Rome. The emperor, Nero, pushed the blame onto the Christians and launched a terrible persecution against them. They were burnt alive or thrown into the arena to be torn apart by animals. It was probably during this persecution that Peter himself lost his life. "When people say bad things to you because you follow Christ," he wrote in this letter, "consider it a blessing. When that happens, it shows that God's Spirit, the Spirit of glory, is with you" (4:14).

QUICK TOUR ▶ 1 PETER

Hope 1:1–12
God's people 1:13 – 2:17

Don't be surprised 4:12–19

"But you are his chosen people, the King's priests. You are a holy nation, people who belong to God. He chose you to tell about the wonderful things he has done. He brought you out of the darkness of sin into his wonderful light."

1 Peter 2:9

1 Greetings from Peter, an apostle of Jesus Christ.

To God's chosen people who are away from their homes—people scattered all over the areas of Pontus, Galatia, Cappadocia, Asia and Bithynia. [2]God planned long ago to choose you and to make you his holy people, which is the Spirit's work. God wanted you to obey him and to be made clean by the blood sacrifice[a] of Jesus Christ.

I pray that you will enjoy more and more of God's grace and peace.

A Living Hope

[3]Praise be to the God and Father of our Lord Jesus Christ. God has great mercy, and because of his mercy he gave us a new life. This new life brings us a living hope through Jesus Christ's resurrection from death. [4]Now we wait to receive the blessings God has for his children. These blessings are kept for you in heaven. They cannot be ruined or be destroyed or lose their beauty.

[5]God's power protects you through your faith, and it keeps you safe until your salvation comes. That salvation is ready to be given to you at the end of time. [6]I know the thought of that is exciting, even if you must suffer through different kinds of troubles for a short time now. [7]These troubles test your faith and prove that it is pure. And such faith is worth more than gold. Gold can be proved to be pure by fire, but gold will ruin. When your faith is proven to be pure, the result will be praise and glory and honour when Jesus Christ comes.

[8]You have not seen Christ, but still you love him. You can't see him now, but you believe in him. You are filled with a wonderful and heavenly joy that cannot be explained. [9]Your faith has a goal, and you are reaching that goal—your salvation.

[10]The prophets studied carefully and tried to learn about this salvation. They spoke about the grace that was coming to you. [11]The Spirit of Christ was in those prophets. And the Spirit was telling about the suffering that Christ would have and about the glory that would come after that suffering. The prophets tried to learn about what the Spirit was showing them—when it would happen and what the world would be like at that time. [12]It was made clear to them that their service was not for themselves. They were serving you when they told people about the things you have now heard. You heard them from those who told

you the Good News with the help of the Holy Spirit sent from heaven. Even the angels would like very much to know more about these things you were told.

A Call to Holy Living

[13]So prepare your minds for service. With complete self-control put all your hope in the grace that will be yours when Jesus Christ comes. [14]In the past you did not have the understanding you have now, so you did the evil things you wanted to do. But now you are children of God, so you should obey him and not live the way you did before. [15]Be holy in everything you do, just as God is holy. He is the one who chose you. [16]In the Scriptures God says, "Be holy, because I am holy."[b]

INSIGHT

Wow, that's a pretty tall order – be holy just as God is holy! But remember, holy simply means "set apart". We are to follow Christ's example, pursuing a lifestyle that at times may seem radically different to those around us.

1 Peter 1:15–16

---

[17]You pray to God and call him Father, but he will judge everyone the same way—by what they do. So while you are visiting here on earth, you should live with respect for God. [18]You know that in the past the way you were living was useless. It was a way of life you learned from those who lived before you. But you were saved from that way of living. You were bought, but not with things that ruin like gold or silver. [19]You were bought with the precious blood of Christ's death. He was a pure and perfect sacrificial Lamb. [20]Christ was chosen before the world was made, but he was shown to the world in these last times for you. [21]You believe in God through Christ. God is the one who raised him from death and gave honour to him. So your faith and your hope are in God.

[22]You have made yourselves pure by obeying the truth. Now you can have true love for your brothers and sisters. So love each other deeply— with all your heart. [23]You have been born again. This new life did not come from something that dies. It came from something that cannot die. You

---

[a] **1:2 made clean . . . sacrifice** Or "sprinkled with the blood", which probably compares the beginning of the new agreement by the blood sacrifice of Christ (Mark 14:24) with Moses' sprinkling the blood of animal sacrifices on the people of Israel to seal the agreement God made with them (Exod. 24:3–8). See also Heb. 9:15–26.
[b] **1:16** Quote from Lev. 11:44–45; 19:2; 20:7.

GOD'S SPECIAL PEOPLE

"Special" is not always meant as a compliment these days, is it? "Ah, you're *special*!" someone might say. What they may actually mean is you're odd!

"Special" means "different" to the average, ordinary person. Sometimes this comes with benefits, often not. The new church was finding out that in their case it means both.

DIG IN

READ 1 Peter 1:22 – 2:12

- Peter writes of being "born again" (v.23). What is different about this new life?
- Why do you think Peter uses so many quotations from the Old Testament in this section?

Peter's first letter is concerned with helping these young churches deal with the suffering that they have to contend with living in the first-century Roman world. We get a hint of this in 1 Peter 1:6. But before we get to his more detailed teaching on suffering, Peter takes time to remind the believers of their identity – their new identity in Christ.

In the early part of the letter, Peter is reminding his readers that they are very special to God and that he is using them to build a "spiritual temple" (2:5): the place where God lives, the church.

He finds scriptures from the Old Testament that root this baby church deep in the historical promises of God. It's as if he's saying, "Understand the history. This is not some new idea; it's been in the pipeline for thousands of years and now you're fulfilling it." Even though the readers are non-Jews, because they have faith in Jesus, they now share in the history that belongs to the Jews. That must have been an encouragement to these churches.

But with that privilege comes some responsibilities to one another and to the world around them.

- What responsibilities do they have to each other (1:22; 2:1–2)?
- How should they behave towards the world around them (2:11–12)?

They need to show deep love to each other, love which is worked out in very practical ways. For example, telling the truth, speaking well of each other and supporting each other through trials.

To the world, they need to see themselves as "foreigners and strangers", taking great care how they live.

DIG THROUGH

- Think of what it means to be a visitor or a stranger in someone else's home. How does it alter your behaviour, compared to being in your own home? So how is Peter asking Christians to think of themselves?
- Don't you just love it when you're chosen – for a sports team, a play, or invited to a party? And isn't it crushing when you're not? Read 2:9–10 again. These words are for you too. You might feel quite ordinary but you have been chosen by God!

DIG DEEPER

- Do you find it particularly significant that Peter should be writing about "living stones"? You may know that Jesus gave him a special name. Read Matthew 16:13–20.

Peter prepares the way for the rest of what he has to say in 1 Peter 2:4. People rejected Jesus, the original living stone. He will go on to say that just like Jesus we will be rejected too.

were born again through God's life-giving message that lasts forever. ²⁴The Scriptures say,

> "Our lives are like the grass of spring,
>   and any glory we enjoy is like the beauty of
>   a wild flower.
> The grass dries up and dies,
>   and the flower falls to the ground.
> ²⁵But the word of the Lord lasts forever."
>
> *Isaiah 40:6–8*

And that word is the Good News that was told to you.

The Living Stone and the Holy Nation

2 So then, stop doing anything to hurt others. Don't lie any more, and stop trying to fool people. Don't be jealous or say bad things about others. ²Like newborn babies hungry for milk, you should want the pure teaching that feeds your spirit. With it you can grow up and be saved. ³You have already tasted the goodness of the Lord.

⁴The Lord Jesus is the living stone.*ᵃ* The people of the world decided that they did not want this stone. But he is the one God chose as one of great value, so come to him. ⁵You also are like living stones, and God is using you to build a spiritual temple.*ᵇ* You are to serve God in this temple as holy priests, offering him spiritual sacrifices that he will accept because of Jesus Christ. ⁶The Scriptures say,

> "Look, I have chosen a cornerstone of great
>   value,
>   and I put that stone in Zion.
> Anyone who trusts in him will never be put to
>   shame."
>
> *Isaiah 28:16*

⁷So, that stone brings honour to you who believe. But for those who don't believe he is

> "the stone that the builders refused to accept,
>   which became the most important stone."
>
> *Psalm 118:22*

⁸For them he is

> "a stone that makes people stumble,
>   a rock that makes people fall."
>
> *Isaiah 8:14*

They refused to accept God's message, and so they stumbled. This is what God planned for them.

⁹But you are his chosen people, the King's priests. You are a holy nation, people who belong to God. He chose you to tell about the wonderful things he has done. He brought you out of the darkness of sin into his wonderful light.

> ¹⁰In the past you were not a special people,
>   but now you are God's people.
> Once you had not received mercy,
>   but now God has given you his mercy.*ᶜ*

Live for God

¹¹Dear friends, you are like foreigners and strangers in this world. So I beg you to keep your lives free from the evil things you want to do, those desires that fight against your true selves. ¹²People who don't believe are living all around you. They may say that you are doing wrong. So live such good lives that they will see the good you do, and they will give glory to God on the day he comes.

Obey Every Human Authority

¹³Be willing to serve the people who have authority*ᵈ* in this world. Do this for the Lord. Obey the king, the highest authority. ¹⁴And obey the leaders who are sent by the king. They are sent to punish those who do wrong and to praise those who do good. ¹⁵When you do good, you stop ignorant people from saying foolish things about you. This is what God wants. ¹⁶Live like free people, but don't use your freedom as an excuse to do evil. Live as those who are serving God. ¹⁷Show respect for all people. Love your brothers and sisters in God's family. Respect God, and honour the king.

Slaves, Follow the Example of Christ

¹⁸Slaves, be willing to serve your masters. Do this with all respect. You should obey the masters who are good and kind, and you should obey the masters who are bad. ¹⁹One of you might have to suffer even when you have done nothing wrong. If you think of God and bear the pain, this pleases God. ²⁰If you are punished for doing wrong, there is no reason to praise you for bearing that punishment. But if you suffer for doing good and you are patient, this pleases God. ²¹This is what you were chosen to do. Christ gave you an

---

ᵃ **2:4 *stone*** The most important stone in God's spiritual temple or house (his people).
ᵇ **2:5 *temple*** Literally, "house", meaning God's house—the place where God's people worship him. Here, it means that believers are the spiritual temple where God lives.
ᶜ **2:10 *In the past . . . his mercy*** See Hos. 2:23.
ᵈ **2:13 *people . . . authority*** Literally, "every human creation", meaning rulers, governors, presidents or other government leaders.

example to follow. He suffered for you. So you should do the same as he did:

22"He never sinned,
and he never told a lie."

Isaiah 53:9

23People insulted him, but he did not insult them back. He suffered, but he did not threaten anyone. No, he let God take care of him. God is the one who judges rightly. 24Christ carried our sins in his body on the cross. He did this so that we would stop living for sin and live for what is right. By his wounds you were healed. 25You were like sheep that went the wrong way. But now you have come back to the Shepherd and Protector of your lives.

Wives and Husbands

3 In the same way, you wives should be willing to serve your husbands. Then, even those who have refused to accept God's teaching will be persuaded to believe because of the way you live. You will not need to say anything. 2Your husbands will see the pure lives that you live with respect for God. 3It is not fancy hair, gold jewellery or fine clothes that should make you beautiful. 4No, your beauty should come from inside you—the beauty of a gentle and quiet spirit. That beauty will never disappear. It is worth very much to God.

5It was the same with the holy women who lived long ago and followed God. They made themselves beautiful in that same way. They were willing to serve their husbands. 6I am talking about women like Sarah. She obeyed Abraham, her husband, and called him her master. And you women are true children of Sarah if you always do what is right and are not afraid.

7In the same way, you husbands should live with your wives in an understanding way, since they are weaker than you. You should show them respect, because God gives them the same blessing he gives you—the grace of true life. Do this so that nothing will stop your prayers from being heard.

Suffering for Doing Right

8So all of you should live together in peace. Try to understand each other. Love each other like brothers and sisters. Be kind and humble. 9Don't do wrong to anyone to pay them back for doing wrong to you and don't insult anyone to pay them back for insulting you. But ask God to bless them. Do this because you yourselves were chosen to receive a blessing. 10The Scriptures say,

"If you want to enjoy true life
and have only good days,
then avoid saying anything hurtful,
and never let a lie come out of your
mouth.
11Stop doing what is wrong, and do good.
Look for peace, and do all you can to help
people live peacefully.
12The Lord watches over those who do what
is right,
and he listens to their prayers.
But he is against those who do evil."

Psalm 34:12–16

13If you are always trying to do good, no one can really harm you. 14But you may suffer for doing right. If that happens, you have God's blessing. "Don't be afraid of the people who make you suffer; don't be worried."*a* 15But keep the Lord Christ holy in your hearts. Always be ready to answer everyone who asks you to explain about the hope you have. 16But answer them in a gentle way with respect. Keep your conscience clear. Then people will see the good way you live as followers of Christ, and those who say bad things about you will be ashamed of what they said.

17It is better to suffer for doing good than for doing wrong. Yes, it is better if that is what God wants.

18Christ himself suffered when he died for
you,
and with that one death he paid for your
sins.
He was not guilty,
but he died for people who are guilty.
He did this to bring all of you to God.
In his physical form he was killed,
but he was made alive by the Spirit.*b*

19And by the Spirit he went and preached to the spirits in prison. 20Those were the spirits who refused to obey God long ago in the time of Noah. God was waiting patiently for people while Noah was building the big boat. And only a few—eight in all—were saved in the boat through the floodwater. 21And that water is like baptism, which now saves you. Baptism is not the washing of dirt from the body. It is asking God for a clean conscience. It saves you because Jesus Christ was raised from death. 22Now he has gone into heaven. He is at God's right side and rules over angels, authorities and powers.

---

a **3:14** Quote from Isa. 8:12.
b **3:18** *by the Spirit* Or "in the spirit". Also in verse 19.

KEEP CALM AND CARRY ON

The main point of Peter's letter is to address the question of suffering. This short passage brings together his argument so far. The fact that Peter took the time to write this letter shows that this must have been a major issue for these young churches. The fact that it made it into the Bible we still have today means it applies to us too.

DIG IN

READ 1 Peter 4:12–19

- How should these new Christians react to the suffering they are undergoing?
- Why should they be glad about it (vv.13,19)?

Life in the first-century Roman Empire was not always easy for Christians (check out 2:12,19; 3:9,14,16 and 4:4). Becoming a Christian in those times meant a radical change in lifestyle.

Their faith in Jesus brought them into direct conflict with the culture because they refused to take part in Roman customs, like giving worship to Caesar. They also stood up against immoral practices like abortion. They showed themselves to be different by showing honour to women, and by regularly meeting for prayer and the Lord's Supper.

For these and other reasons, Christians were often targets of discrimination and abuse, both verbal and physical. So how should they respond?

Earlier in his letter, Peter says Christians need to respect and honour these authorities (2:13–17). Servants were sometimes treated harshly by their masters but Christian servants should serve to a high standard whatever the circumstances (2:18–25). Peter even suggests that there will be times when those close to us – like husbands and wives (3:1–7) – might cause us to suffer. Again we should show honour and respect.

Peter says that we should fully expect some measure of suffering for being a Christ-follower. This might look like being made fun of, being excluded or having bad things said about us. But more than just expect it, we should embrace it. We should consider it a blessing (4:14) and we should certainly not be ashamed of it (4:16).

DIG THROUGH

- Yikes! That's a tall order isn't it? How do we deal with that mentally? The keys are in 1 Peter 4:12–13. It's doing us good, refining our faith and making it more pure. And we are in a mysterious way sharing in Christ's own suffering.
- To become a Christian in those times meant a radical change in lifestyle. Very practically, in what ways do you now live differently from how you did before? Has that attracted any comments or criticism from people who are or were your friends?

DIG DEEPER

- It's clear that God allows us to go through suffering for our own good. Elsewhere the Bible teaches that the more you suffer, the more you will be able to rejoice: study, for example, Acts 5:41, Romans 5:3–5, Colossians 1:24 and Hebrews 10:34.

Peter teaches that we will rejoice greatly when we see Jesus. To suffer is a kind of invitation to enter that rejoicing early. It's proof that you've got God's Spirit inside you – proof that you are truly a follower of Christ.

Changed Lives

4 Christ suffered while he was in his body. So you should strengthen yourselves with the same kind of thinking Christ had. The one who accepts suffering in this life has clearly decided to stop sinning. 2Strengthen yourselves so that you will live your lives here on earth doing what God wants, not the evil things that people want to do. 3In the past you wasted too much time doing what those who don't know God like to do. You were living immoral lives, doing the evil things you wanted to do. You were always getting drunk, having wild drinking parties and doing shameful things in your worship of idols.

4Now those "friends" think it is strange that you no longer join them in all the wild and wasteful things they do. And so they say bad things about you. 5But they will have to face God to explain what they have done. He is the one who will soon judge everyone—those who are living now and those who have already died. 6Some were told the Good News before they died. They were criticized by others in their life here on earth. But it was God's plan that they hear the Good News so that they could have a new life through the Spirit.[a]

Be Good Managers of God's Gifts

7The time is near when all things will end. So keep your minds clear, and control yourselves. This will help you in your prayers. 8Most important of all, love each other deeply, because love makes you willing to forgive many sins. 9Open your homes to each other and share your food without complaining. 10God has shown you his grace in many different ways. So be good servants and use whatever gift he has given you in a way that will best serve each other. 11If your gift is speaking, your words should be like words from God. If your gift is serving, you should serve with the strength that God gives. Then it is God who will be praised in everything through Jesus Christ. Power and glory belong to him for ever and ever. Amen.

Suffering as a Follower of Christ

12My friends, don't be surprised at the painful things that you are now suffering, which are testing your faith. Don't think that something strange is happening to you. 13But you should be happy that you are sharing in Christ's sufferings. You will be happy and full of joy when Christ shows his glory. 14When people say bad things to you because you follow Christ, consider it a blessing. When that happens, it shows that God's Spirit, the Spirit of glory, is with you. 15You may suffer, but don't let it be because you murder, steal, make trouble or try to control other people's lives. 16But if you suffer for being a "Christ-follower," don't be ashamed. You should praise God for that name. 17It is time for judging to begin. That judging will begin with God's family. If it begins with us, then what will happen to those who don't accept the Good News of God?

18"If it is hard for even a good person to be
     saved,
     what will happen to the one who is against
     God and full of sin?"

Proverbs 11:31 (Greek version)

19So if God wants you to suffer, you should trust your lives to him. He is the one who made you, and you can trust him. So continue to do good.

The Flock of God

5 Now I have something to say to the elders in your group. I am also an elder. I myself have seen Christ's sufferings. And I will share in the glory that will be shown to us. I beg you to 2take care of the group of people you are responsible for. They are God's flock.[b] Watch over that flock because you want to, not because you are forced to do it. That is how God wants it. Do it because you are happy to serve, not because you want money. 3Don't be like a ruler over those you are responsible for. But be good examples to them. 4Then when Christ the Ruling Shepherd comes, you will get a crown—one that will be glorious and never lose its beauty.

5Young people, I have something to say to you too. You should accept the authority of the elders. You should all have a humble attitude in dealing with each other.

"God is against the proud,
     but he is kind to the humble."

Proverbs 3:34

---

[a] **4:6 through the Spirit** Or "in the spirit", meaning in the spiritual or heavenly realm.
[b] **5:2 God's flock** God's people. They are like a flock of sheep that need to be cared for.

6So be humble under God's powerful hand. Then, when the right time comes, he will reward you with honour. 7Give all your worries to him, because he cares for you.

8Control yourselves and be careful! The devil is your enemy, and he goes around like a roaring lion looking for someone to attack and eat. 9Refuse to follow the devil. Stand strong in your faith. You know that your brothers and sisters all over the world are having the same sufferings that you have.

10Yes, you will suffer for a short time. But after that, God will make everything right. He will make you strong. He will support you and keep you from falling. He is the God who gives all grace. He chose you to share in his glory in Christ. That glory will last forever. 11All power is his forever. Amen.

Final Greetings

12Silas will bring this letter to you. I know that he is a faithful brother in Christ. I wrote this short letter to encourage you. I wanted to tell you that this is the true grace of God. Stand strong in that grace.

13The church in Babylon*a* send you greetings. They were chosen just as you were. Mark, my son in Christ, also sends his greetings. 14Give each other our special greeting*b* of love when you meet.

Peace to all of you who are in Christ.

---

a **5:13 The church in Babylon** Literally, "She in Babylon".
b **5:14 special greeting** Literally, "kiss".

2 PETER

Who
"Simon Peter, a servant and apostle of Jesus Christ" (1:1). This is his "second letter" (3:1), so presumably he wrote it to the same churches that received 1 Peter.

When
Peter probably wrote this letter from Rome not too long before his martyrdom, sometime during AD 64–67. It is addressed to a wide circle of early Christians: "God's people who are scattered all over the world" (James 1:1).

What
False teachers were corrupting the true message of God. It is a time of darkness. Peter urges his readers to keep their eyes on the prophecies and promises which shine like "a light shining in a dark place" (1:19).

We don't know who these false teachers were who were leading people astray, but they were mocking traditional teaching, and exploiting the churches to satisfy their greed. They hold out promises of freedom, but they themselves are "slaves to a mind that has been ruined by sin" (2:19). And there are those who deny that Jesus is coming back.

Peter asks the believers to have patience – Jesus will return. "But don't forget this one thing, dear friends," he reminds them. "To the Lord a day is like a thousand years, and a thousand years is like a day" (3:8).

This is a kind of farewell letter from Peter. "The things we told you were not just clever stories that people invented," he tells his readers. "No, we saw the greatness of Jesus with our own eyes" (1:16). This is a man who saw the power of Jesus. And he's writing a final message to remind Christians of the need to live in God's power and hold fast to his promises.

The letter also contains memorable descriptions of the day of the Lord's return, and practical instructions for living: keep to the real faith and put it into practice; look for understanding, self-control and patience; and wrap everything in love.

QUICK TOUR — 2 PETER

"The Lord is not being slow in doing what he promised – the way some people understand slowness. But God is being patient with you. He doesn't want anyone to be lost. He wants everyone to change their ways and stop sinning."

2 Peter 3:9

1 Greetings from Simon Peter, a servant and apostle of Jesus Christ.

To all of you who share in the same valuable faith that we have. This faith was given to us because our God and Saviour Jesus Christ always does what is good and right.

[2]Grace and peace be given to you more and more, because now you know God and Jesus our Lord.

God Has Given Us Everything We Need

[3]Jesus has the power of God. And his power has given us everything we need to live a life devoted to God. We have these things because we know him. Jesus chose us by his glory and goodness, [4]through which he also gave us the very great and rich gifts that he promised us. With these gifts you can share in being like God. And so you will escape the ruin that comes to people in the world because of the evil things they want.

[5]Because you have these blessings, do all you can to add to your life these things: to your faith add goodness; to your goodness add knowledge; [6]to your knowledge add self-control; to your self-control add patience; to your patience add devotion to God; [7]to your devotion add kindness towards your brothers and sisters in Christ, and to this kindness add love. [8]If all these things are in you and growing, you will never fail to be useful to God. You will produce the kind of fruit that should come from your knowledge of our Lord Jesus Christ. [9]But those who don't grow in these blessings are blind. They cannot see clearly what they have. They have forgotten that they were cleansed from their past sins.

[10]My brothers and sisters, God called you and chose you to be his. Do your best to live in a way that shows you really are God's called and chosen people. If you do all this, you will never fall. [11]And you will be given a very great welcome into the kingdom of our Lord and Saviour Jesus Christ, a kingdom that never ends.

[12]You already know these things. You are very strong in the truth you have. But I am always going to help you remember them. [13]While I am still living here on earth, I think it is right for me to remind you of them. [14]I know that I must soon leave this body. Our Lord Jesus Christ has shown me that. [15]I will try my best to make sure you remember these things even after I am gone.

We Saw Christ's Glory

[16]We told you about the power of our Lord Jesus Christ. We told you about his coming. The things we told you were not just clever stories that people invented. No, we saw the greatness of Jesus with our own eyes. [17]Jesus heard the voice of the great and glorious God. That was when he received honour and glory from God the Father. The voice said, "This is my Son, the one I love. I am very pleased with him." [18]And we heard that voice. It came from heaven while we were with Jesus on the holy mountain.[a]

[19]This makes us more sure about what the prophets said. And it is good for you to follow closely what they said, which is like a light shining in a dark place. You have that light until the day begins and the morning star brings new light to your minds. [20]Most important of all, you must understand this: no prophecy in the Scriptures comes from the prophet's own understanding. [21]No prophecy ever came from what some person wanted to say. But people were led by the Holy Spirit and spoke words from God.

False Teachers

2 In the past there were false prophets among God's people. It is the same now. You will have some false teachers in your group. They will teach things that are wrong—ideas that will cause people to be lost. And they will teach in a way that will be hard for you to see that they are wrong. They will even refuse to follow the Master who bought their freedom. And so they will quickly destroy themselves. [2]Many people will follow them in the morally wrong things they do. And because of them, others will say bad things about the way of truth we follow. [3]These false teachers only want your money. So they will use you by telling you things that are not true. But the judgement against these false teachers has been ready for a long time. And they will not escape God who will destroy them.

[4]When angels sinned, God did not let them go free without punishment. He sent them to hell. He put those angels in caves of darkness, where they are being held until the time when God will judge them.

[5]And God punished the evil people who lived long ago. He brought a flood to the world that was full of people who were against God. But he saved Noah and seven other people with him. Noah was a man who told people about living right.

[6]God also punished the evil cities of Sodom and Gomorrah. He burned them until there was nothing left but ashes. He used those cities as an example of what will happen to people who are against God. [7]But he saved Lot, a good man who lived there. Lot was greatly troubled by the

---

[a] **1:17–18** This event is described in the Gospels. See Matt. 17:1–8; Mark 9:2–8; Luke 9:28–36.

TIME TO GROW UP . . . IN GOD

The Christian life cannot be static. In fact, in some of Paul's letters, he frequently refers to living as a God-follower as a "race". It is a journey onwards and upwards, with a great prize at the end (Philippians 3:14).

In Peter's second letter, he is writing to churches that have become infected with false teaching and unholy living. His remedy? To show up with a pair of heavy boots and kick out the corrupting influence? No, his solution is less violent but better: to encourage his people to keep on growing in God.

DIG IN

READ 2 Peter 1:3–15

- What gift has God given all believers in Jesus (vv.3–4)?
- What does Peter expect from people who call themselves Christians (vv.5–8)?

Peter's emphasis in this letter is to encourage us to keep on growing in God, and specifically in our knowledge of God. (The word or idea of "knowledge" appears 16 times in this short book.) How we understand God and the Good News of Jesus is so important in living to please him.

But before we get a chance to protest – about not being very academic maybe, or not being able to understand our Bibles very well – Peter makes a bold statement. He says that God has already given us everything we need to do it.

He gives us a list of the things he is looking for in mature followers of Christ: faith, goodness, knowledge, self-control, patience, devotion to God, kindness to others and finally, love. The way he lists them might suggest they come in a specific order, e.g. you have to master faith before you get on to goodness. But no – there's no order. What's important is that we're growing in all of them.

- What does Peter say about those who are not growing in God (v.9)?
- What does he say he's going to keep doing (vv.12–15)?

If you're not producing fruit, Peter says, you're not growing. And the reason you're not growing? Because you've forgotten something very important – that your sins have been forgiven. So Peter commits himself to keep helping them to remember. We easily forget important things.

DIG THROUGH

- What things can help us remember that we are sinners in need of forgiveness? What daily, weekly or yearly events or habits can help keep us reminded of all the blessings God has poured out on our lives?
- Thankfulness that God has saved us and involved us in being like him is an important starting place. In what ways can you grow thankfulness in your heart?

DIG DEEPER

- Is it possible for someone to become a Christian, by praying a prayer of repentance, and then never grow or change? Would that person still be a Christian?
- This is the build-up to Peter's attack on the false teachers who are having such a negative influence on these churches. Read on to the end of chapter 2 to understand what he is dealing with here.

A BAD INFLUENCE

Things started to change in the Christian Union when Gary Carter arrived. He seemed to know the Bible back to front, loved to talk about God and had all the girls swooning after him. Because of his popularity, he was elected President within weeks.

But something wasn't quite right. Although he seemed impressive in public, questions arose about how he behaved out of the public eye. He couldn't deal with being corrected. And rumours began to circulate about his private life. Yet people like Gary have been around Christians from the start.

DIG IN

READ 2 Peter 2:1–19

- Who should Peter's readers expect to show up in their churches?
- How will these people behave (vv.10–14)?
- What does Peter say will happen to them in the end (vv.1,3,9–10)?

Peter says that history shows that wherever God's people are, at some point false teachers will appear. Motivated by greed, seeing an opportunity to exploit gentle people, they will move in with their wrong teaching.

They will be obvious not so much for what they teach but for how they live. Peter says that what they say will sound right (v.1), but the way they live – the fruit of their lives – will give them away.

Peter uses a tough word to describe what will happen to them (vv.1,3): they will face destruction, which they have brought upon themselves. Historically God has never allowed false teaching to go unpunished.

READ 2 Peter 3:17–18

- What is Peter's closing message to the churches?

Peter tells them to "be careful". He acknowledges that these are not "lightweight" Christians – they have a strong faith. Yet even mature Christians need to keep on their guard against heresy and teaching that undermines the true Good News message.

What's our best defence against this kind of destructive teaching? Books and websites claiming to expose heresy? Warnings from our own vicars, pastors and leaders? Actually, no. Peter says it's important to grow in "grace and knowledge" of Jesus. Rather than giving the advice to kick out false teachers, he says that the antidote to false teaching is actually to dig deeper into truth.

DIG THROUGH

- Are we safe from false teachers today? Are we better at spotting them? Not likely. Our modern world is at least as tolerant as the Roman world. They may not come in the form of spiritual teachers, of course. They could be influential people – leaders, artists, musicians, writers – anyone with a platform who strays from the truth revealed in Scripture.
- Christians today take shots at each other over matters of theology and style of worship. It's much harder to make a positive contribution. What would Peter encourage us to do?

DIG DEEPER

- As Peter points out, false teaching was (and is) a common disease in the church. Read how Paul dealt with it in Acts 20:29–31.
- In our world, many people see truth as a private matter. People talk about there being many ways to God. Yet this contrasts sharply with the Good News of Jesus, which says that he is the only way to God (John 14:6).

morally bad lives of those evil people. [8]This good man lived with those evil people every day, and his good heart was hurt by the evil things he saw and heard.

INSIGHT

Any loving father would do everything he could to make sure his children knew of the dangers of listening to bad advice or mingling with the wrong people. Peter is doing the same thing here. He's not trying to scare his audience; he's simply warning them.

2 Peter 2:4–10

---

[9]So you see that the Lord God knows how to save those who honour him. He will save them from their troubles. And the Lord will hold those who are evil so that he can punish them on the day of judgement. [10]That punishment is for those who are always doing the evil that their sinful selves want to do. It is for those who hate the Lord's authority.

These false teachers do whatever they want, and they are so proud of themselves. They are not afraid even to say bad things against the glorious ones.[a] [11]The angels are much stronger and more powerful than these beings. But even the angels don't accuse them and say bad things about them to the Lord.

[12]But these false teachers speak evil against what they don't understand. They are like animals that do things without really thinking—like wild animals that are born to be caught and killed. And, like wild animals, they will be destroyed. [13]They have made many people suffer. So they themselves will suffer. That is their pay for what they have done.

They think it is fun to do evil where everyone can see them. They enjoy the evil things that please them. So they are like dirty spots and stains among you—they bring shame to you in the meals you eat together. [14]Every time they look at a woman, they want her. They are always sinning this way. And they lead weaker people into the trap of sin. They have taught themselves well to be greedy. They are under a curse.[b]

[15]These false teachers left the right way and went the wrong way. They followed the same way that the prophet Balaam went. He was the son of Beor, who loved being paid for doing wrong. [16]But a donkey told him that he was doing wrong. A donkey cannot talk, of course, but that donkey spoke with a man's voice and stopped the prophet from acting like a madman.

[17]These false teachers are like springs that have no water. They are like clouds that are blown by a storm. A place in the deepest darkness has been kept for them. [18]They boast with words that mean nothing. They lead people into the trap of sin. They find people who have just escaped from a wrong way of life and lead them back into sin. They do this by using the evil things people want to do in their human weakness. [19]These false teachers promise those people freedom, but they themselves are not free. They are slaves to a mind that has been ruined by sin. Yes, people are slaves to anything that controls them.

[20]People can be made free from the evil in the world. They can be made free by knowing our Lord and Saviour Jesus Christ. But if they go back into those evil things and are controlled by them, then it is worse for them than it was before. [21]Yes, it would be better for them to have never known the right way. That would be better than to know the right way and then to turn away from the holy teaching that was given to them. [22]What they did is like these true sayings: "A dog vomits and goes back to what it threw up."[c] And, "After a pig is washed, it goes back and rolls in the mud again."

Jesus Will Come Again

3 My friends, this is the second letter I have written to you. I wrote both letters to you to help your honest minds remember something. [2]I want you to remember the words that the holy prophets spoke in the past. And remember the command that our Lord and Saviour gave us. He gave us that command through your apostles.

[3]It is important for you to understand what will happen in the last days. People will laugh at you. They will live following the evil they want to do. [4]They will say, "Jesus promised to come again. Where is he? Our fathers have died, but the world continues the way it has been since it was made."

[5]But these people don't want to remember what happened long ago. The skies were there, and God made the earth from water and with water. All this happened by God's word. [6]Then the world was flooded and destroyed with water. [7]And that same word of God is keeping the skies and the earth that we have now. They are being

---

[a] **2:10 *the glorious ones*** Literally, "the glories". These seem to be some kind of angelic beings.
[b] **2:14 *under a curse*** Literally, "children of a curse", meaning that God will punish them.
[c] **2:22** Quote from Prov. 26:11.

kept to be destroyed by fire. They are kept for the day of judgement and the destruction of all people who are against God.

8But don't forget this one thing, dear friends: to the Lord a day is like a thousand years, and a thousand years is like a day. 9The Lord is not being slow in doing what he promised—the way some people understand slowness. But God is being patient with you. He doesn't want anyone to be lost. He wants everyone to change their ways and stop sinning.

INSIGHT

This is truly remarkable. God's desire is for everyone on planet earth to be saved! It's the job of Christians – as workers with the Holy Spirit – to share the Good News about Jesus with other people in a way that makes sense to them.

2 Peter 3:9

10But the day when the Lord comes again will surprise everyone like the coming of a thief. The sky will disappear with a loud noise. Everything in the sky will be destroyed with fire. And the earth and everything in it will be burned up.[a] 11Everything will be destroyed in this way. So what kind of people should you be? Your lives should be holy and bring honour to God. 12You should be looking forward to the day of God, wanting more than anything else for it to come soon. When it comes, the sky will be destroyed with fire, and everything in the sky will melt in the heat. 13But God made a promise to us. And we are waiting for what he promised—a new sky and a new earth. That will be the place where goodness lives.

14Dear friends, we are waiting for this to happen. So try as hard as you can to be without sin and without fault. Try to be at peace with God. 15Remember that we are saved because our Lord is patient. Our dear brother Paul told you the same thing when he wrote to you with the wisdom that God gave him. 16That's what he says in all his letters when he writes about these things. There are parts of his letters that are hard to understand, and some people give a wrong meaning to them. These people are ignorant and weak in faith. They also give wrong meanings to the other Scriptures. But they are destroying themselves by doing that.

17Dear friends, you already know about this. So be careful. Don't let these evil people lead you away by the wrong they do. Be careful that you do not fall from your strong faith. 18But grow in the grace and knowledge of our Lord and Saviour Jesus Christ. Glory be to him, now and forever! Amen.

---

[a] 3:10 **will be burned up** Among the other readings of this text in early Greek copies, many have "will be found", and one has "will disappear".

1 JOHN

Who
The author is not mentioned in the book, but the early Church believed that John the Apostle wrote this letter, as well as 2 and 3 John, the Gospel of John and Revelation. It was written to the churches in Asia Minor (now Turkey).

When
It was probably written in the late first century AD, sometime after the Gospel of John had been written, while John was a leader of the church at Ephesus.

What
The churches were clearly worried by teachers of strange ideas. John writes to combat false teaching and call for pure, loving, light-filled lives. He stresses the certainty that Christians have, repeatedly saying "we know".

The early Church had to counter the teachings of the people who had changed the message of the Bible in several key ways. John exposes these false teachers and their lack of morality. He assures his readers that they have been saved. John had seen Christ, had known Christ, so he knows that Jesus wasn't some kind of spirit being, but a real man and the real God.

He was writing to Christian communities who had lost members to false teachers and leaders (2:19). They were probably Gnostics – people who promised special, secret knowledge (the name comes from the Greek word *gnosis* meaning knowledge). John urges those who remain to stick to the truth. There is no special knowledge – they know what they should do: "You have the gift that the Holy One gave you. So you all know the truth" (2:20).

What they have to do is show love. Love is the great theme which pulses through this letter. "Love one another," he keeps saying. "Dear friends, we should love each other, because love comes from God. Everyone who loves has become God's child. And so everyone who loves knows God. Anyone who does not love does not know God, because God is love" (4:7–8). This is the real proof of who are God's children. Not special knowledge or secret ideas, but love and obedience. Simple.

 1 JOHN

The Word of life 1:1–4
God is light 1:5–10
Jesus our helper 2:1–6
A new command 2:7–14
Not the world 2:15–17
Enemies of Christ 2:18–29

God's children 3:1–10
Love one another 3:11–24
False teachers 4:1–6
God is love 4:7–21
Be sure 5:1–21

"If we obey what God has told us to do, then we are sure that we know him. If we say we know God but do not obey his commands, we are lying. The truth is not in us."

1 John 2:3–4

1 We want to tell you about the Word*a* that gives life—the one who existed before the world began. This is the one we have heard and have seen with our own eyes. We saw what he did, and our hands touched him. ²Yes, the one who is life was shown to us. We saw him, and so we can tell others about him. We now tell you about him. He is the eternal life that was with God the Father and was shown to us. ³We are telling you about what we have seen and heard because we want you to have fellowship*b* with us. The fellowship we share together is with God the Father and his Son Jesus Christ. ⁴We write these things to you so that you can be full of joy with us.

INSIGHT

One of the main heresies facing the early Church involved the gnostic understanding of evil. Gnostics believed that evil was just an error due to ignorance and that those who did wrong were not responsible for their actions. Many people today still believe this. John sets the record straight here.

1 John 1:5 – 2:2

God Forgives Our Sins

⁵We heard the true teaching from God. Now we tell it to you: God is light, and in him there is no darkness. ⁶So if we say that we share in life with God, but we continue living in darkness, we are liars, who don't follow the truth. ⁷We should live in the light, where God is. If we live in the light, we have fellowship with each other, and the blood sacrifice of Jesus, God's Son, washes away every sin and makes us clean.

⁸If we say that we have no sin, we are fooling ourselves, and the truth is not in us. ⁹But if we confess our sins, God will forgive us. We can trust God to do this. He always does what is right. He will make us clean from all the wrong things we have done. ¹⁰If we say that we have not sinned, we are saying that God is a liar and that we don't accept his true teaching.

Jesus Is Our Helper

2 My dear children, I write this letter to you so that you will not sin. But if anyone sins, we have Jesus Christ to help us. He always did what

was right, so he is able to defend us before God the Father. ²Jesus is the way our sins are taken away. And he is the way all people can have their sins taken away too.

³If we obey what God has told us to do, then we are sure that we know him. ⁴If we say we know God but do not obey his commands, we are lying. The truth is not in us. ⁵But when we obey God's teaching, his love is truly working in us. This is how we know that we are living in him. ⁶If we say we live in God, we must live the way Jesus lived.

Jesus Told Us to Love Others

⁷My dear friends, I am not writing a new command to you. It is the same command you have had since the beginning. This command is the teaching you have already heard. ⁸But what I write is also a new command. It is a true one; you can see its truth in Jesus and in yourselves. The darkness is passing away, and the true light is already shining.

⁹Someone might say, "I am in the light," but if they hate any of their brothers or sisters in God's family, they are still in the darkness. ¹⁰Those who love their brothers and sisters live in the light, and there is nothing in them that will make them do wrong. ¹¹But whoever hates their brother or sister is in darkness. They live in darkness. They don't know where they are going, because the darkness has made them blind.

¹²I write to you, dear children,
    because your sins are forgiven through
        Christ.
¹³I write to you, fathers,
    because you know the one who existed
        from the beginning.
I write to you, young people,
    because you have defeated the Evil One.
¹⁴I write to you, children,
    because you know the Father.
I write to you, fathers,
    because you know the one who was there
        from the beginning.
I write to you, young people,
    because you are strong.
The word of God lives in you,
    and you have defeated the Evil One.

¹⁵Don't love this evil world or the things in it. If you love the world, you do not have the love of the Father in you. ¹⁶This is all there is in the world: wanting to please our sinful selves,

---

a **1:1 Word** The Greek word is "*logos*", meaning any kind of communication. Here, it means Christ—the way God told people about himself.

b **1:3 fellowship** Associating with people and sharing things together with them. Believers in Christ share love, joy, sorrow, faith and other things with each other and with God. Also in verse 7.

SMALL DIFFERENCE, IMPORTANT DIFFERENCE

Have your friends ever said to you, "I believe in God, I'm not sure about this Jesus stuff though"? How has that made you feel? Does it confuse you as to whether they're a Christian or not? John might be able to help.

DIG IN

READ 1 John 1:1-4

Does it seem confusing that John wants to tell people in his letter about "the Word that gives life" (v.1)? What could he mean?

- What does he say about both the Word that gives life and who *is* the life?
- How has John experienced the Word that gives life?

The Word that gives life existed before anything else (Gospel of John 1:4), is able to be touched, seen, experienced . . . John is talking about Jesus Christ, the Son of God. Jesus is called the Word that gives life because it was through him that God told people about himself.

- Why is John telling people about Jesus (v.3)?
- What gives "fellowship" (relationship of togetherness)?

There were some in the churches who didn't believe that Jesus was God. They didn't believe God could associate with the "stuff" of this world – that it was all evil. But that creates a problem: if God didn't become a man, then Jesus' death on the cross wouldn't give us fellowship with God. This is what sets Christianity apart from other religions!

John wants those reading his letter and us to know that Jesus is the Son of God who lived as a man, and nothing binds us to God except believing this, and nothing qualifies us to belong to the church except this.

READ 1 John 2:18-25

- Can you see who the enemies of God are and who are friends?
- Why is knowing the truth so important (vv.21–22)?

This is how we know we are on the right path and how we know God: we believe Jesus is God's Son. Denying this makes us enemies of God. For those who believe and accept Jesus there is the promise of life forever with him.

DIG THROUGH

- Whatever happens we need to continue believing that Jesus is God's Son and the only way we can know God (2:24). Are you ever tempted to believe something else is more important to being a Christian than accepting Jesus for who he is? Are you ever tempted to think that Jesus isn't enough and you need something more? Stick with him – if you've got him, you've got everything!
- Spend time reading one of the Gospels, as it will help you to get to know Jesus. Ask the Holy Spirit to help you learn more about Jesus and love him more.

DIG DEEPER

- John isn't one of those writers to say one thing and then move on to another. He keeps coming back to the same ideas and adding new layers. Why not read through the rest of the letter and pick out all the times he talks about Jesus being God's Son. What does he want to get across each time?

LIVING IN THE LIGHT

Do you feel guilty for the stuff you do wrong, or don't you care? Would you like to know once and for all whether you're friends with God and forgiven by him? John's words make things reassuringly clear.

Here is an opportunity to think about the words you might use if your friends confront you with some typical everyday scenarios.

DIG IN   READ 1 John 1:5–7; 2:3–6

"It doesn't matter how I live," says Katy. She is a Christian but recently she's started sleeping with her boyfriend. When her youth worker spoke to her about it she said, "It's okay, it's not a big deal. I'm still really close to God and to everyone at church. We love each other so I'm sure God's fine with it. He knows rules are there to be broken."

- What would you say to Katy?
- How does the image of light and darkness help (1:5–7)?

John is really firm – if we claim to follow God and live in the light we won't just go on sinning as if it doesn't matter. If we carelessly keep on disobeying God then we can't say we belong to him. Just as light and darkness can't exist together so sin and God can't. On the other hand, when we obey God we can be sure we have a real relationship with him.

READ 1 John 1:8–10

"There's nothing wrong with me – I've done nothing wrong," is Matthew's usual response when Giovanni tries to share the Good News with him. Matthew listens to what Giovanni has to say about Jesus and God, but refuses to believe there is anything wrong with him. "Sure, I'm not perfect . . . but a sinner? That's a term reserved for murderers, right?"

- How should Giovanni understand the position Matthew is in?
- What might you say to Matthew?

John is really clear – if we say we aren't sinners we're lying to ourselves and saying God is a liar! We are born as sinners and we sin – this is the truth and anything else is a lie. One day we will reach perfection – but not in this life!

READ 1 John 1:9; 2:1–3

"I know I've done wrong," is Susannah's guilty cry. Susannah feels really bad. She is a Christian but doesn't always find it easy and over the weekend she went out with her friends and got drunk. She wonders if God still loves her.

- What does Susannah need to do?
- What has Jesus done (2:2)?

It's great news for those of us who know we have done wrong – we can be forgiven. Jesus lived a perfect life and then died in our place – God put all our sin on him – he was punished instead of us. If we say sorry to him we can be certain he will forgive us because Jesus has already done everything that needs to be done.

READ 1 John 3:4–6

"All she wants to do is sin," Jared says about his friend Petra. Jared feels really sad – Petra said she was a Christian and seemed to want to live for God but now all she wants to do is everything God doesn't want her to.

- Bringing everything we've read so far together, what would you say to Jared?
- What else does this say?

DIG THROUGH

- Who are you most like? What do you need to do?
- Think about 1 John 1:9 – especially the last bit – do you feel clean? Ask God to help you believe that if you have said sorry for your sin you are clean before God – the best news ever!

wanting the sinful things we see and being too proud of what we have. But none of these comes from the Father. They come from the world. [17]The world is passing away, and all the things that people want in the world are passing away. But whoever does what God wants will live forever.

Don't Follow the Enemies of Christ

[18]My dear children, the end is near! You have heard that the enemy of Christ is coming. And now many enemies of Christ are already here. So we know that the end is near. [19]These enemies were in our group, but they left us. They did not really belong with us. If they were really part of our group, they would have stayed with us. But they left. This shows that none of them really belonged with us.

[20]You have the gift[a] that the Holy One[b] gave you. So you all know the truth. [21]Do you think I am writing this letter because you don't know the truth? No, I am writing because you do know the truth. And you know that no lie comes from the truth.

[22]So who is the liar? It is the one who says Jesus is not the Messiah. Whoever says that is the enemy of Christ—the one who does not believe in the Father or in his Son. [23]Whoever does not believe in the Son does not have the Father, but whoever accepts the Son has the Father too.

[24]You must continue to follow the teaching you heard from the beginning. If you do that, you will always be in the Son and in the Father. [25]And this is what the Son promised us—eternal life.

[26]I am writing this letter about those who are trying to lead you into the wrong way. [27]Christ gave you a special gift. You still have this gift in you. So you don't need anyone to teach you. The gift he gave you teaches you about everything. It is a true gift, not a false one. So continue to live in Christ, as his gift taught you.

[28]Yes, my dear children, live in him. If we do this, we can be without fear on the day when Christ comes again. We will not need to hide and be ashamed when he comes. [29]You know that Christ always did what was right. So you know that all those who do what is right are God's children.

We Are God's Children

3 The Father has loved us so much! This shows how much he loved us: we are called children of God. And we really are his children. But the people in the world don't understand that we are God's children, because they have not known him. [2]Dear friends, now we are children of God. We have not yet been shown what we will be in the future. But we know that when Christ comes again, we will be like him. We will see him just as he is. [3]He is pure, and everyone who has this hope in him keeps themselves pure like Christ.

[4]Anyone who sins breaks God's law. Yes, sinning is the same as living against God's law. [5]You know that Christ came to take away people's sins. There is no sin in Christ. [6]So whoever lives in Christ does not continue to sin. If they continue to sin, they have never really understood Christ and have never known him.

[7]Dear children, don't let anyone lead you into the wrong way. Christ always did what was right. So to be good like Christ, you must do what is right. [8]The devil has been sinning since the beginning. Anyone who continues to sin belongs to the devil. The Son of God came for this: to destroy the devil's work.

[9]Those who are God's children do not continue to sin, because the new life God gave them[c] stays in them. They cannot keep sinning, because they have become children of God. [10]So we can see who God's children are and who the devil's children are. These are the ones who are not God's children: those who don't do what is right and those who do not love their brothers and sisters in God's family.

> # INSIGHT
>
> *You can't get away from the theme of this letter – all the apostle John wants to talk about is love! In fact the word "love" occurs more than forty times in a book of just five chapters!*
>
> **1 John 3:11–24**

We Must Love Each Other

[11]This is the teaching you have heard from the beginning: we must love each other. [12]Don't be like Cain. He belonged to the Evil One. Cain killed his brother. But why did he kill him? Because what Cain did was evil, and what his brother did was good.

[13]Brothers and sisters, don't be surprised when the people of this world hate you. [14]We know that we have left death and have come into life. We know this because we love each other as brothers

---

[a] **2:20** *gift* Literally, "anointing". This might mean the Holy Spirit. Or it might mean teaching or truth as in verse 24. Also in verse 27.
[b] **2:20** *Holy One* God or Christ.
[c] **3:9** *the new life God gave them* Literally, "his seed".

and sisters. Anyone who does not love is still spiritually dead. [15]Anyone who hates a fellow believer is a murderer.[a] And you know that no murderer has eternal life.

[16]This is how we know what real love is: Jesus gave his life for us. So we should give our lives for each other as brothers and sisters. [17]Suppose a believer who is rich enough to have all the necessities of life sees a fellow believer who is poor and does not have even basic needs. What if the rich believer does not help the poor one? Then it is clear that God's love is not in that person's heart. [18]My children, our love should not be only words and talk. No, our love must be real. We must show our love by the things we do.

[19-20]That's how we know we belong to the way of truth. And when our hearts make us feel guilty, we can still have peace before God, because God is greater than our hearts. He knows everything.

[21]My dear friends, if we don't feel that we are doing wrong, we can be without fear when we come to God. [22]And God gives us what we ask for. We receive it because we obey God's commands and do what pleases him. [23]This is what God commands: that we believe in his Son Jesus Christ, and that we love each other as he commanded. [24]All who obey God's commands live in God. And God lives in them. How do we know that God lives in us? We know because of the Spirit he gave us.

John Warns Against False Teachers

4 My dear friends, many false prophets are in the world now. So don't believe every spirit, but test the spirits to see if they are from God. [2]This is how you can recognize God's Spirit. One spirit says, "I believe that Jesus is the Messiah who came to earth and became a man." That Spirit is from God. [3]Another spirit refuses to say this about Jesus. That spirit is not from God. This is the spirit of the enemy of Christ. You have heard that the enemy of Christ is coming, and now he is already in the world.

[4]My dear children, you belong to God, so you have already defeated these false prophets. That's because the one who is in you is greater than the one who is in the world. [5]And they belong to the world, so what they say is from the world too. And the world listens to what they say. [6]But we are from God. So the people who know God listen to us. But the people who are not from God don't listen to us. This is how we know the Spirit that is true and the spirit that is false.

Love Comes From God

[7]Dear friends, we should love each other, because love comes from God. Everyone who loves has become God's child. And so everyone who loves knows God. [8]Anyone who does not love does not know God, because God is love. [9]This is how God showed his love to us: he sent his only Son into the world to give us life through him. [10]True love is God's love for us, not our love for God. He sent his Son as the way to take away our sins.

[11]That is how much God loved us, dear friends! So we also must love each other. [12]No one has ever seen God. But if we love each other, God lives in us. If we love each other, God's love has reached its goal—it is made perfect in us.

[13]We know that we live in God and God lives in us. We know this because he gave us his Spirit. [14]We have seen that the Father sent his Son to be the Saviour of the world, and this is what we tell people now. [15]Anyone who says, "I believe that Jesus is the Son of God," is a person who lives in God, and God lives in that person. [16]So we know the love that God has for us, and we trust that love.

God is love. Everyone who lives in love lives in God, and God lives in them. [17]If God's love is made perfect in us, we can be without fear on the day when God judges the world. We will be without fear, because in this world we are like Jesus.[b] [18]Where God's love is, there is no fear, because God's perfect love takes away fear. It is his punishment that makes a person fear. So his love is not made perfect in the one who has fear.

[19]We love because God first loved us. [20]If we say we love God but hate any of our brothers or sisters in his family, we are liars. If we don't love someone we have seen, how can we love God? We have never even seen him. [21]God gave us this command: if we love God, we must also love each other as brothers and sisters.

God's Children Win Against the World

5 The people who believe that Jesus is the Messiah are God's children. And anyone who loves the Father also loves the Father's children. [2]How do we know that we love God's children? We know because we love God and we obey his commands. [3]Loving God means obeying his commands. And God's commands are not too hard for us, [4]because everyone who is a child of God has the power to win against the world. [5]It is our faith that has won the victory against the

LOVE GOD? LOVE OTHERS!

Fiona said she was a Christian and that she loved God but she had fallen out with one of the other Christian girls in her youth group. She wouldn't talk to her, de-friended her on Facebook and wrote in her journal about how much she hated her.

So far in 1 John we've discovered that believing that Jesus is God's Son and living in God's forgiving light are two of the three major signs that we know God. There's one more . . .

DIG IN    READ 1 John 4:7–21

What is love?
- You know what it's like when you have to do an in-depth study of a person or animal for a project. You have to ask questions, find out where they come from, what they're like, and so on. Make "love" the subject of a little project and jot down all your findings about it from this passage.

Did you notice that God is love? Often we talk about attributes or qualities that we possess – however, John tells us that love isn't a quality God merely possesses but that his very nature is love. We'll never be able to fully grasp this but it helps us understand what John says in verse 7 – God is the source of love and so we should love others.

- If God is love then all our understanding of love has to come from him. What does John say God shows true love to be (vv.9–10)?
- What is challenging about the type of love Jesus showed?
- What should we do? What is our motivation (vv.11–12)?

Often we think of love as a feeling – something that comes and goes. We do things for people we feel good about. But Jesus showed his love in dying for us – it was a sacrificial, painful love-action – I doubt he felt like it! Check out Romans 5:10 – that's the kind of love we're to imitate!

It's amazing to think that when we show love for each other it's as if God becomes visible – people can see what God is like by the way we treat those around us. Because God is love, when we show that love he is living in us and our love becomes more and more perfect. That's a mark of being a true Christian.

READ 1 John 3:11–18

What if I don't love?
- Jot down the differences between Cain and Jesus. Who are we to be like?
- What is shocking about verse 15? Do you think about hate like that?
- Read 4:7–8 and 19–20. Now what would you say to Fiona?

Both Cain's story and that of Jesus' crucifixion involve a brutal death – only they couldn't be more different. Cain killed his brother because he hated him for being loved by God (Genesis 4). Jesus died willingly for us so we could have a relationship with God and each other.

- What kinds of life, thoughts or words make us like Cain?
- How can we be more like Jesus? If we say we love God but can't be bothered to love others, or just simply don't love them, then we have to ask whether we love or know God at all.

DIG THROUGH

- Can you relate to Fiona's story? Ask God to help you understand the love he showed you, so that you might be able to show it to others.
- How can you show your practical love to another Christian this week?

world. So who wins against the world? Only those who believe that Jesus is the Son of God.

God Told Us About His Son

[6]Jesus Christ is the one who came. He came with water and with blood.[a] He did not come by water only. No, Jesus came by both water and blood. And the Spirit tells us that this is true. The Spirit is the truth. [7]So there are three witnesses that tell us about Jesus: [8]the Spirit, the water and the blood. These three witnesses agree.

[9]We believe people when they say something is true. But what God says is more important. And this is what God told us: he told us the truth about his own Son. [10]Whoever believes in the Son of God has the truth that God told us. But people who do not believe God make God a liar, because they do not believe what God told us about his Son. [11]This is what God told us: God has given us eternal life, and this life is in his Son. [12]Whoever has the Son has life, but whoever does not have the Son of God does not have life.

We Have Eternal Life Now

[13]I write this letter to you who believe in the Son of God. I write so that you will know that you have eternal life now. [14]We can come to God with no doubts. This means that when we ask God for things (and those things agree with what God wants for us), God cares about what we say. [15]He listens to us every time we ask him. So we know that he gives us whatever we ask from him.

[16]Suppose you see your fellow believer sinning (sin that does not lead to eternal death). You should pray for them. Then God will give them life. I am talking about people whose sin does not lead to eternal death. There is sin that leads to death. I don't mean that you should pray about that kind of sin. [17]Doing wrong is always sin. But there is sin that does not lead to eternal death.

[18]We know that those who have been made God's children do not continue to sin. The Son of God keeps them safe.[b] The Evil One cannot hurt them. [19]We know that we belong to God, but the Evil One controls the whole world. [20]And we know that the Son of God has come and has given us understanding. So now we can know the one who is true, and we live in that true God. We are in his Son, Jesus Christ. He is the true God, and he is eternal life. [21]So, dear children, keep yourselves away from false gods.

---

[a] **5:6** *water, blood* Probably meaning the water of Jesus' baptism and the blood he shed on the cross.
[b] **5:18** *The Son . . . safe* Literally, "The one who was born from God keeps him safe" or ". . . keeps himself safe".

Who
Traditionally attributed to John the Apostle, the son of Zebedee, but the author refers to himself as "the Elder". The language is similar to that of the Gospel of John, so it was probably the same author.

When
It was probably written in the late first century AD, sometime after the Gospel of John and 1 John had been written. It is thought that John was a leader in the Ephesian church at the time.

What
This second letter of John takes up some of the themes found in 1 John. Again, John warns against false teaching and talks about holding fast to the truth, loving one another and obedience.

This time John is writing to "the lady chosen by God and to her children". The "lady" is probably a church: in Greek, the word for the congregation is feminine. And elsewhere the Church is described as the "bride of Christ" (Revelation 21:2,9; 22:17). Also at the end of the letter he refers to "the children of your sister" – her sister church as it were. John is probably writing from the church in Ephesus to one of its sister churches.

Gnostics were propagating the belief that Christ was not fully human. John warns the church about being deceived by this teaching. "Jesus Christ came to earth and became a man" (verse 7) and anything taught contrary to that is a lie.

In the early Church the Good News was spread by travelling evangelists, who would stay in the homes of followers. But, John argues, if they are teaching rubbish, then they should be evicted.

QUICK TOUR ▶ 2 JOHN

Greetings verses 1–3
Defend the faith verses 4–9

Beware of false teachers verses 10–11
Farewells verses 12–13

"I tell you: we should all love each other. This is not a new command. It is the same command we had from the beginning. And loving means living the way he commanded us to live. And God's command is this: that you live a life of love. You heard this command from the beginning."

2 John verses 5–6

¹Greetings from the Elder.*a*

To the lady*b* chosen by God and to her children. I truly love all of you. And I am not the only one. All those who know the truth*c* love you in the same way. ²We love you because of the truth—the truth that lives in us. That truth will be with us forever.

³Grace, mercy and peace will be with us from God the Father and from his Son, Jesus Christ, as we live in truth and love.

⁴I was very happy to learn about some of your children. I am happy that they are following the way of truth, just as the Father commanded us. ⁵And now, dear lady, I tell you: we should all love each other. This is not a new command. It is the same command we had from the beginning. ⁶And loving means living the way he commanded us to live. And God's command is this: that you live a life of love. You heard this command from the beginning.

⁷Many false teachers are in the world now. They refuse to say that Jesus Christ came to earth and became a man. Anyone who refuses to accept this fact is a false teacher and the enemy of Christ. ⁸Be careful! Don't lose the reward we*d* have worked for. Make sure you receive that reward in full.

⁹Everyone must continue to follow only the teaching about Christ. Whoever changes that teaching does not have God. But whoever continues to follow the teaching about Christ has both the Father and his Son. ¹⁰Don't accept those who come to you but do not bring this teaching. Don't invite them into your house. Don't welcome them in any way. ¹¹If you do, you are helping them with their evil work.

INSIGHT

With only 13 verses, 2 John is more of a postcard than a letter. John says that he has much to say but would rather say it in person than write it down. This is just a quick note to remind them to keep walking in the truth and not to associate with false teachers.

2 John

¹²I have much to say to you. But I don't want to use paper and ink. Instead, I hope to come and visit you. Then we can be together and talk. That will make us very happy. ¹³The children of your sister*e* who was chosen by God send you their love.

---

a **1 Elder** This is probably John the apostle. "Elder" means an older man or a special leader in the church (as in Titus 1:5).
b **1 lady** This might mean a woman. Or, in this letter, it might mean a church. If it is a church, then "her children" would be the people of the church. Also in verse 5.
c **1 truth** The truth or "Good News" about Jesus Christ that joins all believers together.
d **8 we** Some Greek copies have "you".
e **13 sister** Sister of the "lady" in verse 1. This might be another woman or another church.

A TALE OF TWO MEN

Do you want to know whether you're really a Christian? Are you confused about what being a Christian is supposed to look like? Well, in 1 John, John gave us three tests to determine whether we really know and love God. As we get stuck into 2 and 3 John we discover some pretty major similarities but we meet two pretty different men . . .

DIG IN

READ 2 John verse 1 – 3 John verse 15

In 3 John, John writes to his friend, Gaius, who seems to be ticking the boxes as far as the Christian life is concerned. He's really living it out. Let's see how he was doing it . . .

- What is John happy about in Gaius's life (vv.3–4)?
- The people John wrote to in 2 John were also living pretty well in truth. Check out 2 John verses 1 and 2. What does the truth do?

Gaius was following the way of truth and this was making John happy because it meant he was walking with God, believing in Jesus. It is the truth about Jesus and what he has done that brings Christians together.

- What else is Gaius doing (3 John 5–8)?
- What does this suggest about him (2 John 5–6)?

Gaius is doing a great job of loving and helping other believers and so John asks him to do more! We discovered in 1 John that our love for other Christians shows whether we know God or not. This isn't just about feelings but about doing practical, kind, thoughtful things for people even when it's hard, because this is the kind of love Jesus showed to us.

In contrast let's look at Diotrephes – not your ideal church leader!

- What is Diotrephes doing (3 John 9–10)?
- What is Diotrephes not doing?
- What was the warning in 2 John 7–11?

He couldn't be more different from Gaius if he tried! He doesn't love the truth and he doesn't love others. This isn't good news.

Did you notice how strongly John speaks about those who don't teach truth? John wants the believers and us to be sure we are following only the Bible's teachings about Jesus.

DIG THROUGH

John wrote his three letters at a time when there were people who wanted to add and take things away from the teaching of Jesus. Among other weird ideas they had, they didn't think God could become a man and this was unsettling the believers. John writes to reassure them that trusting in Jesus, wanting to obey God and loving others are the marks of a true follower of God.

- Do you sometimes feel you need to do more to be loved and accepted by God? Ask God to help you feel clean, loved and free from fear.
- John says truth is really important, so get stuck into your Bible – it's the only way to know truth and go on believing.
- God commands us to love because he is love – how are you doing with this? For example, at school/youth group/church do you make an effort to hang out with lonely people, or do you look down your nose at them and only spend time with your mates? Don't be a "too cool for school" Christian, having your own little trendy Christian clique (that may in fact not be that Christian after all, 3 John 9–10).

Who
As with 1 and 2 John, this letter is traditionally attributed to John the Apostle, the son of Zebedee, brother of Andrew and disciple of Jesus. Like 2 John, the author refers to himself as "the Elder".

 When
Probably near the end of the first century AD, soon after 2 John was written. John was probably a leader in the church in Ephesus at the time.

 What
John writes to a follower and trusted friend called Gaius, who was probably a leader in a "sister" church. John praises him for the way he stands by the truth and his faithful hospitality.

John has received encouraging reports from fellow believers who have been recipients of Gaius's hospitality and practical love whilst visiting his church, and tells him to keep up the good work.

He encourages him to keep faithful and promises that he will come to sort out the split in the church – a split caused by the gossip of a troublemaker called Diotrephes. He urges true Christians to keep to the truth.

In verse 9, John reveals that he has written "to the church" (this may be the letter known as 2 John) but that Diotrephes would not acknowledge the authority of John. In contrast to Gaius, he is refusing hospitality to the itinerant teachers of the church, and anyone found helping these people is made to "leave the church" (v.10).

He urges Gaius to keep supporting and welcoming those who speak the truth. Jesus' followers are those who are "following the way of truth" (vv.3–4).

QUICK TOUR ▶ **3 JOHN**

Greetings verses 1–2
Good reports verses 3–4
Keep up the good work verses 5–8

Diotrephes verses 9–11
Demetrius verse 12
I'll be there soon verses 13–14

"My dear friend, don't follow what is bad; follow what is good. Whoever does what is good is from God. But whoever does evil has never known God."

3 John verse 11

¹Greetings from the Elder.ᵃ

To my dear friend Gaius, a person I truly love.

²My dear friend, I know that you are doing well spiritually. So I pray that everything else is going well with you and that you are enjoying good health. ³Some believers came and told me about the truthᵇ in your life. They told me that you continue to follow the way of truth. This made me very happy. ⁴It always gives me the greatest joy when I hear that my children are following the way of truth.

INSIGHT

One of the hallmarks of the Christians in the early Church was their hospitality. They would invite travelling believers to stay in their homes even if they didn't know them. John commends this.

3 John verses 5–8

---

⁵My dear friend, it is good that you continue to help the believers. They are people you don't even know. ⁶They told the church about the love you have. Please help them to continue their trip.

Help them in a way that will please God. ⁷They went on their trip to serve Christ. They did not accept any help from people who are not believers. ⁸So we should help them. When we help them, we share with their work for the truth.

⁹I wrote a letter to the church, but Diotrephes will not listen to what we say. He always wants to be the leader. ¹⁰When I come, I will talk with him about what he is doing. He lies and says evil things about us, but that is not all. He refuses to welcome and help the believers who travel there. And he will not let others help them. If they do, he stops them from meeting with the church any more.

¹¹My dear friend, don't follow what is bad; follow what is good. Whoever does what is good is from God. But whoever does evil has never known God.

¹²Everyone says good things about Demetrius, and the truth agrees with what they say. Also, we say good about him. And you know that what we say is true.

¹³I have many things I want to tell you. But I don't want to use pen and ink. ¹⁴I hope to visit you soon. Then we can be together and talk. ¹⁵Peace to you. The friends here with me send their love. Please give our love to each one of the friends there.

ᵃ **1** *Elder* This is probably John the apostle. "Elder" means an older man or a special leader in the church (as in Titus 1:5).

ᵇ **3** *truth* The truth or "Good News" about Jesus Christ that joins all believers together. Also in verses 8,12.

Who The book is traditionally attributed to Jude (or Judas), brother of James and Jesus (Matthew 13:55; Mark 6:3). He may have been an itinerant preacher who was accompanied on his travels by his wife (1 Corinthians 9:5).

 When The situation in the letter seems similar to that of 2 Peter, so it may well have been written around the same time. If so, that would set it in the mid-60s AD. However, it may have been written as late as AD 80.

 What The letter of Jude was written to encourage Christians to stay strong in the faith and to reject false teaching and failing leadership. He condems those who mislead others by their wrong teaching.

There are infiltrators in the Christian communities: ungodly people, who "have used the grace of our God in the wrong way – to do sinful things. They refuse to follow Jesus Christ, our only Master and Lord" (v.4). It doesn't take a genius to work out or guess at some of the activities that the false teachers were introducing. Jude says that they "criticize things they don't understand" (v.10). They are more like animals. There is an emphasis on the dirtiness, the almost physical manifestation of their sin which indicates that they were abusing their authority by luring others into their depravity – a sad feature of cults and false teaching throughout the ages.

Jude rebukes them with some harsh language. They are "dirty spots", "clouds without rain", "trees that have no fruit", "dirty foam on the wild waves", "stars that wander in the sky" (vv.12–13). Jude draws on Old Testament imagery and on Jewish religious writings about the end times (he refers to non-biblical books called *1 Enoch* and *The Testament of Moses*). As you'd expect from the brother of James and Jesus, it's a very Jewish letter.

After all these strong words, the letter ends with a fantastic prayer to the one who is "strong and can keep you from falling . . . Jesus Christ our Lord for all time past, now and forever" (vv.24–25). Amen!

QUICK TOUR ▶ JUDE

"But you, dear friends, use your most holy faith to build yourselves up even stronger. Pray with the help of the Holy Spirit. Keep yourselves safe in God's love, as you wait for the Lord Jesus Christ in his mercy to give you eternal life."

Jude verses 20–21

¹Greetings from Jude, a servant of Jesus Christ and a brother of James.

To those who have been chosen and are loved by God the Father and have been kept safe in Jesus Christ.

²Mercy, peace and love be yours more and more.

God Will Punish Those Who Do Wrong

³Dear friends, I wanted very much to write to you about the salvation we all share together. But I felt the need to write to you about something else: I want to encourage you to fight hard for the faith that God gave his holy people. God gave this faith once, and it is good for all time. ⁴Some people have secretly entered your group. These people have already been judged guilty for what they are doing. Long ago the prophets wrote about them. They are against God. They have used the grace of our God in the wrong way—to do sinful things. They refuse to follow Jesus Christ, our only Master and Lord.

⁵I want to help you remember some things you already know: remember that the Lord[a] saved his people by bringing them out of the land of Egypt. But later he destroyed all those who did not believe. ⁶And remember the angels who lost their authority to rule. They left their proper home. So the Lord has kept them in darkness, bound with everlasting chains, to be judged on the great day. ⁷Also, remember the cities of Sodom and Gomorrah and the other towns around them. They were like those evil angels. They were guilty of sexual sin, even preferring kinds of sex that are not normal. And they also suffer the punishment of eternal fire, an example for us to see.

⁸It is the same way with these people who have entered your group. They are guided by dreams. They make themselves dirty with sin. They reject God's authority and say bad things against the glorious ones.[b] ⁹Not even the archangel Michael did this. Michael argued with the devil about who would have the body of Moses. But Michael did not dare to condemn even the devil for his false accusations. Instead, Michael said, "The Lord punish you!"

¹⁰But these people criticize things they don't understand. They do understand some things. But they understand these things not by thinking, but by feeling, the way dumb animals understand things. And these are the things that destroy them. ¹¹It will be bad for them. They have followed the way that Cain went. To make money, they have given themselves to following the wrong way that Balaam went. They have fought against God like Korah[c] did. And like Korah, they will be destroyed.

¹²These people are like dirty spots among you—they bring shame to you in the special meals you share together. They eat with you and have no fear. They take care of only themselves. They are like clouds without rain. The wind blows them around. They are like trees that have no fruit at harvest time and are pulled out of the ground. So they are twice dead. ¹³Like the dirty foam on the wild waves in the sea, everyone can see the shameful things they do. They are like stars that wander in the sky. A place in the blackest darkness has been kept for them forever.

¹⁴Enoch, the seventh descendant from Adam, said this about these people: "Look, the Lord is coming with thousands and thousands of his holy angels ¹⁵to judge everyone. He will punish all those who are against him for all the evil they have done in their lack of respect for him. Yes, the Lord will punish all these sinners who don't honour him. He will punish them for all the evil things they have said against him."

¹⁶These people always complain and find wrong in others. They always do the evil things they want to do. They boast about themselves. The only reason they say good things about others is to get what they want.

INSIGHT

To make his point, Jude is quoting from Jewish writings that don't form part of the Old Testament we use today. The story of the archangel Michael (v.9) may be from a lost section of a book called The Testament of Moses. The quotation from Enoch (vv.14–15) is taken from a work known as 1 Enoch from the first or second century BC.

Jude verses 9–15

A Warning and Things to Do

¹⁷Dear friends, remember what the apostles of our Lord Jesus Christ said would happen. ¹⁸They told you, "In the last times there will be people who laugh at God and do only what they want to

---

[a] **5 the Lord** Some of the oldest and best Greek manuscripts of Jude have "Jesus" here. If "Jesus" is accepted as the original reading, it should replace "the Lord" in verse 6 as well.
[b] **8 the glorious ones** Literally, "the glories". These seem to be some kind of angelic beings.
[c] **11 Korah** He turned against Moses. See Num. 16:1–40.

BEWARE FALSE TEACHERS!

Sometimes you don't need to use a lot of words to make a powerful point. If the people you're talking to know who you are and where you're coming from, you can say a lot in a short space of time.

That's the case with Jude. It's a book that doesn't get a lot of attention because it's short, tucked away at the back of the Bible, and it assumes quite a lot of Jewish background knowledge. But as always, ask for God's help to see it, and there will be something there for you.

DIG IN

READ Jude verses 1–25

- Who does Jude say he is (v.1)?
- Why does he say he's writing (vv.3–4)?

Jude is the brother of James, and therefore of Jesus, though he chooses not to make this point. Now he sees himself first and foremost as a servant of Christ.

He's writing with a serious warning about false teachers. Across the early churches, certain people had gained positions of influence and were spreading teaching "under the radar" that distorted the true Good News message.

Knowing that he is mostly writing to fellow Jews, Jude makes lots of references to Jewish history and legend. You may recognize the references to the Exodus (v.5) or to Sodom and Gomorrah (v.7) but you might wonder about the story of the archangel Michael arguing with the devil over Moses' body (v.9). This is taken from Jewish writings that didn't make it into the Bible but would have been familiar to the readers of this letter.

Why is he so harsh? To emphasize the seriousness of the judgement that these false teachers are bringing upon themselves, not just with their teaching but also their complaining, fault-finding spirit, their boasting and their manipulation of other followers of Christ.

- How does Jude say the believers should respond individually (vv.20–21)?
- How should they help one another (vv.22–23)?

Jude's recommendation for dealing with false teachers isn't to show them the door. (Perhaps he knew that even if you did manage to remove the poison, it would soon come back again.) Instead, Jude recommends that believers build themselves up in holiness and focus on prayer. They should pay particular attention to building up doubters and those who are weak in their faith.

DIG THROUGH

- Jude points out that false teachers spread their negative influence through both their words and their actions. In what ways can our behaviour teach people about Jesus and the Good News message? How can our actions undermine that truth?
- "These people always complain and find wrong in others. They always do the evil things they want to do. They boast about themselves. The only reason they say good things about others is to get what they want" (v.16). For some of us, these words may be a little close to home! How about you?

DIG DEEPER

- *The letter of Jude goes hand in hand with Peter's second letter – just a few books back in the New Testament. Jude shares a similar theme and suggests the same solution: "grow in the grace and knowledge of our Lord and Saviour Jesus Christ" (2 Peter 3:18).*

do—things that are against God." [19]These are the people who divide you. They are not spiritual, because they don't have the Spirit.

[20]But you, dear friends, use your most holy faith to build yourselves up even stronger. Pray with the help of the Holy Spirit. [21]Keep yourselves safe in God's love, as you wait for the Lord Jesus Christ in his mercy to give you eternal life.

[22]Help those who have doubts. [23]Rescue those who are living in danger of hell's fire. There are others you should treat with mercy, but be very careful that their filthy lives don't rub off on you.[a]

Praise God

[24]God is strong and can keep you from falling. He can bring you before his glory without any wrong in you and give you great joy. [25]He is the only God, the one who saves us. To him be glory, greatness, power and authority through Jesus Christ our Lord for all time past, now and forever. Amen.

---

[a] **23** *that . . . on you* Literally, "hating even their undershirt that is defiled from the flesh".

The author is "John", a prisoner on the prison-island of Patmos (1:9). As early as AD 140 Justin Martyr attributed Revelation to "a certain man, whose name was John, one of the Apostles of Christ".

The book was probably written around AD 95. John was in exile on a small, rocky island called Patmos (off the coast of present-day Turkey), where he had been sent during the reign of the emperor Domitian (AD 81–96).

John is a prisoner on the isle of Patmos. There he sees a vision and is told to write it down. It consists of a series of high-intensity images which are both about the times in which John was living and the times which are to come.

Revelation was written at a time when the churches were facing persecution of a type they had not experienced before. Initially Rome, the great Imperial power, didn't take much notice of Christianity: the authorities dismissed this new movement as just another strange Jewish sect. But by the time Revelation was written, things had changed. The Roman authorities viewed Christianity as something antisocial, if not criminal, and they brutally persecuted the Church.

But the message of Revelation is: "These powers don't really have the victory." The book gives a vision of the future in which Christ is triumphant, not the powers of the world.

Revelation is full of symbols and code words which would no doubt have been understood by the first Christians, but which present even today's experts with a number of problems. So we have to take care with this book and beware of any literal interpretations. Revelation is not a timetable. It's a vision.

Despite the difficulties, there is a lot in Revelation that speaks to us now. Jesus, through John, addresses the churches of the day, and the messages he gives them are as much about the need for Christians to stand against idolatry, sin and oppression as they are about the future of the planet.

We don't know how and we don't know when – but in the end, God will create a new heaven and a new earth. Whoever is in charge at the moment, whichever petty little worldly power thinks it has the victory, in the end, God wins!

QUICK TOUR  REVELATION

The vision 1:1–20	Fall of Babylon 18:1 – 19:10
Letters to churches 2:1 – 3:22	Satan's downfall 19:11 – 20:10
Worship 4:1 – 5:14	New heaven and earth 20:11 – 22:5
All nations 7:9–17	Christ will return 22:6–21
Woman and beasts 12:1 – 13:18	

"I heard a loud voice from the throne. It said, 'Now God's home is with people. He will live with them. They will be his people. God himself will be with them and will be their God. He will wipe away every tear from their eyes. There will be no more death, sadness, crying or pain. All the old ways are gone.'"

Revelation 21:3–4

John Tells About This Book

1 This is a revelation[a] from Jesus Christ, which God gave him to show his servants what must happen soon. And Christ sent his angel to show it to his servant John, ²who has reported everything he saw. It is the truth that Jesus Christ told him; it is the message from God. ³Great blessings belong to the person who reads the words of this message from God and to those who hear this message and do what is written in it. There is not much time left.

John Writes to the Churches

⁴From John,

To the seven churches in the province of Asia:

Grace and peace to you from the one who is, who always was and who is coming; and from the seven spirits before his throne; ⁵and from Jesus Christ. Jesus is the faithful witness. He is first among all who will be raised from death. He is the ruler of the kings of the earth.

Jesus is the one who loves us and has made us free from our sins with his blood sacrifice. ⁶He made us his kingdom and priests who serve God his Father. To Jesus be glory and power for ever and ever! Amen.

⁷Look, Jesus is coming with the clouds! Everyone will see him, even those who pierced[b] him. All peoples of the earth will cry loudly because of him. Yes, this will happen! Amen.

⁸The Lord God says, "I am the Alpha and the Omega.[c] I am the one who is, who always was and who is coming. I am the All-Powerful one."

⁹I am John, your fellow believer. We are together in Jesus, and we share these things: suffering, the kingdom and patient endurance. I was on the island of Patmos[d] because I was faithful to God's message and to the truth of Jesus. ¹⁰On the Lord's Day, the Spirit took control of me. I heard a loud voice behind me that sounded like a trumpet. ¹¹It said, "Write down in a book what you see, and send it to the seven churches: to Ephesus, Smyrna, Pergamum, Thyatira, Sardis, Philadelphia and Laodicea."

¹²I turned to see who was talking to me. When I turned, I saw seven gold lampstands. ¹³I saw someone among the lampstands who looked like the Son of Man. He was dressed in a long robe, with a gold sash tied around his chest. ¹⁴His head and hair were white like wool—wool that is white as snow. His eyes were like flames of fire. ¹⁵His feet were like brass that glows hot in a furnace. His voice was like the noise of flooding water. ¹⁶He held seven stars in his right hand. A sharp two-edged sword came out of his mouth. He looked like the sun shining at its brightest time.

¹⁷When I saw him, I fell down at his feet like a dead man. He put his right hand on me and said, "Don't be afraid! I am the First and the Last. ¹⁸I am the one who lives. I was dead, but look, I am alive for ever and ever! And I hold the keys of death and Hades. ¹⁹So write what you see. Write the things that happen now and the things that will happen later. ²⁰Here is the hidden meaning of the seven stars that you saw in my right hand and the seven gold lampstands that you saw: the seven lampstands are the seven churches; the seven stars are the angels of the seven churches.

INSIGHT

All seven churches lay within a 200-kilometre radius, which is roughly the equivalent of the area within the M25 around London. Revelation may have been sent as a circular letter.
Revelation 1:11

Jesus' Letter to the Church in Ephesus

2 "Write this to the angel of the church in Ephesus. Here is a message from the one who holds the seven stars in his right hand and walks among the seven gold lampstands:

²"I know what you do, how hard you work and never give up. I know that you don't accept evil people. You have tested those who say they are apostles but are not. You found that they are liars. ³You never stop trying. You have endured troubles for my name and have not given up.

⁴"But I have this against you: you have left the love you had in the beginning. ⁵So

---

[a] 1:1 *revelation* An opening up (making known) of truth that was hidden.
[b] 1:7 *pierced* When Jesus was killed, he was stabbed with a spear in the side. See John 19:34.
[c] 1:8 *Alpha . . . Omega* The first and last letters in the Greek alphabet, meaning the beginning and the end.
[d] 1:9 *Patmos* A small island in the Aegean Sea, near the coast of modern-day Turkey.

THE REASON FOR REVELATION

Did you know that around 200,000 Christians are killed for their faith every year? And many more of our brothers and sisters around the world face horrendous persecution for what they believe. If you live in the Western world, it's unlikely you face this sort of suffering but life can still be tough.

What we need to know in these times is: it's going to be all right . . . everything's going to be okay. And it's to give us hope that the apostle John put pen to paper to write what we now know as Revelation.

DIG IN

READ Revelation 1:9 – 2:3

- John is writing from the island of Patmos. Why has he been exiled there?
- What is he told to do?

As Revelation is being written, John and the churches are undergoing an intense period of persecution (v.9). He has been exiled for preaching the Good News, but others have been beaten, imprisoned or even executed for being Christians under the sometimes brutal Roman regime of the first century AD.

The only way he can reach other believers is by letter. But it's a different kind of letter to those earlier in the New Testament. Although, like them, it does contain encouragement and instruction, it's mainly a long, symbolic prophecy – John's attempt to write down a mind-blowing vision that God has given to him.

If you feel a little confused by all the talk of lampstands and golden sashes, don't worry – everybody does! The way Revelation is written is poetic and not very literal. Revelation requires our imagination. It's a letter that can fill your senses, get your heart racing and recharge your "faith batteries".

- Who is the person John falls down before?
- What is he like? How does this compare with the way people might normally think of him?
- How do you think his words in verses 17 and 18 would have made John feel?

It's a stunning picture of Jesus isn't it? By stating he is the "First and Last" he's saying he's the beginning and end of history, and the ruler of everything in between! And, having conquered death, he rules the realm of the dead too! As Jesus walks in the midst of the seven churches we're reminded that he knows exactly what's going on. And it's the same with us right now, which can be comforting in the midst of troubles and challenging when we're getting lazy (1:13,20; 2:1–3).

When your world is falling apart it's easy to give up. God, speaking through John, wants to remind his people of the big picture. He wants to reassure them that he's got everything under control and, though it may be a struggle for a while, Jesus will have the victory in the end.

DIG THROUGH

- Jesus is just who we need to encourage us through tough times as a Christian. Pick out one thing about him from this passage that you find encouraging. Keep this in mind for the next few days, reminding yourself that that's what Jesus is like – and hang on in there!
- In the same way that God used John to bring comfort to the churches under pressure in AD 95, he may want to use you to bring hope and reassurance to someone today. Who in your life needs to hear that God has everything under control?

DIG DEEPER

- Read the apostle Paul's words in 2 Corinthians 4:16–18. In Revelation, God invites us to look beyond what Paul calls "small troubles" in comparison to the greater things to come. Here, he helps us to see "what we cannot see" – the cosmic war going on hidden from our eyes.
- Read on in Revelation and allow John's vision to show you how Satan is defeated and the world is renewed.

remember where you were before you fell. Change your hearts and do what you did at first. If you don't change, I will come to you and remove your lampstand from its place. [6]But there is something you do that is right—you hate the things that the Nicolaitans[a] do. I also hate what they do.

[7]"Everyone who hears this should listen to what the Spirit says to the churches. To those who win the victory I will give the right to eat the fruit from the tree of life,[b] which is in God's paradise.

Jesus' Letter to the Church in Smyrna

[8]"Write this to the angel of the church in Smyrna. Here is a message from the one who is the First and the Last, the one who died and came to life again:

[9]"I know your troubles, and I know that you are poor, but really you are rich! I know the insults you have suffered from people who say they are Jews. But they are not true Jews. They are a group[c] that belongs to Satan. [10]Don't be afraid of what will happen to you. I tell you, the devil will put some of you in prison. He will do this to test you. You will suffer for ten days, but be faithful, even if you have to die. If you continue to be faithful, I will give you the reward[d] of eternal life.

[11]"Everyone who hears this should listen to what the Spirit says to the churches. Those who win the victory will not be hurt by the second death.

Jesus' Letter to the Church in Pergamum

[12]"Write this to the angel of the church in Pergamum. Here is a message from the one who has the sharp two-edged sword:

[13]"I know where you live. You live where Satan has his throne, but you are true to me. You did not refuse to tell about your faith in me even during the time of Antipas. Antipas was my faithful witness[e] who was killed in your city, the city where Satan lives. [14]"But I have a few things against you. You have people there who follow the teaching of Balaam. Balaam taught Balak how to make the people of Israel sin. They sinned by eating food offered to idols and by

committing sexual sins. [15]It is the same in your group. You have people who follow the teaching of the Nicolaitans. [16]So change your hearts! If you don't change, I will come to you quickly and fight against these people with the sword that comes out of my mouth.

[17]"Everyone who hears this should listen to what the Spirit says to the churches!

"I will give the hidden manna to everyone who wins the victory. I will also give each one a white stone that has a new name written on it. And no one will know this name except the one who gets the stone.

Jesus' Letter to the Church in Thyatira

[18]"Write this to the angel of the church in Thyatira. Here is a message from the Son of God, the one who has eyes that blaze like fire and feet like shining brass:

[19]"I know what you do. I know about your love, your faith, your service and your patience. I know that you are doing more now than you did at first. [20]But I have this against you: you let that woman Jezebel do what she wants. She says that she is a prophet,[f] but she is leading my people away with her teaching. Jezebel leads my people to commit sexual sins and to eat food that is offered to idols. [21]I have given her time to change her heart and turn away from her sin, but she does not want to change.

[22]"So I will throw her on a bed of suffering. And all those who commit adultery with her will suffer greatly. I will do this now if they don't turn away from the things she does. [23]I will also kill her followers. Then all the churches will see that I am the one who knows what people feel and think. And I will repay each of you for what you have done.

[24]"But others of you in Thyatira have not followed her teaching. You have not learned the things they call 'Satan's deep secrets'. This is what I say to you: I will not put any other burden on you. [25]Only hold on to the truth you have until I come.

[26]"I will give power over the nations to all those who win the victory and continue until the end to do what I want. [27]They will rule the nations with an iron rod. They will break them to pieces like clay pots.[g] [28]They

---

[a] **2:6 Nicolaitans** A religious group that followed wrong ideas. Also in verse 15.
[b] **2:7 tree of life** The tree whose fruit gives people the power to live forever. See Gen. 2:9; 3:22 and Rev. 22:1–2.
[c] **2:9 group** Literally, "synagogue".
[d] **2:10 reward** Literally, "wreath", a ring of leaves or branches that was placed on the head of the winners of athletic contests to honour them. It is a symbol of victory and reward.
[e] **2:13 faithful witness** A person who speaks God's message truthfully, even in times of danger.
[f] **2:20 prophet** Jezebel was a false prophet. She claimed to speak for God, but she didn't really speak God's truth.
[g] **2:26–27** These verses are almost the same as Ps. 2:8–9.

will have the same power I received from my Father, and I will give them the morning star. [29]Everyone who hears this should listen to what the Spirit says to the churches.

Jesus' Letter to the Church in Sardis

3 "Write this to the angel of the church in Sardis. Here is a message from the one who has the seven spirits and the seven stars:

"I know what you do. People say that you are alive, but really you are dead. [2]Wake up! Make yourselves stronger before what little strength you have left is completely gone. I find that what you do is not good enough for my God. [3]So don't forget what you have received and heard. Obey it. Change your hearts and lives! You must wake up, or I will come to you and surprise you like a thief. You will not know when I will come.

[4]"But you have a few people in your group there in Sardis who have kept themselves clean. They will walk with me. They will wear white clothes, because they are worthy. [5]Everyone who wins the victory will be dressed in white clothes like them. I will not remove their names from the book of life. I will say that they belong to me before my Father and before his angels. [6]Everyone who hears this should listen to what the Spirit says to the churches.

Jesus' Letter to the Church in Philadelphia

[7]"Write this to the angel of the church in Philadelphia. Here is a message from the one who is holy and true, the one who holds the key of David. When he opens something, it cannot be closed. And when he closes something, it cannot be opened:

[8]"I know what you do. I have put before you an open door that no one can close. I know you are weak, but you have followed my teaching. You were not afraid to speak my name. [9]Listen! There is a group[a] that belongs to Satan. They say they are Jews, but they are liars. They are not true Jews. I will make them come before you and bow at your feet. They will know that you are the people I have loved. [10]You followed my command to endure patiently. So I will keep you from the time of trouble that will come to the world—a time that will test everyone living on earth.

[11]"I am coming soon. Hold on to the faith you have, so that no one can take away your crown. [12]Those who win the victory will be pillars in the temple of my God. I will make that happen for them. They will never again have to leave God's temple. I will write on them the name of my God and the name of the city of my God. That city is the new Jerusalem.[b] It is coming down out of heaven from my God. I will also write my new name on them. [13]Everyone who hears this should listen to what the Spirit says to the churches.

Jesus' Letter to the Church in Laodicea

[14]"Write this to the angel of the church in Laodicea. Here is a message from the Amen,[c] the faithful and true witness, the ruler of all that God has made:

[15]"I know what you do. You are not hot or cold. I wish that you were hot or cold! [16]But you are only warm—not hot, not cold. So I am ready to spit you out of my mouth. [17]You say you are rich. You think you have become wealthy and don't need anything. But you don't know that you are really miserable, pitiful, poor, blind and naked. [18]I advise you to buy gold from me—gold made pure in fire. Then you will be rich. I tell you this: buy clothes that are white. Then you will be able to cover your shameful nakedness. I also tell you to buy medicine to put on your eyes. Then you will be able to see.

[19]"I correct and punish the people I love. So show that nothing is more important to you than doing what is right. Change your hearts and lives. [20]Here I am! I stand at the door and knock. If you hear my voice and open the door, I will come in and eat with you. And you will eat with me.

[21]"I will let everyone who wins the victory sit with me on my throne. It was the same with me. I won the victory and sat down with my Father on his throne. [22]Everyone who hears this should listen to what the Spirit says to the churches."

John Sees Heaven

4 Then I looked, and there before me was an open door in heaven. And I heard the same voice that spoke to me before. It was the voice that sounded like a trumpet. It said, "Come up here, and I will show you what must happen after this." [2]Immediately the Spirit took control of me,

---

[a] **3:9 group** Literally, "synagogue".
[b] **3:12 new Jerusalem** The spiritual city where God's people live with him.
[c] **3:14 Amen** Used here, as a name for Jesus, it means to agree strongly that something is true.

YOUR REPORT CARD

Does this have mainly As or mainly Cs? Any pesky Ds or Fs in there too? Report cards are one of the unfortunate necessities of getting a school education. Our teachers get a chance to tell our parents or carers how they think we're really doing. Usually, they're a mix of "Excellent", "Satisfactory" and "Must Try Harder"!

Revelation is a long, prophetic vision sent as a letter written to seven of the churches John has helped in the past (check out 1:11). But before launching into the main prophecy, John passes on some short, specific messages for each of the churches. Some are very positive; others are not.

DIG IN
READ Revelation 3:14–22

- What is Jesus' main observation about this church (vv.15–16)?
- What does he suggest is the main reason for this (vv.17–18)?

The church at Laodicea is lukewarm – neither hot nor cold. What does this mean? During his ministry, Jesus talked about people as being hot or cold; he described John the Baptist as "a lamp that burned and gave light" (John 5:35) and predicted that "the love of most believers will grow cold" (Matthew 24:12).

But these guys are neither hot nor cold – like that last sip of tea you don't want to drink or the fizzy drink that's been out in the sun too long. They got this way by losing their need for God. They have become rich (Laodicea was famous as a successful manufacturing city) and have forgotten that their real need is for God. This has led to a kind of spiritual blindness.

- What does Jesus suggest they do (v.18)? Why?
- What is the reward for doing as he says (vv.20–21)?

Jesus talks in the language of shopping – perhaps it's the only language he thinks they can understand! With these examples he is encouraging them to take their focus off accumulating stuff and be more concerned about the condition of their hearts. He says they need spiritual riches rather than material things: clothes of white (indicating purity), not the latest designer fashions, and for their eyes to be healed by the truth, not by expensive medications.

Jesus may be disappointed with this church, but he's by no means given up on them. He's right there waiting for them to return to him. If they do, he promises a great reward which will far surpass the little luxuries they are used to in this life (v.21).

DIG THROUGH

- These "mini-letters" to the seven churches are there for more than historical interest. They are meant to make us ask, "How are we doing?" What might Jesus' report card say to you personally? Why not read the rest of the letters and ask if one is a particularly good match for you?
- The Laodiceans had become materialistic. Do your possessions ever get in the way, coming between you and God? Is your "shopping fix" a cover-up for what you really need – more of God himself?

DIG DEEPER

The church at Laodicea has become fooled into thinking they are rich when really they are poor – in spirit. This is a contrast with the church at Smyrna (Revelation 2:8–11), whose people face poverty but are described as being rich. Elsewhere in the Bible, Jesus makes it clear that often the poor will be blessed more than the rich because they are more aware of their need for him (e.g. Luke 6:20–21).

and there in heaven was a throne with someone sitting on it. [3]The one sitting there was as beautiful as precious stones, like jasper and carnelian. All around the throne was a rainbow with clear colours like an emerald.

INSIGHT

Seven has always been considered the number of perfection or completeness – from India to China and across the Middle East – and it crops up over six hundred times in the Bible. The seven churches are a kind of shorthand for "all churches" and, of course, in this vision of heaven, where everything is perfect – there's seven of nearly everything.

Revelation 4:5

[4]In a circle around the throne were 24 other thrones with 24 elders sitting on them. The elders were dressed in white, and they had gold crowns on their heads. [5]Lightning flashes and noises of thunder came from the throne. Before the throne there were seven lamps burning, which are the seven Spirits of God. [6]Also before the throne there was something that looked like a sea of glass, as clear as crystal.

In front of the throne and on each side of it there were four living beings. They had eyes all over them, in front and behind. [7]The first living being was like a lion. The second was like a bull. The third had a face like a man. The fourth was like a flying eagle. [8]Each of these four living beings had six wings. They were covered all over with eyes, inside and out. Day and night they never stopped saying,

"Holy, holy, holy is the Lord God All-Powerful.
    He always was, he is and he is coming."

[9]These living beings were giving glory and honour and thanks to the one who sits on the throne, the one who lives for ever and ever. And every time they did this, [10]the 24 elders bowed down before the one who sits on the throne. They worshipped him who lives for ever and ever. They put their crowns down before the throne and said,

[11]"Our Lord and God!
    You are worthy to receive glory and honour
        and power.

You made all things.
    Everything existed and was made because
        you wanted it."

Who Can Open the Scroll?

5 Then I saw a scroll in the right hand of the one sitting on the throne. The scroll had writing on both sides and was kept closed with seven seals. [2]And I saw a powerful angel, who called in a loud voice, "Who is worthy to break the seals and open the scroll?" [3]But there was no one in heaven or on earth or under the earth who could open the scroll or look inside it. [4]I cried and cried because there was no one who was worthy to open the scroll or look inside. [5]But one of the elders said to me, "Don't cry! The Lion[a] from the tribe of Judah has won the victory. He is David's descendant. He is able to open the scroll and its seven seals."

[6]Then I saw a Lamb standing in the centre near the throne with the four living beings around it. The elders were also around the Lamb. The Lamb looked as if it had been killed. It had seven horns and seven eyes, which are the seven spirits of God that were sent into all the world. [7]The Lamb came and took the scroll from the right hand of the one sitting on the throne. [8]After the Lamb took the scroll, the four living beings and the 24 elders bowed down before the Lamb. Each one of them had a harp. Also, they were holding golden bowls full of incense, which are the prayers of God's holy people. [9]And they all sang a new song to the Lamb:

"You are worthy to take the scroll
    and to open its seals,
because you were killed,
    and with your blood sacrifice you bought
        people for God
    from every tribe, language, race of people
        and nation.
[10]You made them to be a kingdom and to be
        priests for our God.
    And they will rule on the earth."

[11]Then I looked, and I heard the voices of many angels. The angels were around the throne, the four living beings and the elders. There were thousands and thousands of angels—10,000 times 10,000. [12]The angels said in a loud voice,

"All power, wealth, wisdom and strength
    belong to the Lamb who was
        killed.
He is worthy to receive
    honour, glory and praise!"

[a] **5:5** *Lion* Used here to refer to Jesus.

¹³Then I heard every created being that is in heaven and on earth and under the earth and in the sea, everything in all these places, saying,

"All praise and honour
   and glory and power for ever and ever
   to the one who sits on the throne and to
      the Lamb!"

¹⁴The four living beings said, "Amen!" And the elders bowed down and worshipped.

The Lamb Opens the Scroll

6 Then I watched as the Lamb opened the first of the seven seals. Then I heard one of the four living beings speak with a voice like thunder. It said, "Come!" ²I looked, and there before me was a white horse. The rider on the horse held a bow and was given a crown. He rode out to defeat the enemy and win the victory.

³The Lamb opened the second seal. Then I heard the second living being say, "Come!" ⁴Then another horse came out, a red one. The rider on the horse was given power to take away peace from the earth so that people would kill each other. He was given a big sword.

⁵The Lamb opened the third seal. Then I heard the third living being say, "Come!" I looked, and there before me was a black horse. The rider on the horse held a pair of scales in his hand. ⁶Then I heard something that sounded like a voice. The voice came from where the four living beings were. It said, "A litre*a* of wheat or three litres of barley will cost a full day's pay. But don't harm the supply of olive oil and wine!"

⁷The Lamb opened the fourth seal. Then I heard the voice of the fourth living being say, "Come!" ⁸I looked, and there before me was a pale-coloured horse. The rider on the horse was death, and Hades was following close behind him. They were given power over a quarter of the earth—power to kill people with the sword, by starving, by disease and by the wild animals of the earth.

⁹The Lamb opened the fifth seal. Then I saw some souls under the altar. They were the souls of those who had been killed because they were faithful to God's message and to the truth they had received. ¹⁰These souls shouted in a loud voice, "Holy and true Lord, how long until you judge the people of the earth and punish them for killing us?" ¹¹Then each one of them was given a white robe. They were told to wait a short time longer. There were still some of their brothers and sisters in the service of Christ who must be killed

as they were. These souls were told to wait until all the killing was finished.

¹²Then I watched while the Lamb opened the sixth seal. There was a great earthquake, and the sun became as black as sackcloth.*b* The full moon became red like blood. ¹³The stars in the sky fell to the earth like a fig tree dropping its figs when the wind blows. ¹⁴The sky was split in the middle and both sides rolled up like a scroll. And every mountain and island was moved from its place.

¹⁵Then all the people—the kings of the world, the rulers, the army commanders, the rich people, the powerful people, every slave and every free person—hid themselves in caves and behind the rocks on the mountains. ¹⁶They said to the mountains and the rocks, "Fall on us. Hide us from the face of the one who sits on the throne. Hide us from the anger of the Lamb! ¹⁷The great day for their anger has come. No one can stand against it."

The 144,000 People of Israel

7 After this happened I saw four angels standing at the four corners of the earth. The angels were holding the four winds of the earth. They were stopping the wind from blowing on the land or the sea or on any tree. ²Then I saw another angel coming from the east. This angel had the seal of the living God. The angel called out in a loud voice to the four angels. These were the four angels that God had given the power to hurt the earth and the sea. The angel said to them, ³"Don't harm the land or the sea or the trees before we mark the foreheads of those who serve our God."

⁴Then I heard how many people had God's mark on their foreheads. There were 144,000. They were from every tribe of the people of Israel:

⁵from the tribe of Judah	12,000
from the tribe of Reuben	12,000
from the tribe of Gad	12,000
⁶from the tribe of Asher	12,000
from the tribe of Naphtali	12,000
from the tribe of Manasseh	12,000
⁷from the tribe of Simeon	12,000
from the tribe of Levi	12,000
from the tribe of Issachar	12,000
⁸from the tribe of Zebulun	12,000
from the tribe of Joseph	12,000
from the tribe of Benjamin	12,000

The Great Crowd

⁹Then I looked, and there was a large crowd of people. There were so many people that no one

---

a **6:6 litre** Literally, "*choinix*", the amount of the daily ration of grain for a soldier.
b **6:12 sackcloth** Literally, "sackcloth of hair". See "SACKCLOTH" in the Word List.

could count them all. They were from every nation, tribe, race of people and language of the earth. They were standing before the throne and before the Lamb. They all wore white robes and had palm branches in their hands. 10They shouted loudly, "Victory belongs to our God, who sits on the throne, and to the Lamb."

11The elders and the four living beings were there. All the angels were standing around them and the throne. The angels bowed down on their faces before the throne and worshipped God. 12They said, "Amen! Praise, glory, wisdom, thanks, honour, power and strength belong to our God for ever and ever. Amen!"

13Then one of the elders asked me, "Who are these people in white robes? Where did they come from?"

14I answered, "You know who they are, sir."

And the elder said, "These are the ones who have come out of the great suffering. They have washed their robes*a* with the blood of the Lamb, and they are clean and white. 15So now these people are before the throne of God. They worship God day and night in his temple. And the one who sits on the throne will protect them. 16They will never be hungry again. They will never be thirsty again. The sun will not hurt them. No heat will burn them. 17The Lamb in front of the throne will be their shepherd. He will lead them to springs of water that give life. And God will wipe away every tear from their eyes."

INSIGHT

Seals were a sign that the message was one of authority, that it belonged to the one whose name was on the seal (in this case God) and that the message was authentic. A seal also made sure that the document was secure.

Revelation 8:1

The Seventh Seal

8 The Lamb opened the seventh seal. Then there was silence in heaven for about half an hour. 2And I saw the seven angels who stand before God. They were given seven trumpets.

3Another angel came and stood at the altar. This angel had a gold holder for incense. The angel was given much incense to offer with the prayers of all God's holy people. The angel put this offering on the golden altar before the throne. 4The smoke from the incense went up from the angel's hand to God. The smoke went up with the prayers of God's people. 5Then the angel filled the incense holder with fire from the altar and threw it down on the earth. Then there were flashes of lightning, thunder and other noises and an earthquake.

The First of Seven Trumpet Blasts

6Then the seven angels with the seven trumpets prepared to blow their trumpets.

7The first angel blew his trumpet. Then hail and fire mixed with blood was poured down on the earth. And a third of the earth and all the green grass and a third of the trees were burned up.

8The second angel blew his trumpet. Then something that looked like a big mountain burning with fire was thrown into the sea. And a third of the sea became blood. 9And a third of the created beings in the sea died, and a third of the ships were destroyed.

10The third angel blew his trumpet. Then a large star, burning like a torch, fell from the sky. It fell on a third of the rivers and on the springs of water. 11The name of the star was Bitterness.*b* And a third of all the water became bitter. Many people died from drinking this bitter water.

12The fourth angel blew his trumpet. Then a third of the sun and a third of the moon and a third of the stars were struck. So a third of them became dark. A third of the day and night was without light.

13While I watched, I heard an eagle that was flying high in the air. The eagle said in a loud voice, "Terrible! Terrible! How terrible for those who live on the earth! The terrible trouble will begin after the sounds of the trumpets that the other three angels will blow."

The Fifth Trumpet Begins the First Terror

9 The fifth angel blew his trumpet. Then I saw a star fall from the sky to the earth. The star was given the key to the deep hole that leads down to the bottomless pit. 2Then the star opened the hole leading to the pit. Smoke came up from the hole like smoke from a big furnace. The sun and sky became dark because of the smoke from the hole.

3Then locusts came out of the smoke and went down to the earth. They were given the power to sting like scorpions. 4They were told not to damage the fields of grass or any plant or tree.

---

a **7:14 washed their robes** Meaning that they had believed in Jesus and had been made clean from sin by his blood sacrifice. See Rev. 5:9; Heb. 9:14; 10:14–22; Acts 22:16; 1 John 1:7.
b **8:11 Bitterness** Literally, "Wormwood", a very bitter plant; here, it is a symbol of bitter sorrow.

They were to hurt only those who did not have God's mark on their foreheads. [5]They were not given the power to kill them but only to cause them pain for five months—pain like a person feels when stung by a scorpion. [6]During those days people will look for a way to die, but they will not find it. They will want to die, but death will hide from them.

[7]The locusts looked like horses prepared for battle. On their heads they wore something that looked like a gold crown. Their faces looked like human faces. [8]Their hair was like women's hair. Their teeth were like lions' teeth. [9]Their chests looked like iron breastplates. The sound their wings made was like the noise of many horses and chariots hurrying into battle. [10]The locusts had tails with stingers like scorpions. The power they had to give people pain for five months was in their tails. [11]They had a ruler, who was the angel of the bottomless pit. His name in Hebrew is Abaddon.[a] In Greek it is Apollyon.[b]

[12]The first terror is now past. There are still two other terrors to come.

The Sixth Trumpet Blast

[13]The sixth angel blew his trumpet. Then I heard a voice coming from the horns on the four corners of the golden altar that is before God. [14]It said to the sixth angel who had the trumpet, "Free the four angels who are tied at the great river Euphrates." [15]These four angels had been kept ready for this hour and day and month and year. The angels were set free to kill a third of all the people on the earth. [16]I heard how many troops on horses were in their army. There were 200,000,000.

[17]In my vision, I saw the horses and the riders on the horses. They looked like this: They had breastplates that were fiery red, dark blue and yellow like sulphur. The heads of the horses looked like heads of lions. The horses had fire, smoke and sulphur coming out of their mouths. [18]A third of all the people on earth were killed by these three plagues coming out of the horses' mouths: the fire, the smoke and the sulphur. [19]The horses' power was in their mouths and also in their tails. Their tails were like snakes that have heads to bite and hurt people.

[20]The other people on earth were not killed by these plagues. But these people still did not change their hearts and turn away from worshipping the things they had made with their own hands. They did not stop worshipping demons and idols made of gold, silver, bronze, stone and wood—things that cannot see or hear or walk. [21]They did not change their hearts and turn away from killing other people or from their evil magic, their sexual sins and their stealing.

The Angel and the Little Scroll

10 Then I saw another powerful angel coming down from heaven. The angel was dressed in a cloud. He had a rainbow around his head. The angel's face was like the sun, and his legs were like poles of fire. [2]The angel was holding a small scroll. The scroll was open in his hand. He put his right foot on the sea and his left foot on the land. [3]He shouted loudly like the roaring of a lion. After he shouted, the voices of seven thunders spoke.

[4]The seven thunders spoke, and I started to write. But then I heard a voice from heaven that said, "Don't write what the seven thunders said. Keep those things secret."

[5]Then the angel I saw standing on the sea and on the land raised his right hand to heaven. [6]The angel made a promise by the power of the one who lives for ever and ever. He is the one who made the skies and all that is in them. He made the earth and all that is in it, and he made the sea and all that is in it. The angel said, "There will be no more waiting! [7]In the days when the seventh angel is ready to blow his trumpet, God's secret plan will be completed—the Good News that God told to his servants, the prophets."

[8]Then I heard the same voice from heaven again. It said to me, "Go and take the open scroll that is in the angel's hand. This is the angel who is standing on the sea and on the land."

[9]So I went to the angel and asked him to give me the little scroll. He said to me, "Take the scroll and eat it. It will be sour in your stomach, but in your mouth it will be sweet like honey." [10]So I took the little scroll from the angel's hand and ate it. In my mouth it tasted sweet like honey, but after I ate it, it was sour in my stomach. [11]Then I was told, "You must prophesy again about many races of people, many nations, languages and rulers."

The Two Witnesses

11 Then I was given a measuring rod as long as a walking stick. I was told, "Go and measure the temple[c] of God and the altar, and count the people worshipping there. [2]But don't

---

[a] **9:11** *Abaddon* A Hebrew name meaning "death" or "destruction", used as a name for the place of death. See Job 26:6 and Ps. 88:11.
[b] **9:11** *Apollyon* A name that means "destroyer".
[c] **11:1** *temple* God's house—the place where God's people worship and serve him. Here, John sees it pictured as the special building in Jerusalem for Jewish worship. Also in verse 19.

measure the courtyard outside the temple. Leave it alone. It has been given to those who are not God's people. They will show their power over the holy city for 42 months. ³And I will give power to my two witnesses. And they will prophesy for 1,260 days. They will be dressed in sackcloth."

⁴These two witnesses are the two olive trees and the two lampstands that stand before the Lord of the earth. ⁵If anyone tries to hurt the witnesses, fire comes from the mouths of the witnesses and kills their enemies. Anyone who tries to hurt them will die like this. ⁶These witnesses have the power to stop the sky from raining during the time they are prophesying. These witnesses have power to make the water become blood. They have power to send every kind of plague to the earth. They can do this as many times as they want.

⁷When the two witnesses have finished telling their message, the beast will fight against them. This is the beast that comes up from the bottomless pit. It will defeat and kill them. ⁸The bodies of the two witnesses will lie in the street of the great city. This city is named Sodom and Egypt. These names for the city have a special meaning. This is the city where the Lord was killed. ⁹People from every race of people, tribe, language and nation will look at the bodies of the two witnesses for three and a half days. The people will refuse to bury them. ¹⁰Everyone on the earth will be happy because these two are dead. They will have parties and send each other gifts. They will do this because these two prophets brought much suffering to the people living on earth.

¹¹But after three and a half days, God let life enter the two witnesses again. They stood on their feet. All those who saw them were filled with fear. ¹²Then the two witnesses heard a loud voice from heaven say, "Come up here!" And both of them went up into heaven in a cloud. Their enemies watched them go.

¹³At that same time there was a great earthquake. A tenth of the city was destroyed. And 7,000 people were killed in the earthquake. Those who did not die were very afraid. They gave glory to the God of heaven.

¹⁴The second terror is now past. The third terror is coming soon.

The Seventh Trumpet Blast

¹⁵The seventh angel blew his trumpet. Then there were loud voices in heaven. The voices said,

"The kingdom of the world has now become
    the kingdom of our Lord and of his Messiah.
And he will rule for ever and ever."

¹⁶Then the 24 elders bowed down on their faces and worshipped God. These are the elders who sit on their thrones before God. ¹⁷The elders said,

"We give thanks to you, Lord God All-
    Powerful.
You are the one who is and who always
    was.
We thank you because you have used your
    great power
    and have begun to rule.
¹⁸The people of the world were angry,
    but now is the time for your anger.
Now is the time for the dead to be
    judged.
It is time to reward your servants, the
    prophets,
    and to reward your holy people,
    the people, great and small, who respect
    you.
It is time to destroy those people who destroy
    the earth!"

¹⁹Then God's temple in heaven was opened. The Box of the Agreement could be seen in his temple. Then there were flashes of lightning, noises, thunder, an earthquake and a great hailstorm.

The Woman Giving Birth and the Dragon

12 And then a great wonder appeared in heaven: a woman who was clothed with the sun, and the moon was under her feet. She had a crown of twelve stars on her head. ²She was pregnant and cried out with pain because she was about to give birth.

³Then another wonder appeared in heaven: a giant red dragon. The dragon had seven heads with a crown on each head. It also had ten horns. ⁴Its tail swept a third of the stars out of the sky and threw them down to the earth. It stood in front of the woman who was ready to give birth to the baby. It wanted to eat the woman's baby as soon as it was born.

⁵The woman gave birth to a son, who would rule all the nations with an iron rod. And her child was taken up to God and to his throne. ⁶The woman ran away into the desert to a place that God had prepared for her. There she would be taken care of for 1,260 days.

⁷Then there was a war in heaven. Michael[a] and his angels fought against the dragon. The dragon and its angels fought back, ⁸but they were not strong enough. The dragon and its angels lost their place in heaven. ⁹It was thrown down out of heaven. (This giant dragon is that old snake, the

---

[a] **12:7 Michael** The archangel—leader of God's angels. See Jude 9.

one called the devil or Satan, who leads the whole world into the wrong way.) The dragon and its angels were thrown to the earth. [10]Then I heard a loud voice in heaven say,

"The victory and the power and the kingdom
  of our God
  and the authority of his Messiah have now
  come,
because the accuser of our brothers and
  sisters
  has been thrown out.
He is the one who accused them
  day and night before our God.
[11]They defeated him by the blood sacrifice of
  the Lamb
  and by the message of God that they told
  people.
They did not love their lives too much.
  They were not afraid of death.
[12]So rejoice, you heavens
  and all who live there!
But it will be terrible for the earth and sea,
  because the devil has gone down to you.
He is filled with anger.
  He knows he doesn't have much time."

[13]The dragon saw that he had been thrown down to the earth. So he chased the woman who had given birth to the child. [14]But the woman was given the two wings of a great eagle. Then she could fly to the place that was prepared for her in the desert. There she would be taken care of for three and a half years. There she would be away from the dragon.[a] [15]Then the dragon poured water out of its mouth like a river. It poured the water towards the woman so that the flood would carry her away. [16]But the earth helped the woman. The earth opened its mouth and swallowed the river that came from the mouth of the dragon. [17]Then the dragon was very angry with the woman. It went away to make war against all her other children. Her children are those who obey God's commands and have the truth that Jesus taught. [18]The dragon stood on the seashore.

The Beast From the Sea

13 Then I saw a beast coming up out of the sea. It had ten horns and seven heads. There was a crown on each of its horns. It had an evil name written on each head. [2]This beast looked like a leopard, with feet like a bear's feet. It had a mouth like a lion's mouth. The dragon gave the beast all of its power and its throne and great authority.

[3]One of the heads of the beast looked as if it had been wounded and killed, but the death wound was healed. All the people in the world were amazed, and they all followed the beast. [4]People worshipped the dragon because it had given its power to the beast, and they also worshipped the beast. They asked, "Who is as powerful as the beast? Who can make war against it?"

[5]The beast was allowed to boast and speak insults against God. It was allowed to use its power for 42 months. [6]The beast opened its mouth to insult God—to insult his name, the place where he lives, and all those who live in heaven. [7]It was given power to make war against God's holy people and to defeat them. It was given power over every tribe, race of people, language and nation. [8]Everyone living on earth would worship the beast. These are all the people since the beginning of the world whose names are not written in the Lamb's book of life. The Lamb is the one who was killed.

[9]Anyone who hears these things should listen to this:

[10]Whoever is to be a prisoner,
  will be a prisoner.
Whoever is to be killed with a sword,
  will be killed with a sword.

This means that God's holy people must have patience and faith.

The Beast From the Earth

[11]Then I saw another beast coming up out of the earth. He had two horns like a lamb, but he talked like a dragon. [12]This beast stood before the first beast and used the same power the first beast had. He used this power to make everyone living on the earth worship the first beast. The first beast was the one that had the death wound that was healed. [13]The second beast did great miracles.[b] He even made fire come down from heaven to earth while people were watching.

[14]This second beast fooled the people living on earth by using the miracles that he had been given the power to do for the first beast. He ordered people to make an idol to honour the first beast, the one that was wounded by the sword but did not die. [15]The second beast was given power to give life to the idol of the first beast. Then the idol could speak and order all those who did not worship it to be killed. [16]The second beast also forced all people, small and great, rich and poor, free and slave, to have a mark put on their right hand or on their forehead. [17]No one

---

[a] **12:14** *dragon* Here and in verse 15 literally, "snake". See verse 9 above.
[b] **13:13** *miracles* False miracles—amazing acts done by the power of the devil.

A BATTLE FOR WORSHIP

Have you ever considered what things are most successful at drawing you away from God? What things stop you praying, trusting, obeying God's word?

Whatever they are, those things are idols, and today the biggest rivals to God are probably our possessions and our comfort. When theologian John Calvin described the human heart as an "idol factory", he was referring to our natural tendency to make counterfeit gods out of comparatively worthless things.

DIG IN

READ Revelation 13:1–18

- Take a moment and let the descriptions you've just read sink in. Imagine the scene in your mind's eye.
- How are the beasts trying to influence the people of the earth?
- What do they want?

You might be surprised by the one thing the beasts crave and demand from the people of the earth: worship. And that's the key to "getting into" Revelation and its mysterious beasts, dragons, riders on horses and legions of angels.

All through the vision, starting at Revelation 4 in the very throne room of Almighty God, you'll find interspersed beautiful songs of worship to him. In the midst of all the carnage, songs of praise are being sung to Jesus. It tells us that what's being played out is a battle for worship.

- What outward signs do the beasts display to suggest authority?
- Do any aspects of the beasts' behaviour remind you of anything?
- How about the words "crown" (v.1), "throne" and "authority" (v.2), "tribe, race of people, language and nation" (v.7)?

It's really interesting that these hideous forces of evil all have a striking resemblance to things we associate with God himself. Many of their attributes and actions are feeble imitations of who God is and how he works.

And there it is, clear as anything. Satan's trick is to try and make us trade the real thing for a cheap imitation. He'll try and sell us any idol he can if it will tear us away from Jesus. The idol might start small and apparently harmless, but one day, some people will be so sucked into the lie that they'll worship pure evil.

DIG THROUGH

- Do you recognize your own heart as an "idol factory"? Who or what are the lesser gods in your own heart? A sport or a team? An instrument or a band? A boy or girl at school? Do you pursue anything or anyone harder than you chase after God?
- What does this mean for us? Should we choose to live in poverty and hardship? Should we wipe our music collection and sell our season ticket? Perhaps not. But we must make sure that the most important thing is the most important thing. When we choose to fix our worship on God, and make him the central authority of our lives, everything else falls into place. Our lives become simpler. The things that we own no longer own us.

DIG DEEPER

- What's going to be important to you as you grow older? Are your ambitions simply to be comfortably off, with a nice house, a nice car and nice holidays? Check out Matthew 6:19–34 for some good advice, especially for those starting out in life.
- In his letter to the Romans, Paul teaches about how human beings "traded the truth of God for a lie. They bowed down and worshipped the things God made instead of worshipping the God who made those things" (Romans 1:25). Take another look at Revelation 13 and take in what an awful, disgusting thing that beast is. Remember how loving, forgiving and pure Jesus is in comparison and ask him to help you worship him instead.

could buy or sell without this mark. (This mark is the name of the beast or the number of its name.)

[18]Anyone who has understanding can find the meaning of the beast's number. This requires wisdom. This number is the number of a man. It is 666.

God's People Sing a New Song

14 Then I looked, and there before me was the Lamb, who was standing on Mount Zion.[a] There were 144,000 people with him. They all had his name and his Father's name written on their foreheads.

[2]And I heard a sound from heaven as loud as the crashing of floodwaters or claps of thunder. But it sounded like harpists playing their harps. [3]The people sang a new song before the throne and before the four living beings and the elders. The only ones who could learn the new song were the 144,000 who had been bought from the earth. No one else could learn it.

[4]These are the ones who did not do sinful things with women. They kept themselves pure. Now they follow the Lamb wherever he goes. They were bought from among the people of the earth as the first to be offered to God and the Lamb. [5]They are not guilty of telling lies; they are without fault.

The Three Angels

[6]Then I saw another angel flying high in the air. The angel had the eternal Good News to announce to the people living on earth—to every nation, tribe, language and race of people. [7]The angel said in a loud voice, "Fear God and give him praise. The time has come for God to judge all people. Worship God. He made the heavens, the earth, the sea and the springs of water."

[8]Then the second angel followed the first angel and said, "She is destroyed! The great city of Babylon is destroyed! She made all the nations drink the wine of her sexual sin and of God's anger."

[9]A third angel followed the first two angels. This third angel said in a loud voice, "God will punish all those who worship the beast and the beast's idol and agree to have the beast's mark on their forehead or on their hand. [10]They will drink the wine of God's anger. This wine is prepared with all its strength in the cup of God's anger. They will be made to suffer pain with burning sulphur before the holy angels and the Lamb. [11]And the smoke from their burning pain will rise for ever and ever. There will be no rest, day or night, for those who worship the beast and its idol or who wear the mark of its name." [12]This means that God's holy people must be patient. They must obey God's commands and keep their faith in Jesus.

[13]Then I heard a voice from heaven. It said, "Write this: From now on there are great blessings for those who belong to the Lord when they die."

The Spirit says, "Yes, that is true. They will rest from their hard work. What they have done will stay with them."

The Earth Is Harvested

[14]I looked and there before me, sitting on a white cloud, was one who looked like the Son of Man. He had a gold crown on his head and a sharp sickle in his hand. [15]Then another angel came out of the temple. This angel called to the one who was sitting on the cloud, "Take your sickle and gather from the earth. The time to harvest has come, and the fruit on the earth is ripe." [16]So the one who was sitting on the cloud swung his sickle over the earth. And the earth was harvested.

[17]Then another angel came out of the temple in heaven. This angel also had a sharp sickle. [18]And then another angel, one in charge of the fire, came from the altar. He called to the angel with the sharp sickle and said, "Take your sharp sickle and gather the bunches of grapes from the earth's vine. The earth's grapes are ripe." [19]The angel swung his sickle over the earth. He gathered the earth's grapes and threw them into the great winepress of God's anger. [20]The grapes were squeezed in the winepress outside the city. Blood flowed out of the winepress. It rose as high as the heads of the horses for a distance of 300 kilometres.[b]

The Angels With the Last Plagues

15 Then I saw another wonder in heaven. It was great and amazing. There were seven angels in charge of seven plagues. These are the last plagues because after these, God's anger is finished.

[2]I saw what looked like a sea of glass mixed with fire. All those who had won the victory over the beast and his idol and over the number of its name were standing by the sea. These people had harps that God had given them. [3]They sang the song of Moses, the servant of God, and the song of the Lamb:

"Great and wonderful are the things you do,
   Lord God All-Powerful.

---

[a] 14:1 *Mount Zion* Another name for Jerusalem, here meaning the spiritual city where God's people live with him.
[b] 14:20 *300 kilometres* Literally, "1,600 *stadia*".

Right and true are your ways,
　Ruler of the nations.
[4]All people will fear you, O Lord.
　All people will praise your name.
　Only you are holy.
All people will come and worship before you,
　because it is clear that you do what is
　　right."

[5]After this I saw the temple, the holy place of God's presence,[a] in heaven. It was opened, [6]and the seven angels in charge of the seven plagues came out. They were dressed in clean, shining linen cloth. They wore gold bands tied around their chests. [7]Then one of the four living beings gave seven gold bowls to the seven angels. The bowls were filled with the anger of God, who lives for ever and ever. [8]The temple was filled with smoke from the glory and the power of God. No one could enter the temple until the seven plagues of the seven angels were finished.

The Bowls Filled With God's Anger

16 Then I heard a loud voice from the temple. It said to the seven angels, "Go and pour out the seven bowls of God's anger on the earth." [2]The first angel left. He poured out his bowl on the land. Then all those who had the mark of the beast and who worshipped its idol got sores that were ugly and painful.

[3]The second angel poured out his bowl on the sea. Then the sea became blood like a dead man's blood. And everything living in the sea died.

[4]The third angel poured out his bowl on the rivers and the springs of water. The rivers and the springs of water became blood. [5]Then I heard the angel of the waters say to God,

"You are the one who is and who always was.
　You are the Holy One.
You are right in these judgements you have
　made.
[6]The people have spilled the blood
　of your holy people and your prophets.
Now you have given those people blood to
　drink.
　This is what they deserve."

[7]And I heard the altar say,

"Yes, Lord God All-Powerful,
　your judgements are true and right."

[8]The fourth angel poured out his bowl on the sun. The sun was given power to burn the people with fire. [9]The people were burned by the great heat. They cursed the name of God, who had control over these plagues. But they refused to change their hearts and lives and give glory to God.

[10]The fifth angel poured out his bowl on the throne of the beast. And darkness covered the beast's kingdom. People bit their tongues because of the pain. [11]They cursed the God of heaven because of their pain and the sores they had. But they refused to change their hearts and turn away from the evil things they did.

[12]The sixth angel poured out his bowl on the great river Euphrates. The water in the river was dried up. This prepared the way for the rulers from the east to come. [13]Then I saw three evil spirits that looked like frogs. They came out of the mouth of the dragon, out of the mouth of the beast and out of the mouth of the false prophet. [14]These evil spirits are the spirits of demons. They have power to do miracles.[b] They go out to the rulers of the whole world to gather them for battle on the great day of God All-Powerful.

[15]"Listen! I will come at a time you don't expect, like a thief. Great blessings belong to those who stay awake and keep their clothes with them. They will not have to go without clothes and be ashamed for people to see them."

INSIGHT

The battle of Armageddon has become one of the myths of Revelation – the idea of a massive battle on earth resulting in the destruction of the planet. But it is a spiritual battle, for it is fought against God and the kings are gathered by evil spirits.

Revelation 16:16

[16]Then the evil spirits gathered the rulers together to the place that in Hebrew is called Armageddon.

[17]The seventh angel poured out his bowl into the air. Then a loud voice came out of the temple from the throne. It said, "It is finished!" [18]Then there were flashes of lightning, noises, thunder and a big earthquake. This was the worst earthquake that has ever happened since people have been on earth. [19]The great city split into three parts. The cities of the nations were destroyed. And God did not forget to punish

---

[a] **15:5** *holy place of God's presence* Literally, "tent of the testimony". See "HOLY TENT" in the Word List. Read Exod. 25:8–22.
[b] **16:14** *miracles* False miracles—amazing acts done by the power of the devil.

Babylon the Great. He gave that city the cup filled with the wine of his terrible anger. [20]Every island disappeared and there were no more mountains. [21]Giant hailstones fell on the people from the sky. These hailstones weighed almost 40 kilogrammes[a] each. People cursed God because of this plague of the hail. It was terrible.

The Woman on the Red Beast

17 One of the seven angels came and spoke to me. This was one of the angels that had the seven bowls. The angel said, "Come, and I will show you the punishment that will be given to the famous prostitute. She is the one sitting over many waters. [2]The rulers of the earth sinned sexually with her. The people of the earth became drunk from the wine of her sexual sin."

[3]Then the angel carried me away by the Spirit to the desert. There I saw a woman sitting on a red beast. The beast was covered with evil names. It had seven heads and ten horns. [4]The woman was dressed in purple and red. She was shining with the gold, jewels and pearls that she was wearing. She had a gold cup in her hand. This cup was filled with terribly evil things and the filth of her sexual sin. [5]She had a title written on her forehead. This title has a hidden meaning. This is what was written:

THE GREAT BABYLON
MOTHER OF PROSTITUTES
AND THE EVIL THINGS OF THE EARTH

[6]I saw that the woman was drunk. She was drunk with the blood of God's holy people. She was drunk with the blood of those who told people about their faith in Jesus.

When I saw the woman, I was fully amazed. [7]Then the angel said to me, "Why are you amazed? I will tell you the hidden meaning of this woman and the beast she rides—the beast with seven heads and ten horns. [8]The beast you saw was once alive, but now it is not. However, it will come up out of the bottomless pit and go away to be destroyed. The people who live on the earth will be amazed when they see the beast, because it was once alive, is no longer living, but will come again. These are the people whose names have never been written in the book of life since the beginning of the world.

[9]"You need wisdom to understand this. The seven heads on the beast are the seven hills where the woman sits. They are also seven rulers. [10]Five of the rulers have already died. One of the rulers lives now, and the last ruler is coming. When he comes, he will stay only a short time.

[11]The beast that was once alive but is no longer living is an eighth ruler. This eighth ruler also belongs to the first seven rulers. And he will go away to be destroyed.

[12]"The ten horns you saw are ten rulers. These ten rulers have not yet received their kingdom, but they will receive power to rule with the beast for one hour. [13]All ten of these rulers have the same purpose. And they will give their power and authority to the beast. [14]They will make war against the Lamb. But the Lamb will defeat them, because he is Lord of lords and King of kings. And with him will be his chosen and faithful followers—the people he has called to be his."

[15]Then the angel said to me, "You saw the waters where the prostitute sits. These waters are the many peoples, the different races, nations and languages in the world. [16]The beast and the ten horns you saw will hate the prostitute. They will take everything she has and leave her naked. They will eat her flesh and destroy her with fire. [17]God put the idea in their minds to do what would complete his purpose. They agreed to give the beast their power to rule until what God has said is completed. [18]The woman you saw is the great city that rules over the kings of the earth."

Babylon Is Destroyed

18 Then I saw another angel coming down from heaven. This angel had great power. The angel's glory made the earth bright. [2]The angel shouted with a powerful voice,

"She is destroyed!
    The great city of Babylon is destroyed!
She has become a home for demons.
    That city has become a place for every
        unclean spirit to live.
She is a city filled with all kinds of unclean
        birds.
    She is a place where every unclean and
        hated animal lives.
[3]All the peoples of the earth have drunk the
        wine
    of her sexual sin and of God's anger.
The rulers of the earth sinned sexually with her,
    and the merchants of the world grew rich
        from the great wealth of her luxury."

[4]Then I heard another voice from heaven say,

"Come out of that city, my people,
    so that you will not share in her sins.
    Then you will not suffer any of the terrible
        punishment she will get.
[5]That city's sins are piled up as high as heaven.

<hr>

[a] **16:21** *almost 40 kilogrammes* Literally, "*talanton*" or "*talent*".

God has not forgotten the wrongs she has
done.
[6]Give that city the same as she gave to others.
Pay her back twice as much as she did.
Prepare wine for her that is twice as strong
as the wine she prepared for others.
[7]She gave herself much glory and rich living.
Give her that much suffering and sadness.
She says to herself, 'I am a queen sitting on
my throne.
I am not a widow;
I will never be sad.'
[8]So in one day she will suffer
great hunger, mourning and death.
She will be destroyed by fire,
because the Lord God who judges her is
powerful.

[9]"The rulers of the earth who sinned sexually
with her and shared her wealth will see the
smoke from her burning. Then they will cry and
be sad because of her death. [10]The rulers will be
afraid of her suffering and stand far away. They
will say,

'Terrible! How terrible, O great city,
O powerful city of Babylon!
Your punishment came in one hour!'

[11]"And the merchants of the earth will cry and
be sad for her. They will be sad because now there
is no one to buy the things they sell—[12]gold,
silver, jewels, pearls, fine linen cloth, purple cloth,
silk and scarlet cloth, all kinds of citron wood and
all kinds of things made from ivory, expensive
wood, bronze, iron and marble. [13]They also sell
cinnamon, spice, incense, frankincense, myrrh,
wine, olive oil, fine flour, wheat, cattle, sheep,
horses, carriages and slaves—yes, even human
lives. The merchants will cry and say,

[14]'O Babylon, the good things you wanted have
left you.
All your rich and fancy things have
disappeared.
You will never have them again.'

[15]"The merchants will be afraid of her suffering
and will stand far away from her. They are the
ones who became rich from selling those things
to her. They will cry and be sad. [16]They will say,

'Terrible! How terrible for the great city!
She was dressed in fine linen;
she wore purple and scarlet cloth.

She was shining with gold, jewels and
pearls!
[17]All these riches have been destroyed in one
hour!'

"Every sea captain, all those who travel on
ships, the sailors and all those who earn money
from the sea stood far away from Babylon. [18]They
saw the smoke from her burning. They cried out,
'There was never a city like this great city!' [19]They
threw dust on their heads and cried loudly to
show the deep sorrow they felt. They said,

'Terrible! How terrible for the great city!
All those who had ships on the sea became
rich because of her wealth!
But she has been destroyed in one hour!'
[20]Be happy because of this, O heaven!
Be happy, God's holy people and apostles
and prophets!
God has punished her because of what she did
to you.'"

[21]Then a powerful angel picked up a large
rock. This rock was as big as a large millstone.
The angel threw the rock into the sea and said,

"That is how the great city of Babylon will be
thrown down.
It will never be found again.
[22]O Babylon, the sound of harps, singers, flutes
and trumpets
will never be heard in you again.
No worker doing any job
will ever be found in you again.
The sound of a millstone
will never be heard in you again.
[23]The light of a lamp
will never shine in you again.
The voices of a bridegroom and bride
will never be heard in you again.
Your merchants were the world's great people.
All the nations were tricked by your magic.
[24]You are guilty of the death of the prophets, of
God's holy people,
and of all those who have been killed on
earth."

People in Heaven Praise God

19 After this I heard what sounded like a
large crowd of people in heaven. The
people were saying,

"Hallelujah![a]
Victory, glory and power belong to our God.

---

[a] **19:1** *Hallelujah* This means "Praise God!" Also in verses 3,4,6.

CHRIST TRIUMPHANT!

The armies of God assemble for the final battle, when evil and all its effects will be wiped out forever . . . Out in front of the legions of angels dressed for battle is a fearsome warrior, dressed all in white.

God's son, Jesus, came to earth in mind-blowing humility, setting aside all material power and glory to be born in a dirty shed and live among the poor. But now we see him as he truly is – almighty, all glorious, ready to take back the universe for good.

DIG IN

READ Revelation 19:11–21

- List all the names of Jesus used in this passage (vv.11,13,16).
- What do they tell you about him?

We know Jesus by many names and each name tells us something about his character and nature: "Good Shepherd" (John 10:11), "Lamb of God" (John 1:29), "Prince of Peace" (Isaiah 9:6). Sometimes perhaps we forget that Jesus also goes by names like "King of Kings" and "Lord of Lords"! No other person or power can match his strength or his authority to rule. And although God has allowed evil to reign in history, now the King returns to take his throne.

- Who has gathered to fight against Jesus and his army (v.19)?
- How does the battle go (v.20)?

The beast (Revelation 13:1–18) and all those who have deceived and ruled over the earth have assembled in vain. Victory by the sword of Jesus is so swift that the armies of heaven don't even need to fight (why else would they turn up in white clothes?)! Read on into chapter 20 for the last battle, the final defeat of Satan and judgement of the people of the world.

DIG THROUGH

- Is the Jesus you know smaller than the Jesus we read about in Revelation? When you come to Jesus to pray, do you acknowledge that he is "King of Kings and Lord of Lords" (19:16) with the ability to do whatever he pleases? Reading Revelation keeps us full of awe at the staggering power and authority of the Lord Jesus.
- The sword that comes out of the rider's mouth is what defeats the enemy (19:21), and is believed to be a symbol of the word of God. How can we use the word of God to overcome the enemy in our lives? Check out Ephesians 6:17 and Hebrews 4:12.

DIG DEEPER

- Cast your mind back: can you remember the last time we read of Jesus riding on the back of an animal? Read Mark 11:1–11 to relive the scene. Then he entered Jerusalem in total humility on the back of the most humble of animals (a donkey); now he is riding triumphantly on the back of a powerful white horse.

These scenes in Revelation 19 fulfil many Old Testament prophecies about Christ's return to reign over the earth forever. For example, Isaiah, written around 800 years before Revelation, points to this day, including details like the winepress and the clothes dipped in lifeblood (Isaiah 63:1–6).

2His judgements are true and right.
Our God has punished the prostitute.
>   She is the one who ruined the earth with
>   her sexual sin.
God has punished the prostitute to pay her
>   back for the death of his servants."

3These people also said,

"Hallelujah!
>   She is burning and her smoke will rise for
>   ever and ever."

4Then the 24 elders and the four living beings bowed down. They worshipped God, who sits on the throne. They said,

"Amen! Hallelujah!"

5Then a voice came from the throne and said,

"Praise our God,
>   all you who serve him!
Praise our God,
>   all you small and great who honour him!"

6Then I heard something that sounded like a large crowd of people. It was as loud as crashing waves or claps of thunder. The people were saying,

"Hallelujah!
>   Our Lord God All-Powerful rules.
7Let us rejoice and be happy
>   and give God glory!
Give God glory, because the wedding of the
>   Lamb has come.
>   And the Lamb's bride has made herself
>   ready.
8Fine linen was given to the bride for her to
>   wear.
>   The linen was bright and clean."

(The fine linen means the good things that God's holy people did.)

9Then the angel said to me, "Write this: Great blessings belong to those who are invited to the wedding meal of the Lamb!" Then the angel said, "These are the true words of God."

10Then I bowed down before the angel's feet to worship him. But the angel said to me, "Don't worship me! I am a servant like you and your brothers and sisters who have the truth of Jesus. So worship God! Because the truth of Jesus is the spirit of prophecy."

The Rider on the White Horse

11Then I saw heaven open. There before me was a white horse. The rider on the horse was called Faithful and True, because he is right in his judging and in making war. 12His eyes were like burning fire. He had many crowns on his head. A name was written on him, but he was the only one who knew its meaning. 13He was dressed in a robe dipped in blood, and he was called the Word of God. 14The armies of heaven were following the rider on the white horse. They were also riding white horses. They were dressed in fine linen, white and clean. 15A sharp sword came out of the rider's mouth, a sword that he would use to defeat the nations. And he will rule the nations with a rod of iron. He will crush the grapes in the winepress of the terrible anger of God All-Powerful. 16On his robe and on his leg was written this name:

KING OF KINGS AND LORD OF LORDS

17Then I saw an angel standing in the sun. In a loud voice the angel said to all the birds flying in the sky, "Come together for the great supper of God. 18Come together so that you can eat the bodies of rulers and army commanders and famous men. Come to eat the bodies of the horses and their riders and the bodies of all people— free, slave, small and great."

19Then I saw the beast and the rulers of the earth. Their armies were gathered together to make war against the rider on the horse and his army. 20But the beast was captured, and the false prophet was also captured. He was the one who did the miracles*a* for the beast. He had used these miracles to trick those who had the mark of the beast and worshipped its idol. The false prophet and the beast were thrown alive into the lake of fire that burns with sulphur. 21Their armies were killed with the sword that came out of the mouth of the rider on the horse. All the birds ate these bodies until they were full.

The 1,000 Years

20 I saw an angel coming down out of heaven. The angel had the key to the bottomless pit. The angel also held a large chain in his hand. 2The angel grabbed the dragon, the old snake that is also known as the devil or Satan. The angel tied the dragon with the chain for 1,000 years. 3Then the angel threw the dragon into the bottomless pit and closed it. The angel locked it over the dragon. The angel did this so that the dragon could not trick the people of the

---

a **19:20** *miracles* False miracles—amazing acts done by the power of the devil.

earth until the 1,000 years were ended. After 1,000 years the dragon must be made free for a short time.

⁴Then I saw some thrones and people sitting on them. These were the ones who had been given the power to judge. And I saw the souls of those who had been killed because they were faithful to the truth of Jesus and the message from God. They did not worship the beast or its idol. They did not receive the mark of the beast on their foreheads or on their hands. They came back to life and ruled with Christ for 1,000 years. ⁵(The rest of the dead did not live again until the 1,000 years were ended.)

This is the first resurrection. ⁶Great blessings belong to those who share in this first resurrection. They are God's holy people. The second death has no power over them. They will be priests for God and for Christ. They will rule with him for 1,000 years.

The Defeat of Satan

⁷When the 1,000 years are ended, Satan will be made free from his prison. ⁸He will go out to trick the nations in all the earth, the nations known as Gog and Magog. Satan will gather the people for battle. There will be more people than anyone can count, like sand on the seashore. ⁹I saw Satan's army march across the earth and gather around the camp of God's people and the city that God loves. But fire came down from heaven and destroyed Satan's army. ¹⁰And Satan, the one who tricked these people, was thrown into the lake of burning sulphur with the beast and the false prophet. There they would be made to suffer pain day and night for ever and ever.

People of the World Are Judged

¹¹Then I saw a large white throne. I saw the one who was sitting on the throne. Earth and sky ran away from him and disappeared. ¹²And I saw those who had died, great and small, standing before the throne. Some books were opened. And another book was opened—the book of life. The people were judged by what they had done, which is written in the books.

¹³The sea gave up the dead who were in it. Death and Hades gave up the dead who were in them. All these people were judged by what they had done. ¹⁴And Death and Hades were thrown into the lake of fire. This lake of fire is the second death. ¹⁵And anyone whose name was not found written in the book of life was thrown into the lake of fire.

The New Jerusalem

21 Then I saw a new heaven and a new earth. The first heaven and the first earth had disappeared. Now there was no sea. ²And I saw the holy city, the new Jerusalem,ᵃ coming down out of heaven from God. It was prepared like a bride dressed for her husband.

³I heard a loud voice from the throne. It said, "Now God's home is with people. He will live with them. They will be his people. God himself will be with them and will be their God. ⁴He will wipe away every tear from their eyes. There will be no more death, sadness, crying or pain. All the old ways are gone."

⁵The one who was sitting on the throne said, "Look, I am making everything new!" Then he said, "Write this, because these words are true and can be trusted."

⁶The one on the throne said to me, "It is finished! I am the Alpha and the Omega,ᵇ the Beginning and the End. I will give free water from the spring of the water of life to anyone who is thirsty. ⁷All those who win the victory will receive all this. And I will be their God, and they will be my children. ⁸But those who are cowards, those who refuse to believe, those who do terrible things, those who kill, those who sin sexually, those who do evil magic, those who worship idols and those who tell lies—they will all have a place in the lake of burning sulphur. This is the second death."

⁹One of the seven angels came to me. This was one of the angels who had the seven bowls full of the seven last plagues. The angel said, "Come with me. I will show you the bride, the wife of the Lamb." ¹⁰The angel carried me away by the Spirit to a very large and high mountain. The angel showed me the holy city, Jerusalem. The city was coming down out of heaven from God.

¹¹The city was shining with the glory of God. It was shining bright like a very expensive jewel, like a jasper. It was clear as crystal. ¹²The city had a large, high wall with twelve gates. There were twelve angels at the gates. On each gate was written the name of one of the twelve tribes of Israel. ¹³There were three gates on the east, three gates on the north, three gates on the south and three gates on the west. ¹⁴The walls of the city were built on twelve foundation stones. On the stones were written the names of the twelve apostles of the Lamb.

¹⁵The angel who talked with me had a measuring rod made of gold. The angel had this rod to measure the city, its gates and its wall. ¹⁶The city was built in a square. Its length was equal to its

---

ᵃ **21:2 new Jerusalem** The spiritual city where God's people live with him.
ᵇ **21:6 Alpha . . . Omega** The first and last letters in the Greek alphabet, meaning the beginning and the end.

NOT AN ENDING, A NEW BEGINNING

Our human lives are full of sad endings. Loved ones, people we respect, even pets, die and leave us bereft. We throw ourselves into projects and jobs that all come to an end eventually. Our own bodies – once we're out of our teens – gradually become weaker and decay.

Every good story (we're told at school) has a beginning, a middle and an end. But the Bible doesn't fit that pattern. God's story doesn't end with an ending. It ends with a beginning.

DIG IN

READ Revelation 21:1–27

- After the previous twenty chapters of turmoil, how does this passage make you feel?
- Think for a moment: where was the last place God lived freely among his people?
- What's the obvious contrast with the new place in which he'll live with us?

"Then I saw a new heaven and a new earth" (v.1) are some of the most hopeful words ever written. God has a powerful promise for us: his perfect creation, ruined by sin in Genesis, is going to be renewed and once again made perfect. And, once again, God will take up residence with all his people (v.3).

But things are going to be different this time. In Genesis, God lived with Adam and Eve in a garden. Now, the new dwelling place of God is a city. This might be a little surprising, especially considering the fate of the city of Babylon, just a few chapters earlier. Why a city? Because two people have now become a multitude!

- How will life in the new heaven and the new earth differ to now?
- What specifically are you not going to miss?

The things that make life hard to bear – pain, tears and death – will all be gone (v.4). The tragic effects of sin will be no more.

- How does this passage differ from traditional or "storybook" descriptions of heaven?

When the Bible talks of "the heavens and the earth" together, the implication is "everything" – all that is seen and unseen, above, below, around. God is telling us that he's not restricting his renewal of creation to a few "sacred" things. Heaven will be a living, breathing, tangible and concrete reality.

Our bodies will be resurrected, working perfectly and beautiful. The Bible teaches that we will eat, play, learn, even work, but all those things will be free of the way that sin has corrupted them in this life.

DIG THROUGH

- God's nature is to redeem and restore. It's what he loves doing. And he's going to renew everything. Is there anything you've secretly given up on God being able to renew and restore to you?
- Be honest: how much are you longing for heaven? Or does earth feel pretty good right now? Are you excited about being with Jesus forever?

DIG DEEPER

- You'll find an Old Testament preview of the future in Isaiah 65:17 – 66:24. Read it and savour the promises God makes, particularly 65:17–25.
- "What happens to us when we die?" is surely one of the questions everyone on the planet asks at some point in their lives; some people think about it all the time. Do you feel you know enough of God's word to answer that question from a Christian perspective? A good place to start is with the words of Jesus in Matthew 25:31–46.

width. The angel measured the city with the rod. The city was 2,200 kilometres[a] long, 2,200 kilometres wide and 2,200 kilometres high. [17]The angel also measured the wall. It was 72 metres[b] high. (The angel was using the same measurement that people use.) [18]The wall was made of jasper. The city was made of pure gold, as pure as glass.

[19]The foundation stones of the city walls had every kind of expensive jewel in them. The first foundation stone was jasper, the second was sapphire, the third was chalcedony, the fourth was emerald, [20]the fifth was onyx, the sixth was carnelian, the seventh was yellow quartz, the eighth was beryl, the ninth was topaz, the tenth was chrysoprase, the eleventh was jacinth and the twelfth was amethyst. [21]The twelve gates were twelve pearls. Each gate was made from one pearl. The street of the city was made of pure gold, as clear as glass.

[22]I did not see a temple in the city. The Lord God All-Powerful and the Lamb were the city's temple. [23]The city did not need the sun or the moon to shine on it. The glory of God gave the city light. The Lamb was the city's lamp. [24]The peoples of the world will walk by the light given by the Lamb. The rulers of the earth will bring their glory into the city. [25]The city's gates will never close on any day, because there is no night there. [26]The greatness and the honour of the nations will be brought into the city. [27]Nothing unclean will ever enter the city. No one who does shameful things or tells lies will ever enter the city. Only those whose names are written in the Lamb's book of life will enter the city.

INSIGHT

In the new Jerusalem there is no temple. But why would it need one? God is everywhere and living with his people. The gates will always be open because all the enemies have been defeated. There will be food for all, healing for all and peace for all.

Revelation 21:22–27

22 The angel showed me the river of the water of life, clear as crystal. The river flows from the throne of God and the Lamb. [2]It flows down the middle of the street of the city. The tree of life is on each side of the river, and it produces fruit every month, twelve times a year. The leaves of the tree are for healing the nations.

[3]Nothing that God judges guilty will be there in that city. The throne of God and the Lamb will be in the city. God's servants will worship him. [4]They will see his face. God's name will be written on their foreheads. [5]There will never be night again. People will not need the light of a lamp or the light of the sun. The Lord God will give them light. And they will rule like kings for ever and ever.

[6]Then the angel said to me, "These words are true and can be trusted. The Lord, the God of the spirits of the prophets, has sent his angel to show his servants what must happen soon: [7]'Listen, I am coming soon! Great blessings belong to the one who obeys the words of prophecy in this book.'"

[8]I am John. I am the one who heard and saw these things. After I heard and saw them, I bowed down to worship at the feet of the angel who showed them to me. [9]But the angel said to me, "Don't worship me! I am a servant like you and your brothers the prophets. I am a servant like all those who obey the words in this book. You should worship God!"

[10]Then the angel told me, "Don't keep secret the words of prophecy in this book. The time is near for these things to happen. [11]Let anyone who is doing wrong continue to do wrong. Let anyone who is unclean continue to be unclean. Let anyone who is doing right continue to do right. Let anyone who is holy continue to be holy."

[12]"Listen, I am coming soon! I will bring rewards with me. I will repay everyone for what they have done. [13]I am the Alpha and the Omega,[c] the First and the Last, the Beginning and the End.

[14]"Great blessings belong to those who have washed their robes.[d] They will have the right to eat the food from the tree of life. They can go through the gates into the city. [15]Outside the city are all those who live like dogs—those who do evil magic, those who sin sexually, those who murder, those who worship idols and those who love to lie and pretend to be good.

[16]"I, Jesus, have sent my angel to tell you these things for the churches. I am the descendant from the family of David. I am the bright morning star."

[17]The Spirit and the bride say, "Come!" Everyone who hears this should also say, "Come!"

---

[a] **21:16 *2,200 kilometres*** Literally 12,000 *stadia*.

[b] **21:17 *72 metres*** Literally, 144 *cubits*. A *cubit* is the length of a man's arm from the elbow to the tip of the little finger, about half a metre.

[c] **22:13 *Alpha . . . Omega*** The first and last letters in the Greek alphabet, meaning the beginning and the end.

[d] **22:14 *washed their robes*** Meaning that they had believed in Jesus and had been made clean from sin by his blood sacrifice. See Rev. 5:9; 7:14; Heb. 9:14; 10:14–22; Acts 22:16; 1 John 1:7.

All who are thirsty may come; they can have the water of life as a free gift if they want it.

[18]I warn everyone who hears the words of prophecy in this book: if anyone adds anything to these, God will give that person the plagues written about in this book. [19]And if anyone takes away from the words of this book of prophecy,

God will take away that person's share of the tree of life and of the holy city, which are written about in this book.

[20]Jesus is the one who says that all of this is true. Now he says, "Yes, I am coming soon."

Amen! Come, Lord Jesus!

[21]The grace of the Lord Jesus be with all people.

WEIGHTS AND MEASURES

Biblical Unit	Metric Equivalent*
Length	
Cubit, long**.............	50 centimetres
Cubit, short**...........	44 centimetres
Span	22 centimetres
Handbreadth	75 millimetres
Finger	18 millimetres
Milion (8 stadia).........	1.5 kilometres
Stadion (1/8 milion)	185 metres

Biblical Unit	Metric Equivalent*
Weights	
Talent (60 minas)........	34 kilogrammes
Mina (50 or 60 shekels)	600 grammes
Shekel (2 bekas)	11.5 grammes
Pim (2/3 shekel)............	8 grammes
Beka (10 gerahs)...........	5 grammes
Gerah (1/20 shekel).........	0.58 gramme
Litra	327 grammes

Biblical Unit	Metric Equivalent*
Capacity, Dry Measure*	
Cor [homer] (10 ephahs)........	220 litres
Letek (1/2 homer).............	110 litres
Ephah (10 omers).............	22 litres
Seah (1/3 ephah)	7 litres
Omer (1/10 ephah).............	2 litres
Cab (1/18 ephah)	1 litre

Biblical Unit	Metric Equivalent*
Capacity, Liquid Measure	
Bath (1 ephah)	22 litres
Hin (1/6 bath)	4 litres
Log (1/72 bath)...............	0.3 litres
Cor (10 baths).................	220 litres
Double Bath (2 ephahs)	44 litres
Metretes......................	40 litres

*The metric equivalents in this chart are approximate and should not be used to calculate precise figures. Also, the precise amounts for some biblical units, such as the mina, varied in different times and places.

**Cubit (short/long) The long cubit seems to be the standard for temple measurements (as found in Ezekiel) and the short cubit the standard of the royal or civil (non-priestly) system.

***The biblical units for dry measure actually indicate capacity or volume, but in the text of the translation approximate weight equivalents have been given. These take into consideration the specific material being measured.

A **Aaron** Moses' brother, who was chosen as the first high priest of Israel.

Abel The son of Adam and Eve who was killed by his brother Cain. Read Gen. 4:1–16.

Abib Or "Nisan", the first month of the ancient Hebrew calendar. The name means "young heads of grain". It was the beginning of spring, about mid-March to mid-April.

Abraham The most respected ancestor of the Jewish people. Through him God promised to make a great nation and bless all the people of the earth. Read Gen. 12:1–3.

Achaia The region in the southern part of Greece where the ancient cities of Athens and Corinth were located.

Adriatic Sea The sea between Greece and Italy, including the central part of the Mediterranean Sea.

adultery Breaking a marriage promise by committing sexual sin.

agreement A contract or agreement from God to his people. The agreement that God gave his people at Mount Sinai, based on the Law of Moses, became the most important for the Israelites or Jews. It replaced or renewed all other agreements, such as that given earlier to Abraham. In the New Testament it is referred to as the "old" or "first" agreement. After Jesus Christ came and offered his life as payment for the sins of all people, God was able to offer a "new" and "better" agreement based on Christ's sacrifice.

agreement (first agreement) The contract God gave to the Israelites when he gave them the Law of Moses. See "agreement".

agreement (new agreement) The "better agreement" that God has given to his people through Jesus Christ. See "agreement".

Agreement Literally "Testimony", a word that usually refers to the flat stones with the Ten Commandments written on them, which were evidence or "proof" of the agreement between God and Israel.

Agreement (Box of the Agreement, Box of God's Agreement, Box of the Lord's Agreement) Or traditionally, "Ark of the Covenant". The special box kept in the Most Holy Place of the Israelite Holy Tent and, later, the Jerusalem Temple. It contained the stone tablets with the Ten Commandments written on them, which were evidence or "proof" of the agreement between God and his people. In some passages it is literally, "Box of the Testimony" or simply, "Testimony" (see "Agreement"). See Exod. 25:10–22; 1 Kgs 8:1–9.

Agreement (Tent of the Agreement) Literally, "Tent of the Testimony", the tent where the Box of the Agreement was kept. See "Holy Tent".

Agrippa Herod Agrippa II, great-grandson of Herod the Great. See Acts 12:1–23.

Ahaz A king of Judah who ruled with his father Jotham from 735 to 732 BC, and then alone from 732 to 715 BC.

alabaster A beautiful kind of stone that can be carved.

aloes The oil from a sweet-smelling wood that was used to make perfume (Ps. 45:8; Prov. 7:17) or the bitter juice from a cactus-like plant that was used to prepare bodies for burial (John 19:39).

altar A raised area, pile of stones or table that people used to offer sacrifices on. An important altar was the one in front of the Temple in Jerusalem. See also "golden altar".

altar (golden altar) The table made from acacia wood and covered with gold that was used in the Holy Tent for burning incense as a gift to God.

altar (horns of the altar) The horn-shaped corners of the altar (see "altar") used for burning sacrifices that was in the courtyard of the Holy Tent (see "Holy Tent") and Temple (see "Temple"). See Exod. 27:2; 38:2. The incense altar inside the Holy Tent also had corners shaped like horns. See Exod. 30:2; 37:25. The law said that a person accused of killing someone (except wilful murder) who ran into the Holy Place (see "Holy Place") and took hold of these horns should not be punished. See Exod. 21:12–14.

Amen A Hebrew word meaning "That's right", "True" or "Yes". It is used to express strong agreement with what has been said.

Anakites Descendants of Anak. They were a family famous for tall and powerful fighting men. See Num. 13:33.

ancestors Literally, "fathers", meaning a person's parents, grandparents and all the other people that person is descended from. In the New Testament it usually refers to people who lived during Old Testament times.

angels (Cherub angels) Winged beings like angels that serve God, usually as guards around his throne or other holy places. Two statues of these beings were on the cover of the Box of the Agreement that represented God's presence. See Exod. 25:10–22.

angels (Seraph angels) Special angels that God used as messengers. The name might mean that they were bright like fire.

anoint To pour a special oil on people or things to show that they have been chosen by God and set apart for a special work or purpose.

apostle A follower of Jesus chosen to represent him in a special way. During his earthly ministry, Jesus named twelve men as apostles. They had the specific responsibility and authority to represent him and proclaim his message throughout the world. Later, he appeared to Paul and gave him a similar commission, especially to non-Jewish people. Barnabas, Paul's missionary companion, and James, the brother of Jesus, are also called apostles, as well as several others in the New Testament. Some of these occurrences of the word, however, have the more general sense of "messenger" or "representative".

aqueduct A ditch or pipe that carries water from one place to another.

Aram A country north of Israel that included much of modern-day Syria. See Isa. 7:1; 17:3.

Aramaic The language of the Arameans, which became the main language of trade and diplomacy in the ancient Near East during the Assyrian, the Neo-Babylonian and Persian empires. Similar to Hebrew, it later became the common language of many Jews and is the spoken "Hebrew" referred to in the New Testament.

Ararat The ancient country of Urartu, an area in eastern Turkey.

archangel The leader among God's angels.

archer A person skilled in using a bow to shoot arrows.

armour The special clothes soldiers wore to protect themselves in war.

Artaxerxes The king of Persia about 465–424 BC. He was the son of Xerxes. See Ezra 4:7; 7:1.

Asherah An important Canaanite goddess, the wife of the Canaanite god El and possibly Baal. People thought she could help them have children.

Asherah pole A wooden pole (originally, perhaps, a tree trunk) that was set up to honour the goddess Asherah.

Ashtoreth Or "Astarte", an important Canaanite goddess, the wife of the Canaanite god Baal and possibly El. Called the "Queen of Heaven", she was the goddess of love and war.

Asia The geographical area, sometimes called Asia Minor, that is now the western part of modern-day Turkey.

Assyria A powerful nation north-east of Israel.

B **Baal** A false god worshipped by the Canaanites. They believed he brought rain and storms and made the land produce good crops.

Balaam A non-Israelite prophet in the Old Testament who was hired by Balak, king of Moab, to curse his enemy Israel. Read Num. 22 – 24.

baptism A Greek word usually referring to the act of dipping or "burying" a person briefly in water, connected with their decision to change their life and turn to God, trusting him to forgive their sins. For people coming to faith in Jesus Christ it was an expression of their trust in his death as the sacrifice God accepted to pay for their sins. Described as a sharing in the death, burial and resurrection of Christ, it marked the beginning of their new life in Christ as part of God's people. See

Acts 2:38; Rom. 6:3,4; Gal. 3:26–28; Col. 2:12,13.

baptize To perform the act of baptism. See "baptism".

Bashan The northern part of Israel east of the Jordan River.

Bel One of the names of the god Marduk, the most important god of the Babylonians.

believer Literally "brother", a term used by followers of Jesus Christ to refer to fellow members of God's family. See Acts 1:15; 2:41; 9:30; 10:23; 11:1; 14:2; 15:1,3,32,33,36; 16:2,40; 17:6,10,14; 18:18,27; 21:7; 28:14,15; Rom. 16:14; 1 Cor. 6:5; 15:6; Phil. 1:14; 1 Thess. 4:6; Jas 1:9; 3 John 3,5; Rev. 1:9.

Bernice King Agrippa's sister, the oldest daughter of Herod Agrippa I.

Bethsaida A town by Lake Galilee that Jesus visited during his teaching ministry and where he performed many miracles.

blacksmith A person who makes weapons, tools or other things from iron.

boomerang A curved stick used in hunting birds. When thrown properly, it flies low to the ground and suddenly curves upward, often returning to the thrower. Literally, "a bow of throwing" or "a bow of deception".

Bozrah A city or an area in Edom, sometimes meaning the whole nation.

bridegroom A man who is getting married.

bronze A type of metal made from copper mixed with tin. The Hebrew word can mean "copper", "brass" or "bronze".

C **Caesar** The name or title given to the emperor (ruler) of Rome.

Cain The son of Adam and Eve who killed his brother Abel. Read Gen. 4:1–16.

Canaan The land where the Canaanites lived. At first, their land was along the coast at the eastern edge of the Mediterranean Sea, but later it included a much larger territory. In the time of Joshua, it was generally the same area that was later called Palestine and included what are now Israel and Lebanon.

Capernaum A town on the northern shore of Lake Galilee where Jesus often spent time and taught.

capital A decorated cap made of stone or wood and placed on top of each of the columns that support the roof of a building.

captive One of those who have been defeated in battle and are taken away as prisoners.

caravan A group of traders with their animals that carried products from one place to another.

Carmel A famous mountain (or high hill) in northern Israel that had good soil and plenty of rain. The name means "God's vineyard". See Isa. 33:9; 35:2.

cassia The fragrant dried flowers of the ancient cinnamon tree that were used in anointing oil and as perfume.

chaff The seed coverings or husks separated from the seeds of plants like wheat or barley. Farmers saved the seeds but let the wind blow the useless chaff away.

Chaldeans An important tribe in Babylon. Sometimes this name means simply "people from Babylonia". King Nebuchadnezzar was from this tribe, as were other kings of Babylon. Well-educated people, they studied science, history, languages and astronomy, but they also believed they could do magic and look at the stars to learn what would happen in the future.

chariot A small, two-wheeled cart pulled by horses and used in war.

Chemosh The national god of the country of Moab.

Cherub See "Cherub angels".

Christ Literally, "Anointed", a title that comes from the Old Testament ceremony in which perfumed oil was poured or rubbed on someone being appointed to a high office, especially that of prophet, priest or king, to show that this person was chosen by God for that role. The Hebrew word is "Messiah", a title used for Old Testament kings and for the one God would send as prophet, priest and king to bring people back to a good relationship with him.

church Literally, "assembly" or "community", the people who have been brought together as God's family through their common faith in Jesus Christ. The word often refers to a group of believers who meet together or who live in the same area, but it is also used to mean the worldwide community of all believers in Christ.

circumcise, circumcision Cutting off the foreskin of the male sex organ. This was done to every Jewish baby boy as a mark of the agreement God made with Abraham. Read Gen. 17:9–14. Sometimes "circumcision" is used with "heart" in the figurative sense of true devotion to God. See Jer. 9:26; Rom. 2:28. In the New Testament "circumcision" is also used in a spiritual sense to refer to the changed life of believers who have come to share in the new agreement God gave his people through Jesus. See Phil. 3:3; Col. 2:11.

Claudius The emperor (ruler) of Rome, AD 41–54.

clean Pure or acceptable. When it refers to animals, it means fit to be eaten. When it refers to things, it means fit to be used. When it refers to people, it means fit to participate in the worship of God at the Holy Tent (Tabernacle) or Temple. See Lev. 11 – 15 for the Old Testament rules about clean and unclean things.

coral A hard, stone-like substance, usually pink, red or black, that is formed from the skeletons of tiny sea animals and covers the ocean floor in certain areas.

cornerstone The first and most important stone of a building.

council (Areopagus council) A group of important leaders in Athens who served like judges.

courtyard The large open area around a king's palace or outside the Temple.

cross The wooden post that Romans used to execute criminals. It is a symbol of shame, suffering and death. Just as Jesus was willing to suffer death on a cross for all people, so he asks his followers to be willing to give up their lives for him.

crown Literally, "wreath", a ring of leaves or branches that was placed on the head of the winners of athletic contests to honour them. It was a symbol of victory and reward.

cud The food that is brought up from the stomach

of some animals (like cattle) and chewed again. See Lev. 11.

curse To ask for bad things to happen to a person or thing. As a noun it is a request for or warning about bad things to come.

curtain The curtain that separated the inner sanctuary (Most Holy Place) from the front room in the Tabernacle (see "Holy Tent") and in the Jerusalem Temple. It represented the spiritual barrier that kept people from entering God's presence. When Jesus died, the curtain was torn open (Matt. 27:51), which was a symbol to show that in the heavenly temple the way into God's presence had been opened. See Heb. 10:19,20.

cymbals A pair of circular metal plates that are hit against each other to make a loud sound.

Cyprus Literally, "the land of Kittim". This could be either Cyprus or Crete.

Cyrus A king of Persia who ruled about 550–530 BC.

D **Dagon** A false god worshipped by the Canaanites in the hope that he would give them a good harvest of grain. When the Philistines settled in Canaan, they adopted Dagon as their most important god.

darkness A symbol for the kinds of things that describe Satan's kingdom, such as sin and evil.

David Israel's greatest king, who ruled about 1,000 years before Christ. Besides being a great military and political leader, he was a deeply spiritual man and a gifted musician, who wrote many of the psalms. He made plans and arrangements for the building of the first Temple in Jerusalem (the city of David), which was actually completed by his son Solomon. The Scriptures said that a descendant of David would be God's chosen messiah (king), who would establish an eternal kingdom. For that reason, Jesus is sometimes called "the Son of David".

David (City of David) Jerusalem, especially the south-eastern and oldest part of the city.

David (Son of David) A name for the Messiah (Christ) because it was prophesied that he would come from the family of David. See "David".

David (son of David) Any person from the family of David. See "David".

David (song of David) This phrase (or a variation of it) is found at the beginning of many of the psalms. It could also mean "a song dedicated to David".

day A symbol for the kinds of things that describe God's kingdom, such as goodness and truth.

Day The day Christ will come to judge everyone and take his people to live with him.

Day of Atonement Also called "Yom Kippur", a very important holy day for the people of Israel. On this day the high priest went into the Most Holy Place and performed the ceremony that made it pure and atoned for (covered or erased) the sins of the people. See Lev. 16:1–34; 23:26–32.

dedicate To offer something to God with a promise that it will be used only for him, or to set apart something for a special purpose, which means it can then be used only for that purpose.

dedication The act of dedicating something to God. See "dedicate".

deed A written record that proves who owns a certain piece of property. See Jer. 32.

demon An evil spirit from the devil.

director This title is part of a phrase found at the beginning of many of the psalms. It could also mean "performer".

discharge Fluid from a person's body, including pus from sores, a man's semen or a woman's period flow.

dungeon A deep pit in the ground, like a cave, used as a prison.

dysentery A very bad intestinal sickness that causes pain and diarrhoea.

E Edom A country south-east of Judah. It is also known as Seir after the mountain range by that name in Edom. The Edomites are descendants of Esau, Jacob's twin brother. At times, they were enemies of the Israelites.

elders (in Revelation) The 24 elders in Revelation could be the great leaders of God's people under both the Old Testament and New Testament periods, combining the leaders of the twelve tribes of Israel and Jesus' twelve apostles. Or they could be angels as leaders of heavenly worship, corresponding to the 24 groups of priests in charge of worship in the Old Testament.

elders Men chosen to lead a local group of believers (church). Also called "overseers" and "pastors" (shepherds), they have the work of caring for God's people. See Acts 14:23; 20:17,28; Eph. 4:11; Phil. 1:1; 1 Tim. 3:1–7; Titus 1:5–9; 1 Pet. 5:1–3.

Elijah A very important Israelite leader and prophet who spoke for God during a 25-year period ending about 850 BC. In the time of Jesus, the Jews were expecting Elijah to come again before the Messiah. See Mal. 4:5–6.

Elisha A prophet who served as an assistant to the prophet Elijah and carried on Elijah's ministry after about 850 BC.

emperor Caesar, the ruler (leader) of the Roman empire.

ephod A special vest (coat) worn by the Israelite high priest (see Exod. 28:6–14; 39:1–7). Sometimes it is a garment worn by people in other kinds of priestly service, such as the boy Samuel (1 Sam. 2:18), or by others like David (2 Sam. 6:14). It is also something used to get answers from God (1 Sam. 23:6–12; 30:7–8). This is why some people think the high priest's garment had a pocket for carrying lots (see "lots"). In Judg. 8:27 Gideon uses gold to make an ephod. In such places, it seems to be an idol, but it may be a garment covering an idol.

Ephraim The second son of Joseph and the name of one of the tribes of Israel. Sometimes it is used as the name for the northern kingdom of Israel, since Ephraim was most often the leading tribe.

Esau Jacob's twin brother. Also, another name for Edom. The Edomites were descendants of Esau.

Ethiopia Or "Cush", a country in Africa by the Red Sea.

eunuch A man who had been castrated so that he could not have sex or one who was physically unable to have children. Often, such men were chosen to be in charge of the women in a ruler's household or served as public officials.

Euphrates One of the two large rivers flowing through the countries of Babylonia and Assyria.

Evil One The devil or Satan, the ruler of demons and enemy of God.

exile Living away from one's home country, usually by force.

F famine A time when there is not enough rain for crops to grow, causing people and animals to die without enough food or water.

fast To live without food for a time of prayer or mourning.

fathers Important ancestors of the Jewish people, especially the leaders of the tribes of Israel.

fawn A baby deer.

Festival of Harvest A one-day celebration of the wheat harvest in the spring, fifty days after Passover, during which the first part of the new crop was offered to God. Often called "Festival of Weeks", it was later known as "Pentecost" (from the Greek word meaning "fifty").

Festival of Shelters A special week each year when the Israelites, and later the Jews, lived in tents to remember God's protection during the time their people wandered in the desert for 40 years with Moses. Also called "Festival of Ingathering" (Exod. 23:16; 34:22). Read Lev. 23:33–36,39–43.

Festival of Unleavened Bread An important and holy week for the people of Israel and their descendants. In the time of the Old Testament it began the day after Passover, but by New Testament times the two festivals had become one. To prepare for it, the people threw out all their yeast and ate only bread without yeast for seven days.

firepan A small shovel used for removing ashes from an altar.

firstborn The first child born into a family. The first son was very important in ancient times and became the head of the family at the father's death. It can also mean a person of special importance. In reference to Christ, it means that he is the first and most important of God's children, the first to share his glory.

fortress A building or city with tall, strong walls for protection.

fortune-teller A person who tries to use magic to learn what will happen in the future.

frankincense Special dried tree sap that was burned to make a sweet-smelling smoke and offered as a gift to God. See "incense".

furnace Or "kiln", an oven for baking bricks to make them hard.

G gazelle A small, fast kind of antelope, an animal like a deer.

Gibeah A place where some men from the tribe of Benjamin committed a terrible sin. See Judg. 19 and 20.

Gilead The area east of the Jordan River where the tribes of Reuben, Gad and half the tribe of Manasseh lived. See Num. 26:29.

Gilgal A city in Israel where people had worshipped God but later became known as a place where people worshipped false gods.

gittith This might be a type of instrument, a tune, a music style or a performer in the Temple orchestra such as Obed Edom from Gath (the Gittite). See 1 Chr. 15:21; 16:4–7.

glory A word that refers to the special qualities of God. The expression "Glory of the Lord" refers to one of the forms God used when he appeared to people. It was like a bright, shining light. In the book of Numbers, it might have been a bright light or a tall cloud. Sometimes glory means majesty or power, referring to a kind of greatness that cannot be compared to anything in human experience. It can also include the ideas of wealth, honour, fame or respect, especially in expressions of praise.

goad A sharp stick that a person used to make animals go the right way.

goldsmith A person who makes things from gold.

Gomorrah A city that God destroyed, together with the city of Sodom, because the people living there were so evil. See Gen. 19.

Good News In the Gospels this is usually the news

about the coming of God's kingdom (see "kingdom (God's kingdom)") or its representative Jesus the Messiah. In other places it is, more specifically, the news or message of God's grace that he has made a way through Jesus Christ for people to be made right with him and enjoy his blessings now and forever.

grace The love and kindness that God shows in his complete willingness to give people favours he does not owe them and blessings they don't deserve.

grave Or "Sheol", the home of the dead. This word is often used as a metaphor for death.

Great Sea Or the Mediterranean Sea.

greatness (divine greatness) Literally, "glory", a word that refers to the special qualities of God. See "glory".

Greek A non-Jewish person anywhere throughout the first-century world who was influenced by Greek language and culture.

H **Hades** The Greek word for "Sheol", the home of the dead. It is often used as a metaphor for death.

Hermes A Greek god. The Greeks believed he was a messenger for the other gods.

Herod (1) Herod I (the Great), king of Judea and all of Palestine (40–4 BC), Matt. 2:1–22; Luke 1:5; Acts 23:35. **(2)** Herod Antipas, son of Herod the Great, tetrarch (ruler) of Galilee and Perea (4 BC–AD 39), Matt. 14:1–6; Mark 6:14–22; 8:15; Luke 3:1,19; 8:3; 9:7,9; 13:31; 23:7–15; Acts 4:27; 13:1. **(3)** Herod Agrippa I, grandson of Herod the Great, king of Palestine (AD 37–44), Acts 12:1,6–21.

Herodians Members of a Jewish political group who were supporters of Herod and co-operated with the Pharisees in finding a way to stop Jesus from teaching.

Hezekiah A king of Judah who ruled about 715–686 BC.

high place A place of worship usually on top of a hill, a mountain or a man-made platform. Although high places were sometimes used for the worship of God, they are most often associated with pagan worship of false gods.

holy When referring to people or things, holy means set apart or chosen for a special use; especially, belonging to God or used only for him. It can also mean pure or perfect, worthy of God and fit for his service. When God is called holy, in addition to the idea of pure and perfect, it often means he is completely separate or different from and above everything else that exists. In the New Testament God's people are holy because they have been made perfect and pure through Christ and, with the help of the Holy Spirit, keep themselves away from sin and live only for God.

Holy Box See "Agreement (Box of the Agreement)".

holy bread This was the special bread that was set out on a table in the Holy Tent as an offering to God. It is also called "showbread" or "bread of the Presence". Normally, only the priests were allowed to eat this bread. See Lev. 24:5–9.

holy people Literally, "saints" or "holy ones", a term used in the New Testament to describe followers of Jesus Christ as God's special people. They are holy because they have been made pure through Christ and belong only to God. See "holy".

Holy Place The room in the Holy Tent (Tabernacle) and in the Temple that was used by the Israelite priests to do their daily service for God.

Holy Spirit Also called the Spirit of God, the Spirit of Christ, and the Comforter. In union with God and Christ, he does God's work among people in the world.

Holy Tent Or "Tabernacle", the special tent described in the Law of Moses, where God lived among his people and where the Israelite priests performed their worship duties. It was often called the "Meeting Tent" because it was where the Israelites went to meet with God. It was used until Solomon built the Temple in Jerusalem.

hypocrisy Pretending to be good while hiding wrong motives.

hypocrite A person with wrong motives who pretends to be good.

hyssop A plant with fine branches and leaves used for sprinkling blood or water in cleansing ceremonies.

idol A statue of a false god that people worship. It can also mean anything that is more important to a person than God.

Illyricum A Roman province north and west of Greece.

incense Special spices that were burned to make a sweet-smelling smoke and offered as a sacrifice. See Exod. 30:34–38.

Isaac The son of Abraham and one of the most important ancestors of the Israelites or Jews.

Israel Another name for Jacob (see Gen. 32:24–28) and for the nation God chose to accomplish his plan of blessing the world through the Messiah (see "Messiah"). The people of Israel were the descendants of Jacob's twelve sons. In the New Testament this name is sometimes used in a broader sense to mean all of God's people.

Israelite Belonging to the nation of Israel (see "Israel").

jackal A kind of wild dog that stays where there are no people. Jackals usually hunt together in a pack.

Jacob Or "Israel", ancestor of the people of Israel (also called Israelites and, later, Jews). See Gen. 32:24–28 for the story of how Jacob was given the name Israel. He was the father of twelve sons from whom the twelve tribes of Israel descended, and the name Jacob continued to be used for the nation or people of Israel.

Jeremiah A man who spoke for God about 600 BC.

John the Baptizer The man God chose to tell people about Christ's coming and to prepare them by warning them to change their lives and by baptizing them (see "baptize") as a sign of their decision to change. Read Matt. 3; Mark 1:1–11; Luke 1:5–25,57–80; 3:1–18.

John See "John the Baptizer".

Joshua The Israelite military captain who, after Moses died, took his place as the leader of the Israelites and led them into the land that God had promised them.

Jotham A king of Judah who ruled with his father Uzziah from 750 to 740 BC, and then alone from 740 to 732 BC.

Jubilee A special horn and the festival marked by the blowing of it to announce that the time had come for slaves to be set free and land returned to the original owners. See Lev. 25:9.

Judah One of the 12 sons of Jacob (Israel); also the tribe and, later, the nation named after him. Described as the "southern kingdom", it was made up of the Israelite tribes that occupied the southern part of Palestine, while the northern tribes were united into a "northern kingdom" known as Israel.

judge One of the civic leaders who judged, led and protected the people of Israel before their first king was appointed.

Kedar An Arabian tribe that lived in the desert south-east of the land of Judah.

kingdom (God's kingdom) The "reign" or "rule" of God over all people who accept Jesus as the Messiah (the chosen king). Jesus' life and teachings show what it means for God to be King on earth. Jesus fulfilled the King's mission of love and justice by setting people free from the control of the devil, the temporary ruler of this world. Through Jesus, God offers his enemies forgiveness for their rebellion against him. And when people are freed from their slavery to sin, they can give control of their lives to Jesus. Then they become part of God's kingdom and gladly accept his mission. Just as Jesus did, they too invite God's enemies to change their hearts and lives, become God's friends, and enjoy the benefits of his just rule, both now and in the future. (Note that in Matthew this term also translates the Greek word "kingdom" by itself or the phrase, "the kingdom of the heavens", which was used by Jews as a way to avoid saying the divine name.)

Lamb A symbolic name for Jesus Christ. It means that he was an offering for sin like the lambs that were offered as a sacrifice to God in the Old Testament.

law This usually refers to God's law as it is represented in the Mosaic Law, the rules he gave to the Israelites through Moses (See Exod. 34:29–32). Sometimes it may mean the principle of law rather than a specific law or set of laws.

leatherworker Or "tanner", a person who makes leather from animal skins.

Lebanon A country north of Israel, famous for its great cedar and pine trees.

leper A person who has leprosy. See "leprosy".

leprosy A very bad skin disease. The word in the text has a broad sense, which may include many different types of skin disease.

Levi The tribe of Israel from which the priests (descendants of Aaron) and the priests' helpers were chosen.

Levite An Israelite from the tribe of Levi. The Levites from the family of Aaron served as priests. All the other descendants of Levi served as helpers of the priests in the Holy Tent (Tabernacle) and Temple. In later periods, some Levites worked for the government as civil servants.

light A symbol for the kinds of things that describe God or his kingdom, such as goodness and truth.

lily A kind of flower. In the Song of Solomon, it is probably a red flower.

linen Thread or cloth made from the fibres of the flax plant.

locusts Insects like grasshoppers that could destroy a large crop very quickly. See Exod. 10. The Law of Moses said that locusts could be eaten. See Lev. 11:21–22.

loom A machine used for making cloth.

lots Stones, sticks or bones used like dice for making decisions. See Prov. 16:33.

lyre A musical instrument with strings, like a harp.

M Macedonia The northern part of Greece, where Thessalonica and Philippi were.

make . . . pure Or "make atonement for . . . " The Hebrew word means "to cover" or "to erase" a person's sins.

man of God Another title for a prophet. See "prophet".

manna The special food provided by God that the Israelites gathered daily from the ground during the 40 years they wandered through the desert. See Exod. 16:4–36.

Marduk The most important god of the Babylonian people.

maskil The meaning of this word is uncertain. It might mean "a poem of meditation", "a poem of instruction" or "a skilfully written poem".

mast The tall pole to which the sail is tied on a sailing boat.

Medes People of the Medo-Persian Empire (also called Media), which defeated the Neo-Babylonian Empire in 539 BC. See Isa. 13:17.

mediator A person who helps one person talk to or give something to another person.

medium A person who tries to talk with the spirits of people who have died.

Meeting Tent See "Holy Tent".

Melchizedek A priest and king who lived in the time of Abraham. See Gen. 14:18–24.

mercy-cover The top part of the Box of the Agreement. The Hebrew word can mean "lid", "cover" or "the place where sins are atoned (covered, erased or forgiven)".

message See "Good News".

Messiah A Hebrew word that has the same meaning as the Greek word Christ (see "Christ"). It was a title for the kings of God's people in the Old Testament and for the special king God promised to send as a "saviour" to defeat evil and establish the reign of God. Many prophets made it clear that this new kingdom would be eternal; that is, not only would the promised Messiah bring about a time of justice and right living among God's people here on earth, but also his kingdom would extend beyond this world to life forever with God. However, most Jews of the first century expected the Messiah to be a political ruler here on earth who would defeat the other nations and return the nation of Israel to a position of great glory and power. But God intended his Messiah to establish a new "Israel", an eternal kingdom that would bless all the nations.

miktam The meaning of this word is uncertain. It might mean "a well-arranged song".

Milcom A god worshipped by the Ammonites, probably the same as the god Molech. See 1 Kgs 11:5,7.

mildew A kind of fungus that often grows on cloth, leather or wood that is in a warm, damp place. The Hebrew word also means "leprosy" or "skin disease".

mill Two large, flat rocks used for grinding grain to make flour.

Millo Probably the stone foundation walls that were built on the steep slopes south-east of the Temple area in Jerusalem.

millstone A large, round stone used for grinding grain.

miracle An amazing act done by the power of God.

Moab A country east of the Dead Sea, named after one of Lot's sons. See Gen. 19:37.

Molech A false god. This name is like the Hebrew word meaning "king".

Moses One of the most important leaders of the Israelites during the time of the Old Testament. God used him to give the people his law, which is often called "the Law of Moses".

Most Holy Place Literally, "holy of holies", the most important room in the Holy Tent or the Temple, where the Box of the Agreement was kept. It was like a throne room where God sat as king of Israel and where the high priest entered into his presence on the Day of Atonement.

Mount Horeb Another name for Mount Sinai.

Mount of Olives A hill east of the city of Jerusalem from which a person could see the Temple area.

Mount Paran This is probably an important mountain west of the Gulf of Aqaba and north of Mount Sinai.

Mount Sinai The mountain located somewhere on the Sinai Peninsula (the eastern part of modern-day Egypt) where God gave his laws to Moses and the Israelites. Also called Mount Horeb. See Exod. 19 and 20.

Mount Zion See "Zion".

mourn, mourners To express sorrow for someone who has died or for something lost. In ancient Israel people often put on special clothes, cried very loudly, and put ashes on their head to show their sadness. Professional "mourners" were sometimes paid to do this at a funeral.

mustard A plant that has a very small seed but grows taller than a man.

myrrh Sweet-smelling sap from the bark of trees or other plants that was used for perfume and also to prepare bodies for burial. Mixed with wine, it was probably used to relieve pain (Mark 15:23).

N **nard** Very expensive oil from the root of the nard plant. It was used as a perfume.

Nazirite A person who has made a special vow of dedication to God. This name is from the Hebrew word meaning "to separate" or "to consecrate" and refers to the promise Nazirites made to separate themselves from others and dedicate themselves to God by following certain requirements. See Num. 6:1–21.

Negev The desert area in the southern part of Judah.

Nephilim A kind of superhuman race that appeared before the flood. Sometimes translated "giants", the name might come from a Hebrew word meaning "people who have fallen". Later, the Nephilim were a famous family whose men were tall and powerful fighters. See Gen. 6:2–4; Num. 13:32–33.

New Moon The first day of the month for Israelites or Jews, which they celebrated as a special day of rest and worship. The people met together and shared in the fellowship offerings like those described in Lev. 7:16–21.

night A symbol for the kinds of things that describe Satan's kingdom, such as sin and evil.

Nisan See "Abib".

oath A strong declaration that one will tell the truth or keep a promise, often using the name of God or something else known to be real or important. It may include a wish to be punished if the promise is not kept.

offering (burnt offering) This was usually an animal that was killed and completely burned on an altar as a sacrifice.

offering (fellowship offering) An offering to God that was also eaten by the person giving the sacrifice and shared with others, especially during New Moon celebrations.

offering (sin offering) Or "purification offering", a sacrifice that was offered to God to remove impurities from sin and make a person fit to worship God.

offering (thank offering) A special fellowship offering that people gave to praise God and thank him for doing good things for them. A part of the animal being offered was burned on the altar, but the people ate most of it in a fellowship meal at the Temple. See Lev. 7:11–26.

official measure Literally, "shekel of the Holy Place", the standard measure of weight used in the Tabernacle and the Temple.

officer (army officer) A centurion, a Roman army officer who had authority over 100 soldiers.

onyx A precious stone with layers of blue or grey.

ostrich A fast-running bird with very long legs and neck. The largest and most powerful of all birds, it commonly lives in the desert.

papyrus A reed-like plant used to make a type of paper used for writing. It was also used to make many other things, such as baskets, rope, sandals, roofing material, and even boats.

paradise A wonderful place of blessing, where God's people go when they die.

parchment Something like paper made from the skins of sheep and used for writing on.

Passover A very important holy day for the people of Israel and their descendants. They ate a special meal on this day every year to remember that God freed them from slavery in Egypt in the time of Moses. The name may come from the word in Exod. 12:13,23 and 27 that means "to pass over" or "to protect".

Pentecost An Israelite or Jewish festival celebrating the wheat harvest fifty days after Passover. See "Festival of Harvest".

persecute To hurt, cause trouble for or do bad things to someone, especially because of their beliefs.

persecution The act of persecuting or being persecuted. See "persecute".

Persians See "Medes".

Pharaoh A title for the king of Egypt.

Pharisee A person who belonged to a Jewish religious group that claimed to follow carefully all Jewish laws and customs.

Philistines The people who lived in an area along the coast of Palestine. They occupied the land of Canaan (see "Canaan") before the Israelites entered it and were their strongest enemy.

philosopher A person who spends much time studying, thinking, talking or writing about different ideas and trying to gain wisdom.

Pilate, Pontius The Roman governor of Judea, AD 26–36. Read Luke 23:1–3.

pillar One of the tall, carved stones used to hold up the roof of a building.

pomegranate A red fruit filled with tiny seeds, each covered with a sweet, juicy part of the fruit.

potter Someone who makes pottery (pots, jars, bowls) from clay. The Hebrew word also means "creator" or "a person who makes new things".

pouch (judgement pouch) A piece of clothing like a bib or an apron that covered the high priest's chest. See Exod. 28:15–30.

prefect An important government official.

priest (high priest) The most important priest and leader of the Israelites or the Jews, God's people under the "old agreement". Under the "new agreement" the high priest for God's people is Jesus Christ. Read Heb. 7:11 – 8:13.

Preparation day Friday, the day before the Sabbath day.

prize See "crown".

prophecy A message or teaching from God. Also, the ability and authority from God to speak for him.

prophesy To speak or teach things from God.

prophet A person who speaks a message from God. Many of the books in the Old Testament are messages spoken or written by "the prophets", who were some of those God chose to speak for him. God often used dreams or visions to tell or show his prophets what they should say.

prophet (false prophet) A person who claims to speak for God but does not really speak God's truth.

prophetess A woman prophet.

proverb A wise saying or short story that teaches a lesson.

pure See "make . . . pure".

Q Queen of Heaven Probably the false goddess Astarte. She was the goddess of sex and war, worshipped by the people of Mesopotamia. They thought she was the planet Venus, which looks like a star in the sky.

quiver A bag or container for carrying arrows.

R Rahab A dragon or sea monster that people thought controlled the sea. Rahab is often a symbol for God's enemies or for anything evil.

ram A male sheep. A very important animal in ancient times, often used in sacrifices. See Gen. 22:13.

resurrection Being raised from death to live again.

Rezin A king of Aram who ruled about 740–731 BC.

Rock A name for God that means he is a place where people can find safety, like a high mountain or the strong wall of a fortress.

S Sabbath Saturday, the seventh day of the week and a special day for Israelites or Jews. By God's command it was set aside as a time for the people to rest and honour God.

sackcloth A rough cloth made from animal hair that people sometimes wore to show sadness.

sacrifice To offer a gift to God (or to any god) as an expression of worship, thanksgiving or payment for sin. Also, the gift that is offered. In the Old Testament it was usually a special animal that was killed and burned on an altar. The Old Testament sacrifices offered for sins were symbolic of the perfect sacrifice that God himself would provide through Jesus Christ. Jesus gave his own life as a sacrifice to pay for the sins of all people. See Heb. 10:1–14.

Sadducees A leading Jewish religious group. They accepted only the first five books of the Old Testament and believed that people will not live again after death.

Samaria During Old Testament times, the capital city of Israel, the northern Israelite kingdom. In New Testament times, the name refers to the central hill country, the general area that had been occupied by the northern kingdom.

Samaritans During New Testament times, the people who lived in Samaria, the region north of Judea. They were part Jewish and followed the Law of Moses, but the Jews of Judea did not accept them as pure descendants of Israel.

Samuel The last judge (leader) and first prophet of Israel.

sapphire A rare and valuable blue stone.

Satan A name for the devil meaning "the enemy" or "the accuser".

satrap An official who ruled over a Persian province.

sceptre A special stick carried by kings to show their authority.

scribe Originally, an educated man who was skilled in reading and writing. By New Testament times scribes had become a distinct social and political group. Because of their work in copying the Scriptures and writing down explanations of the Law of Moses, many became experts in the law and were respected as teachers, lawyers or judges.

Scripture Part of the Scriptures or "Holy Writings" – the Old Testament.

scroll A long roll of paper or leather used for writing on.

seal A small stone or ring with a picture carved in it

that was pressed into wet clay or hot wax to hold down the loose end of a scroll. It left a special mark, also called a seal, that was like a signature to keep anyone from opening the scroll except the right person.

seer A kind of prophet (see "prophet") who received messages from God in visions.

Selah A word appearing in Psalms and Habakkuk that was apparently an instruction for the singers or musicians, perhaps meaning to pause or to get louder.

Sennacherib A king of Assyria who ruled about 706–681 BC.

Sharon Valley The lowlands along the coast of Palestine.

sheath A leather or metal case for carrying a sword or knife.

sheminith The meaning of this word is uncertain, but it may refer to a type of instrument, a special way of tuning an instrument or one of the groups that played harps in the Temple orchestra. See 1 Chr. 15:21.

Sheol The place where people go when they die. This usually means the grave, but it can mean the place where spirits go.

Sheshbazzar A governor of Judah mentioned several times in the book of Ezra. He is possibly the same person as the one named Zerubbabel, mentioned in Ezra 2:2 and elsewhere. If they are not the same man, then Sheshbazzar was the first governor of Judah, and Zerubbabel was the second.

sickle A tool with a curved blade for harvesting grain and other crops.

Sidon A non-Jewish city on the coast of Phoenicia (modern Lebanon).

sign (miraculous sign) An amazing act that demonstrates the power of God.

signet ring A type of seal that was worn on the finger. See "seal".

silver coin Or "denarius", a Roman coin that was worth the average pay for one day's work.

skin disease Traditionally translated "leprosy", the Hebrew word means any of several diseases that cause rashes or sores on the skin.

slave woman Or "concubine", a woman who was owned by a man and treated like a wife.

sling A strip of leather used for throwing rocks.

snuffers Tools used to put out the flame on lamps.

Sodom A city that God destroyed, together with the city of Gomorrah, because the people living there were so evil. See Gen. 19.

Solomon's Porch An area on the east side of the Temple, covered by a roof.

son of man This was usually just a way of saying "a person" or "a human being". In the book of Ezekiel, it is a way of addressing Ezekiel, as one the Lord chose to be his prophet.

Son of Man The name that Jesus most often used for himself. The phrase in Hebrew or Aramaic means "human being" or "mankind", but in Dan. 7:13–14 it is used of a future saviour and king, and this was later understood to be the Messiah, the one God would send to save his people.

sorcery When a person tries to use the power of demons and evil spirits to do magic.

special servant The Greek word is *diakonos*, which is usually translated "servant"; however, in three places (Rom. 16:1; Phil. 1:2; 1 Tim. 3:8–13) the service of those so described is associated with a local church, indicating that they were chosen to serve in some special way. Compare Acts 6:1–6.

spelt A kind of grain like wheat.

Spirit See "Holy Spirit".

stone (memorial stone) A stone that was set up to help people remember something special. In ancient Israel, people often set up stones at places where they worshipped false gods.

strong love The Hebrew word can mean strong feelings such as zeal, jealousy or love.

synagogue A place in many cities where Jews gathered for prayer, study of the Scriptures, and other public meetings.

Syrtis A shallow area in the sea near the Libyan coast.

tar Or "pitch", a thick oil that becomes liquid when heated and hard again when it cools. It was used to seal the boards on ships. It could also be used in place of mortar in buildings.

Tarshish A city far away from Israel, probably in Spain, famous for its large ships that sailed the Mediterranean Sea.

tax collector A Jew hired by the Romans to collect taxes. Tax collectors often cheated, and the other Jews hated them.

Teman An area in the northern part of Edom, although the name means "South".

Temple The permanent building in Jerusalem that replaced the portable "Holy Tent" that was used by the Israelites from the time of their wandering in the desert to the reign of King Solomon, when the first Temple was built. Like the Holy Tent, the Temple was the centre of Israelite worship, although provision was made for it to be "a house of prayer for all nations" (Isa. 56:7).

Ten Towns Greek, "Decapolis", an area on the east side of Lake Galilee that once had ten main towns.

Tent See "Holy Tent".

the Way A symbolic name used by followers of Jesus Christ to describe their faith as "the way" to God through Jesus.

threshing Putting newly harvested wheat or other grain on a hard floor and walking on it or beating it with special tools to separate the husks (see "chaff") from the grain.

Thummim See "Urim".

Tigris One of the two large rivers that flow through the countries of Babylonia and Assyria.

tomb A grave cut out of a wall of rock or a building where a dead body is buried. It can also be a small building made to show respect for important people who had died.

torture To hurt or cause someone pain, often to force them to say something against their will.

traitor A person who turns against his or her own country, friends or family and does anything to help their enemy.

tribute Money paid to a foreign king or nation for protection.

tunic A piece of clothing like a long undershirt.

turban A head covering made by wrapping a long piece of cloth around the top part of the head or around a cap worn on the head.

Tyre A non-Jewish city on the coast of Phoenicia (modern Lebanon).

unclean Impure or unacceptable. When it refers to animals, it means not fit to be eaten. When it refers to things, it means not pure or fit to be used, especially in the worship of God. When it refers to people, it means not fit to be in the area of the Holy Tent (Tabernacle) or Temple or to participate in the worship of God there. See Lev. 11 – 15 for the Old Testament rules about what was clean and unclean.

Urim The Urim and Thummim were probably small stone, metal or wooden pieces that the high priest kept in the judgement pouch he wore. They were used, perhaps like dice, to get answers from God. See Exod. 28:30.

Uzziah A king of Judah who ruled with his father Amaziah from 792 to 767 BC, and then alone from 767 to 740 BC.

virgin A woman, especially a young woman, who is not married and has never had sex.

vision Something like a dream used by God to speak to people.

vow A very strong promise that a person makes, sometimes to God and often using the name of God or something else known to be real or important. It may include a wish to be punished if the promise is not kept.

vulture Or "eagle", a bird of prey that eats dead animals.

wafer A thin bread, like a cracker, made without yeast.

watchman A guard who stood on the city wall,

looked for enemy soldiers, and warned the people of the city if he saw trouble coming.

will The legal paper that people sign to give instructions about what should be done with their possessions after they die.

winepress A place dug out of rock used to mash grapes and collect the juice for making wine.

wineskin A bag made from the skin of an animal and used for storing wine.

wise men Literally, "magi", probably meaning pagan religious scholars who studied the stars to predict future events.

witchcraft Using magic or the power of Satan.

witch A person who uses the power of Satan or evil spirits to do magic.

wonders Miracles that cause people to react with amazement and fear of God.

Y **YAHWEH** A Hebrew name for God that is usually translated LORD. It is like the Hebrew word meaning "He is" or "He makes things exist".

yeast The part of bread dough that makes it rise. Sometimes it is used as a symbol of bad influence.

yoke A pole that was put across the shoulders of men, usually slaves, or animals and used in pulling or carrying heavy loads.

Z **Zealot** A term used to describe Jews who had an enthusiastic desire or "zeal" to maintain the purity of Judaism – the land, the Temple, observance of the law and the traditions. This desire included a willingness to do whatever necessary to protect this purity against any outside threat, such as Roman control. This kind of spirit eventually brought about the formation of a group of Jewish patriots known as the Zealots. (Note that in Matt. 10:4 and Mark 3:18 "Zealot" is used to translate the Aramaic term "Cananaean", which had the same meaning.)

Zeus The most important of the gods in which the ancient Greeks believed.

Zion The south-eastern part of the mountain that Jerusalem is built on. Sometimes it means the city of Jerusalem, the people of God living there, or the Temple.

MAPS

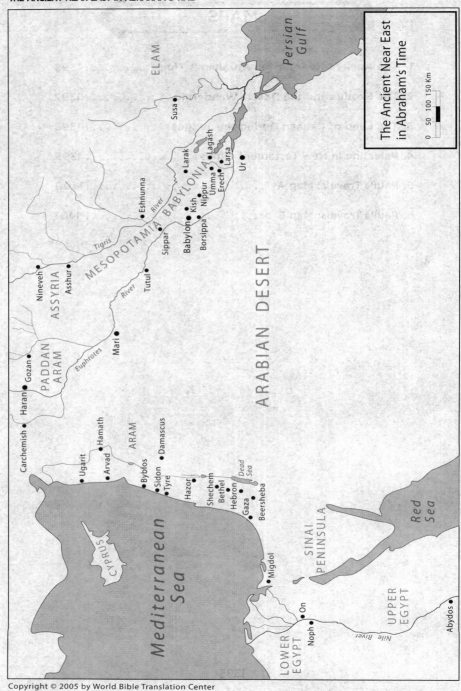

The Ancient Near East
in Abraham's Time

0   50   100 150 Km

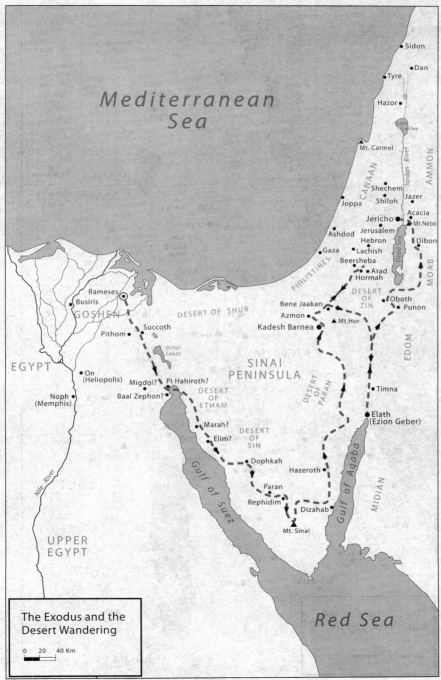

The Exodus and the
Desert Wandering

0   20   40 Km

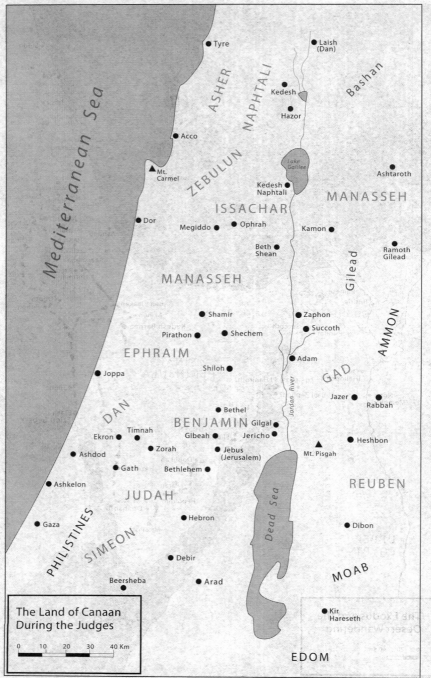

The Land of Canaan
During the Judges

0   10   20   30   40 Km

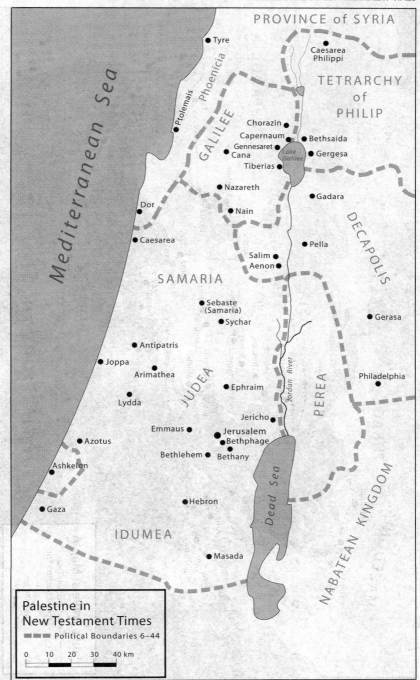

PROVINCE of SYRIA

Mediterranean Sea

● Tyre

● Caesarea Philippi

Phoenicia

Ptolemais

GALILEE

TETRARCHY of PHILIP

● Chorazin
● Capernaum
● Gennesaret
● Cana
● Bethsaida
Lake Galilee
● Gergesa
● Tiberias

● Nazareth

Dor ●

● Nain

● Gadara

DECAPOLIS

Caesarea ●

● Pella

SAMARIA

● Salim
● Aenon

● Sebaste (Samaria)
● Sychar

● Gerasa

● Antipatris

Joppa ●

Arimathea ●

Jordan River

PEREA

● Philadelphia

JUDEA

● Ephraim

Lydda ●

● Jericho

Emmaus ●

● Jerusalem
● Bethphage

Azotus ●

Bethlehem ● ● Bethany

Ashkelon ●

Dead Sea

Gaza ●

● Hebron

IDUMEA

NABATEAN KINGDOM

● Masada

Palestine in New Testament Times

▬▬ Political Boundaries 6–44

0   10   20   30   40 km

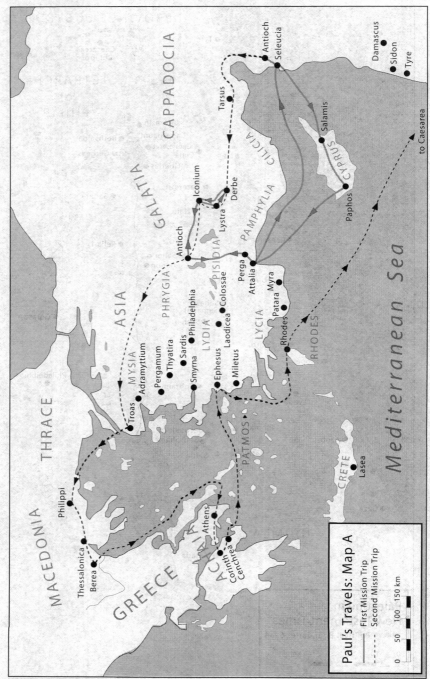

Paul's Travels: Map A

First Mission Trip
Second Mission Trip

0 50 100 150 km

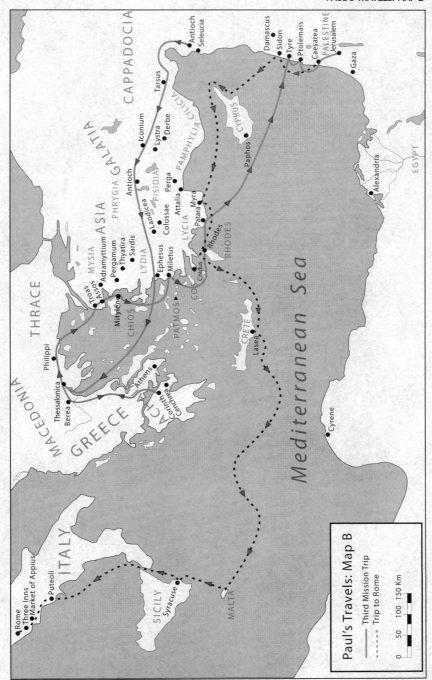

Paul's Travels: Map B

——— Third Mission Trip

········· Trip to Rome

0   50   100   150 Km